HUXFORD'S
OLD BOOK
VALUE GUIDE

Tenth Edition

25,000 Listings of Old Books with Current Values

COLLECTOR BOOKS
A Division of Schroeder Publishing Co., Inc.

The current values in this book should be used only as a guide. They are not intended to set prices, which vary from one section of the country to another. Auction prices as well as dealer prices vary greatly and are affected by condition as well as demand. Neither the Editors nor the Publisher assumes responsibility for any losses that might be incurred as a result of consulting this guide.

Searching For A Publisher?

We are always looking for knowledgeable people considered to be experts within their fields. If you feel that there is a real need for a book on your collectible subject and have a large comprehensive collection, contact Collector Books.

On the Cover:

Wegner, Robert. *Deer & Deer Hunting: The Serious Hunter's Guide*. Stackpole Books. 1984. F/VG. $12.50

Parker, Dorothy. *Dorothy Parker Stories*. NY: Wings Books. 1992. 1st thus. F/F. $8.00

St. Aubin de Teran, Lisa. *The Tiger*. NY: Franklin Watts. 1985. 1st. F/F. $8.50

Grimm, Herman. *Life of Michaelangelo*. Boston: Little Brown. 1900. new ed. 2 vols. gilt. VG with scuffed cloth jackets and slipcase. $40.00

Books featured on cover courtesy of:
David & Nancy Haines
Vintage Books
181 Hayden Rowe St.
Hopkington, MA 01748
(508) 435 – 3499
Editing and Research: Linda Holycross

Cover design: Beth Summers

Additional copies of this book may be ordered from:

COLLECTOR BOOKS
P.O. Box 3009
Paducah, KY 42002-3009

@ $19.95. Add $2.00 for postage and handling.

INTRODUCTION

This book was compiled to help the owner of old books evaluate his holdings and find a buyer for them. Most of us have a box, trunk, stack, or bookcase of old books. Chances are they are not rare books, but they may have value. Two questions that we are asked most frequently are 'Can you tell me the value of my old books?' and 'Where can I sell them?' *Huxford's Old Book Value Guide* will help answer both of these questions. Not only does this book place retail values on nearly 25,000 old books, it also lists scores of buyers along with the type of material each is interested in purchasing. Note that we list retail values (values that an interested party would be willing to pay to obtain possession of the book). These prices are taken from dealers' selling lists that have been issued within the past year. All of the listings are coded (A1, S7, etc.) before the price. This coding refers to a specific dealer's listing for that book. When two or more dealers have listed the same book, their codes will be listed alphabetically in the description line. Please refer to the section titled 'Book Sellers' for codes.

If you were to sell your books to a dealer, you should expect to receive no more than 50% of the values listed in this book, unless the dealer has a specific buyer in mind for some of your material. In many cases, a dealer will pay less than 50% of retail for a book to stock.

Do not ask a dealer to evaluate your old books unless you intend to sell them to him. Most antiquarian book dealers in the larger cities will appraise your books and ephemera for a fee that ranges from a low of $10.00 per hour to $50.00 per hour (or more). If you have an extensive library of rare books, the $50.00-an-hour figure would be money well spent (assuming, of course, the appraiser to be qualified and honest).

Huxford's Old Book Value Guide places values on the more common holdings that many seem to accumulate. You will notice that the majority of the books listed are in the $20.00 to $50.00 range. Many such guides list only the rare, almost non-existent books that the average person will never see. The format is very simple: listings are alphabetized first by the name of the author, translator, editor, or illustrator; if more than one book is listed for a particular author, each title is listed alphabetically under his or her name. When pseudonyms are known, names have been cross-referenced. (Please also see the section titled 'Pseudonyms' for additional information.) Dust jackets or wrappers are noted when present, and sizes (when given) are approximate. Condition is noted as well.

Fine condition refers to books that are perfect, in as-issued condition with no defects. Books in near-fine condition are perfect, but not as crisp as those graded fine. Near-fine condition books show only a little wear from reading (such as very small marks on binding); they are not as crisp as those graded fine, but they still have no major defects. Books rated very good may show wear but must have no tears on pages, binding, or dust jacket (if issued). A rating of good applies to an average used book that has all of its pages and yet may have small tears and other defects. The term reading copy (some dealers also use 'poor') describes a book having major defects; however, its text must be complete. Ex-library books are always indicated as such; they may be found in any condition. This rule also applies to any Book Club edition. Some of our booksellers indicate intermediate grades with a + or ++, or VG-EX. We have endeavored to use the grade that best corresponded to the description of condition as given in each dealer's listing. If you want to check further on the condition of a specific book, please consult the bookseller indicated. Please note that the condition stated in the description is for the book and then the dust jacket. (Dust jackets on many modern first editions may account for up to 80% of their value.)

In the back of the book we have listed buyers of books and book-related material. When you correspond with these dealers, be sure to enclose a self-addressed, stamped envelope if you want a reply. Please do not send lists of books for an appraisal. If you wish to sell your books, quote the price that you want or negotiate price only on the items the buyer is interested in purchasing. When you list your books, do so by author, full title, publisher and place, date, and edition. Indicate condition, noting any defects on cover or contents.

When shipping your books, first wrap each book in paper such as brown kraft or a similar type of material. Never use newspaper for the inner wrap, since newsprint tends to rub off. (It may, however be used as a cushioning material within the outer carton.) Place your books in a sturdy corrugated box and use a good shipping tape to seal it. Tape reinforced with nylon string is preferable, as it will not tear. Books shipped by parcel post may be sent at a special fourth class book rate, which may be lower than regular parcel post zone rates.

LISTING OF STANDARD ABBREVIATIONS

/ .and, also, with, or indicates dual-title book
aeg ....all edge gilt
AJA.......American Jewish Archives
AJC ......American Jewish Congress
AJHS...American Jewish Historical Society
Am ....American
AN ....as new
AP ..proof, advance proof, advance uncorrected proof, or galley
ARC .....advance reading or review copy
bdg..........................binding, bound
b&w........................black & white
bl ....blue
blk ....black
BC ....any book club edition
brd ....boards
c ....copyright
ca ....circa
cb ....cardboard
cbdg..........................comb binding
chip ....chipped
clip ....clipped price
CMG.Coward McCann Geoghegan
decor...........decoration, decorated
dk ....dark
dj ....dust jacket
DIF ....Donald I. Fine
DSP ....Duell Sloan Pearce
dtd..................................dated
E ....east, eastern
edit................................editor
ed ....edition
emb.............embossed, embossing
Eng................England, English
ep ....end pages
ERB ....Edgar Rice Burroughs Inc.
ES................................errata slip
F ....fine
ffe ....front free endpaper
fld.................folding, folder
ftspc.......................frontispiece
FSC..........Farrar, Straus & Cudahy
FSG ....Farrar, Straus & Giroux
fwd.................................forward
G ....good
GPO ...Government Printing Office

gr ....green
HBJ .....Harcourt Brace Jovanovich Inc.
HBW............Harcourt Brace World
hc ....hard cover
hist ....history
HRW ....Holt Rinehart Winston
ils ....illustrated
imp ....imprint, impression
intl................................initialed
inscr ....inscribed
Inst................................Institute
Internat ....International
intro...........................introduction
LEC...............Limited Edition Club
lg ....large
Lib ....library
lt ....light
ltd...................................limited
mc ....multicolor
MIT .....MA Institute of Technology
MOMA.....Museum of Modern Art
mtd...............................mounted
MTI ....movie tie-in
Mus.................................museum
N ....north, northern
NAL ....New American Library
Nat.................................national
NEL...............New English Library
nd ....no date
ne...........................no edition given
NF.......................................near fine
NGS..National Geographic Society
np............................no place given
NYGS ...New York Graphic Society
obl ....oblong
orig.................................original
OUP..........Oxford University Press
p ....page, pages
pc.......................................piece
pict..................................pictorial
pl ....plate, plates
Pr...press
pref ....preface
pres.............................presentation
promo............................promotion
prt.............................print, printing
pub ....publisher, publishing
rem mk..................remainder mark

repro ....reproduction
rpl.................................replaced
rpr.....................................repair
rpt.....................................reprint
RS.................................review slip
S ....south, southern
S&S ....Simon & Schuster
sans ....none issued
sbdg..........................spiral binding
sc ....softcover
SF........................San Francisco
sgn...............signature, signed
sm ....small
sq ....square
stp ....stamp, stamped
supp ....supplement
swrp ....shrink wrap
TB....................................textbook
teg ....top edge gilt
trans ....translated
TVTI ....TV tie-in
U ....University
unp ....unpaged
UP.................uncorrected proof
VG.................................very good
W ....west, western
w/ ...with, indicates laid in material
wht.......................................white
wrp....................................wrappers
xl ....ex-library
yel.......................................yellow
#d ....numbered
12mo ....about 7" tall
16mo ....6" to 7" tall
24mo ....5" to 6" tall
32mo ....4" to 5" tall
48mo ....less than 4" tall
64mo ....about 3" tall
sm 8vo ....7½" to 8" tall
8vo........................8" to 9" tall
sm 4to ....about 10" tall, quarto
4to..............between 11" to 13" tall
folio ....13" or large
elephant folio ....23" or larger
atlas folio ....25"
double elephant folio ....larger than 25"

A'BECKETT, Gilbert Abbott. *Comic Blackstone.* 1887. London. Bradbury Agnew. revised/expanded. 324p. gilt bl cloth. G. M20. $35.00

A'BECKETT, Gilbert Abbott. *Comic History of Rome.* nd. London. Bradbury Evans. 1st. 10 parts in 9. 308p. gr morocco solander case. T10. $650.00

A PASSENGER. *Narrative of the Loss of the Kent East Indiaman, by Fire...* 1825. Edinburgh. Waugh Innes. 78p. brd. P4. $250.00

AARDEMA, Verna. *Bringing the Rain to Kapiti Plain.* 1981. NY. Dial. 1st. sm 4to. F/F. C8. $20.00

AARON, Hank. *Aaron.* 1968. World. 1st. sgn. F/F. A23. $75.00

AARON, Hank. *I Had a Hammer. The Hank Aaron Story.* 1991. Harper Collins. 1st. sgn. F/F. A23. $75.00

AAS, Ingebret. *Roald Amundsen's Stampfedre. Den Gamle Skipperslektpa...* 1941. Sarpsborg. photos. 36p. prt wrp. P4. $35.00

ABBE, Cleveland. *Mechanics of the Earth's Atmosphere.* 1910. Smithsonian. 617p. xl. K5. $40.00

ABBEY, Edward. *Abbey's Road.* 1979. Dutton. 1/1250. NF/NF+. B3. $750.00

ABBEY, Edward. *Appalachian Wilderness.* 1970. Dutton. 1st. NF/NF clip. B3. $150.00

ABBEY, Edward. *Black Sun.* 1971. S&S. 1st. F/VG. B3. $250.00

ABBEY, Edward. *Cactus Country.* 1973. Time Life. 1st. photos. F/sans. A18/M25. $35.00

ABBEY, Edward. *Desert Images.* 1979. HBJ. 1st. NF/case. B3. $200.00

ABBEY, Edward. *Jonathan Troy.* 1954. Dodd Mead. 1st. inscr/dtd 1982. author's 1st book. NF/VG. L3. $3,000.00

ABBEY, Edward. *Monkey Wrench Gang.* 1975. Lippincott. 1st. F/F. B4. $500.00

ABBEY, Edward. *Monkey Wrench Gang.* 1975. Lippincott. 1st. F/VG. B3. $150.00

ABBEY, Edward. *One Life at a Time, Please.* 1988. Holt. 1st. F/F. B3. $100.00

ABBEY, Edward. *Outlet.* 1905. Houghton Mifflin. 1st. ils EB Smith. F. A14. $75.00

ABBEY, Edward. *Slumgullion Stew.* 1984. Dutton. 1st. sgn. F/F. B4. $150.00

ABBEY, Edward. *Texas Matchmaker.* 1904. Houghton Mifflin. 1st. ils EB Smith. VG+. A18. $60.00

ABBEY, Mrs. A. *Practical Goat-Keeping.* ca 1940. London. photos. sc. G+. E6. $12.00

ABBEY & Blaustein. *Hidden Canyon, a River Journey.* 1978. Viking. 136p. blk cloth. NF/VG. F7. $110.00

ABBEY & HYDE. *Slickrock: Endangered Canyons of the Southwest.* 1971. Sierra Club. 1st. tan cloth. NF/dj. F7. $200.00

ABBEY & NICHOLS. *In Praise of Mountain Lions.* 1984. Sierra Club. 1st. sgns. F/wrp. B3. $250.00

ABBOT, Anthony. *Shudders.* 1943. NY. Farrar Rhinehart. 1st. F/F. M15. $150.00

ABBOT, Anthony. *These Are Strange Tales.* 1948. Winston. 1st. NF/dj. M2. $15.00

ABBOT, Willis J. *Panama & the Canal in Picture & Prose.* 1913. NY. Syndicate. 4to. 412p. red cloth/watercolor pl. VG. K7. $45.00

ABBOTT, Bruce. *Sign of the Scorpion.* 1970. Grove. 1st. F/F. P3. $20.00

ABBOTT, Frederick H. *Administration of Indian Affairs in Canada.* 1915. WA, DC. Brd Indian Comm. 30p photos. 148p. gilt stp cloth. D11. $30.00

ABBOTT, I.A. *Laau Hawaii: Traditional Hawaiian Uses of Plants.* 1992. Bishop Mus. 163p. F. B1. $36.00

ABBOTT, Jack Henry. *In the Belly of the Beast: Letters From Prison.* 1981. Random. 1st. inscr Toni Morrison to James Baldwin. F/NF. B4. $650.00

ABBOTT, Jacob. *Harper Establishment; or, How the Storybooks Are Made.* 1855. Harper. 1st. 3-quarter red morocco. M24. $350.00

ABBOTT, Jacob. *History of Xerxes the Great.* 1854. Harper. 16mo. 302p. cloth. VG. W1. $30.00

ABBOTT, Jane. *Laughing Last.* 1924. Grosset Dunlap. 1st thus. ils EC Pauli. 282p. VG. A25. $15.00

ABBOTT, John S.C. *Napoleon at St Helena.* 1855. Harper. G. P3. $85.00

ABBOTT, L.W. *Law Reporting in England, 1485-1585.* 1973. London. Athlone. VG/dj. M11. $85.00

ABBOTT, Lee K. *Living After Midnight.* 1991. Putnam. 1st. F/NF. B3. $25.00

ABBOTT, Lee K. *Living After Midnight.* 1991. Putnam. 1st. sgn. F/F. R14. $40.00

ABBOTT, Lee K. *Strangers in Paradise.* 1987. Putnam. 1st. sgn/dtd 1994. NF/NF. R14. $50.00

ABBOTT, Marguerite. *Syllabus of Occupational Therapy Procedures & Techniques...* 1957. Dubuque. WC Brn. 1st. ils. 95p. VG+. A25. $10.00

ABBOTT, Maude. *Atlas of Congenital Cardiac Disease.* 1954. NY. rpt. folio. 62p. A13. $100.00

ABBOTT, P.L. *Cretaceous Stratigraphy Western North America.* 1986. CA. 233p. ils wrp. B1. $22.50

ABBOTT, R.T. *Compendium of Land Shells.* 1989. Melbourne. Am Malacologists. 1st. 240p. F/F. B1. $50.00

ABBOTT, R.T. *Kingdom of the Seashell.* 1982. Bonanza. ils. 4to. 256p. F/dj. B1. $25.00

ABBOTT & BRECKINRIDGE. *Truancy & Non-Attendance in Chicago Schools...* 1917. Chicago. 1st. 472p. VG+. A25. $40.00

ABBOTT & DICKINSON. *Guide To Reading Books.* 1925. Doubleday Page. VG. P3. $15.00

ABBOTT & GREEN. *I Am Eskimo, Aknik My Name.* 1959. Juneau. Northwest Pub. 1st. sgn Abbott/Ahgupuk. NF/VG. w/card. L3. $150.00

ABBOUSHI, W.F. *Angry Arabs.* 1974. Westminster. 285p. VG/VG. S3. $23.00

ABDUL-JABBAR, Kareem. *Black Profiles in Courage.* 1996. Morrow. 1st. sgn. F/F. A23. $60.00

ABDUL-JABBAR & KNOBLER. *Giant Steps.* 1983. Bantam. photos. F/VG+. P8. $15.00

ABDULLAH, Achmed. *Bungalow on the Roof.* 1931. Mystery League. 1st. VG. N4. $25.00

ABDULLAH, Achmed. *Flower of the Gods.* 1936. Green Circle. 1st. VG/VG. M2. $50.00

ABE, Kobo. *Face of Another.* 1966. Knopf. 1st Am. sgn in Japanese. F/F. B4. $300.00

ABE, Kobo. *Ruined Map.* 1969. Knopf. 1st. VG/VG. P3. $25.00

ABEL, Annie H. *American Indian As Slaveholder & Secessionist. Vol 1.* ca 1970. Scholarly. 394p. A17. $20.00

ABEL, Charles. *Commercial Photographic Lightings.* 1948. NY. 272p. lg 8vo. A17. $15.00

ABEL, Charles. *Professional Portrait Lightings.* 1951. Greenberg. 4th. 272p. dj. A17. $18.50

ABERCROMBIE, W.R. *Alaska, 1899, Copper River Exploring Expedition.* 1900. WA. GPO. 1st. 168 photo pl. 169p. red cloth. VG. P4. $250.00

ABERLE, George P. *From the Steppes to the Prairies.* 1963. Bismark, ND. VG/dj. A19. $45.00

ABERNATHY, T.P. *Burr Conspiracy.* 1954. Oxford. VG/VG. M17. $25.00

ABERT, James W. *Through the Country of Comanche Indians in Fall Year 1845.* 1970. SF. John Howell. folio. ils/pl. 77p. buff cloth. as new/plain wrp. K7. $50.00

ABERT, James W. *Western America in 1846-1847.* 1966. SF. John Howell. 1/3000. ils/2 fld maps. 116p. as new. K7. $50.00

ABISH, Walter. *Alphabetical Africa.* 1974. New Directions. 1st. author's 1st novel. F/F. D10. $65.00

ABISH, Walter. *How German Is It.* 1980. New Directions. 1st. F/F. B4. $85.00

ABISH, Walter. *Minds Meet.* 1975. New Directions. 1st. author's 3rd book. NF/dj. D10. $50.00

ABOLUTION SOCIETY OF NEW YORK. *Constitutional Duty...To Abolish African Slavery...* 1855. NY. Abolution Soc. 1st. 16p. NF/prt wrp. M8. $65.00

ABRAHAM, Max. *Electromagnetische Theorie der Strahung.* 1908. Teubner. 2nd. 8vo. 8vo. VG. K3. $75.00

ABRAHAMS, Gerald. *Brains in Bridge.* 1964. NY. 262p. VG/dj. S1. $12.00

ABRAHAMS, Israel. *Campaigns in Palestine From Alexander the Great.* 1967. Chicago. Argonaut. ils. 55p. VG. S3. $25.00

ABRAHAMS, Israel. *Jewish Life in the Middle Ages.* 1896. London. Macmillan. 1st. 452p. VG. W3. $52.00

ABRAHAMS, Peter. *Fury of Rachel Monette.* 1980. Macmillan. 1st. author's 1st book. NF/NF. H11. $35.00

ABRAHAMS, Peter. *Hard Rain.* 1988. Dutton. 1st. F/F. H11. $25.00

ABRAHAMS, Peter. *Tongues of Fire.* 1982. Evans. 1st. VG/VG. P3. $20.00

ABRAHAMS, Peter. *Tongues of Fire.* 1982. NY. Evans. 1st. F/F. M15. $65.00

ABRAHAMSON, Harold A. *LSD: My Problem Child.* 1983. Los Angeles. Tarcher. 1st. VG/wrp. B2. $35.00

ABRAMOVICH, S.J. *Learn To Do Well.* 1969. NY. Yivo. Yiddish/Hebrew text. VG+. S3. $35.00

ABRAMS, Albert. *Transactions of the Antiseptic Club.* 1902. NY. 205p. A13. $100.00

ABRAMS, Elliott. *Undue Process.* 1993. NY. Free Pr. 1st. inscr. VG/VG. A23. $42.00

ABRAMS, LeRoy. *Flora of Los Angeles & Vicinity.* 1917. Stanford. 1st. 12mo. VG. O4. $20.00

ABRAVANEL, Judah. *Dialoghi di Amore.* 1558. Venice. Giglio. 8vo. title device. quarter calf. R12. $825.00

ABSHIRE, Richard. *Dallas Drop.* 1989. Morrow. 1st. F/F. A20. $10.00

ABSOLON, Karel. *Surgeon, Theodor Billroth, 1829-1894. Vol I.* 1979. Lawrence, KS. 1st. ils. 282p. A13. $25.00

ACCARIAS DE SERIONNE, Jacques. *Les Intrets des Nations de l'Europe, Developes Relativement.* 1766. Paris. 2 vol in 1. 1st. 434p+387p. contemporary mottled calf. G. R15. $650.00

ACKER, Kathy. *Literal Madness.* 1988. Grove. 1st. F/dj. A24. $35.00

ACKERKNECHT, Erwin. *Rudolf Virchow: Doctor, Statesman, Anthropologist.* 1953. Madison. 1st. assn copy/sgn Ralph Major. 304p. A13. $125.00

ACKERMAN, C. *George Eastman.* 1930. Boston. 1st. ils/index. 522p. VG. B5. $35.00

ACKERMAN, Diane. *Lady Faustus.* 1983. Morrow. ARC. RS. F/dj. V1. $20.00

ACKERMAN, Forest. *Gernsback Awards 1926.* 1982. Triton. 1st. sgn. F/dj. M2. $30.00

ACKROYD, Peter. *First Light.* 1989. Grove Weidenfeld. 1st. F/F. B35. $25.00

ACKROYD, Peter. *First Light.* 1989. Grove Weidenfeld. 1st. VG/dj. P3. $20.00

ACKROYD, Peter. *First Light.* 1989. Hamish Hamilton. 1st. F/F. M19. $25.00

ACKROYD, Peter. *Hawksmoor.* 1985. London. Hamish Hamilton. 1st. F/dj. Q1. $150.00

ACKROYD, Peter. *Notes for a New Culture.* 1976. NY. Barnes Noble. 1st Am. author's 2nd book. F/NF. L3. $125.00

ACKWORTH, Robert C. *Dr Kildare Assigned to Trouble.* 1963. Whitman. TVTI. VG. P3. $10.00

ACOSTA, Oscarzeta. *Autobiography of a Brown Buffalo.* 1972. SF. Straight Arrow. 1st. 200p. gilt cloth. dj. D11. $40.00

ADALBERT, Prince of Prussia. *Aus Meinem Tagebuche, 1842-1843.* 1847. Berlin. Deckershen Geheimen Ober-Hofbuchdruckerei. 1st. 1/100. R15. $3,500.00

ADAMCZEWSKI, Jan. *Nicolaus Copernicus & His Epoch.* nd. Phil/WA. Copernius Coc of Am. ils. 162p. VG/dj. K3. $20.00

ADAMI, J. George. *Inflammation.* 1909. London. 4th. 254p. A13. $75.00

ADAMIC, Louis. *Native's Return. An American Immigrant Visits Yugoslavia...* 1934. NY/London. Harper. 1st. 8vo. 32 pl/map ep. 370p. cloth. VG. W1. $10.00

ADAMIC, Louis. *Robinson Jeffers, a Portrait.* 1929. Seattle. 1st. F/orange prt wrp. M24. $50.00

ADAMS, Alice. *After You're Gone.* 1989. Knopf. 1st. sgn. F/F. B3. $40.00

ADAMS, Alice. *Beautiful Girl.* 1978. Knopf. 1st. sgn. F/NF. B3. $45.00

ADAMS, Alice. *Caroline's Daughters.* 1991. Knopf. 1st. sgn. NF/F. B3. $40.00

ADAMS, Alice. *Families & Survivors.* 1974. Knopf. 1st. author's 2nd novel. F/NF. M25. $45.00

ADAMS, Alice. *Return Trips.* 1980. Knopf. 1st. sgn. F/F. B3. $40.00

ADAMS, Alice. *Superior Women.* 1984. Knopf. 1st. sgn. F/NF. R14. $35.00

ADAMS, Alice. *To See You Again.* 1982. Knopf. 1st. sgn. F/NF. B3. $50.00

ADAMS, Andy. *Log of a Cowboy.* 1967. NE U. rpt. A19. $10.00

ADAMS, Andy. *Log of a Cowboy: Narrative of Old Trail Days.* 1931. Houghton Mifflin. 1st thus. ils E Boyd Smith. F/VG. A18. $35.00

ADAMS, Andy. *Mystery of the Arabian Stallion.* 1964. Grosset Dunlap. 1st. 176p. pict brd. VG. M20. $45.00

ADAMS, Ansel. *Letters & Images 1916-1984.* 1988. NGS. 1st. 402p. dj. A17. $37.50

ADAMS, Ansel. *Singular Images.* 1974. Morgan. 1st. sgn. 8vo. 60p. sc. A8. $40.00

ADAMS, Ansel. *Yosemite & the Range of Light.* 1981. Boston. later prt. sgn. lg folio. F/VG. C6. $100.00

ADAMS, B.M.G. *England.* 1923. Three Mtn. 1st. 1/150. floral brd. uncut. M24. $150.00

ADAMS, Bess Porter. *About Books & Children: Historical Survey...* 1954. 1st. ils. 589p. F/VG. A4. $45.00

ADAMS, Carsbie. *Space Flight.* 1958. 1st. VG+/dj. S13. $12.00

ADAMS, Charles Francis. *Autobiography.* 1920. Boston. Houghton Mifflin. 7th. 224p. VG. T10. $30.00

ADAMS, Charles Francis. *Chapter of Erie.* 1869. Boston. James Osgood. 1st. NF/prt wrp. M24. $600.00

ADAMS, Charlotte. *Cooking With Style.* 1967. Gramercy. VG/dj. A16. $8.00

ADAMS, Charlotte. *Four Seasons Cookbook.* 1971. NY. Ridge Pr. ils/photos. 319p. F/VG+ clip. A16. $15.00

ADAMS, Charlotte. *Old Original Bookbinders' Restaurant Cookbook.* 1961. Crowell. 11th. 184p. B10. $6.00

ADAMS, Charlotte. *Singles' First Menu Cookbook.* 1975. Dodd Mead. G/dj. A16. $12.00

ADAMS, Cleve F. *Decoy.* 1945. Books Inc. 2nd. VG/VG. P3. $20.00

ADAMS, Clinton. *Fritz Scholder, Lithographs.* 1975. NYGS. 1st. lithos. F/F. L3. $85.00

ADAMS, Clinton. *Printmaking in New Mexico 1880-1990.* 1991. NM U. 1st. 167p. lg 4to. wrp. A17. $16.50

ADAMS, Douglas. *Dick Gently's Holistic Detective Agency.* 1987. S&S. 1st. NF/NF. M2. $15.00

ADAMS, Douglas. *Dirk Gently's Holistic Detective Age.* 1987. S&S. 1st. F/F. P3. $20.00

ADAMS, Douglas. *Hitchhiker's Guide to the Galaxy.* 1979. Harmony. 1st. F/F. W2. $30.00

ADAMS, Douglas. *Life, the Universe & Everything.* 1982. Harmony Books. 1st. 227p. NF/dj. M20. $25.00

ADAMS, Douglas. *Long Dark Tea-Time of the Soul.* 1988. Stoddart. 1st. VG/dj. P3. $20.00

ADAMS, Douglas. *More Than Complete Hitchhiker's Guide.* 1989. Bonanza. 1st. F/F. M2. $15.00

ADAMS, Douglas. *So Long, & Thanks for All the Fish.* 1985. Harmony. 1st. NF/dj. P3. $20.00

ADAMS, Edwin Plimpton. *Quantum Theory.* 1923. WA, DC. Nat Academy of Sciences. 2nd. VG/wrp. K3. $25.00

ADAMS, Eustace L. *Air Combat Stories for Boys: Doomed Demons (#5).* 1935. Grosset Dunlap. lists 11 titles. VG/dj. M20. $15.00

ADAMS, Eustace L. *Andy Lane: Across the Top of the World (#11).* Grosset Dunlap. bl bdg. VG. N1. $12.00

ADAMS, Eustace L. *Andy Lane: Racing Around the World (#3).* 1928. Grosset Dunlap. 219p. VG/dj lists 12 titles. M20. $25.00

ADAMS, F.D. *Birth & Development of the Geological Sciences.* 1938. Williams Wilkins. 1st. cloth. NF/dj. D8. $55.00

ADAMS, F.W. *Theological Criticims; or, Hints of Philosophy of Man...* 1843. Montpelier, VT. 1st. 12mo. 216p. cloth. M1. $125.00

ADAMS, Foster. *John LaFarge.* 1987. 1st. exhibit catalogue. VG. M17. $25.00

ADAMS, Francis C. *Life & Adventures of Maj Roger Sherman Potter...* 1858. NY. Stanford/Delisser. 1st. 12mo. 522p. cloth. M1. $250.00

ADAMS, Frank. *Simple Simon.* ca 1920. Dodge. 1st Am. 4to. pict label/cloth brd. R5. $200.00

ADAMS, Frank. *Tom, the Piper's Son.* ca 1920. Dodge. 1st Am. 4to. 12 mc pl. red cloth spine/paper brd. VG. M5. $135.00

ADAMS, Frederick Upham. *President John Smith.* 1897. Kerr. 1st. VG. M2. $50.00

ADAMS, Frederick. *Conquest of the Tropics.* 1914. Doubleday. 1st. photos. 368p. gilt gr cloth. F3. $25.00

ADAMS, Gail Galloway. *Purchase of Order.* 1988. Athens, GA. 1st. inscr. author's 1st book. F/F. R13. $45.00

ADAMS, George Burton. *Council & Courts in Anglo-Norman England.* 1965. NY. Russell. reissue of Yale 1926. M11. $45.00

ADAMS, Grace. *Workers on Relief.* 1939. New Haven. Yale. 1st. photos. 344p. xl. VG+. A25. $10.00

ADAMS, Harold. *Barbed Wire Noose.* 1987. Mysterious. 1st. VG/dj. P3. $18.00

ADAMS, Harold. *Man Who Missed the Party.* 1989. Mysterious. 1st. sgn. F/F. P3. $25.00

ADAMS, Harrison. *Pioneer Boys of the Colorado.* 1926. Boston. LC Page. 12mo. tan coth. VG/dj. F7. $37.50

ADAMS, Henry. *Democracy, an American Novel.* 1880. NY. Holt. 1st/1st issue (all points). 12mo. 374p+ads. cloth. M1. $750.00

ADAMS, Henry. *Democracy, an American Novel.* 1882. NY. Holt. 12mo. 374p+ads. prt wrp. M1. $200.00

ADAMS, Herbert. *Mystery & Minette.* 1934. Lippincott. 1st. VG. P3. $35.00

ADAMS, J. Howe. *History of the Life of D Hayes Agnew.* 1892. Phil. 1st. 376p. A13. $75.00

ADAMS, Jill. *Wild Flowers of the Northern Cape.* 1976. Cape Town. ils. 152p. as new. B26. $27.50

ADAMS, John Quincy. *Oration on Life & Character of Gilbert Motier DeLafayette.* 1835. WA. 1/10,000. 94p. cloth. G. B5. $100.00

ADAMS, L.H. *Mink Raising: A Book of Practical Information...* (1935). Columbus, OH. AR harding. 226p. G. H7. $13.50

ADAMS, Ramon F. *Come an' Get It.* 1952. Norman. 1st. ils Nick Eggenhofer. VG/VG. O3. $65.00

ADAMS, Ramon F. *Cowman Says It Salty.* 1971. U AZ. 1st. 163p. VG/VG. J2. $65.00

ADAMS, Ramon F. *Horse Wrangler & His Remuda.* 1971. Encino. 1/850. 51p. pict ep. VG. J2. $215.00

ADAMS, Ramon F. *More Burs Under the Saddle: Books & Histories of the West.* 1979. Norman, OK. 1st. M/dj. A18. $40.00

ADAMS, Ramon F. *Old-Time Cowhand.* 1961. Macmillan. dj. A19. $30.00

ADAMS, Ramon F. *Rampaging Herd: A Bibliography.* 1982. rpt. F/F. A4. $75.00

ADAMS, Ramon F. *Rampaging Herd: Bibliography of Books...* 1959. Norman, OK. 1st. 463p. F/dj. A17. $150.00

ADAMS, Ramon F. *Six-Guns & Saddle Leather.* 1954. Norman. 1st. 8vo. F/NF. T10. $250.00

ADAMS, Ramon F. *Western Words.* 1956. Norman. dj. A19. $30.00

ADAMS, Richard. *Day Gone By.* 1990. London. Hutchinson. 1st. F/F. R14. $30.00

ADAMS, Richard. *Iron Wolf & Other Stories.* 1980. Allen Lane. 1st. F/F. P3. $25.00

ADAMS, Richard. *Plague Dogs.* 1978. Knopf. 1st. VG/dj. P3. $18.00

ADAMS, Richard. *Ryger Voyage.* 1976. Knopf. 1st Am. ils Nicola Bayley. 30p. NF/dj. D1. $45.00

ADAMS, Richard. *Shardik.* 1974. S&S. 1st. sgn. rem mk. VG/VG. R14. $60.00

ADAMS, Richard. *Ship's Cat.* 1977. London. Cape. 1st. sgn. 32p. F/F. D4. $65.00

ADAMS, Richard. *Traveller.* 1988. Knopf. 1st. F/F. M23. $30.00

ADAMS, Richard. *Tyger Voyage.* 1976. 1st. ils Baylor. NF/NF. S13. $15.00

ADAMS, Richard. *Watership Down.* 1972. NY. Macmillan. 1st Am. author's 1st book. F/dj. Q1. $75.00

ADAMS, Sherman. *First-Hand Report: Story of the Eisenhower Administration.* 1961. Harper. 1st. NF/VG+. A20. $30.00

ADAMS, Sherman. *First-Hand Report: Story of the Eisenhower Administration.* 1961. Harper. 1st. sgn. 481p. bl cloth. F/VG+. B22. $82.50

ADAMS, Tom. *Agatha Christie: The Art of Her Crimes.* 1981. Everest. 1st. NF/dj. P3. $35.00

ADAMS, W.H. Davenport. *Lighthouses & Lightships.* 1871. London. Nelson. ils. 322p. gr cloth. xl. K3. $75.00

ADAMS, William Y. *Ninety Years of Glen Canyon Archaeology, 1868-1959.* 1960. Flagstaff. Mus N AZ Bulletin 33. 4to. VG+/stiff wrp. F7. $15.00

ADAMS & ADAMS. *Michael & Anne in the Yosemite Valley.* 1941. NY/London. Studio. photos. 54p. brd/rebacked. D11. $200.00

ADAMS & DAYTON. *Steamboat Days.* 1939. NY. Tudor. ils. 436p. T7. $35.00

ADAMS & HOLCOMBE. *Account of Battle of Wilson's Creek Fought...Aug 10, 1861.* 1961. Springfield. 111p. F. M4. $35.00

ADAMS & NEWHALL. *This Is the American Earth.* 1960. Sierra Club. 2nd. 89p. VG. A17. $40.00

ADAMS & SMITH. *Appalachian Portraits.* 1993. Jackson, MS. 1st. sgns. F/F. R13. $75.00

ADAMS & TAYLOR. *Yosemite Trails & Tales.* 1934. SF. HS Crocker. 24 full-p photos. 78p. cloth. D11. $200.00

ADAMS. *Tom & Jerry: 50 Years of Cat & Mouse.* 1991. ils. F/dj. M13. $30.00

ADAMSON, H.C. *Lands of the New World.* 1941. World. 1st. inscr. Vg/dj. S13. $20.00

ADAMSON, James B. *James: Man & His Message.* 1989. Eeerdmans. 553p. as new. B29. $11.00

ADAMSON & FOLLAND. *Sir Harry Vane: His Life & Times...1662.* 1973. Gambit. 1st. 498p. VG+/clip. M20. $20.00

ADCOCK, Thomas. *Sea of Green.* 1989. Mysterious. 1st. F/NF. H11. $30.00

ADDAMS, Charles. *Charles Addams' Mother Goose.* 1967. NY. 1st. VG/VG. B5. $50.00

ADDAMS, Charles. *Drawn & Quartered.* 1942. Random. hc. G. P3. $25.00

ADDINGTON, Sarah. *Tommy Tingle-Tangle.* (1927). Volland. ils Gertrude Kay. 39p. VG/pict wrp. D1. $50.00

ADDINSELL & DANE. *Come of Age.* 1938. London. Heinemann. 1st Eng. F/clip. B4. $85.00

ADDISON, Joseph. *Free-Holder; or, Political Essays.* 1758. London. J&R Tonson. tall 8vo. 392p. full early mottled calf. F. H13. $195.00

ADDISON, Joseph. *Works...* 1730. London. 4 vol. 2nd. 4to. ils. A15. $225.00

ADDISON & STEELE. *Spectator.* 1749. London. Prt for J Tonson. 8 vol. 8vo. contemporary calf. VG. A4. $1,250.00

ADELL & KLEIN. *Guide to Non-Sexist Children's Books.* 1976. 1st. ils/bibliography. 160p. F. A4. $35.00

ADEMA, Marcel. *Apollinaire.* 1955. Grove. 1st. F/NF. B2. $40.00

ADLEMAN, Robert H. *Annie Deanne.* 1971. World. 1st. VG/dj. P3. $20.00

ADLER, Avraham. *Righteous Man & the Holy City: Aharon of Belz...* nd. Israel. Jerusalem Lib. 343p. VG/G+. S3. $27.00

ADLER, Bill. *Murder in Manhattan.* 1986. Morrow. 1st. VG/dj. P3. $16.00

ADLER, Elmer. *Breaking Into Print.* 1937. NY. 1st. F/dj. B18. $45.00

ADLER, Renata. *Pitch Dark.* 1983. Knopf. 1st. F/F. B35. $12.00

ADLER, Renata. *Reckless Disregard: Westmoreland v CBS et al...* 1986. Knopf. 1st. rem mk. F/F. B4. $75.00

ADLER, Renata. *Speedboat.* 1976. Random. 1st. F/F. B35. $14.00

ADLER, Warren. *Blood Ties.* 1979. Putnam. 1st. VG/dj. P3. $15.00

ADLER & KAMINS. *Fantastic Life of Walter Murray Gibson.* 1986. Honolulu. 1st. photos/map. M/dj. P4. $25.00

ADLERBERT, Elna. *Cooking the Scandinavian Way.* 1961. London. Spring Books. BC. G/dj. A16. $10.00

ADNEY & CHAPELLE. *Bark Canoes & Skin Boats of North America.* 1964. Smithsonian. ils/photos. 242p. VG. M12. $60.00

ADOCK, Thomas. *Drown All the Dogs.* 1994. Pocket. 1st. sgn. F/F. M15. $35.00

ADOFF, Arnold. *All the Colors of the Race.* 1982. NY. 1st. ils John Steptoe. 56p. F/F. D4. $45.00

ADOFF, Arnold. *Big Sister Tells Me That I'm Black.* 1976. HRW. 1st. ils Lorenzo Lynch. 24p. F/F. D4. $35.00

ADOFF, Arnold. *Birds: Poems by...* 1982. Lippincott. 1st. wide sm 8vo. NF/VG+. C8. $30.00

ADOFF, Arnold. *Black Out Loud. An Anthology of Modern Poems...* 1970. Macmillan. 1st. 86p. NF/dj. D4. $45.00

ADOFF, Arnold. *Ma Nda La.* 1971. Harper. 1st. lg 8vo. F/F. C8. $25.00

ADOFF, Arnold. *Poetry of Black America.* 1973. Harper Row. 1st. NF/dj. M25. $25.00

ADOMEIT. *Three Centuries of Thumb Bibles: A Checklist.* 1980. describes 296 Bibles/400 photos. 430p. F. A4. $150.00

ADORNO, T.W. *Stars Down to Earth: Los Angeles Times Astrology Column.* 1957. Heidelberg. Carl Winter/Universitatsverlag. offprt. wrp. D11. $25.00

ADRICH, Chilson D. *Real Log Cabin.* 1945. Macmillan. ils. 278p. VG/dj. H7. $30.00

AEBI, Ernst. *Seasons of Sand: One Man's Quest To Save a Dying Sahara.* 1993. S&S. 1st. 8vo. 236p. NF/dj. W1. $20.00

AESOP. *Aesop's Fables.* 1933. Viking. ils Boris Artzybasheff. F/VG. A20. $45.00

AESOP. *Aesop's Fables.* 1971. Hallmark. ils Fritz Kredel. 61p. F/dj. B24. $95.00

AESOP. *Aesop's Fables.* 1982. Franklin Lib. leather. F. P3. $20.00

AESOP. *Baby's Own Aesop.* (1886). London/NY. Warne. ils Walter Crane. 12mo. VG. D1. $275.00

AESOP. *Fables of Aesop, With a Life of the Author...* 1793. London. John Stockdale. 1st thus. 4to. aeg. full leather. R5. $1,200.00

AESOP. *Fables of Aesop.* 1909. Hodder Stoughton. 1/694. ils/sgn Detmold/25 tipped-in pl. gilt red cloth. D1. $1,250.00

AFANASYEV, V. *Marxist Philosophy: A Popular Outline.* 1965. Progress Pub. 2nd. VG/dj. V4. $15.00

AFTEREM, George. *Silken Threads: A Detective Story.* ca 1890. Alexander Gardner. decor brd. fair. P3. $45.00

AGASSIZ, L. *Geological Sketches.* 1876 (1873). Boston. Osgood. 2 vol. ils/figures. cloth. VG. M12. $95.00

AGASSIZ, L. *Journey in Brazil.* 1868. Boston. Ticknor Fields. 8vo. 20 repro wood engravings. 540p. cloth/rebound. M12. $75.00

AGASSIZ & GOULD. *Principles of Zoology.* 1848. Boston. Gould Kendall Lincoln. 216p. gilt cloth. F. B14. $45.00

AGEE, James. *Lettes of James Agee to Father Flye.* 1962. Braziller. 1st Am. F/NF. D10. $50.00

AGNEW, A.D.Q. *Upland Kenya Wild Flowers.* 1974. London. Oxford. lg 8vo. 827p. F/dj. A22. $60.00

AGNEW, Derek. *Bevin Boy.* 1947. Allen Unwin. 1st. VG/VG. V4. $25.00

AGUIAR, Walter. *Maya Land in Color*. 1978. hastings. 1st. 32 mc pl/map. 96p. dj. F3. $10.00

AHLBERG & AHLBERG. *Funnybones*. 1980. Greenwillow. qst Am. sm 4to. unp. NF/NF. T5. $20.00

AHLBERG & AHLBERG. *Peek-A-Boo!* 1981. Viking. 1st Am. 32p. NF. D4. $30.00

AHLBORN, Richard. *Man Made Mobile: Early Saddles of Western North America*. 1980. SMithsonian. 1st. 147p. VG. O3. $45.00

AI. *Cruelty*. 1973. Houghton Mifflin. ARC. assn copy. RS. F/dj. V1. $40.00

AI. *Greed*. 1993. Norton. 1st. sgn. F/F. R14. $75.00

AICKMAN, Robert. *Cold Hand in Mine*. 1975. Scribner. 1st. F/dj. M2/P3. $40.00

AICKMAN, Robert. *Model*. 1987. Arbor. 1st. NF/dj. P3. $20.00

AICKMAN, Robert. *Painted Devils*. 1979. Scribner. 1st. F/F. M2. $37.00

AIKEN, Conrad. *Blue Voyage*. 1927. NY. 1st. VG/G. B5. $60.00

AIKEN, Conrad. *Punch, the Immortal Liar, Documents in His History*. 1921. Knopf. 1st. VG. M19. $35.00

AIKEN, Conrad. *Seizure of Limericks*. 1964. NY. HRW. 1st. sm 8vo. F/F clip. B4. $85.00

AIKEN, Joan. *Castle Barebane*. 1976. Viking. 1st. Vg/VG. P3. $15.00

AIKEN, Joan. *Cuckoo Tree*. 1971. Doubleday. 1st. 314p. cloth. VG/dj. M20. $35.00

AIKEN, Joan. *Green Flash & Other Tales of Horror, Suspense & Fantasy*. 1971. HRW. 1st. VG/dj. M20. $25.00

AIKEN, Joan. *Kingdom Under the Sea & Other Stories*. 1971. Cape. 1st. ils Jan Pienkowski. F/dj. M5. $70.00

AIKEN, Joan. *Last Slice of Rainbow*. 1985. Harper Row. 1st Am. gr brd. F/NF. T5. $30.00

AIKEN, Joan. *Midnight Is a Place*. 1974. Viking. 1st Am. 287p. VG/G+. P2. $30.00

AIKEN, Joan. *Skin Spinners*. 1976. Viking. 83p. F/F. D4. $35.00

AINSLIE, Kathleen. *Catharine Susan & Me's Coming Out*. 1910. London. Castell Bros. 12mo. pict bdg/silk ribbon. R5. $100.00

AINSLIE, Kathleen. *Oh! Poor Amelia Jane!* ca 1900. London. Castell Bros. ils Ainslie. VG/pict wrp/silk ribbon. D1. $95.00

AINSWORTH & AINSWORTH. *In the Shade of the Juniper Tree*. 1970. NY. Doubleday. 1st. VG/G. O4. $15.00

AINSWORTH & AINSWORTH. *Practical Corn Culture*. 1914. Ainsworth. 166p. VG. A10. $45.00

AIRTH, Rennie. *Once a Spy*. 1981. London. Jonathan Cape. 1st. VG/VG. P3. $18.00

AITKEN, J.R. *In a City Garden*. 1913. London. TN Foulis. 1st. ils Katharine Cameron. 8vo. tan brd. R5. $150.00

AKERS, Dwight. *Drivers Up*. 1938. NY. 1st. VG/VG. B5. $35.00

AKERS, Dwight. *Drivers Up*. 1938. Putnam. 1st. 8vo. NF/dj. T10. $50.00

AKERS, Dwight. *Sleepy Tom*. 1939. NY. 1st. VG/VG. B5. $25.00

AKINSIDE, Mark. *Pleaseures of Imagination. A Poem. In Three Books*. 1744. London. Dodsley. 3rd. tall 8vo. 142p. early mottled calf. H13. $295.00

AKUTAGAWA, Ryunosuke. *Japanese Short Stories*. 1961. NY. Liveright. ils. 224p. VG/dj. W3. $42.00

AKUTAGAWA, Ryunosuke. *Rashomon & Other Stories*. 1952. Tokyo. 1st. intro Howard Hibbett. 95p. VG/worn. W3. $60.00

AL-FARSY, Fouad. *Modernity & Tradition: The Saudi Equation*. 1990. London/NY. Kegan Paul. 1st. 9 pl/4 maps. 337p. NF/dj. W1. $45.00

AL-YOSIFI, Adel Easa. *Evidence*. 1993. Kuwait. self pub. 1st. obl folio. 286p. VG/dj. W1. $45.00

ALBAUGH, William. *Confederate Edged Weapons*. 1960. 1st. 198p. O8. $75.00

ALBAUGH, William. *Confederate Handguns*. 1963. 1st. 4to. dj. O8. $55.00

ALBAUGH, William. *Photographic Supplement of Confederate Swords*. 1963. private prt. 1st. xl. 205p. O8. $75.00

ALBEE, Edward. *Delicate Balance*. 1968. London. 1st. VG/VG. T9. $28.00

ALBEE, Edward. *Malcolm*. 1966. NY. Atheneum. 1st. NF/VG. A24. $40.00

ALBEE, Edward. *Three Tall Women*. 1995. Dutton. later prt. sgn. F/F. A23. $36.00

ALBEE & MCCULLERS. *Ballad of the Sad Cafe*. 1963. Houghton Mifflin. 1st. inscr/dtd Albee. F/NF. D10. $150.00

ALBERT, A.H. *Record of American Uniform & Historical Buttons 1775-1976*. nd. private prt. photos. 511p. F. M4. $55.00

ALBERT, Lillian. *Button Collector's Journal*. 1941. Hightstown, NJ. sgn. 111p. cloth. VG. M20. $35.00

ALBERT, Marvin H. *Gargoyle Conspiracy*. 1975. Doubleday. 1st. VG/clip. P3. $15.00

ALBERT, Susan Wittig. *Hangman's Root*. 1994. Scribner. 1st. sgn. F/F. A23. $32.00

ALBERT, Susan Wittig. *Witches' Bane*. 1993. Scribner. 1st. author's 2nd book. NF/NF. B3. $30.00

ALBERT & BENAGH. *Krazy About the Knicks*. 1971. Hawthorn. photos. VG/VG. P8. $30.00

ALBION, Robert Greenhalgh. *Makers of Naval Policy 1798-1947*. 1980. Naval Inst. 747p. F. A17. $15.00

ALBION & POPE. *Sea Lanes in Wartime*. 1942. NY. Norton. 367p. T7. $60.00

ALBRAND, Martha. *Door Fell Shut*. 1966. NAL. 1st. 214p. VG/dj. M20. $9.00

ALBRAND, Martha. *Manhattan North*. 1971. GMG. 1st. VG/dj. P3. $20.00

ALBRAND, Martha. *Taste of Terror*. 1977. Putnam. 1st. NF/dj. P3. $20.00

ALBRECHT, William A. *Soil Fertility & Animal Health*. 1958. Columbia. Mizzou. 232p. cloth. VG. A10. $16.00

ALBRIGHT, Horace M. *Oh, Ranger!* 1928. Stanford. 2nd. 8vo. gr cloth. VG/G. F7. $35.00

ALBUQUERQUE DE OLIVEIRA, P.E. *Pathogenesia Homoeopathica Brasiliera, Contendo Descripcao*. 1856. Rio de Janerio. Nicolau Lobo Vianna Filhos. 1st/only. 288p. R15. $1,800.00

ALCOCK, John. *Kookaburras' Song*. 1988. AZ U. 27 essays. ils/maps. 218p. F/dj. S15. $15.00

ALCOCK, Vivien. *Cuckoo Sister*. 1986. Delacorte. UP. 8vo. 160p. NF/wrp. C14. $8.00

ALCOTT, Bronson. *Journals*. 1938. edit Odell Shepard. VG. M17. $30.00

ALCOTT, Louisa May. *Aunt Jo's Scrap Bag, Vol 1, My Boys...* 1872. Roberts. 1st. gilt royal blue. VG. M5. $170.00

ALCOTT, Louisa May. *Aunt Jo's Scrap Bag. Shawl-Straps*. 1873. Boston. Roberts. 1st/2nd prt. 12mo. gilt bl cloth. B14. $125.00

ALCOTT, Louisa May. *Behind a Mask: Unknown Thrillers*. 1995. Morrow. 1st collection previously unknown works. 4to. dj. R12. $23.00

ALCOTT, Louisa May. *Eight Cousins.* 1919. Little Brn. ils Harriet Roosevelt Richards. teg. olive cloth. NF. M5. $40.00

ALCOTT, Louisa May. *Flower Fables.* 1855. Boston. George W Briggs. 1st. author's 1st book. 8vo. 182p. gilt brn cloth. F. B2. $1,850.00

ALCOTT, Louisa May. *Flower Fables.* 1855. Boston. GW Briggs. 1st. author's 1st book. gilt brn cloth w/vignette. VG. M24. $1,250.00

ALCOTT, Louisa May. *Hidden Louisa May Alcott.* 1984. Avenel. VG/VG. P3. $15.00

ALCOTT, Louisa May. *Hole in the Wall.* 1899. Boston. Little Brn. 12mo. 62p+8p ads. decor yel cloth. VG. B14. $110.00

ALCOTT, Louisa May. *Hole in the Wall.* 1899. Little Brn. 1st separate ed. gilt yel pict cloth. F. M24. $165.00

ALCOTT, Louisa May. *Jo's Boys.* 1925. Little Brn. 1st thus. 8vo. blk cloth/mc pl. VG+. M5. $42.00

ALCOTT, Louisa May. *Little Men.* 1871. Boston. Roberts Bros. 1st/early issue. gilt maroon cloth. M24. $300.00

ALCOTT, Louisa May. *Little Men.* 1933. Garden City. ils Harve Stein. blk cloth/mc pl. F/VG+. M5. $50.00

ALCOTT, Louisa May. *Little Women.* 1868. Boston. Roberts Bros. 1st/1st state. gilt maroon cloth. F. M24. $10,000.00

ALCOTT, Louisa May. *Little Women.* 1922 (1915). Little Brn. ils JW Smith. blk cloth/mc pl. VG. M5. $75.00

ALCOTT, Louisa May. *Modern Magic.* 1995. NY. Modern Lib. intro Stern. 8vo. cloth. dj. R12. $13.50

ALCOTT, Louisa May. *Old-Fashioned Girl.* 1870 (1870). Roberts. 2nd (ads on copyright p). 378p. red cloth. G+. M20. $40.00

ALCOTT, Louisa May. *Old-Fashioned Girl.* 1928. 1st. ils Clara Burd. VG. S13. $15.00

ALCOTT, Louisa May. *Rose in Bloom.* 1876. Boston. Roberts Bros. 1st/1st state. gilt gr cloth. G. M24. $125.00

ALCOTT, Louisa May. *Rose in Bloom.* 1933. Winston. 1st thus. 8vo. F/VG-. M5. $65.00

ALCOTT, Louisa May. *Under the Lilacs.* 1885. Roberts Bros. G. P3. $35.00

ALCOTT, Louisa May. *Under the Lilacs.* 1934. Winston. 1st thus. 8vo. F/G. B3. $65.00

ALDAN, Daisy. *Poems From India.* 1969. Crowell. 1st. 158p. F/F. D4. $30.00

ALDANOV, Mark. *For Thee the Best.* 1945. Scribner. 1st. VG/G. P3. $15.00

ALDEMAN, Robert H. *Bloody Benders.* 1970. Stein Day. 1st. 247p. VG/dj. M20. $20.00

ALDEMAN & WALTON. *Rome Fell Today.* 1968. Boston. 1st. maps/notes/index. 336p. VG/VG. S16. $21.50

ALDEN, John D. *Submarine Attacks During World War II.* 1989. maps/index. 320p. VG/VG. S16. $21.50

ALDEN, Mary. *Mary Alden's Cake & Cookie Cook Book for Children.* 1956. Wonder. ils Jules Gottlieb. VG. M5. $25.00

ALDEN, Mary. *Mary Alden's Cook Book for Children.* 1955. Wonder. ils Dorothy King. VG+. M5. $35.00

ALDEN & GUERNSEY. *Harper's Pictorial History of Great Rebellion.* 1866-68. harper. 1st. 2 vol. later cloth. NF. M8. $250.00

ALDERSON, Brian. *Cakes & Custard, Children's Rhymes.* 1975. Morrow. 1st Am. ils Helen Oxenbury. VG/worn. D4. $50.00

ALDERSON, Brian. *Peck of Pepper.* 1974. Chatto Windus. 1st. ils Faith Jaques. F/F. D4. $45.00

ALDIN, Cecil. *Just Among Friends.* 1934. Scribner. 1st Am. lg 4to. 27 pl. F/VG. P2. $225.00

ALDIN, Cecil. *Mac.* 1912. Hodder Stoughton. 1st Am. 4to. pict cloth brd. R5. $685.00

ALDIN, Cecil. *Mrs Tickler's Caravan.* 1931. London. Eyre Spottiswoode. 1st. 4to. R5. $150.00

ALDIN, Cecil. *Romance of the Road.* 1986. London. Bracken. facsimile 1928 Eyre Spottiswoode 1st. as new/dj. O3. $45.00

ALDIN, Cecil. *Scarlet to MFH.* 1933. Scribner. 1st Am. VG. O3. $125.00

ALDIN, Cecil. *White Kitten Book.* 1909. London. Hodder Stoughton. 4to. 12 full-p pl. cloth brd. R5. $300.00

ALDING, Peter. *Man Condemned.* 1981. Walker. 1st. VG/dj. P3. $15.00

ALDINGTON, Richard. *Two Stories.* 1930. London. 1/530. sgn. dj. T9. $60.00

ALDIS, Dorothy. *Any Spring.* 1933. NY. Minton Balch. 1st. sgn. 52p. VG+/dj. D4. $45.00

ALDISS, Brian W. *Bury My Heart at WH Smith's.* 1990. London. Hodder Stoughton. 1st. F/F. M23. $30.00

ALDISS, Brian W. *Earthworks.* 1966. Doubleday. 1st. VG/dj. P3. $35.00

ALDISS, Brian W. *Eighty Minute Hour.* 1974. Doubleday. 1st. F/F. M2. $25.00

ALDISS, Brian W. *Hand-Reared Boy.* 1970. McCall. 1st Am. F/F. M2. $25.00

ALDISS, Brian W. *Helliconia Winter.* 1985. Atheneum. 1st. F/dj. M2/P3. $30.00

ALDISS, Brian W. *Last Orders.* 1977. Jonathan Cape. 1st. F/F. P3. $28.00

ALDISS, Brian W. *Malacia Tapestry.* 1976. Harper. 1st Am. sgn. F/F. B2. $45.00

ALDISS, Brian W. *Nebula Award Stories Two.* 1967. Doubleday. 1st. F/dj. M2. $75.00

ALDISS, Brian W. *New Arrivals, Old Encounters.* 1979. Jonathan Cape. 1st. F/F. P3. $25.00

ALDISS, Brian W. *Pile: Petals From Klaed's Computer.* 1979. London. Cape. 1/250. sgns Aldiss/ils Mike Wilks. F/sans. T2. $45.00

ALDISS, Brian W. *Report on Probability A.* 1969. Doubleday. 1st. VG/dj. P3. $25.00

ALDISS, Brian W. *Rude Awakening.* 1978. Random. 1st. VG/VG. P3. $25.00

ALDISS, Brian W. *Saliva Tree.* 1981. Gregg. 1st Am. F. M2. $30.00

ALDISS, Brian W. *Soldier Erect.* 1971. CMG. 1st. VG/dj. P3. $35.00

ALDOUS & MENDALL. *Ecology & Management of the American Woodcock.* 1943. Orono. ils/tables/figures. 201p. xl. G. M12. $22.50

ALDRICH, Ann; see Meaker, Marijane.

ALDRIDGE, Alan. *Peacock Party.* 1979. Viking. 1st. ils Harry Willock. NF/sans. D4. $30.00

ALDRIDGE, James. *Cairo: Biography of a City.* 1969. Little Brn. 1st. ils/maps. 370p. VG. W1. $24.00

ALDRIDGE, Janet. *Meadow-Brook Girls Afloat; or, Stormy Cruise of Red Rover.* 1913. Saalfield. 1st. ils. 250p. VG/dj. A25. $20.00

ALDRIDGE, Janet. *Meadow-Brook Girls Under Canvas; or, Fun & Frolic...* 1913. Phil. Altemus. 1st. ils. 256p. VG. A25. $12.00

ALDRIN, Edeard E. *Return to Earth.* 1973. Random. 2nd. VG/VG. K5. $30.00

ALDROVANDI, U. *Aldrovandi on Chickens: Ornithology of Ulisse Aldrovandi...* 1963. Norman, OK. Vol II only. 8vo. ils. 447p. NF/NF. M12. $30.00

ALEX, Nicholas. *Black in Blue: Study of the Negro Policeman.* 1969. Appleton Century Crofts. 1st. 210p. VG/wrp. B4. $35.00

ALEXANDER, A.F. *Planet Uranius: A History of Observations...* 1965. NY. Am Elsevier. 316p. VG/dj. K5. $90.00

ALEXANDER, C. Edward. *Knowledge for Mother & Daughter.* 1961. Alexander Enterprises. 1st? ils/photos. 64p. VG+. A25. $12.00

ALEXANDER, David. *Pennies From Hell.* 1960. Lippincott. 1st. VG/VG. P3. $25.00

ALEXANDER, Edwin P. *American Locomotives: A Pictorial Record of Steam Power...* 1950. Bonanza. 254p. VG+/dj. M20. $20.00

ALEXANDER, Edwin P. *Pennsylvania Railroad, a Pictorial History.* 1947. NY. ils. 248p. VG. B18. $25.00

ALEXANDER, Karl. *Papa & Fidel.* 1989. Tor. 1st. F/F. M2. $20.00

ALEXANDER, Karl. *Time After Time.* 1979. Delacorte. 1st. inscr. NF/dj. M21. $75.00

ALEXANDER, Lloyd. *Castle of Llyr.* 1966. HRW. 1st. 8vo. 201p. bl cloth. VG. D1. $45.00

ALEXANDER, Lloyd. *Coll & His White Pig.* 1965. HRW. 1st. sq 8vo. unp. gray brd. G/G. T5. $35.00

ALEXANDER, Lloyd. *House Gobbaleen.* 1995. Dutton. 1st. ils Diane Goode. thin 4to. F/dj. T10. $75.00

ALEXANDER, Lloyd. *Marvelous Misadventures of Sebastian.* 1970. Dutton. 1st. VG+/VG. P2. $45.00

ALEXANDER, Lloyd. *Marvelous Misadventures of Sebastian.* 1970. Dutton. 1st. 8vo. 204p. VG+. T5. $35.00

ALEXANDRE E SILVA, Elias. *Relacao, ou Noticia Particular da Infeliz Viagem...* 1778. Lisbon. Regia Officina Typografica. 1st. recent morocco. F. R15. $1,500.00

ALEXIE, Sherman. *First Indian on the Moon.* 1993. Hanging Loose. 1/500. F/sans. A24. $125.00

ALEXIE, Sherman. *Lone Ranger & Tonto Fistfight in Heaven.* 1993. Atlantic Monthly. 1st. rem mk. VG/VG. L1. $45.00

ALEXIE, Sherman. *Lone Ranger & Tonto Fistfight in Heaven.* 1993. Atlantic Monthly. 1st. sgn. F/F. B3. $60.00

ALFORD, John A. *Piers Plowman, a Glossary of Legal Diction.* 1988. Cambridge. VG/dj. M11. $45.00

ALGEO, Sara M. *Story of a Sub-Pioneer.* 1925. Providence. Sonow/Farnham. 1/1000. inscr. 359p. VG+. A25. $95.00

ALGER, Horatio. *In a New World; or, Among the Gold Fields of Australia.* nd (1893). rpt. 12mo. VG+. C8. $15.00

ALGER, Horatio. *Ragged Dick; or, Street Life in New York With Book-Blacks.* (1868). Boston. Loring. 1st/1st issue. 12mo. 296p. purple cloth. M1. $3,750.00

ALGREN, Nelson. *Chicago: City on the Make.* 1951. Doubleday. 1st. sgn. F/NF. B2. $100.00

ALGREN, Nelson. *Galena, Illinois.* 1937. 1st. VG/wrp. A15. $50.00

ALGREN, Nelson. *Notes From a Sea Diary: Hemingway All the Way.* 1965. Putnam. 1st. NF/worn clip. M25. $25.00

ALGREN, Nelson. *Walk on the Wild Side.* 1956. FSC. 1st. F/NF. D10. $65.00

ALI, Muhammad. *Greatest: My Own Story.* 1975. Random. 1st. VG/G+. P8. $25.00

ALI, Salim. *Book of Indian Birds.* 1941. Bombay. 192 pl. 395p. VG. S15. $27.00

ALIBERT & BALOUET. *Extinct Species of the World.* 1990. Barron's NY. 192p. cloth. as new/dj. D8. $30.00

ALICE & JERRY READER. *Five-And-A-Half Club.* 1957. Row Peterson. Parallel 3rd Reader. VG+. M5. $25.00

ALICE & JERRY READER. *Friendly Village.* 1957. Row Peterson. 2nd Reader. M5. $30.00

ALICE & JERRY READER. *New Friendly Village.* 1950. Row Peterson. 2nd Reader. VG. M5. $30.00

ALICE & JERRY READER. *New High on a Hill.* 1943. Row Peterson. 4th Pre-Primer. M5. $22.00

ALICIATUS, Andreas. *Omnia Emblemata Cum Commentariis+Notae per Claudius Minois.* 1589 (1588). Paris. 213 woodcut border emblems+14 botanical. calf. VG. B14. $1,250.00

ALIGHERI, Dante. *New Life.* ca 1915. Harrap. 1st Am. ils Evelyn Paul. trans Rosetti. NF. M19. $85.00

ALIKI. *King's Day, Louis XIV of France.* 1989. NY. Crowell. 1st. 4to. unp. bl brd. NF/dj. T5. $32.00

ALLAN, James G. *Eagle Flies Free.* 1983. 1/5000. inscr. F/F. W2. $125.00

ALLAN, John B.; see Westlake, Donald E.

ALLARD, Noel. *Speed, the Biography of Charles W Holman.* 1976. NM. 1st. inscr. ils/map. VG+/dj. B18. $45.00

ALLARDICE & TRAPNELL. *Atomic Energy Commission.* 1974. NY. Praeger. 1st. Tapnell's copy. VG/dj. K3. $30.00

ALLARDYCE, Paula. *Adam's Rib.* 1963. Hodder Stoughton. 1st. F/F. B35. $30.00

ALLBEURY, Ted. *Girl From Addis.* 1984. Granada. 1st. F/F. P3. $30.00

ALLBEURY, Ted. *Other Side of Silence.* 1981. London. Granada. 1st. VG/dj. M25. $25.00

ALLBEURY, Ted. *Snowball.* 1974. Lippincott. 1st. VG/G. P3. $20.00

ALLBROOK, P. *Tasmanian Odonata.* 1979. Hobart. TAsmania. ils/figures/distribution maps. F/wrp. M12. $15.00

ALLEMAN & WALTON. *Champagne Campaign: Airborne Invasion of Southern France...* 1973. NY. ils. 298p. VG/VG. S16. $35.00

ALLEN, Betsy. *Connie Blair: Brown Satchel Mystery (#9).* 1954. Grosset Dunlap. lists to Ruby Queens. VG/dj. M20. $40.00

ALLEN, Betsy. *Connie Blair: Clue in Blue (#1).* nd. Grosset Dunlap. brn cloth. F/NF. N1. $15.00

ALLEN, Betsy. *Connie Blair: Gray Menace.* Grosset Dunlap. 1st. F/fair. N1. $17.50

ALLEN, Betsy. *Connie Blair: Green Island Mystery (#5).* 1949. Grosset Dunlap. VG/dj. M20. $25.00

ALLEN, Betsy. *Connie Blair: Mystery of the Ruby Queens (#12).* 1958. Grosset Dunlap. lists to this title. VG/dj. M20. $85.00

ALLEN, Betsy. *Connie Blair: Riddle in Red (#2).* nd. Grosset Dunlap. F/dj. N1. $15.00

ALLEN, Betsy. *Connie Blair: Secret of Black Cat Gulch (#4).* nd. Grosset Dunlap. F/dj. N1. $15.00

ALLEN, Betsy. *Connie Blair: Silver Secret (#11).* 1956. Grosset Dunlap. lists to Ruby Queens. VG/mc copy dj. M20. $65.00

ALLEN, Betsy. *Connie Blair: Yellow Warning (#7).* 1951. Grosset Dunlap. lists to Silver Secret. VG/dj. M20. $40.00

ALLEN, Carleton Kemp. *Law in the Making. Sixth Edition.* 1958. Oxford. 645p. prt wrp. M11. $20.00

ALLEN, Carroll. *Local & Regional Anesthesia.* 1915. Phil. 1st/2nd prt. 625p. A13. $50.00

ALLEN, Catherine Ward. *Chariot of the Sun.* 1976. Denver. Sage Books. sgn. hc. dj. A19. $30.00

ALLEN, Douglas. *NC Wyeth.* 1972. Crown. 4to. 335p. VG+/dj. P2. $85.00

ALLEN, Edward. *Dancing Tails & Other Fishy Jingles.* 1951. Seattle, WA. Mitchell. 1/1000. sgn. ils Dorman Smith. VG. D4. $35.00

ALLEN, Elizabeth. *Silent Harp; or, Fugitive Poems.* 1832. Burlington, NJ. Edward Smith. 1st. 12mo. 119p. M1. $125.00

ALLEN, Everett S. *Arctic Odyssey: Life of Admiral Donald B MacMillan.* 1963. NY. Dodd Mead. 4th. inscr Donald MacMillan. w/ephemera. P4. $125.00

ALLEN, G.M. *Bats.* 1962. Dover. 12mo. 368p. B1. $18.50

ALLEN, G.R. *Butterfly & Angelfishes of the World. Vol 2.* 1985. Mentor, OH. 3rd. 352p. F/F. B1. $35.00

ALLEN, G.R. *Pacific Marine Fishes, Book 9: Fishes of Western Australia.* 1985. Neptune City. phtos. pict brd. F. M12. $30.00

ALLEN, Gardner. *Our Navy & the Barbary Corsairs.* 1905. Houghton Mifflin. ils. 354p. T7. $70.00

ALLEN, George. *George Allen's New Handbook of Football Drills.* 1974. Parker. later prt. ils. VG/G. P8. $15.00

ALLEN, H. Warner. *Claret.* 1924. Fisher Unwin. 44p. VG. B10. $25.00

ALLEN, Harris Stearns. *Trail of Beauty.* 1940. SF. Allen. 1/100. sgn. w/orig watercolor by Wm Gaskin. Wm Wheeler brd. F. B24. $1,000.00

ALLEN, Helena G. *Sanford Ballard Dole, Hawaii's Only President 1844-1922.* 1988. Clark. 1st. F/VG. J2. $50.00

ALLEN, Hervey. *Anthony Adverse.* 1935. Farrar Rhinehart. NF/VG. M19. $45.00

ALLEN, Hervey. *Israfel: Life & Times of Edgar Allen Poe.* 1926. Doran. 1st. 2 vol. 8vo. gilt maroon cloth. F. T10. $75.00

ALLEN, Hugh. *House of Goodyear.* 1936. Akron. 2nd. 416p. dj. A17. $20.00

ALLEN, Ida Bailey. *Modern Method of Preparing Delightful Foods.* 1920s. NY. Corn Products Refining Co. A16/H1. $10.00

ALLEN, Ida Bailey. *Round the World Cook Book.* 1934. 2nd. G+/G-. E6. $20.00

ALLEN, James Lane. *Kentucky Cardinal.* 1899. Harper. ils. 16mo. 138p. gilt bdg. G. H1. $12.00

ALLEN, John. *Biosphere 2: Human Experiment.* 1991. Viking. 1st. ils/index. 186p. B19. $40.00

ALLEN, L. David. *Science Fiction: An Introduction.* 1973. Englewood Cliffs. 1st. F/wrp. M2. $12.00

ALLEN, Lewis F. *Rural Architecture, Farm Houses, Cottages & Out Buildings.* 1882. Orange Judd. 378p. cloth. A10. $75.00

ALLEN, Lucy G. *Book of Hors D'Oeuvres.* 1941. NY. Bramhall. VG/dj. A16. $9.00

ALLEN, Lucy. *Book of Hors D'oeuvres.* 1925. 1st. photos. VG/dj. E6. $25.00

ALLEN, Maury. *Voices of Sport.* 1971. Grosset Dunlap. 1st. VG+/dj. P8. $15.00

ALLEN, Paula Gunn. *Coyote's Daylight Trip.* 1978. Albuquerque. La Confluencia. 1st. author's 2nd book. F/wrp. L3. $225.00

ALLEN, Raymond Macdonald. *Why the Chimes Rang & Other Stories.* 1945. Bobbs Merrill. 1st thus. ils Evelyn Copelman. VG+/G. M5. $25.00

ALLEN, Robert Porter. *Whooping Crane.* 1952. NY. Nat Audubon Soc. ils/fld maps. 246p. NF/pict wrp. M12. $45.00

ALLEN, Robert Porter. *Wooping Crane.* 1952. Nat Audubon Soc. Research Report 3. 246p. xl. S15. $12.00

ALLEN, Robert Thomas. *Grass Is Never Greener.* 1956. McClelland Stewart. 1st. VG/dj. P3. $25.00

ALLEN, Robert. *Lucky Forward: History of Patton's Third US Army.* 1947. NY. maps/photos/index. 424p. VG/torn. S16. $50.00

ALLEN, Samuel. *Poems From Africa.* 1973. Crowell. 1st. ils Romare Bearden. F/F. D4. $30.00

ALLEN, Shirley W. *Introduction to American Forestry.* 1988. McGraw Hill. 1st/3rd prt. Am Forestry series. 122 figures. VG. B26. $25.00

ALLEN, W.E.D. *Russian Embassies to the Georgian Kings (1589-1605).* 1970. Cambridge. 2 vol. ils/maps. F/dj. M4. $35.00

ALLEN, Warner. *Uncounted Hour.* 1936. London. Constable. 1st. VG. P3. $30.00

ALLEN, Woody. *Don't Drink the Water.* 1967. Random. 1st hc/author's 1st book. F/dj. Q1. $300.00

ALLEN, Woody. *Play It Again, Sam.* 1969. Random. 1st. VG/G. P3. $30.00

ALLEN, Woody. *Without Feathers.* 1975. Random. 1st. author's 2nd book. NF/NF. H11. $45.00

ALLEN & ALLEN. *NC Wyeth, the Collected Paintings, Ils & Murals.* 1972. NY. Crown. 4to. 335p. F/dj. B24. $85.00

ALLENDE, Isabel. *Eva Luna.* 1988. Knopf. 1st. author's 3rd book. F/F. B3. $35.00

ALLENDE, Isabel. *Eva Luna.* 1988. Knopf. 1st. inscr. F/F. A23. $46.00

ALLENDE, Isabel. *Eva Luna.* 1989. Hamish Hamilton. 1st. F/F. B3. $30.00

ALLENDE, Isabel. *House of Spirits.* 1985. Knopf. 1st. sgn. author's 1st novel. F/F. B3. $125.00

ALLENDE, Isabel. *House of Spirits.* 1985. NY. Knopf. 1st Am. author's 1st book. F/F. L3. $75.00

ALLENDE, Isabel. *Infinite Plan.* 1991. Harper Collins. 1st. sgn. F/F. A23. $40.00

ALLENDE, Isabel. *Of Love & Shadows.* 1987. Knopf. 1st Am. sgn. F/F. R14. $90.00

ALLENDE, Isabel. *Of Love & Shadows.* 1987. Knopf. 1st. F/F. M19. $25.00

ALLENDE, Isabel. *Paula.* 1994. Harper Collins. 1st. sgn. F/F. A23. $40.00

ALLENDE, Isabel. *Stories of Eva Luna.* 1991. Atheneum. 1st. sgn. F/F. A23. $40.00

ALLINGHAM, Margery. *Cargo of Eagles.* 1968. Morrow. 1st. VG/VG. P3. $22.00

ALLINGHAM, Margery. *China Governess.* 1962. Doubleday. 1st. VG/VG. P3. $30.00

ALLINGHAM, Margery. *Estate of the Beckoning Lady.* 1955. Doubleday. 1st. VG/VG. P3. $40.00

ALLINGHAM, Margery. *More Work for the Undertaker.* 1948. London. Heinemann. 1st. F/NF. M15. $100.00

ALLINGHAM, William. *Dirty Old Man.* 1965. Prentice Hall. 1st. ils Erik Blegvad. 30p. F/NF. D4. $30.00

ALLINSON, William J. *Memorials of Rebecca Jones.* 1849. Phil. Longstreth. 2nd. 372p. xl. V3. $20.00

ALLISON, Clyde; see Knowles, William.

ALLISON, Dorothy. *Bastard Out of Carolina.* 1992. Dutton. 1st. author's 1st novel. F/F. B4. $150.00

ALLISON, Dorothy. *Bastard Out of Carolina.* 1992. Dutton. 1st. NF/NF. B2. $100.00

ALLISON, Sam. *Wells Fargo & Danger Station.* 1958. Whitman. TVTI. NF. P3. $20.00

ALLISON. *Horoscope Cook Book.* 1971. VG/VG. E6. $10.00

ALLMENDINGER, Blake. *Cowboy: Representations of Labor in an American Culture.* 1992. Oxford. 1st. ils/notes/index. M/dj. A18. $32.50

ALLRED & DYKES. *Flat Top Ranch, the Story of a Grassland Venture.* 1957. Norman, OK. 1st. 232p. VG/dj. J2. $95.00

ALLSTON, Washington. *Outlines & Sketches.* 1850. Boston. 1st. obl folio. cloth. VG. M1. $500.00

ALMON, John. *Biographical, Literary & Political Anecotes of Several...* 1797. London. Longman Seeley. 2 vol. 1st. tall 8vo. orig tree calf/rebacked. H13. $395.00

ALMOND, Linda Stevens. *When Peter Rabbit Went A-Fishing.* 1923. Altemus Wee Book. apparent 1st. 16mo. ils MC Hoopes. VG/worn. M5. $85.00

ALMQUIST & HEIZER. *Other Californians: Prejudice & Discrimination Under Spain.* 1971. Berkeley. 1st. ils. gilt teal cloth. F. R3. $35.00

ALONSO, Harriet Hyman. *Women's Peace Union & the Outlawry of War 1921-42.* 1989. TN U. 1st. F/F. V4. $15.00

ALPHABET. *ABC Nursery Rhyme & Fairy Tale Puzzle Picture Book.* ca 1950. London. Juvenile Productions Ltd. obl 4to. stiff wrp. as new. R5. $100.00

ALPHABET. *ABC Nursery Rhymes & Fairy Tales.* ca 1950. England. BB Ltd. 4to. pict covers/stapled bdg. as new. R5. $100.00

ALPHABET. *ABC of Nursery Rhymes.* ca 1950. England. BB Ltd. 4to. as new. R5. $125.00

ALPHABET. *ABC of Nursery Rhymes.* nd. McLaughlin. lg 4to. 12p text. stiff pict soft cover. VG+. M5. $135.00

ALPHABET. *Alphabet de ma Petite Fille.* ca 1900. Paris. Paul Bernadin Libraire. 6p chromos on linen-like paper. D1. $85.00

ALPHABET. *Alphabet of Old Friends.* ca 1900. John Lane. 4to. 6 mc pl by Crane. VG. M5. $95.00

ALPHABET. *Alphabetum Herbraicum.* 1771. Rome. Congregation Prapaganda of Faith. 8vo. stitched. R12. $500.00

ALPHABET. *Animal & Train ABC.* ca 1908. London. Dean. gilt gr cloth. NF. D1. $250.00

ALPHABET. *Circus & Menagerie ABC.* 1897. McLoughlin. 4to. mc stiff paper wrp/resewn spine. R5. $300.00

ALPHABET. *Comic Alphabet.* 1836. London. Chas Tilt. ils Cruikshank. yel paper bdg/rebacked orig spine. D1. $320.00

ALPHABET. *Doings of the Alphabet.* ca 1890. McLoughlin. sq 4to. 20p. VG/wrp. T10. $65.00

ALPHABET. *Grandmama Easy's Stories About the Alphabet.* nd. Gray Sprague & Co. 8vo. 8p. sc. M5. $110.00

ALPHABET. *Happy Bears ABC.* ca 1920. NY. Chas Graham. 25p. mc pict brd. R5. $350.00

ALPHABET. *Kindergarten First Book, ABC of Objects for Home & School.* nd. McLoughlin. lg 4to. 12p text. VG. M5. $75.00

ALPHABET. *Our Navy ABC.* 1898. Raphael Tuck. tall narrow 4to. mc stiff paper wrp. R5. $125.00

ALPHABET. *Picture Show of ABC.* ca 1950. London. Juvenile Productions Ltd. stiff wrp. R5. $85.00

ALPHABET. *Pumpkin Pie ABC Linen Book.* 1900. McLoughlin. 4to. mc paper wrp. R5. $110.00

ALPHABET. *Snooty's ABC & Counting Book.* ca 1950. England. Ariel Prod Ltd. 4to. 20p. pict brd. R5. $35.00

ALPHABET. *Work & Play ABC.* 1920. Raphael Tuck. 4to. mc paper wrp. R5. $60.00

ALSOP, Guielma F. *My Chinese Days.* 1918. Little Brn. 1st. photos. VG. A25. $22.00

ALSOP, Richard. *Echo.* (1807). NY. Porcupine. 1st. 8vo. 8 engraved pl. full contemporary tree calf. M1. $375.00

ALSTHELER, Joseph A. *Forest of Swords.* 1915. Appleton. 11th. cloth/pict label. 316p. VG. M20. $35.00

ALSTHELER, Joseph A. *Rock of Chickamauga.* 1915. Appleton. 1st. 328p. cloth/pict label. VG. M20. $35.00

ALTER, Lisa. *Original Sins.* 1981. Knopf 1st. VG/NF. R14. $25.00

ALTIERI, James. *Spearheaders: Personal History of Darby's Rangers.* 1960. Indianapolis. 1st. photos. 318p. VG. S16. $35.00

ALTMAN, Jack. *Born To Raise Hell.* 1967. Grove. 1st. VG/VG. P3. $15.00

ALTMAN, Stuart A. *Japanese Monkeys.* 1965. private prt. 151p. VG. S15. $20.00

ALTON, John. *Painting With Light.* 1949. Macmillan. photos. 192p. cloth. dj. D11. $150.00

ALVAREZ, A. *Feeding the Rat: Profile of a Climber.* 1988. NY. Atlantic Monthly. 1st. rem mk. F/F. B4. $45.00

ALVAREZ, Julia. *How the Garcia Girls Lost Their Accent.* 1991. Algonquin. ARC. F/pict wrp. w/promo material. B3. $75.00

ALVAREZ, Julia. *In the Time of the Butterflies.* 1994. Algonquin. 1st. sgn. F/F. A23. $46.00

ALVAREZ, Luis W. *Alvarez: Adventures of a Physicist.* 1987. NY. Basic. 1st. 8vo. 282p. VG/dj. K3. $18.00

ALVAREZ, Luis W. *Discovering Alvarez.* 1987. Chicago. 1st. 4to. 272p. F/dj. K3. $30.00

ALVAREZ CORREA, Luis. *Execucion de Politicas, y Brevedad de Despachos...* 1629. Madrid. En la Imprenta del Reyno. 1st. contemporary vellum. R15. $1,800.00

ALVERSON, Charles. *Fighting Back.* 1973. Bobbs Merrill. 1st. VG/VG. P3. $20.00

ALVERY, Al. *Yankee Flier in Italy (#12).* 1944. Grosset Dunlap. 212p. VG/dj. M20. $25.00

ALVERY, Al. *Yankee Flier in Normandy (#14).* 1945. Grosset Dunlap. lists to Rescue Mission. 209p. cloth. VG/dj. M20. $25.00

ALVERY, Al. *Yankee Flier in North Africa (#11).* 1943. Grosset Dunlap. 214p. VG/dj. M20. $20.00

ALVERY, Al. *Yankee Flier in the Far East (#9).* 1942. Grosset Dunlap. 216p. VG/dj. M20. $22.00

ALVERY, Al. *Yankee Flier Over Berlin (#13).* 1944. Grosset Dunlap. 212p. VG/dj. M20. $25.00

ALVERY, Al. *Yankee Flier With the RAF (#8).* 1941. Grosset Dunlap. 214p. VG/dj. M20. $22.00

ALVIA DE CASTRO, Fernando. *Panegirico Genealogico y Moral des Excelent...* 1628. Lisbon. Pedro Craesbeeck. 1st/only. woodcut Duque de Barcelos. contemporary bdg. R15. $4,000.00

AMADO, Jorge. *Tereza Batista: Home From the Wars.* 1975. Knopf. 1st Am. rem mk. NF/VG. B4. $65.00

AMARAL, A. *Mustang: Life & Legends of Nevada's Wild Horses.* 1977. Reno. NV U. sgn pres. cloth. NF/F. M12. $25.00

AMARIA, BRUNEAU & LAPP. *Arctic Systems.* 1977. NY. 956p. dj. A17. $50.00

AMBLER, C.H. *Transportation in the Ohio Valley.* 1932. 1st. NF. A15. $150.00

AMBLER, Eric. *Care of Time.* 1981. FSG. 1st. VG/VG. P3. $15.00

AMBLER, Eric. *Cause for Alarm.* 1940. Knopf. 1st. VG. P3. $15.00

AMBLER, Eric. *Dark Frontier.* 1990. Mysterious. 1st Am. F/F. M15. $35.00

AMBLER, Eric. *Dirty Story.* 1967. Bodley Head. 1st. F/NF. M19. $45.00

AMBLER, Eric. *Dirty Story.* 1967. Bodley Head. 1st. VG/G. P3. $20.00

AMBLER, Eric. *Doctor Frigo.* 1974. Atheneum. 1st. VG/VG. P3. $20.00

AMBLER, Eric. *Intercom Conspiracy.* 1969. Atheneum. 1st. VG/VG. P3. $25.00

AMBLER, Eric. *Kind of Anger.* 1964. Bodley Head. 1st. VG/G. P3. $30.00

AMBLER, Eric. *Light of Day.* 1963. Knopf. 1st Am. F/VG. N4. $25.00

AMBROSE, Stephen E. *Crazy Horse & Custer.* 1975. Doubleday. 1st. 486p. VG/dj. J2. $110.00

AMBROSINI & WILLIS. *Secret Archives of the Vatican.* 1969. Little Brn. 1st. 366p. F/dj. H1. $25.00

AMEND, Ottlie. *Jolly Jungle Jingles.* 1929. Volland. 1st. obl 4to. VG-. P2. $55.00

AMERICAN CULINARY SOCIETY. *Cooking & Preserving Vegetables Cookbook.* 1974. NY. Crescent. VG. A16. $7.00

AMERICAN CULINARY SOCIETY. *Desserts for All Occasions.* 1974. NY. Crescent. VG. A16. $7.00

AMERICAN DIABETES ASSOCIATION. *Family Bookbook.* 1980. NY. Prentice Hall. G/dj. A16. $9.50

AMERICAN FRIENDS OF FRANCE. *Specialities de la Maison.* 1949. NY. Am Friends of France. revised. VG/dj. A16. $17.50

AMERICAN HEART ASSOCIATION. *Cooking Without Your Salt Shaker.* 1978. 145p. spbg. VG. B10. $10.00

AMERICAN HERITAGE EDITORS. *American Heritage Cookbook & Ils Hist Am Eating & Drinking.* 1964. S&S. 2 vol. B10. $25.00

AMERICAN SODA FOUNTAIN CO. *American Soda Books of Receipts & Suggestions Cookbook.* nd. fair. A16. $50.00

AMERINE & OUGH. *Methods for Analysis of Musts & Wines.* 1980. NY. ils. 341p. B26. $20.00

AMES, Charles Edgar. *Pioneering the Union Pacific, a Reappraisal of Builders...* 1969. Appleton Century Crofts. 1st. 591p. VG/VG. J2. $70.00

AMES, Clyde; see Knowles, William.

AMES, Jennifer. *Flight Into Fear.* 1954. Collins. 1st. VG/VG. P3. $20.00

AMES, Joseph B. *Bladed Barrier.* 1929. Century. 1st. VG. M2. $50.00

AMES, Mary Clemmer. *Memorial of Alice & Phoebe Cary With Some Later Poems.* 1873. NY. Hurd Houghton. 1st. ils. VG. A25. $35.00

AMES, Mary Ellis. *Balanced Recipes.* 1933. MN. Pillsbury Flour Mills ed. A16. $75.00

AMIS, Kingsley. *Alternation.* 1977. Viking. 1st. F/F. M2. $20.00

AMIS, Kingsley. *Eygptologists.* 1966. Random. 1st. VG/G. P3. $23.00

AMIS, Kingsley. *Girl, 20.* 1971. Jonathan Cape. 1st. VG/VG. P3. $20.00

AMIS, Kingsley. *Green Man.* 1970. HBW. 1st. VG/VG. P3. $30.00

AMIS, Kingsley. *I Like It Here.* 1958. Harcourt Brace. 1st Am. 208p. F/dj. H1. $30.00

AMIS, Kingsley. *Memoirs.* 1991. Hutchinson. 1st. F/F. P3. $30.00

AMIS, Kingsley. *On Drink.* 1973. HBJ. 1st Am. F/clip. B4. $65.00

AMIS, Kingsley. *Riverside Villas Murder.* 1973. HBJ. 1st. VG/VG. P3. $20.00

AMIS, Kingsley. *Russian Hide & Seek.* 1980. Hutchinson. 1st. VG/VG. P3. $20.00

AMIS, Martin. *Dead Babies.* 1975. Knopf. 1st. NF/NF. P3. $75.00

AMIS, Martin. *Dead Babies.* 1976. Knopf. ARC/1st. sgn. author's 2nd novel. RS. F/NF. D10. $135.00

AMIS, Martin. *Einstein's Monsters.* 1987. Harmony. 1st. F/F. M23. $40.00

AMIS, Martin. *Information.* 1995. Harmony. 1st. sgn. F/F. A23. $48.00

AMIS, Martin. *London Fields.* 1989. Harmony. 1st. F/F. B35. $20.00

AMIS, Martin. *Moronic Inferno & Other Visits to America.* 1987. Viking. 1st. sgn. F/F. D10. $60.00

AMIS, Martin. *Rachel Papers.* 1974. Knopf. 1st Am. sgn. author's 1st book. F/NF. D10. $185.00

AMIS, Martin. *Success.* 1987. Harmony. 1st Am. F/F. R14. $25.00

AMIS, Martin. *Success.* 1987. Harmony. 1st Am. sgn. F/dj. B24. $50.00

AMIS, Martin. *Time's Arrow.* 1991. Harmony. 1st. F/F. B35. $18.00

AMORY, Cleveland. *Cat & the Curmudgeon.* 1990. Little Brn. 1st. sgn. F/F. A23. $35.00

AMORY, Robert. *Treatise on Electrolysis & Its Applications...* 1886. NY. 1st. woodcuts. 307p. A13. $150.00

AMRAM, David. *Makers of Hebrew Books in Italy.* 1963. london. ils/index. 417p. F/F. W3. $42.00

AMSDEN, Charles. *Navaho Weaving, Its Technic & Its History.* 1974. Rio Grande. 5th. fld mc pl/123 b&w pl. 261p. VG. J2. $85.00

AMUNDSEN, Roald. *Gjennem Luften Til 88 (degrees) Nord.* 1925. Oslo. Gyldendal Norsk. 8vo. bl cloth/leather spine. P4. $135.00

AMUNDSEN, Roald. *Nordvest-Passagen. Beretning Om Gjoa-Ekspeditionen 1903-07.* 1907. Kristiana. Aschehoug. photos/3 maps. 511p. gilt red cloth. P4. $285.00

AMUNDSEN, Roald. *Plan for en Polarfaerd 1910-1917; Foredrag Tirsdad...* 1908-09. Aarbok. VG/plain wrp. P4. $35.00

AN ANGLER. *Salmonia: Of Days of Fly Fishing...Account of Habits...* 1970. Freshet. facsimile 1828 ed. 16mo. M/case. A17. $22.50

ANATOLE, Ray; see Weiss, Joe.

ANAYA, Rudolfo A. *Silence of the Llano.* 1982. Berkeley. Tonatiuh-Quinto Sol. 1st. inscr. F/tan wrp. M25. $60.00

ANDERS, Curt. *Fighting Confederates.* 1968. NY. Putnam. 1st. 315p. NF/dj. M8. $35.00

ANDERS, Leslie. *Eighteenth Missouri.* 1968. IN. 1st ed. 404p. F/F. A17. $30.00

ANDERS, Nedda Casson. *Casserole Specialties.* 1965. Gramercy. VG/dj. A16. $10.00

ANDERSEN, Allen C. *Beagle As an Experimental Dog.* 1970. IA. 1st ed. 616p. A17. $30.00

ANDERSEN, Hans Christian. *Ardizzone's Hans Andersen.* 1978. London. Deutsch. 1st. 191p. NF/F. P2. $55.00

ANDERSEN, Hans Christian. *Fairy Tales.* 1924. Doran. 1st Am. ils Kay Nielsen/12 tipped-in pl. 280p. VG. D1. $650.00

ANDERSEN, Hans Christian. *Fairy Tales.* 1945. Oxford. 1st thus. ils Tasha Tudor. 273p. VG-/G+. P2. $225.00

ANDERSEN, Hans Christian. *Fairy Tales.* 1961. Oxford. 1st thus. ils Ernest Shepard. 327p. NF/VG. P2. $45.00

ANDERSEN, Hans Christian. *Hans Andersen's Fairy Tales.* 1921. London. Humphrey Milford. 1st. ils MR Cramer. top edge tinted. gr cloth. R5. $400.00

ANDERSEN, Hans Christian. *Hans Andersen's Fairy Tales.* 1927. Hodder Stoughton. ils HW Robinson. 4to. gilt red cloth. red dj. R5. $275.00

ANDERSEN, Hans Christian. *Little Mermaid.* 1935. Holiday House. 1st thus. ils Pamela Bianco. 8vo. 53p. VG/dj. D1. $50.00

ANDERSEN, Hans Christian. *Little Mermaid.* 1939. Macmillan. 1st thus. ils Dorothy Lathrop. gilt bl cloth. VG/dj. D1. $295.00

ANDERSEN, Hans Christian. *Little Mermaid.* 1939. Macmillan. 1st. ils Dorothy Lathrop. 4to. gilt gr cloth. dj. R5. $250.00

ANDERSEN, Hans Christian. *Snow Queen.* 1972. Scribner. ils/sgn Marcia Brown. F/F. C8. $60.00

ANDERSEN, Hans Christian. *Snow Queen.* 1972. Scribner. 95p. cloth. VG/dj. M20. $25.00

ANDERSEN, Hans Christian. *Thumbelina.* 1979. Dial. 1st. ils Susan Jeffers. bl brd. F/VG. D1. $45.00

ANDERSON, Alice Sloane. *Our Garden Heritage.* 1961. NY. ils Redoute/Edwards/Catesby/Thornton. VG/dj. B26. $22.00

ANDERSON, Anne. *Anne Anderson Fairy-Tale Book.* 1923. Thomas Nelson. 1st. lg 4to. red cloth/mc label. R5. $335.00

ANDERSON, Anne. *Children's Wonder Book.* nd (1933). Collins. 4to. ils Harry Rountree/Anne Anderson. NF. M5. $75.00

ANDERSON, Anne. *Dandy-Andy Book.* ca 1912. Thomas Nelson. 12 full-p mc pl. orange lettered wheat cloth. R5. $200.00

ANDERSON, Anne. *Maisie-Daisie Book.* ca 1912. London. Nelson. 12 full-p pl. maroon lettered wheat cloth. R5. $200.00

ANDERSON, Anne. *Old English Nursery Songs.* ca 1920. London. Harrap. music arranged by Horace Mansion. tan brd/label. dj. R5. $150.00

ANDERSON, Bertha C. *Tinker's Tom & the Witches.* 1954. Little Brn. Weekly Reader BC. 147p. V3. $7.50

ANDERSON, C.W. *Big Red.* 1943. 1st. VG/VG. S13. $55.00

ANDERSON, C.W. *Billy & Blaze.* 1936. Macmillan. 1st. VG/G. O3. $45.00

ANDERSON, C.W. *Blaze & the Forest Fire.* 1938. Macmillan. 1st. sm 4to. NF/VG-. P2. $55.00

ANDERSON, C.W. *Blaze & Thunderbolt.* 1955. Macmillan. stated 1st. 4to. VG/worn. M5. $60.00

ANDERSON, C.W. *CW Anderson's Complete Book of Horses & Horsemanship...* 1963. Macmillan. 1st. VG. O3. $35.00

ANDERSON, C.W. *CW Anderson's Favorite Horse Stories.* 1967. Dutton. 1st. VG/G. O3. $30.00

ANDERSON, C.W. *Deep Through the Heart.* 1940. NY. Macmillan. 1st. obl 4to. VG/G. O3. $45.00

ANDERSON, C.W. *Salute.* 1940. Macmillan. 1st. 63p. VG/dj. M20. $32.00

ANDERSON, C.W. *Thoroughbreds.* 1942. Macmillan. 1st. sgn. VG/G. P2. $50.00

ANDERSON, C.W. *Tomorrow's Champion.* 1946. Macmillan. 1st. F/VG. P2. $50.00

ANDERSON, Carl. *How To Draw Cartoons Successfully.* Feb 1936. Greenberg. dj. A19. $20.00

ANDERSON, Charles B. *Bookselling in America & the World.* 1975. np. 1st. ils. VG/dj. K3. $15.00

ANDERSON, D.L. *Theory of the Earth.* 1989. Boston. Blackwell Scientific. 366p. wrp. B1. $26.50

ANDERSON, Dave. *Countdown to Super Bowl.* 1969. Random. 1st. ils. VG/dj. P8. $30.00

ANDERSON, Edgar. *Plants, Man & Life.* 1952. Boston. Little Brn. 1st ed. 245p. dj. A10. $22.00

ANDERSON, Edward F. *Peyote: The Divine Cactus.* 1996 (1980). Tucson. revised. ils/index. M. B26. $20.00

ANDERSON, Eugene N. *First Moroccan Crisis.* 1966. Hamden, CT. 8vo. 420p. xl. VG. W1. $12.00

ANDERSON, Florence. *Magic Whistle & Other Stories.* 1920. Dodd Mead. 1st. 4to. bl cloth/mc pl. VG. M5. $125.00

ANDERSON, Frank J. *Do Not Despair, by Frank J Anderson.* 1969. Spartanburg. 1/100. 54x47mm. red cloth. F/prt dj. B24. $75.00

ANDERSON, Frank J. *Outrageous Cat Tales.* 1988. Spartanburg. Kitemaug. 1st ltd. ils F Anderson. miniature. NF. D1. $35.00

ANDERSON, Frank. *Ils Treasury of Cultivated Flowers.* 1979. NY. Crown. 50 full-p pl. dj. A10. $40.00

ANDERSON, Janice. *Marilyn Monroe.* 1983. Royce. 1st. VG/VG. P3. $25.00

ANDERSON, Jervis. *This Was Harlem.* 1982. FSG. 1st. F/F. M25. $35.00

ANDERSON, Kenneth. *Black Panther of Sivanipalli.* 1961. McNally. 1st Am. 247p. VG/dj. M20. $20.00

ANDERSON, Kent. *Sympathy for the Devil.* 1987. Doubleday. ARC. NF/wrp. B4. $250.00

ANDERSON, Kent. *Sympathy for the Devil.* 1987. Doubleday. 1st. sgn. F/F. T2. $125.00

ANDERSON, Laurie. *Package.* 1971. Bobbs Merrill. 1st. author's 1st book. F/F. L3. $350.00

ANDERSON, Maxwell. *Anne of the Thousand Days.* 1948. Wm Sloane. 1st. lt bl cloth. F/NF black-lettered dj. w/TLS. M24. $275.00

ANDERSON, Maxwell. *Key Largo.* 1939. WA, DC. Anderson House. 1st. maroon lettered gray cloth. F/NF. M24. $250.00

ANDERSON, Nels. *Right To Work.* 1938. Modern Age. 1st. NF/wrp. B2. $35.00

ANDERSON, Poul. *Avatar.* 1978. Berkley Putnam. 1st. F/F. P3. $20.00

ANDERSON, Poul. *Boat of a Million Years.* 1989. Easton. 1st. sgn. leather. F/sans/swrp. P3. $75.00

ANDERSON, Poul. *Broken Sword.* 1954. Abelard. 1st. F/NF. w/sgn bookplate. M2. $175.00

ANDERSON, Poul. *Ensign Flandry.* 1966. Chilton. 1st. NF/dj. M2. $60.00

ANDERSON, Poul. *High Crusade.* 1982. London. Severn. 1st Eng hc. F/clip. T2. $20.00

ANDERSON, Poul. *Homeward & Beyond.* 1975. Doubleday. 1st. F/dj. M2. $18.00

ANDERSON, Poul. *Infinite Voyage.* 1969. Crowell Collier. 1st. VG/VG. P3. $25.00

ANDERSON, Poul. *Inheritors of the Earth.* 1974. Chilton. 1st. VG/VG. P3. $20.00

ANDERSON, Poul. *Is There Life on Other Worlds?* 1963. Crowell. 1st. F/dj. M2. $35.00

ANDERSON, Poul. *Merman's Children.* 1979. Berkley/Putnam. 1st. F/F. T2. $20.00

ANDERSON, Poul. *Orion Shall Rise.* 1983. Phantasia. 1st. 1/600. sgn/#d. F/dj/box. M2/P3. $45.00

ANDERSON, Poul. *Perish the Sword.* 1959. Macmillan. 1st. F/NF. M15. $100.00

ANDERSON, Poul. *Seven Conquests: An Adventure in Science Fiction.* 1969. Macmillan. 1st. sgn. F/F. T7. $45.00

ANDERSON, Poul. *Tauz Zero.* 1970. Doubleday. 1st. F/F. M2. $200.00

ANDERSON, Poul. *Three Hearts & Three Lions.* 1961. Doubleday. 1st. sgn. F/dj. M2. $450.00

ANDERSON, Poul. *Vault of the Ages.* 1952. Winston. 1st. F/frayed. M2. $125.00

ANDERSON, R.C. *Naval Wars in the Levant, 1559-1853.* 1952. Princeton. ils/19 plans/map. 618p. T7. $75.00

ANDERSON, Robert Bowie. *Supplement to Beale's Bibliography of Early English Law...* 1943. Cambridge. maroon cloth. M11. $50.00

ANDERSON, Sherwood. *Hellow Towns.* 1929. Horace Liveright. 1st. VG/poor. M23. $50.00

ANDERSON, Sherwood. *Modern Writer.* 1945. Lantern. 1/1000. 44p. G. M20. $45.00

ANDERSON, Sherwood. *New Testament.* 1927. Boni Liveright. 1st. F/G. M23. $100.00

ANDERSON, Sherwood. *No Swank.* 1934. Phil. Centaur. 1/50. sgn/#d. F. B4. $225.00

ANDERSON, Sherwood. *Perhaps Women.* 1931. Liveright. 1st. 144p. cloth. VG/dj. M20. $100.00

ANDERSON, Sherwood. *Poor White.* 1920. NY. Huebsch. 1st. G. M23. $40.00

ANDERSON, Sherwood. *Story Teller's Story.* 1924. Huebsch. 1st. VG/ragged. M20. $200.00

ANDERSON, Sherwood. *TAR: A Midwest Childhood.* 1926. NY. Boni Liveright. 1st. VG/fair. M23. $50.00

ANDERSON, Sherwood. *Winesburg, Ohio.* 1978. NY. LEC. 1/1600. ils/sgn BF Stahl. 152p. quarter leather. F/VG case. B18. $75.00

ANDERSON, Sherwood. *Winesburg, Ohio: A Group of Tales of Ohio Small Town Life.* 1921. NY. Huebsch. 3rd. F/dj. Q1. $250.00

ANDERSON, Terry A. *Den of Lions: Memoirs of Seven Years.* 1993. Crown. 1st. 8vo. 16 pl. 356p. G. W1. $10.00

ANDERSON, V.S. *King of the Roses.* 1983. Macmillan. 1st. F/NF. P3. $20.00

ANDERSON, W. *Strawberry: World Biography 1920-1966.* 1969. Scarecrow. 731p. cloth. F. M12. $45.00

ANDERSON, Wayne. *Cezanne's Portrait Drawings.* 1970. MIT. ils. G+. M17. $25.00

ANDERSON, William K. *Malarial Psychoses & Neuroses With Chapters Medico-Legal...* 1927. London. Humphrey Miltord/Oxford. 4to. prt panelled red cloth. G1. $50.00

ANDERSON & ANDERSON. *Two in the Kitchen.* 1974. WA. Acropolis Books. G/rpr dj. A16. $10.00

ANDERSON & DICKSON. *Earthman's Burdern.* 1947. Gnome. 1st. F/dj. M2. $100.00

ANDERSON & HEWLETT. *New World 1939-1946. Vol 1.* 1962. University Park, PA. ils. VG/dj. K3. $55.00

ANDERSON & KIMBALL. *Art of American Indian Cooking.* 1965. Doubleday. 1st. fwd Will Rogers Jr. ils. F/VG. L3. $65.00

ANDERSON & PACK. *Geology & Oil Resources of West Border of San Joaquin...* 1915. Dept Interior. 220p+rear pocket map. D11. $30.00

ANDERSON & WOOLWORTH. *Through Dakota Eyes: Narrative Accounts of MN Indian War...* 1988. MN Hist Soc. 316p. cloth. M. A17. $25.00

ANDRAL, Gabriel. *Medical Clinic; or, Reports of Medical Cases...* 1838. Paris. Haswell Barrington. 3 vol in 1. 1st Am. 6 lithos. VG. G1. $350.00

ANDREAS, Walter. *Fix und Fax.* ca 1930. Leipzig. ils Fritz Koch. G. M5. $30.00

ANDREW, Christopher. *KBG: The Inside Story.* 1990. Hodder Stoughton. 1st. VG. P3. $35.00

ANDREW, Felicia; see Grant, Charles L.

ANDREW, R.J. *Neural & Behavioural Plasticity: Use of Domestic Chick...* 1991. Oxford/NY/Tokyo. Oxford. 570p. bl cloth. G1. $65.00

ANDREWS, Allen. *Pig Plantagenet.* 1981. Viking. 1st. VG/G. P3. $15.00

ANDREWS, J.R.H. *Southern Ark. Zoological Discovery in New Zealand 1769-1900.* 1986. Honolulu. ils/index. 237p. F/dj. S15. $20.00

ANDREWS, Jane. *Seven Little Sisters Who Live on the Round Ball That Floats.* 1861. Ticknor Fields. 1st. author's 1st book. gilt brn pict cloth. M24. $275.00

ANDREWS, John Williams. *AD Twenty-One Hundred: A Narrative of Space.* 1969. Boston. Brandon. 8vo. 54p. VG/dj. K5. $20.00

ANDREWS, Lynn. *Star Woman.* 1986. Warner. F/dj. M2. $10.00

ANDREWS, R.C. *On the Trail of Ancient Man.* 1929. Garden City. ils. 375p. F/rpr. W3. $40.00

ANDREWS, R.C. *Quest of the Snow Leopard.* 1955. Viking. ils K Wiese. 190p. pict cloth. NF. M12. $22.50

ANDREWS, Stephen Pearl. *Discoveries in Chinese or Symbolism of Primitive Characters.* 1854. NY. 1st. 12mo. 137p. cloth. xl. VG. M1. $150.00

ANDREWS, T.S. *World Sporting Annual Record Book.* 1928. Milwaukee. 320p. stiff wrp. A17. $22.50

ANDREWS, V.C. *Fallen Hearts.* 1988. Poseidon. 1st. VG/VG. P3. $20.00

ANDREWS, V.C. *Flowers in the Attic.* 1979. S&S. 1st. G/F. P3. $25.00

ANDREWS, William Loring. *Iconography of the Battery & Castle Garden.* 1901. Scribner. 1/135. 20 pl/text ils. teg. F/patterned brd case. O7. $395.00

ANDREWS, William. *Old-Time Punishments.* nd. London. Tabard Pr Ltd. VG/dj. M11. $45.00

ANDREWS & DAVENPORT. *Guide to Manuscript Materials for History of US to 1783...* 1908. WA. Carnegie Inst. 500+p. F/stiff prt wrp. O7. $100.00

ANDREWS & SHAKER. *Furniture: Craftsmanship of the American Communal Sect.* nd. Dover. rpt. VG. M17. $25.00

ANDRIST, R.K. *George Washington: Biography in His Own Words.* 1972. NY. 2 vol. ils. padded leatherette. F/dj. M4. $35.00

ANDRY, Nicholas. *Orthopaedia.* 1961 (1743). Phil. 2 vol. leatherette. case. A13. $100.00

ANGEL, Andriana. *Tiger's Milk.* 1987. NY. Seaver. 1st Am. photos/map. 142p. dj. F3. $10.00

ANGEL, Joan. *Angel of the Navy: Story of a Wave.* 1943. Hastings. 3rd. ils Betty Utley St John. 200p. VG/dj. A25. $28.00

ANGELL, Roger. *Season Ticket: A Baseball Compaion.* 1988. Houghton Mifflin. 1st. NF/dj. M25. $35.00

ANGELL, Roger. *Summer Game.* 1972. Viking. 1st. NF/dj. M25. $60.00

ANGELOU, Maya. *All God's Children Need Traveling Shoes.* 1986. Franklin Lib. 1st/ltd. sgn. full leather. F. Q1. $150.00

ANGELOU, Maya. *All God's Children Need Traveling Shoes.* 1986. Random. 1st. F/NF. B3. $45.00

ANGELOU, Maya. *Heart of a Woman.* 1982. Random. 1st. rem mk. VG/VG. B2. $25.00

ANGELOU, Maya. *I Know Why the Caged Bird Sings.* 1969. Random. 1st. F/F. B4. $250.00

ANGELOU, Maya. *I Know Why the Caged Bird Sings.* 1969. Random. 1st. F/NF. A24. $225.00

ANGELOU, Maya. *Just Give Me a Cool Drink of Water 'Fore I Die.* 1971. Random. 1st. author's 2nd book. NF/NF. B3. $120.00

ANGELOU, Maya. *Life Doesn't Frighten Me.* 1993. NY. Tabori Chang. 1st. ils Basquiat. pict brd. F/F. C8. $40.00

ANGELOU, Maya. *My Painted House, My Friendly Chicken & Me.* 1994. Clarkson Potter. 1st. F/clip. Q1. $30.00

ANGELOU, Maya. *Now Sheba Sings the Song.* 1987. Dutton/Dial. 1st. juvenile. F/F. B2. $30.00

ANGELOU, Maya. *Wouldn't Take Nothing for My Journey Now.* 1993. Random. 1st. F/F. B3. $40.00

ANGLAND, Joan Walsh. *Spring Is a New Beginning.* 1963. Harcourt Brace. 1st. 16mo. F/NF. C8. $25.00

ANGLE, Paul M. *New Letters & Papers of Lincoln.* 1930. 387p. O8. $21.50

ANGLE, Paul M. *Pioneers, Narratives of Noah Harris Letts & TA Banning...* 1972. Lakeside Classic. ils/maps. 284p. F. M4. $18.00

ANGLE, Paul M. *Portrait of Abraham Lincoln in Letters by His Oldest Son.* 1968. Chicago Hist Soc. 92p. VG+/dj. M20. $20.00

ANGLO, Michael. *Nostalgia Spotlight on the Fifties.* 1977. Jupiter. hc. F/F. P3. $20.00

ANGLO. *Penny Dreadfuls & Other Victorian Horrors.* 1977. London. 1st. ils. 125p. F/F. A4. $35.00

ANGLUND, Joan Walsh. *Brave Cowboy.* 1959. Harcourt. 1st. sq sm 8vo. F/VG. M5. $65.00

ANGLUND, Joan Walsh. *Cowboy & His Friend.* 1961. Harcourt. 1st. sq sm 8vo. F/NF. M5. $60.00

ANGLUND, Joan Walsh. *Do You Love Someone?* 1971. Harcourt. 1st. F/VG. M5. $45.00

ANGLUND, Joan Walsh. *In a Pumpkin Shell: A Mother Goose ABC.* 1960. Harcourt. stated 1st. sm 4to. F/VG+. M5. $120.00

ANGLUND, Joan Walsh. *Morning Is a Little Child.* 1969. Harcourt. stated 1st. sm 4to. F/VG. M5. $85.00

ANGLUND, Joan Walsh. *Pocketful of Proverbs.* 1964. London. Collins. 1st Eng. 32p. VG/case. D4. $25.00

ANGLUND, Joan Walsh. *Year Is Round.* 1966. Harcourt. stated 1st. 12mo. F/VG. M5. $30.00

ANGUS, Jacob B. *Evolution of Jewish Thought From Biblical Times...* 1973 (1959). NY. Arno. 442p. VG. S3. $28.00

ANKIN, A. *Gold...the Yellow Devil.* 1983. NY. Internat'l. 1st Am. F/NF. B2. $25.00

ANNAN, David. *Catastrophe! The End of the Cinema.* nd. Bounty Books. 1st. VG/VG. P3. $10.00

ANNEQUIN, Guy. *Civilization of Maya.* (1978). Geneva. Editions Ferni. 1st Eng. 234p. pict cloth. F3. $20.00

ANNERINO, John. *Running Wild Through the Grand Canyon on the Ancient Path.* 1992. Tucson. Harbinger. 8vo. 204p. stiff wrp. F7. $12.00

ANNESLEY, Maude. *Shadow-Shapes.* 1911. London. 1st. G. M2. $25.00

ANNO, Mitsumasa. *Anno's Aesop.* 1989. Orchard. 1st Am. sm 4to. 63p. F/VG+. C14. $18.00

ANNO, Mitsumasa. *Anno's Alphabet.* 1975. Crowell. 1st Am. ils. unp. VG/clip. M20. $25.00

ANNO, Mitsumasa. *Anno's Alphabet: An Adventure in Imagination.* 1975. Crowell. 1st Am. sq 4to. F/dj. D10. $50.00

ANNO, Mitsumasa. *Anno's Britain.* 1982. Philomel. stated 1st. 4to. F/dj. M5. $25.00

ANNO & ANNO. *Anno's Mysterious Multiplying Jar.* 1983. NY. Philomel. 1st Am. sq 4to. prt paper brd. F/dj. T10. $50.00

ANOBILE, Richard J. *Fine Mess...Crazy World of Laurel & Hardy.* 1975. NY. Crown. NF. T12. $25.00

ANOBILE, Richard J. *Godfrey Daniels!* 1975. Crown. ne. VG/VG. P3. $15.00

ANONYMOUS. *Alpine Climbing: Narratives of Recent Ascents of Mont Blanc.* 1881. London. 237p. 12mo. gilt cloth. A17. $35.00

ANONYMOUS. *Bunty: Book for Girls 1979.* 1978. London. DC Thomsom. sm 4to. 127p. VG+/clip. C14. $14.00

ANONYMOUS. *Kentucky Twins, Black Sally & Sambo.* ca 1944. London. Raphael Tuck. ils M Tayler. expertly rpr pict paper brd. C8. $175.00

ANONYMOUS. *Les Musiques de la Guerre-Allied Hymnes.* (1915). Paris. Tolmer & Cie. ils Paulet Thevenaz. VG. D1. $285.00

ANONYMOUS. *Old Mother Goose Nursery Rhyme Book.* nd. Thomas Nelson. ils Ann Anderson. 96p. 16mo. pict brd. G. D1. $75.00

ANONYMOUS. *Original Mother Goose Melodies.* 1880. Lee Shepard/Dillingham. ils JF Goodridge/50 silhouettes. VG. D1. $95.00

ANONYMOUS. *Pets & Toys.* (1918). Akron. Saalfield Muslin Book 242G. 16mo. 6p. VG+/self wrp. D1. $42.00

ANONYMOUS. *Woman's Faith, a Tale of Southern Life.* 1856. NY. Derby Jackson. 1st. gilt brn cloth. F. M24. $225.00

ANOUILH, Jean. *Legend of Lovers.* 1952. Coward McCann. 1st. F/VG. M19. $50.00

ANSA, Tina McElroy. *Ugly Ways.* 1993. Harcourt Brace. 1st. author's 2nd book. F/F. B3. $50.00

ANSON, Jay. *666.* 1981. S&S. 1st. VG/VG. P3. $15.00

ANSON, Lindsay. *Hung by an Eyelash.* 1939. Collins Crime Club. 1st. VG/VG. P3. $20.00

ANSTEY, F. *Humor & Fantasy.* 1931. London. 1st. VG. M2. $35.00

ANSTIE, Francis. *Stimulants & Narcotics: Their Mutual Relations...* 1865. Phil. 1st Am. 414p. A13. $250.00

ANTHOLOGY. *American Omnibus.* 1933. Doubleday Doran. 1st. VG. N4. $20.00

ANTHOLOGY. *American Poetry Observed: Poets & Their Work.* 1984. Urbana. 1st. edit Joe David Bellamy. F/F. B4. $85.00

ANTHOLOGY. *An Apple for My Teacher.* 1987. Algonquin. 1st. sgn Chappell/Spencer/Rubin. F/dj. R13. $45.00

ANTHOLOGY. *Best Short Stories of 1926.* 1926. Dodd Mead. 1st. edit Edward O'Brien. F/VG. B4. $200.00

ANTHOLOGY. *Best Short Stories 1937.* 1937. Houghton Mifflin. F/VG+. B4. $125.00

ANTHOLOGY. *Elephant Stories Retold From St Nicholas.* 1919. Century. 1st. 188p. pict cloth. VG. H7. $25.00

ANTHOLOGY. *I Never Saw Another Butterfly...* 1976 (1971). McGraw Hill. ils. 81p. F/VG+. D4. $45.00

ANTHOLOGY. *New Directions 15: Anthology of New Directions in Prose...* 1955. New Directions. 1st. F/dj. B4. $85.00

ANTHOLOGY. *Prize Stories of 1951.* 1951. Doubleday. 1st. F/worn. B4. $100.00

ANTHOLOGY. *Spoofs.* 1933. NY. McBride. 1st. edit Richard Butler Glaenzer. F/VG+ clip. B4. $100.00

ANTHOLOGY. *World of Good Eating: Collection of Old & New Recipes...* 1951. Phillips Pub. VG/box. A16. $20.00

ANTHON, Charles. *Xenophon's Memorabilia of Socrates, With English Notes...* 1854. NY. 8vo. 438p. orig sheep/red label. F. B14. $60.00

ANTHONY, Edward. *Pussycat Princess.* 1922. NY. Century. 1st. 4to. red pict cloth. dj. R5. $350.00

ANTHONY, Evelyn. *Anne Boleyn.* 1986. Century. VG/VG. P3. $15.00

ANTHONY, Evelyn. *Avenue of the Dead.* 1981. Hutchinson. 1st. NF/NF. P3. $18.00

ANTHONY, Evelyn. *Company of Saints.* 1983. Hutchinson. 1st. F/F. P3. $20.00

ANTHONY, Evelyn. *Grave of Truth.* 1979. Hutchinson. 1st. F/F. P3. $18.00

ANTHONY, Evelyn. *Janus Imperative.* 1980. Coward McCann. 1st. VG/fair. P3. $14.00

ANTHONY, Evelyn. *Stranger at the Gates.* 1973. CMG. 1st. VG/VG. P3. $20.00

ANTHONY, Katherine. *Susan B Anthony: Her Personal History & Her Era.* 1954. Doubleday. 1st. 521p. 8vo. F/dj. H1. $22.50

ANTHONY, Piers. *And Eternity.* 1990. Morrow. 1st. VG/VG. P3. $16.00

ANTHONY, Piers. *Being a Green Mother.* 1987. Del Rey. 1st. F/F. M2. $20.00

ANTHONY, Piers. *Firefly.* 1990. Morrow. 1st. F/F. P3. $20.00

ANTHONY, Piers. *Ghost.* 1986. Tor. 1st. F/F. M2. $22.00

ANTHONY, Piers. *Out of Phaze.* 1987. Ace/Putnam. 1st. NF/dj. P3. $18.00

ANTHONY, Piers. *Pornucopia.* 1989. Tafford. 1st. F/F. P3. $25.00

ANTHONY, Piers. *Rings of Ice.* 1975. London. Millington. 1st hc. F/NF. T2. $30.00

ANTHONY, Piers. *Unicorn Point.* 1989. Ace/Putnam. 1st. F/dj. M21/P3. $15.00

ANTHONY, Piers. *With a Tangled Skein.* 1985. Del Rey. 1st. F/F. M2. $20.00

ANTHONY & KORNWISE. *Through the Ice.* 1989. Underwood Miller. 1st. F/F. M2. $35.00

ANTHONY & MARGROFF. *Chimaera's Copper.* 1990. Tor. 1st. F/F. P3. $18.00

ANTHONY & MARGROFF. *Serpent's Silver.* 1988. Tor. 1st. F/F. P3. $18.00

APEL, Willi. *Harvard Dictionary of Music.* 1958. Harvard. 833p. G. B29. $6.50

APPEL, Benjamin. *Hell's Kitchen.* 1977. Pantheon. 1st. F/F. H11. $40.00

APPEL, Willa. *Cults in America: Programmed for Paradise.* 1983. HRW. 204p. F/dj. B29. $7.50

APPEL, William. *Widowmaker.* 1994. Walker. 1st. F/F. M22. $15.00

APERTURE. *Aperture History of Photography Series.* 1976-1980. Millerton. Aperture. 15 vol (complete). photos. 3 cb cases. D11. $200.00

APPIANUS OF ALEXANDRIA. *Romanorum Historiarum.* 1670. Amsterdam. Janssonii. 2 vol. 8vo. engraved title p. contemporary vellum. T10. $300.00

APPLE, Max. *Free Agents.* 1984. Harper. 1st. author's 3rd book. F/F. B4. $45.00

APPLEBY, John. *Bad Summer.* 1958. Washburn. 1st. VG. P3. $10.00

APPLEFELD, Aharon. *Tzili: Story of a Life.* 1983. Dutton. 1st. F/F. B35. $25.00

APPLER, A.C. *Younger Brothers.* 1955. Frederick Fell. 245p. VG/dj. M20. $28.00

APPLETON, E.V. *Thermionic Vacuum Tubes.* 1933. London. Methuen. 2nd. sgn HO Richardson. 12mo. 117p. VG/worn. K3. $35.00

APPLETON, John Howard. *Beginners' Hand-Book of Chemistry.* 1888. NY. Chautauqua. 256p+14 mc pl. gilt cloth. A17. $20.00

APPLETON, Victor. *Don Sturdy Across the North Pole (#4).* 1925. GRosset Dunlap. 214p. VG+/dj. M20. $55.00

APPLETON, Victor. *Don Sturdy in the Land of Volcanoes (#5).* 1925. Grosset Dunlap. 214p+ads. VG+/dj. M20. $50.00

APPLETON, Victor. *Don Sturdy in the Port of Lost Ships (#6).* 1926. Grosset Dunlap. 214p. VG/dj. M20. $40.00

APPLETON, Victor. *Don Sturdy in the Tombs of Gold (#3).* 1925. Grosset Dunlap. lists to Harpoon Hunters (#15). VG/dj. M20. $50.00

APPLETON, Victor. *Don Sturdy With the Harpoon Hunters (#15).* 1935. Grosset Dunlap. 216p. VG. M20. $40.00

APPLETON, Victor. *Moving Picture Boys in the Jungle (#4).* 1913. Grosset Dunlap. lists 5 titles. VG/tattered. M20. $35.00

APPLETON, Victor. *Moving Picture Boys on the War Front (#9).* 1918. Grosset Dunlap. 218p. VG/tattered. M20. $35.00

APPLETON, Victor. *Tom Swift & His Aerial Warship.* 1915. Grosset Dunlap. 1st. NF. M2. $25.00

APPLETON, Victor. *Tom Swift & His Big Dirigible (#33).* 1930. Grosset Dunlap. lists to House on Wheels. VG/dj. M20. $100.00

APPLETON, Victor. *Tom Swift & His Cosmotron Express (#32).* 1970. Grosset Dunlap. 1st. 180p+ad. pict brd. VG (lists to this title). M20. $35.00

APPLETON, Victor. *Tom Swift & His Deep-Sea Hydrodome (#11).* Grosset Dunlap. 1st. bl bdg. NF/G+. N1. $22.00

APPLETON, Victor. *Tom Swift & His Electric Rifle.* 1911. Grosset Dunlap. 1st. VG. M2. $20.00

APPLETON, Victor. *Tom Swift & His Electric Runabout (#5).* 1910. Grosset Dunlap. lists to House on Wheels. 216p. VG/dj. M20. $45.00

APPLETON, Victor. *Tom Swift & His Electronic Retroscope (#14).* 1959. Grosset Dunlap. 1st. 184p. cloth. VG/dj (lists to this title). M20. $25.00

APPLETON, Victor. *Tom Swift & His Flying Boat.* 1923. Grosset Dunlap. 1st. VG. M2. $20.00

APPLETON, Victor. *Tom Swift & His Giant Magnet (#35).* 1932. Grosset Dunlap. lists to this title. 216p. orange cloth. VG/dj. M20. $200.00

APPLETON, Victor. *Tom Swift & His Giant Telescope (#39).* 1939. Whitman. Big Little Book. 434p. pict brd. VG. M20. $90.00

APPLETON, Victor. *Tom Swift & His Great Oil Gusher.* 1924. Grosset Dunlap. 1st. VG. M2. $20.00

APPLETON, Victor. *Tom Swift & His Jetmarine (#2).* Grosset Dunlap. 1st. F/G. N1. $5.50

APPLETON, Victor. *Tom Swift & His Magnetic Silencer (#40).* 1941. Whitman. Big Little Book. 424p+ads. pict brd. VG. M20. $175.00

APPLETON, Victor. *Tom Swift & His Ocean Airport (#37).* 1934. Grosset Dunlap. lists to Television Detector. orange cloth. VG/dj. M20. $400.00

APPLETON, Victor. *Tom Swift & His Sky Train (#34).* 1931. Grosset Dunlap. lists to Giant Magnet. 218p. tan cloth. VG/dj. M20. $150.00

APPLETON, Victor. *Tom Swift & His Space Solartron (#1).* 1958. Grosset Dunlap. 1st. 183p. VG/dj (lists to this title). M20. $25.00

APPLETON, Victor. *Tom Swift & His Television Detector.* 1933. Racine. Whitman. 217p. G/dj. B18. $25.00

APPLETON, Victor. *Tom Swift & Repelatron Skywalk (#22).* Grosset Dunlap. 1st. VG+. N1. $15.00

APPLETON, Victor. *Tom Swift & the Cosmic Astronauts (#16).* 1960. Grosset Dunlap. 1st. 184p. cloth. VG/dj (lists to this title). M20. $25.00

APPLETON, Victor. *Tom Swift Among the Diamond Makers (#7).* 1911. Grosset Dunlap. 216p. cloth. VG/dj. M20. $45.00

APPLETON, Victor. *Tom Swift Among the Firefighters.* 1921. Grosset Dunlap. 1st. VG. M2. $20.00

APPLETON, Victor. *Tom Swift Circling the Globe.* 1927. Grosset. 1st. NF. M2. $25.00

APPLETON, Victor. *Tom Swift in the Race to the Moon (#12).* 1958. Grosset Dunlap. 1st. 180p. VG/dj (lists to this title). M20. $20.00

APPLEWHITE, Karen Miller. *On the Road to Nowhere: History of Greer, AZ 1879-1979.* 1979. private prt. 1st. sgn. 122p. F/wrp. B19. $20.00

ARAGON, Jane Chelsea. *Major & the Mousehole Mice.* 1990. S&S. 1st. pict brd. VG/dj. M20. $18.00

ARAUJO CARNEIRO, Heliodoro. *Cartas, e Factos, Para Servirem de Introducam...* 1811. London. Cox Filho Baylis. 1st. 172p. contemporary crimson half calf. R15. $3,500.00

ARBIB, Michael A. *Metaphorical Brain: An Introduction to Cybernetics...* 1972. NY. Wiley-Interscience. tall 8vo. 244p. prt purple brd. VG/dj. G1. $50.00

ARBUCKLE, Clyde. *Santa Clara County Ranchos.* 1978. San Jose. Rosecrucian. 2nd. ils/fld map. 47p. simulated leather. F. K7. $30.00

ARBUCKLE, John Twobirds. *Singing Words.* 1978. Lincoln. Word Services. 1st. author's 1st book. F. L3. $85.00

ARCHBOLD, Rick. *Hindenburg, an Ils History.* 1994. NY. 1st. ils. 229p. F/dj. B18. $38.00

ARCHER, Gleason L. *Encyclopedia of Bible Difficulties.* 1982. Zondervan. fwd Kenneth Kantzer. 476p. VG/torn. B29. $13.00

ARCHER, Jeffrey. *First Among Equals.* 1984. Hodder Stoughton. 1st. F/F. P3. $20.00

ARCHER, Jeffrey. *Not a Penny More, Not a Penny Less.* 1976. Doubleday. 1st Am. author's 1st book. NF/NF. B2. $75.00

ARCHER, Jeffrey. *Not a Penny More, Not a Penny Less.* 1976. London. Cape. true 1st. author's 1st book. NF/dj. D10. $110.00

ARCHER, Jeffrey. *Shall We Tell the President?* 1977. Viking. 1st. VG/VG. P3. $20.00

ARCHER, Jeffrey. *Twist in the Tale.* 1988. S&S. 1st. NF/dj. P3. $20.00

ARCHER, John Clark. *Faiths Men Live By.* 1945. Ronald. 497p. VG. B29. $7.00

ARCHIBALD, Edward H.H. *Art & the Seafarer.* 1968. Viking. 4to. 292p. dj. T7. $95.00

ARCINIEGAS, German. *Germans in the Conquest of America.* 1943. Macmillan. 1st. 217p. map ep. dj. F3. $30.00

ARCTIC INSTITUTE OF NORTH AM. *Arctic Bibliography. Vol 5.* 1955. WA, DC. GPO. 1268p. bl cloth. xl. P4. $45.00

ARD, William. *Don't Come Crying to Me.* 1954. Rinehart. 1st. VG/VG. P3. $35.00

ARD, William. *Private Party.* 1953. Rinehart. 1st. VG/VG. P3. $45.00

ARDEN, William. *Die to a Distant Drum.* 1972. Dodd Mead. 1st. VG/VG. P3. $20.00

ARDION, John. *Callas Legacy.* 1977. NY. VG/VG. B5. $25.00

ARDITTI, Joseph. *Orchid Biology.* 1977. Cornell. 1st. tall 8vo. ils. cloth. VG/dj. A22. $60.00

ARDIZZONE, Edward. *Little Tim & the Brave Sea Captain.* 1936. Oxford. 1st. folio. professional rpr spine. VG+. P2. $450.00

ARDIZZONE, Edward. *Sarah & Simon & No Red Paint.* 1966. Delacorte. 1st Am. 48p. pict brd. mc dj. R5. $85.00

ARDIZZONE, Edward. *Tale of Ali Baba & the Forty Thieves.* 1949. LEC. 1/2500. ils/sgn Ardizzone. tall 4to. yel cloth. R5. $125.00

ARDIZZONE, Edward. *Young Ardizzone.* 1970. 1st. ils. NF/NF. S13. $25.00

ARDIZZONE & REEVES. *Arcadian Ballads.* 1977. England. Whittington. 1/200. sgns. 50p. pict cloth. F/F case. D4. $175.00

ARDIZZONE & REEVES. *Wandering Moon.* 1960. Dutton. 1st Am. 74p. NF/dj. D4. $35.00

ARDREY, Robert. *Worlds Beginning.* 1944. Duell. 1st. F/dj. M2. $20.00

ARENAS, Reinaldo. *Farewell to the Sea.* 1986. Viking. 1st Am. trans Andrew Hurley. F/F. R14. $40.00

ARENDT, Hannah. *Eichmann in Jerusalem.* 1963. NY. 1st. VG/VG. B5. $25.00

ARENDT, Hannah. *Truth About Oberlander.* 1960. Berlin. 1st. ils Jewish Holocaust photos. 224p. VG/VG. B5. $65.00

ARFMANN, Florence. *Time Reader's Book of Recipes.* 1949. Dutton. 1st. 252p. dj. B10. $10.00

ARGALL, G.O. *Coal Explorations, Proceedings of 2nd Internat Coal...* 1979. SF, CA. Miller Freeman. Vol 2. 560p. F. D8. $40.00

ARGICOLA, Georgius. *De re Metallica.* 1950. NY. Dover. 4to. 638p. K3. $50.00

ARGUS, M.K. *Moscow-on-the-Hudson.* 1951. Harper. 1st. F/F. B4. $150.00

ARIDJIS, Homer. *Exaltation of Light.* 1981. BOA Ed. 1/10 (of 1200). sgn. w/holograph poem. F. V1. $95.00

ARIOSTO. *Vita di Lodovico Ariosto E Dichiarazioni...* 1773. Ferrara. Stamperia Camerale. 4to. brd. R12. $225.00

ARIS, Ernest. *Bad Little Bear.* ca 1915. London. Frowde/Hodder Stoughton. 12 pl. VG-. M5. $85.00

ARIS, Ernest. *Story of the Yellow Duckling (Uncle Toby Tales).* ca 1937. London. Ward Lock. 8vo. 6 full-p pl. pict brd. mc dj. R5. $200.00

ARISTOPHANES. *Birds.* 1959. LEC. 1st thus. 1/1500. ils/sgn Marian Parry. F/glassine/double case. Q1. $100.00

ARKIN, Alan. *Lemming Condition.* 1976. Harper Row. 1st. 48p. VG+/VG. P2. $25.00

ARKIN, Marcus. *Aspects of Jewish Economic History.* 1975. JPS. 271p. VG/dj. S3. $21.00

ARMER, Laura Adams. *Cactus.* 1934. NY. ils Sidney Armer. VG/torn. B26. $34.00

ARMER, Laura Adams. *Forest Pool.* 1938. Longman Gr. 1st. thin 4to. ils. orange cloth. NF. T10. $75.00

ARMER, Laura Adams. *Forest Pool.* 1938. Longman Gr. 1st. 4to. 40p. G+. P2. $30.00

ARMER, Laura Adams. *In Navajo Land.* 1962. David McKay. 1st. NF/VG. L3. $25.00

ARMITAGE, Angus. *William Herschel.* nd (1962). London. Thomas Nelson. 24 pl/14 text figures. 158p. VG/dj. K5. $30.00

ARMITAGE, Christopher. *Sir Walter Raleigh, an Annotated Bibliography.* 1987. London/Chapel Hill. 1st. 8vo. 236p. gray cloth. P4. $35.00

ARMITAGE, Ethel. *Country Garden.* 1936. Macmillan. 1st Am. 8vo. ils. cloth. G+/torn. A22. $35.00

ARMITAGE, Shelley. *John Held Jr: Illustrator of the Jazz Age.* 1987. Syracuse. 1st. F/F. A11. $40.00

ARMOR & WRIGHT. *Manzanar.* 1988. NY. 1st. ils Ansel Adams. 167p. VG/dj. B18. $17.50

ARMORY, Cleveland. *Man Kind?* 1974. Harper. sgn. 372p. VG/VG. B11. $18.00

ARMOUR, Richard. *All Sizes & Shapes of Monkeys & Apes.* 1970. McGraw Hill. 1st. 37p. F/F. D4. $30.00

ARMOUR, Richard. *Gold Is a Four-Letter Word.* 1962. McGraw Hill. 1st. ils Leo Hershfield. VG/VG. P8. $30.00

ARMOUR, Richard. *Insects All Around Us.* 1981. McGraw Hill. 1st. inscr. 40p. F/F. D4. $25.00

ARMSTRONG, Anthony. *Trail of the Lotto.* 1930. Macrae Smith. 1st. 319p. cloth. VG/ragged. M20. $30.00

ARMSTRONG, Campbell. *White Lights.* 1988. Morrow. 1st. VG/dj. P3. $20.00

ARMSTRONG, Margaret. *Blue Santo Murder Mystery.* 1941. Random. 1st. VG. P3. $30.00

ARMSTRONG, Margaret. *Fanny Kemble: A Passionate Victorian.* 1938. Macmillan. 1st. ils. 387p. VG. A25. $10.00

ARMSTRONG & LUDLOW. *Hampton & Its Students.* 1875. Putnam. 1st. fld ftspc. NF. B2. $150.00

ARNASON, Eleanor. *Woman of the Iron People.* 1991. Morrow. 1st. author's 3rd novel. F/F. M21. $30.00

ARNETT, Carroll. *Through the Woods.* 1971. New Rochelle. Elizabeth Pr. 1/400. sgn. F/F case. L3. $125.00

ARNETT, R.H. *Entomological Information Storage & Retrieval.* 1970. Baltimore. Bio-Rand. 1st. 8vo. 210p. F. B1. $18.00

ARNO, Peter. *Whoops Dearie!* 1927. NY. 1st. sgn. author's 1st book. VG+/VG+. A11. $165.00

ARNOLD, Edmund. *Trailblazers: Story of 70th Infantry Division.* 1989. Richmond. ils/maps. 299p. VG. S16. $65.00

ARNOLD, Edwin. *Seas & Lands.* 1891. Longman Gr. 1st book ed. 8vo. teg. pict cloth. NF. T10. $100.00

ARNOLD, L.B. *American Dairying.* 1879 (1876). Rochester. Rural Home. 354p. cloth. VG. A10. $35.00

ARNOLD, Lloyd. *High on Wild With Hemingway.* 1977. NY. VG/VG. B5. $30.00

ARNOLD, Matthew. *Essays in Criticism.* 1865. London/Cambridge. 1st. 16mo. 302p. old calf-backed brd. M1. $200.00

ARNOLD, Matthew. *Merope, a Tragedy.* 1858. London. Longman Gr. 1st. 32p+November 1857 ads. dk gr cloth. M24. $200.00

ARNOLD, Matthew. *Scholar Gypsy.* 1933. London. 1st. 4to. ils Frnk Adams. VG+. M5. $150.00

ARNOLD, Michael. *Against the Fall of Night.* 1975. Doubleday. 1st. 699p. NF/G. W2. $30.00

ARNOLD, O. *Wild Life in the Southwest: Informal Intro...* 1935. Dallas. Banks Upshaw. 8vo. ils/photos/drawings. 274p. decor gilt cloth. F/NF. M12. $30.00

ARNOLD, Oren. *Sun in Your Eyes: New Light on the Southwest.* 1947. NM U. 1st. ils/bibliography. 253p. VG/dj. B19. $20.00

ARNOLD, R. *Book of the .22.* 1962. NY. 1st. 188p. VG/VG. B5. $25.00

ARNOLD, Schuyler. *Wayside Marketing.* 1929. NY. DeLaMare. 123p. VG/dj. A10. $28.00

ARNOLD & CLARK. *History of Whittier.* 1933. Whittier. self pub. 396p. gilt cloth. D11. $45.00

ARNOLD & HALE. *Hot Irons: Heraldry of the Range.* 1940. Macmillan. 1st. VG. O3. $58.00

ARNOLD & WEST. *Native Trees of Florida.* 1956. Gainesville. revised. tall 8vo. 218p. NF. A22. $35.00

ARNOU, F. *Art of the Faker: 3,000 Years of Deception, Art Forgery.* 1961. Boston. 1st. ils. 364p. VG/G. B5. $25.00

ARON, Robert. *France Reborn: History of the Liberation June 1944-May 1945.* 1964. NY. photos/maps/biblio/index. 490p. VG. S16. $18.50

ARRIGA & MARTINEZ. *Voyage of the Frigate Princesa to Southern California...* 1982. Santa Barbara. 1st. NF/sans. O4. $20.00

ARTHUR, Elizabeth. *Thunder Bay District. 1821-1892. A Collection of Documents.* 1973. Toronto. Champlain Soc. 307p. map ep. gilt red cloth. P4. $115.00

ARTHUR, Stanley Clisby. *Jean Laffite, Gentleman Rover.* 1952. New Orleans. Harmanson. 1/750. sgn. 282p. red cloth. VG/dj. P4. $125.00

ARTHUR & WHITNEY. *Barn: A Vanishing Landmark in North America.* 1981. NY. Garland. 256p. dj. A10. $30.00

ARTISS, Percy. *Market Gardening.* 1949. London. Collingridge. 2nd. 127p. VG. A10. $22.00

ARTSCHWAGER & SMILEY. *Dictionary of Botanical Equivalents.* 1925 (1921). Baltimore. 2nd. 12mo. VG. B26. $40.00

ASBERY, John. *As We Know.* 1979. Viking. 1st. sgn. F/F. D10. $50.00

ASBJORNSEN. *East of the Sun & West of the Moon.* 1914. Hodder Stoughton. 1st. ils Kay Nielsen/25 tipped-in mc pl. VG. D1. $2,500.00

ASBURY, Herbert. *Barbary Coast.* 1949. Long Beach, CA. 1st. VG/G. O4. $15.00

ASCH, Sholem. *Passage in the Night.* 1953. Putnam. 1st. 8vo. 367p. F/VG. H1. $22.50

ASCHAM, Roger. *English Works of...* (1761). London. rto. marbled ep. A15. $75.00

ASH, Brian. *Visual Encyclopedia of Science Fiction.* 1977. Harmony. 1st. NF/dj. M2. $35.00

ASH, Brian. *Who's Who in Science Fiction.* 1976. Taplinger. 1st. F/F. P3. $25.00

ASH, Christopher. *Whaler's Eye.* 1962. NY. 1st. photos. 245p. NF/dj. S15. $15.00

ASH, Mary Kay. *People Management.* 1984. Warner. 1st. NF/NF. W2. $20.00

ASHBERY, John. *April Galleons.* 1987. Viking. 1st. sgn. F/dj. D10. $45.00

ASHBERY, John. *Flow Chart.* 1991. Knopf. 1st. inscr/dtd 1996. NF/F. R14. $40.00

ASHBERY, John. *Some Trees.* 1956. New Haven. 1st. sgn. F/F. B4. $300.00

ASHBERY & SCHUYLER. *Nest of Ninnies.* 1969. Dutton. 1st. inscr Ashbery. F/NF. B4. $250.00

ASHBROOK, F.G. *How To Raise Rabbits for Food & Fur.* 1951. Orange Judd. 256p. cloth. B1. $22.50

ASHBROOK, Frank. *Fur Farming for Profit.* 1951. Orange Judd. revised. 429p. VG/dj. A10. $22.00

ASHBROOK, H. *Murder of Cecily Thane.* 1930. Coward McCann. 1st. VG. P3. $25.00

ASHDOWN, C.H. *Arms & Armour.* nd. NY. 42 pl/450 text figures. 384p. teg. pict cloth. NF. M4. $50.00

ASHE, Geoffrey. *Discovery of King Arthur.* 1985. Debrett's Peerage. 1st. VG/VG. P3. $25.00

ASHE, Gordon; see Creasey, John.

ASHE & DEFORD. *Arthur Ashe: Portrait in Motion.* 1975. Houghton Mifflin. 1st. photos. VG+/dj. P8. $20.00

ASHER, Marty. *Shelter.* 1986. Arbor. 1st. RS. F/dj. M2. $13.00

ASHFORD, Jeffrey. *Honourable Detective.* 1988. St Martin. 1st. VG/VG. P3. $15.00

ASHFORD, Jeffrey. *Question of Principle.* 1986. St Martin. 1st. VG/VG. P3. $15.00

ASHLEY, Clifford W. *Yankee Whaler.* 1926. Houghton Mifflin. 1/1625. ils 379p. F. T7. $400.00

ASHLEY, Michael. *History of the Science Fiction Magazine Vol 1, 1926-1935.* 1976. Regnery. 1st Am. F/NF. M2. $22.00

ASHLEY, Michael. *Souls in Metal.* 1977. St Martin. 1st. F/F. P3. $18.00

ASHLEY, Mike. *History of the Science Fiction Magazine Vol 3: 1946-1955.* 1977. Contemporary Books. 1st Am. VG/G. R10. $10.00

ASHRAF PAHLAVI, Princess. *Faces in a Mirror. Memoirs From Exile.* 1980. Prentice Hall. 238p. 32 pl. VG/torn. W1. $18.00

ASHTON, Francis. *Breaking of the Seals.* 1946. London. 1st. F/dj. M2. $35.00

ASHTON, John. *Humour, Wit & Satire of the Seventeenth Century.* 1883. Chatto Windus. 1st/lg paper ed. tall/wide 4to. gr pebbled cloth. H13. $195.00

ASHTON & ASHTON. *Wrong Side of the Moon.* 1952. London. 1st. VG/dj. M2. $35.00

ASHTON & GRAY. *Chinese Art.* 1945. London. Faber. 3rd. ils/photos. 366p. VG. W3. $38.00

ASHTON-WARNER, Sylvia. *Bell Call.* 1964. S&S. 1st. 317p. VG+/VG+. A25. $30.00

ASHURST, Henry Fountain. *Homage to the Santa Fe.* 1973. Manzanita. ils. 141p. NF/NF. B19. $50.00

ASHWORTH, William. *Penguins, Puffins & Auks: Their Lives & Behavior.* 1993. NY. Crown. 1st. 4to. 208p. M/dj. P4. $45.00

ASIMOV, GREENBERG & WAUGH. *Science-Fictional Solar System.* 1979. Harper Row. 1st. F/NF. M21. $20.00

ASIMOV, Isaac. *Asimov Chronicles.* 1989. Arkham. 1st. 1/500. sgn/#d. F/dj/case. M2. $100.00

ASIMOV, Isaac. *Asimov's Sherlockiana Limericks.* 1978. Mysterious. 1st. F/frayed. M2. $25.00

ASIMOV, Isaac. *Beginning & the End.* 1977. Doubleday. 1st. VG/VG. M2/P3. $22.00

ASIMOV, Isaac. *Best Of Isaac Asimov.* 1974. Doubleday. 1st. VG/VG. P3. $25.00

ASIMOV, Isaac. *Bicentennial Man.* 1976. Doubleday. 1st. VG/VG. P3. $25.00

ASIMOV, Isaac. *Change!* 1981. Houghton Mifflin. 1st. F/NF. A24. $30.00

ASIMOV, Isaac. *Counting the Eons.* 1984. Granada. 1st. VG/VG. P3. $20.00

ASIMOV, Isaac. *End of Eternity.* 1955. Doubleday. 1st. F/dj. M2. $250.00

ASIMOV, Isaac. *Exploring the Earth & the Cosmos.* 1982. Crown. 1st. F/F. M2. $20.00

ASIMOV, Isaac. *Exploring the Earth & the Cosmos.* 1982. Crown. 1st. VG/VG. P3. $15.00

ASIMOV, Isaac. *Eyes on the Universe.* 1975. Houghton Mifflin. xl. dj. K5. $20.00

ASIMOV, Isaac. *Fantastic Voyage II: Destination Brain.* 1987. Doubleday. 1st. F/F. M2. $25.00

ASIMOV, Isaac. *Fantastic Voyage II: Destination Brain.* 1987. Doubleday. 1st. F/NF. N4. $22.50

ASIMOV, Isaac. *Fantastic Voyage II: Destination Brain.* 1987. Doubleday. 1st. VG/VG. P3. $20.00

ASIMOV, Isaac. *Foundation & Empire.* 1952. Gnome. 1st. VG/2nd state dj. M2. $250.00

ASIMOV, Isaac. *Foundation's Edge.* 1982. Whispers. 1/1000. sgn/#d. F/sans. M2. $100.00

ASIMOV, Isaac. *Gods Themselves.* 1972. Doubleday. 1st. NF/dj. M2. $50.00

ASIMOV, Isaac. *Have You Seen These?* 1974. NESFA. 1st. F/F. M2. $75.00

ASIMOV, Isaac. *Intelligent Man's Guide to Science.* 1960. Basic. 2 vol. 1st. VG. M2. $35.00

ASIMOV, Isaac. *Is Anyone There?* 1967. Doubleday. 1st. NF/VG. M19. $35.00

ASIMOV, Isaac. *Is Anyone There?* 1967. Doubleday. 1st. VG/VG. P3. $25.00

ASIMOV, Isaac. *Life & Time.* 1978. Doubleday. 1st. F/F. M2. $20.00

ASIMOV, Isaac. *Lucky Starr & Pirates of Asteroids.* 1978. Gregg. 1st. VG/VG. P3. $20.00

ASIMOV, Isaac. *Lucky Starr & the Rings of Saturn.* 1958. Doubleday. 1st. VG/worn. M2. $125.00

ASIMOV, Isaac. *Microcosmic Tales.* 1980. Taplinger. 1st. F/F. M2. $20.00

ASIMOV, Isaac. *Nemesis.* 1989. Doubleday. 1st. F/dj. M21. $20.00

ASIMOV, Isaac. *Opus 100.* 1969. Houghton Mifflin. 1st. VG/VG. P3. $50.00

ASIMOV, Isaac. *Opus 200.* 1979. Houghton Mifflin. 1st. F/VG. M19. $25.00

ASIMOV, Isaac. *Pebble in the Sky.* 1950. Doubleday. 1st. F/worn. M2. $200.00

ASIMOV, Isaac. *Robots of Dawn.* 1983. Doubleday. 1st. F/NF. N4. $25.00

ASIMOV, Isaac. *Robots of Dawn.* 1983. Doubleday. 1st. NF/VG. A24. $20.00

ASIMOV, Isaac. *Sun Shines Bright.* 1981. Doubleday. 1st. NF/dj. M2. $22.00

ASIMOV, Isaac. *Tomorrow's Children.* 1966. Doubleday. 1st. F/NF. M2. $50.00

ASIMOV, Janet. *Mind Transfer.* 1988. Walker. 1st. F/F. M2. $18.00

ASIMOV & JEPPSON. *Laughing Space.* 1983. Houghton Mifflin. 1st. VG/VG. P3. $20.00

ASIMOV & MCCALL. *Our World in Space.* 1974. NYGS. 1st. NF/dj. M2. $30.00

ASIMOV & SILVERBERG. *Ugly Little Boy.* 1992. Doubleday. 1st. F/F. A20. $15.00

ASINOFF, Eliot. *Eight Men Out.* 1963. HRW. 1st. F/dj. M25. $100.00

ASINOFF, Eliot. *Man on Spikes.* 1955. McGraw Hill. 1st. F/NF. B4. $250.00

ASKINS, Charles. *American Shotgun.* 1910. NY. Outing Pub. 1st. 321p. teg. VG. H7. $65.00

ASKINS, Charles. *Wing & Trap Shooting.* 1911. NY. Outing Pub. 1st. 174p. VG. H7. $35.00

ASPRIN, Robert. *Bug Wars.* 1979. St Martin. 1st. VG/VG. P3. $20.00

ASPRIN, Robert. *Cold Cash War.* 1977. St Martin. 1st. VG/VG. P3. $20.00

ASQUITH, Cynthia. *Book of Modern Ghosts.* 1953. Scribner. 1st Am. F/frayed. M2. $30.00

ASQUITH, Cynthia. *Flying Carpet.* 1925. Scribner. 1st Am. sm 4to. 200p. VG. C14. $30.00

ASQUITH, Cynthia. *King's Daughters.* 1938. Dutton. 1st. photos. 107p. VG/dj. M20. $25.00

ASQUITH, Cynthia. *Not Long for This World.* 1936. Telegraph. 1st. VG/dj. M2. $65.00

ASQUITH, Cynthia. *This Mortal Coil.* 1947. Arkham. 1st. F/F. M2. $110.00

ASQUITH, Cynthia. *Treasure Cave: Book of New Prose & Verse.* 1928. Scribner. 1st Am. 144p. G+. C14. $25.00

ASQUITH & BIGLAND. *Princess Elizabeth Gift Book: In Aid...York Hospital...* ca 1945. Hodder Stoughton. 1st. ils. 224+p. VG. A25. $50.00

ASSMANN, Herbert. *Die Klinische Rontgendiagonstick der Inneren Erkrankungen.* 1929. Leipzig. 4th. 1071p. half leather. A13. $30.00

ASSO Y DEL RIO. *Cortex Celebradas en los Reynaldos de D Sancho IV...* 1775. Madrid. Joachin Ibarra. 1st/only. folio. 42p. recent morocco. R15. $650.00

ASTLEY & GREEN. *New General Collection of Voyages.* 1745-1747. London. Astley. 4 vol. 232 pl/maps/plans. quarter calf/rebacked spines. T7. $2,500.00

ASTON, F.W. *Mass Spectra & Isotopes.* 1942. London. Arnold. 2nd. 8vo. xl. K3. $30.00

ASTOR, Gerald. *Last Nazi.* 1985. NY. ils. 305p. VG/VG. S16. $21.50

ASTOR, John Jacob. *Journey to Other Worlds.* 1894. Appleton. 1st. new ep. VG. M2. $90.00

ATCHISON, Stewart. *Wilderness Called Grand Canyon.* 1991. MN. Voyageur. 4to. 127p. VG/VG. F7. $40.00

ATENBAUGH, Richard J. *Education for the Struggle: American Lagor Colleges...* 1990. Temple U. 1st. F/F. V4. $22.50

ATHANAS, Verne. *Proud Ones.* 1952. S&S. 1st. F/F. B4. $125.00

ATHEARN, R. *Forts of Upper Missouri.* 1967. Englewood Cliffs. 1st. VG/dj. B5. $37.50

ATHERTON, Faxon Dean. *California Diary of Faxon Dean Atherton 1836-1839.* 1964. SF/Los Angeles. CA hist Soc. 1/1550. 8vo. 246p. F/NF. K7. $20.00

ATHERTON, Gertrude. *Conqueror.* 1902. Macmillan. 1st/1st state. 546p. maroon cloth. VG. M20. $50.00

ATHERTON, Gertrude. *Jealous Gods.* 1928. 1st. inscr. F/NF. M19. $35.00

ATHERTON, Gertrude. *My San Francisco: A Wayward Biography.* 1946. Indianapolis, IN. 1st. VG/G+. O4. $15.00

ATHERTON & HUNIS. *California Diary of Faxon Dean Atherton 1836-1839.* 1964. SF. CA Hist Soc. deluxe ed. 1/325. sgn. 8vo. ils. bl buckram. F/box. R3. $125.00

ATKEY, Bertram. *Midnight Mystery.* 1928. Appleton. 1st. VG. M2. $10.00

ATKINSON, Eleanor. *Greyfriar's Bobby.* 1912. 1st. VG. S13. $15.00

ATKINSON, Eleanor. *Loyal Love.* 1912. Boston. Badger. 1st. F/F. B4. $100.00

ATKINSON, Margaret. *How To Raise Your Puppy.* 1944. Greenberg. 1st. obl 8vo. VG/dj. M5. $20.00

ATLEE, Philip; see Philips, James Atlee.

ATTANASIO, A.A. *Beast Marks.* 1984. Ziesing. 1st. F/F. M2. $25.00

ATTANASIO, A.A. *Beast Marks.* 1984. Ziesing. 1st. sgn. F/F. P3. $45.00

ATTANASIO, A.A. *Hunting the Ghost Dancer.* 1991. Harper Collins. 1st. F/F. P3. $22.00

ATTANASIO, A.A. *In Other Worlds.* 1984. Morrow. 1st. VG/VG. P3. $20.00

ATTANASIO, A.A. *Wyvern.* 1988. Ticknor Fields. 1st. NF/dj. M21. $20.00

ATTAR, Farid un-Din. *Conference of the Birds. A Sufi Fable.* 1971. Boulder, CO. Shambala. 8vo. 147p. VG/wrp. W1. $10.00

ATTAWAY, William. *Calypso Song Book.* 1957. McGraw Hill. 1st. music/lyrics to 25 songs. F/dj. Q1. $350.00

ATTENBOROUGH, F.L. *Laws of the Earlist English Kings.* 1963. Russell. M11. $65.00

ATWATER, Caleb. *Writings of Caleb Atwater.* 1833. Columbus. 1st. 408p. leather. G. B18. $125.00

ATWATER, Mary. *Shuttle Craft Book of American Hand-Weaving.* 1975. 1st. ils. VG/VG. S13. $35.00

ATWELL, Lucie. *Lucie Atwell's Book of Verses.* 1960. London. Dean. 1st. 4to. pict brd. F/dj. R5. $150.00

ATWELL, Lucie. *Lucie Atwell's Jolly Book.* ca 1950. London. Dean. 4to. pict brd. F. R5. $150.00

ATWELL, Lucie. *Lucie Atwell's Painting Book 2.* 1963. London. Dean. 1st. 4to. F. R5. $150.00

ATWELL, Lucie. *Story for a Poppet.* 1961. London. Dean. Dean's Little Poppet series. 12mo. F. R5. $60.00

ATWOOD, Margaret. *Bluebeard's Egg.* 1983. McClelland Stewart. 1st. author's 2nd story collection. F/F. M25. $45.00

ATWOOD, Margaret. *Bodily Harm.* 1982. S&S. 1st Am. sgn. F/F. B2/M25. $40.00

ATWOOD, Margaret. *Bodily Harm.* 1982. S&S. 1st. F/F. B3. $30.00

ATWOOD, Margaret. *Cat's Eye.* 1988. McClelland Stewart. 1st Canadian. F/F. B3/T12. $40.00

ATWOOD, Margaret. *Cat's Eye.* 1989. Doubleday. 1st. NF/NF. P3. $20.00

ATWOOD, Margaret. *Cat's Eye.* 1989. London. Bloomsbury. 1st. NF/NF. M23. $25.00

ATWOOD, Margaret. *Dancing Girls & Other Stories.* 1977. McClelland Stewart. 1st. VG/VG. P3. $35.00

ATWOOD, Margaret. *Edible Woman.* 1969. Toronto. McClelland. true 1st Canadian. sgn. author's 1st novel. NF/NF. L3. $500.00

ATWOOD, Margaret. *For the Birds.* 1991. Buffalo. Firefly. 1st Am. F/pict wrp. R13. $15.00

ATWOOD, Margaret. *Good Bones.* 1992. Bloomsbury. 1st. bl brd. F/F. A24. $25.00

ATWOOD, Margaret. *Handmaid's Tale.* 1985. McClelland Stewart. 1st. VG/VG. P3. $30.00

ATWOOD, Margaret. *Lady Oracle.* 1976. S&S. 1st. sgn. rem mk. NF/dj. D10. $65.00

ATWOOD, Margaret. *Life Before Man.* 1979. S&S. 1st. sgn. F/VG. B3. $40.00

ATWOOD, Margaret. *Life Before Man.* 1979. S&S. NF/F. A20. $35.00

ATWOOD, Margaret. *Life Before Man.* 1980. London. Cape. 1st Eng. F/F. R14. $40.00

ATWOOD, Margaret. *Surfacing.* 1972. S&S. 1st Am. author's 2nd novel. F/F. M25. $60.00

ATWOOD, Margaret. *Two-Headed Poems.* 1978. S&S. 1st Am. sgn. rem mk. F/dj. D10. $65.00

AUBERT, Jacques-F. *Papillons d'Europe.* 1949. Paris. 2 vol. ils/pl. French text. NF/VG. S15. $30.00

AUBERTIN, Ernest. *Recherches Cliniques sur les Maladies de Coeur...* 1855. Paris. 276p. B14. $250.00

AUBREY, Edmund. *Sherlock Holmes in Dallas.* 1980. Dodd Mead. 1st. F/F clip. N4. $30.00

AUBREY, Frank. *Devil Tree of El Dorado.* 1897. New Amsterdam Book Co. 1st. VG. M2. $125.00

AUBREY, Frank. *Queen of Atlantis.* 1899. London. 1st. VG. M2. $200.00

AUCHINCLOSS, Louis. *Rector of Justin.* 1964. Houghton Mifflin. 1st. inscr. VG/VG. R14. $75.00

AUCHINCLOSS, Louis. *Reflections of a Jacobite.* 1961. 1st. F/NF. M19. $25.00

AUCHINCLOSS, Louis. *Watchfires.* 1982. Houghton Mifflin. 1st. gilt maroon cloth. NF/dj. T11. $25.00

AUCHINCLOSS, Louis. *Winthrop Covenant.* 1976. Franklin Pr. true 1st. ils Jerry Pinkney. aeg. gilt leather. F. T11. $40.00

AUDEMARS, Pierre. *Now Dead Is Any Man.* 1980. Walker. 1st. F/F. P3. $15.00

AUDEN, W.H. *Double Man.* 1941. Random. 1st. F/dj. B24. $125.00

AUDEN, W.H. *Epistle to a Godson & Other Poems.* 1972. London. Faber. 1st. F/NF. B2. $45.00

AUDEN, W.H. *Mountains.* 1954. London. Faber. 1st. F/wrp/pub envelope. Q1. $40.00

AUDEN, W.H. *Nones.* 1952. London. 1st. dj. T9. $75.00

AUDEN & KALLMAN. *Magic Flute.* 1956. Random. 1st. NF/NF. B2/M19. $75.00

AUDOT, L. *La Cuisiniere de la Campagne et de la Ville...* 1882. Paris. ils. 701p. G+. E6. $65.00

AUDUBON, John James. *Delineations of American Scenery & Character.* 1926. GA Baker. intro FH Herrick. 349p. VG. S15. $30.00

AUDUBON, John James. *Delineations of American Scenery & Character.* 1926. NY. Baker. 8vo. 349p. gilt blk cloth. NF. T10. $75.00

AUDUBON, John James. *Imperial Collection of Audubon Animals.* 1967. 1st thus. lg 4to. mc ils. VG+. S13. $25.00

AUDUBON, John James. *Original Watercolours Paintings by...* 1966. American Heritage. 2 vol. 431 mc pl (some fld). F/VG case. S15. $140.00

AUDUBON, John Woodhouse. *Drawings of..., Illustrating His Adventures Through Mexico.* 1957. SF. BC of CA. Grabhorn. 1/400. 34 pl. decor brd/cloth spine. D11. $200.00

AUDUBON, Maria. *Life of John James Audubon.* 1909. Putnam. 1st. VG. M19. $25.00

AUEL, Jean M. *Clan of The Cave Bear.* 1980. Crown. 1st. F/NF. T11. $65.00

AUEL, Jean M. *Clan of the Cave Bear.* 1980. Crown. 1st. author's 1st book. F/F. H11. $100.00

AUEL, Jean M. *Mammoth Hunters.* 1985. Crown. 1st. VG/VG. P3. $25.00

AUEL, Jean M. *Plains of Passage.* 1990. Crown. 1st. NF/NF. P3/T12. $25.00

AUEL, Jean M. *Plains of Passage.* 1990. Crown. 1st. sgn. F/F. A23. $50.00

AUEL, Jean M. *Valley of the Horses.* 1982. Crown. 1st. sgn. F/F. B35. $40.00

AUERBACH, Ann Hagedorn. *Wild Ride: Rise & Tragic Fall of Calumet Farm.* 1994. Holt. 1st. VG/VG. O3. $25.00

AUERBACH & FITZGERALD. *Red Auerbach: An Autobiography.* 1977. Putnam. VG+/G+. P8. $25.00

AUGUSTA, J. *Prehistoric Animals.* nd. London. Spring. tall folio. 45p+pl. pict cloth. VG. M12. $45.00

AUGUSTUS, Albert Jr.; see Nuetzel, Charles.

AUNT FANNY. *Junior Jewish Book Book.* 1956. NY. Ktav. ils Cyla London. F. C8. $22.50

AUNT LAURA; see Barrow, Frances Elizabeth.

AUPHAN & MORDAL. *French Navy in World War II.* 1959. photos. VG. M17. $30.00

AURELIUS, Marcus. *Meditations of Marcus Aurelius.* 1956. LEC. 1st thus. 1/1500. ils/sgn Hans Alexander Mueller. F/case. Q1. $75.00

AURTHUR, Robert. *Third Marine Division.* 1988. Nashville. maps/photos. 399p. VG. S16. $40.00

AURTHUR & COHLMIA. *Third Marine Division.* 1948. WA. Infantry Pr. 1st. pres from Gen Allen Hal Turnage. 8vo. 335p. C6. $250.00

AUSTEN, Jane. *Fragment of a Novel (Sanditon).* 1925. Oxford. Clarendon. 1st. quarter linen/bl brd. F. M24. $150.00

AUSTEN, Jane. *Love & Friendship & Other Early Writings.* (1922). NY. Stokes. 1st. edit GK Chesterton. gray cloth/label. fabric dj/label. $125.00

AUSTEN, Jane. *Novels of Jane Austen: In Ten Volumes.* 1892. London. Dent. 1st thus. edit RB Johnson. ils WC Cooke. VG. Q1. $750.00

AUSTEN, Jane. *Sense & Sensibility.* 1957. LEC. 1st thus. 1/1500. ils Helen Sewell. F/case. Q1. $125.00

AUSTEN, John. *Hamlet: Prince of Denmark.* 1922. London. Selwyn Blount. 1st. 4to. decor brd. dj. R5. $250.00

AUSTEN-LEIGH, R.A. *Bygone Eton.* 1922. Eton College. 3rd. lg thin 4to. gilt wht cloth/leather label. F. T10. $50.00

AUSTER, Paul. *Ghosts.* 1986. LA. Sun & Moon. 1st. sgn. F/F. D10. $125.00

AUSTER, Paul. *In the Country of Last Things.* 1987. Viking. 1st. F/F. B3. $30.00

AUSTER, Paul. *In the Country of Last Things.* 1987. Viking. 1st. sgn. author's 4th novel. F/F. D10. $65.00

AUSTER, Paul. *Leviathan.* 1992. Viking. 1st. F/F. B4. $85.00

AUSTER, Paul. *Leviathan.* 1992. Viking. 1st. sgn. F/F. B4. $125.00

AUSTER, Paul. *Moon Palace.* 1969. Viking. 1st. sgn. F/F. B4. $150.00

AUSTER, Paul. *Music of Chance.* 1990. NY. Viking. 1st. sgn. F/dj. D10. $50.00

AUSTER, Paul. *Music of Chance.* 1990. Viking. UP. sgn. F/wrp. B4. $200.00

AUSTER, Paul. *Music of Chance.* 1991. London. Faber. 1st. F/NF. A24. $15.00

AUSTIN, A.B. *We Landed at Dawn: Story of the Dieppe Raid.* 1943. NY. sgn James Roosevelt. 217p. VG. S16. $125.00

AUSTIN, Alicia. *Age of Dreams.* 1978. Donald Grant. 1st. F/dj. M2. $40.00

AUSTIN, Alicia. *Age of Dreams.* 1978. Donald Grant. 1st. VG/VG. P3. $35.00

AUSTIN, Jane G. *Cipher: A Romance.* 1869. NY. Sheldon. 1st. author's 4th book. gilt purple cloth. M24. $225.00

AUSTIN, Leonard. *Around the World in San Francisco.* 1940. Stanford. James Ladd Delkin. 1/500. 112p. NF. K7. $85.00

AUSTIN, M. *Gabriel Churchkitten & the Moths.* 1948. 1st. VG. S13. $30.00

AUSTIN, Margot. *Trumpet.* 1943. Dutton. 1st. sq 4to. VG+/VG. P2. $45.00

AUSTIN, Mary. *Experiences Facing Death.* 1931. Bobbs Merrill. 1st. F. A18. $60.00

AUSTIN, Richard L. *Yearbook of Landscape Architecture.* 1985. NY. ils. 4to. VG+/dj. B26. $35.00

AUSTIN, Sarah. *Story Without End.* 1868. London. Sampson Low. 1st. ils EV Boyle/15 chromolithos. gilt pict bdg. G+. P2. $500.00

AUSTIN & SHORT. *Germ Cells & Fertilization. Book 1: Reproduction in Mammals.* 1978. Cambridge. rpt. 133p. F. B1. $22.50

AUTRY, Gene. *Back in the Saddle Again.* 1978. Garden City. sgn. VG/VG. B5. $50.00

AVARY, Myrta Lockett. *Dixie After the War.* 1937. Houghton Mifflin. 2nd. 435p. cloth. VG/dj. M8. $85.00

AVEDON, Richard. *In the American West.* 1985. NY. Abrams. 1st. VG/glassine. B5. $100.00

AVEDON & BALDWIN. *Nothing Personal.* 1964. Atheneum. 1st. VG/poor box. B5. $100.00

AVELLAR BROTERO, Felix. *Compendio de Botanica, ou Nacoens Elementares Desta...* 1788. Paris. Paul Martin. 2 vol. 1st. 31 engraved pl. contemporary French calf. R15. $750.00

AVERILL, Esther. *How the Brothers Joined the Cat Club.* 1953. Harper. 1st. 32p. G+. P2. $40.00

AVERILL, Esther. *Powder.* 1933. Domino. 1st. ils Rojankovsky. sm 4to. VG+. P2. $85.00

AVERILL, Esther. *Voyages of Jacques Cartier.* 1937. NY. Domino. 1st. 1/3000. 4to. F/G. M5. $125.00

AVERY, Al. *Air Combat Stories for Boys: A Yankee Flier in N Am (#11).* 1943. Grosset Dunlap. 213p. VG/dj (lists to this title). M20. $25.00

AVERY, Catherine. *New Century Handbook of Greek Art & Architecture.* 1972. Appleton Century Crofts. 213p. VG/dj. B29. $8.50

AVERY, Kay. *Wee Willow Whistle.* (1947). Knopf. ils Winifred Bromhall. sm 4to. yel pict cloth. T5. $15.00

AVILA, George C. *Pairpoint Glass Story.* 1968. New Bedford. self pub. 1st. sgn. 238p. VG. H1. $120.00

AVNI, Haim. *Spain, the Jews & Franco.* 1982. PA. JPS. 268p. VG+/VG. S3. $26.00

AVRICH, Paul. *Sacco & Vanzetti: The Anarchist Background.* 1991. Princeton. 1st. F/F. B2. $25.00

AWIAKTA, Marilou. *Rising Fawn & the Fire Mystery.* 1983. St Luke's Pr. 1st. laminated brd. F. L3. $55.00

AXELROD & BURGESS. *Fishes of Southern Japan & the Ryukyus.* 1973. Hong Kong. 2nd. Pacific Marine Fishes series. photos. F/dj. W3. $65.00

AXFORD, Joseph. *Around Western Campfires.* 1969. AZ U. 266p. VG/VG. B19. $7.50

AXTON, David; see Koontz, Dean R.

AYALA, Mitzi. *Farmer's Cookbook: Collection of Favorite Recipes...* 1981. SF. Harbor. intro/index. VG/dj. A16. $16.00

AYDELOTTE, Dora. *Green Gavel.* 1937. Appleton Century. 1st. inscr. 249p. VG/G. P2. $35.00

AYKROYD, W.R. *Three Philosophers.* 1935. London. Heinemann. 1st. 8vo. 227p. VG. K3. $25.00

AYLING, Keith. *Semper Fidelis: US Marines in Action.* 1943. Boston. 1st. 194p. VG. S16. $30.00

AYRES, Leonard P. *War With Germany, a Statistical Summary.* 1919. GPO. 2nd. 154p. tan buckram. xl. F. K7. $50.00

AYRES, Ruby M. *Feather.* 1935. Doubleday Doran. 1st. 298p. as new/F. H1. $20.00

AYRES DO CASAL, Manuel. *Corografia Brazilica, ou Relacao Historico...Brazil...* 1817. Rio de Janeiro. Impressao Regia. 1st. contemporary mottled calf. R15. $1,500.00

AZIZ, Philippe. *Mysteries of the Great Pyramid.* 1977. Fermil decor brd. VG. P3. $15.00

B, E.V. see Boyle, E.V.

BAADE, Fritz. *Race to the Year 2000.* 1963. Cresset. VG/VG. P3. $15.00

BAARS, D.L. *Geology of the Canyons of the San Juan River.* 1981. 4 Corners Geological Soc. 2nd. 8vo. 94p. stiff wrp. F7. $17.50

BAARS & STEVENSON. *San Juan Canyons: A River Runner's Guide & Natural Hist...* 1991. Canon Pub. revised. sbdg. VG. F7. $12.50

BAAY, Henry Van L. *Boats, Boat Yards & Yachtsmen.* 1961. Van Nostrand. 1st. ils. 211p. dj. T7. $20.00

BABB, T.A. *In the Bosom of the Comanches, a Thrilling Tale...* 1923. TA Babb. 2nd. 146p. VG. J2. $225.00

BABBITT, George Jr. *Arizona Mosaic.* 1977. B&H Pub. 1st. sgn. 180p. F/NF. B19. $35.00

BABCOCK, Ernest B. *Genus Crepis.* 1947. Berkeley. ils. 1030p. new cloth. B26. $87.50

BABCOCK, George. *Yezad: Romance of the Unknown.* 1922. Cooperative. 1st. G+. M2. $35.00

BABCOCK, Havilah. *Education of Pretty Boy.* 1960. Holt. 1st. inscr. F/NF. B4. $350.00

BABER, D.F. *Longest Rope.* 1940. Caxton. dj. A19. $75.00

BABINGTON. *Records of Fife Foxhounds.* 1883. Edinburgh. Blackwood. 1st. 4to. G. O3. $95.00

BABITZ, Eve. *Eve's Hollywood.* 1974. Delacorte. 1st. F/NF. M25. $45.00

BABITZ, Eve. *Sex & Rage.* 1979. Knopf. 1st. F/F. H11. $25.00

BABSON, Marian. *There Must Be Some Mistake.* nd. St Martin. 1st. F/F. P3. $15.00

BABULA, William. *According to St John.* 1989. Lyle Stuart. 1st. Vg/VG. P3. $18.00

BABYAK, Jolene. *Eyewitness of Alcatraz.* 1988. Berkeley. Ariel Vamp. 128p. VG/wrp. B11. $14.50

BACALL, Lauren. *Now.* 1994. Knopf. 1st. sgn. VG/VG. A23. $40.00

BACH, Richard. *Bridge Across Forever.* 1984. Morrow. 1st. VG/VG. P3. $20.00

BACHELLER, Irving. *Eben Holden's Last Day A-Fishing.* 1907. Harper. 1st. F/VG+. H7. $40.00

BACHMAIR, John James. *Complete German Grammar, in Two Parts.* 1772. London/Phil. Henry Miller. 1st Am. 12mo. recent half leather. M1. $375.00

BACHMAN, Richard; see King, Stephen.

BACKEBERG, Curt. *Cactus Lexicon.* 1977. Poole. 3rd. ils/18 maps. 838p. VG+/dj. B26. $135.00

BACKEBERG, Curt. *Das Kakteenlexikon.* 1966. Jena. 1st. ils/18 full-p maps. 741p. VG/dj. B26. $55.00

BACKEBERG, Curt. *Wunderwelt Kakteen.* 1961. Jena. 1st. ils. 242p. yel cloth. VG. B26. $125.00

BACKHOUSE, Deborah. *Memoir of..., of York; Who Died...1827...* 1828. York. W Alexander & Son. 1st. worn. V3. $28.00

BACKHOUSE & BLAND. *Annals & Memoirs of the Court of Peking.* 1914. Houghton Mifflin. 1st. photos/index. 531p. VG. W3. $110.00

BACKUS, Anna Jean. *Mountain Meadows Witness.* 1995. Clark. 1st. 302p. M. J2. $85.00

BACON, Francis. *Essays, Moral, Economical & Political.* 1807. Boston. Oliver Munroe. 1st Am. tree sheep/red morocco label. M24. $275.00

BACON, Francis. *Essays of Bacon.* 1927. Cleveland. Fined Eds. 140p. leather spine/cloth brds. VG. A10. $30.00

BACON, Francis. *Works of..., Lord Chancellor of England.* 1856. Phil. Parry McMillan. 4to. 455p. xl. K3. $40.00

BACON, Harry. *Cancer of the Colon, Rectum & Anal Canal.* 1964. Phil. 1st. 956p. A13. $30.00

BACON, John. *Forging: A Practical Treatise on Hand Forging...* 1938. Chicago. Am Technical Soc. 116p. VG. O3. $40.00

BACON, Peggy. *Magic Touch.* 1968. Little Brn. 1st. 112p. VG-/G+. P2. $35.00

BADARACCO, Claire. *American Culture & the Marketplace: RR Donnelley...* 1992. Lib of Congress. 67p. 4to. stiff wrp. A17. $15.00

BADASH, Lawrence. *Radioactivity in America.* 1976. Baltimore/London. 1st. 327p. VG. K3. $45.00

BADER. *American Picturebooks From Noah's Ark to the Beast Within.* 1976. 1st. 4to. 700 ils. 623p. F/F. A4. $135.00

BADER. *Bibliography of British Book Illustrators 1860-1900.* 1978. 1/1000. 4to. ils. 197p. F/G. A4. $125.00

BAECK, Leo. *Judaism & Christianity.* 1958. PA. JPS. 292p. VG/G+. S3. $22.00

BAECK, Leo. *Pharisees & Other Essays.* 1947. Schocken. 164p. VG. S3. $30.00

BAEDEKER, Karl. *Baedeker's Touring Guide to Yugoslavia.* 1964. Stuttgart. Baedeker's. tall 8vo. tables/plans/maps/ils. VG/dj. W1. $16.00

BAEDEKER, Karl. *Mediterranean Sea Port & Sea Routes Including Madeira...* 1911. Leipzig. Baedeker. 1st. 12mo. 38 maps/49 plans. 607p. VG. W1. $50.00

BAEDEKER, Karl. *Western Norway.* nd. Leipsic. private prt. ils/fld maps/42p index. full leather. VG. M12. $30.00

BAER, Helene G. *Heart Is Like Heaven: Life of Lydia Maria Child.* 1964. PA U. 1st. 339p. cloth. NF/dj. M20. $28.00

BAER, Ludwig. *History of the German Steel Helmet 1916-1945.* 1985. San Jose. 1st. mc pl/photos. 448p. VG. S16. $40.00

BAERS, Henri. *Les Tables Astronomiques de Louvain, 1528.* 1976. Brussels. Culture et Civililasion. facsimile. F/dj. T10. $25.00

BAERS, Joannes. *Olinda, Ghelegen int Landt van Brasil, inde Capitania...* 1630. Amsterdam. Laurentsz. 1st. woodcut vignette. modern limp vellum. R15. $2,800.00

BAGBY, George. *Cop Killer.* 1956. Crime Club. 1st. NF/dj. M25. $15.00

BAGBY, George. *Dead Wrong.* 1957. Crime Club. 1st. G/G. P3. $12.00

BAGG, Rufus Mather. *Pliocene & Pleistocene Foraminifera From Southern CA.* 1912. WA. Dept Interior. 28 pl. 153p. prt wrp. D11. $20.00

BAGGLEY & MCDOUGALL. *Plants of Yellowstone National Park.* 1956. Yellowstone Lib/Mus. 2nd. 8vo. VG. A22. $20.00

BAGLEY, Desmond. *Bahama Crisis.* 1980. Summit. 1st. VG/VG. P3. $18.00

BAGLEY, Desmond. *Enemy.* 1978. Doubleday. 1st. VG/VG. P3. $18.00

BAGLEY, Desmond. *Flyaway.* 1978. Collins. 1st. VG/VG. P3. $20.00

BAGLEY, Desmond. *Spoilers.* 1970. Doubleday. 1st. VG/G. P3. $15.00

BAGLEY, Desmond. *Windfall.* 1982. Collins. 1st. NF/VG. P3. $18.00

BAGNELL, Kenneth. *Canadese: Portrait of the Italian Canadians.* 1989. Toronto. 1st. sgn. photos. T12. $12.00

BAHR, Edith-Jane. *Nice Neighborhood.* 1973. Collins Crime Club. 1st. VG/G. P3. $15.00

BAIGELL, Matthew. *Charles Burchfield.* 1976. Watson Guptill. 46 mc pl/100+ b&w ils. 208p. cloth. dj. D2. $225.00

BAILEY, Arthur Scott. *Tale of Billy Woodchuck.* 1916. 1st. ils L Brehm. NF. M19. $25.00

BAILEY, Arthur Scott. *Tale of Henrietta Hen.* 1921. Grosset Dunlap. 12mo. ils Harry L Smith. VG+. C8. $35.00

BAILEY, Carolyn Sherwin. *Little Rabbit Who Wanted Red Wings.* 1945. Platt Munk. ils Dorothy Grider. red cloth. VG+/dj. M20. $25.00

BAILEY, Carolyn. *Lil' Hannibal.* 1938. Platt Munk. ils. cloth/pict label. C8. $75.00

BAILEY, Carolyn. *Tops & Whistles.* 1937. Viking. 1st. 193p. F/VG. P2. $45.00

BAILEY, Daniel. *Essex Harmony Containing a New & Concise Introduction...* 1770. Newbury Port, MA. 1st. 16mo. 22p. old calf. M1. $1,500.00

BAILEY, F.M. *Comprehensive Catalogue of Queensland Plants.* 1909. Brisbane. Cumming. 2nd. 879p. B1. $120.00

BAILEY, Flora L. *Some Sex Beliefs & Practices in Navaho Community.* 1950. Harvard. 4to. 108p. F. F7. $35.00

BAILEY, H.C. *Case for Mr Fortune.* 1932. Canada. Doubleday Doran. VG/VG. P3. $45.00

BAILEY, H.C. *Mr Fortune Wonders.* 1933. Crime Club. 1st. VG. P3. $40.00

BAILEY, H.J. *Reminiscences of a Christian Life.* 1885. Portland, ME. Hoyt Fogg & Donham. 2nd. 419p. aeg. xl. V3. $16.00

BAILEY, Howard. *ABC's of Play Producing.* 1955. McKay. 1st. sgn. VG/VG. B11. $18.00

BAILEY, J.O. *Pilgrims Through Time & Space.* 1947. Argus. 1st. NF/dj. M2. $40.00

BAILEY, Kenneth P. *Ohio Company of Virginia...* 1939. Glendale. Arthur Clark. 1st. 5 maps. teg. G+. B18. $125.00

BAILEY, L.H. *Cyclopedia of American Horticulture.* 1904. NY. Macmillan. 3rd. 4 vol. A10. $150.00

BAILEY, L.H. *First Lessons With Plants.* 1898. Macmillan. 1st. 117p. xl. A10. $30.00

BAILEY, L.H. *How To Make a Flower Garden.* 1905. Doubleday. 370p. VG. A10. $25.00

BAILEY, L.H. *Manual of Cultivated Plants.* 1975. NY. Macmillan. 1116p. VG/dj. A10. $45.00

BAILEY, L.H. *Manual of Cultivated Plants.* 1977. Macmillan. revised/16th prt. 1116p. NF. W2. $25.00

BAILEY, L.H. *Nursery Manual.* 1944. Macmillan. 456p. dj. A10. $22.00

BAILEY, L.H. *Outlook to Nature.* 1924 (1905). Macmillan. 195p. dj. A10. $40.00

BAILEY, L.H. *Plant-Breeding.* 1902. NY. Macmillan. 354p. gr cloth. VG. B14. $45.00

BAILEY, L.H. *Principles of Agriculture.* 1910. Macmillan. 16th. 336p. cloth. A10. $28.00

BAILEY, L.H. *Principles of Vegetable Gardening.* 1919. Macmillan. 17th. 458p. A10. $30.00

BAILEY, L.H. *Standard Cyclopedia of Horticulture.* 1917 (1914). NY. 2nd. 6 vol. ils. 3639p. B26. $200.00

BAILEY, Lee. *Lee Bailey's Soup Meals: Main Event Soups...* 1989. NY. 1st. 4to. mc photos. VG/dj. A16. $17.50

BAILEY, Pearce. *Accident & Injury: Their Relations to Diseases of Nervous...* 1898. NY. 1st. 430p. half leather. A13. $250.00

BAILEY, Pearl. *Pearl's Kitchen.* 1973. HBJ. 1st. sgn. F/dj. D10/Q1. $50.00

BAILEY, William W. *Botanizing: A Guide to Field-Collecting & Herbarium Work.* 1899. Providence. Preston Rounds. 142p. cloth. A10. $45.00

BAILEY & BAILEY. *Hortus Second.* 1959. Macmillan. 10th. 778p. VG. B1. $40.00

BAILEY & BISHOFF. *Tin Woodman.* 1979. Doubleday. 1st. sgn. NF/dj. M2. $30.00

BAILEY & CHALMERS. *Report on Surface Geology...New Brunswick.* 1898. Ottawa. photos/map. disbound. A17. $15.00

BAILEY & CHILDERS. *Applied Mineral Exploration With Special Reference...* 1977. Boulder. Westview. 542p. NF/dj. D8. $45.00

BAILEY & COOKE. *Birds of New Mexico.* 1928. np. ils/figures/60 maps. 807p. NF. M12. $195.00

BAIN, F.W. *Digit of the Moon.* 1905. Putnam. 1st. G+. M2. $25.00

BAIN & HARRIS. *Mickey Mouse: Fifty Happy Years.* 1977. Harmony. 1st. F/lg wrp. M2. $20.00

BAINBRIDGE, Beryl. *Birthday Boys.* 1994. NY. Carroll Graf. 8vo. 189p. M/dj. P4. $18.95

BAINBRIDGE, Beryl. *Bottle Factory Outing.* 1975. Brazillier. 1st Am. NF/dj. A24. $30.00

BAINBRIDGE, Beryl. *Injury Time.* 1977. Brazillier. 1st Am. F/F. A24. $30.00

BAINUM, Peter M. *International Space Year in the Pacific Basin.* 1992. San Diego. Am Astronautical Soc. 4to. 782p. VG/wrp. K5. $40.00

BAIRD, Joseph Armstrong. *California's Pictorial Letter Sheets 1849-1869.* 1967. SF. David Magee. 1/475 prt Grabhorn/Hoyem. folio. ils. wht dj. R3. $250.00

BAIRD, W.D. *Quapa People: A History of the Downstream People.* 1980. OK U. ils/maps. F. M4. $18.00

BAIREI. *Vogel und Blumen.* 1952. Leipzig. Wunderlich. 1st. ils. pict brd/cloth spine. VG. W3. $110.00

BAKARICH, Sarah Grace. *Gunsmoke: True Story of Old Tombstone.* 1962. Gateway. 196p. wrp. B19. $15.00

BAKER, Carroll. *Roman Tale.* 1986. DIF. 1st. NF/dj. M25. $25.00

BAKER, Charles H. *Esquire Culinary Companion.* 1959. NY. Crown. VG/dj. A16. $13.00

BAKER, Denys Val. *Face in the Mirror.* 1971. Arkham. 1st. F/F. M2. $40.00

BAKER, Denys Val. *Family at Sea.* 1981. Wm Kimber. 1st. F/F. P3. $20.00

BAKER, Denys Val. *Phantom Lovers.* 1984. Wm Kimber. 1st. VG/VG. P3. $20.00

BAKER, Denys Val. *Waterwheel Turns.* 1982. Wm Kimber. 1st. VG/VG. P3. $20.00

BAKER, G.S. *Ship Design, Resistance & Screw-Propulsion Vol 1 & Vol 2.* 1948 & 1951. Liverpool. Journal of Commerce. 2nd. 2 vol. ils/tables. T7. $110.00

BAKER, J.H. *Legal Profession & the Common Law, Historical Essays.* 1986. London. Hambledon. only collected ed. M11. $65.00

BAKER, J.H. *Manual of Law French. Second Edition.* 1990. Aldershot. Scholar Pr. M11. $65.00

BAKER, Kevin. *Sometimes You See It Coming.* 1993. NY. Crown. 1st. F/clip. B4. $35.00

BAKER, LaFayette. *United States Secret Service in the Late War.* 1889. 1st. 398p. O8. $18.50

BAKER, Mark. *Women.* 1990. S&S. 1st. F/F. A20. $10.00

BAKER, Michael. *Doyle Diary.* 1978. Paddington. VG/VG. P3. $20.00

BAKER, Nicholson. *Mezzanine.* 1988. Weidenfeld Nicolson. 1st. F/F. B3/D10. $100.00

BAKER, Nicholson. *Vox.* 1992. Random. 1st. F/F. B3. $60.00

BAKER, Pearl. *Trail on the Water.* nd (1970). Boulder. sgn. ils/5 fld maps. 134p. VG/VG. F7. $60.00

BAKER, R. Robin. *Evolutionary Ecology of Animal Migration.* 1978. NY. ils. 1012p. F/NF. S15. $35.00

BAKER, Richard M. *Death Stops the Rehearsal.* 1937. Scribner. 1st. VG/G. P3. $35.00

BAKER, Roger. *Marilyn Monroe.* 1990. Portland. VG/VG. P3. $25.00

BAKER, Russell. *Good Times.* 1989. Morrow. 1st. sgn. F/F. W2. $35.00

BAKER, Samuel W. *Wild Beasts & Their Ways.* 1988. Prescott. facsimile 1890 ed. 1/1000. leatherette. F. A17. $17.50

BAKER, Scott. *Night Child.* 1979. Berkley. 1st. author's 2nd novel. F/F. M21. $30.00

BAKER & BAKER. *Doctor Who: Ultimate Foe.* 1988. WH Allen. hc. F/F. P3. $14.00

BAKER & BAKER. *Reindeer's Shoe & Other Stories.* 1988. Austin, TX. 1st. 4to. 112p. NF/dj. C14. $18.00

BAKER & BERTHOZ. *Control by Brain Stem Neurons.* 1977. Amsterdam. Elsevier/North-Holland Biomedical Pr. 8vo. red cloth. G1. $65.00

BAKER & MURPHY. *Handbook of Marine Science.* 1981. Boca Raton. CRC Pr. 223p. F. B1. $65.00

BAKKER, Elna. *Great Southwest.* 1972. Palo Alto. AM West Pub. hc. dj. A19. $20.00

BAKKER, R.T. *Dinosaur Heresies.* 1986. Morrow. 481p. cloth. F/dj. D8. $36.00

BALABAN, John. *After Our War.* 1974. Pittsburgh. 1st. author's 1st book. F/F. B4. $85.00

BALABAN, John. *Remembering Heaven's Face. A Moral Witness in Vietnam.* 1991. Poseidon. 1st. photos. F/F. R14. $30.00

BALCH, Glenn. *Lost Horse.* 1950. Crowell. 1st. VG. O3. $18.00

BALCHIN, Nigel. *Seen Dimly Before Dawn.* 1964. Rpt Soc. VG/VG. P3. $8.00

BALCOM, Mary G. *Ketchikan: Alaska's Totemland.* 1974. Chicago. Adams. 3rd. 8vo. 139p. P4. $25.00

BALDERSTON, Lydia Ray. *Housekeeping Workbook — How To Do It.* 1935. Lippincott. sbdg. B10. $15.00

BALDICK, Cris. *Oxford Book of Gothic Tales.* 1991. Oxford. 1st. F/F. P3. $25.00

BALDRIDGE, M. *Reminiscence of Parker H French Expedition Through TX...* 1959. LA. private prt. 1/17 (of 300 total). special sgns. fld map. 52p. brd. D11. $75.00

BALDWIN, C.H. *Fifth Annual Report State Entomologist of Indiana.* 1912. Indianapolis. Burford. 324p. VG. A10. $25.00

BALDWIN, Faith. *Private Duty.* 1943. Triangle. 9th. 338p. VG/dj. A25. $12.00

BALDWIN, Faith. *Self-Made Woman.* 1932. Farrar Rhinehart. 1st. F/F. B4. $85.00

BALDWIN, Hanson W. *Sea Fights & Shipwrecks. True Tales of the Seven Seas.* 1955. Garden City. Hanover. 8vo. 315p. VG/dj. P4. $30.00

BALDWIN, James. *Cesar: Compressions D'Or.* 1973. np. Hachette. 1st. photos. 93p. F/VG+. B4. $450.00

BALDWIN, James. *Devil Finds Work.* 1976. Dial. 1st. F/F. H11. $55.00

BALDWIN, James. *Evidence of Things Not Seen.* 1985. Holt Rinehart. 1st. sm 8vo. F/F. C8. $60.00

BALDWIN, James. *Go Tell It on the Mountain.* 1953. Knopf. 1st. author's 1st book. F/NF clip. B4. $1,800.00

BALDWIN, James. *Going To Meet the Man.* 1965. Dial. 1st. F/NF. M19. $45.00

BALDWIN, James. *If Beale Street Could Talk.* 1974. Dial. 1st. F/F. H11. $70.00

BALDWIN, James. *Just Above My Head.* 1979. Dial. 1/500. sgn/#d. F/case. M25. $150.00

BALDWIN, James. *Nobody Knows My Name.* 1961. NY. Dial. 1st. VG/VG. R14. $75.00

BALDWIN, James. *Nobody Knows My Name.* 1964. London. 1st. dj. T9. $45.00

BALDWIN, James. *Notes of a Native Son.* 1955. Boston. Beacon. 1st. F/NF. B4. $750.00

BALDWIN, James. *Price of the Ticket.* 1985. St Martin/Marek. 1st. F/dj. Q1. $40.00

BALDWIN, James. *Tell Me How Long the Train's Been Gone.* 1968. NY. Dial. 1st. F/NF. B2/M25. $35.00

BALDWIN, Leland D. *Keelboat Age on Western Waters.* 1941. Pittsburgh. ils. 268p. dj. T7. $50.00

BALDWIN, Leland D. *Pittsburgh: Story of a City.* 1937. Pittsburgh. 3rd. 387p. as new/dj. H1. $20.00

BALDWIN, Victor & Jeane. *Little Kitten, Big World.* 1956. Morrow. 1st. ils. G+/G+. P2. $25.00

BALDWIN & CAZAC. *Little Man, Little Man.* 1976. Michael Joseph. correct 1st. F/NF. B2. $65.00

BALET, Jan. *What Makes an Orchestra.* nd (1951). NY. OUP. 1st. sm 4to. 41p. VG+. C14. $14.00

BALFOUR, Michael. *Royal Baby Book: For the Prince & Princess of Wales.* 1981. London. Pan. 1st. T12. $45.00

BALINT, Alice. *Early Years of Life: A Psychoanalytic Study.* 1954. Basic. 1st. 149p. VG/VG. A25. $15.00

BALKOSKI, Joseph. *Beyond the Beachhead: 29th Infantry Division in Normandy.* 1989. Stackpole. 1st. 304p. VG/dj. M20. $10.00

BALL, Berenice M. *Barns of Chester County Pennsylvania.* 1974. W Chester. Chester County Hospital. 1st/ltd. sgn. VG/VG. O3. $95.00

BALL, Brian N. *Baker Street Boys.* 1983. BC. 1st. VG/VG. P3. $20.00

BALL, John. *Cop Cade.* 1978. Crime Club. 1st. VG/VG. P3. $15.00

BALL, John. *Johnny Get Your Gun.* 1969. Little Brn. 1st. F/NF. Q1. $75.00

BALL, John. *Kiwi Target.* 1989. Carroll Graf. 1st. F/F. P3. $16.00

BALL, John. *Singapore.* nd. Dodd Mead. 2nd. VG/VG. P3. $15.00

BALL, M.W. *Fascinating Oil Business.* 1940. Bobbs Merrill. 420p. F. D8. $20.00

BALL & BREEN. *Murder California Style.* 1987. St Martin. 1st. F/F. P3. $18.00

BALLANCE & EDMUNDS. *Treatise on Ligation of Great Arteries...* 1891. London. 1st. xl. rpr head/tail spine. A13. $550.00

BALLANTINE, Betty. *American Celebration: Art of Charles Wysocki.* 1985. Greenwich. 1st. 192p. NF/NF. M20. $30.00

BALLARD, Allen B. *Education of Black Folk: Afro-American Struggle...* 1973. Harper. 1st. 173p. F/F. B4. $75.00

BALLARD, Frank. *Christian Findings After Fifty Years.* 1927. Epworth. 246p. G/dj. B29. $6.00

BALLARD, G.A. *Rulers of the Indian Ocean.* 1928. Houghton Mifflin. ils/map ep. F. O7. $75.00

BALLARD, George. *Memoirs of British Ladies, Who Have Been Celebrated...* 1775. London. Evans. 2nd. tall 8vo. 320p. rebound full mottled calf. H13. $395.00

BALLARD, J.G. *Crash.* 1973. Farrar. 1st Am. F/dj. M2. $65.00

BALLARD, J.G. *Day of Creation.* 1988. FSG. 1st Am. NF/dj. M21. $12.00

BALLARD, J.G. *Drowned World.* 1981. Dragon's Dream. F/dj. M2. $30.00

BALLARD, J.G. *Empire of the Sun.* 1984. S&S. 1st. F/F. M19. $25.00

BALLARD, J.G. *Hello America.* 1988. Carroll Graf. 1st. F/F. P3. $18.00

BALLARD, J.G. *High-Rise.* 1975. HRW. 1st. F/VG. M19. $25.00

BALLARD, J.G. *Kindness of Women.* 1991. FSG. 1st. F/F. P3. $20.00

BALLARD, J.G. *Memories of the Space Age.* 1988. Arkham. 1st. F/F. M2. $17.00

BALLARD, J.G. *Running Wild.* 1988. London. Hutchinson. 1st. F/F. A24. $30.00

BALLARD, J.G. *Unlimited Dream Company.* 1979. HRW. 1st. VG/VG. P3. $25.00

BALLARD, Robert D. *Discovery of the Bismarck.* 1990. Warner. 1st. sgn. 232p. VG/VG. B11. $65.00

BALLARD, Todhunter. *Californian.* 1971. Doubleday. 1st. VG/VG. P3. $20.00

BALLARD, W.T. *Say Yes to Murder.* 1942. Putnam. 1st. VG. M25. $50.00

BALLEM, John. *Judas Conspiracy.* 1976. Musson. VG/VG. P3. $13.00

BALLEM, John. *Moon Pool.* 1978. McClelland Stewart. 1st. VG/VG. P3. $20.00

BALLENTINE, G. *Autobiography of an English Soldier in the US Army.* 1986. Lakeside Classic. ils. 347p. F. M4. $35.00

BALLINGER, John. *Williamsburg Forgeries.* 1989. St Martin. 1st. sgn. 276p. M/dj. K3. $15.00

BALLINGER, W.A. *Rebellion.* 1967. Howard Baker. 1st. F/F. P3. $15.00

BALLOU, Maturin. *Equatorical America.* 1900 (1892). Houghton Mifflin. 371p. gilt bl cloth. xl. F3. $15.00

BALMER, Edwin. *Wild Goose Chase.* 1915. Duffield. 1st. F/NF. B4. $200.00

BALZER, Richard. *Optical Amusements: Magic Lanterns & Other Transforming...* 1987. self pub. sgn. 81p. F/wrp. H1. $36.00

BAMONTE, Tony. *Sheriffs, 1911-1989. A History of Murders in the Wilderness.* 1991. Clark. 1st. ils. 251p. M. J2. $75.00

BANARD & PEPPER. *Christian Barnard: One Life.* 1970. NY. 1st Am. 402p. dj. A13. $25.00

BANCROFT, A.L. *Author's Carnival Album.* 1880. SF. ils/line drawings. dk gr cloth. VG. K7. $150.00

BANCROFT, Edith. *Jane Allen, Center.* 1920. Cupples Leon. 1st. ils Thelma Gooch. 310p. VG+. A25. $30.00

BANCROFT, Hubert Howe. *Bancroft's History of Utah 1540-1886.* 1982. NV Pub. 8vo. blk cloth. F7. $35.00

BANCROFT, Hubert Howe. *History of California.* 1963. Santa Barbara. Wallace Hebberd. 7 vol. cloth. djs. D11. $325.00

BANCROFT, Hubert Howe. *History of Central America 1501-1887.* 1883-1887. Bancroft. 2 vol. maps. M4. $55.00

BANCROFT, Hubert Howe. *Native Races, Vol IV: Antiquities.* 1886. SF. History Co Pub. ils/fld map. 3-quarter calf. VG. K7. $25.00

BANDELIER, Adolf F. *Delight Makers.* 1890. Dodd Mead. 8vo. 490p. brn cloth. VG-. F7. $145.00

BANDELIER, Adolf F. *Delight Makers.* 1942. Dodd Mead. rpt. VG/G. O4. $15.00

BANDELIER & HEWETT. *Indians of the Rio Grande Valley.* 1937. Albuquerque. 1st. VG/fair. B5. $55.00

BANFIELD, E.J. *My Tropic Isle.* 1913. London. 3rd. 315p. A17. $15.00

BANGS, John Kendrick. *House-Boat on the Styx.* 1896. Harper. decor brd. VG. P3. $50.00

BANGS, John Kendrick. *Mr Bonaparte of Corsica.* 1895. Harper. 1st. ils HW McVicakr. 265p. G. H1. $35.00

BANGS, John Kendrick. *Over the Plum Pudding.* 1901. Harper. 1st. VG. M2. $50.00

BANGS, John Kendrick. *R Holmes & Co.* 1906. Arthur F Bird. 1st. G. P3. $75.00

BANISTER, Judith. *English Silver.* 1969. London. Hamlyn. 1st. 12mo. 71 mc pl. as new/dj. H1. $16.00

BANKO, W.E. *Trumpeter Swan.* 1980. Lincoln, NE. 214p. ils wrp. B1. $22.50

BANKS, Carolyn. *Darkroom.* 1980. Viking. 1st. F/F. P3. $15.00

BANKS, Charles Edward. *Planters of the Commonwealth.* 1930. Houghton Mifflin. 1/787. ils. F. O7. $225.00

BANKS, Iain M. *Consider Phlebas.* 1988. St Martin. 1st Am. F/dj. A24. $25.00

BANKS, Iain M. *Player of Games.* 1988. Macmillan. 1st. F/F. P3. $30.00

BANKS, Iain M. *State of the Art.* 1989. Ziesing. 1st. F/F. P3. $25.00

BANKS, Iain M. *Walking on Glass.* 1985. Macmillan. 1st. F/F. P3. $30.00

BANKS, Iain M. *Wasp Factory.* 1984. Houghton Mifflin. 1st Am. sgn. author's 1st book. F/NF. A24. $45.00

BANKS, Louis Albert. *Story of the Hall of Fame.* 1902. NY. Christian Herald. A19. $25.00

BANKS, Lynne Reid. *Airy Rebel.* 1985. NY. Doubleday. 1st. sgn. VG/VG. A23. $32.00

BANKS, Lynne Reid. *I, Houdini.* 1988. Doubleday. 1st. sgn. VG/VG. A23. $32.00

BANKS, Lynne Reid. *Return of the Indian.* 1986. Doubleday. 5th. sgn. VG/VG. A23. $32.00

BANKS, Roger. *Unrelenting Ice.* 1962. London. Constable. 8vo. 197p. VG/worn. P4. $45.00

BANKS, Russell. *Affliction.* 1989. Harper Row. 1st. F/F. A20. $20.00

BANKS, Russell. *Affliction.* 1989. Harper Row. 1st. sgn. F/F. A23. $32.00

BANKS, Russell. *Continental Drift.* 1985. Hamish Hamilton. 1st. sgn. F/F. A23. $42.00

BANKS, Russell. *Relationship of My Imprisonment.* 1983. Sun Moon. 1st. F/F. R14. $40.00

BANKS, Russell. *Success Stories.* 1986. NY. Harper Row. 1st. F/dj. Q1. $25.00

BANKS, Russell. *Sweet Hereafter.* 1991. Harper Collins. 1st. sgn. F/F. A23. $42.00

BANKS & READ. *History of the San Francisco Disaster & Mt Vesuvius Horror.* nd. SF. self pub. ils. 8vo. VG. O4. $25.00

BANN & HUBBARD. *Impressions: Short Sketches & Intimacies...Elbert Hubbard.* 1927 (1921). Roycrofters. 2nd. 12 tipped-in photos. teg. F/G. H3. $85.00

BANNATYNE, Gilbert. *Rheumatoid Arthritis: Its Pathology, Morbid Anatomy...* 1896. Bristol. ils. 173p. A13. $300.00

BANNERMAN, Helen. *Little Black Sambo.* ca 1920s. Chicago. Whitman. Just Right Books. enlarged prt ed. ils Shinn. 63p. D1. $400.00

BANNERMAN, Helen. *Little Black Sambo.* 1932. Whitman. ils Nina Jordan. 16mo. pict brd. R5. $150.00

BANNERMAN, Helen. *Little Black Sambo.* 1942. Saalfield. ils Ethel Hays. 16p. VG. M5. $125.00

BANNERMAN, Helen. *Story of Little Black Mingo.* 1901. London. Nesbit. 2nd. 16mo. gray textured cloth. R5. $225.00

BANNERMAN, Helen. *Story of Little Black Mingo.* 1902. NY. Stokes. 1st Am. 16mo. 144p. gr cloth. R5. $350.00

BANNERMAN, Helen. *Story of Little Black Quibba.* 1903. NY. Stokes. 1st Am. 16mo. R5. $350.00

BANNERMAN, Helen. *Story of Little Black Sambo.* 1919. Donohue. Peter Rabbit series. ils. 8vo. red brd/pict label. G. D1. $200.00

BANNERMAN & NEILL. *Peter Rabbit & Black Sambo Painting Book.* 1908. Reilly Britton. sm 12mo. VG. C8. $35.00

BANNING, G.H. *In Mexican Waters.* 1925. Boston. Lauriat. 8vo. ils/photos/map. cloth. VG. M12/O4. $65.00

BANNING, Kendall. *Pirates! or, Cruise of the Black Revenge, a Tale...* 1918 (1916). Chicago. Woodworth. rpt. ils Gustave Baumann. F/mailing envelope. D4. $95.00

BANNING, William. *Heritage Years: Second Marine Division Commememorative...* 1988. Paducha. 1st. 1/1000. 191p. VG. S16. $50.00

BANNING & HUGH. *Six Horses.* 1930. Century. VG. O3. $35.00

BANNION, Della; see Sellers, Con.

BANNON, Laura. *Nemo Meets the Emperor.* 1957. Whitman. ils Katherine Evans. 4to. NF. P2. $35.00

BANTA, R.E. *Ohio.* 1949. Rinehart. 1st. 592p. VG/dj. M20. $45.00

BANVILLE, John. *Book of Evidence.* 1989. London. 1st. dj. T9. $20.00

BANVILLE, John. *Long Lankin.* 1970. London. Secker Warburg. UP. sgn. NF/wrp. B4. $850.00

BAPTIST, R. Hernekin. *Cargo of Parrots.* 1937. Boston. Little Brn. 1st. F/F. B4. $85.00

BARAGA, Frederic. *Dictionary of the Ojibway Language.* 1992. MN Hist Soc. rpt 1878 ed. 736p. M/wrp. A17. $25.00

BARAKA, Amiri. *Dikt for Viderekomne.* 1983. Oslo. 1st Norwegian. author's sgn copy. VG/wrp. B4. $125.00

BARBEAU & HORNYANSKY. *Golden Phoenix & Other Tales.* 1963. Oxford. 4th. VG/VG. P3. $15.00

BARBER, Dulan. *Monsters Who's Who.* 1974. Crescent. VG/VG. P3. $18.00

BARBER, Edwin A. *American Glassware.* 1900. McKay. 1st. 112p. VG. M20. $25.00

BARBER, N. *Sinister Twilight: Fall of Singapore, 1942.* 1968. MA. map/index. 364p. VG/VG. S16. $20.00

BARBER, Noel. *Sultans.* 1973. S&S. 1st. 8vo. ils/pl. 304p. cloth. VG/dj. W1. $18.00

BARBIER, Dominique. *Dressage for the New Age.* 1990. Prentice Hall. 1st. F/F. O3. $22.00

BARBOUR, John. *Footprints on the Moon.* 1969. Assoc Pr. 216p. lg 4to. dj. A17. $12.50

BARCLAY, Bill; see Moorcock, Michael.

BARCLAY, Florence L. *Wall of Partition.* 1914. Putnam. 1st. 421p. VG. W2. $40.00

BARCLAY, Glen St. John. *Anatomy of Horror: Masters of Occult Fiction.* 1978. St Martin. 1st. F/dj. M2. $25.00

BARCLAY, John. *Apology for the True Christian Divinity...* 1789. Phil. Joseph James. 574p. leather/rpl leather spine. V3. $55.00

BARCLAY, John. *Memoirs of the Rise, Progress & Persecutions...Quakers...* 1835. Phil. Nathan Kite. 354p. leather. V3. $32.00

BARCLAY, John. *Truth Triumphant Through the Spiritual Warfare.* 1831. Phil. BC Stanton. 3 vol. G. V3. $165.00

BARCLAY, William. *Daily Study Bible: Revelation Vol 1 & 2.* 1975-76. Westminster. VG. B29. $8.00

BARCLAY, William. *Ethics in a Permissive Society.* 1971. Harper. 223p. VG. B29. $7.50

BARDACH, J.E. *Aquaculture: Farming & Husbandry of Fresh-Water & Marine...* 1972. NY. Wiley. photos/figures/tables. 868p. cloth. F. M12. $37.50

BARDIN, John Franklin. *Purloining Tiny.* 1978. Harper Row. 1st. VG/VG. P3. $35.00

BARDWELL, Harrison. *Girl Sky Pilot: Roberta's Flying Courage (#1).* 1930. Saalfield. 1st thus. ils. VG/dj. A25. $30.00

BARENHOLZ, Edith F. *George Brown Toy Sketchbook.* 1971. Princeton. Pyne. 1st. ils George Brn. 60p. NF/case. D1. $125.00

BARFIELD, Owen. *Owen Barfield on CS Lewis.* 1989. Wesleyan U. 1st. edit GB Tennyson. M/clip. A18. $20.00

BARHLOTT, Wilhelm. *Cacti.* 1979. Cheltenham. 249p. F/dj. B26. $29.00

BARING-GOULD, Sabine. *Domitia.* 1898. Stokes. VG. P3. $25.00

BARING-GOULD, William S. *Annotated Sherlock Holmes.* 1972. Clarkson Potter. 2nd/8th prt. 2 vol. 4to. F/VG case. H1. $60.00

BARING-GOULD & BARING-GOULD. *The Annotated Mother Goose.* 1962. Clarkson Potter. 1st. 900 rhymes. cloth brd. F/dj. B24. $125.00

BARJAVEL, Rene. *Immortals.* 1974. Morrow. 1st. VG/VG. P3. $20.00

BARKER, A.J. *Dunkirk: Great Escape.* 1977. NY. 1st Am. 240p. VG/VG. S16. $22.50

BARKER, Catherine. *Yesterday Today.* 1941. Caxton. 1st. ils. 263p. VG/dj. B5. $25.00

BARKER, Cicely Mary. *Fairies of the Trees.* 1940. London. Blackie. 4 full-p pl. 16mo. tan pict brd/mc label. dj. R5. $125.00

BARKER, Cicely Mary. *Flower Fairies of the Summer.* 1925. London. Blackie. 16mo. tan brd/pict label. dj. R5. $125.00

BARKER, Cicely Mary. *Little Book of Old Rhymes.* 1976. London. Blackie. sm 4to. unp. NF/dj. C14. $10.00

BARKER, Cicely Mary. *Summer Songs With Music From Flower Fairies...* ca 1925. London. Blackie. 12 mtd pl. 4to. cloth brd. R5. $135.00

BARKER, Clive. *Books of Blood Volume 1.* 1991. MacDonald. F/F. P3. $25.00

BARKER, Clive. *Cabal.* 1988. Poseidon. ARC/1st. sgn. F/F. D10. $75.00

BARKER, Clive. *Cabal.* 1988. Poseidon. 1st. F/F. P3. $25.00

BARKER, Clive. *Damnation Game.* 1987. Ace Putnam. 1st. sgn. F/NF. B3. $65.00

BARKER, Clive. *Everville.* 1994. Harper Collins. 1st. inscr. F/F. M19. $25.00

BARKER, Clive. *Great & Secret Show.* 1990. Harper Row. 1st. F/F. P3. $20.00

BARKER, Clive. *Imajica.* 1991. Harper Collins. 1st. sgn. F/VG. B3. $50.00

BARKER, Clive. *In the Flesh.* 1986. Poseidon. 1st. sgn. F/F. B3. $75.00

BARKER, Clive. *In the Flesh.* 1986. Poseidon. 1st. F/F. P3. $30.00

BARKER, Clive. *Inhuman Condition.* 1986. Poseidon. 1st Am. sgn. F/F. D10. $85.00

BARKER, Clive. *Weaveworld.* 1987. Collins. 1st. F/F. P3. $25.00

BARKER, Lady. *Station Amusements in New Zealand.* 1953. Christchurch, NZ. Whitcombe Tombs. 1st thus. ils/map. 236p. VG/dj. A25. $18.00

BARKER, M.H. *Tough Yarns.* 1835. London. Effingham Wilson. ils George Cruikshank. 351p. older half calf. T7. $110.00

BARKER, Pat. *Ghost Road.* 1995. London. Viking. 1st. F/F. B2. $150.00

BARKER, Ralph. *Small Fruits.* 1954. NY. Rinehart's Garden Lib. ils. photo brd. B26. $11.00

BARKER, Shirley. *Liza Bowe.* 1956. Random. ARC. RS. F/F clip. B4. $50.00

BARKER, Shirley. *Peace, My Daughters.* 1949. Crown. NF/dj. M2. $15.00

BARKER, Shirley. *Swear by Apollo.* 1958. Random. 1st. VG/VG. P3. $35.00

BARKER, William P. *Everyone in the Bible.* 1966. Revell. 370p. VG. B29. $9.00

BARKOW, Al. *Golf's Golden Grind.* 1974. HBJ. 1st. photos. F/VG+. P8. $25.00

BARKOW, Al. *Golf's Golden Grind.* 1974. HBJ. 1st. sgn Lee Trevino. VG/VG. A23. $45.00

BARKWORTH, S. *Nijmegen Proof.* 1988. Phil. Holmes. 1st. 1/650. sgn. F/dj. K3. $40.00

BARLAY, Stephen. *Tsunami.* 1986. Hamish Hamilton. 1st. NF/NF. P3. $22.00

BARLOW, Jean. *End of Elfintown.* 1894. London. Macmillan. 1st. 77p. aeg. G+. P2. $150.00

BARLOW, Joel. *Vision of Columbus: A Poem, in Nine Books.* 1787. Hartfor. NE Prt. 1st. 16mo. 244p. contemporary calf/lacks label. M1. $350.00

BARLOW, Roger. *Brief Summe of Geographie.* 1932. London. Hakluyt Soc. 1st. 8vo. gilt bl cloth. P4. $150.00

BARLOW, Roger. *Sandy Steele: Black Treasure (#1).* 1959. S&S. 1st. VG/G. P3. $10.00

BARLOWE, Wayne-Douglas. *Star Wars: A Popup Book.* 1978. Random. 1st. VG. M2. $25.00

BARMEY, Libeus. *Letters of the Pike's Peak Gold Rush.* 1959. San Jose, CA. Talisman. 1/975. red/gray bdg. M/F. K7. $85.00

BARNARD, Charles. *$2000 a Year on Fruits & Flowers...* 1892. Phil. Potter. 421p. VG. A10. $30.00

BARNARD, J. Laurens. *Abyssal Crustacea.* 1962. Columbia. ils. 223p. xl. VG. S15. $22.00

BARNARD, Robert. *Bodies.* 1986. Scribner. 1st. VG/VG. P3. $14.00

BARNARD, Robert. *Cherry Blossom Corpse.* 1987. Scribner. 1st. VG/VG. P3. $15.00

BARNARD, Robert. *Death in a Cold Climate.* 1980. London. Collins Crime Club. 1st. F/dj. M15. $200.00

BARNARD, Robert. *Political Suicide.* 1986. Scribner. 1st. VG/VG. P3. $14.00

BARNES, Albert. *Notes on the Old & New Testaments: Minor Prophets.* 1977. Baker. 2 vol. VG/dj. B29. $18.00

BARNES, Arthur K. *Interplanetary Hunter.* 1956. Gnome. 1st. NF/dj. M2. $25.00

BARNES, F.A. *Utah Canyon Country.* 1986. Salt Lake City. UT Geographic Series. 4to. 117p. stiff wrp. F7. $17.00

BARNES, Joanna. *Silverwood.* 1985. Linden. 1st. VG/VG. P3. $12.00

BARNES, John. *Man Who Pulled Down the Sky.* 1986. Cogdon Weed. 1st. VG/VG. P3. $20.00

BARNES, Julian. *Duffy.* 1980. London. Jonathan Cape. 1st. author's 2nd book. F/clip. D10. $90.00

BARNES, Julian. *Flaubert's Parrot.* 1985. Knopf. 1st. F/NF. A24. $45.00

BARNES, Julian. *Going to the Dogs.* 1987. London. Viking. 1st. F/dj. M25. $45.00

BARNES, Julian. *History of the World in 10 1/2 Chapters.* 1989. Knopf. 1st. F/dj. A24. $25.00

BARNES, Julian. *Talking It Over.* 1991. London. Cape. 1st. sgn. F/F. R14. $45.00

BARNES, Julian. *Talking It Over: A Novel.* 1991. NY/Toronto. 1st Canadian. F/dj. Q1. $30.00

BARNES, Linda. *Cities of the Dead.* 1986. London. Severn. 1st. sgn. F/NF. T2. $25.00

BARNES, Linda. *Snake Tattoo.* 1989. St Martin. 1st. NF/NF. A24. $27.50

BARNES, Linda. *Snake Tattoo.* 1989. St Martin. 1st. sgn. F/NF. T2. $35.00

BARNES, Linda. *Snake Tattoo.* 1989. St Martin. 1st. VG/dj. N4. $25.00

BARNES, Linda. *Snapshot.* 1993. Delacorte. 1st. F/dj. Q1. $35.00

BARNES, Linda. *Steel Guitar.* 1991. Delacorte. 1st. F/F. B3. $30.00

BARNES, Linda. *Trouble of Fools.* 1987. St Martin. 1st. author's 5th novel. F/dj. C2/D10. $75.00

BARNES, Madeline. *Stirabout Stories.* 1929. London. Blackie. 1st. ils Anderson. 4to. cloth. R5. $225.00

BARNES, Trevor. *Pound of Flesh.* 1991. Morrow. 1st Am. F/F. M22. $10.00

BARNETT, Correlli. *Desert Generals.* 1961. NY. ils/maps. 320p. VG/VG. S16. $25.00

BARNETT, Lincoln. *Treasure of Our Tongue.* 1964. Knopf. 1st. F/F. B35. $28.00

BARNETT, Lincoln. *Universe & Dr Einstein.* 1950. NY. Sloane. sgn. 127p. F/F. B11. $25.00

BARNEY, Maginel Wright. *Valley of the God Almighty Joneses.* 1965. NY. 1st. VG/dj. B5. $40.00

BARNHOUSE, Donald G. *Invisible War.* 1965. Zondervan. 288p. VG/torn. B29. $9.00

BARNSTONE, H. *Galveston That Was.* 1966. NY/Houston. 1st. photos HC Bresson. VG/VG. B5. $75.00

BARNUM, Richard. *Slico the Jumping Squirrel.* 1915. Barse Hopkins. ils Harriet H Tooker. 120p. VG/dj. M20. $15.00

BARON, Virginia. *Sunset in the Spider Web.* 1974. HRW. 1st. 82p. F/F. D4. $30.00

BARON & CARVER. *Bud Stewart: Michigan's Legendary Lure Maker.* 1990. Marceline, MO. 1st. 227p. w/price list. M. A17. $75.00

BARR, Donald. *Space Relations.* 1973. Charterhouse. 1st. F/dj. M2. $15.00

BARR, George. *Upon the Winds of Yesterday.* 1976. Donald Grant. 1st. sgn. F/F. P3. $40.00

BARR, Nevada. *Ill Wind.* 1995. Putnam. ARC. sgn. F/F. D10. $45.00

BARR, Nevada. *Superior Death.* 1994. Putnam. 1st. author's 2nd mystery. rem mk. F/F. B2. $85.00

BARR, Nevada. *Track of the Cat.* 1993. Putnam. 1st. author's 1st mystery. F/F. M15. $175.00

BARR, Roseanne. *My Life As a Woman.* 1989. Harper Row. 1st. F/F. A20. $15.00

BARR & WILLIAMS. *Voyages in Search of a Northwest Passage 1741-1747...* 1995. London. Hakluyt Soc. 2nd Series #181. 8vo. bl cloth. P4. $65.00

BARRAS DE ARAGON, Francisco. *Documentos Referentes a Mutis y su Tiempo.* 1933. Madrid. 35p. F3. $20.00

BARRATT, Glynn. *Southern & Eastern Polynesia.* 1988. Vancouver. 1st. 8vo. 302p. as new/dj. P4. $57.00

BARRET, Richard Carter. *Bennington Pottery & Porcelain.* 1958. Bonanza. ils/index/457 pl. 342p. dk gr cloth. F/dj. H1. $45.00

BARRETT, Andrea. *Lucid Stars.* 1988. Delta Fiction. ARC/author's 1st book. VG/wrp. Q1. $50.00

BARRETT, Andrea. *Middle Kingdom.* 1991. Pocket. 1st. NF/F. H11. $30.00

BARRETT, C.K. *St John: Introduction With Commentary & Notes on Greek Text.* 1956. SPEK. 531p. G. B29. $13.00

BARRETT, Michael. *Antarctic Secret.* 1966. NY. Roy Pub. 2nd. 170p. VG/dj. P4. $25.00

BARRETT, Neal Jr. *Hereafter Gang.* 1991. Zeising. 1st. sgn. F/dj. A24. $50.00

BARRETT, S.A. *Pomo Indian Basketry.* 1970 (1908). Rio Grande Classic. rpt. 31 pl/231 figures. F. M4. $30.00

BARRETT, T.J. *Harnessing the Earthworm: Practical Inquiry Into Soil...* 1955. Boston. Humphries. ils/pl/drawing. 166p. brd. NF/VG. M12. $20.00

BARRIE, James M. *Farewell Miss Julie Logan.* 1932. Scribner. 1st. VG. P3. $20.00

BARRIE, James M. *Jess.* 1898. Dana Estes. 1st. NF. M19. $45.00

BARRIE, James M. *Little White Bird; or, Adventures in Kensington Gardens.* 1902. 1st. VG+. S13. $18.00

BARRIE, James M. *Peter Pan & Wendy.* 1911. Scribner. 1st Am. ils FD Bedford. 267p. gilt gr cloth. VG. D1. $200.00

BARRIE, James M. *Peter Pan & Wendy.* 1921. Scribner. 1st thus. ils ML Attwell. 4to. olive cloth. M5. $275.00

BARRIE, James M. *Peter Pan & Wendy.* 1927 (1921). Scribner. ils Mabel L Attwell. VG. B15. $115.00

BARRIE, James M. *Peter Pan in Kensington Gardens.* 1906. London. Hodder Stoughton. ils Rackham/50 tipped-in pl. G+. B5. $450.00

BARRIE, James M. *Peter Pan in Kensington Gardens.* 1908. Scribner. ils Rackham/50 mtd mc pl. gold stp gr cloth. dj. R5. $600.00

BARRIE, James M. *Peter Pan in Kensington Gardens.* 1910. London. Hodder Stoughton. 7th. ils Rackham/50 mtd pl. 125p text. gilt cloth. VG. D1. $450.00

BARRIE, James M. *Peter Pan.* 1957. Random. ils Marjorie Torrey. 4to. F. M5. $45.00

BARRIE, James M. *Quality Street.* ca 1913. Hodder Stoughton. 4to. 22 tipped-in pl. gilt purple cloth. 198p. NF. T10. $275.00

BARRIENTOS, Bartolome. *Pedro Menendez de Aviles.* 1965. Gainesville, FL. 1st Eng trans. 1/1000. gilt bdg. F. O7. $125.00

BARRINGTON, Daines. *Possibility of Approaching the North Pole Asserted.* 1818. London. Allman. fld frontis/map. 257p. older full calf. T7. $325.00

BARRON, George L. *Genera of Hyphomycetes From Soil.* 1968. NY. Mershon. 12mo. 221p. gilt bl cloth. VG. A22. $16.00

BARROW, A.H. *Fifty Years in Western Africa: Being a Record of Work...* 1969 (1900). NY. Negro U. rpt. 8vo. map/ils. 157p. cloth. VG. W1. $25.00

BARROW, Frances Elizabeth. *Bird Stories, by Aunt Laura.* 1863. Buffalo. Breed & Butler. 47x37mm. aeg. gilt gr pub cloth. F. B24. $165.00

BARROW, Frances Elizabeth. *Carl's Visit to the Child Island, by Aunt Laura.* 1863. Buffalo. Breed & Butler. 47x36mm. 61p. aeg. gilt pub cloth. B24. $140.00

BARROW, Frances Elizabeth. *Doll's Surprise, by Aunt Laura.* 1863. Buffalo. Breed & Butler. 47x36mm. 64p. aeg. gilt pub cloth. F. B24. $200.00

BARROW, Frances Elizabeth. *Morsels of History, by Aunt Laura.* 1863. Buffalo. Breed & Butler. 40x32mm. 64p. aeg. gilt brn cloth. B24. $164.00

BARROW, Frances Elizabeth. *New Testament Stories, by Aunt Laura.* 1862. Buffalo. Breed & Butler. 53x40mm. 64p. aeg. gilt cloth. B24. $135.00

BARROW, Joe Louis Jr. *Joe Louis: 50 Years an American Hero.* 1988. McGraw Hill. lg 8vo. F/F. C8. $30.00

BARROW, Terence. *Illustrated Guide to Maori Art.* 1984. New Zealand. Methuen. 104p. VG+/prt wrp. P4. $25.00

BARROWS, J.H. *World's Parliament of Religions.* 1983. 2 vol. ils. VG. M17. $35.00

BARROWS, W.B. *English Sparrow in North America.* 1889. USDA. 405p. B1. $24.50

BARROWS, Walter Bradford. *Michigan Bird Life.* 1912. MI Agric College. 822p. lg 8vo. wrp. A17. $50.00

BARRY, James P. *Fate of the Lakes: Portrait of the Great Lakes.* 1972. Grand Rapids. Baker. ils. 192p. dj. T7. $28.00

BARRY, Jerome. *Fall Guy.* 1960. Crime Club. 1st. VG/G. P3. $18.00

BARRY, Jerome. *Murder With Your Malted.* 1941. Doubleday Crime Club. 1st. F/clip. M15. $90.00

BARRY, Patrick. *Barry's Fruit Garden.* 1872. Orange Judd. 491p. cloth. A10. $22.00

BARRY & LIBBY. *Confessions of a Basketball Gypsy.* 1972. Prentice Hall. photos. VG+/dj. P8. $25.00

BARSOCCHINI, Peter. *Ghost.* 1989. Dutton. 1st. F/F. T12. $25.00

BARTH, John. *Chimera.* 1972. Random. 1st. sgn. VG/VG. R14. $50.00

BARTH, John. *Floating Opera.* 1956. Appleton Century Crofts. 1st. author's 1st book. NF/NF. L3. $450.00

BARTH, John. *Friday Book.* 1984. Putnam. 1st. NF/VG. B3. $30.00

BARTH, John. *Giles Goat-Boy.* 1967. Secker Warburg. 1st. VG/VG. P3. $20.00

BARTH, John. *Last Voyage of Somebody the Sailor.* 1991. Little Brn. 1st. sgn. F/F. A23. $32.00

BARTH, John. *Sabbatical.* 1982. Putnam. 1st. NF/NF. B3. $20.00

BARTH, Karl. *Church Dogmatics: Doctrine of Creation Vol III, Part 4.* 1985. T&T Clark. 740p. VG. B29. $21.00

BARTHELME, Donald. *Amateurs.* 1976. FSG. 1st. F/F. B35. $30.00

BARTHELME, Donald. *Come Back, Dr Caligari.* 1964. Boston. Little Brn. 1st. F/NF. B2. $150.00

BARTHELME, Donald. *Great Days.* 1979. FSG. 1st. F/F. B35. $25.00

BARTHELME, Donald. *King.* 1990. Harper Row. 1st. NF/NF. A20. $20.00

BARTHELME, Donald. *Snow White.* 1967. Atheneum. 1st. F/dj. Q1. $100.00

BARTHOLOMEW, Ed. *Wyatt Earp, the Man & the Myth.* 1964. Frontier Book. 1st. photos. 335p. VG/VG. J2. $195.00

BARTLETT, Dana W. *Bush Aflame.* 1923. Grafton Pub. 1st. VG/sans. O4. $25.00

BARTLETT, David Vandewater G. *Life & Public Services of Hon Abraham Lincoln...* 1860. NY. Derby Jackson. 1st. 354p. cloth. NF. M8. $250.00

BARTLETT, Frederick Orin. *Web of the Spider.* 1909. Sm Maynard. 1st. VG. M2. $35.00

BARTLETT, J. Henry. *John H Dillingham 1839-1910, Teacher, Minister, Editor.* 1911. Knickerbocker. 190p. VG. V3. $14.00

BARTLETT, John Russell. *Personal Narrative of Explorations & Incidents in TX, NM...* 1965. Rio Grande Pr. 2 vol. ils/maps. F/sans. B19. $95.00

BARTLETT, W.H. *Walks About the City & Environs of Jerusalem.* ca 1850. London. Hall Virtue. 2nd. 8vo. 24 hand-colored steel engravings. teg. F. B24. $500.00

BARTLEY, William. *Iwo Jima: Amphibious Epic.* 1954. WA. fld maps/photos/index. 253p. VG. S16. $85.00

BARTON, Benjamin Smith. *Collections for an Essay Towards Materia Medical of US.* 1810. Phil. 3rd. 2 parts. contemporary tree sheep. B14. $150.00

BARTON, Bruce. *Boy Nobody Knows & the Man Nobody Knows.* 1925 & 1926. Indianapolis. 1st. sgn pres. VG/dj/G box. B5. $40.00

BARTON, George A. *Miscellaneous Babylonian inscriptions, Part I, Sumarian...* 1918. New Haven/Yale. 1st. 61 pl. half cloth. VG. W1. $55.00

BARTON, George. *Adventures of World's Greatest Detectives.* 1909. Phil. Winston. 1st. VG/dj. M15. $45.00

BARTON, May Hollis. *Barton Books for Girls: Kate Martin's Problem (#10).* 1929. Cupples Leon. lists 15 titles. VG/dj. M20. $40.00

BARTON, Ralph. *Science in Rhyme Without Reason.* 1924. Putnam. 1st. 147p. VG. D4. $25.00

BARTON, Rebecca Chalmers. *Witnesses For Freedom.* 1948. Harper. 1st. 294p. VG+/VG. B4. $85.00

BARTRAM, George. *Job Abroad.* 1975. Macmillan. 1st. VG/VG. P3. $20.00

BARTRAM, John. *Travels in Pennsylvania & Canada.* 1966. Ann Arbor. Micro. 94p. F. A10. $45.00

BARTRAM, William. *Travels Through North & South Carolina, Georgia...* 1973 (1792). Savannah. Beehive. 535p. VG/dj. A10. $115.00

BARTRUM, Douglas. *Growing Cacti & Succulents.* 1973. NY. 12 mc pl. F/dj. B26. $12.50

BARTRUM, Douglas. *Rhododendrons & Magnolias.* 1957. London. Garden BC. 176p. dj. A10. $28.00

BARTSCH & NICHOLS. *Fishes & Shells of the Pacific World.* 1945. NY. Macmillan. 1st. 201p. bl cloth. P4. $22.50

BARUCH & MONTGOMERY. *Sally Does It.* 1940. Appleton. 13th. ils Robb Beebe. 73p. cloth. VG. M20. $125.00

BARUK, Henri. *Tsedek.* 1972. Swan House. 291p. VG/G+. S3. $21.00

BARZUN, Jacques. *Catalogue of Crime.* 1971. Harper Row. 1st. xl. VG+/dj. N4. $30.00

BARZUN, Jacques. *Delights of Detection.* 1961. Criterion. 1st. VG. M2. $10.00

BASCOM, John. *Problems in Philosophy.* 1885. Putnam. 1st. 222p. purple silk-type cloth. VG. B22. $9.50

BASCULE. *Royal Spades Auction Bridge With Laws...1909.* 1913. London. 180p. VG. S1. $20.00

BASHO. *Back Roads to Far Towns.* 1968. NY. Bilingual ed. trans Corman/Susumu. VG+/wrp. W3. $15.00

BASIE, Count. *Count Basie's Piano Styles.* 1940. NY. Bregman Vocco Conn. F/wrp. B2. $40.00

BASINGER, J. Martin. *Artistry in Silver & Steel, the Adolph Bayers Legend.* 1st. ils Ben Miller. J2. $85.00

BASINGER, Jeanine. *Woman's View: How Hollywood Spoke to Women 1930-1960.* 1993. Knopf. 1st. F/F. V4. $17.50

BASKERVILLE, Peter. *Bank of Upper Canada. A Collection of Documents.* 1987. Toronto. Champlain Soc. 400p. gilt red cloth. F. P4. $95.00

BASKIN, Leonard. *Hosie's Alphabet.* 1972. Viking. 1st. 4to. VG/G. P2. $65.00

BASKIN, Leonard. *Imps, Demons, Hobgoblins, Witches, Fairies & Elves.* 1984. Pantheon. 1st. F/dj. M2. $10.00

BASS, Charlotta A. *Forty Years: Memoirs From the Pages of a Newspaper.* 1960. Los Angeles. self pub. 1st. insct/dtd 1960. ils. VG. B4. $175.00

BASS, Rick. *Deer Pasture.* 1985. TX A&M. 1st. author's 1st book. F/NF. D10. $125.00

BASS, Rick. *Fathers & Sons.* 1992. Grove Weidenfeld. 1st. sgn. F/F. B3. $60.00

BASS, Rick. *Oil Notes.* 1989. Houghton Mifflin. 1st. sgn. F/F. B3. $75.00

BASS, Rick. *Watch.* 1989. Norton. 1st. author's 3rd book. F/F. T11. $50.00

BASS, Rick. *Watch.* 1989. Norton. 1st. author's 3rd book. VG/VG. L1. $40.00

BASS, Rick. *Watch.* 1989. Norton. 1st. sgn. F/F. R14. $90.00

BASS, Rick. *Wild to the Heart.* 1987. Stackpole. 1st. author's 2nd book. F/F. D10. $85.00

BASS, Rick. *Wild to the Heart.* 1987. Stackpole. 1st. sgn. author's 2nd book. VG/VG. L1. $150.00

BASS, T.J. *Godwhale.* 1975. Methuen. 1st. NF/NF. P3. $40.00

BASSANI, Giorgio. *Garden of the Finzi-Continis.* 1965. Atheneum. 1st Am. NF/clip. D10. $125.00

BASSETT, Marnie. *Realms & Islands. World Voyage of Rose DeFreycinet...1820.* 1962. London. Oxford. 8vo. 275p. bl-gray cloth. VG/worn. P4. $100.00

BASSIN, Moshe. *American Yiddish Poetry, Anthology.* 1940. NY. sm 4to. Yiddish text. 601p. VG. S3. $40.00

BASSO, Hamilton. *Beauregard the Great Creole.* 1933. NY. 1st. VG/VG. B5. $65.00

BASTABLE, Bernard; see Barnard, Robert.

BATCHELDER, Robert C. *Irreversible Decision 1939-1950.* 1962. Boston. Houghton Mifflin. 1st. inscr. NF. K3. $35.00

BATCHELOR, John Calvin. *Birth of the People's Republic of Antarctica.* 1985. NY. Dial. 1st. 1/6000. author's 2nd novel. F/F. D10. $65.00

BATEMAN, Donald. *Berkeley Moynihan, Surgeon.* 1940. NY. 1st. 354p. A13. $20.00

BATEMAN, G.C. *Vivarium, Being Practical Guide to Construction...Vivaria...* 1897. London. Gill. ils/fld front engraving/figures. 424p. pict cloth. VG. M12. $75.00

BATEMAN, Robert. *When the Whites Went.* 1963. Walker. 1st. F/NF. B2. $25.00

BATES, Edward. *Diary of Edward Bates 1859-1866 Edited by Howard K Beale.* 1933. GPO. 1st. 685p. cloth. NF. M8. $65.00

BATES, Frank. *How To Make Old Orchards Profitable.* 1912. Boston. Ball. 123p. VG. A10. $30.00

BATES, Joseph D. *Atlantic Salmon Flies & Fishing.* 1970. Stackpole. 1st. 362p. VG/dj. M20. $80.00

BATES, Joseph D. *Streamer Fly Tying & Fishing.* 1966. Stackpole. 1st. 368p+8 mc pl. NF/dj. A17. $60.00

BATES, M. Searle. *Religious Liberty: An Inquiry.* 1945. Harper. 604p. G/torn. B29. $7.00

BATES, Marston. *Land & Wildlife of South America.* (1968). NY. Time. 4to. 200p. pict brd. F3. $10.00

BATES, Robert. *Mountain Man, The Story of Belmore Browne, Hunter,...* 1988. Amwell. 1st. 424p. as new/case. J2. $350.00

BATTEN, Jack. *Crang Plays the Ace.* 1987. Canada. Macmillan. 1st. F/F. P3. $20.00

BATTEN, Jack. *Straight No Chaser.* 1989. Canada. Macmillan. 1st. F/F. P3. $20.00

BAUDISSIN & GORNY. *Ein Hundebuch.* 1951. Munchen. 2nd. 120p. 4to. A17. $25.00

BAUDOIN, Simonne. *Fables of la Fontaine.* 1957. NY. trans Marie Ponsot. NF/fair. M5. $25.00

BAUDOUIN, Frans. *PP Rubens.* 1989. ils. VG/VG. M17. $40.00

BAUER, C. Max. *Yellowstone: Its Underworld.* 1953. NM U. ils/photos/maps. 122p. VG/wrp. J2. $45.00

BAUER, K. Jack. *Mexican War, 1846-1848.* 1974. Macmillan. 1st. ils. 454p. dj. D11. $40.00

BAUER, Steven. *Satyrday.* 1980. Berkley Putnam. 1st. NF/NF. P3. $15.00

BAUGHMAN, T.H. *Before the Heroes Came. Antarctica in the 1890s.* 1994. Lincoln/London. 8vo. 160p. dk bl cloth. M/dj. P4. $22.95

BAUM, L. Frank. *Annotated Wizard of Oz.* 1973. 1st. ils Denslow. biblio MP Hearn. VG/VG. M17. $50.00

BAUM, L. Frank. *Dorothy & the Wizard of Oz.* 1920. Reilly Lee. hc. G. P3. $75.00

BAUM, L. Frank. *Glinda of Oz.* pre 1935. Reilly Lee. ils JR Neill/12 mc pl. brick cloth/pict label. G+. D1. $175.00

BAUM, L. Frank. *Journeys Through Oz.* 1982. Galley Pr. VG/VG. P3. $12.00

BAUM, L. Frank. *Junior Edition Oz Books.* 1939. Chicago. Rand McNally. Jr ed/complete set of 9 vol. lg 16mo. VG. C8. $350.00

BAUM, L. Frank. *Land of Oz.* nd. Reilly Lee. Popular ed. VG. M2. $40.00

BAUM, L. Frank. *Lost Princess of Oz.* 1939. Rand McNally. Jr Ed. abridged/1st state. 12 mc pl. 62p. pict brd. T10. $50.00

BAUM, L. Frank. *Master Key.* 1974 (1901). Hyperion. rpt. F. M2. $30.00

BAUM, L. Frank. *Patchwork Girl of Oz.* 1913. Reilly Britton. 1st/later state. ils JR Neill. olive gr cloth. R5. $685.00

BAUM, L. Frank. *Queen Zixi of Ix.* 1905. NY. Century. 1st/2nd state. ils Richardson. gr cloth. R5. $400.00

BAUM, L. Frank. *Rinkitink in Oz.* pre 1935. Chicago. Reilly Lee. ils John R Neill. 314p. red cloth/pict label. NF/torn. D1. $400.00

BAUM, L. Frank. *Rinkitink in Oz.* 1939. Rand McNally. Jr Ed. abridged/1st state. 12mo. 62p. VG. T10. $50.00

BAUM, L. Frank. *Rinkitink in Oz.* 1965. Reilly Lee. VG/G. P3. $25.00

BAUM, L. Frank. *Road to Oz.* 1941. Reilly Lee. NF/NF. P3. $100.00

BAUM, L. Frank. *Tik-Tok of Oz.* ca 1940. Reilly lee. ils JR Neill. F/G. M19. $75.00

BAUM, L. Frank. *Wizard of Oz.* (1944). Saalfield. animated Julian Wehr/6 moveables. VG. D1. $200.00

BAUM, L. Frank. *Wizard of Oz.* 1939 (1903). Bobbs Merrill. photoplay ed w/all 1st issue points. F/VG+. B4. $550.00

BAUM, L. Frank. *Wizard of Oz.* 1982. HRW. 1/500. ils/sgn Hague. gilt emerald cloth. cloth case. R5. $350.00

BAUM, L. Frank. *Wonderful Wizard of Oz/Marvelous Land of Oz.* 1966. Dover. 2 vol. ils WW Denslow. half cloth/brd. G+/case. B18. $35.00

BAUM, Richard. *Planets: Some Myths & Realities.* 1973. Halsted. 8vo. 200p. VG/dj. K5. $25.00

BAUMAN, Janina. *Winter in the Morning: Young Girl's Life in Warsaw Ghetto...* 1986. NY. Free Pr. 195p. VG/dj. S3. $25.00

BAUMAN, Louis S. *Light From the Bible.* 1940. Revell. 169p. VG. B29. $5.50

BAUMAN, Louis S. *Russian Events in Light of Bible Prophecy.* 1942. Revell. 191p. VG. B29. $6.00

BAUMER, William. *Sports As Taught & Played at West Point.* 1939. Military Service Pub. 1st. ils/photos. G+. P8. $20.00

BAUMGARTEN, E. Lee. *Price Guide for Children's & Illustrated Books 1880-1945.* 1991. self pub. 2 vol. 4to. unp. 4313 entries. VG. H1. $27.50

BAUR, John E. *Dogs on the Frontier.* 1964. San Antonio. Naylor. hc. dj. A19. $35.00

BAUSCH, Edwin. *Manipulation of the Microscope.* 1891. Rochester. Bausch Lomb. 12mo. 127p. cloth. K3. $20.00

BAUSCH, Richard. *Take Me Back.* 1981. NY. Dial. 1st. sgn. rem mk. F/F. R14. $75.00

BAUSCH, Richard. *Violence.* 1992. Houghton Mifflin. 1st. F/F. M22. $25.00

BAXENDALE, Walter. *Dictionary of Illustrations for Pulpit & Platform.* 1955. Moody. 690p. VG/dj. B29. $13.00

BAXT, George. *Neon Graveyard.* 1979. St Martin. 1st. VG/VG. P3. $30.00

BAXTER, Charles. *First Light.* 1987. NY. Viking. 1st. author's 5th book overall. F/NF. L3. $50.00

BAXTER, Charles. *Relative Stranger.* 1990. Norton. 1st. F/F. B4. $50.00

BAXTER, Doreen. *Woodland Frolics.* 1952. Leicester. Brockhampton. 1st. 4to. gr lettered wheat cloth. R5. $200.00

BAXTER, E.M. *California Cactus.* 1935. Los Angeles. 1/1000. ils/photos. blk cloth. VG. B26. $75.00

BAXTER, J.P. *Introduction of the Ironclad Warship.* 1968 (1933). NY. rpt. ils. 398p. F. M4. $30.00

BAXTER, L. *Housekeeper's Handy Book.* 1931. 1st. photos. VG. E6. $30.00

BAXTER, Lorna. *Eggchild.* 1979. Dutton. 1st. VG/VG. P3. $18.00

BAXTER, Walter. *Look Down in Mercy.* 1952. Putnam. 1st Am. NF/VG. B4. $85.00

BAYARD, Samuel J. *Sketch of Life of Com Robert F Stockton.* 1856. NY. Derby Jackson. VG. T7. $185.00

BAYER, William. *Blind Side.* 1989. Villard. 1st. VG/VG. P3. $20.00

BAYER, William. *Peregrine.* 1981. Congdon Lattes. 1st. F/dj. A20/P3. $25.00

BAYLEY, Barrington. *Garments of Caean.* 1976. Doubleday. 1st. F/dj. M2. $10.00

BAYLEY, Nicola. *As I Was Going Up & Down & Other Nonsense Rhymes.* 1986. Macmillan. 1st Am. 24p. VG+/F. D4. $35.00

BAYLEY & DAVIS. *Less-Than-Perfect Rider.* 1994. NY. Howell. 1st. VG/VG. O3. $20.00

BAYLOR, Byrd. *When Clay Sings.* 1972. Scribner. 1st. 4to. NF/VG+. P2. $95.00

BAYLOR, Byrd. *Yes Is Better Than No.* 1977. Scribner. 1st. F/NF. M25. $45.00

BAYLOR, Frances Courtenay. *Juan & Juanita.* 1926. Houghton Mifflin. ils Gustaf Tenggren. VG+/G. M5. $40.00

BAYNTON-WILLIAMS. *Investing in Maps.* 1969. London. 4to. ils. 160p. VG/VG. A4. $65.00

BAZELON, Irwin. *Knowing the Score: Notes on Film Music.* 1975. NY. 1st. 352p. xl. F/F. A17. $15.00

BAZIN, Germain. *Paradeisos: Art of the Garden.* 1990. Boston. 1st Am. ils/photos/glossary/index. F/dj. B26. $32.00

BEACH, Edward. *Cold Is the Sea.* 1978. Holt. 1st. F/F. H11. $20.00

BEACH, Edward. *Run Silent, Run Deep.* 1955. NY. sgn/dtd 1955. 364p. VG. S16. $55.00

BEACH, S.A. *Apples of New York.* 1905. Albany. Lyon. 2 vol. gilt bdg. A10. $200.00

BEACH, Sylvia. *Shakespeare & Company.* 1959. Harcourt. 1st. 230p. VG/dj. A17. $25.00

BEACHER. *Miss Beacher's Domestic Receipt Book.* 1855 (1846). VG. E6. $140.00

BEADLE, J.H. *Brigham's Destroying Angel, Being the Life, Confession...* 1904. Shepard. 1st. 221p. VG. J2. $285.00

BEADLE, J.H. *Life in Utah; or, Mysterious & Crimes of Mormonism.* 1870. National Pub. 1st. ils/fld map/rear ads. 540p. VG. J2. $135.00

BEADLE & HOLLISTER. *Polygamy; or, Mysteries & Crimes of Mormonism...* 1882. Phil. Nat Pub Co. 8vo. 572p. gr cloth. F7. $95.00

BEAGLE, Peter S. *Fantasy Worlds of...* 1978. Viking. 1st. F/dj. M2. $25.00

BEAGLE, Peter S. *Fine & Private Place.* 1960. Viking. 1st. F/NF. M2. $175.00

BEAGLE, Peter S. *Folk of the Air.* 1986. Ballantine. 1st. F/NF. M21. $20.00

BEAGLE, Peter S. *Folk of the Air.* 1986. London. Headline. 1st ed. F/F. B3. $40.00

BEAGLE, Peter S. *Last Unicorn.* 1968. Viking. 1st. F/NF/custom box. M21. $150.00

BEAGLEHOLE, J.C. *Exploration of the Pacific.* 1975. London. Blk. 3rd. 346p. VG/clip. P4. $75.00

BEAHM, George. *Stephen King Story.* 1991. Andrews McMeel. 1st. F/F. P3. $20.00

BEAL, Fred E. *Proletarian Journey: Fugitive in Two Worlds...* 1937. Hillman Curl. 1st. VG/dj. V4. $35.00

BEAL, Merrill D. *Grand Canyon: Story Behind the Scenery.* 1967. Flagstaff. KC Pub. 1st. 4to. 38p. mc wrp. F7. $10.00

BEALE, Joseph Henry. *Bibliography of Early English Law Books.* 1926. Cambridge. maroon cloth. M11. $150.00

BEALE & WILLISTON. *Harvard Legal Essays.* 1967. Freeport. Books for Libraries Pr. facsimile. M11. $75.00

BEALS, Carleton. *Dawn Over the Amazon.* 1943. DSP. NF. P3. $13.00

BEAN, L.L. *Hunting, Fishing & Camping.* 1957. Freeport, ME. self pub. A19. $15.00

BEAN & FOWLER. *Fishes of the Series of Capriformes, Ephippiformes...* 1929. Smithsonian. 351p. VG. S15. $30.00

BEAR, Fred. *Fred Bear's Field Notes.* 1993. Derrydale. 1/1250. 288p. gilt leather. F. A17. $35.00

BEAR, Greg. *Eon.* 1985. Bluejay. 1st. F/dj. M2. $85.00

BEAR, Greg. *Eternity.* 1988. Warner. 1st. F/F. M21/P3. $17.00

BEAR, Greg. *Forge of God.* 1987. Tor. 1st. VG/VG. P3. $18.00

BEAR, Greg. *Heads.* 1991. St Martin. 1st. NF/NF. P3. $15.00

BEAR, Greg. *Tangents.* 1989. Warner. 1st Am. F/dj. M2. $25.00

BEAR, Greg. *Wind From a Burning Woman.* 1983. Arkham. 1st. F/dj. M2. $125.00

BEARD, Charles Austin. *Office of Justice of Peace in England, in Its Origin...* nd. NY. Burt Franklin. orig cloth. xl. M11. $65.00

BEARD, D.C. *American Boy's Handy Book.* 1909. Scribner. expanded. 441p. G. H7. $20.00

BEARD, J.S. *Natural Vegetation of Trinidad.* 1946. London. ils/fld map. 152p. B26. $40.00

BEARD, James. *American Cookery.* 1972. Boston. Little Brn. 1st. VG/dj. A16. $37.50

BEARD, James. *Great Cooks Cookbook.* 1974. NY. Ferguson/Doubleday. VG/dj. A16. $20.00

BEARD, James. *New James Beard.* 1981. Knopf. 1st. VG+/dj. A16. $22.50

BEARD, James. *Theory & Practice of Good Cooking.* 1977. Knopf. 5th. VG/dj. A16. $12.00

BEARD, James. *Treasury of Outdoor Cooking.* 1960. Ridge. 282p. G+/fair. B10. $15.00

BEARDEN & HENDERSON. *6 Black Masters of American Art.* 1972. Zenith/Doubleday. 1st. 119p. pict brd. F/F. B4. $125.00

BEARE, George. *Snake on the Grave.* 1974. Houghton Mifflin. 1st. VG/VG. P3. $15.00

BEART, Charles A. *President Roosevelt & the Coming of the War 1941.* 1948. Yale. 1st. 614p. VG. M19. $18.00

BEASLEY, Conger. *Hidalgo's Beard.* 1979. Andrews McMeel. 1st. VG/VG. P3. $20.00

BEASLEY, Norman. *Freighters of Fortune.* 1930. NY. 1st. ils. 311p. G. B18. $45.00

BEATER, Jack. *Tales of South Florida & the Ten Thousand Islands.* 1965. Ft Myers. self pub. 192p. VG/VG. B11. $45.00

BEATON, Cecil. *Face of the World: An International Scrapbook...* (1957). John Day. 1st Am. 240p. VG. H1. $20.00

BEATON, Cecil. *Far East.* 1945. London. Batsford. 1st. photos. VG/dj. A25. $45.00

BEATSON & MEISS. *Belles Heures of Jean, Duke of Berry.* 1974. NY. 1st. ils. gilt bl cloth. F/F case. H3. $75.00

BEATTIE, Ann. *Alex Katz.* 1987. Abrams. 1st. sgn. F/F. R14. $40.00

BEATTIE, Ann. *Burning House.* 1982. Random. 1st. F/NF. R13. $40.00

BEATTIE, Ann. *Burning House.* 1982. Random. 1st. sgn. author's 5th book. F/dj. A24. $48.00

BEATTIE, Ann. *Chilly Scenes of Winter.* 1976. Doubleday. 1st. author's 1st novel. F/NF. L3. $150.00

BEATTIE, Ann. *Chilly Scenes of Winter.* 1976. Doubleday. 1st. NF/NF. B35. $75.00

BEATTIE, Ann. *Distortions.* 1976. Doubleday. 1st. sgn. F/F. B35. $125.00

BEATTIE, Ann. *Love Always.* 1985. Random. 1st. F/dj. B4. $45.00

BEATTIE, Ann. *Picturing Will.* 1989. Random. 1st. sgn. F/F. R13. $35.00

BEATTIE, Ann. *Secrets & Surprises.* 1978. Random. 1st. author's 3rd book. F/F. D10. $40.00

BEATTIE, Ann. *Secrets & Surprises.* 1979. Random. 1st. sgn. author's 3rd book. F/dj. A24. $60.00

BEATTIE, Ann. *What Was Mine.* 1991. Random. 1st. F/F. B35. $15.00

BEATTIE, Ann. *What Was Mine.* 1991. Random. 1st. sgn. NF/dj. R13. $35.00

BEATTIE, Ann. *Where You'll Find Me.* 1986. S&S. 1st. inscr. F/F. R13. $45.00

BEATTIE, William. *Switzerland. Vol II.* 1839. London. fld map. half leather. B18. $195.00

BEATTIE & GEIGER. *Frozen in Time: Unlocking Secrets of Franklin Expedition.* 1987. London. Bloomsbury. 1st Eng. 180p. NF/dj. P4. $49.00

BEATTY, Jerome Jr. *Clambake Mutiny.* 1964. Young Scott Books. 1st. 66p. VG/dj. M20. $20.00

BEATTY, John. *Acoluans: Narrative of Sojourn & Adventure...* 1902. McClelland. 423p. gilt burgundy cloth. M20. $75.00

BEAUCHAMP, Loren; see Silverberg, Robert.

BEAUCLERK, Helen. *Green Lacquer Pavilion.* 1926. Doran. 1st Am. F/NF. B4. $150.00

BEAUMONT, Charles. *Selected Stories.* 1988. Dark Harvest. 1st. F/dj. M2. $45.00

BEAUMONT, William. *Experiments & Observations on the Gastric Juice...* 1833. Plattsburgh. 1st. recent half leather/marbled brd. F. A13. $2,500.00

BEAUMONT, William. *Physiology of Digestion...* 1847. Burlington, VT. Goodrich. 2nd. sm 8vo. 303p. VG. M1. $550.00

BEAUS & RAWSON. *Carboniferous Statigraphy in Grand Canyon Country...* 1979. Am Geol Inst. AGI Selected Guidebook Series 2. 4to. stiff wrp. F7. $45.00

BEBEL, August. *Bebel's Reminiscences, Part 1.* 1911. NY. Socialist Literature Co. 1st. NF. B2. $35.00

BECHDOLT, Jack. *Torch.* 1948. Prime. 1st. F/dj. M2. $15.00

BECHERVAISE, John. *Blizzard & Fire: Year at Mawson, Antarctica.* 1963. Sydney. Angus Robertson. 1st. 252p. VG/dj. P4. $125.00

BECHERVAISE, John. *Far South.* 1961. Sydney. Angus Robertson. 1st. 8vo. 103p. map ep. VG/dj. P4. $75.00

BECHTEREV, Vladimir M. *General Principles of Human Reflexology: An Introduction...* 1928 (1917). NY. Internat Pub. 1st Eng-language/Am issue. 467p. blk cloth. G1. $85.00

BECK, Henry Houghton. *History of South Africa & the British-Boer War.* 1900. Phil. 493p+2p fld map. gilt leather. G. A17. $20.00

BECK, L. Adams. *Garden of Vision.* 1929. Cosmopolitan. 1st. VG. M2. $10.00

BECK, Melissa. *Typographic Bookplates of Ward Ritchie.* 1990. Karamole. 1st. fwd/sgn Ward Ritchie. 96p. F. B19. $40.00

BECK, Phineas. *Clementine in the Kitchen.* 1943. Hastings. ils Henry Stahlhut. VG/dj. B10. $12.00

BECK, Phineas. *Clementine in the Kitchen.* 1943. NY. Hastings. G/dj. A16. $10.00

BECKE, Louis. *Rodiman the Boatsteerer.* 1898. Lippincott. 1st. VG. M2. $15.00

BECKER, Bob. *Devil Bird.* 1933. Reilly Lee. 1st. VG. M2. $35.00

BECKER, Charlotte. *Three Little Steps.* 1947. Scribner. 1st/A. 8vo. VG/dj. M5. $38.00

BECKER, Charlotte. *Unlike Twins.* 1943. Scribner. lg 12mo. VG/dj. M5. $22.00

BECKER, Ethel A. *Treasury of Alaskana.* 1969. NY. Superior. rpt. 4to. 183p. half cloth. VG/dj. P4. $35.00

BECKER, John. *New Feathers for the Old Goose.* 1956. Pantheon. 1st. 63p. cloth. F/NF. D4. $25.00

BECKER, May. *Louisa Alcott's People.* 1936. 1st. ils Thomas Fogarty. VG+. S13. $55.00

BECKER, Peter. *Dingane, King of the Zulus, 1828-1840.* 1965. NY. Crowell. 1st. ils. 283p. NF/dj. W1. $18.00

BECKER, Robert H. *Thomas Christy's Road Across the Plains.* 1969. Sacramento. Old West Pub. 1st. F/F. O4. $35.00

BECKER, Stephen. *Chinese Bandit.* 1975. Random. 1st. VG/VG. P3. $25.00

BECKER, Stephen. *Dog Tags.* 1973. Random. 1st. VG/VG. P3. $25.00

BECKER, Stephen. *Last Mandarin.* 1979. Random. 1st. VG/VG. P3. $25.00

BECKER & LINSCOTT. *Bedside Book of Famous French Stories.* 1945. NY. 1st. VG/sans. T12. $15.00

BECKER & MARTIN. *Report on Geology of Philippine Islands...* 1901 (1895). WA. USGS. royal 8vo. ils/photos/map. NF/wrp. M12. $30.00

BECKETT, Elspeth. *Wild Flowers of Majorca, Minorca & Ibiza...* 1988. Rotterdam. Balkema. ils. 221p. M. B26. $60.00

BECKETT, Samuel. *Cascando.* 1970. Grove. 1st. F/F. M19. $35.00

BECKETT, Samuel. *Poems in English.* 1961. London. John Calder. 1st. F/dj. Q1. $200.00

BECKETT, Samuel. *Rockaby & Other Short Pieces.* 1981. Grove. 1st. F/F. B35. $22.00

BECKETT, Samuel. *Three Novels. Malloy/Malone Dies/The Unnamable.* 1959. Grove. 1st. trans Patrick Bowles. F/F. D10. $150.00

BECKFORD, William. *Vathek.* 1928. John Day. 1st Am. 229p. NF/dj/case. M20. $65.00

BECKWITH, Henry. *Lovecraft's Providence & Adjacent Parts.* 1986. Donald Grant. 2nd revised. F/dj. M2. $15.00

BECKWITH, Lillian. *Hills Is Lonely.* 1962. London. Hutchinson. 10th. ils. VG+/G+. H7. $15.00

BECQUERL, Henri et Deslandres. *Contribution a l'Edude du Phenomene de Zeeman.* 1898. Paris. Gauthier-Villars et Fils. xl. K3. $45.00

BECQUERL, Henri et Deslandres. *Sur le Rayonnement de l'Uranium...* 1900. Paris. Gauthier-Villars et Fils. xl. K3. $50.00

BECVAR, Antonin. *Atlas of the Heavens II.* 1964. Cambridge, MA. Sky. 4th. VG. K5. $25.00

BEDDOME, R.H. *Handbook to the Ferns of British India.* 1892. Calcutta. Thacker Spink. 1st ed thus. 300 pl. NF. A22. $85.00

BEDELL, L. Frank. *Quaker Heritage: Friends Coming Into Heartland of America...* 1966. Cono. 306p. VG. V3. $22.00

BEDELL, Mary Crehore. *Modern Gypsies: Story fo 12,000-Mile Motor Camping Trip...* 1924. Brentano. ils. VG. K3. $20.00

BEDFORD, Annie North. *Susie's New Stove.* 1950. Little Golden. 1st. VG. M5. $55.00

BEDFORD, Denton R. *Foxes & the Lumwoods.* 1977. Vantage. 1st. F/VG. L3. $125.00

BEDFORD, Francis D. *Book of Nursery Rhymes.* 1897. London. Methuen. 8vo. all edges red. R5. $250.00

BEDFORD, Ruth. *Fairies & Fancies.* 1929. London. Blk. 1st. ils Mela Koehler Broman/8 full-p mc pl. R5. $285.00

BEDFORD, Sybille. *Aldous Huxley Vol I: 1894-1939.* 1973. Chatto Windus. VG/VG. P3. $25.00

BEDFORD-JONES, H. *Years Between.* 1928. Longman. 2 vol. F/dj/case. M2. $60.00

BEDIER, J. *Romance of Tristan & Iseult.* 1960. LEC. 1/1500. ils Serge Ivanoff. quarter morocco/paper brd. F/case. T10. $130.00

BEDINGFIELD, James. *Compendium of Medical Practice Ils...* 1823. Greenfield, MA. 1st Am from last London ed. 192p. sheep/marbled brd. B14. $175.00

BEDNAR, Kamil. *Puppets & Fairy Tales.* 1958. Prague. 52p. dj. A17. $20.00

BEE, Clair. *Chip Hilton: Backcourt Ace (#19).* 1961. Grosset Dunlap. 182p. lists to #20. VG. M20. $45.00

BEE, Clair. *Chip Hilton: Blackboard Fever (#10).* 1953. Grosset Dunlap. 210p. lists to #20. VG. M20. $16.00

BEE, Clair. *Chip Hilton: Buzzer Basket (#20).* 1962. Grosset Dunlap. 1st. 175p. VG+/dj (last title listed). M20. $95.00

BEE, Clair. *Chip Hilton: Comeback Cagers (#21).* 1963. Grosset Dunlap. 1st. 170p. lists to this title. pict brd. G+ $85.00

BEE, Clair. *Chip Hilton: Dugout Jinx (#8).* 1952. Grosset Dunlap. lists 23 titles. VG. M20. $12.50

BEE, Clair. *Chip Hilton: Fence Busters (#11).* 1953. Grosset Dunlap. 208p. lists to #20. pict brd. VG. M20. $16.00

BEE, Clair. *Chip Hilton: Fourth Down Showdown (#13).* 1956. Grosset Dunlap. lists 23 titles. VG-. M20. $20.00

BEE, Clair. *Chip Hilton: Fourth Down Showdown (#13).* 1956. Grosset Dunlap. 213p. lists to #20. VG. M20. $20.00

BEE, Clair. *Chip Hilton: Harcourt Upset.* 1957. Grosset Dunlap. 181p. lists to #20. VG+. M20. $30.00

BEE, Clair. *Chip Hilton: Hardcourt Upset (#15).* 1957. Grosset Dunlap. lists 18 titles. 181p. cloth. VG/dj. M20. $25.00

BEE, Clair. *Chip Hilton: Home Run Fued (#22).* 1964. Grosset Dunlap. 1st. 176p. lists to #21. VG+. M20. $200.00

BEE, Clair. *Chip Hilton: Hungry Hurler (#23).* 1966. Grosset Dunlap. 1st. 184p. last title in series. pict brd. M20. $625.00

BEE, Clair. *Chip Hilton: No-Hitter (#17).* 1959. Grosset Dunlap. lists 18 titles. 182p. VG/dj. M20. $35.00

BEEBE, B.F. *American Wolves, Coyotes & Foxes.* 1967. McKay. ils JR Johnson. 151p. cloth. F/VG. M12. $20.00

BEEBE, Lucius. *American West.* 1955. Bonanza. dj. A19. $35.00

BEEBE, Lucius. *Mixed Train Daily: Book of Short-Line Railroads.* 1947. Dutton. 2nd. 365p. cloth. VG/dj. M20. $45.00

BEEBE, Lucius. *When Beauty Rode the Rails.* 1962. Garden City. 1st. VG/VG. B5. $45.00

BEEBE, W. *Nonesuch: Land of Water.* 1932. NY. Brewer Warren. ils/photos. 259p. F/VG. M12. $30.00

BEEBE, William. *Arcturus Adventure.* 1926. Putnam. ils/maps. 439p. T7. $60.00

BEEBE, William. *Half Mile Down.* 1934. Harcourt Brace. 1st. 8vo. 344p. VG/dj. K3. $45.00

BEEBE & CLEGG. *Hear the Train Blow.* 1952. EP Dutton. 1st. 414p. pict buckram. VG/torn. B18. $27.50

BEEBE & CLEGG. *San Francisco's Golden Era...* 1960. Howell North. 1st. 255p. VG+. B18. $35.00

BEEBEE, Chris. *Hub.* 1987. MacDonald. F/F. P3. $22.00

BEECHER, Elizabeth. *Roy Rogers on the Double-R Ranch.* 1951. S&S. VG. P3. $15.00

BEECHEY, Frederick W. *Narrative of Voyage to the Pacific & Bering Strait.* 1832. Phil. Carey Lea. 1st Am. 8vo. 493p. linen cloth. xl. T7. $375.00

BEECROFT, john. *Rocco Came In.* 1959. Dodd Mead. 1st. ils Kurt Wiese. 4to. VG/VG. P2. $50.00

BEEDING, Francis. *Death Walks in Eastrepps.* 1931. Mystery League. 1st. VG. N4. $27.50

BEEDING, Francis. *Spellbound.* 1945. Tower. MTI. VG/VG. P3. $20.00

BEEDING, Francis. *Thee Are Thirteen.* 1946. Harper. 1st. VG. P3. $18.00

BEEHLER, B.M. *Birds of New Guinea.* 1986. Princeton. 8vo. ils Zimmerman/Coe. 21 maps. 293p. VG+/stiff wrp. M12. $30.00

BEEKMAN, W. Boerhave. *Elsevier's Wood Dictionary. Vol 1.* 1964. Amsterdam. Elsevier. 8vo. VG/torn. A22. $50.00

BEER, George Louis. *African Questions at the Paris Peace Conference...* 1969 (1923). NY. Negro Universities. rpt. 8vo. fld map. 628p. VG. W1. $30.00

BEERBOHM, Max. *Christmas Garland.* 1912. London. Heinemann. 198p. gilt bl cloth. VG. B14. $45.00

BEERBOHM, Max. *Happy Hypocrite.* 1915. NY. John Lane. 1st. ils Sheringham. VG. M19. $50.00

BEERBOHM, Max. *Mainly on the Air.* 1958. Knopf. 1st Am. F. B14. $45.00

BEERBOHM, Max. *Zuleika Dobson; or, An Oxford Love Story.* 1960. LEC. 1st thus. 1/1500. ils/sgn George Him. F/case. Q1. $100.00

BEERS. *Bibliographies in American History: Guide to Materials...* 1938. HW Wilson. 1st. 339p. xl. VG. A4. $35.00

BEERY, Jesse. *Saddle-Horse Instructions: Horse Training, ...Breeding...* 1940s Pleas. ant Hill. 23 pamphlets+ephemera. orig case. A17. $22.50

BEESTON, Diane. *Of Wind, Fog & Sail.* 1972. SF. Chronicle. obl 4to. ils. dj. T7. $36.00

BEETLE, David H. *Up Old Forge Way: Central Adirondack Story.* 1948. Utica Observer-Dispatch. 1st. 183p. VG/G. H7. $25.00

BEETLE, David H. *West Canada Creek.* 1946. Utica Observer-Dispatch. 1st. 159p. VG. H7. $20.00

BEETON, Isabella. *Book of Household Management.* 1889. London. 1,644p. VG. B5. $105.00

BEEVOR, Anthony. *Faustian Pact.* 1983. London. Cape. 1st. VG/VG. P3. $20.00

BEGAY, Shonto. *Ma'ii & Cousin Horned Toad.* 1992. Scholastic Inc. 1st. inscr. thin 4to. F/dj. T10. $50.00

BEGLEY, Louis. *Wartime Lies.* 1991. London. 1st. F/F. R14. $75.00

BEHME, R.L. *Bonsai, Saikei & Bonkei: Japanese Dwarf Trees...* 1969. Morrow. ils. 255p. F. W3. $42.00

BEHN, Noel. *Shadowboxer.* 1969. S&S. 1st. VG. P3. $12.00

BEHRENS, Helen Kindler. *Diplomatic Dining.* 1974. NY Times. G/dj. A16. $12.50

BEILENSON, Peter. *Little Treasury of Haiku.* 1980. NY. Avenel. 96p. F/NF. W3. $12.00

BEILHARZ, Peter. *Trostky, Troskyism & Transition to Socialism.* 1987. Barnes Noble. 1st. as new/dj. V4. $20.00

BEILHARZ & LOPEZ. *We Were Forty-Niners.* 1976. Pasadena, CA. 1st. F/VG. O4. $15.00

BEINHART, Larry. *No One Rides for Free.* 1986. NY. Morrow. 1st. F/dj. M15. $60.00

BEINHART, Larry. *You Get What You Pay For.* 1988. Morrow. 1st. author's 2nd novel. F/NF. A24. $30.00

BEINHART, Larry. *You Get What You Pay For.* 1988. Morrow. 1st. NF/NF. P3. $23.00

BEISER, Arthur. *Proper Yacht.* 1970. London. 2nd. 307p. F/dj. A17. $20.00

BEITO, Gretchen Umes. *Coya Come Home: A Congresswoman's Journey.* 1990. Pomegranate. 1st. 334p. VG/dj. A25. $15.00

BELIAEV, Alexander. *Professor Dowell's Head.* 1980. Macmillan. 1st. VG/VG. P3. $15.00

BELKNAP, Charles Eugene. *History of the Michigan Organizations at Chickamauga...* 1899. Lansing, MI. Robert Smith. 2nd. 374p. cloth (bookplate removed). M8. $65.00

BELKNAP, E. McCamly. *Milk Glass.* 1949. Crown. 1st. 324p. cloth. VG/dj. M20. $35.00

BELKNAP, E. McCamly. *Milk Glass.* 1958. Crown. 5th. 327p. F/VG. H1. $52.00

BELKNAP, George. *Letters of Captain George Hamilton Perkins, USN.* 1970 (1886). 533p. O8. $18.50

BELKNAP, Jeremy. *Foresters, an American Tale: Being a Sequel...* 1792. Boston. Thomas/Andrews. 1st separate. 12mo. 216p. contemporary tree calf. M1. $275.00

BELL, Anne Oliver. *Diary of Virginia Wolf.* 1984. HBJ. 1st. Am. NF/NF. W2. $30.00

BELL, Bob. *Hunting the Long-Tailed Bird.* 1975. Freshnet. 212p. M/dj. A17. $15.00

BELL, C.I. *They Knew Franklin Pierce.* 1980. VG. M17. $15.00

BELL, Charles. *Engravings of the Brain & Nerves.* 1982. Birmingham. facsimile of 3 eds/1st collected. 4to. full leather. A13. $150.00

BELL, Charles. *Essays on Anatomy of Expression in Painting.* 1806. London. 1st. folio. full leather. A13. $1,500.00

BELL, Charles. *Essays on Anatomy of Expression in Painting.* 1806. London. Longman Hurst. 1st. lg 4to. 186p. contemporary bdg. M1. $850.00

BELL, Charles. *Essays on Anatomy of Expression in Painting.* 1984. Birmingham. facsimile 1806 London. 4to. 186p. full leather. A13. $100.00

BELL, Charles. *Nervous System of the Human Body.* 1988 (1830). Birmingham. Classics of Neurology/Neurosurgery Lib. facsimile. G1. $85.00

BELL, Charles. *System of Dissections, Explaining Anatomy...* 1814. Baltimore. Samuel Jefferis. 1st Am. 18mo. contemporary bdg. M1. $325.00

BELL, Christine. *Perez Family.* 1990. Norton. 1st. F/dj. A24. $25.00

BELL, Christine. *Saint.* 1985. Englewood. Pineapple. 1st. author's 1st book. F/F. H11. $110.00

BELL, Edward I. *Political Shame of Mexico.* 1914. McBride. 1st. VG. V4. $30.00

BELL, Eric. *Seeds of Life.* 1951. Fantasy. 1st. 255p. brn cloth. NF/fair. B22. $12.50

BELL, Gordon B. *Golden Troubadour.* 1980. McGraw Hill. F/F. P3. $13.00

BELL, H.E. *Introduction to History & Records of Court of Wards...* 1953. CAmbridge. M11. $75.00

BELL, H.E. *Maitland, a Critical Examination & Assessment.* 1965. London. Blk. M11. $35.00

BELL, Horace. *Reminiscences of a Ranger; or, Early Times in S CA...* 1881. LA. Yarnell Caystile Mathes. 1st. 457p. gilt gr cloth. D11. $450.00

BELL, Isaac. *Foxiana.* 1929. Country Life. 1st. VG. O3. $40.00

BELL, Josephine. *In the King's Absence.* 1973. Bles. 1st. F/F. P3. $20.00

BELL, Josephine. *New People at the Hollies.* 1961. Macmillan. 1st. VG/VG. P3. $25.00

BELL, Josephine. *No Escape.* 1966. Macmillan. 1st. VG/G. P3. $13.00

BELL, Josephine. *Wolf! Wolf!* 1980. Walker. 1st. VG/VG. P3. $15.00

BELL, Katie. *Legend of Kohl's Ranch.* 1985. Central AZ Pub. 1st. sgn. ils/maps/bibliography. NF. B19. $25.00

BELL, Landon Covington. *Robert E Lee.* ca 1929. Columbua, OH. 1st. 27p. NF/stiff prt wrp. M8. $27.50

BELL, Madison Smartt. *Barking Man & Other Stories.* 1990. NY. Ticknor. 1st. F/F. H11. $30.00

BELL, Madison Smartt. *Barking Man & Other Stories.* 1990. Ticknor Fields. 1st. sgn. F/VG. B3. $45.00

BELL, Madison Smartt. *Dr Sleep.* 1991. HBJ. 1st. F/F. R14. $30.00

BELL, Madison Smartt. *Soldier's Joy.* 1989. Ticknor Fields. 1st. sgn. F/F. B3. $50.00

BELL, Madison Smartt. *Straight Cut.* 1986. NY. Ticknor. 1st. F/F. H11. $35.00

BELL, Madison Smartt. *Waiting for the End of the World.* 1985. NY. Ticknor. 1st. F/NF. H11. $60.00

BELL, Madison Smartt. *Waiting for the End of the World.* 1985. Ticknor Fields. 1st. author's 2nd book. F/VG. A24. $45.00

BELL, Madison Smartt. *Waiting for the End of the World.* 1985. Ticknor Fields. 1st. author's 2nd novel. F/F. B35/D10. $85.00

BELL, Madison Smartt. *Washington Square Ensemble.* 1983. London. Deutsch. 1st. F/NF. R14. $100.00

BELL, Madison Smartt. *Washington Square Ensemble.* 1983. Viking. 1st. author's 1st novel. NF/VG. A24. $80.00

BELL, Madison Smartt. *Washington Square Ensemble.* 1983. Viking. 1st. sgn/dtd. F/dj. M25. $150.00

BELL, Madison Smartt. *Year of Silence.* 1987. Ticknor Fields. 1st. author's 5th book. F/F. D10. $50.00

BELL, Madison SmartT. *Year of the Silence.* 1987. Ticknor Fields. 1st. VG/VG. L1. $40.00

BELL, Madison Smartt. *Zero DB & Other Stories.* 1987. Ticknor Fields. 1st. sgn. F/F. B3. $50.00

BELL, Peggy Kirk. *Woman's Way to Better Golf.* 1972. np. 3rd. sgn. VG/VG. B11. $35.00

BELL, Syndey. *Wives of the Prophet.* 1935. NY. Macaulay. 1st. F/VG+. B4. $125.00

BELL, Thelma Harnington. *Pawnee.* 1950. Viking. 1st. 63p. VG/G+. P2. $25.00

BELL, Vereen M. *Achievement of Cormac McCarthy.* 1988. Baton Rouge. LSU. 1st. F/F. R13. $45.00

BELL, William Dixon. *Moon Colony.* 1937. Goldsmith. VG. P3. $10.00

BELL & MACKENZIE. *Mexican West Coast & Lower California...* 1923. WA. Dept Commerce. ils/10p photos/fld map. 340p. stp buckram. D11. $50.00

BELLAH, James Warnar. *Ward 20.* 1946. Doubleday. 1st. cloth. VG/dj. M20. $35.00

BELLAIRS, George. *Intruder in the Dark.* 1966. John Gifford. 1st. VG/G. P3. $20.00

BELLAMY, Edward. *Equality.* 1897. Appleton. NF. M22. $35.00

BELLAMY, Edward. *Looking Backward 2000-1887.* 1888. Houghton Mifflin. 1st. G. V4. $45.00

BELLAMY, Edward. *Looking Backward.* 1941. Hollywood. Merle Armitage/Ward Ritchie. ils/sgn Elise. VG. T10. $90.00

BELLAMY, Edward. *Looking Backward.* 1945. Tower. 1st. VG/VG. P3. $20.00

BELLAMY, J.G. *Crime & Public Order in England & the Later Middle Ages.* 1973. London. Kegan Paul. M11. $50.00

BELLAMY, J.G. *Criminal Law & Society in Late Medieval & Tudor England.* 1984. Gloucester. M11. $65.00

BELLI, Melvin. *Blood Money.* 1956. NY. 1st. author's 1st book. F/dj. A17. $15.00

BELLOC, Hilaire. *Cautionary Tales for Children.* nd. London. Duckworth. 8vo. ils. 79p. gray brd. G+. T5. $45.00

BELLOC, Hilaire. *Joan of Arc.* 1929. London. 1st. VG/dj. T9. $60.00

BELLOC, Hilaire. *Matilda Who Told Lies & Was Burned To Death.* 1970. Dial. 1st thus. 32p. cloth. F/F. D4. $40.00

BELLONI, Gian Guido. *Prehistoric to Classical Painting.* 1962. London. Hamlyn. 1st. folio. 24 mc pl. VG. W1. $10.00

BELLOW, Saul. *Dean's December.* 1982. Harper Row. 1st. F/F. H11. $35.00

BELLOW, Saul. *Dean's December.* 1982. Harper Row. 1st. F/VG. B3. $25.00

BELLOW, Saul. *Henderson the Rain King.* 1959. Viking. 1st. VG/VG+. B4. $125.00

BELLOW, Saul. *Him With His Foot in His Mouth.* 1984. Harper. 1st. sgn. F/F. R14. $60.00

BELLOW, Saul. *Humboldt's Gift.* 1975. Viking. ARC. RS. F/F. B4. $350.00

BELLOW, Saul. *Humboldt's Gift.* 1975. Viking. 1st. author's 8th novel. F/NF. D10. $75.00

BELLOW, Saul. *Humboldt's Gift.* 1975. Viking. 1st. NF/VG. B35. $35.00

BELLOW, Saul. *Last Analysis.* 1969. 1st. NF/NF. S13. $16.00

BELLOW, Saul. *More Die of Heartbreak.* 1987. Morrow. 1st. F/F. B3. $20.00

BELLOW, Saul. *Mosby's Memoirs & Other Stories.* 1968. Viking. 1st. F/F. B2. $45.00

BELLOW, Saul. *Mr Sammler's Planet.* 1970. NY. Viking. 1st. F/VG+ clip. A24. $30.00

BELLOW, Saul. *Mr Sammler's Planet.* 1970. Viking. 1st. VG/VG. P3. $15.00

BELLOW, Saul. *To Jerusalem & Back.* 1976. Viking. 1st. VG/dj. B35. $18.00

BELLOW, Saul. *Victim.* 1948. London. Lehmann. 1st Eng. author's 2nd book. F/F. B4. $300.00

BELLOY. *Recveil Des Edicts de Pacification.* 1599. np. Chouet. 1st. 2 parts in 1. 8vo. quarter calf. R12. $695.00

BELLROSE, Frank C. *Ducks, Geese & Swans of North America.* 1980. ils. VG/VG. M17. $20.00

BELLWOOD, Peter. *Man's Conquest of the Pacific.* 1979. NY. Oxford. 1st Am. 4to. 462p. VG/dj. P4. $85.00

BELMONT, Bob; see Reynolds, Mack.

BELOFF, Max. *Foreign Policy & the Democratic Process.* 1955. Johns Hopkins. 1st. sm 8vo. xl. VG/dj. W1. $8.00

BELOTE, T.T. *American & European Sword in Collection of US National Mus.* 1932. WA. photos. 163p. VG. M4. $35.00

BELOUS & WEINSTEIN. *Will Soule: Indian Photographer at Ft Sill, OK 1869-1874.* 1969. Ward Ritchie. 120p. cloth. dj. D11. $150.00

BEMELMANS, Ludwig. *Blue Danube.* 1945. Viking. 1st. F/dj. B35. $60.00

BEMELMANS, Ludwig. *Dirty Eddie.* 1947. Viking. 1st. NF/dj. M25. $35.00

BEMELMANS, Ludwig. *Eye of God.* 1949. Viking. 1st. F/VG+. B4. $65.00

BEMELMANS, Ludwig. *High World.* 1954. Harper. 1st. ils. 8vo. 113p. VG/VG. D1. $40.00

BEMELMANS, Ludwig. *Hotel Splendide.* 1941. Viking. 1st. F/NF. M19. $45.00

BEMELMANS, Ludwig. *Madeline & the Bad Hat.* 1956. Viking. 1/885. sgn. 54p. F/G+ case. P2. $350.00

BEMELMANS, Ludwig. *Madeline & the Gypsies.* 1958. McCall's. obl 4to. F. M5. $95.00

BEMELMANS, Ludwig. *Madeline & the Gypsies.* 1959. Viking. 1st. ils. 56p. F/VG. D1. $250.00

BEMELMANS, Ludwig. *Madeline & the Gypsies.* 1959. Viking. 1st. pict cloth. xl. reading copy/dj. C8. $25.00

BEMELMANS, Ludwig. *Madeline's Christmas.* 1956. McCall's. 1st. 12mo. sc. M5. $75.00

BEMELMANS, Ludwig. *Madeline's Christmas.* 1956. McCall's. 1st. 12mo. supplement for Christmas issue. wrp/envelope. P2. $110.00

BEMELMANS, Ludwig. *Madeline's Christmas.* 1985. Viking. 1st thus. NF/F. P2. $50.00

BEMELMANS, Ludwig. *Madeline's Rescue.* 1953. Viking. 1st. lg 4to. red cloth. dj. R5. $385.00

BEMELMANS, Ludwig. *Quito Express.* 1938. Viking. 1st. obl 4to. dj. R5. $125.00

BEMELMANS, Ludwig. *Sunshine.* 1950. S&S. 1st. ils. 42p. NF/NF. D1. $200.00

BEMELMANS, Ludwig. *World of Bemelmans.* 1955. Viking. 1st. F/VG. M19. $25.00

BEMIS, Samuel Flagg. *John Quincy Adams & Foundations of American Policy.* 1949. Knopf. 1st. 588p. F/dj. H1. $28.00

BEMMANN, Hans. *Stone & the Flute.* 1986. Viking. 1st. VG/VG. P3. $20.00

BEN-ZVI, Itzhak. *Exile & the Redeemed.* 1958. London. 1st. photos/notes/index. 334p. F. W3. $38.00

BENAGH, Jim. *Terry Bradshaw: Superarm of Pro Football.* 1976. Putnam. 1st. VG. P8. $20.00

BENARY-ISBERT, Margot. *Wicked Enchantment.* 1955. Harcourt Brace. 1st. 181p. VG/G. P2. $35.00

BENCHLEY, Nathaniel. *Monument.* 1966. McGraw Hill. 1st. VG/VG. P3. $20.00

BENCHLEY, Nathaniel. *Visitors.* 1965. McGraw Hill. 1st. VG/VG. P3. $25.00

BENCHLEY, Peter. *Deep.* 1976. Andre Deutsch. 1st. F/F. P3. $20.00

BENCHLEY, Peter. *Girl of the Sea of Cortez.* 1982. Andre Deutsch. 1st. VG/VG. P3. $20.00

BENCHLEY, Peter. *Island.* 1979. Doubleday. 1st. F/NF. H11. $40.00

BENCHLEY, Peter. *Island.* 1979. Doubleday. 1st. VG/VG. P3. $18.00

BENCHLEY, Peter. *Jaws.* 1974. Doubleday. 1st. F/NF. H11. $100.00

BENCHLEY, Peter. *Jaws.* 1974. London. Deutsch. 1st Eng. NF/clip. Q1. $125.00

BENDER, Lauretta. *Visual Motor Gestalt Test & Its Clinical Use.* (1938). Am Orthopsychiatric Assn. tall 8vo. 176p. prt blk cloth. G1. $22.50

BENDER, Morris B. *Oculomotor System.* (1964). Hoeber Medical Division. 8vo. 556p. gr cloth. VG/dj. G1. $50.00

BENDER, Texas Bix. *Don't Squat With Yer Spurs On!* 1992. Gibbs Smith. A19. $8.00

BENDER & TAYLOR. *Uniforms, Organization & History of the Waffen SS.* 5 vol. S16. $85.00

BENEDICT, Pickney. *Town Smokes.* 1987. Princeton. Ontario Review. 1st. F/wrp. B2. $75.00

BENEDICT, Ruth. *In Henry's Backyard.* 1948. 1st. VG/clip. S13. $25.00

BENEDITTI, Mario. *Unstill Life, an Intro to Spanish Poetry of Latin America.* 1969. HBW. 1st. 127p. cloth. F/NF. D4. $45.00

BENES, MAREK & TUREK. *Fossils of the World.* 1989. Arch Cape. 4to. 495p. F/F. B1. $65.00

BENET, Laura. *Hidden Valley.* 1940 (1938). Dodd Mead. 8vo. 207p. VG. T5. $20.00

BENET, Stephen V. *Tales Before Midnight.* 1939. Farrar. 1st. VG. M2. $27.00

BENET & BENET. *Book of Americans.* 1933. Farrar Rhinehart. 1st. 115p. cloth. VG+. D4. $25.00

BENETAR, Judith. *Admissions: Notes From a Woman Psychiatrist.* 1974. NY. Charterhouse. 1st. inscr. 219p. VG/VG. A25. $20.00

BENFORD, Gregory. *Artifact.* 1985. Tor. 1st. F/F. P3. $17.00

BENFORD, Gregory. *At the Double Solstice.* 1986. New Castle, VA. Cheap Street. 1st. sgn. F. T2. $65.00

BENFORD, Gregory. *Centigrade 233.* 1990. New Castle, VA. Cheap Street. 1st. sgn. pub/sgn O'Nale. F. T2. $60.00

BENFORD, Gregory. *Great Sky River.* 1987. Bantam. hc. F/F. P3. $18.00

BENFORD, Gregory. *In Alien Flesh.* 1986. Tor. 1st. F/F. M2. $20.00

BENFORD, Gregory. *Of Space, Time & the River.* 1985. Cheap Street. ltd. sgn/#d. F/dj/case. from $125 to $150.00

BENFORD, Gregory. *Stars in Shroud.* 1978. Berkley Putnam. 1st. F/dj. M2/T2. $25.00

BENFORD, Gregory. *Tides of Light.* 1989. Bantam. 1st. F/F. P3. $18.00

BENFORD & BRIN. *Heart of the Comet.* 1986. Bantam. 1st. F/NF. M2. $20.00

BENGTSSON, F.G. *Long Ships: Saga of Viking Age.* 1954. Knopf. 2 maps. 503p. T7. $22.00

BENINCASA, Francesco. *Observations sur la Conduite du Ministre de Portugal...* 1761. np. 2 parts in 1. woodcut tailpcs/vignettes. 19th-C bdg. R15. $650.00

BENITEZ, Conrado. *History of the Philipines.* 1940. Ginn. VG. P3. $20.00

BENJAMIN, David. *Idol.* 1979. Putnam. 1st. F/clip. M25. $25.00

BENJAMIN, Mary. *Autographs: A Key to Collecting.* 1st. 305p. O8. $32.50

BENJAMIN, Paul; see Auster, Paul.

BENKOVITZ, Miriam J. *Rolfe: A Biography.* 1977. NY. 1st. VG. T9. $20.00

BENNER, Samuel. *Benner's Prophecies of Future Ups & Downs in Prices.* 1888. Cincinnati. Clarke. 181p. VG. A10. $35.00

BENNET, Robert Ames. *Bowl of Baal.* 1973. Donald Grant. VG/VG. P3. $20.00

BENNETT, Arnold. *From the Log of the Velsa.* 1920. Chatto Windus. assn copy. sgn. 209p. VG. B11. $75.00

BENNETT, Arnold. *Imperial Palace.* 1931. Doubleday Doran. 769p. VG/dj. H1. $12.00

BENNETT, Arnold. *Loot of Cities.* 1972. Oswald Train. 1st Am. F/dj. M2. $10.00

BENNETT, Geoffrey D.S. *Famous Harness Horses Vol I 1900-1915; Vol II 1916-1931.* 1926. London. Welbecson. 2 vol. 1/600. 4to. VG. O3. $975.00

BENNETT, Geoffrey. *Death in the Dog Watches.* 1974. Wht Lion. VG/VG. P3. $15.00

BENNETT, H.E. *Gold Robbers. A Story of Australia.* 1863. Boston. Elliott Thomes Talbot. 8vo. pink prt wrp. R12. $75.00

BENNETT, Hall. *Wilderness of Vines.* 1966. Doubleday. 1st. author's 1st book. F/F. B4. $250.00

BENNETT, James. *Overland to California: Journal of James Bennett...* 1987. Ye Galleon. 1st thus. ils/index. 91p. F/sans. A18. $17.50

BENNETT, Jill. *Teeny Tiny.* 1986. Putnam. 1st Am. F/NF. P2. $35.00

BENNETT, John. *Doctor to the Dead.* 1946. Rinehart. 1st. VG/dj. M2. $22.00

BENNETT, John. *Master Skylark.* 1922. Century. 1st. thick 4to. F/VG. M5. $65.00

BENNETT, John. *Pigtails of Ah Lee Ben Loo.* 1928. Longman Gr. 1st. ils J Bennett. 8vo. 298p. orange cloth. VG. D1. $40.00

BENNETT, Kay. *Kaibah: Recollection of a Navajo Girlhood.* 1964. Los Angeles. Westernlore. 1st. ils. F/NF. L3. $65.00

BENNETT, Lerone. *Black Power USA.* 1967. Chicago. Johnson. 1st. F/NF. B4. $85.00

BENNETT, Lerone. *Challenge of Blackness.* 1972. Chicago. Johnson. 1st. inscr. 312p. F/NF. B4. $200.00

BENNETT, Logan J. *Blue-Winged Teal.* 1966 (1938). Ames. rpt. ils. 144p. VG. S15. $24.00

BENNETT, Whitman. *Practical Guide to American Book Collecting.* 1941. NY. Bennett. 1st. 1/1250. cream cloth. F. M24. $75.00

BENNETT, Whitman. *Practical Guide to American 19th-C Color Plate Books.* 1949. NY. Bennett. 8vo. 132p. red cloth. NF. B24. $100.00

BENNETT. *Horatio Alger Jr: A Comprehensive Bibliography...* 1980. 1st. ils. 224p. F. A4. $125.00

BENNY & BENNY. *Sunday Nights at Seven.* 1990. Warner. 1st. F/F. W2. $35.00

BENSAUDE, Joaquim. *Lacunes et Surprises l'Historie des Decouvertes Maritimes.* 1930. Coimbra. Imprensa. Samuel Eliot Morison's copy. 194p. VG. O7. $65.00

BENSON, Ben. *Ninth Hour.* 1956. MS Mill. VG/G. P3. $25.00

BENSON, Donald. *And Having Writ...* 1978. Bobbs Merrill. 1st. F/dj. M2. $12.00

BENSON, E.F. *Angel of Pain.* nd. Lippincott. VG. P3. $40.00

BENSON, E.F. *Secret Lives.* 1932. Hodder Stoughton. xl. VG. P3. $20.00

BENSON, E.F. *Sir Francis Drake.* 1927. London. Harper. 8vo. ils/ads. 315p. bl cloth. VG. P4. $35.00

BENSON, E.F. *Visible & Invisible.* 1924. Doran. 1st Am. F/NF. B4. $250.00

BENSON, Irene Eliott. *Campfire Girls in the Forest; or, Lost Trail Found.* 1918. Chicago. Donohue. 1st. ils. 149p. VG+. A25. $15.00

BENSON, Lyman. *Cacti of Arizona.* 1950. AZ U. 2nd/revised. ils. 134p. NF/VG. B19. $40.00

BENSON, Lyman. *Cacti of Arizona.* 1950. Tucson. 2nd. ils/39 pl. F. B26. $22.50

BENSON, Lyman. *Native Cacti of California.* 1969. Stanford. 16 mc pl/distribution maps. 243p. VG+/dj. B26. $29.00

BENSON, Lyman. *Plant Classification.* 1957. Boston. ils/photos/drawings. 688p. B26. $37.50

BENSON, Robert H. *Necromancers.* 1910. Tauchnitz. VG. M2. $50.00

BENSON, Stella. *Kwan-Yin.* 1922. SF. Grabhorn. 1/100. 8vo. inscr Benson/Grabhorn. F. T10. $100.00

BENSON & DARROW. *Manual of Southwestern Desert Trees & Shrubs.* 1944. U AZ Bulletin. 8vo. 411p. stiff wrp. F7. $30.00

BENT, Arthur Cleveland. *Life Histories of North American Birds of Prey.* 1937-38. WA. Smithsonian. 2 vol. ils. VG. S15. $60.00

BENT, Arthur Cleveland. *Life Histories of North American Gallinaceous Birds.* 1932. Smithsonian. ils/pl. 490p. VG. S15. $25.00

BENT, Arthur Cleveland. *Life Histories of North American Wood Warblers.* 1953. Smithsonian. 83 pl. 734p. VG. S15. $27.00

BENT, Newell. *American Polo.* 1929. NY. 1st. 8vo. 407p. gilt gr cloth. F. H3. $90.00

BENTLEY, BURGIS & SLATER. *Dickens Index.* 1990. Oxford. VG/VG. P3. $45.00

BENTLEY, E.C. *Trent's Last Case.* 1946. Tower. VG/VG. P3. $13.00

BENTLEY, James. *Secrets of Mt Sinai.* 1986. Garden City. 1st Am. ils. VG/dj. K3. $20.00

BENTLEY, John. *Great American Automobiles...Their Achievements...* 1957. Englewood Cliffs. 374p. dj. A17. $17.50

BENTLEY, KHOSLA & SECKLER. *Agroforestry in South Asia.* 1993. Internat'l Sci Pub. 367p. dj. B1. $35.00

BENTLEY, Nicolas. *Floating Dutchman.* 1951. DSP. 1st. VG/G. P3. $25.00

BENTLEY & HUMPHREYS. *Snow Crystals.* 1962. rpt orig 1931. ils. VG. D8. $15.00

BENTLEY & NURMI. *Blake Bibliography, Annotated List of Works...* 1964. MN U. 393p. VG/worn. A4. $85.00

BENTON, Arthur Lester. *Right-Left Discrimination & Finger Localization.* 1979. NY. Hoeber-Harper. 185p. prt bl cloth. G1. $50.00

BENTON, Kenneth. *Level.* 1970. Dodd Mead. VG/VG. P3. $13.00

BENTON, Kenneth. *Sole Agent.* 1974. Walker. 1st. NF/NF. H11. $15.00

BENTON, Kenneth. *Spy in Chancery.* 1972. Collins Crime Club. 1st. VG/VG. P3. $20.00

BENTZ, D.O. *Tuners' Handbook & Manual.* 1908. Lima, OH. 74p. 12mo. A17. $15.00

BENWELL, H.A. *History of the Yankee Division.* 1919. photos. VG. M17. $25.00

BERANI & DUTOIT. *Forms of Violence: Narrative in Assyrian Art...* 1985. NY. 1st. 136p. F/F. W3. $36.00

BERBER, Thomas. *Reinhart in Love.* 1962. Scribner. 1st. author's 2nd book. F/dj. M25. $75.00

BERCKMAN, Evelyn. *She Asked for It.* 1969. Doubleday. 1st. VG/VG. P3. $20.00

BERCOVICI, Konrad. *Volga Boatman.* nd. Groset Dunlap. 1st thus/photoplay. VG/dj. M2. $30.00

BERE, R. *World of Animals: The African Elephant.* 1966. London. Barker. ils/photos/distribution maps. 94p. NF/VG. M12. $12.50

BERENDA, Ruth W. *Influence of the Group on the Judgements of Children.* 1950. King's Crown. tall 8vo. 186p. VG. H1. $17.50

BERENDT, John. *Midnight in the Garden of Good & Evil.* 1994. Random. 1st. author's 1st book. F/F. M19. $125.00

BERESFORD, Elisabeth. *Vanishing Garden.* 1965. Funk Wagnalls. 1st Am. 160p. cloth. VG+/dj. M20. $18.00

BERESFORD, Elisabeth. *Wombles at Work.* 1974 (1973). London. Ernest Benn. 2nd. 8vo. 191p. gr brd. VG/G+. T5. $25.00

BERETARIO, P. Sebastiano S.J. *Vida del Padre Joseph de Ancheta de la Compania de Iesus...* 1618. Salamanca. Antonia Ramierez. 1st Spanish language. 430p. R15. $7,500.00

BERG, Elizabeth. *Durable Goods.* 1993. Random. 1st. sgn. F/F. B3. $75.00

BERG, Stephen. *Nothing in the Word.* 1972. Grossman. 1st. assn copy. F/wrp/dj. V1. $20.00

BERGALA & NARBONI. *Orson Welles.* 1982. Cahiers Du Cinema. French Text. 142p. NF. C9. $50.00

BERGAUST, Erik. *Planet for Conquest.* 1967. Putnam. 8vo. 95p. VG/dj. K5. $20.00

BERGER, Alwin. *Mesembrianthemen und Portulacaceen.* 1908. Stuttgart. ils. 328p. B26. $60.00

BERGER, J. *Wild Horses of the Great Basin: Social Competition...* 1986. Chicago. 8vo. ils/photos/figures. 326p. cloth. F/VG. M12. $22.50

BERGER, Phil. *Miracle on 33rd Street.* 1970. S&S. 1st. photos. VG+/dj. P8. $25.00

BERGER, Thomas. *Changing the Past.* 1989. Little Brn. 1st. F/F. H11. $30.00

BERGER, Thomas. *Crazy in Berlin.* 1958. Scribner. 1st. author's 1st book. F/NF. B2. $250.00

BERGER, Thomas. *Meeting Evil.* 1992. Little Brn. 1st. F/F. A20. $15.00

BERGER, Thomas. *Neighbors.* 1980. Delacorte. 3rd. NF/NF. P3. $13.00

BERGER, Thomas. *Reinhart's Women.* 1981. Delacorte. 1st. NF/F. A20. $30.00

BERGER, Thomas. *Reinhart's Women.* 1981. Delacorte. 1st. VG/VG. P3. $20.00

BERGER & CASWELL. *Glendale: A Pictorial History.* 1983. Norfolk. Conning. sgns. silver stp fabricoid. D11. $40.00

BERGERHOFF, Walther. *Atlas of Normal Radiographs of the Skull.* 1961. BErlin. 1st. folio. 57p. A13. $30.00

BERGERSON, Victor. *Trader Vic's Pacific Island Cookbook.* 1968. Doubleday. VG/G. A16. $15.00

BERGHOLD, Alexander. *Indians Revenge or Days of Horror.* 1891. Thomas Pub. 1st Am. VG. J2. $250.00

BERGLAND, Martha. *Farm Under a Lake.* 1989. Graywolf. 1st. F/dj. R13. $20.00

BERGMAN, Andrew. *Big Kiss-Off of 1944.* 1974. HRW. 1st. VG/VG. P3. $25.00

BERGMAN, Andrew. *Hollywood & Levine.* 1975. Holt. 1st. NF/dj. M25. $35.00

BERGMAN, Deborah. *Southern Cross.* 1990. NY. 1st. F/F. T12. $15.00

BERGMAN, Peter M. *Chronological History of the Negro in America.* 1969. NY. Harper Row. 1st. F/dj. Q1. $50.00

BERGMAN, Ray. *Fresh-Water Bass.* 1942. Penn. 1st. 436p+10 mc pl. A17. $30.00

BERGMAN, Ray. *With Fly, Plug & Bait.* 1947. NY. 1st. 640p. F/dj. A17. $45.00

BERKELEY, Anthony. *Poisoned Chocolate Case.* 1929. Crime Club. G. P3. $18.00

BERKELEY, Anthony. *Silk Stocking Murders.* nd. Canada. Doubleday Doran. VG. P3. $35.00

BERKELEY, Henry J. *Treatise on Mental Disease Based on Lecture Course...* 1900. Appleton. 8vo. 15 pl. panelled gr buckram. xl. G1. $65.00

BERKELEY & BERKELEY. *George Wm Featherstonhaugh, 1st US Government Geologist.* 1988. Tuscaloosa. AL U. 357p. F/dj. D8. $35.00

BERKLEY & STEBBINS. *Comparative Perception Vol 1: Basic Mechanisms.* (1990). NY. Wiley-Interscience. 528p. Lib Congress duplicate stp. VG/dj. G1. $40.00

BERKOW, Ira. *Pitchers Do Get Lonely.* 1988. Atheneum. 1st. F/F. P8. $15.00

BERKOWITZ, David Sandler. *John Selden's Formative Years, Politics & Society...* 1988. WA. Folger Books. M11. $65.00

BERLE, A.A. *World Significance of a Jewish State.* 1981. Mitchell Kennerley. 47p. VG+. S3. $25.00

BERLINSKI, David. *Black Mischeif, Mechanics of Modern Science.* 1986. Morrow. 1st. 344p. VG/VG. W2. $20.00

BERLITZ, Charles. *Atlantis: The Eighth Continent.* 1984. Putnam. 1st. VG/VG. P3. $20.00

BERLITZ, Charles. *Atlantis: The Lost Continent Revealed.* 1984. Macmillan. 1st. VG. P3. $15.00

BERLITZ, Charles. *Lost Ship of Noah.* 1987. Putnam. VG/dj. A19. $25.00

BERMANT, Chaim. *Jews.* 1977. NY. Times Books. 278p. VG/dj. S3. $23.00

BERNADOTTE, Folke. *Curtain Falls, Eyewitness Account of Last Days 3rd Reich.* 1945. 1st. F/VG. E6. $25.00

BERNARD, Desire. *De l'Aphasie et de ses Diverses Formes.* 1889. Paris. 2nd. ils. contemporary brd. xl. VG. G1. $125.00

BERNARD, Raymond. *Hollow Earth.* 1979. Bell. VG/VG. P3. $12.00

BERNHARDT, P. *Wily Violets & Underground Orchids.* 1989. NY. Morrow. 1st. 255p. F/F. B1. $19.00

BERNHEIMER, Charles L. *Rainbow Bridge. Circling Navajo Mountain...* 1926. Doubleday Page. 8vo. 3 maps/62 photos. 182p. VG. F7. $40.00

BERNIER, Francois. *Voyages...Contenant la Description des Etats du Grand Mogol.* 1699. Amsterdam. Marret. 2 vol. 8vo. 13 engraved pl/maps. vellum. R12. $750.00

BERNINGER, Ernst. *Otto Hahn: Ein Bild-Dokumentation.* 1969. Munchen. 137 ils. NF. K3. $45.00

BERNSTEIN, Leonard. *Young People's Concerts.* 1962. ils. w/records. VG/VG cases. M17. $20.00

BEROALDUS, Philippus. *Oratio Prouerbiorum.* 1505. Paris. Petit. 4to. Tamburini/De Guinzbourg bookplates. brd. R12. $475.00

BEROLZHEIMER, Ruth. *June's Daily Cookbook*. 1951. Culinary Arts Inst. 1st. VG/G. E6. $20.00

BEROLZHEIMER, Ruth. *Victory Binding of American Woman's Cook Book Wartime Ed.* 1943. Chicago. Culinary Arts Inst. A16. $20.00

BERRIAN & BROEK. *Bibliography of Women Writers From Caribbean (1831-1986)*. 1989. 371p. NF/wrp. A4. $85.00

BERRIAULT, Gina. *Descent*. 1960. Atheneum. 1st. VG/dj. M2. $13.00

BERRIAULT, Gina. *Lights of Earth*. 1984. SF. Northpoint. 1st. F/NF. R13. $25.00

BERRIDGE, Jesse. *Tudor Rose*. 1925. London. 1st. VG. M2. $12.00

BERRIE, BERRIE & EZE. *Tropical Plant Science*. 1987. Longman. 410p. F. B1. $25.00

BERRIGAN, Daniel. *Time Without Number. Selected Poems*. 1957. Macmillan. 1st. F/NF. R13. $25.00

BERRIGAN, Daniel. *World for Wedding Ring*. 1962. 1st. VG/VG. M19. $25.00

BERROW, Norman. *Ghost House*. 1979. St Martin. 1st Am. F/dj. M2. $15.00

BERROW, Norman. *Words Have Wings*. 1946. Ward Lock. 1st. F/clip. M15. $100.00

BERRY, Carole. *Year of the Monkey*. 1988. St Martin. 1st. F/F. P3. $17.00

BERRY, Don. *Majority of Scoundrels, an Informal History...* 1961. Harper. 1st. 432p. VG/dj. J2. $125.00

BERRY, Don. *Moontrap*. 1962. Viking. 1st. F/VG+. A18. $40.00

BERRY, Don. *Trask*. 1961. Viking. 1st. F/VG. A18. $50.00

BERRY, Erick. *Girls in Africa*. 1928. Macmillan. 1st. ils. 128p. VG/VG. D1. $65.00

BERRY, Mike; see Malzberg, Barry.

BERRY, R.J.A. *Stoke Park Monographs on Mental Deficiency & Other Problems*. 1933. London. macmillan. 29 half-tones. 249p. gr cloth. G1. $50.00

BERRY, Rose V.S. *Dream City: Its Art in Story & Symbolism*. 1915. self pub. 8vo. ils/drawings, 335p. brn cloth. NF. K7. $30.00

BERRY, Wendell. *Collected Poems 1957-1982*. 1985. Northpoint. 1st. F/F. D10. $35.00

BERRY, Wendell. *Continuous Harmony*. 1972. HBJ. 1st. F/F. D10. $45.00

BERRY, Wendell. *Sabbaths*. 1987. SF. Northpoint. 1st. sgn. F/F. R14. $50.00

BERRY, Wendell. *Wild Birds*. 1986. Northpoint. 1st. pres. pub slip. F/F. D10. $35.00

BERRY & FLOYD. *History of Eton College Hunt 1857-1969*. 1968. London. Collins. 1st. VG/G. O3. $40.00

BERRY & KELLERT. *Bibliography of Human-Animal Relations*. 1985. Yale. lists 3800 items. F. S15. $30.00

BERRY & MASON. *Mineralogy, Concepts, Descriptions, Determinations*. 1959. SF. Freeman. 630p. cloth. VG. T11. $25.00

BERRYMAN, John. *Delusions, Etc.* 1972. FSG. 1st. 8vo. F/dj. T10. $50.00

BERRYMAN, John. *Homage to Mistress Bradstreet*. 1956. FSC. 1st. 61p. F/F. D4. $145.00

BERRYMAN, John. *Recovery*. 1973. FSG. 1st. VG+/dj. A20. $20.00

BERTHOLLET, C.L. *Researches Into Laws of Chemical Affinity*. 1809. Baltimore. Nicklin. 1st. 12mo. 212p. contemporary calf. M1. $225.00

BERTIN, Jack. *Interplanetary Adventures*. 1970. Lenox Hill. VG. P3. $10.00

BERTO, Giusseppe. *Sky Is Red*. 1948. New Directions. 1st. NF/dj. B35. $20.00

BERTON, Pierre. *Impossible Railway*. 1972. Knopf. dj. A19. $45.00

BERTRAND, A. *Succulent Plants*. 1959 (1953). London. 2nd. ils/photos. VG/dj. B26. $20.00

BERVEILER, David. *Strategic Solitaire*. 1984. NC. 142p. VG. S1. $8.00

BESHLIE. *Snailsleap Lane*. 1977. England. Granada Pub Ltd. 1st. sm 4to. 60p. NF/VG. T5. $35.00

BESKOW, Elsa. *Children of the Forest*. (1969). Delacorte. 1st Am. ils. VG/dj. D1. $65.00

BESKOW, Elsa. *Hanschen im Blaubeerenwald*. nd (1903). Stuttgart. Ferdinand Carl. obl 4to. red bdg. VG. M5. $115.00

BESKOW, Katja. *Astonishing Adventures of Patrick the Mouse*. 1965. Delacorte. 1st Am. 84p. cloth. VG/dj. M20. $25.00

BESSEMER, Henry, of London. *Improvement in Manufacture of Iron & Steel*. 1865. US Patent Office. VG/wrp. K3. $65.00

BESSIE, Alvah. *One for My Baby*. 1980. HRW. 1st. NF/VG+. A24. $20.00

BESSIE, Alvah. *Symbol*. 1966. Random. 1st. M25/V4. $25.00

BESSIE, Alvah. *Un-Americans*. 1957. Cameron Assoc. 1st. Vg/dj. M25. $35.00

BEST, Marc. *Those Endearing Young Charms*. 1971. AS Barnes. 278p. VG/dj. M20. $16.00

BESTER, Alfred. *Computer Connection*. 1975. Berkley. 1st. F/NF. M2. $15.00

BESTER, Alfred. *Demolished Man*. 1953. Shasta. 1st. sgn subscriber copy. F/dj. M2. $450.00

BESTER, Alfred. *Golem 100*. 1980. S&S. 1st. F/dj. M2. $15.00

BESTER, Alfred. *Light Fantastic*. 1976. Berkley Putnam. 1st. VG/VG. P3. $20.00

BESTER, Alfred. *Light Fantastic*. 1977. Gollancz. VG/VG. P3. $25.00

BESTER, Alfred. *Star Light, Star Bright*. 1976. Berkley Putnam. 1st. NF/NF. P3. $20.00

BESTON, Henry. *Songs of Kai: Story of the Indian Told*. 1926. Macmillan. 1st. ils. 55p. VG+. B19. $45.00

BETTEN, H.L. *Upland Game Shooting*. 1940. Phil. 2nd. 450p. gilt cloth. A17. $20.00

BETTER COOKING LIBRARY. *Complete Everyday Cookbook*. 1971. VG/dj. A16. $25.00

BETTER HOMES & GARDENS. *Better Homes & Gardens Complete Step-By Step Cook Book*. 1978. Meredith. 1st. 384p. G+/dj. A16. $12.00

BETTER HOMES & GARDENS. *Encyclopedia of Cooking*. 1973. Meredith. 20 vol. G. A16. $30.00

BETTER HOMES & GARDENS. *New Cook Book*. 1968. Meredith. VG. A16. $12.00

BETTER HOMES & GARDENS. *Step-By-Step Kids' Cook Book*. 1948. Des Moines, IA. Meredith. 1st. ils. VG. C8. $15.00

BETTER HOMES & GARDENS. *Step-By-Step Microwave Cook Book*. 1987. Meredith Corp. 1st/1st prt. M/dj. A16. $12.00

BETTMANN & LANG. *Pictorial History of Music*. 1966. NY. 1st. inscr Lang. VG/VG. T9. $45.00

BETTY CROCKER. *Betty Crocker's Cook Book*. 1970. Golden. looseleaf p. VG. A16. $15.00

BETTY CROCKER. *Betty Crocker's Picture Cook Book*. 1950. McGraw Hill. 1st/2nd prt. G. A16. $50.00

BETTY CROCKER. *Betty Crocker's Picture Cook Book*. 1950. McGraw Hill. 1st/7th prt. looseleaf. G/dj. A16. $50.00

BETTY CROCKER. *Betty Crocker's Picture Cook Book.* 1956. McGraw Hill. 2nd/1st prt. G. A16. $45.00

BETTY CROCKER. *Vitality Demands Energy: 190 Smart New Ways to Serve Bread.* 1934. General Mills. 52p. VG. B10. $35.00

BEVIS, H.U. *Alien Abductors.* 1971. Lenox Hill. G/G. P3. $10.00

BEWICK, John. *Proverbs Exemplified & Ils by Pictures From Real Life...* 1790. London. Rev J Trusler. 1st. 16mo. 196p. rebound/leather spine. R5. $400.00

BEWICK, Thomas. *General History of Quadrupeds.* 1790. Newcastle-Upon-Tyne. Hodgson Beilly Bewick. 1st. tall 8vo. 456p. recent bdg. H13. $895.00

BEWICK, Thomas. *Poetical Works of Robert Burns; With His Life.* 1808. Wm Davison. 1st thus. 2 vol. 8vo. full-p pl. later 19th-C morocco. F. B24. $950.00

BEWICK & BEWICK. *Poems by Goldsmith & Parnell.* 1795. London. Bulmer. 1st thus. 4to. 76p. marbled brd/tooled leather spine. B24. $1,250.00

BEYER, Harold. *History of Norwegian Literature.* 1956. NYU. 1st ed. 370p. F/dj. A17. $15.00

BEYER, William Gray. *Minions of the Moon.* 1950. Gnome. 1st. F/VG. P3. $35.00

BIANCHI, Leonardo. *Mechanism of the Brain & Function of the Frontal Lobes.* 1922. Edinburgh. Livingston. 1st Eng-language. 348p. purple cloth. xl. G1. $200.00

BIANCO, Margery. *House That Grew Smaller.* 1931. Macmillan. 1st. 8vo. gr cloth. dj. R5. $100.00

BIANCO, Margery. *Hurdy-Gurdy Man.* 1933. Oxford. 1st. sq 8vo. VG+. P2. $75.00

BIANCO, Pamela. *Beginning With A.* 1947. Oxford. 1st. bl cloth. F/dj. R5. $150.00

BIANCO, Pamela. *Beginning With A.* 1947. Oxford. 1st. VG+/dj. M5. $95.00

BIANCO, Pamela. *Doll in the Window.* 1953. Oxford. 1st. sq 8vo. VG/VG-. P2. $75.00

BIANCO, Pamela. *Little Houses of Far Away.* 1951. Oxford. 1st. 8vo. gilt lettered gr cloth. dj. R5. $100.00

BIANCO, Pamela. *Paradise Square.* 1950. Oxford. 1st. 96p. VG+/G+. P2. $60.00

BIANCO, Pamela. *Playtime in Cherry Street.* 1948. NY. Oxford. 1st. 8vo. brn-gray cloth. dj. R5. $100.00

BIANCO, Pamela. *Starlit Journey.* 1933. Macmillan. 1st. pres. 12mo. bl cloth. dj. R5. $200.00

BIART, Lucien. *Aztecs: Their History, Manner & Customs.* 1887. Chicago. ils/fld map. 343p. B18. $45.00

BIBB, Henry. *Puttin' on Ole Massa: Slave Narratives of Henry Bibb.* 1969. 1st. edit Osofsky. VG/VG. M17. $25.00

BIBBY, Geoffrey. *Looking for Dilum.* 1969. Knopf. ils/maps. 383p. xl. NF/dj. W1. $22.00

BIBLE. *Bible Atlas Containing Nine Maps With Explanations...* 1827. Phil. Am Sunday School. 1st. sq 18mo. orig engraved yel wrp. M1. $275.00

BIBLE. *Bible in Miniature; or, Concise Hist of Old/New Testaments.* 1780. London. Newbery. 1st/3rd state. 45x30mm. brn leather. F. B24. $550.00

BIBLE. *Bible: Designed To Be Read As Living Literature.* 1943. S&S. King James Version. edit ES Bates. 1285p. VG/torn. B29. $11.00

BIBLE. *Biblia. Nuremberg: Anton Koberger.* Apr 14, 1478. folio. 468 leaves. 16th-C stp leather/wood brd. C6. $10,500.00

BIBLE. *Book of Ecclesiastes.* 1968. NY. LEC. RKJ. Hebrew/Eng text. ils/sgn Edgar Miller. leather. S3. $65.00

BIBLE. *Book of Ruth.* 1947. LEC. 1/1950. ils/sgn Arthur Szyk. VG/case. D1. $225.00

BIBLE. *Child's Bible.* 1834. Phil. Fisher & Brother. 57x48mm. full-p pl. 192p. gilt lavender cloth. NF. B24. $85.00

BIBLE. *Daily Devotional Bible.* nd. Nelson. KJV. arranged for daily devotion for 1 year. swrp. B29. $10.50

BIBLE. *Dakota Wowapi Woken Sioux Holy Bible.* 1919. NY. Am Bible Soc. A19. $250.00

BIBLE. *God's Victorious Army Bible.* nd. Morris Cerullo. KJV. F. B29. $6.50

BIBLE. *Gospel According to Saint Luke, Translated Into Seneca...* 1829. NY. Am Bible Soc. 1st. trans TS Harris. 16mo. 149p. contemporary bdg. M1. $425.00

BIBLE. *History of the Bible.* 1822. Albany. Shaw. 54x36mm. 15 woodcuts. 255p. gilt full blk calf. F. B24. $200.00

BIBLE. *History of the Bible.* 1850. New London. Bolles. 54x45mm. 24 woodcuts. 192p. full calf. B24. $185.00

BIBLE. *History of the Bible.* 1890. Lansingburgh, NY. Disturnell. 52x36mm. 15 woodcuts. 256p. gilt calf. B24. $325.00

BIBLE. *History of the Bible.* 1954. LA. Dudie Studio. facsimile. 56x40mm. 231p. gilt full brn leather. B24. $100.00

BIBLE. *Holy Bible, Containing the Old & New Testaments...* 1919. NY. Oxford/Am Branch. 44x30mm. aeg. limp maroon leather. w/magnifying glass. B24. $225.00

BIBLE. *Holy Bible, Containing the Old & New Testaments...Apocrypha.* 1823. NY. Daniel D Smith. Stereotyped White. lg/thick 4to. 770p. contemporary bdg. M1. $750.00

BIBLE. *Holy Bible.* 1972. Nelson. RSV. reference/concordance/maps. leatherette. VG. B29. $12.00

BIBLE. *Holy Bible.* 1975. Falwell Ministries. Am Bicentennial Ed. ils. wht w/Liberty Bell bdg. VG. B29. $10.50

BIBLE. *Holy Bible.* 1976. Regency. KJV. Giant Prt. red letter/reference. 1855p. VG. B29. $10.50

BIBLE. *Layman's Parallel Bible.* 1980. Zondervan. KJV/MLB/LB/RSV. 3037p. VG/dj. B29. $17.00

BIBLE. *Le Nouveau Testament de Notre Seigneur Jesus-Christ...* 1810. Boston. Buckingham. 1st. thick 8vo. 2-toned brd. uncut. M1. $375.00

BIBLE. *Lord Is My Shepherd: The Twenty-Third Psalm.* 1965. Henry Z Walck. ils Tony Palazzo. VG. B15. $50.00

BIBLE. *New Open Bible.* 1982. Nelson. KJV. Lg Prt ed. references/trans/indexes. leather. G. B29. $15.50

BIBLE. *New Testament in Four Versions.* 1964. Versen-Ford. KJV/RSV/Phillips/NEB. 831p. VG. B29. $15.00

BIBLE. *New Testament.* nd. Am Bible Soc. RSV. photos. 260p. VG. B29. $6.50

BIBLE. *One Year Bible.* 1986. Tyndale. NIV arranged in 365 daily readings. VG/dj. B29. $10.50

BIBLE. *Pentateuch With Haftaroth & Five Megiloth.* 1928. Hebrew Pub. Eng trans revised by Alexander Harkavy. G. B29. $13.00

BIBLE. *Reader's Digest Bible.* 1982. Reader's Digest. RSV. 799p. VG/torn. B29. $7.00

BICKEL, Lennard. *Deadly Element.* 1979. Stein Day. 1st. ils. 312p. VG/dj. K3. $20.00

BICKEL, Walter. *Hering's Dictionary of Classical & Modern Cookery.* nd. London. Virtue. 7th Eng. VG. A16. $30.00

BICKERMAN, Elias. *Maccabees.* 1947. Schocken. 125p. VG/G. S3. $23.00

BIDDLE, A.J. Drexel. *Word for Word & Letter for Letter.* 1898. London. VG. M2. $22.00

BIDDLE, Shelia. *Bolingbroke & Harley.* 1974. Knopf. 1st. 307p. VG+/clip. M20. $12.00

BIDLOO, Govert. *Anatomia Humani Corporis, Centum et Quinque Tabulis...* 1685. Amsterdam. 1st. lg folio. ftspc/pl. contemporary vellum. xl. VG. A13. $13,500.00

BIDWELL, John. *First Emigrant Train to California.* 1966. Menlo Park. Penlitho. 1/500. ils Remington. 52p. whit buckram. F. K7. $35.00

BIDWELL, John. *Life in California Before the Gold Discovery.* 1966. Palo Alto. Lewis Osborne. 1/1950. gilt sage cloth. M. K7. $45.00

BIEN, H.M. *Ben-Beor.* 1891. Friedenwald. 1st. G+. M2. $50.00

BIERCE, Ambrose. *Black Beetles in Amber.* 1892. SF. Western Authors. 1st. sgn. prt wrp. M24. $650.00

BIERCE, Ambrose. *Enlarged Devil's Dictionary.* 1967. Doubleday. 1st. F/dj. M2. $25.00

BIERCE, Ambrose. *Tales of Soldiers & Civilians.* 1891. SF. ELG Steele. 1st. 12mo. 300p. gr cloth. M1. $1,500.00

BIERCE, Ambrose. *Vision of Doom.* 1980. Donald Grant. 1st. F/dj. M2. $12.00

BIERMAN, John. *Dark Safari: Life Behind Legend of Henry Morton Stanley.* 1990. NY. 1st. ils/maps. 401p. F/dj. M4. $20.00

BIERMAN, John. *Odyssey.* 1984. S&S. 255p. F/VG. S3. $25.00

BIERNE, F.F. *War of 1812.* 1949. NY. 1st. 11 maps. F/G. M4. $25.00

BIERSTADT, Edward Hale. *Dunsany the Dramatist.* 1917. Little Brn. 1st. NF. R10. $25.00

BIESTERVELD, Betty. *Peter's Wagon.* 1968. Racine. Whitman. lg 32mo. ils Nagel. as new. C8. $20.00

BIGELOW, Henry J. *Insensibility During Surgical Operations...Inhalation.* 1846. Boston. 1st. 544p. half leather/marbled brd. VG. A13. $5,000.00

BIGELOW, Henry J. *Memoir of Henry Jacob Bigelow.* 1900. Boston. 1st. 297p. A13. $75.00

BIGELOW, John. *Life of Benjamin Franklin Written by Himself.* 1879. Lippincott. 2nd/revised/corrected. 2 vol. bl cloth. VG. T10. $45.00

BIGELOW, John. *Memoir of the Life & Public Services of John Chas Fremont.* 1856. NY. 1st. 480p. O8. $32.50

BIGELOW, John. *Retrospections of an Active Life.* 1909. NY. 1st. 2000p. O8. $27.50

BIGELOW, Melville Madison. *History of Procedure in England From Norman Conquest...* 1880. London. Macmillan. xl. M11. $150.00

BIGELOW, Melville Madison. *Placita Anglo-Normannica, Law Cases of William I...* 1970. S Hackensack. Rothman. facsimile 1881 Soule & Bugbee. M11. $50.00

BIGELOW, Poultney. *Borderland of Czar & Kaiser.* 1895. NY. Harper. 1st. ils Remington. 343p. tan cloth. NF. K7. $80.00

BIGELOW, Wilfred Abram. *Forceps, Fin & Feather.* (1969). Altona, Manitoba. DW Friesen. 1st. 116p. NF/VG+. H7. $20.00

BIGGERS, Earl Derr. *Black Camel.* 1929. Bobbs Merrill. VG. M22. $15.00

BIGGERS, Earl Derr. *Celebrated Cases of Charlie Chan.* 1985. New Orchard. MTI. VG/VG. P3. $20.00

BIGGERS, Earl Derr. *Charlie Chan Carries On.* 1930. Indianapolis. 1st. VG/VG. B5. $60.00

BIGGERS, Earl Derr. *House Without a Key.* 1925. Bobbs Merrill. VG. M2. $15.00

BIGGERS, Earl Derr. *Keeper of the Keys.* 1932. McClelland Stewart. 1st. VG. P3. $35.00

BIGGLE, Jacob. *Biggle Berry Book.* 1913. Atkinson. 144p. cloth. A10. $32.00

BIGGLE, Jacob. *Biggle Horse Book.* 1907. Phil. Atkinson. 136p. VG. A10. $30.00

BIGGLE, Jacob. *Biggle Swin Book.* 1899. Phil. Atkinson. 144p. VG. A10. $25.00

BIGGLE, Jacob. *Poultry Book, a Concise Practical Treatise on Farm Poultry.* 1906 (1895). Biggle Farm Lib. 32mo. 16 chromos. VG. E6. $20.00

BIGGLE, Lloyd. *Light That Never Was.* 1974. London. 1st. F/dj. M2. $12.00

BIGGLE, Lloyd. *Metallic Muse.* 1972. Doubleday. 1st. xl. VG/VG. P3. $8.00

BIGGLE, Lloyd. *Monument.* 1974. Doubleday. 1st. F/F. M2. $20.00

BIGGLE, Lloyd. *Monument.* 1975. NEL. F/F. P3. $17.00

BIGHAM, Madge. *Merry Animal Tales, a Book of Old Fables in New Dresses.* 1935. Little Brn. sgn. sm 8vo. ils Clara Atwood Fitts. VG+. $65.00

BILENKIN, Dmitri. *Uncertainty Principle.* 1978. Macmillan. F/F. P3. $15.00

BILEZIKIAN, Gilbert. *Christianity 101: Your Guide to Eight Basic Christian...* 1993. Zondervan. 287p. F/dj. M4. $6.50

BILLIAS, George Athan. *George Washington's Opponents.* 1969. Morrow. 1st. 362p. VG/dj. M20. $20.00

BILLIK & KAUFMAN. *Brunch Cookbook.* 1972. Hawthorn. 334p. VG/VG. B10. $10.00

BILLING & MANNERING. *South - Man & Nature in Antarctica - A New Zealand View.* 1969. Wellington. Reed. revised. 4to. 86p. cloth. VG/dj. P4. $50.00

BILLINGS, John S. *Description of Johns Hopkins Hospital.* 1890. Baltimore. 1st. 56 pl. 116p. quarter leather/marbled brd. A13. $1,500.00

BILLINGS, John S. *National Medical Dictionary: Including English, French...* 1890. Edinburgh. 2 vol. 1st. A13. $200.00

BILLINGS, Josh. *Old Probability. Rain...Perhaps Not.* 1879. NY. GW Carleton. 1st. 8vo. cloth. M1. $175.00

BILLINGS, M.P. *Structural Geology.* 1972. Englewood Cliffs. 3rd. NF. D8. $16.00

BILLINGTON, C. *Shrubs of Michigan.* 1977. Bloomfield Hills. Cranbrook. 2nd/3rd prt. 339p. F/NF. B1. $27.50

BILROTH, Theodor. *General Surgical Pathology & Therapeutics.* 1871. NY. 1st Eng trans. 676p. A13. $250.00

BILYEU, Richard. *Tanelorn Archives.* 1981. Pandora. 1/250. sgn. ils Steve Leialoha. F/sans. P3. $25.00

BIMBA, Anthony. *History of the American Working Class.* 1927. Internat Pub. 1st. VG/dj. V4. $40.00

BINDER, Eando. *Enslaved Brains.* 1965. Avalon. 1st. F/dj. M2. $25.00

BINDER, Eando. *Lords of Creation.* 1949. Prime. 1st. F/VG. P3. $80.00

BINDER, Otto O. *Victory in Space.* 1962. Walker. 8vo. 211p. G/dj. K5. $25.00

BING, Robert. *Textbook of Nervous Diseases.* 1939. St Louis. Mosby Co. 1st prt. inscr. 8vo. 838p. bl-gr cloth. VG. G1. $125.00

BINGHAM, Clifton. *Animals' School-Treat.* date not legible. London. Deans Rag Books. 4to. cloth. fair. M5. $75.00

BINGHAM, Clifton. *Something New for Little Folk.* 1899. London. Nister. 7 round movable transformation pl. R5. $1,000.00

BINGHAM, Hiram. *Across South America.* (1911). Houghton Mifflin. ils/maps. 405p. gilt gr cloth. F3. $45.00

BINGHAM, Hiram. *Lost City of the Incas.* 1948. NY. sgn pres. VG/G. B5. $125.00

BINGHAM, Hiram. *Lost City of the Incas.* 1962. NY. VG/VG. B5. $30.00

BINGHAM & SCHOLT. *Fifteen Centuries of Children's Litarature...* 1980. 1st. ils. 590p. VG. A4. $145.00

BINKOSKI & PLANT. *115 Infantry Regiment in WWII.* 1948. WA. 1st. photos/maps/map ep. G+. B18. $125.00

BINNIE, G.M. *Early Victorian Water Engineers.* 1981. ils. VG/VG. M17. $35.00

BINNS, Archie. *Northwest Gateway: Story of Port of Seattle.* 1941. Doubleday. ils. 313p. dj. T7. $30.00

BINNS, Archie. *Roaring Land.* 1942. McBride. 1st. sgn. 284p. VG/VG. B11. $40.00

BINNS, Henry Bryan. *Life of Abraham Lincoln.* 1927. 1st. 379p. O8. $9.50

BINYON, Laurence. *William Blake: Illustrations of the Book of Job.* 1906. London. Methuen. 21 engraved pl. cloth. T10. $150.00

BINYON, Lawrence. *Engraved Designs of William Blake.* 1926. London. Ernest Benn. 140p. teg. NF. B24. $250.00

BIRCH, A.G. *Moon Terror.* 1927. Popular Fiction. 1st. VG/facsimile Canon dj. M2. $75.00

BIRCHLEY, W. *British Birds for Cages, Aviaries & Exhibition.* 1909. London. Sherratt Hughes. 2 vol. royal 8vo. ils/pl. xl. VG. M12. $60.00

BIRD, Annie Laurie. *Boise, the Peace Valley.* 1934. CAxton. 1st. 408p. VG/VG. J2. $450.00

BIRD, Larry. *Drive.* 1989. Doubleday. 1st. photos. fwd Magic Johnson. F/F. P8. $80.00

BIRDSALL, L.E. *Animal Pictures & Rhymes.* 1934. Edward Stern. photos Newton Hartman/Richard Dooner. sc. M5. $30.00

BIRINGUCCIO, Vannoccio. *Pyroctechnia.* 1959 (1943). NY. Basic. facsimile. VG/worn case. K3. $95.00

BIRKENHEAD, Earl. *Prof in Two Worlds.* 1961. London. Collins. 1st. 8vo. 382p. VG/dj. K3. $25.00

BIRKENHEAD, Earl. *World in 2030.* 1930. Brewer Warren. 1st Am. VG. M2. $40.00

BIRKENHEAD, J. *Ferns & Fern Culture.* 1897 (1892). Manchester. 2nd. 128p. gilt cloth. B26. $24.00

BIRKLEY, Dolan. *Unloved.* 1965. Crime Club. 1st. VG/VG. P3. $18.00

BIRNBAUM, Martin. *Jacovleff & Other Artists: Alexandre Jacovleff, Wm Blake...* 1946. NY. Paul Struk. 1/2000. 249p. cloth. D2. $75.00

BIRNBAUM, Salomo. *Life & Sayings of the Baal-Shem.* 1933. Hebrew Pub. edit Maximilian Hurwitz. 120p. VG. S3. $24.00

BIRNEY, Hoffman. *Zealots of Zion.* 1931. Phil. 1st. ils. 317p. VG/dj. B5. $50.00

BIRRELL, Anne. *Popular Songs & Ballads of Han China.* 1988. London. Unwin Hayman. 1st. 226p. F/dj. W3. $46.00

BISCHOF, Werner. *Japan.* 1954. NY. 1st/1st prt. photos. NF. W3. $55.00

BISHER, Furman. *Stolen Faces.* 1977. Harper Row. 1st. F/F. P3. $15.00

BISHER, Furman. *Strange But True Baseball Stories.* 1976. Harper Row. 1st. F/F. P3. $15.00

BISHOP, Charles. *Journal & Letters of Capt Chas Bishop on NW Coast America...* 1967. Cambridge. Hakluyt Soc. 2nd series #131. 8vo. 6 maps (1 fld). 341p. bl cloth. P4. $60.00

BISHOP, Claire Huchet. *Pancakes-Paris.* 1947. Viking. 1st. ils Georges Schreiber. 62p. VG. T5. $30.00

BISHOP, Elizabeth. *Ballad of the Burglar of Babylon.* 1968. NY. 1st. ils Ann Grifalconi. unp. VG. B18. $75.00

BISHOP, Elizabeth. *Brazil.* 1962. NY. Time Incorp. 1st. 4to. pict brd. F/sans. B4. $85.00

BISHOP, Elizabeth. *Diary of Helena Morley.* 1957. FSC. 1st. VG/VG. R14. $35.00

BISHOP, Elizabeth. *Geography III.* 1976. NY. 1st. F/F. A11. $75.00

BISHOP, Frank. *Delphinium: A Flower Monograph.* 1949. London. Garden BC. 144p. dj. A10. $25.00

BISHOP, M.S. *Subsurface Mapping.* 1960. John Wiley. 198p. cloth. F/G. D8. $22.50

BISHOP, Michael. *And Strange at Ecbatan the Trees.* 1976. Harper. 1st. sgn. F/F. M2. $30.00

BISHOP, Michael. *Blooded on Arachine.* 1982. Arkham. 1st. F/dj. M2. $14.00

BISHOP, Michael. *Little Knowledge.* 1977. Berkeley. 1st. F/NF. M2. $20.00

BISHOP, Michael. *One Winter in Eden.* 1983. Arkham. 1st. F/dj. M2. $25.00

BISHOP, Michael. *Stolen Faces.* 1977. Harper. 1st. F/dj. M2. $20.00

BISHOP, Zealia. *Curse of Yig.* 1953. Arkham. 1st. F/dj. M2. $200.00

BISHOP & COBLENTZ. *American Decorative Arts: 360 Years of Creative Designs.* 1982. Abrams. ils. VG/VG. M17. $75.00

BISHOP & WATSON. *Under Heaven's Bridge.* 1980. London. Gollancz. ARC/1st. inscr Bishop. RS. F/F. T2. $85.00

BISLAND, Elizabeth. *Japanese Letters of Lafcadio Hearn.* 1910. Houghton Mifflin. 1st. ils. 468p. teg. cloth. NF. W3. $135.00

BISS & MITCHELL. *Gambit Book of Children's Songs.* 1970. Boston. Gambit. 1st. ils Errol LeCain. 159p. VG+/dj. D4. $45.00

BISSETT, Clark Prescott. *Abraham Lincoln: A Universal Man.* 1923. Grabhorn. 1/125. sgn/#d. O8. $75.00

BITTMAN, S. *Seeds.* 1989. NY. Bantam. 243p. F/F. B1. $40.00

BIXBY-SMITH, Sarah. *Adobe Days: Being the Truthful Narrative of Events...* 1931. LA. Jake Zeitlin. 3rd. inscr Zeitlin. photos. 148p. w/prospectus. D11. $100.00

BJERRE, Jens. *Kalahari.* 1960. Hill Wang. 8vo. ils. 227p. NF/dj. W1. $18.00

BJORN, Thyra Ferre. *Home As a Heart.* 1968. NY. HRW. 1st. sgn. F/VG. B11. $25.00

BLAAUW & SCHMIDT. *Galactic Structure.* 1965. Chicago U. sm 4to. 606p. VG/dj. K5. $60.00

BLACK, Campbell. *Brainfire.* 1979. Morrow. 1st. VG/G. P3. $15.00

BLACK, Campbell. *Letters From the Dead.* 1985. Villard. 1st. NF/NF. P3. $16.00

BLACK, Gavin. *Bitter Tea.* 1971. Harper Row. 1st. xl. VG/VG. P3. $6.00

BLACK, Gavin. *Dead Man Calling.* 1962. Random. 1st. 186p. VG+/dj. M20. $15.00

BLACK, Gavin. *Golden Cockatrice.* 1975. Harper Row. 1st. VG/VG. P3. $20.00

BLACK, Gavin. *You Want To Die, Johnny?* 1966. Harper Row. 1st. VG/VG. P3. $20.00

BLACK, Henry Campbell. *Black's Law Dictionary.* 1968. St Paul. W Pub Co. gilt gr buckram. M11. $75.00

BLACK, Hugh. *Work.* 1903. Revell. 1st. VG. V4. $25.00

BLACK, John J. *Cultivation of the Peach & the Pear.* 1887 (1886). NY. ils. 397p. B26. $55.00

BLACK, Lionel. *Breakaway.* 1970. Collins Crime Club. VG/VG. P3. $15.00

BLACK, Lionel. *Flood.* 1971. Stein Day. VG/VG. P3. $13.00

BLACK, Lionel. *Life & Death of Peter Wade.* 1974. Stein Day. 1st. VG/VG. P3. $13.00

BLACK, Mary Martin. *Summerfield Farm.* 1951. Viking. 1st. ils Wesley Dennis. 143p. VG+/dj. M20. $30.00

BLACK, William. *Strange Adventures of a Phaeton.* nd. Harper. VG. M2. $50.00

BLACK & BLACK. *Florence.* 1905. London. 75 mc ils. VG. B5. $75.00

BLACK HAWK. *Life of Ma-Ka-Tai-Me-She-Kia-Kiak or Black Hawk.* 1834. Boston. JB Patterson. 2nd (lacks photo ftspc). G. L3. $350.00

BLACKBURN, Isaac Wright. *Intracranial Tumors Among the Insane.* 1903. GPO. assn copy. 71 pl. w/author's complimentary slip. G1. $125.00

BLACKBURN, John. *Bury Him Darkly.* 1970. Putnam. 1st. VG/VG. P3. $45.00

BLACKBURN, John. *Gaunt Woman.* 1962. Hill Morrow. 1st. VG/VG. P3. $30.00

BLACKBURN, William. *Under Twenty-Five: Duke Narrative & Verse, 1945-1962.* 1963. Durham. Duke. 1st. intro William Styron. F/dj. B4. $175.00

BLACKETT, P.M.S. *Fear War & the Bomb.* 1949. NY. G+. K3. $15.00

BLACKLEDGE, S.D. *Open Book on Hidden Mysteries.* 1925. Elkton, MD. self pub. 1st. 123p. stiff cloth brd. VG/sans. B4. $250.00

BLACKMON, Anita. *Murder a la Richelieu.* 1937. Crime Club. 1st. VG. P3. $30.00

BLACKMORE, Howard L. *Guns & Rifles of the World.* 1965. Viking. 1st. 134p. cloth. VG+/dj. M20. $50.00

BLACKMORE, Jane. *Perilous Waters.* 1957. Collins. VG/VG. P3. $15.00

BLACKMORE, R.D. *Perlycross.* 1894. Harper. 1st. VG. M19. $25.00

BLACKSTOCK, Charity. *Briar Patch.* 1973. Hodder Stoughton. G/VG. P3. $10.00

BLACKSTOCK, Lee. *All Men Are Murderers.* 1958. Collins Crime Club. 1st. VG/VG. P3. $15.00

BLACKSTONE, WIlliam. *Great Charter & Charter of the Forest, With Other...* 1759. Oxford. Clarendon. modern 3-quarter calf. VG. M11. $3,500.00

BLACKWOOD, Algernon. *Best Supernatural Tales of Blackwood.* 1973. Causeway. VG/VG. P3. $30.00

BLACKWOOD, Algernon. *Doll & One Other.* 1946. Arkham. 1st. F/F. M2. $60.00

BLACKWOOD, Algernon. *Doll & One Other.* 1946. Arkham. 1st. F/VG. M19. $45.00

BLACKWOOD, Algernon. *Dudley & Gilderoy.* 1929. Dutton. 1st. VG/VG. P3. $75.00

BLACKWOOD, Algernon. *John Silence.* 1962. London. VG. M2. $17.00

BLACKWOOD, Algernon. *Promise of Air.* 1918. Dutton. 1st. VG/dj. M2. $175.00

BLACKWOOD, Algernon. *Tales of the Mysterious & Macabre.* 1967. Spring Books. 1st. VG. P3. $15.00

BLACKWOOD, Algernon. *Tales of the Uncanny & Supernatural.* 1952. London. VG/dj. M2. $25.00

BLACKWOOD, Andrew. *Preparations of Sermons.* 1948. Abingdon-Cokesbury. 272p. G/torn. B29. $6.50

BLACKWOOD & PEARN. *Karma.* 1918. Dutton. 1st. VG. M2. $40.00

BLAGOWIDOW, George. *Last Train From Berlin.* 1977. Doubleday. 1st. VG/VG. P3. $13.00

BLAINE, John. *Rick Brant's Science Projects.* 1960. Grosset Dunlap. 247p. VG/dj. M20. $450.00

BLAINE, John. *Rick Brant: Egyptian Cat Mystery (#16).* 1961. Grosset Dunlap. 1st. 182p. VG/dj (lists to this title). M20. $50.00

BLAINE, John. *Rick Brant: Flaming Mountain (#17).* 1962. Grosset Dunlap. lists to this title. 172p. VG. M20. $20.00

BLAINE, John. *Rick Brant: Flaming Mountain (#17).* 1962. Grosset Dunlap. 1st. 172p. lists to this title. VG. M20. $30.00

BLAINE, John. *Rick Brant: Magic Talisman (#24).* 1989. Manuscript. 1st. 1/500. M/as issued. N1. $75.00

BLAINE, John. *Rick Brant: Pirates of Shan (#14).* 1958. Grosset Dunlap. 1st. 181p. lists to this title. VG/dj. M20. $35.00

BLAINE, John. *Rick Brant: Rocket's Shadow.* 1947. Grosset Dunlap. 1st. F/F. M2. $40.00

BLAINE, John. *Rick Brant: Veiled Raiders (#20).* 1965. Grosset Dunlap. 1st. 178p. lists to this title. VG+. M20. $85.00

BLAINE, Marge. *Terrible Thing That Happened at Our House.* 1975. Parent's Magazine. 1st. ils JC Wallner. unp. VG/dj. M20. $18.00

BLAIR, Clay. *Atomic Submarine & Admiral Rickover.* 1954. NY. xl. K3. $15.00

BLAIR, Henry. *Biological Effects of External Radiation.* 1954. NY. 1st. 508p. A13. $100.00

BLAIR, John M. *Control of Oil.* 1976. Pantheon. 1st. charts/tables. 441p. NF/dj. W1. $25.00

BLAIR, Millard F. *Practical Tree Surgery.* 1937. Boston. ils. 297p. B26. $65.00

BLAIR, Robert. *Grave: A Poem.* 1808. London. 1st Wm Blake ils ed. lg 4to. VG. C6. $1,550.00

BLAIR, Sam. *Dallas Cowboys Pro or Con?* 1970. Doubleday. later prt. 418p. VG+/G. P8. $30.00

BLAIR, Sam. *Earl Campbell: Driving Force.* 1980. World. 1st. F/VG. P8. $20.00

BLAIR & SEHPLEY. *Hydrogen Bomb.* 1954. NY. 2nd. VG. K3. $15.00

BLAKE, Arlyn. *I Love To Cook Book.* 1971. NY. Essandess. VG/dj. A16. $9.00

BLAKE, Forrester. *Johnny Christmas.* 1948. Morrow. 1st. map ep. F/VG. A18. $50.00

BLAKE, Nelson. *William Mahone of Virginia.* 1935. Richmond. 1st. VG. B5. $50.00

BLAKE, Pamela. *Peep Show.* 1973. Macmillan. 1st Am. 32p. F/F. D4. $25.00

BLAKE, Peter. *God's Own Junkyard: The Planned Deterioration...* 1964. photos. VG/VG. M17. $17.50

BLAKE, William. *Book of Urizen.* 1958. London. Trianon. 4to. 1/526. teg. F/case. B24. $325.00

BLAKE, William. *Jerusalem.* 1951. London. Trianon. 1/250 (of 516). bl cloth brd. clamshell box. B24. $1,000.00

BLAKE, William. *Land of Dreams.* 1928. Macmillan. 1st. ils Pamela Bianco. VG. D4. $35.00

BLAKE, William. *Land of Dreams.* 1928. Macmillan. 1st. 42p. VG/G+. P2. $75.00

BLAKE & COMSTOCK. *Conversations on Chemistry...* 1826. Hartford. OD Cooke. tall 12mo. ils. 348p. VG. M12. $60.00

BLAKEMORE, Colin. *Mechanics of the Mind.* 1977. Cambridge. tall 8vo. 208p. VG/dj. G1. $40.00

BLAKENEY, John. *Heroes: US Marine Corps 1861-1955.* 1957. WA. 1st. ils. 621p. VG/dj. B5. $45.00

BLAKEY, E.S. *Tulsa Spirit.* 1979. Tulsa. ils. 192p. F/NF/case. M4. $20.00

BLAKEY, George C. *Gambler's Companion.* 1979. Paddington. 1st. NF/NF. P3. $20.00

BLANC, Suzanne. *Rose Window.* 1968. Cassell. VG/VG. P3. $15.00

BLANCHARD, Amy E. *My Own Dolly.* ca 1900. Dutton. ils Ida Waugh. 64p. VG. D1. $160.00

BLANCHARD, Charles. *With Heaps O'Love.* 1925. Des Moines. Nichols Book & Travel. inscr. 12mo. 288p. gilt cloth. B11. $25.00

BLANCHARD, Frank N. *Revision of the King Snakes: Genus Lampropeltis.* 1921. Smithsonian. 260p. S15. $22.00

BLANCHARD & WELLMAN. *Life & Times of Sir Archie 1805-1833.* 1958. Chapel Hill. 1st. VG/VG. O3. $45.00

BLANCHET, Francois Norbert. *Notices & Voyages of Famed Quebec Mission to Pacific...* 1961. Portland. OR Hist Soc. 1/1000. ils/lg fld map. F. O7. $65.00

BLANCK. *Harry Castlemon: Boy's Own Author, Appreciation & Biblio...* 1941. 1/750. 159p. VG/VG. A4. $135.00

BLANCK. *Peter Parley to Penrod, a Bibliographical Description...* 1938. 1/500. 1st. 159p. F. A4. $225.00

BLAND, Alexander. *Nureyev Valentino, Portrait of a Film.* 1977. Delta. ils/photos. NF/lg wrp. C9. $35.00

BLANDING, Don. *Songs of the Seven Senses.* 1931. Dodd Mead. 1st. sgn. 12mo. VG. B11. $35.00

BLANK, Clair. *Beverly Gray, Junior (#3).* 1934. AL Burt. lists 4 titles. 254p. VG/dj. M20. $60.00

BLANK, Clair. *Beverly Gray, Junior (#3).* 1934. Grosset Dunlap. lists 8 titles. VG/dj. M20. $30.00

BLANK, Clair. *Beverly Gray at the World's Fair.* 1934. NY. AL Burt. 1st. ils. 250p. G. A25. $8.00

BLANK, Clair. *Beverly Gray's Assigment (#17).* 1947. Grosset Dunlap. 1st. 212p. lists to #16. VG/dj. M20. $20.00

BLANK, Clair. *Beverly Gray's Challenge (#15).* 1945. Grosset Dunlap. 1st. 207p. cloth. VG/dj (lists to #14). M20. $15.00

BLANK, Clair. *Beverly Gray's Journey (#16).* 1946. Grosset Dunlap. lists to this title. VG/dj. M20/N1. $20.00

BLANK, Clair. *Beverly Gray's Scoop (#24).* 1954. Clover. lists 25 titles. 184p. VG. M20. $20.00

BLANKO, Winston E. *Trumpeter Swan: Its History, Habits & Population in US.* 1963 (1960). WA. N Am Fauna 63. ils/maps. 214p. NF. S15. $18.00

BLANSHARD, Frances. *Frank Aydelotte of Swathmore.* 1970. Wesleyan U. 1st. 429p. VG/dj. V3. $18.00

BLASINGAME, Ike. *Dakota Cowboy, My Life in the Old Days.* 1958. Putnam. 1st. ils. 317p. map ep. VG/VG. J2. $145.00

BLATH, MIDDLETON & MURRY. *Origin of Sedimentary Rocks.* 1980. Englewood Cliffs. 2nd. 782p. NF. D8. $30.00

BLATTY, William Peter. *Exorcist.* 1971. Harper Row. 1st. F/F. H11. $130.00

BLATTY, William Peter. *I, Billy Shakespeare!* 1965. Doubleday. 1st. sgn. ils Victoria Chess. F/VG+ clip. B4. $200.00

BLATTY, William Peter. *Legion.* 1983. S&S. 1st. VG/VG. P3. $15.00

BLATTY, William Peter. *Ninth Configuration.* 1978. Harper. 1st. F/F. N4. $30.00

BLAU, Bela. *Presidents of the United States.* 1986. LA. 2 vol. each w/36 tipped-in postage stamps. 59x42mm. M/case. B24. $150.00

BLAUNER, Peter. *Slow Motion Riot.* 1991. Morrow. 1st. author's 1st book. F/F. A24. $35.00

BLAUNER, Peter. *Slow Motion Riot.* 1991. Morrow. 1st. NF/NF. P3. $20.00

BLAYLOCK, James P. *Homunculus.* 1988. Morrigan. 1st. F/F. P3. $30.00

BLAYLOCK, James P. *Last Coin.* 1988. Ace. 1st trade. F/NF. M21. $10.00

BLAYLOCK, James P. *Magic Spectacles.* 1991. Morrigan. 1st. F/F. P3. $30.00

BLECH, Gustavus. *Clinical Electrosurgery.* 1938. London. 1st. 389p. A13. $150.00

BLEDSOE, T. *Brown Bear Summer: Life Among Alaska's Giants.* 1987. Dutton. ils E Mills. 249p. cloth. NF/F. M12. $27.50

BLEDSOE & BROWNE. *Southern Review. Vol 1, #1.* 1867. Baltimore. 256p. 8vo. string-tied wrp. chip/uncut. A17. $25.00

BLEECK, Oliver; see Thomas, Ross.

BLEEDING, Francis. *Hidden Kingdom.* 1927. Little Brn. 1st. VG. M2. $22.00

BLEGVAD & BLEGVAD. *Parrot in the Garret & Other Rhymes About Dwellings.* 1982. Atheneum. 1st. 32p. F/F. D4. $30.00

BLEGVAD & CRAFT. *Winter Bear.* 1974. Atheneum. 1st Am. 25p. F/F. D4. $30.00

BLEILER, E.F. *Best Science Fiction Stories 1950.* 1950. Fell. F/dj. M2. $25.00

BLEILER, E.F. *Checklist of Fantastic Literature.* 1948. Shasta. 1st. NF/rpr. M2. $135.00

BLEILER, E.F. *Year's Best Science Fiction Novels 1954.* 1954. Fell. 1st. F/dj. M2. $40.00

BLESH, Rudi. *O Susanna.* 1960. Grove. 1st. 54p. brd. NF. D4. $35.00

BLESH, Rudi. *Shining Trumpets.* 1946. Knopf. 1st. VG/VG. B2. $40.00

BLESH & JANIS. *They All Played Ragtime.* 1966. NY. Oak. 3rd. NF/wrp. B2. $25.00

BLEVINS, Winfred. *Dictionary of the American West.* 1993. Facts on File. 400p. F/dj. A17. $15.00

BLEVINS, Winfred. *Misadventures of Silk & Shakespeare.* 1985. Ottawa. Jameson Books. 1st. sgn. F. R14. $35.00

BLEYER, W.G. *How To Write Special Feature Articles.* 1920. Houghton Mifflin. 1st. gilt brn cloth. M24. $45.00

BLIER, Bertrand. *Going Places.* 1974. Lippincott. 1st Am. F/F clip. B4. $125.00

BLIGH, William. *Voyage to the South Seas...* 1975. LEC. sgns. 4 mc pl. gilt homespun linen. w/prospectus. as new/case. O7. $195.00

BLISH, James. *Anywhen.* 1970. Doubleday. 1st. NF/dj. M2. $30.00

BLISH, James. *Best Science Fiction Stories of James Blish.* 1965. London. Faber. 1st. inscr. F/NF. T2. $75.00

BLISH, James. *Black Easter.* 1968. Doubleday. 1st. NF/NF. M21. $100.00

BLISH, James. *Doctor Mirabilis.* 1971. Dodd Mead. 1st Am. F/dj. M2. $35.00

BLISH, James. *Frozen Year.* 1957. Ballantine. 1st. VG. M2. $50.00

BLISH, James. *Frozen Year.* 1957. Ballantine. 1st. VG/G. P3. $75.00

BLISH, James. *Jack of Eagles.* 1952. Greenberg. 1st. VG/VG. P3. $85.00

BLISH, James. *Mission to the Heart Stars.* 1965. Putnam. 1st. F/NF. T2. $100.00

BLISH, James. *Quincunx of Time.* 1975. London. Faber. 1st hc. F/NF. T2. $20.00

BLISH, James. *Star Trek Reader III.* 1977. Dutton. 1st. VG/VG. P3. $25.00

BLISH, James. *Tale That Wags the God.* 1987. Advent. 1st. F/dj. M2. $17.00

BLISH, James. *They Shall Have Stars.* 1974. Faber. F/dj. M2. $35.00

BLISH & LOWNDES. *Duplicated Man.* 1959. Avalon. 1st. F/dj. M2. $30.00

BLISHEN, Edward. *Oxford Book of Poetry for Children.* 1963. London. Oxford. 1st. 168p. NF/NF. D4. $65.00

BLIVEN, Bruce Jr. *American Revolution (Landmark Book No 83).* 1960. Random. 1st. 8vo. NF/VG+. C8. $20.00

BLIXEN, B. *African Letters.* 1988. St Martin. ils/photos. 197p. F/NF. M12. $30.00

BLOCH, Eugene B. *Fabric of Guilt.* 1968. Doubleday. 1st. VG/VG. P3. $20.00

BLOCH, Robert. *Cold Chills.* 1977. Doubleday. 1st. RS. F/F. P3. $45.00

BLOCH, Robert. *Dead Beat.* 1960. Inner Sanctum. 1st. VG/VG. M20. $25.00

BLOCH, Robert. *Dead Beat.* 1960. S&S. 1st. VG/dj. M2. $80.00

BLOCH, Robert. *Dragons & Nightmares.* 1968. Mirage. 1st. 1/1000. F/dj. M2. $75.00

BLOCH, Robert. *Eighth Stage of Fandom.* 1962. Advent For World SF Convention. 1/125. sgn/#d. F/sans. M2. $425.00

BLOCH, Robert. *Last Rites.* 1987. Underwood Miller. 1st. NF. P3. $40.00

BLOCH, Robert. *Lori.* 1989. Tor. 1st. F/F. M2/P3. $20.00

BLOCH, Robert. *Night of the Ripper.* 1984. Doubleday. 1st. F/dj. M2. $25.00

BLOCH, Robert. *Night-World.* 1972. S&S. 1st. VG/VG. P3. $30.00

BLOCH, Robert. *Opener of the Way.* 1948. Arkham. 1st. F/dj. M2. $400.00

BLOCH, Robert. *Out of the Mouths of Graves.* 1978. Mysterious. 1st. F/dj. M2. $35.00

BLOCH, Robert. *Pleasant Dreams.* 1960. Arkham. 1st. sgn. F/dj. M2. $175.00

BLOCH, Robert. *Psycho II.* 1982. Whispers. 1st. F/F. N4. $40.00

BLOCH, Robert. *Psycho.* 1959. S&S. 1st. F/F. B4. $950.00

BLOCH, Robert. *Screams.* 1989. Underwood Miller. 1st. F/dj. M2. $50.00

BLOCH, Robert. *Strange Eons.* 1979. Whispers. 1st. F/dj. M2/P3. $30.00

BLOCH, Robert. *Todd Dossier.* 1969. Delacorte. 1st. xl. F/dj. M2. $75.00

BLOCH & MUNGER. *Angel.* 1977. Ward Ritchie. F/F. P3. $8.00

BLOCK, Lawrence. *Ariel.* 1980. Arbor. 1st. NF/NF. P3. $30.00

BLOCK, Lawrence. *Ariel.* 1980. Arbor. 1st. sgn. F/G. A23. $36.00

BLOCK, Lawrence. *Burglar Who Liked to Quote Kipling.* 1979. Random. 1st. sgn. F/NF. M15. $125.00

BLOCK, Lawrence. *Burglar Who Painted Like Mondrian.* 1983. Arbor. 1st. F/dj. Q1. $50.00

BLOCK, Lawrence. *Burglar Who Traded Ted Williams.* 1984. Dutton. 1st. sgn. VG/VG. A23. $42.00

BLOCK, Lawrence. *Burglars Can't Be Choosers.* 1977. Random. 1st. F/dj. M15. $125.00

BLOCK, Lawrence. *Dance at the Slaughterhouse.* 1991. NY. Morrow. 1st. sgn. F/F. T2. $30.00

BLOCK, Lawrence. *Deadly Honeymoon.* 1967. Macmillan. 1st. F/F. M15. $200.00

BLOCK, Lawrence. *Devil Knows You're Dead.* 1993. Morrow. 1st. sgn. as new/dj. N4. $35.00

BLOCK, Lawrence. *Random Walk.* 1988. Tor. 1st. F/dj. M2. $22.00

BLOCK, Lawrence. *Sins of the Father.* 1992. Dark Harvest. 1/400. sgn Block/Stephen King. F/dj/case. M15. $200.00

BLOCK, Lawrence. *Sometimes They Bite.* 1983. Arbor. 1st. F/VG. M19. $45.00

BLOCK, Lawrence. *Telling Lies for Fun & Profit: Manual for Fiction Writers.* 1981. NY. Arbor. 1st. sgn. F/F. T2. $55.00

BLOCK, Lawrence. *Walk Among the Tombstones.* 1992. Morrow. 1st. sgn. F/F. A23. $42.00

BLOCK, Lawrence. *Walk Among the Tombstones.* 1992. NY. Morrow. 1st. sgn. F/F. T2. $25.00

BLOCK, Libbie. *Hills of Beverly.* 1957. Doubleday. 1st. NF/dj. M25. $20.00

BLOCK, Thomas H. *Airship Nine.* 1984. Putnam. 1st. VG/VG. P3. $17.00

BLOCK & WOOLRICH. *Into the Night.* 1987. Mysterious. 1st. F/F. M15. $35.00

BLOCKSON, Charles L. *Pennsylvania's Black History.* 1975. Phil. Portfolio Assoc. 1/5000. inscr/#d. F/NF. B4. $100.00

BLODGETT, Mabel Fuller. *Giant's Ruby.* 1903. 1st. ils Katherine Pyle. NF. M19. $75.00

BLOFELD, John. *I Ching: Book of Change.* 1968. Dutton. trans of ancient text. 228p. F/dj. W3. $32.00

BLOM, K. Arne. *Moment of Truth.* 1977. Harper Row. 1st Am. 147p. VG/dj. M20. $10.00

BLOND, Georges. *Elephants.* 1962. London. trans from French. photos. 180p. VG/worn. S15. $12.00

BLOND, Georges. *Great Story of Whales.* 1954-55. NY/London. 1st. 26 photos. 251p. T7. $25.00

BLONDELL, Joan. *Center Door Fantasy.* 1972. Delacorte. 1st. NF/dj. M25. $35.00

BLOOD, Benjamin Paul. *Bridge of the Iconoclast. A Poem.* 1854. Cambridge. James Munroe. 1st. 12mo. 131p. cloth. M1. $250.00

BLOODSTONE, John; see Byrne, Stuart.

BLOOM, Alan. *Come You Here, Boy!* 1995. Surrey. Aidan Ellis. 1st. 154p. M/dj. A10. $25.00

BLOOM, Amy. *Come To Me.* 1993. Harper Collins. 1st. sgn. author's 1st book. F/dj. A24/R13. $60.00

BLOT, P. *Handbook of Practical Cookery for Ladies...* 1867 (1868). VG. E6. $65.00

BLOUNT, Roy Jr. *About Three Bricks Shy of a Load.* 1974. Little Brn. 1st. inscr. photos. VG/dj. P8. $25.00

BLOUNT, T.P. *Essays on Several Subjects.* 1697. London. 3rd imp. G. A15. $30.00

BLOUT, Thomas. *Fragmenta Antiquitates; or, Antient Tenures of Land...* 1784. York. W Blanchard. tall 8vo. 363p. full early calf. VG. H13. $295.00

BLOWER & KORACH. *The NOT & L Story.* 1966. Chicago. 1st. ils/charts/diagrams. 268p. VG/dj. B18. $65.00

BLUDEN, Edmund. *Shepherd & Other Poems of Peace & War.* 1922. Knopf. 1st thus. 86p. decor brd/cloth spine. VG. B22. $18.00

BLUE, Allan G. *B-24 Liberator.* ca 1975. NY. 1st Am. 223p. VG/VG. B18. $25.00

BLUE, Ron. *Master Your Money: Step-By-Step Plan for Financial Freedom.* 1986. Nelson. 236p. Vg/dj. B29. $7.50

BLUM, Daniel. *Pictorial History of the American Theatre 1900-1956.* 1956. NY. 320p. dj. A17. $22.50

BLUM, Daniel. *Pictorial Treasury of Opera in America.* 1954. NY. 320p. lg 4to. A17. $17.50

BLUMENTHAL, Joseph. *Art of the Printed Book, 1455-1955...* 1978. Pierpont Morgan Lib. 3rd. 125 pl. 192p. gilt blk cloth. F/NF. T10. $50.00

BLUMLEIN, Michael. *Movement of Mountains*. 1987. St Martin. 1st. author's 1st book. F/F. M21. $25.00

BLUNDELL, Michael. *Wild Flowers of Kenya*. 1982. London. 160p. F/NF. B26. $42.50

BLUNDELL, Nigel. *World's Greatest Crooks & Conmen*. 1982b. Octopus. 1st. F. P3. $13.00

BLUNT, Joseph. *Shipmaster's Assistant & Commercial Digest*. 1970s. NY/London. facsimile of 1837 ed. 672p. T7. $50.00

BLUNT, Wilfrid. *Cockerell*. 1965 (1964). Knopf. 1st Am. 385p. VG/clip. M20. $30.00

BLUNT, Wilfrid. *My Diaries: Part Two 1900-1914*. 1922. Knopf. 2nd. 484p. G. A17. $17.50

BLY, Robert. *Crooked Hearts*. 1987. Knopf. 1st. sgn. F/F. R14. $60.00

BLY, Robert. *Loving a Woman in Two Worlds*. 1985. Dial. 1st. NF/dj. B2. $30.00

BLY, Robert. *Loving a Woman in Two Worlds*. 1985. Dial. 1st. sgn. F/NF. V1. $35.00

BLY, Robert. *Man in the Black Coat Turns*. 1981. Dial. 1st. sgn. F/F. R14. $45.00

BLY, Robert. *Old Man Rubbing His Eyes*. 1975. Greensboro. Unicorn. 1st. sgn. prt brd. F/sans. R14. $50.00

BLYTH, R.H. *Senryu: Japanese Satirical Verses*. 1949. Tokyo. 1st. 230p. VG/dj. W3. $86.00

BLYTON, Enid. *Five Go Down to the Sea*. 1961. Reilly Lee. 1st Am. 8vo. VG/dj. M5. $35.00

BLYTON, Enid. *Noddy & His Car*. (1951). London. Sampson Low. 8vo. ils Beek. 61p. G+. T5. $35.00

BLYTON, Enid. *Noddy & Tessie Bear*. 1961. London. Sampson Low. 8vo. 60p. VG. T5. $30.00

BLYTON, Enid. *Ship of Adventure*. 1950. Macmillan. stated 1st. 8vo. VG/dj. M5. $65.00

BLYTON, Enid. *Shock for the Secret Seven*. 1961. Brockhampton. 1st. sm 8vo. NF/VG. M5. $45.00

BLYTON, Enid. *Tales After Tea*. 1963. Collins. VG. P3. $10.00

BLYTON, Enid. *Valley of Adventure*. 1955 (1947). Macmillan. 2nd. ils Stuart Tresilian. NF/dj. M5. $48.00

BOADT, Lawrence. *Reading the Old Testament: An Introduction*. 1984. Paulist. 571p. F. B29. $8.50

BOARDER, Arthur. *Starting With Cacti*. 1968. London. 1st. ils/pl/drawings. 96p. VG/dj. B26. $22.50

BOARDMAN, Elizabeth Jelinek. *Phoenix Trip: Notes on a Quaker Mission to Haiphong*. 1985. Burnsville, NC. Celo. 174p. VG. V3. $12.00

BOARDMAN, Tom. *Science Fiction Stories*. 1979. Octopus. 1st. VG/VG. P3. $15.00

BOAS, I. *Diseases of the Intestines*. 1901. NY. 1st Eng trans. 562p. A13. $75.00

BOATRIGHT, Mody C. *From Hell to Breakfast*. 1944. TX Folk-Lore Soc. inscr. VG. A19. $45.00

BOBA, Antonio. *Hypothermia for the Neurosurgical Patient*. 1960. Springfield. 1st. 124p. A13. $20.00

BOCCACCIO. *Concerning Famous Women*. 1964. London. VG/VG. M17. $20.00

BOCHER, T.W. *Gronlands Flora*. 1966 (1957). Copenhagen. 2nd. Danish text. ils/map. 307p. decor cloth. dj. B26. $32.50

BODE, Vaughn. *Deadbone*. 1975. N Comford Communications. 1st. VG/VG. P3. $100.00

BODE, William. *Lights & Shadows of Chinatown*. 1896. np. HS Crocker. 1st. 32 mtd ils on tissue. F. R3. $500.00

BODECKER, N.M. *Hurry, Hurry Mary Dear & Other Nonsense Poems*. 1976. Atheneum. 1st. 118p. cloth. F/dj. D4. $45.00

BODECKER, N.M. *Let's Marry Said the Cherry & Other Nonsense Poems*. 1974. Atheneum. 1st. F/NF. D4. $45.00

BODELSEN, Anders. *Straus*. 1974. Harper Row. F/F. P3. $13.00

BODENHEIM, Maxwell. *My Life & Loves in Greenwich Village*. 1954. 1st. VG/clip. S13. $45.00

BODGER, Joan. *How the Heather Looks, a Joyous Journey to British Sources*. 1965. Viking. 1st. 8vo. 276p. beige/olive cloth. VG/VG. T5. $48.00

BODIN, Alvin. *Influence of Matthew Baillie's Morbid Anatomy...* 1973. Springfield. 1st. 293p. A13. $150.00

BOESE, Donald L. *John C Greenway & the Opening of Western Mesabi*. 1975. Itasca Community College. ils/index/bibliography. 222p. NF/ragged. B19. $50.00

BOETTNER, Loraine. *Immortality*. 1957. Eerdmans. 159p. G. B29. $5.00

BOETTNER, Loraine. *Roman Catholicism*. 1962. np. 466p. G/dj. B29. $7.50

BOETZEL & CLOCK. *Light in the Sky*. 1929. Coward. 1st. VG. M2. $60.00

BOGAN, Phebe M. *Yaqui Indian Dances of Tucson, AZ*. 1925. Archeological Soc. 1st. ils. 69p. VG. B19. $45.00

BOGDANOVICH, Peter. *Killing of the Unicorn*. 1984. Morrow. 1st. NF/VG. A20. $15.00

BOGEL, GOLDMAN & MARKS. *Birds & Flowers*. 1988. Braziller. 1st. 192p+91 full-p mc pl. F/dj. A17. $45.00

BOGOSIAN, Eric. *Sex, Drugs & Rock 'n Roll*. 1992. Harper Perennial. sgn. NF. C9. $35.00

BOHM, David. *Quantum Theory*. 1951. Prentice Hall. 1st. xl. K3. $40.00

BOICE, James. *Christ of the Empty Tombs*. 1985. Moody. 126p. VG/dj. B29. $7.00

BOISGILBERT, Edmund. *Caesar's Column*. nd. Ward Lock. decor brd. G. P3. $40.00

BOISSEAU, Edmonde. *Les Maladies Simulees et des Moyens de les Reconnaitre...* 1870. Libraires Academie Imperiale Medecine. 15 woodcuts. G1. $475.00

BOISSEVAIN & DAVIDSON. *Colorado Cacti*. 1940. Pasadena. 1/2000. ils. tan buckram. VG B26. $55.00

BOKER, Ben Zion. *From the World of the Cabbalah: Philosophy of Rabbi Loew...* 1954. Philosophical Lib. 210p. VG/dj. S3. $23.00

BOLCOM & KIMBALL. *Reminiscing With Sissle & Blake*. 1973. Viking. 1st. NF/dj. M25. $50.00

BOLITHO, Hector. *Batsford Century: A Record of a Hundred Years...* 1943. London. Batsford. 1st. ils. VG/dj. K3. $18.00

BOLL, Heinrich. *Safety Net*. 1982. Knopf. 1st trade. VG/dj. B35. $16.00

BOLL, Heinrich. *Women in a River Landscape*. 1988. Knopf. 1st. NF/dj. B35. $18.00

BOLLAND, William Craddock. *General Eyre, Lectures Delivered...* 1922. CAmbridge. cloth-backed brd/paper label. M11. $125.00

BOLLAND, William Craddock. *Manual of Year Book Studies*. 1925. Cambridge. M11. $85.00

BOLLINGER, E. *Rails That Climb: Story of the Moffat Road*. 1950. Santa Fe. 2nd. sgn. ils. 402p. VG/G. B5. $50.00

BOLT, Robert. *Flowering Cherry: A Play in Two Acts*. 1958. London. Heinemann. 1st. NF/dj. Q1. $60.00

BOLTON, Herbert Eugene. *Anza's California Expeditions*. 1930. BErkeley. 1st. 5 vol. 8vo. ils/maps. bl cloth. F. R3. $650.00

BOLTON, Herbert Eugene. *Padre on Horseback.* 1963. Loyola. 1st. 91p. F/NF. B19. $25.00

BOLTON, Herbert Eugene. *Plate of Brass: Evidence of Visit of Francis Drake...1579.* 1953. CA Hist Soc. 2 vol. 4to. ils. gilt brn cloth. F. R3. $40.00

BOMBACK, R.H. *Basic Leica Technique.* 1954. London. Fountain. dj. A19. $20.00

BONANNO, Joseph. *Man of Honor: Autobiography of Joseph Bonanno.* 1983. S&S. 1st. ils/index. F/NF. B19. $35.00

BOND, Carrie Jacobs. *Perfect Day & Other Poems.* (1926). Chicago. Volland. unp. F/F box. D4. $50.00

BOND, Francis. *Gothic Architecture in England.* 1906. Batsford/Scribner. 1st. 792p. G+. H1. $55.00

BOND, Geoffrey. *Lakonia.* 1966. London. Oldbourne. ils. 199p. dj. T7. $28.00

BOND, Gladys Baker. *Buffy Finds a Star.* 1970. Whitman. TVTI. VG. P3. $8.00

BOND, Michael. *Paddington Marches On.* 1965. Houghton Mifflin. 1st Am. ils Peggy Fortnum. VG+/dj. M5. $30.00

BOND, Michael. *Thursday in Paris.* 1971. Harrap. 1st. ils Leslie Wood. 128p. NF/VG. P2. $25.00

BOND, Nelson. *Exiles of Time.* 1949. Prime. 1st. F/dj. M2. $35.00

BOND, Nelson. *Lancelot Biggs: Spaceman.* 1950. Doubleday. 1st. NF/VG. P3. $85.00

BOND, Nelson. *Mr Mergenthwirker's Lobblies.* 1946. Coward McCann. 1st. VG/dj. M2. $50.00

BOND, Nelson. *Nightmares & Daydreams.* 1968. Arkham. 1st. F/dj. M2. $45.00

BOND, Nelson. *Thirty-First of February.* 1949. Gnome. 1st. F/rpr. M2. $13.00

BONDY, Louis W. *Miniature Books, Their History From the Beginnings...* 1981. London. Sheppard Pr. 8vo. 221p. F/dj. B24. $125.00

BONDY, Louis. *Miniature Books: Their History From the Beginnings...* 1981. ils. 227p. F/F. A4. $165.00

BONDY, Ruth. *Israelis: Profile of a People.* 1969. Sabra Books/Funk Wagnall. 1st. inscr. 8vo. 320p. VG/dj. T10. $50.00

BONE, Muirhead. *Western Front, Drawings by... Part III.* 1917. London. Authority of War Office. 20 pl. F/dj. K7. $75.00

BONES, Jim Jr. *Texas West of the Pecos.* 1981. TX A&M. 1st. ils. 136p. F/F. B22. $40.00

BONESTEEL, Georgia. *More Lap Quilting With Georgia Bonesteel.* 1985. NY. Oxmoor. 1st. sgn. 132p. VG/G. B11. $25.00

BONFIGLIOLI, Kyril. *After You With the Pistol.* 1979. Secker Warburg. 1st. F/F. P3. $20.00

BONHOEFFER, Dietrich. *Cost of Discipleship.* 1961. Macmillan. 285p. VG/dj. B29. $6.50

BONHOEFFER, Dietrich. *Theology of Dietrich Bonhoeffer.* 1960. Westminster. 299p. VG. B29. $14.00

BONICA, John J. *Advances in Pain Research & Therapy Vol 1.* 1976. NY. Raven. heavy 8vo. 1012p. blk cloth. VG/dj. G1. $85.00

BONINGTON & CLARKE. *Everest: The Unclimbed Ridge.* 1984. NY/London. Norton. 1st. 132p. F/dj. W3. $38.00

BONKER & THORNBER. *Sage of the Desert & Other Cacti.* 1930. Boston. 1st. 8 full-p photos. 106p. NF. B26. $32.50

BONNARD, Abel. *In China 1920-1921.* 1926. Routledge. 361p. VG. W3. $46.00

BONNER, T.D. *Life & Adventures of James P Beckwourth, Mountaineer...* 1965 (1856). rpt. 1/1500. ils. F/dj. M4. $40.00

BONNER, Willard Hallam. *Pirate Laureate: Life & Legends of Captain Kidd.* 1947. New Brunswick. 1st. 239p. gr cloth. VG/worn. P4. $45.00

BONNET, Theodore. *Dutch.* 1955. Doubleday. 1st. VG/VG. P3. $20.00

BONTLY, Thomas. *Celestial Chess.* 1979. Harper Row. 1st. VG/VG. P3. $18.00

BOONE & CROCKETT CLUB. *North American Big Games.* 1939. Scribner. ils/pl. 533p. VG+/fair. M12. $395.00

BOONE & CROCKETT CLUB. *19th Big Game Awards 1983-1985.* 1986. Dumfries. 410p. lg 8vo. F/dj. A17. $30.00

BOORMAN, John. *Emerald Forest Diary.* 1985. FSG. 1st. F/F. P3. $15.00

BOOTH, George. *Rehearsal's Off!* 1976. Dodd Mead. 1st. F/clip. M25. $45.00

BOOTH, Martin. *Winters Night: Knotting.* 1979. Sceptre. 1/50. sgn. hand-tied wrp. F. V1. $35.00

BOOTH, Nicholas. *Space: Next 100 Years.* nd. Orion. 1st Am. F/dj. M2. $20.00

BOOTH, Vincent Ravi. *Dedication of Restored Old First Church of Bennington...* 1937. np. 1/500. sgn. ils. VG. B18. $35.00

BOOTH & WRIGHT. *Flora of Montana: Part II, Dictyledons.* 1966 (1959). Bozeman. revised. ils/maps. 305p. sbdg. B26. $22.50

BOOTHBY, Guy. *Fascination of the King.* nd. Ward Lock. VG. P3. $20.00

BOOTHBY, Guy. *My Indian Queen.* nd. Ward Lock. VG. P3. $35.00

BOOTHBY, Guy. *Sherah McLeod.* 1897. London. 1st. VG. M2. $75.00

BORCHERT, Wolfgang. *Sad Geraniums.* 1973. Ecco. 1st. F/F. B35. $10.00

BORDEAUX, Henry. *Pathway to Heaven.* 1952. Pellegrini Cudahy. 1st Am. F/NF. Q1. $100.00

BORDELEAU, Jean-Marc. *Systeme Extra-Pyramidal et Neuroleptiques.* 1960. Montreal. Psychiatriques. 574p. red cloth. G1. $50.00

BORDEN, Norman E. *Sear Sarah.* 1966. Freeport, ME. Wheelwright. 9 photos/ils. 204p. dj. T7. $24.00

BOREL, Antoine Jr. *San Francisco Is No More.* 1963. Menlo Park. 1/200. prt paper brd/bl cloth spine. F. K7. $75.00

BORER, Eva Maria. *Tante Heidi's Swiss Kitchen.* 1965. Gramercy. VG/dj. A16. $10.00

BORG, Bjorn. *Bjorn Borg Story.* 1975. Henry Regency. 1st Am. photos. F/F. P8. $30.00

BORG, John. *Cacti. A Gardener's Handbook.* (1937). London. 3rd. photos. F/dj. B26. $24.00

BORGENICHT, Miriam. *Bad Medicine.* 1984. Macmillan. 1st. F/F. P3. $15.00

BORGENICHT, Miriam. *False Colors.* 1985. St Martin. 1st. VG/VG. P3. $15.00

BORGENICHT, Miriam. *No Bail for Dalton.* 1985. Bobbs Merrill. 1st. VG/VG. P3. $18.00

BORGENICHT, Miriam. *Roadblock.* 1973. Bobbs Merrill. 1st. VG/VG. P3. $18.00

BORGES, Jorge Luis. *Book of Sand.* 1979. Allen Lane. 1st. VG/VG. P3. $20.00

BORGES & CASARES. *Extraordinary Tales.* 1971. Herder. VG/VG. P3. $25.00

BORIE, Lysbeth Boyd. *Poems for Peter (Set to Music by Ada Richter).* 1940. Phil. Theodore Presser. 1st. sm 4to. VG+/VG. C8. $22.50

BORN, Max. *La Constitution de la Matiere.* 1922. Paris. Blanchard. ils. 8vo. 84p. prt wrp. K3. $45.00

BORN, Max. *Optik. Ein Lehrbuch der Elektromagnetischen...* 1933. Berlin. Springer. ils Allen Property Custodian. 4to. 591p. xl. K3. $40.00

BORNEMAN, Henry. *Pennsylvania Greman Illuminated Manuscripts.* 1927. Norristown. PA German Soc. 1st. obl folio. VG. C6. $175.00

BORODINI, George. *Spurious Sun.* 1948. London. 1st. F/dj. M2. $20.00

BOROWITZ, Eugene B. *How Can a Jew Speak of Faith Today?* 1969. Westminster. 221p. VG/dj. S3. $21.00

BORSTEIN, Larry. *Len Dawson: Superbowl Quarterback.* 1970. Grosset Dunlap. 1st. photos. F/VG. P8. $20.00

BORTHWICK, J.D. *Three Years in California.* 1857. Edinburgh/London. Blackwood. 1st. 8vo. 8 tinted ils. gilt red cloth. case. R3. $1,500.00

BORTHWICK, J.D. *Three Years in California.* 1948. Biobooks. 1/1000. lg 8vo. 318p. NF. K7. $55.00

BORTON, Helen. *Jungle.* 1968. HBW. stated 1st. sm 4to. unp. F/G+. C14. $10.00

BORTSTEIN, Larry. *Superjoe: The Joe Namath Story.* 1969. Grosset Dunlap. 1st. VG/dj. P8. $30.00

BORUP, George. *Tenderfoot With Peary.* 1911. NY. Stokes. 8vo. 317p. pict cloth. worn. P4. $40.00

BORWN, EDGERTON & MCCORKLE. *Algonquin Sampler.* 1990. Algonquin. 1st. F. B3. $30.00

BORYCZKA, Raymond. *No Strength Without Union: Ils History of Ohio Workers...* 1982. OH Hist Soc. 1st. VG/dj. V4. $45.00

BOSE, Jagadis Chunder. *Le Mecanisme Nerveux des Plantes.* 1931. Paris. Gauthier-Villars. 1st French-language ed. ils. 228p. VG. G1. $50.00

BOSNAN, Richard. *Captivity Narrative of Hannah Duston.* 1987. Arion. 1/425. sgn. folio. 56p. hand-made paper brd/backed cloth. M. B24. $425.00

BOSSON, M. *Aunt Mena's Recipe Book.* 1888. erd. VG. E6. $50.00

BOSTON, Lucy. *River at Green Knowe.* 1959. Harcourt Brace. 1st. ils Peter Boston. 153p. NF/VG. P2. $60.00

BOSTON, Lucy. *Treasure of the Green Knowe.* 1958. Harcourt Brace. 1st. ils Peter Boston. 185p. VG/VG. P2. $60.00

BOSTWICK, Arthur E. *Librarian's Open Shelf.* 1920. NY. Wilson. 1st. 8vo. 344p. VG. K3. $15.00

BOSWELL, Hazel. *French Canada.* 1938. Viking. 1st. ils. NF/NF. D1. $75.00

BOSWELL, James. *Journal of Tour to Hebrides With Samuel Johnson, LLD.* (1852). London. nat Ils Lib. 8vo. 361p. Seton Mackenzie bdg. F. H13. $1,250.00

BOSWELL, James. *Life of Johnson.* 1924. London. 3 vol. ils. w/facsimile letter. VG. M17. $50.00

BOSWELL, James. *Life of Samuel Johnson.* 1826. Oxford/London. Tallboy Wheeler Pickering. Oxford Eng Classic. 4 vol. H13. $795.00

BOSWELL, James. *Life of Samuel Johnson.* 1897. London. Dent. Temple Classics. 6 vol. NF. A24. $125.00

BOSWELL, James. *Life of Samuel Johnson... In Three Volumes.* 1793. London. Chas Dilly. 2nd/revised/augmented. period bdg. F. H13. $950.00

BOSWELL, James. *Research Edition of Life of Samuel Johnson, Vol I 1709-65.* 1994. Edinburgh/Yale. 1st. edit Marshall Waingrow. 518p. bl linen. M/dj. H13. $225.00

BOSWELL, Robert. *Crooked Hearts.* 1987. Knopf. 1st. F/F. A15/H11. $60.00

BOSWELL, Tom. *Strokes of Genius.* 1987. Doubleday. 1st. inscr. F/F. P8. $45.00

BOTELHO, Sebastiano Jose X. *Historia Verdadeira dos Acontecimentos da Ilha de Maderia...* 1821. Lisbon. Antonio Rodrigues Galhardo. 1st. modern full calf. VG+. R15. $300.00

BOTKIN, B.A. *Treasury of Southern Folklore.* 1949. NY. 1st. sgn. VG/dj. B5. $25.00

BOUCHARD, Charles Jaques. *Study of Some Points in Pathology of Cerebral...* 1990. Birmingham. Classics Neurology/Neurosurgery Lib. facsimile. G1. $65.00

BOUCHARILAT, J.L. *Elements de Mecanique.* 1861. Paris. Mallet-Bachelier. 4th. 8vo. 364p. xl. K3. $75.00

BOUCHER, Anthony. *Best Detective Stories of the Year.* 1968. Dutton. 1st. F/NF. M25. $25.00

BOUCHER, Anthony. *Best Detective Stories.* 1964. Dutton. 1st. VG/VG. P3. $25.00

BOUCHER, Anthony. *Case of the Baker Street Irregulars.* 1942. Tower. VG. P3. $25.00

BOUCHER, Anthony. *Great American Detective Stories.* 1945. World. 1st. G+. N4. $25.00

BOUCHER, Anthony. *Quintessence of Queen.* 1962. Random. 1st. VG/VG. P3. $40.00

BOUCHER, Jean. *Sermons de la Simvlee Conversion...de Henry de Bourbon.* 1594. Ivxte Paris. Chaudiere. thick 8vo. quarter calf. R12. $800.00

BOUCSEIN, Wolfram. *Electrodermal Activity. Plenum Series...* 1992. NY. Plenum. 442p. prt blk cloth. G1. $40.00

BOULDING, Kenneth E. *Sonnets From Later Life, 1981-1993.* 1994. Wallingford, PA. Pendle Hill. 179p. VG. V3. $10.00

BOULLE, Pierre. *Good Leviathan.* 1978. Vanguard. 1st. F/dj. M2. $15.00

BOUNASSISI, Vincenzo. *Pasta.* 1976. Lyceum. BC. nearly 650 recipes. VG/VG. B10. $10.00

BOUNDS, Sydney J. *Dimension of Horror.* 1953. Hamilton Panther. VG/G. P3. $35.00

BOUQUET, A.G.B. *Cauliflower & Broccoli Culture.* 1929. Orange Judd. 125p. dj. A10. $40.00

BOURGUIGNON, Georges. *La Chronaxie Chez l'Homme...* 1923. Paris. Masson et Cie. ils/192 tables. 417p. prt stiff brn wrp. G1. $65.00

BOURJAILY, Vance. *Great Fake Book.* 1986. Franklin Lib. 1st/ltd. sgn. full leather. Q1. $35.00

BOURKE-WHITE, Margaret; see White, Margaret Bourke.

BOURNE, Eulalia. *Nine Months Is a Year at Baboquivari School.* 1968. AZ U. 1st. ils/maps/notes. NF/NF. B19. $30.00

BOURNE, Eulalia. *Ranch Schoolteacher.* 1974. AZ U. 1st. ils/map. 312p. NF/VG+. B19. $30.00

BOURNE, G.H. *Behavior, Growth & Pathology of Chimpanzees.* 1971. Baltimore. ils/figures/tables. 407p. cloth. VG/VG. M12. $45.00

BOURNE, Gwen. *Wonder World Fairy Tale Book.* 1931. London. Cecil Palmer. 1st. 4to. pict cloth. dj. R5. $375.00

BOURNE, Peter. *Flames of Empire.* 1949. Putnam. 1st. VG/G. P3. $18.00

BOURNE, Peter. *Twilight of the Dragon.* 1954. Putnam. 1st. VG/VG. P3. $20.00

BOURNE, William. *Regiment for the Sea & Other Writings on Navigation.* 1963. Cambridge. Hakluyt Soc. 2nd series #121. 8vo. 464p. bl cloth. P4. $75.00

BOUSFIELD, E.L. *Shallow-Water Gammaridean Amphipoda of New England.* 1973. Ithaca. 312p. F. S15. $22.50

BOUSSEL, Patrice. *Leonardo Da Vinci.* nd. Chartwell. F/F. P3. $75.00

BOUTON, Jim. *Ball Four Plus Five.* 1981. Stein Day. 1st. sgn. F/F. B11. $50.00

BOUTON, Jim. *Ball Four: My Life & Hard Times Throwing the Knuckleball...* 1970. NY. World. 1st. F/F. B4. $150.00

BOUTON, John. *Enchanted.* 1891. Cassell. 1st. VG. M2. $50.00

BOVA, Ben. *Aliens.* 1977. St Martin. 1st. F/dj. M2. $20.00

BOVA, Ben. *As on a Darkling Plain.* 1972. NY. Walker. 1st. sgn. F/NF. T2. $50.00

BOVA, Ben. *Cyberbooks.* 1989. Tor. 1st. F/F. M2/P3. $20.00

BOVA, Ben. *Dueling Machine.* 1971. Faber. 1st. sgn. F/F. P3. $35.00

BOVA, Ben. *End of Exile.* 1975. Dutton. 1st. RS. F/F. P3. $35.00

BOVA, Ben. *Kingsman Saga.* 1989. Easton. leather. F. M2. $40.00

BOVA, Ben. *Kinsman.* 1979. Dial. 1st. F/F. P3. $20.00

BOVA, Ben. *Millenium.* 1976. Random. 1st. NF/NF. P3. $30.00

BOVA, Ben. *Multiple Man.* 1976. Bobbs Merrill. 1st. NF/NF. P3. $25.00

BOVA, Ben. *Peacekeepers.* 1988. Tor. 1st. F/F. P3. $18.00

BOVA, Ben. *Vengeance of Orion.* 1988. Tor. 1st. F/F. P3. $18.00

BOVA, Ben. *Viewpoint.* 1977. Cambridge, MA. NESFA. 1/800. sgn. F/F. T2. $25.00

BOVA, Ben. *Winds of Altair.* 1973. Dutton. 1st. VG. P3. $13.00

BOVILL, E.W. *Missions to the Niger.* 1964-1966. Hakluyt Soc. 4 vol. 26 maps/33 pl/fld pocket map. NF. O7. $150.00

BOVILL, E.W. *Missions to the Niger. Vol 1.* 1962. Cambridge. Hakluyt Soc. 1st. 8vo. pl/maps. cloth. VG/dj. W1. $50.00

BOWDEN, Charles. *Killing the Hidden Waters.* 1977. Austin. TX U. 1st. author's 1st book. F/VG. L3. $350.00

BOWDITCH, Nathaniel. *Discourse on the Life & Character of Hon Nathaniel Bowditch.* 1838. Boston. Little Brn. 1st. 8vo. 119p. xl. K3. $35.00

BOWEN, Abel. *Naval Monument: Containing Official & Other Accounts...* ca 1816. Boston. Phillips Sampson. 23 engravings. full calf. T7. $325.00

BOWEN, B.V. *Faster Than Thought.* 1963. London. Pitman. 18 pl. 416p. VG. K3. $30.00

BOWEN, Elizabeth. *House in Paris.* 1936. Knopf. 1st. VG/VG. P3. $20.00

BOWEN, Elizabeth. *Ivy Gripped the Steps.* 1946. Knopf. 1st Am. VG. M2. $32.00

BOWEN, Peter. *Imperial Kelly.* 1992. Crown. 1st. sgn. author's 3rd book. F/F. B3. $60.00

BOWEN, Peter. *Yellowstone Kelly.* 1982. Ottawa. Jameson. 1st. F/F. D10. $65.00

BOWEN, R. Sidney. *Airport: Our Link to the Sky.* 1961. Whitman. Learn About Book series. decor brd. G. P3. $10.00

BOWEN, R. Sidney. *Dave Dawson in Libya.* nd. Saalfield. VG/VG. P3. $15.00

BOWEN, R. Sidney. *Dave Dawson With the Commandos (#9).* 1942. Crown. 1st. 248p. VG+/dj. M20. $22.00

BOWEN, R. Sidney. *Dave Dawson With the Pacific Fleet (#7).* 1942. Crown. 1st. lists to this title. VG/dj. M20. $20.00

BOWEN, R. Sidney. *Hawaii Five-O Top Secret.* 1969. Whitman. TVTI. VG. P3. $10.00

BOWEN, R. Sidney. *Red Randall at Pearl Harbor (#1).* 1944. Grosset Dunlap. lists 3 titles. VG/dj. M20. $20.00

BOWEN, R. Sidney. *Red Randall on Active Duty (#2).* 1944. Grosset Dunlap. 211p. VG/dj. M20. $16.00

BOWEN, R. Sidney. *Red Randall on New Guinea (#5).* 1944. Grosset Dunlap. lists 3 titles. 208p. VG/worn. M20. $16.00

BOWEN, R.H. *Frenchman in Lincoln's America.* 1974. Lakeside Classic. 2 vol. ils/map. F. M4. $25.00

BOWEN & JUX. *Afro-Arabian Geology.* 1987. London. Chapman Hall. 295p. F. B1. $42.50

BOWER, B.M. *Dark Horse.* 1943. Triangle. VG. P3. $12.00

BOWER, B.M. *Her Prairie Knight.* 1907. Dillingham. A19. $10.00

BOWER, F.O. *Plants & Man.* 1925. London. Macmillan. 365p. cloth. A10. $45.00

BOWER, F.O. *Sixty Years of Botany in Britain (1875-1935).* 1938. London. Macmillan. 112p. dj. A10. $75.00

BOWER & SWANBOROUGH. *United States Navy Aircraft Since 1910.* 1968. NY. 1st. ils/diagrams, 518p. VG/dj. B18. $37.50

BOWERS, Alfred W. *Mandan Social & Ceremonial Organization.* 1950. Chicago U. Social Anthropological series. 407p. NF/dj. K7. $95.00

BOWERS, Elisabeth. *No Forwarding Address.* 1991. Seal. F/F. P3. $20.00

BOWERS, Janice Emily. *Mountains Next Door.* 1991. AZ U. 1st. inscr. 147p. F/F. B19. $35.00

BOWES, Anne LaBastille. *Bird Kingdom of the Mayas.* 1967. Van Nostrand. 1st. 90p. dj. F3. $15.00

BOWIE, Walter Russell. *Story of the Bible.* 1962. Abingdon. 557p. VG/dj. B29. $7.50

BOWKER, Richard. *Marlborough Street.* 1987. Doubleday. 1st. RS. F/F. P3. $18.00

BOWLBY, J. *Charles Darwin: A New Life.* 1990. Norton. 1st. cloth. F/dj. D8. $30.00

BOWLES, E.A. *Handbook of Crocus & Colchicum.* 1952. Van Nostrand. 222p. xl. A10. $25.00

BOWLES, E.A. *My Garden in Spring.* ca 1914. Dodge Pub. 8vo. 24 halftone/16 mc pl. teg. VG. A22. $65.00

BOWLES, Jane. *Collected Works of Jane Bowles.* 1966. Farrar. 1st ed. F/F. B2. $40.00

BOWLES, Paul. *Days Tangier Journal: 1987-1989.* 1991. Ecco. 1st. F/dj. A24. $25.00

BOWLES, Paul. *Let It Come Down.* 1980. Blk Sparrow. 1st. 1/350. sgn. author's 2nd novel. F/acetate dj. D10. $85.00

BOWLES, Paul. *Their Heads Are Green & Their Hands Are Blue...* 1963. Random. 1st. F/F. B4. $225.00

BOWLES, Paul. *Too Far From Home.* 1994. London. Peter Owen. 1/100. sgn. F/F tissue. B2. $125.00

BOWLES, Samuel. *Across the Continent: Summer's Journey to Rocky Mountains...* 1866. Springfield, MA. Bowles. 2nd. 8vo. fld map. gilt brn cloth. xl. R3. $35.00

BOWMAN, Gerald. *From Scott to Fuchs.* 1958. London. Evans Bros. 1st. 8vo. 191p. VG/dj. P4. $40.00

BOWMAN, Isaiah. *Pioneer Fringe.* 1931. NY. 1st ed. 361p. A17. $25.00

BOWMAN, John J. *Modern Watch Repairing & Adjusting.* 1941. Chicago. Henry Paulson. 3rd. ils. 188p. VG. K3. $20.00

BOWMAN, P.B. *Little Brown Bowl With Other Tales & Verse.* 1928. NY. Nelson. sgn. 311p. G. B11. $100.00

BOWMAN, Sheridan. *Radiocarbon Dating.* 1990. Berkeley. ils. 64p. M/wrp. K3. $18.00

BOWMAN & CARTEN. *Busy Bodies: The Busy ABC's.* 1959. Rand McNally. 1st. unp. VG. C14. $9.00

BOWMAN & IRWIN. *Sherman & His Campaigns: A Military Biography.* 1865. NY. Richardson. 1st. maps. 512p. cloth/rebacked/recased. VG. M8. $65.00

BOWREY, Thomas. *Papers of Thomas Bowrey 1669-1713 Discovered in 1913...* 1927. London. Hakluyt Soc. 1st. 8vo. 398p. bl cloth. P4. $95.00

BOWYER & MALINA. *Extreme Ultraviolet Astronomy.* 1991. NY. Pergamon. ils. 520p. VG. K5. $35.00

BOX, Edgar; see Vidal, Luther.

BOXER, C.R. *Dutch in Brazil, 1624-1654.* 1957. Clarendon. 4 maps+ftspc portrait. F/rpr. O7. $100.00

BOXER, C.R. *Great Ship From Amacon: Annals of Macao...1555-1640.* 1963. Lisbon. ils/fld map. VG/wrp. W3. $145.00

BOXER, C.R. *Jan Compagnie in Japan 1600-1850.* 1950. The Hague. 2nd revised/expaned. 198p. F/NF. W3. $256.00

BOXER, C.R. *Portuguese Embassy to Japan (1644-1647).* 1928. London. Kegan Paul. 8vo. 2 ils. prt brd/cloth spine. O7. $350.00

BOXER, C.R. *Tragic History of the Sea.* 1957. Cambridge. Hakluyt Soc. 2nd series #112. 8vo. 170p. bl cloth. P4. $75.00

BOYCE, Chris. *Catchworld.* 1977. Doubleday. F/F. P3. $15.00

BOYD, Andrew. *Chinese Architecture.* 1962. 1st Am. 144 pl/84 drawings. 166p. VG/G. A8. $75.00

BOYD, Frank; see Kane, Frank.

BOYD, John. *Girl With the Jade Green Eyes.* 1978. Viking. 1st. VG/VG. P3. $25.00

BOYD, John. *Gordon Festival.* 1972. Weybright Talley. 1st. VG/VG. P3. $18.00

BOYD, John. *Rakehells of Heaven.* 1969. Weybright Talley. 1st. VG/VG. P3. $18.00

BOYD, Malcolm. *Runner.* 1974. Waco. Word. 1st. sgn. 8vo. 203p. F/VG. B11. $18.00

BOYD, Thomas. *Through the Wheat.* 1923. Scribner. 1st. NF. B2. $35.00

BOYD, William. *Good Man in Africa.* 1982. Morrow. 1st Am. sgn. F/F. B4. $175.00

BOYD, William. *Ice-Cream War.* 1983. Morrow. 1st Am. F/F. B4. $100.00

BOYD, William. *New Confessions.* 1988. Morrow. 1st. F/dj. Q1. $40.00

BOYD, William. *On the Yankee Station.* 1984. Morrow. 1st Am. sgn. F/F. B4. $125.00

BOYD, William. *School Ties.* 1985. Morrow. 1st Am. NF/NF. R14. $40.00

BOYDEN, Polly. *Pink Egg.* 1942. Truro, MA. Pamet. 1st. NF/VG. B2. $125.00

BOYER, Dwight. *Strange Adventures of the Great Lakes.* 1974. Dodd Mead. 1st. 248p. VG+/dj. M20. $25.00

BOYER, Dwight. *True Tales of the Great Lakes.* 1971. Dodd Mead. 1st. 340p. VG/clip. M20. $20.00

BOYER, Glenn. *I Married Wyatt Earp, Recollections of Josephine Sarah...* 1976. 1st. photos. 277p. VG/VG. J2. $350.00

BOYER, Glenn. *Illustrated Life of Doc Holliday.* 1966. Reminder Pub. 1st. ils. wrp. B19. $40.00

BOYER, Richard O. *Legend of John Brown.* 1973. Knopf. 1st. 627p. F/dj. H1. $28.00

BOYER, Richard. *Giant Rat of Sumatra.* 1991. Mysterious. 1st. F/F. M2. $25.00

BOYER, Rick. *Moscow Metal.* 1987. Boston. 1st. NF/sans. T12. $20.00

BOYERS & BOYERS. *Murder by Proxy.* 1945. Crime Club. 1st. VG/rpr. M25. $60.00

BOYINGTON, Gregory 'Pappy.' *Tonya.* 1960. Bobbs Merrill. 1st. inscr. F/NF. B4. $175.00

BOYKIN, FRANKLIN & YATES. *Research Directions of Psychologists.* 1979. NY. Russell Sage. 1st. 440p. F/NF clip. B4. $65.00

BOYLE, E.V. *Beauty & the Beast.* 1875. Sampson Low. 1st. 4to. aeg. deluxe bdg. R5. $675.00

BOYLE, Kay. *My Next Bride.* 1934. HBJ. 1st. 327p. VG. A25. $10.00

BOYLE, Louis M. *Out West Growing Cymbidium Orchids.* 1952. LA. self pub. 8vo. ils/photos. 526p. F/VG. A22. $35.00

BOYLE, Martin. *Yanks Don't Cry: A Marine's-Eye View of 4 Heroic Years...* 1963. NY. 1st. 250p. VG/VG. S16. $35.00

BOYLE, T. Coraghessan. *Budding Prospects.* 1984. Viking. 1st. author's 3rd book. NF/dj. A24. $50.00

BOYLE, T. Coraghessan. *East Is East.* 1990. Viking. 1st. F/F. B3. $30.00

BOYLE, T. Coraghessan. *East Is East.* 1990. Viking. 1st. sgn. author's 4th novel. F/F. D10/M25. $50.00

BOYLE, T. Coraghessan. *Greasy Lake & Other Stories.* 1985. London. Viking. 1st. F/NF. B3. $50.00

BOYLE, T. Coraghessan. *If the River Was Whiskey.* 1989. NY. Viking. 1st. sgn. F/F. D10. $60.00

BOYLE, T. Coraghessan. *If the River Was Whiskey.* 1989. Viking. 1st. sgn/dtd 1993. rem mk. F/F. R14. $50.00

BOYLE, T. Coraghessan. *Road to Wellville.* 1993. Viking. 1st. sgn. F/F. A23. $40.00

BOYLE, T. Coraghessan. *Tortilla Curtain.* 1995. NY. Viking. 1st. sgn. F/F. A23. $45.00

BOYLE, T. Coraghessan. *Water Music.* 1981. Little Brn. 1st. NF/F. B3. $50.00

BOYLE, T. Coraghessan. *World's End.* 1987. Viking. 1st. sgn. author's 3rd novel. F/F. D10. $85.00

BOYLSTON, Elise-Reid. *Atlanta: Its Life, Legends & Laughter.* 1968. Foote Davies. 1st. sgn. F. A23. $25.00

BOYLSTON, Helen Dore. *Sue Barton, Neighborhood Nurse (#6).* 1952 (1949). Little Brn. 236p. VG/dj. M20. $30.00

BOYLSTON, Helen Dore. *Sue Barton, Rural Nurse (#4).* 1953 (1939). Little Brn. 254p. VG/dj. M20. $30.00

BOYLSTON, Helen Dore. *Sue Barton, Senior Nurse (#2).* 1952 (1937). Little Brn. 220p. VG/dj. M20. $30.00

BOYLSTON, Helen Dore. *Sue Barton, Staff Nurse (#7).* 1953 (1952). Little Brn. 204p. VG/dj. M20. $40.00

BOYLSTON, Helen Dore. *Sue Barton, Student Nurse (#1).* 1953 (1936). Little Brn. 244p. VG/dj. M20. $25.00

BOYLSTON, Helen Dore. *Sue Barton: Superintendent of Nurses (#5).* 1952 (1940). Little Brn. 239p. VG/dj. M20. $22.00

BRACE, Charles Loring. *New West; or, California 1867-1868.* 1869. NY. Putnam. 1st. 8vo. gilt brn cloth. VG. R3. $50.00

BRACE, G. *Farm Shop Work.* 1915. 1st. xl. G+. E6. $22.00

BRACE, Timothy. *Murder Goes Fishing.* 1936. Dutton. 1st. VG. N4. $20.00

BRACEGIRDLE & MILES. *Atlas of Plant Structure, Vol 2.* 1978 (1973). London. photos. 107p. F. B26. $9.00

BRACKEN, Peg. *But I Wouldn't Have Missed It for the World...* 1973. HBW. 1st. 270p. VG/G. A25. $10.00

BRACKETT, Leigh. *Book of Skaith.* 1976. Nelson Doubleday. 1st. F/dj. M2. $10.00

BRACKETT, Leigh. *Long Tomorrow.* 1955. Doubleday. 1st. F/NF. P3. $125.00

BRACKETT, Leigh. *Starmen.* 1952. Gnome. 1st. F/dj. M2. $125.00

BRACKMAN, Arnold C. *Search for the Gold of Tutankhamen.* 1976. NY. Mason Charter. 1st. 8vo. VG/dj. W1. $18.00

BRADBURN, John. *Breeding & Developing the Trotter.* 1905. Boston. 1st. VG. O3. $58.00

BRADBURY, Edward P.; see Moorcock, Michael.

BRADBURY, Ray. *Death Is a Lonely Business.* 1985. Knopf. 1st. NF/NF. P3. $25.00

BRADBURY, Ray. *Golden Apples of the Sun.* 1953. Doubleday. 1st. NF/VG. M2. $185.00

BRADBURY, Ray. *Graveyard for Lunatics.* 1990. Knopf. 1st. F/dj. M2. $20.00

BRADBURY, Ray. *Halloween Tree.* 1972. Knopf. 1st. F/dj. M2. $75.00

BRADBURY, Ray. *I Sing the Body Electric.* 1969. Knopf. 1st. F/dj. M2. $85.00

BRADBURY, Ray. *Martian Chronicles.* 1950. Doubleday. 1st. VG/dj. M2. $325.00

BRADBURY, Ray. *Medicine for Melancholy.* 1959. Doubleday. 1st. F/NF clip. A24. $175.00

BRADBURY, Ray. *S Is for Space.* 1966. Doubleday. 1st. F/dj. M2. $75.00

BRADBURY, Ray. *Stories of...* 1980. Knopf. 1st. F/F. M2. $60.00

BRADBURY, Ray. *Switch on the Night.* 1955. Pantheon. P3. $150.00

BRADBURY, Ray. *Toynbee Convector.* 1988. Knopf. 1st. F/F. P3. $18.00

BRADBURY, Ray. *Toynbee Convector.* 1988. NY. 1st. sgn. F/F. A23. $60.00

BRADBURY, Ray. *Toynbee Convector.* 1992. Atlanta. Turner. 1st thus. inscr. F. A23. $45.00

BRADBURY, Ray. *Where Robot Mice & Robot Men Run Round in Robot Towns.* 1977. Knopf. 1st. F/F. A23. $60.00

BRADBURY, Ray. *Wonderful Ice Cream Suit.* 1973. Hart Davis/MacGibbon. 1st. NF/NF. P3. $35.00

BRADBURY, Will. *Into the Unknown.* 1981. Reader's Digest. P3. $15.00

BRADDON, George. *Microbe's Kiss.* 1940. Faber. 1st. G/G. P3. $30.00

BRADDON, Russell. *When the Enemy Is Tired.* 1969. Viking. ne. 251p. NF/VG. W2. $15.00

BRADEN, James A. *Centennial History of Akron 1825-1925.* 1925. Akron. 666p. half leather. B18. $47.50

BRADFORD, Barbara Taylor. *Remember.* 1991. Random. 1st. sgn. F/F. A23. $36.00

BRADFORD, Richard. *Red Sky at Morning.* 1968. Phil. 1st. VG/VG. B5. $45.00

BRADFORD, Roark. *John Henry, a Play.* 1939. Harper. ils/6 pl. 100p. NF. A4. $95.00

BRADFORD, Roark. *Ol' Man Adam an' His Chillun.* 1928. Harper. early prt. 12mo. NF/NF. C8. $75.00

BRADFORD, Roark. *Ol' Man Adam an' His Chillun.* 1928. Harper. VG. P3. $45.00

BRADFORD & BRADFORD. *Boston's Locke-Ober Cafe: Illustrated Social History...* 1978. ils/recipes. VG/VG. M17. $20.00

BRADFORD & WOODRUFF. *Keep Singing Keep Humming.* 1946. NY. Wm Scott. 1st. 46p. VG/torn. D4. $35.00

BRADLEY, Alice; see Sheldon, Alice Bradley.

BRADLEY, Bill. *Life on the Run.* 1976. Quadrangle. 1st. VG/VG. P8. $25.00

BRADLEY, David. *Chaneysville Incident.* 1981. Harper Row. ARC. sgn. F/dj. D10. $50.00

BRADLEY, David. *Chaneysville Incident.* 1981. NY. Harper Row. 1st. author's 2nd novel. F/F. T11. $45.00

BRADLEY, David. *No Place To Hide.* 1948. BOMC. VG/dj. K3. $10.00

BRADLEY, James H. *March of the Montana Column, a Prelude to Custer Disaster.* 1961. Norman, OK. photos/map. 182p. VG. J2. $135.00

BRADLEY, Marion Zimmer. *Best of Marion Zimmer Bradley.* 1985. Chicago. F/F. P3. $17.00

BRADLEY, Marion Zimmer. *Catch Trap.* 1979. Ballantine. 1st. NF/VG. P3. $23.00

BRADLEY, Marion Zimmer. *Firebrand.* 1987. S&S. 1st. F/F. N4. $25.00

BRADLEY, Marion Zimmer. *Heirs of Hammerfell.* 1989. DAW. 1st. F/dj. M2. $30.00

BRADLEY, Marion Zimmer. *Mists of Avalon.* 1982. Knopf. 1st. F/dj. M2. $75.00

BRADLEY, Marion Zimmer. *Star of Danger.* 1979. Gregg. 1st. F/sans. P3. $30.00

BRADLEY, Mary Hastings. *On the Gorilla Trail.* 1922. NY/London. Appleton. 8vo. 47 pl/map ep. cloth. VG. W1. $20.00

BRADLEY, Michael. *Communion in Solitude.* 1975. Scrimshaw. 1st. 96p. dj. F3. $15.00

BRADLEY, Omar. *Soldier's Story.* 1951. NY. sgn. maps/photos/index. VG. S16. $125.00

BRADLEY & JONES. *International Diary of Thoughts.* 1969. FErguson. 1146p. VG. B29. $13.00

BRADLEY & PACKER. *Checklist of the Rare Vascular Plants in Alberta.* 1984. Edmonton. Alberta Culture. 112p. wrp. B1. $15.00

BRADNER, Enos. *Northwest Angling.* 1950. NY. 239p. dj. A17. $20.00

BRADSHAW, Gillian. *Hawk of May.* 1980. S&S. 1st. F/dj. M2. $30.00

BRADSHAW, Gillian. *Kingdom Summer.* 1981. S&S. 1st. F/F. M2. $25.00

BRADSHAW, Marion J. *Maine Land: A Portfolio of Views...* 1941. Bangor, ME. 1/1000. 2nd prt. sgn. ils. 176p. T7. $35.00

BRADSHAW, Marion J. *Nature of Maine.* 1945. Bangor, ME. self pub. 1/1000. sgn. gilt blk cloth. B11. $65.00

BRADSHAW, Percy V. *Brother Savages & Guests.* 1958. London. inscr. 162p. G/dj. B18. $27.50

BRADY, Cyrus Townsend. *Indian Fights & Fighters.* Dec 1904. McClure Phillips. hc. A19. $65.00

BRADY, Cyrus Townsend. *Sir Henry Morgan, Buccaneer.* 1903. Dillingham. 1st. VG. M2. $35.00

BRADY, Leo. *Edge of Doom.* 1949. Dutton. 1st. VG/G. P3. $13.00

BRADY, Ryder. *Instar.* 1976. Doubleday. F/F. P3. $13.00

BRAGADIN, Marc. *Italian Navy World War II.* 1957. Annapolis. 1st. maps/photos/index. 380p. VG/VG. S16. $30.00

BRAGDON, Elspeth. *New Adventures of Peter Rabbit.* ca 1950. Cincinnati. Artcraft. ils LV Schmeing/5 3-D popups. 8vo. pict brd. R5. $125.00

BRAGG, Bill. *Campbell Country, the Slumbering Giant.* 1978. Gilette, WY. 1st. inscr. ils/photos. 20p. VG. J2. $65.00

BRAGG, Lawrence. *Crystalline State: A General Survey.* 1949. London. Bell. rpt. ils. xl. VG. K3. $35.00

BRAGG, Lawrence. *Determination of Crystal Structures.* 1957. London. Bell. 2nd. 8vo. VG/dj. K3. $35.00

BRAGG, Melvyn. *Richard Burton: A Life.* 1989. Little Brn. 1st Am. NF. W2. $25.00

BRAGG & BRAGG. *X-Rays & Crystal Structure.* 1916. London. BEll. 2nd. ils. 228p. cl. VG. K3. $35.00

BRAHAM & BYERS. *Thunderstorm: Report of the Thunderstorm Project.* 1950 (1949). WA, DC. Weather Bureau. 287p. cloth. G. K5. $40.00

BRAIDER, Donald. *Life, History & Magic of the Horse.* 1973. Grosset Dunlap. dj. A19. $30.00

BRAIN, Russell. *Nature of Experience: Riddell Memorial Lectures...* 1959. London. Oxford. 12mo. 73p. bl cloth. VG/clip. G1. $35.00

BRAINE, John. *Life at the Top.* 1962. Houghton Mifflin. 1st Am. author's 3rd book. F/NF. D10. $50.00

BRAINE, Sheila. *To Tell the King the Sky Is Falling.* ca 1898. Scribnr. ils Alice Woodward. 171p. aeg. VG. P2. $50.00

BRAKHAGE, Stan. *Metaphors on Vision.* 1976. Film Culture. 2nd. intro/edit PA Sitney. NF/stiff cb wrp. C9. $35.00

BRAMAH, Ernest. *Kai Lung's Golden Hours.* 1923. Doran. 1st. VG. M2. $60.00

BRAMAH, Ernest. *Mirror of Kong Ho.* 1930. Doubleday. 1st. VG/dj. M2. $150.00

BRAMAH, Ernest. *Transmutation of Ling.* 1912. NY. Brentano. 1/500. ils Ilbery Lynch/12 pl. 80p. VG. W3. $86.00

BRAMBLE, Forbes. *Strange Case of Deacon Brodie.* 1975. Hamish Hamilton. 1st. F/F. P3. $20.00

BRAMHALL, Marion. *Tragedy in Blue.* 1945. Crime Club. 1st. VG. P3. $18.00

BRAMWELL, Byron. *Diseases of the Spinal Cord.* 1985 (1885). Birmingham. Classics Neurology/Neurosurgery Lib. facsimile. F. G1. $75.00

BRAND, Christianna. *Death in High Heels.* 1954. Scribner. 1st. VG/G. P3. $30.00

BRAND, Christianna. *Heaven Knows Who.* 1960. Michael Joseph. 1st. VG/VG. P3. $35.00

BRAND, Max; see Faust, Fredrick S.

BRANDEIS, Madeline. *Little Rose of the Mesa.* 1935. Grosset Dunlap. 8vo. 155p. dj. F7. $35.00

BRANDENBURG & STEGER. *North to the Pole: 5 Men & a Woman Make Arctic History.* Sept 1986. NGS. Vol 170, No 3. P4. $18.50

BRANDER, Michael. *Hunting & Shooting From Earlist Times to Present Day.* 1971. NY. 255p. lg 8vo. A17. $20.00

BRANDES & DOUGLAS. *Immigrants to Freedom: Jewish Communities in Rural NJ...* 1971. PA U. ils. 424p. VG. S3. $26.00

BRANDNER, Gary. *Doomstalker.* 1990. UK. Severn. 1st hc ed. NF/dj. M21. $20.00

BRANDNER, Gary. *Hellborn.* 1988. Severn. F/F. P3. $24.00

BRANDO, Anna. *Brando for Breakfast.* 1979. Crown. 1st. F/NF. A20. $20.00

BRANDON, J. Campbell. *Concise History of Butler County, PA, 1800-1950.* 1962. Butler, PA. 1st. 176p. G+. B18. $35.00

BRANDON, Jay. *Fade the Heat.* 1990. Pocket. 1st. F/NF. P3. $19.00

BRANDON, R. *Life & Many Deaths of Harry Houdini.* 1993. NY. 1st. photos. 355p. F/dj. M4. $25.00

BRANDT, Angelika. *Antarctic Valviferans.* 1990. Leiden. EJ Brill. 176p. VG/wrp. P4. $58.00

BRANDT, Herbert. *Arizona & Its Bird Life.* 1951. Bird Research Found. 1st. ils/index/ map ep. 724p. NF. B19. $175.00

BRANDT, Johanna. *Grape Cure.* 1950. NY. Harmony Centre. 17th. VG/dj. A10. $26.00

BRANDT, Karl. *Management of Agriculture & Food in German-Occupied...* 1953. Stanford. 707p. VG/dj. A10. $45.00

BRANDT, Tom; see Dewey, Thomas B.

BRANLEY, Franklyn. *Lodestar Rocket Ship to Mars.* 1951. Crowell. 1st. VG/VG. P3. $18.00

BRANNEN & ELLIOT. *Festive Wine: Ancient Japanese Poems...* 1969. NY/Tokyo. 1st. ils H Maki. F/dj. W3. $42.00

BRANNER, Robert. *Gothic Architecture.* 1961. Brazillier. 1st. 125p. VG/VG. A8. $12.00

BRANSON, Oscar T. *Hopi Indian Kachina Dolls.* 1992. Treasure Chest. 1st. ils. 244p. as new/sans. B19. $40.00

BRANT, Beth. *Mohawk Trail.* 1985. Ithaca. Firebrand Books. 1st. author's 1st book. F/wrp. L3. $45.00

BRANTLEY, Rabun Lee. *Georgia Journalism of the Civil War Period.* 1929. Nashville. George Peabody College for Teachers. 1st. pres. NF/wrp. M8. $250.00

BRASHEAR, John A. *Man Who Loved the Stars.* 1988 (1924). Cambridge. 8vo. 190p. VG. K5. $10.00

BRASHEAR, Minnie. *Mark Twain, Son of Missouri.* 1934. NC U. 1st. gilt bl cloth. NF/VG. M24. $100.00

BRASHER, Rex. *Birds & Trees of North America.* 1961. NY. Rowan Littlefield. 4 vol. folio. 875 mc pl. quarter leatherette/cloth. F. B24. $250.00

BRASHLER, William. *Josh Gibson: Life in the Negro Leagues.* 1978. Harper Row. 1st. F/dj. M25. $60.00

BRATHWAITE, Richard. *Barnabae Intinerarium; or, Barnabee's journal...* 18761928). London. Reeves Turner. new/ revised. 1/525. 8vo. 400+p. Ballantyne bdg. H13. $185.00

BRAUDY, Susan. *Who Killed Sal Mineo?* 1982. Wyndham. 1st. F/dj. M25. $25.00

BRAUN, Ernest. *Grand Canyon of the Living Colorado.* 1970. Ballantine. 8vo. 144p. VG+. F7. $25.00

BRAUN, Lilian Jackson. *Cat Who Knew a Cardinal.* 1991. NY. 1st. F/dj. A17. $12.50

BRAUN, Lilian Jackson. *Cat Who Talked to Ghosts.* 1990. Putnam. 1st. F/F. P3. $20.00

BRAUNE, Wilhelme. *Atlas of Topographical Anatomy After Plane Sections...* 1877. Phil. 1st Eng trans. 4to. 31 pl. 200p. A13. $450.00

BRAUTIGAN, Richard. *Dreaming of Babylon.* 1977. Delacorte. 1st. NF/NF. P3. $30.00

BRAUTIGAN, Richard. *Hawkline Monster: A Gothic Western.* 1974. S&S. 1st. F/F. P3. $25.00

BRAUTIGAN, Richard. *June 30th, June 30th.* 1978. Delacorte. 1st. rem mk. F/F. B4. $150.00

BRAUTIGAN, Richard. *So the Wind Won't Blow It All Away.* 1982. Delacorte. 1st. F/dj. Q1. $50.00

BRAUTIGAN, Richard. *Sombrero Fallout.* 1976. S&S. 1st. F/F. H11. $50.00

BRAUTIGAN, Richard. *Willard & His Bowling Trophies.* 1975. S&S. 1st. F/F. H11. $50.00

BRAVERMAN, Kate. *Lithium for Medea.* 1979. Harper. 1st. F/NF. M19. $25.00

BRAVERMAN, Kate. *Lithium for Medea.* 1979. Harper. 1st. sgn. author's 1st novel. NF/dj. R13. $45.00

BRAWNER & SCALZO. *Indy 500 Mechanic.* 1975. Chilton. photos. VG. P8. $40.00

BRAY, Warwick. *Meeting of Tow Worlds: Europe & the Americas 1492-1650.* 1993. Oxford. British Academy. ils/maps. as new/dj. O7. $35.00

BRAYMER, Marjorie. *Atlantis: Biography of a Legend.* 1983. Atheneum. 1st. VG/VG. P3. $20.00

BRAYNARD, Frank. *Leviathan, the World's Greatest Ship.* 1972. NY. 6 vol. ltd 1st. sgn pres. VG/VG. B5. $250.00

BRAZIER, Mary A.B. *Electrical Activity of the Nervous System.* 1977. Turnbridge Wells, Kent. Pitman Medical. 4th. 248p. prt laminated brd. G1. $65.00

BREAKENRIDGE, William M. *Helldorado: Bringing the Law to the Mesquite.* 1982. Lakeside. ils/notes/index. 454p. teg. brn cloth. F/sans. B19. $35.00

BREARLEY, harry C. *Time Telling Through the Ages.* 1919. Doubleday Page. 1st. ils. 8vo. 294p. K3. $40.00

BRECHER & SETTI. *High Energy Astrophysics & Its Relation to Elementary...* 1975 (1974). MIT. 2nd. VG/dj. K5. $45.00

BRECHT, Bertolt. *Seven Plays.* 1961. Grove. 1st. F/NF. B2. $30.00

BRECKINRIDGE, S.P. *Marriage & the Civic Rights of Women...* 1931. Chicago. 1st. 158p. xl. VG+. A25. $40.00

BRECKINRIDGE, S.P. *New Homes for Old.* 1921. Harper. 1st. photos. xl. VG. A25. $25.00

BREDES, Don. *Muldoon.* 1982. Holt. 1st. F/F. M25. $15.00

BREITENBACH, Louise M. *Eleanor of the Houseboat.* 1927. Boston. Page. 2nd. ils CE Meister. VG/VG. A25. $20.00

BRENAN, Gerald. *Personal Record 1920-72.* 1975. NY. 1st. VG/dj. T9. $25.00

BRENDEL, Frederick. *Flora Peoriana.* 1887. Peoria. Franks. 89p. cloth. A10. $100.00

BRENNAN, Buddy. *Witness to the Execution. Odyssey of Amelia Earnhart.* 1988. Frederick. Renaissance. 1st. inscr. F/F. A23. $40.00

BRENNAN, Joseph P. *Borders Just Beyond.* 1986. Donald Grant. 1/750. sgn/#d. F/dj. M2. $45.00

BRENNAN, Joseph P. *Chronicles of Lucius Leffing.* 1977. Donald Grant. 1st. F/F. M2. $30.00

BRENNAN, Joseph P. *Nightmare Need.* 1964. Arkham. 1st. F/NF. M2. $250.00

BRENNAN, Joseph P. *Nine Horrors & a Dream.* 1958. Arkham. 1st. F/dj. M2. $150.00

BRENNAN, Joseph P. *Scream at Midnight.* 1963. Macabre. 1st. inscr. F. M2. $300.00

BRENNAN, Joseph P. *Stories of Darkness & Dread.* 1973. Arkham. 1st. F/dj. M2. $40.00

BRENNAN, Noel-Anne. *Winter Reckoning.* 1986. Donald Grant. 1st. 1/650. sgn. F/dj. M2. $30.00

BRENNER, Anita. *Timid Ghost.* 1966. Wm Scott. 1st. inscr w/original drawing Jean Chalot. G+/G. P2. $65.00

BRENNER, Anita. *Wind That Swept Mexico.* (1971). Austin, TX. new ed. 310p. dj. F3. $30.00

BRENNER, Gary. *Naked Grape.* 1975. Bobbs Merrill. VG/dj. A16. $8.00

BRENNERT, Alan. *Her Pilgrim Soul & Other Stories.* 1990. Tor. 1st. VG/VG. P3. $18.00

BRENT, Madeleine; see O'Donnell, Peter.

BRENT, P. *Charles Darwin: Man of Enlarged Curiosity.* 1981. harper Row. 1st. 536p. F/dj. D8. $22.00

BRERETON, F.S. *Great Aeroplane.* nd. Blackie & Son. decor brd. VG. P3. $35.00

BRESKIN, Adelyn. *Graphic Art of Mary Cassatt.* 1967. 1st. ils. NF/VG+. S13. $40.00

BRESLIN, Howard. *Silver Oar.* 1954. Crowell. 1st. VG/VG. P3. $15.00

BRESLIN, Jimmy. *Sunny Jim: Life of America's Most Beloved Horseman.* 1962. Garden City. Doubleday. 1st. VG/VG. O3. $45.00

BRESSCIANNI, Loretta. *Original Prints III: New Writings From Scottish Women.* 1989. Edinburgh. Polygon. 1st. 125p. sc. VG+. A25. $15.00

BRETNOR, Reginald. *Modern Science Fiction.* 1953. Coward McCann. 1st. VG/dj. M2. $15.00

BRETNOR, Reginald. *Modern Science Fiction.* 1979. Advent. 1st thus. F/dj. M2. $16.00

BRETON, Andre. *Ode to Charles Fourier.* 1970. Cape Goliard/Grossman. 1st. F/NF. B2. $45.00

BRETSCHNEIDER, E. *Medieval Researches From Eastern Asiatic Sources.* 1887. London. Kegan Paul. 2 vol. ils/bibliographies/index/etc. F. W3. $385.00

BRETT, Bill. *Stolen Steers.* 1977. TX A&M. 3rd. sgn. VG/G. A23. $30.00

BRETT, David. *Ten Little Niggers With Music.* ca 1910. London. Dean & Son. obl 4to. mc brd. R5. $300.00

BRETT, Leo. *Alien Ones.* 1969. Arcadia. VG/VG. P3. $10.00

BRETT, Simon. *Amateur Corpse.* 1978. Scribner. 1st. VG/VG. P3. $20.00

BRETT, Simon. *Box of Tricks.* 1985. Gollancz. 1st. F/F. P3. $25.00

BRETT, Simon. *Comedian Dies.* 1979. Scribner. 1st. VG/VG. P3. $15.00

BRETT, Simon. *Shock to the System.* 1985. Scribner. 1st. NF/NF. P3. $14.00

BRETT, Simon. *So Much Blood.* 1976. Scribner. 1st Am. VG/G+. N4. $17.50

BRETT, Simon. *What Bloody Man Is That?* 1987. London. Gollancz. 1st. sgn. F/F. M15. $65.00

BRETTELL, R.R. *Paper & Light: Calotype in France & Great Britain 1839-70.* 1984. NY. 1st. 4to. ils. F/dj. M4. $25.00

BREUER, W. *Operation Torch: Allied Gamble to Invade North Africa.* 1983. NY. 1st. ils. 272p. VG/VG. S16. $20.00

BREWER, Gay. *Gay Brewer Shows You How To Score Better...* 1968. S Norwalk, CT. Golf Digest. 1st. sgn. VG/VG. B11. $25.00

BREWER, Reginald. *Delightful Diversion.* 1934. Macmillan. rpt. ils. VG/dj. K3. $20.00

BREWER, Stella. *Chimps of Mt Asserik.* 1978. NY. ils. 302p. VG/VG. S15. $10.00

BREWER & FARQUHAR. *Up & Down California in 1860-1864: Journal of WH Brewer...* 1930. New Haven. Yale. 1st. inscr Farquhar. 8vo. gilt bl cloth. F. R3. $200.00

BREWER & FARQUHAR. *Up & Down California in 1860-1864: Journal of WH Brewer...* 1966. Berkeley. 3rd. 8vo. gilt gr cloth. as new/dj. R3. $35.00

BREWINGTON, M.V. *Chesapeake Bay: Pictorial Maritime History.* 1953. Cambridge, MD. Cornell Maritime. 1st. ils. 229p. dj. T7. $50.00

BREWINGTON, M.V. *Peabody Museum Collection of Navigating Instruments...* 1963. Gloucester/Staten Island. rpt. 56 pl. lk cloth. F. P4. $125.00

BREWINGTON & BREWINGTON. *Marine Paintings & Drawings in Peabody Museum.* 1968. Salem, MA. 4th. 1/3000. ils. 530p. NF. O7. $185.00

BREWSTER, David. *Treatise on Optics.* 1931. London. Longman Gr. new ed. 383p. G. K5. $90.00

BREWSTER, George. *Western Literary Magazine.* 1954. Cleveland. 400p. gilt cloth. B18. $37.50

BREWTON & BREWTON. *America Forever New.* 1968. Crowell. 1st. 269p. cloth. F/F. D4. $35.00

BREWTON & BREWTON. *My Tang's Tungled & Other Ridiculous Situations.* 1973. Crowell. 1st. 111p. cloth. F/NF. D4. $35.00

BREWTON & BREWTON. *Sing a Song of Seasons.* 1955. Macmillan. 1st prt. 200p. cloth. VG+/dj. D4. $45.00

BREWTON. *Index to Children's Poetry: Title, Subject, Author...* 1951-1969. 3 vol. 1/1000. w/2 supp. xl. VG. A4. $125.00

BREYER & POLMAR. *Guide to the Soviet Navy.* 1977. Annapolis. 610p. F. A17. $25.00

BRIANS, Paul. *Nuclear Holocausts: Atomic War in Fiction 1895-1984.* 1987. Kent Sate. 1st. F/dj. M2. $30.00

BRICKDALE, Eleanor Fortescue. *Sweet & Touching Tale of Fleur & Blanchefleur.* 1922. London. 1st thus. 4to. VG. M5. $65.00

BRICKHILL, Paul. *Dam Busters.* 1951. London. Evans. 1st. F/F clip. B4. $175.00

BRICKLIN, Mark. *Natural Healing Cookbook.* 1981. PA. Rodale. G. A16. $15.00

BRICKMAN, Richard P. *Bringing Down the House.* 1972. Scribner. 1st. F/NF. H11. $25.00

BRIDGEMAN, L.J. *Guess.* 1901. DOdge. unp. pict brd. VG. M20. $140.00

BRIDGES, Robert. *Testament of Beauty.* 1930. 1st Am. NF. M19. $25.00

BRIDGMAN, L.J. *Guess.* 1901. Caldwell. ils Bridgman. 4to. G+. P2. $125.00

BRIDWELL, E. Nelson. *Shazam!* 1977. Harmony. 1st. F/dj. M2. $25.00

BRIDWELL, E. Nelson. *Superman from the '30s to the '80s.* 1983. Crown. 1st. F/dj. M2. $30.00

BRIGGS, Barbara. *Licorice.* 1949. Aladdin, NY. pre ISBN ed. sm 4to. pict brd. C8. $20.00

BRIGGS, Peter. *200,000,000 Years Beneath the Sea.* 1972. HRW. 2nd. 8vo. 227p. gr cloth. P4. $25.00

BRIGGS, Philip. *Escape From Gravity.* 1955. Lutterworth. 1st. VG/VG. P3. $15.00

BRIGGS, Raymond. *Father Christmas.* 1973. CMG. 1st Am. sq 4to. F/NF. P2. $40.00

BRIGGS, Raymond. *Father Christmas.* 1973. London. Hamish Hamilton. 1st. F/F. C8. $55.00

BRIGGS, Raymond. *Ring-A-Ring O' Roses: Picture Book of Nursery Rhymes.* nd (1962). Coward McCann. probable 1st. 8vo. 48p. G/clip. C14. $12.00

BRIGGS, Walter. *Without Noise of Arms: The 1776 Dominguez...* 1976. Northland. 1st. ils. 212p. F/F. B19. $65.00

BRIGHAM, William T. *Ka Hana Kapa: Making of Bark-Cloth in Hawaii.* 1911. Honolulu. Bishop Mus Pr. 48 full-p photos. 277p. prt wrp. D11. $300.00

BRIGHT, John. *History of Israel.* 1959. Westminster. 500p+16 mc maps. G. B29. $8.00

BRIGHT, Robert. *Georgie's Halloween.* (1958). Doubleday. 10th. unp. pict brd. VG/dj. T5. $40.00

BRIGHT-HOLMES, John. *Lord's & Commons.* 1988. Deutsch. 1st. F/F. P8. $15.00

BRIN, David. *Postman.* 1985. Bantam. 1st. F/NF. M19. $35.00

BRIN, David. *River of Time.* 1986. Dark Harvest. 1/400. sgn/#d. F/dj/case. M2. $100.00

BRIN, David. *Uplift War.* 1987. Phantasia. 1st. F/dj. M2. $75.00

BRINCARD, Marie-Therese. *Sounding Forms: African Musical Instruments.* 1989. Am Fed of Arts. 205p. 4to. glossy wrp. A17. $22.50

BRINDWELL, E. Nelson. *Batman: From the '30s to the '70s.* 1971. Crown. 1st. F/dj. M2. $30.00

BRINE, Mary D. *Happy Little People.* 1898. Lee Shepard. ils Paul King. 4to. VG. M5. $120.00

BRININSTOOL, E.A. *Fighting Indian Warriors.* 1953. Stackpole. 353p. RS. cloth. VG/dj. M20. $50.00

BRINK, Andre. *Act of Terror.* 1991. Summit. 1st. F/F. P3. $25.00

BRINK, Carol. *Andy Buckram's Tin Men.* 1966. Viking. 1st. 8vo. 192p. xl. G. T5. $20.00

BRINK, Carol. *Caddie Woodlawn.* 1935. Macmillan. 1st. ils Kate Seredy. 270p. gr cloth. VG. D1. $80.00

BRINK, Carol. *Lad With a Whistle.* 1941. Macmillan. 1st. ils Robert Ball. 235p. VG+/VG. P2. $40.00

BRINKERHOFF, Zula C. *God's Chosen People of America.* 1971. private prt. 1st. 259p. VG+/sans. B19. $45.00

BRINKLEY, Frank. *Japan & China.* 1901-1902. Boston. Author's ed. 12 vol. 1/1000. tall 8vo. ils. teg. red cloth. F. H3. $300.00

BRINKMAN, H.C. *Zur Quantenmechanik der Multipolstrahlung.* 1932. Groningen. Nordoff. 8vo. 59p. VG/wrp. K3. $15.00

BRINKMANN, Karl-Heinz. *Die Gattung Sulcorebutia.* 1976. Titisee-Neustadt. German text. 79p. F. B26. $38.00

BRION, Patrick. *Tex Avery.* 1986. Schuler. Herrsching. German text. ils/fld drawing. NF/dj. C9. $150.00

BRIQUET. *Les Filigranes, Dictionnaire Historique...* nd. 4 vol. rpt (2nd Leipzig). 1/150. watermark reference. F. A4. $295.00

BRISCOE, D. Stuart. *Taking God Seriously: Major Lessons From the Minor Prophets.* 1986. Word. 190p. F/dj. B29. $6.50

BRISCOE, Rufus J. *Two Oldest Trees: One Dead, One Living.* 1914. Riverside, CA. 12mo. 20 full-p halftones. 63p. heavy brd/ties. B26. $17.50

BRISSAUD, Edouard. *Kecons sur les Maladies Nerveuses.* L895 & 1899. Paris. Masson. 2 vol. 8vo. xl. G1. $250.00

BRISTOL, Margaret Cochran. *Handbook of Social Case Recording.* 1937. Chicago. 2nd. 219p. VG. A25. $15.00

BRISTOW, Gwen. *Tomorrow Is Forever.* 1944. Consolidated Book Pub. BC. NF/dj. M25. $45.00

BRISTOWE, John. *Diseases of the Intestines & Peritoneum.* 1879. NY. 1st Am. 243p. A13. $25.00

BRITE, Poppy Z. *Lost Souls.* 1992. Delacorte. 1st. author's 1st novel. F/F. M21. $30.00

BRITO, Silvester J. *Man of a Rainbow.* 1983. Marvin. Bl Cloud Quarterly. F/wrp. L3. $45.00

BRITSCH, R. Lanier. *Unto the Islands of the Sea. A History of Latter-Day Saints.* 1986. Salt Lake City. Deseret. 1st. 8vo. 585p. VG/dj. P4. $35.00

BRITTON & ROSE. *Cactaceae.* 1937. Pasadena. vol 1-3 (of 4). 100 pl. A22. $160.00

BRITTON & ROSE. *Cactaceae.* 1963. NY. 2 vol. ils. M/djs. B26. $75.00

BRITTON & ROSE. *Cactaceae: Descriptions & Ils of Plants of Cactus Family.* 1930s. Los Angeles. Abbey Garden Pr. 4 vol. gr cloth. VG. B26. $225.00

BRITTON & ROSE. *New or Noteworthy North American Crassulacae.* 1903. NY. 45p. wrp. B26. $20.00

BROADUS, John A. *On the Preparation & Delivery of Sermons.* 1944. Harper. new/revised by Weatherspoon. 392p. VG. B29. $8.00

BROBECK, Florence. *Chafing Dish Cookery.* nd. NY. Barrows. G/dj. A16. $10.00

BROCK, Emma L. *Plug-Horse Derby.* 1955. Knopf. 1st. VG/G. O3. $20.00

BROCK, H.I. *Colonial Churches in Virginia.* 1972. Port Washington. 4to. 39 photos. 95p. NF. M4. $25.00

BROCK, Ray. *Blood, Oil & Sand.* 1952. London. Bodley Head. 1st. 256p. cloth. VG/torn. W1. $16.00

BROCK, Rose; see Hansen, Joseph.

BROCKETT, I.P. *Men of Our Day.* 1972. ils. VG. M17. $35.00

BROCKLESBY, John. *Elements of Meteorology...* 1849. NY. Pratt Woodford. revised/stereotyped ed. ils. 8vo. 240p. K3. $65.00

BROD, Max. *Redemption of Tycho Brahe.* 1928. Knopf. 1st Am. F/NF. B4. $175.00

BRODER, Patricia Janis. *Hopi Painting: World of the Hopis.* 1979. Brandywine. ils/notes/index. 318p. F/NF. B19. $125.00

BRODHEAD, John Romeyn. *Documents Relative to the Colonial History of State of NY.* 1855. Albany. Weed Parsons. thick 4to. new cloth. VG. T10. $100.00

BRODIE, Benjamin Collins. *Lectures Illustrative of Certain Local Nervous Affections.* 1837. London. Longman Rees Gr. thin 8vo. 88p. contemporary sheep. VG. G1. $750.00

BRODIE, Fawn M. *Richard Nixon: The Shaping of His Character.* 1981. Norton. 1st. 574p. VG/dj. V3. $12.50

BRODIE & BURTON. *City of the Saints.* 1963. NY. 1st thus. ils/index. 654p. VG/dj. B5. $55.00

BRODSKY, Joseph. *Less Than One. Selected Essays.* 1986. FSG. 1st. F/F. D10. $45.00

BRODY, J.J. *Anasazi & Pueblo Painting.* 1991. NM U. 1st. 191p. F/dj. A17. $25.00

BROEL, Albert. *Frog Raising for Pleasure & Profit.* 1953. Detroit. Marlboro. 182p. VG. A10. $30.00

BROGAN, James; see Hodder-Williams, C.

BROGAN & ZARCA. *Deadly Business: Sam Cummings Intrarms & Arms Trade.* 1983. NY. 1st. sgn Wm Bill Colby/Sam Cummings. 384p. VG/VG. S16. $45.00

BROGDON, B.G. *Opinions, Comments & Reflections on Radiology.* 1982. Los Angeles. 1st. ils. 249p. A13. $15.00

BROHL, Ted. *In a Fine Frenzy Rolling.* 1992. Vantage. 1st. sgn. F/F. P3. $20.00

BROMER. *35 Miniature Books in Designer Bindings.* 1987. ils/pl. 78p. F/wrp/custom case. A4. $95.00

BROMFIELD, Louis. *Few Brass Tacks.* 1946. Harper. 1st. 303p. VG/dj. M20. $25.00

BROMFIELD, Louis. *From My Experience.* 1955. Harper. 1st. sgn. VG+/dj. M20. $85.00

BROMFIELD, Louis. *New Pattern for a Tired World.* 1954. Harper. 1st. 314p. VG/dj. M20. $30.00

BROMFIELD, Louis. *Pleasant Valley.* 1945. Harper. 1st. ils Kate Lord. VG/VG. R14. $40.00

BROMFIELD, Louis. *Strange Case of Miss Annie Spragg.* 1928. Stokes. 1st. G. P3. $25.00

BROMFIELD, Louis. *Twenty-Four Hours.* 1930. Grosset Dunlap. 5th prt. inscr. NF. T12. $20.00

BROMFIELD, Louis. *Wild Is the River.* 1941. Harper. 1st. 326p. VG/dj. M20. $35.00

BROMMEL, Bernard. *Eugene V Debs: Spokesman for Labor & Socialism.* 1978. Chicago. Kerr. 1st. sgn. F/F. B2. $35.00

BRONK, William. *Life Supports.* 1981. Northpoint. 1st. F/dj. V1. $40.00

BRONSON, William. *Las Grand Adventure: Story of the Klondike Gold Rush...* 1977. McGraw Hill. 1st. 4to. map ep. 232p. VG/dj. P4. $45.00

BRONTE, BRONTE & BRONTE. *Poems by Currer, Ellis & Acton Bell.* 1848. Phil. Lea Blanchard. 1st Am. authors' 1st book. drab brd/rebacked. M24. $850.00

BRONTE, Emily. *Wuthering Heights.* 1967. NY. Portland House. 1st prt. ils Clare Leighton. F. T12. $30.00

BROOKE, Iris. *English Children's Costumes Since 1771.* 1930 (nd). London. lg 8vo. NF. C8. $80.00

BROOKE, Iris. *English Costume in the 17th Century.* 1964. NY. ils. 89p. F/dj. M4. $20.00

BROOKE, Keith. *Keepers of the Peace.* 1990. Gollancz. 1st. F/F. P3/T2. $20.00

BROOKES, Owen. *Gatherer.* 1982. HRW. 1st. M2/P3. $20.00

BROOKS, Amy. *Randy & Her Friends (#3).* 1902. Lee Shepard. 253p. gilt cloth. VG. M20. $25.00

BROOKS, Amy. *Randy's Good Times (#5).* 1904. Lee Shepard. 265p. VG. M20. $25.00

BROOKS, Amy. *Randy's Luck (#6).* 1905. Lee Shepard. 238p. VG. M20. $25.00

BROOKS, Amy. *Randy's Prince (#8).* 1907. Lee Shepard. 244p. G+. M20. $25.00

BROOKS, Charles H. *Official History of the First African Baptist Church...* 1922. Phil. self pub. 1st. photos. 167p. VG. B4. $350.00

BROOKS, Elisha. *Pioneer Mother in California: Written for His Grandchildren.* 1922. SF. Harr Wagner. 2nd. 8vo. gr buckram. VG. R3. $60.00

BROOKS, Gwendolyn. *Street in Bronzville.* 1945. Harper. 1st. F/F. B4. $550.00

BROOKS, Jennifer. *Princess Jessica Rescues a Prince.* 1993. Nadja. 1st. sgn. glossy brd. VG/dj. M20. $20.00

BROOKS, John Graham. *American Syndicalism: The IWW.* 1913. Macmillan. 1st. F. B2. $50.00

BROOKS, John. *Small Garden.* 1978. Macmillan. 1st Am. 256p. dj. A10. $28.00

BROOKS, Juanita. *Mountain Meadows Massacre.* 1962 (1950). Norman. rpt. 318p. VG. F7. $35.00

BROOKS, Lake. *Science of Fishing: Most Practical Book...* (1912). Columbus, OH. Harding. 1st. 258p. gr pict cloth. VG+. H7. $35.00

BROOKS, Maurice. *Appalachians.* 1965. Houghton Mifflin. 3rd. sgn. VG/VG. B11. $25.00

BROOKS, Patricia. *Meals That Can Wait.* 1970. Gramercy. G/dj. A16. $10.00

BROOKS, Richard. *Brick Foxhole.* 1946. NY. 238p. VG. S16. $30.00

BROOKS, Terry. *Elfstones of Shannara.* 1982. Del Rey. 1st. F/dj. M2. $20.00

BROOKS, Terry. *Wizard at Large.* 1988. Ballantine. 1st. sgn. F/NF. B3. $35.00

BROOKS, Walter R. *Freddy & the Baseball Team From Mars.* 1955. NY. Knopf. 1st. ils Kurt Wiese. 8vo. red cloth. R5. $150.00

BROOKS, Walter R. *Freddy & the Flying Saucer Plans.* 1957. Knopf. stated 1st. ils Kurt Wiese. VG. M5. $135.00

BROOKS, Walter R. *Freddy & the Perilous Adventure.* 1942. Knopf. stated 1st. ils Kurt Wiese. rebound. xl. G. M5. $48.00

BROOKS, Walter R. *Freddy Goes to the North Pole.* 1951 (1930). Knopf. 8th. lg 12mo. NF/VG+. C8. $100.00

BROOKS, Walter R. *Freddy Plays Football.* 1949. Knopf. 1st. ils Kurt Wiese. gray cloth. R5. $200.00

BROOKS, Walter R. *Freddy's Cousin Weedly.* 1940. Knopf. stated 1st. ils Kurt Wiese. VG. M5. $175.00

BROOKS, Walter R. *Freddy the Cowboy.* 1950. Knopf. stated 1st. ils Kurt Wiese. VG/dj. M5. $325.00

BROOKS, Walter R. *Freddy the Cowboy.* 1952 (1950). Knopf. 2nd. 12mo. xl. G. C8. $35.00

BROOKS, Walter R. *Freddy the Detective.* 1944 (1932). Knopf. ils Kurt Wiese. VG. M5. $40.00

BROOKS, Walter R. *Wiggins for President.* 1939. Knopf. 1st. ils Kurt Weise. VG+/dj. D8. $150.00

BROOKS, William Allan. *Girl Gangs: Survey of Teen-Age Drug Addicts...* 1952. NY. Padell. 1st. 244p. VG/dj. A25. $35.00

BROOKS & CLELAND. *Morman Chronicle: Diaries of John D Lee 1848-1876.* 1955. Huntington Lib. 2 vol. VG. F7. $155.00

BROOM, Winston. *Gone the Sun.* 1988. Doubleday. 1st. F/F. M19. $25.00

BROOME, Samuel. *Culture of the Chrysanthemum As Practiced in Temple Gardens.* 1858. London. Florist Office. 2nd. 59p. disbound. A10. $40.00

BROSBT & PRATT. *United States Mineral Resources, Geological Survey...820.* 1973. GPO. 722p. cloth. F. D8. $24.00

BROSNAN, Jim. *Long Season.* 1960. Harper. 1st. F/G. B4. $75.00

BROSNAN, John. *War of the Sky Lords.* 1989. Gollancz. 1st. NF/NF. P3. $20.00

BROUN, Heywood. *It Seems To Me: 1925-1935.* 1935. NY. Harcourt. 1st. 335p. F/partial dj. B14. $45.00

BROUN, Maurice. *Index to North American Ferns.* 1938. Orleans, MA. self pub. 12mo. 217p. VG. A22. $25.00

BROWER, Brock. *Late Great Creature.* 1972. Atheneum. 1st. VG/dj. M2. $25.00

BROWER, Brock. *Late Great Creature.* 1972. Atheneum. 1st. sgn. F/F clip. B11. $30.00

BROWER, Gary. *Haiku in Western Languages.* 1972. NY. Scarecrow. 1st. 133p. NF. W3. $38.00

BROWER, Kenneth. *Starship & the Canoe.* 1978. HRW. 1st. 8vo. 270p. VG/dj. K3. $15.00

BROWER, Kenneth. *Wake of the Whale.* ca 1979. SF. Friends of Earth. photos WR Curtsinger. 160p. NF/dj. P4. $75.00

BROWN, Alan K. *Sawpits in the Spanish Redwoods 1787-1849.* 1966. San Mateo, CA. County Hist Assoc. 1/750. ils/map. 27p. dk gr cloth. M. K7. $60.00

BROWN, Alec. *Angelo's Moon.* 1955. London. 1st. F/dj. M2. $22.00

BROWN, Alfred. *Old Masterpieces in Surgery.* 1928. Omaha. 1st. sgn. 263p. A13. $350.00

BROWN, Bernard J. *From Pharaoh to Hitler: What Is a Jew?* 1933. Chicago. Consolidated Book Pub. 1/2000. inscr. 217p. VG. S3. $30.00

BROWN, Beth. *Universal Station.* 1944. Regent. 1st. NF/dj. M2. $27.00

BROWN, C.W. *Salt Dishes.* 1937. Ashland, MA. sgn. 148p. VG. M20. $45.00

BROWN, CAROTHERS & JOHNSON. *Grand Canyon Birds.* 1987. Tucson. 8vo. 302p. orange cloth. F/dj. F7. $22.00

BROWN, Charles H. *Insurrection at Magellan.* 1854. Boston. VG. 07. $55.00

BROWN, Clair A. *Wildflowers of LA & Ajoining States.* 1972. Baton Rouge. ils/photos/map. 247p. F/dj. B26. $24.00

BROWN, D.A. *Grierson's Raid.* 1954. Urbana. 1st. sgn. VG/dj. B5. $45.00

BROWN, Dale. *Flight of the Old Dog.* 1987. np. 1st. author's 1st novel. F/F. N4. $40.00

BROWN, Dale. *Hammerheads.* 1990. 1st. NF/F. N4. $25.00

BROWN, Dale. *Silver Tower.* 1988. DIF. 1st. author's 2nd novel. NF/dj. M21. $25.00

BROWN, David Jr. *Marine From Virginia: Letters 1941-1945* 1947. Chapel Hill. 105p. VG/G. S16. $45.00

BROWN, Dee. *Bury My Heart at Wounded Knee.* 1970. HRW. 1st/1st prt (pub date code 0171). NF/VG. L3. $175.00

BROWN, Dee. *Conspiracy of Knaves.* 1987. Holt. 1st. F/F. B3. $20.00

BROWN, Dee. *Creek Mary's Blood.* 1980. HRW. 1st trade. F/NF. L3. $35.00

BROWN, Dee. *Fetterman Massacre.* 1972. Barie Jenkins. 1st. F/F. P3. $20.00

BROWN, Dee. *Hear the Lonesome Whistle Blow.* 1977. HRW. 1st. photos/maps. 311p. map ep. VG/VG. J2. $40.00

BROWN, Dee. *They Went Thataway.* 1960. Putnam. 1st. ils Robert Galster. F/VG+. A18. $35.00

BROWN, Dee. *Wonderous Times on the Frontier.* 1991. 324p. F/NF. A4. $25.00

BROWN, Dee. *Yellowhorse.* 1956. Houghton Mifflin. 1st. F/NF. B4. $350.00

BROWN, Douglas; see Gibson, Walter B.

BROWN, Edward. *Poultry Keeping As an Industry for Farmers...* 1904. London. Arnold. 5th/revised. 205p. VG. A10. $22.00

BROWN, Eve. *Plaza Cookbook.* 1972. Prentice Hall. G/dj. A16. $30.00

BROWN, Frank E. *Roman Architecuture.* 1961. Brazillier. 1st. 125p. VG/VG. A8. $12.00

BROWN, Fred R. *History of the Ninth US Infantry, 1799-1909.* 1909. Chicago. 1st. 842p. VG. B18. $295.00

BROWN, Fredric. *Case of the Dancing Sandwiches.* 1985. Volcano, HI. Dennis McMillan. 1st. 1/400. sgn/#d. F/dj. M15. $100.00

BROWN, Fredric. *Compliments of a Friend.* 1950. Dutton. 1st. NF/VG. Q1. $250.00

BROWN, Fredric. *Dead Ringer.* 1948. Dutton. 1st. VG/poor. H11. $135.00

BROWN, Fredric. *Gibbering Hight.* 1991. Dennis McMillan. 1st. 1/425. intro/sgn Joe Lansdale. F/dj. M2. $50.00

BROWN, Fredric. *Here Comes a Candle.* 1950. Dutton. 1st. F/NF. M15. $250.00

BROWN, Fredric. *Martians, Go Home.* 1955. Dutton. 1st. F/NF. P3. $350.00

BROWN, Fredric. *Murderers.* 1958. Dutton. 1st. F/NF. M15. $200.00

BROWN, Fredric. *Office.* 1958. Dutton. 1st. VG/G. P3. $250.00

BROWN, Fredric. *Paradox Lost.* 1973. Random. 1st. NF/NF. P3. $60.00

BROWN, Fredric. *Pardon My Ghoulish Laughter.* 1986. Macmillan. 1st. F/F. P3. $75.00

BROWN, Fredric. *Rogue in Space.* 1957. Dutton. 1st. F/dj. M2. $400.00

BROWN, Fredric. *Screaming Mimi.* 1949. Dutton. 1st. 12mo. yel prt brd. dj. T10. $275.00

BROWN, Fredric. *Selling Death Short.* 1988. Dennis McMillan. 1/450. intro/sgn Francis Nevins. F/dj. M2. $65.00

BROWN, Fredric. *Space on My Hands.* 1951. Shasta. 1st. VG/dj. M2. $100.00

BROWN, Fredric. *What Mad Universe.* 1949. Dutton. 1st. G+. M2. $45.00

BROWN, Fredric. *What Mad Universe.* 1978. Pennyfarthing. 1st thus. F/dj. M2. $30.00

BROWN, G.W. *Baltimore & the 19th of April, 1861.* 1887. Baltimore. 1st. 176p. O8. $42.50

BROWN, Geoff. *I Want What I Want.* 1967. Putnam. 1st Am. F/F. B4. $85.00

BROWN, George T. *Fragments of Life.* 1946. Batavia. Clarmont. 1st. gilt ribbed cloth. F. B4. $275.00

BROWN, Gerald A. *Hazard.* 1973. Arbor. VG/VG. P3. $13.00

BROWN, Harrison. *Bibliography on Meteorites.* 1953. Chicago. 8vo. 608p. xl. K5. $150.00

BROWN, Helen E. *West Coast Cook Book.* 1952. Little Brn. G. A16. $15.00

BROWN, Henry Collins. *Valentine's Manual of Old New York.* 1921. Valentine's Manual. 12mo. 271p. VG. H1. $30.00

BROWN, Hugh Victor. *History of Education of Negros in North Carolina.* 1961. Raleigh, NC. 1st. sgn. 167p. pebble grain cloth. NF. B4. $125.00

BROWN, J. Moray. *Polo.* 1895. London. Vinton. 1st. VG. O3. $85.00

BROWN, J.R. *Unusual Plants: 110 Spectacular Photographs of Succulents.* 1954. Pasadena. 110 full-p photos. 230p. decor cloth. VG. B26. $40.00

BROWN, Jimmy. *Off My Chest.* 1964. Garden City. 1st. sgn pres. VG/VG. A4. $50.00

BROWN, John K. *Baldwin Locomotive Works.* 1995. Johns Hopkins. 1st. 8vo. 328p. F/dj. T10. $45.00

BROWN, John. *Elements of Medicine.* 1804. Portsbouth, NH. New/Revised. 2 vol in 1. fld chart. rebacked. VG. T10. $175.00

BROWN, John. *Rab & His Friends & Marjorie Fleming.* 1876. Osbood. 12mo. 93p. emb gr cloth. NF. T10. $65.00

BROWN, Joseph Epes. *Sacred Pipe.* 1953. Norman, OK. 1st. F/VG. L3. $450.00

BROWN, Larry. *Big Bad Love.* 1990. Algonquin. 1st. F/F. R14. $35.00

BROWN, Larry. *Big Bad Love.* 1990. Algonquin. 1st. sgn. F/dj. R13. $45.00

BROWN, Larry. *Dirty Work.* 1989. Algonquin. 1st. author's 2nd book. F/dj. A24/H11. $40.00

BROWN, Larry. *Dirty Work.* 1989. Algonquin. 1st. sgn. F/F. R13. $50.00

BROWN, Larry. *Facing the Music.* 1988. Algonquin. 1st. sgn. author's 1st book. F/F. R13. $125.00

BROWN, Larry. *Joe.* 1991. Algonquin. 1st. sgn. F/NF. R13. $40.00

BROWN, Larry. *On Fire.* 1994. Algonquin. 1st. F/F. B4. $45.00

BROWN, M.L. *Firearms in Colonial America: Impact on History...1492-1792.* 1980. WA. 1st. ils. 448p. F/dj. M4. $40.00

BROWN, M.L.T. *Gems for the Taking.* 1971. Macmillan. 193p. VG/dj. D8. $12.00

BROWN, Marcia. *Felice.* 1958. Scribner. 1st. 4to. NF/G+. P2. $65.00

BROWN, Margaret Wise. *Baby Animals.* 1950. Random. ils Mary Cameron. NF/dj. M5. $60.00

BROWN, Margaret Wise. *Big Dog Little Dog.* 1943. Doubleday Doran. early prt. sq 4to. VG/G-. P2. $40.00

BROWN, Margaret Wise. *Golden Egg Book.* 1975. NY. Golden. rpt. ils Leonard Weisgard. glazed brd. C14. $14.00

BROWN, Margaret Wise. *House of a Hundred Windows.* 1945. Harper. probable 1st. ils Robert deVeyrac. VG/VG. P2. $95.00

BROWN, Margaret Wise. *Little Fireman.* 1938. Wm Scott. reissue. sq 8vo. VG/G+. P2. $65.00

BROWN, Margaret Wise. *Nibble Nibble: Poems for Children.* 1959. Young Scott. 1st. ils Leonard Weisgard. F. M5. $70.00

BROWN, Margaret Wise. *Night & Day.* 1942. Harper. 1st. ils Leonard Weisgard. tan cloth. dj. R5. $300.00

BROWN, Margaret Wise. *Punch & Judy.* 1940. Wm Scott. 1st. ils Leonard Weisgard. G+. P2. $40.00

BROWN, Margaret Wise. *Pussycat's Christmas.* 1949. Crowell. 1st. sq 8vo. NF/VG. P2. $110.00

BROWN, Margaret Wise. *Red Light Green Light.* 1944. Doubleday Doran. 1st thus. ils Leonard Weisgard. F/G. P2. $110.00

BROWN, Marion. *Pickles & Preserves.* 1960. Avenel. G/dj. A16. $15.00

BROWN, Michael. *Santa Mouse.* 1968. NY. ils Elfrieda DeWitt. VG. M5. $15.00

BROWN, Milton W. *Story of the Armory Show.* 1963. NY. Joseph Hirschhorn Found. 1st. F/clip. Q1. $75.00

BROWN, Monty. *Where Giants Trod.* 1989. Quiller. ils/fld map. 431p. F/F. S15. $30.00

BROWN, Norman O. *Love's Body.* 1966. Random. 1st. F/F. B4. $85.00

BROWN, Palmer. *Hickory.* 1978. Harper Row. 1st. 42p. VG/VG. P2. $40.00

BROWN, Paul. *Insignia of the Services.* 1941. Scribner. 1st Am. G. O3. $40.00

BROWN, Philip. *Return of the Osprey.* 1962. London. 223p. VG. S15. $15.00

BROWN, Riley. *Men, Wind & Sea.* 1939. NY. Carlyle. 1st. ils. 266p. T7. $35.00

BROWN, Rita Mae. *Bingo.* 1988. Bantam. 1st. sgn. F/F. B3. $35.00

BROWN, Rita Mae. *High Hearts.* 1986. Bantam. 1st. F/NF. B3/Q1. $40.00

BROWN, Rita Mae. *In Her Day.* 1976. Plainfield, VT. Daughters. 1st. author's 2nd book. VG+. A24. $30.00

BROWN, Rita Mae. *Plain Brown Wrapper.* 1976. Oakland. Diana. 1st. F/wrp. B4. $125.00

BROWN, Rita Mae. *Rubyfruit Jungle.* (1973). Plainfield, VT. Daughters Inc. 1st. F/wrp. M24. $100.00

BROWN, Rita Mae. *Rubyfruit Jungle.* 1988. Putnam. 1st Am hc. author's 1st book. F/dj. A24. $30.00

BROWN, Rita Mae. *Six of One.* 1978. Harper. 1st. F/NF. B3. $75.00

BROWN, Rita Mae. *Southern Discomfort.* 1982. Harper Row. 1st. F/NF clip. A24. $30.00

BROWN, Rita Mae. *Sudden Death.* 1983. Bantam. 1st. F/NF. B3. $45.00

BROWN, Roselle George. *Sybil Sue Blue.* 1966. Doubleday. 1st. F/dj. M2. $35.00

BROWN, Rosellen. *Autobiography of My Mother.* 1976. Doubleday. ARC. F/NF. M19. $45.00

BROWN, Rosellen. *Autobiography of My Mother.* 1976. Doubleday. 1st. F/NF. M25. $35.00

BROWN, Rosellen. *Before & After.* 1992. FSG. 1st. F/F. B3. $25.00

BROWN, Rosellen. *Cora Fry.* 1977. Norton. 1st. F/F. M19. $25.00

BROWN, S. *Alpine Flora of the Canadian Rocky Mountains.* 1907. Putnam. ils/pl. 353p. VG. M12. $37.50

BROWN, W.R. *Horse of the Desert.* 1967. Springville. J Shuler. Deluxe/ltd. ils/photos/maps. 295p. VG+. M12. $95.00

BROWN, Warren. *Rockne.* 1931. Reilly Lee. 1st. photos. VG. P8. $20.00

BROWN, William A. *Christian Hope.* 1912. Scribner. 216p. VG. B29. $8.50

BROWN, William Moseley. *Freemasonry in Winchester, VA.* 1949. McClure. sgn. 284p. B11. $50.00

BROWN, William R. *Last Crusade: A Negotiator's Middle East Handbook.* 1980. Chicago. Nelson Hall. 399p. VG/wrp. W1. $10.00

BROWN, William W. *Narrative of... a Fugitive Slave. Written by Himself.* 1847. Boston. Anti-Slavery Office. 1st. 12mo. 110p. cloth. M1. $425.00

BROWN & BROWN. *America Cooks: Favorite Recipes From the 48 States.* 1949. Halcyon. rpt. 986p. fair/torn dj. B10. $15.00

BROWN & CONTENTO. *Science Fiction in Print: 1985.* 1986. Locus. VG. P3. $80.00

BROWN & KIRKMAN. *Trees of Georgia & Adjacent States*. 1990. Portland. Timber. 292p. dj. B1. $36.50

BROWN & MIERS. *Gettysburg*. 1948. New Brunswick. ils/maps. 308p. G+/dj. B18. $17.50

BROWN-SEQUARD, Charles Eduard. *Course of Lectures on Physiology & Pathology of Nervous...* 1860. Phil. Collins. 276p. panelled Victorian brn cloth/ rebacked. G1. $585.00

BROWNE, Arline M. *In the Wake of the Topinabee*. 1967. Hubbard Map Service. sgn. 139p. VG+/dj. M20. $22.00

BROWNE, Belmore. *Frozen Barrier: Story of...Behring Sea*. 1921. NY. Putnam. 5th imp. 267p. bl cloth. VG/worn. P4. $40.00

BROWNE, Borden P. *Introduction to Psychological Theory*. 1886. NY. Harper. 329p. gilt bl cloth. F. B14. $75.00

BROWNE, Harold. *Return of Tharn*. 1956. Donald Grant. 1st. sgn. F/VG. M2. $150.00

BROWNE, Howard. *Pork City*. 1988. St Martin. 1st. VG/VG. P3. $17.00

BROWNE, Howard. *Warrior of the Dawn*. 1943. Reilly Lee. 1st. NF/dj. M2. $125.00

BROWNE, J. Ross. *Adventures in Apache Country*. 1974. Promontory. ils. 535p. NF/clip. B19. $25.00

BROWNE, J. Ross. *Report of the Debates in Convention of California...* 1850. np (WA, DC). 1st. 8vo. gilt brn cloth. NF. R3. $350.00

BROWNE, Thomas. *Religio Medici*. 1939. Eugene. LEC. 1/1500. sgn/#d. 113p. B11. $65.00

BROWNE, Thomas. *Tydrotapha: Urne-Buriall or a Discource of Sepulchrall...* 1907. Riverside. 1/385. 8vo. red leather. VG. T10. $145.00

BROWNELL, Baker. *Other Illinois*. 1958. NY. 1st. VG/G. B5. $30.00

BROWNELL, Charles De Wolf. *Indian Races of North & South America*. 1853. Boston. Horace Westworth. 40 hand-colored pl. 640p. gilt rebacked calf. K7. $295.00

BROWNING, Elizabeth Barrett. *Essays on the Greek Christian Poets & the English Poets*. 1863. James Miller. 1st Am. VG. M19. $35.00

BROWNING, Elizabeth Barrett. *Poetical Works of Elizabeth Barrett Browning*. (1920). probable 1st thus/deluxe ed. 12mo. F. C8. $35.00

BROWNING, Robert. *Pied Piper of Hamelin*. 1910. Rand McNally. 1st thus. ils Hope Dunlap. tall 4to. VG. M5. $85.00

BROWNING, Robert. *Pied Piper of Hamelin*. 1939. London. Harrap. 1st trade. ils Rackham. 37p. M/pict wrp. B24. $125.00

BROWNING, Robert. *Ring & the Book*. 1949. LA. Plantin Pr. 1/1500. ils/sgn Carl Schultheiss. F/case. T10. $125.00

BROWNLOW, W.G. *Sketches of the Rise, Progress & Decline of Secession*. 1862. Phil. 1st. 458p. O8. $27.50

BROWNSON, Orestes A. *New Views of Christianity, Society & the Church*. 1836. Boston. James Munroe. 1st. 12mo. 116p. cloth. M1. $175.00

BROXON, Mildred Downey. *Too Long a Sacrifice*. 1984. Bluejay. 1/350. sgn/#d. F/case. M2. $75.00

BROYARD, Anatole. *Men, Women & Other Anticlimaxes*. 1980. Meuthuen. 1st. F/F clip. B4. $650.00

BROYLES, Frank. *Hogwild*. 1979. Memphis. 1st. sgn. F/G. A23. $40.00

BRUCCOLI, Matthew J. *Kenneth Millar/Ross MacDonald: A Checklist*. 1971. Gale Research. 1st. xl. F. A17. $15.00

BRUCCOLI, Matthew J. *Raymond Chandler: A Checklist*. 1968. Kent State. 1st. 35p. cloth. A17. $15.00

BRUCE, F.F. *In Retrospect: Remembrance of Things Past*. 1993. Baker. 336p. VG. B29. $10.00

BRUCE, Jean. *Deep Freeze*. 1963. Cassell. 1st. VG. P3. $12.00

BRUCE, Lenny. *How To Talk Dirty & Influence People*. 1965. Chicago. Playboy. 1st. VG/dj. B5. $25.00

BRUCHAC, Joseph. *Ancestry*. 1980. Ft Kent. Great Raven. 1st. sgn. F/stapled vinyl wrp. L3. $65.00

BRUCHAC, Joseph. *Native American Sweat Lodge*. 1993. Freedom. Crossing Pr. 1st. sgn. F/sans. L3. $50.00

BRUCHAC, Joseph. *Turtle Meat & Other Stories*. 1992. Duluth. Holy Cow! 1st. sgn. F. L3. $100.00

BRULLER, Jean. *21 Delightful Ways of Committing Suicide*. 1930. Covici Friede. 21 full-p mc ils. 92p. VG. B14. $55.00

BRUMBAUGH, R.S. *Most Mysterious Manuscript*. 1978. Carbondale, IL. 1st. ils. VG/dj. K3. $30.00

BRUN & WHEAT. *Maps & Charts Published in America Before 1800*. 1985. London. Holland. 2nd. ils. 215p. F/dj. K3. $60.00

BRUNDAGE, Burr. *Empire of the Inca*. (1969). Norman, OK. 2nd. 396p. dj. F3. $20.00

BRUNDAGE, Burr. *Lords of Cuzco*. (1967). Norman, OK. 1st. 458p. dj. F3. $30.00

BRUNDAGE, Frances. *Three Bears*. 1928. Saalfield. 1st. 16p. VG+. M5. $75.00

BRUNDAGE, Frances. *What Happened to Tommy*. (1921). Rochester. STecher Lithographic. 8vo. VG/pict wrp. D1. $65.00

BRUNELLESCHI. *Studies of His Technology & Inventions*. 1970. Cambridge/London. MIT. ils. 152p. VG. K3. $15.00

BRUNNER, Emil. *Christian Doctrine of Creation & Redemption*. 1952. Westminster. 386p. G. B29. $8.00

BRUNNER, Emil. *Christian Doctrine of God: Dogmatics Vol I*. 1950. Westminster. 361p. VG. B29. $8.00

BRUNNER, John. *Dreaming Earth*. 1972. London. Sidgwick Jackson. 1st hc. F/clip. T2. $35.00

BRUNNER, John. *From This Day Forward*. 1972. Doubleday. 1st. NF/dj. M2. $20.00

BRUNNER, John. *Long Result*. 1965. Faber. 1st. VG/VG. P3. $30.00

BRUNNER, John. *Maze of Stars*. 1991. Del Rey. 1st. F/F. P3. $18.00

BRUNNER, John. *Quicksand*. 1967. Doubleday. 1st. xl. VG/VG. P3. $8.00

BRUNNER, John. *Stone That Never Came Down*. 1973. Doubleday. 1st. F/F. M2. $15.00

BRUNNER, John. *Times Without Number*. 1974. Elmfield. VG/VG. P3. $20.00

BRUNNER, John. *Timescoop*. 1972. London. Sidgwick Jackson. 1st hc. F/clip. T2. $35.00

BRUNNER, John. *Total Eclipse*. 1974. Doubleday. 1st. F/F. M2. $15.00

BRUNNER, John. *Whole Man*. 1964. Walker. 1st. F/F. P3. $20.00

BRUNNER, Robert K. *Shocking Tales*. 1946. Wynn. 1st. VG. M2. $20.00

BRUNNER & SUDDARTH. *Lippincott Manual of Nursing Practice*. 1974. Lippincott. 1st. 1457p. VG. W2. $55.00

BRUNO, Anthony. *Bad Luck*. 1990. Delacorte. 1st. VG/VG. P3. $19.00

BRUNS, Ludwig. *Die Traumatiscen Neurosen. Unfallsneurosen*. 1901. Wien. Alfred Holder. thin 8vo. contemporary bdg. VG. G1. $65.00

BRUNTON, Paul. *Hidden Teaching Beyond Yoga*. 1946. Dutton. revised. 431p. VG/dj. W3. $42.00

BRUNTON, Paul. *Quest of the Overself*. 1953. NY. 304p. F/dj. W3. $40.00

BRUNTON, Paul. *Search in Secret Egypt*. 1953. Dutton. 5th. 287p. VG. W3. $42.00

BRUSH, D.H. *Growing Up in Southern Illinois 1820 to 1861*. 1944. Lakeside Classic. 265p. F. M4. $10.00

BRUST, Stephen. *To Reign in Hell*. 1984. Steeldragon. 1/1000. sgn/#d. F/dj. M2. $25.00

BRUST & LINDHOLM. *Gypsy*. 1992. Tor. 1st. F/F. P3. $19.00

BRUTON, Eric. *Clocks & Watches*. 1968. Feltham, Middlesex. Hamilyn. lg 4to. 138p. VG/dj. K3. $35.00

BRUTON, Eric. *Dictionary of Clocks & Watches*. 1963. Archer. ils. 201p. VG/dj. K3. $22.00

BRUTON, Eric. *Long Case Clock*. 1968. NY. Praeger. 1st Am. dj. xl. K3. $15.00

BRYAN, Ashley. *Ox of the Wonderful Horns & Other African Folktales*. 1971. Atheneum. 1st. sm 4to. F/F. C8. $25.00

BRYAN, C.D.B. *PS Wilkinson*. 1965. Harper Row. 1st. sgn. NF/VG. R14. $60.00

BRYAN, Christopher. *Night of the Wolf*. 1983. Harper Row. 1st. VG/VG. P3. $15.00

BRYAN, John E. *Bulbs*. 1989. Portland. Timber. 2 vol. A10. $120.00

BRYAN, William Alanson. *Natural History of Hawaii. Being Account of Hawaiian People*. 1915. Honolulu. Hawaiian Gazette. 1st. 117 pl. 596p. cloth. P4. $200.00

BRYAN & BRYAN. *Johnny Penguin*. 1931. Doubleday Doran. 1st stated. ils. F/VG. B15. $55.00

BRYAN & CASTLE. *Edible Ornamental Garden*. 1974. SF. ils/plans. 192p. sc. B26. $12.50

BRYANT, Anita. *Bless This Food: The Anita Bryant Family Cookbook*. 1975. Doubleday. 1st. dj. A16. $15.00

BRYANT, Edward. *Among the Dead*. 1973. Macmillan. 1st. F/dj. M2. $27.00

BRYANT, John. *Convalescence, Historical & Practical*. 1927. NY. ils. 269p. A13. $125.00

BRYANT, Marguerite. *Heights*. 1924. Duffield. F. P3. $8.00

BRYANT, Sara Cone. *Epaminodas & His Auntie*. 1938 (1907). ils Inez Hogan. F/NF. C8. $150.00

BRYANT, William Cullen. *New Library of Poetry & Song*. 1883. NY. 2 vol. Memorial ed. 1st. 4to. ils/engravings. aeg. VG. H3. $100.00

BRYANT, William Cullen. *Odyssey of Homer*. 1873. Boston. 2 vol. 12mo. half brn leather/marbled brd. VG. H3. $75.00

BRYCE, David. *My Tiny Alphabet book*. 1896. Glasgow. David Bryce. 29x21mm. 52 mc pl. limp red leather. F. B24. $485.00

BRYDEN, H. Anderson. *Gun & Camera in South Africa*. 1988. Wolf. 535p+33p photos & map. leatherette. F. A17. $20.00

BRYSON, W.H. *Equity Side of Exchequer, Its Jurisdiction, Administration*. 1975. Cambridge. dj. M11. $75.00

BUBER, Martin. *Tales of Rabbi Nachman*. 1956. Horizon. 214p. VG/G. S3. $23.00

BUCHAN, James. *Golden Plough*. 1995. FSG. 1st Am. F/F. B4. $45.00

BUCHAN, John. *Far Islands*. 1984. Donald Grant. 1st. F/dj. M2. $17.00

BUCHAN, John. *John Buchan by His Wife & Friends*. 1947. Hodder Stoughton. 1st. VG/G. P3. $30.00

BUCHAN, John. *Memory Hold the Door*. 1940. Musson. 1st. VG. P3. $30.00

BUCHAN, John. *Sick Heart River*. 1941. Musson. 1st. VG. P3. $20.00

BUCHANAN, A. Russell. *David S Terry of California*. 1956. San Marino, CA. Huntington Lib. 1st. NF/G. O4. $15.00

BUCHANAN, Edna. *Nobody Lives Forever*. 1990. Random. 1st. inscr. F/F. B3. $50.00

BUCHANAN, Edna. *Nobody Lives Forever*. 1990. Random. 1st. VG/VG. P3. $18.00

BUCHANAN, Hayle. *Living Color*. 1979 (1974). Bryce Canyon, UT. 2nd. ils/125 mc photos. 65p. wrp. B26. $14.00

BUCHANAN, Joseph R. *Outline of Lectures on Neurological System of Anthropology*. 1854. Cincinnati. 1st. 8vo. 384p. cloth. M1. $250.00

BUCHANAN, Marie. *Dark Backward*. 1975. Hart Davis/MacGibbon. 1st. VG/VG. P3. $20.00

BUCHANAN, Marie. *Morgana*. 1977. Doubleday. 1st. VG/VG. P3. $15.00

BUCHANAN & ROBISON. *Fishes of Arkansas*. 1992. Fayetteville. 536p. F. S15. $30.00

BUCHER, Elmer E. *Practical Wireless Telegraphy*. 1918 (1917). NY. Wireless Pr. revised. 8vo. 336p. G. K5. $45.00

BUCHNER, Alexander. *Mechanical Musical Instruments*. nd. London. Batchworth. 174p of pl. VG/dj. K3. $90.00

BUCHNER, Georg. *Plays*. 1927. London. 1st. trans G Dunlop. VG. T9. $18.00

BUCK, Margaret Waring. *Where They Go in Winter*. 1968. ils. VG/VG. M17. $17.50

BUCK, Pearl S. *All Men Are Brothers*. 1957. Grove. corrected/amended ed. 2 vol. 1279p. F/NF/box. W3. $65.00

BUCK, Pearl S. *All Under Heaven*. 1973. John Day. 1/1000 special bdg. facsimile sgn. VG/dj. W3. $42.00

BUCK, Pearl S. *Bridge for Passing*. 1962. NY. John Day. 1st. sgn. NF/NF. T11. $100.00

BUCK, Pearl S. *East Wind, West Wind*. 1944. Cleveland/NY. World. 277p. dj. W3. $20.00

BUCK, Pearl S. *Letter From Peking*. 1957. John Day. 1st. NF/VG. M19. $25.00

BUCK, Pearl S. *Patriot*. 1939. NY. 1st. 372p. VG/dj. W3. $36.00

BUCK, Pearl S. *People of Japan*. 1966. S&S. 1st prt. 255p. VG/dj. W3. $36.00

BUCK, William J. *History of the Indian Walk...* 1886. Phil. 1st. 1/210. xl. B18. $125.00

BUCKE, R.M. *Cosmic Consciousness: A Study in Evolution...* 1901. Phil. Innes. 1st. 1/500. sgn. gray cloth/spine label. uncut. M24. $1,000.00

BUCKERIDGE, Anthony. *Stories for Boys*. 1957. Faber. 1st. VG/VG. P3. $25.00

BUCKINGHAM, Bruce. *Boiled Alive*. 1957. Michael Joseph. 1st. VG/VG. P3. $30.00

BUCKINGHAM, Nash. *Blood Lines: Tales of Shooting & Fishing*. (1947). Putnam. 1st trade. 192p. VG. H7. $35.00

BUCKINGHAM, Nash. *De Shootinest Gent'man*. 1941. NY. 1st trade. 24p. F/clip. A17. $75.00

BUCKINGHAM, Nash. *De Shootinest Gent'man*. 1992. Derrydale. 1/2500. gilt leather. F. A17. $25.00

BUCKINGHAM, Nash. *Ole Miss*. (1946). Putnam. 1st trade. 178p. VG/damaged. H7. $45.00

BUCKLAND & MCNAIR. *Roman Law & Common Law, a Comparison in Outline*. 1936. Cambridge. maroon cloth. M11. $125.00

BUCKLEY, Arabella B. *Fairy-Land of Science*. ca 1900. NY. AL Burt. 1st thus. ils. 298p. VG. A25. $20.00

BUCKLEY, Cornelius M. *Nicolas Point...Life & Northwest Indian Chronicles.* 1989. Loyola. 520p. F/dj. A17. $22.50

BUCKLEY, William F. *Mongoose, RIP.* 1987. Random. 1st. F/F. P3. $20.00

BUCKLEY, William F. *Saving the Queen.* 1976. Doubleday. 1st. VG/VG. P3. $13.00

BUCKLEY, William F. *See You Later Alligator.* 1985. NY. Doubleday. 1st. inscr. NF/dj. Q1. $50.00

BUCKLEY, William F. *Stained Glass.* 1978. Doubleday. 1st. F/dj. T10. $45.00

BUCKLEY, William F. *Story of Henri Tod.* 1984. Franklin Lib. 1st. sgn. full leather. B4/Q1. $50.00

BUCKLEY, William F. *Up From Liberalism.* 1968. Arlington. VG/G. P3. $20.00

BUCKLEY, William F. *Who's on First.* 1980. Doubleday. 1st. VG/VG. P3. $20.00

BUCKMASTER, Henrietta. *Women Who Shaped History.* 1966. Collier. 1st thus. 152p. VG/VG. V3. $10.00

BUCOVICH, Mario. *Manhattan Magic.* 1937. photos. sc/sbdg. VG. M17. $50.00

BUDAY, G. *History of the Christmas Card.* 1965. London. ils. 304p. VG. M4. $30.00

BUDD, George. *On the Organic Diseases & Functional Disorders of Stomach.* 1856. NY. 1st Am. 283p. A13. $150.00

BUDGE, E.A. Wallis. *Hittite Texts in Cuneiform Character From Tablets...* 1920. London. Oxford. folio. 50 pl. VG. W1. $65.00

BUDRYS, Algis. *Iron Thorn.* 1969. British SF BC. VG/VG. P3. $12.00

BUECHER, Thomas S. *Norman Rockwell: Artist & Illustrator.* 1970. Abrams. 328p. cloth. VG+/dj. M20. $125.00

BUECHNER, Frederick. *Entrance to Porlock.* 1970. Atheneum. ARC. F/NF. R13. $45.00

BUECHNER, Frederick. *Long Day's Dying.* 1950. Knopf. 1st. author's 1st book. F/NF. R13. $125.00

BUECHNER, Frederick. *Open Heart.* 1972. Atheneum. ARC. RS. F/dj. R13. $40.00

BUECHNER, Frederick. *Return of Ansel Gibbs.* 1958. Knopf. 1st. sgn/dtd 1994. NF/VG. R14. $45.00

BUECHNER, Frederick. *Season's Difference.* 1952. Knopf. ARC. F/dj. R13. $85.00

BUECHNER, Helmut. *Bighorn Sheep in the United States.* 1960. Wildlife Monographs 4. 1974. VG. S15. $15.00

BUEDELER, Werner. *Geschichte der Raumfahrt.* 1979. Kunzelsau. Sigloch. German text. 4to. 498p. VG. K5. $150.00

BUEL, J.W. *Story of Man: History of the Human Race.* 1889. ils. VG. M17. $35.00

BUELL, John. *Playground.* 1976. FSG. 1st. VG/VG. P3. $20.00

BUELL, John. *Shrewsdale Exit.* 1972. FSG. 1st. VG/VG. P3. $23.00

BUFF, Mary Marsh. *Dancing Cloud.* 1945. Viking. 3rd prt. ils Conrad Buff. VG/tattered. D1. $32.00

BUFF & BUFF. *Colorado: River of Mystery.* 1968. Ward Ritchie. 1st. 86p. F/NF. B19. $45.00

BUFF & BUFF. *Magic Maize.* 1953. Houghton Mifflin. 1st. inscr/sgn twice by Mary & once Conrad. NF/G+. P2. $85.00

BUFFETT, Jimmy. *Tales From Margaritaville.* 1989. Harcourt Brace. 1st. F/F. B35. $22.00

BUHLER, W.K. *Gauss: A Biographical Study.* 1987 (1981). Berlin. Springer. corrected 2nd. 8vo. 208p. F. K5. $45.00

BUIE, Louis. *Practical Proctology.* 1938. Phil. 1st. 512p. A13. $50.00

BUIST, Robert. *American Flower Garden Directory.* 1845. Phil. Carey Hart. 3rd. 345p. VG. A10. $85.00

BUIST, Robert. *Family Kitchen Gardener.* 1867 (1847). ils. VG. E6. $50.00

BUKOWSKI, Charles. *Art, by Charles Bukowski.* 1977. Santa Barbara. Blk Sparrow. 1st. 1/50. 68x51mm. gr silk/label. F. B24. $250.00

BUKOWSKI, Charles. *War All the Time.* 1984. Santa Barbara. Blk Sparrow. 1st trade. 1/500. 8vo. F/acetate dj. T10. $100.00

BULEY, R.C. *Old Northwest. Pioneer Period 1815-1940.* 1964. IU. 2 vol. ils/maps. F/case. M4. $45.00

BULEY & PICKARD. *Midwest Pioneer: His Ills, Cures & Doctors.* 1946. ils. VG. M17. $20.00

BULFINCH, Thomas. *Age of Fables; or, Stories of Gods & Heroes.* 1958. LEC. 1st thus. 1/1500. ils/sgn Joe Mugnaini. F/glassine/case. Q1. $100.00

BULFINCH, Thomas. *Bulfinch's Mythology.* 1991. Harper Collins. P3. $23.00

BULGAKOV, Mikhail. *Master & Margarita.* 1967. Harper Row. 1st. VG/VG. P3. $30.00

BULKLEY, R.J. *At Close Quarters.* 1962. DC. ils/maps. 573p. VG. S16. $35.00

BULL, Peter. *Bear With Me, the Teddy Bear: A Symposium.* 1969. London. Hutchinson. 1st. 8vo. 200p. VG/dj. T5. $55.00

BULL & LEE. *Faces of Hollywood.* 1968. AS Barnes. photos. 256p. VG/dj. M20. $15.00

BULLA, Clyde R. *Viking Adventure.* 1963. ils. VG/VG. M17. $15.00

BULLARD, F.M. *Volcanoes: In History, in Theory, in Eruption.* 1973. Austin, TX. 6nd. 441p. F/dj. D8. $45.00

BULLEN, K.E. *Introduction to Theory of Seismology.* 1965. Cambridge. 3rd. cloth. F/torn. D8. $22.00

BULLER, Francis. *Introduction to the Law, Relative to Trials of Nisi Prius.* 1775. London. Strahn Woodfall. 2nd. contemporary calf. M11. $250.00

BULLFINCH, Thomas. *Legends of Charlemagne.* 1924. Cosmopolitan. 1st thus. ils NC Wyeth. teg. maroon cloth/mc pl. VG+. M5. $175.00

BULLIET, C.J. *Apples & Madonnas.* 1933. Covici Friede. dj. A19. $35.00

BULLOCK, H. *Williamsburg Art of Cookery.* ca 1938 (1742). rpt. VG. E6. $15.00

BULLOCK, Wynn. *Wynn Bullock.* 1971. SF. Scrimshaw. ils. 142p. cloth. acetate dj. D11. $200.00

BULLY, PRATT & SMITH. *Yours in Struggle: 3 Feminist Perspectives...* 1984. Brooklyn. Long Haul. 1st. 233p. sc. VG+. A25. $15.00

BULWER-LYTTON, Edward. *Athens: Its Rise & Fall.* 1843. Tauchnitz. G. P3. $40.00

BULWER-LYTTON, Edward. *Coming Race.* 1873. Hinton. VG. M2. $30.00

BULWER-LYTTON, Edward. *New Timon.* 1847. Carey Hart. 2nd Am. spine missing o/w VG. M2. $100.00

BUNN, Thomas. *Closing Costs.* 1990. Holt. 1st. F/F. P3. $10.00

BUNNELL, Peter C. *Harry Callahan.* 1978. NY. Internat Exhibitions Comm Am Federation of Arts. 80p. D11. $30.00

BUNYAN, John. *Complete Works...* 1881. Brantford, Ontario. Bradley Garretson. Ils Ed. 1015p. aeg. blk morocco. T10. $150.00

BUNYAN, John. *Pilgrim's Progress.* ca 1910. Dutton. 8 mc pl by Byam Shaw. gilt cloth/mc pl. VG. M5. $65.00

BUNYAN, Paul. *Wonderful Adventures of...* 1945. LEC. 1/1500. ils/sgn EG Jackson. 8vo. quarter leather. F/case. T10. $60.00

BOOL, S.W. *Soil Genesis & Classification.* 1973. Ames, IA. 360p. VG. A10. $20.00

BUPP, Walter; see Garrett, Randall.

BURBANK, Luther. *Luther Burbank: His Methods & Discoveries...* 1914-15. NY. Luther Burbank. 12 vol. 8vo. VG. A22. $250.00

BURBANK & HALL. *Harvest of the Years.* 1927. Houghton Mifflin. ils. 296p. gilt cloth. VG+. M12. $20.00

BURBIDGE & GRAY. *Flora of the Australian Capital Territtory.* 1960. Canberra. 409 line drawings. 447p. VG/dj. B26. $59.00

BURCHARD, Peter. *River Queen.* 1957. Macmillan. 1st. 4op. VG+/G+. C14. $14.00

BURCK, Jacob. *Hunger & Revolt: Cartoons by Burck.* nd. Daily Worker. 2nd. VG. V4. $75.00

BURCKHARDT, Jacob. *Civilization of the Renaissance in Italy.* 1944. London. Phaidon. 1st thus. ils. 12mo. 462p. F/dj. H1. $20.00

BURDEKIN, Kay. *Burning Ring.* 1929. Morrow. 1st Am. VG. M2. $30.00

BURDETTE, Robert Jones. *Drums of the 47th.* 1914. Bobbs Merrill. 1st. 212p. cloth. NF. M8. $125.00

BURES, Jan. *Brain & Behavior: Paradigms for Research Neural Mechanisms.* 1988. Chichester. John Wiley. 304p. red cloth. VG/dj. G1. $50.00

BURFORD, E.J. *In the Clink.* 1977. London. NEL. VG/dj. M11. $65.00

BURGESS, Alan. *Small Woman.* 1957. Dutton. 1st. photos/2 maps. 256p. VG/dj. W3. $32.00

BURGESS, Anthony. *Any Old Iron.* 1989. Random. 1st. F/F. B35/P3. $20.00

BURGESS, Anthony. *Coaching Days of England.* 1966. London. full-p mc pl. VG+/dj. B18. $75.00

BURGESS, Anthony. *Devil's Mode.* 1989. Hutchinson. 1st. NF/NF. P3. $25.00

BURGESS, Anthony. *Devil's Mode.* 1989. Random. 1st. F/F. B35. $30.00

BURGESS, Anthony. *Earthly Powers.* 1980. S&S. 1st. F/F. B35. $25.00

BURGESS, Anthony. *Enderby's Dark Lady.* 1984. McGraw Hill. 1st. NF/NF. P3. $15.00

BURGESS, Anthony. *Kingdom of the Wicked.* 1985. Arbor. 1st. NF/NF. W2. $30.00

BURGESS, Anthony. *Kingdom of the Wicked.* 1985. Franklin Lib. ltd. sgn. leather. F. B35. $55.00

BURGESS, Anthony. *Little Wilson & Big God.* 1986. Weidenfeld Nicolson. 1st. VG. P3. $25.00

BURGESS, Anthony. *Long Trip to Teatime.* 1976. Dempsey Squires. F/F. P3. $15.00

BURGESS, Anthony. *Pianoplayers.* 1986. Arbor. 1st. F/F. B35. $18.00

BURGESS, Anthony. *Pianoplayers.* 1986. Hutchinson. 1st. F/F. P3. $18.00

BURGESS, Anthony. *1985* 1978. Little Brn. 1st. VG/dj. M2/P3. $18.00

BURGESS, Gelett. *Goop Encyclopedia: Containing Every Child Fault.* 1916. ils. VG. M17. $50.00

BURGESS, Gelett. *Heart Line: Drama of San Francisco.* 1907. Bobbs Merrill. 1st. 584p. cloth/pict label. D11. $50.00

BURGESS, Gelett. *Purple Cow & Other Poems.* 1968. Pasadena. Castle. facsimile. 4to. 14p. NF. C14. $10.00

BURGESS, Glenn. *Mt Graham Profiles: Graham County, Arizona 1870-1977.* 1977. Graham Co Hist Soc. 1st. ils. 416p. VG+/sans. B19. $120.00

BURGESS, J. *Rock-Temples of Elephanta or Gharapuri.* 1871. Bombay. DH Skykes. pres. ils/plans. 4to. 80p. K3. $75.00

BURGESS, Thornton W. *Adventures of Chatterer the Red Squirrel.* nd. McClelland Stewart. VG. P3. $10.00

BURGESS, Thornton W. *Adventures of Chatterer the Red Squirrel.* 1934. Little Brn. ils Harrison Cady. sm 8vo. stp gray cloth. F/dj. M5. $40.00

BURGESS, Thornton W. *Adventures of Peter Cottontail.* 1958. London. MacDonald. ils Phoebe Erickson. 4to. dj. R5. $85.00

BURGESS, Thornton W. *Adventures of Reddy Fox.* 1946. Little Brn. inscr. ils Harrison Cady. VG/VG. D1. $185.00

BURGESS, Thornton W. *At the Smiling Pool.* 1945. Little Brn. stated 1st. ils Harrison Cady. VG/dj. M5. $65.00

BURGESS, Thornton W. *Aunt Sally's Friends in Fur.* 1955. Little Brn. stated 1st. F/dj. M5. $65.00

BURGESS, Thornton W. *Bowser the Hound.* 1920. Little Brn. 1st. ils Harrison Cady. decor gr cloth. M5. $90.00

BURGESS, Thornton W. *Boy Scouts of Woodcraft Camp.* 1914 (1912). Penn. ils CS Corson. G. M5. $42.00

BURGESS, Thornton W. *Burgess Flower Book for Children.* 1923. 1st. ils. decor brd. VG. M17. $40.00

BURGESS, Thornton W. *Lightfoot the Deer.* 1923. Little Brn. Green Forest series. VG. M5. $75.00

BURGESS, Thornton W. *Little Red's Adventure.* 1942. McLoughlin. Little Color Classics. 12mo. VG. M5. $40.00

BURGESS, Thornton W. *Littlest Christmas Tree.* 1954. Wonder. ils Mary/Carl Hauge. VG. M5. $20.00

BURGESS, Thornton W. *Mother West Wind When Stories.* 1937. Little Brn. ils Harrison Cady. tan cloth. VG. M5. $45.00

BURGESS, Thornton W. *Mrs Peter Rabbit.* 1920. Little Brn. Green Meadow series. ils Harrison Cady. 8vo. VG. M5. $75.00

BURGESS, Thornton W. *Old Granny Fox.* 1920. Little Brn. Green Meadow series. ils Harrison Cady. VG+. M5. $125.00

BURGESS, Thornton W. *Old Mother West Wind Why Stories.* (1915). Grosset Dunlap. rpt. 12mo. NF/VG+. C8. $40.00

BURGESS, Thornton W. *Tales From the Story Teller's House.* 1937. Little Brn. ils Lemuel Palmer. 195p. beige cloth. VG. D1. $65.00

BURGESS, Thornton W. *While the Story-Log Burns.* 1938. Little Brn. stated 1st. ils Lemuel Palmer. lg 8vo. VG+. M5. $75.00

BURKE, Edmund. *Conciliation With the Colonies & Other Papers...* 1975. Stinehour/ LEC. 1/2000. ils Lynd Ward/26 ful-p pl. gilt bdg. F/case. H13. $195.00

BURKE, James Lee. *Black Cherry Blues.* 1989. Little Brn. 1st. F/dj. M15. $85.00

BURKE, James Lee. *Black Cherry Blues.* 1989. Little Brn. 1st. rem mk. F/F. B2. $75.00

BURKE, James Lee. *Black Cherry Blues.* 1989. Little Brn. 1st. sgn. F/F. D10. $110.00

BURKE, James Lee. *Burning Angel.* 1995. Hyperion. 1st. F/F. P3. $25.00

BURKE, James Lee. *Burning Angel.* 1995. Hyperion. 1st. sgn. F/F. A23. $42.00

BURKE, James Lee. *Cadillac Jukebox.* 1996. Hyperion. 1st. sgn. F/F. Q1. $40.00

BURKE, James Lee. *Dixie City Jam.* 1994. Hyperion. special ed. sgn/#d. F/case. P3. $100.00

BURKE, James Lee. *Dixie City Jam.* 1994. Hyperion. 1st. sgn. F/F. D10. $40.00

BURKE, James Lee. *Half of Paradise.* 1965. Houghton Mifflin. 1st. author's 1st book. F/NF. P3. $1,250.00

BURKE, James Lee. *Heaven's Prisoners.* 1988. NY. Holt. 1st. F/dj. M15/M25. $100.00

BURKE, James Lee. *Heaven's Prisoners.* 1988. NY. Holt. 1st. sgn. F/F. D10. $140.00

BURKE, James Lee. *In the Electric Mist With Confederate Dead.* 1993. Hyperion. 1st. sgn. F/F. A23. $50.00

BURKE, James Lee. *Lost Get-Back Boogie.* 1986. LSU. UP. F/wrp. B4. $1,250.00

BURKE, James Lee. *Lost Get-Back Boogie.* 1986. LSU. 1st. sgn. F/F clip. B4. $600.00

BURKE, James Lee. *Morning for Flamingos.* 1990. Little Brn. 1st. sgn. F/F. T2. $100.00

BURKE, James Lee. *Neon Rain.* 1986. Holt. 1st. F/F. M23. $150.00

BURKE, James Lee. *Neon Rain.* 1989. London. Century/Mysterious. 1st. F/F. T2. $50.00

BURKE, James Lee. *Stained White Radiance.* 1992. Hyperion. 1st. sgn. F/F. A23/R13. $60.00

BURKE, James Lee. *Texas City, 1947.* 1992. Lord John. 1/275. sgn. F/sans. B3. $125.00

BURKE, Jan. *Goodnight, Irene.* 1993. S&S. 1st. F/F. B2. $35.00

BURKE, Jan. *Goodnight, Irene.* 1993. S&S. 1st. sgn. author's 1st book. F/F. A23. $42.00

BURKE, John. *Roman England.* 1984. photos. VG/VG. M17. $22.50

BURKE, Jonathan. *Pursuit Through Time.* 1956. Ward Lock. 1st. VG/VG. P3. $30.00

BURKE, Thomas. *Bloomsbury Wonder.* 1929. London. Mandrake. 1st. F/NF. M15. $100.00

BURKE, Thomas. *East of Mansion House.* 1926. Doran. 1st. F/NF. M2. $50.00

BURKETT, Larry. *Coming Economic Earthquake.* 1991. Moody. 230p. F/dj. B29. $8.00

BURKHARDT, V. *Chinese Creeds & Customs.* 1959 & 1972. Hong Kong. 3 vol. ils. F/dj. W3. $92.00

BURKS, Arthur J. *Black Medicine.* 1966. Arkham. 1st. F/dj. M2. $60.00

BURLAND, Cottie. *Aztecs.* (1980). Galahad. 1st this. 4to. 128p. dj. F3. $15.00

BURLAND, Cottie. *Eskimo Art.* 1973. London. Hamlyn. 100 ils. 96p. map ep. VG/VG. P4. $65.00

BURLEY, Andrew S. *Uncle Sam's Army Boys.* 1919. Donohue. A19. $10.00

BURLEY, W.J. *Charles & Elizabeth.* 1981. Walker. 1st. NF/NF. P3. $13.00

BURLINGAME, John K. *History of Fifth Regiment of Rhode Island Heavy Artillery...* 1892. Providence. Snow Farnham. 1st. ils/maps. 382p. cloth. VG. M8. $225.00

BURLINGAME, Roger. *Of Making Many Books.* 1946. Scribner. 1st. 8vo. 347p. gilt beige cloth. NF. T10. $35.00

BURMAN, Ben Lucien. *Steamboat Round the Bend.* 1933. Farrar Rhinehart. 1st. F/VG+ clip. B4. $150.00

BURMEISTER, Eugene. *Golden Empire: Kern County, California.* 1977. Beverly Hills. Autograph Pr. photos. 168p. D11. $25.00

BURNABY, Nigel. *Secret of Matchams.* 1934. Ward Lock. 1st. xl. VG. P3. $20.00

BURNE-JONES, Edward. *Letters to Katie.* 1988. London. 1st. intro J Christian. VG/dj. T9. $12.00

BURNET, James. *Antient Metaphysics.* 1779-1799. Edinburgh. 6 vol in 3. modern buckram. C6. $450.00

BURNETT, Frances Hodgson. *Editha's Burglar.* 1888. Jordan March. 1st. NF. M19. $35.00

BURNETT, Frances Hodgson. *In the Closed Room.* 1904. McClure Phillips. 1st. ils JW Smith. TEG. VG. B15. $155.00

BURNETT, Frances Hodgson. *Land of the Blue Flower.* 1913. Moffat Yard. G+. M2. $20.00

BURNETT, Frances Hodgson. *Little Lord Fauntleroy.* 1886. Scribner. 1st/1st state (DeVinne imp). missing ep o/w VG. M19. $75.00

BURNETT, Frances Hodgson. *Little Lord Fauntleroy.* 1887 (1886). Scribner. ils RB Birch. G+. B15. $80.00

BURNETT, Frances Hodgson. *Little Princess.* 1914 (1905). Scribner. ils Ethel Franklin Betts. teg. VG+. B15. $150.00

BURNETT, Frances Hodgson. *Little Princess.* 1963. Lippincott. ils Tasha Tudor. VG. B15. $50.00

BURNETT, Frances Hodgson. *Little Princess.* 1963. Lippincott. 1st thus. ils Tasha Tudor. 240p. VG/G+. P2. $65.00

BURNETT, Frances Hodgson. *Little Saint Elizabeth & Other Stories.* ca 1889-90. London. Warne. 1st (preceding Am). pict red S cloth. M24. $150.00

BURNETT, Frances Hodgson. *Louisiana/Pretty Sister of Jose.* 1914. Scribner. VG. P3. $15.00

BURNETT, Frances Hodgson. *Secret Garden.* 1911. Stokes. 1st. teg. G. M5. $95.00

BURNETT, Frances Hodgson. *Two Little Pilgrims' Progress.* 1895. Scribner. 1st. ils Reginald Birch. 191p. aqua cloth. VG. D1. $50.00

BURNETT, Hallie. *Brain Pickers.* 1957. Messner. 1st. VG+/VG. B4. $85.00

BURNETT, I. Compton. *Pastors & Masters: A Study.* 1925. London. Heath Cranton. 1st. NF/dj. Q1. $300.00

BURNETT, Jim. *High Lonesome: Tales of Bisbee & Southern Arizona.* 1990. private prt. 1st. ils. 278p. F/F. B19. $30.00

BURNETT, Virgil. *Towers at the Edge of a World.* 1980. St Martin. 1st. F/F. P3. $15.00

BURNETT, W.R. *Goodhues of Sinking Creek.* 1934. Harper. 1st. ils JJ Lankes. F/dj. Q1. $150.00

BURNETT, W.R. *Iron Man.* 1930. Lincoln Mac Veagh/Dial. NF/G. M22. $30.00

BURNETT, W.R. *It's Always Four O'Clock.* 1956. Random. 1st. NF/dj. M25. $25.00

BURNETT, W.R. *Little Caesar.* 1929. Dial. VG. M22. $45.00

BURNETT, W.R. *Mi Amigo.* 1959. Knopf. 1st. NF/VG clip. B4. $125.00

BURNETT, W.R. *Pale Moon.* 1956. Knopf. 1st. F/VG+. B4. $150.00

BURNETT, W.R. *Quick Brown Fox.* 1942. Knopf. 1st. F/VG+. B4. $250.00

BURNETT, W.R. *Roar of the Crowd.* 1964. Clarkson Potter. 1st. VG. P3. $20.00

BURNETT, W.R. *Romelle.* 1946. Knopf. 1st. VG+/dj. M25. $25.00

BURNETT, W.R. *Saint Johnson.* 1930. NY. Dial. 1st. NF/dj. Q1. $200.00

BURNETT, W.R. *Underdog.* 1957. Knopf. 1st. VG/VG. P3. $30.00

BURNEY, Charles. *Account of the Musical Performances in Westminster...* 1785. London. Payne Robinson. lg 4to. 8 full-p pl. quarter calf. R12. $450.00

BURNEY, Charles. *Memoirs of Life & Writings of Abate Metastasio...* 1796. London. Robinson. 3 vol. 1st. gilt red morocco. xl. H13. $295.00

BURNEY, Frances. *Evelina; or, History of a Young Lady's Entrance Into World.* 1779. London. Lowndes. 3 vol. 8vo. orig tree calf/rebacked raised bands. H13. $495.00

BURNEY, Joseph John. *Familiar Letters to Henry Clay of Kentucky...* 1840. NY. Mahlon Day. gilt bdg. xl. VG. O7. $75.00

BURNFORD, Sheila. *Incredible Journey: Tale of 3 Animals.* 1961. Atlantic Monthly. stated 1st. 8vo. F/VG. M5. $125.00

BURNHAM, S.W. *Report to Trustees of James Lick Trust...* 1880. Chicago. Knight Leonard. xl. K5. $100.00

BURNHAM & RAY. *Children of the Stones.* 1977. Scribner. 1st Am. F/dj. M2. $15.00

BURNNER, Lousene Rousseau. *Casserole Magic.* 1953. Harper. 1st. 180p. ils Stephen Voorhies. sbdg. B10. $12.00

BURNS, B. Delisle. *Uncertain Nervous System.* 1968. London. Arnold. ils. 194p. bl cloth. VG/dj. G1. $30.00

BURNS, John H. *Memoirs of a Cow Pony, As Told by Himself.* 1906. Eastern Pub. 1st. sgn Adams Herd. 178p. VG. J2. $1,975.00

BURNS, John. *Burns's Obstetrical Works...* 1809. NY. 3 vol in 1. contemporary sheep. B14. $275.00

BURNS, Margery. *Nottingham System of Contact Bridge.* 1969. London. 3rd. VG. S1. $10.00

BURNS, Robert. *Hand in Hand We'll Go, Ten Poems.* 1965. Crowell. 1st. 31p. cloth. F/F. D4. $30.00

BURNS, Robert. *Poems Chiefly in the Scottish Dialect.* ca 1900. Glasgow. Bryce. 30x22mm. reduced facsimile. 240p. aeg. limp maroon leather. B24. $125.00

BURNS, Robert. *Poems Chiefly in the Scottish Dialect.* nd. Glasgow. Robert Gibson. facsimile 1st 1786 Kilmarnock. tall 8vo. double box. H13. $165.00

BURNS, Tex; see L'Amour, Louis.

BURNS, Walter Noble. *Year With a Whaler.* 1913. NY. Outing. 1st. ils. 250p. T7. $65.00

BURNSHAW, Stanley. *Caged in an Animal's Mind.* 1963. HRW. 1st. inscr. F/NF. B4. $125.00

BURR, Anna R. *West of the Moon.* 1926. Duffield. 1st. VG/dj. M2. $25.00

BURR, Fearing. *Field & Garden Vegetables of America.* 1865. Boston. Tilton. 667p. cloth. A10. $85.00

BURR, Fearing. *Field & Garden Vegetables of America.* 1994. Chillicothe, IL. Am Botanist. 664p. M. A10. $35.00

BURR, G.L. *Narratives of the Witchcraft Cases 1648-1706.* 1914. VG. M17. $50.00

BURR, Harold Saxton. *Neural Basis of Behavior.* 1960. Springfield. 262p. gr cloth. VG/dj. G1. $28.50

BURRAGE, Albert C. *Catalogue of Library of Albert C Burrage, Esq...* 1930. Manchester, MA. 97p. xl. B26. $75.00

BURRELL, Maurice. *Wide of the Truth: Mormons, What They Believe.* 1972. Marshall Morgan Scott. 148p. xl. VG/dj. B29. $6.50

BURRELL & STRAND. *Second Colloquium in Biological Sciences.* 1986. NY Academy of Sciences. 422p. F. S15. $20.00

BURRIS, Marcus L. *Chips & Whetstones.* 1913. NY. Every Where Pub. sgn. gr cloth. G. B11. $18.00

BURRIS-MYER & COLE. *Theatres & Auditoriums.* 1949. Reinhold. photos/plans/diagrams. NF. C9. $125.00

BURROUGHS, Alan. *Art Criticism From a Laboratory.* 1936. Little Brn. 1st. ils. 277p. VG/dj. K3. $30.00

BURROUGHS, Edgar Rice. *Apache Devil.* nd. Grosset Dunlap. NF. P3. $30.00

BURROUGHS, Edgar Rice. *Beasts of Tarzan.* 1917. AL Burt. VG. P3. $35.00

BURROUGHS, Edgar Rice. *Carson of Venus.* 1939. ERB. 1st. F/NF. M2. $350.00

BURROUGHS, Edgar Rice. *Cave Girl.* 1926. Grosset Dunlap. VG. P3. $35.00

BURROUGHS, Edgar Rice. *Cave Girl.* 1962. Canaveral. NF/dj. M2. $25.00

BURROUGHS, Edgar Rice. *Chessman of Mars.* 1924. Grosset Dunlap. 3rd. VG. P3. $30.00

BURROUGHS, Edgar Rice. *Chessmen of Mars.* 1922. McClurg. 1st. VG/mc Canon dj. M2. $200.00

BURROUGHS, Edgar Rice. *Escape on Venus.* 1946. ERB. 1st. F/NF. M2. $150.00

BURROUGHS, Edgar Rice. *Escape on Venus.* 1946. ERB. 1st. ils John Coleman Burroughs. VG/dj. P3/S13. $125.00

BURROUGHS, Edgar Rice. *Fighting Man of Mars.* 1932. Grosset Dunlap. 1st. 319p. blk lettered red cloth. VG/dj. H1. $45.00

BURROUGHS, Edgar Rice. *Gods of Mars.* 1962. Canaveral. 1st. VG/VG. P3. $50.00

BURROUGHS, Edgar Rice. *Jungle Tales of Tarzan.* 1919. McClurg. 3rd. VG. P3. $150.00

BURROUGHS, Edgar Rice. *Lad & the Lion.* 1964. Canaveral. F/dj. M2. $95.00

BURROUGHS, Edgar Rice. *Lad & the Lion.* 1964. Canaveral. VG/VG. P3. $60.00

BURROUGHS, Edgar Rice. *Land That Time Forgot.* 1924. McClurg. 1st. VG/mc Canon dj. M2. $100.00

BURROUGHS, Edgar Rice. *Land That Time Forgot.* 1962. Canaveral. VG/VG. P3. $60.00

BURROUGHS, Edgar Rice. *Llana of Gathol.* 1948. ERB. 1st. F/dj. M2. $145.00

BURROUGHS, Edgar Rice. *Llana of Gathol.* 1948. ERB. 1st. G/G. P3. $100.00

BURROUGHS, Edgar Rice. *Lost on Venus.* 1935. ERB. 1st. ils St John. VG. S13. $85.00

BURROUGHS, Edgar Rice. *Mastermind of Mars.* 1929. Grosset Dunlap. 1st. 8vo. 312p. blk lettered red cloth. VG/dj. H1. $65.00

BURROUGHS, Edgar Rice. *Mastermind of Mars.* 1948. ERB. F/NF. M2. $40.00

BURROUGHS, Edgar Rice. *Monster Men.* 1962. Canaveral. VG/VG. P3. $50.00

BURROUGHS, Edgar Rice. *Moon Maid.* 1927. Grosset Dunlap. G. P3. $25.00

BURROUGHS, Edgar Rice. *Moon Men.* 1962. Canaveral. NF/NF. P3. $50.00

BURROUGHS, Edgar Rice. *Mucker.* 1922. Grosset Dunlap. VG. P3. $30.00

BURROUGHS, Edgar Rice. *New Adventures of Tarzan.* 1935. Chicago. Pleasure Books. 3 popups. ils brd. R5. $450.00

BURROUGHS, Edgar Rice. *Oakdale Affair & the Rider.* 1937. Grosset Dunlap. G/mc Canon dj. M2. $85.00

BURROUGHS, Edgar Rice. *Outlaw of Torn.* 1927. McClurg. 1st. F/sm chips at top. M2. $2,000.00

BURROUGHS, Edgar Rice. *Pellucidar.* 1924. Grosset Dunlap. VG/VG. P3. $60.00

BURROUGHS, Edgar Rice. *Pellucidar.* 1924. Methuen. 1st. VG/mc Canon dj. M2. $95.00

BURROUGHS, Edgar Rice. *Princess of Mars.* 1917. McClurg. 1st. ils Frank Schoonover. VG. M22. $300.00

BURROUGHS, Edgar Rice. *Princess of Mars.* 1952. Methuen. 13th. VG. P3. $20.00

BURROUGHS, Edgar Rice. *Return of Tarzan.* 1916. AL Burt. VG. P3. $35.00

BURROUGHS, Edgar Rice. *Science Fiction Classics*. nd. Castle. 3rd. VG/VG. P3. $15.00

BURROUGHS, Edgar Rice. *Son of Tarzan*. 1917. Chicago. McClurg. 1st. VG. T12. $125.00

BURROUGHS, Edgar Rice. *Son of Tarzan*. 1917. McClurg. 1st. VG/mc Canon dj. M2. $185.00

BURROUGHS, Edgar Rice. *Son of Tarzan*. 1918. AL Burt. VG/G. P3. $45.00

BURROUGHS, Edgar Rice. *Tales of Three Planets*. 1964. Canaveral. 1st. F/F. M2. $100.00

BURROUGHS, Edgar Rice. *Tanar of Pellucidar*. 1931. Metropolitan. 1st. VG/mc Canon dj. M2. $150.00

BURROUGHS, Edgar Rice. *Tarzan, Lord of the Jungle*. 1929. Grosset Dunlap. VG. P3. $25.00

BURROUGHS, Edgar Rice. *Tarzan & the Ant Men*. 1924. Grosset Dunlap. F/VG. M2. $95.00

BURROUGHS, Edgar Rice. *Tarzan & the Ant Men*. 1940. Grosset Dunlap. VG. P3. $20.00

BURROUGHS, Edgar Rice. *Tarzan & the City Gold*. 1948. ERB. VG. P3. $35.00

BURROUGHS, Edgar Rice. *Tarzan & the Foreign Legion*. 1948. ERB. 1st. VG/dj. M2. $80.00

BURROUGHS, Edgar Rice. *Tarzan & the Golden Lion*. 1923. McClurg. 1st. VG/mc Canon dj. M2. $75.00

BURROUGHS, Edgar Rice. *Tarzan & the Golden Lion*. 1927. Grosset Dunlap. MTI. VG/VG. P3. $650.00

BURROUGHS, Edgar Rice. *Tarzan & the Jewels of Opar*. 1918. McClurg. 1st. VG/mc Canon dj. M2. $150.00

BURROUGHS, Edgar Rice. *Tarzan & the Jewels of Opar*. 1919. McClurg. 2nd. VG. P3. $90.00

BURROUGHS, Edgar Rice. *Tarzan & the Jewels of Opar*. 1920. Methuen. Cheap ed. VG. P3. $13.00

BURROUGHS, Edgar Rice. *Tarzan & the Leopard Men*. 1935. ERB. 1st. VG/mc Canon dj. M2. $100.00

BURROUGHS, Edgar Rice. *Tarzan & the Lost Empire*. 1931. Grosset Dunlap. VG/fair. P3. $30.00

BURROUGHS, Edgar Rice. *Tarzan & the Lost Safari*. 1966. Whitman. decor brd. G. P3. $10.00

BURROUGHS, Edgar Rice. *Tarzan at the Earth's Core*. (1923). Grosset Dunlap. later prt. 277p. blk lettered red cloth. G/dj. H1. $65.00

BURROUGHS, Edgar Rice. *Tarzan at the Earth's Core*. 1923. Grosset Dunlap. VG. P3. $25.00

BURROUGHS, Edgar Rice. *Tarzan at the Earth's Core*. 1930. Metropolitan. 1st. G+/mc Canon dj. M2. $165.00

BURROUGHS, Edgar Rice. *Tarzan at the Earth's Core*. 1962. Canaveral. NF/NF. P3. $50.00

BURROUGHS, Edgar Rice. *Tarzan of the Apes*. 1915. AL Burt. VG/heavy chip. M2. $75.00

BURROUGHS, Edgar Rice. *Tarzan of the Apes*. 1964. Whitman. decor brd. VG. P3. $15.00

BURROUGHS, Edgar Rice. *Tarzan the Terrible*. 1923. Grosset Dunlap. VG/VG. P3. $75.00

BURROUGHS, Edgar Rice. *Tarzan the Untamed*. 1920. McClurg. 1st. G+/mc Canon dj. M2. $50.00

BURROUGHS, Edgar Rice. *Thuva, Maid of Mars*. 1920. McClurg. 1st. VG. M2. $175.00

BURROUGHS, Edgar Rice. *War Chief*. 1928. Grosset Dunlap. VG. P3. $40.00

BURROUGHS, Edgar Rice. *Warlord of Mars*. 1919. McClurg. VG/mc Canon dj. M2. $250.00

BURROUGHS, Edgar Rice. *Warlord of Mars*. 1919. McClurg. 1st. G. P3. $75.00

BURROUGHS, Edward. *Memorable Works of a Son of Thunder & Consolation...* 1672. 1st. 896p. poor leather. V3. $400.00

BURROUGHS, John Rolfe. *Guardian of the Grasslands, the First Hundred Years...* 1971. Pioneer. 1st. sgn. 430p. map ep. VG/VG. J2. $185.00

BURROUGHS, John. *Camping & Tramping With Roosevelt*. 1907. Houghton Mifflin. 1st. 111p. VG. J2. $75.00

BURROUGHS, Paul H. *Southern Antiques*. 1967 (1931). Bonanza. facsimile. 117 pl. 191p. F/dj. H1. $28.00

BURROUGHS, Polly. *Great Ice Ship Bear: 89 Years in Polar Seas*. 1970. NY. Van Nostrand. 1st. 104p. VG/dj. P4. $45.00

BURROUGHS, William S. *Cities of the Red Night*. 1981. HRW. 1st. sgn. F/F. R14. $90.00

BURROUGHS, William S. *Exterminator!* 1973. Viking. 1st. F/clip. H11. $80.00

BURROUGHS, William S. *Exterminator!* 1973. Viking. 1st. xl. VG/VG. P3. $20.00

BURROUGHS, William S. *Last Words of Dutch Schultz*. 1975. Viking. 1st. F/NF. H11. $75.00

BURROUGHS, William S. *Nova Express*. 1964. Grove. 1st. NF/dj. M2. $50.00

BURROUGHS, William S. *Ticket That Exploded*. 1967. NY. Grove. 1st. sgn/dtd 1995. NF/NF. R14. $150.00

BURROUGHS, William S. *Western Lands*. 1987. 1st. sgn. F/F. M19. $50.00

BURROUGHS, William S. *Western Lands*. 1987. Viking. 1st. inscr/sgn/dtd 1996. F/F. R14. $90.00

BURROUGHS & ODIER. *Job*. 1970. NY. Grove. 1st. F/VG. M19. $65.00

BURROWS, George Man. *On Disorders of Cerebral Circulation...* 1994 (1846). NY. Classics Neurology/Neurosurgery Lib. facsimile. G1. $65.00

BURROWS, Jack. *John Ringo: Gunfighter Who Never Was*. 1987. AZ U. 1st. 242p. F/clip. B19. $20.00

BURROWS, Larry. *Larry Burrows: Compassionate Photographer*. 1972. Time-Life. 156p. cloth. cb case. D11. $150.00

BURROWS, Millar. *More Light on the Dead Sea Scrolls*. 1958. Viking. 1st. 8vo. 434p. VG/dj. W1. $12.00

BURRUS, Ernest J. *Kino & the Cartography of Northwestern New Spain*. 1965. AZ Pioneers Hist Soc. 1/750. ils/notes/bibliography/index. NF. B19. $200.00

BURSEY, Jack. *Antarctic Night*. 1957. NY. Rand McNally. 1st prt. photos/map. 256p. dj. P4. $40.00

BURT, Edward Angus. *North American Species of Clavaria...* 1922. MO Botanical Garden. tall 8vo. wrp. A22. $12.00

BURT, J.C. *Nashville, Its Life & Times*. 1959. Nashville. 1st. ils. 182p. F/dj. M4. $20.00

BURT, Struthers. *Powder River, Let'er Buck*. 1938. Farrar Rinehart. 1st. 398p. VG/dj. J2. $125.00

BURTIS, Thomson. *Air Combat Stories for Boys: Four Aces (#2)*. 1932. Grosset Dunlap. 216p. VG+/dj (lists 7 titles). M20. $25.00

BURTIS, Thomson. *Air Combat Stories for Boys: Wing for Wing (#3)*. 1932. Grosset Dunlap. lists 11 titles. VG/dj. M20. $15.00

BURTIS, Thomson. *Rex Lee: Gypsy Flyer (#1)*. 1928. Grosset Dunlap. lists 3 titles. 248p. ep removed. VG/dj. M20. $25.00

BURTON, Hal. *Walton Boys & Gold in the Snow*. 1958. Whitman. VG. P3. $12.00

BURTON, J. Hill. *Book Hunter.* 1863. NY. Sheldon. 1st. 8vo. 411p. K3. $40.00

BURTON, Jack. *Blue Book of Hollywood Musicals.* 1953. Century House. photos. cloth. NF. C9. $50.00

BURTON, Jean. *Sir Richard Burton's Wife.* 1941. Knopf. 1st. 12 pl. VG/dj. W1. $55.00

BURTON, Richard. *Arabian Nights Entertainments.* 1954. Ipswich. LEC. 1st thus. 4 vol. 1/1500. ils Arthur Szyk. F/glassine/2 cases. Q1. $300.00

BURTON, Richard. *Book of the Thousand Nights & a Night.* 1962. Heritage. LEC. 6 vol in 3. 8vo. ils Valenti Angelo. W1. $65.00

BURTON, Richard. *Christmas Story.* 1964. Morrow. 2nd. VG/VG. P3. $10.00

BURTON, Richard. *City of the Saints & Across the Rocky Mountains to CA...* 1963. Knopf. 1st. 654p. VG/VG. J2. $65.00

BURTON, Richard. *Little Essays in Literature & Life.* 1914. NY. Century. 1st. yel lettered gr cloth. VG. M24. $45.00

BURTON, Richard. *Meeting Mrs Jenkins.* 1966. Morrow. 1st. F/NF. B4. $100.00

BURTON, Richard. *Perfumed Garden of the Shaykh Nefzawi.* 1964. Putnam. 1st Am. 8vo. 271p. VG/dj. W1. $20.00

BURTON, Richard. *Tales From the Arabian Nights.* nd. Avenel. 2nd. VG/VG. P3. $15.00

BURTON, Robert. *Bird Migration.* 1992. Facts on File. ils/photos. 160p. F/dj. S15. $12.00

BURTON, Walter. *Coal Mine Fires.* 1938. Akron. 17 photos & typed title p. w/typed sheet. VG. B18. $75.00

BURWASH, N. *Wesley's Doctrinal Standards Part I.* 1881. BMP. 523p. fair. B29. $8.00

BUSBY, F.M. *Long View.* 1976. Berkley Putnam. 1st. F/dj. M2. $20.00

BUSBY, F.M. *Rissa Kerguelen.* 1976. Berkley. 1st. F/dj. M2. $25.00

BUSCEMA & LEE. *How To Draw Comics the Marvel Way.* 1978. ils. 160p. F. M13. $24.00

BUSCH, Briton Cooper. *Alta California. 1840-1842. Journal & Observations...* 1983. Glendale. Arthur Clark. 8vo. 364p. NF. P4. $50.00

BUSCH, Frederick. *Breathing Trouble & Other Stories.* 1973. London. Calder Boyars. 1st. sgn. F/F. R14. $75.00

BUSCH, Frederick. *Hardwater Country.* 1979. Knopf. 1st. NF/dj. A24. $20.00

BUSCH, Frederick. *I Wanted a Year Without Fall.* 1971. London. Calder Boyars. 1st. author's 1st book. F/clip. L3. $125.00

BUSCH, Frederick. *Too Late American Boyhood Blues.* 1984. Boston. Godine. 1st. F/dj. A24. $20.00

BUSCH, Mortiz. *Bismark in the Franco-German War.* 1879. Chicago. Belfords Clarke. 8vo. gild tan cloth. VG. B14. $45.00

BUSH, Barbara. *A Memoir.* 1994. Scribner. 1st. sgn. F/F. A23. $55.00

BUSH, Barbara. *Barbara Bush: A Biography.* 1992. St Martin. 1st. sgn. F/F. A23. $65.00

BUSH, Barbara. *C Fred's Story.* 1984. Doubleday. 1st. sgn. F/F. A23. $65.00

BUSH, Barbara. *Millie's Book.* 1990. Morrow. 1st. Millie's bookplate/sgn Barbara Bush. F/F. A23. $65.00

BUSH, Christopher. *Case of the Heavenly Twin.* 1964. Macmillan. 1st. VG/VG. P3. $20.00

BUSH, Christopher. *Case of the Triple Twist.* 1958. Macmillan. 1st. F/VG. T12. $20.00

BUSH, Vannevar. *Modern Arms & Free Men.* 1949. S&S. VG/dj. K3. $15.00

BUSH, Vannevar. *Pieces of the Action.* 1970. Morrow. 1st. VG/dj. K3. $15.00

BUSHELL, R. *Netsuke Masks.* 1985. Tokyo/NY. Kodansha. 1st. ils/glossary/index. F/F case. W3. $165.00

BUSHELL, R. *Wonderful World of Netsuke.* 1969. Tuttle. ils. 72p. F/dj. W3. $42.00

BUSHELL, Stephen. *Description of Chinese Pottery & Porcelain.* 1910. Clarendon. 1st. 222p. VG. W3. $125.00

BUSHNELL, David I. *Choctaw of Bayou Lacomb, St Tammany Parish, Louisiana.* 1909. GPO. 8vo. 3-quarter morocco. VG. K7. $50.00

BUSS, Irven O. *Elephant Life. Fifteen Years of High Population Density.* 1990. IA State. 191p. F/F. S15. $20.00

BUSS, Kate. *Studies in the Chinese Drama.* 1922. Boston. Four Seasons. 1/1000. 77p. cloth. W3. $87.00

BUTCHART, Harvey. *Grand Canyon Treks.* 1970. La Siesta. 72p. VG/stiff wrp. F7. $12.50

BUTENKO, R.G. *Plant Cell Culture.* 1985. Moscow. MIR Pub. 207p. VG/wrp. B1. $21.00

BUTLER, Bonnibel. *Cupids & Kisses: A Book of Delights.* ca 1910. Donohue. tall 8vo. heavy linen. VG. M5. $75.00

BUTLER, C. *American Gentleman.* 1839. G+. M17. $20.00

BUTLER, Gwendoline. *Coffin in Fashion.* 1987. St Martin. 1st. VG/VG. P3. $15.00

BUTLER, Jack. *Jujitsu for Christ.* 1986. Little Rock. August. ARC. NF/F. w/pub letter. R14. $30.00

BUTLER, James. *American Bravery Displayed in Capture of 1400 Vessels...* 1816. self pub. 1st. full leather. G+. E6. $195.00

BUTLER, Lollie. *Erni Cabat's Magical World of Dinosaurs.* 1989. AZ. Great Imp. 1st. fwd Stanley Olson. 55p. F/F. D4. $35.00

BUTLER, M. *Valley of the Ohio.* 1971. KY Hist Soc. 302p. F/dj. M4. $30.00

BUTLER, Margaret Manor. *Pictorial History of Western Reserve 1796 to 1860.* 1963. Cleveland. Western Reserve Hist Soc. sgn. VG/VG. B11. $45.00

BUTLER, Octavia E. *Dawn.* 1987. NY. Warner. 1st. F/F. A24. $30.00

BUTLER, Octavia E. *Dawn.* 1987. Warner. 1st. inscr. F/dj. M2. $60.00

BUTLER, Octavia E. *Wild Seed.* 1980. Doubleday. 1st. F/F. M23. $125.00

BUTLER, Robert Olen. *Alleys of Eden.* 1981. Horizon. 1st. F/NF. B4. $85.00

BUTLER, Robert Olen. *Alleys of Eden.* 1981. Horizon. 1st. sgn. author's 1st book. F/NF. A15/A24. $150.00

BUTLER, Robert Olen. *Countrymen of Bones.* 1983. Horizon. 1st. sgn. F/NF. Q1. $125.00

BUTLER, Robert Olen. *Countrymen of Bones.* 1983. Horizon. 1st. sgn. F/VG+. A24. $95.00

BUTLER, Robert Olen. *Deuce.* 1989. S&S. 1st. rem mk. F/F. B2. $30.00

BUTLER, Robert Olen. *Deuce.* 1989. S&S. 1st. sgn. F/F. A24. $60.00

BUTLER, Robert Olen. *Good Scent From a Strange Mountain.* 1992. Holt. 1st. sgn. F/F. A23. $50.00

BUTLER, Robert Olen. *On Distant Ground.* 1985. Knopf. 1st. F/F. H11. $55.00

BUTLER, Robert Olen. *Sun Dogs.* 1982. Horizon. 1st. sgn. author's 2nd book. F/F. B2/B3. $150.00

BUTLER, Robert Olen. *Sun Dogs.* 1982. Horizon. 1st. sgn. author's 2nd book. F/NF. A24. $95.00

BUTLER, Robert Olen. *Wabash: A Novel.* 1987. Knopf. 1st. F/F. H11. $35.00

BUTLER, Robert Olen. *Wabash: A Novel.* 1987. Knopf. 1st. sgn. F/dj. Q1. $75.00

BUTLER, Robert Olen. *Whisper.* 1994. Holt. 1st. sgn. F/F. A23. $32.00

BUTLER, Samuel. *Atlas of Ancient Geography.* 1826-27. London. Longman Rees. 7000+ entries in index. half calf/marbled brd. T7. $150.00

BUTLER, Samuel. *Way of All Flesh.* 1936. NY. LEC. 1/1500. ils/sgn RW Johnson. 2 vol. teg. full leahter. case. T10. $100.00

BUTLER, T.B. *Philosophy of the Weather.* 1856. Appleton. sm 8vo. 414p. K5. $95.00

BUTLER. *Bibliographical Check List...American Indian Linguistics...* 1941. Chicago. Newberry. 2 vol. unp. VG. A4. $495.00

BUTT, Archie. *Taft & Roosevelt: The Intimate Letters of Archie Butt.* 1930. Garden City. 2 vol. 1st. VG/G. B5. $45.00

BUTTERFIELD, H. *Origins of Modern Science 1300-1800.* 1956. Macmillan. 187p. VG/dj. B14. $30.00

BUTTERWORTH, Michael. *Festival.* 1976. Collins Crime Club. 1st. VG/G. P3. $15.00

BUTTERWORTH, Michael. *Virgin on the Rocks.* 1985. Collins Crime Club. 1st. NF/NF. P3. $13.00

BUXBAUM, Franz. *Cactus Culture Based on Biology.* 1958. London. ils/photos/fld maps. 224p. B26. $44.00

BUXTON, J. *Redstart.* 1950. London. Collins. 8vo. ils/20 maps. 180p. cloth. VG. M12. $15.00

BUYRON & GORDON. *Works in Eight Vols.* 1825. Phil. RW Pomeroy. 8 vol. 1st thus. sm 8vo. ils Westall. uncut. orig pub brd. H13. $495.00

BUZAKI & VANDERWOLF. *Electrical Activity of Archicortex.* 1985. Budapest. Akademiai Kiado. 404p. prt bl brd. G1. $65.00

BUZZATI, Dino. *Bears Famous Invasion of Sicily.* 1947. Pantheon. 1st Am. 16 full-p mc ils. VG/poor. P2. $90.00

BYATT, A.S. *Angels & Insects.* 1992. London. Chatto Windus. true 1st. sgn. NF/dj. D10. $50.00

BYATT, A.S. *Possession.* 1990. Random. 1st Am. sgn. F/dj. D10. $60.00

BYATT, Antonia. *Still Life.* 1985. Scribner. 1st Am. sgn/dtd 1996. F/dj. Q1. $100.00

BYE, John O. *At the End of the Rainbow.* 1959. Seattle. 1st inscr. 474p. VG. B11. $100.00

BYE, John O. *Back Trailing in the Heart of Short Grass Country.* 1956. Seattle. 1st. inscr. 2 fld-map. VG. B11. $150.00

BYERS, D.E.L. *Lone Gambler: Autobiography of DEL Byers of Casper, WY.* nd. np. pl. 163p. cloth. F. D8. $35.00

BYI, Charlot. *Christmas on Stage.* 1950. Polygraphic Company Am. obl 4to. stiff paper wrp/sbdg. R5. $75.00

BYINGTON, Eloise. *Pancake Brownies.* 1928. Chicago. Whitman. 8vo. bl cloth. R5. $100.00

BYJ, Charlot. *Christmas on Stage.* 1950. Polygraphic Co of Am. obl 8vo. stiff sbdg. T10. $150.00

BYKOV, Konstantin M. *Cerebral Cortex & Internal Organs.* 1959. Moscow. Foreign Languages Pub. 1st Russian/2nd Eng-language. G1. $30.00

BYNNER, Witter. *Book of Lyrics.* 1955. 1/1750. #d. F/NF. M19. $45.00

BYNNER & FORT. *Snickerty Nick.* 1919. Moffat Yard. 1st. sgns. ils/bookplate design Rackham. bl cloth. R5. $575.00

BYRD, Martha. *Chennault: Giving Wings to the Tiger.* 1987. Tuscaloosa. ils/photos/biblio/index. 451p. VG/VG. S16. $24.00

BYRD, Richard E. *Alone.* nd. Garden City. Internat Collectors Lib. 221p. VG. P4. $22.00

BYRD, Richard E. *Alone.* 1995. NY. Kodansha. facsimile. 8vo. 309p. sc. VG. P4. $19.50

BYRD, Richard E. *Big Aviation Book for Boys.* 1929. Springfield, MA. 285p. F/dj. A17. $25.00

BYRD, Richard E. *Little America.* 1930. NY. 1st. sgn. 422p. dj. A17. $35.00

BYRD, Richard E. *Skyward.* 1928. Putnam. 1st. 8vo. map ep. bl cloth. VG. P4. $45.00

BYRD & PECKHAM. *Bibliography of Indiana Imprints 1804-1853.* 1955. Indianapolis. IN Hist Bureau. 501p. NF. A4. $195.00

BYRNE, Edward. *Along the Dark Shore.* 1977. BOA Ed. 1/26. sgn. fwd/sgn Ashbery. w/poem card. F. V1. $125.00

BYRNE, H.W. *Christian Education for the Local Church.* 1984. Academie. revised. 379p. VB/dj. B29. $7.50

BYRNES, Gene. *Complete Guide to Professional Cartooning.* 1950. Drexel Hill. 1st. 255p. VG. A17. $25.00

BYRON, May. *Land of Nod.* ca 1909. Hodder Stoughton. ils Rosa Petherick/12 full-p pl. pict brd. R5. $300.00

BYRON, May. *Little Yellow Duckling.* 1928. Nelson. 1st. ils Rudge. NF. M5. $95.00

BYRON, May. *Peek-A-Boo Farmers.* ca 1920. London. Humphrey-Milford/Oxford. 6 full-p pl. sq 4to. brd/label. R5. $350.00

BYRON, May. *Peek-A-Boos in War Time.* ca 1917. London. Henry Frowde (Hodder Stoughton). 6 full-p pl. brd. R5. $225.00

CABBAGE PATCH CIRCLE. *Famous Kentucky Recipes.* 1956. Louisville, KY. sbdg. G. A16. $20.00

CABELL, James Branch. *Letter of...* 1975. OK U. 1st. NF/dj. M2. $25.00

CABELL, James Branch. *Music Behind the Moon.* 1926. NY. John Day. 1/3000. ils Leon Underwood. VG. T10. $75.00

CABELL, James Branch. *Preface to the Past.* 1936. McBride. VG/dj. M2. $35.00

CABELL, James Branch. *Silver Stallion.* 1926. McBride. 1st. G. P3. $30.00

CABELL, James Branch. *Silver Stallion.* 1926. McBride. 1st. ils Frank Pape. F. M19. $65.00

CABELL, James Branch. *Silver Stallion.* 1926. McBride. 1st. 358p. cloth. VG. M20. $45.00

CABELL, James Branch. *Something About Eve.* 1927. McBride. 1st. VG/VG. P3. $75.00

CABELL, James Branch. *These Restless Heads.* 1932. Literary Guild. 2nd. G. P3. $20.00

CABELL, James Branch. *Way of Ecben.* 1929. NY. McBride. 1st. F/torn glassine dj/NF blk case. M23. $40.00

CABELL, James Branch. *Way of Ecben.* 1929. NY. McBride. 1st. NF. P3. $35.00

CABEZA DE VACA, Alvar Nunez. *Narrative of...* 1972. Barre, MA. Imp Soc. ils Michael McCurdy. as new/case. O7. $75.00

CABLE & FRENCH. *Gobi Desert.* 1950. Westminster. Readers Union. ils 305+p. VG. A25. $16.00

CABOT, Calvin. *Year of Regeneration: 1933.* 1932. Harper. F/dj. M2. $25.00

CABRERA, Luis. *Tragic Bomb.* 1964. Mexico. 49x37mm. Eng text. 39p. gilt full tan leather. F. B24. $65.00

CADBURY, Henry J. *George Fox's Book of Miracles.* 1948. Cambridge. 162p. VG/dj. V3. $60.00

CADE, Leland P. *Well, I Guess I Was Lucky.* 1992. Cade. 1st. 243p. as new. J2. $45.00

CADIGAN, Pat. *Mindplayers.* 1988. London. 1st. F/dj. M2. $25.00

CADOGAN, Mary. *Women With Wings.* 1992. London. 1st. 280p. F/dj. B18. $25.00

CADUTO, M.J. *Pond & Brook: Guide to Nature Study...* 1985. Prentice Hall. 276p. rem mk. dj. B1. $14.50

CADY, Annie Cole. *History of Ohio in Words of One Syllable.* 1888. NY. 208p. G. B18. $25.00

CADY, Edwin H. *John Woolman: Mind of the Quaker Saint.* 1966. NY. WA Square Pr. 182p. G. V3. $15.00

CADY, Harrison. *Caleb Cottontail.* 1921. Houghton Mifflin. 1st. 8vo. orange-yel pict cloth. R5. $175.00

CADY, Jack. *Singleton.* 1981. Seattle, WA. Madrona. 1st. author's 4th book. NF/dj. M21. $25.00

CADY, Jack. *Well.* 1980. Arbor. 1st. NF/dj. M21. $45.00

CADY, John H. *Arizona's Yesterday.* 1916. private prt. 1st. sgn. ils. 120p. F. B19. $40.00

CADZOW, Donald A. *Achaeological Studies of Susquehannock Indians of PA.* 1936. Harrisburg. 1st. 8vo. ils/pl/maps. VG. H1. $40.00

CAESAR, C. Julius. *Commentaries of C Julius Caesar, of His Wars in Gallia...* 1677. London. 1st thus. sm folio. 332p. contemporary bdg. C6. $475.00

CAESAR, Julius. *Ancient State Authoritie & Proceedings of Court of Requests.* 1975 (1597). London. edit/intro LM Hill. M11. $85.00

CAESAR, Sid. *Where Have I Been?* 1982. Crown. sgn. photos. VG+. C9. $40.00

CAGNEY, Peter. *Grave for Madam.* 1961. Herbert Jenkins. 1st. VG/G. P3. $18.00

CAHILL, James. *Hills Beyond a River.* 1976. NY/Tokyo. Weatherhill. 1st. ils. 198p. F/dj. W3. $85.00

CAHILL, Tim. *Road Fever.* 1991. Random. 1st. sgn. F/F. B3. $45.00

CAIANELLO, E.R. *Physics of Cognitive Processes.* 1987. NY. World Scientific. 463p. prt gr laminated brd. G1. $75.00

CAIDIN, Martin. *Destination Mars.* 1972. Doubleday. 1st. VG/VG. P3. $22.00

CAIDIN, Martin. *Devil Take All.* 1966. Dutton. 1st. NF/VG. N4. $15.00

CAIDIN, Martin. *Rendezvous in Space, Story of Projects Mercury...* 1962. NY. 1st. ils. VG/dj. B18. $20.00

CAILLE, Augustus. *Differential Diagnosis & Treatment of Disease.* 1906. NY. 1st. ils. 867p. half leather. A13. $100.00

CAILLET. *Manual Bibliographique des Sciences, Psychiques ou Occultes.* nd. 3 vol. 1/100. rpt. 11648 entries. F. A4. $175.00

CAIN, James M. *Baby in the Icebox & Other Short Fiction.* 1981. Holt. 1st. F/VG. B3. $30.00

CAIN, James M. *Body in the Icebox & Other Short Fiction.* 1981. HRW. 1st. F/F. M15. $45.00

CAIN, James M. *Butterfly.* 1947. Knopf. 1st. VG/G. M19. $35.00

CAIN, James M. *Cloud Nine.* 1984. Mysterious. 1st. VG/VG. P3. $18.00

CAIN, James M. *Galatea.* 1953. Knopf. 1st. NF/NF. M15/M22. $45.00

CAIN, James M. *Institute.* 1976. Mason Charter. 1st. F/NF. M19. $35.00

CAIN, James M. *Love's Lovely Counterfeit.* 1942. Knopf. 1st. VG. P3. $100.00

CAIN, James M. *Love's Lovely Counterfeit.* 1945. Tower. 2nd. VG/dj. M22. $15.00

CAIN, James M. *Moth.* 1948. Knopf. F/F. M22. $45.00

CAIN, James M. *Postman Always Rings Twice.* 1934. Knopf. 3rd. NF. M22. $15.00

CAIN, James M. *Rainbow's End.* 1975. Mason/Charter. 1st. inscr/dtd 1975. F/NF. R14. $150.00

CAIN, James M. *Serenade.* 1937. Knopf. VG/G+. M22. $90.00

CAIN, James M. *Serenade.* 1937. Knopf. 1st. VG. P3. $35.00

CAIN, Paul. *Fast One.* 1978. S IL U. 1st thus. VG/VG. M22. $60.00

CAIN, Paul. *Seven Slayers.* 1987. Los Angeles. Blood & Guts. 1st hc. sgn. F/F. T2. $25.00

CAIN & SHARP. *Bryophytic Unions of Certain Forest Types...* 1938. Notre Dame. rpt. G/wrp. B1. $14.00

CAIRD, G.B. *Revelation of St John the Divine.* 1966. Harper. 316p. VG/dj. B29. $11.50

CAIRNS, Bob. *Pen Men: Baseball's Greatest Bullpen Stories...* 1992. St Martin. 1st. F/F. T12. $25.00

CAJORI, F. *Sir Isaac Newton's Mathematical Principles...* 1947. Berkeley, CA. 680p. cloth. F. D8. $20.00

CALADO, Manoel. *O Valeroso Lucideno, e Triumpho da Liberdalde...* 1668. Lisbon. Domingos Carneiro. 1st. folio. modern morocco. R15. $15,000.00

CALAHAN, H.A. *Ship's Husband: Guide to Yachtsmen in Care of Their Craft.* 1937. NY. 1st. 323p. VG. A17. $15.00

CALBE & FRENCH. *Gobi Desert.* 1944. Macmillan. ils/fld map. 302p. VG. W3. $38.00

CALDECOTT, Andrew. *Fires Burn Blue.* 1948. London. 1st. VG/dj. M2. $35.00

CALDECOTT, Moyra. *Tall Stones.* 1977. Hill Wang. 1st. VG/VG. P3. $20.00

CALDECOTT, Randolph. *Caldecott's Picture Books (8 One Shilling Eds in 1 Vol).* nd. London. Routledge. 1st probable. cloth/quarter leather. VG+. C8. $450.00

CALDWELL, E. *Fairy Ship.* ca 1890. London. Marcus Ward. ltd. sq 12mo. pict wrp. R5. $75.00

CALDWELL, Erskine. *Annette.* 1973. NAL. 1st. F/NF. M19. $25.00

CALDWELL, Erskine. *Gulf Coast Stories.* 1956. Little Brn. 1st. F/NF. D10. $35.00

CALDWELL, Erskine. *Molly Cottontail.* 1958. Little Brn. stated 1st. sm 4to. VG/dj. M5. $75.00

CALDWELL, Erskine. *Sure Hand of God.* 1947. DSP. 1st. F/NF. D10. $40.00

CALDWELL, George W. *Ghost Stories of the California Missions & Rhymes...* 1939. Hollywood, CA. 1st. NF/G+. O4. $15.00

CALDWELL, Taylor. *Balance Wheel.* 1951. Scribner. 1st. VG/VG. P3. $20.00

CALDWELL, Taylor. *Pillar of Iron.* 1965. Doubleday. 1st. 649p. VG/G. W2. $40.00

CALDWELL, Taylor. *There Was a Time.* 1947. Scribner. 1st. VG/VG. P3. $25.00

CALHOUN, Alfred R. *Lost in the Canyon.* 1888. NY. AL Burt. 8vo. 267p. gr cloth. G+. F7. $30.00

CALHOUN, Frances Boyd. *Miss Minerva & William Green Hill.* 1911 (1909). Reilly Britton. 212p. pict cloth. VG. M20. $20.00

CALHOUN, Mary. *Katie John.* 1960. Harper. possible 1st prt. 8vo. 134p. gr cloth. xl. G. T5. $22.00

CALHOUN & McCAFFERY. *Flower Mother.* 1972. Morrow. 1st. sm 4to. unp. NF/dj. C14. $14.00

CALISHER, Hortense. *Journal From Ellipsia.* 1965. Little Brn. 1st. NF/dj. B35. $20.00

CALISHER, Hortense. *Kissing Cousins.* 1988. Weidenfeld Nicholson. 1st. NF/dj. B35. $12.00

CALISHER, Hortense. *Tale for the Mirror.* 1962. Little Brn. 1st. NF/dj. B35. $18.00

CALLAHAN, Daniel. *Abortion: Law, Choice & Morality.* 1970. Macmillan. 1st. 524p. VG/dj. A25. $15.00

CALLAHAN, North. *Henry Knox: General Washington's General.* 1958. NY. Rinehart. 1st. sgn. 404p. VG/G. B11. $25.00

CALLAHAN & O'HANLON. *Christianity Divided: Protestant & Roman Catholic...* 1961. Sheed Ward. 335p. G/dj. B29. $6.50

CALLAN, John F. *Military Laws of the United States 1776-1858...* nd. np. 8vo. 484p. full leather. VG. K7. $75.00

CALLAWAY, Lew L. *Montana's Righteous Hangmen: Vigilantes in Action.* 1973. Norman. 1st. inscr edit. F/NF. T11. $65.00

CALLOWAY, Cab. *Of Minnie the Moocher & Me.* 1976. Crowell. 1st. F/NF. B2. $35.00

CALNAN, Denis. *Knights in Durance.* 1966. Malta. 1st. 32 pl. VG/dj. K3. $20.00

CALVAN & HIRSHBERG. *Gardening for All Seasons.* 1893. Andover, MA. Brick House. 309p. VG. A10. $35.00

CALVERT, George H. *Charlotte Von Stein: A Memoir.* 1877. Boston. Lee Shepard. 1st. ils. 280p. teg. VG+. A25. $25.00

CALVERTON, V.F. *Man Inside.* 1936. Scribner. 1st. Vg/dj. M2. $35.00

CALVIN, Jack. *Sitka.* 1936. Arrowhead. 1st. 40p+photos. G/wrp. A17. $25.00

CALVIN, Ross. *River of the Sun: Stories of the Storied Gila.* 1946. ils. VG/partial. M17. $25.00

CALVIN, William H. *How the Shaman Stole the Moon.* 1991. NY. Bantam. 1st. 223p. M/wrp. K3. $13.00

CAM, Helen. *Law-Finders & Law-Makers in Medieval England...* 1962. London. Merlin. maroon cloth. M11. $65.00

CAM, Helen. *Selected Historical Essays of FW Maitland.* 1957. Cambridge. G/dj. M11. $85.00

CAMERON, Agnes Deans. *New North: Being Some Account of a Woman's Journey...* 1910. NY/London. Appleton. 2nd. 8vo. 398p. gr cloth. P4. $85.00

CAMERON, Eleanor. *Room Made of Windows.* 1971. Little Brn. 1st. 271p. NF/VG+. P2. $30.00

CAMERON, Eleanor. *Spell Is Cast.* 1964. Atlantic Monthly. 1st. 271p. VG/G. P2. $35.00

CAMERON, Owen. *Butcher's Wife.* 1954. S&S. 1st. VG/G. P3. $20.00

CAMERON, Peter. *One Way or Another.* 1986. Harper Row. 1st. sgn. F/F. R13. $45.00

CAMERON, Polly. *Child's Book of Nonsense.* 1960. NY. Coward McCann. 1st. 32p. F/dj. D4. $35.00

CAMERON, Thomas W.M. *Internal Parasites of Domestic Animals.* 1934. London. Blk. 1st. VG. O3. $35.00

CAMM, F.J. *Watches: Adjustment & Repair.* nd. Brooklyn. Chemical Pub. 166p. dj. K3. $18.00

CAMP, Charles L. *Desert Rats.* 1866. Berkeley. Bancroft Lib. Friends Bancroft Lib #14. 55p. gilt red cloth. F. K7. $30.00

CAMP, John; see Sandford, John.

CAMP, Raymond R. *All Seasons Afield With Rod & Gun.* 1939. Whittlesey. 1st. sgn. 352p. VG. B11. $50.00

CAMP, Samuel G. *Art of Fishing.* 1911. NY. Outing. 1st. 177p. VG. H7. $25.00

CAMP, Walter. *Custer in '76.* 1976. Bringham Young U. 1st. 303p. VG/VG. J2. $95.00

CAMP, William Martin. *San Francisco.* 1947. Doubleday. 1st. VG/G. O4. $15.00

CAMP & WAGNER. *Plains & the Rockies.* 1937. Grabhorn. 1/600. 308p. VG. A4. $175.00

CAMPANA, Michele. *Oriental Carpets.* 1969. London. Hamlyn. 1st Eng language prt. 12mo. 66 mc pl. as new/dj. H1. $12.50

CAMPANELLA, Roy. *It's Good To Be Alive.* 1959. Boston. 1st. VG/dj. B5. $20.00

CAMPANELLA, Tommaso. *De Sensv Rervm, et Magia.* 1637. Paris. DuBray. 4to. bellum. R12. $1,175.00

CAMPBELL, A.B. *When I Was in Patagonia.* (1953). London. Christopher Johnson. 1st. 202p. F3. $15.00

CAMPBELL, Alfred Walter. *Histological Studies on Localization of Cerebral Function.* 1905. Cambridge. assn copy. sm folio. 29 pl. 360p. G1. $500.00

CAMPBELL, Alice. *Click of the Gate.* 1931. Farrar Rhinehart. 1st. F/dj. M15. $75.00

CAMPBELL, Bebe Moore. *Successful Women, Angry Men: Backlash in 2-Career Marriage.* 1986. NY. Random. 1st. author's 1st book. F/NF. B4. $250.00

CAMPBELL, Bruce. *Ken Holt: Mystery of Sultan's Scimitar (#18).* 1963. Grosset Dunlap. 1st. 177p. last title in series. VG. M20. $350.00

CAMPBELL, Craig S. *Water in Landscape Architecture.* 1978. NY. ils. 128p. F/dj. B26. $17.50

CAMPBELL, Elizabeth. *Encyclopedia of World Cookery.* 1968. London. Hamlyn. G/dj. A16. $15.00

CAMPBELL, H.J. *Beyond the Visible.* 1952. Hamish Hamilton. 1st. VG/VG. P3. $25.00

CAMPBELL, J. *Mythic Image.* 1974. Princeton. ils. 552p. F/rpr. M4. $45.00

CAMPBELL, John Lord. *Lives of the Chief Justices of England.* 1894. Long Island. Ed Thompson. 3 vol (of 5). M11. $85.00

CAMPBELL, John W. *Analog 8.* 1971. Doubleday. 1st. VG/VG. P3. $18.00

CAMPBELL, John W. *Best of...* nd. SF BC. F/dj. M2. $15.00

CAMPBELL, John W. *Black Star Passes.* 1953. Fantasy. 1st. F/dj. M2. $125.00

CAMPBELL, John W. *Cloak of Aesir.* 1952. Shasta. 1st. sgn subscriber copy. F/dj. M2. $200.00

CAMPBELL, John W. *Cloak of Aesir.* 1952. Shasta. 1st. VG/VG. P3. $75.00

CAMPBELL, John W. *Cloak of Aesir.* 1976 (1952). Hyperion. rpt. F. M2. $35.00

CAMPBELL, John W. *Incredible Planet.* 1949. Fantasy. 1st. F/dj. M2. $100.00

CAMPBELL, John W. *Islands of Space.* 1956. Fantasy. F/dj. M2. $100.00

CAMPBELL, John W. *Mightiest Machine.* 1947. Hadley. 1st. VG/VG. P3. $250.00

CAMPBELL, John W. *Moon Is Hell.* 1951. Fantasy. 1st. sgn/#d. F/NF. P3. $200.00

CAMPBELL, Julie. *Rin Tin Tin's Rinty.* 1954. Whitman. Authorized ed. VG. W2. $30.00

CAMPBELL, Karen. *Wheel of Fortune.* 1973. Bobbs Merrill. 1st. VG/VG. P3. $15.00

CAMPBELL, Maria. *Halfbreed.* 1973. Saturday Review. 1st. F/NF. L3. $45.00

CAMPBELL, Mary Mason. *New England Butt'ry Shelf Almanac.* 1970. World. 1st. ils Tasha Tudor. 302p. cloth. VG+/dj. M20. $55.00

CAMPBELL, Mary Mason. *New England Butt'ry Shelf Cookbook.* 1968. World. 1st. ils/sgn Tasha Tudor. 192p. VG/dj. M20. $125.00

CAMPBELL, R. Wright. *Killer of Kings.* 1979. Bobbs Merrill. 1st. NF/dj. M25. $35.00

CAMPBELL, R. Wright. *Malloy's Subway.* 1981. NY. Atheneum. 1st. F/dj. M15. $45.00

CAMPBELL, Ramsey. *Ancient Images.* 1989. Scribner. 1st Am. NF/VG+. M21. $15.00

CAMPBELL, Ramsey. *Dark Companions.* 1982. Macmillan. 1st. F/F. P3. $60.00

CAMPBELL, Ramsey. *Dark Feasts.* 1987. London. 1st. F/dj. M2. $30.00

CAMPBELL, Ramsey. *Demons by Daylight.* 1973. Arkham. 1st. F/dj. M2. $60.00

CAMPBELL, Ramsey. *Doll Who Ate His Mother.* 1976. Bobbs Merrill. 1st author's 1st novel. F/F. P3. $125.00

CAMPBELL, Ramsey. *Fantasy Readers Guide to Ramsey Campbell.* 1980. Cosmos/Borgo. 62p. NF/sans. R10. $15.00

CAMPBELL, Ramsey. *Incarnate.* 1983. Macmillan. 1st. F/NF. N4. $40.00

CAMPBELL, Ramsey. *Inhabitant of the Lake.* 1964. Arkham. 1st. inscr. F/dj. M2. $185.00

CAMPBELL, Ramsey. *Parasite.* 1980. Macmillan. 1st. F/dj. M2. $30.00

CAMPBELL, Robert. *Alice in La-La Land.* 1987. Poseidon. 1st. VG/VG. P3. $17.00

CAMPBELL, Robert. *In a Pig's Eye.* 1991. Pocket. 1st. as new/dj. N4. $20.00

CAMPBELL, Robert. *In La-La Land We Trust.* 1986. Mysterious. 1st. F/F. M25. $35.00

CAMPBELL, Robert. *Nibbled to Death by Ducks.* 1989. Pocket. 1st. F/F. P3. $18.00

CAMPBELL, Ruth. *Small Fry & the Winged Horse.* 1927. Volland. later. ils Gustaf Tenggren. NF/G. M5. $85.00

CAMPBELL, Sam. *Beloved Rascals.* 1957. Bobbs Merrill. 1st. sgn. VG. B11. $25.00

CAMPBELL, Thomas J. *Jesuits 1534-1921.* 1921. Encyclopedia Pr. 937p. gilt cloth. A17. $25.00

CAMPBELL, Thomas. *Gertrude of Wyoming.* 1809. London. Longman. 1st. wide folio. 134p. uncut. orig pub brd. ES. H13. $295.00

CAMPBELL, Thomas. *Life of Mrs Siddons.* 1972. NY. Blom. 378p. wrp. A17. $12.50

CAMPBELL & GARNETT. *Life of James Clerk Maxwell.* 1884. London. Macmillan. new abridged/revised. 8vo. 421p. teg. leather. K5. $200.00

CAMPEN, Richard N. *Architecture of the Western Reserve, 1800-1900.* 1971. Cleveland. 1st. 260p. VG+/dj. B18. $75.00

CAMPION, Lynn. *Training & Showing the Cutting Horse.* 1990. Prentice Hall. 1st. F/F. O3. $19.00

CAMPION & PULLINGER. *Piano.* 1994. NY. Miramax/Hyperion. 1st. F/F. B4. $50.00

CAMPOLO, Tony. *How To Rescue the Earth Without Worshiping Nature.* 1992. Nelson. 1st. sgn. VG/dj. B29. $8.50

CAMPUZANO, Francisco Maria. *Oracion que en la Abertura de Sesiones del Dia Quince...* 1815. Logrono. Antonio Jose Delgado. 1st/only. contemporary bdg. R15. $650.00

CAMRASS, Zoe. *Essential Cookbook.* 1985. Bonanza. dj. A16. $12.00

CAMUS, Albert. *Exile & the Kingdom.* 1958. Knopf. 1st. F/NF. B35. $40.00

CAMUS, Albert. *Happy Death.* 1972. Knopf. 1st. trans Richard Howard. F/dj. Q1. $60.00

CAMUS, Albert. *Outsider.* 1946. London. Hamish Hamilton. 1st Eng trans. author's 1st book. F/dj. Q1. $400.00

CANCIAN, Frank. *Change & Uncertainty in Peasant Economy.* 1972. Stanford. 1st. 208p. dj. F3. $20.00

CANFIELD, Cook. *Lucky Terrell: Secret Mission (#3).* 1943. Grosset Dunlap. 210p. cloth. VG+/dj (lists to #2). M20. $16.00

CANFIELD, Cook. *Lucky Terrell: Springboard to Tokyo (#5).* 1943. Grosset Dunlap. 210p. VG/dj (lists to #6). M20. $20.00

CANIFF, W. *History of the Province of Ontario.* 1872. Toronto. 672p. new cloth. NF. M4. $30.00

CANIN, Ethan. *Blue River.* 1991. Houghton Mifflin. 1st. author's 2nd novel. VG/VG. L1. $35.00

CANIN, Ethan. *Blue River.* 1991. Houghton Mifflin. 1st. sgn. author's 2nd book. NF/F. B3. $55.00

CANIN, Ethan. *Emperor of the Air.* 1988. Houghton Mifflin. 1st. author's 1st book. F/dj. A24. $75.00

CANNADINE, David. *Pleasure of the Past.* 1989. NY. 1st. dj. T9. $16.00

CANNE & BROWNE. *Treasury of Scripture Knowledge.* 1982. MacDonald. VG. B29. $9.50

CANNING, John. *50 Great Horror Stories.* 1971. Bell. 1st. F/dj. M2. $18.00

CANNING, Victor. *Dragon Tree.* 1958. Sloane. 1st. NF/NF. P3. $45.00

CANNING, Victor. *Mr Finchley Goes to Paris.* 1938. Carrick Evans. 1st. VG/fair. P3. $25.00

CANNING, Victor. *Rainbird Pattern.* 1972. Morrow. 1st Am. NF/VG. M22. $15.00

CANNON, Curt; see Hunter, Evan.

CANNON & GRIFFITHS. *Oxford Illustrated History of British Monarchy.* 1988. ils. VG/VG. M17. $30.00

CANNON & ROSENBLEUTH. *Supersensitivity of Denervated Structures.* 1949. Macmillan. 245p. prt panelled gr cloth. VG/dj. G1. $75.00

CANSLER, Charles W. *Three Generations: Story of a Colored Family in E TN.* 1939. private prt. 1st. NF. B4. $300.00

CANTINE, Marguerite. *Beggar T Bear.* 1981. Cantine Kilpatrick. photos. 62p. F/wrp. H1. $17.50

CANTWELL, R. *Alexander Wilson: Naturalist & Pioneer.* 1961. 1st. VG/VG. M17. $35.00

CANTY, Kevin. *Stranger in This World.* 1994. Doubleday. 1st. F/F. R14. $35.00

CANTY, Thomas. *Monster at Christmas.* 1985. Donald Grant. 1st. 1/1050. sgn. F/dj. M2. $30.00

CAPE, Tony. *Cambridge Theorem.* 1990. Doubleday. 1st. NF/NF. P3. $20.00

CAPEK, Abe. *Chinese Stone Pictures.* 1962. London. Spring. ils. gilt cloth. F/F/case. W3. $65.00

CAPEK, Karel. *Absolute at Large.* 1974 (1927). Hyperion. rpt. F. M2. $25.00

CAPON, Edward. *Chinese Painting.* 1979. NY. Phaidon/Dutton. ils. F/wrp. W3. $32.00

CAPOTE, Truman. *Answered Prayers: Unfinished Novel.* 1987. Random. 1st. NF. T12. $15.00

CAPOTE, Truman. *Dogs Bark.* 1973. Random. 1st. F/dj. Q1. $60.00

CAPOTE, Truman. *Grass Harp.* 1951. Random. 1st. 2nd issue bdg (fine-grained beige cloth). F/clip. Q1. $100.00

CAPOTE, Truman. *Grove Day.* 1969. NY. 1st. fwd James Michener. VG/VG. B5. $40.00

CAPOTE, Truman. *In Cold Blood.* 1965. Random. 1st. F/F. Q1. $75.00

CAPOTE, Truman. *In Cold Blood.* 1965. Random. 1st. F/NF. D10. $60.00

CAPOTE, Truman. *In Cold Blood.* 1965. Random. 1st. F/VG. M19. $25.00

CAPOTE, Truman. *One Christmas.* 1983. Random. 1st. 1/500. sgn. F/sans/case. Q1. $350.00

CAPOTE, Truman. *Other Voices, Other Rooms.* 1948. Random. 1st. author's 1st book. VG+/G. D10. $175.00

CAPOTE, Truman. *Other Voices, Other Rooms.* 1948. Random. 1st. sgn. author's 1st book. F/dj. Q1. $750.00

CAPOTE, Truman. *Thanksgiving Visitor.* 1967. NY. 1st. F/box. B5. $35.00

CAPPE, Jeanne. *Blanche-Neige et Autres Contes de Grimm.* 1947. Casterman. 1st. lg 4to. VG. M5. $60.00

CAPPER, Mary. *Memoir of..., Late of Birmingham, England, a Minister...* nd. Phil. Assn Friends Diffusion Religious & Useful Knowledge. V3. $16.00

CAPPON, Lester J. *History of Expedition Under Command of Capts Lewis & Clark.* 1970. NY. Columbia. as new/stiff wrp. O7. $25.00

CAPPS, Benjamin. *Great Chiefs.* 1980. Time Life. 4th. A19. $20.00

CAPPS, Benjamin. *Indians.* 1975. Time Life. A19. $20.00

CAPPS, Benjamin. *Warren Wagon Train Raid, the First Complete Account...* 1974. Dial. 1st. 304p. VG/VG. J2. $70.00

CAPPS, Benjamin. *Woman of the People.* 1966. DSP. 1st. F/VG+. B4. $25.00

CAPUTO, Philip. *Horn of Africa.* 1980. Holt. 1st. F/F. H11. $45.00

CAPUTO, Philip. *Horn of Africa.* 1980. HRW. 1/250. sgn. F/acetate dj/case. R14. $100.00

CARAS, Roger A. *North American Mammals.* 1967. NY. ils/pl. 577p. VG. S15. $12.00

CARAS, Roger A. *Panther.* 1969. Little Brn. 1st. sgn. VG/VG. B11. $40.00

CARD, Orson Scott. *Abyss.* 1989. London. Legend/Century. 1st hc. F/F. M21. $35.00

CARD, Orson Scott. *Lost Boys.* 1992. Harper Collins. 1st. F/F. N4. $30.00

CARD, Orson Scott. *Lost Boys.* 1993. ARC. F/wrp. M19. $25.00

CARD, Orson Scott. *Prentice Alvin.* 1989. Tor. 1st. sgn. F/F. M23. $45.00

CARD, Orson Scott. *Red Prophet.* 1988. Tor. 1st. sgn. F/F. M23. $50.00

CARD, Orson Scott. *Seventh Son.* 1987. NY. Tor. 1st. sgn. F/F. M23. $55.00

CARD, Orson Scott. *Songmaster.* 1980. NY. Dial. 1st. rem mk. NF/VG+. M23. $100.00

CARD, Orson Scott. *Speaker for the Dead.* 1986. NY. Tor. 1st. sgn. xl. VG/NF. M23. $75.00

CARDINALL, A.W. *Natives of the Northern Territories of Gold Coast...* 1969 (1920). NY. Negro U. rpt. 8vo. ils. 158p. VG. W1. $25.00

CARDOSO, Jorge. *Agiologio Lusitano dos Sanctos e Varoens Illustres...* 1652-1744. Lisbon. various prts. complete 4 vol set. R15. $4,250.00

CARDOSO DE MIRANDO, Joao. *Relacao Circurgica, e Medica, na Qual se Trata...* 1752? (1741). Lisbon. Manoel Soares. 2nd. contemporary bdg. R15. $2,000.00

CARELL, Paul. *Scorched Earth.* 1966. Boston. 1st. VG/VG. B5. $75.00

CAREY, Arthur A. *Memoirs of a Murder Man.* 1930. Doubleday Doran. 1st. VG. P3. $20.00

CAREY, Mary. *Gremlins Storybook.* 1984. Golden. 1st. as new. T12. $16.00

CAREY, Peter. *Fat Man in History & Other Stories.* 1980. Random. 1st Am. F/NF. M25. $45.00

CAREY, Peter. *Illywhacker.* 1985. Harper Row. 1st. F/F. M19. $25.00

CAREY, Peter. *Oscar & Lucinda.* 1988. Harper Row. ARC. sgn. F/wrp. B3. $40.00

CAREY, Peter. *Unusual Life of Tristan Smith.* 1995. Knopf. 1st. sgn. F/dj. Q1. $45.00

CAREY, Rosa Nouchette. *Our Bessie.* ca 1900. AL Burt. 1st thus. ils. 343p. VG+. A25. $12.00

CARFAX, Catherine. *Silence With Voices.* 1969. Macmillan. 1st. VG/VG. P3. $20.00

CARGILL, Morris. *Ian Fleming Introduces Jamaica.* 1965. Andre Deutsch. 1st. VG/G. P3. $30.00

CARIGAN, William. *Staves for Louisville.* 1981. Lexington. Juniper. 1st. inscr. F/F. B11. $55.00

CARKEET, David. *Greatest Slump of All Time.* 1984. Harper Row. 1st. F/F. M25. $35.00

CARLETON, Mark A. *Small Grains.* 1920. Macmillan. 699p. VG. A10. $28.00

CARLEY, K. *Minnesota in the Civil War.* 1961. Minneapolis. 1st. ils/maps. 168p. F/dj. M4. $20.00

CARLIN, J.W. *Naval Encyclopedia...Together With Descriptions...* 1971 (1884). Detroit. Gale Research. rpt. F. O7. $35.00

CARLISLE, D.T. *Belvidere Hounds.* 1935. Derrydale. 1st. G. O3. $75.00

CARLISLE & STYRON. *Modern Russian Poetry.* 1972. Viking. 1st. 210p. cloth. F/F. D4. $35.00

CARLSON, E.A. *Genes, Radiation & Society. Life & Work of HJ Muller.* 1981. Cornell. 1st. ils. 457p. VG. K3. $15.00

CARLSON, Ed. *Look Back Once in Awhile.* 1981. Phoenix, AZ. self pub. sgn. A19. $20.00

CARLSON, John Roy. *Plotters.* 1946. Dutton. 1st. F/VG. B2. $30.00

CARLSON, John Roy. *Under Cover: My Four Years in Nazi Underworld of America.* 1943. Dutton. 17th prt. 544p. VG. S3. $23.00

CARLSON, Natalie Savage. *Family Under the Bridge.* (1958). Harper Row. 8vo. ils Garth Williams. 97p. G+. T5. $25.00

CARLSON, Raymond. *Flowering Cactus.* 1954. NY. ils/photos. 96p. VG/dj. B26. $20.00

CARLSON, Ron. *News of the World.* 1987. Norton. 1st. F/F. H11. $45.00

CARLSON, Victor I. *Matisse As a Draughtsman.* 1971. Baltimore Mus Art. 191p. 83 full-p pl. G. A17. $20.00

CARLSON, William. *Sunrise West.* 1981. Doubleday. 1st. F/dj. M2. $12.00

CARLTON, Charles. *Court of the Orphans.* 1974. Leicester. G. M11. $45.00

CARLYE, Thomas. *French Revolution: A History.* 1956. LEC. 1st thus. 1/1500. ils/sgn Bernard Lamotte. F/glassine/case. Q1. $75.00

CARLYON, RIchard. *Dark Lord of Pengersick.* 1980. FSG. 1st. F/F. P3. $15.00

CARMEL, Herman. *Black Days, White Nights.* 1984. Hippocrene. 323p. VG/dj. S3. $25.00

CARMER, Carl. *Susquehanna.* 1955. Rinehart. 2nd. sm 8vo. 493p. F/G. H1. $22.50

CARMICHAEL, Harry; see Creasey, John.

CARNEGIE, Andrew. *American Four-in-Hand in Britain.* 1884. NY. ils. 338p. G. B18. $35.00

CARNEGIE, D. *Among the Matabele.* 1970 (1894). Negro U. rpt. 128p. VG. W1. $25.00

CARNELL, John. *New Writings in Science Fiction 15.* 1969. Dennis Dobson. 1st. VG/VG. P3. $30.00

CARNER, Gary. *Jazz Performers: An Annotated Bibliography...* 1990. Westport. Greenwood. 1st. 364p. F/sans. B2. $50.00

CARNOT, S. *Reflections on the Motive Power of Heat.* 1943. NY. Am Soc Mechanical Engineers. 107p. box. K3. $30.00

CAROLL, HARGROVE & LUMMIS. *Women of the Cloth: A New Opportunity for the Churches.* 1983. Harper Row. 276p. F/dj. B14. $35.00

CARPENTER, Edward. *Angel's Wings: Series of Essays on Art...Relation to Life.* 1908. Swan Sonnenschein. 1st. VG. w/letter. V4. $75.00

CARPENTER, Edward. *From Adam's Peak to Elephanta: Sketches in Ceylon & India.* (1910). London. Swan. new revised. ils/photos. 370p. VG. M12. $30.00

CARPENTER, Edwin H. *Printers & Publishers in Southern California 1850-1876.* 1964. La Siesta. 1st. inscr. ils/index. 48p. F. B19. $60.00

CARPENTER, F.B. *Six Months at the White House.* 1866. NY. 1st. F. O8. $32.50

CARPENTER, Frances. *Holiday in Washington.* 1958. Knopf. 1st. sgn. 207p. VG/dj. M20. $20.00

CARPENTER, Frances. *People From the Sky.* 1972. Doubleday. 1st. ils. 107p. F/dj. W3. $46.00

CARPENTER, Frank G. *Cairo to Kisumu: Egypt, the Sudan, Kenya Colony.* 1925. Doubleday Page. 96 pl/2 fld maps. 313p. teg. G. W1. $12.00

CARPENTER, Humphrey. *Tolkien: A Biography.* 1977. Houghton Mifflin. 1st. VG/VG. P3. $20.00

CARPENTER, Iris. *No Woman's World.* 1946. Houghton Mifflin. 1st. 378p. VG. A25. $28.00

CARPENTER, R.A. *Assessing Tropical Forest Lands.* 1981. Dublin. Tycooly Internat'l. 1st. 337p. dj. B1. $30.00

CARPENTER, William B. *Microscopes & Its Revelations.* 1881. London. Churchill. 6th. 882p. VG. K3. $60.00

CARPENTER & GROSSBERG. *Neutral Networks for Vision & Image Processing.* 1992. Cambridge, MA. MIT. lg 8vo. 467p. prt stiff wrp. G1. $40.00

CARPENTER & NASMYTH. *Moon: Considered As a Planet, a World, A Satellite.* 1874. London. John Murray. 408p. VG/VG. K5. $400.00

CARPENTER. *History of American Schoolbooks.* 1963. PA U. 322p. VG/VG. A4. $165.00

CARPENTIER, Alejo. *Kingdom of This World.* 1957. Knopf. 1st. NF/dj. M25. $150.00

CARR, Archie. *Handbook of Turtles.* 1983 (1952). Cornell. 9th. 542p. F. S15. $40.00

CARR, Caleb. *Alienist.* 1994. Random. 1st. F/F. B4. $100.00

CARR, Caleb. *Casing the Promised Land.* 1980. Harper Row. 1st. sm stp B on half title. F/NF. L3. $150.00

CARR, Charles. *Colonists of Space.* 1954. Ward Lock. VG/VG. P3. $20.00

CARR, Frank G.G. *Sailing Barges.* 1931. London. Hodder Stoughton. 1st. 68 pl. 328p. T7. $85.00

CARR, Jayge. *Treasure in the Heart of the Maze.* 1985. Doubleday. 1st. F/dj. M2. $15.00

CARR, Jayge. *Treasure in the Heart of the Maze.* 1985. Doubleday. 1st. RS. F/F. P3. $18.00

CARR, John Dickson. *Bride of Newgate.* 1950. Harper. 1st. VG/G. P3. $25.00

CARR, John Dickson. *Captain Cut-Throat.* 1955. Hamish Hamilton. 1st. VG. P3. $40.00

CARR, John Dickson. *Captain Cut-Throat.* 1955. Harper. 1st. F/F. P3. $80.00

CARR, John Dickson. *He Wouldn't Kill Patience.* 1944. Morrow. 1st. NF/dj. M15. $250.00

CARR, John Dickson. *Scandal at High Chimneys.* 1959. Hamish Hamilton. 1st. NF/NF. P3. $35.00

CARR, Robert Spencer. *Beyond Infinity.* 1951. Fantasy. 1/350. sgn/#d. F/dj. M2. $100.00

CARR, SAUNDERS & STOM. *Geology of the Terrestrial Planets.* 1984. NASA SP-469. 317p. G. D8. $25.00

CARR, Terry. *Fellowship of the Stars.* 1974. S&S. 1st. F/NF. M2. $25.00

CARR, Terry. *Infinite Arena.* 1977. Thomas Nelson. 1st. VG/VG. P3. $18.00

CARR, Terry. *Universe 13.* 1983. Doubleday. 1st. F/F. P3. $25.00

CARR, Terry. *Year's Finest Fantasy.* 1979. Berkley Putnam. 1st. F/F. P3. $20.00

CARR, William H. *Desert Parade.* 1947. NY. 1st. ils. map ep. VG/rpr. B26. $15.00

CARR & CARR. *Fox-Hunting.* 1982. Oxford. 1st. F/F. O3. $10.00

CARRASCO, David. *To Change Place.* 1991. Niwot. CO U. 1st. 254p. dj. F3. $30.00

CARREL, Alexis. *Voyage to Lourdes.* 1950. NY. 1st. 52p. cloth. G. B5. $25.00

CARRICK, Valery. *Valery Carrick's Picture Folk-Tales.* 1928. Stokes. ils. 90p. VG/tattered dj. D1. $85.00

CARRIER, Jim. *Down the Colorado.* 1989. Rinehart. 8vo. 141p. stiff wrp. F7. $17.50

CARRIER, Robert. *Connoisseur's Cookbook.* 1954. Hanover. 1st Am. VG/G. B10. $35.00

CARRIER, Robert. *Cooking for You.* 1973. Viking. 1st. 4to. mc photos. dj. A16. $17.50

CARRIER, Robert. *Great Dishes of the World.* 1964. Random. 1st Am. photos. 297p. VG/fair. B10. $25.00

CARRIGHAR, Sally. *Wild Heritage.* 1965. Houghton Mifflin. dj. A19. $20.00

CARRILLO, Leo. *California I Love.* 1961. Englewood Cliffs. Prentice Hall. 1st. 8vo. 280p. half cloth. F/VG. T10. $35.00

CARRINGTON, Grant. *Time's Fool.* 1981. Doubleday. 1st. F/F. P3. $13.00

CARROLL, Alice. *Complete Guide to Modern Knitting & Crocheting.* 1943. NY. Wise. 1st. ils/photos. 310p. VG+. A25. $18.00

CARROLL, James. *Supply of Heroes.* 1986. Dutton. ne. F/F. W2. $20.00

CARROLL, John. *Benteen-Golden Letters on Custer & His Last Battle.* 1974. Liveright. 1st ltd. 1/27. sgn. 312p. VG. J2. $875.00

CARROLL, John. *Black Experience in the American West.* 1971. Liveright. 1st. ils. 591p. VG/VG. J2. $325.00

CARROLL, John. *Custer Trail, a Narrative of the Line of March of Troops...* 1983. Clark. 1/350. sgn. map/photos. 148p. VG. J2. $135.00

CARROLL, John. *To Set the Record Straight! Real Story of Wounded Knee.* nd. np. 1st. 1/50. sgn. 178p. typewritten. VG/stiff wrp. J2. $395.00

CARROLL, John. *Two Battles of the Little Big Horn.* 1974. Liveright. 1/1000. sgn. 214p. w/fld painting by Bjorklund. as new/case. J2. $275.00

CARROLL, Jonathan. *Land of Laughs.* 1980. 1st. author's 1st book. F/NF. M19. $45.00

CARROLL, Kay. *Han Solo's Rescue.* 1983. Random Pop-Up Book. F. P3. $10.00

CARROLL, Lewis. *Adventures in Wonderland.* 1932. Lippincott. reduced format ed. ils Gertrude Kay/John Tenniel. cloth. R5. $100.00

CARROLL, Lewis. *Alice in Wonderland, Through the Looking-Glass & Other...* 1929. London. ils Carroll. 335p. VG. B18. $25.00

CARROLL, Lewis. *Alice in Wonderland Novelty Cut-Outs.* ca 1940s. London. Juvenile Prod. 4to. mc glazed ils. stiff paper wrp. F. R5. $300.00

CARROLL, Lewis. *Alice in Wonderland.* (1945). Grosset Dunlap. animated Julian Wehr/4 movables. VG/dj. D1. $475.00

CARROLL, Lewis. *Alice in Wonderland.* ca 1915. London. Blackie. ils Frank Adams. 12mo. top edge gr. gr cloth. R5. $100.00

CARROLL, Lewis. *Alice in Wonderland.* ca 1950. London. Juvenile Prod. ils AA Nash/24 mc pl. 4to. dj. R5. $125.00

CARROLL, Lewis. *Alice in Wonderland.* 1921. London. Raphael Tuck. 1st thus. ils AL Bowley. gr cloth/pict label. R5. $125.00

CARROLL, Lewis. *Alice in Wonderland.* 1932. Hodder Stoughton for Boot s Pure Drug Co. Centenary ed. ils GM Hudson. red dj. R5. $250.00

CARROLL, Lewis. *Alice in Wonderland.* 1934. Rand McNally. ils. VG. P3. $20.00

CARROLL, Lewis. *Alice in Wonderland.* 1969. London. Dean. 1st thus. ils/retold Rene Cloke. 4to. pict brd. unused. R5. $150.00

CARROLL, Lewis. *Alice's Adventures in Wonderland & Through Looking Glass.* 1957 (1954). London. Dent. ils Tennell/Stanley. VG+/G+. N1. $7.50

CARROLL, Lewis. *Alice's Adventures in Wonderland & Through Looking Glass.* 1966 (1954). London. Dent. ils Tennell/Stanley. xl. F. T12. $12.00

CARROLL, Lewis. *Alice's Adventures in Wonderland.* (1922). Dodd Mead. 1st Am thus. ils G Hudson. 81p. VG. D1. $375.00

CARROLL, Lewis. *Alice's Adventures in Wonderland.* 1869. Lee Shepard. 1st Am. ils CL Dodgson. aeg. gilt apricot cloth. M24. $600.00

CARROLL, Lewis. *Alice's Adventures in Wonderland.* 1907. London. Heinemann. 1st thus. ils Rackham/13 mc pl. 8vo. gilt gr cloth. R5. $275.00

CARROLL, Lewis. *Alice's Adventures in Wonderland.* 1908. London. Thomas Nelson. 1st. ils Harry Rountree. 4to. teg. bl cloth. F. R5. $150.00

CARROLL, Lewis. *Alice's Adventures in Wonderland.* 1919. London. Humphrey Milford. ils AE Jackson. 8vo. teg. gr pict cloth. R5. $200.00

CARROLL, Lewis. *Alice's Adventures in Wonderland.* 1922. London. Ward Lock. ils MW Tarrant. 8vo. gray cloth. dj. R5. $200.00

CARROLL, Lewis. *Alice's Adventures in Wonderland.* 1929. EP Dutton. 1st thus. ils Willy Pogany. 8vo. gilt purple cloth. dj. R5. $350.00

CARROLL, Lewis. *Alice's Adventures in Wonderland.* 1945. London. Arthur Barron. 1st. ils Harry Riley. 12mo. gray cloth. dj. R5. $150.00

CARROLL, Lewis. *Alice's Adventures in Wonderland.* 1980. Franklin. leather. NF. P3. $20.00

CARROLL, Lewis. *Alice's Adventures in Wonderland/Through the Looking Glass.* 1950. Paris. ES Wood. 2 vol. 1st thus. ils Tenniel. half morocco. miniature/F/box. H13. $295.00

CARROLL, Lewis. *Alice's Adventures in Wonderland/Through the Looking Glass.* 1993. London. Folio Soc. 8th. 2 vol. gilt red cloth. F/case. T10. $60.00

CARROLL, Lewis. *Hunting of the Snark & Other Poems & Verses.* 1903. Harper. 1st thus. ils/sgn Peter Newell. 4to. gilt wht brd. stiff gr dj. R5. $300.00

CARROLL, Lewis. *Hunting of the Snark & Other Poems & Verses.* 1903. NY. 1st. ils/sgn Newell. 248p. teg. F. H3. $100.00

CARROLL, Lewis. *Hunting of the Snark.* 1970. NY. Watts. 1st Am. 48p. NF/dj. D4. $55.00

CARROLL, Lewis. *Hunting of the Snark.* 1981. Los Altos. Kaufmann. Centenary ed. 1/1955. 43 pl/Henry Holiday. linen. A17. $35.00

CARROLL, Lewis. *Philosopher's Alice.* 1974. St Martin. intro Heath. xl. VG. N1. $12.00

CARROLL, Lewis. *Pig-Tale.* 1975. Little Brn. 1st thus. 30p. VG+/dj. M20. $25.00

CARROLL, Lewis. *Through the Looking-Glass & What Alice Found There.* 1909. NY. Dodge. 1st. ils Bessie Pease Guttman. 8vo. bl cloth. dj. R5. $300.00

CARROLL, Lewis. *Through the Looking-Glass & What Alice Found There.* 1931. NY. Cheshire. 1/1200. ils Franklin Hughes. 4to. top edge brn. wht silk. R5. $200.00

CARROLL, Lewis. *Useful & Instructive Poetry.* 1954. Macmillan. 1st. F/F. D4. $45.00

CARROLL, Lewis. *Verses From Alice.* (1944). London. Collins. 1st thus. ils GL Sherwood. VG/VG. D1. $225.00

CARROLL, Lewis. *Walt Disney's Alice in Wonderland.* 1951. London. Dean. 1st Eng thus. 4to. pict brd. R5. $275.00

CARROLL, Lewis. *Walt Disney's Alice in Wonderland.* 1951. Whitman. Cozy Corner series. ils Walt Disney Studio. VG. M5. $25.00

CARROLL, Paul. *Poem in Its Skin.* 1968. Follett. 1st. F/NF. V1. $25.00

CARROLL & CARROLL. *Danny & the Poi Pup.* 1965. Walck. 1st. F/VG. M5. $22.00

CARROLL & COLEMAN. *New Singing Time: Book of Songs for Little Children.* 1950. John Day. 1st. sm 4to. 32p. tan cloth. NF. C14. $14.00

CARROLL & DIPPIE. *Bards of the Little Big Horn.* 1978. Guidon. 1st. 1/350. sgn/ils Dave Powell. 344p. VG. J2. $115.00

CARROLL & GARDNER. *More Annotated Alice.* 1990. Random. 1st. 4to. 400p. F/dj. T10. $50.00

CARROLL & PRICE. *Roll Call on the Little Big Horn, 28 June 1876.* 1974. Old Army. 1st ltd. 1/75. sgn Carroll/Price/Clendenen. 168p. as new. J2. $695.00

CARRUTH, Hayden. *For You — Poems.* 1970. New Directions. 1st. sgn. F/F. R14. $60.00

CARRUTH, Vance. *Teton Sketches of Summer.* 1969. Johnson Pub. 1st. sgn. 30p. VG/torn. J2. $35.00

CARRYL, Charles E. *Davy & the Goblin or What Followed Reading Alice...* (1913). Houghton Mifflin/Riverside. ils EB Bensell. G. B15. $85.00

CARRYL, Charles. *Admiral's Caravan.* 1892. Century. 1st. ils Reginald Birch. VG. M5. $95.00

CARSON, Gerald. *Social History of Bourbon.* 1963. NY. 1st. ils. 280p. VG/dj. B18. $17.50

CARSON, James. *Saddle Boys in the Grand Canyon.* 1913. Cupples Leon. 12mo. VG. F7. $37.50

CARSON, John F. *Boys Who Vanished.* 1959. DSP. 1st. 212p. cloth. VG/dj. M20. $15.00

CARSON, Mina. *Settlement Folk.* 1990. Chicago. 1st. as new/dj. V4. $20.00

CARSON, Rachel. *Edge of the Sea.* 1956. Houghton Mifflin. 1st. ils Bob Hines. VG+/dj. A25. $22.00

CARSON, Rachel. *Edge of the Sea.* 1956. Houghton Mifflin. 1st. NF/VG. M19. $25.00

CARSON, Rachel. *Sea Around Us.* 1951. Oxford. 1st. gr pict brd. NF/NF later state. M24. $100.00

CARSON, Rachel. *Silent Spring.* 1962. Houghton Mifflin. 1st. F/NF. Q1. $150.00

CARSON, Rachel. *Under the Sea-Wind: A Naturalist's Picture of Ocean Life.* 1952. NY. Oxford. revised. 314p. VG/dj. A25. $18.00

CARSON, Robin. *Dawn of Time.* 1957. Holt. 1st. VG/worn. M2. $18.00

CARTER, Angela. *Fireworks.* 1981. Harper Row. 1st Am. F/NF. A24. $25.00

CARTER, Angela. *Love.* 1971. Hart Davis. 1st. VG/VG. P3. $50.00

CARTER, Angela. *Nights at the Circus.* 1985. Viking. 1st. F/NF. A24. $25.00

CARTER, Angela. *Shadow Dance.* 1966. Heinemann. 1st. VG/VG. P3. $100.00

CARTER, Angela. *Shadow Dance.* 1966. London. Heinemann. true 1st. author's 1st book. NF/dj. A24. $185.00

CARTER, Clarence Edwin. *Territorial Papers of the US, Territory of Michigan 1805-37.* 1942-1945. GPO. 3 vol. D11. $100.00

CARTER, G.S. *General Zoology of the Invertebrates.* 1948. London. Sidgwick Jackson. 3rd. 13 pl. clip dj. B1. $35.00

CARTER, Henry. *Methodist Heritage.* 1951. Abingdon-Cokesbury. 246p. VG/dj. B29. $9.00

CARTER, Herbert R. *Spinning & Twisting of Long Vegetable Fibres.* 1919. London. Griffin. 434p. cloth. A10. $45.00

CARTER, Howard. *Tomb of Tut-Akka-Amen.* 1923. Doran. A19. $30.00

CARTER, Howard. *Tomb of Tutankhamen.* 1972. NY. Excalibur. 1st Am. 238p. NF/dj. W1. $22.00

CARTER, Jared. *Work for the Night Is Coming.* 1980. Macmillan. 1st. assn copy. F/dj. V1. $25.00

CARTER, Jimmy & Rosalynn. *Everyting To Gain: Making the Most of Rest of Your Life.* 1987. Random. 1st. sgn Rosalynn Carter bookplate. VG/VG. A23. $60.00

CARTER, Jimmy. *Always a Reckoning.* 1995. Times Books. 1st. sgn. F/F. S13. $55.00

CARTER, Jimmy. *Blood of Abraham: Insights to the Middle East.* 1985. Houghton Mifflin. 1st. sgn. VG/VG. A23. $75.00

CARTER, Jimmy. *Blood of Abraham: Insights to the Middle East.* 1985. Houghton Mifflin. 1st. 8vo. maps. 257p. NF/dj. W1. $18.00

CARTER, Jimmy. *Living Faith.* 1996. Times Books. 1st. sgn. F/F. A23. $75.00

CARTER, Jimmy. *Outdoor Journal.* 1988. Bantam. 1st. VG/VG. A23. $75.00

CARTER, Jimmy. *Talking Peace: A Vision for the Next Generation.* 1993. Dutton. 1st. sgn. VG/VG. A23. $75.00

CARTER, Jimmy. *Turning Point.* 1992. Times Books. 1st. sgn. F/F. A23. $75.00

CARTER, Lin. *Dreams From R'lyeh.* 1975. Arkham. 1st. F/dj. T2. $35.00

CARTER, Lin. *Invisible Death.* 1975. Doubleday. 1st. F/F. P3. $15.00

CARTER, Lin. *Man Who Loved Mars.* 1973. Wht Lion. hc. VG/G. P3. $17.00

CARTER, Lin. *Valley Where Time Stood Still.* 1974. Doubleday. 1st. NF/NF. P3. $20.00

CARTER, Lin. *Volcano Ogre.* 1976. Doubleday. 1st. F/F. M2/P3. $15.00

CARTER, M. *Isabella Stewart Gardner & Fenway Court.* 1972. photos. VG/VG. M17. $20.00

CARTER, Nick (a few); see Avallone, Mike.

CARTER, Paul. *Road to Botany Bay.* 1988. NY. Knopf. 1st Am. 384p. half cloth. as new/dj. P4. $23.00

CARTER, Samuel. *Final Fortress.* 1980. 354p. O8. $12.50

CARTER, W.H. *From Yorktown to Santiago With the Sixth US Calvery.* 1900. Lord Baltimore. 1st. frontis/tissue. ils Remington. roster. 317p. VG. J2. $1,575.00

CARTER, William Harding. *Horses of the World.* 1923. NGS. ils. VG. O3. $45.00

CARTER, Youngman. *Mr Campion's Quarry.* 1971. Morrow. 1st. VG/VG. P3. $18.00

CARTIER, Ed. *Known & the Unknown.* 1977. De La Ree. NF/NF. P3. $35.00

CARTIER, John O. *Getting the Most Out of Modern Wildfowling.* 1974. NY. 396p. dj. A17. $15.00

CARTIN, Hazel. *Elijah.* 1980. St Martin. 1st. inscr. F/NF clip. L3. $75.00

CARTWRIGHT, H. Mills. *Photogravure: A TB on the Machine & Hand-Prt Processes.* 1930. Boston. 142p. A17. $12.50

CARUS, Titus Lucretius. *Of the Nature of Things.* 1957. LEC. 1st thus. 1/1500. ils/sgn Paul Landacre. F/remnant glassine/case. Q1. $125.00

CARUTHERS, William. *Loafing Along Death Valley Trails.* 1951. Death Valley Pub. 1st. VG/sans. O4. $15.00

CARVEL, John L. *Stephen of Linthouse.* 1950. Glasgow. Stephen & Sons. ils. 311p. torn dj. T7. $50.00

CARVER, Jeffrey A. *Infinity Link.* 1984. Bluejay Internat. 1st. NF/dj. M21. $15.00

CARVER, Jeffrey A. *Infinity Link.* 1984. Bluejay. 1st. sgn. F/F. P3. $25.00

CARVER, Jeffrey A. *Rapture Effect.* 1987. Tor. 1st. RS. F/F. P3. $20.00

CARVER, Raymond. *Carver Country: World of Raymond Carver.* 1990. Scribner. 1st. F/torn. A18. $35.00

CARVER, Raymond. *My Crow.* 1984. Ewert. 1/150. ils Thomas Berwick. F/wrp. V1. $30.00

CARVER, Raymond. *New Path to the Waterfall.* 1989. Atlantic Monthly. 1st. ils Tess Gallagher. F/NF. B3. $50.00

CARVER, Raymond. *Put Yourself in My Shoes.* 1974. Capra. 1st trade. sgn. F/wrp. B2. $300.00

CARVER, Raymond. *River.* 1986. Concord, NH. 1/26. sgn. w/sgn broadside by John Jagel. F. V1. $250.00

CARVER, Raymond. *Ultramarine.* 1986. Random. 1st. sgn. F/F. D10. $175.00

CARVER, Raymond. *What We Talk About When We Talk About Love.* 1981. Knopf. 1st. F/dj. B4/Q1. $200.00

CARVER, Raymond. *Where I'm Calling From.* 1988. Franklin Lib. 1st/ltd. sgn. full burgundy leather. F. Q1. $200.00

CARVER, Raymond. *Where I'm Calling From: New & Selected Stories.* 1988. Atlantic Monthly. 1st. F/dj. A18. $40.00

CARVER, Raymond. *Where Water Comes Together With Other Water.* 1985. Random. 1st. NF/dj. D10. $75.00

CARVIC, Heron. *Miss Seeton Sings.* 1973. Harper Row. VG. P3. $22.00

CARVIC, Heron. *Picture Miss Seeton.* 1968. Geoffrey Bles. 1st. VG/G. P3. $25.00

CARY, Diana Serra. *Hollywood Posse: Story of a Gallant Band of Horsemen...* 1975. Houghton Mifflin. 1st. 268p. VG/VG. J2. $75.00

CARY, Gillie. *Uncle Jerry's Platform & Other Christmas Stories.* 1895. Boston. 1st. lg 12mo. VG. C8. $60.00

CARY, Joyce. *Cock Jarvis.* 1974. London. Michael Joseph. true 1st. author's last/unfinished novel. F/F. D10. $50.00

CARY, Joyce. *Prisoner of Grace.* 1952. Michael Joseph. 1st. 398p. VG+/dj. M20. $38.00

CARYLE, Thomas. *Oliver Cromwell's Letters & Speeches.* 1871. Chapman Hall. 5 vol. 8vo. decor brn cloth. VG. B22. $15.00

CASAL, U. *Some Notes on the Sakazuki.* 1940. Tokyo. Asiatic Soc Japan. rpt. 186p. VG/wrp. W3. $135.00

CASE, David. *Third Grave.* 1981. Arkham. 1st. F/dj. M2. $25.00

CASE, Shirley J. *Origins of Christian Supernaturalism.* 1946. Chicago. 239p. VG/torn. B29. $7.00

CASEWIT, Curtis. *Peacemakers.* 1960. Avalon. 1st. F/dj. M2. $15.00

CASEY, John. *American Romance.* 1977. Atheneum. 1st. VG/dj. A20. $25.00

CASEY, John. *Spartina.* 1989. Knopf. 1st. inscr. F/F. D10. $85.00

CASEY, John. *Testimony & Demeanor.* 1979. Knopf. 1st. F/F. B3. $75.00

CASEY, Robert J. *Baghdad & Points East.* ca 1930. London. Hutchinson. 8vo. 16 pl. xl. VG. W1. $24.00

CASEY, Robert J. *Black Hills.* 1949. Bobbs Merrill. map. VG. A19. $55.00

CASEY, Robert J. *Easter Island: Home of the Scornful Gods.* 1931. Bobbs Merrill. 8vo. 43 photos. 337p. bl cloth. P4. $36.00

CASEY, Robert J. *Mr Clutch, Story of George William Borg.* 1948. Indianapolis. 1st. inscr. 258p. VG/dj. B18. $27.50

CASEY, Robert J. *Torpedo Junction: With the Pacific Fleet From Pearl Harbor.* 1942. Indianapolis. 1st. photos/map. 423p. VG/G. S16. $27.50

CASHIN, Hershel V. *Under Fire With the 10th Calvary.* 1970. NY. Bellwether. rpt. 361p. F/VG+. B4. $65.00

CASHMAN, A.W. *Vice-Regal Cowboy.* 1957. Edmonton. 1st prt. inscr. 199p. P4. $35.00

CASIMER & VAN VLECK. *Cherwell-Simon Memorial Lectures 1961 & 1962.* 1962. London. Oliver Boyd. 1st. VG. K3. $20.00

CASPARY, Vera. *Weeping & the Laughter.* 1950. Little Brn. 1st. VG/VG. P3. $35.00

CASS, Bevan. *History of the Sixth Marine Division.* 1948. WA, DC. 1st. ils/maps/awards. 262p. VG. S16. $95.00

CASSANDRA, Knye; see Disch, Thomas.

CASSERLY, Gordon. *Elephant God.* 1921. Putnam. 1st. VG. M2. $15.00

CASSIDAY, Bruce. *Floater.* 1960. Abelard Schuman. VG/VG. P3. $20.00

CASSIDY, S.M. *Elements of Practical Coal Mining.* 1973. NY. Soc Mining Engineers Am Inst Mining. 614p. cloth. NF/dj. D8. $35.00

CASSILL, R.V. *Eagle on the Coin.* 1950. 1st. author's 1st book. F/VG. M19. $35.00

CASSIN, J. *Illustrations of California, Texas, Oregon...* 1991 (1856). Austin. TX Hist Assn. 1/250. facsimile. 8vo. 298p. half leather. F/F case. M12. $150.00

CASSIRER, Ernst. *Substance & Function & Einstein's Theory of Relativity.* 1923. Open Court. 8vo. 465p. G/tattered. K5. $25.00

CASSON, Herbert N. *History of the Telephone.* 1910. McClurg. 1st. ils. 8vo. 315p. VG. K3. $20.00

CASSON, Lionel. *Ancient Egypt.* 1978. NY. Time. 11th. 191p. VG. W1. $10.00

CASSON, Lionel. *Ancient Mariners: Seafarers & Sea Fighters...* 1968. Macmillan. 286p. VG/dj. P4. $30.00

CASTANEDA, Carlos. *Fire From Within.* 1984. S&S. 1st. F/dj. B4. $45.00

CASTANEDA, Carlos. *Tales of Power.* (1974). S&S. 1st. 207p. VG/dj. F3. $20.00

CASTANEDA, Pedro. *Journey of Coronado.* 1966. Readex Microprint. rpt. 8vo. F. F7. $30.00

CASTIGLIONI, Arturo. *History of Medicine.* 1941. NY. 1st. 1013p. A13. $175.00

CASTLE, Frederick. *Gilbert Green: The Real Right Way To Dress For Spring...* 1986. McPherson. 1st. F/VG+. A20. $20.00

CASTLE, Jeffery Lloyd. *Satelite E One.* 1954. Eyre Spottiswoode. VG/G. P3. $10.00

CASTLE, Lewis. *Cactaceous Plants: Their History & Culture.* 1974 (1884). Annapolis. ils. 94p. B26. $15.00

CASTLE & CASTLE. *Our Sentimental Garden.* 1914. Phil. Lippincott. 1st Am. ils Chas Robinson. 4to. gilt gr cloth. dj. R5. $275.00

CASTRO, Michael. *Interpreting the Indian.* 1983. Albuquerque. NM U. 1st. F/dj. L3. $50.00

CASWELL, J.E. *Arctic Frontiers. United States Explorations in Far North.* 1956. Norman, OK. 1st. photos/maps. 232p. F/dj. M4. $20.00

CATANZARO, Angela. *Italian Desserts & Antipasto.* 1958. NY. Liveright. VG/dj. A16. $15.00

CATESBY, Mark. *Natural History of Carolina, Florida & Bahama Islands.* 1974. Savannah, GA. Beehive. 1/500. folio. 107p+suite loose pl. as new/cloth box. C6. $800.00

CATHER, Willa. *April Twilights.* 1923. NY. Knopf. 1st trade. quarter gr cloth/patterned brd. F/sans. M24. $100.00

CATHER, Willa. *Death Comes for the Archbishop.* 1927. Knopf. 1st. F/dj. Q1. $350.00

CATHER, Willa. *Death Comes for the Archbishop.* 1927. Knopf. 1st/1st prt. 1st bdg (gr cloth). F. M24. $200.00

CATHER, Willa. *December Night: Scene From Willa Cather's Novel...* 1933. Knopf. 1st. ils. fancy brd. F/NF. A18. $40.00

CATHER, Willa. *Lucy Gayheart.* 1935. 1/749. sgn/#d. 231p. ribbon marker bdg in. VG. A4. $350.00

CATHER, Willa. *Lucy Gayheart.* 1935. Knopf. 1st. 1/25000. F/NF. M24. $100.00

CATHER, Willa. *Obscure Destinies.* 1932. Knopf. 1st. gr cloth. F/VG clip (lowered before pub). M24. $100.00

CATHER, Willa. *Sapphira & the Slave Girl.* 1940. Knopf. ARC. F/F. D10. $175.00

CATHER, Willa. *Sapphira & the Slave Girl.* 1940. Knopf. 1st. F/NF. M24. $75.00

CATHER, Willa. *Shadows on the Rock.* 1931. Knopf. 1st. NF/VG. M23. $75.00

CATHERINE II OF RUSSIA. *Memoirs of the Empress Catherine II of Russia by Herself.* 1859. London. 12mo. full dk red leather/raised bands. F. H3. $125.00

CATICH, Edward M. *Eric Gill, His Social & Artistic Roots.* 1964. IA City. Prairie Pr. 1st. M/dj. B24. $100.00

CATLIN, George. *Breath of Life; or, Mal-Respiration & Its Effects...* 1872. NY. John Wiley. 8vo. 76p. cloth. M1. $150.00

CATLIN, George. *Catlin's North American Indian Portfolio.* 1970. Chicago. Sage. 1/1000. facsimile 1844 London. stiff portfolio. B24. $500.00

CATLIN, George. *North American Indians: Being Letters & Notes...* 1926. Edinburgh. Jonn Grant. 2 vol. ils/fld map. maroon T-grain cloth. F. K7. $950.00

CATTELL, Ann. *Mind Juggler & Other Ghost Stories.* 1966. Exposition. 1st. VG/VG. P3. $15.00

CATTELL, Henry. *Post-Mortem Pathology: A Manual...* 1903. Phil. 1st. ils. 372p. A13. $100.00

CATTON, Bruce. *Glory Road: Bloody Route From Fredericksburg to Gettysburg.* 1952. Doubleday. 1st. 416p. cloth. NF/dj. M8. $35.00

CATTON, Bruce. *Mr Lincoln's Army.* 1951. Doubleday. 1st. 372p. NF/VG. M8. $35.00

CATTON, Bruce. *Mr Lincoln's Army.* 1951. Doubleday. 1st. 372p. VG/dj. O8. $21.50

CATTON, Bruce. *Reflections on the Civil War.* 1981. NY. 1st. ils John Geyser. F/dj. M4. $30.00

CATTON, Bruce. *Waiting for the Morning Train: An American Boyhood.* 1972. Doubleday. 1/250. sgn/#d. F/sans/case. Q1. $75.00

CAUDILL, Rebecca. *Come Along!* 1969. HRW. 1st. 32p. F/F. D4. $25.00

CAUFFMAN, Stanley. *Witchfinders.* 1934. Penn. 1st. VG. M2. $22.00

CAUMERY. *Becassine Voyage.* 1923 (1921). Paris. Gautier. Semaine de Suzette. ils Pinchon. VG. M5. $90.00

CAUNITZ, William J. *Exceptional Clearance.* 1991. Crown. 1st. F/F. N4. $20.00

CAUNITZ, William J. *One Police Plaza.* 1984. Crown. 1st. author's 1st book. F/F. H11. $50.00

CAUNITZ, William J. *Suspects.* 1986. Crown. 1st. inscr. F/F. H11. $50.00

CAUNITZ, William J. *Suspects.* 1986. Crown. 1st. NF/NF. P3. $22.00

CAUNITZ, William J. *Suspects.* 1986. NY. Crown. 1st. F/F. R14. $25.00

CAUSLEY, Charles. *Early in the Morning.* 1986. Viking. 1st. ils Michael Foreman/music Anthony Castro. F/F. D4. $30.00

CAVALLERO, Gene. *Colony Cookbook.* 1972. Bobbs Merrill. VG/dj. A16. $17.50

CAVALLO, A.S. *Tapestries of Europe & of Colonial Peru in Mus of Fine Arts.* 1967. Boston. 2 vol. ils. VG/VG case. M17. $25.00

CAVANNA, Betty. *Accent on April.* (1960). Morrow. BC. 8vo. 188p. bl brd. G+/dj. T5. $14.00

CAVANNA, Betty. *Boy Next Door.* 1956. Morrow. 1st. 253p. VG/dj. M20. $30.00

CAVANNA, Betty. *Passport to Romance.* 1955. Morrow. 1st. 249p. VG/dj. M20. $15.00

CAVANNA, Betty. *Pick of the Litter.* (1952). Phil. Westminster. 8vo. 222p. brn cloth. VG. T5. $15.00

CAVANNA, Betty. *Puppy Stakes.* 1948. Phil. Westminster. 1st. ils. G. O3. $18.00

CAVE, Emma. *Blood Bond.* 1979. Harper Row. 1st. F/F. P3. $25.00

CAVE, Henry. *Golden Tips: Descriptive of Ceylon & Its Great Tea Industry.* 1904. London. Cassell. 3rd. photos. teg. 476p. VG. W3. $185.00

CAVE, Hugh. *Cross on the Drum.* 1959. Doubleday. VG. M2. $12.00

CAVE, Hugh. *Long Were the Nights: Saga of PT Squadron X in Solomons.* 1943. NY. sgn pres. map/roster. 220p. VG/VG. S16. $45.00

CAVERLY, Carol. *All the Old Lions.* 1994. Aurora, CO. Write Way. 1st. sgn. F/F. B3. $35.00

CAWEIN, Madison. *Myth & Romance.* 1899. NY/London. 1st. 12mo. cloth. M1. $200.00

CAWTHORN & MOORCOCK. *Fantasy: 100 Best Books.* 1988. Carroll Graf. 1st Am. F/F. R10. $10.00

CAYTON & MITCHELL. *Black Workers & the New Unions.* 1939. Chapel Hill. 1st. inscr. 473p. NF/VG. B4. $200.00

CAZALET-KEIR, Thelma. *Homage to PG Wodehouse.* 1973. Barrie Jenkins. 1st. VG/VG. P3. $25.00

CECIL, David. *Two Quiet Lives.* 1948. London. 1st. VG/dj. T9. $20.00

CECIL, Henry. *Brief to Counsel.* 1958. Michael Joseph. 1st. VG. P3. $20.00

CECIL, Henry. *Unlawful Occasions.* 1962. London. Michael Joseph. 1st. F/NF. M22. $25.00

CEDERGREN, H.R. *Seepage, Drainage & Flow Nets.* 1967. John Wiley. 489p. F/dj. D8. $25.00

CELEHAR, Jane H. *Kitchens & Kitchenware.* 1985. Wallace-Homestead. 1st. 208p. VG/glossy ils wrp. H1. $32.00

CELLI, Rose. *Picture Play Book.* 1935. Artists Writers Guild. folio. stiff sc. VG. M5. $110.00

CELY, Michael. *Canada Calling.* nd. Frederick Warne. 240p. VG/ragged. M20. $17.50

CENDRARS, Blaise. *Shadow.* 1982. Scribner. 1st. 4to. VG+/NF. P2. $95.00

CERAM, C.W. *Gods, Graves & Scholars.* 1953. Knopf. 415p. G. B29. $9.00

CERAM, C.W. *Hands on the Past. Pioneer Archaeologists Tell Their Story.* 1966. Knopf. 1st. 31 pl. 434p. VG/dj. W1. $15.00

CERF, Bennett. *Favorite One Act Plays.* 1958. Doubleday. dj. A19. $20.00

CERF, Leon. *Letters of Napoleon to Josephine.* (1928). Paris. 12mo. French text. ils. 188p. 3-quarter leather. H3. $50.00

CERISE, Laurent-Alexis-P. *Des Fonctions et des Maladies Nerveuses...* 1870 (1842). Paris. Victor Masson. 2nd. 508p. prt gr wrp. G1. $100.00

CERNY & NOVAK. *Tales of the Uncanny.* 1976. Hamlyn. 1st. VG/G. P3. $15.00

CERVANTES. *Don Quixote.* 1906. 2 vol. ils Gustave Dore. VG. M17. $45.00

CH'ANG, Lo-huang. *Ming-Hsien Mo-Chi.* 1971. Shanghai. Commercial Pr. 2 vol. VG/bl wrp. W3. $65.00

CHABER, M.E. *Acid Nightmare.* 1967. HRW. 1st. VG/VG. P3. $22.00

CHABER, M.E. *Green Grow the Graves.* 1970. HRW. 1st. F/F. P3. $15.00

CHABER, M.E. *Wanted: Dead Men.* 1965. HRW. 1st. VG/VG. P3. $18.00

CHABON, Michael. *Model World.* 1991. Morrow. 1st. author's 2nd book. F/F. B4. $45.00

CHABON, Michael. *Mysteries of Pittsburgh.* 1988. Morrow. 1st. author's 1st novel. F/F. D10. $50.00

CHABON, Michael. *Mysteries of Pittsburgh.* 1988. Morrow. 1st. NF/dj. A20. $30.00

CHADWICK, Douglas. *Fate of the Elephant.* 1993. Viking. 1st. 492p. F. S15. $10.00

CHADWICK, Lester. *Baseball Joe Around the World (#8).* 1918. Cupples Leon. 246p. cloth. VG/dj (lists to #14). M20. $37.50

CHAFER, Lewis Sperry. *Kingdom in History & Prophecy.* 1943. Dunham. 167p. VG/torn. B29. $6.50

CHAFETS, Zev. *Inherit the Mob.* 1991. Random. 1st. F/dj. M22. $20.00

CHAFETZ, Henry. *Legend of Befana.* 1958. Houghton Mifflin. 1st possible ed. 8vo. F/F. C8. $17.50

CHAHINIAN, B. Juan. *Sansevieria Trifasciata Varieties.* 1986. Reseda, CA. photos. 109p. F/dj. B26. $17.50

CHAILLEY, Jacques. *40,000 Years of Music: Man in Search of Music.* 1964. FSG. 1st Am. 229p. VG/dj. M20. $22.00

CHAIS, Pamela. *Final Cut.* 1981. S&S. 1st. F/dj. M25. $25.00

CHALFONT, Lord. *Waterloo.* 1979. Knopf. 1st Am. 239p. VG/dj. M20. $30.00

CHALK, Ocania. *Black College Sport.* 1976. Dodd Mead. 1st. photos. F/VG. P8. $30.00

CHALKER, Jack L. *Demons at Rainbow Bridge.* 1989. Ace. 1st. F/F. P3. $18.00

CHALMER, Patrick. *Kenneth Graham: Life, Letters & Unpublished Work.* 1933. London. Methuen. 1st. ils/photos/letters/facsimilies. bl cloth. VG. D1. $125.00

CHALMERS, Audrey. *Fancy Be Good.* 1941. Viking. 1st. 8vo. VG+/dj. M5. $20.00

CHALMERS, Mary. *Throw a Kiss, Harry.* 1958. Harper. probable 1st. 12mo. 32p. VG/VG. P2. $50.00

CHALMERS, Stephen. *Affair of the Gallows Tree.* 1930. Crime Club. 1st. VG. P3. $30.00

CHALMERS, Thomas. *On the Power, Wisdom & Goodness of God...* 1853. London. Bohn. later ed. rebound/red label. VG. K3. $30.00

CHAMALES, Tom. *Never So Few.* 1957. NY. 1st. VG/VG. B5. $35.00

CHAMBERLAIN, Allen. *Beacon Hill: Its Ancient Pastures & Early Mansions.* 1925. photos. VG. M17. $30.00

CHAMBERLAIN, George Agnew. *Scudda A-Hoo! Scudda-Hay!* 1946. Bobbs Merrill. 1st. VG/VG. O3. $48.00

CHAMBERLAIN, Hope Summerell. *Old Days in Chapel Hill Being Life & Letters CP Spencer.* 1926. Chapel Hill. 1st. 325p. cloth. NF. M8. $45.00

CHAMBERLAIN, Joseph W. *Physics of the Aurora & Airglow.* 1961. Academic. 8vo. 704p. VG/dj. K5. $60.00

CHAMBERLAIN, Samuel. *Bouquet de France.* 1960. NY. Gourmet. G+. A16. $20.00

CHAMBERLAIN, Samuel. *British Bouquet.* 1973. Gourmet. G+. A16. $25.00

CHAMBERLAIN, Sarah. *Beasts From Belloc.* 1982-1858. Chamberlain. 1/125. sgn. 17 wood engravings. Blumenthal bdg. w/2 sgn postcards. B24. $500.00

CHAMBERLAIN, Sarah. *Bremen Town Musicians. A Grimm Fairy Tale.* 1978. Chamberlain. 1/120. sgn. 10 wood engravings. Gray Parrot bdg. F. B24. $300.00

CHAMBERLAIN, Sarah. *Frog He Would A-Wooing Go.* 1981. Chamberlain. 1/125. sgn. 7 full-p wood engravings. Oriental-style bdg. F. B24. $300.00

CHAMBERLAIN, Sarah. *Selection of Aesop's Fables.* 1984. Chamberlain. 1/150. sgn. trans Artzybasheff. w/prospectus & sgn postcard. F. B24. $350.00

CHAMBERLAIN & SHAW. *Wilt.* 1973. Macmillan. 1st. VG/G+. P8. $15.00

CHAMBERLIN, Charles. *Methods in Plant Histology.* 1928. Chicago. 4th. 349p. dj. A10. $28.00

CHAMBERLIN, F. *Private Character of Queen Elizabeth.* 1922. NY. ils. VG. M17. $17.50

CHAMBERLIN, Harry D. *Training Hunters, Jumpers & Hacks.* 1969. NY. Van Nostrand Reinhold. later rpt. VG/G. O3. $25.00

CHAMBERLIN & HOFFMAN. *Checklist of the Millipeds of North America.* 1958. Smithsonian. 236p. wrp. B1. $18.50

CHAMBERS, Dana. *Death Against Venus.* 1946. Dial. VG/VG. P3. $23.00

CHAMBERS, G.F. *Story of the Solar System.* 1905 (1895). NY. Appleton. ils. 188p. cloth. G. K5. $12.00

CHAMBERS, G.F. *Story of the Weather.* 1897. London. George Newnes. 232p. G. K5. $18.00

CHAMBERS, Peter; see Phillips, Dennis.

CHAMBERS, Robert E.S. *John Tom Alligator & Others.* 1937. Dutton. 1st. VG/dj. M2. $12.00

CHAMBERS, Robert W. *In Search of the Unknown.* 1974 (1904). Hyperion. rpt. F. M2. $30.00

CHAMBERS, Robert W. *Slayer of Souls.* 1920. Doran. 1st. VG/facsimile mc Canon dj. M2. $45.00

CHAMBERS, Robert W. *Streets of Ascalon.* 1912. Appleton. 1st. VG. P3. $25.00

CHAMBERS, Whitman. *Invasion!* 1943. Dutton. 1st. VG. P3. $20.00

CHAMBERS & SONNICHSEN. *San Agustin: First Cathedral Church in Arizona.* 1974. AZ Historical Soc. 1st. 1/100. inscr/sgns. ils/notes. 56p. F/F case. B19. $110.00

CHAMPOMIER, P.A. *Statement of the Sugar Crop Made in Louisiana in 1851-52...* 1852. New Orleans. Cook Young. 1st. 16mo. 52p. prt wrp. M1. $400.00

CHAN, Sucheng. *This Bittersweet Soil: Chinese in California Agriculuture...* 1986. Berkeley. 8vo. ils. burgundy cloth. F/dj. R3. $40.00

CHANDLER, A. Bertram. *Bring Back Yesterday.* 1981. Allison Busby. 1st. F/F. P3. $20.00

CHANDLER, Ann C. *Pan the Piper & Other Marvelous Tales.* 1923. Harper. 1st. ils. 234p. gilt bl cloth. VG. D1. $40.00

CHANDLER, David. *Campaigns of Napoleon.* 1966. 1st. ils/maps. VG/VG. M17. $50.00

CHANDLER, Edna Walker. *Cowboy Sam & Big Bill.* 1960. Chicago. Benefic. ils Jack Merryweather. xl. VG. C8. $15.00

CHANDLER, Edna Walker. *Cowboy Sam & Freckles.* 1960. Chicago. Benefic. ils Merryweather. xl. G. C8. $12.50

CHANDLER, Edna Walker. *Cowboy Sam & the Fair.* 1953. Chicago. Berkley-Cardy. lg 12mo. VG. C8. $15.00

CHANDLER, Edna Walker. *Cowboy Sam & the Rodeo.* 1959. Chicago. Benefic. 8vo. VG. C8. $15.00

CHANDLER, John Greene. *Remarkable History of Chicken Little.* 1979. Boston. Bromer/Hyder. 1/150. 59x50mm. ils Janet Hobbs. marbled brd. F. B24. $65.00

CHANDLER, Melbourne C. *Of Gerryowen in Glory, the History of the 7th US Calvary.* 1960. Turnpike. 1st. photos/maps. 463p. VG/VG. J2. $245.00

CHANDLER, Raymond. *Big Sleep.* 1939. Knopf. 1st. author's 1st book. apricot cloth. NF. M24. $300.00

CHANDLER, Raymond. *High Window.* 1942. Knopf. 1st. NF/VG. M15. $1,250.00

CHANDLER, Raymond. *High Window.* 1942. Knopf. 1st. xl. VG. P3. $125.00

CHANDLER, Raymond. *Lady in the Lake.* 1944. London. Hamish Hamilton. 1st. G. M22. $45.00

CHANDLER, Raymond. *Long Goodbye.* 1953. London. Hamish Hamilton. true 1st. VG. M22. $60.00

CHANDLER, Raymond. *Midnight Raymond Chandler.* 1971. Houghton Mifflin. 1st. VG. M22. $15.00

CHANDLER, Raymond. *Midnight Raymond Chandler.* 1971. Houghton Mifflin. 1st. VG+/dj. M25. $30.00

CHANDLER, Raymond. *Playback.* 1958. London. Hamish Hamilton. 1st. NF/VG. M15. $100.00

CHANDLER, Raymond. *Playback.* 1958. Thriller BC. VG/G. P3. $15.00

CHANDLER, Raymond. *Red Wind.* 1946. World. 1st. VG. M22. $15.00

CHANDLER, Raymond. *Spanish Blood.* 1946. World. 1st. VG. M22. $15.00

CHANDLER & PARKER. *Poodle Springs.* 1989. Putnam. 1st. F/F. M22. $15.00

CHANEY, Jack. *Foolish Questions, Yellowstone Best.* 1924. Woodruff. 3rd. 104p. VG/wrp. J2. $165.00

CHANG, Garma. *Hundred Thousand Songs of Milarepa.* 1962. U Books. 1st. 2 vol. ils/index. F/VG box. W3. $125.00

CHANG, Kwang-chih. *Archeology of Ancient China.* 1963. Yale. 1st. 346p. F/VG. W3. $75.00

CHANG, Kwang-chih. *Shang Civilization.* 1980. Yale. 1st. ils/charts/tables. 417p. F. W3. $68.00

CHANG & SHEFTS. *Manual of Spoken Tibetan.* 1964. WA U. 286p. NF. W3. $72.00

CHANIN & CHANIN. *This Land These Voices: A Different View of AZ History...* 1977. Northland. 1st. ils/index. 266p. F/NF. B19. $50.00

CHANNING, Steven. *Crisis of Fear.* 1972. 315p. O8. $7.50

CHANNING, W.E. *Thoreau: Poet-Naturalist.* 1873. Boston. Roberts Bros. 1st. 1/1500. gilt gr cloth. M24. $100.00

CHANSLOR, Roy. *Ballad of Cat Ballou.* 1956. Little Brn. 1st. F/F. B4. $175.00

CHANSLOR, Roy. *Johnny Guitar.* 1953. NY. S&S. 1st. F/F. B4. $200.00

CHANTER, Charlotte. *Ferny Combes.* 1856. London. Lovell Reeve. 2nd. 16mo. A22. $85.00

CHAO, Yuen-ren. *Aspects of Chinese Socio-Linguistics.* 1976. Stanford. 1st. F/F. W3. $52.00

CHAPDELAINE, Perry A. *Laughing Terran.* 1977. London. Hale. 1st. sgn. F/VG. B11. $35.00

CHAPEL, Charles Edward. *Art of Shooting.* 1960. Barnes. 409p. dj. A17. $15.00

CHAPEL, Charles Edward. *Guns of the Old West, the Definitive Book on Firearms...* 1961. Coward McCann. 1st. VG/dj. J2. $65.00

CHAPELLE, Howard I. *History of American Sailing Ships.* (1935). NY. Norton. later prt. 400p. VG/worn. P4. $35.00

CHAPELLE, Howard I. *History of the American Sailing Navy: Ships & Developement.* (1949). Bonanza. later prt. 558p. VG/worn. P4. $40.00

CHAPIN, Howard Millar. *Tartar: Armed Sloop of the Colony of Rhode Island...* 1922. Providence. Soc of Colonial Wars. 7 pl. 67p. T7. $50.00

CHAPIN, James Henry. *From Japan to Granada.* 1889. Putnam. 1st. inscr. 12mo. gr cloth. G. B11. $25.00

CHAPIN & CHAPIN. *Stories of Pioneer Days; or, Advance Guard of Civilization.* 1894. Oriental Pub. 1st. VG. M19. $35.00

CHAPLIN, Charles. *My Autobiography.* 1966. London. 545p. F/dj. A17. $25.00

CHAPLIN, Ralph. *Somewhat Barbaric.* 1944. Seattle. McCaffrey Dogwood. 1st. inscr. F/NF. B2. $125.00

CHAPMAN, Allen. *Radio Boys at Mountain Pass (#4).* 1922. Grosset Dunlap. 218p+ads. VG/dj (lists to #5). M20. $35.00

CHAPMAN, Allen. *Radio Boys at Ocean Point.* 1922. NY. VG/G. B5. $17.50

CHAPMAN, Allen. *Radio Boys to the Rescue (#13).* 1930. Grosset Dunlap. 1st. 220p. last title in series. VG/dj (lists to #12). $150.00

CHAPMAN, Allen. *Radio Boys With the Iceberg Patrol (#7).* 1924. Grosset Dunlap. 218p. cloth. VG/dj (lists to #11). M20. $45.00

CHAPMAN, Charles. *Piloting Seamanship & Small Boat Handling.* 1968-69. NY. 664p. 4to. F. A17. $17.50

CHAPMAN, Clark R. *Planets of Rock & Ice: From Mercury to Moons of Saturn.* 1982. Scribner. 1st. F/dj. M2. $15.00

CHAPMAN, Frank M. *Handbook of Birds of Eastern North America.* 1966. NY. rpt (2nd). ils. 581p. VG. S15. $15.00

CHAPMAN, Frank. *Life in an Air Castle.* 1938. Appleton. 1st. 250p. xl. F3. $20.00

CHAPMAN, John Jay. *Treason & Death of Benedict Arnold.* 1910. Moffat Yard. 1st. 76p. brd/paper label. M1. $75.00

CHAPMAN, John Jay. *Two Greek Plays.* 1928. Houghton Mifflin. 1st. 12mo. 118p. salmon brd. dj. M1. $85.00

CHAPMAN, John Ratcliffe. *Instructions to Young Marksmen...Improved American Rifle.* 1848. NY. 1st. 160p. rebound. VG. B18. $225.00

CHAPMAN, John Ratcliffe. *Instructions to Young Marksmen...Improved American Rifle.* 1848. NY. Appleton. 1st. 12mo. 160p. orig cloth. M1. $250.00

CHAPMAN, Kenneth M. *Pottery of the Santo Domingo Pueblo.* 1936. Santa Fe, NM. Laboratory of Anthropology. 191p. VG. K7. $225.00

CHAPMAN, Lee; see Bradley, Marion Zimmer.

CHAPMAN, Paul H. *Spirit Runestones: A Study of Linguistics.* 1994. SF. Epigraphic Soc. 60p. F/prt wrp. P4. $22.50

CHAPMAN, Robert D. *Universe at Ultraviolet Wave Lengths...* 1981. NASA. 823p. VG/wrp. K5. $40.00

CHAPMAN & PRATT. *Methods of Analysis for Soils, Plants & Waters.* 1982. Berkeley. rpt. ils. new cloth. B1. $22.50

CHAPPELE, F.J. *Heather Garden.* 1952. London. ils. 180p. VG/torn. B26. $25.00

CHAPPELL, Fred. *Inkling.* 1965. HBW. 1st. author's 2nd book. F/NF. B3. $100.00

CHAPPELL, Fred. *More Shapes Than One.* 1991. St Martin. 1st. sgn. F/F. R13. $45.00

CHAPUT, Don. *Virgil Earp, Western Peace Officer.* 1994. Affiliated Writers of Am. 1st. photos/maps. 255p. as new. J2. $39.00

CHAPUT, W.J. *Dead in the Water.* 1991. St Martin. 1st. VG/VG. P3. $16.00

CHARBNEAU, Jules. *Jules Carbneau's World of Miniatures.* ca 1970. SF. 37x27mm. 44p. F/red wrp/plastic case. B24. $75.00

CHARBONNEAU, Louis. *Way Out.* 1966. Barrie Rockliff. 1st. VG/VG. P3. $25.00

CHARCOT, Jean Martin. *Clinical Lectures on Senile & Chronic Diseases.* 1881. New Sydenham Soc. 1st Eng. 6 pl. 308p. emb brn cloth. G1. $250.00

CHARCOT, Jean Martin. *Clinique des Maladies du Systeme Nerveaux...* 1892. Paris. Aux Bureaux Progres Medical/Veuve Babe. 468p. xl. G1. $285.00

CHARCOT, Jean Martin. *Lectures on Diseases of the Nervous System...2nd Series.* 1881. London. New Sydenham Soc. 1st Eng-language. 17 pl. 400p. emb brn cloth. VG. G1. $200.00

CHARDIN, John. *Sir John Chardin's Travels in Persia.* 1927. London. Argonaut. 1/975. ils. as new/unopened. O7. $225.00

CHARGAFF, Erwin. *Heraclitean Fire.* 1978. Rockefeller U. 1st. 252p. xl. VG. K3. $15.00

CHARLES, R.H. *Apocrypha & Pseudepigrapha of Old Testament in English.* 1963. Oxford. 2 vol. NF/dj. W3. $625.00

CHARLES, Robert H. *Roundabout Turn.* 1930. London. Warne. unp. cloth. G+/VG+. D4. $35.00

CHARLES, V.K. *Introduction to Mushroom Hunting.* 1974. Dover. 48p. VG/stiff wrp. B1. $12.50

CHARLESWORTH, J.K. *Historical Geology of Ireland.* 1963. London. Oliver Boyd Ltd. 565p. VG/dj. D8. $30.00

CHARLIP, Remy. *Arm in Arm: Collection of Connections, Endless Tales...* nd (1969). Parents Magazine. probable 1st. sm 4to. unp. NF/G+. C14. $17.00

CHARLIP & MOORE. *Hooray for Me!* 1975. NY. Parents. 1st. ils Vera Williams. F. C8. $20.00

CHARLOT, Jean. *Charlot Murals in Georgia.* 1945. Athens. 1st. VG/VG. B5. $65.00

CHARLOT, Jean. *Picture Book. Images & Verses by Jean Charlot.* 1974. LA. Dawson's Book Shop. 1/300. 54x42mm. sgns. prt brd. F/dj/case. B24. $250.00

CHARRIERE, Henri. *Papillon.* 1970. Morrow. 1st Am. NF/NF. M22. $15.00

CHARTERIS, Leslie. *Enter the Saint.* nd. Detective Story Club. NF/G. P3. $30.00

CHARTERIS, Leslie. *Saint Goes West.* 1942. Canada. Musson. VG/G. P3. $25.00

CHARTERIS, Leslie. *Saint on the Spanish Main.* 1955. Doubleday Crime Club. 1st. NF/rpr. M15. $65.00

CHARTERIS, Leslie. *Saint Sees It Through.* 1947. Canada. Musson. VG/G. P3. $20.00

CHARTERIS, Leslie. *Saint Vs Scotland Yard.* 1953. Doubleday. VG/VG. P3. $25.00

CHARTERIS, Leslie. *Senor Saint.* 1959. Hodder Stoughton. 1st. VG/VG. P3. $35.00

CHARTERIS, Leslie. *Vendetta for the Saint.* 1964. Crime Club. 1st. F/NF. M19. $25.00

CHARTERS, Ann. *Kerouac.* 1973. Straight Arrow. 1st. VG/VG. P3. $40.00

CHARUDATTAN & WALKER. *Biological Control of Weeds With Plants.* 1982. NY. Walker. 293p. dj. A10. $22.00

CHARUSHIN, E. *Baby Bears.* 1945. Macmillan. 8vo. ils George Korff. VG/fair. M5. $45.00

CHARYN, Jerome. *Darlin' Bill.* 1980. Arbor. 1st. F/F. T11. $30.00

CHARYN, Jerome. *Isaac Quartet.* 1984. Zomba. 1st. F/F. P3. $30.00

CHARYN, Jerome. *Once Upon a Droshky.* 1964. McGraw Hill. 1st. sgn. author's 1st book. F/F. L3. $150.00

CHARYN, Jerome. *Pinocchio Nose.* 1983. Arbor. 1st. F/NF. T12. $20.00

CHARYN, Jerome. *Seventh Babe.* 1979. Arbor. 1st. author's 13th book. F/F. T11. $40.00

CHASE, Glen; see Fox, Gardner F.

CHASE, James Hadley. *Figure It Out for Yourself.* nd. Robert Hale. VG/G. P3. $20.00

CHASE, James Hadley. *Twelve Chinks & a Woman.* nd. Jarrolds. VG. P3. $25.00

CHASE, Pearl. *Cacti & Other Succulents.* 1930. Santa Barbara. 107p. sc. B26. $21.00

CHASE, Richard. *Old Songs & Singing Games.* 1938. Chapel Hill. 42p. VG+/wrp. D4. $35.00

CHASE, Robert. *Atlas of Hand Surgery.* 1973. Phil. 1st. 438p. A13. $150.00

CHASE, W.H. *Pioneers of Alaska.* 1951. KS City. sgn. ils/photos. 203p. F. M4. $30.00

CHASE, William C. *Front Line General: Command of Wm C Chase...* 1974. Houston. Gulf Pub. 1st. sgn. F/F. A23. $32.00

CHASTAIN, Thomas. *Pandora's Box.* 1974. Mason Lipscomb. 1st. VG/VG. P3. $20.00

CHATHAM, Russell. *Angler's Coast.* 1976. Doubleday. 1st. author's 1st book. F/VG clip. B3. $100.00

CHATTERTON, E. Keble. *Down Channel in the Vivette.* 1910. London. ils. G+. M17. $15.00

CHATTERTON, E. Keble. *English Seamen & the Colonization of America.* 1930. London. 1st. 326p. G. B18. $22.50

CHATTERTON, E. Keble. *Fore & Aft Craft & Their Story.* 1922-27. Phil/London. ils/plans. 347p. T7. $70.00

CHATTERTON, E. Keble. *On the High Seas.* 1929. London. Philip Allan. 16 half-tone pl/32 plans. 319p. gilt bl cloth. P4. $30.00

CHATTERTON, E. Keble. *Ship-Models.* 1923. London. The Studio. 1/1000. 142 pl. gilt bdg. P4. $225.00

CHATTERTON, E. Keble. *Windjammers & Shellbacks: Strange True Stories of the Sea.* 1926. London. Fisher Unwin. 254p. bl cloth. P4. $65.00

CHATTERTON, Fenimore C. *Yesterday's Wyoming.* 1957. Powder River. dj. A19. $100.00

CHATWIN, Bruce. *In Patagonia.* 1978. Summit. 1st Am. author's 1st book. F/F. D10. $125.00

CHATWIN, Bruce. *On the Black Hill.* 1983. Viking. 1st Am. author's 3rd book. F/F. D10. $50.00

CHATWIN, Bruce. *Songlines.* 1987. Viking. 1st. F/dj. A24. $35.00

CHATWIN, Bruce. *Utz.* 1988. Viking. 1st. F/F. H11. $25.00

CHATWIN, Bruce. *Viceroy of Ouidah.* 1980. Summit. 1st. F/F. H11. $65.00

CHAUCER, Geoffrey. *Tales From Chaucer, Canterbury Tales by Geoffrey Chauncer...* 1947. Heritage Pr. ils Szyk. tall 8vo. 182p. F. H1. $55.00

CHAVOOR & DAVIDSON. *50-Meter Jungle.* 1973. Coward McCann. 1st. VG/VG. P8. $20.00

CHAYEFSKY, Paddy. *Altered States.* 1978. Harper Row. 1st. NF/NF. M22. $20.00

CHEADLE & MILTON. *North-West Passage by Land: Being Narrative of Expedition...* nd. London. Cassell Petter Galpin. 394p. gilt gr cloth. P4. $55.00

CHEATHAM FOUNDATION. *Dali: A Study of His Art-in-Jewels.* 1959. Greenwich. NYGS. 8vo. 28 tipped-in pl. 67p. NF/case. T10. $100.00

CHEATLE & CUTLER. *Tumors of the Breast: Their Pathology, Symptoms, Diagnosis.* 1931. Phil. 1st Am. 596p. A13. $150.00

CHEESMAN, Evelyn. *Islands Near the Sun: Off the Beaten Track...* 1927. London. Witherby. 1st. ils. 304p. VG/VG. S25. $50.00

CHEETHAM, Anthony. *Science Against Man.* 1971. MacDonald. 1st. VG/VG. P3. $28.00

CHEEVER, John. *Wapshot Chronicle.* 1957. NY. Harper. 1st. author's 3rd book. F/NF. L3. $200.00

CHEEVER, John. *Wapshot Scandal.* 1964. Harper. 1st. assn copy. cloth. F/F. M24. $300.00

CHEEVER, John. *Way Some People Live.* 1943. Random. 1st. 1/2750. author's 1st book. G. L3. $400.00

CHEEVER, John. *Way Some People Live.* 1943. Random. 1st. author's 1st book. F/dj. B24. $950.00

CHEIRO, Louis Hamon. *Cheiro's Guide to the Hand.* 1900. Rand McNally. 1st cloth-bdg ed/Am issue. wht pict cloth. VG. M24. $100.00

CHEKHOV & MOSER. *Kashtanka.* 1991. Putnam. 1st. F/NF. C14. $17.00

CHENAK, Susan. *Smithereens.* 1995. Doubleday. 1st. sgn. F/F. A23. $34.00

CHENAULT, John Cabell. *Old Cane Springs.* 1937. Louisville, KY. 2nd. 257p. G. B18. $45.00

CHENEVIX-TRENCH, Charles. *History of Horsemanship.* 1970. Doubleday. 1st Am. VG/VG. O3. $45.00

CHENEY, E. *Farm Woodlot, a Handbook of Forestry for the Farmer.* 1926 (1914). xl. VG. E6. $25.00

CHENEY, Margaret. *Tesla: Man Out of Time.* 1981. Dorset. 320p. F/dj. K3. $15.00

CHENEY, Warren. *Yosemite Illustrated in Colors.* (1890). SF. HS Crocker. ils WH Hansen/Carl Dahlgren (13 full-p pl). rebound. R3. $750.00

CHENG, Chen-to. *Great Heritage of Chinese Art, Illustrated.* nd. np. 2 vol. 12 sets ils pl. emb gilt bdg. F/F. W3. $425.00

CHENG, Chu-yuan. *Scientific & Engineering Manpower in Communist China...* 1965. National Science Found. 588p. VG/stiff wrp. W3. $95.00

CHERF, John Frank. *Studies in the Text Tradition of St Jerome's 'Vitae Patrum.'* 1943. Urbana, IL. 1st. thick 4to. 566p. VG. T10. $75.00

CHERNIN, Kim. *Obsession.* 1981. Harper Row. 1st. author's 1st book. F/NF. M19. $25.00

CHERNIN, Milton. *Convict Road Work in California.* 1929. Los Angeles. 4to. typed dissertation. gilt bl lib cloth. NF. R3. $75.00

CHERRY, Kelly. *My Life & Dr Joyce Brothers.* 1990. Algonquin. 1st. F/F. B35. $15.00

CHERRY-GARRARD, Apsley. *Worst Journey in the World.* 1994. London. Picador. 4 maps. 607p. NF/dj. P4. $40.00

CHERRYH, C.J. *Chanur's Venture.* 1984. Phantasia. 1st. sgn. F/dj. M2. $30.00

CHERRYH, C.J. *Chernevog.* 1991. Methuen. 1st. F/F. P3. $25.00

CHERRYH, C.J. *Cyteen.* 1988. Warner. 1st. F/F. M21. $60.00

CHERRYH, C.J. *Glass & Amber.* 1987. NESFA. 1st. F/dj. M2. $15.00

CHERRYH, C.J. *Kif Strike Back.* 1985. Phantasia. 1st. F/F. P3. $25.00

CHERRYH, C.J. *Rimrunners.* 1989. Warner. 1st. F/F. W2. $20.00

CHERRYH, C.J. *Rusalka.* 1989. Easton. 1st. sgn. leather. F/sans/swrp. P3. $100.00

CHESBRO, George C. *Second Horseman Out of Eden.* 1989. Atheneum. 1st. F/F. N4. $35.00

CHESBRO, George C. *Shadow of a Broken Man.* 1977. S&S. 1st. NF/dj. M25. $35.00

CHESBRO, George C. *Shadow of a Broken Man.* 1977. S&S. 1st. VG/VG. P3. $30.00

CHESEBROUGH, Caroline. *Foe in the Household.* 1871. Boston. Osgood. 1st. author's 8th/final book. gilt terra-cotta cloth. F. M24. $100.00

CHESELDEN, William. *Anatomy of the Human Body.* 1806. Boston. 2nd Am. 352p. half leather. A13. $400.00

CHESHIRE, Giff. *Stronghold.* 1963. Doubleday. 1st. F/NF clip. B4. $65.00

CHESLER, Ellen. *Woman of Valor: Margaret Sanger & Birth Control Movement.* 1992. S&S. 2nd. VG/VG. B4. $35.00

CHESMAN & JOAN. *Guide to Women's Publishing.* 1978. Paradise, CA. Dustbooks. 1st. sc. VG+. A25. $20.00

CHESNUTT, Charles W. *Colonel's Dream.* 1905. Doubleday Page. 1st thus. 1st. 1st state bdg (name misspelled). VG. M24. $1,500.00

CHESNUTT, Charles W. *Conjure Tales.* 1975. London. Collins. 1st thus. 1st. ils Ross/Romano. 8vo. NF/VG. C8. $17.50

CHESNUTT, Charles W. *Conjure Woman.* 1899. Boston. 1st thus. 1st trade. 229p. pict cloth. VG. B18. $225.00

CHESNUTT, Charles W. *Conjure Woman.* 1899. Cambridge. Riverside. 1st thus. lg paper ed. 1/250. 229p. buckram. G. B18. $450.00

CHESNUTT, Charles W. *House Behind the Cedars.* 1900. Houghton Mifflin. 1st. author's 4th book. silver/gilt stp gr pict cloth. VG. M24. $275.00

CHESS & GOREY. *Fletcher & Zenobia.* 1967. Meredith. 1st. ils Victoria Chess. 12mo. VG/VG. P2. $25.00

CHESTER, Peter; see Phillips, Dennis.

CHESTERTON, G.K. *Annotated Innocence of Father Brown.* 1987. Oxford. 1st. F. M2. $20.00

CHESTERTON, G.K. *Collected Poems of GK Chesterton.* 1927. Great Britain. Cecil Palmer. 1st. G+. M23. $25.00

CHESTERTON, G.K. *Common Man.* 1950. Sheed Ward. 1st. VG/VG. P3. $30.00

CHESTERTON, G.K. *Gloria in Profundis.* nd. 1/350. ils Eric Gill. yel brd. VG+. S13. $20.00

CHESTERTON, G.K. *Heretics.* 1960. London. VG. M2. $12.00

CHESTERTON, G.K. *Man Who Was Thursday.* 1908. Bristol/London. 1st. G-. M23. $50.00

CHESTERTON, G.K. *Paradoxes of Mr Pond.* 1945. 1st Am. F/NF. M19. $45.00

CHESTERTON, G.K. *St Francis of Assisi.* 1926. London. 1st. VG/dj. T9. $75.00

CHETWODE, Penelope. *Two Middle-Aged Ladies in Adalusia.* 1963. London. John Murray. 3rd. photos. VG/VG. A25. $18.00

CHETWYND-HAYES, R. *Quiver of Ghosts.* 1984. Wm Kimber. 1st. F/F. P3. $25.00

CHEUNG, D. *Isle Full of Noises.* 1987. Columbia. 1st. 257p. F. W3. $38.00

CHEUSE, Alan. *Grandmother's Club.* 1986. Peregrine Smith. 1st. F/F. A20. $20.00

CHEVALIER, Haakon. *Last Voyage of the Schooner Rosamond.* 1970. London. Deutsch. 248p. dj. T7. $35.00

CHEVALIER, Haakon. *Oppenheimer, the Story of a Friendship.* 1965. NY. 1st. xl. VG. K3. $15.00

CHEVALIER, Maurice. *Mome a Cheveux Blancs.* 1969. Paris. inscr. 280p. F/dj. B14. $60.00

CHEVIGNY, Hector. *Lost Empire: Life & Adventures of Nikolai Petrovich Rezanov.* 1937. Macmillan. 1st. 8vo. 356p. gray cloth. P4. $65.00

CHEW, Peter. *Kentucky Derby: The First 100 Years.* 1974. Houghton Mifflin. 1st. 4to. VG. O3. $45.00

CHEYNEY, Peter. *Curiosity of Etienne MacGregor.* 1952. 1st Eng. NF/VG. M19. $25.00

CHEYNEY, Peter. *Dames Don't Care!* nd. Coward McCann. 2nd Am imp. 250p. cloth. VG/dj. M20. $35.00

CHEYNEY, Peter. *Dark Bahama.* 1950. Collins. VG/VG. P3. $15.00

CHEYNEY, Peter. *Uneasy Terms.* 1947. Dodd Mead. 1st. VG/G. P3. $25.00

CHI, Wen-shun. *Readings in Chinese Communist Documents.* 1963. CA U. 478p. F. W3. $45.00

CHI & SERVICE. *Chinese-English Dictionary of Contemporary Usage.* 1977. CA U. 484p. F/F. W3. $135.00

CHIANG, Yee. *Chinese Calligraphy: An Introduction...* 1955. Harvard. 230p. VG/dj. W3. $52.00

CHIANG & WOLF. *Indians of North & South America: Supplement.* 1988. Scarecrow. 8vo. 3542 works described. F. T10. $50.00

CHICKERING, Carol. *Flowers of Guatemala.* 1973. Norman, OK. 128p. VG. A10. $25.00

CHIDAMIAN, Claude. *Book of Cacti & Other Succulents.* 1958. Garden City. BC. 243p. VG/dj. B26. $12.50

CHIDESTER, Otis. *Brand Book 1 of the Tucson Corral of the Westerners...* 1967. Tucson. Corral of Westerners. 1st. ils. 204p. F/sans. B19. $65.00

CHIDSEY, Donald Barr. *Captain Adam.* 1953. Crown. 1st. VG/VG. P3. $20.00

CHIKAMATSU, Shigenori. *Stories From a Tearoom Window.* 1982. Tuttle. ils. 191p. F/dj. W3. $38.00

CHILD, Frank. *Colonial Witch.* 1897. Baker Taylor. VG. M2. $75.00

CHILD, Georgie Boynton. *Efficient Kitchen.* 1914. McBride Nast. G. A16. $25.00

CHILD, Julia. *Julia Child & Company.* 1978. Knopf. 1st. 243p. B10. $10.00

CHILD, Julia. *Mastering the Art of French Cooking.* 1950. Knopf. BC. ils. 622p. VG/fair. B10. $15.00

CHILD, Julia. *Mastering the Art of French Cooking.* 1966 (1961). Knopf. 13th. 684p. VG/G. B10. $15.00

CHILD, Lydia Maria. *Appeal in Favor of That Class of Americans Called Africans.* 1833. Boston. Ticknor. 1st. 232p. ES. bl muslin brd. VG. B4. $3,750.00

CHILD, Theodore. *Spanish-American Republics.* 1891. Harper. 1st. 444p. xl. F3. $25.00

CHILD STUDY ASSN. OF AMERICA. *Read Me More Stories.* (1951). NY. Crowell. 8vo. ils Barbara Cooney. 166p. G. T5. $18.00

CHILDE, Harold. *Child's Book of Abridged Wisdom.* 1905. SF. Elder/Tomoye. ils. gr cloth spine. VG. B14. $60.00

CHILDERS & RUSSO. *Nightshades & Health.* 1977. Somerville. Horticultural Pub. 189p. xl. B1. $16.50

CHILL, Abraham. *Mizvot: Commandments & Their Rationale.* 1974. Jerusalem. Keter. 508p. VG/dj. S3. $34.00

CHILLS, Marquis W. *This Is Democracy: Collective Bargaining in Scandinavia.* 1938. Yale. 1st. VG. V4. $22.50

CHIN, Ann-Ping. *Children of China: Voices From Recent Years.* 1988. Knopf. 1st. F/dj. W3. $42.00

CHIN, Art. *Anything, Anytime, Anywhere: Legacy of Flying Tiger Line.* 1993. Seattle. 293p. 4to. wrp. A17. $17.50

CHIN, S.S. *Missile Configuration Design.* 1961. McGraw Hill. 8vo. 279p. VG/dj. K5. $45.00

CHINA ART PUBLICATIONS. *Costumes of the Minority Peoples of China.* 1981. Kyoto. 362 mc pl. 244p. F/dj/case. W3. $165.00

CHINIQUY, Charles. *Fifty Years in the Church of Rome.* 1960. Baker. 597p. G. B29. $20.00

CHINNOCK & HEATH. *Ferns & Fern Allies of New Zealand.* 1974. Wellington. Reed. 8vo. cloth. VG/dj. A22. $15.00

CHIPAULT, Antoine Maxime. *Travaux de Neurologie Chirugicle.* 1896. Paris. Vigot Freres. 352p+208 woodcuts. contemporary bdg. xl. G1. $100.00

CHIPMAN, Frank W. *Romance of Old Sandwich Glass.* 1932. Sandwich Pub. 158p. VG. M20. $35.00

CHIPMAN, William Pendleton. *Roy Gilbert's Search: Tale of the Great Lakes.* 1889. AL Burt. 277p. bl cloth. VG. M20. $16.00

CHIRENJE, J. Mutero. *History of Northern Botswana 1850-1910.* 1977. Rutherford, NJ. Farleigh Dickinson. 1st. 8vo. ils. NF/dj. W1. $25.00

CHITTENDEN, Alfred K. *Red Gum.* 1905. WA, DC. ils/fld map. 56p. tan wrp. B26. $15.00

CHITTENDEN, H.M. *History of Early Steamboat Navigation on Missouri River.* 1962 (1903). Minneapolis. 2 vol in 1. 1/1500. F/dj. M4. $55.00

CHITTENDEN, H.M. *History of the American Fur Trade of the Far West.* 1954. Academic. 2 vol. VG/dj. J2. $195.00

CHITTENDEN, L.E. *Personal Reminiscences 1840-1890.* 1893. NY. 434p. O8. $12.50

CHITTENDEN & COLSON. *Children's Letters: A Collection...* 1905. NY. sm 8vo. gilt wine cloth. VG. M5. $85.00

CHITTENDEN & SYNGE. *RHS Dictionary of Gardening.* 1977. Oxford. Clarendon. 2nd. 4 vol+supplement. xl. F. A10. $300.00

CHIVERS, T.H. *Nacoochee; or, Beautiful Star, With Other Poems.* 1837. NY. WE Dean. 1st. 12mo. 143p. reddish-brn cloth. M1. $425.00

CHOLMELEY & MELLAND. *Through the Heart of Africa: Being an Account...* 1912. Houghton Mifflin. 1st. ils/fld map. 305p. teg. VG+. H7. $125.00

CHOMSKY, William. *Hebrew: Eternal Language.* 1957. JPS. ils. 321p. VG/dj. S3. $22.00

CHOPIN, Kate. *Bayou Folk.* 1894. Houghton Mifflin. 1st. 1/1000. gilt gr sateen cloth. G. M24. $125.00

CHOPPING, Richard. *Fly.* 1965. FSG. 1st. author's 1st book. NF/F. H11. $40.00

CHORAO, Kay. *Lester's Overnight.* 1977. Dutton. 1st. lg 8vo. unp. F/VG. C14. $17.00

CHORIS, Louis. *San Francisco One Hundred Years Ago.* 1913. SF. Robertson. ils/drawings. 20p. F/dj. K7. $45.00

CHOURAQUI, Andre. *Between East & West: Brief History of Jews in North America.* 1968. Phil. Jewish Pub Soc. 1st. 376p. NF. W3. $46.00

CHOW & COLLISON. *Gin Chow's First Annual Almanac.* 1932. Los Angeles. Wetzel. 2nd. 12mo. ils. red/blk/tan brd. F. R3. $20.00

CHRISMAN, Miriam Usher. *Bibliography of Strasbourg Imprints, 1480-1599.* 1982. New Haven. Yale. 1st. 8vo. gilt purple cloth. F/sans. T10. $45.00

CHRISTENSEN, Edwin O. *Index of American Design.* 1950. Macmillan. 1st. 229p. VG. A8. $26.50

CHRISTENSEN, Lars. *Such Is the Antarctic.* 1935. London. Hodder Stoughton. 1st. 45 photo pl. 8vo. map ep. bl cloth. NF. P4. $265.00

CHRISTENSEN, Lillian Langseth. 1959. Gourmet. 599p. B10. $45.00

CHRISTIANSEN, Harry. *Lake Shore Electric, Interurban Days 1893-1938.* 1963. Cleveland. photos. unp. VG/wrp. M20. $20.00

CHRISTIE, Agatha. *Agatha Christie Hour.* 1982. Collins. 1st. VG/VG. P3. $20.00

CHRISTIE, Agatha. *And Then There Were None.* 1945. Grosset Dunlap. photoplay ed. VG/VG. M22. $30.00

CHRISTIE, Agatha. *By the Pricking of My Thumbs.* 1968. Dodd Mead. 1st. VG/G. P3. $25.00

CHRISTIE, Agatha. *Caribbean Mystery.* 1964. Collins. 1st. NF/dj. M25. $25.00

CHRISTIE, Agatha. *Elephants Can Remember.* 1972. Collins. 1st. F/NF. M25. $25.00

CHRISTIE, Agatha. *Hercule Poirot: Clocks.* 1963. Dodd Mead. 1st Am. 276p. VG/dj. M20. $25.00

CHRISTIE, Agatha. *Miss Marple: In Mirror Cracked/Nemesis/Body in Library...* 1983. NY. Avenel. 3rd. F/F. T12. $25.00

CHRISTIE, Agatha. *Murder of Roger Ackroyd.* Oct 1926. Dodd Mead. 5th. VG. M22. $25.00

CHRISTIE, Agatha. *Nemesis.* 1971. Collins Crime Club. 1st. VG/fair. P3. $18.00

CHRISTIE, Agatha. *Passenger to Frankfurt.* 1970. London. Collins. Crime Club. 1st. F/dj. Q1. $75.00

CHRISTIE, Agatha. *Postern of Fate.* 1973. Dodd Mead. 1st. VG/VG. P3. $25.00

CHRISTIE, Agatha. *Sad Express.* 1940. Dodd Mead. 1st Am. VG. N4. $40.00

CHRISTIE, Agatha. *Sleeping Murder.* 1976. Collins Crime Club. 1st. NF/NF. P3. $20.00

CHRISTIE, Agatha. *Taken at the Flood.* 1948. London. Collins Crime Club. 1st. VG/dj. M15. $45.00

CHRISTIE, Agatha. *Third Girl.* 1966. London. Collins Crime Club. 1st. F/NF. N4. $50.00

CHRISTIE, Agatha. *Third Girl.* 1967. Dodd Mead. 1st. VG/VG. P3. $20.00

CHRISTIE, Agatha. *Triple Threat.* 1943. Dodd Mead. omnibus ed. F/NF. M15. $150.00

CHRISTINA OF SWEDEN. *Histoire des Intrigues Galantes de la Reine Christine...* 1697. Amsterdam. Henri. 8vo. ftspc portrait. quarter calf. R12. $175.00

CHRISTISON, Robert. *Dispensatory; or, Commentary on the Pharmacopoeias...* 1848. Phil. Lee Blanchard. 2nd. rebound modern cloth. xl. K3. $75.00

CHRISTOPHER, John. *Little People.* 1966. S&S. 1st. VG/dj. M2. $15.00

CHRISTOPHER, John. *Pendulum.* 1968. S&S. 1st. VG/VG. P3. $15.00

CHRISTOPHER, John. *Ragged Edge.* 1965. S&S. 1st. VG/dj. M2. $25.00

CHRISTOPHER, John. *Scent of White Poppies.* 1959. 1st. NF/VG. M19. $25.00

CHRISTY, Howard Chandler. *Our Girls.* 1907. NY. 1st. VG. B5. $95.00

CHRISTY, Thomas. *Thomas Christy's Road Across the Plains...* 1969. Denver. Rosenstock. 1st. 94 maps. F. M4. $40.00

CHUBIN, Barry. *Feet of a Snake.* 1984. Arbor. 1st. VG/VG. P3. $18.00

CHUKOVSKY, Kornei. *Telephone.* 1977. Delacorte. 1st Am. 48p. F/F. D4. $45.00

CHUNG, Kyung-cho. *New Korea.* 1962. NY. ils. 274p. VG/dj. W3. $32.00

CHUNG, Wa Nan. *Art of Chinese Gardens.* 1982. Hong Kong U. sm obl 4to. 251p. F. S15. $20.00

CHURCH, Alfred J. *With the King at Oxford.* 1896. London. Seeley. 16 full-p ils. 298p. bl cloth. F. T10. $45.00

CHURCH, Archibald. *Diseases of the Nervous System.* 1908. NY. Appleton. 1st Eng-language. 8vo. 1205p. rebound. G1. $65.00

CHURCH, Peggy Pond. *Wind's Trail: Early Life of Mary Austin.* 1990. Mus of NM Pr. 1st. F/dj. A18. $20.00

CHURCH & PETERSON. *Nervous & Mental Diseases.* 1904. Phil. Saunders. 4th revised/2nd prt. 922p+ads. VG. G1. $50.00

CHURCHILL, Fleetwood. *On the Theory & Practice of Midwifery.* 1946. Phil. 2nd Am. 525p. full leather. A13. $200.00

CHURCHILL, Winston S. *Blood, Sweat & Tears.* 1941. NY. 1st Am. VG. M17. $20.00

CHURCHILL, Winston S. *London to Ladysmith Via Pretoria.* 1900. NY. 1st Am. VG. M17. $250.00

CHURCHILL, Winston S. *Marlborough: His Life & Times.* 1933. NY. 6 vol. 1st Am. VG. M17. $350.00

CHURCHILL, Winston S. *Secret Session Speeches.* UK. 1st. VG. M17. $30.00

CHURCHILL, Winston S. *Unrelenting Struggle.* 1942. NY. 1st Am. VG/G+. M17. $50.00

CHURCHWARD, William B. *My Consulate in Samoa: A Record of Four Years Sojourn...* 1887. London. Richard Bentley. 1st. 8vo. 403p. teg. gilt bdg. xl. H1. $125.00

CHUTE, Carolyn. *Beans.* 1985. Chatto Windus/Hogarth. 1st Eng. author's 1st book. F/1st issue dj. R13. $60.00

CHUTE, Carolyn. *Beans.* 1985. Chatto Windus/Hogarth. 1st Eng. rem mk. F/F. R14. $35.00

CHUTE, Carolyn. *Beans.* 1985. Chatto Windus/Hogarth. 1st. sgn. author's 1st book. F/2nd issue. Q1. $100.00

CHUTE, Carolyn. *Letourneau's Used Auto Parts.* 1988. Ticknor Fields. 1st. sgn. F/F. B3. $45.00

CIARDI, John. *Alphabestiary.* 1966. Lippincott. 1st. 56p. cloth. F/VG. D4. $75.00

CIARDI, John. *Monster Den; or, Look What Happened at My House — And To It.* 1966. Lippincott. ils Edward Gorey. 64p. VG+/dj. D4. $45.00

CIARDI, John. *You Know Who.* 1964. Lippincott. 1st. 63p. VG/dj. M20. $50.00

CIARDI, John. *You Read to Me, I'll Read to You.* 1962. Phil. Lippincott. 1st. 64p. F/dj. D4. $75.00

CIBBER, Colley. *Another Occasional Letter From Mr Cibber to Mr Pope.* 1744. London. W Lewis. tall 8vo. 56p. VG. H13. $265.00

CIMENT, Jill. *Small Claims.* 1986. NY. 1st. author's 1st book. NF/dj. R13. $25.00

CINTRON, Lola. *Goddess of the Bullring...Story of Conchita Cintron.* (1960). Bobbs Merrill. 1st. 349p. dj. F3. $25.00

CIPOLLA, Carlo M. *Clocks & Culture 1300-1700.* 1967. Walker. 1st. 8vo. 192p. ils. VG/dj. K3. $20.00

CISNEROS, Sandra. *Woman Hollering Creek.* 1991. Random. 1st. F/F. B3. $75.00

CIST, Henry M. *Army of the Cumberland.* 1882. NY. 1st. 289p. F. O8. $21.50

CLAGETT, Marshall. *Critical Problems in History of Science.* 1959. Madison, WI. 8vo. 547p. wrp. K3. $10.00

CLAIR, Maxine. *Coping With Gravity.* 1988. WA Writer's Pub. 1st. author's 1st book. F/wrp. A24. $75.00

CLAIRE, Mabel. *Crowley Milner's Cookbook.* 1932. NY. Greenberg. fair. A16. $20.00

CLAIRMONTE, Glenn. *Calamity Was the Name for Jane, a Distinguished Biography...* 1959. Sage Books. 1st. sgn pres. ils. 215p. VG/dj. J2. $135.00

CLAIRON, Claire Hyppolite. *Memoires...Et Reflections sur l'Art Dramatique.* 1799. Paris. Buisson, An VII. 8vo. calf/brd. R12. $250.00

CLAMPITT, John W. *Echoes From the Rocky Mountains.* 1889. ils. 671p. O8. $55.00

CLANCY, Tom. *Cardinal of the Kremlin.* 1988. Putnam. 1st. F/F. H11. $35.00

CLANCY, Tom. *Cardinal of the Kremlin.* 1988. Putnam. 1st. VG/VG. P3. $25.00

CLANCY, Tom. *Clear & Present Danger.* 1989. Putnam. 1st. NF/NF. P3. $40.00

CLANCY, Tom. *Hunt for Red October.* 1985. Annapolis. Naval Inst. 1st. author's 1st book. F/NF. L3. $650.00

CLANCY, Tom. *Patriot Games.* 1987. Putnam. 1st. VG/VG. P3. $45.00

CLANCY, Tom. *Red Storm Rising.* 1986. Putnam. 1st. F/F. D10. $50.00

CLANCY, Tom. *Red Storm Rising.* 1986. Putnam. 1st. sgn. F/F. A23. $90.00

CLANCY, Tom. *Sum of All Fears.* 1991. Harper Collins. 1st Eng. F/dj. Q1. $60.00

CLANCY, Tom. *Sum of All Fears.* 1991. Putnam. 1/600. sgn/#d. F/sans. M15. $225.00

CLANCY, Tom. *Sum of All Fears.* 1991. Putnam. 1st. NF/NF. P3. $25.00

CLANCY, Tom. *Without Remorse.* 1993. Putnam. 1st. sgn. F/F. A23. $75.00

CLAPESATTLE, Helen. *Doctors Mayo.* 1941. Minneapolis. 1st. 822p. A13. $30.00

CLARE, John. *Dwellers in the Wood.* 1967. Macmillan. ARC/1st. 43p. F/F. D4. $35.00

CLARK, A. *Barbarossa: Russian German Conflict, 1941-1945.* 1950. NY. ils/maps. 500p. VG/VG. S16. $30.00

CLARK, Ann Nolan. *Bear Cub.* 1965. Viking. 1st. 62p. F/F. D4. $45.00

CLARK, Ann Nolan. *Blue Canyon Horse.* 1954. Viking. 1st. tall 8vo. F/VG. M5. $85.00

CLARK, Ann Nolan. *Little Herder in Spring/Daago Na'Nilkaadi Yazhi.* 1940. US Office Indian Affairs. 1st. ils. 114p. VG. B19. $35.00

CLARK, Ann Nolan. *Magic Money.* 1950. Viking. 1st. 121p. VG/VG. P2. $80.00

CLARK, Ann Nolan. *Secret of the Andes.* 1953 (1952). Viking. 3rd. 8vo. 130p. VG/G+. T5. $25.00

CLARK, Ann Nolan. *Slim Butte Raccoon.* 1942. US Dept Interior. ils Andrew Standing Soldier. obl 4to. VG+. M5. $45.00

CLARK, Ann Nolan. *Tia Maria's Garden.* 1966 (1963). NY. Viking. 3rd. ils Ezra Jack Keats. xl. VG/NF. C8. $15.00

CLARK, Anna Morris. *Sylvia of the Hills.* 1936. Custer, SD. Chronicle Shop. box. A19. $45.00

CLARK, Arthur. *History of Yachting 1600-1815.* 1904. NY. Putnam. ils. 249p. teg. rebound. T7. $210.00

CLARK, B.F. *How Many Miles From St Jo?* 1929. SF. private prt. sm 8vo. marbled brd/maroon cloth. VG. O4. $45.00

CLARK, B.L. *Fauna of the San Pablo Group of Middle California.* 1915. Berkeley. CA U. pres. ils/pl. VG+/wrp. M12. $37.50

CLARK, Badger. *Sun & Saddle Leather.* 1920. Boston. Gorham. A19. $35.00

CLARK, C.M. *Picturesque Ohio: Historical Monograph.* (1887). Cincinnati. Cranston Curts. Columbian ed. ils. 238p. cloth. VG. M12. $45.00

CLARK, Carol. *Thomas Moran: Watercolors of the American West.* 1980. Austin. 4to. cream cloth. F/NF. F7. $60.00

CLARK, Curt; see Westlake, Donald E.

CLARK, Dorothy. *Little Joe.* 1940. Lee Shepard. 1st. ils Leonard Weisgard. VG+/G. P2. $50.00

CLARK, Douglas. *Big Grouse.* 1986. Gollancz. 1st. NF/NF. P3. $25.00

CLARK, Douglas. *Sick to Death.* 1971. Stein Day. 1st. VG/VG. P3. $20.00

CLARK, E.E. *Poetry: An Interpretation of Life.* 1935. Farrar Rhinehart. 1st. 584p. VG. W2. $30.00

CLARK, Eleanor. *Oysters of Locmariaquer.* 1964. Pantheon. 1st. 203p. F/VG. H1. $25.00

CLARK, Ellery H. *Red Sox Fever.* 1979. Hicksville. Exposition. inscr to Bob Watson. G/G. A23. $30.00

CLARK, Elmer T. *Arthur James Moore, World Evangelist.* 1960. NY. Methodist Church. sgn. 45p. marbled brd/brn spine. B11. $18.00

CLARK, Emma Chickester. *Story of Horrible Hilda & Henry.* 1988. Little Brn. 1st. glossy pict brd. VG/dj. M20. $18.00

CLARK, Francis E. *In Christ's Own Country.* 1914. Grosset Dunlap. 1st. 8vo. 25 pl. VG. W1. $12.00

CLARK, H.H. *Lost in Pompeii.* 1883. Lothrop Lee Shepard. 1st. VG. M2. $30.00

CLARK, John Willis. *Liber Memorandorum Ecclesie de Bernewelle.* 1907. Cambridge. M11. $150.00

CLARK, Kate. *Maori Tales & Legends.* 1896. London. Nutt. 1st. 18 woodcuts. 186p. VG. W3. $86.00

CLARK, Leonard. *Flutes & Cymbals.* 1969. Crowell. ARC/1st. ils Shirley Hughes. 104p. F/F. D4. $35.00

CLARK, Mary Higgins. *All Around Town.* 1992. S&S. 1st. sgn. F/F. A23. $25.00

CLARK, Mary Higgins. *Cradle Will Fall.* 1980. S&S. 1st. F/F. T12. $25.00

CLARK, Mary Higgins. *Cry in the Night.* 1982. S&S. 1st. F/clip. P3. $20.00

CLARK, Mary Higgins. *Loves Music, Loves To Dance.* 1991. S&S. 1st. sgn. F/F. A23. $25.00

CLARK, Mary Higgins. *Stranger Is Watching.* 1977. S&S. 1st. F/F. M15. $50.00

CLARK, Mary Higgins. *While My Pretty One Sleeps.* 1989. S&S. 1st. sgn. F/F. A23. $30.00

CLARK, Mary Higgins. *While My Pretty One Sleeps.* 1989. S&S. 1st. F/F. H11. $25.00

CLARK, Neil. *Campfires & Cattle Trails, Recollections of the Early West.* 1970. Caxton. 1st. 912p. VG/wrp. J2. $95.00

CLARK, O.S. *Clay Allison of the Washita, First Cowman...* 1922. Clark. 1st thus. ils/map. 135p. VG. w/3 orig photos. J2. $2,350.00

CLARK, Ronald W. *Einstein, the Life & Times.* 1984. Abrams. lg 4to. VG+/dj. K3. $20.00

CLARK, Ronald W. *JBS: The Life & Work of JBS Haldane.* 1969. Coward McCann. 1st Am. ils. 326p. VG/dj. K3. $15.00

CLARK, Rufus W. *Review of the Reverand Moses Stuart's Pamphlet on Slavery...* 1850. Boston. CCP Moody. 1st. 8vo. 103p. M1. $85.00

CLARK, Sterling B.F. *How Many Miles From St Jo?* 1988. Ye Galleon. 1st thus. F/sans. A18. $17.50

CLARK, Walter Van Tilborg. *Grove Day.* 1969. NY. 1st. VG/VG. B5. $45.00

CLARK, Walter Van Tilborg. *Watchful Gods.* 1950. NY. 1st. VG/G. B5. $40.00

CLARK, Walter. *Two Lamaistic Pantheons.* 1965. NY. Harvard. Paragon Repr of Harvard ed. 2 vol in 1. F/VG. W3. $145.00

CLARK, William. *Field Notes of Captain William Clark.* 1964. Yale. sgn. 335p. NF/dj. O7. $275.00

CLARK & DEFENDORF. *Neurological & Mental Diagnosis: Manual of Methods.* 1908. Macmillan. assn copy. 12mo. 188p. panelled bl cloth. xl. G1. $50.00

CLARK & HAM. *Pleasant Hill & Its Shakers.* 1968. Pleasant Hill. Shakertown Pr. ils/16 photos. 88p. VG+/dj. B18. $25.00

CLARK & LE GETTE. *Echo in My Soul.* 1962. Dutton. 1st. 243p. NF/VG. B4. $85.00

CLARK & STARN. *Geological Evolution of North America.* 1960. Ronald Pr. 1st. ils/figures, 434p. VG. D8. $15.00

CLARK. *Children's Annual: A History & Collector's Guide.* 1988. London. 4to. 160p. F/NF. A4. $95.00

CLARKE, Anna. *Legacy of Evil.* 1976. Collins Crime Club. 1st. VG/VG. P3. $20.00

CLARKE, Arthur C. *Deep Range.* 1957. Harcourt. 1st. F/dj. M2. $200.00

CLARKE, Arthur C. *Expedition to Earth.* 1955. London. 1st. F/dj. M2. $100.00

CLARKE, Arthur C. *Exploration of Space.* 1951. Harper. 1st. author's 3rd book. VG/VG. M19. $50.00

CLARKE, Arthur C. *Fall of Moondust.* 1961. Harcourt Brace. 1st. NF/VG. M19. $50.00

CLARKE, Arthur C. *Fountains of Paradise.* 1979. HBJ. 1st. VG/VG. P3. $25.00

CLARKE, Arthur C. *Ghost From the Grand Banks.* 1990. Bantam. 1st. F/F. P3. $20.00

CLARKE, Arthur C. *Imperial Earth.* 1975. London. 1st. F/dj. M2. $55.00

CLARKE, Arthur C. *Imperial Earth.* 1976. Harcourt Brace. 1st. NF/dj. M2. $37.00

CLARKE, Arthur C. *Lion of Commare & Against the Fall of Night.* 1968. Harcourt Brace. 1st. F/VG. M19. $45.00

CLARKE, Arthur C. *Other Side of the Sky.* 1957. Harcourt Brace. 1st. VG/dj. M2. $100.00

CLARKE, Arthur C. *Promise of Space.* 1968. Harper. sgn. F/dj. M2. $40.00

CLARKE, Arthur C. *Reach for Tomorrow.* 1970. HBW. 1st. VG/VG. P3. $20.00

CLARKE, Arthur C. *Songs of Distant Earth.* 1986. Del Rey. 1/500. sgn/#d. F/case. M2. $85.00

CLARKE, Arthur C. *Songs of Distant Earth.* 1986. Del Rey. 1st. NF/VG+. N4. $20.00

CLARKE, Arthur C. *Songs of Distant Earth.* 1986. Del Rey. 1st. 256p. NF/clip. M20. $25.00

CLARKE, Arthur C. *2010: Odyssey Two.* 1982. Del Rey. 1st. F/dj. M2. $25.00

CLARKE, Covington. *For Valor.* 1928. Chicago. 264p. VG. B18. $25.00

CLARKE, Covington. *Mystery Flight of the Q2.* 1932. Reilly Lee. 270p. cloth. VG/dj. M20. $25.00

CLARKE, Donald Henderson. *That Mrs Renney.* 1937. Vanguard. 1st. F/NF. M19. $25.00

CLARKE, Edward H. *Visions: Study of False Sight.* 1878. Boston. Houghton Osgood. 1st. 12mo. cloth. xl. M1. $125.00

CLARKE, John Henrik. *Harlem, USA.* 1964. Seven Seas. ne. VG/wrp. M25. $45.00

CLARKE, Sara. *Lord Will Love Thee.* 1959. 1st. ils Tasha Tudor. VG+. S13. $25.00

CLARKE, T.E.B. *Murder at Buckingham Palace.* 1981. Hale. 1st. VG/VG. P3. $20.00

CLARKE, Walter E. *Alaska.* 1910. Boston. 207p. gilt cloth. F. A17. $30.00

CLARKE, William M. *Secret Life of Wilkie Collins.* 1991. Chicago. Ivan R Dee. 1st. 8vo. 239p. F/dj. T10. $50.00

CLARKE & LEE. *Cradle.* 1988. Warner. 1st. F/dj. M2. $20.00

CLARKE & LEE. *Garden of Rama.* 1991. Bantam. 1st Am. rem mk. NF/dj. M21. $10.00

CLARKE & LEE. *Garden of Rama.* 1991. Bantam. 1st. F/F. N4. $22.50

CLARKE & LEE. *Rama II.* 1989. Bantam. 1st. F/F. N4. $25.00

CLARKSON, Henry E. *Yachtsman's A-Z.* 1979. Arco. 1st. 160p. F/F. W2. $20.00

CLARKSON, Rosetta E. *Herbs: Their Culture & Uses.* 1951. Macmillan. 10th. 226p. VG. A10. $20.00

CLARKSON, Rosetta E. *Magic Gardens.* 1939. Macmillan. 1st. 8vo. cloth. VG. A22. $30.00

CLARKSON, Thomas. *Memoirs of the Private & Public Life of William Penn.* 1813. London. Longman. 2 vol. 1st. thick 8vo. modern bdg. F. H13. $365.00

CLAUDE, Blair. *Pistols of the World.* 1968. Viking. 205p. cloth. VG+/dj. M20. $50.00

CLAUDE, Henri. *Maladies du Cervelet et de l'Isthme de l'Encephale...* 1922. Paris. JB Bailliere et Fils. pres. 439p. VG. G1. $75.00

CLAUDINE. *Flight of the Animals.* 1971. NY. Parents. 1st. ils Claudine. F. C8. $15.00

CLAUSEN, Jens. *Stages in the Evolution of Plant Species.* 1951. Ithaca. Cornell. 206p. VG. A10. $24.00

CLAUSSEN & FRIS. *Descriptive Catalog of Maps Published by Congress 1817-1843.* 1941. WA. private prt. 429 maps. 104p. F. M4. $35.00

CLAVELL, James. *King Rat, a Novel.* 1962. 1st. author's 1st book. NF/VG. A4. $200.00

CLAVELL, James. *Noble House.* 1981. Delacorte. 1st. F/NF. H11. $35.00

CLAVELL, James. *Shogun.* 1983. Delacorte. 1st. NF/F. H11. $45.00

CLAVELL, James. *Whirlwind.* 1986. Morrow. 1st. NF/NF. P3/T12. $35.00

CLAVER, Scott. *Under the Lash.* 1954. London. 1st. ils. 288p. G. B18. $15.00

CLAY, Catherine Lee. *Season of Love.* 1968. Atheneum. 1st. inscr. F/dj. T10. $45.00

CLAY & HUBBARD. *Trees for Hawaiian Gardens.* 1962. Honolulu. inscr. photos. 101p. sc. B26. $22.50

CLAYMORE, Tod. *Appointment in New Orleans.* 1950. Cassell. 1st. VG/G. P3. $30.00

CLAYTON, Edward T. *Negro Politician: His Success & Failure.* 1964. Chicago. Johnson. 1st. F/NF. B4. $85.00

CLEARY, Beverly. *Ramona & Her Mother.* 1979. Morrow. 1st. 208p. VG/VG. P2. $25.00

CLEARY, Jon. *Beufort Sisters.* 1979. Collins. 1st. VG/VG. P3. $23.00

CLEARY, Jon. *Fall of an Eagle.* 1964. Morrow. 1st. VG/G. P3. $25.00

CLEARY, Jon. *Faraway Drums.* 1982. Morrow. 1st. VG/VG. P3. $20.00

CLEARY, Jon. *Liberators.* 1971. Morrow. 1st. VG/VG. P3. $25.00

CLEARY, Jon. *Man's Estate.* 1972. Collins. 1st. VG/VG. P3. $20.00

CLEARY, Jon. *Very Private War.* 1980. Collins. 1st. NF/NF. P3. $25.00

CLEAVER, Kathleen. *Release Eldrige Cleaver!* nd (1969). Berkeley. Blk Panther Party/CA Peace & Freedom Movement. F/wrp. B4. $100.00

CLEAVER & RODMAN. *Horace Pippin: The Artist As a Black American.* 1972. Doubleday. 1st. NF/dj. M25. $50.00

CLEEVE, Brian. *Death of a Painted Lady.* 1962. Hammond Hammond. 1st. VG/VG. P3. $25.00

CLELAND, Hugh. *George Washington in the Ohio Valley.* 1955. Pittsburgh. 1st. 405p. as new/dj. H1. $32.00

CLELAND, Robert Glass. *Cattle on a Thousand Hills.* 1941. Huntington Lib. 1st. VG. O4. $40.00

CLELAND, Robert Glass. *Irvine Ranch of Orange Country.* 1952. San Marino. Huntington Lib. 1st. VG/sans. O4. $25.00

CLELAND, Robert Glass. *Irvine Ranch.* 1966. San Marino. 2nd. NF/VG. O4. $15.00

CLEMENS, Samuel L. *Adventures of Huckleberry Finn.* 1912. Harper. new ed from new pl. 405p. VG. W2. $900.00

CLEMENS, Samuel L. *Adventures of Tom Sawyer.* 1876. Hartford. Am Pub Co. 1st/3rd prt. gilt bl cloth. M24. $1,500.00

CLEMENS, Samuel L. *Adventures of Tom Sawyer.* 1879. Hartford. Am Pub. early rpt. gilt bl cloth/recased. M24. $100.00

CLEMENS, Samuel L. *Adventures of Tom Sawyer.* 1879. Toronto. Rose-Belford. 1st thus. sewn self-wrp. M24. $650.00

CLEMENS, Samuel L. *Adventures of Tom Sawyer.* 1920. Grosset Dunlap. Prt in USA. ne. 292p. G. W2. $500.00

CLEMENS, Samuel L. *Christian Science.* 1907. Harper. 1st. VG. M19. $35.00

CLEMENS, Samuel L. *Conversations As It Was by Social Fire-Side...* July 1913. Private Prt for Bruno. 1/75 on Japan vellum. F/uncut wrp. M24. $600.00

CLEMENS, Samuel L. *Conversations As It Was by Social Fire-Side...* 1920. Private Prt for Johnson. 1st. 1/110. gilt quarter cloth/gray brd. F. M24. $225.00

CLEMENS, Samuel L. *Dog's Tale.* 1904. Harper. 1st. red pict cloth. VG. M24. $60.00

CLEMENS, Samuel L. *Editorial Wild Oats.* 1905. Harper. 1st. pink cloth. VG. M24. $60.00

CLEMENS, Samuel L. *Eve's Diary.* 1906. NY. Harper. 1st. red pict cloth. VG. M24. $65.00

CLEMENS, Samuel L. *Extract From Captain Stormfield's Visit to Heaven.* 1909. NY. 1st. VG. B5. $30.00

CLEMENS, Samuel L. *Extracts From Adam's Diary.* 1904. Harper. 1st. ils. 89p. pict cloth. G+. B18. $35.00

CLEMENS, Samuel L. *Extracts From Adam's Diary.* 1904. Harper. 1st. red pict cloth. NF. M24. $100.00

CLEMENS, Samuel L. *Following the Equator.* 1897. Hartford. Am Pub. 1st/single imp. teg. 3-quarter maroon morocco. M24. $300.00

CLEMENS, Samuel L. *Gilded Age.* 1873. Hartford/Chicago. 1st/early state+1st state ads. gilt blk cloth. M24. $350.00

CLEMENS, Samuel L. *Letters From the Sandwich Islands.* 1937. Grabhorn. 1st. 1/550. dk bl cloth. F. M24. $350.00

CLEMENS, Samuel L. *Life on the Mississippi.* 1883. Boston. Osgood. 1st Am/2nd state (points p441/443). NF. Q1. $600.00

CLEMENS, Samuel L. *Mark Twain's Letter to the California Pioneers.* 1911. Oakland. DeWitt Snelling. 1st/1st issue. F/prt wrp. M24. $125.00

CLEMENS, Samuel L. *Mark Twain's Letters.* (1917). Harper. 1st trade. 2 vol. teg. gilt red cloth. M24. $100.00

CLEMENS, Samuel L. *Mark Twain's Perforated Interleaved Scrap Book...* (1892). NY. Daniel Slote. lg 8vo. 100p. 3-quarter cloth/marbled sides. VG. M1. $300.00

CLEMENS, Samuel L. *Mark Twain's Sketches, New & Old.* 1875. Hartford. Am Pub. 1st/2nd. aeg. gilt bl cloth/recased. VG. M24. $85.00

CLEMENS, Samuel L. *More Tramps Abroad.* 1897. London. Chatto Windus. 1st. gilt maroon cloth. w/1897 catalogue. M24. $275.00

CLEMENS, Samuel L. *Old Times on the Mississippi, by Mark Twain.* 1876. Toronto. Belford. 1st. 12mo. 157p. purple cloth. M1. $300.00

CLEMENS, Samuel L. *Personal Recollections of Joan of Arc.* 1896. London. Chatto Windus. 1st. teg. pict bl cloth. NF. M24. $200.00

CLEMENS, Samuel L. *Prince & the Pauper.* 1937. Winston. 1st thus. ils Lawson. gilt red cloth. VG. M5. $45.00

CLEMENS, Samuel L. *Roughing It.* 1872. Hartford. Am Pub. 1st/1st issue. gilt 3-quarter brn morocco. M24. $1,000.00

CLEMENS, Samuel L. *Stolen White Elephant.* 1882. Chatto Windus. 1st/1st prt. 8vo. G. T10. $185.00

CLEMENS, Samuel L. *Tom Sawyer Abroad, Tom Sawyer Detective.* 1896. Harper. 1st/1st prt (date present on title p). 1/1000. gilt red cloth. M24. $650.00

CLEMENS, Samuel L. *Tragedy of Pudd'nhead Wilson & Comedy of Extraordinary...* 1894. Hartford. Am Pub. 1st/1st prt. gilt tan decor cloth. M24. $1,650.00

CLEMENS, Samuel L. *Tramp Abroad.* 1880. Hartford. Am Pub. 1st/1st state sheets/state A portrait ftspc. M24. $450.00

CLEMENS, Samuel L. *What Is Man?* 1906. NY. DeVinne Pr. 1st. 1/250. gray brd/morocco label. F/cloth case. M24. $1,250.00

CLEMENS, Will. *Ken of Kipling.* 1899. NY. New Amsterdam Book. 1st. gilt orange cloth. M24. $100.00

CLEMENT, Hal. *Cycle of Fire.* 1957. Ballantine. 1st. F/NF. M2. $750.00

CLEMENT, Hal. *Mission of Gravity.* 1954. Doubleday. 1st. F/F. P3. $225.00

CLEMENT, Hal. *Mission of Gravity.* 1954. Doubleday. 1st. sgn. VG/dj. M2. $225.00

CLEMENT, Hal. *Needle.* 1950. Doubleday. 1st. VG/VG. P3. $60.00

CLEMENTE & LINDSLEY. *Aggression & Defense: Neural Mechanisms & Social Patterns.* 1967. Berkeley. 4to. 361p. wht/red cloth. VG/dj. G1. $40.00

CLEMENTS, F.E. *Minnesota Plant Studies I-III.* 1909-10. tall 8vo. VG/wrp. A22. $50.00

CLEMENTS, F.E. *Plant Succession & Indicators.* 1928. Wilson. ils/pl/figures. 453p. cloth. VG. A22. $65.00

CLERKE, Agnes M. *Familiar Studies in Homer.* 1892. London. Longman Gr. 8vo. 302p. xl. K5. $45.00

CLERKE, Agnes M. *Problems in Astrophysics.* 1903. London. Black. 1st/only. 567p. G. K5. $90.00

CLEVE, John; see Offutt, Andrew.

CLEVELAND, Anne. *It's Better With Your Shoes Off.* 1958. Rutland. Tuttle. 4th. ils. 94p. VG+. A25. $15.00

CLIFFORD, A.G. *Conquest of North Africa.* 1943. MA. 1st. 450p. VG. S16. $25.00

CLIFFORD, Francis. *Amigo, Amigo.* 1973. CMG. 1st. F/NF. H11. $25.00

CLIFFORD, Francis. *Amigo, Amigo.* 1973. CMG. 1st. VG/VG. P3. $20.00

CLIFFORD, Francis. *Battle Is Fought To Be Won.* 1961. Coward. 1st. F/NF. H11. $35.00

CLIFFORD, Francis. *Wild Justice.* 1972. CMG. 1st. VG/VG. P3. $25.00

CLIFFORD, Hugh. *Further Side of Silence.* 1916. Doubleday. 1st. F. M2. $50.00

CLIFTON, Bud; see Stacton, David.

CLIFTON, James. *Prairie People (Potawatomi, 1665-1965).* 1977. KS U. 1st. NF/NF. A20. $30.00

CLIFTON, Lucille. *Everett Anderson's Christmas Coming.* 1971. Holt Rinehart. 1st. sm 4to. F/F. C8. $25.00

CLIFTON, Lucille. *Good Woman.* 1969-80. BOA Ed. 1st. sgn/dtd 1997. F/dj. V1. $45.00

CLIFTON, Lucille. *My Friend Jacob.* 1980. Dutton. 1st. F/F. C8. $35.00

CLIFTON, Lucille. *Some of the Days of Everett Anderson.* 1970. HRW. 1st. ils Evaline Ness. F/F. B4. $100.00

CLIFTON, Mark. *Eight Keys to Eden.* 1960. Doubleday. 1st. VG/VG. P3. $40.00

CLIFTON, Oliver Lee. *Camp Fire Boys in Muskrat Swamp (#2).* 1923. Barse Hopkins. lists 3 titles. VG/G. M20. $35.00

CLIFTON, V. *Book of Talbot.* 1933. NY. 1st. ils/fld maps. 439p. VG/dj. B5. $45.00

CLINE, Isaac Monroe. *Storms, Floods & Sunshine.* 1945. New Orleans. Pelican. 1st. sgn. 290p. VG/G. B11. $35.00

CLINE, John. *Forever Beat.* 1990. Dutton. 1st. VG/VG. P3. $20.00

CLINE, Platt. *They Came to the Mountain.* 1976. N AZ U. 1st. ils/index. 364p. NF/NF. B19. $35.00

CLINE, Platt. *They Came to the Mountain.* 1986. Flagstaff. 4th. 8vo. blk cloth. F/F. F7. $25.00

CLINTON, Catherine. *Plantation Mistress.* 1982. Pantheon. 1st. 331p. VG/dj. M20. $22.00

CLINTON, Henry. *Narrative of Lt-Gen Sir Henry Clinton...* 1783. London. Debrett. 4th. NF/wrp. O7. $175.00

CLISE, Michele Durkson. *Ophelia's World. Memoirs of Parisian Shop Girl.* 1984. Clarkson Potter. 1st. sgn. F/clip. A23. $40.00

CLISE, Michelle Durkson. *Ophelia's Voyage to Japan.* 1986. Potter. 1st. 4to. F/dj. M5. $65.00

CLIVE, William. *Tune That They Play.* 1973. Macmillan. 1st. VG/VG. P3. $15.00

CLOUD, P. *Cosmos, Earth & Man: A Short History of the Universe.* 1978. Yale. 372p. F. D8. $25.00

CLOUSTON, J. Storer. *Man From the Clouds.* 1919. Doran. 1st. VG. M2. $25.00

CLUTE, Nelson. *Our Ferns in Their Haunts.* 1901. Stokes. 332p. VG. A10. $48.00

CLUTESI, George. *Potlatch.* 1969. Sydney, BC. Gray's. 1st. ils. F/NF. L3. $85.00

CLUTESI, George. *Son of Raven, Son of Deer.* 1967. Sidney, BC. Gray's. ARC. sgn. ils. VG. L3. $125.00

CLYMER, Theodore. *Four Corners of the Sky: Poems, Chants & Oratory.* 1975. Little Brn. 1st. 48p. cloth. F/NF. D4. $35.00

CLYNE, Densey. *Australian Ground Orchids.* 1970. Melbourne. ils/photos. 112p. sc. VG. B26. $27.50

COAD. *New Jersey in Travelers' Accounts 1524-1971, Descriptive...* 1972. 633 entries. 221p. F. A4. $75.00

COATES, R.M. *Outlaw Years: History of Land Pirates of Natchez Trace.* 1930. Literary Guild. ils. VG. M17. $20.00

COATES, Walter John. *Land of Allen & Other Verse.* 1928. N Montpelier. Recluse. inscr assn copy. F. B11. $75.00

COATES & TUPPER. *Vermont Verse.* 1931. Brattleboro. Stephen Daye. sgn assn copy. gray cloth. VG. B11. $18.00

COATS, Alice. *Plant Hunters.* 1969. McGraw Hill. 400p. VG/dj. A10. $48.00

COATS, Alice. *Travels of Maurice.* 1939. London. ils. Vg/G+. M17. $20.00

COATSWORTH, Elizabeth. *Cat Who Went to Heaven.* 1930. Macmillan. 1st. ils Lynd Ward. 57p. cloth. VG+/dj. M20. $325.00

COATSWORTH, Elizabeth. *Children Come Running.* 1960. Golden Pr/Western Pub. 1st. 8vo. VG+/VG+. C8. $15.00

COATSWORTH, Elizabeth. *Door to the North.* (1950). Winston. Land of the Free series. 1st. brn bdg. F/VG+. N1. $10.00

COATSWORTH, Elizabeth. *Down Half the World.* 1968. Macmillan. 1st. 98p. F/F. D4. $35.00

COATSWORTH, Elizabeth. *Mouse Chorus.* 1955. pantheon. 1st. ils Geneive Vaughn-Jackson. VG+/VG. P2. $35.00

COATSWORTH, Elizabeth. *Princess & the Lion.* 1963. Pantheon. 1st. 78p. NF/VG. P3. $35.00

COATSWORTH, Elizabeth. *Silky.* 1953. Pantheon. 1st. ils John Carroll. 142p. bl brd/brn spine. VG/G+. T5. $35.00

COATSWORTH, Elizabeth. *Trudy & the Tree House.* 1944. Macmillan. 1st. 114p. VG/G. P2. $25.00

COBB, Irvin S. *Cobb's Bill of Fare.* 1913. NY. Doran. 1st. ils Peter Newell/James Preston. pict brd. F/dj. M24. $125.00

COBB, Irvin S. *Roughing It Deluxe.* 1914. NY. Doran. 1st. 12mo. 219p. gray cloth. VG. F7. $30.00

COBB, J.H. *Manual Containing Information Respecting Growth of Mulberry.* 1833. Boston. Carter Hendee. hand-colord pl. 98p. VG. B5. $100.00

COBBETT, William. *American Gardener.* ca 1830s. Claremont, NH. 16mo. 230p. A22. $125.00

COBLEIGH, Rolfe. *Handy Farm Devices & How To Make Them.* 1912. Orange Judd. 288p. VG. A10. $50.00

COBLENTZ, Stanton A. *After 12,000 Years.* 1950. Fantasy. 1st. F/dj. M2. $20.00

COBLENTZ, Stanton A. *After 12,000 Years.* 1975 (1950). Garland. rpt. F. M2. $20.00

COBLENTZ, Stanton A. *Decline of Man.* 1925. Minton Balch. 1st. VG. M2. $35.00

COBLENTZ, Stanton A. *Sunken World.* 1948. Fantasy. 1st. sgn. F/dj. M2. $50.00

COBLENTZ, Stanton A. *Under Triple Suns.* 1955. Fantasy. 1/300. sgn/#d. F/M. M2. $160.00

COBLENTZ, Stanton A. *Villains & Vigilantes: Story of James King...* 1957. NY. Yoseloff. rpt. VG/G+. O4. $15.00

COBLENTZ, Stanton A. *When the Birds Fly South.* 1945. Wings. 1st. F/NF. M2. $50.00

COBLENTZ, Stanton A. *Winds of Chaos.* 1942. Wings. 1st. inscr. NF/G. M19. $25.00

COBURN, Andrew. *Sweetheart.* 1985. Secker Warburg. 1st. VG/VG. P3. $20.00

COBURN, Walt. *Barbwire.* 1931. Chicago. AL Burt. dj. A19. $30.00

COBURN, Walt. *Pioneer Cattleman in Montana, the Story of Circle C Ranch.* 1968. Norman, OK. 1st. sgn. 338p. VG/dj. J2. $145.00

COCHISE, Ciye Nino. *First Hundred Years of Nino Cochise: Untold Story...* 1971. Abelard Schuman. ils/map ep. 346p. VG/NF. B19. $45.00

COCHRAN, Johnnie. *Journey to Justice.* 1996. Ballantine. 1st. sgn bookplate. F/F. A23. $50.00

COCHRAN, Keith. *American West Historical Chronology.* 1992. Cochran. photos. 464p. dj. A19. $35.00

COCHRAN, Mike. *And Deliver Us From Evil.* 1989. TX Monthly. 1st. 213p. F/F. W2. $20.00

COCHRAN, Robert. *Vance Randolph, an Ozark Life.* 1985. U IL. 1st. VG/VG. V4. $15.00

COCKBURN, J.S. *Crime in England 1550-1800.* 1977. London. Methuen. 11 essays. M11. $45.00

COCKCROFT, G.L. *Index to the Weird Fiction Magazines.* 1975. Arno. 1st hc. VG. M2. $50.00

COCKERELL, Sidney. *Psalter & Hours.* 1905. London. Chiswick. 1st/only. obl folio. 25 full-p gravure pl. w/ALS. H13. $285.00

COCKRILL, Pauline. *Ultimate Teddy Bear Book.* 1991. NY. Kindersley. 1st Am. 128p. F/dj. H1. $22.50

CODDINGTON, Edwin. *Gettysburg Campaign.* 1968. NY. 1st. VG/dj. B5. $50.00

CODMAN, C.R. *Drive.* 1957. MA. 1st. ils. 335p. VG/VG. S16. $30.00

CODMAN, C.R. *Years & Years: Some Vintage Years in French Wines.* 1932. private prt. inscr. 25p. stapled bdg. G+. B10. $65.00

CODRESCU, Andrei. *Craving for Swan.* 1986. Columbus. OH State. 1st. sgn. NF/NF. B4. $85.00

CODRESCU, Andrei. *History of the Growth of Heaven.* 1973. Braziller. 1st. photo Tom Veitch. F/NF. V1. $30.00

CODRINGTON, Robert. *Ten Books of Quintus Curtius Rufus...* 1652. London. Alsop. 1st this trans. sm 4to. 303p. modern bdg. C6. $350.00

COE, Michael D. *Maya.* (1986). Thames Hudson. 3rd. 190p. wrp. F3. $15.00

COE, Michael D. *Mexico.* 1977. Praeger. 2nd. 216p. NF/VG. W2. $15.00

COE, Tucker. *Don't Lie to Me.* 1972. Random. 1st. 181p. NF/NF. W2. $10.00

COELHO, Paul. *Valkyries: An Encounter With Angels.* 1992. Harper Collins. 1st. F/F. B3. $25.00

COETZEE, J.M. *Age of Iron.* 1990. Random. 1st. sgn. author's 7th book. F/F. D10. $35.00

COETZEE, J.M. *From the Heart of the Country.* 1977. Harper Row. 1st Am. sgn. author's 2nd novel. F/F. D10. $75.00

COETZEE, J.M. *Life & Times of Michael K.* 1984. NY. Viking. 1st Am. sgn. F/F. D10. $50.00

COETZEE, J.M. *Life & Times of Michael K.* 1984. Viking. 1st. F/NF. M23. $20.00

COFFEEN, J.A. *Seismic Exploration Fundamentals.* 1978. Tulsa, OK. Petroleum Pub. 277p. VG/dj. D8. $30.00

COFFEY, Brian; see Koontz, Dean R.

COFFEY, D.J. *Dolphins, Whales & Porpoises.* 1977. NY. 223p. VG/VG. S15. $15.00

COFFEY, Timothy. *History & Folklore of North American Wildflowers.* nd. Facts on File. 356p. dj. A10. $32.00

COFFIN, Charles Carleton. *Our New Way Round the World.* 1869. Boston. Osgood. 524p. VG. W1. $35.00

COFFIN, Charles Carleton. *Redeeming the Republic.* 1890. NY. ils 478p. O8. $14.50

COFFIN, Geoffrey; see Mason, Van Wyck.

COFFIN, Margaret. *American Country Tinware 1700-1900.* 1968. photos. NF/VG. S13. $18.00

COFFMAN, Virginia. *From Satan, With Love.* 1983. Piatkus. F/F. P3. $15.00

COGGER & SWEIFEL. *Reptiles & Amphibians.* 1992. Smithmark. 1st. F/F. B1. $40.00

COGGESHALL, George. *History of American Privateers.* 1861 (1856). aeg. half leather/raised bands. VG. E6. $175.00

COGGESHALL, George. *Voyages to Various Parts of the World...1799 & 1844.* 1851. NY. 1st. 8vo. ils. 213p. cloth. M1. $200.00

COGGINS & PRATT. *Rockets, Satellites & Space Travel.* 1958. Random. 2nd. 4to. 64p. VG. K5. $12.00

COGNIAT, Raymond. *XXth Century Drawings & Watercolors.* nd. NY. Crown. trans from French by Anne Ross. ils/list of artists. dj. D2. $75.00

COGSWELL, H.L. *Water Birds of California.* 1977. Berkeley. 399p. F/F. B1. $30.00

COHAN, George. *Broadway Jones.* 1913. Dillingham. 1st. F/NF. B4. $350.00

COHANE, Tim. *Great College Football Coaches of the Twenties & Thirties.* 1973. Arlington. 1st. photos. VG/dj. P8. $20.00

COHEN, Bernard. *Sensing & Controlling Motion: Vestibular & Sensorimotor...* 1992. NY Academy of Sciences. 1st. thick 8vo. 989p. F/wrp. G1. $65.00

COHEN, Bernard. *Sociocultural Changes in American Jewish Life...* 1972. Fairleigh Dickinson. 282p. VG/dj. S3. $20.00

COHEN, David William. *Womunafu's Bunafu: A Study of Authority...* 1977. Princeton. 1st. 216p. cloth. NF/dj. W1. $18.00

COHEN, Herman. *History of the English Bar & Attornatus to 1450.* 1967. London. Wildy & Sons Ltd. facsimile. cloth. M11. $125.00

COHEN, I. Bernard. *Newtonian Revolution...* 1980. Cambridge. inscr. 404p. VG/dj. K5. $45.00

COHEN, I. Bernard. *Some Early Tools of American Science.* 1950. Cambridge, MA. 1st. 8vo. 201p. VG. K3. $35.00

COHEN, Octavius Roy. *Bullet for My Love.* 1950. Macmillan. 1st. VG/dj. M25. $45.00

COHEN, Octavius Roy. *Eric Peters, Pullman Porter.* 1930. Appleton. 1st. 12mo. VG+/G. C8. $75.00

COHEN, Peter Zachary. *Bee.* 1975. Atheneum. 1st. VG/VG. O3. $18.00

COHEN, Robert. *Organ Builder.* 1988. Harper. 1st. F/NF. R13. $35.00

COHEN, Sam. *Truth About the Neutron Bomb.* 1983. NY. 1st. F/dj. K3. $10.00

COHEN, Stanley. *Man in the Crowd.* 1981. Random. 1st. VG+/dj. P8. $10.00

COHEN, Stanley. *Park.* 1977. Putnam. 1st. F/F. P3. $15.00

COHEN & SMOLAN. *Day in the Life of America.* 1986. Collins. 272p. cloth. dj. D2. $65.00

COHN, Isadore. *Rudolph Matas: Biography of One Great Pioneers in Surgery.* 1960. Garden City. 1st. 431p. A13. $30.00

COHN, Norma. *Little People in a Big Country.* 1945. Oxford. 1st. sm 12mo. F/VG. M5. $45.00

COHN, Roy. *How To Fight for Your Rights & Win.* 1981. S&S. 1st. F/F. A20. $30.00

COHN & FINKE. *Power Defenisve Bidding.* 1988. Louisville, KY. 1st. 204p. VG. S1. $8.00

COHNHEIM, Julius. *Lectures on General Pathology.* 1889-1890. London. 1st Eng trans. 3 fol. 1434p. A13. $400.00

COHON, Samuel S. *Essays in Jewish Theology.* 1987. HUC Pr. 366p. VG/dj. S3. $25.00

COKE, Edward. *First Part of the Institutes of Laws of England...* 1703. London. contemporary calf/rebacked. M11. $650.00

COKER, Elizabeth Boatwright. *Bees.* 1968. Dutton. 1st. sgn. VG/VG. B11. $40.00

COKER, ELizabeth Boatwright. *India Allan.* 1953. Dutton. 1st. VG/G. P3. $15.00

COLACELLO, Bob. *Holy Terror: Andy Warhol Close Up.* 1990. Harper Collins. 1st. F/F. P3. $23.00

COLBERG, Nancy. *Wallace Stegner: Descriptive Bibliography.* 1990. Confluence. 1st. M/sans. A18. $50.00

COLBERT, E.H. *Age of Reptiles.* 1965. Norton. ils/drawings. 228p. F/NF. D8. $25.00

COLBERT, E.H. *Fosssil Hunter's Notebook.* 1980. Dutton. dj. A19. $25.00

COLBERT, E.H. *Men & Dinosaurs: Search in Field & Laboratory...* 1968. Dutton. 1st. ils. 283p. VG/dj. D8. $20.00

COLBERT, E.H. *Wandering Lands & Animals.* 1973. NY. Dutton. 1st. ils. 323p. NF/dj. D8. $22.00

COLBRY, Vera L. *Diagnostic Characteristics of Fruits & Florets...* 1957. WA, DC. ils. 24p. wrp. B26. $10.00

COLBY, C.B. *Moon Exploration.* 1970. Coward McCann. 4to. 48p. xl. K5. $10.00

COLBY, John. *Life, Experience & Travels of John Colby, Preacher...* 1918. Andover. Ebenezer Chase. 1st. 16mo. contemporary wrp. M1. $250.00

COLBY & VAN DEN BERGHE. *Ixil Country: A Plural Society in Higland Guatemala.* 1969. Berkeley. 1st. 218p. dj. F3. $25.00

COLBY. *Children's Book Field.* 1952. 246p. VG. A4. $45.00

COLCHIE, Thomas. *Hammock Beneath the Mangoes.* 1991. Dutton. 1st. F/dj. M2. $30.00

COLE, Adrian. *Place Among the Fallen.* 1987. Arbor. 1st. NF/NF. P3. $20.00

COLE, Burt. *Quick.* 1989. Morrow. 1st. NF/NF. P3. $20.00

COLE, Duane. *Vagabond Club.* 1967. Ken Cook Pub. 1st. sgn pres. 183p. VG/dj. B5. $30.00

COLE, G.D.H. *Last Will & Testament.* 1985. Collins Crime Club. VG/VG. P3. $15.00

COLE, H. *Heraldry: Decoration & Floral Forms.* 1988. ils. VG/VG. M17. $15.00

COLE, Helen R. *100 Years in Thatcher, 1883-1983.* 1983. Thatcher. 1st. ils. 384p. F. B19. $75.00

COLE, Maria. *Nat King Cole: An Intimate Biography.* 1971. Morrow. 1st. F/F. M25. $35.00

COLE, S.W. *American Fruit Book.* 1849. Boston. John P Jewett. 288p. leather. VG. M20. $50.00

COLE, S.W. *American Fruit Book.* 1866. Orange Judd. 276p. cloth. VG. A10. $30.00

COLE, S.W. *Soil Management for Conservation & Production.* 1962. NY. Wiley. 527p. dj. A10. $20.00

COLE, W.R. *Checklist of Science Fiction Anthologies.* 1964. Cole. 1st. F/F. P3. $100.00

COLE, William. *Book of Animal Poems.* 1973. Viking. ARC/1st. 288p. F/F. D4. $35.00

COLE, William. *Book of Nature Poems.* 1969. Viking. 1st. ils RA Parker. F/NF. D4. $35.00

COLE, William. *Oh What Nonsense!* 1966. Viking. 1st. 80p. F/NF. D4. $45.00

COLE, William. *Poems From Ireland.* 1972. Crowell. 1st. ils Wm Stobbs. 237p. F/F. D4. $30.00

COLE, William. *Sea, Ships & Sailors.* 1967. Viking. 1st. ils Robin Jacques. 236p. F/NF. D4. $40.00

COLE & MALTZMAN. *Handbook of Contemporary Soviet Psychology.* 1969. Basic. thick 8vo. 887p. VG/dj. G1. $35.00

COLEMAN, E.L. *New England Captives Carried to Canada Between 1677...* 1925. Portland. 2 vol. gilt maroon cloth. VG. M4. $60.00

COLEMAN, Ken. *So You Want To Be a Sportscaster.* 1973. Hawthorn. 1st. photos. VG+/dj. P8. $25.00

COLEMAN, McAlister. *Eugene V Debs: Man Unafraid.* 1930. Greenberg. 1st. VG/VG. V4. $50.00

COLEMAN, Satis N. *Book of Bells.* 1938. NY. 177p. xl. A17. $45.00

COLERIDGE, Anthony. *Chippendale Furniture: Work of Thomas Chippendale...* 1968. Clarkson Potter. 1st Am. 229p. cloth. VG/dj. M20. $60.00

COLERIDGE, S.T. *Phantasmion.* 1874. Roberts Bros. G. M2. $150.00

COLERIDGE, S.T. *Poems.* 1848. NY/Boston. CS Francis. 1st thus. intro HT Tuckerman. full blk morocco. M24. $275.00

COLERIDGE, S.T. *Rime of the Ancient Mariner.* 1877. NY. Harper. 1st Am. ils Gustave Dore. gilt red cloth. F/NF/box. B24. $500.00

COLES, Manning. *All That Glitters.* 1954. Doubleday/Crime Club. 1st. VG+/dj. M20. $35.00

COLES, Manning. *Dangerous by Nature.* 1950. Doubleday. 1st. VG/VG. N4. $30.00

COLES, Manning. *Drink To Yesterday.* 1944. Canada. Musson. VG/VG. P3. $30.00

COLES, Manning. *Without Lawful Authority.* 1944. Canada. Musson. 1st. VG/G+. P3. $20.00

COLES, P. Catherine. *King's Command.* (1958). Victory Pr. bl bdg. VG/fair. N1. $8.50

COLETTA, Paolo. *Annotated Bibliography of US Marine Corps History.* 1986. Lanham. 1st. 417p. VG. S16. $45.00

COLETTE. *Cat.* 1936. Farrar Rhinehart. 1st. NF/NF. B4. $85.00

COLETTE. *Chats.* 1945. Lausanne. 1st. photos. natural linen. F/VG+. A11. $135.00

COLLEDGE & DITTMAR. *British Warships, 1914-1919.* 1972. London. Ian Allan. 150 photos. dj. T7. $35.00

COLLEDGE & LENTON. *Warships of World War II.* 1964. London. Ian Allan. 425 photos. 638p. dj. T7. $40.00

COLLETT, Marjorie. *Elizabeth in Toyland.* 1925. Harrap. 1st. ils Tarrant. 12mo. beige brd. pict dj. R5. $150.00

COLLIDGE, Mary Roberts. *Chinese Immigration: American Public Problems.* 1909. NY. Holt. thick 8vo. gilt bl cloth. F. R3. $125.00

COLLIE & FRASER. *George Borrow: A Bibliographical Study.* 1984. 1/750. 23 pl. 239p. F/VG. A4. $125.00

COLLIER, John. *Fancies & Goodnights.* 1951. Doubleday. 1st. F/dj. M2. $100.00

COLLIER, John. *Green Thoughts.* 1932. London. 1/550. sgn/#d. VG. M2. $125.00

COLLIER, John. *His Monkey Wife.* 1931. Appleton. 1st. VG. P3. $35.00

COLLIER, John. *Patterns & Ceremonies of the Indians of the Southwest.* 1949. Dutton. 1/1475. sgn/#d. ils/sgn Ira Moskowitz. 192p. NF/dj. K7. $150.00

COLLIER, Peter. *Kennedy's: An American Drama.* 1984. Summit. 1st. sgn. VG/VG. A23. $32.00

COLLIER, Richard. *House Called Memory.* 1961. Dutton. 1st. VG/VG. P3. $15.00

COLLIER, S. *Mount Desert: Most Beautiful Island in the World.* 1952. photos. VG. M17. $30.00

COLLIER, V.W.F. *Dogs of China & Japan in Nature & Art.* 1921. London. Heinemann. ils. 207p. remnant rear xl pocket. VG. W3. $95.00

COLLIER & EATON. *Roland, the Warrior.* (1934). Harcourt Brace. ils Frank Schoonover. G+. B15. $45.00

COLLIER. *Collier's Photographic History of World War II.* 1945. NY. 800+ photos/map ep. gilt/red stp brn cloth. VG. K7. $50.00

COLLING, Susan. *Frogmorton.* 1956. Knopf. 1st Am. 148p. gr cloth/red spine. VG/torn. T5. $30.00

COLLINGWOOD, W.G. *Life & Works of John Ruskin.* 1893. Houghton Mifflin. 2 vol. 1st. 8vo. aeg. dk red ribbed cloth. H13. $95.00

COLLINS, A. Frederick. *Amateur Mechanic.* 1919 (1918). Appleton. 8vo. 208p. G. K5. $20.00

COLLINS, Clella R. *Army Woman's Handbook.* 1942. Whittlesey. revised. 239p. VG+. A25. $32.00

COLLINS, Erroll. *Mariners of Space.* 1949. London. VG. M2. $15.00

COLLINS, Freda. *Shrove-tide Fair.* 1960. Faith Pr. 1st. F/F. N1. $4.00

COLLINS, G.B. *Wildcats & Shamrocks.* 1977. Mennonite Pr. 2nd. inscr. VG/dj. D8. $12.00

COLLINS, Gary. *Magnificent Mind.* 1985. World. 262p. VG/dj. B29. $8.00

COLLINS, Gilbert. *Valley of Eyes Unseen.* 1924. McBride. 1st Am. VG. M2. $37.00

COLLINS, Hunt; see Hunter, Evan.

COLLINS, Jackie. *Lady Boss.* 1990. S&S. 1st. NF/F. T12. $20.00

COLLINS, Larry. *Maze.* 1989. S&S. 1st. VG/VG. P3. $20.00

COLLINS, Mary. *Sister of Cain.* 1943. Scribner. 1st. VG. P3. $20.00

COLLINS, Michael; see Lynds, Dennis.

COLLINS, Nancy. *Midnight Blue: Sonia Blue Collection.* 1995. Stone Mtn. 1st collection. VG+/dj. M21. $20.00

COLLINS, Paul. *Alien Worlds.* 1979. Void Pub. 1st. NF/NF. P3. $30.00

COLLINS, Randall. *Case of the Philosophers' Ring.* 1980. Harvester. 1st. VG/VG. P3. $30.00

COLLINS, Richard L. *Thunderstorms & Airplanes.* 1982. Delacorte. 1st. 8vo. 280p. VG/dj. K5. $15.00

COLLINS, Wilkie. *Man & Wife.* 1870. NY. Harper. 1st Am. gilt purple cloth. M24. $75.00

COLLINS, Wilkie. *Moonstone.* 1959. NY. LEC. 1st thus. 1/1500. ils/sgn Andre Dignimont. F/dj/case. Q1. $100.00

COLLINS, Wilkie. *Queen of Hearts.* 1859. NY. Harper. 1st Am. gilt brick-brn pebbled cloth. F. M24. $375.00

COLLINS & ERIKSSON. *Ann of Green Gable's Treasury.* 1991. Viking. 1st. 243p. F/dj. T10. $35.00

COLLINS & LAPIERRE. *Fifth Horseman.* 1980. S&S. 1st. NF/NF. M22. $15.00

COLLIS, LOUISE. *Soldier in Paradise: Life of Capt John Stedman 1744-97.* (1966). Harcourt Brace. 1st Am. 231p. F3. $20.00

COLLIS, Maurice. *Grand Peregrination.* 1959. London. Faber. 2nd. cloth. VG/dj. M20. $20.00

COLLODI, Carlo. *Adventures of Pinocchio.* nd. NY. Macmillan. 3rd. ils Attilio Mussino. 404p. dk bl cloth. VG. D1. $225.00

COLLODI, Carlo. *Adventures of Pinocchio.* 1939. London. Collins. 1st thus. ils AH Watson. 8vo. red textured cloth. dj. R5. $135.00

COLLODI, Carlo. *Pinocchio's Adventures in Wonderland.* 1898. Boston. Jordan Marsh. 1st Am. 12mo. M5. $275.00

COLLODI, Carlo. *Pinocchio.* (1932). Garden City. ils Petersham. G. B15. $40.00

COLLODI, Carlo. *Pinocchio.* 1904. Ginn. full-p mc pl. gilt cloth/mc pl. VG. M5. $75.00

COLLODI, Carlo. *Pinocchio.* 1904. Ginn. Once Upon A Time series. 12mo. gilt gr cloth. M5. $55.00

COLLODI, Carlo. *Pinocchio.* 1919. Dent Dutton. 2nd. thick 8vo. VG. M5. $110.00

COLLODI, Carlo. *Pinocchio.* 1933. Blue Ribbon. ils Harold Lentz/4 popups. 96p. VG+. D1. $650.00

COLLODI, Carlo. *Walt Disney's Pinocchio. A Giant Golden Punch-Out.* 1962. England. Purnell. adapted from movie. lg 4to. unpunched. R5. $150.00

COLMAN, Miss. *Bijou Alphabet.* 1846. Phil. 12mo. 111p. gilt cloth. VG. B14. $100.00

COLMONT, Marie. *Down the River.* 1940. NY/London. Harper. 1st. mc litho. B24. $185.00

COLMONT, Marie. *Le Roi Chat.* 1944. Flammarion. 1st. ils Andre Paul. sq 12mo. VG+. M5. $65.00

COLNETT, James. *Voyage to the South Atlantic & Round Cape Horn...* 1968. Amsterdam. rpt. fld maps/charts. 179p. P4. $110.00

COLOMBO, John Robert. *Not To Be Taken at Night.* 1981. Lester Denys. F/NF. P3. $20.00

COLTMAN, Paul. *Tog the Ribber; or, Granny's Tale.* 1985. London. Deutsch. 1st. 29p. F/F. D4. $25.00

COLTMAN, Paul. *Witch Watch.* 1989. FSG. 1st. unp. VG/dj. M20. $20.00

COLTON, James; see Hansen, Joseph.

COLTON, Walter. *Deck & Port; or, Incidents of Cruise in US Frigate Congress.* 1850. NY. AS Barnes. 1st. 5 pl. 408p. gray-gr cloth. VG. K7. $150.00

COLTON, Walter. *Three Years in California.* 1850. NY. Barnes. 456p. red cloth. VG. K7. $175.00

COLTON, Walter. *Three Years in California.* 1886. Boston. Cleaves Macdonald. 12mo. 456p. gilt cloth. VG. T10. $75.00

COLUM, Padraic. *Collected Poems.* 1953. NY. Devin-Adair. 1st thus. sgn. F/VG. B4. $85.00

COLUM, Padraic. *Six Who Were Left in a Shoe.* 1923. Chicago. Volland. ils Dugald Stewart Walker. 40p. NF. A4. $65.00

COLUM, Padraic. *Voyager, Legends & History of Atlantic Discoveries.* 1925. Macmillan. 1st. ils Winfred Jones. 188p. VG/worn. D1. $50.00

COLVILLE, Jessie. *Kentucky Woman's Handy Cookbook.* 1912. self pub. VG. E6. $45.00

COLVIN, Verna Rae. *Garden & How It Grew: Eden 1881-1981.* nd (1981). private prt. 1st. 1/200. ils. 206p. F/sans. B19. $95.00

COLWELL & WAKELEY. *Introduction to Study of X-Rays & Radium.* 1926. London. 1st. 203p. A13. $35.00

COLWIN, Laurie. *Passion & Affect.* 1974. NY. Viking. 1st. author's 1st book. NF/VG. L3. $50.00

COMANCHO, El. *Old Timer's Tale.* 1929. Canterbury. 1st. pl. 114p. VG. J2. $95.00

COMBE, William. *Three Tours of Dr Syntax...* 1823. London. Ackerman. 3 vol. 1st thus. 78 hand-colored aquatints. Birdsall bdg. H13. $1,295.00

COMBE, William. *Tour of Doctor Syntax Through London.* 1820. London. Johnson. 1st. 19 hand-colored pl. 319p. tan brd. VG. D1. $800.00

COMENIUS, Joannes Amos. *Orbis Sensualium Pictus (Visible World...).* 1810. NY. T&J Swords. 1st Am. based on 12th London. 12mo. rebound leather. R5. $2,500.00

COMENIUS, Joannes Amos. *Orbis Sensualium Pictus...* 1777. London. Leacroft. 12th. 150 woodcuts. rebound/rpl ep/marbled brd/label. R5. $285.00

COMLY, John. *Epistle, or Salutation in Gospel Love...* 1832. Phil. J Richards. 1st. 36p. V3. $25.00

COMLY & COMLY. *Friends' Miscellany: Being Collection of Essays...* 1833-1835. Phil. J Richards. 2nd. 6 vol. full leather. V3. $185.00

COMMAGER, Henry Steele. *Blue & the Gray.* 1950. Indianapolis. 2 vol. 1st. VG/dj. B5. $125.00

COMMAGER. *St Nicholas Anthology.* (1948). Random. 3rd. ils. VG. B15. $40.00

COMMANDER SCOTT. *Romance of the Highways of California.* 1945. Pasadena. Commander Scott Prod. 1st ltd/sgn. G+/poor. O4. $20.00

COMMELIN, Isaac. *Histoire de la Vie & Acts Memorables de Frederic Henry...* 1656. Amsterdam. Vefve & Heritiers Judocus Jansson. 1st. 39 double-p pl. R15. $3,500.00

COMPARETTI, Andre. *Occursus Medici de Vaga Aegritudine Infirmitatis Nervorum.* 1780. Venetiis. Typis Francisci ex Nicolao Pezzana. 396p. F. G1. $650.00

COMPERTZ, M. *Corn From Egypt: Beginning of Agriculuture...* 1928. 87p. xl. VG. E6. $15.00

COMPTON, Arthur Holly. *Cosmos of Arthur Holly Compton.* 1967. Knopf. 1st. VG/dj. K3. $20.00

COMPTON, D.G. *Windows.* 1979. Berkley Putnam. 1st. VG/VG. P3. $13.00

COMPTON, R.R. *Manual of Field Geology.* 1962. John Wiley. 378p. G. D8. $12.00

COMPTON-BURNETT, I. *First & the Last.* 1971. Knopf. 1st Am. F/NF. B4. $50.00

COMSTOCK, J.L. *Elements of Chemistry.* 1850. Pratt Woodford. 32nd ed from the 54th. 422p. full leather. G+. H1. $35.00

COMSTOCK, Sarah. *Moon Is Made of Green Cheese.* 1929. Doubleday. 1st. VG. M2. $12.00

CON, J. *American Orders & Societies & Their Decorations.* 1917. Phil. ils. VG. E6. $125.00

CONANT, Charles A. *History of Modern Banks of Issue.* 1896. Putnam. 1st. 8vo. 595p. teg. gilt brn cloth. VG. T10. $75.00

CONCHA, Joseph L. *Lonely Deer.* 1969. Taos Pueblo Council. 1st. sgn. NF/wrp. L3. $250.00

CONCIDINE, J. Francis. *Singing Rails.* 1934. Blk Cat. 1st. 1/300. unp. VG. D4. $45.00

CONDIT & TURNBLADH. *Hold High the Torch: History of 4th Marines.* 1989. Nashville. rpt. maps/biblio/index. 458p. VG. S16. $40.00

CONDON, Richard. *Ecstasy Business.* 1967. Dial. 1st. VG/VG. M22. $20.00

CONDON, Richard. *Infirmity of Mirrors.* 1964. Random. 1st. F/NF. H11. $30.00

CONDON, Richard. *Prizzi's Family.* 1986. Putnam. 1st. F/F. H11. $20.00

CONDON, Richard. *Prizzi's Honor.* 1982. Coward. 1st. F/NF. H11. $35.00

CONDON, Richard. *Trembling Upon Rome.* 1983. Michael Joseph. 1st. F/F. P3. $25.00

CONDON, Richard. *Vertical Smile.* 1971. Dial. 1st. VG/VG. P3. $25.00

CONEY, Michael G. *Celestial Steam Locomotive.* 1983. Houghton Mifflin. 1st. F/dj. M2. $15.00

CONEY, Michael G. *Fang the Gnome.* 1988. NAL. 1st/1st prt. 8vo. 345p. F/F. T10. $75.00

CONEY, Michael G. *Gods of the Greataway.* 1984. Houghton Mifflin. 1st. VG/VG. P3. $16.00

CONGER, A. *Rise of US Grant.* 1931. 390p. xl. F. O8. $18.50

CONGREVE, William. *Way of the World & Love for Love.* 1929. Dodd Mead. 1st. ils John Kettelwell. NF. M19. $45.00

CONGREVE, William. *Way of the World: Comedy in Five Acts.* 1959. LEC. 1st thus. 1/1500. ils/sgn TM Cleland. F/glassine/ case. Q1. $75.00

CONKLIN, E. *Picturesque Arizona: Being Result of Travels & Observations.* 1878. Mining Record Prt Establishment. 1st. 390p. B19. $200.00

CONKLIN, Groff. *Omnibus of Science Fiction.* 1952. Crown. 1st. F/dj. M2. $37.00

CONKLIN, Groff. *Science Fiction in Mutation.* 1955. Vanguard. 1st. VG/dj. P3. $35.00

CONKLIN, Groff. *Treasury of Science Fiction.* 1948. Crown. 1st. VG/NF. M2. $30.00

CONLEY, Robert J. *Back to Malachi.* 1986. Doubleday. 1st. inscr. F/F. L3. $125.00

CONLEY, Robert J. *Saga of Henry Starr.* 1989. Doubleday. 1st. F/NF. L3. $65.00

CONNELL, Evan S. *Mrs Bridge.* 1960. London. Heinemann. 1st Eng. F/VG+ clip. B4. $225.00

CONNELL, Evans. *Anatomy Lesson.* 1957. 1st. sgn. F/VG. M19. $85.00

CONNELL, Will. *In Pictures: A Hollywood Satire.* 1937. NY. TJ Maloney. 106p. wrp/sbdg/cb case. D11. $500.00

CONNELLY, Marc. *Souvenir From Qam.* 1965. Holt. 1st. F/F. H11. $30.00

CONNELLY, Michael. *Black Echo.* 1992. Little Brn. ARC. F/F. D10. $50.00

CONNELLY, Michael. *Black Ice.* 1993. Boston. Little Brn. 1st. VG/VG. P3. $20.00

CONNELLY, Michael. *Black Ice.* 1993. Little Brn. 1st. F/dj. M22. $25.00

CONNELLY, Michael. *Black Ice.* 1993. Little Brn. 1st. sgn. F/F. A23. $40.00

CONNELLY & KAUFMAN. *Beggar on Horseback.* 1924. Boni Liveright. 1st. F/NF. B4. $300.00

CONNER, Howard. *Spearhead: World War II History of the 5th Marine Division.* 1950. WA, DC. 1st. photos/maps/casualty lists. VG. S16. $125.00

CONNINGTON, J.J. *No Past Is Dead.* 1942. Little Brn. 1st Am. Vg/dj. M15. $50.00

CONNOLLY, Cyril. *Condemned Playground, Essays.* 1945. London. 1st. VG. T9. $20.00

CONNOLLY. *Children's Modern First Editions, Their Value...* 1988. ils. 335p. F/F. A4. $165.00

CONNOR, Ralph. *Foreigner: A Tale of Saskatchewan.* 1909. Hodder Stoughton. dj. A19. $20.00

CONRAD, Barnaby. *How To Fight a Bull.* 1968. Doubleday. 1st. 224p. dj. F3. $20.00

CONRAD, Barnaby. *La Fiesta Brava.* 1953. Houghton Mifflin. later prt. photos. VG. P8. $20.00

CONRAD, Earl. *Invention of the Negro.* 1966. NY. Ericksson. 1st. NF/VG. B4. $45.00

CONRAD, Henry S. *How To Know the Mosses & Liverworts.* 1956. Dubuque. revised 2nd. Picture-Keyed Nature series. F. B26. $17.50

CONRAD, Joseph. *Almayer's Folly.* 1895. London. Fisher Unwin. 1st/1st issue. author's 1st book. teg. gilt gr cloth. M24. $1,650.00

CONRAD, Joseph. *Conrad Argosy.* 1942. Doubleday Doran. 4to. 713p. T7. $40.00

CONRAD, Joseph. *Dover Patrol, a Tribute.* 1922. Canterbury. Prt for Private Circulation/ 1st. 1/75. NF/prt wrp. M24. $375.00

CONRAD, Joseph. *Lord Jim: A Tale.* 1959. LEC. 1st thus. 1/1500. ils/sgn Lynd Ward. F/NF case. Q1. $150.00

CONRAD, Joseph. *Marcel Proust, an English Tribute.* 1923. Chatto Windus. 1st/lg paper issue. 1/150. quarter parchment. uncut. M24. $250.00

CONRAD, Joseph. *Outcast of the Islands.* 1896. Appleton. 1st Am. 3-quarter maroon roan. teg. pub bdg. M24. $600.00

CONRAD, Joseph. *Secret Agent.* 1907. Harper. 1st Am. 372p. gilt bl bdg. G+. H1. $40.00

CONRAD, Joseph. *Secret Agent: A Drama in Three Acts.* 1923. London. 1/1000. sgn/#d. NF/VG. A11. $400.00

CONRAD, Joseph. *Some Reminiscences.* 1912. London. Eveleigh Nash. 1st. 1/1000. gilt bl cloth. F. M24. $225.00

CONRAD, Joseph. *Suspense: A Napoleonic Novel.* 1925. Doubleday. 1st. 1/377. gilt cream brd/bl trim. inner & outer dj/case. B24. $250.00

CONRAD, Joseph. *Tremolino.* 1942. NY. Duschnes. 1st separate. ils/sgn EA Wilson. F/case. B24. $150.00

CONRAD, Joseph. *Victory.* 1921. Modern Lib. ne. G. W2. $250.00

CONRAD & DEMAREST. *Religion & Empire.* (1984). Cambridge. 1st. 2656p. reading copy. F3. $10.00

CONRAD & PATTERSON. *Scottsboro Boy.* 1950. Doubleday. 1st. G/dj. M25. $35.00

CONRAN, Shirley. *Savages.* 1987. S&S. 1st. F/F. T12. $25.00

CONRAN, Terence. *Vegetable Book.* 1976. Crescent. VG/dj. A16. $6.00

CONRNSWEET, Tom N. *Visual Perception.* 1970. Academic. 3rd. tall 8vo. 475p. blk cloth. G1. $65.00

CONROY, Albert; see Albert, Marvin H.

CONROY, Frank. *Midair.* 1985. Dutton. 1st. NF/F. H11. $25.00

CONROY, Frank. *Stop-Time.* 1967. Viking. 1st. F/F. B4. $150.00

CONROY, Pat. *Great Santini.* 1976. Houghton Mifflin. 1st. author's 3rd book. F/F. L3/Q1. $150.00

CONROY, Pat. *Great Santini.* 1976. Houghton Mifflin. 1st. G/G. M19. $65.00

CONROY, Pat. *Great Santini.* 1976. Houghton Mifflin. 1st. sgn. F/NF. B4. $300.00

CONROY, Pat. *Lords of Discipline.* 1980. Houghton Mifflin. 1st. author's 4th novel. F/NF. D10. $85.00

CONROY, Pat. *Lords of Discipline.* 1980. Houghton Mifflin. 1st. sgn. F/F. B4/Q1. $200.00

CONROY, Pat. *Prince of Tides.* 1986. Houghton Mifflin. 1st. inscr. F/dj. Q1. $75.00

CONROY, Pat. *Prince of Tides.* 1986. Houghton Mifflin. 1st. NF/NF. A24/T11. $35.00

CONSIDINE, Bob. *Toots.* 1969. NY. inscr Toots Shor. 214p. VG. B14. $45.00

CONSIDINE, Shaun. *Barbra Streisand: Woman, Myth, Music.* 1985. Delacorte. 1st. photos. 335p. VG/G. A25. $10.00

CONSTANTINE, K.C. *Man Who Liked Slow Tomatoes.* 1982. Godine. 1st. NF/NF. M22. $75.00

CONSTANTINE, K.C. *Upon Some Midnight's Clear.* 1985. Godine. 1st. NF/NF. M22. $25.00

CONWAY, Tom (a few); see Avallone, Mike.

CONWELL, Russell H. *Magnolia Journey: A Union Veteran Revisits...* 1974. AL U. 1st. 190p. cloth. VG/dj. M20. $25.00

CONYBEARE & HOWSON. *Life & Epistles of St Paul.* 1893. Longman Gr. 850p. fair. B29. $11.00

CONYBEARE & HOWSON. *Life & Epistles of St Paul.* 1980. Eerdmans. 850p. VG/dj. B29. $13.00

COOK, A.H. *Physics of the Earth & Planets.* 1973. Wiley. 8vo. 316p. VG/VG. K5. $20.00

COOK, Allyn Austin. *Diseases of Tropical & Subtropical Fruits & Nuts.* 1975. Hafner. 8vo. 317p. xl. A22. $22.00

COOK, Canfield. *Lucky Terrell: Lost Squadron (#4).* 1943. Grosset Dunlap. 1st. lists to this title. 216p. VG/dj. M20. $22.50

COOK, Canfield. *Lucky Terrell: Secret Mission (#3).* 1943. Grosset Dunlap. 1st. lists 2 titles. 210p. VG/dj. M20. $20.00

COOK, Canfield. *Lucky Terrell: Springboard to Tokyo (#5).* 1943. Grosset Dunlap. 210p. cloth. VG/rpr. M20. $20.00

COOK, Canfield. *Lucky Terrell: Wings Over Japan (#6).* 1944. Grosset Dunlap. 1st. lists 5 titles. VG/dj. M20. $25.00

COOK, Frederick A. *To the Top of the Continent: Discovery, Exploration...* 1996. Hurleyville. 1/200. 19th Anniversary ed. 312p. P4. $50.00

COOK, Harold J. *Tales of the 04 Ranch.* 1968. U NE. 1st. 221p. VG/VG. J2. $90.00

COOK, James. *Explorations of Capt James Cook in the Pacific...* nd (1955). Heritage. 292p. gilt bdg. VG/poor case. P4. $45.00

COOK, James. *Explorations of Capt James Cook in the Pacific...1779.* 1957. LEC. 1st thus. 1/1500. ils/sgn Geoffrey Ingleton. F/glassine/case. Q1. $250.00

COOK, Marc. *Wilderness Cure.* 1881. NY. 153p. pict cloth. VG. B14. $95.00

COOK, Robin. *Brain.* 1981. Putnam. 1st. VG/VG. P3. $25.00

COOK, Robin. *Coma.* 1977. Little Brn. 1st. NF/clip. M22. $20.00

COOK, Robin. *Coma.* 1977. Little Brn. 1st. NF/NF. M19. $45.00

COOK, Robin. *Fever.* 1982. Putnam. 1st. sgn. NF/NF. M19. $25.00

COOK, Robin. *Mindbend.* 1985. Putnam. 1st. VG/VG. P3. $15.00

COOK, Robin. *Private Parts in Public Places.* 1969. Atheneum. 1st. VG/VG. P3. $40.00

COOK, Robin. *Sphinx.* 1979. Putnam. 1st. VG/VG. P3. $23.00

COOK, Thomas H. *Night Secrets.* 1990. Putnam. 1st. F/F. P3. $20.00

COOK, Thomas H. *Orchids.* 1982. Houghton Mifflin. 1st. F/F. T2. $45.00

COOK, Warren L. *Flood Tide of Empire: Spain & Pacific Northwest 1543-1819.* 1973. New Haven. Yale. Yale W Am series 24. 4to. 620p. F. O7. $35.00

COOK & GLEASON. *Ecological Survey of the Flora of Porto Rico.* 1928. Rio Piedras. Insular Experiment Station. 8vo. G+/wrp. A22. $50.00

COOK-LYNN, Elizabeth. *Badger Said This.* 1977. NY. Vantage. 1st. author's 1st book. NF/VG. L3. $350.00

COOK-LYNN, Elizabeth. *Power of Horses & Other Stories.* 1990. NY. Arcade/Little Brn. AP. wrp. R13. $30.00

COOKE, Alistair. *America.* 1974. Knopf. dj. A19. $25.00

COOKE, Alistair. *Americans: Fifty Letters From America.* 1979. London. 1st. VG/dj. T9. $20.00

COOKE, Alistair. *Patient Has the Floor.* 1986. Franklin Lib. 1st/ltd. sgn. full leather. F. Q1. $35.00

COOKE, Alistair. *Patient Has the Floor.* 1986. Knopf. 1st trade. F/F. B35. $16.00

COOKE, D.E. *Firebird.* 1939. Winston. 1st. ils. red cloth. VG. M5. $45.00

COOKE, David C. *Best Detective Stories of the Year 1950.* 1950. Dutton. 1st. VG/G+. P3. $20.00

COOKE, David C. *My Best Murder Story.* 1955. Merlin. 1st. VG+/G. N4. $20.00

COOKE, Donald. *For Conspicuous Gallantry: Winners of Medal of Honor.* 1966. Maplewood. ils/roster/index. 93p. VG/VG. S16. $15.00

COOKE, G. Walter. *Death Is the End.* 1965. Geoffrey Bles. 1st. VG/VG. P3. $18.00

COOKE & MCQUEEN. *Girls of Silver Spur Ranch.* ca 1950. Chicago. Goldsmith. 1st. unp. VG/dj. A25. $20.00

COOL, Joyce. *Kidnapping of Courtney Van Allen & What's-Her-Name.* (1982). Knopf. 8vo. 175p. VG. T5. $18.00

COOLIDGE, Calvin. *Extracts From the Autobiography of...* 1930. Kingsport, TN. 21x15mm. 129p. aeg. full bl leather. B24. $150.00

COOLIDGE, Olivia. *George Bernard Shaw.* 1968. Houghton Mifflin. 1st. VG/dj. V4. $20.00

COOLIDGE, Olivia. *Greek Myths.* (1949). Houghton Mifflin. 8vo. 244p. VG. T5. $20.00

COOLIDGE, Susan. *What Katy Did.* (1936). Little Brn. ils Ralph Pallen Coleman. 271p. VG/dj. T5. $17.00

COOMBS, Charles. *Andy Burnett on Trial.* 1958. Whitman. TVTI. VG. P3. $15.00

COOMBS, Charles. *Maverick.* 1959. Whitman. TVTI. VG. P3. $15.00

COOMBS, John Hartley. *Dr Livingstone's 17 Years' Explorations & Adventures...* 1857. Phil/Chicago. Lloyd/Bronson Fobes. 1st. sm 8vo. 334p. VG. W1. $30.00

COOMBS, Patricia. *Molly Mullett.* 1975. Lee Shepard. 1st. sm 4to. unp. brn cloth. F/NF. T5. $25.00

COON, Carleton S. *Living Races of Man.* 1965. Knopf. 1st. NF/VG. A20. $15.00

COON, Carleton S. *Seven Caves: Archaeological Explorations in Middle East.* 1957. Knopf. 1st. 8vo. 31 pl. VG. W1. $18.00

COONEY, Barbara. *Chanticleer & the Fox.* 1958. Crowell. 1st. Caldecott Medal. VG+/VG. P2. $125.00

COONEY, Barbara. *Courtship, Merry Marriage & Feast of Cock Robin.* 1965. Scribner. 1st. 32p. cloth. F/VG. D4. $35.00

COONTS, Stephen. *Flight of the Intruder.* 1986. Naval Inst. 1st. author's 1st book. F/F. N4. $35.00

COONTS, Stephen. *Minotaur.* 1989. Doubleday. 1st. NF/NF. P3. $20.00

COONTS, Stephen. *Minotaur.* 1989. NY. 1st. F/F. T2. $25.00

COOPER, Basil. *Great White Space.* 1975. St Martin. 1st Am. F/dj. M2. $85.00

COOPER, Basil. *House of the Wolf.* 1983. Saulk City. Arkham. 1st. ils/sgn Stephen Fabian. VG. B11. $50.00

COOPER, Dennis. *Wrong.* 1980. Knopf. 1st. F/F. B35. $15.00

COOPER, Douglas. *Great Private Collections.* 1961. 1st. lg 4to. ils. NF/VG. S13. $18.00

COOPER, Edmund. *Prisoner of Fire.* 1974. Walker. 1st. F/dj. M2. $12.00

COOPER, Irving S. *Cerebellum, Epilepsy & Behavior.* 1974. NY. Plenum. 401p. brn cloth. G1. $50.00

COOPER, James Fenimore. *Last of the Mohicans.* 1919. Scribner. 1st. ils NC Wyeth. VG. M17. $85.00

COOPER, James Fenimore. *Last of the Mohicans.* 1919. Scribner. 1st. ils NC Wyeth. 4to. pict dj. R5. $750.00

COOPER, James Fenimore. *Last of the Mohicans.* 1977. Franklin Lib. ils NC Wyeth. aeg. F. A18. $50.00

COOPER, James Fenimore. *Pathfinder.* 1965. LEC. into Robert E Spiller. Ils Richard Powers. F/case. A18. $60.00

COOPER, James Fenimore. *Pioneers; or, Sources of the Susquehanna...* 1823. NY. Chas Wiley. 2 vol. 1st/1st prt vol 1 (2nd state vol 2). 12mo. M1. $1,250.00

COOPER, James Fenimore. *Prairie, a Tale, by the Author of The Spy, the Pilot...* 1827. London. Henry Colburn. 1st. 3 vol. 12mo. contemporary polished calf. M1. $350.00

COOPER, James Fenimore. *Wing-And-Wing; or, Le Feu-Follet, a Tale.* 1842. Lee Blanchard. 1st. 2 vol. unusual variant pub bdg. M24. $450.00

COOPER, Jefferson; see Fox, Gardner F.

COOPER, John R. *Mel Martin: Mystery at the Ball Park (#1).* 1947. Cupples Leon. 1st. 208p. VG/dj. M20. $35.00

COOPER, Lenna Frances. *New Cookery.* 1924. Battle Creek. Modern Medicine. G. A16. $25.00

COOPER, Merian C. *Grass.* 1925. Putnam. 2nd. inscr. VG/dj. B4. $450.00

COOPER, Nelle Grant. *Australians All. Bush Folk in Rhyme.* 1934. Australia. Angus Robertson. 1st. ils Dorothy Wall. 30p. pict brd. R5. $200.00

COOPER, Susan Rogers. *Funny As a Dead Relative.* 1994. St Martin. 1st. sgn. F/F. A23. $42.00

COOPER, Susan Rogers. *Gray King.* 1975. Atheneum. 1st. Newbery Medal. ils Michael Heslop. 208p. NF/VG+. P2. $145.00

COOPER, Susan Rogers. *Gray King.* 1975. NY. Atheneum. 1st. ils Michael Heslop. 8vo. 208p. gray-gr cloth. VG/VG. R5. $110.00

COOPER, Susan Rogers. *Houston in the Rear View Mirror.* 1990. St Martin. 1st. sgn. author's 2nd book. NF/F. A24. $90.00

COOPER, Susan Rogers. *One, Two, What Did Daddy Do?* 1992. St Martin. 1st. sgn. F/F. A23. $42.00

COOPER, Susan Rogers. *Other People's Houses.* 1990. St Martin. 1st. sgn. author's 3rd book. F/NF. A24. $55.00

COOPER, Susan Rogers. *Seaward.* 1983. Atheneum. 1st. 167p. NF/NF. P2. $35.00

COOPER, Will. *Death Has a Thousand Doors.* 1976. Bobbs Merrill. 1st. VG/VG. P3. $15.00

COOPER & DOURISH. *Neurobiology of Stereotyped Behavior.* 1990. Oxford. 297p. navy cloth. G1. $50.00

COOPER & GASKELL. *North Sea Oil: The Great Gamble.* 1966. Bobbs Merrill. 179p. VG/dj. T11. $14.00

COOPER & RATNER. *Many Hands Cooking.* 1974. Crowell/Unicef. 1st. ils Tony Chen. VG. M5. $20.00

COOPER & TRAVERS. *Surgical Essays.* 1821. Phil. 1st Am. 409p. A13. $300.00

COOPER & TREAT. *Man O'War.* 1950. photos. G. M17. $30.00

COOTE, Stephen. *Byron, the Making of a Myth.* 1988. London. 1st. as new. T9. $16.00

COOVER, Robert. *Origin of the Brunists.* 1966. Putnam. 1st. author's 1st book. F/dj. D10. $165.00

COOVER, Robert. *Pricksongs & Descants.* 1969. Dutton. 1st. author's 3rd book. F/NF. D10. $70.00

COOVER, Robert. *Public Burning.* 1977. Viking. 1st. F/F. A20. $25.00

COPE, Myron. *Broken Cigars.* 1968. Prentice Hall. 1st. VG/G+. P8. $25.00

COPE, Zachary. *Clinical Researches in Acute Abdominal Disease.* 1925. London. 1st. 148p. A13. $150.00

COPELAND, Bonnie. *Lady of Moray.* 1979. Atheneum. 1st. 313p. F/NF. W2. $25.00

COPELAND, Richard. *No Face in a Mirror.* 1980. Macmillan. 1st. VG/VG. P3. $15.00

COPEMAN, Edward. *Report of Cerebral Affections of Infancy...* 1995 (1873). NY. Classics Neurology/Neurosurgery Lib. facsimile. G1. $65.00

COPP, DeWitt S. *Forged in Fire.* 1982. Garden City, NY. 1st. 521p. quarter cloth. VG/dj. B18. $19.50

COPPARD, A.E. *Collected Tales of...* 1951. Knopf. VG/dj. M2. $30.00

COPPARD, A.E. *Nixey's Harlequin.* 1932. Knopf. 1st Am. VG. M2. $25.00

COPPEE, Henry. *Grant & His Campaigns.* 1866. NY. ils/maps. G. M17. $20.00

COPPEL, Alfred. *Apocalypse Bridge.* 1981. HRW. 1st. sgn. F/F. T12. $25.00

COPPEL, Alfred. *Apocalypse Brigade.* 1981. HRW. 1st. VG/VG. P3. $15.00

COPPEL, Alfred. *Dragon.* 1977. HBJ. 1st. VG/VG. P3. $15.00

COPPER, Basil. *From Evil's Pillow.* 1973. Arkham. 1st. F/dj. M2/M19. $25.00

COPPER, Basil. *Necropolis.* 1980. Arkham. 1st. F/dj. M2. $100.00

COPPER, Edmund. *All Fools' Day.* 1966. Hodder Stoughton. 1st. VG/VG. P3. $20.00

COPPER, Edmund. *Kronk.* 1971. Putnam. 1st. VG/VG. P3. $20.00

COPPER, Edmund. *Transit.* 1964. Faber. 1st. VG/VG. P3. $30.00

COPPIN, Glorgio. *Bears: Art, Legend, History.* 1993. Boston. 112p. F/F. S15. $8.00

COPWAY, George. *Kah-Ge-Ga-Gah-Bowh. Running Sketches of Men & Places...* 1851. NY. JC Riker. 1st. author's 3rd/last book. G. L3. $375.00

COQUIA, Jorge R. *Legal Status of the Church of the Philippines.* 1950. WA. Catholic U of Am Pr. 224p. F. P1. $20.00

CORBETT, A. *Poultry Yard & Market.* 1877. Orange Judd. 96p. gilt bdg. VG. A10. $30.00

CORBETT, Bertha L. *Sun-Bonnet Babies.* 1900. Minneapolis. 1st. sq 8vo. pale gr pict brd. R5. $200.00

CORBETT, Helen. *Helen Corbett Cooks for Company.* 1974. Houghton Mifflin. 1t. dj. A16. $10.00

CORBETT, Helen. *Helen Corbett's Cookbook.* 1962. Houghton Mifflin. VG/partial. A16. $8.00

CORBETT, James. *Death Pool.* 1936. Herbert Jenkins. 1st. VG/VG. P3. $75.00

CORBETT, James. *Merrivale Mystery.* 1931. Mystery League. 1st. NF. P3. $20.00

CORBETT, James. *Roar of the Crowd.* 1925. Garden City. VG/VG. B5. $40.00

CORBETT, Scott. *Hairy Horror Trick.* 1969. Little Brn. 1st. 8vo. F/VG+. C8. $17.50

CORBETT & CORBETT. *Pot Shots From a Grosse Ile Kitchen Cookbook.* 1947. Harper. 1st. G. A16. $12.00

CORBETT & CORBETT. *Pot Shots From a Grosse Ile Kitchen Cookbook.* 1947. Harper. 1st. 214p. VG/fair. B10. $20.00

CORDAN, Wolfgang. *Secret of the Forest.* 1963. London. Gollancz. 1st. 163p. F3. $25.00

CORDELL, Alexander. *Fire People.* 1972. Hodder Stoughton. 1st. VG/VG. P3. $15.00

CORDELL, Alexander. *Rape of the Fair Country.* 1959. Doubleday. VG/VG. P3. $10.00

CORDELL, L.S. *Prehistory of the Southwest.* 1984. Orlando. Academic. 50 maps/photos/drawings. 490p. VG/wrp. M12. $30.00

CORDER, Eric. *Murder, My Love.* 1973. Playboy. 1st. VG/G+. P3. $12.00

CORDIER, Henri. *Bibliotheca Sinica: Dictionnaire Bibliographique...* 1904. Paris. 2nd/revised/corrected. 5 vol. NF. W3. $725.00

CORELLI, Marie. *Secret Power.* 1961. London. VG/dj. M2. $15.00

CORELLI, Marie. *Young Diana.* 1918. Doran. 1st. F/NF. M2. $50.00

COREVON, Henry. *Fleurs des Champ et des Bois des Haies et des Murs.* 1911. Geneva. Albert Kundig. 8vo. VG. A22. $65.00

CORK, Barry. *Dead Ball.* 1989. Scribner. 1st. F/F. P8. $12.50

CORLE, Edwin. *Gila: River of the Southwest.* 1951. Rinehart. 1st. ils/map/bibliography. 402p. VG+. B19. $30.00

CORLE, Edwin. *Listen, Bright Angel.* 1946. DSP. 1st. 8vo. 312p. brn cloth. VG/VG. F7. $35.00

CORLE, Edwin. *Story of the Grand Canyon.* nd. London. Sampson Low. 8vo. 312p. VG+/G+. F7. $35.00

CORLEY, Edwin. *Farewell, My Slightly Tarnished Hero.* 1971. Dodd Mead. 1st. VG/dj. M25. $35.00

CORLISS, Philip G. *Hemerocallis.* 1951. SF. self pub. 1/1000. 8vo. red cloth. NF. A22. $35.00

CORLISS, William R. *Moon & the Planets.* 1985. Glen Arm, MD. Sourcebook Project. 4to. 377p. VG. K5. $30.00

CORLISS, William R. *Propulsion Systems for Space Flight.* 1960. McGraw Hill. 1st. lg 8vo. 300p. VG. K5. $60.00

CORLISS, William R. *Radioisotopic Power Generation.* 1964. Englewood Cliffs. 8vo. 304p. VG/dj. K5. $60.00

CORNELIUS, Mrs. *Young Housekeeper's Friend.* Brn Taggard Chase. facsimile 1859 revised ed. 254p. B10. $12.00

CORNELL, John J. *Essays on the View of Friends...* 1884. Friends Book Assn. 2nd. 95p. V3. $12.00

CORNELL, Ralph D. *Conspicuous California Plants.* 1938. Pasadena. 1st. 1/1500. inscr. 192p. VG. B26. $65.00

CORNER, George. *Anatomy.* 1930. NY. 1st. 82p. A13. $60.00

CORNEY, Peter. *Voyages in Northern Pacific. Narratives...Trading Voyages...* 1965. Fairfield. Ye Galleon. rpt. 8vo. 238p. tan cloth. P4. $75.00

CORNEY, Peter. *Voyages in the Northern Pacific.* 1896. Honolulu. Thos G Thrum. 1st separate. 3-quarter leather/raised bands. P4. $600.00

CORNFORD, L. Cope. *Lord High Admiral & Others.* 1915. London. VG. M2. $35.00

CORNING, James Leonard. *Treatise on Headache & Neuralgia...* 1894. NY. EB Treat. 3rd enlarged. 12mo. pebbled mauve cloth. G. G1. $50.00

CORNISH & DIXON. *Chickory: Young Voices From the Black Ghetto.* 1969. NY. Assn Pr. 1st. xl. NF/VG. B4. $45.00

CORNWELL, Bernard. *Killer's Wake.* 1989. Putnam. 1st. NF/NF. P3. $20.00

CORNWELL, Bernard. *Sharpe's Devil.* 1992. Harper Collins. 1st. sgn. F/dj. Q1. $60.00

CORNWELL, Bernard. *Sharpe's Eagle.* 1981. NY. Viking. 1st Am. F/F. M23. $50.00

CORNWELL, Bernard. *Sharpe's Honour.* 1985. Viking. 1st Am. F/dj. T11. $65.00

CORNWELL, Bernard. *Sharpe's Regiment.* 1986. London. Collins. 1st. sgn. F/dj. Q1. $250.00

CORNWELL, Bernard. *Wildtrack.* 1988. Putnam. 1st. NF/F. T12. $30.00

CORNWELL, Patricia D. *All That Remains.* 1992. Scribner. 1st. F/F. M22. $35.00

CORNWELL, Patricia D. *All That Remains.* 1992. Scribner. 1st. sgn. F/F. D10. $50.00

CORNWELL, Patricia D. *Body of Evidence.* 1991. Scribner. 1st. F/NF. A20. $85.00

CORNWELL, Patricia D. *Body of Evidence.* 1991. Scribner. 1st. NF/dj. Q1. $75.00

CORNWELL, Patricia D. *Body of Evidence.* 1991. Scribner. 1st. sgn. NF/dj. D10. $100.00

CORNWELL, Patricia D. *Cruel & Unusual.* 1993. Scribner. 1st. NF/dj. Q1. $40.00

CORNWELL, Patricia D. *Cruel & Unusual.* 1993. Scribner. 1st. sgn. F/F. M15. $50.00

CORNWELL, Patricia D. *Postmortem.* 1990. Scribner. 1st. blk cloth. NF/dj. D10. $600.00

CORRAL, Jesus C. *Caro Amigo: Autobiography of Jesus C Corral.* 1984. Westernlore. 1st. sgn. 238p. F/VG+. B19. $50.00

CORREA DE MELLO, Jose. *Allegacao do Brigadeiro Jose Correa de Mello...* 1822. Lisbon. Antonio Rodrigues Galhardo. 1st. contemporary wrp. R15. $1,800.00

CORREARD & SAVIGNY. *Narrative of a Voyage to Senegal in 1816.* 1818. London. Colburn. 2nd. hand-colored ftspc. 360p. half calf/marbled brd. T7. $350.00

CORREDOR-MATHEOS, Jose. *Miro's Posters.* 1987. Barcelona. Poligrafa. 119 pl. 269p. dj. D2. $150.00

CORRELL, D.S. *Potato & Its Wild Relatives.* 1962. TX Research Found. 606p. cloth. dj. B1. $45.00

CORREVON, Henry. *Rock Gardens & Alpine Plants.* 1930. NY. ils/pl. 544p. VG. B26. $25.00

CORRIGAN, J.D. *Working With the Microscope.* 1971. McGraw Hill. 418p. F. D8. $15.00

CORRIN & CORRIN. *Pied Piper of Hamelin.* 1988. London. Faber. 1st. ils/sgn Errol LeCain. pict brd. dj. R5. $175.00

CORROTHERS, James D. *Black Cat Club.* 1902. NY. ils JK Bryans. 264p. pict cloth. B18. $45.00

CORROZET, Gilles. *Le Thresor des Histoires de France.* 1615. Paris. Jean Corrozet. 8vo. title device. calf. R12. $325.00

CORTWRIGHT, Edgar. *Exploring Space With a Camera.* 1968. NASA. F. M2. $15.00

CORVO, Baron. *Without Prejudice.* 1963. London. Allen Lane. 1st. 1/600. F/salmon dj. Q1. $250.00

CORY, Charles B. *Birds of Illinois & Wisconsin.* 1909. Field Mus Natural Hist. ils. 764p. VG. S15. $55.00

CORY, David. *Little Jack Rabbit & the Big Brown Bear.* 1921. Grosset Dunlap. 128p. cloth. VG/dj. M20. $12.50

CORY, Desmond. *Bennett.* 1977. Crime Club. 1st. VG/VG. P3. $15.00

CORY, Fanny. *Fanny Cory Mother Goose.* 1917. Bobbs Merrill. 12 mc full-p pl. 4to. cloth. R5. $300.00

CORY, H.T. *Imperial Valley & the Salton Sink.* 1915. SF. John J Newgegin. ils/fld maps/plans. gilt stp cloth. D11. $150.00

COSBY, Bill. *Fatherhood.* 1986. Doubleday. 1st. F/F. W2. $30.00

COSELL, Howard. *Cosell.* 1973. Playboy. 1st. sgn. VG/G. B11. $18.00

COSTAIN, Thomas B. *Below the Salt.* 1957. Doubleday. 1st. VG/VG. P3. $35.00

COSTAIN, Thomas B. *High Towers.* 1949. Doubleday. 1st. VG/VG. P3. $15.00

COSTAIN, Thomas B. *Silver Chalice.* 1952. Doubleday. 1st. inscr. VG. T12. $18.00

COTE, Phyllis. *Rabbit-Go-Lucky.* 1944. Doubleday Doran. 1st. 175p. VG/dj. M20. $15.00

COTT. *Pipers at the Gates of Dawn: Wisdom Children's Literature.* 1983. ils. 351p. NF/F. A4. $75.00

COTTER, Clay. *Mystery & Adventure Stories: Hidden Peril (#8).* 1939. Cupples Leon. 204p. cloth. VG+/dj. M20. $10.00

COTTON, Charles. *Poetical Works...* 1734. London. 34d. half leather/brd. A15. $25.00

COTTON, Charles. *Scaronides; or, Virgil Travestie...* 1776. Whitehaven. Dunn Evans. tall 12mo. 144p. early polished calf/rebacked. H13. $195.00

COTTON, Robert. *Exact Abridgement of Records in Tower of London...* 1657. London. early tree calf/rebacked. G. M11. $650.00

COTTRELL, Edwin A. *Pasadena Social Agencies Survey.* 1940. Pasadena. 378p+4p ES. wrp/cloth spine (as issued). D11. $40.00

COTTRILL, GREENBERG & WAUGH. *Science Fiction & Fantasy Series & Sequels.* 1986. Garland. 1st. F. P3. $45.00

COTUGNO, Domenico Felice A. *Treatise on Nervous Sciatica; or, Nervous Hip Gout.* 1993 (1775). NY. Classics Neurology/Neurosurgery Lib. facsimile. G1. $65.00

COUCH, Houston B. *Disease of Turfgrasses.* 1962. Rheinhold. 289p. NF/dj. A22. $25.00

COULTER, E. Merton. *South During Reconstruction 1865-1877.* 1947. LSU. later prt. 426p. cloth. NF/NF. M8. $25.00

COULTER, E. Merton. *Travels in the Confederate States.* nd. Broadfoot. facsimile 1st. 289p. index. F. A17. $30.00

COUNSELMAN, Mary Elizabeth. *Half in Shadow.* 1978. Arkham. 1st. F/dj. Q1. $30.00

COUNTER, S. Allen. *North Pole Legacy: Black, White & Eskimo.* 1991. Amherst. 8vo. 222p. blk cloth. P4. $45.00

COUPER, Greta Elena. *American Sculptor on Grand Tour...William Couper.* 1988. LA. TreCavalli. ils/photos/footnotes. 157p. dj. D2. $45.00

COUPPEY, Madeleine. *Rumor of the Forest.* 1947. Scribner. 1st. VG/VG. A4. $15.00

COURANT, Maurice. *Bibliographie Coreene.* 1894-1896. NY. Burt Franklin. 4 vol in 3. ils/charts/tables. French/Chinese text. F. W3. $525.00

COURET, Pierre. *Joyas de las Orquideas Venezolanas.* 1977. Caracas. ils/photos. 104p. VG+/dj. B26. $52.50

COURLANDER & SAKO. *Heart of the Ngoni: Heroes of African Kingdom of Segu.* 1982. NY. Crown. 1st. 178p. VG. W1. $18.00

COURT DE GEBELIN. *Histoire Naturelle de la Parole.* 1776. Paris. self pub. 8vo. ftspc Marillier/fld table of alphabets. half calf. R12. $1,600.00

COURTNEY, W. *Farmers' & Mechanics' Manual.* 1868. revised. ils. 505p. G+. E6. $95.00

COURTRIGHT, G. *Tropicals.* 1988. Timber. 155p. B1. $38.00

COUSINS, Geoffrey. *Golfers at Law.* 1959. Knopf. 1st. VG/VG. P8. $30.00

COUSY & LINN. *Last Loud Roar.* 1964. Prentice Hall. 1st. photos Robert Riger. VG/G+. P8. $30.00

COUTANT, F. *ABC of Goat-Keeping.* 1946. photos. sc. G+. E6. $12.00

COUTINHO, Gago. *Nautica dos Descubrimentos Maritimos Vistos por Navegador.* 1969. Lisboa. Agencia-Geral Ultramar. lg 4to. 14 maps/50 ils. F/wrp. O7. $75.00

COVARRUBIAS, M. *Eagle, Jaguar & Serpent.* 1954. NY. 1st. dj. F3. $125.00

COVARRUBIAS, M. *Indian Art of Mexico & Central America.* 1957. NY. 1st. VG/G. B5. $65.00

COVENTRY, George. *Critical Inquiry Regarding the Real Authorship of Letters...* 1825. London. Wm Philips/G Woodfall. 1st. tall 8vo. 382p. H13. $195.00

COVERT & ELLSWORTH. *Water Supply Investigations in the Yukon-Tanana Region...* 1909. GPO. 8vo. 3 fld maps/ils/photos. 108p. new cloth. F. T10. $75.00

COVINGTON, Vicki. *Bird of Paradise.* 1990. S&S. 1st. sgn. F/F. B3. $45.00

COVINGTON, Vicki. *Gathering Home.* 1988. S&S. 1st. author's 1st book. F/F. B3. $60.00

COVVIN & PRUIT. *Energy Resources of the Denver Basin.* 1978. Rocky Mtn Assn Geol. 272p. 10 pocket maps. F. D8. $30.00

COWAN, James. *Daybreak, a Romance of an Old World.* 1896. Richmond. 1st. VG. M2. $50.00

COWAN, James. *Maori Folk-Tales of Port Hills.* 1923. Auckland. Whitcombe Tombes. 73p. gray wrp. P4. $50.00

COWAN, L. *Wit of the Jews.* 1970. VG/VG. E6. $8.00

COWAN, May. *Inverewe: Garden in the NW Highlands.* 1964. London. ils/photos/map/plan. 152p. VG/dj. B26. $15.00

COWAN, Paul. *Orphan in History: Retrieving a Jewish Legacy.* 1982. Doubleday. 246p. VG/dj. S3. $24.00

COWAN, Robert G. *Ranchos of California.* 1977. Los Angeles. rpt. VG. H1. $20.00

COWAN, Sam. *Sergeant York.* 1928. NY. 1st. sgn Alvin York. VG/torn. S16. $450.00

COWAN & DUNLAP. *Bibliography of the Chinese Question in the United States.* 1909. SF. Robertson. 4to. inscr Dunlap/sgn Cowan. ES. tan brd. F. R3. $250.00

COWAN. *Bibliography of History of California, 1510-1930.* 1964 (1933). 4 vol in 1. rpt. w/supp. VG. A4. $295.00

COWARD, Noel. *Play Parade.* 1933. NY. 1st. VG. T9. $20.00

COWARD, Noel. *Pretty Polly & Other Stories.* 1965. Doubleday. 1st Am. 8vo. NF/clip. T10. $40.00

COWARD, Noel. *Pretty Polly & Other Stories.* 1965. Doubleday. 1st. sgn. F/dj. Q1. $250.00

COWDRY, E.V. *Special Cytology: Form & Functions of Cell in Health...* 1828. NY. 1st. 2 vol. 1348p. A13. $150.00

COWELL, John. *Instivtiones Ivris Anglicani.* 1630. Frankfurt. Fitzer. 8vo. vellum. R12. $475.00

COWLEY, Cecil. *Schiwikkard of Natal & Old Transvaal.* 1974. Cape Town. Struik. 1st. 8vo. ils Paul Wiles. VG/dj. W1. $12.00

COWLEY, John D. *Bibliography of Abridgments, Digests, Dictionaries...* 1979 (1932). Holmes Beach. Wm Gaunt. facsimile. M11. $85.00

COWLEY, Stewart. *Spacewreck: Ghostships & Derelicts.* 1979. Exeter. 1st. F/dj. M2. $15.00

COWPER, Richard. *Breakthrough.* 1967. London. Dennis Dobson. 1st. F/F. T2. $30.00

COWPER, Richard. *Clone.* 1972. London. Gollancz. 1st. F/F. T2. $45.00

COWPER, Richard. *Clone.* 1973. Doubleday. 1st. F/F. P3. $20.00

COWPER, Richard. *Custodians & Other Stories.* 1972. London. Gollancz. 1st. F/clip. T2. $30.00

COWPER, Richard. *Dream of Kinship.* 1981. London. Gollancz. 1st. F/F. T2. $25.00

COWPER, Richard. *Kuldesak.* 1972. Doubleday. 1st Am. F/NF. T2. $20.00

COWPER, Richard. *Profundis.* 1979. London. Gollancz. 1st. F/F. T2. $40.00

COWPER, Richard. *Shades of Darkness.* 1986. Salisbury, Wilts. Kerosina Books. 1st. F/F. T2. $25.00

COWPER, Richard. *Tapestry of Time.* 1982. London. Gollancz. 1st. F/F. T2. $25.00

COWPER, Richard. *Tithonian Factor.* 1984. Gollancz. 1st. F/F. P3. $25.00

COWPER, Richard. *Twilight of Briareus.* 1974. Day. 1st Am. F/dj. M2. $35.00

COWPER, Richard. *Web of the Magi.* 1980. London. 1st. F/dj. M2/T2. $40.00

COWPER, William. *Poems, of William Cowper, of the Inner Temple, Esq.* 1823. Boston. Bedlington. 3 vol. leather. VG. M20. $40.00

COWPER, William. *Task, a Poem in Six Books.* 1787. Phil. Thos Dobson. 1st Am. 12mo. 218p. contemporary calf/red label. H13. $295.00

COWPER, William. *Task.* 1856. NY. Robert Carter. ils Birket Foster. 263p. aeg. bl cloth. NF. B24. $100.00

COX, A.E. *Potato: A Practical & Scientific Guide.* 1967. London. Collingridge. 176p. dj. A10. $38.00

COX, Betty J. *New Sexuality.* 1969. NY. Medical Pr of NY. 1st. ils. 256p. VG/tattered. A25. $8.00

COX, C.B. *Biogeography: Ecological & Evolutionary Approach.* 1977. Oxford. Blackwell Scientific. 2nd/2nd prt. 194p. wrp. B1. $18.50

COX, E.H. *Plant Hunting in China.* 1945. London. 1st. ils/maps. 230p. VG/dj. W3. $95.00

COX, Erle. *Missing Angel.* 1947. Australia. 1st. VG. M2. $35.00

COX, Isaac. *Annals of Trinity County.* 1940. Eugene, OR. Nash. 1/350. 4to. 265p. NF/NF. T10. $250.00

COX, J. Charles. *Pulpits, Lecterns & Organs in English Churches.* 1915. London. 8vo. ils. 228p. xl. VG. B14. $45.00

COX, J. Charles. *Royal Forests of England.* 1905. London. Methuen. red cloth. VG. M11. $65.00

COX, J. Randolph. *Man of Magic & Mystery: A Guide to Work of Walter Gibson.* 1988. Scarecrow. 383p. F/sans. M21. $40.00

COX, Jacob D. *Atlanta.* 1882. NY. 274p. O8. $21.50

COX, Jacob D. *Franklin & Nashville: The March to the Sea.* 1882. NY. 1st. 265p. O8. $23.50

COX, James. *My Native Land.* 1903. ils. 400p. O8. $18.50

COX, Palmer. *Another Brownie Book.* 1890. Century. 1st. pict brd. R5. $275.00

COX, Palmer. *Brownies & Prince Florimel.* 1918. Century. 1st. ils. 8vo. gray cloth/mc pl. VG. M5. $110.00

COX, Palmer. *Brownies at Home.* 1893. NY. Century. 1st. 4to. 144p. pict brd. R5. $250.00

COX, Palmer. *Frolic on Wheels.* 1895. Hubbard. 4to. VG. M5. $110.00

COX, Palmer. *Queer Stories About Queer Animals Told in Rhymes & Jingles.* 1905. Phil. unp. decor cloth. G+. B18. $65.00

COX, R. *Columbia River or Scenes & Adventures During a Residence...* 1957. OK U. 1st. ils/maps. 396p. F/dj. M4. $45.00

COX, Samuel S. *Three Decades of Federal Legislation 1855 to 1885.* 1885. Providence. Reid. 726p. brn cloth. VG+. M20. $50.00

COX, Thomas R. *Park Builders: History of State Parks in Pacific Northwest.* 1988. WA U. 248p. F/F. S15. $15.00

COX, Wally. *Mr Peepers: A Sort of Novel.* 1955. S&S. 1st. NF/VG. B4. $85.00

COX & FUJII. *Three Treasures: Myths of Old Japan.* 1964. Harper. ils. 256p. pict wht cloth. F. W3. $38.00

COX & STOIKO. *Spacepower: What It Means to You.* 1958. Winston. 1st. F/VG. M2. $17.00

COX-MCCORMACK, Nancy. *Peeps: The Really Truly Sunshine Fairy.* 1918. Volland. 1st. ils Katharine Sturges Dodge. 8vo. pict brd. R5. $75.00

COXE, George Harmon. *Butcher, Baker, Murder-Maker.* 1954. Knopf. 1st. VG. P3. $25.00

COXE, George Harmon. *Double Identity.* 1970. Knopf. 1st. NF/NF. N4. $25.00

COXE, George Harmon. *Fenner.* 1971. Knopf. 1st. NF/NF. P3. $15.00

COXE, George Harmon. *Impetuous Mistress.* 1958. Knopf. 1st. VG/VG. N4. $25.00

COXE, George Harmon. *Inside Man.* 1974. Knopf. 1st. VG/VG. P3. $18.00

COXE, George Harmon. *Mrs Murdock Takes a Case.* 1941. Knopf. 1st. VG/NF. M19. $35.00

COXE, George Harmon. *Ring of Truth.* 1966. Knopf. 1st. 176p. VG/dj. M20. $15.00

COXE, George Harmon. *Silent Witness.* 1973. Knopf. 1st. VG/VG. P3. $20.00

COYLE, William. *Ohio Authors & Their Books, 1796-1950.* 1962. World. ARC/1st. 741p. VG/dj. M20. $50.00

COYLE & ROBERTS. *Field Guide to Common & Interesting Plants of Baja CA.* 1975. La Jolla. 1st. 206p. bl cloth. F/dj. B26. $25.00

COYNE, John. *Hobgoblin.* 1981. Putnam. 1st. F/dj. M2. $25.00

COYNE, John. *Piercing.* 1979. Putnam. 1st. inscr. F/dj. M2. $40.00

COZZENS, James Gould. *Children & Others.* 1964. HBW. 1st. 343p. VG. W2. $30.00

COZZENS, S.W. *Marvelous Country; or, Three Years in Arizona & New Mexico..* 1967 (1873). Minneapolis. rpt. 1/1500. ils. 540p. F/dj. M4. $30.00

CRABB & MACKAY. *Tristan da Cunha: Its Postal History & Philately.* 1965. Ewell. self pub. 21 pl/list of ships. 72p. P4. $175.00

CRABBE, George. *Borough: A Poem, in Twenty-Four Letters.* 1820. London. Murray. 8vo. 347p. detailed fore-edge painting. red morocco. F. B24. $950.00

CRACE, Jim. *Continent.* 1986. Harper Row. 1st. NF/F. M11. $25.00

CRADDOCK, Harry. *Savoy Cocktail Book.* 1934. S&S. 287p. B10. $35.00

CRADDOCK, LOVELESS & VIERIMA. *Antarctic Geoscience.* 1982. Madison. 1st. 1172p. bl cloth. M/dj. P4. $65.00

CRADOCK, Mrs. H.C. *Josephine, John & the Puppy.* nd. London. Blackie. ils Appleton. brn lettered cloth brd/pict label. R5. $150.00

CRADOCK, Mrs. H.C. *Josephine Keeps House.* nd. London. Blackie. ils Appleton/8 full-p pl. cloth/pict label. dj. R5. $150.00

CRADOCK, Mrs. H.C. *Josephine's Pantomime.* nd. London. Blackie. ils Appleton/8 full-p pl. cloth/pict label. dj. R5. $150.00

CRAIG, David. *Albion Case.* 1975. Macmillan. 1st. VG/VG. P3. $20.00

CRAIG, Gordon. *Henry Irving.* 1930. ils. VG. M17. $15.00

CRAIG, Helen. *Angelena on Stage.* 1986. Clarkson Potter. 1st. ils Katherine Holabird. F. C8. $25.00

CRAIG, John A. *Judging Live Stock.* 1906. Austin. self pub. 193p. photos. cloth. NF. A10. $10.00

CRAIG, Robert T. *Mammillaria Handbook With Descriptions...* 1945. Pasadena. 1st. 390p. VG+. B26. $75.00

CRAINE, E.J. *Conquistador.* 1931. Duffield Green. 1st. VG. M@. $17.00

CRAINE & REINDORP. *Chronicles of Michoacan.* 1970. OK U. 1st. 259p. cloth. dj. D11. $35.00

CRAIS, Robert. *Freefall.* 1993. Bantam. 1st. sgn. F/F. A23. $42.00

CRAIS, Robert. *Lullaby Town.* 1992. Bantam. 1st. sgn. F/dj. D10. $175.00

CRAIS, Robert. *Stalking the Angel.* 1989. Bantam. 1st. F/F. M15. $45.00

CRAIS, Robert. *Stalking the Angel.* 1989. NY. Bantam. 1st. sgn. F/F. D10. $85.00

CRAM, Mildred. *Promise.* 1949. Knopf. 1st. VG/VG. P3. $30.00

CRAM, Ralph Adams. *Impressions of Japanese Architecture & Allied Arts.* 1905. NY. Baker Taylor. 1st. 227p. NF. W3. $165.00

CRAMER, Maurice. *Phoenix in East Hadley.* 1941. Houghton Mifflin. 1st. NF/dj. M2. $30.00

CRAMOND, Mike. *Killing Bears.* 1982. Outdoor Life. 2nd. 312p. VG/VG. S15. $15.00

CRAMP, Arthur J. *Nostrums & Quackery, Vol 2.* 1921. Chicago. AMA. 8vo. 832p. gilt dk gr cloth. H1. $37.50

CRAMP, H. *Institute Cookbook, Planned for a Family of Four.* 1913. ils/photos. 507p. G. E6. $25.00

CRAMP & PERRINS. *Birds of the Western Palearctic.* 1980. Oxford. 96 mc pl. 695p. NF/dj. S15. $100.00

CRAMPTON, C. Gregory. *Ghosts of Glen Canyon.* 1988. St George. 2nd. 4to. 135p. VG+/stiff wrp. F7. $25.00

CRAMPTON, C. Gregory. *Land of Living Rock: Grand Canyon & the High Plateaus.* 1972. Knopf. 1st. ils/index. 268p. F/NF. B19. $50.00

CRAMPTON, C. Gregory. *Path on the Rainbow.* 1918. NY. Boni Liveright. 8vo. 347p. blk cloth. G+. F7. $110.00

CRAMPTON, C. Gregory. *Sharlot Hall on the Arizona Strip.* 1975. Flagstaff. 1st. 8vo. gr cloth. VG+. F7. $35.00

CRAMPTON, C. Gregory. *Standing Up Country: Canyon Lands of Utah & Arizona.* 1964. Knopf. 1st. ils. 191p. NF/VG+. B19. $60.00

CRAMPTON, J. *Falling Stars.* nd (ca 1866). London. Macintosh. xl. K5. $35.00

CRAN, Marion. *Garden of Experience.* ca 1920s. Herbert Jenkins. 6th. 8vo. 316p. VG. A22. $25.00

CRAN, Marion. *Gardens of Character.* 1939. Herbert Jenkins. 1st. 8vo. 284p. G. A22. $30.00

CRAN, Marion. *Story of My Ruin.* 1924. London. Herbert Jenkins. 1st. 8vo. 320p. G. A22. $25.00

CRANE, Aimee. *Marines at War.* 1943. NY. ils. 182p. S16. $28.50

CRANE, Clinton H. *Clinton Crane's Yachting Memories.* 1952. Van Nostrand. ils. 216p. T7. $35.00

CRANE, Frances. *Coral Princess Murders.* 1954. Random. 1st. 235p. cloth. VG+/dj. M20. $30.00

CRANE, J. *Fiddler Crabs of the World.* 1975. Princeton. 50 pl. cloth. dj. B1. $75.00

CRANE, Joan. *Willa Cather: A Bibliography.* 1982. NE U. 440p. F/F. A4. $45.00

CRANE, Laura Dent. *Automobile Girls at Chicago (#4).* 1912. Altemus. lists 6 titles. VG/ragged. M20. $20.00

CRANE, Laura Dent. *Automobile Girls at Palm Beach (#5).* 1913. Altemus. lists 6 titles. VG/ragged. M20. $20.00

CRANE, Leo. *Indians of the Enchanted Desert.* 1925. Little Brn. 1st. 8vo. 32 pl/fld map. pict bl cloth. VG. T10. $75.00

CRANE, Paul. *Korean Patterns.* 1967. Seoul. Hollyn. 1st. Royal Asiatic Soc Handbook series. VG/dj. W3. $38.00

CRANE, Stephen. *George's Mother.* 1896. NY/London. 1st. 12mo. 177p. cloth. M1. $150.00

CRANE, Stephen. *Great Battles of the World.* 1901. London. Chapman Hall. 1st Eng. gilt brick red cloth. NF. M24. $225.00

CRANE, Stephen. *Maggie, a Girl of the Streets.* 1896. Appleton. 1st trade/2nd state. gilt cloth. VG/dj. M24. $1,250.00

CRANE, Stephen. *Whilomville Stories.* 1900. NY. Harper. 1st. ils Peter Newell. gilt gr cloth. NF. M24. $165.00

CRANE, T. *Architectural Construction: Choice of Structural Design.* 1947. NY. Wiley. 1st. ils/index. 414p. VG/dj. B5. $20.00

CRANE, Walter. *Beatrice Crane: Her Book.* 1983. Toronto. Osborne Collection. facsimile. 12mo. gilt blk cloth. VG. D1. $45.00

CRANE, Walter. *Masque of Days.* 1901. London. Cassell. 1st. 44p. NF/dj. B24. $350.00

CRANE, Walter. *Princess Belle Etoile.* ca 1900. John Lane. 4to. stiff wrp. M5. $75.00

CRANE, Walter. *Sing a Song of Sixpence.* ca 1900. John Lane. reissue. 8 pl. VG. M5. $65.00

CRANE & DRESSES. *Masque of Days.* 1901. London. Cassell. 1st. 4to. unp. VG. D1. $325.00

CRANSTON, Edwin. *Izumi Shikibu Diary: Romance of the Heian Court.* 1969. Harvard. 1st. notes/bibliography. 332p. NF/NF. W3. $67.00

CRASE, Douglas. *Revisionist.* 1981. Little Brn. 1st. assn copy. F/F. V1. $15.00

CRAVEN, Avery O. *Soil Exhaustion As a Factor in Agricultural History...* 1965. Gloucester. Smith. rpt. 179p. VG. A10. $25.00

CRAVEN, J.B. *Doctor Robet Fludd: English Rosicrucian.* nd. Occult Research. 1/300. VG. M17. $25.00

CRAVEN, J.H. *Chiropractic Orthopedy.* 1922. Davenport. 2nd. ils. 399p. VG. B5. $45.00

CRAVEN, Thomas. *Treasury of American Prints.* 1939. S&S. 100 b&w pl. sbdg. D2. $65.00

CRAVEN, Tunis. *Naval Campaign in the Californias 1846-1849: Journal of...* 1973. SF. BC of CA. 1/400. edit/inscr/sgn Kemble. as new/plain dj. O7/R3. $125.00

CRAVENS, Gwyneth. *Speed of Light.* 1979. S&S. 1st. F/dj. M2. $17.00

CRAWFORD, F. Marion. *Adam Johnstone's Son.* 1896. Macmillan. 1st. VG. M2. $25.00

CRAWFORD, F. Marion. *Lady of Rome.* 1906. Macmillan. 1st. VG. M2. $25.00

CRAWFORD, F. Marion. *Saracinesca.* 1893. Macmillan. VG. M2. $25.00

CRAWFORD, F. Marion. *Zoroaster.* 1885. Macmillan. 1st Am. VG. M2. $50.00

CRAWFORD, Hubert. *Crawford's Encyclopedia of Comic Books.* 1978. David. 1st. F/dj. M2. $40.00

CRAWFORD, Isabel. *Kiowa.* 1915. NY. Revell. G. A19. $75.00

CRAWFORD, Lewis F. *Medora-Deadwood Stage Line.* 1925. Capital Book. 1st. sgn. 17p. VG/wrp. J2. $55.00

CRAWFORD, M.H. *Methods & Theories of Anthropoligical Genetics.* (1973). Albuquerque. 1st. 509p. dj. F3. $15.00

CRAWFORD, Samuel. *Kansas in the Sixities.* 1911. McClurg. 1st. 438p. VG. J2. $285.00

CRAWFORD & CRAWFORD. *Missionary Adventures in the South Pacific.* 1967. Rutland. Tuttle. 1st. 8vo. 280p. P4. $35.00

CRAWLEY, Rayburn. *Chattering Gods.* 1931. Harper. 1st. G. M2. $17.00

CREASEY, John. *Alibi.* 1971. Scribner. 1st. VG/VG. P3. $15.00

CREASEY, John. *As Merry As Hell.* 1973. Hodder Stoughton. 1st. VG/VG. P3. $18.00

CREASEY, John. *Baron & the Chinese Puzzle.* 1966. Scribner. 1st. VG/VG. P3. $20.00

CREASEY, John. *Croaker.* 1973. HRW. 1st. VG/VG. P3. $15.00

CREASEY, John. *Dissemblers.* 1967. Scribner. 1st. F/F. H11. $30.00

CREASEY, John. *Executioners.* 1967. Scribner. 1st. NF/NF. N4. $20.00

CREASEY, John. *Gallows Are Waiting.* 1973. David McKay. 1st. VG/VG. P3. $20.00

CREASEY, John. *Gideon's Staff.* 1959. Harper. 1st. VG/NF. M19. $25.00

CREASEY, John. *Hang the Little Man.* 1963. Hodder Stoughton. 1st. NF/NF. P3. $25.00

CREASEY, John. *Inspector West Alone.* 1975. Scribner. 1st. VG/VG. P3. $15.00

CREASEY, John. *Lame Dog Murder.* 1972. Cleveland. World. 1st. F/F. H11. $25.00

CREASEY, John. *Life for a Death.* 1973. HRW. 1st. NF/NF. P3. $15.00

CREASEY, John. *Make-Up for the Toff.* 1956. Walker. 1st. 189p. VG/dj. M20. $15.00

CREASEY, John. *Most Deadly Hate.* 1974. Dutton. 1st. VG/VG. P3. $18.00

CREASEY, John. *Sly As a Serpent.* 1967. Macmillan. 1st. 183p. cloth. VG/dj. M20. $12.00

CREASEY, John. *So Young To Burn.* 1968. Scribner. 1st. VG/VG. P3. $15.00

CREASEY, John. *Take a Body.* 1972. Cleveland. World. 1st. F/F. H11. $25.00

CREASEY, John. *Theft of Magna Carta.* 1973. Scribner. 1st. VG/VG. P3. $15.00

CREASEY, John. *Toff Proceeds.* 1968. Walker. 1st. F/F. P3. $15.00

CREASY, R. *Complete Book of Edible Landscaping.* 1983. Sierra Club. 3rd. 379p. dj. A10. $30.00

CREDLE, Ellis. *Flop-Eared Hound.* 1938. Oxford. 3rd. ils Chas Townsend. VG/VG. P2. $75.00

CREEL, H.G. *Studies in Early Chinese Culture.* 1938. Baltimore. 1st. 266p. F. W3. $125.00

CREELEY, Robert. *Charm.* 1971. Calder Boyars. 1st Eng. F/F. M19. $25.00

CREELEY, Robert. *Numbers.* 1968. Stuttgart/Dusseldorf. Domberger/Galerie Sc. 1st. 1/2500. ils/sgn Indiana. F. B4. $750.00

CREELEY, Robert. *Thanks.* 1977. Deerfield/ Gallery. 1/250. sgn/#d. F/F. B2. $75.00

CREIGHTON, Helen. *Maritime Folk Songs.* 1979. np. Breakwater. Canada's Atlantic Folklore Series 5. 210p. dj. T7. $25.00

CREMER, Jan. *I Jan Cremer.* 1965. 1st. VG/VG. S13. $35.00

CRESPELLE, Jean-Paul. *Fauves.* 1962. NYGS. 100 b&w pl. 351p. dj. D2. $150.00

CRESSON, W.P. *Francis Dana.* 1930. Dial. 1st. 397p. VG/clip. M24. $20.00

CRESSWELL, Helen. *Bagthorpes Abroad.* 1984. London. Faber. 1st. ils Jill Bennett. 186p. xl. VG. T5. $25.00

CRESWICK, Alice M. *Red Book of Fruit Jars No 3.* 1978. Collector Books. ils. 224p. lib bdg w/orig ils cover. xl. H1. $45.00

CREVECOEUR. *Letters d'un Cultivateru Americain.* 1784. Paris. Cuchet. 2 vol. 8vo. mottled calf. R12. $975.00

CREWS, Donald. *Light.* 1981. Bodley Head. 1st. sm 4to. NF. C8. $25.00

CREWS, Donald. *Ten Black Dots Redesigned & Revised.* 1986. Greewnwillow. 1st. ils. F/NF. C8. $25.00

CREWS, Harry. *All We Need of Hell.* 1987. Harper Row. 1st. F/F. M23. $50.00

CREWS, Harry. *Body.* 1990. NY. Poseidon. 1st. sgn. F/F. B11. $75.00

CREWS, Harry. *Childhood: The Biography of a Place.* 1978. Harper Row. 1st. F/dj. Q1. $150.00

CREWS, Harry. *Karate Is a Thing of the Spirit.* 1972. Secker Warburg. 1st. F/NF. B3. $125.00

CREWS, Harry. *Scarlover.* 1992. Poseidon. 1st. sgn. F/F. B11/R13. $55.00

CRICHTON, Michael. *Andromeda Strain.* 1969. Knopf. 1st. F/F. D10. $200.00

CRICHTON, Michael. *Congo.* 1980. Knopf. 1st. author's 5th novel. F/F. D10. $50.00

CRICHTON, Michael. *Congo.* 1980. Knopf. 1st. VG/clip. P3. $30.00

CRICHTON, Michael. *Disclosure.* 1993. Knopf. 1st. sgn. F/F. A23. $50.00

CRICHTON, Michael. *Eaters of the Dead.* 1976. NY. Viking. 1st. author's 4th novel. F/clip. D10. $50.00

CRICHTON, Michael. *Electronic Life.* 1983. Knopf. 1st. NF/NF. T11. $40.00

CRICHTON, Michael. *Electronic Life.* 1983. Knopf. 1st. sgn. F/F. A23. $75.00

CRICHTON, Michael. *Five Patients.* 1970. Knopf. 1st. VG/VG. S13. $20.00

CRICHTON, Michael. *Great Train Robbery.* 1975. Knopf. 1st. NF/NF. A24. $40.00

CRICHTON, Michael. *Jurassic Park.* 1990. Knopf. 1st. F/F. D10. $50.00

CRICHTON, Michael. *Jurassic Park.* 1990. Knopf. 1st. NF/NF. M19. $35.00

CRICHTON, Michael. *Lost World.* 1995. Knopf. 1st. inscr. F/F. A23. $50.00

CRICHTON, Michael. *Odds On.* 1966. NAL. 1st. author's 1st book. F/wrp. Q1. $150.00

CRICHTON, Michael. *Rising Sun.* 1992. Knopf. 1st. F/F. P3. $22.00

CRICHTON, Michael. *Rising Sun.* 1992. Knopf. 1st. sgn. F/F. A23. $45.00

CRICHTON, Michael. *Sphere.* 1987. Knopf. 1st. F/dj. B3/D10. $40.00

CRICHTON, Michael. *Sphere.* 1987. Knopf. 1st. sgn. F/VG. A23. $60.00

CRICHTON, Michael. *Terminal Man.* 1972. Knopf. F/dj. M2/T11. $75.00

CRICHTON, Michael. *Terminal Man.* 1972. Knopf. 1st. NF/NF. B3/P3. $60.00

CRICHTON, Michael. *Travels.* 1988. Knopf. 1st. F/F. B35. $35.00

CRICK, Francis. *What Mad Pursuit.* 1988. Basic Books. 8vo. ils. NF/dj. K3. $10.00

CRIDER, Bill. *Galveston Gunman.* 1988. Evans. 1st. VG/VG. P3. $15.00

CRIDER, Bill. *Time for Hanging.* 1989. Evans. 1st. F/F. M22. $15.00

CRILE, George. *Anoci-Association.* 1914. Phil. 1st/1st prt. 259p. A13. $200.00

CRILE, George. *Hemorrhage & Transfusion: Experimental & Clinical Research.* 1909. NY. 1st. sgn. 560p. xl. A13. $350.00

CRILE & LOWER. *Surgical Shock & Shockless Operation Through Anoci-Assoc.* 1921. Phil. 272p. A13. $100.00

CRIPPEN, David. *Two Sides of the River.* 1976. Nashville. Abingdon. 1st probable. obl sm 4to. as new/dj. C8. $25.00

CRIPPEN, T.G. *Christmas & Christmas Lore.* 1923. London. Blackie. ils. 221p. G-. B18. $30.00

CRIPPS, Richard S. *Critical & Exegetical Commentary on Book of Amos.* 1955. SPCK. 365p. G/torn. B29. $10.00

CRIPPS, Wilfred Joseph. *Old English Plate.* 1967. London. Spring Books. rpt of 1926 11th. 8vo. ils. 540p. F/VG. H1. $22.50

CRISLER, Lois. *Arctic Wild.* 1958. Harper. 1st. 301p. VG/G. W2. $30.00

CRISP, Frank. *Medieval Gardens.* 1924. London. Lane. 2 vol. A10. $150.00

CRISP, N.J. *Brink.* 1982. Viking. 1st. F/F. P3. $15.00

CRISP, N.J. *London Deal.* 1978. St Martin. 1st. VG/VG. P3. $18.00

CRISP, William. *Compleat Agent.* 1984. Macmillan. 1st. F/F. P3. $15.00

CRISPIN, Edmund. *Best of Science Fiction Three.* 1958. London. F/dj. M2. $20.00

CRISPIN, William Frost. *Bibliographical & Historical Sketch of Capt Wm Crispin...* 1901. Akron. ils. 144p. fair. B18. $22.50

CRISPIN & NORTON. *Gryphon's Eyrie.* 1984. NY. Tor. 1st. sgn. VG/VG. B11. $45.00

CRISTABEL. *Mortal Immortals.* 1971. Walker. 1st. VG/G+. P3. $20.00

CRITCHFIELD & LITTLE. *Geographic Distribution of Pines of the World.* 1966. USDA. 97p. wrp. B1. $28.50

CROCKER, Betty; see Betty Crocker.

CROCKETT, Lucy Herndon. *Kings Without Castles.* 1957. Rand McNally. 1st. sgn. VG/VG. B11. $18.00

CROCKETT, S.R. *Adventurer in Spain.* 1903. Isibster. VG. P3. $20.00

CROCKETT, S.R. *Black Douglas.* 1899. Doubleday. 1st Am. VG. M2. $35.00

CROCKETT, S.R. *Flower O'the Corn.* 1902. London. 1st. VG. M2. $20.00

CROCOMBE & CROCOMBE. *Works of Ta'Unga. Records of a Polynesian Traveller...* 1968. Canberra. Australian Nat U. 1st. ils. 164p. P4. $45.00

CROFT, Terrell. *Library of Practical Electricity.* 1924. NY. 8 vol. 4th. limp cloth. A17. $30.00

CROFT-COOKE, Rupert. *Exotic Food.* 1971. NY. Herder. G/dj. A16. $20.00

CROFTON, Algernon. *Goat's Hoof.* 1928. Covici Friede. 1st. F. w/pub brochure. M2. $25.00

CROFTS, Freeman Wills. *Purple Sickle Murders.* 1929. Harper. 1st Am. G. N4. $25.00

CROFTS, Freeman Wills. *Tragedy in the Hollow.* 1939. Dodd Mead. 1st. VG. P3. $35.00

CROFUT, William. *Moon on the One Hand.* 1975. Atheneum. 1st. 80p. F/NF. D4. $45.00

CROLL, James. *Climate & Time, in Their Geological Relations.* 1893. NY. Appleton. 8vo. 577p. K5. $85.00

CROLY, George. *May Fair. In Four Cantos.* 1827. London. Ainsworth. 1st. 8vo. 194p. Riviere bdg. H13. $295.00

CROLY, George. *Salathiel.* nd. Funk Wagnall. NF. M2. $25.00

CROLY, George. *Tarry Thou Till I Come; or, Salathiel, the Wandering Jew.* 1901. Funk Wagnall. 1st. 8vo. 17 pl. 588p. VG. W1. $15.00

CROMARTIE, Countess. *Temple of the Winds.* 1925. London. 1st. VG. M2. $15.00

CROMBIE, Deborah. *Share in Death.* 1993. Scribner. 1st. author's 1st mystery. F/NF. A24. $40.00

CROMIE, Robert. *From the Cliffs of Croaghaun.* 1904. Saalfield. 1st. VG. M2. $27.00

CRONIN, Leonard. *Key Guide to Australian Palms, Ferns & Allies.* 1989. NSW. ils. 192p. as new/dj. B26. $20.00

CRONIN, Michael. *Night of the Party.* 1958. Ives Washburn. 1st. VG/VG. P3. $13.00

CRONKITE, Walter. *Reporter's Life.* 1996. Knopf. 1st. sgn bookplate. F/F. A23. $46.00

CRONLEY, Jay. *Quick Change.* 1981. Doubleday. 1st. VG/VG. M22. $35.00

CRONQUIST, Arthur. *Evolution & Classification of Flowering Plants.* 1968. Boston. ils. 396p. B26. $30.00

CRONQUIST, Arthur. *Intermountain Flora.* 1986. NY Botanical Garden. rpt. 270p. B1. $37.50

CRONQUIST & GLEASON. *Natural Geography of Plants.* 1964. Columbia. 420p. B1. $65.00

CROOKES, Marguerite. *New Zealand Ferns.* 1963. Whitcombe Tombs. 6th. 8vo. cloth. VG/dj. A22. $40.00

CROSBY, Bing. *Call Me Lucky.* 1953. S&S. 1st. VG/clip. A20. $40.00

CROSBY, Edward. *Radiana.* 1906. Ivy. 1st. VG. M2. $40.00

CROSBY, Ernest. *Captain Jinks, Hero.* 1902. Funk Wagnall. 1st. 393p. VG. M20. $20.00

CROSBY, John. *Company of Friends.* 1977. Stein Day. 1st. VG/VG. P3. $13.00

CROSLAND, Margaret. *Colette: Difficulty of Loving.* 1973. Bobbs Merrill. 1st Am. photos. VG/dj. A25. $18.00

CROSLAND, Margaret. *Madame Colette: A Provincial in Paris.* 1953. London. Peter Own. 1st. photos. 22p. VG/dj. A25. $18.00

CROSS, Amanda; see Heilbrun, Carolyn G.

CROSS, Helen Reid. *Simple Simon.* 1908. London. Chatto Windus. Dumpy Books. 24 full-p pl. 95p. brn cloth. R5. $200.00

CROSS, John Kier. *Angry Planet.* 1946. Coward McCann. NF/dj. M2. $25.00

CROSS, John Kier. *Best Black Magic Stories.* 1960. London. 1st. F/dj. M2. $30.00

CROSS, Melinda. *Bloomsbury Needlepoint: From Tapestries at Charleston...* 1992. ils. VG/VG. M17. $25.00

CROSS & PARKIN. *Captain Gray in the Pacific Northwest.* 1987. Bend, OR. Maverick. 2nd. sgn. VG/VG. B11. $25.00

CROSSEN, Kendell Foster. *Adventures in Tomorrow.* 1950. Greenberg. VG/VG. P3. $40.00

CROSSEN, Kendell Foster. *Future Tense.* 1952. Greenberg. 1st. NF/VG. P3. $45.00

CROTHER, Ruth. *Manly Manners.* 1946. Encee Pub. ils Ethel Hays. 115p. VG+/G. P2. $35.00

CROUCH, D.E. *Carl Rungius: Complete Prints.* 1989. Missoula. ils/figures. 203p. F/dj. M4. $55.00

CROUCH, Tom D. *Eagle Aloft: Two Centuries of the Balloon in America.* 1983. Smithsonian. thick 8vo. 770p. F/dj. T10. $60.00

CROWDER, Herbert. *Ambush at Osirak.* 1988. Presidio. 1st. F/NF. W2. $25.00

CROWDER, William. *Naturalist at the Seashore.* 1928. NY. 384p. VG. S15. $25.00

CROWE, Earle. *Men of El Tejon: Empire in the Tehachapis.* 1957. Ward Ritchie. 1st. NF/VG. O4. $25.00

CROWE, Jack. *Hopalong Cassidy Lends a Helping Hand.* 1950. John Martin's House. Bonnie Book. pict brd. VG+. M20. $40.00

CROWE, John; see Lynds, Dennis.

CROWE, Samuel. *Halsted of Johns Hopkins: Man & His Men.* 1957. Springfield. 1st. 247p. A13. $75.00

CROWE & CROWE. *Heaven, Hell & Salt Water.* 1955-57. London. Hart Davis. Mariners Lib 35. photos/maps. 221p. dj. T7. $24.00

CROWELL, Ann. *Hogan for the Bluebird.* 1969. NY. Scribner. 1st/Weekly Reader BC. VG. L3. $30.00

CROWELL, Pers. *First Horseman.* 1948. Whittlesey. 1st. obl 4to. VG/fair. O3. $30.00

CROWELL, Pers. *What Can a Horse Do That You Can't Do?* 1954. Whittlesey. 1st. 27p. G. O3. $20.00

CROWEN, T. *American Lady's Cookbook.* 1861 (1847). 15th thousand. VG. E6. $125.00

CROWLEY, John. *Deep.* 1977. London. NEL. 1st. author's 1st book. F/F. L3. $150.00

CROWLEY, John. *Engine Summer.* 1979. Doubleday. 1st. F/F. M2. $125.00

CROWLEY, John. *Love & Sleep.* 1994. Bantam. 1st. F/F clip. B4. $45.00

CROWNINSHIELD, Ethel. *For You: Stories, Songs, Rhythm & Dramatization.* nd (1956). Boston, MA. Boston Music Co. 8vo. 35p. VG. C14. $10.00

CROWNSHIELD, Mrs. Schuyler. *Lattitude 19 Degrees.* 1898. Appleton. 1st. VG. M2. $30.00

CROWTHER, Charles. *Steamboat Bill.* nd. London. pre WWII ed. ils Chas Crowther. NF. C8. $95.00

CROWTHER, Samuel. *Romance & Rise of the American Tropics.* 1929. Doubleday. 1st. 390p. F3. $15.00

CROZIER, M.J. *Landslides, Causes, Consequences & Environment.* 1986. np. 252p. xl. F/dj. D8. $20.00

CRUIKSHANK, George. *Jack & the Beanstalk From the George Cruikshank Fairy Lib.* 1854. London. David Bogue. 1st/1st issue. 12mo. prt paper wrp. R5. $350.00

CRUM, H. *Focus on Peatlands & Peat Moses.* 1988. Ann Arbor. 306p. F. B1. $50.00

CRUMBO, Kim. *River Runner's Guide to the History of the Grand Canyon.* 1988. Boulder, CO. 3rd. sm 8vo. 61p. VG/pict wrp. F7. $12.00

CRUMLEY, James. *Last Good Kiss.* 1978. Random. 1st. author's 3rd book. F/F. D10. $85.00

CRUMLEY, James. *Last Good Kiss.* 1978. Random. 1st. NF/VG+. M22. $50.00

CRUMLEY, James. *Mexican Tree Duck.* 1993. Mysterious 1st. sgn. F/F. D10. $40.00

CRUMLEY, James. *Mexican Tree Duck.* 1993. Mysterious. 1st. F/dj. M23. $25.00

CRUMLEY, James. *One to Count Cadence.* 1969. Random. 1st. author's 1st book. rem mk. F/NF. H11. $260.00

CRUMLEY, James. *Pigeon Shoot.* 1987. Neville. 1st. 1/350. sgn. F/sans. M15. $125.00

CRUMLEY, James. *Wrong Case.* 1975. Random. 1st. author's 1st mystery. G/VG. M22. $250.00

CRUMMELL, Alex. *Relations & Duties of Free Colored Men in America...* 1861. Hartford. 1st. 8vo. 54p. prt wrp. M1. $450.00

CRUMP, Irving. *Boy's Book of Mounted Police.* 1917. Dodd Mead. sgn/dtd 1917. 297p. cloth. VG. M20. $75.00

CRUMP, Irving. *Boys Book of Airmen.* 1927. Dodd Mead. 278p. VG+/dj. M20. $35.00

CRUMP, J. *Chinese Theatre in the Days of Kublai Khan.* 1980. AZ U. 1st. ils. 429p. F/NF. W3. $62.00

CRUSE, Amy. *Englishman & His Books in the Early 19th Century.* nd99. NY. Crowell. 8vo. 311p. VG/dj. K3. $35.00

CRUSO, Solomon. *Last of the Jews & the Japs.* 1933. Lefkowitz. 1st. VG. M2. $75.00

CRUSO, Solomon. *Messiah on the Horizon.* 1940. Audobon. 1st. F/dj. M2. $45.00

CRUTCH & GREENE. *Lewis Carroll Handbook, Being a New Version...* 1979. revised. 12 pl. F/F. A4. $165.00

CSONKA, Larry. *Always on the Run.* 1973. Random. 1st. VG/dj. P8. $15.00

CUBIERES-PALMEZEAUX. *Le Calendrier Republicain, Poeme.* 1799. Paris. Merigot Chemin. 8vo. disbound. R12. $85.00

CUBITT, G. *Portraits of the African Wild.* 1986. Chartwell. ils/200+ mc photos. 208p. brd. VG. M12. $25.00

CUDDIHY, John Murray. *Ordeal of Civility: Freud, Marx, Levi-Strauss...* 1974. Basic. 272p. VG/dj. S3. $25.00

CULINARY ARTS INSTITUTE. *Pennsylvania Dutch Cook Book.* 1936. Culinary Arts Pr. VG/wood covers. A16. $15.00

CULLEN, Countee. *Color.* 1925. Harper. 1st. author's 1st book. 3-pc cover. VG. M25. $200.00

CULLEN, Countee. *One Way to Heaven.* 1932. Harper. 1st. cloth. VG. M25. $75.00

CULLEN, Thomas S. *Early Medicine in Maryland.* 1927. Baltimore. ils. 15p. brd. K3. $15.00

CULLEN & MURRAY-ROBERTSTON. *Exploring the Poles.* 1988. Needham. Schoolhouse. 48p. VG. P4. $25.00

CULLMAN, Willy. *Kakteen. Einfuhrung in die Kakteenkunde und Anleitung...* 1976 (1963). Stuttgart. photos. 280p. F/dj. B26. $30.00

CULLMAN & GRONER. *Encyclopedia of Cacti.* 1987. Portland. ils. M/dj. B26. $55.00

CULLMANN, Oscar. *Christology of the New Testament.* 1963. Westminster. revised. 331p. VG/dj. B29. $13.00

CULLUM, Albert. *You Think Just Because You're Big You're Right.* 1976. Harlin Quist. obl 8vo. F/F. C8. $37.50

CULPAN, Maurice. *Minister of Injustice.* 1966. Walker. 1st. VG/VG. P3. $10.00

CULVER, Francis Barnum. *Blooded Horses of Colonial Days.* 1922. Baltimore. self pub. 1st. VG. O3. $65.00

CULVER, Timothy; see Westlake, Donald E.

CUMBERLAND, Charles. *Mexican Revolution.* 1972. Austin, TX. 1st. 449p. dj. F3. $20.00

CUMMING, Primrose. *Ben: Story of a Cart Horse.* 1940. Dutton. 1st Am. VG. O3. $25.00

CUMMING, W.P. *Exploration of North America 1630-1776.* 1974. NY. 400 pl/5 maps. 272p. VG+/dj. B26. $75.00

CUMMINGS, D. Duane. *William Robinson Leigh, Western Artist.* 1980. Norman. OK U. 1st. sm 4to. VG/VG. O3. $65.00

CUMMINGS, E.E. *One Times One.* 1944. NY. Henry Holt. 1st. gray cloth. dj. M24. $100.00

CUMMINGS, E.E. *Six Nonlectures.* 1954. Harvard. 2nd prt. sgn/dtd. w/poem & drawing on Christmas card. B35. $75.00

CUMMINGS, Ray. *Insect Invasion.* 1967. Avalon. 1st. RS. F/dj. M2. $40.00

CUNARD STEAMSHIP COMPANY. *Royal Mail Steamships.* nd (1893). Liverpool. Cunard. 5 fld charts/maps. 82p. T7. $95.00

CUNNINGHAM, E.V. *Case of Kidnapped Angel.* 1982. Delacorte. 1st. F/NF. M25. $25.00

CUNNINGHAM, Frank. *Sky Master, the Story of Donald Douglas.* 1943. Phil. 1st. 321p. G/dj. B18. $65.00

CUNNINGHAM, J. Morgan; see Westlake, Donald E.

CUNNINGHAM, Jere. *Abyss.* 1981. Wyndham. 1st. VG/VG. P3. $20.00

CUNNINGHAM, Michael. *Flesh & Blood.* 1995. FSG. 1st. author's 2nd novel. F/F. B3. $25.00

CUNNINGHAM, Virginia. *What Happened to Fluffy.* 1948. Whitman. Fuzzy Wuzzy Book. pict brd. VG/dj. M20. $25.00

CUNNINGHAM, W. *Christianity & Social Questions.* 1910. Scribner. 232p. VG. B29. $7.50

CUNY, Hilaire. *Man & His Theories (Einstein).* 1965. NY. Erikson. 1st Am. ils. VG/dj. K3. $15.00

CURCIO, Vincent. *Suicide Blond, the Life of Gloria Grahame.* 1989. Morrow. 37 photos. cloth. NF/dj. C9. $30.00

CURIE, Eve. *Journey Among the Warriors.* 1943. NY. sgn/dtd 1943. 501p. VG. S16. $25.00

CURIE, Marie. *Pierre Curie.* 1926. Macmillan. 2nd. ils. VG-. K3. $35.00

CURIE, Marie. *Sur le Poids Atomique de Baryum Radifere.* 1898. Paris. xl. wrp. K3. $95.00

CURRAN, Bob. *Violence Game.* 1966. Macmillan. 1st. photos. F/VG+. P8. $35.00

CURRAN, Terrie. *All Booked Up.* 1987. Dodd Mead. 1st. NF/NF. P3. $16.00

CURREY, L.W. *Science Fiction & Fantasy AUthors.* 1979. GK Hall. VG/sans. P3. $75.00

CURREY & KRUSKA. *Bibliography of Yosemite, the Central & High Sierra...* 1992. Dawson's Book Shop. 1/300. ils. gray brd/bl cloth spine. F. R3. $300.00

CURRIE, Barton. *Fishers of Books.* 1931. 1st. VG/G. K3. $20.00

CURRIE, Ellen. *Available Light.* 1986. Summit. 1st. F/NF. M23. $40.00

CURRIE & MCHUGH. *Officer 666.* 1912. AL Burt. VG. M2. $12.00

CURRIER & TILTON. *Bibliography of Oliver Wendell Holmes.* 1953. NY. 1st. gilt brn cloth. F. M24. $65.00

CURRINGTON, O.J. *Breath-Out.* 1978. Andre Deutsch. 1st. VG/VG. P3. $18.00

CURRY, Jane. *Miss Sniff.* 1945. Whitman. Fuzzy Wuzzy Book. pict brd. VG/dj. M20. $25.00

CURRY, Larry. *American West: Painters From Catlin to Russell.* 1972. Viking. 1st. 132 pl. F/clip. A14. $40.00

CURRY, W.L. *Ohio, the Buckeye State.* 1915. Columbus. 64p. decor wrp. B18. $15.00

CURTIES, Henry. *Out of the Shadows.* 1911. Greening. decor brd. VG. P3. $35.00

CURTIS, Anna L. *Stories of the Underground Railroad.* 1941. Island Workshop Pr Co-op. 1st. sgn. F/NF. B4. $85.00

CURTIS, Charles. *Orchids: Their Description & Cultivation.* 1950. London. Putnam. 1st. 274p. dj. A10. $125.00

CURTIS, George William. *Equal Rights for All.* 1967. Rochester. 8vo. stitched. R12. $60.00

CURTIS, Jack. *Glory.* 1988. Dutton. 1st. VG/VG. P3. $25.00

CURTIS, M.M. *Book of Snuff & Snuff Boxes With 119 Rare & Unusual...* 1935. NY. 1st. 119 photos. 137p. F. M4. $35.00

CURTIS, Mary. *Stories in Trees.* 1925. Chicago. Lyons. 224p. VG. A10. $25.00

CURTIS, Wardon. *Strange Adventures of Mr Middleton.* 1903. Stone. 1st. G+. M2. $30.00

CURTISS, Ursula. *Noonday Devil.* 1953. Eyre Spottiswoode. 1st. VG/VG. P3. $25.00

CURWOOD, James O. *Baree, Son of Kazan.* nd. Grossett. G+. M2. $20.00

CURWOOD, James O. *Country Beyond.* 1922. Cosmopolitan. 1st. ils Walt Louderback. VG+/dj. A18. $50.00

CURZON, Clare. *Three-Core Lead.* 1988. Collins Crime Club. 1st. F/F. P3. $20.00

CURZON OF KEDLESTON, Marquess. *Tales of Travel.* 1923. Hodder Stoughton. 1st. 27 tipped-in pl. 344p. VG. W1. $50.00

CUSHING, Harvey. *Consecratio Medici & Other Papers.* 1928. Boston. 1st/1st prt. 276p. A13. $150.00

CUSHING, Harvey. *Medical Career & Other Papers.* 1940. Boston. 1st. 302p. A13. $100.00

CUSHING, Harvey. *Meningiomas: Their Classification, Regional Behavior...* 1988 (1938). NY. Classics Neurology/Neurosurgery Lib. facsimile. G1. $100.00

CUSHING, Harvey. *Pituitary Body & Its Disorders.* 1912. Phil. 1st/1st prt. 341p. A13. $600.00

CUSHING, Harvey. *Pituitary Body & Its Disorders: Clinical States...* 1988 (1912). Birmingham. Classics Neurology/ Neurosurgy Lib. facsimile. G1. $100.00

CUSHION, John P. *Animals in Pottery & Porcelain.* 1974. Crown. 1st. VG/G. O3. $35.00

CUSHMAN, Dan. *Brothers in Kickapoo.* 1962. McGraw Hill. 1st. F/NF. M25. $35.00

CUSHMAN, J.A. *Foraminifera.* 1948. Harvard. 4th. 478p. VG. D8. $30.00

CUSSLER, Clive. *Dragon.* 1990. S&S. 1st. F/F. T2. $20.00

CUSSLER, Clive. *Inca Gold.* 1994. S&S. 1st. F/F. T2. $25.00

CUSSLER, Clive. *Raise the Titanic!* 1976. Viking. 1st. F/NF. B2/B3/M15. $65.00

CUSSLER, Clive. *Raise the Titanic!* 1976. Viking. 1st. sgn. VG/VG. P3. $150.00

CUSSLER, Clive. *Sahara.* 1992. S&S. 1st. F/F. T2. $35.00

CUSSLER, Clive. *Treasure.* 1988. S&S. 1st. F/F. H11/T2. $25.00

CUSSLER, Clive. *Vixen O3.* 1978. Viking. 1st. F/dj. P3/T2. $35.00

CUSTER, Elizabeth. *Boots & Saddles.* 1885. 1st. 312p. O8. $37.50

CUT-CAVENDISH. *Complete Bridge Player.* 1905. London. 232p. VG. S1. $20.00

CUTAK, Ladislaus. *Cactus Guide.* 1956. Princeton. ils. VG/dj. B26. $15.00

CUTBUSH, James. *American Artist's Manual; or, Dictionary...* 1814. Phil. 1st. 2 vol. thick 8vo. contemporary calf. M1. $425.00

CUTLER, Carl C. *Queens of Western Ocean: Story of America's Mail...Lines.* 1961. ils. VG/VG. M17. $25.00

CUTLER, Thomas. *Surgeon's Practical Guide in Dressing...* 1838. Phil. Barrington Haswell. 1st Am. 16mo. 208p. cloth. M1. $250.00

CUTLER. *Sir James M Barrie: A Bibliography...* 1968. 1st. 254p. F. A4. $35.00

CUVIER, Georges. *Le Regne Animal Distribue d'Apres son Organisation...* 1817. Paris. 1st. 4 vol. ils. quarter leather. A13. $1,250.00

D'ALBAS, Andrieu. *Death of a Navy: Japanese Naval Action in World War II.* 1957. NY. 1st. 362p. VG/VG. S16. $25.00

D'AMATO & D'AMATO. *African Animals Through African Eyes.* 1971. NY. Messner. 1st. sm 4to. F/F. C8. $25.00

D'ARBLEY, Madame. *Diary & Letters of..., Edited by Her Niece.* 1854. London. Henry Colburn. New Ed. 7 vol. 12mo. teg. half maroon calf/marbled brd. T10. $500.00

D'AUBIGNE, J.H. Merle. *Germany, England & Scotland.* 1848. London. Simpkin Marshall. 1st. 8vo. full marbled calf/gilt spine. VG. T10. $125.00

D'AUBIGNE, J.H. Merle. *History of the Reformation in Europe in Time of Calvin.* 1863-69. London. Longman Gr. 4 vol. 8vo. marbled ep. full tree calf. VG. T10. $250.00

D'AULAIRE & D'AULAIRE. *Columbus.* 1955. Doubleday. 1st. lg 4to. F/VG. P2. $95.00

D'AULAIRE & D'AULAIRE. *D'Aulaire's Trolls.* (1972). Doubleday. 4th. F/VG. B15. $35.00

D'AULAIRE & D'AULAIRE. *George Washington.* 1936. Doubleday. 1st. ils. unp. VG. D1. $45.00

D'AULAIRE & D'AULAIRE. *Lord's Prayer.* 1934. Doubleday Doran. 1st. VG/G+. P2. $110.00

D'AULAIRE & D'AULAIRE. *Magic Meadow.* 1958. Doubleday. 1st. lg 4to. F/VG+. P2. $135.00

D'AULAIRE & D'AULAIRE. *Trolls.* 1972. Doubleday. 1/200. sgns. F/VG+ case. P2. $250.00

D'AULAIRE & D'AULAIRE. *Wings for Per.* 1944. Doubleday Doran. 1st. ils. unp. bl cloth. VG/dj. D1. $85.00

D'AULAIRE & PARIN. *Buffalo Bill.* 1952. Doubleday. probable 1st (date title p). ils. unp. G+. T5. $35.00

D'AULAIRE & PARIN. *Lord's Prayer. Catholic Edition.* 1934. Doubleday. 1st. 32p. VG+/frayed. D4. $65.00

D'AULAIRE & PARIN. *Star Spangled Banner.* 1942. Doubleday Doran. 1st. 39p. NF/VG. D4. $65.00

D'AURE, Le Comte. *Cours d'Equitation.* 1883. Paris. Librarie Militaire de L Baudoin. French text. 324p. VG. O3. $125.00

D'ERMO, Dominique. *Chef's Dessert Cookbook.* 1976. Atheneum. 1st. VG/dj. A16. $15.00

D'ESSEN, Lorrain. *Kangaroos in the Kitchen.* 1959. NY. McKay. 1st. sgn. 306p. VG/G. B11. $25.00

D'HARONCOURT, Rene. *Mexicana: Book of Pictures.* 1946. 3rd. VG/G+. S13. $20.00

D'HERBELOT, Barthelemi. *Bibliotheque Orientale, ou Dictionnaire Universel...* 1781-83. Paris. Moutard. Nouvelle ed. 6 vol. new lib buckram. VG. W1. $600.00

D'OYLEY, Enid. *Between Sea & Sky.* ca 1979. Toronto. Williams Wallace. 1st. inscr. ils Albert Huie. F/NF. B4. $85.00

D'URFEY, Thomas. *Wit & Mirth; or, Pills To Purge Melancholy.* nd. np. 6 vol. facsimile rpt 1719 Tonson. F. H13. $485.00

D'URVILLE, Jules S-C Dumont. *Two Voyages to the South Seas.* 1988. Honolulu. 1st Am. lg 8vo. beige cloth/labels. P4. $90.00

DA SILVA FIGUERIREDO, Antonio. *Descripcam Antilogica Physio-moral do Terremoto...* 1756. Lisbon. Patriarcal Francisco Luiz Ameno. 1st/only. 32p. R15. $400.00

DAANE, James. *Freedom of God: Study of Election & Pulpit.* 1973. Eerdmans. 208p. VG/dj. B29. $7.50

DABNEY, Robert Lewis. *Life & Campaigns of Lt-Gen Thoms J (Stonewall) Jackson.* 1866. NY. Blelock. 1st. 742p. half leather/marbled brd. G+. M8. $150.00

DABNEY, V. *Richmond: Story of a City.* 1976. Garden City. ils/map/photos. NF/G. M4. $20.00

DACUS, J.A. *Ils Lives & Adventures of Frank & Jesse James...* 1881. St Louis. enlarged. ils. 442p. G-. B18. $25.00

DADANT, C. *Longstretch on the Hive & Honey Bee.* 1902 (1888). 20 pl/197 text ils. 521p. VG. E6. $40.00

DADSWELL, M.J. *Common Strategies of Anadromous & Catadromous Fishes.* 1987. Bethesda. Am Fisheries Soc. 561p. VG. B1. $45.00

DAGLISH, Eric. *How To See Plants.* 1932. NY. Morrow. 122p. VG. A10. $20.00

DAGLISH, Eric. *Life Story of Birds.* 1930. Morrow. 1st. 8vo. woodcuts. gilt blk cloth. F/case. T10. $300.00

DAGMAR, Peter. *Alien Skies.* 1967. Arcadia. 1st. VG/dj. M2. $25.00

DAGUE, R.A. *Henry Ashton.* 1903. Alameda. self pub. 1st. F. B2. $100.00

DAHL, Roald. *Bottom Dogs.* 1930. S&S. 1st Am. F/NF. B2. $150.00

DAHL, Roald. *Boy, Tales of Childhood.* 1984. ils. 160p. F/F. A4. $45.00

DAHL, Roald. *Charlie & the Chocolate Factory.* 1964. Knopf. 1st. 162p. VG/G. P2. $100.00

DAHL, Roald. *Danny, the Champion of the World.* 1975. Knopf. 1st. F/NF. T12. $35.00

DAHL, Roald. *Danny, the Champion of the World.* 1975. Knopf. 1st. ils Jill Bennett. 196p. G+/dj. P2. $28.00

DAHL, Roald. *Esio Trot.* 1990. Viking. 1st Am. 8vo. 62p. F/VG. T5. $35.00

DAHL, Roald. *Kiss Kiss.* 1960. Knopf. 1st. F/F. M2. $50.00

DAHL, Roald. *Kiss Kiss.* 1960. Knopf. 1st. VG/VG. M22. $35.00

DAHL, Roald. *My Uncle Oswald.* 1980. Knopf. 1st. VG/VG. P3. $20.00

DAHL, Roald. *Some Time Never.* 1948. Scribner. 1st. NF/dj. M2. $85.00

DAHL, Roald. *Someone Like You.* 1953. Knopf. 1st. F/F. M2. $85.00

DAHL, Roald. *Switch Bitch.* 1974. Knopf. 1st. VG/VG. P3. $20.00

DAHL, Roald. *Two Fables.* 1986. London. Viking. 1st. ils Graham Dean. F/F. B3. $50.00

DAHL, Roald. *Witches.* 1983. FSG. 1st. ils Quentin Blake. 202p. VG/dj. D1. $35.00

DAHL, Roald. *Wonderful Story of Henry Sugar & Six More.* 1977. London. Cape. 1st. 8vo. F/VG+. C8. $50.00

DAHL, Roald. *Wonderful Story of Henry Sugar.* 1977. Knopf. 1st. F/F. M2. $25.00

DAHL & THYGESEN. *Garden Pests & Diseases.* 1974. London. ils. 223p. VG/dj. B26. $9.00

DAHLBERG, Edward. *Bottom Dogs.* 1929. London. Putnam. 1/500. intro DH Lawrence. F/NF. L3. $450.00

DAHLBERG, Edward. *From Flushing to Calvary.* 1932. Harcourt. F/F. B2. $125.00

DAICHES, David. *Virginia Woolf.* 1942. New Directions. 1st. 169p. VG/VG. A25. $30.00

DAILEY, Janet. *Aspen Gold.* 1991. Little Brn. 1st. sgn. F/F. W2. $160.00

DAILEY, Janet. *Heiress.* 1987. Little Brn. 1st/3rd prt. inscr. F/F. W2. $200.00

DAILEY, Janet. *Rivals.* 1989. Little Brn. 1st. sgn. G. W2. $40.00

DAILY, R.A. *Igneous Rocks & the Depths of the Earth.* 1933. McGraw Hill. 598p. G. D8. $30.00

DAITCH, Susan. *LC.* 1987. San Diego. HBJ. 1st. author's 1st book. F/NF. D10. $60.00

DALE, Harrison. *Great Ghost Stories.* 1951. London. 1st. VG. M2. $45.00

DALEY, Arthur. *Dangerous Edge.* 1983. S&S. VG/VG. P3. $25.00

DALEY, Arthur. *Fast One.* 1978. Crown. 1st. VG/VG. P3. $20.00

DALEY, Arthur. *Inside Baseball.* 1950. Grosset Dunlap. VG/VG. P3. $20.00

DALEY, Arthur. *Man With a Gun.* 1988. Hutchinson. 1st. NF/NF. P3. $22.00

DALEY, Robert. *Hands of a Stranger.* 1986. S&S. 1st. F/F. H11. $25.00

DALEY, Robert. *Year of the Dragon.* 1981. S&S. 1st. F/F. H11. $25.00

DALGLIESH, Alice. *Adam & the Golden Cock.* 1959. Scribner. 1st. ils Leonard Weisgard. 64p. F/VG+. P2. $50.00

DALGLIESH, Alice. *Ride on the Wind.* 1956. Scribner. 1st. 4to. unp. VG/dj. S13/T5. $25.00

DALGLIESH & MILHOUS. *Once on a Time.* 1938. Scribner. 1st. sm 4to. 70p. G+. C14. $15.00

DALL, Caroline. *Romance of the Association; or, One Last Glimpse...* 1875. Cambridge, MA. 1st. 12mo. 102p. cloth. M1. $125.00

DALLAS, Sandra. *Buster Midnight's Cafe.* 1990. Random. 1st. F/F. H11. $35.00

DALLAWAY, James. *Anecotes of the Arts in England...* 1800. London. Cadell Davies. 1st. tall thick 8vo. orig pub brd. H13. $395.00

DALMAS, Herbert. *Exit Screaming.* 1966. Walker. 1st. VG/VG. P3. $18.00

DALMAT, Herbert T. *Black Flies (Diptera, Simuliidae) of Guatemala...* 1955. Smithsonian. 44 pl/fld map. 425p. S15. $20.00

DALTON, Priscilla; see Avallone, Mike.

DALY, Eileen. *Huckleberry Hound Giant Story Book.* 1961. Whitman. TVTI. VG. P3. $25.00

DAMMANN, George H. *Illustrated History of Ford, 1903-1970.* nd. Sarasota. Crestline. ils. 320p. VG. B18. $19.50

DAMON, Valerie Hubbard. *Grindle Lamfoon & the Procurnious Fleekers.* 1978. Star. 1st. sgn. unp. cloth. VG/dj. M20. $22.00

DAMS, Jeanne. *Body in the Transept.* 1995. NY. Walker. 1st. sgn. F/F. A23. $60.00

DANA, Richard henry. *Two Years Before the Mast.* 1930. Chicago. Lakeside. 1/1000. woodcuts. 524p. teg. gilt bdg. VG. T7. $85.00

DANA, S. *Muck Manual for Farmers.* 1856 (1855). VG. E6. $35.00

DANBY, J.M. *Fundamentals of Celestial Mechanics.* 1988 (1962). Richmond, VA. Willmann-Bell. 2nd. 8vo. 466p. VG. K5. $20.00

DANBY, Mary. *Realms of Darkness.* 1988. Chartwell. VG/VG. P3. $15.00

DANDY, Walter. *Benign Tumors in the Third Ventricle of the Brain...* 1991 (1933). Birmingham. Classics Surgery Lib. facsimile. 171p. F. G1. $75.00

DANDY, Walter. *Intracranial Arterial Aneurysms.* 1944. Ithaca. 1st. ils/fld charts. 147p. A13. $275.00

DANE, Clemence. *Arrogant History of White Ben.* 1939. Doubleday. 1st. NF/dj. M2. $27.00

DANE, Clemence. *Arrogant History of White Ben.* 1939. Literary Guild. VG/VG. P3. $20.00

DANE, Clemence. *Enter Sir John.* 1971. Tom Stacey. VG/VG. P3. $15.00

DANE, Clemence. *Flower Girls.* 1955. Norton. 1st. VG. P3. $10.00

DANFORTH, Mildred. *Quaker Pioneer: Laura Haviland.* 1961. NY. Exposition. 1st. 260p. VG/dj. V3. $15.00

DANGERFIELD, Rodney. *I Couldn't Stand My Wife's Cooking So I Opened a Restaurant.* 1972. Middle Village, NY. Jonathan David. 1st. ils Lil Goldstein. F/F. B4. $150.00

DANIEL, C.H.O. *Daniel Press: Memoirs of CHO Daniel.* 1921. Oxford. Daniel Pr. 1/500. 200p. w/ephemera. F/glassine wrp/double case. B24. $300.00

DANIEL, Dorothy. *Cut & Engraved Glass 1771-1905.* 1950. Barrows. 6th. 441p. F/VG. H1. $65.00

DANIEL, J.F. *Elasmobranch Fishes.* (1928). Berkeley. 2nd. ils/figures. 332p. VG. M12. $45.00

DANIEL, Yuli. *This Is Moscow Speaking & Other Stories.* 1968. London. 1st. trans S Hood. VG/dj. T9. $15.00

DANIELS, F.J. *Japanese Prose.* 1944. London. Eng/Japanese text. 97p. W3. $32.00

DANIELS, Guy. *Falcon Under the Hat, Russian Fairy Tales & Merry Tales.* 1969. NY. 1st. ils Rojankovsky. F/VG. M5. $45.00

DANIELS, Jonathan. *Clash of Angels.* 1930. Brewer Warren. 1st. VG. M2. $20.00

DANIELS, Les. *Black Castle.* 1978. Scribner. 1st. NF/NF. P3. $25.00

DANIELS, Les. *Silver Skull.* 1979. Scribner. 1st. VG/VG. P3. $30.00

DANIELS & MURANE. *Uphill All the Way: Documentary Hist of Women in Australia.* 1980. St Lucia. 8vo. 335p. M/dj. P4. $25.00

DANIELS. *Comix: History of Comic Books in America.* 1971. ils. F/dj. M13. $25.00

DANIELSSON, Bengt. *Love in the South Seas.* 1956. Reynal. 8vo. 240p. map ep. bl cloth. P4. $30.00

DANISH, Max D. *World of David Dubinsky.* 1957. World. 347p. VG/G. S3. $26.00

DANK, Milton. *Albert Einstein.* 1983. NY. Franklin Watts. 1st. ils. VG/dj. K3. $10.00

DANN, Jack. *Future Power.* 1976. Random. NF/VG. P3. $15.00

DANN, Jack. *Starhiker.* 1977. Harper. 1st. F/F. M2. $17.00

DANN, John C. *Nagle Journal: Diary of Life of Jacob Nagle, Sailor...1775.* 1988. NY. 1st. 402p+20: mc pl. F/dj. A17. $20.00

DANN & DOZOIS. *Future Power.* 1976. Random. 1st. F/F. M2. $17.00

DANSEREAU, Pierre. *Biogeography: An Ecological Perspective.* 1957. NY. Ronald. 394p. dj. A10. $25.00

DANTAS PEREIRA, Jose Maria. *Memoria Sobre Hum Projecto de Pasigrafia...* 1800. Lisbon. Casa Litteraria do Arco do Cego. 1st/only. folio. 34p. R15. $900.00

DANTE. *Inferno.* nd. Collier. stp New Ed. folio. trans Henry Francis Cary/ils Gustave Dore. aeg. H1. $36.00

DAR, Bashir Ahmad. *Religious Thought of Sayyid Ahmad Khan.* 1971. Lahore. Inst Islamic Culture. 2nd. 304p. VG/dj. W1. $14.00

DARBY, J.N. *Murder in the House With Blue Eyes.* 1939. Bobbs Merrill. 1st. VG. P3. $35.00

DARE, Ann. *Clockwatchers' Cookbook.* 1973. NY. Hamlyn. G/dj. A16. $9.00

DARLING & DARLING. *Bird.* 1962. Boston. 2nd. 261p. worn dj. A17. $27.50

DARLING & NEUMEYER. *Image & Maker.* 1984. obl 4to. 72p. F/F. A4. $125.00

DARLINGTON, C.D. *Chromosome Botany & the Origins of Cultivated Plants.* 1964. London. Allen. 2nd. 231p. cloth. VG. A10. $40.00

DARLINGTON, Charles. *1943 Year Book of Dentistry.* 1943. Chicago. Year Book Medical Pub. 1st. photos. VG/dj. A25. $18.00

DARRAH, John. *Real Camelot: Paganism & the Arthurian Romances.* 1980. VG/VG. M17. $20.00

DART. *GA Henty: A Bibliography.* 1971. ils. 201p. F/NF. A4. $150.00

DARTON & HARVEY. *Emma & the Little Silk-Makers. A True & Wonderful Story.* 1836. London. 12mo. prt 1 side only. pink prt wrp. B24. $525.00

DARTON. *Children's Books in England, Five Centuries of Social Life.* 1958. Cambridge. 2nd/corrected. ils. VG. A4. $75.00

DARWIN, Charles. *Effects of Cross & Self Fertilization in Vegetable Kingdom.* 1877. NY. Apple. ils/tables. 482p+12p ads. decor cloth. VG. M12. $175.00

DARWIN, Charles. *Geological Observations: On Volcanic Islands...* 1915. Appleton. 1st of 3rd authorized. 12mo. 648p. brn-orange cloth. H1. $25.00

DARWIN, Charles. *Journal of Researches Into Geology & Natural History...* 1952 (1839). NY. Hafner. facsimile 1st ed. 8vo. ils/map ep. 615p. cloth. P4/T7. $60.00

DARWIN, Charles. *Life & Letters of Charles Darwin.* 1896. NY. Appleton. authorized ed. 2 vol in 3. 3-quarter leather. P4. $125.00

DARWIN, Charles. *Movement & Habits of Climbing Plants.* (1888). London. Murray. 3rd. ills/figures. 208p. cloth. VG+. M12. $60.00

DARWIN, Charles. *Origin of Species by Means of Natural Selection.* nd. NY. AL Burt. rpt from 6th London. 538p. VG. D8. $8.00

DARWIN, Charles. *Voyage of Charles Darwin.* 1979. NY. Mayflower. 1st Am. 183p. bl cloth. P4. $25.00

DARWIN, Charles. *Voyage of HMS Beagle.* 1946. LEC. 1st thus. 1/1500. ils/sgn Robert Gibbings. F/case. Q1. $350.00

DARY, David. *Entrepreneurs of the Old West.* 1987. Lincoln/London. NE U. A19. $15.00

DASHIELL, B. Francis. *Popular Guide to Radio.* 1927. Baltimore. Williams Wilkins. 8vo. 286p. xl. K5. $25.00

DAUBENMIRE & DAUBENMIRE. *Forest Vegetation of Eastern Washington & Northern Idaho.* 1968. Pullman. ils. sc. B26. $17.50

DAUDET, Alphonse. *Port Tarascon.* 1891. Harper. 1st Am. 359p. teg. F. H1. $85.00

DAUMAS, E. *Horses of the Sahara.* 1969. Austin. trans Sheila M Ohlendorf. F/F. O3. $65.00

DAUSEY, Gary. *Youth Leader's Source Book.* 1983. Zondervan. 332p. VG/dj. B29. $8.50

DAVENPORT, Basil. *Inquiry Into Science Fiction.* 1955. Longman. 1st. F/dj. M2. $35.00

DAVENPORT, Basil. *Science Fiction Novel.* 1959. Advent. 1st. F/F. P3. $40.00

DAVENPORT, Basil. *13 Ways To Kill a Man.* 1966. Faber. 1st. NF/NF. P3. $18.00

DAVENPORT, Cyril. *Royal English Bookbindings.* 1896. London. Seeley. 1st. pres w/correction in Epilogue. tall 4to. 93p. teg. H13. $350.00

DAVENPORT, Guy. *Eclogues.* 1981. Northpoint. 1st. F/F. B35. $20.00

DAVENPORT, Guy. *Resurrection in Cookham Courtyard.* 1982. Jordan Davies. 1/230. sgn/#d. F/F. B2. $125.00

DAVENPORT, Guy. *Trois Caprices.* 1982. Louisville. Pace Trust. 1/75. sgn. F/sans. B2. $85.00

DAVENPORT, Homer. *Country Boy.* 1910. NY. Dillingham. 1st. VG. O3. $45.00

DAVENPORT, L. *Bride's Cook Book.* 1908. 1st. 12 tabbed title p. VG. E6. $135.00

DAVENPORT, Marc. *Visitors From Time.* 1992. Wild Flower. 1st. sgn. 280p. VG. B11. $18.00

DAVENPORT, Marcia. *Mozart.* 1932. Scribner. 1st Am. NF/VG. W2. $125.00

DAVENPORT, Spencer. *Rushton Boys in the Saddle (#2).* 1916. Sully. 244p. VG. M20. $18.00

DAVENTRY, Leonard. *Man of Double Deed.* 1965. Doubleday. VG/VG. P3. $20.00

DAVENTRY, Leonard. *Twenty-One Billionth Paradox.* 1971. Doubleday. 1st. F/F. M2. $15.00

DAVEY, Norman. *Judgment Day.* 1928. Bobbs Merrill. 1st. VG/dj. M2. $30.00

DAVID, Jay. *Inside Joan Collins.* 1988. Caroll Graf. 1st. F/F. T12. $15.00

DAVIDOFF, Zino. *Connoisseur's Book of the Cigar.* 1967. McGraw Hill. 1st of Eng trans. trans Lawrence Grow. 32 pl. 92p. G. H1. $75.00

DAVIDSON, Avram. *Best From Fantasy & Science Fiction 13th Series.* 1964. Doubleday. 1st. F/F. M2. $30.00

DAVIDSON, Avram. *Redward Edward Papers.* 1978. Doubleday. 1st. VG/VG. P3. $20.00

DAVIDSON, Bill. *Cut Off.* 1972. Stein Day. 1st. VG/VG. P3. $15.00

DAVIDSON, F. *New Bible Commentary.* 1958. Eerdmans. 1199p. G. B29. $9.50

DAVIDSON, J. Brownlee. *Agricultural Engineering.* 1917. St Paul. Webb. revised. 554p. VG. A10. $25.00

DAVIDSON, K.L. *Unheated Greenhouse.* 1907. London. Country Life. 248p. VG. A10. $20.00

DAVIDSON, Lionel. *Menorah Men.* 1966. Harper Row. VG/VG. P3. $20.00

DAVIDSON, Lionel. *Rose of Tibet.* 1962. Harper. 1st. NF/dj. M2. $25.00

DAVIDSON, Lionel. *Sun Chemist.* 1976. Knopf. 1st. VG/VG. P3. $25.00

DAVIDSON, Lionel. *Under Plum Lake.* 1980. Knopf. 1st. F/NF. P3. $20.00

DAVIDSON, Orlando. *Deadeyes: Story of the 96th Infantry Division.* 1947. WA, DC. 1st. ils/maps. 310p. VG. S16. $95.00

DAVIDSON & LIBBY. *Breaking the Game Wide Open.* 1974. Atheneum. 1st. VG+/VG. P8. $35.00

DAVIE, Oliver. *Nests & Eggs of North American Birds.* 1989. Columbus, OH. 423p. xl. rebound. A17. $10.00

DAVIES, Charles B. *Report on Interoceanic Canals & Railroads...* 1867. GPO. 8vo. 14 fld maps. 37p. blk cloth. P4. $250.00

DAVIES, David B. *Structural Molecular Biology: Methods & Applications...* 1981. NY. Plenum. 530p. red cloth. VG/dj. G1. $50.00

DAVIES, Howell. *South American Handbook.* 1939. London. lg fld map/maps. 694p. gilt red cloth. F3. $10.00

DAVIES, John. *History of the Tahitian Mission 1799-1830.* 1974. Nendeln. Kraus for Hakluyt Soc. 8vo. 392p. bl cloth. P4. $75.00

DAVIES, K.G. *North Atlantic World in the 17th Century. Vol IV...* 1974. Minneapolis. MN U. 1st. F/dj. O7. $30.00

DAVIES, L.P. *Land of Leys.* 1979. Doubleday. 1st Am. NF/NF. N4. $25.00

DAVIES, L.P. *What Did I Do Tomorrow?* 1972. Barrie Jenkins. 1st. NF/NF. P3. $30.00

DAVIES, Margaret Gay. *Enforcement of English Apprenticeship, a Study...* 1956. Cambridge. Harvard Economics Studies, Vol XCVII. M11. $50.00

DAVIES, Pete. *Dollarville.* 1989. Random. 1st. F/F. P3. $18.00

DAVIES, Rhys. *Withered Root.* 1927. London. Holden. 1st. sgn. VG/G. M23. $50.00

DAVIES, Robertson. *High Spirits.* 1983. Viking. 1st. author's only collection of short fiction. F/F. D10. $75.00

DAVIES, Robertson. *Jig for the Gypsy.* 1954. Toronto. Clarke Irwin. 1st. F/dj. Q1. $250.00

DAVIES, Robertson. *Lyre of Orpheus: A Novel.* 1988. Toronto. Macmillan. 1st. F/dj. Q1. $50.00

DAVIES, Robertson. *Murther & Walking Spirits.* 1991. Toronto. 1st trade. F/F. T12. $20.00

DAVIES, Robertson. *Murther & Walking Spirits.* 1991. Viking. 1st. rem mk. F/F. M22. $15.00

DAVIES, Robertson. *Papers of Samuel Marchbanks.* 1986. Viking. 1st. F/NF. A24. $35.00

DAVIES, Robertson. *Reading & Writing.* 1993. Salt Lake City. special trade. 64p. brd/leather spine. F/sans. D10. $50.00

DAVIES, Robertson. *Rebel Angels.* 1981. Toronto. Macmillan. 1st. sgn. F/NF. Q1. $150.00

DAVIES, Robertson. *Tempest-Tost.* 1952. Rinehart. 1st. F/G. M19. $100.00

DAVIES, Robertson. *What's Bred in the Bone.* 1985. Viking. 1st. F/dj. A24. $35.00

DAVIES, Valentine. *It Happens Every Spring.* 1949. NY. ARC. VG/wrp. B4. $250.00

DAVILA OREJON Y GASTON, F. *Excelencias del Arte Militar, y Varones Ilustres.* 1683. Madrid. Julian deParedes. 1st/only. contemporary limp vellum. R15. $4,800.00

DAVIS, Andrew Jackson. *Principles of Nature, Her Divine Revelations...* 1847. NY. Lyon Fishbough. 3rd. 8vo. 782p. cloth. M1. $375.00

DAVIS, B. *Get Yamamoto.* 1969. NY. 1st. ils/map. 231p. VG/VG. S16. $30.00

DAVIS, Burke. *Civil War: Strange & Fascinating Facts.* 1982. NY. later prt. 249p. cloth. F/F. M8. $25.00

DAVIS, C.C. *Marine & Fresh-Water Plankton.* 1955. Lansing. ils. 562p. cloth. VG. M12. $25.00

DAVIS, C.H. *Telegraphic Determination of Longitudes in Mexico...* 1885. GPO. fld pl. 151p. K3. $65.00

DAVIS, Charles G. *Shipping & Craft in Silhouette.* 1929. Salem. Marine Research Soc. 1/950. 102 silhouettes. red cloth. P4. $95.00

DAVIS, Charles G. *Ships of the Past.* 1929. Marine Research Soc. 170p. VG+/tattered. M20. $90.00

DAVIS, Dorothy Salisbury. *Death in the Life.* 1976. Scribner. 1st. VG/VG. P3. $18.00

DAVIS, Dorothy Salisbury. *Shock Wave.* 1974. Scribner. 1st. VG/VG. P3. $18.00

DAVIS, Eva. *Court Square Recipes: Southern Cooking...* 1950. Vicksburg. Warren County Hist Soc. G/wp. A16. $15.00

DAVIS, Fitzroy. *Through the Doors of Brass.* 1974. Dodd Mead. 1st. F/NF. M25. $35.00

DAVIS, Frederick C. *Lilies in Her Garden Grew.* 1951. Doubleday/Crime Club. 1st. 223p. VG/dj. M20. $25.00

DAVIS, Grania. *Moonbird.* 1986. Doubleday. 1st. RS. F/F. P3. $20.00

DAVIS, H.L. *Honey in the Horn.* 1977. Franklin Lib. ils Uldis Klavins. gilt brn leather. F. A18. $50.00

DAVIS, Harriet Eager. *Elmira, the Girl Who Loved Poe.* 1966. Houghton Mifflin. 1st. VG/VG. P3. $20.00

DAVIS, Helen Burns. *Life & Work of Cyrus Guernsey Pringle.* 1936. Burlington, VT. 8vo. 756p. G. A22. $35.00

DAVIS, J.K. *High Altitude.* 1962. Parkville. 1st. 292p. Gr cloth. VG/dj. P4. $95.00

DAVIS, Jefferson. *Rise & Fall of the Confederate Government.* 1881. Appleton. 2 vol. 1st. cloth. VG. M8. $300.00

DAVIS, Jefferson. *Rise & Fall of the Confederate Government.* 1881. NY. 2 vol. 1st. full leather. G+. B5. $250.00

DAVIS, Joe Lee. *James Branch Cabell.* 1962. Twayne US Authors #21. 1st. F/VG. R10. $15.00

DAVIS, John Gordon. *Taller Than Trees.* 1975. Doubleday. 1st. F/F. P3. $15.00

DAVIS, John W. *Vast Amount of Trouble.* 1993. Niwot, CO. dj. A19. $30.00

DAVIS, L.J. *Walking Small.* 1974. Braziller. 1st. F/F. T12. $15.00

DAVIS, Lindsey. *Iron Hand of Mars.* 1992. London. Heinemann. 1st. sgn. F/F. M15. $100.00

DAVIS, Lindsey. *Shadows in Bronze.* 1991. Crown. 1st. F/F. A20. $30.00

DAVIS, Lindsey. *Silver Pigs.* 1989. Crown. ARC/1st Am. author's 1st book. F/wrp. Q1. $100.00

DAVIS, Lindsey. *Silver Pigs.* 1989. Crown. 1st Am. author's 1st novel. F/clip. D10. $75.00

DAVIS, Lindsey. *Venus in Copper.* 1991. Hutchinson. 1st. F/dj. Q1. $75.00

DAVIS, Loyal. *Intracranial Tumors Roentgenologially Considered.* 1933. NY. 1st. 277p. A13. $200.00

DAVIS, Loyal. *JB Murphy: Stormy Petrel of Surgery.* 1938. NY. 1st. 311p. A13. $25.00

DAVIS, M.E.M. *Queen's Garden.* 1900. Houghton Mifflin. 1st. Knoxville Encampment bookplate. F. M24. $165.00

DAVIS, Mrs. Jefferson. *Jefferson Davis: Ex President of Confederate States.* 1890. NY. 2 vol. 1st. ils. G. B5. $145.00

DAVIS, Nuel Pharr. *Lawrence & Oppenheimer.* 1968. S&S. 1st. VG/dj. K3. $25.00

DAVIS, Patti. *House of Secrets.* 1991. NY. Birchlane. 1st. F/F. T12. $10.00

DAVIS, Ray J. *Flora of Idaho.* 1955 (1952). Dubuque. 828p. B26. $45.00

DAVIS, Reginald. *Royal Family Album.* 1979. London. Pitkin. 1st. F. T12. $40.00

DAVIS, Richard Harding. *In the Fog.* 1901. Russell. 1st. VG. M2. $17.00

DAVIS, Richard Harding. *Soldiers of Fortune.* 1917. Scribner. 358p. gr cloth. F3. $10.00

DAVIS, Richard Harding. *West From a Car Window.* 1892. Harper. ils Frederick Remington. VG. K3. $35.00

DAVIS, Richard. *Space 3.* 1976. Abelard. 1st. VG/VG. P3. $22.00

DAVIS, S.T. *Caribou Shooting in Newfoundland.* 1895. Lancaster, PA. New Era Pub House. 1st. double-p map. 212p. G. H7. $150.00

DAVIS, William C. *Image of War: 1861-1865.* 1981. Doubleday. Nat Hist Soc. 6 vol. cloth. VG+/djs. M20. $350.00

DAVIS, William Heath. *Sixty Years in California...* 1889. SF. AJ Leary. 1st. 639p. maroon cloth. VG. K7. $175.00

DAVIS, William M. *Nimrod of the Sea or the American Whaleman.* 1972. North Quincy. Christopher Pub. 405p. NF/dj. P4. $45.00

DAVIS, Winfield J. *History of Political Conventions in California 1849-1892.* 1893. Sacramento. CA State Lib. 1st. 8vo. gilt brn buckram. NF. R3. $250.00

DAVIS & DOLLARD. *Children of Bondage.* 1946. WA, DC. Am Council Edu. 4th. 299p. VG. B4. $85.00

DAVIS & FOSTER. *Home Front.* 1986. Crown. 1st. 231p. F/F. W2. $30.00

DAVIS & HELLYER. *Nature's Clown, the Penguin.* 1952. NGS. sgn Hellyer. fld map. VG+. P4. $27.50

DAVIS & HORNE. *All-Lover All-Star Team & 50 Other Improbable Baseball...* 1990. Morrow. 1st. F/F. B4. $35.00

DAVIS. *Comprehensive Guide to Children's Literature...* 1981. 550 titles. 187p. F/VG. A4. $30.00

DAVISON, Grace L. *Gates of Memory.* 1955. Solvang, CA. Santa Ynez Valley News. 1st. inscr. VG. O4. $20.00

DAVISON, Peter. *Praying Wrong.* 1984. Atheneum. 1st. F/F. B35. $16.00

DAVISON, Ralph. *Concrete Pottery & Garden Furniture.* 1917. NY. Munn. 196p. cloth. A10. $50.00

DAWE, Carlton. *Live Cartridge.* 1937. Ward Lock. 1st. xl. VG. P3. $20.00

DAWE, R.D. *Collation & Investigation of Manuscripts of Aeschylus.* 1964. Cambridge. 352p. xl. dj. A17. $12.00

DAWSON, Conningsby. *Vanishing Point.* 1922. Cosmopolitan Book. 1st. ils JM Flagg. 350p. VG/dj. M20. $20.00

DAWSON, E. Yale. *Cacti of California.* 1966. Berkeley. ils/photos. gr cloth. F. B26. $17.50

DAWSON, E. Yale. *How To Know the Cacti.* 1963. Dubuque, IA. photos/line drawings. hc. VG+. B26. $22.50

DAWSON, Elmer A. *Garry Grayson's Football Rivals.* 1926. Grosset Dunlap. ne. 218p. G. W2. $40.00

DAWSON, Elmer A. *Garry Grayson's Winning Kick (#6).* 1928. Grosset Dunlap. 218p. cloth. VG/dj (lists 10 titles). M20. $30.00

DAWSON, James. *Hell Gate.* 1971. McKay. VG/VG. P3. $10.00

DAWSON, John P. *History of Lay Judges.* 1960. Harvard. VG/dj. M11. $125.00

DAWSON, L.H. *Stories From the Faerie Queen Retold.* 1914. Harrap. VG. P3. $25.00

DAWSON & FOSTER. *Seashore Plants of California.* 1982. Berkeley. 12mo. 226p. VG/VG. B1. $26.50

DAY, Clarence. *Life With Father.* 1947. Sun Dial. MTI. VG/VG. P3. $20.00

DAY, David. *Tolkien Bestiary.* 1979. Ballantine. 1st. VG/VG. P3. $25.00

DAY, Gina. *Tell No Tales.* 1967. Hart Davis. 1st. F/F. P3. $15.00

DAYTON, William A. *Notes on Western Range Forest.* 1960. UDSA/Forest Service. 8vo. 254p. VG. A22. $18.00

DAYTON, William A. *United States Tree Books.* 1952. GPO. 8vo. xl. A22. $10.00

DE ACOSTA, Jose. *Historia Natural y Moral de las Indias.* 1940 (1590). Mexico. Fondo Cultura Economica. ils. F. O7. $75.00

DE ALARCON, Pedron Antonio. *Three-Cornered Hat.* 1959. Los Angeles. LEC. 1st thus. 1/1500. ils/sgn R Duvoisin. F/glassine/case. Q1. $75.00

DE ALBUQUERQUE, Luis. *Astronomical Navigation.* 1988. Lisboa. National Brd Celebration Portuguese Discoveries. VG/F. O7. $45.00

DE ALPOIM, Jose Fernandes P. *Exame de Bombeiros, que Comprehende de Tratados...* 1748. Madric. Francisco Martinez Abad. 1st. 20 fld pl/1 fld table. R15. $4,500.00

DE AMICIS, Edmondo. *Holland.* 1894. Phil. 2 vol. teg. VG/dj. B18. $35.00

DE AMICIS, Edmondo. *Spain & the Spaniards.* 1895. Phil. 2 vol. gilt cloth. VG/cloth dj. B18. $35.00

DE ANGELI, Marguerite. *Book of Nursery & Mother Goose Rhymes.* nd (1954). Doubleday. 4to. 192p. VG. C14. $18.00

DE ANGELI, Marguerite. *Butter at the Old Price.* 1971. Doubleday. 5th. 258p. VG+/VG. P2. $20.00

DE ANGELI, Marguerite. *Door in the Wall.* 1949. Doubleday. 1st. Newbery Medal. 112p. NF/VG+. P2. $110.00

DE ANGELI, Marguerite. *Just Like David.* 1951. Doubleday. 1st. 8vo. 122p. G+. T5. $28.00

DE ANGELI, Marguerite. *Marguerite DeAngeli's Book of Favorite Hymns.* 1963. Doubleday. 1st. 64p. VG+. D4. $35.00

DE ANGELI, Marguerite. *Old Testament.* 1959. 1st. inscr. VG/G. S13. $75.00

DE ANGELI, Marguerite. *Skippack School.* 1939. Doubleday. 1st. VG+/VG. P2. $90.00

DE ANGELI, Marguerite. *Summer Day With Ted & Nina.* 1940. Doubleday. sq 8vo. VG. M5. $65.00

DE ANGELI, Marguerite. *Turkey for Christmas.* 1st. sgn. VG/VG. M17. $75.00

DE ANGELIS & FRANCIS. *Early Ford V-8.* 1982. South Lyon. Motor Cities. 50th Anniversary Commemorative Prt. VG/dj. B18. $17.50

DE ANGULO, Jaime. *Indian Tales.* 1953. NY. AA Wyn. 1st. NF/VG. L3. $150.00

DE BEAUMONT, Madame LePrince. *Beauty & the Beast.* 1963. Macmillan. 1st thus. ils Hilary Knight. folio. F. M5. $60.00

DE BEAUVOIR, Simone. *Memoirs of a Dutiful Daughter.* 1959. VG/G+. M17. $17.50

DE BEER, Gavin. *Hannibal: Challenging Rome's Supremacy.* 1969. ils. VG/VG. M17. $25.00

DE BENNEVILLE, James. *Saito Musashi-bo Benkei: Tales of Wars of the Genpei...* 1910. Yokohama. 1st. 2 vol. ils. fld map. gilt gr cloth. F/dj. W3. $575.00

DE BERARD, Frederick B. *Famous Tales of Wonder.* 1899. Internat Book Co. 1st. VG. M2. $50.00

DE BERNIERES, Louis. *War of Don Emmanuel's Nether Parts.* 1990. London. Secker Warburg. 1st. author's 1st book. NF/F. B3. $125.00

DE BISSCHOP, Eric. *Tahiti-Nui.* 1959. Obolensky. 284p. T7. $24.00

DE BOISSIERE, Jean. *Cooking Creole: Suggestions on Making Creole Food.* nd. Port of Spain. Cosmopolitan Printery. 4th. 44p. B10. $15.00

DE BOLT, Joseph W. *Happening Worlds of John Brunner.* 1975. Kennikat. 1st. F/F. P3. $20.00

DE BONNEFOUX & PARIS. *Dictionnaire de Marine a Voiles et a Vapeur.* 1847-1848. Paris. 2nd. 2 vol. 24 fld pl/ils. half cloth/calf. T7. $450.00

DE BOSSCHERE, Jean. *Marthe & the Madmen.* 1928. Covici Friede. 1st. author's 1st novel. blk cloth. F/case. B35. $75.00

DE BOTHEZAT, George. *Back to Newton.* 1936. NY. Stechert. 1st. 8vo. 152p. VG. K3. $20.00

DE BRACTON, Henrici. *Bracton on the Laws & Customs of England.* 1968. Harvard. 4 vol. edit George Woodbine. M11. $650.00

DE BRACTON, Henrici. *De Legibus et Consuetudinibus Angliae. Six Volumes.* 1878-83. London. Longman. 1st trans/1st modern ed. usable only. M11. $450.00

DE BRAGANZA. *Hill Collection of Pacific Voyages.* 1974-83. Castle. 3 vol. ltd ed. ils. VG. A4. $750.00

DE BRUNHOFF, Jean. *Babar the King.* 1935. NY. Random. 1st. 8vo. yel brd. dj. R5. $200.00

DE BRUNHOFF, Jean. *Babar the King.* 1935. Smith Haas. 1st. 3rd in Babar series. ils. 47p. VG. D1. $700.00

DE BRUNHOFF, Jean. *Le Voyage de Babar.* 1932. Jardin Des Modes. 1st. author's 2nd book. folio. 48p. G+. P2. $225.00

DE BRUNHOFF, Laurent. *Babar's Mystery.* nd (1978). Random. 2nd. 4to. unp. NF. C14. $12.00

DE BRUTELLE, C.-L. L'Hertier. *Sertum Anglicum.* 1963 (1788). Pittsburgh. Hunt Botanical. facsimile. 4to. 34 full-p pl. B1. $40.00

DE BUSSCHERE, Dave. *Open Man.* 1970. Random. 1st. photos. VG/dj. P8. $25.00

DE CAMP, Catherine Crook. *Creatures of the Cosmos.* 1977. Westminster. 1st. VG/G+. P3. $20.00

DE CAMP, L. Sprague. *Ancient Engineers.* 1963. Doubleday. ils. 8vo. 408p. NF/dj. K3. $20.00

DE CAMP, L. Sprague. *Carnelian Cube.* 1948. Gnome. 1st. F/VG. P3. $75.00

DE CAMP, L. Sprague. *Castle of Iron.* 1950. Gnome. 1st. VG/G+. P3. $75.00

DE CAMP, L. Sprague. *Continent Makers.* 1953. Twayne. VG. P3. $25.00

DE CAMP, L. Sprague. *Continent Makers.* 1953. Twayne. 1st. sgn. F/dj. M2. $45.00

DE CAMP, L. Sprague. *Demons & Dinosaurs.* 1970. Arkham. 1st. F/dj. M2. $325.00

DE CAMP, L. Sprague. *Heroic Age of American Invention.* 1961. Doubleday. 1st. F/dj. M2. $50.00

DE CAMP, L. Sprague. *Honorable Barbarian.* 1989. Easton. 1st. sgn. leather. F/sans/swrp. P3. $80.00

DE CAMP, L. Sprague. *Incomplete Enchanter.* 1941. Holt. 1st. sgn. VG/dj. M2. $150.00

DE CAMP, L. Sprague. *Lest Darkness Fall.* 1949. Prime Pr. 1st. NF/VG. M19. $45.00

DE CAMP, L. Sprague. *Man & Power.* 1961. Golden. VG. P3. $20.00

DE CAMP, L. Sprague. *Miscast Barbarian: Biography of Robert E Howard.* 1975. Gerry de la Ree. 1st. 1/900. F/wrp. R10. $15.00

DE CAMP, L. Sprague. *Purple Pterodactyls.* 1979. Huntington Woods, MI. Phantasia. 1st. 1/200. sgn. F/F/case. T2. $45.00

DE CAMP, L. Sprague. *Tales From Gavagan's Bar.* 1953. Twayne. 1st. F/F. M2. $50.00

DE CAMP, L. Sprague. *Tritonian Ring.* 1953. Twayne. 1st. VG/dj. M2. $40.00

DE CAMP, L. Sprague. *Unbeheaded King.* 1983. Ballantine. 1st. 8vo. F/dj. T10. $50.00

DE CAMP & DE CAMP. *Day of the Dinosaur.* 1985. NY. Bonanza. rpt. 319p. VG+/dj. M21. $10.00

DE CAMP & LEY. *Lands Beyond.* (1952). NY. Rinehart. 1st thus. 214p. F3. $15.00

DE CANDOLLE, Alphonse. *Origin of Cultivated Plants.* 1884. London. Kegan Paul. 12mo. VG. A22. $55.00

DE CARLE, Donald. *Practical Watch Repairing.* 1964 (1946). London. NAG Pr. 2nd. 303p. VG/torn. K5. $45.00

DE CASTRO, Joao Bautista. *Roteiro Terrestre de Portugal, em que se Enisnao...* 1748. Lisbon. Miguel Manescal da Costa. 1st. contemporary calf. R15. $300.00

DE CASTRO ALVES, Antonio. *A Cachoeira de Paulo-Affonso.* 1876. Bahia. Imprensa Economica. modern morocco/orig wrp bdg in. R15. $1,250.00

DE CHATEAUBRIAND, F.A. *Travels in Greece, Palestine, Egypt & Barbary...* 1814. NY. Van Winkle Wiley. trans from French. 471p. full leather. lacks map. K3. $95.00

DE CHIRICO, Giorgio. *Hebdomeros.* 1966. Four Seasons Book Soc. 1st Eng. 1/500. F/NF. B2. $75.00

DE COMBRAY, Richard. *Caravansary: Alone in Moslem Places.* 1978. Doubleday. 1st. 179p. VG/dj. W1. $18.00

DE COMINES, Philippe. *Historie.* 1614. London. Bill. sm folio. 17 genealogical tables at end. gilt goat. R12. $475.00

DE CREBILLON, C.P.J. *Divan.* 1927. np. private prt. 1/1470. #d. VG. M2. $75.00

DE ESPINOSA Y TELLO, Jose. *Spanish Voyage to Vancouver & NW Coast of America...* 1930 (1802). London. Argonaut. 1/525. ils/double-p fld map. orange brd/vellum spine. F. O7. $375.00

DE FELITTA, Frank. *Entity.* 1978. Putnam. 1st. VG/VG. P3. $15.00

DE FOE, Daniel. *History of the Devil, As Well Ancient As Modern.* 1727. London. Warner. 2nd. 8vo. 408p. 18th-C panelled calf/rebacked. C6. $250.00

DE FOE, Daniel. *Life & Adventures of Robinson Crusoe.* ca 1796. London. C Cooke. 3 vol. engravings dtd 1793-1796. gilt full leather. R5. $300.00

DE FOE, Daniel. *Life & Strange Adventures of Robinson Crusoe.* 1895. London. Nister. 6 chromolithos/80 b&w ils. 328p. gilt red coth. VG. D1. $100.00

DE FOE, Daniel. *Life & Strange Adventures of Robinson Crusoe.* 1979. London. Basilisk. 1/500. ils EG Craig. quarter bl morocco. bevelled cloth case. B24. $500.00

DE FOE, Daniel. *Moll Flanders.* 1929. 1st. ils John Austen. VG/VG. M19. $45.00

DE FOREST, Charlotte. *Prancing Pony.* 1967. NY/Tokyo. Walker/Weatherhill. 1st Am. 63p. VG+/VG+. D4. $35.00

DE FOREST, J.W. *Miss Ravenel's Conversation From Secession to Loyalty.* 1867. NY. Harper. 1st. 521p+ads. G+. B5. $60.00

DE GERLACHE, Adriene. *Voyage de la Belgica Quinze Mois Dans l'Antarctique...* 1902. Bruxelles. Imprimerie Scientifique Ch Bulens. 310p. bl cloth. P4. $650.00

DE GRAAFF, Robert M. *Book of the Toad.* 1991. Park Street. ils. 208p. F. S15. $15.00

DE GRAFF, Phil. *Birches, Beaches & Belches.* 1962. Matlacha. 1st. sgn. sbdg. VG. A16. $35.00

DE GRAFF & TILGHMAN. *Management of W Forests & Grasslands for Nongame Birds.* 1980. Ogden. 535p. VG. S15. $16.00

DE GRAMONT, S. *Strong Brown God: Story of the Niger River.* 1976. Boston. 1st. ils/map. 350p. F/dj. M4. $15.00

DE GROOT, Roy Andries. *Feast for All Seasons.* 1966. Knopf. 730p+index. VG/dj. A16. $12.00

DE GROTTE, Roger. *Olympic Sports Album: Montreal, 1976.* 1975. Little Brn. 1st Am. Eng/French text. ils. VG+/VG. P8. $25.00

DE GRUMMOND, Jan Lucas. *Renato Beluche.* (1983). LSU. 1st. 300p. dj. F3. $20.00

DE GRUYTER, Julius A. *Drum Beats on the Sandusky.* 1969. Carlton. 265p. VG/dj. M20. $20.00

DE HAAS, Elsa. *Antiquities of Bail, Origin & Historical Development...* 1940. NY. Columbia. pres copy. maroon cloth. M11. $65.00

DE HAAS, Jacob. *Theodor Herzl: A Biographical Study...* 1927. NY. Leonard Co. 2 vol. VG/dj. S3. $48.00

DE HARTOG, Jan. *Artist.* 1963. Atheneum. 1st. 167p. VG/clip. V3. $16.00

DE HARTOG, Jan. *Children: A Personal Record for Use of Adoptive Parents.* 1969. Atheneum. 1st. 265p. VG/G. V3. $12.00

DE HARTOG, Jan. *Waters of the New World.* 1961. Atheneum. 1st. 276p. G/clip. V3. $14.00

DE HAVEN, Tom. *Freaks Amour.* 1979. Morrow. 1st. sgn. F/NF. B4. $150.00

DE HAVEN, Tom. *Funny Papers.* 1985. Viking. 1st. F/F. H11. $35.00

DE ILINCHETA, Jose. *Officio de Don Jose de Ilincheta al Exm Sir Capital General.* 1813. Havana. Imprenta Liberal. 1st/only. 28p. contemporary plain wrp. R15. $650.00

DE ISABA, Marcos. *Cuerpo Enfermo de la Milicia Espanola...* 1594. Madrid. Guillermo Druy. 1st. full-p woodcut. new ep. R15. $4,200.00

DE JONG, Meindert. *Big Goose & the Little White Duck.* 1938. Harper. 1st. ils Edna Potter. 160p. VG/G. P2. $75.00

DE JONG, Meindert. *Horse Came Running.* (1970). Macmillan. 3rd. 8vo. 147p. bl cloth. xl. G+. T5. $12.00

DE JONG, Meindert. *Last Little Cat.* 1961. Harper. probable 1st. ils Jim McMullan. 66p. VG/VG. P2. $30.00

DE JONG, Meindert. *Wheel on the School.* (1954). Harper. early ed (A on dj). 8vo. 298p. VG/G. T5. $35.00

DE KATZLEBEN, Baroness. *Cat's Tail: Being the History of Childe Merlin.* 1831. Edinburgh. Blackwood. 8vo. 32p. etched George Cruikshank. F. B24. $325.00

DE KOVEN, Mrs. Reginald. *By the Waters of Babylon.* 1901. Stone. 1st. VG. M2. $25.00

DE LA CAMPA, Miguel. *Journal of Explorations Northward Along Coast of Monterey...* 1964. SF. John Howell. 1/1000. 9 mc pl/2 full-p maps. 67p. as new. K7. $50.00

DE LA COSTA, H.S.J. *Jesuits in the Philippines 1581-1768.* 1967. Cambridge. Harvard. ils/7 maps. F. O7. $75.00

DE LA FALAISE, Maxime. *Food in Vogue.* 1980. Doubleday. VG/dj. A16. $20.00

DE LA FRESNAYE, J.F. *Brain Mechanisms & Learning: A Symposium...* 1961. Oxford. Blackwell/Macmillan. 8vo. 702p. navy cloth. stp. VG. G1. $37.50

DE LA LOUPE, Vincent. *Premier et Second Livre des Dignitez, Magistrats...* 1564. Paris. Le Noir. 3 parts in 1. 8vo. gilt calf. R13. $850.00

DE LA MARE, Walter. *Beginning & Other Stories.* 1955. London. VG/dj. M2. $17.00

DE LA MARE, Walter. *Bells & Grass.* 1942. Viking. 1st. ils Dorothy Lathrop. 8vo. VG/dj. D1. $35.00

DE LA MARE, Walter. *Ding Dong Bell.* 1924. London. Selwyn Blount. 1/300. sgn. 76p. NF/dj. D4. $125.00

DE LA MARE, Walter. *Down-Adown-Derry, a Book of Fairy Poems.* 1922. London. Constable. 1st. ils DP Lathrop. 4to. gilt gr cloth. VG/VG. R5. $225.00

DE LA MARE, Walter. *Down-Adown-Derry, a Book of Fairy Poems.* 1922. London. Constable. 1st. 190p. gilt cloth. VG. D1/D4. $100.00

DE LA MARE, Walter. *Dutch Cheese.* 1931. Knopf. 1st Am. ils Dorothy Lathrop. 75p. VG/G+. P2. $145.00

DE LA MARE, Walter. *Flora. A Book of Drawings.* 1919. London. Heinemann. 1st. 4to. ivory brd. dj. R5. $200.00

DE LA MARE, Walter. *Memoirs of a Midget.* 1921. Knopf. 1st Am. G+. M2. $10.00

DE LA MARE, Walter. *Molly Whuppie.* 1983. Farra. 1st Am. ils LeCain. F/dj. M5. $48.00

DE LA MARE, Walter. *Peacock Pie.* 1913. London. Constable. 1st. 122p. cloth. F/professional rpr. D4. $150.00

DE LA MARE, Walter. *Peacock Pie.* 1961. Knopf. 1st thus. 117p. cloth. VG+/worn. D4. $45.00

DE LA MARE, Walter. *Stuff & Nonsense.* 1927. NY. Holt. 1st. ils Bold. 112p. gilt cloth. F/tape rpr. D4. $45.00

DE LA MARE, Walter. *Veil & Other Poems.* (1921). London. Constable. 1st. 8vo. 91p. cloth/leather label. M1. $100.00

DE LA MARE, Walter. *Warmit.* 1976. Scribner. 1st. unp. VG/dj. M20. $20.00

DE LA NEZIERE, R. & S. *Nos Amis Les Animaux. Alphabet par R De La Neziere...* ca 1920s. Paris. Hachette. 4to. F/self wrp. B24. $125.00

DE LA PARRA, Macro. *Chile: From Within, by Chilean Photographers 1973-1986.* 1990. Norton. 1st. VG. V4. $12.50

DE LA RUE, Louise. *Cardboard Court. Essay by Louise de la Rue.* nd. Mill Valley. Figment. 1/65. 76x59mm. prt/inscr Diana Weiss. 40p. red cloth. B24. $135.00

DE LA TORRE, Lilian. *Detections of Dr Sam: Johnson.* 1960. Crime Club. 1st. sgn. F/F. P3. $50.00

DE LA VEGA, Garcilaso. *Florida of the Inca: History of Adelantado, Hernando DeSoto.* 1951. Austin. trans/edit Varner. F. O7. $50.00

DE LAET, Joannes. *L'Histoire du Nouveau Monde, ou Description des Indes...* 1640. Leyden. Bonaventure & Abraham Elsevier. 1st. folio. later bdg. R15. $6,500.00

DE LAET, Joannes. *Novus Orbis Seu Descriptionis Indiae Occidentalis.* 1633. Leiden. Elzevir. folio. 14 double-p maps. 690p. full vellum. complete. C6. $5,000.00

DE LAUNAY, L. *La Science Geologique. Ses Methodes, Results, Problemes...* 1905. Paris. Armand Colin. 1st. ils/fld maps. 750p. VG. K3. $80.00

DE LEEUW, Adele. *Nobody's Doll.* 1946. Little Brn. 1st. 86p. VG/dj. P2. $80.00

DE LILLO, Don. *Americana.* 1971. Houghton Mifflin. 1st. VG/worn. B2. $175.00

DE LILLO, Don. *Day Room.* 1987. Knopf. 1st. sgn. F/F. D10. $60.00

DE LILLO, Don. *End Zone.* 1972. Houghton Mifflin. 1st. author's 2nd book. NF/dj. M25. $75.00

DE LILLO, Don. *Great Jones Street.* 1973. Houghton Mifflin. 1st. author's 3rd book. F/NF. B2/M25. $65.00

DE LILLO, Don. *Great Jones Street.* 1973. Houghton Mifflin. 1st. sgn. author's 3rd novel. F/NF. D10. $125.00

DE LILLO, Don. *Mao II.* 1991. Viking. 1st. F/F. D10. $45.00

DE LILLO, Don. *Names.* 1982. Knopf. 1st. F/dj. Q1. $60.00

DE LILLO, Don. *Names.* 1982. Knopf. 1st. sgn. F/F. D10. $75.00

DE LILLO, Don. *Players.* 1977. Knopf. 1st. sgn. F/dj. D10. $125.00

DE LILLO, Don. *Ratner's Star.* 1976. Knopf. 1st. sgn. F/F. D10. $110.00

DE LILLO, Don. *Ratner's Star.* 1976. Knopf. 1st. F/F clip. D10. $75.00

DE LILLO, Don. *Running Dog.* 1978. Knopf. 1st. NF/NF. H11. $45.00

DE LILLO, Don. *White Noise.* 1985. Viking. 1st. author's 8th novel. F/F. D10. $75.00

DE LUBAC, Henri. *Un-Marxian Socialist: Study of Proudhon.* 1948. London. 1st. 304p. dj. A17. $10.00

DE LUCCHI, M.R. *Stereotaxic Atlas of the Chimpanzee Brain.* 1965. Berkeley/Los Angeles. obl folio. VG/dj. G1. $125.00

DE MARINIS, Rick. *Coming Triumph of the Free World.* 1988. Viking. 1st. sgn. F/F. A23. $40.00

DE MARINIS, Rick. *Scimitar.* 1977. Dutton. 1st. VG/VG. P3. $25.00

DE MARINIS, Rick. *Year of the Zinc Penny.* 1989. Norton. 1st. F/F. B3. $25.00

DE MAUPASSANT, Guy. *Woman's Life (Une Vie).* 1952. NY. LEC. 1st thus. 1/1500. ils Edy Legrand. NF/case. Q1. $60.00

DE MAURIER, Daphne. *Don't Look Now.* 1971. Doubleday. 1st. VG/dj. M2. $30.00

DE MAURIER, Daphne. *Echoes of the Macabre.* 1947. Doubleday. 1st AM. F/dj. M2. $40.00

DE MESQUITA, Luiz Manoel. *Conta a Sua Magestade o Senhor D Joao VI do Orgulhoso...* 1822. Lisbon. Impressao Liberal. 1st/only. 27p. stitched early wrp. R15. $1,500.00

DE MILLE, James. *Strange Manuscript Found in a Copper Cylinder.* 1900. Harper. VG. M2. $35.00

DE MILLE, Nelson. *By the Rivers of Babylon.* 1978. HBJ. 1st. author's 1st book. NF/dj. M25. $60.00

DE MILLE, Nelson. *Charm School.* 1988. Warner. 1st. NF/NF. N4. $25.00

DE MILLE, Nelson. *Talbot Odyssey.* 1984. Delacorte. 1st. NF/dj. M25. $100.00

DE MONT, John. *Custer Battle Guns.* 1974. Old Army. 1st. 1/250. sgn. ils/photos. 113p. VG/VG. J2. $295.00

DE MONVEL, Maurice Boutet. *Veielles Chansons.* Paris. Plon-Nourrit et Cie. obl 4to. VG. M5. $65.00

DE MORGAN, William. *When Ghost Meets Ghost.* 1914. Holt. 1st. VG. M2. $30.00

DE MUSSET, Paul. *Mr Wind & Madam Rain.* 1904. Putnam/Knickerbocker. ils Chas Bennett. aeg. VG. B15. $250.00

DE NADAILLAC, Marquis. *Pre-Historic America.* 1884 (1883). NY. Putnam. ils/index. 566p. teg. F3. $75.00

DE NEMETHY, Bertalan. *De Nemethy Method: Modern Techniques for Training...* 1988. NY. Doubleday. 1st. VG/VG. O3. $25.00

DE NOON, Christopher. *Posters of the WPA 1935-1943.* 1987. Wheatley. 1st. F/F. V4. $35.00

DE PAOLA, Tomie. *Legend of the Bluebonnet.* 1983. Putnam. 1st. sgn. F/NF. P2. $45.00

DE PAOLA, Tomie. *Little Friar Who Flew.* 1980. Putnam. 1st. VG+/VG+. A20. $20.00

DE PAOLA, Tomie. *Tomie dePaola's Mother Goose.* 1985. NY. Putnam. 1st ltd. 1/300. sgn/#d. 128p. F/F box. D4. $100.00

DE PINEDO, Francesco. *Il Mio Vola Attreverso l'Antlantico e le due Americhe...* 1928. Milano. Ulrico Hoepli. ils/fld maps. gilt bdg. F. K3. $85.00

DE POL, John. *Patterns: Drawn & Engraved on Wood.* 1986. Council Bluffs, IA. Yel Barn. 1st. 1/150. 8vo. patterned brd. F. T10. $250.00

DE PROFT, Melanie. *American Family Cookbook.* 1974. Chicago. ils. 4to. VG/tattered. A16. $15.00

DE PROFT, Melanie. *My Favorite Recipes.* 1959. Chicago. Spencer. G. A16. $10.00

DE PUY, Henry. *Ethan Allen & the Green-Mountain Heroes of '76.* 1858. Buffalo. 428p. O8. $18.50

DE REGNIER, Henri. *L'Escapade.* 1927. Paris. Henri Cyral. 1/1021. ils Daniel-Girard. NF/wrp/glassine. T10. $100.00

DE REGNIERS, Beatrice Schenk. *Red Riding Hood.* 1974 (1972). NY. Atheneum. 3rd. 8vo. ils Edward Gorey. tan cloth. VG. T5. $30.00

DE REGNIERS, Beatrice. *Sing a Song of Popcorn.* 1988. NY. Scholastic. 1st. 142p. F/F. D4. $35.00

DE SADE, Marquis. *120 Days of Sodom & Other Writings.* 1966. Grove. 1st. F/NF. B2. $35.00

DE SAINT REAL, Cesar Vichard. *Dom Carlos Novvelle Historiqve.* 1673. Amsterdam. Commelin. 12mo. calf. R12. $145.00

DE SAINT-EXUPERY, Antoine. *Le Petit Prince.* 1946. French text. VG/G. M17. $20.00

DE SAO BOAVENTURA, Fortunato. *Summario da Vida Accoens e Gloriosa Morte Senhor D Fernando.* 1836. Modena. Impressao Regia Cameral. 1st/only. 61p. R15. $500.00

DE SCHWEINTZ, Edmund. *Life & Times of David Zeisberger...* 1870. Phil. 1st. 474p. G+. B18. $150.00

DE SEGUR, Philip. *History of Expedition to Russia Undertaken by Napoleon 1812.* 1825. Phil. 2 vol. 24mo. full leather. E6. $75.00

DE SEVIGNE, Marchioness. *Letters to Her Daughter the Countess of de Grignon.* 1927. London. Spurr Swift. 10 vol. 1/1000. 1st thus. tall 8vo. brn linen. H13. $495.00

DE SITTER, L.U. *Structural Geology.* 1959. McGraw Hill. 552p. VG. D8. $15.00

DE SMET, Pierre Jean. *Letters & Sketches, With a Narrative of Year's Residence...* 1843. Phil. Fithian. 1st/1st issue. ftspc/pl/fld ils. 252p. D11. $1,250.00

DE SMITH, L. *Cocina Moderna y Practica.* 1919. 4to. ils. 574p. G+. E6. $25.00

DE SOLIS Y RIVADENEIRA, A. *Historica de la Conquista de Mexico, Poblacion, Progressos.* 1684. Madrid. Imprenta Bernardo deVilla-Diego. 1st. folio. 548p. R15. $5,000.00

DE SOUSA DE ALMADA, Francisco. *Satyra Moral Contra os Vicios em Commum...* 1736. Lisbon. Miguel Rodrigues. 1st. 16p. modern marbled wrp. R15. $150.00

DE TAKATS, Geza. *Vascular Surgery.* 1959. Phil. 1st. 726p. A13. $75.00

DE TARDE, Gabriel. *Underground Man.* 1974 (1905). Hyperion. rpt. F. M2. $25.00

DE TENA, Torcuato. *Second Life of Captain Contreras.* 1960. Houghton Mifflin. 1st. NF/dj. M2. $10.00

DE TERRE, H. *Humboldt: Life & Times of Alexander Von Humboldt 1769-1859.* 1955. NY. 1st. ils/maps. F/dj. M4. $23.00

DE TOLNAY, Charles. *Michelangelo: Sculptor, Painter, Architect.* 1975. Princeton. 283p. cloth. dj. D2. $75.00

DE TORRES, Pedro. *Excelencias de S Joseph, Varon Divino, Patriarca Grande...* 1710. Seville. Herederos Thoms Lopez deHaro. 1st/only. folio. R15. $850.00

DE VALDES, Francisco. *Specchio, et Disciplina Militare...Nel Quale si Tratta...* 1598. Venice. Cornelio Arrivabene. 1st Italian language. woodcuts. R15. $2,000.00

DE VARGAS, Don Juan. *Les Adventurers de Don Juan deVargas, Racontees Lui-Meme.* 1853. Paris. Jannett. 184p. cloth. D11. $100.00

DE VASCONCELOS, Jose Mauro. *My Sweet-Orange Tree.* 1971. London. 1st. trans EH Miller. VG/VG. T9. $12.00

DE VAUCOULEURS, Gerard. *L'Exploration des Galaxies Voisines...* 1958. Paris. Masson et Cie. ils. 151p. G. K5. $25.00

DE VEAUX, Alexis. *Don't Explain: Song of Billie Holiday.* 1980. Harper. 1st. F/clip. B4. $85.00

DE VEAUX, Alexis. *Na-Ni.* 1973. Harper. 1st. ils. F/F clip. B4. $85.00

DE VELLEZ GUERREIRO, Joao T. *Jornada, que Qntonio de Albuquerque Coelho...* 1732. Lisbon. Officina da Musica. 1st. 427p. contemporary calf. R15. $2,250.00

DE VERE, M. Schele. *Stray Leaves From Nature.* 1856. NY. Putnam. 291p. VG. A10. $20.00

DE VOGEL, E.F. *Seedlings of Dicotyledons.* 1980. Wgeningen, Netherlands. Agric Pub. 465p. cloth. A10. $40.00

DE VOS, L. *Atlas of Sponge Morphology.* 1991. Smithsonian. 117p. cloth. F. B1. $26.50

DE VOTO, Bernard. *Across the Wide Missouri.* Bonanaza. rpt. VG. A19. $20.00

DE VOTO, Bernard. *Across the Wide Missouri.* 1947. NY. 81 pl. 483p. F/dj. M4. $30.00

DE VOTO, Bernard. *Course of Empire.* 1952. Houghton Mifflin. 1st. 8vo. 647p. VG/dj. K7. $45.00

DE VOTO, Bernard. *Journals of Lewis & Clark.* 1953. Houghton Mifflin. 1st. 504p. as new/F. H1. $32.50

DE VRIES, Hugo. *Species & Varieties: Their Origin by Mutation.* 1906. Chicago. Open Court. 2nd. 8vo. 847p. scarce. K3. $95.00

DE VRIES, Leonard. *Flowers of Delight From the Osborne Collection...1765-1830.* 1965. sm 4to. ils/woodcuts/engravings. 232p. NF/VG. A4. $50.00

DE VRIES, Leonard. *Flowers of Delight. An Agreeable Garland of Prose...* 1965. Pantheon. 8vo. 232p. F/dj. B24. $55.00

DE VRIES, Leonard. *Little Wide-Awake/Anthology From Victorian Children's Books.* 1967. ils. 240p. F/F. A4. $45.00

DE WAAL, Ronald Burt. *World Bibliography of Sherlock Holmes.* 1974. NYGS. 1st. VG. P3. $60.00

DE WITT, Howard A. *Chuck Berry Rock 'n' Roll Music.* 1985. Ann Arbor. Pierian. 291p. cloth. A17. $15.00

DE WITT & ERICKSON. *Littlest Reindeer.* nd (1946). Chicago. Children's Pr. probable 1st. 8vo. unp. VG. C14. $8.00

DEACON, Richard. *Spyclopedia.* 1988. Silver Arrow/Morrow. 1st Am. F/F. N4. $20.00

DEAKIN, F.W. *Brutal Friendship: Mussolini, Hitler & Fall Italian Fascism.* 1962. London. notes/index. 896p. VG/poor. S16. $28.50

DEAN, Amber. *Dower Chest.* 1970. Putnam. 1st. VG/VG. P3. $20.00

DEAN, Amber. *Wrap It Up.* 1946. Crime Club. 1st. VG/fair. P3. $20.00

DEAN, James. *Catalog James Dean.* 1991. Haga. Japanese text. photos. NF/dj. C9. $85.00

DEAN, Spencer. *Murder After a Fashion.* 1960. Doubleday. 1st. VG/VG. P3. $25.00

DEAN'S RAG BOOK COMPANY. *Railway Rag Book.* ca 1900. London. #150. 16mo. VG. D1. $200.00

DEANDREA, William L. *Killed in Paradise.* 1988. Mysterious. 1st. F/F. P3. $16.00

DEANDREA, William L. *Lunatic Fringe.* 1980. Evans. 1st. VG/VG. P3. $15.00

DEANE, Norman; see Creasey, John.

DEANS, Samuel. *New England Farmer...* 1822. Boston. Wells Lilly. 3rd. 532p. full leather. scarce. A10. $115.00

DEAR, Ian. *Early Challenges of the America's Cup.* 1986. London. Columbus Books. 1st. 160p. NF/worn. P4. $65.00

DEASON, Wilborn J. *Nature's Silent Call.* (1925). Waukegan. Bunting Pub. 1st. 405p. NF. H7. $60.00

DEAVER, John B. *Surgical Anatomy. Vol 1.* 1899. Blakiston's Son. 4to. 151 engraved pl. 632p. leather. G. H1. $36.00

DEBO, Angie. *Prairie City: Story of an American Community.* 1944. Knopf. 1st. photos. VG/VG. A25. $28.00

DEBS, Eugene V. *Writings & Speeches of Eugene V Debs.* 1948. Hermitage. 1st. NF. B2. $30.00

DEBUIGNE, Gerard. *Larousse Dictionary of Wines of the World.* 1976. Larousse. 1st. F/F. W2. $30.00

DECARPENTRY, Colonel. *Piaffer & Passage.* 1961. SF. John Howell. 1/1000. inscr. 8vo. cream cloth. F. R3. $100.00

DECHANT, John. *Modern United States Marine Corps.* 1966. Princeton. 230p. VG/VG. S16. $35.00

DECKER, John W. *Cheese Making.* 1900. Columbus, OH. 192p. VG. A10. $30.00

DECKER, Peter. *George W Solitay Collection of Western Americana.* nd. rpt. 1/100. F. A4. $125.00

DECKER, Siegfried. *Lebensbilder aus der Flora Brasiliens.* ca 1932. Sao Leopoldo. Rotemund. 8vo. ils. cloth. VG. A22. $30.00

DECKER & DECKER. *Volcanoes & the Earth's Interior.* 1982. SF. Freeman. ils/figures. 141p. VG/wrp. D8. $9.00

DECKER & HAMMOND. *Christian Mother Goose Book.* 1980. Grand Junction. Christian Mother Goose Book Co. 3rd. 111p. VG+. C14. $12.00

DEDERA, Don. *Mile in His Moccasins.* 1960. McGrew. 1st. sgn. F/VG+. A24. $25.00

DEE, Jonathan. *Lover of History.* 1990. Ticknor Fields. 1st. author's 1st novel. F/F. A24. $25.00

DEEPING, Warwick. *I Live Again.* 1942. London. 1st. VG. M2. $25.00

DEEPING, Warwick. *King Behind the King.* 1914. McBride. 1st. VG. M2. $20.00

DEFORD, Frank. *Five Strides on the Banked Track.* 1971. Little Brn. 1st. photos. VG/VG. P8. $30.00

DEFORD, Frank. *There She Is.* 1971. Viking. 1st. photos. VG/dj. P8. $15.00

DEGENER, Otto. *Ils Guide to More Common or Noteworthy Ferns...* 1930. Honolulu Star. 1st. 8vo. ils/figures/map ep. G+. A22. $30.00

DEGENHARDT, Richard K. *Belleek: Complete Collector's Guide & Ils Reference.* 1978. Portfolio. 4to. 207p. gilt khaki cloth. H1. $85.00

DEIGHTON, L. *ABC of French Food.* 1989. London. 1st. pref Egon Ronay/intro Jacques Pepin. VG/dj. T9. $15.00

DEIGHTON, Len. *Battle of Britain.* 1980. Clark Irwin. F/F. P3. $25.00

DEIGHTON, Len. *Berlin Game.* 1983. Knopf. 1st. F/F. A20. $25.00

DEIGHTON, Len. *Berlin Game.* 1983. London. Hutchinson. 1st. F/NF. B3. $30.00

DEIGHTON, Len. *Berlin Game.* 1984. Knopf. 1st Am. F/VG+. N4. $17.50

DEIGHTON, Len. *Billion Dollar Brain.* 1968. London. Cape. true 1st. NF/NF clip. M22. $65.00

DEIGHTON, Len. *Close-Up.* 1972. Clarke Irwin. 1st. VG/G+. P3. $25.00

DEIGHTON, Len. *Eleven Declarations of War.* 1971. HBJ. 1st. F/F. T12. $45.00

DEIGHTON, Len. *Expensive Place To Die.* 1967. Jonathan Cape. 1st. VG/VG. P3. $35.00

DEIGHTON, Len. *Funeral in Berlin.* 1965. Putnam. 1st. F/NF. H11. $50.00

DEIGHTON, Len. *London Match.* 1985. Knopf. 1st. F/NF. A20. $25.00

DEIGHTON, Len. *Mamista.* 1991. Century. 1st Eng. VG/dj. A20. $25.00

DEIGHTON, Len. *Spy Hook.* 1988. Knopf. 1st Am. F/F. N4. $20.00

DEIGHTON, Len. *Spy Line.* 1989. Hutchinson. 1st. F/F. P3. $23.00

DEIGHTON, Len. *Spy Sinker.* 1990. Harper Collins. 1st. F/F. N4. $20.00

DEIGHTON, Len. *Spy Story.* 1974. HBJ. 1st. VG/VG. P3. $20.00

DEIGHTON, Len. *SS-GB.* 1978. Jonathan Cape. 1st. VG/VG. P3. $25.00

DEIGHTON, Len. *SS-GB.* 1979. Knopf. 1st Am. F/VG. N4. $20.00

DEIGHTON, Len. *Winter.* 1987. Knopf. 1st. NF/F. H11. $20.00

DEIGHTON, Len. *Xpd.* 1981. Knopf. 1st. F/F. P3. $20.00

DEJERINE & GAUCKLER. *Les Manifestations Fonctionelles des Psychonevroses...* 1911. Paris. Masson. thick 8vo. later bdg. G1. $125.00

DEL CASTILLO, Bernal Diaz. *Discovery & Conquest of Mexico.* 1956. VG/VG. M17. $20.00

DEL MONTE, H.D. *Life of Chief Washakie & Shoshone Indians.* 1947. self pub. 1st. 20p. VG. J2. $18.00

DEL REY, Lester. *Best Science Fiction Stories of the Year #3.* 1974. Dutton. 1st. VG/dj. P3. $10.00

DEL REY, Lester. *Infinite Worlds of Maybe.* 1966. Holt. 1st. F/F. P3. $35.00

DEL REY, Lester. *Moon of Mutiny.* 1979. Gregg. 1st. F/F. P3. $20.00

DEL REY, Lester. *Pstalemate.* 1971. Putnam. 1st. F/NF. M19. $25.00

DEL REY, Lester. *Step to the Stars.* 1954. Phil. 1st. F/NF. B14. $95.00

DEL REY, Lester. *Tunnel Through Time.* 1966. Westminister. 1st. VG/dj. M2. $20.00

DEL REY, Maria. *Safari by Jet Through Africa & Asia.* 1962. NY. Scribner. 1st. 8vo. 32 pl/map. 308p. VG. W1. $10.00

DEL REY & KESSLER. *Once Upon a Time: Treasury of Modern Fairy Tales.* 1991. Del Rey. 1st. F/NF. P3. $25.00

DEL VECCHIO, John. *13th Valley.* 1982. Bantam. 1st. NF/VG. R14. $40.00

DELACOUR & MAYR. *Birds of the Philippines.* 1946. Macmillan. ils. 309p. VG+. M12. $37.50

DELAFIELD, R. *Report on the Art of War in Europe 1854-1856.* 1861. WA. 4to. 11 tinted pl. G+. E6. $195.00

DELANEY, John. *Blue Devils in Italy: History of 88th Infantry Division...* 1947. WA, DC. 1st. ils/maps. 360p. VG. S16. $75.00

DELANO, Alonzo. *Miner's Progress; or, Scenes in Life of California Miner.* 1853. Sacramento. Daily Union Office. 1st. 8vo. pict wrp. M1. $1,000.00

DELANY, Mary. *Letters From Mrs Delany to Mrs Francis Hamilton...* 1820. London. Longman Hurst. 1st. 8vo. 106p. full polished calf/raised bands. H13. $295.00

DELANY, Samuel. *Stars in My Pocket Like Grains of Sand.* 1984. Bantam. 1st. F/dj. M2. $20.00

DELANY, V.T.H. *Frederic William Maitland Reader.* 1957. NY. Oceana. 256p. sewn wrp. M11. $45.00

DELBANCO, Nicholas. *Writers' Trade & Other Stories.* 1990. Morrow. 1st. F/F. B4. $45.00

DELCOURT, Pierre. *Miaou-Miaou.* ca 1910. French. 5 full-p tab movables. R5. $900.00

DELDOTTO, Dave. *How To Make Nothing But Money.* 1990. S&S. 1st. 271p. F/F. W2. $25.00

DELGADO, James P. *Pearl Harbor Recalled.* 1991. Annapolis, MD. 1st. ils. 160p. F/VG. B18. $27.50

DELGADO, Jose M.R. *Physical Control of the Mind: Toward a Psychocivilized Soc.* 1969. Harper Row. 280p. VG/dj. G1. $25.00

DELISLE, Guillaume. *Atlante Novissimo Che Contiene Tuttle Le Parti Del Mondo.* 1740-1750. Venice. 2 vol. 1st. folio. 78 double-p maps. C6. $8,000.00

DELKIN, James Ladd. *Flavor of San Francisco: A Guide to the City.* 1946. Stanford. JL Delkin. ils CA artists. 128p. VG/prt wrp. K7. $20.00

DELL, William. *Works of..., Minister of the Gospel & Master of Gonvil...* 1816. Phil. Sharpless. 592p. modern bdg. V3. $125.00

DELLBRIDGE, John. *Unfit To Plead.* 1949. Hurst Blackett. 1st. VG/fair. P3. $18.00

DELLENBAUGH, Frederick S. *Canyon Voyage.* 1988. Tucson. 2nd. VG+. F7. $9.00

DELLENBAUGH, Frederick S. *Romance of the Colorado River.* 1962. Rio Grande Pr. VG. F7. $20.00

DELLENBAUGH, Frederick S. *Romance of the Colorado River...* 1909. NY. ils/fld maps. teg. pict cloth. VG-. B18. $45.00

DELMAN, David. *Nice Murders.* 1977. Morrow. 1st. NF/NF. P3. $20.00

DELMAR, Vina. *Freeways.* 1971. HBJ. 1st. F/dj. M25. $35.00

DELMAS, D.M. *Speeches & Addresses.* 1901. SF. AM Robertson. 8vo. 363p. leather. T10. $60.00

DELORIA, Ella. *Speaking of Indians.* 1944. NY. Friendship. 1st hc. VG. L3. $375.00

DELORIA, Vine Jr. *We Talk, You Listen.* 1970. Macmillan. 1st. NF/NF. L3. $75.00

DELORIA, Vine. *Custer Died for Your Skins.* 1969. Macmillan. 8vo. 279p. yel cloth. xl. VG/dj. K7. $16.00

DELPAR, Helen. *Encyclopedia of Latin America.* 1974. McGraw Hill. 1st. 650p. xl. F. O7. $45.00

DEMAREST, Ann. *Murder on Every Floor.* 1939. NY. Hillman Curl. 1st. F/VG. M15. $45.00

DEMEREC & KAUFMANN. *Drosophila Guide.* 1978. WA. rpt. 8vo. wrp. B1. $16.00

DEMI. *Demi's Count the Animals 1 2 3.* 1986. Grosset Dunlap. 1st. sm 4to. unp. NF/NF clip. C14. $18.00

DEMIJOHN, Thomas; see Disch, Thomas.

DENEVI, D. *Earthquakes.* 1977. Millbrae, CA. Celestial Arts. 1st. 230p. F/dj. D8. $15.00

DENEVI, Marco. *Secret Ceremony.* 1961. Time. ltd ed. F/NF. B35. $30.00

DENHARDT, Robert Moorman. *Horse of the Americas.* 1947. Norman, OK. 1st. 386p. VG/dj. J2. $115.00

DENING, Greg. *Mr Bligh's Bad Language. Passion, Power & Theatre...* 1992. Cambridge. 1st. 8vo. blk cloth. gilt bdg. P4. $35.00

DENISON, Edmund Beckett. *Astronomy Without Mathematics.* 1871. Putnam. from 4th London. xl. cloth. K5. $30.00

DENISON & HERBERT. *Hancock the Superb.* 1880. Phil. 431p. G. B18. $27.50

DENKER, Henry. *Experiment.* 1976. S&S. 1st. F/F. P3. $10.00

DENLINGER, Milo G. *Complete Cocker Spaniel.* nd. Silver Spring, MD. Denlingers. ils Paul Brown. VG. O3. $35.00

DENMAN, E. *Animal Africa.* 1957. London. Hale. ils/photos. 208p. NF/VG. M12. $30.00

DENNIS, C.A. *Aquatic Gastropods of the Bass Island Region of Lake Erie.* 1928. Columbus, OH. 8vo. 34p. B1. $18.00

DENNIS, C.J. *Glugs of Gosh.* 1917. Sydney. Angus Robertson. 1st. 12mo. 130p. dj. R5. $275.00

DENNIS, Jan. *Walk Beside the Sea: History of Manhattan Beach.* 1987. Manhattan Beach. Janstan Studio. 208p. dj. D11. $40.00

DENNIS, Lane T. *Letters of Francis A Schaeffer.* 1985. Crossway Books. 1st. 264p. as new/dj. B29. $9.00

DENNIS, Morgan. *Morgan Dennis Dog Book, With Some Special Cats.* 1946. Viking. 1st. 68p. NF/G+. C14. $18.00

DENNIS, Patrick. *Around the World With Auntie Mame.* 1958. Harcourt Brace. 1st. F/F. B35. $26.00

DENNIS, Patrick. *Genius.* 1962. HBW. 1st. F/dj. M25. $75.00

DENNIS, Wesley. *Flip & the Cows.* 1944. Viking. 3rd. 8vo. unp. VG. C14. $10.00

DENNIS, Wesley. *Flip.* 1941. Viking. 1st. sm 4to. VG+/G+. P2. $40.00

DENNISON, C.S. *Around the World With Texaco.* 1925. Houston. TX Co. 165p. cloth. VG. D8. $60.00

DENNISON, Tim. *American Negro & His Amazing Music.* 1963. Vintage. 1st. NF/dj. M25. $35.00

DENNY, George H. *Dread Fishwish & Other Tales.* 1975. Freshet. 222p. F/dj. A17. $15.00

DENSLOW, W.W. *Billy Mounce.* 1906. NY. Dillingham. 1st. 4to. 16 full-p pl. yel cloth/label. R5. $375.00

DENSLOW, W.W. *Denslow's Mother Goose.* 1901. NY. McClure Phillips. 1st. 4to. dk gr cloth. R5. $1,250.00

DENTINGER, Jane. *Death Mask.* 1988. Scribner. 1st. NF/NF. N4. $20.00

DENUCE, Jean. *Magellan: La Question des Moluques...* 1911. Brussles. Academies Royales. lg format. inscr pres. maps. NF. O7. $350.00

DEPEW, Chauncey. *My Memories of Eighty Years.* 1922. NY. Scribner. 1st/2nd prt. maroon cloth. VG. M24. $30.00

DER LING. *Kowtow.* 1930. Dodd Mead. 322p. F/VG. W3. $48.00

DERAUL, A. *History of Secret Societies.* 1962. Citadel. 1st Am. 256p. NF. W3. $42.00

DERHAM, William. *Physico-Theology; or, Demonstration of Being...God.* nd. np. 3rd/corrected. tall 8vo. 447p. full calf. H13. $295.00

DERLETH, August. *Beast in Holger's Woods.* 1968. CRowell. 1st. F/F. M2. $25.00

DERLETH, August. *Beyond Time & Space.* 1950. Payson Clarke. 1st. F/VG. M2. $40.00

DERLETH, August. *Chronicles of Solar Pons.* 1973. Arkham. 1/4000. F/F. R10. $10.00

DERLETH, August. *County Growth.* 1940. Scribner. 1st. inscr. NF. R10. $50.00

DERLETH, August. *Far Boundaries.* 1951. Pelligrini Cudahy. 1st. VG/VG. P3. $45.00

DERLETH, August. *Man Track Here.* 1939. Rittenhouse. 1st. sgn/dtd 1939. NF/VG. R10. $75.00

DERLETH, August. *Mischief in the Lane.* 1944. Scribner. 1st. G/G. N4. $65.00

DERLETH, August. *Moon Tenders.* 1958. DSP. 1st. inscr/dtd 1958. VG+. R10. $35.00

DERLETH, August. *Mr Fairlie's Final Journey.* 1968. Mycroft Moran. 1st. 1/3493. VG/VG. P3. $40.00

DERLETH, August. *New Poetry Out of Wisconsin.* 1969. Stanton Lee. 1st. F/F. P3. $50.00

DERLETH, August. *Other Side of the Moon.* 1949. NY. 1st. VG/VG. B5. $30.00

DERLETH, August. *Outer Reaches.* 1951. Payson Clarke. 1st. F/F. M2. $35.00

DERLETH, August. *Portals of Tomorrow.* 1954. Rinehart. 1st. NF/VG. P3. $35.00

DERLETH, August. *Strange Ports of Call.* 1948. Pelligrini Cadahy. 1st. VG/VG. P3. $35.00

DERLETH, August. *Village Daybook.* 1947. Pellegrini Cudahy. 1st. inscr/dtd 1947. ils/sgn Frank Utpatel. NF/VG. R10. $100.00

DERLETH, August. *When Evil Wakes.* 1963. Souvenir. 1st. sgn. VG/VG. P3. $75.00

DERLETH, August. *Who Knocks? Twenty Tales of Spectral for the Connoisseur.* 1946. Rinehart. 1st. NF/dj. M2. $45.00

DERLETH, August. *Who Knocks? Twenty Tales of Spectral for the Connoisseur.* 1946. Rinehart. 1st. 391p. cloth. G. A17. $17.50

DERLETH, August. *Wind Over Wisconsin.* 1938. Scribner. 1st. VG. M2. $40.00

DERRICK, Thomas. *Everyman.* 1930. London. Dent. 1/200. sgn. lacks woodcut. full vellum. VG. T10. $50.00

DERRY, Joseph T. *Address Delivered by Joseph T Derry...* ca 1913. np. 1st. 11p. VG/prt wrp. M8. $85.00

DERVAL, Paul. *Folies Bergere.* 1955. London. 1st. pref Maurice Chevalier. VG/dj. T9. $20.00

DES BARRES, Pamela. *I'm With the Band: Confessions of a Groupie.* 1987. Beech Tree/Morrow. 1st. F/F. B4. $50.00

DES CARS, A. *Treatise on Pruning Forest & Ornamental Trees.* 1906 (1881). ils. 65p. VG. E6. $15.00

DESANI, G.V. *Hali, a Play.* 1950. London. Saturn House. 1st. red cloth. dj. M24. $35.00

DESCARTES, Rene. *Geometry of...* 1925. Chicago/London. Open Court. 1st. ils. 246p. VG/dj. K3. $65.00

DESCHNER, Ramy. *Evolution of Sports & Cultural Implications of Physical Edu.* 1946. Medart Mfg. 1st. ils. VG. P8. $15.00

DESCOURTILZ, J.T. *Tropical American Birds.* 1960. HRW. facsimile. folio. 60 pl. cloth brd. F/dj/case. B24. $200.00

DESMEDT, John E. *Visual Evoked Potentials in Man: New Developments.* 1977. Oxford. Clarendon. 588p. blk cloth. G1. $65.00

DESMOND, A.J. *Hot-Blooded Dinosaurs, a Revolution in Palaeontology.* 1976. Dial. 238p. D8. $18.00

DESMOND, Adrian. *Archetypes & Ancestors.* 1982. Chicago. 287p. F/F. S15. $22.00

DESMOND, Hugh. *Terror Walks by Night.* 1945. Wright Brn. VG/VG. P3. $20.00

DESMOND, Ray. *Kew: The History of the Royal Botanic Gardens.* 1995. Kew, Harvill & RBG. 466p. A10. $25.00

DESMOND & MOORE. *Darwin: Life of a Tormented Evolutionist.* 1992. NY. Warner. 1st Am. 8vo. 808p. half cloth. NF/dj. P4. $45.00

DESROCHES-NOBLECOURT, C. *Life & Death of a Pharoah, Tutankhamen.* 1963. NGS. 1st. ils. 312p. VG/dj. W1. $22.00

DESSART, Gina. *Cry for the Lost.* 1959. Harper. 1st. VG/VG. P3. $10.00

DETECTION CLUB. *Floating Admiral.* 1981. Macmillan. F/F. P3. $25.00

DETMOLD, E.J. *Arabian Nights. Tales From the Thousand & One Nights.* 1924. Hodder Stoughton. 1st trade. 240p. 12 tipped-in pl. gilt cream cloth. B24. $400.00

DETMOLD, E.J. *Book of Baby Beasts.* 1911. London. Henry Frowde/Hodder Stoughton. 1st. 19 pl. R5. $375.00

DETROIT FREE PRESS. *Twentieth Century Cook Book.* 1925. Chicago. H&H Periodical Service Co. fair. A16. $27.50

DETWEILER, Frederick G. *Negro Press in the United States.* 1922. Chicago. 1st. 274p. NF/VG. B4. $225.00

DETZER & HARRISON. *Culture Under Canvas: Story of Chatauqua.* 1958. NY. 1st. ils. 287p. VG/dj. B5. $25.00

DEUEL, Leo. *Conquistadors Without Swords.* 1967. St Martin. 1st. 647p. F3. $25.00

DEUEL, Leo. *Testaments of Time.* 1965. Knopf. 1st. ils. VG/dj. K3. $25.00

DEUEL, Leo. *Treasures of Time.* 1961. World. 1st. ils/map ep. 318p. VG/dj. W1. $20.00

DEUTSCH, Helene. *Psychology of Women: A Psychoanalytic Interpretation. Vol 1.* 1946. London. Research Books. 1st. 312p. VG. A25. $10.00

DEUTSCH, Hermann B. *Brennan's New Orleans Cookbook.* 1974. Robert Crager. 4th. 244p. VG/VG. B10. $15.00

DEUTSCH & HANAU. *Provincetown: Story of the Theatre.* 1931. NY. Farrar. 1st. VG. B2. $65.00

DEUTSCHMAN, Deborah. *Signals.* 1978. Seaview Books. 1st. VG/VG. P3. $15.00

DEVAL, Jacqueline. *Reckless Appetites: A Culinary Romance.* 1993. Hopewell. Ecco. 1st. author's 1st book. F/dj. R13. $20.00

DEVANEY, John. *Tinyl: Story of Nate Archibald.* 1977. Putnam. 1st. phtos. F/clip. P8. $30.00

DEVANEY & GROSSO. *Murder at the Harlem Mosque.* 1977. NY. 1st. VG/dj. B5. $20.00

DEVERAUX, Roy. *Side Lights on South Africa.* 1899. Scribner. 8vo. 273p. xl. VG. W1. $22.00

DEVERDUN, Alfred. *True Mexico.* (1928). Menasha, WI. Banta. 1st. sgn. 304p. tattered dj. F3. $35.00

DEVERELL, WIlliam. *Platinum Blues.* 1988. McClelland Stewart. 1st. VG/VG. P3. $20.00

DEVEREUX, James. *Story of Wake Island.* 1947. NY. photos/roster. 252p. VG. S16. $35.00

DEVEREUX, W.B. *Position & Team Play in Polo.* 1924. NY. Brooks Bros. 1st. VG. O3. $65.00

DEVILLERS & EXBRAYAT. *Ecotoxicity of Chemicals to Amphibians.* 1992. Gordon Breach. 351p. F. S15. $30.00

DEVINE, Dominic. *This Is Your Death.* 1982. St Martin. VG/VG. P3. $15.00

DEVLIN, R.M. *Plant Physiology.* 1975. Van Nostrand. 3rd. 600p. B1. $32.00

DEVON, Gary. *Lost.* 1986. Knopf. 1st. VG/VG. P3. $18.00

DEWAR, James. *Preliminary Note on Liquifaction of Hydrogen & Helium.* 1898. Proceedings of Royal Soc. VG/wrp. K3. $50.00

DEWAR, James. *T O'Conor Sloane: Liquid Air & Liquifaction of Gases.* 18993). NY. Henley. 1st. sgn. K3. $95.00

DEWEES, William. *Essay on the Means of Lessening Pain...* 1819. Phil. 2nd. 156p. brd/paper backstrip. A13. $300.00

DEWES, Simon. *Panic in Pursuit.* 1944. Rich Cowan. VG. P3. $20.00

DEWEY, John. *Experience & Nature.* 1925. Chicago. Open Court. 1st. gilt gray-gr cloth. NF. M24. $100.00

DEWEY, Lyster H. *Fiber Production in the Western Hemisphere.* 1943. GPO. 8vo. G/wrp. A22. $40.00

DEWEY, Orville. *Works of Orville Dewey, DD, With a Biographical Sketch.* 1899 (1883). Am Unitarian Assoc. New ed. 8vo. 803p. gilt brn cloth. H1. $30.00

DEWEY, Thomas B. *Brave Bad Girls.* 1956. Inner Sanctum. 1st. VG/F. M25. $25.00

DEWEY, Thomas B. *Case of the Chased & the Unchased.* 1959. Random. 1st. NF/dj. M25. $45.00

DEWEY, Thomas B. *How Hard To Kill.* 1962. S&S. 1st. VG/VG. P3. $20.00

DEWEY, Thomas. *Journey to the Far Pacific.* 1952. NY. 335p. VG. S16. $17.50

DEXTER, Colin. *Jewel That Was Ours.* 1991. London. Macmillan. 1st. sgn. F/F. M15. $75.00

DEXTER, Colin. *Morse's Greatest Mystery & Other Stories.* 1993. London. Macmillan. 1st. F/F. T12. $22.00

DEXTER, Colin. *Wench Is Dead.* 1989. St Martin. 1st Am. F/dj. Q1. $40.00

DEXTER, Colin. *Wench Is Dead.* 1989. St Martin. 1st Am. NF/NF clip. M22. $15.00

DEXTER, John (some); see Bradley, Marion Zimmer.

DEXTER, Pete. *Deadwood.* 1986. Random. 1st. F/NF. T11. $50.00

DEXTER, Pete. *Fish Trout.* 1988. Random. 1st. F/F. M19. $25.00

DEXTER, Pete. *God's Pocket.* 1983. Random. ARC. author's 1st book. F/dj. D10. $135.00

DEXTER, Pete. *God's Pocket.* 1983. Random. 1st. author's 1st book. F/NF. B3. $85.00

DEXTER, Pete. *Paris Trout.* 1988. Random. 1st. F/F. T11. $45.00

DEXTER, Pete. *Paris Trout.* 1988. Random. 1st. F/NF. B3. $35.00

DHLOMO, R.R. *African Tragedy: A Novel in English by a Zulu Warrior.* nd (1928). Johannesburg. Lovedale Inst. 1st. author's 1st novel. F. B4. $250.00

DI CHIARA, Robert. *Dick & the Devil.* 1989. Tor. 1st. F/F. M2. $20.00

DI CHIRO, Giovanni. *Atlas of Detailed Norman Pneumoencephalographic Anatomy.* 1961. Springfield, IL. Chas Thoms. obl 4to. 328p. pict yel cloth. G1. $75.00

DI MONA, Joseph. *Last Man at Arlington.* 1973. NY. Fields. 1st. NF/F. H11. $20.00

DIAZ DEL CASTILLO, Bernal. *Discovery & Conquest of Mexico 1517-1521.* 1928. London. Routlege. 1st. Broadway Travellers series. ils/4 maps. F. O7. $45.00

DIAZ DEL CASTILLO, Bernal. *Discovery & Conquest of Mexico 1517-1521.* 1956. FSC. 8vo. 478p. VG/dj. K7. $15.00

DIBDIN, Michael. *Ratking.* 1989. Bantam. 1st. sgn. F/NF. T2. $25.00

DIBDIN, Michael. *Vendetta.* 1991. Doubleday. 1st Am. as new/F. N4. $25.00

DIBNER, Bern. *Agricola on Metals.* 1958. Norwalk, CT. Burndy Lib. 70 woodcuts. 128p. VG/wrp. K3. $30.00

DIBNER, Bern. *Alessandro Volta & the Electric Battery.* (1964). Franklin Watts. 2nd. 135p. VG/dj. K5. $12.00

DIBNER, Bern. *Darwin of the Beagle.* 1960. Norwalk, CT. Burndy Lib. facsimile manuscript p. ils. VG/wrp. K3. $25.00

DIBNER, Bern. *Luigi Galvani.* 1971. Norwalk, CT. Burndy Lib. 3 fld pl. VG/wrp. K3. $25.00

DICK, Erma Biesel. *Old House: Holiday & Party Cook Book.* 1969. NY. 1st. ils/index. VG/dj. A16. $25.00

DICK, Philip K. *Beyond Lies the Wub.* 1988. Gollancz. 1st. F/F. P3. $25.00

DICK, Philip K. *Broken Bubble.* 1989. Gollancz. 1st. F/F. P3. $30.00

DICK, Philip K. *Flow My Tears, the Policeman Said.* 1974. Doubleday. 1st. NF/dj. M2. $185.00

DICK, Philip K. *Man in the High Castle.* 1962. Putnam. 1st. F/torn. M2. $400.00

DICK, Philip K. *Maze of Death.* 1970. Doubleday. 1st. VG/NF. M2. $475.00

DICK, Philip K. *Maze of Death.* 1970. Doubleday. 1st. xl. VG/NF. M23. $60.00

DICK, Philip K. *Radio Free Albemuth.* 1985. Arbor House. 1st. F/F. P3. $20.00

DICK, Philip K. *Transmigration of Timothy Archer.* 1982. Timescape. 1st. F/F. M2. $20.00

DICK, Stewart. *Arts & Crafts of Old Japan.* 1923. Edinburgh/London. ils. 153p. VG. W3. $38.00

DICK & JANE READER. *Guess Who.* 1951. Scott Foresman. Special Junior Primer. VG. M5. $60.00

DICK & JANE READER. *Guess Who.* 1951. Scott Foresman. 95p. cloth. G+. M20. $30.00

DICK & JANE READER. *Our Big Book.* 1951. Scott Foresman. teacher ed. folio. 3 ring bdg w/6 sections/easel stand. R5. $850.00

DICK & ZELAZNY. *Deus Irae.* 1976. Doubleday. 1st. F/dj. M2. $30.00

DICKENS, Charles. *Barnaby Rudge.* 1987. Folio Soc. VG. P3. $30.00

DICKENS, Charles. *Child-Wife From the David Copperfield of Charles Dickens.* (1855). NY. Redfield. 1st. gilt blk cloth. M24. $250.00

DICKENS, Charles. *Christmas Carol.* nd (1911). Hodder Stoughton. ils AC Michael. gilt red/gold cloth. VG. M5. $75.00

DICKENS, Charles. *Christmas Carol.* 1963. NY. 1st. ils/inscr John Groth. F/F. A11. $265.00

DICKENS, Charles. *Christmas Carol.* 1989. Heinemann. F/F. P3. $20.00

DICKENS, Charles. *Great Expectations.* 1987. Oxford. 1st. F/F. P3. $11.00

DICKENS, Charles. *Haunted Man & the Ghost's Bargain.* 1848. Bradbury Evans. orig cloth/newer spine. VG. M19. $85.00

DICKENS, Charles. *Is She His Wife?* 1877. Boston. Osgood. 1st Am. gilt gr cloth. F. M24. $200.00

DICKENS, Charles. *Life of Our Lord.* 1934. 1st Am. F/G. M19. $35.00

DICKENS, Charles. *Mystery of Edwin Drood.* 1870. London. Chapman Hall. 1st/1st issue text/1st state ads. 1st state bdg. M24. $350.00

DICKENS, Charles. *Oliver Twist.* 1984. Folio Soc. VG. P3. $30.00

DICKENS, Charles. *Sissy Jupe.* 1855. NY. Redfield. 1st. gilt dk gr cloth. VG. M24. $250.00

DICKENS, Charles. *Tale of Two Cities.* 1911. Am Books. ne. 331p. G. W2. $80.00

DICKER, Laverne Mau. *Chinese in San Francisco: Pictorial History.* 1979. Dover. 1st. 4to. photos. F/wrp. R3. $30.00

DICKEY, Christopher. *With the Contras.* 1985. S&S. 1st. 327p. F3. $10.00

DICKEY, Glenn. *Jock Empire.* 1974. Chilton. 1st. sgn. F/VG. P8. $25.00

DICKEY, Herbert. *Misadventures of a Tropical Mexico.* 1929. Dodd Mead. 1st. photos. 304p. F3. $20.00

DICKEY, James. *Bronwen, the Traw & the Shape-Shifter.* 1986. HBJ. 1st. ils/sgn Richard Jessee Watson. F/F. D4. $45.00

DICKEY, James. *Deliverance.* 1970. Houghton Mifflin. 1st. author's 1st novel. F/NF. H11. $70.00

DICKEY, James. *Deliverance.* 1970. Houghton Mifflin. 1st. F/F. B35. $80.00

DICKEY, James. *Deliverance: A Screenplay.* 1982. Carbondale. S IL U. inscr. F/F. R14. $150.00

DICKEY, James. *Eye-Beaters, Blood, Victory, Madness, Buckhead & Mercy.* 1970. Doubleday. 1st. F/VG+. B4. $125.00

DICKEY, James. *Helmets.* 1964. Longman. 1st Eng. VG/VG. M19. $50.00

DICKEY, James. *Night Hurdling.* 1983. Bruccoli Clark. 1st. F/dj. V1. $20.00

DICKEY, James. *To the White Sea.* 1993. Houghton Mifflin. 1st. inscr/sgn. F/F. A23. $60.00

DICKEY, James. *To the White Sea.* 1993. Houghton Mifflin. 1st. sgn. F/dj. R13. $45.00

DICKEY, James. *Tucky the Hunter.* 1978. Crown. 1st. 44p. F/F. D4. $40.00

DICKEY, James. *Zodiac.* 1976. Dougleday. 1st. inscr. NF/NF. B3. $75.00

DICKEY & SHUPTRINE. *Jericho, the South Beheld.* 1974. Birmingham. 1st. sgns. obl folio. F/NF. C6. $200.00

DICKINSON, Emily. *Letters of Emily Dickinson.* 1894. Boston. Roberts Bros. 1st/1st prt. 2 vol. 1/1000. gilt gr cloth (1st bdg). M24. $400.00

DICKINSON, Emily. *Poems, Second Series.* 1892. Boston. Roberts Bros. 1st/2nd issue. 1/1000. teg. gilt gr cloth (B bdg). M24. $800.00

DICKINSON, Emily. *Poems...Edited by Two of Her Friends.* 1891. Boston. Roberts. 1st. 12mo. 230p. silk marker/not bevelled. F. M1. $1,000.00

DICKINSON, H.W. *James Watt: Craftsman & Engineer.* 1935. Cambridge. 1st. ils. 207p. K3. $55.00

DICKINSON, H.W. *Mathew Boulton.* 1936. Cambridge. 1st. 14 pl/ils. 218p. K3. $55.00

DICKINSON, H.W. *Robert Fulton: Engineer & Artist.* 1913. Bodley Head. 1st. assn sgn. 333p. K3. $75.00

DICKINSON, LAIRD & MAXWELL. *Voices From the Southwest.* 1976. Northland. 1st. ils/notes/bibliography. 156p. B19. $25.00

DICKINSON, Lawrence S. *Lawn: Culture of Turf in Park, Golfing & Home Areas.* 1936 (1931). NY. 2nd revised. ils. 128p. VG/torn. B26. $26.00

DICKINSON, Peter. *Annerton Pit.* 1977. Atlantic/Little Brn. 1st. F/F. P3. $23.00

DICKINSON, Peter. *Blue Hawk.* 1976. Little Brn. 1st Am. NF/dj. M2. $15.00

DICKINSON, Peter. *Cold Giant.* 1984. Dutton. 1st Am. ils Alan E Cober. 69p. as new/VG. H1. $12.00

DICKINSON, Peter. *Lizard in the Cup.* 1972. Harper Row. 1st. VG/VG. P3. $20.00

DICKINSON, Peter. *Old English Peep Show.* 1969. Harper Row. 1st. VG/VG. P3. $20.00

DICKINSON, Peter. *Poison Oracle.* 1974. Pantheon. VG/VG. P3. $18.00

DICKINSON, Robert. *Human Sex Anatomy.* 1949. Baltimore. 2nd. 145p. A13. $75.00

DICKINSON & TITLEY. *Richard Trevithick: The Engineer & the Man.* 1934. Cambridge. 2nd imp. ils. 290p. VG. K3. $60.00

DICKINSON & WOOD. *Harmony in Marriage.* 1960. Manhasset. Round Table. 34th. 122p. VG+/wrp/box. A25. $12.00

DICKS, Terrance. *Doctor Who: Wheel in Space.* 1988. WH Allen. TVTI. F. P3. $14.00

DICKSON, Carter; see Carr, John Dickson.

DICKSON, Gordon R. *Alien Art.* 1973. Dutton. 1st. F/F. P3. $25.00

DICKSON, Gordon R. *Dragon & the George.* 1976. SFBC. 1st. F/dj. M2. $15.00

DICKSON, Gordon R. *In Iron Years.* 1980. Doubleday. 1st. VG/VG. P3. $15.00

DICKSON, Gordon R. *In Iron Years.* 1980. Doubleday. 1st. F/F. M2. $17.00

DICKSON, Gordon R. *Mutants.* 1970. Macmillan. 1st. VG/VG. P3. $20.00

DICKSON, Gordon R. *Outposter.* 1972. Lippincott. 1st. VG/dj. M2. $15.00

DICKSON, Gordon R. *Pritcher Mass.* 1972. Doubleday. 1st. F/F. M2. $50.00

DICKSON, Gordon R. *R-Master.* 1973. Lippincott. 1st. VG/dj. M2. $17.00

DICKSON, Gordon R. *Spacepaw.* 1969. Putnam. 1st. VG/VG. P3. $30.00

DICKSON, Gordon R. *Star Road.* 1975. Robert Hale. 1st. VG/VG. P3. $15.00

DICKSON, Gordon R. *Time Storm.* 1977. St Martin. 1st. F/dj. M2. $25.00

DICKSON, Grierson. *Traitors' Market.* 1936. Hutchinson. 1st. G+. P3. $20.00

DIDEROT, Denis. *Dialogues.* 1927. London. 1st thus. trans Birrell. A17. $15.00

DIDEROT, Denis. *Rameu's Nephew & Other Works.* 1926. London. Chapman Hall. 1st thus. 1/1000. VG. A17. $15.00

DIDIER, Eugene L. *Life & Letters of Madame Bonaparte.* 1879. Scribner. 1st. 276p. stp cloth. H1. $27.50

DIDION, Joan. *Book of Common Prayer.* 1977. S&S. 1st. F/dj. A24. $35.00

DIDION, Joan. *Democracy.* 1984. S&S. 1st. F/F. A20. $20.00

DIDION, Joan. *Play It As It Lays.* 1970. FSG. 1st. author's 3rd book. F/NF. A24. $45.00

DIDION, Joan. *Play It As It Lays.* 1971. Weidenfeld Nicolson. 1st. NF/dj. M25. $15.00

DIDION, Joan. *Run River.* 1963. NY. Obolensky. 1st. sgn/dtd 1994. NF/VG. R14. $125.00

DIDION, Joan. *Run River.* 1963. Obolensky. 1st. author's 1st book. F/NF. D10. $95.00

DIDION, Joan. *Salvador.* 1983. S&S. 1st. sgn/dtd 1997. F/F. R14. $45.00

DIDION, Joan. *White Album.* 1979. S&S. 1st. NF/NF. A24. $10.00

DIEHL, C. Lewis. *National Formulary of Unofficial Preparations.* 1906. Baltimore. Am Pharm Assn. 3rd. 267p. VG. A10. $28.00

DIEHL, William. *Chameleon.* 1981. Random. 1st. sgn. F/F. D10. $60.00

DIEHL, William. *Sharky's Machine.* 1978. Delacorte. 1st. sgn. F/NF. D10. $85.00

DIETRICH, Marlene. *Marlene.* 1989. NY. 1st. trans S Attanasio. VG/VG. T9. $12.00

DIETZ, Marjorie. *Complete Guide to Successful Gardening.* 1978. Mayflower. 1st. NF. W2. $20.00

DIGBY, Kenelm Edward. *Introduction to History of Law of Real Property...* 1897. Oxford. Clarendon. later blk buckram. M11. $125.00

DIGBY, Kenelm. *Two Treatises: Nature of Bodies...Nature of Man's Soul...* 1658. London. Williams. 4to. diagrams. panelled calf. R12. $825.00

DIKTY, Alan S. *Boy's Book Collector.* nd. Starmont. hc. F. P3. $75.00

DILLARD, Annie. *American Childhood.* 1987. Harper Row. 1st. F/NF. B3. $40.00

DILLARD, Annie. *Encounters With Chinese Writers.* 1984. Wesleyan U. 1st. F/NF. T11. $55.00

DILLARD, Annie. *Holy the Firm.* 1977. Harper Row. 1st. sgn. author's 3rd book. F/dj. D10. $65.00

DILLARD, Annie. *Living.* 1992. Harper Collins. 1st ltd of 300. sgn. F/case. A18/R13. $125.00

DILLARD, Annie. *Living.* 1992. Harper Collins. 1st. sgn. 1st fiction book. NF/dj. D10. $40.00

DILLARD, Annie. *Teaching a Stone To Talk.* 1982. Harper Row. 1st. sgn. author's 5th nonfiction book. F/F. D10. $50.00

DILLARD, Annie. *Teaching a Stone To Talk.* 1982. Harper Row. 1st. F/F. R14. $40.00

DILLARD, Annie. *Tickets for a Prayer Wheel.* 1974. MO U. 1st. author's 1st book. NF/NF. L3. $650.00

DILLARD, J.M. *Lost Years.* 1989. Pocket. 1st. TVTI. VG/VG. P3. $18.00

DILLARD, R.H.W. *Horror Films.* 1976. NY. 1st. inscr. 132p. F/wrp. A11. $65.00

DILLON, Eilis. *Death in the Quadrangle.* 1956. Faber. 1st. VG/VG. P3. $40.00

DILLON, Richard H. *Embarcadero: Being a Chronicle of True Sea Adventures...* 1959. Coward McCann. 1st sgn. 313p. F/dj. K7. $30.00

DILLON, Richard H. *Hatchet Men: Story of the Tong Wars in San Francisco...* 1962. Coward McCann. 1st. 16p photo section. 375p. gilt cloth. D11. $60.00

DILLON, Richard H. *Images of Chinatown: Louis J Stellman's Chinatown Photos.* 1976. BC of CA. 1/450. 8vo. inscr. decor brd/red cloth spine. F. R3. $135.00

DILLON, Richard H. *Maynard Dixon; or, From Coronado to Canon de Chelly.* 1976. SF. Lester Lloyd. 1/200. sgn/pub sgn. 28p. as new/heavy paper wrp. K7. $25.00

DILLON, Richard H. *San Francisco: Adventures & Visionaries.* 1983. Tulsa. Continental Heritage. 224p. as new/dj. M8. $45.00

DILLWYN, George. *Occasional Reflections, Offered Principally for Use...* 1815. Burlington, NJ. David Allinson. 1st. 205p. V3. $20.00

DILNOT, George. *Scotland Yard.* 1929. Geoffrey Bles. VG. P3. $40.00

DILTS, Marion May. *Telephone in a Changing World.* 1941. Longman Gr. 1st. rebound. K3. $15.00

DIMAND, M.S. *Handbook of Muhammadan Art.* 1958. ils. VG/VG. M17. $20.00

DIMENT, Adam. *Dolly, Dolly Spy.* 1967. Dutton. F/F. P3. $15.00

DIMMOCK, Charles H. *Modern: A Fragment.* 1866. Richmond, VA. Davies. 1st. 8vo. 24p. prt wrp. M1. $225.00

DIMONA, Joseph. *To the Eagle's Nest.* 1980. Morrow. 1st. VG/VG. P3. $15.00

DINESEN, Isak. *Babettes Gaestebud.* 1952. Copenhagen. Forlaget Fremad. 1st book ed. NF/self wrp. B4. $600.00

DINESEN, Isak. *Carnival.* 1975. 1st. NF/NF. S13. $20.00

DINESEN, Isak. *Winter's Tales.* 1942. Random. 313p. VG. A25. $10.00

DINGLE, A.E. *Island Woman.* 1928. Chelsea House. 1st. VG. M2. $15.00

DINGMAN, Larry. *Bibliography of Limited & Signed Editions in Literature.* 1973. VG. K3. $20.00

DINNERSTEIN, Harvey. *Artist at Work.* 1978. Watson Guptil. ils. VG/VG. M17. $20.00

DIODORUS. *Historical Library of Diodorus, in Fifteen Books.* 1814. London. M'Dowell. 2 vol. 8vo. half morocco. W1. $125.00

DIPPER, Alan. *Golden Virgin.* 1973. Walker. 1st. VG/VG. P3. $20.00

DISCH, Thomas M. *Bad Moon Rising.* 1973. Harper Row. 1st. VG/VG. P3. $28.00

DISCH, Thomas M. *Businessman.* 1984. Harper Row. 1st. VG/VG. P3. $20.00

DISCH, Thomas M. *Camp Concentration.* 1969. Doubleday. 1st. xl. VG/dj. M2. $35.00

DISCH, Thomas M. *Getting Into Death & Other Stories.* 1976. Knopf. 1st. F/NF. M19. $25.00

DISCH, Thomas M. *MD.* 1991. Knopf. 1st. F/F. H11/W2. $35.00

DISCH, Thomas M. *New Improved Sun.* 1975. Harper Row. 1st. VG/G+. P3. $22.00

DISCH, Thomas M. *Tale of Dan de Lion.* 1986. Minneapolis. Coffee House. 1st Am. sgn. 28p. F/F. D4. $45.00

DISDIN, Michael. *Cabal.* 1992. London. 1st. F/F. T12. $45.00

DISHER, M. Willson. *Fairs, Circuses & Music Halls.* 1942. London. Britain in Pictures series. yel decor brd. F/NF. A11. $30.00

DISNEY, Doris Miles. *Departure of Mr Gaudette.* 1964. Crime CLub. 1st. VG/VG. P3. $30.00

DISNEY STUDIOS. *Adventures of Mickey Mouse, Book 1.* 1931. Phil. McKay. 1st. mc ils ep. paste-down over cloth. A17. $400.00

DISNEY STUDIOS. *Adventures of Mickey Mouse, Book 2.* 1932. Phil. McKay. sm 8vo. pict brd. VG. D1. $400.00

DISNEY STUDIOS. *Blancaneve ei Sette Nani (Snow White...).* 1940. Milano. Casa Editrice Carroccio. obl 4to. pict paper wrp. R5. $375.00

DISNEY STUDIOS. *Cooking With Mickey Around Our World.* nd. recipes from Walt Disney World/Disneyland. A16. $20.00

DISNEY STUDIOS. *Danny the Little Black Lamb.* 1948. Whitman Story Hour. VG+. N1. $15.00

DISNEY STUDIOS. *Donald & Mickey Cub Scouts.* 1950. Whitman. Cozy Corner Book. G+. N1. $17.50

DISNEY STUDIOS. *Donald Duck & His Nephews.* nd (1940). Boston. VG. M17. $40.00

DISNEY STUDIOS. *Donald Duck & the Lost Mesa Ranch.* 1966. Whitman. Tween Age Book. pict bdg. VG. N1. $15.00

DISNEY STUDIOS. *Donald's Day at the Farm.* ca 1955. England. Birn Bros. 4to. 10p. mc pict wrp. R5. $125.00

DISNEY STUDIOS. *Donald's Inventory.* 1938. England. Collins. Donald w/robot on bdg. VG. N1. $100.00

DISNEY STUDIOS. *Dumbo of the Circus.* 1948. Boston. Heath. 1st. VG. B5. $20.00

DISNEY STUDIOS. *Elmer Elephant.* 1936. Phil. McKay. 1st. 48p. pict cloth. R5. $300.00

DISNEY STUDIOS. *Here They Are.* nd (1940). Boston. ils. VG. M17. $40.00

DISNEY STUDIOS. *Lion King.* 1994. Mouse Works. 96p. F. N1. $8.00

DISNEY STUDIOS. *Little Pigs Picnic.* 1939. 1st. ils Margaret Wise Brown. NF. S13. $55.00

DISNEY STUDIOS. *Mickey Mouse, the Miracle Maker.* nd. Whitman. 24mo. 96p. pict paper label. VG. D1. $50.00

DISNEY STUDIOS. *Mickey Mouse & Bobo the Elephant.* 1934. Racine. Whitman. 1st. Big Little Book format. 428p. NF. A11. $75.00

DISNEY STUDIOS. *Mickey Mouse Annual (Back Again!).* 1930s. Dean & Son. Mickey w/bow on bdg. G+ (no spine). N1. $60.00

DISNEY STUDIOS. *Mickey Mouse Annual (Out Again!).* ca 1930s. Dean & Son. Mickey w/bat on bdg. G+ (no spine). N1. $70.00

DISNEY STUDIOS. *Mickey Mouse Magic Water Colour Book.* 1939. London. Dean. 1st Eng. 4to. mc pict wrp. R5. $285.00

DISNEY STUDIOS. *Mickey Mouse Medley.* ca 1950. London. Dean. 16p. mc pict stiff paper wrp. R5. $100.00

DISNEY STUDIOS. *Mickey Mouse Story Book.* 1931. Phil. McKay. 8vo. 62p. blk lettered cloth/pict label. R5. $575.00

DISNEY STUDIOS. *Mickey Mouse Tales.* 1953. London. Dean. 4to. 45p. mc pict brd. R5. $150.00

DISNEY STUDIOS. *Mickey Sees the USA.* 1944. Heath. 138p. pict cloth. VG. M20/P2. $40.00

DISNEY STUDIOS. *Minnie Mouse & the Antique Chair.* nd. Whitman. 24mo. 96p. VG. D1. $50.00

DISNEY STUDIOS. *Nutcracker Suite, From Walt Disney's Fantasia.* 1940. Collins. ils w/6 piano arrangements. ils brd. C9. $150.00

DISNEY STUDIOS. *Pinocchio.* ca 1940. Milano. Casa Editrice Carroccio. lg sq 4to. mc paper wrp. R5. $350.00

DISNEY STUDIOS. *Pinocchio.* 1940. DC Heath. 51 mc ils. brd. NF/sans. C9. $75.00

DISNEY STUDIOS. *Pinocchio.* 1940. London. Dean. 4to. 48p. pict paper wrp. R5. $175.00

DISNEY STUDIOS. *Pop-Up Minnie Mouse.* 1933. Blue Ribbon. 1st 8vo. 3 popups/wht ils. pict brd. complete. VG. from $700 to $775.00

DISNEY STUDIOS. *Robber Kitten.* 1935. Whitman. obl 4to. G+. P2. $180.00

DISNEY STUDIOS. *Sketchbook.* 1993. Old Sturbridge, CT. Applewood. 1st Am trade. facsimile 1938 British. F/F. T10. $75.00

DISNEY STUDIOS. *Sneeuwwije en de Zeven Dwergen (Snow White...).* ca 1940. Amsterdam. 64p. pict brd. dj. R5. $150.00

DISNEY STUDIOS. *Snow White & the Seven Dwarfs.* 1938. Grosset Dunlap. obl 8vo. mc cloth pict brd. dj. R5. $125.00

DISNEY STUDIOS. *Three Caballeros.* 1944. NY. Random. 1st. lg 4to. mc pict brd. dj. R5. $675.00

DISNEY STUDIOS. *Three Orphan Kittens.* 1935. Whitman. obl 4to. VG/G+. P2. $250.00

DISNEY STUDIOS. *Victory March; or, The Mystery of the Treasure Chest.* 1942. Random. 1st. 4to. pict brd. R5. $450.00

DISNEY STUDIOS. *Walt Disney's Christmas Parade.* ca 1955. London. Juvenile Prod. 4to. mc pict brd. unused. R5. $125.00

DISNEY STUDIOS. *Walt Disney's Circus.* 1944. S&S. 1st. 8vo. unp. VG/VG. D1. $225.00

DISNEY STUDIOS. *Walt Disney's Snow White & the Seven Dwarfs Stamp Book.* 1957. London. Adprint. 4to. mc pict paper covers. R5. $100.00

DISNEY STUDIOS. *Walt Disney's Version of Pinocchio.* 1989 (1939). Abrams. facsimile. 174 drawings/34 mc pl/2 fld ils. NF. C9. $50.00

DISNEY STUDIOS. *Walt Disney's Visit to Disneyland.* 1965. Whitman. Big Tell-a-Tale. VG+. N1. $12.00

DISNEY STUDIOS. *Who's Afraid of the Big Bad Wolf.* (1933). Phil. McKay. 12mo. 31p. VG/pict wrp. D1. $85.00

DISNEY STUDIOS. *101 Dalmatians.* 1961. Big Golden Book. pict bdg. VG. N1. $9.00

DISRAELI, Isaac. *Curiosities of Literature...* 1864. Riverside. 4 vol. 8vo. half brn morocco. VG. H13. $295.00

DITMARS, Raymond L. *Book of Prehistoric Animals...* 1935. Lippincott. ils Helene Carter. T10. $35.00

DIVINE, A.D. *Dunkirk.* 1948. NY. 1st. 311p. VG/dj. B18. $22.50

DIVINE, David. *Opening of the World.* 1973. Putnam. 1st Am. cloth. VG/dj. M20. $30.00

DIVINE, Robert A. *Blowing on the Wind: The Nuclear Test Ban Debate...* 1978. Oxford. 1st. VG/VG. V4. $10.00

DIX & HOOD. *Vertigo.* 1984. Chichester, Eng. Wiley. 491p. prt decor yel laminated brd. G1. $50.00

DIXON, Don. *Universe.* 1978. Houghton Mifflin. 1st. F/dj. M2. $35.00

DIXON, Franklin W. *Hardy Boys' Detective Handbook.* 1959. Grosset Dunlap. VG. P3. $10.00

DIXON, Franklin W. *Hardy Boys: Clue of the Broken Blade (#21).* 1942. Grosset Dunlap. 1st. 218p. VG/dj (lists to this title). M20. $25.00

DIXON, Franklin W. *Hardy Boys: Firebird Rocket (#57).* nd. Grosset Dunlap. lists to this title. bl pict bdg. F. N1. $7.00

DIXON, Franklin W. *Hardy Boys: Ghost at Skeleton Rock (#37).* 1957. Grosset Dunlap. lists to this title. VG/torn. M20. $25.00

DIXON, Franklin W. *Hardy Boys: Great Airport Mystery (#9).* 1930. Grosset Dunlap. 210p. tan cloth. VG/dj (lists 16 titles). M20. $125.00

DIXON, Franklin W. *Hardy Boys: House on the Cliff (#2).* 1927. Grosset Dunlap. lists 21 titles. VG/dj. M20. $50.00

DIXON, Franklin W. *Hardy Boys: House on the Cliff (#2).* 1953. Grosset Dunlap. tan bdg. F/VG. N1. $20.00

DIXON, Franklin W. *Hardy Boys: Hunting for Hidden Gold (#5).* 1928. Grosset Dunlap. 214p+ads. cloth. VG/dj (lists 18 titles). M20. $135.00

DIXON, Franklin W. *Hardy Boys: Mark on the Door (#13).* 1934. Grosset Dunlap. 219+ad. cloth. VG/dj (lists 18 titles). M20. $40.00

DIXON, Franklin W. *Hardy Boys: Secret of Old Mill (#3).* 1927. Grosset Dunlap. thick ed. lists to Footprints Under Window. VG/dj. M20. $100.00

DIXON, Franklin W. *Hardy Boys: Secret of the Lost Tunnel (#29).* 1950. Grosset Dunlap. 1st. 210p. cloth. VG+/dj. M20. $30.00

DIXON, Franklin W. *Hardy Boys: Shore Road Mystery (#6).* 1928. Grosset Dunlap. lists 20 titles. VG/dj. M20. $100.00

DIXON, Franklin W. *Hardy Boys: Sign of the Crooked Arrow (#28).* 1949. Grosset Dunlap. 1st. 214p. VG/dj. M20. $35.00

DIXON, Franklin W. *Hardy Boys: Sign of the Crooked Arrow (#28).* 1958. Grosset Dunlap. F/VG. N1. $15.00

DIXON, Franklin W. *Hardy Boys: Tower Treasure (#1).* 1927. Grosset Dunlap. 214p+ads. red cloth. VG/dj (lists 3 titles). M20. $375.00

DIXON, Franklin W. *Hardy Boys: While the Clock Ticked (#11).* 1932. Grosset Dunlap. lists 20 titles. VG/dj. M20. $135.00

DIXON, Franklin W. *Ted Scott: Across the Pacific (#7).* 1928. Grosset Dunlap. 1st. 216p. VG/dj (lists to this title). M20. $35.00

DIXON, Franklin W. *Ted Scott: Danger Trails of the Sky (#14).* 1931. Grosset Dunlap. 1st. lists 18 titles. 216p. VG/dj. M20. $40.00

DIXON, Franklin W. *Ted Scott: Hunting the Sky Spies (#19).* 1941. Grosset Dunlap. 1st. 216p. VG/dj (lists 18 titles). M20. $65.00

DIXON, Franklin W. *Ted Scott: Lost at the South Pole.* 1930. Grosset Dunlap. VG. P3. $15.00

DIXON, Franklin W. *Ted Scott: Pursuit Patrol (#20).* 1943. Grosset Dunlap. 1st. last in series. VG/rpr. M20. $65.00

DIXON, Franklin W. *Ted Scott: Rescued in the Clouds (#2).* 1927. Grosset Dunlap. lists 18 titles. VG/dj. M20. $25.00

DIXON, Franklin W. *Ted Scott: Through the Air to Alaska (#12).* 1930. Grosset Dunlap. lists 18 titles. VG/dj. M20. $30.00

DIXON, GRINNELL & LINSDALE. *Fur-Bearing Mammals of California: Their Natural History...* 1937. Berkeley. 1st. 2 vol. 8vo. gilt brn cloth. NF. R3. $150.00

DIXON, Joseph S. *Wildlife Portfolio of the Western National Parks.* 1942. GPO. 1st. 4to. 121p. VG. T10. $50.00

DIXON, Maynard. *Images of the Native American.* 1981. CA Academy of Sciences. 42 mc pl/photos. 96p. w/prospectus. F. K7. $75.00

DIXON, Roger. *Noah II.* 1975. Harwood Smart. F/F. P3. $15.00

DIXON, Ruth. *Three Little Bunnies.* 1950. Rand McNally. ils Dale Rooks. unp. glossy brd. VG+. M20. $15.00

DIXON, Stephen. *Fall & Rise.* 1985. Northpoint. 1st. F/dj. A24. $35.00

DIXON, Stephen. *Fall & Rise.* 1985. SF. Northpoint. 1st. sgn. author's 8th book. F/dj. D10. $50.00

DIXON, Stephen. *Love & Will.* 1989. Latham. Paris Review Ed. 1st. sgn. F/F. D10. $40.00

DIXON, William Scarth. *Fox-Hunting in the Twentieth Century.* 1925. NY. Dingwall-Rock. 1st Am. VG. O3. $45.00

DIXON, Winifred Hawkridge. *Westward Hoboes, Ups & Downs of Frontier Motoring.* 1921. Scribner. 1st. 377p. VG+. F7. $45.00

DIXON & FITCH. *Personality of Plants.* 1923. NY. ils. 229p. VG+. B26. $24.00

DJERASSI, Carl. *Cantor's Dilemma.* 1989. 1st. inscr. author's 1st novel. F/F. M19. $25.00

DOANE, Pelagie. *Three Prayers.* 1941. Grosset Dunlap. 32p. VG. P3. $30.00

DOBBIN, Muriel. *Taste for Power.* 1980. Malek. 1st. F/F. M2. $17.00

DOBBINS, Paul H. *Death Trap.* 1951. Phoenix. 1st. VG/fair. P3. $15.00

DOBBS, Caroline C. *Men of Champoeg: A Record of the Lives of Pioneers...* 1932. Portland. Metropolitan. 1st. sgn/dtd. cloth. D11. $50.00

DOBEREINER, Peter. *Down the Nineteenth Fairway.* 1983. Atheneum. 1st. F/VG+. P8. $15.00

DOBIE, Charles Caldwell. *San Francisco's Chinatown.* 1936. Appleton Century. 1st. ils/sgn EH Suydam. gilt red cloth. F/dj. R3. $75.00

DOBIE, Charles Caldwell. *San Francisco's Chinatown.* 1936. NY. Appleton Century. 1st. ils/sgn Suydam. G+. O4. $20.00

DOBIE, J. Frank. *Ben Lilly Legend.* 1952. London. Hammond. ils/photos/pl. 273p. NF. M12. $27.50

DOBIE, J. Frank. *Bulwark.* 1946. Doubleday. 1st. F/F. B35. $30.00

DOBIE, J. Frank. *Mustangs.* 1952. Bramhall. 376p. VG/dj. J2. $55.00

DOBIE, J. Frank. *Texan in England.* 1945. Little Brn. dj. A19. $35.00

DOBREE, Bonamy. *Unacknowledged Legislator.* 1942. Allen Unwin. 1st. VG. P3. $20.00

DOBSON, Austin. *Story of Rosina & Other Verses.* 1895. Dodd Mead. 1st. ils Hugh Thomson. NF. M19. $75.00

DOBSON, Austin. *Story of Rosina.* 1895. London. Kegan Paul. ils Hugh Thomson. 8vo. aeg. gr cloth. T10. $100.00

DOBYNS, Stephen. *Boat Off the Coast.* 1987. Viking. 1st. VG/VG. P3. $18.00

DOBYNS, Stephen. *Concurring Beasts.* 1972. Atheneum. 1st. author's 1st book. F/NF. M23. $75.00

DOBYNS, Stephen. *Dancer With One Leg.* 1983. Dutton. 1st. sgn. F/F. R14. $40.00

DOBYNS, Stephen. *Saratoga Headhunter.* 1985. Viking. 1st. F/F. H11. $40.00

DOBYNS, Stephen. *Saratoga Longshot.* 1976. Atheneum. 1st. NF/dj. M25. $50.00

DOBYNS, Stephen. *Saratoga Snapper.* 1986. Viking. 1st. F/F. H11. $35.00

DOCK, Phyllis. *Little Hawk: Story of a Morgan Stallion.* 1967. Hampden Highlands, ME. Highland Pr. 1st. VG. O3. $58.00

DOCKSTADER, Frederick J. *American Indian in Graduate Studies: A Bibliography...* 1957. NY. Mus of Am Indian. 399p. prt wrp. D11. $30.00

DOCKSTADER, Frederick J. *Kachina & the White Men.* 1954. Bloomfield Hills. Cranbrook Inst Science. 1st. NF/VG. L3. $200.00

DOCTOROW, E.L. *American Anthem.* 1982. NY. Stewart Tabori Chang. 1st. sgn. F/sans. R14. $100.00

DOCTOROW, E.L. *Billy Bathgate.* 1989. Random. UP. F/wrp. D10. $75.00

DOCTOROW, E.L. *Billy Bathgate.* 1989. Random. 1st. F/F. H11. $30.00

DOCTOROW, E.L. *Billy Bathgate.* 1989. Random. 1st. NF/NF. A20. $20.00

DOCTOROW, E.L. *Book of Daniel.* 1971. Random. 1st. rem mk. NF/NF. M22. $40.00

DOCTOROW, E.L. *Book of Daniel.* 1971. Random. 1st. sgn. author's 3rd novel. F/NF. D10. $150.00

DOCTOROW, E.L. *Loon Lake.* 1980. Random. 1/350. sgn/#d. F/F case/swrp. B2. $75.00

DOCTOROW, E.L. *Loon Lake.* 1980. Random. 1st. inscr. F/F. R14. $40.00

DOCTOROW, E.L. *Ragtime.* 1975. Random. 1st. F/NF. H11. $40.00

DOCTOROW, E.L. *Ragtime.* 1975. Random. 1st. 1/150. sgn/#d. F/case. B4. $400.00

DOCTOROW, E.L. *World's Fair.* 1985. Random. 1st. F/F. h11. $30.00

DODD, C.H. *Interpretation of the Fourth Gospel.* 1954. Cambridge. 478p. VG. B29. $26.00

DODD, C.H. *Moffatt Commentary: Romans.* 1932. Harper. 246p. G/torn. B29. $8.00

DODD, William. *Sisters; or, History of Lucy & Caroline Sanson.* 1791. London. Harrison. 2 vol in 1. sm 4to. 169p. recent bdg. H13. $265.00

DODGE, David. *Angel's Ransom.* 1956. Random. 1st. VG/VG. P3. $25.00

DODGE, David. *Long Escape.* 1948. Random. 1st. F/dj. M15. $45.00

DODGE, David. *20,000 Leagues Behind the 8 Ball.* 1951. Random. 1st. VG/VG. P3. $25.00

DODGE, Ernest S. *Thirty Years of the American Neptune.* 1972. Cambridge. 8vo. ils. 300p. bl cloth. P4. $40.00

DODGE, Katherine Sturges. *Dodge's Red Picture Book, Fairy Tales for Little Folk.* nd. Dodge. 4to. red brd/mc pl. VG. M5. $65.00

DODGE, Katherine Sturges. *Peeps, the Really Truly Sunshine Fairy.* 1918. Volland. 1st. VG. M5. $65.00

DODGE, Louis. *Sandman's Mountain.* 1920. Scribner. 1st. gilt gr cloth. VG+. M5. $55.00

DODGE, Theodore Ayrault. *Bird's-Eye View of Our Civil War.* 1897. Boston. new revised. 8vo. 348p. VG. B14. $45.00

DODMAN, Frank E. *Observer's Book of Ships.* 1952-66.. London. Warne. ils. 190p. T7. $18.00

DODOENS, De Rembert. *Histoire des Plantes. Petit Recueil...Et Liqueurs...* 1978. Brussels. Cent Nat Hist Sci. 622p. sm folio. A10. $150.00

DODRILL, William Christian. *Moccasin Tracks & Other Imprints.* 1974. Parson, WV. rpt 1915. 298p. VG. B18. $22.50

DODWELL, Christina. *Traveller on Horseback in Eastern Turkey & Iran.* 1989. NY. Walker. 1st Am. 8vo. 3 maps. 191p. NF/dj. W1. $18.00

DOERR, Harriet. *Stones for Ibarra.* 1984. Viking. 1st. author's 1st book. NF/NF. B3. $50.00

DOERR, Harriet. *Stones for Ibarra.* 1984. Viking. 1st. inscr/dtd 1995. F/F. R14. $150.00

DOGGETT, Frank. *Cigarette Cards & Novelties.* 1981. Michael Joseph. ils. NF. C9. $45.00

DOIG, Ivan. *Dancing at the Rascal Fair.* 1987. Atheneum. 1st. NF/dj. R14. $35.00

DOIG, Ivan. *Dancing at the Rascal Fair.* 1987. Atheneum. 1st. sgn. F/NF. B3. $40.00

DOIG, Ivan. *Dancing at the Rascal Fair.* 1987. Atheneum. 1st. sgn. M/dj. A18. $60.00

DOIG, Ivan. *English Creek.* 1984. Atheneum. 1st. F/NF clip. T11. $60.00

DOIG, Ivan. *English Creek.* 1984. Atheneum. 1st. sgn. M/dj. A18. $80.00

DOIG, Ivan. *Heart Earth.* 1993. Atheneum. 1st. sgn. M/dj. A18. $35.00

DOIG, Ivan. *House of Sky: Landscapes of a Western Mind.* 1978. HBJ. 1st. sgn. author's 1st book. M/dj. A18. $175.00

DOIG, Ivan. *Ride With Me, Mariah Montana.* 1990. Atheneum. 1st. sgn. F/F. B3. $45.00

DOIG, Ivan. *Ride With Me, Mariah Montana.* 1990. Atheneum. 1st. sgn. M/dj. A18. $50.00

DOIG, Ivan. *Sea-Runners.* 1982. Atheneum. ARC/1st. author's 3rd book. F/NF. D10. $135.00

DOIG, Ivan. *Sea-Runners.* 1982. Atheneum. 1st. sgn. M/dj. A18. $100.00

DOIG, Ivan. *Winter Brothers: Season at the Edge of America.* 1980. HBJ. 1st. author's 2nd book. F/F. D10. $85.00

DOIG, Ivan. *Winter Brothers: Season at the Edge of America.* 1980. HBJ. 1st. NF/clip. M25. $75.00

DOIG, Ivan. *Winter Brothers: Season at the Edge of America.* 1980. HBJ. 1st. sgn. M/dj. A18. $100.00

DOLAN, J.R. *English Ancestral Names: Evolution of Surname...* 1972. VG/VG. M17. $17.50

DOLINGER, Jane. *Inca Gold: Find It If You Can...* 1968. Chicago. Regnery. 1st. photos. 189p. dj. F3. $15.00

DOLLFUS, A. *Surfaces & Interiors of Planets & Satellites.* 1970. NY. Academic. 8vo. 569p. xl. G. K5. $40.00

DOLMETSCH, Carl R. *Smart Set.* 1966. Dial. 1st. sgn. VG/VG. B11. $75.00

DOLPHIN, Rex. *Driven To Kill.* 1969. Howard Baker. 1st. VG/VG. P3. $25.00

DOLSON, Hildegarde. *Great Oildorado.* 1959. Random. sgn. 300p. B11. $35.00

DOMANSKA, J. *Best of the Bargain.* 1977. Greenwillow. 1st. sm 4to. unp. VG+. C14. $14.00

DOMANSKA, J. *Whizz!* 1974. Hamish Hamilton. 1st Eng. 33p. F/NF. D4. $35.00

DOMATILLA, John. *Last Crime.* 1984. Atheneum. 1st. VG/VG. P3. $20.00

DOMBHART, J.M. *History of Walker County.* 1937. VG. M17. $25.00

DOMHOFF, G. William. *Bohemian Grove & Other Retreats. A Study...* 1974. Harper Row. 1st. F/F. O4. $20.00

DOMICO, T. *Bears of the World.* 1988. NY. ils author/M Newman. distribution maps. 189p. NF/NF. M12. $30.00

DOMINGO, Xavier. *Villa Milo.* 1962. Brazillier. 1st. F/NF. B2. $30.00

DOMINIC, R.B. *Epitaph for a Lobbyist.* 1974. Doubleday Crime Club. 1st. VG/G+. P3. $20.00

DOMINIC, R.B. *Unexpected Developments.* 1984. St Martin. 1st. VG/VG. P3. $20.00

DONAHEY, Mary Dickerson. *Adventures of a Happy Dolly.* 1914. Barse Hopkins. 1st. ils Grace Evans. 4to. gr cloth/label. dj. R5. $175.00

DONAHEY, William. *Teenie Weenie Town.* 1942. Whittlesey. 1st. red cloth. VG. M5. $110.00

DONAHEY, William. *Teenie Weenies in the Wildwood.* 1923. Reilly Lee. orig ed. 4to. cloth/mc pl. G. M5. $165.00

DONALDSON, Frances. *PG Wodehouse, the Authorized Biography.* 1982. Weidenfeld Nicolson. 1st. F/F. P3. $25.00

DONALDSON, Gerald. *Books.* 1981. NY. 1st. 128p. F/dj. A17. $17.50

DONALDSON, Gerald. *Books.* 1981. Van Nostrand. 2nd. ils. VG/dj. K3. $15.00

DONALDSON, Henry Herbert. *Growth of the Brain. Contemporary Science Series.* 1895. London. Walter Scott. 1st/Am issue. 374p. G1. $65.00

DONALDSON, J.K. *Surgical Disorders of the Chest: Diagnosis & Treatment.* 1944. Phil. 1st. 364p. A13. $35.00

DONALDSON, Professor. *Rudimentary Treatise on Clay Lands & Loamy Soils.* 1852. London. Weale. 140p. A10. $25.00

DONALDSON, Samuel. *Roentgenologist in Court.* 1937. Springfield. 1st. 230p. xl. A13. $20.00

DONALDSON, Stephen. *Chronicles of Thomas Covenant.* 1977. Holt. 3 vol. 1st. F/dj. M2. $145.00

DONALDSON, Stephen. *Daughter of Regals.* 1984. Del Rey. 1st. F/F. P3. $15.00

DONALDSON, Stephen. *Lord Foul's Bane.* 1977. Holt. 1st. F/F. M2. $40.00

DONALDSON, Stephen. *Mirror of Her Dreams.* 1986. Del Rey. 1st. VG/VG. P3. $25.00

DONALDSON, Stephen. *One Tree.* 1982. Del Rey. 1st. VG/VG. P3. $20.00

DONALDSON, Stephen. *Power That Preserves.* 1977. Holt. 1st. F/F. M2. $40.00

DONALDSON, Stephen. *Real Story.* 1991. Bantam. 1/350. sgn/#d. F. M2. $125.00

DONALDSON, Thomas. *Public Domain: Its History, With Statistics.* 1884. WA. House of Representatives. 19 (of 20) fld maps. 1343p. D11. $250.00

DONATO, Nicolo. *L'Homme d'Etat.* 1767. Plomteux. 3 vol. 8vo. vellum. R12. $375.00

DONLEAVY, J.P. *Fairy Tales of NY.* 1961. Random. 1st. F/NF. M19. $45.00

DONLEAVY, J.P. *Further in the Destinies of Darcy Dancer...* 1983. Franklin Lib. 1st/ltd. sgn. full leather. Q1. $60.00

DONLEAVY, J.P. *Ginger Man.* 1958. Paris. Olympia. Traveller's Companion series. 1/500. F/F. B3. $225.00

DONNEL, C.P. *Murder-Go-Round.* 1945. McKay. VG. P3. $15.00

DONNELLY, Ignatius. *Atlantis: The Antediluvian World.* 1882. Harper. 1st. VG. B2. $125.00

DONNELLY, Ignatius. *Atlantis: The Antediluvian World.* 1949. NY. Gramercy. revised. ils. 355p. dj. K3. $20.00

DONNELLY, Ignatius. *Ragnarok.* 1883. Appleton. VG. M2. $30.00

DONNELLY, M. *Chinese Junks & Other Native Craft.* (1939). Shanghai. Kelly Walsh. 3rd. ils/pl. 142. pict brd. VG. M12. $60.00

DONNELLY, T. *Rocky Mountain Politics.* 1940. Albuquerque. 1st. 304p. VG. B5. $30.00

DONOFRIO, Beverly. *Riding in Cars With Boys.* 1990. Morrow. 1st. author's 1st book. F/F. R13. $25.00

DONOGHUE & WHEELER. *Save the Dolphins.* 1990. Sheridan. 119p. F/F. S15. $12.00

DONOVAN, Robert J. *PT 109.* 1961. McGraw Hill. 1st. sgn. 248p. G-. B11. $100.00

DONOVAN & DRURY. *Fatso: Football When Men Were Really Men.* 1987. Morrow. 1st. F/F. B4. $35.00

DOOB, Leonard. *Crocodile Has Me by the Leg.* 1967. NY. Walker. 1st. 56p. cloth. NF/dj. D4. $45.00

DOOLEY, Dennis. *Dashiell Hammett.* 1984. NY. Ungar. 1st. F/F. M15. $45.00

DOOLEY & TANIS. *Lewis Carroll's Hunting of the Snark...* 1981. trade ed. 1/5000. ils. 266p. F/F. A4. $85.00

DOOLITTLE, Hilda. *Palimpsest.* 1968. Carbondale. S IL U. 1st. 268p. xl. VG/dj. A25. $15.00

DOOLITTLE, Jerome. *Bombing Officer.* 1982. Dutton. 1st. F/F. B4. $150.00

DOPAGNE, Jacques. *Dali.* 1974. Leon Amiel. 1st. VG/VG. P3. $15.00

DORAN, Adelaide L. *Pieces of Eight Channel Islands.* 1980. Glendale, CA. Clark. 1st. VG/sans. O4. $40.00

DORDON-AINE. *Bibliotheca Esoterica: Catalogue Annote et Illustre...* nd. rpt. 1/100. 6707 entries. F. A4. $95.00

DORIAN, Emil. *Quality of Witness: A Romanian Diary.* 1982. JPS. 350p. VG/dj. S3. $30.00

DORIAN & WILSON. *Trails West & the Men Who Made Them.* 1955. McGraw Hill. 8th. lg 8vo. xl. VG/dj. C8. $17.50

DORN, Michael. *Tycoons in the Kitchen.* 1968. NY. Dorn. 1st. VG/dj/box. A16. $25.00

DORNBUSCH, Charles H. *Pennsylvania German Barns.* 1958. PA German Folklore Soc. 1st. scarce. O3. $165.00

DORRIS, Michael. *Broken Cord.* 1989. Harper Row. 1st. F/NF. D10. $45.00

DORRIS, Michael. *Broken Cord.* 1989. Harper Row. 1st. sgn. F/F. B3. $75.00

DORRIS, Michael. *Morning Girl.* 1992. Hyperion. 1st. F/F. B4. $65.00

DORRIS, Michael. *Yellow Raft in Blue Water.* 1987. Holt. ARC. sgn. F/wrp. B4. $150.00

DORRIS, Michael. *Yellow Raft in Blue Water.* 1987. Holt. 1st. inscr/sgn. F/F. L3. $125.00

DORRIS, Michael. *Yellow Raft in Blue Water.* 1987. Holt. 1st. sgn. F/F. R14. $90.00

DORRIS, Michael. *Yellow Raft in Blue Water.* 1987. NY. Holt. 1st. author's 1st novel. NF/dj. L3. $50.00

DORRIS & ERDRICH. *Crown of Columbus.* 1991. Harper Collins. 1st. inscr Dorris/sgn Erdrich. F/NF. L3. $65.00

DORSEY, G.A. *Cheyenne. I. Ceremonial Organization. II. The Sun Dance.* 1971 (1905). Rio Grande Classic. rpt. ils. 186p. F. M4. $35.00

DORSON, R.M. *Jonathan Draws the Log Bow: New England Popular Tales...* 1946. Harvard. VG/VG. M17. $15.00

DORST, Jean. *Life of Birds.* 1974. Columbia. 2 vol. NF/VG. S15. $55.00

DORST, Jean. *Migrations of Birds.* 1963. Houghton Mifflin. 1st Am. 476p. bl cloth. B22. $15.00

DORST, Jean. *South American & Central America: A Natural History.* 1967. Random. 1st. 298p. dj. F3. $25.00

DOS PASSOS, John. *Airways Inc.* 1928. Macaulay. 1st. VG/fair. M23. $50.00

DOS PASSOS, John. *Garbage Man.* 1926. Harper. 1st. VG/poor. M23. $75.00

DOS PASSOS, John. *Grand Design.* 1949. Houghton Mifflin. 1st. 440p. red cloth. F/fair. B22. $12.00

DOS PASSOS, John. *Orient Express.* 1927. NY. 1st. ils. VG/VG. B5. $60.00

DOS PASSOS, John. *42 Parallel.* 1930. Harper. 1st. NF/fair. M23. $75.00

DOS REIS (QUITA), Domingos. *Sylva no Lamentavel Terremoto do Primeiro Novembro 1755...* 1756. Lisbon. Patriarcal Francisco Luiz Ameno. 1st. marbled brd. R15. $500.00

DOSS, James. *Shaman Laughs.* 1995. St Martin. 1st. sgn. F/F. A23. $45.00

DOSTOEVSKY, Fyodor. *Idiot.* 1956. LEC. 1st thus. 1/1500. ils/sgn Fritz Eichenberg. F/remnant dj/case. Q1. $150.00

DOSTOEVSKY, Fyodor. *Possessed.* 1959. LEC. 1st thus. 1/1500. ils/sgn Fritz Eichenberg. F/glassine/case. Q1. $175.00

DOTEN, Dana. *Art of Bundling.* 1938. Countryman/Farrar Rinehart. 1st. 190p. VG+/dj. M20. $30.00

DOTY, Richard. *Photography in America...* 1974. NY. 255p. lg 4to. dj. A17. $35.00

DOUBLEDAY, Abner. *Chancellorsville & Gettysburg.* 1882. 1st. 243p. O8. $21.50

DOUCETTE, Earle. *Fisherman's Guide to Maine.* (1951). Random. stated 1st. 13maps/map ep. 308p. VG. H7. $20.00

DOUGALL, William H. *Off for California: Letters, Log & Sketches of...* 1949. Oakland. Biobooks. CA Centennial ed. 1/600. bl cloth. as new. K7. $50.00

DOUGHTY, A.G. *Quebec of Yester-Year.* 1932. Thomas Nelson. 1st. 198p. VG/VG. M20. $35.00

DOUGHTY, Charles M. *Travels in Arabia Deserta.* 1953. NY. Heritage. intro TE Lawrence. ils Edy Legrand. 453p. VG. W1. $35.00

DOUGLAS, Alan. *For the King.* 1926. Macrae Smith. 1st. F/dj. M2. $100.00

DOUGLAS, Amanada. *Clover's Princess.* 1904. ils John Rea Neill. VG+. S13. $25.00

DOUGLAS, Arthur. *Last Rights.* 1986. St Martin. 1st. F/F. P3. $15.00

DOUGLAS, Kirk. *Dance With the Devil.* 1990. Random. 1st. sgn. VG/VG. A23. $35.00

DOUGLAS, Kirk. *Gift.* 1992. Warner. 1st. inscr. VG/VG. A23. $30.00

DOUGLAS, Marjory Stoneman. *Nine Florida Stories by Marjory Stoneman Douglas.* 1990. Jacksonville. 1st. sgn. F/F. B11. $85.00

DOUGLAS, Norman. *Fountains in the Sand.* 1921. London. Secker. 1st. 8vo. 336p. VG. W1. $9.00

DOUGLAS, R. Alan. *John Prince: A Collection of Documents.* 1980. Toronto. Champlain Soc. 229p. red cloth. P4. $95.00

DOUGLASS, Benjamin Wallace. *Every Step in Beekeeping.* 1921. Bobbs Merrill. VG. P3. $20.00

DOUGLASS, Frederick. *Narrative of Life of Frederick Douglass, an American Slave.* 1845. Boston Anti-Slavery Office. 1st. 125p. VG. B4. $1,500.00

DOUTHIT, Mary Osborn. *Souvenir of Western Women.* 1905. Anderson Duniway. 1st. full-p repro Remington painting. 200p. VG/pict wrp. J2. $255.00

DOVE, Rita. *Darker Face of the Earth.* 1994. Brownsville. Storyline. 1/250. sgn. F/sans. R14. $125.00

DOW, Ethel C. *Diary of a Birthday Doll.* 1908or. NY. Barse Hopkins. 1st. ils Florence Nosworthy/LC Smith. gr cloth. dj. R5. $200.00

DOW & EDMONDS. *Pirates of the New England Coast 1630-1730.* 1923. Salem. Marine Research Soc. 1st. 8vo. 394p. red buckram. P4. $165.00

DOWELL, Coleman. *One of the Children Is Crying.* 1968. NY. Random. 1st. inscr. author's 1st book. F/dj. Q1. $75.00

DOWNER, Jane. *Happy Dieter.* 1974. Regional Ent. G. A16. $10.00

DOWNER, L.J. *Leges Henrici Primi.* 1972. Oxford. 1st Eng trans. M11. $85.00

DOWNES, Donald. *Red Rose for Maria.* 1959. Rinehart. 1st. VG/G+. P3. $15.00

DOWNEY, Fairfax. *Cannonade: Great Artillery Actions of History...* 1966. 1st. VG/VG. M17. $30.00

DOWNEY, Fairfax. *Free & Easy.* 1951. Scribner. 1st. 8vo. NF/dj. M5/O3. $25.00

DOWNEY, Glansville. *Ancient Antioch.* 1963. Princeton. ils/maps. 298p. VG. W1. $22.00

DOWNEY, HALFORD & KEELER. *Militant Methodism: Story of 1st National Convention...* 1913. Methodist Book Concern. 379p. VG. B29. $7.00

DOWNEY, Joesph T. *Cruise of the Portsmouth 1845-1847.* 1963. New Haven/London. 2nd issue. 8vo. 246p. VG/dj. P4. $45.00

DOWNIE, William. *Hunting for Gold.* 1971 (1893). Palo Alto. rpt. ils. 412p. VG/dj. B18. $25.00

DOWNIE & ROBERTSON. *Wind Has Wings, Poems From Canada.* 1968. NY. Walck. ARC/1st. 95p. F/NF. D4. $35.00

DOWNING, A.J. *Cottage Residences; or, Series of Designs Rural Cottages...* 1844. Wiley Putnam. 2nd. 187p. A10. $75.00

DOWNING, A.J. *Fruits & Fruit Trees of America.* 1852. NY. Wiley. 594p. A10. $90.00

DOWNING, A.J. *Horticulturist & Journal of Rural Art & Rural Taste.* 1847. Albany. Tucker. 12 vol. complete w/all pl. A10. $10.00

DOWNING, A.J. *Treatise on Theory & Practice on Landscape Gardening...* 1849. Putnam. 4th. lg 8vo. 532p. gilt gr cloth. VG. C6. $225.00

DOWNING, C.T. *Neuralgia: Its Various Forms, Pathology & Treatment.* 1851London.. 1st. 375p. cloth/rebacked. A13. $300.00

DOWNING, Todd. *Cat Screams.* 1934. Garden City. Crime Club. 1st. author's 2nd book. NF. L3. $275.00

DOWNING, Todd. *Murder on the Tropic.* 1935. Garden City. Crime Club. 1st. VG. L3. $125.00

DOWNING, Todd. *Night Over Mexico.* 1937. Garden City. Crime Club. 1st. author's 7th novel. G. L3. $75.00

DOWNING, Todd. *Vultures in the Sky.* 1935. Garden City. Crime Club. 1st. NF. L3. $125.00

DOWNS, Joseph. *American Furniture. Queen Ann & Chippendale Periods...* 1977 (1952). Viking/Bonanza. ils/pl. cloth. dj. D2. $75.00

DOWNS, Karl E. *Meet the Negro.* 1943. Login. later prt. red cloth. VG-. M25. $25.00

DOXIADIS, Constaninos. *Ekistics: An Intro to Science of Human Settlements.* 1968. OUP. 527p. dj. A10. $85.00

DOYLE, Arthur Conan. *Adventures of Sherlock Holmes.* 1892. London. Newnes. 1st. VG. M15. $950.00

DOYLE, Arthur Conan. *Captain of the Polestar.* nd. Homewood. G+. P3. $35.00

DOYLE, Arthur Conan. *Complete Sherlock Holmes Long Stories.* 1987. Galley. F/F. P3. $15.00

DOYLE, Arthur Conan. *Duet.* 1899. Appleton. 1st. VG. P3. $50.00

DOYLE, Arthur Conan. *Hound of the Baskervilles.* 1902. McClure Phillips. 1st Am/2nd state (R on c p). ils Paget. G. H1. $65.00

DOYLE, Arthur Conan. *Later Adventures of Sherlock Holmes.* 1952. LEC. 1st thus. 1/1500. edit Edgar W Smith. F/glassine/case. Q1. $150.00

DOYLE, Arthur Conan. *Man From Archangel & Other Tales of Adventure.* 1919. NY. 256p. 12mo. orange cloth. G. A17. $20.00

DOYLE, Arthur Conan. *Micah Clarke.* 1894. Harper. NF. M2. $35.00

DOYLE, Arthur Conan. *Rodney Stone.* 1896. Appleton. 1st. VG. P3. $150.00

DOYLE, Arthur Conan. *Sir Nigel.* 1906. McClure Phillips. 1st. VG. P3. $85.00

DOYLE, Arthur Conan. *Songs of Action.* 19898. NY. 1st. VG. M17. $35.00

DOYLE, Arthur Conan. *Stark Munro Letters.* 1934. John Murray. VG/G+. P3. $35.00

DOYLE, Arthur Conan. *Tragedy of the Korosko.* 1898. London. Smith Elder. 1st. gilt stp bdg. NF. M15. $200.00

DOYLE, Arthur Conan. *Uncle Bernac.* 1897. London. Smith Elder. 1st. G. M23. $60.00

DOYLE, Arthur Conan. *Vital Message.* 1919. Doran. 1st. VG. P3. $60.00

DOYLE, Arthur Conan. *Works of...* 1937. Garden City. 5 vol. VG. M2. $50.00

DOYLE, James E. *Chronicle of England, BC 55-AD 1485.* 1864. London. Longman Gr. 4to. 462p. aeg. half morocco. F. B24. $650.00

DOYLE & MCDIARMID. *Baker Street Dozen.* 1987. Congdon Weed. F/F. P3. $20.00

DOZOIS, Gardner. *Day in the Life.* 1972. Harper. 1st. F/F. M2. $20.00

DR. SEUSS; see Geisel, Theodor Seuss.

DRABBLE, Margaret. *Needle's Eye.* 1972. Knopf. 1st Am. F/dj. A24. $35.00

DRABBLE, Margaret. *Radiant Way.* 1987. Weidenfeld Nicholson. 1st. NF/dj. A24. $30.00

DRABBLE, Margaret. *Realms of Gold.* 1975. Knopf. 1st Am. NF/dj. A24. $25.00

DRACO, F. *Devil's Church.* 1951. Rinehart. 1st. VG/VG. P3. $30.00

DRAGO, Henry Sinclair. *Great American Cattle Trails.* 1945. Bramhall. dj. A19. $30.00

DRAGO, Henry Sinclair. *Steamboaters, from Early Side-Wheelers to Big Packets.* 1967. Dodd Mead. 1st. 269p. VG/dj. M20. $35.00

DRAGSTED, O. *Gems & Jewelry in Color.* 1975. Macmillan. 1st Am. 232p. F/dj. D8. $24.00

DRAKE, Alexander. *Three Midnight Stories.* 1916. Century. 1st. 1/500. F/dj/box. M2. $100.00

DRAKE, Joseph Rodman. *Culprit Fay & Other Poems.* 1835. NY. George Dearborn. 1st. contemporary bdg. M1. $150.00

DRAKE, Robert L. *Boy Allies in the Baltic (#2).* 1916. AL Burt. lists 6 titles. 252p. G/tattered. M20. $15.00

DRAKE, S. *Particular History of the 5 Years French & Indian War.* 1870. 1st. lg 8vo. VG. E6. $60.00

DRAKE, Samuel Adams. *Making of New England.* 1886. ils. VG. M17. $35.00

DRAKE & HALLECK. *Croakers.* 1860. NY. Bradford Club. 1st complete. lg 8vo. 191p. cloth. M1. $225.00

DRAPE, Joe. *In the Hornets' Nest.* 1989. St Martin. 1st. photos. F/F. P8. $12.50

DREADSTONE, Carl; see Campbell, Ramsey.

DREANY, E. Joseph. *Cowboys in Pop-Up Action.* 1951. London. Publicity Prod. 5 double-p popups. obl 4to. stiff pict sbdg. R5. $150.00

DREER, Henry. *Dreer's Garden Book 1932.* 1931. Phil. Dreer. 225p. NF. A10. $30.00

DREER, Henry. *Dreer's Vegetables Under Glass.* 1896. Phil. Dreer. 96p. gilt cloth. A10. $40.00

DREIFUSS, Jerome. *Catherine & Potemkin.* 1937. Covici Friede. 1st. 343p. cloth. VG/dj. M20. $28.00

DREISER, Theodore. *Genius.* 1915. NY/ London. 1st. gilt red cloth. NF. M24. $100.00

DREISER, Theodore. *Plays of the Supernatural.* 1916. John Lane. 1st. VG. B2. $75.00

DREISER, Theodore. *Traveler at Forty.* 1913. NY. Century. 1st. teg. gilt red cloth. F. M24. $85.00

DREISS, Joseph G. *Gari Melchers: His Works in the Belmont Collection.* 1984. Charlottesville. 221p. cloth. dj. D2. $85.00

DRESNER, Samuel H. *Zaddik: Doctrine of Zaddik According to Writings...* 1960. London. Abelard Schuman. 312p. VG/G. S3. $26.00

DREW, Katherine Fischer. *Laws of the Salian Franks.* 1991. Phil. PA U. 261p. prt sewn wrp. M11. $15.00

DREXLER, Arthur. *Drawings of Frank Lloyd Wright.* 1962. Horizon. 1st. 320p. VG/VG. A8. $95.00

DRIGGS & LEWINE. *Black Beauty, White Heat: A Pictorial History...Jazz...* 1982. Morrow. 1st. F/F. B2. $200.00

DRINKARD, Michael. *Green Bananas.* 1989. Knopf. 1st. author's 1st novel. VG/VG. L1. $45.00

DRINKWATER, John. *Robert Burns.* 1925. Houghton Mifflin. 1st. 12mo. red cloth. NF. T10. $50.00

DROTNER. *English Children & Their Magazines 1751-1945.* 1988. Yale. ils. 282p. F/F. A4. $35.00

DRUCKER-COLIN & MCGAUGH. *Neurobiology of Sleep & Memory.* 1977. Academic. 456p. panelled bl fabricoid. VG/dj. G1. $50.00

DRUETT, Joan. *She Was a Sister Sailor: Whaling Journals of Mary Brewster.* 1992. Mystic Seaport Mus. 449p. gilt rose cloth. P4. $40.00

DRUITT, Robert. *Principles & Practice of Modern Surgery.* 1844. Phil. 153 woodcuts. 568p. full leather. A13. $100.00

DRUMMOND, Henry. *Tropical Africa.* 1888. Scribner/Welford. authorized ed. sm 8vo. 5 maps. VG. W1. $25.00

DRUMMOND, John. *Charter for the Soil.* 1944. London. Faber. 219p. dj. A10. $25.00

DRUMMOND, Walter; see Silverberg, Robert.

DRURY, Allen. *God Against the Gods.* 1976. Franklin Pr. 1st. aeg. gilt leather. F/sans/cb enclosure. T11. $40.00

DRURY, Clifford Merrill. *Diaries & Letters of Henry H Spalding & Asa Bowen.* 1958. Clark. 1st. Northwest Hist Series IV. 1st. sgn. ils/maps. VG. J2. $185.00

DRURY, Clifford Merrill. *Marcus Whitman, MD: Pioneer & Martyr.* 1937. Caxton. 1st. ils. 473p. gilt cloth. D11. $50.00

DRURY, Clifford Merrill. *My Road From Yesterday.* 1984. Clark. 1st. 354p. VG. J2. $115.00

DRUSE, Ken. *Natural Garden.* 1989. NY. 400+ mc photos/plans. 296p. F/dj. B26. $25.00

DRUXMAN, Michael B. *Paul Mini, His Life & His Films.* 1974. Barnes. photos. NF/dj. C9. $40.00

DRY, Florence Swinton. *Sources of Wuthering Heights.* 1937. Cambridge. W Heffer. 1st. 48p. cloth. VG/dj. M20. $30.00

DRYDEN, Cecil P. *Give All to Oregon! Missionary Pioneers of the Far West.* 1968. Hastings. 1st. 256p. cloth. VG+/dj. M20. $35.00

DRYDEN, John. *Fables, From Boccaccio & Chaucer.* 1822. Chiswick. Whittingham. sm 8vo. 267p. aeg. full calf/raised bands/ labels. B24. $200.00

DRYDEN, Ken. *Game.* 1983. Canada. Macmillan. later prt. F/F. P8. $15.00

DU BOIS, Ellen Carol. *Feminism & Suffrage: Emergence of Independent Woman...* 1994. AZ U. 1st. as new/dj. V4. $20.00

DU BOIS, Theodora. *Listener.* 1953. Crime Club. 1st. VG/VG. P3. $15.00

DU BOIS, Theodora. *Murder Strikes an Atomic Unit.* 1946. Crime Club. 1st. VG/rpr. M2. $17.00

DU BOIS, Theodora. *Solution T-25.* 1951. Doubleday. 1st. NF/dj. M2. $18.00

DU BOIS, W.E.B. *Quest of the Silver Fleece.* 1911. Chicago. McClurg. 1st. ils HS DeLay. NF. B4. $500.00

DU BOIS, W.E.B. *Reader.* 1970. Harper Row. 1st. NF/dj. M25. $25.00

DU BOIS, William Pene. *Elizabeth the Ghost Cow.* 1936. Viking. true 1st/rpt author's 1st children's book. 41p. VG/VG. P2. $45.00

DU BOIS, William Pene. *Gentleman Bear.* 1985. FSG. 1st. 78p. VG+/dj. M20. $15.00

DU BOIS, William Pene. *Lion.* 1956. Viking. 1st. lg 8vo. NF/NF. C8. $35.00

DU BOIS, William Pene. *Mother Goose for Christmas.* 1973. Viking. stated 1st. VG+/VG. M5. $65.00

DU BOIS, William Pene. *Peter Graves.* 1950. Macmillan. 1st. 168p. VG/G+. P2. $50.00

DU BOIS, William Pene. *Twenty-One Balloons.* 1947. Viking. 1st (cloth backed/ wicker patterned brd). NF. A4. $50.00

DU BOIS, William Pene. *Twenty-One Balloons.* 1947. Viking. 1st. 8vo. 180p. VG. D1. $35.00

DU BOURDIEU, William J. *Baby on Her Back: History of Huguenot Family DuBourdieu.* 1967. private prt. 1st. 358p. bl-gr cloth. B22. $10.00

DU CHAILLU, Paul. *My Apingi Kingdom: With Life in Great Sahara & Sketches...* 1871. Harper. ils/engravings. 254p. VG. W1. $45.00

DU CHAILLU, Paul. *My Apingi Kingdom: With Life in the Great Sahara.* 1928. NY. 263p. A17. $17.50

DU GUAY-TROUIN, Rene. *Memoires de Monsieur DuGuay-Trouin, Lieutenant General...* 1740. Paris? CFS. 1st authorized. 6 engravings. 284p. recent morocco. R15. $1,400.00

DU MAURIER, Daphne. *Glass-Blowers.* 1963. Doubleday. 1st Am. gilt gray cloth. NF. T12. $150.00

DU MAURIER, Daphne. *I'll Never Be Young Again.* 1932. Doubleday. 1st. author's 2nd book. VG. M22. $25.00

DU MAURIER, Daphne. *Parasites.* 1949. Canada. Ryerson. 1st. VG/VG. P3. $20.00

DU MAURIER, Daphne. *Rule Britannia.* 1972. Gollancz. 1st. VG/VG. P3. $25.00

DU MAURIER, Daphne. *Scapegoat.* 1957. Doubleday. 1st. VG/VG. P3. $30.00

DU MAURIER, George. *Martian.* 1897. Harper. VG. P3. $75.00

DU MAURIER, George. *Trilby.* (1894). Grosset Dunlap. photoplay. 464p. cloth. VG/dj. M20. $20.00

DU MAURIER, George. *Trilby.* 1894. Harper. G+. P3. $35.00

DU MAURIER, George. *Trilby.* 1894. Harper. 1st. VG. M2/P3. $35.00

DU PETIT-THOUARS, Abel. *Voyage of the Venus: Sojourn in California.* 1956. Los Angeles. Dawson. 10 pl. 113p. patterned brd. K7. $165.00

DU RAY, Carel. *Art of the Ancient Near & Middle East.* 1969. NY. Abrams. 1st. 291 pl/maps. 264p. F/F. W3. $38.00

DU SOLIER, W. *Indumentataria Antigua Mexicana.* 1950. Mexico. Ediciones Mexicanas. lg 4to. 110p. gray cloth. VG. K7. $95.00

DUBNOW, S.M. *Jewish History: Essay in Philosophy of History.* 1927 (1903). JPS. 184p. VG. S3. $19.00

DUBOS, Rene J. *Professor, the Institute & DNA.* 1976. Rockefeller U. 1st. ils. 8vo. 238p. xl. K3. $15.00

DUBUS, Andre. *Adultery & Other Choices.* 1977. Boston. Godine. 1st. F/NF. D10. $110.00

DUBUS, Andre. *Broken Vessels.* 1991. Boston. Godine. 1st. sgn. F/F. R14. $50.00

DUBUS, Andre. *Finding a Girl in America.* 1980. Boston. Godine. 1st. sgn. author's 4th book. F/NF. D10. $90.00

DUBUS, Andre. *Last Worthless Evening.* 1986. Boston. Godine. 1st. F/F. D10. $50.00

DUBUS, Andre. *Lieutenant.* 1967. NY. Dial. 1st. author's 1st book. F/VG. L3. $350.00

DUBUS, Andre. *Selected Stories.* 1988. Boston. Godine. 1st. F/F. D10. $45.00

DUBUS, Andre. *Selected Stories.* 1988. Godine. 1st. NF/F. A20. $30.00

DUBUS, Andre. *Voices From the Moon.* 1984. Boston. Godine. 1st. sgn. F/F. R13. $50.00

DUC DE SAINT-SIMON, Louis. *Memoirs of...* 1959. NY. LEC. 1st thus. 1/1500. 2 vol. ils/sgn Pierre Brissaud. F/glassine/case. Q1. $75.00

DUCA, Lo. *Technique de l'Erotisme.* 1958. Pauvert Editeur. French text. ils/photos. w/pub card. dj. C9. $85.00

DUCASSE, Isadore. *Maldoror (Les Chants de Maldoror).* 1943. New Directions. 1st. 8vo. NF/NF case. B2. $85.00

DUCHENNE DE BOULOGNE, G.B.A. *Treatise on Localized Electrization...* 1992 (1871). NY. Classics Neurology/Neurosurgery Lib. facsimile. G1. $65.00

DUCHESNE, Andre. *Histoire d'Angleterre, d'Escosse, et d'Irlande.* 1666. Paris. Iolly. 2 vol. folio. title devices. calf. R12. $400.00

DUCKED, James H. *Men of the Steel Rails: Workers on the Atchison, Topeka...* nd. NE U. 1st. VG/VG. V4. $35.00

DUCKETT, Margaret. *Mark Twain & Bret Harte.* 1964. Norman, OK. 1st. gilt gray cloth. F/dj. M24. $65.00

DUDA & LUBOS. *Minerals of the World.* 1989. Arch Cape. 4to. 520p. F/F. B1. $65.00

DUDA & LUBOS/FA & SOUTHWICK. *Ecology & Behavior of Food-Enhanced Primate Group.* 1988. NY. 355p. F/F. B1. $52.00

DUDENAY, Henry Ernest. *536 Puzzles & Curious Problems.* 1967. NY. 428p. VG/dj. S1. $15.00

DUDLEY, A.T. *Phillips Exeter: Making the Nine (#2).* 1904. Lee Shepard. 332p. G. M20. $22.50

DUDLEY, Elizabeth. *Unity of Evolutionary Biology.* 1991. Portland. 2 vol. F/F. S15. $40.00

DUERRENMATT, Friedrich. *Pledge.* 1959. Knopf. 1st. F/F. B35. $60.00

DUFF, Hector. *Ivory Graves.* 1926. Doubleday. 1st. VG. M2. $25.00

DUFF, James. *Fruits of Ontario.* 1914. Toronto. Cameron. 320p. gr cloth. A10. $65.00

DUFFIELD, Anne. *Stamboul Love.* 1934. Knopf. 1st Am. NF/VG. B4. $85.00

DUFFIELD, Anne. *Stamboul Love.* 1934. Knopf. 1st. VG. P3. $15.00

DUFFIELD, Kenneth G. *Four Little Pigs, Didn't Have a Mother.* (1919). Phil. Altemus. Wee Book For Wee Folks. ils KG Duffield. 24mo. 60p. VG. D1. $12.50

DUFFIELD, Kenneth G. *Little Wise Chicken That Knew It All.* 1918. Altemus Wee Book. 16mo. 29 pl. red cloth. VG. M5. $65.00

DUFFUS, R.L. *Tower of Jewels: Memories of San Francisco.* 1960. Norton. 1st. VG/G+ clip. O4. $15.00

DUFFY, Margaret. *Rook-Shoot.* 1991. St Martin. 1st Am. VG/VG. M22. $10.00

DUFFY & HOLIDAY. *Lady Sings the Blues.* 1956. Doubleday. 1st. F/VG+. B4. $100.00

DUFIEF, N.G. *Nature Displayed in Her Mode of Teaching Language to Man...* 1806. Phil. John Watts. 2 vol. full contemporary calf. M1. $300.00

DUFRENE, Maurice. *Florilegium. A Collection of Flower Initials...* 1988. Utrecht. Catharijne. 1/15. 59x47mm. hand-colored Luce Thurkow. limp suede. B24. $250.00

DUFRESNE, John. *Louisiana Power & Light.* 1994. Norton. ARC. author's 1st novel. F/F. D10. $60.00

DUFRESNE, John. *Way That Water Enters Stone.* 1991. Norton. 1st. sgn. F/F. R14. $150.00

DUGDALE, Florence. *Book of Baby Pets.* ca 1910. London. Hodder Stoughton. 1st. lg 4to. cloth. R5. $375.00

DUGDALE, William. *Antient Usage in Bearing Such Ensigns of Honour...* 1682. Oxford. Prt at Theater for Moses Pitt. contemporary sheep. M11. $350.00

DUGDALE, William. *Baronage of England; or, Historical Account of Lives...* 1675-76. London. 3 vol in 2. contemporary calf. M11. $850.00

DUGDALE, William. *Life, Diary & Correspondence of..., With Appendix...* 1827. Pall-Mall E. London. Harding Lepard. contemporary diced calf. M11. $450.00

DUGDALE, William. *Monasticon Anglicanum; or, History of Ancient Abbies...* 1693. London. Samuel Keble at Turks-Head. contemporary calf. usable. M11. $750.00

DUGMORE, A.R. *In the Heart of the Northern Forests.* 1930. London. ils/photos. 243p. cloth. G+. M12. $45.00

DUGUE-TROUIN, Rene. *Memoires de Monsieur Dugue, Chef d'Escadre des MIC...* 1730. Amsterdam. Pierre Mortier. unauthorized 1st. 12mo. wrp/fld case. O7. $2,000.00

DUKAS & HOFFMANN. *Albert Einstein, the Human Side.* 1981. Princeton. 1st pb prt. NF. K3. $10.00

DUKE, Alton. *When the Colorado River Quit the Ocean.* 1974. SW Printers. 1st. 122p. VG/dj. F7. $40.00

DUKE, Donald. *Water Trails West.* 1978. Doubleday. 1st. VG/VG. P3. $20.00

DUKE, Kate. *Aunt Isabel Tells a Good One.* 1992. Dutton Children's Books. 1st. sm 4to. unp. F/F. C14. $15.00

DUKE, Marc. *Du Ponts.* 1976. Dutton. 1st. F/NF. W2. $40.00

DULAC, Edmund. *Edmund Dulac's Fairy-Book: Fairy Tales of Allied Nations.* 1916. Hodder Stoughton. 4to. 15 mtd pl. wht coth. VG. T10. $350.00

DULAC, Edmund. *Golden Cockerel.* nd. Heritage. tall 4to. gilt royal bl silk. VG. M5. $45.00

DULL, Mrs. S.R. *Southern Cooking.* 1972 (1928). Grosset Dunlap. rpt. photos. index. VG. A16/B10. $12.50

DULL, Paul. *Battle History of the Imperial Japanese Navy 1941-1945.* 1978. Annapolis. photos/maps/notes/biblio/index. VG/VG. S16. $25.00

DULLES, Foster Rhea. *Eastward Ho!* 1931. London. John Lane. 199p. T7. $45.00

DULLES, John W.F. *Sao Paulo Law School & the Anti-Vargas Resistance (1938-45).* 1986. TX U. 1st. VG/VG. V4. $17.50

DUMAS, Alexandre. *Memoirs of a Physician.* 1879. Routledge. G. M2. $20.00

DUMAS, Charles Robert. *Contes de Nacre de ma Mere Grand.* 1937. Paris. Boivin & Cie. 1st. ils Felix Lorioux/8 tipped-in pl. 160p. VG. D1. $350.00

DUMAS, Claudine; see Malzberg, Barry.

DUMAS, J. *Codex Medicamentarius Pharmocopee...* 1866. Paris. royal 8vo. 784p+ads. cloth. VG. M12. $60.00

DUMMELOW, J.R. *One Volume Bible Commentary.* 1937. Macmillan. 1092p. G. B29. $8.00

DUNAWAY, Wayland Fuller. *Reminiscences of a Rebel.* 1913. NY. Neale. 1st. 133p. cloth. VG. M8. $275.00

DUNBAR, Anthony P. *Against the Grain: Southern Radicals & Prophets 1929-59.* 1982. VA U. 2nd. as new/dj. V4. $30.00

DUNBAR, C.O. *Earth.* 1967. World. 252p. VG/dj. D8. $25.00

DUNBAR, C.O. *Historical Geology.* 1949. John Wiley. 567p. VG. D8. $15.00

DUNBAR, Charles S. *Buses, Trolleys & Trams.* 1967. London. 141p. dj. A17. $17.50

DUNBAR, Paul Laurence. *Howdy Honey Howdy.* 1905. Dodd Mead. 1st. ils Leigh Miner. sm 8vo. VG+. C8. $375.00

DUNBAR, Paul Laurence. *Li'l Gal.* 1904. Dodd Mead. 1st. photos Leigh Richmond Miller. NF. B4. $350.00

DUNBAR, Paul Laurence. *Little Brown Baby: Poems for Young People.* 1957 (1940). np. ils Erick Berry. lg 12mo. xl. C8. $45.00

DUNBAR, Paul Laurence. *Lyrics of Lowly Life.* 1899. Dodd Mead. later prt. gr-gray cloth. VG. Q1. $75.00

DUNBAR, Paul Laurence. *Lyrics of the Hearthside.* 1899. NY. 1st. 12mo. teg. VG. A11. $250.00

DUNBAR, Paul Laurence. *Speakin' O' Christmas.* 1914. Dodd Mead. 1st. NF. B4. $500.00

DUNBAR & RODGERS. *Principles of Stratigraphy.* 1957. John Wiley. 356p. VG. D8. $20.00

DUNCAN, Bob. *Buffalo Country.* 1959. NY. 256p. F. S15. $22.00

DUNCAN, David. *Another Tree in Eden.* 1956. Heinemann. 1st. NF/NF. P3. $40.00

DUNCAN, David. *Beyond Eden.* 1955. Ballantine. 1st. VG/rpr. M2. $35.00

DUNCAN, Robert Clifton. *Dynamics of Atmosphereic Entry.* 1962. McGraw Hill. 8vo. 306p. Vg. K5. $45.00

DUNCAN, Robert L. *Day the Sun Fell.* 1970. Morrow. 1st. VG/torn. K3. $15.00

DUNCAN, Robert L. *Temple Dogs.* 1977. Morrow. 1st. VG/VG. P3. $18.00

DUNCAN, Sara Jeanette. *Social Departure: How Orthodocia & I Went Round the World...* 1891. Appleton. 1st. ils FH Townsend. 417p. VG+. A25. $30.00

DUNCOMBE, Frances. *High Hurdles.* 1941. NY. Jr Literary Guild. VG/VG. O3. $18.00

DUNHAM, Jacob. *Journal of Voyages.* 1850. NY. self pub. 12 engravings. 243p. T7. $325.00

DUNHAM, Katherine. *Journey to Accompong.* 1946. NY. Holt. 1st. ils Ted Cook. 162p. VG/dj. A25. $30.00

DUNHILL, Alfred. *Gentle Art of Smoking.* 1954. Putnam. 1st. NF/dj. N4. $60.00

DUNLAP, Susan. *Not Exactly a Brahmin.* 1985. St Martin. 1st. sgn. F/dj. A24. $50.00

DUNLOP, Richard. *Wheels West 1590-1900.* 1977. Chicago. Rand McNally. 1st. sgn. VG. O3. $45.00

DUNLOP, William. *Recollections of the American War, 1812-1814.* 1905. Toronto. variant ed. 1/1000. 112p. G. B18. $125.00

DUNN, Arthur Wallace. *Gridiron Nights: Humorous & Satirical Views...* 1915. NY. ils. VG. M17. $20.00

DUNN, Dorothy. *Murder's Web.* 1950. Harper. sgn. VG/VG. P3. $30.00

DUNN, Jacob Piatt. *Negro Issue: An Address.* 1904. Indianapolis. Sentinel Prt. 1st. 8vo. 22p. prt self-wrp. M1. $175.00

DUNN, Katherine. *Geek Love.* 1989. Knopf. 1st. F/F. B2/D10. $50.00

DUNN, Nell. *Up the Junction.* 1966. Lippinoctt. 1st Am. F/NF. B4. $65.00

DUNN, Stephen. *Work & Love.* 1981. Carnegie-Mellon. 1st. sgn. F/NF. V1. $35.00

DUNN, Stephen. *5 Impersonations.* 1971. Marshall, MN. Ox Head. 1/350. sgn. F/bl wrp. V1. $45.00

DUNN & DUNN. *Papers of William Penn, Vol 3, 1685-1700.* 1986. PA U. 794p. VG. V3. $25.00

DUNN & DUNN. *World of William Penn.* 1986. PA U. 1st. 421p. F/dj. V3. $25.00

DUNN & MILLER. *Atlantic Hurricanes.* 1960. LSU. 1st. v8o. 326p. dj. K5. $35.00

DUNN & TORIGOE. *Actors' Analects.* 1969. Columbia. 1st. 306p. F/F. W3. $85.00

DUNNE, Dominick. *Inconvenient Woman.* 1990. Franlkin Lib. 1st. sgn. full leather. F. Q1. $40.00

DUNNE, Dominick. *Two Mrs Grenvilles.* 1985. Crown. 1st. inscr/dtd 1985. VG/VG. M22. $30.00

DUNNE, John Gregory. *Delano: Story of the California Grape Strike.* 1967. FSG. 1st. F/dj. M19. $50.00

DUNNE, John Gregory. *Studio.* 1969. FSG. 1st. F/NF. M19. $35.00

DUNNE, John Gregory. *Studio.* 1969. NY. 1st. sgn. author's 2nd book. NF/VG+. A11. $75.00

DUNNE, John Gregory. *True Confessions.* 1977. Dutton. 1st. F/NF. A20. $30.00

DUNNE, John Gregory. *True Confessions.* 1977. Dutton. 1st. NF/NF. M19. $25.00

DUNNE, John Gregory. *Vegas: A Memoir of a Dark Season.* 1974. Random. 1st. NF/NF. M19. $25.00

DUNNE, John Gregory. *Vegas: A Memoir of a Dark Session.* 1974. Random. 1st. author's 3rd book. F/F. H11. $40.00

DUNNE, Peter Masten. *Juan Antonio Balthasar, Padre Visitador...1744-1745.* 1957. AZ Pioneer Hist Soc. 1st. fld map/index. 129p. NF/sans. B19. $75.00

DUNNETT, Dorothy. *Dolly & the Nanny Bird.* 1982. Knopf. 1st. F/F. M19. $35.00

DUNNETT, Dorothy. *Dolly & the Nanny Bird.* 1982. Knopf. 1st. VG/VG. P3. $25.00

DUNNETT, Dorothy. *Spring of the Ram.* 1988. Knopf. 1st. F/F. M19. $25.00

DUNNETT, Harding McGregor. *Shackleton's Boat: Story of the James Caird.* 1996. Benenden. Neville Harding. 150p. NF/dj. P4. $65.00

DUNNING, John. *Bookman's Wake.* 1995. Scribner. 1st. F/F. D10/M19/Q1. $50.00

DUNNING, John. *Holland Suggestions.* 1975. Bobbs Merrill. 1st. author's 1st novel. xl. VG/F. M23. $60.00

DUNNING, John. *Tune in Yesterday: Ultimate Encyclopedia...* 1976. Prentice Hall. 2nd. 703p. cloth. VG+/dj. M20. $45.00

DUNNING, LUDERS & SMITH. *Reflections on a Gift of Watermelon Pickle...* 1966. Scott Foresman. 5th. sm 4to. VG+. C8. $25.00

DUNNING, LUEDERS & SMITH. *Some Haystacks Don't Even Have Any Needle...* 1969. Scott Foresman. 1st. 192p. cloth. F/NF. D4. $30.00

DUNPHY, Eamon. *Unforgettable Fire.* 1988. Warner. 1st. F/F. W2. $25.00

DUNSANY, Lord. *Curse of the Wise Woman.* 1933. Longman. 1st Am. VG. M2. $40.00

DUNSANY, Lord. *Five Plays.* 1917. Little Brn. VG. P3. $30.00

DUNSANY, Lord. *Five Plays.* 1931 (1914). Little Brn. rpt. VG. M22. $12.00

DUNSANY, Lord. *Tales of War.* 1918. Little Brn. 1st. VG. M2. $35.00

DUNSANY, Lord. *Time & the Gods.* 1922. London. Putnam. 1/250. sgn. ils/sgn Sidney Sime. half vellum/leather label. B24. $250.00

DUNTHORNE, Gordon. *Flower & Fruit Prints of the 18th & Early 19th Centuries...* 1938. WA, DC. 1st. 275p. VG. B26. $375.00

DUNTHORNE, Gordon. *Flower & Fruit Prints of the 18th & Early 19th Centuries...* 1970. Da Capo. folio. ils. 275p. NF/dj. A22. $200.00

DUPLAIX, Georges. *Pee-Gloo.* 1935. Harper. 1st. ils. VG. D1. $200.00

DUPUNY, R. Ernest. *5 Days to War: April 2-6, 1917.* 1967. Stackpole. 1st. 192p. VG/dj. M20. $20.00

DUPY, Ernest. *St Vith Lion in the Way: 106th Infantry Division in WWII.* 1949. WA, DC. 1st. ils/maps. 253p. VG/VG. S16. $95.00

DURAND, Edward. *Ponies' Progress.* 1935. Scribner. 1st Am. G. O3. $30.00

DURAND & SCHINZ. *Conspectus Florae Africae.* 1895. Bruxelles. 8vo. teg. xl. A22. $95.00

DURANT, C.F. *Exposition; or, New Theory of Animal Magnetism...* 1837. Wiley Putnam. 1st. 12mo. 225p. modern cloth. M1. $200.00

DURANT, Will. *Story of Philosophy.* 1928. NY. 8vo. ils. teg. 3-quarter dk bl leather/raised bands. H3. $50.00

DURANT & DURANT. *Pictorial History of the American Circus.* 1957. photos. leather. VG. M17. $25.00

DURAS, Claire Lechat. *Ourika; a Tale, From the French.* 1829. Boston. Carter Hendee. 1st Am. 18mo. 84p. contemporary calf. M1. $250.00

DURAS, Marguerite. *Malady of Death.* 1986. Grove. 1st Am. 60p. VG/dj. A25. $12.00

DURBRIDGE, Francis. *Man Called Harry Brent.* 1970. Hodder Stoughton. 1st. TVTI. F/F. P3. $25.00

DURER, Albrecht. *Brothers, by Terence.* 1968. Kentfield, CA. Allen. 1/140. ils brd/decor cloth. F/case. w/prospectus. B24. $400.00

DURER, Albrecht. *Designs of the Prayer Book.* 1817. London. Ackermann. folio. full-p portrait Durer/43 pl. quarter morocco. R12. $575.00

DURICK, Agnes York. *Baby Bear.* 1932. Harter. 1st. VG. M5. $55.00

DURLAND, Kellogg. *Red Reign.* 1907. Century. 1st. inscr. 8vo. 533p. red cloth. w/prospectus. T10. $100.00

DURRELL, C. *History of Feather River Country, CA.* 1987. Berkeley. 337p. NF. D8. $45.00

DURRELL, Lawrence. *Antrobus Complete.* 1985. London. 1st. VG/dj. T9. $18.00

DURRELL, Lawrence. *Balthazar.* 1958. London. 1st. VG/frayed. T9. $60.00

DURRELL, Lawrence. *Black Book.* 1938. Paris. Obelisk. G/wrp. B2. $250.00

DURRELL, Lawrence. *Black Book: An Agon.* 1938. Paris. Obelisk. 1st. VG. Q1. $1,000.00

DURRELL, Lawrence. *Cities, Plains & People.* 1946. London. Faber. 1st. NF/VG. M19. $85.00

DURRELL, Lawrence. *Ikons.* 1966. London. Faber. 1st. F/dj. Q1. $75.00

DURRELL, Lawrence. *La Descente du Styx.* 1964. np. La Murene. 1st. 1/250. sgn/#d. F/wht wrp. Q1. $175.00

DURRELL, Lawrence. *Livia or Buried Alive.* London. 1st. F/F. T12. $100.00

DURRELL, Lawrence. *On the Suchness of the Old Boy.* 1972. London. Turret. 1st. 1/226 total. sgn. ils/sgn Sappho Durrell. F/wrp. Q1. $200.00

DURRELL, Lawrence. *Quinx.* 1985. Viking. 1st. NF/NF. A20. $15.00

DURRELL, Lawrence. *Selected Poems.* 1956. London. Faber. 1st. F/dj. Q1. $200.00

DURRELL, Lawrence. *Stiff Upper Lip.* 1958. London. Faber. 1st. F/clip. Q1. $75.00

DURRELL, Lawrence. *Tunc.* 1968. Dutton. 1st Am. sgn. VG/VG. R14. $40.00

DURRELL & SACHS. *Big Book for Peace.* 1990. Dutton Childrens Books. 1st. sm 4to. 120p. NF/NF. C14. $19.00

DURSO, Joseph. *All-American Dollar.* 1971. Houghton Mifflin. 1st. inscr. F/VG. P8. $45.00

DURST, Paul. *Florentine Table.* 1980. Scribner. 1st. F/F. P3. $20.00

DUTHIE, Eric. *Mystery & Adventure Stories for Girls.* 1962. Odhams. 1st. VG/VG. P3. $25.00

DUTOURD, Jean. *Dog's Head.* 1951. John Lehmann. 1st. VG/VG. P3. $40.00

DUTTON, Clarence E. *Tertiary History of the Grand Canyon District.* 1882. GPO. 23 16x20" pl. 246p. orig brd/leather. VG. F7. $4,995.00

DUTTON, Joan Parry. *They Left Their Mark: Famous Passages Through Wine Country.* 1983. St Helena. Illuminations Pr. 1st. tan cloth. as new/dj. K7. $30.00

DUVOISIN, Roger. *Day & Night.* (1960). Knopf. 4to. unp. xl. VG. T5. $15.00

DWIGGINS, W.A. *Millenium 1.* 1945. Knopf. 1st. VG/dj. M2. $30.00

DWIGHT, Thomas. *Anatomy of the Head...* 1876. Boston. 1st. ils/fld pl. 136p. A13. $350.00

DWIGHT, Thomas. *Variations of the Bones of the Hands & Feet.* 1907. Phil. 1st. photos. A13. $250.00

DWYER, Deanna; see Koontz, Dean R.

DWYER, K.R.; see Koontz, Dean R.

DYE, Charles. *Prisoner in the Skull.* 1952. Abelard. 1st. NF/F. P3. $75.00

DYE, Daniel. *Grammar of Chinese Lattice. Vol II.* 1937. Harvard. ils. VG/dj. W3. $62.00

DYE, Eva Emery. *McLoughlin & Old Oregon: A Chronicle.* 1900. McClurg. 2nd. 381p. pict cloth. D11. $40.00

DYE, John Thomas. *Golden Leaves.* 1962. Ward Ritchie. 227p. VG/dj. B18. $22.50

DYER, Cecil. *Newport Cookbook.* 1972. Weathervane. rpt. 250p. dj. B10. $10.00

DYKE, A.L. *Dyke's Automobile & Gasoline Engine Encyclopedia.* 1924. Chicago. Goodheart-Willcox. 13th. 8vo. 1226p. VG/dj. K3. $75.00

DYKES, Jeff. *Billy the Kid: Bibliography of a Legend.* 1952. NM U. 186p. VG. A4. $165.00

DYKES, Jeff. *Fifty Great Western Illustrators.* 1975. Northland. 1st Collector. 1/200. sgn. 96 pl. M/case. A18. $200.00

DYKES, Jeff. *Western High Spots: Reading & Collecting Guides.* 1977. Northland. 1st. inscr. F/F. A18. $75.00

DYLAN, Bob. *Tarantula.* nd (1965). Hibbing, MN. Wimp. pirated before 1st trade. 4to. stapled sheets. NF/wrp. B4. $250.00

DYMOND, Jonathan. *War: Essay, With Intro Words by John Bright.* 1889. Friends Book & Tract. 88p. VG. V3. $15.00

DYSON, Freeman. *Astronomy.* 1918. Dutton. 118p. cloth. K5. $15.00

DYSON, Freeman. *Disturbing the Universe.* 1979. Harper Row. 1st. F/NF. A20. $25.00

DYSON, Freeman. *Infinite in All Directions.* 1988. Harper Row. 1st. F/F. B35. $16.00

DYSON, Freeman. *Symmetry Groups in Nuclear & Particle Physics.* 1966. NY. WA Benjamin. 1st. 320p. xl. K3. $15.00

DYSON, John. *South Seas Dream.* 1982. Boston/Toronto. 1st Am. stp Not for Resale. 242p. P4. $25.00

E-YEH-SHURE. *I Am a Pueblo Indian Girl.* 1939. Morrow. 1st. ils Houser/Martinez/Nailor/Tahoma. VG-. P2. $40.00

EAGER, Edward. *Mouse Manor.* 1952. Ariel. 1st. ils Beryl Bailey-Jones. F/VG. P2. $55.00

EAGER, Edward. *Red Head.* 1951. Houghton Mifflin. 1st. sgn. ils Louis Slobodkin. 24p. VG. P2. $35.00

EAGER, Samuel W. *Outline of History of Orange County...1846-47.* 1846. ST Callahan. 652p. brd/leather spine & corners. worn. M20. $75.00

EAGLE, Dallas Chief. *Winter Count.* 1967. Colorado Springs. Dentan Berkeland. 1st prt. inscr. NF/VG clip. L3. $250.00

EAGLE, Mary Kavanaugh. *Congress of Women Held in Women's Building...* 1894. Chicago. 1st. ils. 824p. G. B5. $95.00

EAGLEMAN, Joe R. *Severe & Unusual Weather.* 1983. Van Nostrand. 1st. VG/torn. K5. $30.00

EALES & SULLIVAN. *Political Context of Law, Proceedings of Seventh British...* 1987. London. Hambledon. 12 essays. M11. $35.00

EAMES, Wilberforce. *Americana Collection of Herschel V Jones, a Checklist...* 1938. Wm Rudge. 1/200. lg 4to. VG. A4. $375.00

EAMES & MACDANIELS. *Introduction to Plant Anatomy.* 1925. NY. McGraw Hill. 1st/6th imp. 364p. B1. $35.00

EAMES & MACDANIELS. *Introduction to Plant Anatomy.* 1947 (1925). McGraw Hill. 2nd. Botanical Sciences series. ils. 427p. cloth. B26. $26.00

EARDMAN, Paul. *Billion Dollar Sure Thing.* 1973. Scribner. 1st. VG/VG. P3. $25.00

EARDMAN, Paul. *Palace.* 1987. Doubleday. 1st. VG/VG. P3. $15.00

EARHART, Amelia. *Fun of It: Random Records of My Own Flying...* 1932. NY. Brewer Warren Putnam. 1st. pink cloth. w/record. M24. $450.00

EARHART, John F. *Color Printer: A Treatise on Use of Colors...* 1892. Cincinnati. Earhart Richardson. 1st. 4to. sample pages. M1. $750.00

EARL, John Prescott. *School Teem in Camp (#2).* 1928 (1909). Penn. 331p. VG+. M20. $15.00

EARL, Stephen. *Hills of the Boasting Woman.* 1963. London. Readers Union. 160p. dj. F3. $15.00

EARL OF CHESTERFIELD. *Letters to His Son on Art of Becoming a Man in the World...* 1917. NY. Chesterfield Pr. 2 vol. uncut/ unopened. teg. 3-quarter leather. VG. H3. $85.00

EARLE, Alice Morse. *Two Centuries of Costume in America 1620-1820.* 1974. Williamstown, MA. Corner House. rpt. 2 vol. F/F. V3. $35.00

EARLE, Ferdinand. *Lyric Year, One Hundred Poems.* 1912. NY. Kennerley. 1st/1st issue. gilt maroon cloth. NF. M24. $100.00

EARLE, W. Hubert. *Cacti of the Southwest.* 1966 (1963). Phoenix. 2nd. ils/photos. VG. B26. $14.00

EARLE, W. Hubert. *Southwest Desert in Bloom.* nd. Phoenix. 32p. F. B26. $6.00

EARLY, Gerald. *Daughters on Family & Fatherhood.* 1994. Reading, MA. Addison Wesley. 1st. 234p. F/F. B4. $35.00

EARLY, Jack; see Scoppetone, Sandra.

EARNSHAW, Brian. *Starclipper & the Song Wars.* 1985. Methuen. decor brd. VG. P3. $13.00

EASEY, Ben. *Practical Organic Gardening.* 1955. London. Faber. 312p. A10. $30.00

EASON, A. *Boom Town: Kilgore, TX.* 1970s. Kilgore. sgn. photos. 144p. F. M4. $20.00

EASTLAKE, William. *Go in Beauty.* 1957. London. Secker Warburg. 1st. F/dj. Q1. $125.00

EASTMAN, Charles A. *Old Indian Days.* 1907. NY. McClure. 1st. cloth. NF. L3. $200.00

EASTMAN, Mary. *Dacotah; or, Life & Legends of the Sioux Around Ft Snelling.* 1849. John Wiley. 1st. 268p. pict cloth. J2. $375.00

EASTMAN, Max. *Love & Revolution.* 1964. Random. 1st. w/sgn leaf. F/NF. B2. $75.00

EASTMAN, Max. *Sense of Humor.* 1921. Scribner. 1st. inscr. VG. B2. $65.00

EASTMAN KODAK CO. *How To Make Good Pictures.* ca 1910. NY. 166p+4 mtd photos. VG. A17. $25.00

EASTMAN. *Index to Fairy Tales, Myths & Legends.* 1926. revised/enlarged. 619p. xl. VG. A4. $85.00

EASTON, Nat. *Bill for Damages.* 1958. Roy. 1st. VG/VG. P3. $18.00

EASTWOOD, T. *Stanford's Geological Atlas of Great Britain.* 1964. London. Edward Stanford Ltd. 288p. NF/dj. D8. $15.00

EATON, A.H. *Handicrafts of New England.* 1949. NY. 1st. 128 photos. 374p. VG/fair. M4. $35.00

EATON, Anne Thaxter. *Treasure for the Taking.* 1967 (1957). Viking. 3rd. 8vo. 322p. NF/NF. T5. $25.00

EATON, Clement. *History of the Southern Confederacy.* 1954. Macmillan. 1st. 351p. cloth. NF/VG. M8. $55.00

EATON, Clement. *Jefferson Davis.* 1977. Free Pr. 1st. tall 8vo. 8 pl. 334p. as new/dj. H1. $25.00

EATON, Daniel Cady. *Ferns of North America.* 1879. Salem/Boston. Cassino. 2 vol. VG. A22. $350.00

EATON, E.H. *Birds of New York.* 1910 & 1914. NYSU. 2nd. 2 vol. lg 4to. xl. VG. M12. $175.00

EATON, Flora McCrea. *Memory's Wall: Autobiography.* 1956. Toronto. Clark Irwin. 1st. sgn. F. T12. $35.00

EATON, Seymour. *Adventures of the Traveling Bears.* 1915. Barse Hopkins. ils V Floyd Campbell. 4to. cloth. mc dj. R5. $110.00

EBERHART, Mignon G. *Alpine Condo Crossfire.* 1984. Random. 1st. NF/NF. P3. $15.00

EBERHART, Mignon G. *Bayou Road.* 1979. Random. 1st. VG/VG. P3. $15.00

EBERHART, Mignon G. *Danger Money.* 1974. Random. F/NF. N4. $25.00

EBERHART, Mignon G. *Fair Warning.* 1936. Doubleday. 1st. VG. M22. $15.00

EBERHART, Mignon G. *Family Affair.* 1981. Random. 1st. VG/VG. P3. $15.00

EBERHART, Mignon G. *Hunt With the Hounds.* 1950. Random. 1st. 247p. cloth. VG/dj. M20. $15.00

EBERHART, Mignon G. *Postmark Murder.* 1956. Random. 1st. NF/NF. M22. $35.00

EBERHART, Mignon G. *Run Scared.* 1965. Random. 1st. VG/VG. P3. $25.00

EBERHART, Mignon G. *White Cockatoo.* 1933. Crime Club. 1st. VG. P3. $40.00

EBERHART, Perry. *Ghosts of the Colorado Plains.* 1986. Athens, OH. Swallow. dj. A19. $50.00

EBERHART, Richard. *Long Reach.* 1984. New Directions. 1st. inscr/dtd 1984. F/F. R14. $300.00

EBERHART, Richard. *Survivors.* 1979. BOA Ed. 1/25. sgn. F. V1. $125.00

EBERLAIN & HUBBARD. *Diary of Independence Hall.* 1948. sgns. ils. VG/VG. M17. $20.00

EBERLE, Irmengarde. *Listen to the Mockingbird.* 1949. Whittlesey. 1st. 64p. VG+/dj. M20. $25.00

EBERS, George. *Egypt: Descriptive, Historical & Picturesque.* 1880-83. London. Cassell. 2 vol. 1st Eng language. folio. ornate gilt cloth. NF. C6. $250.00

EBERSTADT, Edward. *Annotated Eberstadt Catalogs of Americana.* 1965. NY. Argosy-Antiquarian. 4 vol. 1/750. thick 8vo. as new. O7. $300.00

EBON, Martin. *Knew the Unknown.* 1971. World. 1st. NF/VG. P3. $15.00

EBY, Cecil. *Between the Bullet & the Lie.* 1969. Holt. 1st. F/F. B2. $25.00

EBY & FLEMING. *Case of the Malevolent Twin.* 1946. Dutton. 1st. G+. P3. $12.00

ECHEVERRIA, M. Gonzalez. *Reflex Paralysis: Its Pathological Anatomy & Relation...* 1866. NY. 80p. bl cloth. B14. $275.00

ECKER, Alexander. *Cerebral Convolutions of Man.* 1989 (1873). Birmingham. Classics Neurology/Neurosurgery Lib. facsimile. G1. $65.00

ECKERT, Allan W. *Conquerors.* 1970. Little Brn. 1st. 720p. VG+/dj. M20. $40.00

ECKERT, Allan W. *Court-Martial of Daniel Boone.* 1973. Little Brn. 1st. 309p. VG/dj. M20. $60.00

ECKERT, Allan W. *Frontiersmen.* 1967. Little Brn. 1st. 626p. VG+/dj. M20. $60.00

ECKERT, Allan W. *Great Auk.* 1963. Little Brn. 1st. inscr. NF/VG+. T11. $75.00

ECKERT, Allan W. *Incident at Hawk's Hill.* (1971). Little Brn. 2nd. ils John Schoenherr. 173p. VG/G+. T5. $25.00

ECKERT, Allan W. *Silent Sky.* 1965. Little Brn. 1st. sgn. 241p. VG+/clip. M20. $85.00

ECKERT, Allan W. *Twilight of Empire.* 1988. Little Brn. 1st. 587p. VG/dj. M20. $45.00

ECKERT, Allan W. *Wilderness Empire.* 1969. Little Brn. 1st. sgn. 653p. VG/dj. M20. $90.00

ECKHARDT, George H. *Pennsylvania Clocks & Clockmakers.* 1955. Bonanza. ils. 229p. VG/dj. H1/K3. $30.00

ECKLEY & PERRY. *Young French Chef.* 1969. Platt Munk. ils Catherine Cambier. VG/G. M5. $45.00

ECKSTEIN, Gustav. *Canary: History of a Family.* 1936. NY/London. inscr/sgn. VG. S15. $30.00

ECKSTROM, Fannie H. *Penobscot Man.* 1972 (1924). NH Pub. 1st thus. 351p. brn cloth. F/VG. B22. $9.50

ECO, Umberto. *Foucault's Pendulum.* 1989. HBJ. 1st Am. sgn. F/dj. Q1. $75.00

ECO, Umberto. *Foucault's Pendulum.* 1989. HBJ. 1st. F/F. T11. $50.00

ECO, Umberto. *Postscript to the Name of the Rose.* 1984. HBJ. 1st Am. F/F. R14. $35.00

ECO & ZORZOLI. *Picture History of Inventions, From Plough to Polaris.* 1963. Macmillan. 1st Am. 360p. F/dj. T10. $150.00

EDDINGS, David. *Demon Lord of Karanda.* 1988. Del Rey. 1st. F/F. M2. $25.00

EDDINGS, David. *Guardians of the West.* 1987. 1st. NF/NF. S13. $35.00

EDDINGS, David. *King of Murgos.* 1988. Del Rey. 1st. F/F. M2. $30.00

EDDINGS, David. *Sorceress of Darshiva.* 1989. Del Rey. 1st. VG/VG. P3. $20.00

EDDINGTON, A.S. *From Paracelsus to Newton.* 1982. Cambridge. 1st. VG/dj. K3. $15.00

EDDINGTON, A.S. *Fundamental Theory.* 1949. Cambridge. rpt. VG. K3. $40.00

EDDINGTON, A.S. *New Pathways in Science.* 1934. NY. Macmillan. 1st. VG/dj. K3. $30.00

EDDINGTON, A.S. *Philosophy of Physical Science.* 1938. Tarner. 1st. NF. K3. $35.00

EDDINGTON, A.S. *Philosophy of Physical Science.* 1941. Macmillan. rpt. VG/dj. K3. $20.00

EDDY, Mary Baker Glover. *Poems.* 1911. Allison Stewart. 1st. NF/case. M19. $35.00

EDDY, Mary Baker Glover. *Science & Health With Key to the Scriptures.* 1887. self pub. 29th ed. 8vo. 590p. gilt tan bdg. G+. H1. $85.00

EDE, Basil. *Wild Birds of America: Art of Basil Ede.* 1991. Abrams. ils. 125p. F/dj. S15. $30.00

EDEL, Leon. *Bloomsbury, a House of Lions.* 1979. London. 1st. VG/dj. T9. $20.00

EDELMAN, G.M. *Neural Darwinism: Theory of Neural Group Selection.* 1987. Basic. ils/fld pl/figure/tables. 371p. cloth. NF/F. M12. $30.00

EDELMAN, Lily. *Face to Face: Primer in Dialogue.* 1967. Crown. 122p. VG/G+. S3. $18.00

EDELSON, Edward. *Visions of Tomorrow.* 1975. Doubleday. 1st. F/F. M2. $12.00

EDELSON, Edward. *Who Goes There? Search for Intelligent Life in Universe.* 1979. NY. Doubleday. 1st. F/G. T12. $20.00

EDEN, Dorothy. *Important Family.* 1982. Morrow. 1st. F/F. P3. $14.00

EDEN, Dorothy. *Time of the Dragon.* 1975. Hodder Stoughton. 1st. VG/VG. P3. $18.00

EDEN, Dorothy. *Whistle for the Crows.* 1962. Hodder Stoughton. 1st. VG/VG. P3. $25.00

EDERSHEIM, Alfred. *Life & Times of Jesus the Messiah, Vol I & II.* 1896. Longmans. 8th. 2 vol. VG. B29. $17.00

EDERSHEIM, Alfred. *Life & Times of Jesus the Messiah.* 1953. Eerdmans. 2 vol. VG. B29. $17.00

EDGECOMBE, Winnie S. *Weeds of Lebanon.* 1970 (1959). Beirut. 3rd/revised enlarged. 214 pl. 457p. sc. B26. $32.50

EDGERTON, Clyde. *Floatplane Notebooks.* 1988. Algonquin. 1st. inscr. F/F. A23. $45.00

EDGERTON, Clyde. *Walking Across Egypt.* 1987. Algonquin. 1st. F/clip. M25. $45.00

EDGERTON, Clyde. *Walking Across Egypt.* 1987. Chapel Hill. Algonquin. 1st/1st issue (blue t-shirt p164). F/F. H11. $60.00

EDGEWORTH, Maria. *Tales & Novels.* 1832-34. NY. Harper. 18 vol in 9. 12mo. contemporary bdg. M1. $500.00

EDGEWORTH & EDGEWORTH. *Essay on Irish Bulls.* 1808. London. Johnson. 3rd/corrected. 280p. early tree calf. H13. $225.00

EDGLEY, Leslie. *Angry Heart.* 1947. Crime Club. 1st. VG/dj. M25. $45.00

EDGLEY, Leslie. *Fear No More.* 1946. S&S. 1st. VG/VG. P3. $18.00

EDINGER, Ludwig. *Twelve Lectures on Structure of Central Nervous System...* 1891. Phil. FA Davis. 1st Eng-language/later issue. 230p. panelled brn cloth. G1. $75.00

EDMAN, Irwin. *Candle in the Dark.* 1939. Viking. 1st. F/F. B35. $22.00

EDMINSTER, Frank C. *Ruffed Grouse: Its Life Story, Ecology & Management.* 1947. Macmillan. stated 1st. 385p. VG. H7. $40.00

EDMONDS, Emma E. *Nurse & Spy in the Union Army.* 1865. ils. G. M17. $27.50

EDMONDS, I.G. *Magic Brothers.* 1979. Elsevier/Nelson. 1st. VG/VG. P3. $15.00

EDMONDS, I.G. *Universal in the Silent Days.* 1977. Barnes. ils/photos. NF/dj. C9. $50.00

EDMONDS, Walter. *Chad Hanna.* 1940. Boston. 1st. VG/VG. B5. $35.00

EDMONDS, Walter. *Matchlock Gun.* 1941. Dodd Mead. 1st. inscr. Newbery Medal. VG/VG. P2. $150.00

EDMONDSON, G.C. *THEM.* 1974. Doubleday. 1st. VG/dj. M2. $16.00

EDMONSON, Munro. *Ancient Future of Itzas: Book of Chilam Balam of Tizimun.* 1982. Austin, TX. 1st. ils/index. 220p. dj. F3. $50.00

EDNEY, Andrew. *Complete Cat Care Manual.* 1992. Dorling Kindersley. 1st Am. 192p. F/F. W2. $30.00

EDRICH, Louise. *Love Medicine.* 1984. HRW. 1st. author's 1st novel. NF/NF clip. B3. $125.00

EDSALL, F.S. *World of Psychic Phenomena.* 1958. McKay. 1st. VG/dj. P3. $20.00

EDSON, Lee. *Worlds Around the Sun.* 1969. Am Heritage/Smithsonian. 159p. VG/dj. K5. $15.00

EDWARD, E.I. *Desert Voices.* 1958. Los Angeles. Westernlore. 1st. 1/500. NF/G. O4. $75.00

EDWARD, E.I. *Enduring Desert.* 1969. Ward Ritchie. 1st. F/F case. O4. $125.00

EDWARD, William B. *Story of Colt's Revolver, the Biography of Col Samuel Colt.* 1983. Stackpole. 1st. 470p. VG/dj. J2. $245.00

EDWARDES, Allen. *Jewel in the Lotus: Historical Survey of Sexual Culture...* 1959. NY. Julian. 8th. 293p. VG/dj. A25. $25.00

EDWARDES & MASTERS. *Cradle of Erotica: Study of Afro-Asian Sexual Expression...* 1963. NY. Julian. 4th. 362p. VG. A25. $15.00

EDWARDS, Amelia B. *Thousand Miles Up the Nile.* ca 1888. NY. Lovell Coryell. 2nd. ils. 468p. teg. VG. W1. $30.00

EDWARDS, Deltus Malin. *Toll of the Arctic Seas.* 1910. London. Chapman Hall. ils/maps. 448p. T7. $50.00

EDWARDS, Frank. *Flying Saucers: Serious Business.* 1966. Lyle Stuart. 1st. sgn. VG/VG. B11. $35.00

EDWARDS, Frank. *Flying Saucers: Serious Business.* 1966. Lyle Stuart. 1st. VG/dj. P3. $20.00

EDWARDS, George Wharton. *Vanished Towers & Chimes of Flanders.* 1916. Penn Pub. 1st. mc pl. F. M19. $75.00

EDWARDS, Gladys Brown. *Arabian War Horse to Show Horse.* 1980. Denver. Arabian Horse Trust. 3rd. VG/VG. O3. $125.00

EDWARDS, Gladys Brown. *Photographic History of the Polish Arabian.* 1978. Rockville, MD. 1st. 4to. O3. $85.00

EDWARDS, Harry. *Revolt of the Black Athlete.* 1969. Free Pr. 1st. photos. 201p. F/F. B4. $85.00

EDWARDS, Jesse. *Atlas of Congenital Anomalies of the Heart & Great Vessels.* 1954. Springfield. 1st. 4to. 202p. xl. A13. $50.00

EDWARDS, Julie Andrews. *Last of the Really Great Whangdoodles.* 1974. author's 2nd book. F/F. A4. $25.00

EDWARDS, Julie Andrews. *Mandy.* 1971. author's 1st book. F/F. A4. $30.00

EDWARDS, Leo. *Jerry Todd, Editor-in-Grief (#10).* 1930. Grosset Dunlap. lists to Caveman. 246p. VG/dj. M20. $60.00

EDWARDS, Leo. *Jerry Todd, Pirate (#8).* 1928. Grosset Dunlap. lists to Buffalo Bill Bathtub. VG/partial. M20. $45.00

EDWARDS, Leo. *Jerry Todd & the Bob-Tailed Elephant (#9).* 1929. Grosset Dunlap. lists to Flying Flapdoodle. 331p. VG/dj. M20. $60.00

EDWARDS, Leo. *Jerry Todd & the Buffalo Bill Bathtub (#13).* 1936. Grosset Dunlap. lists to this title. VG/dj. M20. $75.00

EDWARDS, Leo. *Jerry Todd & the Buffalo Bill Bathtub (#13).* 1936. Grosset Dunlap. lists to this title. VG/dj. M20. $75.00

EDWARDS, Leo. *Jerry Todd & the Oak Island Treasure (#3).* 1925. Grosset Dunlap. lists 8 titles. 233p. VG/dj. M20. $55.00

EDWARDS, Leo. *Jerry Todd & the Purring Egg (#6).* 1925. Grosset Dunlap. lists to Buffalo Bill Bathtub. VG/dj. M20. $60.00

EDWARDS, Leo. *Jerry Todd & the Rose Colored Cat (#2).* 1921. Grosset Dunlap. lists to Whispering Cave. VG/dj. M20. $60.00

EDWARDS, Leo. *Jerry Todd & the Talking Frog (#5).* 1925. Grosset Dunlap. lists to Buffalo Bill Bathtub. VG/dj. M20. $60.00

EDWARDS, Leo. *Jerry Todd & the Waltzing Hen (#4).* 1924. Grosset Dunlap. lists to Buffalo Bill Bathtub. VG/dj. M20. $60.00

EDWARDS, Leo. *Jerry Todd in the Whispering Cave (#7).* 1927. Grosset Dunlap. lists to this title. VG/dj. M20. $60.00

EDWARDS, Leo. *Jerry Todd's Poodle Parlor (#15).* 1938. Grosset Dunlap. lists 13 titles. 203p. VG/partial. M20. $60.00

EDWARDS, Leo. *Poppy Ott & the Freckled Goldfish (#5).* 1928. Grosset Dunlap. lists 7 titles. VG/dj. M20. $65.00

EDWARDS, Leo. *Poppy Ott & the Galloping Snail (#3).* 1927. Grosset Dunlap. lists 8 titles. 238p. VG/dj. M20. $65.00

EDWARDS, Leo. *Poppy Ott & the Monkey's Paw (#10).* 1938. Grosset Dunlap. lists 8 title. VG. M20. $85.00

EDWARDS, Leo. *Poppy Ott & the Prancing Pancake (#7).* 1930. Grosset Dunlap. 298p. cloth. VG/dj. M20. $65.00

EDWARDS, Leo. *Poppy Ott & the Stuttering Parrot (#1).* 1926. Grosset Dunlap. lists 8 titles. 220p. VG/dj. M20. $55.00

EDWARDS, Leo. *Poppy Ott & the Tittering Totem.* 1929. NY. 1st. VG/G. B5. $25.00

EDWARDS, Leo. *Poppy Ott's Pedigreed Pickles (#4).* 1927. Grosset Dunlap. lists 8 titles. VG/VG. M20. $60.00

EDWARDS, Lionel. *Leicestershire Sketchbook.* 1935. Scribner. 1st. VG. O3. $95.00

EDWARDS, Lionel. *Seen From the Saddle.* 1937. Scribner. 1st Am. VG. O3. $95.00

EDWARDS, Peter. *Blood Brothers.* 1990. Key Porter Books. 1st. NF/NF. P3. $25.00

EDWARDS, Philip. *Story of the Voyage: Sea Narratives in 18th-C England.* 1994. Cambridge. 1st. ils/pl/index. 244p. M/dj. P4. $55.00

EDWARDS, Tickner. *Bee-Keeping for All.* 1930. Dutton. 221p. VG. A10. $12.00

EDWARDS, William H. *Football Days.* (1916). Moffat Yard. later prt. photos. G. P8. $40.00

EDWARDS, William H. *Football Days.* 1916. Moffat Yard. 1/250. inscr pres. VG/dj front laid in. B4. $225.00

EDWARDS & HOLDSTOCK. *Tour of the Universe.* 1980. Mayflower. 1st. F/F. M2. $25.00

EFFINGER, George Alec. *Heroics.* 1979. Doubleday. 1st. VG/dj. P3. $20.00

EFFINGER, George Alec. *Irrational Numbers.* 1976. Doubleday. 1st. F/NF. M2. $35.00

EFFINGER, George Alec. *Mixed Feelings.* 1974. Harper Row. 1st. F/F. P3. $20.00

EFFINGER, George Alec. *Relatives.* 1973. Harper. 1st. NF/dj. M2. $20.00

EFFINGER, Geroge Alec. *Exile Kiss.* 1991. Doubleday. 1st. sgn. F/F. B11. $35.00

EFFINGER, Geroge Alec. *Fire in the Sun.* 1989. Doubleday. 1st. inscr. F/F. B11. $35.00

EFFINGER, Geroge Alec. *When Gravity Fails.* 1987. NY. Arbor. 1st. inscr. F/F. B11. $50.00

EGAN, Constance. *Rustie Has a Holiday.* ca 1941. London. Hutchinson. 4to. R5. $200.00

EGAN, Lesley. *Wine of Life.* 1986. Gollancz. 1st. F/F. P3. $22.00

EGAN, Major Howard. *Pioneering the West 1846-1878.* 1917. Richmond, UT. private prt. A19. $150.00

EGAN, Pierce. *Tom & Jerry: Life in London.* 1874. ils George Cruikshank/37 full-p ils. VG. S13. $85.00

EGAN, R. *Fremont: Explorer for a Restless Nation.* 1977. Garden City. 1st. sgn. 582p. F/dj. M4. $35.00

EGERTON, Clement. *Golden Lotus: A Trans From Chinese Original...* 1939. London. Routledge. 1st. 4 vol. gr cloth. NF. W3. $450.00

EGGENHOFER, Nick. *Wagons, Mules & Men, How the Frontier Moved West.* 1961. Hastings. 1st. VG/dj. J2. $225.00

EGGLESTON, Edward. *End of the World. A Love Story.* (1872). Orange Judd. 1st. 12mo. 299p. cloth. M1. $85.00

EGGLESTON & SEELYE. *Pocahantas.* 1879. NY. 310p. gilt wht cloth. G. A17. $20.00

EGLETON, Clive. *Seven Days to a Killing.* 1973. CMG. 1st. VG/dj. P3. $18.00

EGLETON, Clive. *Seven Days to a Killing.* 1973. CMG. 1st. F/VG. H11. $20.00

EHLE, John. *Changing of the Guard.* 1974. Random. 1st. NF/dj. M25. $35.00

EHLE, John. *Road.* 1967. NY. 1st. VG/VG. B5. $45.00

EHRENREICH, Barbara. *Witches, Midwives & Nurses: A History of Woman Healers.* 1973. NY. Feminist. 2nd/3rd prt. photos. 45p. VG+. A25. $10.00

EHRHART, W.D. *Unaccustomed Mercy: Soldier-Poets of the Vietnam War.* 1989. TX Tech. 1st. F/F. B4. $50.00

EHRLICH, Gretel. *Arctic Heart: Poem Cycle.* 1992. Santa Barbara. 1st. 65p. wrp. P4. $12.95

EHRLICH, Gretel. *Heart Mountain.* 1988. NY. Viking. 1st. inscr. F/F. R14. $75.00

EHRLICH, Gretel. *Words From the Land.* 1988. Salt Lake City. Peregrin Smith. 1st. inscr/dtd 1992. F/F. R14. $75.00

EHRLICH, Gretel. *Wyoming Stories.* 1986. Santa Barbara. Capra. 1st. author's 2nd book. F/wrp. B3. $50.00

EHRLICH, Max. *Big Eye.* 1949. Doubleday. 1st. VG/dj. M2. $20.00

EHRLICH, Max. *Deep Is the Blue.* 1964. Doubleday. 1st. VG/dj. P3. $15.00

EHRLICH, Max. *Reincarnation in Venice.* 1979. S&S. 1st. VG/dj. P3. $15.00

EHRLICH, Yigal. *Modulators, Mediators & Specifiers in Brain Function.* 1979. NY. Plenum. tall 8vo. xl. VG/dj. G1. $45.00

EHRLICHMAN, John. *Whole Truth.* 1979. S&S. 1st. NF/VG. A20. $10.00

EHRLICHMAN, John. *Witness to Power.* 1982. S&S. 1st. F/F. W2. $30.00

EICHELBERGER, R. *Our Jungle Road to Tokyo.* 1950. NY. ils. 306p. VG/G. S16. $45.00

EICHENBERG, Fritz. *Wood & the Graver: Work of Fritz Eichenberg.* 1977. Clarkson Potter. intro Alan Fern. 130 full-p pl. 199p. M/dj. B24. $75.00

EICHHOLZ, Georg. *Landscapes of the Bible.* ca 1963. Harper Row. 1st. ils. 152p. VG/torn. W1. $9.00

EICHLER, Alfred. *Election by Murder.* 1947. Lantern. 1st. 224p. cloth. VG/dj. M20. $12.00

EIDLITZ, Walther. *Zodiak.* 1931. London. 1st. VG. M2. $75.00

EIDSMOE, John. *God & Caesar: Christian Faith & Political Action.* 1984. Crossway. 239p. F/dj. B29. $6.50

EILKINS, Aaron. *Icy Clutches.* 1990. Mysterious. 1st. sgn. F/dj. A24. $30.00

EINSTEIN, Albert. *Out of My Later Years.* 1950. Philosophical Lib. 1st. F. B35. $42.00

EINSTEIN, Albert. *Out of My Later Years.* 1950. Philosophical Lib. 1st. 282p. VG. S3. $25.00

EINSTEIN, Albert. *World As I See it.* 1934. Covici. 1st Am. 390p. gray cloth. VG+. B22. $12.00

EINSTEIN, Phyllis. *Sorcerer's Son.* 1989. London. 1st. F/F. M2. $25.00

EISELEN & LEWIS. *Abingdon Bible Commentary.* 1929. Abingdon-Cokesbury. 1452p. G. B29. $9.50

EISELEY, Loren. *Francis Bacon & the Modern Dilemma.* 1962. Lincoln. 1st. inscr. F. B4. $450.00

EISENBERG, Azriel. *Jewish Historical Treasures.* 1968. NY. photos. 207p. VG/G+. S3. $43.00

EISENBERG, Deborah. *Under the 82nd Airborne.* 1992. FSG. 1st. F/F. A20. $25.00

EISENBERG, James. *Bacteriological Diagnosis: Tabular Aids for Use...* 1892. Phil. 1st Eng trans. 184p. A13. $60.00

EISENHOWER, David. *Eisenhower at War: 1943-1945.* 1986. NY. photos/maps. 977p. VG/VG. S16. $25.00

EISENHOWER, Dwight D. *Crusade in Europe.* 1948. Doubleday. 1st. VG+/VG+. A20. $30.00

EISENHOWER, Dwight D. *Crusade in Europe: Personal Account of WWII.* 1952. NY. sgn. photos/maps/index. 559p. VG/torn. S16. $325.00

EISENHOWER, Dwight D. *In Review: Pictures I've Kept.* 1969. Doubleday. 1st. sm 4to. 236 photos. 237p. F/dj. T10. $50.00

EISENHOWER, J.S.D. *Bitter Woods: Hitler's Suprise Ardennes Offensive.* 1969. NY. 506p. VG/VG. S16. $25.00

EISENSCHIML, Otto. *American Iliad.* 1947. 1st. ils/index. 720p. F. O8. $21.50

EISENSTADT, Jill. *From Rockaway.* 1987. Knopf. 1st. F/F. A20. $25.00

EISENSTEAIN, Sergei. *Notes of a Film Director.* nd. Moscow. Foreign Languages Pub. 207p. VG/dj. M20. $45.00

EISENSTEIN, Judith Kaplan. *Heritage of Music: Music of the Jewish People.* 1973. UAHC. 2nd prt. 4to. 339p. VG/G. S3. $30.00

EISENSTEIN, Sergei. *Film Sense.* 1947. Harcourt Brace. revised. cloth. VG+/dj. C9. $75.00

EISENSTEIN & SINCLAIR. *Making & Unmaking of Que Viva Mexico.* 1970. IN U. photos/glossary. cloth. VG+/dj. C9. $50.00

EISLER, Steven. *Alien World: Complete Illustrations. A Guide.* 1980. NY. Crescent. 1st. ils. F/F. T12. $18.00

EISNER, Simon; see Kornbluth, Cyril.

EISNER, Will. *Spirit Casebook.* 1990. Kitchen Sink. 1st. sgn. F. M19. $25.00

EISNER, Will. *Spirit Color Album Vol 3.* 1983. Kitchen Sink. 1st. F. M2. $15.00

EITEL, W. *Structural Conversions in Crystalline Systems...* 1958. Geological Soc of Am. Special paper 66. 183p. cloth. F. D8. $24.00

EKLUND, Gordon. *Beyond the Resurrection.* 1973. Doubleday. 1st. VG/VG. P3. $15.00

EL-SADAT, Anwar. *In Search of Identity.* 1978. Harper Row. 1st. 8vo. 369p. NF/dj. W1. $18.00

ELBERT & ELBERT. *Miracle Houseplants.* 1984. Crown. 272p. dj. B1. $25.00

ELDREDGE, Charles C. *Charles Walter Setson: Color & Fantasy.* 1982. Lawrence, KS. 13 mc pl/b&w ils/photos/footnotes. D2. $35.00

ELDREDGE, N. *Fossils.* 1991. Abrams. 1st. 160 photos. 220p. M/dj. D8. $30.00

ELDREDGE, Zoeth. *March of Portola & Discovery of the Bay of San Francisco...* 1909. SF. CA Promotion Comm. ils. F. O7. $55.00

ELDRIDGE, Elleanor. *Elleanor's Second Book.* 1839. Providence. BT Albo. 1st. quarter muslin/marbled brd/bl paper label. F. M24. $450.00

ELDRIDGE, Fred. *Wrath in Burma, the Uncensored Story...* 1946. Garden City. 1st. ils/map ep. 320p. VG/torn. B18. $22.50

ELDRIDGE, Roger. *Shadow of the Gloom-World.* 1977. London. Gollancz. 1st. F/F. P3. $15.00

ELDRIDGE, Roger. *Shadow of the Gloom-World.* 1977. NY. Dutton. 1st. F/F. M2. $15.00

ELEGANT, Robert. *Manchu.* 1980. McGraw Hill. 1st. 560p. F/F. W2. $40.00

ELEGANT, Robert. *Mandarin.* 1983. S&S. 1st. F/F. P3. $20.00

ELGIN, Kathleen. *Quakers: Religious Society of Friends.* 1968. NY. McKay. 1st. 96p. V3. $9.50

ELGIN, Suzette Haden. *Grand Jubilee.* 1981. Doubleday. 1st. VG/VG. P3. $15.00

ELGIN, Suzette Haden. *Star-Anchored, Star-Angered.* 1979. Doubleday. 1st. F/F. M2. $15.00

ELGOOD, Cyril. *Medical History of Persia & the Eastern Capiphate...* 1951. Cambridge. 617p. gr cloth. VG/dj. B14. $100.00

ELIACH, Yaffa. *Hasidic Tales of the Holocaust.* 1982. Oxford. 1st collected. 266p. VG/dj. S3. $25.00

ELIAS, T.S. *Conservation & Management of Rare & Endangered Plants.* 1986. Sacramento. 630p. NF. B1. $25.00

ELIOT, Ethel Cook. *House Above the Trees.* 1921. London. Butterworth. 1st. ils Anderson. bl cloth/mc label. dj. R5. $250.00

ELIOT, George. *Impressions of Theophrastus Such.* 1879. Edinburgh. Blackwood. 1st. gilt mauve cloth. w/pub slip. M24. $150.00

ELIOT, George. *Middlemarch.* 1873. Harper. 1st Am. 8vo. cloth. T10. $200.00

ELIOT, George. *Silas Marner: The Weaver of Raveloe.* 1861. Harper. 1st Am. gilt pebble-grain brn cloth. M24. $200.00

ELIOT, Gwen. *Colour Your Garden With Australian Plants.* 1984. Melbourne. 80 photos. as new/dj. B26. $23.00

ELIOT, T.S. *Aims of Poetic Drama.* 1949. London. Poets Theatre Guild. 1st. F/stapled self-wrp. M24. $100.00

ELIOT, T.S. *Animula.* 1929. London. 1st. 1/400. sgn. ils Gertrude Hermes. NF/sans. A11. $400.00

ELIOT, T.S. *Dry Salvages.* 1941. London. Faber. 1st. VG. Q1. $100.00

ELIOT, T.S. *Elder Statesman, a Play.* 1959. London. 1st. VG. T9. $35.00

ELIOT, T.S. *Essays Ancient & Modern.* 1936. London. Faber. 1st. gilt bl cloth. F/dj. M24. $100.00

ELIOT, T.S. *Family Reunion.* 1939. Harcourt Brace. 1st. NF/G. M19. $45.00

ELIOT, T.S. *For Lancelot Andrews, Essays on Style & Order.* 1929. Doubleday Doran. 1st Am. mauve cloth. F/VG. M24. $150.00

ELIOT, T.S. *Journey of the Magi.* 1991. Baarn, Holland. Arethusa. 1st thus. 1/100. ils/sgns. 8vo. 26p. M/gray wrp. B24. $275.00

ELIOT, T.S. *Little Gidding.* 1942. London. Faber. 1st/1st issue (hand-sewn wrp). NF. Q1. $85.00

ELIOT, T.S. *Music of Poetry.* 1942. Glasgow. Jackson. 1st. F/wrp. M24. $85.00

ELIOT, T.S. *Old Possum's Book of Practical Cats.* 1939. London. Faber. 1st. NF/dj. Q1. $950.00

ELIOT, T.S. *Sweeney Among the Nightingales.* 1983. Como. 1/60. ils/sgn Christopher Chapman. loose/portfolio. B24. $650.00

ELIOT, T.S. *Triumphal March.* 1931. London. Faber. 1st. 1/300. sgn. ils McKnight Kauffer. gilt gray brd. F/wrp. B24. $500.00

ELIOT, T.S. *Use of Poetry & the Use of Criticism.* 1933. London. Faber. 1st. gilt rust cloth. F/dj. M24. $150.00

ELIOT, Thomas Stearns. *Family Reunion.* 1939. Harcourt Brace. 1st Am. 131p. NF/NF. H1. $65.00

ELIOT & HOELLERING. *Film of Murder in the Cathedral.* 1952. London. Faber. 1st/1st issue in mauve brd. F/NF. B4. $100.00

ELIOTT, E.C. *Kemlo & the Zombie Men.* 1958. Thomas Nelson. 1st. VG/dj. P3. $20.00

ELIZABETH, D. *Glory of Israel; or, Letters to Jewish Children...* 1842. Nat Sunday School Union. E6. $15.00

ELKIN, Benjamin. *King's Wish.* 1960. 1st. ils Leonard Shortall. VG/dj. S13. $30.00

ELKIN, Stanley. *Boswell.* 1964. Random. 1st. author's 1st book. F/NF. L3. $175.00

ELKIN, Stanley. *Boswell.* 1964. Random. 1st. author's 1st book. NF/NF. B2. $125.00

ELKIN, Stanley. *Dick Gibson Show.* 1971. Random. 1st. VG+/dj. A20. $30.00

ELKIN, Stanley. *Eighth Circle.* 1979. Mysterious. 1st thus. NF/NF. M22. $25.00

ELKIN, Stanley. *George Mills.* 1982. Dutton. 1st. NF/dj. B35. $20.00

ELKIN, Stanley. *Luxembourg Run.* 1977. Random. 1st. NF/NF. P3. $30.00

ELKIN, Stanley. *Luxembourg Run.* 1977. Random. 1st. VG/dj. N4. $20.00

ELKIN, Stanley. *Searches & Seizures.* 1973. Nonpareil. 1st. VG/wrp. M22. $25.00

ELKIN, Stanley. *Star Light Star Bright.* 1979. Random. 1st. NF/NF. P3. $20.00

ELKIN, Stanley. *Valentine Estate.* 1968. Random. 1st. F/F. M19. $25.00

ELKIN, Stanley. *Winter After This Summer.* 1960. Random. 1st. VG/dj. P3. $35.00

ELKINS, Aaron J. *Deceptive Clarity.* 1987. NY. Walker. 1st. F/dj. M15. $100.00

ELKINS, Aaron J. *Fellowship of Fear.* 1982. Walker. 1st. xl. VG. N4. $40.00

ELKINS, Aaron J. *Icy Clutches.* 1990. Mysterious. 1st. NF/NF. H11/N4. $25.00

ELLENSON, Gene. *Coaching Linebackers & the Perimeter Defense.* 1972. Parker. 1st. ils. VG/G+. P8. $12.50

ELLER, John. *Charlie & the Ice Man.* 1981. St Martin. 1st. VG/dj. P3. $13.00

ELLIK & EVANS. *Universes of EE Smith.* 1966. Advent. 1st. F/F. P3. $45.00

ELLIN & SCHIER. *Anagram Detectives.* 1979. Mysterious. 1st. 1/250. sgn/#d Ellin & Schier. F/dj/case. Q1. $50.00

ELLINGTON, Mercer. *Duke Ellington in Person.* 1978. Houghton Mifflin. 1st. NF/dj. M25. $25.00

ELLIOT, Donald. *Frogs & the Ballet.* 1979. GAmbit. 1st. ils Clinton Arrowood. 57p. G+/VG. P2. $35.00

ELLIOT, Elizabeth. *Through Gates of Splendour.* 1957. Harper. 1st. F/VG. T12. $25.00

ELLIOT, James Francis. *Jumbo Elliot: Maker of Milers, Maker of Men.* 1982. St Martin. 1st. photos. F/VG+. P8. $20.00

ELLIOT, James. *Poetical & Miscellaneous Works of James Elliot...* 1798. Greenfield, MA. 1st. 12mo. 271p. contemporary sheep. M1. $1,850.00

ELLIOT & KERR. *Rings: Discoveries From Galileo to Voyager.* 1984. MIT. 8vo. 209p. VG/dj. K5. $17.00

ELLIOTT, Charles W. *Remarkable Characters & Places of the Holy Land...* 1867. Hartford, CT. Burr. 1st. ils/mc map. 640p. aeg. cloth. VG. W1. $45.00

ELLIOTT, Don (some); see Silverberg, Robert.

ELLIOTT, Francis P. *Haunted Pajamas.* 1911. Bobbs Merrill. 1st. VG. M2. $30.00

ELLIOTT, H. Chandler. *Reprieve From Paradise.* 1955. Gnome. 1st. NF/NF. P3. $35.00

ELLIOTT, James. *Transport to Disaster.* 1962. NY. 1st. VG/dj. B5. $32.50

ELLIS, Bret Easton. *Informers.* 1994. Knopf. 1st. sgn. F/F. A23. $40.00

ELLIS, Bret Easton. *Rules of Attraction.* 1987. S&S. 1st. NF/NF. P3. $18.00

ELLIS, E. *Dewey & Other Naval Commanders.* 1899. 1st. ils. NF. E6. $25.00

ELLIS, George W. *Negro Culture in West Africa...* 1914. NY. Neale. 1st. 290p. NF. B4. $200.00

ELLIS, Havelock. *Psychology of Sex: A Manual for Students.* 1946. NY. Emerson Books. 2nd/11th prt. 377p. VG. A25. $8.00

ELLIS, Richard. *Men & Whales.* 1991. NY. Knopf. 542p. blk cloth. P4. $40.00

ELLIS, T.P. *Welsh Tribal Law & Custom in Middle Ages.* 1926. Oxford. Clarendon. 2 vol. VG/djs. M11. $250.00

ELLISON, Emily. *Picture Makers.* 1990. Morrow. 1st. F/dj. R13. $20.00

ELLISON, Harlan. *Again Dangerous Visions.* 1972. Doubleday. 1st. F/dj. M2. $175.00

ELLISON, Harlan. *Approaching Oblivion.* 1974. Walker. sgn. F/F. P3. $100.00

ELLISON, Harlan. *Dangerous Visions.* 1967. Doubleday. 1st. F/NF clip. P3. $225.00

ELLISON, Harlan. *Harlan Ellison Hornbook.* 1990. NY. Penzler. 1st. inscr. VG/VG. A23. $46.00

ELLISON, Harlan. *Harlan Ellison's Watching.* 1989. Underwood Miller. 1st. F/F. P3. $50.00

ELLISON, Harlan. *Harlan Ellison's Watching.* 1989. Underwood Miller. 1st. inscr. VG/VG. A23. $50.00

ELLISON, Harlan. *Shatterday.* 1980. Houghton Mifflin. 1st. NF/dj. P3. $50.00

ELLISON, Harlan. *Strange Wine.* 1978. Harper Row. 1st. F/F. P3. $75.00

ELLISON & PRICE. *Life & Adventures in California of Don Augustin Janssens...* 1953. Huntington Lib. 1st. F/F. O4. $15.00

ELLROY, James. *Big Nowhere.* 1988. Mysterious. 1st. F/F. R14. $40.00

ELLROY, James. *Big Nowhere.* 1988. Mysterious. 1st. sgn. F/F. D10. $45.00

ELLROY, James. *Blood on the Moon.* 1984. Mysterious. 1st. NF/dj. M25. $45.00

ELLROY, James. *Blood on the Moon.* 1984. Mysterious. 1st. sgn. F/NF. B2/D10. $65.00

ELLROY, James. *Clandestine.* 1984. London. Allison Busby. 1st hc/1st Eng. F/F. M22. $120.00

ELLROY, James. *LA Confidential.* 1990. Mysterious. 1st. sgn. NF/F. D10. $65.00

ELLROY, James. *LA Confidential.* 1990. Mysterious. 1st. VG/dj. A24/P3. $20.00

ELLROY, James. *Suicide Hill.* 1986. Mysterious. 1st. F/F. M15. $75.00

ELLROY, James. *White Jazz.* 1992. Knopf. 1st. F/F. M19. $25.00

ELLROY, James. *White Jazz.* 1992. Knopf. 1st. sgn. F/F. B3. $40.00

ELLSBERG, Edward. *Hell on Ice: Saga of the Jeannette.* 1938. Dodd Mead. 1st. 8vo. 421p. map ep. K3. $25.00

ELLSWORTH, J. Lewis. *57th Annual Report MA State Board of Agriculture.* 1909. Boston. Wright. 357p+257p report. VG. A10. $15.00

ELLWANGER, W.D. *Oriental Rug.* 1903. Dodd Mead. 1st. 12 full-p pl. 8vo. 154p. VG. T10. $60.00

ELMAN, Robert. *Atlantic Flyway.* 1972. NY. 200p. F/dj. A17. $35.00

ELMSLIE, W.A. *Among the Wild Njoni.* 1899. NY. ils/index. 320p. G+. B5. $30.00

ELON, Amos. *Herzl.* 1975. HRW. 1st. tall 8vo. 448p. as new/VG. H1. $20.00

ELSBERG, Charles A. *Diagnois & Treatment of Surgical Diseases...* 1916. Phil. Saunders. heavy 4to. ils. panelled crimson cloth. G1. $300.00

ELSENBERG, J.M. *Collector's Guide to Seashells of the World.* 1989. NY. rpt. 239p. F/F. S15. $20.00

ELSTON, Allan Vaughan. *Treasure Coach From Deadwood.* 1962. Lippincott. dj. A19. $15.00

ELTON, G.R. *FW Maitland.* 1985. London. Weidenfeld Nicolson. M11. $45.00

ELVAS, Gentleman of. *Discovery of Florida. Being True Relation of Vicissitudes...* 1946. SF. BC of CA/Grabhorn. 1/280. folio. gilt decor brd. F/plain dj. O7. $500.00

ELVERSON, Virginia T. *Cooking Legacy.* 1975. NY. Walker. 1st. G/dj. A16. $15.00

ELWOOD, Roger. *Continuum 1.* 1974. Putnam. 1st. VG/VG. P3. $30.00

ELWOOD, Roger. *Continuum 3.* 1974. Putnam. 1st. F/dj. M2. $20.00

ELWOOD, Roger. *Dystopian Visions.* 1975. Prentice Hall. 1st. VG/VG. P3. $20.00

ELWOOD, Roger. *Future Kin.* 1974. Doubleday. 1st. F/dj. P3. $15.00

ELWOOD, Roger. *Many Worlds of Andre Norton.* 1974. NY. Chilton. 1st. sgn. G/fair. B11. $40.00

ELWOOD, Roger. *New Mind.* 1973. Macmillan. 1st. F/F. P3. $20.00

EMANUEL, Cedric. *Southwest Pacific Sketchbook.* 1945. NY. ils. unp. G. S16. $35.00

EMBERLEY, Barbara. *Drummer Hoff.* (1967). S&S. 17th. sm 8vo. unp. VG/NF. T5. $20.00

EMBERLEY, Barbara. *Simon's Song.* 1969. Prentice Hall. 1st. 32p. F/NF. D4. $35.00

EMBERLEY, Ed. *Ed Emberley's ABC.* 1978. Little Brn. 1st. ils. NF/VG. P2. $40.00

EMBERLY, Michael. *Dinosaurs! A Drawing Book & More Dinosaurs!* 1983. Little Brn. 1st. NF/dj. C8. $27.50

EMBREE, Ainslie. *Hindu Tradition: Readings in Oriental Thought.* 1966. Random/Modern Lib. 1st. 363p. F/VG. W3. $36.00

EMERSON, Alice B. *Ruth Field in the Red Cross (#13).* 1918. Cupples Leon. 204p. cloth. VG/dj (lists to #25). M20. $15.00

EMERSON, Alice B. *Ruth Fielding & Her Double (#28).* 1932. Cupples Leon. ils Bert Salg. 298p. cloth. VG/dj (lists 8 titles). M20. $65.00

EMERSON, Alice B. *Ruth Fielding at Golden Pass (#21).* 1925. Cupples Leon. 205p. cloth. VG/dj (lists to #25). M20. $17.50

EMERSON, Earl W. *Black Hearts & Slow Dancing.* 1988. Morrow. 1st. F/dj. M25. $25.00

EMERSON, Earl W. *Deviant Behavior.* 1988. Morrow. 1st. F/F. P3. $18.00

EMERSON, Earl W. *Deviant Behavior.* 1988. Morrow. 1st. sgn. F/F. N4. $40.00

EMERSON, Earl W. *Fat Tuesday.* 1987. Morrow. 1st. F/F. M22. $30.00

EMERSON, Earl W. *Yellow Dog Party.* 1991. Morrow. 1st. as new/dj. N4. $25.00

EMERSON, Gloria. *Winners & Losers: Battles, Retreats, Gains, Losses...* 1976. Random. UP. VG/tall wrp. B4. $125.00

EMERSON, Harry. *Is Your Cosmic Radio Working?* 1972. Coral Gables. Your Cosmic Radio. sgn. 192p. dj. B11. $35.00

EMERSON, Jill; see Block, Lawrence.

EMERSON, R.W. *Conduct of Life.* 1860. Ticknor Fields. 1st/1st prt/A bdg. gilt brn cloth. M24. $225.00

EMERSON, R.W. *Conduct of Life. Author's Edition.* 1860. Smith Elder. 1st. 12mo. 203p. cloth. M1. $275.00

EMERSON, R.W. *Essays.* 1841-44. Boston. James Munroe. 2 vol. 1st/1st prt/1st bdg. gilt blk cloth. M24. $3,500.00

EMERSON, R.W. *Essays.* 1910. London. Macmillan. 8vo. fore-edge painting. 538p. full crushed morocco. H13. $695.00

EMERSON, R.W. *Fortune of the Republic.* 1878. Houghton Osgood. 1st. 1/504. gilt dk brn cloth. M24. $165.00

EMERSON, S. *American Horse of Aud, Secret Petrodollar Connection.* 1985. Franklin Watts. inscr. VG/dj. D8. $25.00

EMERSON, Sarah Hopper. *Life of Abby Hopper Gibbons, Told Chiefly Through...* 1897. Putnam. 1st. 2 vol. V3. $35.00

EMERY, Walter B. *Nubian Treasure: Account of Discoveries at Ballana...* 1948. London. Methuen. 1st. ils/maps/plan. 168p. VG/dj. W1. $45.00

EMETT, Rowland. *New World for Nellie.* 1952. Harcourt Brace. 1st. 4to. unp. VG/G. C14. $15.00

EMHARDT, William Chauncey. *Religion in Soviet Russia: Anarchy.* 1929. Morehouse. 1st. NF/VG. B2. $100.00

EMMART, Emily. *Badianus Manuscript: An Aztec Herbal of 1552.* 1940. Baltimore. Hopkins. 200p. VG. A10. $200.00

EMME, Eugene M. *History of Space Flight.* 1965. HRW. 8vo. 224p. VG. K5. $25.00

EMMETT, Chris. *Ft Union & the Winning of the Southwest.* 1965. Norman, OK. 1st. 436p. VG/VG. J2. $95.00

EMMISON, F.G. *Elizabethan Life: Disorder, Mainly From Essex Sessions...* 1970. Chelmsford. Essex County Council. M11. $65.00

EMMITT, Robert. *Last War Trail, the Utes & Settlement of Colorado.* 1954. Norman, OK. 1st. Civilization of Am Indian #40. 333p. VG/VG. J2. $95.00

EMMONS, W.H. *Principles of Economic Geology.* 1940. NY. McGraw Hill. 2nd/2nd imp. 529p. VG. D8. $20.00

EMORY, W.H. *Notes of Military Reconnoissance From Ft Leavenworth...* 1848. WA, DC. 1st. thick 8vo. 62 lithos/6 maps (3 fld)+lg pocket map. modern bdg. R3. $600.00

EMORY, W.H. *Notes of Military Reconnoissance From Ft Leavenworth...* 1848. Wendell Van Benthuysen. 43 engravings/3 maps (lacks 1 fld). 416p. brn cloth. K7. $195.00

EMTSEV & EMTSEV. *World Soul.* 1978. Macmillan. 1st. F/dj. M2. $25.00

ENAN, Muhammad Abdullah. *Ibn Khaldun, His Life & Work.* 1969. Lahore. Ashraf. 5th. 193p. VG. W1. $18.00

ENARI, Leonid. *Ornamental Shrubs of California.* 1962. Arcadia. ils. 214p. VG/dj. B26. $12.50

ENDE, Michael. *Momo.* 1985. Doubleday. 1st. F/NF. M19. $100.00

ENDE, Michael. *Neverending Story.* 1983. Doubleday. 1st. F/NF. M19. $65.00

ENDICOTT, W. *Adventures in Alaska & Along the Trail.* 1928. NY. Stokes. ils/photos/map. 344p. VG. M12. $60.00

ENDICOTT & JENKINS. *Wrecked Among the Cannibals in the Fijis.* 1923. Salem. Marine Research Soc. ils. 76p. T7. $120.00

ENGEBRETSON, Doug. *Empty Saddles, Forgotten Names.* 1984. North Plains. A19. $25.00

ENGEL, Howard. *City Called July.* 1986. Viking. 1st. VG/VG. P3. $20.00

ENGEL, Howard. *Murder Sees the Light.* 1984. Viking. 1st. NF/NF. P3. $18.00

ENGEL, Howard. *There Was an Old Woman.* 1973. Toronto. Viking. 1st. VG/VG. T12. $18.00

ENGEL, Lyle. *Incredible AJ Foyt.* 1970. Arco. 1st. inscr. A23. $40.00

ENGELS, Friedrich. *Condition of the Working Class in England in 1844.* 1887. NY. Lovell. 1st Am. gilt brn cloth. VG. M24. $275.00

ENGEN, Rodney. *Kate Greenaway.* 1976. 4to. ils. 68p. F/F. A4. $65.00

ENGLAND, George Allan. *Air Trust.* 1976 (1915). Hyperion. rpt. F. M2. $35.00

ENGLAND, George Allan. *Alibi.* 1916. Small Maynard. 1st. VG. M2. $50.00

ENGLAND, George Allan. *Darkness & Dawn.* 1974 (1914). Hyperion. rpt. F. M2. $40.00

ENGLEBERT, Omer. *Last of the Conquistadors.* 1956. Harcourt Brace. 1st. trans from French by Katherine Woods. VG. O4. $15.00

ENGLEHARD, Jack. *Horsemen: The Thoroughbred Racing World...* 1974. Chicago. Regnery. VG. O3. $25.00

ENGLEMAN, Roy A. *Autocraft.* 1915. Cincinnati. Am Chauffeur. 12mo. 240p. K3. $20.00

ENGLES, Frederick. *Peasant War in Germany.* 1956. Foreign Languages Pub. ne. VG/VG. V4. $12.50

ENGLISH, Barbara. *War for a Persian Lady.* 1971. Houghton Mifflin. 1st. 192p. VG/dj. M20. $18.00

ENGLISH, Charles; see Nuetzel, Charles.

ENGLISH, David. *Excalibat.* 1987. London. Barker. 1st. obl 4to. 30p. F. T10. $10.00

ENGLISH, E. Schuyler. *Things Surely To Be Believed: Primer of Bible Doctrine...* 1956. Loizeaux. 307p. VG/dj. B29. $7.50

ENGLISH, G.L. *Getting Acquainted With Minerals.* 1934. McGraw Hill. 1st/14th imp. ils. 324p. VG. D8. $20.00

ENGLISH, William Hayden. *Conquest of the Country Northwest of River Ohio, 1778-1783.* 1896. Bowen Merrill. 1st. 2 vol. pict cloth. VG+. B18. $295.00

ENGSTROM, Elizabeth. *When Darkness Loves Us.* 1985. Morrow. 1st. VG/VG. P3. $20.00

ENNES, James M. *Assault on the Liberty.* 1979. Random. 299p. VG/dj. S3. $26.00

ENOCK, C. Reginald. *Andes & the Amazon: Life & Travel in Peru.* 1910. 4th. ils. G+. M17. $25.00

ENOCK, C. Reginald. *Great Pacific Coast: Twelve Thousand Miles in Golden West.* 1909. London. Grant Richards. fld pocket map. 356p. gilt cloth. D11. $50.00

ENRIGHT, Elizabeth. *Christmas Tree.* 1951. Rinehart. 1st. inscr. 38p. F/NF. P2. $40.00

ENRIGHT, Elizabeth. *Gone-Away Lake.* (1957). London. Heinemann. 8vo. ils Krush. maroon brd. VG/G. T5. $20.00

ENRIGHT, Elizabeth. *Tatsinda.* 1963. HBW. 1st. inscr. ils Irene Haas. F/VG+. P2. $60.00

ENRIQUEZ & MIRANDE. *La Chicana: The Mexican-American Woman.* 1979. Chicago. 1st. ils. 283p. VG/VG. A25. $40.00

EPHRON, Nora. *Heartburn.* 1983. Knopf. 1st. F/F. B4. $65.00

EPSTEIN, Sarah G. *Prints of Edvard Munch, Mirror of His Life.* 1983. Allen Memorial Art Mus. 208p. F/wrp. H1. $22.50

EPSTEIN & EPSTEIN. *Andrews Raid; or, The Great Locomotive Chase.* (1956). Coward McCann. 8vo. ils RM Powers. 253p. G+/torn. T5. $12.00

EQUIANO, Olaudah. *Kidnapped Prince.* 1995. Knopf. 1st. F/F. B4. $35.00

ERDMAN, Paul. *Swiss Account.* 1982. NY. Tor. 1st. F/F. T12. $20.00

ERDRICH, Louise. *Baptism of Desire.* 1989. Harper. 1st. F/F. R13. $25.00

ERDRICH, Louise. *Beet Queen.* 1986. Holt. 1st. author's 2nd novel. F/dj. from $25 to $35.00

ERDRICH, Louise. *Beet Queen.* 1986. Holt. 1st. sgn. F/F. from $45 to $60.00

ERDRICH, Louise. *Beet Queen.* 1987. London. Hamish Hamilton. 1st. sgn. F/dj. Q1. $100.00

ERDRICH, Louise. *Love Medicine.* 1984. HRW. 1st. author's 1st novel. F/dj. from $150 to $175.00

ERDRICH, Louise. *Love Medicine.* 1984. HRW. 1st. author's 1st novel. NF/clip. L3. $125.00

ERDRICH, Louise. *Love Medicine.* 1984. HRW. 1st. sgn. author's 1st novel. F/F. L3. $250.00

ERDRICH, Louise. *Love Medicine.* 1984. HRW. 2nd. sgn. G/G. A23. $40.00

ERDRICH, Louise. *Love Medicine.* 1985. London. Deutsch. 1st. sgn. author's 1st novel. F/dj. Q1. $250.00

ERDRICH, Louise. *Tracks.* 1988. London. Hamish Hamilton. 1st. sgn. F/dj. Q1. $75.00

ERDTMAN, G. *Introduction to Pollen Analysis.* 1943. NY. 28 pl/15 figures/3 portraits. 239p. VG. B26. $36.00

ERICKSON, John R. *Devil in Texas & Other Cowboy Tales.* 1982. Perryton, TX. Maverick Books. F. A19. $15.00

ERICKSON, John R. *Modern Cowboy.* 1981. Lincoln, NE. A19. $15.00

ERICKSON, Steve. *Days Between Stations.* 1985. NY. Poseidon. 1st. sgn. author's 1st book. F/NF. L3. $175.00

ERICKSON, Steve. *Days Between Stations.* 1985. Poseidon. 1st. sgn. rem mk. F/F. R14. $75.00

ERICKSON, Steve. *Rubicon Beach.* 1986. Poseidon. 1st. F/F. R14. $50.00

ERICKSON, Steve. *Tours of the Black Clock.* 1989. Poseidon. 1st. sgn. F/F. R14. $50.00

ERICSON, Eric. *Woman Who Slept With Demons.* 1980. St Martin. 1st Am. F/dj. M2. $25.00

ERNSBERGER, George. *Mountain King.* 1978. Morrow. 1st. NF/NF. P3. $25.00

ERSKINE, John. *Adam & Eve.* 1927. Bobbs Merrill. 1st. F/dj. M2. $20.00

ERSKINE, John. *Venus: The Lonely Goddess.* 1949. Morrow. 1st. F/F. M2. $30.00

ERSKINE, Laurie York. *Renfrew's Log Trail (#5).* 1933. Grosset Dunlap. 302p. VG/dj. M20. $35.00

ERSKINE, Margaret. *Brood of Folly.* 1971. Crime Club. 1st. VG/VG. P3. $20.00

ERSKINE, Margaret. *Fatal Relations.* 1955. Hammond Hammond. 1st. VG. P3. $30.00

ERSKINE, Margaret. *Old Mrs Ommanney Is Dead.* 1955. Crime Club. 1st. VG/VG. P3. $30.00

ERVIN, Jean Adams. *Twin Cities Perceived.* 1976. Minneapolis. dj. A19. $25.00

ERWIN, Allen A. *Southwest of John Horton Slaughter, Cattleman, Sheriff.* 1965. Clark. 1st. 368p. VG/VG. J2. $325.00

ERWIN, Betty. *Summer Sleigh-Ride.* 1966. Little Brn. 1st. ils Paul Kennedy. 154p. VG/dj. P2. $20.00

ERWIN, James Jay. *Naval Reserves of Ohio in War With Spain, 1898-99.* ca 1900. Cleveland. ils. 96p. G. B18. $95.00

ERWIN, Marie H. *Wyoming Historical Blue Book.* 1946. Denver, CO. Bradford Robinson. inscr. A19. $150.00

ESAU, K. *Plant Anatomy.* 1965. John Wiley. 2nd. 767p. B1. $50.00

ESCOFFIER, A. *Kochkunst Fuhrer; Le Guide Culinaire, Deutsche Ausgabe...* 1904. Frankfurt. 806p. emb leather spine. VG. E6. $250.00

ESENWEIN, J. Berg. *Adventures To Come.* 1937. McLoughlin. 1st. VG. M2. $22.00

ESHBACH, Lloyd Arthur. *Of Worlds Beyond.* 1965. London. 1st. F/dj. M2. $25.00

ESHBACH, Lloyd Arthur. *Tyrant of Time.* 1955. Fantasy. 1st. F/F. P3. $20.00

ESHLEMAN, L.W. *Victorian Rebel.* 1940. NY. 1st. VG/VG. B5. $27.50

ESKELUND, Karl. *Vagabond Fever: A Gay Journey in Land of the Andes.* 1954. Chicago. Rand McNally. 1st. 240p. dj. F3. $15.00

ESKENAZI, Gerald. *Thinking Man's Guide to Pro Hockey.* 1972. Dutton. 1st. sgn. F/F. P8. $40.00

ESKRIDGEM, Robert Lee. *Umi: Hawaiian Boy Who Became King.* 1937. ils. VG/VG. M17. $20.00

ESPOSITO, V.J. *West Point Atlas of American Wars.* 1960. NY. 2 vol. maps. NF. M4. $75.00

ESPOSITO & MORIARTY. *Brothers Espositio.* 1971. Hawthorn. 1st. photos. VG+/dj. P8. $25.00

ESPY, Hilda. *Another World: Central America.* (1970). Viking. 1st. 311p. dj. F3. $15.00

ESQUIRE. *Esquire Cook-Book.* 1955. McGraw Hill. 1st. ils. sm 4to. dj. A16. $15.00

ESQUIVEL, Laura. *Like Water for Chocolate.* 1991. 1st. F/clip. M19. $50.00

ESTEN, John. *Manhattan Style.* 1990. Little Brn. photos George Chinsee. 223p. cloth. dj. D2. $55.00

ESTERHAZY, Peter. *Helping Verbs & Heart.* 1991. Grove. 1st. F/F. B35. $15.00

ESTES, Eleanor. *Ginger Pye.* (1951). Harcourt Brace. 8vo. 250p. VG. T5. $20.00

ESTES, Eleanor. *Hundred Dresses.* (1944). Harcourt Brace. early prt. 8vo. ils/sgn Louis Slobodkin. VG/G. T5. $85.00

ESTES, Eleanor. *Moffats.* 1941. Harcourt. 1st/pub review. ils Louis Slobodkin. cloth. G+. M5. $60.00

ESTEY, Paul C. *Woodchuck Hunter.* (1936). Onslow County, NC. Sm Arms Pub. VG. H7. $35.00

ESTIENNE, Henri. *Discours Merveilleux de la Vie...* 1663. 12mo. calf. R12. $150.00

ESTLEMAN, Loren D. *Any Man's Death.* 1986. Mysterious. 1st. VG/dj. P3. $20.00

ESTLEMAN, Loren D. *Bloody Season.* 1988. Bantam. 1st. 231p. VG/dj. J2. $110.00

ESTLEMAN, Loren D. *Downriver.* 1986. Houghton Mifflin. 1st. F/F. P3. $25.00

ESTLEMAN, Loren D. *Downriver.* 1988. Houghton Mifflin. 1st. NF/NF. M22. $15.00

ESTLEMAN, Loren D. *Lady Yesterday.* 1987. Houghton Mifflin. 1st. F/F. H11/P3. $25.00

ESTLEMAN, Loren D. *Motor City Blue.* 1980. Houghton Mifflin. 1st. sgn. F/NF. H11. $175.00

ESTLEMAN, Loren D. *Sugartown.* 1984. Houghton Mifflin. 1st. sgn. F/NF. A20. $25.00

ESTLEMAN, Loren D. *Sweet Women Lie.* 1990. Houghton Mifflin. 1st. F/F. P3. $20.00

ETCHISON, Dennis. *Dark Country.* 1982. Scream. 1st. VG/VG. P3. $100.00

ETHRIDGE, Willie Snow. *Summer Thunder.* 1958. NY. Coward. 1st. sgn. VG/VG. B11. $40.00

ETS, Marie Hall. *Jay Bird.* 1974. Viking. 1st. ils. 40p. F/NF. D4. $35.00

ETS, Marie Hall. *Mister Penny.* 1935. Viking. 1st. 12mo. 48p. VG. D1. $150.00

EUGENIDES, Jeffrey. *Virgin Suicides.* 1993. FSG. 1st. F/F. M25. $45.00

EUNSON, Dale. *Up on the Rim.* 1970. NY. FSG. A19. $35.00

EUSEBIUS PAMPHILI, Bishop. *Chronicon...* 13 June 1512. Paris. Henricus Stephanus. 1st Estienne ed. recent bdg. R15. $4,000.00

EUSTACHI, Bartolomeo. *Tabulae Anatomicae.* 1714. Rome. 1st. folio. half leather/marbled brd. A13. $12,500.00

EUSTIS, Helen. *Fool Killer.* 1954. Doubleday. 1st. VG/dj. P3. $20.00

EVANOVICH, Janet. *One for the Money.* 1994. Scribner. 1st. inscr/dtd 1994. F/wht dj. Q1. $100.00

EVANS, Bergen. *Spoor of Spooks & Other Nonsense.* 1954. Knopf. 1st. VG/VG. P3. $10.00

EVANS, C.S. *Sleeping Beauty.* 1920. London. Heinemann. ils Rackham/1 mtd mc pl/silhouettes. pict brd. rose dj. R5. $225.00

EVANS, Clement Anselm. *Confederate Military History.* 1976. Syracuse, NY. Bl & Gray Pr. 1st. 13 vol. cloth. VG. M8. $150.00

EVANS, Clement Anselm. *Confederate Military History: Kentucky & Missouri.* 1899. Atlanta. Confederate Pub. 1st. xl. VG. M8. $35.00

EVANS, Donald P. *Still Hooked on Harness Racing.* 1905. Phil. Winston. 1st. VG/G. O3. $12.00

EVANS, Donald. *Big Bum: Story of Bret Hanover.* 1969. NY. 1st. ils. 220p. VG/dj. B5. $35.00

EVANS, E.N. *Judah P Benjamin: The Jewish Confederate.* 1988. VG/VG. M17. $22.50

EVANS, Elizabeth. *Weathering the Storm: Women of the American Revolution.* 1975. Scribner. 1st. sm 4to. 372p. as new/dj. H1. $22.50

EVANS, Eva Knox. *Jerome Anthony.* 1936. Putnam. ils Erick Berry. 8vo. VG/dj. M5. $75.00

EVANS, G.B. *Troubles With Bird Dogs & What To Do About Them...* 1975. NY. Winchester. ils/photos. 307p. F/NF. M12. $45.00

EVANS, Gladys. *Journey Across Three Worlds.* 1973. Moscow. 1st. F/dj. M2. $10.00

EVANS, John W. *Solar Corona.* 1963. NY. Academic. xl. K5. $40.00

EVANS, Larry. *Chess: Beginner to Expert.* 1967. MA. 226p. VG/dj. S1. $6.00

EVANS, Max. *Rounders.* 1960. Macmillan. 1st. NF/NF. B4. $145.00

EVANS, Oliver. *Young Mill-Wright's & Miller's Guide. In Five Parts...* 1807. Octoraro, PA. Francis Bailey. 2nd. 8vo. 25 pl. contemporary calf. M1. $650.00

EVANS, Thomas. *Old Ballads, Historical & Narrative...* 1784. London. Evans. 1st collected. 4 vol. 8vo. full tree calf. H13. $495.00

EVANS & EVANS. *Friends' Lib.* 1841. Phil. Joseph Rakestraw. 14 vol. modern bdg. V3. $365.00

EVANS & SHOEMAKER. *International Symposium on Hydrometallurgy.* 1973. NY. Am Inst Mining/Petroleum Engineers. 1184p. cloth. NF. D8. $37.50

EVANS-WENTZ, W.Y. *Tibet's Great Yogi, Milarepa...* 1928. Oxford. 1st. index. 315p. VG. W3. $86.00

EVASHEVSKI & NELSON. *Scoring Power With the Winged T Offense.* 1957. Brown. 1st. inscr. VG/G+. P8. $50.00

EVELYN, John. *Miscellaneous Writings.* 1825. London. Colburn. 1st. tall thick 4to. 875p. tan morocco. H13. $395.00

EVERETT, Susanne. *Slaves.* 1978. Putnam. G. A19. $35.00

EVERITT, Charles P. *Adventures of a Treasure Hunter.* 1951. Little Brn. 1st. G+/dj. K3. $20.00

EVERMANN & JORDAN. *American Food & Game Fishes.* 1902. Doubleday Page. 1st. 4to. ils/photos. gilt gr cloth. w/letter. T10. $300.00

EVERS & PETERS. *For Us, the Living.* 1967. Doubleday. 1st. photos. VG/VG. A25. $10.00

EVERSON, William. *Veritable Years, 1949-1966.* 1978. Santa Barbara. Blk Sparrow. 1/500. D11. $50.00

EVERSON & POWELL. *Take Hold Upon the Future: Letters on Writers...* 1994. Scarecrow. 1st. sgn Powell. edit WR Eshelman. 603p. M. B19. $70.00

EVERSON MUSEUM OF ART. *New Works in Clay by Contemporary Painters & Sculptors.* 1976. Syracuse. 1/3000. ils/photos. D2. $30.00

EWALD, Carl. *Old Willow-Tree & Other Stories.* ca 1921. NY. Stokes. 1st. ils Helen Jacobs. 8vo. 157p. tan cloth. R5. $100.00

EWAN, Joe. *From Seed to Flower: Philadelphia 1681-1876.* 1976. Penn Hort Soc. 120p. A10. $28.00

EWAN & EWAN. *John Banister & His Natural History of Virginia 1678-92.* 1970. Urbana. 485p. F/NF. S15. $30.00

EWBANK, Thomas. *Report of Commissioner of Patents, Agriculture.* 1851. WA. House Prt. 579p. leather spine/marbled brd. VG. A10. $28.00

EWEN, C. L'Estrange. *Witch Hunting & Witch Trials...* 1971 (1929). London. Frederick Muller. facsimile. M11. $85.00

EWING, Frederick R.; see Sturgeon, Theodore.

EWING, James. *Causation, Diagnosis & Treatment of Cancer.* 1831. Baltimore. 1st. 87p. A13. $75.00

EWING, Joseph H. *29 Let's Go!* 1948. WA. 1st. 315p. VG. B18. $95.00

EWING & HAGEMAN. *Archeological & Restoration Study of Mission La Purisima...* 1980. Santa Barbara. Trust for Historic Preservation. ils/notes. 307p. NF. B19. $45.00

EXLEY, Frederick. *Fan's Notes.* 1968. Harper Row. 1st. author's 1st book. NF/NF. A15. $60.00

EXLEY, Frederick. *Pages From a Cold Island.* 1975. Random. 1st. NF/NF. R14. $30.00

EYLES. *World of Oz: Historical Expedition Over the Rainbow.* 1985. London. 4to. ils. 96p. F/F. A4. $35.00

EYRE, Alice. *Famous Fremonts & Their America.* 1961. Boston. rpt. inscr. VG. O4. $25.00

EYRE, S.R. *Vegetation & Soils: A World Picture.* 1963. Chicago. Aldine. 324p. dj. A10. $30.00

EZELL & EZELL. *On Mars: Exploration of the Red Planet 1958-1978.* 1984. NASA. sm 4to. 535p. VG/wrp. K5. $40.00

FABES, Gilbert H. *John Galsworth: His First Editions, Points & Values.* 1932. London. Foyle. 1st. sgn. 12mo. VG. A17. $25.00

FABIAN, Stephen. *Fantasy of Fabian.* 1978. De La Ree. 1st. NF/NF. P3. $35.00

FABRE, D.G. *Beyond the River of the Dead.* (1963). London. Travel BC. 191p. F3. $15.00

FABRE, Jean Henri. *Fabre's Book of Insects.* 1921. Dodd Mead. 1st Am. 271p. gr decor cloth. VG. T10. $200.00

FABRO BREMUNDAN, Francisco. *Historia de los Hechos del Serenissimo Senor Don Juan...* 1673. Zaragoza. Diego Dormer. 1st/only. folio. 458p. contemporary vellum. R15. $3,000.00

FACKENHEIM, Emil L. *Quest for Past & Future: Essays in Jewish Theology.* 1968. IU. 336p. VG/G+. S3. $22.00

FACKLER, Elizabeth. *Arson.* 1984. Dodd Mead. 1st. author's 1st novel. F/F. T2. $20.00

FACKLER, Elizabeth. *Barbed Wire.* 1986. St Martin. 1st. F/F. T2. $15.00

FADIMAN, Clifton. *Joys of Wine.* 1975. Abrams. lg 4to. 449p. F/torn. T10. $75.00

FAEGRI & PIJL. *Principles of Pollination Ecology.* 1966. London. Pergamon. 1st. 248p. dj. A10. $25.00

FAGES, Pedro. *Diary of Pedro Fages: Colorado River Campaign 1781-82.* 1913. CA U. 1st. edit HI Priestley. 101p. F/wrp. B19. $40.00

FAIR, A.A.; see Gardner, Erle Stanley.

FAIR, Charles M. *Dying Self.* 1969. Middletown, CT. Wesleyan U. 240p. gray cloth. VG/dj. G1. $25.00

FAIR, Charles M. *Physical Foundations of the Psyche.* 1963. Wesleyan U. 287p. gr cloth. G1. $25.00

FAIRBAIRN, Henry. *Defence of William Penn, From Charges Contained...* 1849. Phil. Rakestraw. 1st. 38p. V3. $20.00

FAIRBAIRN, Roger; see Carr, John Dickson.

FAIRBURN, William Armstrong. *Merchant Sail.* 1945-55. Center Lovell. Fairburn Marine Edu Found. mixed eds. NF. P4. $750.00

FAIRCHILD, David. *Garden Islands of the Great East.* 1943. Scribner. 1st. 8vo. 239p. F. A22. $30.00

FAIRFAX, Virginia. *Girl Scouts: Curious Quest (#5).* 1934. AL Burt. 1st. 250p. cloth. VG/dj (last title listed). M20. $45.00

FAIRLEIGH, Runa. *Old-Fashioned Mystery.* 1983. Denys. 1st. VG/dj. M2. $20.00

FAIRLEY & ISRAEL. *True North: Story of Captain Joseph Bernier.* 1957. Toronto. Macmillan. 160p. map ep. VG/dj. P4. $25.00

FAIRMONT, Ethel. *Rhymes for Kindly Children.* 1927. Volland. 46th. 8vo. ils brd. R5. $125.00

FAISS, Fritz. *Roster Mond Weisses Wild: Leider der Indianer.* 1955. Wolfgang Rothe. 1st. sgn. 38p. NF/VG. B19. $35.00

FAKHRY, Ahmed. *Pyramids.* 1969. Chicago. 1st. ils/maps. VG/dj. W1. $10.00

FALK, Edwin A. *Fighting Bob Evans.* 1931. ils. VG. M17. $17.50

FALK, K. George. *Chemistry of Enzyme Actions.* 1924. NY. Chemical Catalog Co. 249p. cloth. A10. $8.00

FALKNER, J. Meade. *Last Stradivarius.* 1896. Appleton. 1st. VG. M2. $75.00

FALL, Bernard B. *Hell in a Very Small Place: Siege of Dien Bien Phu.* 1967. Phil. ils/photos/maps. 515p. G. B18. $22.50

FALL, Thomas. *Ordeal of Running Standing.* 1970. NY. McCall. 1st. F/VG clip. L3. $50.00

FALLON, Martin; see Patterson, Henry.

FALLOWELL, Duncan. *Drug Tales.* 1979. Hamish Hamilton. 1st. F/F. P3. $20.00

FALLOWS & TRUITT. *Know Thyself, a Word at the Right Time.* 1911. SA Mulliken. salesman's copy. full leather. G-. B18. $22.50

FALS-BORDA, Orlando. *Peasant Society in the Columbian Andes.* 1962. Gainesville. 1st. 377p. dj. F3. $15.00

FALWELL, Jerry. *Aflame for God.* 1979. Nashville. Nelson. 2nd. inscr. A23. $32.00

FANNER, Janet. *Cubical City: With an Afterword by the Author.* 1974. Carbondale. S IL U. Lost American Fiction series. 1st thus. F/clip. Q1. $40.00

FANNIN, Cole. *Leave It To Beaver.* 1962. Whitman. TVTI. VG. P3. $15.00

FANNIN, Cole. *Rin Tin Tin & the Ghost Wagon Train.* 1958. Whitman. TVTI. VG. P3. $10.00

FANNIN, Cole. *Sea Hunt.* 1960. Whitman. TVTI. F. P3. $20.00

FANNING, Edmund. *Voyages & Discoveries in South Seas 1792-1832.* 1924. Salem. Marine Research Soc. 32 pl. 355p. P4. $135.00

FANNING, L.M. *Our Oil Resources.* 1945. NY. McGraw Hill. 331p. NF. D8. $10.00

FANTE, John. *Brotherhood of the Grape.* 1977. Houghton. 1st. F/NF. M25. $45.00

FANTE, John. *Dreams From Bunker Hill.* 1982. Blk Sparrow. 1st. F/dj. M25. $45.00

FARAGO, L. *Game of Foxes.* 1971 (1971). 696p. F/G+. E6. $13.00

FARAGO, Ladislas. *Abyssinia on the Eve.* 1935. Putnam. 4th. 8vo. ils/map ep. 286p. VG. W1. $22.00

FARBER, Eduard. *Nobel Prize Winners in Chemistry 1901-1950.* 1953. NY. Henry Schumann. 1st. ils. 291p. xl. dj. K3. $15.00

FARBER, Norma. *How Does It Feel To Be Old?* 1979. Dutton. 1st. ils TS Hyman. 34p. NF/worn. D4. $40.00

FARBER, Seymour. *Cytologic Diagnosis of Lung Cancer.* 1950. Springfield. 1st. sgn. 4to. 59p. A13. $50.00

FARHI, Moris. *Last of Days.* 1983. Crown. 1st. VG/VG. P3. $18.00

FARINA, Richard. *Been Down So Long It Looks Like Up to Me.* 1966. Random. 1st. author's 1st book. F/NF. M25. $100.00

FARINA, Richard. *Long Time Coming & Long Time Gone.* 1969. Random. 1st. F/dj. Q1. $50.00

FARIS, John T. *Old Churches & Meeting Houses in & Around Philadelphia.* 1926. Lippincott. 1st. 261p. VG. V3. $24.00

FARIS, John T. *Old Roads Out of Philadelphia.* 1917. Lippincott. VG. O3. $35.00

FARJEON, Eleanor. *Cherrystones.* nd (1942). Lippincott. 1st Am. sm 8vo. 61p. VG+/G+. C14. $25.00

FARJEON, Eleanor. *Children's Bells.* 1960. NY. Walck. 1st Am. ils Peggy Fortum. 212p. coth. NF/dj. D4. $45.00

FARJEON, Eleanor. *Gipsy & Ginger.* 1920. London. Dent. 1st. 151p. VG. P2. $55.00

FARJEON, Eleanor. *Martin Pippin in the Apple Orchard.* 1922 (1921). Stokes. 1st Am. 8vo. gr cloth. VG/G+. T5. $60.00

FARJEON, Eleanor. *Then There Were Three.* 1965. Lippincott. 174p. cloth. F/dj. D4. $40.00

FARJEON & FARJEON. *Kings & Queens.* nd (1932). London/NY. Gollancz/Dutton. 1st. 79p. VG/dj. D4. $75.00

FARLEY, Jim. *Jim Farley's Story: The Roosevelt Years.* (1948). McGraw. 3rd. inscr. 388p. VG/fair. B22. $9.00

FARLEY, Walter. *Black Stallion & Satan.* 1949. RAndom. 1st. VG/G. O3. $58.00

FARLEY, Walter. *Black Stallion's Courage.* 1956. Random. 1st. VG/VG. O3. $45.00

FARLEY, Walter. *Black Stallion's Filly.* 1952. Random. 1st. ils Milton Menasco. 307p. VG+/dj. M20. $35.00

FARLEY, Walter. *Black Stallion's Filly.* 1952. Random. 1st. 309p. VG/dj. M20. $30.00

FARLEY, Walter. *Island's Stallion's Fury.* 1951. Random. 1st. 243p. VG/dj. M20. $35.00

FARLEY, Walter. *Island Stallion Races.* 1955. Random. 1st. 256p. VG/dj. M20. $22.50

FARMER, Bernard J. *Gentle Art of Book Collecting.* 1950. Thorsons. 1st. VG/G. P3. $25.00

FARMER, E.J. *Resources of the Rocky Mountains...* 1883. Cleveland. 196p. VG. B18. $30.00

FARMER, Fannie Merritt. *Boston Cooking-School Cook Book.* 1924. Little Brn. fair. A16. $12.00

FARMER, Philip Jose. *Dark Is the Sun.* 1979. Del Rey. 1st. F/F. P3. $20.00

FARMER, Philip Jose. *Dayworld Rebel.* 1987. Putnam. 1st. F/F. H11. $20.00

FARMER, Philip Jose. *Dayworld.* 1985. Putnam. 1st. F/F. H11. $25.00

FARMER, Philip Jose. *Flesh.* 1968. Doubleday. 1st. sgn. F/F. M2. $325.00

FARMER, Philip Jose. *Lord Tyger.* 1970. Doubleday. 1st. sgn. NF/dj. M2. $150.00

FARMER, Philip Jose. *Love Song.* 1983. McMillan. 1st. 1/500. sgn. F/F. M2/P3. $85.00

FARMER, Philip Jose. *Magic Labyrinth.* 1980. Berkley. 1st. F/F. M2. $13.00

FARMER, Philip Jose. *Night of Light.* 1975. Garland. 1st hc. F/sans. M2. $60.00

FARMER, Philip Jose. *Unreasoning Mask.* 1981. Putnam. 1st. VG/VG. P3. $20.00

FARNHAM, Eilza A. *Woman & Her Era.* 1864. NY. AJ Davis. 1st. gilt blk cloth. M24. $250.00

FARNOL, Jeffery. *Shadow.* 1929. Little Brn. 1st Am. VG. M2. $27.00

FARR, Finis. *Margaret Mitchell of Atlanta.* 1965. Morrow. 1st. 244p. cloth. VG/dj. M20. $50.00

FARR, John; see Webb, Jack.

FARR, Robert. *Electronic Criminals.* 1975. McGraw Hill. 1st. VG/VG. P3. $15.00

FARRAR, Frederick M. *Fred Farrar's Type Book.* 1927. Harper. 1st. ils. VG/dj. K3. $20.00

FARRAR, Mrs. John. *Recollections of Seventy Years.* 1866. Ticknor Fields. 331p. V3. $12.00

FARRAR, Timothy. *Report of the Case of Trustees of Dartmouth College...* 1819. Portsmouth, NH. 1st. 8vo. 406p. uncut. M1. $275.00

FARRARS, E.X. *Neck in a Noose.* 1943. Doubleday Crime Club. 1st Am. F/VG. M15. $45.00

FARRELL, James T. *Brand New Life.* 1968. Doubleday. 1st. F/VG+. A24. $30.00

FARRELL, James T. *Fate of Writing in America.* 1946. New Directions. 1st. inscr. NF/stapled wrp. B4. $125.00

FARRELL, James T. *Gas-House McGinty.* 1933. Vanguard. 1st. NF/dj. Q1. $450.00

FARRELL, James T. *Guillotine Party & Other Stories.* 1935. Vanguard. 1st. VG/dj. M22. $140.00

FARRELL, James T. *Lonely for the Future.* 1966. Doubleday. 1st. 263p. G. W2. $15.00

FARRELL, James T. *Note on Literary Criticism.* 1937. Vanguard. 1st. F/NF. B2. $75.00

FARRELL & KOCH. *Talking to the Sun.* 1985. HRW/Metro Mus Art. 1st. 112p. F/F. D4. $30.00

FARRER, Reginald. *English Rock Garden.* 1922 (1919). London. 2 vol. 2nd imp. photos/fld map. VG. B26. $165.00

FARRIER, Denis. *Country Vet.* 1973. NY. Taplinger. 1st Am. VG/G. O3. $15.00

FARRIS, John. *Fury.* 1976. Playboy. 1st. VG/fair. P3. $20.00

FARRIS, John. *Sacrifice.* nd (1994). Forge. UP. sgn. F/prt wrp. M22. $65.00

FARRIS, John. *Scare Tactics.* 1988. Tor. 1st. VG/VG. P3. $18.00

FARRIS, John. *Sharp Practice.* 1974. S&S. 1st. 286p. half red cloth/gray brd. F/dj. H1. $28.00

FARRIS, John. *Uninvited.* 1982. Delacorte. 1st. F/F. M21. $25.00

FARSHLER, Earl R. *Riding & Training.* 1959. Van Nostrand. 2nd. 340p. VG/clip. M20. $15.00

FARWELL, George. *Mask of Asia: Philippines Today.* 1967. NY. Praeger. sm 4to. 227p. as new/VG. P1. $8.00

FARWELL, Willard B. *Chinese at Home & Abroad; Together With Report...* 1885. SF. Bancroft. 8vo. fld Chinatown street map. burgundy cloth. NF. R3. $600.00

FASSET, Norman C. *Sping Flora of Wisconsin.* 1938. Madison. 12mo. VG. A22. $10.00

FASSETT & OGDEN. *Manual of Aquatic Plants.* (1957). Madison. revised ed. ils/figures. 405p. cloth. VG/VG. M12. $25.00

FAST, Howard. *Max.* 1982. Houghton Mifflin. 1st. F/F. B35. $18.00

FAST, Howard. *Outsider.* 1984. Houghton Mifflin. 1st. VG/VG. P3. $15.00

FAST, Howard. *Pledge.* 1988. Houghton Mifflin. 1st. VG/VG. P3. $18.00

FAST, Howard. *Pledge.* 1988. Houghton Mifflin. 1st. 324p. F/F. W2. $35.00

FAST, Howard. *Spartacus.* 1951. NY. self pub. 1st. sgn. F/VG. B4. $250.00

FAST, Jonathan. *Mortal Gods.* 1978. Harper Row. 1st. F/F. P3. $15.00

FAST, Jonathan. *Mortal Gods.* 1989. Easton. leather. F. M2. $40.00

FAST, Julius. *Model for Murder.* 1956. Rinehart. 1st. F/dj. M15. $45.00

FATOUT, Paul. *Mark Twain in Virginia City.* 1964. IU. 1st/1st prt. cream cloth. NF/dj. M24. $30.00

FATOUT, Paul. *Meadow Lake Gold Town.* 1969. Bloomington. IU. 1st. 8vo. 178p. gilt brn cloth. as new/dj. K7. $40.00

FAULCONER & KEYS. *Foundations of Anesthesiology.* 1965. Springfield. 1st. 2 vol. A13. $250.00

FAULK, John Henry. *Fear on Trial: Story of His Six-Year Battle...* 1964. S&S. 1st. F/F. V4. $20.00

FAULK, Odie B. *Arizona: Short History.* 1970. OK U. 1st. ils/bibliography. 265p. F/NF. B19. $20.00

FAULK, Odie B. *Land of Many Frontiers.* 1968. Oxford. 1st. 8vo. brn cloth. dj. F7. $35.00

FAULK, Odie B. *Tombstone, Myth & Reality.* 1972. Oxford. 1st. 242p. VG. J2. $69.00

FAULKNER, Georgene. *Old English Nursery Tales.* 1916. Chicago. 1st. ils Milo Winter. 8vo. blk cloth/label. R5. $125.00

FAULKNER, William. *Afternoon of a Cow.* 1991. Windover. 1/200. 1st separate appearance. F/wrp. B2. $75.00

FAULKNER, William. *Big Woods.* 1955. NY. 1st. VG/VG. B5. $125.00

FAULKNER, William. *Faulkner & Race.* 1987. Jackson, MS. 1st. edit Fowler/Abadie. F/F. B3. $25.00

FAULKNER, William. *Light in August.* 1932. Smith Haas. 1st. 480p. cloth. VG/dj/glassine dj cover. M20. $750.00

FAULKNER, William. *Mansion.* (1959). Random. 1st/1st prt. gilt bl cloth. F/F. M24. $150.00

FAULKNER, William. *Marble Faun/Green Bough.* 1965. Random. 1st thus. F/VG clip. B4. $65.00

FAULKNER, William. *Marble Faun/Green Gough.* 1965. NY. 1st combined. NF/NF. A11. $65.00

FAULKNER, William. *Mirrors of Chartres Street.* 1953. Minneapolis. Faulkner Studies. 1st. 1/1000. F/dj. B24. $325.00

FAULKNER, William. *Miss Zilphia Gant.* 1932. Dallas. BC of Texas. 1st. 1/300. gilt rust cloth. F. M24. $2,250.00

FAULKNER, William. *New Orleans Sketches.* 1958. Rutgers. 1st Am. gilt quarter maroon cloth. F/dj. M24. $100.00

FAULKNER, William. *Reivers.* 1962. Random. 1st. F/VG+. T11. $50.00

FAULKNER, William. *Sanctuary.* 1931. Cape/Smith. 1st/1st prt. gray/magenta brd. M24. $200.00

FAULKNER, William. *Santuari.* 1970. Barcelona. 1st Spanish. NF/wrp. A11. $40.00

FAULKNER, William. *Sartoris.* 1929. Harcourt Brace. 1st. top edge red. red titled blk bdg. G. B24. $200.00

FAULKNER, William. *Selected Letters...Edited by Joseph Blotner.* 1976. Franklin Lib. 1st. intro Albert Erskine. full leather. F. B4. $150.00

FAULKNER, William. *Sherwood Anderson & Other Famous Creoles.* 1926. New Orleans. Pelican Bookshop. 1st/1st issue. 1/250. gr brd. M24. $4,500.00

FAULKNER, William. *Spotted Horses.* 1989. U of SC. 1st separate of 600 deluxe. ils/sgn Saunders. F/case. A24. $195.00

FAULKNER, William. *Stallion Road.* 1989. MS U. 1st. F/dj. A24. $30.00

FAULKNER, William. *Town.* 1957. Random. 1st. gilt rust cloth. VG. M24. $35.00

FAULKNER, William. *Town.* 1957. Random. 1st. F/G. M19. $45.00

FAUST, Frederick S. *Notebooks & Poems of Max Brand.* 1957. Dodd Mead. 1/750. #d. F/box. M2. $75.00

FAUST, Fredrick S. *Futitives' Fire.* 1991. Putnam. 1st. F/F. P3. $19.00

FAUST, Fredrick S. *On the Trail of Four.* 1967. Dodd Mead. rpt. F/NF. M15. $35.00

FAUST, Fredrick S. *Thunderer.* 1933. Derrydale. VG. O3. $85.00

FAUST, Ron. *Tombs of Blue Ice.* 1974. Bobbs Merrill. 1st. VG/VG. P3. $20.00

FAUSTE, Jeane. *Historie Prodigieuse et Lamentable de Jeane Fauste.* 1712. Cologne. Heirs of Marteau. 12mo. quarter calf. R12. $425.00

FAUSTER, Carl U. *Libby Glass Since 1918.* 1979. Len Beach Pr. 4to. 1300+ pieces ils on 71 mc pl. 415p. as new/dj. H1. $300.00

FAUSTO DA LONGIANO. *Histoire de la Vie & Faits D'Ezzelin III.* 1644. Paris. Prome. 8vo. armorial bookplate. vellum. R12. $150.00

FAVOR, E.H. *Fruit-Growers Guide-Book.* 1911. St Joseph MO Fruit Grower. 285p. cloth. VG. A10. $20.00

FAVOUR, Alpheus H. *Old Bill Williams, Mountain Man.* 1936. NC C. Southwestern Century #30. 229p. VG/dj. J2. $175.00

FAWAD, D. *Victory Denied: Rise of Air Power & Defeat of Germany 1920.* 1987. 1st Am. F/VG. E6. $12.00

FAWCETT, Clara Hallard. *Dolls: A Guide for Collectors.* 1947. NY. Linquist. 1st. sgn. 194p. VG. B11. $45.00

FAWCETT, Clara Hallard. *Paper Dolls: A Guide to Costume.* 1951. HL Lindquist. 1st probable. lg 8vo. VG+. C8. $50.00

FAWCETT, E. Douglas. *Hartmann the Anarchist.* 1893. Arnold. 1st. VG. P3. $200.00

FAWCETT, P.H. *Lost Trails, Lost Cities.* 1953. Funk Wagnalls. 1st. 332p. VG/dj. F3. $25.00

FAWCETT, P.H. *Lost Trails, Lost Cities.* 1953. NY. 1st Am. 332p. VG. B18. $17.50

FAX, Elton C. *Through Black Eyes: Journeys of a Black Artist...* 1974. Dodd Mead. 1st. 203p. F/NF. B4. $100.00

FAY, Charles Edey. *Mary Celeste: Odyssey of an Abandoned Ship.* 1942. Salem. Peabody Mus. ltd (not abridged). 1/1000. VG. O7. $150.00

FEATHERS, Davis L. *Camellia.* 1978. Columbia, SC. 8vo. 476p. cloth. VG/dj. A22. $30.00

FEATHERSTONHAUGH, G.W. *Canoe Voyage Up the Minnay Sotor.* 1970. MN Hist Soc. facsimile 1847 ed. cloth/case. A17. $25.00

FEATHERSTONHAUGH, G.W. *Excursion Through the Slave States.* 1844. London. John Murray. 1st. 2 vol. fld map. aeg. rebound half morocco. Q1. $750.00

FEELEY, Pat. *Best Friend.* 1977. Dutton. 1st. F/F. P3. $20.00

FEIBLEMAN, Peter S. *Charlie Boy.* 1980. Little Brn. 1st. VG/VG. P3. $15.00

FEID, Richard. *Upper Ottawa Valley to 1855: A Collection of Documents.* 1990. Toronto. Champlain Soc. 354p. gilt red cloth. F. P4. $95.00

FEIERBERG, M.Z. *Whither? And Other Stories.* 1972-73. JPS. 240p. VG/dj. S3. $23.00

FEIFER, George. *Tennozan: Battle of Okinawa & the Atomic Bomb.* 1992. nY. photos/map/index. 622p. VG/VG. S16. $27.50

FEIFER. *Great Comic Book Heroes.* 1965. 1st. ils. 189p. F/dj. M13. $38.00

FEIFFER, Jules. *Carnal Knowledge.* 1971. NY. 1st. inscr. F/NF clip. A11. $80.00

FEIGENBAUM, Edward A. *Fifth Generation.* 1983. Addison-Wesley. 1st. 275p. NF/NF. W2. $25.00

FEIKEMA, Feike; see Manfred, Frederick.

FEINBLATT, Henry. *Transfusion of Blood.* 1926. NY. 1st. 137p. A13. $60.00

FEINGOLD, Henry L. *Zion in America: Jewish Experience in Colonial Times...* 1974. Twayne. 357p. VG/G+. S3. $21.00

FEIS, Herbert. *Japan Subdued.* 1961. VG/dj. K3. $20.00

FEIST, Bertha E. *Grunty Grunts & Smiley Smile Indoors.* 1920. Altemus. ils MP Brater. 12mo. cloth brd/mc label. dj. R5. $125.00

FEIST, Raymond. *Silverthorn.* 1985. Doubleday. 1st. F/dj. M2. $35.00

FEJES, Claire. *People of the Noatak.* 1966. Knopf. 1st. inscr. 8vo. 368p. F/dj. P4. $45.00

FELDBORG, A.A. *Tour of Zealand.* 1807. Phil. Bartram Reynolds. 1st. 16mo. 131p. contemporary calf. M1. $200.00

FELDMAN, Anette. *Handmade Lace & Patterns.* 1975. NY. Harper Row. 1st. 4to. 208p. F/dj. T10. $75.00

FELDMAN & HATA. *Josephus, Judaism & Christianity.* 1987. Wayne State. 1st. 448p. F/dj. W3. $48.00

FELICE, Cynthia. *Downtime.* 1985. Bluejay. 1st. F/F. P3. $20.00

FELLER, Bob. *How To Pitch.* 1948. NY. 1st. VG/fair. B5. $20.00

FELLER, John Quentin. *Dorflinger: America's Finest Glass, 1852-1921* 1988. Antique Publications. 550+ photos. 374p. as new/dj. H1. $85.00

FELLINI, Frederico. *La Dolce Vita.* 1961. Ballantine. 1st. wrp. A17. $15.00

FELSKI, Elsa. *Blumen-Fibel.* 1959. Berlin. FA Herbig. 2 vol. 8vo. cloth. VG/djs/case. A22. $65.00

FELSKI, Elsa. *Book of wild Flowes.* 1956. Yoseloff. 1st Am. 8vo. 160 full-p pl. VG/dj. A22. $35.00

FELTOE, Charles. *Memorials of John Flint South...1841-63.* 1884. London. 1st. 216p. A13. $45.00

FELTON, C.N. *Contested Election in California.* 1887. Santa Clara. 45 full-p photos. 3-quarter brn morocco/mottled brd. K7. $295.00

FENELON. *Selections From Writings of Fenelon...By a Lady.* 1829. Boston. Hilliard Gray Little. 283p. gr leather. G. V3. $35.00

FENN, George Manville. *Seven Frozen Sailors.* 1896. New Amsterdam Book Co. 1st. VG. M2. $40.00

FENNER, Phyllis R. *Cowboys, Cowboys, Cowboys.* 1950. Franklin Watts. dj. A19. $15.00

FENNER. *Something Shared: Children & Books...* 1959. ils/cartoons. NF/G. A4. $30.00

FENTON, Robert W. *Big Swingers.* 1967. Prentice Hall. VG/VG. P3. $50.00

FENTON & FENTON. *Rock Book.* 1950. Doubleday. 357p. cloth. NF. D8. $20.00

FENWICK, Robert W. *Red Fenwick's West.* 1956. Denver. Sage Books. sgn. dj. A19. $30.00

FERBER, Edna. *Giant.* 1952. Doubleday. 1st. sgn. F/F. B4. $275.00

FERBER, Edna. *No Room at the Inn.* 1941. Doubleday. 1st. F. B4. $85.00

FERBER, Edna. *Showboat.* 1926. Doubleday Page. 1st. 1/201. sgn/#d. white Japanese vellum. F. B4. $600.00

FERBER, Nat. *One Happy Jew.* 1934. 1st. VG. E6. $20.00

FERDON, Edwin N. *Early Observations of Marquesan Culture 1595-1813.* 1993. Tucson/London. 1st. 184p. burgundy cloth. P4. $40.00

FERDON, Edwin N. *Early Tonga: As the Explorers Saw It: 1616-1810.* 1987. Tucson. 8vo. 339p. VG. P4. $40.00

FERE, Charles. *Les Epilepsies et les Epileptiques.* 1890. Paris. Gailliere. heavy 8vo. photos/ils. 636p. contemporary bdg. G1. $650.00

FERENCZI, Sandor. *Sex in Psychoanalysis.* 1950. NY. Basic. 6th. authorized trans. 338p. VG/dj. A25. $8.00

FERGUSON, Blanche E. *Countee Cullen & the Negro Renaissance.* 1966. Dodd Mead. 1st. NF/dj. M25. $35.00

FERGUSON, David L. *Cleopatra's Barge: Crowninshield Story.* 1976. Little Brn. 1st. 293p. cloth. VG/dj. M20. $22.00

FERGUSON, Delancey. *Mark Twain, Man & Legend.* 1943. Bobbs Merrill. 1st. gilt red cloth. F/dj. M24. $85.00

FERGUSON, Helen. *Julia & the Bazooka.* 1970. Knopf. 1st. F/F. B35. $45.00

FERGUSON, James. *Astronomy Explained Upon Sir Isaac Newton's Principles.* 1817. Phil. Abraham Small. 2 vol. enlarged. rebacked. K5. $150.00

FERGUSON, James. *Astronomy Explained Upon Sir Isaac Newton's Principles...* 1778. London. Strahan. tall thick 8vo. fld ftspc/17 full-p fld pl. tree calf. H13. $350.00

FERGUSON, John C. *Survey of Chinese Art.* 1940. Shanghai. Commercial Pr. 200+ pl. 153p. VG/dj. W3. $65.00

FERGUSSON, Bruce. *Shadow of His Wings.* 1987. Arbor. 1st. F/F. P3. $17.00

FERGUSSON, Harvey. *Wolf Song.* 1927. Knopf. 1st. 1/100. sgn/#d. F/glassine dj. A18. $300.00

FERLANTTE, William J. *Flora of the Trinity Alps of Northern California.* 1974. Berkeley. 8vo. 206p. cloth. F. A22. $30.00

FERLINGHETTI, Lawrence. *Coney Island of the Mind.* 1968. New Directions. 1st. cloth. F/case. B2. $45.00

FERLINGHETTI, Lawrence. *Leaves of Life (Vol 2): Thirty Drawings From the Model.* 1995. Charleston, WV. 1st. sgn. F/saddle-stiched wrp/blk envelope. Q1. $50.00

FERLINGHETTI, Lawrence. *Secret Meaning of Things.* 1969. New Directions. 1st. sgn. NF/NF. R14. $35.00

FERLINGHETTI & PETERS. *Literary San Francisco: A Pictorial History...* 1980. Harper Row. 1st. F/F. A18. $35.00

FERMAN, Edward L. *Best From Fantasy & Science Fiction 17th Series.* 1968. Doubleday. 1st. NF/dj. M2. $20.00

FERMAN, Edward L. *Best From Fantasy & Science Fiction: 40th Anniversary...* 1989. St Martin. 1st. F/F. P3. $20.00

FERMI, Laura. *Atoms in the Family. My Life With Enrico Fermi.* 1969. Chicago. ils. 8vo. 267p. wrp. K3. $9.00

FERMI, Laura. *Atoms of the World.* 1957. Chicago. 1st. VG/VG. A20. $20.00

FERNALD & PATTON. *Water Resources Atlas of Florida.* 1984. FL State. 291p. D8. $35.00

FERRARS, Elizabeth X. *Alibi for a Witch.* 1952. Crime Club. 1st. VG. P3. $20.00

FERRARS, Elizabeth X. *Decayed Gentlewoman.* 1963. Crime Club. 1st. F/NF. P3. $35.00

FERRARS, Elizabeth X. *Murder Too Many.* 1989. Doubleday. 1st. F/F. P3. $16.00

FERRARS, Elizabeth X. *Thinner Than Water.* 1982. Doubleday. 1st. VG/VG. P3. $15.00

FERREIRA CARDOSO DA COSTA, V. *Theses ex Jurisprudentia Naturali, Sacra & Civili...* 1785. Coimbra. Academico-Regia. 1st. 29p. stitched wrp. R15. $1,500.00

FERRERO, Guglielmo. *Characters & Events of Roman History, From Ceasar to Nero...* 1922. Putnam/Knickerbocker. 8vo. 275p. VG. W1. $12.00

FERRIER, David. *Functions of the Brain.* 1886. Putnam. 2nd Am. 137 woodcuts. emb Victorian cloth. VG. G1. $475.00

FERRIS, Helen. *Love's Enchantment.* 1944. Doubleday. 1st. inscr. 120p. NF/dj. D4. $30.00

FERRIS, James Cody. *X Bar X Boys on Big Bison Trail (#4).* 1927. Grosset Dunlap. 216p. cloth. NF/dj. M20. $40.00

FERRIS, W.A. *Life in the Rocky Mountains, a Diary of Wanderings...* 1940. Old West Pub. 1st. ils/maps. 365p. VG. J2. $475.00

FERSON & FERSON. *Yesterday's Milk Glass Today.* 1987. self pub. 2nd. ils. 188p. w/separate 4p price guide. as new. H1. $90.00

FESBACH, Norma D. *Early Schooling in England & Israel.* 1973. McGraw Hill. 127p. VG. S3. $21.00

FESSENDEN, Thomas Green. *Terrible Tractoration!! A Poetical Petition...* 1804. NY. Stansbury. 16mo. 192p. ES. disbound. M1. $175.00

FETRIDGE, W.P. *Paris Commune.* 1871. Harper. 1st. gilt bl cloth. NF. B2. $150.00

FEUCHTWANGER, L. *Fermented Liquors: Brewing, Distilling, Rectifying...* 1858. 1st. xl. G+. E6. $125.00

FEUCHTWANGER, Lion. *Proud Destiny.* 1947. Viking. 1st. VG/VG. P3. $18.00

FEVAL, Paul; see Bedford-Jones, H.

FEWKES, Jesse Walter. *Hopi Katchinas Drawn by Native Artists.* 1904. GPO. sgn. 63 mc pl. 126p. 3-quarter red morocco. VG. K7. $550.00

FICHTE (Johann Gottlieb). *Reden an die Deutsche Nation.* 1808. Berlin. Realschulbuchhandlung. 8vo. quarter calf. R12. $675.00

FICOWSKI, Jerzy. *Sister of the Birds & Other Gypsy Tales.* 1976. Abingdon. 1st Am. ils Chas Mikolaycak. VG+/G+. P2. $20.00

FIELD, Eugene. *Love Affairs of a Bibliomaniac.* 1896. Scribner. 1st. VG. K3. $30.00

FIELD, Eugene. *Lullaby-Land.* 1897. Scribner. 1st. ils Chas Robinson. 231p. teg. gr cloth. R5. $175.00

FIELD, Eugene. *Poems of Childhood.* ca 1922 (1904). Scribner. later prt. ils Parrish/8 mc pl. 199p. VG. D4. $75.00

FIELD, Eugene. *Poems of Childhood.* 1904. Scribner. 1st. ils Maxfield Parrish/8 full-p pl. 199p. VG. D1. $175.00

FIELD, Eugene. *Sugar Plum Tree & Other Verses.* 1930. Saalfield. ils FB Peat. pink spine. VG. B15. $65.00

FIELD, Eugene. *Writings in Prose & Verse.* 1896-1901. Scribner. 1st. 12 vol. 1/100. 12mo. teg. uncut. M1. $375.00

FIELD, Henry M. *History of the Atlantic Telegraph.* 1866. Scribner. 1st. ils. 364p. VG. K3. $55.00

FIELD, Henry M. *Old Spain & New Spain.* 1888. Scribner. 1st. 8vo. 303p. gilt gr cloth. T10. $100.00

FIELD, Kate. *Drama of Glass.* ca 1895. Libby Glass Co. 16mo. ils. 46p. gilt decor brd. G. H1. $50.00

FIELD, Michael. *Culinary Classics & Improvisations.* 1968. Knopf. 2nd. ils Mozelle Thompson. VG/dj. A16. $10.00

FIELD, Rachel. *Christmas Time.* 1941. Macmillan. probable 1st. 16mo. F/VG+. M5. $25.00

FIELD, Rachel. *General Store.* 1988. Little BRn. 1st. ils Giles Laroche. F/F. C8. $25.00

FIELD, Rachel. *Hitty, Her First Hundred Years.* 1929. Macmillan. 3rd. inscr/dtd 1936. ils DP Lathrop. VG/later dj. M5. $65.00

FIELD, Rachel. *Prayer for a Child.* 1944. Macmillan. 1st. ils Elizabeth Orton Jones. 32p. VG. D4. $35.00

FIELD, Rachel. *Yellow Shop.* 1931. Doubleday Doran. 1st. 12mo. yel cloth. dj. R5. $100.00

FIELD, William B.O. *John Leach on My Shelves.* 1970 (1930). rpt. ils. F. K3. $25.00

FIELDER, Mildred. *Guide to Black Hills Ghost Mines.* 1972. Aberdeen, SD. N Plains. photos. dj. A19. $35.00

FIELDER, Mildred. *Railroads of the Black Hills.* 1960. NY. Bonanza. dj. A19. $45.00

FIELDER, Mildred. *Treasure of Homestake Gold.* 1970. Aberdeen, SD. N Plains. dj. A19. $35.00

FIELDING, A. *Eames-Erskine Case.* 1925. Knopf. 1st. NF/G. M19. $25.00

FIELDING, Henry. *Joseph Andrews.* 1939. Random. VG/VG. P3. $20.00

FIELDING, Howard. *Straight Crooks.* 1927. Chelsea House. 1st. VG. P3. $25.00

FIELDMAN, Walter. *Alphabet Book...WWII. A Short History of Second World War...* 1996. Providence, RI. Ziggurat. 1/35. 2 vol. 4to. ils. M/case. B24. $500.00

FIELDS, Annie. *How To Help the Poor.* 1884. Boston. Houghton Mifflin. 1st. gray-gr prt wrp. M24. $85.00

FIELDS, James T. *Boston Book.* 1850. Ticknor Reed Fields. 1st. gilt blk cloth. M24. $100.00

FIERZ & WEISSKOPF. *Theoretical Physics in the 20th Century.* 1960. NY. Interscience. 1st. VG/dj. K3. $35.00

FIFTOOT, C.H.S. *English Law & Its Background.* 1932. London. BEll. bl cloth. M11. $65.00

FIFTOOT, C.H.S. *Frederic William Maitland, a Life.* 1971. Harvard. M11. $45.00

FIGUEROA, Jose. *Manifesto Which the General of Brigade...* 1855. SF Herald. 1st Eng-language ed. 8vo. full gilt brn calf. box. R3. $1,350.00

FIGUIER, Louis. *Ocean World, Being a Description of the Sea...* 1869. Appleton. revised/enlarged ed. 8vo. 615p. rebound leather. H1. $40.00

FILLIS, James. *Breaking & Riding.* 1977. London. Allen. rpt. VG/VG. O3. $20.00

FILM DAILY COMPANY. *1934 Film Daily Year Book of Motion Pictures, 16th Annual.* 1934. ads/articles/info/statistics. 1000+p. NF. C9. $150.00

FINCH, C. *Of Muppets & Men.* 1981. NY. 1st. VG/VG. B5. $40.00

FINCH, Christopher. *Art of Walt Disney.* 1973. Abrams. 1st. NF/VG+. T11. $110.00

FINCH, Henry. *Law; or, A Discovrse Therof, in Foure Bookes.* 1627. London. Societie of Stationers. 12mo. calf. R12. $500.00

FINCH, Simon. *Slave Island.* 1983. Souvenir. 1st. VG/VG. P3. $15.00

FINCHAM, John. *Introductory Outline to the Practice of Shipbuilding.* 1825. Portsea. Woodward. 2nd. 3 tables. 3-quarter calf. T7. $350.00

FINDLATER, Richard. *Emlyn Williams.* 1956. Macmillan. 112p. dj. A17. $12.50

FINDLATER, Richard. *Grimaldi, King of Clowns.* 1955. MacGibbon Kee. 1st. 240p. cloth. VG/dj. M20. $20.00

FINDLEY, Ferguson. *Waterfront.* 1951. DSP. 1st. VG. P3. $15.00

FINDLEY, Francine. *Treeless Eden.* 1934. NY. King. 1st. VG/clip. B4. $85.00

FINDLEY, James S. *Bats: A Community Perspective.* 1993. Cambridge. 167p. F/F. S15. $17.00

FINEBERG, S. Andhil. *Rosenberg Case: Fact & Fiction.* 1953. Oceana Pub. 1st. VG/VG. V4. $20.00

FINGER, Charles J. *Spreading Stain.* 1927. Doubleday. 1st. NF. M2. $37.00

FINGER & HALDEMAN-JULIUS. *Oscar Wilde in Outline.* 1923. Girard, KS. Haldeman-Julius. 1st. Little Bl Book 442. VG+. A25. $10.00

FINLAY, Virgil. *Astrology Sketch Book.* 1975. Donald Grant. 1st. VG/dj. P3. $25.00

FINLEY, J.P. *Report of the Tornadoes of May 29 & 30, 1879...* 1881. WA, DC. US War Dept. xl. K5. $95.00

FINLEY, James B. *Autobiography of Rev James B Finley...* 1861. Cincinnati. later prt. 455p. half leather. VG-. B18. $45.00

FINLEY, Martha. *Elise at Home (#22).* 1897. Dodd Mead. 295p. cloth w/pansy design. lists to #27. M20. $15.00

FINN, Sidney B. *Clinical Pedodontics.* 1962. Phil. Saunders. 2nd. photos. VG+. A25. $15.00

FINNEY, Charles G. *Unholy City.* 1927. Vanguard. 1st. VG. M2. $22.00

FINNEY, Jack. *Assault on a Queen.* 1960. Eyre Spottiswoode. 1st. VG/dj. M2. $50.00

FINNEY, Jack. *Forgotten News.* 1983. Doubleday. 1st. NF/dj. M2. $20.00

FINNEY, Jack. *Good Neighbor Sam.* 1963. S&S. 1st. VG/dj. M2. $65.00

FINNEY, Jack. *Night People.* 1977. Doubleday. 1st. F/dj. M2. $35.00

FINNEY, Jack. *Night People.* 1977. Doubleday. 1st. VG/dj. P3. $30.00

FINNEY, Jack. *Time & Again.* 1970. S&S. stated 1st. NF/NF. M22. $10.00

FINNEY, Jack. *Woodrow Wilson Dime.* 1968. S&S. 1st. F/F. B2. $60.00

FINNIE, Richard. *Lure of the North.* 1940. Phil. 56 photos. A17. $25.00

FINSTAD, Suzanne. *Sleeping With the Devil.* 1991. Morrow. 1st. 382p. F/F. W2. $30.00

FIRBANK, Ronald. *Extravaganzas.* 1935. Coward McCann. 1st Am. F/dj. Q1. $125.00

FIRBANK, Ronald. *Odette: A Fairy Tale for Weary People.* 1916. London. Grant Richards. 1st separate ils ed. VG. Q1. $200.00

FIRBANK, Ronald. *Princess Zoubaroff: A Commedy.* 1920. London. Grant Richards. 1st. 1/513. NF/dj. Q1. $600.00

FIRSOFF, V.A. *Ski Track on the Battlefield.* 1943. photos. VG/VG. M17. $25.00

FIRTH, Anthony. *Tall, Balding, Thirty-Five.* 1967. Harper Row. 1st. F/NF. H11. $20.00

FIRTH, M.J. *Native Orchids of Tasmania.* 1965. Devonport, Tasmania. ils/drawings/ index. 90p. F/dj. B26. $32.50

FISCHEL, Walter J. *Ibn Khaldun in Egypt. His Public Functions...* 1967. LA. 1st. 217p. VG/dj. W1. $32.00

FISCHER, Bruno. *More Deaths Than One.* 1947. Ziff-Davis. 1st. NF/VG. B4. $250.00

FISCHER, Bruno. *Quoth the Raven.* 1944. Crime Club. 1st. VG. P3. $25.00

FISCHER, Martin H. *Nephritis.* 1912. NY. 1st. 203p. A17. $15.00

FISCHER, Tibor. *Art of Eating.* 1954. World. 1st. F/VG. B3. $75.00

FISCHER, Tibor. *Dubious Honors.* 1988. Northpoint. 1st. F/F. B3. $35.00

FISCHL & RUE. *After Your Deer is Down: Care & Handling of Big Game.* 1981. Tulsa. ils/photos. 137p. brd. F/F. M12. $17.50

FISCHLER, Stan. *Hockey's Great Rivalries.* 1974. Random. 1st. G+. P8. $6.00

FISH, John Perry. *Unfinished Voyages.* 1989. Lower Cape Pub. 1st. ils. 299p. dj. T7. $40.00

FISH, Robert L. *Pursuit.* 1978. Doubleday. 1st. VG/VG. P3. $20.00

FISHER, Aileen. *Feathered Ones & Furry.* 1971. Crowell. ARC/1st. 39p. F/F. D4. $45.00

FISHER, Aileen. *In the Woods in the Meadow in the Sky.* 1965. Scribner. 1st. ils Margot Tomes. 64p. F/F. D4. $45.00

FISHER, Carrie. *Postcards From the Edge.* 1987. S&S. 1st. inscr. F/F. B4. $125.00

FISHER, Clay. *Yellowstone Kelly.* 1957. Houghton Mifflin. 1st. F/VG+. B4. $175.00

FISHER, Frederick Vining. *Transformation of a Job: A Tale of the High Sierras.* 1900. Chicago. David C Cook. 96p. 3-quarter brn cloth/marbled brd. VG. K7. $50.00

FISHER, H.A.L. *Collected Papers of Frederic William Maitland...* 1911. Cambridge. 3 vol. orig cloth. M11. $350.00

FISHER, Harrison. *American Belles.* 1911. Dodd Mead. 1st. 16 full-p mtd mc pl. folio. teg. rose brd/label. R5. $800.00

FISHER, John. *Reform & Insurrection in Bourbon New Granada & Peru.* 1990. LSU. 1st. 356p. dj. F3. $20.00

FISHER, L.H. *Territorial Governors of Oklahoma.* 1975. OK Hist Soc. 1st. inscr. photos. 150p. F. M4. $30.00

FISHER, M.F.K. *Boss Dog.* 1991. Berkeley. ARC. inscr/dtd 1991. author's last novel. F/wrp. A11. $165.00

FISHER, M.F.K. *Boss Dog: A Story.* 1991. SF. Northpoint. 1st trade. F/NF. R13. $20.00

FISHER, M.F.K. *Gastronomical Me.* 1948. World. 1st thus. 295p. VG/G. H1. $15.00

FISHER, M.F.K. *Map of Another Town.* 1964. Boston. 1st. VG/VG. B5. $45.00

FISHER, M.F.K. *With Bold Knife & Fork.* 1969. NY. 1st. VG/VG. B5. $45.00

FISHER, Marjorie. *Food & Flowers for Informal Entertaining.* 1965. Hearthside. G/dj. A16. $10.00

FISHER, Paul R. *Hawks of Fellheath.* 1980. Atheneum. 1st. VG/dj. P3. $18.00

FISHER, Robert Lewis. *Odyssey of Tobacco.* 1939. Litchfield, CT. Prospect. 1st. 8vo. 93p. G. T10. $45.00

FISHER, Robert Moore. *How About the Weather?* 1951. NY. Harper. 1st. 8vo. 186p. G/dj. K5. $10.00

FISHER, Rudolph. *Conjure-Man Dies.* 1971. NY. Arno/NY Times. 1st thus. 316p. F/NF. B4. $85.00

FISHER, Steve. *Big Dream.* 1970. Doubleday. 1st. NF/dj. M25. $35.00

FISHER, Steve. *Destroyer.* 1941. Appleton. 1st. NF/VG. B4. $475.00

FISHER, Steve. *Giveaway.* 1954. Random. 1st. F/VG. B4. $100.00

FISHER, Sydney George. *True William Penn.* 1900. Lippincott. 392p. V3. $12.50

FISHER, Vardis. *Adam & the Serpent.* 1947. Vanguard. 1st. VG. M2. $20.00

FISHER, Vardis. *Children of God.* 1939. Harper. 1st. VG/VG. P3. $45.00

FISHER, Vardis. *City of Illusion.* 1941. Harper. 1st. VG. P3. $45.00

FISHER, Vardis. *Golden Rooms.* 1944. NY. 1st. VG/VG. B5. $35.00

FISHER, Vardis. *Idaho: A Guide in Word & Picture.* 1937. Caxton. 1st. F. A18. $200.00

FISHER, Vardis. *Mountain Man.* 1965. NY. 1st. VG/VG. B5. $35.00

FISHER, Vardis. *No Villain Need Be.* 1936. Caxton. 1st. F/dj. A18. $75.00

FISHER, Vardis. *Orphans in Gethsemane: A Novel of the Past in the Present.* 1960. Swallow. 1st. 1/200. sgn. VG/dj. A18. $250.00

FISHER, Vardis. *Pemmican: A Novel of the Hudson Bay Company.* 1956. Doubleday. 1st. F/dj. Q1. $50.00

FISHER, Vardis. *Toilers of the Hills.* 1928. Houghton Mifflin. 1st. NF/dj. A18. $80.00

FISHER, W.S. *Revision of the North American Species of Buprestid Beetles.* 1928. Smithsonian. 347p. NF. S15. $18.00

FISHER & FISHER. *Shackleton & the Antarctic.* 1958. Boston. ils/maps/photos. F/G. M4. $25.00

FISHER & HOLMES. *Gold Rushes & Mining Camps of the Early American West.* 1968. Caxton. 1st. inscr/sgns. F/dj. A18. $125.00

FISKE, Dorsey. *Bound to Murder.* 1987. St Martin. 1st. NF/NF. P3. $18.00

FISKE & LUMMIS. *Charles F Lummis: Man & His West.* 1975. Norman, OK. 1/200. sgn. F/F. O4. $65.00

FITCH, Florence Mary. *Book About God.* July 1956. Lee Shepard. 4th. sm 4to. unp. NF/VG clip. C14. $12.00

FITZ, Grancel. *North American Head Hunting.* 1957. NY. Oxford. 1st. 188p. F/F. H7. $30.00

FITZ & ODLUM. *Lady Sourdough.* 1941. NY. 1st. VG/VG. B5. $25.00

FITZGERALD, Edward. *Rubaiyat of Omar Khayyam.* 1878. Boston. Osgood. 1st Am. gilt terra-cotta decor cloth. F. M24. $250.00

FITZGERALD, F. Scott. *Afternoon of an Author.* 1957. Princeton. 1/1500. NF/dj. M25. $150.00

FITZGERALD, F. Scott. *Afternoon of an Author.* 1957. Princeton. 1st. 1/1500. F/clip. Q1. $175.00

FITZGERALD, F. Scott. *Great Gatsby.* 1925. Scribner. 1st/all points present. dk gr brd. VG. M25. $450.00

FITZGERALD, F. Scott. *Great Gatsby.* 1925. Scribner. 1st/1st prt (points on p60/119/205/211). F. Q1. $1,000.00

FITZGERALD, F. Scott. *Great Gatsby.* 1974. Franklin Lib. 1st thus/ltd. aeg. full leather. F. Q1. $75.00

FITZGERALD, F. Scott. *John Jackson's Arcady.* 1928. Walter Baker. 1st. F/stapled orange wrp. B4. $2,000.00

FITZGERALD, F. Scott. *Pat Hobby Stories.* 1962. Scribner. 1st. NF/dj. M25. $60.00

FITZGERALD, F. Scott. *Princeton Bric-a-Brac, XXXVIII.* 1914. Phil. EA Wright. 1st. teg. gilt blk morocco. M24. $225.00

FITZGERALD, F. Scott. *Tales of the Jazz Age.* 1922. 1st/3rd issue. VG. S13. $30.00

FITZGERALD, F. Scott. *This Side of Paradise.* 1920. Scribner. 1st. 1/3000. inscr/dtd 1920. author's 1st book. NF. L3. $7,500.00

FITZGERALD, Joe. *Championship Feeling.* 1975. Scribner. 1st. photos. F/F. P8. $35.00

FITZGERALD, John D. *Great Brain.* 1967. Dial. 1st. ils Mercer Mayer. 175p. NF/VG. P2. $25.00

FITZGERALD, John D. *More Adventures of Great Brain.* 1969. NY. Dial. 1st. 142p. VG/worn. M20. $22.50

FITZGERALD, Kevin. *Quiet Under the Sun.* 1954. Little Brn. 1st. VG/VG. P3. $20.00

FITZGERALD, Michael. *Universal Pictures: Panoramic History in Words.* 1977. New Rochelle. 766p. dj. A17. $20.00

FITZGERALD, Percy. *Sheridans.* nd (1937). NY. Atheneum. 2 vol. 8vo. tan cloth. H13. $125.00

FITZGERALD, Robert. *In the Rose of Time: Poems 1931-1956.* 1956. New Directions. 1st. F/dj. Q1. $75.00

FITZGERALD & FITZGERALD. *Bits of Paradise.* 1973. Scribner. 1st. F/clip. M25. $35.00

FITZHUGH, Louise. *Long Secret.* 1965. Harper. sm 8vo. VG/VG. C8. $20.00

FITZHUGH, Percy Keese. *Pee-Wee Harris FOB Bridgeboro (#6).* 1923. Grosset Dunlap. lists to Darkest Africa. VG/dj. M20. $30.00

FITZHUGH, Percy Keese. *Roy Blakely: Lost, Strayed or Stolen (#7).* 1921. Grosset Dunlap. 207p+ads. VG/dj (lists 11 titles). M20. $25.00

FITZLYON, Kyril. *Before the Revolution: Russia & Its People Under the Czar...* 1978. Overlook. 1st. VG/dj. V4. $25.00

FITZPATRICK, T.J. *Rafinesque: A Sketch of His Life With Bibliography.* 1911. Des Moines. Hist Dept IA/Torch. 241p. A10. $175.00

FITZPATRICK, Wendy. *Practical Sailing.* 1979. Mayflower. 1st Am ed. F/F. W2. $25.00

FITZSIMONS, Bernard. *Illustrated Encyclopedia of Weapons & Warfare.* 1977. NY. 24 vol. photos. VG. S16. $140.00

FLACH, Frederic F. *Fridericus.* 1980. Lippincott Crowell. 1st. VG/dj. P3. $13.00

FLACK, Marjorie. *Angus & the Cat.* 1931. Doubleday Doran. 1st. VG. P2. $65.00

FLACK, Marjorie. *Walter the Lazy Mouse.* 1937. Doubleday Doran. 1st. 4to. VG/VG. P2. $90.00

FLAGG, Fannie. *Fried Green Tomatoes at the Whistle Stop Cafe.* 1987. Random. 1st. F/F. T11. $95.00

FLAGG, Fannie. *Fried Green Tomatoes at the Whistle Stop Cafe.* 1987. Random. 1st. sgn bookplate. author's 2nd book. VG/NF. B3. $40.00

FLAMMARION, Camille. *Atmosphere.* 1873. Harper. 4to. 453p. gilt cloth. K5. $125.00

FLAMMARION, Camille. *Mysterious Psychic Forces.* 1907. Small Maynard. 1st. VG. M2. $75.00

FLAMMARION, Camille. *Popular Astronomy: A General Description of the Heavens.* 1931. NY. Appleton. new imp/revised, 698p. K5. $80.00

FLANAGAN, E.M. *Corregidor: Rock Force Assault, 1945.* 1988. SF. Presidio. sm 4to. 331p. M/F. P1. $14.00

FLANAGAN, Edward Jr. *Angels: History of the 11th Airborne Division 1943-1946.* 1948. WA, DC. 1st. photos/maps. 176p. VG. S16. $125.00

FLANAGAN, Thomas. *Tenants of Time.* 1988. Dutton. 1st. F/F. T12. $25.00

FLAUBERT, Gustave. *Salambo.* 1931. Golden Cockrel. 1/500. ils R Gibbings. VG. T9. $100.00

FLAVELL, Geoffrey. *Oesophagus.* 1963. London. 1st. 168p. A13. $50.00

FLAVELL, M. Kay. *George Grosz: A Biography.* 1988. Yale. 1st. F/dj. V4. $45.00

FLEET, Simon. *Clocks: Pleasures & Treasures.* 1961. NY. Putnam. 1st. 8vo. 128p. pict cloth. VG/box. K3. $15.00

FLEETWOOD, Hugh. *Beast.* 1978. Hamish Hamilton. 1st. VG/dj. P3. $20.00

FLEETWOOD, Hugh. *Painter of Flowers.* 1972. Viking. 1st. VG/VG. P3. $22.00

FLEISCHMAN, Harry. *Norman Thomas: A Biography.* 1964. Norton. 2nd. VG/G. V4. $40.00

FLEISCHMAN, J. *Art of Blending & Compounding Liquors & Wines.* 1885. 1st. VG. E6. $45.00

FLEISCHMAN, Sid. *Chancy & the Grand Rascal.* 1966. Atlantic/Little Brn. 8vo. 179p. VG. T5. $15.00

FLEISHER. *Batman.* 1976. ils. 387p. F. M13. $30.00

FLEITMANN, Lida L. *Horse in Art: From Primitive Times to the Present.* 1931. London. Medici Soc. 1st. VG/G. O3. $95.00

FLEMING, Alice. *America Is Not All Traffic Lights.* 1976. Little Brn. 1st. 68p. cloth. F/NF. D4. $30.00

FLEMING, Alice. *Hosannah the Home Run!* 1972. Little Brn. ARC/1st. 68p. F/F. D4. $35.00

FLEMING, Archibald Lang. *Archibald the Arctic.* 1956. Appleton Century Crofts. 1st. 8vo. 399p. F/dj. T10. $25.00

FLEMING, Berry. *Lucinderella.* 1967. NY. John Day. 1st. F/F. T12. $30.00

FLEMING, Denise. *Barnyard Banter.* 1994. Holt. 1st. unp. F. C14. $14.00

FLEMING, Ian. *Bonded Fleming.* 1965. Viking. 1st. NF/NF. M19. $50.00

FLEMING, Ian. *Bonded Fleming.* 1965. Viking. 1st. VG/dj. P3. $40.00

FLEMING, Ian. *Casino Royale.* 1954. NY. Macmillan. 1st Am. F/NF. M15. $800.00

FLEMING, Ian. *Chitty Chitty...* 1964. Random. 1st. 8vo. gilt red cloth. F/NF. R5. $275.00

FLEMING, Ian. *Diamond Smugglers.* 1957. London. Cape. 1st. F/F. M15. $250.00

FLEMING, Ian. *Diamonds Are Forever.* 1956. London. Cape. 1st issue (emb diamond brd). author's 4th book. F/VG+. A24. $600.00

FLEMING, Ian. *Diamonds Are Forever.* 1956. London. Cape. 1st. F/dj. M15. $1,250.00

FLEMING, Ian. *Dr No.* 1958. London. Cape. 1st. F/F. M15. $750.00

FLEMING, Ian. *For Your Eyes Only.* 1960. London. Jonathan Cape. 1st. F/NF. M15. $350.00

FLEMING, Ian. *Goldfinger.* 1959. London. Cape. 1st. F/dj. M15. $650.00

FLEMING, Ian. *Live & Let Die.* 1954. London. Cape. 1st. F/clip. M15. $3,750.00

FLEMING, Ian. *Live & Let Die.* 1955. Macmillan. 1st Am. letter C stp on bottom page edges. F/NF. M15. $450.00

FLEMING, Ian. *Man With the Golden Gun.* 1965. London. Cape. 1st/1st imp. F/dj. M15. $100.00

FLEMING, Ian. *Man With the Golden Gun.* 1965. London. Cape. 1st/3rd imp. F/F. T12. $50.00

FLEMING, Ian. *Man With the Golden Gun.* 1965. NAL. 1st Am. NF/dj. M2. $50.00

FLEMING, Ian. *Man With the Golden Gun.* 1965. NAL. 1st Am. VG/G. M22. $20.00

FLEMING, Ian. *Man With the Golden Gun.* 1965. NAL. 1st. 183p. cloth. VG/dj. M20/P3. $35.00

FLEMING, Ian. *Octopussy & the Living Daylights.* 1966. Johnathan Cape. 1st. VG/dj. P3. $23.00

FLEMING, Ian. *Octopussy & the Living Daylights.* 1966. London. Cape. F/F. M15. $45.00

FLEMING, Ian. *Octopussy.* 1965. NAL. 1st Am. F/NF. M2. $30.00

FLEMING, Ian. *On Her Majesty's Secret Service.* 1963. NAL. 1st Am. F/NF. M22. $60.00

FLEMING, Ian. *Spy Who Loved Me.* 1962. London. Cape. 1st. F/F. M15. $175.00

FLEMING, Ian. *You Only Live Twice.* 1964. London. Cape. true 1st. VG/VG. M22. $45.00

FLEMING, Ian. *You Only Live Twice.* 1964. London. Cape. 1st. F/dj. M15. $125.00

FLEMING, Ian. *You Only Live Twice.* 1964. NAL. 1st. VG/dj. P3. $35.00

FLEMING, Joan. *Good & the Bad.* 1953. Crime Club. 1st. NF/VG. P3. $25.00

FLEMING, Joan. *In the Red.* 1961. Ives Washburn. 1st. author's 5th novel. VG/VG. M22. $15.00

FLEMING, Joan. *Malice Matrimonial.* 1959. Ives Washburn. 1st. NF/NF. P3. $25.00

FLEMING, Joan. *Nothing Is the Number When You Die.* 1965. London. Collins. 1st. NF/VG. M22. $15.00

FLEMING, Joan. *Too Late! Too Late! the Maiden Cried.* 1975. Putnam. 1st. VG/VG. P3. $20.00

FLEMING, Joan. *You Won't Let Me Finish.* 1973. Collins Crime Club. 1st. VG/dj. P3. $20.00

FLEMING, Peter. *Flying Visit.* 1940. London. 1st. ils David Low. VG/dj. S13. $35.00

FLEMING. *Sinclair Lewis: A Reference Guide.* 1980. 240p. VG. A4. $45.00

FLETCHER, Colin. *Man Who Walked Through Time.* 1968. Knopf. 4th. 8vo. 239p. dj. F7. $20.00

FLETCHER, David. *Raffles.* 1977. Putnam. 1st. F/F. P3. $15.00

FLETCHER, Inglis. *Cormorant's Brood.* 1959. Lippincott. 1st. VG/dj. P3. $15.00

FLETCHER, Inglis. *Roanoke Hundred.* 1948. Bobbs Merrill. 1st. sgn. gilt bl cloth. B11. $50.00

FLETCHER, John Gould. *Japanese Prints.* 1918. Boston. Four Seas. 1st. 1/1000. ils Dorothy Lathrop. F. Q1. $75.00

FLETCHER, N.H. *Physics of Rainclouds.* 1962. Cambridge. 1st. 8vo. 396p. VG/dj. K5. $40.00

FLETCHER, R.A. *Steam-Ships.* 1910. London. Sidgwick Jackson. ils. 421p. rebacked. T7. $85.00

FLETCHER, Robert Howe. *Ten Drawings in Chinatown by Ernest C Peixotto.* (1898). SF. Robertston. 1/750. folio. pict brd/cloth spine/gr ribbon ties. R3. $850.00

FLETCHER, Robert Samuel. *History of Oberlin College From Its Foundation...* 1943. Oberlin, OH. 2 vol. sgn. F. B4. $175.00

FLETCHER, S. *Strawberry in North America.* 1917. np. 1st. xl. VG. E6. $20.00

FLETCHER, Stevenson Whitcomb. *Pennsylvania Agriculture & Country Life 1640-1840.* 1950. PA Hist & Mus Comm. 8vo. 605p. rebound buckram. VG. H1. $25.00

FLEW, R. Newton. *Jesus & His Church.* 1949. Epworth. 192p. G. B29. $13.50

FLICK, Art. *Master Fly-Tying Guide.* 1972. NY. 207p. dj. A17. $35.00

FLINT, C. *Milch Cows & Dairy Farming.* 1867 (1858). ils. VG. E6. $20.00

FLINT, L. *Practical Treatise on Grasses & Forage Plants.* 1858 (1857). ils. VG. E6. $50.00

FLINT, Timothy. *Recollections of Last Ten Years in Valley of Mississippi.* 1968. S IL U. 1st. 337p. VG/clip. M20. $40.00

FLINT & NORTH. *Tiger Bridge.* 1970. NY. 1st. 191p. VG/dj. S1. $10.00

FLINT & RIMINGTON. *Grand Slam: International Bridge Tournament...* 1983. Eng. 1st. 174p. F/dj. S1. $12.00

FLOHERTY, J.J. *High, Wide & Deep.* 1952. Phil/Lippincott. ils/photos/pict ep. 154p. cloth. F/VG+. M12. $15.00

FLOOD, Charles Bracelen. *Lee, the Last Years.* 1981. Boston. later prt. cloth. F/F. M8. $25.00

FLOOD, Charles. *Hitler: Path to Power.* 1969. Boston. 1st. photos/notes/biblio/index. 686p. VG/VG. S16. $22.50

FLOOD, John Henry. *Rare Historical Document Biography of Wyatt Earp...* 1926. np. 1st. maps. 258p. as new. J2. $165.00

FLOOK, Maria. *Family Night.* 1993. Pantheon. ARC. author's 1st novel. RS. NF/dj. R13. $35.00

FLORA, Fletcher. *Irrepressible Peccadilo.* 1962. Macmillan. 1st. VG/dj. P3. $20.00

FLORA, Snowden D. *Tornadoes of the United States.* 1953. Norman, OK. 1st. 194p. G/dj. K5. $20.00

FLORENTIN, Eddie. *Battle of the Falaise Gap.* 1965. Hawthorn. 1st. 362p. cloth. VG/ragged. M20. $15.00

FLORES, Ivan. *Assemblers & Bal.* 1971. Prentice Hall. 1st. 420p. dj. A17. $15.00

FLORESCU, Radu. *In Search of Frankenstein.* 1975. NYGS. 1st. VG/VG. P3. $20.00

FLORIN, Lambert. *Western Wagon Wheels, a Pictorial Memorial...* 1970. Bonanza. rpt. 185p. VG/VG. O3. $35.00

FLORIS, Maria. *Bakery Cakes & Simple Confectionary.* 1968. Bonanza. G/dj. A16. $20.00

FLORNEY, Bertram. *World of the Inca.* (1956). Vanguard. 1st. 212p. dj. F3. $20.00

FLORY, Jane. *Faraway Dream.* 1968. Houghton Mifflin. 2nd. 8vo. 219p. gold cloth. VG/dj. T5. $22.00

FLOURNOY, Theodora. *From India to the Planet Mars.* 1900. Harper. 1st Am. G. M2. $35.00

FLOWER, John. *Moonlight Serenade: A Biodiscography of Glenn Miller Band.* 1972. NY. 1st. ils/photos. VG/VG. B5. $35.00

FLOWER, Pat. *Crisscross.* 1976. Collins Crime Club. 1st. F/F. P3. $13.00

FLOWER, William Henry. *Diagrams of the Nerves of the Human Body...* 1872. London. Churchill. 2nd. 6 double-p lithos. emb brn cloth. G. G1. $150.00

FLOWERS, A.R. *De Monjo Blues.* 1985. Dutton. 1st. F/F. B2. $60.00

FLOWERS & FLOWERS. *Finches: Their Care & Breeding.* nd. Reseda. Bird Haven. 8vo. ils/drawings. 80+p. pict brd. VG. M12. $37.50

FLOYD, Olive. *Doctora in Mexico: Life of Dr Katherine Neel Dale.* 1944. Putnam. 1st. 270p. VG+. A25. $30.00

FLUGUM, Charles T. *Birding From a Tractor Seat.* 1973. St Paul. 435p. NF/VG. S15. $18.00

FLYMAN, Rose. *51 New Nursery Rhymes.* 1932. Doubleday Doran. 1st stated. ils Dorothy Burroughes. VG. B15. $85.00

FLYNN, Lucine Hansz. *Antique & Deadly.* 1988. Walker. 1st. F/F. H11. $20.00

FLYNT, Candace. *Mother Love.* 1987. Random. 1st. inscr. F/F. R13. $35.00

FLYNT, Candace. *Sins of Omission.* 1984. Random. 1st. inscr. F/dj. R13. $35.00

FOCK, H. *Fast Fighting Boats 1870-1945: Their Design...* 1978. Naval Inst. 304p. F/dj. A17. $45.00

FODOR, Laszlo. *Argentina.* 1941. Hastings. 1st. 23p. dj. F3. $15.00

FODOR, M.W. *Revolution Is On.* 1940. Houghton Mifflin. 1st. sgn. NF. B2. $30.00

FOGG, H.G. Witham. *Coloured Leaved & Berried Plants, Shrubs & Trees.* 1972. GBC. ils/drawings. VG/dj. B26. $19.00

FOHRER, Stellin. *Introduction to Old Testament.* 1978. Abingdon. trans David Green. 540p. VG/torn. B29. $15.00

FOLDES, Francis F. *Narcotics & Narcotic Antagonists.* 1964. Springfield. Charles Thomas. 1st. F/F. B2. $50.00

FOLEY, James. *Songs of Schooldays.* 1906. Doubleday. 1st. 12mo. VG. M5. $35.00

FOLEY, Martha. *Best American Short Stories.* 1965. MacGibbon Kee. 1st. VG/dj. P3. $20.00

FOLEY, Rae. *Last Gamble.* 1956. Dodd Mead. 1st. VG/dj. P3. $29.00

FOLEY, Rae. *Trust a Woman?* 1973. Dodd Mead. 1st. VG/VG. P3. $15.00

FOLEY & THOMPSON. *Siberian Husky.* 1962. Alderwood Manor. Raymond Thompson. 69p. P4. $40.00

FOLLETT, Helen. *Third Class Ticket to Heaven: A Black Forest Adventure.* 1938. Phil. Winston. 1st. ils Floethe. VG. A25. $15.00

FOLLETT, Ken. *Key to Rebecca.* 1980. Morrow. 1st. F/clip. N4. $25.00

FOLLETT, Ken. *Key to Rebecca.* 1980. Morrow. 1st. F/F. H11. $40.00

FOLLETT, Ken. *Man From Saint Petersburg.* 1986. Morrow. 1st Am. sgn. F/F. R14. $60.00

FOLLETT, Ken. *On Wings of Eagles.* 1983. Morrow. 1st. sgn. F/F. T11. $55.00

FOLLETT, Ken. *On Wings of Eagles.* 1983. Morrow. 1st. 444p. VG/torn. W1. $20.00

FOLLETT, Ken. *Pillars of the Earth.* 1989. NY. Morrow. 1st. F/F. T12. $30.00

FOLLETT, Ken. *Triple.* 1979. NY. Arbor. 1st. F/F. H11. $40.00

FONDA, Jane. *Jane Fonda's Workout Book.* 1981. S&S. 1st. sgn. F/NF. W2. $30.00

FONER, Philip. *Jack London. American Rebel.* 1947. Citadel. 1st. NF/NF. B2. $30.00

FONTANA, John M. *Mankind's Greatest Invention...* 1964. NY. Fontana. ils. 8vo. 112p. xl. K3. $20.00

FONTANINI, Giusto. *Biblioteca Dell'Eloquenza Italiana.* 1753. Venice. Giambatista Pasquali. 2 vol. VG. T10. $450.00

FOOTE, E.B. *Sammy Tubbs, the Boy Doctor & Sponsie, Troublesome Monkey.* 1874. Murray Hill. 12mo. 245p. VG-. P2. $135.00

FOOTE, Edward. *Text-Book of Minor Surgery.* 1908. NY. 1st. 752p. half leather. A13. $40.00

FOOTE, Horton. *Courtship, Valentine's Day, 1918.* 1987. Grove. 1st. sgn. F/dj. A24. $35.00

FOOTE, Horton. *Harrison, Texas.* 1956. Harcourt Brace. 1st. sgn. author's 1st book. F/NF. A24. $125.00

FOOTE, Horton. *Roots in a Parched Ground, Convicts, Lilly Dale...* 1988. Grove. 1st. sgn. F/dj. A24. $40.00

FOOTE, John Taintor. *Look of Eagles.* 1916. Appleton. 1st. VG/dj. H7. $35.00

FOOTE, Sam. *Dramatic Works of...* ca 1795. London. 4 vol. leather. VG. A15. $100.00

FOOTE. *American Imprints Inventory No 19, Bibliography...* 1942. 4to. 597p. VG. A4. $165.00

FOOTNER, Hulbert. *Rivers of the Eastern Shore, Seventeen Maryland Rivers.* 1944. Farrar Rhinehart. 4th. sm 8vo. 375p. F/G. H1. $16.00

FORBES, Alexander. *California: History of Upper & Lower California.* 1937. SF. John Henry Nash. rpt. 1/650. ils/fld map. marbled brd. as new. K7/O7. $275.00

FORBES, Alexander. *California: History of Upper & Lower California...* 1839. London. Smith Elder. 1st w/ES at p 339. litho ftspc. 9 lithos/fld map. R3. $2,250.00

FORBES, Alexander. *Radio Gunner.* 1924. Houghton Mifflin. 1st. VG. M2. $25.00

FORBES, Allan. *Sport in Norfolk Country.* 1938. Houghton Mifflin. 1/665. sgn/#d. VG. O3. $95.00

FORBES, Colin. *Target Five.* 1973. Collins. 1st. VG/VG. P3. $18.00

FORBES, Colin. *Year of the Golden Ape.* 1974. Dutton. 1st. NF/NF. P3. $20.00

FORBES, Edgar Allen. *Leslie's Photographic Review of the Great War.* 1920. Leslie-Judge. G+. P3. $40.00

FORBES, Eric G. *Gersham Lectures of John Flamsteed.* 1975. London. Mansell. 8vo. 479p. F. K5. $55.00

FORBES, Graham B. *Boys of Columbia High in Winter Sports (#7).* 1915. Grosset Dunlap. 1st. 236p. VG/dj (lists to this title). M20. $40.00

FORBES, Hugh. *Extracts From the Manual for the Patriotic Volunteer...* 1857. NY. Tinson. 1st. 16mo. 198p. prt wrp. M1. $1,750.00

FORBES, Jack D. *Apache, Navaho & Spaniard.* 1971. Norman. 3rd. 8vo. VG/stiff wrp. F7. $8.00

FORBES, Jack D. *Native Americans of California & Nevada.* 1969. Healdsburg. Naturegraph pub. 8vo. 200p. F/wrp. K7. $15.00

FORBES, Robert B. *Personal Reminiscences.* 1970. NY. Lib Eds. facsimile of 2nd 1882 ed. ils. 412p. T7. $40.00

FORBES, Robert B. *Voyage of the Jamestown on Her Errand of Mercy.* 1847. Boston. Eastburn's Pr. ftspc litho Fitz Hugh Lane. O7. $1,500.00

FORBES, Rosita. *Secret of the Sahara: Kufara.* 1921. Doran. 1st Am. ils. 356p. VG. A25. $38.00

FORBES, Stanton. *Deadly Kind of Lonely.* 1971. Crime Club. 1st. VG/VG. P3. $20.00

FORBES, Stanton. *Terror Touches Me.* 1966. Collins Crime Club. 1st. VG/dj. P3. $15.00

FORBES, Thomas A. *Guide to Better Archery.* (1955). Harrisburg. 1st. 307p. F/VG. H7. $25.00

FORBIS, William. *Cowboys.* 1974. Time-Life. leather. A19. $20.00

FORBUSH, Bliss. *Elias Hicks: Quaker Liberal.* 1956. Columbia. 1st. sgn. 355p. VG/dj. V3. $25.00

FORBUSH, Edward H. *Birds of Massachusetts & Other New England States, Vol I.* 1925. MA Dept Agriculture. 481p. VG. B1. $75.00

FORBUSH, Edward H. *Birds of Massachusetts & Other New England States.* 1925-27. Boston. 3 vol. 1st. 4to. ils. NF. C6. $250.00

FORBUSH, Edward H. *History of Game Birds, Wild-Fowl & Shore-Birds of MA...* 1912. Boston. 1st. 4to. 622p. F. C6. $125.00

FORCE, M.F. *From Ft Henry to Corinth (Mississippi)...* 1881. 204p. O8. $21.50

FORD, Betty. *Betty: A Glad Awakening.* 1987. Doubleday. 1st. sgn. VG/VG. A23. $50.00

FORD, Corey. *Short Cut to Tokyo.* 1934. NY. 1st. VG/G. B5. $35.00

FORD, E.B. *Butterflies.* 1957. London. 3rd. ils/maps. 368p. VG. S15. $25.00

FORD, Florence. *Shadow on the House.* 1974. Hamish Hamilton. 1st. VG/VG. P3. $20.00

FORD, Madox. *Communist.* 1987. Babcock Koontz. 1st. 1/200. sgn. F/gr Roma wrp. Q1. $75.00

FORD, Madox. *Independence Day.* 1995. Knopf. 1st. sgn. F/dj. Q1. $75.00

FORD, Madox. *Portraits of My Life.* 1937. Houghton Mifflin. 1st. F/dj. Q1. $75.00

FORD, Gerald. *Humor & the Presidency.* 1987. Arbor. 1st. sgn. F/F. A23. $90.00

FORD, Gerald. *Portrait of the Assassin.* 1965. S&S. 1st. sgn. G/G. A23. $90.00

FORD, Gerald. *Time To Heal.* 1979. Harper Row. 1st. sgn. F/F. A23. $125.00

FORD, Grace Horney. *Button Collector's History.* 1943. Springfield, MA. sgn. 238p. VG/dj. M20. $40.00

FORD, Henry Chapman. *Artist Records the California Missions.* 1989. BC of CA. obl 4to. ils. decor beige bdg. F/dj. w/prospectus. R3. $175.00

FORD, Hilary; see Silverberg, Robert.

FORD, James L. *Hypnotic Tales.* 1891. Keppler Schwarzmann. 1st. VG. M2. $40.00

FORD, James. *Comparison of Formative Cultures in the Americas.* 1969. Smithsonian. 1st. 4to. 211p. F3. $45.00

FORD, John M. *Dragon Waiting.* 1983. Timescape. 1st. F/dj. M2. $65.00

FORD, Leslie. *Woman in Black.* 1947. Scribner. 1st. VG/G. N4. $25.00

FORD, Marcia; see Radford, R.L.

FORD, Marilyn C. *Wildflowers of Mount Shasta: Lone Giant of the Cascades.* 1981. Klamath Falls. ils/photos/maps. 72p. F/dj. B26. $65.00

FORD, Richard. *Independence Day.* 1995. Knopf. 1st. F/F. R14. $60.00

FORD, Richard. *Independence Day.* 1995. Knopf. 1st. inscr. F/F. D10. $125.00

FORD, Richard. *Independence Day.* 1995. Knopf. 1st. sgn/dtd July 4 1995. F/F. A11. $175.00

FORD, Richard. *Independence Day.* 1995. London. Harvill. 1st. F/F. B3. $60.00

FORD, Richard. *Piece of My Heart.* 1976. Harper Row. 1st. inscr. author's 1st book. F/NF. L3. $450.00

FORD, Richard. *Piece of My Heart.* 1976. Harper Row. 1st. rem mk. F/VG+ clip. T11. $200.00

FORD, Richard. *Piece of My Heart.* 1987. London. Harvill. 1st. sgn. F/F. T2. $85.00

FORD, Richard. *Rock Springs.* 1987. Atlantic Monthly. 1st. sgn. F/dj. D10/M23. $60.00

FORD, Richard. *Rock Springs.* 1988. London. Collins Harvill. 1st. sgn. F/F. T2. $55.00

FORD, Richard. *Sportswriter.* 1996. Knopf. 1st Am hc. sgn. F/F. D10. $50.00

FORD, Richard. *Ultimate Good Luck.* 1981. Houghton Mifflin. 1st. sgn. author's 2nd novel F/dj. D10. $350.00

FORD, Richard. *Ultimate Good Luck.* 1989. London. Collins Harvill. 1st. sgn. F/F. T2. $65.00

FORD, Richard. *Wildlife.* 1990. Atlantic Monthly. 1/200. sgn. M/case/swrp. B4. $200.00

FORD, Richard. *Wildlife.* 1990. Atlantic Monthly. 1st. F/F. S13. $20.00

FORD, Richard. *Wildlife.* 1990. Atlantic Monthly. 1st. sgn. F/F. A23/D10. $50.00

FORD, Richard. *Wildlife.* 1990. London. Collins Harvill. 1st. F/F. T2. $65.00

FORD, Tirey L. *California State Prisons: Their History, Development...* 1910. SF. Star Pr. 1st. 8vo. ils. w/complimentary slip. F/gray wrp. R3. $100.00

FORD, Tirey L. *Dawn & the Dons: Romance of Monterey.* 1926. San Francisco. 1st. ils/pict label. VG. O4. $25.00

FORD & MARTIN. *Musical Fantasies of L Frank Baum.* 1969. 1/1000. sgn/#d. F. A4. $95.00

FORD. *Bibliotheca Hamiltoniana: List of Books Written...* 1969 (1886). rpt. 165p. F. A4. $45.00

FORDHAM, Mary Weston. *Magnolia Leaves.* 1897. Charleston, SC. Walker Evans Cogswell. 1st. intro BT Washington. NF. B4. $450.00

FOREMAN, Grant. *Last Trek of the Indians.* 1946. Chicago. 1st. 8 fld maps. 382p. pict cloth. D11. $30.00

FOREMAN, Grant. *Pathfinder in the Southwest: Itinerary of Lt AW Whipple...* 1941. OK U. 1st. 7 full-p ils. cloth. dj. D11. $40.00

FOREMAN, L.L. *Farewell to Texas.* 1964. Doubleday. 1st. F/F. B4. $75.00

FORESTER, C.S. *Age of Fighting Sail, Story of the Naval War of 1812.* 1956. NY. 1st. 284p. G+/dj. B18. $27.50

FORESTER, C.S. *Barbary Pirates.* 1953. Random. 1st. ils Charles Mazoujian. red cloth. F/NF. T11. $125.00

FORESTER, C.S. *Captain From Connecticut.* 1942. Clipper Books. VG/dj. P3. $30.00

FORESTER, C.S. *Commodore Hornblower.* 1945. 1st Am. VG/VG. M17. $45.00

FORESTER, C.S. *General.* 1936. Little Brn. 1st. VG. P3. $35.00

FORESTER, C.S. *Hornblower & the Atropos.* 1953. London. Michael Joseph. 1st. NF/dj. Q1. $100.00

FORESTER, C.S. *Hornblower & the Hotspur.* 1962. Michael Joseph. 1st. 286p. VG/dj. M20. $70.00

FORESTER, C.S. *Josephine, Napoleon's Empress.* 1925. London. Methuen. 1st. 1/2000. gr cloth. G+. T11. $250.00

FORESTER, C.S. *Long Before Forty.* 1967. Little Brn. 1st. F/NF. B2. $30.00

FORESTER, C.S. *Lord Hornblower.* 1946. Little Brn. 1st. VG. P3. $25.00

FORESTER, C.S. *Lord Hornblower.* 1946. Little Brn. 1st/11th prt. F/F. T12. $20.00

FORESTER, C.S. *Lord Nelson.* 1929. Bobbs Merrill. 1st Am. F/NF. T11. $400.00

FORESTER, C.S. *Louis XIV: King of France & Navarre.* 1928. Dodd Mead. 1st Am. 1/1700. VG+. T11. $175.00

FORESTER, C.S. *Lt Hornblower.* 1952. Little Brn. 1st Am. 306p. cloth. VG/dj. M20. $30.00

FORESTER, C.S. *Lt Hornblower.* 1952. London. Michael Joseph. 1st. VG/dj. Q1. $125.00

FORESTER, C.S. *Nightmare.* 1954. Michael Joseph. 1st. VG/VG. P3. $35.00

FORESTER, C.S. *Poo-Poo & the Dragon.* 1942. Little Brn. 1st. ils Robert Lawson. 143p. VG/VG. P2. $450.00

FORESTER, C.S. *Sky & the Forest.* 1948. Michael Joseph. 1st. VG/VG. P3/S13. $20.00

FORESTER, C.S. *To the Indies.* 1940. Canada. Saunders. 1st. VG. P3. $30.00

FORESTER, Frank. *Warwick Woodlands.* 1990. Derrydale. 1/2500. aeg. gilt leather. F. A17. $25.00

FORMAN, George. *By George.* 1995. Villard. 1st. sgn. F/F. A23. $50.00

FORMAN, H. Buxton. *Books of William Morris.* 1969. Frnklin. 224p. cloth. A17. $25.00

FORRER, Eric. *From the Nets of a Salmon Fisherman.* 1973. NY. 1st. 158p. wrp. A17. $7.50

FORREST, D.W. *Francis Galton: Life & Work of a Victorian Genius.* 1974. Taplinger. 1st. ils. 340p. VG/dj. K3. $15.00

FORRESTER, Glenn. *Falls of Niagara.* 1928. NY. 1st. ils/27 maps. 155p. VG. B5. $35.00

FORST, Sigmund. *Book of Hanukkah, Incorporating Album of Illustrations...* 1958. NY. Schlusinger Bros. 27 full-p pl. F. E6. $60.00

FORSTER, E.M. *Battersea Rise.* 1955. Harcourt Brace. 1st. decor brd/label. F. M24. $65.00

FORSTER, E.M. *Hill of Devi.* 1953. London. 1st. VG/dj. T9. $45.00

FORSTER, E.M. *Pharos & Pharillon.* 1923. Richmond. Hogarth. 1st. assn copy. VG. T9. $125.00

FORSTER, E.M. *Virginia Woolf.* 1942. Cambridge. 1st. 1/5000. F/prt wrp. M24. $100.00

FORSYTH, Frederick. *Day of the Jackal.* 1971. Viking. 1st. NF/dj. D10. $75.00

FORSYTH, Frederick. *Dogs of War.* 1974. Viking. 1st. VG/VG. M22. $15.00

FORSYTH, Frederick. *Dogs of War.* 1974. Viking. 1st Am. F/F. M15. $40.00

FORSYTH, Frederick. *Fourth Protocol.* 1984. Hutchinson. 1st. F/dj. A24. $45.00

FORSYTH, Frederick. *Fourth Protocol.* 1984. Viking. 1st Am. VG+/dj. N4. $20.00

FORSYTH, Frederick. *Negotiator.* 1989. Bantam. 1st Am. NF/VG+. N4. $17.50

FORSYTH, Frederick. *Odessa File.* 1972. Viking. 1st. NF/NF. M22. $30.00

FORSYTH, Frederick. *Odessa File.* 1972. Viking. 1st Am. F/F. M15. $50.00

FORT, Charles. *Lo!* 1931. Kendall. 1st. VG. M2. $50.00

FORT, Charles. *Outcast Manufacturers.* 1909. Dodge. 1st. VG+. M2. $75.00

FORTESCUE, John. *Governance of England: Otherwise Called the Difference...* 1926. London. Oxford. 2nd imp. M11. $125.00

FORTIER, Y.O. *Geology of North-Central Part of Arctic Archipelago...* 1963. Geol Survey Canada Memoir 320. 671p. VG/torn box. D8. $25.00

FORTMAN, Edmund J. *Everlasting Life: Towards a Theology of the Future Life.* 1986. Alba House. 369p. G/wrp. B29. $7.50

FORTUINE, Robert. *Chills & Fever: Health & Disease in Early History of Alaska.* 1989. np. 1st. inscr. 8vo. 393p. gray cloth. NF/dj. P4. $45.00

FORTUNE, Dion. *Moon Magic.* 1972. Weiser. NF/dj. M2. $12.00

FORTUNE, T. Thomas. *Black & White: Land, Labor & Politics in the South.* 1884. NY. Fords Howard Hulbert. 1st. 310p. coth. VG. B4. $600.00

FORWARD & TORRES. *Men Who Hate Women & the Women Who Love Them.* 1986. Bantam. 294p. VG/dj. B29. $10.50

FOSTER, Alan Dean. *Day of the Dissonance.* 1984. Phantasia. 1st. 1/375. sgn/#d. F/F. P3. $40.00

FOSTER, Alan Dean. *Icerigger.* 1976. London. 1st. F/dj. M2. $45.00

FOSTER, Alan Dean. *Moment of the Magician.* 1984. Phantasia. 1/375. sgn/#d. F/dj/case. P3. $40.00

FOSTER, Alan Dean. *Star Wars.* 1976. NY. Del Rey BC. ghostwriter/sgn Alan Dean Foster. F/NF. A11. $275.00

FOSTER, Alan Dean. *Star Wars: From the Adventures of Luke Skywalker.* 1977. Ballantine. 1st hc/MTI. F/NF. B4. $250.00

FOSTER, Alan Dean. *To the Vanishing Point.* 1988. Warner. 1st. NF/NF. P3. $16.00

FOSTER, Charles H.W. *Eastern Yacht Club Ditty Box, 1870-1900.* 1932. Norwood, MA. Plimpton. 317p. T7. $65.00

FOSTER, Genevieve. *Abraham Lincoln's World.* 1944. Scribner 1st/A ed. sgn. 347p. cloth. VG+/clip. M20. $75.00

FOSTER, Genevieve. *Augustus Caesar's World.* 1947. Scribner. 1st/A ed. 4to. 330p. VG. T5. $40.00

FOSTER, Genevieve. *Year of the Flying Machine, 1903.* 1977. NY. 1st. 96p. half cloth. VG/dj. B18. $12.50

FOSTER, Hal. *Prince Valiant in the New World.* 1956. Hastings. VG/VG. P3. $35.00

FOSTER, M.S. *Causes of Spatial & Temporal Patterns...* 1988. CA Academy of Sci. 45p. pict wrp. B1. $15.00

FOSTER, Michael. *Claude Bernard.* 1899. NY. 1st. 245p. A13. $60.00

FOSTER, Mulford B. *Brazil: Orchid of the Tropics.* 1946 (1945). NY. 2nd. ils/photos. dj. B26. $46.00

FOSTER, Pearl Byrd. *Classic American Cooking.* 1983. S&S. G/dj. A16. $15.00

FOSTER, R.F. *Moat House Mystery.* 1930. MacAulay. G+. P3. $20.00

FOSTER, R.F. *Practical Poker.* 1905. Brentano. 1st. 253p. pict cloth. VG. J2. $125.00

FOSTER, Robert V. *Systematic Theology.* 1898. Cumberland Presb. 868p. xl. VG. B29. $11.00

FOSTER & GIFFORD. *Comparative Morphology of Vascular Plants.* 1974. Freeman. 2nd. ils. 751p. VG+. S15. $11.00

FOUQUE, DeLaMotte. *Undine.* (1909). London. 1st. ils Rackham/15 tipped-in pl. cloth. VG. S13. $150.00

FOUQUE, DeLaMotte. *Undine.* 1909. 19th. 15 tipped-in pl. VG+. S13. $40.00

FOURNIER, Pierre Simon. *Manuel Typographique.* 1764-1766. Paris. Fournier. 2 vol. 8vo. fld/double-p pl. aeg. full brn morocco. R12. $7,500.00

FOWLER, Christopher. *Rune.* 1991. Ballantine. 1st. author's 2nd novel. F/F. M22. $30.00

FOWLER, Connie May. *Sugar Cage.* 1992. Putnam. 1st. sgn. F/F. R13. $50.00

FOWLER, Guy. *Dawn Patrol.* 1930. Grosset Dunlap. MTI. 241p. VG+/dj. B18. $25.00

FOWLER, H. Alfred. *Lincolniana Book Plates & Collections.* 1913. Kansas City. unp. quarter cloth. VG-. B18. $75.00

FOWLER, John M. *Fallout: Study of Superbombs, Strontium 90 & Survival.* 1960. NY. 2nd. 235p. F/dj. A17. $15.00

FOWLER, Karen Joy. *Sara Canary.* 1991. NY. Holt. 1st. sgn/dtd 1991. author's 1st novel. F/F. M23. $50.00

FOWLER, Manley B. *Prophecy; or, Love & Friendship...* 1821. NY. Murden Thomson. 1st. 18mo. 34p. M1. $150.00

FOWLER & WEST. *Food for Fifty.* 1937. Whiley. photos/diagrams. 384p. B10. $45.00

FOWLER & WRIGHT. *Moving Frontier.* 1972. np. Great Explorers series. 348p. VG+/torn. B18. $22.50

FOWLER & WRIGHT. *West & by North.* 1971. Delacorte. 1st. VG/dj. K3. $20.00

FOWLES, John. *Brief History of Lyme.* 1981. Lyme Regis. Friends of the Mus. sgn. F/stapled wrp. B4. $125.00

FOWLES, John. *Collector.* 1963. London. Cape. 1st issue (no blurbs on dj). VG/dj. A24. $375.00

FOWLES, John. *Daniel Martin.* 1977. Jonathan Cape. 1st Eng. NF/VG. M19. $25.00

FOWLES, John. *Ebony Tower.* 1974. London. Cape. VG/clip. A24. $45.00

FOWLES, John. *Enigma.* 1987. Helsinki. Eurographica. 1st. 1/350. sgn. F/F. B4. $150.00

FOWLES, John. *Maggot.* 1985. Little Brn. BC. 408p. VG/VG. V3. $8.50

FOWLES, John. *Magus.* 1963. Little Brn. 1st Am (before Eng). VG/clip. Q1. $100.00

FOWLES, John. *Magus.* 1966. London. Cape. 1st. NF/dj. A24. $150.00

FOWLES, John. *Mantissa.* 1982. Little Brn. 1st. F/F. P3. $20.00

FOWLES, John. *Mantissa.* 1982. Toronto. Collins. 1st. NF/F. B3. $20.00

FOWLES, John. *Poems.* 1973. Ecco. 1st. NF/NF. M19. $35.00

FOWLES, John. *Swan Song of the European Wild.* 1965. Venture. 1st. NF. B3. $20.00

FOX, D.L. *Animal Biochromes & Structural Colours: Physical...* 1976. Berkeley. 2nd revised. ils/pl/figures/tables. 433p. F/VG+. M12. $37.50

FOX, Frances L. *San Jose's Luis Maria Peralta & His Adobe.* 1975. San Jose. Smith-Mckay. sgn. 92p. orange cloth. as new/dj. K7. $35.00

FOX, Frances Margaret. *Little Bear's Adventures.* 1923. Rand McNally. 1st. ils Frances Beem. bl cloth/mc pl. VG. M5. $75.00

FOX, George Henry. *Photographic Ils of Skin Diseases.* 1880. NY. 48 pl. 102p. brn cloth. B14. $375.00

FOX, George. *Amok.* 1978. S&S. 1st. VG/VG. P3. $15.00

FOX, George. *Concerning Persecution in All Ages To This Day.* 1682. London. John Bringhurst. 1st. V3. $140.00

FOX, George. *Gospel Truth Demonstrated in Collection Doctrinal Books.* 1706. London. Sowle. 1090p. full leather. V3. $185.00

FOX, George. *Journal or Historical Account of Life, Travels, Sufferings.* 1832. Phil. Kimber Sharpless. 672p. worn leather. V3. $50.00

FOX, George. *Warlord's Hill.* 1982. Times Books. 1st. VG+/VG+. N4. $17.50

FOX, Helen Morgenthau. *Patio Gardens.* 1929. NY. ils/fld plans. 228p. yel/bl cloth. VG. B26. $72.50

FOX, James M. *Iron Virgin.* 1951. Little Brn. 1st. VG/dj. M25. $45.00

FOX, James M. *Shroud for Mr Bundy.* 1952. Little Brn. 1st. VG. P3. $15.00

FOX, John Jr. *Little Shepherd of Kingdom Come.* 1931. Scribner. 1st. ils NC Wyeth/14 full-p pl. 322p. VG. D1. $200.00

FOX, Larry. *New England Patriots.* 1979. Atheneum. 1st. photos. VG+/dj. P8. $25.00

FOX, Norman A. *Arizona Stranger.* 1973. Collins. VG/VG. P3. $12.00

FOXBURGH, William. *Flora Indica; or, Descriptions of Indian Plants...* 1975. NY. facsimile 1st ed. intro DH Nicolson. NF/dj. B26. $59.00

FOXE, Arthur N. *Plague: Laennec (1782-1826)...* 1947. NY. Hobson. 122p. VG. K3. $25.00

FOXON, David. *Libertine Literature in England 1660-1745.* 1965. NY. U Books. 70p+13 pl. F. A17. $17.50

FOXX, Jack; see Pronzini, Bill.

FRACKELTON & SEELY. *Sagebrush Dentist, Old WY in Days of Buffalo Bill...* 1947. Trails End. 1st revised. 258p. VG/dj. J2. $175.00

FRADKIN, Philip L. *River No More.* 1981. Knopf. 1st. 8vo. 360p. bl/blk cloth. VG+. F7. $35.00

FRAIGNEAU, Andre. *Jean Cocteau on the Film, a Conversation Recorded.* 1954. Roy Pub. ils. VG+/dj. C9. $75.00

FRANCATELLI, C. *Modern Cook; a Practical Guide to Culinary Art.* 1846 (1880). lg 8vo. 80p of menus. VG. E6. $75.00

FRANCE, Anatole. *At the Sign of the Queen Pedauque.* 1933. LEC. 1st. ils LA Patterson. F. M19. $45.00

FRANCE, Anatole. *Filles et Garcons. Scenes de la Ville et des Champs.* nd. Paris. Librairie Hachett. ils DeMonvel. 24p. pict brd. R5. $100.00

FRANCE, Anatole. *Golden Tales of Anatole France.* 1927. Dodd Mead. 1st. ils LA Patterson. F. M19. $45.00

FRANCIS, Dick. *Blood Sport.* 1967. London. Michael Joseph. 1st. NF/dj. Q1. $350.00

FRANCIS, Dick. *Bolt.* 1986. Michael Joseph. 1st. F/F. M25. $35.00

FRANCIS, Dick. *Bolt.* 1986. Michael Joseph. 1st. F/NF. P3. $22.00

FRANCIS, Dick. *Bonecrack.* 1972. Harper. 1st Am. NF/NF. N4. $60.00

FRANCIS, Dick. *Break In.* 1986. Michael Joseph. 1st. VG/VG. P3. $18.00

FRANCIS, Dick. *Break In.* 1986. Putnam. 1st Am. F/F. T12. $20.00

FRANCIS, Dick. *Danger.* 1983. Putnam. 1st. VG/VG. P3. $20.00

FRANCIS, Dick. *Dead Cert.* 1989. NY. Armchair Detective. 1/26 lettered. sgn. F/case. M15. $150.00

FRANCIS, Dick. *Driving Force.* 1992. London. Michael Joseph. true 1st. sgn. F/dj. D10. $40.00

FRANCIS, Dick. *Edge.* 1988. London. Michael Joseph. true 1st. sgn. NF/NF. D10. $45.00

FRANCIS, Dick. *Edge.* 1988. Michael Joseph. 1st. F/NF. B3. $40.00

FRANCIS, Dick. *Edge.* 1988. NY. Putnam. 1st Am. F/F. T12. $45.00

FRANCIS, Dick. *For Kicks.* 1965. London. Michael Joseph. 1st. NF/dj. Q1. $1,000.00

FRANCIS, Dick. *High Stakes.* 1975. Harper. 1st Am. VG/VG. M22. $30.00

FRANCIS, Dick. *Hot Money.* 1987. Michael Joseph. 1st. F/F. B3/Q1. $60.00

FRANCIS, Dick. *Hot Money.* 1987. Michael Joseph. 1st. VG/VG. P3. $20.00

FRANCIS, Dick. *In the Frame.* 1976. Harper Row. 1st Am. 8vo. F/NF. T10. $45.00

FRANCIS, Dick. *Jockey's Life.* 1986. Putnam. later prt. F/VG. P8. $25.00

FRANCIS, Dick. *Knockdown.* 1974. Harper. 1st. VG/G. M19. $35.00

FRANCIS, Dick. *Nerve.* 1964. London. Michael Joseph. 1st. F/NF. M15. $850.00

FRANCIS, Dick. *Proof.* 1984. London. Joseph. 1st. NF/F. H11. $50.00

FRANCIS, Dick. *Proof.* 1984. London. Michael Joseph. 1st. F/F. M15/T12. $75.00

FRANCIS, Dick. *Proof.* 1984. Michael Joseph. 1st. VG/VG. P3. $20.00

FRANCIS, Dick. *Rat Race.* 1971. Harper Row. 1st. F/VG. M19. $35.00

FRANCIS, Dick. *Risk.* 1977. Harper. 1st. NF/NF. M19. $45.00

FRANCIS, Dick. *Risk.* 1977. London. Michael Joseph. 1st. F/F. M15. $75.00

FRANCIS, Dick. *Slay-Ride*. 1973. Michael Joseph. 1st. NF/dj. M25. $50.00

FRANCIS, Dick. *Smokescreen*. 1972. Harper Row. 1st Am. 8vo. F/NF. T10. $75.00

FRANCIS, Dick. *Smokescreen*. 1973. Harper Row. 1st. VG/VG. P3. $35.00

FRANCIS, Dick. *Sport of Queens*. 1969. Harper Row. 1st Am. author's 1st book. F/VG+. A24. $150.00

FRANCIS, Dick. *Sport of Queens*. 1969. Harper Row. 1st Am. F/F. M15. $250.00

FRANCIS, Dick. *Straight*. 1989. London. Michael Joseph. true 1st. sgn. F/dj. D10. $45.00

FRANCIS, Dick. *Trial Run*. 1978. London. Michael Joseph. 1st. NF/NF. T12. $85.00

FRANCIS, Dick. *Twice Shy*. 1981. Michael Joseph. 1st. NF/NF. P3. $30.00

FRANCIS, Philip W. *Remarkable Adventures of Little Boy Pip*. 1907. SF. Paul Elder. 1st. ils Merle Johnson. 4to. pict brd. dj. R5. $300.00

FRANCIS, Richard H. *Whispering Gallery*. 1984. Norton. 1st. VG/VG. P3. $15.00

FRANCK, Harry. *Vagabonding Down the Andes*. 1917. NY. Century. 1st. 612p. teg. F3. $20.00

FRANCKENAU, Gerhard Ernst. *Bibliotheca Hispanica Historico-Genealogico-Heraldica*. 1724. Leipzig. Maur Georg Weidmann. 1st/only. 412p. VG. R15. $450.00

FRANCL, Joseph. *Overland Journey of Joseph Francl, First Bohemian...* 1968. SF. Wm Wreden. 1/540. ils. 59p. pict brd. D11. $60.00

FRANCOIS, Yves. *Citz Paradigm*. 1975. Doubleday. 1st. F/dj. M2/P3. $15.00

FRANCOISE. *Fanchette & Jeannot*. 1937. Grosset Dunlap. ils. VG. P2. $50.00

FRANCOISE. *Springtime for Jeanne-Marie*. 1955. Scribner. 1st/A. 4to. VG+/dj. M5. $25.00

FRANCOISE. *Story of Colette*. 1940. Scribner. 1st/A. VG/G. M5. $110.00

FRANCOME & MACGREGOR. *Eavesdropper*. 1986. London. Macdonald. 1st. sgn. author's 1st novel. F/dj. M25. $60.00

FRANGSMYR, Tore. *Linnaeus: The Man & His Work*. 1983. Berkeley. ils. 203p. F/dj. B26. $29.00

FRANK, Alan. *Galactic Aliens*. 1979. Chartwell. 1st. F/F. M2. $12.00

FRANK, Alan. *Horror Movies*. 1974. Octopus. 1st. VG/VG. P3. $20.00

FRANK, Anne. *Anne Frank: The Diary of a Young Girl*. 1952. Doubleday Doran. 1st Am. 285p. VG/G+. P2. $250.00

FRANK, Benis. *Brief History of the 3rd Marines*. 1968. WA. maps/notes. sc. VG. S16. $25.00

FRANK, Bruno Z. *Man Called Cervantes*. 1935. Viking. 1st. F/F. M19. $25.00

FRANK, C.W. *Anatomy of a Waterfowl*. 1982. Gretna. Pelican. ils/mc pl/lg fld mc pl. 297p. cloth. NF. M12. $37.50

FRANK, Gerold. *Boston Strangler*. 1967. Jonathan Cape. 1st. VG/fair. P3. $18.00

FRANK, Niklas. *In the Shadow of the Reich*. 1991. Knopf. 371p. VG/dj. S3. $25.00

FRANK, Pat. *Forbidden Area*. 1956. Lippincott. 1st. inscr. VG/VG. B11. $65.00

FRANK, Pat. *Mr Adam*. 1946. Lippincott. 13th prt. 252p. G. W2. $10.00

FRANKAU, Pamela. *Pen to Paper: A Novelist's Notebook*. 1961. London. 1st. inscr. VG/dj. T9. $30.00

FRANKE, Herbert. *Zone Null*. 1974. Seabury. 1st. F/dj. M2. $25.00

FRANKLIN, G.C. *Wild Animals of the Five River Country*. (1947). Houghton Mifflin. ils MO Abbott. 271p. cloth. NF/VG+. M12. $15.00

FRANKLIN, H. Bruce. *Future Perfect*. 1968. Oxford. F/dj. M2. $20.00

FRANKLIN, John Hope. *Racial Equality in America*. 1976. Chicago. 1st. inscr. 113p. F/NF. B4. $150.00

FRANKLIN, John. *Narrative of 2nd Expedition to Shores of Plar Sea*. 1969 (1829). NY. Greenwood. facsimile. 4to. 6 fld maps. 320p. T7. $90.00

FRANKLIN, K.J. *Monograph on Veins*. 1937. Springfield. 1st. 410p. A13. $75.00

FRANKLIN, Stephen. *Knowledge Park*. 1972. Toronto. 1st. F/F. T12. $95.00

FRANKLYN, Irwin R. *Flight: An Epic of the Air*. 1929. Grosset Dunlap. photoplay ed. 245p. VG+/dj. B18. $25.00

FRANKLYN, Robert Alan. *Developing Bosom Beauty*. 1959. Frederick Fell. 1st. ils. 141p. VG+. A25. $18.00

FRANKS, K.A. *Early Oklahoma Oil: Photographic History 1859-1936*. 1981. TX A&M. 1st. 325 photos. F/dj. M4. $30.00

FRANKS, K.A. *Oklahoma Petroleum Industry*. 1980. OK U. 1st. 150 photos. F/dj. M4. $25.00

FRANZEN, Jonathan. *Twenty-Seventh City*. 1988. FSG. ARC. author's 1st book. NF/wrp. A24. $25.00

FRANZEN, Jonathan. *Twenty-Seventh City*. 1988. FSG. 1st. F/NF. P3. $20.00

FRANZEN, Jonathan. *Twenty-Seventh City*. 1988. FSG. 1st. sgn. author's 1st book. F/F. D10. $50.00

FRASER, Antonia. *Quiet As a Nun*. 1977. Viking. 1st. VG/VG. P3. $18.00

FRASER, Antonia. *Your Royal Hostage*. 1987. Weidenfeld Nicolson. 1st. VG/VG. P3. $19.00

FRASER, C.L. *Pirates*. 1922. 1st. ils. VG+. S13. $45.00

FRASER, Claud Lovat. *Book of Simple Toys*. 1982. Bryn Mawr. 1st thus. 8vo. red textured cloth/label. R5. $100.00

FRASER, Colin. *Harry Ferguson: Inventor & Pioneer*. 1972. London. Murray. 294p. dj. A10. $35.00

FRASER, Donald. *Autobiography of an African Retold in Biographical Form...* 1970 (1925). Negro U. rpt. VG. W1. $25.00

FRASER, George MacDonald. *Flashman & the Dragon*. 1986 (1985). Knopf. 1st Am. 320p. NF/dj. M20. $55.00

FRASER, George MacDonald. *Flashman & the Mountain of Light*. 1990. London. Collins. true 1st. F/clip. D10. $45.00

FRASER, George MacDonald. *Flashman & the Redskins*. 1982. Knopf. 1st. F/dj. Q1. $50.00

FRASER, George MacDonald. *Flashman in the Great Game*. 1975. Knopf. 1st Am. F/NF. Q1. $60.00

FRASER, George MacDonald. *Flashman in the Great Game*. 1975. London. Barrie Jenkins. true 1st. F/clip. D10. $50.00

FRASER, George MacDonald. *Flashman's Lady*. 1978. Knopf. 1st Am. F/dj. M15/Q1. $50.00

FRASER, George MacDonald. *Flashman*. 1969. London. Jenkins. 1st Eng. F/NF clip. T11. $125.00

FRASER, George MacDonald. *Flashman*. 1969. World. 1st Am. F/clip. Q1. $150.00

FRASER, George MacDonald. *General Danced at Dawn*. 1970. London. Barrie Jenkins. 1st. F/F. B4. $150.00

FRASER, George MacDonald. *McAusland in the Rough*. 1974. Knopf. 1st Am. F/dj. B4/Q1. $100.00

FRASER, George MacDonald. *Mr American*. 1980. S&S. 1st. rem mk. F/dj. Q1. $50.00

FRASER, George MacDonald. *Pyrates*. 1983. Collins. 1st. F/F. P3. $35.00

FRASER, George MacDonald. *Pyrates*. 1984. Knopf. 1st. F/F. P3. $30.00

FRASER, George MacDonald. *Royal Flash*. 1970. Knopf. 1st Am. F/NF. Q1. $150.00

FRASER, George MacDonald. *Steel Bonnets.* 1972. VG. M17. $30.00

FRASER, Kathleen. *Stilts, Somersaults & Headstands: Game Poems...* 1968. Atheneum. 1st. 37p. F/F. D4. $35.00

FRASER, Kathleen. *Stilts, Somersaults & Headstands: Game Poems...* 1968. Atheneum. 1st. 8vo. 37p. VG/VG clip. C14. $15.00

FRASER, R. *Once Round the Sun, Story of International Geophysical Year.* 1957. Macmillan. 160p. xl. G/dj. D8. $12.50

FRASER, Samuel. *Potato.* 1915. NY. Orange Judd. 185p. VG. A10. $22.00

FRASER, Samuel. *Strawberry: Culture, Harvesting, Marketing.* 1926. ils. xl. E6. $15.00

FRASSANITO, William A. *Grant & Lee: Virginia Campaigns 1864-1865.* 1983. Scribner. 1st. 442p. VG/dj. M20. $40.00

FRAYLING, Christopher *Vampyre: A Bedside Companion.* 1978. Scribner. 1st Am. F/F Gorey ils. B2. $45.00

FRAYN, Michael. *Landing on the Sun.* 1991. Viking. 1st. F/F. P3. $22.00

FRAYNE, Trent. *Mad Men of Hockey.* 1974. Dodd Mead. 1st. F/VG. P8. $30.00

FRAZAR, Douglas. *Perserverance Island.* 1899. Lee Shepard. VG. M2. $40.00

FRAZEE, Steve. *Sky Block.* 1953. Rinehart. 1st. F/F. B4. $125.00

FRAZER, Deryk. *Reptiles & Amphibians in Britain.* 1989 (1983). London. New Naturalist series. 254p. F/F. S15. $25.00

FRAZER, J.G. *Golden Bough.* 1951. Macmillan. G+. P3. $20.00

FRAZIER, E. Franklin. *Negro Family in the United States.* 1939. Chicago. 1st. charts/tables. 686p. VG. B4. $100.00

FRAZIER, Ian. *Dating Your Mom.* 1986. FSG. 1st. author's 1st book. F/F. M23. $30.00

FRAZIER, Ian. *Nobody Better, Better Than Nobody.* 1987. NY. FSG. 1st. F/NF. M23. $20.00

FRAZIER, Robert Caine; see Creasey, John.

FRAZIER & JARES. *Clyde.* 1970. HRW. 1st. photos. F/VG. P8. $30.00

FRAZIER & OFFEN. *Walt Frazier.* 1988. Times. 1st. sgn Frazier. F/F. P8. $50.00

FREDE, Richard. *Secret Circus.* 1967. Random. 1st. VG/VG. P3. $25.00

FREDERICKS, J. Paget. *Miss Pert's Christmas Tree.* 1929. Macmillan. 1st. lg 4to. VG. M5. $65.00

FREDERICS, Diana. *Diana, a Strange Autobiography.* 1939. NY. Dial. 1st. flexible gray cloth. F/dj. M24. $400.00

FREDMAN, John. *False Joanna.* 1970. Bobbs Merrill. F/F. P3. $15.00

FREE, John B. *Insect Pollination of Crops.* 1970. NY. Academic. 544p. VG/dj. A10. $35.00

FREEBORN, Brian. *Good Luck Mister Cain.* 1976. St Martin. 1st. VG/G+. P3. $12.00

FREEHAND, Julianna. *Seafaring Legacy: Photographs, Diaries, Letters...1859-1908.* 1981. Random. 1st. 209p. NF/NF. P4. $38.00

FREELAND, Humphrey. *Fountain of Youth.* 1866. London. 1st. VG. M2. $100.00

FREELING, Nicolas. *Tsing-Boum.* 1969. Harper Row. 1st. VG/VG. P3. $20.00

FREELING, Nicolas. *Wolfnight.* 1982. Pantheon. 1st. F/VG. P3. $15.00

FREEMAN, Bud. *You Don't Look Like a Musician.* 1974. Detroit. Balamp. 1st. F/F. B2. $50.00

FREEMAN, Don. *Seal & the Slick.* 1974. Viking. 1st. obl 4to. F/VG+. P2. $55.00

FREEMAN, Don. *Space Witch.* 1959. Viking. 1st. 48p. VG/G+. P2. $135.00

FREEMAN, Douglas Southall. *Lee's Lieutenants.* 1946. 3 vol. ils. VG. M17. $150.00

FREEMAN, Douglas Southall. *Robert E Lee: A Biography.* 1934. Scribner. 4 vol. 1st. sgn. gilt red cloth. VG. M20. $230.00

FREEMAN, Douglas Southall. *Robert E Lee: A Biography.* 1934-35. NY. 4 vol. red cloth. VG. A4. $90.00

FREEMAN, Douglas Southall. *Robert E Lee: A Biography.* 1946. 4 vol. ils. VG. M17. $125.00

FREEMAN, Douglas Southall. *South to Posterity: An Intro to Writing Confederate Hist.* 1983. Broadfoot. facsimile 1951 Scribner. F/F. A17. $30.00

FREEMAN, Estelle B. *Their Sisters' Keepers: Women's Prison Reform in America.* 1981. MI U. 1st. VG/VG. V4. $17.50

FREEMAN, Ira M. *Look-It Up Book of Space.* 1969. Random. 4to. 129p. G. K5. $13.00

FREEMAN, James Dillet. *Once Upon a Christmas.* 1978. Unity. 1st. 173p. NF. W2. $20.00

FREEMAN, Joseph. *Long Pursuit.* 1947. Rinehart. 1st. VG/VG. B4. $85.00

FREEMAN, Lois M. *Betty Crocker's Parties for Children.* 1964. Golden/Western. 2nd. ils Martin. VG+. C8. $17.50

FREEMAN, Margaret B. *Story of the Three Kings.* 1955. MOMA. woodcuts. VG. M17. $25.00

FREEMAN, R. Austin. *Dr Thorndyke Omnibus.* 1933. Dodd Mead. later prt. VG+. N4. $30.00

FREEMAN, R. Austin. *Dr Thorndyke's Crime File.* 1941. Dodd Mead. 1st. G. N4. $45.00

FREEMAN, R. Austin. *John Thorndyke's Cases.* 1909. London. Chatto Windus. 1st. pict cloth. F. M15. $800.00

FREEMAN, R. Austin. *Mr Pottermack's Oversight.* 1930. Dodd Mead. 1st. F/NF. M15. $175.00

FREEMAN, R. Austin. *Silent Witness.* 1915. Winston. 1st. VG. M22. $65.00

FREEMAN, R. Austin. *Stoneware Monkey.* 1938. Hodder Stoughton. 1st. G+. P3. $35.00

FREEMAN, Walter Jackson. *Neuropathology: Anatomical Foundation of Nervous Diseases.* 1933. Phil. Saunders. 349p. panelled bl-gr cloth. VG. G1. $75.00

FREEMAN & PITCAIRN. *Adventures of Romney Pringle.* 1968. Train. 1st. xl. VG/VG+. N4. $25.00

FREEMANTLE, Anne. *Protestant Mystics.* 1964. Weidenfeld Nicolson. 1st. VG. A20. $25.00

FREEMANTLE, Brian. *Blind Run.* 1986. Bantam. 1st. VG/VG. P3. $16.00

FREEMANTLE, Brian. *November Man.* 1976. London. Cape. 1st. F/dj. M15. $75.00

FREEMANTLE, Brian. *O'Farrell's Law.* 1990. Tor. 1st. NF/NF. P3. $18.00

FREEMANTLE, Brian. *Run Around.* 1989. Bantam. 1st. F/F. P3. $17.00

FREID, Jacob. *Judaism & Community: New Directions in Jewish Social Work.* 1968. Yoseloff. 22 articles. 248p. VG/dj. S3. $23.00

FREIDEL, Frank. *Over There, Story of America's 1st Great Overseas Crusade.* 1964. Bramhall. 1st. 300+ photos. 385p. gr cloth. VG/dj. K7. $45.00

FREIDENREICH, Harriet Pass. *Jews of Yugoslavia: Quest for Community.* 1979. JPS. 323p. VG/dj. S3. $40.00

FREMONT, John Charles. *Report of Exploring Expedition to the Rocky Mountains...* 1845. WA, DC. Blair Rives. 1st. ils/2 fld maps (lacks 1). gilt brn cloth. R3. $750.00

FRENCH, Albert. *Holly.* 1995. Viking. 1st. F/F. R13. $35.00

FRENCH, Joseph Lewis. *Great Ghost Stories.* 1918. Dodd Mead. 1st. VG. M2. $40.00

FRENCH, Marilyn. *Bleeding Heart.* 1980. Summit. 1st. F/F. T12. $12.50

FRENCH & KENNEDY. *Niels Bohr. A Centenary Volume.* 1985. Cambridge, MA. Harvard. ils. VG/dj. K3. $30.00

FRENEAU, Phillip. *Some Account of Capture of the Ship Aurora.* 1899. NY. Mansfield Wessels. 49p. VG. T7. $50.00

FRERE, Thomas. *Hoyle's Games With a Brief History of Playing Cards.* 1857. Boston. Improved ed. 356p. VG. S1. $30.00

FRESHNEY, R.I. *Animal Cell Culture, a Practical Approach.* 1986. IRL PR. 248p. pict brd. F. B1. $35.00

FREUD, Sigmund. *Collected Papers.* 1950. London. Hogarth. 5 vol. 5th & 6th imp. F/dj. H1. $125.00

FREUD, Sigmund. *Psychopathology of Everyday Life.* 1914. NY. 1st authorized. trans VG. M17. $250.00

FREYER, Fredric. *Black Black Hearse.* 1955. St Martin. 1st. VG/G+. P3. $25.00

FRICKE. *Wizard of Oz: Official 50th Anniversary Pictorial History.* 1989. 400 photos. 255p. F/F. A4. $85.00

FRIED, Henry B. *Watch Repairer's Manual.* 1949. Van Nostrand. 1st. ils. VG/dj. K3. $20.00

FRIED, John J. *Life Along the San Andreas Fault.* 1973. Saturday Review. 1st. sgn. NF/NF. O4. $15.00

FRIEDBERG, Gertrude. *Revolving Boy.* 1966. Gollancz. 1st. NF/NF. P3. $45.00

FRIEDEBERG, S. *Joshua: Annotated Hebrew Text With Introduction...* 1913. London. Heinemann. 245p. G+/poor. S3. $24.00

FRIEDENWALD, Harry. *Jews & Medicine, Essays.* 1944-1946. Baltimore. 1st. 2 vol. 817p. A13. $250.00

FRIEDHOFF, Richard Mark. *Visualization: Second Computer Revolution.* 1989. Abrams. 1st. F/dj. M2. $20.00

FRIEDLANDER, Saul. *Prelude to Downfall: Hitler & the United States 1939-41.* 1967. Knopf. 1st Am. 328p. VG/dj. M20. $10.00

FRIEDMAN, Bruce Jay. *Dick.* 1970. Knopf. 1st. sgn. VG/VG. R14. $35.00

FRIEDMAN, Bruce Jay. *Let's Hear It for a Beautiful Guy.* 1984. DIF. 1st. F/F. A20. $25.00

FRIEDMAN, Bruce Jay. *Let's Hear It for a Beautiful Guy.* 1984. DIF. 1st. NF/NF. P3. $20.00

FRIEDMAN, H. *Sun & Earth.* 1986. Scientific Am Books. ils/pl. 251p. F/dj. D8. $12.00

FRIEDMAN, Herbert. *Parasitic Weaverbirds.* 1960. WA. 15 pl. 196p. VG. S15. $28.00

FRIEDMAN, Jake. *Jake Friedman's Common Sense Candy Teacher.* 1915 (1911). w/supp by Wm Kennedy. VG. E6. $75.00

FRIEDMAN, Kinky. *Case of Lone Star.* 1987. NY. Morrow. 1st. sgn. author's 2nd book. NF/F. A24. $60.00

FRIEDMAN, Kinky. *Frequent Flier.* 1989. Morrow. 1st. F/F. M19. $25.00

FRIEDMAN, Kinky. *Frequent Flyer.* 1989. Morrow. 1st. as new/dj. N4. $30.00

FRIEDMAN, Kinky. *Frequent Flyer.* 1989. Morrow. 1st. sgn. F/F. A23. $40.00

FRIEDMAN, Kinky. *God Bless John Wayne.* 1995. S&S. 1st. sgn. F/F. A23. $40.00

FRIEDMAN, Kinky. *Greenwich Killing Time.* 1986. Morrow. 1st. inscr/dtd 1986. author's 1st book. F/NF. A24. $85.00

FRIEDMAN, Kinky. *When the Cat's Away.* 1988. Beech Tree. 1st. F/F. N4. $35.00

FRIEDMAN, Kinky. *When the Cat's Away.* 1988. Morrow. 1st. sgn. F/F. A23. $40.00

FRIEDMAN, M. *Jewish Life in Philadelphia 1830-1940.* 1983. ils. VG/VG. E6. $15.00

FRIEDMAN, Mickey. *Temporary Ghost.* 1989. Viking. 1st. VG/VG. P3. $18.00

FRIEDMAN, Norman. *US Aircraft Carriers: Illustrated Design History.* 1983. Annapolis. photos/drawings/notes. 427p. VG/VG. S16. $30.00

FRIEDMAN, Philip. *Roads to Extinction: Essays on the Holocaust.* 1980. JPS. 24 essays. 610p. VG/dj. S3. $39.00

FRIEDMANN, Marion. *I Will Still Be Moved: Reports From South Africa.* 1963. Quadrangle. later prt. NF/dj. M25. $25.00

FRIEDRICH, Otto. *Going Crazy.* 1976. S&S. 1st. F/F. B35. $20.00

FRIEL, Arthur O. *Mountains of Mystery.* 1954. Harper. 1st. G+. P3. $50.00

FRIEND, Esther. *Topsy Turvey & Tin Clown.* 1934 (1932). pict brd. VG+. S13. $25.00

FRIENDLY, A. *Beaufort of the Admiralty: Life of Sir Francis Beaufort...* 1977. ils. VG/VG. M17. $20.00

FRIER, Jane Eayre. *Mary Frances Housekeeper.* 1914. Phil. Winston. 1st. VG. B5. $175.00

FRIES, R. *Empire in Pine: Story of Lumbering in Wisconsin 1830-1930.* 1951. Madison. 1st. 285p. VG/G. B5. $35.00

FRINK, Maurice. *Cow Country Cavalcade, 80 Years of WY Stock Growers Assn.* 1954. Old West Pub. 1st. ils/brand/maps/photos. 243p. VG/dj. J2. $75.00

FRINK, Maurice. *When Grass Was King.* 1956. CO U. 1st. ils/pl. 465p. VG/VG. J2. $315.00

FRISCH, Ephraim. *Historical Survey of Jewish Philanthropy...* 1969. Cooper Sq. 196p. VG+. S3. $24.00

FRISON-ROCHE, R. *Lost Trail of the Sahara.* 1952. Prentice Hall. 1st Am. trans Paul Bowles. F/dj. Q1. $75.00

FRITZ, Jean. *China Homecoming.* 1985. Putnam. 1st. sgn. VG/VG. B11. $25.00

FRITZ, Jean. *Homesick.* 1982. Putnam. 2nd. sgn. VG/VG. B11. $25.00

FRITZ, Samuel. *Journal of Travels & Labours of Father Samuel Fritz.* 1992. London. Hakluyt Soc. 2nd series. 164p. P4. $135.00

FRITZSCH, H. *Quarks, the Stuff of Matter.* 1983. Basic Books. 1st Eng. F/dj. D8. $15.00

FRODERSTROM, H. *Genus Sedum.* 1930-35. Goteborg. English text in 4 parts as 1. brn buckram. NF. B26. $195.00

FROND & LEE. *Faeries.* 1978. NY. Abrams. 1st. inscr. F/F. T12. $20.00

FROSSARD, Jean. *Guide to Basic Dressage.* 1978. London. Pelham Horsemaster series. prt. VG/VG. O3. $15.00

FROST, Frances. *American Caravan.* 1944. Whittlesey. 1st. 4to. VG/G. P2. $20.00

FROST, Frances. *Christmas in the Woods.* 1942. Harper. stated 1st. ils Aldren Watson. F/VG. M5. $22.00

FROST, John. *Indian Wars of the United States.* 1859. NY. CM Saxton. 300p. gilt brn cloth. VG. K7. $125.00

FROST, John. *Thrilling Incidents of the Wars of the United States.* 1853. NY. Robert Sears. 8vo. 600p. brn brd. G. K7. $65.00

FROST, Kent. *My Canyon Lands.* 1971. Abelard-Schuman. sgn. 8vo. orange cloth. NF/VG+. F7. $30.00

FROST, Lawrence A. *Custer Album.* 1964. Seattle. Superior. 1st. A19. $50.00

FROST, Lawrence A. *General Custer's Libbie.* 1976. Seattle, WA. Superior. dj. A19. $45.00

FROST, Richard H. *Mooney Case: San Francisco Preparedness Day Bombing of 1916.* 1968. Stanford. 1st. VG/VG. V4. $35.00

FROST, Robert. *Accidentally on Purpose.* 1960. NY. HRW. 1st. F/wrp. Q1. $35.00

FROST, Robert. *Birches.* 1988. NY. Holt. 1st. 32p. F/F. D4. $30.00

FROST, Robert. *Boy's Will.* 1915. NY. 1st Am/1st state/1st bdg. bl silk. VG. w/ephemera. A11. $225.00

FROST, Robert. *Boy's Will.* 1915. NY. Henry Holt. 1st Am/2nd state text/1st bdg (gilt bl cloth). F. M24. $1,000.00

FROST, Robert. *Complete Poems.* 1949. NY. Henry Holt. 1st. 1/500. sgn. gilt cream cloth. F/NF box. M24. $550.00

FROST, Robert. *In the Clearing.* 1962. HRW. 1st. F/F. B35. $45.00

FROST, Robert. *Letters of Robert Frost to Louis Untermeyer.* 1963. Holt Rinehart. 1st. F/clip. Q1. $40.00

FROST, Robert. *Letters of Robert Frost to Louis Untermeyer.* 1963. HRW. UP/1st. F/pink wrp. B24. $175.00

FROST, Robert. *Neither Out Far Nor in Deep: A Poem.* 1935. Holt. 1st. F/wrp. Q1. $125.00

FROST, Robert. *Poetry.* 1971. Barre, MA. Imp Soc. 1/1950. 2 vol. 8vo. sgn Rudolph Ruzicka. F/case. B24. $225.00

FROST, Robert. *You Come Too: Favorite Poems for Young Readers.* 1959. NY. Holt. 1st. 94p. F/dj. D4. $45.00

FROUD, Brian. *Goblins.* 1983. Macmillan. 1st Am. popup. VG+. P2. $35.00

FROUD & LEE. *Faeries.* 1979 (1978). Abrams/Peacock Pr. 1st thus. 4to. unp. wht cloth. NF/dj. T5. $48.00

FRY, Christopher. *Boat That Mooed.* 1965. Macmillan. 1st. ils Leonard Weisgard. obl 4to. 32p. VG/VG-. P2. $35.00

FRY, J. *Combat Soldier.* 1968. DC. sgn. ils/maps. VG/G. S16. $35.00

FRY, Rosalie. *Wind Call.* 1955. Dutton. 1st. VG/G. M5. $65.00

FRYATT. *Horn Book Sampler on Children's Books & Reading...* 1969. 261p. F/F. A4. $35.00

FRYE, D.E. *12th Virginia Cavalry.* 1988. Lynchburg. 1st ltd. 1/1000. sgn. 188p. F/dj. M4. $40.00

FRYER, J.E. *Easy Steps in Cooking or Mary Frances Among Kitchen People.* 1912. 1st. ils. VG. E6. $95.00

FRYER, J.E. *Mary Frances Cook Book.* 1912. Phil. Winston. ils Hays/Boyer. 175p. bl cloth/pict label. VG. D1. $160.00

FRYER, J.E. *Mary Frances Housekeeper: Adventures Among the Doll People.* 1914. Phil. 1st. all paper dolls present. VG. B5. $190.00

FRYER, J.E. *Mary Frances Knitting & Crocheting Books...* (1918). Winston. ils JA Boyer. VG. B15. $130.00

FRYER, J.E. *Mary Francis First Aid Book.* 1916. Phil. Winston. 1st. 8vo. bl cloth/pict label. dj. R5. $285.00

FU, Li-Kuo. *China Plant Red Data Book. Rare & Endangered Plants Vol I.* 1992. Beijing. 1st. ils/photos. 741p. as new/dj. B26. $195.00

FUCHIDA & OKUMIYA. *Midway: Battle That Doomed Japan.* 1955. ils. VG/G+. M17. $25.00

FUCHIDA & OKUMIYA. *Midway: Battle That Doomed Japan.* 1971. MD. ils/maps. 266p. VG/VG. S16. $25.00

FUCHS, Erich. *Journey to the Moon.* nd. NY. Delacorte. 1st Am. xl. dj. K5. $8.00

FUENTES, Carlos. *Buried Mirror.* 1992. Houghton Mifflin. 1st. 4to. 399p. F3. $30.00

FUENTES, Carlos. *Burnt Water.* 1980. FSG. 1st Am. sgn. F/F. D10. $50.00

FUENTES, Carlos. *Christopher Unborn.* 1989. FSG. 1st. F/F. A20. $20.00

FUENTES, Carlos. *Hydra Head.* 1978. FSG. 1st Am. sgn. F/F. D10. $50.00

FUENTES, Carlos. *Old Gringo.* 1985. FSG. 1st. F/F. T11. $20.00

FUENTES, Carlos. *Terra Nostra.* 1976. FSG. 1st. F/dj. A24. $50.00

FUENTES, Norberto. *Hemingway in Cuba.* 1984. Secaucus. Lyle Stuart. 1st. photos. F/F. D10. $50.00

FUERTES, Louis Agassiz. *Louis Agassiz Fuertes & the Singular Beauty of Birds.* 1971. NY. 1st. ils/edit Frederick G Marcham. 220p. NF/dj. S15. $95.00

FUJIKAWA, Gyo. *Child's Book of Poems.* nd (1969). Grosset Dunlap. 125p. VG+. C14. $20.00

FUJIKAWA, Gyo. *Mother Goose.* 1968. NY. early or 1st. 125p. VG. M5. $35.00

FULFORD, Margaret *Cladoniae of Eastern Kentucky.* 1938. Cincinnati. 8vo. stiff wrp. VG. A22. $17.00

FULGHUM, Robert. *It Was on Fire When I Lay Down on It.* 1989. Villard. 1st. 218p. F/dj. H1. $18.00

FULLER, Andrew. *Grape Culturist.* 1865 (1864). ils. VG. E6. $40.00

FULLER, Andrew. *Practical Forestry.* 1908. Orange Judd. 299p. VG. A10. $28.00

FULLER, Andrew. *Small Fruit Culturist.* 1867. 1st. ils. VG. E6. $35.00

FULLER, Bucky. *Tetrascroll: Goldilocks & the Three Bears.* 1982. FSG. 1st. F/F. A20. $25.00

FULLER, Jean Overton. *Double Webs.* 1958. Putnam. 1st. 256p. VG/dj. M20. $12.00

FULLER, Mabel Louise. *In Poppy Land.* 1890. ils. G+. M17. $15.00

FULLER, Roger; see Tracy, Don.

FULLER, Roy. *Fantasy & Fugue.* 1954. London. Derek Verschoyle. 1st. F/dj. M15. $80.00

FULLERTON, Hugh S. *Jimmy Kirkland & the Plot for the Pennant.* 1915. Winston. 341p. G+/ragged. M20. $50.00

FULLERTON, Hugh S. *Jimmy Kirland of the Shasta Boys Team.* 1915. Winston. 270p. cloth. VG. M20. $30.00

FULOP-MILLER, Rene. *Triumph Over Pain.* 1938. Bobbs Merrill. 1st. sm 4to. 438p. G+. H1. $8.50

FULTON, James. *Peach Culture.* 1870. Orange Judd. 190p. beveled brd. A10. $35.00

FULTON, John F. *Functional Localization in Relation to Frontal Lobotomy.* 1949. NY. Oxford. 1st Am. 140p. red cloth. VG. G1. $75.00

FULTON, John F. *Harvey Cushing: A Biography.* 1991. NY. Classics Neurology/Neurosurgery Lib. facsimile. G1. $75.00

FULTON, Robert. *Tratado do Melhoramento da Navegacao por Canaes...* 1800. Lisbon. Litteraria do Arco do Cego. 1st Portugese language. R15. $2,200.00

FUMENTO, Rocco. *Tree of Dark Reflection.* 1962. NY. Knopf. 1st. F/dj. Q1. $50.00

FUNK, Michael. *Ruckenmarks-Entzundung.* 1832. Bamberg. Dresch. 3rd. 12mo. contemporary drab yel brd. G1. $125.00

FUNT, Allen. *Eavesdropper at Large: Adventures in Human Nature...* 1952. Vanguard. 1st. F/VG clip. B4. $85.00

FURBAY, James R. *Along Life's Trail: One Quaker's Experiences...* 1978. Dublin, IN. 157p. VG. V3. $14.00

FURCHTOTT, Ernest. *Pharmacological & Biophysical Agents & Behavior.* 1971. Academic. 402p. tan cloth. VG/dj. G1. $35.00

FURLONG, Charles Wellington. *Gateway to the Sahara.* 1914. Scribner. 2nd. ils/maps. 306p. VG. W1. $18.00

FURNIVALL, Frederick J. *Fifty Earliest English Wills in Court of Probate, London...* 1964 (1882). London. Oxford. facsimile. M11. $50.00

FUSSELL, Betty. *Food in Good Season.* 1988. Knopf. VG/dj. A16. $15.00

FUSSELL, Betty. *Story of Corn.* 1992. NY. 1st. ils. F/clip. B26. $27.50

FUTRELLE, Jacques. *Diamond Master.* 1909. Bobbs Merrill. 1st. F. M15. $150.00

FYFE, Andrew. *Compendium of the Anatomy of the Human Body...* 1802. Phil. John Humphreys. 1st Am. 16mo. contemporary calf. M1. $250.00

FYFE, Thomas Alexander. *Who's Who in Dickens Books.* 1971. Haskell House. VG. P3. $75.00

FYLEMAN, Rose. *Fairy Flute.* 1921. Methuen. 1st. VG. M5. $22.00

GACHET, Jacqueline. *Ladybug*. 1970. McCall. 1st. pict cloth. VG/dj. M20. $15.00

GADD, L. *Deadly Beautiful: World's Most Poisonous Animals & Plants*. 1980. Macmillan. ils/photos. 208p. cloth/brd. VG+/NF. M12. $25.00

GADEN & SERANNE. *Sandwich Book: Modern Art of Sandwich Making...* 1964. Doubleday. 1st. 151p. VG/VG. B10. $10.00

GADER, June Rose. *LA Live: Profiles of a City*. 1980. St Martin. ARC. F/NF. O4. $15.00

GADNEY, Reg. *Cry Hungary! Uprising 1956*. 1986. Atheneum. 1st. VG/VG. V4. $17.50

GAEDDERT, Lou Ann. *Split-Level Cookbook: Family Meals to Cook*. 1967. NY. TY Crowell. 1st. 228p. VG/dj. A25. $15.00

GAER, Joseph. *Bibliography of California Literature*. 1970. Burt Franklin. rpt. F. O4. $25.00

GAG, Flavia. *Sing a Song of Seasons*. 1936. Coward McCann. 1st. 4to. 30p. pict brd. VG. T5. $55.00

GAG, Wanda. *Funny Thing*. 1929. Coward McCann. 1st. author's 2nd children's book. 32p. VG. D1. $325.00

GAG, Wanda. *Gone Is Gone*. 1935. Coward McCann. 1st. 16mo. unp. gr cloth. VG/dj. D1. $60.00

GAG, Wanda. *Growing Pains*. 1940. Coward McCann. 1st. ils. 179p. beige cloth. VG/VG. D1. $150.00

GAG, Wanda. *Millions of Cats*. 1928. Coward McCann. 1st. obl 8vo. VG. M5. $175.00

GAGE, Jack R. *Tensleep & No Rest*. 1958. Prairie Pub. 1st. sgn. map/pl/facsimiles. 222p. VG/dj. J2. $145.00

GAGNON, Maurice. *Inner Ring*. 1985. Collins Crime Club. 1st. VG/VG. P3. $18.00

GAIGELL, Matthew. *Thomas Hart Benton*. 1981. Abrams. 229 pl. 279p. sand-colored cloth. F/dj. B24. $200.00

GAIL & GAIL. *Shot Into Infinity*. 1975. Garland. 1st. F/sans. M2. $45.00

GAILHARD, Jean. *Present State of the Republick of Venice*. 1669. London. 12mo. pub list at end. calf. R12. $385.00

GAINES, Ernest J. *Autobiography of Miss Jane Pittman*. 1973. Michael Joseph. 1st. NF/NF clip. B3. $75.00

GAINES, Ernest J. *In My Father's House*. 1978. Knopf. 1st. NF/dj. D10. $55.00

GAINES & SWAN. *Weeds of Eastern WA & Adjacent Areas*. 1972. Davenport, WA. Camp-Na-Bor-Lee Assn. 349p. cloth. VG. A10. $30.00

GAINHAM, Sarah. *Appointment in Vienna*. 1958. Dutton. 1st. VG/dj. P3. $15.00

GAINHAM, Sarah. *Cold Dark Night*. 1961. Walker. VG/dj. P3. $15.00

GAITHER, Frances. *Double Muscadine*. 1949. Toronto. Macmillan. 1st. VG. T12. $20.00

GAITO, John. *Macromolecules & Behavior*. 1966. Appleton Century. 197p. bl cloth. VG/dj. G1. $27.50

GAITSKILL, Mary. *Bad Behavior*. 1989. London. Hodder Stoughton. 1st Eng. F/F. R14. $50.00

GALBRAITH, John K. *Affluent Society*. 1958. Houghton Mifflin. 1st. author's 6th book. tan cloth. dj. M24. $45.00

GALDONE, Paul. *Frog Prince*. (1975). McGraw Hill. rpt. ils Galdone. VG. C8. $15.00

GALDONE, Paul. *King of the Cats*. 1980. Houghton Mifflin/Clarion. probable 1st sm 8vo. red cloth. F/VG+. T5. $25.00

GALE, Oliver Marble. *Carnack: Lifebringer*. 1928. Wise. 1st. NF/dj. M2. $35.00

GALE, Zona. *Preface to a Life*. 1926. Appleton. 1st. 346p. VG+. A25. $10.00

GALET, Pierre. *Grapevine Identification*. 1979. Cornell. 1st. VG/dj. W2. $35.00

GALLAGHER, C.H. *Nutritional Factors & Enzymological Disturbances...* 1964. Phil. Lippincott. 181p. F. B1. $28.50

GALLAGHER, Stephen. *Boat House*. 1991. NEL. 1st. F/dj. P3. $28.00

GALLAGHER, Stephen. *Down River*. 1989. NEL. 1st. F/F. P3. $25.00

GALLAGHER, Tess. *Lover of Horses & Other Stories*. 1989. London. Hamish Hamilton. 1st. F/dj. Q1. $60.00

GALLAGHER, Tess. *Lover of Horses*. 1986. NY. Harper Row. 1st. F/F. D10. $40.00

GALLAGHER. *Jules Verne: A Primary & Secondary Bibliography*. 1980. 387p. F. A4. $65.00

GALLANCE, George. *In Her Birthday Dress*. 1977. Paisley, Scotland. Gleniffer. 1/150. 51x52mm. prt/sgn Ian MacDonald. box. B24. $45.00

GALLANT, Roy A. *Man's Reach Into Space*. 1959. Garden City. 4to. 152p. G. K5. $12.00

GALLANT, T. Grady. *On Valor's Side: A Marine's Own Story of Parris Island...* 1963. NY. 364p. VG/VG. S16. $35.00

GALLICO, Paul. *Abandoned*. 1950. Knopf. 1st. VG/dj. M2. $20.00

GALLICO, Paul. *Boy Who Invented the Bubble Gun*. 1974. Delacorte. 1st Am. F/NF. A24. $25.00

GALLICO, Paul. *Hand of Mary Constable*. 1964. Doubleday. 1st. VG/VG. P3. $25.00

GALLICO, Paul. *Lonely*. 1949. Knopf. 1st. NF/NF. M19. $25.00

GALLICO, Paul. *Love, Let Me Not Hunger*. 1963. Doubleday. 1st. VG/dj. P3. $15.00

GALLICO, Paul. *Man Who Was Magic*. 1966. Doubleday. 1st. NF/dj. P3. $20.00

GALLICO, Paul. *Mrs 'Arris Goes to New York*. 1960. Doubleday. 1st Am. NF/VG+ clip. A24. $40.00

GALLICO, Paul. *Mrs 'Arris Goes to Parliament*. 1965. Doubleday. 1st. 152p. cloth. VG/clip. M20. $15.00

GALLICO, Paul. *Poseidon Adventure*. 1969. Coward. 1st. F/NF clip. H11. $40.00

GALLICO, Paul. *Revealing Eye: Personalities of the 1920s...* 1967. NY. 307p. xl. dj. A17. $60.00

GALLISON, Kate. *Death Tape*. 1987. Little Brn. 1st. VG/VG. P3. $15.00

GALLOWAY, Janice. *Blood*. 1991. Random. ARC. author's 1st story collection. F/F. w/promo material. R13. $35.00

GALLUP, Donald. *TS Eliot: A Bibliography*. 1952. London. Faber. 1st. gilt gray cloth. F/VG. M24. $65.00

GALLUP, George. *Adventures in Immortality: A Look Beyond Threshold of Death*. 1982. McGraw. 226p. VG. B29. $8.00

GALSWORTHY, John. *Arthur & Critic*. 1933. NY. House of Books Ltd. 1/300. F. A17. $30.00

GALSWORTHY, John. *Modern Comedy*. 1929. Heinemann. 1st Eng. NF/G. M19. $25.00

GALSWORTHY, John. *Modern Comedy*. 1929. Scribner. 1st. VG. P3. $30.00

GALSWORTHY, John. *White Monkey*. nd (1924). London. Heinemann. 1st. sgn. VG+. B4. $125.00

GALTON, Francis. *Hereditary Genius: An Inquiry Into Its Laws & Consequences*. 1871. Appleton. new/revised. 8vo. 390p. VG. K3. $60.00

GAMOW, George. *My World Line: An Informal Autobiography.* 1970. Viking. 1st. VG/dj. K3. $15.00

GAMOW, George. *Planet Called Earth.* 1963. Viking. 8vo. 257p. Vg/dj. K5. $15.00

GANACHILLY, Alfred. *Whispering Dead.* 1920. Knopf. 1st. VG. M2. $15.00

GANN, Ernest K. *Gentlemen of Adventure.* 1984. NY. Arbor. 1st. NF/F. H11. $25.00

GANN, Ernest K. *In the Company of Eagles.* 1966. S&S. 1st. F/NF. H11. $35.00

GANN, Ernest K. *Magistrate.* 1982. Arbor. 1st. F/F. B35. $15.00

GANN, Ernest K. *Trouble With Lazy Ethel.* 1958. Sloane. 1st. NF/VG. M19. $25.00

GANN, Thomas. *Discoveries & Adventures in Central America.* 1929. Scribner. 1st. xl. reading copy. F3. $20.00

GANN, W.D. *Tunnel Thru the Air.* 1927. Financial Guardian. 1st. VG. P3. $40.00

GANNETT, Ruth Stiles. *My Father's Dragon.* (1948). Random. reset 1986 ed/1st thus prt. 8vo. pict brd. F/dj. C8. $17.50

GANPAT. *Mirror of Dreams.* 1928. Doubleday. 1st. VG. M2. $25.00

GANTHER, MARTIN & SPALLHOLZ. *Selenium in Biology & Medicine.* 1981. AVI Pub. 8vo. cloth. F. B1. $67.50

GANZEL, Dewey. *Fortune & Men's Eyes.* 1982. Oxford. ils 8vo. F/dj. K3. $40.00

GARCES & GALVIN. *Record of Travels in Arizona & California 1775-1776.* 1965. SF. John Howell. 1/1250. folio. tan cloth. F. R3. $100.00

GARCES & GALVIN. *Record of Travels in Arizona & California 1775-1776.* 1965. SF. John Howell. 4to. 113p. VG+. F7. $75.00

GARCIA, Andrew. *Tough Trip Through Paradise 1878-1879.* 1967. Houghton Mifflin. 1st. 446p. map ep. VG/dj. J2. $265.00

GARCIA, Cristina. *Dreaming in Cuban.* 1992. Knopf. 1st. sgn. F/F. R13. $75.00

GARCIA ICAZBALCETA, Joaquin. *Bibliografia Mexicana del Siglo XVI: Catalogo Razonado...* 1954 (1886). Mexico. Fondo Cultura. lg format. 581p. F/rpr dj. O7. $225.00

GARCIA LORCA, Federico. *Five Plays: Comedies & Tragicomedies.* 1963. New Directions. 1st Am. F/dj. Q1. $60.00

GARCIA MARQUEZ, Gabriel; see Marquez, Gabriel Garcia.

GARD, Robert. *Horse Named Joe.* 1956. Little Brn. 1st. ils CW Anderson. 237p. VG/VG-. P2. $30.00

GARD, Wayne. *Retracing the Chisholm Trail.* 1956. TX State Hist Assn. 24p. VG. J2. $45.00

GARDEN, J.F. *Bugaboos.* 1987. Revelstoke. 1st. 156p. F/dj. A17. $25.00

GARDENIER, Andrew A. *Hand-Book of Ready Reference.* 1897. Springfield. King-Richardson Pub. 1st. VG. O3. $65.00

GARDINER, Dorothy. *Great Betrayal.* 1949. Doubleday. 1st. VG/VG. P3. $20.00

GARDINER, Howard C. *In Pursuit of the Golden Dream.* 1970. Stoughton, MA. Western Hemisphere. 390p. gilt red cloth. as new. K7. $50.00

GARDINER, Linda. *Rare, Vanishing & Lost British Birds.* 1923. London. 25 mc pl. 120p. NF. S15. $25.00

GARDINER, Linda. *Sylvia in Flowerland.* early 1900s. Dutton. ils HE Butler. wine cloth. VG. M5. $60.00

GARDNER, Alexander. *Gardner's Photographic Sketch Book of the Civil War.* 1959. Dover. 8vo. 100+ pl. cloth. F/G. H1. $60.00

GARDNER, C.A. *Flora of Western Australia, Vol I, Part I.* 1952. Gramineae. ils/pl/diagrams. 400p. red cloth. F. B26. $65.00

GARDNER, E.S. *Desert Is Yours: Spirited Account of Adventure in Present...* 1963. NY. Morrow. ils/photos. 256p. cloth. VG+/VG+. M12. $30.00

GARDNER, E.S. *Hunting Lost Mines by Helicopter.* 1965. Morrow. photos. 387p. VG/G. M12. $30.00

GARDNER, Erle Stanley. *Beware the Curves.* 1956. Morrow. 1st. NF/dj. M25. $25.00

GARDNER, Erle Stanley. *Case of the Beautiful Beggar.* 1965. Morrow. 1st. F/F. H11. $50.00

GARDNER, Erle Stanley. *Case of the Bigamous Spouse.* 1961. NY. Morrow. 1st. F/F. M15. $45.00

GARDNER, Erle Stanley. *Case of the Borrowed Brunette.* 1946. Morrow. 1st. F/NF. H11. $65.00

GARDNER, Erle Stanley. *Case of the Cautious Coquette.* 1949. Morrow. 1st. NF/VG. H11. $70.00

GARDNER, Erle Stanley. *Case of the Demure Debutant.* 1956. NY. Morrow. 1st. F/F. M15. $50.00

GARDNER, Erle Stanley. *Case of the Duplicate Daughter.* 1960. NY. Morrow. 1st. F/NF. M15. $45.00

GARDNER, Erle Stanley. *Case of the Glamorous Ghost.* 1955. Morrow. 1st. VG/G+. P3. $45.00

GARDNER, Erle Stanley. *Case of the Lonely Heiress.* 1948. Morrow. 1st. NF/dj. P3. $70.00

GARDNER, Erle Stanley. *Case of the Lucky Legs.* 1946. Tower. 2nd. VG/dj. P3. $20.00

GARDNER, Erle Stanley. *Case of the Stuttering Bishop.* 1946. Tower. VG/dj. P3. $20.00

GARDNER, Erle Stanley. *Case of the Troubled Trustee.* 1965. Morrow. 1st. F/NF. H11. $45.00

GARDNER, Erle Stanley. *Count of Nine.* 1958. Morrow. 1st. G+/torn. M25. $15.00

GARDNER, Erle Stanley. *DA Tries a Case.* 1940. Morrow. 1st. VG. M22. $20.00

GARDNER, Erle Stanley. *Off the Beaten Track in Baja.* 1967. Morrow. 1st. ils. F/F. O4. $25.00

GARDNER, Erle Stanley. *Shills Can't Cash Chips.* 1961. Morrow. 1st. NF/dj. M25. $15.00

GARDNER, Erle Stanley. *Traps Need Fresh Bait.* 1967. Morrow. 1st. inscr. F/NF. M15. $175.00

GARDNER, Erle Stanley. *Up for Grabs.* 1964. Morrow. 1st. inscr. F/F. M15. $175.00

GARDNER, Ethel. *Soarings.* 1990. Cherokee. 1st. sgn. 120p. F/wrp. B11. $18.00

GARDNER, John. *Amber Nine.* 1966. Viking. 1st. F/NF. H11. $35.00

GARDNER, John. *Cornermen.* 1976. Doubleday. 1st. F/F. M19/P3. $35.00

GARDNER, John. *For Special Services.* 1982. Coward McCann. 1st. F/F. P3. $18.00

GARDNER, John. *Grendel.* 1971. Knopf. 1st. author's 3rd book. F/dj. D10. $125.00

GARDNER, John. *In the Suicide Mountains.* 1977. Knopf. 1st. F/dj. Q1. $60.00

GARDNER, John. *License Renewed.* 1981. Jonathan Cape. 1st. VG/dj. P3. $25.00

GARDNER, John. *Life & Times of Chaucer.* 1977. Knopf. 1st. F/clip. D10. $45.00

GARDNER, John. *Nickel Mountain.* 1973. Knopf. 1st. author's 6th novel. F/VG+. A24. $45.00

GARDNER, John. *Nickel Mountain.* 1973. Knopf. 1st. VG/dj. P3. $30.00

GARDNER, John. *No Deals, Mr Bond.* 1987. Putnam. 1st. VG/dj. P3. $15.00

GARDNER, John. *Nobody Lives Forever.* 1986. Putnam. 1st. VG/dj. P3. $15.00

GARDNER, John. *October Light.* 1976. Knopf. 1st. ils Elaine Raphael/Don Bolognese. NF/VG. A24. $25.00

GARDNER, John. *Role of Honour.* 1984. Jonathan Cape. 1st. VG/dj. P3. $25.00

GARDNER, John. *Secret Families.* 1989. Putnam. 1st Am. NF/dj. A24. $25.00

GARDNER, John. *Secret Generations.* 1985. Putnam. 1st Am. inscr. F/dj. A24. $30.00

GARDNER, John. *Secret Houses.* 1987. Putnam. 1st Am. inscr. F/dj. A24. $30.00

GARDNER, John. *Stillness & Shadows.* 1986. Knopf. 1st. F/F. Q1. $35.00

GARDNER, John. *Sunlight Dialogues.* 1972. Knopf. 1st. author's 4th novel. red cloth. NF/VG+. A24. $55.00

GARDNER, John. *Understrike.* 1965. Viking. 1st. F/NF clip. H11. $25.00

GARDNER, John. *Vlemk the Box Painter.* 1979. Northridge. 1st. sgn. F/F. R14. $75.00

GARDNER, Martin. *Annotated Snark.* 1962. S&S. 1st. 111p. VG/worn. M20. $35.00

GARDNER, Mary. *Boat People.* 1995. Norton. 1st. sgn. F/F. A23. $40.00

GARDNER, Miriam; see Bradley, Marion Zimmer.

GARDNER, Paul V. *Glass of Frederick Carder.* 1971. Crown. 4th. 400 photos. 373p. VG. H1. $350.00

GARDNER, Richard A. *Objective Diagnosis of Minimal Brain Dysfunction.* 1979. Cresskill, NJ. Creative Therapeutics. 452p. gray cloth. VG/dj. G1. $22.50

GARETH, Jones. *Sovereignty of the Law, Selections From Blackstone's...* 1973. Toronto. M11. $50.00

GARFIELD, Brian. *Death Sentence.* 1975. Evans. 1st. VG/VG. P3. $30.00

GARFIELD, Brian. *Death Sentence.* 1975. NY. Evans. 1st. F/F. M15. $45.00

GARFIELD, Brian. *Death Wish.* 1972. NY. McKay. 1st. inscr. F/F. M15. $125.00

GARFIELD, Brian. *Line of Succession.* 1972. Delacorte. 1st. VG/dj. P3. $23.00

GARFIELD, Brian. *Paladin.* 1980. Macmillan. 1st. NF/dj. P3. $20.00

GARFIELD, Brian. *Recoil.* 1977. Morrow. 1st. VG/dj. P3. $40.00

GARFIELD, Brian. *Romanov Succession.* 1974. Evans. 1st. VG/dj. P3. $25.00

GARFIELD, Brian. *West Times.* 1978. S&S. dj. A19. $30.00

GARFIELD, Brian. *What of Terry Conniston?* 1971. World. 1st. VG/dj. P3. $20.00

GARFIELD, Brian. *Wild Times.* 1978. S&S. 1st. 477p. NF/NF. W2. $50.00

GARFINKLE, Richard. *Celestial Matters.* 1986. Tor. 1st. F/dj. P3. $25.00

GARIS, Cleo F. *Arden Blake: Orchard Secret (#1).* 1934. AL Burt. 250p. VG/dj. M20. $35.00

GARIS, Howard R. *Uncle Wiggily & Alice in Wonderland.* 1918. Donohue. ils Edward Bloomfield. 8vo. dk bl cloth/label. R5. $150.00

GARIS, Howard R. *Uncle Wiggily & His Flying Rug.* 1940. Racine. NF/NF. C8. $45.00

GARIS, Howard R. *Uncle Wiggily & His Friends.* 1939. Platt Munk. post ISBN prt. sm 8vo. VG+. C8. $25.00

GARIS, Howard R. *Uncle Wiggily & His Funny Auto.* 1940. Whitman. 1st. ils Campbell. VG. S13. $20.00

GARIS, Howard R. *Uncle Wiggily on Roller Skates.* (1940). Racine. Whitman. ils. NF/NF. C8. $45.00

GARIS, Howard R. *Uncle Wiggily on the Farm.* 1939. Platt Munk. 6 full-p mc pl. 185p. ils gr cloth. F. B14. $40.00

GARIS, Howard R. *Uncle Wiggily's Arabian Nights.* 1917. Fenno. 1st. ils Edward Bloomfield. VG. M5. $150.00

GARIS, Howard R. *Uncle Wiggley Stories.* 1977 (1965). Grosset Dunlap. ils Art Seiden. NF. C8. $15.00

GARLAND, Hamlin. *Book of the American Indian.* 1923. NY/London. Harper. 1st thus. 274p. NF. K7. $200.00

GARLAND, Hamlin. *Boy Life on the Prairie.* 1899. Macmillan. 1st. F. A18. $75.00

GARLAND, Hamlin. *Trail-Makers of the Middle Border.* 1927. Grosset Dunlap. A19. $10.00

GARLAND, Joseph E. *Great Pattillo.* 1966. Little Brn. 1st. 342p. cloth. VG/dj. M20. $25.00

GARN. *Tommy on the Train.* 1946. Saalfield. 4 popups. obl 4to. sbdg. VG/VG-. P2. $100.00

GARNER, Alan. *Elidor.* 1966. London. VG/dj. M2. $20.00

GARNER, Alan. *Red Shift.* 1973. Macmillan. 1st. VG/fair. P3. $13.00

GARNER, Bess. *Mexico.* 1937. Houghton Mifflin. 1st. ils. 164p. F3. $15.00

GARNER, Harry. *Chinese & Japanese Cloisonne Enamels.* 1977. London/Boston. Faber. 2nd revised. ils. F/NF. W3. $65.00

GARNER, William. *Think Big, Think Dirty.* 1983. St Martin. 1st. VG/dj. P3. $16.00

GARNETT, Bill. *Down Bound Train.* 1973. Doubleday. 1st. F/dj. M2. $12.00

GARNETT, David. *Letters of TE Lawrence.* 1939. Doubleday Doran. 1st Am. ils/maps. 896p. VG. K3. $40.00

GARNETT, Garet. *Blue Wound.* 1921. Putnam. 1st. VG. M2. $20.00

GARNETT, Louise A. *Muffin Shop.* 1908. Rand McNally. 1st. ils Hope Dunlap. 80p. VG. D1. $150.00

GARRARD, Lewis H. *Wah-To-Ya...Taos Trail; or, Prairie Travel & Scalp Dances.* 1850. Derby. 1st. inscr pres. 349p. w/LC Powell bookplate. B19. $2,500.00

GARRARD, Lewis H. *Wah-To-Yah & the Taos Trail.* 1936. Grabhorn. 1/500. 290p. as new. K7. $130.00

GARRARD & HANNAU. *Tropical Flowers.* 1973. Miami. ils/photos. pict brd. F. B26. $20.00

GARRETT, Annette. *Counseling Methods for Personnel Workers.* 1945. NY. Family Welfare Assn. 1st. 187p. xl. VG. A25. $16.00

GARRETT, George. *Death of the Fox.* 1971. Doubleday. 1st. sgn. F/F. D10. $65.00

GARRETT, George. *Entered From the Sun.* 1990. Doubleday. 1st. sgn. F/F. D10. $40.00

GARRETT, George. *Succession.* 1983. Doubleday. 1st. F/NF. D10. $40.00

GARRICK, David. *Memoirs of the Life of..., Esq.* 1808. London. Longman Hurst. 2 vol. 8vo. all edges marbled. later brn leather. H13. $285.00

GARRICK, David. *Private Correspondence of...* 1831. London. 2 vol. 4to. A15. $40.00

GARRISON, Jim. *Heritage of Stone.* 1970. NY. VG/G. B5. $45.00

GARRISON, Jim. *Star Spangled Contract.* 1976. McGraw Hill. 1st. F/dj. P3. $18.00

GARRISON, R.E. *Dolomites of the Monterey Formation...* 1984. Los Angeles. 215p. F/stiff wrp. B1. $18.50

GARSIDE, E. *Cranberry Red.* 1938. Boston. 1st. VG/VG. B5. $35.00

GARST, Shannon. *Cowboy-Artist: Charles M Russell.* 1966. Messner. A19. $20.00

GARTHWAITE, Jimmy. *Puddin' an' Pie.* 1929. Harper. 1st. 93p. cloth. VG. D4. $30.00

GARTON, Ray. *Lot Lizards.* 1991. Ziesing. 1st. as new/dj. N4. $45.00

GASH, Jonathan. *Fire Fly Gadroon.* 1982. St Martin. 1st. F/NF. M19. $65.00

GASH, Jonathan. *Gondola Scam.* 1984. St Martin. 1st. F/VG. M19. $45.00

GASH, Jonathan. *Grail Tree.* 1979. Harper. 1st Am. VG/VG. M22. $20.00

GASH, Jonathan. *Grail Tree.* 1979. London. Collins Crime Club. 1st. inscr. F/clip. M15. $400.00

GASH, Jonathan. *Great California Game.* 1991. St Martin. 1st. F/F. M19. $25.00

GASH, Jonathan. *Jade Woman.* 1989. St Martin. 1st. F/dj. P3. $18.00

GASH, Jonathan. *Spend Game.* 1981. Ticknor Fields. 1st. VG/dj. P3. $40.00

GASH, Jonathan. *Tartan Sell.* 1986. St Martin. 1st. F/dj. P3. $25.00

GASK, Arthur. *Silent Dead.* 1950. Herbert Jenkins. 1st. VG. P3. $25.00

GASK, Lilian. *Fairies & the Christmas Child.* 1912. Harrap. 1st. ils Pogany/21 full-p ils. teg. gilt cloth. R5. $285.00

GASKELL, E.C. *Life of Charlotte Bronte.* 1857. Appleton. 2 vol. 1st. rear ep removed o/w VG. M20. $125.00

GASKELL, Jane. *City.* 1978. St Martin. 1st Am. F/dj. M2. $20.00

GASKELL, Jane. *Strange Evil.* 1958. Dutton. 1st Am. VG. M2. $20.00

GASKELL, Mrs. *Cranford.* 1907. Macmillan. 1st. ils Hugh Thomson. NF. M19. $35.00

GASPARD, Helen. *Doctor Dan the Bandage Man.* 1950. Little Golden. 1st. no bandaids o/w VG. M5. $28.00

GASS, William H. *Fiction & Figures on Life.* 1970. Knopf. 1st. sgn. NF/NF. R14. $65.00

GASS, William H. *Tunnel.* 1995. Knopf. 1st. sgn. F/F. B2. $50.00

GASSER, M. *Self-Portraits.* 1963. ils. VG/VG. M17. $25.00

GASTINE, Louis. *L' ABC de l'Aviation.* 1911. Paris. ils/diagrams, 248p. G/pict wrp. B18. $150.00

GASTON, Mary Frank. *American Belleek.* 1984. Collector Books. 1st. 127p. VG. H1. $45.00

GATENBY, Rosemary. *Fugitive Affair.* 1976. Dodd Mead. 1st. VG/dj. P3. $15.00

GATES, Betsey. *Colton Letters: Civil War Period, 1861-65.* 1993. McLane. 1st. 393p. NF/NF. M20. $40.00

GATES, Doris. *Sensible Kate.* 1943. Viking. 1st. 189p. F/G+. P2. $35.00

GATES, Henry Louis. *Loose Canons.* 1992. NY. Oxford. 1st. sgn. F/F. R13. $35.00

GATES, MacBurney. *Aloma of the South Seas.* 1926. Grosset Dunlap. 235p. cloth. VG/dj. M20. $15.00

GATEWOOD, Charles. *Photographs.* 1993. SF. Flash. 1/2000. sgn. F/F. B4. $85.00

GATLAND, Kenneth. *Ils Encyclopedia of Space Technology.* 1984. NY. Harmony. revised. 4to. 301p. K5. $35.00

GATLAND, Kenneth. *Manned Spacecraft.* 1967. Macmillan. 256p. VG/VG. K5. $12.00

GATS, HUBER & SALISBURY. *Ted & Sally.* 1952. Macmillan. 2nd. 8vo. 144p. red cloth. T5. $30.00

GATT, G. *Oskar Kokoschka.* 1970. ils. Italian text. VG/VG. M17. $12.50

GATTY. *Juliana Horatia Ewing & Her Books...* 1885. London. ils. 88p. VG. A4. $75.00

GAUL, Albro. *Wonderful World of Insects.* 1953. Rinehart. 219p. dj. A10. $18.00

GAULKNER, Georgene. *Little Peachling & Other Tales From Old Japan.* 1928. Volland. 1st. ils Frederick Richardson. 8vo. cloth. pict box. R5. $250.00

GAULT, William Campbell. *Cat & Mouse.* 1988. St Martin. 1st. F/F. M25. $25.00

GAULT, William Campbell. *Come Die With Me.* 1959. Random. 1st. VG. P3. $20.00

GAULT, William Campbell. *Dead Hero.* 1963. Dutton. 1st. F/NF. B2. $35.00

GAULT, William Campbell. *Death in Donegal Bay.* 1984. Walker. 1st. F/dj. M25. $25.00

GAULT, William Campbell. *Death in Donegal Bay.* 1984. Walker. 1st. NF/dj. P3. $15.00

GAVIN, J. *War & Peace in the Space Age.* 1959. 1st. F/VG. E6. $18.00

GAVRON, Jeremy. *King Leopold's Dream.* 1993. NY. 288p. F/F. S15. $10.00

GAWRON, Jean Mark. *Apology for Rain.* 1974. Doubleday. 1st. F/dj. M2/P3. $17.00

GAY, Carl W. *Productive Horse Husbandry.* 1914. Lippincott. Lippincott's Farm Manual series. VG. O3. $25.00

GAY, John. *Trivia; or, Art of Walking the Streets of London.* 1924. London. Daniel O'Connor. 16 full-p pl. NF. M19. $45.00

GAY, Peter. *Bourgeois Experience.* 1984 & 1986. NY. 2 vol. 1st. VG/dj. T9. $38.00

GAY, Romney. *Romney Gay Mother Goose.* 1936. Grosset Dunlap. 1st. sq 4to. 56p. VG-/G. P2. $50.00

GAY, Zhenya. *Bits & Pieces.* 1958. Viking. 1st. VG. M5. $22.00

GAY, Zhenya. *Who Is It?* 1955. Viking. 1st. 47p. F/dj. D4. $45.00

GAYLIN, Willard. *In the Service of Their Country: War Registers in Prison.* 1970. Viking. 1st. 344p. dj. V3. $10.00

GAYTON, Bertram. *Gland Stealers.* 1922. Herbert Jenkins. 1st. G. P3. $25.00

GAZE, Harold. *Coppertop: The Queer Adventures of a Quaint Child.* 1924. Harper. 1st. 11 full-p pl. 4to. gilt bl cloth. R5. $250.00

GAZE, Harold. *Goblin's Glen.* 1924. Little Brn. 1st. 6 full-p pl. 8vo. dk bl cloth. R5. $125.00

GAZZANIGA, Michael S. *Handbook of Cognitive Neuroscience.* 1984. NY. Plenum. 416p. prt brn cloth. F. G1. $50.00

GAZZANIGA, Michael S. *Mind Matters: How Mind & Brain Interact To Create...* 1988. Houghton Mifflin. 256p. VG/dj. G1. $22.50

GEDGE, Pauline. *Stargate.* 1982. NY. 1st. NF/dj. M2/P3. $20.00

GEE, Ernest R. *Early American Sporting Books 1734 to 1844.* 1971. NY. facsimile 1928 ed. 13 pl+4p Derrydale ads. F. A17. $27.50

GEGAN, Phyllis. *Dick Whittington & His Cat.* 1957. London. Purnell. 1st. ils Willy Schermele. pict brd. as new. R5. $85.00

GEHLEN, Reinhard. *Service: Memoirs of General Reinhard Gehlen.* 1972. NY. 1st. photos/glossary. 386p. VG/VG. S16. $25.00

GEIKIE, A. *Landscape in History.* 1905. NY/Glasgow. Macmillan. 352p. G. D8. $12.00

GEIKIE, James. *Glacial Geology.* 1891. GPO. removed (p221-230) annual report. VG. P4. $9.50

GEIOGAMAH, Hanay. *New Native American Drama: Three Plays.* 1980. Norman, OK. 1st. F/NF. L3. $85.00

GEISEL, Theodore Seuss. *Boners.* 1931. Viking. 1st. 12mo. VG. M5. $75.00

GEISEL, Theodore Seuss. *Butler Battle Book.* 1984. Random. 1/500. sgn. M/case. B4. $750.00

GEISEL, Theodore Seuss. *Cat's Quizzer.* 1976. Random. 1st. 4to. 62p. VG/sans. P2. $125.00

GEISEL, Theodore Seuss. *Dr Seuss's Sleep Book.* 1962. Random. 1st. 4to. VG/VG. D1. $60.00

GEISEL, Theodore Seuss. *Dr Suess's Sleep Book.* 1962. Random. 1st. 4to. glazed brd. NF/NF 1st issue. B4. $750.00

GEISEL, Theodore Seuss. *Happy Birthday to You!* (1959). Random. 1st. 4to. VG/VG. D1. $650.00

GEISEL, Theodore Seuss. *Horton Hears a Who!* 1954. Random. 1st. 4to. pict brd. F. B4. $650.00

GEISEL, Theodore Seuss. *How the Grinch Stole Christmas!* 1957. Random. 1st. 4to. glazed pict brd. F/NF. B4. $1,200.00

GEISEL, Theodore Seuss. *How the Grinch Stole Christmas!* 1957. Random. 1st. 4to. VG/dj. D1. $800.00

GEISEL, Theodore Seuss. *I Had Trouble in Getting to Solla Sollew.* 1965. Random. 1st. thin folio. F/clip 1st issue. B4. $650.00

GEISEL, Theodore Seuss. *I Had Trouble in Getting to Solla Sollew.* 1965. Random. 1st. 4to. VG/G+. P2. $450.00

GEISEL, Theodore Seuss. *If I Ran the Zoo.* (1950). Random. early ed. VG/$2.50 dj. D1. $250.00

GEISEL, Theodore Seuss. *McElliot's Pool.* (1947). Random. 56p. VG/NF. D1. $600.00

GEISEL, Theodore Seuss. *More Boners.* 1931. Viking. 1st. 12mo. dk gr cloth. pict dj. R5. $400.00

GEISEL, Theodore Seuss. *Oh, the Places You'll Go!* (1990). Random. 1st. VG/dj. D1. $50.00

GEISEL, Theodore Seuss. *One Fish Two Fish Red Fish Blue Fish.* (1960). Random. 1st. sm 4to. 63p. VG/VG. D1. $500.00

GEISEL, Theodore Seuss. *Seven Lady Godivas.* 1939. Random. 1st. 4to. VG/G-. P2. $350.00

GEISEL, Theodore Seuss. *Sneetches & Other Stories.* 1961. NY. Random. 1st. 4to. glazed brd. F/NF. B4. $550.00

GEISEL, Theodore Seuss. *Sneetches & Other Stories.* 1961. Random. 1st. 4to. VG/dj. M5. $175.00

GEISEL, Theodore Seuss. *Yertle the Turtle & Other Stories.* 1958. Random. 1st. 4to. glazed brd. F/NF clip. B4. $500.00

GEISEL, Theodore Seuss. *You're Only Old Once!* 1986. Random. 1/500. sgn. gr cloth. F/NF gr case. R5. $600.00

GEISEL, Theodore Seuss. *500 Hats of Bartholomew Cubbins.* (1938). Vanguard. early ed. NF/clip. D1. $250.00

GEIST, Valerus. *Mule Deer Country.* 1990. North Word. photos Michael Francis. 176p. F/F. S15. $20.00

GEIST & RAINEY. *Archaeological Excavations at Kukulik...* 1936. GPO. 8vo. 391p. blk cloth. P4. $150.00

GELB, Ignace J. *Hittite Hieroglyphs.* 1931. Chicago. 3 parts. 1st. VG/wrp. W1. $65.00

GELHORN & LOOFBOURROW. *Emotions & Emotional Disorders: A Neurophysiological Study.* 1963. NY. Hoeber/Harper Row. 496p. 2-toned gr cloth. VG/dj. G1. $50.00

GELLER, Stephen. *Gad.* 1979. Harper Row. 1st. NF/dj. P3. $20.00

GELLERT, Hugo. *Comrade Gulliver.* 1935. Putnam. 1st. VG. B2. $50.00

GELMAN, Rita Golden. *Dumb Joey.* 1973. HRW. 1st. 55p. pict brd. NF/dj. M20. $18.00

GEMMELL, David. *Last Guardian.* 1989. Legend. 1st. F/dj. P3. $25.00

GENDERS, Roy. *Collecting Hardy Plants for Interest & Profit.* 1959. London. Stanley. 1st. 191p. dj. A10. $22.00

GENDERS, Roy. *Greenhouse for Pleasure & Profit.* 1955. London. Museum. 189p. dj. A10. $20.00

GENDERS, Roy. *Vegetables for the Epicure.* 1956. London. Museum. 187p. VG/dj. A10. $25.00

GENDZIER, Irene L. *Frantz Fanon: A Critical Study.* 1973. Pantheon. 300p. xl. Vg/dj. W1. $12.00

GENERAL FOODS CORPORATION. *All About Home Baking.* 1933. G. A16. $10.00

GENERAL FOODS CORPORATION. *General Foods Kitchens Cookbook.* 1959. NY. Random. 1st. 8vo. 436p. VG/dj. A16. $10.00

GENET, Jean. *Miracle of the Rose.* 1966. Grove. 1st Am. F/F. M19. $25.00

GENIN, Sylvester. *Selections From Works of..., in Poetry, Prose...* 1855. NY. Maigne Hall. 1st. 8vo. 252p. cloth. M1. $300.00

GENT, Peter. *North Dallas Forty.* 1973. Morrow. 1st. VG+/VG+. P8. $25.00

GENTHE, Arnold. *Old China Town.* 1913. NY. Mitchell Kennerly. G+. B5. $75.00

GENTHE, Arnold. *Old China Town: Photographic Calendar for Year 1946.* 1945. Oakland. Mills College. 2nd/enlarged. 8vo. ils. sbdg. F. R3. $50.00

GENTILLET. *Commentariorvm De Regno Recte Administrando, Libri Tres.* 1655. Utopia. thick 12mo. calf. R12. $475.00

GENTILLET. *Discours, Svr Les Moyens de Bien Govverner et Maintenir...* 1576. Geneva. Stoer? 8vo. vellum. R12. $1,250.00

GENTLE, Mary. *Rats & Gargoyles.* 1990. Bantam (British). 1st. F/dj. P3. $30.00

GENTRY, A.H. *Field Guide to the Families & Genera of Woody Plants...* 1993. WA. Conservation Internat'l. 895p. F/wrp. B1. $38.00

GENTRY, Curt. *Madams of San Francisco.* 1964. Doubleday. 1st. VG/VG. O4. $15.00

GENTRY, Howard S. *Agaves of Baja California.* 1978. SF. ils/figures/tables/pl. F/wrp. B26. $30.00

GEORGE, Elizabeth. *Great Deliverance.* 1988. Putnam. 1st. author's 1st novel. F/dj. A24. $65.00

GEORGE, Peter. *Commander-1.* 1965. Delacorte. 1st. VG/dj. P3. $20.00

GEORGE, R.D. *Minerals & Rocks: Their Nature, Occurrence & Uses.* 1943. Appleton Century. 1st. 595p. G. D8. $20.00

GEORGE, Theodore. *Murders on the Square.* 1971. Dodd Mead. 1st. VG/VG. P3. $15.00

GERARD, Francis. *Secret Sceptre.* 1971. Tom Stacey. VG/VG. P3. $15.00

GERARD, Louise. *Golden Centipede.* 1927. Dutton. 1st. VG. M2. $15.00

GERHARD & GULICK. *Lower California Guidebook.* 1970. Arthur H Clark. 4th (reissue). NF/poor. O4. $15.00

GERLACH, Don R. *Philip Schuyler & the American Revolution.* 1964. NE U. 1st. 358p. as new/dj. H1. $40.00

GERLACH, Rex. *Fly Fishing for Rainbows.* 1988. Stackpole. 1st. sgn. M/dj. A17. $30.00

GERMANN, Georg. *Gothic Revival in Europe & Britain.* 1973 (1972). Cambridge. MIT. 1st Am. 98 pl. 263p. brd. dj. D2. $85.00

GERNSHEIM, Helmut. *Incunabula of British Photographic Literature...* 1984. 4to. 180 ils. 1261 entries. 159p. F/F. A4. $95.00

GERROLD, David. *Chess With a Dragon.* 1987. Walker. 1st. F/dj. M2/P3. $22.00

GERROLD, David. *Deathbeast.* 1981. London. Robert Hale. 1st. sgn. F/F. T2. $45.00

GERROLD, David. *War Against the Chtorr, Book 1: A Matter of Men.* 1983. NY. Timescape. 1st. sgn. F/F. T2. $50.00

GERROLD, David. *Yesterday's Children.* 1974. London. Faber. 1st hc. sgn. F/F. T2. $40.00

GERSI, Douchan. *Explorer.* 1987. Tarcher. 1st. 285p. F/F. W2. $30.00

GERSON, Noel B. *Neptune.* 1976. Dodd Mead. 1st. VG/dj. P3. $18.00

GERSTACKER, Frederick. *How a Bride Was Won; or, Chase Across the Pampas.* 1869 (1868). Appleton. 274p. F3. $45.00

GERSTER, Arpad. *Rules of Aseptic & Antiseptic Surgery.* 1888. NY. 2nd. 332p. leather. A13. $125.00

GEST, John. *Selection of Masonic Oaths & Penalities...* 1835. Phil. WK Boden. 1st. 12mo. 8p. disbound. xl. M1. $200.00

GETTY, Estelle. *If I Knew Then What I Know Now...So What?* 1988. Chicago. Contemporary Books. 1st. inscr. A23. $40.00

GETTY, J.P. *My Life & Fortunes.* 1963. DSP. 1st. 300p. F/clip. D8. $18.00

GHITELMAN, David. *Space Telescope.* 1987. Mitchell. 1st. F/F. T12. $60.00

GIACOMINI, Carlo. *Guida Allo Studio Delle Circonvoluzioni Cerebrali...* 1884. Torino. Ermanno Loescher. 2nd revised. 47 woodcuts. G. G1. $150.00

GIANOLI, Luigi. *Horses & Horsemanship Through the Ages.* 1969. NY. Crown. 1st Am. VG/VG. O3. $48.00

GIBB, H.A.R. *Arabic Literature: An Introduction.* 1926. London. Oxford. 1st. 12mo. 128p. cloth. VG. W1. $20.00

GIBBINGS, Robert. *Blue Angels & Whales: Record of Personal Experiences...* 1946. Dutton. 1st. offset from laid-in review. VG/worn. P4. $35.00

GIBBINGS, Robert. *Charm of Birds.* 1927. NY. Stokes. 1st Am. 8vo. 286p. F/NF. T10. $50.00

GIBBINGS, Robert. *Over the Reefs & Far Away.* 1948. Dutton. 1st. 240p. burgundy cloth. P4. $65.00

GIBBINGS, Robert. *Wood Engravings of...* 1959. Chicago. Quadrangel. 1st Am. edit Patience Empson. gilt cloth. M/Lucite dj. B24. $125.00

GIBBON, David. *Old South.* 1979. Crescent. 1st Am. VG/VG clip. A8. $10.00

GIBBON, Edward. *History of the Decline & Fall of the Roman Empire.* 1804-05. Phil. Birch Sm. 1st Am. 8vo. fld map/plans. contemporary calf. M1. $1,000.00

GIBBON, J.M. *Romantic History of the Canadian Pacific.* 1937. NY. photos/fld map. 423p. F. M4. $25.00

GIBBONS, Hannah. *Memoir of Hannah Gibbons, Late, of West Chester, PA.* 1873. Phil. WH Pile. inscr June Gibbons. 220p. VG. V3. $16.00

GIBBONS, Kaye. *Cure for Dreams.* 1991. Algonquin. Special pres ed. F. R14. $50.00

GIBBONS, Kaye. *Cure for Dreams.* 1991. Algonquin. 1st. author's 3rd book. VG/VG. L1. $30.00

GIBBONS, Kaye. *Cure for Dreams.* 1991. Algonquin. 1st. sgn. F/F. A24/R13. $45.00

GIBBONS, Kaye. *Ellen Foster.* 1987. Algonquin. 1st. author's 1st book. F/F. B3/L1. $175.00

GIBBONS, Kaye. *Ellen Foster.* 1987. Algonquin. 1st. sgn. author's 1st book. F/clip. A24. $125.00

GIBBONS, Kaye. *Family Life.* 1990. NC Wesleyan. 1/500. sgn/#d. F/wrp. R13. $50.00

GIBBONS, Kaye. *Sights Unseen.* 1995. Putnam. 1st. sgn. F/F. A23. $40.00

GIBBONS, Kaye. *Virtuous Woman.* 1989. Algonquin. 1st. sgn. author's 2nd book. VG/VG. L1. $100.00

GIBBONS, Stella. *Cold Comfort Farm.* 1957 (1932). Longman Gr. 17th. 307p. VG/dj. A25. $12.00

GIBBS, Joe. *Fourth & One.* 1991. Nashville. Nelson. 1st. sgn. VG/VG. A23. $40.00

GIBBS, May. *Gum-Blossom Babies.* ca 1917. Angus Robertson. 11 full-p sepias. brn paper wrp/label/ribbon bdg. R5. $275.00

GIBBS, May. *Gum-Blossom Babies.* 1916. Sydney. Angus Robertson. 1st. 8vo. brn paper wrp/label. R5. $400.00

GIBBS, May. *Gum-Nut Babies.* ca 1917. Angus Robertson. 11 full-p sepias. 8vo. brn paper wrp/label/ribbon bdg. R5. $275.00

GIBBS, May. *Scotty in Gumnut Land.* 1950 (1941). Sydney. Angus Robertson. VG/G. M5. $60.00

GIBBS, Philip. *Out of the Ruins.* 1928. Doubleday. 1st Am. VG. M2. $20.00

GIBRAN, Kahlil. *Prophet.* 1942. Knopf. sm 8vo. 12 pl. 107p. cloth. VG. W1. $10.00

GIBRAN, Kahlil. *Sand & Foam.* 1926. Knopf. 1st. VG. M19. $25.00

GIBRAN, Kahlil. *Tear & a Smile.* 1950. Knopf. 1st. F. M19. $25.00

GIBRAN, Kahlil. *Tears & Laughter.* 1947. Phil Lib. 1st. F/VG. M19. $25.00

GIBSON, A.M. *Kickapoos: Lords of the Middle Border.* 1963. OK U. ils. 391p. cloth. dj. D11. $35.00

GIBSON, Charles. *Spain in America.* 1966. Harper Row. 25 ils/4 maps. F/rpr. O7. $35.00

GIBSON, Edward. *Reach.* 1989. Doubleday. 1st. F/dj. M2. $10.00

GIBSON, Eva Katharine. *Zauberlinda the Witch.* 1901. Robert Smith. 255p. VG. P2. $75.00

GIBSON, Robert. *Theory & Practice of Surveying.* 1828. Harper. 14 fld pl/ils/frontis. T7. $120.00

GIBSON, Walter Murray. *Diaries of Walter Murray Gibson 1886, 1887.* 1973. HI U. 1st. tall 8vo. 199p. P4. $30.00

GIBSON, Walter. *Magic With Science.* 1974. Collins. 3rd. NF. P3. $18.00

GIBSON, William Hamilton. *Our Native Orchids.* 1905. Doubleday. 158p. VG. A10. $85.00

GIBSON, William. *Mona Lisa Overdrive.* 1988. Bantam. 1st. F/NF. A20. $25.00

GIBSON & STERLING. *Difference Engine.* 1991. Bantam. 1st Am. 1/350. sgn/#d. F. M2. $125.00

GIBSON & STERLING. *Difference Engine.* 1991. Bantam. 1st. F/F. P3. $20.00

GIDDINGS, J.L. *Forest Eskimos: An Ethnographic Sketch of Kobuk River...* 1956. Phil. Vol 20, June 1956, No 2. F/gr wrp. P4. $25.00

GIDE, Andre. *Amyntas.* 1958. London. 1/1500. trans V David. VG/dj. T9. $30.00

GIDE, Andre. *Corydon.* 1950. Farrar. 1st Am. F/NF. M19. $25.00

GIDE, Charles. *Communist & Co-Operative Societies.* nd. Crowell. 1st. G. V4. $15.00

GIERASCH & KING. *Protein Folding.* 1990. WA. AAAS. 8vo. 334p. VG. B1. $35.00

GIERKE, Otto. *Natural Law & Theory of Society 1500 to 1800.* 1957. Boston. Beacon. 423p. prt wrp. M11. $50.00

GIERKE, Otto. *Political Theories of the Middle Ages.* 1938. Cambrige. G/dj. M11. $85.00

GIESEY, Ralph E. *If Not, Not, the Oath of Aragonese & Legendary Laws...* 1968. Princeton. inscr. M11. $50.00

GIESY, J.U. *Mystery Woman.* 1929. Whitman. 1st. VG/dj. P3. $60.00

GIFFEN, Guy J. *California Expedition. Stevenson's Regiment of 1st NY...* 1951. Oakland. 1/650. 4to. tipped-in frontis. gilt red cloth. F. H3. $60.00

GIFFORD, Barry. *Night People.* 1992. Grove. 1st. NF/NF. B3. $20.00

GIFFORD, Barry. *Wild at Heart.* 1990. Grove Weidenfeld. 1st. F/dj. A24/M22. $30.00

GIFFORD, Thomas. *Man From Lisbon.* 1977. McGraw Hill. 1st. VG/dj. P3. $25.00

GIFFORD, Thomas. *Wind Chill Factor.* 1975. NY. Putnam. 1st. author's 1st novel. F/clip. M15. $65.00

GIKES, Lillian. *Cora Crane: Biography of Mrs Stephen Crane.* 1960. IN U. 1st. cloth. VG/dj. M20. $25.00

GILBERT, A.W. *Potato.* 1917. 2nd. 16 pl. VG. E6. $18.00

GILBERT, A.W. *Potato.* 1917. Macmillan. Rural Science Series. 12mo. 318p. B1. $45.00

GILBERT, Anthony. *By Hook or by Crook.* 1947. AS Barnes. 1st. 186p. cloth. VG/dj. M20. $15.00

GILBERT, Anthony. *Murder Anonymous.* 1968. Random. 1st. VG/dj. P3. $20.00

GILBERT, Arthur. *Jew in Christian America.* 1966. Sheed Ward. 235p. VG+/VG. S3. $17.00

GILBERT, B. *Trailblazers.* 1979. Time-Life. 3rd. leather. A19. $20.00

GILBERT, George. *Bucking With Bar C.* 1928. Chelsea House. A19. $15.00

GILBERT, George. *Quick Draw Kid.* 1927. Chelsea. VG/dj. M2. $20.00

GILBERT, Henry. *Robin Hood & the Men of the Greenwood.* 1912. NY. Stokes. 1st Am. ils Walter Crane. 1st Am. teg. gr cloth. R5. $150.00

GILBERT, J. Warren. *Blue & Gray.* 1922. np. A19. $40.00

GILBERT, Jack. *Kochan.* 1984. Tamarack. 1st. 1/300 (of 376). F/handmade hemp wrp. V1. $125.00

GILBERT, Jack. *Monolihos Poems 1962 & 1982.* 1982. Knopf. 1st. assn copy. F/dj. V1. $55.00

GILBERT, MARTIN & SAVAGE. *Avian Osteology.* 1985. Flagstaff. 2nd. 252p. B1. $25.00

GILBERT, Michael. *Body of a Girl.* 1972. Harper Row. 1st. VG/VG. P3. $13.00

GILBERT, Michael. *Flash Point.* 1974. Harper Row. 1st. VG/VG. P3. $18.00

GILBERT, Michael. *Petrella at Q.* 1977. Harper Row. 1st. VG/dj. P3. $13.00

GILBERT, Paul. *Bertram & His Funny Animals.* 1937. Chicago. Rand McNally. VG/G. B5. $45.00

GILBERT, Paul. *Egbert & His Marvelous Adventures.* 1944. Harper. 1st. 103p. VG/G. P2. $30.00

GILBERT, Paul. *With Bertram in Africa.* 1940 (1939). Rand McNally. 8vo. ils. VG. M5. $30.00

GILBERT, Sarah. *Hairdo.* 1990. NY. Warner. 1st. author's 1st book. F/F. H11. $25.00

GILBERT, Stephen. *Ratman's Notebook.* 1969. Viking. 1st. F/F. B4. $300.00

GILBERT, W.S. *Complete Plays of Gilbert & Sullivan.* 1938. Garden City. tall 8vo. 711p. VG+/dj. H1. $20.00

GILBERT & JEFFERYS. *Crossties Through Carolina...* 1969. Raleigh. 1st. 88p. VG. A17. $30.00

GILBERT & SULLIVAN. *Her Majesty's Ship Pinafore; or, Lass That Loved a Sailor.* 1879. NY. AS Seer. 1st Am. sewn gr prt wrp. M24. $450.00

GILBRETH, Frank. *Cheaper by the Dozen.* 1948. Crowell. 1st. F/NF clip. B4. $275.00

GILCHRIST, Ellen. *Drunk With Love.* 1986. Little Brn. 1st. inscr. VG/VG. A23. $50.00

GILCHRIST, Ellen. *Drunk With Love.* 1987. London. Faber. 1st. author's 4th book. F/dj. A24. $20.00

GILCHRIST, Ellen. *In the Land of Dreamy Dreams.* 1982. London. Faber. 1st. sgn. F/F. R14. $75.00

GILCHRIST, Ellen. *Light Can Be Both Wave & Particle.* 1989. Little Brn. 1st. F/F. A20/A24/M23. $25.00

GILCHRIST, Ellen. *Light Can Be Both Wave & Particle.* 1989. Little Brn. 1st. sgn. F/F. R14. $35.00

GILCHRIST, Ellen. *Starcarbon: A Meditation on Love.* 1994. London. Faber. 1st Eng. F/F. R13. $20.00

GILCHRIST, Ellen. *Victory Over Japan.* 1984. Little Brn. 1st. F/NF. H11. $45.00

GILCHRIST, Ellen. *Victory Over Japan.* 1984. Little Brn. 1st. VG+/VG. A20. $20.00

GILDEN, Mel. *Harry Newberry & the Raiders...* 1989. Holt. 1st. F/dj. P3. $15.00

GILDER, George. *Men & Marriage.* 1986. Pelican. 219p. F/dj. B29. $6.00

GILDER & GILDER. *Authors at Home.* 1888. NY. Cassell. 1st. bl cloth. NF. M24. $100.00

GILDERSLEEVE, Virginia C. *Many a Good Crusade: Memories of...* 1955. Macmillan. 1st. 434p. VG+/clip. A25. $20.00

GILES, H. *GI Journal of Sgt Giles.* 1965. MA. ils. 399p. VG/VG. S16. $27.50

GILES, Herbert A. *Chinese Poetry in English Verse.* 1898. Shanghai. Kelly Walsh. 1st. 8vo. 212p. contemporary calf. M1. $125.00

GILES, Herbert. *Glossary of Reference...Connected With Far East.* 1974. London. Curzon. 328p. F. W3. $56.00

GILES, Kenneth. *Death Among the Stars.* 1969. Walker. 1st. F/dj. P3. $10.00

GILES, Kenneth. *Provenance of Death.* 1966. S&S. 1st. VG/fair. P3. $15.00

GILES, Molly. *Rough Translations.* 1985. Athens, GA. 1st. author's 1st book. F/F. R13. $35.00

GILFILLAN, Archer B. *Goat's Eye-View of the Black Hills.* 1953. Rapid City, SD. Dean. A19. $20.00

GILKEY, Helen M. *Handbook of Northwest Flowering Plants.* 1951. Portland. 2nd. 412p. B26. $12.50

GILL, B.M.; see Trimble, Barbara Margaret.

GILL, Brendan. *Here at the New Yorker.* 1975. Random. 1st. inscr/dtd 1975. VG/NF. B4. $200.00

GILL, Brendan. *Malcontents.* 1973. HBJ. ltd. inscr w/drawing. F/unprt tissue dj. B4. $125.00

GILL, Brendan. *Trouble of One House.* 1950. Doubleday. 1st. author's 1st novel. F/NF. B4. $175.00

GILL, Eric. *Social Justice & the Stations of the Cross.* 1939. London. James Clarke. 1st. 12mo. 21p. F. B24. $125.00

GILL, Patrick; see Creasey, John.

GILLELAN, Howard G. *Complete Book of the Bow & Arrow.* 1994. Derrydale. 1/1250. gilt leather. F. A17. $22.00

GILLENSON, Lewis. *Fabulous Yesterday: Coronet Magazine's 25th Anniversary...* 1961. NY. 1st. F/G. A17. $20.00

GILLESPIE, Noel. *Endotrachael Anesthesia.* 1941. Madison. 1st. 187p. A13. $125.00

GILLESPIE, W.M. *Treatise on Land-Surveying.* 1855. Appleton. 6th. 424p+84p tables. G. A17. $45.00

GILLETT, Eric. *Film Fairyland.* nd. London. lg 8vo. ils. cloth. G. C8. $15.00

GILLETT, James B. *Six Years With the Texas Rangers 1875-1881.* 1921. Austin. Von Boeckmann-Jones. 1st. 8 full-p photos. 332p. D11. $100.00

GILLIAM, Harold. *San Francisco Bay.* 1957. Doubleday. 1st. sgn. 8vo. 336p. bl cloth. M/VG. K7. $25.00

GILLIARD, E. Thomas. *Living Birds of the World: 1500 Species Described.* 1958. NY. 400p. dj. A17. $22.50

GILLIES, Ed. *My Own Sea Kingdom.* 1994. Chicago. Aspen. as issued. P4. $20.00

GILLIGAN, Edmund. *Gaunt Woman.* 1943. Scribner. 1st. VG/VG. P3. $20.00

GILLIS, Charles. *Yellowstone Park & Alaska.* 1893. np. sgn. 76p. VG. J2. $175.00

GILLIS, J.M. *US Naval Astonomical Expedition to the Southern Hemisphere.* 1855. WA. Vol 2 only. ils. 300p. VG. B5. $150.00

GILLIS, Leon. *Amputations.* 1954. London. 1st. 423p. A13. $100.00

GILLMAN & GILLMAN. *Collar the Lot! How Britain Interned & Expelled...Refugees.* 1980. London. 1st. VG/VG. T9. $15.00

GILLSTATER, S. *Wave After Wave.* 1964. London. ils/maps. brd. F/NF. M12. $20.00

GILMAN, A. *Practical Bee Breeding.* 1929. NY. 1st. 264p. VG/VG. B5. $17.50

GILMAN, Charlotte P. Stetson. *In This Our World.* 1893. Oakland, CA. McCombs Vaughn. 1st. 12mo. 120p. cloth. M1. $3,000.00

GILMAN, Dorothy. *Mrs Polifax & the Golden Triangle.* 1988. Doubleday. 1st. VG/dj. P3. $16.00

GILMAN, Dorothy. *Tightrope Walker.* 1979. Doubleday. 1st. 186p. cloth. VG/clip. M20. $12.00

GILMAN, Kay Iselin. *Inside the Pressure Cooker.* 1973. Berkley. 1st. VG/G+. P8. $20.00

GILMAN, Laselle. *Red Gate.* 1953. Ballantine. 1st. VG/dj. P3. $30.00

GILMAN, Robert C. *Navigator of Rhada.* 1969. Harcourt. 1st. F/dj. M2. $25.00

GILMORE, C.W. *Contributions to Vertebrate Paleontology.* 1924. Ottowa. 89p. wrp. B1. $19.00

GILPIN, Laura. *Enduring Navaho.* 1968. Austin. TX U. 1st. photos. F/F. L3. $65.00

GILPIN, Laura. *Enduring Navaho.* 1971. Austin. 2nd. 4to. photos. gr cloth. F/NF. T10. $60.00

GILSON, Etienne. *History of Christian Philosophy in the Middle Ages.* 1955. Random. 1st Am. 829p. F/VG. H1. $48.00

GILSVIK, Bob. *Modern Trapline.* 1980. Radnor, PA. Chilton. dj. A19. $20.00

GINN & HEATH. *Classical Atlas.* ca 1880. Boston/NY/Chicago. Ginn & Heath. 23 maps (most double-p). VG. W1. $85.00

GINSBERG, Allen. *Empty Mirror.* 1961. NY. Cornith/Totem. 1st. sgn/dtd 1963. NF/wrp. B4. $350.00

GINSBERG, Allen. *Kaddish & Other Poems 1958-1960.* 1961. SF. City Lights. 1st prt. NF/wrp. B4. $250.00

GINSBERG, Allen. *TV Baby Poems.* 1967. London. Cape Goliard. 1/100. sgn/#d. w/Ginsberg photo. F/F. B2. $250.00

GINSBERG, H.L. *Book of Isaiah: A New Translation.* 1972-73. JPS. 1st. sm 4to. 116p. VG+/G. S3. $23.00

GINSBERG, Louis. *Photographers in Virginia 1839-1900: A Checklist.* 1986. Petersburg, VA. self pub. 1st. 1/200. pres. 64p. cloth. NF. M8. $85.00

GINSBURG, Mirra. *Last Door to Aiya.* 1968. SG Phillips. 1st. F/dj. P3. $23.00

GINSBURG, Mirra. *Ultimate Threshold.* 1970. Holt. 1st. VG/dj. M2. $10.00

GINZBERG, Louis. *On Jewish Law & Lore.* 1955. JPS. 262p. VG/G+. S3. $22.00

GIPSON, Morrell. *Mr Bear Squash-You-All-Flat.* 1950. Wonder. ils Angela. VG. M5. $145.00

GIPSON, Morrell. *Surprise Doll.* 1949. Wonder. 1st. ils Steffie Lerch. VG. M5. $35.00

GIRAUD, S. Louis. *Bookano Stories.* 1946. London. Strand Pub. Pot-Pourri ed. 5 double-p popups. 4to. pict brd. R5. $275.00

GIRAUD, S. Louis. *Daily Express Children's Annual No 4.* ca 1930s. London. Lane. 7 pop-ups. NF. T10. $200.00

GIRLING, Richard. *Forest on the Hill.* 1982. Viking. 1st. F/F. M2. $15.00

GIRODIAS, Maurice. *Best of Olympia, an Anthology.* 1966. London. 1st. VG/dj. T9. $45.00

GIROUARD, Mark. *Cities & People: A Social Architectural History.* 1986. ils. VG/VG. M17. $22.50

GISBON & STERLING. *Difference Engine.* 1991. Bantam. 1st. F/F. M22. $35.00

GISH, Franklin. *First Horses.* 1993. Reno. NV U. 1st. F/F. L3. $35.00

GITLER, Ira. *Blood on the Ice.* 1974. Regenry. 1st. photos. F/VG. P8. $25.00

GITTINGER, Roy. *Formation of the State of Oklahoma, 1803-1906.* 1917. Berkeley. 256p. gilt cloth. D11. $50.00

GITTINGS, Robert. *Peach Blossom Forest & Other Chinese...* 1951. Oxford. 1st. VG/dj. P3. $20.00

GIVEN, James Buchanan. *Society & Homicide in 13th-Century England.* 1977. Stanford. ES. dj. M11. $50.00

GIVENS, Charles J. *Financial Self-Defense.* 1990. S&S. 1st. 488p. F/F. W2. $25.00

GLADSTONE, Bernard. *Complete Book of Garden & Outdoor Lighting.* 1956. NY. photos/drawings. 120p. VG/dj. B26. $14.00

GLADSTONE, William E. *Female Suffrage.* 1892. np. Am Women Remonstrants. 8vo. stitched. R12. $75.00

GLADSTONE, William E. *Might of Right.* 1898. Boston. Lee Shepard. New ed/1st thus. 302p. gray cloth. B22. $8.50

GLADWIN, Thomas. *East Is a Big Bird.* 1970. Cambridge. Harvard. photos/9 maps/diagrams. 241p. dj. T7. $45.00

GLANCY, Diane. *Firesticks.* 1993. Norman, OK. 1st. F/F. L3. $45.00

GLANCY, Diane. *Trigger Dance.* 1990. Boulder. Fiction Collective Two. 1st hc. F/F. L3. $75.00

GLANTZ, David M. *When Titans Clashed: How the Red Army Stopped Hitler.* 1995. Kansas City. 1st. F/F. V4. $17.50

GLANVILL. *De Legibus et Consuetudinibus Regni Angliae...* 1932. New Haven. cloth-backed brd. VG. M11. $150.00

GLASS, C. *Family Album: Cactus & Succulent Journal 1966 Yearbook.* 1966. Resda. photos. 296p. VG. B26. $35.00

GLASS, David C. *Neurophysiology & Emotion.* 1967. Rockefeller. 234p. gr/gray cloth. VG. G1. $25.00

GLASS, INNES & SCHNECK. *Identifying Cacti.* 1996. Edison, NJ. 80 mc photos. M/dj. B26. $8.00

GLASS & FOSTER. *1975 Yearbook.* 1975. Reseda. ils/photos. 104p. F. B26. $25.00

GLASS-GRAY, Charles. *Off at Sunrise: Overland Journal of Charles Glass-Gray.* 1976. San Marino. Huntington Lib. 1st. F/F. O4. $25.00

GLASSER, Otto. *Physical Foundations of Radiology.* 1944. NY. 1st. 426p. A13. $20.00

GLATZER, Nahum. *Dynamics of Emancipation: Jew in the Modern Age.* 1965. Beacon. 70 essays. 320p. VG/dj. S3. $23.00

GLATZER, Nahum. *In Time & Eternity: A Jewish Reader.* 1946. Schocken. 255p. VG. S3. $22.00

GLAZER, Lynn. *Engraved America: Iconography of America Through 1800.* 1970. Phil. Ancient Orb. lg folio. 1/1000. 232p pl/maps. M. O7. $575.00

GLAZIER, Willard Worchester. *Three Years in the Federal Cavalry.* 1870. NY. Ferguson. 1st. 339p. cloth. VG. M8. $65.00

GLAZIER, Willard. *Heroes of Three Wars.* 1884. Phil. ils. gilt cloth. VG. B18. $25.00

GLEASON, Duncan. *Islands & Ports of California.* 1958. NY. Devin-Adair. 1st. ils. 201p. as new/dj. K7. $50.00

GLEASON, Duncan. *Islands of California.* 1951. Sea Pub. 1st. inscr. NF/G. O4. $30.00

GLEASON, Henry Allan. *Vegetational History of the Middle West.* 1923. NY. offprint. tall 8vo. wrp. A22. $25.00

GLEASON & GLEASON. *Beloved Sister: Letters of James Henry Gleason 1841-1859.* 1978. Arthur H Clark. 1st. F/F. O4. $15.00

GLEASON & GLEASON. *Rough & the Righteous.* 1970. Babloa Island. Piasano. 1st. inscr. F/sans. O4. $20.00

GLENN, Lois. *Charles WS Williams: A Checklist.* 1975. Kent State. 128p. cloth. A17. $12.50

GLESSING, Robert J. *Underground Press in America.* 1970. Bloomington. 1st. F/F. B4. $125.00

GLEYE, Paul. *Behind the Wall: American in East Germany 1988-1989.* 1991. S IL U. 1st. as new/dj. V4. $12.50

GLOAG, Julian. *Only Yesterday.* 1986. Holt. 1st. F/F. A20. $10.00

GLOAG & GLOAG. *Simple Furnishing & Arrangement.* 1922. Stokes. 1st. 165p. VG/tattered. M20. $25.00

GLOBE, Alexander. *Peter Stent, London Printseller, ca 1642-1665.* 1985. Vancouver. catalogue raisonne. 4to. 268p. F/dj. T10. $80.00

GLOSER & HUSAK. *Sukulenti Rostliny.* 1987. Prague. 118p. M. B26. $11.00

GLOSTER, Hugh Morris. *Negro Voices in American Fiction.* 1948. Chapel Hill. 1st. F/VG. B2. $85.00

GLOVER, Richard. *Leonidas. A Poem.* 1737. London. Dodsley. 1st. tall wide 4to. 335p. ES. H13. $245.00

GLUCK, Louise. *Firstborn.* 1969. Anvil. 1st Eng. assn copy. NF/dj. V1. $40.00

GLUCK, Sinclair. *Dragon in Harness.* 1932. Dodd Mead. 1st. VG. M2. $15.00

GLUECK, N. *Rivers in the Desert: History of Negev & Account...* 1959. 1st. ils. VG/G+. E6. $13.00

GLUECKEL. *Memoirs.* 1932. Harper. 1st Am. 8vo. 295p. VG. T10. $75.00

GLYN, Elinor. *Three Weeks.* 1924. Macaulay. 1st thus. F/F. B4. $85.00

GOBLE, Neil. *Asimov Analyzed.* 1972. Mirage. 1st. VG/dj. P3. $45.00

GOBLE, Warwick. *Folk Tales of Bengal.* 1912. Macmillan. 1st. 32 mtd pl. 274p. VG. P2. $300.00

GOBRIGHT & PRATT. *Union Sketch-Book: A Reliable Guide.* 1860. Pudney Russell. 8vo. aeg. gilt bl cloth. F. T10. $150.00

GODDARD, Anthea. *Aztec Skull.* 1977. Walker. 1st. F/dj. M2. $15.00

GODDARD, Donald. *Joey (Gallo).* 1974. Harper Row. 1st. F/NF. A20. $25.00

GODDARD, Kenneth. *Balefire.* 1983. Bantam. 1st. F/VG. N4. $20.00

GODDARD, Kenneth. *Prey.* 1992. Tor. NF/dj. P3. $22.00

GODDARD, Paul Beck. *Plates of Cerebro-Spinal Nerves, With References...* 1991. NY. Classics Neurology/Neurosurgery. facsimile. G1. $85.00

GODDARD, Robert H. *Rockets, Comprising a Method of Reaching Extreme Altitudes.* 1946. NY. ils. VG/dj. B18. $295.00

GODDARD, Robert. *In Pale Battalions.* 1988. Poseidon. 1st. sgn. author's 2nd novel. F/F. T2. $45.00

GODDEN, Geoffrey A. *Illustrated Encyclopedia of British Pottery & Porcelain.* 1966. Crown. 1st Am. 390p. gilt bl cloth. F/VG. H1. $40.00

GODDEN, Rumer. *Candy Floss.* 1960. Viking. 1st. ils Adrienne Adams. 64p. VG/dj. P2. $75.00

GODDEN, Rumer. *China Court.* 1961. Viking. 1st. F/NF. M19. $25.00

GODDEN, Rumer. *Creatures' Choir.* 1965. Viking. 1st Am. 25 poems. F/NF. D4. $30.00

GODDEN, Rumer. *Miss Happiness & Miss Flowers.* 1961. Viking. 1st. ils Jean Primrose. 82p. VG/dj. P2. $60.00

GODDEN, Rumer. *River.* 1946. Little Brn. 1st. F/VG. M19. $35.00

GODDEN, Rumer. *St Jerome & the Lion.* 1961. Viking. 1st. 32p. F/F. D4. $30.00

GODDEN, Rumer. *Woman Who Lived in a Vinegar Bottle.* 1970. Viking. 1st. sm 4to. unp. VG/VG. T5. $30.00

GODEY, John. *Nella.* 1981. Delacorte. 1st. G+/dj. N4. $17.50

GODEY, John. *Never Put Off Till Tomorrow What You Can Kill Today.* 1970. Random. 1st. VG/dj. P3. $25.00

GODEY, John. *Talisman.* 1976. Putnam. 1st. VG/dj. P3. $20.00

GODEY & HALE. *Lady's Book.* 1869. Phil. Godey. ils. 522p. G. D1. $200.00

GODFREY, Henry. *Your Yucatan Guide.* 1967. Funk Wagnalls. 1st. 196p. dj. F3. $15.00

GODFROY, Chief Clarence. *Miami Indian Stories.* 1961. Winona Lake. Light/Life Pr. 1st. VG. L3. $150.00

GODOLPHIN, Mary. *Robinson Crusoe, in Words of One Syllable.* nd. London. Shoe Lane. sm 4to. ils John Harris. VG. C8. $22.50

GODWIN, Gail. *Finishing School.* 1984. Franklin Lib. ltd. sgn. leather. F. B35. $45.00

GODWIN, Gail. *Finishing School.* 1985. London. Heinemann. 1st Eng. NF/dj. R13. $25.00

GODWIN, Gail. *Violet Clay.* 1978. Knopf. 1st. F/dj. Q1. $50.00

GODWIN, Joan. *Baffling World.* 1968. Hart. 1st. NF/dj. M2. $17.00

GODWIN, Parke. *Firelord.* 1979. Doubleday. 1st. F/dj. M2. $25.00

GODWIN, Parke. *Waiting for the Galactic Bus.* 1988. Doubleday. 1st. F/dj. P3. $20.00

GODWIN, William. *History of Commonwealth of England.* 1824-1828. London. Colburn. 4 vol. 8vo. contemporary full polished gilt calf. R12. $1,075.00

GOEDICKE, Patricia. *Wind of Our Going.* 1985. Copper Canyon. inscr. assn copy. NF/wrp. V1. $15.00

GOELET, Francis. *Voyages & Travels of Francis Goelet, 1746-1758.* 1970. Queens College/Gregg. ils/maps/pl. VG. K3. $25.00

GOEMER, Fred. *Search for Amelia Earhart.* 1966. London. Bodley Head. 1st Eng. photos. 286p. VG/clip. A25. $18.00

GOETHE; see Von Goethe.

GOFF, Frederick. *John Dunlap Broadside: First Printing of Declaration...* 1976. Lib Congress. 4to. ils/tipped-in portrait. F/F case. A4. $45.00

GOFF, John S. *George WP Hunt & His Arizona.* 1972. Socio Technical Pub. 1st. ils/notes/index. 286p. NF/NF. B19. $45.00

GOFF, John S. *Governors 1863-1912: Arizona Territorial Officials II.* 1978. Blk Mtn Pr. 1st. 212p. F/sans. B19. $30.00

GOFF, McCAFFREE & STERBENZ. *Centennial Brand Book, Famous Brands & Biographies...* 1967. Cattlemen's Centennial. 1st. 2 vol. sgn. VG. J2. $325.00

GOLB, Norman. *Who Wrote the Dead Sea Scrolls?* 1995. Scribner. 1st. 446p. NF/dj. W1. $20.00

GOLD, H.L. *Fifth Galaxy Reader.* 1961. BC. VG/VG. P3. $30.00

GOLD, H.L. *Mind Partner & 8 Other Novelettes From Galaxy.* 1961. Doubleday. 1st. F/dj. M2. $25.00

GOLD, H.L. *Old Die Rich.* 1955. Crown. 1st. VG/dj. M2. $50.00

GOLD, M. *Jews Without Money.* 1941 (1930). ils Howard Simon. G+. E6. $22.00

GOLDBERG, Elkhonon. *Contemporary Neuropsychology & Legacy of Luria.* 1990. Hillsdale, NJ. Lawrence Erlbaum Assoc. 287p. prt bl cloth. F. G1. $50.00

GOLDEN, Marita. *Long Distance Life.* 1989. Doubleday. 1st. F/F. B4. $45.00

GOLDIN, Hayman E. *Jewish Woman & Her Home.* 1941. Hebrew Pub. ils Nota Koslowsky. 354p. VG/dj. S3. $22.00

GOLDIN, Stephen. *World Called Solitude.* 1981. Doubleday. 1st. F/dj. P3. $15.00

GOLDING, Harry. *Wonder Book of Nature.* 1934 (1934). London. Ward. 5th. inscr. NF. T12. $50.00

GOLDING, Harry. *Zoo Days.* 1919. Ward Lock. 1st. 8vo. red cloth. R5. $175.00

GOLDING, Louis. *Jewish Problem.* 1939. Penguin. 5th. 213p. sc. VG. S3. $19.00

GOLDING, William. *Brass Butterfly: A Play in Three Acts.* 1958. London. Faber. 1st. F/dj. Q1. $150.00

GOLDING, William. *Darkness Visible.* 1979. FSG. 1st. F/F. B35. $18.00

GOLDING, William. *Lord of the Flies.* 1955. Coward McCann. 1st Am. author's 1st book. NF/VG. L3. $650.00

GOLDING, William. *Lord of the Flies.* 1960. London. Faber. 5th imp. sgn. F. B4. $200.00

GOLDING, William. *Paper Men.* 1984. FSG. 1st. F/dj. P3. $15.00

GOLDING, William. *Spire.* 1964. Harcourt. 1st Am. F/dj. M2. $25.00

GOLDMAN, Albert. *Lives of John Lennon.* 1988. Morrow. 1st. F/F. A20. $15.00

GOLDMAN, Alex J. *Giants of Faith: Great American Rabbis.* 1964. NY. Citadel. 349p. VG/G+. S3. $24.00

GOLDMAN, Emma. *Living My Life.* 1931. Knopf. 2 vol. 993p. S3. $45.00

GOLDMAN, Emma. *Syndicalism.* 1913. Mother Earth. 1st. VG/wrp. B2. $60.00

GOLDMAN, Francisco. *Long Night of White Chickens.* 1992. Atlantic Monthly. 1st. author's 1st novel. F/NF. D10. $45.00

GOLDMAN, Laurel. *Sounding the Territory.* 1982. Knopf. 1st. F/dj. M25. $15.00

GOLDMAN, William. *Brothers.* 1986. Warner. 1st. inscr. F/F. A23. $40.00

GOLDMAN, William. *Color of Light.* 1984. Granada. 1st. VG/dj. P3. $23.00

GOLDMAN, William. *Control.* 1982. Delacorte. 1st. VG/dj. P3. $25.00

GOLDMAN, William. *Heat.* 1985. Warner. 1st. F/F. A20. $20.00

GOLDMAN, William. *Heat.* 1985. Warner. 1st. NF/NF. M22. $12.00

GOLDMAN, William. *Marathon Man.* 1974. Delacorte. 1st. sgn. F/VG. A23. $40.00

GOLDMAN, William. *Marathon Man.* 1974. Delacorte. 1st. VG/dj. P3. $30.00

GOLDMAN, William. *Princess Bride.* nd. BC. F/dj. M2. $15.00

GOLDMAN, William. *Temple of Gold.* 1957. NY. 1st. sgn. NF/NF. A11. $125.00

GOLDOWSKY, Seebert. *Yankee Surgeon: Life & Times of Usher Parsons...* 1988. Canton, MA. 1st. 450p. dj. A13. $30.00

GOLDSBOROUGH, Robert. *Murder in E Minor.* 1986. Bantam. 1st. F/dj. P3. $15.00

GOLDSCHEIDER, Ludwig. *Sculptures of Michelangelo.* 1950. London. Phaidon. 2nd. ils/pl/footnotes/bibliography. cloth. dj. D2. $60.00

GOLDSCHMIDT, Sidney G. *Eye for a Horse: A Guide to Buying & Judging.* 1933. Scribner. 1st Am. VG/fair. O3. $35.00

GOLDSMITH, Oliver. *Deserted Village.* 1857. NY. Appleton. 8vo. 46p. aeg. gilt gr morocco. B24. $100.00

GOLDSMITH, Oliver. *History of Little Goody Two Shoes.* 1925. Macmillan. ils Alice Woodward. 16mo. VG. D1. $35.00

GOLDSMITH, Oliver. *Miscellaneous Works of Oliver Goldsmith.* 1850 (1837). Putnam. rpt. 4 vol. G. H1. $85.00

GOLDSMITH, Oliver. *Poems of...* 1859. London. Routledge. edit RA Willmott. ils after Birket Foster. 158p. aeg. B24. $200.00

GOLDSMITH, Oliver. *She Stoops to Conquer; or, The Mistake of a Night.* nd (1912). Hodder Stoughton. 25 mtd pl. thick 4to. VG. M5. $125.00

GOLDSMITH, Oliver. *Traveller, a Poem.* 1770. London. Carman Newberry. 4to. recent bdg. H13. $395.00

GOLDSMITH, Oliver. *Traveller. A Poem by...* ca 1856. London. David Bogue. 8vo. ils Birket Foster. 39p. aeg. gilt pub cloth. NF. B24. $150.00

GOLDSMITH, Oliver. *Vicar of Wakefield.* nd. Phil. McKay. 1st Am. ils Rackham/12 mc pl. 231p. NF/dj. M20. $175.00

GOLDSMITH, Oliver. *Vicar of Wakefield.* 1929. London. Harrap. 1/775. ils/sgn Rackham. 232p. teg. gilt vellum. F. B24. $700.00

GOLDSMITH, Oliver. *Vicar of Wakefield.* 1929. London. Harrap. 1st. ils Rackham/12 full-p pl. 232p. VG/torn. D1. $120.00

GOLDSTEIN, Joseph. *Government of British Trade Unions: A Study...* 1952. Allen Unwin. VG/VG. V4. $25.00

GOLDSTEIN, Lisa. *Dream Years.* 1985. Bantam. 1st. F/dj. P3. $15.00

GOLDSTEIN, Milton. *Magnificent West: Grand Canyon.* 1980. NY. Bonanza. 4to. ils. 201p. gr brd. dj. F7. $25.00

GOLDSTONE & PAYNE. *John Steinbeck Bibliography.* 1974. Austin, TX. HRC. 1st. 1/1200. tan cloth. F. M24. $300.00

GOLDTHWAIT, R.P. *Till, a Symposium.* 1971. OH State. 402p. cloth. F/dj. D8. $45.00

GOLDTHWAITE, Eaton K. *Cat & Mouse.* 1946. DSP. 1st. VG/dj. P3. $25.00

GOLDWASSER, Janet. *Huan-Ying: Workers' China.* 1975. Monthly Review. 1st. VG/dj. V4. $25.00

GOLDWATER, Barry. *Goldwater.* 1988. Doubleday. 1st. sgn. F/F. A23. $50.00

GOLDWATER & MUENCH. *Arizona.* 1978. Chicago. Rand McNally. 1st. 128p. VG/dj. F7. $35.00

GOLDWORTH, Bella. *Across the Border: Short Stories.* 1971. Yiddisher Kultur. 269p. VG/G+. S3. $29.00

GOLLANCZ, Victor. *Devil's Repertoire or Nuclear Bombing & the Life of Man.* 1959. VG/dj. K3. $10.00

GOLLER, Nicholas. *Tomorrow's Silence.* 1979. Macmillan. 1st. VG/VG. P3. $15.00

GOLOVANOV, Yaroslav. *Our Gagarin.* 1978. Moscow. Progress. lg 4to. 317p. VG. K5. $100.00

GOLOVIN, Pavel N. *End of Russian America: Capt PN Golovin's Last Report 1862.* 1979. Portland. OR Hist Soc. 4to. 8 maps. as new/dj. O7. $35.00

GOMBROWICZ, Witold. *Ferdydurke.* 1961. HRW. 1st Am. F/NF clip. B4. $200.00

GOMES, Bernardino Antonio. *Ensaio Dermosographico ou Succinta e Systematica...* 1820. Lisbon. Typ de Academia Real das Sciencias. 1st. mc pls. 171p. R15. $1,800.00

GONCALVES DOS SANTOS, Luis. *Impiedade Confundida, ou Refutacao da Carta de Talleyrand...* 1830. Rio de Janeiro. Torres. 1st. 324p. modern blk calf. R15. $1,500.00

GONDOR, Emery J. *You Are... A Puzzle Book for Children.* (1937). Modern Age. 1st. ils Emery J Gondor. VG/VG. D1. $135.00

GONZALES & HAWK. *Tennis.* 1962. Fleet. 1st. ils/photos. G+/dj. P8. $15.00

GONZALES DAVILA, Francisco. *Ancient Cultures of Mexico.* (1968). Mexico. INAH. ils. 80p. wrp. F3. $10.00

GONZALES-GERTH, Miguel. *Ruben Dario Centennial Studies.* 1972. Austin, TX. 120p. dj. F3. $10.00

GOOD, John Mason. *Book of Nature.* 1831. NY. 467p. full calf. A17. $20.00

GOOD HOUSEKEEPING INSTITUTE. *Good Meals & How To Prepare Them.* 1929. NY. 8th. G. A16. $10.00

GOODALL, A. *Wandering Gorillas.* 1979. London. Collins. ils/photos. F/F. M12. $27.50

GOODALL, Jane. *Chimpanzees of Gombe.* 1986. Harvard. ils. F/NF. S15. $35.00

GOODALL, John. *Sleeping Beauty.* 1979. London. Macmillan. 1st. ils. 20p. F. P2. $20.00

GOODCHILD, George. *Splendid Crime.* 1930. Houghton Mifflin. 1st Am. F/dj. M15. $60.00

GOODE, G.B. *Origins of Natural Science in America.* 1991. WA. ils. F/dj. M4. $35.00

GOODE BROTHERS. *Miniature History of England.* ca 1910. London. 35x31mm. 78p. ils/italic calligraphy. dk red calf. F. B24. $375.00

GOODERS, J. *Birds of Canada.* 1984. Limps. Dragons World. ils Pledger/Boyer. 159p. brd. NF/NF. M12. $37.50

GOODFELLOW. *Collector's Guide to Games & Puzzles.* 1991. 4to. photos. 128p. F/F. A4. $55.00

GOODICH, Michael. *Unmentionable Vice, Homosexuality in Later Medieval Period.* 1979. Dorset. M11. $50.00

GOODING, James Henry. *On the Altar of Freedom: A Black Solder's Civil War Letters.* 1991. Amherst. 1st. edit VM Adams. 139p. F/F. B4. $50.00

GOODIS, David. *Of Missing Persons.* 1950. Morrow. 1st. NF/NF. B4. $650.00

GOODIS, David. *Retreat From Oblivion.* 1939. Dutton. 1st F/VG+. B4. $2,000.00

GOODMAN, A.J. *Jurassic & Carboniferous of Western Canada.* 1958. Tulsa. AAGA John Andrew Allan Memorial Vol. 514p. xl. D8. $15.00

GOODMAN, Benny. *Kingdom of Swing.* 1939. Stackpole. 1st. sgn by 13 members of Goodman's band. NF/G+. B4. $350.00

GOODMAN, Edward J. *Exploration of South America: Annotated Bibliography.* 1983. NY. Garland. 174p. F. O7. $35.00

GOODMAN, Paul. *Growing Up Absurd.* 1960. NY. 1st. VG/VG. T9. $32.00

GOODMAN, W.L. *British Planemakers From 1700.* 1978. Suffolk, Eng. Arnold Walker. 2nd. 182p. gilt brn cloth. as new/F. H1. $65.00

GOODRICH, A.J. *Goodrich's Analytical Harmony: Theory Musical Composition.* nd (1893). Cincinnati. John Church. 1st. 404p. purple buckram. F. B22. $7.00

GOODRICH, Frank B. *Women of Beauty & Heroism...* 1861. NY. HW Derby. engravings. 400p. teg. VG+. A25. $100.00

GOODRICH, Lloyd. *Thomas Eakins.* 1970. Whitney Mus. ils. VG/VG. M17. $20.00

GOODRICH, S.G. *Johnson's Natural History.* 1874. NY. 2 vol. ils. 3-quarter leather. VG. M17. $60.00

GOODRICH, Ward L. *Modern Clock: A Study of Time Keeping Mechanism...* 1905. Chicago. Hazlitt Walker. 1st. ils. 502p. VG. K3. $55.00

GOODRUM, Charles A. *Best Cellar.* 1987. St Martin. 1st. VG/VG. P3. $15.00

GOODRUM, Charles A. *Dewey Decimated.* 1977. NY. Crown. 1st. F/F. T2. $35.00

GOODSPEED, Charles E. *Nathaniel Hawthorne & Museum of Salem East India Marine Soc.* 1946. Peabody Mus. ils. 32p. wrp. T7. $24.00

GOODSPEED, Charles E. *Yankee Bookseller.* 1937. Houghton Mifflin. 1st. ils. G+. K3. $35.00

GOODSPEED, Thomas H. *Genus Nicotiana.* 1954. Waltham, MA. ils/50 tables. 536p. VG/dj. B26. $62.50

GOODSTONE, Tony. *Pulps.* 1970. Chelsea House. 1st. VG/dj. P3. $35.00

GOODWIN, John. *Idols & the Prey: A Novel of Haiti.* 1953. NY. Harper. 1st. F/NF. B4. $85.00

GOOSE, Phillip Henry. *Evenings at the Microscope.* 1860. Appleton. VG. K3. $60.00

GOOSMAN, Bessie. *History of Old Northfield Township.* 1973. Northfield, OH. 169p. VG. B18. $15.00

GORDIMER, Nadine. *Burger's Daughter.* 1979. Viking. 1st. F/F. M19. $25.00

GORDIMER, Nadine. *Conservationist.* 1975. Viking. 1st. F/F. M19. $35.00

GORDIMER, Nadine. *Lying Days.* 1953. London. Gollancz. 1st. sgn. NF/VG. B3. $150.00

GORDIMER, Nadine. *Occasion for Loving.* 1963. Gollancz. 1st. F/NF. Q1. $150.00

GORDIMER, Nadine. *Soft Voice of the Serpent & Other Stories.* 1952. S&S. 1st Am. author's 1st book. NF/dj. D10/L3. $200.00

GORDIMER, Nadine. *Sport of Nature.* 1987. London. Cape. 1st. F/F. R13. $25.00

GORDINIER, H.C. *Gross & Minute Anatomy of Central Nervous System.* 1899. Phil. Blakiston. 8vo. 48 full-p pl/213 text ils. VG. G1. $85.00

GORDON, Donald. *Star-Raker.* 1962. Hodder Stoughton. 1st. VG/dj. P3. $20.00

GORDON, Elizabeth. *Buddy Jim.* 1922. Volland. 1st. ils John Rae. pict brd. VG. M20. $22.00

GORDON, Elizabeth. *Four Footed Folk or the Children of the Farm & Forest.* 1914. Whitman. 1st. 8vo. pict cloth. R5. $125.00

GORDON, Elizabeth. *King Gum Drop or Neddie's Visit to Candyland.* (1916). Whitman. ils Hazel Frazee. VG+. B15. $175.00

GORDON, Elizabeth. *Mother Earth's Children.* 1914. Volland. 2nd. ils MT Ross. 8vo. pict brd. R5. $100.00

GORDON, Elizabeth. *Watermelon Pete & Others.* 1914. Rand McNally. 1st. ils Clara Powers Wilson. red cloth. VG. M5. $250.00

GORDON, Frederick. *Fairview Boys at Camp Mystery (#4).* 1914. Chas E Graham. 126p. cloth. VG. M20. $10.00

GORDON, G.B. *Notes on the Western Eskimo.* 1906. Phil. Dept Archaeology. 18 pl. F. P4. $45.00

GORDON, Howard. *African in Me.* 1993. Brazille. 1st. sgn. F/F. B4. $45.00

GORDON, Jean. *Rose Recipes: Customs, Facts, Fancies.* 1959 (1958). Woodstock, VT. 2nd. ils. 100p. ils red cloth. B26. $22.50

GORDON, John B. *Reminiscences of the Civil War.* 1903. NY. 1st. VG. B5. $125.00

GORDON, John B. *Reminiscences of the Civil War.* 1981. Time-Life. rpt. 474p. aeg. gilt bl leather. F. M4. $30.00

GORDON, John Steele. *Scarlet Woman of Wall Street.* 1988. Weidenfeld. 1st. F/F. W2. $40.00

GORDON, Mary. *Final Payments.* 1978. Random. 1st. sgn. F/NF. R14. $75.00

GORDON, Mary. *Temporary Shelter.* 1987. Random. 1st. sgn. NF/F. R14. $60.00

GORDON, Nikki. *Gemini: An Extended Autobiographical Statement...* 1972. Bobbs Merrill. 1st. F/dj. M25. $45.00

GORDON, Patricia. *Not-Mrs Murphy.* 1942. Viking. 1st. ils Ralph Boyer. 122p. F/VG. P2. $30.00

GORDON, Pearl Scott. *Simply Elegant.* sgn. VG/G. A16. $14.00

GORDON, Richard. *Captain's Table.* 1954. Michael Joseph. 1st. VG/dj. P3. $30.00

GORDON, Richard. *Doctor at Large.* 1955. Michael Joseph. 1st. VG/dj. P3. $30.00

GORDON, Richard. *Doctor in the Swim.* 1962. Michael Joseph. 1st. VG/dj. P3. $20.00

GORDON, Roxy. *Breeds.* 1984. Austin. Place of Herons. 1st hc issue. F. L3. $125.00

GORDON, Stuart. *Suane & the Crow God.* 1975. NEL. 1st. F/dj. M2. $17.00

GORDON, Stuart. *Two-Eyes.* 1975. Sidgwick Jackson. 1st. VG/dj. P3. $20.00

GORDON & MEDARIS. *Countdown for Decision.* 1960. NY. 1st. inscr Medaris. 303p. F/dj. B18. $35.00

GORDON & MILLER. *Lost Heritage of Alaska.* 1967. Bonanza. 289p. VG/dj. P4. $35.00

GORDON-BOWE, Nicolas. *Harry Clarke: His Graphic Art.* 1982. Dolmen. 1st. 1/250. w/extra suite ils. F/dj. M2. $200.00

GOREAU, Laurraine. *Just Mahalia, Baby: The Mahalia Jackson Story.* 1975. Waco, TX. World. 1st. photos. 611p. NF/VG+. B4. $75.00

GOREN, Arthur. *New York Jews & Quest for Community: Kehillah Experiment...* 1970. Columbia. 361p. VG/G+. S3. $24.00

GOREN, Charles H. *Contract Bridge in a Nutshell.* 1946. Doubleday. 1st. 128p. VG. H1. $18.00

GOREN, Charles H. *Goren's Bridge: Complete, New & Expanded Edition.* 1980. NY. 2nd. 706p. VG/dj. S1. $8.00

GOREN, Charles H. *Goren's Easy Steps to Winning Bridge: Programmed Textbook.* 1963. NY. 1st. 287p. dj. S1. $10.00

GORENSTEIN, Shirley. *Not Forever on Earth.* 1975. Scribner. 1st. ils/index. 153p. dj. F3. $15.00

GORES, Joe. *Come Morning.* 1986. Mysterious. 1st. F/dj. P3. $20.00

GORES, Joe. *Come Morning.* 1986. Mysterious. 1st. sgn. F/F. T2. $35.00

GORES, Joe. *Dead Man.* 1993. Mysterious. 1st. F/F. N4. $25.00

GORES, Joe. *Dead Skip.* 1973. London. Gollancz. 1st Eng. NF/dj. Q1. $75.00

GORES, Joe. *Interface.* 1974. NY. Evans. 1st. F/dj. M15. $65.00

GORES, Joe. *Mostly Murder.* 1992. Mystery Scene. 1/50. sgn/#d. leather. F. P3. $50.00

GOREY, Edward. *Amphigorey.* 1972. Putnam. 1st. VG. M2. $20.00

GOREY, Edward. *Awdrey-Gore Legacy.* 1972. Dodd Mead. 1st. unp. pict brd. VG/dj. M20. $85.00

GOREY, Edward. *Broken Spoke.* 1976. Dodd Mead. 1st. F/F. A11. $80.00

GOREY, Edward. *Die Sehr Gute Uhr.* 1971. Zurich. Diogenes. 1st German. 12mo. unp. F/F. D1. $75.00

GOREY, Edward. *Dwindling Party: A Pop-Up Book.* 1982. Random. 1st. glossy ils brd. F. A11. $125.00

GOREY, Edward. *Fletcher & Zenobia.* 1967. Meredith. stated 1st. ils Victoria Chess. VG. M5. $25.00

GOREY, Edward. *Gilded Bat.* 1966. S&S. 1st stated. VG. D1. $60.00

GOREY, Edward. *Glorious Nosebleed.* 1974. Dodd Mead. 1st. 26 full-p ils. unp. orange brd. F/F. D1. $25.00

GOREY, Edward. *Gorey Posters.* 1979. Abrams. folio. VG. P2. $100.00

GOREY, Edward. *Hapless Child.* 1980. Dodd Mead. 1st thus. unp. VG/dj. M20. $45.00

GOREY, Edward. *Red Riding Hood.* 1972. Atheneum. 1st. 43p. gray cloth. F/F. D1. $37.50

GOREY, Edward. *Secrets: Vol 1, the Other Statue.* 1968. S&S. 1st. ils Gorey. pict brd. VG. D1. $40.00

GOREY, Edward. *Unstring Harp; or, Mr Earbrass Writes a Novel.* 1953. DSP/Little Brn. 1st. NF/NF. B4/D1. $300.00

GOREY, Edward. *Utter Zoo.* 1967. Meredith. 1st. unp. VG/dj. M20. $95.00

GOREY, Edward. *Willowdale Handcar.* 1979. Dodd Mead. 1st. ils Gorey. F/F. D1. $25.00

GORKY, Maxim. *Life of a Useless Man.* 1972. Andre Deutsch. 1st. NF/dj. P3. $25.00

GORMAN, Ed. *Modern Treasury of Great Detective...* 1984. Carroll Graf. 1st. sgn. F/dj. P3. $27.00

GORMAN, Ed. *Murder Straight Up.* 1986. NY. 1st. F/F. H11. $30.00

GORMAN, John C. *Lee's Last Campaign...Stonewall Jackson's Last Wound.* 1866. Raleigh. WB Smith. 2nd/enlarged. 71p. half leather/marbled brd. NF. M8. $1,750.00

GORMAN & GREENBERG. *Solved.* 1991. Carroll Graf. 1st. F/dj. P3. $22.00

GORMAN & GREENBERG. *Stalkers.* 1989. Dark Harvest. 1st. 1/750. sgn/#d. F/case. P3. $90.00

GORNICK, Vivian. *In Search of Ali Mahmould. An American Woman in Egypt.* 1973. Dutton. 1st. 8vo. 343p. VG. W1. $10.00

GORSKI & WHALEN. *Brain & Behavior: Brain & Donadal Function.* 1966. Berkeley, CA. tall 8vo. 290p. tan/red bdg. G1. $40.00

GORZALKA, Ann. *Saddlemakers of Sheridan, Wyoming.* 1984. Pruett. 1st. photos. 91p. VG. J2. $295.00

GOSLING, Paula. *Fair Game.* 1978. CMG. 1st. author's 1st novel. F/F. M23. $45.00

GOSLINGA, Cornelis C. *Dutch in the Caribbean & on the Wild Coast 1580-1680.* 1971. Gainesville. thick 8vo. 12 fld maps/map ep. F/dj. O7. $55.00

GOSNER, Kenneth. *Working Decoys of the Jersey Coast & Delaware Valley.* 1985. Phil. 184p+16p mc pl. M/dj. A17. $27.50

GOSSE, Philip. *History of Piracy.* 1976. Detroit. Gale. rpt. 4 maps. F. O7. $35.00

GOSWAMI, Amil. *Cosmic Dancers.* 1983. Harper. 1st. F/dj. M2. $18.00

GOTHEIN, Marie Luise. *History of Garden Art.* 1928. London. Dent. 2 vol. A10. $350.00

GOTLIEB, Judy. *Wife of...: An Irreverent Account of Life in Washington.* 1985. Toronto. Macmillan. 1st. F/F. T12. $20.00

GOTLIEB, Phyllis. *O Master Caliban!* 1976. Harper Row. 1st. F/dj. P3. $20.00

GOTSHALL, D.W. *Marine Animals of Baja California.* 1982. Los Osos. Sea Challengers. 112p. NF/wrp. B1. $18.50

GOTTEHRER, Barry. *Giants of New York.* 1963. Putnam. 1st. photos/records/stats. VG/G+. P8. $30.00

GOTTLIEB, Hinko. *Key to the Great Gate.* 1947. S&S. 1st. F/dj. M2. $10.00

GOTTLIEB, Phyllis. *Heart of Red Iron.* 1989. St Martin. 1st. F/dj. M2. $17.00

GOUCOT & GRAY. *Historical Biogeography...* 1979. OR State. 500p. F/dj. D8. $55.00

GOUDEY, Alice E. *Here Come the Elephants!* 1955. Scribner. 1st. ils MacKenzie. VG/G+. C8. $15.00

GOUDGE, Elizabeth. *Castle on the Hill.* 1949 (1942). London. Duckworth. sm 8vo. 296p. VG/dj. T5. $30.00

GOUDGE, Elizabeth. *Dean's Watch.* (1960). Coward McCann. 8vo. ils AR Whitear. 383p. G+. T5. $30.00

GOUDGE, Elizabeth. *Little White Horse.* 1946. London. 1st. sm 8vo. VG. M5. $120.00

GOUGH, Barry M. *Northwest Coast: British Navigation, Trade & Discoveries...* 1992. Vancouver. 8vo. 265p. P4. $45.00

GOUGH, J.W. *Fundamental Law in English Constitutional History.* 1955. Clarendon. M11. $85.00

GOUGH, John. *Memoirs of Life, Religious Experiences & Labors...* 1886. Phil. Friends Bookstore. 149p. VG. V3. $14.00

GOUGH, Laurence. *Hot Shots.* 1989. Gollancz. 1st. NF/NF. P3. $22.00

GOUGH, Laurence. *Hot Shots.* 1989. Viking. 1st. rem mk. as new/dj. N4. $15.00

GOULART, Ron. *Brinkman.* 1981. Doubleday. 1st. NF/dj. M2. $20.00

GOULART, Ron. *Broke Down Engine.* 1971. Macmillan. 1st. VG/VG. P3. $30.00

GOULART, Ron. *Cowboy Heaven.* 1979. Doubleday. 1st. F/dj. M2. $20.00

GOULART, Ron. *Land of Terror.* 1933. Street Smith. 1st. F. M2. $175.00

GOULART, Ron. *Odd Job #101.* 1975. Scribner. 1st. F/dj. P3. $20.00

GOULD, C.N. *Covered Wagon Geologist.* 1959. Norman. 282p. VG. D8. $25.00

GOULD, Chester. *Dick Tracy.* 1943. Whitman. ils. VG/VG. S13. $30.00

GOULD, Frank W. *Grasses of Texas.* 1975. College Sta. 1st. inscr. ils/map. F/dj. B26. $62.50

GOULD, John. *Monstrous Depravity.* 1963. Morrow. G/dj. A16. $10.00

GOULD, Lewis. *Wyoming, a Political History 1868-1896.* 1968. Yale. 1st. map ep. VG/VG. J2. $65.00

GOULD, Nat. *Fast As the Wind.* 1918. AL Burt. 265p. cloth. VG/ragged. M20. $15.00

GOULD, Rupert T. *Oddities: A Book of Unexplained Facts.* 1965. University Books. 1st. 228p. cloth. VG/clip. M20. $22.00

GOULD, S.J. *Bully for Brontasaurus Reflections in Natural History.* 1991. Norton. 1st. 540p. F/dj. D8. $22.00

GOULD, Stephen J. *Wonderful Life.* 1989. NY. 347p. F/NF. S15. $13.00

GOULDEN, Shirley. *Royal Book of Ballet.* 1962. Follett. 2nd. folio. F/VG. M5. $20.00

GOULDING, M. *Fishes & the Forest.* 1980. Berkeley. 379p. dj. B1. $20.00

GOULDSBURY, G.E. *Tiger Slayer by Order.* 1916. London. Chapman Hall. 2nd. tall 8vo. 240p. gilt bl cloth. VG. H7. $65.00

GOURARD, Aimee. *Moon-Madness.* 1928. Broadway. VG. M2. $25.00

GOVER, Robert. *Here Goes Kitten.* 1964. Grove. 1st. sgn. F/F. B11. $65.00

GOVERNMENT PRINTING OFFICE. *Annual Report of Secretary of Navy for Year 1863.* 1863. WA, DC. 1st. 1109p. later cloth. xl. VG. M8. $65.00

GOVERNMENT PRINTING OFFICE. *Bibliography of State Participation in Civil War 1861-66.* 1913. WA, DC. 3rd/enlarged. 1140. later cloth. NF. M8. $450.00

GOVERNMENT PRINTING OFFICE. *Condition of Affairs in the Southern States.* 1871. WA, DC. 1st. 426p. later cloth. NF. M8. $45.00

GOVERNMENT PRINTING OFFICE. *Effects of Atomic Weapons.* Los Alamos. 1950. 456p. VG/wrp. E6. $35.00

GOVERNMENT PRINTING OFFICE. *Index to the Official Records.* 1901. WA. 1st. 1242p. O8. $75.00

GOVERNMENT PRINTING OFFICE. *Instructions for Voluntary Observers of Signal Service.* 1882. 108p. gilt blk cloth. VG. K7. $20.00

GOVERNMENT PRINTING OFFICE. *Low Dams.* 1939. 1st. 8vo. 421p. VG. A8. $20.00

GOVERNMENT PRINTING OFFICE. *Poisonous Snakes of the World.* 1965. WA. 212p. G. B1. $25.00

GOVERNMENT PRINTING OFFICE. *Report of Adjutant General of State of Arkansas...1866.* 1867. WA, DC. 1st. 278p. later cloth. VG. M8. $150.00

GOVERNMENT PRINTING OFFICE. *Report of the Secretary of War 1865.* 1865. WA, DC. 1st. 2 vol. later cloth. VG. M8. $125.00

GOVERNMENT PRINTING OFFICE. *Report on Treatment of Prisoners of War by Rebel Authorities...* 1869. WA, DC. 1st. 1205p. later cloth. xl. VG. M8. $65.00

GOVERNMENT PRINTING OFFICE. *Testimony Taken...To Inquire...Affairs of Late Insurrection.* 1872. 14 vol. 1st. 8vo. contemporary half brn calf. VG. C6. $750.00

GOWER, Charlotte. *Northern & Southern Afflictions on Antillean Culture.* 1927. Menasha, WI. Am Anthrop Assn Memoirs 35. 4to. 60p. wrp. F3. $30.00

GOWERS, William R. *Border-Land of Epilepsy: Faints, Vagal Attacks, Vertigo...* 1907. Phil. Blakiston's Son. 1st Am. 122p. gilt emb gr cloth. VG. G1. $150.00

GOWERS, William R. *Lectures on Diagnosis of Diseases of Brain...* 1887. Phil. Blakiston. 2nd revised/1st Am prt. 254p. olive cloth. NF. G1. $175.00

GOWERS, William R. *Subjective Sensations of Sight & Sound, Abiotraphy...* 1904. Phil. Blakiston. 1st Am. 250p+32p catalog. gr cloth. G1. $150.00

GOWING, Margaret. *Britain & Atomic Energy 1939-1945.* 1965. London. Macmillan. 2nd. ils. 464p. VG/dj. K3. $45.00

GOYEN, William. *Arcadio.* 1983. Potter. 1st. F/NF. A24. $25.00

GOYNE, Richard. *Overnight.* 1953. London. Stanley Paul. 1st. F/F. M15. $45.00

GRACE, Peter. *Polo.* 1991. NY. 1st Am. VG/VG. O3. $40.00

GRACQ, Julien. *Balcony in the Forest.* 1959. Braziller. 1st. F/NF. B2. $30.00

GRADY, James. *Six Days of the Condor.* 1974. Norton. 1st. VG/NF. M22. $40.00

GRADY, James. *Steeltown.* 1989. Bantam. 1st. VG/VG. P3. $20.00

GRAFTON, C.W. *My Name Is Christopher Nagel.* 1947. Rinehart. 1st. F/VG. B4. $200.00

GRAFTON, Sue. *A Is for Alibi.* 1982. HRW. 1st. F/3 sm closed tears. P3. $700.00

GRAFTON, Sue. *A Is for Alibi.* 1982. HRW. 1st. sgn. author's 3rd book. F/F. D10. $1,250.00

GRAFTON, Sue. *B Is for Burglar.* 1985. HRW. 1st. F/NF. Q1. $750.00

GRAFTON, Sue. *C Is for Corpse.* May 1986. Holt. ARC. inscr twice/sgn/dtd 1986. VG. M22. $225.00

GRAFTON, Sue. *C Is for Corpse.* 1986. NY. Holt. ARC. F/wht glossy wrp. D10. $275.00

GRAFTON, Sue. *D Is for Deadbeat.* 1987. Holt. 1st sgn. F/dj. from $280 to $325.00

GRAFTON, Sue. *E Is for Evidence.* 1988. HRW. 1st. F/F. M15. $150.00

GRAFTON, Sue. *F Is for Fugitive.* 1989. Holt. ARC. sgn/dtd 1989. NF/wrp. B3. $100.00

GRAFTON, Sue. *F Is for Fugitive.* 1989. Holt. 1st. NF/F. B2. $50.00

GRAFTON, Sue. *F Is for Fugitive.* 1989. Holt. 1st. F/F. D10. $65.00

GRAFTON, Sue. *F Is for Fugitive.* 1989. Holt. 1st. sgn. F/F. A23. $90.00

GRAFTON, Sue. *G Is for Gumshoe.* 1990. Holt. 1st. sgn. F/F. A23/A24. $60.00

GRAFTON, Sue. *G Is for Gumshoe.* 1990. HRW. 1st. F/F. B2. $35.00

GRAFTON, Sue. *H Is for Homicide.* 1991. HRW. 1st. sgn. F/F. A23/A24. $50.00

GRAFTON, Sue. *H Is for Homicide.* 1991. London. Macmillan. 1st Eng. F/dj. Q1. $40.00

GRAFTON, Sue. *H Is for Homocide.* 1991. Holt. 1st. F/F. M15. $35.00

GRAFTON, Sue. *I Is for Innocent.* 1992. Holt. 1st. F/dj. from $25 to $30.00

GRAFTON, Sue. *I Is for Innocent.* 1992. Holt. 1st. sgn. F/F. from $40 to $50.00

GRAFTON, Sue. *I Is for Innocent.* 1992. London. Macmillan. 1st Eng. F/NF. Q1. $35.00

GRAFTON, Sue. *J Is for Judgement.* 1993. Holt. 1st. NF/clip. P3. $25.00

GRAFTON, Sue. *J Is for Judgement.* 1993. Holt. 1st. sgn. F/F. from $40 to $50.00

GRAFTON, Sue. *J Is for Judgement.* 1993. London. Macmillan. 1st Eng. F/dj. Q1. $40.00

GRAFTON, Sue. *K Is for Killer.* 1994. Holt. 1st. VG/VG. P3. $20.00

GRAFTON, Sue. *K Is for Killer.* 1994. Holt. 1st. sgn. F/F. A23/A24. $40.00

GRAFTON, Sue. *Keziah Dane.* 1967. Macmillan. 1st. author's 1st book. F/F. H11. $750.00

GRAHAM, Anthony. *Death Business.* 1967. Boardman. 1st. VG/VG. P3. $25.00

GRAHAM, Billy. *Hope for the Troubled Heart.* 1991. Word. 230p. F/dj. B29. $7.50

GRAHAM, David. *Down to the Sunless Sea.* 1981. S&S. 1st. F/dj. M2. $12.00

GRAHAM, Don. *No Name on the Bullet.* 1989. NY. 1st. VG/VG. B5. $42.50

GRAHAM, Duff. *How Peter Rabbit Went to Sea.* 1935 (1917). Platt Munk. lg 24mo. F/VG+. C8. $75.00

GRAHAM, Ethel. *Creative Wok Cooking.* 1976. Weathervane. VG/dj. A16. $15.00

GRAHAM, James; see Patterson, Henry.

GRAHAM, Otto. *Otto Graham: T Quarterback.* 1963. Prentice Hall. 1st. photos. VG. P8. $25.00

GRAHAM, R.B. Cunninghame. *Horses of the Conquest.* 1949. Norman, OK. edit RM Denhardt. ils JC Sheppard. F/dj. O7. $75.00

GRAHAM, R.B. Cunninghame. *Mogreb-El-Acksa. A Journey to Morocco.* 1930. Viking. 1st. 8vo. 358p. VG. W1. $12.00

GRAHAM, Robert; see Haldeman, Joe.

GRAHAM, Sheilah. *Garden of Allah.* 1970. Crown. 1st. F/NF. H11. $40.00

GRAHAM, Shirley. *There Was Once a Slave.* 1947. Messner. 1st. NF/remnant. M25. $15.00

GRAHAM, Tim. *Royal Review.* 1984. Michael Joseph. 1st. F/F. T12. $40.00

GRAHAM, Victor. *Growing Succulent Plants.* 1987. Newton Abbot. Devon. 200p. VG/dj. B26. $35.00

GRAHAM, W.A. *Custer Myth.* 1953. Stackpole. dj. A19. $40.00

GRAHAM, W.A. *Story of the Little Big Horn.* 1926. Century. 1st. 174p. VG/VG. J2. $265.00

GRAHAM, Whidden. *Crimson Hairs: An Erotic Mystery.* 1970. Grove. 1st. F/dj. P3. $20.00

GRAHAM, Winston. *Merciless Ladies.* 1979. Bodley Head. 1st. VG/dj. P3. $20.00

GRAHAM, Winston. *Woman in the Mirror.* 1975. Bodley Head. 1st. VG/VG. P3. $18.00

GRAHAM & GRAHAM. *Only Human.* 1932. Vanguard. 1st. F/NF. B4. $275.00

GRAHAM & MCMINN. *Ornamental Shrubs & Woody Vines of the Pacific Coast.* 1941. Berkeley. ils. 259p. VG/dj. B26. $26.00

GRAHAM & TELEK. *Leaf Protein Concentrates.* 1983. Westport. AVI Pub. 844p. cloth. F. B1. $125.00

GRAHAME, Kenneth. *Bertie's Escapade.* 1949. Lippincott. 1st thus. ils Ernest Shepard. VG+/VG. P2. $65.00

GRAHAME, Kenneth. *Bertie's Escapade.* 1949. Methuen. 1st. ils EH Shepard. 12mo. pink pict brd. dj. R5. $150.00

GRAHAME, Kenneth. *Le Vent Dans les Saules.* 1983. Fernand Nathan. popup. ils Babette Cole. 4to. NF. P2. $35.00

GRAHAME, Kenneth. *Wind in the Willows.* (1929). London. 12mo. heavy gilt tooled full red leather. F. H3. $55.00

GRAHAME, Kenneth. *Wind in the Willows.* 1940. Heritage. 1st thus. ils Rackham/12 full-p mc pl. dj/case. R5. $150.00

GRAHAME, Kenneth. *Wind in the Willows.* 1940. Heritage. 1st thus. ils Rackham. VG+/G. P2. $65.00

GRAHAME, Kenneth. *Wind in the Willows.* 1983. London. Methuen. 1st popup ed. ils Babette Cole. F. T10. $40.00

GRAN, Trggve. *Norwegian With Scott.* 1984. London. Nat Maritime Mus. 1st Eng. 8vo. 258p. F/dj. T10. $35.00

GRAND, Gordon. *Colonel Weatherford & His Friends.* 1991. Derrydale. 1/1450. gilt leather. F. A17. $25.00

GRAND, Gordon. *Millbeck Hounds.* 1947. Scribner. 1st. VG. O3. $40.00

GRAND, Gordon. *Old Man & Other Colonel Weatherford Stories.* 1991. Derrydale. 1/2500. aeg. gilt bdg. F. A17. $25.00

GRANGER, Bill. *British Cross.* 1983. Crown. 1st. F/F. A20. $20.00

GRANGER, Bill. *Hemingway's Notebook.* 1986. Crown. 1st. VG/dj. P3. $16.00

GRANGER, Bill. *Infant of Prague.* 1987. Warner. 1st. VG/dj. P3. $17.00

GRANGER, Bill. *Man Who Heard Too Much.* 1989. Warner. 1st. F/F. N4. $25.00

GRANGER, Bill. *There Are No Spies.* 1986. Warner. 1st. VG/VG. P3. $17.00

GRANGER, Bill. *Zurich Numbers.* 1984. Crown. 1st. F/NF. N4. $25.00

GRANGER, Byrd H. *Grand Canyon Place Names.* 1960. Tucson. 1st. 8vo. stiff magenta wrp. F7. $10.00

GRANICH, Louis. *Guide To Retaining.* 1947. NY. Gurne Stratton. 108p. prt bl-gray cloth. xl. G1. $20.00

GRANOVSKY, Abraham. *Land Policy in Palestine.* 1940. NY. Bloch. 208p. VG/dj. S3. $24.00

GRANT, Anne. *Memoirs of an American Lady: With Sketches of Manners...* 1808. London. 2 vol. 1st. 12mo. teg. 3-quarter leather/raised bands. F. H3. $850.00

GRANT, Bruce. *Cowboy Encyclopedia.* 1951. ils. VG. M17. $17.50

GRANT, Bruce. *Trip in Space.* 1968. Rand McNally. 8vo. 20p. G. K5. $8.00

GRANT, Charles L. *Last Call of Mourning.* 1979. Doubleday. 1st. NF/dj. P3. $80.00

GRANT, Charles L. *Nightmare Seasons.* 1982. Doubleday. 1st. F/dj. P3. $50.00

GRANT, Charles L. *Ravens of the Moon.* 1978. Doubleday. 1st. VG/dj. P3. $20.00

GRANT, Charles L. *Shadows 2.* 1979. Doubleday. 1st. NF/dj. P3. $25.00

GRANT, Charles L. *Sound of Midnight.* 1978. Doubleday. 1st. F/dj. P3. $30.00

GRANT, Hugh Duncan. *Cloud & Weather Atlas.* 1944. Coward McCann. 4to. 294p. G/dj. K5. $65.00

GRANT, Joan. *Lord of the Horizon.* 1948. London. F/dj. M2. $15.00

GRANT, Joan. *Winged Pharoah.* 1938. Harper. 1st. VG. M2. $20.00

GRANT, John W. *Watt & the Steam Age.* 1917. London. St Bride. sgn. K3. $25.00

GRANT, Michael. *Founders of the Western World.* 1991. Scribner. 1st. F/dj. P3. $28.00

GRANT, Michael. *Rise of the Greeks.* 1988. Scribner. 1st. F/F. P3. $28.00

GRANT, P.J. *Gulls: A Guide to Identification.* 1982. Vermillion. photos. 280p. xl. VG. S15. $20.00

GRANT, Robert. *History of Physical Astronomy.* nd (1852). London. Henry Bohn. inscr/dtd 1869. 637p. gilt full leather. VG. K5. $150.00

GRANT, Roderick. *Private Vendetta.* 1978. Scribner. 1st. F/dj. P3. $15.00

GRANT, Ulysses S. *Personal Memoirs of US Grant. Edited With Notes...EB Long.* 1952. NY. World. 1st thus. 608p. cloth. NF/VG. M8. $35.00

GRANT, Verne. *Plant Speciation.* 1971. NY. ils/figures. 435p. dj. B26. $37.50

GRANT, Vernon. *Tinker Tim, the Toy Maker.* 1934. Whitman. 1st. ils Vernon Grant. 29p. pict brd. VG/VG. D1. $200.00

GRANVILLE, A.B. *Spas of England/Principal Sea-Bathing Places.* 1971 (1841). Bath. Adams Dart. 2 vol. facsimile. 8vo. F/djs. H13. $185.00

GRASS, Gunther. *Cat & Mouse.* 1963. HBW. 1st Am. 189p. VG/dj. M20. $30.00

GRASS, Gunther. *Dog Years.* 1963. HBW. 1st. NF/NF. B35. $25.00

GRASS, Gunther. *Flounder.* 1977. HBJ. 1st. NF/dj. B35. $20.00

GRASS, Gunther. *Local Anaesthetic.* 1970. HBW. 1st. F/F. B35. $32.00

GRASS, Gunther. *Meeting at Telgte.* 1981. NY. 1st. trans R Manheim. VG/dj. T9. $15.00

GRASS, Gunther. *Rat.* 1986. HBJ. 1st. F/F. B35. $32.00

GRASSI, Joseph S. *Grassi Block Substitution Test for Measuring Organic...* 1953. Springfield, IL. Chas Thomas. sm 8vo. flexible blk cloth. 75p. G1. $17.50

GRATACAP, L.P. *Benjamin the Jew.* 1913. NY. ils Thomas Benton. 492p. VG. S3. $25.00

GRATTAN-SMITH, T.E. *Cave of a Thousand Columns.* 1938. London. 1st. VG. M2. $25.00

GRAU, Shirley Ann. *House on Coliseum Street.* 1961. Knopf. 1st. author's 2nd novel. NF/dj. D10. $65.00

GRAU, Shirley Ann. *Keepers of the House.* 1964. Knopf. inscr/dtd 1964. author's 3rd novel. F/NF. D10. $85.00

GRAU, Shirley Ann. *Keepers of the House.* 1964. Knopf. 1st. NF/NF. M23. $50.00

GRAU, Shirley Ann. *Wind Shifting West.* 1973. Knopf. 1st. NF/dj. Q1. $35.00

GRAUMONT, Raoul. *Encyclopedia of Knots & Fancy Rope Work.* 1970. Cambridge, MD. Cornell Maritime. A19. $45.00

GRAVELL & MILLER. *Catalogue of American Watermarks 1690-1835.* 1979. 4to. ils/checklist. 253p. F. A4. $250.00

GRAVELL & MILLER. *Catalogue of Foreign Watermarks Found on Paper...1700-1835.* 1983. rto. ils. 305p. F. A4. $195.00

GRAVER, Elizabeth. *Have You Seen Me?* 1991. Pittsburgh. 1st. author's 1st book. F/NF. R13. $25.00

GRAVES, Charles Burr. *Catalogue of the Flowering Plants & Ferns of Connecticut.* 1910. Hartford. 1st. 8vo. 567p. xl. A22. $40.00

GRAVES, Henry S. *Principles of Handling Woodlands.* 1911. NY. 1st. 1/1000. ils. 325p. xl. B26. $35.00

GRAVES, J.A. *California Memories 1857-1930.* 1930. Times-Mirror. 1st. VG. O4. $20.00

GRAVES, J.A. *My Seventy Years in California 1857-1927.* 1927. Los Angeles. Times-Mirror. 1st. VG. O4. $20.00

GRAVES, J.A. *Out of Doors in California & Oregon.* 1912. Los Angeles. inscr. 122p. O8. $21.50

GRAVES, John. *Last Running.* 1974. Austin. Encino Pr. ils John Groth. 47p. brd/cloth spine. D11. $50.00

GRAVES, Richard. *Spiritual Quizote; or, Summer's Ramble...* 1783. London. Dodsley. 3 vol. new/corrected/improved. lg 12mo. ils Grignion. H13. $395.00

GRAVES, Robert. *Ann at Highwood Hall, Poems for Children.* 1964. London. Cassell. 1st. gilt bl brd. F. M24. $75.00

GRAVES, Robert. *Claudius the God.* 1935. Smith Haas. 1st. G+. P3. $25.00

GRAVES, Robert. *Collected Poems (1914-1947).* 1948. London. Cassell. 1st. 1/2962. gilt bl cloth. F/NF. M24. $125.00

GRAVES, Robert. *Collected Poems.* 1961. Doubleday. 1st. F/F. B35. $32.00

GRAVES, Robert. *Isles of Unwisdom.* 1950. London. Cassell. 1st Eng. 1/14988. gilt blk cloth. F/dj. M24. $65.00

GRAVES, Robert. *Man Does, Woman Is.* 1964. Doubleday. 1st Am. NF/VG+. T11. $60.00

GRAVES, Robert. *More Poems.* 1961. London. Cassell. 1st. 1/3913. gilt red cloth. F/NF. M24. $45.00

GRAVES, Robert. *Mrs Fisher; or, The Future of Humour.* 1928. London. Kegan Paul. 1st. magenta brd. VG. M24. $50.00

GRAVES, Robert. *New Poems.* 1963. Doubleday. 1st Am. NF/clip. D10. $35.00

GRAVES, Robert. *No More Ghosts.* 1940. London. Faber. 1st. 1/2000. tan prt brd. F/dj. M24. $100.00

GRAVES, Robert. *Poems, 1926-1930.* 1931. London. Heinemann. 1st. 1/1000. decor brd. F. M24. $75.00

GRAVES, Robert. *Poems (1914-26).* 1927. London. Heinemann. 1st. 1/1000. VG/dj. Q1. $500.00

GRAVES, Robert. *Poor Boy Who Followed His Star & Children's Poems.* 1968. Doubleday. 1st Am. 43p. cloth. F/F. D4. $175.00

GRAVES, Robert. *Sergeant Lamb of the Ninth.* 1940. London. Methuen. 1st. 1/10,000. wht lettered red cloth. F. M24. $45.00

GRAVES, Robert. *Sergeant Lamb of the Ninth.* 1940. Methuen. 1st. VG. P3. $30.00

GRAVES, Robert. *Sergeant Lamb's America.* 1940. NY. 1st. 380p. map ep. VG+/dj. B18. $37.50

GRAVES, Robert. *Treasure Box.* nd (1919). London. Chiswick. 1st. 1/200. inscr. F/clamshell box. Q1. $3,000.00

GRAVES, Robert. *Wife to Mr Milton.* 1944. Creative Age. 1st Am. F/NF. B2. $35.00

GRAVES, Valerie; see Bradley, Marion Zimmer.

GRAVESON, S. *History of Life of Thomas Ellwood...* 1906. London. Headley Bros. 372p. V3. $28.00

GRAY, A.W. *Man Offside.* 1991. Dutton. 1st. VG/VG. P3. $20.00

GRAY, Charles Wright. *Sporting Spirit: An Anthology.* 1925. NY. 1st. 319p. gilt cloth. A17. $30.00

GRAY, David F. *Lectures on Spectral-Line Analysis: F, G & K Stars.* 1988. Arva, ON, Canada. The Pub. 328p. VG. K5. $30.00

GRAY, Elizabeth Janet. *Adam of the Road.* 1942. Viking. 1st. ils Marguerite DeAngeli. 317p. NF/VG. P2. $125.00

GRAY, Elizabeth Janet. *Cheerful Heart.* 1959. Viking. 1st. 176p. xl. dj. V3. $8.50

GRAY, Elizabeth Janet. *I Will Adventure.* 1962. Viking. 1st. 208p. VG/G. V3. $15.00

GRAY, Henry. *Gray's Anatomy.* 1977. Bounty. Classic Collector. 1257p. F/NF. W2. $250.00

GRAY, James Kendricks;   see Fox, Gardener F.

GRAY, James. *Intro to Arithmetic.* 1827. Edinburgh. 26th. 108p. 16mo. full leather. G. A17. $20.00

GRAY, John P. *Responsibility of the Insane. Homicide of Insanity.* 1875. Utica. 57p. wrp. B14. $100.00

GRAY, Joseph. *Navajo Sunrise.* 1976. Corte Madera, CA. Omega. sgn. 166p. VG. K7. $15.00

GRAY, Millicent Ethelreda. *Treasure Book of Children's Verse.* nd. Doran. 20 mtd mc pl. F. M5. $95.00

GRAYSMITH, Robert. *Sleeping Lady.* 1990. Dutton. 1st. VG/VG. P3. $20.00

GRAZIANO, Rocky. *Somebody Down Here Likes Me Too.* 1981. Stein Day. 1st. photos. F/VG+. P8. $20.00

GREAVES, Griselda. *Burning Thorn.* 1971. Macmillan. ARC/1st. 201p. cloth. F/NF. D4. $35.00

GREBANIER, Bernard. *Great Shakespeare Forgery.* 1965. Norton. ils. 8vo. 308p. xl. dj. K3. $20.00

GREELEY, Andrew. *Happy Are the Merciful.* 1992. Jove. 1st. F/F. W2. $30.00

GREELEY, Horace. *American Conflict: History of Great Rebellion in USA...* 1869. Hartford. OD Case. 1st. 2 vol. cloth. NF. M8. $125.00

GREELY, Adolphus W. *Handbook of Polar Discoveries.* 1910. Boston. 5th/revised/enlarged. 336p+maps. G. A17. $30.00

GREELY, Adolphus W. *Report on Proceedings US Expedition to Lady Franklin Bay...* 1888. GPO. 2 vol. 4to. blk cloth. P4. $500.00

GREEN, Anna Katharine. *Chief Legatee.* 1916. Dodd Mead. 1st. VG. P3. $50.00

GREEN, Anna Katharine. *Circular Study.* 1902. Ward Lock. 1st. decor brd. VG. P3. $60.00

GREEN, Anna Katharine. *Filigree Ball.* 1902. Bobbs Merrill. 1st. NF. P3. $60.00

GREEN, Arthur. *Tormented Maste: Life of Rabbi Nahman of Bratslav.* 1979. AL U. 395p. S3. $26.00

GREEN, Ben K. *Horse Conformation.* 1982. Northland. VG/VG. O3. $25.00

GREEN, Ben K. *Last Trail Drive Through Downtown Dallas.* 1971. Northland. 1/100. sgn Beeler/Green. half leather. as new. J2. $1,200.00

GREEN, C.E. *Plant Tissue & Cell Culture.* 1987. NY. ils/index. F. B26. $36.00

GREEN, Garrett. *Imagining God: Theology & the Religious Imagination.* 1980s. Harper. 1st. 179p. VG/dj. B29. $11.50

GREEN, Gate. *Night Angel.* 1989. Delacorte. 1st. F/NF. N4. $17.50

GREEN, George Dawes. *Caveman's Valentine.* 1994. Warner. 1st. F/F. N4. $55.00

GREEN, Gerald. *Artists of Terezin.* 1978. Hawthorn. ils. 191p. VG+. S3. $50.00

GREEN, Gerald. *Last Angry Man.* 1956. 1st. author's 1st book. VG/VG. S13. $25.00

GREEN, Gilbert G. *Cacti & Succulents.* 1953. London. 17 mc pl/166 photos/ils. 240p. B26. $25.00

GREEN, Hannah. *In the City of Paris.* 1980. Doubleday. 1st. sm 4to. F/VG+. C8. $45.00

GREEN, Henry. *Back.* 1946. London. 1st. author's 6th novel. VG+/VG. A11. $125.00

GREEN, J. *Sasquatch: Apes Among Us.* 1978. Seattle. Hancock. ils/map/photo. 492p. F/F. M12. $37.50

GREEN, Joseph. *Conscience Interplanetary.* 1973. Doubleday. 1st. F/dj. P3. $15.00

GREEN, Judith. *Laughing Souls.* 1969. San Diego Mus of Man. 1st. 4to. 27p. wrp. F3. $10.00

GREEN, N.W. *Mormonism Rise Progress.* 1870. Hartford. 1st. 472p. 3-quarter leather. B5. $50.00

GREEN, Peter. *Kenneth Grahame.* 1959. World. 1st. 400p. VG/VG. D1. $45.00

GREEN, Roger Lancelyn. *Andrew Lang; Critical Biography With Short Title Biblio...* 1946. Leicester, England. ils. 276p. NF/VG. A4. $65.00

GREEN, S.G. *Pictures From Bible Lands.* 1879. ils Edward Whymper/others. VG. M17. $25.00

GREEN, Thomas Andrew. *Verdict According to Conscience, Perspectives on English...* 1985. Chicago. M11. $45.00

GREEN, Thomas J. *Flowered Box.* 1980. Beaufort. 1st. VG/dj. P3. $15.00

GREEN, Thomas. *John Woolman: A Study for Young Men.* 1885. Manchester. Brook Chrystal. 126p. VG. V3. $14.00

GREEN, William M. *Salisbury Manuscript.* 1973. Bobbs Merrill. 1st. F/dj. P3. $15.00

GREEN & HIRSBERG. *High Stick.* 1971. Dodd Mead. 1st. photos. VG/dj. P8. $27.50

GREEN & WRIGHT. *Native Son: A Play.* 1941. Harper. 1st. VG/dj. M25. $200.00

GREENAWAY, Kate. *Almanack for 1884.* nd. London. Routledge. 1st. 12mo. professionally rpr spine. G+. P2. $90.00

GREENAWAY, Kate. *Kate Greenaway Pictures.* 1921. London. Warne. 1st. VG/torn. D1. $300.00

GREENAWAY, Kate. *Language of Flowers.* nd. Routledge. 1st. 12mo. VG. M5. $95.00

GREENBERG, Eric Rolfe. *Celebrant.* 1983. Everest. 1st. F/F. B4. $250.00

GREENBERG, Martin H. *Dawn of Time.* 1979. Elsevier/Nelson. 1st. F/dj. M2. $15.00

GREENBERG & GREENBERG. *Whiskey in the Kitchen.* 1968. Weathervane. G/dj. A16. $12.00

GREENBERG & GREENBERG. *Whiskey in the Kitchen: Lively Art of Cooking...* 1968. Bobbs Merrill. 1st. 315p. VG/G. B10. $25.00

GREENBLATT, Milton H. *Studies in Lobotomy.* 1950. NY. Grune Stratton. heavy 8vo. ils. 495p. pebbled red cloth. xl. G1. $50.00

GREENE, F.V. *Mississippi.* 1882. np. 1st. fld maps. O8. $21.50

GREENE, Graham. *Burnt-Out Case.* 1961. London. Heinemann. 1st. F/clip. Q1. $60.00

GREENE, Graham. *Burnt-Out Case.* 1961. Viking. 1st. NF/NF. A11/B35. $45.00

GREENE, Graham. *Captain & the Enemy.* 1988. Toronto. Dennys. 1st. F/NF. A24. $25.00

GREENE, Graham. *Carving a Statue.* 1964. London. Bodley Head. 1st. inscr. F/NF. B4. $1,500.00

GREENE, Graham. *Collected Essays.* 1969. Bodley Head. 1st. NF/VG+. A24. $70.00

GREENE, Graham. *Comedians.* 1966. Bodley Head. 1st. VG+/VG+. A24. $65.00

GREENE, Graham. *Comedians.* 1966. Viking. 1st. VG. P3. $15.00

GREENE, Graham. *Doctor Fischer of Geneva; or, The Bomb Party.* 1980. S&S. 1st Am. F/F. A24/B35. $25.00

GREENE, Graham. *Doctor Fischer of Geneva; or, The Bomb Party.* 1980. S&S. 1st Am. 1/500. sgn. F/case. B4. $350.00

GREENE, Graham. *Doctor Fischer of Geneva; or, The Bomb Party.* 1980. S&S. 1st. NF/NF. P3. $15.00

GREENE, Graham. *End of the Affair.* 1951. Viking. 1st. NF/NF. P3. $100.00

GREENE, Graham. *Essais Catholiques.* 1953. Paris. 1st/only. NF/uncup wrp/pub band. A11. $135.00

GREENE, Graham. *Getting To Know the General.* 1984. Canada. Dennys. 1st. NF/F. A24. $30.00

GREENE, Graham. *Getting To Know the General.* 1984. S&S. 1st. F/F. P3. $18.00

GREENE, Graham. *Heart of the Matter.* 1948. Canada. Viking. 1st. VG. P3. $50.00

GREENE, Graham. *Heart of the Matter.* 1948. Viking. 1st Am/2nd prt before pub. inscr. VG. B4. $950.00

GREENE, Graham. *Human Factor.* 1978. Bodley Head/Clarke Irwin. 1st. VG/dj. P3. $25.00

GREENE, Graham. *In Search of a Character.* 1961. Bodley Head. 1st. F/F. P3. $25.00

GREENE, Graham. *Last Word.* 1990. Toronto. Dennys. 1st Canadian. F/dj. Q1. $40.00

GREENE, Graham. *Little Horse Bus.* 1954. Lee Shepard. 1st. ils Dorothy Craigie. 35p. VG/G. P2. $100.00

GREENE, Graham. *Little Steamroller.* 1974 (1940). Doubleday. 1st Am. obl 8vo. unp. VG/G+. T5. $40.00

GREENE, Graham. *Lord Rochester's Monkey.* 1974. Viking. 1st. 4to. 231p. gilt brn cloth. F/dj. H13. $85.00

GREENE, Graham. *Loser Takes All.* 1955. London. Heinemann. 1st. F/NF. B2. $125.00

GREENE, Graham. *Lost Childhood & Other Essays.* 1951. London. Eyre Spottiswoode. 1st. inscr/dtd 1951. F/NF. B4. $1,950.00

GREENE, Graham. *Monsignor Quixote.* 1982. Lester/Orpen Denys. 1st. G+/dj. P3. $15.00

GREENE, Graham. *Our Man in Havana.* 1958. Heinemann. 1st. VG/VG. A24. $75.00

GREENE, Graham. *Our Man in Havana.* 1958. Viking. 1st Am. F/VG. M22. $75.00

GREENE, Graham. *Quiet American.* 1955. Heinemann. 1st. G+. A24. $50.00

GREENE, Graham. *Shipwrecked.* 1953. Viking. 1st thus. NF/VG. M22. $35.00

GREENE, Graham. *Tenth Man.* 1985. S&S. 1st. F/dj. P3. $20.00

GREENE, Graham. *Travels With My Aunt.* 1969. Bodley Head. 1st. inscr. F/F. B4. $850.00

GREENE, Graham. *Travels With My Aunt.* 1969. London. Bodley Head. 1st. F/dj. Q1. $75.00

GREENE, Harry Washington. *Holders of Doctorates Among American Negroes.* 1946. Boston. Meador. 1st. 275p. NF. B4. $225.00

GREENE, Horace. *General Grant's Last Stand.* 1936. np. 334p. O8. $21.50

GREENE, Hugh. *American Rivals of Sherlock Holmes.* 1976. Bodley Head. 1st. VG/dj. P3. $30.00

GREENE, Hugh. *Victorian Villanies.* 1984. London. 1st. F/dj. M2. $15.00

GREENE, Jacob W. *Greene Brothers' Clinical Course in Dental Prosthesis.* 1910. self pub. 1st. 210p. G+. H1. $45.00

GREENE, Julia. *Flash Back.* 1983. Severn. VG/dj. P3. $20.00

GREENE & MARTIN. *Oz Scrapbook.* 1977. Random. 1st. ils. 182p. VG/dj. P2. $75.00

GREENEWALT, Crawford H. *Hummingbirds.* 1960. NY. Doubleday. 4to. NF. T10. $100.00

GREENEWOOD, Edwin. *Deadly Dowager.* 1937. Doubleday. VG/dj. M2. $25.00

GREENFELD & MAZURSKY. *Harry & Tonto.* 1974. Saturday Review. 1st. NF/NF. B4. $125.00

GREENFIELD, Arthur II. *Anatomy of a Bullfight.* 1961. Longman Gr. 1st. ils. VG. P8. $20.00

GREENFIELD, Eloise. *She Came Bringing Me That Little Baby Girl.* (1974). Lippincott. 8vo. unp. mauve cloth. rem mk. VG+/dj. T5. $20.00

GREENLEAF, Stephen. *Fatal Obsession.* 1983. Dial. 1st. F/F. M15. $45.00

GREENLEAF, Stephen. *Fatal Obsession.* 1983. Dial. 1st. NF/dj. N4. $30.00

GREENLEAF, Stephen. *Toll Call.* 1987. Villard. 1st. F/F. M15. $45.00

GREENLEAF & PENINOU. *Directory of California Wine Growers & Wine Makers in 1860.* 1957. Berkeley, CA. 1st. 1/450. NF. O4. $15.00

GREENMAN, J. *Diary of a Common Soldier in the American Revolution...* 1978. N IL U. ils. 333p. F/dj. M4. $30.00

GREENSBERG, Martin. *Coming Attractions.* 1957. Gnome. 1st. VG/dj. P3. $25.00

GREENSBERG, Martin. *Robot & the Man.* 1953. Gnome. 1st. VG. P3. $25.00

GREENSTEIN, Mrs. Saul. *Flavor of Dubuque.* 1971. Dubuque. dj. A19. $15.00

GREENWALD, Norman. *Mideast in Focus.* 1960. WA. Public Affairs. 1st. 8vo. 86p. cloth. VG. W1. $12.00

GREENWOOD, James. *Philadelphia Vocabulary, English & Latin...* 1787. Phil. Carey. 1st Am. 16mo. 123p. old calf/crudely rebacked. M1. $1,250.00

GREENWOOD, John. *Mists Over Mosley.* 1986. Walker. 1st. F/NF. P3. $18.00

GREENWOOD, L.B. *Sherlock Holmes & the Case of Sabina Hall.* 1988. S&S. 1st. VG/dj. P3. $20.00

GREENWOOD, Marianne. *Tattooed Heart of Livingston.* 1965. Stein Day. 1st. 187p. dj. F3. $20.00

GREENWOOD, Robert. *California Imprints 1833-1862: A Bibliography.* 1961. Los Gatos. Talisman. 1/750. facsimile ils. red cloth. NF. R3. $100.00

GREER, Germaine. *Female Eunuch.* 1971. McGraw Hill. 1st Am. NF/VG. R14. $35.00

GREER, Germaine. *Female Eunuch.* 1971. McGraw Hill. 1st. author's 1st book. F/NF. H11. $80.00

GREER, H.E. *Greer's Guide Book to Available Rhododendrons...* 1982. Eugene. Offshoot. 152p. G/pict wrp. $28.00

GREER & WARD. *Richmond During the Revolution 1775-83.* 1977. VA U. ils/map. F/dj. M4. $25.00

GREGG, Joshua. *Commerce of the Prairies.* 1968. Citadel. rpt. VG/G. O3. $45.00

GREGG, Linda. *Sacraments of Desire.* 1991. Graywolf. 1st. sgn. F/dj. V1. $30.00

GREGOIRE, Henri-Baptiste. *Historie du Mariage des Pretres en France...1789.* 1826. Paris. Baudouin. 1st. 8vo. cloth. R12. $485.00

GREGOIRE, Henri-Baptiste. *Rapport Sur la Bibliographie.* 1794. Paris. Quiber-Pallissaux. 8vo. stitched. R12. $375.00

GREGOIRE, Henri-Baptiste. *Rapport Sur les Encouragemens, Recompenses et Pensions...* 1795. Paris. Imprimerie Nationale. 8vo. wrp. R12. $200.00

GREGOIRE. *Rapport Sur la Necessite & les Moyens d'Aneantir Patois...* 1794. Paris. Imprimerie Nationale. 8vo. caption title. stitched. R12. $285.00

GREGORY, Dick. *Dick Gregory's Political Primer.* 1972. Harper Row. 1st. NF/dj. M25. $35.00

GREGORY, Dick. *No More Lies: Myth & Reality of American History.* 1971. Harper Row. 1st. NF/dj. M25. $35.00

GREGORY, Joseph W. *Gregory's Guide for California Travellers via Isthmus...* 1949. BC of CA. 1/300. 8vo. ils. F/pict orange cloth. w/prospectus. R3. $75.00

GREGORY, Lady. *Spreading the News, a Play in One Act.* 1904. NY. John Quinn. 1st. 1/50. sgn. F/wrp. B24. $950.00

GREGORY, Olinthus. *Lessons, Astronomical & Philosophical...* 1824 (1793). London. Holdsworth. 6th. 330p. half leather/marbled brd. K5. $110.00

GREGORY & ZATURENSKA. *Crystal Cabinet.* 1962. HRW. 1st. 225p. cloth. F/NF. D4. $35.00

GREGORY & ZATURENSKA. *Silver Swan.* 1966. HRW. 1st. 221p. F/NF. D4. $35.00

GRENDON, Stephen; see Derleth, August.

GRESHAM, William Lindsay. *Nightmare Alley.* 1946. NY. 1st. w/sgn letter dtd 1959. VG/VG+. A11. $100.00

GRESHAM, William Lindsay. *Nightmare Alley.* 1946. Rinehart. 1st. VG. M2. $17.00

GRESS, Kathryn. *Ninety Years Cow Country, a Factural History of Wyoming...* 1963. WY Stock Growers Assn. 1st. 85p. VG/wrp. J2. $85.00

GREY, Harry. *Hoods.* 1952. Crown. 1st. F/VG+. B4. $250.00

GREY, Zane. *Black Mesa.* 1955. Harper. 1st. NF/dj. P3. $25.00

GREY, Zane. *Fighting Caravans.* 1929. Toronto. Musson. 1st. inscr/dtd 1931. G. T12. $100.00

GREY, Zane. *Fighting Caravans.* 1930. Grosset Dunlap. 1st thus/photoplay. VG. M2. $25.00

GREY, Zane. *Ken Ward in the Jungle.* 1912. Grosset Dunlap. A19. $20.00

GREY, Zane. *Light of Western Stars.* 1914. Grosset Dunlap. A19. $15.00

GREY, Zane. *Nevada.* 1928. Harper. 1st. VG. P3. $40.00

GREY, Zane. *Redheaded Outfield & Other Baseball Stories.* 1920. Grosset Dunlap. 1st. NF/dj. B4. $150.00

GREY, Zane. *Redheaded Outfield & Other Baseball Stories.* 1920. Grosset Dunlap. 238p. VG/dj. M20. $125.00

GREY, Zane. *Redheaded Outfield & Other Baseball Stories.* 1948. Grosset Dunlap. 238p. VG/dj. B18. $45.00

GREY, Zane. *Reef Girl.* 1977. NY. 1st. VG/VG. B5. $35.00

GREY, Zane. *Roping Lions in the Grand Canyon.* (1922). Grosset Dunlap. 1st. NF. T12. $100.00

GREY, Zane. *Tales of Southern Rivers.* (1924). Grosset Dunlap. rpt from Harper 1st ed pl. 4to. 249p. VG/dj. H7. $75.00

GREY, Zane. *Tales of Southern Rivers.* 1924. Grosset Dunlap. 249p. VG+/rpr. M20. $95.00

GREY, Zane. *Tales of Swordfish & Tuna.* 1991. Derrydale. 1st thus. 1/2500. sgn/#d by Grey's son. leather. F. Q1. $75.00

GREY, Zane. *Thundering Herd.* 1925. Grosset Dunlap. VG+. M2. $40.00

GREY, Zane. *Vanishing American.* 1925. Canada. Musson. 1st. VG/fair. P3. $35.00

GREY, Zane. *Wanderer of the Wasteland.* 1923. Harper. 1st. VG. M2. $35.00

GREY, Zane. *Wanderer of the Wasteland.* 1923. NY. Harper. 1st. VG/VG. B5. $60.00

GREY, Zane. *Young Pitcher.* 1911. Grosset Dunlap. 248p+ads. cloth. VG/dj. M20. $50.00

GREY, Zane. *Zane Grey Fishing Library.* 1990-91. 1st ltd of 2500 10-vol sets. sgn Grey's son. leather. A18. $750.00

GRIERSON, H.J.C. *William Blake's Designs for Gray's Poems Reproduced...* 1922. Oxford. 1st. 1/650. folio. 122 pl. rust cloth. VG. C6. $375.00

GRIESBACH, Marc. *Combat History of the 8th Infantry Division in WWII.* 1946. Baton Rouge. 98p. sc. VG. S16. $85.00

GRIESS, Thomas. *Atlas for the Second World War: Asia & the Pacific.* 1985. Wayne. 53p. sbdg. VG. S16. $22.00

GRIFFIN, George Butler. *California Coast: Documents From Sutro Collection.* 1969 (1891). Norman, OK. Bilingual ed. maps. as new/dj. O7. $50.00

GRIFFIN, John Howard. *Devil Rides Outside.* 1953. London. Collins. 1st. VG/VG. B4. $100.00

GRIFFIN, Marjorie. *How To Cook.* 1944. Hall. 223p. B10. $12.00

GRIFFIN, Susan. *Sink.* 1974. San Lorenzo. Shameless Hussy. 1st. ils. 48p. VG+. A25. $20.00

GRIFFIS, William E. *Verbeck of Japan.* 1900. NY. Fleming Revell. 1st. photos/index. 376p. VG. W3. $245.00

GRIFFITH, Corinne. *Eggs I Have Known.* 1955. 1st. VG/G+. E6. $20.00

GRIFFITH, Corinne. *Papa's Delicate Condition.* 1952. Houghton Mifflin. 1st. inscr. F/VG. B4. $175.00

GRIFFITH, George. *Angel of the Revolution.* 1974 (1894). Hyperion. rpt. F. M2. $35.00

GRIFFITH, J.W. *Elementary Text-Book of the Microscope.* 1864. London. Van Voorst. 1st. 12mo. 192p. cloth. VG. T10. $100.00

GRIFFITH, Samuel. *Battle for Guadalcanal.* 1979. Baltimore. maps/notes/index. 282p. VG. S16. $22.50

GRIFFITH & JONES. *Descriptive Catalogue of an Exhibition of Manuscripts...* 1924. Austin, TX. 1st. 1/307. gilt bl cloth. w/16p supplement. M24. $100.00

GRIFFITHS, A.B. *Treatise on Manures; or, Philosophy of Manuring.* 1889. London. Whittaker. 399p. cloth. VG. A10. $40.00

GRIFFITHS, Ella. *Murder on Page Three.* 1984. Quartet Crime. NF/dj. P3. $18.00

GRIFFITHS, Julia. *Autographs for Freedom.* 1854. Auburn/Rochester. Alden Beardsley. 1st. gilt brn cloth. M24. $165.00

GRIFFITHS & THOMPSON. *Cacti.* 1929. WA, DC. 24 mc pl/photos/2 figures. brd. B26. $17.50

GRIGSON, Geoffrey. *Cherry Tree.* 1959. Pantheon. 1st. 517p. cloth. F/NF. D4. $35.00

GRILLOT DE GIURY, Emile. *Pictorial Anthology of Witchcraft, Magic & Alchemy.* 1958. University Books. 1st Am. F/dj. M2. $30.00

GRIMEK, H.C.B. *Grimek's Animal Life Encyclopedia. Vol 3.* 1972. Van Nostrand. 541p. F/F. B1. $60.00

GRIMES, J. Stanley. *Compend of the Phreno-Philosophy of Human Nature.* 1853. Boston/Cambridge. 1st. 8vo. 121p. cloth. M1. $125.00

GRIMES, Martha. *Anodyne Necklace.* 1983. Little Brn. 1st. F/NF. D10. $75.00

GRIMES, Martha. *Dirty Duck.* 1984. Little Brn. 1st. NF/dj. M25. $35.00

GRIMES, Martha. *End of the Pier.* 1992. Knopf. 1st. sgn. F/F clip. A23. $35.00

GRIMES, Martha. *Five Bells & Bladebone.* 1987. Little Brn. 1st. VG/dj. P3. $16.00

GRIMES, Martha. *I Am the Only Running Footman.* 1986. Little Brn. 1st. F/NF. N4. $17.50

GRIMES, Martha. *Man With a Load of Mischief.* 1990. London. Michael O'Mara. 1st Eng. F/dj. Q1. $60.00

GRIMES, Martha. *Old Contemptibles.* 1991. Little Brn. 1st. F/F. A23/T12. $35.00

GRIMES, Martha. *Old Fox Deceiv'd.* 1982. London. Michael O'Mara. 1st Eng. F/dj. Q1. $50.00

GRIMES, Martha. *Old Silent.* 1989. Little Brn. 1st. sgn. F/F. A23. $35.00

GRIMES, Martha. *Send Bygraves.* 1989. Putnam. 1st. decor brd. VG. P3. $15.00

GRIMM & GRIMM. *Fairy Tales of the Brothers Grimm.* 1909. Doubleday Page. 1st Am. ils Rackham/40 tipped-in mc pl. 325p. brd. R5. $1,400.00

GRIMM & GRIMM. *Fairy Tales.* 1913. ils Hope Dunlap. VG. M17. $40.00

GRIMM & GRIMM. *German Popular Stories.* 1868. London. JC Hotten. 1st thus. gilt gr cloth. M24. $150.00

GRIMM & GRIMM. *Grimm's Fairy Tales.* 1909. London. Constable. 1st thus. ils Rackham/40 full-p ils & 55 b&w. 325p. VG. D1. $1,150.00

GRIMM & GRIMM. *Grimm's Fairy Tales.* 1914. Cupples Leon. 1st. ils Gruelle. 4to. wine cloth/pict label. R5. $385.00

GRIMM & GRIMM. *Hansel & Gretel.* 1985. Weathervane. ils Kay Nielsen. F/dj. M2. $17.00

GRIMM & GRIMM. *Household Stories.* 1979. London. ils Walter Crane. NF/dj. M2. $17.00

GRIMM & GRIMM. *King Grisly-Beard.* 1973. FSG. 1st. ils Sendak. glazed brd. VG. D1. $45.00

GRIMM & GRIMM. *Snowdrop & Other Tales.* 1920. London. Constable. 1st. ils Rackham/20 mtd mc pl. bl cloth. R5. $400.00

GRIMMILL, W.N. *Salem Witch Trials.* 1924. Chicago. 1st. ils. 240p. VG. B5. $32.50

GRIMSHAW, Beatrice. *Sorcerer's Stone.* 1914. Winston. 1st. VG. M2. $15.00

GRIMSHAW, William Robinson. *Grimshaw's Narrative.* 1964. Sacramento Book Collectors Club. tall 8vo. as new. K7. $45.00

GRIMWOOD, Ken. *Replay.* 1986. Arbor. 1st. F/dj. M2. $35.00

GRIMWOOD, Ken. *Replay.* 1986. Arbor. 1st. VG/dj. P3. $20.00

GRINDON, Leo H. *Phenomena of Plant Life.* 1866. Boston. 93p. gilt emb cloth/beveled brd. VG+. B26. $22.50

GRINKO, G.T. *5-Year Plan of the Soviet Union: A Political Interpretation.* 1930. Internat Pub. 1st. G. V4. $22.50

GRINNELL, David; see Wollheim, Don.

GRINNELL, George Bird. *American Duck Shooting.* 1918 (1901). NY. Forest/Stream. 2nd. ils. 627p. VG. H7. $75.00

GRINNELL, George Bird. *American Game Bird Shooting.* 1910. Forest/Stream. 1st. ils. 558p. VG. H7. $75.00

GRINNELL, George Bird. *Fighting the Cheyennes.* 1995 (1915). np rpt. map. 431p. F/dj. M4. $20.00

GRINNELL, Joseph. *Distributional Summation of the Ornithology of Lower CA.* 1928. Berkeley. CA U Pub Zoology Vol 32 #1. 300p. VG. S15. $22.00

GRIS, Henry. *New Soviet Psychic Discoveries.* 1979. Souvenir. 1st. F/NF. P3. $20.00

GRISANTI, Mary Lee. *Art of the Vatican.* 1983. Excalibur. 1st Am. 4to. 70 mc pl. 143p. F/dj. T10. $20.00

GRISET, Ernest. *Funny Picture-Book.* 1874. London. Wm Nimmon. 4to. gilt emb pict brn cloth. R5. $400.00

GRISEWOOD, R. Norman. *Zariah the Martian.* 1909. Fenno. copyright p removed o/w G+. P3. $50.00

GRISHAM, John. *Client.* March 1993. Doubleday. 1st ltd. 422p. NF. W2. $300.00

GRISHAM, John. *Firm.* 1991. Doubleday. 1st. F/F. B2/M19. $175.00

GRISHAM, John. *Firm.* 1991. Doubleday. 1st. NF/F. H11. $140.00

GRISWOLD, John. *Fuels.* 1946. McGraw Hill. 1st/3rd. 496p. VG. H1. $20.00

GRIVAS, Theodore. *Military Governments in California, 1846-1850...* 1963. Clark. 1st. 247p. VG. J2. $165.00

GRIZZARD & SMITH. *Glory, Glory.* 1981. Atlanta. 1st. VG/VG. B5. $35.00

GROAT, Dick. *World Champion Pittsburgh Pirates.* 1961. NY. 1st. sgn. VG/dj. B5. $40.00

GROBANI, Anton. *Guide to Football Literature.* 1975. GAle. 1st. VG+. P8. $65.00

GROGNARD, C. *Tattoo: Graffiti for the Soul.* 1994. Sanford. ils/photos. 132p. F/dj. M4. $30.00

GROLIER CLUB. *One Hundred Influential American Books.* 1947. Grolier. 1st. 1/600 prt by Colish. teg. F. M24. $300.00

GROMME, Owen J. *Birds of Wisconsin.* 1963. Madison. sgn. 220p. gr cloth. B11. $75.00

GRONDAL, Florence Armstrong. *Romance of Astronomy.* 1942 (1926). Macmillan. 24 pl. 334p. K5. $18.00

GRONOWICZ, A. *Orange Full of Dreams.* 1971. Dodd Mead. 1st. F/dj. B4. $200.00

GROOM, Winston. *Better Times Than These.* 1978. NY. Summit. 1st. inscr. author's 1st book. F/NF. L3. $150.00

GROOM, Winston. *Better Times Than These.* 1978. Summit. 1st. author's 1st book. F/clip. Q1. $85.00

GROOM, Winston. *Gone the Sun.* 1988. Doubleday. 1st. F/F. A24. $20.00

GROOMS, Red. *Ruckus Rodeo.* 1988. Abrams. 6 popups. 4to. P2. $40.00

GROSE, Francis. *Olio: Being a Collection of Essays, Dialogues, Letters...* 1793. London. Hooper. 1st. 8vo. 321p. H13. $295.00

GROSE, Francis. *Provincial Glossary, With a Collection of Local Proverbs...* 1811. London. Edward Jeffrey. tall 12mo. H13. $245.00

GROSS, Joel. *Sarah.* 1987. Morrow. 1st. F/F. H11. $25.00

GROSS, Leonard. *Last Jews in Berlin.* 1982. S&S. 1st. F/VG+. S3. $22.00

GROSS, Louis S. *Redefining the American Gothic.* 1989. Umi Research. 1st. F/dj. P3. $35.00

GROSS, Milt. *Dear Dollink.* 1945. NY. 1st. w/orig ink drawing. VG/VG. A11. $135.00

GROSS, Milt. *Dun't Esk!!* 1927. Doran. 1st/MTI. VG. P3. $30.00

GROSS, Robert. *Elements of Pathological Anatomy.* 1845. Phil. 2nd. ils. 822p. full leather. A13. $400.00

GROSS, Robert. *Surgery of Infancy & Childhood.* 1953. Phil. 1st/2nd prt. 1000p. A13. $125.00

GROSS, S. *I Am Blind & My Dog Is Dead.* 1977. Dodd Mead. 1st. VG/VG. P3. $18.00

GROSS, Samuel D. *Autobiography of..., MD With Sketches of His Contemporaries.* 1887. Phil. 1st. 2 vol. A13. $250.00

GROSS, Samuel W. *Practical Treatise on Tumors of the Mammary Gland.* 1880. NY. 246p. gr cloth. B14. $350.00

GROSSBACK, Robert. *Never Say Die.* 1979. Harper. 1st. F/dj. M2. $12.00

GROSSMAN & GROSSMAN. *Italian Kosher Cookbook.* 1964. 1st. F/F. E6. $15.00

GROUP, Larry. *Treat American Deer Hunt.* 1992. Boulder. 1st. 226p. M/dj. A17. $27.50

GROVE, Harriet Pyne. *Betty Lee, Freshman.* 1931. Cleveland. World. 1st. 254p. VG/dj. A25. $20.00

GROVE, Lee Edmonds. *Of Brooks & Books.* 1945. 1/1500. VG/dj. K3. $20.00

GROVER, Eulalie Osgood. *Mother Goose Rhymes.* 1953. Platt Munk. ils. unp. cloth. VG. M20. $25.00

GROVER, Eulalie Osgood. *Mother Goose.* 1915. Volland. 1st. ils Frederick Richardson. lg 4to. bl cloth. M5. $250.00

GROVER, Eulalie Osgood. *Sunbonnet Babies A-B-C Book.* 1934 (1929). Rand McNally. ils BC Melcher. 64p. VG. M20. $75.00

GROVER, Eulalie Osgood. *Sunbonnet Babies in Holland.* 1929. 1st thus. ils Melcher. VG+. S13. $55.00

GROVER, Eulalie Osgood. *Sunbonnet Babies in Mother Goose Land.* 1928 (1927). Rand McNally. 115p. cloth. VG. M20. $60.00

GROVER & GROVER. *Art Glass Nouveau.* 1967. Tuttle. 1st. 231p. bl cloth. VG/dj. H1. $75.00

GROVER & GROVER. *Carved & Decorated European Art Glass.* 1980. Tuttle. 1st/4th. 244p. gr cloth. F. H1. $95.00

GROVES, J. Walton. *Edible & Poisonous Mushrooms of Canada.* 1962. Ottawa. Canada Dept Agric. 298p. dj. A10. $28.00

GRUBB, Davis. *Golden Sickle.* 1968. World. 1st. ils Vosburgh. F/dj. Q1. $75.00

GRUBB, Davis. *Shadow of My Brother.* 1966. Hutchinson. 1st. NF/dj. P3. $25.00

GRUBB, Davis. *Voices of Glory.* 1962. Scribner. 1st. F/NF. Q1. $60.00

GRUBB, Edward. *What Is Quakerism?* ca 1917. London. Headley Bros. 244p. worn. V3. $10.00

GRUBB & GUILFORD. *Potato.* 1912. Doubleday. 545p. xl. A10. $25.00

GRUBER, Frank. *Brass Knuckles.* 1977. Sherbourne. 1st. VG/dj. P3. $45.00

GRUBER, Frank. *Buffalo Grass.* 1956. NY. Rhinehart. 1st. F/rpr. M15. $45.00

GRUBER, Frank. *Pulp Jungle.* 1967. Sherbourne. 1st. F/dj. M2. $50.00

GRUBER, Frank. *Run, Fool, Run.* 1966. Dutton. 1st. VG/dj. P3. $30.00

GRUELLE, Johnny. *Friendly Fairies.* 1919. Volland. 27th. 8vo. mc pict brd. R5. $125.00

GRUELLE, Johnny. *Funny Little Book.* 1917. Volland. Sunny Book. 8vo. VG+. M5. $75.00

GRUELLE, Johnny. *Little Sonny Stories.* 1919. Volland. 30th. pict brd. R5. $125.00

GRUELLE, Johnny. *Magical Land of Noom.* (1922). Chicago. Donohue. 12 full-p ils+other b&w. 157p. bl-gr cloth. VG. D1. $300.00

GRUELLE, Johnny. *My Very Own Fairy Stories.* (1949). Johnny Gruelle. 8vo. unp. VG/dj. D1. $125.00

GRUELLE, Johnny. *Nobody's Boy.* 1916. Cupples Leon. 1st. gilt mint gr cloth/circular mc pl. VG. M5. $65.00

GRUELLE, Johnny. *Orphant Annie Story Book.* (1921). Bobbs Merrill. ils. VG. B15. $175.00

GRUELLE, Johnny. *Paper Dragon.* (1926). Volland. 3rd. unp. pict brd. M20. $16.00

GRUELLE, Johnny. *Paper Dragon.* 1926. Volland. VG/box. B5. $145.00

GRUELLE, Johnny. *Raggedy Andy Stories.* 1920. Volland. 37th. 8vo. pict brd. orig pub box. R5. $135.00

GRUELLE, Johnny. *Raggedy Ann & Andy & the Nice Fat Policeman.* 1942. Johnny Gruelle. 8vo. 95p. VG/torn. D1. $100.00

GRUELLE, Johnny. *Raggedy Ann & Andy & the Nice Fat Policeman.* 1942. NY. Gruelle. 1st. 8vo. ils Worth Gruelle. 95p. F/dj. T10. $150.00

GRUELLE, Johnny. *Raggedy Ann & Betsy Bonnet String.* 1943. 1st. F/VG. M19. $75.00

GRUELLE, Johnny. *Raggedy Ann & Betsy Bonnet String.* 1943. NY. Gruelle. 1st. 8vo. 95p. VG. T10. $50.00

GRUELLE, Johnny. *Raggedy Ann & the Golden Butterfly.* 1940. Gruelle Co. ils. VG. M17. $45.00

GRUELLE, Johnny. *Raggedy Ann in the Deep Woods.* 1930. Donohue. 8vo. unp. VG/G. D1. $100.00

GRUELLE, Johnny. *Raggedy Ann's Magical Wishes.* ca 1930s. Donohue. rpt. 94p. VG+/dj. M20. $65.00

GRUELLE, Johnny. *Raggedy Ann's Magical Wishes.* 1928. Chicago. Donohue. 8vo. 95p. pict brd. VG/dj. D1. $125.00

GRUELLE, Johnny. *Raggedy Ann's Wishing Pebble.* 1925. Volland. later prt. 8vo. VG+. M5. $55.00

GRUEN, John. *Erik Bruhn Danseur Noble.* 1979. Viking. 1st. sgn Erik Bruhn. VG/VG. A23. $30.00

GRUENBERG, Sidonie Mastner. *Let's Hear a Story.* (1961). Doubleday. ils Dagmar Wilson. 160p. beige cloth. VG. T5. $24.00

GRUGER, Herbert. *Liederfibel, Kinderlieder in Bildernoten.* 1927. Breslau. Ostdeutsche. 1st. ils J Gruger. song primer. D1. $150.00

GRUNFELD, F. *Hitler File, a Social History of Germany & the Nazis...* ca 1974. 1st Am. 4to. ils. F/F. E6. $25.00

GRUNFELD, Frederic V. *Vienna.* 1981. NY. Newsweek. dj. A19. $20.00

GRUNWALD, Henry Anatole. *Salinger: A Critical & Personal Portrait.* 1962. Harper. 1st. F/clip. Q1. $100.00

GRUZINSKI, Serge. *Painting the Conquest.* 1992. France. Flammerion. 1st. 239p. dj. F3. $65.00

GUADALUPI & MANGUEL. *Dictionary of Imaginary Places.* 1980. Macmillan. 1st. 438p. NF/clip. M21. $45.00

GUDDE, Erwin G. *California Place Names.* 1962. Berkeley. 2nd. NF/VG. O4. $25.00

GUEDEL, Arthur. *Inhalation Anesthesia.* 1947. NY. 1st. 172p. A13. $30.00

GUENON, F. *Treatise on Milch Cows.* 1856. 63rd thousand. 88p. VG. E6. $60.00

GUERARD, Michael. *Cruisine Minceur.* 1976. Morrow. 1st. VG/dj. A16. $10.00

GUERRA, Tonino. *Equilibrium.* 1970. NY. Walker. 1st Am. F/NF. B4. $100.00

GUEST, C.Z. *First Garden.* nd. ils/sgn Cecil Beaton. intro Truman Capote. VG/VG. M17. $35.00

GUEST, Judith. *Killing Time in St Cloud.* 1988. Delacorte. 1st. F/NF. T11. $10.00

GUEST, Judith. *Killing Time in St Cloud.* 1988. Delacorte. 1st. G+/dj. P3. $8.00

GUEVARA, Che. *Reminiscences of the Cuban Revolutionary War.* 1968. Monthly Review. 1st. VG/VG. V4. $40.00

GUIDROZ, Myriam. *Adventures in French Cooking.* 1970. London. Macmillan. G/dj. A16. $7.50

GUILD, Nicholas. *Chain Reaction.* 1983. St Martin. 1st. VG/dj. P3. $15.00

GUILIANO. *Lewis Carroll Observed: A Collection...* 1976. 4to. ils/photos. 224p. F/NF. A4. $125.00

GUILIANO. *Lewis Carroll: Annotated International Bibliography.* 1977. 261p. F/F. A4. $65.00

GUILLAIN, Georges. *J-M Charcot 1825-1893: His Life-His Work.* 1959. NY. Hoeber. 1st English. 202p. tan Naugahide. G1. $65.00

GUILLEMIN, Amedee. *Heavens: An Ils Yearbook of Popular Astronomy.* 1868. London. Richard Bentley. 3rd. rebacked. K5. $100.00

GUILLEMIN, Amedee. *Sun.* 1870. Scribner. Ils Lib of Wonder series. 8vo. gilt cloth. K5. $70.00

GUILLOU, Charles F.B. *Oregon & California Drawings 1841 & 1847.* 1961. BC of CA. 1/450. sm rolio. ils. stp gilt cream cloth. F. w/prospectus. R3. $100.00

GUINNESS, Benjamin. *Guinness Book of World Records.* 1988. Sterling. special ed. 447p. F. W2. $45.00

GUITERMAN, Arthur. *Ballads of Old New York.* 1920. Harper. sgn. 12mo. G. B11. $18.00

GUIZOT, Francois. *Popular History of France, From Earliest Times.* (1880). Boston. 6 vol. royal 8vo. teg. uncut. 3-quarter leather. F. H3. $450.00

GULL, William Withey. *Collection of Published Writings of Wm Withey Gull.* 1894. London. New Sydenham. 2 vol. 8vo. 19 lithos. emb brn cloth. NF. G1. $350.00

GULLIVER, P.H. *Social Control in an African Society.* 1963. Boston. 1st. 8vo. VG/dj. W1. $18.00

GULVIN, Harold E. *Farm Engines & Tractors.* 1953. McGraw Hill. later prt. 397p. gilt cloth. VG. H1. $20.00

GUMMERE, Amelia Mott. *Friends in Burlington.* 1884. Phil. Collins. 100p. VG. V3. $25.00

GUMMERMAN, Jay. *We Find Ourselves in Moontown.* 1989. Knopf. 1st. NF/NF. M23. $20.00

GUMMINGS, D. Duane. *William Robinson Leigh, Western Artist.* 1980. Norman, OK. 1st. 204p. G/dj. J2. $85.00

GUMP, Richard. *Jade, Stone of Heaven.* 1962. Doubleday. 1st. ils/map/bibliography. 256p. VG/dj. W3. $42.00

GUNN, James. *Alternate Worlds.* 1975. Prentice Hall. VG/dj. P3. $35.00

GUNN, James. *Breaking Point.* 1972. Walker. 1st. F/dj. M2. $25.00

GUNN, James. *Dreamers.* 1980. S&S. 1st. VG/dj. N4. $17.50

GUNN, T. *Moly.* 1971. London. Faber. 1st. sgn. F/NF. R14. $100.00

GUNN, T. *Poem After Chaucer.* 1971. Albondocani. 1/300. sgn/dtd April 1997. F/wrp. R14. $75.00

GUNN & GUNN. *Tegucigalpa, Honduras.* 1966. Tegucigalpa. 1st. 1/1500. 27p. wrp. F3. $10.00

GUNSTON, Bill. *Illustrated Guide to Modern Airborne Missiles.* nd. NY. Arco. 8vo. 159p. VG. K5. $15.00

GUNTHART, Lotte. *Kinger Golden Light.* 1984. Hunt Inst Bot Docu. 245p. Vg/stiff wrp. A10. $40.00

GUNTHER, John. *Eden for One.* 1927. Harper. 1st. VG. M2. $27.00

GUNTHER, Max. *Doom Wind.* 1986. Contemporary. 1st. VG/dj. P3. $18.00

GUPPY, Estella L. *Cypress of Monterey: Historical Sketch.* 1922. np. 1st. ils M DeNeale Morgan. F/stiff tan wrp. B26. $35.00

GURDJIEFF, G.I. *Meetings With Remarkable Men.* 1963. Dutton. 1st. F/NF. B2. $50.00

GURDON, J.E. *Secret of the South.* 1950. London. 1st. NF/dj. M2. $25.00

GURGANUS, Allan. *Oldest Living Confederate Widow Tells All.* 1989. Knopf. 1st. author's 1st book. F/dj. Q1. $35.00

GURGANUS, Allan. *White People.* 1991. Knopf. 1st. F/F. A20. $20.00

GURGANUS, Allan. *White Poeple.* 1991. Knopf. AP. sgn. F/prt wrp. R13. $35.00

GURION, Itzhak. *Triumph on the Gallows.* Sept 1950. Brooklyn. ils Arthur Szyk. 200p. bl cloth. VG. B14. $45.00

GURLEY, Ralph Randolph. *Life of Jehudi Ashun...* 1969 (1835). Negro U. rpt. 2 parts in 1. 8vo. cloth. VG. W1. $25.00

GURNEY, C.S. *Portsmouth: Historic & Picturesque.* 1902. ils. VG. M17. $75.00

GURNEY, David. *F Certificate.* 1968. Bernard Geis. 1st. F. P3. $10.00

GURNEY, E.R. *Messages to Boys.* 1929. Yankton, SD. private prt. A19. $30.00

GURNEY, Gene. *Rocket & Missile Technology.* 1964. Franklin Watts. 1st. 394p. VG/dj. K5. $50.00

GURNEY, Gene. *Space Technology Spinoffs.* 1979. Franklin Watts. 1st. 8vo. 88p. VG. K5. $12.00

GURNEY, Joseph John. *Declaration, by the Late Joseph John Gurney of His Faith...* 1847. Phil. Longstreth. 44p. V3. $27.50

GUTERSON, David. *Country Ahead of Us, the Country Behind.* 1989. Harper Row. 1st. NF/dj. M25. $150.00

GUTERSON, David. *Country Ahead of Us, the Country Behind.* 1989. Harper Row. 1st. sgn. authors 1st book of fiction. NF/F. L3. $225.00

GUTERSON, David. *Country Ahead of Us, the Country Behind.* 1989. NY. Harper. 1st. F/F. B4. $200.00

GUTERSON, David. *Family Matters: Why Home Schooling Makes Sense.* 1992. HBJ. 1st. author's 2nd book. F/NF. R13. $25.00

GUTHELIM, F. *Illustrated Rivers of America: The Potomac.* 1968. Grosset Dunlap. revised. ils/maps. pict brd. NF/VG+. M12. $25.00

GUTHELIM, Frederick. *In the Cause of Architecture.* 1975. 1st/2nd prt. 246p. VG/VG. A8. $35.00

GUTHRIE, A.B. *Big It.* 1960. Houghton Mifflin. 1st. F/NF. T11. $45.00

GUTHRIE, A.B. *Big Sky, Fair Land: Environmental Essays.* 1988. Northland. 1st. sgn. F/F. A18. $100.00

GUTHRIE, A.B. *Big Sky.* 1947. NY. Sloane. 1st. NF/VG clip. H11. $80.00

GUTHRIE, A.B. *Big Sky.* 1947. Wm Sloane. 1st ltd of 500. sgn. F/dj. A18. $250.00

GUTHRIE, A.B. *Last Valley.* 1975. Houghton Mifflin. 1st. F/NF. T11. $40.00

GUTHRIE, A.B. *Murder in the Cotswolds.* 1989. Houghton Mifflin. 1st. F/F. D10. $30.00

GUTHRIE, A.B. *These Thousand Hills.* 1956. Houghton Mifflin. 1st. inscr. F/VG clip. A18. $100.00

GUTHRIE, Donald. *New Testament Theology.* 1981. IVP. 1064p. VG/dj. B29. $18.00

GUTHRIE, Douglas. *Lord Lister, His Life & Doctrine.* 1949. Edinburgh. 1st. 128p. A13. $60.00

GUTHRIE, George. *On Diseases & Injuries of Arteries...* 1830. London. 1st. 416p. half leather. xl. A13. $1,000.00

GUTHRIE, George. *On Wounds & Injuries of the Abdomen & Pelvis.* 1847. London. 1st. 73p. xl. A13. $200.00

GUTHRIE, MOTYER & STIBBS. *New Bible Commentary Revised.* 1976. IVP. 1310p. VG/dj. B29. $12.50

GUTMAN, Bill. *Pistol Pete Maravich.* 1972. Grosset Dunlap. 1st. photos. VG/G. P8. $22.50

GUTTERIDGE, Lindsay. *Killer Pine.* 1973. Putnam. 1st. VG/dj. P3. $18.00

GUZINA, Vijislav. *Genetics of European Aspen.* 1981. Aagreb. map. 38p. wrp. B26. $15.00

GUZMAN, D.J. *Expecies Utiles de la Flora Salvadorena...* (1947). San Salvador. Segunda ed. Spanish text. ils/photos. 691p. VG. M12. $60.00

GUZMAN, Jessie Parkhurst. *1952 Negro Year Book, a Review of Events...* 1952. NY. Wm Wise. 424p. VG/torn. B18. $45.00

GWALTNEY, John Langston. *Drylongso: A Self-Portrait of Black America.* 1980. NY. Random. 1st. F/F. B2. $35.00

GWYNNE, Fred. *Chocolate Moose for Dinner.* 1976. Prentice Hall. 1st. 4to. NF/NF. C8. $50.00

GWYNNE, Fred. *Little Pigeon Toad.* 1988. S&S. 1st. glazed brd. rem mk. F/F. C8. $35.00

GWYNNE, Fred. *Sixteen Hand Horse.* 1980. NY. Windmill/Wanderer. 1st. 48p. NF/NF. D4. $35.00

GYLES & SAYER. *Of Gods & Men.* 1980. NY. Harper. 1st. F3. $25.00

HAAGE, Walther. *Cacti & Succulents: A Practical Handbook.* 1963. London/NY. 1st Am. ils/221 mc photos. decor cloth. B26. $38.00

HAAGE, Walther. *Cacti As House Plants.* 1969 (1965). Chester Springs, PA. ils/photos. B26. $25.00

HAASE, John. *Seasons & Moments.* 1971. S&S. 1st. inscr. F/F. B11. $30.00

HABENSTEIN & LAMERS. *Funeral Customs in World Over.* 1960. Bulfin. ils. 973p. VG/dj. B29. $25.00

HABER, Joyce. *Users.* 1976. Delacorte. 1st. NF/dj. M25. $25.00

HABER, Julius. *Odyssey of an American Zionist: 50 Years of Zionist History.* 1956. Twayne. inscr. 415p. VG. S3. $24.00

HABERLY, L. *Farewells.* 1927. Long Crendon. Seven Acres. 1/300 hand-prt. VG. T9. $145.00

HABERLY, L. *Pursuit of the Horizon.* 1948. Macmillan. 1st. 8vo. 239p. gilt brn cloth. F. K7. $48.00

HABERSTEIN & LERNESS. *History of American Funeral Directing.* 1963. Bulfin. F/dj. M2. $15.00

HACHIYA, Michihiko. *Hiroshima Diary: Journal of Japanese Physician Aug 6...1945.* Sept 1945. Chapel Hill. sgn. VG/dj. K3. $65.00

HACKETT, John. *Third World War.* 1978. Sidgwick Jackson. 1st. VG/dj. P3. $20.00

HACKLEMAN, Charles W. *Commercial Engraving & Printing.* 1924. 2nd. 820p. VG. K3. $40.00

HADDAM, Jane; see Papazoglou, Orania.

HADDOX, John. *Antonio Caso: Philosopher of Mexico.* 1971. Austin, TX. 1st. 128p. dj. F3. $20.00

HADEN & KAISER. *Pat Haden.* 1977. Morrow. 1st. inscr. photos. F/VG. P8. $25.00

HADER & HADER. *Cat & the Kitten.* 1940. Macmillan. 1st/2nd prt. 8vo. 98p. gr cloth. VG/dj. D1. $85.00

HADER & HADER. *Midget & Bridget.* 1934. Macmillan. 1st. ils EB Hader. VG/dj. D1/P2. $45.00

HADER & HADER. *Mighty Hunter.* 1947 (1943). London. Hale. 1st. ils. NF/VG. C8. $35.00

HADER & HADER. *Quack Quack.* 1961. Macmillan. 1st. 4to. 47p. NF/VG+. P2. $40.00

HADER & HADER. *Rainbow's End.* 1945. Macmillan. VG. B15. $50.00

HADFIELD, R.L. *Phantom Ship.* 1973. Geoffrey Bles. 1st. G+. P3. $18.00

HADLEY, Arthur. *Joy Wagon.* 1958. Viking. 1st. F/dj. M2. $25.00

HADVIELD, Robert A. *Work & Position of the Metallurgical Chemist.* 1921. Sheffield. 8vo. 97p. VG. K3. $35.00

HAECKEL, Ernst. *Evolution of Man: Popular Exposition of Principle Points...* 1896 & 1897. Appleton. 2 vol. leather/marbled brd. G. H1. $110.00

HAEUSSLER, Armin. *Story of Our Hymns.* 1952. Eden. 1099p. G. B29. $7.00

HAFEZ, E.S.E. *Reproduction in Farm Animals.* 1987. Lea Febiger. 5th. 649p. B1. $22.50

HAGANS & SEIBEL. *Complicated Watches.* 1945. Denver. Roberts. 136p. decor cloth. VG. K3. $25.00

HAGBERG, David. *Crossfire.* 1991. Tor. 1st. NF/dj. P3. $22.00

HAGEDORN, Hermann. *Leonard Wood, a Biography.* 1931. NY. 2 vol. 1st. ils/photos/appendix/index. B5. $60.00

HAGEDORN, Hermann. *Roosevelt in the Badlands.* 1921. Houghton Mifflin. dj. A19. $65.00

HAGEN, Gretchen L. *Atlas of Open Cluster Colour-Magnitude Diagrams.* 1970. Toronto. David Dunlap Observatory. complete boxed set. K5. $70.00

HAGER, Jean. *Grandfather Medicine.* 1989. St Martin. 1st. author's 1st mystery. F/F. L3. $200.00

HAGER, Jean. *Night Walker.* 1990. St Martin. 1st. sgn. F/NF. A24. $60.00

HAGER, Jean. *Redbird's Cry.* 1994. Mysterious. 1st. F/F. L3. $45.00

HAGERMANN, E.R. *Fighting Rebels & Redskins...Col Geo B Sanford 1861-62.* 1969. OK U. 1st. maps. 355p. F/dj. M4. $25.00

HAGGARD, H. Rider. *Allan & the Ice Gods.* 1927. Doubleday. 1st AM. VG. M2. $75.00

HAGGARD, H. Rider. *Allan Quatermain.* 1926. Hodder Stoughton. VG/dj. P3. $35.00

HAGGARD, H. Rider. *Ayesha: The Return of She.* 1905. Doubleday Page. 1st. G+. P3. $40.00

HAGGARD, H. Rider. *Classic Adventures.* 1986. New Orchard. 1st. F/dj. P3. $20.00

HAGGARD, H. Rider. *Cleopatra.* 1889. London. VG. M2. $95.00

HAGGARD, H. Rider. *Finished.* 1917. Longman Gr. 1st. VG. M19. $35.00

HAGGARD, H. Rider. *Heart of the World.* 1896. London. 1st. F. M2. $150.00

HAGGARD, H. Rider. *Jess & King Solomon's Mines.* 1899. Newnes. VG. P3. $30.00

HAGGARD, H. Rider. *Jess.* 1896. Smith Elder. G+. P3. $60.00

HAGGARD, H. Rider. *Joan Haste.* 1895. Longmans. 1st Am. VG-. M2. $60.00

HAGGARD, H. Rider. *Margaret.* 1907. NY. Longman Gr. 1st Am. ribbed cloth. F. B24. $100.00

HAGGARD, H. Rider. *Montezuma's Daughter.* 1894. Longmans. 1st Am. VG. M2. $100.00

HAGGARD, H. Rider. *Nada the Lily.* 1892. London. 1st. VG. M2. $200.00

HAGGARD, H. Rider. *Stella Fregelius.* 1903. Longmans. 1st. VG. P3. $125.00

HAGGARD, H. Rider. *Wanderer's Necklace.* 1914. Longmans. 1st. VG/dj. M2. $90.00

HAGGARD, H. Rider. *Yellow God.* 1908. Cupples Leon. 1st. VG. M2. $125.00

HAGGARD, William. *Arena.* 1961. Washburn. 1st. VG/dj. P3. $15.00

HAGGARD, William. *Hard Sell.* 1965. Cassell. 1st. NF/dj. P3. $25.00

HAGGARD, William. *Median Line.* 1979. Cassell. NF/dj. P3. $20.00

HAGUE, Michael. *Cinderella & Other Tales From Perrault.* 1989. 4to. 23 full-p pl. 88p. F/F. A4. $25.00

HAGUE, Michael. *Magic Moments.* 1990. Little Brn. 1st. sgn. as new/sans. A20. $40.00

HAGUE, Michael. *Michael Hague's Favourite Hans Christian Andersen Fairy...* 1981. HRW. 1/350. sgn. bl cloth/label. as new/case. w/sgn drawing. R5. $350.00

HAHN, Emily. *Eve & the Apes.* 1988. NY. 1st. 180p. F/NF. S15. $10.00

HAHNEMANN, Samuel. *Organon of Homoeopathic Medicine.* 1843. NY. 2nd Am. 8vo. 212p. cloth. VG. M1. $250.00

HAIG-BROWN, Roderick L. *Return to the River.* 1946. Toronto. McClelland Stuart. 1st. F/VG+. A18. $80.00

HAIG-BROWN, Roderick L. *Silver: Life Story of an Atlantic Salmon.* 1931. London. Black. ils JP Moreton. 96p. cloth. VG. M12. $45.00

HAIG-BROWN, Roderick L. *Western Angler.* 1939. Derrydale. 2 vol. 1/950. gilt red cloth. VG+. M20. $500.00

HAIGH & NEWTON. *Wools of Britain.* 1950. London. Pitman. 78p. cloth. VG. A10. $22.00

HAILE & OAKES. *Beautyway: A Navajo Ceremonial.* 1957. Pantheon. 1st. Bollingen series 53. mc pl. F/NF. w/supp. L3. $600.00

HAILEY, Arthur. *Airport.* 1968. Doubleday. 1st. NF/VG. N4. $27.50

HAILEY, Arthur. *Strong Medicine.* 1984. Doubleday. 1st. NF/NF. N4. $17.50

HAINES, John. *Stone Harp.* 1971. Wesleyan U. 1st. assn copy. F/NF. V1. $45.00

HAINING, Peter. *Lucifer Society.* 1972. Taplinger. 1st. F/dj. M2. $35.00

HAINING, Peter. *Mystery!* 1977. Stein Day. 1st. F/dj. M2. $20.00

HAINING, Peter. *Nightmare Reader.* 1973. Doubleday. 1st. F/dj. M2. $15.00

HAINING, Peter. *Werewolf! Horror Stories of the Man-Beast.* 1987. London. Severn. 1st. F/F. M21. $20.00

HAIRE, Frances. *Folk Costume Book.* 1937. 1st. ils Gertrude Moser. VG+. S13. $20.00

HAITES, Erik F. *Western River Transportation.* 1975. Johns Hopkins. 209p. T7. $45.00

HAITT, Ben. *Fish Poems.* 1968. Sacramento. Runcible Spoon. 1/200. 12mo. F/wrp. A17. $15.00

HAKLUYT, Richard. *Hakluyt's Collection of the Early Voyages, Travels...* 1809-12. Evans McKinlay Priestley. marked A New Ed. 5 vol. leather/raised spine bands. P4. $2,500.00

HAKLUYT, Richard. *Hakluyt's Voyages: Principal Navigations, Voyages...* 1965. Viking. 8vo. 522p. brn cloth. P4. $45.00

HALACY, D.S. *Colonization of the Moon.* 1969. Van Nostrand Reinhold. xl. K5. $10.00

HALBERSTAM, David. *Breaks of the Game.* 1981. Knopf. 1st. VG+/VG+. P8. $20.00

HALBERSTAM, David. *Noblest Roman.* 1961. Houghton Mifflin. 1st. F/F. B4. $250.00

HALBERT, Sherrill. *In Re, Dr Morse's History.* 1965. Sacramento Book Collectors Club. 1/300. as new. K7. $15.00

HALCOMB & SARIS. *Headgear of Hitler's Germany Vol 1: Heer-Kriegsmarine...* 1989. San Jose. 1st. ils. 348p. VG. S16. $40.00

HALDANE, Charlotte. *Last Great Empress of China.* 1963. Bobbs Merrill. 1st. 304p. F. W3. $38.00

HALDANE, J.B.S. *Last Judgment.* 1927. Harper. 1st. VG/dj. M2. $17.00

HALDEMAN, Joe. *Buying Time.* 1989. Morrow. 1st. F/F. H11. $25.00

HALDEMAN, Joe. *Mindbridge.* 1976. St Martin. 1st. sgn. F/F. B11. $45.00

HALE, Christopher. *Murder in Tow.* 1943. Doubleday Crime Club. 1st. F/NF. M15. $45.00

HALE, Edward Everett. *Brick Moon.* 1971. Barre, MA. Imp Soc. ils/sgn Michael McCurdy. 2-tone gilt cloth. F/case. T10. $60.00

HALE, James. *After Midnight Ghost Book.* 1981. Watts. 1st Am. VG/dj. M2. $22.00

HALE, Janet Campbell. *Jailing of Cecelia Capture.* 1985. Random. 1st. author's 2nd novel. F/F. L3. $45.00

HALE, Kathleen. *Puss in Boots.* nd. Fld Books Ltd. Peepshow Book. fld 3-D panorama. VG+. M20. $150.00

HALE, Louise Closser. *American's London.* 1920. Harper. 1st. ils. 349p. VG/dj. A25. $18.00

HALE, Mason E. Jr. *Monograph of the Lichen Relicina.* 1975. WA, DC. ils/figures. wrp. B26. $12.50

HALE, Sarah Jospheha. *Ladies' New Book of Cookery: A Practical System...* 1852. NY. Long. 3rd. 474p. lib buckram. B10. $100.00

HALE, Sarah Jospheha. *Mrs Hale's New Cookbook.* 1857. 1st. VG. E6. $125.00

HALE, William Harlan. *Horizon Cookbook & Ils History of Eating & Drinking...* 1968. Am Heritage. 768p. VG/G. B10. $35.00

HALEY, Alex & Malcolm X. *Autobiography of Malcolm X.* 1965. NY. Grove. 1st. VG/clip. B4. $850.00

HALEY, Alex. *Queen: Story of an American Family.* 1992. NY. Morrow. 1st. F/F. T12. $50.00

HALEY, Alex. *Roots.* 1976. Doubleday. 1st. F/NF. D10. $100.00

HALEY, Alex. *Roots.* 1976. Doubleday. 1st. VG/VG. R14. $25.00

HALEY, Alex. *Roots.* 1977. London. Hutchinson. 1st Eng. F/dj. Q1. $75.00

HALEY, Gail. *Wonderful, Magical World of Marguerite.* 1964. Sayre Ross. 1st. ils. w/uncut paper doll. NF/VG/box. P2. $175.00

HALEY, Nelson Cole. *Whale Hunt.* 1948. NY. 1st. 304p. map ep. A17. $12.50

HALIFAX, Lord. *Lord Halifax's Ghost Book.* 1944. Didier. 1st. VG. P3. $20.00

HALKER, Clark D. *For Democracy, Workers & God: Labor-Song Poems...* 1991. IL U. 1st. F/F. V4. $25.00

HALL, A. Daniel. *Genus Tulipa.* 1940. London. 1st. 171p. A10. $125.00

HALL, Baynard R. *Frank Freeman's Barber Shop: A Tale.* 1853. Auburn. Alden Beardsley. ils Rush B Hall. 8vo. 343p. G. K7. $60.00

HALL, C. *Introduction to Electron Microscopy.* 1983. Malabar. 2nd. 397p. F. B1. $35.00

HALL, C.A. *Evolution of the Echinoid Genus Astrodapsis.* 1962. Berkeley. CA. ils/5 pocket maps & charts. F/wrp. M12. $25.00

HALL, Charles A.M. *Common Quest.* 1965. Westminster. 332p. VG/dj. B29. $6.50

HALL, Donald. *Principal Products of Portugal.* 1995. Beacon. 1st. sgn. F/dj. V1. $30.00

HALL, Donald. *Their Ancient, Glittering Eyes.* 1992. Ticknor Fields. F/F. A20. $25.00

HALL, Edward T. *Dance of Life: Other Dimension of Time.* 1983. Anchor. 232p. VG/dj. B29. $13.00

HALL, Eliza Calvert. *Aunt Jane of Kentucky.* 1907. Little Brn. 1st. 12mo. VG+. C8. $75.00

HALL, Eliza Calvert. *Land of Long Ago.* 1909. Little Brn. 1st. 295p. VG+. H1. $15.00

HALL, Hal. *Cinematographic Annual 1930. Vol 1.* 1930. Am Soc Cinematographers. photos. 600+. NF/sans. C9. $175.00

HALL, James Norman. *Doctor Dogbody's Leg.* 1940. Boston. 1st. G/dj. B5. $35.00

HALL, James W. *Bones of Coral.* 1991. Knopf. 1st. sgn. F/F. T2. $30.00

HALL, James W. *Tropical Freeze.* 1989. Norton. 1st. sgn. F/F. M15/T2. $45.00

HALL, James W. *Under Cover of Daylight.* 1987. Norton. 1st. F/F. M15. $75.00

HALL, James W. *Under Cover of Daylight.* 1987. Norton. 1st. sgn. author's 1st novel. F/F. L3. $150.00

HALL, James. *Racers to the Sun.* 1960. Obolensky. 1st. F/dj. M2. $15.00

HALL, Manly D. *Shadow Forms.* 1925. Hall. 1st. VG. M2. $30.00

HALL, Marshall. *Lectures on the Nervous System & Its Diseases.* 1836. Phil. Carey Hart. 1st Am. 240p. contemporary calf. VG. G1. $325.00

HALL, Melvin. *Journey to the End of an Era: An Autobiography.* 1947. Scribner. 1st. 438p. cloth. W1. $24.00

HALL, Parnell. *Detective.* 1987. DIF. 1st. sgn. author's 1st book. F/F. A24. $65.00

HALL, Parnell. *Strangler.* 1989. 1st. F/F. N4. $25.00

HALL, Radclyffe. *Well of Loneliness.* 1928. Paris. Pegasus. 1st French (in Eng). gilt cloth. M24. $85.00

HALL, Ruth. *Passionate Crusader: Life of Marie Stopes.* 1977. HBJ. 1st Am. photos. 351p. VG+/dj. A25. $20.00

HALL, S.C. *Book of Hand-Woven Coverlets.* 1931. Boston. ils. 278p. VG. M4. $25.00

HALL, Trowbridge. *Egypt in Silhouette.* 1928. McMillan. 1st. 8vo. 378p. VG. W1. $18.00

HALL, William. *Christmas Pony.* 1948. Knopf. 1st. ils Roger Duvoisin. 4to. VG/G. P2. $35.00

HALL & HOWE. *Story of the First Decade in Imperial Valley, CA.* 1910. Imperial. Howe. photos. 282p. gilt buckram/leather spine. D11. $200.00

HALL & NORDHOFF. *Bounty Trilogy.* (1962). Boston. Wyeth Ed/later prt. 633p. P4. $40.00

HALL & SHARP. *Wolf & Man: Evolution in Parallel.* 1978. Academic. ils/photo/map/drawings. 210p. F/VG+. M12. $37.50

HALL-DUNCAN, Nancy. *History of Fashion Photography.* 1979. NY. Alpine Book Co. 240p. cloth. dj. D11. $100.00

HALLAHAN, William H. *Keeper of the Children.* 1978. Morrow. 1st. F/F. M21. $55.00

HALLAHAN, William H. *Ross Forgery.* 1973. Bibliomystery. 1st. xl. VG/dj. K3. $10.00

HALLAHAN, William H. *Search for Joseph Tully.* 1974. Bobbs Merrill. 1st. F/F. M21. $65.00

HALLECK, Fitz-Greene. *Fanny.* 1819. NY. 1st. 8vo. 49p. prt wrp. G. M1. $525.00

HALLECK, R.P. *History of American Literature.* 1911. Am Book Co. 1st/later issue. VG gilt bl cloth. M24. $25.00

HALLENBECK, Cleve. *Alvar Nunez Cabeza de Vaca: Journey & Route...1534-1536.* 1940. Glendale. AH Clark. 9 maps/charts/14p index. teg. NF. O7. $275.00

HALLET, Jean-Pierre. *Congo Kitabu.* 1966. Random. 5th. sgn pres. 16 pl/map ep. 436p. VG/dj. W1. $25.00

HALLIBURTON, Richard. *New Worlds To Conquer.* 1929. Bobbs Merrill. ils. 368p. F3. $15.00

HALLIBURTON, Richard. *Royal Road to Romance.* 1930. NY. sgn. VG. B14. $30.00

HALLIDAY, F.E. *Cult of Shakespeare.* 1960. Yoseloff. 1st Am. 218p. VG/dj. M20. $22.00

HALLIDAY, Samuel B. *Lost & Found; or, Life Among the Poor.* 1860. Phinney Blakeman Mason. 8vo. 356p. cloth. M1. $85.00

HALLIGAN, James. *Fundamentals of Agriculture.* 1911. Boston. Heath. 492p. cloth. VG. A10. $6.00

HALLOWELL, Priscilla. *Dinah & Virginia.* 1956. Viking. 1st. 8vo. NF/dj. M5. $35.00

HALPER, Albert. *Only an Inch From Glory.* 1943. Harper. 1st. F/NF. B2. $50.00

HALPERIN, Irving. *Here I Am: A Jew in Today's Germany.* 1971. Westminster. 140p. VG/dj. S3. $22.00

HALPERN, Jay. *Jade Unicorn.* 1979. Macmillan. 1st. F/dj. M2. $20.00

HALPERN, Joseph. *History of Our People in Bible Times.* 1939. London. Shapiro Vallentine. 2nd. ils/charts/plans. 299p. VG. S3. $20.00

HALSEY, Francis W. *Authors of Our Day in Their Homes.* 1902. NY. James Pott. 1st/1st state. teg. F. M24. $75.00

HALSEY, Francis W. *Forgotten Books of the American Nursery.* 1911. Boston. Goodspeed. 1/700. ils. xl. VG. A4. $75.00

HALSEY, Mina Deane. *Tenderfoot in Southern California.* 1914. NY. Little Ives. 1st. ils. 162p. VG. A25. $32.00

HALSMAN, Philippe. *Photographs.* 1979. Internat Center Photography. ils. NF/lg wrp. C9. $75.00

HALSTEAD, Bruce W. *Poisonous & Venomous Marine Animals of the World.* 1965. WA. 3 vol. VG+. S15. $295.00

HALSTED, William. *Results of Operations for Cure of Cancer to Breast...* 1894. Baltimore. 1st. ils. 54p. A13. $150.00

HALTER, Jon C. *Bill Bradley: One To Remember.* 1975. Putnam. 1st. F/VG+. P8. $30.00

HAMADA, Shoji. *Catalogue of 77 Tea Bowls by Hamada Shoji.* 1972. Japan Folk Arts Mus. 1st. Japanese text. 77 full-p mc pl. 177p. F/F case. W3. $245.00

HAMBIDGE, G. *Hunger Signs in Crops.* 1941. WA. 1st. tall 8vo. 327p. cloth. NF. A22. $30.00

HAMBURGER, Michael. *Variations: Travelling in Suffolk.* 1981. Blk Swan. 1st. F/F. B4. $65.00

HAMBY, W.B. *Case Reports & Autopsy Records of Ambroise Pare.* 1960. Springfield. 1st Eng trans. 214p. A13. $150.00

HAMILL, Katherine. *Swamp Shadow.* 1936. Knopf. 1st. F/NF. B4. $85.00

HAMILL, Pete. *Gift.* 1973. Random. 1st. author's 2nd novel. F/F. D10. $35.00

HAMILTON, Alexander. *Works of..., Comprising His Most Important Offical Reports.* 1810. NY. Williams Whiting. 1st. 3 vol in 1. thick 8vo. new half calf. F. M1. $950.00

HAMILTON, Allan McLane. *Nervous Diseases: Their Description & Treatment.* 1878. Phil. Henry Lea. heavy 8vo. 512p+catalog. panelled brn cloth. xl. G1. $175.00

HAMILTON, Angus. *Korea.* 1904. Scribner. 1st. ils. 313p. xl. G+. W3. $42.00

HAMILTON, Charles. *Bench & the Ballot.* 1973. Oxford. 1st. 258p. F/VG+. B4. $60.00

HAMILTON, Charles. *Braddock's Defeat: Journal of Capt Robert Cholmey...* 1959. Norman, OK. 1st. 134p. as new/clip. H1. $65.00

HAMILTON, Charles. *Collecting Autographs & Manuscripts.* 1970. OK U. 2nd. F/VG. M24. $50.00

HAMILTON, Clarence. *Outlines of Music History.* 1913. Oliver Ditson. 308p. VG. B29. $6.50

HAMILTON, Edith. *Mythology.* 1942. Little Brn. 38th prt. 497p. F/NF. W2. $30.00

HAMILTON, Frank. *Treatise on Military Surgery & Hygiene.* 1865. NY. 648p. A13. $750.00

HAMILTON, Franklin; see Silverberg, Robert.

HAMILTON, Henry W. *Sioux of the Rosebud.* 1971. Norman, OK. photos John Anderson. F. A19. $35.00

HAMILTON, Henry. *History of the Homeland: Story of British Background.* 1947. London. Allen Unwin. 1st. maps. gr buckram. VG. B22. $15.00

HAMILTON, Jane. *Book of Ruth.* 1988. Ticknor Fields. 1st. author's 1st book. F/F. T11. $175.00

HAMILTON, Joyce. *White Water: Colorado Jet Boat Expedition 1960.* 1963. Caxton. 2nd. 8vo. VG/dj. F7. $80.00

HAMILTON, K.G.A. *Leafhoppers of Ornamental & Fruit Trees in Canada.* 1985. Ottawa. Agriculture Canada. 193 mc photos. 71p. VG/wrp. B1. $18.50

HAMILTON, Luther. *Reasons for the Unitarian Belief.* 1830. Boston. Bowles. 1st. 12mo. 137p. cloth. M1. $100.00

HAMILTON, Mary E. *Policewoman: Her Service & Ideals.* 1924. Stokes. 1st. sgn pres. 200p. VG/fair. A25. $22.00

HAMILTON, Robert. *WH Hudson: The Vision of Earth.* 1946. London. Dent. 1st. F/dj. Q1. $40.00

HAMILTON, Roberts. *Mayflower.* 1846. Saxton Kelt. 1st. aeg. gilt emb blk morocco. F. M24. $275.00

HAMILTON, Virginia. *All Jahdu Storybook.* 1991. HBJ. 1st. sgn. F/F. B3. $35.00

HAMILTON, Virginia. *In the Beginning: Creation Stories From Around the World.* 1988. HBJ. 1st. sm 4to. 161p. F/F clip. C14. $30.00

HAMILTON, Virginia. *MC Higgins, the Great.* 1974. Macmillan. 1st. F/F. B4. $150.00

HAMILTON, Virginia. *Paul Robeson: Life & Times of a Free Black Man.* 1974. Harper Row. 1st prt. NF/dj. M25. $25.00

HAMILTON, Virginia. *WEB DuBois: A Biography.* 1972. NY. Crowell. 4th. 8vo. F/F. C8. $25.00

HAMILTON, W.C. *Statistics in Physical Science.* 1964. Ronald. 1st. 230p. F. D8. $20.00

HAMILTON, William Rowan. *Mathematical Papers. Vol III. Algebra.* 1967. Cambridge. 1st. sgn RE Ingram. 672p. VG. K3. $90.00

HAMILTON-PATERSON, James. *That Time in Malomba.* 1990. Soho. 1st Am. F/F. M25. $25.00

HAMLIN, Augustus Choate. *Battle of Chancellorsville.* 1896. Bangor, ME. 9 mc maps. rebound. G. B18. $125.00

HAMLIN, Talbot. *Greek Revival Architecture in America.* 1947 (1944). London/NY. Oxford. 2nd. ils/pl/figures. cloth. D2. $65.00

HAMMEL, Eric. *Guadalcanal: Decision at Sea, Naval Battle of Guadalcanal...* 1988. NY. 1st. maps. 480p. VG/VG. S16. $25.00

HAMMEL & LANE. *76 Hours: Invasion of Tarawa.* 1985. Pacifica. 1st. sgns. 266p. VG/VG. S16. $35.00

HAMMER, Victor. *Theory of Architecture.* 1952. NY. Wittenborn Schultz. ARC/1st. 1/250. inscr. prt brd. F/dj. B24. $225.00

HAMMET, Evelyn Allen. *I, Priscilla.* 1960. Macmillan. 1st. sgn. 202p. VG/dj. M20. $25.00

HAMMETT, Dashiell. *Adventures of Sam Spade.* 1945. World. 1st. VG/VG. M22. $45.00

HAMMETT, Dashiell. *Battle of Aleutians.* 1944. Adak. Intelligence Section, US Infantry. 1st. F/stapled wrp. M15. $300.00

HAMMETT, Dashiell. *Big Knockover.* 1966. Random. 1st. F/dj. M15. $100.00

HAMMETT, Dashiell. *Maltese Falcon.* 1934. Modern Lib. 1st thus. NF. M22. $30.00

HAMMETT, Dashiell. *Novels of...* 1965. NY. Knopf. Omnibus ed. F/dj. M15. $100.00

HAMMETT, Dashiell. *Red Harvest.* 1929. Knopf. 1st. author's 1st book. NF. C2. $400.00

HAMMETT, Dashiell. *Red Harvest.* 1931. Grossett Dunlap. rpt. VG. M22. $10.00

HAMMETT, Dashiell. *Woman in the Dark.* 1988. Knopf. 1st thus. F/F. T11. $55.00

HAMMILL, Joel. *Trident.* 1981. Arbor. 1st. F/dj. M2. $12.00

HAMMITZSCH, Horst. *Zen in the Art of the Tea Ceremony.* 1981. St Martin. 104p. F/dj. W3. $28.00

HAMMOND, Dorothy. *Confusing Collectibles: Guide to Identification of Repros.* 1969. Mid-America Book Co. 475 mc pl/714 b&w ils. 224p. orange cloth. F/VG. H1. $52.00

HAMMOND, G.P. *Adventures of Alexander Barclay, Mountain Man...1845-1850.* 1976. Denver. Rosenstock. ils/photos/3 fld pocket maps. 246p. F. M4. $50.00

HAMMOND, G.P. *Digging for Gold Without a Shovel. Letters of Daniel W Coit.* 1967. Denver. Rosenstock. 1/1250. ils. 116p. F. M4. $45.00

HAMMOND, Gerald. *Stray Shot.* 1989. St Martin. 1st Am. F/F. N4. $15.00

HAMMOND, L.H. *In the Vanguard of a Race.* 1922. NY. Council of Women for Home Missions. xl. clip ep. G+. B2. $25.00

HAMMOND, William A. *Sleep & Its Derangements.* 1873. Lippincott. 318p. bevelled ruled gr cloth. G. G1. $135.00

HAMMOND, William A. *Spinal Irritation.* 1870. Appleton. 1st separate. 42p. VG/prt olive wrp. G1. $100.00

HAMMOND & MORGAN. *Captain Charles M Weber: Pioneer of San Joaquin...* 1966. Bancroft Lib #1. 1/700. folio. 3 maps. 118p. as new. K7. $65.00

HAMMOND & MORGAN. *Weber Era in Stockton History.* 1982. Berkeley. Friends of Bancroft Lib. 170p. as new/wrp. K7. $20.00

HAMNER, Earl Jr. *Fifty Roads to Town.* 1953. Random. 1st. F/VG. B4. $200.00

HAMPE, Theodor. *Crime & Punishment in Germany...* 1929. London. Routledge. trans Malcolm Letts. ils. gr cloth. M11. $50.00

HAMPSON, John. *Man About the House.* 1935. London. 1/285. sgn. F/F. T9. $45.00

HANAUER, J. *Folk-Lore of the Holy Land: Moslem, Christian & Jewish.* 1910. London. Duckworth. 326p. teg. NF/NF. W3. $135.00

HANAWALT, Barbara A. *Crime & Conflict in English Communities 1300-1348.* 1979. Cambridge. VG/dj. M11. $45.00

HANBURY, Harold Greville. *Vinerian Chair & Legal Education.* 1958. Oxford. Basil Blackwell. M11. $85.00

HANCHETT, William. *Lincoln Murder Conspiracies.* 1983. 303p. dj. O8. $9.50

HANCOCK, H. Irving. *Making the Last Stand for Old Glory.* 1916. Altemus. 1st. VG/dj. M2. $100.00

HANCOCK, Thomas. *Principles of Peace Exemplified...* 1830. Providence. HH Brn. 315p. worn. V3. $25.00

HAND, G.J. *English Law in Ireland 1290-1324.* 1967. Cambridge. M11. $85.00

HAND, Sherman. *Collector's Encyclopedia of Carnival Glass.* 1978. Collector Books. 256p. mc pl. w/price guide. F/F. H1. $65.00

HANDLER, David. *Boy Who Never Grew Up.* 1992. Doubleday. 1st. sgn. F/dj. M15. $40.00

HANDLIN & LAYTON. *Let Me Hear Your Voice: Portraits of Aging Immigrant Jews.* 1983. WA U. photos Rochelle Casserd. 110p. VG/dj. S3. $25.00

HANEY, Lynn. *Naked at the Feast.* 1981. Dodd. 1st. F/F. B2. $25.00

HANFF, Helene. *84 Charling Cross Road.* 1975 (1970). NY. Deluxe ed. F/F. C8. $30.00

HANKE, Lewis. *Spanish Struggle for Justice in the Conquest of America.* 1959. PA U. 2nd. 217p. dj. F3. $25.00

HANKE, W. *Biology & Physiology of Amphibians.* 1990. Stuttgart. 413p. F. S15. $40.00

HANKINS, Maude McGehee. *Daddy Gander.* 1928. Volland. 1st. ils VE Cadie. 8vo. ils brd. pict box. R5. $200.00

HANLE & VON DEL CHAMBERLAIN. *Space Science Comes of Age.* 1981. Smithsonian. 194p. VG/dj. K5. $17.00

HANLEY, Sylvanus. *Caliphs & Sultans, Being Tales Omitted in Usual Editions...* 1869. Appleton. 1st. 363p. cloth. VG. W1. $45.00

HANNA, A.J. *Prince in Their Midst.* 1947. Norman. 2nd. sgn. 276p. VG. B11. $25.00

HANNA, Phil Townsend. *California Through Four Centuries: Handbook of...Dates.* 1935. Farrar Rinehart. 1st. sgn. ils/index. 212p. VG. B19. $40.00

HANNA, Phil Townsend. *Libros Californianos; or, Five Feet of California Books.* 1932. Jake Zeitlin/Primavera. 1st. 74p. VG. B19. $70.00

HANNA, Warren L. *Lost Harbor: Controversy Over Drake's California Anchorage.* 1979. Berkeley. 1st. inscr. 8vo. map ep. bl cloth. F/dj. P4. $45.00

HANNAH, Barry. *Airships.* 1978. Knopf. 1st. author's 3rd book. F/F. D10. $85.00

HANNAH, Barry. *Airships.* 1978. Knopf. 1st. inscr. NF/NF. R14. $90.00

HANNAH, Barry. *Boomerang.* 1989. Houghton Mifflin. 1st. as new. A20. $25.00

HANNAH, Barry. *Captain Maximus.* 1985. Knopf. 1st. F/F. H11. $30.00

HANNAH, Barry. *Captain Maximus.* 1985. Knopf. 1st. sgn. author's 6th book. F/F. D10. $45.00

HANNAH, Barry. *Geronimo Rex.* 1972. Viking. 1st. inscr. author's 1st book. NF/dj. L3. $175.00

HANNAH, Barry. *Hey Jack!* 1987. Dutton. 1st. F/F. H11. $35.00

HANNAH, Barry. *Nightwatchmen.* 1973. Viking. 1st. F/NF. B2. $85.00

HANNAH, Barry. *Ray.* 1980. Knopf. 1st. sgn. author's 3rd novel. F/F. D10. $55.00

HANNAH, Barry. *Tennis Handsome.* 1983. Knopf. 1st. sgn. author's 5th novel. F/F. D10. $45.00

HANNAM, Alberta. *Paint the Wind.* 1959. London. Michael Joseph. 1st Eng. 192p. F/NF. K7. $45.00

HANNEMAN, Audre. *Ernest Hemingway.* 1967. Princeton. 1st. F/dj. Q1. $100.00

HANNOCK, Ralph. *Rainbow Republics: Central America.* 1947. Coward McCann. 1st. 305p. dj. F3. $25.00

HANNON, Ezra; see Hunter, Evan.

HANNUM, Anna Paschall. *Quaker Forty-Niner: Adventures of Chas Edward Pancoast...* 1930. Phil. PA U. 2nd. 402p. G+. V3. $30.00

HANRAHAN, Joyce Y. *Works of Maurice Sendak 1947-1994.* 1995. Portsmouth. Peter Randall. 1st. F/dj. Q1. $45.00

HANS, Fred. *Great Sioux Nation, a Complete History of Indian Life...* 1907. Donohue. 1st. ils. 575p. VG. J2. $475.00

HANSBERRY, Lorraine. *Movement: Documentary of a Struggle for Equality.* 1964. S&S. later prt. photos. F/dj. M25. $75.00

HANSBERRY, Lorraine. *Sign in Sidney Brustein's Window.* 1965. Random. 1st. F/F. B4. $225.00

HANSBERRY, Lorraine. *Sign in Sidney Brustein's Window.* 1965. Random. 1st. NF/dj. M25. $60.00

HANSEN, Chuck. *US Nuclear Weapons.* 1988. NY. Orion. 1st. ils. 232p. NF/dj. K3. $25.00

HANSEN, James R. *Engineer in Charge.* 1987. Washington, DC. 4to. 620p. VG. K5. $50.00

HANSEN, Joseph. *Obedience.* 1988. Mysterious. 1st Am. NF/VG. M22. $10.00

HANSEN, Joseph. *Strange Marriage.* 1965. Los Angeles. Argyle Books. ne. 8vo. 176p. F/VG. H1. $45.00

HANSEN, MELDGAARD & NORDQVIST. *Greenland Mummies.* 1991. London. Trustees of British Mus. 192p. VG/dj. P4. $50.00

HANSEN, Ron. *Assassination of Jesse James.* 1983. Knopf. 1st. F/F. T11. $85.00

HANSEN, Ron. *Desperadoes.* 1979. Knopf. 1st. author's 1st book. F/F. T11. $110.00

HANSEN & MILLER. *Wild Oats in Eden.* 1962. Santa Rosa. self pub. photos Ansel Adams/John Lebaron/Beth Winter. 147p. NF. K7. $50.00

HANSFORD, S.H. *Chinese Jade Carving.* nd. London. Humphries. 1st/2nd imp. photos. 145p. F/F. W3. $86.00

HANSON, Earl Parker. *South From the Spanish Main.* 1967. NY. Delacorte. 1st. maps. VG/dj. K3. $20.00

HANSON, Margaret Brock. *Powder River Country.* 1981. Frontier Prt. sgn. dj. A19. $65.00

HANSON, Maurice F. *College Reunion.* 1955. Coward McCann. 1st. VG. O3. $25.00

HARANG, L. *Aurorae.* 1951. John Wiley. sm 4to. 166p. VG. K5. $30.00

HARBECK, Charles T. *Contribution to Bibliography of History of United States.* 1906. Riverside. 1/350. 4to. T7. $125.00

HARBISON, POTTERTON & SHEEHY. *Irish Art & Architecture.* 1978. Thames Hudson. 1st. 4to. 272p. F/dj. T10. $75.00

HARCOURT, Helen. *Florida Fruits & How To Raise Them.* 1886. Louisville. revised/enlarged. 347p. gilt cloth. VG. B26. $65.00

HARCOURT, L.W. Vernon. *His Grace the Steward & Trial of Peers, a Novel Inquiry...* 1907. London. Longman Gr. gilt bl cloth. VG. M11. $175.00

HARCOURT-SMITH, Simon. *Last of Uptake; or, The Estranged Sisters.* 1942. London. Batsford. 1/100. ils/sgn Rex Whistler. F. B24. $650.00

HARDENOFF, Jeanne. *Sing Song Scuppernong.* 1974. HRW. 1st. 59p. F/F. D4. $25.00

HARDIN, John Wesley. *Life of John Wesley Hardin From Original Manuscript...* 1896. Smith Moore. 1st. 144p. G/dj. J2. $195.00

HARDING, A.R. *Deadfalls & Snares: A Book of Instruction for Trappers...* (1907). Columbus, OH. Harding. 218p. H7. $15.00

HARDING, A.R. *Fur Farming: Book of Information on Raising Animals...* (1909). Columbus. private prt. ils/photos. 278p. pict cloth. VG. M12. $20.00

HARDING, A.R. *Fur Farming: Book of Information...* (1909). Columbus, OH. Harding. revised. 278p. G. H7. $15.00

HARDING, A.R. *Mink Trapping: Book of Instruction...* (1906). Columbus, OH. Harding. 171p+15p appendix. G. H7. $15.00

HARDING, Alan. *Law-Making & Law-Makers in British History...* 1980. London. Royal Historical Soc. M11. $45.00

HARDING, Anthony. *Racer's & Driver's Reader.* 1972. Arco. photos. F/F. P8. $35.00

HARDING, Bertia. *Phantom Crown.* 1934. Bobbs Merrill. 1st. sgn. 381p. VG. B11. $25.00

HARDING, Christopher. *Imprisonment in England & Wales, a Concise History.* 1985. London. Croom Helm. VG/dj. M11. $45.00

HARDING, G. Lankester. *Antiquities of Jordan.* 1967. NY. Praeger. revised. 8vo. ils/pl/maps. 215p. VG/dj. W1. $24.00

HARDING, George L. *Brief History of the California Spanish Press.* nd. Grabhorn. 1/100. lg folio fld once. ils. NF/self wrp. R3. $150.00

HARDWICH, T. Fredrick. *Manual of Photographic Chemistry...* 1858. NY. 4th. G. M17. $50.00

HARDWICK & HARDWICK. *Charles Dickens Encyclopedia.* 1973. Scribner. 531p. M/dj. H1. $25.00

HARDWICK & HARDWICK. *Sherlock Holmes Companion.* 1963. Doubleday. 1st Am. VG/dj. M2. $30.00

HARDY, Adam; see Bulmer, Kenneth.

HARDY, Alice Dale. *Riddle Club at Home (#1).* 1924. Grosset Dunlap. 246p. cloth. VG/dj. M20. $25.00

HARDY, Alister. *Great Waters: Voyage of Natural History to Study Whales...* 1967. NY. Harper Row. 1st Am. VG/dj. P4. $65.00

HARDY, Forsyth. *Scandinavian Film.* 1952. London. Falcon. 62p+32p photos. A17. $15.00

HARDY, Helen Henriques. *Louisiana's Fabulous Foods & How To Cook Them.* nd. LA. Hope Pub. G/wrp. A16. $17.50

HARDY, James. *Surgery of the Aorta & Its Branches.* 1960. Phil. 1st. 386p. A13. $50.00

HARDY, Thomas. *Changed Man.* 1913. London. Macmillan. 1st. map/etching. gr cloth. VG. S13. $75.00

HARDY, Thomas. *Changed Man.* 1913. London. Macmillan. 1st. teg. bl cloth. F/dj. M24. $600.00

HARDY, Thomas. *Famous Tragedy of the Queen of Cornwall.* 1923. London. Macmillan. 1st. NF/G. M23. $50.00

HARDY, Thomas. *Far From Madding Crowd.* 1937. 1st thus. VG+. S13. $15.00

HARDY, Thomas. *Human Shows Far Phantasies.* 1925. London. Macmillan. 1st. 8vo. gr brd. VG/NF. M23. $75.00

HARDY, Thomas. *Jude the Obscure.* 1896. London. Osgood McIlvaine. 1st/mixed states. 517p. gilt gr cloth. B24. $150.00

HARDY, Thomas. *Late Lyrics & Earlier.* 1922. London. 1st. VG. S13. $50.00

HARDY, Thomas. *Life's Little Ironies.* 1894. Harper. 1st. gilt gr cloth. VG. M24. $100.00

HARDY, Thomas. *Poems of the Past & Present.* 1902. Harper 1st Am. gilt gr cloth. M24. $165.00

HARDY, Thomas. *Tess of the D'Urbervilles.* 1892. NY. Harper. 1st Am. gilt tan cloth. M24. $450.00

HARDY, Thomas. *Woodlanders.* 1887. NY. 1st Am hc. 12mo. bl half cloth/marbled brd. VG. A11. $185.00

HARDY & PINNEY. *Vineyards & Wine Cellars of California: Essay...* 1994. BC of CA. 1/450. 4to. ils. purple brd. F/box. R3. $200.00

HARE, Augustus J. *Gurneys of Earlham.* 1895. Dodd Mead. 2 vol. G+. V3. $32.00

HARE, Augustus J. *Life & Letters of Baroness Bunsen.* 1880s. NY. Routledge. thick 8vo. 2 vol in 1. gilt blk cloth. VG. T10. $50.00

HARE, Cyril. *English Murder.* 1951. Little Brn. 1st Am. F/dj. M15. $70.00

HARGRAVE, Lydon Lane. *Report on Archaeological Reconnaissance...* 1935. Berkeley. 8vo. 56p. stiff wrp. F7. $75.00

HARGREAVES, Bruce J. *Succulent Spurges of Malawi.* 1987. np. ils/maps/drawings. cbdg. F. B26. $20.00

HARING, C.H. *Spanish Empire in America.* 1947. NY. Oxford. map ep. F. O7. $75.00

HARING, C.H. *Trade & Navigation Between Spain & Indies...* 1964 (1918). Gloucester. Peter Smith. double-p map. F. O7. $55.00

HARIOT, Thomas. *Brief & True Report of the New Found Land of Virginia.* 1951. Ann Arbor. Clements Lib. facsimile 1588 ed. 1/500. 8vo. unp. M/case. H13. $65.00

HARJO, Joy. *In Mad Love & War.* 1990. Middletown. Wesleyan U. 1st. author's 2nd book. F/F clip. L3. $75.00

HARJO, Joy. *She Had Some Horses.* 1983. NY/Chicago. Thunder's Mouth. 1st hc issue. F/F. L3. $250.00

HARJO, Joy. *Woman Who Fell From the Sky.* 1994. Norton. 1st. inscr/dtd. F/clip. L3. $75.00

HARKER, A. *Metamorphism: A Study of Transformations of Rock-Masses.* 1939. Dutton. 2nd. 185 diagrams. 362p. F. D8. $20.00

HARLAND, Marion. *Complete Cookbook.* 1906 (1903). ils. 709p. VG. E6. $65.00

HARLAND, Marion. *House & Home: A Complete Housewife's Guide.* ca 1889. Clawson Bros. 532p. fair. B10. $65.00

HARLOW, A. *Road of the Century.* 1947. NY. 1st. VG/G. B5. $50.00

HARMAN, F. Ward. *Ship Models Illustrated, With Working Guide to Modeling.* 1943. NY. Marine Model Co. 1st. 128p. VG/dj. P4. $45.00

HARMAN, H.H. *Modern Factor Analysis.* 1967. Chicago. 474p. NF/dj. D8. $30.00

HARMER, Jenny. *North Australian Plants. Part 1: Wildflowers...* 1970s. np. photos. 132p. glossy photo brd. as new. B26. $21.00

HARMETZ, Aljean. *Making of the Wizard of Oz.* 1977. Knopf. ils/photos. 350p. F/F. A4. $75.00

HARMETZ, Aljean. *Making of the Wizard of Oz.* 1977. Knopf. photos. NF/dj. C9. $40.00

HARMON, Harry. *Picasso for Children.* 1962. 1st. ils. VG/VG. S13. $20.00

HARNSBERGER, Caroline. *Mark Twain, Family Man.* 1960. Citadel. 1st. cloth. F/dj. M24. $45.00

HARNSBERGER, Caroline. *Mark Twain's Clara.* 1982. Evanston, IL. Ward Schori. 1st. gr cloth. F/dj. M24. $20.00

HAROLD, Childe. *Child's Book of Abridged Wisdom.* 1905. Paul Elder. 1st. French fld p/cords. VG. P2. $100.00

HARPENDING, Asbury. *Great Diamond Hoax.* 1958. Norman, OK. 1st thus. Western Frontier Lib series. VG/dj. M24. $15.00

HARPER, Michael. *Photographs, Negatives: History As Apple Tree.* 1972. SF. Scarab. 1st. assn copy. F/dj. V1. $25.00

HARPER, Wilhellmina. *Gunniwolf & Other Merry Tales.* 1936. McKay/Jr Literary Guild. 1st thus. 104p. G+/G. P2. $65.00

HARPER, Wilhelmina. *Gunniwolf & Other Merry Tales.* 1937. London. Harrap. 1st. lg 8vo. G+. C8. $20.00

HARPER, Wilhelmina. *Little Book of Necessary Ballads.* 1930. Harper. 1st. 86p. NF. D4. $35.00

HARPER, Wilhelmina. *Selfish Giant & Other Stories.* 1935. McKay. probable 1st. ils Kate Seredy. 86p. VG/G+. P2. $80.00

HARPER, Wilhelmina. *Uncle Sam's Story Book.* 1944. McKay/Jr Literary Guild. 1st thus. 144p. NF/VG-. P2. $20.00

HARRE, T. Everett. *Behold the Woman.* 1916. Lippincott. NF. M2. $15.00

HARRIGAN, Edward. *Ten Little Mulligan Guards.* 1874. McLoughlin. 10 mc pl. pict wrp. M1. $225.00

HARRING, Harro. *Dolores: Novel of South America.* 1846. NY/Montevideo. 4 parts as issued. inscr. 4to. R12. $675.00

HARRINGTON, Alan. *Paradise 1.* 1978. Little Brn. 1st. F/dj. M2. $15.00

HARRINGTON, H.D. *Manual of Plants in Colorado.* 1964 (1954). Chicago. 2nd. map. 666p. gilt emb tan cloth. F. B26. $63.00

HARRINGTON, James. *Aphorismes Politiques.* 1795. Paris. Didot Jeune. 8vo. ftspc. brd. R12. $475.00

HARRINGTON, Ollie. *Bootsie & Others.* 1958. Dodd Mead. 1st. NF. M25. $75.00

HARRINGTON, William. *Cromwell File.* 1986. St Martin. 1st. NF/VG. N4. $17.50

HARRINGTON, William. *Virus.* 1991. Morrow. 1st. F/F. M22. $15.00

HARRINGTON. *Southwest in Children's Books, a Bibliography.* 1952. LSU. 143p. VG. A4. $65.00

HARRIS, Albert W. *Blood of the Arab.* 1941. Chicago. private prt. 1st. VG. O#. $125.00

HARRIS, Beth Coombe. *In the Grip of the Druids.* 1930s. London. VG. M2. $50.00

HARRIS, Burton. *John Colter, His Years in the Rockies.* 1952. Scribner. 1st. 180p. VG/dj. J2. $225.00

HARRIS, Clare. *Away From Here & Now.* 1947. Dorrance. 1st. F/dj. M2. $35.00

HARRIS, Credo. *Motor Rambles in Italy.* 1912. Moffat Yard. 1st. photos. VG. K3. $20.00

HARRIS, Dorothy Joan. *House Mouse.* 1974. London. Warne. 1st Eng. 8vo. ils Barbara Cooney. 46p. VG/dj. T5. $30.00

HARRIS, Frank. *Contemporary Portraits.* 1915. NY. Mitchell Kennerley. 1st Am. inscr Joseph Conrad. teg. gilt gr cloth. F. M24. $1,350.00

HARRIS, Frank. *Oscar Wilde, His Life & Confessions.* 1918. NY. 1st trade. 2 vol. gilt gr cloth. VG. K7. $65.00

HARRIS, Helena J. *Southern Sketches. Cecil Gray; or, The Soldier's Revenge.* 1866. New Orleans. 1st. 12mo. 20p. emb lib stp on title. prt wrp. M1. $300.00

HARRIS, Henry. *California's Medical Story.* 1932. SF. JW Stacey. inscr pres. ils. NF. R3. $100.00

HARRIS, Jessie W. *Everyday Foods.* 1939. Houghton Mifflin. G. A16. $10.00

HARRIS, Joel Chandler. *Chronicles of Aunt Minervy Ann.* 1899. London. Dent. 1st Eng. ils AB Frost. 12mo. VG+. C8. $250.00

HARRIS, Joel Chandler. *Chronicles of Aunt Minervy Ann.* 1899. Toronto. Wm Briggs. 1st Canadian. ils AB Frost. VG+/wrp. C8. $150.00

HARRIS, Joel Chandler. *Daddy Jake, the Runaway & Other Stories.* 1889. NY. Century. 1st. 4to. 145p. glazed brd. G. D1. $200.00

HARRIS, Joel Chandler. *Stories From Uncle Remus.* 1934. Saalfield. sm 4to. F/VG. M5. $125.00

HARRIS, Joel Chandler. *Tales From Uncle Remus.* 1935. Houghton Mifflin. sgn by daughter-in-law/dtd 1948. red brd. VG. B11. $100.00

HARRIS, Joel Chandler. *Uncle Remus & Brer Rabbit.* 1907. Stokes. 1st thus. obl 4to. gr cloth/label. R5. $375.00

HARRIS, Joel Chandler. *Uncle Remus Returns.* Sept 1918. Boston. Houghton Mifflin. 1st. ils AB Frost. pict cloth. F. B14. $75.00

HARRIS, Joel Chandler. *Uncle Remus.* nd. Nelson. ils Harry Rountree. 12mo. VG. M5. $45.00

HARRIS, Joel Chandler. *Uncle Remus: His Songs & Sayings.* 1957. NY. LEC. 1/1500. ils/sgn Seong Moy. F/case. T10. $90.00

HARRIS, Joel Chandler. *Uncle Remus: New Stories of the Old Plantation.* 1905. NY. McClure Phillips. 1st. ils Frost/Conde/Verbeck. teg. red textured cloth. R5. $275.00

HARRIS, John W. *Africa: Slave or Free?* 1969 (1919). NY. Negro U. rpt. 8vo. 244p. VG. W1. $25.00

HARRIS, John. *Chapter of Kings by Mr Collins Illustrated by 38 Engravings.* 1818. London. J Harris. 1st. 16mo. gilt red leather. R5. $485.00

HARRIS, John. *Scenes in America for the Amusement & Instruction...* 1822. London. J Harris. 2nd. 85 #d engravings/fld map. leather-backed pict brd. R5. $225.00

HARRIS, Joseph. *Gardening for Young & Old.* 1905 (1882). Orange Judd. 191p. gilt bdg. A10. $50.00

HARRIS, MacDonald. *Hemingway's Suitcase.* 1990. S&S. 1st. NF/F. A20. $20.00

HARRIS, R.J. *Primer of Multivariate Statistics.* 1975. NY. Academic. 1st. 332p. NF. D8. $30.00

HARRIS, Robert. *Selling Hitler.* 1986. Pantheon. 1st Am. ils. 8vo. 402p. F/dj. K3. $20.00

HARRIS, Rosemary. *Child in the Bamboo Grove.* 1971. Faber. 1st. sm 4to. F/dj. M5. $65.00

HARRIS, Rosemary. *Tower of the Stars.* 1980. London. 1st. F/jd. M2. $12.00

HARRIS, Seale. *Woman's Surgeon, J Marion Sims.* 1950. NY. 1st. VG/VG. B5. $35.00

HARRIS, Thomas A. *I'm OK — You're OK.* 1969. Harper Row. author's 1st book. 278p. NF/NF. W2. $30.00

HARRIS, Thomas L. *Conversation in Heaven. A Wisdom Song.* 1984. Fountaingrove, CA. private prt. 1st. 8vo. cloth. M1. $125.00

HARRIS, Thomas L. *Star-Flowers, a Poem of the Woman's Mystery.* 1986. Fountaingrove, CA. private prt. 1st. 8vo. 121p. cloth. M1. $85.00

HARRIS, Thomas. *Black Sunday.* 1975. Putnam. 1st. author's 1st book. F/NF. H11. $165.00

HARRIS, Thomas. *Black Sunday.* 1975. Putnam. 1st. NF/NF. B2. $150.00

HARRIS, Thomas. *Black Sunday.* 1975. Putnam. 1st. VG/dj. Q1. $100.00

HARRIS, Thomas. *Red Dragon.* 1981. Putnam. 1st. F/dj. B3. $60.00

HARRIS, Thomas. *Red Dragon.* 1981. Putnam. 1st. NF/NF. D10/T11. $50.00

HARRIS, Thomas. *Red Dragon.* 1981. Putnam. 1st. NF/VG. M19/M22. $25.00

HARRIS, Thomas. *Silence of the Lambs.* 1988. St Martin. 1st. F/F. B3. $60.00

HARRIS, Thomas. *Silence of the Lambs.* 1988. St Martin. 1st. NF/F. T11. $45.00

HARRIS, Thomas. *Silence of the Lambs.* 1988. St Martin. 1st. NF/clip. A24. $35.00

HARRIS, W.S. *Life in a Thousand Worlds.* nd (1905). Beaver Springs, PA. Am Pub. 8vo. 344p. H1. $30.00

HARRIS, Wilfred. *Neuritis & Neuralgia.* 1926. London. Milford/Oxford. 418p. pebbled bl cloth. VG. G1. $50.00

HARRIS & HARRIS. *Blackfellow Bundi: A Native Australian Boy.* 1939. Whitman. 1st. ils Kurt Wiese. 63p. F/VG. P2. $65.00

HARRIS & HARRIS. *Complete Etchings of Rembrandt.* 1970. Bounty Books. VG/VG. M17. $20.00

HARRIS & HARRIS. *Eldon House: 5 Women's Views of the 19th Century.* 1994. Toronto. Champlain Soc. 1st. 8vo. 517p. red cloth. F. P4. $125.00

HARRIS & WEEKS. *X-Raying the Pharoahs: Most Important Breakthrough...* 1973. NY. 1st. ils. 195p. dj. A13. $100.00

HARRISON, Chip; see Block, Lawrence.

HARRISON, Colin. *Bodies Electric.* 1993. NY. Crown. 1st. F/F. B3. $30.00

HARRISON, Edith Ogden. *Princess of Sayrane.* 1910. McClurg. 1st. VG. M2. $45.00

HARRISON, Edith. *Below the Equator.* 1918. McClurg. 1st. photos. 288p. red cloth. F3. $20.00

HARRISON, Everett F. *Introduction to the New Testament.* 1982. Eerdmans. 507p. VG/dj. B29. $8.50

HARRISON, Fairfax. *Belair Stud 1747-1761.* 1929. Richmond. 1st. w/card. O3. $175.00

HARRISON, Gordon. *Mosquitoes, Malaria & Man: A History...* 1978. NY. 314p. F/NF. S15. $15.00

HARRISON, Grace Clergue. *Allied Cookery: British, French, Italian, Belgian, Russian.* 1916. Putnam. G. A16. $30.00

HARRISON, Harry. *Bill, the Galactic Hero.* 1965. Doubleday. 1st. NF/dj. M2. $135.00

HARRISON, Harry. *Spaceship Medic.* 1970. London. Faber. 1st. sgn. F/F. T2. $125.00

HARRISON, Harry. *Stainless Steel Rat's Revenge.* 1970. Walker. 1st. NF/dj. M2. $40.00

HARRISON, Harry. *Two Tales & 8 Tomorrows: Science Fiction Stories.* 1965. London. Gollancz. 1st. sgn. F/NF. T2. $95.00

HARRISON, Harry. *West of Eden.* 1984. Bantam. 1st. F/dj. M2. $22.00

HARRISON, Harry. *Year 2000.* 1970. Doubleday. 1st. F/dj. M2. $20.00

HARRISON, Jamie. *Edge of Crazies.* 1995. Hyperion. 1st. sgn. author's 1st book. F/F. A23. $45.00

HARRISON, Jim. *Dalva.* 1988. Dutton/Lawrence. 1st. author's 7th novel. F/F. D10. $45.00

HARRISON, Jim. *Farmer.* 1976. Viking. 1st. inscr. author's 3rd novel. F/F. D10. $150.00

HARRISON, Jim. *Good Day To Die.* 1973. S&S. 1st. F/F. D10. $250.00

HARRISON, Jim. *Julip.* 1994. Boston. 1st. sgn. F/F. A11. $75.00

HARRISON, Jim. *Legends of the Fall.* 1979. Delacorte. trade ed (1 vol). wht linen. F/F. T11. $130.00

HARRISON, Jim. *Legends of the Fall.* 1979. Delacorte. 1st. rem mk. NF/NF clip. H11. $60.00

HARRISON, Jim. *Legends of the Fall.* 1979. Delacorte. 1st. VG/dj. Q1. $75.00

HARRISON, Jim. *Legends of the Fall.* 1979. Delacorte. 1st. 3 vol. wht cloth. F/sans/case. T11. $250.00

HARRISON, Jim. *Letters to Yesenin & Returning to Earth.* 1979. Los Angeles. Sumac Poetry series. NF/sans/wrp. T11. $75.00

HARRISON, Jim. *Locations.* 1968. NY. 1st. sgn. F/wrp. A11. $135.00

HARRISON, Jim. *Selected & New Poems: 1961-1981.* 1982. Delacorte. 1st. ils Russell Chatham. F/dj. V1. $110.00

HARRISON, Jim. *Sundog.* 1984. Dutton. 1st. sgn. F/F. H11. $80.00

HARRISON, Jim. *Sundog.* 1984. Dutton. 1st. sgn. NF/VG. R14. $50.00

HARRISON, Jim. *Sundog.* 1984. NY. Dutton. 1st. author's 6th novel. F/dj. D10. $50.00

HARRISON, Jim. *Warlock.* 1981. Delacorte. 1st. F/F. T11. $75.00

HARRISON, Jim. *Wolf.* 1971. S&S. 1st. sgn. author's 1st novel. F/NF. L3. $275.00

HARRISON, Kathryn. *Thicker Than Water.* 1991. Random. 1st. author's 1st book. F/F. R13. $35.00

HARRISON, Orlando. *How To Grow & Market Fruit.* 1911. Berlin, MD. 142p. VG. A10. $28.00

HARRISON, Paul Carter. *Drama of Mommo.* 1972. NY. Grove. 1st. 245p. F/F. B4. $50.00

HARRISON, Peter. *Brick Pavement: The Architects' & Builders' Companion.* 1994. Raleigh. self pub. 167p. M. A10. $30.00

HARRISON, Peter. *Seabirds: An Identification Guide.* 1893. Boston. 1st. 88 mc pl. 448p. F/F. S15. $38.00

HARRISON, R.K. *Archaeology of the New Testament.* 1964. Assn. 138p. VG/dj. B29. $8.00

HARRISON, Richard E. *Know Your Garden Series: Climbers & Trailers.* 1973. Cape Town. photos. 115p. VG/dj. B26. $37.50

HARRISON, Robert. *Dublin Dissector; or, Manual of Anatomy.* 1835. Phil. 1st Am. 314p. wrp. A13. $45.00

HARRISON, Whit; see Whittington, Harry.

HARRISON, William. *Roller Ball Murder.* 1974. Morrow. 1st. NF/dj. P3. $20.00

HARRISON, William. *Roller Ball Murder.* 1974. NY. 1st. sgn. F/NF. A11. $60.00

HARRISON & HARRISON. *Trees & Shrubs.* 1965. Rutland/Tokyo. Tuttle. 4to. 582 mc pl. F/VG. A22. $20.00

HARRISON & LOBBAN. *Seaweed Edology & Physiology.* 1994. Cambridge. 8vo. 366p. NF. B1. $45.00

HARRON, Robert. *Rockne: Idol of American Football.* 1931. Burt. 1st. photos/scores/rosters. G. P8. $20.00

HARRY, Eric. *Arc Light.* 1994. S&S. 1st. sgn. F/F. A23. $36.00

HARSHBERGER, John W. *Botanists of Philadelphia & Their Work.* 1899. Phil. 457p. gilt bl cloth. VG. B26. $295.00

HART, Carolyn. *Scandal in Fair Haven.* 1994. Bantam. 1st. sgn. VG/VG. A23. $35.00

HART, Carolyn. *Southern Ghost.* 1992. Bantam. 1st. sgn. F/F. A23. $35.00

HART, Cyril. *Verderers & Forest Laws of Dean.* 1971. Newton Abbot. David & Charles. M11. $45.00

HART, Francis Russell. *Admirals of the Caribbean.* 1922. Houghton Mifflin. inscr. 203p. map ep. P4. $60.00

HART, Henry H. *Venetian Adventurer...Life & Times of Marco Polo.* 1942. Stanford. ils/maps/index/bibliography.   284p. bl/rust cloth. P4. $65.00

HART, James. *Man Who Invented Hollywood...DW Griffith.* 1972. Louisville. 1st. 170p. VG. A17. $18.50

HART, Jerome. *In Our Second Century.* 1931. Pioneer. 1st ed. 454p. G. A17. $20.00

HART, Josephine. *Damage.* 1991. Knopf. 1st. sgn. F/F. R14. $50.00

HART, Liddell. *Colonel Lawrence: Man Behind the Legend.* 1937. Dodd Mead. 6th. 406p. VG. W1. $32.00

HART, R. *Leavening Agents: Yeast, Leaven, Salt-Rising...* 1912. VG. E6. $20.00

HART, Robert W. *Philippines Today.* 1928. Dodd Mead. photos. 191p. VG. P1. $25.00

HART, William. *Told Under a White Oak Tree by Bill Hart's Pinto Pony.* 1922. Houghton Mifflin. 1st. ils J Montgomery Flagg. 51p. VG/dj. J2. $65.00

HARTE, Bret. *Echoes of the Foothills.* 1875. 1st Am. VG. S13. $45.00

HARTE, Bret. *Jack Hamilton's Meditation.* 1899. 1st Am. VG. S13. $45.00

HARTE, Bret. *Lectures of Bret Harte.* 1909. NY. Chas Kozlay. 1st/trade issue. gilt brn cloth. M24. $75.00

HARTE, Bret. *Luck of Roaring Camp & Other Sketches.* 1899. Grosset Dunlap. ne. 256p. xl. G. W2. $95.00

HARTE, Bret. *Sally Dows & Other Stories.* 1893. 1st Am. VG. S13. $45.00

HARTE, Bret. *Trent's Trust.* 1903. 1st Am. VG. S13. $45.00

HARTE, Bret. *Under the Redwoods.* 1901. 1st Am. VG. S13. $45.00

HARTER & THOMPSON. *John Irving.* 1986. Twayne. 1st. F/F. T11. $30.00

HARTFORD, John. *Steamboat in a Cornfield.* 1986. NY. Crown. 1st. photos. F/F. D4. $25.00

HARTHAN, John P. *Bookbindings.* 1961. London. 2nd. VG. T9. $20.00

HARTLEY, Cecil B. *Heroes & Patriots of the South.* 1860. Phil. Evans. 320p. dk gr cloth. VG. K7. $50.00

HARTLEY, L.P. *Arm of Mrs Egan.* 1951. London. 1st. VG. M2. $20.00

HARTLEY, L.P. *Hireling.* 1957. London. 1st. VG/dj. T9. $35.00

HARTLEY, Margaret L. *Southwest Review Reader.* 1974. SMU. 242p. VG/VG. B19. $25.00

HARTLEY & INGILBY. *Vanishing Folkways.* 1971. S Brunswick. 1st Am. ils. 128p. VG/dj. B18. $15.00

HARTMAN, David. *Maimonides: Torah & Philosophic Quest.* 1977. JPS. 2nd imp. 296p. VG+/G+. S3. $25.00

HARTMAN, Joan. *Chinese Jade of Five Centuries.* 1969. 1st. photos. NF/clip. S13. $35.00

HARTMANN, Ernest L. *Biology of Dreaming.* 1967. Springfield, IL. C Thomas. 206p. VG/dj. G1. $50.00

HARTMANN, William. *Desert Heart: Chronicles of the Sonoran Desert.* 1989. Fisher Books. 1st. ils/index/notes. 216p. F/F. B19. $50.00

HARTMANN, William. *In the Stream of Stars: Soviet/American Space Art Book.* 1990. Workman. 1st. F/dj. M2. $30.00

HARTMANN & KESTER. *Plant Propagation Principles & Practices.* 1968. Prentice Hall. 2nd. 702p. dj. A10. $28.00

HARTNEY, Harold E. *Up & at 'Em.* 1940. Harrisburg. 2nd. inscr. 333p. G+. B18. $65.00

HARTNOLL, Phyllis. *Oxford Companion to the Theatre.* 1951. London. 1st. VG/dj. T9. $25.00

HARTUNG, Marion T. *First Book of Carnival Glass...Tenth Book of Carnival Glass.* 1962-1973. Emporia, KS. self pub. 10 vol. 8vo. 100 patterns per book. VG or better. H1. $175.00

HARUF, Kent. *Tie That Binds.* 1984. HRW. 1st. inscr/dtd 1984. F/F. B3. $50.00

HARVESTER, Simon. *Nameless Road.* 1969. Walker. 1st. 199p. VG/dj. M20. $15.00

HARVEY, Henry. *History of the Shawnee Indians From Year 1681 to 1854.* 1855. Cincinnati. Ephraim Morgan. 1st/2nd issue. 316p. D11. $250.00

HARVEY, Peggy. *Great Recipes From the World's Great Cooks.* 1964. Gramercy. VG/dj. A16. $10.00

HARVEY, Peggy. *Horn of Plenty.* 1964. Boston. Little Brn. 1st. ils. VG/dj. A16. $10.00

HARVEY, Samuel. *History of Hemostasis.* 1929. NY. 1st. 128p. A13. $50.00

HARVEY, W.F. *Debatable Tumours in Human & Animal Pathology.* 1940. Edinburgh. 1st. 124p. dj. A13. $25.00

HARVEY-GIBSON, R.J. *Outlines of the History of Botany.* 1919. London. 274p. xl. B26. $49.00

HARWELL, Richard. *Margaret Mitchell's Gone With the Wind Letters 1936-1949.* 1976. Macmillan. dj. A19. $20.00

HASAN, Sana. *Enemy in the Promised Land.* 1986. Pantheon. 1st. tall 8vo. 335p. cloth. VG/dj. W1. $20.00

HASELTON, Scott E. *Cacti for the Amateur.* 1958 (1938). Pasadena. ils. 132p. brn cloth. B26. $17.50

HASKELL, W.E. *News Print: Origina of Papermaking & Manufacturing...* 1921. Int'l Paper Co. 72p. G. A17. $30.00

HASLUCK, Paul. *Greenhouse & Conservatory Construction & Heating.* 1907. London. Cassell. 160p. VG. A10. $40.00

HASSALL, John. *Our Diary or Teddy & Me.* ca 1905. London. Thomas Nelson. 4to. pict brd. R5. $335.00

HASSE, Carl. *Hand-Atlas der Sensiblen und Motorischen Gebiete...* 1895. Wiesbaden. Bergmann. 36 mc lithos. xl. VG. G1. $150.00

HASSELL, M.P. *Dynamics of Arthropod Predator-Prey Stystems.* 1978. Princeton. 237p. F/wrp. B1. $20.00

HASSIN, George B. *Histopathology of the Peripheral & Central Nervous System.* 1933. Baltimore. Wm Wood. heavy 8vo. 491p. panelled pebbled bl cloth. VG. G1. $50.00

HASSLER, Jon. *Love Hunter.* 1988. Morrow. 1st. NF/dj. M25. $50.00

HASSLER, Jon. *Simon's Night.* 1979. Atheneum. 1st. NF/dj. M25. $75.00

HASSRICK, P.H. *Frederic Remington: Paintings, Drawings & Sculpture...* 1973. Abrams. ils. 218p. F/dj. M4. $45.00

HASTINGS, George T. *Trees of Santa Monica.* 1956. Santa Monica. self pub. 1st. VG/sans. O4. $25.00

HASTINGS, Howard L. *Top Horse of Crecent Ranch.* 1942. Cupples Leon. 1st. VG. O3. $18.00

HASTINGS, Margaret. *Court of Common Pleas in 15th-Century England...* 1971 (1947). Hamden. Archon. facsimile. M11. $45.00

HASTINGS, Max. *Das Reich: March of the 2nd Panzer Division Through France.* 1981. NY. 1st. photos/notes/index. 264p. VG/VG. S16. $30.00

HASTINGS, Max. *Overlord: D-Day, June 6, 1944.* 1984. S&S. 1st Am. 368p. VG/dj. M20. $15.00

HASTINGS, Milo. *City of Endless Night.* 1974 (1920). Hyperion. rpt. F. M2. $35.00

HATA & IZAWA. *Japanese Naval Aces & Fighter Units in World War II.* 1989. Annapolis. photos/index. 442p. VG/VG. S16. $25.00

HATCH, Eric. *Year of the Horse.* 1960. Crown. 1st. VG/VG. O3. $22.00

HATCH, Gardner. *American Ex-Prisoners of War.* 1988. Paducah. 184p. VG. S16. $50.00

HATCHER, Harlan. *Western Reserve: Story of New Connnecticut in Ohio.* 1949. Bobbs Merrill. 1st. 365p. VG+/dj. M20. $25.00

HATFIELD, Bud. *Wealth Within Reach.* 1992. Dallas. World. 1st. inscr. F/F. A23. $36.00

HATFIELD, Mrs. Mark O. *More Remarkable Recipes.* 1970. Beaverton. Criterion. 1st. sgn. F/F. A23. $36.00

HATHAWAY, B.A. *1001 Questions & Answers on Arithmetic.* 1887. Lebanon, OH. 161p. G+. B18. $25.00

HATHAWAY, N. *Unicorn.* 1980. Viking. ils/photos. 191p. F/VG+. M12. $45.00

HATT, D.E. *Sitka Spruce: Songs of Queen Charlotte Islands.* 1919. Vancouver. RP Latta. 51p. VG/prt wrp. P4. $25.00

HATTERAS, Owen; see Menken, H.L.

HATZAN, A. Leon. *True Story of Hiawatha & History of the Six Nation Indians.* 1925. Toronto. 1st. 8vo. ils. 298p. gilt red cloth. F/VG. H3. $85.00

HAUSER, Hillary. *Women in Sports: Scuba Diving.* 1976. NY. Harvey House. 1st. photos. 80p. VG+. A25. $8.00

HAUSTEIN, Erik. *Cactus Handbook.* 1988. Seacaucus, NJ. 320p. F/dj. B26. $22.50

HAVIARAS, Stratis. *Crossing the River.* 1976. Cleveland. 1st. sgn. NF/decor gray wrp. A11. $55.00

HAVIGHURST, Walter. *Voices on the River.* 1964. Macmillan. 1st. ils. 310p. T7. $28.00

HAVILAND, Virginia. *Favorite Fairy Tales Told in Denmark.* 1971. Little Brn. 1st. 90p. F/G. P2. $25.00

HAVILAND, Virginia. *Favorite Fairy Tales Told in England.* 1959. Little Brn. 1st. 88p. F/VG. P2. $25.00

HAVILAND, Virginia. *Favorite Fairy Tales Told in France.* 1959. Little Brn. 1st. ils Roger Duvoisin. 92p. NF/VG-. P2. $30.00

HAVILAND. *Samuel Langhorne Clemens: A Centennial for Tom Sawyer.* 1976. ils. 95p. F. A4. $45.00

HAVLICEK & RYAN. *Hondo: Celtic Man in Motion.* 1977. Prentice Hall. 1st. VG/dj. P8. $35.00

HAWES, Charles Boardman. *Dark Frigate.* 1923. Atlantic Monthly. 1st. 8vo. VG+. M5. $75.00

HAWGOOD, J.A. *America's Western Frontiers. Exploration & Settlement...* 1967. NY. 1st. ils. 440p. F/dj. M4. $20.00

HAWKER, C.E. *Chats About Wine.* 1907. London. Daly. 154p. fair. B10. $25.00

HAWKES, Jacquetta. *Province Island.* 1959. RAndom. 1st. NF/dj. M2. $20.00

HAWKES, John. *Adventures in the Alaskan Skin Trade.* 1985. NY. S&S. 1st prt. rem mk. VG/dj. P4. $25.00

HAWKES, John. *Death, Sleep & the Traveler.* 1974. New Directions. 1st. F/dj. D10. $50.00

HAWKES, John. *Passion Artist.* 1979. Harper Row. 1st. F/F. B35. $30.00

HAWKESWORTH, Ed. *Adventurer.* 1788. Dublin. Moore. 4 vol. new/corrected. tall 12mo. tree calf. H13. $325.00

HAWKEY, Raymond. *Evolution.* 1987. Putnam. 1st Am. popup/ils Christos Kondeatis. 4to. F. P2. $35.00

HAWKING, Stephen W. *Brief History of Time: From Big Bang to Black Holes.* 1988. Bantam. 1st. intro Carl Sagan. F/F. B4. $250.00

HAWKINS, Daisy Waterhouse. *Old Point Lace & How To Copy It.* 1878. London. Chatto Windus. 12mo. 17 fld charts. gilt cloth. VG. T10. $175.00

HAWKINS, John. *General History of the Science & Practice of Music.* 1853. London. Novello. New Ed. 3 vol. cloth. VG. T10. $150.00

HAWKINS & WHITE. *Stonehenge Decoded.* 1966 (1965). Doubleday. revised. G/dj. K5. $20.00

HAWKSWORTH & WIENS. *Biology & Classification of Dwarf Mistletoes.* 1972. WA. Forest Service. tall 8vo. 234p. VG. A22. $25.00

HAWLEY, R. *Practice of Silvaculture.* 1946 (1921). VG/torn. E6. $15.00

HAWLEY, Walter A. *Oriental Rugs.* 1913. John Lane. 1st. 11 full-p pl/80 pl/4 maps. 4to. 320p. teg. buckram. T10. $200.00

HAWORTH, P.L. *Trailmakers of the Northwest.* 1921. Harcourt. ils. 277p. cloth. VG. M12. $30.00

HAWTHORNE, Hildegarde. *Life of Thomas Paine.* 1949. Longmans. 1st. VG/dj. W2. $15.00

HAWTHORNE, Julian. *Nathaniel Hawthorne & His Wife.* 1884. Cambridge. Riverside. 1st. 2 vol. 1/350 on lg paper. uncut. M24. $300.00

HAWTHORNE, Nathaniel. *House of the Seven Gables, a Romance.* 1851. Boston. 1st. 8vo. 344p. cloth/rebacked. M1. $750.00

HAWTHORNE, Nathaniel. *House of the Seven Gables, a Romance.* 1851. Ticknor Reed Fields. 1st/2nd prt. gilt brn cloth. M24. $500.00

HAWTHORNE, Nathaniel. *Marble Faun; or, The Romance of Monte Beni.* 1931. LEC. 2 vol. 1/1500. ils/sgn Sarl Straus. NF. M19. $50.00

HAWTHORNE, Nathaniel. *Our Old Home: A Series of English Sketches.* 1863. Ticknor Fields. 1st/1st state. gilt brn cloth. NF. M24. $150.00

HAWTHORNE, Nathaniel. *Snow Image: A Childish Miracle.* 1854. NY. James Gregory. thin 12mo. 31p. gilt bl cloth. VG. T10. $300.00

HAWTHORNE, Nathaniel. *Tales of the White Hills.* 1877. Boston. Osgood. 1st thus. gilt gr cloth. M24. $100.00

HAWTHORNE, Nathaniel. *Tanglewood Tales.* 1853. Ticknor Reed Fields. 1st/1st prt. gilt brn cloth (1st bdg). G. M24. $300.00

HAWTHORNE, Nathaniel. *Tanglewood Tales.* 1921. Phil. Penn. 1st thus. ils Sterrett/10 mc pl. 261p. VG. D1. $285.00

HAWTHORNE, Nathaniel. *Twice-Told Tales.* 1842. Boston. James Munroe. 1st thus/1st issue. pub pres. 2 vol. blk cloth. M24. $3,500.00

HAWTHORNE, Nathaniel. *Wonder-Book for Girls & Boys.* 1852. Ticknor Reed Fields. 1st/2nd prt. gilt bl cloth. VG. M24. $500.00

HAWTHORNE, Nathaniel. *Wonder-Book for Girls & Boys.* 1893. Riverside. 1/250. ils Walter Crane. 210p. teg. VG/dj. D1. $700.00

HAXARD, F. *Profitable Pigeon Breeding.* 1922. 1st. ils. VG. E6. $25.00

HAY, Henry. *Cyclopedia of Magic.* 1949. Phil. 498p. VG/dj. S1. $10.00

HAY, Thomas Robson. *Hood's Tennessee Campaign.* 1929. NY. Neale. 1st. 272p. cl. cloth. NF. M8. $125.00

HAY. *Sambo Sahib: Story of Little Black Sambo & Helen Bannerman.* 1981. 1st. 205p. F/F. A4/D1. $75.00

HAYAT, M.A. *Principles & Techniques of Electron Microscopy.* 1978. Van Nostrand. 318p. F/F. B1. $40.00

HAYCRAFT, Howard. *Murder for Pleasure: Life & Times of Detective Story.* 1941. Appleton Century. 1st. NF/G+. N4. $40.00

HAYDEN, Robert. *Kaleidoscope: Poems by American Negro Poets.* 1967. HBW. 1st. VG/dj. M25. $50.00

HAYDEN, Robert. *Night-Blooming Cereus.* 1972. London. 1st. 1/150. sgn Hayden/Paul Breman. F/wrp. w/prospectus. A11. $185.00

HAYDEN & WAKE. *Bonnie & Clyde Book.* 1972. S&S. 69 photos. cloth. F/dj. C9. $45.00

HAYES, Helen. *Gathering of Hope.* 1983. Phil. Fortress. sgn. VG/VG. B11. $18.00

HAYES & YOUNG. *Norman & the Nursery School.* nd (1949). Platt Munk. sm 4to. unp. NF/VG. C14. $18.00

HAYLEY & SMITH. *Life on the Texas Range.* 1952. TX Pr. 1st. 112p. VG/VG case. J2. $235.00

HAYMAKER, Webb. *Bing's Local Diagnosis in Neurological Diseases.* 1956. St Louis. Mosby. 2nd Eng-language. 478p. xl. G1. $65.00

HAYMAKER & WOODHALL. *Peripheral Nerve Injuries: Principles of Diagnosis.* 1945. Phil. Saunders. 1st. 227p. prt gray cloth. G1. $100.00

HAYS, H.R. *Dangerous Sex: Myth of Feminine Evil.* 1964. Putnam. 1st. 316p. VG. A25. $10.00

HAYTHORNTHWAITE, Philip F. *British Infantry of the Napoleonic Wars.* 1987. ils. VG/VG. M17. $25.00

HAYWOOD, Carolyn. *Eddie Makes Music.* 1957. Morrow. 1st. 191p. VG/G+. P2. $30.00

HAYWOOD, Carolyn. *Taffy & Melissa Molasses.* 1969. Morrow. 1st. sgn. F/VG+. P2. $35.00

HAYWOOD, Gar Anthony. *Fear of the Dark.* 1988. St Martin. 1st. author's 1st book. F/NF. A24. $75.00

HAYWOOD, Gar Anthony. *Fear of the Dark.* 1988. St Martin. 1st. sgn. F/NF. M15. $100.00

HAYWOOD, Gar Anthony. *Not Long for This World.* 1990. St Martin. 1st. F/NF. A24/M23. $50.00

HAYWOOD & OSTLER. *Spencer Haywood: Rise, Fall & Recovery.* 1992. Amistad. ARC. F/F. w/promo material. B4. $35.00

HAZARD, Caroline. *Brief Pilgrimage in the Holy Land...* 1909. Houghton Mifflin. 1st. 138p. VG. V3. $17.50

HAZARD, Caroline. *Scallop Shell of Quiet.* 1908. Houghton Mifflin. 1st. VG. V3. $14.00

HAZARD, Paul. *Books, Children & Men.* 1972. Boston. Horn Book. 1/3000. 202p. VG/VG. A4. $45.00

HAZARD. *Frontier in American Literature.* 1941 (1927). rpt. 328p. F/VG. A4. $45.00

HAZELTINE, H.D. *Maitland, Selected Essays.* 1936. Cambridge. gilt bl cloth. VG. M11. $85.00

HAZELTON, Harry. *Ocean Spectres; or, Brides of the Bahamas.* 1863. Boston. Elliott Thomes Talbot. 8vo. bl prt wrp. R12. $75.00

HAZO, Samuel. *Past Won't Stay Behind You. Poems.* 1993. Fayetteville, AR. 1st. F/F. R13. $15.00

HAZZARD, Shirley. *Bay of Noon.* 1970. Little Brn. 1st. F/F. B35. $16.00

HAZZARD, Shirley. *Transit of Venus.* 1980. Viking. 1st. sgn. F/dj. Q1. $50.00

HEACOX, K. *Alaska's National Parks.* 1990. Portland. Graphic Arts. ils Hirschmann. 160p. NF. M12. $30.00

HEAD, Francis. *Life in Germany; or, Visit to Springs of Germany...* 1848. NY. Leavitt Trow. 228p. lacks rear ep. A17. $25.00

HEAD, Henry. *Aphasia & Kindred Disorders of Speech.* 1963 (1926). NY/London. Hafner. rpt. 2 vol. tan cloth. VG/dj. G1. $200.00

HEADLEY & JOHNSON. *HM Stanley's Wonderful Adventures in Africa.* nd (1890). ils. VG. M17. $35.00

HEAL, Edith. *Robin Hood.* 1928. Rand McNally. Windemere series. 1st thus. gilt bl cloth/mc pl. VG. M5. $75.00

HEALD, C.B. *Injuries & Sport.* 1931. London. 1st. 543p. A13. $200.00

HEALY, Jeremiah. *Right To Die.* 1991. Pocket. 1st. F/F. P3. $20.00

HEALY, Jeremiah. *Right To Die.* 1991. Pocket. 1st. sgn. NF/dj. A24. $30.00

HEALY, Jeremiah. *So Like Sleep.* 1987. Harper Row. 1st. sgn. author's 3rd book. F/dj. A24. $40.00

HEALY, Jeremiah. *Staked Goat.* 1986. Harper Row. 1st. F/F. A20. $25.00

HEALY, Jeremiah. *Staked Goat.* 1986. Harper Row. 1st. sgn. author's 2nd book. F/dj. A24. $45.00

HEALY, Raymond. *New Tales of Time & Space.* 1951. Holt. 1st. VG/dj. M2. $12.00

HEANEY, Howell J. *Thirty Years of Bird & Bull: A Bibliography 1958-1988.* 1988. Newtown. Bird & Bull. 1/300. 4to. 106p. w/portfolio. case/box. B24. $400.00

HEANEY, Seamus. *Haw Lantern.* 1987. FSG. 1st. F/F. A24. $30.00

HEANEY, Seamus. *Haw Lantern.* 1987. London. Faber. 1st. inscr/dtd 1988. F/F. w/ephemera. R14. $190.00

HEANEY, Seamus. *Sweeney Ashtray.* 1983. Derry. Field Day Pub. 1st. F/dj. Q1. $200.00

HEARD, H.F. *Lost Cavern.* 1948. Vanguard. 1st. F/dj. M2. $40.00

HEARN, Lafcadio. *Chin Chin Kobakama.* (1905). Tokyo. Hasegawa. 1st. trans Kate James. crepe paper/silk tie/glassine wrp. D1. $300.00

HEARN, Lafcadio. *Exotics & Retrospectives.* 1898. Boston. Little Brn. 1st. teg. olive pict cloth. F. M24. $250.00

HEARN, Lafcadio. *Gleanings in Buddha Fields, Studies of Hand & Soul...* 1897. Houghton Mifflin. 1st. teg. gilt bl cloth. M24. $225.00

HEARN, Lafcadio. *Historical Sketchbook & Guide to New Orleans...* 1885. NY. WH Coleman. 1st/1st prt. map A. bdg A. F/brick-red prt cb wrp. M24. $1,250.00

HEARN, Lafcadio. *In Ghostly Japan.* 1899. Boston. Little Brn. 1st. photos/ils. 241p. VG. W3. $155.00

HEARN, Lafcadio. *Japan's Religions: Shinto & Buddhism.* 1966. New Hyde Park. 1st. 356p. NF/VG. W3. $65.00

HEARN, Lafcadio. *Japan: An Interpretation.* 1904. Macmillan. 1st. ils/notes/index. 541p. VG. W3. $125.00

HEARN, Lafcadio. *Japanese Miscellany.* 1901. Little Brn. 1st. teg. gilt gr cloth. F. M24. $250.00

HEARN, Lafcadio. *Letters From the Raven.* 1970. Brentano. 1st. teg. gilt quarter blk cloth. F. M24. $75.00

HEARN, Lafcadio. *Out of the East, Reveries & Studies in New Japan.* 1895. Houghton Mifflin. 1st/1st prt. silver stp yel cloth. F. M24. $150.00

HEARN, Lafcadio. *Romance of the Milky Way.* 1905. Houghton Mifflin. 1st. gray decor cloth. NF. M24. $125.00

HEARN, Michael. *Wizard of Oz, the Critical Heritage Series.* 1983. 320p. F/wrp. A4. $45.00

HEARTMAN, C. *Cuisinne d'Amour: A Cookbook for Lovers.* 1952 (1942). VG/G. E6. $20.00

HEARTMAN, Charles F. *Census of First Editions & Source Materials by Edgar A Poe.* 1932. Metuchen, NJ. private prt. 1st. 2 vol. gr brd/label. VG. M24. $300.00

HEAT-MOON, William Least. *Blue Highways.* 1982. Atlantic/Little Brn. 1st. NF/VG. H11. $55.00

HEATH, Dunbar Isidore. *Phoenician Inscriptions. Part I.* 1873. London. Quaritich. 1st. 8vo. 103p. VG. W1. $65.00

HEATH, Francis. *Fern Paradise: Plea for Culture of Ferns.* 1880. London. Low Searle. 474p. VG. A10. $50.00

HEATH, Robert Galbraith. *Studies in Schizophrenia: Multidisciplinary Approach...* 1954. Harvard. thick 8vo. 620p. gr cloth. G1. $50.00

HEATH-STUBBS & WRIGHT. *Faber Book of Twentieth Century Verse.* 1953. London. 1st. VG/dj. T9. $20.00

HEATTER, Maida. *Maida Heatter's Book of Desserts.* 1973. 1st. F/G+. E6. $12.00

HEBDEN, Mark. *Killer for the Chairman.* 1972. HBJ. 1st. F/NF. H11. $20.00

HEBDEN, Mark. *Pel Under Pressure.* 1983. NY. Walker. 1st. F/F. H11. $25.00

HECHT, Ben. *Cat That Jumped Out of the Story.* 1947. Winston. 1st. VG-. P2. $50.00

HECHT, Ben. *Kingdom of Evil.* 1924. Covici Friede. 1st. 1/2000. #d. ils Angarola/12 full-p ils. VG. M19. $100.00

HECKSCHER, Morrison. *American Rococo, 1750-1775: Elegance in Ornament.* 1991. NY. Abrams. 4to. 288p. F/wrp. T10. $25.00

HEDIN, Sven. *Riddles of the Gobi Desert.* 1933. nY. ils. 382p. VG+. W3. $96.00

HEDREN, Paul. *With Crook in the Black Hills, Stanley J Morrow's 1876...* 1985. Pruett. 1st. photos/maps. 90p. VG/dj. J2. $225.00

HEDRICK, U.P. *Grapes & Wines From Home Vineyards.* 1946. NY. OUP. 2nd. 326p. VG+/dj. A10. $30.00

HEDRICK, U.P. *History of Agriculture in State of New York.* 1933. Geneva, NY. 1st. ils. 462p. gilt gr cloth. xl. B26. $65.00

HEDRICK, U.P. *Pears of New York.* 1921. JB Lyon/Dept Agric. 29th Annual Report. 80 mc pl. 636p. gilt gr cloth. A10. $185.00

HEGARTY, Reginald B. *Birth of a Whaleship.* 1964. Free Public Lib. sgn. photos/plans/drawings. 159p. T7. $60.00

HEGEMANN, Elizabeth Compton. *Navaho Trading Days.* 1966. NM U. ils/bibliography. 288p. VG. B19. $20.00

HEGGEN, Thomas. *Mister Roberts.* 1946. Houghton Mifflin. 1st. NF/dj. B4. $275.00

HEGI, Ursula. *Floating in My Mother's Palm.* 1990. Poseidon. 1st. NF/F. H11. $50.00

HEGLAR, Mary Schnall. *Grand Prix Champions.* 1973. Bond/Parkhurst. photos. VG. P8. $35.00

HEIDE, Florence Parry. *Treehorn's Treasure.* 1981. Holiday House. 1st. ils Edward Gorey. unp. VG/clip. M20. $60.00

HEIGHWAY, O. *Leila Ada, the Jewish Convert.* 1853. Phil. VG. E6. $60.00

HEILBRUN, Carolyn G. *No Word From Winifred.* 1986. Dutton. 1st. NF/NF. P3. $20.00

HEILBRUN, Carolyn G. *Question of Max.* 1976. Knopf. 1st. NF/dj. M25. $25.00

HEILBRUN, Carolyn G. *Sweet Death, Kind Death.* 1984. Dutton. 1st. F/dj. M25. $15.00

HEILBRUN, Carolyn G. *Writing a Woman's Life.* 1988. Norton. 1st. F/NF. R13. $20.00

HEIM, Katherine. *True Story of Mary, Wife of Lincoln.* 1928. London/NY. A19. $30.00

HEIMER, Mel. *Long Count.* 1969. Atheneum. 1st. photos. VG+/dj. P8. $25.00

HEIN, Wolfgang-Hagen. *Alexander Von Humboldt: Life & Work.* 1987. Ingelheim Rhein. ils. 334p. F/dj. B26. $45.00

HEINDEL, Max. *Rosicrucian Mysteries: The Rosicrucian Fellowship.* 1916. London. 12mo. 228p+14p catalog. gilt/blk pict gr cloth. VG. H3. $45.00

HEINE, Heinrich. *Poems of...* 1957. LEC. 1st thus. 1/1500. intro Louis Untermeyer. ils Fretz Kredel. F/case. Q1. $150.00

HEINE, Heinrich. *Poetry & Prose of Heinrich Heine.* 1948. Citadel. 1st thus. 8vo. 874p. F/dj. H1. $22.50

HEINE, Susanne. *Women & Early Christianity.* 1988. Augsburg. 182p. VG. B29. $8.00

HEINEMANN, Larry. *Close Quarters.* 1977. FSG. 1st. author's 1st book. F/NF. A24. $100.00

HEINEMANN, Larry. *Paco's Story.* 1986. FSG. 1st. F/F. A20. $35.00

HEINIGER, Ernst A. *Grand Canyon.* 1975. WA/NY. Luce. 1st. folio. wht brd. dj+3-D glasses. F7. $60.00

HEINLEIN, Robert A. *Assignment in Eternity.* 1955. London. SF Club. 1st Eng. author's 2nd book. VG/dj. Q1. $200.00

HEINLEIN, Robert A. *Cat Who Walks Through Walls.* 1985. Putnam. 1st. NF/NF. N4. $25.00

HEINLEIN, Robert A. *Door Into Summer.* 1957. Doubleday. 1st. VG/dj. M2. $325.00

HEINLEIN, Robert A. *Farmer in the Sky.* 1962. London. Gollancz. 1st Eng. VG/dj. Q1. $125.00

HEINLEIN, Robert A. *I Will Fear No Evil.* 1970. Putnam. 1st. VG/dj. M2. $95.00

HEINLEIN, Robert A. *Job: A Comedy of Justice.* 1984. Ballantine. 1st. NF/F. A20. $15.00

HEINLEIN, Robert A. *Space Cadet.* 1954 (1948). Scribner. 8vo. ils Clifford N Geary. 252p. VG/G+. T5. $24.00

HEINLEIN, Robert A. *Starship Troopers.* 1959. Putnam. 1st. VG/dj. M2. $500.00

HEINLEIN, Robert A. *Stranger in a Strange Land.* 1961. Putnam. 1st. F/VG. Q1. $750.00

HEINLEIN, Robert A. *Time for the Stars.* 1956. Scribner. 1st. VG/dj. M2. $75.00

HEINRICH, B. *Bumble-Bee Economics.* 1979. Harvard. sgn pres. ils/tables. 245p. pict cloth. F/NF. M12. $30.00

HEINRICH, Willi. *Cross of Iron.* 1956. Bobbs Merrill. 1st. VG+/dj. A20. $35.00

HEINS, Henry H. *Golden Anniversary Bibliography.* 1964. Donald Grant. revised. 8vo. 418p. F/dj. B24. $200.00

HEINSOHN & LEWIN. *Heinsohn Don't You Ever Smile?* 1976. Doubleday. 1st. VG/G+. P8. $15.00

HEINTZ, Wulff D. *Double Stars.* 1978. Dordrecht, Holland. Reidel. revised. 174p. K5. $20.00

HEISENBERG, Werner. *Cosmic Radiation.* 1946. NY. Dover. 192p. NF. K3. $50.00

HEISENBERG, Werner. *Nuclear Physics.* 1953. NY. Philosophical Lib. 1st Eng language. 8vo. 225p. VG/dj. K3. $25.00

HEISENFELT, Kathryn. *Shirley Temple & the Spirit of Dragonwood.* 1945. Whitman. 248p. cloth. VG/dj. M20. $25.00

HEITLER, W. *Quantum Theory of Radiation.* 1966. Oxford/Clarendon. 3rd. 8vo. 430p. K3. $20.00

HEIZER, Robert. *Sources of Stones Used in Prehistoric Mesoamerican Sites.* 1976. Ramona. Bellena. rpt. maps/photos. F3. $20.00

HEKKING, Johanna M. *Pigtails.* 1937. Stokes. 1st. ils Molly Castle. VG/VG. D1. $60.00

HELD, Peter; see Vance, Jack.

HELL, Richard. *Across the Years.* 1991. Amsterdam. Soyo. 1/500. sgn. 12mo. w/CD. M/wooden box. B4. $150.00

HELL, Richard. *Go Now.* 1996. Scribner. 1st. sgn. F/F. B4. $100.00

HELLER, Joseph. *God Knows.* 1984. Franklin Lib. 1st/ltd. sgn. full leather. F. Q1. $75.00

HELLER, Joseph. *God Knows.* 1984. Knopf. 1st. F/VG+. A20. $25.00

HELLER, Joseph. *Picture This.* 1988. Putnam. 1st. F/F. T12. $25.00

HELLER, Joseph. *Something Happened.* 1974. Knopf. ARC. author's 2nd novel. RS. F/F. w/promo material. B4. $125.00

HELLER, Joseph. *Something Happened.* 1974. Knopf. 1st. F/F. N4. $40.00

HELLMAN, Lillian. *Maybe.* 1980. Little Brn. 1st. VG+/dj. A20. $20.00

HELLMAN, Lillian. *Scoundrel Time.* 1976. Little Brn. 1st. F/F. B35. $30.00

HELLMAYR, Charles E. *Birds of the James Simpson-Roosevelts Asiatic Expedition.* 1929. Chicago. Field Mus Natural Hist Pub 263. 144p. VG. S15. $15.00

HELLSTROM & RYWELL. *Smith & Wesson: Story of the Revolver.* (1953). Harriman, TN. Pioneer. stated 1st. 136p. VG. H7. $12.50

HELM, MacKinlay. *Angel Mo' & Her Son, Roland Hayes.* 1942. Little Brn. 1st. VG. M25. $35.00

HELME & PAUL. *Jerry: Story of an Exmoor Pony.* 1930. Scribner. 1st Am. VG. O3. $48.00

HELMS, Mary. *Middle America.* 1975. NY. Prentice Hall. 1st. 367p. dj. F3. $30.00

HELPER, Hinton Rowan. *Impending Crises of the South.* (1860). NY. AB Burdick. 50th thousand. 418p. cloth. VG. M20. $75.00

HELPER, Hinton Rowan. *Three Americas Railway.* 1881. St Louis. WS Bryan. 1st. 8vo. 473p. cloth. xl. M1. $125.00

HELPRIN, Mark. *Dove of the East.* 1975. Knopf. 1st. author's 1st book. NF/dj. D10/Q1. $75.00

HELPRIN, Mark. *Soldier of the Great War.* 1991. HBJ. 1st. F/F. A24. $35.00

HELPRIN, Mark. *Swan Lake.* 1989. Houghton Mifflin/Ariel. 1st. sm 4to. 81p. F/F. A24. $35.00

HELPRIN, Mark. *Winter's Tale.* 1983. HBJ. 1st. author's 4th book/2nd novel. F/NF. D10. $35.00

HELPRIN, Mark. *Winter's Tale.* 1983. HBJ. 1st. NF/dj. M2. $12.00

HELVETIUS, Claude Adrien. *Oeuvres Completes.* 1777. London. 4 vol. 8vo. engraved ftspc portrait. quarter calf. R12. $750.00

HELWEG-LARSEN, Kjeld. *Columbus Never Came.* 1964. London. Jarrolds. 2nd. inscr. 240p. map ep. dj. F3. $20.00

HEMINGWAY, Ernest. *By-Line: Ernest Hemingway: Selected Articles...* 1967. NY. 1st. edit Wm White. F/F. A11. $55.00

HEMINGWAY, Ernest. *Dangerous Summer.* 1985. London. Hamish Hamilton. 1st. F/dj. Q1. $50.00

HEMINGWAY, Ernest. *Dangerous Summer.* 1985. Scribner. 1st. F/clip. A24. $35.00

HEMINGWAY, Ernest. *Dateline: Toronto.* 1985. NY. 1st. edit Wm White. F/F. A11. $45.00

HEMINGWAY, Ernest. *Death in the Afternoon.* 1932. Scribner. 1932A/1st. G+/G-. B5. $250.00

HEMINGWAY, Ernest. *Farewell to Arms.* 1947. Paris. Albatross. 1st. VG-/dj. A11. $55.00

HEMINGWAY, Ernest. *Fifth Column.* 1969. Scribner. 1st thus. F/dj. Q1. $125.00

HEMINGWAY, Ernest. *For Whom the Bell Tolls.* 1940. 1st/1st state. VG/G. M19. $100.00

HEMINGWAY, Ernest. *For Whom the Bell Tolls.* 1940. Scribner. 1st/1st prt. beige cloth. F/2nd state dj. M24. $275.00

HEMINGWAY, Ernest. *For Whom the Bell Tolls.* 1942. LEC. 1/1500. ils/sgn Lynd Ward. NF/damaged box. B2. $125.00

HEMINGWAY, Ernest. *Garden of Eden.* 1986. Scribner. 1st. F/dj. A24/M19. $25.00

HEMINGWAY, Ernest. *Islands in the Stream.* 1970. Scribner. 1st. F/F clip. D10. $60.00

HEMINGWAY, Ernest. *Islands in the Stream.* 1970. Scribner. 1st. VG/NF. A24. $35.00

HEMINGWAY, Ernest. *Kiki's Memoirs.* 1930. Paris. Blk Manikin. 1st. VG/lg wrp/acetate dj/prt band. B5. $450.00

HEMINGWAY, Ernest. *Moveable Feast.* 1964. NY. Scribner. 1st. photos. NF/dj. Q1. $75.00

HEMINGWAY, Ernest. *Moveable Feast.* 1964. Scribner. 1st. F/dj. D10. $175.00

HEMINGWAY, Ernest. *Moveable Feast.* 1964. Scribner. 1st. VG/VG. B5. $50.00

HEMINGWAY, Ernest. *Sun Also Rises.* 1926. Scribner. 1st/1st prt/1st issue. blk cloth/gold labels. F. M24. $850.00

HEMINGWAY, Ernest. *Sun Also Rises.* 1954. Scribner. ne. NF. W2. $150.00

HEMINGWAY, Ernest. *Winner Take Nothing.* 1933. Scribner. 1st. VG/dj. Q1. $750.00

HEMMING, John. *Red Gold: Conquest of the Brazilian Indians, 1500-1760.* 1978. Harvard. 1st. tall 8vo. 677p. as new/dj. H1. $25.00

HEMMING, John. *Search for El Dorado.* (1978). London. Micheal Joseph. 1st. 4to. 223p. dj. F3. $25.00

HEMPEL, Amy. *At the Gates of the Animal Kingdom.* 1990. Knopf. 1st. F/NF. R13. $20.00

HEMPEL, Amy. *Reasons To Live.* 1985. Knopf. 1st. author's 1st book. F/F. M25. $35.00

HEMSLEY, H. *Rock & Alpine Gardens.* 1910. London. Simpkin. 2nd. 92p. brd. A10. $32.00

HENDERSON, Alice Corbin. *Turquoise Trail.* 1928. Houghton Mifflin. 1st. VG/G. L3. $100.00

HENDERSON, Andrew. *Field Guide to the Palms of the Americas.* 1995. Princeton. ils/photos/maps. M. B26. $75.00

HENDERSON, Frank D. *Official Roster of Soldiers of American Revolution...* 1929. Columbus. 447p. buckram. VG. B18. $35.00

HENDERSON, Mariana. *DG Rossetti.* 1973. London/NY. Academy/St Martin. 104p. brd. dj. D2. $35.00

HENDERSON, Mrs. L.R. *Magic Aeroplane.* (1911). Reilly Britton. ils Emile a Nelson. 96p. G/torn. D1. $185.00

HENDERSON, Peter. *Garden & Farm Topics.* 1884. Henderson. 1st. 244p. A10. $28.00

HENDERSON, Peter. *Gardening for Profit.* 1893. Orange Judd. revised. 376p. VG. A10. $28.00

HENDERSON, Peter. *Gardening for Profit.* 1991. Chillicothe, IL. Am Botanist. rpt. 496p. M. A10. $26.00

HENDERSON, Peter. *Practical Floriculture, Cultivating Plants...* 1869. NY. inscr. 249p. VG. B14. $55.00

HENDERSON, Peter. *Practical Floriculture, Cultivating Plants...* 1869. NY. 1st. VG. E6. $25.00

HENDERSON, Randall. *Sun, Sand & Solitude.* 1968. Los Angeles. 1st. tan cloth. VG+. F7. $40.00

HENDERSON, W. *Modern Domestic Receipt Book.* 1857. ils. G+. E6. $135.00

HENDERSON, Zenna. *Pilgrimage: Book of the People.* 1978. Gregg. 1st thus. F. M2. $35.00

HENDRICK, George. *To Reach Eternity: Letters of James Jones.* 1989. Random. 1st. NF/NF. A20. $20.00

HENKE, Jack. *Sylvan Beach: On the Lake Oneida, a History.* 1980. North Country Books. 1st thus. 219p. bl cloth. B22. $10.00

HENNESSEY, William J. *Russel Wright, American Designer.* 1983. MIT Pr. 2nd. 1985. 96p. F. H1. $35.00

HENRI, Florette. *Black Migration: Movement North 1900-1920.* 1975. Anchor/Doubleday. 1st. 419p. F/NF. B4. $65.00

HENRI, Raymond. *Iwo Jima: Springboard to Final Victory.* 1945. NY. 96p. VG/VG. S16. $75.00

HENRIQUES, H.S.Q. *Jews & the English Law.* 1974 (1908). Clifton. Augustus M Kelley. facsimile. M11. $75.00

HENRY, B.C. *Cross & the Dragon.* 1885. NY. Randolph. 2nd. ils/map. 482p. VG. W3. $110.00

HENRY, Charles. *Hostage.* 1959. Random. 1st. 237p. VG/dj. M20. $12.00

HENRY, Clark W. *Cross & the Eternal Order: A Study of Atonement...* 1944. Macmillan. 1st. fwd CH Dodd. 319p. xl. VG. B29. $14.00

HENRY, Gordon Jr. *Light People.* 1994. Norman. 1st. Am Indian Literature Critical Studies series. F/F. L3. $35.00

HENRY, H.M. *Police Control of the Slave in South Carolina.* 1914. Emory, VA. 1st. 216p. VG. B4. $50.00

HENRY, Marguerite. *Birds at Home.* 1942. Donohue. 12 full-p pl. NF. A17. $20.00

HENRY, Marguerite. *Born To Trot.* 1950. Rand McNally. 1st. sgn. F/VG. C8. $65.00

HENRY, Marguerite. *Dear Readers & Riders.* 1969. Rand McNally. 1st. VG. O3. $35.00

HENRY, Marguerite. *Justin Morgan Had a Horse.* 1945. Chicago. Wilcox Follett. 1st. folio. F/NF. B4. $175.00

HENRY, Marguerite. *Justin Morgan Had a Horse.* 1945. Wilcox Follett. 1st. ils Wesley Dennis. 4to. VG/dj. from $50 to $65.00

HENRY, Marguerite. *Misty of Chincoteague.* 1947. Rand McNally. 1st. ils Wesley Dennis. NF/G+. C8. $65.00

HENRY, Marguerite. *Stormy, Misty's Foal.* 1963. Rand McNally. 1st. ils Wesley Dennis. NF/VG. M19. $35.00

HENRY, Marguerite. *Stormy, Misty's Foal.* 1963. Rand McNally. 1st. lg 8vo. F/NF. C8. $50.00

HENRY, Marguerite. *White Stallions of Lipizza.* 1964. Rand McNally. 3rd. sgn. 116p. VG/ragged. M20. $35.00

HENRY, R.S. *Story of Reconstruction: 1865-1877*. 1938. NY. Grosset. ils. 633p. VG/dj. B5. $40.00

HENRY, R.S. *Story of the Confederacy*. 1931. 1st. ils/index/map ep. 514p. O8. $18.50

HENRY, Samuel. *Foxhunting Is Different*. 1938. Derrydale. 1/950. ils Paul Brown. VG. T10. $100.00

HENRY, Will. *San Juan Hill*. 1962. Random. 1st. F/VG. B4. $100.00

HENRY, Will. *Sons of the Western Frontier*. 1967. Chilton. 2nd. F/VG+. T11. $20.00

HENRY VII (King of England). *Assertio Septem Sacramentorum Adversus Mart*. 1562. Paris. Desboys. 16mo. early calf. R12. $875.00

HENSEL, W.U. *Christina Riots & the Treason Trials of 1851...* 1911. Lancaster, PA. New Era. 2nd/revised. 4to. 158p. VG+. B4. $500.00

HENSHALL, J.A. *Bass, Pike, Perch & Other Game Fishes of America*. 1923. Stewart Kidd. 1st/3rd prt. 410p. VG. W2. $120.00

HENSHALL, J.A. *Camping & Cruising in Florida*. 1884. Cincinnati. R Clarke. 8vo. ils. 248p. pict cloth. G. M12. $95.00

HENSHAW, Henry W. *Book of Birds*. 1921. NGS. ils LA Fuertes. 195p. VG. S15. $20.00

HENSLEY, Joe L. *Fort's Law*. 1987. Doubleday. 1st. NF/NF. M22. $10.00

HENSLOW, T. Geoffrey. *Garden Instruction*. 1940. London. Quality. 1st. 324p. VG. A10. $25.00

HENSLOW, T. Geoffrey. *Gardens of Fragrance*. 1928. London. Warne. 224p. dj. A10. $28.00

HENSON, Matthew A. *Negro Explorer at the North Pole*. 1912. NY. Stokes. 8vo. 200p. bl cloth. P4. $750.00

HENTHOFF, Nat. *Boston Boy*. 1986. KNopf. 1st. F/F. A20. $20.00

HENTY, G.A. *In the Heart of the Rockies*. nd. London. Foulsham Henty Lib. 12mo. 223p. bl cloth. NF/torn. F7. $20.00

HENTZ, Caroline Lee. *Planter's Northern Bride*. 1854. Phil. TB Peterson. 8vo. 579p. cloth. VG. K7. $45.00

HEPBURN, Andrew. *Great Houses of American History*. 1974. Bramhall. 1st. 244p. VG. A8. $20.00

HEPBURN, Katherine. *Making of African Queen*. 1987. Knopf. 1st. F/F. A20. $25.00

HEPBURN, Katherine. *Me*. 1991. Knopf. 1st. F/NF. A20. $20.00

HEPBURN & JACOBSON. *World's 72 Toughest Golf Holes*. 1985. Price Stern Sloan. 1st. ils. F/G+. P8. $20.00

HEPPER, F. Nigel. *Royal Botanic Gardens, Kew*. 1982. Owings Mills, MD. ils. 195p. F/dj. B26. $24.00

HERBERSTAIN, Sigismund. *Rervm Moscoviticarvm Commentarij*. 1571. Basle. Oporin. folio. 6 full-p pl/3 double-p maps. brd. R12. $2,250.00

HERBERT, A.G. *Throne of David: Study of Fulfillment of Old Testament...* 1956. Faber. 275p. G/torn. B29. $9.50

HERBERT, Frank. *Heretics of Dune*. 1984. Putnam. ltd ed. 480p. VG. W2. $40.00

HERBERT, Frank. *Nebula Winners Fifteen*. 1981. Harper. 1st. F/dj. M2. $25.00

HERBERT, Frank. *White Plague*. 1982. Putnam. 1st. F/dj. M2. $15.00

HERBERT, H.W. *Captains of the Old World*. 1852. Scribner. 8vo. 364p. bl brd. G. K7. $40.00

HERBERT, H.W. *Frank Forester's Field Sports of the United States...* 1849. NY. Stringer Townsend. 1st Am. 2 vol. 12 full-p pl. 3-quarter blk calf. K7. $195.00

HERBERT, H.W. *Frank Forester's Fish & Fishing of the United States...* 1850. NY. Stringer Townsend. 1st Am. 43 pl. 359+16p. gilt red cloth. NF. H7. $125.00

HERBERT, H.W. *Hints to Horse-Keepers, a Complete Manual...* 1863. NY. 425p. stp cloth. G. B18. $37.50

HERBERT, James. *Sepulchre*. 1988. Putnam. 1st Am. NF/dj. M2. $15.00

HERBERT & RANSOM. *Jesus Incident*. 1979. Putnam. ne. 405p. VG/VG. W2. $30.00

HERFORD, Oliver. *Child's Primer of Natural History*. 1899. Scribner. 1st. all edges tinted. pict brd. R5. $150.00

HERFORD, Oliver. *Most Timid in the Land*. 1992. SF. Chronicle. 2nd. thin obl 4to. ils/sgn Sylvia Long. F/dj. T10. $50.00

HERGE. *Adventures of Tintin, Flight 714*. 1968. Methuen. 1st ed. hc. glazed pict brd. VG. M5. $40.00

HERGESHIMER, Joseph. *Balisand*. 1924. Knopf. 1st. F/VG+. B4. $150.00

HERGESHIMER, Joseph. *Cytherea*. 1922. London. Heinemann. 1st Eng. F/F. B4. $135.00

HERGESHIMER, Joseph. *San Cristobal de la Habana*. 1927. Knopf. photos. 255p. dj. M20. $20.00

HERLEY, Richard. *Earth Goddess*. 1984. Morrow. 1st Am. F/dj. M2. $17.00

HERLIHY, James Leo. *Midnight Cowboy*. 1965. S&S. 1st. F/F. B4. $150.00

HERM, Gerhard. *Celts: People Who Came Out of the Darkness*. 1976. St Martin. 1st Am. ils/maps. 312p. as new/F. H1. $15.00

HERMANN, Armin. *German Nobel Prizewinners*. 1968. Munich. Heinz Moos. 1st. 3 mc pl/162 portraits/vignettes. 172p. VG/wrp. K3. $25.00

HERMANN, Paul. *Conquest by Man*. 1954. Harper. 1st. 455p. dj. F3. $15.00

HERR, Charlotte B. *Wise Mamma Goose*. 1913. Volland. early. ils Frances Beem. 12mo. NF. M5. $55.00

HERR, Michael. *Dispatches*. 1977. Knopf. 1st. author's 1st book. NF/clip. D10. $90.00

HERR, Michael. *Winchell*. 1990. Knopf. 1st. F/F. A20. $25.00

HERRESHOFF, L. Francis. *Sensible Cruising Designs*. 1973. diagrams/notes. VG/VG. M17. $45.00

HERRIES, J.W. *Storm Island & Other Stories*. 1947. London. 1st. inscr. F/NF. M2. $35.00

HERRIMAN, G. *Krazy Kat*. 1946. NY. Holt. 1st. ils. VG/worn. B5. $85.00

HERRING, D.W. *Lure of the Clock*. 1963. NY. Crown. ils. 121p. K3. $25.00

HERRIOT, James. *James Herriot's Cat Stories*. 1994. St Martin. 1st. 161p. F/F. W2. $15.00

HERRON, Carolivia. *Thereafter Johnnie*. 1991. Random. 1st. author's 1st novel. NF/NF. R13. $25.00

HERSCHEL, John F.W. *Outlines of Astronomy*. 1881 (1849). London. Longman Gr. new ed. xl. rebound. K5. $100.00

HERSEY, John. *Call*. 1985. Knopf. 1st. F/F. B4. $45.00

HERSEY, John. *Fling*. 1990. Knopf. 1st. F/F. B4. $45.00

HERSEY, John. *Hiroshima*. 1946. Knopf. VG/worn. K3. $20.00

HERSEY, John. *Hiroshima*. 1946. Knopf. 1st. NF/VG. M19. $35.00

HERSEY, John. *Hiroshima: Story of Six Human Beings Who Survived...* 1946. NY. 118p. VG/G. S16. $17.50

HERSEY, John. *Into the Valley*. 1943. Knopf. 1st. NF/VG. M19. $25.00

HERSEY, John. *Marmot Drive*. 1953. Knopf. 1st. NF/dj. B35. $25.00

HERSEY, John. *Wall*. 1957. LEC. 1st thus. 1/1500. ils/sgn Raymond Holden. wht buckram. F/case. Q1. $75.00

HERSEY, John. *War Lover*. 1959. Knopf. 1st. G/VG. B35. $18.00

HERSHEY, Scott F. *Science of National Life...Wealth of Nations*. 1885. Chicago. 547p. full calf. A17. $20.00

HERT, C. *Tracking the Big Cats*. 1955. Caxton. ils/photos/map ep. cloth. VG. M12. $45.00

HERTER, Christian A. *Diagnosis of Organic Nervous Diseases*. 1892. Putnam. 12mo. 628p. gr cloth. xl. VG. G1. $50.00

HERTER & HERTER. *Bull Cook & Authentic Historical Recipes & Practices*. 1963 (1960). VG. E6. $20.00

HERTRICH, William. *Palms & Cycads: Their Culture in Southern California...* 1960 (1951). San Marino, CA. 2nd. ils. VG/dj. B26. $59.00

HERTZLER, Arthur. *Surgical Operations With Local Anesthesia*. 1912. NY. 1st. 209p. A13. $100.00

HERTZLER, Arthur. *Surgical Pathology of the Diseases of the Neck*. 1937. Phil. 1st. 237p. A13. $40.00

HERTZLER, Arthur. *Ventures in Science of a Country Surgeon*. 1944. private prt. 1st. 304p. A13. $35.00

HERVEY, John. *American Harness Racing. Book I*. 1948. NY. Hartenstein. 206p. VG. O3. $58.00

HERZOG, Arthur. *IQ 83*. 1978. S&S. 1st. NF/F. H11. $20.00

HERZOG, Arthur. *Make Us Happy*. 1978. Crowell. 1st. F/rpr. B35. $25.00

HERZOG, Yaacov. *People That Dwells Alone*. 1975. Sanhedrin. 283p. VG/G. S3. $23.00

HESLIP, Malcolm. *Nostalgic Happenings in Three Bands of John Philip Sousa*. 1983. Laguna Hills, CA. Heslip. 2nd. 8vo. ils/photo/facsimiles. F/NF. T10. $45.00

HESS, H.H. *Stillwater Igneous Complex, Montana*. 1960. GSA Memoir 80. 6 pocket maps. 230p. NF. D8. $22.00

HESS, Joan. *Much Ado in Maggody*. 1989. St Martin. 1st. F/F. M22. $30.00

HESS, Joan. *O Little Town of Maggody*. 1993. Dutton. 1st. sgn. F/F. A23. $38.00

HESS & PETROVICH. *Imprinting*. 1977. Stroudsburg. 333p. F. S15. $45.00

HESSE, Herman. *Beneath the Wheel*. 1968. FSG. 1st. F/VG. B35. $38.00

HESSLER & PISCO. *Lehrbuch der Technischen Physik*. 1866. Wein. Wilhelm Braumiller. ils. half leather/marbled brd. K3. $75.00

HESTON, Charlton. *Actor's Journals 1956-1976*. 1978. Dutton. 1st. sgn. G/G clip. A23. $25.00

HESTON, Charlton. *Beijing Diary*. 1990. S&S. 1st. sgn. A23. $36.00

HETH, Edward Harris. *Wonderful World of Cooking*. 1956. S&S. VG/dj. A16. $16.00

HETRICH, William. *Camellias in the Huntington Gardens*. 1954-59. San Marino. Huntington Botanical Gardens. 1st. 3 vol. ils. F/djs. T10. $150.00

HETRICH, William. *Camellias in the Huntington Gardens*. 1954-59. San Marino. Huntington Lib. 3 vol. VG/djs. A22. $95.00

HETSCH, Rolf. *Paula Modersohn-Becker. Ein Buch der Freudschaft*. 1932. Berlin. Rembrandt. Die Zeichner des Volkes, Band IV series. 112p. cloth. D2. $55.00

HEUMAN, William. *Girl From Frisco*. 1955. Morrow. 1st. F/NF. B4. $65.00

HEUVELMANS, B. *In the Wake of Sea Serpents*. 1968. NY. ils/map. 645p. F/VG. M12. $37.50

HEWARD, Constance. *Ameliaranne Goes Touring*. 1941. London. Harrap. 1st. ils Pearse. 8vo. cloth. dj. R5. $125.00

HEWETT, Edgar L. *Ancient Life in the American Southwest*. 1930. Bobbs Merrill. 1st. 392p. map ep. bl cloth. VG/G+. F7. $45.00

HEWETT, Edgar L. *Chaco Canyon & Its Monuments*. 1936. Albuquerque. 1st. VG/G. B5. $55.00

HEWETT & MAUZY. *Landmarks of New Mexico*. 1940. Albuquerque. 1st. VG/G. B5. $55.00

HEWETT-BATES, J.S. *Bookbinding for Schools*. 1935. Peoria. Manual Arts. 2nd revised. VG/dj. K3. $20.00

HEWINS, Jack. *Borleske: Never Far From Hope*. 1966. Superior. 1st. photos. VG+/VG. P8. $20.00

HEWITT, Foster. *Hello Canada! And Hockey Fans in the United States*. 1950. Thomas Allen. 1st. VG. P8. $25.00

HEWITT, Foster. *Hockey Night in Canada*. 1968. Ryerson. revised/later prt. VG+/VG. P8. $35.00

HEWITT, Jean. *NY Natural Foods Cookbook*. 1971. NY. Quadrangle. VG/dj. A16. $15.00

HEWLETT, Maurice. *Earthwork Out of Tuscany*. 1911. Portland. 1st. 1/700. VG/dj. T9. $15.00

HEY, William. *Practical Observations in Surgery, Illustrated...* 1805. Phil. 1st Am. 332p. A13. $300.00

HEYDT, Henry J. *Studies in Jewish Evangelism*. 1951. Am Brd Missions to Jews. 237p. VG/G. S3. $25.00

HEYER, Georgette. *April Lady*. 1957. Putnam. 1st Am. 254p. VG/dj. M20. $45.00

HEYER, Georgette. *Bath Tangle*. 1955. Putnam. 1st. 312p. VG/dj. M20. $45.00

HEYER, Georgette. *Black Sheep*. 1967. Dutton. 1st Am. 255p. VG/dj. M20. $25.00

HEYER, Georgette. *Death in the Stocks*. 1970. Dutton. 1st Am. 263p. cloth. VG/dj. M20. $25.00

HEYER, Georgette. *My Lord John*. 1975. Dutton. 1st. VG/VG. P3. $20.00

HEYER, Georgette. *Simon & the Coldheart*. 1979. Dutton. VG/VG. P3. $20.00

HEYER, Georgette. *Sprig Muslin*. 1956. Putnam. 1st. 276p. VG/dj. M20. $45.00

HEYER, Georgette. *Sylvester*. 1957. Putnam. 1st. 309p. VG/dj. M20. $45.00

HEYERDAHL, Thor. *American Indians in the Pacific: Theory Behind Kon-Tiki...* 1953. Rand McNally. 4to. 820p. brn cloth. VG. K7. $150.00

HEYLINGER, William. *Don Strong: Patrol Leader*. 1918. Grosset Dunlap. 287p. VG/dj. M20. $22.50

HEYLYN, Peter. *Cosmographie in Four Books, Containing the Chrographie...* 1657. London. For Henry Seile. 2nd. 5 parts in 1. 1100+p. full calf. H13. $595.00

HEYMANS, Margriet. *Cats & Dolls*. 1976. Addison-Wesley. 1st. unp. VG/dj. M20. $25.00

HEYWARD, DuBose. *Porgy*. 1925. 1st. gilt blk cloth. VG. S13. $50.00

HIAASEN, Carl. *Double Whammy*. 1987. Putnam. 1st. F/F. M22. $70.00

HIAASEN, Carl. *Native Tongue*. 1991. Knopf. 1st. NF/NF. A20. $35.00

HIAASEN, Carl. *Native Tongue*. 1991. Knopf. 1st. sgn. F/F. D10. $60.00

HIAASEN, Carl. *Native Tongue*. 1991. Knopf. 1st. sgn. NF/dj. N4. $50.00

HIAASEN, Carl. *Skin Tight.* 1989. Putnam. 1st. sgn. F/F. M15. $75.00

HIAASEN, Carl. *Stormy Weather.* 1995. Knopf. 1st. sgn. F/F. A23. $40.00

HIAASEN, Carl. *Strip Tease.* 1993. Knopf. 1st. F/F. from $25 to $30.00

HIAASEN, Carl. *Tourist Season.* 1986. Putnam. 1st. inscr. F/dj. M15. $175.00

HIAASEN & MONTALBANO. *Powder Burn.* 1981. Atheneum. 1st. F/F. M15. $500.00

HIBBARD & HULME. *Familiar Garden Flowers.* 1900. London. Cassell. 5 vol. A10. $125.00

HICHENS, Robert. *Barbary Sheep. A Novel.* 1907. Harper. 1st. ils. 253p. VG. W1. $18.00

HICHENS, Robert. *Black Spaniel.* 1905. Stokes. 1st. VG. M2. $25.00

HICKERSON, Thomas F. *Highway Curves & Earthwork.* 1926. McGraw Hill. aeg. 12mo. 382p. limp bdg. A8. $12.00

HICKES, John Edwards. *Adventures of a Tramp Printer.* 1950. KS City. 1st. 285p. VG/G. B5. $40.00

HICKEY, D.R. *War of 1812: Forgotten Conflict.* 1989. IL U. 1st. ils/maps. F/dj. M4. $30.00

HICKEY & SMITH. *Operation Avalanche: Salerno Landings.* 1983. NY. ils/maps. 379p. VG/VG. S16. $25.00

HICKS, Elias. *Journal of the Life & Religious Labours.* 1832. NY. Isaac T Hopper. 1st. 451p. worn leather. V3. $55.00

HICKS, Granville. *Only One Storm.* 1942. Macmillan. 1st. author's 1st novel. F/F. B4. $125.00

HICKS, Granville. *Small Town.* 1946. Macmillan. 1st. F/NF. B4. $85.00

HICKS, Jimmie. *WW Robinson: Biography & Bibliography.* 1970. Zamarano Club. 1st. ils/bibliography. 83p. F. B19. $75.00

HICKS, Sam. *Desert Plants & People.* 1966. San Antonio. Naylor. 1st. 8vo. cloth. G+/dj. A22. $30.00

HIEB, David. *Fort Laramie, National Monument, Wyoming.* 1954. GPO. 1st. photos/maps. VG. J2. $25.00

HIELSCHER, Kurt. *Italia Natura ed Arte.* 1925. Milan. 304 full-p sephia photos. gilt cloth. VG. A17. $25.00

HIEMEYER, Fritz. *Flora Von Augsburg.* 1978. Augsburg. Naturwissenschaftlicher. 8vo. cloth. VG. A22. $15.00

HIGGERS, Jim. *Adventures of Theodore...* 1901. Chicago. 1st. 210p. pict cloth. G+. B18. $95.00

HIGGINS, D.S. *Rider Haggard: A Biography.* 1983. Stein Day. 1st Am. NF/dj. M2. $35.00

HIGGINS, Ethel Bailey. *Our Native Cacti.* 1931. NY. ils. 170p. pict cloth. B26. $20.00

HIGGINS, George V. *Cogan's Trade.* 1974. Knopf. 1st. F/F. N4. $25.00

HIGGINS, George V. *Defending Billy Ryan.* 1992. Holt. 1st. F/F. B4. $45.00

HIGGINS, George V. *Friends of Eddie Coyle.* 1972. Knopf. 1st. bl cloth (assumed 2nd issue). F/dj. Q1. $40.00

HIGGINS, George V. *Friends of Richard Nixon.* 1975. Atlantic/Little Brn. 1st. NF/NF. M22. $15.00

HIGGINS, George V. *On Writing.* 1990. Holt. 1st. F/F. M22. $15.00

HIGGINS, George V. *Patriot Game.* 1982. Knopf. 1st. sgn. NF/VG. R14. $35.00

HIGGINS, George V. *Trust.* 1989. Holt. 1st. NF/VG+. A20. $20.00

HIGGINS, George V. *Wonderful Years, Wonderful Years.* 1988. Holt. 1st. F/NF. M22. $10.00

HIGGINS, J.W. *Guide to Geology & Oil Fields of Los Angeles...* 1958. Los Angeles. 2 pocket maps. 204p. NF. D8. $40.00

HIGGINS, Jack; see Patterson, Henry.

HIGGINSON, A.H. *Foxhunting: Theory & Practice.* 1948. photos. VG/VG. M17. $25.00

HIGGINSON, John. *Working Class in the Making: Belgian Colonial Labor Policy.* 1989. WI U. 1st. as new. V4. $12.50

HIGGINSON, T.W. *Army Life in a Black Regiment.* 1935. MI U. 235p. F/G. M4. $35.00

HIGHAM, Charles. *Adventures of Conan Doyle.* 1976. NY. Norton. 1st. F/NF. M23. $25.00

HIGHAM, Charles. *Adventures of Conan Doyle: Life of Creator Sherlock Holmes.* 1976. Norton. 1st?/3rd prt. VG/NF. R10. $10.00

HIGHAM, Charles. *Elizabeth & Phillip.* 1991. Doubleday. ne. F/NF. W2. $25.00

HIGHSMITH, Patricia. *Found in the Street.* 1986. London. Heinemann. 1st. F/dj. Q1. $60.00

HIGHSMITH, Patricia. *Ripley Under Ground.* 1970. Doubleday. 1st. NF/VG. M22. $20.00

HIGHSMITH, Patricia. *Tales of Natural & Unnatural Catastrophes.* 1987. Atlantic. 1st. F/F. B35. $18.00

HIGHSMITH, Patricia. *Tremor of Forgery.* 1969. Doubleday. 1st Am. VG/VG. M22. $20.00

HIGHTOWER, Florence. *Ghost of Follonsbee's Folly.* (1958). Houghton Mifflin. 7th. 8vo. 218p. G+. T5. $12.00

HIGHWATER, Jamake. *Anpao: An American Indian Odyssey.* 1977. Lippincott. 1st. author's 4th book using Indian name. F/NF. L3. $100.00

HIGHWATER, Jamake. *Fodor's Indian America.* 1975. NY. McKay. 1st/only. NF/NF. L3. $100.00

HIGHWATER, Jamake. *I Wear the Morning Star.* 1986. Harper Row. 1st. F/F clip. L3. $65.00

HIGHWATER, Jamake. *Song From the Earth: American Indian Painting.* 1976. Boston. NYGS. 1st. NF/dj. L3. $350.00

HIJIKATA, Hisakatsu. *Society & Life in Palau.* 1993. Tokyo. Sasakawa Peace Found. 1st. ils. 273p. F. W3. $38.00

HIJORTSBERG, William. *Falling Angel.* 1978. Harper. 1st. VG/dj. M2. $50.00

HIJUELOS, Oscar. *Mambo Kings Play Songs of Love.* 1989. FSG. 1st. F/F. from $40 to $45.00

HIJUELOS, Oscar. *Mambo Kings Play Songs of Love.* 1989. FSG. 1st. inscr. F/dj. B3. $80.00

HIJUELOS, Oscar. *Mambo Kings Play Songs of Love.* 1989. FSG. 1st. inscr. NF/dj. M25. $50.00

HIJUELOS, Oscar. *Mambo Kings Play Songs of Love.* 1989. FSG. 1st. sgn. G/G. A23. $30.00

HIJUELOS, Oscar. *Mr Ives' Christmas.* 1995. Harper Collins. 1st. sgn. F/F. A23. $40.00

HIJUELOS, Oscar. *Our House in the Last World.* 1983. NY. Persea. 1st. author's 1st book. F/F. D10. $185.00

HIJUELOS, Oscar. *Our House in the Last World.* 1983. Persea. 1st. sgn. F/F. B4. $250.00

HILBERG, Raul. *Destruction of the European Jews.* 1961. London. WH Allen. 788p. VG/G+. S3. $35.00

HILDRETH, Richard. *White Slave; or, Memoirs of a Fugitive.* 1852. Tappan Whittemore/Rood Whittemore. 1st complete. M1. $200.00

HILEGAS, Mark. *Future As Nightmare: HG Wells & the Anti-Utopians.* 1967. Oxford. 1st. NF/dj. M2. $35.00

HILL, Alice P. *Tales of the Colorado Pioneers.* 1884. Pierson Gardner. 1st. 319p. VG. J2. $325.00

HILL, Douglas. *Day of the Starwind.* 1980. Atheneum. 1st. F/dj. M2. $15.00

HILL, Geoffrey. *Tenebrae.* 1978. London. 1st. sgn. F/NF. A11. $125.00

HILL, George. *Yearbook of the Dept of Agriculture 1899.* 1900. GPO. 880p. cloth. A10. $30.00

HILL, Grace Brooks. *Corner House Girls' Odd Find (#5).* 1916. Barse Hopkins. lists 8 titles. 252p. VG+/dj. M20. $30.00

HILL, Herbert. *Anger & Beyond: Negro Writer in the United States.* 1966. Harper Row. 1st. F/F. M25. $45.00

HILL, Ingrid. *Dixie Church Interstate Blues.* 1989. Viking. ARC. author's 1st book. RS. F/F. w/promo material. R13. $25.00

HILL, John; see Koontz, Dean R.

HILL, Joseph. *Bookmakers of Old Birmingham.* 1971. Burt Franklin. rpt. ils. VG. K3. $15.00

HILL, Ray. *OJ Simpson.* 1975. Random. revised/1st prt. phtos. F/VG+. P8. $30.00

HILL, Reginald. *No Man's Land.* 1985. London. 1st. VG/VG. T9. $45.00

HILL, Sallie F. *Progressive Farmer's Southern Cookbook.* 1961. Progressive Farmer. 470p. G. B10. $12.00

HILL, W.E. *Among Us Cats.* 1926. Harper Row. 1st. mtd mc frontis/full-p ils. VG/poor. P2. $125.00

HILL & WHEELER. *Grassland Seeds.* 1957. Van Nostrand. 734p. VG/dj. A10. $30.00

HILLARY, Louise. *Yak for Christmas.* 1968. Hodder Stoughton. 1st. sgn pres. ils/map ep. 208p. VG/dj. W3. $54.00

HILLER, Brett. *Voyages of Torres: Discovery of Southern Coastline..* 1980. St Lucia. U Queensland. 194p. VG/dj. P4. $50.00

HILLER, L. *Surgery Through the Ages: Pictorial Chronicle.* 1944. NY. 1st. 177p. A13. $75.00

HILLER, Mary. *Automata & Mechanical Toys.* 1988. London. Bloomsbury. 200p. NF/dj. K3. $25.00

HILLERMAN, Tony. *Best of the West.* 1991. Harper Collins. 1st. sgn. F/F. A23/B3. $60.00

HILLERMAN, Tony. *Blessingway.* 1990. Armchair Detective. 1st. sgn. F/F. A23. $50.00

HILLERMAN, Tony. *Blessingway.* 1970. Harper Row. 1st. F/NF. M15. $1,250.00

HILLERMAN, Tony. *Blessingway.* 1970. Harper Row. 1st. VG/VG. M19. $750.00

HILLERMAN, Tony. *Coyote Waits.* 1990. Harper Row. 1st. F/F. R14. $30.00

HILLERMAN, Tony. *Coyote Waits.* 1990. Harper Row. 1st. sgn. F/F/case. B3. $350.00

HILLERMAN, Tony. *Coyote Waits.* 1991. London. Michael Joseph. 1st. F/dj. M15. $45.00

HILLERMAN, Tony. *Dance Hall of the Dead.* 1991. Armchair Detective. 1st trade. M/dj. A18. $25.00

HILLERMAN, Tony. *Fly on the Wall.* 1971. Harper Row. 1st. F/dj. M15. $800.00

HILLERMAN, Tony. *Great Taos Bank Robbery.* 1973. Albuquerque. NM U. 1st/1 of 2 states. gray bdg. F/dj. M15. $500.00

HILLERMAN, Tony. *Joe Leaphorn Mysteries.* 1989. Harper Row. Omnibus ed. F/dj. M15. $35.00

HILLERMAN, Tony. *New Mexico, Rio Grande & Other Essays.* 1992. Graphic Arts Center. 1st. M/dj. A18. $35.00

HILLERMAN, Tony. *Skinwalkers.* 1986. Harper Row. 1st. F/F. M15. $75.00

HILLERMAN, Tony. *Skinwalkers.* 1986. Harper Row. 1st. inscr to John Ball. F/dj. M15. $200.00

HILLERMAN, Tony. *Talking God.* 1989. Harper Row. 1st. F/dj. M15. $45.00

HILLERMAN, Tony. *Talking God.* 1989. Harper Row. 1st. inscr. NF/NF. A23. $50.00

HILLERMAN, Tony. *Talking God.* 1989. Harper Row. 1st. sgn. F/F. M25. $60.00

HILLERMAN, Tony. *Talking God.* 1989. Harper Row. 1st. 1/300 special bdg. sgn. F/case. M15. $150.00

HILLERMAN, Tony. *Thief of Time.* 1988. Harper Row. 1st. inscr. NF/dj. M25/S13. $50.00

HILLERMAN, Tony. *Thief of Time.* 1988. Harper Row. 1st. NF/F. A20. $30.00

HILLERMAN, Tony. *Thief of Time.* 1988. Harper Row. 1st. 1/250 special bdg. sgn. F/case. M15. $200.00

HILLERMAN, Tony. *Thief of Time.* 1988. Harper Row. 1st. 209p. NF. W2. $20.00

HILLERMAN, Tony. *Words, Weather & Wolfmen.* 1989. Gallup. Southwesterner Books. 1st. 1/350. sgns. F/dj. M15. $150.00

HILLES, M.W. *Pocket Anatomist: Being Complete Description of Anatomy...* 1860. Phil. 1st Am. 12mo. 263p. A13. $50.00

HILLESUM, Etty. *Interrupted Life: Diaries of Etty Hillesum 1941-43.* 1981. Pantheon. 1st Am. 226p. VG/VG. A25. $15.00

HILLESUM, Etty. *Letters From Westerbork.* 1986. Pantheon. 1st Am. 156p. VG/dj. A25. $15.00

HILLIER & SHINE. *Walt Disney's Mickey Mouse Memorabilia.* 1986. NY. Abrams. 4to. 235 mc ils. 180p. F/F. A4. $75.00

HILLIS, Newell Dwight. *Quest of John Chapman. Story of a Forgotten Hero.* 1904. NY. 349p. G. B18. $32.50

HILLS, Marjorie. *Live Alone & Like It: A Guide for the Extra Woman.* 1936. Bobbs Merrill. 1st/later prt. ils Cipe Pineless. 149p. VG/dj. A25. $18.00

HILLS, Rick. *Limbo River.* 1990. Pittsburgh. 1st. author's 1st story collection. F/F. R13. $20.00

HILTON, James. *Lost Horizon.* 1936. Grosset Dunlap. MTI. VG/VG. B5. $35.00

HILTON, James. *Nothing So Strange.* 1947. Atlantic/Little Brn. 1st. NF/torn. M25. $25.00

HILTON, James. *Nothing So Strange.* 1947. Atlantic/Little Brn. 1st. 308p. beige cloth. F/VG. H1. $22.50

HIMES, Chester. *Case of Rape.* 1980. Targ. 1/350. sgn. F/glassine dj. A24. $100.00

HIMES, Chester. *Cast the First Stone.* 1952. Coward McCann. 1st. VG. M25. $100.00

HIMES, Chester. *Cast the First Stone.* 1952. Coward-McCann. 1st. F/dj. M15. $200.00

HIMES, Chester. *Cotton Comes To Harlem.* 1965. Putnam. 1st. NF/dj. M25. $100.00

HIMES, Chester. *Pinktoes.* 1965. Putnam/Stein Day. 1st. NF/VG. M19. $65.00

HIMES, Chester. *Quality of Hurt.* 1972. NY. ARC. sgn assoc copy w/TLS. RS. F/F. A11. $675.00

HIMES, Chester. *Real Cool Killers.* 1985. London. Allison Busby. 1st hc ed. F/dj. M15. $45.00

HIMES, Joshua V. *Views of the Prophecies & Prophetic Chronology...* 1841. Boston. Moses Dow. 1st. 16mo. 252p. cloth. M1. $125.00

HINCKLEY, F. Lewis. *Directory of Antique Furniture.* 1963. photo. VG/VG. S13. $25.00

HIND, Robert. *Ruby Pendant: Story of Texas Life.* ca 1880. London. James B Knapp. 1st. mc stp bl pict cloth. M24. $125.00

HINDE, Thomas. *Lewis Carrol: Looking-Glass Letters.* 1991. NY. Rizzoli. 1st Am. sm 8vo. 160p. F/F. T5. $35.00

HINDS, Dudley S. *International Real Estate Investing.* 1983. Real Estate Edu. 1st. 315p. NF/VG. W2. $25.00

HINDS, John. *Veterinary Surgeon.* 1846. Phil. Grigg Elliot. leather. G. O3. $58.00

HINDS, N.E.A. *Geomorphology: The Evolution of Landscape.* 1943. Prentice Hall. 1st. ils. 894p. VG. D8. $20.00

HINDUS, Milton. *Worlds of Maurice Samuel: Selected Writings.* 1977. JPS. 444p. VG/dj. S3. $25.00

HINE, L. *Baptists in Southern California.* 1966. Judson. 1st. VG/sans. O4. $15.00

HINE, Robert F. *William Andrew Spalding.* 1961. San Marino, CA. Huntington Lib. 1st. F/F. O4. $15.00

HINE, Robert V. *Bartlett's West, Drawing the Mexican Boundary.* 1968. New Haven/London. Yale. ils. 155p. F/VG. K7. $30.00

HINE, Robert V. *California's Utopian Colonies.* 1966. New Haven/London. Yale. 8vo. 209p. VG. K7. $8.00

HINES, Alan. *Square Dance.* 1984. Harper. 1st. sgn. author's 1st book. NF/dj. R13. $30.00

HINKE. *Oz in Canada, a Bibliography.* 1982. 1/1000. intro Peter E Hanff. F. A4. $135.00

HINTON, Alan. *Shells of New Guinea & Central Indo-Pacific.* 1975. Hong Kong. rpt 1972 Australian. 44 full-p pl. 94p. VG/VG. S15. $24.00

HINTON, Richard J. *John Brown & His Men.* 1894. index/ils. 752p. O8. $12.50

HINTZ, Howard W. *Quaker Influence in American Literature.* 1940. Revell. 90p. G. V3. $12.00

HIROKAWA, Taishi. *Sonomama Sonomama: High Fashion in Japanese Countryside.* 1987. SF. Chronicle. wrp. D11. $60.00

HIRSCH, Edwin W. *Power To Love: A Psychic & Physiologic Study...* 1935. Knopf. 3rd. ils. 363p. VG/dj. A25. $20.00

HIRSCH, Joe. *Kentucky Derby: Chance of a Lifetime.* 1988. NY. McGraw Hill. 1st. 4to. 221p. VG/VG. O3. $45.00

HIRSCH, Susan E. *Roots of the American Working Class.* 1978. Pittsburgh. 1st. VG/worn. V4. $15.00

HIRSCHFELD, Al. *Show Business Is No Business.* 1951. S&S. 1st. 8vo. 141p. F/NF. T10. $50.00

HIRSCHFELD, Burt. *Masters Affair.* 1971. Arbor. 1st. author's 2nd book. F/F. H11. $20.00

HIRSCHFELD, Florence Kerr. *Cooking With Love.* 1965. Houghton Mifflin. VG/dj. A16. $12.50

HIRSCHFELDER, J.O. *Effects of Atomic Weapons.* August 1950. Combat Forces Pr. VG/dj. K3. $50.00

HIRST, Stephen. *Havsuw'Baaja: People of the Blue Green Water.* 1985. Supai, AZ. 8vo. 259p. F/dj. F7. $45.00

HIRST, Stephen. *Life in a Narrow Place.* 1976. NY. McKay. 1st/2nd prt. 8vo. photos. yel cloth. dj. F7. $35.00

HISSEY, James John. *Through Ten English Countries.* 1894. London. Bentley. 1st. VG. O3. $95.00

HISSEY, Jane. *Little Bear Lost.* nd (1989). Hutchinson. 1st. sm 4to. unp. VG. C14. $12.00

HITCHCOCK, Alfred. *My Favorites in Suspense.* 1959. Random. 1st. blk cloth. NF/VG. A24. $30.00

HITCHCOCK, Alfred. *Stories My Mother Never Told Me.* 1963. Random. 1st. NF/VG. A24. $25.00

HITCHCOCK, E.C. *Saddle Up.* 1937. Scribner. 304p. gilt cloth. VG. M20. $25.00

HITCHCOCK & STANDLEY. *Flora of the District of Columbia & Vicinty.* 1919. GPO. 327p. VG. A10. $45.00

HITLER, Adolf. *Mein Kampf.* 1939. Stackpole. 1st unexpurgated in Eng language. VG. M19. $85.00

HITLER, Adolf. *Mein Kampf.* 1939. Munich. pres Mayor of Heidelberg in 1940. teg. leather. case. B18. $95.00

HITTELL, John S. *History of City of San Francisco & Incidentally of...CA.* 1878. SF. Bancroft. 1st. pres to JW Dwinelle. 8vo. gilt brn cloth. F. R3. $900.00

HITTI, Philip K. *Near East in History, a 5000 Year Story.* 1961. Princeton. Van Nostrand. 1st rpt. 8vo. 574p. VG/dj. W1. $35.00

HJORTSBERG, William. *Alp.* 1969. S&S. 1st. author's 1st book. NF/NF. L3. $85.00

HJORTSBERG, William. *Falling Angel.* 1978. HBJ. 1st. F/dj. M21. $60.00

HJORTSBERG, William. *Gray Matters.* 1971. S&S. 1st. author's 3rd novel. NF/NF. M22. $40.00

HO & TSOU. *China in Crisis.* 1968. Chicago. 3 vol in 2. F. W3. $48.00

HOAGLAND, Edward. *Heart's Desire.* 1988. Summit. 1st. F/NF clip. T11. $60.00

HOAGLAND, Edward. *Notes From the Century Before.* 1969. Random. 1st. NF/F clip. T11. $35.00

HOAI-TRINH, Minh-Duc. *This Side...the Other Side.* 1980. WA, DC. Occidental. 1st. F/F. B4. $150.00

HOBAN, Lillian. *Arthur's Honey Bear.* 1974. Harper Row. 1st. 64p. F/VG. P2. $25.00

HOBAN, Russell. *Bread & Jam for Frances.* 1964. Harper Row. probable 1st. 31p. VG/VG. P2. $65.00

HOBAN, Russell. *Egg Thoughts & Other Frances Songs.* 1972. Harper Row. 1st. 32p. F/F. D4. $35.00

HOBAN, Russell. *Medusa Frequency.* 1987. Atlantic Monthly. 1st Am. F/dj. Q1. $30.00

HOBAN, Russell. *Ridley Walker.* 1980. SUmmit. 1st Am. F/dj. M2. $50.00

HOBAN, Tana. *A, B, See.* (1982). NY. Greenwillow. stated 1st. unp. VG+/VG. C14. $10.00

HOBAN, Tana. *Look! Look! Look!* 1988. Greenwillow. 1st. F/F. C8. $35.00

HOBART, Lois. *Mexican Mural: Story of Mexico, Past & Present.* 1963. NY. Harcourt Brace. 1st. 224p. dj. F3. $10.00

HOBBIE & HOBBIE. *Art of Holly Hobbie, Drawing on Affection.* 1986. 1st collected. 100 mc pl. 127p. F/F. A4. $35.00

HOBBS, Lois Zortmann. *Corny Cornpicker Finds a Home.* 1959. John Deere. 1st. Golden format. sq 8vo. M8. $75.00

HOBBS, MEANS & WILLIAMS. *Outline of Structural Geology.* 1976. John Wiley. 1st. 571p. VG/dj. D8. $15.00

HOBBS, Robert. *Robert Smithson: Sculpture.* 1981. Cornell. ils/photos/bibliography/index. cloth. dj. D2. $125.00

HOBBS, William Herbert. *Peary.* 1936. NY. Macmillan. 1st. 27 maps/13 halftones/10 records. bl cloth. P4. $95.00

HOBBS & PASCHALL. *Teacher's Bible Commentary.* 1972. Broadman. 817p. VG/dj. B29. $16.00

HOBBS & WHALLEY. *Beatrix Potter: V&A Collection, the Leslie Linder Bequest.* nd. London. 4to. ils. 240p. F/F. A4. $145.00

HOCHWALT, A.F. *Farmer's Dog: For Work, for Profit & for Sport.* 1922. Cincinnati. Sportsmen's Digest. 1st. 12mo. VG. H7. $15.00

HOCHWALT, A.F. *Working Dog & His Education: A Treatise...* 1921. Cincinnati. Sportsmen's Review. 1st. 116p. VG. H7. $15.00

HOCKING, Charles. *Dictionary of Disasters at Sea.* 1990. London Stp Exchange. rpt. 4to. 779p. dj. T7. $145.00

HOCKING, D. *Trees for Drylands.* 1993. Internat Sci Pub. 370p. NF/dj. B1. $60.00

HODGE, Frederick Webb. *Handbook of American Indians, North of Mexico.* 1907. Smithsonian. 1st. 2 vol. ils. VG/VG. J2. $475.00

HODGE, Frederick Webb. *History of Hawikuh.* 1937. Ward Ritchie. A19. $55.00

HODGE & UMARU. *Hausa. Basic Course.* 1963. WA. Foreign Service Inst. 399p. xl. VG. W1. $12.00

HODGES, George W. *Swamp Angel.* 1958. New Voice. 1st. inscr. F/F. B4. $150.00

HODGES, Henry. *Technology in the Ancient World.* 1974. London. BC Assoc. 4to. ils. 260p. NF/VG. K3. $65.00

HODGES, Margaret. *Little Humpbacked Horse.* 1980. FSG. 1st. 8vo. unp. F/NF clip. C14. $14.00

HODGKISS & TATHAM. *Keyguide to Information Sources in Cartography.* 1986. 253p. NF. A4. $195.00

HODGSON, Fred T. *Estimating Frame & Brick Houses, Barns, Stables...* 1910. NY. David Williams. 12mo. VG. O3. $40.00

HODGSON, Fred T. *Up-To-Date Hardwood Finisher, in Two Parts.* 1904. Chicago. Drake. 1st. ils. 209p. B18. $22.50

HODGSON, Moira. *Cooking With Fruits & Nuts.* 1973. NY. Crowell. 1st. VG/dj. A16. $17.50

HODGSON, William Hope. *Ghost Pirates.* 1976 (1909). Hyperion. rpt. F. M2. $45.00

HODGSON & WILLIAMS. *Growing Bromeliads.* 1990. Portland. ils/photos. F/dj. B26. $25.00

HODSON, Geoffrey. *Kingdom of the Gods.* 1952. Madras. Theosophical Pub. 1st. 8vo. 247p. F. T10. $50.00

HODSON, J.L. *Annual Report of Adjutant General of State of Maine...1866.* 1867. Augusta. 588p. leather spine/marbled brd. M4. $55.00

HOEHLING, A.A. *Jeannette Expedition: Ill-Fated Journey to the Arctic.* 1969. London. Abelard Schuman. 8vo. 224p. VG/dj. P4. $45.00

HOEHLING, A.A. *They Sailed Into Oblivion.* 1962. NY. VG/VG. B5. $15.00

HOEHN, Reinhardt. *Curiosities of the Plant Kingdom.* 1980. Universe. 4to. 212p. NF/dj. A22. $30.00

HOEKEMA, Anthony A. *Created in God's Image.* 1988. Eerdmans. 264p. VG/dj. B29. $17.00

HOEXTER, Corrine K. *From Canton to California: Epic of Chinese Immigration.* 1976. Four Winds. 1st. 8vo. ils. gilt red cloth. F. R3. $40.00

HOFFAMNN, Heinrich. *King Nut-Cracker; or, Dream of Poor Reinhold.* 1853. London. Wm Tegg. 1st Eng. 28 hand-colored p. 8vo. rose-orange brd. box. R5. $1,600.00

HOFFMAN, Alice Spencer. *Children's Shakespeare.* 1911. London. 1st thus. ils Chas Folkard. VG. M5. $145.00

HOFFMAN, Alice. *Drowning Season.* 1979. Dutton. 1st. author's 2nd book. VG/dj. A24. $75.00

HOFFMAN, Alice. *Drowning Season.* 1979. Dutton. 1st. sgn. author's 2nd book. F/NF. D10. $110.00

HOFFMAN, Alice. *Fortune's Daughter.* 1985. Putnam. 1st. sgn. F/F. D10. $50.00

HOFFMAN, Alice. *Illumination Night.* 1987. Putnam. 1st. F/dj. B4. $45.00

HOFFMAN, Alice. *Illumination Night.* 1987. Putnam. 1st. sgn. F/F. B3. $75.00

HOFFMAN, Alice. *Property of...* 1977. FSG. 1st. sgn. author's 1st book. F/NF. D10. $110.00

HOFFMAN, Alice. *Property of...* 1977. FSG. 1st. VG/NF. M25. $35.00

HOFFMAN, Alice. *Turtle Moon.* 1992. Putnam. 1st. inscr. F/F. R13. $35.00

HOFFMAN, Alice. *White Horses.* 1982. Putnam. ARC. sgn. author's 4th novel. F/F. D10. $65.00

HOFFMAN, Alice. *White Horses.* 1982. Putnam. 1st. sgn. F/F. D10. $50.00

HOFFMAN, Andrew Jay. *Twain's Heroes, Twain's Worlds.* 1988. Phil. PA U. 1st. bl cloth. F/dj. M24. $20.00

HOFFMAN, B.R. *Luther & the Mystics.* 1976. Augsburg. 285p. VG/dj. B29. $8.50

HOFFMAN, Bob. *High Protein Road to Better Nutrition.* 1961 (1940). York. Strength & Health Magazine. 7th. photos. 255p. VG/dj. A25. $8.00

HOFFMAN, Carl. *Saipan: Beginning of the End.* 1950. WA. fld mc maps/charts/photos. 286p. VG. S16. $85.00

HOFFMAN, Carl. *Seizure of Tinian.* 1951. WA. fld mc maps/photos/index. VG. S16. $85.00

HOFFMAN, E.T.A. *Selected Writings of ETA Hoffman.* 1969. Chicago. 2 vol. ils. xl. VG/VG case. A4. $45.00

HOFFMAN, F.J. *Little Magazine: A History & a Bibliography.* 1946. Princeton. 1st ed. NF/dj. B2. $60.00

HOFFMAN, Felix. *Bearskinner.* 1978. Atheneum. 1st Am. lg 4to. F/F. P2. $25.00

HOFFMAN, G.W. *Geography of Europe Including Asiatic USSR.* 1969. Ronald. ils. cloth. 669p. VG. D8. $10.00

HOFFMAN, Heinrich. *Adolf Hitler. Bilder Aus dem Leben des Fuhrers.* 1936. Hamburg. photos. 132p. VG-/tattered. B18. $125.00

HOFFMAN, Heinrich. *Der Struwwelpeter.* pre-1900. Frankfurt. Literarifche Anftalt Rutten & Loening. 24p. VG. M20. $60.00

HOFFMAN, Heinrich. *Der Struwwelpeter.* ca 1960s. London. Blackie. 8vo. 24p. pict brd. VG/VG. D1. $40.00

HOFFMAN, Heinrich. *Slovenly Peter (Der Struwwelpeter).* 1935. NY. LEC. 1st thus. 1/1500. 4to. VG/case. D1. $500.00

HOFFMAN, Heinrich. *Slovenly Peter.* nd. Winston. ils. gilt wine cloth. VG. M5. $75.00

HOFFMAN, Malvina. *Heads & Tales.* 1936. Scribner. 1st. inscr pres. photos. VG/dj. w/TLS+ephemera. A25. $175.00

HOFFMAN, Malvina. *Heads & Tales.* 1936. Scribner. 1st. photos. 416p. teg. VG+/VG. A25. $80.00

HOFFMAN, W.S. *Paul Mellon, Portrait of an Oil Baron.* 1974. Chicago. 1st. 204p. NF/dj. D8. $18.50

HOFFMAN, Walter James. *Graphic Art of the Eskimos.* 1897. GPO. 8vo. ils/figures/82 pl. professionally rebound. P4. $225.00

HOFFMAN & HOFFMAN. *We Married an Englishman.* 1938. NY. Carrick Evans. 1st. sgns. 8vo. 314p. cloth. VG. W1. $35.00

HOFFMAN & JOHNSON. *Reports of Land Cases Determined...1853...* 1975. SF. Yosemite Collections. rpt. 1/50. sgn/edit Johnson. 8vo. cloth. F. R3. $100.00

HOFFMANN, E.T. *Nutcracker.* 1984. Crown. ltd. 1/250. 4to. ils/sgn/#d Sendak. 102p. w/orig litho. M/case. D1. $1,200.00

HOFFMANN, E.T. *Tales of Hoffmann.* 1943. Heritage. ils Hugo Steiner-Prag. 344p. F/VG case. H1. $20.00

HOFFMANN, Professor. *Modern Magic: A Practical Treatise on Art of Conjuring.* nd. Phil. ils. 563p. decor cloth. dj. B18. $37.50

HOFFMEISTER, Donald F. *Mammals of the Grand Canyon.* 1971. Chicago. 8vo. 183p. stiff wrp. VG. F7. $12.00

HOFMANN, Charles. *American Indians Sing.* 1967. John Day. ils. 96p. xl. VG. K7. $25.00

HOFSINDE, Robert (Gray-Wolf). *Indian Sign language.* 1972 (1956). Morrow. 14th prt. 8vo. xl. VG/VG. C8. $15.00

HOFSTAETTER, Hans H. *Art Nouveau. Prints, Illustrations & Posters.* 1984. NY. Greenwich. ils/biographies/bibliographies/index. 295p. cloth. D2. $175.00

HOGAN, Desmond. *Link With the River.* 1989. FSG. 1st. F/NF. R13. $15.00

HOGAN, Inez. *Monkey Twins, They Saw It All!* 1944 (1943). Dutton. 2nd. sm 8vo. NF. C8. $30.00

HOGAN, Inez. *Mule Twins.* 1939. Dutton. probable 1st. 8vo. 49p. VG/VG. D1. $60.00

HOGAN, Inez. *Nicodemus Runs Away.* 1946. Shakespeare Head Pr. 1st thus. 12mo. VG+. C8. $125.00

HOGAN, Inez. *Twin Deer.* 1943 (1941). Dutton. 2nd. 12mo. G+. C8. $27.50

HOGAN, James. *Code to the Lifemaker.* 1983. Del Rey. 1st. sgn. F/dj. M2. $35.00

HOGAN, Linda. *Mean Spirit.* 1990. Atheneum. 1st. F/dj. A24. $30.00

HOGAN, Linda. *Seeing Through the Sun.* 1985. Amherst. MA U. 1st. NF/wrp. L3. $45.00

HOGBIN, H. Ian. *Experiments in Civilization: Effects of European Culture...* 1970. NY. Schocken. ils/2 maps. 268p. VG/worn. P4. $35.00

HOGES, Margaret. *Saint George & the Dragon.* 1984. Little Brn. stated 1st. ils Hyman. F/dj. M5. $52.00

HOGG, Ian. *Fighting Tanks.* 1977. NY. ils. 160p. VG/VG. S16. $25.00

HOGG, James. *Jabobite Relics of Scotland.* 1819. Edinburgh. Blackwood Cadell Davies. 1st. tall 8vo. 424p. H13. $295.00

HOGNER, Dorothy Childs. *Summer Roads to Gaspe.* 1939. Dutton. 1st. ils Nils Hogner. 288p. VG. A25. $15.00

HOGUE, Arthur R. *Origins of the Common Law.* 1966. Bloomington. IU. 1st. M11. $45.00

HOHLER, Robert T. *I Touch the Future.* 1986. Random. 1st. 8vo. 262p. VG/dj. K5. $17.00

HOHMAN, Elmo Paul. *American Whaleman: Study of Life & Labor in Whaling...* 1928. Longmans. photos. 355p. VG. S15. $70.00

HOIG, Stan. *Western Odyssey of John Simpson Smith, Frontiersman...* 1974. Clark. 1st. 254p. VG/VG. J2. $155.00

HOKE, Helen. *Doctor the Puppy Who Learned.* 1944. Messner. 1st. NF/VG-. P2. $45.00

HOKOLA, John W. *Frontier Omnibus.* 1962. Missoula/Helena. ils. 436p. buckskin. D11. $100.00

HOLABIRD, Katherine. *Angelina at the Fair.* 1985. NY. Potter. 1st/1st prt. sm 4to. F/F. C8. $30.00

HOLBEIN, Hans. *Celebrated Hans Holbein's Alphabet of Death.* 1856. Paris. Prt for Edwin Tross. gilt gr cloth. Q1. $250.00

HOLBEIN. *Selected Drawings From Collection of Her Majesty...* 1954. ils. stp for USAF/For Salvage Only. VG/G. M17. $15.00

HOLBERG, Ruth. *Hester & Timothy Pioneers.* 1937. Doubleday Doran. 1st. 128p. VG/VG. P2. $30.00

HOLBROOK, James G. *Survey of Metropolitan Trial Courts.* 1956. LA. 434p. gilt fabricoid. D11. $30.00

HOLBROOK, M.L. *Parturition Without Pain: Code of Directions...* 1871. NY. 1st. 159p. A13. $125.00

HOLBROOK, Stewart H. *Old Post Road.* 1962. McGraw Hill. 1st. American Trails series. 8vo. 273p. VG. T10. $25.00

HOLBROOK, Stewart H. *Wild Bill Hickok Tames the West.* 1952. Random. dj. A19. $20.00

HOLCOMB, William Hartley. *Old Mission Rhymes.* 1900. San Diego. Frye Garrett Smith. A19. $40.00

HOLDEN, George Parker. *Idyl of the Split-Bamboo.* 1920. Cincinnati. Stewart Kidd. 1st. ils. 278p. VG. B18. $150.00

HOLDEN, George Parker. *Idyl of the Split-Bamboo.* 1934. NY. 2nd. 278p+11 photos. NF. A17. $135.00

HOLDEN, Reuben. *Yale in China.* 1964. New Haven. 1st. photos/addenda/9 appendix. 327p. NF. W3. $68.00

HOLDEN, William Curry. *Spur Ranch, a Study...* 1934. Christopher Pub. 1st. 229p. VG. J2. $275.00

HOLDER, C.F. *Life in the Open: Sport With Rod, Gun, Horse & Hound...* 1906. Putnam. 8vo. photos. 401p. gilt pict cloth. NF. M12. $60.00

HOLDSTOCK, Robert. *Eye Among the Blind.* 1977. Doubleday. 1st Am. F/dj. M2. $22.00

HOLDSWORTH, W.S. *Charles Dickens As a Legal Historian.* 1929. Yale. 2nd. maroon cloth/morocco label. M11. $85.00

HOLDSWORTH, W.S. *Historians of Anglo-American Law.* 1966 (1928). Hamden. Archon. facsimile. M11. $75.00

HOLDSWORTH, W.S. *Sources & Literature of English Law.* 1952. Clarendon. gilt crimson cloth. M11. $125.00

HOLE, S. Reynolds. *Book About Roses: How To Grow & Show Them.* 1932 (1869). London. ils EF Daglish. 276p. gr cloth. B26. $17.50

HOLL, Adelaide. *Sylvester, the Mouse With the Musical Ear.* 1973 (1961). Golden/Western. 1st thus. lg 4to. VG+/VG. C8. $45.00

HOLLAND, Isabelle. *God, Mrs Muskrat & Aunt Dot.* 1983. Phil. Westminster. 1st. 8vo. 77p. VG. T5. $25.00

HOLLAND, Ray P. *Now Listen, Warden.* 1946. NY. Barnes. A19. $15.00

HOLLAND, Ray P. *Shotgunning in the Lowlands.* 1945. NY. AS Barnes. stated 1st. 1/3500. 4to. 213p. F/VG box. H7. $60.00

HOLLAND, Rupert Sargent. *Historic Railroads.* (1927). Macrae Smith. 1st probable. lg 8vo. NF. C8. $60.00

HOLLEY, Marietta. *Samatha Among the Colored Folks.* 1894. NY. ils. G+. M17. $45.00

HOLLEY, O.L. *Life of Benjamin Franklin.* 1848. Boston. 468p. O8. $12.50

HOLLICK, Frederick. *Outlines of Anatomy & Physiology...* ca 1846. Phil. TB Peterson. 4to. orig leather/pict brd. M1. $150.00

HOLLIDAY, J.S. *World Rushed In.* 1981. S&S. 1st. 8vo. 559p. brn leatherette. VG. K7. $25.00

HOLLIDAY, J.S. *World Rushed In: California Gold Rush Experience.* 1981. S&S. 2nd. F/NF clip. O4. $25.00

HOLLIDAY, Laurel. *Heart Songs: Intimate Diaries of Young Girls.* 1978. Guerneville. Bluestocking Books. 1st. 191p. sc. VG+. A25. $20.00

HOLLIDAY, Michael; see Creasey, John.

HOLLIDAY, Robert Cortes. *Literary Lanes & Other Byways.* 1925. Doran. 1st. 219p. gr cloth. NF/dj. B22. $18.00

HOLLING, Holling C. *Book of Cowboys.* 1936. Platt Munk. 1st. F/dj. C8/M19. $65.00

HOLLING, Holling C. *Book of Indians.* 1935. Platt Munk. 1st. VG/G. O3. $45.00

HOLLING, Holling C. *Minn of the Mississippi.* 1951. Houghton Mifflin. 1st. ils. 87p. VG/VG. J2. $185.00

HOLLING, Holling C. *Paddle to the Sea.* 1945 (1941). London. Collins. 1st. VG/VG. C8. $75.00

HOLLING, Holling C. *Seabird.* 1948. Houghton Mifflin. 1st. ils. 4to. VG+/dj. P2. $80.00

HOLLING, Holling C. *Seabird.* 1948. Houghton Mifflin. 1st. ils/27 full-p ils. 63p. VG/torn. D1. $75.00

HOLLING, Holling C. *Twins Who Flew Around the World.* (1931). Platt Munk. very early ed. lg 4to. VG+. C8. $50.00

HOLLINGSHEAD, M. *Hawking Ground Quarry: A Treatise on Hawking.* 1993. Blainbe. Hancock. ils/photos. 168p. brd. F/F. M12. $30.00

HOLLINGSWORTH, Adelaide. *Home Cook Book.* 1895. ils. G+. M17. $25.00

HOLLO, Anselm. *Heavy Jars.* 1977. W Branch. Toothpaste. 1/100. sgn. F. B2. $35.00

HOLLON, W.E. *Beyond the Cross Timbers. Travels of Randolph B Marcy.* 1955. OK U. 1st. ils. F/dj. M4. $40.00

HOLLON, W.E. *Great American Desert.* 1966. Oxford. 1st. ils/notes/index. 284p. NF/VG. w/2 TLS. B19. $35.00

HOLLOWAY, David. *Stalin & the Bomb.* 1994. New Haven. Yale. ils. M/dj. K3. $30.00

HOLLOWAY, Laura C. *Mothers.* 1891. Baltimore. RH Woodward Co. A19. $35.00

HOLMAN, Felice. *I Hear You Smiling & Other Poems.* 1973. Scribner. 1st. 62p. F/F. D4. $30.00

HOLMAN, Russell. *Freshman.* 1925. Grosset Dunlap. 1st/photoplay. F/VG. B4. $185.00

HOLMAN, William. *Library Publications.* 1965. SF. Roger Beacham. 1st. 1/350. folio. M24. $350.00

HOLMAN & MARKS. *Pioneering in Northwest. Niobrara-Virginia City Wagon Road.* 1924. Sioux City. Deitch Lamar. 150p. prt cloth. D11. $40.00

HOLME, Bryan. *Enchanted Garden.* 1982. NY. Oxford. 8vo. ils. F/clip. A22. $20.00

HOLME, Bryan. *Horses.* 1951. Studio. 1st. photos. VG. O3. $35.00

HOLME. *Kate Greenaway Book, a Collection of Illustrations, Verse...* 1976. 144p. F/VG. A4. $45.00

HOLMER, W.J. *Undersea Victory: Influence of Submarine Operations...* 1966. Garden City. 1st. ils/maps. 595p. VG/dj. B5. $35.00

HOLMES, Bruce T. *Anvil of the Heart.* 1983. Haven. 1st. F/dj. M2. $20.00

HOLMES, Charles M. *Principles & Practice of Horse-Shoeing.* 1949. Leeds, England. Farriers Journal. 1st. VG. O3. $38.00

HOLMES, James William. *Voyaging: 50 Years on the Seven Seas in Sail.* 1972. Dodd Mead. 8vo. 207p. silvered gr cloth. NF/VG. P4. $25.00

HOLMES, John Clellon. *Go.* 1952. Scribner. 1st. inscr. VG/VG+. B4. $1,350.00

HOLMES, John Clellon. *Horn.* 1958. Random. 1st. F/NF. B2. $100.00

HOLMES, John Clellon. *Nothing More To Declare.* 1967. NY. 1st. Holme's copy. F/NF. A11. $65.00

HOLMES, Kenneth. *Covered Wagon Women, Diaries & Letters...1840-1890.* 1983-93. Arthur H Clarke. 11 vol. 1st. fld maps. F. w/prospectus. A4. $595.00

HOLMES, L.P. *Black Sage.* 1950. Doubleday. 1st. F/NF. B4. $100.00

HOLMES, L.P. *Hill Smoke.* 1959. Dodd Mead. 1st. F/VG. B4. $65.00

HOLMES, Maurice. *Captain James Cook, RN, FRS: A Bibliographical Excursion.* 1952. London. Francis Edwards. 1/500. 11 full-p photos. 103p. cloth. D11. $100.00

HOLMES, Oliver Wendell. *Astraea: Balance of Illusions.* 1850. Ticknor Reed Fields. 1st/2nd prt/state A (B?). gilt brn wavy-grain cloth. F. M24. $125.00

HOLMES, Oliver Wendell. *Common Law. Edited by Mark DeWolfe Howe.* 1968. Macmillan. VG/dj. M11. $75.00

HOLMES, Oliver Wendell. *Dedication of New Building & Hall of Boston Medical Lib...* 1881. Boston. Riverside. bl cloth/bl-gray wrp bdg in. NF. M24. $200.00

HOLMES, Oliver Wendell. *One Hoss Shay.* 1905. Houghton Mifflin. 1st thus. ils Howard Pyle. VG/G-. P2. $100.00

HOLMES, Samuel Jackson. *Negro's Struggle for Survival: A Study in Human Ecology.* 1937. Berkeley, CA. 1st. 296p. cloth. cl. VG. M8. $85.00

HOLMES, W.J. *Undersea Victory.* 1966. Garden City. 1st. VG/VG. B5. $40.00

HOLMES, William. *National Gallery of Art in Washington: Catalogue of...* 1922. GPO. 25 full-p pl w/tissue guards. bl cloth. VG/VG+. B22. $12.00

HOLST, Adolf. *Die Glucklichen Mausleut.* (1929). Oldenburg. Cerhard Stalling. orange cloth. G. D1. $150.00

HOLST, Adolf. *Die Wunderwiese.* ca 1920s. Koln. Hermann Schaffstein. ils Ritter. VG. D1. $350.00

HOLT, Samuel; see Westlake, Donald E.

HOLTE, Clarence L. *Nubian Baby Book.* 1971. Nubian. 1st. ils Robert Pious. wht cloth. F/wrp band. B4. $100.00

HOLTON, Isaac. *New Granada.* (1967). Carbondale, IL. 1st this. 223p. dj. M20. $15.00

HOLTON, Leonard. *Flowers by Request.* 1964. Dodd Mead. 1st. xl. NF/dj. M25. $45.00

HOLWAY, John. *Voices From the Great Black Baseball Leagues.* 1975. Dodd Mead. 1st. photos. F/dj. B4. $100.00

HOLWAY, John. *Voices From the Great Black Baseball Leagues.* 1975. Dodd Mead. 1st. 363p. cloth. NF/dj. M20. $85.00

HOLWAY, Mary Gordon. *Art of the Old World in New Spain & Mission Days of Alta...* 1922. SF. AM Robertson. 1/1000. 8vo. ils/photos. tan cloth. VG. K7. $25.00

HOLYBAND, Claudius. *French Litteton (A Most Easie, Perfect & Absolute Way...* 1953. Cambridge. only modern ed. M11. $65.00

HOLZMAN & LEONARD. *View From the Bench.* 1980. Norton. 1st. photos. VG/dj. P8. $25.00

HOME, H.H. *Citrus Fruits & Their Culture.* 1904. Jacksonville. 1st. ils. 597p. VG. B5. $60.00

HOME, Henry (of Kames). *Elements of Criticism.* 1883. NY. revised. 486p. NF. A17. $10.00

HOMER. *Iliad.* 1962. Chicago. 1st thus. ils Baskin. 526p. F/VG. H1. $30.00

HOMER. *Illustrated Odyssey.* 1980. London. 1st. VG/VG. T9. $20.00

HOMEWOOD, Harry. *O God of Battles.* 1983. Morrow. 1st. F/F. H11. $25.00

HOMSHER, Lola A. *History of Albany County, Wyoming to 1880.* 1965. The Lusk Herald. 1st. 110p. VG/pict wrp. J2. $95.00

HONCE. *Vincent Starrett Library: Astonishing Result...* 1941. Golden Eagle. 1/100. ils. 85p. VG. A4. $350.00

HONEY, W.B. *Dresden China.* 1946. Troy, NY. Rosenfeld. 1st. 61 pl. 223p. F. T10. $100.00

HONNYWILL, Eleanor. *Challenge of Antarctica.* 1969. London. Methuen. 1st. 160p. VG/dj. P4. $30.00

HONNYWILL, Eleanor. *To Stand at the Pole: Dr Cook-Admiral Peary North Pole...* 1981. NY. Stein Day. 8vo. 288p. half cloth. P4. $20.00

HONORE, Tony. *Tribonian.* 1978. London. Duckworth. VG/dj. M11. $75.00

HONOUR, Hugh. *European Vision of America...* 1975. Cleveland Mus of Art. ils. 389p. ES. as new/dj. O7. $85.00

HONOUR, Hugh. *New Golden Land: European Images of America...* 1975. Pantheon. ils/12 3-column p of notes. as new/dj. O7. $50.00

HOOD, Hugh. *Strength Down Centre.* 1970. Prentice Hall. 1st. photos. VG/G+. P8. $27.50

HOOD, Thomas. *New Comic Annual, for 1831.* (1831). London. Hurst Chance. 1st. 16mo. 192p. full contemporary calf. M1. $200.00

HOOD, Thomas. *Poems by...* 1871. London. Moxon. lg paper ed. ils Birket Foster. 109p. half gr morocco. B24. $300.00

HOOKER, J.D. *Life & Letters of Sir Joseph Hooker.* 1918. London. 2nd. 2 vol. ils/map/4 portraits. gilt navy cloth. VG. B26. $200.00

HOOPES, Chad L. *What Makes a Man: Annie E Kennedy & John Bidwell Letters...* 1973. Fresno, CA. Valley Pub. 1st. F/NF. O4. $25.00

HOOPES, Donelson. *Winslow Homer Watercolors.* 1969. 4to. ils. VG/VG. S13. $25.00

HOOPES, Roy. *Cain: The Biography of James M Cain.* 1982. NY. 1st. 684p. F/dj. A17. $30.00

HOOTON, Earnest H. *Apes, Men & Morons.* 1937. Putnam. 1st. sgn. F. B14. $45.00

HOOVER, H.M. *Rains of Zenda.* 1977. Viking. 1st. F/dj. M2. $20.00

HOOVER, Herbert Clark. *Remedy for Disappearing Game Fishes.* 1930. NY. Huntington. 1st. 1/990. ils Harry Cimino. 42p. NF. H7. $65.00

HOOVER, Herbert T. *South Dakota Leaders.* 1989. Vermillion, SD. SD U. A19. $22.00

HOOVER, J. Edgar. *Study of Communism.* 1962. HRW. 1st. F/VG+. A20. $25.00

HOPE, Bob. *Confessions of a Hooker. My Lifelong Love Affair With Golf.* 1985. Doubleday. 1st. Gerald Ford sgn/dtd 1997. VG/VG. A23. $80.00

HOPE, Bob. *Don't Shoot, It's Only Me.* 1990. Putnam. 1st. sgn. F/F. A23. $45.00

HOPE, Bob. *Five Women I Love.* 1966. Doubleday. 1st. 255p. F. W2. $15.00

HOPE, Brian; see Creasey, John.

HOPE, Christopher. *White Boy Running.* 1988. FSG. 1st. F/F. B3. $30.00

HOPE, Laura Lee. *Blythe Girls: Helen, Margy & Rose; or, Facing Great World.* 1925. Grosset Dunlap. 1st. ils Thelma Gooch. 214p. VG/dj. A25. $18.00

HOPE, Laura Lee. *Bobbsey Twins, or Merry Days Indoors & Out.* nd. Grosset Dunlap. rpt/pre 1943 prt. 12mo. VG+/NF. C8. $22.50

HOPE, Laura Lee. *Bobbsey Twins at the Seashore (#3).* nd. Chicago. Goldsmith. 1st. F/poor. T12. $19.00

HOPE, Laura Lee. *Bobbsey Twins in Echo Valley (#36).* (1943). Grosset Dunlap. early ed. 12mo. VG+/VG. C8. $22.50

HOPE, Laura Lee. *Bobbsey Twins on a Ranch.* 1935. Grosset Dunlap. 1st. inscr. VG/poor. T12. $10.00

HOPE, Laura Lee. *Bobbsey Twins on an Airplane Trip (#26).* (1933). Grosset Dunlap. pre-1943 prt. 12mo. VG/VG. C8. $35.00

HOPE, Laura Lee. *Outdoor Girls Around the Campfire.* 1923. Grosset Dunlap. 1st. 214p. pict bdg. VG/VG. H1. $20.00

HOPE, Laura Lee. *Outdoor Girls in a Winter Camp.* 1913. Grosset Dunlap. 8vo. 208p. pict cloth. lists to Outdoor Girls in FL. VG. T10. $25.00

HOPKINS, Charles H. *Rise of the Social Gospel in American Protestantism.* 1950. Yale. 352p. VG. B29. $12.00

HOPKINS, Edward J. *Organ: Its History & Construction.* 1855. London. Robert Cocks. 1st. thick 4to. 600p. cloth/rebacked orig spine. T10. $150.00

HOPKINS, Lee Bennett. *Hey-How for Halloween!* 1974. HBJ. 7th. sgn. 8vo. 31p. VG/G. T5. $24.00

HOPKINS, Lee Bennett. *Me! A Book of Poems.* 1970. NY. Seabury. 1st. 32p. F/NF. D4. $30.00

HOPKINS, Lee Bennett. *Side by Side.* 1988. S&S. 1st. sgn. F/F. D4. $45.00

HOPKINS, Lee Bennett. *This Street's for Me!* 1970. NY. Crown. 1st. ils Ann Grifalconi. F/F. D4. $30.00

HOPKINS, Robert. *Darwin's South America.* 1969. John Day. 1st. 224p. dj. F3. $20.00

HOPMAN, Harry. *Lobbing Into the Sun.* 1975. Bobbs Merrill. 1st. ils. F/VG. P8. $15.00

HOPWOOD, John A. *Pussy Cat Dirty Nose.* 1928. McLoughlin. 4to. pict brd. R5. $85.00

HORAN, James D. *Across the Cimarron.* 1956. Crown. 1st. 301p. cloth. VG/dj. M20. $30.00

HORAN, James D. *Confederate Agent.* 1960. 326p. O8. $18.50

HORAN, James D. *Desperate Women.* 1952. Putnam. 1st. 336p. cloth. VG/dj. M20. $25.00

HORAN, James D. *Pictorial History of the Wild West.* 1954. NY. Crown. dj. A19. $45.00

HORAN, James D. *Pinkertons: Detective Dynasty That Made History.* 1967. NY. ARC/1st. photos. 564p. F/dj. M4. $40.00

HORDER, Thomas. *Clinical Pathology in Practice With Short Account Vaccine...* 1910. London. 1st. 216p. A13. $75.00

HORDER, W. Garrett. *Quaker Worthies.* 1896. London. Headley Bros. 224p. V3. $15.00

HORGAN, J.J. *City of Flight: History of Aviation in St Louis.* 1984. Gerald. 1/175. sgn/#d. photos/ils. leather. F. M4. $90.00

HORGAN, Paul. *Centuries of Santa Fe.* 1956. Dutton. 1st. VG+/VG+ clip. T11. $30.00

HORGAN, Paul. *Devil in the Desert.* 1952. Longman Gr. 1st. F/VG. A18. $30.00

HORGAN, Paul. *Everything To Live For.* 1968. FSG. 1st. F/NF. T11. $25.00

HORGAN, Paul. *Josiah Gregg & His Vision of the Early West.* 1979. FSG. 1st. 116p. VG+/dj. M20. $20.00

HORGAN, Paul. *Lamy of Santa Fe.* 1975. FSG. 1st. F/F. T11. $60.00

HORGAN, Paul. *Lamy of Santa Fe: His Life & Times.* 1975. NY. FSG. 1st. sgn. 523p. VG/VG. B14. $55.00

HORGAN, Paul. *Memories of the Future.* 1966. FSG. 1st. F/dj. Q1/T11. $45.00

HORGAN, Paul. *Mexico Bay.* 1982. FSG. 1st ed. inscr. NF/NF. T11. $65.00

HORGAN, Paul. *One Red Rose for Christmas.* 1952. Longman Gr. 1st. VG+/VG. A18. $30.00

HORGAN, Paul. *Thin Air Mountain.* 1977. FSG. 1st. F/VG+. T11. $35.00

HORLER, Sidney. *Peril.* 1930. Mystery League. 1st. VG. M2. $20.00

HORN, Huston. *Pioneers.* 1975. Time-Life. leather. A19. $20.00

HORN, M.A. *Digest of Hygiene for Mother & Daughter...* 1947. Wilmington. Hygienic Prod. 39th prt. ils. 93p+ads. VG+. A25. $20.00

HORN, Stanley Fitzgerald. *Decisive Battle of Nashville.* 1956. LSU. 1st. inscr. 181p. cloth. NF. M8. $35.00

HORN. *World Encyclopedia of Cartoons.* 1980. 4to. ils. 676p. F/F. A4. $50.00

HORNE, John. *Diversions of an Autograph-Hunter by John Horne.* 1894. London. Elliot Stock. 1st. gilt dk purple-brn cloth. uncut. F. M24. $150.00

HORNELL, James. *British Coracles.* 1936. Greenwich. 2 parts. 21 pl/13 drawings. wrp. T7. $50.00

HORNER, Harlan Hoyt. *Lincoln & Greeley.* 1953. 1st. 432p. O8. $18.50

HORNUNG, Clarence P. *Treasury of American Design.* (1976). Abrams. 2 vol. 4to. F/dj (Mylar w/end sleeves). H1. $50.00

HORNUNG, E.W. *Mr Justice Raffles.* 1909. NY. 1st Am. gilt cloth. G. A17. $20.00

HORNUNG, E.W. *Raffles.* 1901. Scribner. 1st Am. NF. M22. $35.00

HORNUNG, E.W. *Thief in the Night.* 1905. Raffles. 1st. VG. M22. $20.00

HOROWITZ, David. *First Frontier.* 1978. S&S. hc. dj. A19. $25.00

HORRISON, Samuel Elliot. *John Paul Jones: A Sailor's Biography.* 1959. Little Brn. 1st. 453p. F/dj. H1. $16.00

HORSCHI, Josef. *Steinzeug.* 1978. German text. photos. VG/VG. M17. $25.00

HORSLEY, Terrence. *Sporting Pageant: A Gun, a Rifle & an Aeroplane.* (1947). London. Witherby Ltd. 1st. photos. 205p. VG. H7. $15.00

HORT, Alfred. *Via Nicaragua: Sketch of Travel.* 1987. Conway, NH. facsimile. 267p. F3. $25.00

HORTENSE, Queen. *Memoirs...* 1927. 2 vol. stp Sample Copy. G+. M17. $30.00

HORTON, John J. *Jonathan Hale Farm, a Chronicle...* 1961. Cleveland. Western Reserve Hist Soc. 1st. photos/map. 160p. VG. B18. $12.50

HORTON, Richard. *Complete Measurer.* 1862. London. Weale. 319p. cloth. A10. $25.00

HORTON & JACKSON. *Ohio Valley Flood of March-April 1913.* 1913. WA. ils/fld map/charts/fld panorama. 96p. wrp. B18. $22.50

HOSILLOS, Lucilla. *Philippine-American Literary Relations, 1898-1941.* 1969. Quezon City. U Philippines. 4to. VG+. P1. $15.00

HOSMER, George L. *Practical Astronomy.* 1948 (1910). John Wiley. 4th. 355p. K5. $20.00

HOTMAN, Francois. *Franco-Gallia; or, Account of Ancient Free State of France.* 1711. London. Goodwin. 8vo. calf. R12. $475.00

HOUEL, J. *Elements de la Theorie des Quaternions.* 1874. Paris. Gauthier. half leather. xl. K3. $35.00

HOUGEN, John. *Story of the Famous 34th Infantry Division.* 1949. San Angelo. 1st. maps/photos. 981p. VG. S16. $125.00

HOUGH, Emerson. *Covered Wagon.* nd. Grosset Dunlap. 1st thus/photoplay. NF/dj. M2. $30.00

HOUGH, Emerson. *Maw's Vacation.* 1921. St Paul. 1st. ils. 62p. G+. B5. $35.00

HOUGH, Frank O. *If Not Victory.* 1939. NY. Carrick Evans. 1st. F/NF. B4. $85.00

HOUGH, Franklin. *Elements of Forestry.* 1882. Cincinnati. Clarke. 381p. cloth. VG. A10. $35.00

HOUGH, George A. *Disaster on Devil's Bridge.* 1963. Marine Hist Assn. 146p. VG/prt wrp. P4. $30.00

HOUGH, J.L. *Geology of the Great Lakes.* 1958. Urbana. 313p. cloth. VG. D8. $25.00

HOUGH, Richard. *Buller's Victory.* 1984. Morrow. 1st Am. F. T11. $25.00

HOUGH, Stella V. *Woman's Exchange Recipes.* 1946. Detroit. Arnold Powers. G. A16. $17.50

HOUGH, Walter. *Antiquities of the Upper Gila & Salt River Valleys in AZ...* 1907. GPO. 8vo. ils. 96p. VG. K7. $50.00

HOUGHTON, George. *Golf Addict Among the Scots.* 1967. Country Life. 1st. ils Houghton. F/VG+. P8. $35.00

HOUGHTON, Norris. *Moscow Rehearsals.* 1936. Harcourt Brace. 1st. sgn. 291p. G. H1. $25.00

HOUK, R. *Eastern Wildflowers.* 1989. SF. Chronicle. 108p. F/F. B1. $27.50

HOUNIHAN. *Hounihan's Baker's & Confectioner's Guide & Treasure...* ca 1877. Staunton, VA. self pub. ils. G+. E6. $100.00

HOURANI, Albert. *History of the Arab Peoples.* 1991. Cambridge. Belknap Pr of Harvard. 39 ils/12 maps. as new/dj. O7. $35.00

HOUSE, E.M. *Philip Dru: Administrator.* 1912. Huebsch. 1st. VG. M2. $100.00

HOUSE, Edward J. *Hunter's Camp-Fires.* 1909. Harper. 1st. 402p. F. H7. $250.00

HOUSEHOLD, Geoffrey. *Salvation of Pablo Gabar & Other Stories.* 1940. Little Brn. 1st Am. F/dj. B4. $175.00

HOUSEHOLD, Geoffrey. *Sending.* 1980. Little Brn. 1st. F/F. M21. $40.00

HOUSEHOLD, Geoffrey. *Third Hour.* 1938. Little Brn. 1st Am. F/VG. B4. $200.00

HOUSEMAN, A.E. *More Poems.* 1936. London. Cape. 1st. NF/NF. B2. $45.00

HOUSEMAN, John. *Final Dress.* 1982. S&S. 1st. sgn. F/NF. M25. $45.00

HOUSEMAN, Laurence. *Arabian Nights.* 1921. Phil. Penn. ils Sterrett/16 mc pl. 308p. bl cloth/pict label. D1. $385.00

HOUSEMAN, Laurence. *Echo de Paris, a Study From Life.* 1923. London. Cape. sm 8vo. 60p. VG. K7. $195.00

HOUSEMAN, Laurence. *Princess Badoura.* nd (1913). London. Hodder Stoughton. ils Dulac/10 tipped-in pl. 4to. whit pict cloth. VG. T10. $400.00

HOUSHOLDER, B. *Grand Slam of North American Wild Sheep.* 1974. Phoenix. N Am Sheep Hunt Assn. sgn pres. 220p. F. M12. $95.00

HOUSTON, Edwin J. *Elements of Physical Geography.* 1884 (1875). Phil. Eldredge. 4to. woodcuts/maps. 160p. quarter leather. G. K5. $30.00

HOUSTON, James. *Gig.* 1969. Dial. 1st. author's 2nd novel. F/NF. B4. $100.00

HOUSTON, James. *Men in My Life.* 1987. Creative Arts. F/dj. M2. $15.00

HOUSTON, James. *Songs of the Dream People.* 1972. Atheneum. 1st. 83p. F/F. D4. $35.00

HOUSTON, S.D. *Maya Glyps.* 1990. Berkeley. 2nd. 4to. wrp. F3. $15.00

HOVELL, Mark. *Rats & How To Destroy Them.* 1924. London. John Bale. 466p. VG. H7. $35.00

HOW, R.W. *Adventures at Friendly Farm.* 1952. Coward McCann. VG/G. O3. $18.00

HOWARD, Albert. *Farming & Gardening for Health & Disease.* 1945. London. Faber. 2nd. 282p. VG. A10. $25.00

HOWARD, Cecil. *Pizarro & the Conquest of Peru.* 1968. Am Heritage. 2nd. 153p. F3. $15.00

HOWARD, Clark. *Arm.* 1967. LA. Sherbourne. 1st. F/F. H11. $40.00

HOWARD, Elizabeth. *North Winds Blow Free.* 1949. Morrow. 1st. 8vo. 192p. G+. T5. $20.00

HOWARD, George E. *On Development of King's Peace & English Local Peace...* early 1890s. 65p. prt/sewn wrp. M11. $65.00

HOWARD, Hamilton G. *Civil War Echoes.* 1907. 1st. 298p. O8. $35.00

HOWARD, J.H. *Childhood Delight.* ca 1880s. McLoughlin. 4to. sc. VG. M5. $150.00

HOWARD, Joseph Kinsey. *Strange Empire.* 1952. Morrow. 1st. 601p. cloth. VG/dj. M20. $40.00

HOWARD, Maureen. *Not a Word About Nightingales.* 1962. Atheneum. 1st Am. author's 1st book. F/NF. L3. $65.00

HOWARD, O.O. *My Life & Experiences Among Our Hostile Indian.* 1907. AD Worthington. sgn. ils. 570p. VG. J2. $575.00

HOWARD, Robert E. *Red Nails.* 1979. Berkley Putnam. 1st. NF/dj. M2. $20.00

HOWARD, Robert West. *Waggonmen.* 1964. Putnam. 1st. VG/G. O3. $48.00

HOWARTH, David. *D-Day: The Sixth of June, 1944.* 1959. McGraw Hill. 1st. 251p. VG/dj. M20. $15.00

HOWE, Henry. *Historical Collections of Ohio...* 1848 (1847). Cincinnati. 599p+ads. w/fld map. VG. M20. $150.00

HOWE, Henry. *History of Wayne County, Ohio.* 1977. Knightstown, IN. The Bookmark. A19. $15.00

HOWE, Irving. *UAW & Walter Reuther.* 1949. Random. 1st. F/F. V4. $35.00

HOWE, Mark DeWolfe. *Holmes-Pollock Letters, Correspondence of Mr Justice Holmes.* 1941. Cambridge. 1st. 2 vol. crimson cloth. box. M11. $100.00

HOWE, Walter. *Mining Guild of New Spain & Its Tribunal General.* 1968 (1949). Greenwood. rpt. 534p. F3. $30.00

HOWE & MARKHAM. *Paul Outerbridge Jr: Photographs.* 1980. NY. Rizzoli. ils. 160p. cloth. dj. D11. $175.00

HOWELL, A.B. *Aquatic Mammals: Their Adaptations to Life in the Water.* 1930. Springfield. Thomas. ils/figures. 338p. gilt pict cloth. F/VG. M12. $60.00

HOWELL, Arthur H. *Birds of Arkansas.* 1911. WA. USDA. 4 pl. 100p. VG. S15. $15.00

HOWELL, John Thomas. *Marin Flora: Manual of Flowering Plants & Ferns...* 1949. Berkeley, CA. 1st. inscr. VG/G+. O4. $20.00

HOWELL, William. *William E Howell's Real Estate Tract Directory...* 1888. LA. Times-Mirror Prt House. 279p. orange brd. D11. $1,000.00

HOWELLS, John Mead. *Architectural Heritage of the Piscataqua.* 1937. NY. 240p. bl cloth. VG. B14. $125.00

HOWELLS, John Mead. *Architectural Heritage of the Piscataqua.* 1965. Architectural Pub. VG/VG. B5. $37.50

HOWELLS, Victor. *Naturalist in Palestine.* 1956. London. 180p. VG/dj. S15. $18.50

HOWELLS, W.D. *Certain Delightful English Towns...* 1906. NY. 1st trade. ils. 290p. teg. VG. B18. $35.00

HOWELLS, W.D. *Italian Journeys.* 1867. NY. Hurd Houghton. 1st. gilt maroon cloth. VG. M24. $75.00

HOWELLS, W.D. *Literary Friends & Acquaintances.* 1900. NY. Harper. 1st. teg. gilt sage gr cloth. M24. $65.00

HOWELLS, W.D. *Questionable Shapes.* 1903. Harper. 1st. VG. M2. $30.00

HOWES, Edith. *Cradle Ship.* 1916. London. Cassell. 1st. ils FM Anderson. 8vo. bl cloth. dj. R5. $175.00

HOWES, Paul Griswold. *Giant Cactus Forest & Its World.* 1954. NY. DSP. ils/drawings. VG/dj. from $25 to $30.00

HOWITT, S. *Orme's Collection of British Field Sports...* 1955. Guildford. Chas Traylen. facsimile 1807 London. obl folio. half leather. B24. $850.00

HOWLAND, Mrs. E. *American Economical Housekeeper & Family Receipt Book.* 1850 (1845). self pub. rebacked. E6. $150.00

HOWSE, Derek. *Francis Place & the Early History of Greenwich Observatory.* 1975. NY. Science Hist Pub. 1st. pl. VG/dj. K3. $30.00

HOWSE & THROWER. *Buccaneer's Atlas: Basil Ringrose's South Sea Waggoner.* 1992. Berkeley. 1st. 107 charts. 314p. as new/dj. P4. $95.00

HOYLE, Trevor. *Last Gasp.* 1983. Crown. 1st. F/dj. M2. $15.00

HOYNE, Thomas Temple. *Intrigue on the Upper Level.* 1934. Reilly Lee. 1st. VG/mc Canon dj. M2. $50.00

HOYT, A.M. *Toto & I: Gorilla in the Family.* 1941. Lippincott. ils/photos. 238p. cloth. F/NF. M12. $27.50

HOYT, E.P. *Battle of Leyte Gulf: Death Knell of Japanese Fleet.* 1972. NY. ils. 314p. VG. S16. $25.00

HOYT, E.P. *Japan's War: Great Pacific Conflict.* 1986. NY. 514p. VG/VG. S16. $25.00

HOYT, E.P. *Peabody Influence: How a Great Family Helped To Build Am.* 1968. photos. VG/VG. M17. $25.00

HOYT, Edwin J. *Buckskin Joe.* 1966. NE U. 1st. edit Glenn Shirley. cloth. VG+/dj. M20. $45.00

HOYT, Edwin. *Guadalcanal.* 1982. NY. maps/photos/index. VG/VG. S16. $25.00

HOYT, Henry. *Frontier Doctor.* 1929. Houghton Mifflin. 1st. 260p. VG. J2. $185.00

HOYT, Richard. *Manna Enzyme.* 1982. Morrow. 1st. NF/VG+. N4. $20.00

HOYT, Richard. *Marimba.* 1992. Tor. 1st. NF/NF. N4. $15.00

HUANG, Dorothy. *Dorothy Huang's Chinese Cooking.* 1980. Houston. Pinewood. 1st. sgn. VG/VG. A23. $30.00

HUARD, Frances Wilson. *My Home in the Field of Mercy.* 1917. NY. Doran. 1st. ils Chas Huard. 269p. VG+. A25. $20.00

HUBBARD, B. *Mush You Malemutes.* 1938 (1932). lg 8vo. photos. VG. E6. $20.00

HUBBARD, Elbert. *Ali Baba.* 1926 (1913). East Aurora, NY. ltd. ils/pl. 114p. teg. 3-quarter leather. F/fair. H3. $125.00

HUBBARD, Elbert. *Little Journeys to the Homes of Eminent Painters.* 1902 (1899). Putnam. 16mo. 497p. gilt full suede. VG. H1. $35.00

HUBBARD, Elbert. *Little Journeys to the Homes of Famous Women.* 1928. Roycrofters. A19. $20.00

HUBBARD, Elbert. *Little Journeys to the Homes of the Great.* 1928. Roycrofters. A19. $20.00

HUBBARD, Elbert. *Selected Writings of...* 1928. NY. Wm H Wish Co. Memorial ed. VG/dj. A19. $350.00

HUBBARD, Eleanore Mineah. *Peter Piper's Playmates.* 1930. Chicago. Whitman. 8vo. 62p. F. B24. $150.00

HUBBARD, Harlan. *Shantyboat.* 1954. NY. VG/VG. B5. $37.50

HUBBARD, Jim. *American Refuges.* 1991. MN U. 1st. as new/dj. V4. $25.00

HUBBARD, L. Ron. *Dianetics.* 1950. NY. 1st. VG. B5. $60.00

HUBBARD, L. Ron. *Mission Earth Vol 1, Invaders Plan.* 1985. Bridge. 1st. F/NF. W2. $30.00

HUBBARD, L. Ron. *Mission Earth Vol 6, Death Quest.* 1986. Bridge. 1st. F/F. W2. $30.00

HUBBARD, L. Ron. *Science of Survival: Simplified, Faster Dianetic Techniques.* 1951. Wichita, KS. Hubbard Dianetic Found. 4th. inscr. VG/shabby. B4. $2,500.00

HUBBARD, L. Ron. *Scientology Handbook Based on Works of...* 1994. Bridge. 871p. as new. B29. $35.00

HUBBARD, William. *Narrative of Indian Wars in New England.* 1801. Worcester. leather. A15. $40.00

HUBBARD & KIMBALL. *Introduction to Study of Landscape Design.* nd. np. ils HG Ripley. 36 pl. 406p. decor cloth. xl. G. B18. $37.50

HUCK. *Children's Literature in the Elementary School.* 1979. 3rd. 4to. 813p. VG. A4. $45.00

HUCKER, Charles. *China's Imperial Past.* 1975. Stanford. 1st. 474p. F/F. W3. $46.00

HUDSON, Christopher. *Playing in the Sand.* 1989. London. 1st. VG/VG. T9. $10.00

HUDSON, Derek. *Arthur Rackham: His Life & Work.* 1916. Scribner. 4to. 181p. F/dj. B24. $65.00

HUDSON, Derek. *Lewis Carroll.* 1977. Clarkson Potter. 1st. ils/photos. 271p. A4/D1. $65.00

HUDSON, Harry K. *Bibliography of Hard-Cover Boys' Books.* 1977. self pub. revised/enlarged. 280p. G+/wrp. H1. $85.00

HUDSON, Norman. *American Antiques.* 1972. 1st. ils. NF/VG. S13. $25.00

HUDSON, Travis. *Breath of the Sun.* 1980. Banning, CA. Malki Mus Pr. 1st. F/F. O4. $20.00

HUDSON, W.H. *Green Mansions.* 1976. Heritage. 1st. F/case. M2. $20.00

HUDSON, W.H. *Purple Land: Being Narrative...Richard Lamb's Adventures...* (1911). London. Duckworth. 8vo. 355p. decor cloth. NF. M12. $20.00

HUESTON, Ethel. *Coasting Down East.* 1924. Dodd Mead. 26 pl/text drawings. 304p. T7. $48.00

HUFFAKER, Clair. *Flaming Lance.* 1958. S&S. 1st. VG/clip. B4. $125.00

HUFFMAN, Eugene Henry. *Now I Am Civilized.* 1930. Los Angeles. Wetzel. 1st. sgn. ils Herbert Rasche. F/VG. B4. $850.00

HUGEL, Avon Chew. *Chew Bunch in Browns Park.* 1970. Scrimshaw. 1st. 1/1000. 103p. VG. J2. $185.00

HUGGINS, Nathan Irvin. *Harlem Renaissance.* 1971. Oxford. 1st. NF/dj. M25. $35.00

HUGGLER, Tom. *Grouse of North America.* 1990. Minocqua. 1/4000. sgn. M/dj. A17. $45.00

HUGHES, Colin; see Creasey, John.

HUGHES, Graham. *Modern Silver Throughout the World 1880-1967.* 1967. World. 480 ils. 256p. cloth. dj. D2. $115.00

HUGHES, J.P. *How You Got Your Name: Origin & Meaning of Surnames.* 1959. London. VG/VG. M17. $15.00

HUGHES, Langston. *Ask Your Mama: 12 Moods for Jazz.* 1961. Knopf. 1st. NF/dj. M8. $200.00

HUGHES, Langston. *Big Sea.* 1940. Knopf. 1st. gr brd. VG. M25. $50.00

HUGHES, Langston. *Black Misery.* 1969. Eriksson. 1st. NF/dj. M25. $75.00

HUGHES, Langston. *Black Misery.* 1969. Paul Eriksson. 1st. 57p. VG/dj. D4. $65.00

HUGHES, Langston. *Laughing To Keep From Crying.* 1952. Holt. later prt. NF/dj. M25. $60.00

HUGHES, Langston. *Montage of a Dream Deferred.* 1951. Holt. 1st. blk brd. G. M25. $45.00

HUGHES, Langston. *One Way Ticket.* 1949. NY. 1st. VG/VG. B5. $100.00

HUGHES, Langston. *Simple Speaks His Mind.* 1950. S&S. 1st. VG/VG. M19. $175.00

HUGHES, Langston. *Simple Takes a Wife.* 1953. S&S. 1st. decor brd. sans. A24/M25. $200.00

HUGHES, Langston. *Simple Takes a Wife.* 1954. London. Gollancz. 1st. NF/dj. Q1. $150.00

HUGHES, Langston. *Tambourines to Glory.* 1958. John Day. 1st. inscr/dtd 1963. F/NF. B4. $650.00

HUGHES, Langston. *Ways of White Folks.* 1934. Knopf. 1st. sgn/dtd 1934. orange/blk brd. VG. M25. $250.00

HUGHES, Monica. *Isis Pedlar.* 1983. Atheneum. 1st Am. F/dj. M2. $17.00

HUGHES, Robert R. *Introduction to Clinical Electro-Encephalography.* 1961. Bristol. John Wright. 4to. ils. 118p. panelled red cloth. VG. G1. $30.00

HUGHES, Suckey. *Washi: World of Japanese Paper.* 1978. Tokyo. 1st. 227 pl/maps/glossary. 360p. F/VG. W3. $185.00

HUGHES, Ted. *Cave Birds, an Alchemical Cave Drama.* 1978. Viking. 1st. 62p. coth. NF/NF. D4. $35.00

HUGHES, Ted. *Earth-Owl & Other Moon-People.* 1963. London. Faber. 1st. sgn. 46p. F/F. D4. $100.00

HUGHES, Ted. *Five Autumn Songs for Children's Voices.* 1968. Devonshire. Gilbertston. 1st. 1/150 (of 500 total). sgn. 10p. F/wrp. D4. $165.00

HUGHES, Ted. *Moon-Whales & Other Moon Poems.* 1976. Viking. 1st. 80p. NF/NF. D4. $40.00

HUGHES, Ted. *Rain-Charm for the Duchy.* 1992. London. Faber. 1st. FNF. A24. $25.00

HUGHES, Ted. *Season Songs.* 1975. Viking. 1st. ils Leonard Baskin. 77p. F/F. D4. $65.00

HUGHES, Ted. *Season Songs.* 1976. London. Faber. 1st. 75p. NF/dj. D4. $45.00

HUGHES, Ted. *Under the North Star.* 1981. Viking. 1st. ils Leonard Baskin. 47p. F/F. D4. $35.00

HUGHES, Thomas. *Scouring of the White Horse.* 1859. Cambridge. Macmillan. 8vo. ils Richard Doyle. aeg. gilt cloth. B24. $185.00

HUGHES & ROWE. *Colouring, Bronzing & Patination of Metal.* 1991. Watson Guptill. 372p. cloth. dj. D2. $75.00

HUGO, Victor. *Hunchback of Notre Dame.* nd. AL Burt. 416p. VG/tattered. M20. $40.00

HUGO, Victor. *Les Miserables.* nd. Donohue. ne. 1000p. VG. W2. $350.00

HUGO, Victor. *Notre-Dame de Paris.* 1955. LEC. 1st thus. 1/1500. ils/sgn Bernard Lamotte. F/glassine/case. Q1. $100.00

HUGO, Victor. *Toilers of the Sea.* 1960. LEC. 1st thus. 1/1500. ils/sgn Tranquillo Marangoni. F/dj/case. Q1. $125.00

HUIE, William Bradford. *He Slew the Dreamer.* 1970. Delacorte. 1st. sgn. F/F. B35. $45.00

HUIE, William Bradford. *Hiroshima Pilot.* 1964. xl. G/dj. K3. $10.00

HULBACH, Vladimir. *Sinbad the Sailor, Retold From the Classic...* 1975. London. Hamlyn. ils Vladimir Jachaj. 56p. cloth. VG. W1. $15.00

HULFISH, David S. *Cyclopedia of Motion Picture Work.* 1911. Chicago. 1st hc. 600+p. VG+. A11. $165.00

HULL, Burling. *Thirty-Three Rope Ties & Chain Releases.* ca 1930s. NY. Magno Novelty. 8vo. 46p. F/ils wrp. B24. $75.00

HULL, E. Mayne. *Planets for Sale.* 1954. Fell. 1st. VG/dj. M2. $25.00

HULL, F.M. *Bee Flies of the World.* 1973. Smithsonian. 687p. clip dj. B1. $50.00

HULL, Robert Charlton. *Search for Adele Parker.* 1974. Libra. 1st. 188p. VG/VG. J2. $95.00

HULTGREN, Arland J. *Christ & His Beliefs: Christology & Redemption in New Test.* 1987. Fortress. 285p. VG. B29. $12.00

HULTON & QUINN. *American Drawings of John White, 1577-1590.* 1964. Chapel Hill. NC U. 2 vol. 1st. 1/600. 160 pl. gilt red cloth. F/cloth case. C6. $850.00

HUME, H. Harold. *Camellias in America.* 1955. Harrisburg. McFarland. revised. 422p. A10. $75.00

HUME, H. Harold. *Camellias.* 1951. Macmillan. 1st. 8vo. ils/pl. 271p. VG/torn. A22. $20.00

HUME, H. Harold. *Gardening in the Lower South.* 1968. Macmillan. revised. 8vo. 377p. F/dj. A22. $25.00

HUME, Robert E. *World's Living Religions.* 1958. Scribner. 335p. as new. B29. $9.00

HUMMEL, Arthur. *Eminent Chinese of the Ch'ing Period 1644-1912.* 1970. Taipei. 1103p. F. W3. $68.00

HUMPHREY, George. *Human Foot & Human Hand.* 1861. London. 1st. 216p. A13. $250.00

HUMPHREY, Zephine. *'Allo Good-By.* 1940. Dutton. 1st. 284p. VG/dj. A25. $10.00

HUMPHREYS, A.A. *Virginia Campaign of 1864 & 1865.* 1883. 1st. 9 lg fld maps. 451p. O8. $21.50

HUMPHREYS, Henry Noel. *Origin & Progress of Art of Writing.* 1855. London. Day. 4to. 28 pl. mid-Victorian papier-mache bdg. R12. $475.00

HUMPHREYS, W.J. *Ways of the Weather.* 1942. Lancaster, PA. Cattell. 4to. 400p. G/dj. K5. $18.00

HUMPHRIES, Jefferson. *Conversations With Reynolds Price.* 1991. Jackson, MS. 1st. sgn Reynolds Price. F/F. R13. $35.00

HUMPHRIES, Sydney. *Oriental Carpets, Runners & Rugs & Some Jacquard Repros.* 1910. London. Adam/Chas Blk. 1st. thick 4to. 427p. polished wht linen. VG. T10. $200.00

HUNG, William. *Tu Fu: China's Greatest Poet.* 1952. Harvard. 1st. 300p. F/VG. W3. $65.00

HUNGERFORD, Edward. *Wells Fargo Advancing the American Frontier.* 1949. Random. 1st. 274p. pict cloth. VG. B14. $45.00

HUNGERFORD, Edwin. *Men of Eire: Story of Human Effort.* 1946. NY. 2nd. 346p. map ep. VG/dj. B18. $20.00

HUNGERFORD, James. *Falcon Rover.* 1866. NY. Beadle. Beadle Dime Novel #112. 8vo. orange wrp. R12. $60.00

HUNNICUTT, Ellen. *In the Music Library.* 1987. Pittsburgh. 1st. NF/NF. R13. $20.00

HUNNICUTT, R.P. *Firepower: History of the American Heavy Tank.* 1988. Novato. 224p. VG/VG. S16. $45.00

HUNNISETT & POST. *Medieval Coroner.* 1961. Cambridge. M11. $85.00

HUNNISETT & POST. *Medieval Legal Records, Edit in Memory of CAF Meekings.* 1978. London. Her Majesty's Stationary Office. M11. $75.00

HUNT, Barbara. *Little Night Music.* 1947. Rinehart. 1st. F/VG. B4. $75.00

HUNT, C.B. *Natural Regions of the United States & Canada.* 1974. SF. Freeman. 725p. pict brd. VG. D8. $20.00

HUNT, D.C. *Lithographs of Charles Banks Wilson.* 1989. OK U. 1st. 118 lithos. 270p. F/F. M4. $45.00

HUNT, Edward Eyre. *Greathouse.* 1937. Harcourt. 1st. NF/dj. M2. $20.00

HUNT, Frazier. *Untold Story of Douglas MacArthur.* 1954. Devin Adair. 1st. sgn. VG/G. A23. $40.00

HUNT, Irene. *Trail of Apple Blossoms.* 1968. Chicago. Follett. 1st. 8vo. 64p. VG/VG. T5. $24.00

HUNT, John M. *Creating an Australian Garden.* 1986. Kenhurst, NSW. ils/photos. 168p. F/dj. B26. $24.00

HUNT, John. *Ascent of Everest.* 1953. London. 1st. 300p. F/G. A17. $20.00

HUNT, Kyle; see Creasey, John.

HUNT, Mabel Leigh. *Benjie's Hat.* 1938. Stokes. 1st. ils Grace Paull. 119p. VG/dj. P2. $35.00

HUNT, Mabel Leigh. *Johnny-Up & Johnny-Down.* 1962. Lippincott. Weekly Reader BC. 1st. 94p. VG. V3. $8.50

HUNT, Mabel Leigh. *Michael's Island.* 1940. Stokes. 1st. ils Kate Seredy. 266p. VG/dj. P2. $50.00

HUNT, Mabel Leigh. *Young Man of the House.* 1944. Lippincott. 1st. 171p. VG/dj. V3. $22.00

HUNT, Rockwell D. *Fifteen Decisive Events of California History.* 1959. Los Angeles. 1st. F. O4. $25.00

HUNT, Thomas. *Ghost Trails of California.* 1974. Palo Alto, CA. 1st. Images of Am series. 4to. ils. F/VG. O4. $25.00

HUNT, W.R. *Alaska: A Bicentennial History.* 1976. NY. 1st. photos/maps. 200p. F/dj. M4. $20.00

HUNT, W.R. *Arctic Passage: Turbulent History of the Land & People...* (1975). NY. 1st. ils/map. gr cloth. VG/clip. H3. $40.00

HUNT & MOORE. *Atlas of Neptune.* 1994. Cambridge. F/F. K5. $20.00

HUNT & SANCHEZ. *Short History of California.* 1929. NY. Crowell. 8vo. 671p. gilt red cloth. xl. VG. K7. $50.00

HUNT & THOMPSON. *North to the Horizon: Arctic Doctor & Hunter 1913-1917.* 1980. Camden. 117p. F/dj. A17. $20.00

HUNTER, Ben. *Baja Feeling.* nd. Ontario, CA. Brasch. 1st. F/F. O4. $20.00

HUNTER, Cyrus Lee. *Sketches of Western NC, Historical & Biographical...* 1877. Raleigh News Steam Job. 1st. 357p. cloth. VG+. M8. $250.00

HUNTER, D'Allard; see Ballard, W.T.

HUNTER, Dard. *Papermaking by Hand in America.* 1950. Chillicothe. Mtn House. 1st. 1/210. folio. F/box/leather label. M1. $9,500.00

HUNTER, Evan. *Another Part of the City.* 1986. Mysterious. 1st. NF/NF. M22. $15.00

HUNTER, Evan. *Beauty & the Beast.* 1983. Holt. 1st. F/F. N4. $35.00

HUNTER, Evan. *Cinderella.* 1986. Holt. 1st. F/F. B4. $50.00

HUNTER, Evan. *Cut Me In.* 1954. Abelard Schuman. 1st. VG. M25. $25.00

HUNTER, Evan. *Downtown.* 1991. Morrow. 1st Am. F/F. N4. $25.00

HUNTER, Evan. *Easter Man.* 1972. Doubleday. 1st. VG/VG. M22. $15.00

HUNTER, Evan. *Every Little Crook & Nanny.* 1972. Doubleday. 1st. inscr. VG/VG. M22. $35.00

HUNTER, Evan. *Ice.* 1983. Arbor. 1st. sgn. F/NF. B3. $50.00

HUNTER, Evan. *Jigsaw.* 1970. Doubleday. 1st. VG/dj. M25. $25.00

HUNTER, Evan. *Let's Hear It for the Deaf Man.* 1973. Doubleday. 1st. F/F. M25. $17.50

HUNTER, Evan. *Mischief: A Novel of the 87th Precinct.* 1993. Morrow. 1st. sgn. VG/VG. A23. $40.00

HUNTER, Evan. *Pusher.* 1991. Armchair Detective. 1st in hc. as new/dj. N4. $30.00

HUNTER, Evan. *Puss in Boots.* 1987. Holt. 1st. F/dj. M15. $35.00

HUNTER, Evan. *Rumplestiltskin.* 1981. Viking. 1st. F/F. N4. $45.00

HUNTER, Evan. *Snow White & Rose Red.* 1985. HRW. 1st. F/dj. M15. $30.00

HUNTER, Evan. *Strangers When We Meet.* 1958. S&S. 1st. F/NF. B4. $100.00

HUNTER, Evan. *Streets of Gold.* 1974. Harper Row. 1st. VG+/F. A20. $30.00

HUNTER, Evan. *Tricks.* 1987. Arbor. 1st. F/F. A20. $25.00

HUNTER, J.A. *Hunter's Tracks.* 1947. Appleton Century Croft. 1st. 8vo. photos. 240p. F/VG. H1. $55.00

HUNTER, J.A. *Hunter.* 1952. Harper. A19. $25.00

HUNTER, J.M. *Trail Drivers of Texas.* 1925. 2nd/revised. 1044p. VG. A15. $175.00

HUNTER, Jim Catfish. *Catfish: My Life in Baseball.* 1988. McGraw Hill. 1st. F/F. T12. $70.00

HUNTER, John. *Treatise on Blood, Inflammation & Gun-Shot Wounds.* 1840. Phil. 611p. half leather. A13. $200.00

HUNTER, Kristin. *Landlord.* 1966. Scribner. 1st. NF/NF. M25. $60.00

HUNTER, Louis. *Steamboats on the Western Rivers.* 1949. Cambridge. ils/pl/tables. 684p. dj. T7. $85.00

HUNTER, Robert. *Violence & the Labor Movement.* 1914. Macmillan. 1st. F. V4. $25.00

HUNTER, Stephen. *Black Light.* 1996. Doubleday. 1st. sgn. F/F. A23. $40.00

HUNTER, Stephen. *Day Before Midnight.* 1989. Bantam. 1st. F/F. H11. $60.00

HUNTER, Stephen. *Spanish Gambit.* 1985. Crown. 1st. 389p. F/F. W2. $35.00

HUNTER, W.S. *Hunter's Eastern Townships Scenery, Canada East.* 1860. Montreal. John Lovell. 1st. lg 4to. cloth. VG. M1. $1,750.00

HUNTER & FERGUSON. *Ancient America & the Book of Mormon.* 1950. Oakland, CA. Kolob Book. 1st. 8vo. 448p. VG/dj. K7. $45.00

HUNTER & ROSE. *Album of Gun-Fighters.* 1951. Hunter Rose. 1st. 236p. ES. VG/dj. J2. $475.00

HUNTFORD, Roland. *Amundsen Photographs.* 1987. NY. 199p. F/dj. A17. $30.00

HUNTINGTON, Dwight W. *Our Wild Fowl & Waders.* (1910). NY. Amateur Sportsman. 1st. sgn pres. 207p. red cloth. VG. H7. $60.00

HUNTINGTON, James. *On the Edge of Nowhere: A Thrilling True Story...Alaska.* 1966. NY. Crown. 8vo. 183p. VG/worn. P4. $25.00

HUNTINGTON, Nathaniel G. *System of Modern Geography...* 1835. Hartford. 306p. prt brd/leather spine. G. B14. $55.00

HURD, Clement. *Race Between the Monkey & the Duck.* 1946 (1940). Wonder. lg 8vo. NF. C8. $35.00

HURD, Edith Thacher. *Dinosaur My Darling.* 1978. Harper Row. 1st. ils Don Freeman. 32p. NF/VG+. P2. $35.00

HURD, Edith Thacher. *Faraway Christmas.* 1958. lee Shepard. 1st. ils Clement Hurd. NF/VG. P2. $40.00

HURLBUT, C.S. *Dana's Manual of Mineralogy, 18th Edition.* 1971. John Wiley. 579p. VG. D8. $22.00

HURLEY, Frank. *Pearls & Savages: Adventures in the Air, on Land & Sea...* 1924. London. Putnam. Imperial 8vo. ils/map. gilt gr cloth. VG. P4. $250.00

HURLEY & LEGG. *Once More on My Adventure: Life of Frank Hurley.* 1966. Sydney/London. Ure Smith Pty Ltd. 8vo. 227p. VG/dj. P4. $85.00

HURLEY & PONTING. *Antarctic Photographs.* 1979. Macmillan. photos. 129p. dj. P4. $85.00

HURLIMANN, Bettina. *Picture-Book World.* 1968. London. Oxford. 1st Eng. 4to. red/wht pict brd. dj. R5. $100.00

HURLIMANN, Bettina. *Seven Houses: My Life With Books.* 1976. London. Bodley Head. photos. 216p. F/NF. A4. $65.00

HURLIMANN, Bettina. *Three Centuries of Children's Books in Europe.* 1967. London. Oxford. ils. 297p. F/F. A4. $60.00

HURLIMANN, Martin. *Frankreich Landschaft und Baukunst.* 1931. Berlin-Zurich. 1st. 304 full-p photos. lg 4to. A17. $35.00

HURNARD, Noami D. *King's Pardon for Homicide Before AD 1307.* 1969. Clarendon. VG/dj. M11. $65.00

HURRELL, George. *Portfolios of George Hurrell.* 1991. Graystone. photos. wht cloth. dj. O3. $85.00

HURST, Earl Oliver. *Big Book of Space.* 1959 (1953). Grosset Dunlap. 4to. 26p. VG. K5. $12.00

HURST, Fannie. *Every Soul Hath It's Song.* 1916. NY. Harper. 1st. F/F. B4. $400.00

HURST, Fannie. *Star-Dust: Story of an American Girl.* 1921. Harper. 1st. F/NF. B4. $400.00

HURST, S.B.H. *Commera Ali.* 1922. Harper. 1st. VG. M2. $25.00

HURSTON, Zora Neale. *Complete Stories.* 1995. Harper. 1st. F/F. R13. $25.00

HURSTON, Zora Neale. *Gilded Six-Bits.* 1986. Redpath. 1st thus. Perfect Present series. F/wrp/envelope. Q1. $40.00

HURSTON, Zora Neale. *Moses, Man of the Mountain.* 1939. Lippincott. 1st. NF/VG. B4. $750.00

HURSTON, Zora Neale. *Tell My Horse.* 1938. Phil. 2nd. VG/dj. B5. $165.00

HURT, Wesley. *El Abra Rockshelters, Savana de Bogota, Columbia, S Am.* 1976. Bloomington. Monograph No 2. 1st. 4to. 56p. wrp. F3. $10.00

HUSKISSON, William. *Substance of Two Speeches, Delivered in House of Commons...* 1825. London. Hatchard. 1st. inscr. 88p. stitched. R15. $350.00

HUSMANN, George. *American Grape Growing & Wine Making.* 1907. Orange Judd. 4th. 269p. A10. $55.00

HUSSEY, A. *Voyage of the Racoon: A Secret Journal of Visit to Oregon...* 1958. SF. BC of CA. 1/400. ils H Gusk. marbled brd/morocco spine. F. w/prospectus. R3. $135.00

HUSSEY, Christopher. *Eton College.* 1923. London. 2nd. lg 4to. ES. half leather. VG. T10. $100.00

HUSTE, Annemarie. *Annemarie's Cooking School Cookbook.* 1974. Houghton Mifflin. 1st. sgn. VG/dj. A16. $12.00

HUSTON, James. *Out of the Blue: US Army Airborne Operations in WWII.* 1982. TN. ils/maps. 327p. VG/VG. S16. $21.50

HUTCHENS, Alma R. *Indian Herbology of North America.* 1983 (1969). Windsor, Ontario. 9th. ils/glossary/index. 382p. B26. $47.50

HUTCHENSON, Horace G. *Life of Sir John Lubbock.* 1914. London. Lord Avebury. 2 vol. ils/2 pl/fld pedigree. bl cloth. VG. B26. $69.00

HUTCHEON, Wallace S. *Robert Fulton: Pioneer of Undersea Warfare.* 1981. Annapolis. Naval Inst. ils. 191p. dj. T7. $25.00

HUTCHINS, Pat. *Wind Blew.* 1974. Macmillan. 1st. 32p. NF/dj. D4. $40.00

HUTCHINSON, I.W. *Calling of Bride.* nd. Stirling. Eneas Mackay. inscr. 32p. VG. P4. $75.00

HUTCHINSON, Jonathan. *Extracts From the Letters of Jonathan Hutchinson...* 1844. London. Harvey Darton. 2nd. 376p. V3. $15.00

HUTCHINSON, Veronica S. *Chimney Corner Poems.* 1929. Minton Balch. 1st. ils Lois Lenski. 4to. G. P2. $30.00

HUTCHINSON, Veronica S. *Henny Penny.* 1976. Little Brn. 1st thus. ils Leonard B Lubin. unp. F/F. T5. $45.00

HUTCHINSON, W.H. *California: Two Centures of Man, Land & Growth Golden State.* 1969. Palo Alto. Am W Pub. ils/collated John Barr Tompkins. 352p. F/NF. K7. $25.00

HUTCHINSON, William T. *Cyrus Hall McCormick, Harvest, 1856-1884.* 1935. Appleton. 1st. photos/charts/maps. 793p. VG. K3. $20.00

HUTSON, Curtis. *Great Preaching on Thanksgiving.* 1992. Sword of the Lord. 247p. F/dj. B29. $7.00

HUTT & GIBBY. *Patterns of Abnormal Behavior.* 1957. Boston. Allyn Bacon. 1st. ils. 452p. VG+. A25. $20.00

HUTTON, Harold. *Vigilante Days.* 1978. Chicago. Swallow. dj. A19. $45.00

HUTTON, Laurence. *From the Books of Laurence Hutton.* 1892. NY. Harper. 1st. teg. dk gr cloth. M24. $35.00

HUXFORD & HUXFORD. *Collector's Encyclopedia of Brush-McCoy Pottery.* 1978. Collector Books. 1st. 4to. 87 mc pl+10p catalog rpts. 190p. G. H1. $30.00

HUXLEY, Aldous. *After Many a Summer Dies the Swan.* 1939. Chatto Windus. 1st. VG. M25. $45.00

HUXLEY, Aldous. *After Many a Summer Dies the Swan.* 1939. Harper. 1st Am. VG/G torn. M25. $60.00

HUXLEY, Aldous. *Ape & Essence.* 4948. Harper. 1st. F/NF. M25. $45.00

HUXLEY, Aldous. *Art of Seeing.* 1942. Harper. 1st. F/VG. M19. $35.00

HUXLEY, Aldous. *Brave New World.* 1932. Chatto Windus. 1st. gilt bl cloth. NF. M24. $165.00

HUXLEY, Aldous. *Brave New World.* 1932. Doubleday. 1st Am. VG/dj. B4. $350.00

HUXLEY, Aldous. *Devils of Loudon.* 1952. Harper. 1st. F/VG. T12. $75.00

HUXLEY, Aldous. *Devils of Loudon.* 1952. London. 1st. VG/VG. T9. $45.00

HUXLEY, Aldous. *Ends & Means.* 1937. NY. Harper. 1st Am. NF. B24. $50.00

HUXLEY, Aldous. *Gioconda Smile. A Play.* 1948. Chatto Windus. AP. gray-gr plain wrp. B24. $65.00

HUXLEY, Aldous. *Leda.* (1920). NY. Doran. 1st Am. 1/500. sgn. linen-backed lavender brd. M24. $225.00

HUXLEY, Aldous. *Leda.* 1920. Chatto Windus. 1st. 1/748 (Chatto title p). sgn/dtd 1921. NF. B24. $200.00

HUXLEY, Aldous. *Limbo.* 1920. Chatto Windus. 1st. G+. M25. $35.00

HUXLEY, Aldous. *Little Mexican & Other Stories.* 1924. Chatto Windus. 1st. inscr. F/NF. B24. $300.00

HUXLEY, Aldous. *Music at Night & Other Essays.* 1931. NY. Fountain. 1st. 1/842. sgn. quarter blk cloth/marbled brd. F. M24. $150.00

HUXLEY, Aldous. *On the Margin.* 1923. Chatto Windus. 1st. gray-gr cloth. F/NF. M24. $125.00

HUXLEY, Anthony. *Plant & Planet.* 1974. Readers Union. 428p. F/VG. S15. $10.00

HUXLEY, E. *Whipsnade: Captive Breeding for Survival.* 1981. London. Collins. ils/photos. 159p. F/F. M12. $17.50

HUXLEY, Elspeth. *Out in the Midday Sun: My Kenya.* 1987. Viking. 1st Am. 8vo. 262p. NF/dj. W1. $25.00

HUXLEY, Francis. *Raven & the Writing Desk.* 1976. ils. 191p. F/F. A4. $85.00

HUXLEY, Francis. *Way of the Sacred.* 1989. London. 1st. VG/VG. T9. $15.00

HUXLEY, Julian. *From an Antique Land. Ancient & Modern in the Middle East.* 1955. London. Parrish. 3rd. 8vo. 66 pl/maps. 310p. VG. W1. $14.00

HUXLEY, Thomas H. *American Address With a Lecture on Study of Biology.* 1877. Appleton. 1st. ils. 164p. G. K3. $35.00

HUXLEY & LEARY. *Visionary Experience & How To Change Behavior.* 1962. Copenhagen. Munksgaard. 2nd separate prt. 8vo. 39p. wht self-wrp. M1. $750.00

HUYGHE, Rene. *Watteau's Universe.* 1968. Paris/Woodbury. Screpel/Barron. ils. 118p. clear plastic dj. D2. $40.00

HYAMS, Edward. *Astrologer.* 1950. London. Lognman. 1st. F/VG+. B4. $100.00

HYAMS, Joe. *Flight of the Avenger.* 1993. Harcourt Brace. 1st. inscr George Bush. F/F. A23. $125.00

HYAMS, Paul R. *King, Lords & Peasants in Medieval England...* 1980. Clarendon. M11. $65.00

HYATT, T. Hart. *Hyatt's Hand-Book of Grape Culture...* 1867. SF. inscr. ils/diagrams. 279p+ads. cloth. B26. $115.00

HYDE, George. *Pawnee Indians.* 1951. Denver, CO. dj. A19. $45.00

HYDE, George. *Sioux Chronicle.* 1956. Norman, OK. 1st. 334p. VG/dj. J2. $80.00

HYDE, George. *Spotted Tail's Folk, a History of the Brule Sioux.* 1961. Norman, OK. 1st. 329p. VG/VG. J2. $95.00

HYDE, J.A. Lloyd. *Oriental Lowestoft, With Special Reference to Trade China...* 1936. Scribner. 1st. 4to. 30 collotype pl. teg. VG. T10. $200.00

HYDE, J.A. Lloyd. *Oriental Lowestoft Chinese Export Porcelains...* 1954. Newport, Eng. Ceramic Book Co. 2nd. 1/1500. ils. 166p. VG. W3. $150.00

HYDE, Joe. *Love, Time & Butter.* 1971. NY. Richard Baron. VG/dj. A16. $12.00

HYDE, Robert. *McTodd.* 1903. Macmillan. 1st. VG. M2. $22.00

HYDE, Robert. *Winds of Gobi.* 1930. Brewer Warren. 1st. VG. M2. $25.00

HYDE & JETT. *Navajo Wildlands.* 1969. Sierra Club. 8vo. 158p. VG. F7. $20.00

HYDEN, Dorothea Hoaglin. *These Pioneers.* 1938. Los Angeles. 1st. inscr. VG. O4. $20.00

HYGINUS, Gaius Julius. *Poeticon Astronomicon.* 1985. Greenbrae, CA. Allen. 1/140. trans Livingston/Smith. F/case. w/prospectus. B24. $350.00

HYLAND & LOCKWOOD. *Estates of Beverly Hills, Holmby Hills, Bel-Air...* 1984. Beverly Hills. Margrant Pub. 1st. ils. 161p. dj. D11. $125.00

HYLANDER, C.J. *Cruisers of the Air.* 1931. NY. 1st. photos/drawings. 308p. B18. $95.00

HYLL, Thomas. *First Garden Book.* 1946. Herrin, IL. 3rd. 98p. cloth. A10. $40.00

HYMAN, Marc. *No Time for Sergeants.* 1954. 1st. author's 1st book. NF/VG. S13. $50.00

HYMAN, Susan. *Edward Lear's Birds.* 1980. Secaucus, NY. Wellfleet. lg 4to. 96p. F/dj. T10. $145.00

IACOCCA & NOVAK. *Iacocca.* 1984. Bantam. 1st Canadian/14th prt. F/NF. T12. $15.00

IACOPI, Robert. *Earthquake Country.* 1973. Lane Books. A19. $20.00

IBANEZ, V. Blasco. *Sonnica.* 1918. Duffield. NF. M2. $10.00

IBERLIN, Dollie. *Basque Web.* 1982. Buffalo, WY. sgn. photos. A19. $35.00

IBSEN, Henrik. *Little Eyolf.* 1894. Chicago. Stone Kimball. 1st Am. 1/500. trans Wm Archer. teg. gr pict cloth. M24. $100.00

IBSEN, Henrik. *Peer Gynt.* 1955. Oslo. LEC. 1st thus. 1/1500. ils/sgn Per Krohg. F/glassine/dj. Q1. $75.00

IBUSE, Masuji. *Black Rain.* 1987. Tokyo. pb. 300p. K3. $20.00

IDE, Simeon. *Biographical Sketch of Life of Wm B Ide...* (1880). Claremont, NH. Prt for Subscribers. 1st. 12mo. 3-quarter gr morocco. R3. $1,750.00

IDONE, Christopher. *Glorious American Food.* 1985. NY. Random. 1st. VG/dj. A16. $37.50

IGNATOW, David. *Sunlight.* 1979. BOA Ed. 1/25. sgns. F. V1. $125.00

ILLER, Lawrence R. *Shots at Whitetails.* 1970. Knopf. dj. A19. $20.00

ILLMAN, Harry R. *Unholy Toledo.* 1985. Polemic. 361p. cloth. VG+/dj. M20. $45.00

ILOWITE, Sheldon. *Centerman From Quebec.* 1974. Hastings. 1st. ils. F/F. P8. $25.00

IMANISHI, S. *Chiao-Chu I-Yu-Lu.* 1965. tenri. Oyasato Research Inst. ils. 400p. F/VG. W3. $265.00

IMES, Birney. *Juke Joint.* 1990. Jackson, MS. 1st. 1/26 lettered. sgn Imes/Ford. sq folio. cloth/case. B4. $750.00

IMLACH & YOUNG. *Hockey Is a Battle.* 1969. Canada. Macmillan. 1st. VG/G. P8. $30.00

IMMROTH. *Texas in Children's Books, an Annotated Bibliography.* 1986. 207p. F. A4. $30.00

IMPEY, Oliver. *Chinoiserie: Impact of Oriental Styles on Western Art...* 1977. Scribner. ils. 208p. F. W3. $52.00

INALCIK, Halil. *Ottoman Empire: Classical Age 1300-1600.* 1973. ils. VG. M17. $20.00

INDICK, Ben P. *George Alec Effinger From Entrophy to Budayeen.* 1993. San Bernadino. Borgo. 1st. sgn. F/wrp. B11. $20.00

ING, Dean. *Ransom of Black Stealth One.* 1989. St Martin. 1st. F/dj. M2. $22.00

INGALLS, Eleazar Stillman. *Journal of a Trip To California by Overland Route...* 1979. Ye Galleon. 1st thus. F/sans. A18. $17.50

INGE, William. *Faith & Its Psychology.* 1910. Scribner. 248p. VG. B29. $6.50

INGE, William. *Four Plays.* 1958. Random. 1st. F/VG. M19. $35.00

INGE, William. *Good Luck, Miss Wyckoff.* 1970. Atlantic/Little Brn. 1st. F/NF. H11. $35.00

INGE, William. *Summer Brave: And Eleven Short Plays.* 1962. Random. 1st. F/dj. Q1. $60.00

INGENTHRON, E. *Indians of the Ozark Plateau.* 1970. Point Lookout. inscr. ils. 182p. F. M4. $15.00

INGERSOL, R. *Battle Is the Pay Off.* 1943. TN. 1st. 217p. VG/G. S16. $18.50

INGERSOLL, Chester. *Overland to California in 1847...* 1970. Ye Galleon. 1st. M/sans. A18. $17.50

INGERSOLL, Ernest. *Crest of the Continent.* 1885. Chicago. ils. 344p. O8. $18.50

INGHAM, Vicki. *Christmas With Southern Living.* 1991. Oxmoor. VG. A16. $15.00

INGLIS, William. *George F Johnson & His Industrial Democracy.* 1935. Huntington. 1st. 306p. gr cloth. F/dj. B22. $6.50

INGOLD, C.T. *Spore Discharge in Land Plants.* 1939. London. Oxford. 1st. 12mo. ils. NF. A22. $15.00

INGOLDSBY, Thomas. *Jackdaw of Rheims.* 1914. Phil. Winston. 1st Am. 12 pl/tissue guards. teg. F. B24. $250.00

INGRAM, Rex. *Mars in the House of Death.* 1939. Knopf. 1st. ils Carlos Ruano Llopis. VG. P8. $25.00

INGWERSEN, Will. *Classic Garden Plants.* 1975. London. Hamlyn. 192p. dj. A10. $35.00

INN & LEE. *Chinese Houses & Gardens.* 1950. Bonanza. revised. ils/photos. 140+p. F/dj. W3. $145.00

INN & LEE. *Chinese Houses & Gardens.* 1950. Bonanza. 2nd. 148p. F. B1. $115.00

INNES, Clive. *Cacti & Succulents.* 1990. NY. ils/28 photos. M. B26. $20.00

INNES, Hammond. *North Star.* 1974. London. Collins. 1st. VG/VG. P3. $22.00

INNES, Hammond. *Sea & Island.* 1967. Knopf. 1st. 288p. cloth. VG+/dj. M20. $15.00

INNES, Hammond. *Strange Land.* 1954. London. 1st. VG/dj. T9. $25.00

INNES, Michael. *Appleby Intervenes.* 1965. Dodd Mead. Omnibus ed. F/dj. M15. $35.00

INNES, Michael. *Long Farewell.* 1958. Dodd Mead. 1st. NF/NF. M22. $30.00

INNES, Michael. *Weight of the Evidence.* 1943. Dodd Mead. 1st (precedes Eng). F/NF. M15. $85.00

INOGUCHI & NAAJIMA. *Divine Wind: Japan's Kamikaza Force in WWII.* 1958. ils. VG/VG. M17. $30.00

IOLAS, Alexandre. *Victor Brauner: Peintures 1963-1964.* jan 1965. paris. photo. unp. stiff paper. D2. $35.00

IONESCO, Eugene. *Story Number 1.* 1968. Harlinquist. probable 1st. ils Delessert. VG/dj. P2. $45.00

IONIDES, C.J.P. *Mambas & Man Eaters.* 1965. NY. 1st. VG/dj. B5. $35.00

IPCAR, Dahlo. *Dark Horn Blowing.* 1978. Viking. 1st. F/dj. M2. $60.00

IRELAND, Orlin L. *Plants of the Three Sisters Region, Oregon Cascade Range.* 1968. Eugene. photos/drawings. 130p. sc. F. B26. $15.00

IRELAND, Tom. *Great Lakes-St Lawrence: Deep Waterway to the Sea.* 1934. Putnam. 1st. 223p. cloth. NF/dj. M20. $40.00

IRELAND, William. *Scribbleomania; or, Printer's Devil's Polychronicon...* 1815. London. Sherwood. 1st. tall 8vo. 320p. polished calf. H13. $295.00

IRONSIDE, R.L. *Adventure Called Skelly...1919-1969.* 1970. Appleton Century Crofts. 147p. cloth. G. D8. $25.00

IRVINE, Joan. *How To Make Pop-Ups.* 1987. 4to. ils. F/F. A4. $65.00

IRVINE, Van. *Anybody Can Be Slow.* 1989. NY. Irvine Pub. dj. A19. $35.00

IRVING, Alexander. *Bitter Ending.* 1946. Dodd Mead. 1st. 216p. cloth. VG/tape rpr dj. M20. $15.00

IRVING, David. *Trail of the Fox: Search for True Field Marshal Rommel.* 1977. NY. 1st. photos/biblio/index. 496p. xl. dj. S16. $20.00

IRVING, John. *Cider House Rules.* 1985. Franklin Lib. 1st/ltd. sgn. aeg. full leather. F. B3/Q1. $150.00

IRVING, John. *Cider House Rules.* 1985. Morrow. 1st trade. F/F. T11. $30.00

IRVING, John. *Crider House Rules.* 1985. Morrow. 1/750 (Not for Sale). sgn pres. F/glassine dj. M25. $60.00

IRVING, John. *Hotel New Hampshire.* 1981. Dutton. 1st. F/NF. N4. $40.00

IRVING, John. *Hotel New Hampshire.* 1981. NY. Dutton. 1st. sgn. F/F. T11. $65.00

IRVING, John. *Prayer for Owen Meany.* 1989. Morrow. 1st trade. NF/NF. A20/B3. $25.00

IRVING, John. *Prayer for Owen Meany.* 1989. Morrow. 1st. F/F. T11. $35.00

IRVING, John. *Prayer for Owen Meany.* 1989. Morrow. 1st. 1/250. sgn. F. Q1. $200.00

IRVING, John. *Setting Free the Bears.* 1968. NY. Random. 1st. inscr/dtd 1969. author's 1st book. NF/NF. L3. $1,250.00

IRVING, John. *Setting Free the Bears.* 1968. Random. 1st. author's 1st book. VG/VG. T11. $300.00

IRVING, John. *Trying To Save Piggy Sneed.* 1993. London. Bloomsbury. true 1st. F/F. D10. $165.00

IRVING, John. *Water-Method Man.* 1972. Random. 1st. NF/NF. B2/T11. $150.00

IRVING, John. *World According to Garp.* 1977. 1st. VG/VG. S13. $30.00

IRVING, John. *World According to Garp.* 1978. Dutton. 1st. F/dj. H11. $115.00

IRVING, John. *World According to Garp.* 1978. Dutton. 1st. NF/dj. from $75 to $100.00

IRVING, Laurence. *Birds of Anaktuvuk Pass, Kobuk & Old Crow.* 1960. Smithsonian. 409p. VG+. S15. $27.50

IRVING, Washington. *Crayon Miscellany.* 1895. Putnam. Holly Ed. 2 vol. ils. teg. maroon cloth. NF. T10. $45.00

IRVING, Washington. *History of New-York...By Diedrich Knickerbocker.* 1809. NY. Inskeep Bradford. 1st. 2 vol. fld map. full tree sheep/gilt bands. case. M24. $2,250.00

IRVING, Washington. *Legend of Sleepy Hollow.* 1906. Indianapolis. 1st. ils Arthur Keller. VG/dj/worn mc box. B5. $45.00

IRVING, Washington. *Legend of Sleepy Hollow.* 1928. London. 1/250. ils/sgn Rackham/8 tipped-in pl. teg. full vellum. case. T10. $2,000.00

IRVING, Washington. *Legend of Sleepy Hollow.* 1990. NY. Stewart Tabori Chang. 1st Kelley Ed. 4to. 63p. gilt gr cloth. M/dj. T10. $25.00

IRVING, Washington. *Oliver Goldsmith, a Biography.* 1872. Lippincott. 8vo. 427p. teg. maroon cloth/bevelled brd. H13. $175.00

IRVING, Washington. *Tales From Washington Irving's Traveller.* 1913. Lippincott. 1st. ils George Hood. 235p. G+. P2. $65.00

IRVING, Washington. *Tales of a Traveller.* 1824. London. Murray. 1st Eng/1st state. 2 vol. old brd. M24. $375.00

IRVING, Washington. *Washington Irving's Tales of the Supernatural.* 1982. Stemmer. 1st. F/dj. M2. $18.00

IRVINS, W.M. Jr. *Wood-Engravings of Rudolph Ruzicka.* 1917. Newark. Merrymount. 8vo. 9p. F/NF. B24. $85.00

IRVWIN, Wallace. *North Shore.* 1932. Houghton Mifflin. 1st. inscr. bl cloth. NF/VG. B4. $150.00

IRWIN, Constance. *Fair Gods & Stone Faces.* 1963. St Martin. 1st. 346p. dj. F3. $25.00

IRWIN, Frank. *Blocksberg Tryst.* 1963. Franklin, NH. Hillside. 1/310. 60x48mm. sgn author/pub. F. B24. $46.00

IRWIN, Frank. *Sound Track.* 1969. Franklin, NH. 1/350. 60x51mm. sgn. yel cloth. F. B24. $35.00

IRWIN, Hale. *Play Better Golf Than Hale Irwin.* 1980. London. Octopus. 1st. inscr. VG. A23. $45.00

IRWIN, Inez Haynes. *Maida's Little Camp.* (1940). Grosset Dunlap. pre-1943 prt. NF/VG. C8. $25.00

IRWIN, Inez Haynes. *Maida's Little House Boat.* 1947 (1943). Grosset Dunlap. 12mo. VG+/dj. C8. $35.00

IRWIN, Inez Haynes. *Maida's Little House.* (1921). Grosset Dunlap. 8vo. 264p. pict ep. G+. T5. $25.00

IRWIN, Inez Haynes. *Maida's Little Island.* (1939). Grosset Dunlap. 8vo. 251p. bl tweed. 251p. VG/dj. T5. $30.00

IRWIN, Inez Haynes. *Maida's Little School.* (1926). Grosset Dunlap. pre-1963 prt. 12mo. VG/rpr. C8. $22.50

IRWIN, J.R. *Guns & Gunmaking Tools of the Southern Appalachia.* 1983. Exton. photos. 118p. F. M4. $15.00

IRWIN, R. *British Bird Books: An Index to British Ornithology AD 1481.* 1951. London. Grafton. 8vo. 398p. cloth spine. VG+. M12. $60.00

IRWIN, Will. *House That Shadows Built.* 1928. Doubleday Doran. 15 photos. NF/dj. C9. $75.00

ISAACS, A.C. *Ascent of Mount Shasta: 1856.* 1952. LA. Glen DAwson. 1/250. decor brd/cloth spine. D11. $125.00

ISAACS, Edith J.R. *Negro in the American Theatre.* 1947. Theatre Arts. 1st. VG/dj. M25. $125.00

ISAACS, Susan. *Compromising Positions.* 1978. Times. 1st. author's 1st book. F/F. H11. $30.00

ISADORA, Rachel. *Lili on Stage.* 1995. NY. Putnam. 1st. sm 4to. F/F. C8. $25.00

ISH-KISHOR, Shulamith. *Boy of Old Prague.* 1963. Pantheon. 1st. 8vo. F/NF. C8. $75.00

ISHAM, Fredric A. *Social Buccaneer.* 1910. Grosset Dunlap. VG. M2. $12.00

ISHERWOOD, Christopher. *Condor & the Cows.* 1949. Random. 1st. xl. F/NF. B2. $35.00

ISHERWOOD, Christopher. *Lions & Shadows.* 1947. New Directions. 1st Am. NF/dj. M25. $60.00

ISHERWOOD, Christopher. *Lions & Shadows.* 1947. New Directions. 1st. F/NF. M19. $65.00

ISHERWOOD, Christopher. *Meeting by the River.* 1967. S&S. 1st. F/NF. M25. $40.00

ISHERWOOD, Christopher. *Memorial.* 1946. New Directions. 1st. F/VG. M19/T9. $65.00

ISHERWOOD, Christopher. *People One Ought To Know.* 1982. Doubleday. 1st. ils Sylvain Mangeot. F/dj. M25. $25.00

ISHERWOOD, Christopher. *People One Ought To Know.* 1982. London. 1st. VG/VG. T9. $20.00

ISHERWOOD, Christopher. *Prater Violet.* 1945. Random. 1st. F/NF. M25. $60.00

ISHERWOOD, Christopher. *Single Man.* 1964. S&S. 1st. NF/dj. M25. $45.00

ISHIGURO, Kazuo. *Artist of the Floating World.* 1986. London. Faber. true 1st. author's 2nd book. F/F. B3. $150.00

ISHIGURO, Kazuo. *Artist of the Floating World.* 1986. London. Faber. 1st. F/NF. Q1. $100.00

ISHIGURO, Kazuo. *Artist of the Floating World.* 1986. Putnam. 1st Am. author's 2nd book. F/F. D10. $90.00

ISHIGURO, Kazuo. *Artist of the Floating World.* 1986. Putnam. 1st Am. author's 2nd book. NF/dj. M25. $75.00

ISHIGURO, Kazuo. *Pale View of the Hills.* 1982. Putnam. 1st Am. author's 1st book. F/F. B3. $225.00

ISHIGURO, Kazuo. *Remains of the Day.* 1989. Knopf. 1st Am. author's 3rd novel. F/clip. D10. $100.00

ISHIGURO, Kazuo. *Unconsoled.* 1995. Knopf. 1st. sgn. F/F. A23. $45.00

ISHIGURO, Kazuo. *Unconsoled.* 1995. London. Faber. 1st. F/dj. A24. $45.00

ISRAEL, Lee. *Estee Lauder Beyond the Magic.* 1985. Macmillan. 1st. NF/NF. W2. $30.00

ISSAWI, Charles. *Egypt: An Economic & Social Analysis.* 1947. London/NY/Toronto. Oxford. 1st. 219p. G. W1. $25.00

ISSERMAN, Maurice. *Which Side Were You On? American Communist Party...* 1982. Wesleyan U. 1st. F/F. V4. $27.50

ISSLER, Anne Roller. *Happier for His Presence.* 1949. Stanford. 1st. sgn. VG. O4. $25.00

ITTEN, Hans. *Alpine Garden of Schynige Platte.* 1955. Berne. photos. 48p. sc. dj. B26. $15.00

IVANOFF, Pierre. *Monuments of Civilization: Maya.* 1973. Grosset Dunlap. 2nd. 191p. dj. F3. $40.00

IVES, Halsey C. *Dream City, Portfolio of Photographic Views...* nd (1893). Thompson Pub. intro Prof HC Ives. 4to. unp. G+. H1. $50.00

IVES, Joseph Christmas. *Report Upon the Colorado River of the West...* 1861. GPO. 4to. 5 parts. 12 full-p engravings/7 Indian pl/maps. F7. $675.00

IVES, Morgan; see Bradley, Marion Zimmer.

IVES, Paul. *Domestic Geese & Ducks.* 1947. Orange Judd. 372p. cloth. VG. A10/M12. $25.00

IVES & MANCHESTER. *Law, Litigants & the Legal Profession...* 1983. London. Royal Historical Soc. M11. $65.00

IVINS, Molly. *Molly Ivins Can't Say That, Can She?* 1991. Random. 1st. inscr. F/VG. A23. $40.00

IZENBERG, Jerry. *Great Latin Sports Figures.* 1976. Doubleday. 1st. F/VG. P8. $20.00

IZZEDDIN, Nejla. *Arab World: Past, Present & Future.* 1953. Chicago. Regnery. 412p. VG/dj. W1. $22.00

IZZI, Eugene. *Bad Guys.* 1988. St Martin. 1st. sgn. author's 2nd novel. F/dj. A24. $85.00

IZZI, Eugene. *Invasions.* 1990. Bantam. 1st. sgn. F/F. A24. $65.00

IZZI, Eugene. *Take.* 1987. St Martin. 1st. NF/dj. M25. $45.00

IZZI, Eugene. *Take.* 1987. St Martin. 1st. sgn. author's 1st novel. NF/VG+. A24. $65.00

JABLONSKI, Stanley. *Illustrated Dictionary of Eponymic Syndromes & Diseases...* 1969. Phil. 1st. 335p. A13. $75.00

JABLOWSKI, David. *Behold the Mighty Dinosaur.* 1980. Elsevier Nelson. 1st. F/dj. M2. $25.00

JACK, Florence. *Cookery for Every Household.* ca 1925. ils. 711p. VG. E6. $25.00

JACK, Robert L. *History of the National Assn for Advancement Colored People.* 1943. Boston. Meador. 1st. 110p. dj. B18. $25.00

JACKMAN, E.R. *Oregon Desert.* 1967. Caldwell. Caxton. G. A19. $45.00

JACKS, L.P. *All Men Are Ghosts.* 1913. London. 1st. VG. M2. $50.00

JACKS, L.P. *Magic Formula.* 1927. Harper. 1st. VG. M2. $32.00

JACKS, L.P. *Sir Arthur Eddington, Man of Science & Mystic.* 1949. Cambridge. NF/wrp. K3. $25.00

JACKSON, Aurilda. *Untangled.* 1956. Vantage. 1st. F/VG. B4. $100.00

JACKSON, Charles. *Second-Hand Life.* 1967. Macmillan. 1st. F/NF. H11. $30.00

JACKSON, Clarence S. *Picture Maker of the Old West: William H Jackson.* 1947. Scribner. 1st. 4to. brn cloth. VG+. F7. $70.00

JACKSON, D. *Thomas Jefferson & the Story Mountains...* 1981. IL U. 15 maps. 339p. F/dj. M4. $20.00

JACKSON, Donald. *Custer's Gold.* 1966. Yale. 1st. 152p. VG/dj. M20. $30.00

JACKSON, G. Gibbard. *World's Aeroplanes & Airships.* nd (1929). Sampson Low. ils. 244p. VG-. B18. $65.00

JACKSON, Gabrielle E. *Peggy Stewart at School.* ca 1920. Chicago. Goldsmith. 1st thus. 285p. VG/dj. A25. $22.00

JACKSON, Helen Hunt. *Ramona.* 1959. LA. LEC. 1st thus. 1/1500. ils/sgn EG Jackson. F/glassine/case. Q1. $125.00

JACKSON, Herbert J. *European Hand Firearms of the 16th, 17th & 18th Centuries.* nd (1923). Bramhall. rpt. ils. VG/VG. M17. $35.00

JACKSON, J. Denis. *Black Commandos.* 1967. Atlanta. Cultural Inst. 1st. gilt blk cloth. F. B4. $250.00

JACKSON, James C. *Consumption: How To Prevent It & How To Cure It.* 1862. Boston. 400p. cloth. G. A17. $35.00

JACKSON, James C. *Sexual Organism & Its Healthful Management.* 1862. Boston. Emerson. 1st. 8vo. 279p. cloth. M1. $175.00

JACKSON, John G. *Introduction to African Civilizations.* 1970. NY. U Books. 384p. cloth. NF/dj. W1. $20.00

JACKSON, John. *Reflections on Peace & War.* 1846. Phil. Ellwood Chapman. 78p. V3. $20.00

JACKSON, Jon A. *Diehard.* 1977. Random. 1st. author's 1st book. NF/dj. L3. $200.00

JACKSON, Jon A. *Grootka.* 1990. Woodstock. Countryman. 1st. F/dj. M15. $75.00

JACKSON, Joseph. *Mexican Interlude.* 1937. Grosset Dunlap. 246p. F3. $15.00

JACKSON, K.C. *Textbook of Lithology.* 1970. McGraw Hill. 552p. cloth. G. D8. $20.00

JACKSON, O.B. *Southpaw in the Mighty Mite League.* 1965. McGraw Hill. 1st. 128p. VG/clip. M20. $15.00

JACKSON, Reggie. *Reggie.* 1984. Villard. 1st. F/F. B4. $35.00

JACKSON, S. *13th Annual Report on Introduction Domestic Reindeer...* 1904. WA. US Senate. 8vo. ils/fld map. 192p. VG. M12. $37.50

JACKSON, Shirley. *Lottery.* 1949. FSG. 1st. VG/G. M22. $95.00

JACKSON, Shirley. *Sundial.* 1958. FSC. 1st. author's 7th book. F/F. D10. $135.00

JACKSON, Stanley. *Sassoons: Fascinating Story of a Fabulous Family...* 1968. Dutton. 2nd. 8vo. 20 pl/genealogical tables. 304p. NF/dj. W1. $28.00

JACKSON, Turrentine. *Wells Fargo & Co in Idaho Territory.* 1984. Boise, ID. ID State Hist Soc. A19. $35.00

JACKSON, William Henry. *Time Exposure: Autobiography of William Henry Jackson.* 1940. NY. Putnam. ils. 341p. cloth. dj. D11. $175.00

JACKSON & JACKSON. *Jerry at School.* 1950. S&S. 1st/A ed. pict brd. VG. T5. $18.00

JACKSON & PAIGE. *Blitz.* 1987. Contemporary. 1st. fwd Dan Reeves. F/VG+. P8. $17.50

JACKSON. *Engines of Instruction: Mischief & Magic.* 1989. NE U. ils. 304p. F/NF. A4. $75.00

JACOB, Giles. *Common Law Common-Plac'd: Containing Substance & Effect...* 1733. London. Nutt/Gosling. contemporary calf. M11. $450.00

JACOB, Joseph. *More English Fairy Tales.* 1894. Putnam. 1st. ils JD Batten. VG. P2. $85.00

JACOBELLIS, William. *Sports Photo Album.* 1951. McKay. 1st. photos. VG/G. P8. $10.00

JACOBI, Carl. *Disclosures in Scarlet.* 1972. Arkham. 1st. F/NF. Q1. $50.00

JACOBI, Carl. *Portraits in Moonlight.* 1964. Arkham. 1st. F/NF. Q1. $75.00

JACOBS, Flora Gill. *Doll House Mystery.* 1958. Coward McCann. 1st. ils Chuck Gruen. VG/dj. M20. $15.00

JACOBS, Frances E. *Finger Plays & Action Rhymes.* 1941. Lee Shepard. photos Lura/Courtney Owen. VG+/dj. M5. $85.00

JACOBS, Joseph. *Indian Fairy Tales.* 1892. London. 1st. ils John Batten. M5. $125.00

JACOBS, Joseph. *Tom Tit Tot, an English Folk Tale.* 1966 (1965). Scribner. 2nd/B prt. 4to. beige cloth. VG/G+. T5. $40.00

JACOBS, Lynn. *Waste of the West: Public Lands Ranching.* 1991. private prt. 1st. ils/index. 602p. F/wrp. B19. $35.00

JACOBS, Michael William. *Notes on the Rebel Invasion of MD & PA...1863.* 1864. Lippincott. 1st. fld map. 47p. cloth. VG. M8. $85.00

JACOBS, W.R. *Francis Parkman, Historian As Hero: Formative Years.* 1991. TX U. 1st. ils. F/F. M4. $20.00

JACOBS, W.W. *Lady of the Barge.* 1906. London. VG. M2. $27.00

JACOBS & JEFFERS. *Buried Moon.* nd (1969). Englewood Cliffs. Bradbury. stated 1st. unp. NF. C14. $12.00

JACOBS-BOND, Carrie. *Tales of Little Dogs.* (1921). Volland. 29th. ils Katharine Dodge. 12mo. G. D1. $40.00

JACOBSEN, Hermann. *Handbook of Succulent Plants.* 1960. London. revised/enlarged. 3 maps. 1441p. B26. $155.00

JACOBSEN, Hermann. *Lexicon of Succulent Plants.* 1974. London. Blandford. 1st Eng. 200 pl. 664p. G+/worn. A22. $75.00

JACOBSEN, Hermann. *Succulent Plants.* 1946 (1935). Pasadena. 2nd. 293p. VG. B26. $44.00

JACOBSON, B.S. *Meditations of the Torah: Topical Discourses...* 1956. Tel-Aviv. Sinai Pub. 322p. VG. S3. $24.00

JACOBSON, W.H.A. *Operations of Surgery.* 1895. Phil. 1st Am. 199 woodcuts. 1006p. quarter leather. A13. $75.00

JACOBY, N.H. *Multinational Oil, a Study of Industrial Dynamics.* 1974. Macmillan. 323p. xl. VG. D8. $12.50

JACQUES, M. *Colette's Best Recipes, a Book of French Cookery.* 1923. 1st. VG/dj. E6. $25.00

JAEGER, Edmund C. *California Deserts: A Visitor's Handbook.* 1946. Stanford. 4th. VG/sans. O4. $15.00

JAKES, John. *California Gold.* 1989. Random. 1st. F/F. T12. $25.00

JAKES, John. *Secrets of Stardeep.* 1969. Westminster. 1st. F/dj. M2. $20.00

JAKOB, A. *Die Extrapyramidalen Erkrankungen mit Besonderer...* 1923. Berlin. Julius Springer. heavy 8vo. 419p. VG. G1. $100.00

JAKOBOVITS, Immanuel. *Jewish Medical Ethics: A Comparative & Historical Study...* 1962. Bloch. 2nd. 389p. VG/G. S3. $35.00

JAKUBOWSKI, Maxim. *Travelling Towards Epsilon.* 1976. NEL. 1st. F/dj. M2. $15.00

JAKUBOWSKI, Maxim. *100 Great Detectives.* 1991. Carroll Graf. 1st Am. F/clip. M22. $25.00

JALLINGS, John J. *Elevators.* 1919. Chicago. 5 vol. G. A17. $20.00

JAMES, C.L.R. *Mariners, Renegades & Castaways: Story of Herman Melville...* 1953. NY. self pub. 1st. sgn+sgn Alfred Kazin. G/wrp. B4. $750.00

JAMES, C.L.R. *World Revolution 1917-1936.* 1937. Secker Warburg. 1st. sgn. 429p. F/VG. B4. $1,500.00

JAMES, George Wharton. *Arizona the Wonderland.* 1918. Boston. Page. 2ns. teg. brn cloth. G+. F7. $65.00

JAMES, George Wharton. *California: Romantic & Beautiful.* 1921. Boston. Page. ils/72 photos/1 fld map. 433p. NF. K7. $95.00

JAMES, George Wharton. *Grand Canyon of Arizona: How To See It.* 1918. Boston. Little Brn. 12mo. 265p. teg. G+. F7. $42.50

JAMES, George Wharton. *In & Around the Grand Canyon.* 1907. Little Brn. 8vo. gr cloth. VG. F7. $70.00

JAMES, George Wharton. *Indian Basketry/How To Make Indian & Other Baskets.* 1972. Rio Grande Classic. rpt. 2 vol in 1. ils. F. M4. $35.00

JAMES, Harry. *Dahlias for Garden & Exhibition.* 1963. London. ils. VG/dj. B26. $14.00

JAMES, Henry. *Awkward Age.* 1899. NY. Harper. 1st Am/1st prt/1st bdg. 1/1000. gilt brn cloth. M24. $125.00

JAMES, Henry. *Finer Grain.* 1910. London. Methuen. 1st Eng. gilt rust brn cloth. F. M24. $850.00

JAMES, Henry. *Gabrielle de Bergerac.* 1918. Boni Liveright. 1st. 1/1300. VG/dj. M24. $300.00

JAMES, Henry. *Hawthorne.* 1879. London. Macmillan. 1st. wht cloth. F. M24. $450.00

JAMES, Henry. *Heiress: Washington Square.* 1949. NY. United Book Guild. 1st. F/F. B4. $175.00

JAMES, Henry. *Little Tour in France.* 1900. London. Heinemann. 1st Eng. 1/150 on Japan vellum. gilt full vellum. M24. $450.00

JAMES, Henry. *Outcry.* 1911. NY. 1st. 261p. G. B18. $35.00

JAMES, Henry. *Question of Our Speech, the Lesson of Balzac.* 1905. Houghton Mifflin. 1st/trade issue. teg. dk gray cloth. VG. M24. $85.00

JAMES, Henry. *Sense of the Past.* 1917. Scribner. 1st. 1/1500. plain top edge. gilt tan cloth. F/NF. M24. $600.00

JAMES, Henry. *Transatlantic Sketches.* 1875. Boston. Osgood. 1st/1st bdg. author's 2nd book. gilt gr cloth. F. M24. $600.00

JAMES, Henry. *Washington Square.* 1881. Harper. 1st. ils Geo DuMaurier. gilt olive cloth. VG. M24. $350.00

JAMES, Juliet. *Sculpture of the Exposition Palaces & Courts.* 1915. SF. HS Crocker Co. tan cloth. VG. O4. $30.00

JAMES, Lawrence. *War With Russia in Contemporary Photographs.* 1981. photos. VG/VG. M17. $25.00

JAMES, M. *Texaco: Story of the First 50 Years, 1902-1952.* 1953. 1st. 118p. cloth. dj. D8. $36.00

JAMES, M.R. *Warning to the Curious.* 1927. London. VG. M2. $25.00

JAMES, Margaret. *Black Glass.* 1981. Collector Books. 8vo. 80p. VG/glossy wrp. H1. $27.50

JAMES, Marquis. *Cherokee Strip.* 1945. Viking. 1st. 294p. VG/dj. M20. $20.00

JAMES, Marquis. *Life of Andrew Jackson.* 1938. Indianapolis. Bobbs Merrill. A19. $35.00

JAMES, Neill. *Petticoat Vagabond Among the Nomads.* 1939. Scribner. 1st. ils. 350p. VG. A25. $20.00

JAMES, P.D. *Black Tower.* 1975. London. Faber. true 1st. F/F. D10. $195.00

JAMES, P.D. *Children of Men.* 1993. Knopf. 1st. sgn. VG/VG. A23/O4. $40.00

JAMES, P.D. *Cover Her Face.* 1962. Scribner. 1st Am. author's 1st book. NF/dj. Q1. $375.00

JAMES, P.D. *Death of an Expert Witness.* 1977. London. Faber. 1st. sgn. F/F. M15. $145.00

JAMES, P.D. *Devices & Desires.* 1989. London. Faber. 1st. sgn. F/dj. M15. $100.00

JAMES, P.D. *Devices & Desires.* 1990. Franklin Lib. 1st. sgn. full leather. F. Q1. $75.00

JAMES, P.D. *Devices & Desires.* 1990. Knopf. 1st Am trade. VG/VG. M22. $10.00

JAMES, P.D. *Devices & Desires.* 1990. Knopf. 1st Am. sgn. F/dj. M25. $35.00

JAMES, P.D. *Innocent Blood.* 1980. Scribner. 1st. VG/VG. A20. $20.00

JAMES, P.D. *Original Sin.* 1995. Knopf. 1st. sgn. VG/VG. A23. $40.00

JAMES, P.D. *Skull Beneath the Skin.* 1982. Scribner. 1st Am. F/F. D10. $35.00

JAMES, P.D. *Taste for Death.* 1986. Knopf. 1st Am. F/F. P3/T12. $20.00

JAMES, P.D. *Taste for Death.* 1986. London. 1st. sgn. VG. T9. $60.00

JAMES, Peter. *Possession.* 1988. Doubleday. 1st Am. NF/NF. N4. $25.00

JAMES, Philip. *Children's Books of Yesterday.* 1933. London. The Studio. edit CG Holme. ils. 4to. 128p. gr cloth. VG/dj. R5. $150.00

JAMES, Philip. *Children's Books of Yesterday.* 1933. London. The Studio. 4to ils. 132p. VG. A4. $90.00

JAMES, Robert. *Board Stiff.* 1951. Doubleday Crime Club. 1st. 185p. cloth. VG/dj. M20. $15.00

JAMES, T. *Three Years Among the Indians & Mexicans.* 1953. Lakeside Classic. ils. 294p. F. M4. $30.00

JAMES, Will. *Flint Spears: Cowboy Rodeo Contestant.* 1951 (1938). World. 2nd. 269p. VG/dj. M20. $30.00

JAMES, Will. *Lone Cowboy.* 1930. NY. Scribner. 1st. sgn. G. B5. $50.00

JAMES, Will. *Scorpion, a Good Bad Horse.* ca 1948. Grosset Dunlap. lg 12mo. NF/VG+. C8. $22.50

JAMES, Will. *Smoky.* 1926. AL Burt. photoplay ed. 308p. VG/dj. M20. $75.00

JAMES, Will. *Sun Up.* 1931. ils James. VG+. S13. $35.00

JAMES, Will. *Uncle Bill.* 1932. NY. 1st. VG. B5. $50.00

JAMES, William. *Psychology.* 1892. Holt. 1st abridged. 12mo. 478p. cloth. M1. $150.00

JAMES & STEPHENS. *In Praise of Hunting.* 1960. London. Hollis Carter. 1st. VG/G. O3. $40.00

JAMES I, KING OF SCOTLAND. *Poetical Remains.* 1783. Edinburgh. Balfour. 1st collected. edit Wm Tytler. 246p. teg. VG. H13. $195.00

JAMESON, Horatio. *Case of Tumour of the Superior Jaw.* 1821. Phil. 1st. 790p. full leather. A13. $200.00

JAMESON, William. *Wandering Albatross.* 1959. NY. ils/photos/maps. VG/dj. S15. $13.00

JAMIESON, Paul F. *Adirondack Canoe Waters, North Flow.* 1977. Glen Falls. Adirondack Mtn Club. 300p. sbdg. VG. H7. $12.50

JANCE, J.A. *Hour of the Hunter.* 1991. Morrow. 1st. sgn. F/NF. A23. $40.00

JANE, Cecil. *Spanish Voyage to Vancouver & North-West Made in Year 1792.* 1971. Amsterdam. N Israel. rpt. ils/fld maps. 156p. as new. P4. $50.00

JANICK, J. *Horticultural Science.* 1963. SF. Freeman. 472p. dj. B1. $35.00

JANIK, Carolyn. *Barn Book.* 1990. NY. Gallery Books. 1st. folio. ils. VG/G. O3. $35.00

JANIK & REINIS. *All America's Real Estate Book.* 1986. Viking. 2nd. 851p. NF/NF. W2. $40.00

JANNEY, Samuel M. *Summary of Christian Doctrines As Held by...Friends.* 1871. Phil. Friends Book Assn. 2nd. 64p. V3. $10.00

JANOWITZ, Tama. *Cannibal in Manhattan.* 1987. Crown. 1st. F/F. B35. $20.00

JANOWITZ, Tama. *Slaves of New York.* 1986. Crown. 1st. F/NF. B35. $22.00

JANSSON, Tove. *Book About Moomin Mymble & Little My.* 1953. London. Benn. 1st. ils. 4to. VG-. P2. $225.00

JANVIER, Thomas. *Aztec Treasure House.* 1890. Harper. 1st. VG. M2. $100.00

JAQUES, F.P. *Francis Lee Jaques: Artist of the Wilderness World.* 1973. Garden City. 1st. ils. 370p. F/NF case. M4. $250.00

JAQUES, H.E. *How To Know the Beetles: Picture Keys for Identifying...* 1951. Dubuque. Brn. ils/figures. 372p. gilt pict cloth. VG. M12. $45.00

JAQUISH, O.W. *Short Talk on Covers.* ca 1917. np. sgn. VG. B11. $85.00

JARES, Joe. *Basketball: American Game.* 1971. Rutledge. 1st. photos. VG/dj. P8. $20.00

JARMAN, Derek. *Derek Jarman's Caravaggio: Complete Film Strip...* 1986. Thames Hudson. ils. VG+. C9. $50.00

JARMAN, Derek. *Modern Nature.* 1994. Woodstock. 1st. VG/dj. T9. $15.00

JARRELL, Randall. *Fly By Night.* 1976. FSG. 1st. ils/sgn/dtd Maurice Sendak. 12mo. blk cloth. dj. R5. $150.00

JARRELL, Randall. *Jerome: A Biography of a Poem.* 1971. Grossman. 1st. sgn. NF/dj. R13. $50.00

JASPER, Herbert Henry. *Reticular Formation of the Brain.* 1958. Little Brn. heavy 8vo. 766p. bl cloth. G. G1. $50.00

JASTROW, Robert. *Journey to the Stars.* 1989. Bantam. 1st. F/F. W2. $30.00

JASZI, Jean. *Everybody Has Two Eyes.* 1956. NY. Lee Shepard. 1st. sgn. ils Mariana. 36p. F/worn. D4. $35.00

JAUFFRET, Louis Francois. *Historie Impartiale du Proces de Louis XVI...* 1793. Paris/Lausanne. Perlet/Mourer. 8 vol. 8vo. fld chart. quarter calf. R12. $975.00

JAY, K.E.B. *Atomic Energy at Harwell.* 1955. Philosophical Lib. 1st. xl. VG. K3. $15.00

JAY, Mae Foster. *Rag-House Tales.* 1927. Wilde. 8vo. cloth. VG. M5. $22.00

JAY, Ricky. *Learned Pigs & Fireproof Women.* 1986. 343p. dj. O8. $14.50

JAYNES, Julian. *Origin of Consciousness in Breakdown of Bicameral Mind.* 1976. Houghton Mifflin. later prt. 467p. VG/dj. G1. $30.00

JEAN, Marcel. *History of Surrealist Painting.* 1960. Grove. 1st. F/die-cut dj. B2. $250.00

JEAN-AUBREY, G. *Joseph Conrad in the Congo.* 1926. Little Brn. 1st/Am issue. 1/225 (of 470). teg. gilt gr cloth. F. M24. $125.00

JEANS, J.H. *Dynamical Theory of Gases.* 1921. CAmbridge. 3rd. 4to. 442p. VG. K3. $30.00

JEANS, J.H. *Problems of Cosmogony & Stellar Dynamics.* 1919. Cambridge. 1st. 293p. G. K5. $110.00

JEBB, Samuel. *Life of Robert Earl of Leicester, Favourite of Queen...* 1727. London. Woodman Lyon. 8vo. full calf. R12. $225.00

JEFFERIS, Edith. *Memoir of...* 1849. Phil. Kite Walton. 76p. V3. $15.00

JEFFERS, Robinson. *Be Angry at the Sun.* 1941. NY. Random. 1st. inscr. gilt blk cloth. F. M24. $250.00

JEFFERS, Robinson. *Double Axe & Other Poems.* 1948. Random. 1st/2nd prt. inscr. gilt bl cloth. F/dj. M24. $150.00

JEFFERS, Robinson. *Double Axe & Other Poems.* 1977. NY. Liveright. 197p. brd/cloth spine. dj. D11. $40.00

JEFFERS, Robinson. *Hungerfield & Other Poems.* 1954. Random. 1st. inscr/dtd 1955. F/F. w/sgn postcard. M24. $250.00

JEFFERS, Robinson. *Medea.* 1946. Random. 1st. F/F. B35. $60.00

JEFFERS, Robinson. *Such Counsels You Gave to Me.* 1937. Random. 1st trade. inscr. gilt maroon cloth. F/NF. M24. $250.00

JEFFERS, Susan. *If Wishes Were Horses.* 1979. Dutton. 1st. 32p. VG+/dj. D4. $45.00

JEFFERSON, Floyd W. *Iamic & Dactylic.* 1954. NY. private prt. inscr. VG. B11. $55.00

JEFFERSON, Robert B. *Crimson Joy.* 1988. Delacorte. 1st. F/F. M22. $20.00

JEFFRESS, Lloyd A. *Cerebral Mechanisms of Behavior: Hixon Symposium.* 1951. NY. John Wiley. 311p. VG/dj. G1. $75.00

JEFFREY, Arthur. *Koran: Selected Suras.* 1958. NY. LEC. 1st thus. 1/1500. ils/sgn Valenti Angelo. F/glassine/case. Q1. $300.00

JEFFREY, Grant R. *Messiah: War in the Middle East & Road to Armageddon.* 1991. Frontier. 332p. as new. B29. $7.50

JEKYLL, Francis. *Gertrude Jekyll: A Memoir.* 1935. Northampton, MA. Bookshop Roundtable. 248p. A10. $40.00

JEKYLL, Gertrude. *Some English Gardens.* 1905. London. 3rd. ils after GS Elgood. gilt stp cloth. B26. $200.00

JELLEY, S.M. *Voice of Labor.* 1888. Phil. HJ Smith. revised/enlarged. 402p. gilt leather. VG+. B2. $100.00

JELLICOE & JELLICOE. *Modern Private Gardens.* 1968. ils. VG/VG. M17. $25.00

JEN, Gish. *Typical American.* 1991. Houghton Mifflin. 1st. F/F. R14. $35.00

JEN, Gish. *Typical American.* 1991. Houghton Mifflin. 1st. sgn. author's 1st book. G/VG. L1. $30.00

JENKINS, A.O. *Olive's Last Roundup.* nd. Sherman County Times. 1st. 98p. VG/wrp. J2. $395.00

JENKINS, Dafydd. *Law of Hywel Dda, Law Texts From Medieval Wales.* 1986. Llandysul. Gomer. M11. $75.00

JENKINS, Dan. *Dead Solid Perfect.* 1974. NY. 1st. sgn pres. VG/VG. B5. $40.00

JENKINS, Dan. *Sports Illustrated's Best 18 Golf Holes in America.* 1966. Delacorte. 1st. photos. VG. P8. $40.00

JENKINS, Dan. *You Call It Sports, But I Say It's a Jungle Out There.* 1989. S&S. 1st. as new/dj. P8. $15.00

JENKINS, Frank S. *I Didn't Start Out To Be a Poet.* 1977. LA. Shockley. ne. inscr. NF/wrp. M25. $25.00

JENKINS, John. *Cracker Barrel Chronicles.* 1965. 539p. F/VG. A4. $375.00

JENKINS, Will F. *Great Stories of Science Fiction.* 1951. Random. 1st. F/dj. M2. $30.00

JENKINS, Will F. *Last Starship.* 1949. Fell. 1st. F/dj. M2. $50.00

JENKS, Almet. *Huntsman at the Gate.* 1952. Lippincott. 1st. VG. O3. $35.00

JENNETT, Sean. *Making of Books.* 1951. London. Pantheon. 1st. ils. VG. K3. $25.00

JENNEWEIN, J. Leonard. *Calamity Jane of the Western Trails.* 1953. Dakota Books. 1st. 46p. VG/stiff wrp. J2. $145.00

JENNEWEIN, J. Leonard. *Dakota Panorama.* 1961. Sioux Falls. Brevet. A19. $25.00

JENNINGS, Dana Close. *Cattle on a Thousand Hills.* 1968. Aberdeen. N Palins. dj. A19. $35.00

JENNINGS, Frances. *Tour in a Donkey Cart.* 1921. Bodley Head. 1st. sm 4to. VG. O3. $65.00

JENNINGS, John. *Golden Eagle.* 1958. Putnam. sgn. VG/VG. B11. $22.50

JENNINGS, Preston J. *Book of Trout Flies.* 1935. Crown. 190p+13p pl. cloth. A17. $30.00

JENYNS, Soame. *View of the Internal Evidence of the Christian Religion.* 1793. Boston. Thomas/Andrews. 12mo. 162p. H13. $195.00

JEPPSON, J.O. *Last Immortal.* 1980. Houghton Mifflin. 1st. F/dj. M2. $13.00

JEPSON, Edgar. *Emerald Tiger.* 1928. Macy-Macius. 1st. VG. M@. $20.00

JEPSON, Willis L. *Flora of the Economic Plants of California.* 1924. Berkeley. ils. 223p. VG+. B26. $21.00

JERMAN, Sylvia Paul. *Set Free.* 1934. Smith Haas. 1st. F/VG+. B4. $85.00

JERNBERG, John. *Forging, Manual of Practical Instruction...* 1919. Chicago. Am Technical Soc. 131p. G. B18. $19.50

JERNINGHAM, Edward. *Poems.* 1779. London. Robson. 8vo. 170p. full polished calf. H13. $195.00

JEROLD, Walter. *Michael Faraday, Man of Science.* nd. NY. Revell. ils. K3. $10.00

JEROME, Irene E. *Sun Prints in Sky Tints, Original Designs...* 1893. Lee Shepard. 1st. 4to. aeg. gilt quarter bl linen. M24. $150.00

JEROME, Jerome K. *My First Book.* 1894. Chatto Windus. 1st. bl cloth. M24. $150.00

JESPERSON & TANING. *Studies in Bird Migration.* 1950. Copenhagen. 272p. VG. S15. $30.00

JESSE, F. Tennyson. *Beggars on Horseback.* 1915. London. 1st. VG. M2. $22.00

JESSUP, Elon. *Motor Camping Book.* 1921. Putnam. 1st. ils. VG. K3. $25.00

JESSUP, Richard. *Threat.* 1981. Viking. 1st. 281p. F/NF. W2. $25.00

JESSYE, Eva A. *My Spirituals.* 1927. NY. Robbins-Engel. ne. inscr. 17 spirituals from author's life. VG. M25. $300.00

JETER, K.W. *Farewell Horizontal.* 1989. St Martin. 1st. F/dj. M2. $30.00

JETER, K.W. *Infernal Devices.* 1987. St Martin. 1st. inscr. F/F. M19. $25.00

JEWELL, Nancy. *Snuggle Bunny.* 1972. Harper Row. 1st. 16mo. 32p. G+. T5. $30.00

JEWETT, Charles C. *Notices of Public Libraries.* 1851. Smithsonian. 1st. gilt modern quarter morocco. F. M24. $300.00

JEWETT, John Howard. *Bunnies, Birds & Blossoms.* ca 1910. London. Nister. 16mo. pict brd. R5. $125.00

JEWETT, Sara Orne. *White Heron.* 1963. Crowell. 1st. ils Barbara Cooney. 35p. VG/VG. P2. $38.00

JEX-BLAKE, A.J. *Gardening in East Africa.* 1957 (1934). Longman Gr. 4th. tall 8vo. teg. VG+. A22. $45.00

JHABVALA, Ruth Prawer. *Amrita.* 1956. Norton. 1st. F/VG. M19. $45.00

JHABVALA, Ruth Prawer. *Heat & Dust.* 1976. Harper Row. 1st Am. F/clip. D10. $50.00

JHABVALA, Ruth Prawer. *How I Became a Holy Mother & Other Stories.* 1976. Harper Row. 1st Am. author's 4th collection short fiction. F/clip. D10. $50.00

JHABVALA, Ruth Prawer. *How I Became a Holy Mother & Other Stories.* 1976. Harper Row. 1st. xl. VG/dj. A25. $20.00

JHABVALA, Ruth Prawer. *How I Became a Holy Mother & Other Stories.* 1976. London. 1st. inscr. F/F. A11. $70.00

JHABVALA, Ruth Prawer. *How I Became a Holy Mother & Other Stories.* 1976. London. Murray. 1st. F/NF. A24. $35.00

JIMENEZ, Juan Ramon. *Selected Writings of...* 1957. FSC. 1st. trans HR Hays. 260p. F/F. H1. $18.00

JOAN, Natalie. *Ameliaranne in Town.* 1930. London. Harrap. 1st. ils Susan Pearse. 8vo. tan brd. R5. $125.00

JOAN, Natalie. *Tales for Teeny Wee.* ca 1935. Whitman. ils Ann Anderson/Alan Wright. thick 4to. pict brd. R5. $250.00

JOELS, Kerry Mark. *Mars One Crew Manual.* 1985. Ballantine. 4to. 158p. VG/glossy wrp. K5. $10.00

JOFFE, Judah A. *Elia Bachur's Poetical Works, Vol I...* 1949. Joffe Pub Comm. facsimile 1541 1st. Eng/Yiddish text. S3. $50.00

JOHANNSEN, Albert. *Phiz, Illustrations From Novels of Charles Dickens.* 1956. Chicago. obl 4to. ils/516 variant etchings. 442p. VG. A4. $350.00

JOHANSEN & LIDE. *Ood-Le-Uk the Wanderer.* 1930. Jr Literary Guild. ils Raymond Lufkin. 265p. purple cloth. P4. $35.00

JOHANSON, Donald. *Lucy: The Beginning of Humanity.* 1981. S&S. 1st. VG/F. A20. $20.00

JOHANSON & SHREEVE. *Lucy's Child: Discovery of a Human Ancestor.* 1989. Morrow. 318p. F/dj. D8. $10.00

JOHL, Janet. *Still More About Dolls.* 1950. 1st. sgn. photos. VG/worn. S13. $30.00

JOHN, Brian S. *Winters of the World: Earth Under the Ice Ages.* 1979. NY. John Wiley. 1st. 8vo. gilt bl cloth. VG/dj. P4. $35.00

JOHNS, Anne Page. *Fir Tree Prays.* 1943. Richmond, VA. Dietz. 1st. sgn. VG/VG. B11. $20.00

JOHNS, Francis A. *Bibliography of Arthur Waley.* 1968. Rutgers. 1st ed. 187p. F. A17. $17.50

JOHNS, Rowland. *Our Friend the Cocker Spaniel.* 1932. NY. 85p. dj. A17. $15.00

JOHNSON, A.F. *Bibliography of Ghana.* 1964. Evanston, IL. Northwestern. 8vo. 210p. xl. VG. W1. $35.00

JOHNSON, Arthur M. *Taxonomy of Flowering Plants.* 1931. NY. ils. 864p. VG. B26. $75.00

JOHNSON, Betty. *Complete Western Cookbook.* 1964. NY. Castle. VG/dj. A16. $10.00

JOHNSON, Bryan. *Four Days of Courage: Untold Story of People...* 1987. NY. Free Pr. 1st. 280p. F/VG+. P1. $15.00

JOHNSON, Burges. *Beastly Rhymes.* 1906. NY. Crowell. 1st. ils EW Blaisdell. 72p. VG. D4. $35.00

JOHNSON, Charles S. *Patterns of Negro Segregation.* 1943. Harper. 1st. 332p. VG+. B4. $225.00

JOHNSON, Charles. *Oxherding Tale.* 1982. IU. 1st. F/NF. M25. $100.00

JOHNSON, Claude. *Little Knights & Jacko & Minnie.* 1919. London. private prt. VG/dj. C8. $15.00

JOHNSON, Clifton. *Farmer's Boy.* 1894. Appleton. 1st. sm 4to. 116p. gilt cloth. T10. $25.00

JOHNSON, Denis. *Angels.* 1983. Knopf. 1st. sgn. author's 1st novel. F/F. D10. $100.00

JOHNSON, Denis. *Resuscitation of a Hanged Man.* 1990. FSG. 1/500 uncorrected galley proofs. sgn. F/pict wrp/box. R13. $30.00

JOHNSON, Denis. *Resuscitation of a Hanged Man.* 1990. FSG. 1st. F/F. B3. $40.00

JOHNSON, Denis. *Resuscitation of a Hanged Man.* 1991. London. Faber. 1st. F/F. A20. $15.00

JOHNSON, Denis. *Stars at Noon.* 1986. Knopf. 1st. F/F. B2. $40.00

JOHNSON, Denis. *Stars at Noon.* 1986. Knopf. 1st. sgn. author's 3rd novel. F/F. from $50 to $60.00

JOHNSON, Diane. *Dashiell Hammett: A Life.* 1983. Random. 1st. F/dj. M2. $18.00

JOHNSON, Diane. *Health & Happiness.* 1990. Knopf. 1st. F/F. R14. $25.00

JOHNSON, Dorothea. *Entertaining & Etiquette.* 1979. WA, DC. Acropolis. 2nd. sgn. VG/VG. B11. $18.00

JOHNSON, Dorothy M. *Bloody Bozeman: Perilous Trail to Montana's Gold.* 1971. McGraw Hill. 1st. 366p. VG+/worn. M20. $38.00

JOHNSON, Dorothy M. *Hanging Tree.* 1957. NY. 1st. VG/VG. B5. $45.00

JOHNSON, E. Pauline. *Flint & Feather.* 1912. Toronto. Musson. 1st. cloth. NF/VG. L3. $850.00

JOHNSON, Edward. *Domestic Practice of Hydropathy With 15 Engraved Ils...* 1849. NY. John Wiley. 1st Am. 8vo. 467p. cloth. M1. $100.00

JOHNSON, Edward. *Marine Corps Aviation: Early Years 1912-1940.* 1977. wA. photos/notes/index. 106p. VG. S16. $35.00

JOHNSON, Elmer S. *At Least Once.* 1983. Vintage. 1st. sgn. F/F. B11. $18.00

JOHNSON, Emile Fendall. *Umbrella Bird & Other Verses.* 1939. Falmouth. 1st. ils Lucretia Malcher. 83p. VG/G+. P2. $65.00

JOHNSON, Ernest D. *In Search of Ghosts.* 1989. Boise. Jet Pub. sgn. 192p. VG. B11. $22.50

JOHNSON, Florence Ridgely. *Welcome Aboard: Service Manual for Naval Officer's Wife.* 1951. Annapolis. 1st. 243p. xl. VG. A25. $15.00

JOHNSON, G.M.T. *Practical Poultry Keeping.* 1886. Binghamton, NY. Carl. 5th. 120p. VG/wrp. A10. $25.00

JOHNSON, Henry P. *Story of Stony Point on the Hudson.* 1900. NY. fld map/ils. xl. VG. M17. $25.00

JOHNSON, Hugh. *Modern Encyclopedia of Wine.* 1985. S&S. 1st. F/F. W2. $55.00

JOHNSON, Hugh. *Wine.* 1973. S&S. 8th. F/F. W2. $45.00

JOHNSON, James Weldon. *Black Manhattan.* 1930. Knopf. 1st. NF. B2. $150.00

JOHNSON, James Weldon. *Book of American Negro Poetry.* 1922. Harcourt Brace. 1st. VG. B4. $125.00

JOHNSON, James Weldon. *Creation.* 1993. Little Brn. 1st thus. sm 4to. unp. F/F. C14. $18.00

JOHNSON, James Weldon. *God's Trombones: Seven Negro Sermons in Verse.* 1927. Viking. later prt. VG/dj. M25. $35.00

JOHNSON, James Weldon. *Negro Americans, What Now?* 1934. Viking. 1st. 103p. F/VG+. B4. $525.00

JOHNSON, James Weldon. *Negro Americans, What Now?* 1934. Viking. 1st. 12mo. NF. C8. $100.00

JOHNSON, Joyce. *In the Night Cafe.* 1989. Dutton. 1st. 231p. VG/dj. A25. $15.00

JOHNSON, Kenneth M. *Champagne & Shoes.* 1962. SF. Porpoise Bookshop. 1/76. sm volio. ils. F/box. R3. $250.00

JOHNSON, M.L.; see Malzberg, Barry.

JOHNSON, Magic. *My Life.* 1992. Random. 1st. F/F. A23. $40.00

JOHNSON, Martin. *Lion: African Adventure With the King of Beasts.* 1929. NY/London. Putnam. tall 8vo. 63p. xl. VG. W1. $25.00

JOHNSON, Martin. *Over African Jungles: Record of Glorious Adventure...* 1935. NY. 1st. photos. VG/G. M17. $20.00

JOHNSON, Mary. *Croatan.* 1923. Little Brn. 1st. VG. M2. $17.00

JOHNSON, Mary. *Wanderers.* 1917. Houghton Mifflin. 1st. VG. M2. $15.00

JOHNSON, Mel; see Malzberg, Barry.

JOHNSON, Merle. *Bibliography of the Works of Mark Twain.* 1935. Harper. 1st/1st prt. rust brn cloth. F. M24. $150.00

JOHNSON, Osa. *Bride in the Solomons.* 1944. Houghton Mifflin. 1st. sgn. 249p. VG/tattered. M20. $35.00

JOHNSON, Osa. *Four Years in Paradise.* Garden City. rpt. sgn. 345p. VG/dj. M20. $25.00

JOHNSON, Pamela Hansford. *Error of Judgement.* 1962. London. 1st. VG/dj. T9. $15.00

JOHNSON, Richard William. *Shoot-Down.* 1986. Viking. 1st. 335p. F/F. W2. $30.00

JOHNSON, Robert. *Nova Britannia: Offering Most Excellent Fruits by Planting.* 1867 (1609). NY. Sabin. 4to. unopened/VG. O7. $150.00

JOHNSON, Ronald. *Songs of the Earth.* 1970. Grabhorn Hoyem. 1st. 1/150. F. B2. $65.00

JOHNSON, Rossiter. *Little Classics: Volume 8, Mysteries.* nd. Houghton Mifflin. VG. M2. $12.00

JOHNSON, Samuel. *Deformities of Dr Samuel Johnson...* 1971. Augustan Rpt Soc. facsimile. 8vo. 89p. F/heavy tan paper wrp. H13. $45.00

JOHNSON, Samuel. *Diaries, Prayers & Annals.* 1958. New Haven. Yale. 1st. tall 8vo. gilt bl cloth. F/dj. H13. $95.00

JOHNSON, Samuel. *Dictionary of English Language...* 1805. Phil. Jacob Johnson. 8vo. 883p. orig tree calf. F. B14. $555.00

JOHNSON, Samuel. *Dictionary of the English Language.* 1755. London. Strahan. 2 vol. 1st. folio. 18th-C full calf. C6. $8,500.00

JOHNSON, Samuel. *Fountains.* 1927. London. Mathews Marrot. 1/510. sm 8vo. 48p. gilt marbled brd. NF. H13. $65.00

JOHNSON, Samuel. *Harleian Miscellany; or, Collection of Scarce, Curious...* 1744-46. London. T Osborne. 8 vol. tall 4to. subscriber list each vol. VG. H13. $2,250.00

JOHNSON, Samuel. *Johnson's Last Literary Project.* 1948. New Haven. 1/200. sm 8vo. F/heavy bl paper wrp. H13. $85.00

JOHNSON, Samuel. *Lives of the Most Eminent English Poets...* 1800-1801. London. Baldwin Johnson. 4 vol. apparent rpt 1783. sm 8vo. VG. H13. $495.00

JOHNSON, Samuel. *Prayers & Meditations...* 1807. London. Cadell Davis. 4th. tall 8vo. 230p. full polished morocco. H13. $295.00

JOHNSON, Samuel. *Rambler.* 1820. London. 3 vol. leather. A19. $150.00

JOHNSON, Samuel. *Some Unpublished Letters to & From Dr Johnson.* 1932. Manchester. sm 4to. 55p. NF. H13. $65.00

JOHNSON, Samuel. *Works of Samuel Johnson.* nd (ca 1915). Cambridge. 16 vol in 8. 1/500. sgn/pub Bigelow. NF. B4. $300.00

JOHNSON, Samuel. *Works... New Edition.* 1809-1812. Boston/NY. 12 vol. 12mo. all orig bdg. M1. $850.00

JOHNSON, Stanley. *Doomsday Deposit.* 1980. Dutton. ne. 217p. F/F. W2. $20.00

JOHNSON, Virginia M. *Unregimented General, a Biography of Nelson A Miles.* 1962. Houghton Mifflin. 1st. 401p. VG/VG. J2. $95.00

JOHNSON, W. Fletcher. *Life of Sitting Bull & History of the Indian War of 1890-91.* 1891. Edgewood Pub. 1st. 544p. VG. J2. $235.00

JOHNSON, Wayne. *Snake Game.* 1990. Knopf. 1st. F/F. L3. $30.00

JOHNSON, William G. *Overland to California: A Member of the Wagon Train...* 1948. Biobooks. 1st. 1/1000. M/sans. A18. $30.00

JOHNSON, William Weber. *Forty-Niners.* 1976. Time-Life. 3rd. leather. A19. $20.00

JOHNSON & JOHNSON. *Second Book of Negro Spirituals.* 1926. Viking. 1st. 4to. 189p. F/VG. B4. $485.00

JOHNSON & LEWIN. *Magic.* 1983. Viking. 1st. photos. F/F. P8. $25.00

JOHNSON & LOSSING. *Dixie Dobie, a Sable Island Pony.* 1945. Harcourt Brace. 1st. wide sm 8vo. VG/G. C8. $17.50

JOHNSON & PALMER. *Murder.* 1928. Covici Friede. 1st. VG. M2. $20.00

JOHNSON & STRAAYER. *Book of One's Own: Guide to Self-Publishing.* 1979. Chicago. Metis. 1st. ils. VG/wrp. A25. $15.00

JOHNSON & WINTER. *Route Across the Rocky Mountains...* 1982. Ye Galleon. 1st thus. M/sans. A18. $17.50

JOHNSTON, Annie Fellows. *Little Colonel's Christmas Vacation (#6).* 1905. Page. 19th imp. 333p+ads. w/flyer. VG+/ragged. M20. $40.00

JOHNSTON, Annie Fellows. *Little Colonel.* 1896. Joseph Knight. 1st/2nd issue. 12mo. gilt lettered red cloth. VG. M5. $95.00

JOHNSTON, Annie Fellows. *Mary Ware's Promised Land.* 1912. Page. 1st. tan pict cloth. VG. M5. $45.00

JOHNSTON, Basil. *Tales the Elders Told.* 1981. Toronto. Royal Ontario Mus. 1st. ils/sgn Shirley Cheechoo. NF. L3. $85.00

JOHNSTON, Charles M. *Famous Indian Chiefs.* 1909. Boston. Page. 1st. ils. 458p. pict cloth. G. B18. $22.50

JOHNSTON, Charles M. *Valley of the Six Nations. Collection of Documents...* 1964. Toronto. Champlain Soc. 8vo. 344p. gilt red cloth. F. P4. $125.00

JOHNSTON, Johanna. *Penguin's Way.* 1962. np. Doubleday. 1st. ils Leonard Weisgaard. unp. bl cloth. P4. $22.00

JOHNSTON, Joseph Eggleston. *Narrative of Military Operations, Directed During Late War.* 1874. Appleton. 1st. 602p. later cloth. NF. M8. $125.00

JOHNSTON, Mary. *Lewis Rand.* 1908. Houghton Mifflin. 4th. ils FC Yohn. 510p. VG. A25. $12.00

JOHNSTON, Mary. *To Have & To Hold.* 1900. Houghton Mifflin. 1st. ils. 403p. VG+. A25. $8.00

JOHNSTON, Paul Forsythe. *Ship & Boat Models in Ancient Greece.* 1985. Naval Inst. 1st. 187p. VG/torn. M20. $22.00

JOHNSTON, S. *Queen of the Flat-Tops: USS Lexington & Coral Sea Battle.* 1942. later prt. photos. VG. M17. $17.50

JOHNSTON, W.G. *Overland to California.* 1948. Oakland. 1/1000. 272p. NF. M4. $45.00

JOLIVET, P. *Insects & Plants.* 1986. NY. Brill/Flora & Fauna. 197p. VG/wrp. B1. $22.50

JOLLEY, Elizabeth. *Miss Peabody's Inheritance.* 1984. Viking. 1st AM. 157p. VG+/VG. A25. $15.00

JOLLY, Allson. *Lemurs.* 1974. Chicago. ils/maps. VG. S15. $17.50

JONES, A.E. *Extracts From the History of Cincinnati & Territory of OH.* 1888. Cincinnati. 1 map/10 views. 133p. leather. VG. B18. $125.00

JONES, A.G.E. *Antarctica Observed: Who Discovered the Antarctic Continent?* 1982. Whitby. 8vo. 118p. NF/dj. P4. $62.00

JONES, Bobby. *Golf Is My Game.* 1960. Garden City. 1st. VG/VG. B5. $65.00

JONES, Charles H. *Africa: History of Exploration & Adventures...* 1970 (1875). Negro U. rpt. 8vo. ils/fld map. 496p. VG. W1. $35.00

JONES, Christopher. *Deciphering Maya Hieroglyphs.* 1984. Phil U Mus. ils. 78p. sbdg. F3. $25.00

JONES, D.F. *Fall of Colossus.* 1974. Putnam. 1st. F/dj. M2. $20.00

JONES, D.F. *Fall of Colossus.* 1974. Putnam. 1st. NF/VG. M22. $12.00

JONES, Donald F. *Selective Fertilization.* 1928. Chicago. 1st. 163p. A10. $30.00

JONES, Douglas C. *Arrest Sitting Bull.* 1977. Scribner. hc. dj. A19. $25.00

JONES, Douglas C. *Barefoot Brigade.* 1981. HRW. 1st. F/F. T11. $55.00

JONES, Douglas C. *Court-Martial of George Armstrong Custer.* 1976. NY. dj. A19. $35.00

JONES, E. Stanley. *Christ of the American Road.* 1944. Abingdon Cokesbury. 16mo. 255p. gilt bl brd. F/VG. H1. $9.00

JONES, Franklin D. *Ingenious Mechanisms for Designers & Inventors.* 1944 (1930). NY. Industrial Pr. 2 vol. 5th prt. sm 4to. F. H1. $22.50

JONES, Franklin D. *Ingenious Mechanisms for Designers & Inventors.* 1957-1969. Industrial Pr. 4 vol. A17. $35.00

JONES, Gareth Elwyn. *People, Protest & Politics: Case Studies in 19th-C Wales.* 1987. Llandysul. Gomer. 1st. photos. 136p. VG+. A25. $18.00

JONES, George Neville. *Annotated Bibliography of Mexican Ferns.* 1966. Urbana, IL. 8vo. 297p. NF. A22. $30.00

JONES, Helen. *Robert Lawson, Illustrator.* 1972. Little Brn. 1st. sm 4to. 121p. NF/VG. P2. $80.00

JONES, Herschel V. *Adventures in Ameriana, 1491-1897, Romance of Voyage...* 1928. Wm Rudge. 2 vol. 1/200. lg 4to. VG. A4. $595.00

JONES, Hettie. *Coyote Tales.* 1974. HRW. 1st. sm obl 4to. F/F. L3. $100.00

JONES, Hettie. *Trees Stand Shining, Poetry of the North American Indians.* 1971. NY. Dial. 1st. ils Robert Andrew Parker. 32p. NF/NF. D4. $45.00

JONES, Idwal. *Ark of Empire: San Francisco's Montgomery Block.* 1951. Doubleday. sgn. ils AJ Camille. 253p. gr cloth/ivory spine. VG/dj. K7. $45.00

JONES, James. *From Here to Eternity.* 1952. Scribner. 1st. F/NF. M25. $150.00

JONES, James. *Some Came Running.* 1957. Scribner. 1st. NF/dj. M25. $30.00

JONES, James. *Thin Red Line.* 1962. NY. Scribner. 1st. NF/VG+. T11. $40.00

JONES, James. *Thin Red Line.* 1962. Scribner. 1st. author's 4th book. F/clip. D10. $45.00

JONES, James. *Whistle.* 1978. Delacorte. 1st. NF/NF. T11. $35.00

JONES, James. *World War II.* 1975. NY. ils/maps. VG/VG. S16. $25.00

JONES, Katharine. *Plantation South.* 1957. Bobbs Merrill. 1st. 8vo. 412p. as new/dj. H1. $45.00

JONES, L. Meyer. *Veterinary Pharmacology & Therapeutics.* 1954. Ames, IA. VG. O3. $25.00

JONES, LeRoi. *Blues People: Schwarze und Ihre Musik im Weiben Amerika.* nd. Weisbaden. Fourier Verlag. 1st German. sgn. 319p. F/F. B4. $250.00

JONES, LeRoi. *Moderns: Anthology of New Writing in America.* 1963. NY. Cornith. 1st. NF/dj. Q1. $75.00

JONES, Lloyd. *US Fighters: Army-Airforce 1925-1980s.* 1975. Fallbrook. ils/diagrams. 352p. VG/G. S16. $35.00

JONES, Louis B. *Ordinary Money.* 1990. Viking. 1st. inscr. F/F. R14. $35.00

JONES, Louis T. *Quakers of Iowa.* 1914. State Hist Soc. 1st. 360p. VG. V3. $30.00

JONES, Marcus E. *Revision of North-American Species of Astragalus.* 1923. Salt Lake City. 78 pl. 288p. wrp. B26. $29.00

JONES, N.E. *Squirrel Hunters of Ohio.* 1898 (1897). Robert Clarke 363p. gilt gr cloth. VG+. M20. $185.00

JONES, Neil R. *Planet of the Double Sun.* 1975. Garland. 1st hc. F/sans. M2. $35.00

JONES, Neville. *Stone Age in Rhodesia.* 1969 (1926). Negro U. 8vo. 120p. VG. W1. $25.00

JONES, O.S. *Fresh-Water Protection From Pollution Arising in Oil Fields.* 1950. Lawrence. 132p. cloth. F. D8. $10.00

JONES, Patricia. *Columbine the White Cat.* 1955. Container Corp. 1st. ils Jan Balet. 31p. NF/VG. P2. $75.00

JONES, Peter. *Kahkewaquonaby: History of the Ojebway Indians...* 1861. London. AW Bennett. rpr joints/modest foxing. G. L3. $850.00

JONES, R.S. *Force of Gravity.* 1991. Viking. 1st. author's 1st book. F/F. R13. $30.00

JONES, Rufus. *Boy Jesus & His Companions.* 1922. Macmillan. 1st. 189p. xl. V3. $12.50

JONES, Rufus. *Eli & Sibyl Jones: Their Life & Work.* 1889. Porter Coates. 316p. VG. V3. $27.00

JONES, Rufus. *George Fox, an Autobiography.* 1903. Ferris Leach. 1st. 2 vol. 484p. xl. V3. $35.00

JONES, Rufus. *Later Period of Quakerism.* 1921. London. Macmillan. 2 vol. G+. V3. $65.00

JONES, S.A. *Thoreau: A Glimpse.* 1903. Concord. Erudite. 1st trade. quarter gr linen/brd. M24. $250.00

JONES, Thomas. *Pugilist at Rest.* 1993. Little Brn. 1st. sgn. author's 1st book. F/NF. A24. $65.00

JONES, Tim. *Last Great Race: Iditarod Sled Dog Race.* 1982. Seattle. Madrona. 1st. 8vo. 266p. map ep. VG/dj. P4. $30.00

JONES, Tristan. *Yarns: Articles & Stories by the Man Who Logged...* 1983. Boston. Sail Books. 272p. dj. T7. $18.00

JONES, W. Unite. *Button Industry.* 1946. London. Pitman. 113p. VG. M20. $20.00

JONES, Walter. *Heating by Hot Water.* 1894. London. Lockwood. 2nd. 12mo. 220p. VG. T10. $50.00

JONES, Walter. *Sandbar.* 1981. Casper, WY. BASCO Inc. sgn. w/ephemera. A19. $40.00

JONES, William. *Works of Sir William Jones.* 1799. London. Robinson Evans. 6 vol. 1st. 4to. ils. 19th-C half morocco/bl cloth. C6. $425.00

JONES & KELLEY. *Admiral Arleigh (31 Knot) Burke.* 1962. NY. 1st. 203p. VG. S16. $23.50

JONES & WARNER. *Rebound.* 1986. Quinlan. 1st. F/F. P8. $15.00

JONES & WASHINGTON. *Black Champions Challenge American Sports.* 1972. McKay. 1st. 180p. F/NF. B4. $65.00

JONES & WILLIAMS. *Household Elegancies: Suggestions in Household Art.* 1875. NY. Williams. 2nd. 8vo. 300p. gilt gr cloth. F. T10. $75.00

JONES. *Children's Literature Awards & Winners: A Directory...* 1983. 4to. 495p. F. A4. $95.00

JONG, Erica. *Any Women's Blues.* 1990. Harper Row. 1st. inscr/dtd 1992. NF/NF. R14. $35.00

JONG, Erica. *Fear of Flying.* 1973. HRW. 1st. author's 1st novel. F/F. D10. $70.00

JONG, Erica. *Fruits & Vegetables.* 1971. HRW. 1st hc. author's 1st book. F/F. L3. $50.00

JONG, Erica. *Loveroot.* 1975. HRW. ARC. inscr/dtd 1992. RS. F/clip. R14. $50.00

JONG, Erica. *Megan's Book of Divorce.* 1984. NAL. 1st. F/G. T12. $15.00

JONG, Erica. *Witches.* 1981. Abrams. 1st. F/dj. M2. $30.00

JONSON, Ben. *Volpone; or, The Foxe.* 1898. 1/1000. 4to. ils Aubrey Beardsley. NF. S13. $150.00

JONSON, Ben. *Volpone; or, The Foxe.* 1898. London. Leonard Smithers. 1/100 deluxe. ils Beardsley. full vellum. w/extra ils. B24. $2,750.00

JONSON, Ben. *Volpone; or, The Foxe.* 1952. Oxford. LEC. 1st thus. 1/1500. ils/sgn RB Sussan. F/dj/case. Q1. $150.00

JOOS & WELLS. *Golden Prince.* 1928. Duffield. probable 1st. sm 4to. 129p. VG. C14. $20.00

JORDAN, David Starr. *Fishes.* 1925. Appleton. revised. ils. 771p. VG. S15. $50.00

JORDAN, Don. *Songs of the Fire Circles.* 1977. Newcastle. Bl Oak. 1st. 1/100. F/F. L3. $200.00

JORDAN, J. *Give Me the Wind.* 1972. Englewood Cliffs. 253p. F/dj. M4. $25.00

JORDAN, Pat. *Black Coach.* 1971. Dodd Mead. 1st. F/VG+. P8. $40.00

JORDAN, Pat. *Chase the Game.* 1979. Dodd Mead. 1st. VG+/VG. P8. $25.00

JORDAN, Pat. *False Spring.* 1975. Dodd Mead. 1st. 277p. cloth. VG/dj. M20. $30.00

JORDAN, S. *Confectionary Standards for Chocolate, Nougat, Marshmallows.* 1933. Am Sugar Labs. G+. E6. $28.00

JORDAN & HEARON. *Barbara Jordan.* 1979. Doubleday. 1st. sgn. F/F. W2. $20.00

JORDAN & SHAW. *Story of a Pioneer.* 1915. Harper. 1st. photos. 338p. teg. VG+. A25. $40.00

JORDAN-SMITH, Paul. *For the Love of Books.* 1934. 1st. sgn. VG. K3. $25.00

JOSCELYN, Archie. *Golden Bowl.* 1931. Internat Fiction Lib. 246p. cloth. VG/dj. M20. $30.00

JOSEPHS, Jeremy. *Swastika Over Paris.* 1989. NY. 1st. VG/VG. T9. $12.00

JOSEPHY, Alvin M. *American Heritage Book of Indians.* 1961. NY. 3rd. 424p. dj. A17. $18.50

JOSEPHY, Alvin M. *Civil War in the American West.* 1991. NY. 1st. 448p. F/dj. M4. $40.00

JOSEPHY, Alvin M. *Nez Perce Indians & the Opening of the Northwest.* 1965. Yale. 1st. 705p. VG/dj. J2. $125.00

JOSLIN, Sesyle. *What Do You Do, Dear.* 1961. Wm Scott. 1st. ils Sendak. NF/VG+. P2. $250.00

JOY, Charles R. *Music in the Life of Albert Schweitzer.* 1951. NY. 1st. inscr. ils. VG. T12. $25.00

JOYCE, James. *Cat & the Devil.* 1964. Dodd Mead. 1st. ils Richard Erdoes. VG/dj. P2. $65.00

JOYCE, James. *Chamber Music.* 1918. NY. Huebsch. 1st authorized Am. F/NF. B4. $4,500.00

JOYCE, James. *Letters.* 1957. edit Stewart Gilbert. VG. M17. $25.00

JOYCE, James. *Portrait of the Artist As a Young Man.* 1930. Leipzig. Tauchnitz. 1st. VG+/wrp. A11. $125.00

JOYCE, James. *Today: Essays on the Major Works.* 1966. edit TF Staley. VG/VG. M17. $15.00

JOYCE, James. *Ulysses.* 1928. Paris. Shakespeare. 1st/10th prt. VG/bl wrp. Q1. $600.00

JOYCE, John Alexander. *Jewels of Memory.* 1896. WA, DC. Gibson Bros. 2nd. pres. 245p. cloth. xl. NF. M8. $75.00

JOYCE, Robert. *White Mouse. A Story in Pictures.* ca 1940. Brd Edu & Federal Works Agency. 4to. ils wrp. B24. $225.00

JOYCE & THOMAS. *Women of All Nations: Record of Their Characteristics...* 1942. NY. Metro Pub. 2nd revised. 663p. G+. A25. $10.00

JOYNER, Tim. *Magellan.* 1992. Camden, ME. Internat Marine. ils/maps. as new/dj. O7. $25.00

JOYS, J. *Wild Animal Trainer in America.* 1983. Boulder. Pruitt. ils/photos. 327p. F/NF. M12. $60.00

JUDAH, Samuel B.H. *Gotham & the Gothamites, a Medley.* 1823. NY. self pub. 1st. narrow 16mo. 93p. prt brd/rebacked/uncut. M1. $375.00

JUDD, B.I. *Handbook of Tropical Forage Grasses.* 1979. Garland STPM Pr. 116p. F. B1. $20.00

JUDD, Cyril. *Gunner Cade.* 1952. S&S. 1st. F/NF. M2. $30.00

JUDD, Mary Catherine. *Wigwam Stories Told by North American Indians.* 1911. Boston. 278p. tan brd. B14. $55.00

JUDSON, Clara Ingram. *Child Life Cook Book.* (1929). Rand McNally. silhouettes. glazed pict brd. F/NF. D1. $60.00

JUDSON, Clara Ingram. *Mr Justice Holmes.* (1956). Chicago. Follett. 192p. xl. G+. T5. $18.00

JUDSON, Horace Freeland. *Eighth Day of Creation.* 1979. S&S. rpt. 686p. wrp. K3. $12.00

JUDSON, Katharine B. *Myths & Legends of California & Old Southwest.* 1912. Chicago. McClurg. 51 photos. 193p. gr cloth. VG. K7. $45.00

JUDSON & JUDSON. *Let's Go to Colombia.* (1949). Harper. 1st. 332p. dj. F3. $15.00

JUETTNER, Otto. *Daniel Drake & His Followers.* 1909. Cincinnati. 1st. 496p. VG. B5. $145.00

JULL, Morley. *Raising Turkeys, Ducks, Geese, Game Birds.* 1947. McGraw Hill. 467p. VG. A10. $24.00

JUMONVILLE. *Bibliography of New Orleans Imprints 1764-1864.* 1989. 1/1000. 800p. F. A4. $60.00

JUNG, Leo. *Jewish Leaders 1750-1940.* 1964 (1953). Boys Town Jerusalem Pub. 25 essays. 564p. VG. S3. $47.00

JUNG, Richard. *Visual Centers of the Brain.* 1973. NY. Springer. heavy 8vo. 738p. bl cloth. xl. VG. G1. $65.00

JUNGK, Robert. *Brighter Than a Thousand Suns.* 1956. NY. Harcourt. 1st Am. dj. K3. $25.00

JUNIOR LEAGE OF CORPUS CRISTI. *Fiesta: Favorite Recipes of South Texas.* 1976. The League. 4th. 310p. VG. B10. $10.00

JUNIOR LEAGUE OF PASADENA. *California Heritage Cookbook.* 1976. 16th. 424p. VG/dj. B10. $15.00

JUNIUS. *Letters.* 1801. London. Bensley for Vernor & Hood. 2 vol. tall 8vo. H13. $350.00

JUPTNER, Joseph P. *US Civil Aircraft, Vol 1.* 1962. LA. Aero Pub. ils. covers 1927-1929. 247p. brd. VG/dj. B18. $45.00

JURMAIN, Suzanne. *Once Upon a Horse: History of Horses...* 1989. Lee Shepard. 1st. VG/VG. O3. $25.00

JUSTER, Norton. *As, a Surfeit of Similes.* 1989. Morrow. 1st. sgn. as new. D4. $30.00

JUSTICE, Donald. *Summer Anniversaries.* 1960. Wesleyan U. 1st. sgn. NF/dj. V1. $90.00

JUSTUS, May. *At the Foot of Windy Low.* 1930. Volland. 1st. ils Carrie Dudley. gr cloth. G. M5. $45.00

JUSTUS, May. *Fiddle Away.* 1942 (1936). Grosset Dunlap. 8vo. unp. pict brd. VG/torn. T5. $25.00

JUSTUS, May. *Fiddler's Fair.* (1945). Chicago. Whitman. pict cloth. 32p. G+. T5. $30.00

JUSTUS, May. *Honey Jane.* 1935. Doubleday Doran. 1st. 202p. NF/VG-. P2. $35.00

JUSTUS, May. *Near-Side-And-Far.* 1936. LA. Suttonhouse. 1st. 8vo. 148p. aqua cloth. VG/G. T5. $35.00

JUSTUS, May. *Toby Has a Dog.* 1949. Whitman. 1st. ils Sanford Tousey. cloth/mc pl. F/VG. M5. $45.00

JUTA, J. *Look Out for the Ostriches: Tales of South Africa.* 1949. Knopf. ils H Pitz. 177p. pict cloth. F/VG+. M12. $12.50

KABERRY, Charles. *Book of Baby Dogs.* nd (1914). Frowde/Hodder Stoughton. ils EJ Detmold. 120p. VG. D1. $365.00

KABERRY, Charles. *Our Little Neighbors.* 1921. London. Milford/Oxford. 1st. ils Detmold. 4to. blk lettered rose cloth. R5. $375.00

KABOTIE, Fred. *Designs From the Ancient Mimbrenos With Hopi Interpretation.* 1949. Grabhorn. 1/250. inscr. 38 full-p ils. F. K7. $375.00

KABOTIE, Fred. *Hopi Indian Artist.* 1977. Flagstaff. Mus N AZ. 1st. obl 4to. 2-tone cloth. F/dj. T10. $75.00

KADAR. *Motoring Through Europe: Europe Travel Guide.* 1957. Zurich. 400p/fld mc maps. G. A17. $20.00

KAEWERT, Julie Wallin. *Unsolicited.* 1994. St Martin. 1st. sgn. author's 1st book. F/F. B3. $35.00

KAFAROFF, Bruce. *Deadwood Gulch.* 1941. Knopf. dj. A19. $35.00

KAFKA, Barbara. *Microwave Gourmet.* 1987. Morrow. 1st. M/dj. A16. $15.00

KAGAWA, Toyohiko. *Before the Dawn.* 1924. Doran. 1st Am. F/VG+. B4. $175.00

KAGAWA, Toyohiko. *Grain of Wheat.* 1916. Harper. 150p. VG/dj. W3. $38.00

KAGAWA, Toyohiko. *Songs From the Slums.* 1935. Nashville, TN. VG/dj. W3. $36.00

KAHANE, Meir. *They Must Go.* 1981. Grosset Dunlap. 1st. 282p. VG/G+. S3. $25.00

KAHL, Virginia. *Maxie.* 1956. Scribner. 1st. VG/dj. M5. $30.00

KAHN, David. *Codebreakers.* 1967. NY. 1st. VG/VG. B5. $40.00

KAHN, Douglas. *John Heartfield & Mass Media.* 1985. NY. Tanam. 1st. F/F. B2. $50.00

KAHN, E.J. Jr. *Fighting Divisions: Histories of Each US Army Combat...* 1980. WA. maps/order of battle. 218p. VG. S16. $30.00

KAHN, Edgar M. *Cable Car Days in San Francisco.* 1940. Stanford. 8vo. 124p. as new/dj. K7. $35.00

KAHN, James. *Timefall.* 1987. St Martin. 1st. F/dj. M2. $15.00

KAHN, Roger. *Season in the Sun.* 1977. Harper Row. 1st. sgn. F/F. A23. $40.00

KAHN, Roger. *Seventh Game.* 1982. NAL. 1st. NF/NF. A20. $20.00

KAI-SHEK, Chaing. *Soviet Russia in China.* 1957. FSC. 1st. NF/dj. B35. $22.00

KAINS, Josephine; see Goulart, Ron.

KAINS, M.G. *Ginseng.* 1910. Orange Judd. revised. 144p. A10. $28.00

KAINS, M.G. *Plant Propagation.* 1927. Orange Judd. 322p. VG. A10. $24.00

KAISER, Charles. *In America.* 1988. Weidenfeld Nicolson. 1st. F/VG. T12. $20.00

KAKONIS, Tom. *Criss Cross.* 1990. St Martin. 1st. author's 2nd novel. VG/dj. P3. $20.00

KAKONIS, Tom. *Criss Cross.* 1990. St Martin. 1st. sgn. author's 2nd novel. F/F. N4. $40.00

KAKONIS, Tom. *Double Down.* 1991. Dutton. 1st. F/dj. N4. $27.50

KAKONIS, Tom. *Michigan Roll.* 1988. NY. 1st. author's 1st book. F/F. H11. $45.00

KAKUZO, Okakura. *Book of Tea.* 1912 (1906). Duffield. 160p. B10. $10.00

KALES, Anthony. *Sleep: Physiology & Pathology, a Symposium.* 1969. Lippincott. 360p. prt bl cloth. G1. $28.50

KALPAKIAN, Laura. *Beggars & Choosers.* 1978. Little Brn. 1st. F/F. H11. $15.00

KALTON, M. *To Become a Sage: 10 Diagrams on Sage Learning by Yi Yoegye.* 1988. Columbia. 1st. annotated trans. 278p. F/dj. W3. $52.00

KAMINSKY, Stuart M. *Cold Red Sunrise.* 1988. Scribner. 1st. VG/F. M25. $15.00

KAMINSKY, Stuart M. *Exercise in Terror.* 1985. St Martin. 1st. F/dj. M15. $45.00

KAMINSKY, Stuart M. *Fala Factor.* 1984. NY. 1st. F/F. H11. $40.00

KAMINSKY, Stuart M. *Opening Shots.* 1991. Eugene. Mystery Scene. 1st. 1/300. sgn. F/F. M15. $45.00

KAMINSKY, Stuart M. *You Bet Your Life.* 1978. St Martin. 1st. F/VG. M19. $25.00

KAMM, Minnie Watson. *Fifth Pitcher Book.* 1956. Century. 2nd/2nd prt. 209p. VG. H1. $32.50

KAMM, Minnie Watson. *Second Two Hundred Pattern Glass Pitchers.* 1940. Detroit. Motschall. 1st. 135p. sbdg. VG. H1. $27.50

KANAMATSU, Kenryo. *Amitabha: Life of Naturalness.* 1949. Kyoto. Otani. sgn. 75p. navy brd. VG. B11. $35.00

KANE, Elisha Kent. *Adrift in the Arctic Ice Pack.* 1916. Outing. 420p. F. A17. $20.00

KANE, Elisha Kent. *Arctic Explorations in the Years 1853-55. Vol 1.* 1856. Phil. Childs Peterson. 464p. cloth. VG. M20. $35.00

KANE, Elisha Kent. *Arctic Explorations: Second Grinnell Expection... Vol 1.* 1857. Phil. Childs Peterson. 2nd. 8vo. fld map. emb bdg. G. H1. $35.00

KANE, Frank. *Bullet Proof.* 1951. Washburn. 1st. VG/VG. M22. $55.00

KANE, Harnet T. *New Orlean's Woman.* 1946. Doubleday. sgn. VG/VG. B11. $20.00

KANE, Henry. *Report for a Corpse.* 1948. S&S. 1st. 245p. VG/dj. M20. $15.00

KANIEL, Michael. *Judaism.* 1979. Blandford. 160p. VG/dj. S3. $23.00

KANT, Immanuel. *Kritik Der Reinen Vernunft.* 1781. Riga. 1st. 8vo. 856p. contemporary brd. C6. $5,000.00

KANTOR, Alfred J. *Book of Alfred J Kantor.* 1971. McGraw Hill. 1st. F/F. B35. $15.00

KANTOR, MacKinlay. *Andersonville.* 1955. 1st. full-p map. 279p. O8. $12.50

KANTOR, MacKinlay. *Arouse & Beware.* 1936. Coward McCann. 1st. NF/NF. B4. $100.00

KANTOR, MacKinlay. *God & My Country.* 1954. Cleveland. 1st. inscr. F/F. B4. $150.00

KANTOR, MacKinlay. *Lobo.* 1957. NF/NF. A4. $20.00

KANTOR, MacKinlay. *Signal 32.* 1950. Random. 1st. NF/VG. M22. $20.00

KAO, George. *Chinese Wit & Humor.* 1974. NY. intro Lin Yutang. 347p. F. W3. $45.00

KAPLAN, Aryeh. *Rabbi Nachman's Stories...Rabbi Nachman of Breslov.* 1983. Breslov Research Inst. 1st. 552p. VG+/dj. S3. $26.00

KAPLAN, Howard. *Chopin Express.* 1978. Dutton. 1st. author's 2nd book. F/F. H11. $25.00

KAPLAN, Mordecai M. *Meaning of God in Modern Jewish Religion.* 1947. Jewish Reconstructionist. 2nd. 381p. G+/fair. S3. $21.00

KAPPERS & SCHADE. *Structure & Function of the Epiphysis Cerebri.* 1965. Amsterdam. Elsevier. 4to. ils. 694p. VG. G1. $55.00

KAPPES, Alfred. *Mother Goose's Melodies; or, Songs for the Nursery.* 1879. Houghton Osgood. 186p. VG. D4. $95.00

KAPUSCINSKI, Ryszard. *Shah of Shahs.* 1985. HBJ. 1st Am. 8vo. 152p. VG/dj. W1. $18.00

KARAMANSKI, Theodore J. *Fur Trade & Exploration, Opening the Far Northwest 1821-52.* 1983. Norman, OK. 1st. 330p. VG/dj. J2. $75.00

KARDINER, Abram. *Bio-Analysis of the Epileptic Reaction.* 1932. NY. Psychoanalytic Quarterly. 1st separate. inscr. VG. G1. $75.00

KAREN, Ruth. *Song of the Quail.* 1972. Four Winds. 222p. dj. F3. $15.00

KARIG, Walter. *War in the Atomic Age.* 1946. Wm Wise. 63p+ads. VG/wrp. K3. $10.00

KARIG, Walter. *Zotz!* 1947. Rinehart. 1st. NF/dj. M2. $15.00

KARLGREN, Bernhard. *Book of Odes: Chinese Text, Transcription & Translation.* 1950. Stockholm. Mus Far East Antiq. 270p. VG/wrp. W3. $110.00

KARNOVSKY & WILLIAMS. *Romper Room Bedtime Storybook.* 1984. Garden City. 1st. 63p. NF. C14. $15.00

KAROLEVITZ, Robert F. *Challenge, the South Dakota Story.* 1975. Sioux Falls. Brevet. sgn. dj. A19. $25.00

KAROLEVITZ, Robert F. *Yankton: A Pioneer Past.* 1972. Aberdeen, SD. North Plains. dj. A19. $65.00

KARPF, Fay B. *Psychology & Psychotheraphy of Otto Rank.* 1953. Philosophical Lib. 129p. F/dj. H1. $20.00

KARPINSKI, Louis Charles. *History of Arithmetic.* 1925. Rand McNally. 1st. 8vo. 200p. VG/dj. K3. $50.00

KARR, Mary. *Liar's Club.* 1995. Viking. 1st. sgn. F/F. A23. $50.00

KARSH, Yousef. *Faces of Our Time.* 1971. Toronto. 48 full-p portraits. gilt bl buckram. dj. B14. $250.00

KARSH, Yousuf. *Faces of Our Time.* 1971. Toronto. 1st. 48 portraits. 203p. G/G. A8. $50.00

KARSH, Yousuf. *In Search of Greatness.* 1962. np. 1st. 8vo. 210p. VG/G. A8. $50.00

KARSH, Yousuf. *Karsh American Legends.* 1992. 1st. 88 photos. 159p. F/F. A8. $45.00

KARSH, Yousuf. *Karsh Portfolio.* 1967. 1st. 203p. VG/worn. A8. $50.00

KARSH, Yousuf. *Karsh: Fifty Year Perspective.* 1983. Boston. 1st. sgn. VG/VG. B5. $75.00

KARSH, Yousuf. *Portraits of Greatness.* 1959. Toronto. 1st. folio. 96 portraits. 208p. F/G+. A8. $120.00

KARSNER, David. *Debs: His Authorized Life & Letters From Woodstock Prison...* 1919. Boni Liveright. 1st. VG. V4. $50.00

KARSNER, David. *Talks With Debs in Terre Haute.* 1922. NY. NY Call. 1st. VG. B2. $65.00

KASDAN, Sara. *Mazel Tov Y'All.* 1968. Vanguard. G/dj. A16. $15.00

KASER, David. *Book for a Sixpence: Circulating Lib in America.* 1980. Beta Phi Mu. 1/3000. 194p. A17. $17.50

KASHNER, Rita. *Bed Rest.* 1981. Macmillan. 1st. author's 1st novel. F/F. R13. $25.00

KASTNER, Erich. *Der Gestiefelte Kater (Puss in Boots).* 1950. Munchen. Europaischer Kulturkreis. ils Walter Trier. pres. dj. R5. $150.00

KASTNER, Erich. *Puss in Boots.* 1957. Messner. 1st Am. ils Walter Trier. 66p. VG+/VG-. P2. $55.00

KATES, George. *Chinese Household Furniture.* 1948. Harper. 1st. 125p. VG. W3. $86.00

KATO, Ken. *Yamata: A Rage in Heaven.* 1990. NY. Warner. 1st. F/F. T12. $15.00

KATZ, D. Mark. *Custer in Photographs.* 1990. NY. Bonanza. 2nd. ils. 141p. brd. dj. D11. $60.00

KATZ, Friedrich. *Ancient American Civilizations.* 1972. NY. Praeger. 1st Eng. 386p. dj. F3. $30.00

KATZ, John. *Death by Station Wagon.* 1993. Doubleday. 1st. F/dj. M15. $45.00

KATZ, Jonathan. *Resistance at Christiana: Fugitive Slave Rebellion...* 1974. NY. Crowell. 1st. 359p. F/F. B4. $75.00

KATZ, Sali Barnett. *Hispanic Furniture: An American Collection From Southwest.* 1986. Architectural Book Pub. 4to. 224p. M/dj. T10. $35.00

KATZ, Sander. *Freud on Sex & Neurosis.* 1949. Garden City. rpt. 216p. VG. A25. $8.00

KATZ, Steve. *Saw.* 1972. Knopf. 1st. F. M2. $10.00

KATZENBACH, John. *Day of Reckoning.* 1989. Putnam. 1st. NF/F. T12. $15.00

KATZENBACH, John. *Traveler.* 1987. Putnam. 1st. F/F. T12. $15.00

KAUCHER, Dorothy. *James Duval Phelan, a Portrait 1861-1930.* 1965. Saratoga. Montalvo Assoc. sgn. 53p. VG/prt wrp. K7. $15.00

KAUFFMAN, Henry J. *American Pewterer.* 1970. 1st. photos. NF/VG+. S13. $20.00

KAUFFMAN, Henry J. *American Pewterer.* 1970. NY. Nelson. 1st. sgn. F/F. B11. $35.00

KAUFFMAN, Janet. *Body in Four Parts.* 1993. Graywolf. 1st. F/F. R13. $20.00

KAUFFMAN, Janet. *Collaborators.* 1986. Knopf. 1st. F/F. R13. $20.00

KAUFFMAN, Janet. *Obscene Gestures for Women.* 1989. Knopf. 1st. F/NF. R13. $15.00

KAUFFMAN, Janet. *Places in the World a Woman Could Walk.* 1983. Knopf. 1st. F/F. R13. $40.00

KAUFFMAN, Reginald Wright. *Share & Share Alike.* 1925. Chelsea. 1st. VG/dj. M2. $25.00

KAUFFMAN, Russell. *Chihuahua.* 1952. Judy. 1st. 158p. dj. A17. $15.00

KAUFMAN, Fred S. *Custer Passed Our Way.* nd. Aberdeen, SD. North Plains. sc. A19. $15.00

KAUFMAN, Frederick. *Forty-Two Days & Nights on Iberian Peninsula...* 1987. HBJ. 1st. F/F. H11. $40.00

KAUFMAN, William I. *Art of Creole Cookery.* 1962. NY. Doubleday. ils Margot Tomes. VG/dj. A16. $12.00

KAULA, Edna Mason. *First Book of Australia.* 1960. Franklin Watts. 2nd. 8vo. VG/dj. M5. $18.00

KAVANAGH, Dan; see Barnes, Julian.

KAVANAUGH, James. *Crooked Angel.* 1970. LA. Nash. 1st. ils Elaine Havelock. 48p. F/F. D4. $30.00

KAWABATA, Yasunari. *Snow Country & Thousand Cranes.* 1969. Knopf. Novel Prize ed. 147p. VG/dj. W3. $52.00

KAWABATA, Yasunari. *Sound of the Mountain.* 1970. Knopf. 1st. 276p. F/dj. W3. $42.00

KAY, Gertrude Alice. *Adventures in Geography.* 1930 (1929). Volland. 1st. 157p. VG+/ragged. M20. $40.00

KAY, Gertrude Alice. *Helping the Weatherman.* 1920. Volland. 1st. 8vo. ils brd/matching pub box. R5. $200.00

KAY, Gertrude Alice. *Us Kids & the Circus.* 1927. Buzza (Gordon Volland). 3rd. 8vo. pict brd. pict pub box. R5. $200.00

KAY, Terry. *After Eli.* 1981. Houghton Mifflin. 1st. inscr. F/F. B4. $100.00

KAY, Terry. *To Dance With the White Dog.* 1990. Peachtree. 1st. F/F. B4. $65.00

KAY, William J. *Complete Book of Dog Health.* 1985. Macmillan. 1st. F/F. W2. $30.00

KAYE, Mollie. *Willow Witches Brook.* 1944. London. Collins. 1st. ils Margaret Tempest. 12mo. 46p. pict brd. R5. $100.00

KAYS, John M. *Horse: A Complete Guide to Its Care & Handling.* 1982. NY. Arco. 3rd. VG/G. O3. $22.00

KAYSER, Jacques. *Dreyfus Affair.* 1931. Covici Friede. 1st. 432p. G. B14. $45.00

KAZAN, Elia. *Acts of Love.* 1978. Knopf. sgn. NF/dj. C9. $75.00

KAZANTZAKIS, Nikos. *Spain.* 1963. S&S. 1st. F/NF. M19. $35.00

KAZANTZAKIS, Nikos. *Symposium.* 1974. Crowell. 1st. F/F. B35. $18.00

KEAN, Robert Garlick Hill. *Inside the Confederate Government.* 1957. 1st. 241p. dj. O8. $21.50

KEARNEY, Julian; see Goulart, Ron.

KEARNEY & PEEBLES. *Flowering Plants & Ferns of Arizona.* 1942. GPO. 1st. 8vo. gr buckram. VG. A22. $45.00

KEARNS, Frank. *Rin Tin Tin.* 1953. Whitman. 1st. 8vo. unp. pict brd. G+. T5. $15.00

KEARSE, Amalya. *Bridge Conventions Complete Revised & Expanded...* 1984. Louisville. 813p. VG. S1. $12.00

KEARTON, C. *My Friend Toto: Adventures of a Chimpanzee...* 1926. NY. Dodd Mead. 12mo. ils/photos. 110p. cloth. VG. M12. $15.00

KEARTON, Richard. *With Nature & a Camera: Being Adventures & Observations...* 1899. London. Cassell. 5th thousand. ils Cherry Kearton. teg. VG. H7. $35.00

KEATING, Bern. *Illustrated History of the Texas Rangers.* 1908 (1975). Promontory. 4to. F/VG+. C8. $25.00

KEATING, Bern. *Invaders of Rome.* 1966. Putnam. dj. A19. $15.00

KEATING, H.R.F. *Underside.* 1974. London. Macmillan. 1st. F/F. T12. $20.00

KEATING, H.R.F. *Whodunit? A Guide to Crime, Suspense & Spy Fiction.* 1982. Van Nostrand Reinhold. 1st Am. F/dj. M15. $35.00

KEATING, William. *By Laws: Philadelphia Society for Promoting Agriculture.* ca 1819. Phil Soc. disbound. A10. $20.00

KEATINGE, Maurice. *True History of Conquest of Mexico.* 1927. rpt 1800 London 1st. ils. 562p. cloth. F3. $25.00

KEATS, Ezra Jack. *Snowy Day.* 1962. Viking. 1st/12th prt. obl 4to. VG. T5. $17.00

KEATS, John. *Collected Sonnets of...* 1930. Maastricht. Halcyon. 1/35. ils/sgn John Buckland Wright. unbound as issued. B24. $1,250.00

KEATS, John. *Letters of John Keats to Fanny Brawne.* 1878. Scribner Armstrong. 1st Am. teg. bl cloth. M24. $275.00

KEATS, John. *Poems of..., Selected, Edited & Introduced by Aileen Ward.* 1966. Cambridge. LEC. 1/1500. ils/sgn David Gentleman. F/case. B24. $85.00

KEATS, John. *Poetical Works...* 1920. London. facsimile title p of early works. 12mo. teg. leather. H3. $75.00

KEBABIAN, John S. *Henry S Taylor Collection.* 1971. Yale. gilt bdg. F. O7. $20.00

KEEL, B.C. *Cherokee Archaeology: Study of Appalachian Summit.* 1987. TN U. ils/maps. 312p. F. M4. $25.00

KEEL-SMITH, Hilda. *My Drawing Book Step One.* 1929. 1st. ils. VG+. S13. $20.00

KEELER, Harry Stephen. *Sing Sing Nights.* nd (1928). London. Hutchinson. 1st. VG. A17. $15.00

KEELING, J. *Ask of the Beasts.* 1960. London. Blond. ils/photos. 203p. NF/VG. M12. $15.00

KEEN, Mary. *Garden Border Book.* 1987. Deer Park, WI. ils. 153p. F/dj. B26. $21.00

KEEN, Mary. *Glory of the English Garden.* 1989. 1st Am. photos. VG/VG. M17. $30.00

KEEN, Sam. *Faces of the Enemy: Reflections of the Hostile Imagination.* 1986. Harper Row. 1st. VG/VG. V4. $17.50

KEEN, W.W. *Surgery: Its Principles & Practice by Various Authors.* 1906-1921. Phil. 1st/1st prt. 8 vol (includes index/2 supp vol). A13. $400.00

KEENAN, Brian. *Evil Cradling: Five-Year Ordeal of a Hostage.* 1992. Viking. 1st Am. 297p. VG/dj. W1. $18.00

KEENE, Carolyn. *Dana Girls: In the Shadow of the Tower (#3).* 1934. Grosset Dunlap. 1st. purple cloth. VG/ragged. M20. $95.00

KEENE, Carolyn. *Dana Girls: Light of the Study Lamp (#1).* 1934. Grosset Dunlap. 214p. VG/dj (lists 9 titles). M20. $35.00

KEENE, Carolyn. *Dana Girls: Riddle of the Frozen Fountain (#26).* 1964. Grosset Dunlap. 173p. lists 25 titles. VG. M20. $20.00

KEENE, Carolyn. *Nancy Drew Cookbook.* 1973. Grosset Dunlap. 1st. F. A16/T12. $20.00

KEENE, Carolyn. *Nancy Drew: Clue in the Ancient Disguise (#60).* 1982. Wanderer. 1st. 206p. VG/dj. M20. $25.00

KEENE, Carolyn. *Nancy Drew: Clue in the Old Stagecoach (#37).* 1960. Grosset Dunlap. 1st. 180p. cloth. VG+/dj. M20. $125.00

KEENE, Carolyn. *Nancy Drew: Clue of the Black Keys (#28).* 1954 (1951). Grosset Dunlap. B prt. 214p. VG/dj (lists 31 titles). M20. $25.00

KEENE, Carolyn. *Nancy Drew: Haunted Bridge (#15).* 1939 (1937). Grosset Dunlap. B prt. 220p. VG+/dj. M20. $85.00

KEENE, Carolyn. *Nancy Drew: Haunted Showboat (#35).* 1957. Grosset Dunlap. 2nd. 184p. cloth. VG/dj (lists to this title). M20. $55.00

KEENE, Carolyn. *Nancy Drew: Mystery at the Ski Jump (#29).* 1952. Grosset Dunlap. 1st. 212p. VG/dj. M20. $60.00

KEENE, Carolyn. *Nancy Drew: Mystery of the Fire Dragon (#38).* 1961. Grosset Dunlap. 2nd. 182p. cloth. VG/dj. M20. $50.00

KEENE, Carolyn. *Nancy Drew: Nancy's Mysterious Letter (#8).* (1932). Grosset Dunlap. 7th (1933C). 209p. VG/dj. M20. $250.00

KEENE, Carolyn. *Nancy Drew: Secret of Red Gate Farm (#6).* 1931. Grosset Dunlap. 1st. 208p. VG+. M20. $50.00

KEENE, Carolyn. *Nancy Drew: Secret of Shadow Ranch (#5).* 1931. Grosset Dunlap. 1st. VG+. M20. $50.00

KEENE, Carolyn. *Nancy Drew: Secret of the Old Clock (#1).* 1930. Grosset Dunlap. 4th (1930D)/blank ep format. VG/tattered. M20. $350.00

KEENE, Carolyn. *Nancy Drew: Sign of the Twisted Candles (#9).* 1933. Grosset Dunlap. 217p. VG/dj (lists 12 titles). M20. $300.00

KEENE, Carolyn. *Nancy Drew: Witch Tree Symbol (#33).* 1955. Grosset Dunlap. 1st. 213p. VG/dj (lists to this title). M20. $85.00

KEENE, Donald. *Landscapes & Portraits.* 1971. Tokyo. Kodansha. 1st/2nd prt. 343p. F/dj. W3. $45.00

KEENE, Donald. *World Within Walls: Japanese Literature...1600-1867.* 1976. NY. 1st. 606p. F/dj. W3. $65.00

KEENE, James. *Iron Man, Iron Horse.* 1960. Doubleday. 1st. F/F. B4. $75.00

KEENEY, M. *Cow Philosophy: The Art of Practical Dairy Practice.* 1949 (1940). VG. E6. $20.00

KEEP, Rosalind A. *Fourscore Years: History of Mills College.* 1932. Mills College. 1st. 1/990. inscr. F. O4. $30.00

KEEPING, Charles. *Joseph's Yard.* 1969. Franklin Watts. 1st Am. ils. 4to. VG+/VG. P2. $35.00

KEEPING, Charles. *Joseph's Yard.* 1969. Franklin Watts. 1st Am. NF. C8. $22.50

KEEPING, Charles. *Tinker Tailor Folk Song Tales.* 1969. World. stated 1st Am. sm 4to. unp. F/NF clip. C14. $25.00

KEESE, John. *Floral Keepsake, With 30 Engravings...* nd. NY. Leavitt Allen. 111p. gilt cloth. VG. M20. $150.00

KEESE, John. *Poets of America.* 1840. NY. Samuel Colman. 1st/1st prt/1st state title p (gold). 1st bdg. M24. $300.00

KEETON, George W. *English Law, the Judicial Contribution.* 1974. Newton Abbot. M11. $50.00

KEHRER, Daniel M. *Profits in Precious Metals.* 1985. Times. 1st. 302p. NF/NF. W2. $30.00

KEILLOR, Garrison. *Book of Guys.* 1993. Viking. 1st. sgn. F/F. R13. $35.00

KEILLOR, Garrison. *Lake Wobegon Days.* 1985. Viking. 1st. F/dj. N4/R14. $40.00

KEIM, D.B.R. *Sheridan's Troopers on Borders: Winter Campaign on Plains.* 1870. Claxton Remsen Haffelfinger. 308p. cloth. VG. M20. $50.00

KEIR, James. *Account of the Life & Writings of Thomas Day, Esq.* 1791. London. Stockdale. 8vo. 144p. H13. $95.00

KEITH, Agnes. *Bare Feet in the Palace.* 1955. Little Brn. 370p. NF/VG. W3. $38.00

KEITH, Harold. *Rifles for Waitie.* 1957. Crowell. 1st. Newbery Medal. NF/VG+. P2. $125.00

KEITH, Lloyd. *Wildlife's Ten-Year Cycle.* 1963. WI. 201p. F/VG. S15. $15.00

KEITHLEY, George. *Donnor Party.* 1972. Braziller. 1st. VG/G+. O4. $15.00

KELEMEN, P. *Art of the Americas.* 1969. NY. Crowell. G. A19. $15.00

KELLAND, Clarence Budington. *Mark Tidd, Editor.* 1934 (1917). Harper. 8vo. 286p. red cloth. VG+/G+. t5. $15.00

KELLAR, P.H. *Seth Bullock's Founding of a County.* 1986. Deadwood, SD. Dakota Graphics. A19. $15.00

KELLEMS, Vivien. *Toil, Taxes & Trouble.* 1952. NY. Dutton. 1st. sgn. NF/NF-. T11. $45.00

KELLER, A.G. *Theatre of Machine.* 1965. Macmillan. 1st thus. 52 woodcuts. xl. K3. $30.00

KELLER, David H. *Death & the Doctor.* 1940. S&S. 1st. VG. M2. $45.00

KELLER, Frances Ruth. *Curious Little Owl.* nd (1957). Platt Munk. unp. NF/VG+. C14. $20.00

KELLER, Kenneth. *Seth Bullock, Frontier Marshall.* 1972. North Plains. 1st. 191p. VG/dj. J2. $65.00

KELLERMAN, Faye. *Ritual Bath.* 1986. Arbor. 1st. author's 1st book. F/F. N4. $125.00

KELLERMAN, Jonathan. *Butcher's Theater.* 1986. Bantam. 1st. F/NF. N4. $35.00

KELLERMAN, Jonathan. *When the Bough Breaks.* 1985. Atheneum. 1st. NF/dj. M25. $100.00

KELLERMAN, Jonathan. *When the Bough Breaks.* 1985. NY. Atheneum. 1st. author's 1st book. F/F. H11. $140.00

KELLEY, Kitty. *Nancy Reagan.* 1991. S&S. 1st. NF/NF. W2. $35.00

KELLEY, Leo P. *Time 110100.* 1972. Walker. 1st. NF/dj. M2. $15.00

KELLEY, William Melvin. *Different Drummer.* 1962. Garden City. 1st. F/NF. A11. $125.00

KELLOGG, Charles. *Driving the Horse in Harness.* 1980. Brattleboro. Stephen Greene. VG/VG. O3. $18.00

KELLOGG, Charlotte. *Women of Belgium: Turning Tragedy to Triumph.* 1917. Funk Wagnalls. 3rd. ils. 210p. A25. $35.00

KELLOGG, Edward. *New Monetary System: Only Means of Securing...Rights...* 1861. NY. Rudd Carleton. 1st. 12mo. 366p. cloth. M1. $175.00

KELLOGG, Robert H. *Giving a Complete History of Inhuman & Barbarous Treatment.* 1965. Hartford, CT. Stebbens. 399p. gilt leather. G+. M20. $40.00

KELLOGG, Stephen. *Aster Aardvark's Alphabet Adventures.* nd. Morrow. 1st. inscr. F/dj. M25. $25.00

KELLOGG, Steven. *Johnny Appleseed: A Tale Retold & Ils by Steven Kellogg.* 1988. Morrow Jr Books. 1st. 4to. unp. F/F. C14. $18.00

KELLOGG, Steven. *Liverwurst Is Missing.* 1981. Four Winds. 1st. VG+/VG. P2. $30.00

KELLOGG, Vernon. *Muova the Bee.* 1920. Houghton Mifflin. ils Milo Winter/14 b&w pl. VG-. P2. $40.00

KELLOGG & THWAITES. *Documentary History of Dunmore's War 1774.* 1905. Madison. 1st. 1/1000. ils/fld map. 472p. G+. B18. $125.00

KELLOGG & THWAITES. *Revolution on the Upper Ohio, 1775-1777.* 1908. Madison. 1st. 275p. VG. B18. $125.00

KELLY, C. *Journal of Fray Martin de Munills...* 1966. Cambridge. 2 vol. ils/maps. F/dj. M4. $35.00

KELLY, Charles. *Holy Murder: Porter Rockwell, Chief of Danites.* 1934. NY. Minton Balch. 1st. ils/index. 313p. VG. B5. $35.00

KELLY, Eric. *Treasure Mountain.* 1937. Macmillan. 1st. 211p. VG/G. P2. $20.00

KELLY, J. Reaney. *Quakers in the Founding of Anne Arundel County, MD.* 1963. Baltimore. MD Hist Soc. 1st. 146p. VG/dj. V3. $40.00

KELLY, J.B. *Arabia, the Gulf & the West.* 1980. NY. Basic. 1st Am. 8vo. 5 maps. cloth. xl. VG. W1. $30.00

KELLY, J.M. *Roman Litigation.* 1966. Clarenton. M11. $85.00

KELLY, John. *All Soul's Night.* 1947. Harcourt Brace. 1st. author's 1st book. F/NF. B4. $125.00

KELLY, Walt. *Deck Us All With Boston Charlie.* 1962. NY. 1st. NF/wrp. A11. $50.00

KELLY, Walt. *Pogo Primer for Parents.* 1961. WA. 1st. 24p. VG+/wrp. A11. $60.00

KELLY, Walt. *Songs of Pogo.* 1956. NY. 1st hc. inscr pres. 152p. NF/NF. A11. $375.00

KELLY, Walt. *Songs of Pogo.* 1956. NY. 1st. VG/VG. B5. $60.00

KELMAN, James. *Chancer.* 1985. Polygon. 1st. sgn. F/F. A24. $85.00

KELMAN, James. *Disaffection.* 1989. FSG. 1st Am. F/dj. A24. $40.00

KELSEY, Charles. *Diseases of the Rectum & Anus.* 1882. NY. 1st. 483p. A13. $100.00

KEMAL, Yashar. *Seagull.* 1981. NY. 250p. F/dj. W3. $30.00

KEMBLE, Edward W. *Blackberries & Their Adventures.* 1897. NY. Russell. 1st. obl 4to. pict brd. R5. $975.00

KEMELMAN, Harry. *Day the Rabbi Resigned.* 1992. Fawcett. 1st. F/F. N4. $20.00

KEMELMAN, Harry. *Nine Mile Walk.* 1967. Putnam. 1st. F/dj. M15. $60.00

KEMELMAN, Harry. *Nine Mile Walk.* 1967. Putnam. 1st. VG+/NF. N4. $15.00

KEMELMAN, Harry. *Thursday the Rabbi Walked Out.* 1978. Putnam. 1st. F/F. T12. $35.00

KEMP, J.F. *Handbook of Rocks for Use Without the Microscope...* 1911. Van Nostrand. 272p. G. D8. $22.00

KENAN, Randall. *Visitation of Spirits.* 1989. Grove. 1st. author's 1st book. dj. A24/L1. $35.00

KENDALL, Phebe Mitchell. *Maria Mitchell: Life, Letters, Journals.* 1896. Lee Shepard. 300p. cloth. G. K5. $150.00

KENDELL, Elizabeth. *Wayfarer in China.* 1913. Houghton Mifflin. 1st. gilt cloth. VG. W3. $115.00

KENDRAKE, Carleton; see Gardner, Erle Stanley.

KENDRICK, Dolores. *Women of Plums: Poems in Voices of Slave Women.* 1989. Morrow. 1st. NF/prt wrp. M25. $35.00

KENDRICK, Douglas. *Blood Program in World War II: Medical Dept, US Army.* 1964. WA, DC. 1st. 922p. A13. $75.00

KENEALLY, Thomas. *Family Madness.* 1986. S&S. 1st Am. rem mk. F/F. R14. $25.00

KENEALLY, Thomas. *Ned Kelly & the City of Bees.* 1981. Godine. 1st Am. 120p. VG/VG. P2. $30.00

KENEALLY, Thomas. *Schindler's List.* 1982. S&S. 1st Am. F/clip. D10. $125.00

KENEALLY, Thomas. *Season in Purgatory.* 1977. HBJ. 1st Am. F/F. D10. $40.00

KENEALLY, Thomas. *Victim of the Aurora.* 1978. HBJ. 1st. author's 11th novel. NF/clip. D10. $40.00

KENG, Hsuan. *Orders & Families of Malayan Seed Plants.* 1978. Singapore. revised. 8vo. 437p. A22. $35.00

KENNAN, A. *Phoenix of the West, a Study...* 1961. 1st Am. VG/VG. E6. $13.00

KENNEALY, Jerry. *Polo Anyone?* 1988. NY. 1st. F/F. H11. $35.00

KENNEDY, A.E. *Somebody's Darlings.* ca 1925. London. Juvenile Prod. 4to. 40p. dj. R5. $85.00

KENNEDY, A.E. *Ten Little Kittens & Ten Little Dogs.* ca 1952. London. Juvenile Prod. pict brd. dj. R5. $85.00

KENNEDY, J.P. *Horse-Shoe Robinson.* 1839. London. TL Holt. 8vo. plain wrp/prt paper label. M1. $150.00

KENNEDY, Jimmy. *Teddy Bears' Picnic.* 1983. La Jolla. Gr Tiger. 1st/1st prt. ils/sgn Alexandra Day. 32p. F/sans. D4. $30.00

KENNEDY, John F. *Burden & the Glory.* 1964. Harper. 1st. VG+/dj. A20. $25.00

KENNEDY, William. *Ink Truck.* 1984. Viking. 1st thus. sgn. F/F. B3. $40.00

KENNEDY, William. *Ironweed.* 1983. Viking. 1st. F/NF. B4. $150.00

KENNEDY, William. *Ironwood.* 1983. Viking. 1st. author's 4th novel. F/F. D10. $200.00

KENNEDY, William. *Legs.* 1975. CMG. 1st. author's 2nd novel. VG/G. M22. $50.00

KENNEDY, William. *Legs.* 1975. CMG. 1st. sgn. author's 2nd novel. F/clip. D10. $175.00

KENNEDY, William. *Legs.* 1975. NY. CMG. 1st. author's 2nd novel. F/F. R13. $175.00

KENNEDY, William. *O Albany!* 1983. Viking. 1st. sgn. F/F. D10. $110.00

KENNEDY, William. *Sport in the Navy & Naval Yarns.* 1902. Westminster. Constable. 8vo. 317p. gilt bl cloth. VG/NF. T10. $75.00

KENNEDY, William. *Very Old Bones.* 1992. Viking. 1st. sgn. F/F. R13. $45.00

KENNEDY, X.J. *Forgetful Wishing Well.* 1985. Atheneum. 1st. ils Monica Incisa. NF/dj. D4. $35.00

KENNEDY, X.J. *One Winter Night in August & Other Nonsense Jingles.* 1975. Atheneum. 1st. ils David McPhail. F/F. D4. $40.00

KENNEDY & KENNEDY. *Charlie Malarky & the Belly Button Machine.* 1986. Atlantic Monthly. 1st. sgn. F/NF. B3. $75.00

KENNEDY CENTER. *Kennedy Center Performing Artists Cookbook.* 1973. VG/VG. A16. $15.00

KENNEY, Susan. *In Another Country.* 1984. Viking. 1st. VG. T12. $15.00

KENRICK, Baynard. *Florida Trails to Turnpikes 1914-1964.* 1964. Gainesville. inscr. VG/G acetate dj/VG gold case. B11. $85.00

KENSHALO, Dan R. *Skin Sense: Proceedings of First International Symposium...* 1968. Springfield, IL. Chas Thomas. 636p. VG/dj. G1. $50.00

KENT, Austin. *Free Love; or, Philosophical Demonstration...* 1857. Hopkinton, NY. 1st. 16mo. 140p. cloth. M1. $400.00

KENT, Henry Watson. *What I Am Pleased To Call My Education.* 1949. NY. Grolier. 1/1025. is. VG. K3. $20.00

KENT, Jack. *Christmas Pinata.* 1975. Parents. 1st. obl 8vo. NF. C8. $22.50

KENT, Patricia. *American Woman & Alcohol.* 1967. HRW. 1st. 184p. VG/dj. A25. $18.00

KENT, Rockwell. *N By E.* 1936. NY. sgn. 281p. VG/dj. B14. $100.00

KENT, Rockwell. *Voyaging: Southward From Straits of Magellan.* 1924. NY. Putnam. 1st. 69 woodcuts. 4to. tan cloth. T7. $120.00

KENTUCKY GENERAL ASSEMBLY. *Acts of the General Assembly of Commonwealth of Kentucky...* 1861. Frankfort, KY. JB Major, State Prt. 1st. 271p. later cloth. VG. M8. $150.00

KEPHART, Horace. *Camp Cookery.* 1910. Outing. 1st. 154p. VG. E6. $25.00

KEPHART, Horace. *Camping & Woodcraft: A Handbook for Vacation Campers...* 1937. Macmillan. 2 vol in 1. VG/dj. H7. $20.00

KEPLER, Angela K. *Proteas in Hawaii.* 1988. Honolulu. photos. sc. as new. B26. $10.00

KEPLER, William. *History of the Three Months' & Three Years' Service.* 1886. Cleveland, OH. 287p. pub cloth. VG. B18. $150.00

KER, N.R. *Medieval Manuscripts in British Libraries: I, London.* 1969. Clarendon. 437p+10 pl. xl. A17. $20.00

KERANS & PHILLIPS. *Escape of the Amethyst.* 1957. London/NY. photos/drawings. 274p. dj. T7. $22.00

KERCHEVER, Edmund. *History: Motives of Literary Forgeries.* 1970 (1891). rpt. 37p. VG+. K3. $15.00

KERENYI, Charles. *Asklepios: Archetypal Image of the Physician's Existence.* 1960. Lodnon. 1st Eng trans. 139p. A13. $125.00

KERFOOT, J.B. *American Pewter.* 1924. Houghton Mifflin. 1st. 4to. 239p. VG. T10. $125.00

KERFOOT & SIH. *Predation.* 1987. U Pr New Eng. 386p. F. S15. $15.00

KERLIN, Robert Thomas. *Negro Poets & Their Poems.* 1935. WA. Assoc Pub. 3rd/revised. 342p. NF/NF. B2. $200.00

KERNER VON MARILAUN, Anton. *Natural History of Plants.* 1895. London. 2 vol in 4. 4to. ils. cloth. B26. $100.00

KERNODLE, George. *From Art to Theatre: Form & Convention in the Renaissance.* 1947. Chicago. 3rd. 255p. A17. $20.00

KEROUAC, Jack. *Book of Dreams.* 1961. San Francisco. 1st. 1/5000. VG+. A11. $115.00

KEROUAC, Jack. *Dharma Bums.* 1958. Viking. 1st. F/NF. D10. $475.00

KEROUAC, Jack. *On the Road.* 1957. Viking. 2nd. sgn. silvered blk cloth. G. B11. $150.00

KERR, Alvin. *Family Cookbook: French.* 1973. Ridge. G/dj. A16. $15.00

KERR, Graham. *Galloping Gourmet.* 1970. Fremantle Internat. G. A16. $7.00

KERR, Jessica. *Shakespare's Flowers.* 1969. ils AO Dowden. ils. VG/VG. M17. $20.00

KERR, Mary Brandt. *America: A Regional Cookbook.* nd. NJ. Chartwell. VG/dj. A16. $15.00

KERR, Philip. *Dead Meat.* 1993. Chatto Windus. true 1st. F/F. B3. $40.00

KERR, Philip. *March Violets.* 1989. Viking. 1st. NF/dj. M25. $35.00

KERR, Philip. *Philosophical Investigation.* 1992. FSG. 1st Am. F/F. M25. $25.00

KERR, William F. *Ministers' Research Service.* 1970. Tyndale. 854p. F. B29. $12.00

KERROD, Robbin. *Mission Outer Space.* 1980 (1979). Minneapolis. Lerner. revised. xl. K5. $5.00

KERSHAW. *Bibliography of Works of Richard Aldington 1915-1948.* 1950. London. 68p. F/F. A4. $175.00

KESEY, Ken. *Further Inquiry.* 1990. Viking. 1st. F/F. B35. $25.00

KESEY, Ken. *One Flew Over the Cuckoo's Nest.* 1962. Viking. 1st. author's 1st book. F/VG+. B4. $1,000.00

KESEY, Ken. *Sailor Song.* 1992. Viking. 1st. sgn. F/F. A18. $50.00

KESHISHIAN, Mark. *Guide to Oriental Rugs.* 1970. self pub. 1st. sgn pres. ils/maps. 134p. VG/dj. W1. $65.00

KESSELL, John L. *Good News From Outer Space.* 1989. Tor. 1st. F/dj. M2. $27.00

KESSELL, John L. *Mission of Sorrows: Jesuit Guevavi & the Pimas 1691-1767.* 1970. AZ U. 1st. ils/notes/index. 224p. NF/VG+. B19. $75.00

KESSLER, Henry H. *Accidental Injuries: Medico-Legal Aspects...* 1932. Phil. lea Febiger. 2nd. heavy 8vo. VG. G1. $85.00

KETCHAM, Henry. *Oriental Fairy Tales.* ca 1915. NY. Burt. sm 8vo. ils/pl. 365p. VG. W1. $20.00

KETCHUM, Richard. *Will Rogers: The Man & His Times.* 1973. Am Heritage. 415p. paisley bdg. as new/dj. H1. $20.00

KETTELL, Russell Hawkes. *Pine Furniture of Early New England.* 1929. photos. VG. M17. $75.00

KETTER, David. *Imprisoned in a Tesseract: Life & Works of James Blish.* 1987. Kent State. 1st. F/dj. M2. $35.00

KEUTNER, Herbert. *Sculpture: Renaissance to Rococo.* 1969. ils. VG/VG. M17. $25.00

KEVLES, Daniel J. *Physicists: History of a Scientific Community...* 1979. Vintage. 489p. NF/wrp. K3. $9.00

KEW, W.S.W. *Cretaceous & Cenozoic Echinoidea of Pacific Coast...* 1920. Berkeley. ils/pl/figures. VG/wrp. M12. $37.50

KEY, Alexander. *Wrath & the Wind.* 1949. Bobbs Merrill. 1st. F/VG+. B4. $75.00

KEY, Astley Cooper. *Narrative of Recovery of HMS Gorgon...* 1847. London. Smith Elder. 8vo. 114p. emb bl cloth. P4. $295.00

KEY, Ted. *Hazel.* 1947. Dutton. 3rd. sgn. VG+/dj. C9. $50.00

KEYES, Frances Parkinson. *All Flags Flying.* 1972. NY. 1st. VG/G. B5. $22.50

KEYES, Frances Parkinson. *All This Is Louisiana.* 1950. Harper. inscr by author to Taylor Caldwell. 317p. VG/dj. M20. $75.00

KEYES, Frances Parkinson. *Joy Street.* 1950. Messner. 1st. 490p. cloth. VG/dj. M20. $25.00

KEYES, Josa. *Teddy Bear Story.* 1985. Gallery Books. stated 1st Am. 96p. glossy brd. F/dj. M5. $22.00

KEYES, Thomas E. *History of Surgical Anesthesia.* 1945. ils. VG. M17. $25.00

KEYHOE, Donald E. *Flying With Lindbergh.* 1928. Putnam. 1st. VG/VG. C8. $22.50

KEYNES, Geoffrey. *Apologie & Treatise of Ambroise Pare.* 1952. Chicago. 1st. 8vo. 227p. VG/dj. K3. $45.00

KEYNES, Geoffrey. *Bibliography of Dr John Donne, Dean of St Paul's.* 1958. Cambridge. 3rd. ils. 315p. xl. VG. A4. $85.00

KEYNES, Geoffrey. *Bibliography of Rupert Brooke.* 1964. London. 3rd/revised. ils. 158p. F/VG. A4. $125.00

KEYNES, Geoffrey. *Blood Transfusion.* 1949. Baltimore. 1st Am. 574p. A13. $75.00

KEYNES, Geoffrey. *Study of Illuminated Books of William Blake, Poet...* 1964. NY/Paris. Trianon. 4to. 31p pl. 103p. F/dj. B24. $100.00

KEYNES, John Maynard. *Keynes, Cambridge & the General Theory.* 1978. Toronto/Buffalo. 8vo. 182p. VG/dj. K3. $15.00

KGOSITILE, Keorapetse. *My Name Is Afrika.* 1971. Doubleday. 1st. F/NF. B4. $125.00

KHAYYAM, Omar. *Rubaiyat.* 1909. NY/London. Hodder Stoughton. ils Dulac/20 tipped-in pl. VG. T10. $350.00

KHERDIAN, David. *Settling America, the Ethnic Expression...* 1974. Macmillan. 1st. 126p. F/NF. D4. $30.00

KHERDIAN, David. *Six Poets of the San Francisco Renaissance.* 1967. Fresno. Giligia. 1st. intro Wm Saroyan. inscr/sgn each of 6 poets. F/F. D10. $265.00

KHOSLA, G. *Himalayan Circuit.* 1956. London. ils/fld map. 233p. VG/dj. W3. $48.00

KICH, C.J. *Year of Living Dangerously.* 1978. St Martin. 1st Am. F/NF. B4. $125.00

KIDD, John. *On the Adaption of External Nature to Physical Condition...* 1852. London. HG Bohn. 6th. 12mo. 332p. VG. K3. $45.00

KIDDER, D.P. *Ancient Egypt: Its Monuments & History.* 1854. NY. Carlton Phillips. 12mo. map ftspc. 214p. VG. T10. $50.00

KIDDER, J. Edward Jr. *Jomon Pottery of Japan.* 1957. Ascona, Switzerland. 51 full-p pl/7 maps. 200p. VG. W3. $325.00

KIDDER, Tracy. *Among School Children.* 1989. Houghton Mifflin. 1st. F/F. A20. $20.00

KIDDER, Tracy. *House.* 1985. Houghton Mifflin. 1st. F/F. A20. $20.00

KIDDER, Tracy. *Road to Yuba City.* 1974. Doubleday. 1st. author's 1st book. NF/VG+. A24. $85.00

KIDDER, Tracy. *Soul of a New Machine.* 1981. Little Brn. 1st. author's 2nd book. F/VG+. A24. $40.00

KIECKEFER, Richard. *European Witch Trials, Their Foundations in...Culture...* 1976. London. Kegan Paul. M11. $50.00

KIEFER. *American Children Through Their Books, 1700-1835.* 1948. PA U. 289p. F/NF. A4. $75.00

KIELTY, Bernardine. *Marie Antoinette (Landmark Book W-20).* 1955. Random. 3rd. sm 8vo. NF/VG. C8. $17.50

KIERAN, John. *American Sporting Scene.* 1941. NY. 1st. 212p. F/G. A17. $15.00

KIES. *Occult in the Western World: Annotated Bibliography.* 1986. 890 entries. 244p. F. A4. $65.00

KIEWE & MARKRICH. *Victorian Fancywork: 19th-Century Needlepoint Patterns...* 1974. Henry Regnery. 1st. 172p. VG+/dj. M20. $25.00

KIGER, Robert. *Kate Greenaway: Catalogue of Exhibition...* 1980. Pittsburgh. Hunt. 106p. VG. A10. $35.00

KIJEWSKI, Karen. *Alley Kat Blues.* 1995. Doubleday. 1st. sgn. F/F. D10. $35.00

KIJEWSKI, Karen. *Copy Kat.* 1992. Doubleday. 1st. F/F. H11/N4. $35.00

KIJEWSKI, Karen. *Kat's Cradle.* 1992. Doubleday. 1st. F/F. N4. $40.00

KIJEWSKI, Karen. *Kat's Cradle.* 1992. Doubleday. 1st. sgn. F/NF. T2. $60.00

KIJEWSKI, Karen. *Katapult.* 1990. NY. 1st. F/F. H11. $90.00

KIJEWSKI, Karen. *Katapult.* 1990. St Martin. 1st. sgn. F/F. M15/M25. $100.00

KIJEWSKI, Karen. *Wild Kat.* 1994. Doubleday. 1st. sgn. VG/VG. A23. $40.00

KIJIMA, Takashi. *Orchids.* 1989. NY. 203 pl. F/dj. S15. $12.00

KIKUCHI, Sadao. *Treasury of Japanese Wood Block Prints: Ukiyo-E.* 1969. NY. Crown. ils. 423p. F/VG. W3. $165.00

KIKUCHI, Takehiko. *Formation & Activities of Kyoto University...* 1970. Hiroshima. ABCC. Historical Note 3. K3. $15.00

KILDUFF, Peter. *That's My Bloody Plane.* 1975. Chester. Pequot. 1st. NF/VG+. T11. $40.00

KILGALLEN, Dorothy. *Girl Around the World.* ca 1936. McKay. 1st. ils. 219p. VG/dj. A25. $22.00

KILLENS, John O. *Cotillion; or, One Good Bull Is Half the Breed.* 1971. Dial. 1st. NF/dj. M25. $60.00

KILLENS, John O. *Youngblood.* 1954. Dial. 1st. inscr/dtd 1955. VG/VG. B4. $225.00

KILLENS, John O. *Youngblood.* 1954. Dial. 1st. 3-pc bdg. VG. M25. $25.00

KILLION, C.E. *Honey in the Comb.* 1951. Paris, IL. Killion. 114p. cloth. B1. $25.00

KILMER, Joyce. *Trees.* 1925. Doran. 1st thus. ils Elizabeth MacKinstry. F/VG. M5. $85.00

KILPATRICK & KILPATRICK. *Shadow of Sequoyah. Social Documents of Cherokees 1862-1964.* 1965. Norman, OK. 1st. F/NF clip. L3. $75.00

KILWORTH, G. *Foxes of First Dark.* 1990. Doubleday. 1st. VG/VG. O3. $15.00

KIM, So-un. *Story Bag: Korean Folktales.* 1955. Rutland/Tokyo. special ed. sgn for Asian BC. 229p. F/VG. W3. $38.00

KIMBALL, Elisabeth. *Cambridgeshire Goal Delivery Roll, 1332-1334.* 1978. Cambridge. Cambridge Antiquarian Records Soc. VG/dj. M11. $50.00

KIMBER, Clarissa. *Martinique Revisited.* 1988. TX A&M. 458p. F. S15. $15.00

KIMBROUGH, Emily. *And a Right Good Crew.* 1958. Harper. 1st. ils Vasiliu. 273p. VG/dj. A25. $12.00

KIMBROUGH, Emily. *Better Than Oceans.* 1976. Harper Row. 1st. 231p. VG/dj. A25. $10.00

KIMBROUGH, Emily. *Floating Island.* 1968. Harper. 1st. sgn. ils Vasiliu. 243p. VG/dj. A25. $20.00

KIMBROUGH, Emily. *Forever Old, Forever New.* 1964. Harper. 1st. ils Vasiliu. 241p. VG/dj. A25. $10.00

KIMBROUGH, Emily. *Now & Then.* 1972. Harper Row. 1st. sgn. ils Vasiliu. 176p. VG/dj. A25. $22.00

KIMES & KIMES. *John Muir: Reading Bibliography.* 1986. Panorama West Books. revised. inscr to LP Powell. ils/index, 179p. VG. B19. $95.00

KIMMEL, Stanley. *Kingdom of Smoke.* 1932. NY. Nicholas Brn. 1st. sgn. VG/VG. B2. $60.00

KIMURA, Motoharu. *Living With Nuclei: 50 Years in the Nuclear Age.* 1993. Sendai Japan. Kimura/Carpenter. ARC/1st. M/wrp. K3. $30.00

KINCAID, Earle H. *History & Cruises of the United States Ship Whipple.* 1920. Constantinople. Zellitch Bros. photos/2 maps. 106p. T7. $45.00

KINCAID, Jamaica. *Annie John.* 1985. FSG. 1st. author's 2nd book. F/NF. B3. $100.00

KINCAID, Jamaica. *At the Bottom of the River.* 1983. FSG. 1st. author's 1st book. F/F. L3. $75.00

KINCAID, Jamaica. *At the Bottom of the River.* 1983. NY. FSG. 1st. sgn. author's 1st book. F/F. D10. $135.00

KINCAID, Jamaica. *Lucy.* 1990. FSG. 1st. F/dj. A24. $35.00

KINCAID, Jamaica. *Lucy.* 1990. FSG. 1st. sgn. F/F. R14. $50.00

KINCAID, Paul. *Camellia Treasury.* 1964. NY. Hearthside. 8vo. 224p. A22. $25.00

KINCAID, Peter. *Rule of the Road: International Guide to History...* 1986. Greenwood. 1st. VG. O3. $35.00

KINCK, Richard E. *Land of Room Enough & Time Enough.* 1953. Albuquerque. 1st. 135p. map ep. pict brd. VG+. F7. $35.00

KINDER, Gary. *Victim.* 1982. Delacorte. 1st. 305p. VG/dj. W2. $20.00

KINDON-WARD, Frank. *Land of the Blue Poppy: Travels of a Naturalist...* 1973. Sakonet, RI. rpt 1913 ed. F/F. W3. $110.00

KING, Alexander. *Peter Altenberg's Evocation of Love.* 1960. S&S. 1st. 175p. F/F. H1. $22.50

KING, Bernard. *Strakadder.* 1985. London. 1st. F/dj. M2. $17.00

KING, Bernard. *Vargr-Moon.* nd. St Martin. 1st. NF/VG. M21. $10.00

KING, Billie Jean. *Billie Jean.* 1974. Harper Row. 1st. photos. VG/VG. P8. $20.00

KING, Blanche Busey. *Under Your Feet: Story of American Mound Builders.* 1948. Dodd Mead. rpt. sgn. VG. B11. $30.00

KING, Charles. *Daughter of the Sioux.* 1903. Hobart. ils Remington. A19. $30.00

KING, Charles. *General's Double.* 1898. Lippincott. A19. $25.00

KING, Charles. *Initial Experience.* 1909. Phil. Lippincott. A19. $35.00

KING, Charles. *Story of Ft Frayne.* 1895. Chicago. F Tennyson Neely. rare. A19. $65.00

KING, Charles. *Tonio, Son of the Sierras.* 1906. Dillingham. 1st. 338p. gray cloth. NF. K7. $45.00

KING, Charles. *Trooper Galahad.* 1899. NF. A4. $25.00

KING, Constance Eileen. *Encyclopedia of Toys.* 1978. Crown. 1st. 272p. NF/clip. C14. $25.00

KING, Coretta Scott. *My Life With Martin Luther King, Jr.* 1969. HRW. 1st. NF/dj. M25. $25.00

KING, David S. *Mountain Meadows Massacre: A Search for Perspective.* 1970. WA. Great Western Series 8. sgn. 8vo. orange brd. VG. F7. $50.00

KING, Dick. *Ghost Towns of Texas.* 1953. Naylor. 1st. cloth. VG/dj. M20. $25.00

KING, Dorothy N. *Take the Children.* 1945. Morrow. 1st. sgn pres. 6 movables. VG. D1. $120.00

KING, Elizabeth T. *Memoir With Extracts From Her Letters & Journal.* 1859. Baltimore. 1st. 128p. G. V3. $18.50

KING, Elmer R. *Handbook of Historical Landmarks of California.* 1938. Los Angeles. 1st. VG/sans. O4. $15.00

KING, Ernest. *Fleet Admiral King: A Naval Record.* 1952. NY. 1st. sgn. 674p. VG/VG. S16. $65.00

KING, H.G.R. *Antarctic.* 1969. NY. Blanford. 8vo. 276p. xl. P4. $16.00

KING, John L. *Trouting on the Brule River.* 1973. Iron Mtn. facsimile 1879 Chicago ed. lib buckram. F. A17. $25.00

KING, Laurie. *Grave Talent.* 1995. London. Harper Collins. 1st. author's 1st book. F/dj. Q1. $100.00

KING, Laurie. *Letter to Mary.* 1996. St Martin. 1st. sgn. F/F. A23. $45.00

KING, Laurie. *Monstrous Regiment of Women.* 1995. St Martin. 1st. sgn. F/F. A23. $50.00

KING, M.J. *William Orlando Darby.* 1981. CT. 1st. ils. 219p. VG/VG. S16. $17.50

KING, Martin Luther Jr. *Trumpet of Conscience.* 1967. NY. Harper. 1st. sgn ML King Sr. 78p. F/NF. B4. $200.00

KING, Martin Luther Jr. *Trumpet of Conscience.* 1968. Harper Row. 1st Am. NF/dj. M25. $50.00

KING, Martin Luther Jr. *Where Do We Go From Here: Chaos or Community?* 1967. Harper Row. 1st. NF/dj. M25. $60.00

KING, Mrs. Francis. *Flower Garden Day by Day.* 1927. NY. Stokes. 1st. 209p. VG+/remnant. A25. $10.00

KING, P.B. *Evolution of North America.* 1977. Princeton. fld map. 197p. NF/dj. D8. $30.00

KING, P.B. *Tectonics of Middle North America, East of Cordilleran...* 1951. princeton. ils/maps. 203p. cloth. G+. M12. $20.00

KING, P.D. *Law & Society in the Visigothic Kingdom.* 1972. Cambridge. orig cloth. remnant dj. M11. $85.00

KING, Rufus. *Murder in the Willett Family.* 1931. Doubleday. 1st/Subscribers Ed. VG/dj. N4. $25.00

KING, Rufus. *Museum Piece No 13.* 1946. Doubleday. 1st. F/NF. M15. $50.00

KING, Stephen. *Bare Bones.* 1988. Underwood Miller. 1st. 1/1000 #d. F/case. M2. $100.00

KING, Stephen. *Carrie.* 1974. Doubleday. 1st. F/NF. B4. $750.00

KING, Stephen. *Carrie.* 1974. Doubleday. 1st. VG-/dj. M2. $200.00

KING, Stephen. *Christine.* 1983. Viking. 1st. VG/VG. P3. $60.00

KING, Stephen. *Cujo.* 1981. Mysterious. 1/750. sgn/#d. F/case. M2. $450.00

KING, Stephen. *Cujo.* 1981. Viking. 1st trade. F/dj. from $50 to $55.00

KING, Stephen. *Cujo.* 1981. Viking. 1st trade. VG/VG. M22. $45.00

KING, Stephen. *Dark Half.* 1989. Viking. 1st. F/F. M22. $30.00

KING, Stephen. *Different Seasons.* 1982. Viking. 1st. F/dj. M2. $75.00

KING, Stephen. *Dolores Claiborne.* 1993. 1st. F/F. W2. $25.00

KING, Stephen. *Eyes of the Dragon.* 1987. Viking. 1st. F/NF. Q1. $35.00

KING, Stephen. *Firestarter.* 1980. Viking. 1st. F/dj. from $65 to $85.00

KING, Stephen. *Firestarter.* 1980. Viking. 1st. NF/VG+. N4. $40.00

KING, Stephen. *Four Past Midnight.* 1990. Viking. 1st. F/F. P3. $25.00

KING, Stephen. *Four Past Midnight.* 1990. Viking. 1st. inscr. F/F. A23. $120.00

KING, Stephen. *Gerald's Game.* 1992. Viking. 1st. inscr. F/F. A23. $90.00

KING, Stephen. *It.* 1986. London. Hodder Stoughton. 1st. F/F. T12. $50.00

KING, Stephen. *It.* 1986. Viking. 1st. F/dj. from $35 to $45.00

KING, Stephen. *Misery.* 1987. Viking. 1st. F/dj. from $40 to $50.00

KING, Stephen. *Needful Things.* 1991. Viking. 1st. F/F. from $25 to $35.00

KING, Stephen. *Needful Things.* 1991. Viking. 1st. inscr. F/F. A23. $120.00

KING, Stephen. *Night Shift.* 1978. Doubleday. 1st. F/F. M2. $675.00

KING, Stephen. *Nightmares in the Sky.* 1988. Viking. 128p. photos Fitzgerald. cloth. VG. A10. $20.00

KING, Stephen. *Pet Sematary.* 1983. Doubleday. 1st. NF/dj. M21/R14. $30.00

KING, Stephen. *Salem's Lot.* 1975. Doubleday. 1st. VG/VG 2nd state. H11. $525.00

KING, Stephen. *Shining.* 1977. Doubleday. 1st. F/F. A4. $250.00

KING, Stephen. *Shining.* 1977. Doubleday. 1st. F/NF. M2. $225.00

KING, Stephen. *Skeleton Crew.* 1985. Scream. 1/1000. sgn/#d. F/case. B4/M2. $400.00

KING, Stephen. *Stand.* 1978. Doubleday. 1st. F/dj. M2. $250.00

KING, Stephen. *Stand.* 1978. Doubleday. 1st. NF/NF. M19/P3. $175.00

KING, Stephen. *Thinner.* 1984. NAL. 1st. NF/dj. Q1. $75.00

KING, Stephen. *Thinner.* 1984. NAL. 1st. VG/VG. M22. $35.00

KING, Stephen. *Thinner.* 1984. NAL. 1st. F/dj. M2. $100.00

KING, Stephen. *Tommyknockers.* 1987. Putnam. 1st. F/NF. N4. $35.00

KING, Stephen. *Tommyknockers.* 1987. Putnam. 1st. VG/VG. P3. $25.00

KING, Stephen. *Tommyknockers.* 1987. Putnam. 1st. F/F. W2. $55.00

KING, Tabitha. *Small World.* 1981. NY. Macmillan. 1st. F/NF. T12. $40.00

KING, Tabitha. *Small World.* 1981. NY. Macmillan. 1st. sgn. author's 1st book. VG/dj. Q1. $75.00

KING, W.C. *Campfire Sketches & Battlefield Echoes of '61-65.* 1889. 624p. ils red bdg. O8. $42.50

KING & STRAUB. *Talisman.* 1984. Donald Grant. 2 vol. 1st semi-ltd w/mc pl. F. M2. $150.00

KING & STRAUB. *Talisman.* 1984. Viking. 1st trade. F/dj. M2. $30.00

KINGLAKE, A.W. *Eothen; or, Traces of Travel Brought Home From the East.* ca 1908. Lippincott. ils Frank Brangwyn. 306p. xl. VG. W1. $22.00

KINGMA, J.T. *Geological Structure of New Zealand.* 1974. Wiley-Interscience. 1 pocket map. 407p. cloth. F/NF. D8. $45.00

KINGSBURN, Emart. *Gems of Promise.* 1924. Chelsea. 1st. F/dj. M2. $27.00

KINGSLEY, Charles. *Hypatia.* 1897. Crowell. ils EH Garrett. 477p. VG+. M20. $35.00

KINGSLEY, Charles. *Two Years Ago.* 1887. Macmillan. 1st. VG. M19. $45.00

KINGSLEY, Charles. *Water Babies.* ca 1915. Stokes. ils Katherine Cameron. 246p. VG. D1. $175.00

KINGSLEY, Charles. *Water Babies.* 1916. Dodd Mead. 1st thus. ils JW Smith/12 full-p ils. 362p. gr cloth/pict label. D1. $450.00

KINGSLEY, Charles. *Water Babies.* 1961. Gollancz. 1st thus. 222p. gr brd. VG. T5. $35.00

KINGSLEY, Charles. *Westward Ho!* 1920. Scribner. 1st. ils NC Wyeth/14 full-p pl. blk cloth/label. pict dj. R5. $750.00

KINGSMILL, Hugh. *Return of William Shakespeare.* 1929. Bobbs Merrill. 1st. VG/dj. M2. $40.00

KINGSOLVER, Barbara. *Animal Dreams.* 1990. Harper Collins. 1st. F/F. T11. $50.00

KINGSOLVER, Barbara. *Animal Dreams.* 1991. London. Scribner. 1st. F/dj. A24. $40.00

KINGSOLVER, Barbara. *Bean Trees.* 1988. Harper Row. ARC. author's 1st novel. F/F. L3. $450.00

KINGSOLVER, Barbara. *Bean Trees.* 1988. Harper Row. 1st. author's 1st novel. F/F. B2. $250.00

KINGSOLVER, Barbara. *Bean Trees.* 1989. London. Virago. 1st. sgn. F/F. B3. $75.00

KINGSOLVER, Barbara. *Homeland & Other Stories.* 1989. Harper Row. 1st. author's 2nd book. F/F. D10. $90.00

KINGSOLVER, Barbara. *Homeland & Other Stories.* 1989. Harper Row. 1st. inscr. F/F. T11. $135.00

KINNELL, Galway. *Black Light.* 1966. Houghton Mifflin. 1st. sgn. VG/VG. R14. $60.00

KINNELL, Galway. *Selected Poems.* 1982. Houghton Mifflin. 1/200. sgn. F/sans/case. R14. $60.00

KINNEY, Charles; see Gardner, Erle Stanley.

KINO, Father. *Kino & the Cartography of Northwestern New Spain.* 1965. AZ Pioneers Hist Soc. 1/750. sm folio. ils. gilt red cloth. as new. R3. $385.00

KINSELLA, W.P. *Box Socials.* 1991. Ballantine. 1st. sgn. F/F. A23. $40.00

KINSELLA, W.P. *Chapter One of a Work in Progress.* 1988. Vancouver. Wm Hoffer. 1st. 1/300. sgn/#d. F/sans/wrp. T11. $150.00

KINSELLA, W.P. *Dance Me Outside.* 1986. Boston. Godine. 1st Am. F/NF clip. R14. $35.00

KINSELLA, W.P. *Dixon Cornbelt League.* 1993. Harper Collins. 1st. sgn. F/F. A23. $40.00

KINSELLA, W.P. *Iowa Baseball Confederacy.* 1986. Houghton Mifflin. 1st. F/F. T11. $30.00

KINSELLA, W.P. *Iowa Baseball Confederacy.* 1986. Houghton Mifflin. 1st. sgn. rem mk. F/F. A23. $36.00

KINSELLA, W.P. *Rainbow Warehouse.* 1989. Nova Scotia. Pottersfield Pr. 1st. sgn author/wife. F/sans. T11. $100.00

KINSELLA, W.P. *Red Wolf, Red Wolf.* 1987. Toronto. 1st. rem mk. NF/F. B3. $20.00

KINSELLA, W.P. *Shoeless Joe.* 1982. Houghton Mifflin. 1st. assn/MTI. NF/dj. D10. $145.00

KINSELLA, W.P. *Shoeless Joe.* 1982. Houghton Mifflin. 1st. F/dj. from $200 to $250.00

KINSEY, Alfred C. *Sexual Behavior in the Human Female.* 1953. Phil. WB Saunders. 1st. F/dj. Q1. $125.00

KINSLEY, D.A. *Favor the Bold: Custer: The Indian Fighter.* 1968. Promotory. rpt. NF/NF. L3. $25.00

KINYON, Jeannette K. *Incredible Gladys Pyle.* 1985. Vermillion, SD. SD U. A19. $15.00

KINZIE, Mary. *Autumn Eros & Other Poems.* 1991. Knopf. 1st. F/NF. R13. $15.00

KIPLING, Rudyard. *Captains Courageous.* 1897. London. 1st. VG. T9. $100.00

KIPLING, Rudyard. *Diversity of Creatures.* 1917. Macmillan. 1st. NF. Q1. $75.00

KIPLING, Rudyard. *Feet of the Young Men.* 1920. Garden City. 1/377. sgn. half leather. B5. $500.00

KIPLING, Rudyard. *Jungle Book.* 1894. Century. 1st Am. 303p. VG+. P2. $100.00

KIPLING, Rudyard. *Just-So Stories.* 1929. Doubleday Doran. mc pl. NF. M19. $35.00

KIPLING, Rudyard. *Just-So Stories.* 1952 (1912). Garden City. sm 4to. 84p. VG/poor. T5. $25.00

KIPLING, Rudyard. *Mandalay.* nd (1899). NY. Alex Grosset. 1st separate ed? tan wrp. M24. $45.00

KIPLING, Rudyard. *Phantom Rickshaw.* 1898. Altemus. G+. M2. $10.00

KIPLING, Rudyard. *Puck of Pook's Hill.* 1906. Doubleday Page. 1st Am. ils Rackham. 277p. VG. P2. $100.00

KIPLING, Rudyard. *Sea & Sussex.* 1926. Doubleday Page. 1st. 95p. cloth. VG. D4. $45.00

KIPLING, Rudyard. *Sea Warfare.* 1916. London. Macmillan. 1st. NF/dj. Q1. $150.00

KIPLING, Rudyard. *Soldier Tales.* 1896. London. Macmillan. 1st. NF. Q1. $250.00

KIPLING, Rudyard. *Under the Deodars.* 1891. NY. Geo Munro. early Am ed. Seaside Lib #1809. bl wrp. M24. $64.00

KIPLING, Rudyard. *Wee Willie Winkie/Under the Deodars/Phantom Rickshaw.* 1895. London. Macmillan. 1st collected. NF. Q1. $175.00

KIRALFY, A.K.R. *Potter's Outlines of English Legal History.* 1963. Lonon. Sweet & Maxwell Ltd. 5th/2nd imp. M11. $50.00

KIRBY, Michael. *Happenings.* 1965. Dutton. 1st. F/NF. B2. $35.00

KIRBY, William. *On the Power, Wisdom & Goodness of God...* 1853. London. HG Bohn. new ed. 2 vol. ils. rebound. K3. $50.00

KIRBY-PARRISH, L. *Greta & Peter in the Tea Cup.* 1915. Volland. ils. VG. M5. $38.00

KIRK, J.T.O. *Plastids: Their Chemistry, Structure...* 1967. London. Freeman. 8vo. 608p. rem mk. B1. $250.00

KIRK, Russell. *Watchers at the Strait Gate.* 1984. Arkham. 1st. F/F. R10. $15.00

KIRKLAND, Thomas. *Commentary on Apoplectic & Paralytic Affections.* 1991. Birmingham. Classics Neurology/Neurosurgery Lib. facsimile. G1. $65.00

KIRKPATRICK, B.J. *Bibliography of Virginia Woolf.* 1957. London. Hart Davis. 1st. gilt brick cloth. F/dj. M24. $75.00

KIRKPATRICK, Ivone. *Mussolini: A Study in Power.* 1964. NY. ils/photos/notes. 726p. G/poor. S16. $17.50

KIRKPATRICK, Konstance. *History of Indian Harbor Yacht Club.* 1978. Cincinnati. Young Klein. photos. 445p. T7. $40.00

KIRKPATRICK. *Twentieth-Century Children's Writers.* 1983. 2nd. 4to. 1024p. F/F. A4. $145.00

KIRKWOOD, Edith Brown. *Animal Children.* 1913. Volland. 10th. ils MT Ross. 8vo. mc pict brd. pub box. R5. $250.00

KIRKWOOD, James. *PS Your Cat Is Dead.* 1972. Stein Day. 1st. VG/dj. M25. $25.00

KIRKWOOD, James. *Some Kind of Hero.* 1975. Crowell. 1st. sgn. MTI. F/F. M25. $50.00

KIRN, Walter. *My Hard Bargain.* 1990. Knopf. 1st. F/F. B35. $30.00

KIRSCH, Abby Gail. *Teen Cuisine.* 1969. NY. Parents Magazine. G. A16. $5.00

KIRSCH & MURPHY. *West of the West: Story of California From Conquistadores...* 1967. Dutton. 1st. F/F. O4. $20.00

KIRSHENBAUM, David. *Mixed Marriage & the Jewish Future.* 1958. Bloch. 2nd. 144p. VG/VG. S3. $25.00

KIRST, Hans Hellmut. *Nights of the Long Knives.* 1976. London. 1st. dj. T9. $18.00

KISCH & MAPP. *Separate Cinema: 50 Years of Black Cast Posters.* 1992. NY. 168p. 4to. glossy wrp. A17. $14.50

KISSELL, M.L. *Basketry of the Papago & Pima Indians.* 1972. Rio Grande Classic. ils/photos. 264p. F. M4. $25.00

KISSINGER, Henry. *Years of Upheaval.* 1982. Little Brn. 1st. NF/NF. W2. $45.00

KITCHELL, Joseph. *Earl of Hell.* 1924. Century. 1st. F/dj. M2. $85.00

KITCHINER, W. *Cook's Oracle, Containing Receipts for Plain Cookery...* 1836 (1823). new ed. half leather. VG. E6. $165.00

KITELEY, Brian. *Still Life With Insects.* 1989. Ticknor Fields. 1st. author's 1st book. F/F. L3. $35.00

KITT, Eartha. *Thursday's Child.* 1956. DSP. later prt. VG/dj. M25. $25.00

KITTEREDGE, William. *We Are Not in This Together.* 1984. Graywolf. 1st. gilt blk quarter cloth. F/F. T11. $95.00

KITTON, F.G. *Minor Writings of Charles Dickens, a Bibliography...* 1900. London. Elliot Stock. 1st. gilt gr cloth. uncut. F. M24. $85.00

KITZINGER, Shelia. *Experience of Childbirth.* 1962. London. Gollancz. 1st. ils. VG/G. A25. $12.00

KIZZIA, Tom. *Wake of the Unseen Object.* 1991. Holt. 1st. F/NF. M23. $25.00

KJELGAARD, Jim. *Explorations of Pere Marquette.* (1951). Random/Landmark. 6th. 8vo. 179p. rebound. xl. G+. T5. $12.00

KLAR, M. *Technology of Wood Distillation.* 1925. Van Notrand. 496p. VG. H1. $25.00

KLARMANN, Andrew. *Fool of God.* 1912. Pustet. 1st. VG. M2. $10.00

KLATELL & MARCUS. *Sports for Sale.* 1988. Oxford. 1st. F/F. P8. $15.00

KLAUBER, L.M. *Rattlesnakes: Their Habits, Life Histories, Etc.* 1956. Berkeley. ils/figures/tables. 476p. cloth. VG+/G+. M12. $375.00

KLAUSNER, Betty. *Focus Santa Barbara.* 1985. Santa Barbara. Santa Barbara Contemporary Arts Forum. 58p. wrp. D11. $25.00

KLAVAN, Andrew. *Darling Clementine.* 1988. Permanent. ltd. 1/2000. F/dj. M22. $50.00

KLAVAN, Andrew. *Face of the Earth.* 1980. Viking. 1st. F/F. H11. $35.00

KLAVAN, Andrew. *Son of Man.* 1988. Sag Harbor. Permanent. 1st. F/F. H11. $40.00

KLEES, F. *Pennsylvania Dutch.* 1950. NY. 1st. VG/VG. B5. $32.50

KLEHR, Harvey. *Secret World of American Communism.* 1995. yale. 1st. F/F. V4. $15.00

KLEIN, Carol. *Credo of Maimonides: A Synthesis.* 1958. Philosophical Lib. 143p. VG/dj. S3. $26.00

KLEIN, Herman. *Herman Klein & the Gramophone.* 1990. Portland. Amadeus. 618p. F/dj. A17. $25.00

KLEIN, Herman. *Star Atlas.* 1893. London. 2nd. trans Edmund McClure. 72p. disbound. K5. $20.00

KLEIN, T.E.D. *Ceremonies.* 1984. Viking. 1st. VG/dj. R10. $10.00

KLEIN, T.E.D. *Dark Gods.* 1985. Viking. 1st. NF/VG+. M21. $30.00

KLEIN & FISHER. *First Down & a Billion.* 1987. Morrow. 1st. VG+/VG. P8. $15.00

KLEINPELL, R.M. *Miocene Stratigraphy of California.* 1938. Tulsa. 1st. 5 pocket maps. 450p. VG. D8. $25.00

KLIMA, Ivan. *Love & Garbage.* 1991. Knopf. 1st. F/F. A20. $15.00

KLINE, Herbert. *New Theatre & Film 1934-1937, an Anthology...* 1985. HBJ. 1st. VG/VG. V4. $20.00

KLINEFELTER, Lee M. *Bookbinding Made Easy.* 1952. Milwaukee, WI. dj. A19. $20.00

KLINEFELTER, Lee M. *Illustrations in Miniature, Postal Designs...* 1939. Blk Cat. 1/500. ils. 26p. F. A4. $175.00

KLINEFELTER, Lee M. *Small Display of Old Maps & Plans.* 1962. Prairie Pr. 1/550. 83p. F/F. A4. $175.00

KLINEFELTER, Walter. *Christmas Books.* 1936. Portland, ME. Southworth-Anthoenson. 8vo. 28p. F. F. B24. $325.00

KLINGMAN, Peter D. *Josiah Walls: Florida's Black Congressman of Reconstruction.* 1976. Gainsville. 1st. 157p. F/F. B4. $65.00

KLIPPART, John. *Wheat Plant.* 1860. Cincinnati. Moore. 706p. G+. A10. $50.00

KLOPPENBURG, Jack R. *Seeds & Sovereignty.* 1988. Durham. 368p. F/dj. B26. $40.00

KLUCKOHN, Clyde. *Navajo Witchcraft.* nd. Beacon. rpt 1944 ltd ed. 8vo. brn brd. dj. F7. $75.00

KNAPP, Arthur Jr. *Race Your Boat Right.* 1952. Van Nostrand. 1st. sgn. 296p. VG. B11. $35.00

KNAPP, H.S. *History of the Maumee Valley.* 1872. Toledo. ils. 667p. rebound. B18. $95.00

KNEBEL, Fletcher. *Bottom Line.* 1974. Doubleday. 1st. G+/dj. N4. $17.50

KNEELAND, Samuel. *Annual of Scientific Discovery.* 1868. Boston. Gould Lincoln. 8vo. brn cloth. K3. $25.00

KNIGGE, K.M. *Brain-Endocrine Interation II: Venticular System...* 1975. Basel. Karger. 406p. gray cloth. VG/dj. G1. $50.00

KNIGHT, Charles. *Half Hours With the Best Authors.* (1859). London. 4 vol. 12mo. woodcuts. 3-quarter leather. VG. H3. $125.00

KNIGHT, Charles. *Old England: Pictorial Museum of Regal, Ecclesiastical...* nd (1844). London. James Sangster. 2 vol. tall 4to. aeg. red pebbled linen. H13. $295.00

KNIGHT, Damon. *In Deep.* 1964. London. Gollancz. 1st hc. sgn. F/NF. T2. $45.00

KNIGHT, Damon. *Off Centre.* 1969. London. Gollancz. 1st hc. collects 8 stories. F/VG. T2. $35.00

KNIGHT, Damon. *Orbit 20.* 1978. Harper. 1st. F/dj. M2. $20.00

KNIGHT, Damon. *Other Foot.* 1966. London. Whiting Wheaton. 1st hc. F/clip. T2. $50.00

KNIGHT, Damon. *Turning On.* 1967. London. Gollancz. 1st. collects 14 stories. F/F. T2. $25.00

KNIGHT, Damon. *Two Novels: Earth Quarter/Double Meaning.* 1974. London. Gollancz. 1st. F/F. T2. $45.00

KNIGHT, Damon. *World & Thorinn.* 1980. Berkley. 1st. F/dj. M2. $20.00

KNIGHT, Frank. *Clipper Ship.* 1973. London. Collins. photos/maps. 95p. dj. T7. $35.00

KNIGHT, Joseph. *Pipe & Pouch: Smoker's Own Book of Poetry.* 1897. Boston. LC Page. 182p. full suede. VG. H7. $25.00

KNIGHT, Marjorie. *Land of Lost Hankerchiefs.* 1954. Dutton. stated 1st. ils Rosalie K Fry. VG/dj. M5. $45.00

KNIGHT, Mrs. H. *Breakfast, Dessert, Supper: 400 Practical Recipes.* 1884. Auburn, NY. 1st. 97p. VG. E6. $75.00

KNIGHT, Mrs. S.B. *Minnie Maverick; or, Man's Wrongs & Woman's Foibles.* 1870. NY. Broughton Wyman. 1st. 12mo. 272p. cloth. M1. $125.00

KNIGHT, Oliver. *Frontier Army.* 1978. Norman, OK. dj. A19. $25.00

KNIGHT, R. Baker. *Chronicle of Kings of England.* 1660. London. 3rd. 500p+catalog of nobility/index. A15. $50.00

KNIPE & KNIPE. *Story of Old Ironsides.* 1928. Dodd Mead. 1st. ils Mead Schaeffer. 321p. VG. T5. $35.00

KNIPLING, E.F. *Basic Principles of Insect Population Suppression...* 1979. GPO. USDA Handbook 512. 659p. VG. A10. $20.00

KNITTLE, Rhea Mansfield. *Early American Glass.* 1937 (1927). Century. sgn. 496p. VG/ragged. M20. $25.00

KNOEDLER. *Derain.* 1971. 12 b&w pl. 32p. D2. $25.00

KNOEPFMACHER, Hugo. *Outer Mongolia: Selection of References.* 1944. NY Public Lib. VG/wrp. W3. $32.00

KNOPF, Mildred O. *Around the World Cookbook for Young People.* 1966. Knopf. G/dj. A16. $10.00

KNOPF, Olga. *Successful Aging: Facts & Fallacies of Growing Old.* 1975. Viking. 1st. 229p. VG/dj. A25. $18.00

KNOWLES, James S. *Dramatic Works of...* 1856. London. 2 vol. 1st? VG. A15. $30.00

KNOWLES, John. *Separate Peace.* 1960. Macmillan. 1st Am. NF/2nd state. T11. $150.00

KNOX, Calvin; see Silverberg, Robert.

KNOX, Dudley W. *Naval Sketches of the War in California.* 1939. Random. sm folio. ils. marbled brd/vellum spine. F. R3. $300.00

KNOX, Rawle. *Work of EH Shepard.* (1980). NY. Schocken. 1st. ils Shepard. 256p. VG/VG. D1. $65.00

KNOX, Ronald. *Memories of the Future.* 1923. London. 1st. F/dj. M2. $50.00

KNOX, Thomas. *Overland Through Asia...Siberian, Tartar & Chinese Life.* 1870. Hartford. 1st. 200 engravings/map. 608p. VG. W3. $275.00

KNOX. *Work of EH Shepard.* 1980. ils. 256p. F/F. A4. $85.00

KNYSTAUTAS, A. *Natural History of the USSR.* 1987. McGraw Hill. 275 mc photos. cloth. F/F. B1. $38.50

KOCH, Dorothy. *I Play at the Beach.* 1955. Holiday House. 1st. ils Rojankovsky. 8vo. VG/dj. P2. $110.00

KOCH, Robert. *Louis C Tiffany: Rebel in Glass.* 1964. Crown. 1st/1st prt. sgn. 4to. 246p. as new/F. H1. $65.00

KOCH, Robert. *Louis Tiffany's Glass, Bronzes, Lamps.* 1971. Crown. 8th. 208p. F/plastic dj. H1. $65.00

KOCHER, Theodor. *Text-Book of Operative Surgery.* 1895. London. 1st Eng trans. 303p. A13. $350.00

KOEBEL, W.H. *Central America.* 1925. London. Fisher Unwin. 3rd. 382p. F3. $20.00

KOEBEL, W.H. *South America.* nd (1912). London. A&C Blk. 8vo. ils/fld map. 230p. pict gr cloth. VG. H3. $75.00

KOEHN, Ilse. *Mischling, Second Degree, My Childhood in Nazi Germany.* 1977. 1st. intro Harrison Salisbury. VG. E6. $15.00

KOEPCKE, Maria. *Birds of the Department of Lima, Peru.* 1983. Harrowood. 3rd. trans from Spanish. ils. 144p. F/VG+. S15. $15.00

KOESTLER, Arthur. *Act of Creation.* 1964. Macmillan. 1st Am. NF/clip. Q1. $60.00

KOHLSTEDT & ROSSITER. *Historical Writing on American Science.* 1986. Johns Hopkins. 8vo. ils. NF/wrp. K3. $12.00

KOHN, Marek. *Narcomania. On Heroin.* 1987. London. Faber. 1st. VG+/wrp. B2. $25.00

KOHN, Susan E. *Conduction Aphasia.* 1992. Hillsdale, NJ. Lawrence Erlbaum Assoc. bl cloth. G1. $38.00

KOLB, E.L. *Through the Grand Canyon From Wyoming to Mexico.* 1946. NY. Macmillan. inscr/dtd 1947. 76 pl. F. B14. $55.00

KOLB, E.L. *Through the Grand Canyon From Wyoming to Mexico...* 1967. NY. inscr by author's brother. ils/map. 344p. F/dj. M4. $30.00

KOLB & SLEDD. *Reynolds Copy of Johnson's Dictionary.* 1955. Manchester. tall 8vo. 29p. F/heavy tan wrp. H13. $45.00

KOLLEK, Teddy. *Jerusalem, Sacred City of Mankind.* 1975 (1968). Jerusalem. sm 4to. ils. VG/VG. E6. $15.00

KOLLER, E.L. *Artistic Show-Cards, How To Design & Make Them.* 1924. Scranton, PA. Internat Lib Technology. ils. VG. B18. $22.50

KOLLONTAI, Alexandra. *Autobiography of a Sexually Emancipated Communist Woman.* 1971. NY. Herder. 1st Am. 138p. VG/dj. A25. $20.00

KOLTUN, Frances. *Frances Koltun's Complete Book for the Intelligent Woman...* 1967. S&S. 3rd. sgn. 507p. VG/dj. A25. $18.00

KONDO, Yumiko. *Moontoo the Cat.* 1978. Barron's. 1st Am. ils. F/F. P2. $25.00

KONVITZ, Jeffrey. *Sentinel.* 1974. S&S. 1st. sgn. F/F. M21. $55.00

KOONTZ, Dean R. *Bad Place.* 1990. Putnam. 1st. NF/NF. N4. $22.50

KOONTZ, Dean R. *Chase.* 1972. Random. 1st. F/F. H11. $240.00

KOONTZ, Dean R. *Cold Fire.* 1990. Putnam. 1st. F/dj. M2. $25.00

KOONTZ, Dean R. *Dragon Tears.* 1993. Putnam. 1st ltd. 377p. F/F. W2. $75.00

KOONTZ, Dean R. *Dragonfly.* 1975. Random. 1st. NF/NF. from $125 to $150.00

KOONTZ, Dean R. *Hanging On.* 1973. NY. 1st. sgn bookplate. NF/NF. A11. $165.00

KOONTZ, Dean R. *Night Chills.* 1976. Atheneum. 1st. NF/NF. B2. $150.00

KOONTZ, Dean R. *Shattered.* 1973. Random. 1st. xl. VG/VG. P3. $30.00

KOONTZ, Dean R. *Shattered.* 1973. Random. 1st. NF/dj. M2. $250.00

KOONTZ, Dean R. *Surrounded.* 1974. Bobbs Merrill. 1st. VG/dj. from $175 to $200.00

KOONTZ, Dean R. *Wall of Masks.* 1975. Bobbs Merrill. 1st. F/dj. P3. $275.00

KOONTZ, Dean R. *Wall of Masks.* 1975. Bobbs Merrill. 1st. NF/dj. M2. $200.00

KOOP, C. Edward. *Memoirs of America's Family Doctor.* 1991. Random. 1st. sgn. F/F. A23. $40.00

KOOP & SCHAEFFER. *Whatever Happened to the Human Race?* 1979. Revell. 256p. F/dj. B29. $7.50

KOPAL, Zdenek. *Realm of the Terrestrial Planets.* 1979. NY. Halstead. 9 mc pl. 223p. VG/dj. K5. $20.00

KOPLOS, Janet. *Contemporary Japanese Sculpture.* 1991. NY/London/Paris. 1st. ils. 175p. F/dj. W3. $72.00

KOPPANY, B. *Tempting Letters...Experienced Demon to a Novice.* 1995. Striking Imp. 338p. F/dj. B29. $10.00

KORCZAK, Janusz. *Ghetto Diary.* 1978. Holocaust Lib. ils. 181p. VG/G+. S3. $26.00

KOREIN, Julius. *Brain Death: Interrelated Mecial & Social Issues.* 1978. NY. Academy of Sciences. 454p. prt bl wrp. G1. $42.00

KORNBLATT, Joyce Reiser. *White Water.* 1985. Dutton. 1st. author's 2nd book. F/NF. R13. $20.00

KORNBLUTH, C.M. *Best of...* 1976. SFBC. 1st. F/dj. M2. $15.00

KORNBLUTH, C.M. *Takeoff.* 1952. Doubleday. 1st. VG. M2. $17.00

KORNBLUTH, C.M. *Takeoff.* 1952. Doubleday. 1st. VG/G. P3. $60.00

KORNBLUTH & POHL. *Space Merchants.* 1953. Ballantine. 1st. VG/dj. M2. $100.00

KORTH, William W. *Tertiary Record of Rodents in North America.* 1994. Plenum. 319p. F. S15. $35.00

KOSINSKI, Jerzy. *Being There.* 1970. Harcourt Brace. 1st. F/NF. B4. $85.00

KOSINSKI, Jerzy. *Being There.* 1970. Harcourt Brace. 1st. quarter cloth. VG/dj. M24. $50.00

KOSINSKI, Jerzy. *Future Is Ours, Comrade: Conversations With the Russians.* 1960. Bodley Head. 1st Eng. VG+/VG. B4. $125.00

KOSINSKI, Jerzy. *Steps.* 1968. Random. 1st. F/NF. M19. $35.00

KOSTER, Henry. *Travels in Brazil.* 1816. London. Longman Hurst Rees Orme Brn. 1st. 8 aquatints. 501p. R15. $3,800.00

KOTSCH, William J. *Weather for the Mariners.* 1977. Naval Inst. 2nd. F/VG. S15. $18.00

KOTSUJI, Abram. *Origin & Evolution of Semitic Alphabets.* 1937. Tokyo. sgn pres. ils/bibliography/index. 229p. VG/dj. W3. $125.00

KOTZWINKLE, William. *Fan Man.* 1974. Harmony. 1st. F/dj. M2. $45.00

KOTZWINKLE, William. *Great World Circus.* 1983. Putnam. 1st. ils Joe Sefello. F/F. R14. $30.00

KOTZWINKLE, William. *Jewel of the Moon.* 1985. Putnam. ARC. F/F. w/promo materials. R14. $40.00

KOTZWINKLE, William. *Midnight Examiner.* 1989. Houghton Mifflin. 1st. F/F. P3. $20.00

KOTZWINKLE, William. *Queen of Swords.* 1983. Putnam. 1st. F/F. R14. $30.00

KOUES, Helen. *How To Beautify Your Home & Be Your Own Decorator.* 1930. Good Housekeeping. 2nd. ils. 224p. VG. A25. $12.00

KOVACS, Ernie. *Zoomar.* 1957. Doubleday. 1st. NF/dj. M25. $60.00

KOVEL, Joel. *Against the State of Nuclear Terror.* 1984. Boston. South End Pr. 1st Am. VG/wrp. K3. $5.00

KOVIC, Ron. *Born on the Fourth of July.* 1976. McGraw Hill. 1st. F/F. H11. $80.00

KRAEPELIN, Emil. *General Paresis: Nervous & Mental Disease...* 1913. NY. Monograph 14/Journal Nervous Mental Disease Pub. G1. $150.00

KRAISER. *Peter Porter: A Biography 1954-1986.* 1990. complete info. F. A4. $65.00

KRAKEL, Dean. *Adventures in Western Art.* 1977. Lowell. 1st. 377p. VG/VG. J2. $89.00

KRAMER, Dale. *Ross & the New Yorker.* 1951. Doubleday. 1st. F/VG+ clip. B4. $85.00

KRAMER, Jack. *Bromeliads.* 1981. NY. 1st. ils/photos. 179p. F/dj. B26. $44.00

KRAMER, Jack. *Cacti & Other Succulents.* 1977. NY. ils. 160p. VG+/dj. B26. $15.00

KRAMER, Jack. *Philodendrons.* 1974. NY. ils. 87p. VG/dj. B26. $14.00

KRAMER, Jerry. *Distant Replay.* 1985. Putnam. 1st. 236p. F/NF. W2. $25.00

KRAMER, Kathryn. *Rattlesnake Farming.* 1992. Knopf. 1st. author's 2nd novel. F/dj. A24. $20.00

KRAMISH, Arnold. *Atomic Energy in the Soiet Union.* 1959. Stanford. 1st. xl. VG/dj. K3. $50.00

KRANTZ, Judith. *Dazzle.* 1990. Crown. 1st. F/F. W2. $30.00

KRANZ & FRANZ. *Gardening Under Lights.* 1971. Viking. revised/BC. 8vo. 269p. blk cloth. VG/VG. H1. $12.00

KRAUS, H. *Work Relief in Germany.* 1934. NY. Russell Sage Found. 1st. photos. VG. A25. $18.00

KRAUS, Hans P. *Sir Francis Drake: Pictorial Biography.* 1970. Amsterdam. N Israel. folio. 133 ils/maps/addendum sheet. as new. O7. $125.00

KRAUS, Karl. *Traumtheater. Spiel in Einem Akt.* 1924. Vienna. Die Fackel. 1st. NF. B2. $150.00

KRAUS, Robert. *Amanda Remembers.* nd (1965). Harper Row. early prt. sm 4to. 32p. VG. C14. $12.00

KRAUS, Robert. *King's Trousers.* 1981. Windmill. ils Fred Gwynne. F/NF. C8. $45.00

KRAUS & NICOLAI. *Das Elektrokardiogramm des Gesunden und Kranken Menschen.* 1910. Leipzig. 322p. bl cloth. B14. $200.00

KRAUSE, Lawrence A. *Money Go Round.* 1985. S&S. 1st. 202p. F/F. W2. $30.00

KRAUSE. *Mark Twain As Critic.* 1967. Baltimore. Johns Hopkins. 308p. F/VG. A4. $75.00

KRAUSKOPF, J. *Rabbi's Impression of the Oberammergau Play.* 1901. 1st. VG. E6. $20.00

KRAUSS, Ruth. *Big World & the Little House.* 1949. Henry Schuman. 1st. ils Marc Simont. VG+/VG. P2. $50.00

KRAUSS, Ruth. *Cantilever Rainbow.* 1965. Pantheon. probable 1st. VG+/VG. P2. $35.00

KRAUSS, Ruth. *Hole Is To Dig.* 1952. Harper. 1st. ils Sendak. 12mo. NF/clip. P2. $165.00

KRAUSS, Ruth. *Open House for Butterflies.* 1960. Harper. 1st. VG+/VG. B3. $75.00

KRAVITZ, Nathaniel L. *3000 Years of Hebrew Literature From Earliest Time...* 1972. Swallow. biblio/index. 586p. VG/G+. S3. $28.00

KREDEL, Fritz. *Big Golden Book of Bible Stories.* 1958. Golden. ils Kredel/Schnorr von Carolsfeld. pict brd. F. B24. $100.00

KREDEL, Fritz. *Dolls & Puppets of the 18th Century...* 1958. Lexington, KY. Gravesend. 1/500. sgn. sm 8vo. gilt cloth/morocco label. F/case. B24. $200.00

KREDEL & TODD. *Soldiers of the American Army 1775-1954.* 1954. Chicago. 32 full-p pl. F/poor. M4. $35.00

KREDENSER, Gail. *ABC of Bumptious Beasts.* 1966. Harlin Quest. 1st. sgn. ils/sgn Stanley Mack. VG+/VG. P2. $30.00

KREIG, Margaret B. *Green Medicine. Search for Plants That Heal.* 1964. Chicago. Rand McNally. 1st. 8vo. cloth. F/VG. A22. $30.00

KREISLER, Fritz. *Four Weeks in the Trenches.* 1915. Houghton Mifflin. 1st. inscr. gr cloth. F. B14. $200.00

KREMENTZ, Jill. *How It Feels When a Parent Dies.* 1981. Knopf. 1st. sm 8vo. F/F. C8. $30.00

KREPS, E. *Science of Trapping: Describes the Fur Bearing Animals...* (1909). Columbus, OH. Harding. 229p. VG. H7. $15.00

KRESH, Paul. *Isaac Bashevis Singer: Magician of W 86th St.* 1979. Dial. 1st. sgn Singer. rem mk. F/NF. B2. $85.00

KRESS, Nancy. *Alien Light.* 1988. Arbor. 1st. F/dj. M25. $25.00

KREUTZWEISER, Erwin E. *Red River Insurrection.* ca 1960. Quebec. Garden City. 8vo. 166p. gr cloth. VG/dj. T10. $50.00

KREY, O. *Ship's Cook & Baker.* 1944 (1942). Cornell Maritime Pr. VG. E6. $20.00

KRIEG, Saul. *What's Cooking in Portugal.* 1974. Macmillan. 1st. VG/dj. A16. $10.00

KRIEGER, L.C.C. *Mushroom Handbook.* 1967. Dover. 12mo. 32 mc pl. 560p. wrp. B1. $20.00

KROEBER, Theodora. *Ishi, Last of His Tribe.* 1964. Berkeley. Parnassus. 1st. NF/VG clip. L3. $250.00

KROLL, Harry Harrison. *Their Ancient Grudge.* 1946. Bobbs Merrill. 1st. 8vo. bl cloth. VG/dj. T10. $25.00

KROLL, Steven. *Hand-Me-Down Doll.* 1983. Holiday. 1st. sq 8vo. unp. lilac brd/bl spine. F/NF. T5. $30.00

KROMM & WHITE. *Groundwater Exploitation in the High Plains.* 1992. Lawrence, KS. 240p. F/dj. D8. $20.00

KRUGER, Rayne. *Goodbye Dolly Gray.* 1960. Phil. VG/VG. B5. $30.00

KRUMBEIN & SLOSS. *Stratigraphy & Sedimentation.* 1951. SF. Freeman. 1st. 497p. G. D8. $14.00

KRUPP, Edwin C. *Echoes of the Ancient Skies.* 1983. Harper. 1st. 386p. VG/VG. K5. $35.00

KRUSEN, Frank. *Physical Medicine & Rehabilitation for the Clinician.* 1951. Phil. 1st. sgn. 371p. A13. $150.00

KRYZHANOVSKII, O.L. *Lepidopterous Fauna of the USSR & Adjacent Countries.* 1988. Smithsonian. 405p. F/NF. B1. $48.00

KUBASTA, V. *Jolly Jim.* 1969. Frick. 1st Am. popup. obl 4to. VG. P2. $125.00

KUBASTA, V. *Puss in Boots.* 1961. London. Bancroft. 1st. popup. obl 4to. VG-. P2. $125.00

KUBASTA, V. *Tip, Top, Tap Go.* 1964. London. Bancroft. 6 double-p popups. sq 4to. pict brd. R5. $250.00

KUBE-MCDOWELL, Michael. *Quiet Pools.* 1990. Ace. 1st. F/dj. M2. $25.00

KUECHLER, A.W. *Vegetation Mapping.* 1967. Ronald. 8vo. 472p. cloth. G. A22. $35.00

KUHLMAN, Charles. *Custer & the Gall Saga, Some Interesting Deductions...* 1876. Kuhlman. 1st ltd. sgn. fld map. 46p. VG/wrp. J2. $235.00

KUHN, Franz. *King Ping Meh.* ca 1939. leipzig. 920p. VG. W3. $38.00

KUHN, Joy. *Elephant Man, the Book of the Film.* 1980. Virgin. 100+ photos. NF. C9. $75.00

KUHN, LAMPHREY & SHEER. *Ultrafine Particles.* 1963. John Wiley. 561p. NF. D8. $35.00

KULIKOV, K.A. *Fundamental Constants of Astronomy.* 1964. Jerusalem. Israel program for Scientific Trans. xl. K5. $14.00

KUMAR, Shiv K. *British Victorian Literature: Recent Revaluations.* 1969. NY U. 1st. tall 8vo. 510p. xl. F/plastic dj. H1. $30.00

KUMIN, Maxine. *Nightmare Factory.* 1970. Harper Row. 1st. inscr. NF/NF. B3. $60.00

KUMIN, Maxine. *Our Ground Time Here Will Be Brief.* 1983. Viking. AP. F/wrp. R14. $35.00

KUMIN, Maxine. *Why Can't We Live Together Like Civilized Human Beings.* 1982. Viking. 1st. inscr. NF/VG. B3. $45.00

KUMIN, Maxine. *Wonderful Babies of 1809 (And Other Years).* 1968. Putnam. ARC/1st. ils. NF/F. D4. $35.00

KUMMEL & TEICHERT. *Stratigraphic Boundary Problems: Permian & Triassic...* 1970. Lawrence, KS. 474p. as new/dj. D8. $30.00

KUMMER, Frederic Arnold. *Gentlemen in Hades.* 1930. Sears. 1st. VG. M2. $22.00

KUNDEERA, Milan. *Life Is Elsewhere.* 1974. Knopf. 1st Eng trans. author's 3rd book. F/F. D10. $85.00

KUNDERA, Milan. *Art of the Novel.* 1988. NY. Grove. 1st Eng language. F/F. R14. $35.00

KUNDERA, Milan. *Immortality.* 1991. Grove Weidenfeld. 1st. F/F. M23. $25.00

KUNDERA, Milan. *Unbearable Lightness of Being.* 1984. Harper Row. 1st. F/NF. A24. $50.00

KUNDERA, Milan. *Zert.* 1967. Prague. Zatva. true 1st. author's 1st book. VG/VG. L3. $650.00

KUNETKA & STRIEBER. *Day War.* 1984. HRW. 1st. NF/NF. N4. $30.00

KUNHARDT, C.P. *Steam Yachts & Launches: Their Machinery & Management.* 1887. Forest Stream. 1st. 239p+ads. G. A17. $45.00

KUNHARDT, Dorothy. *Brave Mr Buckingham.* 1935. Harcourt Brace. 1st. 8vo. unp. VG. D1. $95.00

KUNHARDT. *Lincoln: An Illustrated Biography.* 1992. 415p. O8. $18.50

KUNITZ & HAYCRAFT. *Twentieth Century Authors.* 1944. NY. Wilson. 2nd. 1577p. xl. G+. M21. $15.00

KUNKEL, Fritz. *Let's Be Normal! The Psychologist Comes to His Senses.* 1929. Ives Washburn. 1st. 240p. VG/dj. A25. $15.00

KUNTZLEMAN, Charles T. *Well Family Book.* 1985. Here's Life. 266p. F/dj. B29. $7.50

KUNZ, George Frederick. *Gems & Precious Stones of North America.* 1892. NY. ils Louis Prang. 367p. F. B14. $250.00

KUNZ, George Frederick. *Rings for the Finger.* 1917. Lippincott. 1st. ils. 381p. F. B14. $275.00

KUNZ, Jeffrey R.M. *AMA Family Medical Guide.* 1982. Random. ne. 832p. F. W2. $75.00

KUPPER, Walter. *Das Kakteenbuch.* 1928. Berlin/Westend. Gartenschoenheit. 8vo. 201p. G. A22. $45.00

KUPPER, Walter. *Das Kakteenbuch.* 1929 (1928). Berlin/Westend. ils/10 mc pl. 201p. yel cloth. VG. B26. $50.00

KUPPER & ROSHARDT. *Cacti.* 1960. NY. ils/photos. 127p. VG/dj. B26. $30.00

KUREISHI, Hanif. *Black Album.* 1995. London. Faber. 1st. F/F. A24. $35.00

KUROSAWA, Akira. *Ran.* 1986. Shambhala. ils. NF/lg wrp. C9. $75.00

KUROSAWA, Akira. *Something Like an Autobiography.* 1982. Knopf. ils. 205p. F/F. W3. $38.00

KURTEN, B. *Innocent Assassins: Biological Essays on Life in Present...* 1991. Columbia. ils Nystrom. 206p. F/F. M12. $20.00

KURTEN, Nancy Noland. *Needlepoint in Miniature.* 1979. Scribner. 1st. 4to. 146p. F/dj. T10. $75.00

KURZ, Louis. *Battles of the Civil War 1861-1865.* 1976. Birmingham. Oxmoor. 1st. obl folio. F/dj. B24. $250.00

KURZMAN, D. *Day of the Bomb.* 1986. 1st. 544p. VG/VG. E6. $12.00

KURZMAN, D. *Race for Rome.* 1975. NY. 1st. ils/maps. 488p. VG/VG. S16. $23.50

KURZWEIL, Allen. *Case of Curiosities.* 1992. HBJ. 1st. author's 1st/only novel. F/dj. D10. $45.00

KUSHNAREV, Evgenii. *Bering's Search for the Strait: First Kamchatka Expedition.* 1990. Portland. OR Hist Soc. 1st. 214p. map ep. gilt wine cloth. F/dj. P4. $45.00

KUSHNER, Ellen. *Thomas the Rhymer.* 1990. Morrow. 1st. F/F. M21. $40.00

KUSKIN, Karla. *Near the Window Tree.* 1975. Harper Row. 1st. 63p. F/VG. D4. $30.00

KUSKIN, Karla. *Roar & More.* 1956. Harper. early ed. inscr. 48p. pict brd. D4. $75.00

KUSS, Johanna. *Die Holsteinische Kueche Oder Anleitung zur Fuehrung...* 1881. Hamburg. 347p. gr cloth. B14. $95.00

KUTCHIN, Howard M. *Report of the Special Agent for Protection of AK Salmon...* 1900. GPO. remobed. 71p. VG. P4. $37.50

KUTTNER, Henry. *Man Drowning.* 1952. Harper. 1st. F/dj. M2. $50.00

KYSERLING, Hermann. *Travel Diary of a Philosopher.* 1929. VG/VG. M17. $20.00

L'AMOUR, Louis. *Education of a Wandering Man.* 1989. Bantam. 1st. F/F. A20. $15.00

L'AMOUR, Louis. *Guns of the Timberlands.* 1955. Jason. 1st. F/NF. B4. $2,250.00

L'AMOUR, Louis. *Jubal Sackett.* 1985. Bantam. 1st. 375p. VG+/clip. M20. $30.00

L'AMOUR, Louis. *Sitka.* 1957. Appleton-Century-Crofts. 1st. F/NF. B4. $1,500.00

L'ENGLE, Madeleine. *Acceptable Time.* 1989. FSG. 1st. F/F. B3. $20.00

L'ENGLE, Madeleine. *House Like a Lotus.* 1984. FSG. 1st. NF/NF clip. B3. $25.00

L'ENGLE, Madeleine. *Other Side of the Sun.* 1971. FSG. 1st. NF/NF. B3. $60.00

L'ENGLE, Madeleine. *Ring of Endless Light.* 1980. FSG. 1st. 324p. F/VG+. P2. $50.00

L'ENGLE, Madeleine. *Young Unicorns.* 1968. FSG. 1st. NF/VG. B3. $75.00

L'HEUREUX, John. *No Place for Hiding.* 1971. Doubleday. 1st. sgn. NF/VG. R14. $35.00

L'HEUREUX, John. *Woman Run Mad.* 1988. Viking. 1st. sgn. rem mk. NF/F. R14. $30.00

L'HOTE, Henri. *Search for the Tassili Frescoes...* 1959. NY. 1st Am. ils/maps. 236p. decor cloth. VG/dj. B18. $25.00

LA CHAPELLE, Mary. *House of Heros & Other Stories.* 1988. Crown. 1st. inscr. author's 1st book. F/NF. R13. $35.00

LA CLAIR, Earl E. *Wood & the Wool.* 1966. Francestown, NH. Golden Quill. inscr/orig poem. F/F. B11. $18.00

LA FLESCHE, Francis. *Middle Five.* 1900. Boston. Sm Maynard. 1st. author's 1st book. NF. L3. $250.00

LA FONTAINE. *Fables of La Fontaine.* (1940). NY. Harper. 1st. ils Andre Helle. 39p. VG. D1. $100.00

LA FONTAINE. *Fables.* 1893. Paris. ils. VG. M17. $30.00

LA GARGE, Oliver. *Enemy Gods.* 1937. Boston. 1st ed. F/taped. A17. $20.00

LA LANNE, Jack. *Abundant Health & Vitality After 40.* 1962. Prentice Hall. 1st. sgn. 224p. VG/VG. B11. $35.00

LA MOTTA, Jake. *Raging Bull: My Story.* 1970. Prentice Hall. 1st. F/F. B4. $200.00

LA POINT, James. *Legends of the Lakota.* 1976. SF. Indian Historian Pr. 1st. F. L3. $100.00

LA RAME, Louis. *Bimbi.* 1910. Lippincott. 1st thus. ils Maria Kirk. gilt red cloth. F. M5. $35.00

LABADIE, Emile L. *Native Plants for Use in California Landscape.* 1978. Sierra City, CA. 2nd. ils. 244p. as new. B26. $16.00

LABAT, Gaston. *Regional Anesthesia.* 1928. Phil. 2nd. 567p. A13. $100.00

LABOCETTA, Mario. *Tales of Hoffmann.* nd. NY. Dodd Mead/H Piazza. 10 full-p ils. G+. C14. $20.00

LACH, Alma. *Campbell Kids at Home.* 1954. Rand McNally. 1st Elf (#493). VG. P2. $20.00

LACHAMBRE & MACHURON. *Andree's Balloon Expedition in Search of North Pole.* 1898. NY. Stokes. 1st Am. 306p. P4. $145.00

LACHOUQUE, Henry. *Waterloo.* 1972. ils. VG/VG. M17. $27.50

LACK, D. *Population Studies of Birds.* 1966. Clarendon. ils/figures/photos. 341p. cloth. VG. M12. $45.00

LACKINGTON, J. *Confessions of J Lackington, Late Bookseller...* 1808. NY. Wilson Hitt. 16mo. 189p. F. T10. $250.00

LACOUTURE, Jean. *Ho Chi Min: A Political Biography.* 1968. Random. 1st Am. VG/VG. V4. $25.00

LACY, Ed. *Hotel Dwellers.* 1966. Harper Row. 1st. F/dj. M15. $45.00

LADA-MOCARSKI, Valerian. *Bibliography of Books on Alaska Published Before 1868.* 1969. Yale. ils. 567p. cloth. dj. D11. $250.00

LADD, George Eldon. *Theology of the New Testament.* 1975. Eerdmans. 661p. G. B29. $9.00

LAFEVER, Minard. *Modern Builder's Guide: Ils by 87 Copperplate Engravings.* 1833. Sleight/Collins Hannaay. 1st. lg 4to. 146p. full contemporary calf. M1. $1,000.00

LAFFERTY, R.A. *Does Anyone Else Have Anything Further To Add?* 1974. Scribner. 1st. F/dj. M2. $25.00

LAFFERTY, R.A. *Not To Mention Camels.* 1976. Bobbs Merrill. 1st. F/dj. M2. $25.00

LAGARDE, Andre. *Latin Church in the Middle Ages.* 1915. Scribner. 600p. VG. B29. $8.50

LAGERBERG, Torsten. *Vare Ville Planter.* 1950-1958. Oslo. revised/enlarged. 8 vol in 9. ils. xl. half morocco. B26. $185.00

LAGUARDIA, Robert. *Red Tempestuous Life of Susan Hayward.* 1985. Macmillan. 1st. VG/VG. W2. $25.00

LAHR, Bert. *Notes on a Cowardly Lion: Biography of Bert Lahr.* 1969. 408p. F/NF. A4. $35.00

LAI, LIM & YUNG. *Island: Poetry & History of Chinese Immigrants...1910-40.* 1980. SF. Hoc Doi. sgns. 8vo. F/paper wrp. R3. $20.00

LAJITHA, E. *March of Japan.* ca 1938. ils. xl. G+. E6. $15.00

LAKE, Nancy. *Daily Dinners.* 1892. London. Warne. G. A16. $35.00

LAMB, Brian M. *Guide to Cacti of the World.* 1991. NY. ils/photos/map. M/dj. B26. $40.00

LAMB, Bruce. *Wild Bunch.* 1993. Worland, WY. High Plains. A19. $30.00

LAMB, Charles. *Essays of Elia.* 1899. E Aurora. Roycroft. 1/100 (of 970). 14 hand-colord initials. full suede. B24. $200.00

LAMB, Charles. *Prince Dorus; or, Flattery Put Out of Countenance.* 1889 (1881). London. Field Tuer. rpt. 8vo. 3-quarter vellum/gilt bl brd. H13. $135.00

LAMB, E. *Flowering of Your Cacti.* 1955. London. ils/photos. 12mo. glossy pict brd. B26. $17.50

LAMB, Frank W. *Indian Baskets of North America.* 1972. Riverside. 1st. ils/maps/photos. 155p. NF/dj. K7. $50.00

LAMB, Harold. *Curved Saber.* 1964. Doubleday. 1st. NF/dj. M2. $75.00

LAMB, Harold. *Durandal.* 1931. Doubleday. 1st. F/dj. M2. $50.00

LAMB, Harold. *Nur Mahal.* 1935. Doubleday Doran. 325p. VG/dj. W1. $18.00

LAMB, Hugh. *Terror by Gaslight: More Victorian Tales.* 1976. Taplinger. 1st Am. F/dj. M2. $22.00

LAMB, S.H. *Native Trees & Shrubs of the Hawaiian Islands.* 1987. Sunstone. 2nd. 159p. NF. B1. $26.50

LAMB, Ursula. *Martin Fernandez dei Navarrete Clears the Deck...* 1980. Coimbra. 17p. as new/wrp. O7. $15.00

LAMB, Wally. *She's Come Undone.* 1992. Pocket. 1st. F/F. H11. $40.00

LAMB, Wally. *She's Come Undone.* 1992. Pocket. 1st. NF/clip. A24. $35.00

LAMB & LAMB. *Ils Reference on Cacti & Other Succulents.* 1974-79. London. Blanford. 5 vol. 8vo. cloth. F/djs. A22. $150.00

LAMB & LAMB. *Pocket Encyclopedia of Cacti in Colour.* 1969. Poole. ARC. sgns. 326 mc photos. 217p. F/dj. B26. $15.00

LAMB & LARRICK. *To Ride a Butterfly: Original Pictures, Stories...* 1991. NY. Doubleday/Dell Pub Group. 1st. 96p. F/NF. C14. $16.00

LAMBERT, Darwin. *Gold Strike in Hell.* 1964. Doubleday. 1st. F/F. B4. $65.00

LAMBERT, Gerard B. *Yankee in England.* 1957. ils. xl. VG. M17. $25.00

LAMBERT, Janet. *Candy Kane.* (1943). Grosset Dunlap. rpt. 8vo. 185p. G. T5. $14.00

LAMBERT, Janet. *Parri MacDonald: That's My Girl.* 1964. Dutton. 1st. 190p. VG+/dj. M20. $30.00

LAMBERT, Janet. *Penny Parish: Up Goes the Curtain.* 1946. Dutton. 2nd. 189p. VG/dj. M20. $20.00

LAMBERT, Janet. *Practically Perfect.* (1947). Grosset Dunlap. 8vo. 192p. gray tweed brd. VG/VG. T5. $15.00

LAMBERT, Janet. *Star Dream.* (1951). Grosset Dunlap. 8vo. 190p. VG. C8/T5. $12.50

LAMBERT, Oscar D. *Pioneer Leaders of Western Virginia.* 1935. Parkersburg, WV. 10 biographies. 226p. gilt cloth. G+. B18. $22.50

LAMBERT, Reita. *Right to the Heart.* 1939. Caxton. 1st. F/F clip. B4. $175.00

LAMMERS & VERHEY. *On Moral Medicine: Theological Perspectives...* 1987. Eerdmans. 657p. VG. B29. $18.50

LAMON, H. *Turkey Raising.* 1924 (1922). photos. VG. E6. $25.00

LAMONT, Helen Otis. *Story of Shelter Island in the Revolution.* 1975. Shelter Island. Hist Soc. sgn. 64p. VG/wrp. B11. $18.00

LAMOTT, Anne. *Hard Laughter.* 1980. NY. Viking. 1st. author's 1st book. VG+/clip. B4. $100.00

LAMOTT, Anne. *Joe Jones.* 1985. SF. Northpoint. 1st. F/NF. M23. $30.00

LAMPELL, Millard. *The Wall.* 1961. Knopf. 1st. F/NF. B2. $35.00

LAMPORT, Felicia. *Light Metres.* 1982. Everest House. ils Gorey. 122p. VG/dj. M20. $50.00

LAMPORT, Felicia. *Scrap Irony.* 1961. Houghton Mifflin. 1st. 128p. F/NF. D4. $45.00

LAMSON, Peggy. *Roger Baldwin, Founder of Am Civil Liberties Union.* 1976. Houghton Mifflin. 1st. F/NF. B2. $30.00

LAMSON & VANDERZWAAG. *Challenge of Arctic Shipping...* 1990. Montreal/Kingston. McGill-Queen's U. 282p. bl cloth. P4. $35.00

LANCASTER, Roy. *Travels in China: A Plantsman's Paradise.* 1993 (1989). Woodbridge, Suffolk. ils. 520p. as new/dj. B26. $80.00

LANCASTER-BROWN, Peter. *Halley & His Comet.* 1985. Poole. Blanford. 1st. ils. NF/dj. K3. $20.00

LANCIANI, Rodolfo. *Ancient Rome in Light of Recent Discoveries.* 1889. Boston. 3rd. 329p. gilt cloth. A17. $25.00

LANCMAN, E. *Chinese Portraiture.* 1966. Tokyo. Tuttle. 1st. 188p. F/dj. W3. $65.00

LANCOUR, Gene. *Globes of Llarun.* 1980. Doubleday. 1st. inscr. F/F. T12. $15.00

LANCOUR, Gene. *War Machines of Kalinth.* 1977. Doubleday. 1st. F/dj. M2. $10.00

LANDA, M.J. *Jew in Drama.* 1927. Morrow. 1st. 340p. VG+. S3. $24.00

LANDE, Carl H. *Rebuilding a Nation.* 1987. WA Inst Pr. 592p. M/VG. P1. $15.00

LANDELS, J.G. *Engineering in the Ancient World.* 1978. Berkeley. 1st. 8vo. 224p. F/dj. K3. $20.00

LANDESBERGER, Franz. *Rembrandt, the Jews & the Bible.* 1961. JPS. 2nd. ils/biblio/index. 190p. VG. S3. $33.00

LANDIS, C.S. *Woodchucks & Woodchuck Rifles.* 1951. NY. 1st. VG/G. B5. $45.00

LANDOR, A. Henry Savage. *Across Widest Africa.* 1907. NY. Scribner. 1st. 2 vol. 150+ pl/missing fld map. teg. VG. W1. $95.00

LANDOR, A. Henry Savage. *Explorer's Adventures in Tibet.* 1910. Harper. 1st. ils. pict cloth. VG. W3. $120.00

LANDOR, A. Henry Savage. *In the Forbidden Land: Account of Journey Into Tibet.* 1899. NY/London. Harper. 1st. 2 vol. photos/pl/lg fld map. VG. W3. $245.00

LANDOR, Walter Savage. *Imaginary Conversations.* 1936. Verona. Officina Bodoni. 1/1500. sgn Hans Mardersteig. VG. T10. $60.00

LANDSMAN, Anne Cheek. *Needlework Designs From American Indians.* 1977. Barnes/Yoseloff. 4to. 122 full-p designs+36p text. as new/dj. K7. $35.00

LANDSTROM, Bjorn. *Bold Voyages & Great Explorers.* 1964. Doubleday. 1st. F/rpr. O7. $30.00

LANE, Edward William. *Thousand & One Nights, Commonly Called, in England...* 1865. Warne Routledge. new ed. 3 vol. 8vo. ils. cloth. VG. W1. $175.00

LANE, Ronald. *Rudder's Rangers: The Second US Ranger Battalion.* 1979. Manassas. Ranger Assoc. 1st. sgn Margaret Rudder. F/F. A23. $40.00

LANE, Rose Wilder. *Discovery of Freedom.* 1943. NY. 1st. VG/dj. B5. $45.00

LANE, Walter Paye. *Adventures & Recollections of Gen Walter P Lane...* 1970 (1887). Austin, TX. Pemberton. rpt. 180p. cloth. F/NF. M8. $45.00

LANE, Wheaton J. *Commodore Vanderbilt: An Epic of the Steam Age.* 1942. NY. Knopf. ils/maps. 357p. T7. $45.00

LANE-POOLE, Stanley. *Speeches & Table-Talk of the Prophet Mohammad.* 1882. Macmillan. 16mo. 196p. cloth. VG. W1. $45.00

LANES, Selma G. *Art of Maurice Sendak.* 1980. Abrams. 1st. obl 4to. ils. 278p. F/prt plastic. from $150 to $165.00

LANG, Andrew. *Arabian Nights Entertainment.* 1898. Longman Gr. 1st. ils HJ Ford. aeg. 424p. gilt bl cloth. F. D1. $850.00

LANG, Andrew. *Arabian Nights.* 1968. Santa Rose, CA. Classic. 1st. ils Wm Dempster. 218p. VG. W1. $15.00

LANG, Andrew. *Ballads & Lyrics of Old France.* 1898. Postland, ME. Mosher. 1/925. 12mo. teg. full blk leather/raised bands. NF. H3. $125.00

LANG, Andrew. *Blue Fairy Book.* 1889. London. Longman Gr. 1st. ils HJ Ford/GP Jacomb Hood. aeg. gilt bl cloth. R5. $220.00

LANG, Andrew. *Books & Bookmen.* 1892. Longman Gr. new ed. ils. 177p. G. K3. $20.00

LANG, Andrew. *Cock Lane & Common-Sense.* (1894). London. Longman Gr. 8vo. 357p+24p ads. gilt red cloth. VG. D1. $125.00

LANG, Andrew. *Library.* 1881. London. Macmillan. 1st. mc pl/woodcuts. 184p. VG. K3. $30.00

LANG, Andrew. *Price Prigio & Prince Ricardo.* 1961. 1st thus. ils Watkins-Pitchford. VG/VG. S13. $16.00

LANG, Andrew. *Princess Nobody: A Tale of Fairyland.* 1884. London. Longman Gr. 1st thus. 4to. ils Richard Doyle. 56p text. cloth. R5. $475.00

LANG, Andrew. *True Story Book.* (1893). Longman Gr. 2nd. ils Bogle/Davis/etc. 337p. VG. D1. $85.00

LANG, Daniel. *From Hiroshima to the Moon.* 1959. S&S. ils. 496p. VG. K3. $20.00

LANG, Mrs. Andrew. *Book of Saints & Heroes.* 1912. Longman Gr. 1st. edit Andrew Lang. VG. M19. $45.00

LANG, Rev. Dr. *On the Origin & Migrations of the Polynesian Nation...* nd. np. 8vo. VG. P4. $55.00

LANGBEIN, John H. *Torture & the Law of Proof, Europe & England...* 1977. Chicago. M11. $65.00

LANGDON, Philip. *Orange Roofs, Golden Arches.* 1986. photos. VG. M17. $17.50

LANGDON, Stephen. *Sumerian Grammatical Texts.* 1917. Phil. U Mus. 1st. 44p. VG/wrp. W1. $45.00

LANGDON-DAVIES, John. *Behind the Spanish Barricades.* 1936. Secker Warburg. 1st. G. V4. $30.00

LANGE, John; see Crichton, Michael.

LANGE & TAYLOR. *American Exodus.* 1939. NY. Reynal Hitchcock. ils. 158p. cloth. D11. $250.00

LANGER, Susanne. *Cruise of the Little Dipper.* 1923. Norcross. ils Helen Sewell. 176p. G. P2. $25.00

LANGERLOF, Selma. *Story of Gosta Berling.* 1928. Doubleday Doran. Marbacka ed. 473p. VG. A25. $10.00

LANGFORD, N.P. *Discovery of Yellowstone Park, 1879, Diary...* 1905. Langford. 1st. sgn. 122p. VG. J2. $375.00

LANGLEY, Noel. *Tale of the Land of Green Ginger.* 1937. Morrow. 1st. 4to. 143p. VG/VG. D1. $135.00

LANGLOIS, Dora. *In the Shadow of Pa-Menkh.* 1908. London. VG. M2. $50.00

LANGMAN, Ida K. *Selected Guide to Literature on Flowering Plants of Mexico.* 1964. Phil. 1015p. as new/dj. B26. $62.50

LANGMORE, Diane. *Missionary Lives: Papua, 1874-1914.* 1989. Honolulu. 8vo. 408p. map ep. as new/sans. P4. $35.00

LANGSETH-CHRISTENSEN, Lillian. *Look & Cook Cookbook.* 1958. NM. Brn Bigelow. G/box. A16. $40.00

LANGSTAFF, J. Brett. *Oxford 1914.* 1965. NY. 1st. inscr. 317p. VG+/dj. B18. $25.00

LANGSTAFF, John. *Over in the Meadow.* 1957. Harcourt Brace. 1st. VG/G. C8. $25.00

LANGSTAFF & LANGSTAFF. *Jim Along, Josie.* 1970. HBJ. 1st. 127p. cloth. F/F. D4. $50.00

LANGTON, Jane. *Dark Nantucket Noon.* 1975. Harper Row. 1st. F/dj. M15. $100.00

LANGTON, Jane. *Memorial Hall Murder.* 1978. Harper Row. 1st. F/F. M15. $50.00

LANGTON, Jane. *Transcendental Murder.* 1964. Harper Row. 1st. author's 1st novel. VG/dj. M15. $175.00

LANIER, Sidney. *Boy's King Arthur.* 1968 (1924). ils NC Wyeth. VG/dj. S13. $30.00

LANKS, Herbert. *By Pan American Highway Through S Am.* 1942. Appleton. 1st. xl. F3. $10.00

LANNER & LANNER. *Pinon Pine: A Natural & Cultural History...* 1981. Reno, NV. ils/map/photo. F/NF. M12. $22.50

LANNING, George. *Pedestal.* 1967. London. Michael Joseph. 1st. VG/NF. Q1. $40.00

LANNING, John. *Pedro de la Torre.* 1974. LSU. 1st. 145p. dj. F3. $25.00

LANNING, John. *18th-Century Enlightenment in University of San Carlos...* 1956. Cornell. 1st. 372p. F3. $20.00

LANSDALE, Joe R. *Magic Wagon.* 1986. Doubleday. 1st. xl. G+/VG+. M21. $40.00

LANSDALE, Joe R. *Savage Season.* 1990. Ziesing. 1st hc. F/F. M22. $50.00

LANTZ, Sherlee. *Pageant of Pattern for Needlepoint Canvas.* 1973. Atheneum. 1st. 4to. 509p. 16 mc pl/150 photos/351 diagrams. F/dj. T10. $125.00

LANVAL, Marc. *Inquiry Into Intimate Lives of Women.* 1950 (1937). NY. Cadillac. 1st Am. chart. 243p. VG. A25. $12.00

LANZMAN, Claude. *Shoah: Oral History of the Holocaust, Complete Text of Film.* 1985. Pantheon. ils. 200p. VG/dj. S3. $24.00

LAO TZU. *Way of Life.* 1944. John Day. 1st. VG/dj. M25. $45.00

LAPIDE, Phinn E. *Prophet of San Nicandro.* 1953. Beechhurst. ils. 240p. VG/VG. S3. $25.00

LAQUEUR, W. *Struggle for the Middle East.* 1969. Macmillan. 1st Am. 360p. VG/dj. W1. $22.00

LAQUIAN, Aprodicio A. *Slums Are for People.* 1971. Honolulu. 245p. cloth. M/VG. P1. $15.00

LARDNER, Dionysius. *Popular Astronomy.* 1856. London. Walton Maberly. ils. 369p. gilt cloth. K5. $60.00

LARDNER, Dionysius. *Treatise on Hydrostatics & Pneumatics.* 1832. Phil. Carey Lea. 1st Am from 1st London. lg 12mo. 273p. rebound. K3. $40.00

LARDNER, Ring. *Bib Ballads.* 1915. Volland. 1st. presumed 1/500. teg. ils tan cloth. VG. M24. $100.00

LARDNER, Ring. *Ecstasy of Owen Muir.* 1954. Cameron Kahn. 1st. F/NF. B2. $35.00

LARDNER, Ring. *Say It With Oil.* 1923. Doran. 1st. NF/F. B4. $300.00

LARDNER, Ring. *Some Champions: Sketches & Fiction.* 1976. NY. 1st. F/F. A11. $85.00

LARGE, E.C. *Asleep in the Afternoon.* 1939. Holt. 1st. F/dj. M2. $90.00

LARKIN, David. *Fantastic Creatures of Edward Julius Detmold.* intro Keith Nicholson. 4to. 40 full-p pl. M/dj. B24. $75.00

LARKIN, Margaret. *Seven Shapes in a Gold Mine.* 1960. London. Readers Union. 213p. F3. $15.00

LARKIN, Philip. *All What Jazz.* 1985. Farrar Straus. reissue w/new intro. F/dj. Q1. $40.00

LARKINS, William. *US Navy Aircraft 1921-1941 & US Marine Corps Aircraft...* 1988. NY. 2 vol in 1. ils/index. VG/VG. S16. $35.00

LARMOTH, Jeanine. *Murder on the Menu.* 1972. Scribner. VG/dj. A16. $35.00

LAROUSSE. *Larousse Encyclopedia of Mythology.* 1959. photos. VG/VG. M17. $30.00

LAROUSSE. *Larousse Encyclopedia of Renaissance & Baroque Art.* 1967. ils. VG/VG. M17. $22.50

LAROUSSE. *Wines & Vineyards of France.* 1991. NY. 1st. VG/VG. T9. $26.00

LARSEN, Jeanne. *Silk Road.* 1989. Holt. 1st. F/dj. M2. $20.00

LARSEN, Lucinda Christenson. *Lucinda's Party Foods.* 1960. Caxton. VG. A16. $12.00

LARSON, Arthur. *Eisenhower: The President Nobody Knew.* 1968. Scribner. 1st. NF/clip. A20. $20.00

LARSON, Dewey B. *Quasars & Pulsars.* 1971 (1959). Portland, OR. 180p. Vg/dj. K5. $25.00

LARSON, Jennifer. *Leaf From Francisco Palou's Noticias de la Nueva California.* 1990. Orinda. Golden Key. 1/150. pict wrp. D11. $50.00

LARSON, Roger K. *Controversial James: An Essay on Life & Work of Geo W James.* 1991. BC of CA/Yolla Bolly. 1st. 1/400. ils/notes/bibliography. 98p. F/F case. B19. $250.00

LARSON, T.A. *History of Wyoming.* 1965. NE U. 1st. 619p. VG/VG. J2. $135.00

LARTEGUY, Jean. *Centurions.* 1962. Dutton. 2nd. NF/VG+. A20. $20.00

LASANSKY, Mauricio. *Nazi Drawings.* 1976. IA. revised. 16p+30 full-p pl. cloth. A17. $27.50

LASCELLES, G. *Falconry With Coursing by Harding Cox.* (1901). London. Longman. new imp. 2 vol in 1. ils GE Lodge. gilt polished calf. M12. $125.00

LASH, Joseph P. *Eleanor & Franklin.* 1971. Norton. 1st. tall 8vo. 32 pl. 765p. F/dj. H1. $22.50

LASH, Joseph P. *World of Love.* 1984. Franklin Lib. 1st. sgn. full leather. F. Q1. $35.00

LASKER, David. *Boy Who Loved Music.* 1979. Viking. 1st. ils Joe Lasker. VG/dj. T5. $35.00

LASKI, Marghanita. *Little Boy Lost.* 1949. London. 1st. VG/dj. w/sgn Christmas card. T9. $35.00

LASSWELL, Mary. *Mrs Rassmusson's One-Arm Cookery.* 1946. Boston. VG/VG. B5. $30.00

LASSWELL, Mary. *One on the House.* 1949. Houghton Mifflin. 1st. ils George Price. 263p. VG. A25. $8.00

LATH, J.A. *Adventure & Mystery: Cortez Emerald Mystery.* 1935. Cupples Leon. 189p. VG/dj. M20. $20.00

LATH, J.A. *Lost City of the Aztecs.* 1934. Cupples Leon. 1st. NF. M2. $35.00

LATHAM, Aaron. *Crazy Sundays: F Scott Fitzgerald in Hollywood.* 1971. Viking. 1st. NF/dj. M25. $35.00

LATHAM, Hiram. *Trans-Missouri Stock Raising.* 1962. Old West Pub. rpt. A19. $30.00

LATHEM, E.C. *Robert Frost 100.* 1974. Boston. Godine. 1st. pict wrp. M24. $25.00

LATHEN, Emma. *Longer the Thread.* 1971. S&S. 1st. F/NF. B2. $35.00

LATHEN, Emma. *Pick Up Sticks.* 1970. Inner Sanctum. 1st. NF/dj. M25. $22.50

LATHROP, Dorothy. *Animals of the Bible.* 1937. Stokes. 1st. 4to. gr cloth. G+. D1. $150.00

LATHROP, Dorothy. *Animals of the Bible.* 1937. Stokes. 1st/1st issue. sgn pres/ils Dorothy Lathrop. R5. $850.00

LATHROP, Dorothy. *Hide & Go Seek.* 1938. Macmillan. 1st. pres/sgn. teal-gr cloth. dj. R5. $200.00

LATHROP, Dorothy. *Puffy & the Seven Leaf Clover.* 1954. Macmillan. 1st. 34p. VG/VG. P2. $75.00

LATHROP, Dorothy. *Skittle-Skattle Monkey.* 1945. Macmillan. 12mo. ils. VG/dj. D1. $150.00

LATHROP, Dorothy. *Sung Under the Silver Umbrella.* 1935. NY. 1st. VG/fair. B5. $30.00

LATHROP, Elise. *Early American Inns & Taverns.* 1935 (1926). Tudor. 365p. VG/ragged. M20. $20.00

LATHROP, Elise. *Historic Houses of Early America.* 1933. NY. 110 photos. 464p. VG. M4. $30.00

LATHROP, Elise. *Historic Houses of Early America.* 1935 (1927). Tudor. 464p. NF/dj/box. M20. $45.00

LATHROP, Leonard. *Farmer's Library; or, Essays...* 1826. Windsor. Spooner. 2nd. 300p. leather brd. VG. A10. $200.00

LATOURETTE, Kenneth. *Christianity in Revolutionary Age...* 1976. Zondervan. 2 vol. VG. B29. $40.00

LATOURETTE, Kenneth. *History of Christian Missions in China.* 1929. Macmillan. 1st. bibliography/fld map. 930p. F/VG. W3. $145.00

LATROB, C.J. *Rambler in Oklahoma: Latrobe's Tour With Washington Irving.* 1955. OK City. ils/maps. 92p. VG. M4. $20.00

LATTA, Estelle. *Controversial Mark Hopkins.* 1963. Duke. Cothran Hist Research Found. 2nd revised. NF/G+. O4. $15.00

LATTA, F.F. *Black Gold in the Joaquin.* 1949. Caldwell. 1st. VG. O4. $15.00

LATTAUER, V.S. *Commonsense Horsemanship.* 1974. NY. Arco. rpt. VG/G. O3. $25.00

LATTAUER, V.S. *More About the Forward Seat.* 1939. London. Hurst Blackett. 1st. VG. O3. $45.00

LATTAUER & KOURNAKOFF. *Defense of the Forward Seat.* 1934. Boots & Saddles Riding School. ltd. sgns. half leather. O3. $150.00

LATTIMORE, Eleanor Frances. *More About Little Pear.* 1971. Morrow. 1st. lg 12mo. VG/VG+. C8. $22.50

LATTIMORE, Eleanor Frances. *Two Helens.* 1967. Morrow. 1st. 8vo. 128p. VG/G. T5. $25.00

LATTIMORE & LATTIMORE. *Silks, Spices & Empire.* 1968. Delacorte. 1st. maps. VG/dj. K3. $20.00

LATYMER, Hugo. *Mediterranean Gardener.* 1990. Barron's. tall 8vo. F/dj. A22. $30.00

LAUBER, Lynn. *White Girls.* 1990. Norton. 1st. author's 1st book. F/F. R13. $25.00

LAUBER, Lynn. *21 Sugar Street.* 1993. Norton. 1st. inscr. F/F. R13. $35.00

LAUBER, Patricia. *Runaway Flea Circus.* 1958. Random. 1st. 72p. VG/dj. M20. $30.00

LAUBIN & LAUBIN. *American Indian Archery.* 1990. OK U. ils/photos. 179p. F/dj. M4. $12.00

LAUFE, Leonard. *Obstetric Forceps.* 1968. NY. 1st. ils. 141p. A13. $75.00

LAUFER, Berthold. *Chinese Pottery of the Han Dynasty.* 1970. Rutland/Tokyo. 2nd (rpt 1909). 339p. F/dj. W3. $86.00

LAUGHLIN, Clara E. *So You're Going to France!* 1927. Houghton Mifflin. 1st. ils. 611p. VG. A25. $10.00

LAUGHLIN, Clarence John. *Ghosts Along the Mississippi.* 1961. NY. Bonanza. sgn. 220p. cloth. dj. D11. $150.00

LAUGHLIN, Robert. *Of Wonders Wild & New.* 1976. Smithsonian. 4to. xl. wrp. F3. $15.00

LAUMER, Keith. *Nine by Laumer.* 1967. Doubleday. 1st. F/NF. M2. $50.00

LAUMER, Keith. *Star Colony.* 1981. St Martin. 1st. F/dj. M2. $25.00

LAURENCE, Dan H. *Shaw, Books & Libraries.* 1976. Austin. HRC. 1st. 1/500. red cloth/label. F. M24. $30.00

LAURENTS, Arthur. *Way We Were.* 1972. Harper Row. 1st. sgn. F/VG. M19. $25.00

LAURITZEN, Jonreed. *Ordeal of the Young Hunter.* 1954. Little Brn. 1st. 246p. cloth. VG+/dj. M20. $25.00

LAUSANNE, Edita. *Great Book of Wine.* 1974. Galahad. revised. F/F. W2. $95.00

LAUT, Agnes C. *Through Our Unknown Southwest.* 1925. McBride. 5th. 271p. blk cloth. G+. F7. $22.50

LAVELL, Edith. *Linda Carlton's Ocean Flight (#2).* 1931. AL Burt. 283p. cloth. VG/dj (lists 3 titles). M20. $85.00

LAVENDER, David. *River Runners of the Grand Canyon.* 1986. Tucson. 2nd. sm 4to. bl cloth. F. F7. $35.00

LAVENDER, David. *Rockies.* 1968. Harper Row. 1st. 404p. VG/dj. M20. $25.00

LAVER, James. *Adventures in Monochrome: Anthology of Graphic Art.* ca 1950. London. Studio. 128p. G. A17. $15.00

LAVIN, Mary. *House in Clewe Street.* 1945. Little Brn. 21st. sgn. author's 2nd book. F/VG. L3. $200.00

LAVIN, Mary. *Shrine & Other Stories.* 1977. London. 1st. VG/VG. T9. $25.00

LAWES & MILTON. *Mask of Comus.* 1937. Nonesuch. 1/950. ils MRH Farrar. VG/worn box. B5. $95.00

LAWLISS, Chuck. *Civil War Sourcebook: A Traveler's Guide.* 1991. NY. Harmony. 1st. 308p. stiff prt wrp. M8. $20.00

LAWRENCE, A.B. *History of Texas; or, Emigrant's Guide...* 1844. NY. Nafis Cornish. 12mo. 275p. old calf. M1. $500.00

LAWRENCE, D.H. *Collected Letters of...* 1962. NY. Viking. 1st. 2 vol. edit HT Moore. F/djs. Q1. $100.00

LAWRENCE, D.H. *Lady Chatterly's Lover.* 1959. Grove. 1st Am Complete/Authorized from 3rd Manuscript Version. W2. $1,500.00

LAWRENCE, D.H. *Love Poems & Others.* 1915. NY. Mitchell Kennerly. 1st Am prt. gilt bl-purple cloth. VG. M24. $250.00

LAWRENCE, D.H. *Man Who Died.* 1931. London. 1/2000. VG/partial laid in. T9. $85.00

LAWRENCE, D.H. *Mornings in Mexico.* 1927. Knopf. 1st Am. 189p. VG. A4. $75.00

LAWRENCE, D.H. *My Skirmish With Jolly Roger.* 1929. Random. 1st. 1/600. F/F glassine dj as issued. D10. $300.00

LAWRENCE, D.H. *Reflections on the Death of Porcupine & Other Essays.* 1925. Phil. Centaur. 1st. 1/925. VG. Q1. $150.00

LAWRENCE, G.H.M. *B-P-H: Botanico-Periodicum-Huntianum.* 1968. Pittsburgh. Hunt Botanical Lib. 1063p. NF. B1. $35.00

LAWRENCE, George. *Adanson: Bicentennial Michel Adanson's Familles des Plantes.* 1963 & 1965. Pittsburgh. Hunt. 2 vol. F. A10. $55.00

LAWRENCE, Louise. *Star Lord.* 1978. Harper. 1st. F/dj. M2. $15.00

LAWRENCE, Mildred. *Crissy at the Wheel.* 1966 (1952). HBW. ils Marvin Bileck. 200p. VG/dj. T5. $22.00

LAWRENCE, T.E. *Letters of...* 1939. Doubleday Doran. 1st. edit David Garnett. VG. W1. $30.00

LAWRENCE, T.E. *Minorities.* 1971. London. 1st. edit JM Wilson/pref C Day Lewis. VG/VG. T9. $35.00

LAWRENCE, T.E. *Mint: A Day-Book of the RAF Depot...* 1955. London. Jonathan Cape. 1st/1st under his own name. F/dj. Q1. $100.00

LAWRENCE, W.G. *Ceramic Science for the Potter.* 1972. Chilton. 1st. 239p. F. D8. $30.00

LAWRENCE, W.J.C. *Practical Plant Breeding.* 1937. London. ils. 155p. cloth. B26. $10.00

LAWRENCE, W.J.C. *Practical Plant Breeding.* 1951. Allen Unwin. 3rd/6th imp. 12mo. 161p. B1. $19.00

LAWRENCE, William. *Treatise on Ruptures, Containing Anatomical Description...* 1811. Phil. 1st Am. 412p. full leather. A13. $350.00

LAWRENCE & MAYBEE. *Barbie, Midge & Ken (#9).* 1964. Random. 181p. VG+. M20. $25.00

LAWRENCE & MAYBEE. *Here's Barbie (#1).* 1962 (1958). Random. 186p. glossy brd. VG/dj. M20. $20.00

LAWSON, A.C. *Atlas of Maps & Seismograms Accompanying Report...1906.* 1970. WA. Carnegie. rpt 1908 ed. sbdg. NF. B1. $45.00

LAWSON, John Howard. *Processional! A Jazz Symphony of American Life.* 1925. NY. Seltzer. 1st. NF. B2. $40.00

LAWSON, Marie A. *Sea Is Blue.* 1946. Viking. 1st. ils. cloth. VG/dj. M20. $25.00

LAWSON, Robert. *Fabulous Flight.* 1949. Little Brn. 1st. 8vo. 152p. bl cloth. VG. T5. $35.00

LAWSON, Robert. *I Hear America Singing.* 1937. Winston. 1st. VG. M5. $30.00

LAWSON, Robert. *Rabbit Hill.* 1944. Viking. 1st. 128p. VG/G. P2. $95.00

LAWSON, Robert. *Rabbit Hill.* 1944. Viking. 1st. 8vo. VG+. M5. $50.00

LAWSON, Robert. *Robbut, a Tale of Tails.* 1948. Viking. 1st. 8vo. VG+/dj. M5. $60.00

LAWSON, Robert. *Smeller Martin.* 1950. Viking. 1st. 157p. VG/G. P2. $65.00

LAWSON, Robert. *Tough Winter.* 1954. Viking. 1st. ils. 8vo. 128p. VG/torn. D1. $60.00

LAWTON, Manny. *Some Survived: Epic Account of Japanese Captivity WWII.* 1984. Algonquin. 3rd. 295p. as new/dj. P1. $14.00

LAWTON, Thomas. *Chinese Figure Painting.* 1973. Freer Gallery. 1st. ils. 236p. F. W3. $125.00

LAYCOCK, Thomas. *Essay on Hysteria: Being Analysis of Irregular & Aggravated.* 1840. Phil/New Orleans. Haswell. 2 vol in 1. 1st Am. 8vo. 192p. G1. $300.00

LAYDEN & SNYDER. *It Was a Different Game.* 1969. Prentice Hall. 1st. photos. P8. $15.00

LAYMAN, Richard. *Dashiell Hammett: A Descriptive Bibliography.* 1979. Pittsburgh. 1st. 185p. cloth. F. A17. $30.00

LAYNE, J. Gregg. *Western Wayfaring: Routes of Exploration & Trade...* 1954. Automobile Club S CA. 1st. 1/100. ils/index. 63p. NF/sans. B19. $100.00

LAZZARO, G. Di San. *Klee.* 1957. Praeger. 1st Am. 12mo. 304p. F/dj. H1. $25.00

LE BLANC, Maurice. *Arsene Lupin: Super-Sleuth.* 1927. NY. Macaulay. 1st Am. NF/VG. B4. $100.00

LE BLANC, Maurice. *Crystal Stopper.* 1913. Doubleday. 1st. VG. M2. $25.00

LE CARRE, John. *Call for the Dead.* 1962. Walker. 1st. F/F. B35. $250.00

LE CARRE, John. *Clandestine Muse.* 1986. Newark, VT. Janus. 1st. 1/250. sgn. F/handmade wrp. Q1. $275.00

LE CARRE, John. *Honorable Schoolboy.* 1977. Hodder Stoughton. 1st. VG/VG clip. M22. $45.00

LE CARRE, John. *Little Drummer Girl.* 1983. Knopf. 1st Am (precedes Eng). 1/1048 special bdg. sgn. F/case. M15. $350.00

LE CARRE, John. *Little Drummer Girl.* 1983. Knopf. 1st. F/F. from $40 to $50.00

LE CARRE, John. *Little Drummer Girl.* 1983. Knopf. 1st. NF/dj. P3. $25.00

LE CARRE, John. *Looking-Glass War.* 1965. Heinemann. 1st. VG/dj. A24. $80.00

LE CARRE, John. *Naive & Sentimental Lover.* 1971. Hodder Stoughton. 1st. F/clip. M15. $100.00

LE CARRE, John. *Night Manager.* 1993. Knopf. 1st. F/NF. A20. $20.00

LE CARRE, John. *Perfect Spy.* 1986. Hodder Stoughton. 1st. sgn. F/F. M15. $175.00

LE CARRE, John. *Perfect Spy.* 1986. Knopf. 1st Am. sgn. F/F. M15. $150.00

LE CARRE, John. *Russia House.* 1989. Knopf. 1st. F/F. B35. $30.00

LE CARRE, John. *Russia House.* 1989. London Ltd Eds. 1/250 special bdg. sgn. F/tissue dj. M15. $200.00

LE CARRE, John. *Secret Pilgrim.* 1991. Knopf. 1st. F/F. B35. $22.00

LE CARRE, John. *Small Town in Germany.* 1968. Coward McCann. 1st Am. F/dj. M15. $50.00

LE CARRE, John. *Small Town in Germany.* 1968. Coward McCann. 1st Am. VG/VG. M22. $25.00

LE CARRE, John. *Small Town in Germany.* 1968. London. Heinemann. 1st. NF/dj. A24. $50.00

LE CARRE, John. *Spy Who Came in From the Cold.* 1964. Coward McCann. 1st Am. sgn. 256p. F/F. W2. $450.00

LE CARRE, John. *Tinker, Tailor, Soldier, Spy.* 1974. Knopf. 1st Am. NF/NF. N4. $30.00

LE CONTE, J. *Journal of Ramblings Through High Sierra of California...* 1930 (1875). SF. Sierra Club. rpt. 1/1500. ils. 152p. cloth/brd. F/VG. M12. $125.00

LE FANU, J. Sheridan. *Uncle Silas.* 1947. London. F/dj. M2. $35.00

LE GALLIENE, Richard. *Quest of the Golden Girl.* 1896. London/NY. John Lane/Bodley Head. 1st Am. gilt dk gr cloth. NF. M24. $150.00

LE GALLIENNE, Eva. *At 33.* 1940 (1934). Longman Gr. sgn ep. 262p. gilt bl cloth. G. H1. $18.00

LE GALLIENNE, Richard. *Old Country House.* 1902. Harper. 144p. leather. A10. $25.00

LE GALLOIS, Julien Jean Cesar. *Experiments on Principle of Life...* 1994. NY. Classics Neurology/Neurosurgery. facsimile. F. G1. $75.00

LE GEAR. *List of Geographical Atlases in Library of Congress...* nd. 9 vol. rpt of 1958-92 eds. 1/150. F. A4. $325.00

LE GRAND. *Augustus Rides the Border.* 1947. Bobbs Merrill. 1st. 134p. VG/dj. M20. $30.00

LE GUIN, Ursula K. *Buffalo Gals, Won't You Come Out Tonight.* 1994. Pomegranate. 1st. sgn. ils/sgn SS Boulet. F/dj. A24. $45.00

LE GUIN, Ursula K. *City of Illusions.* 1971. London. Gollancz. 1st. NF/dj. Q1. $100.00

LE GUIN, Ursula K. *Compass Rose.* 1982. Harper. 1st. F/dj. M2. $25.00

LE GUIN, Ursula K. *Dispossessed.* 1986. Easton. 1st thus. F/sans. M21. $40.00

LE GUIN, Ursula K. *Eye of the Heron.* 1983. Harper Row. 1st. F/VG. B3. $20.00

LE GUIN, Ursula K. *Gwilan's Harp.* 1981. Lord John. 1/300. sgn/#d. VG. M2. $50.00

LE GUIN, Ursula K. *Malafrena.* 1979. Putnam. 1st. sgn. F/F. R14. $45.00

LE GUIN, Ursula K. *Rocannon's World.* 1975. Garland. 1st hc. F/sans. M2. $50.00

LE GUIN, Ursula K. *Rocannon's World.* 1979. Gollancz. 1st. author's 1st book. F/dj. Q1. $75.00

LE GUIN, Ursula K. *Tehanu, the Last Book of Earthsea.* 1990. Atheneum. 1st. F/F. B3. $25.00

LE HURAY, Peter. *Treasury of English Church Music Vol 2 1545-1650.* 1965. Blandford. 282p. VG/dj. B29. $10.50

LE LIONNAIS, Francois. *Encyclopedie Essentielle.* 1959. Paris. Robert Delpire. 112p. NF. K3. $15.00

LE MAIR, Willebeek. *Old Dutch Nursery Rhymes.* 1917. London. Augener. obl 4to. 42p. gilt bl cloth/pict label. VG. D1. $200.00

LE MASTER, Richard. *Wildlife in Wood.* 1978. 1st. photos. VG/VG. M2. $35.00

LE MAY, Alan. *Unforgiven.* 1957. 1st. VG/VG. S13. $50.00

LE NEVE FOSTER, C. *Text-Book of Ore & Stone Mining.* 1901. Chas Griffin. 4th/revised. 700+ ils. 765p. cloth. D8. $60.00

LE NOBLE, Pierre. *La Cassette Ouverte de L'Illustre Criole...* 1691. Villefranche. Du Four. 12mo. brd. R12. $225.00

LE QUEUX, William. *Closed Box.* 1908. Dodge. G+. M2. $17.00

LE QUEUX, William. *Golden Tree.* 1931. Fiction League. 1st Am. F/NF. M15. $50.00

LE QUEUX, William. *Great White Queen.* nd. Shaw. VG. M2. $95.00

LE ROUX, Hugues. *Acrobats & Mountebanks.* 1890. London. trans AP Morton. ils Jules Garnier. gilt gr silk. VG. A11. $175.00

LE VAYER DE BOUTIGNY, R.-R. *Dissertations sur l'Autorite des Rois...* 1682. Cologne. Marteau. 12mo. brd. R12. $300.00

LEA, Henry Charles. *Ordeal, With Additional Original Documents in Translation...* 1973. Phil. 199p. sewn wrp. M11. $20.00

LEA, Tom. *Hands of Cantu.* 1964. Little Brn. 1st. F/VG+ clip. T11. $45.00

LEA, Tom. *Selection of Paintings & Drawings From the Nineteen-Sixties.* 1969. Encino. 1st ltd Rio Bravo of 200. sgns. F/case. A18. $175.00

LEA, Tom. *Wonderful Country.* 1952. Little Brn. 1st. NF/VG+. T11. $75.00

LEA & MASTERS. *Sex Crimes in History: Evolving Concepts...* 1966. NY. Matrix House. 1st thus. 323p. VG/dj. A25. $20.00

LEACH, Brownie. *Kentucky Derby Diamond Jubilee.* 1949. NY. 1st. 192p. lg 4to. F. A17. $25.00

LEACH, C. *Aids to Goatkeeping.* 1946 (1926). G+. E6. $12.00

LEACH, D.G. *Rhododendrons of the World & How To Grow Them.* 1961. Scribner. 1st. 544p. dj. B1. $100.00

LEACH, David G. *Rhododendrons of the World.* 1962. Allen Unwin. 4to. 544p. VG/torn. A22. $65.00

LEACH, Julian G. *Insect Transmission of Plant Diseases.* 1940. McGraw Hill. ils. 615p. F/dj. B26. $37.50

LEACH, Maria. *God Had a Dog.* 1961. Rutgers. 1st. VG/G. B5. $45.00

LEACH, Sally. *Scholar at Work, an Exhibit.* 1970. Austin. 1st. bl cloth. F. M24. $65.00

LEAF, Munro. *Arithmetic Can Be Fun.* (1949). Lippincott. 11th. 4to. red cloth. VG/G. T5. $30.00

LEAF, Munro. *Arithmetic Can Be Fun.* 1949. Lippincott. stated 1st. 4to. VG. M5. $20.00

LEAF, Munro. *Manners Can Be Fun.* 1936. Lippincott. 31st imp. 45p. cloth. VG/dj. M20. $22.00

LEAF, Munro. *Story of Ferdinand.* 1936. Viking. 3rd. VG+/VG. M5. $42.00

LEAF, Munro. *Story of Ferdinand.* 1936. Viking. 1st. ils Robert Lawson. cloth. dj. R5. $875.00

LEAKEY, John. *West That Was.* 1967. Lincoln, NE. A19. $10.00

LEAR, Edward. *Book of Nonsense.* 1980. Viking/Met Mus Art. sm 4to. unp. F/G+ clip. C14. $20.00

LEAR, Edward. *Dong With the Luminous Nose.* 1969. NY. Young Scott. 1st. ils/sgn Edward Gorey. obl 8vo. mauve cloth. dj. R5. $45.00

LEAR, Edward. *Jumblies.* 1968. NY. Young Scott Books. 1st. ils/sgn Edward Gorey. tan pict cloth. dj. as new. R5. $45.00

LEAR, Edward. *Jumblies.* 1972. 2nd. ils Gorey. VG/VG. M17. $40.00

LEAR, Edward. *Le Hibou et la Poussiquette.* 1961. Little Brn. 1st. 31p. NF/VG clip. C14. $20.00

LEAR, Edward. *New Vestments.* 1970. NJ. Bradbury. 1st. ils Arnold Lobel. 32p. F/NF. D4. $35.00

LEAR, Edward. *Nonsense Songs.* nd. London/NY. Warne. ne. ils LL Brooke. unp. cloth. F/F. D4. $50.00

LEAR, Edward. *Owl & the Pussycat.* 1983. Macmillan. 1st. unp. NF/dj. M20. $25.00

LEAR, Edward. *Quangle Wangle's Hat.* 1969. Heinemann. 1st. ils Helen Oxenbury. 32p. VG+/VG+. D4. $65.00

LEAR, Edward. *Teapots & Quails.* 1953. MA. Harvard. 1st. ils. intro/edit Angus Davidson/Philip Hofer. VG+/dj. D4. $35.00

LEAR, Floyd Seyward. *Treason in Roman & Germanic Law, Collected Papers.* 1965. Austin. VG/dj. M11. $65.00

LEARNARD, Rachel. *Mrs Roo & the Bunnies.* 1953. Houghton Mifflin. ARC/1st. ils Tom Funk. 31p. F/NF. D4. $35.00

LEARY, Timothy. *Jail Notes.* 1970. NY. 1st. intro Allen Ginsberg. VG/VG. B5. $45.00

LEARY. *Book-Peddling Parson: Account of Life & Works of Mason Lock.* 1984. 158p. F/F. A4. $35.00

LEASON & SUTTON. *Big Book of Dogs.* nd (1952). Grosset Dunlap. 4to. unp. NF. C14. $12.00

LEAVITT, David. *Equal Affections.* 1989. Weidenfeld Nicholson. 1st. sgn. F/F. R14. $40.00

LEAVITT, David. *Family Dancing.* 1984. Knopf. 1st. sgn. F/F. L3. $125.00

LEAVITT, Gertrude Stevens. *Story of Frances E Willard.* 1905. Portland. HL Nelson. 1st. photos. 32p. VG+. A25. $22.00

LEAVITT, Robert Greenleaf. *Forest Trees of New England.* 1932. Jamaica Plain. Arnold Arboretum. 8vo. G+. A22. $15.00

LEBARON, Anthony; see Laumer, Keith.

LEBAS, F. *Rabbit: Husbandry, Health & Production.* 1986. Rome. ils. 235p. NF. S15. $13.50

LECKY, W.E.H. *History of Ireland in the 18th Century.* 1972. Chicago. 8vo. 494p. gilt bl/red cloth. F/dj. H13. $85.00

LEDERER, William J. *Mirages of Marriages.* 1968. Norton. 1st. 473p. NF/NF. W2. $55.00

LEDOUX, Louis. *Art of Japan.* 1927. NY. Japan Soc. 85p. VG. W3. $42.00

LEDYARD, Gleason H. *And to the Eskimos.* 1962. Chicago. 4th. 254p. F/dj. A17. $15.00

LEE, Anna. *Natural Foods Cookbook.* 1972. London. Hamlyn. VG/dj. A16. $7.00

LEE, Charles E. *Blue Riband.* ca 1935. London. Sampson Low. 67 halftones. VG. T7. $50.00

LEE, Fred J. *Casey Jones: True Story of John Luther Casey Jones.* 1939. Southern Pub. 1st. 298p. pict cloth. VG/dj. M20. $50.00

LEE, Frederic P. *Azalea Book.* 1958. Van Nostrand. 324p. VG. A10. $22.00

LEE, Frederic P. *Azalea Book.* 1958. Van Nostrand. 8vo. 324p. VG/torn. A22. $35.00

LEE, Frederic P. *Azalea Handbook.* 1953. Am Horticultural Soc. tall 8vo. cloth. VG/tattered. A22. $20.00

LEE, Gus. *China Boy.* 1991. Dutton. 1st. sgn. F/F. R14. $60.00

LEE, Hanna. *Memoir of Pierre Toussaint, Born a Slave in St Domingo.* 1854. Boston. Crosby Nichols. 2nd. 124p. NF. B4. $375.00

LEE, Harper. *To Kill a Mockingbird.* 1960. London. Heinemann. 1st Eng. NF/dj. B4. $500.00

LEE, Harper. *To Kill a Mockingbird.* 1993. Harper Collins. 35th Anniversary/later prt. inscr. F/F. A23. $250.00

LEE, Mary Catherine. *Lois Mallet's Dangerous Gift.* 1902. Houghton Mifflin. 1st. 116p. V3. $15.00

LEE, Mrs. N.K.M. *Cook's Own Book, Being Complete Culinary Encyclopedia.* 1972. NY. Arno. G/dj. A16. $10.00

LEE, Mrs. N.K.M. *Cook's Own Book, Being Complete Culinary Encyclopedia.* 1972 (1832). rpt. F/VG. E6. $15.00

LEE, Nathaniel. *Lee's Plays.* 1726-1734. London. 3 vol. leather. VG. A15. $50.00

LEE, Norman E. *Harvests & Harvesting Through the Ages.* 1960. London. ils. 208p. F/dj. B26. $20.00

LEE, Rebecca Lawrence. *Concha: My Dancing Saint.* 1966. Riverside, CA. 1st. 1/300. inscr/sgn/#d. xl. VG. O4. $25.00

LEE, Robert E. *Recollections & Letters of General Robert E Lee.* 1926. 471p. O8. $14.50

LEE, Robert. *Victory at Guadalcanal.* 1981. Novato. photos/map/index. 260p. VG/VG. S16. $17.50

LEE, Ruth Webb. *Antique Fakes & Reproductions.* 1966. Lee Publications. enlarged/revised 8th. 317p. gilt bl cloth. F/clip. H1. $45.00

LEE, Ruth Webb. *Early American Pressed Glass.* 1931. Pittsford. self pub. 630p. VG. M20. $25.00

LEE, Ruth Webb. *Victorian Glass.* 1944. Northboro. self pub. 1st. sgn. 608p. VG. M20. $35.00

LEE, Stan. *Bring on the Bad Guys.* 1976. 253p. F. M13. $16.00

LEE, Stan. *Marvel Masterworks, X-Men 1-10.* 1987. Marvel Comics. 1st. F/dj. M2. $35.00

LEE, Tanith. *Dreams of Dark & Light.* 1986. Arkham. 1st. collects 23 stories. F/F. T2. $45.00

LEE, Vincent. *Building of Sacsayhuaman & Other Papers.* 1987-89. Wilson, WY. 1st. sgn. 4to. 108p. wrp. F3. $25.00

LEE, Vincent. *Investigations in Bolivia.* 1992. Wilson, WY. 1st. sgn. 105p. wrp. F3. $25.00

LEE, Vincent. *Vira Vira: A New Chachapoyas Site.* 1993. Wilson, WY. sgn. 40p text+maps/photos. F3. $20.00

LEE, W. Storrs. *Great California Deserts.* 1963. Putnam. 1st. NF/VG clip. O4. $15.00

LEE, W. Storrs. *Great California Deserts.* 1963. Putnam. 1st. 8vo. 306p. F/dj. T10. $25.00

LEE, W. Storrs. *Sierra.* 1962. Putnam. 1st. ils Edward Sanborn. VG/VG. O4. $15.00

LEE, William F. *Stan Kenton, Artist in Rhythm.* 1980. Los Angeles. Creative Pr. 1st. 727p. VG/dj. M20. $35.00

LEECH, M. *Reveille in Washington.* 1941. 1st. 483p. O8. $9.50

LEECH, Samuel. *Thirty Years From Home; or, Voice From the Main Deck...* 1844. Boston. Tappan Dennet. 12mo. 305p. brn cloth. P4. $150.00

LEEDALE, G.F. *Euglenoid Flagellates.* 1967. Prentice Hall. 242p. dj. B1. $32.00

LEESE & LEESE. *Desert Plants: Cacti & Succulents in the Wild...* 1959. London. photos/drawings. 220p. VG. B26. $20.00

LEFANU, W.R. *Bio-Bibliography of Edward Jenner 1749-1823.* 1951. London. Harvey Blythe. 1st. 1/1000. 29 pl. 176p. NF. K3. $95.00

LEFCOURT, Peter. *Deal.* 1991. Random. 1st. F/F. M22. $20.00

LEFFINGWELL, William Bruce. *Shooting on Upland, Marsh & Stream.* 1890. Rand McNally. 1st. 473p. gilt bdg. VG. H7. $150.00

LEGGE, James. *Record of Buddhist Kingdoms: Being Account by Chinese Monk.* 1975 (1886). SF. rpt. notes/index. 123p. F/NF. W3. $48.00

LEGMAN, G. *Love & Death: Study in Censorship.* 1949. Breaking Point. 1st? 95p. G/wrp. A17. $15.00

LEGRAND, Edy. *Petite Histoire de Lafayette.* ca 1935. Paris. Tolmer. obl 4to. pict brd. VG. D1. $165.00

LEGSTRAND & ROLEN. *Long Pony Race.* 1966. Knopf. 1st Am. VG/G. O3. $10.00

LEHANE, Dennis. *Drink Before the War.* 1994. Harcourt Brace. 1st. sgn. F/F. D10. $60.00

LEHMANN, John. *Edward Lear & His World.* 1977. Scribner. 1st. sm 4to. bl brd. NF/dj. T5. $45.00

LEHY, Frank. *Notre Dame Football: The T Formation.* 1949. Prentice Hall. 1st. photos/diagrams. VG. P8. $25.00

LEIBER, Fritz. *Knight & Knave of Swords.* 1988. Morrow. 1st. F/dj. M2. $20.00

LEIBERT, Herman W. *Dr Johnson's First Book.* 1950. New Haven. Yale. 1/150. 8vo. F/heavy paper wrp. H13. $85.00

LEICHHARDT, F.W. Ludwig. *Letters of...* 1968. Cambridge. Hakluyt Soc. 8vo. 1175p. bl cloth. VG. P4. $70.00

LEICHMAN, Seymour. *Boy Who Could Sing Pictures.* 1968. Doubleday. 1st. sm 4to. VG/NF. C8. $35.00

LEIGH, Randolph. *Forgotten Waters: Adventures in Gulf of California.* 1941. Lippincott. 1st. VG. O4. $25.00

LEIGHTEN, Peter. *Moon Travelers.* nd. London. Oldbourne. 8vo. 240p. NF/dj. K3. $20.00

LEINSTER, Murray; see Jenkins, Will F.

LEIPOLD, L. Edmond. *Famous Scientists & Astronauts.* 1968 (1967). Minneapolis. TS Denison. 4th. 8vo. 80p. xl. K5. $14.00

LEIRIS, Galerie Louise. *Picasso.* 1960. France. self pub. French text. A19. $10.00

LEITER, S. *Art of Kabuki: Famous Plays in Performance.* 1979. CA U. photos/trans/bibliography/index. F/VG. W3. $38.00

LEITHAUSER, Brad. *Hence.* 1989. Knopf. 1st. NF/dj. M21. $20.00

LEITHAUSER, Joachim. *World Beyond the Horizon.* 1955. Knopf. 1st. 412p. dj. F3. $20.00

LEITNER, Irving. *Baseball Diamond in the Rough.* 1972. NY. 1st. VG/dj. B5. $30.00

LEJARD, Andre. *Art of the French Book, From Early Manuscripts to Present.* 1947. Paris. ils. 166p. G+. B18. $37.50

LEJEUNE, Anthony. *Gentlemen's Clubs of London.* 1979. photos. VG. M17. $25.00

LEM, Stanislaw. *Chain of Chance.* 1978. Harcourt. 1st. F/dj. M2. $15.00

LEMAITRE, Canon Georges. *Primeval Atom.* 1950. Van Nostrand. 186p. cloth. K5. $25.00

LEMAITRE, Georges. *Four French Novelists.* 1969. Kennikat. 419p. F. A17. $7.50

LEMAN, A.E. *Diseases of Swine.* 1986. IA State. 6th. 930p. cloth. F. B1. $60.00

LEMAN, Rhoda. *Book of the Night.* 1984. HRW. 1st. F/NF. M21. $25.00

LEMMON, Ken. *Cool Greenhouse Plants.* 1967. London. Garden BC. 192p. VG/dj. A10. $22.00

LEMOINE, Ann. *Wild Girl of the Wood.* nd (ca 1812). London. Roe Lemoine. Chapbook. 28p. Sawyer bdg. H13. $95.00

LEMPRIERE, J. *Universal Biography.* 1810. NY. Sargeant. 2 vol. 1st Am. thick tall 8vo. contemporary full calf. H13. $250.00

LENARD, Philipp. *Great Men of Science.* 1933. Macmillan. trans from 2nd German. 8vo. 389p. G. K5. $30.00

LENIN, N. *Imperialism: The State & Revolution.* 1926. Vanguard. VG/dj. V4. $30.00

LENIN, V.I. *Toward the Seizure of Power.* 1932. NY. Intern'l. 1st. 2 vol. F/dj. B2. $60.00

LENK, Torsten. *Flintlock: Its Origin & Development.* 1965. Bramhall. photos. VG/VG. M17. $40.00

LENNON, Florence Becker. *Victoria Through the Looking Glass: Life of Lewis Carroll.* 1945. S&S. 1st. 387p. F/G. H1. $18.00

LENNOX, Charlotte Ramsey. *Female Quixote; or, Adventures of Arabella.* 1810. London. 2 vol. new ed. 12mo. full tan calf/rebacked. H13. $395.00

LENNOX, Charlotte Ramsey. *Memoirs for the History of Madame deMaintenon & Last Age.* 1757. London. 5 vol. 1st. 12mo. full early speckled calf. H13. $595.00

LENOTRE, G. *Paris Revolutionnaire.* 1908. Paris. 4 vol. Premiere Serie. 12mo. ils. teg. 3-quarter red leather. H3. $150.00

LENSKI, Lois. *Cotton in My Sack.* 1949. Lippincott. 1st 191p. VG/G+. P2. $120.00

LENSKI, Lois. *I Like Winter.* (1950). NY. Walck. 24mo. unp. bl cloth. G+. T5. $35.00

LENSKI, Lois. *Journey Into Childhood: Autobiography of Lois Lenski.* 1972. Lippincott. 1st. 208p. VG/clip. M20. $25.00

LENSKI, Lois. *Little Airplane.* (1938). London. Oxford. 1st. 8vo. beige cloth. VG. D1. $60.00

LENSKI, Lois. *Little Sail Boat.* 1944 (1937). Oxford. 8th. sq 12mo. unp. G. T5. $35.00

LENSKI, Lois. *Surprise for Davy.* 1947. Oxford. 1st. 12mo. VG. M5. $55.00

LENSKI, Lois. *Susie Mariar.* (1939). Oxford. obl 8vo. unp. G. T5. $20.00

LENSKI, Louis. *Songs of Mr Small.* 1954. 1st. VG. M17. $25.00

LENSKI, R.C.H. *Interpretation of St John's Gospel.* 1956. Warburg. 1444p. G. B29. $9.50

LENT, Henry B. *Full Steam Ahead!* 1933. Macmillan. 1st. ils Earle Winslow. pict cloth. VG. C8. $40.00

LENTRICCHIA, Melissa. *No Guarantees.* 1990. Morrow. 1st. inscr. F/NF. R13. $40.00

LENTZ, Harold B. *Sleeping Beauty.* 1933. Bl Ribbon. 1 double-p popup at center. 8vo. mc pict brd. R5. $250.00

LENZ, Ellis Christian. *Rifleman's Progress.* 1946. Huntington, WV. Standard pub. 1st. 4to. 162p. F/VG. H7. $50.00

LENZ, Sidney. *Lenz on Bridge: Volume Two.* 1927. NY. 2nd. 456p. VG. S1. $15.00

LENZNER, R. *Great Getty: Life & Loves of J Paul Getty...* 1985. Crown. 283p. NF/G. D8. $22.00

LEONARD, Charles. *Stolen Squadron.* 1942. Doubleday Crime Club. 1st. F/dj. M15. $45.00

LEONARD, Elmore. *Bandits.* 1987. Arbor. 1st. NF/NF. N4/T12. $28.00

LEONARD, Elmore. *Bandits.* 1987. Arbor. 1st. sgn. F/NF. B2. $35.00

LEONARD, Elmore. *City Primeval. High Noon in Detroit.* 1980. Arbor. 1st. F/NF. Q1. $60.00

LEONARD, Elmore. *Double Dutch Treat.* 1986. Arbor. 1st. F/F. A20. $25.00

LEONARD, Elmore. *Dutch Treat.* 1977. Arbor. 1st. VG/VG. A20. $25.00

LEONARD, Elmore. *Dutch Treat.* 1985. NY. Mysterious. Omnibus. F/sans/case. M15. $75.00

LEONARD, Elmore. *Fifty-Two Pickup.* 1974. Delacorte. 1st. VG/dj. M15. $150.00

LEONARD, Elmore. *Get Shorty.* 1990. Delacorte. 1st. F/F. from $25 to $30.00

LEONARD, Elmore. *Glitz.* 1985. Arbor. 1st. NF/NF. M22. $15.00

LEONARD, Elmore. *Glitz.* 1985. Mysterious. 1st. 1/500 special bdg. sgn. F/sans/case. M15. $60.00

LEONARD, Elmore. *Hombre.* 1989. Armchair Detective. 1st thus. M/dj. A18. $20.00

LEONARD, Elmore. *Hombre.* 1989. NY. Armchair Detective. 1st Am hc. 1/26 lettered. sgn. F/case. M15. $100.00

LEONARD, Elmore. *Killshot.* 1989. Arbor. 1st. VG+/NF. N4. $22.50

LEONARD, Elmore. *LaBrava.* 1983. Arbor. 1st. F/F. B35. $40.00

LEONARD, Elmore. *LaBrava.* 1983. Arbor. 1st. sgn. F/NF. M15. $65.00

LEONARD, Elmore. *Maximum Bob.* 1991. Delacorte. 1st. F/F. B35. $25.00

LEONARD, Elmore. *Split Images.* 1981. NY. Arbor. 1st. F/F. M15. $65.00

LEONARD, Elmore. *Swag.* 1976. Delacorte. 1st. NF/dj. M25. $75.00

LEONARD, Elmore. *Touch.* 1987. Arbor. 1st. F/F. M22/P3. $20.00

LEONARD, Elmore. *Unknown Man No 89.* 1977. London. Secker Warburg. 1st Eng. F/dj. M15. $150.00

LEONARD, Elmore. *Unknown Man No 89.* 1993. Armchair Detective. 1/100. sgn/#d. F/case. M19. $50.00

LEONARD, George. *Ultimate Athlete.* 1975. Viking. 1st. ils. F/VG. P8. $17.50

LEONARD, Jonathan. *Ancient America.* 1967. Time. 1st. 4to. 192p. F3. $15.00

LEONARD, L.L. *International Regulation of Fisheries.* 1944. WA. Carnegie. ils/maps/figures. 201p. VG. M12. $22.50

LEONARDO, Richard. *History of Surgery.* 1943. NY. 1st. 100 pl. 504p. A13. $350.00

LEONIS, Shelia. *Thread in the Maze.* ca 1965. London. Rider. 1st. 12mo. 96p. NF/dj. W1. $12.00

LEOPOLD, Aldo. *Aldo Leopold's Wilderness: Selected Early Writings.* 1990. Harrisburg. 1st. ils. F/dj. M4. $18.00

LEOPOLD, Aldo. *Sand County Almanac, Etc.* 1949. Oxford. ils CW Schwartz. 226p. cpict cloth. NF. M12. $125.00

LEOPOLD, Aldo. *Wildlife of Mexico.* 1959. Berkeley. ils CW Schwartz. 568p. cloth. xl. VG. M12. $60.00

LERICHE, Rene. *Surgery of Pain.* 1939. London. 1st. 512p. A13. $300.00

LERNER, J. *Review of Amino Acid Transport Processes in Animal Cells...* 1978. Orono. 234p. B1. $35.00

LEROY, L.W. *Biostratigraphy of the Majfi Section, Egypt.* 1953. GSA Memoir 54. 73p. cloth. F. D8. $16.00

LESBERG, Sandy. *Great Classic Recipes of Europe.* 1972. NJ. Prentice Hall. G/dj. A16. $20.00

LESBERG, Sandy. *Specialty of the House.* 1970. Prentice Hall. G/fair. A16. $15.00

LESCOVET. *Remonstrances Prononcees avx Ovvertvres Pvbliqves...* 1619. Paris. Cramoisy. 8vo. quarter vellum. R12. $350.00

LESIEUTRE, Alain. *Spirit & Splendour of Art Deco.* 1974. NY. Paddington. 1st. ils. 304p. VG/VG. B5. $37.50

LESLEY, Craig. *River Song.* 1989. Houghton Mifflin. 1st. sgn. M/dj. A18. $50.00

LESLEY, Craig. *Sky Fisherman.* 1995. Houghton Mifflin. 1st. sgn. M/dj. A18. $35.00

LESLIE, Eliza. *Directions for Cookery in Its Various Branches.* 1839. Phil. Carey Hart. 8th. 468p. modern lib buckram. B10. $250.00

LESLIE, Eliza. *Maid of Canal Street & the Bloxhams. By Miss Leslie.* 1851. Phil. Hart. 1st. 8vo. 115p. later calf-backed cloth. M1. $125.00

LESLIE, Eliza. *75 Receipts for Pastry, Cake, Sweetmeats.* 1835 (1827). G. E6. $150.00

LESLIE, Frank. *Report on the Fine Arts.* 1868. GPO. pres. folio. purple prt wrp. R12. $225.00

LESLIE, John. *Narrative of Discovery & Adventure in Polar Seas & Regions.* 1833. NY. Harper. ils/fld chart. 373p. full calf. T7. $115.00

LESLIE, R.F. *Miracle at Square Top Mountain.* 1979. Dutton. ils/maps. 243p. cloth/brd. F/VG. M12. $15.00

LESSA, William A. *Drake's Island of Thieves, Ethnological Sleuthing.* 1975. Honolulu. 1st. ils/maps/tables. 289p. NF/dj. P4. $30.00

LESSING, Doris. *Briefing for a Descent Into Hell.* 1971. London. Cape. 1st. sgn. F/clip. D10. $125.00

LESSING, Doris. *Fifth Child.* 1988. Knopf. 1st. NF/VG+. M21. $10.00

LESSING, Doris. *In Pursuit of the English.* 1961. S&S. 1st. sgn. author's 4th book pub in US. NF/VG. D10. $75.00

LESSING, Doris. *Memoirs of a Survivor.* 1975. Knopf. 1st Am. 8vo. F/dj. T10. $100.00

LESTER, Julius. *Falling Pieces of the Broken Sky.* 1990. NY. Arcade. 1st. rem mk. F/F. B4. $35.00

LESTER, Julius. *Long Journey Home: Stories From Black History.* 1972. 156p. VG/VG. A4. $75.00

LESTER, Pauline. *Marjorie Dean: College Freshman.* 1922. NY. AL Burt. 1st. ils. 278p. VG+. A25. $16.00

LESTER, Pauline. *Marjorie Dean: High School Senior.* 1917. AL Burt. 1st. ils. 302p. VG. A25. $15.00

LESTER, Pauline. *Marjorie Dean: High School Sophomore.* 1917. NY. AL Burt. 1st. 256p. VG/dj. A25. $20.00

LESY, Michael. *Wisconsin Death Trip.* 1973. NY. 1st. VG/VG. B5. $50.00

LETCHER, Owen. *Big Game Hunting in North-Eastern Rhodesia.* 1987. NY. rpt. F/F. S15. $12.00

LEUPOLD, H.C. *Exposition of Genesis. Vol 1: Chapters 1-19.* 1950. Baker. 578p. G. B29. $9.50

LEVANDER, F.W. *Total Solar Eclipse 1905.* 1906. London. Eyre Spottiswoode. 8vo. 64p. K5. $60.00

LEVEL, Maurice. *Tales of Mystery & Horror.* 1920. McBride. VG. M2. $32.00

LEVENSON, Sam. *Sex & the Single Child.* 1969. S&S. 1st. lg 8vo. VG+/VG. C8. $15.00

LEVERTOV, Denise. *Pig Dreams.* 1981. Countryman Pr. 1st. 47p. F/F. D4. $30.00

LEVI, Carlo. *Words Are Stones.* 1958. Farrar Straus. 1st. F/VG. M19. $25.00

LEVI & REGGE. *Dialoggo.* 1989. Princeton. 1st. F/clip. B35. $20.00

LEVIATAN. *Collection of References Pertaining to Miniature Books.* 1985. 1/500. 459 entries. 76p. F. A4. $85.00

LEVICK, James J. *Early Friends & Their Services in America.* 1883. Phil. WH Pile. 36p. V3. $20.00

LEVIEN, Michael. *Naval Surgeon: Voyages of Dr Edward H Cree, Royal Navy...* 1982. NY. 1st Am. 276p. A13. $45.00

LEVIN, Ira. *Boys From Brazil.* 1976. Random. 1st. NF/NF. M22. $50.00

LEVIN, Ira. *Boys From Brazil.* 1976. Random. 1st. VG/NF. R14. $40.00

LEVIN, Ira. *Perfect Day.* 1970. Random. 1st. F/NF. R14. $25.00

LEVIN, Ira. *Rosemary's Baby.* 1967. Random. 1st. author's 2nd novel. F/dj. D10/H11. $100.00

LEVIN, Ira. *This Perfect Day.* 1970. Random. 1st. F/dj. M2. $25.00

LEVIN, Meyer. *Beginnings of Jewish Philosophy.* 1971. Behrman. ils. 192p. VG. S3. $25.00

LEVIN, Meyer. *Citizens.* 1940. Viking. 1st. NF/NF. B4. $200.00

LEVINE, Daniel. *Bird: Making of an American Sports Legend.* 1988. McGraw Hill. 1st. photos. F/F. P8. $25.00

LEVINE, Israel. *Francis Bacon (1561-1626).* 1925. London. Parsons. 1st. sm 8vo. 181p. VG/dj. K3. $12.00

LEVINE, Philip. *5 Detroits.* 1970. Unicorn. 1st. 1/500. F/sans. R14. $125.00

LEVINGER, Lee J. *Jewish Chaplain in France.* 1921. Macmillan. 220p. VG. S3. $25.00

LEVINSOHN, John L. *Frank Morrison Pixley of the Argonaut.* 1989. SF. BC of CA. 1/450. 8vo. gray linen. R3. $90.00

LEVINSON, Edward. *I Break Strikes! Technique of Pearl L Bergoff.* 1936. Robert McBride. 2nd. VG/VG. V4. $30.00

LEVISON, Eric. *Eye Witness.* 1921. Bobbs Merrill. 1st. F/VG. M15. $65.00

LEVITAN, Tina. *Laureates: Jewish Winners of the Nobel Prize.* 1960. Twayne. ils/biblio/index. 236p. VG/G. S3. $22.00

LEVORSEN, A. *Geology of Petroleum.* 1967. Freeman. 2nd. F/dj. D8. $20.00

LEVY, Barry. *Quakers & the American Family.* 1988. NY. Oxford. 1st. 340p. VG/dj. V3. $15.50

LEVY, Deborah. *Ophelia & the Great Idea.* 1989. NY. Viking. ARC. author's 1st story collection. F/F. w/promo material. R13. $25.00

LEVY, Ferdinand. *Flashes From the Dark.* 1941. Dublin. Sgn of 3 Candles. 1st. F/NF. B4. $225.00

LEVY, Newman. *Sandy MacPherson: Book Collector.* 1940. 1/750. sgn. wrp. K3. $15.00

LEWANDOWSKY, Max Heinrich. *Untersuchungen Uber die Leitungsbahnen...* 1904. Jena. Gustav Fischer. folio. assn copy. 13 photo pl. G/cloth case. G1. $250.00

LEWIN, Michael Z. *Hard Line.* 1982. Morrow. 1st. F/F. B2. $35.00

LEWIN, R.S. *Elements of Mining.* 1941. John Wiley. 2nd/2nd prt. 579p. G. D8. $18.00

LEWIN, Ralph A. *Genetics of Algae.* 1976. Berkeley. ils. 360p. F/dj. B26. $37.50

LEWIN, Ronald. *Rommel As Military Commander.* 1968. Batsford/Van Nostrand. 1st. 262p. VG/dj. M20. $15.00

LEWINSOHN, Richard. *Science, Prophecy & Preditiction.* 1961. NY. Bell. 318p. xl. dj. K3. $15.00

LEWIS, Alfred Henry. *Confessions of a Detective.* 1906. NY. AS Barnes. 1st. F/case. M15. $75.00

LEWIS, Arthur H. *It Was Fun While It Lasted.* 1973. Trident. 1st. F/F. B4. $85.00

LEWIS, Bernard. *Islam & the Arab World.* 1976. Knopf/Am Heritage. 1st Am. 360p. VG/torn. W1. $65.00

LEWIS, C.S. *All My Road Before Me: The Diary, 1922-27.* edit W Hooper. VG/VG. M17. $25.00

LEWIS, C.S. *Case for Christianity.* 1943. VG. M17. $20.00

LEWIS, C.S. *Case for Christianity.* 1974. Macmillan. 56p. VG. B29. $7.50

LEWIS, C.S. *Christian Behaviour: Further Series of Broadcast Talks.* 1943. Geoffrey Bles. 1st. F/VG. A18. $50.00

LEWIS, C.S. *English Literature in the 16th Century Excluding Drama.* 1954. Oxford. 1st. F/VG. A18. $75.00

LEWIS, C.S. *English Literature in the 16th Century Excluding Drama.* 1965. Oxford. Clarendon. later prt. 8vo. 696p. xl. T10. $25.00

LEWIS, C.S. *Horse & His Boy.* 1956 (1954). London. Bles. 2nd. sm 8vo. VG. C8. $35.00

LEWIS, C.S. *Last Battle.* 1962. Macmillan. F/dj. M2. $17.00

LEWIS, C.S. *Letters to an American Lady.* 1967. Eerdmans. 1st Am. F/clip. A18. $35.00

LEWIS, C.S. *Letters to Malcolm: Chiefly on Prayer.* 1964. Geoffrey Bles. 1st. F/clip. A18. $35.00

LEWIS, C.S. *Magician's Nephew.* 1960 (1955). London. Bodley Head. 3rd. sm 8vo. NF/G+. C8. $35.00

LEWIS, C.S. *Prince Caspian: Return to Narnia.* 1951. Geoffrey Bles. 1st. ils Pauline Baynes. VG. A18. $150.00

LEWIS, C.S. *Reflections on the Psalms.* 1958. Geoffrey Bles. 1st. F/F. A18. $60.00

LEWIS, C.S. *Screwtape Letters & Screwtape Proposes a Toast.* 1961 (1942). 1st thus. lg 12mo. VG/dj. C8. $45.00

LEWIS, C.S. *Silver Chair.* 1961 (1953). Macmillan. 3rd. 8vo. 208p. VG/VG. T5. $45.00

LEWIS, C.S. *Surprised by Joy: The Shape of My Early Life.* 1955. Geoffrey Bles. 1st. F/clip. A18. $125.00

LEWIS, C.S. *Voyage of the Dawn Trader.* nd. London. Bles. 1st. ils Pauline Baynes. 223p. bl cloth. VG. D1. $250.00

LEWIS, C.S. *Voyage of the Dawn Trader.* 1960 (1952). Macmillan. 2nd. 210p. bl cloth. VG/G. T5. $65.00

LEWIS, C.S. *Voyage of the Dawn Trader.* 1970 (1952). Macmillan. 9th. NF/VG+. C8. $35.00

LEWIS, Cecil Day. *Otterbury Incident.* 1948. Putnam. 1st. ils Ardizzone. 148p. VG/VG. P2. $70.00

LEWIS, Charles Lee. *Famous Old-World Sea Fighters.* 1929. Boston/London. ils. 362p. T7. $35.00

LEWIS, D.B. Wyndham. *Francois Villon.* 1928. Coward McCann. 1st Am. gilt bdg. NF/dj. Q1. $40.00

LEWIS, David. *We, the Navigators.* 1972. Honolulu. 345p. bl cloth. VG. P4. $45.00

LEWIS, Deborah; see Grant, Charles L.

LEWIS, Edward R. Jr. *Reflections of Canton in Pharmacist's Show Globe.* 1967. Canton. self pub. sgn. 256p. F/VG. B11. $65.00

LEWIS, G.R. *Stannaries: A Study of Medieval Tin Miners of Cornwall...* 1965 (1908). Truro. Bradford Barton Ltd. facsimile. M11. $75.00

LEWIS, George Andrew. *Origin & Treatment of Stammering.* 1910. Akron. 8th. 199p. G. A17. $15.00

LEWIS, H. Spencer. *Thousand Years of Yesterday.* 1935. Amorc. VG. M2. $22.00

LEWIS, Henry. *Valley of the Mississippi Illustrated.* 1967. Minneapolis. 1/2000. ils/pl. 423p. F/dj. M4/O7. $60.00

LEWIS, Isabel Martin. *Handbook of Solar Eclipses.* 1925. NY. Duffield. 1st. ils. VG/torn. K3. $25.00

LEWIS, Jerry D. *Tales of Our People: Great Stories of the Jew in America.* 1969. Bernard Geis. 332p. VG/dj. S3. $23.00

LEWIS, John N.C. *Small Boat Conversions.* 1951. London. Hart Davis. ils/plans/photos. 207p. T7. $25.00

LEWIS, Lange. *Juliet Dies Twice.* 1943. Bobbs Merrill. 1st. NF. M25. $35.00

LEWIS, Lange. *Passionate Victims.* 1952. Bobbs Merrill. 1st. VG/rpr. M25. $45.00

LEWIS, Lloyd. *Sherman: Fighting Prophet.* 1932. Harcourt Brace. 1st. 690p. VG/dj. M20. $40.00

LEWIS, Oscar. *Death in the Sanchez Family.* 1969. Random. 1st. 8vo. F/NF. T10. $35.00

LEWIS, Oscar. *Life in a Mexican Village: Tepoztlan Restudied.* 1951. Urbana. 2nd. 512p. F3. $15.00

LEWIS, Oscar. *Sacramento River.* nd. HRW. 1st. ils Michael Hampshire. NF/VG clip. O4. $15.00

LEWIS, Preston. *Lady & Doc Holliday.* 1989. Diamonds. 197p. as new/dj. J2. $95.00

LEWIS, R.B. *Light & Truth: Collected From the Bible...& Modern History.* 1844. Boston. Comm of Colored Gentlemen. 2nd. contemporary bdg. F. L3. $850.00

LEWIS, Ralph. *Inductive Preaching: Helping People Listen.* 1983. Crossway. 223p. G/dj. B29. $7.50

LEWIS, Richard. *In a Spring Garden.* 1965. Dial. 1st. ils Ezra Jack Keats. 32p. cloth. NF/dj. D4. $35.00

LEWIS, Richard. *Still Waters of the Air: Poems by 3 Modern Spanish Poets.* 1970. NY. Dial. 1st. ils/sgn bookplate Ed Young. F/F. D4. $25.00

LEWIS, Richard. *There Are Two Lives: Poems by Children of Japan.* 1970. S&S. 1st. trans Kimura. F/F. W3. $36.00

LEWIS, Shari. *One-Minute Greek Myths.* 1987. Doubleday. 1st. 48p. F. C14. $10.00

LEWIS, Sinclair. *Ann Vickers.* 1933. Doubleday Doran. 1st. 1/2350 on rag paper. 562p. cloth. VG+/dj. M20. $185.00

LEWIS, Sinclair. *Bethel Merraday.* 1940. NY. 1st. VG/VG. B5. $40.00

LEWIS, Sinclair. *Cass Timberlane.* 1945. Random. 1st. F/VG. M19. $35.00

LEWIS, Sinclair. *Dodsworth.* 1929. Harcourt Brace. 1st. F/G. M23. $200.00

LEWIS, Sinclair. *Elmer Gantry.* 1927. NY. Harcourt. 1st. 8vo. cloth/bl brd. G. M23. $50.00

LEWIS, Sinclair. *God-Seeker.* 1949. Random. 1st. F/VG. M19. $45.00

LEWIS, Sinclair. *It Can't Happen Here.* 1935. Doubleday Doran. 1st. F/F. B4. $175.00

LEWIS, Sinclair. *It Can't Happen Here.* 1935. Doubleday Doran. 1st. 458p. VG+/dj. M20. $30.00

LEWIS, Sinclair. *Keep Out of the Kitchen.* 1929. ARC (of article for Cosmopolitan). 34p. bl brd. VG. M20. $425.00

LEWIS, Sinclair. *Man From Main Street.* 1953. Random. 1st. 317p. VG/dj. M20. $35.00

LEWIS, Sinclair. *Man Who Knew Coolidge.* 1928. Harcourt Brace. 1st. NF/VG. M23. $100.00

LEWIS, Sinclair. *Prodical Parents.* 1938. Doubleday Doran. 1st. VG/VG. M19. $45.00

LEWIS, Sinclair. *World So Wide.* 1951. Random. 1st. NF/NF. B35. $30.00

LEWIS, Sinclair. *World So Wide.* 1951. Random. 1st. VG/VG. M19. $25.00

LEWIS, Thomas. *Pain.* 1942. Macmillan. 1st Am. 192p. panelled pebbled red buckram. G1. $75.00

LEWIS, Thomas. *Vascular Disorders of the Limbs.* 1936. London. 1st. 111p. A13. $75.00

LEWIS, Wilmarth Sheldon. *Three Tours Through London...1748-1776.* 1941. Yale. sgn. ils. VG. M17. $20.00

LEWIS, Wilmarth. *Collector's Progress.* 1951. Knopf. 1st. ils. VG/dj. K3. $25.00

LEWIS & LEWIS. *Jayhawker: A Play.* 1935. Doubleday. 1st. 163p. VG/dj. M20. $125.00

LEWIS & LITAI. *China Builds the Bomb.* 1991. Stanford. rpt. M/wrp. K3. $20.00

LEWIS & MURAKAMI. *R MacDonald: Narrative of His Early Life on the Columbia...* 1923. Spokane. 1st. 1/1000. 8vo. 333p. red cloth. NF. P4. $250.00

LEWIS & PACELLA. *Modern Trends in Child Psychiatry.* 1945. NY. Internat U. 1st. ils. 341p. VG+. A25. $20.00

LEWIS & SCHARY. *Storm in the West.* 1963. Stein Day. 1st. 192p. VG/dj. M20. $45.00

LEWISOHN, Ludwig. *Last Days of Shylock.* 1931. Harper. 1st. 221p. VG. S3. $30.00

LEY, Willy. *Conquest of Space.* 1950. Viking. VG. M2. $20.00

LEY, Willy. *Events in Space.* 1969. McKay. 8vo. 180p. dj. K5. $13.00

LEY, Willy. *Harnessing Space.* 1963. Macmillan. 8vo. 314p. VG/dj. K5. $15.00

LEY, Willy. *Rockets, Missiles & Men in Space.* 1968. Viking. sm 4to. 557p. xl. dj. K5. $20.00

LEYARD, John. *Journal of Capt Cook's Last Voyage...* 1963. Chicago. Quadrangle. facsimile. F. O7. $55.00

LEYDET, Francois. *Coyote: Defiant Sondog of the West.* 1977. OK U. 224p. F/F. S15. $25.00

LEYDET, Francois. *Time & the River Flowing.* 1968. Ballantine/Sierra Club. 8vo. 160p. VG/wrp. F7. $12.00

LEYMARIE, Jean. *Fauvism.* 1959. d'Art Albert Skira. 71 tipped-in mc pl. F/F. H1. $47.50

LI, H.L. *Trees of Pennsylvania, the Atlantic States & Lake States.* 1972. Phil. 8vo. 276p. F/wrp. B1. $20.00

LI CHIIAO-P'ING. *Chemical Arts of Old China.* 1948. Easton, PA. Journal Chemical Ed. 1st. tall 8vo. 215p. xl. VG. H1. $35.00

LIANG, Yen. *Tommy & Dee-Dee.* 1953. Oxford. 1st. sq 8vo. F/VG. M5. $35.00

LIBBY, Bill. *Great American Race Drivers.* 1970. Cowles. photos/records/stats. VG/G+. P8. $45.00

LIBBY, Bill. *We Love You Lakers.* 1972. Sports Magazine Pr. 1st. photos. VG+. P8. $15.00

LIBBY & WEST. *Basketball My Way.* 1973. Prentice Hall. 1st. photos. VG/G+. P8. $30.00

LICHAUCO, Alejandro. *Lichauco Paper: Imperialism in the Philippines.* 1973. Monthly Review. 1st. 111p. cloth. M/VG. P1. $8.00

LICHINE, Alex. *Wines of France.* 1951. Knopf. 1st. 316p. VG/G+. B10. $45.00

LICHT, Hans. *Sexual Life in Ancient Greece.* 1956. London. Routledge Kegan. 8th. photos. 557p. VG. A25. $20.00

LICHTENBERG, G.G. *Lichtenberg Reader.* 1959. trans Mautner/Hatfield. VG/VG. M17. $17.50

LICHTENBERG, Jacqueline. *Mahogany Rose.* 1981. Doubleday. 1st. F/dj. M2. $20.00

LICHTENBERG, Jacqueline. *Unto Zeor, Forever.* 1978. Doubleday. 1st. NF/dj. M2. $20.00

LIDA. *Bourru, L'Ours Brun.* 1936. Flammarion. Albums du Pere Castor. ils Rojankovsky. VG. M5. $55.00

LIDA. *Martin Pecheur.* 1938. Flammarion. ils Rojankovsky. obl 8vo. VG. M5. $42.00

LIDA. *Spiky the Hedgehog.* 1938. Harper. 1st. sq 4to. VG+/dj. P2. $75.00

LIDDEL-HART, B.H. *Rommel Papers.* 1953. NY. fld maps/index. 454p. VG/torn. S16. $35.00

LIDDELL & LIDDELL. *Greek-English Lexicon: A Supplement.* 1968. Oxford. edit EA Barber. 153p. VG. B29. $30.00

LIDDIC & HARBAUGH. *Camp on Custer, Transcribing the Custer Myth.* 1995. Clark. 1/500. sgn Liddic. 189p. as new. J2. $325.00

LIDE & JOHANSES. *Thord Firetooth.* 1937. Lee Shepard. 1st. 236p. VG/G. P2. $20.00

LIDELL, John A. *Treatise on Apoplexy, Cerebral Hemorrhage, Cerebral...* 1990. NY. Classics Neurology/Neurosurgery Lib. facsimile. G1. $65.00

LIDTKE, Vernon L. *Alternative Culture: Socialist Labor in Imperial Germany.* 1985. Oxford. 1st. VG/VG. V4. $25.00

LIE, F. *Military History of Modern China 1924-49.* 1965. Princeton. 1st. F/F. E6. $18.00

LIEBERMAN, William S. *Nelson A Rockefeller Collection: Masterpieces of Modern Art.* 1981. NY. Hudson Hills. photos Lee Boltin. 255p. cloth. dj. D2. $65.00

LIEBHERR, James K. *Zoogeography of Caribbean Insects.* 1988. Cornell. 285p. F. S15. $20.00

LIEBIG, Justus. *Address to Agriculturists of Great Britain.* 1845. Liverpool. Baines. 32p. wrp. A10. $25.00

LIEBKNECHT, Karl. *Briefe aus Dem Felde, aus der Untersuchungshaft...* 1919. Berlin. Wochenschrift Die Aktion. 1st. VG. B2. $125.00

LIEBLING, A.J. *Normandy Revisited.* 1958. S&S. 1st. 243p. VG/dj. M20. $8.00

LIFF, Flora Gregg. *Peoples of the Blue Water.* 1954. Harper. 1st. 271p. VG/G+. F7. $27.50

LIFTON, B.J. *Place Called Hiroshima.* 1985. Tokyo. 1st. ils E Hosoe. F/dj. K3. $20.00

LIGHTMAN, Alan. *Einstein's Dreams.* 1993. Pantheon. 1st. inscr. F/F. B2. $75.00

LIGHTNER, Otto. *History of Business Depressions.* 1932. NY. 1st. VG. B5. $25.00

LIGHTNER, Theodore A. *Highlights of the Culbertson System.* 1931. NY. 1st. 238p. VG. S1. $15.00

LIGOTTI, Thomas. *Nocturary.* 1994. Carroll Graf. 1st Am. F/NF. R10. $10.00

LIKINS, Mrs. J.W. *Six Years' Experience As a Book Agent in California.* 1992. SF. BC of CA. tall 8vo. ils. terra-cotta cloth. R12. $50.00

LIKINS, William M. *Trail of the Serpent.* 1928. Uniontown, PA. Watchman. 1st. 123p. stiff prt wrp. M8. $250.00

LILIENTHAL, Alfred H. *There Goes the Middle East.* 1957. NY. Devin Adair. 1st. 8vo. 12 pl. 300p. VG. W1. $12.00

LILIENTHAL, Howard. *Thoracic Surgery: Surgical Treatment of Thoracic Disease.* 1925. Phil. 1st. 2 vol. A13. $250.00

LILLIGRIDGE, Will. *Ben Blair.* 1907. NY. AL Burt. A19. $25.00

LILLYS, William. *Persian Miniatures: Story of Rustam.* 1958. Rutland/Tokyo. Art Treasures of Asia series. VG. W3. $28.00

LIMNELIUS, George. *Medbury Fort Murder.* 1929. Doubleday Crime Club. 1st Am. F/dj. M15. $90.00

LIMOJON DE SAINT-DIDIER. *La Ville et la Republique de Vnise.* 1680. Lyne. 12mo. vellum. R12. $450.00

LINCOLN, Abraham. *Addresses of Abraham Lincoln.* 1929. Kingsport, TN. 22x16mm. 139p. aeg. gilt red leather. B24. $150.00

LINCOLN, Abraham. *Discoveries & Inventions: A Lecture...1860.* 1915. SF. John Howell. 1/1000. 24p. gilt brd. D11. $30.00

LINCOLN, Abraham. *His Talk With Lincoln.* 1922. Riverside. 1/530. 33p. F. O8. $27.50

LINCOLN, Abraham. *President's Words.* 1865. Boston. Walker Fuller. 186p. F. O8. $21.50

LINCOLN, Almira H. *Familiar Lectures on Botany...* 1829. Hartford. Huntington. 1st. 338p. tree calf. A10. $95.00

LINCOLN, Joseph. *Back Numbers.* 1932. NY. 1st. VG/VG. B5. $45.00

LINCOLN, Joseph. *Old Home House.* 1907. NY. 1st. VG. B5. $55.00

LINCOLN, Joseph. *Storm Girl.* 1937. NY. 1st. sgn pres. VG/VG. B5. $35.00

LINDBERG. *Annotated McGuffey, Selections From...Readers 1836-1920.* 1976. 4to. ils. 380p. xl. VG/VG. A4. $50.00

LINDBERGH, Anne Morrow. *Flower & the Nettle: Diaries & Letters 1936-39.* 1976. Harcourt. 1st. 605p. white cloth/bl spine. as new/dj. B22. $12.00

LINDBERGH, Anne Morrow. *Gifts From the Sea.* 1955. Pantheon. 1st. F/F case. B35. $55.00

LINDBERGH, Anne. *Three Lives To Live.* 1992. Little Brn. 1st. sm 8vo. NF/NF. C8. $30.00

LINDBERGH, Charles A. *Of Flight & Life.* 1948. Scribner. 1st. VG/dj. B4. $85.00

LINDBERGH, Charles A. *We.* 1927. Putnam. 1st trade. VG/VG. B4. $150.00

LINDBERGH, Charles. *We.* 1927. Scribner. 1st. VG/dj/box. B5. $50.00

LINDBURG, D.C. *Macaques.* 1980. Van Nostrand. 8vo. 384p. F/F. B1. $25.00

LINDEMAN, E.B. *Space: A New Direction for Mankind.* 1969. Harper. sgn. F/dj. M2. $15.00

LINDER, Kurt. *Hunting Book of Wolfgang Birkner.* 1969. Winchester. 1/250. facsimile. plates loose as issued. box w/20p booklet. B24. $200.00

LINDER. *History of the Writings of Beatrix Potter.* 1979. ils. 472p. F/F. A4. $165.00

LINDGREN, Astrid. *Springtime in Noisy Village.* 1966. Viking. 1st Am. sm 4to. VG+/G+. C8. $35.00

LINDGREN & WILDES. *Century of Electrical Engineering & Computer Science at MIT.* 1985. Cambridge, MA. 1st. ils. 4to. 423p. VG/dj. K3. $25.00

LINDLEY, Harlow. *History of the Ordinance of 1787 & Old Northwest Territory.* 1937. Marietta. 95p. VG/wrp. B18. $15.00

LINDMAN, M. *Snipp, Snapp, Snurr & the Magic Horse.* 1933. Whitman. 1st. 4to. cloth. VG. M5. $60.00

LINDOP, Audrey. *Sight Unseen.* 1969. Doubleday. 1st. F/dj. M2. $13.00

LINDSAY, Alexander J. *Survey & Excavations North & East of Navajo Mountain...* 1968. Flagstaff. ils/79 tables. 399p. F/orange wrp. F7. $45.00

LINDSAY, Cynthia. *Dear Boris: Life of William Henry Pratt, aka Boris Karloff.* 1975. Knopf. photos. NF/dj. C9. $50.00

LINDSAY, Vachel. *General William Booth Enters Heaven & Other Poems.* 1916 (1913). Macmillan. rpt. sgn/dtd 1916. VG+. B4. $85.00

LINDSAY, Vachel. *Springfield Town Is Butterfly Town...* 1969. Kent State. 1st. ils. pref Louis Untermeyer. unp. F/F. D4. $125.00

LINDSAY & MAMET. *Owl: Story for Children.* 1987. NY. Kipling. 1st. ils Stephen Alcorn. F/NF. R13. $25.00

LINDSAY & POULSSON. *Joyous Guests.* 1921. Boston. 1st. ils WM Berger. cloth. VG. M5. $65.00

LINDSELL, Harold. *Battle for the Bible.* 1976. Zondervan. 218p. VG/dj. B29. $8.00

LINDSEY, A.A. *Natural Areas in Indiana & Their Preservation.* 1969. Purdue. 594p. xl. NF. S15. $17.00

LINDSEY, David. *Cold Mind.* 1983. Harper Row. 1st. NF/F. A20. $35.00

LINDSEY, David. *Heat From Another Sun.* 1984. Harper Row. 1st. F/F. N4. $30.00

LINDSEY, David. *Heat From Another Sun.* 1984. Harper Row. 1st. sgn. VG/VG. A23. $42.00

LINDSEY, David. *Spinal.* 1986. Atheneum. 1st. NF/F. A20. $30.00

LINDSEY, Robert. *Gathering of Saints.* 1988. S&S. 1st. 397p. VG/VG. J2. $85.00

LINEBARGER, Paul. *Instrumentality of Mankind.* 1989. Gollancz. F/dj. P3. $30.00

LINEBARGER, Paul. *Quest of the Three Worlds.* 1989. Gollancz. 1st. F/dj. P3. $25.00

LINEBARGER, Paul. *Rediscovery of Man.* 1988. Gollancz. 1st. F/dj. P3. $30.00

LINFORTH, James. *Route From Liverpool to Great Salt Lake Valley.* (1855). Los Angeles. Westernlore. facsimile. 1/350. fld map. 120p. VG/dj. K7. $145.00

LING, Max Freedom. *Growing Into the Light.* 1955. DeVorss. 1st. 177p. F. H1. $20.00

LINGENFELTER, Richard E. *Presses of the Pacific Islands 1817-1867: A History...* 1967. LA. Plantin. 1/500. photos/woodcuts/fld map. 131p. D11. $75.00

LINGO, Ada E. *Murder in Texas.* 1935. Houghton Mifflin. 1st. inscr. F/clip. M15. $125.00

LININGTON, Elizabeth. *Greenmask!* 1964. Harper. 1st. author's 1st book. F/VG. M19. $45.00

LININGTON, Elizabeth. *Something Wrong.* 1967. Harper Row. 1st. NF/NF. M19. $25.00

LINK, P.S. *Basic Petroleum Geology.* 1987. OGCI Pub. 493 figures. 425p. F/dj. D8. $30.00

LINKE, Lilo. *Peoples of the Amazon.* 1965. London. Adventurers Club. 189p. dj. F3. $20.00

LINKLATER, Eric. *Voyage of the Challenger.* 1972. Doubleday. ils/photos. 288p. VG/dj. P4/S15. $30.00

LINSDALE, Jean. *Natural History of Magpies.* 1937. Cooper Ornithological Club. ils. 234p. F. S15. $40.00

LINTON, Calvin D. *Bicentennial Almanac.* 1975. Thomas Nelson. dj. A19. $35.00

LIONNI, Leo. *Alphabet Tree.* 1968. Pantheon. 1st. 4to. unp. VG/G+. T5. $32.00

LIONNI, Leo. *Fish Is Fish.* 1970. Pantheon. 1st. ils. VG/G+. P2. $30.00

LIPMAN, Jean. *American Folk Painters of Three Centuries.* 1980. 1st. ils. F/F. S13. $55.00

LIPMAN, Jean. *Rufus Porter: Rediscovered Artist, Inventor, Journalist.* 1980. NY. Potter/Crown. photos/ils/genealogy/checklist. 212p. cloth. dj. D2. $65.00

LIPMAN & WINCHESTER. *Flowering of American Folk Art 1776-1876.* 1974. ils. VG/VG. M17. $45.00

LIPOWSKI, Z.J. *Delirium: Acute Brain Failure in Man.* 1980. Springfield, IL. Chas Thomas. thick 8vo. 568p. VG/worn. G1. $50.00

LIPP & VON REIS. *New Plant Sources of Drugs & Foods From NY Botanical...* 1982. Cambridge. Harvard. 1st. 8vo. 363p. F/dj. A22. $25.00

LIPPINCOTT, David. *Salt Mine.* 1979. Viking. 1st. NF/F. H11. $15.00

LIPPINCOTT, Mary S. *Life & Letters of Mary S Lippincott.* 1893. Phil. WH Pile. 294p. V3. $12.00

LIPSCHITZ, Max A. *Faith of a Hassid.* 1967. NY. Jonathan David. ils Steinsnyder/Yanich. 346p. VG/G+. S3. $30.00

LIPSCOMB, Ken. *Duke Casanova.* 1958. NY. Exposition. 1st. F/NF. B4. $125.00

LIPSON. *NY Times, Parent's Guide to Best Books for Children.* 1988. 4to. ils. 421p. F/F. A4. $45.00

LIPTON, Morris A. *Psychopharmacology: Generation of Progress.* 1978. NY. Raven. 1732p. bl-gr cloth. G1. $50.00

LIPTZIN, S. *Germany's Stepchildren.* 1944. 1st. VG/VG. E6. $15.00

LISH, Gordon. *Dear Mr Capote.* 1983. HRW. 1st. F/F. B35. $35.00

LISH, Gordon. *Dear Mr Capote.* 1983. HRW. 1st. sgn. author's 1st book. F/F. L3. $125.00

LISH, Gordon. *Mourner at the Door.* 1988. Viking. 1st. F/F. B35. $25.00

LISH, Gordon. *What I Know So Far.* 1984. HRW. 1st. F/F. R14. $25.00

LISS, Howard. *Strange But True Hockey Stories.* 1972. Random. Pro Hockey Lib series. photos. VG. P8. $10.00

LISTER, Raymond. *Craftsman in Metal.* 1968. AS Barnes. 1st Am. 208p. VG+/dj. M20. $15.00

LISTER & LISTER. *Those Who Came Before: SW Archeology in National Park...* 1983. AZ U. 1st. ils/bibliography/index. 184p. B19. $45.00

LISTON, Robert. *Elements of Surgery.* 1837. Phil. 1st Am. 540p. full leather. A13. $200.00

LITTAUER, Vladimir S. *Development of Modern Riding.* 1991. Howell. 1st. VG/VG. O3. $25.00

LITTLE, George. *American Cruisers Own Book.* 1859. Phil. JB Smith. 384p. emb cloth. P4. $75.00

LITTLE, Jean. *When the Pie Was Opened.* 1968. Little Brn. 1st. 83p. cloth. NF/dj. D4. $25.00

LITTLE, W.J. *On the Nature & Treatment of Deformities of Human Frame...* 1993. NY. Classics Neurology/Neurosurgery Lib. facsimile. G1. $75.00

LITTLE & WADSWORTH. *Common Trees of Puerto Rico & the Virgin Islands.* 1964. USDA. 548p. VG. B1. $68.00

LITTLEJOHN, D. *Hitler Youth.* 1987. SC. ils. 377p. VG/VG. S16. $22.50

LITTLER, Gene. *Real Score.* 1976. Waco. Word. 1st. inscr. VG/VG. A23. $50.00

LITTLETON, Thomas. *Littleton's Tenures, in French & English.* 1671. London. John Streater/James Flesher. contemporary calf. M11. $850.00

LITVAG, Irving. *Master of Sunnybank: Biography of Albert Payson Terhune.* 1977. Harper Row. 1st. VG/dj. M20. $40.00

LIVEING, Edward. *On Megrim, Sick-Headache & Some Allied Disorders...* 1986. Birmingham. Classics Neurology/Neurosurgery Lib. facsimile. G1. $85.00

LIVELY, Penelope. *Moon Tiger.* 1988. Grove. 1st Am. F/F. R13/R14. $25.00

LIVELY, Penelope. *Next to Nature, Art.* 1982. Heinemann. 1st. F/F. A24. $45.00

LIVELY, Penelope. *Pack of Cards.* 1989. Grove. 1st. F/NF. R13. $15.00

LIVELY, Penelope. *Pack of Cards.* 1989. NY. Grove. 1st Am. F/F. R14. $20.00

LIVELY, Penelope. *Passing On.* 1990. NY. 1st Am. F/dj. R13. $15.00

LIVELY, Penelope. *Revenge of Samuel Stokes.* 1981. London. Heinemann. 1st. F/NF. R13. $25.00

LIVERMOORE, Mary. *My Story of the War.* nd. np. 1st ed. mc pl of Civil War battle flags. F. O8. $22.50

LIVERSIDGE, Douglas. *Prince Charles: Monarch in the Making.* 1975. London. Barker. 1st. F/F. T12. $35.00

LIVERSIDGE, Douglas. *Whale Killers.* 1963. London. Jarrolds. ils. 191p. dj. T7. $24.00

LIVINGSTON, Armstrong. *Monster in the Pool.* 1929. AL Burt. F/NF. M2. $25.00

LIVINGSTON, F.V. *Bibliography of the Works of Rudyard Kipling.* 1927. NY. Edgar Wells. 1st. teg. gilt brn cloth. F. M24. $75.00

LIVINGSTON, Myra. *Child As Poet: Myth or Reality?* 1984. Boston. Horn Book. 1st. inscr. 354p. F/F. D4. $30.00

LIVINGSTON, Myra. *Higgledy-Piggledy.* 1986. NY. McElderry. 1st. inscr. ils Peter Sis. 32p. F/F. D4. $35.00

LIVINGSTON, Myra. *Learical Lexicon.* 1985. Atheneum. 1st. sgn. 64p. F/F. D4. $30.00

LIVINGSTON, Myra. *Listen, Children, Listen.* 1972. HBJ. 1st. 96p. F/F. D4. $35.00

LIVINGSTON, Myra. *Way Things Are & Other Poems.* 1974. Atheneum. 1st. 40p. NF/NF. D4. $30.00

LIVINGSTON, Myra. *4-Way Stop & Other Poems.* 1976. Atheneum. 1st. 40p. F/F. D4. $30.00

LIVINGSTON & WEST. *Hybrids & Hybridizers.* 1978. Newton Square, PA. ils/photos. 256p. F/dj. B26. $29.00

LIVINGSTONE, David. *Livingstone's Travel & Researches in South Africa...* 1859. Phil. Bradley. 8vo. 440p. cloth. G. W1. $28.00

LLOYD, B.E. *Lights & Shades in San Francisco.* 1876. SF. AL Bancroft. 1st. thick 4to. ils. aeg. gilt blk calf. F. R3. $600.00

LLOYD, Hugh. *Hal Keen: Copperhead Trail Mystery (#3).* 1930s. Grosset Dunlap. 218p. orange cloth. VG/dj (lists 6 titles). M20. $60.00

LLOYD, J. Ivester. *Beagling.* 1954. London. Herbert Jenkins. 1st. VG/G. O3. $45.00

LLOYD, J.W. *Muskmelon Production.* 1928. Orange Judd. 12mo. 10 pl. 126p. B1. $14.00

LLOYD & LLOYD. *Lloyd on Lloyd.* 1985. Beaufort. 1st. sgn. A23. $48.00

LOBECK, A.K. *Geomorphology: An Introduction...* 1939. NY. McGraw Hill. 1st/7th imp. 731p. VG. D8. $35.00

LOBEL, Arnold. *Arnold Lobel's Little Library of Nursery Rhymes.* 1986. Random. 1st. 3 vol. F/F case. D4. $35.00

LOBEL, Arnold. *Book of Pigericks.* 1983. Harper Row. 1st. sgn. 48p. F/F. D4. $75.00

LOBEL, Arnold. *Comic Adventures of Mother Hubbard & Her Dog.* 1968. Bradbury. 1st. 32p. F/F. D4. $35.00

LOBEL, Arnold. *Days With Frog & Toad.* 1979. Harper. 1st. 8vo. NF/VG. C8. $50.00

LOBEL, Arnold. *Gregory Griggs & Other Nursery Rhyme People.* 1978. Greenwillow. 1st. sgn pres+sgn drawing on title p. cloth. dj. R5. $175.00

LOBEL, Arnold. *Gregory Griggs & Other Nursery Rhyme People.* 1978. Greenwillow. 1st. 48p. F/F. D4. $45.00

LOBEL, Arnold. *Mouse Soup.* 1977. Harper Row. 1st. 64p. F/NF. P2. $45.00

LOBEL, Arnold. *Rose in My Garden.* 1984. Greenwillow. 1st. 39p. F/F. D4. $50.00

LOBLEY, Douglas. *Ships Through the Ages.* 1972. London. Octopus. ils. 144p. dj. T7. $20.00

LOCK, M. *East Asian Medicine in Urban Japan.* 1980. CA U. 1st. ils/figures/tables. F/F. W3. $58.00

LOCK & SCHALLY. *Hypothalamus & Pituitary in Health & Disease.* 1972. Springfield, IL. Chas Thomas. lg 8vo. red cloth. VG/dj. G1. $75.00

LOCKE, A. *Tigers of Trengganu.* (1954). Scribner. 1st. 181p. F/clip. H7. $35.00

LOCKE, David R.; see Nasby, Petroleum.

LOCKE, E.W. *Three Years in Camp & Hospital.* 1870. Boston. 408p. O8. $18.50

LOCKE, Edwin A. *Food Values: Practical Tables for Use in Private Practice.* 1928. NY. Appleton. 2nd. 110p. VG/dj. A25. $25.00

LOCKE, George. *Worlds Apart.* 1972. London. 1st. F. M2. $15.00

LOCKE, John. *Some Thoughts Concerning Education.* 1809. London. Sherwood Neely. lg 12mo. 255p. G. H13. $195.00

LOCKE, William J. *Golden Journey of Mr Paradyne.* 1924. Dodd Mead. 1st. VG. M2. $27.00

LOCKE & STERN. *When Peoples Meet: Race & Culture Contacts.* 1949. Hinds Hayden Eldredge. rpt. 825p. NF/VG clip. B4. $150.00

LOCKHART, James L. *Porkey, an Arkansas Razorback.* 1939. Whitman. ils. NF/VG. M5. $40.00

LOCKHART, Robert Bruce. *Scotch: The Whiskey of Scotland in Fact & Story.* 1951. Putnam. 1st. 184p. VG. B10. $35.00

LOCKHART, Theodore. *In Search of Roots.* 1970. Dorrance. 1st. F/VG clip. B4. $100.00

LOCKRIDGE, Richard. *Death on the Hour.* 1974. Lippincott. 1st. inscr. NF/dj. Q1. $75.00

LOCKRIDGE, Richard. *Inspector's Holiday.* 1971. Lippincott. 1st. inscr. VG/dj. Q1. $50.00

LOCKRIDGE, Richard. *Murder in False-Face.* 1968. Phil/NY. Lippincott. 1st. F/NF. Q1. $60.00

LOCKRIDGE, Richard. *Preach No More.* 1971. Lippincott. 1st. inscr. NF/dj. Q1. $50.00

LOCKRIDGE, Richard. *Something Up a Sleeve.* 1972. Lippincott. 1st. inscr. VG/dj. Q1. $50.00

LOCKRIDGE, Richard. *Twice Retired.* 1970. Lippincott. 1st. inscr. NF/dj. Q1. $50.00

LOCKRIDGE & LOCKRIDGE. *Cats & People.* 1950. Phil. inscr. 286p. gr cloth. VG. B14. $35.00

LOCKRIDGE & LOCKRIDGE. *Norths Meet Murder.* 1946. World/Tower. 1st thus. VG/VG. M22. $30.00

LOCKRIDGE & LOCKRIDGE. *Voyage Into Violence.* 1956. Lippincott. 1st. 191p. VG/dj. M20. $12.00

LOCKWOOD, Charles. *Hell at 50 Fathoms.* 1962. NY. 1st. VG/VG. B5. $40.00

LOCKWOOD, Douglas. *Front Door: Darwin 1869-1969.* 1969. London/Adelaide. Angus Robertson/Rigby. 1st. 8vo. 288p. map ep. VG. P4. $25.00

LOCKWOOD, Frank C. *Pioneer Portraits: Selected Vignettes.* 1968. AZ U. 1st. ils/index. 240p. F/F. B19. $25.00

LOCKYER, Herbert. *All the Apostles of the Bible.* 1972. Zondervan. 278p. VG/dj. B29. $9.00

LOCKYER, Herbert. *All the Miracles of the Bible.* 1961. Zondervan. 316p. F. B29. $9.50

LOCKYER, J. Norman. *Dawn of Astronomy.* 1973. Cambridge. MIT. facsimile 1894 London. VG/dj. K5. $75.00

LOCKYER & LOCKYER. *Life & Work of Sir Norman Lockyer.* 1928. London. Macmillan. 17 pl. 474p. G. K5. $125.00

LOCSIN & LOCSIN. *Oriental Ceramics Discovered in the Philippines.* 1967. Rutland/Tokyo. 1st. ils/pl. gray line. NF/VG. W3. $585.00

LODEWIJK, Tom. *Book of Tulips.* 1979. Vendome. 4to. ils. 128p. F/NF. A22. $30.00

LODEWIJKS, J.M. *Tropical Fish in the Aquarium.* 1974. London. Blandford. revised. ils/drawings. 127p. pict brd. NF. M12. $15.00

LODGE, O.R. *Recapture of Guam.* 1954. WA. ils/fld maps. 214p. VG. S16. $85.00

LODGE, Oliver. *Past Years: An Autobiograpy.* 1931. London. Hodder Stoughton. 1st. ils. 364p. VG. K3. $35.00

LODGE & SPENS. *Terms & Vacations.* 1938. London. Oxford. 1st. 250p. VG/dj. A25. $40.00

LOEB, Charles. *Future Is Yours.* 1947. Cleveland. Future Outlook League. 1st. F/VG. B2. $45.00

LOEHR, Max. *Chinese Painting After Sung.* 1967. Yale U Art Gallery. ils. 38p. silk bdg. F. W3. $42.00

LOEHR, Max. *Ritual Vessels of Bronze Age China.* 1968. NYGS. ils. 183p. gilt gray cloth. NF/VG. W3. $52.00

LOFTING, Hugh. *Doctor Dolittle & the Green Canary.* (1950). Lippincott. 1st thus. 276p. VG/VG. D1. $85.00

LOFTING, Hugh. *Doctor Dolittle's Circus.* (1924). Stokes. 1st. 8vo. 379p. VG. from $80 to $125.00

LOFTING, Hugh. *Gub Gub's Book.* 1932. London. Cape. 1st Eng. orange-yel cloth. dj. R5. $200.00

LOFTING, Hugh. *Story of Mrs Tubbs.* 1923. Stokes. 1st. 92p. VG. P2. $150.00

LOFTUS, Agustus. *Diplomatic Reminiscences of Lord Augustus Loftus PC, GCB.* 1892. London. Cassell. 1st. 2 vol. half morocco. xl. VG. W1. $95.00

LOGAN, John. *Great Conspiracy.* 1886. 1st. inscr. 806p. O8. $87.50

LOGAN, Rayford W. *Negro in American Life & Thought: Nadir 1877-1901.* 1954. Dial. 1st. 380p. F/F. B4. $125.00

LOGAN, S.A. *Old Saint Jo: Gateway to the West 1799-1932.* 1979. St Joseph. ils/photos. 464p. NF. M4. $20.00

LOGSDON, Gene. *Gardener's Guide to Better Soil.* 1975. Emmaus. Rodale. 1st. 246p. dj. A10. $16.00

LOGUE, Christopher. *Children's Book of Comic Verse.* 1979. London. Batsford. 1st. 162p. NF/F. D4. $25.00

LOHMAN, Fred. *Mother Goose.* 1938. Saalfield. 116p. VG+/dj. D4. $85.00

LOKEN, Marty. *Davis Boats.* 1981. Seattle, WA. Center for Wooden Boats. photos/plans/drawings. wrp. T7. $10.00

LOMASK, Milton. *Aaron Burr.* 1979-1982. NY. 1st. 2 vol. ils. VG+/djs. B18. $37.50

LOMAX, Louis E. *Negro Revolt.* 1962. Harper. 1st. NF/dj. M25. $25.00

LOMBARDI, Felipe Rojas. *A-To-Z No-Cookbook.* 1972-. RL Creations. ils Dorothy Ivens. VG/VG. B10. $15.00

LONDON, A. *Complete American-Jewish Cookbook.* 1971 (1952). 3,500 recipes. F/VG. E6. $15.00

LONDON, Charmian. *Book of Jack London.* 2 vol. 1st. inscr. NF. M19. $850.00

LONDON, Jack. *Adventure.* 1911. Macmillan. 1st. inscr/dtd 1913. VG/lacks dj/custom case. B4. $2,500.00

LONDON, Jack. *Before Adam.* 1907. Macmillan. 1st. VG. M19. $125.00

LONDON, Jack. *Burning Daylight.* 1910. Macmillan. 1st. G. M19. $75.00

LONDON, Jack. *Call of the Wild.* 1903. London. Heinemann. 1st Eng. VG. B2. $75.00

LONDON, Jack. *Call of the Wild.* 1903. Macmillan. 1st/1st prt/Eng issue. teg. gilt bl cloth. M24. $225.00

LONDON, Jack. *Call of the Wild.* 1960. LA. LEC. 1st thus. 1/1500. ils/sgn HV Poor. F/case. Q1. $150.00

LONDON, Jack. *Chinago.* 1911. Leslie Judge. 1st. VG. M19. $125.00

LONDON, Jack. *Dream of Debs.* nd. Chicago. Kerr. 1st. VG/wrp. B2. $150.00

LONDON, Jack. *Essays of Revolt.* 1926. Vanguard. 1st. NF. M19. $75.00

LONDON, Jack. *Game.* 1905. Macmillan. 1st. Metro stp. VG. M19. $100.00

LONDON, Jack. *Game.* 1905. Macmillan. 1st. no Metro stp. VG. M19. $125.00

LONDON, Jack. *John Barleycorn.* 1913. Century. 1st. NF. M19. $200.00

LONDON, Jack. *John Barleycorn.* 1913. NY. Century. 1/5342. G+. B2. $150.00

LONDON, Jack. *Mutiny of the Elsinore.* 1914. Macmillan. 1st. VG. M19. $150.00

LONDON, Jack. *Red One.* 1918. Macmillan. 1/5342. G+. B2. $300.00

LONDON, Jack. *Sea-Wolf.* 1904. Macmillan. 1st. VG. B2. $60.00

LONDON, Jack. *Smoke & Shorty.* 1920. 1st Eng (no Am issued). VG. M19. $175.00

LONDON, Jack. *Smoke Bellew.* 1912. Century. 1st. VG. M19. $85.00

LONDON, Jack. *South Sea Tales.* 1911. Macmillan. 1st. G. M19. $100.00

LONDON, Jack. *Star Rover.* 1915. Macmillan. 1st. F/NF. B4. $750.00

LONDON, Jack. *Tales of the Fish Patrol.* (1905). NY. Internat Fiction Lib. sm 8vo. blk stp gr cloth. F/pict dj. R3. $50.00

LONDON, Jack. *Tales of the Fish Patrol.* 1906. 1st Eng. NF. M19. $250.00

LONDON, Jack. *When God Laughs.* nd. Internat Fiction Lib. F/dj. M2. $27.00

LONDON, Rose. *Cinema of Mystery.* 1975. Bounty. F/NF. M2. $12.00

LONG, Esmond. *History of American Pathology.* 1962. Springfield. 1st. 460p. A13. $75.00

LONG, Frank Belknap. *In Mayan Splendor.* 1977. Arkham. 1st. 1/3000. ils Stephen Fabian. NF/F. M19. $25.00

LONG, Frank Belknap. *Rim of the Unknown.* 1972. Arkham. 1st. NF/dj. Q1. $75.00

LONG, Haniel. *Cabeza de Vaca: His Relation of the Journey...* 1988. Okeanos. 18p. F/sans. B19. $40.00

LONG, Huey. *My First Days in the White House.* 1935. Harrisburg. 1st. VG/VG. B5. $95.00

LONG, John Luther. *Madame Butterfly.* 1898. NY. Century. 1st. quarter gr cloth/pict label. uncut. M24. $250.00

LONG, John Luther. *Madame Butterfly.* 1903. NY. Century. 1st separate ed. teg. bl-gr cloth. M24. $175.00

LONG, Joseph W. *American Wild-Fowl Shooting.* 1879. Orange Judd. 330p. G. H7. $50.00

LONG, Lydia Belknap; see Long, Frank Belknap.

LONG LANCE, Chief Buffalo Child. *Long Lance.* 1928. NY. Cosmopolitan. 1st. NF. L3. $85.00

LONG LANCE, Chief Buffalo Child. *Long Lance: Autobiography of a Blackfoot Indian Chief.* 1956. London. Faber. 1st. 241p. VG/dj. M20. $25.00

LONGFELLOW, Henry Wadsworth. *Courtship of Miles Standish & Other Poems.* 1858. Boston. Ticknor Fields. 1st/1st prt. 12mo. gilt cloth. M24/T10. $450.00

LONGFELLOW, Henry Wadsworth. *Courtship of Miles Standish.* 1920. Houghton Mifflin. 1st. 4to. gilt gray-gr cloth. dj. R5. $275.00

LONGFELLOW, Henry Wadsworth. *Divine Tragedy.* 1871. Osgood. 1st. 150p. 12mo. emb gilt bdg. VG. H1. $35.00

LONGFELLOW, Henry Wadsworth. *Estray.* 1847. Boston. Wm Ticknor. 1st. aeg. unrecored pub gift bdg (bl-gr cloth). M24. $400.00

LONGFELLOW, Henry Wadsworth. *Hanging of the Crane.* 1907. Houghton Mifflin. Centennial/1st thus. 1/1000. unp. F/VG. D4. $45.00

LONGFELLOW, Henry Wadsworth. *Hiawatha's Childhood.* 1984. FSG. 1st Am. ils Errol LeCain. F/F. D4. $30.00

LONGFELLOW, Henry Wadsworth. *Nuremberg.* 1888. Phil. Gebbie. 1st Am. pub sgn/#d. full vegetable vellum. M24. $125.00

LONGFELLOW, Henry Wadsworth. *Song of Hiawatha.* nd. Merson. ne. 262p. NF/VG. W2. $75.00

LONGFELLOW, Henry Wadsworth. *Song of Hiawatha.* 1855. Ticknor Fields. 1st/1st prt. 1/5250. gilt brn cloth. M24. $450.00

LONGFELLOW, Henry Wadsworth. *Song of Hiawatha.* 1911. Chicago. Rand McNally. lg 8vo. 242p. M/glassine wrp/box. B24. $325.00

LONGFELLOW, Henry Wadsworth. *Song of Hiawatha.* 1960. Dent/Dutton. 1st thus. 214p. F/F. D4. $35.00

LONGFELLOW, Henry Wadsworth. *Tales of a Wayside Inn.* 1863. Boston. Ticknor Fields. 1st/1st prt/1st state ads. teg. gr cloth. M24. $225.00

LONGFELLOW, Samuel. *Few Verses of Many Years.* 1887. Cambridge. private prt. 1st. 16mo. 104p. prt wrp. M1. $150.00

LONGFORD, Elizabeth. *Elizabeth.* 1983. Toronto. Musson. 1st. NF. T12. $35.00

LONGFORD, Elizabeth. *Royal House of Windsor.* 1974. London. Weidenfeld Nicolson. 1st. F/F. T12. $50.00

LONGGOOD, William. *Poisons in Your Food.* 1960. S&S. 1st. 277p. VG+/dj. H1. $12.50

LONGRIGG, Roger. *History of Horse Racing.* 1972n. Stein Day. 1st. photos. G+. P8. $50.00

LONGSTREET, Stephen. *War Cries on Horseback.* 1970. Doubleday. 1st. 8vo. 335p. xl. VG/dj. K7. $18.00

LONGSTRETH, T.M. *Missouri Clipper.* 1941. Appleton. 1st. 282p. cloth. VG/dj. M20. $40.00

LONGSTRETH, T.M. *Reading the Weather.* 1941 (1915). Macmillan. 8vo. 195p. G. K5. $12.00

LONGUEVILLE, Peter. *English Hermit; or, Adventurers of Philip Quarll.* 1799. Hartford, CT. John Babcock. 1st Am. 18mo. M1. $675.00

LONGUS. *Daphnis & Chloe.* 1931. 1st. ils John Austen. VG. M19. $25.00

LONGYEAR, Barry B. *City of Baraboo.* 1980. Berkley Putnam. 1st. F/dj. M2. $15.00

LONGYEAR, Barry B. *City of Baraboo.* 1980. Berkley Putnam. 1st. sgn. F/F. P3. $25.00

LONSDALE, G. *20 Years in Soviet Secret Service.* 1965. 1st Am. VG/VG. E6. $13.00

LONTZ, Vernon E. *Arctic Interlude: True Stories of Alaska.* 1900. NY. Vantage. photos. VG/dj. P4. $25.00

LOOFBOUROW, Leon L. *In Search of God's Gold.* 1950. Stockton, CA. 1st. G/fair. O4. $15.00

LOOK, A. *U-Boom: Uranium on the Colorado Plateau.* 1956. Bell pr. 224p. G/dj. D8. $20.00

LOOMIS, Elias. *Treatise on Meteorology.* 1868. Harper. 8vo. 305p. contemporary leather. K5. $75.00

LOOMIS & PARMALEE. *Decoys & Decoy Carvers of Illinois.* 1969. N IL U. 1st. 426 photos. 506p. F/F case. M4. $175.00

LOOSE, G. *Guide to American Bird Names, Origins, Meanings...* 1989. Virginia Beach. 146p. F/wrp. B1. $14.00

LOPEZ, Barry. *Crossing Open Ground.* 1988. Scribner. 1st. sgn. M/dj. A18. $40.00

LOPEZ, Barry. *Crow & Weasel.* 1990. Northpoint. 1st state w/gold stp bdg. sgn. ils Pohrt. M/dj. A18. $100.00

LOPEZ, Barry. *Desert Notes: Reflections in the Eye of a Raven.* 1976. Sheed Andrews & McMeel. 1st. F/NF. B4. $350.00

LOPEZ, Barry. *Field Notes: Grace Note of the Canyon Wren.* 1994. Knopf. 1st. sgn. M/dj. A18. $35.00

LOPEZ, Barry. *Of Wolves & Men.* 1978. Scribner. 1st. F/NF. B2. $100.00

LOPEZ, Barry. *Of Wolves & Men.* 1978. Scribner. 1st. sgn. F/clip. A18. $150.00

LOPEZ, Barry. *River Notes: Dance of Herons.* 1979. Andrews McMeel. 1st. sgn. F/dj. A18. $100.00

LOPEZ, Barry. *Winter Count.* 1981. Scribner. 1st. F/NF. T11. $65.00

LOPEZ, Barry. *Winter Count.* 1981. Scribner. 1st. sgn. F/F. A18. $80.00

LOPEZ, Salvador P. *Literature & Society: Essays on Life & Letters.* 1940. Manila. Philippine Book Guild. 224p. cloth. VG/G. P1. $10.00

LOPEZ ENGUIDANOS, Jose. *Coleccion de Vaciados de Estatuas Antiguas Que Posee...* 1794. Madrid. 1st/only. folio. 84 engravings. contemporary bdg. R15. $4,500.00

LORAND, Rhoda L. *Love, Sex & the Teenager.* 1968. Macmillan. 5th. 243p. VG. A25. $8.00

LORANT, Stefan. *New World: First Pictures of America...* 1946. Duell Sloan. 1st. 4to. 292p. F3. $50.00

LORD, Bette Bao. *Legacies.* 1990. Knopf. 1st. F/F. A20. $15.00

LORD, Ernest E. *Shrubs & Trees for Australian Gardens.* 1978 (1948). Melbourne. 4th. photos. VG+/dj. B26. $54.00

LORD, Isabel Ely. *Everybody's Cookbook.* 1924. Holt. 1925 prt. 916p. recent red cloth. T10. $35.00

LORD, John. *Beacon Lights of History. First Series: Jewish Heroes...* 188. NY. Fords Howard Hulbert. 524p. fair. B29. $10.00

LORD, Sheldon; see Block, Lawrence.

LORD, W. *Miracle of Dunkirk.* 1962. NY. 1st Am. 323p. VG/VG. S16. $20.00

LORD & LORD. *Forever the Land.* 1950. Harper. 1st. 394p. dj. A10. $25.00

LORENTZ, H.A. *Einstein Theory of Relativity.* 1920. NY. Brentano. 8vo. 64p. VG. K3. $22.00

LORIMER, Norma. *By the Waters of Egypt.* ca 1910. Stokes. 1st. ils/maps. 314p. G. W1. $10.00

LORIMER, Norma. *There Was a King in Egypt.* 1918. Brentanos. 1st. NF/dj. M2. $35.00

LORING, Brent; see Worts, George F.

LOSE, Phyllis. *No Job for a Lady.* 1979. NY. Macmillan. 1st. sgn. VG/VG. O3. $35.00

LOSKE, Lothar M. *Die Sonnenuhren.* 1959. Berlin. Springer. ils. 12mo. 88p. VG+. K3. $22.00

LOSSING, Benson J. *Our Great Continent.* 1889. NY. Gay Bros. A19. $50.00

LOSSING, Benson J. *Pictorial Field-Book of Revolution; or, History...* 1969 (1860). rpt. 2 vol. 1100 ils. F. M4. $55.00

LOTI, Pierre. *Iceland Fisherman.* 1931. Stockholm. LEC. 1/1500. ils/sgn Yngve Berg. NF. M19. $35.00

LOTT, Bret. *Man Who Owned Vermont.* 1987. Viking. 1st. sgn. NF/NF. R14. $45.00

LOTTMAN, Herbert R. *Left Bank.* 1982. London. 1st. VG/VG. T9. $25.00

LOUGHBOROUGH, Mary Ann. *My Life in Vicksburg With Letters of Trial & Travel.* 1864. NY. Appleton. 1st. 196p. cloth. NF. M8. $250.00

LOUGHRAN, Peter. *Dearest.* 1983. Stein Day. 1st. F/dj. M2. $20.00

LOUIRIE, Dick. *Stumbling.* 1973. Crossing. sgn pres. 8vo. 111p. VG/glossy wrp. H1. $35.00

LOUIS, Joe. *How To Box.* 1948. McKay. 1st. ils/photos. VG. P8. $75.00

LOUSLEY, J.E. *Flora of the Isles of Scilly.* 1971. Newton Abbott. 8vo. 336p. F/F. A22. $25.00

LOVE, Jeannette F. *Fall & Rise of Cushan & Other Poems.* 1911. Stoneman. 1st. NF. B4. $650.00

LOVECRAFT, H.P. *Dunwich Horror.* 1963. Salk City. 1st. VG/VG. B5. $35.00

LOVECRAFT, H.P. *Something About Cats & Other Pieces.* 1949. Arkham. 1st. F/dj. w/sgn postcard. B24. $225.00

LOVELACE, Maud Hart. *Betsy-Tacy.* 1940. Crowell. ils Lenski. VG+/G+. M5. $75.00

LOVELACE, Maud Hart. *Early Candlelight.* 1929 (1929). John Day. 3rd. 322p. VG. T5. $45.00

LOVELACE & RICE. *Music & Worship in the Church.* 1960. Abingdon. 220p. G/dj. B29. $6.50

LOVELL, J. *Flower & the Bee, Plant Life & Pollination.* 1918. 1st. photos. VG. E6. $25.00

LOVELL, Mary S. *Sound of Wings: Life of Amelia Earhart.* 1989. St Martin. 1st. photos. 420p. VG/VG. A25. $18.00

LOVESEY, Peter. *Last Detective.* 1991. Doubleday. 1st. F/F. M23. $30.00

LOVETT, C. *Lewis Carroll's Alice: Annotated Checklist...* 1990. ils. 556p. F. A4. $225.00

LOVETT, C. *Robinson Crusoe: Bibliographical Checklist...* 1991. 1198 entries. 322p. F. A4. $125.00

LOVETT, Sarah. *Dangerous Attachments.* 1995. Villard. 1st. sgn. author's 1st book. F/F. A23. $50.00

LOW, Frances H. *Queen Victoria's Dolls.* 1894. London. sm 4to. ils Alan Wright. VG. C8. $125.00

LOW, Joseph. *Mother Goose Riddle Rhymes.* 1953. Harcourt Brace. 1st. 48p. VG+/dj. D4. $45.00

LOWE, Samuel. *New Story of Peter Rabbit.* 1926. Whitman. legal pirated ed. ils Wright/Vetsch. VG. D1. $75.00

LOWE & STEENBERGH. *Ecology of the Saguaro: II.* 1977. Tucson. 8vo. 243p. G. A22. $30.00

LOWELL, James Russell. *Branded Hand.* 1845. Salem, OH. Anti-Slavery Bugle. 1st/variant issue. F. M24. $165.00

LOWELL, James Russell. *Conversations on Some of the Old Poets.* 1845. Cambridge. John Owen. 1st. 16mo. contemporary calf. M1. $475.00

LOWELL, James Russell. *Conversations on Some of the Old Poets.* 1845. Cambridge. John Owen. 1st/wrp state D (no priority). M24. $375.00

LOWELL, James Russell. *Impressions of Spain.* 1899. Houghton Mifflin. 1st/2nd prt. teg. quarter vellum (2nd state). M24. $225.00

LOWELL, James Russell. *Liberty Bell.* 1844. Boston. Anti-Slavery Fair. 1st. yel glazed prt brd/rebacked. M24. $125.00

LOWELL, Percival. *Occult Japan; or, The Way of the Gods.* ca 1894. Houghton Mifflin. 4th. 379p. VG. W3. $125.00

LOWELL, Robert. *History.* 1973. FSG. 1st. F/dj. M25. $45.00

LOWELL, Robert. *Old Glory.* 1965. NY. 1st. F/VG+. A11. $35.00

LOWERY, George H. *Louisana Birds.* 1955. LSU. 3rd. sgn. VG/VG. B11. $40.00

LOWRY, Robert. *Find Me in Fire.* 1948. Garden City. 1st. sgn. NF/VG+. A11. $250.00

LOWRY, Shannon. *Northern Lights: Tales of Alaska's Lighthouses...* 1992. Harrisburg. Stackpole. 1st. 118p. M/dj. P4. $30.00

LOWRY & WHITE. *Century of Speed the Red Mile 1875-1975.* 1975. Lexington Trots Breeders. 1st. sgn pres from White. VG. O3. $65.00

LOZOWICK, Louis. *William Gropper.* 1983. Phil. Art Alliance. 1st. F/NF. B2. $75.00

LUARD, Nicholas. *Gondar.* 1988. Gondor. 1st. VG/VG. T9. $10.00

LUBBOCK, Basil. *Blackwall Frigates.* 1924. ils. VG. M17. $15.00

LUBBOCK, Basil. *Log of the Cutty Sark.* 1974. Glasgow. Brn, Son & Ferguson. later ed. 332p. bl cloth. VG. P4. $65.00

LUBBOCK, John. *Pre-Historic Times, As Illustrated by Ancient Remains...* 1872. Appleton. New Ed. 8vo. 649p. emb cloth. T10. $150.00

LUCANUS, Marcus Annaeus. *Annei Lucani Bellorum Ciuilium Scriptoris Accuratissimi...* 4 June 1511. Venice. Augustino de Zanni for Melchior Sessa. 1st ils ed. R15. $3,500.00

LUCAS, A. *Ancient Egyptian Materials & Industries.* 1934. London. Arnold. 8vo. 447p. VG. W1. $65.00

LUCAS, Annabelle. *Wild Flowers of the Witwatersrand.* 1987. Cape Town. ils Barbara Pike. 113p. F. B26. $22.50

LUCAS, Dione. *Cordon Bleu Cook Book.* 1951 (1947). Little Brn. sgn. 322p. VG/worn. M20. $30.00

LUCAS, E.V. *Another Book of Verses for Children.* 1925. Macmillan. 1st reissue. 8vo. 431p. gray cloth. NF. M5. $35.00

LUCAS, E.V. *Four & Twenty Toilers.* 1900. NY. McDevitt-Wilson. 1st. obl 4to. pict cloth. R5. $285.00

LUCAS, E.V. *If Dogs Could Write: Second Canine Miscellany.* 1930. Lippincott. ne. 16mo. 95p. G/dj. H7. $20.00

LUCAS, E.V. *Lucas' Annual.* 1914. Macmillan. 1st. VG. M2. $15.00

LUCAS, E.V. *Verena in the Midst.* 1920. Doran. 1st Am. F/pict dj. B4. $125.00

LUCAS, Frederic A. *Expedition to Funk Island, With Observations...* 1890. GPO. removed. p493-529+2 pl/map/tables/charts. VG. P4. $30.00

LUCAS, George; see Foster, Alan Dean.

LUCAS, Jerry. *Remember the Word: Bible Memorization System. Vol 1.* 1975. Memory Ministries. 291p. w/memory cards. xl. VG. B29. $9.00

LUCAS, Jim G. *Dateline: Viet Nam.* 1966. NY. Award. 1st. F/F. H11. $45.00

LUCAS, Robert Irwin. *Tarentum Pattern Glass.* 1981. self pub. 1st. 422p. ES. as new/dj. H1. $35.00

LUCAS, Walter A. *Popular Picture & Plan Book of Railroad Cars & Locomotives.* 1951. Simmons-Boardman. 1st. 4to. 288p. H1. $45.00

LUCE, Edward. *Keogh, Comanche & Custer.* 1939. np. ltd. sgn. facsimiles/photos. 127p. G. J2. $785.00

LUCIE-SMITH, Edward. *Art Deco Painting.* 1990. ils. VG/VG. M17. $35.00

LUCIW & LUCIW. *Ahapius Honcharenko & the Alaska Herald.* 1963. Toronto. Slavia Lib. 120p. VG/prt wrp. P4. $32.50

LUCKINGHAM, Bradford. *Phoenix: History of Southwestern Metropolis.* 1989. AZ U. 1st. ils/index/notes. 316p. F/F. B19. $20.00

LUCRETIUS, Carus Titius. *Titi Lucretii Cari de Rerum Natura.* 1773. Birminghamiae. Johannis Baskerville. 12mo. 214p. new bdg. K3. $90.00

LUDECKE, Heinz. *Albrech Durer.* 1970. ils. VG/G. M17. $20.00

LUDLOW, Fitz Hugh. *Hasheesh Eater.* 1857. NY. Harper. 1st. author's 1st book. gilt purple-brn cloth. F. M24. $400.00

LUDLUM, Robert. *Bourne Supremacy.* 1986. Franklin Lib. 1st. sgn. ils Hodges Soileau. full leather. F. Q1. $75.00

LUDLUM, Robert. *Bourne Supremacy.* 1986. Random. 1st. 597p. NF/NF. W2. $20.00

LUDLUM, Robert. *Bourne Ultimatum.* 1990. Random. 1st. 611p. F/F. W2. $30.00

LUDLUM, Robert. *Chancellor Manuscript.* 1977. Dial. 1st. VG/NF. T11. $55.00

LUDLUM, Robert. *Chancellor Manuscript.* 1977. NY. Dial. 1st. F/VG. Q1. $75.00

LUDLUM, Robert. *Cry of the Halidon.* 1974. Delacorte. 1st. F/VG+. T11. $65.00

LUDLUM, Robert. *Gemini Contenders.* 1976. Dial. 1st. F/dj. Q1. $60.00

LUDLUM, Robert. *Gemini Contenders.* 1976. Dial. 1st. F/NF clip. N4. $35.00

LUDLUM, Robert. *Gemini Contenders.* 1976. NY. Dial. 1st. F/NF. T11. $40.00

LUDLUM, Robert. *Holcroft Covenant.* 1978. NY. Richard Marek. 1st. F/dj. Q1. $75.00

LUDLUM, Robert. *Icarus Agenda.* 1988. Random. 1st. F/F. T12. $25.00

LUDLUM, Robert. *Icarus Agenda.* 1988. Random. 1st. NF/NF. B35. $18.00

LUDLUM, Robert. *Matarese Circle.* 1979. Richard Marek. 1st. F/dj. Q1. $40.00

LUDLUM, Robert. *Matlock Paper.* 1973. NY. Dial. 1st. F/dj. M15. $100.00

LUDLUM, Robert. *Road to Gandolfo.* 1975. Dial. 1st. F/all 3 djs present. from $125 to $150.00

LUDLUM, Robert. *Road to Omaha.* 1992. Random. 1st. F/dj. Q1. $25.00

LUDLUM, Robert. *Scarlatti Inheritance.* 1971. World. 1st. author's 1st book. VG+/fair. N4. $75.00

LUDLUM, Robert. *Scarlatti Inheritance.* 1971. World. 1st. F/VG+ clip. T11. $95.00

LUDLUM, Robert. *Scorpio Illusion.* 1993. Bantam. 1st. NF/dj. Q1. $25.00

LUDWIG, Emil. *Cleopatra: Story of a Queen.* 1937. Viking. 1st. 8vo. 342p. VG. W1. $18.00

LUDWIG, Emil. *Goethe: History of a Man 1749-1832.* 1928. NY. 1st. 8vo. ils. teg. 3-quarter leather. F. H3. $50.00

LUEDERS, Edward. *Clam Lake Papers.* 1977. NY. 1st. VG/dj. B5. $25.00

LUGARD, Lord. *Dual Mandate in British Tropical Africa.* 1965. London. Cassell. 5th. 8vo. cloth. NF/dj. W1. $35.00

LUGER, Richard. *Letters to the Next President.* 1988. S&S. 1st. F/F. B35. $16.00

LUI, Garding. *Inside Los Angeles Chinatown.* 1948. np. 8vo. ils. blk stp red cloth. F. R3. $85.00

LUKEMAN, Tim. *Koren.* 1981. Doubleday. 1st. F/dj. M2. $17.00

LUKENBILL & STEWART. *Youth Literature, Interdisciplinary, Annotated Guide...* 1988. 481p. VG. A4. $125.00

LUMAN, Duncan. *New Worlds for Old.* 1979. Morrow. 1st. F/dj. M2. $15.00

LUMLEY, Brian. *Blood Brothers.* 1992. Tor. 1st. F/dj. M2. $30.00

LUMMIS, Charles F. *Bullying the Moque.* 1968. Flagstaff, AZ. 1st. NF/VG. O4. $20.00

LUMMIS, Charles F. *Flowers of Our Lost Romance.* 1929. Houghton Mifflin. 1st. VG. O4. $60.00

LUMMIS, Charles F. *Land of Poco Tiempo.* 1893. Scribner. 1st. 310p. decor cloth. D11. $100.00

LUMMIS, Charles F. *Land of Poco Tiempo.* 1902. Scribner. later prt. ils. VG. O4. $30.00

LUMMIS, Charles F. *Man Who Married the Moon & Other Pueblo Indian Folk-Stories.* 1894. Century. 1st. ils. VG+. A18. $125.00

LUMMIS, Charles F. *Mesa, Canon & Pueblo.* 1925. Century. 1st. G. O4. $25.00

LUNA, Kris. *Steller Radium Discharge.* 1952. London. 1st. F/dj. M2. $10.00

LUNDAHL, Gene. *Jargon's Journey.* 1966. Denver. 1st. 1/300. sgn. F/dj. A17. $15.00

LUNDQUIST, Carl. *United We Stood.* 1985. Todd Honeywell. 1st. F/VG+. P8. $20.00

LUNGWITZ, A. *Text-Book of Horseshoeing for Horseshoers & Veterinarians.* 1902. Phil. ils. 168p. G-. B18. $25.00

LUPOFF, Richard. *Forever City.* 1987. Walker. 1st. F/dj. M2. $20.00

LUPOFF & THOMAS. *All in Color All for a Dime.* 1970. New Rochelle. 1st. VG/VG. A4. $25.00

LURIA, A.R. *Higher Cortical Functions in Man.* 1977. NY. Basic. 1st Eng-language/5th prt. blk cloth. VG/dj. G1. $50.00

LURIA, A.R. *Nature of Human Conflicts or Emotion, Conflict & Will...* 1932. NY. Liveright. 321p. bl cloth. VG/dj. G1. $65.00

LURIE, Alison. *Don't Tell the Grown-Ups.* 1990. Little Brn. 1st. F/dj. A24. $25.00

LURIE, Alison. *Foreign Affairs.* 1984. Franklin Lib. ltd. sgn. leather. F. from $40 to $50.00

LURIE, Alison. *Real People.* 1969. Random. 1st. F/NF. M19. $35.00

LURIE, Alison. *Truth About Lorin Jones.* 1988. Little Brn. 1st trade. F/F. T12. $35.00

LURIE, Alison. *Women & Ghosts.* 1994. Doubleday. 1st. sgn. F/F. A23. $40.00

LUSK, Clayton R. *Revolutionary Radicalism: Its History, Purpose & Tactics.* 1920. Albany. JB Lyon. 4 vol. B2. $150.00

LUSTBADER, Eric V. *French Kiss.* 1989. Fawcett. 1st. F/dj. M2. $20.00

LUTHER, Martin. *Acta...Agust(ana).* 1518. Leipzig. Lotter. 4to. woodcut. vellum/manuscript brd. R12. $875.00

LUTHER, Martin. *An die Pfarrherrn Wider den Wucher zu Predigen.* 1540. Wittenberg. Klug. 4to. woodcut title border. brd. R12. $1,675.00

LUTHER, Martin. *Luther's Works, Vol 26: Lectures on Galatians Chapters 1-4.* nd. np. Am ed. as new/dj. B29. $15.00

LUTHER, Seth. *Address on Origin & Progress of Avarice...* 1834. Boston. self pub. 1st. 8vo. 43p. modern cloth. M1. $1,000.00

LUTHER, Tal. *High Spots of Custer & Battle of the Little Big Horn.* 1967. KS City Posse Westerners. 1st. 1/250. sgn. VG. J2. $145.00

LUTRELL, Estelle. *Mission of San Xavier Del Bac: An Historical Guide.* 1922. Kimball. 1st? LC Powell bookplate. F/wrp. B19. $25.00

LUTZ, W.J. *William D Wittliff: Bibliography.* 1975. Dallas. sgn. 49p. F. M4. $35.00

LUTZE, Eberhard. *Veit Stoss.* 1940. Berlin. Keutscher Kunstverlag. 2nd. ils. D2. $35.00

LUXFORD, Nola. *Kerry Kangaroo.* 1957. Whittlesey. 1st. sm 4to. cloth. dj. M5. $22.00

LUYS, Jules Bernard. *Brain & Its Functions. International Scientific Series 39.* 1882. NY. Appleton. 1st Eng-language/1st prt/Am issue. 327p. xl. VG. G1. $85.00

LUYTEN, Willem J. *Search for Faint Blue Stars, I-XXX.* 1956-1962. Minneapolis. The Observatory. 161p. cloth. K5. $30.00

LYBACK, Johanna R.M. *Indian Legends.* 1925. Lyons Carnahan. ils Alexander Key. M5. $45.00

LYDON, Sandy. *Chinese Gold: Chinese in Monterey Bay Region.* 1985. Capitola book Co. lg obl 8vo. ils. gilt bl cloth. F/dj. R3. $40.00

LYLE, R.C. *Royal Newmarket.* 1945. London. Putnam. 1st. ils Lionel Edwards/10 mc pl. VG/fair. O3. $145.00

LYNCH, Kenneth. *Benches.* 1971. Canterbury, CT. Arch Handbook. 80p. VG. A10. $30.00

LYNCH, Kenneth. *Garden Ornaments.* 1974. Canterbury, CT. Arch Handbook. 768p. VG. A10. $35.00

LYNCH, Patricia. *Brogeen & the Bronze Lizard.* 1970. Macmillan. 1st Am. 8vo. ils HB Vestal. F/dj. T10. $25.00

LYND & LYND. *Middletown: A Study in American Culture.* 1929. Harcourt Brace. 1st. gilt cloth. dj. M24. $75.00

LYNDE, Francis. *Flight of the Gray Goose.* 1927. Scribner. 1st. 216p. VG/dj. M20. $45.00

LYNDE, Francis. *Scientific Sprague.* nd. AL Burt. VG. M2. $17.00

LYNDS, Dennis. *Deadly Innocents.* 1986. Walker. 1st. F/F. P3. $15.00

LYNN, Elizabeth. *Dancers of Arun.* 1979. Berkley. 1st. F/dj. M2. $25.00

LYNN, Elizabeth. *Sardonyx Net.* 1981. Putnam. 1st. F/dj. M2. $25.00

LYNN, F.J. *Ecology & Economic Impact of Poisonous Plants...* 1988. Westview. 428p. B1. $26.50

LYNN. *Fantasy Literature for Children & Young Adults...* 1989. 3rd. 818p. NF. A4. $145.00

LYON, G.F. *Brief Narrative of Unsuccessful Attempt to Reach Repulse...* 1825. London. John Murray. 1st. 198p. rebound. P4. $395.00

LYON, W.E. *Youth in the Saddle.* nd (1955). Barnes. VG/VG. O3. $10.00

LYONS, A.B. *Plant Names Scientific & Popular...* 1900. Detroit. Nelson Baker. 469p. A10. $45.00

LYONS, James R. *Intellectual Legacy of Paul Tillich.* 1969. Wayne State. 4 essays. 115p. VG/G+. S3. $22.00

LYONS, Mary E. *Sorrow's Kitchen. Life & Folklore of Zora Neale Hurston.* 1990. Scribner. 1st. F/NF. R13. $15.00

LYONS & NOGUCHI. *Physical Evidence.* 1990. Putnam. 1st. F/F. N4. $22.50

LYONS & WOODHALL. *Atlas of Peripheral Nerve Injuries.* 1949. Phil. 1st. 4to. 339p. A13. $200.00

LYSAGHT, A.M. *Joseph Banks in Newfoundland, 1766: His Diary...* 1971. Berkeley. 4to. 12 mc pl/9 charts/91 b&w pl. ES. M/protected dj. O7. $100.00

LYSAGHT, A.M. *Joseph Banks in Newfoundland & Labrador, 1766.* 1971. LA. CA U. 1st. ils/pl/maps. VG. K3. $65.00

LYTLE, Andrew. *Novel, Novella & Four Stories.* 1958. NY. 1st. sgn pres. VG/dj. B5. $125.00

M'CLELLAND, J. *Calcutta Journal of Natural History.* 1985 (1841-45). Dehra Dun. rpt. 5 vol. djs. B26. $165.00

MAAS, Peter. *Manhunt.* 1986. Random. 1st. F/F. M22. $10.00

MAASS, Walter. *Country Without a Name: Austria Under Nazi Rule 1938-45.* 1979. NY. maps/biblio/index. 178p. VG/VG. S16. $17.50

MABEY, Richard. *Oxford Book of Nature Writing.* 1995. Oxford. 260p. as new/dj. S15. $15.00

MABIE, Hamilton W. *Fairy Tales Every Child Should Know.* 1926. Doubleday. ils MH Frye. VG. M5. $55.00

MABIE, Hamilton W. *Myths Every Child Should Know.* 1914. Doubleday Page. ils Mary Hamilton Frye. F. M19. $35.00

MABIE, Peter. *A to Z Book.* (1929). Whitman. 4to. NF/pict wrp. D1. $60.00

MABIE, Peter. *Parade of the Toy Soldiers.* 1931. Whitman. 8vo. cb stock. VG. D1. $95.00

MACAPAGAL, Diosdado. *Democracy in the Philippines.* 1976. Manila. photos/index. 216p. F. P1. $20.00

MACARTHUR, Arthur. *After the Afternoon.* 1941. Appleton. NF. M2. $25.00

MACARTHUR, D. Wilson. *They Sailed for Senegal.* 1938. Stokes. 1st. F/VG. B4. $100.00

MACARTHUR, David. *Thunderbolt Man.* 1947. London. 1st. F. M2. $22.00

MACARTHUR, John. *Our Sufficiency in Christ: Three Deadly Influences...* 1991. Word. 282p. VG/dj. B29. $9.00

MACARTNEY, Carol. *Easy Stages Cook Book.* 1972. London. Octopus. G/dj. A16. $15.00

MACASKILL, Wallace R. *Out of Halifax.* 1937. NY. Derrydale. 1st. sgn/#d. 98 pl. F. B11. $185.00

MACAULAY, David. *Underground.* 1976. Houghton Mifflin. 1st. sgn. 112p. VG+/VG. P2. $40.00

MACAULEY, Robie. *Secret History of Time To Come.* 1979. Knopf. 1st. F/dj. M2. $15.00

MACBRIDE, Roger Lee. *West From Home.* 1974. Harper. dj. A19. $35.00

MACCARGO, J.T.; see Rabe, Peter.

MACCOBY, Eleanor E. *Development of Sex Differences.* 1966. Stanford. 1st. 351p. VG+. A25. $15.00

MACCREAGH, G. *White Waters & Black.* 1926. Grosset Dunlap. 8vo. ils/photos/map ep. decor cloth. F/VG. M12. $25.00

MACDONALD, Aeneas. *Whiskey.* 1934. Duffield Gr. 1st Am. 135p. VG. B10. $35.00

MACDONALD, Betty. *Mrs Piggly-Wiggle's Farm.* (1954). Lippincott. 1st. ils Sendak. 128p. VG/rpr. D1. $325.00

MACDONALD, Betty. *Nancy & Plum.* 1952. Lippincott. 1st. sm 8vo. VG+/dj. C8. $75.00

MACDONALD, Charles. *Mighty Endeavor: American Armed Forces in the European...* 1969. NY. photos/maps/notes/biblio/index. 564p. VG/VG. S16. $25.00

MACDONALD, Dwight. *Masscult & Midcult.* 1961. NY. Partisan Review. 1st. F/stapled wrp. B4. $75.00

MACDONALD, G.A. *Volcanoes.* 1972. Prentice Hall. 510p. F. D8. $18.00

MACDONALD, George. *At the Back of the North Wind.* 1871. NY. Routledge. 1st Am/later prt. gilt pict red cloth. VG. M24. $350.00

MACDONALD, George. *At the Back of the North Wind.* 1909. ils Maria Kirk. NF. M19. $35.00

MACDONALD, George. *At the Back of the North Wind.* 1924. Macmillan. 1st thus. ils Francis Bedford. VG. M5. $30.00

MACDONALD, George. *Golden Key.* 1976. FSG. 1st. ils Sendak. 86p. bl brd. F/F. D1. $75.00

MACDONALD, George. *Princess & Curdie.* nd (1883). Lippincott. 1st Am. 8vo. VG. M5. $75.00

MACDONALD, George. *Princess & Curdie.* 1908. Lippincott. ils Maria Kirk. gold lettered red cloth. VG. M5. $45.00

MACDONALD, George. *Princess & the Goblin.* 1920. McKay. early ed. ils JW Smith. 4to. top edge orange. gr cloth. R5. $250.00

MACDONALD, Golden; See Brown, Margaret Wise.

MACDONALD, Gordon. *Restoring Your Spiritual Passion.* 1986. Nelson. 223p. VG/dj. B29. $6.00

MACDONALD, John D. *Barrier Island.* 1986. Knopf. 1st. F/F. N4. $27.50

MACDONALD, John D. *Barrier Island.* 1986. Knopf. 1st. VG. P3. $18.00

MACDONALD, John D. *Blue City.* 1st. VG/NF. M22. $200.00

MACDONALD, John D. *Cinnamon Skin.* 1982. Harper. 1st. F/NF. N4. $27.50

MACDONALD, John D. *Condominium.* 1977. Lippincott. 1st. F/NF. N4. $35.00

MACDONALD, John D. *Dress Her in Indigo.* 1971. Lippincott. 1st Am hc. F/NF. M15. $350.00

MACDONALD, John D. *Empty Copper Sea.* 1978. London. Robert Hale. 1st. F/NF. Q1. $50.00

MACDONALD, John D. *Free Fall in Crimson.* 1981. Harper. 1st. VG. P3. $30.00

MACDONALD, John D. *Ivory Grin.* 1952. Knopf. 1st. VG. M25. $50.00

MACDONALD, John D. *Lonely Silver Rain.* 1985. Knopf. 1st. F/F. from $20 to $30.00

MACDONALD, John D. *One More Sunday.* 1984. Knopf. 1st. 311p. NF/VG. W2. $20.00

MACDONALD, John D. *Scarlet Ruse.* 1980. Lippincott Crowell. 1st Am hc. F/dj. M15. $100.00

MACDONALD, John D. *Three for McGee.* 1967. Doubleday. 1st. VG/VG+ clip. B4. $250.00

MACDONALD, John D. *Wine of the Dreamers.* 1951. NY. Greenberg. 1st. author's 1st hc book. F/dj. B4/L3. $250.00

MACDONALD, John Ross; see Millar, Kenneth.

MACDONALD, Ross; see Millar, Kenneth.

MACDONALD, Wilson. *Miracle Songs of Jesus.* 1921. Toronto. Ryerson. 2nd. VG. T12. $100.00

MACDONELL, Anne. *Italian Fairy Book.* 1911. London. Fisher Unwin. 1st. ils Morris Williams. 8vo. gr cloth. R5. $375.00

MACDOUGAL, A. *Secret of Successful Restaurants.* 1929. 1st. VG. E6. $25.00

MACEWEN, William. *Pyogenic Infective Diseases of the Brain & Spinal Cord.* 1893. Glasgow. Maclehouse. heavy 8vo. 354p. pebbled gr cloth. G1. $500.00

MACEY, Peter. *Alien Culture.* 1977. London. 1st. F/dj. M2. $12.00

MACFALL, Haldane. *Beautiful Children.* ca 1910. TC Jack. 33 mc pl. VG. M19. $45.00

MACFARLAN, Allan. *American Indian Legends.* 1968. LEC/Ward Ritchie. 1/1500. ils/sgn Everett jackson. w/prospectus. M/box. K7. $140.00

MACGRATH, Harold. *Cellini Plaque.* 1925. Grosset Dunlap. 252p. VG/dj. M20. $15.00

MACGREAGOR-MORRIS, Pamela. *World's Show Jumpers.* 1967. Barnes. 1st Am. VG/G. O3. $25.00

MACGREGOR, Alexander. *Highland Superstitions.* 1922. Enease MacKay. VG. B2. $30.00

MACGREGOR, Geddes. *Bible in the Making.* 1959. Lippincott. 447p. VG/dj. B29. $12.00

MACGREGOR, James. *Father Lacombe.* 1975. Hurtig. 1st. F/F. T12. $20.00

MACH, Ernest. *Space & Geometry in Light of Physiological...Inquiry.* 1943. Lasalle. Open Court. 8vo. 148p. K3. $18.00

MACHADO DE CASTRO, Joaquim. *Ao Rey Fidelissimo Dom Jose I Nosso Senhor, Collocando...* 1775. Lisbon. Regia Off Typografica. 1st/only. unbound. R15. $650.00

MACHEN, Arthur. *Chronicle of Clemedy.* 1923. Soc Pantagruelists. 1/1050. sgn/#d. 331p. VG. B11. $85.00

MACHEN, Arthur. *Hill of Dreams.* 1907. Estes. 1st Am. VG. M2. $75.00

MACHEN, Arthur. *100 Merrie Tales.* 1924. Carbonnell. 2 vol. 1/1250. sgn. ils/sgn Clara Tice. VG/dj. B5. $150.00

MACHEN, J. Gresham. *Christianity & Liberalism.* 1974. Eerdmans. 189p. VG. B29. $7.00

MACHIAVELLI, Niccolo. *Prince.* 1954. NY. LEC. 1st thus. 1/1500. full leather. NF/case. Q1. $200.00

MACHIAVELLI. *Tvtte le Opere.* 1650 (1550). np. 5 works in 1. 4to. double-p woodcut. calf. R12. $650.00

MACINNES, Helen. *Above Suspicion.* 1941. Little Brn. 1st. VG. N4. $20.00

MACINNES, Helen. *Hidden Target.* 1980. HBJ. 1st. F/G. T12. $10.00

MACINNES, Helen. *I & My True Love.* 1953. Harcourt Brace. 1st. F/NF. B4. $85.00

MACINTYRE, Donald. *Narvik.* 1959. London. 1st. ils/maps. 224p. VG/VG. S16. $25.00

MACINTYRE, Donald. *Wings of Neptune, Story of Naval Aviation.* 1964. NY. 1st Am. 268p. VG/dj. B18. $22.50

MACK, Burton L. *Lost Gospel: Book of Q & Christian Origins.* 1993. Harper Collins. 275p. F/wrp. B29. $9.00

MACK, Burton L. *Mack & Christian Origins: Myth of Innocence.* 1988. Fortress. 432p. VG. B29. $13.50

MACK, Connie. *Connie Mack's Baseball Book.* 1950. NY. 1st. sgn. VG/VG. B5. $40.00

MACK, R.E. *From Lace to Leaf, a Volume of Poems With Illustrations.* ca late 1800s. NY. ils. VG. M17. $20.00

MACKAY, Douglas. *Honourable Company: History of Hudson's Bay Company.* 1936. Bobbs Merrill. 8vo. blk cloth. VG/worn. P4. $75.00

MACKELLAR, Thomas. *American Printer: A Manual of Typography.* 1870. Phil. Mackellar Smith. 5th. ils. VG. K3. $60.00

MACKENZIE, Compton. *Santa Claus in Summer.* 1924. Constable. 1st. 298p. VG/G. P2. $30.00

MACKENZIE, D.R. *Movement & Dispersal of Agriculturally Important Biotic...* 1985. Baton Rouge. Claitor's Pub. 611p. F. B1. $45.00

MACKENZIE, Norman. *Secret Societies.* 1967. NY. 1st Am. ils. 350p. F/F. W3. $135.00

MACKENZIE, Robert. *19th Century: A History.* 1880. London. Nelson. 1st. 8vo. 463p. brn cloth. VG. T10. $50.00

MACKENZIE. *Mackenzie's Five Thousand Receipts in All Useful...Arts.* 1853. Phil. Troutman Hayes. rebound. A16. $70.00

MACKEY, Sandra. *Saudis: Inside the Desert Kingdom.* 1987. Houghton Mifflin. 1st. 433p. VG. W1. $22.00

MACKEY & SOOY. *Early California Costumes 1769-1850.* 1949. Stanford. 2nd. 8vo. xl. VG. O4. $15.00

MACKINSTRY, Elizabeth. *Aladdin & the Wonderful Lamp.* 1935. Macmillan. 1st. 4to. unp. NF/G+ clip. C14. $38.00

MACLACHLAN, Colin. *Criminal Justice in 18th-Century Mexico.* 1974. Berkeley. 1st. 141p. dj. F3. $30.00

MACLAREN, Malcom. *Rise of the Electrical Industry in the 19th Century.* 1943. Princeton. 1st. 225p. VG/dj. B5. $45.00

MACLAREN, Sherrill. *Braehead.* 1986. Toronto. McClelland Stewart. dj. A19. $40.00

MACLAURIN, C. *Mere Mortals.* 1925. Doran. 8vo. 291p. VG/dj. K3. $15.00

MACLAURIN, C. *Post Mortem.* nd. Doran. 8vo. 260p. K3. $15.00

MACLAURIN, Colin. *Account of Sir Isaac Newton's Philosophical Discoveries.* 1750 (1748). London. Millar. 2nd. 8vo. 412p. rebound modern leather. K5. $450.00

MACLAY, Edgar Stanton. *History of the United States Navy.* 1894. NY. Appleton. 2 vol. ils. rebacked. T7. $125.00

MACLEAN, A.D. *Winter's Tales 24.* 1974. St Martin. 1st Am. F/dj. M2. $15.00

MACLEAN, Alistair. *Athabasca.* 1980. Doubleday. 1st Am. F/F. N4. $25.00

MACLEAN, Alistair. *Bear Island.* 1971. Collins. 1st. F/F. N4. $30.00

MACLEAN, Alistair. *Bear Island.* 1971. London. Collins. 1st. VG/dj. P3. $25.00

MACLEAN, Alistair. *Breakheart Pass.* 1974. Doubleday. 1st Am. F/F. N4. $25.00

MACLEAN, Alistair. *Captain Cook.* 1972. Doubleday. 1st. F/dj. B26/M19. $25.00

MACLEAN, Alistair. *Carvan to Vaccares.* 1970. London. Collins. 1st Am. F/dj. Q1. $35.00

MACLEAN, Alistair. *Force 10 From Navarone.* 1968. Doubleday. 1st Am. VG+/VG. N4. $25.00

MACLEAN, Alistair. *Guns for Navarone.* 1957. Doubleday. 1st. VG/VG. R14. $35.00

MACLEAN, Alistair. *HMS Ulysses.* 1955. London. Collins. 1st Eng (true 1st). gilt red cloth. F/VG+. T11. $95.00

MACLEAN, Alistair. *Last Frontier.* 1959. London. Collins. 1st. F/VG+. T11. $50.00

MACLEAN, Alistair. *Puppet on a Chain.* 1969. Doubleday. 1st Am. NF/VG. N4. $25.00

MACLEAN, Alistair. *Seawitch.* 1977. Doubleday. 1st Am. F/NF. N4. $25.00

MACLEAN, Alister. *Seawitch.* 1977. London. Collins. 1st. F/poor. T12. $25.00

MACLEISH, Archibald. *Collected Poems, 1971-1952.* 1952. Houghton Mifflin. rpt. sgn. F/dj. M24. $65.00

MACLEISH, Archibald. *Fall of the City: A Verse Play for Radio.* 1937. Farrar Rinehart. 8vo. 33p. orange brd. NF/torn glassine dj. T10. $45.00

MACLEISH, Archibald. *Songs for Eve.* 1954. Houghton Mifflin. 1st. sgn. gilt red cloth. F/dj. M24. $75.00

MACLEISH, Roderick. *Prince Ombra.* (1982). Congdon Weed. 3rd. F/NF. M21. $7.50

MACLEISH & VAN DOREN. *Dialogues.* 1964. Dutton. 1st. edit Warren Bush. F/F. B35. $35.00

MACLEOD, Barbara. *Children's Twilight Tales.* 1942. NY. Henry Harrison. 1st. inscr/dtd 1942. NF. C14. $25.00

MACLEOD, Charlotte. *An Owl Too Many.* 1991. Mysterious. 1st. F/F. N4. $20.00

MACLEOD, Charlotte. *Recycled Citizen.* 1988. Mysterious. 1st. F/F. N4. $20.00

MACLEOD, Charlotte. *Silver Ghost.* 1988. Mysterious. 1st. F/F. N4. $20.00

MACLEOD, Charlotte. *Something the Cat Dragged in.* 1983. Doubleday. 1st. F/NF. Q1. $30.00

MACLEOD, Fiona. *Dominion of Dreams.* 1900. Stokes. 1st Am. VG. M2. $50.00

MACLEOD. *Moral Tale: Children's Fiction & American Culture 1820-60.* 1975. 196p. F. A4. $30.00

MACMANUS, Seamus. *Ballads of a Country Boy.* 1905. MH Gill. 1st. inscr/dtd 1909. 100p. gilt gr cloth. H1. $75.00

MACMANUS, Seamus. *Top O' the Mornin'.* 1920. Stokes. 1st. VG. M2. $20.00

MACMICHAEL, William. *Gold Headed Cane.* 1953. Springfield, IL. 7th. 186p. uncut. VG/worn. K3. $25.00

MACMINN, George R. *Theater of the Golden Era in California.* 1941. Caxton. ils. 529p. yel stp blk cloth. D11. $60.00

MACNEICE, Louis. *One for the Grave.* 1968. Oxford. ARC. RS. dj. V1. $25.00

MACNEIL, Neil; see Ballard, W.T.

MACOBOY, S. *Ultimate Rose Book.* 1993. Abrams. folio. ils. 472p. F/F. E6. $25.00

MACPHERSON, James. *Fingal, an Ancient Epic Poem in Six Books...* 1762. London. Beckett DeHondt. 2nd. tall 4to. 270p. full polished calf/rebacked. H13. $375.00

MACPHERSON, Margaret L. *Australia Calling.* 1946. Dodd Mead. 1st. sgn. 197p. VG/VG. M20. $20.00

MACPHERSON & STUART-WORTLEY. *Partridge: Natural History, Shooting, Cookery.* 1894. Longman Gr. 2nd. 276p. pict bdg. xl. VG. H7. $20.00

MACQUITTY, William. *Tutankhamun: The Last Journey.* 1978. NY. Quartet Books. BC. 5th. ils. 50p. NF/dj. W1. $18.00

MACRAE, Stuart. *Winston Churchill's Toyshop: Invention & Making...* 1971. NY. photos/index. 228p. VG/VG. S16. $24.00

MACSHERIDAN, C. *Stag Cook Book: Man's Cook Book for Men.* 1922. Doran. 197p. B10. $25.00

MACSWIGGAN, A.E. *Fairy Lamps.* 1962. Fountainhead. 1st. sgn. 170p. VG/dj. M20. $45.00

MACSWIGGAN, A.E. *Fairy Lamps.* 1962. Fountainhead. 1st. 20 pl/prices. 170p. F/dj. H1. $37.50

MACVEY, John. *Colonizing Other Worlds.* 1984. Stein Day. 1st. F/dj. M2. $15.00

MADAULE, Jacques. *Albigensian Crusade.* 1967. NY. Fordham. 8vo. 177p. VG/dj. W1. $22.00

MADDAMS, W.F. *Interesting Newer Mammillarias.* nd. np. Mammillarian Soc. photos. brn cloth. F. B26. $17.50

MADDEN, Betty I. *Art, Crafts & Architecture in Early Illinois.* 1974. Urbana. 1st. ils. 297p. VG/dj. B18. $22.50

MADDEN, Henry Miller. *German Travellers in California.* 1958. Roxburghe Club. 1/125. 39p. prt brd/cloth spine. as new. K7. $50.00

MADDEN, John. *First Book of Football.* 1988. Crown. 1st. sgn. F/F. A23. $40.00

MADDEN, John. *One Size Doesn't Fit All.* 1988. Villard. 1st. sgn. F. A23. $40.00

MADDISON, Francis. *Sir William Dugdale 1605-1686.* 1953. Warick. Warwickshire County Council. 92p. prt sewn wrp. M11. $45.00

MADISON, Charles A. *Yiddish Literature: Its Scope & Major Writers.* 1968. NY. Ungar. 540p. VG/G+. S3. $28.00

MADISON, Lucy Foster. *Washington.* 1925. Phil. Penn Pub. 1st. 8vo. 399p. G+. C14. $17.00

MADS, George. *Winchester Book.* 1985. Brownesboro, TX. sgn. 655p. M. A17. $50.00

MAE, Verta. *Vibration Cooking; or, Travel Notes of a Geechee Girl.* 1970. Doubleday. 1st. 190p. F/F. B4. $85.00

MAETERLINCK, Maurice. *Hours of Gladness.* 1912. London. Allen. 1st. ils Detmold. lg 4to. gilt wht cloth. R5. $400.00

MAETERLINCK, Maurice. *Inner Beauty.* 1910. London. 1st. half leather. VG+. S13. $50.00

MAETERLINCK, Maurice. *Life of the Bee.* nd. Bl Ribbon. rpt. VG. E6. $12.00

MAGEE, David. *Infinite Riches: Adventures of a Rare Book Dealer.* 1973. NY. Eriksson. 1st. ils. 274p. VG+/dj. K3. $25.00

MAGEE, David. *Jam Tomorrow.* 1941. Houghton Mifflin. 1st. author's 1st book. F/dj. Q1. $75.00

MAGNAN, Valentin. *Recherches sur les Centres Nerveux...* 1893. Paris. Masson. 8vo. 572p. xl. VG. G1. $175.00

MAGNER, D. *Magner's Standard Horse & Stock Book.* 1900. Akron. Saalfield. 1st. 1181p. rebacked. VG. O3. $95.00

MAGNI, Laura. *Goodnight Stories From the Big Tree.* 1990. Derrydale. 1st Am. 192p. NF. C14. $20.00

MAGNIAUX, Phillippe. *Adventures of Charlie Chaplin, the Gold Rush.* 1975. Drake. ils. lg laminated brd. NF/sans. C9. $75.00

MAGOUN, F. Alexander. *Frigate Constitution & Other Historic Ships.* 1928. Marine Research Soc. 154p. cloth. VG. M20. $200.00

MAGOUN, H.W. *Neurophysiology. Handbook of Physiology.* 1959. WA, DC. Am Physiological Soc. 3 vol. later prt. VG/dj. G1. $150.00

MAGRIEL, P. *Backgammon.* 1976. NY. 1st. VG/VG. B5. $60.00

MAGRIEL, P. *Pavlova: Illustrated Monograph.* 1948. photos. VG/G+. M17. $25.00

MAHAN, A.T. *Gulf & Inland Waters.* 1883. Scribner. 1st. 12mo. 267p. VG. M1. $125.00

MAHAN, A.T. *Types of Naval Officers.* 1902. London. Sampson Low. 7 pl. 500p. T7. $80.00

MAHAN, D.H. *Summary of the Course of Permanent Fornication...* 1850. West Point, NY. Lith at US Mill Academy. 1st. 372p. M1. $550.00

MAHARAJAH OF COOCH BEAR. *37 Years of Big Game Shooting in Cooch Bear, the Duars...* 1993. Wolf. 471p+4p fld map. aeg. gilt leatherette. A17. $45.00

MAHFOUZ, Naguib. *Atlas of Mahfouz's Obstetric & Gynaecological Museum.* 1949. Altricham, Eng. 1st. 3 vol. 1276p. A13. $200.00

MAHLER, Raphael. *History of Modern Jewry 1780-1815.* 1971. Schocken. 742p. VG/dj. S3. $40.00

MAHONEY, Latimer. *Illustrators of Children's Books 1744-1945.* 1947. ltd. 4to. ils. 544p. VG. A4. $145.00

MAHONEY, Latimer. *Illustrators of Children's Books 1744-1945.* 1947. Horn Book. 1st. 4to. VG/home-made case. D1. $175.00

MAHONEY & WHITNEY. *Realms of Gold.* 1929. Doubleday Doran. various ils. 796p. VG. P2. $50.00

MAILER, Norman. *Advertisements for Myself.* 1959. Putnam. 1st. VG/VG. R14. $40.00

MAILER, Norman. *American Dream.* 1965. Dial. 1st. NF/dj. Q1. $60.00

MAILER, Norman. *Ancient Evenings.* 1983. Little Brn. 1st. F/F. B35. $35.00

MAILER, Norman. *Barbary Shore.* 1951. NY. Rinehart. 1st. NF/dj. from $110 to $150.00

MAILER, Norman. *Cannibals & Christians.* 1966. Dial. 1st. VG/VG. R14. $35.00

MAILER, Norman. *Deer Park.* 1967. NY. Dial. 1st. F/clip. Q1. $100.00

MAILER, Norman. *Executioner's Song.* 1979. Little Brn. 1st. F/F. H11. $60.00

MAILER, Norman. *Genius & Lust.* 1976. Grove. 1st. F/dj. Q1. $40.00

MAILER, Norman. *Harlot's Ghost.* 1991. Random. 1st. sgn. F/F. R14. $60.00

MAILER, Norman. *Harlot's Ghost.* 1991. Random. 1st. VG+/F. A20. $20.00

MAILER, Norman. *Naked & the Dead.* 1948. 1st. author's 1st book. rem mk. VG/torn. A15. $75.00

MAILER, Norman. *Naked & the Dead.* 1948. NY. Rinehart. ARC. author's 1st book. F/wrp/clamshell case. Q1. $1,000.00

MAILER, Norman. *Naked & the Dead.* 1948. Rinehart. 1st. G/G. M19. $175.00

MAILER, Norman. *Of a Fire on the Moon.* 1970. Little Brn. 1st. NF/clip. Q1. $40.00

MAILER, Norman. *Oswald's Tale: An American Mystery.* 1995. Random. 1st. sgn. VG/VG. A23. $50.00

MAILER, Norman. *Pieces & Pontifications.* 1983. NEL. 1st. sgn. F/dj. A24. $45.00

MAILER, Norman. *Prisoner of Sex.* 1971. Boston. 1st. VG/VG. T9. $20.00

MAILER, Norman. *St George & the Godfather.* 1983. Arbor. 1st. F/F. A24. $35.00

MAILER, Norman. *Tough Guys Don't Dance.* 1984. Random. 1st. F/F. A20. $25.00

MAILER, Norman. *Tough Guys Don't Dance.* 1984. Random. 1st. sgn. F/F. A23. $32.00

MAILLET. *Telliamed; or, World Explain'd.* 1797. Baltimore. Pechin for Porter. 8vo. calf. R12. $250.00

MAILS, Thomas E. *Fools Crow.* 1979. Doubleday. 1st. F/dj. A19. $50.00

MAINE, Charles Eric. *Crisis 2000.* 1956. London. 1st. F/dj. M2. $25.00

MAINE, Henry Sumner. *Ancient Law, Its Connection With Early History of Society...* 1908. London. gilt gr cloth. G. M11. $50.00

MAIR, John. *Fourth Forger.* 1938. London. Cobden Sanderson. 1st. ils. VG. K3. $45.00

MAITLAND, F.W. *Bracton's Note Book: A Collection of Cases...* 1983 (1887). Littleton. facsimile. M11. $350.00

MAITLAND, F.W. *Constitutional History of England.* 1908. Cambridge. 1st. cloth. M11. $125.00

MAITLAND, F.W. *Domesday Book & Beyond, Three Essays in Early History...* 1921. Cambridge. bl cloth. M11. $85.00

MAITLAND, F.W. *English Law & the Renaissance.* 1901. London. Cambridge. gilt crimson cloth. M11. $100.00

MAITLAND, F.W. *Equity, a Course of Lectures...* 1969. Cambridge. VG/dj. M11. $85.00

MAITLAND, F.W. *Forms of Action at Common Law.* 1965. Cambridge. VG/dj. M11. $65.00

MAITLAND, F.W. *Roman Canon Law in the Church of England, Six Essays.* 1968 (1898). Burt Franklin. facsimile. M11. $75.00

MAITLAND, F.W. *Why the History of English Law Is Not Written.* 1888. London. 20p. sewn wrp. M11. $125.00

MAJDALANY, Fred. *Cassino: Portrait of a Battle.* 1957. London. ils/biblio/index. 270p. VG/VG. S16. $24.00

MAJNO, Guido. *Healing Hand: Man & Wound in the Ancient World.* 1975. Cambridge. 1st. 571p. A13. $50.00

MAJOR, Clarence. *All-Night Visitors.* 1969. Olympia. 1st. f/VG clip. B4. $100.00

MAJOR, Clarence. *Painted Turtle: Woman With Guitar.* 1988. Sun Moon. 1st. sgn. F/F. R14. $40.00

MAJOR, John. *Oppenheimer Hearing.* 1971. Stein Day. ils. 8vo. 336p. VG/ils wrp. K3. $15.00

MAJOR, Ralph H. *Classic Descriptions of Disease.* 1932. Thomas. 630p. dj. A17. $30.00

MAJORS, Simon; see Fox, Gardner F.

MAKEMSON, Maud. *Book of the Jaguar Priest.* 1951. NY. Schuman. 1st. 238p. dj. F3. $45.00

MAKSHEV, O.A. *Patriotic War of 1812 in Paintings.* 1912. Paris. Lapina. folio. crimson cloth portfolio. F. B24. $250.00

MAKUCK, Peter. *Where We Live.* 1982. BOA Ed. 1/10 (of 1200). sgns. w/holograph poem. F. V1. $100.00

MALAMUD, Bernard. *Dubin's Lives.* 1979. Franklin Lib. 1st. decor gr leather. F/sans. T11. $40.00

MALAMUD, Bernard. *Natural.* 1963. Eyre Spottiswoode. 1st Eng. author's 1st book. F/dj. Q1. $450.00

MALAMUD, Bernard. *Pictures of Fidelman.* 1969. Farrar. 1st. NF/clip. M25. $25.00

MALAMUD, Bernard. *Tenants.* 1971. FSG. 1st. NF/NF. R14. $35.00

MALAMUD, Bernard. *Two Fables.* 1978. Pawlet, VT. 1/320. sgn/#d. F. B2. $100.00

MALAURIE, Jean. *Last Kings of Thule: Year Among the Eskimos of Greenland.* 1956. ils/photos. VG/VG. M17. $30.00

MALCOLM, Fiona. *Child's Own Visions.* 1916. London. Harrap. 1st. ils Anderson/4 mtd pl. cloth. R5. $175.00

MALET, Andre. *Thought of Rudolf Bultmann.* 1969. Doubleday. 440p. VG/torn. B29. $8.50

MALET, Lucas. *Gateless Barrier.* 1900. Dodd Mead. 1st. VG. M2. $50.00

MALET, Lucas. *Tall Villa.* 1919. Doran. 1st. VG. M2. $25.00

MALING, Arthur. *Taste of Treason.* 1983. Harper Row. 1st. F/F. H11. $20.00

MALL, Thomas. *History of the Martyrs Epitomised...* 1747. Boston. Rogers Fowle. 1st Am. 2 vol. later bdg. M1. $225.00

MALLAN, Lloyd. *Men, Rockets & Space Rats.* 1956 (1955). NY. Messner. 2nd. 8vo. 335p. G/dj. K5. $30.00

MALLARD, Robert Q. *Plantation Life Before Emancipation.* 1892. Richmond, VA. Whittet Shepperson. 1st. 237p. cloth. NF. M8. $250.00

MALLARME, Stephane. *Selected Letters.* 1988. Chicago. 1st. trans R Lloyd. VG/dj. T9. $15.00

MALLET, Thierry. *Glimpses of the Barren Lands.* 1930. NY. Fevillon Freres. 1st. 142p. VG. H7. $15.00

MALLONEE, R.C. *Naked Flagpole.* 1980. CA. 1st. ils/maps. 204p. VG/VG. S16. $25.00

MALLORY, William Wyman. *Geologic Atlas of the Rocky Mountain Region, US of Am.* 1972. Rocky Mtn Assn Geolog. full-p maps. 331p. gilt cloth. D11. $40.00

MALM, William. *Japanese Music & Musical Instruments.* 1974. Rutland/Tokyo. ils/pl/figures/4 append/glossary. 299p. F/F. W3. $56.00

MALONE, Michael. *Painting the Roses Red.* 1974. Random. ARC. author's 1st novel. RS. F/F. B4. $250.00

MALONE, Michael. *Psychetypes: A New Way of Exploring Personality.* 1977. Dutton. 1st. F/F. B4. $250.00

MALONE, Michael. *Uncivil Seasons.* 1983. Delacorte. 1st. F/F. M22. $65.00

MALONEY, Richard C. *Fifty Notable Ship Portraits at Mystic Seaport.* 1963. Marine Hist Assn. ils. 63p. P4. $25.00

MALORY, Thomas. *Le Morte d'Arthur.* 1955. NY. Heritage. 4to. 757p. patterned brd/blk linen spine. F/G case. H13. $65.00

MALOUF, David. *Johnno.* 1975. Queensland. correct 1st. author's 1st novel. NF/NF. L3. $150.00

MALTBY, Lucy Mary. *It's Fun To Cook.* (1938). Phil. Winston. 8vo. 399p. VG/G+. T5. $25.00

MALZBERG, Barry. *Herovit's World.* 1973. Random. 1st. F/dj. M2. $25.00

MAMET, David. *Cabin.* 1992. NY. Turtle Bay. 1st. sgn. F/F. D10. $40.00

MAMET, David. *Some Freaks.* 1989. NY. Viking. 1st. F/F. R14. $35.00

MAMET, David. *Some Freaks.* 1989. Viking. 1st. F/NF. B3. $30.00

MAMET, David. *Some Freaks.* 1989. Viking. 1st. sgn. author's 2nd essay collection. F/F. D10. $50.00

MAMET, David. *Village.* 1994. Little Brn. 1st. F/F. R13. $20.00

MAMET, David. *Writing in Resturants.* 1986. Viking. 1st. sgn. F/F. D10. $60.00

MAMMANA, Dennis. *Star Hunters.* 1990. Phil. Running Pr. 160p. F/F. K5. $20.00

MANCHESTER, William. *Death of a President November 20-November 25, 1963.* 1967. Harper Row. 1st. F/F. H11. $25.00

MANCHESTER, William. *Death of a President November 20-November 25, 1963.* 1967. Harper Row. 1st. 710p. F/VG. H1. $20.00

MANDERS, Olga Sarah. *Mrs Manders' Cook Book.* 1968. NY. Viking. G/dj. A16. $15.00

MANFRED, Frederick. *Man Who Looked Like the Prince of Wales.* 1965. Trident. 1st. NF/dj. M25. $45.00

MANFRED, Frederick. *Riders of Judgment.* 1957. Random. 1st. VG/dj. w/author's photo. M25. $35.00

MANFRED, Frederick. *Sons of Adam.* 1980. Crown. 1st. NF/dj. M25. $25.00

MANFRED, Frederick. *This Is the Year.* 1947. Doubleday. 1st. VG/dj. M25. $45.00

MANFRED, Frederick. *Wanderlust: A Trilogy.* 1962. Swallow. 1st thus. NF/dj. A18. $50.00

MANGAN, F. *Pipeliners: Story of El Paso Natural Gas.* 1977. El Paso. Guynes. ils/photos. 354p. cloth. NF/dj. D8. $35.00

MANGAN, Terry William. *Colorado on Glass...As Seen by the Camera.* 1975. Denver. Sundance Ltd. 1st. 1/250. sgn. 406p. brd. cloth case. w/contact prt. D11. $500.00

MANGELSDORF, Paul. *Corn: Its Origin, Evolution & Improvement.* 1974. Cambridge. Harvard. 262p. VG/dj. A10. $20.00

MANGLAPUS, Raul S. *Philippines: Silenced Democracy.* 1976. Maryknoll, NY. Orbis Books. 203p. cloth. M/VG. P1. $10.00

MANGUEL, Alberto. *Seasons.* 1987. Doubleday. ils Warabe Aska. 48p. F/F. D4. $30.00

MANKOWITZ, Wolf. *Wedgwood.* 1966 (1953). Spring Books. 284p. gilt bl cloth. NF/plastic dj. H1. $65.00

MANLEY, William Lewis. *Death Valley in '49.* 1894. San Jose, CA. Pacific Tree & Vine. 1st. 498p. VG. K7. $250.00

MANLOVE. *Impulse of Fantasy Literature.* 1983. 188p. F/F. A4. $45.00

MANN, Arthur. *Baseball Confidential.* 1951. NY. 1st. VG/VG. B5. $25.00

MANN, Edward Andrew. *Portals.* 1974. S&S. 1st. F/dj. M2. $10.00

MANN, Felix. *Acupuncture: Ancient Chinese Art of Healing.* 1963. Random. fwd Aldous Huxley. 174p. F/VG. W3. $42.00

MANN, Heinrich. *Henry, King of France.* 1939. Knopf. 1st Am. F/VG+. B4. $125.00

MANN, Heinrich. *Small Town Tyrant.* 1944. Creative Age. 1st Am. VG/VG. B4. $250.00

MANN, M.T. *Rev JT Mann of Fitzgerald, Georgia...* ca 1907. np. 1st. NF/prt wrp. M8. $1,250.00

MANN, Thomas. *Doctor Faustus.* 1948. Knopf. 1st. NF/VG. M19. $25.00

MANN, Thomas. *Holy Sinner.* 1951. Knopf. 1st. 336p. blk cloth. F/VG. B22. $12.00

MANN, Thomas. *Sketch of My Life.* 1930. Harrison of Paris. 1/695. F/partial box. B2. $85.00

MANN, Thomas. *Sketch of My Life.* 1960. Knopf. 1st. F/VG. M19. $25.00

MANN, Thomas. *Transposed Heads: A Legend of India.* 1977. Kentfield, CA. Allen. 1/140. 4to. 108p. Indian cloth. F. B24. $475.00

MANNIN, Ethel. *Lovely Land: Hashemite Kingdom of Jordan.* 1965. London. Hutchinson. 1st. 17 pl. VG/dj. W1. $24.00

MANNING, Elise W. *Farm Journal's Friendly Food Gifts From Your Kitchen.* 1978. Doubleday. G/dj. A16. $7.50

MANNING, J. Russell. *Illustrated Stock Doctor.* 1882. Phil. Hibbard. leather. G. O3. $48.00

MANNING, Paul. *Boy. Merry-Go-Rhymes.* 1987. Macmillan. 1st. ils Nicola Bayley. 18p. F/F D4. $25.00

MANNING, R. *What Kinda Cactus Izzat?* 1957 (1941). Phoenix. 7th or later. 108p. VG. B26. $6.00

MANNING-SANDERS, Ruth. *Book of Sorcerers & Spells.* 1975 (1973). London. Methuen. rpt. sm 4to. 125p. VG. T5. $25.00

MANO, D. Keith. *Horn.* 1969. Houghton Mifflin. 1st. sgn. NF/NF. R14. $45.00

MANSFIELD, Katherine. *Dove's Nest.* 1923. Knopf. 1st Am. gr cloth/label. M24. $250.00

MANSFIELD, Katherine. *Dove's Nest.* 1923. London. Constable. 1st/2nd issue. gr cloth. F. M24. $85.00

MANSFIELD, Katherine. *In a German Pension.* 1926. Knopf. 1st Am. gr cloth/label. F. M24. $75.00

MANSFIELD, Katherine. *Poems.* 1924. Knopf. 1st Am. gr linen/orange decor brd/label. F/dj. M24. $200.00

MANSO, Peter. *Mailer: His Life & Times.* 1985. S&S. 1st. F/F. T12. $20.00

MANTEGAZZA, Paolo. *Sexual Relations of Mankind.* 1932. Anthropological Pr. 1st. 1/1500. sm 4to. handmade/untrimmed paper. F. H1. $35.00

MANTEL, Hilary. *Fludd.* 1989. London. Viking. 1st. F/NF. B3. $15.00

MANTHEY, Gerda. *Fuchsias.* 1991. Portland. ils. 204p. as new/dj. B26. $39.00

MANTZ & MURRY. *Life of Katherine Mansfield.* 1933. London. Constable. 1st. 349p. VG. A25. $15.00

MANVILL, Mrs. P.D. *Lucinda; or, Mountain Mourner. Being Recent Facts...* 1807. Johnstown, NY. Child. 1st. 12mo. 150p. contemporary sheep. M1. $1,250.00

MANWOOD, John. *Treatise of the Laws of the Forest, Wherein Is Declared...* 1665. London. Prt for Co of Stationers. 3-quarter sheep. M11. $650.00

MANZONI, Alessandro. *I Promessi Sposi (The Betrothed).* 1951. Verona. Officina Bodoni. LEC. 1/1500. sgn Hans Mardersteig/Bramanti. F/VG case. T10. $150.00

MARA, Bernard; see Moore, Brian.

MARACOTTA, Lindsay. *Everything We Wanted.* 1984. Crown. 1st. 356p. NF/NF. W2. $20.00

MARAMOROSCH, K. *Invertebrate Tissue Culture.* 1976. Academic. 393p. cloth. VG. B1. $65.00

MARASCO, Robert. *Burnt Offerings.* 1973. Delacorte. 1st. author's 1st book. 260p. F/F. W2. $30.00

MARAT, Jean-Paul. *Discours...Sur la Defense of Louis XVI.* 1792. Paris. Impirmerie de Marat. 8vo. brd. R13. $550.00

MARBURY, Mary Orvis. *Favorite Flies & Their Histories.* 1988. Secaucus. facsimile 1892 ed. F/F. A17. $25.00

MARCEL, Pierre. *Biblical Doctrine of Infant Baptism.* 1959. James Clarke. 256p. VG/torn. B29. $7.50

MARCET, Jane Haldimand. *Conversations on Vegetable Physiology...* 1829. London. Longman Rees. 2 vol. A10. $95.00

MARCH, Daniel. *Home Life in the Bible.* 1873. ils. VG. M17. $25.00

MARCH & TAMBIMUTTU. *TS Eliot: A Symposium.* 1949. Chicago. 1st. 259p. F/dj. A17. $35.00

MARCOS, Ferdinand E. *Today's Revolution: Democracy.* 1971. Manila. sm 8vo. 152p. M/VG. P1. $15.00

MARCOSSON, I.F. *Anaconda.* 1957. Dodd Mead. 370p. cloth. VG. D8. $18.00

MARCUS, G.J. *Naval History of England.* 1961. Little Brn. 18 maps. 494p. T7. $35.00

MARCUS, J.S. *Art of Cartography.* 1991. Knopf. 1st. author's 1st book. F/F. A24. $35.00

MARCUS, J.S. *Art of Cartography.* 1991. Knopf. 1st. VG/VG. L1. $30.00

MARCUS, Joyce. *Inscriptions of Calakmul.* 1987. Ann Arbor. 1st. 4to. 205p. wrp. F3. $25.00

MARECHAUX, Pascal. *Arabia Felix: Images of Yemen & Its People.* 1980. NY. Barron. 1st Am. NF/dj. W1. $45.00

MAREK, George. *Opera As Theater.* 1962. NY. 1st. inscr. VG/VG. T9. $50.00

MAREY, E.J. *Animal Mechanism: Treatise Terrestrial & Aerial Locomotion.* 1874. London. King. 1st Eng-language ed. 12mo. 283p+32p catalog. red cloth. G1. $125.00

MARGOLIN & WYLIE. *Ring of Dancers: Images of Faroese Culture.* 1981. Phil. 1st. 182p. rust cloth. P4. $25.00

MARGOLIS & SENDAK. *Some Swell Pup.* 1976. FSG. 1st. unp. VG/VG. D1. $55.00

MARGULIES, Leo. *Flying Wildcats.* 1943. Hampton. 1st. VG. M2. $35.00

MARIA, Father Vincent. *San Francisco Bay 1775.* 1971. SF. John Howell. A19. $45.00

MARIANA. *Miss Flora McFlimsey & Little Red Schoolhouse.* 1957. Lee Shepherd. 1st. unp. VG/tattered. M20. $40.00

MARIANA. *Miss Flora McFlimsey's Christmas Eve.* 1949. Lee Shepard. 1st. F/VG. M5. $60.00

MARIANO & MOZINO. *Noticias de Nutka.* 1913. Mexico City. Imprenta Y Fototipia Secretaria Fomento. 117p. wrp. P4. $500.00

MARIE, Pierre. *Lectures on Diseases of the Spinal Cord.* 1892. London. Sydenham Soc. 1st Eng-language. 512p. emb brn cloth. NF. G1. $350.00

MARINO. *La Francia Consolata.* 1619. Venice/Torino. 10 parts in 1. 16mo. vellum. R12. $350.00

MARIO, Queena. *Murder in the Opera House.* 1934. NY. 1st. VG/VG. B5. $50.00

MARIO, Thomas. *Playboy's Host & Bar Book.* 1971. Chicago. Playboy. VG. A16. $15.00

MARION, Frances. *Powder Keg.* 1953. Little Brn. 1st. inscr. F/VG+. B4. $275.00

MARIS, Jesse. *Remembering.* 1951. np. 1st. sgn pres. ils/photos. 84p. VG. B5. $50.00

MARITAIN, Jacques. *France My Country, Through the Disaster.* 1941. Longman Gr. 1st trans ed. 8vo. 117p. VG/dj. T10. $50.00

MARK, Stuart A. *Southern Hunting in Black & White: Nature, History...* 1991. Princeton. 1st. 327p. M/dj. A17. $15.00

MARK, Yudel. *Grammar of Standard Yiddish.* 1978. Congress Jewish Culture. Yiddish text. 394p. VG+. S3. $27.00

MARKBREIT & STEINBERG. *Born to Referee.* 1988. Morrow. 1st. photos. F/VG. P8. $12.50

MARKENS, Isaac. *Hebrew in America, a Series of Historical...Sketches.* 1888. self pub. VG. E6. $100.00

MARKHAM, Clements R. *Narrative of Proceedings of Pedrarias Davila...* 1865. London. Hakluyt Soc. 8vo. fld map. 88p. gilt bl cloth. P4. $395.00

MARKHAM, Edwin. *Man With the Hoe & Other Poems.* 1899. Doubleday McClure. 1st collected/2nd issue. 8vo. 134p. cloth. case. M1. $200.00

MARKHAM, Edwin. *Man With the Hoe & Other Poems.* 1900. Doubleday. inscr to RJ Hinton/dtd 1900. NF. Q1. $125.00

MARKHAM, Edwin. *Shoes of Happiness & Other Poems.* 1913. Doubleday Page. sgn. VG. M20. $25.00

MARKHAM, Ernest. *Raspberries & Kindred Fruits.* 1936. London. Macmillan. 68p. VG/dj. A10. $28.00

MARKMAN & MARKMAN. *Flayed Gods.* 1992. Harper. 1st. 456p. xl. dj. F3. $15.00

MARKMANN & SHERWIN. *Book of Sports Cars.* 1959. Putnam. 1st. 323p. cloth. VG/clip. M20. $30.00

MARKOFF, Alexander. *Russians on the Pacific Ocean.* 1955. LA. Glen Dawson. 1/300. decor cloth. D11. $75.00

MARKS, David. *Treatise on Faith of Freewill Baptists...* 1834. Dover. 1st. 18mo. 156p. F. M1. $200.00

MARKS, J.; see Highwater, Jamake.

MARKS, Lis. *Ghostly Towers.* 1986. Dial. 1st. ils Angela Barrett. F. T10. $50.00

MARKS, Paul Mitchell. *And Die in the West.* 1989. Morrow. 1st. 480p. VG/VG. J2. $225.00

MARKS, Richard Lee. *Three Men of the Beagle.* 1991. Knopf. 1st. 8vo. index/bibliography/map ep. NF/dj. P4. $35.00

MARKS-HIGHWATER, J.; see Highwater, Jamake.

MARKSON, David. *Ballad of Dingus Magee.* 1965. Bobbs Merrill. 1st. sgn. F/dj. Q1. $60.00

MARKSON, David. *Going Down.* 1970. HRW. 1st. sgn. F/dj. Q1. $50.00

MARKSON, David. *Malcolm Lowry's Volcano.* 1978. Times Books. 1st. sgn. F/F. Q1. $60.00

MARKSON, David. *Springer's Progress.* 1977. HRW. 1st. sgn. F/dj. Q1. $50.00

MARKSON, David. *Wittgenstein's Mistress.* 1988. Elmwood Park, IL. Dalkey Archive. 1st. sgn. F/dj. Q1. $50.00

MARKUS, Kurt. *Buckaroon.* 1987. Little Brn. 1st. 127p. VG/VG. J2. $195.00

MARKUS, Rixi. *Common-Sense Bridge.* 1972. NY. 1st Am. 171p. VG/dj. S1. $6.00

MARLIN, J. *Appeal to the Heart.* 1985. Putnam. 1st. 138p. F/F. W2. $15.00

MARLOWE, Dan J. *Operation Flashpoint.* 1972. London. Wht Lion. 1st hc. F/dj. M15. $45.00

MARLOWE, Derek. *Dandy in Aspic.* 1966. Putnam. 1st. author's 1st book. F/NF. H11. $25.00

MARLOWE, Hugh; see Patterson, Henry.

MAROGER, Jacques. *Secret Formulas & Techniques of the Masters.* 1948. Studio. trans from French. 200p. gray cloth. B14. $45.00

MAROIS, Blanche. *Le Premier Livre.* 1928. Neuvieme Ed/Pour Les Petis Enfants. ils. VG. M17. $30.00

MARON, Margaret. *Bootlegger's Daughter.* 1992. Mysterious. 1st. F/F. D10. $55.00

MARON, Margaret. *Bootlegger's Daughter.* 1992. Mysterious. 1st. NF/dj. Q1. $50.00

MARON, Margaret. *Corpus Christmas.* 1989. Doubleday. 1st. F/F. D10. $45.00

MARON, Margaret. *Death of a Butterfly.* 1984. Doubleday Crime Club. 1st. VG+/VG+. N4. $50.00

MARON, Margaret. *Past Imperfect.* 1991. Doubleday. 1st. F/F. D10. $35.00

MARON, Margaret. *Shooting at Loons.* 1994. Mysterious. 1st. sgn. F/F. R13. $35.00

MARON, Margaret. *Southern Discomfort.* 1993. Mysterious. 1st. sgn. F/F. A23. $40.00

MARQUEZ, Gabriel Garcia. *Autumn of the Patriarch.* 1976. Harper Row. 1st Am. F/NF. D10. $75.00

MARQUEZ, Gabriel Garcia. *Collected Stories.* 1984. Harper Row. 1st. F/F. B3/D10. $45.00

MARQUEZ, Gabriel Garcia. *El Amor en los Tiempos de Colera.* 1985. Mexico. 1st/Editorial Diana issue. F/F. A11. $65.00

MARQUEZ, Gabriel Garcia. *El Otono del Patriarca.* 1975. Buenos Aires. Editorial Sudamericana. 1st Latin Am. F/NF wrp. B4. $450.00

MARQUEZ, Gabriel Garcia. *General in His Labyrinth.* 1990. NY. 1st. VG/VG. T9. $15.00

MARQUEZ, Gabriel Garcia. *Innocent Erendira & Other Stories.* 1978. Harper Row. 1st. author's 5th book. F/F clip. H11. $65.00

MARQUEZ, Gabriel Garcia. *La Hojarasca.* 1955. Bogota. Ediciones SLB. 1st. author's 1st book. VG/self wrp. L3. $25.00

MARQUEZ, Gabriel Garcia. *Love in the Time of Cholera.* 1988. London. Cape. 1st. F/F. D10. $50.00

MARQUEZ, Gabriel Garcia. *Of Love & Other Demons.* 1995. Knopf. 1st Am. trans Edith Grossman. F/dj. Q1. $25.00

MARQUIS, Thomas B. *Keep the Last Bullet for Yourself.* 1976. Two Continents. 1st. 203p. cloth. VG/dj. M20. $28.00

MARQUIS, Thomas B. *Rain-in-the-Face, Curley, the Crow.* 1934. Cactus Pony Pub. VG/wrp. J2. $28.00

MARR-JOHNSON, Diana. *Rainbow's Pop-Up Book.* 1960. London. Dean. ils Janet/Anne Grahame-Johnstone. pict brd. unused. R5. $75.00

MARRIC, J.J.; see Creasey, John.

MARRINER, John. *Black Sea & Blue River.* 1968. Hart Davis. 16 pl/28 maps. 240p. VG. W1. $20.00

MARSDEN, Brian G. *Catalog of Cometary Orbits.* 1983. Hillside, NJ. Enslow. 1st trade. VG/glossy wrp. K5. $15.00

MARSDEN, C. *Grow Cacti: A Practical Handbook.* 1958 (1955). London. enlarged 2nd. 4 mc pl. 178p. VG/dj. B26. $24.00

MARSDEN, C. *Mammillaria.* 1957. London. ils. VG/dj. B26. $40.00

MARSDEN, John. *Fury of the Northmen: Saints & Shrines & Sea-Raiders...* 1995. NY. St Martin. 1st Am. M/dj. P4. $25.00

MARSH, Andrew. *Marsh's Manual of Reformed Phonetic Short-Hand.* 1868. SF. Bancroft. 1st. gilt blk cloth. NF. M24. $850.00

MARSH, Dave. *Glory Days.* 1986. Pantheon. 1st. F/F. A20. $10.00

MARSH, George P. *Lectures on the English Language.* 1860. NY. Scribner. 1st. 8vo. 697p. cloth. M1. $225.00

MARSH, George. *Toilers of the Trails.* 1921. Penn Pub. 1st. 245p. VG. J2. $65.00

MARSH, J.B.L. *Story of the Jubilee Singers.* 1877. 7th. VG. M17. $35.00

MARSH, Ngaio. *Colour Scheme.* 1943. London. Collins. 1st. NF/worn. B2. $80.00

MARSH, Ngaio. *Death at the Bar.* 1940. Little Brn. 1st Am. F/VG. M15. $125.00

MARSH, Ngaio. *Death of a Peer.* 1940. Little Brn. 1st. NF/VG. M22. $75.00

MARSH, Ngaio. *When in Rome.* 1970. Little Brn. 1st. F/NF. M19. $25.00

MARSH, O.C. *Dinocerata: Monograph of Extinct Order of Gigantic Mammals.* 1886. USGS. ils/55 pl/fld pl/200 figures. 243p. xl. VG. M12. $95.00

MARSHALIS & STEWART. *Sweet Swing Blues on the Road.* 1994. Norton. 1st. inscr. 190p. F/F. B4. $85.00

MARSHALL, A.J. *Biology & Comparative Physiology of Birds.* 1960-61. NY/London. 2 vol. VG. S15. $65.00

MARSHALL, Alan; see Westlake, Donald E.

MARSHALL, Catherine. *Friends With God: Stories & Prayers of the Marshall Family.* 1956. Whittlesey. 1st. 48p. NF/VG clip. C14. $18.00

MARSHALL, Don B. *California Shipwrecks.* 1978. Seattle. Superior Pub. 1st. inscr. ils. 175p. dj. T7. $35.00

MARSHALL, Edison. *Love Stories of India.* 1950. Farrar. 1st. VG/dj. M2. $20.00

MARSHALL, John A. *American Bastille: Hist of Illegal Arrests & Imprisonment...* 1870. Phil. Evans Stoddart. 4th. 728p. cloth. NF. M8. $85.00

MARSHALL, Marguerite Mooers. *Arms & the Girl.* 1942. Triangle/Blakiston. 1st thus/4th prt. 285p. VG/VG. A25. $20.00

MARSHALL, Mel. *Delectable Egg & How To Cook It.* 1968. NY. Trident. 1st. G/dj. A16. $15.00

MARSHALL, Paule. *Daughters.* 1991. Atheneum. 1st. sgn. author's 6th book. F/F. D10. $45.00

MARSHALL, Paule. *Soul Clap Hands & Sing.* 1961. NY. Atheneum. 1st. sgn. author's 2nd book. F/NF. D10. $165.00

MARSHALL, R. *Arctic Wilderness.* 1956. Berkeley. ils/photos/fld map. 171p. decor cloth. VG/VG. M12. $30.00

MARSHALL, Roger. *Race To Win.* 1980. NY. Norton. 1st. 8vo. 370p. F/VG. P4. $15.00

MARSHALL, S.L. *Pork Chop Hill.* nd. Nashville. BC. 22 maps/index. 315p. F/NF. W3. $28.00

MARSHALL, S.L.A. *Crimsoned Prairie: Indian Wars on the Great Plains.* 1972. Scribner. 1st. 256p. VG/worn. M20. $20.00

MARSHALL, W. Taylor. *Cataceae With Ils Keys of All Tribes...* 1941. Pasadena. 1st. ils. 227p. VG+. B26. $95.00

MARSHALL & WOODS. *Glossary of Succulent Plant Terms.* 1945 (1938). Pasadena. 2nd. ils/photos. 112p. maroon cloth. B26. $35.00

MARSHALL. *America's Great Comic Strip Artists.* nd. mc ils. 295p. F. M13. $85.00

MARSTEN, Richard; see Hunter, Evan.

MARTENS & SISSON. *Jack London, First Editions, Illustrated...* 1979. 1/1000. ils. 167p. NF. A4. $625.00

MARTIN, A.E. *Bridal Bed Murders.* 1953. S&S. 1st. NF/VG. H11. $15.00

MARTIN, Albro. *James J Hill & the Opening of the Northwest.* 1992. MN Hist Soc. 676p. M/wrp. A17. $22.50

MARTIN, Alfred. *First Corinthians.* 1989. Loizeaux. 152p. F/dj. B29. $90.00

MARTIN, C.L. *Sketch of Sam Bass, the Bandit...* 1956 (1880). OK U. new ed/1st prt. ils. 166p. F/dj. M4. $35.00

MARTIN, Christopher. *Amistad Affair.* 1970. London. Abelard Schuman. 240p. dj. T7. $20.00

MARTIN, David. *Crying Heart Tatoo.* 1982. HRW. 1st. F/F. T12. $20.00

MARTIN, Douglas D. *Yuma Crossing.* 1954. Albuquerque. 1st. 8vo. VG+/dj. F7. $30.00

MARTIN, Douglas. *Telling Line: Essays on 15 Contemporary Book Illustrators.* 1989. London. Julia MacRae. 1st. 4to. 320p. F/dj. T10. $75.00

MARTIN, Edward W. *Secrets of the Great City.* 1868. Phil. 522p+2p ads. G. A17. $35.00

MARTIN, Edward. *Always Be on Time.* 1959. Harrisburg. 1st. inscr. 183p. VG/torn. B18. $27.50

MARTIN, Franklin. *South America From a Surgeon's Point of View.* 1922. NY. 1st. 325p. A13. $50.00

MARTIN, Fred. *Travel Book.* 1976. SF. Arion. 1/200. sgn. prt/sgn Andrew Hoyem. F/Lucite case. B24. $400.00

MARTIN, George. *Fevre Dream.* 1950. Farrar. 1st. VG/dj. M2. $45.00

MARTIN, George. *Verdi: His Music, Life & Times.* 1963. Dodd Mead. tall 8vo. 633p. as new/dj. H1. $20.00

MARTIN, Henry Byam. *Polynesian Journal.* 1981. Salem. ils. VG/VG. M17. $20.00

MARTIN, Jack; see Etchison, Dennis.

MARTIN, James E. *95 File.* 1973. S&S. 1st. sgn. 247p. VG+/dj. M20. $20.00

MARTIN, John. *Heirs of Hippocrates.* 1980. IA City. Friends of U IA Lib. 4to. 474p. F. K3. $65.00

MARTIN, L.C. *Theory of the Microscope.* 1967 (1966). London. Blackie. lg 8vo. 488p. VG/dj. K5. $55.00

MARTIN, Linda. *Way We Wore: Fashion Ils of Children's Ware...1870-1970.* 1978. ils. VG/VG. M17. $30.00

MARTIN, Percy. *Mexico's Treasure House (Guanajuato).* 1906. NY. Cheltenham. 1st. 256p. silvered/gilt red cloth. F3. $55.00

MARTIN, Pete. *Hollywood Without Make-Up.* 1948. Lippincott. 1st. VG. M25. $25.00

MARTIN, Robert Bernard. *Accents of Persuasion: Charlotte Bronte's Novels.* 1966. Faber. 2nd. cloth. VG+/dj. M20. $25.00

MARTIN, Robert. *Judas Journey.* 1956. Dodd Mead. 1st. 212p. cloth. VG/dj. M20. $25.00

MARTIN, Steve. *Cruel Shoes.* 1979. Putnam. 1st. F/F. H11. $35.00

MARTIN, Thomas Commerford. *Inventions, Researches & Writings of Nikola Tesla.* 1952. Milwaukee. rpt 1894 ed. 496p. A17. $20.00

MARTIN, Valerie. *Set in Motion.* 1978. FSG. 1st. author's 2nd book. NF/dj. L3. $75.00

MARTIN, William W. *Manual Ecclesiastical Architecture.* 1897. Jennings Graham. ils. 429p. fair. B29. $8.00

MARTIN, William. *Nerve Endings.* 1984. Crown. 1st. sgn. F/G. B11. $25.00

MARTIN, William. *These Were God's People: Bible History.* 1966. Southwest Co. 506p. G. B29. $7.00

MARTIN & MARTIN. *Black Extended Family.* 1978. Chicago. 1st. 129p. F/VG clip. B4. $45.00

MARTIN & MARTIN. *Lightning, a Cowboy's Colt.* 1948. Kansas City, MO. 4to. VG+. C8. $17.50

MARTIN & SACHS. *Electric Boats & Navigation.* 1894. NY. Shelley. ils. 224p. VG. T7. $145.00

MARTINEAU, Alice. *Herbaceous Garden.* 1913. Williams Norgate. 2nd imp. 8vo. 298p. A22. $60.00

MARTINEAU, Mrs. Philip. *Reminiscences of Hunting & Horses.* 1930. London. Benn. 1st. VG. O3. $58.00

MARTINEZ, Buck. *From Worst to First: Toronto Blue Jays in 1980.* 1985. Toronto. 1st. F. T12. $25.00

MARTINEZ, Oscar J. *Border People: Life & Society in the US-Mexican Borderlands.* nd. AZ U. 1st. as new/dj. V4. $20.00

MARTINEZ, Raymond J. *Mysterious Marie Laveau Voodoo Queen & Folk Tales... ca 1980s.* Jefferson, LA. Hope Pub. rpt. ils. 96p. VG+. A25. $10.00

MARTINS DE SIQUEIRA, Luis. *Informacao em Direito com Que se Satisfas per Parte...* 1630. Lisbon. Rodriguez. 1st/only. sm folio. 18th-C mottled calf. R15. $650.00

MARTONE, Michael. *Alive & Dead in Indiana.* 1984. Knopf. 1st. author's 1st book. F/F. H11. $35.00

MARTY, Martin E. *Health & Medicine in the Lutheran Tradition.* 1986. Crossroad. 178p. G/dj. B29. $7.00

MARUKI, Toshi. *Hiroshima No Pika.* nd. np. 1st Am. ils. F/dj. K3. $25.00

MARUKI & MARUKI. *Art of Ira Maruki & Toshiko Maruki.* 1985. 1st. photos. 128p. M/dj. K3. $50.00

MARUKI & MARUKI. *Atomic Bomb.* 1959. Niji Shobo. Eng/Japanese text. 18 repro paintings. 22p. K3. $75.00

MARX, Groucho. *Beds.* 1930. NY. 1st. VG. B5. $75.00

MARX, Harpo. *Harpo Speaks.* 1961. NY. 1st. VG/VG. B5. $40.00

MARX, Joseph Laurence. *Nagasaki, the Necessary Bomb.* 1971. 1st. VG/dj. K3. $20.00

MARX, Karl. *Poverty of Philosophy.* 1920. Charles Kerr. 1st. VG. V4. $22.50

MARX, Karl. *Salaires Prix, Profits.* 1899. Paris. Girard Briere. 8vo. orig prt wrp. R12. $60.00

MARX, Karl. *World Without Jews.* 1959. Philosophical Lib. VG/VG. V4. $17.50

MARX, Robert F. *Shipwrecks of the Western Hemisphere.* 1970s. NY. World. ils. 482p. dj. T7. $35.00

MARYANSKI, Richard A. *Antique Picture Frame Guide.* 1973. Cedar Forest. 80p. cloth. VG/dj. M20. $25.00

MARYE, George Thomas. *From '49 to '83 in California & Nevada.* 1923. SF. Robertson. pre-pub copy (pastebrd cover/cloth tape spine). K7. $50.00

MARZALEK, J.J. *Sherman: Soldier's Passion for Order.* 1993. NY. 1st. 635p. F/dj. M4. $20.00

MARZIO, Peter C. *Democratic Art.* 1979. Boston. Godine. 4to. 357p. M/dj. B24. $50.00

MASEFIELD, John. *South & East.* 1929. 1st. ils J Parsons. NF/G. M19. $35.00

MASELLA, Jack. *Racing Cancer.* 1963. Exposition. 1st. inscr. VG+. P8. $35.00

MASO, Carole. *Ghost Dance.* 1986. Northpoint. 1st. sgn. author's 1st book. F/F. L3. $75.00

MASON, Arthur. *Wee Men of Ballwooden.* 1930. Doubleday. stated 1st. ils Lawson. VG. M5. $38.00

MASON, Bobbie Ann. *Girl Sleuth.* 1975. Old Westbury. Feminist. 1st. inscr. prt wrp. R14. $175.00

MASON, Bobbie Ann. *In Country.* 1985. Harper Row. 1st. author's 1st novel. NF/NF. T11. $40.00

MASON, Bobbie Ann. *In Country.* 1985. Harper Row. 1st. inscr. F/F. R14. $60.00

MASON, Bobbie Ann. *Shiloh & Other Stories.* 1982. Harper Row. 1st. author's 1st fiction book. NF/dj. L3. $85.00

MASON, Bobbie Ann. *Spence & Lila.* 1988. Harper Row. 1st. F/NF. T11. $25.00

MASON, Charles. *Report of the Commissioner of Patents for Year 1855.* 1856. Nicholson. 488p. cloth. A10. $30.00

MASON, F. Van Wyck. *Harpoon in Eden.* 1969. Doubleday. 1st. 430p. bl cloth. H1. $20.00

MASON, F. Van Wyck. *Spider House.* 1932. Mystery League. 1st. NF/VG. M22. $75.00

MASON, Grace Sartwell. *His Wife's Job.* 1919. Appleton. 1st. F/F. B4. $125.00

MASON, J. Monck. *Comments on Plays of Beumont & Fletcher.* 1798. London. Harding. 1st. half leather/brd. VG. K3. $90.00

MASON, Mike. *Mystery of Marriage: As Iron Sharpens Iron.* 1985. Multnomah. 185p. F/dj. B29. $6.00

MASON, R.H. *Photography Yearbook.* 1979. Argus. 1st. 276p. F/NF. W2. $60.00

MASON, Susanna. *Selections From Letters & Manuscripts...* 1836. Phil. Rackliff Jones. 1st. 312p. V3. $30.00

MASON, Theodore C. *Battleship Sailor.* 1982. ils. VG. M17. $15.00

MASON, William M.A. *Poems.* 1771. York. new ed. VG. A15. $50.00

MASON & PACKER. *Illustrated Dictionary of Jewelery.* 1974. ils. VG/VG. M17. $30.00

MASPERO, Gaston. *Art in Egypt.* 1912. London. Heinemann. 12mo. 4 mc pl/photos. 314p. gilt gr cloth. VG. T10. $25.00

MASPERO, Gaston. *Popular Stories of Ancient Egypt.* 1967. New Hyde Park, NY. U Books. 316p. VG. W1. $30.00

MASQUERIER, Lewis. *Sociology; or, Reconstruction of Society...* 1877. NY. self pub. 1st. 12mo. cloth. M1. $325.00

MASSEY, A.B. *Orchids in Virginia.* 1953. Blacksburg, VA. 8vo. wrp. A22. $10.00

MASSMAN. *Bibliomidgets of Achille J St Onge: Memorial & Bibliography.* 1979. 1/1000. sgn. 100p. F/case. A4. $225.00

MASSON, Madeleine. *Birds of Passage.* 1950. Cape Town. HB Timmins. 1st. ils. 190p. VG. A25. $12.00

MASTERS, Anthony. *Literary Agents, the Novelist As Spy.* 1987. Oxford. 1st. VG/VG. T9. $20.00

MASTERS, Edgar Lee. *Fate of the Jury.* 1929. Appleton. 1st. F/VG. M23. $50.00

MASTERS, Edgar Lee. *Lee: A Dramatic Poem.* 1926. Macmillan. 1st. VG. M23. $50.00

MASTERS, Edgar Lee. *Maximilian: A Play in Five Acts.* 1902. Boston. Badger/Gorham. 1st. 12mo. 154p. xl. M1. $125.00

MASTERS, Edgar Lee. *Skeeters Kirby.* 1923. Macmillan. 1st. NF/VG+. M23. $75.00

MASTERS, John. *Deceivers.* 1952. Viking. 1st Am. F/dj. Q1. $60.00

MASTERS, John. *High Command.* 1983. Morrow. 1st Am. 404p. F/F. W2. $30.00

MASTERSON, Elsie. *Blueberry Hill Cookbook.* 1959. Crowell. 1st. sgn. VG/clip. M20. $75.00

MASTERSON, V.V. *Katy Railroad & the Last Frontier.* 1952. Norman, OK. dj. A19. $50.00

MASTERSON, William H. *William Blount.* 1954. Baton Rouge. LSU. 1st. 378p. cloth. NF/dj. M8. $65.00

MATEER, Mrs. A.H. *Handbook of New Terms & Newspaper Chinese.* 1917. Shanghai. 309p. VG. W3. $58.00

MATERA, Lia. *Prior Convictions.* 1991. S&S. 1st. as new/dj. N4. $25.00

MATHER, Berkely. *Spy for a Spy.* 1968. Scribner. 1st. F/F. H11. $35.00

MATHER, Cotton. *Essays To Do Good.* 1822. Lexington, KY. Skillman. 1st thus. 12mo. w/subscriber list. full calf. case. T10. $400.00

MATHER, Fred. *Men I Have Fished With: Sketches of Character...* 1897. NY. Forest/Stream. 1st. 371p. gilt gr cloth. G. H7. $65.00

MATHER, Helen. *Light Horsekeeping: How To Get a Horse & How To Keep It.* 1970. Dutton. 1st. G/G. O3. $15.00

MATHES, W. Michael. *Mexico on Stone: Lithography in Mexico, 1826-1900.* 1984. SF. BC of CA. 1/550. ils. pict brd/cloth spine. D11. $75.00

MATHESON, Donald H. *Something New in Model Boat Building.* 1950s. London. Hutchinson. ils. 80p. T7. $38.00

MATHESON, Richard. *Earthbound.* 1989. NY. Tom Doherty. 1st. inscr. F/F. A23. $50.00

MATHESON, Richard. *Earthbound.* 1994. Tor. 1st. as new/F. N4. $20.00

MATHESON, Richard. *What Dreams May Come.* 1978. Putnam. 1st. F/dj. M2. $65.00

MATHESON, Richard. *7 Steps to Midnight.* 1993. NY. Forge. 1st. sgn. F/F. A23. $50.00

MATHEWS, Jack. *Memoirs of a Bookman.* 1990. Athens, OH. 1st. NF/dj. K3. $15.00

MATHEWS, John Joseph. *Sundown.* 1934. Longman Gr. 1st. inscr. author's 2nd book. NF. L3. $750.00

MATHEWS, John Joseph. *Talking to the Moon.* 1945. Chicago. 1st. author's 3rd book. NF/G. L3. $175.00

MATHEWS, John Joseph. *Wah'Kon-Tah.* 1932. OK U. 1st. 539p. VG/dj. M20. $35.00

MATHIAS & MATHIAS. *Revision of the Andean Genus Niphogrton.* 1951. Berkeley. ils. 22p. VG/wrp. B26. $9.00

MATHIEU, Bertrand. *Rimbaud's Illuminations.* 1979. BOA Ed. 1/26 (of 1200). fwd/sgn/+1 sgn mc litho Henry Miller. F. V1. $350.00

MATLES, James J. *Them & Us: Struggles of a Rank-and-File Union.* nd. Prentice Hall. 1st. VG/VG. V4. $25.00

MATOS MOCTEZUMA, Eduardo. *Great Temple of the Aztecs.* 1988. Thames Hudson. 1st. 4to. 192p. dj. F3. $35.00

MATSCHAT, Cecile. *Seven Grass Huts: An Enginner's Wife in Central...America.* 1939. NY. ils. 218p. F3. $10.00

MATTES, Merrill J. *Platte River Narratives: A Descriptive Bibliography...* 1988. IL U. 1st. lg format. 632p. M/sans. A18. $95.00

MATTHES, F.E. *Incomparable Valley...Yosemite.* 1950. Berkeley. 1st paper-bound ed. photos Ansel Adams. 160p. VG. D8. $22.00

MATTHEWS, Basil. *Clash of Color: A Study in Problem of Race.* 1924. Missionary Ed Movement of US/Canada. G/G. V4. $15.00

MATTHEWS, Brander. *Americanisms & Criticisms.* 1892. NY. Harper. 1st. gilt dk gr cloth. F. M24. $35.00

MATTHEWS, Brander. *Intro to the Study of American Literature.* 1896. NY. Am Book Co. 1st/later issue. gilt sage gr cloth. VG. M24. $15.00

MATTHEWS, David. *Feel of Feeling.* 1976. Vantage. 1st. inscr dedication to Nikki Giovanni. F/NF. B4. $150.00

MATTHEWS, Greg. *Further Adventures of Huckleberry Finn.* 1983. NY. Crown. 1st. author's 1st book. F/F. T11. $45.00

MATTHEWS, Janet Snyder. *Edge of the Wilderness.* 1983. Tulsa, OK. Caprine. inscr. 464p. F/F. B11. $40.00

MATTHEWS, John. *Grail: Quest for the Eternal.* 1981. ils. VG/VG. M17. $30.00

MATTHEWS, Kevin; see Fox, Gardner F.

MATTHEWS, L. Harrison. *Life of Mammals.* 1969. Universe. 2 vol. VG. S15. $40.00

MATTHEWS, Mrs. M.M. *10 Years in Nevada.* 1880. Buffalo. 1st. ils. 343p. G+. B5. $175.00

MATTHEWS, William. *Sleek for the Long Flight.* 1972. 1st. F/NF. V1. $35.00

MATTHIESSEN, Peter. *African Silences.* 1991. Random. 1st. F/F. M23. $25.00

MATTHIESSEN, Peter. *African Silences.* 1991. Random. 1st. sgn. F/F. D10. $50.00

MATTHIESSEN, Peter. *At Play in the Fields of the Lord.* 1965. Random. 1st. F/dj. Q1. $125.00

MATTHIESSEN, Peter. *At Play in the Fields of the Lord.* 1965. Random. 1st. sgn. VG/VG. R14. $200.00

MATTHIESSEN, Peter. *At Play in the Fields of the Lord.* 1965. Random. 1st. VG/G. B5. $40.00

MATTHIESSEN, Peter. *Baikal.* 1992. London. Thames Hudson. 1st Eng. F/F. T11. $50.00

MATTHIESSEN, Peter. *Far Tortuga.* 1975. Random. 1st. sgn. author's 5th fiction book. F/F. D10. $75.00

MATTHIESSEN, Peter. *In the Spirit of Crazy Horse.* 1983. NY. Viking. 1st. sgn. F/F. D10. $200.00

MATTHIESSEN, Peter. *In the Spirit of Crazy Horse.* 1983. Viking. 1st. NF/NF. M19. $125.00

MATTHIESSEN, Peter. *Killing Mr Watson.* 1990. Random. 1st. sgn. F/F. D10. $60.00

MATTHIESSEN, Peter. *Men's Lives: The Surfmen & Baymen of the South Fork.* 1986. Random. 1st. sgn. F/F. D10. $110.00

MATTHIESSEN, Peter. *Nine-Headed Dragon River.* 1986. Boston. Shambala. 1st. NF/NF. D10. $40.00

MATTHIESSEN, Peter. *Nine-Headed Dragon River.* 1986. Boston. Shambala. 1st. sgn. F/F. R14. $100.00

MATTHIESSEN, Peter. *On the River Styx & Other Stories.* 1989. Collins Harvill. 1st. F/F. B3. $35.00

MATTHIESSEN, Peter. *On the River Styx.* 1989. Random. 1st. sgn. F/F. D10. $60.00

MATTHIESSEN, Peter. *Oomingmak: Expedition to Musk Ox Island in Bering Sea.* 1967. Hastings. ils/photos. 85p. silvered pict cloth. VG. M12. $20.00

MATTHIESSEN, Peter. *Oomingmak: Expedition to Musk Ox Island in Bering Sea.* 1967. Hastings. 1st. F/F. C6. $60.00

MATTHIESSEN, Peter. *Race Rock.* 1954. Harper. 1st. inscr. author's 1st book. NF/VG+. T11. $400.00

MATTHIESSEN, Peter. *Race Rock.* 1954. London. 1st. author's 1st novel. F/NF clip. L3. $300.00

MATTHIESSEN, Peter. *Sand Rivers.* 1981. Viking. 1st. photos. F/dj. Q1. $75.00

MATTHIESSEN, Peter. *Shorebirds of North America.* 1967. NY. 1st. folio. F/F. C6. $275.00

MATTHIESSEN, Peter. *Shorebirds of North America.* 1967. NY. 1st. NF/VG clip. B4. $250.00

MATTHIESSEN, Peter. *Snow Leopard.* 1978. Franklin Lib. 1st (preceeds trade). sgn. F/sans. R14. $150.00

MATTHIESSEN, Peter. *Snow Leopard.* 1978. Viking. 1st. sgn. F/F. D10. $95.00

MATTHIESSEN, Peter. *Under the Mountain Wall: A Chronicle of Two Seasons...* 1962. Viking. 1st. 256p. VG/dj. W1. $25.00

MATTHIESSEN, Peter. *Wildlife in America.* 1959. Viking. 1st. 8 mc pl/ils/ F/dj. T10. $150.00

MATTHIESSEN & PORTER. *Tree Where Man Was Born/The African Experience.* 1972. Dutton. 1st. NF/NF. M19. $65.00

MATTHIESSEN & PORTER. *Tree Where Man Was Born/The African Experience.* 1972. Viking. true 1st. sgn. F/F. D10. $100.00

MATTISON, Alice. *Great Wits.* 1988. Morrow. 1st. sgn. F/F. R14. $45.00

MATTISON, Christ. *A-Z of Snake Keeping.* 1991. NY. ils. 143p. F/F. S15. $20.00

MATTISON, Ray H. *Army Post of the Northern Plains 1865-1885.* 1965. OR Trail Mus Assn. 27p. as new. J2. $25.00

MAUCHLINE, John. *Introductory Hebrew Grammar.* 1967. Clark. 192p. VG. B29. $10.00

MAUDSLAY & MAUDSLAY. *Glimpse at Guatemala & Some Notes on Ancient Monuments...* 1992. Flo Silver. rpt of 1899 ed. ils/pl/fld map. F3. $40.00

MAUGHAM, W. Somerset. *Ashenden; or, The British Agent.* 1928. Doubleday Doran. 1st Am. orange stp bl cloth. VG. M24. $100.00

MAUGHAM, W. Somerset. *Cakes & Ale & 12 Short Stories.* 1967. Doubleday. 1st Am. F/F. B4. $125.00

MAUGHAM, W. Somerset. *Christmas Holiday.* 1939. Doubleday. 1st Am. F/NF clip. B4. $150.00

MAUGHAM, W. Somerset. *Ex Libris.* 1936. NY Times 1st Nat Book Fair. 1st. VG. K3. $15.00

MAUGHAM, W. Somerset. *France at War.* 1940. London. Heinemann. 1st. xl. K3. $10.00

MAUGHAM, W. Somerset. *Magician.* 1909. Duffield. 1st Am. NF. B4. $300.00

MAUGHAM, W. Somerset. *Mr Maugham Himself.* 1954. Doubleday. ne. 688p. NF. W2. $60.00

MAUGHAM, W. Somerset. *Princess September & the Nightingale.* 1939. London. Oxford. 1st thus. 8vo. F/VG. C8. $50.00

MAUGHAM, W. Somerset. *Razor's Edge.* 1944. Doubleday Doran. ne. 343p. NF. W2. $200.00

MAUGHAM, W. Somerset. *Razor's Edge.* 1944. Doubleday Doran. true 1st/precedes Eng. sgn. NF/worn pub case. B4. $750.00

MAUGHAM, W. Somerset. *Razor's Edge.* 1944. Doubleday Doran. 1st. 1/750. sgn. gilt maroon cloth. F. M24. $250.00

MAUGHAM, W. Somerset. *Summing Up.* 1938. Doubleday. 1st Am. F/NF. B4. $150.00

MAUGHAM, W. Somerset. *Theatre.* 1937. NY. Doubleday. 1st. F/NF clip. B4. $150.00

MAUGHAM, W. Somerset. *Then & Now.* 1946. Doubleday. 1st. F/VG. M35. $35.00

MAUGHAM, W. Somerset. *Unconquered.* 1944. NY. House of Books. only ed. 1/300. sgn. NF/NF. B4. $275.00

MAULDIN, Henry K. *Your Lakes, Valleys & Mountains: History of Lake Co.* 1960. SF. East Wind Prt. ils/map. 64p. NF/wrp. K7. $20.00

MAUNDY, Talbot. *Cock O' the North.* 1929. Bobbs Merrill. 1st. VG. M2. $35.00

MAUNDY, Talbot. *Winds of the World.* 1932. London. VG. M2. $10.00

MAUPIN, Armstead. *Sure of You.* 1989. Harper Row. 1st. F/F. R14. $25.00

MAURER, M. *World War II Combat Squadrons of the USAF: Official...* 1992. NY. rpt. 841p. VG/VG. S16. $35.00

MAURICEAU, A.M. *Married Woman's Private Medical Companion.* 1855. NY. 16mo. cloth. F. M1. $200.00

MAURO, Frederic. *Portugal et l'Atlantique au XVIIme Siecle 1570-1670...* 1960. Paris. SEVPEN. 22 maps. 550p. F/wrp. O7. $55.00

MAUROIS, Andre. *Country of 36 Thousand Wishes.* 1930. Appleton. 1st Am. ils Adrienne Segur. 66p. VG. D1. $75.00

MAUROIS, Andre. *Fatapoufs & Thinifers.* 1940. Holt. 1st. ils Jean Bruller. 92p. G. P2. $30.00

MAUROIS, Andre. *My Latin American Diary.* 1953. London. Falcon. 1st. 89p. dj. F3. $15.00

MAUROIS, Andre. *Private Universe.* 1932. London. 1st. inscr by trans. VG. T9. $30.00

MAUS, Cynthia P. *Old Testament & the Fine Arts.* 1954. Harper. 826p. VG/dj. B29. $7.00

MAVOR, James W. *Voyage to Atlantis.* 1969. Putnam. 8vo. 320p. bl cloth. VG/dj. P4. $30.00

MAWSON, T. *Art & Craft of Garden Making.* 1901. London. 2nd enlarged. ils/pl. VG. E6. $100.00

MAXIMOV, N.A. *Plant in Relation to Water.* 1929. Allen Unwin. 1st. 8vo. VG. A22. $40.00

MAXON, William R. *Studies of Tropical American Ferns Nos 1 to 7.* 1908-22. WA, DC. 7 parts. 298p. B26. $68.00

MAXWELL, A.E. *Frog & the Scorpion.* 1986. Doubleday. 1st. F/dj. M15. $100.00

MAXWELL, Alice. *Recipes of Guam.* 1954. Agana. self pub. ils. VG. E6. $30.00

MAXWELL, Arthur. *Uncle Arthur's Bedtime Stories.* 1950. 5 vol. orange bdg. VG+. S13. $75.00

MAXWELL, Gavin. *Ring of Bright Water.* 1960. London. 1st. VG/VG. T9. $30.00

MAXWELL, Margaret F. *Passion for Freedom: Life of Sharlot Hall.* 1982. Tucson. 8vo. 234p. F/VG. F7. $35.00

MAXWELL, William. *Old Man at the Railroad Crossing & Other Tales.* 1966. Knopf. 1st. NF/dj. D10. $65.00

MAXWELL, William. *Outermost Dream.* 1989. Knopf. 1st. F/F. D10. $35.00

MAXWELL, William. *Over by the River & Other Stories.* 1977. Knopf. 1st. sgn. F/F. R14. $90.00

MAXWELL, William. *So Long, See You Tomorrow.* 1980. Knopf. 1st. F/F. D10. $50.00

MAXWELL & MAXWELL. *Legal Bibliography of British Commonwealth of Nations...* 1955. London. Sweet & Maxwell. 2nd. M11. $150.00

MAXXE, Robert; see Rosenblum, Robert.

MAY, Robert L. *Rudolph, the Red-Nosed Reindeer.* 1939. Montgomery Ward. 1st. 1/200. ils Denver Gillen. 8vo. 32p. pres bdg. R5. $485.00

MAY, Robert L. *Rudolph, the Red-Nosed Reindeer.* 1939. NY. Maxton Pub. 1st commercial (after MW). inscr. 8vo. red pict brd. dj. R5. $975.00

MAY, Robin. *Gold Rushes: From California to the Klondike.* 1977. London. Wm Luscombe. 1st Eng. F/F. O4. $20.00

MAY, Walter. *Die Geschichte vom Rotkappchen (Little Red Riding Hood).* 1940. Zurich. Albert Miller. sm 4to. pict brd. F/dj. B24. $350.00

MAYARD, L. *Tropical Cooking (Cuisine des Pays Clauds).* nd. ca 1962. Haiti. VG/G+. E6. $25.00

MAYBEE, Betty Lou. *Barbie's Fashion Success (#3).* 1962. Random. 188p. glossy brd. VG/ragged. M20. $12.50

MAYBEE, Betty Lou. *Barbie's Hawaiian Holiday (#6).* 1963. Random. 172p. pict brd (lists 6 titles). VG. M20. $18.00

MAYER, Marianna. *Iduna & the Magic Apples.* 1988. Macmillan. 1st. obl 8vo. unp. burgundy brd. VG. T5. $20.00

MAYER, Marianna. *Unicorn & the Lake.* 1982. Dial. 1st. ils Michael Hague. unop. VG+. T5. $35.00

MAYER, MAYER & MAYER. *Clockwork Universe.* 1980. NY. Neale Watson. ils. 321p. VG/dj. K3. $40.00

MAYER, Mercer. *Ah-Choo.* 1976. Dial. 1st. obl 12mo. VG/VG. P2. $30.00

MAYER, Mercer. *Boy, a Dog & a Frog.* 1967. Dial. 1st. 24mo. unp. whit brd. VG+. T5. $35.00

MAYHAR, Ardath. *Lords of the Triple Moons.* 1983. Atheneum. 1st. F/dj. M2. $20.00

MAYHAR, Ardath. *World Ends in Hickory Hollow.* 1985. Doubleday. 1st. F/dj. M2. $27.00

MAYHEW & MAYHEW. *Greatest Plague of Life.* 1847. London. David Bogue. 12mo. ils Cruikshank. contemporary half leather. T10. $350.00

MAYLE, Peter. *Dog's Life.* 1995. Knopf. 1st. sgn. F/F. A23. $35.00

MAYLE, Peter. *Hotel Pastis.* 1993. Knopf. 1st. sgn. VG/VG. A23. $40.00

MAYNARD, Kenneth. *Lamb's Mixed Fortunes.* 1987. Weidenfeld Nicolson. 1st. F/NF. Q1. $50.00

MAYNARD, Olga. *Bird of Fire.* 1962. Dodd Mead. 2nd prt. sgn. F/NF. L3. $45.00

MAYNE, Peter. *Alleys of Marrakesh.* 1954. London. Travel Book. 8vo. 172p. VG. W1. $12.00

MAYNE, William. *Swarm in May.* 1955. London. Oxford. 1st 199p. VG/G. P2. $35.00

MAYO, Eleanor. *Forever Strangers.* 1958. Norton. 1st. F/dj. B4. $45.00

MAYO, Herbert. *Nervous System & Its Functions.* 1992. NY. Classics Neurology/Neurosurgery. facsimile. F. G1. $65.00

MAYO, Herbert. *Observations on Injuries & Diseases of the Rectum.* 1833. London. 1st. 220p. quarter leather. VG. A13. $150.00

MAYO, Jim; see L'Amour, Louis.

MAYONE DIAS, Eduardo. *Cantares de Alem-Mar.* 1982. Coimbre. Ordem DeUniversidade. 1/1000. 223p. wrp. F3. $10.00

MAYOR, Joseph B. *Epistle of St James.* 1978. Baker. 2nd (rpt 1897). Greek text. 256p. G. B29. $11.00

MAYR, Ernst. *Growth of Biological Thought.* 1982. Harvard. 8vo. 974p. F/wrp. K3. $15.00

MAYS, Benjamin E. *Negro's God, As Reflected in His Literature.* 1938. Boston. Chapman Grimes. 269p. G. B18. $35.00

MAYS & SIMMONS. *People of the Sun.* 1979. Albuquerque. 1st. 4to. F/NF. L3. $35.00

MAZZUCHELLI. *La Vita di Pietro Aretino.* 1741. Padua. Comino. 8vo. quarter calf. R12. $350.00

MCAFEE, John. *Slow Walk in a Sad Rain.* 1993. NY. Warner. 1st. author's 1st book. F/F. R13. $35.00

MCALMON, Robert. *Not Alone Lost.* 1937. New Directions. 1st. F/F clip. B4. $500.00

MCALPINE, J.F. *Manual of Nearctic Diptera, Vol 2.* 1987. Canadian Gove Pub Center. 287 pl. B1. $68.50

MCANDREW, H.J. *History of Critical Conservation North American Waterfowl.* 1950. Berkeley. private prt. 2 vol. 160 tipped-in mc photos/drawings. 429p. VG. M12. $125.00

MCBAIN, Ed; see Hunter, Evan.

MCBANE, Susan. *Know Your Pony.* 1992. Ward Lock Riding School. 1st. VG. O3. $15.00

MCBETH, George. *Poems From Oby.* 1983. Atheneum. 1st. 1/750. F/F. B35. $60.00

MCBRIDE, Barrie St. Clair. *Farouk of Egypt: A Biography.* 1968. Barnes. 1st Am. 8vo. 238p. NF/dj. W1. $22.00

MCBRIDE, Mary Margaret. *Encyclopedia of Cooking. 12 Volumes.* 1960. Evanston. Homeakers Inst. G. A16. $30.00

MCCABE, James Dabney. *Life & Campaigns of General Robert E Lee.* (1866). Atlanta, National Pub. 1st. 717p. later cloth. VG. M8. $125.00

MCCABE, Olivia. *Rose Fairies.* 1911. Rand McNally. 1st. ils Hope Dunlap. 4to. gilt gr cloth/label. R5. $200.00

MCCAFFREY, Anne. *Coelura.* 1983. CA. Underwood Miller. 1st. F/F. A24. $35.00

MCCAFFREY, Anne. *White Dragon.* 1978. Del Rey. 1st. VG/dj. M2. $45.00

MCCAGUE, J. *Cumberland.* 1973. NY. 1st. Rivers of Am series. VG/VG. B5. $32.50

MCCALL, Anthony; see Kane, Henry.

MCCALLEY & MILLER. *From Here to Obscurity.* 1975. np. ils. ils ep. VG+/torn. B18. $25.00

MCCALLUM & MCCALLUM. *Wire That Fenced the West.* 1979. Norman, OK. A19. $15.00

MCCAMMON, Robert R. *Mine.* 1990. Pocket Books. 1st. NF/NF. N4. $30.00

MCCAMMON, Robert R. *Usher's Passing.* 1984. HRW. 1st. NF/dj. N4. $35.00

MCCANDLESS & SENZAKI. *Buddhism & Zen.* 1953. NY. Philos Lib. 90p. VG/dj. W3. $30.00

MCCANN, Edson. *Preferred Risk.* 1955. S&S. 1st. F/dj. M2. $35.00

MCCANN, Lee. *Nostradamus.* 1941. Creative Age. 1st. VG/dj. M2. $15.00

MCCARRY, Charles. *Last Supper.* 1983. Dutton. 1st. NF/NF. A20. $25.00

MCCARRY, Charles. *Last Supper.* 1983. Dutton. 1st. 389p. F/F. W2. $30.00

MCCARRY, Charles. *Miernik Dossier.* 1973. Saturday Review. 1st. NF/dj. M25. $45.00

MCCARTHY, Cormac. *All the Pretty Horses.* 1992. Knopf. UP. F/wrp. B3. $350.00

MCCARTHY, Cormac. *All the Pretty Horses.* 1992. Knopf. 1st. F/dj. from $200 to $250.00

MCCARTHY, Cormac. *All the Pretty Horses.* 1993. London. Picador/Pan. 1st Eng. F/dj. from $100 to $150.00

MCCARTHY, Cormac. *Child of God.* 1973. Random. 1st. author's 3rd book. F/dj. Q1. $850.00

MCCARTHY, Cormac. *Child of God.* 1973. Random. 1st. VG/clip. C6. $500.00

MCCARTHY, Cormac. *Crossing.* 1994. Knopf. 1st. 1/1000. sgn. F/dj. Q1. $350.00

MCCARTHY, Cormac. *Outer Dark.* 1968. Random. 1st. author's 2nd novel. F/NF. D10. $850.00

MCCARTHY, Cormac. *Stonemason.* 1994. Hopewell. Ecco. 1/350. sgn. F/case. B3. $325.00

MCCARTHY, Cormac. *Suttree.* 1979. Random. 1st. author's 4th novel. NF/dj. Q1. $850.00

MCCARTHY, Cormac. *Suttree.* 1979. Random. 1st. F/NF. C2. $900.00

MCCARTHY, Mary. *Group.* 1963. HBW. 1st. F/NF. H11. $60.00

MCCARTHY, Mary. *Ideas & the Novel.* 1980. HBJ. 1st. F/F. B35. $28.00

MCCARTHY, Mary. *Memories of a Catholic Girlhood.* 1957. Harcourt Brace. 1st. 245p. blk cloth. F/VG. H1. $20.00

MCCARTHY James Remington. *Matter of Time.* 1947. NY. Harper. ils. 8vo. 230p. K3. $35.00

MCCAUSLAND, Elizabeth. *AH Mauerer: Biography of America's First Modern Painter.* 1951. Wyn. 1st. 289p. VG/ragged. M20. $35.00

MCCAUSLAND, Hugh. *Old Sporting Characters & Occasions From Sporting & Road...* 1948. Batchworth. 1st. 172p. cloth. VG/dj. M20. $30.00

MCCLANE, A.J. *McLane's New Standard Fishing Encyclopedia.* 1974. NY. 1156p. dj. A17. $27.50

MCCLANE, A.J. *Practical Fly Fisherman.* 1953. NY. 1st. 257p. NF/taped. A17. $85.00

MCCLELLAN, Edwin. *Woman in the Crested Kimono: Life of Shibue Io...* 1985. New Haven. Yale. 1st. 192p. VG/dj. A25. $15.00

MCCLELLAN, George B. *McClellan's Own Story.* 1887. NY. 1st. 678p. O8. $65.00

MCCLELLAND, Lucille Hudin. *Textbook for Psychiatric Technicians.* 1967. St Louis. Mosby. 1st. ils. VG+. A25. $15.00

MCCLINTON, K.M. *Chromolithographs of Louis Prang.* 1973. NY. 1st. ils. 246p. F/dj. M4. $30.00

MCCLINTON, K.M. *Lalique for Collectors.* 1975. Scribner. 1st. 152p. as new/dj. H1. $48.00

MCCLOSKEY, Robert. *Blueberries for Sal.* 1949. Viking. 3rd. sgn pres. obl 4to. pict brd. dj. R5. $225.00

MCCLOSKEY, Robert. *Lentil.* 1946. Viking. 2nd. sgn pres. lg 4to. gray cloth. dj. R5. $150.00

MCCLOSKEY, Robert. *Make Way for Ducklings.* 1941. Viking. 2nd. 4to. VG/G. P2. $100.00

MCCLOSKEY, Robert. *Make Way for Ducklings.* 1950. NY. Viking. 10th. sgn pres. brn cloth. dj. R5. $250.00

MCCLOSKEY, Robert. *One Morning in Maine.* Jan 1953. Viking. 2nd. 1953 Caldecott Honor. lg 4to. gray cloth. dj. R5. $75.00

MCCLOSKEY, Robert. *One Morning in Maine.* 1952. Viking. 1st. lg 4to. 64p. VG/VG. P2. $250.00

MCCLURE, Alfred J.P. *Steamin' to Bells Around the Middle Sea.* 1900. self pub. 1/350. sgn. VG. B11. $150.00

MCCLURE, James. *Artful Egg.* 1984. Pantheon. 1st. F/F. H11. $25.00

MCCLURE, James. *Four & Twenty Virgins.* 1973. London. Gollancz. 1st. F/dj. M15. $85.00

MCCLURE, James. *Song Dog.* 1991. Mysterious. 1st Am. F/F. A24. $15.00

MCCLURE, James. *Steam Pig.* 1971. Harper Row. 1st. author's 1st book. F/F. H11. $35.00

MCCLURE, Michael. *Gargoyle Cartoons.* 1971. Delacorte. 1st. inscr. NF/VG. R14. $40.00

MCCLURE, Michael. *Jaguar Skies.* 1975. New Directions. 1st. inscr. F/NF. R14. $45.00

MCCLURE, Robert. *Diseases of the American Horse, Cattle & Sheep.* 1890. Phil. Keystone. G. O3. $38.00

MCCLURE, Roy. *Burns, Shock, Wound Healing & Vascular Injuries.* 1943. Phil. 1st. 272p. A13. $75.00

MCCLURE. *With Stanley in Africa.* 1891. ils. VG. M17. $40.00

MCCLURKEN, James M. *Gah-Baeh-Jhagwah-Buk: The Way It Happened.* 1992. Lansing. 1st. photos/maps. 130p. M/dj. A17. $25.00

MCCOMAS & TUOHY. *Collector's Guide & History to Lionel Trains.* TM Prod/Chilton. 6 vol (complete). VG to F. H1. $145.00

MCCONNELL, Duncan. *Granpappy's Pistol; or, To Hell With Gun Collecting.* 1956. Coward McCann. 1st. sgn. 152p. VG/dj. M20. $50.00

MCCONNELL, James V. *Worm Returns.* 1965. Prentice Hall. ils. VG/worn. K3. $20.00

MCCORKLE, Jill. *Cheerleader.* 1984. Algonquin. 1st. sgn. VG/VG. L1. $200.00

MCCORKLE, Jill. *Ferris Beach.* 1990. Algonquin. 1st. sgn. VG/VG. L1. $75.00

MCCORKLE, Jill. *July 7.* 1984. Algonquin. 1st. author's 1st book. F/dj. from $150 to $175.00

MCCORKLE, Jill. *Tending to Virginia.* 1987. Algonquin/Taylor Pub. 1st. sgn. VG/VG. L1. $85.00

MCCORMICK, Charles H. *Nest of Vipers: McCarthyism & Higher Education...* 1989. IL U. 1st. M/dj. V4. $20.00

MCCORMICK, Donald. *Blood on the Sea.* 1962. London. Muller. ils. 158p. dj. T7. $22.00

MCCORMICK, Harriet Hammond. *Landscape Art Past & Present.* 1923. Scribner. 1/1200. A10. $200.00

MCCORMICK, Richard C. *Arizona: Its Resources & Prospects.* 1865. NY. Van Nostrand. fld map. 22p. prt wrp. D11. $150.00

MCCORMICK, Wilfred. *Rocky McCune: Phantom Shortstop.* 1963. McKay. 1st. cloth. 178p. Vg/dj. M20. $45.00

MCCOWEN, Alec. *Young Gemini.* 1979. London. Elm Tree. 1st. F/F. T12. $20.00

MCCOY, Horace. *Scalpel.* 1952. Appleton Century. 1st. F/dj. from $50 to $85.00

MCCOY, Horace. *They Shoot Horses, Don't They?* 1935. S&S. 1st. inscr/dtd 1935. author's 1st book. NF/VG. L3. $2,000.00

MCCOY, J.J. *Hunt for the Whooping Cranes.* 1966. NY. photos/maps/drawings. 223p. VG/VG. S15. $20.00

MCCOY, John T. *Airplanes.* 1936. Rand McNally. ils/drawings. VG/stiff wrp. B18. $45.00

MCCRACKEN, Harold. *Frederic Remington: Artist of the Old West...* (1947). 4to. full-p pl. 205p. xl. VG/VG. A4. $65.00 M4.

MCCRACKEN, Harold. *God's Frozen Children: Animals, Men & Mummies...* 1930. NY. 1st ed. inscr. 291p. dj. B5. $45.00 M4.

MCCRACKEN, Harold. *Portrait of the Old West With Bibliographical Checklist...* 1952. NY. 1st. ils. 232p. F/dj. T10. $125.00

MCCRUMB, Sharyn. *Hangman's Beautiful Daughter.* 1992. Scribner. 1st. F/F. D10. $40.00

MCCRUMB, Sharyn. *If Ever I Return, Pretty Peggy-O.* 1990. Scribner. 1st. F/F. D10. $50.00

MCCRUMB, Sharyn. *Missing Susan.* 1991. Ballantine. 1st. F/F. D10. $50.00

MCCRUMB, Sharyn. *She Walks These Hills.* 1994. Scribner. 1st. sgn. F/F. A23. $42.00

MCCRUMB, Sharyn. *Windsor Knot.* 1990. Ballantine. 1st. F/F. B3/Q1. $50.00

MCCRUMB, Sharyn. *Zombies of the Gene Pool.* 1992. S&S. 1st. F/F. A23. $42.00

MCCULLERS, Carson. *Mortgaged Heart.* 1971. Houghton Mifflin. 1st. F/NF. D10. $50.00

MCCULLOCH, Hugh. *Men & Measures of Half a Century.* 1889. np. 1st. 542p. O8. $21.50

MCCULLOUGH, Colleen. *Creed for the Third Millenium.* 1985. NY. Harper Row. 1st. F/F. T12. $12.50

MCCULLOUGH, Colleen. *First Man in Rome.* 1990. Morrow. 1st. F/F. T12. $20.00

MCCULLY, Emily Arnold. *Mirette on the High Wire.* 1992. Putnam. 1st. 1993 Caldecott Award. pict brd. dj. R5. $65.00

MCCUNE, Shannon. *Korea: Land of Broken Calm.* 1966. Princeton. ils/maps. 221p. VG/dj. W3. $38.00

MCCURRACH, James C. *Palms of the World.* 1970. Stuart. Horticultural Books. rpt. 4to. cloth. G. A22. $55.00

MCCUTCHEON, George B. *Prince of Graustark.* 1914. 1st. ils Keller. NF. M19. $35.00

MCDANIEL, Bruce W. *Dune & Desert Folk.* nd. Los Angeles. ils. unp. cloth/vignette. B26. $24.00

MCDERMOTT, Alice. *Bigamist's Daughter.* 1982. Random. 1st. F/F. B4. $125.00

MCDERMOTT, Alice. *That Night.* 1987. FSG. 1st. F/NF. R14. $30.00

MCDERMOTT, Gerald. *Anansi the Spider, a Tale from the Ashanti.* 1973 (1972). Holt Rinehart. 2nd. obl 8vo. F/NF. C8. $22.50

MCDERMOTT, Gerald. *Stone-Cutter, a Japanese Folk Tale.* 1975. Viking. 1st. 4to. unp. red cloth. NF/VG. T5. $30.00

MCDEVITT, Jack. *Talent for War.* 1989. London. 1st hc. F/dj. M2. $25.00

MCDONALD, Edward D. *Bibliography of Writings of Norman Douglas.* 1927. Phil. Centaur Book Shop. 1/300. VG. K3. $25.00

MCDONALD, Gregory. *Brave.* 1991. Barricade. 1st. F/dj. M22. $30.00

MCDONALD, Gregory. *Fletch Too.* 1986. Warner. 1st. F/F. N4. $25.00

MCDONALD, Gregory. *Flynn's In.* 1984. Mysterious. 1st. F/F. A20. $25.00

MCDONALD, Gregory. *Running Scared.* Obolensky. 1964 1st. VG/VG. A20. $45.00

MCDONALD, Lucile. *Search for the Northwest Passage.* 1958. Portland. Binford Mort. 8vo. 137p. VG. P4. $45.00

MCDONELL, Katherine. *Journals of William Lindsay: An Ordinary 19th-C Physician...* 1989. Indianapolis. 216p. A13. $30.00

MCDOUGALL, Bonnie. *Popular Chinese Literature & Performing Arts...1949-1979.* 1984. CA U. 450p. F/F. W3. $48.00

MCDOUGALL, W.B. *Grand Canyon Wild Flowers.* 1964. Flagstaff. 8vo. cloth. NF. A22. $20.00

MCDOUGALL & MOIR. *Selected Correspondence of Glasgow Colonial Society...1840.* 1994. Toronto. Champlain Soc. 8vo. 1272p. red cloth. F. P4. $85.00

MCDOWELL, Roddy. *Double Exposure.* 1966. NY. 1st. VG/VG. B5. $30.00

MCELRATH, Jean. *Aged in Sage.* 1964. NV U. A19. $25.00

MCELROY, John. *Struggle for Missouri.* 1913. WA, DC. National Tribune. A19. $45.00

MCELROY, Joseph. *Ancient History: A Paraphase.* 1971. Knopf. 1st. NF/dj. M25. $35.00

MCELWEE, William. *Murder of Sir Thomas Overbury.* 1952. Faber. 1st. 280p. VG/dj. M20. $35.00

MCEWAN, Ian. *Child in Time.* 1987. Houghton Mifflin. 1st. F/F. B35. $18.00

MCEWAN, Ian. *Comfort of Strangers.* 1981. S&S. ARC/1st. author's 4th book. F/F. w/pub promo material. D10. $50.00

MCEWAN, Ian. *First Love, Last Rites.* 1975. Random. 1st Am. author's 1st book. F/F. L3. $85.00

MCEWAN, Ian. *In Between the Sheets.* 1979. S&S. 1st Am. NF/NF. R14. $30.00

MCEWAN, Ian. *Innocent.* 1990. Doubleday. 1st. F/F. H11. $30.00

MCEWAN, Ian. *Innocent.* 1990. Doubleday. 1st. NF/NF. A20. $20.00

MCEWEN, J.D. *Brazil: Description of People, Country & Happenings...* 1915. np. Witness Pr. 1st. ils. 259p. F3. $30.00

MCFADYEN, Ella. *Pegmen Tales.* 1946. Sydney. Angus Robertson. 1st. 4to. pict brd. NF/dj. R5. $275.00

MCFARLAND, Dennis. *Music Room.* 1990. Houghton Mifflin. 1st. author's 1st novel. F/dj. A24. $40.00

MCFARLAND, J. Horace. *How To Grow Roses.* 1946. Harrisburg. Horace McFarland. 21st. 192p. VG. H1. $15.00

MCFARLANE, Brian. *Stanley Cup.* 1971. Scribner. 1st Am. photos. VG/VG. P8. $30.00

MCFEE, William. *Law of the Sea.* 1950. Lippincott. VG. M11. $50.00

MCFIE, H. *Wasa-Wasa: Tale of Trails & Treasure in Far North.* 1951. NY. 288p. F/dj. M4. $20.00

MCGARGAR & COLBY. *Lost Victory: A Firsthand Account...Vietnam.* 1989. Chicago. 438p. map ep. VG+/dj. B18. $17.50

MCGARRITY, Mark. *Death on a Cold, Wild River.* 1993. Morrow. 1st. F/dj. Q1. $40.00

MCGARRITY, Mark. *Lucky Shuffles.* 1973. Grossman. 1st. F/F. M25. $25.00

MCGAUGH, James L. *Psychobiology: Behavior From Biological Perspective.* 1971. Academic. 366p. gray cloth. G1. $50.00

MCGIFFERT, Arthur C. *Protestant Thought Before Kant.* 1911. Scribner. 261p. VG. B29. $7.50

MCGINLEY, Phyllis. *Love Letters of Phyllis McGinley.* 1954. Viking. sgn. VG/VG. B11. $8.50

MCGINNIS, R.A. *Beet-Sugar Technology.* 1971 (1951). Ft Collins. 2nd. ils. 835p. VG+. B26. $14.00

MCGINNIS, Vera. *Rodeo Road: My Life As a Pioneer Cowgirl.* 1974. Hastings. 1st. 225p. VG+/dj. M20. $35.00

MCGINNISS, Joe. *Dreaming Team.* 1972. Random. 1st. F/F. A20. $20.00

MCGLASHAN, C.F. *History of the Donner Party: A Tragedy of the Sierra.* 1881. Bancroft. 4th. ils. 261p. D11. $250.00

MCGLASHAN, C.F. *History of the Donner Party: A Tragedy of the Sierra.* 1973 (1880). Fresno, CA. rpt. F/F. O4. $15.00

MCGOVERN, William Montgomery. *Jungle Paths & Inca Ruins.* 1927. NY. Century. 1st. 8vo. 526p. F. T10. $75.00

MCGOWAN, Edward. *Narrative of..., Including Full Account Author's Adventures.* 1857. SF. self pub. 1st. 7 full-p woodcuts. rebound brd/prt wrp. R3. $900.00

MCGOWEN, Tom. *Album of Spaceflight.* 1983. Chicago. Rand McNally. 1st. VG. K5. $12.00

MCGRATH, Patrick. *Blood & Water & Other Tales.* 1988. Poseidon. 1st. author's 1st book. F/F. D10. $50.00

MCGRATH, Patrick. *Blood & Water & Other Tales.* 1988. Poseidon. 1st. inscr. F/F. R14. $60.00

MCGRATH, Patrick. *Grotesque.* 1989. Poseidon. 1st Am. NF/dj. M25. $35.00

MCGRATH, Patrick. *Grotesque.* 1989. Poseidon. 1st. F/F. M22. $45.00

MCGRATH, Patrick. *Spider.* 1990. Poseidon/S&S. 1st. sgn. F/dj. A24. $35.00

MCGROATRY, John S. *California of the South.* 1933. Los Angeles. 1st. 5 vol. NF. O4. $150.00

MCGROATRY, John S. *California Plutarch Vol 1.* 1935. Los Angeles. 1st. 4to. half leather. U xl. G+. O4. $60.00

MCGROATRY, John S. *California: Its History & Romance.* 1911. Los Angeles. 8th. inscr. VG. O4. $20.00

MCGROATRY, John S. *Wander Songs.* 1908. Los Angeles. Grafton. VG. O4. $20.00

MCGUANE, Thomas. *Bushwhacked Piano.* 1971. S&S. 1st. author's 2nd book. NF/NF clip. T11. $120.00

MCGUANE, Thomas. *Keep the Change.* 1989. Houghton Mifflin. 1st. F/NF. R13. $20.00

MCGUANE, Thomas. *Ninety-Two in the Shade.* 1973. FSG. 1st. author's 3rd book. F/F. Q1. $75.00

MCGUANE, Thomas. *Nobody's Angel.* 1982. Random. 1st. author's 5th novel. F/dj. D10. $60.00

MCGUANE, Thomas. *Nothing But Blue Skies.* 1992. Houghton Mifflin. 1st. 1/300. sgn/#d. F/case. Q1. $125.00

MCGUANE, Thomas. *Outside Chance.* 1990. Houghton Mifflin. 1st. F/NF. A20. $20.00

MCGUANE, Thomas. *Panama.* 1978. FSG. 1st. author's 4th novel. F/F. D10. $50.00

MCGUANE, Thomas. *Panama.* 1978. FSG. 1st. F/NF. B3. $40.00

MCGUANE, Thomas. *Something To Be Desired.* 1984. Random. 1st. author's 6th novel. F/F. from $30 to $40.00

MCGUANE, Thomas. *Sporting Club.* 1968. S&S. 1st. sgn. author's 1st book. NF/dj. R13. $250.00

MCGUANE, Thomas. *Sporting Club.* 1968. S&S. 1st. sgn. rem mk. F/F. B4. $200.00

MCGUANE, Thomas. *Sporting Club.* 1969. S&S. 1st. author's 1st book. F/dj. Q1. $75.00

MCGUANE, Thomas. *To Skin a Cat.* 1986. Dutton/Lawrence. 1st. F/F. R13. $25.00

MCGUANE, Thomas. *To Skin a Cat.* 1987. Secker Warburg. 1st Eng. F/F. T11. $30.00

MCGUCKIN, Jack. *Split Second From Hell.* 1979. Perkasie. 1st. photos. 197p. VG/VG. S16. $30.00

MCGUFFEY READER. *McGuffey's New Fifth Eclectic Reader.* 1866. leather. torn ep o/w VG. A4. $35.00

MCGUFFEY READER. *McGuffey's Readers.* facsimile. 7 vol. F/VG case. A4. $75.00

MCGUFFEY READER. *McGuffey's Smaller Eclectic Primer.* 1867 (1849). VanAntwerp. 34p. sc. M5. $110.00

MCGUGAN, B.M. *Forest Lepidoptera of Canada.* 1958-1965. Dept Forestry of Canada. 4 vol in 1 (orig covers bdg in). 840p. F. S15. $35.00

MCHENRY, George. *Cotton Trade: Negro Slavery in the Confederate States.* 1863. London. Saunders Otley. inscr. 292p. xl. B11. $200.00

MCHENRY & ROPER. *Smith & Wesson Hand Guns.* 1958. Stackpole. 1st. 233p. VG/torn. J2. $195.00

MCHUGH, Tom. *Time of the Buffalo.* 1972. NY. 339p. VG/VG. S15. $30.00

MCHUGH, Vernon. *From Hell to Heaven: Memoirs From Patton's 3rd Army.* 1980. Ardmore. 35p. VG/VG. S16. $15.00

MCILVANNEY, William. *Big Man.* 1985. Morrow. 1st Am. F/F. M25. $25.00

MCILVANNEY, William. *Papers of Tony Veitch.* 1983. Pantheon. 1st Am. F/dj. M25. $35.00

MCILVANNEY, William. *Strange Loyalties.* 1991. Morrow. 1st Am. F/dj. M25. $25.00

MCILVOY, Kevin. *Fifth Station.* 1988. Algonquin. 1st. F/F. B35. $12.00

MCINERNEY, Jay. *Bright Lights, Big City.* 1984. Vintage Contemporaries. 1st. F/wrp. B2. $50.00

MCINERNEY, Jay. *Story of My Life.* 1988. Atlantic Monthly. 1st. F/F. B35/P3. $20.00

MCINERNY, Ralph. *Seventh Station.* 1977. Vanguard. 1st. VG/VG. M22. $30.00

MCINTOSH, J.T. *One in Three Hundred.* 1954. Doubleday. 1st. VG/dj. M2. $25.00

MCINTYRE, John T. *Ashton-Kirk, Special Detective.* 1914. Phil. 1st. VG+. B2. $50.00

MCINTYRE, Nancy Fair. *It's a Picnic!* 1969. Viking. G/dj. A16. $15.00

MCINTYRE, Vonda N. *Search for Spock.* 1984. Boston. Gregg. 1st. sgn. F/F. B11. $40.00

MCISSAC, F.J. *Tony Sarg Marionette Book.* 1921. NY. Huebsch. 1st. 12mo. 58p. NF. D1. $85.00

MCKAY, Claude. *Harlem Shadows.* 1922. Harcourt Brace. 1st. VG+. B4. $300.00

MCKAY, Martha Nicholson. *When the Tide Turned in the Civil War.* 1929. Indianapolis. Hollenbeck. 1st. 66p. F/F. B4. $100.00

MCKAY, Paul. *Pilgrim & the Cowboy.* 1989. NY. 1st. 214p. F/dj. S15. $25.00

MCKEARIN & MCKEARIN. *American Glass.* 1941. Crown. 1st. 622p. G/dj. H1. $65.00

MCKEARIN & WILSON. *American Bottles & Flasks & Their Ancestry.* 1978. Crown. 1st/1st prt. 779p. gilt bl cloth. F/dj. H1. $150.00

MCKECHNIE, Hector. *Judicial Process Upon Brieves, 1219-1532.* 1956. Glasgow. Jackson. 31p. prt stapled wrp. M11. $35.00

MCKEE, Alexander. *King Henry VIII's Mary Rose.* 1974. Stein Day. 346p. VG/clip. P4. $25.00

MCKEE, Mrs. *Royal Cookery Book.* 1983. Arlington. 1st. 239p. photos. clip dj. B10. $15.00

MCKEE, Ruth Eleanor. *Lord's Anointed: A Novel of Hawaii.* 1935. Doubleday Doran. 1st. VG/VG. A25. $20.00

MCKEE. *McKee's Price Guide to Children's Literature.* 1970. 82p. VG. A4. $55.00

MCKELVEY, Blake. *Urbanization of America.* 1963. Rutgers. 2nd. 8vo. 370p. red cloth. T10. $25.00

MCKELVEY, Susan Delano. *Botanical Exploration of Trans-Mississippi West 1790-1850.* 1955. Jamaica Plain. Arnold Arboretum of Harvard. 10 fld maps. 1144p. D11. $200.00

MCKENDRY, Maxine. *Seven Centuries Cookbook.* 1973. McGraw Hill. G/dj. A16. $25.00

MCKENNA, Dolores. *Tom Mitten's Cousins.* 1923. NY. Samuel Gabriel. 8vo. pict brd. box. R5. $200.00

MCKENNA, Richard. *Left-Handed Monkey Wrench.* 1984. Annapolis. Naval Inst. 1st. F/dj. Q1. $50.00

MCKENNA, Richard. *Sand Pebbles.* 1962. Harper Row. 1st. F/NF. T11. $85.00

MCKENNA, Rollie. *Portrait of Dylan.* 1982. Owings Mills. Stemmer. inscr/dtd. photos. 112p. cloth. dj. D11. $60.00

MCKENNON, Joe. *Horse Dung Trail: Sage of American Circus.* 1975. Carnival Pub. sgn. 528p. VG/dj. M20. $50.00

MCKEOWN, Martha Ferguson. *Alaska Silver.* 1951. NY. Macmillan. 2nd. 274p. map ep. dj. P4. $23.00

MCKILLUP, Patricia. *Stepping From the Shadows.* 1982. Atheneum. 1st. F/dj. M2. $30.00

MCKINLEY, Clare. *Misty the Wonder Pony.* nd (1956). Rand McNally. lg 4to. unp. VG+. C14. $17.00

MCKINLEY, Robin. *Door in the Hedge.* 1981. Greenwillow. 1st. 8vo. 216p. NF/NF. T5. $30.00

MCKNIGHT, Reginald. *I Get on the Bus.* 1990. Little Brn. 1st. sgn/dtd 1993. F/F. R13. $40.00

MCKOWN, Robin. *Congo: River of Mystery.* 1968. NY. McGraw Hill. 1st. lg 8vo. ils. 144p. VG/dj. W1. $18.00

MCKUEN, Rod. *Lonesome Cities.* 1967. NY. special deluxe sgn ed. VG/box. B5. $45.00

MCLAGLEN, Victor. *Express to Hollywood.* 1934. London. Jerrold. 1st. inscr. G+. B4. $250.00

MCLANATHAN, Richard. *Brandywine Heritage.* 1971. Brandywine River Mus. 1st. 121p+18 mc pl. sq 4to. dj. A17. $25.00

MCLAREN, Moray. *Bonnie Prince Charlie.* 1972. Saturday Review. 1st. 224p. VG/dj. M20. $18.00

MCLAREN, Samuel Bruce. *Scientific Papers.* 1925. Cambridge. 1st. xl. K3. $30.00

MCLAURIN, Tim. *Keeper of the Moon.* 1991. Norton. 1st. sgn. F/F. R13. $35.00

MCLAURIN, TIm. *Woodrow's Trumpet.* 1989. Norton. 1st. sgn. NF/NF. R13. $40.00

MCLEAN, Joseph E. *William Rufus Day, Supreme Court Justice From Ohio.* 1946. John Hopkins. 172p. G/wrp. B18. $12.50

MCLEAN, Rauri. *Joseph Cundall, a Victorian Publisher, Notes on His Life...* 1976. 4to. ils. 104p. F/NF. A4. $65.00

MCLEAN, Rauri. *Victorian Publishers' Bookbindings in Paper.* 1983. 4to. ils. 112p. F/F. A4. $135.00

MCLEAN, Ruari. *Modern Book Design From William Morris to Present Day.* 1959. Essential Books. 116p+16 pl. xl. F/dj. A17. $15.00

MCLENNAN, William E. *Settlement Men's Clubs.* 1917. np. 20p. VG. A25. $15.00

MCLEOD, Alexander. *Pigtails & Gold Dust: Panorama of Chinese Life...* 1947. Caxton. 1st. VG. O4. $35.00

MCLEOD, Alexander. *Pigtails & Gold Dust: Panorama of Chinese Life...* 1948. Caxton. 2nd. 8vo. gilt bl cloth. F/dj. R3. $50.00

MCLEOD, George. *Notes on Surgery of the War in the Crimea...* 1858. London. 1st. 439p. xl. A13. $450.00

MCLEOD, Robert R. *In the Acadian Land: Nature Studies.* 1899. Boston. Bralee Whidden. 1st. ils. 166p. cloth. K3. $30.00

MCLEOD & REHBOCK. *Darwin's Laboratory: Evolutionary Theory & Natural History.* 1994. Honolulu. 1st. 540p. bl cloth. P4. $45.00

MCLINTOCK, Barbara. *Heartaches of a French Cat.* 1989. Boston. Godine. 1st. thin 4to. F/clip. T10. $50.00

MCLINTOCK, Elizabeth. *Japanese Tea Garden, Golden Gate Park, San Francisco, CA.* 1977. SF. John McLaren Soc. 8vo. ils. F/wrp. R3. $10.00

MCLOUGHLIN BROTHERS. *All About Santa.* 1896. NY. narrow 4to. stiff die-cut covers. R5. $275.00

MCLOUGHLIN BROTHERS. *Doings of Kriss Kringle.* 1897. NY. 8vo. 10p. mc paper wrp. R5. $150.00

MCLOUGHLIN BROTHERS. *Kriss Kringle.* 1897. NY. 4to. 14p. mc pict self-wrp. R5. $250.00

MCLOUGHLIN BROTHERS. *Little Pigs.* ca 1890s. ils anonymously. heavy cb stock. G. D1. $75.00

MCLOUGHLIN BROTHERS. *Object Teacher.* (1884). NY. 1st. ils CJ Howard. 12p. VG. D1. $285.00

MCLOUGHLIN BROTHERS. *Old Woman & Her Pig.* (1890). NY. Little Pig series. unp. G/wrp. D1. $40.00

MCLOUGHLIN BROTHERS. *Rip Van Winkle.* ca 1880. NY. ils Thomas Nast. VG/pict wrp. D1. $285.00

MCLOUGHLIN BROTHERS. *Snapshots at Santa Claus.* 1906. NY. Mistletoe series. 4to. mc pict paper cover. R5. $150.00

MCLOUGHLIN BROTHERS. *Tempest. Shakspearian (sic) Tales in Verse.* 1882. NY. 4to. pict wrp. R5. $50.00

MCLOUGHLIN BROTHERS. *Ten Little Mulligan Guards.* ca 1870. obl 4to. pict wrp. R5. $285.00

MCLOUGHLIN BROTHERS. *Three Blind Mice.* ca 1860. NY. Aunt Jenny series. 8vo. pict wrp. R5. $150.00

MCLOUGHLIN BROTHERS. *Visit From Santa Claus.* ca 1899. McLoughlin. 4to. pict wrp. R5. $300.00

MCLOUGHLTIN BROTHERS. *Jolly Jump-Ups See the Circus.* (1944). NY. 8 popups. VG. D1. $185.00

MCLOUGHTLIN BROTHERS. *Jolly Jump-Ups Vacation Trip.* (1942). Springfield. ils Geraldyne Clyne. 5 popups. VG. D1. $85.00

MCLUHAN, Marshall. *War & Peace in the Global Village.* 1966. 1st. F/NF. M19. $50.00

MCLUHAN, T.C. *Dream Tracks, the Railroad & the American Indian 1890-1930.* 1985. Harry Adams. 1st. 208p. VG/dj. J2. $75.00

MCLUHAN, T.C. *Touch the Earth.* 1971. Toronto. New Pr. 1st. inscr/dtd 1971. F/VG clip. L3. $275.00

MCMANUS, Edgar J. *Black Bondage in the North.* 1973. Syracuse. 1st. 236p. F/F. B4. $50.00

MCMATH, Robert C. *Populist Vanguard: A History of Southern Farmer's Alliance.* 1975. Norton. trade pb. VG/dj. V4. $12.50

MCMILLAN, Carol. *Our Own Mother Goose.* 1934. Reid/Koehne Studios. 36p. lg sc. VG. M5. $42.00

MCMILLAN, George. *Old Breed: History of First Marine Division in WWII.* 1949. WA, DC. 1st. ils/maps. 483p. VG. S16. $150.00

MCMILLAN, George. *Uncommon Valor: Marine Divisions in Action.* 1986. Nashville. photos/maps. 256p. VG/VG. S16. $27.50

MCMILLAN, Priscilla Johnson. *Marina & Lee.* 1977. Harper. 1st. inscr. NF/F. B4. $125.00

MCMILLAN, Terry. *Disappearing Acts.* 1989. Viking. 1st. F/F. B2. $175.00

MCMILLAN, Terry. *Mama.* 1987. Houghton Mifflin. 1st. inscr/dtd 1987. author's 1st book. F/dj. Q1. $350.00

MCMURRICH, J. Playfair. *Leonardo Da Vinci: Anatomist (1452-1519).* 1930. Baltimore. 1st. 265p. A13. $125.00

MCMURTRY, Larry. *All My Friends Are Going To Be Strangers.* 1972. S&S. 1st. F/clip. H11. $135.00

MCMURTRY, Larry. *All My Friends Are Going To Be Strangers.* 1972. S&S. 1st. NF/NF. T11. $135.00

MCMURTRY, Larry. *Anything for Billy.* 1988. S&S. 1st. F/F. A23. $42.00

MCMURTRY, Larry. *Anything for Billy.* 1989. London. Collins. 1st. sgn. F/F. from $50 to $60.00

MCMURTRY, Larry. *Buffalo Girls.* 1990. S&S. 1st. sgn. F/F. A23/D10/R14. $60.00

MCMURTRY, Larry. *Cadillac Jack.* 1982. S&S. 1st. F/F. M19. $45.00

MCMURTRY, Larry. *Cadillac Jack.* 1982. S&S. 1st. rem mk. F/F. D10. $40.00

MCMURTRY, Larry. *Cadillac Jack.* 1982. S&S. 1st. rem mk. NF/NF. M23. $30.00

MCMURTRY, Larry. *Cadillac Jack.* 1992. S&S. 1st. sgn. F/F. A23. $75.00

MCMURTRY, Larry. *Daughter of the Tejas.* 1965. Greenwich. NYGS. 1st/2nd state. NF/NF clip 2nd state. T11. $125.00

MCMURTRY, Larry. *Desert Rose.* 1983. S&S. 1st. F/dj. D10/T11. $50.00

MCMURTRY, Larry. *Desert Rose.* 1983. S&S. 1st. sgn. F/F. A23. $75.00

MCMURTRY, Larry. *Evening Star.* 1992. S&S. 1st. sgn. F/F. A23. $40.00

MCMURTRY, Larry. *Flim Flam.* 1987. S&S. 1st. F/F. D10. $45.00

MCMURTRY, Larry. *Flim Flam.* 1987. S&S. 1st. rem mk. F/F. T11. $40.00

MCMURTRY, Larry. *Horseman, Pass By.* 1961. Harper. 1st. inscr. author's 1st book. NF/NF. L3. $1,750.00

MCMURTRY, Larry. *Late Child.* 1995. S&S. ARC. sgn. F/F. D10. $50.00

MCMURTRY, Larry. *Lonesome Dove.* 1985. S&S. 1st. F/F. T11. $200.00

MCMURTRY, Larry. *Moving On.* 1970. S&S. 1st. NF/dj. M25/T11. $75.00

MCMURTRY, Larry. *Pretty Boy Floyd.* 1994. S&S. 1st. sgn. F/F. A23. $42.00

MCMURTRY, Larry. *Some Can Whistle.* 1989. S&S. 1st. F/F. T11/T12. $20.00

MCMURTRY, Larry. *Some Can Whistle.* 1989. S&S. 1st. sgn. F/F. A23. $40.00

MCMURTRY, Larry. *Somebody's Darling.* 1978. S&S. 1st. F/dj. Q1. $60.00

MCMURTRY, Larry. *Somebody's Darling.* 1978. S&S. 1st. rem mk. NF/F. D10. $40.00

MCMURTRY, Larry. *Somebody's Darling.* 1978. S&S. 1st. sgn. F/F. A23. $90.00

MCMURTRY, Larry. *Streets of Laredo.* 1993. NY. S&S. 1st. F/F. T12. $25.00

MCMURTRY, Larry. *Streets of Laredo.* 1993. S&S. 1st. sgn. F/F. A23. $45.00

MCMURTRY, Larry. *Terms of Endearment.* 1975. S&S. 1st. F/dj. B24. $400.00

MCMURTRY, Larry. *Terms of Endearment.* 1975. S&S. 1st. inscr. NF/NF. R14. $225.00

MCMURTRY, Larry. *Texasville.* 1987. S&S. 1st. F/dj. Q1. $30.00

MCMURTRY, Larry. *Texasville.* 1987. S&S. 1st. inscr. NF/NF. R14. $50.00

MCMURTRY, Larry. *Texasville.* 1987. S&S. 1st. sgn. F/F. A23. $40.00

MCNAIRN, Jack. *San Francisco's Celestial Sons.* 1980. Boonville, CA. self pub. ils/map Chinatown. F/stapled wrp. R3. $15.00

MCNALLY, Dennis. *Desolate Angel: A Biography of Jack Kerouac...* 1979. Random. 1st. F/clip. Q1. $40.00

MCNALLY, Raymond. *Clutch of Vampires.* 1974. NYGS. 1st. 8vo. F/dj. T10. $50.00

MCNALLY, Raymond. *Dracula Was a Woman.* 1983. McGraw Hill. 1st. F/dj. M2. $30.00

MCNALLY & MCNALLY. *This Is Mexico.* 1947. Dodd Mead. 1st. 4to. dj. F3. $15.00

MCNARRY, Donald. *Ship Models in Miniature.* 1975. Praeger. ils. 176p. dj. T7. $25.00

MCNEER, May. *Story of the Southern Highlands.* nd (1945). Harper. 4to. unp. VG+. C14. $18.00

MCNEIL, Marion. *Round the Mulberry Bush.* 1933. Saalfield. ils Fern Bisel Peat. VG. from $55 to $75.00

MCNEILL, Elizabeth. *Nine & a Half Weeks: A Memoir of a Love Affair.* 1978. Dutton. 1st. F/F. B4. $150.00

MCNICKLE, D'Arcy. *Surrounded.* 1936. Dodd Mead. 1st. author's 1st book. NF. L3. $750.00

MCNICKLE & FEY. *Indians & Other Americans.* 1959. Harper. 1st. G/G. L3. $75.00

MCNULTY, John. *Third Avenue, New York.* 1946. Little Brn. 1st. F/VG+ clip. B4. $125.00

MCPEEK & MCPEEK. *Verlys of America Decorative Glass 1935-1951.* 1972. self pub. 1st. 66p. VG. H1. $45.00

MCPHAIL, David. *Oh, No, Go.* 1973. Atlantic/Little Brn. 1st. 4to. NF/G+. P2. $35.00

MCPHEE, John. *Alaska: Images of the Country.* 1981. Sierra Club. 1st. folio. F/F. B4. $100.00

MCPHEE, John. *Basin & Range.* 1981. FSG. 1st. F/F. T11. $45.00

MCPHEE, John. *Basin & Range.* 1981. FSG. 1st. 216p. F. D8. $20.00

MCPHEE, John. *Coming Into the Country.* 1977. Farrar Straus. 1st. F/clip. Q1. $60.00

MCPHEE, John. *Crofter & Laird.* 1970. FSG. 1st. NF/NF clip. T11. $100.00

MCPHEE, John. *Deltoid Pumpkin Seed.* 1973. Farrar Straus. 1st. F/clip. Q1. $30.00

MCPHEE, John. *Deltoid Pumpkin Seed.* 1973. Farrar Straus. 1st. F/F. H11. $45.00

MCPHEE, John. *Deltoid Pumpkin Seed.* 1973. FSG. 1st. sgn. NF/NF. R14. $100.00

MCPHEE, John. *Giving Good Weight.* 1979. FSG. 1st. F/F. D10. $40.00

MCPHEE, John. *Giving Good Weight.* 1979. FSG. 1st. NF/dj. H11. $30.00

MCPHEE, John. *Headmaster.* 1966. FSG. 1st. author's 2nd book. F/NF. B3. $300.00

MCPHEE, John. *Headmaster.* 1966. NY. 1st. VG/dj. B5. $95.00

MCPHEE, John. *La Place de la Concorde Suisse.* 1984. FSG. 1st. F/F. D10. $45.00

MCPHEE, John. *Levels of the Game.* 1969. FSG. 1st. VG+/dj. P8. $35.00

MCPHEE, John. *Levels of the Game.* 1970. London. Macdonald. 1st Eng. F/dj. Q1. $75.00

MCPHEE, John. *Pieces of the Frame.* 1975. FSG. 1st. F/F. B4. $200.00

MCPHEE, John. *Roomful of Hovings & Other Profiles.* 1968. FSG. 1st. NF/NF. B3. $125.00

MCPHEE, John. *Sense of Where You Are.* 1965. FSG. 1st. photos. VG. P8. $45.00

MCPHEE, John. *Wimbledon, a Celebration.* 1972. Viking. 1st. inscr association copy. F/F. D10. $200.00

MCPHEE, John. *Wimbledon, a Celebration.* 1972. Viking. 1st. photos Alfred Eisenstaedt. VG/VG. R14. $60.00

MCPHERSON, James Alan. *Atlas of the Civil War.* 1994. 223p. O8. $18.50

MCPHERSON, James Alan. *Hue & Cry.* 1969. Atlantic/Little Brn. 1st. F/NF. B4. $150.00

MCQUADE, James. *Misty.* 1972. Sherbourne. 1st. sgn. VG/dj. M2. $25.00

MCQUAID, Clement. *Gamblers Digest.* 1971. Northfield, IL. 320p. VG/dj. S1. $8.00

MCQUARRIE, Ralph. *Star Wars, Return of the Jedi Portfolio.* 1983. Ballantine. ils. oversize portfolio. NF. C9. $100.00

MCQUINN, Donald E. *Targets.* 1980. Macmillan. 1st. F/F. H11. $35.00

MCQUOWN, F.R. *Fine-Flowered Cacti.* 1965. London. 1st. 30 photos/8 drawings. VG/dj. B26. $25.00

MCRAVEN, Charles. *Building With Stone.* 1990. Alpine. 2nd. 192p. VG. A8. $10.00

MCTAGGART, M.F. *Mount & Man: A Key to Better Horsemanship.* 1925. Country Life. 1st. ils Lionel Edwards. VG. O3. $20.00

MCTEER, May. *Story of the Great Plains.* 1943. 1st. lithos CH DeWitt. VG+/worn. S13. $20.00

MCTIGUE. *Child's Garden of Delights: Pictures, Poems & Stories...* 1987. ils. 271p. F/F. A4. $35.00

MCVAUGH, Rogers. *Edward Palmer: Plant Explorer of American West.* 1956. Norman. photos/lists/2 maps. 430p. VG+/dj. B26. $29.00

MCWHINEY, Grady. *Braxton Bragg & Confederate Defeat. Vol 1.* 1969. NY. 1st. ils/map. 421p. VG/dj. B18. $20.00

MCWHORTER, L.V. *Hear Me, My Chiefs, Nez Perce Legend & History.* 1952. Caxton. 1st. photos. 640p. VG/dj. J2. $295.00

MCWHORTER, L.V. *Yellow Wolf: His Own Story.* 1940. Caxton. 1st. sgn. NF. L3. $450.00

MCWHORTER, L.V. *Yellow Wolf: His Own Story.* 1940. Caxton. 1st. 324p. VG. J2. $95.00

MEACHUM, Walter E. *Old Oregon Trail, the Road That Won an Empire.* 1924. Ryder Bros. 1st. 33p. VG. J2. $55.00

MEACHUM, Walter E. *Old Oregon Trail, the Road That Won an Empire.* 1948. Am Pioneer Trails Assn. G. A19. $35.00

MEAD, J.R. *Hunting & Trading on the Great Plains 1859-1875.* 1986. OK U. 1st. photos/maps. F/dj. M4. $30.00

MEAD, Margaret. *Continuities in Cultural Evolution.* 1964. New Haven. Yale. 1st. 8vo. VG/dj. w/card: Compliments of Author. T10. $50.00

MEAD, Margaret. *Growing Up in New Guinea: Comparative Study...* 1930. Morrow. 1st. F/NF. B4. $275.00

MEAD, Richard. *Medical Precepts & Cautions.* 1755. London. Brindley. 2nd. 8vo. 311p. F. T10. $200.00

MEAD, Sheperd. *Big Ball of Wax.* 1954. S&S. 1st. F/dj. M2. $20.00

MEAD. *Thomas Pynchon: Biography of Primary & Secondary Materials.* 1989. 1/957. ils. 184p. F/F. A4. $125.00

MEADE, L.T. *Bad Little Hannah, a Story of Girls.* ca 1908. NY. AL Burt. 373p. VG. A25. $15.00

MEADE, L.T. *Bunch of Cousins & the Barn Boys.* nd (1923). London. Chambers. 12mo. VG+. C8. $25.00

MEADE, L.T. *Frances Kane's Fortune.* ca 1900. Chicago. Donohue. 1st thus? 72p+ads. G+. A25. $10.00

MEADE, L.T. *Gay Charmer.* ca 1916. NY. AL Burt. 1st? 317p+ads. VG/dj. A25. $20.00

MEADE, L.T. *Girl of the People.* ca 1915. NY. Hurst. 1st thus? 271p. VG. A25. $10.00

MEADE, L.T. *World of Girls.* (1886). London. Cassell. 39 Thousand prt. 12mo. VG. C8. $45.00

MEADE, Martha L. *Recipes From the Old South.* 1961. Bramhall. G/dj. A16. $12.00

MEADE, Mary. *Mary Meade's Cooking Fun.* 1965. Chicago. Tribune. ils Becky Krehbiel. 4to. 32p. VG+. M5. $20.00

MEADOWCRAFT, Enid La Monte. *By Wagon & Flatboat.* 1938. Crowell. 1st. 170p. VG/G+. P2. $35.00

MEADOWS & MILLS. *Antarctic.* 1994. Oxford/Santa Barbara. Clio. 8vo. 383p. M/sans. P4. $87.50

MEAGHER, Maude. *Green Scamander.* 1933. Houghton Mifflin. 1st. VG/dj. M2. $35.00

MEANS, Philip Ainsworth. *Ancient Civilizations of the Andes.* 1931. Scribner. 1st. 586p. G. F3. $45.00

MEANS, Philip Ainsworth. *Spanish Main.* 1935. Scribner. ils. 278p. T7. $45.00

MEANY, Tom. *Incredible Giants.* 1955. Barnes. sgn. VG/VG. B11. $65.00

MEAR & SWAN. *In the Footsteps of Scott.* 1987. London. Cape. 1st Eng. 306p. map ep. gilt bl. P4. $35.00

MEARS, Eliot Grinnell. *Resident Orientals on the American Pacific Coast...* 1928. Chicago U. 8vo. gilt red cloth. F. R3. $90.00

MEASE, James. *Memoirs of Philadelphia Society for Promoting Agriculture.* 1816. Phil. Warner. 543p. leather spine missing pieces. scarce. A10. $75.00

MEBANE, John. *Collecting Brides' Baskets & Other Glass Fancies.* 1976. Wallace-Homestead. ne. 174p. VG/glossy wrp. H1. $45.00

MECHI, John J. *Series of Letters on Agricultural Improvements.* 1845. London. Longman. 122p. cloth. A10. $45.00

MEDINA, J.T. *Discovery of the Amazon According to Account Friar Gaspar...* 1934. Am Geog Soc. trans from 1894 ed. 467p. M4. $35.00

MEDUNA, Ladislas. *Die Entwicklung der Zirbeldruse im Sauglingsalter...* 1925. Munchen/Berlin. Bergmann/Springer. 1st separate. inscr. 547p. G1. $85.00

MEDWAY, Lord. *Wild Mammals of Malaya & Offshore Islands...* 1969. London. Oxford. ils. 127p. cloth. VG. M12. $60.00

MEE, John L. *Three Little Frogs.* 1924. Chicago. Volland. 1st. ils John Rae. sq 12mo. mc brd. R5. $75.00

MEEKINGS, C.A.F. *1235 Surrey Eyre, Vol I, Introduction.* 1979. Guildford. Surrey Record Soc. M11. $65.00

MEERPOL & MEERPOL. *We Are Your Sons: Legacy of Ethel & Julius Rosenberg...* 1975. Houghton Mifflin. 419p. VG/dj. S3. $24.00

MEEUSE, A.D.J. *All About Angiosperms.* 1987. Eburon. 8vo. 212p. F/wrp. B1. $25.00

MEGAW & MEGAW. *Celtic Art: From Its Beginnings to the Book of Kells.* 1989. photos. VG/VG. M17. $27.50

MEGGENDORFER, Lothar. *All Alive: A Moveable Toybook.* ca 1890. London. Grevel. 8 moveable hand-colord pl. paper brd/cloth spine. T10. $1,800.00

MEGGENDORFER, Lothar. *Militarisches Ziehbilderbuch.* 1890. Munchen. Braun Schneider. 8 tab-controlled moveables. pict brd. R5. $3,000.00

MEIGHN, Moira. *Little Book of Conceited Secrets & Delights...* 1928. London. Medici Soc. 1st. ils. 79p. VG+. A25. $20.00

MEIGNAN, Victor. *From Paris to Pekin Over Siberian Snows...* 1889. London. Swann. 2nd. ils/notes. 428p. gilt pict cloth. VG. W3. $265.00

MEIGS, Charles. *Obstetrics: Science & the Art.* 1849. Phil. 1st. 685p. recent leatherette/orig label. A13. $250.00

MEIGS, Cornelia. *Trade Wind.* 1955 (1927). Little Brn. 8vo. 309p. xl. VG. T5. $12.00

MEIGS. *Critical History of Children's Literature, a Survey...* 1953. ils. 648p. VG/VG. A4. $95.00

MEIJER, W. *Spinoza een Levensbeeld.* nd. Amsterdam. sm 4to. Dutch text. 34p. wrp in brd. S3. $19.00

MEIR, Golda. *My Life.* 1975. Putnam. 1st. F/F. B35. $15.00

MEIROWSKY, Arnold M. *Neurological Surgery of Trauma.* 1965. WA, DC. Office Surgeon General. 4to. gray cloth. G1. $50.00

MELANCHTHON, Philipp. *Oratio Vber der Leich des Ehrwirdigen Herrn Martini Lutheri.* 1546. Wittenberg. Rhaw. 4to. woodcut. modern manuscript brd. R12. $1,250.00

MELKONIAN, Michael. *Algal Cell Mobility.* 1992. NY. ils. 236p. as new. B26. $29.00

MELLIN, Jeanne. *Horseback Riding.* 1970. Grosset Dunlap. rpt. VG. O3. $25.00

MELLIN, Jeanne. *Morgan Horse Handbook.* 1973. Brattleboro. Stephen Green. ARC/1st. F/F. O3. $45.00

MELLING, Elizabeth. *Crime & Punishment, a Collection of Examples...* 1969. Maidstone. Kent County Council. M11. $50.00

MELLOW, James R. *Charmed Circle: Gertrude Stein & Company.* 1974. Praeger. 1st. 528p. red brd/gray cloth. B22. $10.00

MELVILLE, George W. *In the Lena Delta: A Narrative...* 1884. Boston. Houghton Mifflin. 8vo. 497p. brn cloth. P4. $225.00

MELVILLE, Herman. *Billy Budd & Other Prose Pieces.* 1924. London. Constable. 1st. F/torn. B4. $400.00

MELVILLE, Herman. *Moby Dick.* 1851. Harper. 1st/1st prt. slate morocco-grain cloth (1st bdg). half morocco case. M24. $15,000.00

MELVILLE, Herman. *Moby Dick.* 1851. NY. Harper. 1st/1st prt/1st bdg. orange ep/gilt brn cloth. M24. $6,000.00

MELVILLE, Herman. *Moby Dick.* 1930. Chicago. Lakeside. 1/1000. 3 vol. ils R Kent. F/cloth & aluminum case. B4. $2,750.00

MELVILLE, Herman. *Redburn: His First Voyage.* 1849. NY. Harper. 1st/2nd state (18p ads dated Oct 1849). glt brn cloth. M24. $750.00

MELVIN, Jean Sutherland. *American Glass Paperweights & Their Makers.* 1967. Thomas Nelson. 192p. as new/dj/Fcase. H1. $80.00

MENCKEN, H.L. *Book of Prefaces.* 1917. Knopf. 1st. VG. A20. $50.00

MENCKEN, H.L. *Christmas Story.* 1946. Knopf. 1st. F/dj. Q1. $75.00

MENCKEN, H.L. *Prejudices.* 1926. Knopf. 1st. F/NF. B4. $450.00

MENCKEN, H.L. *Prejudices.* 1926. Knopf. 1st. VG/fair. M23. $50.00

MENDEL, Gregor. *Experiments in Plant-Hybridisation.* 1925. Cambridge. rpt. 41p. VG/wrp. B26. $9.00

MENDELL, Ronald. *Who's Who in Basketball.* 1973. Arlington. 1st. VG+/dj. P8. $25.00

MENDELL & PHARES. *Who's Who in Football.* 1974. Arlington. 1st. biographical sketches. VG+. P8. $20.00

MENDELSSOHN, Kurt. *Riddle of the Pyramids.* 1975. London. BC Assoc. ils. 224p. NF/dj. W1. $12.00

MENDELSSOHN, Moses. *Phedon, ou Entretiens sur la Spiritualite...* 1772. Paris/Bayeux. Saillant Lepelley. tall 8vo. gilt calf. R12. $375.00

MENDOZA, George. *Inspector.* 1970. Doubleday. 1st. ils Peter Parnall. obl 4to. VG+/dj. P2. $35.00

MENDOZA & ROCKWELL. *Norman Rockwell's Americana ABC.* nd (1975). Dell/Abrams. unp. NF. C14. $8.00

MENGE, J.J. *Erstes Lese-, Lehr- und Vebungsbuch fur Deutsche...* 1874. NY/Cincinnati. 1st. 8vo. 64p. G. T10. $75.00

MENGEL, Willi. *Ottmar Mergenthaler & the Printing Revolution.* 1954. 1st. ils. decor bdg. VG. K3. $18.00

MENKE, Frank G. *All-Sports Record Book.* 1950. Barnes. 1st. G+/G. P8. $6.00

MENKE, Frank G. *Down the Stretch.* 1945. Smith Durell. 1st. 209p. VG/dj. M20. $30.00

MENKEN, Alice Davis. *On the Side of Mercy: Problems in Social Readjustment.* 1933. Convici Friede. 1st. ils. 224p. VG/dj. A25. $15.00

MENNINGER, Edwin A. *Flowering Trees of the World...* 1962. Hearthside. 1st. 8vo. F/VG. A22. $75.00

MENPES, Mortimer. *Japan: Record in Color.* 1904. London. 200 full-p engravings. 207p. teg. gold-tooled cloth. NF. W3. $75.00

MERCER, Alexander Gardiner. *Bible Characters.* 1885. Putnams. 335p. VG. B29. $8.00

MERCER, F.A. *Gardens & Gardening.* 1937. London. Studio. 134p. VG. A10. $22.00

MERCER, Samuel A.B. *Sumero-Babylonian Year-Formulae.* 1946. London. Luzac. 1st. 4to. 2 fld charts. 121p. VG. W1. $35.00

MERCHANT, Paul; see Ellison, Harlan.

MEREDITH, D. *Grasses & Pastures of South Africa.* 1955. np. ils/figures/maps. 771p. VG/dj. B26. $122.50

MEREDITH, D. *Search at Lock Ness: Expedition of the NY Times...* (1977). NY. ils/map/drawings. 183p. cloth/brd. NF/F. M12. $25.00

MEREDITH, De Witt. *Voyages of the Velero III. Pictorial Version...* 1939. Los Angeles. private prt. 1st. inscr. 286p. P4. $165.00

MEREDITH, George. *Last Poems.* Oct 1909. Scribner. 1st Am. 64p. teg. gilt bdg. G. H1. $16.00

MEREDITH, George. *Shaving of Shagpat.* 1955. NY. LEC. 1st thus. 1/1500. ils/sgn Honore Guilbeau. F/glassine/case. Q1. $125.00

MEREDITH, Isabel. *Girl Among the Anarchists.* 1903. London. Duckworth. 1st. B2. $85.00

MEREDITH, Owen. *Lucile.* 1868. Ticknor Fields. ils George DuMaurier. aeg. gilt brn cloth. G. H1. $28.00

MEREDITH, Scott. *Bar 1 Roundup of Best Western Stories.* 1952. Dutton. 1st. VG/dj. M2. $12.00

MEREDITH, William. *Earth Walk.* 1970. Knopf. 1st. F/dj. V1. $45.00

MERILLAT, Herb. *Guadalcanal Remembered.* 1982. NY. maps/photos/notes/biblio/index. 298p. VG/VG. S16. $15.00

MERINO, Jose Maria. *Beyond the Ancient Cities.* 1987. FSG. 1st Am. F/F. B4. $45.00

MERRELL, David J. *Ecological Genetics.* 1981. NM U. 1st. as new/dj. V4. $12.50

MERRIAM, D.F. *Computer Applications in the Earth Sciences.* 1981. NY. Plenum. 385p. F/G. D8. $25.00

MERRIAM, D.F. *Geostatistics, a Colloquium.* 1970. NY. Plenum. 177p. F/G. D8. $25.00

MERRIAM, Eve. *Emma Lazarus: Woman With a Torch.* 1956. Citadel. 160p. G+/fair. S3. $20.00

MERRIAM, Harold. *Montana Adventure, the Recollections of Frank B Linderman.* 1968. NE U. 1st. 224p. VG/VG. J2. $125.00

MERRIEN, Jean. *Lonely Voyages.* 1954. London. 1st. 8vo. 280p. map ep. VG/dj. P4. $35.00

MERRILL, Anthony F. *Rammed-Earth House.* 1947. Harper. 1st. 230p. dj. A10. $40.00

MERRILL, Dean. *Clergy Couples in Crisis: Impact of Stress...* 1985. Word. 216p. VG/dj. B29. $7.50

MERRILL, Judith. *Path Into the Unknown.* 1968. Delacorte. 1st Am. VG/dj. M2. $10.00

MERRILL, Judith. *9th Annual Year's Best Science Fiction.* 1964. S&S. 1st. F/dj. M2. $25.00

MERRIMAN, Charles E. *Who's It in America.* 1906. NY. Dodge. 1st. cream pict cloth. NF/VG. M24. $65.00

MERRIMAN, Henry Seton. *Vultures.* 1902. Harper. 1st Am. F/NF. B4. $125.00

MERRYMAN, Mildred Plew. *Bonbon & Bonbonette.* 1924. Rand McNally. 1st. 96p. VG+. P2. $95.00

MERSAND, Joseph. *Traditions in American Literature: A Study of Jewish...* 1939. Modern Chapbooks. biblio/index. 247p. VG. S3. $25.00

MERSERVE & SANDBURG. *Photographs of Abraham Lincoln.* 1944. Harcourt Brace. 1st. photos. 126p. F/dj. H1. $60.00

MERTENS, J.M. *Living Snakes of the World.* 1987. Sterling. 480p. dj. B1. $50.00

MERTON, Robert K. *On the Soulders of Giants.* 1985. HBJ. 8vo. 300p. F/dj. K3. $15.00

MERTON, Robert K. *Sociology of Science.* 1974. Chicago. 2nd. VG/dj. K3. $40.00

MERTON, Thomas. *Alaskan Journal of Thomas Merton.* 1988. Isla Vista, CA. Turkey Pr. 1st. 1/140 deluxe. Japanese linen. F/case. Q1. $250.00

MERTON, Thomas. *Disputed Questions.* 1960. NY. 1st. 297p. F/VG. W3. $45.00

MERTON, Thomas. *Seasons of Celebration.* 1965. Farrar. 1st. F/NF. B2. $35.00

MERTON, Thomas. *Seeds of Contemplation.* 1949. New Directions. 1st. F/dj. Q1. $250.00

MERTON, Thomas. *Silent Life.* 1957. FSC. 1st. F/NF. B3. $60.00

MERTON, Thomas. *Thomas Merton on Peace.* 1971. NY. 1st. VG/VG. B5. $40.00

MERTZ, Barbara Gross. *Into the Darkness.* 1990. S&S. 1st. 298p. F/NF. W2. $20.00

MERTZ, Barbara Gross. *Jackal's Head.* 1968. Meredith. 1st. VG/VG. P3. $40.00

MERTZ, Barbara Gross. *Lion in the Valley.* 1986. Warner. 1st. sgn. VG/VG. A23. $42.00

MERTZ, Barbara Gross. *Naked Once More.* 1989. Warner. 1st. F/F. H11. $25.00

MERTZ, Barbara Gross. *Night Train to Memphis.* 1994. Warner. 1st. sgn. VG/VG. A23. $40.00

MERTZ, Barbara Gross. *Sea King's Daughter.* 1975. Dodd Mead. VG/VG. P3. $25.00

MERTZ, Barbara Gross. *Search the Shadows.* 1987. Atheneum. ARC. NF/wrp. B3. $30.00

MERYMAN, Richard. *Andrew Wyeth.* 1968. 1st. folio. NF/VG. S13. $150.00

MESERVE & SANDBURG. *Photographs of Abraham Lincoln.* 1944. NY. Harcourt Brace. photos. 30p. cloth. dj. D11. $75.00

MESSICK, Dale. *Brenda Starr, Girl Reporter.* 1943. Racine. Whitman. authorized ed. ils. 248p. VG. A25. $8.00

MESSNER, Reinhold. *Antarctica: Both Heaven & Hell.* 1991. Seattle. Mountaineers. 1st Am. 8vo. 381p. M/dj. P4. $35.00

METALIOUS, Grace. *Peyton Place.* 1956. S&S. 1st. 378p. VG. W2. $140.00

METCALF, Arthur. *Arm's Length.* 1930. Scribner. 1st. VG. M2. $22.00

METCALF, Arthur. *Green Devil.* 1912. Pilgrim. 1st. sgn. VG. M2. $35.00

METCALF & FLINT. *Destructive & Useful Insects.* 1951. McGraw Hill. 3rd. 1071p. A10. $22.00

METCALFE, C.R. *Anatomy of the Monocotyledons.* 1960. Oxford. Clarendon. 731p. VG/dj. A10. $65.00

METCHNIKOFF, Elie. *Prolongation of Life: Optimistic Studies.* 1908. NY. 1st Am. 343p. A13. $75.00

METHVEN, Barbara. *Microwaving for One & Two.* 1981. Cy DeCosse. VG. B10. $10.00

METRAUX, Alfred. *History of the Incas.* 1969. Pantheon. 1st Am. 205p. dj. F3. $20.00

METTLER, Frederick Albert. *Neuroanatomy.* 1948. St Louis. Mosby. 2nd revised/enlarged. tall 8vo. ils. 536p. VG. G1. $65.00

METZ, Alice Hulett. *Early American Pattern Glass.* 1961 (1958). self pub. 3rd. sgn. 243p. sbdg. G. H1. $25.00

METZ, Alice Hulett. *Much More Early American Pattern Glass.* 1965. self pub. 1st. sgn. 232p. sbdg. G. H1. $48.00

METZGER & RUBIN. *Shaker Industries.* 1977. Butternut. 1/225. 68x60mm. M/prt wrp. B24. $100.00

MEW, Egan. *Chelsea & Chelsea-Derby China.* nd. Jack/Dodd Mead. 92p. cloth/pict label. VG. M20. $22.00

MEWSHAW, Michael. *Blackballed.* 1986. Atheneum. 1st. F/F. A20. $10.00

MEYER, Elise. *You Can Be a Better Cook Than Mama Ever Was.* 1968. Doubleday. A16. $10.00

MEYER, F.B. *Our Daily Homily.* 1966. Revell. 469p. fair. B29. $8.00

MEYER, J.B. *William Carey: Shoemaker Who Became Father & Founder...* nd. Partridge. 160p. xl G. B29. $9.50

MEYER, Milton W. *Diplomatic History of the Philippine Republic.* 1965. Honolulu. 321p. M/VG. P1. $35.00

MEYER, Nicholas. *Seven-Per-Cent Solution.* 1974. Dutton. 1st. VG/VG. P3. $25.00

MEYER, Nicholas. *West End Horror.* 1976. Dutton. 1st. VG/dj. M2. $15.00

MEYER, Roy W. *History of the Santee Sioux.* 1967. Lincoln, NE. 8vo. 434p. bl cloth. NF. K7. $48.00

MEYER. *Treasury of Great Children's Book Illustrators.* 1987. 4to. ils/93 mc pl. 272p. F/VG. A4. $85.00

MEZZROW & WOLFE. *Really the Blues.* 1946. Random. 1st. sgn Mezzrow. VG/NF. B2. $350.00

MIAN, Mary. *Take Three Witches.* 1971. Houghton Mifflin. 1st. sgn. F/F. B11. $40.00

MICHAEL, Barbara; see Mertz, Barbara Gross.

MICHAEL, Bryan; see Moore, Brian.

MICHAEL, Paul. *American Movies Reference Book, the Sound Era.* 1969. Prentice Hall. 600+p. NF/dj. C9. $50.00

MICHAEL, W.H.C. *Mississippi Flotilla: What the Gunboats Accomplished...* 1886. Omaha, NE. 1st. 19p. VG/prt wrp. M8. $250.00

MICHAEL. *Musical Instruments in the Dayton C Miller Flute Collection.* 1982. Lib of Congress. 349p. 4to. F. A17. $22.50

MICHAELS, Leonard. *Going Places.* 1969. FSG. 1st. inscr. author's 1st book. F/F. L3. $125.00

MICHAELS, Leonard. *I Would Have Saved Them If I Could.* 1975. FSG. 1st. author's 2nd book. F/F. B4. $75.00

MICHAELS, Leonard. *Shuffle.* 1990. FSG. 1st. F/F. B35. $12.00

MICHAUX, F.A. *Travels to the West of Alleghany Mountains...* 1805. London. Shury. 294p. VG. A10. $350.00

MICHEAUX, Oscar. *Story of Dorothy Stanfield.* 1946. Book Supply. 1st. F/F. B4. $200.00

MICHEL, Henri. *Second World War.* 1975. NY. 947p. VG/VG. S16. $45.00

MICHELET, Jules. *Bird.* 1879. London. revised. ils Giacomelli. 350p. VG. S15. $80.00

MICHELET, M. *Life of Martin Luther.* 1856. NY. Kelley. 314p. gr cloth. VG. M20. $40.00

MICHELMORE, Peter. *Swift Years: The Robert Oppenheimer Story.* 1969. Dodd Mead. ils. 8vo. 273p. VG/dj. K3. $15.00

MICHENER, E.A. *How To Grow Food for Your Family.* 1942. NY. Barnes. 139p. xl. A10. $13.00

MICHENER, James A. *About Centennial: Some Notes on the Novel.* 1974. Random. 1/3200 mk Not for Sale. F/NF. M25. $100.00

MICHENER, James A. *About Centennial: Some Notes on the Novel.* 1974. Random. 1st. NF/NF. T11. $75.00

MICHENER, James A. *Alaska.* 1988. Random. ltd. 868p. NF/NF. W2. $50.00

MICHENER, James A. *Bridge at Andau.* 1957. Random. 1st. NF/G+. M19. $50.00

MICHENER, James A. *Caravans.* 1963. Random. 1st. sgn/dtd 1995. NF/NF. R14. $175.00

MICHENER, James A. *Caribbean.* 1989. Random. 1st. F/F. A20. $20.00

MICHENER, James A. *Centennial.* 1974. Random. 1st. F/NF. B2. $65.00

MICHENER, James A. *Centennial.* 1974. Random. 1st. F/clip. D10. $50.00

MICHENER, James A. *Century of Sonnets.* 1977. Austin. State House. sgn. M/dj. R14. $125.00

MICHENER, James A. *Chesapeake.* 1978. Random. 1st. sgn on tipped-in leaf. F/F. B2. $125.00

MICHENER, James A. *Covenant.* 1980. Random. 1st. F/dj. Q1. $60.00

MICHENER, James A. *Drifters.* 1971. Random. 1st. NF/dj. A24. $60.00

MICHENER, James A. *Eagle & the Raven.* 1990. Austin. State House. sgn. F/F. B3. $45.00

MICHENER, James A. *Fires of Spring.* 1949. Random. 1st. NF/VG. B4. $600.00

MICHENER, James A. *Firstfruits: Harvest of 25 Years of Israeli Writing.* 1973. JPS. F/NF. H11. $55.00

MICHENER, James A. *Firstfruits: Harvest of 25 Years of Israeli Writing.* 1973. JPS. 15 stories. 346p. VG/fair. S3. $21.00

MICHENER, James A. *Floating World.* 1954. Random. 1st/4th prt. ils. 403p. F/clear plastic dj. W3. $75.00

MICHENER, James A. *Fodor's Modern Guides/Hawaii 1961.* 1961. McKay. intro Michener. F/NF pink dj. A24. $50.00

MICHENER, James A. *Iberia.* 1968. Random. 1st. F/dj. Q1. $75.00

MICHENER, James A. *Japanese Prints: From the Early Masters to the Modern.* 1959. Rutland/Tokyo. Tuttle. 1st. VG/VG. B5. $110.00

MICHENER, James A. *Japanese Prints: From the Early Masters to the Modern.* 1959. Rutland/Tokyo. Tuttle. 1st. 257 pl. silk brd. F/dj/case. Q1. $500.00

MICHENER, James A. *Legacy.* 1987. Random. 1st. F/F. N4. $25.00

MICHENER, James A. *Michener Miscellany.* 1973. Random. 1st. F/NF. T11. $75.00

MICHENER, James A. *Miracle in Seville.* 1995. Random. 1/500. sgn. ils John Fulton. F/sans/F case. R14. $175.00

MICHENER, James A. *Modern Japanese Print.* 1968. Tuttle. 1st trade. ils. 57p. F. W3. $110.00

MICHENER, James A. *My Lost Mexico.* 1992. Austin. State House. 1/350. sgn. F/case. B3. $150.00

MICHENER, James A. *Novel.* 1991. Random. 1st. F/dj. Q1. $30.00

MICHENER, James A. *Pilgrimage.* 1990. Rodale. 1st. 119p. NF/F. W2. $15.00

MICHENER, James A. *Presidential Lottery.* 1969. NY. 1st. VG/VG. B5. $40.00

MICHENER, James A. *Presidential Lottery.* 1969. NY. Random. 1st. blk cloth. F/NF. T11. $75.00

MICHENER, James A. *Rascals in Paradise.* 1957. NY. Random. 1st. NF/VG+. T11. $95.00

MICHENER, James A. *Recessional.* 1994. Random. 1st trade. 484p. F/F. W2. $45.00

MICHENER, James A. *Sayonara.* 1954. Random. 1st. NF/NF. M19. $50.00

MICHENER, James A. *Sayonara.* 1954. Random. 1st. VG/VG. B3/P3. $45.00

MICHENER, James A. *Sayonara.* 1954. VT/Japan. Tuttle. 1st thus. prt for Am occupation forces. NF/dj. D10. $90.00

MICHENER, James A. *Space.* 1982. Random. ltd 1st. 622p. F/NF. W2. $120.00

MICHENER, James A. *Tales of the South Pacific.* 1947. NY. 4-line inscr/dtd May 29, 1947. salmon cloth. VG. B14. $250.00

MICHENER, James A. *Tales of the South Pacific.* 1951. London. Collins. 1st Eng. F/VG+. B4. $450.00

MICHENER, James A. *Voice of Asia.* 1951. Random. 1st/1st state. NF/NF. T11. $165.00

MICHENER, James A. *Watermen.* 1979. Random. 1st. ils John Moll. NF/NF. A24. $50.00

MICHENER, James A. *Watermen.* 1979. Random. 1st. ils Moll. NF/VG+. S13. $35.00

MICKLETHWAIT & PEPPIN. *Dictionary of British Book Illustrations, the 20th Century.* 1983. London. 1st. VG/VG. T9. $50.00

MIDDENDORF, John William. *Henley Royal Regatta.* 1964. Baltimore. Barton Cotton. 1/1000. ils. unp. T7. $35.00

MIDDLEKAUFF, R. *Glorious Cause: American Revolution 1763-1789.* 1982. Oxford. 1st prt. ils/map. 696p. F/dj. M4. $30.00

MIDDLETON, Christopher. *Vindication of Conduct of Capt Christopher Middleton...* 1967. Wakefield. rpt (London 1742). 206p. 48p. xl. P4. $25.00

MIDDLETON, Christopher. *Voyages in Search of a Northwest Passage 1741-1747...* 1994. London. Hakluyt Soc. 2nd Series #177. 8vo. 333p. bl cloth. P4. $50.00

MIDDLETON, Don. *Roy Rogers & the Gopher Creek Gunman.* 1945. Racine. Whitman. Ils Erwin Hess. sm 8vo. VG+/dj. C8. $22.50

MIDDLETON, W.E. Knowles. *History of the Barometer.* 1964. Johns Hopkins. sm 4to. 489p. dj. K5. $125.00

MIDGLEY, John. *Goodness of Beans, Peas & Lentils.* 1992. Random. 1st Am. VG/VG. B10. $9.00

MIDGLEY, John. *Goodness of Olive Oil.* 1992. Random. 65p. VG/VG. B10. $10.00

MIERS, Earl Schenck. *Career Coach.* 1941. Westminster. 1st. ils. VG/G+. P8. $25.00

MIERS, Earl Schenck. *Composing Sticks & Mortar Boards.* 1941. Rutgers. 1st trade. 97p. A17. $12.50

MIERS, Earl Schenck. *General Who Marched to Hell.* 1990. Dorset. A19. $20.00

MIGHELS, Ella Sterling. *Fairy Tale of the White Man, Told From Gates of Sunset by...* 1915. SF. Pacific Pub. 8vo. 72p. VG/wrp. K7. $45.00

MIHALAS, D. *Galactic Astronomy.* 1968. SF. Freeman. 1st. 257p. VG. D8. $10.00

MIKI, Fumio. *Haniwa: Clay Sculpture of Protohistoric Japan.* 1960. Tuttle. 1st. 12 full-p mc pl/80 full-p gravure. 161p. F/NF. W3. $135.00

MILAN, Galleria del Levante. *Il Contributo Russo Alle Avanguardie Plastiche.* 1964. Curato. Carlo Belloi. Italian text. 117p. xl. D2. $45.00

MILES, Babe. *Bluebells & Bittersweet Gardening...* 1969. Van Nostrand. 168p. cloth. VG. A10. $20.00

MILES, Barry. *Ginsberg: A Biography.* 1989. NY. 1st. 588p+photos. F/dj. A17. $15.00

MILES, Keith; see Tralins, Bob.

MILES, Miska. *Annie & the Old One.* (1971). Little Brn. 3rd. NF/NF. C8. $22.50

MILES, Miska. *Apricot ABC.* (1969). Little Brn. 3rd. obl 4to. wht cloth. VG. T5. $15.00

MILES, Miska. *Apricot ABC.* 1969. Atlantic/Little Brn. 1st. ils Peter Parnall. VG+/VG+. P2. $35.00

MILES, Miska. *Pony in the Schoolhouse.* 1964. Little Brn. 1st. F/VG. C8. $22.50

MILES, Nelson. *Personal Recollections & Observations of General...Miles...* 1896. Werner Co. 1st. ils Fredrick Remington. 590p. VG. J2. $475.00

MILES, William. *Horse's Foot & How To Keep It Sound.* 1856. NY. Saxton. G. O3. $45.00

MILHAM, Willis I. *Meteorology: A Text-Book on the Weather...* 1925 (1912). NY. Macmillan. 8vo. 549p. cloth. G. K5. $15.00

MILHAM, Willis I. *Time & Timekeepers.* 1941. Macmillan. Imperial ed. 339 figures. 616p. VG. K3. $40.00

MILL, James. *Analysis of the Phenomena of the Human Mind.* 1869. London. new ed. 2 vol. red cloth. B14. $125.00

MILL, John Stuart. *Dissertations & Discussions Political, Philosophical...* 1859. London. John Parker. 1st. 8vo. cloth. M1. $175.00

MILLAIS, J.G. *Far Away Up the Nile.* 1924. London. Longman. ils/drawings. 254p. cloth. VG. M12. $150.00

MILLAR, C.E. *Soil Fertility.* 1955. NY. Wiley. 436p. dj. A10. $20.00

MILLAR, David P. *From Snowdrift to Shellfire.* 1984. Sydney. David Ell. 1st. 4to. 160p. VG/dj. P4. $110.00

MILLAR, Kenneth. *Barbarous Coast.* 1956. Knopf. 1st. VG+/VG+. B2. $200.00

MILLAR, Kenneth. *Chill.* 1964. Knopf. 1st. F/NF. M15. $125.00

MILLAR, Kenneth. *Goodbye Look.* 1969. Knopf. 1st. F/dj. M25. $60.00

MILLAR, Kenneth. *Lew Archer.* 1977. Mysterious. 1st hc. 1/250. sgn. F/dj/case. Q1. $250.00

MILLAR, Kenneth. *On Crime Writing.* 1973. Santa Barbara. Capra. 1st. 1/250. sgn. F. Q1. $250.00

MILLAR, Kenneth. *Self-Portrait.* 1981. Santa Barbara. Capra. 1st. 1/250. sgn. fwd/sgn Eudora Welty. F. Q1. $200.00

MILLAR, Margaret. *Banshee.* 1983. Morrow. 1st. F/F. M22. $20.00

MILLAR, Margaret. *Iron Gates.* 1945. Random. 1st. VG. M22. $12.00

MILLARD, S.T. *Goblets & Goblets II.* c 1938. Topeka, KS. Central Pr. 1st. sgn/dtd 1940. 8vo. 177 pl. unp. ES. G+. H1. $90.00

MILLAY, Edna St Vincent. *Collected Sonnets.* 1941. Harper. 1st. 8vo. 161p. VG+. H1. $15.00

MILLAY, Edna St. Vincent. *Buck in the Snow.* 1928. Harper. 1st. F/NF. M23. $40.00

MILLAY, Edna St. Vincent. *Conversations at Midnight.* 1937. Harper. 1st. NF/dj. B35. $28.00

MILLAY, Edna St. Vincent. *Conversations at Midnight.* 1937. NY. Harper. 1st trade. gilt bl full flexible calf. NF. M24. $65.00

MILLAY, Edna St. Vincent. *Fatal Interview.* 1931. Harper. 1st. F/F. Q1. $75.00

MILLAY, Edna St. Vincent. *Fatal Interview.* 1931. Harper. 1st. F/VG+. M23. $50.00

MILLER, A.K. *Ordovician Cephalopod Fauna of Baffin Island.* 1954. Geological Soc of Am. 8vo. 234p. gilt cloth. P4. $65.00

MILLER, Albert G. *Fury & the Mustangs.* nd. Grosset Dunlap. pict brd. VG. O3. $10.00

MILLER, Anne Archbold. *Little Old Outlaws.* 1910. McClurg. 1st. ils HG Reed/WN Peoples. VG. M5. $85.00

MILLER, Arthur. *Enemy of the People.* 1951. Viking. 1st. sgn. VG/VG. R14. $90.00

MILLER, Arthur. *Situation Normal.* 1944. Reynal Hitchcock. 1st. sgn. NF/VG. R14. $225.00

MILLER, Arthur. *Timebends.* 1987. Grove. 1st. sgn. NF/NF. R14. $75.00

MILLER, Basil. *Ten Slaves Who Became Famous.* 1951. Zondervan. 1st. 71p. F/NF. B4. $85.00

MILLER, Charlotte. *50 Drawings of Canaletto From the Royal Lib Windsor Castle.* 1983. Johnson Rpt Co. 1/520. atlas folio. 44p+50 facsimile pl. A17. $350.00

MILLER, Daniel. *Early History of the Reformed Church in Pennsylvania.* 1906. self pub. 12mo. 280p. gilt cloth. G. H1. $30.00

MILLER, Debbie S. *Midnight Wilderness: Journeys in Alaska's Arctic...* 1990. SF. Sierra Club. 8vo. 238p. half cloth. P4. $20.00

MILLER, E.D. *Modern Polo.* 1902. London/NY. Hurst Blackett/Scribner. 2nd. G. O3. $25.00

MILLER, Edgar G. *American Antique Furniture.* 1966. Dover. 2 vol. rpt. VG. M17. $45.00

MILLER, F.T. *Photographic History of the Civil War.* 1910. 10 vol. 4to. orig cloth. VG. A4. $650.00

MILLER, F.T. *Photographic History of the Civil War.* 1912. NY. Review of Reviews. 10 vol. G/VG. B5. $300.00

MILLER, Gloria Bley. *Thousand Recipe Chinese Cookbook.* 1988. NY. Weathervane. M/dj. A16. $18.00

MILLER, H. *Old Red Sandstone; or, New Walks in Old Field...* (1878). NY. Carter. new enlarged. ils. 403p. VG. M12. $30.00

MILLER, Henry. *Crazy Cock.* 1991. Grove Weidenfeld. 1st. F/F. B35. $16.00

MILLER, Henry. *Dear, Dear Brenda.* 1986. Morrow. 1st. F/F. T11. $20.00

MILLER, Henry. *Moloch; or, This Gentile World.* 1992. Grove. 1st. F/F. B35. $16.00

MILLER, Henry. *Opus Pistorum.* 1983. Grove. 1st. F/F. D10. $45.00

MILLER, Henry. *Remember To Remember.* 1947. New Direcitons. 1st. F/F. D10. $250.00

MILLER, Henry. *Remember To Remember.* 1952. London. Grey Walls. 2nd Eng. yel brd. VG/dj. Q1. $50.00

MILLER, Henry. *Tropic of Cancer.* 1961. Grove. 1st thus. intro Karl Shapiro. VG/VG. R14. $40.00

MILLER, Henry. *Tropic of Capricorn.* 1964. Calder. 1st Eng. NF/VG. M19. $25.00

MILLER, Henry. *13 California Towns From the Original Drawings.* 1947. SF. BC of CA. 1/300. obl 4to. marbled brd/gray cloth. NF. R3. $150.00

MILLER, Janet. *Jungles Preferred.* 1931. Houghton Mifflin. 1st. 8vo. 321p. cloth. VG. W1. $9.00

MILLER, Joaquin. *True Bear Stories.* 1990. Rand McNally. ils. NF. M19. $65.00

MILLER, Judith. *Antiques Directory.* 1985. 4to. ils. NF/NF. S13. $25.00

MILLER, Lynn R. *Work Horse Handbook.* 1981. np. Mill Pr. 224p. VG. O3. $25.00

MILLER, Max. *Harbor of the Sun.* 1940. Doubleday Doran. 1st. VG. O4. $15.00

MILLER, Maxine Adams. *Bright Blue Beads. An American Family in Persia.* 1965. Caldwell. Caxton. 4th. 8vo. 11 pl. VG. W1. $12.00

MILLER, Merle. *On Being Different: What It Means To Be Homosexual.* 1971. Random. 1st. F/VG+. B4. $50.00

MILLER, Nolan. *Why I Am So Beat.* 1954. Putnam. 1st. F/NF. B4. $125.00

MILLER, Olive Beaupre. *Engines & Brass Bands.* 1933. Doubleday Doran. 1st. 376p. VG/dj. M20. $30.00

MILLER, Olive Beaupre. *Engines & Brass Bands.* 1933. Doubleday Doran. 376p. VG/G. A4. $20.00

MILLER, Olive Thorne. *Bird-Lover in the West.* 1894. Boston/NY. 1st. 277p. gr cloth. VG. S15. $30.00

MILLER, Ray. *Real Corvette, an Illustrated History...* 1975. Oceanside, CA. 1st. ils. 320p. VG/dj. B18. $35.00

MILLER, Ray. *V-8 Affair.* 1972. Avalon. Evergreen. ils. 303p. VG/dj. B18. $35.00

MILLER, Raymond C. *Kilowatts at Work: History of Detroit Edison Company.* 1957. Wayne. 467p. F/dj. A17. $20.00

MILLER, Richard Gordon. *History & Atlas of Fishes of the Antarctic Ocean.* 1993. Carson City. Foresta Inst Ocean/Mtn Studies. 792p. M/dj. P4. $95.00

MILLER, Richard L. *Truth About Big-Time Football.* 1953. Sloane. 1st. G+. P8. $17.50

MILLER, Robert Ryal. *For Science & National Glory.* 1968. Norman, OK. 1st. ils. VG/dj. K3. $35.00

MILLER, Samuel. *Dilemma of Modern Belief.* 1963. Harper. 1st. sgn. F/VG. B11. $18.00

MILLER, Samuel. *Notes on Hospital Practice: Phil & NY Hospitals.* 1881. Phil. 1st. 3 vol in 1. A13. $75.00

MILLER, Sue. *Family Pictures.* 1990. Harper Row. 1st. F/F. R14. $25.00

MILLER, Sue. *Family Pictures.* 1990. Harper Row. 1st. F/NF. B3. $20.00

MILLER, Sue. *Good Mother.* 1986. Harper Row. 1st. sgn. NF/NF. M22. $40.00

MILLER, Sue. *Inventing the Abbotts.* 1981. Harper Row. 1st. F/F. R14. $40.00

MILLER, Sue. *Inventing the Abbotts.* 1987. Harper Row. 1st. NF/dj. Q1. $35.00

MILLER, T. *Castles & the Crown.* 1963. NY. 1st. VG/VG. B5. $25.00

MILLER, Thomas W. *Chronic Man.* 1990. Madison, CT. International U. 2 vol. 8vo. blk cloth. VG/dj. G1. $65.00

MILLER, Walter M. *Canticle for Leibowitz.* 1960. Lippincott. VG/dj. M2. $50.00

MILLER, Warren H. *Camping Out.* (1918). NY. Doran. 1st. 322p. VG. H7. $15.00

MILLER & SNELL. *Why the West Was Wild, a Contemporary Look.* 1963. KS State Hist Soc. 1st. ils/pl/map. 685p. VG/dj. J2. $495.00

MILLET, Allan. *Semper Fidelis: History of the US Marine Corps.* 1982. NY. 782p. VG/VG. S16. $35.00

MILLETT, Kate. *Basement: Meditations on Human Sacrifice.* 1979. S&S. 1st. ils. VG/G. A25. $20.00

MILLETT, Kate. *Going to Iran.* 1982. GMG. 1st. ils. rem mk. VG/G. A25. $8.00

MILLHAUSER, Steven. *Barnum Museum.* 1990. Poseidon. 1st. F/F. R14. $35.00

MILLHAUSER, Steven. *Barnum Museum.* 1990. Poseidon. 1st. NF/dj. A24/B3. $25.00

MILLHAUSER, Steven. *Edwin Mullhouse.* 1972. Knopf. 1st. author's 1st book. F/NF. B2. $175.00

MILLHAUSER, Steven. *From the Realm of Morpheus.* 1986. Morrow. 1st. F/F. R14. $35.00

MILLHAUSER, Steven. *From the Realm of Morpheus.* 1986. Morrow. 1st. F/VG. B3. $20.00

MILLHAUSER, Steven. *In the Penny Arcade.* 1986. Knopf. 1st. author's 3rd book. F/F. D10. $50.00

MILLIGAN, David. *Color Book of Wine.* 1974. Octopus. 1st. F/F. W2. $20.00

MILLIKAN, Robert A. *Autobiography of Robert A Millikan.* 1950 (1950). Prentice Hall. 2nd. 8vo. 311p. G. K5. $40.00

MILLIKEN, R. *No Conceivable Injury.* 1986. Australia. Penguin. 1st. VG/wrp. K3. $20.00

MILLIN, Sarah Gertrude. *God's Stepchildren.* 1927. Grosset Dunlap. 1st thus/10th prt. 319p. VG. A25. $15.00

MILLIS, Walter. *Martial Spirit.* 1931. Cambridge. Literary Guild of Am. 8vo. 427p. gilt maroon cloth. T10. $25.00

MILLS, C. Wright. *Sociological Imagination.* 1959. Oxford. 1st. 234p. F/dj. H1. $22.50

MILLS, E.A. *Watched by Wild Animals.* 1922. Doubleday. ils W James. 243p. cloth. VG+. M12. $30.00

MILLS, J.V.G. *Ying-Yai Sheng-Lan: Overall Surveys of Ocean Shores.* 1970. Cambridge. ils/maps. 393p. F/dj. M4. $25.00

MILLS, William Stowell. *Story of the Western Reserve of Connecticut.* 1900. NY. 1st. 134p. VG. B18. $37.50

MILNE, A.A. *Chloe-Mar.* 1946. 1st. VG/VG. S13. $40.00

MILNE, A.A. *Christopher Robin Verses.* 1932. Dutton. stated 1st. ils Ernest Shepard. gilt bl cloth. G. M5. $65.00

MILNE, A.A. *Christopher Robin Verses.* 1932. Dutton. 1st. VG+. T10. $100.00

MILNE, A.A. *Enchanted Places.* 1975. Dutton. 1st Am. 169p. F/G. M5. $75.00

MILNE, A.A. *House at Pooh Corner.* 1928. London. Methuen. 1st. F/VG+. B4. $500.00

MILNE, A.A. *House at Pooh Corner.* 1928. Methuen. 1st. gilt pink silk. VG. M5. $135.00

MILNE, A.A. *House at Pooh Corner.* 1928. Methuen. 1/350. sgn Milne/Shepard. 4to. bl cloth/wht brd/label. dj. F5. $3,000.00

MILNE, A.A. *Now We Are Six.* 1927. London. Methuen. 1st Eng. ils Ernest Shepard. teg. maroon cloth. dj. D1. $350.00

MILNE, A.A. *Now We Are Six.* 1927. London. Methuen. 1st. ils EH Shepard. orig gilt red cloth. F. B14. $250.00

MILNE, A.A. *Now We Are Six.* 1927. London. Methuen. 1st. ils/sgn/dtd Shepard. Bayntum Riviere bdg. F. B24. $1,350.00

MILNE, A.A. *Now We Are Six.* 1927. London. Methuen. 1st. 103p. VG+/VG. P2. $600.00

MILNE, A.A. *Winnie the Pooh/House at Pooh Corner (titled in Russian).* 1965. Moscow. 1st thus. ils Diodorov/Kalinovskiy. 8vo. gilt wheat cloth. dj. R5. $125.00

MILNE, Caleb. *I Dream of the Day...: Letters From Caleb Milne...* 1945. Longman. 1st. intro Marjorie Kinnan Rawlings. F/clip. B4. $100.00

MILORADOVICH, Milo. *Art of Fish Cookery.* 1949. Doubleday. 1st. 457p. G-. B10. $10.00

MILSOM, S.F.C. *Historical Foundations of the Common Law.* 1969. London. Butterworths. 1st. M11. $125.00

MILSOM, S.F.C. *Legal Framework of English Feudalism.* 1976. Cambridge. M11. $125.00

MILSOM, S.F.C. *Studies in History of Common Law.* 1985. London. Hambledon. M11. $45.00

MILTON, John. *Complete Poetical Works...* 1899. Boston. 8vo. 417p. teg. 3-quarter leather. VG. H3. $45.00

MILTON, John. *Comus.* 1921. London. Heinemann. 1st. 1/550. ils/sgn Rackham. teg. VG. B24. $950.00

MILTON, John. *Histoire Entiere & Veritable Dv Procez de Charles Stuart...* 1650. London. JG. 4to. full calf. gilt bdg. R12. $750.00

MILTON, John. *L'Allegro & Il Penseroso.* 1954. NY. LEC. 1st thus. 1/1780. ils Wm Blake. F/glassine/case. Q1. $150.00

MILTON, John. *Masque of Comus.* 1954. Cambridge. LEC. 1st thus. 1/1500. ils Edmund Dulac. F/case. Q1. $175.00

MILTON, John. *Paradise Lost.* 1905. London/NY. Routledge. ils Wm Strang. VG. B5. $60.00

MILTON, Nancy. *Giraffe That Walked to Paris.* 1992. Crown. 1st. obl 4to. unp. NF/F. T5. $24.00

MINAMIKI, George. *Chinese Rites Controversy: From Beginnings to Modern Times.* 1985. Loyola. 1st. 353p. F/F. W3. $40.00

MINAMOTO, Toyomune. *Daitokuji.* 1958. Tokyo. 1st. Japanese text. ils Sakamoto. 205p. F/NF. W3. $125.00

MINER, Earl. *Intro to Japanese Court Poetry.* 1968. Stanford. notes/glossary. 173p. F/F. W3. $58.00

MINER, Ellis D. *Uranus: The Planet, Rings & Satellites.* 1990. NY. Ellis Horwood. 334p. VG. K5. $25.00

MINER, V. Alchech. *From My Grandmother's Kitchen, a Sephardic Cookbook.* 1984. photos. sc. VG. E6. $18.00

MINGUS, Charles. *Beneath the Underdog.* 1971. Knopf. 1st. F/NF. B2. $50.00

MINGUS, Charles. *Beneath the Underdog.* 1971. Knopf. 1st. NF/dj. M25. $45.00

MINKOFF, George. *Bibliography of the Black Sun Press.* 1970. Great Neck. self pub. 1st. F/sans. B2. $75.00

MINNEY, R. *Next Stop-Peking: Record of a 16,000-Mile Journey...* 1957. London. 1st. ils/photos. 192p. VG/VG. W3. $36.00

MINNICH, J.W. *Inside Rock Island Prison From December 1863 to June 1865.* 1908. Nashville. ME Church. 1st. 59p. NF/prt wrp. M8. $350.00

MINNICK, Sylvia Sun. *Samfow: San Goaquin Chinese Legacy.* 1988. Fresno. panorama W Pub. 4to. sgn. gilt red cloth. F/dj. R3. $30.00

MINNIGH, L.W. *Gettysburg, What They Did Here.* 1924. Gettysburg. NA Meligakes. w/map. A19. $50.00

MINOT, Susan. *Lust & Other Stories.* 1989. Houghton Mifflin. 1st. NF/F. A20. $25.00

MINOT, Susan. *Lust & Other Stories.* 1989. Houghton Mifflin. 1st. sgn. F/F. R14. $40.00

MINTON & MINTON. *Venomous Reptiles.* 1969. Scribner. 275p. NF/VG. S15. $30.00

MINTZ, M. *Martial Arts Films.* 1978. NY. ils/index/notes. 243p. F/VG. W3. $36.00

MIRABEAU. *Considerations sur l'Ordre de Cincinnatus/Memoire.* 1784. London/np. 2 works in 1. tall 8vo. calf. R12. $750.00

MIRABEAU. *Plan de Division du Royaume.* 1798. Paris. Baudouin. 8vo. wrp. R12. $225.00

MIRABEAU. *Sur La Liberte de La Presse, Imite De L'Anglois, De Milton.* 1789. London. unrecorded 2nd. 8vo. stitched. R12. $650.00

MIRALLIE, Charles. *De l'Aphasie Sensorielle.* 1896. Paris. Steinheil. 220p. ils/woodcuts. contemporary brd. xl. VG. G1. $125.00

MIRBEAU, Ken; see Wiess, Joe.

MIRICK, B.L. *History of Haverhill, Massachusetts.* 1832. Haverhill. AW Thayer. 1st. quarter purple muslin/tan brd. M24. $450.00

MIRO, Joan. *Quelques Fleurs Pour des Amis.* 1964. Paris. 1/150. sgn/#d. folio. loose portfolio/wrp/clamshell box/mailer. C6. $2,800.00

MIRSKY, Jeannette. *Elisha Kent Kane & the Seafaring Frontier.* 1954. Little Brn. 1st. 201p. dj. T7. $18.00

MIRSKY, Jeannette. *Western Crossings.* 1946. Balboa Mackenzie. 1st. ils. 365p+13p index. VG+/dj. B18. $22.50

MIRSKY & NIVENS. *World of Eli Whitney.* 1952. Macmillan. 1st. 346p. F/dj. H1. $17.50

MISHIMA, Sumie Seo. *Broader Way: A Woman's Life in New Japan.* 1953. John Day. 1st. 247p. VG/dj. A25. $22.00

MISHIMA, Yukio. *Confessions of a Mask.* 1958. NY. New Directions. 1st. NF/VG. A24. $85.00

MISHIMA, Yukio. *Five Moderns No Plays.* 1957. NY. Knopf. 1st Am. trans from Japanese. F/clip. Q1. $75.00

MISHIMA, Yukio. *Runaway Horses.* 1973. Knopf. 1st Am. trans from Japanese. F/dj. Q1. $50.00

MISHIMA, Yukio. *Temple of the Golden Pavilion.* 1959. Knopf. 1st. ils Fumi Komatsu. F/dj. Q1. $75.00

MISKELLA, William. *Practical Japanning & Enameling.* 1928. Chicago. 256p. A17. $30.00

MISS READ; see Stuart, Dora Jessie.

MISTH, Mary Stuart. *Virginia Cookery-Book.* 1885 (1884). Harper. 352p. orig cloth over modern buckram/new ep. B10. $150.00

MISTRY, Rohanton. *Swimming Lessons.* 1987. Houghton Mifflin. 1st. NF/NF. A20. $30.00

MITCHEL, John. *Jail Journal.* 1913. Dublin. MH Hill. VG+. B2. $150.00

MITCHELL, C. Bradford. *Touching the Adventures & Perils...* 1970. NY. Am Hull Insurance. ils. 234p. dj. T7. $25.00

MITCHELL, David. *Pirates.* 1976. NY. Dial. 1st. ils/index/bibliography. 208p. VG/dj. P4. $25.00

MITCHELL, Don. *Thumb Tripping.* 1970. Little Brn. 1st. F/VG. B4. $85.00

MITCHELL, Ehrman B. *Ponies for Young People.* 1960. Van Nostrand. 1st. VG/VG. O3. $15.00

MITCHELL, Ethelyn. *Nip & Tuck at Play.* 1938. Lyons & Carnaha. 46p. VG/wrp. M20. $12.00

MITCHELL, George. *Little Babs.* 1919. Volland. 1st. ils Arthur Henderson. 12mo. pict brd. pub box. R5. $200.00

MITCHELL, J. Leslie. *Cairo Dawns.* 1931. Bobbs Merrill. 1st Am. VG. M2. $30.00

MITCHELL, Jan. *Cooking a la Longchamps.* 1964. Doubleday. 1st. G/dj. A16. $20.00

MITCHELL, Joseph. *Old Mr Flood.* 1948. DSP. 1st. inscr/dtd 1948. F/VG. B4. $650.00

MITCHELL, Joseph. *Up in the Old Hotel & Other Stories.* 1992. Pantheon. 1st. F/F clip. B4. $55.00

MITCHELL, Juliet. *Psychoanalysis & Feminism.* 1974. NY. Pantheon. 1st. F/VG. B2. $30.00

MITCHELL, Lebbeus. *Bobby in Search of a Birthday.* 1916. Volland. 1st. ils Joseph Pierre Nuyttens. VG. T5. $45.00

MITCHELL, Mairin. *Elcano: First Circumnavigator.* 1958. London. Herder. as new. O7. $35.00

MITCHELL, Margaret. *Gone With the Wind.* 1936. Macmillan. VG. W2. $1,250.00

MITCHELL, Richard. *Thought Control in Pre-War Japan.* 1976. Cornell. 226p. F/dj. W3. $36.00

MITCHELL, S.A. *Eclipses of the Sun.* 1932 (1923). NY. Columbia. 3rd. G/dj. K5. $80.00

MITCHELL, Silas Weir. *Fat & Blood: How To Make Them.* 1879. Lippincott. 2nd revised. 12mo. flexible panelled mauve cloth. G. G1. $185.00

MITCHELL, Silas Weir. *Injuries of Nerves & Their Consequences.* 1872. Phil. 1st. 377p. A13. $600.00

MITCHELL, Silas Weir. *Injuries of Nerves & Their Consequences.* 1983 (1872). Birmingham. Classics Neurology/Neurosurgery. facsimile. G1. $75.00

MITCHELL-HODGES, F.A. *Danger My Ally.* 1954. London. Elek Books. 1st. 255p. dj. F3. $35.00

MITCHENER, C.H. *Ohio Annals.* 1876. Dayton. 358p. G-. B18. $95.00

MITCHUM, S.W. Jr. *Romme's Last Battle.* 1983. NY. 1st. ils. 212p. VG/VG. S16. $22.50

MITFORD, Jessica. *American Way of Death.* 1963. NY. S&S. 1st. F/NF. M24. $65.00

MITSCHERLICH. *Doctors of Infamy: Story of Nazi Medical Crimes.* 1949. Schuman. 172p+16p photos. G. A17. $20.00

MITTEN, Homer H. *Enchanted Canyon Fairy Story.* 1932. LA. Suttonhouse. ltd. 1/400. sgn pres. ils/sgn Eulalie. gilt gr cloth. R5. $350.00

MIX, Tom. *West of Yesterday.* 1923. Times-Mirror Pr. 1st. 162p. VG. J2. $185.00

MIYOSHI, Masao. *As We Saw Them: First Japanese Embassy to the United States.* 1979. Berkeley. 1st. ils. wht cloth brd/bl cloth spine. F. R3. $25.00

MIZWA, Stephen P. *Nicholas Copernicus, 1543-1943.* 1969. Port WA. Kennikat. reissue. ils. VG. K3. $20.00

MIZWA, Stephen P. *Nicholas Copernicus: A Tribute of Nations.* 1945. NY. Kosciuszko Found. ils. VG/dj. K3. $25.00

MO, Timothy. *An Insular Possession.* 1986. Chatto Windus. 1st. F/clip. A24. $40.00

MO, Timothy. *Monkey King.* 1986. Morrow. 1st Am. NF/NF. M23. $35.00

MO, Timothy. *Redundancy of Courage.* 1991. Chatto Windus. 1st Eng. VG/G. A20. $30.00

MO, Timothy. *Redundancy of Courage.* 1991. Chatto Windus. 1st. F/dj. A24. $35.00

MOCHI, Ugo. *Hoofed Mammals of the World.* 1953. Scribner. folio. 40 pl. cloth brd. F. B24. $375.00

MOERMAN, Daniel E. *American Medical Ethnobotany.* 1977. NY. Garland. 527p. xl. A10. $45.00

MOFFAT, James. *Theology of the Gospels.* 1913. Scribner. 220p. VG. B29. $7.50

MOFFAT, Robert U. *John Smitt Moffat CMG Missionary: A Memoir.* 1969 (1921). Negro U. rpt. 8vo. 8 pl/1 map. 388p. VG. W1. $25.00

MOFFETT, Cleveland. *Possessed.* 1920. McCann. 1st. G+. M2. $27.00

MOHAMMAD REZA PAHLAVI, Shah. *Answer to History: Shah of Iran.* 1980. Stein Day. 1st. 8vo. 204p. NF/dj. W1. $16.00

MOHLENBROCK & VOIGT. *Flora of Southern Illinois.* 1959. Carbondale. 390p. dj. A10. $24.00

MOHR, John H. *Medical Guide in Treating All Internal & External Diseases.* 1868. Reading, PA. Owens Steam Pr. 16mo. 262p. G. O3. $125.00

MOHR & ROTH. *Timber Pines of the Southern United States.* 1897 (1896). WA, DC. revised. 176p. new buckram. B26. $75.00

MOJTABAI, A.G. *Stopping Place.* 1979. S&S. 1st. 349p. F/F. W2. $30.00

MOKLER, Alfred James. *Ft Casper, Comprising a Description of Killing Lt Collins...* 1939. Prairie. 1st. 74p. VG/pict wrp. J2. $115.00

MOKLER, Alfred James. *Transition of the West: Portrayal of Indian Problem...* 1927. Lakeside. is. 228p. cloth. D11. $125.00

MOLESWORTH & MOSELEY. *Wing to Wing, Air Combat in China 1943-45.* 1990. NY. 1st. 207p. VG/dj. B18. $32.50

MOLEY, Raymond. *American Century of John C Lincoln.* 1962. Duell Sloan. 1st. sgn. 209p. VG/VG. B11. $25.00

MOLFINO, Francesco. *Fisiopatologia Della Ghiandola Pineale.* 1935. Roma. Luigi Pozzi. 132p. VG/stiff tan wrp. G1. $50.00

MOLIERE. *Tartuffe.* 1930. NY. LEC. 1/1500. sgn/#d. VG/case. B11. $55.00

MOLLEMA, J.C. *De Nederlandsche Vlag op de Wereldzeen...* 1930s. Amsterdam. Scheltens Giltay. ils/maps. NF. O7. $125.00

MOLLISON, P.L. *Blood Transfusion in Clinical Medicine.* 1851. Oxford. 1st. 456p. A13. $35.00

MOLLO, Andrew. *Armed Forces of World War II: Uniforms, Insignia...* 1981. NY. photos/pl/table of ranks/index. 312p. VG/VG. S16. $40.00

MOLLO, Victor. *Bridge in the Menagerie.* 1967. NY. 1st Am. 152p. VG/dj. S1. $8.00

MOLLOY, Hercules. *Oedipus in Disneyland.* 1972. 1st. ils. VG. S13. $18.00

MOLLOY, Robert. *Medical Electrical Equipment: Principles, Installation...* 1958. NY. 1st. 312p. A13. $75.00

MOLONEY, Alfred. *CMG: Sketch of the Forestry of West Africa.* 1887. Sampson Low Marston. 527p. gr cloth. VG. M20. $25.00

MOLONY, E. *Portrait of Rivers: Itchen, Trent, Crouch, Wye, Ouse, Avon.* nd. London. Dobson. ils/photos. 139p. NF/F. M12. $15.00

MOLTMANN, Jurgen. *Gospel of Liberation.* 1974. Word. 136p. VG/dj. B29. $9.50

MOMADAY, Natachee Scott. *Ancient Child.* 1989. Doubleday. ARC. sgn. author's 2nd novel. F/F. D10. $55.00

MOMADAY, Natachee Scott. *Colorado.* 1973. Chicago. Rand McNally. 1st. folio. photos David Muench. F/VG. L3. $100.00

MOMADAY, Natachee Scott. *Gourd Dancer.* 1976. Harper Row. 1st. F/NF. L3. $100.00

MOMADAY, Natachee Scott. *House Made of Dawn.* 1968. Harper Row. 1st. F/NF. L3. $350.00

MOMADAY, Natachee Scott. *Owl in the Cedar Tree.* 1965. np. Ginn. 1st. F. L3. $125.00

MOMADAY, Natachee Scott. *Way to Rainy Mountain.* 1969. Albuquerque. NM U. 1st. F/F. L3. $200.00

MONACHAN, John; see Burnett, W.R.

MONAGHAN, Frank. *French Travellers in the United States 1765-1932.* 1961. NY. Antiquarian. 1/750. ils. F. O7. $55.00

MONAGHAN, Jay. *Book of the American West.* 1969. S&S. new prt. 608p+reading list. F/VG dj. A17. $27.50

MONAGHAN. *Common Heritage, Noah Webster's Blue-Black Speller.* 1983. 304p. F. A4. $35.00

MONDEY, David. *Rockets & Missiles.* 1971. Grosset Dunlap. 1st Am. 4to. 75p. VG. K5. $12.00

MONES & MULL. *Independent Oilman: From Spivey-Grabs to Cheyenne Wells...* 1982. Wichita, KS. 291p. cloth. as new/dj. D8. $25.00

MONETTE, Paul. *Borrowed Time: An Aids Memoir.* 1988. HBJ. 1st. rem mk. NF/F. R14. $25.00

MONRO, Edward. *Sacred Allegories.* 1888. London. Mastes. thick 8vo. full calf. F. T10. $75.00

MONROE, Harriet. *Valeria & Other Poems.* 1892. Chicago. McClurg. trade ed. author's 1st book. VG+. B2. $125.00

MONSARRAT, Nicholas. *East Coast Corvette.* 1943. Lippincott. 1st. 153p. dj. T7. $15.00

MONSON, William. *Sir William Monson's Naval Tracts: In Six Books...* 1703. London. Churchill. folio. modern cloth. P4. $600.00

MONTAGNE, Prosper. *New Larousse Gastronomique.* 1983. London. Hamlyn. VG/dj. A16. $35.00

MONTAGU, Mary Worley. *Works...Including Correspondence, Poems & Essays.* 1803. London. R Phillips. 1st. ils. teg. 3-quarter calf/linen brd. G. H13. $295.00

MONTAGU. *Essay on Writings & Genius of Shakespeare.* 1770. London. Hughs. 8vo. 3-quarter calf. R12. $125.00

MONTAGUE, Richard. *Oceans, Poles & Airman.* 1971. Random. 1st. 307p. G+/dj. B18. $15.00

MONTANA, Joe. *Audibles.* 1986. Morrow. 1st. F/F. P8. $15.00

MONTECINO, Marcel. *Big Time.* 1990. Morrow. 1st. F/F. H11. $30.00

MONTECINO, Marcel. *Crosskiller.* 1988. Arbor. 1st. author's 1st novel. F/F. D10. $65.00

MONTECINO, Marcel. *Crosskiller.* 1988. Arbor. 1st. sgn. author's 1st book. F/F. H11. $140.00

MONTEITH, James. *Manual of Geography.* 1868. BArnes. sm 4to. ils/maps. 124p. G+. H1. $20.00

MONTESQUIEU, C. *Considerations Sur les Causes de la Grandeur Romains.* 1755. Paris. A15. $30.00

MONTESQUIEU. *Reflections on Causes of Grandeur & Declension of Romans.* 1734. London. Innys Manby. 8vo. calf. R12. $750.00

MONTGOMERY, Bernard L. *Eighth Army: El Alamein to River Sangro.* 1946. Berlin. 1/100 pres to US Army. fld maps. 158p. VG/VG. S16. $125.00

MONTGOMERY, Elizabeth Rider. *Three Miles an Hour.* 1952. Dodd Mead. 2nd. 245p. VG/dj. A25. $15.00

MONTGOMERY, Elizabeth. *Land Divided.* 1938. London. Hutchinson. 1st. 2 full-p maps. 288p. VG. W1. $12.00

MONTGOMERY, Field Marshal V. *Normandy to the Baltic List Army Group.* 1948. Boston. 1st. maps. 351p. VG/G. B5. $45.00

MONTGOMERY, Frances Trego. *Billy Whiskers in the South.* 1917. Saalfield. ils Will Fitzgerald. 4to. gr cloth. R5. $135.00

MONTGOMERY, Frances Trego. *On a Lark to the Planets.* 1922. Akron. 186p. pict yel bdg. VG. B14. $45.00

MONTGOMERY, L.M. *Anne of Avonlea.* 1909. Page. 3rd imp (same month as 1st). gilt cloth/mc pl. VG. M5. $65.00

MONTGOMERY, L.M. *Anne of Green Gables.* 1935 (1908). Grosset Dunlap. pre-1963 prt. lg 12mo. VG/dj. C8. $25.00

MONTGOMERY, L.M. *Anne's House of Dreams.* 1917. 1st. VG. M17. $50.00

MONTGOMERY, L.M. *Chronicles of Avonlea.* 1912. Page. 2nd imp. gilt cloth/mc pl. VG. M5. $60.00

MONTGOMERY, L.M. *Emily of New Moon.* 1934. Toronto. 1st. xl. NF/G. T12. $40.00

MONTGOMERY, L.M. *Tangled Web.* 1931. McClelland Stewart. 324p. VG+/dj. M20. $15.00

MONTGOMERY, Rutherford. *Capture of the Golden Stallion.* nd. Grosset Dunlap. Famous Horse Stories series. VG. O3. $12.00

MONTGOMERY, Rutherford. *Golden Stallion & the Wolf Dog.* nd. Grosset Dunlap. Famous Horse Stories series. VG. O3. $15.00

MONTGOMERY, Rutherford. *High Country.* (1938). Derrydale. rpt/ltd. photos. leather. VG. M17. $25.00

MONTGOMERY, Rutherford. *Tom Pittman USAF.* 1957. DSP. 1st. 152p. VG/dj. M20. $20.00

MONTHAN & MONTHAN. *Art & Indian Individualists: Art of 17 Contemporary...* 1975. Northland. 1st. ils. 198p. cloth. dj. D11. $100.00

MONZERT, L. *Independent Liquorist or Art of Preparing Cordials...* 1866. VG. E6. $75.00

MOODEY, Marion McCook. *Here Comes the Peddler.* nd (1947). Holiday. sm 4to. unp. F/VG+. C14. $14.00

MOODIE, Susanna. *Roughing It in the Bush.* Oct 1938. London. Thomas Nelson. A19. $45.00

MOODIE, William. *Old English, Scotch & Irish Songs, With Music.* ca 1900. Glasgow. Bryce. Mite series. 31x22mm. 127p. aeg. Zaehnsdorf bdg. B24. $350.00

MOODY, Ralph. *Stagecoach West.* 1967. Crowell. 1st. VG. O3. $35.00

MOODY, Ralph. *Stagecoach West.* 1967. Crowell. 1st. 341p. as new/dj. H1. $45.00

MOON, Marjorie. *Children's Books of Mary (Belson) Elliott, a Biography.* 1987. 30 pl. 172p. F/F. A4. $95.00

MOON & MOON. *One Little Indian.* 1950. Whitman. 1st. sm 4to. VG/dj. M5. $60.00

MOONEY, James. *Ghost-Dance Religion & the Sioux Outbreak of 1890.* 1973. Rio Grande Classic. rpt. ils/maps/figures. VG. M4. $45.00

MOONEY, James. *Historical Sketch of the Cherokee.* 1975. Chicago. Adeline. ils. 265p. cloth. D11. $35.00

MOONEY & OLBRECHTS. *Swimmer Manuscript: Cherokee Sacred Formulas...* 1932. WA. BAE. ils. 319p. prt wrp. D11. $30.00

MOONEY & SHIPTON. *National Index of American Imprints Through 1800.* 1969. Am Antiquarian Soc. 2 vol. 1028p. F. A4. $200.00

MOORCOCK, Michael. *Cure for Cancer.* 1971. Holt. 1st. F/dj. M2. $30.00

MOORCOCK, Michael. *Land Leviathan.* 1974. Doubleday. 1st Am. F/dj. M2. $30.00

MOORE, Alexander. *Life Cycles in Atchalan.* 1973. NY. Teachers College. 1st. 220p. wrp. F3. $15.00

MOORE, Anne Carroll. *Art of Beatrix Potter.* (1955). London. Warne. ils. F/dj. B15. $75.00

MOORE, Anne Carroll. *Century of Kate Greenaway.* 1946. NY/London. ils Kate Greenaway. VG/glassine dj/wrp. D1. $85.00

MOORE, Anne Carroll. *My Roads to Childhood, Views & Reviews...* 1939. 399p. VG/VG. A4. $55.00

MOORE, Anne Carroll. *Roads to Childhood.* 1920. Doran. probable 1st. narrow 8vo. brn brd. VG. T5. $55.00

MOORE, Bernard. *Wines of North America.* 1983. Chartwell. 1st Am. 192p. VG/VG. B10. $35.00

MOORE, Brian. *Answer From Limbo.* 1962. Little Brn. 1st. sgn. NF/clip. Q1. $150.00

MOORE, Brian. *Black Robe.* 1985. Dutton. 1st. F/F. H11. $45.00

MOORE, Brian. *Catholics.* 1972. McClelland Stewart. UP/1st Canadian. NF/wrp. D10. $75.00

MOORE, Brian. *Catholics.* 1973. HRW. 1st. F/F. B35. $45.00

MOORE, Brian. *Emperor of Ice-Cream.* 1965. McClelland Stewart. 1st. NF/NF. P3. $25.00

MOORE, Brian. *Emperor of Ice-Cream.* 1965. Viking. 1st. VG/dj. M25. $35.00

MOORE, Brian. *Feast of Lupercal.* 1957. Little Brn. 1st. NF/NF. B35. $65.00

MOORE, Brian. *I Am Mary Dunne.* 1968. Toronto. McClelland Stuart. 1st Canadian. sgn. F/clip. Q1. $150.00

MOORE, Brian. *Lies of Silence.* 1990. London. 1st. sgn. VG/VG. T9. $45.00

MOORE, Brian. *Lies of Silence.* 1990. London. Bloomsbury. 1st. sgn. F/F. D10. $50.00

MOORE, Brian. *Lies of Silence.* 1990. London. Bloomsbury. 1st. 1/150. sgn/#d. marbled brd/gilt spine. F/glassine. Q1. $125.00

MOORE, Brian. *Lonely Passion of Judith Hearne.* 1956. Atlantic/Little Brn. ARC/1st Am. RS. F/dj. D10. $225.00

MOORE, Brian. *Luck of Ginger Coffey.* 1960. Atlantic/Little Brn. 1st. NF/dj. M25. $45.00

MOORE, Brian. *Revolution Script.* 1970. HRW. 1st. NF/dj. M25. $50.00

MOORE, Brian. *Revolution Script.* 1971. HRW. 1st. inscr. F/dj. Q1. $100.00

MOORE, Brian. *Temptation of Eileen Hughes.* 1981. Toronto. McClelland Stewart. 1st Canadian. sgn. F/dj. Q1. $75.00

MOORE, Christopher. *Practical Demon-Keeping.* 1992. St Martin. 1st. sgn. author's 1st book. F/dj. A24. $40.00

MOORE, Clement C. *Night Before Christmas.* 1935. Platt Munk. 28 full-p ils. gr cloth. G. B14. $25.00

MOORE, Clement C. *Night Before Christmas.* 1942. Phil. Winston. 1st thus. 4to. dj. R5. $85.00

MOORE, Clement C. *Night Before Christmas.* 1954. Garden City. 1st. ils Roger Duvoisin, pict brd. dj. R5. $100.00

MOORE, Clement C. *Night Before Christmas, or A Visit of St. Nicholas.* 1899 (1896). McLoughlin. prt on linen. VG. M5. $145.00

MOORE, Donald J. *Martin Buber: Prophet of Religious Secularism.* 1974. JPS. biblio. 264p. VG/dj. S3. $24.00

MOORE, Edward C. *Outline of th History of Christian Thought Since Kant.* 1912. Scribner. 249p. VG. B29. $10.00

MOORE, Edward. *Fables for the Female Sex.* 1771. London. Davies Dodsley. 4th. tall 8vo. 173p. contemporary tree calf. H13. $295.00

MOORE, Elaine T. *Winning Your Spurs.* 1954. Little Brn. 1st. VG/fair. O3. $25.00

MOORE, Evelyn. *Sancocho.* 1947. Panama. Star & Herald. 2nd. 214p. pict cloth. F3. $25.00

MOORE, Frank. *Women of the War: Their Heroism & Self-Sacrifice.* 1866. Hartford. Scranton. 1st. 596p. cloth. M8. $85.00

MOORE, George. *Brook Kerith. A Syrian Story.* 1929. Macmillan. 1st thus. 1/500. sgn. ils/sgn Stephen Gooden. F/case. B24. $200.00

MOORE, George. *Sister Teresa.* 1901. London. Fisher Unwin. 1st. teg. gr cloth. untrimmed. F. M24. $35.00

MOORE, Harry T. *Intelligent Heart.* 1954. NY. 1st. VG/VG. T9. $40.00

MOORE, Isabel. *Talks in a Library With Laurence Hutton.* 1909. NY. 458p. VG. A17. $12.50

MOORE, John Hamilton. *New Practical Navigator...* 1800. Newburyport. Edmund M Blunt. 2nd. 8vo. 570p. VG. M1. $550.00

MOORE, John W. *Roster of North Carolina Troops in Civil War.* 1882. Raleigh. 4 vol. 1st. Vol 1-3 in modern buckram. C6. $200.00

MOORE, John William. *Notes on Raiatean Flowering Plants.* 1963. Honolulu. tall 8vo. VG/wrp. A22. $20.00

MOORE, John. *Incian Paul.* 1945. Harcourt Brace. 1st. F/NF. B4. $100.00

MOORE, Lorrie. *Anagrams.* 1986. Knopf. 1st. author's 1st novel. NF/dj. A24. $50.00

MOORE, Lorrie. *Self-Help.* 1985. Knopf. 1st. author's 1st book. F/F. D10. $160.00

MOORE, Margaret. *Dangerous Conceits.* 1989. Walker. 1st Am. as new/dj. N4. $20.00

MOORE, Marianne. *Like a Bulwark.* 1957. London. Faber. 1st. F/dj. Q1. $75.00

MOORE, Marianne. *Marianne Moore Reader.* 1961. Viking. 1st. F/NF. A24. $30.00

MOORE, Marianne. *Nevertheless.* 1944. NY. 1st. VG/G. B5. $100.00

MOORE, Marianne. *Occasionem Cognosce.* 1963. Lunenburg. Stinehour. 1/175. stn/#d. F/sewn wrp. B2. $250.00

MOORE, N. Hudson. *Collector's Manual.* 1935 (1905). Tudor. 329p. VG+/dj/case. M20. $60.00

MOORE, N. Hudson. *Old China Book.* 1935 (1903). Tudor. 300p. cloth. VG/ragged. M20. $20.00

MOORE, N. Hudson. *Old Glass: European & American.* 1935 (1924). Tudor. 394p. cloth. VG+/torn dj/case. M20. $40.00

MOORE, N. Hudson. *Old Pewter, Brass, Copper & Sheffield Plate.* 1905. Stokes. 1st. 229p. cloth/pict label. VG+. M20. $35.00

MOORE, Nancy. *Unhappy Hippotamus.* 1957. Vanguard. 1st. ils Edward Leight. 4to. VG/G+. P2. $30.00

MOORE, Patrick. *Return of Halley's Comet.* 1984. Norton. 1st. F. T12. $15.00

MOORE, Robin. *Country Team.* 1967. NY. Crown. 1st. inscr/dtd 1967. F/VG. B4. $200.00

MOORE, Robin. *French Connection.* 1969. Little Brn. 1st. F/VG. M19. $25.00

MOORE, Robin. *Green Berets.* 1965. NY. Crown. 1st. inscr/dtd 1978. NF/VG+ clip. B4. $275.00

MOORE, Ruth. *Earth We Live On, Story of Geological Discovery.* 1956. Knopf. 416p. D8. $14.50

MOORE, Ruth. *Niels Bohr, the Man, His Science & the World They Changed.* 1966. NY. Knopf. 1st. VG/dj. K3. $20.00

MOORE, Susanna. *My Old Sweetheart.* 1982. Houghton Mifflin. 1st. author's 1st book. F/F. D10. $75.00

MOORE, Susanna. *Sleeping Beauties.* 1993. Knopf. 1st. F/dj. Q1. $25.00

MOORE, Susanna. *Sleeping Beauties.* 1993. Knopf. 1st. sgn. author's 3rd novel. F/F. D10. $35.00

MOORE, Susanna. *Whiteness of Bones.* 1989. NY. Doubleday. 1st. F/NF. B4. $50.00

MOORE, Thomas Jr. *Sky Is My Witness.* 1943. NY. 135p. VG. S16. $60.00

MOORE, Ward. *Bring the Jubilee.* 1955. Heinemann. 1st. VG/dj. M2. $30.00

MOORE. *Checklist of Writings of Daniel DeFoe.* 1971. revised. 299p. F. A4. $65.00

MOOREHEAD, A. *Darwin & the Beagle.* 1969. Harper Row. 1st/5th imp. ils. F/NF. D8. $25.00

MOOREHEAD, Alan. *Fatal Impact.* 1966. Harper Row. 1st. 230p. VG+/dj. M20. $18.00

MOOREHEAD, Alan. *Traitors.* 1952. Hamish Hamilton. 1st. ils. VG/dj. K3. $30.00

MOORHOUSE, Geoffrey. *Fearful Void.* 1974. Lippincott. 1st. 8vo. 20 pl/2 full-p maps. 288p. NF/dj. W1. $18.00

MORA, J. *Californios.* 1949. Doubleday. dj. A19. $35.00

MORA, J. *Trail Dust & Saddle Leather.* 1946. Scribner. A19. $40.00

MORAN, Jim. *US Marine Corps Uniforms & Equipment in WWII.* 1992. London. ils. 138p. VG/VG. S16. $40.00

MORAN DE BUTRON, Jacinto. *La Azucena de Quito.* 1732. Mexico. Imprenta Real Superior Govierno. woodcut. limp vellum. D11. $200.00

MORAND, Paul. *Champions du Monde.* 1930. Abbeville. Grasset. 1/56 on Rives. 4to. F/wrp/cloth case. T10. $90.00

MORAVIA, Alberto. *Five Novels.* 1955. FSG. 1st. F/VG. A20. $15.00

MORAVIA, Alberto. *Times of Desecration.* 1985. FSG. 1st. F/F. A20. $25.00

MORE, Cresacre. *Life of Sir Thomas More, ...By His Great Grandson.* 1726. London. Woodman Lyon. 8vo. engraved ftspc. calf/rebacked. R12. $375.00

MORE, Edward. *Utopia; or, A Philosphical Romance, in Two Books...* 1743. Glasgow. Robert Foulis. sm 4to. 139p. mottled calf/leather label. H13. $285.00

MOREAU, Georges. *Theorie des Moteurs a Gaz.* 1902. Paris. Beranger. 8vo. 224p. orig cloth. VG. K3. $90.00

MOREAU, Jeanne. *Jeanne Moreau.* 1989. Haga. Japanese text. photos. NF/dj. C9. $75.00

MORELOCK, J.D. *Army Times Book of Great Land Battles, From Civil War...* 1994. Berkley Books. 1st. 8vo. 311p. F/dj. T10. $25.00

MORENO, H.J. *Moreno's Cictionary of Spanish-Names California Cities...* 1916. San Luis Obispo. 1st. VG. O4. $25.00

MORES, Edward Rowe. *Dissertation Upon English Typographical Founders...* 1924. NY. Grolier. rpt. tall 8vo. full-/half-p pl. French marbled brd. R12. $350.00

MORETON, C. Oscar. *Old Carnations & Pinks.* 1955. London. Rainbird. 51p. dj. A10. $55.00

MOREY, Sheena. *Pat 'n' Penny.* 1946. Chicago. obl 4to. VG. M5. $30.00

MOREY, Walt. *Scrub Dog of Alaska.* 1971. NY. Dutton. 1st Am. inscr. 8vo. 212p. bl cloth. VG/dj. P4. $30.00

MORFIT, Campbell. *Chemical & Pharmaceutical Manipulations...* 1849. Phil. 482p. blk cloth. VG. B14. $200.00

MORGA, A.D. *Sucesos de las Filipinas.* 1971. Cambridge. edit/trans JS Cummins. ils. 347p. F/dj. M4. $20.00

MORGAN, A.T. *Yazoo; or, On the Picket Line of Freedom in the South.* 1884. WA, DC. self pub. 1st. 512p. ES. later cloth. VG. M8. $350.00

MORGAN, Al. *Cast of Characters.* 1957. Dutton. 1st. F/VG. M25. $25.00

MORGAN, Charles S. *Master in Sail & Steam.* 1981. Concord, MA. self pub. ils. 89p. wrp. T7. $12.00

MORGAN, Dale. *Great Salt Lake.* 1947. Indianapolis. 1st. sgn. VG/G+. B5. $65.00

MORGAN, Dale. *Jedeiah Smith & the Opening of the West.* 1953. Bobbs Merrill. 1st. 458p. VG/torn. J2. $285.00

MORGAN, David P. *Canadian Steam!* 1961. Kalmbach. 1st. unp. cloth. VG/dj. M20. $28.00

MORGAN, Elizabeth. *Making of a Woman Surgeon.* 1980. Putnam. 1st. photos. 368p. VG/dj. A25. $18.00

MORGAN, F.R. *Teddy Bear's House Underground.* 1908. Donohue. 12mo. mc pict brd. R5. $150.00

MORGAN, F.R. *Teddy Bears on Rollers & What Happened.* 1908. Donohue. 12mo. 16p. mc pict brd. R5. $150.00

MORGAN, G. Campbell. *Acts of the Apostles.* 1924. REvell. 547p. G. B29. $11.00

MORGAN, G. Campbell. *Analyzed Bible.* 1909. Revell. 477p. VG. B29. $9.50

MORGAN, G. Campbell. *Peter & the Church.* 1938. Revell. 96p. VG. B29. $7.50

MORGAN, George Hallenbrooke. *Annals, Comprising Memoirs, Incidents & Statistics...* 1858. Harrisburg. 1st/1st prt. 400p. EX. rebound. H1. $95.00

MORGAN, Janet. *Agatha Christie.* 1985. Knopf. 1st Am. NF. W2. $20.00

MORGAN, John Medford; see Fox, Gardner F.

MORGAN, L.H. *American Beaver & His Works.* 1868. Lippincott. 1st. 24 pl/fld map. 330p. B1. $235.00

MORGAN, Lael. *Woman's Guide to Boating & Cooking.* 1968. Freeport, ME. Bond Wheelwright. 1st. ils. 246p. VG/dj. A25. $12.00

MORGAN, Murry. *One Man's Gold Rush: A Klondike Album.* 1967. Seattle/London. 2nd. map 213p. VG/dj. P4. $35.00

MORGAN, Rod; see Fox, Gardner F.

MORGAN, Ruth. *Cooking for Compliments.* 1968. London. Hamlyn. VG/dj. A16. $10.00

MORGAN, Speer. *Whipping Boy.* 1994. Houghton Mifflin. 1st. sgn. F/F. A23. $40.00

MORGAN & STRICKLAND. *Arizona Memories.* 1984. Tucson. sgn pres. 354p. VG/VG. B11. $35.00

MORGAN. *Oxford Illustrated History of Britain.* 1987. ils. VG/VG. M17. $25.00

MORGENSTERN, Christian. *Three Sparrows & Other Nursery Poems.* 1968. Scribner. 1st. ils/sgn Nonny Hogrogian. trans Max Knight. F/NF. D4. $45.00

MORGENSTERN, Soma. *In My Father's Pastures.* 1947. JPS. 369p. G/G. S3. $22.00

MORIN, Edgar. *Rumor in Orleans.* 1971. Pantheon. 1st Am. 276p. VG/G. S3. $26.00

MORISON, Samuel Eliot. *Conservative American Revolution.* 1976. VG. M17. $40.00

MORISON, Samuel Eliot. *European Discovery of America, Vol I & Vol II.* 1971 & 1974. Oxford. 2 vol. F/dj. O7. $35.00

MORISON, Samuel Eliot. *Maritime History of Massachusetts, 1783-1860.* 1941. Houghton Mifflin. 1st thus. 420p. VG/ragged. M20. $20.00

MORISON, Samuel Eliot. *Portuguese Voyages to American in 15th Century.* 1965. NY. Octagon. rpt. 6 maps. as new. O7. $55.00

MORISON, Samuel Eliot. *Spring Tides.* 1965. Houghton Mifflin. 1st. VG/VG. M17. $20.00

MORISON, Samuel Eliot. *Victory in the Pacific 1945.* 1975. Boston. photos/map/index. 407p. VG/VG. S16. $30.00

MORIST, Hugh. *Cat As a Musical Instrument; or, Propagation of Musical Art.* 1984. Westmoreland. 1/30 on hand-made paper. 70x54mm. bl brd/prt label. B24. $95.00

MORLEY, Christopher. *Haunted Bookshop.* 1955. Lippincott. 253p. F. W2. $55.00

MORLEY, Griswold S. *Covered Bridges of California.* 1938. Berkeley. ils/photos. 92p. silvered gray cloth. F. K7. $85.00

MORLEY, Henry. *Ideal Commonwealths.* 1885. Routledge. 1st. VG. M2. $100.00

MORLEY, John. *Edmund Burke: A Historical Study.* 1867. Macmillan. 312p. VG. H1. $65.00

MORLEY, John. *Rousseau.* 1873. London. Chapman Hall. 1st. 2 vol. 8vo. brick cloth. VG. T10. $100.00

MORLEY, Margaret W. *Carolina Mountains.* 1913. Boston. 1st. ils/map ep. pict cloth. VG. B18. $35.00

MORLEY, Sylvanus G. *Excavation of the Cannonball Ruins in Southwestern Colorado.* 1908. np. Archaeological Inst of Am. fld map. prt wrp. D11. $15.00

MORPURGO, J.E. *Barnes Wallis.* 1972. London. 1st. 400p. VG/dj. B18. $47.50

MORRELL, David. *Covenant of the Flame.* 1991. 1st. F/F. H11. $25.00

MORRELL, David. *Covenant of the Flame.* 1991. 1st. sgn/dtd. F/F. A15. $30.00

MORRELL, David. *First Blood.* 1972. Evans. 1st. F/F. C2. $100.00

MORRELL, David. *First Blood.* 1972. Evans. 1st. F/NF. M25. $75.00

MORRELL, David. *League of Night & Fog.* 1987. Dutton. 1st. F/dj. M2/N4. $30.00

MORRELL, David. *Testament.* 1975. NY. Evans. 1st. author's 2nd novel. G+/dj. M21. $15.00

MORRELL, David. *Testament.* 1975. NY. Evans. 1st. F/NF. M15. $45.00

MORRELL, Gipson. *Mr Bear Squash You All Flat.* 1950. Wonder. ils Angela. unp. glossy brd. VG+. M20. $150.00

MORRIS, Alan. *Bloody April.* 1967. London. 1st. ils. map ep. 208p. VG-/dj. B18. $22.50

MORRIS, Charles. *San Francisco Calamity by Earthquake & Fire.* 1906. Phil/Chicago/Toronto. John Winston. salesman sample book. 104p+ad. bl cloth. K7. $75.00

MORRIS, Eugene. *Against the Grain.* 1988. McGraw Hill. 1st. photos. F/VG+. P8. $20.00

MORRIS, Henry. *Human Anatomy: Complete Systematic Treatise...* 1893. Phil. 1st Am. 1286p. full leather. A13. $40.00

MORRIS, Henry. *Omnibus.* 1967. North Hills. Bird & Bull. 1/500. 8vo. Sangorski Sutcliffe bdg. w/prospectus. B24. $400.00

MORRIS, Ivan. *World of the Shining Prince: Court Life in Ancient Japan.* 1964. Knopf. 1st Am. 336p. F/VG. W3. $68.00

MORRIS, J.E. *North Wales.* 1911. London. Blk. Beautiful Britain series. ils. VG. M17. $20.00

MORRIS, James. *Conundrum.* 1974. London. 1st. VG/VG. T9. $25.00

MORRIS, James. *Islam Inflamed: A Middle East Picture.* 1969. NY. Panthon. 1st. 8vo. 7 maps. 326p. VG/torn. W1. $18.00

MORRIS, Jan; see Morris, James.

MORRIS, Jim. *Sheriff of Purgatory.* 1979. Doubleday. 1st. F/dj. M2. $15.00

MORRIS, Josephine. *Household Science & Arts.* 1913. Am Book Co. 256p. VG. B10. $25.00

MORRIS, Mary McGarry. *Dangerous Woman.* 1991. Franklin Lib. 1st/ltd issue. sgn. full leather. F. Q1. $40.00

MORRIS, Phillip Quinn. *Mussels.* 1989. Random. 1st. author's 1st novel. F/F. M23. $25.00

MORRIS, Phillip Quinn. *Thirsty City.* 1990. Random House. 1st. F/F. B4. $45.00

MORRIS, Ronald L. *Wait Until Dark. Jazz & the Underworld, 1880-1940.* 1980. Bowling Gr. Popular. 1st. F/NF. B2. $35.00

MORRIS, Stephen. *King of Vermont.* 1989. Morrow. 1st. F/F. R14. $30.00

MORRIS, W.F. *GB: Story of the Great War.* 1929. Dodd Mead. 1st Am. NF/VG. B4. $100.00

MORRIS, William Alfred. *Medieval English Sheriff to 1300.* 1968 (1927). Manchester. facsimile. M11. $65.00

MORRIS, William. *Doom of King Acrisius.* 1902. NY. RH Russell. 1st. ils Edward Burne-Jones. VG. B2. $75.00

MORRIS, William. *Early Poems of Wm Morris.* 1913. London. Blackie. 4to. 194p. F/glassine/pub cb box. C6. $325.00

MORRIS, William. *News From Nowhere; or, Epoch of Rest...* nd. Humboldt Lib. G. V4. $30.00

MORRIS, Willie. *James Jones: A Friendship.* 1978. Doubleday. 1st. NF/NF. A20. $30.00

MORRIS, Willie. *My Dog Skip.* 1995. Random. 1st. sgn. F/F. A23. $40.00

MORRIS, Willie. *Prayer for the Opening of the Little League Season.* 1995. Harcourt Brace. 1st. sgn. F/F. A23. $40.00

MORRIS, WOOD & WRIGHT. *Persia.* 1969. London. Thames Hudson. 1st. folio. 216p. VG/torn. W1. $45.00

MORRIS, Wright. *About Fiction.* 1975. Harper Row. 1st. inscr. F/F. R14. $45.00

MORRIS, Wright. *Deep Sleep.* 1953. Scribner. 1st. F/NF. B4. $300.00

MORRIS, Wright. *Love Among the Ruins.* 1957. Harcourt Brace. 1st. F/F. B4. $150.00

MORRIS, Wright. *Love Among the Ruins.* 1957. Harcourt Brace. 1st. F/NF. B24. $100.00

MORRIS, Wright. *Will's Boy.* 1981. Harper. 1st. F/F. B4. $50.00

MORRIS & MORRIS. *Men & Pandas.* 1967. NY. ils. 223p. VG. S15. $16.00

MORRISON, Arthur. *Red Triangle.* 1903. LC Page. 1st. VG+. N4. $65.00

MORRISON, Gertrude W. *Girls of Central High on Lake Luna (#2).* 1914. Grosset Dunlap. VG/dj (lists 7 titles). M20. $20.00

MORRISON, J.H. *Streams in the Desert: A Picture of Life in Livingstonia.* ca 1930. Doran. 8vo. 174p. cloth. VG. W1. $10.00

MORRISON, Toni. *Beloved.* Chatto Windus. 1st. sgn. F/F. Q1. $150.00

MORRISON, Toni. *Beloved.* 1987. Knopf. 1st. F/F. B4/C2. $75.00

MORRISON, Toni. *Bluest Eye.* 1979. Chatto Windus. 1st Eng. sgn. author's 1st book. F/dj. Q1. $350.00

MORRISON, Toni. *Jazz.* Chatto Windus. sgn. F/F. Q1. $150.00

MORRISON, Toni. *Jazz.* Franklin Lib. 1st thus. sgn. leather. F. Q1. $150.00

MORRISON, Toni. *Song of Solomon.* 1977. Knopf. 1st. inscr. F/F. D10. $245.00

MORRISON, Toni. *Song of Solomon.* 1977. Knopf. 1st. NF/dj. B4. $100.00

MORRISON, Toni. *Song of Solomon.* 1978. Chatto Windus. 1st Eng. F/F. Q1. $100.00

MORRISON, Toni. *Tar Baby.* 1981. Knopf. ARC. inscr. NF/dj. D10. $160.00

MORRISON, Toni. *Tar Baby.* 1981. Knopf. 1st. F/VG. M19. $35.00

MORRISON, Tony. *Pathways to the Gods.* 1978. Harper. 1st. 208p. dj. F3. $20.00

MORROW, Bradford. *Almanac Branch.* 1991. Linden. 1st. author's 2nd novel. F/F. B3. $40.00

MORROW, Bradford. *Come Sunday.* 1988. Weidenfeld Nicolson. 1st. sgn. F/F. D10. $65.00

MORROW, Bradford. *Posthumes.* 1982. Santa Barbara. Cadmus. 1st. sgn Morrow/Ginzel. 1/150. F/F. D10. $145.00

MORROW, E. Frederic. *Way Down South Up North.* 1973. Pilgrim. 1st. 128p. F/F. B4. $65.00

MORSE, Arthur D. *While Six Million Died: Chronicle of American Apathy.* 1968. Random. BC. 420p. VG/G+. S3. $24.00

MORSE, Benjamin, M.D.; see Block, Lawrence.

MORSE, Howard H. *Historic Old Rhinebeck.* 1908. NY. self pub. 1st. sgn. 448p. G. B11. $18.00

MORSE, Melvin. *Closer to the Light: Learning From Near-Death Experiences...* 1990. Villard. 206p. VG/dj. B29. $9.50

MORSE, Sidney. *Household Discoveries: An Encyclopedia...* 1909. NY. Success Co. G. A16. $50.00

MORSE, Sidney. *New Household Discoveries.* 1917. NY. Success Co. G. A16. $47.50

MORSE, Theresa A. *Best I Ever Tasted.* 1969. Doubleday. VG/dj. A16. $10.00

MORSE. *Beatrix Potter's Americans, Selected Letters.* 1982. 216p. F/VG. A4. $60.00

MORTIMER, John. *Summer's Lease.* 1988. Franklin Lib. 1st. sgn. full leather. F. Q1. $60.00

MORTOFT, Francis. *Francis Mortoft: His Book. Being His Travels...* 1925. London. Hakluyt Soc. 8vo. 216p. bl cloth. P4. $95.00

MORTON, H.V. *Through Lands of the Bible.* 1938. Dodd Mead. 1st. 8vo. 452p. VG. W1. $10.00

MORTON, Harry. *Whale's Wake.* 1982. Honolulu. 8vo. 396p. gilt bdg. M/dj. P4. $32.50

MORTON, Julia F. *Plants Poisonous to People in Florida & Other Warm Areas.* 1977 (1971). Miami. Fairchild Tropical Garden. 8vo. VG/dj. A22. $25.00

MORTON, Leah. *I Am a Woman — And a Jew.* 1926. NY. JH Sears. 362p. VG. S3. $35.00

MORTON, Rosalie Slaughter. *Doctor's Holiday in Iran.* 1940. Funk Wagnall. 8vo. 355p. xl. W1. $10.00

MOSCOW, Alvin. *Collision Course: Andrea Doria & the Stockholm.* 1959. NY. 1st. inscr. 316p. F/dj. B18. $22.50

MOSELEY, H.N. *Notes by a Naturalist: An Account...* 1892. NY/London. Putnam/Murray. 8vo. 540p. tan cloth. P4. $125.00

MOSELEY, Walter. *Red Death.* 1991. Norton. 1st. F/F. T11. $45.00

MOSER, Barry. *Ghost Horse of the Mounties.* 1991. Godine. 1st. VG/NF. B3. $20.00

MOSES, Robert. *Public Works: A Dangerous Trade.* 1970. McGraw Hill. sgn. 952p. full leather. w/ephemera. B11. $150.00

MOSHER, Howard Frank. *Disappearances.* 1977. Viking. 1st. author's 1st novel. F/NF. T11. $75.00

MOSHKIN, V.A. *Castor.* 1986. New Delhi. ils/figures/tables. 315p. F/dj. B26. $22.50

MOSKOWITZ, Sam. *Charles Fort: A Radical Corpuscle.* 1976. Moskwitz. 1/300. NF/stapled wrp. R10. $25.00

MOSKOWITZ, Sam. *Modern Masterpieces of Science Fiction.* 1974 (1966). Hyperion. rpt. F. M2. $25.00

MOSKOWITZ, Sam. *Strange Horizons.* 1976. Scribner. 1st. F/dj. M2. $25.00

MOSLEY, Diana. *Loved Ones, Pen Portraits.* 1985. London. 1st. VG/VG. T9. $25.00

MOSLEY, Walter. *Black Betty.* 1994. Norton. ARC. sgn. F/F. D10. $40.00

MOSLEY, Walter. *Devil in a Blue Dress.* 1990. Norton. 1st. sgn. author's 1st book. F/dj. from $75 to $100.00

MOSLEY, Walter. *Red Death.* 1991. Norton. 1st. author's 2nd book. F/dj. A24. $50.00

MOSLEY, Walter. *Red Death.* 1991. Norton. 1st. sgn. author's 2nd book. F/F. from $60 to $75.00

MOSLEY, Walter. *White Butterfly.* 1992. Norton. 1st. F/dj. B2. $75.00

MOSLEY, Walter. *White Butterfly.* 1992. Norton. 1st. sgn. author's 3rd book. F/dj. A24. $100.00

MOSS, C. *Portraits in Wild: Behavior Studies East African Mammals.* 1975. Houghton Mifflin. ils/pl. 363p. cloth. F/NF. M12. $22.50

MOSS, Howard. *Instant Lives.* 1974. Saturday Review/Dutton. 1st. ils Gorey. 84p. VG/clip. M20. $35.00

MOSS, James A. *Field Service.* Aug 1917. Menasha, WI. George Banta. 186p+ads. tan cloth. F. H1. $20.00

MOSSMAN, Isaac Van Dorsey. *Pony Expressman's Recollections.* 1955. np. Champoeg. 1/500. 55p+fld pocket map. D11. $50.00

MOSZKOWSKI, Alexander. *Einstein: Einblicke in Seine Gedankenwelt.* 1922. Berlin. Fontane. 1st. 240p. K3. $30.00

MOTLEY, John Lothrop. *Life & Death of John of Barneveld...* 1879. NY. 2 vol. VG. A17. $18.50

MOTLEY, Willard. *Let No Man Write My Epitaph.* 1958. Random. 1st. NF/NF. B4. $65.00

MOTT, Valentine. *Ligature of the Arteria Ilica Communis, at Its Origin.* 1827. Phil. 422p. half leather. A13. $150.00

MOTTRAM, R.H. *Castle Island.* 1931. Chatto Windus. 1st. 415p. cloth. VG/dj. M20. $35.00

MOTZ & NATHANSON. *Constellations: An Enthusiast's Guide to the Night Sky.* 1988. Doubleday. 411p. VG/dj. K5. $30.00

MOUNTEVANS, Admiral Lord. *Man Against the Desolate Antarctic.* 1951. NY. Funk. ils. 172p. dj. T7. $22.00

MOUNTFIELD, D. *History of Polar Exploration.* 1974. NY. ils/maps. 208p. VG/dj. M4. $20.00

MOURELLE, Don Francisco A. *Voyage of the Sonora From the 1775 Journal of...* 1987. Fairfield. Ye Galleon. 1/301. facsimile 1920 SF ed. w/fld pocket map. M/sans. P4. $40.00

MOURELLE, Don Francisco A. *Voyage of the Sonora in 2nd Ducareli Expedition...* 1920. SF. TC Russell. 1/230. 2 facsimile maps (1 fld). half bl cloth. VG. K7. $175.00

MOUREY & VALLANCE. *Art Nouveau Jewelry & Fans.* 1973. Dover. rpt. ils. VG. M17. $25.00

MOURNING DOVE. *Co-Ge-We-A. The Half-Blood.* 1927. Boston Four Seas. 1st. edit LV McWhorter. NF. L3. $1,500.00

MOURSE, Hosea Ballou. *Gilds of China.* 1909. London. 1st. 2 photos/notes/bibliography. 92p. VG. W3. $110.00

MOURSE, Hosea Ballou. *Trade & Administration of the Chinese Empire.* 1908. NY/Bombay. Longman Gr. 1st. 451p. xl Cornell Club. VG. W3. $135.00

MOUSSY & TRUFFAUNT. *400 Blows.* 1969. Grove. 100+ photos. VG+. C9. $30.00

MOWAT, Farley. *Black Joke.* 1963. Little Brn. 1st Am. 8vo. 218p. VG. T5. $20.00

MOWAT, Farley. *Grey Seas Under.* 1958. Little Brn. 1st Am. NF/NF. T11. $50.00

MOWAT, Farley. *Polar Passion.* 1967. Toronto. McClelland Stewart. 4to. 302p. gray cloth. VG/dj. P4. $55.00

MOWAT, Farley. *Snow Walker.* 1975. Toronto. McClelland Stewart. 1st. NF/VG. B3. $30.00

MOWBRAY, Jay Henry. *Illustrious Career & Heroic Deeds of Colonel Roosevelt.* 1910. Berton. 1st. 363p. VG. J2. $65.00

MOYER, John W. *Famous Frontiersmen.* nd (1972). Hubbard. probable 1st. 116p. F. C14. $20.00

MOYES, Patricia. *Angel Death.* 1981. HRW. 1st Am. F/dj. N4. $30.00

MOYLE, J.B. *Institutes of Justinian. Fifth Edition.* 1955. Clarendon. 2 vol. VG/dj. M11. $175.00

MOYLE & MOYLE. *Northland Wild Flowers.* 1993. MN U. 6th. ils. 236p. F. S15. $14.00

MOYZISCH, L.C. *Operation Cicero.* 1950. London. Wingate. 1st. NF/VG. B4. $200.00

MOZART. *Grundliche Violinschule.* 1770. Augsburg. Lotter. 4to. 3 full-p pl/fld table prt music. modern calf. R12. $2,750.00

MRAZKOVA, Daniela. *Another Russia: Through the Eyes of New Soviet Photographer.* 1986. Facts on File. 1st. VG/VG. V4. $30.00

MUCHA, Jiri. *Alphonse Maria Mucha.* 1989. ils/fld ils. VG/VG. M17. $40.00

MUCK. *Einhundert Jahre, Berliner Philharmonisches Orchester...* 1982. 3 vol. lg 4to. ils. F. A4. $150.00

MUCKENSTURM, L. *Louis' Salads & Chafing Dishes.* 1906. 1st. tall narrow 4to. VG. E6. $55.00

MUDD, Samuel Alexander. *Life of Dr Samuel A Mudd...* 1955. Marietta, GA. Continental Book. rpt. 363p. cloth. xl. M8. $45.00

MUDIMBE, V.Y. *Between Tides.* 1973. S&S. 1st. F/F. A20. $15.00

MUEGGLER, Walter F. *Aspen Community Types of Intermountain Region.* 1988. Ogden. 32 mc photos/map. 135p. VG/wrp. B26. $14.00

MUELLER, Ralph. *Report After Action: Story of 103rd Infantry Division.* 1945. Innsbruck. 1st. ils/maps. VG/torn. S16. $75.00

MUENCH, J. *Along Yosemite Trails.* 1948. Hastings. ils/photos/map ep. 101p. cloth. VG/G. M12. $17.50

MUENCH, Paul. *Hindenburg's March to London.* 1916. Winston. 1st Am. VG/wrp. M2. $75.00

MUHAMMAD, Elijah. *Message to the Blackman.* 1965. 1st. author's 1st book. F/G. M19. $100.00

MUIR, John. *Our National Parks.* 1909. Boston. 1st. ils/2p map. 382p. G+. B5. $95.00

MUIR, John. *Rambles of a Botanist Among Plants & Climates of CA.* 1974. Mariposa, CA. Rocking K. 1/50. prt/sgn Wm Kimes. gr cloth. F. K7. $85.00

MUIR, John. *South of Yosemite. Selected Writings.* 1968. Garden City, NY. Am Mus Natural Hist. bl cloth brd/blk spine. NF/dj. K7. $45.00

MUIR, John. *Travels in Alaska.* 1915. Boston. 1st. VG/VG. B5. $80.00

MUIR, John. *Travels in Alaska.* 1971. NY. ils/photos. 327p. cloth. F. M12. $20.00

MUIR, Marcie. *Bibliography of Australian Children's Books.* 1970. 1st. ils. 1038p. F/NF. A4. $155.00

MUIR, Percy. *Victorian Illustrated Books.* 1989. London. rpt. F/F. A4. $85.00

MUIRDEN, James. *Sky Watcher's Handbook.* 1993. NY. Freeman. 8vo. ils. 408p. VG/dj. K5. $30.00

MUKERJEE, Radhakamal. *Culture & Art of India.* 1969. NY. Praeger. 1st. photos/bibliography/maps/index. F/NF. W3. $75.00

MUKHERJEE, Bharati. *Holder of the World.* 1993. Knopf. 1st. sgn. F/F. R14. $35.00

MUKHERJEE, Bharati. *Jasmine.* 1989. Grove Weidenfeld. 1st. F/F/wrp band. R14. $30.00

MULDOON, Paul. *Faber Book of Contemporary Irish Poetry.* 1986. London. 1st. VG/VG. T9. $20.00

MULFORD, Clarence E. *Corson of the JC.* 1927. Doubleday Page. 1st. VG. M25. $25.00

MULLAHY & THOMPSON. *Psychoanalysis: Evolution & Development.* 1950. Hermitage. 1st. 250p. VG/dj. A25. $15.00

MULLER, Dan. *My Life With Buffalo Bill.* 1948. Reilly Lee. 1st. 303p. VG/dj. J2. $95.00

MULLER, Katherine K. *Wild Flowers of Santa Barbara.* 1958. Santa Barbara. unp. sbdg. F. B26. $9.00

MULLER, Marcia. *Cavalier in White.* 1986. St Martin. 1st. F/F. M15. $50.00

MULLER, Marcia. *Eye of the Storm.* 1988. Mysterious. UP. NF/beige wrp. Q1. $60.00

MULLER, Marcia. *There Hangs the Knife.* 1988. St Martin. 1st. rem mk. F/VG+. N4. $15.00

MULLER, Marcia. *Trophies & Dead Things.* 1990. Mysterious. 1st. F/F. P3. $18.00

MULLER, Marcia. *Trophies & Dead Things.* 1990. Mysterious. 1st. sgn. F/F. T2. $35.00

MULLER, Orrie. *Orientalisches Tagebuch. Impressionen Rande Dreier Welten.* 1932. Bremen. Leumer. 1st. 8vo. G/torn dj/stiff wrp. W1. $12.00

MULLER, Richard. *American Greenhouse Construction.* 1927. NY. DeLaMare. 143p. VG. A10. $32.00

MULLER, W. Max. *Egyptian Mythology.* 1923. Boston. ils. VG. M17. $20.00

MULLER & PRONZINI. *Chapters & Hearse: Suspense Stories About World of Books.* 1985. Morrow. 1st. sgn. F/dj. M15. $45.00

MULLER & PRONZINI. *Kill or Cure.* 1985. Macmillan. 1st. F/dj. Q1. $30.00

MULLER-BROCKMAN, J. *Grid Systems in Graphic Design.* 1981. Eng/German text. ils. VG/VG. M17. $20.00

MULLETT, J.C. *Five Years' Whaling Voyage 1848-1853.* 1977. Ye Galleon. rpt. ils. 48p. T7. $45.00

MULLIGAN, B.O. *Maples Cultivated in the United States & Canada.* 1958. Am Assn Botanical Gardens & Aboretums. 56p. wrp. $23.00

MULLIKEN, Robert S. *Selected Papers of Robert S Mulliken.* 1975. Chicago/London. 4to. 1127p. VG. K3. $35.00

MULLINS, P. *Rocking Horse: History of Moving Toy Horses.* 1992. Great Britain. 1st. sq 4to. ils. 376p+48p servey. F/case. M4. $90.00

MULLINS & REED. *Union Bookshelf: A Selected Civil War Bibliography.* 1982. Broadfoot. 81p. F. A17. $25.00

MULOCK, Dinah. *Little Lame Prince.* 1909. Rand McNally. 1st thus. ils Hope Dunlap. VG. M5. $60.00

MUMFORD, John Kimberly. *Oriental Rugs.* 1900. Scribner. 1st. 24 tissue-guarded pl/2 maps/table. maroon buckram. T10. $250.00

MUNARI, Bruno. *ABC.* 1960. World. 1st. ils. VG. P2. $35.00

MUNARI, Bruno. *Circus in the Mist.* 1969 (1968). World. 1st Am. NF/NF. C8. $125.00

MUNBY, A.N.L. *Portrait of an Obsession: Life of Sir Thomas Phillips.* 1967. Putnam. 1st. NF/dj. K3. $25.00

MUNDY, Talbot. *C-I-D.* 1932. Century. 1st. NF. M19. $25.00

MUNDY, Talbot. *Winds of the World.* 1917. Bobbs Merrill. 1st. VG. M19. $25.00

MUNK, J.A. *Activities of a Lifetime.* 1924. Times-Mirror. 1st. ils. 221p. NF. B19. $75.00

MUNK, J.A. *Southwest Sketches.* 1920. Putnam/Knickerbocker. 8vo. 311p. VG. F7. $50.00

MUNK, J.A. *Story of the Munk Library...* 1927. LA. Times-Mirror. 1st. 8vo. 78p. brn Victorian cloth. xl. T10. $45.00

MUNN, Henry Toke. *Tales of the Eskimo.* nd. London. 196p+19 photos. dj. A17. $40.00

MUNNINGS, A.J. *Pictures of Horses & English Life.* 1927. London/NY. Eyre Spottiswoode/Scribner. 1st. VG. O3. $750.00

MUNRO, Alice. *Friend of My Youth.* 1990. Knopf. ARC. sgn. F/wrp/box. R13. $45.00

MUNRO, Hugh. *Compendious System of Theory & Practice of Modern Surgery.* 1792. London. 1st. lg fld table. recent quarter leather/new ep. A13. $300.00

MUNROE, David Hoadley. *Grand National, 1839-1930.* 1931. Huntington. 1st regular. 147p. cloth. VG. M20. $50.00

MUNSEY. *Disneyana: Walt Disney Collectibles.* 1974. 4to. ils. 385p. NF/VG. A4. $150.00

MUNTANER, Ramon. *Chronicle of Muntaner.* 1920-21. Hakluyt Soc. 1st Eng. 2 vol. 8vo. gilt bdg. P4. $125.00

MUNTEAN, Michaela. *Runaway Soup & Other Stories.* 1987. Golden. 1st. sm 4to. unp. F. C14. $12.00

MUNTHE, Axel. *Story of San Michele.* 1930. Lodnon. rpt. inscr. VG/VG. T9. $65.00

MUNZ, Philip A. *California Spring Wildflowers.* 1974 (1961). Berkeley. ils/photos. 122p. sc. VG. B26. $7.50

MURAKAMI, Haruki. *Hard-Boiled Wonderland & the End of the World.* 1991. Kodansha. 1st Am. trans Alfred Birnbaum. F/dj. A24. $25.00

MURAKAMI, Haruki. *Wild Sheep Chase.* 1989. Kodansha. 1st Am ed. trans Alfred Birnbaum. NF/dj. A24. $30.00

MURBARGER, Nell. *Ghosts of the Glory Trail.* June 1965. LA. Westernlore. dj. A19. $50.00

MURCOCK, Harold. *Earl Percy Dines Abroad: A Boswellian Episode.* 1924. Boston. 1/550. VG/G case. M17. $45.00

MURCOCK, John R. *Arizona Characters in Silhouette.* 1939. Fray Marcos DeNiza. inscr. 8vo. 151p. F7. $55.00

MURDOCH, Iris. *Good Apprentice.* 1985. London. 1st. VG/VG. T9. $25.00

MURIE, O.J. *Elk of North America.* (1957). Stackpole. 2nd. ils. 376p. gilt pict cloth. F. M12. $37.50

MURIE, O.J. *Jackson Hole With a Naturalist.* 1963. Frontier. 1st. 55p. VG/wrp. J2. $40.00

MURIE & MURIE. *Wapiti Wilderness.* 1966. Knopf. dj. A19. $40.00

MURKY, Norman. *Scottish Hand-Loom Weavers 1790-1850: A Social History.* nd. John Donald Pub. 1st. VG/VG. V4. $15.00

MURPHEY, Robert Cushman. *Bird Islands of Peru.* 1925. Putnam. 1st. 362p. xl. F3. $20.00

MURPHY, Arthur. *Works of Cornelius Tacitus.* 1805. London. Stockdale. 8 vol. tall 8vo. fld maps. H13. $495.00

MURPHY, Dallas. *Apparent Wind.* 1991. Pocket. 1st. as new/dj. N4. $22.50

MURPHY, Dallas. *Lover Man.* 1987. Scribner. 1st. sgn. F/F. M22. $20.00

MURPHY, Edward. *Lectures on Principles & Practice of Midwifery.* 1852. London. 1st. 616p. A13. $500.00

MURPHY, George. *Soviet Mongolia.* 1966. CA U. 1st. 224p. F/dj. W3. $48.00

MURPHY, John. *Roentgen Ray As Therapeutic Force...* 1903. Louisville. 1st. xl. A13. $50.00

MURPHY, Pat. *Falling Woman.* 1986. NY. Tor. 1st. sgn. F/F. T2. $100.00

MURPHY, Robert Cushman. *Fish-Shape Paumanok: Nature & Man on Long Island.* 1964. Am Philosophical Soc. 1st. sgn. ils/pict ep. 67p. VG/dj. B18. $15.00

MURRAY, Bruce. *Journey Into Space.* 1989. Norton. Vg/VG. K5. $24.00

MURRAY, George. *Antarctic Manual for Use of Expedition of 1901.* 1994. Plaistow. Explorer Books. 1/500. 8vo. 586p. M/sans. P4. $75.00

MURRAY, J.W. *Distribution & Ecology of Living Benthic Foraminiferids.* 1973. Heinemann. 274p. VG/dj. D8. $35.00

MURRAY, Janet. *Traditional Scots Recipes: With a Fine Feeling for Food.* 1972. NY. Bramhall. G/dj. A16. $10.00

MURRAY, Jim. *Jim Murray Collection.* 1988. Taylor. 1st. intro Vin Scully. F/F. P8. $20.00

MURRAY, Lindley. *Power of Religion on the Mind...* 1838. NY. Trustees of Residuary Estate of Lindley Murray. 376p. V3. $16.50

MURRAY, Robert. *Ft Laramie: Visions of a Grand Old Post.* 1974. Ft Collins, CO. Old Army. dj. A19. $50.00

MURRAY, Robert. *Military Posts of Wyoming.* 1974. Old Army. 1st. sgn. ils/photos/map. 82p. VG/VG. J2. $195.00

MURRAY, Spencer. *Cuising the Sea of Cortez.* 1963. Desert Southwest Inc. 1st. photos Ralph Poole. VG. O4. $25.00

MURRAY, Thomas Boyles. *Pitcairn: The Island, the People & the Pastor...* ca 1858. London. Soc for Promoting Christian Knowledge. 11th. full calf. P4. $175.00

MURRAY, Thomas Boyles. *Pitcairn: The Island, the People & the Pastor...* 1860. London. The Soc. 12th. ils. 414p. T7. $120.00

MURRAY, V.T. *Fifty Masterpieces of Mystery.* nd. London. 1st. VG. M2. $35.00

MURRAY, William. *Treatise on Emotional Disorders of Sympathetic System...* 1867. NY. Simpson. 1st Am. 95p. prt pebbled ochre cloth. xl. G1. $225.00

MURRAY, William. *When the Fat Man Sings.* 1987. Bantam. 1st. F/clip. M22. $15.00

MURREY, T. *Valuable Cooking Receipts.* 1880. 1st. VG. E6. $45.00

MUSE, Maude B. *Materia Medica Pharmacology & Therapeutics.* 1941. Phil. Saunders. 3rd. 12mo. VG/dj. A22. $25.00

MUSGRAVE, Thomas. *Castaway on the Auckland Isles.* 1866. London. Hutchinson. ils. 251p. dj. T7. $18.00

MUSIAL, Stan. *Stan Musial: The Man's Own Story.* 1964. Doubleday. 1st. 328p. VG/dj. M20. $45.00

MUSTON, Michael. *Manhattan on the Rocks.* 1989. Holt. 1st. F/F. B35. $12.00

MUZIK, T.J. *Weed Biology & Control.* 1970. McGraw Hill. 273p. cloth. B1. $18.50

MYER, Albert J. *Manual of Signals.* 1868. NY. mc pls of signal flags. 417p. O8. $55.00

MYER, F.S. *Handbook of Ornament.* 3rd Am. ils. VG. M17. $20.00

MYERS, Edward H. *Disruption of the Methodist Episcopal Church 1844-46.* 1875. Nashville/Macon. 12mo. 216p. xl. VG. B14. $35.00

MYERS, Gustavus. *History of the Supreme Court.* 1925. Kerr. VG/dj. V4. $25.00

MYERS, Joan. *Santiago: Saint of Two Worlds.* 1991. Albuquerque. 1st. 4to. 73p. 83 photo pl/map. F/dj. T10. $50.00

MYERS, John Myers. *Dead Warrior.* 1956. Little Brn. 1st. VG/dj. M2. $50.00

MYERS, John Myers. *Deaths of the Bravos.* 1962. Little Brn. 1st. 467p. VG/dj. M20. $18.00

MYERS, John Myers. *Doc Holliday, Life...of America's Legendary Desparadoes...* 1955. Little Brn. 1st. 287p. VG/VG. J2. $125.00

MYERS, John Myers. *Print in Wild Land.* 1967. Doubleday. sm 8vo. 274p. as new/dj. K7. $25.00

MYERS, R.D. *Handbook of Drug & Chemical Stimulation of Brain.* 1974. Van Nostrand Reinhold. 8vo. red cloth. VG/dj. G1. $50.00

MYERS, R.M. *Children of Pride.* 1972. New Haven. 1st. VG/G. B5. $50.00

MYERS, R.M. *Children of Pride.* 1972. New Haven. 1st. 1845p. F/dj. A15. $75.00

MYERS, William. *Journal of a Cruise to California & Sandwich Islands...* 1955. BC of CA. 1/400. lg 4to. gilt beige cloth. F. R3. $275.00

MYERS, William. *Sketches of California & Hawaii by...* 1970. BC of CA. 1/450. lg 4to. 2-tone beige cloth. F. R3. $200.00

MYLAR, Isaac L. *Early Days at the Mission San Juan Bautista.* 1929. Watsonville, CA. Evening Pajaronian. 1/300. sgn. gilt maroon cloth. VG. K7. $50.00

MYRER, Anton. *Big War.* 1957. NY. 463p. VG. S16. $28.50

MYRER, Anton. *Once an Eagle.* 1968. HRW. 1st. 817p. VG. W2. $35.00

MYRICK, David F. *San Francisco's Telegraph Hill.* 1972. Howell North. 1st. 4to. ils. NF/VG. O4. $20.00

MYRICK, Herbert. *Sugar: A New & Profitable Industry in the US.* 1897. NY. Orange Judd. 160p. VG. A10. $35.00

MYTINGER, Caroline. *Headhunting in the Solomon Islands Around the Coral Sea.* 1942. Macmillan. 1st. ils. VG/VG. A25. $22.00

MYTINGER, Carolyn. *Headhunting in the Solomon Islands Around the Coral Sea.* 1942. Macmillan. 1st. 8vo. 416p. VG. H1. $15.00

NABOKOV, Peter. *Two Leggings: Making of a Crow Warrior.* 1967. Crowell. 1st. 8vo. 226p. xl. VG/dj. K7. $17.00

NABOKOV, Vladimir. *Book of the Bear.* 1926. Nonesuch. trans Harrison/Mirrlees. ils Garnett. VG. M17. $25.00

NABOKOV, Vladimir. *Defense.* 1964. Putnam. 1st Am. NF/dj. Q1. $75.00

NABOKOV, Vladimir. *Despair.* 1966. Putnam. 1st. blk cloth. F/NF. S24. $100.00

NABOKOV, Vladimir. *Invitation to a Beheading.* 1959. Putnam. 1st. decor brd. F/VG+. S24. $75.00

NABOKOV, Vladimir. *King, Queen, Knave.* 1968. McGraw Hill. 1st. F/NF. A24. $37.50

NABOKOV, Vladimir. *Laughter in the Dark.* 1961. Weidenfeld Nicolson. 1st. NF/clip. A24. $100.00

NABOKOV, Vladimir. *Look at the Harlequins.* 1974. McGraw Hill. 1st. NF/NF. M19. $35.00

NABOKOV, Vladimir. *Nabokov's Dozen.* 1958. Doubleday. 1st. NF/VG. M19. $75.00

NABOKOV, Vladimir. *Nearctic Members of Genus Lycaeides Hubner.* 1949. Cambridge. Mus Comparative Zoology. 1st. 9 pl. F/gr wrp. B4. $1,500.00

NABOKOV, Vladimir. *Transparent Things.* 1972. McGraw Hill. 1st. F/NF. M19. $35.00

NACK, William. *Big Red of Meadow Stable.* 1975. Arthur fields. 1st. VG/VG. P8. $20.00

NADELSON & NOTMAN. *Woman Patient: Aggression, Adaptions & Psychotherapy.* 1982. NY. Plenum. 1st. 314p. VG/dj. A25. $15.00

NAGATA, T. *Rock Magnetism.* 1961. NY. Plenum. 2nd. 350p. F/dj. D8. $30.00

NAGLE, Jacob. *Nagle Journal: Diary of Life of Jacob Nagle, Sailor...* 1988. Weidenfeld Nicholson. 1st. 402p. VG/dj. P4. $27.50

NAGLER, Barney. *Brown Bomber.* 1972. World. 1st. VG/G. P8. $25.00

NAIFEH & SMITH. *Mormon Murders, a True Story of Greed, Forgery, Deceit...* 1988. Weidenfeld Nicolson. 1st. 458p. VG/VG. J2. $95.00

NAIPAUL, V.S. *Among the Believers.* 1981. Knopf. 1st. NF/dj. A24. $35.00

NAIPAUL, V.S. *Guerrillas.* 1983. knopf. 1st. F/NF clip. T11. $35.00

NAIPAUL, V.S. *Return of Eva Peron.* 1980. Knopf. 1st. NF. A24. $35.00

NAIPAUL, V.S. *Turn in the South.* 1989. Franklin Lib. 1st. sgn. gilt full leather. Q1. $75.00

NAIPAUL, V.S. *Turn in the South.* 1989. Knopf. 1st. sgn. F/F. M23. $35.00

NAKAYAMA, Shigeru. *History of Japanese Astronomy.* 1969. Harvard. 1st. 369p. F/NF. W3. $125.00

NANCE, R. Morton. *Sailing-Ship Models.* 1924. London. Halton Truscott. 1/1750. 1st trade. bl cloth. NF. P4. $325.00

NANOVIC, John. *Complete Book of Wines, Vineyards & Labels.* 1979. Ottenheimer. 1st. F/F. W2. $30.00

NAOYA, Shiga. *Paper Door & Other Stories.* 1987. SF. Northpoint. 1st. NF/dj. R13. $15.00

NARAMORE, Earl. *Handloader's Manual.* (1937). Onslow County, NC. Samworth. 1st. 369p. VG/VG. H7. $35.00

NARAYAN, R.K. *Tiger for Malgudi.* 1983. Viking. 1st. F/NF. M23. $20.00

NARDI, Jacopo. *Le Historie Della Citta Di Fiorenza.* 1582. Lyons. Ancelin. 4to. quarter calf. R12. $550.00

NAREMORE, James. *Magic World of Orson Welles.* 1978. Oxford. photos. VG+/dj. C9. $50.00

NARLIKAR, Jayant. *Violent Phenonena in the Universe.* 1982. Oxford. 1st. F/dj. M2. $12.00

NASH, J.A. *Progressive Farmer: Scientific Treatise on Agricultural...* 1861. Saxton Barker. 12mo. xl. K3. $35.00

NASH, Ogden. *Girls Are Silly.* 1962. NY. Watts. 1st. oblong 4to. ils LB Smith. F/NF. B4. $75.00

NASH, Ogden. *Marriage Lines.* 1964. Little Brn. 1st. ils Isador Seltzer. F/VG+. B4. $50.00

NASH, Ogden. *Private Dining Room.* 1953. Little Brn. 1st. F/F. M19. $45.00

NASON, Elias. *Life & Public Services of Henry Wilson.* 1876. Boston. 452p. gilt emb bdg. O8. $14.50

NASSAU, Robert Hamill. *In an Elephant Corral & Other Tales of West Africa...* 1969 (1912). Negro U. rpt. 8vo. 180p. VG. W1. $20.00

NATHAN, George Jean. *Theatre of the Moment.* 1936. Knopf. 1st. 309p. G. H1. $18.00

NATHAN, Robert. *Road of Ages.* 1935. Knopf. 1st. M/orange dj. B4. $100.00

NATHAN, Robert. *Road of Ages.* 1935. Knopf. 1st. VG/dj. P3. $45.00

NATHAN, Robert. *Winter Tide.* 1940. NY. 1st. VG/dj. B5. $30.00

NATIVE OF VIRGINIA. *Rejected Stone; or, Insurrection Vs Resurrection in America.* 1862. Boston. 121p. O8. $27.50

NAUDE, Gabriel. *Science des Princes.* 1752. np. 2 vol in 3. 8vo. calf. R12. $675.00

NAUMOFF, Lawrence. *Night of the Weeping Women.* 1988. Atlantic Monthly. 1st. inscr. author's 1st book. F/NF. R13. $45.00

NAVE, Orville J. *Nave's Topical Bible.* 1974. Moody. 1376p. VG. B29. $12.00

NAYLOR, Gloria. *Bailey's Cafe.* 1991. HBJ. 1st. F/dj. H1. $25.00

NAYLOR, Gloria. *Linden Hills.* 1985. Ticknor Fields. 1st. sgn. NF/VG. R14. $65.00

NAYLOR, Gloria. *Mama Day.* 1988. Ticknor Fields. 1st. sgn/dtd 1997. NF/VG. R14. $60.00

NAYLOR, Gloria. *Women of Brewster Place.* 1983. Hodder Stoughton. 1st Eng. author's 1st book. F/dj. Q1. $200.00

NAYLOR, Phyllis. *Galloping Goat & Other Stories.* 1965. Abingdon. 1st. ils Robert Jefferson. 112p. VG+/VG. P2. $25.00

NAYLOR, Phyllis. *String of Chances.* 1982. Atheneum. 1st. sm 8vo. F/F. C8. $30.00

NAYLOR, Phyllis. *To Make a Wee Moon.* 1969. Follett. 1st. ils Krush. 190p. VG+/dj. P2. $25.00

NEAL, Bill. *Southern Cooking.* 1985. UNC. 233p. VG/VG. B10. $15.00

NEALE, Richard. *Medical Digest.* 1877. London. New Sydenham Soc. 8vo. 650p. K3. $20.00

NEALE, W.T. *Cacti & Other Succulents.* 1935. Newhaven, Sussex. ils/photos. 200p. red buckram. F. B26. $30.00

NEARING, H. *Sinister Researches of CP Ransom.* 1954. Doubleday. 1st. ils Edward Gorey. VG/dj. M2. $20.00

NEARING, Scott. *British General Strike.* 1926. VAnguard. 1st. VG/dj. V4. $15.00

NEARING, Scott. *Freedom, Promise & Menace.* 1961. Social Science Inst. 1st. sgn. VG/worn. V4. $30.00

NEARING & NEARING. *Brave New World.* 1958. Harborside. Social Sci Inst. 1st. sgn. F/NF. B2. $35.00

NEATBY, L.H. *Conquest of the Last Frontier.* 1966. OH U. 1st. 425p+2 maps. F/dj. A17. $20.00

NEBENZAHL, Kenneth. *Atlas of Columbus & the Great Discoveries.* 1990. Rand McNally. BOMC. folio. 100 maps. 168p. gilt bl cloth. F/dj. T10. $50.00

NEEDHAM, David. *Birthright: Christian, Do You Know Who You Are?* 1981. Multnomah. 293p. VG/torn. B29. $8.50

NEEDHAM, Joseph. *Clerks & Craftsmen in China & the West.* 1970. Cambridge. 1st. ils. 470p. xl. K3. $35.00

NEEDHAM, Joseph. *Science, Religion & Reality.* 1955. NY. Braziller. 1st. VG/dj. K3. $30.00

NEEDHAM, Joseph. *Science in Traditional China.* 1981. Cambridge. 1st. 8vo. 134p. VG/dj. K3. $25.00

NEFFLEN, John. *Method of Increasing the Yield of the Milch-Cow.* 1853. Phil. Rogers. 54p. 36p ads. fld mc pl. very scarce. A10. $45.00

NEIHARDT, John G. *Black Elk Speaks.* 1932. Morrow. 1st. NF/VG clip. L3. $1,250.00

NEIHARDT, John G. *Collected Poems of John G Neihardt.* 1926. Macmillan. 1st. cloth. D11. $50.00

NEIHARDT, John G. *Eagle Voice: Authentic Tale of the Sioux Indians.* 1953. London. Andrew Melrose. 1st. NF/VG. A18. $75.00

NEIHARDT, John G. *Splendid Wayfaring.* 1920. NY. Macmillan. 1st. 8vo. gr cloth. F7. $55.00

NEISON, Edmund. *Moon: Condition & Configurations of Its Surface.* 1876. Longman Gr. 1st. 576p. K5. $450.00

NELL, William C. *Services of Colored Americans in Wars of 1776 & 1812.* 1851. Boston. Prentiss Sawyer. 1st. inscr. 24p. F/prt wrp. B4. $2,000.00

NELSON, A.W. *Yankee-Swanson: Chapters From a Life at Sea.* 1913. NY. Sturgis Walton. 8vo. 374p. bl cloth. P4. $35.00

NELSON, Antonya. *Expendables.* 1990. Athens, GA. 1st. author's 1st book. M/dj. A24. $40.00

NELSON, Aven. *First Report of the Flora of Wyoming.* 1896. Laramie. photos. 174p. bl buckram. B26. $56.00

NELSON, Dick J. *Wyoming Has a Distinguished Heritage & the Big Horn Basin...* 1957. Steele Prt. 1st. sgn. photos. 76p. VG/wrp. J2. $85.00

NELSON, E.W. *Smaller North American Mammals.* 1918. NGS. ils after Louis Agassiz. VG. S15. $15.00

NELSON, Edward W. *Wild Animals of North America: Intimate Studies...* (1918). NGS. 1st. ils/fld pl. pliable cloth. VG. H7. $35.00

NELSON, Edward. *Eskimo About Bering Strait.* 1971. NY. Johnson Rpt Corp. 8vo. 518p. mustard cloth. P4. $125.00

NELSON, Harold B. *Sounding the Depths: 150 Years of American Seascape.* 1989. SF. 111p. 4to. wrp. A17. $15.00

NELSON, Richard. *Richard Nelson's American Cooking.* 1983. NAL. 1st. 446p. VG/G. B10. $12.00

NELSON, William. *Laws Concerning Game. Of Hunting, Hawking, Fishing...* 1753. London. contemporary calf. M11. $350.00

NELSON, William. *Lex Maneriorum; or, Law & Customs of England...* 1726. London. Nutt Gosling. 1st. contemporary calf. M11. $350.00

NELSON, Willie. *Willie.* 1988. S&S. 1st. F/clip. A20. $20.00

NEMCEK, Paul. *Films of Nancy Carroll.* 1969. Lyle Stuart. photos. NF/dj. C9. $50.00

NEMEROV, Howard. *Homecoming Game.* 1957. S&S. 1st. NF/VG. B4. $125.00

NENTWIG, W. *Spiders of Panama.* 1993. Gainesville. Sandhill Crane. 274p. VG. B1. $35.00

NERMAN. *Caricature.* 1946. Am Studio Book. ils. VG+. C9. $75.00

NESBIT, E. *Long Ago When I Was Young.* 1966. Franklin Watts. 1st Am thus. NF/NF. C8. $30.00

NESBIT, E. *Long Ago When I Was Young.* 1966. Franklin Watts. 1st Am. 8vo. 127p. aqua cloth. xl. VG/dj. T5. $20.00

NESBIT, E. *Wouldbegoods.* 1901. Harper. 1st Am. 313p. VG. P2. $185.00

NESIS, K.N. *Odphalopods of the World.* 1987. Neptune City. TFH Pub. 8vo. 351p. NF. B1. $50.00

NETTER, Frank H. *CIBA Collection of Medical Illustrations Vol 1.* 1953. Summit, NJ. CIBA Pharmaceutical Products Inc. folio. gr cloth. G1. $30.00

NETTLETON, L.L. *Geophysical Prospecting for Oil.* 1940. McGraw Hill. 1st. 444p. VG. D8. $22.00

NEUGEBAUER & ORENDI. *Handbuch der Orientalischen Teppichkunde.* 1922. Leipzig. Hiersemann. 1st. 16 mc pl/fld map. 246p. NF. T10. $100.00

NEUHAUS, Eugene. *Art of the Exposition.* 1915. SF. Paul Elder. 1st. b&w tipped-in pl. VG. O4. $30.00

NEUHAUSS, Richard. *Lehrbuch der Mikrophotographie.* 1907. Leipzig. Hirzel. 1st. 8vo. ils/3 pl. 289p. cloth. VG. T10. $100.00

NEUMANN, Ruth Vendley. *Conversation-Piece Recipes.* 1962. Reilly Lee. VG/dj. A16. $17.50

NEUMARK, David. *Philosophy of the Bible.* 1918. Ark Pub. index. 326p. VG. S3. $25.00

NEUNZIG, H.H. *Moths of America North of Mexico.* 1990. WA. NMNH. 165p. NF/wrp. B1. $40.00

NEUTRA, Richard. *Survival Through Design.* 1954. Oxford. 393p. cloth. dj. D2. $40.00

NEVE, J.L. *History of Christian Thought Vol 1.* 1946. Muhlenberg. 344p. VG. B29. $8.50

NEVELSON, Louise. *Louise Nevelson: Atmospheres & Environments.* 1980. Clarkson Potter. 1st. intro Edward Albee. 192p. VG+. A25. $35.00

NEVILL, Ralph. *Old English Sporting Books.* 1924. London. The Studio. 1/1500. 4to. teg. rose buckram. F. B24. $225.00

NEVILLE, Emily. *It's Like This, Cat.* (1963). Harper Row. early prt. 8vo. 180p. VG/dj. T5. $25.00

NEVILLE, Henry. *Plato Redivivus; or, Dialogue Concerning Government.* 1681. London. SI. 1st. 8vo. calf. R12. $475.00

NEVILLE, Katherine. *Eight.* 1989. Ballantine. 1st. author's 1st book. F/F. D10. $55.00

NEVILLE, Richard. *Play Power.* 1970. London. Cape. 1st. F/F. B4. $275.00

NEVIN, C.M. *Principles of Structural Geology.* 1931. NY. John Wiley. 1st. G. D8. $15.00

NEVIN, David. *Soldiers.* 1975. Time-Life. leather. A19. $20.00

NEVIN, David. *Texans.* 1948. Bonanza. A19. $25.00

NEVIN, Robert P. *Les Trois Rois.* 1888. Pittsburgh. Eichbaum. 1st. 12mo. gilt gr cloth. NF. w/2 assn pieces. T10. $200.00

NEVINS, Francis M. *Cornell Woolrich: First You Dream, Then You Die.* 1985. Mysterious. 600+p. NF. C9. $50.00

NEVINS, Francis M. *Mystery Writer's Art.* 1970. Bowling Green. 1st. VG. M2. $20.00

NEVINS, Francis M. *Ninety Million Dollar Mouse.* 1987. Walker. 1st. NF/F. M22. $10.00

NEVINS, William Manlius. *Segregation Versus Integration.* nd. Columbus, GA. Tribune. 12mo. VG/plain wrp. C8. $25.00

NEW YORK STATE. *Forest, Fish & Game Commission 8th Annual Report.* 1903. Albany. NYS. 164p. G/wrp. H7. $12.50

NEWARK, Peter. *Cowboys.* 1982. London. Bison Books. dj. A19. $30.00

NEWBERRY, Clare Turlay. *Barkis.* 1938. Harper. 1st. 12mo. 30p. VG/VG. D1. $150.00

NEWBERRY, Clare Turlay. *Mittens.* 1936. Harper. 1st. 4to. VG/VG. R5. $175.00

NEWBERRY, Clare Turlay. *Mittens.* 1936. Harper. 8vo. VG. M5. $35.00

NEWBERRY, Clare Turlay. *Pandora.* 1944. Harper. 1st. lg 4to. NF/VG. C8. $125.00

NEWBERRY, Clare Turlay. *Pandora.* 1944. Harper. 1st. VG/VG. P2. $75.00

NEWBERRY, Clare Turlay. *Smudge.* 1948. Harper. 1st. sgn. dj. R5. $250.00

NEWBERRY, John S. *Later Extinct Floras of North America.* 1898. WA, DC. 68 tinted pl. 295p. gilt brn cloth. VG. B26. $135.00

NEWBY, Elizabeth. *Philosopher's Way: Essays & Address of D Elton Trueblood.* 1978. Nashville, TN. 1st. 136p. VG/dj. V3. $12.00

NEWBY, Leroy. *Target Ploesti.* 1983. Novato. Presidio. 1st. inscr. G/G. A23. $30.00

NEWCOMB, Covelle. *Secret Door: Story of Kate Greenaway.* 1946. Dodd Mead. 1st. ils A Burbank. VG. B15. $40.00

NEWCOMBE, Jack. *Christmas Treasury.* 1982. Viking. 1st. 474p. NF/NF. W2. $89.00

NEWELL, David M. *If Nothin' Don't Happen.* 1975. Knopf. 1st. sgn. 242p. VG/VG. B11. $75.00

NEWELL, Peter. *Hole Book.* 1908. Harper. 1st. 8vo. cloth/pict label. F/rare dj/chemise/case. B24. $3,000.00

NEWELL, Peter. *Hole Book.* 1908. NY. Harper. 1st. bl cloth/pict label. VG. M24. $165.00

NEWELL, Peter. *Peter Newell's Pictures & Rhymes.* 1899. Harper. 1st. obl 4to. tan cloth. R5. $300.00

NEWELL, Peter. *Pictures & Rhymes.* 1900 (1899). Harper. obl 8vo. VG. C8. $125.00

NEWELL, Peter. *Rocket Book.* 1912. Harper. G. M5. $110.00

NEWELL, Peter. *Rocket Book.* 1912. Harper. 1st. VG. P2. $250.00

NEWELL & SMITH. *Mighty Mo, the USS Missouri...* 1969. Seattle. 1/2500. ils. 190p. VG. B18. $45.00

NEWHALL, Beaumont. *Photography: Essays & Images.* 1980. NY. MOMA. 327p. tall 4to. wrp. A17. $15.00

NEWHAM, Paul. *Outlandish Adventures of Orpheus in the Underworld.* 1994. Bath/Boston. Barefoot Books. 1st Am. 31p. F/F. C14. $20.00

NEWHOUSE, S. *Trapper's Guide & Manual of Instructions...* 1894. NY. Forest/Stream. 9th revised. 205+16p. gray cloth. VG+. H7. $150.00

NEWMAN, Anna Pearl Leonard. *Stories of Early Life Along Beautiful Indian River.* 1953. Stuart, FL. self pub. sgn. 89p. VG. B11. $65.00

NEWMAN, Edward. *History of British Ferns.* 1940. London. Van Voorst. 1st. 8vo. 104p. A22. $65.00

NEWMAN, Elias. *Art in Palestine.* 1939. Siebel. 125p. VG. S3. $45.00

NEWMAN, Horatio H. *Evolution, Genetics & Eugenics.* 1921. Chicago. 2nd. 523p. dj. A17. $15.00

NEWMAN, J.P. *From Dan to Beersheba.* 1864. NY. Harper. lg fld map. 485p. xl. VG. T10. $75.00

NEWMAN, Kim. *Anno Dracula.* 1992. London. S&S. 1st. NF/damaged. M21. $60.00

NEWMAN, Nanette. *Fun Food Factory.* 1976. London. Whizzard. unp. VG. B10. $15.00

NEWMAN, Nanette. *Fun Food Factory.* 1977. Harmony. 1st. sm 4to. NF. C8. $17.50

NEWMAN, Robert P. *Cold War Romance of Lillian Hellman & John Melby.* 1989. Chapel Hill. 1st. as new/dj. V4. $15.00

NEWPORT, David. *Eudemon Spiritual & Rational: Apology for a Preacher...* 1901. Lippincott. 527p. V3. $14.00

NEWQUIST, Roy. *Conversations With Joan Crawford.* 1980. Citadel. 1st. NF/NF. T12. $15.00

NEWSOM, John. *Perspectives on John Philip Sousa.* 1983. WA. 1st. ils. 144p. VG/VG. B5. $35.00

NEWSOME, William Monypeny. *Whitetailed Deer.* 1926. Scribner. 1st. 288p. VG. H7. $40.00

NEWTON, A. Edward. *Dr Johnson, a Play.* 1923. Atlantic Monthly. 1st. ils. 120p. VG/dj. K3. $30.00

NEWTON, A. Edward. *Tourist in Spite of Himself.* 1930. Little Brn. 1st. ils Gluyas Williams. VG/rpr. K3. $30.00

NEWTON, A. Edward. *Tourist in Spite of Himself.* 1930. Little Brn. 3rd trade. 8vo. 252p. F/dj. T10. $35.00

NEWTON, Arthur Percival. *Travel & Travellers of the Middle Ages.* 1968. NY. Barnes Noble. rpt. 3 maps. as new/dj. O7. $45.00

NEWTON, Helmut. *White Women.* 1976. Stonehill. 1st. folio. F/NF. B4. $125.00

NEWTON, Huey P. *In Search of Common Ground.* 1973. NY. Norton. 1st. inscr. 143p. F/NF. B4. $375.00

NEWTON, Huey P. *Revolutionary Suicide.* 1973. HBJ. 1st. F/F. M25. $75.00

NEWTON, Isaac. *Papers & Letters on Natural Philosophy.* 1958. facsimiles of pub. VG/VG. M17. $25.00

NEWTON, Robert R. *Ancient Astronomical Observations...* 1970. Johns Hopkins. 8vo. 309p. VG. K5. $40.00

NEYHART, Louise Albright. *Giant of the Yards.* 1952. Boston. Houghton Mifflin. 1st. sgn. F/G. B11. $35.00

NICHOLAS, Barry. *Introduction to Roman Law.* 1965. Clarendon. Clarendon Law series. cloth. M11. $75.00

NICHOLLS, Peter. *Encyclopedia of Science Fiction.* 1981. London. Granada. 1st trade. 8vo. 672p. VG. M21. $20.00

NICHOLLS, Peter. *Foundation: Numbers 1-8.* 1978. Gregg. 1st. NF. M2. $35.00

NICHOLS, Beverley. *Art of Flower Arrangement.* 1967. NY. 1st Am. 239p. VG/rpr. B26. $67.50

NICHOLS, Beverley. *Case of Human Bondage.* 1966. London. 1st. inscr. VG/VG. T9. $45.00

NICHOLS, Beverley. *Laughter on the Stairs.* 1954. Dutton. 254p. VG/dj. A10. $28.00

NICHOLS, Beverley. *Tree That Sat Down.* 1947. London. Cape. 3rd. 8vo. 302p. VG. T5. $30.00

NICHOLS, F.H. *Through Hidden Shensi.* 1902. London. 333p. 2-toned cloth. NF. W3. $48.00

NICHOLS, Henry. *Eastward Around the World on Barque Emerald.* 1973. Salem. Naumkeag. sgn. ils/maps. 184p. dj. T7. $35.00

NICHOLS, Henry. *Voice at Sea.* 1950. Boston. Edinboro. 3rd. sgn. 12mo. VG. B11. $18.00

NICHOLS, J.T. *Representative North American Fresh-Water Fishes.* 1942. Macmillan. 1st. 128p. F/case. H1. $18.00

NICHOLS, John. *American Blood.* 1987. Holt. 1st. sgn. F/dj. A24. $40.00

NICHOLS, John. *Elegy for September.* 1992. Holt. 1st. sgn. F/F. T11. $45.00

NICHOLS, John. *Ghost in the Music.* 1979. Holt Rinehart. 1st. F/NF. M19. $35.00

NICHOLS, John. *Ghost in the Music.* 1979. HRW. 1st. inscr/sgn. VG+/F. A20. $55.00

NICHOLS, John. *Ghost in the Music.* 1979. HRW. 1st. sgn. F/F. T11. $55.00

NICHOLS, John. *Keep It Simple.* 1992. Norton. 1st. sgn. F/F. A20. $40.00

NICHOLS, John. *Milagro Beanfield War.* 1974. Holt. 1st. inscr. F/NF clip. H11. $380.00

NICHOLS, John. *Milagro Beanfield War.* 1974. NY. 1st. VG/dj. B5. $105.00

NICHOLS, John. *Nirvana Blues.* 1981. Holt. 1st. inscr/sgn drawing. VG+/NF. A20. $60.00

NICHOLS, John. *Sterile Cuckoo.* 1965. David McKay. 1st. author's 1st book. F/dj. A18. $80.00

NICHOLS, John. *Wizard of Loneliness.* 1966. Putnam. 1st. F/VG. M19. $125.00

NICHOLS, Leigh; see Koontz, Dean R.

NICHOLS, Robert. *Fantastica.* 1923. Macmillan. 1st. F. M2. $15.00

NICHOLS, Rose Standish. *English Pleasure Gardens.* 1925 (1902). Macmillan. 8vo. 324p. decor cloth. VG. A22. $75.00

NICHOLS, Roy F. *Battles & Leaders of the Civil War.* 1956. Yoseloff. 4 vol. boxed. A19. $100.00

NICHOLS & SHAW. *Okinawa: Victory of the Pacific.* 1955. WA, DC. fld mc maps/photos/index. 332p. VG. S16. $85.00

NICHOLSON, Ian. *Improve Your Own Boat.* 1986. Norton. ils. 241p. dj. T7. $30.00

NICHOLSON, Ian. *Road to the Stars.* 1978. Morrow. ils Andrew Farmer. 224p. VG/dj. K5. $20.00

NICHOLSON, T.R. *Wild Roads, Story of Transcontinental Motoring.* 1969. NY. 1st. ils/amps. 302p. VG/dj. B18. $22.50

NICKLAUS, Jack. *On & Off the Fairway.* 1978. S&S. 1st. photos. F/VG. P8. $40.00

NICKLAUS & WIND. *Greatest Game of All: My Life in Golf.* 1969. NY. 1st. inscr Nicklaus. 416p. VG/dj. B18. $27.50

NICOLAY, John G. *Outbreak of the Rebellion.* 1881. 220p. O8. $21.50

NICOLLIER, Jean. *Collecting Toy Soldiers.* 1967. 1st. photos. VG/VG. S13. $45.00

NIDETCH, Jean. *Weight Watchers Program Cookbook.* 1975 (1973). Hearthside. 11th. 320p. VG/VG. B10. $10.00

NIEBUHR, Carl. *Tell El Amarna Period, the Relations of Egypt & W Asia...* 1903. London. Nutt. 1st. trans Hutchinson. 62p. VG. W1. $22.00

NIEBUHR, Reinhold. *Nature & Destiny of Man.* 1953. Scribner. 2 vol. G. B29. $8.00

NIEBUHR, Reinhold. *Structure of Nations & Empires.* 1959. Scribner. 206p. G/dj. B29. $8.00

NIELSEN, Johannes M. *Agnosia, Apraxia, Aphasia: Their Value...* 1936. Los Angeles. Neurological Soc. 210p. panelled bl cloth. VG. G1. $65.00

NIELSEN, Kay. *East of the Sun & West of the Moon.* 1977. Doubleday. 1st Am thus. ils Kay Nielsen. gr cloth. NF/NF. T5. $55.00

NIELSON, Leslie. *Naked Truth.* 1993. Pocket. 1st. inscr. F/F. A23. $40.00

NIERENBERG, W.A. *Encyclopedia of Earth Science Vol 4, Ri-Z.* 1992. San Diego. Academic. 715p. VG. D8. $20.00

NIETO (or NETO), David. *Matteh Dan y Segunda Parte del Cuzari, Donde se Prueva...* (1714). London. Thomas Ilive. 1st. Spanish/Hebrew text. woodcuts. recent morocco. R15. $3,800.00

NIETZ. *Old Textbooks: Spelling, Grammar, Reading, Arithmetic...* 1961. Pittsburgh. 373p. VG. A4. $145.00

NIJINSKY, Romolo. *Nijinsky & the Last Years of Nijinsky.* 1980. S&S. F/NF. W2. $35.00

NIKOLSKY, G.V. *Ecology of Fishes.* 1978. Neptune City. TFH Pub. 352p. F/wrp. B1. $25.00

NILES, Blair. *Colombia: Land of Miracles.* (1924). Century. 1st. 389p. cloth. F3. $15.00

NILES, Blair. *Condemned to Devil's Island: Biography of Unknown Convict.* 1928. Grosset Dunlap. 1st thus/5th prt. photos Rober Niles. VG. A25. $10.00

NILES, Grace G. *Bog-Trotting for Orchids.* 1904. Putnam. 1st. 310p. VG. A10. $95.00

NILES, John M. *View of South America & Mexico.* 1826. NY. Huntington. 2 vol in 1. leather brd. F3. $95.00

NILSSON, B.E. *Political Socialism: Capturing the Government.* 1913. Portland. self pub. 1st. NF/wrp. B2. $40.00

NIN, Anais. *Diary of...1966-1974.* 1980. Harcourt Brace. 1st. F/dj. Q1. $35.00

NIN, Anais. *Little Birds.* 1979. HBJ. 1st. NF/dj. A24. $30.00

NIN, Anais. *Novel of the Future.* 1968. Macmillan. 1st. NF/VG clip. B3. $60.00

NIVEN, Larry. *Integral Trees.* 1984. Ballantine. 1st. inscr. F/F. R14. $35.00

NIVEN, Larry. *Legacy of Heart.* 1987. S&S. 1st. F/F. P3. $20.00

NIVEN & POURNELLE. *Mote in God's Eye.* nd. SFBC. NF/dj. M2. $15.00

NIXON, Howard M. *Five Centuries of English Bookbinding.* 1978. London. 1st. VG/dj. T9. $45.00

NIZAN, Paul. *Watchdogs.* 1971. Monthly Review. 1st. F/F. B35. $32.00

NOAKES, Vivien. *Painted Edward Lear.* 1991. Newton Abbot. 1st. fwd The Prince of Wales. VG/VG. T9. $75.00

NOBLE, G.P. *Hula Blues: Story of Johnny Noble.* 1948. photos. VG/VG. M17. $20.00

NOBLE, G.P. *On Hawaiian Folk Music.* 1971. ils. VG. M17. $25.00

NOBLE & O'BRIEN. *Sentinels of the Rocks.* 1979. MI U. ils. 61p. wrp. T7. $16.00

NODIER, Charles. *Bibliomaniac.* 1894. JO Wright. 1/150. A19. $30.00

NODIER, Charles. *Luck of the Bean-Row's.* nd. London. Daniel O'Connor. ils CL Fraser. VG-. P2. $20.00

NOEL, J. *Footloose in Arcadia.* 1940. London. 1st. VG/G. B5. $25.00

NOGUERIA DA GAMA, Manoel J. *Memoria Sobre o Loureiro Cinnamomo Vulgo...* 1797. Lisbon. Officina Patriarcal. 1st/only. 38p. contemporary wrp. R15. $1,250.00

NOIR, Julien. *Etude sur les Tics Chez les Degeneres, Imbeciles et Idiots.* 1893. Paris. Bureaux Progres Medical/Felix Alcan. ils. 170p. VG. G1. $125.00

NOLAN, William F. *Dashiell Hammett: A Casebook.* 1969. Santa Barbara. McNally Loftin. 1st. F/dj. M15. $50.00

NOLAN, William F. *Hammett: Life at the Edge.* 1983. Congdon Weed. 1st. F/dj. M2. $20.00

NOLAN, William F. *Hammett: Life at the Edge.* 1983. NY. 1st. sgn. F/F. A11. $45.00

NOLAN, William F. *Logan: A Trilogy.* 1986. Maclay. 1st. F/dj. w/sgn label. M2. $25.00

NOLDE, Eile. *Flowers & Animals: Watercolors & Drawings.* 1966. ils. VG. M17. $50.00

NOLL, Mark A. *History of Christianity in the United States & Canada.* 1992. Eerdmans. 576p. VG. B29. $11.00

NONNE, Max. *Syphilis und Nervensystem: Neunzehn Vorlesungen...* 1909. Berlin. Von S Karger. 2nd revised. 8vo. 699p. early red buckram. G1. $75.00

NOONE, Edwina; see Avallone, Mike.

NORBECK, J. *Encyclopedia of American Steam Traction Engines...* nd. Glen Ellyn. ils. 320p. F. M4. $25.00

NORD, Max. *Thank You Canada.* 1967. Montreal. 1st. F. T12. $15.00

NORDAN, Lewis. *Music of the Swamp.* 1991. Algonquin. 1st. F/F. R14. $50.00

NORDAN, Lewis. *Music of the Swamp.* 1991. Algonquin. 1st. sgn. author's 3rd book. F/F. B3. $75.00

NORDAN, Lewis. *Music of the Swamp.* 1991. Chapel Hill. Algonquin. 1st. sgn. F/F. R13. $50.00

NORDAN, Lewis. *Welcome to the Arrow-Catcher Fair.* 1989. NY. Vintage. 1st thus. sgn. F/wrp. M23. $50.00

NORDAN, Lewis. *Wolf Whistle.* 1993. Algonquin. 1st. sgn. F/F. R13. $45.00

NORDANG, Bruno. *Patagonia Year.* 1938. Knopf. 1st Am. dj. F3. $20.00

NORDHEIMER, Isaac. *Critical Grammar of the Hebrew Language.* 1841-2. NY. Wiley Putnam. 2nd. 2 vol. 8vo. contemporary bdg. M1. $175.00

NORDYKE, Lewis. *John Wesley Hardin, Texas Gunman, the Complete & Fabulous...* 1957. Morrow. 1st. 278p. VG/VG. J2. $125.00

NOREM, Owen J.C. *Timeless Lithuana.* 1943. Chicago. Amerlith. tall 8vo. 299p. silvered red cloth. H1. $20.00

NOREN, Catherine Hanf. *Camera of My Family.* 1976. Knopf. 1st. photos. 238p. VG/G+. S3. $33.00

NORFOLK, Lawrence. *Lempriere's Dictionary.* 1991. Harmony. 1st. F/F. A24. $20.00

NORFOLK, William; see Farmer, Philip Jose.

NORIE, J.W. *New Seaman's Guide & Coaster's Companion.* 1821. London. Norie. 12mo. 414p. recased cloth. T7. $375.00

NORLEY, Alfred. *Letter to Lucian & Other Poems.* 1957. Lippincott. 1st. F/F double dj. V1. $25.00

NORMAN, D. *Illustrated Encyclopedia of Dinosaurs.* 1985. Salamander Books Ltd. 208p. as new/dj. D8. $30.00

NORMAN, D. *Prehistoric Life, Rise of the Vertebrates...* 1994. Macmillan. ils. 246p. NF/dj. D8. $25.00

NORMAN, Howard. *How Glooskap Outwits the Ice Giants.* 1989. Little Brn. 1st. rem mk. VG/F. B3. $50.00

NORMAN, Howard. *Kiss in the Hotel Joseph Conrad.* 1989. Summit. 1st. F/F. from $65 to $75.00

NORMAN, Howard. *Kiss in the Hotel Joseph Conrad.* 1989. Summit. 1st. sgn. F/F. D10/M23. $100.00

NORMAN, Howard. *Northern Lights.* 1987. NY. Summit. 1st. sgn. author's 1st novel. F/NF. L3. $150.00

NORMAN, Howard. *Northern Lights.* 1987. Summit. 1st. sgn. author's 1st novel. F/F. D10. $175.00

NORMAN, Howard. *Owl-Scatterer.* 1986. Atlantic Monthly. 1st. ils Michael McCurdy. F/dj. B4. $175.00

NORMAN, Howard. *Where the Chill Came From.* 1982. Northpoint. 1st. NF/F. L3. $125.00

NORMAN, Marc. *Oklahoma Crude.* 1973. Dutton. 1st. author's 2nd book. F/F. H11. $25.00

NORMAN, Sidney A. *Elements of Natural Philosophy.* 1870. Cincinnati. Wilson Hinkle. 8vo. 468p. quarter leather. K5. $15.00

NORMANTON, Simon. *Tibet: Lost Civilization.* 1989. Viking. 192p. F/dj. W3. $48.00

NORRIS, Clarence. *Last of the Scottsboro Boys: An Autobiography.* 1979. Putnam. 1st. VG/VG. V4. $17.50

NORRIS, Frank. *Blix.* 1899. Doubleday McClure. 1st. cream cloth. F. M24. $100.00

NORRIS, Frank. *Pit.* 1903. Doubleday. 1st/1st prt (Special Pres Ed). top edge gray. gray bdg. M24. $165.00

NORRIS, Frank. *Responsibilities of the Novelist & Other Literary Essays.* 1903. Doubleday Page. 1st. variant bdg. D11. $100.00

NORRIS, George. *Contributions to Practical Surgery.* 1873. Phil. 1st. 318p. A13. $250.00

NORRIS & NORRIS. *History of Zaca Lake.* 1994. Santa Barbara/Los Olivos. ils. 192p. pict wrp. D11. $45.00

NORRIS & WASHINGTON. *Last of the Scottsboro Boys.* 1979. NY. 1st. VG/dj. B5. $25.00

NORSWORTHY & WHITLEY. *Psychology of Childhood.* 1923. NY. 8vo. 375p. brn cloth. VG. B14. $55.00

NORTH, Andrew; see Norton, Andre.

NORTH, Anthony; see Koontz, Dean R.

NORTH, Arthur Walbridge. *Camp & Camino in Lower California.* 1977 (1910). Rio Grande. rpt. F. O4. $25.00

NORTH, Elisha. *Treatise on Malignant Epidemic...Spotted Fever...* 1993. NY. Classics Neurology/Neurosurgery. facsimile. G1. $65.00

NORTH, Oliver. *One More Mission.* 1993. Zondervan. 1st. sgn. F/F. A23. $45.00

NORTHEN, R.T. *Miniature Orchids.* 1980. Van Nostrand. 189p. photos. dj. B1. $25.00

NORTHEND, Charles. *American Speaker, Being a Collection of Pieces in Prose...* 1848. Syracuse. 1st. 252p. cloth/blk leather spine. B22. $17.00

NORTHEND, Mary Harrod. *American Glass.* Jan 1936. Tudor. 2nd. 209p. VG. H1. $30.00

NORTHROP, H.D. *Chinese Horrors & Persecutions of the Christians...* 1900. Phil. World Bible. 1st. ils. 403p. VG. W3. $245.00

NORTHROP, H.D. *Wonders of the Tropics; or, Explorations & Adventures...* 1889. Portland. Downing. ils/808p. gilt pict cloth. VG. M12. $75.00

NORTON, Alice; see Norton, Andre.

NORTON, Andre. *Beast Master.* 1959. Harcourt. 1st. VG/dj. M2. $50.00

NORTON, Andre. *Crystal Gryphon.* 1972. Atheneum. 1st. xl. VG/F. M2. $90.00

NORTON, Andre. *Dare To Go A-Hunting.* 1990. Tor. 1st. VG/VG. P3. $20.00

NORTON, Andre. *Dark Piper.* 1968. HBW. 1st. xl. dj. P3. $13.00

NORTON, Andre. *Dread Companion.* 1970. HBJ. 1st. 8vo. F/dj. T10. $75.00

NORTON, Andre. *Flight in Yiktor.* 1986. Tor. 1st. F/F. P3. $15.00

NORTON, Andre. *Garan the Eternal.* 1972. Fantasy. 1st. F/F. P3. $40.00

NORTON, Andre. *Gate of the Cat.* 1987. Ace. 1st. sgn. F/dj. M2. $45.00

NORTON, Andre. *Gryphon in Glory.* 1981. Atheneum. 2nd. sgn. G/G. B11. $18.00

NORTON, Andre. *Iron Cage.* 1974. Viking. 1st. F/dj. M2/P3. $35.00

NORTON, Andre. *Judgment on Janus.* 1963. Harcourt. 1st. NF/dj. M2. $80.00

NORTON, Andre. *No Night Without Stars.* 1976. London. 1st. inscr. F/dj. M2. $60.00

NORTON, Andre. *Opal-Eyed Fan.* 1977. Dutton. 1st. VG/dj. P3. $20.00

NORTON, Andre. *Opal-Eyed Fan.* 1977. Dutton. 1st. 8vo. F/dj. T10. $50.00

NORTON, Andre. *Operation Time Search.* 1967. Harcourt. 1st. F/dj. M2. $75.00

NORTON, Andre. *Ordeal in Otherwhere.* 1964. World. 1st. NF/dj. M2. $85.00

NORTON, Andre. *Quag Keep.* 1978. Atheneum. 1st. F/dj. M2. $35.00

NORTON, Andre. *Small Shadows Creep.* 1974. Dutton. 1st. F/F. P3. $15.00

NORTON, Andre. *Space Service.* 1953. World. 1st. VG/dj. M2. $125.00

NORTON, Andre. *Star Born.* 1957. World. 1st. xl. VG/dj. M2. $75.00

NORTON, Andre. *Steel Magic.* 1965. World. 1st. F/clip. M21. $45.00

NORTON, Andre. *Victory on Janus.* 1966. HBW. 1st. VG/dj. M20/P3. $80.00

NORTON, Andre. *Wizards' Worlds.* 1989. Tor. 1st. NF/dj. P3. $20.00

NORTON, Andre. *X Factor.* 1965. Harcourt. 1st. F/dj. M2. $85.00

NORTON, Herman. *Record of Facts Concerning Persecutions at Maderia 1843... 1849.* NY. Fanshaw. 1st. full-p ils. 228p. gilt brn cloth. B14. $350.00

NORTON, J.B.S. *North American Species of Euphorbia, Section Tithyalus.* 1899. St Louis. inscr. 52 pl. 60p. wrp. B26. $32.50

NORTON, John P. *Elements of Scientific Agriculture.* 1860. NY. Saxton Barker. ils. 208p. xl. K3. $40.00

NORTON, Mary. *Bed-Knobs & Broom-Sticks.* 1957. Dent. 1st. ils Erik Blegvad. VG. M5. $30.00

NORTON, Mary. *Borrowers Afloat.* 1959. Harcourt Brace. 1st. 191p. cloth. VG/dj. M20. $37.00

NORTON, Mary. *Borrowers Afloat.* 1961. Harcourt. ils Beth/Joe Krush. F/VG+. M5. $45.00

NORTON, Mary. *Borrowers.* 1953. Harcourt Brace. 1st Am. ils Krush. VG-/dj. P2. $85.00

NORTON, Mary. *Magic Bed-Knob.* 1943. Hyperion. 1st Am. ils Waldo Peirce. VG/G+. P2. $125.00

NORTON, T.E. *Fur Trade in Colonial New York 1686-1776.* 1974. WI U. 1st prt. F/dj. M4. $20.00

NORVIL, Manning; see Bulmer, Kenneth.

NORWAK, Mary. *Home Baked Bread & Cakes.* 1973. London. Hamlyn. VG/dj. A16. $10.00

NORWOOD, Hayden. *Marble Man's Wife, Thomas Wolfe's Mother.* 1947. Scribner. 1st. gilt red cloth. F/NF. M24. $50.00

NORWOOD, Robin. *Women Who Love Too Much.* 1985. Tarcher. 266p. F/dj. B29. $6.50

NOTH, Martin. *Exodus.* 1962. Westminster. Old Testament Lib. 283p. G/dj. B29. $13.00

NOTH, Martin. *History of Israel.* 1958. Harper. 479p. G/dj. B29. $10.00

NOURSE, Alan E. *Fourth Horseman.* 1983. Harper Row. 1st. VG/VG. P3. $18.00

NOURSE, Alan E. *Raiders From the Rings.* 1962. McKay. 1st. VG/dj. M2. $30.00

NOVA, Craig. *Good Son.* 1982. Delacorte. 1st. F/F. R14. $30.00

NOVA, Craig. *Incandenscence.* 1979. Harper. 1st. F/dj. M25. $25.00

NOVA, Craig. *Trombone.* 1992. Grove Weidenfeld. 1st. F/F. H11. $20.00

NOVA, Craig. *Turkey Hash.* 1972. Harper Row. 1st. NF/NF. R14. $40.00

NOVAK, Joseph. *Future is Ours, Comrade: Conversations With the Russians.* 1960. Doubleday. ARC/1st. author's 1st book. RS. gray cloth. dj. M24. $200.00

NOVECK, Simon. *Great Jewish Personalities in Modern Times.* 1964. WA, DC. 3rd. 366p. VG/dj. S3. $25.00

NOVIKOV, I.D. *Evolution of the Universe.* 1983. Cambridge. 176p. VG/VG. K5. $25.00

NOVITSKI, Joseph. *Wind Star: Building of a Sailship.* 1987. Macmillan. ils. 242p. dj. T7. $20.00

NOYES, Alfred. *Enchanted Island.* nd. Stokes. inscr. VG. M2. $75.00

NOYES, Alfred. *Highwayman.* 1983. Lee Shepard. 1st. sm 8vo. red cloth. F/NF. T5. $35.00

NOYES, Pierrpoint. *Gentlemen: You Are Mad!* 1946. Barter Feres. 1st thus. F/dj. M2. $35.00

NULAND, Sherwin. *Doctors: Biography of Medicine.* 1988. NY. 1st. 519p. A13. $30.00

NUMBERS, Ronald L. *Creation by Natural Law.* 1977. London. W of WA. NF/dj. K3. $15.00

NUMBERS, Ronald L. *Education of American Physicians.* 1980. Los Angeles. 345p. A13. $35.00

NUNAN, Thomas. *Diary of an Old Bohemian.* 1927. SF. Har Wagner Pub. 1st. VG. O4. $20.00

NUNES DE LIAO, Duarte. *Leis Extravagantes Collegidas e Relatados...* 1569. Lisbon. Antonio Goncalvez. 1st. folio. G. R15. $4,250.00

NUNEZ MELENDEZ, Esteban. *Plantas Medicinales de Puerto Rico.* 1982. Rio Piedras. Folklore Fundamentos Cientificos. photos. 498p. sc. B26. $36.00

NUNN, Kem. *Unassigned Territory.* 1987. Delacorte. 1st. author's 2nd book. F/NF. H11. $35.00

NUNN, Kem. *Unassigned Territory.* 1987. Delacorte. 1st. VG/VG. A20. $25.00

NURA. *Mitty Children Fix Things.* 1946. Jr Lit Guild/Am Studio. lg 4to. VG/G. M5. $42.00

NUSBAUMER, Louis. *Valley of Salt, Memoires of Wine.* 1967. Berkeley. Friends Bancroft Lib #15. 68p. gr cloth. as new. K7. $35.00

NUTT, Frederic. *Complete Confectioner; or, Whole Art of Confectionary...* 1807. NY. Richard Scott. 1st Am. 12mo. 91p. full contemporary calf. M1. $525.00

NUTTING, Wallace. *Clock Book.* 1924. Old Am Co. photos. VG. M17. $50.00

NUTTING, Wallace. *Furniture of the Pilgrim Century 1620-1720.* nd. Dover. 2 vol. rpt. VG. M17. $40.00

NYE, Naomi Shihab. *Hugging the Jukebox.* 1982. Dutton. 1st. sgn. author's 1st book. F/dj. V1. $65.00

NYGREN, Anders. *Commentary on Romans.* 1949. Muhlenberg. 457p. VG. B29. $16.00

O'BRIAN, Patrick. *Men-of-War.* 1974. London. Collins. 1st. F/F clip. w/pub price label present. B4. $375.00

O'BRIEN, Andy. *Fire-Wagon Hockey.* 1967. Ryerson. 1st. photos. VG+/VG+. P8. $35.00

O'BRIEN, Edna. *August Is a Wicked Month.* 1965. S&S. 1st Am. author's 3rd novel. F/NF. D10. $60.00

O'BRIEN, Edna. *Girls in Their Married Bliss.* 1965. S&S. 1st Am. F/F. D10. $50.00

O'BRIEN, Edna. *High Road.* 1988. FSG. 1st. F/F. R14. $30.00

O'BRIEN, Edna. *If I Die in a Combat Zone.* 1973. Delacorte. 1st. author's 1st book. NF/NF. D10. $1,000.00

O'BRIEN, Flann. *At Swim-Two-Birds.* (1939). Pantheon. 1st Am (actually pub in 1951). F/NF. L3. $200.00

O'BRIEN, Flann. *Poor Mouth.* 1974. Viking. 1st. trans PC Power. Ils Ralph Steadman. F/dj. Q1. $75.00

O'BRIEN, Frederick. *Atolls of the Sun.* 1922. NY. Century. 60 photos/map. 508p. T7. $25.00

O'BRIEN, Jack. *Valiant, Dog of the Timberline.* (1935). Grosset Dunlap. pre-1963 prt. ils Kurt Wiese. VG+/dj. C8. $22.50

O'BRIEN, John. *Interviews With Black Writers.* 1973. Liveright. 1st. F/dj. M25. $45.00

O'BRIEN, John. *Leaving Las Vegas.* 1990. Wichita. Watermark. 1st. sgn. author's 1st novel. F/dj. B3/L3. $500.00

O'BRIEN, John. *Twelve Days of Christmas.* 1991. Honesdale. Boyds Mill. 4th. sgn. F/F. A23. $32.00

O'BRIEN, P.J. *Will Rogers, Ambassador of Good Will, Prince of Wit...* 1935. Phil. Winston. A19. $25.00

O'BRIEN, R. Barry. *John Bright: A Monograph.* 1911. Houghton Mifflin. 270p. G+. V3. $40.00

O'BRIEN, Robert. *This Is San Francisco.* 1948. McGraw Hill. ils Antonio Sotomayor. blk cloth. NF/dj. K7. $15.00

O'BRIEN, Tim. *Going After Cacciato.* 1978. London. Cape. 1st. F/NF clip. B3. $125.00

O'BRIEN, Tim. *In the Lake of the Woods.* 1994. Houghton Mifflin. 1st. F/dj. T2. $25.00

O'BRIEN, Tim. *In the Lake of the Woods.* 1994. Houghton Mifflin. 1st. sgn. F/dj. Q1. $50.00

O'BRIEN, Tim. *Nuclear Age.* 1985. Knopf. 1st ed. sgn. rem mk. F/F. B2. $50.00

O'BRIEN, Tim. *Speaking of Courage.* 1980. Santa Barbara. Neville. ltd ed. 1/326. sgn. F/sans. R14. $225.00

O'BRIEN, Tim. *Things They Carried.* 1990. Franklin Lib. 1st. sgn. full leather. F. Q1. $125.00

O'BRIEN, Tim. *Things They Carried.* 1990. Houghton Mifflin. 1st. F/dj. A24/M19/T11. $45.00

O'BRIEN. *TE Lawrence: A Bibliography.* 1988. ils. 754p. F/F. A4. $165.00

O'CASEY, Sean. *Silver Tassie: A Tragi-Comedy in Four Acts.* 1928. Macmillan. 1st. 140p. gr cloth. VG+/F. B22. $10.00

O'CONNELL, Jack. *Box Nine.* 1992. Mysterious. 1st. author's 1st novel. F/F. P3. $40.00

O'CONNOR, Flannery. *Et ce Sont les Violents Qui l'Emportent.* 1965. Paris. Gallimard. 1/27 on lafuma navarre. unopened. NF/wrp. R13. $150.00

O'CONNOR, Flannery. *Habit of Being.* 1979. Farrar Straus. 1st. F/dj. B2/Q1. $75.00

O'CONNOR, Flannery. *La Sagesse Dans le Sang (Wise Blood).* 1959. Paris. Gallimard. 1/35 on lafuma navarre. author's 1st book. NF/wrp. R13. $275.00

O'CONNOR, Flannery. *Les Braves Gens ne Courent Pas les Rues (A Good Man...).* 1963. Paris. Gallimard. 1/26 on lafuma navarre. NF/wrp/tissue dj. R13. $200.00

O'CONNOR, Flannery. *Memoir of Mary Ann.* 1961. FSG. 1st. VG/VG. S13. $85.00

O'CONNOR, Flannery. *Mon Mal Vient de Plus Lion (Everything That Rises...).* 1969. Paris. Gallimard. 1/26 on lafuma navarre. NF/wrp/tissue dj. R13. $125.00

O'CONNOR, Flannery. *Running in the Family.* 1982. FSG. 1st. NF/VG+. S13. $30.00

O'CONNOR, Flannery. *Wise Blood.* 1952. Harcourt Brace. 1st. yel brd. F/dj. M24. $600.00

O'CONNOR, Jack. *Game in the Desert.* (1939). Derrydale. rpt. leather. VG. M17. $25.00

O'CONNOR, Jack. *Hunting Rifle.* 1970. Winchester. 1st. 314p. cloth. VG+/worn. M20. $25.00

O'CONNOR, John. *Adobe Book.* 1973. Santa Fe. 1st. 130p. VG/dj. B5. $45.00

O'CONNOR, Richard. *Sheridan the Inevitable.* 1953. Bobbs Merrill. 1st. 24 pl/7 maps. 400p. F/VG. H1. $60.00

O'DONNELL, Barrett; see Malzberg, Barry.

O'DONNELL, E.P. *Great Big Doorstep.* 1941. Boston. Houghton Mifflin. 1st. F/NF. B4. $250.00

O'DONNELL, K.M.; see Malzberg, Barry.

O'DONNELL, Lillian. *Falling Star.* 1979. Putnam. 1st. F/dj. P3. $20.00

O'DONNELL, Lillian. *Ladykiller.* 1984. Putnam. 1st. VG/dj. P3. $18.00

O'DONNELL, Peter. *Dead Man's Handle.* 1985. London. Souvenir. 1st. sgn. F/F. T2. $55.00

O'DONNELL, Peter. *Dragon's Claw.* 1978. Mysterious. 1/250. sgn/#d. F/case. B11/T2. $65.00

O'DONNELL, Peter. *Modesty Blaise.* 1965. Souvenir. 1st. NF/dj. P3. $30.00

O'DONNELL, Peter. *Moonraker's Bride.* 1973. Souvenir. 1st. NF/NF. P3. $60.00

O'DONOGHUE & SPRINGER. *Adventures of Phoebe Zeit-Geist.* (1968). Grove. 1st. 150p. bl cloth. B22. $12.00

O'DONOVAN, Edmond. *Mern Oasis: Travels & Adventures of Caspian...* 1883. NY. 2 vol. maps. VG. B5. $250.00

O'FAOLAIN, Sean. *Talking Trees & Other Stories.* 1970. Boston. 1st. F/F. A17. $20.00

O'FLAHERTY, Joseph S. *Those Powerful Years: South Coast & Los Angeles 1887-1917.* 1978. Hicksville, NY. 1st. F/F. O4. $15.00

O'FLAHERTY, Liam. *Fairy Goose & Two Other Stories.* 1927. Crosby Gaige. 1/1190. sgn. F/VG. C6. $75.00

O'FLAHERTY, Liam. *Insurrection.* 1950. London. 1st. VG/VG. T9. $45.00

O'GRADY, Timothy. *Motherland.* 1989. Holt. 1st. F/F. A20/W2. $25.00

O'HANLON, Redmond. *Joseph Conrad & Charles Darwin.* 1984. Atlantic Highlands. 1st Am. author's 1st book. NF/VG. L3. $200.00

O'HARA, Frank. *Homage to Frank O'Hara.* 1980. Creative Age. revised. photos. V1. $15.00

O'HARA, John. *Collected Stories of...* 1984. Random. 1st. F/F. D10. $40.00

O'HARA, John. *Farmer's Hotel.* 1951. Random. 1st. VG/VG. P3. $60.00

O'HARA, John. *From the Terrace.* 1958. Random. 1st. F/NF. D10. $50.00

O'HARA, John. *Lockwood Concern.* 1965. NY. 1st. 1/300. sgn. F/case. C2. $150.00

O'HARA, John. *North Frederick.* 1955. Random. 1st. VG/dj. P3. $50.00

O'HARA, John. *Ourselves To Know.* 1963. Random. 1st. NF/VG. R14. $35.00

O'HARA, John. *Pipe Night.* 1946. Faber. 1st. F/F. M19. $85.00

O'HARA, John. *Rage To Live.* 1949. Random. 1st. F/VG. M19. $45.00

O'HARA, John. *Sermons & Soda Water.* 1960. Random. 1st. 3 vol. F/NF. B35. $45.00

O'HARA, John. *Sermons & Soda Water.* 1960. Random. 1st. 3 vol. VG/VG box. A20. $25.00

O'HARA, Kenneth. *Bird Cage.* 1968. Random. 1st. 184p. VG/dj. M20. $15.00

O'HARA, Kenneth. *View to a Death.* 1958. London. Cassell. 1st. VG/VG. P3. $25.00

O'HARRA, Cleophas. *White River Badlands.* 1920. Rapid City, SD. scarce. A19. $40.00

O'LEARY, Brian. *Mars 1999.* 1987. Stackpole. 1st. 8vo. 160p. VG/VG. K5. $30.00

O'MALLEY, C.D. *Andreas Vesalius of Brussels.* 1964. Berkeley. 1st. 480p. A13. $100.00

O'MALLEY, M. *Gone Away With O'Malley.* 1944. Garden City. 1st. ils Paul Brn. VG/VG. B5. $20.00

O'MEARA, W. *Guns at the Forks.* 1965. Englewood Cliffs. American Fort series. 273p. F/dj. M4. $25.00

O'NEAL, Bill. *Encyclopedia of Western Gun-Fighters.* 1983. Norman, OK. dj. A19. $20.00

O'NEIL, Dennis. *Secret Origins of the Super DC Heroes.* 1976. Harmony. 1st. F/dj. M2. $25.00

O'NEIL, George. *American Dream.* 1933. NY. Samuel French. 1st. F/VG. B4. $125.00

O'NEIL, Paul. *End & the Myth.* 1979. Time-Life. leather. A19. $20.00

O'NEILL, Eugene. *All God's Chillun Got Wings & Welded.* 1924. NY. 1st. NF. B4. $75.00

O'NEILL, Eugene. *Anna Christie.* 1930. Liveright. 1st separate. 1/775. sgn. ils Alexander King. dj/case. B24. $350.00

O'NEILL, Eugene. *Dynamo.* 1929. Horace Liveright. 1st. NF/VG. M23. $25.00

O'NEILL, Eugene. *Emperor Jones.* 1928. NY. 1/750. sgn. VG/worn box. B5. $200.00

O'NEILL, Eugene. *Hughie.* 1959. New Haven. Yale. 1st. F/F. B4. $200.00

O'NEILL, Eugene. *Long Day's Journey Into Night.* 1956. New Haven. Yale. 1st. F/dj. B24. $100.00

O'NEILL, Eugene. *Marco Millions.* 1927. Boni Liveright. 1st. F/F. B4. $275.00

O'NEILL, Eugene. *Mourning Becomes Electra: A Trilogy.* 1931. Horace Liveright. 1st. glazed teal cloth. F/dj. B24. $100.00

O'NEILL, Eugene. *Nine Plays.* 1954. Modern Lib. 867p. G. W2. $65.00

O'NEILL, Eugene. *Strange Interlude.* 1928. Boni Liveright. 1st. F/NF. D10. $225.00

O'NEILL, Moira. *Songs of the Glens of Glens of Antrim.* 1911. Portland, ME. Thomas B Mosher. 1st. 1/950. 16mo. VG. H1. $48.00

O'NEILL, Tip. *Man of the House.* 1987. Random. 1st. VG. W2. $20.00

O'NEILL, William L. *Everyone Was Brave: Rise & Fall of Feminism in America.* 1969. Quadrangle. 1st. F/F. B35. $35.00

O'REILLY, Tim. *Frank Herbert: Maker of Dune.* 1987. Berkley. 1st. F. M2. $15.00

O'REILLY, Victor. *Games of the Hangman.* 1991. Grove Weidenfeld. 1st. NF/dj. P3. $20.00

O'SHAUGHNESSY, Michael. *Monster Book of Monsters.* 1988. Bonanza. 1st. F/F. P3. $15.00

O'SHEA, Sean; see Tralins, Bob.

O'SHELL, Patrick. *Semper Fidelis: US Marines in the Pacific 1942-1945.* 1947. NY. 1st. maps/photos. 360p. VG. S16. $45.00

O'SULLIVAN, J.B. *Don't Hang Me Too High.* 1954. Mill Morrow. 1st. 222p. VG/dj. M20. $12.00

O'SULLIVAN, Maurice. *Twenty Years A-Growing.* 1933. 1st. VG/VG. M17. $20.00

OAKESHOTT, E. *Dark Age Warrior.* 1974. Lutterworth. ils/map ep. 135p. brd. F/F. M12. $27.50

OAKLEY, Amy. *Our Pennsylvania, Keys to the Keystone State.* 1950. Bobbs Merrill. 1st. 8vo. ils Thornton Oakley. F/dj. H1. $20.00

OATES, Joyce Carol. *All the Good People I've Left Behind.* 1979. Black Sparrow. 1st. 1/300. sgn. F/glassine. B4. $100.00

OATES, Joyce Carol. *American Appetites.* 1989. Dutton. 1st. F/dj. Q1. $30.00

OATES, Joyce Carol. *American Appetites.* 1989. Dutton. 1st. inscr. rem mk. F/F. R14. $40.00

OATES, Joyce Carol. *Angel of Light.* 1981. Dutton. 1st. VG+/F. A20. $25.00

OATES, Joyce Carol. *Anonymous Sins & Other Poems.* 1969. LSU. 1st. F/NF. A15. $40.00

OATES, Joyce Carol. *Assassins.* 1975. Vanguard. 1st. F/F. H11. $35.00

OATES, Joyce Carol. *Assassins.* 1975. Vanguard. 1st. F/NF. A24. $30.00

OATES, Joyce Carol. *Assassins.* 1975. Vanguard. 1st. F/VG. A20. $25.00

OATES, Joyce Carol. *Childworld.* 1976. Vanguard. 1st. inscr. F/F. B4. $125.00

OATES, Joyce Carol. *Fabulous Beasts.* 1975. LSU. 1st. ils AG Smith. F/F. B4. $125.00

OATES, Joyce Carol. *Garden of Earthly Delights.* 1967. Vanguard. 1st. sgn. NF/dj. B4. $150.00

OATES, Joyce Carol. *Goddess & Other Women.* 1974. Vanguard. 1st. NF/dj. A24. $30.00

OATES, Joyce Carol. *Hungry Ghosts.* 1974. Blk Sparrow. 1st issue in wrp. F. Q1. $35.00

OATES, Joyce Carol. *I Lock My Door Upon Myself.* 1990. Ecco. 1st. F/dj. Q1. $30.00

OATES, Joyce Carol. *I Lock My Door Upon Myself.* 1990. Ecco. 1st. sgn. F/F. B4. $85.00

OATES, Joyce Carol. *In Exile.* 1990. Toronto. Exile Eds. 1st Canadian. F/dj. Q1. $35.00

OATES, Joyce Carol. *Marya: A Life.* 1986. Dutton. 1st. sgn. F/F. R14. $50.00

OATES, Joyce Carol. *Marya: A Life.* 1986. Dutton. 1st. F/F. H11. $25.00

OATES, Joyce Carol. *Mysteries of Winterhurn.* 1984. Dutton. 1st. inscr/dtd 1997. F/F. R14. $50.00

OATES, Joyce Carol. *Mysteries of Winterhurn.* 1984. Dutton. 1st. NF/NF. A20. $25.00

OATES, Joyce Carol. *On Boxing.* 1987. Dolphin/Doubleday. 1st trade. sgn. F/dj. B4. $85.00

OATES, Joyce Carol. *Poisoned Kiss & Other Stories.* 1976. Gollancz. 1st. F/F. P3. $20.00

OATES, Joyce Carol. *Poisoned Kiss.* 1975. Vanguard. 1st. inscr/dtd 1995. VG/NF. R14. $75.00

OATES, Joyce Carol. *Reading the Fights.* 1988. Holt. 1st. F/F. A20. $20.00

OATES, Joyce Carol. *Sentimental Education.* 1981. Dutton. 1st. NF/NF. A20. $25.00

OATES, Joyce Carol. *Snake Eyes.* 1992. NY. Dutton. 1st. F/F. B4. $45.00

OATES, Joyce Carol. *Son of the Morning.* 1978. Vanguard. 1st. VG/dj. P3. $30.00

OATES, Joyce Carol. *Soul/Mate.* 1989. Dutton. 1st. VG/dj. P3. $20.00

OATES, Joyce Carol. *Wonderland.* 1971. Vanguard. 1st. F/F. H11. $45.00

OATES, Wayne E. *Christian Pastor.* 1976. Westminster. 258p. VG/dj. B29. $6.50

OATES, Wayne E. *Practical Handbook for Ministry From Writings of...* 1992. Westminster. 517p. F/dj. B29. $8.50

OBER, Frederick. *Travels in Mexico & Life Among the Mexicans.* (1887). Boston. Estes Lauriat. revised. ils/lacks fld map. 732p. F3. $65.00

OBERHOSLER, Harry C. *Birds of the Natuna Islands.* 1932. Smithsonian. Bulletin 159. 137p. VG. S15. $15.00

OBLIGADO, George. *Gaucho Boy.* 1961. Viking. 1st. ils Lilian Obligado. 63p. VG/G+. P2. $20.00

OBLIGADO, George. *Magic Butterfly & Other Fairy Tales of Central Europe.* 1963. Golden/Western. 1st prt. sm folio. NF. C8. $35.00

OBREGON, Mauricio. *Argonauts to Astronauts.* 1980. Harper. 1st. 205p. dj. F3. $15.00

OCH, Joseph. *Missionary in Sonora. Travel Reports of...1755-1767.* 1965. SF. CA Hist Soc. 8vo. 196p. brn cloth/yel cloth sides. as new/dj. K7. $25.00

OCHROCH, Ruth. *Diagnosis & Treatment of Minimal Brain Dysfunction...* 1981. NY. Human Sciences. 304p. gray cloth. VG/dj. G1. $25.00

OCHSNER, Albert. *Clinical Surgery.* 1904. Chicago. 2nd. 757p. A13. $75.00

ODDO, Sandra. *Home Made.* 1972. Atheneum. VG/dj. A16. $12.00

ODETS, Clifford. *North Star.* 1963. Culver City. Classic Films. 1st revised screenplay. F/wrp. B2. $150.00

ODLUM, Jerome. *Morabilis Diamond.* 1945. Scribner. 1st. NF/dj. M25. $60.00

OEHLER, C.M. *Great Sioux Uprising.* 1959. Oxford. 1st. sgn pres. ils/map/drawings. 272p. VG/VG. J2. $110.00

OELLRICHS, Inez. *Murder Comes at Night.* 1940. Doubleday Crime Club. 1st. F/VG. M15. $40.00

OEMLER, A. *Truck-Farming at the South.* 1883. Orange Judd. 270p. VG. A10. $35.00

OERTEL, Horst. *Special Pathological Anatomy & Pathogenesis of Circulatory.* 1838. Montreal. 1st. 640p. buckram. A13. $40.00

OFFUTT, Chris. *Same River Twice.* 1993. S&S. 1st. author's 2nd book. F/dj. A24. $65.00

OFFUTT, Chris. *Same River Twice.* 1993. S&S. 1st. sgn. F/F. D10. $75.00

OGBURN, C. *Marauders.* 1959. NY. ils/maps. 307p. VG/VG. S16. $23.50

OGDEN, A. *California Sea Otter Trade 1784-1848.* (1975). Berkeley. 251p. cloth. VG+. M12. $30.00

OGDEN, Peter Skeene. *Portraits of American Indian Life & Character.* 1933. Grabhorn. 1st ltd. 1/500. 6 pl. 107p. VG. J2. $175.00

OGDEN, Robert Morris. *Hearing: Illustrated With Diagrams.* 1924. London. Cape. 1st. buckram. G1. $35.00

OGILVY, C. Stanley. *Thoughts on Small Boat Racing.* 1957. Van Nostrand. 148p. F/dj. A17. $12.50

OGRIZEK, Dore. *United States.* 1950. NY. 418p. The World in Color series. G. A17. $10.00

OHIE, Howard Pitcher. *Old Silver & Old Sheffield Plate.* 1928. Doubleday Doran. 1st. 12 full-p ils. 420p. teg. blk buckram. T10. $125.00

OKHOTINA. *Phonology & Morphology of African Languages.* 1972. Moscow. Science Moscow. 12mo. 195p. VG/wrp. W1. $12.00

OKRI, Ben. *Incidents at the Shrine.* 1986. Heinemann. 1st. author's 3rd book. F/dj. A24. $45.00

OKRI, Ben. *Stars of the New Curfew.* 1988. Viking. 1st Am. F/F. B3. $35.00

OKUDAIRA, Hideo. *Emaki: Japanese Picture Scrolls.* 1962. Tuttle. 1st. 241p. F/NF. W3. $150.00

OLAJUWON, Hakeem. *Living the Dream.* 1996. Little Brn. 1st. sgn. F/F. A23. $75.00

OLCOTT, H. *Sorgho & Imphee, the Chinese & African Sugar Canes.* 1857. 1st. VG. E6. $85.00

OLCOTT, William T. *Field Book of the Stars.* nd (1907). Putnam. 8vo. VG/dj. K5. $20.00

OLDER, Julia. *Menus a'Trois.* 1987. NY. Stephen Greene. G/dj. A16. $10.00

OLDER, Mrs. Fremont. *San Francisco Magic City.* 1961. NY/London/Toronto. Longman Gr. 1st. 8vo. 280p. F/NF. K7. $20.00

OLDEROGGE, D.A. *Kamus na Hausa Rashaci (Hausa-Russian Dictionary).* 1963. Moscow. Foreign & Internat Dictionaries. 12mo. 459p. VG. W1. $20.00

OLDFELD, Peter. *Alchemy Murder.* 1929. Washburn. 1st. VG. N4. $22.50

OLDRIN, John. *Chipmunk Terrace.* 1958. Viking. sgn. ils Kurt Wiese. 79p. cloth. VG/dj. M20. $20.00

OLDRIN, John. *Eight Rings on His Tail.* 1956. Viking. 1st. sgn. 79p. VG/dj. M20. $25.00

OLDROYD, Ida Shepard. *Marine Shells of the West Coast of North America.* 1924 & 1927. Stanford. 4 vol. ils. cloth. D11. $125.00

OLDROYD, Osborn. *Assassination of Abraham Lincoln.* 1901. 1st. O8. $47.50

OLDS, Helen Diehl. *Joan of the Journal.* 1930. NY. 1st. ils Robb Beebe. VG/dj. A25. $15.00

OLENDER, Terryst. *For the Prosecution: Miss Deputy DA.* 1961. Phil. Chilton. 380p. dj. D11. $40.00

OLIPHANT, Laurence. *Russian Shores of the Black Sea.* 1854. Edinburgh. Blackwood. 3rd. 380p. rebound. T7. $95.00

OLIPHANT, Margaret. *Lucy Crofton.* 1860. Harper. 1st Am/probable 1st. sm 8vo. 222p. H13. $125.00

OLIVEIRA, Benjamin. *Notes & Correspondence Upon Introduction of Railways...* 1854. London. JC Bridgewater. 1st. 28p. stitched. R15. $250.00

OLIVER, Chad. *Another Kind.* 1955. Ballantine. 1st. F/rpr. M2. $150.00

OLIVER, Chad. *Shadows in the Sun.* 1985. Crown. 1st. F/dj. P3. $14.00

OLIVER, Douglas. *Return to Tahiti: Bligh's Second Breadfruit Voyage.* 1988. Honolulu. 281p. M/dj. P4. $40.00

OLIVER, James. *Abdominal Tumours & Abdominal Dropsy in Women.* 1895. London. 1st. 289p. A13. $100.00

OLIVER, Katherine Elspeth. *Claw.* 1914. Los Angeles. Out West Magazine. 1st. 384p. gilt red cloth. VG. T10. $45.00

OLIVER, Paul. *Shelter in Africa.* 1971. Praeger. F/VG. D1. $65.00

OLIVER, Raymond. *La Cuisine.* 1969. NY. Tudor. G/dj. A16. $30.00

OLIVER, Raymond. *La Cuisine: Secrets of Modern French Cooking.* 1969. Tudor. 1st Am. 896p. bl cloth. F/dj. H1. $32.00

OLIVIER, Charles P. *Meteors.* 1925. Baltimore. Williams Wilkins. assn copy. 276p. VG. K5. $150.00

OLLARD, Richard. *Escape of Charles II After Battle of Worcester.* 1966. ils. VG/VG. M17. $15.00

OLMSTEAD, Denison. *Letters on Astronomy.* 1841 (1841). Boston. Marsh Capen Lyon Webb. 419p. G. K5. $90.00

OLMSTEAD, Robert. *America by Land.* 1993. Random. 1st. F/F. R14. $30.00

OLMSTEAD, Robert. *Trail of Heart's Blood Wherever We Go.* 1990. London. Secker Warburg. 1st Eng. F/F. R14. $35.00

OLMSTED, Gideon. *Journal of Gideon Olmsted, Adventures of a Sea Captain...* 1978. WA. Lib of Congress. 129p. beige cloth. P4. $25.00

OLMSTED & OLMSTED. *Claude Bernard & the Experimental Method in Medicine.* 1952. NY. 1st. 277p. A13. $25.00

OLNEY, Andy. *Rocket Richard.* 1961. Ryerson. later prt. photos. VG. P8. $20.00

OLNEY, Ross. *Out to Launch.* 1979. Lee Shepard. 8vo. 125p. xl. K5. $15.00

OLNEY, Ross. *Winners! Super Champions of Ice Hockey.* 1982. Clarion. 1st. photos. F/VG+. P8. $20.00

OLOTAREFF, Gregoire. *Don't Call Me Little Bunny.* 1988. FSG. 1st Am. 4to. unp. NF. C14. $15.00

OLSCHAK & WANGYAL. *Mystic Art of Ancient Tibet.* 1973. NY. 1st. 224p. F/clear plastic dj. W3. $285.00

OLSEN, D.B. *Bring the Bride a Shroud.* 1945. Doubleday Crime Club. 1st. F/NF. M15. $40.00

OLSEN, D.B. *Death Walks on Cat Feet.* 1956. Doubleday Crime Club. 1st. NF/dj. M15. $45.00

OLSEN, Jack. *Silence on Monte Sole: Italy's Mountain of the Sun...* 1968. NY. 374p. VG/G. S16. $28.50

OLSHAUSEN, George. *American Slavery & After.* 1983. Olema. 1st. VG. V4. $20.00

OLSON, Albert. *Picture Painting for Young Artists.* 1906. Chicago. Thompson Thomas. 1st. 8vo. ils. D1. $65.00

OLSON, Charles. *Charles Olson & Ezra Pound.* 1975. Grossman. 1st. F/dj. V1. $30.00

OLSON, Reuel Leslie. *Colorado River Compact.* 1926. Los Angeles. Neuner Corp. 2nd. 8vo. bl cloth. VG+. F7. $55.00

OLSON, Ted. *Ranch on the Laramie.* 1973. Boston/Toronto. Little Brn. dj. A19. $25.00

OLSON, Toby. *Changing Appearance: Poems 1965-1970.* 1975. Membrane. NF/wrp. V1. $20.00

OLSON, Toby. *Dorit in Lesbos.* 1990. S&S. 1st. NF/F. A20. $20.00

OLSON, Toby. *Seaview.* 1982. New Directions. 1st. F/dj. A24. $40.00

OLSON, Toby. *Utah.* 1987. Linden/S&S. 1st. F/NF. A24. $85.00

OLSVANGER, Immanuel. *L'Chayim — Jewish Wit & Humor.* 1949. Schocken. index. 192p. VG/G+. S3. $21.00

OMAN & STRONG. *Eliabeth R.* 1971. VG/VG. M17. $15.00

OMETEV & STUART. *St Petersburg: Portrait of an Imperial City.* nd. photos. VG/VG. M17. $25.00

OMMANNEY, F.D. *Shoals of Capricorn.* 1952. NY. Harcourt Brace. 1st Am. 8vo. 322p. map ep. gray cloth. P4. $22.50

OMORI, Annie Shepley. *Diaries of Court Ladies of Old Japan.* 1920. Houghton Mifflin. 1st. ils. 199p. VG+. A25. $45.00

OMWAKE, John. *Conestoga Six-Horse Bell Teams of Eastern Pennsylvania.* 1930. Cincinnati. sm 4to. G. O3. $145.00

ONASSIS, Jacqueline. *Firebird & Other Russian Fairy Tales.* 1978. Viking. 1st Am. ils Boris Zvorykin. 112p. F/dj. T10. $50.00

ONDAATJE, Michael. *Coming Through Slaughter.* 1976. Norton. 1st. sgn. author's 1st novel. F/NF. D10. $125.00

ONDAATJE, Michael. *Coming Through Slaughter.* 1979. London. Marion Boyars. 1st Eng. F/F. B2. $85.00

ONDAATJE, Michael. *English Patient.* 1992. Knopf. 1st. F/F. B4. $100.00

ONDAATJE, Michael. *In the Skin of a Lion.* 1987. Knopf. 1st Am. sgn. author's 2nd novel. F/F. D10. $85.00

ONDAATJE, Michael. *Running in the Family.* 1982. Norton. 1st. F/F. D10. $75.00

ONDER, Eleanor Fox. *Plantation Shadows.* 1949. Pelican. 1st. inscr assn copy. G. B11. $65.00

ONIONS, Oliver. *Whom God Hath Sundered.* 1947. London. VG/dj. M2. $25.00

OPEKE, Lawrence K. *Tropical Tree Crops.* 1982. Chichester. ils. 312p. VG/dj. B26. $49.00

OPEZINGA, Pedro. *Pensamientos Militares.* 1670. Rome. Por el Bernabo. 1st. 4 letterpress fld plans. contemporary sgn. R15. $2,500.00

OPIE, John Newton. *Rebel Cavalryman With Lee, Stuart & Jackson.* 1899. Chicago. WB Conkey. 1st. 336p. cloth. VG. M8. $350.00

OPIE & OPIE. *Children & Their Books: Celebration of Work of...* 1990. Clarendon. ils. 440p. F/wrp. A4. $40.00

OPIE & OPIE. *Classic Fairy Tales.* 1974. Oxford. ils. 255p. VG/VG. A4. $85.00

OPIE & OPIE. *Lore & Language of Schoolchildren.* 1976. 437p. F/F. A4. $85.00

OPIE & OPIE. *Nursery Companion.* 1980. Oxford. ils. F/F. A4. $55.00

OPLER, Morris E. *Grenville Goodwin Among the Western Apaches.* 1973. AZ U. ils. 103p. F/F. B19. $25.00

OPPENHEIM, E. Phillips. *Dumb Gods Speak.* 1937. McClelland Stewart. 1st. VG/dj. P3. $30.00

OPPENHEIM, E. Phillips. *Envoy Extraordinary.* 1937. Little Brn. 1st. VG/VG. M19. $45.00

OPPENHEIM, E. Phillips. *Gabriel Samara: Peacemaker.* 1925. McClelland Stewart. 1st. VG. P3. $25.00

OPPENHEIM, E. Phillips. *Golden Beast.* 1926. Little Brn. 1st. VG. P3. $20.00

OPPENHEIM, E. Phillips. *Great Prince Shan.* 1922. Little Brn. 1st. xl. VG. M22. $15.00

OPPENHEIM, E. Phillips. *Lost Leader.* 1907. Little Brn. 1st. VG. M2. $25.00

OPPENHEIM, E. Phillips. *Man Without Nerves.* 1934. 1st. F/G. M19. $45.00

OPPENHEIM, E. Phillips. *Ostrekoff Jewels.* 1932. McClelland Stewart. 1st. VG/VG. P3. $30.00

OPPENHEIM, E. Phillips. *Secret Service Omnibus.* 1941. Blue Ribbon. 1st. F/dj. M2. $12.00

OPPENHEIM, E. Phillips. *Shy Plutocrat.* 1941. Little Brn. 1st. VG. P3. $25.00

OPPENHEIM, E. Phillips. *Tempting of Tavernake.* 1912. Little Brn. 1st. VG. P3. $20.00

OPPENHEIM, E. Phillips. *Wrath To Come.* 1924. Little Brn. 1st. VG. M2/P3. $25.00

OPPENHEIM, Hermann. *Diseases of the Nervous System: Text-Book for Students...* 1900. Lippincott. 1st Eng-language. ils. 899p. panelled bl buckram. G1. $250.00

OPPENHEIMER, J. Robert. *Uncommon Sense.* 1984. Boston. Birkhauser. 1st. ils. 195p. VG/dj. K3. $20.00

OPPENHEIMER, Jane. *New Aspects of John & William Hunter.* 1946. NY. 1st. 188p. A13. $50.00

OPTIC, Oliver. *Blue & the Gray: On the Blockade.* 1891 (1890). Lee Shepard. 355p. VG. M20. $30.00

OPTIC, Oliver. *Fighting for the Right.* 1893 (1892). Lee Shepard. 363p. VG. M20. $25.00

ORBACH, Jack. *Neuropsychology After Lashley: 50 Years...* 1982. Hillsdale, NJ. Erlbaum. 541p. crimson cloth. G1. $50.00

ORCUTT, William Dana. *Book in Italy.* 1928. Harper. 1/750. T10. $100.00

ORCUTT, William Dana. *Kingdom of Books.* 1927. Little Brn. 1st trade. 8vo. brn cloth. F. T10. $45.00

ORCZY, Baroness. *Bronze Eagle.* 1915. Doran. 1st. NF. P3. $30.00

ORCZY, Baroness. *Eldorado.* nd. London. 1st. VG. M2. $35.00

ORD, Angustias de la Guerra. *Occurences in Hispanic California.* 1956. WA, DC. Academy Am Franciscan Hist. 98p. navy cloth. F. K7. $50.00

ORDE, A.J. *Little Neighborhood Murder.* 1989. Doubleday. 1st. author's 1st book. F/F. H11/T2. $25.00

ORDWAY, Frederick I. *Advances in Space Science & Technology.* 1962. Academic. 8vo. 431p. xl. K5. $35.00

ORE, Oystein. *Cardano, the Gambling Scholar.* 1953. Princeton. ils. 249p. VG/dj. K3. $40.00

ORGILL, D. *Gothic Line: Autumn Campaign in Italy 1944.* 1967. London. 1st. ils/maps. 257p. VG/VG. S16. $21.50

ORIARD, Michael. *End of Autumn.* 1982. Doubleday. 1st. VG/G+. P8. $15.00

ORLINSKY, Harry M. *Notes on the New Translation of the Torah.* 1969. JPS. biblio/indexes. 288p. VG/G+. S3. $22.00

ORME, B. *Anthropology for Archaeologists: An Introduction.* nd. Ithaca. Cornell. ils. 300p. cloth. VG+/VG. M12. $22.50

ORMSBY, R. McKinley. *History of the Whig Party.* 1860. 377p. O8. $14.50

ORNITZ, Samuel. *Bride of the Sabbath.* 1951. Rhinehart. 410p. VG. S3. $21.00

ORR, A. *In the King's Palace.* 1986. Tor. 1st. F/F. P3. $16.00

ORR, A. *World in Amber.* 1985. Bluejay. 1st. VG/dj. P3. $20.00

ORR, Bobby. *Bobby Orr: My Game.* 1974. Little Brn. 1st. F/VG. P8. $30.00

ORR, Frank. *Puck Is a Four Letter Word.* 1983. Morrow. 1st. F/VG. P8. $25.00

ORR, James. *International Standard Bible Encyclopedia.* 1937. Howard Severance. 5 vol. VG. B29. $50.00

ORR, James. *Resurrection of Jesus.* nd. Hodder Stoughton. 292p. G. B29. $9.50

ORSTEIN, Robert Evan. *New World New Mind.* 1989. Doubleday. 1st. 302p. F/F. W2. $30.00

ORTEGA, Luis B. *California Hackamore (La Jaquima), an Authentic Story...* 1948. New Pub. 1st. 109 photos/20 pen sketches. 133p. VG. J2. $465.00

ORTIZ, Elisabeth Lambert. *Complete Book of Caribbean Cooking.* 1973. Evans. G+/dj. A16. $10.00

ORTIZ, Simon J. *Fightin'.* 1983. Chicago. Thunder Mouth. 1st. NF/VG. L3. $85.00

ORTIZ, Simon J. *Going for the Rain.* 1976. Harper Row. 1st. author's 1st book. NF/NF. L3. $175.00

ORTLOFF, Henry Stuart. *Garden Bluebook of Annuals & Biennials.* 1931. Doubleday. VG. P3. $8.00

ORTON, Helen Fuller. *Mystery Over the Brick Wall.* 1951. Lippincott. 1st. ils Robert Doremus. 114p. G+/dj. P2. $15.00

ORTON, Joe. *Head to Toe.* 1971. St Martin. 1st. 186p. VG/dj. M20. $25.00

ORTZEN, Len. *Guns at Sea.* 1976. NY. Galahad. 160p. dj. T7. $35.00

ORWELL, George. *Animal Farm.* 1946. Harcourt Brace. 1st Am. VG/dj. M25. $75.00

ORWELL, George. *England, Your England & Other Essays.* 1953. London. Secker Warburg. 1st. 12mo. 224p. cloth. VG/dj. M1. $125.00

ORWELL, George. *Homage to Catalonia.* (1938). London. Secker Warburg. 1st. 8vo. 314p. cloth. F/dj. M1. $1,250.00

ORWELL, George. *Lost Writings.* 1985. Arbor. 1st Am. F/F. B4. $45.00

ORWELL, George. *Nineteen Eighty-Four.* 1949. Harcourt Brace. 1st Am. F/dj. Q1. $125.00

ORWELL, George. *Nineteen Eighty-Four.* 1949. Harcourt Brace. 1st Am. VG/VG. M22. $85.00

ORWELL, George. *Orwell: The War Broadcasts.* 1985. London. Duckworth/BBC. 1st. F/F. B4. $45.00

OSBORN, David. *Love & Treasure.* 1982. NAL. 1st. VG/dj. P3. $15.00

OSBORN, P.G. *Concise Law Dictionary. Fifth Edition.* 1964. London. Sweet & Maxwell. bl cloth. M11. $50.00

OSBORNE, Bertram. *Justices of the Peace 1361-1848.* 1960. Shaftesbury. Sedgehill. cloth. dj. M11. $50.00

OSBORNE, J. *Cardinal.* 1992. Austin, TX. ils/photos G Barland. 108p. cloth. F/F. M12. $17.50

OSBORNE, John. *Better Class of Person.* 1981. Dutton. 1st Am. NF/NF. R14. $25.00

OSBORNE, John. *Look Back in Anger.* 1957. Criterion. 1st Am from Eng sheets. F/F. B4. $125.00

OSBORNE, John. *Patriot for Me.* 1966. London. Faber. 1st. F/dj. B4. $125.00

OSBORNE, Walter. *Thoroughbred World.* nd. np. Amiel. 4to. VG/fair. O3. $20.00

OSHIKAWA, Josui. *Manual of Japanese Flower Arrangement.* 1936. Tokyo. 1st. ils. 322p. VG/VG. B5. $45.00

OSLER, Jerry. *Saint Mike.* 1987. Harper Row. 1st. F/F. A20. $20.00

OSLER, W. *An Alabama Student & Other Biographical Addresses.* 1909. London. 1st/2nd prt. 334p. A13. $100.00

OSLER, W. *Cancer of the Stomach: A Clinical Study.* 1900. Phil. 1st. 157p. A13. $400.00

OSLER, W. *Diagnosis of Abdominal Tumors.* 1895. NY. 1st/2nd prt. 192p. later cloth. A13. $100.00

OSLER, W. *Principles & Practice of Medicine.* 1892. NY. 1st/2nd prt. 1079p. cloth. F. A13. $1,250.00

OSLER, W. *Way of Life.* nd. Baltimore. Remington Putnam. ils. 47p. NF/dj. K3. $20.00

OSLER, William. *Bibliotheca Osleriana, Catalogue of Books...* 1969. Osler Lib/McGill U. 7787 entries. 834p. NF. A4. $365.00

OSLER, William. *Incunabula Medica: A Study of Earlist Prt Medical Books...* nd (1923). 1/150. ils. 217 entries books pub before 1481. F. A4. $95.00

OSLEY, A.S. *Scribes & Sources.* 1980. Boston. Godine. 1st. ils. VG/dj. K3. $15.00

OSOFSKY, Gilbert. *Puttin' on Ole Massa.* 1969. Harper Row. 1st. 8vo. 409p. F/dj. H1. $35.00

OSPITAL, J. *We Wore Jump Boots & Baggy Pants.* 1977. CA. ils. 119p. sc. VG. S16. $18.50

OSSENDOWSKI, Ferdinand. *Fire of the Desert Folk. Account of Journey...Morocco.* 1926. NY. Dutton. 1st. 8vo. 354p. VG. W1. $12.00

OSTERWEIS, Rollin G. *Rebecca Gratz: Study in Charm.* 1935. PUtnam. ils/biblio/index. 244p. VG. S3. $27.00

OSTRANDER, Isabel. *Crimson Blotter.* 1921. White House. G+. M2. $12.00

OSTRANDER, Isabel. *Twenty-Six Clues.* 1919. WJ Watt. 277p. VG/VG. M20. $45.00

OSTRANDER, Sheila. *Festive Food Decoration.* 1969. Gramercy. G/dj. A16. $7.00

OSTROFF, E. *Western Views & Eastern Visions.* 1981. Smithsonian. 1st. photos WH Jackson/TH O'Sullivan/CE Watkins. NF. M4. $20.00

OSTROM, Henry. *Jews & His Mission.* 1923. BICA. 157p. VG. B29. $8.00

OSTROW, Joanna. *In the Highlands Since Time Immemorial.* 1970. Knopf. 1st. author's 1st book. F/NF. H11. $30.00

OSWALD, F.L. *Zoological Sketches: A Contribution to Outdoor Study...* 1883. Phil. Lippincott. pres. ils H Faber. 266p. pict cloth. G+. M12. $25.00

OSWALD, John Clyde. *Printing in the Americas.* 1937. London. Gregg. 1st. VG/dj. K3. $85.00

OTIS, James. *Aeroplane at Silver Fox Farm.* 1911. Crowell. 360p. VG. M20. $25.00

OTIS, James. *Toby Tyler; or, Ten Weeks With the Circus.* 1923. Harper. VG/VG. P3. $15.00

OTIS, James. *With Serman to the Sea.* 1911. AL Burt. 317p. VG. M20. $20.00

OTTLEY, Roi. *No Green Pastures.* 1951. Scribner. 1st. 234p. VG/VG. B4. $85.00

OTTLEY, Roi. *White Marble Lady.* 1965. FSG. 1st. F/NF. M25. $60.00

OTTMAN, Jim. *Hunting on Horseback.* 1987. Paladin. F/F. O3. $15.00

OTTO, Margaret. *Great Aunt Victoria's House.* 1957. Holt. 1st. 122p. VG/G+. P2. $25.00

OTTO, Whitney. *How To Make an American Quilt.* 1991. NY. Villard. 1st. sgn. author's 1st novel. F/F. L3. $85.00

OTTO, Whitney. *How To Make an American Quilt.* 1991. Villard. 1st. inscr/sgn/dtd 1991. F/F. B3. $125.00

OUIDA. *Dog of Flanders (A Story of Noel), & Lampblack.* 1938 (1910). Chicago. Rand McNally. wide sm 16mo. VG+. C8. $17.50

OUSLEY & RUSSELL. *Little White House.* 1961 (1948). Boston. Ginn. revised. 8vo. 191p. probable school xl. G+. T5. $35.00

OUSPENSKY, P.D. *Strange Life of Ivan Osokin.* 1955 (1966). Hermitage. rpt. VG/clip. M25. $35.00

OUTHWAITE, Ida S. Rentoul. *Bunch of Wild Flowers.* 1933. Australia. Angus Robertson. 1st ed. 6 mtd pl/15 full-p pl. tan brd. R5. $485.00

OUTHWAITE, Ida S. Rentoul. *Bunch of Wild Flowers.* 1948. Sydney. Angus Robertson. 1st thus. 8vo. gilt bl cloth. dj. R5. $500.00

OUTHWAITE, Ida S. Rentoul. *Chimney Town by Tarella Quin Daskein.* 1934. London. A&C Black. 1st. 2 mc pl/27 full-p b&w pl. 8vo. bl cloth. R5. $475.00

OUTHWAITE, Ida S. Rentoul. *Fairyland.* 1931. London. A&C Black. 1st Eng. sm folio. bl cloth. R5. $1,875.00

OUTHWAITE, Ida S. Rentoul. *Little Laddie & His Bush-Land Friends.* 1948. Glasgow. Maclaren. 1st. 4to. limp gr brd. dj. R5. $400.00

OUTLAND, Charles. *Mines, Murders & Grizzlies: Tales of California...* 1986. Clark. 1st. 161p. as new/VG. J2. $65.00

OUTLAND, Charles. *Stagecoaching on El Camino Real, Los Angeles...* 1973. Clark. 1st. ils/maps. 339p. VG/VG. J2. $195.00

OVID. *Metamorphoses. In Fifteen Books.* 1958. Verona. LEC. 1st thus. 1/1500. ils/sgn Hans Erni. F/dj/case. Q1. $450.00

OWEN, Catherine. *Catherine Owen's New Cookbook. Part 1 & Part 2.* 1883. revised. pict bdg. G+. E6. $60.00

OWEN, Catherine. *Choice Cookery.* 1889. NY. 1st. 316p. G. B18. $45.00

OWEN, David. *Fantastic Planets.* 1979. Addison. 1st. VG/dj. M2. $12.00

OWEN, Frank. *Murder for the Millions (A Harvest of Horror & Homicide).* 1946. Fell. 1st. NF-/VG. N4. $30.00

OWEN, Iris M. *Conjuring Up Philip.* 1976. Harper Row. 1st. VG. P3. $15.00

OWEN, Maggie. *Book of Maggie Owen.* 1944. NY. VG/VG. M17. $15.00

OWEN, Richard. *On the Nature of Limbs.* 1849. London. 1st. fld pl. 119p. A13. $300.00

OWEN, Robert Dale. *Address Touching the Influence & Progress of Literature...* 1838. Richmond. 1st. 8vo. 38p. prt wrp. xl. VG. M1. $425.00

OWEN, Wilfred. *Thirteen Poems.* 1956. Northampton, MA. 1/35 (of 400). sm folio. sgn Shahn/Baskin. F/case. B24. $1,250.00

OWEN-SMITH, R.N. *Megaherbivores.* 1992. Cambridge. 369p. F. S15. $18.50

OWENS, Bill. *Our Kind of People: American Groups & Rituals.* 1975. SF. Straight Arrow. sgn/dtd. photos. wrp. D11. $75.00

OWENS, Bill. *Suburbia.* 1973. SF. Straight Arrow. 3rd. inscr/dtd. wrp. D11. $125.00

OXBERRY, William. *Actor's Budget of Wit & Merriment...* nd (1820). London. Simpkin Marshall. 1st thus. Morrell bdg. H13. $195.00

OXENHORN, Harvey. *Tuning the Rig: A Journey to the Arctic.* 1990. Harper. 281p+2p ship drawings. M/wrp. A17. $10.00

OZ, Amos. *Hill of Evil Council.* 1978. HBJ. 1st Am. sgn. author's 5th book. F/clip. D10. $60.00

OZ, Amos. *In the Land of Israel.* 1983. HBJ. 1st. F/F. B35. $20.00

OZ, Amos. *Slopes of Lebanon.* 1989. San Diego. HBJ. 1st. sgn. F/clip. D10. $35.00

OZ, Amos. *Touch the Water, Touch the Wind.* 1973. HBJ. 1st. F/F. B35. $20.00

OZ, Amos. *Touch the Water, Touch the Wind.* 1974. HBJ. 1st Am. sgn. author's 3rd novel. F/clip. D10. $60.00

OZAKI, Yukio. *Romances of Old Japan.* 1920. NY. Brentano. 32 full-p ils. 278p. pict cloth. W3. $48.00

OZENFANT, Amedee. *Foundations of Modern Art, Part I & Part II.* 1952. NY. Dover. photo frontis/photos/notes. 364p. cloth. D2. $50.00

OZICK, Cynthia. *Bloodshed.* 1976. Knopf. 1st. sgn. F/clip. D10. $50.00

OZICK, Cynthia. *Cannibal Galaxy.* 1983. Knopf. 1st. F/F. A24/T11. $25.00

OZICK, Cynthia. *Cannibal Galaxy.* 1983. Knopf. 1st. sgn. F/F. D10. $50.00

OZICK, Cynthia. *Messiah of Stockholm.* 1987. Knopf. 1st. F/dj. A24. $25.00

OZICK, Cynthia. *Pagan Rabbi & Other Stories.* 1971. Knopf. 1st. author's 1st book. F/dj. B4. $85.00

OZICK, Cynthia. *Shawl.* 1989. Knopf. 1st. F/NF. B4. $35.00

PABODIE, William J. *Calidore: a Legendary Poem.* 1738. Boston. Marsh Capen Lyon Webb. 1st. 8vo. 48p. plain brd. M1. $200.00

PACHTER, Henry M. *Magic Into Science: Story of Paracelsus.* 1951. Schuman. 1st. VG/dj. M2. $15.00

PACKARD, Francis. *History of Medicine in the United States.* 1963 (1931). NY. facsimile. 2 vol. 1323p. A13. $250.00

PACKER, Vin; see Meaker, Marijane.

PADDEN, R.C. *Hummingbird & the Hawk.* 1967. Columbus, OH. 1st. 319p. dj. F3. $30.00

PADDLEFORD, C. *Best in American Cooking.* 1970. abridged ed. VG. E6. $12.00

PADEN, Irene D. *Prairie Schooner Detours.* 1949. Macmillan. sgn. dj. A19. $40.00

PADGETT, Lewis. *Mutant.* 1953. Gnome. 1st. 210p. brd. VG/dj. P3. $100.00

PADGETT, Ron. *Great Balls of Fire.* nd. HRW. 1st. F/VG+. V1. $20.00

PAGE, Charles N. *Feathered Pets: A Treatise on Food...Canaries, Parrots...* 1898. Des Moines. self pub. 142p. 16mo. A17. $25.00

PAGE, Gerald. *Nameless Places.* 1975. Arkham. 1st. F/NF. M19. $25.00

PAGE, Thomas. *Hephaestus Plague.* 1973. Putnam. 1st. NF/dj. M2. $12.00

PAGE, Victor W. *Model T Ford Car: Its Construction, Operation & Repair.* 1917. NY. ils. 288p. pict cloth. G+. B18. $25.00

PAGE & PAGE. *Space Science & Astronomy.* 1976. NY. Macmillan. 1st. 8vo. 467p. VG/VG. K5. $20.00

PAGE & PAGE. *Starlight: What It Tells About the Stars.* 1967. Macmillan. 1st. 8vo. 377p. VG/dj. K5. $25.00

PAGELS, H.R. *Cosmic Code, Quantum Physics As Language of Nature.* 1982. S&S. 370p. F/dj. D8. $20.00

PAIEWONSKY, Isidor. *Eyewitness Accounts of Slavery in Danish West Indies.* 1987. Virgin Islands. ils. 166p. ils ep. G+/dj. B18. $25.00

PAIGE, Richard; see Koontz, Dean R.

PAINE, Albert Bigelow. *Hollow Tree Nights & Days.* 1944. NY. VG/VG. B5. $40.00

PAINE, Martyn. *Institutes of Medicine.* 1847. NY. 1st. 826p. A13. $150.00

PAINE, Ralph. *First Down, Kentucky!* 1921. Grosset Dunlap. 347p. VG/dj. M20. $25.00

PAINE, Ralph. *Stroke Oar.* 1911. Scribner. ils Enright. pict cloth. VG. B14. $55.00

PAINE, Thomas. *Life & Works of Thomas Paine.* 1925. New Rochelle. Thomas Paine Hist Assn. 10 vol. intro TA Edison. F/NF. B4. $275.00

PAINE & STUART. *Gobolinks or Shadow Pictures.* 1896. Century. 1st. sgn. obl 4to. pict brd. R5. $250.00

PAINTER, George D. *Critical Biography.* 1968. London. 1st. VG/dj. T9. $32.00

PALAZZO, Tony. *Giant Nursery Book.* 1957. ils. VG. M17. $30.00

PALFREY, F.W. *Antietam & Fredericksburg.* 1882. 1st. ils/maps. 228p. O8. $23.50

PALFREY, F.W. *Memoir of William Francis Bartlett.* 1878. Boston. 1st. 309p. O8. $35.00

PALGRAVE & PALGRAVE. *Trees of Central Africa.* 1957 (1956). Salisbury. 2nd. ils/map. 466p. VG. B26. $175.00

PALIN & JONES. *Ripping Yarns (Monty Python).* 1978. Pantheon. photos. NF. C9. $35.00

PALLEY, Reese. *Porcelain Art of Edward Marshall-Boehm.* 1976. Abrams. sgn. 89 tipped-in pl. F/VG. B11. $55.00

PALLISER, Charles. *Quincunx.* 1990. Ballantine. 1st. author's 1st book. NF/F. H11. $25.00

PALLISER, Charles. *Quincunx.* 1990. Ballantine. 1st. F/F. A20. $30.00

PALLISER, Charles. *Sensationalist.* 1991. Ballantine. 1st. author's 2nd book. F/F. H11. $30.00

PALLUCCHINI, Rodolfo. *Sebastian Viniziano: Fra Sebastiano del Piombo.* 1944. Italian text. ils. VG/VG. M17. $20.00

PALMER, A.N. *Palmer Method of Business Writing.* 1915. Palmer. obl 8vo. 95p. cloth spine/limp wrp. T10. $50.00

PALMER, David. *Atlantic Challenge.* 1977. London. Hollis Carter. ils/maps. 186p. dj. T7. $22.00

PALMER, E.L. *Fieldbook of Natural History.* (1949). Whittlesey. ils/figures. 664p. cloth. F. M12. $25.00

PALMER, Joe H. *This Was Racing.* 1953. NY. Barnes. 1/1000. sgn. ils/sgn Willard Mullin. leather. VG/G case. O3. $65.00

PALMER, Joel. *Journal of Travels Over the Rocky Mountains.* 1983. Ye Galleon. 1st thus. M/sans. A18. $17.50

PALMER, John. *George Bernard Shaw: Harlequin or Patriot?* 1915. Century. 1st. VG/VG. V4. $25.00

PALMER, L.S. *Man's Journey Through Time: 1st Step in Physical Culture...* 1959. NY. Phil Lib. ils/figures. 184p. NF/fair. M12. $17.50

PALMER, Ralph S. *Handbook of North American Birds. Vol 1: Loons...Flamingos.* 1978. Yale. 3rd. F/dj. A17. $25.00

PALMER, Robert C. *County Courts of Medieval England, 1150-1350.* 1982. Princeton. M11. $45.00

PALMER, Robert C. *English Law in Age of Black Death, 1348-1381...* 1993. Chapel Hill. M11. $45.00

PALMER, William. *Letters to N Wiseman, DD on the Errors of Romanism.* 1843. Baltimore. Joseph Robinson. 1st Am. 8vo. new cloth. F. T10. $150.00

PALOU, Francisco. *La Vida de Junipero Serro.* 1966. Readex Microprint. prt. NF. O4. $15.00

PANCAKE, Breece D'J. *Stories of Breece D'J Pancake.* 1983. Little Brn. 1st. author's 1st book. F/F. L3. $75.00

PANCHARD, E. *Meats, Pountry & Game: How To Buy, Cook & Carve.* 1919. 30 full-p photos. G+. E6. $20.00

PANGBORN, Edgar. *Mirror for Observers.* 1954. SFBC. VG/dj. M2. $10.00

PANICH & TRULSSON. *Desert Southwest Gardens.* 1990. Bantam. tall 8vo. 245p. cloth. F/dj. A22. $40.00

PANSHIN, Alexei. *Farewell to Yesterday's Tomorrow.* 1975. Berkley/Putnam. 1st. F/F. T2. $25.00

PANTELIDIS, Veronica S. *Arab World: Libraries & Librarianship 1960-1976.* 1979. London. Mansell. 1st. 100p. VG/stiff wrp. W1. $12.00

PAPADAKIS, Elim. *Green Movement in West Germany.* 1984. St Martin. 1st. VG/VG. V4. $12.50

PAPAZOGLOU, Orania. *Sanctity.* 1986. Crown. 1st. author's 3rd novel. F/F. N4. $30.00

PARDEE, R.G. *Complete Manual for Cultivation of Strawberry...* 1863 (1856). NY. Saxton. 157p. A10. $55.00

PARETSKY, Sara. *Bitter Medicine.* 1987. NY. 1st. F/F. C2. $40.00

PARETSKY, Sara. *Blood Shot.* 1988. Delacorte. 1st. F/F. A20/M22. $25.00

PARETSKY, Sara. *Burn Marks.* 1990. Delacorte. 1st. F/F. N4. $30.00

PARETSKY, Sara. *Burn Marks.* 1990. Delacorte. 1st. inscr. F/F. B2. $40.00

PARETSKY, Sara. *Deadlock.* 1984. Dial. 1st. NF/dj. P3. $250.00

PARETSKY, Sara. *Indemnity Only.* 1982. London. Gollancz. 1st. author's 1st book. F/dj. Q1. $400.00

PARETSKY, Sara. *Killing Orders.* 1985. Morrow. 1st. sgn. F/F. C2. $175.00

PARGETER, Edith Mary. *Black Is the Colour of My True Love's Heart.* 1967. Collins Crime Club. 1st. F/dj. M15. $175.00

PARGETER, Edith Mary. *Bloody Field.* 1972. Viking. 1st Am. F/F. B4. $85.00

PARGETER, Edith Mary. *Excellent Mystery.* 1985. London. Macmillan. 1st. F/dj. Q1. $125.00

PARGETER, Edith Mary. *Fallen Into the Pit.* 1990. MacDonald. VG/VG. P3. $30.00

PARGETER, Edith Mary. *Heretic's Apprentice.* 1989. London. Headline. 1st. F/dj. Q1. $65.00

PARGETER, Edith Mary. *Heretic's Apprentice.* 1989. Stoddart. 1st. VG/VG. P3. $30.00

PARGETER, Edith Mary. *Hermit of Eyton Forest.* 1987. Headline. 1st. F/F. M15. $65.00

PARGETER, Edith Mary. *Holy Thief.* nd. Mysterious. 3rd. sgn. VG/VG. P3. $25.00

PARGETER, Edith Mary. *Knocker on Death's Door.* 1970. London. Macmillan. 1st. F/F. M15. $200.00

PARGETER, Edith Mary. *Leper of St Giles.* 1982. Morrow. 1st Am. F/F. B4. $100.00

PARGETER, Edith Mary. *Potter's Field.* 1989. Stoddart. 1st. VG/VG. P3. $30.00

PARGETER, Edith Mary. *Rare Benedictine.* 1989. Mysterious. 1st Am. sgn. F/dj. Q1. $100.00

PARGETER, Edith Mary. *Raven in the Forgate.* 1986. London. Macmillan. 1st. NF/dj. Q1. $75.00

PARGETER, Edith Mary. *Sanctuary Sparrow.* 1983. Morrow. 1st Am. F/F. M15. $55.00

PARGETER, Edith Mary. *Summer of the Danes.* 1991. Mysterious. 1st Am. F/NF. Q1. $35.00

PARINI, Jay. *Anthracite Country.* 1982. Random. 1st. F/F. B2. $45.00

PARINI, Jay. *Patch Boys.* 1986. Holt. 1st. F/NF. R14. $25.00

PARIS, Edmond. *Souvenirs de Marine, 1882-1908.* 1961. Rostock. Hinstorff. 50 pl. 106p. dj. T7. $100.00

PARISH, James Robert. *Film Directors Guide: Western Europe.* 1976. Scarecrow. 73 portraits. NF/sans. C9. $25.00

PARISH, Peggy. *Come Back Amelia Bedelia.* 1971. Harper Row. 1st. ils Wallace Tripp. 64p. F/VG+. P2. $25.00

PARK, Benjamin. *Shakings: Etching From Naval Academy...* 1867. Lee Shepard. 1st. ils. VG. E6. $250.00

PARK, Jordan; see Kornbluth, C.M.

PARK, Mungo. *Travels in the Interior Districts of Africa...1795...* ca 1920. Newnes/Scribner. 12mo. 560p. teg. xl. G. W1. $12.00

PARK, No-Yong. *Oriental View of American Civilization.* 1945. Boston. Hale Cushman Flint. inscr. 12mo. 128p. red cloth. T10. $50.00

PARK, Paul. *Coelestis.* 1993. Harper Collins. 1st. F/F. P3. $30.00

PARK, Roswell. *Sketch of the History & Topography of West Point...* 1840. Phil. Henry Perkins. 1st. 16mo. 140p. cloth. M1. $100.00

PARK, Ruth. *Witch's Thorn.* 1952. Houghton Mifflin. 1st. VG/VG. P3. $35.00

PARKE, T.H. *My Personal Experiences in Equatorial Africa...* 1969 (1891). Negro U. rpt. ils. 526p. F. M4. $20.00

PARKER, B. *Cinderella at the Zoo.* nd. London. Chambers. ltd 1st. ils N Parker/16 full-p mc pl. 4to. pict brd. $775.00

PARKER, Barry. *Colliding Galaxies.* 1990. NY. Plenum. 8vo. 298p. VG/dj. K5. $20.00

PARKER, Courtney. *How To Eat Like a Southerner & Live To Tell the Tale.* 1992. Clarkson Potter. 191p. F/F. B10. $12.00

PARKER, Derek. *God of the Dance.* 1988. Wellingborough. 1st. ils Ninette deValois. VG/VG. T9. $16.00

PARKER, Dorothy. *Sunset Gun.* 1928. Boni Liveright. 1st. F/NF. B4. $950.00

PARKER, Franklin. *Central American Republics.* 1971. London. Oxford. 348p. F3. $20.00

PARKER, Idella. *Idella: Marjorie Rawlings' Perfect Maid.* 1992. Gainesville. 1st. photos. 135p. F/F. B4. $50.00

PARKER, John Henry. *ABC of Gothic Architecture.* 1896. Stand, London. James Parker Co. 18mo. 265p. A8. $30.00

PARKER, John Henry. *Introduction to Gothic Architecture.* 1898. ils. VG. M17. $20.00

PARKER, Lester Shepard. *Nancy MacIntyre: A Tale of the Prairies.* 1911. St Louis, MO. w/promo letter. A19. $30.00

PARKER, Mrs. E.E. *Mrs Parker's Complete Housekeeper...Cookery in All Branches.* 1888. NY. 471p. pict gr cloth. B14. $75.00

PARKER, Robert Allerton. *Transatlantic Smiths.* 1959. Random. 1st. 237p. VG/dj. V3. $12.00

PARKER, Robert B. *All Our Yesterdays.* 1994. Delacorte. 1st. F/F. N4. $25.00

PARKER, Robert B. *All Our Yesterdays.* 1994. Delacorte. 1st. sgn. F/dj. from $35 to $40.00

PARKER, Robert B. *Crimson Joy.* 1988. Delacorte. ltd. 1/250. sgn. F/case. M15. $100.00

PARKER, Robert B. *Crimson Joy.* 1988. Delacorte. 1st. VG/VG. P3. $20.00

PARKER, Robert B. *Double Deuce.* 1992. Putnam. 1st. sgn. F/F. M19. $25.00

PARKER, Robert B. *Early Autumn.* 1981. Delacorte. 1st. NF/dj. P3. $45.00

PARKER, Robert B. *God Save the Child.* 1974. Houghton Mifflin. 1st. sgn. author's 2nd book. F/NF. H11. $350.00

PARKER, Robert B. *God Save the Child.* 1975. London. Deutsch. 1st. author's 2nd book. F/NF. Q1. $125.00

PARKER, Robert B. *Godwulf Manuscript.* 1974. Houghton Mifflin. 1st. sgn. author's 1st book. F/F. H11. $425.00

PARKER, Robert B. *Judas Goat.* 1978. Houghton Mifflin. 1st. F/dj. M15. $85.00

PARKER, Robert B. *Looking for Rachel Wallace.* 1980. Delacorte. 3rd. NF/NF. P3. $20.00

PARKER, Robert B. *Love & Glory.* 1983. Delacorte. 1st. F/NF. A20. $30.00

PARKER, Robert B. *Pale Kings & Princes.* 1987. Delacorte. 1st. F/F. P3. $16.00

PARKER, Robert B. *Pastime.* 1991. Putnam. 1st. sgn. F/F. B11. $35.00

PARKER, Robert B. *Pastime.* 1991. Putnam. 1st. VG/VG. P3. $20.00

PARKER, Robert B. *Perchance To Dream.* 1991. Putnam. 1st. F/F. P3. $20.00

PARKER, Robert B. *Playmates.* 1989. Putnam. 1st. F/F. M22/T12. $20.00

PARKER, Robert B. *Playmates.* 1989. Putnam. 1st. sgn. VG/VG. B11. $35.00

PARKER, Robert B. *Poodle Springs.* 1989. Putnam. 1st. F/F. A20. $20.00

PARKER, Robert B. *Poodle Springs.* 1989. Putnam. 1st. sgn. F/F. T2. $25.00

PARKER, Robert B. *Promised Land*. 1976. Houghton Mifflin. 1st. inscr. F/dj. T2. $150.00

PARKER, Robert B. *Promised Land*. 1976. Houghton Mifflin. 1st. VG/dj. M25. $75.00

PARKER, Robert B. *Promised Land*. 1977. London. Deutsch. 1st. F/dj. Q1. $75.00

PARKER, Robert B. *Stardust*. 1990. Putnam. 1st. F/F. M22. $15.00

PARKER, Robert B. *Stardust*. 1990. Putnam. 1st. sgn. as new/dj. N4. $30.00

PARKER, Robert B. *Taming a Sea-Horse*. 1986. Delacorte. 1st. NF/NF. P3. $16.00

PARKER, Robert B. *Valediction*. 1984. Delacorte. 1st. F/NF. M19. $25.00

PARKER, Robert B. *Valediction*. 1984. Delacorte. 1st. sgn. F/F. M25. $35.00

PARKER, Robert B. *Walking Shadow*. 1994. Putnam. 1st. F/F. P3. $20.00

PARKER, Robert B. *Widening Gyre*. 1983. Delacorte. 1st. F/F. H11. $35.00

PARKER, Robert B. *Widening Gyre*. 1983. Delacorte. 1st. NF/F. A20. $20.00

PARKER, Robert B. *Widening Gyre*. 1983. Delacorte. 1st. sgn. F/F. T2. $45.00

PARKER, Robert B. *Wilderness*. 1979. Delacorte/Lawrence. 1st. F/dj. M15. $85.00

PARKER, Sybil P. *McGraw-Hill Encyclopedia of Ocean & Atmospheric Sciences*. 1980. NY. 580p. F/dj. A17. $20.00

PARKER, T. Jefferson. *Laguna Heat*. 1985. NY. 1st. F/NF. H11. $50.00

PARKER, T. Jefferson. *Laguna Heat*. 1985. St Martin. 1st. VG/VG. R14. $30.00

PARKER, T. Jefferson. *Little Saigon*. 1988. NY. 1st. F/F. H11. $30.00

PARKER, T.J. *Pacific Beat*. 1991. St Martin. 1st. F/F. A20. $12.00

PARKES, Henry. *History of Mexico*. 1960. Houghton Mifflin. 3rd/revised. dj. F3. $15.00

PARKINSON, C. Northcote. *Portsmouth Point*. 1949. Cambridge. Harvard. ils. 154p. dj. T7. $35.00

PARKINSON, James. *Essay on Shaking Palsy*. 1986 (1817). Birmingham. facsimile. 8vo. tooled crimson leather. F. G1. $75.00

PARKINSON, John. *Garden of Pleasant Flowers*. 1976. NY. Dover. 627p. VG/dj. A10. $50.00

PARKINSON, John. *Garden of Pleasant Flowers*. 1976 (1629). Paradisi in Sole. Paradisus Terrestris. facsimile. 612p. dj. B26. $58.00

PARKMAN, Francis. *Oregon Trail*. 1943. LEC. ils/sgn Maynard Dixon. 298p. tan brd. NF. K7. $95.00

PARKS, David. *GI Diary*. 1968. Harper Row. 1st. NF/dj. M25. $35.00

PARKS, Gordon. *Choice of Weapons*. 1966. Harper Row. 1st. NF/dj. M25. $35.00

PARKS, Gordon. *Flash Photography*. 1947. NY. Grosset Dunlap. photos. 96p. wrp. D11. $30.00

PARKS, Gordon. *Learning Tree*. 1963. 1st. author's 1st book. NF/G. M19. $45.00

PARKS, Tim. *Family Planning*. 1989. Grove Weidenfeld. 1st. F/F. H11. $20.00

PARMER, Charles H. *For Gold & Glory*. 1939. NY. Carrick Evans. 1st. VG. O3. $28.00

PARNELL, Thomas. *Poems on Several Occasions*. 1747. London. Lintot Tonson. 8vo. 279p. 3-quarter blk leather. H13. $195.00

PARR, Charles McKew. *Magallanes: Un Noble Capitan*. 1955. Madrid. Sapientia. 572p. F/stiff wrp/dj. O7. $25.00

PARR, Charles McKew. *So Noble a Captain: Life & Times of Ferdinand Magellan*. 1953. Crowell. NF/rpr. O7. $20.00

PARRA, Aquileo. *Memorias de Quileo Parra*. 1912. Bogota. 747p. quarter leather. F3. $15.00

PARRINDER, Patrick. *Science Fiction: Its Criticism & Teaching*. 1980. London. 1st. F/dj. M2. $20.00

PARRISH, Anne D. *Knee High to a Grasshopper*. 1923. Macmillan. 1st. ils. 208p. VG. D1. $75.00

PARRISH, Anne D. *Story of Appleby Capple*. 1950. Harper. 4to. 184p. yel cloth. VG/VG. D1. $75.00

PARRISH, Joseph. *Etherization in Labor*. 1849. Boston. 528p. quarter leather. A13. $100.00

PARRISH, Maxfield. *Arabian Nights*. 1909. NY. Scribner Classic. 1st. 12 mc pl. G+. B5. $60.00

PARRISH, Maxfield. *Arabian Nights*. 1912. Scribner. 1st. 12 mc pl. edit KD Wiggin/NA Smith. 339p. teg. cloth. G. W1. $65.00

PARRISH, Morris. *Supplementary List of Writings of Lewis Carroll*. 1933. NJ. private prt. ils. 125p. full red leather. F. A4. $475.00

PARRISH & PARRISH. *Dream Coach*. 1924. Macmillan. 1st. 8vo. bl cloth. VG. M5. $75.00

PARRY, Albert. *Peter Kapitza on Life & Science*. 1968. NY. Macmillan. 1st. 271p. VG/dj. K3. $15.00

PARRY, Edwin Satterthwaite. *Betsy Ross, Quaker Rebel: Being True Story of Romantic Life*. 1933. Phil. Winston. 252p. G. V3. $15.00

PARRY, J.H. *Discovery of South America*. 1979. Taplinger. 1st. 320p. dj. F3. $35.00

PARRY, J.H. *Trade & Dominion: European Oversea Empires in 18th Century*. 1971. London. Weidenfeld Nicolson. ils/6 maps. F/dj. O7. $50.00

PARSONS, Claudia. *Vagabondage*. 1941. Chatto Windus. 1st. ils. VG/VG. A25. $28.00

PARSONS, Derrick. *Do Your Own Horse*. 1977. London. Allen. 1st. sm 4to. VG. O3. $15.00

PARSONS, F.T. *How To Know the Ferns*. 1927. VG/VG. M17. $20.00

PARSONS, John E. *Firearms in the Custer Battle*. 1953. Stackpole. 1st. A19. $50.00

PARSONS, Kitty. *Ancestral Timber: Ballads Without Music*. 1957. ils. VG/VG. M17. $20.00

PARSONS, R.H. *Steam Turbine & Other Inventions of Sir Charles Parsons*. 1948. Longman Gr. rpt. VG/wrp. K3. $10.00

PARSONS, S. *How To Plan the Home Grounds*. 1899. Doubleday. 249p. cloth. A10. $25.00

PARSONS, Usher. *Directions for Making Anatomical Preparations...* 1831. Phil. 1st. 316p. full leather/new ep. A13. $200.00

PARSONS, William Barclay. *Engineers & Engineering in the Renaissance*. 1968. MIT. revised. 8vo. 661p. NF/dj. K3. $35.00

PARTON, Dolly. *Dolly. My Life & Other Unfinished Business*. 1994. Harper Collins. 1st. sgn bookplate. F/F. A23. $45.00

PARTON, J. *Life of Horace Greeley*. 1855 (1854). NY. Mason Bros. 442p. brn buckram-type cloth w/vignette. VG. B22. $15.00

PARTRIZI, Francesco. *Il Sacro Regno*. 1553. Venice. Sons of Aldus. thick 8vo. vellum. R12. $900.00

PASACHOFF, Jay M. *Contemporary Astronomy*. 1981. Phil. Saunders College. 2nd. 454p. VG. K5. $10.00

PASLEY, Virginia. *Christmas Cookie Book*. 1949. Little Brn. G. A16. $15.00

PASLEY, Virginia. *In Celebration of Food*. 1974. S&S. 1st. G/dj. A16. $17.50

PASSANTINO & PASSANTINO. *Witch Hunt*. 1990. Nelson. 254p. F. B29. $7.50

PASTAN, Linda. *Heroes in Disguise*. 1991. Norton. 1st. NF/F. R13. $20.00

PATCHEN, Kenneth. *Before the Brave*. 1936. Random. 1st. author's 1st book. NF/VG. L3. $450.00

PATCHEN, Kenneth. *Journal of Albion Moonlight*. 1944. NY. United Book Guild. 1st thus. VG/dj. M25. $60.00

PATCHEN, Kenneth. *See You in the Morning.* 1947. NY. Padell. 1st. F/NF. B2. $75.00

PATCHEN, Kenneth. *Sleepers Awake.* 1946. Padell. 1st trade. assn copy. NF/dj. V1. $50.00

PATCHETT, Ann. *Taft.* 1994. Houghton Mifflin. 1st. author's 2nd book. F/dj. A24. $20.00

PATCHETT, M.E. *Space Captives of the Golden Men.* 1953. Bobbs Merrill. 1st Am. F/dj. M2. $50.00

PATENT, Dorothy Hinshaw. *Draft Horses.* 1986. Holiday House. 1st. photos. VG/VG. O3. $18.00

PATER, Walter. *Imaginary Portrait.* 1894. Oxford. Daniel. 1st. 1/250. 12mo. 61p. NF/prt wrp. B24. $200.00

PATER, Walter. *Marriage of Cupid & Psyche.* 1951. LEC. 1st. 1/1500. sgn. 4to. wht Japanese vellum brd. F/VG+. B4. $400.00

PATERSON, John. *Praises of Israel. Studies Literary & Religious in Psalms.* 1950. Scribner. 8vo. 256p. VG. W1. $12.00

PATERSON, Katherine. *Gates of Excellence.* 1981. 127p. F/VG. A4. $45.00

PATERSON, Katherine. *Jacob Have I Loved.* 1980. NY. Crowell. 1st. 1981 Newbery Award. 8vo. gilt cloth. dj. R5. $110.00

PATERSON, Nathaniel. *Manse Garden.* 1838. Glasgow. Collins. 262p. A10. $75.00

PATNER, Andrew. *Stone: A Portrait (IF Stone).* 1988. Pantheon. 1st. as new/dj. V4. $20.00

PATON, Alan. *Cry, the Beloved Country.* 1951. NY. Scribner. 1st/photoplay. F/clip. B4. $85.00

PATRICK, Culbert T. *Lost Civiliation: Story of the Classic Maya.* (1974). Harper Row. 123p. wrp. F3. $20.00

PATRICK, Lucille Nichols. *Candy Kid, James Calvin Kid Nichols 1883-1962.* 1969. Flintlock Pub. 1st. 179p. VG/dj. J2. $95.00

PATRICK, Ted. *Thinking Dog's Man.* 1964. Random. 1st. ils Roy McKie. F/clip. Q1. $50.00

PATRICK, Vincent. *Pope of Greenwich Village.* 1979. NY. Seaview. 1st. author's 1st book. NF/dj. Q1. $35.00

PATTEN, Brian. *Shy Cormorant & the Fishes.* 1977. London. Kestrel. 1st. 64p. F/F. D4. $35.00

PATTEN, Marguerite. *Cake Icing & Decoration.* 1965. Feltham. Hamlyn. G/dj. A16. $25.00

PATTEN, Marguerite. *Cakes & Baking.* 1972. NY. Hamlyn. G/dj. A16. $15.00

PATTEN, Marguerite. *Classic Dishes Made Simple.* 1969. London. Hamlyn. VG/dj. A16. $20.00

PATTEN, Marguerite. *Fish, Meat, Poutry & Game.* 1970. NY. Hamlyn. G/dj. A16. $20.00

PATTERSON, Floyd. *Victory Over Myself.* 1962. NY. Gies. 1st. inscr/dtd 1962. photos. 244p. NF/NF. B4. $400.00

PATTERSON, Harry; see Patterson, Henry.

PATTERSON, Henry. *Confessional.* 1985. Stein Day. 1st. F/VG+. N4. $15.00

PATTERSON, Henry. *Eagle Has Flown.* 1991. S&S. 1st. F/F. N4. $20.00

PATTERSON, Henry. *Storm Warning.* 1976. HRW. 1st. F/F. W2. $30.00

PATTERSON, Henry. *To Catch a King.* 1979. Stein Day. 1st. NF/NF. A20. $25.00

PATTERSON, Howard. *Yachtsman's Kedge Anchor.* 1901. NY. Nautical College. 16mo. ils. 112p. T7. $45.00

PATTERSON, Innis. *Eppworth Case.* 1930. Farrar Rhinehart. 1st. VG/VG. P3. $30.00

PATTERSON, J.H. *Man-Eaters of Tsavo & Other East African Adventures.* 1907. London. ils. VG. M17. $100.00

PATTERSON, J.H. *Man-Eaters of Tsavo & Other East African Adventures.* 1924. London. Macmillan. ils/photo/map. 346p. gilt leather. G+. M12. $45.00

PATTERSON, James. *Along Came a Spider.* 1993. Little Brn. 1st. NF/NF. P3. $22.00

PATTERSON, James. *Black Market.* 1986. S&S. 1st. NF/NF. P3. $20.00

PATTERSON, James. *Jericho Commandment.* 1979. Crown. 1st. author's 2nd novel. F/F. T2. $40.00

PATTERSON, James. *Midnight Club.* 1989. Little Brn. 1st. F/F. T2. $15.00

PATTERSON, James. *Midnight Club.* 1989. Little Brn. 1st. sgn. F/F. A23. $48.00

PATTERSON, James. *Thomas Berryman Number.* 1976. Little Brn. 1st. F/dj. M15. $65.00

PATTERSON, R.M. *Dangerous River.* 1954. Sloane. ils/photos/drawings/map ep. 314p. cloth/brd. VG+. M12. $25.00

PATTERSON, Richard North. *Escape the Night.* 1983. Random. 1st. F/dj. M15. $45.00

PATTIE, J. *Cowboy Spurs & Their Makers.* 1991. TX A&M. ils. 172p. F/dj. M4. $35.00

PATTON, Frances Gray. *Good Morning, Miss Dove.* 1954. NY. Dodd Mead. 1st. F/NF. B4. $200.00

PAUCK, Wilhelm. *Heritage of the Reformation.* 1950. BEacon. sgn. 312p. VG/dj. B29. $12.00

PAUL, Aileen. *Kids Cooking Without a Stove.* (1975). Doubleday. 5th. wide 8vo. VG+/dj. C8. $22.50

PAUL, Austin. *Trumpet Notes in Congo.* 1949. Brooklyn. Africa Inland Mission. F/dj. B2. $35.00

PAUL, Carl. *Golf Clubmaking & Repair.* 1984. Paul Assoc. 1st. photos. VG+/dj. P8. $50.00

PAUL, Elliot. *Murder on Left Bank.* 1951. NY. 1st. VG/VG. B5. $30.00

PAUL, Gunther. *Satellite Spin-Off.* 1975. WA, DC. Robert Luce. 8vo. 272p. dj. K5. $15.00

PAUL, Henry E. *Outer Space Photography for the Amateur.* 1967 (1960). NY. Amphoto. 3rd. VG/VG. K5. $15.00

PAUL, Michel. *Orchids: Care & Growth.* 1964. NY. ils/photos. 135p. flexible photo brd. VG. B26. $11.00

PAUL, Rodman W. *California Gold: Beginning of Mining in the Far West.* 1947. Harvard. 1st. VG/sans. O4. $15.00

PAUL, S. *Economical Cookbook.* 1905. 1st. ils. VG. E6. $35.00

PAUL & QUINTANILLA. *With a Hays Nonny Nonny.* 1942. Random. 1st. VG/VG-. B4. $125.00

PAULI, Hertha. *Silent Night, the Story of a Song.* (1943). Knopf. 1st. sm 8vo. ils. VG/dj. C8. $30.00

PAULI, Wolfgang. *Meson Theory of Nuclear Forces.* 1946. NY. Interscience. 1st. 12mo. 69p. VG/dj. K3. $25.00

PAULI, Wolfgang. *Theoretical Physics in the Twentieth Century.* 1960. London. Interscience. 1st. VG/dj. K3. $50.00

PAULING & WILSON. *Introduction to Quantum Mechanics.* 1935. McGraw Hill. 468p. VG. K3. $40.00

PAULL, Grace. *They Had a Blue Cart.* (1935). Whitman. sm 8vo. VG. C8. $17.50

PAULL, Mrs. George A. *Prince Dimple & His Everyday Doings...* 1890. Anson Randolph. photos. 8vo. VG. M5. $75.00

PAULSEN, Gary. *Winter Room.* 1989. Orchard Books. 1st. 8vo. 103p. F/F. T5. $40.00

PAULSEN, Martha. *Picnic Day.* 1946. Akron. Saalfield. 4 double-p popups. 8vo. pict brd. dj. R5. $125.00

PAUSTOVSKY, Konstantin. *Story of a Life.* 1964. London. 1st. trans M Harari/M Duncan. VG/VG. T9. $18.00

PAVITT, N. *Kenya: First Explorers.* 1989. London. 1st. ils/maps. 207p. F/dj. M4. $25.00

PAVLOV, Ivan Petrovich. *Conditioned Reflexes & Psychiatry.* 1941. NY. Internat Pub. 1st Eng-language ed. inscr. 199p. panelled blk cloth. G1. $100.00

PAXSON, Diana L. *Wolf & the Raven.* 1993. Morrow. 1st. NF/dj. M21. $15.00

PAXTON, June le Mert. *My Life on the Mojave.* 1957. Vantage. 1st. 168p. cloth. dj. D11. $40.00

PAYNE, David. *Confessions of a Taoist on Wall Street.* 1984. 1st. author's 1st book. F/NF. M19/M23. $25.00

PAYNE, David. *Early for the Dance.* 1989. Doubleday. 1st. VG+/F. A20. $25.00

PAYNE, Helen E. *Plant Jewels of the High Country.* 1972. Medford, OR. inscr. 145p. VG/torn. B26. $35.00

PAYNE, R.S. *Baltimore Oriole & Biographical Sketch of Audubon.* 1923. Baltimore. Norman. ils. 55p. pict brd. NF/VG+. M12. $30.00

PAYNE, Robert. *Journey to Persia.* 1951. London/Melbourne. Heinemann. 1st. 8vo. 246p. cloth. VG. W1. $18.00

PAYNE, Robert. *Life & Death of Adolf Hitler.* 1973. NY. photos/maps/notes/index. 623p. VG/worn. S16. $25.00

PAYNE, Theodore. *Life on the Modjeska Ranch in the Gay Nineties.* 1962. self pub. 1st. F/F. O4. $15.00

PAYTIAMO, James. *Flaming Arrow's People.* 1932. Duffield Gr. 1st. VG/dj. L3. $350.00

PAYZANT & PAYZANT. *Like a Weaver's Shuttle.* 1979. Toronto. Nimbus. ils/photos. 214p. dj. T7. $45.00

PAZ, Ireneo. *Life & Adventures of...Joaquin Murrieta...* 1925. Chicago. Regan. 1st. 1/975. 8vo. 174p. red cloth. VG. T10. $45.00

PAZ, Octavio. *On Poets & Others.* 1986. NY. Seaver. 1st Am. F/F. R14. $25.00

PEABODY, Barbara. *Screaming Room: Mother's Journal...* 1986. San Diego. Oak Tree. 1st. 254p. VG/dj. A25. $15.00

PEABODY, Elizabeth P. *Lectures in the Training Schools for Kindergarteners.* 1886. Boston. Heath. 12mo. 266p. cloth. M1. $150.00

PEABODY, Elizabeth P. *Record of a School: Exemplifying General Principles...* 1836. Boston/NY. 2nd. 12mo. 198p. cloth/paper label. M1. $500.00

PEABODY, Josephine Preston. *Portrait of Mrs W: A Play in Three Acts.* 1922. Houghton Mifflin. 1st. xl. VG. A25. $15.00

PEACOCK, Doug. *Grizzly Years.* 1990. Holt. 1st. inscr/dtd 1990. NF/F. T11. $125.00

PEACOCK, Molly. *And Live Apart.* 1980. MO U. 1st. assn copy. F/sans. V1. $55.00

PEAKE, James. *Rudimentary Treatise on Ship Building...* 1849. London. John Weale. 6 fld pl. 132p. gr cloth/pict label. P4. $175.00

PEARCE, Catherine Owens. *William Penn: A Biography.* 1957. Lippincott. 1st. 448p. as new/VG. H1. $30.00

PEARL, R.H. *Successful Mineral Collecting & Prospecting.* 1961. Bonanza. ils. 164p. F/torn. D8. $12.00

PEARMAN, G.I. *Greenhouse.* 1988. Melbourne. 752p. F. B1. $35.00

PEARSON, Edmund. *Murder at Smutty Nose & Other Murders.* 1927. London. Heinemann. 330p. gilt cloth. D11. $45.00

PEARSON, Hesketh. *Bernard Shaw: His Life & Personality.* 1943. Collins. 3rd. VG/dj. V4. $30.00

PEARSON, John. *Wildlife & Safari in Kenya.* ca 1970. E African Pub House. 384p. lg 8vo. A17. $20.00

PEARSON, Patti. *North.* 1993. Pittsburgh. Dorrance. 1st. 8vo. 202p. NF/dj. P4. $30.00

PEARSON, Preston. *Hearing the Noise.* 1985. Morrow. 1st. 303p. NF/VG. W2. $20.00

PEARSON, Ridley. *Angel Maker.* 1993. Delacorte. 1st. sgn. F/F. A23. $40.00

PEARSON, Ridley. *Seizing of Yankee Green Mall.* 1987. NY. 1st. NF/F. H11. $35.00

PEARSON, Thomas G. *Birds of North Carolina.* 1942. Raleigh. ils Brasher/Horsfall/Peterson. 416p. VG. S15. $40.00

PEARSON, Virginia. *Play a Time With Betty & Bill.* nd (1940). Boston Music Co. 21p. NF. C14. $20.00

PEARSON, William. *Chessplayer.* 1984. Viking. 1st. F/F. H11. $40.00

PEARSON & PEARSON. *Study of American Cut Glass Collections.* 1969. self pub. 1st trade. 170 pl. 200p. NF/VG. H1. $185.00

PEARY, R.E. *Nearest the Pole.* 1907. Doubleday Page. 1st. 95 photos/65 pl/2 fld map. gilt gr cloth. 411p. G. H1. $95.00

PEARY, R.E. *Northward Over the Great Ice: A Narrative of Life...* 1898. NY. Stokes. 2 vol. inscr. teg. P4. $375.00

PEASE, Howard. *Tod Moran: Fog Horns.* 1937. Doubleday. 295p. VG/dj. M20. $22.00

PEASE, John. *Address of John Pease to Friends in America.* 1845. NY. Egbert Hovey King. 1st. 16p. V3. $25.00

PEASE, William D. *Playing the Dozens.* 1990. Viking. 1st. F/F. M22. $10.00

PEAT, Fern Bisel. *Cock, the Mouse & the Little Red Hen.* 1931. Saalfield. Calico series. VG. M5. $75.00

PEAT, Fern Bisel. *Picture & Rhyme Book.* 1941. Saalfield. 16p. F. M5. $60.00

PEAT, Fern Bisel. *Rags.* 1929. Saalfield. 12p. sc. VG+. M5. $80.00

PEATTIE, Donald Culross. *Audubon's America.* 1940. Houghton Mifflin. 1/3025. sgn. 16 double-p repros. teg. cream bdg. case. B24. $150.00

PEATTIE, Donald Culross. *Audubon's America.* 1940. Houghton Mifflin. 1st. 16 mc pl. 328p. VG. H1. $35.00

PEATTIE, Donald Culross. *Flora of the Indiana Dunes: A Handbook...* 1930. Chicago. photos/fld map. 432p. flexible gr cloth. VG. B26. $35.00

PEATTIE, Roderick. *Geography of Ohio.* 1923. Columbus. 4th Series Bulletin 27. 137p. VG. B18. $27.50

PECHMEJA, Jean. *Telephe, En XII Livres.* 1784. London. 1 vol in 1. 12mo. quarter calf. R12. $250.00

PECK, Abe. *Uncovering the Sixties.* 1985. Pantheon. 1st. NF/wrp. B2. $25.00

PECK, Anne S. *Flying Over South America.* 1932. Houghton Mifflin. 1st. 255p. map ep. F3. $25.00

PECK, George W. *Grocery Man & Peck's Bad Boy.* 1883. Chicago. Belford Clarke. 240p. G-. B18. $45.00

PECK, George W. *How Private George W Peck Put Down the Rebellion...* 1887. Belford Clarke. 1st. 316p. pict bl cloth. B18. $65.00

PECK, Leigh. *Pecos Bill & Lightning.* 1940. Boston. Houghton Mifflin. 1st. sm 4to. G+/VG. C8. $15.00

PECK, M. Scott. *Different Drum: Community Making & Peace.* 1987. Touchstone. 333p. F. B29. $9.00

PECK, Paula. *Art of Fine Baking.* 1961. S&S. later ed. ils. 8vo. dj. A16. $12.00

PECK, Robert Newton. *Fawn.* 1975. Little Brn. 1st. 143p. VG/clip. M20. $18.00

PECK, William. *Southern Hemisphere Constellations & How To Find Them.* nd. London. Gall Inglis. 13 mc sky maps. xl. K3. $35.00

PECKER & SCHATZMAN. *Astrophysique Generale.* 1959. Paris. Masson et Cie. 756p. VG. K5. $50.00

PEDDIE, Robert A. *Fifteenth-Century Books.* 1969. Burt Franklin. rpt. VG. K3. $15.00

PEDERSEN, Martin. *Graphis Photo 91.* 1991. Zurich. 267p. lg 4to. F/dj. A17. $30.00

PEDERSEN, Martin. *Graphis Publication 1.* 1992. Zurich. 256p. F/dj. A17. $30.00

PEEBLES, Curtis. *Watch the Skies!* 1994. Smithsonian. 2nd. 8vo. 342p. F/F. K5. $20.00

PEEBLES, P.J.E. *Physical Cosmology.* 1974. Princeton. 2nd. 282p. VG. K5. $50.00

PEEL, Colin D. *Hell Seed.* 1979. St Martin. 1st. NF/dj. M21. $15.00

PEET, Bill. *Bill Peet: An Autobiography.* nd (1989). Houghton Mifflin. 2nd. sm 4to. 190p. xl. VG. C14. $10.00

PEET, Bill. *Luckiest One of All.* 1982. Houghton Mifflin. 1st. 4to. 30p. F/F. P2. $60.00

PEGGE, Samuel. *Curialia Miscellanea; or, Anecdotes of Old Times...* 1818. London. Nichols. 1st. tall 8vo. 351p. 3-quarter polished calf. H13. $195.00

PEGLER, Westbook. *Lady Me, Lady I.* 1942. private prt. 1/200. inscr. VG+. B4. $85.00

PEI, Lowry. *Family Resemblances.* 1986. Random. 1st. F/NF. M23. $20.00

PEINS, Maryann. *Contemporary Approaches in Stuttering Therapy.* 1984. Boston. 1st. 304p. A17. $15.00

PEIXOTTO, Ernest. *Pacific Shores From Panama.* 1913. Scribner. 1st. 24 pl/ils. 285p. cloth. F3. $35.00

PELISSERI, Jean. *Histoire de Lorigine de la Royaute, et du Premier...* 1684. Paris. Sercy. thick 8vo. engraved title p/35 half-p engravings. R12. $235.00

PELLAPRAT, H. *Modern French Culinary Art.* 1961. 1st. 752p. VG/VG. E6. $40.00

PELLETIER, Cathie. *Funeral Makers.* 1986. Macmillan. 1st. inscr. author's 1st novel. F/F. M23. $35.00

PELLETT, Frank. *American Honey Plants Including...* 1920. 1st. 8vo. ils. VG. E6. $20.00

PELLETT, Frank. *American Honey Plants.* 1976. Hamilton, IL. Dadant. 5th. 467p. cloth. VG. A10. $32.00

PELLETT, Frank. *Practical Rearing.* 1918. 3rd. ils. VG. E6. $15.00

PELLOWE, William. *Royal Road to Mexico. A Travel Log...* 1937. Detroit. 1st. sgn. 168p. F3. $15.00

PEMBERTON, Christopher. *Practical Treatise on Various Diseases of Abdominal Viscera.* 1815. Worcester. 1st Am. 201p. full leather. A13. $200.00

PEMBERTON, Ebenezer. *Funeral Sermon on Death of That Learned...Samuel Willard...* 1707. Boston. Prt B Green for Benj Eliot. 1st. 18mo. contemporary bdg. M1. $2,250.00

PEMBERTON, Max. *Captain Black.* 1911. Hodder Stoughton. 1st. VG. M2. $30.00

PENDERGAST, David. *Palenque. The Walker-Caddy Expedition...* 1967. Norman, OK. 1st. 213p. dj. F3. $35.00

PENDERGRASS, Eugene. *Head & Neck in Roentgen Diagnosis.* 1956. Springfield, IL. Chas Thomas. 2 vol. 2nd revised. ils. 1759p. VG/dj. G1. $50.00

PENDLETON, Louis. *In Assyrian Tents.* 1904. Jewish Pub Soc. 1st. VG. M2. $35.00

PENFIELD, Wilder. *Cytology & Cellular Pathology of Nervous System.* 1965. NY. Hafner. 3 vol. rpt. 8vo. blk cloth. VG. G1. $175.00

PENINGTON, Isaac. *Letters of..., Son of Alderman Penington of London...* 1842. Phil. Nathan Kite. 292p. worn leather. V3. $45.00

PENN, I. Garland. *Afro-American Press & Its Editors.* 1891. Springfield, MA. Willey. 565p. VG+. B4. $450.00

PENN, Irving. *Worlds in a Small Room.* 1974. NY. Grossman. photos. 96p. cloth. dj. D11. $150.00

PENN, William. *No Cross, No Crown: A Discourse Shewing the Nature...* 1807. Phil. Kimber Conrad. 370p. worn leather. V3. $45.00

PENNAK, R.W. *Fresh-Water Invertebrates of the United States.* 1953. Ronald Pr. 769p. xl. B1. $20.00

PENNANT, Thomas. *History of the Parishes of Whiteford & Holywell.* 1796. Fleet St, London. 1st. 22 pl/etchings/engravings. half leather. H3. $95.00

PENNELL, Joseph. *Adventures of an Illustrator.* 1925. Little Brn. 1st trade. beige cloth. VG. T10. $75.00

PENNINGTON, Robert R. *Stannary Law, a History of Mining Law of Cornwall & Devon.* 1973. Newton Abbot. M11. $65.00

PENNY, Nicholas. *Church Monuments in Romantic England.* 1977. Yale. photos. VG/VG. M17. $30.00

PENNY, Prudence. *Coupon Cookery.* 1943. Murry & Gee. 128p. B10. $25.00

PENNYPACKER, Morton. *General Washington's Spies.* 1939. Brooklyn. Long Island History. NF/VG. T11. $65.00

PENROSE, Boies. *Travel & Discovery in Renaissance 1420-1620.* 1962. Atheneum. 1st. F/wrp. O7. $20.00

PENROSE, Margaret. *Dorothy Dale: Girl of To-Day.* 1908. Cupples Leon. 1st. ils Nuttall. 242p. G. A25. $10.00

PENTECOST, J. Dwight. *Words & Works of Jesus Christ: A Study of Life of Christ.* 1981. Academie. 629p. VG/torn. B29. $13.00

PENZLER, Otto. *Great Detectives.* 1978. Little Brn. 1st. F/dj. M2. $15.00

PEPITONE, Lena. *Marilyn Monroe Confidential.* 1979. S&S. 1st. VG+/NF. A20. $15.00

PEPLOW, Edward H. Jr. *History of Arizona.* 1958. Lewis Hist Pub. 1st. 3 vol. ils/index/bibliography. VG+/sans. B19. $300.00

PEPLOW & PEPLOW. *Pioneer Stories of Arizona's Verde Valley.* 1972. Verde Valley Pioneers. ils. 219p. F/sans. B19. $35.00

PEPOON, H.S. *Annotated Flora of the Chicago Area.* 1927. Chicago. Academy of Sciences/Lakeside. inscr. 8vo. A22. $60.00

PEPPER, Adeline. *Glass Gaffers of New Jersey.* 1971. Scribner. 1st. 332p. turquoise cloth. F/dj. H1. $120.00

PEPPER, Charles. *Life-Work of Louis Klopsch.* nd (1910). NY. Christian Herald. probable 1st. 395p. VG. B22. $15.00

PEPPER, George Wharton. *Philadelphia Lawyer: An Autobiography.* 1944. Lippincott. 1st. pres. 407p. F/dj. H1. $22.50

PEPPER, James. *Letters: Raymond Chandler M Fox.* 1978. Santa Barbara. Neville+Yellin. 1/26. sgn. w/photo. F. R3. $225.00

PEPPER, Robert D. *Oscar Wilde: Irish Poets & Poetry of 19th Century.* 1972. BC of CA. ils. 45p. maroon cloth. as new. K7. $75.00

PEPPER, William. *System of Practical Medicine by American Authors Vol 5.* 1886. Phil. Lea Bros. 8vo. rebound. xl. VG. G1. $100.00

PEPPERCORN, David. *Drinking Wine.* 1979. Harbor House. 1st. F/F. W2. $35.00

PEPPERGRASS, Paul. *Shandy McGuire; or, Tricks Upon Travellers...* 1853. Boston. Patrick Donahoe. 354p. cloth. VG. M20. $35.00

PERCEVAL, Don. *Daynard Dixon Sketch Book.* 1967. Northland. 100p. brd/cloth spine. dj. D11. $100.00

PERCIVAL, Richard. *Assault Heroic 1895-1926.* 1986. London. 1st. VG/dj. T9. $18.00

PERCY, Thomas. *Reliques of Ancient English Poetry...* 1839. London. Lewis. 3 vol. tall 8vo. pebbled cloth brd/blk leather spine. H13. $395.00

PERCY, Walker. *Lancelot.* 1977. FSG. 1st. F/F. B35. $30.00

PERCY, Walker. *Lost in the Cosmos.* 1983. FSG. 1st. sgn. F/NF. R13. $85.00

PERCY, Walker. *Lost in the Cosmos.* 1983. FSG. 1st. F/F. A20. $25.00

PERCY, Walker. *Love in the Ruins.* 1971. FSG. 1st. F/NF. B35. $60.00

PERCY, Walker. *Love in the Ruins.* 1971. FSG. 1st. NF/NF. S13. $45.00

PERCY, Walker. *Questions They Never Asked Me.* 1979. Lord John. 1/326. sgn. F/sans. R14. $100.00

PERCY, Walker. *Second Coming.* 1980. Farrar Straus. 1st. F/clip. Q1. $35.00

PERCY, Walker. *Thanatos Syndrome.* 1987. FSG. 1st trade. 372p. F/NF. W2. $30.00

PERCY, Walker. *Thanatos Syndrome.* 1987. FSG. VG/VG. P3. $15.00

PEREIRA, P. Joao. *Exhortacoens Domesticas Feytas nos Collegios...* 1716 (1715). Coimbra. 1st/only. 2-column text. woodcuts. 503p. R15. $500.00

PEREIRA, William L. *Majestic World of Arabian Horses.* 1986. NY. Abrams. 1st. folio. VG/VG. O3. $65.00

PEREIRA DA SANTA ANNA, Joseph. *Chronica dos Carmelitas da Antiga, e Regular Observancia...* 1745-1751. Lisbon. Antonio Pedrozo Galram. 2 vol. 1st. folio. woodcuts. R15. $3,500.00

PEREIRA DA SILVA, Mathias. *Fenix Renascida, ou Obras Poeticas dos Melhores...* 1746. Lisbon. Antonio Pedrozo Galram. 5 vol. 2nd/corrected. R15. $5,000.00

PERELMAN, S.J. *Rising Gorge.* 1961. S&S. 1st. 8vo. 287p. orange brd/wht cloth spine. F/dj. H1. $45.00

PERETZ, I.L. *Magician.* 1973. Macmillan. 1st. lg 8vo. F/F. C8. $30.00

PEREZ, Nissan N. *Focus East: Early Photography in the Near East 1839-85.* 1988. NY/Jerusalem. Abrams/Domino/Israel Mus. 1st. photos. cloth. NF/dj. W1. $50.00

PEREZ DE LUXAN, Diego. *Expedition Into New Mexico Made by Antonio deEspejo...* 1929. LA. Quivira Soc. 1/500. ils/pl/maps. VG. O7. $350.00

PEREZ-REVERTE, Arturo. *Flanders Panel.* 1994. Harourt Brace. 1st Am. F/dj. A24. $40.00

PERKINS, G. *Summer in Maryland & Virginia; or, Campaigning...* 1911. Chillicothe, OH. 1st. 106p. F. M4. $100.00

PERKINS, Lucy Fitch. *Book of Joys.* 1907. McClurg. 1st. 212p. G+. P2. $40.00

PERKINS, Lucy Fitch. *Dutch Twins.* 1911. Houghton Mifflin. ils. VG+/worn. M5. $45.00

PERKINS, Lucy Fitch. *Puritan Twins.* 1921. Houghton Mifflin. 1st. F/VG. M5. $55.00

PERKINS, LUcy Fitch. *Robin Hood.* 1906. NY. Stokes. 1st thus. 12 full-p mc pl. olive pict cloth. w/sgn card. R5. $150.00

PERKINS, Lucy Fitch. *Swiss Twins.* 1922. Houghton Mifflin. F/G. M5. $52.00

PERKINS, Marlin. *Zoo Parade.* 1954. Rand McNally. 1st. 4to. 95p. VG. C14. $18.00

PERKINS, Michael. *Secret Record. Modern Erotic Literature.* 1976. NY. 1st. sgn. w/sgn poem. A11. $75.00

PERKINS, Steve. *Next Year's Champions.* 1969. World. 1st. photos. F/VG+. P8. $35.00

PERKINS & TANIS. *Native Americans of North America.* 1975. Scarecrow. 558p. F3. $35.00

PERLEMAN, S.J. *Swiss Family Perelman.* 1950. S&S. 1st. F/NF. B2. $60.00

PERLES, Alfred. *Great True Spy Adventures.* 1960. Arco. 2nd. VG. P3. $15.00

PERLEY, M.V.B. *Salem Village Witchcraft.* 1911. Salem. 1st. ils. 76p. VG. B5. $25.00

PERLMAN, Janet. *Cinderella Penguin; or, the Little Glass Flipper.* 1992. NY. Viking. 1st. unp. M/dj. P4. $13.00

PEROTTI. *Important Firsts in Missouri Imprints 1808-1858.* 1967. 1/500. 83p. F/VG. A4. $125.00

PERRAULT, Charles. *Les Hommes Illustres Qui Ont Paru en France...* 1696 & 1700. Paris. Dezallier. 2 vol. folio. 103 full-p pl. contemporary mottled calf. R12. $3,750.00

PERRAULT, Charles. *Sleeping Beauty.* 1919. London. Heinemann. 1/625 on handmade. ils/sgn Rackham. VG/case. D1. $1,500.00

PERRETT, B. *Knights of the Black Cross: Histler's Panzerwaffe...* 1986. NY. BC. ils/maps. 260p. VG/VG. S16. $15.00

PERRONE, Charles. *Masters of Contemporary Brazilian Song.* 1989. Austin, TX. 1st. F/NF. A20. $20.00

PERRY, Anne. *Farriers' Lane.* 1993. Fawcett. 1st. inscr. NF/dj. R13. $35.00

PERRY, Bliss. *Life & Letters of Henry Lee Higginson.* 1921. Boston. Atlantic Monthly. A19. $40.00

PERRY, Bliss. *Life & Letters of Henry Lee Higginson.* 1921. np. 557p. O8. $18.50

PERRY, Charles. *Portrait of a Young Man Drowning.* 1962. S&S. 1st. M/dj. B4. $100.00

PERRY, Frances. *Flowers of the World.* 1972. NY. 1st. ils Leslie Greenwood. 320p. VG/torn. B26. $57.50

PERRY, Frances. *Garden Pool.* 1972. S Brunswick/NY. Great Albion. 8vo. 144p. cloth. VG/dj. A22. $15.00

PERRY, J.R. *Art of Stair Building, With Original Improvements...* 1855. self pub. 1st. 8vo. 28 full-p pl. cloth. M1. $175.00

PERRY, Kenneth. *Binding of Books.* 1940. Peoria. Manual Arts. ils. VG/dj. K3. $15.00

PERRY, Richard. *Polar Worlds.* 1973. Newton Abbot. David & Charles. 8vo. 316p. VG/dj. P4. $30.00

PERRY, Ronald. *Denizens.* 1980. Random. 1st. Nat Poetry Series. F/F. V1. $10.00

PERRY, Thomas. *Butcher's Boy.* 1982. Scribner. 1st. 1/2000. author's 1st book. F/NF. D10. $325.00

PERRY, Thomas. *Metzger's Dog.* 1983. Scribner. 1st. sgn. F/NF. D10. $50.00

PERRY, Thomas. *Vanishing Act.* 1995. Random. 1st. F/F. P3. $23.00

PERRY & PERRY. *Austalian Opals in Colour.* 1969. Sydney. 112p. pict brd. NF. D8. $25.00

PERSAUD, T.V.N. *Early History of Human Anatomy: From Antiquity to Modern...* 1984. Springfield. 1st. 200p. A13. $150.00

PESCE, Angelo. *Colours of the Arab Fatherland.* 1972. Italy. Castelfranco Veneto. 1st. ils. 144p. NF/dj. W1. $35.00

PESEK, Ludek. *Log of a Moon Expedition.* 1969. Knopf. trans Schmidt. 113p. dj. K5. $40.00

PESMAN, M. Walter. *Meet Flora Mexicana.* 1962. Globe, AZ. Dale King. 8vo. 278p. G. A22. $25.00

PETER, John. *Masters of Modern Architecture.* (1958). Bonanza. rpt. VG/G-. A8. $25.00

PETERKIN & ULMANN. *Roll, Jordan, Roll.* 1933. NY. Ballou. 1st trade/1st issue. VG+/VG. B4. $600.00

PETERS, Alan. *Fine Structure of Nervous System...* 1970. Hoeber/Harper Row. lg 8vo. 198p. prt bl cloth. G1. $50.00

PETERS, Elizabeth; see Mertz, Barbara Gross.

PETERS, Ellis; see Pargeter, Edith Mary.

PETERS, Fred J. *Clipper Ship Prints.* 1930. NY. Antique Bulletin Pub. ils. 107p. T7. $95.00

PETERS, John L. *Cry Dignity!* 1976. World Neighbors. 1st. sgn. F/VG. B11. $20.00

PETERS, John. *Treatise on Inflammatory & Organic Diseases of Brain...* 1855. NY. Wm Radde. thin 8vo. 156p. panelled pebbled Victorian brn cloth. G1. $150.00

PETERS, M. *Jew As Patriot.* 1902. 1st. VG. E6. $20.00

PETERS, Zack. *Ten Dreams.* 1927. Winston. 1st. NF/dj. M2. $30.00

PETERSEN, Elly. *Taschenbuch fur den Kakteenfreund.* 1930 (1927). Esslingen. 3rd. 24 pl/12 photos. 180p. B26. $34.00

PETERSEN, William. *Another Hand on Mine: Story of Dr Karl K Becker...* 1967. McGraw Hill. 228p. VG/dj. B29. $6.50

PETERSHAM & PETERSHAM. *American ABC.* 1941. Macmillan. 1st. 4to. unp. gilt bl cloth. VG/torn. T5. $55.00

PETERSHAM & PETERSHAM. *Circus Baby.* 1950. Macmillan. 1st. 4to. pict brd. dj. R5. $125.00

PETERSHAM & PETERSHAM. *Off to Bed. 7 Stories for Wide-Awakes.* 1954. Macmillan. unp. G+/torn. w/ad flyer. B18. $25.00

PETERSHAM & PETERSHAM. *Rooster Crows.* 1945. Macmillan. 1st. 4to. VG. P2. $50.00

PETERSHAM & PETERSHAM. *Story Book of Clothes.* 1933. Chicago. Winston. 1st. F/VG rpr. C8. $55.00

PETERSHAM & PETERSHAM. *Story Book of Foods From the Field.* 1936. Winston. 1st. sq 8vo. gilt gr cloth. VG+/dj. M5. $40.00

PETERSON, Dale. *Deluge & the Ark.* 1989. Boston. 1st. 378p. F/F. S15. $13.50

PETERSON, H.L. *Book of the Continental Soldier Being a Complete Account...* 1968. Harrisburg. 1st. ils. 287p. F/dj. M4. $30.00

PETERSON, H.L. *One Man's Life.* 1969. Vantage. A19. $40.00

PETERSON, Hans. *Magnus in Danger.* nd (1963). Pantheon. stated 1st Am. 135p. VG+. C14. $8.00

PETERSON, Karen. *Women Artists.* 1976. NYU. ils. NF/NF. S13. $35.00

PETERSON, Keith; see Klavan, Andrew.

PETERSON, Mendel. *History Under the Sea.* 1973. Alexandria, VA. self pub. ils. 208p. wrp. T7. $25.00

PETERSON, Roger Tory. *Bird Watcher's Anthology.* 1957. NY. 1st trade. G/worn. S15. $15.00

PETERSON, Roger Tory. *Penguins.* 1979. Boston. Houghton Mifflin. 1st. 238p. NF/dj. P4. $35.00

PETERSON & PETERSON. *Audubon's Birds of America.* 1983 (1981). Artabras. rpt. 435 full-p pl. rem mk. tear cloth/dj. S15. $75.00

PETERSON & SMITH. *Forest Nursery Diseases in the United States.* 1975. GPO. 8vo. 125p. cloth. xl. VG. A22. $20.00

PETIT, Michel. *Variable Stars.* 1987. NY. John Wiley. 257p. VG. K5. $35.00

PETO, Gladys. *Gladys Peto's Children's Book.* ca 1920s. NY. Warne. 7 full-p mc pl/b&w drawings. pict brd. R5. $225.00

PETO, Gladys. *Peto Picture Book.* ca 1920s. London. Sampson Low. ils/pl/19 stories. pict brd/label. dj. R5. $285.00

PETRIE, Sidney. *Martinis & Whipped Cream.* 1966. NY. Parker. G/dj. A16. $10.00

PETROV, G.I. *Conquest of Outer Space in the USSR.* 1973. New Delhi. Amerind for NASA. 8vo. 444p. xl. dj. K5. $50.00

PETRY, Ann. *Drugstore Cat.* 1946. Crowell. 1st. author's 1st book for children. 87p. VG/G+. P2. $35.00

PETRY, Ann. *Narrows.* 1953. Boston. Houghton Mifflin. 1st. NF/VG. B4. $150.00

PETRY, Ann. *Street.* 1947. World. 1st thus. VG. M25. $35.00

PETZINGER, T. *Oil & Honor: Texaco-Pennzoil Wars...* 1987. Putnam. 1st. 495p. F/dj. D8. $28.00

PEYREFITTE, Alan. *Collision of Two Civilizations.* 1993. London. Harvard. 1st. 630p+16p mc pl. F/dj. A17. $17.50

PEYTON, Richard. *At the Track.* 1987. Bonanza. hc. F/F. P3. $15.00

PFEIFFER, Charles F. *Old Testament History.* 1973. Canon. 640p. VG/dj. B29. $15.00

PFEIFFER, Ehrenfried. *Earth's Face & Human Destiny.* 1947. Emmaus. Rodale. 183p. VG/dj. A10. $30.00

PFEIFFER, Ida. *Journey to Iceland & Travels to Sweden & Norway.* 1852. NY. 1st. 273p. VG. A17. $50.00

PHARR, Robert Deane. *Book of Numbers.* 1970. London. Calder Boyars. 1st. author's 1st book. F/clip. Q1. $60.00

PHELPS, Richard 'Digger.' *Coach's World.* 1974. Crowell. 1st. photos. VG/VG. P8. $15.00

PHELPS, William Dane. *Alta, California, 1840-1842. Journal & Observations...* 1983. Clark. 1st. W Land & Waters Series XIII. 346p. VG. J2. $65.00

PHELPS, William Lyon. *Howells, James, Bryant & Other Essays.* 1924. Macmillan. 1st. NF/VG+. A20. $25.00

PHILBRICK, W.R. *Slow Dancer.* 1984. St Martin. 1st. VG/VG. P3. $18.00

PHILBY, Kim. *My Silent War.* 1968. Grove. 1st. F/F. H11. $40.00

PHILELFUS, Franciscus. *Orationes.* 1515. Paris. Petit. sm 4to. vellum. R12. $675.00

PHILIP, K.R. *Indian Self-Rule: First Hand Accounts...* 1986. VG/VG. M17. $30.00

PHILIPPI, Donald. *Songs of Gods, Songs of Humans.* 1979. Princeton/Tokyo. 12 photos. decor cloth. F/F case. W3. $86.00

PHILIPPS, Jayne Anne. *Machine Dreams.* 1984. Dutton Lawrence. 1st. F/F. B35. $42.00

PHILIPS, John. *Poems on Several Occasions.* 1728. London. Thomas Astley. sm 12mo. early full calf/later leather label. H13. $325.00

PHILIPSON, David. *Letters of Rebecca Gratz.* 1929. JPS. 454p. G. S3. $25.00

PHILIPSON, David. *Old European Jewries.* 1894. 1st. VG. E6. $35.00

PHILIPSON, David. *Reform Movement in Judaism.* 1931. Macmillan. revised. inscr. 581p. S3. $25.00

PHILLIPS, C.E. Lucas. *Alamein.* 1962. MA. ils/maps. 434p. VG/VG. S16. $20.00

PHILLIPS, Catherine Coffin. *Cornelius Cole, CA Pioneer & US Senator.* 1929. SF. John Henry Nash. 1st trade. ils/fld pl. marbled cloth. F/marbled box. R3. $65.00

PHILLIPS, Catherine Coffin. *Jessie Benton Fremont: Woman Who Made History.* 1935. SF. John Henry Nash. 1st. from author's personal lib. F/VG. O4. $250.00

PHILLIPS, Catherine. *Memoirs of Life of..., To Which Are Added Some Her Epistles.* 1797. London. James Phillips. 382p. worn leather. xl. V3. $65.00

PHILLIPS, Conrad. *Unrepentant.* 1958. Arthur Barker. 1st. VG/dj. P3. $25.00

PHILLIPS, Dorothy Waldo. *Dear Mrs Bender.* 1937. Phil. Winston. sgn. F/F. C8. $25.00

PHILLIPS, Ethel Calvert. *Calico.* 1937. Houghton Mifflin. 1st. VG. O3. $25.00

PHILLIPS, George A. *Delphiniums: Their History & Cultivation.* 1949 (1933). London. revised. photos. 114p. dj. B26. $22.50

PHILLIPS, Henry. *Germany Today & Tomorrow.* 1935. 1st. G+. E6. $20.00

PHILLIPS, Henry. *New Designs for Old Mexico.* 1939. National Travel Club. 1st. 336p. dj. F3. $15.00

PHILLIPS, Henry. *Plain Mary Smith: A Romance of Red Saunders.* 1905. NY. Century. 1st. pict cloth. F. B4. $150.00

PHILLIPS, James H. *Undercover Wildlife Agent.* 1981. Tulsa. 108p. F/NF. AS15. $10.00

PHILLIPS, Jayne Anne. *Black Tickets.* 1979. Delacorte. 1st. F/F. B4. $200.00

PHILLIPS, Jayne Anne. *Black Tickets.* 1979. Delacorte. 1st. inscr/dtd. author's 1st book. F/F. L3. $350.00

PHILLIPS, Jayne Anne. *Fast Lanes.* 1987. Dutton. 1st. F/F. A20. $30.00

PHILLIPS, Jayne Anne. *Fast Lanes.* 1987. Dutton. 1st. sgn. F/F. D10. $45.00

PHILLIPS, Jayne Anne. *Machine Dreams.* 1984. Dutton. 1st. author's 2nd book. F/dj. A24/H11. $40.00

PHILLIPS, Jayne Anne. *Machine Dreams.* 1984. Dutton. 1st. sgn/dtd. F/F. D10. $60.00

PHILLIPS, Jill M. *Walfords Oak.* 1990. Citadel. 1st. F/F. M21. $25.00

PHILLIPS, John C. *Natural History of Ducks.* 1986. NY. unabridged Dover hc rpt. 4 vol in 2. F/dj. S15. $80.00

PHILLIPS, John C. *Wenham Great Pond.* 1938. Peabody Mus. 1/500. ils. VG. M17. $50.00

PHILLIPS, P. Lee. *List of Geographical Atlases in Library of Congress.* nd. 4 vol. rpt of 1909-20 eds. 1/100. F. A4. $355.00

PHILLIPS, Ulrich Bonnell. *American Negro Slavery, a Survey of the Supply...* 1929 (1918). NY. Appleton. 8vo. VG. C8. $85.00

PHILLIPSE, Robert. *Cruiser of the Chesapeake; or, Pride of the Nansemond.* 1864. NY. Beadle Dime Novel 74. 8vo. orange wrp. R12. $60.00

PHILLPOTTS, Beatrice. *Clem & the Fancy Dress Party.* 1987. London. Laura Ashley/Weidenfeld. 1st. 8vo. F. C8. $15.00

PHILPOTTS, Eden. *Captain's Curio.* 1933. Macmillan. 1st Am. F/NF. M15. $45.00

PHILPOTTS, Eden. *Flower of the Gods.* 1943. Macmillan. 1st. NF/dj. M2. $30.00

PHIN, John. *Open Air Grape Culture: A Practical Treatise.* 1862. NY. Saxton. 1st. 375p. VG. A10. $150.00

PHIN, John. *Open Air Grape Culture: A Practical Treatise.* 1876. NY. ils. 266p. gilt gr cloth. VG. B26. $65.00

PHIPPS, Frances. *Colonial Kitchens, Their Furnishings & Their Gardens.* 1972. NY. Hawthorn. 2nd. sgn. VG/dj. A10. $65.00

PHIPSON, Joan. *Polly's Tiger.* 1974. Dutton. 1st. 8vo. 43p. xl. G+. T5. $14.00

PHISTERER, Frederick. *Statistical Record of the Armies of the United States.* 1883. NY. 1st. 343p. O8. $27.50

PHOENIX, John. *Phoenixiana; or, Sketches & Burlesques.* 1903. Appleton. 1st thus. 8vo. 333p. VG. F7/K7. $55.00

PICANO, Felice. *Mesmerist.* 1977. Delacorte. 1st. F/F. H11. $40.00

PICARD, Jean. *De Prisca Celtopaedia...Quam Vel in Graecia Vel in Italia...* 1556. Paris. David Matthew. only ed. 138 leaves. orig suede w/4 gild devices. B14. $750.00

PICASSO, Pablo. *Desire, Caught by the Tail.* 1950. London. Rider. 1st. ils. author's only play. VG+. D10. $75.00

PICASSO, Pablo. *Picasso, Forty Nine New Lithographs.* 1947. NY. Crown. 1st. sm 4to. F/VG. C8. $95.00

PICCOLOMINI, Aeneas. *Secret Memoirs of a Renaissance Pope.* 1988. London. Folio Soc. 1st. 8vo. ils. vellum paper brd/leather label. F/case. T10. $50.00

PICHUGINA, P. *Women in the USSR.* 1939. Moscow. Foreign Languages Pub. 1st. ils Klering. VG+. A25. $20.00

PICKARD, Nancy. *IOU.* 1991. NY. 1st. F/dj. A24. $25.00

PICKEN, Mary Brooks. *Sewing Materials.* 1924. Women's Inst Domestic Arts & Sciences. 267p. VG. H1. $25.00

PICKENS, T. Boone. *Boone.* 1987. Houghton Mifflin. 304p. F/dj. D8. $18.00

PICKERING, James Sayre. *Stars Are Yours.* 1988. Macmillan. 1st. sgn. VG. K3. $20.00

PICKERING, John. *Vocabulary; or, Collection of Words & Phrases...* 1816. Boston. 1st. 8vo. 206p. ES. ca 1840 bdg. VG. M1. $400.00

PICKERING. *John Locke & Children's Books in 18th-C England.* 1985. TN U. ils. 299p. F. A4. $65.00

PICKFORD, Mary. *Demi-Widow.* 1935. Bobbs Merrill. 1st. NF/NF. B4. $125.00

PICKNEY, Josephine. *My Son & Foe.* 1952. Viking. 1st. F/NF. B4. $100.00

PICKOFF, Louise. *For Serving Four.* 1964. NY. AS Barnes. VG/dj. A16. $10.00

PICKVANCE, Ronald. *Drawings of Gauguin.* 1970. Paul Hamlyn. ils. VG/VG. M17. $25.00

PICKWELL, Gaylor B. *Prairie Horned Lark.* 1931. St Louis. Academy of Science. 33 pl. 160p. VG. S15. $15.00

PICO, Ulde. *Rainbow Goblins.* 1979. Warner. 1st Am. ils. obl 4to. NF/sans. P2. $75.00

PICO DELLA MIRANDOLA. *De Rerum Praenotione Libri Novem.* 1507. Strasbourg. Knobloch for Schurer. folio. contemporary calf. R12. $4,750.00

PIDGEON, Harry. *Around the World Single-Handed.* 1932. NY. Appleton Century. ils. 232p. dj. T7. $40.00

PIENKOWSKI, Jan. *Haunted House.* 1981 (1979). Heinemann. 4th. popup. 4to. VG+. P2. $25.00

PIERCE, A. *Home Canning For Victory: Pickling, Preserving, Dehydrating.* 1942. 2nd. VG/VG. E6. $18.00

PIERCE, Don. *Master in the Kitchen.* 1964. 1st. lg 8vo. VG/VG. E6. $25.00

PIERCE, John. *Greenhouse Grow How: A Reference Book.* 1977. Seattle. Plants Alive. 241p. VG/dj. A10. $28.00

PIERCY, Marge. *Breaking Camp.* 1968. Middletown. Wesleyan U. 1st. author's 1st book. F/NF. L3. $100.00

PIERCY, Marge. *Breaking Camp.* 1968. Wesleyan U. sgn. poet's 1st book. F/NF clip. V1. $65.00

PIERCY, Marge. *Going Down Fast.* 1969. Trident. 1st. F/dj. A24. $85.00

PIERCY, Marge. *Woman on the Edge of Time.* 1976. Knopf. 1st. NF/dj. A24. $40.00

PIERON, Henri. *Thought & Brain.* 1973 (1927). NY. Arno. facsimile. 262p. prt gray cloth. G1. $28.50

PIEROT, Suzanne. *Ivy Book of Growing & Care of Ivy...* 1974. Macmillan. 1st. 164p. dj. A10. $22.00

PIERSALL, Jim. *Fear Strikes Out: The Jim Piersall Story.* 1955. Atlantic/Little Brn. 1st. F/NF. B4. $125.00

PIGAFETTA, Antonio. *Magellan's Voyage: A Narrative Account...* 1969. New Haven. Yale. 2 vol. 1st trans of French text. M/case. O7. $300.00

PIGAFETTA, Antonio. *Magellan's Voyage: A Narrative of 1st Navigation.* 1975. London. Folio Soc. 8vo. ils/map ep. gilt bdg. as new/case. O7. $45.00

PIGAFETTA, Antonio. *Voyage of Magellan: Journal of Antonio Pigafetta.* 1969. Prentice Hall. trans PS Paige/orig French text on versos. NF. O7. $45.00

PIGGOTT, Stuart. *William Stukeley, an Eighteenth-C Antiquary.* 1985. Thames Hudson. revised/enlarged. 8vo. 191p. F/dj. K3. $50.00

PIGOTT, Charles. *Jockey Club; or, Sketch of the Manners of the Age.* 1793. NY. Thomas Greenleaf. 1st Am. 8vo. 205p. old calf. M1. $200.00

PIKE, Donald G. *Anasazi: Ancient People of the Rock.* 1974. American West. 2nd. ils/map ep. 191p. NF/VG. B19. $20.00

PIKE, Luke Owen. *History of Crime in England, Illustrating Changes of Laws...* 1873-76. London. Smith Elder. later maroon cloth. M11. $250.00

PILCHER, Lewis. *Surgical Pilgrim's Progress: Reminiscences of LS Pilcher.* 1925. Phil. 1st. 451p. A13. $40.00

PILCHER, Lewis. *Treatment of Wounds, Its Principles & Practice...* 1883. NY. 1st. 116 engravings. 391p. A13. $100.00

PILCHER, Rosamunde. *Flowers in the Rain & Other Stories.* 1991. NY. 1st. F/F. H11. $30.00

PILCHER, Rosamunde. *September.* 1990. St Martin. 1st. 536p. F/F. W2. $30.00

PILEGGI, Nicholas. *Wiseguy.* 1985. S&S. 1st. NF/NF. M22. $40.00

PILKINGTON, James. *Artist's Guide & Mechanics Own Book...* 1847. Portland. Sanborn Carter. 490p. gilt cloth. VG. B14. $75.00

PINCHON, Edgcumb. *Dan Sickles, Hero of Gettysburg & Yankee King of Spain.* 1945. Doubleday Doran. 1st. 280p. cloth. NF/VG. M8. $45.00

PINCHON, Jerome. *Life of Charles Henry Count Hoym.* 1899. NY. Grolier. 4to. ils. calf/brocade. R12. $175.00

PINCKNEY, Darryl. *High Cotton.* 1992. FSG. 1st. F/F. R14. $45.00

PINCKNEY, Pauline A. *American Figureheads & Their Carvers.* 1969. NY. Kennikat. rpt. ils/pl. 223p. T7. $45.00

PINCUS & THIMANN. *Hormones.* 1948. Academic. 2 vol. F/dj. A17. $35.00

PINDAR, Peter. *Works of...* 1812. London. J Walker. 5 vol. tall 8vo. full tan polished calf. H13. $395.00

PINEROS CORPAS, Joaquin. *El Libro Del Nuevo Reino.* (1966). Bogota. 1st. 179p. F3. $15.00

PINES, Ayala M. *Keeping the Spark Alive.* 1988. St Martin. 1st. 291p. F/F. W2. $25.00

PINKERTON, Allan. *Bucholz & the Detective.* 1880. Careton. 1st. 341p. gilt cloth. VG. M20. $30.00

PINKERTON, Allan. *Model Town & the Detectives.* 1876. NY. Carleton. 1st. gilt gr pict cloth. VG. M24. $250.00

PINKERTON, Robert. *Canoe: Its Selection, Care & Use.* 1959. Macmillan. 162p. NF/VG+. H7. $27.50

PINKERTON, Robert. *First Overland Mail.* 1953. Random. BC. VG/VG. O3. $15.00

PINKNEY, D.W. *Rope Spinning, With Special Chapter on How to Use Lariat.* 1930. London. Jenkins. 1st. 96p. VG. A10. $28.00

PINNER, David. *Ritual.* 1967. New Authors Ltd. 1st. F/F. P3. $15.00

PINSON, Koppel S. *National & History: Essays on Old & New Judaism...* 1958. JPS. notes/index. 385p. VG/dj. S3. $24.00

PINTAURO, Joseph. *Peace Box.* 1970. Harper. 1st. sm sq 8vo. pict brd. F/sans. B4. $85.00

PINTER, Harold. *Mountain Language.* 1988. NY. Grove. 1st Am. F/F. R14. $25.00

PINTER, Harold. *Poems & Prose 1949-1977.* 1978. Grove. 1st. F/F. V1. $20.00

PINTO, O. *Spy Catcher.* 1952. 1st. F/VG. E6. $18.00

PINTO DE AZEREDO, Jose. *Ensaios Sobre Algumas Enfermedades d'Angola.* 1799. Lisbon. Regia Officina Typografica. 1st/only. 149p. F. R15. $4,800.00

PIOZZI, Hester Lynch. *Anecdotes of the Late Samuel Johnson, LLD.* 1786. London. Cadell. 1st. sm 8vo. 306p. H13. $550.00

PIOZZI, Hester Lynch. *Baviad & Maeviad.* 1811. London. John Murray. 8th. tall 8vo. full tree calf. H13. $225.00

PIOZZI, Hester Lynch. *Retrospection; or, Review of the Most Striking Events...* 1801. London. Stockdale. 2 vol. 1/750. 1st. tall 4to. pub cloth/morocco labels. H13. $850.00

PIPER, Evelyn. *Nanny.* 1964. Atheneum. 1st. F/NF. B4. $125.00

PIPER, H. Beam. *Little Fuzzy.* 1983. Platt Munk. 1st. F/dj. M2. $10.00

PIPER, R.G. *Fish Hatchery Management.* 1982. WA. ils/photos/figures/tables. 513p. NF/wrp. M12. $37.50

PIPER, Watty. *Children of Other Lands.* 1933. Platt Munk. thin 4to. ils Holling/Holling. 12 stories. VG. T10. $40.00

PIPER, Watty. *Children of Other Lands.* 1956. 1st thus. ils Holling. VG/VG clip. S13. $25.00

PIPER, Watty. *Children of Other Lands.* 1956. Platt Munk. ils HC Holling. F/VG. M19. $45.00

PIPER, Watty. *Little Engine That Could.* 1954. Platt Munk. probable 1st/Silver Anniversary ed. unp. VG/G+. T5. $25.00

PIPER, Watty. *Stories Children Love.* 1933 (1922). Platt Munk. 4to. unp. pict brd/cloth spine. G+. T5. $35.00

PIPPERT, Wesley. *Land of Promise: Land of Strife: Israel at Forty.* 1988. World. 273p. VG/dj. B29. $8.50

PIPPETT, Aileen. *Moth & the Star: Biography of Virginia Woolf.* 1955. Little Brn. 1st. 368p. 2-toned cloth. VG/poor. B22. $15.00

PIPPETT, Aileen. *Moth & the Star: Biography of Virginia Woolf.* 1955. Little Brn. 2nd. VG/dj. A25. $15.00

PIRANESI, Giovanni Battista. *Magnificence of Rome.* 1962. Harcourt. 1/200. facsimile. 28 double-p pl. maroon brd. F/case. B24. $450.00

PIRIE, David. *Vampire Cinema.* 1977. Crescent. VG/dj. M2/P3. $20.00

PIRNIE, Miles D. *Michigan Waterfowl Management.* 1935. Lansing. 328p. xl. A17. $35.00

PIRSIG, Robert M. *Lila.* 1991. Bantam. 1st. F/F. M23. $25.00

PIRSIG, Robert M. *Zen & the Art of Motorcycle Maintenance.* 1974. 1st. author's 1st book. F/dj. A15. $150.00

PIRSIG, Robert M. *Zen & the Art of Motorcycle Maintenance.* 1984. Morrow. special anniversary ed. 1/1000. sgn. F/case/band. R14. $75.00

PISAR, Samuel. *Of Blood & Hope.* 1979. Little Brn. 311p. VG+/G+. S3. $25.00

PITMAN, Richard. *Good Horses Make Good Jockeys.* 1976. London. Pelham. 1st. VG/VG. O3. $25.00

PITRONE, Jean Maddern. *Trailblazer: Negro Nurse in the American Red Cross.* 1969. HBW. 1st. 191p. F/VG. B4. $65.00

PITT-TAYLOR, Nora. *All About Miss Fluffy Chick.* 1926. Cupples Leon. 16mo. VG. M5. $45.00

PITTENGER, Mark. *American Socialists & Evolutionary Thought, 1870-1920.* 1993. WI U. 1st. as new/dj. V4. $30.00

PITTENGER, Peggy Jett. *Back Yard Foal.* 1967. Barnes. sm 4to. VG. O3. $25.00

PITTENGER, Peggy Jett. *Wonderful World of Ponies.* 1969. Barnes. 1st. VG/VG. O3. $20.00

PITTER, Ruth. *Spirit Watches.* 1940. Macmillan. 1st. F/NF. V1. $35.00

PITTSFORD & PITTSFORD. *Eastward Whoa, 1927.* 1928. Chicago. 1/200. ils. 96p. VG. B5. $30.00

PITZ, Henry. *Drawing Trees.* 1956. 1st. VG/VG. S13. $45.00

PLANCK, Max. *Vorlesungen Uber die Theorie der Warmestrahlung.* 1923. Leipzig. Johan Ambrosius Barth. 221p. VG. K3. $20.00

PLANES-BURGADE, Georges. *Bordeaux.* 1934. Paris. Picquot. 1/54. ils Jacques le Tanneur. NF/wrp. T10. $150.00

PLANK, Sam. *Story of the String & How It Grew.* 1916. NY. Altemas Ward. novelty. obl 8vo. pict brd. R5. $350.00

PLANTE, David. *Catholic.* 1985. Chatto Windus. 1st. F/dj. Q1. $40.00

PLATE, R. *Dinosaur Hunters Othniel C Marsh & Edward D Cope.* 1964. McKay. 281p. xl. VG/dj. D8. $18.00

PLATH, Sylvia. *Ariel.* 1966. Harper Row. 1st. F/F. B35. $200.00

PLATH, Sylvia. *Bed Book.* 1976. Harper. 1st Am. NF/VG. C8. $40.00

PLATH, Sylvia. *Johnny Panic & the Bible of Dreams.* 1979. 1st. NF/VG+. S13. $25.00

PLATH, Sylvia. *Letters Home: Correspondence 1950-1963.* 1975. NY. Harper Row. 1st. photos. NF/F. R14. $25.00

PLATO. *Collected Dialogues of...* 1987. Princeton. 13th. F/F. P3. $35.00

PLATO. *Five Great Dialogues.* 1942. Walter J Blk for Classics Club. 511p. NF. W2. $165.00

PLATT, Colin. *Medieval England: Social History & Archaeology...* 1978. Scribner. 1st. 292p. as new/dj. H1. $22.50

PLAYER & THATCHER. *Gary Player: World Golfer.* 1974. Word. 1st. photos. VG/G+. P8. $22.50

PLEASANTS, William J. *Twice Across the Plains 1849 & 1856.* 1981. Fairfield, WA. 1st. F/F. O4. $15.00

PLENN, J.H. *Mexico Marches.* 1939. Bobbs Merrill. 1st. 386p. F3. $10.00

PLENN, J.H. *Saddle in the Sky: Lone Star State.* 1940. Bobbs Merrill. 1st. 287p. cloth. VG/dj. M20. $35.00

PLIMPTON, George. *Bogey Man.* 1968. Harper Row. 1st. F/NF. B4. $45.00

PLIMPTON, George. *Bogey Man.* 1968. Harper Row. 1st. sgn. F/dj. Q1. $75.00

PLIMPTON, George. *Bogey Man.* 1968. Harper Row. 1st. VG/clip. A20. $25.00

PLIMPTON, George. *Mad Ducks & Bears.* 1973. Random. 1st. VG/VG. P8. $10.00

PLIMPTON, George. *Paper Lion.* ca 1970s. Holtzman. Autographed Sports Classic series. sgn. F. P8. $30.00

PLIMPTON, George. *Paper Lion.* 1966. Harper Row. 1st. F/F. B35. $25.00

PLIMPTON, George. *Rabbit's Umbrella.* 1955. NY. Viking. 1st. sgn. author's 1st regulary pub book. NF/dj. Q1. $200.00

PLOWDEN, David. *Lincoln & His America.* 1970. 1st. 352p. O8. $21.50

PLOWRIGHT, Teresa. *Dreams of an Unseen Planet.* 1986. Arbor. 1st. author's 1st novel. F/F. G10/P3. $20.00

PLUCKNETT, T.F.T. *Concise History of the Common Law.* 1929. Rochester. Lawyers Co-Operative. 1st. gilt brn cloth. M11. $125.00

PLUCKNETT, T.F.T. *Early English Legal Literature.* 1958. Cambridge. M11. $85.00

PLUCKNETT, T.F.T. *Edward I & Criminal Law.* 1960. Cambridge. VG/dj. M11. $65.00

PLUCKNETT, T.F.T. *Statutes & Their Interpretation in First Half of 14th C...* 1986. Holmes Beach. Wm Gaunt. M11. $75.00

PLUCKNETT, T.F.T. *Studies in English Legal History.* 1983. London. Hambledon. M11. $45.00

PLUMLY, Stanley. *Boy on the Step.* 1989. Ecco. 1st. F/dj. V1. $20.00

PLUMPTRE, George. *Royal Gardens.* 1981. London. photos. 224p. F/dj. B26. $24.00

PLUNKETT, Robert. *Love Junkie.* 1992. Harper Collins. 1st. F/F. B4. $45.00

PLUTARCH. *Lives of the Nobel Grecians & Romans.* 1929. Nonesuch. 5 vol. 1st. 1/1550. sm folio. ils. teg. NF. C6. $350.00

PLUTARCH. *Lives of the Noble Grecians & Romans.* 1941. Heritage. 2 vol. thick 8vo. tan linen. F/NF case. H13. $45.00

PLUTARCH. *Lives of the Noble Grecians & Romans.* 1941. NY. LEC. 8 vol. gilt bl cloth. F. T10. $175.00

PODHAJSKY, Alois. *Lipizzaners.* 1970. Doubleday. 2nd Am. VG/VG. O3. $48.00

PODRUG, Junius. *Frost of Heaven.* 1992. Arlington Hts. Dark Harvest. 1st. inscr. F/F. H11. $45.00

POE, Clarence Hamilton. *True Tales of the South War: How Soldiers Fought...1861-65.* 1961. Chapel Hill. Confederate Descendants ed. 208p. cloth. NF. M8. $35.00

POE, Edgar Allan. *Complete Stories & Poems of...* 1966. Doubleday. F. T12. $15.00

POE, Edgar Allan. *Essays & Reviews.* 1984. Lib of Am. 1st. F/dj. M2. $12.00

POE, Edgar Allan. *Poe's Tales of Mystery & Imagination.* 1985. Weathervane. ils Rackham. NF/dj. M2. $30.00

POE, Edgar Allan. *Raven.* 1884. NY. Harper. folio. ils Gustav Dore. G. B5. $310.00

POE, Edgar Allan. *Representative Selections.* 1935. Am Book Co. probable later prt. John Gardner's copy/sgn. VG. B4. $250.00

POE, Edgar Allan. *Tales of Mystery & Imagination.* (1929). NY. Brentano. 1/2500. ils. 412p. VG/G. B5. $125.00

POEBEL, Arno. *Historical & Grammatical Texts.* 1914. Phil. U Mus. 1st. 4to. 125 pl (many fld pl). VG/wrp. W1. $65.00

POGANY, Willy. *Golden Cockerel.* 1938. NY. 1st. 8vo. VG. B5. $45.00

POGANY, Willy. *Gulliver's Travels.* 1917. Macmillan. 1st. 8vo. VG. M5. $75.00

POGANY, Willy. *Water-Color Lessons.* 1950. ils. VG/G+. M17. $15.00

POGANY & POGANY. *Peterkin.* 1940. McKay. 1st. ils Willy Pogany. unp. VG/dj. M20. $110.00

POHL, Frederik. *Beyond the Blue Event Horizon.* 1980. Del Rey. 1st. F/dj. M2. $40.00

POHL, Frederik. *Beyond the Blue Event Horizon.* 1980. Del Rey. 1st. VG/VG. P3. $18.00

POHL, Frederik. *Chernobyl.* 1987. Bantam. 1st. VG/G. P3. $15.00

POHL, Frederik. *Day the Martians Came.* 1989. Easton. 1st. sgn. full leather. F/swrp. P3. $60.00

POHL, Frederik. *Gateway Trip: Tales & Vignettes of the Heechee.* 1990. Ballantine. 1st. F/dj. M21. $15.00

POHL, Frederik. *Jem.* 1979. St Martin. 1st. NF/dj. M2. $20.00

POHL, Frederik. *Jem.* 1979. St Martin. 1st. VG/VG. P3. $15.00

POHL, Frederik. *Merchant's War.* 1984. St Martin. 1st. NF/VG+. N4. $20.00

POHL, Frederik. *Merchants' War.* 1985. Gollancz. 1st. F/F. P3. $20.00

POHL, Frederik. *Midas World.* 1983. St Martin. 1st. F/dj. M2. $35.00

POHL, Frederik. *Narabedla Ltd.* 1988. Ballantine. 1st. F/F. H11. $25.00

POHL, Frederik. *Plague of Pythons.* 1966. London. Gollancz. 1st. F/clip. T2. $200.00

POHL, Frederik. *Second If Reader of Science Fiction.* 1968. Doubleday. 1st. VG/VG. P3. $25.00

POHL, Frederik. *World at the End of Time.* 1990. Ballantine. 1st. F/NF. M21. $15.00

POHL & WILLIAMSON. *Land's End.* 1988. Tor. 1st. F/dj. M2. $20.00

POHL & WILLIAMSON. *Singers of Time.* 1991. Doubleday. 1st. VG/dj. P3. $22.00

POIGNANT, Axel. *Bush Walkabout.* 1974. NY. Addison-Wesley. 60p. VG+. P4. $20.00

POINCARE, H. *Rapport sur le Project de Revision de l'arc Meridiene...* 1898. Pais. Gauthier. xl. wrp. K3. $65.00

POINDEXTER, Miles. *Ayer Incas.* 1930. NY. 2 vol. 1st. ils. VG/G+. B5. $65.00

POIRET, Abbe. *Travels Through Barbary, in a Series of Letters...* ca 1790. London. Prt for C Forster. 12mo. 366p. contemporary morocco. xl. W1. $180.00

POITIER, Sidney. *This Life.* 1980. Knopf. 1st. inscr. F/F. M25. $75.00

POLASEK, Emily. *MK: A Bohemian Girl in America.* 1982. Rollins. inscr. 120p. VG/VG repro dj. B11. $25.00

POLIDORI, John William. *Vampyre.* 1973. Hertfordshire. Gubblecote. 1/1000. 8vo. 42p. F. T10. $100.00

POLING-KEMPES, Lesley. *Harvey Girls: Women Who Opened the West.* 1989. Paragon House. 1st. photos. 252p. VG/clip. A25. $18.00

POLITE, Carlene Hatcher. *Sister X & the Victims of Foul Play.* 1975. FSG. 1st. NF/dj. M25. $40.00

POLITI, Leo. *Moy Moy.* 1960. Scribner. 9th. sm 4to. F/VG+. C8. $40.00

POLITI, Leo. *Three Stalks of Corn.* 1976. Vanguard. 1st. ils. 4to. F/VG. P2. $65.00

POLK, James K. *Diary of a President 1845-1849.* 1952. VG. M17. $25.00

POLLAK, Otto. *Criminality of Women.* 1950. PA U. 1st. 180p. VG/dj. H1. $35.00

POLLARD, Edward Alfred. *First Year of the War.* 1863 (1862). NY. Chas Richardson. 368p. gilt gr cloth. VG. M20. $75.00

POLLARD, Edward Alfred. *Second Year of the War.* 1863. Richmond. West Johnson. 1st. 326p. later cloth. VG. M8. $250.00

POLLARD, William. *Old-Fashioned Quakerism: Its Origins, Results & Future.* 1887. London. Harris. 110p. V3. $10.00

POLLOCK, Frederick. *Jurisprudence & Legal Essays...* 1961. London. Macmillan. reissue. M11. $65.00

POLLOCK, J.C. *Centrifuge.* 1984. Crown. 1st. 276p. F/F. W2. $20.00

POLOCK, Dale. *Skywalking: Life & Films of George Lucas.* 1983. Harmony. 1st. F/dj. M2. $25.00

POLSKY, Ned. *Hustlers, Beats & Others.* 1967. Chicago. Aldine. 1st. F/NF. B2. $45.00

POLUNIN & STAINTON. *Flowers of Himalaya.* 1984. Delhi. photos. 580p. F/dj. B26. $75.00

POLVINEN, Tuomo. *Between East & West: Finland in International Politics...* 1986. NM U. 1st. as new/dj. V4. $15.00

POMERLEAU, Rene. *Mushrooms of Eastern Canada & the United States.* 1951. Montreal. 1st. ils/pl. pict cloth. VG. H3. $45.00

POMEROY, Frank T. *Picturesque Brattleboro.* 1894. Northampton, MA. Picturesque Pub. 1st. gilt br cloth. VG. M24. $300.00

POMFRET, John E. *California Gold Rush Voyages 1848-1849.* 1954. San Marino. 1st. NF/VG. O4. $20.00

POND, George. *Shenandoah Valley in 1864.* 1883. 1st. 287p. O8. $23.50

POND, James B. *Eccentricities of Genius.* 1900. Dillingham. 1st/1st state (no ad leaf). teg. gilt red cloth. G. M24. $85.00

PONICSAN, Darryl. *Unmarried Man.* 1980. Delacorte. 1st. F/F. B4. $65.00

PONSOT, Marie. *Fables of La Fontaine.* (1957). Grosset Dunlap. ils. pict ep. VG. T5. $25.00

PONSOT, Marie. *My Big Book of Cat Stories.* nd. Golden. lg 4to. 108p. VG+. C14. $40.00

PONSOT, Marie. *Russian Fairy Tales.* 1960. Golden. 1st. folio. VG+. M5. $45.00

PONTEY, W. *Profitable Planter: A Treatise...* 1808. Huddersfield. 2nd. 8vo. 222p. brd. VG. C6. $100.00

PONTI, Claude. *Adele's Album.* 1988. Dutton. 1st Am. ils Ponti/Monique Rauscher. VG. T5. $30.00

PONTING, Herbert G. *Great White South; or, Scott in the Antarctic...* 1923. NY. McBride. later imp. 305p. VG+. P4. $200.00

PONZI, Frank. *19th-Century Iceland: Artists & Odysseys.* nd. np. Almenna Bokafelagio. Eng/Icelandic text. 159p. P4. $65.00

POOL, ELizabeth. *Unicorn Was There.* nd. Barre. 1st. ils/sgn James Houston. 48p. VG/dj. M20. $25.00

POOL, Raymond J. *Marching With the Grasses.* 1948. Lincoln. 1st. 8vo. 210p. cloth. VG/dj. A22. $30.00

POOLMAN, Kenneth. *Allied Escort Carriers of World War II.* 1988. Annapolis. maps/photos/biblio/glossary/index. 272p. VG/VG. S16. $25.00

POOLMAN, Kenneth. *Guns Off Cape Ann.* 1965. Mill Valley, CA. self pub. ils. 175p. T7. $24.00

POOR, Henry V. *Manual of the Railroads of the United States 1868-69...* nd. np. rpt 1868. VG+. B18. $25.00

POORTENAAR, Jan. *Dans en Wajang (Dance in Wayang).* 1929. Haarlem. 1/150. 6 sgn etchings. yel brd. F/case. B24. $285.00

POPE, Alexander. *Essai sur l'Homme...* 1772. Strasbourg. Armand Konig. 8vo. 351p. early full calf. H13. $225.00

POPE, Alexander. *Letters of... & Several of His Friends.* 1737. London. 4to. A15. $150.00

POPE, Alexander. *Of the Use of Riches, an Epistle to Lord Bathurst...* 1732. London. J Wright for Laton Gilliver. 1st/1st issue. folio. H13. $395.00

POPE, Alexander. *Works of...* 1806. London. 10 vol. VG. A15. $125.00

POPE, Clifford H. *Reptile World.* 1955. Knopf. 325p. VG. S15. $38.00

POPE, Dudley. *Buccaneer.* 1981. Musson. 1st. F/F. P3. $22.00

POPE, Dudley. *England Expects.* 1959. London. Weidenfeld Nicolson. 1st Eng. VG/VG. P3. $30.00

POPE, Dudley. *Ramage's Prize.* 1974. S&S. 1st Am. F/F. B2. $40.00

POPE, Gustavus. *Journey to Mars.* 1974 (1894). Hyperion. rpt. F. M2. $30.00

POPE, Jessie. *Cat Scouts.* ca 1912. Dodge. 1st Am. ils Louis Wain. G. P2. $250.00

POPE, Jessie. *Cat Scouts.* 1912. London. Blackie. 1st. ils Louis Wain. cloth-backed broad weave cloth/label. F. R5. $1,250.00

POPE, Jessie. *Story of Flip & Fuzzy.* ca 1912. NY. Dodge. 1st Am. ils Macgregor. pict brd. R5. $350.00

POPE, Richard M. *Church & the Culture.* 1965. Bethany. 618p. VG/dj. B29. $10.00

POPE, Saxon. *Adventurous Bowman: Field Notes on African Archery.* 1994. Derrydale. sgn. aeg. gilt leather. F. A17. $20.00

POPE, Saxton. *Hunting With Bow & Arrow.* (1947). Putnam. 6th. 257p. VG. H7. $40.00

POPE, Thomas. *Treatise on Bridge Architecture...* 1811. NY. Alexander Niven. 1st. 8vo. 15 pl/2 vignettes. recent cloth. M1. $1,250.00

POPE-HENNESSY, John. *Portrait in the Renaissance.* 1966. NY. 1st. VG/dj. T9. $30.00

POPE-HENNESSY, Una. *Aristocratic Journey.* 1931. London. Putnam. A19. $45.00

POPOL VUH. *Book of the People.* 1954. LA. LEC. 1st thus. 1/1500. ils/sgn EG Jackson. F/glassine/case. Q1. $100.00

POPOVICH, John A. *Custer, Cavalry & Crows: Story of William White...* 1975. Old Army. 1st. 183p. VG. J2. $195.00

PORCH, Douglas. *Conquest of the Sahara.* 1984. Knopf. 1st. 8vo. 332p. NF/dj. W1. $20.00

PORCUPINE, Peter. *Political Censor; or, Monthly Review...* (1796). Phil. Wm Cobbett. 3rd. 12mo. later brd. M1. $600.00

PORSILD, A.E. *Botanical Excursion to Jasper...* 1959. Ottawa. Alpine/Subalpine Flora. photos. 38p. sc. VG. B26. $12.50

PORTER, Anna. *Hidden Agenda.* 1985. Putnam. 1st. F/F. T12. $20.00

PORTER, Connie. *All-Bright Court.* 1991. Houghton Mifflin. 1st. F/dj. A24. $40.00

PORTER, David D. *Naval History of the Civil War.* 1886. NY. 1st. 843p. O8. $75.00

PORTER, E. *Place No One Knew: Glen Canyon on the Colorado.* 1966. Sierra Club/Ballantine. photos. 159p. G/wrp. D8. $7.50

PORTER, Eleanor H. *Across the Years.* 1919. Houghton Mifflin. 1st. 315p. gilt red cloth. VG. M20. $18.00

PORTER, Eliot. *Forever Wild: The Adirondacks.* 1966. NY. folio. F/dj. M4. $20.00

PORTER, Gene Stratton. *Birds of the Bible.* 1909. Jennings Graham. 467p. pict cloth. VG. A4. $400.00

PORTER, Gene Stratton. *Freckles.* 1916. Grosset Dunlap. later ed. mc frontis/ils ep. 252p. VG+/dj. A25. $15.00

PORTER, Gene Stratton. *Harvester.* ca 1950-60 (1911). Grosset Dunlap. rpt. 12mo. F/VG. C8. $30.00

PORTER, Gene Stratton. *Laddie.* nd. Grosset Dunlap. ne. sm 8vo. 401p. lt gr cloth. F/VG-. H1. $25.00

PORTER, Gene Stratton. *Laddie.* 1915 (1913). Doubleday. 541p. limp suede. VG+. M20. $85.00

PORTER, Gene Stratton. *Laddie: A True Blue Story.* 1913. Doubleday. 1st. ils Herman Pfeifer. gilt bl cloth. F. B14. $55.00

PORTER, Gene Stratton. *Magic Garden.* 1927. Doubleday Page. 1st. ils Lee Thayer. 272p. VG/dj. P2. $175.00

PORTER, Gene Stratton. *Michael O'Halloran.* 1915. Doubleday. 560p. limb suede/orig suede strap. VG+. M20. $95.00

PORTER, Gene Stratton. *Morning Face.* 1916. 1st. 4to. photos. VG+. S13. $150.00

PORTER, Gene Stratton. *Morning Face.* 1916. NY. 1st. royal 8vo. ils. 129p. gilt pict bl cloth. G. H3. $135.00

PORTER, Jane. *Scottish Chiefs.* 1930 (1921). ils NC Wyeth. VG. S13. $35.00

PORTER, Joyce. *Dead Easy for Dover.* 1979. St Martin. VG/VG. P3. $22.00

PORTER, Joyce. *Dover One.* 1964. Scribner. 1st. VG/VG. P3. $40.00

PORTER, Katherine Anne. *Collected Stories.* 1964. London. Cape. true 1st. F/F. B4. $275.00

PORTER, Katherine Anne. *Collected Stories.* 1967. London. Cape. 1st revised. F/F. B4. $125.00

PORTER, Katherine Anne. *Flowering Judas & Other Stories.* 1935. Harcourt Brace. 1st trade. F/dj. B24. $450.00

PORTER, Katherine Anne. *Ship of Fools.* 1962. Atlantic/Little Brn. 1st. F/NF. H11. $60.00

PORTER, Katherine Anne. *Ship of Fools.* 1962. Atlantic/Little Brn. 1st. sgn. F/F. D10. $125.00

PORTER, Katherine Anne. *Ship of Fools.* 1962. Atlantic/Little Brn. 1st. VG/VG. R14. $40.00

PORTER, Richard W. *Versatile Satellite.* 1977. Oxford. lg 8vo. 173p. VG/dj. K5. $26.00

PORTER, Rufus. *Aerial Navigation: Practicability of Traveling...* 1935. SF. Lawton Kennedy. rpt. prt brd. D11. $60.00

PORTER, Sylvia. *Sylvia Porter's New Money Book.* 1975. Doubleday. 1st. 1105p. VG/dj. W2. $60.00

PORTER, W.S. *Cabbages & Kings.* 1904. McClure Phillips. 1st/1st state spine imprint. orange/gr stp blk cloth. M24. $250.00

PORTER, W.S. *Hiding of Black Bill.* 1913. NY. Ridgeway. 1st separate ed. NF/lt bl prt wrp. M24. $100.00

PORTER, W.S. *Strictly Business.* 1910. Doubleday Page. 1st. gilt red cloth. F. M24. $45.00

PORTER, Willard H. *Who's Who in Rodeo.* nd. Powder River Book Co. A19. $20.00

PORTER, Willard H. *13 Flat, the Rodeo, Horses & Riders, Tales...* 1967. AS Barnes. 256p. VG/dj. J2. $69.00

PORTIS, Charles. *Gringos.* 1991. S&S. 1st. F/F. A18. $20.00

PORTIS, Charles. *True Grit.* 1968. S&S. 1st. F/dj. M2. $50.00

POSNER, David. *Sandpipers, Selected Poems 1965-1975.* nd. FL U. 1st. F/VG+. V1. $20.00

POSSEVINO, Antonio. *Moscovia, et, Alia Opera.* 1587. Cologne. Birckmann-Mylius. folio. vellum. R12. $1,500.00

POST, Emily. *Etiquette: Blue Book of Social Usage.* 1941. Funk Wagnall. revised/4th prt. sgn. F/NF. B4. $150.00

POST, Emily. *Personality of a House.* 1937. fld chart/photos. VG/VG. M17. $30.00

POSTL, Karl. *North & South; or, Scenes & Adventures in Mexico.* 1844. NY. Winchester. 1st. tan prt wrp. uncut. M24. $375.00

POSTUMA, J.A. *Manual of Planktonic Foraminifera.* 1971. Elsevier Pub. 420p. NF/torn. D8. $45.00

POTEET, G. Howard. *Tom Swift & His Electric English Teacher.* 1974. Pflaum Pub. 96p. VG. M20. $250.00

POTOCKI, Jan. *Saragossa Manuscript.* 1960. Orion. 1st Am. F/torn. M2. $20.00

POTOK, Chaim. *Davita's Harp.* 1985. Knopf. 1st. F/NF. R14. $25.00

POTOK, Chaim. *My Name Is Asher Lev.* 1972. Knopf. 1st. NF/NF clip. H11. $15.00

POTOK, Chaim. *Promise.* 1969. Knopf. 1st. F/F. H11. $30.00

POTOK, Chaim. *Promise.* 1969. Knopf. 1st. F/NF. S13. $20.00

POTOK, Chaim. *Wanderings, Chaim Potok's History of the Jews.* 1978. Knopf. 1st. ils. VG/VG. E6. $20.00

POTTER, Beatrix. *Dear Ivy, Dear June.* 1977. Toronto Public Lib. NF/case. M20. $30.00

POTTER, Beatrix. *Fairy Caravan.* (1929). Phil. McKay. 1st Am. sm 4to. 225p. dk gr cloth/pict label. VG. D1. $450.00

POTTER, Beatrix. *Isn't It Funny.* ca 1890s. London. Nister. 4to. pict brd. R5. $875.00

POTTER, Beatrix. *Letters to Children From Beatrix Potter.* 1992. London. Warne. 200 photos. 240p. F/F. A4. $65.00

POTTER, Beatrix. *Roly-Poly Pudding.* 1908. Warne. 1st/2nd prt. sq 8vo. red cloth/pict label. VG. D1. $500.00

POTTER, Beatrix. *Tailor of Gloucester.* Dec 1902. private prt. 1/500. 16mo. pink brd/vignette. R5. $6,500.00

POTTER, Beatrix. *Tailor of Gloucester.* nd. Warne. 1/1500. facsimile orig manuscript. F/VG case. M5. $150.00

POTTER, Beatrix. *Tale of Little Pig Robinson.* (1930). Phil. McKay. 1st Am. 8vo. 141p. gr cloth. VG. D1. $375.00

POTTER, Beatrix. *Tale of Mrs Tittlemouse.* 1910. London. Warne. 1st. 16mo. gray-bl brd/hexagonal label. R5. $350.00

POTTER, Beatrix. *Tale of Tom Kitten.* 1907. London. Warne. 1st. 16mo. gray-bl brd/label. R5. $350.00

POTTER, David. *Car of Alloy Spars & Rigging.* 1980. NY. Scribner. ils/photos. 120p. T7. $20.00

POTTER, David. *Impending Crisis.* 1976. new/expanded. 630p. O8. $14.50

POTTER, Dennis. *Ticket To Ride.* 1985. Faber. 1st Am. NF/VG. M22. $30.00

POTTER, E.B. *Bull Halsey: A Bibliography.* 1985. Annapolis. ils/biblio/index. 421p. VG/VG. S16. $23.50

POTTER, Guy D. *Sectional Anatomy & Tomography of the Head.* 1971. NY. Grune Stratton. tall 4to. ils. 334p. blk cloth. VG/dj. G1. $75.00

POTTER, Harold. *Historical Introduction to English Law & Its Institutions...* 1948. London. Sweet & Maxwell. maroon cloth. M11. $35.00

POTTER, John Deane. *Fatal Gallows Tree, an Account of British Habit of Hanging.* 1965. London. Elek Books. M11. $35.00

POTTER, Mariam Clark. *Sally Gabble & the Fairies.* 1930 (1929). NY. Macmillan. Little Library ed/3rd prt. sm 16mo. VG. C8. $35.00

POTTER, Stephen. *Three-Upmanship.* 1962. NY. 1st. 467p. VG/dj. S1. $6.00

POUGET, Marcel. *Franco-American Professional Cookbook.* 1962. Exposition. G/dj. A16. $12.50

POUGH, F.H. *Field Guide to Rocks & Minerals.* 1960. Houghton Mifflin. 3rd. F/dj. D8. $10.00

POUGH, Richard H. *Audubon Water Bird Guide.* 1951. NY. ils Don Edkelberry. 352p. NF/VG. S15. $16.00

POULAILLE, Henry. *La Grande et Belle Bible des Noels Anciens XVII et XVIII...* 1950. Albin Michel. 628p. lg 8vo. pict wrp. A17. $20.00

POULET, Claude. *Cowboys, America's Living Legend.* 1986. Crescent. 1st. photos. VG/dj. J2. $95.00

POULSOM, Neville W. *White Ribbon: Medallic Record of British Polar Expeditions.* 1968. London. BA Seaby. 1st. 8vo. map ep. blk cloth. P4. $195.00

POUND, Ezra. *Literary Essays of Ezra Pound.* 1954. New Directions. 1st Am from eng sheets. intro TS Eliot. F/VG+. B4. $85.00

POUND, Ezra. *Thrones 95-109 De Los Cantares.* 1959. New Direictons. 1st. NF/VG+. B2. $45.00

POUND, Reginald. *Scott of the Antarctic.* 1967. Coward McCann. 1st Am. 327p. bl cloth. P4. $25.00

POUND, Roscoe. *Interpretations of Legal History.* 1930. Cambridge. 1st reissue. gilt olive cloth. M11. $85.00

POURADE, Richard F. *Anaza Conquers the Desert.* 1971. Copley Book. 1st. ils/maps/index. 217p. NF/VG+. B19. $65.00

POURADE, Richard F. *Colorful Butterfield Overland Stage.* 1966. Palm Desert, CA. dj. A19. $40.00

POURADE, Richard F. *Glory Years: History of San Diego.* 1965. San Diego. Union-Tribune. 2nd. F/F. O4. $25.00

POURADE, Richard F. *Silver Dons.* 1966. Union-Tribune. 3rd. 4to. F/F. O4. $25.00

POURNELLE, Jerry. *King David's Spaceship.* 1980. S&S. 1st. F/dj. M2. $17.00

POURNELLE, Jerry. *Step Farther Out.* 1980. WH Allen. 1st. VG. P3. $20.00

POURNELLE, Jerry. *Storms of Victory.* 1987. Ace. 1st. VG/VG. P3. $17.00

POVERMAN, C.E. *Susan.* 1977. Viking. 1st. 254p. NF/NF. W2. $40.00

POVICH, Shirley. *All These Mornings.* 1969. Prentice Hall. 1st. photos. VG/G. P8. $45.00

POWELL, A. Michael. *Grasses of the Trans-Pecos & Adacent Areas.* 1994. Austin. 1st. ils/photos/map. sc. M. B26. $30.00

POWELL, Anthony. *Fisher King.* 1986. Norton. 1st. NF/dj. A24. $20.00

POWELL, Anthony. *John Aubrey & His Friends.* 1948. NY. Scribner. 1st Am from Eng sheets. VG/intact. B4. $85.00

POWELL, Anthony. *Kindly Ones.* 1962. Little Brn. 1st. F/F. B35. $35.00

POWELL, Anthony. *O, How the Wheel Becomes It.* 1983. HRW. 1st. F/F. B35. $12.00

POWELL, Anthony. *Temporary Kings.* 1973. London. Heinemann. 1st. F/F. B4. $85.00

POWELL, Anthony. *Valley of Bones.* 1964. Little Brn. 1st. NF/clip. A24. $20.00

POWELL, Claire. *Meaning of Flowers: A Garland of Plant Lore & Symbolism.* 1977. London. Jupiter. 182p. VG/dj. A10. $30.00

POWELL, Dannye. *Parting the Curtains: Interviews With Southern Writers.* 1994. John F Blair. 1st. photos Jill Krementz. F/F. A20. $30.00

POWELL, Dawn. *Locusts Have No King.* 1948. Scribner. 1st. NF/NF. B4. $250.00

POWELL, Donald M. *Arizona Gathering II, 1950-1969.* 1973. AZ U. 1st. 207p. F/NF. B19. $45.00

POWELL, Donald M. *Arizona Gathering II, 1950-1969.* 1973. Tucson. 8vo. 207p. F/G. F7. $30.00

POWELL, E. Alexander. *In Barbary, Tunisia, Algeria, Morocco & Sahara.* 1926. NY/London. Century. 8vo. 65 pl/2 fld mc maps. 483p. G. W1. $9.00

POWELL, E.P. *Country Home.* 1904. NY. McClure. 1st. 384p. VG. A10. $25.00

POWELL, J.W. *Down the Colorado.* 1969. NY. 2nd. ils. VG/dj. B18. $20.00

POWELL, J.W. *Eighth Annual Report of Bureau of Ethnology...1886-1887.* 1891. GPO. 123 full-p ills/118 text ils. 298p. VG. K7. $175.00

POWELL, J.W. *Fifth Annual Report of Bureau Ethnology...1883-84.* 1887. GPO. 4to. 23 full-p pl/4 double-p lithos. 564p. gilt bdg. K7. $225.00

POWELL, J.W. *First Through the Grand Canyon.* 1928. Macmillan. bl cloth. VG/G+. F7. $25.00

POWELL, J.W. *Report on the Lands of the Arid Region of the United States.* 1962. Cambridge, MA. 202p. w/2 pocket map. VG/dj. B18. $65.00

POWELL, J.W. *Sixth Annual Report of the Bureau of Ethnology 1884.* 1888. WA. 669p. olive cloth. G+. M20. $85.00

POWELL, J.W. *13th Annual Report of the US Geological Survey...1891-92.* 1893. WA. Dept Interior. 74 pl/486p+2 fld pocket maps. T10. $150.00

POWELL, Lawrence Clark. *Arizona: A Bicentennial History.* 1976. Norton. 1st. ils. 154p. NF/NF. B19. $25.00

POWELL, Lawrence Clark. *El Morro.* 1984. Capra. 1st. 129p. VG+. B19. $30.00

POWELL, Lawrence Clark. *Evening Redness.* 1991. Capra. 1/100. sgn/#d. 436p. leather spine. NF/case. B19. $75.00

POWELL, Lawrence Clark. *Holly & the Fleece.* 1995. Capra. 1st. 125p. F. B19. $20.00

POWELL, Lawrence Clark. *Landscape & Literature.* 1990. DeGolyer Lib. 1st. 1/750. sgn. NF/sans. B19. $40.00

POWELL, Lawrence Clark. *My Haydn Commonplace Book.* 1983. private prt. 1st. 1/200 (not intended for sale). 50p. NF. B19. $50.00

POWELL, Lawrence Clark. *Passion for Books.* 1958. World. ltd. 154p. F/NF case. B19. $110.00

POWELL, Lawrence Clark. *Vein of Silk, Vein of Steel.* 1975. private prt. 1st. F/sans. B19. $65.00

POWELL, Lawrence Clark. *Where Water Flows: Rivers of Arizona.* 1980. Northland. 1st. sgn. photos Michael Collier. 64p. NF/NF. B19. $30.00

POWELL, N.V. *American Navies of the Revolutionary War.* 1974. NY. obl 4to. 53 mc pl. VG/dj. M4. $35.00

POWELL, Padgett. *Edisto.* 1984. FSG. 1st. F/dj. B4. $75.00

POWELL, Padgett. *Edisto.* 1984. FSG. 1st. sgn. F/F. B35. $115.00

POWELL, Padgett. *Typical.* 1991. FSG. 1st. sgn. F/F. B35. $50.00

POWELL, Padgett. *Woman Named Drown.* 1987. FSG. 1st. sgn. F/F. B35. $55.00

POWELL, Peter John. *People of the Sacred Mountain: History of N Cheyenne...* 1981. Harper Row. 1st. pl/photos. 1441p. as new. J2. $495.00

POWELL, Richard. *I Take This Land.* 1962. Scribner. 1st. sgn. VG/G. B11. $45.00

POWELL, Talmage. *Smasher.* 1959. Macmillan. 1st. VG/VG. w/sgn label. P3. $35.00

POWELL, Virgil S. *Notable Black Americans.* 1971. Cedar Rapids. WMT Stations. sgn. 87p. VG. B11. $25.00

POWER & WHITLATCH. *Shoot-Out at Dawn: An Arizona Tragedy.* 1981. Bill McCreary. ils. 173p. F/wrp. B19. $12.00

POWERS, J.F. *Look How the Fish Live.* 1975. Knopf. 1st. sgn. F/dj. Q1. $60.00

POWERS, J.F. *Prince of Darkness & Other Stories.* 1947. Doubleday. 1st. author's 1st book. F/NF. C2. $100.00

POWERS, J.L. *Black Abyss.* 1966. Arcadia. VG/VG. P3. $15.00

POWERS, John. *Short Season.* 1979. Harper Row. 1st. photos. F/VG+. P8. $25.00

POWERS, Richard. *Gold Bug Variations.* 1991. Morrow. 1st. F/F. R13. $150.00

POWERS, Richard. *Gold Bug Variations.* 1992. London. Scribner. 1st Eng. F/F. R13. $65.00

POWERS, Richard. *Prisoner's Dilemma.* 1988. Beech Tree Books. 1st. F/dj. B2. $100.00

POWERS, Richard. *Three Farmers on Their Way to a Dance.* 1985. Beech Tree. 1st. author's 1st book. F/dj. B3/B4. $250.00

POWERS, Richard. *Three Farmers on Their Way to a Dance.* 1985. Morrow. 1st. author's 1st book. F/NF. from $175 to $200.00

POWERS, Richard. *Three Farmers on Their Way to a Dance.* 1985. Morrow. 1st. F/F. B4. $250.00

POWERS, Richard. *Three Farmers on Their Way to a Dance.* 1988. London. Weidenfeld Nicolson. 1st. F/F. Q1. $100.00

POWERS, Richard. *Three Farmers on Their Way to a Dance.* 1988. London. 1st Eng. author's 1st book. F/NF. R13. $75.00

POWERS, Robert M. *Planetary Encounters.* 1978. Stackpole. sm 4to. 288p. dj. K5. $20.00

POWERS, Tim. *Drawing of the Dark.* 1991. Hypatia. 1st hc. 1/825. contributors sgn. F/sans. M21. $45.00

POWERS, Tim. *On Stranger Tides.* 1987. Ace. 1st. NF/F. B3. $60.00

POWLES, L.D. *Land of Pink Pearl; or, Recollections of Life in Bahamas.* 1888. London. Sampson Low. 1 fld map. 321p. new ep/orig bdg. T7. $110.00

POYNTER, H. May. *Fair Jacobite: Tale of the Exiled Stuarts.* 1905. London. Nelson. 8vo. 296p. pict bl cloth. F. T10. $50.00

PRAGER & SCAGLIA. *Mariano Taccola & His Book De Ingeneis.* 1972. MIT. ils. VG. K3. $15.00

PRAGER. *Rascals at Large.* 1971. 334p. VG/VG. A4. $55.00

PRAGNELL, Festus. *Green Man of Graypec.* 1950. Greenberg. 1st Am. F/dj. M2. $42.00

PRANGE, Gordon. *Miracle at Midway.* 1982. NY. photos/maps/biblio/index. 469p. VG/G. S16. $27.50

PRATT, Alice Edwards. *Sleeping Princess California.* 1892. SF. Wm Doxey. ils EM Dillaway. unp. aeg. VG. K7. $45.00

PRATT, Ambrose. *Living Mummy.* 1900. Stokes. VG. M2. $50.00

PRATT, Annis. *Archetypal Patterns in Women's Fiction.* 1982. Brighton. 1st. ils. VG+. 211p. A25. $25.00

PRATT, Calvin E. *Oration of Hon Calvin E Pratt at Reunion of Army on Potomac.* ca 1885. np. 1st. 26p. G+/lacks wrp. M8. $15.00

PRATT, E.H. *Official Surgery & Its Application to Treatment...* 1890. Chicago. 2nd. 164p. A13. $200.00

PRATT, Fletcher. *Double in Space.* 1951. Doubleday. 1st. NF/dj. P3. $40.00

PRATT, Fletcher. *Marines' War: Account of Struggle for Pacific...* 1948. NY. maps/index. 456p. VG. S16. $27.50

PRATT, Fletcher. *Night Work.* 1946. Holt. 1st. VG. P3. $30.00

PRATT, Fletcher. *Petrified Planet.* 1952. Twayne. 1st. NF/dj. M2. $60.00

PRATT, Fletcher. *Undying Fire.* 1953. Ballantine. 1st. F/F. P3. $45.00

PRATT, Fletcher. *Well of the Unicorn.* 1975. Garland. F. M2. $25.00

PRATT, Fletcher. *Witches Three.* 1952. Twayne. 1st. VG/dj. P3. $45.00

PRATT, Parley Parker. *Millennium, a Poem. To Which Is Added Hymns & Songs...* 1835. Boston. self pub. 1st. 12mo. 52p. contemporary plain stiff wrp. M1. $15,000.00

PRATT, Parley Parker. *Voice of Warning & Instruction to All People...* 1837. NY. Sandford. 1st. 18mo. 216p. cloth. M1. $4,500.00

PRATT, Richard. *Treasury of Early American Homes.* nd. ne. 136p. VG/G. A8. $15.00

PRENDERGAST, Mabel. *Little Yellow Duckling.* 1907. Leeds. Alf Cooke. 1st. 18 full-p mc pl. obl 4to. pict brd. R5. $250.00

PRENTICE, George. *Biography of Henry Clay.* 1831. NY. 312p. full leather. O8. $37.50

PRENTICE, Harry. *Captured by Apes.* 1892. AL Burt. 1st thus. VG. M2. $50.00

PRESCOTT, Casey. *Assent in Black.* 1985. Arbor. 1st. 396p. F/F. W2. $30.00

PRESCOTT, H.F.M. *Once to Sinai: Further Pilgrimage of Friar Felix Fabri.* 1958. Macmillan. 1st. 8vo. 310p. VG/dj. W1. $12.00

PRESCOTT, William H. *History of the Conquest of Peru: 1524-1550.* 1892. Phil. 2 vol. 12mo. half brn leather. VG. H3. $75.00

PRESCOTT, William H. *History of the Conquest of Peru: 1524-1550.* 1957. Mexico City. LEC. 1st thus. 1/1500. ils/sgn EG Jackson. F/case. Q1. $200.00

PRESLEY, J. *Saga of Wealth: Rise of the Texas Oilmen.* 1978. Putnam. 1st. 464p. cloth. NF/G. D8. $25.00

PREST, Wilfrid R. *Inns of Court Under Elizabeth I & the Early Stuarts...* 1972. London. Longman Group. M11. $65.00

PRESTON, Anthony. *Navies of the American Revolution.* 1975. Prentice Hall. ils. 160p. dj. T7. $30.00

PRESTON, Chloe. *Peek-a-Boos.* nd. Hodder Stoughton. 1st Am. ils Preston. VG. D1. $500.00

PRESTON, Jack. *Heil! Hollywood.* 1939. Chicago. Reilly Lee. 1st. inscr/dtd 1941. F/VG clip. B4. $175.00

PRESTON, Jennifer. *Queen Bess: An Unauthorized Biography of Bess Myerson.* 1990. Contemporary Books. 1st. F/F. W2. $30.00

PRESTON, John Hyde. *Liberals.* 1938. John Day. 1st. NF/NF. B2. $65.00

PRESTON, Tom. *Peek-a-Boos' Holiday.* ca 1915. London. Frowde/Hodder Stoughton. 1st. VG. D1. $600.00

PRESTON, Walter W. *History of Harland County, Maryland.* 1972 (1901). Baltimore. 1st/2nd prt. ils. 379p. gilt red cloth. F. H3. $45.00

PRESTON, William. *Illustrations of Masonry. The First American Improved Ed...* 1804. Portsmouth. Treadwell. 12mo. 400p. full contemporary calf. M1. $175.00

PRIBRAM, Karl H. *Brain & Behavior: Selected Readings...* 1969. Penguin. 4 vol. 16mo. xl. VG. G1. $75.00

PRICE, A. Grenfell. *White Settlers in the Tropics.* 1939. Am Geog Soc. 311p+full-p photos. lg 8vo. A17. $25.00

PRICE, Charles. *Golf Magazine's Pro Pointers & Stroke Savers.* 1960. Harper. 1st. ils. VG/G+. P8. $12.50

PRICE, E. Hoffman. *Far Lands & Other Days.* 1975. Chapel Hill. Carcosa. 1st. F/NF. Q1. $75.00

PRICE, Nancy. *Sleeping With the Enemy.* 1987. S&S. 1st. F/F. H11. $40.00

PRICE, Nancy. *Sleeping With the Enemy.* 1987. S&S. 1st. 249p. F/NF. W2. $35.00

PRICE, Reynolds. *Clear Pictures.* 1989. Atheneum. 1st. sgn. F/dj. from $45 to $50.00

PRICE, Reynolds. *Early Dark.* 1977. Atheneum. 1st. sgn. F/NF. D10. $85.00

PRICE, Reynolds. *Good Hearts.* 1988. Atheneum. 1st. sgn. NF/dj. R13. $40.00

PRICE, Reynolds. *Kate Vaiden.* 1986. Atheneum. 1st. NF/dj. A24. $35.00

PRICE, Reynolds. *Kate Vaiden.* 1986. Atheneum. 1st. sgn. F/NF. R13. $50.00

PRICE, Reynolds. *Long & Happy Life.* 1962. Atheneum. ARC. author's 1st book. RS. F/dj. A24. $150.00

PRICE, Reynolds. *Love & Work.* 1968. Atheneum. 1st. sgn. F/dj. R13. $75.00

PRICE, Reynolds. *New Music. A Trilogy.* 1990. NY. Theater Communications Group. sgn. F/F. D10. $50.00

PRICE, Reynolds. *Nine Mysteries.* 1979. Palaemon. 1/300. sgn. F/sans. A24. $100.00

PRICE, Reynolds. *Palpable God.* 1978. Atheneum. 1st. sgn. F/clip. R13. $35.00

PRICE, Reynolds. *Surface of Earth.* 1975. Atheneum. 1st. sgn. NF/dj. R13. $60.00

PRICE, Reynolds. *Things Themselves.* 1972. Atheneum. 1st. sgn. NF/dj. R13. $65.00

PRICE, Reynolds. *Tongues of Angels.* 1990. Atheneum. 1st. sgn. F/F. A24/R13. $45.00

PRICE, Reynolds. *Use of Fire.* 1990. Atheneum. 1st. F/F. M23. $20.00

PRICE, Reynolds. *Use of Fire.* 1990. Atheneum. 1st. sgn. F/F. R13. $45.00

PRICE, Reynolds. *Vital Provisions.* 1982. Atheneum. 1st. sgn. F/F. D10. $65.00

PRICE, Richard. *Bloodbrothers.* 1976. Houghton Mifflin. 1st. author's 2nd book. VG/VG. H11. $35.00

PRICE, Richard. *Bloodbrothers.* 1976. Houghton Mifflin. 1st. sgn. author's 2nd novel. NF/dj. D10. $65.00

PRICE, Richard. *Bloodbrothers.* 1976. Houghton Mifflin. 1st. sgn/dtd 1995. VG/VG. R14. $50.00

PRICE, Richard. *Breaks.* 1983. S&S. 1st. sgn. author's 4th novel. F/F. D10. $40.00

PRICE, Richard. *Breaks.* 1983. S&S. 1st. sgn. VG/VG. R14. $35.00

PRICE, Richard. *Clockers.* 1992. Houghton Mifflin. 1st. sgn. author's 5th/MTI. F/F. D10. $40.00

PRICE, Richard. *Ladies' Man.* 1978. Houghton Mifflin. 1st. F/NF. M19. $25.00

PRICE, Richard. *Ladies' Man.* 1978. Houghton Mifflin. 1st. sgn. F/NF. D10. $55.00

PRICE, Richard. *Wanderers.* 1974. Houghton Mifflin. 1st. author's 1st novel. F/clip. B35. $60.00

PRICE, Richard. *Wanderers.* 1974. Houghton Mifflin. 1st. sgn. F/F. D10. $90.00

PRICE, Uvedale. *Essay on the Picturesque, As compared With the Sublime...* 1794. London. J Robison. 1st. tall 8vo. 288p. full polished morocco. H13. $495.00

PRICE, Willard. *Amazing Amazon.* 1952. John Day. 1st. 306p. dj. F3. $20.00

PRICE, Willard. *America's Paradise Lost: Strange Story of Secret Atolls.* 1966. NY. John Day. 3rd imp. 8vo. 240p. bl cloth. P4. $25.00

PRICE, Willard. *Negro Around the World.* 1925. NY. Doran for African Methodist Episcopal Church. NF/VG. B4. $225.00

PRICHARD, A.M. *Leage's Roman Private Law, Founded on Institutes of Gaius...* 1964. London. Macmillan. G/dj. M11. $65.00

PRICHARD, Anita. *Complete Candy Book.* 1978. Harmony. G. A16. $12.00

PRIDE, W.F. *History of Ft Riley.* 1926. np. 1st. 339p. VG. J2. $95.00

PRIEST, Christopher. *Anticipations.* 1978. London. Faber. 1st. F/dj. M21. $20.00

PRIEST & SIMMONS. *Chinese Textiles.* 1931. Metrop Mus Art. 1/1000. ils. cloth/brd. F. W3. $58.00

PRIESTLEY, Herbert Ingram. *Exposition: Addressed to Chamber of Deputies of Congress...* 1938. SF. John Henry Nash. 1/650. lg 4to. gr brd/cloth spine. F/dj. R3. $75.00

PRIESTLEY, Herbert Ingram. *Log of the Princesa: By Estevan Jose Martinez.* 1920. Portland. Ivy Pr. 11p. VG/wrp. P4. $37.50

PRIESTLEY, J.B. *Doomsday Men.* 1938. London. true 1st. VG. M22. $20.00

PRIESTLEY, J.B. *Jenny Villiers.* 1947. Heinemann. 1st. F/VG. M19. $35.00

PRIESTLEY, J.B. *Lost Empires.* 1965. Atlantic/Little Brn. 1st Am. VG/VG. M22. $15.00

PRIESTLEY, J.B. *Snoggle.* 1971. Harcourt Brace. 1st/2nd prt. sm 8vo. NF/VG+. C8. $40.00

PRIESTLY, J.B. *Black-Out in Gretley.* 1943. Clipper Books. F/F. P3. $30.00

PRIESTLY, J.B. *Carfitt Crisis.* 1976. Stein Day. 1st. VG/dj. P3. $15.00

PRIESTLY, J.B. *Faraway.* 1932. Macmillan. 1st. VG. P3. $25.00

PRIESTLY, J.B. *Good Companions.* 1929. Harper. 1st. VG. P3. $35.00

PRIESTLY, J.B. *Magicians*. 1954. Harper. 1st. VG/dj. P3. $40.00

PRIESTLY, J.B. *Shapes of Sleep*. 1962. Heinemann. 1st. NF/dj. P3. $25.00

PRINCE, William R. *Pomological Manual; or, Treatise on Fruits*. 1832. NY. Swords. 2nd (2 parts in 1 vol). orig pub brd. A10. $225.00

PRINGLE, Laurence. *Frost Hollows & Other Microclimates*. 1981. Morrow. 4to. 62p. xl. K5. $8.00

PRINZ, J. *Secret Jews (Marranos)*. 1973. 1st. F/G+. E6. $10.00

PRIOR, Matt. *Poems on Several Occasions*. 1766. London. G+. A15. $20.00

PRITCHARD, James B. *Gibeon Where the Sun Stood Still. Discovery Biblical City*. 1962. Princeton. 1st. ils/pl. 176p. VG/dj. W1. $25.00

PRITCHETT, V.S. *Blind Love & Other Stories*. 1969. Chatto Windus. 1st. F/clip. B4. $100.00

PRITCHETT, V.S. *Marching Spain*. 1928. London. Ernest Benn. 1st. author's 1st book. VG/VG. L3. $450.00

PRITZKE, Herbert. *Bedouin Doctor: My Adventurous Years With the Arabs*. 1957. Dutton. 1st. 8vo. 255p. cloth. VG/torn. W1. $30.00

PROCTER, Gil. *People of the Moonlight*. 1958. Pub Pr for Pete Kitchen Mus. 1st. 1/100. sgn. NF/VG+. B19. $35.00

PROCTER & GAMBLE. *Praise for the Cook*. 1959. 120p. sbdg. B10. $8.00

PROCTOR, Richard A. *Light Science for Leisure Hours*. 1886 (1883). London. Longman Gr. new ed. 8vo. 309p. G. K5. $35.00

PROCTOR, Richard A. *Our Place Among Infinities*. 1897. London. Longman Gr. new. 288p. K5. $40.00

PROCTOR, Samuel. *Loves of Nero*. 1902. Homewood. VG. M2. $40.00

PROEHL, Carl. *Fourth Marine Division in WWII*. 1946. WA, DC. 1st. maps/photos. 238p. VG. S16. $125.00

PROGULSKE, Donald R. *Following Custer*. 1974. Brookings, SD. A19. $30.00

PRONZINI, Bill. *Blowback*. 1977. Random. 1st. NF/NF. M22. $65.00

PRONZINI, Bill. *Breakdown*. 1991. Delacorte. 1st. F/F. P3. $20.00

PRONZINI, Bill. *Cat's Paw*. 1983. Richmond. Waves Pr. 1st. 1/150. sgn. F/sewn wrp/dj. M15. $45.00

PRONZINI, Bill. *Crime & Crime Again*. 1990. Bonanza. NF/dj. P3. $12.00

PRONZINI, Bill. *Gun in Cheek*. 1982. CMG. 1st. sgn. F/F. M15. $35.00

PRONZINI, Bill. *Hard-Boiled*. 1995. Oxford. 1st. F/F. P3. $25.00

PRONZINI, Bill. *Jackpot*. 1990. Delacorte. 1st. F/F. B3. $25.00

PRONZINI, Bill. *Masques*. 1981. Arbor. 1st. VG/dj. N4. $30.00

PRONZINI, Bill. *Panic!* 1972. Random. 1st. VG/dj. P3. $40.00

PRONZINI, Bill. *Quicksilver*. 1984. St Martin. 1st. F/F. P3. $25.00

PRONZINI, Bill. *Shattershot*. 1982. St Martin. 1st. F/F. P3. $30.00

PRONZINI, Bill. *Snatch*. 1971. Random. 1st. NF/G. M19. $35.00

PRONZINI, Bill. *Stalker*. 1971. Random. 1st. author's 1st book. NF/NF. H11. $55.00

PROSE, Francine. *Bigfoot Dreams*. 1986. Pantheon. 1st. NF/dj. R13. $20.00

PROSKOURIAKOFF, Tatiana. *Album of Maya Architecture*. 1958. Mexico. Maya Found. 1/1100. 72p+36 pl. F3. $150.00

PROUDFIT, Isabel. *Broom Closet Family*. 1938. McKay. ils Caroline Whitehead. VG/G+. P2. $25.00

PROULX, E. Annie. *Complete Dairy Foods Cookbook*. 1982. Rodale. 1st. F/sans. B3. $200.00

PROULX, E. Annie. *Fences & Gates, Walkways, Walls & Drives*. 1983. Rodale. 1st. NF. A24. $100.00

PROULX, E. Annie. *Heart Songs*. 1988. NY. Scribner. 1st. sgn. F/F. B4. $650.00

PROULX, E. Annie. *Shipping News*. 1993. Scribner. 1st. author's 2nd novel. F/F. D10. $225.00

PROUST, Marcel. *Swann's Way*. 1954. LEC. 1st thus. 1/1500. ils/sgn Bernard Lamotte. F/glassine/case. Q1. $150.00

PROUT, William. *Chemistry, Meteorology & Function of Digestion*. 1855. London. Bohn. 4th. fld map. rebound. K3. $35.00

PROUTY, Olive Higgins. *Home Port*. 1947. Houghton Mifflin. 1st. 285p. VG. W2. $15.00

PROVENSEN & PROVENSEN. *Mother Goose Book*. 1976. Random. 1st. lg 4to. VG+/G+. P2. $28.00

PROVENSEN & PROVENSEN. *Year at Maple Hill Farm*. 1978. Atheneum. 1st. 4to. orange cloth. VG/G+. T5. $45.00

PRYOR, Mrs. Roger A. *My Day: Reminiscences of a Long Life*. 1909. NY. 462p. xl. O8. $18.50

PRYOR, Mrs. Roger A. *Reminiscences of Peace & War*. 1924. 418p. O8. $18.50

PSALTER. *Kiev Psalter*. 1978. Moscow. 2 vol. flexible linen cloth. fld box. A17. $135.00

PSYCHOUNDAKIS, George. *Cretan Runner: His Story of German Occupation*. 1955. London. photos/index. 242p. VG/VG. S16. $21.50

PTACEK, Kathryn. *Women of Darkness*. 1988. Tor. 1st. F/F. N4. $25.00

PUBLIUS. *Works...* 1822. Lincolns Inn Fields. Pickering. miniature. contemporary calf. F. T10. $100.00

PUCH, R.B. *Imprisonment in Medieval England*. 1968. Cambridge. M11. $75.00

PUCH, R.B. *Itinerant Justices in English History*. 1967. Exeter. 30p. prt sewn wrp. M11. $25.00

PUCKETT, Andrew. *Bloodstains*. 1989. Crime Club. 1st. NF/NF. P3. $15.00

PUFFER, J. Adams. *Boy & His Gang*. 1912. Boston. later prt. 187p. VG. B18. $22.50

PUGH, Richard H. *Audubon Bird Guide*. 1949. NY. BC. revised. ils Don Eckelberry. 312p. NF/VG. S15. $12.00

PULLEIN-THOMPSON, Josephine. *Black Beauty's Clan*. 1980. McGraw Hill. 1st Am. ils Elizabeth Grant. 287p. F/dj. T10. $40.00

PULLEN, John J. *Twentieth Maine, a Volunteer Regiment in Civil War*. 1957. Lippincott. 1st. 8vo. 338p. NF/dj. H1. $90.00

PULLING, Pierre. *Principles of Canoeing*. 1954. Macmillan. stated 1st. 217p. VG/dj. H7. $20.00

PULSZKY, Francis. *Tricolor on the Atlas; or, Algeria & the French Conquest*. 1855. NY. Nelson. 1st. 8vo. 4 tinted fld pl. 402p. G. W1. $65.00

PUNSHON, E.R. *It Might Lead Anywhere*. 1949. Gollancz. 2nd. VG/dj. P3. $20.00

PURDY, Carl. *My Life & Times*. 1976. np. ils. VG. B26. $26.00

PURDY, James. *Cabot Wright Begins*. 1964. New Directions. 1st. sgn. VG/VG. R14. $45.00

PURDY, James. *Day After the Fair*. 1977. NY. Note of Hand Pub. 1st. 1/1000. sgn. F/dj. T10. $100.00

PURDY, James. *Malcolm*. 1960. Secker Warburg. 1st. NF/VG. M19. $25.00

PURDY, James. *Mourners Below.* 1981. Viking. 1st. F/F. A20. $20.00

PURI & SARAHIRAN. *Ramakirti: The Thai Version of the Ramayana.* 1949. Bangkok, Siam. Prachandra. 8vo. 129p. VG/prt wrp. B14. $55.00

PUTNAM, Bertha Haven. *Place in Legal History of Sir William Shareshull...* 1950. Cambridge. cloth. G. M11. $85.00

PUTNAM, David Binney. *David Goes Voyaging.* 1926-29. NY. Putnam. later prt. ils. 132p. T7. $22.00

PUTNAM, George Haven. *Books & Their Makers in Middle Ages.* 1962. NY. Hillary House. rpt. VG. K3. $35.00

PUTNAM, George. *Southland of North America.* 1914 (1913). Putnam. 2nd imp. 425p. w/rear fld map. gilt cloth. F3. $30.00

PUTNAM, J. Pickering. *Metric System of Weights & Measures.* 1877. Boston. 2nd. fld chart. VG. M17. $25.00

PUZO, Mario. *Dark Arena.* 1955. Random. 1st. author's 1st book. NF/NF. H11. $75.00

PUZO, Mario. *Fools Die.* 1978. Putnam. 1st. F/F. H11. $40.00

PUZO, Mario. *Godfather.* 1969. Putnam. 1st. NF/VG. H11. $120.00

PYE & SHEA. *Navy Wife.* 1949. Harper. 360p. VG. A25. $15.00

PYLE, Howard. *Book of Pirates.* 1921. 1st. ils. VG. S13. $65.00

PYLE, Howard. *Merry Adventures of Robin Hood.* nd. Grosset. VG. M2. $10.00

PYLE, R.M. *Where Bigfoot Walks: Crossing the Dark Divide.* 1995. Houghton Mifflin. 338p. cloth/brd. F/F. M12. $20.00

PYM, Barbara. *Few Green Leaves.* 1980. Dutton. 1st. F/F. T11. $50.00

PYM, Roland. *Cinderella, a Peepshow Book.* 1950. Houghton Mifflin. 6 interior popups. VG. M5. $95.00

PYNCHON, Thomas. *Crying of Lot 49.* 1966. Lippincott. 1st. F/NF. B2. $125.00

PYNCHON, Thomas. *Gravity's Rainbow.* 1973. Viking. 1st. author's 3rd book. NF/clip. C2. $375.00

PYNCHON, Thomas. *Gravity's Rainbow.* 1973. Viking. 1st. F/NF. B2. $450.00

PYNCHON, Thomas. *Secret Integration.* 1980. London. Aloes. 1st. 1/2500. M24. $100.00

PYNCHON, Thomas. *Slow Learner.* 1984. Little Brn. 1st. F/F. B3. $60.00

PYNCHON, Thomas. *Small Rain.* nd (1982). London. Aloes. 1/2000 (1st separate appearance). F/pict wrp. R13. $25.00

PYNCHON, Thomas. *V.* 1963. London. Jonathan Cape. 1st Eng. NF/clip. Q1. $300.00

PYNCHON, Thomas. *Vineland.* 1990. Little Brn. 1st. F/F. A20. $20.00

PYNE, Stephen J. *Ice: Journey to Antarctica.* 1986. 1st. ils. VG/VG. M17. $20.00

PYRNELLE, Louise Clarke. *Diddie, Dumps & Tot; or, Plantation Child-Life.* 1900. VG. M17. $35.00

QUAIFE, Milo M. *John Askin Papers.* 1928 & 1931. Detroit Lib Comm. 2 vol. 1/1000. thick 8vo. ils. 3-quarter leather. F. O7. $250.00

QUAIN, Richard. *Diseases of the Rectum.* 1854. London. 1st. 4 hand-colored pl. 285p. A13. $200.00

QUALE. *Collector's Book of Children's Books.* 1971. lg 4to. 144p. NF/NF. A4. $155.00

QUAMMEN, David. *Natural Acts.* 1985. NY. Lyons. 1st. F/NF. B3. $50.00

QUAMMEN, David. *To Walk the Line.* 1970. Knopf. 1st. sgn/#d bookplate. author's 1st book. F/NF. B3. $100.00

QUANTIC, Diane Dufva. *Nature of the Place: A Study of Great Plains Fiction.* 1995. NE U. 1st. M/dj. A18. $25.00

QUARLES, Benjamin. *Frederick Douglass.* 1948. WA, DC. Assoc Pub. 1st. F/NF clip. B4. $185.00

QUARRY, Nick; see Albert, Marvin H.

QUARTI & RENAUD. *Neuropsychologie de la Douleur.* 1971. Paris. Hermann. 199p. prt bl wrp. G1. $30.00

QUAYLE, Dan. *Standing Firm.* 1994. Harper Collins. 1st. sgn. VG/VG. A23. $60.00

QUAYLE, Eric. *Collector's Book of Books.* 1971. NY. 144p. F/dj. A17. $20.00

QUAYLE, Eric. *Collector's Book of Boy's Stories.* 1973. London. Studio Vista. 1st. tan cloth. F/dj. M24. $125.00

QUAYLE, Eric. *Collector's Book of Detective Fiction.* 1972. London. Studio Vista. 1st. lg format. F/clip. M15. $145.00

QUAYLE, Eric. *Early Children's Books: A Collector's Guide.* 1983. Totowa, NJ. Barnes Noble. 8vo. gr cloth/label. as new/dj. R5. $85.00

QUAYLE, R.M. *Ballantyne: A Bibliography of First Editions.* 1968. London. Dawson. 1st. 9 pl. 128p. F/F. A4. $125.00

QUEBEDEAUX, Richard. *Worldly Evangelicals.* 1978. Harper. 189p. VG/dj. B29. $8.50

QUEEN, Ellery. *Brown Fox Mystery.* 1948. Little Brn. 1st. 243p. VG/tattered. M20. $20.00

QUEEN, Ellery. *Challenge to the Reader.* 1940. Bl Ribbon. hc. VG. P3. $20.00

QUEEN, Ellery. *Double, Double.* 1950. Little Brn. 1st. VG. M22. $15.00

QUEEN, Ellery. *Egyptian Cross Mystery.* 1932. NY. Stokes. 1st. NF/professional restored dj. Q1. $1,750.00

QUEEN, Ellery. *Ellery Queen's Bureau of Investigation.* 1954. Little Brn. 1st. F/clip. M15. $45.00

QUEEN, Ellery. *Ellery Queen's Champions of Mystery.* 1977. Dial. 1st. F/F. N4. $25.00

QUEEN, Ellery. *Ellery Queen's Circumstantial Evidence.* 1980. Dial. 1st. VG/dj. P3. $16.00

QUEEN, Ellery. *Ellery Queen's Doors to Mystery.* 1981. Dial. 1st. VG/dj. P3. $15.00

QUEEN, Ellery. *Ellery Queen's Poetic Justice.* 1967. NAL. 1st. VG/VG. P3. $20.00

QUEEN, Ellery. *Fourth Side of the Triangle.* 1965. Random. 1st. F/VG. M19. $35.00

QUEEN, Ellery. *Literature of Crime.* 1950. Little Brn. 1st. F/G. M19. $25.00

QUEEN, Ellery. *Murderer Is a Fox.* 1948. London. Gollancz. 1st/2nd imp. VG. T12. $30.00

QUEEN, Ellery. *Origin of Evil.* 1951. Lodnon. 1st. NF/dj. M2. $30.00

QUEEN, Ellery. *Queen's Awards, Sixth Series.* 1951. Little Brn. 1st. VG. M22. $10.00

QUEEN, Ellery. *Siamese Twin Mystery.* 1933. NY. Stokes. 1st. VG/professionally restored. Q1. $1,000.00

QUEEN, Ellery. *To the Queen's Taste.* 1946. Little Brn. 1st. VG. P3. $30.00

QUEEN, Ellery. *101 Years' Entertainment/Great Detective Stories/1841-1941.* 1941. Little Brn. 1st. VG+. N4. $20.00

QUEKETT, John. *Lectures on Histology.* 1852. London. 1st. 215p. A13. $75.00

QUENNELL, Peter. *Mayhew's Characters.* nd. London. Spring Books. 360p. cloth. VG/dj. M20. $15.00

QUENNELL, Peter. *Shakespeare.* 1963. World. 1st. 8vo. 352p. rust cloth. F/VG. H1. $12.00

QUICK, Armand. *Physiology & Pathology of Hemostasis.* 1951. Phil. 1st. 188p. A13. $75.00

QUICK, Herbert. *Invisible Woman.* 1924. Bobbs Merrill. 1st. F/VG. A18. $30.00

QUIGG, Jane. *Polly Peters.* 1942. Oxford. 1st. 8vo. NF/VG. C8. $25.00

QUIGLEY, Martin. *Today's Game.* 1965. Viking. 1st. 176p. VG+/dj. B18. $22.50

QUILLER-COUCH, Arthur. *Twelve Dancing Princesses & Other Fairy Tales.* ca 1913. Doran. 1st Am. ils Kay Nielsen. 244p. gilt bl cloth. VG. D1. $295.00

QUILLER-COUCH, Arthur. *Twelve Dancing Princesses & Other Fairy Tales.* 1923. Doran. ils Kay Nielsen. 8vo. bl cloth. VG/dj. R5. $450.00

QUIN, Bernetta. *Introduction to the Poetry of Ezra Pound.* 1972. Columbia. 1st. F/VG+. V1. $15.00

QUIN-HARKIN, Janet. *Peter Penny's Dance.* 1976. Dial. 1st. lg 8vo. VG/VG. C8. $12.50

QUINBY & STEVENSON. *Catalogue of Botanical Books in Collection RMM Hunt.* 1958-1961. Pittsburgh. 2 vol in 3. 1/750. ils. F/djs. B26. $949.00

QUINBY. *Richard Harding Davis: A Bibliography.* 1924. np. 1/1000. 31 pl. 315p. VG. A4. $135.00

QUINCY, John. *Lexicon Physico-Medicum; or, New Medicinal Dictionary.* 1767. London. 482p. VG. B14. $150.00

QUINCY, Josiah. *Essays on the Soiling of Cattle.* 1866. Boston. Williams. 121p. A10. $35.00

QUINCY, William S. *Three-Masted Schooner James Miller.* 1986. Mystic Seaport Mus. ils/3 fld plans. 48p. wrp. T7. $17.00

QUINN, Dan; see Lewis, Alfred Henry.

QUINN, David. *North America From Earliest Discovery to First Settlements.* 1977. Harper Row. New Am Nation series. 1st. 81 ils/maps. F/dj. O7. $45.00

QUINN, David. *Roanoke Voyages 1584-1590.* 1955. London. Hakluyt Soc. 1st. 2 vol. 8vo. gilt bl cloth. NF. P4. $165.00

QUINN, P.T. *Money in a Garden, a Vegetable Manual.* 1871. 1st. woodcuts. xl. VG. E6. $30.00

QUINN, P.T. *Pear Culture for Profit.* 1869. NY. Tribune. 136p. A10. $38.00

QUINN, Seabury. *Phantom-Fighter.* 1966. Arkham. 1st. VG/dj. P3. $60.00

QUINN, Vernon. *Leaves: Their Place in Life & Legend.* 1937. NY. Stokes. 211p. VG. A10. $32.00

QUINN, Vernon. *Seeds: Their Place in Life & Legend.* 1936. NY. Stokes. 188p. cloth. VG. A10. $28.00

QUINTANILLA, Luis. *Franco's Black Spain.* 1946. Reynal Hitchcock. 1st. 4to. VG/VG. B2. $85.00

QUIRING, Daniel. *Collateral Circulation (Anatomical Aspects).* 1949. Phil. 1st. 142p. xl. A13. $15.00

QUIRK, John. *Hard Winners.* 1965. Random. 1st. VG/VG. P3. $22.00

QUIRK, Lawrence J. *Claudette Colbert, an Illustrated Biography.* 1985. Crown. 1st. 212p. VG+/dj. M20. $15.00

QUISUMBING, E.A. *Complete Writings of... on Philippine Orchids.* 1981. Manila. 2 vol. ils/pl. edit HI Valmayor. as new. B26. $45.00

QUOGAN, Anthony. *Fine Art of Murder.* 1988. St Martin. 1st. VG/VG. P3. $16.00

R

RABAN, Jonathan. *Arabia: A Journey Through the Labyrinth.* 1979. S&S. 1st. 344p. cloth. NF/dj. W1. $20.00

RABAN, Sandra. *Mortmain Legislation & the English Church, 1279-1500.* 1982. Cambridge. M11. $65.00

RABELAIS, Francis. *Works of Mr Francis Rabelais.* nd. London. 2 vol. ils WH Robinson. G. B18. $65.00

RABI, S.S. *Boatbuilding in Your Own Backyard.* 1958. Cambridge, MD. Cornell Maritime. 2nd. 223p. T7. $30.00

RABIER, Benjamin. *Maurice en Nourrice.* nd. Paris. Jules Tallandier. ils. VG. M5. $95.00

RABINOWICZ, Oskar K. *Winston Churchill on Jewish Problems.* 1960. Yoseloff. 231p. VG+/G. S3. $26.00

RACKHAM, Arthur. *Arthur Rackham Fairy Book.* nd. Lippincott. 8 full-p pl. 287p. gray cloth. VG. T5. $45.00

RACKHAM, Arthur. *Fairy Tales From Many Lands.* (1974). Viking/Studio. 8vo. 12 full-p mc pl. 122p. VG/tattered. T5. $35.00

RACKHAM, Arthur. *Mother Goose: The Old Nursery Rhymes.* 1931. London. Heinemann. 1st thus. 1/1130. ils/sgn Rackham/13 full-p mtd pl. VG. D1. $2,100.00

RACKHAM, Arthur. *Some British Ballads.* 1919. London. Constable. 1st. 1/575. sgn. 170p. teg. gilt bdg. case. B24. $1,800.00

RACKHAM, Bernard. *Book of Porcelain.* 1910. London. Adam/Chas Blk. 1st. 28 tipped-in mc pl. VG. T10. $150.00

RACKHAM, John. *Time To Live.* 1969. Lodnon. 1st. NF/dj. M2. $20.00

RADCLIFFE, Ann. *Complete Novels.* 1987. London. Folio Soc. 6 vol. tall 8vo. blk linen spines/decor brd. F/box. H13. $450.00

RADCLIFFE, Charles Bland. *On Diseases of the Spine & of the Nerves.* 1871. Phil. Henry Lea. 1st Am. 196p. contemporary bdg. G1. $135.00

RADER. *South of Forty, From Mississippi to Rio Grande...* 1947. OK U. 1/1000. 4to. 3793 entries. 336p. VG/dj. A4. $225.00

RADFORD, Ruby Lorrainen. *Sandra of the Girl Orchestra.* 1946. Racine. Whitman. 1st. ils Lise Fomenko. 248p. G+. A25. $8.00

RADIGUET, Raymond. *Devil in the Flesh.* 1948. Blk Sun. 1st thus. trans Kay Boyle. VG/VG. M22. $35.00

RADIN, Paul. *Road of Life & Death.* 1945. Pantheon. 1st. 8vo. 345p. VG. K3. $22.00

RADIN, Paul. *Story of the American Indian.* 1937. Garden City. 383p. F3. $15.00

RADLEY, Sheila. *Death in the Morning.* 1979. Scribner. 1st Am. F/NF. M25. $35.00

RADZINOWICZ & TURNER. *Penal Reform in England, Introductory Essays...* 1940. London. King. 1st. red cloth. M11. $45.00

RAE, Hugh C. *Harkfast: Making of the King.* 1976. St Martin. 1st. NF/dj. M21. $35.00

RAE, J.B. *American Automobile: Brief History.* 1969. Chicago. ils. 265p. F/dj. M4. $10.00

RAEDER, Erich. *My Life.* 1960. Annapolis. 1st. VG/VG. B5. $50.00

RAFIZADEH, Mansur. *Witness: From the Shah to the Secret Arms Deal...* 1987. Morrow. 1st. 8vo. ils. 396p. VG/dj. W1. $18.00

RAGLAND, J. Farley. *Little Slice of Living.* 1953. Richmond. Quality Pr. 1st. inscr. F/prt wrp. B4. $175.00

RAIGERSFELD, Jeffrey. *Life of a Sea Officer.* 1929. London. Cassell. 8 pl. 210p. T7. $60.00

RAIM, Ethel. *Freedom Is a Constant Struggle: Songs of Freedom Movement.* 1968. Oak Pub. 2nd. VG/VG. V4. $20.00

RAINE, James. *Wills & Inventories Illustrative of History, Manners...* 1835. London. 1/400. gilt olive cloth. M11. $150.00

RAINE, William McLeod. *Justice Comes to Tomahawk.* 1952. Houghton Mifflin. 1st. F/VG. B4. $200.00

RAINER & RAINER. *Sexual Pleasure in Marriage.* 1959. NY. Messner. 5th. 251p. VG. A25. $10.00

RAINES. *Bibliography of Texas: Being Descriptive List...* nd. rpt. 1/100. F. A4. $95.00

RAINGER, Ronald. *Agenda for Antiquity.* 1991. AL U. 360p. F/F. S15. $13.50

RAINS, Mane. *Lazy Liza Lizard.* 1938. Winston. 1st. sgn. ils V Neville. 184p. VG. P2. $75.00

RAINSFORD, W.S. *Story of a Varied Life.* 1922. Doubleday Page. 481p. NF/dj. H7. $25.00

RAISIN, Jacob S. *Haskalah Movement in Russia.* 1913. JPS. ils. 355p. G+. S3. $24.00

RALLING, C. *Voyage of Charles Darwin: His Autobiographical Writings...* 1979. Mayflower. 1st Am. 183p. F/dj. D8. $12.00

RAMALEY, Francis. *Wild Flowers & Trees of Colorado.* 1909. Boulder. ils/tissue guard frontis/figures. VG. B26. $41.00

RAMIREZ, Anthony Jr. *Romualdo Pacheco: Governor of California.* 1974. SF Pr. 1st. inscr. ils Victor R Anderson. NF. O4. $15.00

RAMIREZ, Jose F. *Statement of the Right & Just Reasons on Part of Government.* 1852. Mexico. Sullivan Nolan. 40p. 2 Lib Congress stps. wrp. F3. $125.00

RAMON, Cajal Santiago. *Histology.* 1933. Baltimore. Wm Wood. 1st Eng-language ed. 8vo. 738p. ruled pebbled gr cloth. G1. $225.00

RAMPLING, Anne; see Rice, Anne.

RAMSAY, Jay; see Campbell, Ramsey.

RAMSAY, Robert. *Rough & Tumble on Old Clipper Ships.* 1930. NY. Appleton. 1st. NF/G. T11. $65.00

RAMSAY, William. *Bearing of Recent Discoveries on Trustworthiness of NT.* 1915. Hodder Stoughton. 427p. VG. B29. $16.00

RAMSBOTHAM, Frances. *Principles & Practice of Obstetric Medicine & Surgery.* 1843. Phil. 2nd Am. 52 engravings. 458p. A13. $150.00

RAMSEY, Frederic Jr. *Been Here & Gone.* 1960. Rutgers. 1st. F/NF. M25. $60.00

RAMSEY & RAMSEY. *This Was Mission Country: Orange County California.* 1973. Laguna Beach, CA. self pub. 1st. sgns. NF/NF. O4. $25.00

RAMSLAND, Katherine. *Prism of the Night: Biography of Anne Rice.* 1991. NY. 1st. 85p. F/dj. A17. $20.00

RANAHAN, Thomas. *Beecher Island Annual.* 1868. Beecher Island Battle Memmorial Assn. 1st. VG/wrp. J2. $175.00

RAND, A. *Philosophy, Who Needs It.* 1982. Indianapolis. 1st. VG/VG. B5. $35.00

RAND, A.L. *Southern Half of the Alaska Highway & Its Mammals.* 1944. Ottawa. Edmond Cloutier. inscr. VG. P4. $40.00

RAND, Addison. *Southpaw Fly Hawk.* 1952. Jr Lit Guild/Longman Gr. 183p. VG/dj. M20. $12.00

RAND, Ayn. *Atlas Shrugged.* 1957. NY. 1st. VG/VG. A15. $200.00

RAND, Clayton. *Sons of the South.* 1961. HRW. 1st. inscr. 212p. NF. T10. $35.00

RANDALL, Charles A. *Extra-Terrestrial Matter.* 1969. DeKalb, IL. N IL U. 331p. VG. K5. $40.00

RANDALL, David A. *Dukedom Large Enough.* 1969. Random. 1st. ils. xl. VG. K3. $15.00

RANDALL, E.O. *Serpent Mound & Adams County Ohio Mystery...* 1907. Columbus. 2nd. ils. 125p. VG. B5. $50.00

RANDALL, J.G. *Mid-Stream: Lincoln the President.* 1952. Dodd Mead. 1st. 467p. bl cloth. F/dj. H1. $25.00

RANDALL, Marta. *Sword of Winter.* 1983. Timescape. 1st. F/dj. M2. $20.00

RANDALL, W.S. *Benedict Arnold: Patriot & Traitor.* 1990. NY. 1st. ils. 667p. F/dj. M4. $25.00

RANDIER, Jean. *Nautical Antiques for the Collector.* 1977. photos. VG/VG. M17. $25.00

RANDISI, Robert J. *Separate Cases.* 1990. Walker. 1st. NF/F. N4. $15.00

RANDOLPH, Clare. *Nautical Ned.* 1948. Chicago. Hollow-Tree House. 1st probable. NF/VG+. C8. $20.00

RANDOLPH, Cornelia. *Parlor Gardener: Treatise on House Culture...* 1861. Boston. Tilton. 158p. VG. A10. $55.00

RANDOLPH, E. *Hell Among the Yearlings.* 1978. Lakeside Classic. photos. F. M4. $15.00

RANDOLPH, Howard. *La Jolla, Year by Year.* 1946. La Jolla. self pub. ils. 150p. prt wrp. D11. $50.00

RANDOLPH, Vance. *Ozark Folksongs.* 1946. Columbia, MO. 4 vol. 1st. ils Benton. VG. B5. $145.00

RANKIN, Louise. *American Cookbook for India.* 1944 (1933). Pub for India Red Cross. VG. E6. $20.00

RANKINE, John. *Bromius Phenomenon.* 1976. Dobson. 1st. NF/NF. N4. $25.00

RANNEY, Ambrose Loomis. *Applied Anatomy of the Nervous System.* 1881. NY. 1st. 500p. A13. $150.00

RANNEY, Ambrose Loomis. *Applied Anatomy of the Nervous System...* 1881. NY. Appleton. ils. 500p. ruled gr cloth. xl. VG. G1. $85.00

RANSMAYR, Christopher. *Terrors of Ice & Darkness.* 1991. Grove Weidenfeld. 1st Am. trans JE Woods. F/F. R14. $30.00

RANSOM, J.E. *Fossils in America.* 1964. Harper Row. 1st. 402p. F/dj. D8. $18.00

RANSOM, J.H. *History of American Saddle Horses.* 1952. Lexington. Ransom. 1st. VG. O3. $195.00

RANSOME, Arthur. *Picts & the Martyrs.* 1943. London. Cape. 1st. 303p. VG/G+. P2. $85.00

RANSOME. *Puppets & Shadows: A Bibliography.* 1931. Boston. 66p. VG. A4. $145.00

RAO, N.S.S. *Biological Nitrogen Fixation.* 1988. Montreaux. Gordon Breach. 337p. F/F. B1. $50.00

RAPER, Howard. *Man Against Pain: Epic of Anesthesia.* 1945. NY. 1st. 337p. A13. $40.00

RAPHAEL DE JESUS. *Castrioto Lusitano Part I...Entrepresa, Restauracao...* 1679. Lisbon. Antonio Craesbeeck deMello. 1st. folio. 701p. R15. $4,500.00

RAPHAEL TUCK. *Dolly in the Country.* ca 1901-10. 12 chromolitho. VG. M5. $150.00

RAPHALL, M.J. *Devotional Exercises, for the Use of Daughters of Israel...* (1852). NY. Joachimssen. 1st. sq 12mo. 139p. cloth. M1. $750.00

RASA, A. *Mongoose Watch.* 1985. London. John Murray. 298p. NF/F. B1. $25.00

RASCOVICH, Mark. *Bedford Incident.* 1963. Atheneum. 1st. F/F. T12. $50.00

RASHID & SHAHEEN. *King Fahd & Saudi Arabia's Great Revolution.* 1987. Joplin. Internat Inst Technology. 1st. 8vo. ils/maps. NF/dj. W1. $28.00

RASKIN, Ellen. *Westing Game.* (1978). Dutton. 2nd. sgn. 185p. VG/G. T5. $45.00

RASKIN, Jonah. *My Search for B Traven.* 1980. Methuen. 1st. NF/NF. A20. $25.00

RASPE, Rudolph Erich. *Singular Adventures of Baron Munchausen.* 1952. LEC. 1st thus. 1/1500. ils/sgn Fritz Kredel. F/case. Q1. $125.00

RASPE, Rudolph Erich. *Surprising Travels & Adventures of Baron Munchausen...* 1792. London. 12mo. copperplates. aeg. rebound Bayntum leather. R5. $485.00

RASTELL, John. *Les Termes de la Ley; or, Certain Difficult & Obscure Words.* 1971. London. Nutt Gosling. contemporary calf. M11. $450.00

RATCLIFFE, J.A. *Physics of the Upper Atmosphere.* 1960. NY. Academic. 8vo. 586p. VG/G. K5. $45.00

RATHBUN & RICHARDSON. *Crustaceans: Harriman Alaska Series. Vol X.* 1910. Smithsonian. 26 pl. 337p. NF/dj. P4. $150.00

RATHENAU, E. *Oskar Kokoschka Drawings, 1906-1965.* 1970. Miami. VG/VG. M17. $22.50

RATHER, Louis J. *Ross Browne, Adventurer.* 1978. Oakland. Rather. 1/150. 111p. pict cloth. D11. $25.00

RATHET & SMITH. *Their Deeds & Dogged Faith.* 1984. Balsam. 1st. inscr. photos. F/F. P8. $30.00

RATHMANN, Peggy. *Officer Buckle & Gloria.* 1995. Putnam. 1st. 1996 Caldecott Award. pict brd. dj. R5. $75.00

RATIGAN, William. *Great Lakes Shipwrecks & Survivals.* 1974. NY. Galahad. ils. 333p. dj. T7. $20.00

RATTRAY, R.F. *Bernard Shaw: A Chronicle.* 1950. Leagrave. 1st. VG/dj. V4. $20.00

RAUCAZ, L.M. *In the Savage Solomons: Story of a Mission.* 1928. Lyon. 1st. ils. 270p. simulated leather. B14. $45.00

RAUCH, Earl Mac. *New York, New York.* 1977. S&S. 1st. F/F. B4. $250.00

RAUCHER, Herman. *Summer of '42.* 1971. Putnam. 1st. F/F. B4. $150.00

RAUH, Werner. *Die Grossartige Welt der Sukkulenten.* 1967. Hamburg. sgn. ils/96 pl. F/dj. B26. $50.00

RAUH, Werner. *Schone Kakteen und Sukkulenten.* 1967. Heidelberg. ils/photos/pl. 221p. F/dj. B26. $22.00

RAUH, Werner. *Succulent & Xerophytic Plants of Madagascar Vol 1.* 1995. Mill Valley. 1011 mc photos. 343p. M/dj. B26. $110.00

RAWLINGS, Marjorie Kinnan. *Cross Creek Cookery.* 1942. NY. 1st. VG/VG. P3. $50.00

RAWLINGS, Marjorie Kinnan. *Cross Creek Cookery.* 1960. Hammond. 1st Eng. 12mo. F/NF clip. T10. $100.00

RAWLINGS, Marjorie Kinnan. *Cross Creek.* 1942. Scribner. 1st. sgn. VG/VG clip. B4. $600.00

RAWLINGS, Marjorie Kinnan. *Cross Creek.* 1942. Scribner. 1st. ils Edward Shenton. 368p. gr cloth. VG/dj. from $50 to $65.00

RAWLINGS, Marjorie Kinnan. *Marjorie Rawlings Reader Selected & Edited...JS Bigham.* 1956. Scribner. 1st. F/NF. B4. $225.00

RAWLINGS, Marjorie Kinnan. *Secret River.* 1955. Scribner. 1st. ils Leonard Weisgard. VG+/dj. P2. $125.00

RAWLINGS, Marjorie Kinnan. *Sojourner.* 1953. Scribner. 1st. NF/VG+. A24. $75.00

RAWLINGS, Marjorie Kinnan. *Yearling.* 1938. Scribner. 1st. ils NC Wyeth/14 full-p mc pl. NF. from $100 to $150.00

RAWLS, W. *Great Civil War Heroes & Their Battles.* 1985. NY. obl 4to. ils. 303p. F/dj. M4. $20.00

RAY, G. Whitfield. *Through Five Republics on Horseback.* ca 1921. Cleveland. Evangelical Pr. 25th/revised. 305p. F3. $15.00

RAY, Isaac. *Contribution to Mental Pathology.* 1873. Boston. 558p. gr cloth. VG. B14. $275.00

RAY, Jim. *Inside Story of the Flying Fortress: Boeing B-17.* 1943. ils. sbdg. VG. E6. $35.00

RAY, Man. *Man Ray: Self Portrait.* 1963. Boston. 1st. 398p. dj. A17. $65.00

RAY, Milton S. *Farallones, the Painted World & Other Poems of California.* 1934. SF. John Henry Nash. 1/200. 2 vol. photos. NF/VG case. O4. $75.00

RAY, Ophelia. *Daughter of Tejas.* 1965. Greenwich. NYGS. 1st. gray cloth. F/wht pict dj. M24. $100.00

RAY, P.H. *Report of International Polar Expedition to Point Barrow...* 1885. GPO. thick 4to. 22 pl/1 map. 695p. T7. $200.00

RAY, Robert. *Cage of Mirrors.* 1980. Lippincott/Crowell. 1st. VG/VG. A20. $20.00

RAYMOND, Alex. *Flash Gordon in the Planet Mongo.* 1974. Nostalgia. 1st. F/dj. M2. $50.00

RAYMOND, Ernest. *Late in the Day.* 1964. London. 1st. VG/VG. T9. $8.00

RAYMOND, Fulgence. *Lecons sur les Maladies du Systeme Nerveux...* 1896. Paris. Octave Doin. heavy 8vo. 2 lithos/ils. contemporary bdg. xl. G. G1. $125.00

RAYMOND, Louise. *Child's Book of Prayers.* (1941). Random. ils Masha. unp. pict brd/gray cloth spine. G. T5. $20.00

RAYMOND & RAYMOND. *Home Gardening Wisdom.* 1982. Garden Way. 1st. NF. W2. $15.00

RAYMONT, J.E.G. *Plankton & Productivity in the Oceans.* 1967. Oxford. Pergamon. 2nd. 660p. B1. $30.00

RAYNAL, Maurice. *Picasso: Biographical & Critical Studies.* 1959. Lausanne. Skira. ils/bibliography/index. 136p. cloth. dj. D2. $30.00

RAYZER, G. *Flowering Cacti: A Color Guide.* 1984. NY. 181p. photo brd. F. B26. $9.00

RAZZI, Silvano. *Vita Di Piero Soderini Gonfaloniere Perpetvo...* 1737. Padua. 4 parts in 1. folio. Salsa/Dudley bookplates. vellum. R12. $750.00

READ, George H. *Last Cruise of the Saginaw.* 1912. Houghton Mifflin. 1/150. 127p. P4. $70.00

READ, Herbert. *This Way, Delight. A Book of Poetry for the Young.* 1956. Pantheon. 1st. 155p. F/NF. D4. $35.00

READ, Kenneth E. *High Valley: Autobiographical Account of 2 Years...* 1965. NY. Scribner. 8vo. 266p. dj. P4. $30.00

READ, Miss (Dora Saint). *Time Remembered.* 1986. Houghton Mifflin. 1st Am/BC prt. sm 8vo. F/F. C8. $15.00

READ, Miss (Dora Saint). *Village Centenary.* 1980. London. Michael Joseph. 1st. 8vo. 236p. VG/VG. T5. $25.00

READ, Miss (Dora Saint). *Village School.* 1956. Houghton Mifflin. 1st Am. 8vo. 238p. VG/G+. T5. $30.00

READ, Piers Paul. *On the Third Day.* 1990. RAndom. 1st. F/F. B35. $16.00

READER'S DIGEST. *Creative Cooking.* 1977. NY. VG. A16. $10.00

READER'S DIGEST. *Reader's Digest Creative Cooking.* 1977. 3rd. 176p. G. B10. $8.00

READY, Alma. *Nogales, Arizona, 1880-1980: Centennial Anniversary.* nd (1980). np. 1st. ils/notes/chronology. 110p. F/wrp. B19. $15.00

REAGAN, Nancy. *My Turn.* 1989. Random. 1st. inscr. F/F. A23. $75.00

REAGAN, Ronald. *American Life.* 1990. S&S. 1st. inscr bookplate. F/F. A23. $150.00

REAGE, Pauline. *Story of O.* 1965. Grove. 1st Am. F/NF. R14. $75.00

REAMY, Tom. *Blind Voices.* 1978. Berkley. 1st. F/dj. M2. $25.00

REARDON, M.M. *Zululand: Wildlife Heritage.* 1984. Cape Town. Struik. ils/photos. 160p. brd. NF/NF. M12. $30.00

REAUGH, F. *Frank Reaugh: Painter to the Longhorns.* 1985. TX A&M. 1st. 61 mc pl. 146p. F/dj. M4. $30.00

RECHY, John. *City of Night.* 1963. Grove. 1st. F/NF. B2. $40.00

RECHY, John. *City of Night.* 1963. Grove. 1st. sgn. NF/VG. R14. $75.00

RECHY, John. *Numbers.* 1967. Grove. 1st. author's 2nd book. F/dj. M25. $35.00

RECLUS, Paul. *L'Anesthesie Localisee par la Cocaine.* 1903. Paris. 1st. 276p. wrp. A13. $300.00

RECORD, Paul. *Tropical Frontier.* 1969. Knopf. 1st. 325p. dj. F3. $15.00

RECORD, S.J. *Economic Woods of the United States.* 1912. John Wiley. 117p. cloth. B1. $25.00

REDDING, Saunders J. *They Came in Chains.* 1950. Phil. 1st. 320p. VG/dj. B5. $40.00

REDFERN, R. *Making of a Continent.* 1983. Times. ils. 242p. NF/dj. D8. $30.00

REDFIELD, J.S. *Mineral Resources in Oklahoma.* 1927. OK Geol Survey Bulletin 42. 130p. VG/prt wrp. D8. $15.00

REDFIELD, James. *Celsetine Prophecy: An Adventure.* 1993. Warner. 1st. M/dj. B4. $200.00

REDFIELD, Robert. *Folk Culture of Yucatan.* 1959. Chicago. 7th. 416p. F3. $20.00

REDLIN, Terry. *Art of Terry Redlin. Opening Windows to the Wild.* 1987. Plymouth, MI. Hadley. 1/2400. sgn. 132p. gilt bdg. M/case. B24. $350.00

REDMAN, L.A. *Einstein Delusion & Other Essays.* 1926. SF. Robertson. 1st. 217p. VG. K3. $20.00

REDOUTE, P.J. *Redoute's Roses.* 1990. London. Wellfleet. 342p. dj. A10. $50.00

REDPATH, James. *Echoes of Harper's Ferry.* 1850. Thayer Eldridge. 1st. gilt bl cloth. F. M24. $250.00

REECE, N.C. *Cultured Pearl: Jewel of Japan.* 1958. Rutland. Tuttle. ils/photos/maps. 107p. F/VG. M12. $25.00

REED, Alma. *Jose Clemente Orozco.* 1932. NY. Delphic Studios. ils/photos/drawings. 16p text. cloth/paper label. D2. $200.00

REED, Chester. *North American Bird Eggs.* 1904. NY. 1st. ils/index. 356p. VG. B5. $35.00

REED, Clyde F. *Ferns & Fern-Allies of Maryland & Delaware...* 1953. Baltimore. Reed Herbarium. 8vo. xl. A22. $25.00

REED, David A. *How To Rescue Your Loved One From the Watchtower.* 1994. Baker. 161p. as new. B29. $7.00

REED, Dorinda Riessen. *Women Suffrage Movement in South Dakota.* 1958. Vermillion, SD. SD U. A19. $15.00

REED, Ishmael. *Conjure.* 1972. Amherst. 1st. F/clip. V1. $20.00

REED, Ishmael. *Flight to Canada.* 1976. Random. 1st. F/dj. A24. $35.00

REED, Ishmael. *Writin' Is Fightin'.* 1988. Atheneum. 1st. sgn. F/F. R14. $40.00

REED, Myrtle. *Book of Clever Beasts.* 1904. Putnam. 1st. ils Peter Newell. VG. B5. $35.00

REED, Myrtle. *Master of the Vineyard.* 1910. Putnam. 2nd. ils. teg. emb bdg. A25. $25.00

REED, Myrtle. *Old Rose & Silver.* 1909. Putnam. 3rd. 364p. teg. VG+. A25. $20.00

REED, S.B. *House Plans for Everybody.* 1894. Orange Judd. 243p. cloth. A10. $75.00

REED, Walt. *Illustrator in America 1900-1960s.* 1966. NY. 1st. VG/G. B5. $35.00

REED, William. *DeGrazia: Irreverant Angel.* 1971. Frontier Heritage. 1st. 191p. F/NF. B19. $100.00

REED & ROBINSON. *War in Eastern Europe.* 1916. NY. Scribner. 1st. ils Robinson. F. B2. $150.00

REEDSTROM, E. Lisle. *Custer's 7th Cavalry.* 1922. NY. Sterling. A19. $20.00

REEDY, William. *Impact: Photography for Advertising.* 1973. 1st/1st prt. inscr. ils. 323p. F/VG. A8. $45.00

REEMAN, Douglas. *HMS Saracen.* 1965. London. Jarrolds. 1st Eng. F/F. T11. $145.00

REEMAN, Douglas. *In Danger's Hour.* 1988. Toronto. Stoddart. 1st Canadian ed. rem mk. F/F. T11. $40.00

REEMAN, Douglas. *Surface With Daring.* 1976. London. Hutchinson. 1st Eng. inscr. NF/NF. T11. $85.00

REES, Arthur. *Threshold of Fear.* 1926. Dodd Mead. VG. M2. $20.00

REES, Ennis. *Fables From Aesop.* 1966. NY. Oxford. 1st. ils Grandville. 210p. F/dj. T10. $40.00

REES, Lucy. *Horse of the Air.* 1980. Methuen. 1st Am. VG/G. O3. $18.00

REESE, A.M. *Alligator & Its Allies.* 1915. Putnam. ils/figures/pl. 358p. cloth. G. M12. $75.00

REESE, David Meredith. *Quakerism, Versus Calvinism, Being a Reply...* 1834. NY. Wm Mercein. 1st. 211p. poor. V3. $20.00

REESE, H.H. *Horses of Today.* 1960. Pomona. Reese. 2nd. VG/fair. O3. $30.00

REESE, H.H. *Kellogg Arabians: Their Background & Influence.* 1958. Alhambra. Borden. 8vo. photos. gilt pict brd. F/VG+. M12. $37.50

REESE, Terence. *Bridge Tips From the Masters.* 1981. NY. 1st Am. 236p. VG/dj. S1. $10.00

REESE, William. *Six Score, the 120 Best Books on the Range Cattle Industry.* 1989. Wm Reese. revised. VG/VG. J2. $60.00

REEVE, Arthur B. *Clutching Hand.* 1934. Reilly Lee. 1st. VG. M2. $25.00

REEVES, Arthur Middleton. *Finding of Wineland the Good: Hist of Icelandic Discovery...* 1960s. NY. Burt Franklin. rpt. as new. O7. $75.00

REEVES, Robert. *Doubting Thomas.* 1985. NY. Arbor. 1st. author's 1st book. F/F. H11. $50.00

REEVES & ROBINSON. *Classic Lines: A Gallery of Great Thoroughbreds.* 1975. Birmingham. Oxmoor. sgn. VG/G. O3. $325.00

REEVES & ROBINSON. *Decade of Champions.* 1980. NY. Fine Arts Ent. 1st trade. sgn pres from Reeves. VG/VG. O3. $295.00

REEVES-STEVENS, Garfield. *Dark Matter.* 1990. Doubleday. 1st. F/F. M21. $25.00

REGAN, Michael. *Mansions of Los Angeles.* 1965. Regan Pub. photos. 80p. gilt fabricoid. D11. $75.00

REGAN, Robert. *Poe: Collection of Critical Essays.* 1967. Prentice Hall. 1st. NF/wrp. M2. $10.00

REGNERY, Dorothy F. *Enduring Heritage.* 1976. Stanford. 124p. xl. F/dj. K7. $35.00

REICHEL-DOLMATOFF. *People of Aritama.* (1961). London. Routledge. 1st. ils/index. 483p. dj. F3. $20.00

REID, Alastair. *Ounce Dice Trice.* 1958. Little Brn. stated 1st. sm 4to. 57p. VG+/G+. C14. $14.00

REID, Alastair. *Supposing.* 1960. Little Brn. 1st. 8vo. 48p. VG+/G+. C14. $9.00

REID, Wynwode. *New Australian Cookery Illustrated.* nd. Membourne, Australia. G. A16. $20.00

REID & VISKOCHIL. *Chicago & Downstate.* 1989. Chicago. 1st. F/F. B2. $25.00

REIGER, Barbara. *Zane Grey Cookbook.* 1976. Prentice Hall. 1st. xl. dj. A16. $15.00

REIK, Theodor. *Compulsion To Confess: On Psychoanalysis of Crime...* 1959. FSC. 1st. 8vo. 493p. as new/dj. H1. $25.00

REILLY, Helen. *Not Me, Inspector.* 1959. Random. 1st. F/VG. N4. $25.00

REINER, Ralph E. *Introducing the Flowering Beauty of Glacier National Park...* 1969. np. 246 mc photos/index. sc. B26. $10.00

REINHARDT, Hans. *Holbien.* 1938. French/European Pub. ils/pl. VG. M17. $25.00

REISER, Morton F. *Memory in Mind & Brain: What Dream Imagery Reveals.* 1990. NY. Basic. 218p. crimson cloth-backed gray brd. VG/dj. G1. $30.00

REISS, Lionel S. *My Models Were Jews: A Painter's Pilgrimage to Many Lands.* 1938. Gordon. 1/1200. 4to. ils. 147p. VG. S3. $95.00

REIT. *Those Fabulous Flying Machines: A History of Flight...* 1985. ils Weidner/Ossmann. 6 popups. F. A4. $30.00

REITLINGER, Gerald. *Economics of Taste: Rise & Fall of Picture Market 1760...* 1961. HRW. 1st Am. 8vo. 518p. F/dj. H1. $60.00

REMARQUE, Erich Maria. *All Quiet on the Western Front.* 1929. Little Brn. 1st. VG. M19. $35.00

REMARQUE, Erich Maria. *All Quiet on the Western Front.* 1929. London. Putnam. 1st Eng. NF/NF. M23. $200.00

REMICK, Grace M. *Sheldon Six: Anne.* 1920. Penn. 366p. cloth. G+. M20. $15.00

REMINGTON, Frederic. *Done in the Open: Drawings...* 1902. Collier. 1st. double-/half-/full-p ils. pict brd. case. D11. $300.00

REMINGTON, Frederic. *Done in the Open: Drawings...* 1903. Collier. folio. unp. quarter tan cloth. G. K7. $95.00

REMINGTON, Frederic. *Remington's Frontier Sketches.* 1898. Chicago. Werner. 1st. obl 4to. 15 pl w/titles. pict vegetable vellum. M1. $600.00

REMINGTON, Frederic. *Selected Writings.* April 1982. Secaucus, NJ. Castle. dj. A19. $30.00

REMINI, Robert V. *Andrew Jackson & the Course of American Empire 1767-1821.* 1977. Harper Row. 1st. tall 8vo. 502p. as new/dj. H1. $30.00

REMOND DE SAINT-SAUVEUR. *Agenda des Auteurs.* 1755. Parnasse. Anomime Fertile. 8vo. brd. R12. $325.00

REMSBURG, John E. *Thomas Paine, the Apostle of...* 1881. Boston. Mindum. A19. $30.00

RENARD, Maurice. *New Bodies for Old; or, Strange Experiments of Dr Lerne.* 1923. NY. Macaulay. 1st Am/1st Eng language. F/F. B4. $750.00

RENAULT, Mary. *Mask of Apollo.* 1966. Longmans. 1st. F/dj. Q1. $50.00

RENAULT, Mary. *Praise Singer.* 1978. Pantheon. 1st. F/dj. Q1. $35.00

RENDELL, Ruth. *Collected Stories.* 1988. Pantheon/Random. 1st omnibus of short fiction (38 stories). NF/dj. A24. $15.00

RENDELL, Ruth. *Crocodile Bird.* 1993. Crown. 1st Am. sgn. F/NF. N4. $40.00

RENDELL, Ruth. *Dark-Adapted Eye.* 1986. Bantam. 1st. F/F. H11. $40.00

RENDELL, Ruth. *Face of Trespass.* 1974. London. Heinemann. 1st. F/F. M15. $300.00

RENDELL, Ruth. *Fever Tree.* 1983. Pantheon. 1st. F/NF. N4. $40.00

RENDELL, Ruth. *Gallowglass.* 1990. Harmony. 1st. sgn. F/F. B3. $40.00

RENDELL, Ruth. *Going Wrong.* 1990. London. Hutchinson. 1st. sgn. F/F. B3. $50.00

RENDELL, Ruth. *Guilty Thing Surprised.* 1970. Hutchinson. 1st. VG/VG+ clip. A24. $250.00

RENDELL, Ruth. *Heartstones.* 1987. Hutchinson. 1st. sgn. F/F. B3. $50.00

RENDELL, Ruth. *House of Stairs.* 1989. NY. Harmony. 1st. sgn. F/NF. w/promo folder. B3. $50.00

RENDELL, Ruth. *Killing Doll.* 1984. London. Hutchinson. 1st. F/dj. A24. $40.00

RENDELL, Ruth. *Killing Doll.* 1984. Pantheon. 1st Am. F/F. W2. $40.00

RENDELL, Ruth. *King Solomon's Carpet.* 1991. NY. Harmony. 1st. sgn. F/F. B3. $40.00

RENDELL, Ruth. *Lake of Darkness.* 1980. Doubleday. 1st Am. NF/VG+. A24. $25.00

RENDELL, Ruth. *Live Flesh.* 1986. London. Hutchinson. 1st. sgn. F/dj. A24. $50.00

RENDELL, Ruth. *Make Death Love Me.* 1979. Doubleday. 1st Am. sgn. F/F. D10. $60.00

RENDELL, Ruth. *One Across, Two Down.* 1971. London. Heinemann. 1st. F/clip. M15/T2. $400.00

RENDELL, Ruth. *Speaker of Mandarin.* 1983. Pantheon. 1st Am. sgn. F/F. B3. $50.00

RENDELL, Ruth. *Talking to Strange Men.* 1987. Pantheon/Random. 1st Am. inscr. F/dj. A24. $25.00

RENDELL, Ruth. *Tree of Hands.* 1985. Pantheon. 1st Am. F/dj. A24. $15.00

RENDELL, Ruth. *Unkindness of Ravens.* 1985. Pantheon. 1st. sgn. NF/NF. B3. $40.00

RENEHAN, E.J. *John Burroughs: An American Naturalist.* 1992. Post Mills. Chelsea Gr. 1st. 356p. F/F. B1. $35.00

RENNER, Frederic G. *Charles M Russell.* nd. NY. Abrams. A19. $85.00

RENNER, Frederic G. *Charles M Russell.* 1966. TX U. 1st. 148p. VG/dj. J2. $200.00

RENNER, G.K. *Joplin From Mining Town to Urban Center: Ils History.* 1985. Joplin Hist Soc. 1st. ils. 128p. F/dj. M4. $25.00

RENNER, L.L. *Pioneer Missionary to the Bering Strait Eskimos.* 1979. Portland. 1st. ils/photos/map. 207p. F/dj. M4. $30.00

RENSE, Paige. *American Interiors.* nd. 1st ed. 1/1000. sgn. folio. aeg. gilt blue leather/silk ep. A8. $85.00

RENTOUL, Annie R. *Lady of the Blue Beads.* 1908. Melbourne. Geo Robertson. 1st. 4to. tan cloth. R5. $600.00

RENTZ, John. *Marines in the Central Solomons.* 1952. WA. fld maps/photos/index. 186p. G. S16. $85.00

RENZI, Renzo. *Era Notte Aroma (It Was a Night in Rome).* 1960. Cappelli. Italian text. photos. VG+/dj. C9. $40.00

REQUA, Richard A. *Old World Inspiration for American Architecture.* 1929. Monolith Portland Midwest Co of Denver. folio. 144 pl. gilt stp bdg. F/dj. A8. $250.00

RESNICK, Michael. *Official Guide to the Fantastics.* 1976. House of Collectibles. 1st. VG/wrp. M2. $10.00

RESNICOW & SEAVER. *Beanball.* 1989. Morrow. 1st. VG/dj. P3. $17.00

RESSMEYER, Roger. *Space Places.* 1990. SF. Collins. 1st. VG/VG. K5. $45.00

RESSNER, Philip. *Jerome.* nd (1967). Parents Magazine. probable 1st. unp. NF. C14. $10.00

RETELI, Ernest. *Captain Knickerbocker.* 1938. London. Edward Arnold. 1st. 4to. pict brd. dj. R5. $250.00

RETTEW, G. Raymond. *Manual of Mushroom Culture.* 1941 (1935). West Chester. 3rd. ils/plans. flexible maroon bdg. VG. B26. $16.00

REVERE, Joseph Warren. *Naval Duty in California.* 1947. Oakland, CA. Biobooks. 1/1000. 245p. gray cloth. as new. K7. $65.00

REVERE, Joseph Warren. *Tour of Duty in California...* 1849. Boston. JH Francis. 305p+ads. gilt brn cloth. VG. K7. $295.00

REVI, Albert Christian. *American Art Nouveau.* 1968. Thomas Nelson. 1st. 4to. 476p. NF/G. H1. $95.00

REXROTH, Kenneth. *Excerpts From a Life.* 1981. Santa Barabara. Conjunction. 1/350. sgn/#d. F/F. D10. $85.00

REXROTH, Kenneth. *Phoenix & the Tortoise.* 1944. New Directions. 1st. VG. M19. $45.00

REY, H.A. *Feed the Animals.* 1944. limp bdg. G+. M17. $45.00

REY, H.A. *Where's My Baby.* (1943). Houghton Mifflin. 1st. G+/pict wrp. D1. $50.00

REY, Margaret. *Pretzel.* 1944. Harper. 1st. ils HA Rey. 4to. VG+/G. P2. $125.00

REYNOLDS, Alfred. *Kiteman of Karanga.* 1985. Knopf. 1st. F/dj. M2. $10.00

REYNOLDS, Cuyler. *New York at the Jamestown Exposition.* 1909. Albany. JB Lyon. 1st. gilt red cloth. M24. $225.00

REYNOLDS, Francis J. *Master Tales of Mystery, Vol I, II, III.* 1915. Collier. 3 vol. VG. N4. $25.00

REYNOLDS, James. *More Ghosts in Irish Houses.* 1956. Farrar. 1st. NF/dj. M2. $35.00

REYNOLDS, Quentin. *Officially Dead.* 1945. NY. 244p. VG. S16. $16.50

REYNOLDS, Quentin. *They Fought for the Sky.* 1957. NY. 1st. VG/VG. B5. $20.00

REYNOLDS, Stephen. *Voyage of New Hazard to the Northwest Coast, HI & China...* nd. np. rpt 1938 ed. 1/437. 12 pl. F. M4. $40.00

REYNOLDS, Stephen. *Voyage of New Hazzard to the Northwest Coast, HI & China...* 1938. Salem. Peabody Mus. 1st. 158p. VG. P4. $135.00

REYNOLDS, V. *Apes.* 1967. Dutton. 1st. 296p. VG/VG. B1. $30.00

REYNOLDS, W.F.R. *Fly & Minnow: Common Problems of Trout & Salmon Fishing.* (1930). Country Life. 1st. sm 4to. 156p. VG. H7. $25.00

REYNOLDS, William J. *Things Invisible.* 1989. Putnam. 1st. sgn. F/F. B2. $40.00

REZANOV, Nickolai Petrovich. *Rezanov Voyage to Nueva California in 1806...* 1926. SF. Private Pr of Thomas C Russell. 1/260. sgn Russell. VG. P4. $300.00

RHIND, William. *History of Vegetable Kingdom.* 1877. London. Blackie. revised. v8o. 744p. w/supplement. A22. $130.00

RHINE, J.B. *New Frontiers of the Mind.* 1937. Farrar. 1st. VG/dj. M2. $20.00

RHODE, John. *Telephone Call.* 1948. London. Bles. 1st. VG/clip. M15. $45.00

RHODE, John. *Three Cousins Die.* 1960. Dodd Mead. 1st. F/NF. N4. $35.00

RHODES, Eugene Manlove. *Bransford in Arcadia; or, The Little Eohippus.* 1914. Holt. 1st. VG. A18. $100.00

RHODES, Eugene Manlove. *Desire of the Moth.* 1916. Henry Hold. 1st. 155p. VG. J2. $225.00

RHODES, Richard. *Making of the Atomic Bomb.* 1986. ils. NF/wrp. K3. $20.00

RHODIUS, Apollonius. *Argonautica.* 1957. Athens. LEC. 1st thus. 1/1500. ils/sgn A Tassos. F/glassine/case. Q1. $125.00

RHYS, Grace. *In Wheel About & Cock Alone.* 1919. London. Harrap. 1st. NF. T12. $60.00

RHYS & RHYS. *English Fairy Tales.* nd (1913). London. Dent. Tales for Children From Many Lands series. VG. M5. $75.00

RIBEIRO DE SEQUEIRA, Angelo. *Livro do Vinde, a Vede, e do Sermam do Dia Juizo Universal.* 1758. Lisbon. Antonio Vincent daSilva. 1st. 255p. contemporary bdg. R15. $2,500.00

RICARD, Robert. *La Conquette Spirituelle du Mexique.* 1933. Paris. Inst D'Ethnologie. 1st in French. 404p. F3. $65.00

RICCIARDI, Lorenzo. *Voyage of the Mir-El-Lah.* 1981. Viking. ils/photos/maps. 256p. gilt bdg. P4. $22.50

RICCIOTTI, Giuseppe. *Life of Christ.* 1951. Milwaukee, WI. Bruce. 5th. 8vo. ils. cloth. VG. W1. $10.00

RICCIUTI, E.R. *American Aligator: Its Life in the Wild.* 1972. Harper Row. ils/photos. 71p. cloth. NF/VG. M12. $15.00

RICCIUTI, E.R. *Devil's Garden.* 1978. NY. ils. 172p. VG+/dj. B26. $27.50

RICE, Anne. *Belinda.* 1986. Arbor. 1st. F/F. B3. $50.00

RICE, Anne. *Belinda.* 1986. Arbor. 1st. sgn. F/dj. B4/D10. $100.00

RICE, Anne. *Belinda.* 1986. Arbor. 1st. VG/VG. P3. $35.00

RICE, Anne. *Claiming of Sleeping Beauty.* 1983. Dutton. 1st pb ed. F/wrp. Q1. $35.00

RICE, Anne. *Cry to Heaven.* 1982. Knopf. 1st. F/F. M2. $75.00

RICE, Anne. *Cry to Heaven.* 1982. Knopf. 1st. F/VG. M19. $65.00

RICE, Anne. *Cry to Heaven.* 1982. Knopf. 1st. inscr/dtd 1995. NF/NF. R14. $100.00

RICE, Anne. *Exit to Eden.* 1985. Arbor. 1st. F/dj. from $100 to $125.00

RICE, Anne. *Exit to Eden.* 1985. Arbor. 1st. NF/F. A24. $75.00

RICE, Anne. *Exit to Eden.* 1985. Arbor. 1st. sgn. F/F. A23. $150.00

RICE, Anne. *Exit to Eden.* 1985. Arbor. 1st. VG/dj. P3. $65.00

RICE, Anne. *Feast of All Saints.* 1979. S&S. 1st. NF/NF. M19. $85.00

RICE, Anne. *Feast of All Saints.* 1979. S&S. 1st. VG/VG. B5. $50.00

RICE, Anne. *Interview With the Vampire.* (1976). NY. Knopf. rpt. sgn. F/VG clip. B11. $35.00

RICE, Anne. *Interview With the Vampire.* 1976. Knopf. ARC. F/glossy wrp. B4. $1,200.00

RICE, Anne. *Interview With the Vampire.* 1976. Knopf. BC. NF/dj. Q1. $35.00

RICE, Anne. *Interview With the Vampire.* 1976. NY. Knopf. 1st. author's 1st book. F/F. L3. $850.00

RICE, Anne. *Interview With the Vampire.* 1976. NY. Knopf. 1st. author's 1st book. NF/dj. Q1. $750.00

RICE, Anne. *Interview With the Vampire.* 1996. Knopf. anniversary ed. sgn. F/F/F case. B11. $75.00

RICE, Anne. *Lasher.* 1993. Knopf. 1st. F/F. B2/H11. $45.00

RICE, Anne. *Lasher.* 1993. Knopf. 1st. sgn. VG/VG. A23. $60.00

RICE, Anne. *Memnoch the Devil.* 1995. Knopf. 1/425. sgn. BE Trice bdg. F/cloth case. B3. $150.00

RICE, Anne. *Memnoch the Devil.* 1995. Knopf. 1st. sgn. F/F. A23. $45.00

RICE, Anne. *Queen of the Damned.* 1988. Knopf. 1st sgn. F/dj. A24. $65.00

RICE, Anne. *Queen of the Damned.* 1988. Knopf. 1st. VG/dj. P3. $25.00

RICE, Anne. *Servant of the Bones.* 1996. Knopf. 1st. sgn. F/F. A23/D10. $45.00

RICE, Anne. *Servant of the Bones.* 1996. Toronto. Knopf. 1st Canadian. F/NF. T12. $40.00

RICE, Anne. *Tale of the Body Thief.* 1992. Knopf. 1st. F/dj. M2. $35.00

RICE, Anne. *Tale of the Body Thief.* 1992. Knopf. 1st. sgn. VG/VG. A23. $60.00

RICE, Anne. *Tale of the Body Thief.* 1992. Knopf. 1st. VG/dj. P3. $25.00

RICE, Anne. *Taltos.* 1994. Knopf. 1st. F/F. M2/M22/P3. $25.00

RICE, Anne. *Taltos.* 1994. Knopf. 1st. sgn. VG/VG. A23. $60.00

RICE, Anne. *Vampire Chronicles.* 1990. Knopf. 1st boxed ed. 3 vol. sgn. F/djs/VG case. Q1. $325.00

RICE, Anne. *Vampire Lestat.* 1985. Knopf. 1st. F/dj. B5. $95.00

RICE, Anne. *Vampire Lestat.* 1985. Knopf. 1st. VG/VG. M19. $75.00

RICE, Anne. *Witching Hour.* 1990. Knopf. 1st. 965p. F/F. W2. $65.00

RICE, Craig. *45 Murderers.* 1952. S&S. 1st. NF/G. M19. $25.00

RICE, Elmer. *Two on an Island.* 1940. Coward McCann. 1st. F/NF. B2. $45.00

RICE, Grantland. *Tumult & Shouting.* 1956. Cassell. 1st Eng. photos. VG/G+. P8. $12.50

RICE, Harvey. *Founder of the City of Cleveland & Other Sketches.* 1892. Boston. 238p. G. B18. $37.50

RICE, Homer. *Homer Rice on Triple Option Football.* 1973. Parker. 1st. diagrams. VG/dj. P8. $10.00

RICE & STOUDT. *Shenandoah Pottery.* 1929. Strasburg. 1st. G+. B5. $100.00

RICH, Adrienne. *Wild Patience Has Taken Me This Far.* 1981. Norton. 1st. assn copy. F/dj. V1. $45.00

RICH, Edwin Gile. *Arabian Nights' Entertainments.* 1921. Sm Maynard. 1st. 347p. VG. W1. $20.00

RICH, Louise Dickinson. *We Took to the Woods.* 1942. Lippincott. 1st. photos. 322p. VG+. A25. $8.00

RICHARD, Mark. *Ice at the Bottom of the World.* 1989. Knopf. 1st. author's 1st book. F/dj. A24. $35.00

RICHARD, Mark. *Ice at the Bottom of the World.* 1989. Knopf. 1st. sgn. F/F. R13. $60.00

RICHARDS, A. *Ennal's Point.* 1977. London. Michael Joseph. 1st Eng. F/F. T11. $45.00

RICHARDS, Alan. *Birds of Prey: Hunters of the Sky.* 1992. Phil. photos. 144p. F/F. S15. $15.00

RICHARDS, Edward A. *Shadows: Selected Poems.* 1933. St Thomas, Virgin Island. 1st. sm 8vo. 20p. cloth. NF. B4. $275.00

RICHARDS, G.M. *Pied Piper of Hamelin.* 1934 (1927). Macmillan. 12mo. VG. P2. $40.00

RICHARDS, Joe. *Princes-New York-Key Biscayne.* 1973. NY. David McKay. 2nd. 346p. T7. $20.00

RICHARDS, L. *Tea Room Recipes, a Book for Homemakers...* 1925. 1st. xl. VG. E6. $25.00

RICHARDS, Larry. *Dictionary of Basic Bible Truths.* 1987. Lamplighter. 384p. as new. B29. $7.50

RICHARDS, Laura E. *Tirra Lirra: Rhymes Old & New.* 1955 (1932). Little Brn. ils Marguerite Davis. 194p. VG. T5. $30.00

RICHARDS, Lawrence O. *Theology of Christian Education.* 1975. Zondervan. 324p. VG/dj. B29. $8.50

RICHARDS, Lela Horn. *Blue Bonnet's Family (#7).* 1929. Page. 1st. 249p. VG+/dj. M20. $45.00

RICHARDS, Vyvyan. *From Crystal to Television: The Electron Bridge.* 1928. London. Black. xl. K5. $30.00

RICHARDSON, A.E. *Old Inns of England.* 1035. London. 2nd/revised. G. O3. $40.00

RICHARDSON, Alfred. *Plants of the Rio Grande Delta.* 1995. Austin. 200 mc photos. 342p. sc. M. B26. $25.00

RICHARDSON, C. *Practical Farriery: A Guide for Apprentices...* 1950. London. Pitman. 1st. VG/VG. O3. $25.00

RICHARDSON, Charles. *Chancellorsville Campaign.* 1907. Neale Pub. 124p. NF. A4. $200.00

RICHARDSON, Joanna. *Rachel.* 1957. Putnam. 222p. VG/fair. S3. $21.00

RICHARDSON, R. *Foods That Make or Break You.* 1928. VG. E6. $20.00

RICHARDSON, R.H. *Wickedness in High Places: A Discourse...* 1851. Chicago. SC Griggs. 1st. 8vo. 43p. modern cloth. M1. $425.00

RICHARDSON, R.S. *Fascinating World of Astronomy.* 1960. McGraw Hill. 1st. 274p. F/dj. D8. $10.00

RICHARDSON, Rupert Norval. *Frontier of Northwest Texas, 1846-1876.* 1963. Clark. 1st. ils/maps. 332p. VG. J2. $225.00

RICHARDSON, S.C. *In Desert Arizona.* 1938. Zion Prt/Pub. inscr. ils. 186p. NF. B19. $75.00

RICHARDSON, Samuel. *History of Sir Charles Grandison.* 1762. London. Rivington. 7 vol. 4th. 12mo. contemporary bdg. H13. $395.00

RICHARDSON, Samuel. *History of Sir Charles Grandison.* 1766. London. 7 vol. 12mo. full calf. C6. $225.00

RICHARDSON, Samuel. *Pamela; or, Virtue Rewarded.* 1785. London. Harrison. 4 vol in 1. thick 8vo. orig blk leather/marbled brd. H13. $295.00

RICHLER, Mordecai. *St Urbain's Horseman.* 1971. Knopf. 1st Am. F/clip. M25. $45.00

RICHTER, Conrad. *Town.* 1950. Knopf. 1st. F/dj. Q1. $60.00

RICHTER, N.B. *Nature of Comets.* 1963. London. Methuen. revised/trans. 8vo. 221p. G/dj. K5. $45.00

RICKARD, T.A. *Mines: A History of American Mining.* 1932. 1st. ils. 419p. O8. $21.50

RICKETT, Harold W. *Wildflowers of the US: The Northeastern States.* 1966. McGraw Hill. 1st ed. 2 vol. folio. A10. $200.00

RICKETT, Harold W. *Wildflowers of the US: The Southwestern States.* 1966. McGraw Hill. 1st. 3 vol. cloth/case. A10. $250.00

RICKETTS, Charles. *Letters to Michael Field.* 1981. Edinburgh. Tragara. 1st. 1/145. VG/VG. T9. $65.00

RICKETTS, R.L. *First Class Polo.* 1928. Aldershot. Gale Polden. 1st. VG. O3. $125.00

RICO, Ulde. *Ring of the Nibelung. Wagner's Epic Drama, Illustrated.* 1980. Thames Hudson. 4to. 204p. 30 glossy pl. cloth brd. M/pict dj. B24. $100.00

RIDDELL, John. *John Riddell Murder Case: Philo Vance Parody.* 1930. Scribner. 1st. VG/dj. M15. $75.00

RIDEOUT, Henry Milner. *Dulcarnon.* 1925. Duffield. 1st. VG. M2. $12.00

RIDER, J.W. *Hot Tickets.* 1987. NY. Arbor. 1st. author's 2nd book. F/F. H11. $25.00

RIDER, J.W. *Jersey Tomatoes.* 1986. NY. Arbor. 1st. author's 1st book. F/F. H11. $50.00

RIDGE, John Rollin. *Trumpet of Our Own.* 1981. BC of CA. 1/650. ils. 128p. gilt blk cloth spine. as new/wrp. K7. $75.00

RIDGWAY, Matthew. *Soldier: Memoirs of Matthew B Ridgway.* 1956. Harper. 1st. inscr. 371p. G+. B11. $100.00

RIDGWAY, Matthew. *Soldier: Memoirs of Matthew B Ridgway.* 1956. NY. 1st. photos/index. 371p. VG/VG. S16. $28.50

RIDLEY, Thomas. *View of Civile & Ecclesiastical Law. Third Edition.* 1662. Oxford. John Forrest. modern 3-quarter calf. M11. $550.00

RIDOLFI, Roberto. *Life of Francesco Guicciardini.* 1968. Knopf. 1st Am. 336p. VG+/dj. M20. $18.00

RIDPATH, Ian. *Illustrated Encyclopedia of Astronomy & Space.* 1976. Crowell. 1st. F/F. M2. $20.00

RIDPATH, Ian. *Messages From the Stars.* 1978. Harper Row. 1st. ils. 241p. VG/dj. K5. $15.00

RIEDER, Hermann. *Atlas of Urinary Sediments: With Special Reference...* 1899. Lonodn. 1st Eng trans. 111p. A13. $200.00

RIEFENSTAHL, Leni. *A Memoir.* 1993. NY. 669p. F/dj. A17. $12.50

RIESENBERG, Felix. *Golden Gate: Story of San Francisco Harbor.* 1940. Knopf. 1st. NF/VG. O4. $15.00

RIESENBERG, Felix. *Golden Gate: Story of San Francisco Harbor.* 1940. NY. Tudor. sm 8vo. ils/photos. 347p. red cloth. NF/NF. K7. $20.00

RIGBY, Ray. *Hill.* 1965. John Day. 1st Am. F/VG+. B4. $75.00

RIGG, Robert B. *How To Say Alive in Vietnam.* 1966. Stackpole. 1st. NF/sans. B4. $100.00

RIGG, Robert B. *Red China's Fighting Hordes.* 1952. Harrisburg. 1st revised. ils/index. 378p. VG/VG. B5. $35.00

RIGGS, S.R. *Dakota-English Dictionary.* 1992. NM Hist Soc. rpt 1890 ed. M/wrp. A17. $25.00

RIGGS, S.R. *Grammar & Dictionary of the Dakota Language.* 1852. Smithsonian. 338p. bl-gray cloth. xl. VG. K7. $550.00

RIGSBY, Olga. *Cook's Quick From Scratch.* 1989. CT. Pennington. VG/dj. A16. $15.00

RIHBANY, Abraham Mitrie. *Syrian Christ.* 1916. Houghton Mifflin. 426p. VG. B29. $9.00

RIKER, Ben. *Pony Wagon Town.* 1948. Indianapolis. 1st. sgn. 312p. G+/dj. B18. $22.50

RILEY, J.H. *Birds From Siam & the Malay Penninsula...* 1938. Smithsonian. ils. 579p. VG. S15. $30.00

RILEY, James Whitcomb. *'Ef You Don't Watch Out.* (1908). Bobbs Merrill. ils Betts. brd. G+. B15. $100.00

RILEY, James Whitcomb. *Flying Islands of the Night.* 1913. Bobbs Merrill. 4to. dj. R5. $250.00

RILEY, James Whitcomb. *Riley Child-Rhymes With Hoosier Pictures.* 1898 (1890). Bobbs Merrill. 188p. gilt cloth. VG. M20. $20.00

RILEY, James Whitcomb. *Riley Farm-Rhymes.* 1883-1901. Bobbs Merrill. 187p. gilt cloth. VG. M20. $20.00

RILEY, James Whitcomb. *Riley Love-Lyrics With Life Pictures by Wm B Dyer.* (1899). Indianapolis. tall 12mo. 191p. gilt gr cloth. VG+. H1. $40.00

RILEY, James Whitcomb. *While the Heart Beats Young.* 1906. Bobbs Merrill. ils Ethel Betts. 110p. gr cloth/pict label. VG. D1. $75.00

RILEY, Pat. *Show Time.* 1988. Bantam. 1st. sgn. phtoos. F/F. P8. $65.00

RILEY, Pat. *Winner Within.* 1993. Putnam. 1st. sgn. F/F. A23. $45.00

RILEY, Ridge. *Road to Number One.* 1977. Doubleday. 1st. VG/G+. P8. $25.00

RILEY. *Poems of Childhood.* 1943. Artists/Writers Guild. sm 4to. VG/G. M5. $35.00

RILING, Ray. *Guns & Shooting, a Selected Bibliography.* 1951. NY. 1st. 1/1500. ils. VG/dj. B18. $125.00

RILKE, Rainer Maria. *Lay of Love & Death of Cornet Christopher Rilke.* 1948. London. Lindsay Drummond. 1st Eng. German/Eng text. F. B14. $75.00

RILKE, Rainer Maria. *Letters to Merline 1919-1922.* 1951. London. 1st Eng. F/VG. M19. $35.00

RIMINGTON, Critchell. *Merchant Fleets.* 1944. Dodd Mead. 293p. torn dj. T7. $25.00

RINEHART, Mary Roberts. *Out Trail.* 1932. NY. McBride. 8vo. 246p. red cloth. F7. $25.00

RING, Alfred A. *Valuation of Real Estate.* 1979. Prentice Hall. 2nd. NF/NF. W2. $30.00

RING, M. *Dentistry: An Illustrated History.* 1985. NY. 1st. 319p. A13. $50.00

RING, Ray. *Telluride Smile.* 1988. Dodd Mead. 1st. author's 1st book. F/NF. H11/M15. $65.00

RINGGOLD, Faith. *Tar Beach.* 1991. NY. Crown. 1st. folio. glossy brd. F/F. B4. $85.00

RINGWALD, Donald C. *Steamboats for Rondout.* 1981. Providence, RI. Steamboat Hist Soc. ils/maps. 145p. dj. T7. $45.00

RINGWALT, J.L. *Development of Transportation Systems in the United States.* 1888. Phil. self pub. 1st. 398p. cloth. xl. M1. $750.00

RINK, Henry. *Tales & Traditions of the Eskimo With a Sketch...* 1875. Edinburgh/London. Wm Blackwood. 472p. recent half morocco. P4. $350.00

RINTOUL, W. *Drilling Ahead, Tapping California's Richest Oil Fields.* 1981. Santa Cruz. Valley Pub. 291p. cloth. NF/dj. D8. $30.00

RIPLEY, Alexandra. *Scarlett.* 1991. Warner. 1st. 823p. NF/dj. W2. $40.00

RIPLEY, Dillon. *Paddling of Ducks.* 1957. 1st. ils. VG/G+. M17. $15.00

RIPLEY, S. Dillon. *Rails of the World.* 1984. Smithsonian. ils/41 unbound mc pl. F/heavy paper portfolio. S15. $30.00

RIPLEY, William Z. *Main Street & Wall Street.* 1927. Little Brn. 1st. 359p. purple cloth. NF. B22. $7.00

RIPPERGER, H. *Coffee Cookery.* 1940. 1st. 94p. VG. E6. $15.00

RISTER, C.C. *Southern Plainsmen.* 1939. OK U. 1st. photos/map. 289p. NF. M4. $35.00

RITCH, Johnny. *Horse Feathers.* 1941. Helena, MT. A19. $40.00

RITCHIE, Carson I.A. *Eskimo & His Art.* 1975. London/New York. 1st. 67 photos. VG/dj. P4. $50.00

RITENOUR, John S. *Old Tom Fossit, a True Narrative...* 1926. Pittsburgh. ils. 269p. G. B18. $19.50

RITTENHOUSE. *Santa Fe Trail: Historical Bibliography.* 1986. 1/500. sgn. map. 718 entries. ES. VG. A4. $85.00

RITTER, Ema I. *Life at the Old Amphibian Airport.* 1970. Santa Ana, CA. 1st. NF/dj. H1. $30.00

RITTER, L.S. *Glory of Their Times: Story of Early Days of Baseball...* 1966. NY. photos. 300p. F/dj. M4. $20.00

RITZ, David. *Blue Notes Under a Green Felt Hat.* 1989. NY. DIF. 1st. NF/F. H11. $20.00

RITZER. *Rainer Maria Rilke, Bibiographie.* 1951. Wein. O Kerry. 344p. VG/wrp. A4. $125.00

RIVERS, Joan. *Still Talking.* 1991. Turtle Bay. 1st. sgn. F/F. A23. $32.00

RIVERS, Thomas. *Miniature Fruit Garden; or, Culture of Pyramidian...* 1859. London. Longman. 8th. 85p. A10. $65.00

RIVERS, Thomas. *Miniature Fruit Garden; or, Culture of Pyramidian...* 1870. 15th. ils. VG. E6. $35.00

RIVERS-COFFEY, Rachel. *Horse Like Mr Ragman.* 1977. Scribner. 1st. VG/G. O3. $20.00

RIVKIN, S. *Mama Meichulim, Traditional Jewish Cooking Made Easy.* 1960. G+. E6. $20.00

RIZK, Salom. *Syrian Yankee.* 1952. Doubleday. sgn. 317p. cloth. VG/torn. W1. $10.00

ROARK, R.J. *Formulas for Stress & Strain.* 1938. McGraw Hill. 1st. 326p. G. D8. $9.00

ROBB, Charles. *Red O'Leary Wins Out.* 1927. NY. 1st. ils. 287p. VG/dj. B5. $25.00

ROBBINS, Archibold. *Journal Comprising Account of Loss of Brig Commerce...* 1825. Hartford. 18th. 275p. G. B5. $60.00

ROBBINS, Clifton. *Mystery of Mr Cross.* 1933. Appleton. VG. N4. $20.00

ROBBINS, Harold. *Memories of Another Day.* 1979. S&S. 1st trade. F/F. T12. $25.00

ROBBINS, John. *Tooth Fairy Is Broke.* 1988. Darnstown, MD. Clark-Davis. 1st. ils/sgn Rae Owings. lg 8vo. F/F. C8. $45.00

ROBBINS, Tom. *Another Roadside Attraction.* 1971. Doubleday. 1st. author's 1st book. F/NF. D10. $495.00

ROBBINS, Tom. *Jitterbug Perfume.* 1984. Bantam. 1st. F/NF. B3. $50.00

ROBBINS, Tom. *Skinny Legs & All.* 1990. Bantam. 1st. F/F. R14. $25.00

ROBERT, Maurice. *Le Katanga Pysique.* 1927. Bruxelles. Lamertin. 1st. 8vo. 29 pl/6 fld maps/plans/ils. VG/wrp. W1. $12.00

ROBERT, Otto. *Outlaws of Cave-in-Rock.* 1924. Clark. 1st. ils/maps/facsimiles. 364p. VG. J2. $900.00

ROBERT & WARDE. *Code for Collector of Beautiful Books.* 1936. LEC. 1st. VG. K3. $20.00

ROBERTS, Brian B. *Chronological List of Antarctic Expeditions.* 1958. Cambridge. Scott Polar Research Inst. prt wrp. P4. $75.00

ROBERTS, Catherine. *Real Book About Making Dolls & Doll Clothes.* (1951). Garden City. 8vo. 191p. G+. T5. $15.00

ROBERTS, Daniel. *Quaker of the Olden Time, Being a Memoir of John Roberts.* 1898. London. Headley Bros. 507p. xl. V3. $25.00

ROBERTS, David. *Cattle Breeds & Origin.* 1916. Waukesha, WI. self pub. 177p. cloth. VG. A10. $48.00

ROBERTS, E.H. *Viability of Seeds.* 1972. Syracuse. 12 separately authored chapters. 448p. F. S15. $12.00

ROBERTS, Edwards. *Shoshone & Other Western Wonders.* 1888. Harper. A19. $35.00

ROBERTS, Gillian. *Penguins & Polar Bears.* 1993. London. Grange. 30 postcards in sc bdg. M. P4. $14.50

ROBERTS, Henry W. *Aviation Radio.* 1945. Morrow. 1st. inscr. ils. VG/dj. K3. $25.00

ROBERTS, Jim. *Gene Autry & the Prairie Fire.* 1950s. London. Adprint Ltd. pub file copy. as new. R5. $200.00

ROBERTS, John. *Manual of Modern Surgery: Exposition of Accepted Doctrines.* 1890. Phil. 1st. 800p. A13. $100.00

ROBERTS, Kenneth. *Antiquamania, Collected Papes of Prof Milton Kilgallen.* 1928. NY. 1st. ils. 260p. G. B18. $25.00

ROBERTS, Kenneth. *Boon Island.* 1956. Doubleday. 1st. F/NF. H11. $25.00

ROBERTS, Kenneth. *Oliver Wiswell.* 1940. Doubleday Doran. 1st. NF/dj. Q1. $50.00

ROBERTS, Lee; see Martin, Robert.

ROBERTS, Ned H. *Muzzle-Loading Cap Lock Rifle.* 1958. Stackpole. 5th. 308p. VG. A17. $32.50

ROBERTS, Norman C. *Baja California Plant Field Guide.* 1989. La Jolla. ils/map/photos. as new/photo wrp. B26. $23.00

ROBERTS, O.W. *Narrative of Voyages & Excursions on East Coast...* 1965 (1827). Gainesville. rpt. ils/fld map. 302p+9p index. gilt cloth. NF. M12. $17.50

ROBERTS, Oral. *Exactly How You May Receive Your Healing Through Faith.* 1958. Oral Roberts Evang Assn. 1st. sgn. 12mo. VG/VG. B11. $15.00

ROBERTS, Susan. *Magician of the Golden Dawn: Story of Aleister Crowley.* 1978. Contemporary Books. 1st. NF/F. R10. $15.00

ROBERTS, Thomas. *Birds of Minnesota.* 1932. Minneapolis. 2 vol. 1st. 4to. ils. F. C6. $185.00

ROBERTS, W. Adolphe. *Haunting Hand.* 1926. Macaulay. 1st. VG/VG. B4. $1,000.00

ROBERTS, W. Adolphe. *Single Star.* 1949. Bobbs Merrill. 1st. F/VG+. B4. $175.00

ROBERTSON, A. Haeworth. *Coming Revolution in Social Security.* 1981. Security. 1st/3rd prt. 376p. F/F. W2. $30.00

ROBERTSON, Don. *Rare Birds of the West Coast.* 1980. Pacific Grove. photos/maps/11 mc pl. 496p. NF/NF. S15. $25.00

ROBERTSON, Frank C. *Ram in the Thicket.* 1950. Hastings. A19. $35.00

ROBERTSON, George. *Discovery of the Tahiti: Journal of the 2nd Voyage...* 1948. London. Hakluyt Soc. 8vo. 292p. gilt bl cloth. P4. $95.00

ROBERTSON, Heather. *Terrible Beauty: Art of Canada at War.* 1977. Toronto. Lorimer. 1st. F/NF. T12. $40.00

ROBERTSON, Keith. *Henry Reed, Inc.* 1958. Viking. 1st. ils Robert McCloskey. VG/VG-. P2. $65.00

ROBERTSON, Mary Elsie. *Clearing.* 1982. Atheneum. 1st. F/F. B4. $45.00

ROBERTSON, Mary Elsie. *What I Have To Tell You.* 1989. Doubleday. 1st. 322p. F/F. W2. $25.00

ROBERTSON, Morgan. *Down to the Sea.* 1905. Harper. 1st. VG. M2. $40.00

ROBERTSON, Morgan. *Where Angels Fear To Tread.* 1889. Century. 1st. VG. M2. $65.00

ROBERTSON, Pat. *New Millennium: 10 Trends That Will Impact You...* 1990. Word. 322p. F. B29. $6.50

ROBESON, Kenneth; see Goulart, Ron.

ROBESON, Paul. *Paul Robeson Speaks: Writings, Speeches, Interviews 1918-74.* 1978. Brunner/Mazel. 1st. edit PS Foner. F/F. M25. $75.00

ROBIE, Virginia. *Historic Styles of Furniture.* 1916. ils. VG. M17. $25.00

ROBIN, Jeff. *Adventure Heroes.* 1994. Facts on File. 1st. F/dj. M2. $35.00

ROBIN, Jeff. *Encyclopedia of Super Villains.* 1987. Facts on File. 1st. F/dj. M2. $35.00

ROBIN, Jeff. *Mars!* 1978. LA. Corwin. 1st. 4to. 244p. VG. K5. $20.00

ROBINSON, Anthony. *Departure From the Rules.* 1960. Putnam. 1st. sgn. 316p. F/dj. B18. $19.50

ROBINSON, Arthur. *Early Thematic Mapping in History of Cartography.* 1982. Chicago. sm 4to. ils. 266p. F/VG. A4. $125.00

ROBINSON, Charles E. *Cruise of the Widgeon: 700 Miles in a Ten Ton Yawl...* 1876. London. Chapman Hall. 4 woodcuts. 268p. T7. $115.00

ROBINSON, Charles N. *Old Naval Prints: Their Artists & Engravers.* 1924. London. The Studio. 1/1500. 4to. 96 pl. teg. gilt buckram. F. B24. $250.00

ROBINSON, Conway. *Account of Discoveries in the West...* 1848. Richmond. Shepard Colin. 491p. T7. $180.00

ROBINSON, Doane. *History of Dakota or Sioux Indians.* 1967. Minneapolis. rpt. 8vo. ils/photos/maps. 523p. F/dj. K7. $195.00

ROBINSON, E.A. *Dionysus in Doubt.* 1925. Macmillan. 1st. 1/350. sgn. quarter cloth/brd/label. uncut. F. M24. $75.00

ROBINSON, Edward Arlington. *Amaranth.* 1934. Macmillan. 1st. 105p. cloth. VG+/dj. M20. $25.00

ROBINSON, Elmo Arnold. *Universalist Church in Ohio.* 1923. OH Universalist Convention. 1st. 275p. VG. B18. $15.00

ROBINSON, F.N. *Complete Works of Geoffrey Chaucer.* nd. London. Oxford. Student Cambridge ed. G/dj. K5. $30.00

ROBINSON, George O. *Oak Ridge Story.* 1950. Kingsport. Southern Pub. 1st. VG/dj. K3. $35.00

ROBINSON, Heath. *Heath Robinson At War.* 1942. London. Methuen. 1st. 48p. prt paper wrp. paper dj. R5. $275.00

ROBINSON, Heath. *Heath Robinson's Book of Goblins.* 1934. London. Hutchinson. 1st. 7 full-p pl. 4to. dk bl cloth. R5. $400.00

ROBINSON, Heath. *Inventions.* 1973. Duckworth. 1st. ils. 147p. VG/VG. D1. $30.00

ROBINSON, Ione. *Wall To Paint On.* 1946. Dutton. 1st. VG/dj. V4. $25.00

ROBINSON, Jackie. *Breakthrough to the Big League.* 1965. Harper. 1st. inscr. 178p. F/NF. B4. $250.00

ROBINSON, Judith. *Tom Cullen of Baltimore.* 1949. NY. 1st. 453p. A13. $30.00

ROBINSON, Kim Stanley. *Escape From Katmandu.* 1989. Tor. 1st trade. F/dj. M2/P3. $20.00

ROBINSON, Kim Stanley. *Remaking History.* 1991. Tor. 1st. F/F. G10. $25.00

ROBINSON, M.S. *MacPherson Collection: Pageant of Sea of Maritime Prints...* 1950. London. Halton. 4to. 16 mc pl/210 halftones. 264p. T7. $150.00

ROBINSON, Marilynne. *Housekeeping.* 1980. Farrar Straus. 1st. author's 1st book. F/dj. Q1. $75.00

ROBINSON, R.J. *Brain & Early Behavior: Development in Fetus & Infant.* 1969. London. Academic. 374p. gr cloth. VG/dj. G1. $32.50

ROBINSON, Robert E. *William Hazlitt's Life of Napoleon Buonaparte.* 1959. Geneva. Librairie Droz. inscr. 8vo. 108p. VG. T10. $25.00

ROBINSON, Thomas. *Common Law of Kent; or, Customs of Gavelkind.* 1741. London. Nutt Gosling. contemporary calf/rebacked. M11. $450.00

ROBINSON, Tom. *In & Out.* 1943. Viking. 1st. ils Marguerite deAngeli. 140p. G+. T5. $25.00

ROBINSON, Victor. *Pathfinders in Medicine.* 1929. NY. 2nd. 810p. A13. $125.00

ROBINSON, W.W. *Lawyers of Los Angeles.* 1959. Los Angeles. 1st. F/G. O4. $15.00

ROBINSON, W.W. *Maps of Los Angeles From Ord's Survey of 1849...* 1966. Dawson's Bookshop. 1/380. sm folio. sgn. gray cloth. F. R3. $400.00

ROBINSON & ROBINSON. *Starseed.* 1991. Ace. 1st. F/F. M2. $25.00

ROBINSON & SCORTIA. *Gold Crew.* 1980. Warner. 1st. VG/dj. P3. $20.00

ROBINSON & SCORTIA. *Prometheus Crisis.* 1975. Doubleday. 1st. VG/dj. P3. $25.00

ROBINSON. *Readings About Children's Literature.* 1966. 444p. xl. VG. A4. $35.00

ROBISON, Mary. *Amateur's Guide to the Night.* 1983. Knopf. 1st. F/F. R13. $25.00

ROBISON, Mary. *Subtraction.* 1991. Knopf. 1st. F/F. R13. $20.00

ROBOTTI, Frances Diane. *Whaling & Old Salem.* 1950. Newcomb Guass. 1st. 192p. VG/ragged. M20. $40.00

ROBSON, A.W. Mayo. *Cancer of the Stomach.* 1907. NY. 1st Am. 218p. A13. $100.00

ROCHE, Henri-Pierre. *Jules & Jim.* 1963. London. Caldar. 1st Eng. F/NF clip. B4. $150.00

ROCHESTER, A. *Nursery Rhymes.* ca 1935. Raphael Tuck. obl 4to. stiff wrp w/diecuts of children. R5. $75.00

ROCHESTER, A. *Why Farmers Are Poor: Agricultural Crisis in the US.* 1940. Internat Pub. 1st. VG/VG. V4. $20.00

ROCHESTER, Earl of. *Works, Containing Poems on Several Occasions, His Letters...* 1714. London. Tonson. 1st collected. 310p. early pub calf. H13. $495.00

ROCK, J.F. *Amnye Ma-Chen Range & Adjacent Regions.* 1956. Rome. 1st. 80 photos/5 fld maps. 194p. NF. W3. $485.00

ROCK, J.F. *Sandalwoods of Hawaii.* 1916. Honolulu. ils. 43p. F/wrp. B26. $26.00

ROCKEFELLER, John D. Jr. *Last Rivet: Story of Rockefeller Center.* 1940. NY. 1st. ils. suede cloth. F. B5. $40.00

ROCKFELLOW, John A. *Log of an Arizona Trail Blazer.* 1933. Acme. 1st. ils 201p. B19. $55.00

ROCKNE, Dick. *Bow Down to Washington.* 1975. Strode. 1st. VG/VG. P8. $30.00

ROCKWELL, Carey. *Tom Corbett: Robot Rocket (#8).* 1956. Grosset Dunlap. 181p. VG/dj (lists to this title). M20. $20.00

ROCKWELL, F.F. *Gardening Under Glass.* 1923. Doubleday. 297p. VG. A10. $25.00

ROCKWELL, Robert F. *Frederick Carder & His Steuben Glass 1903-1933.* 1966. Dexter. sm 4to. 35p. VG. H1. $22.50

ROCKWOOD, Roy. *Dave Dashaway & His Hydroplane (#2).* 1913. Cupples Leon. lists 5 titles. 202p. VG/ragged. M20. $25.00

ROCKWOOD, Roy. *Great Marvel Series: By Air Express to Venus (#8).* 1929. Cupples Leon. lists 9 titles. 248p. VG/dj. M20. $95.00

ROCKWOOD, Roy. *Great Marvel Series: Five Thousand Miles Underground (#3).* 1908. Cupples Leon. lists 6 titles. VG/dj. M20. $85.00

ROCKWOOD, Roy. *Great Marvel Series: Lost on the Moon (#5).* 1911. Cupples Leon. lists 7 titles. 248p. orange cloth. VG/2nd dj art. M20. $125.00

ROCKWOOD, Roy. *Great Marvel Series: On a Torn-Away World (#6).* 1913. Cupples Leon. lists 7 titles. 246p. gr cloth. VG/2nd dj art. M20. $50.00

ROCKWOOD, Roy. *Great Marvel Series: Through Space to Mars (#4).* 1910. Cupples Leon. lists 6 titles. 248p. VG/dj. M20. $60.00

ROCKWOOD, Roy. *Great Marvel Series: Under the Ocean to South Pole (#2).* 1907. Cupples Leon. lists 9 titles. 248p. VG/3rd dj art. M20. $80.00

ROCKWOOD, Roy. *Through Space to Mars; or, The Longest Journey on Record.* 1910. Cupples Leon. 8vo. 248p. T10. $50.00

RODGERS, Andrew D. *Noble Fellow: William Starling Sullivant.* 1940. NY. 1st. 14 pl/3 maps. 361p. VG/dj. B26. $25.00

RODMAN, Seldon. *Caribbean.* 1968. Hawthorne. 1st. 4to. 320p. dj. F3. $15.00

RODRIGUES DA COSTA, Antonio. *Embaixada Que fes o Excellentissimo Senhor Conde deVillar...* 1694. Lisbon. Miguel Manescal. 1st/only. folio. woodcuts. 319p. 18th-C calf. R15. $1,500.00

RODRIGUEZ DA CASTRO, Jose. *Biblioteca Espanola.* 1781-1786. Madrid. Imprenta Real Gazeta. 2 vol. 1st/only. lg folio. F. R15. $3,800.00

RODRIGUEZ DE RIBAS, Ignacio. *Caraquenos: Llego la Epoca Feliz del Desengano...* 1812. Cadiz. Imprenta Real. 1st/only. folio. unbound. R15. $750.00

RODRIQUEZ, Manuel. *Rum & Roosters.* (1957). Crowell. 1st. 256p. dj. F3 $15.00

ROE, Alfred Seelye. *Twenty-Fourth Regiment MA Volunteers 1861-1866.* 1907. Worcester, MA. 24th Veteran Assoc. 1st. 573p. cloth. VG. M8. $175.00

ROE, F. Gordon. *Sporting Prints of the 18th & 19th Centuries.* 1927. Payson Clarke. 4to. 50 pl. teg. gilt red cloth. NF. B24. $75.00

ROE, Francis. *Doctors & Doctor's Wives.* 1990. NAL. 1st. author's 1st book. F/F. W2. $75.00

ROE, Fred. *Old Oak Furniture.* 1907. McClurg. 1st. 8vo. teg. VG. T10. $75.00

ROEBUCK, Carl. *World of Ancient Times.* 1966. Scribner. 8vo. ils/maps. 758p. VG. W1. $10.00

ROEBUCK & STAEHLE. *Photography: Its Science & Practice.* 1942. NY. 1st. 283p. A17. $17.50

ROEDIGER, Virginia More. *Ceremonial Costumes of the Pueblo Indians...* 1941. CA U. 1st. 4to. 40 full-p pl. 251p. buckrum. as new/dj. K7. $275.00

ROESLER, Hugo. *Atlas of Cardio-Roentgenology.* 1940. Springfield. 1st. 124p. A13. $100.00

ROESSEL, Ruth. *Navajo Studies at Navajo Community College.* 1971. Navajo Community College. 1st. ils. 128p. F/sans. B19. $20.00

ROETHKE, Theodore. *Straw for the Fire.* 1972. Doubleday. 1st. NF/NF. R14. $35.00

ROFES, Eric. *Kids Book of Divorce.* 1981. Lexington, MA. Lewis Pub. 3rd. 8vo. F/F. C8. $15.00

ROFF. *Bibliography of the Writings of Charles & Mary Lamb.* 1979. 1/450. 304p. F. A4. $35.00

ROGAN, Helen. *Mixed Company: Women in the Modern Army.* 1981. NY. Putnam. 1st. 333p. rem mk. VG/dj. A25. $18.00

ROGER, J.E. *Shell Book.* 1951. Boston. Branford. revised. 503p. cloth. B1. $35.00

ROGER-MARX, Claude. *Jacques Zucker.* 1969. Paris. Petrides. ils pres/sgn. English/French text. cloth. dj. D2. $100.00

ROGERS, Andrew D. *Bernhard Eduard Fernow: Story of North Am Forestry.* nd. Princeton. 623p. dj. A10. $35.00

ROGERS, David Banks. *Prehistoric Man of the Santa Barbara Coast.* 1929. Santa Barbara. Mus Nat Hist. ils/fld map. 452p. D11. $175.00

ROGERS, Ernest E. *Connecticut's Naval Office at New London.* 1933. New London, CT. New London Co Hist Soc. 1/750. ils. 357p. teg. T7. $55.00

ROGERS, Eugene. *Beyond the Barrier: Story of Byrd's Expedition...* 1990. Annapolis. Naval Inst. 1st/2nd prt. 8vo. M/dj. P4. $28.00

ROGERS, Fairman. *Manual of Coaching.* 1900. Lippincott. 1/1500. rebound quarter leather. VG. O3. $900.00

ROGERS, Francis M. *Europe Informed: An Exhibition of Early Books...* 1966. Harvard/Columbia. ils/index. F/wrp. O7. $45.00

ROGERS, Fred Blackburn. *Filings From an Old Saw: Reminiscences of San Francisco...* 1956. SF. John Howell. 1/750. 8vo. ftspc Stockton. gr cloth. F. R3. $45.00

ROGERS, H.C.B. *Mounted Troops of the British Army 1066-1945.* 1959. London. 1st. ils. 256p. VG/poor. M4. $20.00

ROGERS, Henry M. *Memories of Ninety Years.* 1928. 1st. 409p. O8. $12.50

ROGERS, J.A. *Nature Knows No Color-Line.* 1952. NY. self pub. 1st. 1/2000. 242p. F. B4. $200.00

ROGERS, James E. Thorold. *Six Centuries of Work & Wages: History of English Labour.* nd. Putnam. G. V4. $12.50

ROGERS, Mary. *Rotten Book.* 1969. Harper Row. 1st. ils Steven Kellogg. F/VG. T5. $30.00

ROGERS, Pat. *Oxford Ils History of English Literature.* 1987. Oxford. 528p. F/dj. A17. $25.00

ROGERS, Samuel. *Pleasures of Memory. In Two Parts.* 1805. Portland, ME. Prt for Daniel Johnson. 12mo. 127p. M1. $175.00

ROGERS, Stanley. *Ships & Sailors.* 1928. Little Brn. 1st. 8vo. VG. T10. $45.00

ROGERS, Will. *Ether & Me or Just Relax.* 1929. NY. Putnam. 1st. NF/VG. L3. $125.00

ROGERS, Will. *Illiterate Digest.* 1924. Boni. 1st. author's 2nd book. VG. L3. $85.00

ROGERS, Will. *Letters of a Self-Made Diplomat to His President.* 1926. NY. Boni. 1st. NF/pict dj. L3. $250.00

ROGERS, Will. *Wit & Wisdom.* 1936. NY. Stokes. 1st/2nd prt. photos. NF. L3. $45.00

ROGIN, Gilbert. *Fencing Master & Other Stories.* 1965. Random. 1st. rem mk. NF/F. B4. $50.00

ROGOW, Roberta. *Futurespeak: A Fan's Guide to Language of Science Fiction.* 1991. Paragon. 1st. 408p. NF/dj. M21. $15.00

ROHAN, Michael Scott. *Anvil of Ice.* 1986. Morrow. 1st Am. F/dj. M2. $25.00

ROHAN, Michael Scott. *Hammer of the Sun.* 1988. Morrow. 1st Am. F/dj. M2. $25.00

ROHMER, Sax. *Brood of the Witch Queen.* 1924. Doubleday. 1st. G. P3. $45.00

ROHMER, Sax. *Day the World Ended.* nd. AL Burt. NF/dj. M2. $60.00

ROHMER, Sax. *Dope.* 1925. London. VG. M2. $12.00

ROHMER, Sax. *Drums of Fu Manchu.* 1939. Doubleday Crime Club. 1st. F/NF. M15. $400.00

ROHMER, Sax. *Drums of Fu Manchu.* 1939. Doubleday Crime Club. 1st. VG. P3. $75.00

ROHMER, Sax. *Mask of Fu Manchu.* 1932. Doubleday Crime Club. 1st. F/clip. M15. $450.00

ROHMER, Sax. *Orchard of Tears.* 1969. Bookfinger. 1st Am. F/sans. M2. $25.00

ROHMER, Sax. *She Who Sleeps.* 1928. Doubleday Doran. 1st. VG. M19. $35.00

ROHRBAUGH, John W. *Event-Related Brain Potentials.* 1990. NY. Oxford. 384p. blk cloth. G1. $50.00

ROIPHE, Anne Richardson. *Up the Sandbox!* 1970. S&S. 1st. F/VG+. B4. $65.00

ROJANKOVSKY, Feodor. *Powder: Story of Colt, a Duchess & the Circus.* 1933. Paris. Domino. sgn/#d. 4to. stiff paper wrp. glassine dj. R5. $375.00

ROJANKOVSKY, Feodor. *Tall Book of Nursery Tales.* 1944. Harper. 1st. 120p. VG/dj. D1. $95.00

ROJANKOVSKY, Feodor. *Tall Book of Nursery Tales.* 1944. NY. Harper. early ed. G+/dj. C8. $25.00

ROJAS-LOMBARDI, Felipe. *A to Z No-Cook Cookbook.* 1972. NY. R-L Creations/World. ils Dorothy Ivens. sm 4to. VG+/G+. C8. $20.00

ROLFE. *Nicholas Crabbe.* 1958. London. 1st. intro C Woolf. VG/dj. T9. $65.00

ROLLE, A. *John Charles Fremont.* 1991. OK U. 1st. ils. F/dj. M4. $30.00

ROLLIN, M. *Ancient History of the Egyptians, Assyrians, Bablyonians...* 1851. London. Wm Tegg. ils/maps/engraved ftspc. Riviere bdg. H13. $495.00

ROLLINS & SHAW. *Genus Lesquerella in North America.* 1973. Cambridge. ils/maps/tables. 288p. VG+. B26. $19.00

ROLLYSON, Carl. *Nothing Ever Happens to the Brave: Story of Martha Gellhorn.* 1990. St Martin. 1st. F/F. R13. $15.00

ROLPH, E.H. *Women of the Streets: Sociological Study...* 1955. London. Secker Warburg. 1st. 248p. VG. A25. $18.00

ROLTZ, L.T.C. *Picture History of Motoring.* 1956. Macmillan. 1st. 160p. cloth. VG/dj. M20. $25.00

ROMBAUER, Irma S. *Cookbook for Boys & Girls.* 1946. Bobbs Merrill. 1st. tall 8vo. VG. M5. $75.00

ROMBAUER, Irma S. *Joy of Cooking.* 1972. Bobbs Merrill. G. A16. $20.00

ROMBERGER, J.A. *Meristems, Growth & Development in Woody Plants.* 1963. WA. USDA. 214p. cloth. B1. $26.50

ROME, Anthony; see Albert, Marvin H.

ROMERO, George A. *Dawn of the Dead.* 1978. St Martin. 1st. F/dj. M2. $35.00

ROMILLY, Eric. *Bleeding From the Roman.* 1949. London. 1st. F/dj. M2. $15.00

ROMOLI, Kathleen. *Colombia: Gateway to South America.* 1941. Doubleday. 1st. 4to. 364p. G. M20. $15.00

RONAN, Colin. *Edmund Halley: Genius in Eclipse.* 1970. London. Macdonald. 1st Eng. ils. 251p. VG/dj. K3. $25.00

RONAN, Colin. *Encyclopedia of Astronomy.* ca 1980. Secaucus, NJ. Chartwell. ils. 240p. VG/dj. K5. $20.00

RONNBERG, Erik. *To Build a Whaleboat.* 1985. New Bedford. ODHS Whaling Mus. ils. 150p. dj. T7. $45.00

ROONEY, Andy. *Word for Word.* 1986. Putnam. 1st. F/F. B35. $20.00

ROONEY, Mickey. *Life Is Too Short.* 1991. Villard. 1st. sgn. F/F. $50.00

ROONEY, Mickey. *Search for Sonny Skies.* 1994. Birch Lane. 1st. sgn. F/F. A23. $40.00

ROOSEVELT, Robert Barnwell. *Game Birds of the North Carleton.* 1866. NY. A19. $75.00

ROOSEVELT, Robert Barnwell. *Superior Fishing; or, Striped Bass, Trout & Black Bass...* 1985. NM Hist Soc. facsimile 1865 ed. 310p. F/dj. A17. $22.50

ROOSEVELT, Theodore. *African Game Trails.* 1910. Scribner. 1st. gilt gr bdg. VG+. B5. $95.00

ROOSEVELT, Theodore. *African Game Trails.* 1910. Scribner. 1st. photos/map. 529p. G. H7. $30.00

ROOSEVELT, Theodore. *African Game Trails.* 1910. Scribner. 1st. 8vo. photos. NF. A15. $125.00

ROOSEVELT, Theodore. *Book-Lover's Holidays in the Open.* 1925. Scribner. 8vo. 373p. VG. F7. $30.00

ROOSEVELT, Theodore. *Ranch Life & the Hunting-Trail.* 1907. Century. sm 4to. ils Remington. teg. stp City of Boston. H7. $55.00

ROOSEVELT, Wyn. *Frontier Boys in the Grand Canyon.* 1908. NY. Platt Peck. ils Schneider. white cloth. VG. F7. $30.00

ROOT, Charles P. *Automobile Troubles & How To Remedy Them.* 1916. Chicago. revised. ils. 255p. G+. B18. $15.00

ROOT, Ralph Rodney. *Camouflage With Planting.* 1942. Chicago. Seymour. 79p. VG/self wrp. A10. $35.00

ROOT, Ralph Rodney. *Contourscaping.* 1941. Chicago. Seymour. 246p. dj. A10. $85.00

ROOT, Waverley. *Foods of France.* 1958. Knopf. 2nd. dj. B10. $50.00

ROOT, William Pitt. *Storm & Other Poems.* 1969. Atheneum. 1st. assn copy. poet's 1st book. F/dj. V1. $55.00

ROPER, M. *Feet of Fines for County of York From 1300 to 1314.* 1965. Wakefield. M11. $45.00

ROPER, Stephen. *Engineer's Handy-Book.* 1881. 10th thousand. ils/charts. limp wraparound leather. VG. M17. $30.00

ROPES, John C. *Army Under Pope.* 1881. 1st. ils/maps/index. 229p. O8. $23.50

ROQUELAURE, A.N.; see Rice, Anne.

RORER, Sarah Tyson. *Mrs Rorer's New Cook Book: A Manual of Housekeeping.* 1902. Phil. Arnold. 731p. fair. B10. $15.00

ROSA, Joseph. *West of Wild Bill Hickok.* 1982. Norman, OK. 1st. 223p. VG/VG. J2. $195.00

ROSA, Rodrigo Rey. *Pelcari Project.* 1991. London. Peter Owen. 1st. F/NF. A24. $30.00

ROSE, Elizabeth. *Socerer's Apprentice.* 1968. NY. Walker. 1st Am. sm 4to. unp. VG. C14. $12.00

ROSE, John. *English Vineyard Vindicated.* 1966. Herb Growers. 1/250. facsimile 1675 London ed. 27p. VG. B10. $75.00

ROSE, Mark. *Science Fiction.* 1976. Prentice Hall. 1st. NF/dj. M2. $22.00

ROSE & ROSE. *Shattered Ring.* 1970. Knox. 1st. NF/dj. M2. $12.00

ROSEN, Edward. *Naming of the Telescope.* 1947. NY. Schuman. 1st. 110p. dj. K5. $45.00

ROSEN, Richard. *Fadeaway.* 1986. Harper Row. 1st. F/F. P3/P8. $16.00

ROSEN, Ruth Chier. *Wendy & Chip's Kitchen Debut.* 1956. ASF Ent. sbdg. VG. M5. $45.00

ROSENBACH, A.S.W. *Book Hunter's Holiday.* 1936. Houghton Mifflin. 1/760. sgn. F/glassine dj. T10. $200.00

ROSENBACH, A.S.W. *Books & Bidders: Adventures of a Bibliophile.* 1927. 77 pl. 402p. VG/dj. A4. $65.00

ROSENBACH, A.S.W. *Early American Children's Books, With Bibliographical...* 1966. 4to. ils. 413p. F/NF. A4. $165.00

ROSENBACH, A.S.W. *Unpublishable Memoirs.* 1924. London. CAstle. 1st. VG/dj. K3. $40.00

ROSENBERG, Arthur. *Professor an der Universitat Berlin.* 1931. London. trans from German. VG/dj. B14. $45.00

ROSENBERG, David A. *Marcos & Martial Law in the Philippines.* 1979. Ithaca. Cornell. 315p. F/VG. P1. $14.00

ROSENBERG, Nancy. *Interest of Justice.* 1993. Dutton. 1st. 368p. F/F. W2. $35.00

ROSENBLATT, Frank. *Principles of Neurodynamics: Perceptrons & Theory...* 1962. WA, DC. Spartan. 616p. red cloth. VG. G1. $50.00

ROSENBLATT, Samuel. *Yossele Rosenblatt: Story of His Life As Told By His Son.* 1954. FSY. 371p. G+. S3. $30.00

ROSENE, Walter. *Bobwhite Quail: Its Life & Management.* 1969. Rutgers. 418p+65 photos+5 mc pl+2 maps. F/dj. A17. $50.00

ROSENFELD, Alvin H. *Double Dying: Reflections on Holocaust Literature.* 1980. IU. 210p. VG+/dj. S3. $29.00

ROSENGARTEN, Joseph George. *German Soldier in the Wars of the United States.* 1886. Lippincott. 1st thus. 47p. half leather/marbled brd. M8. $85.00

ROSENTHAL, Jacques. *Bibliotheca Magica et Pneumatica, Geheime Wissenschaften...* 1903-04. 1/150. 8875 entries. 680p. F. A4. $125.00

ROSENTHAL, M.L. *She.* 1977. BOA Ed. 1/14 (pres). sgns. F. V1. $125.00

ROSENTHAL, Stuart. *Cinema of Federico Fellini.* 1976. AS Barnes/Tantivy. ils. NF. C9. $50.00

ROSENZWEIG, Mark R. *Neural Mechanisms of Learning & Memory.* 1976. MIT. 4to. ils. bl cloth. G1. $50.00

ROSIGNOLI, Guido. *Badges & Insignia of WWII: Air Force-Naval-Marine.* 1983. NY. ils. 363p. VG/VG. S16. $25.00

ROSKE, Ralph. *Everyman's Eden: History of California.* 1968. Macmillan. 1st. 8vo. 624p. blk/yel cloth. VG/tattered. T10. $45.00

ROSKIES & ROSKIES. *Shtetl Book.* 1975. Ktav/ADL. 327p. VG. S3. $25.00

ROSKILL, S.W. *Navy at War, 1939-1945.* 1960. London. Collins. 43 photos/24 maps. 480p. T7. $40.00

ROSNER, Fred. *Studies in Torah Judaism: Modern Medicine & Jewish Law.* 1972. Yeshiva. 216p. VG. S3. $25.00

ROSNER, Paul. *Princess & the Goblin.* 1966. Sherbourne. 1st. VG/dj. M25. $35.00

ROSS, Blake. *Golden Crucible.* 1930. SF. 1/1000 (of 1125) on India Antique paper. G+. O4. $25.00

ROSS, D.A. *Introduction to Oceanography.* 1970. NY. Appleton Century Crofts. 384p. VG. D8. $8.50

ROSS, David. *Letters From Foxy.* 1966. Pantheon. 1st Am. 103p. cloth. VG/clip. M20. $18.00

ROSS, James. *They Don't Dance Much.* 1940. Houghton Mifflin. 1st. F/F. B4. $500.00

ROSS, James. *Treatise on the Diseases of the Nervous System.* 1883. NY. Wm Wood. 2 vol. 2nd revised/1st Am prt. ES. xl. G1. $750.00

ROSS, Lillian. *Portrait of Hemingway.* 1961. S&S. 1st. G/G. B35. $16.00

ROSS, Patricia. *In Mexico They Say.* 1946. Knopf. 3rd. 211p. dj. F3. $15.00

ROSS, Roselle. *Kankie Kangaroo...Who Couldn't Hop.* 1945. Maxton. ils Paul Kaloda/Charles E Bracker. die-cut bdg. VG. M5. $65.00

ROSS, Sam. *He Ran All the Way.* 1947. NY. 1st. NF/VG clip. B4. $150.00

ROSS, W. Gillies. *Arctic Whalers Icy Seas.* 1985. Tor. 1st. 263p. F/dj. A17. $25.00

ROSS & KENNEDY. *Bibliography of Negro Migration.* 1934. NY. Columbia. 1st. 251p. cloth. VG+. M8. $75.00

ROSS & ROSS. *Imperial Glass.* 1971. Wallace-Homestead. 8vo. mc pl. sbdg. VG. H1. $26.00

ROSS & ROSS. *Long Road South.* 1968. Mitchell. 1st. 168p. F3. $15.00

ROSSELLINI, Roberto. *War Trilogy.* 1973. Grossman. 1st. 467p. F/dj. A17. $15.00

ROSSETTI, Christina. *Goblin Market.* nd. Lippincott. ils Rackham/4 mc pl. 42p. cloth. VG+/dj. M20. $200.00

ROSSETTI, Christina. *Goblin Market.* nd. London. TC & EC Jack. 1st probable thus. lg 24mo. F. C8. $25.00

ROSSETTI, Christina. *Goblin Market.* 1893. Macmillan. 1st. ils Laurence Housman. tall 12mo. aeg. gr cloth. R5. $550.00

ROSSETTI, Christina. *Goblin Market.* 1933. Lippincott. 1st. ils Rackham/4 full-p mc pl. red cloth/label. R5. $125.00

ROSSETTI, D.G. *Henry the Leper.* 1905. Boston. Bibliophile Soc. 1/10 (of 467). Japanese vellum/deluxe bdg. teg. B24. $950.00

ROSSETTI, D.G. *Poems.* 1873. Leipzig. Tauchnitz. 1st Continental/1st state. full vellum. M24. $100.00

ROSSETTI, D.G. *Poems.* 1881. Ellis White. new ed. gilt bl cloth. M24. $100.00

ROSSETTI, W.M. *Life of John Keats.* 1887. London. Walter Scott. 1st. teg. gilt maroon cloth. F. M24. $75.00

ROSSI, Agnes. *Quick.* 1992. Norton. 1st. author's 1st book. F/dj. A24. $30.00

ROSSNER, Judith. *Looking for Mr Goodbar.* 1975. S&S. 1st/MTI. F/dj. M25. $35.00

ROSTEN, Leo. *Dear Herm.* 1975. WH Allen. 1st Eng. F/F. B35. $18.00

ROSTEN, Norman. *Under the Boardwalk.* 1968. Prentice Hall. 1st. F/F. B4. $100.00

ROSTEN & SHAW. *Marilyn Among Friends.* 1987. Bloomsbury. VG/dj. P3. $20.00

ROSTENBERG, Leona. *English Publishers in the Graphic Arts 1599-1700.* 1963. NY. Franklin. 40 full-p pl. cloth. R12. $65.00

ROSTENBERG, Leona. *Library of Robert Hooke: Scientific Book Trade...* 1989. Santa Monica. Modoc. 8vo. preface Nicolas Barker. R12. $30.00

ROSTENBERG, Leona. *Minority Press & the English Crown: A Study in Repression...* 1971. Nieuwkoop. De Graaf. 4to. ils. cloth. R12. $75.00

ROSTENBERG & STERN. *Old & Rare: Forty Years in the Book Business.* 1988. Santa Monica. Modoc. 8vo. ils. pb. R12. $20.00

ROSTENBERG & STERN. *Old Books in the Old World.* 1996. New Castle. Oak Knoll. ltd ed. sgns. cloth. case. R12. $45.00

ROSVALL, Toivo David. *Very Stupid Folk.* 1938. Dutton. 1st. ils Tibor Gergely. VG+/VG. C8. $45.00

ROTH, Barry. *Annotated Bibliography of Jane Austen Studies.* 1985. VA U. 1st. as new. V4. $25.00

ROTH, Cecil. *Haggadah.* 1957. Jerusalem. Massadah Alumoth. 1st trade. 8vo. ils Szyk. box. B24. $250.00

ROTH, Gunther D. *Amateur Astronomer & His Telescope.* 1963. Van Nostrand. trans Alex Helm. xl. dj. K5. $14.00

ROTH, Henry. *Shifting Landscape: A Composite 1925-1987.* 1987. Jreidh Pub Soc. 2nd. VG/VG. V4. $22.50

ROTH, Philip. *Anatomy Lesson.* 1983. Franklin Lib. 1st. sgn. aeg. full leather. F. Q1. $75.00

ROTH, Philip. *Anatomy Lesson.* 1983. FSG. 1st. F/dj. A24. $25.00

ROTH, Philip. *Breast.* 1972. HRW. 1st. F/F. B35. $35.00

ROTH, Philip. *Deception.* 1990. S&S. 1st. F/F. T12. $15.00

ROTH, Philip. *Facts.* 1988. FSG. ARC. RS. F/dj. Q1. $35.00

ROTH, Philip. *Goodbye, Columbus.* 1959. Houghton Mifflin. 1st. author's 1st book. NF/NF. H11. $450.00

ROTH, Philip. *Goodbye, Columbus.* 1966. Modern Lib. 1st thus. F/NF clip. R14. $30.00

ROTH, Philip. *Our Gang.* 1971. NY. Random. 1st. author's 5th book. NF/F. H11. $30.00

ROTH, Philip. *Our Gang.* 1971. Random. 1st. F/F. B35. $35.00

ROTH, Philip. *Partrimony.* 1991. S&S. 1st. sgn. F/F. R14. $45.00

ROTH, Philip. *Portnoy's Complaint.* 1969. Random. ltd. 1/600. sgn/#d. F/case. B4. $350.00

ROTH, Philip. *Portnoy's Complaint.* 1969. Random. 1st. F/dj. B35. $38.00

ROTH, Philip. *Reading Myself & Others.* 1975. FSG. 1st. F/F. B35. $18.00

ROTHERHAM, E.R. *Flowers & Plants of New South Wales & Southern Queensland.* 1975. Sydney. 556 mc pl/map ep. 191p. F/dj. B26. $65.00

ROTHMAN & SIMEONE. *Spine.* 1975. Phil. Saunders. 2 vol. 8vo. ils. bl cloth. VG. G1. $65.00

ROTHSTEIN, Arden. *Learning Disorders: An Integration of Neuropsychological...* 1989. Internat U. 382p. blk cloth. F/dj. G1. $32.50

ROTHWELL, H.T. *Duet for Three Spies.* 1967. Roy. 1st. F/F. P3. $10.00

ROTSLER, William. *Zandra.* 1973. Doubleday. 1st. F/dj. M2. $25.00

ROTTENSTEINER, Franz. *Science Fiction Book: Illustrated History.* 1975. Seabury. 1st. F/dj. M2. $15.00

ROTZLER, Willy. *Constructive Concepts: History of Constructive Art...* 1989. NY. Rizzoli. revised. 332p. cloth. dj. D2. $60.00

ROUECHE, Berton. *Feral.* 1974. Harper Row. 1st. VG/dj. P3. $18.00

ROUNDS, Glen. *Stolen Pony.* 1948. Holiday House. sgn/sketch. VG/VG. O3. $25.00

ROUQUETTE, Dominique. *Fleurs d'Amerique. Poesies Nouvelles.* 1856. Nouvelle-Orleans. 1st. inscr. 12mo. 303p. M1. $175.00

ROURKE, Constance. *Troupers of the Gold Coast; or, Rise of Lotta Crabtree.* 1928. Harcourt Brace. 1st. G+/sans. O4. $20.00

ROUSE, John E. *Criollo, Spanish Cattle in the Americas.* 1977. Norman, OK. 303p. dj. A10. $40.00

ROUSE, John E. *World Cattle.* 1972. Norman, OK. 2 vol. boxed. A19. $50.00

ROUSE, Parke Jr. *Great Wagon Road: From Philadelphia to the South.* 1973. Am Trails series. ils. VG. M17. $20.00

ROUSE, Parke Jr. *Great Wagon Road: From Philadelphia to the South.* 1973. McGraw Hill. VG/VG. O3. $65.00

ROUSSEAU, Jean-Jacques. *Confessions of Jean-Jacques Rousseau.* 1955. NY. LEC. 1st thus. 1/1500. ils/sgn Wm Sharp. F/glassine/box. Q1. $100.00

ROUSSEAU, Victor. *Messiah of the Cylinder.* 1917. McClurg. 1st. ils Joseph Clement Coll. VG. M2. $150.00

ROUX, Georgette. *Gerda & Peter & Mr Boo.* 1943. Chicago. private prt. 1/50. sgn pres. 8vo. textured cloth. R5. $200.00

ROWAN, A.N. *Of Mice, Models & Men.* 1984. Albany. 8vo. 323p. VG. B1. $26.50

ROWE, John. *Introduction to Archaeology of Cuzco.* 1944. CAmbridge. ils. VG/wrp. O7. $45.00

ROWE, John. *Long Live the King.* 1984. Stein Day. VG/VG. P3. $15.00

ROWE, Nicholas. *Works of...* 1756. London. 2 vol. leather. VG. A15. $50.00

ROWE, Richard. *Jack Afloat & Ashore.* 1875. London. Smith Elder. 268p. T7. $45.00

ROWELL, Galen. *Mountains of the Middle Kingdom: Exploring...China & Tibet.* 1983. Sierra Club. 1st. photos. VG/VG. M17. $30.00

ROWELL, Galen. *Poles Apart: Parallel Visions of Arctic & Antarctic.* 1995. Berkeley. 1st. ils/photos. 183p. map ep. bl cloth. NF/dj. P4. $65.00

ROWELL, Raymond J. *Ornamental Flowering Shrubs in Australia.* 1991. Kensington, NSW. 28 mc photos. 334p. as new. B26. $36.00

ROWLAND, B. *Birds With Human Souls: A Guide to Bird Symbolism.* 1978. Knoxville. ils. 213p. pict cloth. NF/NF. M12. $30.00

ROWLAND, John. *Pro Rege & Populo Anglicano Apologia...* 1651. Antwerp. Verdussen. 12mo. vellum. R12. $375.00

ROWLAND, John. *Rutherford: Atom Pioneer.* 1957. NY. VG/dj. K3. $12.00

ROWLAND, Peter. *Disappearance of Edwin Drood.* 1992. St Martin. 1st Am. F/NF. N4. $25.00

ROWLAND, Phyllis. *Every Day in the Year.* 1959. Little Brn. 1st. sm 4to. unp. VG. C14. $17.00

ROWLANDS, John J. *Cache Lake Country.* 1990. Lyons Burford. rpt. 272p. as new/dj. S15. $15.00

ROWLEY, Gordon D. *Caudiciform & Pachycaul Succulents.* 1987. Mill Valley. ils/photos. 282p. M/dj. B26. $85.00

ROWLEY, Gordon D. *Ils Encyclopedia of Succulents.* 1978. Crown. 4to. 256p. F/VG. A22. $75.00

ROWLEY, Gordon D. *Name That Succulent.* 1980. Cheltenham, Eng. 268p. M/dj. B26. $27.50

ROWLEY, Gordon D. *Repertorium Planatarum Succulentarium. Vols I-XXX.* 1950-1979. Utrecht/Richmond. Surrey. Vols I-XX in 1 vol bdg/balance unbound. ils. F. B26. $140.00

ROWLEY, Gordon D. *Succulent Compositae.* 1994. Mill Valley. photos. M/dj. B26. $35.00

ROWNDREE, Lester. *Flowering Shrubs of California & Their Value...* 1948 (1939). Stanford. 2nd. ils. VG+/torn. B26. $45.00

ROWSE, A.L. *Shakespeare's Southampton.* 1965. Harper Row. 1st Am. 323p. VG/dj. M20. $25.00

ROWSOME, Frank. *Verse by the Side of the Road.* 1965. Brattleboro. 2nd. lg 12mo. cloth. F/F. C8. $20.00

ROXAS, Manuel. *Problems of Philippine Rehabilitation & Trade Relations.* 1947. Manila. Bureau of Prt. 208p. VG. P1. $10.00

ROXBOROUGH, Henry. *Stanley Cup Story.* 1966. Follett. revised/1st prt. photos. VG. P8. $20.00

ROXBURGH, Ronald. *Origins of Lincoln's Inn.* 1963. Cambridge. M11. $85.00

ROY, Gabrielle. *Tin Flute.* 1947. Reynal Hitchcock. 1st. VG. P3. $25.00

ROY, Maurice. *Dynamics of Satellites.* 1963. Academic. 8vo. 335p. xl. K5. $45.00

ROY & SEBAG. *Tunisia.* 1961. NY. Orion. 1st. 164p. G. W1. $10.00

ROYAL, William R. *Man Who Rode Sharks.* 1978. Dodd Mead. 1st. sgn. VG/VG. B11. $35.00

ROYCE, C.C. *Cherokee Nation of Indians.* 1975. Chicago. photos/3 maps. 272p. F. M4. $40.00

ROYCE, Kenneth. *Miniatures Frame.* 1972. S&S. 1st. VG/VG. P3. $15.00

ROYCE. *Balzac Bibliography, Writings Relative to Life & Works...* 1929 & 1930. 2 vol. VG/dj. A4. $95.00

ROYLE, A. *Geostatistics.* 1980. McGraw Hill. 168p. F. D8. $22.00

ROZE, Uldis. *North American Porcupine.* 1989. Smithsonian. 1st. ils. 261p. F/F. S15. $20.00

ROZENBERG, Georgii V. *Twilight.* 1966. NY. Plenum. 8vo. 358p. VG. K5. $55.00

ROZIER, John. *Granite Farm Letters.* 1988. 330p. O8. $9.50

RUARK, Gibbons. *Rescue the Perishing.* 1991. Baton Rouge. LSU. 1st. F/NF. R13. $15.00

RUARK, Robert. *Something of Value.* 1955. 1st. NF/VG+. S13. $55.00

RUARK, Robert. *Uhuru.* 1962. McGraw Hill. 1st. 555p. NF. W2. $20.00

RUARK, Robert. *Use Enough Gun.* 1966. NAL. 1st. F/NF. H11. $55.00

RUARK, Robert. *Use Enough Gun.* 1966. NY. 1st. NF. A17. $30.00

RUBENSTEIN, Leonard. *Great Spy Films.* 1979. Citadel. 1st. VG/VG. P3. $20.00

RUBER, Peter. *Last Bookman.* 1968. NY. Candlelight. 1st. sgn. VG/dj. K3. $35.00

RUBIE, Peter. *Werewolf.* 1991. Longmeadow. 1st. F/F. P3. $16.00

RUBIN & RUGIN. *Old Boston Fare in Food & Pictures.* 1976. 1st. photos. VG/G+. E6. $20.00

RUBY, Robert H. *Ogala Sioux.* 1955. Vantage. VG/dj. A19. $50.00

RUCKER, Rudy. *Hollow Earth.* 1990. NY. Morrow. 1st. 8vo. 308p. half cloth. P4. $35.00

RUCKER, Rudy. *Secret of Life.* 1985. Bluejay. 1st. F/dj. M2. $25.00

RUDD, Hugh R. *Hocks & Moselles.* 1935. Constable. 1st. 165p. fld map. B10. $45.00

RUDD, W.H. *Orrocco Poultry Farm.* 1893. Boston. Rudd. 64p. wrp. A10. $35.00

RUDEAU, Charlotte. *Josie, Jay & Jerri & Yoga.* 1973. np. sgn. 128p. VG/wrp. B11. $18.00

RUDHYAR, Dane. *Astrological Houses.* 1972. Doubleday. 1st. VG. P3. $10.00

RUDORFF, Raymond. *House of Brandersons.* 1973. Arbor. 1st. G/G. M2. $20.00

RUDWICK, M.J.S. *Great Devonian Controversy: Shaping of Scientific Knowledge.* 1985. Chicago. 494p. M/dj. D8. $42.50

RUE, Leonard Lee. *Game Birds of North America.* 1973. Outdoor Life. 490p+25 full-p pl. NF/dj. A17. $17.50

RUFF, Willie. *Call to Assembly: Autobiography of Musical Storyteller.* 1991. Viking. 1st. 432p. F/F. B4. $45.00

RUFFNER, Budge. *All Hell Needs Is Water.* 1972. AZ U. 1st. ils. 96p. F/NF. B19. $25.00

RUGE, Friedrich. *Rommel in Normandy.* 1979. San Rafael. photos/maps/index. 266p. VG/VG. S16. $26.50

RUGGLE, George. *Ignoramus. Comedia.* 1630. London. 2nd. 12mo. engraved ftspc. calf. R12. $325.00

RUGGLERO, Leonard F. *American Marten, Fisher, Lynx & Wolverine in W US.* 1994. USDA Forest Service. lg 8vo. maps. F. S15. $12.00

RUGGLES, Alice McGuffey. *Story of the McGuffeys.* 1950. ils. 141p. VG/VG. A4. $35.00

RUGGLES, R.G. *One Rose.* 1964. Oakland. 1st. sgn. VG/dj. B5. $80.00

RUHL, Arthur. *Central Americans: Adventures & Impressions...* 1928. Scribner. 1st. 284p. F3. $20.00

RULE, Ann. *Small Sacrifices.* 1987. NAL. 1st. F/wht dj. A24. $15.00

RUMER, Thomas A. *Wagon Trains of '44, a Comparative View...* 1990. Clark. 1st. ils/maps. 273p. VG/dj. J2. $75.00

RUNDELL, Maria Eliza. *New System of Domestic Cookery, Formed Upon Principles...* 1807. Boston. Andrews Cummings Blake. 2nd. 297p. contemporary bdg. M1. $225.00

RUNDELL, Maria Eliza. *New System of Domestic Cookery, Formed Upon Principles...* 1864. 32mo. 348p. VG. E6. $75.00

RUNTE, Alfred. *Yosemite: Embattled Wilderness.* 1990. Lincoln, NE. NE U. 1st. ils. lg 8vo. F/NF. O4. $30.00

RUNYON, Charles. *I, Weapon.* 1974. Doubleday. 1st. F/dj. M2. $25.00

RUNYON, Damon. *Rest of Runyon.* 1938. Stokes. 1st. ils Nicholas Bentley. xl. VG/clip. B4. $100.00

RUNYON, Damon. *Take It Easy.* 1938. Stokes. 1st. VG+/VG+ clip. B4. $350.00

RUPPEL, A. *Gutenberg Jahrbuch 1926.* 1926. Mainz. 202p+10 pl & ads. cloth. G. A17. $30.00

RUPPELT, Edward J. *Report on Unidentified Flying Objects.* 1956. Doubleday. 8vo. 243p. VG. K5. $15.00

RUSCH, Kristine Kathryn. *Gallery of His Dreams.* 1991. Axolotl. sgn. F/F. P3. $35.00

RUSE, Gary Alan. *Houndstooth.* 1975. Prentice hall. 1st. NF/dj. M2. $12.00

RUSH, Hanniford. *Man to the Moon.* 1962. Chicago. Rand McNally. 4to. 96p. VG/wrp. K5. $8.00

RUSH, Norman. *Whites.* 1986. Knopf. 1st. F/F. B4. $75.00

RUSH, Norman. *Whites.* 1986. London. Heinemann. 1st. F. B3. $35.00

RUSHDIE, Salman. *East, West.* 1994. London. Cape. 1st. sgn. F/F. B3. $85.00

RUSHDIE, Salman. *Grimus: A Novel.* 1979. NY. Overlook. 1st Am. author's 1st book. F/F. D10. $150.00

RUSHDIE, Salman. *Grimus: A Novel.* 1979. Overlook. 1st Am. author's 1st book. F/clip. Q1. $100.00

RUSHDIE, Salman. *Haroun & the Sea of Stories.* 1990. London. Granta. true 1st. author's 5th novel. F/F. D10. $50.00

RUSHDIE, Salman. *Haroun & the Sea of Stories.* 1990. Viking. ARC. RS. B35. $35.00

RUSHDIE, Salman. *Haroun & the Sea of Stories.* 1990. Viking. 1st. w/sgn bookplate. F/F. B2. $35.00

RUSHDIE, Salman. *Midnight's Children.* 1981. Knopf. 1st. F/dj. B4. $275.00

RUSHDIE, Salman. *Satanic Verses.* 1988. Viking. 1st. F/F. from $50 to $55.00

RUSHER, William A. *Coming Battle for the Media.* 1988. Morrow. 1st. 228p. F/F. W2. $25.00

RUSHING, Lilith. *Cake Cookbook.* 1965. Chilton. 1st. G/dj. A16. $45.00

RUSHKIN, John. *Sesame & Lilies.* nd (1900). NY. 12mo. full dk bl leather. F. H3. $125.00

RUSHKOPF, Douglas. *Cyberia: Life in the Trenchs of Hyper.* 1994. Harper. 1st. F/dj. P3. $22.00

RUSHTON, Charles. *Furnace for a Foe.* 1957. London. 1st. VG/dj. M2. $20.00

RUSHWORTH, William. *Sheep.* 1899. Buffalo. 1st. 496p+14p ads. G. B5. $45.00

RUSK, Ralph Leslie. *Literature of the Middle Western Frontier.* 1962. Frederick Ungar. 2 vol. 1st. VG+/clip. $40.00

RUSKIN, John. *Arrows of the Chace, Being a Collection...* 1880. Orpinton. George Allen. 2 vol. 1st ed. ils. H13. $195.00

RUSKIN, John. *Art of England. Lectures Given at Oxford.* 1884. Orpington. George Allen. 1st. sm 4to. 272p. full blk polished morocco. H13. $295.00

RUSKIN, John. *King of the Golden River.* nd (1945). Hyperion. VG/G. C14. $15.00

RUSKIN, John. *Poems.* 1882 (1882). John Wiley. sm 8vo. 234p. teg. gilt tan cloth. VG. H1. $75.00

RUSKIN, John. *Sesame & Lilies.* ca 1900. Barse Hopkins. 12mo. full dk bl leather. H3. $75.00

RUSS, Joanna. *Extra (Ordinary) People.* 1984. St Martin. 1st. F/dj. P3. $25.00

RUSS, Joanna. *Two of Them.* 1978. Berkley Putnam. 1st. F/F. P3. $20.00

RUSSELL, A.P. *Library Notes.* 1875. NY. Hurd Houghton. 1st. VG. K3. $15.00

RUSSELL, Alan Kinglsey. *Rivals of Sherlock Holmes 2.* 1981. Castle. VG/dj. P3. $15.00

RUSSELL, Alan. *Forest Prime Evil.* 1992. Walker. 1st. sgn. F/dj. A24. $35.00

RUSSELL, Austin. *Charles M Russell, Artist.* 1957. Twayne. 1st. 247p. VG/VG. J2. $145.00

RUSSELL, Austin. *Mr Arrow.* 1947. Veechhurst. 1st. VG/dj. M2. $27.00

RUSSELL, Bertrand. *Authority & the Individual.* 1949. Unwin Bros. 1st. B35. $45.00

RUSSELL, Bertrand. *Autobiography...* 1967-69. Boston. Little Brn. 1st Am/1st prt. bl, red & gr cloth. djs. M24. $75.00

RUSSELL, Bertrand. *Nightmares of Eminent Persons.* 1954. Dutton. 1st. F/NF. M19. $25.00

RUSSELL, Bill. *Go Up for Glory.* 1966. Coward McCann. 1st. photos. VG+/G+. P8. $25.00

RUSSELL, Bill. *Second Wind.* 1979. Random. 1st. VG+/dj. P8. $15.00

RUSSELL, Carl. *Firearms, Traps & Tools of the Mountain Men.* 1967. Knopf. 1st. 448p. VG/VG. J2. $225.00

RUSSELL, Carl. *Guns on the Early Frontier: A History of Firearms...* 1980. NE U. ils. 395p. F. M4. $25.00

RUSSELL, Charles Edward. *A-Rafting on the Mississippi.* 1928. Century. 1st. fld map. VG+. B2. $35.00

RUSSELL, Charles Edward. *Outlook for the Philippines.* 1922. NY. Century. 411p. VG+. P1. $10.00

RUSSELL, Charles M. *Charles M Russell Book.* 1970. 1st. mc pl. F. M19. $45.00

RUSSELL, Charles M. *Trails Plowed Under.* 1927. Doubleday Page. 1st. ils. intro Will Rogers. 212p. brn cloth. VG. K7. $120.00

RUSSELL, Don. *Campaigning With King: Charles King, Chronicler of Old Army.* 1991. NE U. photos. 240p. F/F. A4. $45.00

RUSSELL, Eric Frank. *Dreadful Sanctuary.* 1972. Dobson. VG/VG. P3. $40.00

RUSSELL, Eric Frank. *Men, Martians & Machines.* nd. Roy Pub. 1st Am. F/dj. M2. $75.00

RUSSELL, Eric Frank. *Sinister Barrier.* 1948. Fantasy. 1st. VG/G. P3. $60.00

RUSSELL, Frederick H. *Just War in the Middle Ages... Third Series.* 1977. Cambridge. M11. $75.00

RUSSELL, Howard. *Long, Deep Furror: 3 Centuries of Farming in New England.* 1976. Hanover. 672p. dj. A10. $40.00

RUSSELL, J.H. *Cattle on the Conejo.* 1959. LA. Thomas Litho. A19. $25.00

RUSSELL, Jane. *Jane Russell.* 1985. Franklin Watts. 1st. inscr. F/F. A23. $50.00

RUSSELL, John. *Max Ernst: Life & Work.* 1967. NY. Abrams. 359p. cloth. dj. D2. $235.00

RUSSELL, John. *Paris.* 1983. NY. 1st. ils. VG/VG. T9. $35.00

RUSSELL, Maria. *Beer Makes It Better Cookbook.* 1971. S&S. G/dj. A16. $15.00

RUSSELL, Martin. *Darker Side of Death.* 1985. Collins Crime Club. 1st. VG/dj. P3. $15.00

RUSSELL, Paul. *Salt Point.* 1990. Dutton. 1st. author's 1st book. VG/VG. L1. $30.00

RUSSELL, Ray. *Colony.* 1969. Sherbourne. 1st. NF/dj. M25. $25.00

RUSSELL, Ray. *Colony.* 1969. Sherbourne. 1st. VG/dj. P3. $20.00

RUSSELL, Ray. *Incubus.* 1976. Morrow. 1st. F/dj. M2. $100.00

RUSSELL, Roger W. *Frontiers in Physiological Psychology.* 1966. NY. Academic. 261p. ruled blk cloth. G1. $25.00

RUSSELL, Solveig Paulson. *What Good Is a Tail?* 1962. Bobbs Merrill. 1st. ils Ezra Jack Keats. 4to. F. C8. $25.00

RUSSELL, W. Clark. *Phantom Death.* 1895. Stokes. 1st. VG. M2. $35.00

RUSSO & SULLIVAN. *Bibliography of Booth Tarkington, 1869-1946.* 1949. IN Hist Soc. 322p. VG. A4. $125.00

RUST, Brian. *Complete Entertainment Discography.* 1973. New Rochelle. Arlington. F/NF. B2. $75.00

RUST, Fred Winslow. *Road Ahead & Bypaths.* 1944. Boston. Humphries. 12mo. VG. B11. $18.00

RUST, Fred Winslow. *Unto the Hills.* 1936. Boston. Humphries. 12mo. VG. B11. $18.00

RUTGERS, A. *Birds of Europe.* 1966. London. Methuen. 1st. sm 4to. ils John Gould. F/dj. T10. $50.00

RUTH, Kent. *Great Day in the West, Forts, Posts & Rendezvous...* 1963. Norman, OK. 1st. 308p. VG/VG. J2. $95.00

RUTHERFORD, Douglas. *Black Leather Murders.* 1966. Walker. 1st. VG/VG. P3. $15.00

RUTHERFORD, Douglas. *Collision Course.* 1978. Macmillan. 1st. NF/dj. P3. $16.00

RUTHERFORD, Douglas. *On the Track of Death.* 1959. Abelard Schuman. VG/VG. P3. $15.00

RUTHERFORD, Douglas. *Turbo.* 1980. Macmillan. 1st. NF/NF. P3. $15.00

RUTHERFORD, Ernest. *Radioactive Substances & Their Radiations.* 1913. Cambridge. 1st. 699p. gilt gr cloth. G. H1. $75.00

RUTHERFORD, Ernest. *Radioaktive Substanzen und Ihre Strahlungen.* 1913. Leipzig. Akademische Verlagsgesellschaft. ils. 642p. xl. K3. $65.00

RUTHERFORD, Mildred Lewis. *Address Delivered by Miss Mildred Lewis Rutherford...* ca 1915. Athens. McGregor. 1st. 36p. VG/prt wrp. M8. $22.50

RUTHVEN, Malise. *Torture: The Grand Conspiracy.* 1978. Weidenfeld Nicholson. 1st. 342p. VG+/dj. M20. $20.00

RUTLEDGE, Albert J. *Anatomy of a Park.* 1971. NY. sq 8vo. ils/plans. dj. B26. $29.00

RUTLEDGE, Nancy. *Easy To Murder.* 1951. Crime Club. 1st. VG. P3. $20.00

RUTLEDGE, Nancy. *Frightened Murderer.* 1957. Random. 1st. G/G. P3. $10.00

RUTSALA, Vern. *Window.* 1964. Wesleyan. 1st. poet's 1st book. F/dj. V1. $75.00

RUTTER, John. *Culture & Diseases of the Peach.* 1880. Harrisburg. 95p. cloth. VG. A10. $50.00

RUTTER, Peter. *Sex: In the Forbidden Zone.* 1989. Tarcher. 240p. VG/dj. B29. $9.50

RUTZEBECK, Hjalmar. *Alaska Man's Luck & Other Works by...* 1988. Santa Barbara. Capra. 8vo. 582p. F/dj. P4. $35.00

RUXTON, G.F. *Life in the Far West.* 1951. OK U. 1st. ils. 252p. VG/poor. M4. $25.00

RUZIC, Neil P. *Case for Going to the Moon.* 1965. Putnam. 8vo. 239p. VG/dj. K5. $25.00

RUZICKA, Rudloph. *Walden.* 1930. Lakeside. VG. A20. $35.00

RYAN, Alan. *Bones Wizard.* 1988. Doubleday. 1st. F/dj. M2. $30.00

RYAN, Alan. *Penguin Book of Vampire Stories.* 1991. Bloomsbury Books. F/dj. P3. $20.00

RYAN, Alan. *Reader's Companion to Mexico.* 1995. Harcourt Brace. 1st. 372p. M. F3. $15.00

RYAN, Bob. *Boston Celtics.* 1989. Addison Wesley. 1st. photos. F/F. P8. $27.50

RYAN, Charles C. *Starry Messenger.* 1979. St Martin. 1st. F/F. P3. $20.00

RYAN, Cornelius. *Longest Day: D-Day Story.* 1960. London. photos/maps. 256p. VG/VG. S16. $22.50

RYAN, Ginny. *Margo: Horse Who Wouldn't Stay on the Merry-Go-Round.* 1945. Dietz. 1st. sm 4to. 32p. VG. C14. $14.00

RYAN, J.A. *Town of Milan.* 1928. sgn. 96p. cloth. VG. M20. $40.00

RYAN, Marah Ellis. *Indian Love Letters.* 1911. McClurg. 2nd. 122p. brd. G+. F7. $40.00

RYAN, Nolan. *Throwing Heat.* 1988. Doubleday. 1st. sgn. F/F. A23. $75.00

RYAN, Stella. *Death Never Weeps.* 1992. Harper Collins. 1st. VG/dj. P3. $25.00

RYAN & SMART. *Cooking the French Way.* 1960. Spring Books. revised. VG/fair. B10. $12.00

RYDEN, Hope. *God's Dog.* 1975. NY. photos. 288p. VG/VG. S15. $15.00

RYDER, David Warren. *Men of Rope: Being History of Tubbs Cordage Company...* 1954. SF. Hist Pub. 29 pl. 146p. T7. $35.00

RYDER, J.P. *Breeding Biology of Ross' Goose in Perry River Region...* 1967. Canadian Wildlife. ils. 56p. VG. S15. $7.00

RYDER, Jonathan; see Ludlum, Robert.

RYLANT, Cynthia. *Missing May.* (1992). Orchard Books. 2nd. 8vo. 89p. F/F. T5. $25.00

SAAB, Peter. *Sweetwater Point Motel.* 1981. St Martin. 1st. VG/dj. P3. $15.00

SABARSKY, Serge. *Egon Schiele.* 1985. NY. Rizzoli. 185 mc pl/28 b&w photos. brd. dj. D2. $65.00

SABATINI, Rafael. *Bellarion.* 1926. Houghton Mifflin. 1st Am. NF/VG. B4. $185.00

SABATINI, Rafael. *Hounds of God.* 1928. McClelland Stuart. G. P3. $13.00

SABATINI, Rafael. *Scaramouche.* 1922. McClelland Stewart. VG/dj. P3. $30.00

SABERHAGEN, Fred. *Fifth Book of Lost Swords.* 1989. Tor. 1st. F/F. P3. $17.00

SABERHAGEN, Fred. *Merlin's Bones.* 1995. Tor. 1st. F/dj. P3. $23.00

SABIN, Arthur J. *Red Scare in Court. New York Versus Intern'l Workers Order.* 1993. Phil. 1st. F/F. B2. $30.00

SABLJAK, Mark. *Bloody Legacy.* 1992. Granmercy. 1st. NF/dj. P3. $15.00

SACHAR, Howard M. *Egypt & Israel.* 1981. NY. Richard Marek. 384p. VG/G+. S3. $26.00

SACHAR, Howard M. *Emergence of the Middle East, 1914-1924.* 1969. Knopf. 1st. 518p. VG/dj. W1. $25.00

SACHAR, Howard M. *Israel: Establishment of a State.* 1952. British Book Centre. 332p. VG/fair. S3. $22.00

SACKS, B. *Be It Enacted: Creation of Territory of Arizona.* 1964. Phoenix. A19. $45.00

SACKS, Janet. *Best of Science Fiction Monthly.* 1975. London. 1st. F/dj. M2. $20.00

SACKS, Oliver. *Man Who Mistook His Wife for a Hat & Other Clinical Tales.* 1985. Summit. later prt. 233p. cloth. VG/dj. G1. $22.50

SACKTON, Alexander. *TS Eliot Collection of the University of Texas at Austin.* 1975. Austin. 1st. 1/1500. gilt brn cloth. glassine. M24. $50.00

SACKVILLE-WEST, V. *Saint Joan of Arc.* 1936. London. Cobden Sanderson. 1st. F/VG. B4. $150.00

SACRANIE, Raj. *Stories From Outer Space.* 1979. Chartwell. 1st. F/dj. P3. $10.00

SADAJI & SAITO. *Magic of Trees & Stones. Secrets of Japanese Gardening.* 1965. NY. Japan Pub. 2nd. 282p. dj. A10. $35.00

SADDLEBAGS, Jeremiah. *Journey to the Gold Diggins... Collotype Facsimile...* 1950. Burlingame. Wm Wreden. 1/390. ils Read. F. R3. $65.00

SADEN, Hans. *True History of His Captivity 1557.* 1929. NY. McBride. ils/3 maps. xl. F. O7. $45.00

SADLEIR, Michael. *Anthony Trollope, a Commentary.* 1927. Houghton Mifflin. 1st Am. lg 8vo. 432p. VG. H13. $85.00

SADLEIR, Michael. *XIX Century Fiction: A Bibliographical Record.* nd. 2 vol. rpt. 1/350. ils. F. A4. $185.00

SADLEIR, Michael. *XIX Century Fiction: A Bibliographical Record.* 1951. Cambridge. 1st. 2 vol. 1/1025. inscr/sgn/dtd Christmas 1950. maroon cloth. M24. $450.00

SADLER, Mark; see Lynds, Dennis.

SADOWSKI, Yahya M. *Scuds or Butter? Political Economy of Arms Control...* 1993. WA, DC. Brookings Inst. 1st. 8vo. ils. VG/wrp. W1. $10.00

SAFIRE, William. *Freedom.* 1987. Doubleday. 1st. sgn. 1125p. NF. W2. $30.00

SAFIRE, William. *Full Disclosure.* 1977. Doubleday. 1st. VG/dj. P3. $15.00

SAFRAN, Alexandre. *Kabbalah: Law & Mysticism of Jewish Tradition.* 1975. Feldheim. 339p. VG. S3. $32.00

SAGAN, Carl. *Contact: A Novel.* 1985. S&S. 1st. VG/VG. K5. $20.00

SAGAN, Carl. *Dragons of Eden: Speculations on Evolution...* 1977. Random. 1st. 263p. NF/dj. D8. $10.00

SAGAN, Carl. *Pale Blue Dot.* 1994. Random. 8vo. 429p. G. K5. $15.00

SAGAN, Francoise. *Heart-Keeper.* 1968. Dutton. 1st. NF/dj. P3. $15.00

SAGAN, Francoise. *Painted Lady.* 1983. NY. Dutton. 1st. F/F. T12. $20.00

SAGAN & SHKLOVSKII. *Intelligent Life in the Universe.* 1966. SF. Holden Day. 1st. w/sm tattle tape. F/NF. B4. $250.00

SAGE, Dana. *22 Brothers.* 1950. S&S. G/dj. P3. $20.00

SAGE, Leland L. *William Boyd Allison.* 1956. Iowa City. State Hist Soc IA. A19. $30.00

SAGE, Rufus B. *Rocky Mountain Life.* 1880. Boston. ils. VG. M17. $25.00

SAGGS, H.W.F. *Greatest That Was Babylon.* 1962. Hawthorn. 1st. tall 8vo. 64 b&w pl/line ils. 562p. F/G. H1. $45.00

SAGLE, Lawrence W. *Steam, Diesel & Electric Power of B&O RR, 1829-1964.* 1964. Standard Pr & Pub. 351p. VG/dj. M20. $45.00

SAINSBURY, C.L. *Geology of Lost River Mine Area, Alaska.* 1964. US GPO. 10 pl in pocket fld. 80p. wrp. P4. $38.00

SAINSBURY, Noel. *Billy Smith: Exploring Ace (#1).* 1928. Cupples Leon. 247p. VG+/dj (lists 3 titles). M20. $25.00

SAINSBURY, Noel. *Flying Ace Stories.* nd. Cupples Leon. VG. P3. $20.00

SAINSBURY, Noel. *Gridiron Grit.* 1934. NY. Cupples Leon. 1st. VG. T12. $15.00

SAINT, H.F. *Memoirs of an Invisible Man.* 1987. Atheneum. 1st. sgn. author's 1st novel. NF/NF. M22. $20.00

SAINT-DENIS, Ruth. *Lotus Light.* 1932. Boston. 1st. ils. VG. B5. $25.00

SAINT-GERMAIN, Christopher. *Doctor & Student 1531.* 1970. Menston. Scholar Pr. facsimile. M11. $75.00

SAINT-GERMAIN, Christopher. *Doctor & Student; or, Dialogues Between a Dr of Divinity...* 1721. London. contemporary calf. M11. $450.00

SAINT-JOHN, Bayle. *Village Life in Egypt: With Sketches of the Said, Vol 1.* 1853. Boston. Ticknor Reed Fields. 1st. sm 8vo. W1. $145.00

SAINT-JOHN, H.C. *Notes & Sketches From the Wild Coasts of Nippon.* 1880. Edinburgh. Douglas. 50 engravings/1 fld map. 392p. cloth/leather label. T7. $175.00

SAINT-JOHN, Mrs. H. *Audubon, the Naturalist of the New World...* (1863). Boston. Crosby Nichols. revised corrected w/additions. 12mo. VG. M12. $95.00

SAINT-JOHN. *Osborne Collection of Early Children's Books 1566-1910.* 1958. Toronto Public Lib. 1/1500. 99 pl. 585p. VG. A4. $285.00

SAINT-PIERRE. *Abrege du Projet de Paix Perpetuelle.* 1729. Rotterdam. Beman. 8vo. pub 3-p catalogue at end. quarter calf. R12. $600.00

SAINTE-MARTHE. *Elogia Gallorvm Saecvlo XVI.* 1722. Eisenach. Officina Boetiana. 8vo. vellum. R12. $300.00

SAINTSBURY, George. *Notes on a Cellar-Book.* 1931. Macmillan. 3rd/5th prt. VG/VG. B10. $25.00

SAKI. *Short Stories of Saki.* 1958. Modern Lib. VG/dj. P3. $20.00

SALA, George Augustus. *America Revisited: From the Bay of New York to Gulf...* 1882. London. Vizetelly. 2 vol. 54 pl/400 engravings. 3-quarter gr calf. NF. R3. $300.00

SALE, James. *Few Last Words.* 1970. Macmillan. 1st. NF/dj. P3. $25.00

SALE, Roger. *Seattle, Past to Present.* 1976. Seattle. 2nd. 8vo. 273p. F/dj. T10. $25.00

SALES, Frances. *Ibrahim.* 1989. Lippincott. 1st Am. sm 4to. 31p. F/NF. C14. $17.00

SALGADO, Mathias Antonio. *Monumento do Agradecimiento, Tributo de Veneracam...* 1751. Lisbon. Francisco daSilva. 1st. woodcuts/fld pl. 50p. R15. $4,500.00

SALINGER, J.D. *Catcher in the Rye.* 1951. Little Brn. 1st. author's 1st book. F/F clip. B4. $5,000.00

SALINGER, J.D. *Raise High the Roof Beam, Carpenters.* 1963. Little Brn. 1st/3rd issue. VG/VG. R14. $40.00

SALISBURY, Albert. *Here Rolled the Covered Wagons.* 1948. Superior. dj. A19. $40.00

SALISBURY, Harrison E. *Long March.* 1985. Franklin Lib. 1st. sgn. full leather. F. Q1. $60.00

SALLIS, James. *Black Hornet.* 1994. NY. Carroll Graf. 1st. sgn. F/F. T2. $30.00

SALLIS, James. *Long-Legged Fly.* 1992. NY. Carroll Graf. 1st. sgn. author's 1st novel. F/NF. T2. $45.00

SALMON, Richard. *Trout Flies.* 1975. NY. 1/589. sgn twice. VG/dj/box. B5. $180.00

SALMOND, John A. *Miss Lucy of the CIO: Life & Time of Lucy Randolph Mason...* 1988. Athens, GA. 1st. F/F. B2. $25.00

SALOMONSKY, V.C. *Masterpieces of Furniture in Photographs...* 1953. Dover. rpt. VG. M17. $17.50

SALSBURY & WALSH. *Making of Buffalo Bill: Study in Heroics.* 1928. Bobbs Merrill. 1st. ils. 391p. stp cloth. dj. D11. $50.00

SALSLOW, James M. *Poetry of Michelangelo.* 1991. Yale. 1st. F/F. P3. $45.00

SALTEN, Felix. *Bambi.* July 1928. S&S. 1st Am. sm 8vo. gr pict cloth. VG. C8. $60.00

SALTEN, Felix. *Bambi.* 1942. Grosset Dunlap. 1st. ils Disney Studio. VG/dj. D1. $85.00

SALTER, James. *Arm of Flesh.* 1961. Harper. 1st. sgn. author's 2nd book. F/NF. D10. $365.00

SALTER, James. *Dusk & Other Stories.* 1988. Northpoint. 1st. F/F. from $35 to $45.00

SALTER, James. *Dusk & Other Stories.* 1988. Northpoint. 1st. sgn. F/F. D10. $55.00

SALTER, James. *Hunters.* 1956. Harper. 1st. author's 1st book. F/NF. L3. $750.00

SALTER, James. *Light Years.* 1975. Random. 1st. sgn. author's 4th novel. F/F. D10. $125.00

SALTER, James. *Solo Faces.* 1979. Little Brn. 1st. sgn/dtd. author's 5th novel. F/NF. D10. $110.00

SALTER, James. *Solo Faces.* 1980. London. Collins. 1st. sgn. F/NF clip. R14. $100.00

SALWAY. *Peculiar Gift, Nineteenth Century Writings...* 1976. rpt 40 essays. ils. 573p. F/F. A4. $55.00

SALYER, Alfred Mark. *Salyer's Antics of the Ants Done in Verse & Prose.* 1924. NY. 121p. VG. S15. $25.00

SALZMAN, Mark. *Laughing Sutra.* 1991. Random. 1st. sgn. author's 2nd book. F/F. B3. $60.00

SAMBON, Arthur. *Catalogue des Fresques de Boscoreale.* 1903. Paris. Canessa. 4to. 26p. new cloth spine. xl. T10. $300.00

SAMPLE, Albert Race. *Race Hoss: Big Emma's Boy.* 1984. Austin, TX. Eakin. 2nd. 320p. F/NF clip. B4. $45.00

SAMPLE & SCHWARTZ. *Confessions of a Dirty Ballplayer.* 1970. Dial. 1st. photos. VG+/VG. P8. $20.00

SAMPSON, A. *Seven Sisters: Great Oil Companies & World They Shaped.* 1975. Viking. 334p. NF/G. D8. $25.00

SAMPSON, Emma Speed. *Billy & the Major.* 1918. Reilly Lee. 20th. 299p. VG+/dj. M20. $35.00

SAMPSON, Emma Speed. *Miss Minerva's Problem.* 1936. Reilly Lee. 311p. VG/dj. M20. $35.00

SAMPSON, G. *Historic Churches & Temples of Georgia.* 1987. Mercer U. ils from paintings/drawings. 111p. F/dj. M4. $20.00

SAMPSON, Henry. *History of Advertising: From the Earlies Times.* 1874. London. Chatto Windus. 1st. ils. 616p. red cloth. VG. Q1. $250.00

SAMS, Ferrol. *Widow's Mite.* 1987. Peachtree. 1st. F/F. B35. $32.00

SAMUEL, Maurice. *Jews on Approval.* 1932. 1st. VG+. E6. $25.00

SAMUEL, Maurice. *Whatever Gods.* 1923. Duffield. sgn. 346p. VG. S3. $30.00

SAMUELSEN, Rube. *Rose Bowl Game.* 1951. Doubleday. 1st. inscr. VG. P8. $20.00

SANBORN, Ruth Burr. *Murder on the Aphrodite.* 1935. Macmillan. 1st. xl. VG. P3. $12.00

SANCHEZ, Thomas. *Mile Zero.* 1989. Knopf. ARC. sgn/dtd 1989. F/wrp/box. R14. $40.00

SANCHEZ, Thomas. *Mile Zero.* 1989. Knopf. 1st. inscr. F/F. A20. $30.00

SANCHEZ, Thomas. *Zoot-Suit Murders.* 1978. Dutton. 1st. F/NF. M19. $25.00

SANCHEZ, Thomas. *Zoot-Suit Murders.* 1978. Dutton. 1st. VG+/dj. A20. $20.00

SANCHEZ, Thomas. *Zoot-Suit Murders.* 1978. Dutton. 1st. VG/dj. P3. $18.00

SAND, Algo. *Senor Bum in the Jungle.* 1932. NY. National Travel Club. 319p. F3. $15.00

SAND, George. *Tales of a Grandmother.* 1930. Lippincott. 1st thus. 12 mc pl. 384p. F/dj. H1. $45.00

SANDBORN, F.B. *Genius & Character of Emerson, Lectures at Concord...* 1885. Boston. Osgood. 1st. gilt brn cloth. M24. $125.00

SANDBURG, Carl. *Abraham Lincoln: The War Years.* 1939. Harcourt Brace. 4 vol. 14th prt. gilt bl cloth. F. H1. $50.00

SANDBURG, Carl. *Early Moon.* 1930. Harcourt Brace. 1st. ils James Daugherty. 137p. VG. D4. $50.00

SANDBURG, Carl. *Lincoln Preface.* 1953. NY. 16p. O8. $9.50

SANDBURG, Carl. *More Rootabagas.* 1993. Knopf. 1st. 94p. F/F. C14. $18.00

SANDBURG, Carl. *Poems of the Midwest.* 1946. Cleveland. World. 1st thus. 1/950. #d. VG. Q1. $50.00

SANDBURG, Carl. *Remembrance Rock.* 1948. Harcourt Brace. 1st regular after ltd sgn ed. NF/NF clip. D10. $50.00

SANDBURG, Carl. *Smoke & Steel.* 1920. NY. 1st. sgn. VG. B5. $40.00

SANDERS, Charles W. *Mournful Rides Again.* 1936. Wild West Club. xl. VG. P3. $10.00

SANDERS, Charles W. *Sanders' Pictorial Reader.* 1869. Ivison Phinney Blakeman. enlarged/revised. 12mo. 48p. gr paper brd. T10. $50.00

SANDERS, Dori. *Ideal Land for Farming.* 1990. Alonquin. 1st. sgn. F/wrp. R13. $35.00

SANDERS, Ed. *Tales of Beatnik Glory.* 1975. Stonehill. 1st. NF/VG+. B4. $45.00

SANDERS, George. *Stranger at Home.* 1946. S&S. 1st. VG/dj. P3. $45.00

SANDERS, Lawrence. *Anderson Tapes.* 1970. Putnam. 1st. NF/NF. M19. $25.00

SANDERS, Lawrence. *Capital Crimes*. 1989. Putnam. 1st. F/F. P3. $20.00

SANDERS, Lawrence. *Passion of Molly T.* 1984. Putnam. 1st. VG/dj. P3. $20.00

SANDERS, Lawrence. *Pleasures of Helen*. 1971. Putnam. 1st. F/F. H11. $30.00

SANDERS, Lawrence. *Seduction of Peter S.* 1983. Putnam. 1st. F/F. H11. $35.00

SANDERS, Lawrence. *Sullivan's Sting*. 1990. Putnam. 1st. F/F. T12. $20.00

SANDERS, Lawrence. *Third Deadly Sin*. 1981. Putnam. 1st. NF/dj. P3. $25.00

SANDERS, Lawrence. *Timothy Files*. 1987. Putnam. 1st. F/F. T12. $15.00

SANDERS, T.W. *Fruit & Its Cultivation in Garden & Orchard*. 1945. London. Collingridge. 5th. 288p. VG-. A10. $22.00

SANDERSON, Ivan. *Animal Treasure*. 1937. Viking. 1st. VG/VG. A20. $20.00

SANDERSON, Ivan. *How To Know the American Mammals*. 1951. Boston. ils LA Fuertes. 164p. VG/worn. S15. $20.00

SANDERSON, Ruth. *Story of the First Christmas*. 1994. Atlanta. Turner. 4 3-D mc scenes. ribbon ties. M. T10. $25.00

SANDES, R. *Downtown Jews, Portraits of Immigrant Generation*. 1969. NYC. 1st. photos. VG/VG. E6. $15.00

SANDFORD, John. *Eyes of Prey*. 1991. Putnam. 1st. F/F. H11. $40.00

SANDFORD, John. *Fool's Run*. 1989. Holt. 1st. sgn. F/F. A20. $60.00

SANDLIN, Tim. *Sex & Sunsets*. 1987. Holt. 1st. sgn. author's 1st book. F/dj. A24. $65.00

SANDLIN, Tim. *Sex & Sunsets*. 1987. Holt. 1st. sgn/dtd 1997. F/F. R14. $75.00

SANDLIN, Tim. *Skipped Parts*. 1991. Holt. 1st. sgn. F/F. B3. $40.00

SANDLIN, Tim. *Western Swing*. 1988. Holt. 1st. author's 2nd book. F/dj. A24. $30.00

SANDLIN, Tim. *Western Swing*. 19883. NY. Holt. 1st. sgn. F/F. R14. $45.00

SANDOVAL, Judith Hancock. *Historic Ranches of Wyoming*. 1986. Casper, WY. Nicolaysen Art Mus. A19. $350.00

SANDOZ, Mari. *Beaver Men*. 1964. Hastings. 1st. 1/185. sgn. mc map/photos. 335p. box. J2. $425.00

SANDOZ, Mari. *Beaver Men*. 1964. NY. Hastings. 1st. sgn. NF/VG+ clip. T11. $145.00

SANDOZ, Mari. *Buffalo Hunter*. 1954. Hastings. 1st. NF/VG. T11. $45.00

SANDOZ, Mari. *Capital City*. 1939. Little Brn. 1st. NF/VG. T11. $65.00

SANDOZ, Mari. *Cheyenne Autumn*. 1953. McGraw Hill. 1st. F/NF clip. B4. $200.00

SANDOZ, Mari. *Crazy Horse: Strange Man of the Oglalas*. 1945. Lincoln. dj. A19. $30.00

SANDOZ, Mari. *Old Jules Country*. 1965. Hastings. 1st. VG/VG. P3. $15.00

SANDOZ, Mari. *Story Catcher*. 1968. Phil. Westminster. special ed. dj. A19. $150.00

SANDOZ, Mari. *Winter Thunder*. 1954. Phil. Westminster. A19. $25.00

SANDOZ, Maurice. *Maze*. 1945. Doubleday. ils Salvador Dali. dj. A19. $150.00

SANDOZ, Maurice. *On the Verge*. 1950. Doubleday. 1st. ils Salvador Dali. F/NF. B24. $150.00

SANDS, Oliver Jackson. *Story of Sport & Deep Run Hunt Club*. 1977. Richmond. 1/750. sgn/#d. VG. O3. $165.00

SANDSTROM, Eve. *Death Down River*. 1990. Scribner. 1st. sgn. F/F. A23. $38.00

SANDYS, Charles. *History of Gavelkind & Other Remarkable Customs...* 1851. London. John Russell Kent. fld tables. emb cloth. M11. $175.00

SANFORD, John. *View From the Wilderness: American Literature As History*. 1977. Capra. 1st. inscr. F/dj. T10. $35.00

SANGER, Majory Bartlett. *Checkerback's Journey: Migration of the Ruddy Turnstone*. 1969. Cleveland. 1st. 159p. F/VG. S15. $18.00

SANGER, Richard H. *Arabian Peninsula*. 1954. Cornell. 1st. sgn pres. ils/maps. 295p. VG/dj. W1. $45.00

SANSOM, William. *Last Hours of Sandra Lee*. 1961. Hogarth. 1st. F/clip. A24. $45.00

SANTEE, Ross. *Apache Land*. 1945. Scribner. 1st. inscr/2 mc sketches+hand-colored ils. 216p. VG/worn. B19. $950.00

SANTEE, Ross. *Apache Land*. 1957. Scribner. 1st. 216p. VG/dj. J2. $125.00

SANTEE, Ross. *Cowboy*. 1928. Grosset Dunlap. A19. $45.00

SANTEE, Ross. *Cowboy*. 1977. Lincoln/London. A19. $8.00

SANTESSON, Hans. *Crime Prevention in the 30th Century*. 1970. Walker. VG/dj. M2. $10.00

SANTESSON, Hans. *Fantastic Universe Omnibus*. 1960. Prentice Hall. 1st. VG/torn. M2. $15.00

SANZ, Carlos. *Australia: Su Decubrimiento y Determinacion*. 1973. Madrid. F/stiff wrp. O7. $35.00

SANZ, Carlos. *Bibliografia General de la Carta de Colon*. 1958. Madrid. Victoriano Suarez. 367p. F/wrp. O7. $125.00

SANZ, Charles. *Juan Sebastian Elcano: Autentico Protagonista Prima...* 1973. Madrid. Aguirre. ils/45 maps. NF/prt wrp. O7. $45.00

SAPIENZA, Marilyn. *Cosby Show Scrapbook*. 1986. Weekley Reader BC. TVTI. VG. P3. $4.00

SAPPER. *Island of Terror*. 1931. Musson. 1st. VG. P3. $25.00

SAPPER. *Tiny Carteret*. 1932. Musson/Hodder Stoughton. NF. P3. $15.00

SARAVIA, Antanasio. *Los Missioneros Muertos en el Norte de Nueva Espana*. 1943. Mexico. 2nd. 253p. wrp. F3. $15.00

SARAZEN, Gene. *Better Golf After Fifty*. 1967. NY. 1st. VG/VG. B6. $35.00

SARAZEN, Gene. *Golf Magazine's Your Long Game*. 1964. Harper Row. 1st. sgn. VG/VG. A23. $60.00

SARG, Tony. *Tony Sarg's Savings Book*. 1946. World. 1st. spbdg. NF/VG+. P2. $115.00

SARG, Tony. *Where Is Tommy?* 1932. Greenberg. 1st. obl 4to. VG. M5. $85.00

SARGENT, Charles Sprague. *Trees & Shrubs, Ils of New or Little Known Ligneous Plants*. 1902-1905. Houghton Mifflin. 4 parts in 2 vol. xl. scarce. A10. $95.00

SARGENT, Charles Sprague. *Woods of the United States*. 1885. NY. 7 tables/28p index. 203p. gilt brn cloth. B26. $139.00

SARGENT, F.W. *On Bandaging & Other Operations of Minor Surgery...* 1867. Phil. 3rd. ils. 383p. A13. $350.00

SARGENT, Pamela. *Golden Space*. 1982. Timescape. 1st. F/F. P3. $20.00

SARGENT, Pamela. *Venus of Shadows*. 1988. Doubleday. 1st. F/F. P3. $20.00

SARGENT, Wyn. *People of the Valley. Life With Cannibal Tribe New Guinea*. 1974. NY. 1st/2nd prt. 302p. VG/dj. P4. $35.00

SARNER. *Checklist of Works of Herman Wouk*. 1995. 1/400. sgn. 18 pl. 156p. F/F. A4. $45.00

SAROS, Theodore. *Christmas Lighting & Decorating*. 1954. Van Nostrand. 155p. VG. A10. $25.00

SAROYAN, William. *Hilltop Russians in San Francisco.* 1941. Stanford. JL Delkin. 1/500. 4to. ils. VG/dj. K7. $195.00

SAROYAN, William. *Human Comedy.* 1943. NY. Harcourt Brace. 1st. author's 1st novel. ils Don Freeman. F/VG. T12. $150.00

SAROYAN, William. *My Name Is Aram.* (1940). Harcourt Brace. later prt. sgn. VG/dj. Q1. $40.00

SAROYAN, William. *Sons Come & Go, Mothers Hang in Forever.* 1976. FRanklin Lib. true 1st/ltd. aeg. decor gilt leather. F/sans. T11. $45.00

SARPI, Paolo. *Les Froits des Souverains.* 1721. The Hague. Scheurleer. 2 vol. 8vo. brd. R12. $500.00

SARPI, Paolo. *Rights of Sovereigns & Subjects...* 1707. London. Tonson Barker King. 2 parts in 1. 8vo. gilt calf. R13. $450.00

SARRANTONIO, Al. *Campbell Wood.* 1986. Doubleday. 1st. F/F. P3. $18.00

SARTON, May. *After the Stroke.* 1988. Norton. 1st. F/F. B3. $30.00

SARTON, May. *Anger.* 1982. Norton. 1st. F/F. B3. $40.00

SARTON, May. *As We Are Now.* 1973. Norton. 1st. NF/NF. B3. $45.00

SARTON, May. *As We are Now.* 1973. Norton. 1st. VG/VG. M17. $17.50

SARTON, May. *Faithful Are the Wounds.* 1955. Rinehart. 1st. NF/dj. A24. $55.00

SARTON, May. *Fur Person.* 1957. Rinehart. 3rd. ils Barbara Knox. 106p. VG/dj. A25. $15.00

SARTON, May. *Journal of a Solitude.* 1973. Norton. 1st. F/NF. B3. $75.00

SARTON, May. *Magnificent Spinster.* 1985. Norton. 1st. F/clip. A24. $25.00

SARTON, May. *Mrs Stevens Hears the Mermaids Singing.* 1965. Norton. 1st. NF/dj. A24. $45.00

SARTON, May. *Silence of Now.* 1988. Norton. 1st. F/F. B3. $20.00

SARTON, May. *World of Light: Portraits & Celebrations.* 1976. Norton. 1st. 254p. VG/clip. A25/M17. $18.00

SARTRE, Jean-Paul. *Age of Reason.* 1947. London. Hamish. 1st. NF. T12. $35.00

SARTRE, Jean-Paul. *Troubled Sleep.* 1951. NY. 1st. trans G Hopkins. VG/VG. T9. $15.00

SARVIS, Shirley. *Woman's Day Home Cooking Around the World.* 1978. S&S. 1st. 222p. VG. B10. $10.00

SASEK, M. *This Is Australia.* 1970. Macmillan. 1st. 4to. VG. C8. $30.00

SASEK, M. *This Is Israel.* 1962. Macmillan. 1st. 4to. VG+/dj. C8. $25.00

SASEK, M. *This Is Munich.* 1963. Macmillan. 1st. VG/VG. C8. $30.00

SASEK, M. *This Is Washington DC.* 1969. London. Allen. 1st. 4to. NF/NF. C8. $60.00

SASSON, Jean P. *Princess: True Story of Life Behind Veil in Saudi Arabia.* 1992. Morrow. 1st. 8vo. ils. NF/dj. W1. $20.00

SASSOON, Siegfried. *Memoirs of a Fox-Hunting Man.* 1971. London. Folio Soc. 8vo. ils Lynton Lamb. olive cloth. F/case. T10. $50.00

SATCHELL, G.H. *Circulation in Fishes.* 1971. Cambridge. 131p. VG. S15. $15.00

SATO, Koji. *Zen Life.* 1972. photos. VG/VG. M17. $17.50

SATTERTHWAIT, Walter. *At Ease With the Dead.* 1991. Harper Collins. 1st. F/dj. Q1. $75.00

SATTERTHWAIT, Walter. *Wall of Glass.* 1987. St Martin. 1st. author's 1st book. F/VG clip. B3. $250.00

SATTLER, H.R. *Illustrated Dinosaur Dictionary.* 1983. Lee Shepard. 1st. 315p. VG/dj. D8. $21.00

SATYRE MENIPPEE. *De La Vertv dv Catholicon d'Espagne.* 1594. np. 12mo. 13 full-p woodcuts. brd. R12. $675.00

SAUER, H.W. *Developmental Biology of Physarum.* 1982. London. 237p. dj. B1. $49.00

SAUL, John. *Creature.* 1989. Bantam. 1st. F/F. M21. $12.00

SAUNDERS, Charles Francis. *Finding the Worthwhile in the Southwest.* 1918. NY. McBride. 12mo. 231p. F7. $40.00

SAUNDERS, Charles Francis. *Little Book of California Missions.* 1935. McBride. 5th. VG. O4. $15.00

SAUNDERS, Charles Francis. *With the Flowers & Trees in California.* 1923. NY. ils EH Saunders. 286p. VG. S15. $12.00

SAUNDERS, George. *Civil Wars: Land in Bad Decline.* 1996. Random. 1st. sgn. F/F. A23. $42.00

SAUNDERS, George. *Your Horse: His Selection, Stabling & Care.* 1954. NY. Van Nostrand. 1st. VG/G. O3. $15.00

SAUNDERS, Gill. *Ehret's Flowering Plants.* 1987. London. ils/40 mc pl. 63p. VG. B26. $14.00

SAUNDERS, J.J. *History of Medieval Islam.* 1969. London. Kegan Paul. 3rd. ils/maps. VG/dj. W1. $18.00

SAUNDERS, L.G. *Contract Bridge Primer: 55 Rules With Logical Reasons.* nd. Phil. 198p. VG. S1. $20.00

SAUNDERS, Marshall. *Beautiful Joe's Paradise, a Sequel to Beautiful Joe.* 1903 (1893). np. sm 12mo. ils Chas Livingston Bull. pict cloth. G. C8. $20.00

SAUNDERS, Roy. *Queen of the River.* (1961). London. Osbourne. ne. 160p. VG/dj. H7. $20.00

SAVAGE, Candace. *Aurora: The Mysterious Northern Lights.* 1995. Sierra Club. ils. 144p. VG/glossy wrp. K5. $20.00

SAVAGE, Ernest A. *Old English Libraries.* 1970. Barnes Noble. rpt. ils. 298p. VG. K3. $15.00

SAVAGE, Henry. *Surgery, Surgical Pathology...Female Pelvis Organs...* 1880. NY. 3rd. 32 full-p pl. 115p. A13. $100.00

SAVAGE, Katharine. *People & Power: Story of Four Nations.* 1959. London. Oxford. 1st. F. T12. $20.00

SAVAGE, Les. *Doctor at Coffin Gap.* 1949. Doubleday. 1st. NF/NF. B4. $85.00

SAVAGE, Les. *Hide Hustlers.* 1950. Doubleday. 1st. F/F. B4. $100.00

SAVAGE, Richard. *Strangers' Meeting.* 1957. Mus Pr. 1st. VG/dj. P3. $20.00

SAVAGE, Richard. *Works of..., Esq., Son of the Earl of Rivers...* 1777. London. Evans. 2 vol. new ed. contemporary flame calf. H13. $295.00

SAVAGE, Thomas. *Some Put Their Trust in Chariots.* 1961. Random. 1st. NF/dj. M25. $25.00

SAVAGE, William W. *Cherokee Strip Livestock Association: Federal Regulation...* 1973. U MO Pr. 1st. 154p. cloth. NF/dj. M20. $32.00

SAVAGE, William W. *Comic Books & America 1945-1954.* 1990. Norman, OK. 1st. 8vo. buckram. F/F. C8. $20.00

SAVARIN, Julian J. *Waiters on the Dark.* 1972. St Martin. 1st Am. F/dj. M2. $15.00

SAVCHENKO, Vladimir. *Saucers Over the Moor.* nd. Children's BC. VG/dj. P3. $8.00

SAVELL, Isabelle Keating. *Daughter of Vermont: Biography of Emily Eaton Hepburn.* 1952. N River Pr. 1st. 184p. cloth. VG/dj. M20. $25.00

SAVELLE, Max. *Empires to Nations: Expansion in America 1713-1824...* 1974. MN U. 3 maps. as new/dj. O7. $35.00

SAVORY, J. *George Lodge: Artist Naturalist.* 1986. London. Helm. ils/pl. 118p. F/F. M12. $37.50

SAVOURS, Ann. *Scott's Last Voyage Through the Antarctic Camera...* 1975. NY. Praeger. 160p. VG/dj. P4. $55.00

SAVOY, Gene. *On the Trail of the Feathered Serpent.* 1974. Bobbs Merrill. 1st. 217p. dj. F3. $20.00

SAWARD, Dudley. *Bernard Lovell: A Biography.* 1984. London. Hale. photos. VG/dj. K5. $26.00

SAWYER, Corinne Holt. *Murder by Owl Light.* 1992. DIF. 1st. F/dj. Q1. $35.00

SAWYER, Edith A. *Denise of the Three Pines.* 1922. Page. 1st. 315p. cloth. VG+/dj. M20. $32.00

SAWYER, Edmund Ogden Jr. *Our Sea Saga: Wood Wind Ships.* 1929. SF. self pub. inscr. 205p. VG/VG. B11. $75.00

SAWYER, George S. *Southern Institutes; or, Inquiry Into Origin...Slave Trade.* 1859. Lippincott. 8vo. 393p+6p ads. VG. K7. $125.00

SAWYER, Ruth. *Christmas Anna Angel.* 1944. Viking. 1st. ils Kate Seredy. G+/dj. P2. $50.00

SAWYER, Ruth. *Maggie Rose, Her Birthday Christmas.* 1952. Harper. 1st. 12mo. VG. C8. $135.00

SAWYER, Susan F. *Priestess of the Hills.* 1928. Meador. 1st. NF. M2. $25.00

SAWYER. *Story of Mary & Her Little Lamb As Told by Mary...* 1928. ils. 47p. NF. A4. $65.00

SAXON, Gladys Relyea. *California Camel Adventure.* 1955. Caxton. 1st. 183p. VG+/G+. P2. $15.00

SAXON, John A. *Liability Limited.* 1947. Mill. 1st. VG/dj. M25. $45.00

SAYERS, Dorothy L. *Busman's Honeymoon.* 1955. Gollancz. 16th. NF/dj. P3. $20.00

SAYERS, Dorothy L. *Gaudy Night.* 1935. London. Gollancz. 1st. G. M22. $15.00

SAYERS, Dorothy L. *Hangman's Holiday.* 1954. Gollancz. 18th. NF/dj. P3. $20.00

SAYERS, Dorothy L. *Lord Peter Takes the Case.* nd. BC. F/F. P3. $15.00

SAYERS, Dorothy L. *Mind of the Maker.* 1944. Methuen. 2nd. VG/dj. P3. $35.00

SAYERS, Dorothy L. *Nine Tailors.* 1934. Harcourt Brace. 1st Am. F/NF. M15. $450.00

SAYERS, Dorothy L. *Nine Tailors.* 1939. Gollancz. 11th. VG/dj. P3. $20.00

SAYERS, Dorothy L. *Omnibus of Crime.* 1929. Payson Clarke. 1st. VG. M22/N4. $25.00

SAYERS, Dorothy L. *Three Great Lord Peter Novels.* 1978. Gollancz. TVTI. F/dj. P3. $25.00

SAYERS, Valerie. *Due East.* 1987. 1st. author's 1st book. F/F. M19. $35.00

SAYLES, John. *Anarchists' Convention.* 1979. Little Brn. 1st. F/dj. Q1. $75.00

SAYLOR, Steven. *Arms of Nemesis.* 1992. St Martin. 1st. sgn. F/dj. A24. $40.00

SCALES, Alfred M. *Battle of Fredericksburg.* 1884. WA, DC. Polkinghorn. 1st. 23p. VG+/orig prt wrp in cloth. M8. $350.00

SCANTAMBURLO, Luigi. *Etnologia dos Bijagos da Ilha de Bubaque.* 1991. Lisbon/Bissau. Instituto de Investigacao. sm 4to. ils. 148p. xl. VG. W1. $10.00

SCARLETT, Roger. *Murder Among the Angels.* 1932. Crime Club. VG. P3. $25.00

SCARRY, Richard. *Look & Learn Library.* 1978. Golden/Western. 1st probable. 4 vol. sm 4to. VG+/VG case. C8. $80.00

SCHAAP, Dick. *Massacre at Winged Foot.* 1974. Random. 1st. photos. VG/VG. P8. $20.00

SCHACHNER, Nathan. *Alexander Hamilton.* 1946. Appleton. VG. M2. $10.00

SCHACHNER, Nathan. *Sun Shines West.* 1943. Appleton Century. 1st. VG/dj. P3. $23.00

SCHACHNER, Nathan. *Thomas Jefferson: A Biography.* 1951. NY. 2 vol. ils. VG. M4. $35.00

SCHACHT, Al. *Clowning Through Baseball.* 1941. NY. inscr. ils Mullin. gray cloth. VG. B14. $47.50

SCHACHTER, Norm. *Close Calls.* 1981. Morrow. 1st. VG+/dj. P8. $20.00

SCHAEFER, Jack. *Great Endurance Horse Race: 600 Miles on a Single Mount...* 1963. Statecoach. 1st ltd of 750. F/F clip. A18. $150.00

SCHAFER, Joseph. *History of Agriculture in Wisconsin.* 1922. Madison. State Hist Soc. 1/1600. 212p. VG. A10. $35.00

SCHALDACH, William. *Fish.* 1937. Phil. 1st. 1/1500. VG. B5. $130.00

SCHARF, J. Thomas. *History of the Confederate States Navy.* 1886. Joseph McDonaough. 2nd. 824p. cloth. VG. M20. $135.00

SCHATZKI, Walter. *Children's Books, Old & Rare, Catalogue Number One.* 1974. rpt. 200+ entries. 46p. cloth. VG. A4. $95.00

SCHEIDL, Gerda Marie. *Crystal Ball.* 1993. North-South Books. 1st. 4to. 26p. F/VG+. C14. $14.00

SCHELL, Herbert. *History of South Dakota.* 1961. NE U. 1st. 424p. VG/dj. J2. $75.00

SCHELLING, F.W.J. *Erster Entwurf Eines Systems der Naturphilosophie.* 1799. Jena/Leipzig. Christian Ernst Gabler. 1st. 12mo. contemporary bdg. VG. M1. $750.00

SCHEMBECHLER, Bo. *Bo.* 1989. Warner. 1st. inscr. F/F. A23. $40.00

SCHENCK, Hilbert. *Chronosequence.* 1988. Tor. 1st. F/F. P3. $18.00

SCHENKEN, Howard. *Better Bidding in 15 Minutes — Expert Bidding in a Week.* 1963. NY. sgn. 192p. VG/dj. S1. $8.00

SCHER, Paula. *Brownstone.* 1973. Pantheon. sm 4to. VG+/VG. C8. $17.50

SCHERER, James. *First Forty-Niner & Story of Golden Tea-Caddy.* 1925. NY. Minton Balch. ils. 127p. NF. K7. $45.00

SCHERF, Margaret. *Beautiful Birthday Cake.* 1971. Doubleday. 1st. VG/dj. M20/P3. $20.00

SCHERMELE, Willy. *Bunnikins.* ca 1952. London. Juvenile Prod. 4to. cloth. dj. R5. $125.00

SCHERMELE, Willy. *Fairyland Secrets.* ca 1950s. London. Juvenile Prod. ils. VG-. P2.

SCHERMELE, Willy. *Teddy Bears' Picnic.* ca 1961. London. Purnell. 4to. pict brd. dj. R5. $125.00

SCHERR, George H. *Journal of Irreproducible Results.* 1986. Dorset. 3rd. ils. VG. K3. $25.00

SCHERREN, H. *Ponds & Rock Pools With Hints on Collecting...* 1894. London. Rel Tract Soc. ils/figures. 208p. cloth. VG. M12. $37.50

SCHEVILL, Margaret Erwin. *Beautiful on the Earth.* 1947. Hazel Dreis. 1st. 1/500. sgn. ils. 155p. VG+. B19. $125.00

SCHEWEY, Don. *Caught in the Act: NY Actors Face to Face.* 1986. NY. 1st. 304p+54 full-p photos. xl. F/dj. A17. $17.50

SCHIAPARELLI, G.V. *Le Opere di GV Schiaparelli.* 1969. NY. Johnson Rpt Corp. 11 vol. 8vo. Italian text. gilt cloth. K5. $500.00

SCHICKEL, Richard. *Harold Lloyd: Shape of Laughter.* 1974. NGS. 1st. 218p. dj. A17. $15.00

SCHIEL, Jacob H. *Journey Through the Rocky Mountains...* 1959. Norman, OK. dj. A19. $40.00

SCHIEPS, Paul. *Hold the Fort.* 1971. lg 8vo. 57p. ils bdg. O8. $9.50

SCHIFF, Stuart David. *Whispers II.* 1979. Doubleday. 1st. F/dj. P3. $25.00

SCHIFF, Stuart David. *Whispers III.* 1981. Doubleday. 1st. F/dj. M2. $15.00

SCHILKE, Fritz. *Trakehner Horses: Then & Now.* 1977. Norman. Am Trakehner Assn. VG. O3. $65.00

SCHILLINGS, C.G. *With Flashlight & Rifle.* 1905. NY. 1st. 421p. VG. A17. $35.00

SCHILPP, Paul Arthur. *Albert Einstein: Autobiographical Notes.* 1979. Open Court. Centenial ed. 1st thus. F/dj. K3. $20.00

SCHILPP, Paul Arthur. *Albert Einstein: Philosopher-Scientist.* 1949. Evanston, IL. 1st. ils. VG. K3. $85.00

SCHINDLER, Harold. *Orrin Porter Rockwell.* 1993. Salt Lake City. A19. $16.00

SCHINE, Cathleen. *To the Birdhouse.* 1990. FSG. 1st. author's 2nd book. F/F. B3. $50.00

SCHISGALL, Oscar. *Devil's Daughter.* 1932. Fiction League. 1st. VG/dj. P3. $25.00

SCHIWETZ, E.M. *Buck Schiwetz' Memories: Paintings & Drawings...* 1978. TX A&M. ils/pl/drawings. 112p. F/dj. M4. $25.00

SCHLEE, Susan. *On Almost Any Wind.* 1978. Ithaca. 1st. 310p. VG/dj. P4. $25.00

SCHLERETH, Hewitt. *Common Sense Celestial Navigation.* 1975. Chicago. Regnery. 231p. dj. T7. $20.00

SCHLESINGER, Arthur. *Thousand Days.* 1965. Houghton Mifflin. 1st. inscr. F/price marked out. Q1. $100.00

SCHLESINGER, Max. *Historical Jesus of Nazareth.* 1876. NY. Somerby. 12mo. VG. B14. $55.00

SCHLICKE, C.P. *General George Wright, Guardian of the Pacific Coast.* 1988. OK U. 1st. photos/maps. F/dj. M4. $30.00

SCHMIDT, Nathaniel. *Prophet of Nazareth.* 1905. London/NY. Macmillan. 1st. 8vo. 422p. G. W1. $10.00

SCHMIDT, Stanley. *Alalog's Children of the Future.* 1982. Dial. 1st. NF/dj. M2. $15.00

SCHMIDT, Stanley. *Analog: Writers' Choice Vol 2.* 1984. Dial. 1st. VG/dj. P3. $15.00

SCHMIDT, Stanley. *From Mind to Mind.* 1984. Doubleday. 1st. F/dj. P3. $18.00

SCHMIDT, Stanley. *War & Peace.* 1983. Dial. 1st. VG/VG. P3. $15.00

SCHMITT, Martin F. *Fighting Indians of the West.* 1948. Scribner. 270 photos. dj. A19. $50.00

SCHMITZ, James H. *Best of James H Schmitz.* 1991. NESFA. 1st. F/F. P3. $20.00

SCHMITZ, James H. *Nice Day for Screaming.* 1964. Chilton. 1st. F/dj. M2. $250.00

SCHMITZ, James H. *Tale of Two Clocks.* 1962. Torquil/Dodd Mead. 1st trade. VG/dj. M21. $75.00

SCHMOLLER, Alfredi. *Handkonkordanz zum Griechischen Neuen Testament.* 1982. Bibelgsellschaft. Greek concordance to New Testament. 534p. VG. B29. $14.50

SCHMUTZ, Ervin M. *Livestock-Poisoning Plants of Arizona.* 1968. Tucson. tall 8vo. 176p. F. A22. $20.00

SCHNACKENBERG, G. *Lamplit Answer.* 1985. FSG. 1st. F/dj. V1. $30.00

SCHNAPPER, M.B. *American Labor: Pictorial Social History.* nd. Public Affairs. 1st. VG/VG. V4. $45.00

SCHNELL, D.E. *Carnivorous Plants of the United States & Canada.* 1976. Winston-Salem. Blair. 125p. dj. B1. $27.50

SCHOENBERGER, Guido. *Drawings of Mathis Gothart Nithart.* 1948. NY. Bittner. 64p+44 pl. dj. A17. $35.00

SCHOENER, Allon. *Portal to America: The Lower East Side 1870-1925.* 1967. NY. 1st. photos. 256p. VG/dj. B18. $15.00

SCHOEPFLIN, Johann Daniel. *Vindiciae Typographicae.* 1760. Strasbourg. Bauer. lg 4to. 7 fld pl. gilt vellum. R12. $425.00

SCHOFIELD, Susan Clark. *Refugio, They Named You Wrong.* 1991. Algonquin. 1st. author's 1st book. F/F. B3. $30.00

SCHOLEFIELD, Alan. *Sea Cave.* 1983. Congdon Weed. 1st. VG/dj. P3. $20.00

SCHOLEM, Gershom. *Walter Benjamin: Story of a Friendship.* 1981. JPS. ils. 242p. VG+/VG. S3. $25.00

SCHOLES, Percy A. *Dr Burney's Musical Tours in Europe.* 1959. Oxford. 2 vol. 1st. gilt tan buckram. H13. $195.00

SCHOLES, Robert. *Structural Fabulation.* 1975. Notre Dame. 1st. F/dj. P3. $25.00

SCHONFELDER & SCHONFELDER. *Guide de la Flore Mediterraneene.* 1988. Fribourg, Switzerland. French text. 500 mc photos. 314p. F. B26. $39.00

SCHOOLCRAFT, Henry R. *Travels in Central Portions of the Mississippi Valley.* 1975. Millwood, KS. rpt. as new. O7. $55.00

SCHORR, Mark. *Ace of Diamonds.* 1984. NY. 1st. F/F. H11. $30.00

SCHORR, Mark. *Eye for an Eye.* 1989. St Martin. 1st. F/F. P3. $17.00

SCHORSCH, Ismar. *Jewish Reactions to German Anti-Semitism 1870-1914.* 1972. Columbia/JPS. biblio/notes/index. 291p. VG. S3. $25.00

SCHOW, David J. *Kill Riff.* 1988. Tor. 1st. F/dj. M2/P3. $18.00

SCHRAER, H. *Biological Calcification.* 1970. NY. Appleton Century Crofts. 8vo. 462p. dj. B2. $45.00

SCHRAFT, Constance. *Instead of You.* 1990. Ticknor. ARC. F/NF. w/promo material. R13. $25.00

SCHRANTZ, W.L. *Jasper County, Missouri, in the Civil War.* 1923. Carthage. photos/map/new ep. G. M4. $95.00

SCHREIBER, Flora Rheta. *Sybil.* 1973. Regnery. 1st. 359p. NF. W2. $25.00

SCHREIBER, Martin. *Last of a Breed.* 1982. Cowboy Project. 1st. VG/case. J2. $175.00

SCHREIBER & SCHREIBER. *Vanished Cities.* 1957. Knopf. 1st. 8vo. 344p. VG. W1. $20.00

SCHREINER, Olive. *Trooper Peter Halket of Mashonaland.* 1897. Boston. Roberts Bros. 1st Am. gilt cream cloth. NF. M24. $45.00

SCHROEDER, Doris. *Annette & Mystery of Moonstone Bay.* 1962. Whitman. TVTI. VG. P3. $10.00

SCHROEDER, Doris. *Annie Oakley in the Ghost Town Secret.* 1957. Whitman. 1st. TVTI. VG. P3. $20.00

SCHROEDER, Doris. *Secret of Holiday Island.* 1960. Whitman. TVTI. G. P3. $10.00

SCHROEDER, Doris. *Spin & Marty Trouble at Triple-R.* 1958. Whitman. TVTI. VG. P3. $18.00

SCHROEDER, John Frederick. *Life & Times of Washington...* 1857. NY. Johnson Fry. 1st in 2 vol. 4to. full leather/raised bands. VG. H1. $250.00

SCHROEDINGER, Erwin. *Statistical Thermodynamics.* 1946. Cambridge. 12mo. 88p. VG/torn. K3. $25.00

SCHUBERT, Kurt. *Dead Sea Community: Its Origin & Teachings.* 1959. Harper. 178p. VG/G+. S3. $24.00

SCHUCK, H. *Novel, the Man & His Prizes.* 1950. Stockholm. Sohlmans Forlag. 8vo. 620p. rpr front hinge. K3. $25.00

SCHUELER, Donald. *Temple of the Jaguar.* 1993. Sierra Club Books. 1st. 253p. dj. F3. $25.00

SCHULBERG, Budd. *Disenchanted.* 1983. London. 2nd. sgn. F/F. A11. $60.00

SCHULBERG, Budd. *Waterfront.* 1955. Random. 1st. inscr/dtd 1993. NF/NF. R14. $70.00

SCHULBERG, Budd. *What Makes Sammy Run?* 1941. Random. later prt. 8vo. 303p. F/VG. H1. $22.50

SCHULER, Harold H. *South Dakota Capitol in Pierre.* 1985. Pierre, SC. A19. $20.00

SCHULER, Stanley. *American Barns: In a Class by Themselves.* 1984. photos. VG/VG. M17. $25.00

SCHULKIN, J. *Sodium Hunger: Search for a Salty Taste.* 1991. Cambridge. ils/figures/tables. 192p. F/F. M12. $27.50

SCHULLERY, Paul. *Bear Hunter's Century: Profiles From Golden Age...* 1988. Stackpole. 252p. F/dj. A17. $15.00

SCHULLERY, Paul. *Grand Canyon: Early Impressions.* 1981. Boulder. CO Assoc U Pr. 1st. 195p. orange cloth. F7. $25.00

SCHULLERY, Paul. *Old Yellowstone Days.* 1979. Boulder, CO. CO Assoc U Pr. A19. $15.00

SCHULMAN, J. Neil. *Alongside Night.* 1979. Crown. 1st. F/dj. M2. $15.00

SCHULMAN, Pauline. *Our Merciful Father: Life Story of a Jewish Woman...* 1959. Exposition. 159p. VG/G. S3. $22.00

SCHULTZ, LeRoy. *Barns, Stables & Outbuildings.* 1986. McFarland. 150p. cloth. F. A10. $40.00

SCHULTZ, Samuel J. *Old Testament Speaks: Complete Survey of Old Testament Hist.* 1980. Harper Collins. 3rd. 436p. as new/dj. B29. $10.00

SCHULZ, Charles M. *Charlie Brown Christmas.* 1965. World. F/dj. M13. $25.00

SCHULZ, Ellen D. *Texas Cacti.* 1930. San Antonio. TX Academy of Science. maroon cloth. VG. B26. $47.50

SCHULZ, Fritz. *Classical Roman Law.* 1961. Oxford. M11. $125.00

SCHURZ, Carl. *Abraham Lincoln: A Biographical Essay.* 1907. 1/1040. 134p. O8. $27.50

SCHUTT, Arthur. *Flying Business: A Life of Arthur Schutt.* 1976. Melbourne. Nelson. 1st. inscr. 12mo. 179p. F/F. T10. $35.00

SCHUTZ, Benjamin M. *All the Old Bargains.* 1985. Bluejay. 1st. sgn. F/dj. P3. $25.00

SCHUTZ, Benjamin M. *Embrace the Wolf.* 1985. Bluejay. 1st. F/dj. P3. $18.00

SCHUTZ, Benjamin M. *Fistful of Empty.* 1991. Viking. 1st. F/dj. P3. $18.00

SCHUYLER, George S. *Black No More: Being an Account of the Strange...* 1931. NY. Macaulay. 1st. F. B4. $400.00

SCHUYLER, Robert Livingston. *Frederic William Maitland, Historian...* 1960. Berkeley. 261p. prt sewn wrp. M11. $45.00

SCHWANTES, G. *Cultivation of the Mesembryanthemacae.* 1954. London. photos. VG/dj. B26. $35.00

SCHWARTZ, A. *Butterflies of Hispaniola.* 1989. Gainesville, FL. ils/distribution maps. 580p. pict cloth. F. M12. $27.50

SCHWARTZ, Delmore. *I Am Cherry Alive, the Little Girl Sang.* 1979. Harper Row. 1st. 32p. F/F. D4. $35.00

SCHWARTZ, Hans. *Evil: Historical & Theological Perspective.* 1995. Fortress. 226p. F/wrp. B29. $8.00

SCHWARTZ, John Burnham. *Bicycle Days.* 1989. Summit. 1st. F/F. H11. $25.00

SCHWARTZ, Stephen. *Perfect Peach.* 1977. Little Brn. 1st. 48p. gilt brd. F/G+. C14. $10.00

SCHWARTZ, Urs. *John F Kennedy 1917-1963.* 1964. London. Hamlyn. 1st Eng. ils. F/dj. Q1. $75.00

SCHWARTZ-NOBEL, Loretta. *Engaged to Murder.* 1987. Viking. 2nd. VG. P3. $15.00

SCHWARZ, Jeffrey. *Orang-Utan Biology.* 1988. Oxford. 383p. F. S15. $45.00

SCHWATKA, F. *Summer in Alaska in the 1880s...* 1988. Secaucus. Castle Books. 8vo. 418p. F/F. P4. $25.00

SCHWATKA, F. *Summer in Alaska: Popular Account of Travels in Alaska...* 1894 (1891). ils. VG. E6. $40.00

SCHWATKA, F. *Summer in Alaska: Popular Account of Travels of Alaska...* 1891. Phil. ils. 418p. rebound. F. M4. $80.00

SCHWEBELL, Gertrude C. *Where Magic Reigns.* 1957. Stephen Daye. 1st. 313p. VG/dj. M5. $20.00

SCHWEITZER, Albert. *Psychiatric Study of Jesus.* 1948. Beacon. 1st. VG. M19. $45.00

SCHWEITZER, Byrd Baylor. *Chinese Bug.* 1968. Houghton Mifflin. 1st. sm 4to. F/VG+. C14. $20.00

SCHWEITZER, Jerome M. *Restorative Dentistry: Clinical Photographic Presentation.* 1947. St Louis. 511p. 4to. A17. $27.50

SCHWIEBERT, E.G. *Luther & His Times.* 1950. Concordia. 892p. VG. B29. $15.00

SCITHERS, George. *Isaac Asimov's Marvels of Science Fiction.* 1979. Dial. 1st. VG/dj. P3. $15.00

SCOBEE, Barry. *Ft Davis, TX 1853-1960.* 1963. Hill Prt Co. 1st. sgn. 220p. VG. J2. $110.00

SCOBIE, Alastair. *Kangaroo Shoots Man.* 1949. Cassell. 1st. VG/G. P3. $25.00

SCOGINS, C.E. *Red Gods Call.* 1926. Bobbs Merrill. ARC for Am Booksellers Convention. F/dj. M2. $50.00

SCOOT, Anna Miller. *Flower Babies Book.* 1914. Rand McNally. later prt. 8vo. VG. M5. $85.00

SCOPPETTONE, Sandra. *Everything You Have Is Mine.* 1991. Little Brn. 1st. author's 1st mystery. F/dj. A24. $35.00

SCOPPETTONE, Sandra. *Let's Face the Music & Die.* 1996. Little Brn. 1st. F/dj. P3. $22.00

SCOPPETTONE, Sandra. *Razzamatazz.* 1985. Franklin Watts. 1st. VG/VG. M22. $25.00

SCOPPETTONE, Sandra. *Suzuki Beane.* 1961. Garden City. 1st. VG. B5. $60.00

SCORESBY, William. *Account of Arctic Regions With History & Description...* 1820. Edinburgh. Constable. 2 vol. 20 engravings/4 maps/appendix. polished calf. T7. $1,550.00

SCORTIA, Thomas N. *Artery of Fire.* 1972. Doubleday. 1st. F/dj. M2. $12.00

SCORTIA, Thomas N. *Best of Thomas N Scortia.* 1981. Doubleday. 1st. NF/dj. P3. $20.00

SCOTLAND, Jay; see Jakes, John.

SCOTT, Alastair. *Tracks Across Alaska: A Dogsled Journey.* 1990. NY. Atlantic Monthly. 1st Am. 8vo. 247p. M/dj. P4. $20.00

SCOTT, Alma. *Wanda Gag: Story of an Artist.* 1949. NM U. 1st. photos/ils. VG/VG. D1. $100.00

SCOTT, Anna M. *Year With the Fairies.* (1914). Volland. 1st. ils MT Ross. VG. D1. $275.00

SCOTT, C.A. Dawson. *Haunting.* 1985. Tabb House. NF/dj. P3. $20.00

SCOTT, Charles W. *Pieces of the Game: Human Drama of Americans Held Hostage...* 1984. Atlanta. Peachtree. 1st. F/G. T12. $6.00

SCOTT, Frank J. *Art of Beautifying Suburban Home Grounds of Small Extent.* 1881. NY. ils. 618p. pict cloth. VG. B18. $125.00

SCOTT, Fred. *Saipan Under Fire.* 1982. Foster. rpt. maps. sc. VG. S16. $15.00

SCOTT, Genio C. *Fishing in American Waters.* (1875). Orange Judd. 539p. VG. H7. $75.00

SCOTT, H.A. *Blue & White Devils: 3rd Infantry Division.* 1984. TN. 1st. ils/maps. 173p. VG/VG. S16. $30.00

SCOTT, Jack Denton. *Spargo.* 1971. Cleveland. World. 1st. F/F. H11. $20.00

SCOTT, Jack. *Bill Walton.* 1978. Crowell. 1st. photos. F/VG. P8. $25.00

SCOTT, Joanna. *Arrogence.* 1990. Linden. 1st. author's 3rd book. VG/VG. L1. $40.00

SCOTT, Joanna. *Fading, My Parmacheene Belle.* 1987. Ticknor Fields. 1st. author's 1st novel. VG/VG. L1. $85.00

SCOTT, Justin. *Treasure for Treasure.* 1975. Arthur Barker. 1st. VG/dj. P3. $35.00

SCOTT, Lynn H. *Covered Wagon & Other Adventures.* 1987. Omaha. 1st. F/F. B3. $20.00

SCOTT, Martha B. *Artist & the Sportsman.* 1968. Renaissance Eds. 1st. ils. F/VG+. P8. $25.00

SCOTT, Mary Hurlburt. *Oregon Trail Through Wyoming.* 1958. Powder River. inscr. map. A19. $100.00

SCOTT, Melissa. *Shadow Man.* 1995. Tor. 1st. F/dj. P3. $23.00

SCOTT, Morgan. *Rival Pitchers of Oakdale.* 1911. Hurst. 1st. VG. B2. $50.00

SCOTT, Natalie. *Gourmet's Guide to New Orleans.* 1939. New Orleans. Stafford. G/wrp. A16. $15.00

SCOTT, Paul. *Jewel in the Crown.* 1966. Morrow. 1st Am. NF/dj. M25. $25.00

SCOTT, Paul. *Male Child.* 1957. Dutton. 1st Am. VG/VG+. B4. $85.00

SCOTT, Peter. *Coloured Key to the Wildfowl of the World.* 1961. NY. ils. 91p. NF/dj. S15. $12.00

SCOTT, Renae. *Doing Community Outreach to Third World Women.* 1980. Casa Myrna Vazques. 1st. ils. VG+. A25. $15.00

SCOTT, Reva. *Samuel Brannan & the Golden Fleece.* 1944. Macmillan. 1st. inscr. G+. O4. $15.00

SCOTT, S. Gilbert. *Monograph on Adolescent Spondylitis...* 1942. London. 1st. 132p. A13. $65.00

SCOTT, Thomas. *Vindication of Divine Inspiration of Holy Scriptures...* 1797. NY. Forman for Davis. 8vo. contemporary calf. R12. $275.00

SCOTT, Walter. *Black Dwarf.* nd. Collins. VG. P3. $12.00

SCOTT, Walter. *Complete Poetical & Dramatic Works.* 1883. London. Rutlege. sm 8vo. intro Wm B Scott. ils. leather/marbled brd. G. H1. $35.00

SCOTT, Walter. *Ivanhoe.* 1933. Windermere. ils Milo WInter. F. M19. $35.00

SCOTT, Walter. *Ivanhoe.* 1950. Heritage. F/sans/case. P3. $45.00

SCOTT, Walter. *Lady of the Lake.* 1853. Little Brn. 8vo. 375p. bl cloth. F. B24. $150.00

SCOTT, Walter. *Poetical Works of Sir Walter Scott.* nd. Routledge. decor brd. G. P3. $20.00

SCOTT, Walter. *Talisman.* 1929. ils Rowland Wheelwright. VG/G. M19. $35.00

SCOTT-ELLIOTT, W. *History of Atlantis/Lost Lemuria.* 1925. London. Theosophical Pub. 6 fld pocket maps. F. O7. $75.00

SCRIBNER, Harvey. *My Mysterious Clients.* 1900. Cincinnati. Robert Clarke. 1st. inscr to brother. NF. M15. $125.00

SCRIPPS, John Locke. *Life of Abraham Lincoln.* 1961. 1st. 192p. O8. $9.50

SCRYMSOUR, Ella. *Perfect World.* 1922. Stokes. 1st. VG. M2. $32.00

SCUDDER. *Mr Bodley Abroad.* 1908 (1881). Rare Book Div of Lib of Congress. VG. A4. $45.00

SCULL, Penrose. *Great Ships Around the World.* 1960. NY. Ziff Davis. 4to. 400+ ils. 260p. T7. $35.00

SCULLY, Julia. *Disfarmer: Heber Springs Portraits, 1939-1946.* 1976. Danbury. Addison House. photos. 136p. cloth. dj. D11. $250.00

SCULLY & SCULLY. *Official Motorists' Guide to Mexico.* 1937. Dallas. Turner. 238p. dj. F3. $15.00

SEABORNE, E.A. *Detective in Fiction.* 1937. Clarke Irwin. 4th. VG. P3. $20.00

SEABROOK, W.P. *Modern Fruit Growing.* 1945. London. Benn. 7th. 307p. VG/dj. A10. $22.00

SEABROOK, William. *Dr Wood, Modern Wizard of the Laboratory.* 1941. Harcourt Brace. 1st. ils. 8vo. 335p. VG/dj. K3. $20.00

SEALE, Bobby. *Seize the Time: Story of Black Panther Party...* 1970. Random. 1st. sgn. 429p. F/F. B4. $300.00

SEALE, Patrick. *Abu Nidal, a Gun for Hire. Secret Life of...Terrorist.* 1992. Random. 1st. 339p. NF/dj. W1. $22.00

SEAMAN, Augusta Huiell. *Crimson Patch.* 1920. Century. 1st. 226p. cloth. VG. M20. $20.00

SEAMAN, Augusta Huiell. *Girl Next Door.* 1920 (1917). Century. 260p. cloth. VG/dj. M20. $35.00

SEAMAN, Louise. *Brave Bantam.* 1946. Macmillan. 1st. sgn. ils Helen Sewell. VG/dj. M20. $50.00

SEARGENT, David A. *Comets: Vagabonds of Space.* 1982. NY. Doubleday. 1st. F/F. T12. $25.00

SEARLE, Ronald. *St Trinian's Story.* 1959. London. Perpetua/London House & Maxwell. 1st. F/clip. Q1. $50.00

SEARLES, Baird. *Films of Science Fiction & Fantasy.* 1988. Abrams. 1st. VG. P3. $75.00

SEARS, Edmund. *Zathu, a Tale of Ancient Galilee.* 1925. Cornhill. 1st. VG. M2. $17.00

SEARS, George W. *Woodcraft: Spirit of the Outdoors.* (1936). NY. Nessmuk Lib. 189p. VG. H7. $12.50

SEARS, Robert. *Wonders of the World, in Nature, Art & Mind.* 1853. NY. Edward Walker. New Ed. 8vo. ils. 528p. emb gilt cloth. T10. $125.00

SEARS, Victor H. *Principles & Technics for Complete Denture Construction.* 1949. St Louis. Mosby Co. 1st. 8vo. 416p. gilt bl cloth/red spine. F. H1. $22.50

SEARS. *Sears' New & Complete History of the Bible.* 1846 (1846). np. 6th. 672p. gilt blk cloth. VG. B22. $12.00

SEATON, Albert. *Stalin As Military Commander.* 1975. NY. ils/notes/biblio/index. 312p. VG/VG. S16. $21.50

SEAVER, Jeannette. *Jeannette's Secrets of Everyday Good Cooking.* 1975. Knopf. 1st. ils. 8vo. 309p+index. dj. A16. $12.00

SEAWELL, Molly Elliot. *Twelve Naval Captains.* 1897. Scribner. 233p. gray cloth. F. K7. $35.00

SEBALD, William. *With MacArthur in Japan.* 1965. Toronto. George J McLeod Ltd. inscr. dj. A19. $30.00

SEBASTIAN, Tim. *Spy in Question.* 1988. Toronto. Doubleday. 1st Canadian. F/F. T12. $25.00

SECREST, William. *Lawmen & Desperadoes, a Compendium of Noted & Early...* 1994. Clark. 1st. photos/ils. 343p. as new. J2. $65.00

SEDGWICK, Mabel C. *Garden Month by Month.* 1907. Garden City. 1st. 516p. VG. A10. $30.00

SEEBER, Edward D. *Choix de Pieces Huguenotes (1685-1756).* 1930s. Bloomington, IN. IU. sgn. 80p. VG. B11. $150.00

SEELEY, Mabel. *Chuckling Fingers.* 1941. Crime Club. VG/fair. P3. $15.00

SEELEY, Mabel. *Eleven Came Back.* 1943. Crime Club. 1st. VG. P3. $20.00

SEELEY, Mabel. *Stranger Beside Me.* 1951. Doubleday. 1st. VG/VG. P3. $23.00

SEELEY, Mabel. *Woman of Property.* 1947. Doubleday. 1st. VG/dj. P3. $23.00

SEGAL, Erich. *Fairy Tale.* 1973. Harper Row. 1st. ils Dino Kotopoulis. VG/G+. T5. $20.00

SEGAL, Erich. *Love Story.* 1970. Harper Row. 1st. F/dj. Q1. $200.00

SEGAL, Erich. *Love Story.* 1970. NY. special ltd sgn pres. VG/glassine dj. B5. $50.00

SEGAR, E.C. *Popeye With the Hag of the 7 Seas.* 1935. Chicago. Pleasure Books. 3 pop-ups. pict brd. D1. $500.00

SEIBLE, C.W. *Helium, Child of the Sun.* 1968. Lawrence, KS. 138p. F/dj. D8. $15.00

SEIFERT, Howard. *Space Technology.* 1959. John Wiley. 8vo. 1250p. Vg/dj. K5. $100.00

SEISS, J.A. *Gospel in the Stars.* 1884 (1882). NY. Chas Cook. 4th. 8vo. 522p. cloth. K5. $100.00

SEKOROVA, Dagmar. *European Fairy Tales.* 1971. Lee Shepard. 1st. VG/dj. P3. $12.00

SELA, Owen. *Exchange of Eagles.* 1977. Pantheon. 1st. VG/dj. P3. $15.00

SELBY, Henry. *Zapolic Deviance.* 1974. Austin, TX. 1st. 166p. dj. F3. $10.00

SELBY, Hubert. *Demon.* 1976. Playboy. 1st. NF/VG. A20. $20.00

SELBY, Hubert. *Last Exit to Brooklyn Post-Trial Ed.* 1968. Calder Boyars. 2nd. VG/dj. P3. $25.00

SELBY, Hubert. *Room.* 1972. Calder Boyars. 1st. F/dj. P3. $45.00

SELBY, John. *Eagle & the Serpent.* 1977. Hippocrene Books. 1st. 163p. dj. F3. $15.00

SELDEN, G. *Garden Under the Sea.* 1957. Viking. 1st. VG/G. P2. $20.00

SELDEN, John. *Priviledges of the Barnonage of England...* 1642. London. Prt T Badger for Matthew Wallbanck. contemporary sheep. M11. $650.00

SELDEN, John. *Table-Talk...With a Biographical Preface & Notes...* 1860. London. John Russell Smith. 3rd (Singer) ed. emb gr cloth. M11. $125.00

SELDEN, John. *Titles of Honor. Second Edition.* 1631. London. Prt Wm Stansby for Richard Whitakers. half morocco. M11. $450.00

SELDENI, Ioannis. *Ad Fletam Dissertatio, Reprinted From Edition of 1647...* 1925. Cambridge. cloth. M11. $125.00

SELDENI, Ioannis. *De Lure Naturali & Gentium...* 1640. London. Exudebat Richard Bishopius. 1st. contemporary calf. M11. $850.00

SELDENI, Ioannis. *Historie of Tithes, That Is...Laws Made for Them...* 1618. np (London). contemporary calf. M11. $650.00

SELDES, George. *You Can't Do That.* 1938. Modern Age Services. hc. VG. P3. $25.00

SELF, H. *Environment & Man in Kansas.* 1978. np. ils/maps. 288p. NF/dj. D8. $15.00

SELF, M.C. *American Quarter Horse in Pictures.* 1969. Phil. Smith. ils/photos/drawings. 157p. gilt cloth. F/G+. M12. $17.50

SELF, M.C. *Riding With Mariles.* 1960. McGraw Hill. 1st. VG/G. O3. $25.00

SELF, Will. *Cock & Bull.* 1992. London. Bloomsbury. 1st. F/dj. A24. $45.00

SELIGMAN, Kurt. *History of Magic.* 1948. Pantheon. VG/G. P3. $30.00

SELIGO, Hans. *Morocco.* 1966. Munich. Andermann. 1st. broad 8vo. 30 mc pl. 60p. NF. W1. $10.00

SELL & WEYBRIGHT. *Buffalo Bill & the Wild West.* 1955. Oxford. 1st. ils/photos. 278p. VG/dj. J2. $75.00

SELLINGS, Arthur. *Quy Effect.* 1966. Dobson. 1st. VG/dj. P3. $28.00

SELTZER, Charles Alden. *Land of the Free.* 1927. Gundy. 1st. VG. P3. $30.00

SELTZER, Charles Alden. *So Long, Sucker.* 1941. Doubleday Doran. 1st. G. P3. $20.00

SELVERSTON, Allen I. *Model Neural Networks & Behavior.* 1985. Plenum. tall 8vo. 458p. prt blk brd. G1. $50.00

SELVON, Samuel. *Lonely Londoner.* 1956. St Martin. 1st. NF/dj. M25. $35.00

SELWYN, E.W.H. *Photography in Astronomy.* 1950. Rochester, NY. Eastman Kodak. 1st. VG. K5. $15.00

SENAULT, Louis. *Hevres Nouvelles Dediees a Madame La Davphine.* 1680. Paris. Duval. 8vo. vignettes/borders. contemporary sharkskin/silver clasp. R12. $1,500.00

SENDAK, Maurice. *Caldecott & Co: Notes on Books & Pictures.* 1988. ils. 216p. F/F. A4. $65.00

SENDAK, Maurice. *Cunning Little Vixen.* 1985. Farrar. stated 1st. sm 4to. F/VG. M5. $75.00

SENDAK, Maurice. *Cunning Little Vixen.* 1985. NY. Farrar. 1/250. sgn. as new/box. R5. $200.00

SENDAK, Maurice. *Dear Mili.* 1988. FSG. 1st. unp. cloth. NF/dj. M20. $37.00

SENDAK, Maurice. *In the Night Kitchen.* nd (1970). Harper Row. 4to. unp. F. C14. $18.00

SENDAK, Maurice. *In the Night Kitchen.* 1970. Harper Row. 1st. 4to. unp. VG/$4.95 dj. D1. $395.00

SENDAK, Maurice. *Ten Little Rabbits: A Counting Book.* (1970). Phil. Rosenbach Found. 1st. 32mo. NF. D1. $40.00

SENDAK, Maurice. *We Are All in the Dumps With Jack & Guy.* 1993. Harper Collins. 1st. unp. NF/dj. M20. $25.00

SENDAK & STOCKTON. *Bee-Man of Orn.* (1964). HRW. 1st stated. 8vo. 46p. NF/$3.50 dj. D1. $100.00

SENECA. *Hints & Points for Sportsmen.* 1895. Forest/Stream. 224+16p. VG. H7. $35.00

SENEFELDER, Alois. *Invention of Lithography.* 1911. NY. Fuchs Lang. 1st. 229p. NF. K3. $80.00

SENN, N. *In the Heart of the Arctics.* 1907. Chicago. inscr. ils. G. M4. $15.00

SENNETT, Mack. *King of Commedy.* 1954. Doubleday. 1st. photos. VG+/dj. C9. $75.00

SENOUR, Faunt le Roy. *Morgan & His Captors.* 1865. Cincinnati. CF Vent. 1st. 389p. cloth. VG. M8. $250.00

SEQUIN, E.C. *Medical Thermometry & Human Temperature.* 1876. NY. 1st. 446p. A13. $200.00

SERANNE, Ann. *Complete Book of Desserts.* 1963. Doubleday. G/dj. A16. $10.00

SEREDY, Kate. *Lazy Tinka.* 1962. Harrap. 1st. ils. VG/dj. M20. $30.00

SEREDY, Kate. *Lazy Tinka.* 1962. Viking. 1st. sq 8vo. 56p. VG+/VG. P2. $75.00

SEREDY, Kate. *Open Gate.* 1943. Viking. 1st. 280p. VG/G. P2. $50.00

SERFOZO, Mary. *Rain Talk.* 1990. NY. Margaret K McElderry Books. 1st. 8vo. F/F. C14. $16.00

SERGEANT, Philip. *Last Empress of the French. Life of Empress Eugenie.* nd. Phil. 8vo. ils. teg. 3-quarter dk red leather. F. H3. $75.00

SERLING, Rod. *Season To Be Wary.* 1967. Little Brn. 1st. xl. VG/dj. P3. $10.00

SERRA, Victoria. *Tia Victoria's Spanish Kitchen.* 1963. NY. Weathervane. VG/dj. A16. $15.00

SERVICE, Robert W. *Ballads of a Cheechako.* 1909. NY. Barse Hopkins. 1st. NF/VG. T11. $50.00

SERVICE, Robert W. *Rhymes of a Rebel.* 1952. NY. Dodd Mead. 1st. F/VG. T11. $60.00

SERVICE, Robert W. *Rhymes of a Red Cross Man.* 1916. Barse Hopkins. 192p. gilt gr cloth. P4. $30.00

SERVISS, Garrett P. *Columbus of Space.* 1974 (1911). Hyperion. rpt. F. M2. $30.00

SERVISS, Garrett P. *Second Deluge.* 1974. Hyperion. F/sans. P3. $25.00

SESSONS, Ruth Huntington. *Sixty-Odd: A Personal History.* 1936. Brattleboro. Stephen Daye. 1st. 429p. VG. A25. $12.00

SETH, Vikram. *Suitable Boy.* 1993. Harper Collins. 1st Am. F/F. B4. $45.00

SETLOWE, Richard. *Experiment.* 1980. Holt. 1st. F/dj. M2. $12.00

SETON, Anya. *Dragonwick.* 1944. Houghton Mifflin. 1st. inscr/dtd 1944. F/F clip. B4. $250.00

SETON, Ernest Thompson. *Life-Histories of Northern Animals: Account of Mammals...* 1910. London. Constable. ils/figures/68 maps. 267p. G+. M12. $350.00

SETON, Ernest Thompson. *Trail of the Sandhill Stag.* 1920. Scribner. later prt. VG. A19. $25.00

SETON, Graham. *Eye for an Eye.* 1933. Farrar Rhinehart. 1st Am. F/NF. M15. $80.00

SETTLE, Mary Lee. *Charley Bland.* 1989. Franklin Lib. 1st. sgn. leather. F. B35. $45.00

SETTLE, Mary Lee. *Fight Night on a Sweet Saturday.* 1964. NY. Viking. 1st. F/NF. B4. $85.00

SETTLE, Raymond W. *March of the Mounted Riflemen, First United States...* 1940. Clark. 1st. ils/map. 380p. VG. J2. $325.00

SETTLE, Raymond W. *Saddles & Spurs.* 1972. Lincoln, NE. A19. $15.00

SETTLE & SETTLE. *Empire on Wheels.* 1949. Stanford. 1st. VG/VG. O3. $45.00

SETTLE & SETTLE. *War Drums & Wagon Wheels.* 1966. NE U. 1st. 268p. cloth. VG/dj. M20. $30.00

SEVERIN, Mark F. *Making a Bookplate.* 1949. The Studio. How To Do It series. ils. xl. G+. M17. $20.00

SEVERIN, Tim. *Brendan Voyage.* 1978. NY. McGraw Hill. 292p. cloth. VG/dj. P4. $30.00

SEVERIN, Tim. *Jason Voyage: Quest for the Golden Fleece.* 1985. NY. S&S. BC. 8vo. 263p. half cloth. VG/dj. P4. $25.00

SEVERN, Merlyn. *Ballet in Action.* 1938. Oxford. 1st. 4to. F/dj. w/sgn photo. T10. $50.00

SEWALL, Thomas. *Examination of Phrenology in Two Lectures...1837.* 1839. Boston. DS King. 2nd revised. 6 lithos (5 fld). 110p. brn cloth. G1. $185.00

SEWARD, George F. *Chinese Immigration in Its Social & Economical Aspects.* 1881. Scribner. 1st. stp With Compliments of Author. NF. R3. $275.00

SEWARD, John. *Spirit of Anecdote & Wit.* 1823. London. Walker/Bumpus. 4 vol. 1st. sm 8vo. early Regency-style bdg. H13. $245.00

SEWELL, Anna. *Black Beauty.* 1890. Boston. Geo Angell. 1st. stiff brd. M24. $350.00

SEWELL, Anna. *Black Beauty.* 1946. Garden City. Jr DeLuxe ed. VG. O3. $15.00

SEWELL, Anna. *Black Beauty: His Grooms & Companions.* 1890. Boston. Am Humane Edu Soc. 1st Am. prt brd. VG. B14. $250.00

SEXBY, Edward. *Killing No Murder.* 1749. London. 8vo. title in red/blk. quarter calf. R12. $150.00

SEXBY, Edward. *Killing No Murder.* 1792. London. Ridgway. tall 8vo. disbound. R12. $125.00

SEXBY, Edward. *Traicte Politique, ...Ou il est Prouve...* 1793 (1658). Paris. 16mo. gilt calf. R12. $150.00

SEXTON & SEXTON. *Samuel A Maverick.* 1964. San Antonio. 1st. sgn. VG/VG. B5. $15.00

SEYFFERT, O. *Spielzeug.* ca 1910. Berlin. Ernst Wasmuth. ils W Trier. pink silk ep. pict brd. VG. D1. $200.00

SEYMOUR, Alta Halverson. *Grandma for Christmas.* 1941. Westminster. ils Janet Smalley/Jeanne McLavy. VG. M5. $20.00

SEYMOUR, Charles. *Intimate Papers of Colonel House, Arranged As a Narrative.* 1926. Houghton Mifflin. 4 vol. 8vo. teg. gilt red buckram. VG. T10. $75.00

SEYMOUR, Frank C. *Flora of Vermont.* 1969. Burlington. 4th. 393p. VG. B26. $38.00

SEYMOUR, Gerald. *Glory Boys.* 1976. Random. 1st. VG/dj. P3. $25.00

SEYMOUR, Gerald. *Harry's Game.* 1975. Random. 1st. author's 1st book. F/F. H11. $35.00

SEYMOUR, Gerald. *Home Run.* 1989. Collins Harvill. 1st. NF/F. A20. $30.00

SEYMOUR, Gerald. *Song in the Morning.* 1987. Norton. 1st. VG/dj. P3. $18.00

SEYMOUR, Henry. *Intrigue in Tangier.* 1958. John Gifford. 1st. VG/dj. P3. $18.00

SEYMOUR, John. *Fat of the Land.* 1975. Shocken. 176p. dj. A10. $25.00

SEYMOUR, Peter. *Discovering Our Past.* 1986. Macmillan. popup John Strejan. ils Borje Svensson. NF. P2. $15.00

SEYMOUR, Peter. *Naughty Nineties: A Pop-Up Book for Adults.* 1982. LA. Price Stern Sloan. 10 popups. F. T10. $35.00

SEYMOUR, Ralph Fletcher. *Across the Gulf: Narration of Short Journey...* 1928. Chicago. Alderbrink. 1/425. sgn. fld map. 63p. G+. B11. $85.00

SEYNER, Antonio. *Historica del Levantamiento de Portugal.* 1644. Zaragoza. Pedro Lanaja. 1st. 276p. later speckled calf. R15. $2,000.00

SHAARA, Michael. *Broken Place.* 1968. NY. NAL. 1st. author's 1st book. F/NF. D10. $425.00

SHABAZZ, L. *Cooking for the Champ, Mohammed Ali's Favorite Recipes.* 1979. 1st. 4to. sc. VG. E6. $20.00

SHACOCHIS, Bob. *Next New World.* 1989. Crown. 1st. F/F. B2. $40.00

SHADOIAN, Jack. *Dreams & Dead Ends: American Gangster/Crime Film.* 1977. MIT. 366p. dj. A17. $12.50

SHAFAREVICH, Igor. *Socialist Phenomenon.* 1980. Harper. 1st. VG/dj. V4. $15.00

SHAFER, George D. *Ways of a Mud Daubner.* 1949. Stanford. 78p. NF/VG. S15. $12.00

SHAFFER, E.T.H. *Carolina Gardens.* 1939. Chapel Hill. 326p. cloth. A10. $40.00

SHAGAN, Steve. *Circle.* 1982. Morrow. 1st. VG/dj. P3. $18.00

SHAHN, Ben. *Sweet Was the Song.* 1965 (1956). NY. Odyssey. obl 24mo. NF/VG. C8. $25.00

SHAKESPEARE, William. *Complete Works of Shakespeare.* 1936. NY. Doubleday Doran. 2 vol. 1/750. sgn Kent. edit Wm Wright. B11. $550.00

SHAKESPEARE, William. *Complete Works...* nd (1952). Harcourt. sq tall 8vo. 1666p. bl cloth. B22. $12.00

SHAKESPEARE, William. *Flowers From Shakespeare's Garden.* 1906. London. Cassell. 1st. ils Walter Crane. 40p. VG. D1. $250.00

SHAKESPEARE, William. *Julius Caesar.* 1908. Macmillan. rpt. 201p. G. W2. $1,250.00

SHAKESPEARE, William. *Life of Henry VIII.* 1758. London. D Browne. 1st ils. 8vo. 116p. half calf. B24. $550.00

SHAKESPEARE, William. *Life of King Henry the Fifth.* 1909. Macmillan. rpt. 219p. G. W2. $1,100.00

SHAKESPEARE, William. *Midsummer-Night's Dream.* 1908. London. Heinemann. 1st. 1/1000. sgn Rackham. F. B24. $1,500.00

SHAKESPEARE, William. *Romeo & Juliet: A Tragedy in Five Acts.* 1833. Phil. Turner. 18mo. 65p. sewn. M1. $750.00

SHAKESPEARE, William. *Starlight & Moonshine.* 1988. Orchard Books. 1st thus. glossy brd. F. T5. $20.00

SHALER, N.S. *First Book of Geology.* 1904 (1884). Boston. DC Heath. 8vo. 255p. xl. K5. $15.00

SHALLETT, S. *Old Nameless: Epic of a US Battlewagon.* 1943. NY. 177p. VG. S16. $21.50

SHALLIT, Joseph. *Lady, Don't Die on My Doorstep.* 1951. Lippincott. VG. P3. $15.00

SHAMBURGER, Page. *Tracks Across the Sky.* 1964. Phil. 1st. VG/VG. B5. $35.00

SHAMES, Laurence. *Florida Straits.* 1992. S&S. 1st. sgn. F/F. D10. $60.00

SHAMES, Laurence. *Hunger for More: Searching for Values in an Age of Greed.* 1989. Times Books. 1st. F/F. B4. $100.00

SHAND, P. Morton. *Book of French Wines.* 1928. London. Knopf. 247p. B10. $45.00

SHANGE, Ntozake. *Betsey Brown.* 1985. St Martin. 1st. 207p. NF/NF. W2. $20.00

SHANGE, Ntozake. *Ridn' the Moon in Texas.* 1987. St Martin. 1st. F/F. R14. $35.00

SHANKLAND, E.N. *Bird Book: Observations of Bird Life.* (1931). Saalfield. ils FB Peat. VG. B15. $100.00

SHANKS, Edward. *Dark Green Circle.* 1936. Bobbs Merrill. 1st. G+. M2. $10.00

SHANN, Renee. *Air Force Girl.* 1943. Triangel/Blakiston. 1st thus. 275p. VG/dj. A25. $35.00

SHANN, Renee. *Airman's Wife.* 1944. Phil. Triangle/Blakiston. 1st thus. 202p. VG/dj. A25. $22.00

SHANNON, Dell. *Blood Count.* 1986. Morrow. 1st. VG/dj. P3. $16.00

SHANNON, Dell. *Case Pending.* 1960. Harper. 1st. author's 1st book. VG/dj. M25. $35.00

SHANNON, Dell. *Extra Kill.* 1962. Morrow. 1st. VG/VG. M19. $25.00

SHANNON, Dell. *Felony at Random.* 1979. Morrow. 1st. VG/dj. P3. $20.00

SHANNON, Dell. *Knave of Hearts.* 1962. Morrow. 1st. NF/NF. M19. $25.00

SHANNON, Dell. *Murder by the Tale.* 1987. Morrow. 1st. VG/dj. P3. $20.00

SHANNON, Dell. *With Intent To Kill.* 1972. Morrow. 1st. VG/dj. P3. $20.00

SHANNON, James. *Catholic Colonization on Western Frontier.* 1957. Yale. 1st. sgn. 10 pl. VG/fair. B11. $40.00

SHANNON, Terry. *Little Wolf & the Rain Dancer.* 1954. Whitman. 1st. ils Charles Payzant. VG+. M5. $38.00

SHAPELEY, H. *Climactic Change, Evidence, Causes & Effects.* 1953. Harvard. 1st. 318p. VG. D8. $20.00

SHAPIRO, David. *Introduction to the Poetry (John Ashbery).* 1979. Columbia. 1st. assn copy. F/VG+. V1. $15.00

SHAPIRO, H.L. *Migration & Environment: Study of Physical Characteristics.* 1939. London. Oxford. 168 tables/77 graphs. 594p. cloth. VG/remnant. P4. $45.00

SHAPIRO, H.L. *Peking Man: The Discovery, Disappearance & Mystery...* 1974. S&S. 1st. 190p. VG/dj. D8. $22.00

SHAPIRO, Karl. *Poems 1940-1953* 1953. Random. rpt. sgn. VG/VG. B11. $45.00

SHAPIRO, Lionel. *6th of June.* 1955. Doubleday. 1st. NF. T12. $15.00

SHAPIRO. *Carson McCullers: Descriptive Listings...* 1980. Garland. ils 324p. F. A4. $195.00

SHAPLEN, Robert. *Forest of Tigers.* 1956. Knopf. 1st. F/NF. H11. $40.00

SHAPLEY, Harlow. *Flights From Chaos.* 1930. Whittlesey. 1st. 8vo. 168p. K5. $25.00

SHARMA, P.V. *Geophysical Methods in Geology.* 1983 (1976). Elsevier, NY. 6th. 428p. VG. B1. $26.50

SHARP, Evelyn. *Other Side of the Sun (Fairy Stories).* 1900. Bodley Head. 1st. 8 full-p pl. 8vo. all edges gr. pict cloth. R5. $250.00

SHARP, Margery. *Britannia Mews.* 1946. Little Brn. 1st. VG/dj. P3. $30.00

SHARP, Margery. *Miss Bianca & the Bridesmaids.* 1972. Little Brn. 1st. 123p. VG/VG. P2. $40.00

SHARP, Margery. *Miss Bianca in the Antarctic.* 1971. Little Brn. 1st. ils Eric Blegvard. 134p. VG+/VG. P2. $40.00

SHARP, Margery. *Rescuers.* 1959. Little Brn. 1st. ils Garth Williams. 8vo. bl cloth. dj. R5. $100.00

SHARP, Marilyn. *Sunflower.* 1979. Marek. 1st. F/dj. P3. $15.00

SHARP, Samuel. *Critical Enquiry Into Present State of Surgery.* 1750. London. 2nd. 294p. full leather. A13. $600.00

SHARP, W. Watson. *Australia's Native Orchids.* 1970. Sydney. photos/line drawings. 144p. VG+/dj. B26. $26.00

SHARPE, Dinah. *My Horse; My Love.* 1892. Orange Judd. 1st. G. O3. $58.00

SHARPE, Tom. *Great Pursuit.* 1978. Harper Row. 1st. F/dj. P3. $20.00

SHARPE, Tom. *Riotous Assembly.* 1971. Viking. 1st. author's 1st novel. F/NF. L3. $100.00

SHATRAW, Milton. *Thrashin' Time: Memories of a Montanan Boyhood.* 1970. Am West. 1st. 188p. VG/VG. J2. $55.00

SHAUB & SHAUB. *Treasures From the Earth: World of Rocks & Minerals.* 1975. Crown. 1st prt. 223p. VG. D8. $10.00

SHAW, Albert. *Abraham Lincoln: A Cartoon History.* 1929. 500+p. O8. $27.50

SHAW, Andrew; see Block, Lawrence.

SHAW, Bob. *Cosmic Kaleidoscope.* 1976. Gollancz. 1st. F/dj. P3. $35.00

SHAW, Bob. *Dark Night in Toyland.* 1989. Gollancz. 1st. F/dj. P3. $25.00

SHAW, Bob. *Killer Planet.* 1989. Gollancz. 1st. F/F. P3. $25.00

SHAW, Bob. *Medusa's Children.* 1979. Doubleday. 1st Am. F/dj. M2. $15.00

SHAW, Bob. *Obitsville Judgement.* 1990. Gollancz. 1st. F/F. P3. $25.00

SHAW, Bob. *Wooden Spaceships.* 1988. Gollancz. 1st. F/F. P3. $25.00

SHAW, Bob. *Wreath of Stars.* 1977. Doubleday. 1st. NF/dj. P3. $20.00

SHAW, Ellen Eddy. *Gardening & Farming.* 1919. Toronto. Gundy. 376p. gilt cloth. VG. A10. $40.00

SHAW, Frank H. *Full Fathom Five: Book of Famous Shipwrecks.* 1930. Macmillan. 20 pl. 301p. T7. $35.00

SHAW, George Bernard. *Back to Methuselah, a Metabiological Pentateuch...* 1939. 4to. ils/sgn John Farleigh. 260p. VG. A4. $135.00

SHAW, George. *Roy Rogers Rodeo.* ca 1950s. London. Purnell. pub file copy. 5 double-p popups/ils. R5. $200.00

SHAW, Irwin. *Beggarman, Thief.* 1977. Delacorte. 1st. F/dj. Q1. $50.00

SHAW, Irwin. *Bread Upon the Waters.* 1981. Delacorte. 1st trade. 438p. NF/dj. W2. $10.00

SHAW, Irwin. *Bread Upon the Waters.* 1981. Delacorte. 1st. sgn. F/sans/F case. R14. $100.00

SHAW, Irwin. *Top of the Hill.* 1979. London. 1st. F/F. T12. $30.00

SHAW, Lloyd. *Cowboy Dances, a Collection of Western Square Dances.* 1940. Caldwell, ID. 2nd. sgn. 375p. VG/torn. B18. $17.50

SHAW, Luella. *True History of Some of Pioneers of Colorado.* 1909. Coburn Patterson Shaw. 1st. 268p. VG. J2. $195.00

SHAW, R.E. *Erie Water West: History of the Erie Canal 1792-1854.* 1966. KY U. 1st. ils. F/VG. M4. $25.00

SHAW, Richard J. *Trees & Flowering Shrubs of Yellowstone & Grand Teton...* 1964. Salt Lake City. 72 mc photos. cbdg. B26. $7.50

SHAW, Stanley. *Woman Tamer.* 1923. MacAulay. 1st. VG/dj. P3. $25.00

SHAW, T.E. *Odyssey of Homer.* 1935. London. Oxford. 1st Eng trade. gilt bl buckram. F/dj. Q1. $200.00

SHAW. *Childhood in Poetry: Forty-Year History of a Collection...* 1970. inscr. 28p. cloth. F. A4. $65.00

SHAW(N), Frank S.; see Goulart, Ron.

SHEA, Michael. *Tomorrow's Men.* 1982. Weidenfeld Nicolson. 1st. F/dj. P3. $20.00

SHEARING, Joseph. *Spectral Bride.* 1942. Smith Durrell. 1st. NF. M2. $25.00

SHECKLEY, Robert. *Dramocles.* 1983. HRW. 1st. F/dj. P3. $18.00

SHECKLEY, Robert. *Victim Prime.* 1987. Methuen. 1st. F/dj. P3. $20.00

SHEDLEY, Ethan. *Earth Ship & Star Song.* 1979. Viking. 1st. F/dj. M2. $15.00

SHEDLEY, Ethan. *Medusa Conspiracy.* 1980. Viking. 1st. VG+/dj. N4. $17.50

SHEED, Wilfrid. *Transatlantic Blues.* 1978. Dutton. 1st. 312p. NF/NF. W2. $20.00

SHEEHAN, J. Eastman. *General & Plastic Surgery With Emphasis on War Injuries.* 1945. NY. 1st. ils. 345p. A13. $150.00

SHEEHAN, Michael M. *Will in Medieval England, From Conversion of Anglo-Saxons...* 1963. Toronto. Pontifical Inst Mediaval Studies. 359p. prt wrp. M11. $50.00

SHEEHAN, Neil. *Bright & Shining Lie.* 1988. Random. 1st. NF/F. A20. $20.00

SHEEHAN, Perley Poore. *Abyss of Wonders.* 1953. Polaris. 1st. F/case. P3. $65.00

SHEEHAN, William. *Worlds in the Sky.* 1992. Tucson. 243p. VG. K5. $15.00

SHEERAN, James B. *Confederate Chaplain, a War Journal of James B Sheeran...* 1960. Milwaukee. 1st. 168p. VG. B18. $15.00

SHEETS, K.A. *American Fishing Books 1743-1993.* 1993. Ann Arbor. 1800+ titles. 111p. F/dj. M4. $35.00

SHEFFIELD, Charles. *Divergence.* 1991. Del Rey. 1st. F/dj. P3. $17.00

SHEFFIELD, Charles. *Summertide.* 1990. Del Rey. F/dj. P3. $17.00

SHEFFIELD, J. *Works of..., Duke of Buckingham.* 1729. London. 2 vol. 2nd/corrected. A15. $45.00

SHEFNER, Vadim. *Unman/Kovrigin's Chronicles.* 1980. Macmillan. 1st. VG/dj. P3. $15.00

SHEHADEH, Raja. *Third Way. A Journal of Life in the West Bank...* 1982. London/Melbourne/NY. Quartet Books. 1st. 8vo. 143p. NF/dj. W1. $12.00

SHELDON, Charles. *Wilderness of Denali: Explorations of a Hunter-Naturalist...* 1960. NY. new ed. 412p. F/dj. A17. $45.00

SHELDON, Charles. *Wilderness of North Pacific Coast Islands.* 1912. Scribner. 1st. 45 pl/5 maps. dk gr cloth. teg. F. B14. $250.00

SHELDON, Harold P. *Tranquility Revisited.* 1989. Derrydale. 1/2500. aeg. gilt leather. F. A17. $35.00

SHELDON, Roy. *House of Entropy.* 1953. Hamilton Panther. G/G. P3. $35.00

SHELDON, Sidney. *Doomsday Conspiracy.* 1991. Morrow. 1st. sgn. VG/VG. A23. $30.00

SHELDON, Sidney. *Doomsday Conspiracy.* 1991. Morrow. 1st. 412p. NF/NF. W2. $30.00

SHELDON, Sidney. *Other Side of Midnight.* 1974. Morrow. 1st. F/NF. H11. $35.00

SHELDON, Sidney. *Rage of Angels.* 1980. Morrow. 1st. VG/VG. P3. $20.00

SHELDON, Sidney. *Rage of Angels.* 1980. Morrow. 1st. 504p. NF/NF. W2. $30.00

SHELDON, Sidney. *Sands of Time.* 1988. Morrow. 1st. 412p. F/F. W2. $40.00

SHELL, Jacob. *Lumberman's Ready Calculator...* 1853 (1847). Harrisburg. Scheffer Beck. 41p. cloth. VG. A10. $35.00

SHELLEY, Bruce. *Call to Christian Character...* 1970. Zondervan. 186p. F/dj. B29. $6.00

SHELLEY, E.M. *Hunting Big Game With Dogs in Africa.* 1924. Columbus, MS. self pub. 1st. photos. 215p. F. H7. $100.00

SHELLEY, Mary. *Frankenstein.* 1983. Dodd Mead. 1st. ils Berni Wrightson. intro Stephen King. F/dj. P3. $30.00

SHELLEY, Percy B. *Complete Poetical Works...* 1929. London. 12mo. teg. 3-quarter leather. F. H3. $75.00

SHELLEY, R.M. *Revision of the Milliped Family Eurymerodesmidae.* 1989. Phil. Am Entomological Soc. 112p. F/stiff wrp. B1. $22.00

SHELTON, Ferne. *Southern Appalachian Cookbook: Rare Time-Treated Recipes...* 1964. Hutcraft. 32p. VG. B10. $6.00

SHEN, W.H. *River Mechanics Vol II.* 1971. Ft Collins. VG. D8. $40.00

SHENK & SHENK. *Encyclopedia of Pennsylvania.* 1932. Harrisburg. 593p. gilt bdg. G. H1. $35.00

SHENSTONE, William. *Works of...* 1764. London. 2 vol. 1st collected. ils. A15. $75.00

SHEPARD, E.H. *Everybody's Pepys.* 1926. Harcourt Brace. VG. A20. $25.00

SHEPARD, J.W. *Christ of the Gospels.* 1954. Eerdmans. 650p. G. B29. $10.00

SHEPARD, Leslie. *Dracula Book of Great Vampire Stories.* 1977. Citadel. 1st. NF/dj. P3. $25.00

SHEPARD, Lucius. *Ancient Curse of the Baskervilles.* 1984. Bloomington, IN. Gaslight Pub. reissue/1st thus. F/sans. T2. $12.00

SHEPARD, Lucius. *Beyond the City: Idyll of a Suburb.* 1982. Bloomington, IN. Gaslight Pub. reissue/1st thus. F/sans. T2. $15.00

SHEPARD, Lucius. *Father of Stones.* 1989. Baltimore, MD. WA SF Assn. 1/500. sgn. ils/sgn JK Potter. F/F/case. T2 $65.00

SHEPARD, Lucius. *Jaguar Hunter.* 1988. Kerosina. 1st. F/F. P3. $30.00

SHEPARD, Lucius. *Kalimantan.* 1990. Legend. 1st. F/F. P3. $27.00

SHEPARD, Lucius. *Kalimantan.* 1990. London. Century. 1st. 1/300. sgn/#d. F/F/case. T2. $75.00

SHEPARD, Lucius. *Scalehunter's Beautiful Daughter.* 1988. Willimantic, CT. Ziesing. 1/300. sgn. F/F. T2. $75.00

SHEPARD, O. *Lore of the Unicorn.* 1967. London. Allen Unwin. ils/pl/figures. 312p. brd. F/VG. M12. $30.00

SHEPARD, Sam. *Five Plays.* 1967. Bobbs Merrill. 1st. NF/NF. D10. $235.00

SHEPARD. *Encyclopedia of Occultism & Parapsychology: A Compendium...* 1984. 3 vol. 1/1000. 2nd. F. A4. $250.00

SHEPHERD, John. *Simpson & Syme of Edinburgh.* 1969. Edinburgh. 1st. 288p. dj. A13. $40.00

SHEPHERD, John. *Spencer Wells: Life & Work of Victorian Surgeon.* 1965. Edinburgh. 1st. 132p. A13. $40.00

SHEPHERD, Michael; see Ludlum, Robert.

SHEPHERD & WREN. *Super Summer of Jamie McBride.* 1971. S&S. 1st. inscr Wren. NF/NF. M23. $35.00

SHEPLEY, J. *Hydrogen Bomb: The Men, the Menace, the Mechanism.* 1954. 1st. VG. E6. $20.00

SHERBURNE, Andrew. *Memoirs of Andrew Sherburne: A Pensioner of the Navy...* 1828. Utica. 1st. 12mo. 262p. calf/red label. F. B14. $150.00

SHERBURNE, James. *Hacey Miller.* 1971. Houghton Mifflin. 1st. sgn. VG/VG. B11. $30.00

SHERIDAN, Philip Henry. *Personal Memoirs..., General United States Army.* 1888. NY. Webster. 1st. 2 vol. cloth/shoulder strap insignia spine. M8. $250.00

SHERIDAN, Richard Brinsley. *Rivals.* 1953. London. LEC. 1st thus. 1/1500. ils/sgn RB Sussan. F/remnant glassine/F case. Q1. $100.00

SHERMAN, Dan. *Dynasty of Spies.* 1980. Arbor. 1st. VG/dj. P3. $20.00

SHERMAN, Dan. *Man Who Loved Mata Hari.* 1985. DIF. 1st. VG/dj. P3. $18.00

SHERMAN, Dan. *White Mandarin.* 1982. Arbor. 1st. VG/dj. P3. $20.00

SHERMAN, Eleazer. *Narrative of..., Giving an Account of His Life...* 1828. Providence, RI. Prt for Author. 1st. 16mo. old calf. M1. $200.00

SHERMAN, Fanny Jessop. *Admiral Wags.* 1944. Dodd Mead. sgn. ils Paul Brown. G. O3. $25.00

SHERMAN, Harold M. *Winning Point.* 1936. Saalfield. 1st. G+. P8. $12.50

SHERMAN, S.M. *History of the 133rd Regiment, OVI.* 1896. Columbus. 163p. G. B18. $135.00

SHERMAN, Steve. *Maple Sugar Murders.* 1987. Walker. 1st. VG/dj. P3. $12.00

SHERMAN, William C. *Air Warfare.* 1926. NY. 307p. VG. B18. $65.00

SHERMAN, William Tecumseh. *Memoirs of..., by Himself.* 1957. Bloomington, IN. IU. rpt. 2 vol in 1. NF/VG. M8. $65.00

SHERRINGTON, Charles. *Integrative Action of the Nervous System.* 1906. London. Constable. 1st/Eng issue. 411p. gilt ruled bl cloth. G1. $750.00

SHERROD, Robert. *History of Marine Corps Aviation in World War II.* 1952. WA, DC. 1st. maps/unit sketches/index. 496p. VG. S16. $40.00

SHERROD, Robert. *Tarawa: Story of a Battle.* 1944. NY. map/casualty list. 164p. VG. S16. $18.50

SHERWOOD, Martin. *Maxell's Demon.* 1976. NEL. 1st. F/dj. P3. $15.00

SHERWOOD, Martin. *Survival.* 1975. NEL. 1st. F/dj. P3. $15.00

SHERWOOD, Mrs. *Master Henry's Lesson.* nd (1850s). Troy, NY. Merriam & Moore. 12mo. 24p. 20 woodcuts. VG. T10. $50.00

SHERZER, Joel. *Kuna Way of Speaking.* 1990. Austin. 1st wrp ed. 260p. F3. $15.00

SHETTERLY, Will. *Elsewhere.* 1991. HBJ. 1st. F/dj. P3. $17.00

SHEW, Joel. *Children: Their Hydropathic Management in Health...* 1852. NY. Fowlers Wells. 1st. 8vo. 432p. cloth. F. M1. $200.00

SHEW, Spencer. *Second Companion to Murder.* 1961. Knopf. 1st. VG. P3. $25.00

SHEWAN, Andrew. *Great Days of Sail.* 1927. Boston/London. ils. 240p. T7. $50.00

SHEWEY, Don. *Caught in the Act: NY Actors Face to Face.* 1986. NY. 1st. 304p. xl. F/dj. A17. $17.50

SHIEL, M.P. *Purple Cloud.* 1946. World. NF/dj. P3. $30.00

SHIEL, M.P. *Xelucha.* 1975. Arkham. 1st. 1/4283. F/dj. P3. $25.00

SHIELD, G.O. *Cruisings in the Cascades.* 1889. Chicago. 1st. photos/ads. 339p. VG. B18. $275.00

SHIELDS, Carol. *Orange Fish.* 1990. Viking. 1st Am. F/F. R13. $35.00

SHIELDS, Carol. *Republic of Love.* 1992. Random. 1st Canadian/true 1st. sgn. author's 10th book. F/F. D10. $50.00

SHIELDS, Carol. *Stone Diaries.* 1994. Viking. 1st. F/F. B2. $85.00

SHIELDS, David. *Dead Languages.* 1989. Knopf. 1st. sgn. NF/dj. R13. $35.00

SHIELDS, G.O. *Battle of the Big Hole, a History of General Gibbon...* 1889. Rand McNally. 1st. photos. 120p. VG. J2. $425.00

SHIMA. *Japanese Children's Books at Library of Congress..1946-85.* 1987. 4to. 304 annotated entries. F/wrp. A4. $35.00

SHIMER, J.A. *This Changing Earth: An Intro to Geology.* 1968. Harper Row. 1st. 233p. F/dj. D8. $12.00

SHIMER, R.H. *Squaw Point.* 1972. Harper Row. 1st. F/dj. M15. $65.00

SHINE, Deborah. *Ghost Stories.* 1980. Octopus. VG/dj. P3. $15.00

SHINER, Lewis. *Deserted Cities of the Heart.* 1988. Doubleday. 1st. F/dj. M2. $25.00

SHINER, Lewis. *Slam.* 1990. Doubleday. 1st. NF/NF. M22. $30.00

SHINN, Everett. *Christmas in Dickens.* 1941. NY. Garden City. 1st. 8vo. pict brd. dj. R5. $65.00

SHIPPEN, Katherine. *New Found World.* 1945. Viking/Jr Literary Guild. 1st thus. lg 8vo. 262p. VG/G. T5. $35.00

SHIPPEY, Lee. *Folks Ushud Know.* 1930. Sierra Madre, CA. 1st. sgn. ils AL Ewing. VG. O4. $20.00

SHIPPEY, Lee. *It's an Old California Custom.* 1948. Vanguard. 2nd. inscr. VG. O4. $15.00

SHIRAKAWA, Yoshikazu. *Himalayas. Photos & Text by Yoshikazu Shirakawa.* 1971. NY. Abrams. folio. pl/fld panoramas/fld map. dj/fld case. B24. $250.00

SHIRAS, George. *Hunting Wild Life With Camera & Flashlight.* 1936. NGS. 2nd. 950 photos. 450p. VG. S15. $30.00

SHIRCLIFE, Arnold. *Edgewater Beach Hotel Salad Book.* 1929 (1926). Hotel Monthly. 4th. 306p. B10. $20.00

SHIRLEY, Dame. *Shirley Letters From California Mines 1851-52.* 1922. SF. TC Russell. 1st thus. 8 hand-colored pl. 352p. F/dj. K7. $495.00

SHIRLEY, Orville. *Americans: Story of the 442nd Combat Team.* 1946. WA, DC. 1st. photos/map/roster. 151p. VG. S16. $95.00

SHIRLEY, Rodney W. *Early Printed Maps of the British Isles.* 1980. London. Holland. revised. ils. 188p. NF/dj. K3. $60.00

SHIVERS, Louise. *Here To Get My Baby Out of Jail.* 1983. Random. 1st. F/dj. R13. $50.00

SHOBIN, David. *Seeding.* 1982. Linden. 1st. F/dj. P3. $18.00

SHOCKLEY, Ann Allen. *Afro-American Women Writers 1746-1933: An Anthology...* 1988. Boston. Hall. 1st. pres sgn/dtd 1989. 465p. NF/dj. M8. $45.00

SHOEMAKER, Bill. *Shoemaker: America's Greatest Jockey.* 1988. Doubleday. 1st. photos. F/VG+. P8. $20.00

SHOHET, D. *Jewish Court in the Middle Ages, Studies...* 1931. 1st. G+. E6. $18.00

SHOLOKHOV, Mikhail. *One Man's Destiny & Other Stories, Articles & Sketches...* 1967. Knopf. 1st. F/F. B35. $32.00

SHORE, Dinah. *Dinah Shore Cook Book.* 1983. Doubleday. 1st. sm 4to. pict cloth. F/NF. C8. $40.00

SHORT, Bobby. *Black & White Baby.* 1971. Dodd Mead. 1st. 304p. F/NF. B4. $45.00

SHORT, Christopher. *Blue-Eyed Boy.* 1966. Dodd Mead. 1st. VG/dj. P3. $20.00

SHORT, Luke. *Saddle by Starlight.* 1952. Houghton Mifflin. 1st. NF/dj. P3. $35.00

SHORT, Philip. *Dragon & the Bear.* 1982. Morrow. 1st. 519p. F/F. W2. $45.00

SHOUMATOFF, Alex. *Rivers Amazon.* 1978. Sierra Club. 1st. 258p. dj. F3. $20.00

SHOUP, D. *Marines in China 1927-28.* 1987. Archon. 1st. F/F. E6. $15.00

SHRIBER, Ione Sandberg. *Never Say Die.* 1950. Rhinehart. 1st. VG/dj. P3. $25.00

SHRINER, Charles. *Wit, Wisdom & Foibles of the Great.* 1918. Funk Wagnalls. 1st. sm 4to. 689p. VG. H1. $12.00

SHROCK, R.R. *Sequence in Layered Rocks: A Study of Features...* 1948. McGraw Hill. 1st. 507p. NF. D8. $30.00

SHROCK & TWENHOFEL. *Principles of Invertebrate Paleontology.* 1953. NY. McGraw Hill. 2nd. ils/figures. 816p. G. D8. $37.00

SHRROR, R. *History of Marine Corps Aviation in WWII.* 1952. WA. 1st. VG/G. B5. $25.00

SHUCK, Oscar T. *California Scrap-Book: A Repository of Useful Information...* 1869. SF. Bancroft. 1st. sheep/gilt blk label. M24. $350.00

SHUCK, Oscar T. *History of the Bench & Bar of California.* 1901. LA. Commercial Prt House. ils. 1152p. cloth. D11. $75.00

SHULEVITZ, Uri. *Oh What a Noise.* nd (1971). Macmillan. 1st. sm 4to. unp. G+. C14. $10.00

SHULEVITZ, Uri. *Toodlecreek Post Office.* 1990. FSG. 1st. 4to. unp. F/G+. C14. $14.00

SHULL, A.F. *Principles of Animal Biology.* 1946. McGraw Hill. 6th. 425p. B1. $35.00

SHULMAN, Albert M. *Gateway to Judaism: Encyclopedia Home Reference.* 1971. Yoseloff. 1056p. VG/G+. S3. $52.00

SHULMAN, Irving. *Velvet Knife.* 1959. Doubleday. 1st. VG/dj. M25. $25.00

SHULMAN, Max. *I Was a Teen-Age Dwarf.* 1959. Bernard Geis. 1st. VG/dj. M25. $75.00

SHUMATE, Albert. *San Francisco Scandal: California of George Gordon.* 1994. CA Hist Soc. 1st. photos/maps. as new. J2. $45.00

SHURA, Mary Francis. *In the Valley of the Frost Giants.* 1971. Lee Shepard. 1st. 48p. NF. C14. $17.00

SHURLY, E. *Cacti.* 1962 (1959). London. 2nd. 160p. F/dj. B26. $17.50

SHURTLEFF, Malcolm. *How To Control Plant Diseases in Home & Garden.* 1962. Ames, IA. 520p. dj. A10. $20.00

SHUSTER & SIEGEL. *Superman Archives Vol 1.* 1989. DC Archive Eds. 1st. F/dj. P3. $40.00

SHUTE, Henry A. *Brite & Fair.* 1968. Noone House. 1st thus. ils Tasha Tudor. 286p. VG/dj. M20. $75.00

SHUTE, Nevil. *Chequer Board.* 1947. McClelland Stewart. 1st. VG/G. P3. $25.00

SHUTE, Nevil. *In the Wet.* 1953. NY. 1st. VG/VG. B5. $40.00

SHUTE, Nevil. *Old Captivity.* 1940. Literary Guild. VG/dj. P3. $30.00

SHUTE, Nevil. *Ordeal.* 1939. Morrow. 1st. VG/dj. P3. $40.00

SHUTE, Nevil. *Pastoral.* 1944. Morrow. VG/dj. P3. $18.00

SHUTE, Nevil. *Rainbow & the Rose.* 1958. Morrow. VG/dj. P3. $35.00

SHUTTLESWORTH & WILLIAMS. *Moon: Steppingstone to Outer Space.* 1977. Doubleday. 8vo. 117p. xl. dj. K5. $15.00

SHWARTZ, Susan. *Grail of Hearts.* 1992. Tor. 1st. F/dj. P3. $22.00

SIA, Mary Li. *Chinese Chopsticks.* nd. Peking. Peking Internat Women's CLub. 2nd. G/dj. A16. $25.00

SIAS, Beverlee. *Skier's Cookbook.* 1971. NY. AS Barnes. G/dj. A16. $10.00

SIBLEY, Celestine. *Christmas in Georgia.* 1964. NY. Doubleday. 1st. sgn. F/VG. B11. $40.00

SIDDIQI, Mazheruddin. *Islamic State: Political Writings of Maulana Sayyid...* 1986. Karachi. Islamic Research Academy. 1st. 8vo. 82p. xl. VG. W1. $12.00

SIDDONS, Anne Rivers. *Fox's Earth.* 1981. S&S. 1st. VG/dj. P3. $20.00

SIDDONS, Anne Rivers. *Heartbreak Hotel.* 1976. S&S. 1st. author's 2nd book. F/F. H11. $85.00

SIDDONS, Anne Rivers. *King's Oak.* 1990. Harper Collins. 1st. F/F. H11. $20.00

SIDDONS, Anne Rivers. *Outer Banks.* 1991. Harper Collins. 1st. sgn. VG/VG. A23. $40.00

SIDDONS, Henry. *Practical Ils of Rhetorical Gesture & Action.* 1968. Blom. facsimile 1822 London. 408p. 12mo. F. A17. $20.00

SIDEN, Harry. *Hockey Showdown.* 1972. Canada. Doubleday. 1st. F/VG. P8. $25.00

SIDGWICK, J.B. *Observational Astronomy for Amateurs.* 1982. Hillside, NJ. Enslow. 4th. 348p. VG/VG. K5. $20.00

SIDIS, Boris. *Psychopathological Researches: Studies...* 1802. NY. GE Stechert. tall 8vo. 10 fld pl. 330p. beveled ochre buckram. NF. G1. $175.00

SIDNEY, Margaret. *Five Little Peppers & How They Grew.* 1951. Whitman. ils Roberta Paflin. VG/dj. P3. $15.00

SIDNEY, Sage. *Stand-Ups: Adventures of Alice in Wonderland.* 1939. Saalfield. popups. unp. VG/pict wrp. M20. $60.00

SIEBEN, Hubert. *Tahiti: A Photographic Record of the Pearl of the Pacific...* 1965. London. Proffer. French/Eng/Dutch/Spanish text. 63 mc pl. unp. T7. $35.00

SIEGBAHN, Manne. *Spectroscopy of X-Rays.* 1925. Oxford. 1st Eng text. 8vo. 287p. xl. K3. $30.00

SIEMENS, Georg. *History of the House of Siemens.* 1957. Freiburg. 1st. 2 vol. A13. $65.00

SIENKIEWICZ, Henryk. *Quo Vadis, a Narrative of the Time of Nero.* 1897. Boston. Little Brn. 2 vol. ils Howard Pyle. teg. djs. B24. $125.00

SIENKIEWICZ, Henryk. *Quo Vadis?* 1959. LEC. 1st thus. 1/1500. ils/sgn Salvatore Fiume. F/dj/case. Q1. $175.00

SIKORSKI, Helena. *Dark Side of the Moon.* 1946. London. Faber. 1st. gilt bl cloth. faded dj. M24. $35.00

SILK, J. Frederick. *Manual of Nitrous Oxide Anaesthesia.* 1888. London. 1st. 120p. A13. $150.00

SILK, Joseph. *Big Bang.* 1989. NY. Freeman. 1st thus. ils. 485p. VG/dj. K3. $20.00

SILKO, Leslie Marmon. *Almanac of the Dead.* 1991. S&S. 1st. F/dj. A24. $35.00

SILKO, Leslie Marmon. *Almanac of the Dead.* 1991. S&S. 1st. sgn. F/F. B3. $45.00

SILLER, Van. *Lonely Breeze.* 1965. Crime Club. 1st. VG/dj. P3. $20.00

SILLTOE, Alan. *Storyteller.* 1979. S&S. 1st. F/F. B3. $20.00

SILVA, Joseph; see Goulart, Ron.

SILVER, Eric. *Book of the Just: Unsung Heroes Who Rescued Jews...* 1992. Grove. biblio/index. 175p. VG+/VG+. S3. $28.00

SILVERBERG, Robert. *Auk, the Dodo & the Oryx.* 1967. Crowell. 1st. xl. dj. M2. $17.00

SILVERBERG, Robert. *Book of the Skulls.* 1972. Scribner. 1st. F/F. M2. $25.00

SILVERBERG, Robert. *Calibrated Alligator.* 1969. HRW. 1st. NF/dj. P3. $25.00

SILVERBERG, Robert. *Conglomeroid Cocktail Party.* 1984. Arbor. 1st. F/dj. P3. $15.00

SILVERBERG, Robert. *Galactic Dreamers.* 1977. Random. 1st. NF/dj. P3. $15.00

SILVERBERG, Robert. *Gate of Worlds.* 1978. Gollancz. F/dj. P3. $20.00

SILVERBERG, Robert. *Ghost Towns of the American West.* 1968. Crowell. 1st. sgn. ils Bjorklund. F/VG. O4. $35.00

SILVERBERG, Robert. *Infinite Jests.* 1974. Chilton. 1st. F/dj. P3. $18.00

SILVERBERG, Robert. *Lord Valentine's Castle.* 1979. Harper. 1st. sgn. F/dj. M2. $45.00

SILVERBERG, Robert. *Lost Race of Mars.* 1960. Winston. 1st. VG/dj. M2. $30.00

SILVERBERG, Robert. *New Dimensions 6.* 1976. Harper Row. 1st. F/dj. P3. $20.00

SILVERBERG, Robert. *Project Pendulum.* 1987. Walker. 1st. sgn. F/dj. P3. $25.00

SILVERBERG, Robert. *Recalled to Life.* 1977. Doubleday. 2nd? sgn. F/dj. P3. $35.00

SILVERBERG, Robert. *Robert Silverberg's Worlds of Wonder.* 1987. Warner. 1st. NF/dj. P3. $20.00

SILVERBERG, Robert. *Star of Gypsies.* 1986. DIF. 1st. F/dj. P3. $20.00

SILVERBERG, Robert. *Star of Gypsies.* 1986. DIF. 1st. NF/dj. M21. $15.00

SILVERBERG, Robert. *Thebes of the Hundred Gates.* 1991. Axolotl. sgn. F/dj. P3. $40.00

SILVERBERG, Robert. *Thorns.* 1969. Rapp Whiting. 1st. VG/dj. P3. $20.00

SILVERBERG, Robert. *Time Hoppers.* 1967. Doubleday. 1st. NF/dj. P3. $50.00

SILVERBERG, Robert. *Tom O'Bedlam.* 1985. DIF. 1st. F/F. N4. $25.00

SILVERBERG, Robert. *Treasure Beneath the Sea.* 1960. Whitman. 1st. F. P3. $30.00

SILVERBERG, Robert. *World Inside.* 1971. Doubleday. 1st. NF/NF. M23. $30.00

SILVERBERG, Robert. *World Inside.* 1976. Millington. F/dj. P3. $23.00

SILVERBERG, Robert. *15 Battles That Changed the World.* 1963. Putnam. 1st. inscr. VG/dj. M2. $75.00

SILVERMAN, Kenneth. *Edgar A Poe: Mournful & Never-Ending Romance.* 1991. NY. 1st. 564p. dj. A17. $15.00

SILVIERA DE BRAGANZA, Ronald. *Hill Collection of Pacific Voyages.* 1974, 1982 & 1983. San Diego. U Lib/CA U. 3 vol. 1/1000. gilt cloth. D11. $600.00

SIMAK, Clifford D. *City.* nd. SFBC. Nf/dj. M2. $20.00

SIMAK, Clifford D. *Cosmic Engineers.* 1950. Gnome. 1st. VG/dj. P3. $125.00

SIMAK, Clifford D. *Fellowship of the Talisman.* 1978. Del Rey. 1st. F/dj. P3. $20.00

SIMAK, Clifford D. *Mastodonia.* 1978. Del Rey. 1st. F/dj. P3. $20.00

SIMAK, Clifford D. *Project Pope.* 1981. Del Rey. 1st. F/dj. P3. $20.00

SIMAK, Clifford D. *Skirmish.* 1977. Berkley Putnam. 1st. F/dj. P3. $25.00

SIMAK, Clifford D. *Strangers in the Universe.* 1956. S&S. 1st. VG/dj. M2. $25.00

SIMAK, Clifford D. *Strangers in the Universe.* 1956. S&S. 1st. F/VG. P3. $45.00

SIMAK, Clifford D. *Time & Again.* 1951. S&S. 1st. NF/dj. P3. $90.00

SIMAK, Clifford D. *Visitors.* 1980. Del Rey. 1st. F/NF. M23. $35.00

SIMAK, Clifford D. *Visitors.* 1980. Del Rey. 1st. VG/dj. P3. $20.00

SIMAK, Clifford D. *Where the Evil Dwells.* 1982. Del Rey. 1st. F/dj. P3. $20.00

SIMAK, Clifford D. *Wonder & Glory.* 1969. St Martin. VG/dj. P3. $35.00

SIMENON, Georges. *Blind Alley.* 1946. Reynal Hitchcock. 1st Am. VG/dj. Q1. $75.00

SIMENON, Georges. *Five Times Maigret.* 1964. HBW. 1st. VG/dj. P3. $28.00

SIMENON, Georges. *Glass Cage.* 1973. Harcourt. 1st Am. F/F. M22. $15.00

SIMENON, Georges. *Grandmother.* 1964. HBJ. 1st. VG/dj. P3. $18.00

SIMENON, Georges. *In Case of Emergency.* 1959. Dell. MTI. 11 photos. VG. C9. $25.00

SIMENON, Georges. *Innocents.* 1973. HBJ. 1st. VG/dj. P3. $20.00

SIMENON, Georges. *Letter to My Mother.* 1976. HBJ. 1st. VG/dj. P3. $20.00

SIMENON, Georges. *Magician & the Widow: Two Novels.* 1955. Doubleday. 1st. VG/dj. P3. $30.00

SIMENON, Georges. *Maigret & the Black Sheep.* 1976. Hamish Hamilton. 1st. VG/dj. P3. $18.00

SIMENON, Georges. *Maigret & the Informer.* 1973. HBJ. 1st. VG/dj. P3. $20.00

SIMENON, Georges. *Maigret & the Nabour Case.* 1982. HBJ. 1st. VG/dj. P3. $15.00

SIMENON, Georges. *Maigret Abroad.* 1940. Routledge. 1st. VG. P3. $35.00

SIMENON, Georges. *Man Who Watched the Train Go By.* 1942. London. Routledge. 1st Eng. VG/dj. M15. $100.00

SIMENON, Georges. *Monsieur Monde Vanishes.* 1977. HBJ. 1st. VG/dj. P3. $20.00

SIMENON, Georges. *Move.* 1968. NY. HBW. 1st Am. F/F. T12. $100.00

SIMENON, Georges. *Rich Man.* 1971. HBJ. 1st. VG/VG. P3. $20.00

SIMENON, Georges. *Strangers in the House.* 1954. Doubleday. 1st. VG/dj. P3. $35.00

SIMENON, Georges. *When I Was Old.* 1971. HBJ. 1st. NF/dj. P3. $25.00

SIMMONDS, A. *Horticultural Who Was Who.* 1948. London. inscr. 80p. VG. A10. $40.00

SIMMONDS, N.W. *Evolution of Crop Plants.* 1976. London. ils/maps. VG+. B26. $32.50

SIMMONS, Andre. *Arab Foreign Aid.* 1981. E Brunswick, NY. Assoc U Pr. 1st. 8vo. 196p. G/dj. W1. $10.00

SIMMONS, Dan. *Carrion Comfort.* 1989. Dark Harvest. 1st. NF/NF. M19. $65.00

SIMMONS, Dan. *Hollow Man.* 1992. Bantam. 1st. F/dj. P3. $20.00

SIMMONS, Dan. *Summer of Night.* 1991. Putnam. 1st. F/F. M23. $40.00

SIMMONS, Diane. *Let the Bastards Freeze in the Dark.* 1980. Wyndham. 1st. VG/dj. P3. $15.00

SIMMONS, Geoffrey. *Adam Experiment.* 1978. Arbor. 1st. F/dj. P3. $15.00

SIMMONS, Matty. *Best of the Diners' Club Magazine.* 1962. Regents American. VG/dj. P3. $20.00

SIMO, Melanie L. *Loudon & the Landscape.* 1988. New Haven. 337p. dj. A10. $30.00

SIMON, Andre L. *Noble Grapes & the Great Wines of France.* 1957. McGraw Hill VG/dj. A16. $20.00

SIMON, Carly. *Fisherman's Song.* 1991. Doubleday. 1st. ils Margot Datz. F/F. B3. $30.00

SIMON, Leonard. *Irving Solution.* 1977. Arbor. 1st. F/dj. P3. $15.00

SIMON, Merrill. *God, Allah & the Great Land Grab: Middle East in Turmoil.* 1989. Jonathan David. biblio/index. 385p. VG. S3. $24.00

SIMON, Merrill. *Jerry Falwell & the Jews.* 1984. Jonathan David. 172p. VG/dj. S3. $22.00

SIMON, Paul. *At the Zoo.* 1991. NY. Doubleday. 1st. unp. NF/NF. C14. $17.00

SIMON, Philip J. *Log of the Mayflower.* 1957. Chicago. Priam. 208p. T7. $18.00

SIMON, Roger L. *California Roll.* 1985. Villard. 1st. F/dj. P3. $18.00

SIMON, Roger L. *Mama Tass Manifesto.* 1970. HRW. 1st. VG/dj. P3. $30.00

SIMON, Roger L. *Raising the Dead.* 1988. Villard. 1st. F/dj. p3. $16.00

SIMON, S.J. *Cut for Partners.* 1956. London. rpt. 128p. VG. S1. $20.00

SIMON & SIMON. *Tumblers With a Past.* 1967. np. self pub. 32 mc pl. sbdg. w/price guide. F. H1. $35.00

SIMONS, Arthur. *All About Greenhouses.* 1960. London. Garden BC. 231p. VG/dj. A10. $25.00

SIMPSON, A.W.B. *Biographical Dictionary of the Common Law.* 1984. London. Butterworths. M11. $75.00

SIMPSON, A.W.B. *Legal Theory & Legal History, Essays on Common Law.* 1987. London. Hambledon. M11. $45.00

SIMPSON, Bruce L. *Development of Metal Castings Industry.* 1948. Chicago. Am Foundryman's Assoc. 246p. VG/torn. K3. $25.00

SIMPSON, C.T. *In Lower Florida Wilds: A Naturalist's Observations...* 1920. NY. Putnam. ils/photos/2 fld maps. 404p. pict cloth. VG. M12. $37.50

SIMPSON, Dorothy. *Suspicious Death.* 1988. Michael Joseph. 1st. VG/dj. P3. $20.00

SIMPSON, Dorothy. *Wake the Dead.* 1992. Scribner. 1st. F/F. P3. $20.00

SIMPSON, George. *Narrative of a Voyage to California Ports in 1841-42.* 1930. SF. TC Russell. facimile fld map. 232p. quarter red/navy bdg. as new. K7. $295.00

SIMPSON, George. *Narrative of a Voyage to California Ports in 1841-42.* 1988. Fairfield. Ye Galleon. rpt. 1/271p. ils/map. 270p. P4. $40.00

SIMPSON, George. *Penguins: Past & Present, Here & There.* 1976. New Haven. Yale. ils/photos/tables/distribution maps. F/VG. M12. $20.00

SIMPSON, George. *Splendid Isolation: Curious History of S Am Mammals.* 1980. New Haven. 266p. dj. A10. $25.00

SIMPSON, J. *Wild Rabbit in a New Aspect; or, Rabbit Warrens...* 1908 (1895). VG. E6. $25.00

SIMPSON, John M. *Osier Culture.* 1989. WA, DC. USDA Forestry Bulletin 19. 27p. wrp. B26. $12.50

SIMPSON, Lesley. *Enomienda in New Spain.* 1982. Berkeley. rpt. 263p. F3. $25.00

SIMPSON, Louis. *Riverside Drive.* 1962. Atheneum. 1st. sgn. assn copy. F/dj. V1. $65.00

SIMPSON, Margaret. *Sorry, Wrong Number.* 1973. Andre Deutsch. 1st. F/dj. P3. $22.00

SIMPSON, Mona. *Anywhere But Here.* 1987. Knopf. 1st. author's 1st book. F/F. H11. $75.00

SIMPSON, Mona. *Anywhere But Here.* 1987. Knopf. 1st. author's 1st book. VG/VG. L1. $50.00

SIMPSON, Mona. *Lost Father.* 1992. 1st. author's 2nd book. F/dj. A15/A24/B3. $30.00

SIMPSON, O.J. *OJ: The Education of a Rich Rookie.* 1970. Macmillan. 1st. photos. F/F. B4. $100.00

SIMS, George R. *Nelle's Prayer.* ca 1890. London. Raphael Tuck. ils J Willis Grey. pict brd. NF. T10. $65.00

SIMS, George. *End of the Web.* 1976. Gollancz. 1st. NF/dj. P3. $25.00

SINCLAIR, Andrew. *Project.* 1960. S&S. 1st. F/dj. P3. $10.00

SINCLAIR, Andrew. *Under Milk Wood.* 1972. S&S. 1st Am from Eng sheets. VG/wrp. B4. $75.00

SINCLAIR, Angus. *Development of the Locomotive Engine.* 1970. Cambridge. rpt 1907. ils. VG. B18. $25.00

SINCLAIR, Isabella. *Indigenous Flowers of the Hawaiian Islands.* 1885. London. Sampson Low. folio. 44p+44 chromolitho pl. aeg. gilt olive cloth. A22. $575.00

SINCLAIR, John L. *Death in the Claimshack.* 1947. Denver. Sage Books. 1st. Ils Harold West. F/F. B4. $100.00

SINCLAIR, Mary. *Intercessor & Other Stories.* 1932. Macmillan. 1st. VG. M2. $35.00

SINCLAIR, May. *Three Brontes.* 1912. Houghton Mifflin. 1st/1st prt. gilt gr cloth. NF. M24. $65.00

SINCLAIR, Michael. *Dollar Covenant.* 1973. Gollancz. 1st. VG/fair. P3. $20.00

SINCLAIR, Sally. *Muted Murder.* 1953. Arcadia. 1st. VG/dj. P3. $20.00

SINCLAIR, Upton. *American Outpost: A Book of Reminiscences.* 1932. Upton Sinclair. 1st. G. V4. $20.00

SINCLAIR, Upton. *Another Pamela.* 1950. Viking. 1st. NF/VG. M19. $25.00

SINCLAIR, Upton. *Another Pamela.* 1950. Viking. 1st. VG. P3. $10.00

SINCLAIR, Upton. *Brass Check.* nd. np. self pub. 1st. G. V4. $20.00

SINCLAIR, Upton. *Dragon Harvest.* 1945. Viking. 1st. VG. M2. $10.00

SINCLAIR, Upton. *Flivver King.* 1969. Phaedra. new ed. F/NF. B2. $35.00

SINCLAIR, Upton. *Goslings: A Study of American Schools.* 1924. Pasadena. self pub. 1st. F/fair. M23. $30.00

SINCLAIR, Upton. *Goslings: A Study of American Schools.* 1924. self pub. 1st. VG. V4. $15.00

SINCLAIR, Upton. *Jungle.* 1906. Doubleday Page. 1st. VG. M19. $85.00

SINCLAIR, Upton. *Jungle.* 1906. Jungle Pub. 2nd. G. V4. $20.00

SINCLAIR, Upton. *Little Steel.* 1938. NY. 1st. F/NF. B4. $125.00

SINCLAIR, Upton. *Our Lady.* 1938. Rodale. 1st. VG. M2. $25.00

SINCLAIR, Upton. *World To Win.* 1946. Viking. 1st. F/VG. M19. $25.00

SINCLAIR, Upton. *100%: The Story of a Patriot.* 1920. self pub. 1st. VG. V4. $15.00

SINCLAIR, William A. *Aftermath of Slavery.* 1905. Boston. Sm Maynard. 1st. 358p. NF. B4. $300.00

SINGER, Bant. *Don't Slip, Delaney.* 1954. Collins. 1st. VG/dj. P3. $25.00

SINGER, Charles. *From Magic to Science.* 1928. London. Ernest Benn. 1st. ils. xl. K3. $50.00

SINGER, Charles. *Short History of Scientific Ideas to 1900.* 1959. NY/London. 1st. ils. 8vo. 525p. VG/dj. K3. $30.00

SINGER, Howard. *Wake Me When It's Over.* 1959. Putnam. 1st. F/VG clip. B4. $125.00

SINGER, Isaac Bashevis. *Collected Stories.* nd. BC. VG/dj. P3. $15.00

SINGER, Isaac Bashevis. *Crown of Feathers.* 1973. FSG. 1st. 342p. F/VG. H1. $30.00

SINGER, Isaac Bashevis. *Death of Methuselah.* 1988. Franklin Lib. 1st/ltd. sgn for members. aeg. full leather. F. Q1. $100.00

SINGER, Isaac Bashevis. *Family Moskat.* 1950. NY. Knopf. 1st. F/dj. Q1. $40.00

SINGER, Isaac Bashevis. *Gifts.* 1985. Jewish Pub Soc. 1st. F/case. B35. $85.00

SINGER, Isaac Bashevis. *King of the Fields.* 1988. FSG. 1st. F/F. T12. $15.00

SINGER, Isaac Bashevis. *Naftali the Storyteller & His Horse, Sus.* 1976. FSG. 1st. ils Margot Zemach. 1st. 129p. NF/VG. P2. $35.00

SINGER, Isaac Bashevis. *Old Love.* 1979. Farrar. 1st. inscr. F/F. B2. $125.00

SINGER, Isaac Bashevis. *Penitent.* 1983. FSG. 1st. F/F. B35. $18.00

SINGER, Isaac Bashevis. *Power of Light, Eight Stories for Hanukkah.* 1983 (1980). London. Robson. ils Lieblich. F/F. C8. $25.00

SINGER, Isaac Bashevis. *Scum.* 1991. FSG. 1st. F/F. B4. $45.00

SINGER, Isaac Bashevis. *When Shlemiel Went to Warsaw.* 1968. FSG. 1st. ils Margot Zemach. beige cloth. NF/NF. D1. $50.00

SINGER, Isaac Bashevis. *Why Noah Chose the Dove.* 1974. FSG. 1st. ils Eric Carle. F/NF. P2. $65.00

SINGER, Isaac Bashevis. *Young Man in Search of Love.* 1978. Doubleday. 1/300. sgn/#d. w/ils Raphael Soyer sgn mc prt. F/F case. B2. $250.00

SINGER, Kurt. *Laughton Story.* 1954. Winston. 1st. VG/dj. P3. $15.00

SINGER, Kurt. *More Spy Stories.* 1955. WH Allen. 1st. VG/dj. P3. $25.00

SINGER, Kurt. *Spy Stories From Asia.* 1955. Winfred Funk. VG. P3. $20.00

SINGER, Kurt. *Tales From the Unknown.* 1970. London. 1st. F/dj. M2. $27.00

SINGER, Loren. *Parallax View.* 1970. Doubleday. 1st. rem mk. F/F. B4. $100.00

SINGER, Shelley. *Spit in the Ocean.* 1987. St Martin. 1st. VG/dj. P3. $15.00

SINGERMAN, Philip. *Red Adair: An American Hero.* 1989. London. Bloomsbury. 1st. sgn. VG/VG. A23. $40.00

SINKANKAS, J. *Gem Cutting: A Lapidary's Manual.* 1960. 4th prt. VG/clip. D8. $15.00

SINYARD, Neil. *Directors: The All-Time Greats.* 1985. Gallery Books. 1st. VG/dj. P3. $12.00

SIODMAK, Curt. *City in the Sky.* 1975. Barrie Jenkins. 1st. F/dj. P3. $18.00

SIODMAK, Curt. *Donovan's Brain.* 1944. Triangle. 1st. VG/dj. P3. $20.00

SIODMAK, Curt. *Third Ear.* 1971. Putnam. 1st. NF/dj. P3. $18.00

SIPLE, Paul. *90 (degrees) South: Story of American South Pole Conquest.* 1959. Putnam. 8vo. 384p. VG/dj. P4. $60.00

SIRAGUSA, Charles. *Trail of the Poppy.* 1966. Prentice Hall. 1st. inscr. F/NF. B2. $35.00

SIRINGO, Charles A. *Texas Cowboy.* 1886. Rand McNally. 3rd (from sheets of 2nd). complete. poor. M24. $250.00

SISKIND, Aaron. *Photographs.* 1959. Horizon. intro Harold Rosenberg. 108p. cloth. dj. D11. $150.00

SISKIND, Patrick. *Perfume: The Story of a Murder.* 1986. Knopf. 1st Am. F/F. B4. $75.00

SISLEY, Nick. *Deer Hunting Across North America.* 1975. Freshet. 281p. lg 8vo. VG. A17. $18.50

SISON & WERNING. *Philippine Revolution.* 1989. NY. Crane Russak. 1st. 241p. M. P1. $15.00

SITCHIN, Zecharia. *Lost Realms.* 1990. Santa Fe. Bear. 1st. 298p. dj. F3. $10.00

SITGREAVES, L. *Report of Expedition down the Zuni & Colorado River 1851.* 1962. Chicago. facsimile 1853 Washington. 198p. VG+. F7. $65.00

SITWELL, Edith. *Canticle of the Rose: Poems 1917-1949.* 1949. Vanguard. 1st. F/F. B4. $65.00

SITWELL, Edith. *I Live Under a Black Sun.* 1938. 1st. F/NF. M19. $45.00

SITWELL, Sacheverell. *Fine Bird Books 1700-1900.* 1990. NY. Atlantic Monthly. 1st. 180p. F/dj. A17/S15. $37.50

SITWELL, Sacheverell. *Great Flower Books 1700-1900.* 1990. NY. 1st. 189p. F/dj. A17. $35.00

SJOWALI & WAHLOO. *Fire Engine That Disappeared.* 1970. Pantheon. 1st Am. F/clip. M15. $45.00

SJOWALL & WAHLOO. *Abominable Man.* nd. BC. VG/dj. P3. $8.00

SJOWALL & WAHLOO. *Laughing Policeman.* 1970. Pantheon. 1st Am. F/clip. D10. $85.00

SJOWALL & WAHLOO. *Laughing Policeman.* 1970. Pantheon. 1st Am. VG/F. M22. $40.00

SJOWALL & WAHLOO. *Man on the Balcony.* 1968. Pantheon. 1st Am. F/NF. M15. $35.00

SJOWALL & WAHLOO. *Terrorists.* 1976. Pantheon. 1st. VG/dj. P3. $23.00

SKAF, Robert. *Story of the Planet Candy.* 1990. Vantage. 1st. sgn. VG/dj. P3. $15.00

SKAGGS, Jimmy M. *Clipperton: A History of the Island the World Forgot.* 1989. NY. Walker. 8vo. 318p. gilt bdg. VG/dj. P4. $45.00

SKAL, David. *Antibodies.* 1988. Congdon Weed. 1st. F/F. M2. $15.00

SKAL, David. *Hollywood Gothic: Tangled Web of Dracula...* 1990. Norton. 1st. 4to. F/F. B2. $25.00

SKARMETA, Antonio. *Burning Patience.* 1987. Pantheon. 1st Am. F/F. B4. $125.00

SKAZKA. *Ivan Czarevich, the Firebird & Grey Wolf.* 1901. USSR. 1st. ils Ivan Bilibine. F. D1. $600.00

SKINNER, J.S. *Discourse on the Wants of Agriculture.* 1848. Middlesex Agric Soc. 12p. VG/wrp. A10. $25.00

SKINNER, Margaret. *Old Jim Canaan.* 1990. Algonquin. AP. NF/wrp. R13. $15.00

SKIRVING, R. Scot. *Wire Splicing.* 1953. Glasgow. Brn, Son & Ferguson. rpt. ils. half cloth. VG. P4. $20.00

SKLEPOWICH, Edward. *Death in a Serene City.* 1990. Morrow. 1st. F/F. N4. $25.00

SKOTTSBERG, Carl. *Botanische Ergenisse der Schwedischen Expedition...1907-09.* 1910-1913. Uppsala/Stockholm. 3 vol in 1. ils/figures. mtd in lib-style binder. VG. B26. $110.00

SKUES, G.E.M. *Minor Tactics of the Chalk Stream.* 1910. London. Adam/Chas Blk. 1st. 8vo. gilt cloth. NF. T10. $300.00

SLADE, Irene. *Ring of Bells: Poems Selected for Younger Readers.* 1963. Houghton Mifflin. 1st Am. ils Ardizzone. 129p. NF/NF. D4. $45.00

SLADEK, John. *Bugs.* 1989. Macmillan. 1st. F/dj. P3. $28.00

SLADEK, John. *Reproductive System.* 1968. Gollancz. 1st. VG/dj. P3. $65.00

SLADEN, Douglas. *Younger American Poets.* 1891. NY. Cassell. 1st. gilt bl cloth. F/dj. M24. $75.00

SLATER, Leonard. *Aly: A Biography.* 1965. Random BC. 1st. 8vo. 10 pl. 207p. VG/dj. W1. $18.00

SLATER, Nigel. *Falcon.* 1979. Atheneum. 1st. F/dj. P3. $15.00

SLATER, Philip. *How I Saved the World.* 1985. Dutton. 1st. VG/dj. P3. $17.00

SLATZER, Robert F. *Life & Curious Death of Marilyn Monroe.* 1975. WH Allen. VG/dj. P3. $20.00

SLAUSON, H.W. *Everyman's Guide to Motor Efficiency.* 1920. Leslie Judge. 1st ed. 290p. limp leatherette. A17. $30.00

SLAVITT, David R. *Agent.* 1986. Doubleday. 1st. VG/dj. P3. $15.00

SLAVITT, David R. *Cold Comfort.* 1980. Methuen. 1st. VG/VG. P3. $20.00

SLESAR, Henry. *Gray Flannel Shroud.* 1959. Random. author's 1st book. G+/dj. N4. $20.00

SLETTEBAK, Arne. *Stellar Rotation.* 1970. NY. Gordon Breach. sm 4to. 355p. VG/VG. K5. $65.00

SLEVIN, Joseph R. *Log of the Schooner Academy on a Voyage...* 1931. CA Adademy of Sciences. 162p. VG/prt wrp. P4. $75.00

SLILPER, E.J. *Whales.* 1962. Basic Books. trans from Dutch. 473p. VG. S15. $30.00

SLOANE, Eric. *Age of Barns.* nd. Funk Wagnalls. 1st. VG/G. O3. $65.00

SLOANE, Eric. *Age of Barns.* 1976. NY. Natural Hist. 50p. A10. $20.00

SLOANE, Eric. *Mr Daniels & the Grange.* 1968. NY. 1st. sgn. VG/VG. B5. $40.00

SLOANE, Eric. *Museum of Early American Tools.* 1964. NY. 1st. ils. 108p. F/dj. M4. $25.00

SLOANE, Eric. *Return to Taos.* 1960. Wilfred Funk. 1st. NF/1st state. T11. $130.00

SLOANE, William. *Edge of Running Water.* nd. BC. VG/dj. P3. $10.00

SLOANE, William. *Space, Space, Space.* nd. Grosset. VG/dj. M2. $18.00

SLOBODKIN, Louis. *Gogo, the French Sea Gull.* 1960. Macmillan. 1st. lib bdg. VG/dj. T5. $30.00

SLOBODKIN, Louis. *Horse With High-Heeled Shoes.* 1954. Vanguard. 1st. 32p. NF/VG-. P2. $60.00

SLOBODKIN, Louis. *Seaweed Hat.* 1947. Macmillan. 1st. sq 8vo. VG/VG. P2. $60.00

SLOCHOWER, Harry. *No Voice Is Wholly Lost. Writers & Thinkers in War & Peace.* 1946. London. Dobson. 1st. VG/VG. B2. $30.00

SLOCHOWER, Harry. *Thomas Mann's Joseph Story: An Interpretation.* 1938. Knopf. 1st. F/VG. B4. $55.00

SLOMAN, Larry. *Reefer Madness.* 1979. Bobbs Merrill. 1st. VG/dj. p3. $20.00

SLOSSON, Elvenia. *Pioneer American Gardening.* 1951. NY. Coward. 306p. VG/dj. A10. $12.00

SLOTE, Alfred. *Air in Fact & Fancy.* 1968. Cleveland. World. 8vo. 160p. VG/dj. K5. $16.00

SLOVO, Gillian. *Death by Analysis.* 1988. Crime Club. 1st. VG/dj. P3. $15.00

SLUNG, Michele. *I Shudder at Your Touch.* 1991. Roc. 1st. F/dj. P3. $20.00

SMALL, Austin J. *Avenging Ray.* 1930. Crime Club. VG. P3. $30.00

SMALL, Austin J. *Mystery Maker.* 1930. Crime Club. 1st. G. P3. $20.00

SMALL, Austin J. *Pearls of Desire.* nd. Grosset. F/dj. M2. $15.00

SMALL, Austin J. *Vantine Diamonds.* 1930. Crime Club. 1st. G. P3. $20.00

SMALL, John K. *Monograph of the North American Species of Genus Polygonum.* 1895. Lancaster, PA. 85 pl. 183p. new gr buckram. VG. B26. $95.00

SMALLEY, George H. *My Adventures in Arizona.* 1966. Tucson. sgn. 8vo. 154p. gr wrp. F7. $30.00

SMEDLEY, Agnes. *Portraits of Chinese Women in Revolution.* 1976. Old Westbury. Feminist Pr. 1st. ils. VG+. A25. $10.00

SMILEY, Jane. *Age of Grief.* 1987. Knopf. 1st. sgn. F/F. D10. $95.00

SMILEY, Jane. *At Paradise Gate.* 1981. S&S. 1st. F/F. B4. $300.00

SMILEY, Jane. *Catskill Crafts.* 1988. Crown. 1st. F/F. M19. $25.00

SMILEY, Jane. *Catskill Crafts.* 1988. NY. Crown. 1st. sgn. author's 3rd book. F/F. B3. $45.00

SMILEY, Jane. *Duplicate Keys.* 1984. London. Cape. 1st. F/F. T12. $100.00

SMILEY, Jane. *Greenlanders.* 1988. Crown. 1st. F/F. M19. $45.00

SMILEY, Jane. *Moo.* 1995. Knopf. 1st. F/F. H11. $35.00

SMILEY, Jane. *Moo.* 1995. Knopf. 1st. sgn. F/F. A23. $40.00

SMILEY, Jane. *Ordinary Love & Good Will.* 1989. Knopf. 1st. F/F. H11. $50.00

SMILEY, Jane. *Thousand Acres.* 1991. Knopf. 1st. F/clip. H11. $70.00

SMILEY, jane. *Thousand Acres.* 1991. Knopf. 1st. NF/dj. R13. $45.00

SMILEY, Jane. *Thousand Acres.* 1991. Knopf. 1st. sgn. F/dj. D10. $125.00

SMISS, W.G. *Gift... for 1837.* (1836). Phil. Carey Hart. 1st. aeg. full brn morocco. M24. $125.00

SMISS, W.G. *Opal.* 1848. NY. JC Riker. 1st. hand-mc pres pl. aeg. gilt full blk morocco. VG. M24. $100.00

SMIT, Mary P. Wells. *Boy Captive of Old Deerfield.* 1929. Little Brn. 1st thus. ils Frank Schoonover. gilt blk cloth. NF. T10. $100.00

SMITH, A.C. *British Dogs.* 1947. London. Collins. 48p. VG/VG. H7. $10.00

SMITH, A.C. *Fijian Plant Studies II: Botanical Results...* 1942. Jamaica Plain. Arnold Arboretum of Harvard. 148p. gray wrp. P4. $65.00

SMITH, Alexander. *Mushroom Hunter's Field Guide.* 1967. Ann Arbor. revised/enlarged. ils. 264p. VG. B26. $15.00

SMITH, Alexander. *Veiled Species of Hebeloma in Western United States.* 1983. Ann Arbor. ils. 219p. F. S15. $15.00

SMITH, Alfred E. *Campaign Addresses of Governor Alfred E Smith.* 1929. WA. Democratic Comm. 1st. 322p. cloth. F. B22. $20.00

SMITH, Alice Upham. *Trees in a Winter Landscape.* 1969. NY. Holt. 207p. dj. A10. $20.00

SMITH, Andrew. *Tomato in America.* 1994. Columbia. 224p. dj. A10. $25.00

SMITH, Anthony. *Explorers of the Amazon.* 1990. Viking. 1st. 344p. dj. F3. $20.00

SMITH, Barbara Burnett. *Writers of the Purple Sage.* 1994. St Martin. 1st. sgn. author's 1st book. VG/VG. A23. $45.00

SMITH, Ben. *Design Your Own Yacht.* 1988. London. Coles. ils/31 pl. 204p. dj. T7. $38.00

SMITH, Bernard. *European Vision & the South Pacific.* 1985. London/New Haven. Yale. 2nd. 222 ils. 370p. gilt navy cloth. P4. $85.00

SMITH, Bertha H. *Yosemite Legends.* 1904. SF. Paul Elder. ils. 64p. terra-cotta cloth. F. K7. $150.00

SMITH, Bertha Whitridge. *Only a Dog, Story of the Great War.* (1917). Dutton. 12mo. VG. C8. $17.50

SMITH, C. Fox. *There Was a Ship: Chapters From the History of Sail.* 1930. Hartford. Edwin Valentine Mitchell. ils PW Smith. F/rpr. O7. $45.00

SMITH, C. Ross. *Sinbad the Sailor.* 1972. NY. Good Book/Doubleday. 1st. 4to. ils Alain LeFoll. VG/dj. W1. $15.00

SMITH, C.H. *Ancient Costumes of Great Britain & Ireland...* 1989. London. 85 mc pl. 224p. F/dj. M4. $40.00

SMITH, Carl N. *Inside the Circle of Samuel F & Lulu J Smith Family...* 1977. private prt. 1st. ils. 151p. F/sans. B19. $75.00

SMITH, Charles. *Comprehensive History of Minnehaha County, South Dakota.* 1949. Educator Supply. 504p. VG. J2. $145.00

SMITH, Charlie. *Canaan.* 1984. S&S. 1st. NF/F. B3. $30.00

SMITH, Charlie. *Crystal River.* 1991. NY. Linden. 1st. F/F. B3. $40.00

SMITH, Charlie. *Lives of the Dead.* 1990. S&S. 1st. F/F. H11. $35.00

SMITH, Charlie. *Lives of the Dead.* 1990. S&S. 1st. F/NF. R13. $20.00

SMITH, Clark Ashton. *Strange Shadows.* 1989. Greenwood. 1st. VG/sans. M2. $40.00

SMITH, Cornelius C. *Don't Settle for Second: Life & Times of Cornelius C Smith.* 1977. Presidio. 1st. ils/chronology/bibliography. 229p. F/NF. B19. $25.00

SMITH, Cornelius C. *Emilo Kosterlitsky, Eagle of Sonora & Southwest Border.* 1970. Clark. 1st. 344p. VG. J2. $65.00

SMITH, D.A. *Rocky Mountain Mining Camps: The Urban Frontier.* 1967. IN U. 304p. VG/clip. D8. $30.00

SMITH, D.W. *Silver Spoon Murders.* 1988. Lyle Stuart. 1st. VG/dj. P3. $16.00

SMITH, Dave. *Blue Spruce.* 1981. Tamarack. 1/300. sgn. F/wrp. V1. $35.00

SMITH, Dave. *Gray Soldiers.* 1983. np. Stuart Wright. 1/75. inscr/sgn twice. F/sans. R13. $150.00

SMITH, Dave. *Mean-Rufus-Throw-Down.* 1973. Basilisk. 1/200 (of 600). sgn. VG+/wrp. V1. $35.00

SMITH, David. *Days of His Flesh.* nd. Harper. 549p. VG. B29. $6.50

SMITH, David. *Rara Arithemtica: A Catalogue of Arithmetics...* nd (1908). rpt. 1/100. ils. 532p. F. A4. $95.00

SMITH, Dennis. *Glitter & Ash.* 1980. Dutton. 1st. VG/dj. P3. $13.00

SMITH, Dodie. *Hundred & One Dalmations.* 1956. London. Heinemann. 1st. inscr/dtd 1956. ils Janet/Anne Graham-Johnstone. NF/VG. B4. $2,500.00

SMITH, E. *Official Cookbook of the Hay System.* 1947 (1934). Mt Pocono, PA. G. E6. $18.00

SMITH, E. *Recipes & Menues for 50 As Used in Boston.* 1922 (1915). YMCA. VG. E6. $20.00

SMITH, E. Boyd. *Early Life of Mr Man.* 1914. Houghton Mifflin. 1st. VG. P2. $185.00

SMITH, E. Boyd. *Railroad Book: Bob & Betty's Summer on the Railroad.* 1913. Houghton Mifflin. 1st. 12 full-p mc pl. obl 4to. cloth/label. R5. $200.00

SMITH, E. Boyd. *Run in the Radio World.* 1923. Stokes. 1st. 12 full-p mc pl/b&w ils. gr cloth/label. R5. $200.00

SMITH, E.E. *Skylark of Space.* 1950. FFF. VG/dj. P3. $100.00

SMITH, E.E. *Skylark of Valeron.* 1949. Fantasy. 1st. 1/500. sgn/#d/inscr also. NF/VG. P3. $175.00

SMITH, E.E. *Skylark Three.* 1975. Garland. F. M2. $20.00

SMITH, E.E. *Spacehounds of Ipc.* 1947. Fantasy. 1st. inscr. NF/G. P3. $125.00

SMITH, E.E. *Subspace Explorers.* 1965. Canaveral. 1st. F/dj. M2/M19. $45.00

SMITH, Edgar Newbold. *American Naval Broadsides.* 1974. Clarkson Potter. 4to. 117 pl. 225p. M/dj. B24. $185.00

SMITH, Edgar W. *Profile by Gaslight: An Irregular Reader...Sherlock Holmes.* 1944. S&S. 1st. sm 8vo. 312p. red brd. G. H1. $45.00

SMITH, Edmund Ware. *One-Eyed Poacher of Privilege.* 1991. Derrydale. 187p. aeg. gilt leather. F. A17. $22.50

SMITH, Elihu Hubbard. *Diary of Elihu Hubbard Smith 1771-1798.* 1973. Phil. Am Philosophical Soc. 481p. B18. $45.00

SMITH, Emma. *Emily.* 1959. McDowell/Obolensky. 1st Am. ils Katherine Wigglesworth. 76p. F/VG+. P2. $50.00

SMITH, Ethan. *Daughters of Zion Excelling. A Sermon Preached to Ladies...* 1814. Concord, NH. George Hough. 1st. 12mo. 23p. VG/wrp. M1. $125.00

SMITH, Ethan. *View of the Hebrews; or, Tribes of Israel in America...* 1825. Smith Shute. 12mo. full contemporary calf. VG. M1. $325.00

SMITH, F.G. *Pulsars.* 1977. Cambridge. 8vo. 239p. VG/dj. K5. $30.00

SMITH, Fay Jackson. *Captain on the Phantom Presidio, a History...* 1993. Clark. 1st. 217p. as new. J2. $55.00

SMITH, Florence Pritchett. *These Entertaining People.* 1966. Macmillan. G/dj. A16. $15.00

SMITH, Frances Rand. *Architectural History of Mission San Carlos Borromeo.* 1921. Berkeley. CA Hist Survey Comm. inscr/dtd 1922. F. K7. $95.00

SMITH, Francis Henney. *Introductory Lecture Read Before Corps of Cadets...1864.* 1865. Richmond. McFarlane Fergusson. 1st. VG/prt wrp. M8. $650.00

SMITH, Frank A. *Corpse in Handcuffs.* 1969. Macmillan of Canada. 1st. F/dj. P3. $15.00

SMITH, Frank A. *Dragon's Breath.* 1980. Nelson Foster/Scott General. 1st. VG/dj. P3. $18.00

SMITH, G. Geoffrey. *Gas Turbines & Jet Propulsion for Aircraft.* 1944. Aerosphere. 123p. G. A17. $17.50

SMITH, G. Royde. *History of Bradshaw.* 1939. London/Manchester. Henry Blaylock. 4to. ils. VG. K3. $25.00

SMITH, G.M. *History & Government of South Dakota.* 1904. NY/Cincinnati/Chicago. Am Book Co. A19. $15.00

SMITH, Gary. *Windsinger.* 1976. Ballantine. A19. $15.00

SMITH, George O. *Brain Machine.* 1975. Garland. 1st. F/sans. M2. $50.00

SMITH, George O. *Hellflower.* 1953. Abelard-Schuman. 1st. F/NF. P3. $60.00

SMITH, George O. *Nomad.* 1950. Prime. 1st. VG/fair. P3. $20.00

SMITH, George O. *Pattern for Conquest.* 1949. Gnome. 1st. VG/dj. P3. $30.00

SMITH, H. Allen. *Complete Practical Joker.* 1953. Garden City. 1st. VG/VG. B5. $40.00

SMITH, H. Allen. *Desert Island Decameron.* 1945. Doubleday. VG/dj. P3. $20.00

SMITH, H. Allen. *Rhubarb.* 1946. Doubleday. 1st. VG. P3. $15.00

SMITH, H. Maynard. *Inspector Frost in the City.* 1930. Doubleday. 1st. VG. P3. $28.00

SMITH, Harmon. *Nursing in Diseases of the Eye, Ear, Nose & Throat.* 1927. Phil. Saunders. 4th. ils/photos. 335p. VG. A25. $30.00

SMITH, Harris P. *Farm Machinery & Equipment.* 1937. McGraw Hill. 460p. xl. A10. $20.00

SMITH, Harris P. *Farm Machinery & Equipment.* 1948. McGraw Hill. 520p. cloth. A10. $28.00

SMITH, Harry B. *First Nights & First Editions.* 1931. Little Brn. 1st. ils. 325p. VG/dj. K3. $35.00

SMITH, Hedrick. *New Russians.* 1990. Random. 1st. 621p. F/NF. W2. $35.00

SMITH, Helen V. *Michigan Wildflowers.* 1966. Cranbrook Inst. Bulletin 42. ils/drawings. 468p. F/dj. S15. $10.00

SMITH, Helena Huntington. *War on Powder River.* 1966. NY/London/Toronto. McGraw Hill. dj. A19. $55.00

SMITH, Hervey Garrett. *Marlinspike Sailor.* 1952. NY. Rudder Pub. 2nd enlarged. 115p. G. A17. $22.50

SMITH, Holland. *Coral & Brass: Howlin' Mad Smith's Own Story...* 1949. NY. 1st. 289p. VG. S16. $40.00

SMITH, Ingrid. *When Grandma Was a Little Girl.* nd. DSP. ils Mela Koehler-Broman. VG. M20. $20.00

SMITH, Jack. *Spend All Your Kisses, Mr Smith.* 1978. McGraw Hill. 1st. 8vo. F/dj. T10. $45.00

SMITH, James H. *History of Duchess County, New York.* 1882. Syracuse. 1st. thick 4to. 562p. VG. C6. $150.00

SMITH, Janet Adam. *Children's Illustrated Books.* 1948. London. ils. NF/VG. A4. $45.00

SMITH, Jeff. *Frugal Gourmet.* 1984. NY. Morrow. sm 4to. VG+/VG. A16. $12.00

SMITH, Jessie Wilcox. *Baby's Red Letter Days.* (1901). Syracuse, NY. Justs Food. 1st. VG/emb stiff wht wrp. D1. $160.00

SMITH, John. *Narrative of Some Sufferings, for His Christian...* 1800. Phil. Johnson. 43p. worn. V3. $85.00

SMITH, Joseph S.J. *Biblical Greek.* 1979. Reeditio. Eng ed from 4th Latin. 185p. VG. B29. $8.00

SMITH, Julie. *Axeman's Jazz.* 1991. St Martin. 1st. F/NF. D10. $35.00

SMITH, Julie. *Axeman's Jazz.* 1991. St Martin. 1st. F/VG. B3. $30.00

SMITH, Julie. *Axeman's Jazz.* 1991. St Martin. 1st. VG/VG. M22. $10.00

SMITH, Julie. *Huckleberry Fiend.* 1987. Mysterious. 1st. F/F. D10. $40.00

SMITH, Julie. *New Orleans Mourning.* 1990. St Martin. 1st. sgn. F/F. M22. $60.00

SMITH, Julie. *Tourist Trap.* 1986. Mysterious. 1st. author's 4th book. NF/F. B3. $35.00

SMITH, Julie. *Tourist Trap.* 1986. Mysterious. 1st. sgn. NF/dj. D10. $50.00

SMITH, Julie. *True-Life Adventure.* 1985. Mysterious. 1st. sgn. F/NF. D10. $65.00

SMITH, Kenneth. *Plant Viruses.* 1974. London. Chapman. 5th. 211p. dj. VG. A10. $18.00

SMITH, L. Neil. *Crystal Empire.* 1986. Tor. 1st. F/dj. P3. $18.00

SMITH, L.A. *Catalogue of Pre-Revival Dulcimers.* 1983. MO U. photos. 128p. F/dj. M4. $40.00

SMITH, Lawrence B. *American Game Preserve Shooting.* 1933. NY. Windward. photos/drawing/200p+ pl. pict cloth. VG. M12. $20.00

SMITH, Lawrence B. *Fur or Feather: Days With Dog & Gun.* 1946. Scribner. 1st Am. sgn. ils/sgn Paul Brown. VG/VG. O3. $95.00

SMITH, Lawrence Dwight. *Mystery of the Yellow Tie.* 1939. Grosset Dunlap. 220p. cloth. VG/dj. M20. $30.00

SMITH, Lee. *Cakewalk.* 1981. Putnam. 1st. F/F. D10. $75.00

SMITH, Lee. *Family Linen.* 1985. Putnam. 1st. F/F. B3. $35.00

SMITH, Lee. *Family Linen.* 1985. Putnam. 1st. sgn. F/clip. R13. $50.00

SMITH, Lee. *Me & My Baby View the Eclipse.* 1990. Putnam. 1st. F/F. A20/B3. $25.00

SMITH, Lee. *Me & My Baby View the Eclipse.* 1990. Putnam. 1st. sgn. F/F. R13. $35.00

SMITH, LeRoi. *We Came in Peace.* 1969. Classic Pr. 4to. 77p. G. K5. $10.00

SMITH, Lucy. *Biographical Sketches of Joseph Smith, the Prophet...* 1853. London. 1st. 16mo. 297p. contemporary bdg. xl. M1. $950.00

SMITH, Mark. *Moon Lamp.* 1976. Knopf. 1st. NF/dj. M2. $15.00

SMITH, Martin Cruz. *Canto for a Gypsy.* 1972. NY. Putnam. 1st. VG/G. L3. $85.00

SMITH, Martin Cruz. *Gorky Park.* 1981. Random. 1st. 356p. F/NF. W2. $30.00

SMITH, Martin Cruz. *Nightwing.* 1977. Andre Deutsch. 1st. NF/dj. P3. $30.00

SMITH, Martin Cruz. *Polar Star.* 1989. Random. 1st trade. sgn. NF/NF. B3. $45.00

SMITH, Martin Cruz. *Stallion Gate.* 1986. 1st. NF/dj. K3. $20.00

SMITH, Martin Cruz. *Stallion Gate.* 1986. Random. 1st. F/F. A20. $25.00

SMITH, Mary P. Wells. *Young Puritans in King Phillip's War.* 1920. Little Brn. 373p. G+. V3. $15.00

SMITH, Melville. *Auction Bridge Up-To-Date.* nd. London. 74p+auction scoring table. VG. S1. $15.00

SMITH, Michael L. *Pacific Visions.* 1987. Yale. ils. 243p. F/F. S15. $15.00

SMITH, Mitchell. *Daydreams.* 1987. McGraw Hill. 1st. F/F. H11. $30.00

SMITH, Mitchell. *Daydreams.* 1987. McGraw Hill. 1st. NF/dj. P3. $18.00

SMITH, Mrs. J.G. *Angels & Women.* 1924. AB Abac Co. 1st revised. VG. M2. $27.00

SMITH, Myron. *WWII at Sea: Bibliography of Sources in English.* 1976-1990. Metuchen. 4 vol. VG. S16. $95.00

SMITH, N. Gerard. *Dahlia Cultivation.* ca 1948. NY. ils. 96p. dj. B26. $10.00

SMITH, Nathan. *Case of Ovarian Dropsy, Successfully Removed...* 1822. Phil. 1st. 780p. full leather. A13. $150.00

SMITH, Nora Archibald. *Kate Douglas Wiggin As Her Sister Knew Her.* 1925. 12 pl. 407p. VG. A4. $45.00

SMITH, Perry Michael. *Last Rites.* 1971. Scribner. 1st. F/NF. B4. $85.00

SMITH, Peter C. *Design & Construction of Stables & Ancillary Buildings.* 1967. London. Allen. 1st. VG/G. O3. $40.00

SMITH, Philip. *Mineral Resources of Alaska: Report on Progress...* 1936. GPO. 8vo. gilt burgundy cloth. VG. P4. $45.00

SMITH, Philip. *New Directions in Bookbinding.* 1974. London. 1st. VG/VG. T9. $50.00

SMITH, Red. *Best of Red Smith.* 1963. WAtts. 1st. VG.VG. P8. $30.00

SMITH, Richard Gordon. *Ancient Tales & Folklore of Japan.* 1986. Mitchell. F/dj. P3. $25.00

SMITH, Richard K. *Airships Akron & Macon.* 1972. Annapolis. later prt. 228p. VG/torn. B18. $65.00

SMITH, Robert. *Illustrated History of Pro Football.* 1970. Grosset Dunlap. 1st. photos. VG/VG. P8. $8.50

SMITH, Rosamond; see Oates, Joyce Carol.

SMITH, S. Bayliss. *British Waders in Their Haunts.* 1950. London. photos. VG/VG. M17. $25.00

SMITH, Samuel Stanhope. *Essay on Causes of Variety of Complexion & Figure...* 1810. New Brunswick, NJ. 2nd. 411p. contemporary sheep. VG. B14. $250.00

SMITH, Shelley. *Game of Consequences.* 1978. Macmillan. 1st. F/dj. P3. $20.00

SMITH, Steve. *Hunting Upland Gamebirds.* 1987. Stackpole. 176p. M/dj. A17. $17.50

SMITH, Surrey. *Village That Wandered.* 1960. London. 1st. F/dj. M2. $25.00

SMITH, Thorne. *Bishop's Jaegers.* 1933. Doubleday Doran. VG. P3. $12.00

SMITH, Thorne. *Dreams End.* 1927. NY. 1st. VG. B5. $65.00

SMITH, Truman. *Examination of Question of Anaesthesia, Arising on...* 1859. NY. 1st. 154p. brd/rebacked leather. A13. $300.00

SMITH, W.D.A. *Under the Influence: History of Nitrous Oxide...* 1982. London. 1st. 188p. dj. A13. $75.00

SMITH, Wallace. *Little Tigress.* 1923. Putnam. 1st. ils. 209p. decor cloth. F3. $15.00

SMITH, Wilbur. *Burning Stove.* 1985. Stoddard. VG/dj. P3. $20.00

SMITH, Wilbur. *Hungry As the Sea.* 1978. Heinemann. 1st. VG/dj. P3. $25.00

SMITH, Wilbur. *Men of Men.* 1981. Heinemann. 1st. VG/dj. P3. $20.00

SMITH, Wilbur. *Rage.* 1987. Little Brn. 1st. VG/dj. P3. $18.00

SMITH, Wilbur. *When the Lion Feeds.* 1964. Viking. 1st. NF/dj. P3. $75.00

SMITH, William Gardner. *Last of the Conquerors.* 1948. Farrar Straus. 1st. gray brd. VG. M25. $75.00

SMITH, William Gardner. *South Street.* 1954. FSY. 1st. NF/dj. M25. $60.00

SMITH, William Gardner. *Stone Face.* 1963. Farrar. 1st. NF/NF. B2. $75.00

SMITH, William Jay. *Army Brat.* 1980. NY. Persea. 1st. F/NF. B4. $45.00

SMITH, William Jay. *Ho for a Hat!* 1989. Little Brn. 1st thus. inscr. sm 4to. unp. VG+. C14. $12.00

SMITH, William. *Diary & Selected Papers of Chief Justice Wm Smith 1784-1794.* 1965. Toronto. Champlain Soc. 1/775. 8vo. 335p. red cloth. unopened. P4. $95.00

SMITH, William. *Pseudoic Majesty.* 1903. Liberty Pub. 1st Am. VG. M2. $27.00

SMITH, Winifred. *Children's Singing Games.* 1894. David Nutt. 1st. lg 8vo. M5. $65.00

SMITH & THIERS. *Contribution Toward a Monograph of...Suillus.* 1964. Ann Arbor. Herbarium Papers. 116p. VG. A10. $28.00

SMITH & WEBER. *Field Guide to Southern Mushrooms.* 1985. Ann Arbor. 280p. VG/wrp. B1. $20.00

SMITH & WILCOX. *Farmer's Cyclopedia of Agriculture.* 1922. Orange Judd. 619p. cloth. VG. A10. $25.00

SMITS, Ted. *Game of Soccer.* 1968. Prentice Hall. 1st. photos/stats/index. G+/dj. P8. $15.00

SMOLLETT, Tobias. *Adventures of Gil Blas de Santillane...* 1819. London. Thomas M'Lean. 3 vol. 8vo. 15 aquatint pl. teg. morocco. NF. B24. $850.00

SMOLLETT, Tobias. *Adventures of Peregrine Pickle.* 1936. LEC. 2 vol. 1/1500. tall 4to. ils/sgn John Ansten/24 full-p pl. djs. H13. $225.00

SMOLUCHOWSKI, R. *Solar System.* 1983. Scientific Books. 174p. F/dj. D8. $12.00

SMUCKER, Samuel M. *Life of Col John Charles Fremont & His Narrative...* 1856. Miller Orton Mulligan. G+. M20. $35.00

SMYTH, Henry D. *Atomic Energy for Military Purposes.* 1945. Princeton. 1st commercial. 264p. F/dj. A17. $150.00

SMYTH, W.H. *Sailor's Word-Book.* 1867. London. Blackie. revised. 744p. T7. $110.00

SMYTHE, H. DeWolf. *Atomic Energy for Military Purposes.* 1945. Princeton. 1st hc. VG. E6. $65.00

SNAITH, J.C. *Araminta.* 1923. McLeod. 1st. VG. P3. $20.00

SNAVELY, Joseph Richard. *Intimate Story of Milton S Hershey.* 1957. self pub. sgn/dtd. photos. 549p. F. H1. $95.00

SNEDEKER, Caroline Dale. *Downright Dencey.* (1927). Doubleday. early prt ($3.95 dj). 8vo. 314p. dj. T5. $30.00

SNELGROVE, L.E. *Queen Rearing.* 1946. London. 1st. 344p. VG. B5. $25.00

SNELL, Roy J. *Eskimo Island & Penguin Land.* 1930. Chicago. Albert Whitman. later prt. school xl. P4. $35.00

SNELL, Roy J. *Mystery Stories for Boys: White Fire.* 1922. Reilly Lee. 238p. VG/dj. M20. $25.00

SNELL, Roy J. *Sign of the Green Arrow.* 1939. Reilly lee. VG/dj. P3. $30.00

SNELL, Roy J. *Sparky Ames of the Ferry Command.* 1943. Racine. Whitman. 1st. ils EL Darwin. VG/VG. A25. $22.00

SNELL, Roy J. *Whispers at Dawn.* 1934. Reilly Lee. sgn. 247p. VG/dj. M20. $35.00

SNODGRASS, Melinda. *Very Large Array.* 1987. NM U. 1st. F/dj. P3. $23.00

SNODGRASS, W.D. *Heart's Needle.* 1959. Knopf. 1st. 1/1500. author's 1st book. F/NF. B2. $125.00

SNOW, Dorothea. *Circus Boy Under the Big Top.* 1957. Whitman. TVTI. VG. P3. $20.00

SNOW, Edward Rowe. *Fury of the Seas.* 1964. Dodd Mead. 271p. gr cloth. VG/dj. P4. $25.00

SNOW, Edward Rowe. *Tales of Terror & Tragedy.* 1979. NY. Dodd Mead. 1st. sm 8vo. 250p. VG/dj. P4. $20.00

SNOW, Jack. *Shaggy Man of Oz.* (1949). Reilly Lee. 1st/1st state. ils Frank Kramer. 32p. NF/dj. D1. $300.00

SNOWDEN, J. *Truth About Mormonism.* 1926. NY. 1st. ils/index. 369p. VG/VG. B5. $35.00

SNOWDON. *Snowdon: Personal View.* 1979. London. Weidenfeld Nicholson. 240p. cloth. dj. D2. $125.00

SNYDER, Gary. *Dimensions of a Life.* 1991. Sierra Club. 1st. NF/NF. B3. $40.00

SNYDER, T.E. *Our Enemy the Termite.* 1935. Ithaca. Comstock. ils. 196p. decor cloth. NF/VG+. M12. $45.00

SNYDER, Zilpha Keatley. *Headless Cupid.* 1972 (1971). Atheneum. 2nd. 8vo. orange cloth. NF/VG. T5. $25.00

SOBIN, Harris. *Florence Townsite AT: Final Report of Florence Townsite...* 1977. private prt. 1st. ils/notes/bibliography/maps. 359p. NF/VG+. B19. $100.00

SODERLUND, Jean R. *Quakers & Slavery.* 1988. Princeton. 220p. sc. V3. $14.00

SOGGIN, Alberto. *Introduction to the Old Testament From Its Origins...* 1980. Westminster. 508p. VG. B29. $18.00

SOHL, Jerry. *Altered Ego.* 1954. Rinehart. 1st. VG. P3. $13.00

SOHL, Jerry. *Prelude to Peril.* 1957. Rinehart. 1st. VG/dj. P3. $30.00

SOHL, Jerry. *Spun Sugar Hole.* 1951. S&S. 1st. VG/dj. P3. $15.00

SOLC, V. *Swords & Daggers of Indonesia.* 1970. London. Spring. ils/pl. gilt pict cloth/brass sword closure. VG. M12. $45.00

SOLDATI, Mario. *Malacca Cane.* 1973. NY. 1st. F/F. H11. $20.00

SOLECKI, Ralph S. *Shanidar: The First Flower People.* 1971. Knopf. 1st. 290p. NF/dj. W1. $20.00

SOLLY, S. Edwin. *Handbook of Medical Climatology Embodying Its Principles...* 1897. Phil. 1st. 470p. xl. A13. $175.00

SOLOGUB, F. *Petty Demon.* 1962. NY. 1st. trans A Field. VG/VG. T9. $25.00

SOLOGUB, F. *Sweet-Scented Name & Other Fairy Tales, Fables & Stories.* 1915. Putnam. 1st Am. 8vo. 240p. gilt blue cloth. F. T10. $50.00

SOLOMITA, Stephen. *Bad to the Bone.* 1991. Putnam. 1st. F/dj. P3. $22.00

SOLOMON, David. *LSD: The Consciousness-Expanding Drug.* 1964. Putnam. 1st. 8vo. 273p. F/G. H1. $35.00

SOLOMON, Maury. *Album of Voyager.* 1990. Franklin Watts. 4to. 64p. xl. dj. K5. $15.00

SOLOVYEV, Vladimir. *Meaning of Love.* 1947. Internat U Pr. 2nd (1946 sic) 8vo. 82p. F/VG. H1. $25.00

SOLZHENITSYN, Alexander. *Candle in the Wind.* 1973. Bodley Head/Oxford. 1st Eng. trans from Russian. F/dj. Q1. $50.00

SOLZHENITSYN, Alexander. *Lenin in Zurich.* 1976. FSG. 1st. F/F. B35. $25.00

SOLZHENITSYN, Alexander. *Stories & Prose Poems.* 1971. FSG. 1st. F/F. B35. $26.00

SOMERVILLE, Hugh. *Sceptre.* 1959. NY. Funk. ils/55 photos/charts. 185p. dj. T7. $35.00

SOMERVILLE, J. Alexander. *Man of Color, an Autobiography.* 1949. Los Angeles. Morrison. 1st. NF/VG. B4. $175.00

SOMERVILLE, Mollie. *Washington Walked Here.* 1970. Acropolis. 1st. 256p. cloth. VG/dj. M20. $25.00

SOMERVILLE & ROSS. *Irish RM Complete.* 1962. London. Faber. 1st. VG/VG. O3. $45.00

SOMERVILLE & ROSS. *Wheel-Tracks.* 1934. London. Longman Gr. VG. O3. $35.00

SOMMER, Frederick. *Frederick Sommer at Seventy-Five: A Retrospective.* 1980. Long Beach. CA State. exhibition catalog. 72p. wrp. D11. $50.00

SOMMER, Scott. *Nearing's Grace.* 1979. Taplinger. 1st. sgn. author's 1st book. F/NF. L3. $125.00

SOMMERS, Richard J. *Richmond Redeemed: Siege at Petersburg.* 1981. ils. VG/VG. M17. $27.50

SOMNER, William. *Treatise of Gavelkind, Both Name & Thing...* 1660. London. Prt R&W Leybourn for Author. contemporary bdg. G. M11. $750.00

SONDERN, Fredric. *Brotherhood of Evil: The Mafia.* 1959. FSC. VG. P3. $15.00

SONIN, Eileen. *ESP-Ecially Ghosts.* 1970. Clarke Irwin. 1st. VG/dj. P3. $15.00

SONNICHSEN, C.L. *Billy King's Tombstone, the Private Life of AZ Boom Town.* 1942. Caxton. 1st. 233p. VG. J2. $145.00

SONNICHSEN, C.L. *I'll Die Before I'll Run.* 1951. NY. 1st. 294p. G+/torn. B18. $25.00

SONNICHSEN, C.L. *Tucson: Life & Times of an American City.* 1982. OK U. 1st. inscr. ils/notes/bibliography/index. 369p. F/NF. B19. $50.00

SONTAG, Susan. *Benefactor.* 1963. Farrar Straus. 1st. NF/VG. M19. $45.00

SONTAG, Susan. *Volcano Lover.* 1992. FSG. 1st. sgn. VG/VG. A23. $40.00

SOPHOCLES. *Oedipus the King.* 1955. Haarlem. 1st thus. 1/1500. ils/sgn Demetrois Galanis. F/glassine/case. Q1. $250.00

SORACCO, Sin. *Edge City.* 1992. Dutton. 1st. author's 1st novel. F/F. M22. $15.00

SORACCO, Sin. *Low Bite.* 1989. Black Lizard. 1st. VG/dj. P3. $17.00

SOREL, Charles. *Bibliotheqve Francoise.* 1664. Paris. 8vo. gilt calf. R12. $375.00

SOREL, Stefan. *Tarzan Hat Getraumt.* 1924. Vienna. Carl Stephenson. 242p. VG. M20. $250.00

SORENSON, Theodore C. *Kennedy.* 1965. Harper Row. 1st. F/dj. Q1. $40.00

SORRENTINO, Gilbert. *Darkness Surrounds Us.* 1960. Highlands. Williams. 1st. author's 1st book. F/stapled wrp/dj. R13. $75.00

SOSEKI, Muso. *Sun at Midnight. 23 Poems by...* 1985. NY. Jadja. 1st. 1/226. sgn Merwin/Frasconi. M/striped bl wrp. B24. $165.00

SOUSTELLE, Jacque. *Olmecs.* 1984. Doubleday. 1st. 214p. dj. F3. $30.00

SOUTAR, Andrew. *Kharduni.* 1934. Macauley. 1st. VG. M2. $22.00

SOUTHALL, Eliza. *Brief Memoir With Portions of Diary, Letters...* 1869. Diffusion of Knowledge. 195p. xl. V3. $18.00

SOUTHERN, Terry. *Blue Movie.* 1973. Calder Boyars. 1st. F/F. M19. $35.00

SOUTHERN, Terry. *Flash & Filigree.* 1958. Coward McCann. VG/dj. P3. $35.00

SOUTHERN, Terry. *Magic Christian.* 1960. Random. 1st. F/F. B4. $150.00

SOUTHERN, Terry. *Red-Dirt Marijuana.* 1967. NAL. 1st. NF/NF. H11. $50.00

SOUTHERN, Terry. *Red-Dirt Marijuana.* 1967. NAL. 1st. VG/dj. P3. $45.00

SOUTHERN, Terry. *Texas Summer.* 1991. Arcade. 1st. F/F. A24. $25.00

SOUTHWART, Elizabeth. *Password to Fairyland.* 1920. Stokes. 1st Am. ils Anderson/8 full-p pl. R5. $225.00

SOUTHWICK, L. *Dwarf Trees.* 1948. 1st. ils. VG/dj. E6. $20.00

SOUTHWORTH, J.R. *El Estado de Sinaloa, Mexico: Sus Industrias Commerciales...* 1898. SF. Southworth. Spanish/Eng text. 102p+30p ads. gilt cloth. D11. $100.00

SOWELL, Thomas. *Ethnic America: A History.* 1981. Basic. 1st. 353p. NF/NF. B4. $65.00

SOWERBY, Millicent. *Our Pets' Play Book. Mrs Strang's Play Books.* ca 1925. np. 12p. R5. $125.00

SOWERBY & SOWERBY. *Yesterday's Children.* 1908. London. 1st. 4to. gilt cloth/mc pl. VG. M5. $110.00

SOWLS, L.K. *Peccaries.* 1984. Tucson. 8vo. ils/photos. 251p. F/F. M12. $30.00

SOYER, A. *Modern Housewife; or, Menagere.* 1857 (1849). VG. E6. $125.00

SPAIGHT, J.M. *Aircraft in War.* 1914. London. 1st. 172p. xl. B18. $75.00

SPAIN, John. *Death Is Like That.* 1943. Dutton. 1st. VG. P3. $30.00

SPALDING, H. *Treasure-Trove of American Jewish Humor.* 1978 (1976). VG/VG. E6. $12.00

SPALDING, J.L. *Socialism & Labor & Other Arguments: Social, Political...* 1902. McClurg. 1st. VG/VG. V4. $20.00

SPALDING, Jesse. *War Years of Canada's Bluenose.* 1974. NY. Vantage. 61p. dj. T7. $20.00

SPALDING, W.R. *Music at Harvard: Historical Review.* 1935. ils. VG. M17. $20.00

SPARK, Muriel. *Fanfarlo & Other Verse.* 1952. Hand & Flower. 1st. F/1st issue wrp. Q1. $200.00

SPARK, Muriel. *Only Problem.* 1984. Franklin Lib. 1st. sgn. ils Vivienne Flesher. full leather. F. Q1. $40.00

SPARK & STANFORD. *Emily Bronte: Her Life & Work.* 1960. NY. London House/Maxwell. 1st. photos. 271p. VG/dj. A25. $35.00

SPARKE, Michael. *Truth Brought to Light.* 1692. London. Baldwin. 4 parts in 1. 8vo. disbound. R12. $200.00

SPARKS, Edwin Erle. *Lincoln-Douglas Debates of 1858.* 1908. IL State Hist Lib. 627p. G. A17. $22.50

SPARKS, H.F.D. *Synopsis of the Gospels.* 1964. Fortress. 248p. VG/dj. B29. $14.00

SPARLING, Sharon. *Glass Mountain.* 1986. London. O'Mara. 1st. F/F. T12. $20.00

SPARROW, Walter Shaw. *Angling in British Art.* 1923. London. 1st. ils/index/bibliography. 288p. buckram. B18. $225.00

SPATE, O.H.K. *Spanish Lake.* 1979. NM U. ils/maps. 372p. 372p. F/dj. O7. $50.00

SPAULDING, E.S. *Venison & Breath of Sage.* 1967. Santa Barbara. Genns. ils DR Johnson. 312p. cloth. F/VG+. M12. $45.00

SPAULDING, Karen. *Huarochiri.* 1984. Stanford. 1st. 364p. F3. $20.00

SPAULDING, Perley. *Diseases of North American Forest Trees Planted Abroad.* 1956. WA, DC. USDA Agric Handbook 100. sc. B26. $12.50

SPEAIGHT. *History of English Toy Theatre.* 1969. 2nd/revised. 4to. ils/12 mc pl. F/dj. A4. $95.00

SPEARE, Elizabeth George. *Witch of Blackird Pond.* 1958. Boston. Houghton Mifflin. 19th. 249p. VG/dj. V3. $9.50

SPEARS, John R. *Short History of the American Navy.* 1907. Scribner. 8vo. ils. 134p. P4. $55.00

SPECTOR, R.H. *After Tet, the Bloodiest Year in Vietnam.* 1993. NY. 1st. ils/photos. VG+/dj. B18. $19.50

SPECTOR, R.H. *Eagle Against the Sun: American War With Japan.* 1985. NY. 1st. ils. 589p. VG. S16. $18.50

SPEED, Nell. *Molly Brown's Freshman Days.* 1912. NY. Hurst. 1st. ils CL Wrenn. G+. A25. $8.00

SPEED, Thomas. *Guilty-Covered Clergy-Man Unveiled...* 1657. London. Giles CAlvert. sm 8vo. 79p. recent bdg. H13. $95.00

SPEER, Albert. *Spandau: Secret Diaries.* 1976. NY. photos/index. 463p. VG/VG. S16. $22.50

SPEER, William. *Oldest & Newest Empire: China & the United States.* 1870. Hartford. Scranton. thick 8vo. ils. red fabricoid. F. R3. $225.00

SPEISER & SPEISER. *Changing West.* 1975. Miles City, MT. H&T Quality Prt. $45.00

SPELTZ, Robert. *Real Runabouts II.* 1978. Lake Mills, IA. Graphic Pub. 4to. 800+ ils. 230p. dj. T7. $45.00

SPENCE, Bill. *Harpooned: Story of Whaling.* 1980. Crescent. 192p. VG/dj. P4. $20.00

SPENCE, Lewis. *Myths of the North American Indians.* 1914. London. Harrap. 8vo. ils/map. 393p. F. K7. $95.00

SPENCE, William. *Tracts on Political Economy.* 1933. private prt (Viking). 8vo. rpt from 1822 London. paper brd. VG. T10. $75.00

SPENCER, Colin. *Anarchy of Love.* 1963. Weybright Talley. 1st. VG/dj. P3. $35.00

SPENCER, Cornelia. *Romulo Voice of Freedom.* 1953. John Day. 256p. VG+. P1. $20.00

SPENCER, Ross H. *Fedorovich File.* 1991. DIF. 1st. NF/dj. P3. $20.00

SPENCER, Ross H. *Monastery Nightmare.* 1986. Mysterious. 1st. F/dj. P3. $20.00

SPENCER, Scott. *Last Night at the Brain Thieves Ball.* 1973. Houghton Mifflin. 1st. VG/dj. P3. $25.00

SPENCER, Scott. *Preservation Hall.* 1976. Knopf. 1st. F/clip. M25. $25.00

SPENCER, William Browning. *Maybe I'll Call Anna.* 1990. Permanent Pr. 1st. F/F. M22. $15.00

SPENDER, Michael. *Island-Reefs of the Queensland Coast.* 1930. Royal Geographical Soc. ils/fld maps. wrp. P4. $45.00

SPENDER, Ramon. *Counter-Attack in Spain.* 1937. Houghton Mifflin. 1st. NF/dj. B2. $35.00

SPENDER, Stephen. *Journals 1939-1983.* 1985. London. 1/150. sgn. edit J Goldsmith. VG/case. T9. $150.00

SPENSER, Edmund. *Faerie Queene.* 1953. Oxford. LEC. 1st thus. 2 vol. 1/1500. lils/sgn Agnes Miller. F/djs/case. Q1. $250.00

SPERDUTI, Dominick R. *For You I Commit Murder.* 1956. Christoper. 1st. VG/dj. P3. $20.00

SPERRY, Armstrong. *One Day With Jambi in Sumatra.* (1934). Phil. John Winston. 1st. 8vo. VG. D1. $60.00

SPHYROERAS. *Maps & Map-Makers of the Aegean.* 1985. Athens. Olkos Ltd. 4to. ils/166 maps. 264p. VG/worn. A4. $245.00

SPICE ISLANDS HOME ECONOMICS. *Spice Islands Cookbook.* 1961. Menlo Park, CA. Lane. 1st. 8vo. 208p. cloth. NF/VG. T10. $30.00

SPICER, Edward H. *People of Pascua.* 1988. AZ U. 1st. 331p. F/F. B19. $30.00

SPIELMANN, Mrs. M.H. *Rainbow Book. Tales of Fun & Fancy.* 1909. Chatto Windus. 1st. ils Rackham. B24. $300.00

SPIELMANN. *Catalogue of Library of Miniature Books...* nd (1961). rpt. 1/150. ils. 500+ entries. 304p. F. A4. $85.00

SPIER, Peter. *Peter Spier's Christmas.* 1938. Doubleday. 1st. xl. VG. C8. $25.00

SPIESS, Gerry. *Along Against the Atlantic.* 1981. Control Data Pub. 1st. sgn. VG/VG. B11. $25.00

SPILHAUS, Athelstan F. *Weathercraft.* 1967 (1951). Viking. 10th. xl. dj. K5. $12.00

SPILLANE, Mickey. *Bloody Sunrise.* 1965. Dutton. 1st. F/VG. M19. $45.00

SPILLANE, Mickey. *Day of Ghosts.* 1964. Dutton. 1st. F/F. M15. $50.00

SPILLANE, Mickey. *Death Dealers.* 1965. Dutton. 1st. VG/VG. M22. $20.00

SPILLANE, Mickey. *Deep.* 1961. Dutton. 1st. VG/F. M19. $45.00

SPILLANE, Mickey. *Erection Set.* 1972. WH Allen. 1st. NF/dj. P3. $30.00

SPILLANE, Mickey. *I, the Jury.* 1947. Dutton. 1st. NF/VG. B4. $450.00

SPILLANE, Mickey. *Killing Man.* 1989. Dutton. 1st. inscr. rem mk. F/F. R14. $60.00

SPILLANE, Mickey. *Killing Man.* 1989. Dutton. 1st. VG/dj. T12. $20.00

SPILLANE, Mickey. *Killing Man.* 1989. Franklin Lib. 1st. sgn. full leather. F. Q1. $60.00

SPILLER, Burton L. *More Grouse Feathers.* (1938). Derrydale. 1/950. tall 8vo. ils Lynn Bogue Hunt. NF. H7. $100.00

SPILLMAN, Louis. *So This Is South America.* 1962. VA. 1st. inscr. 140p. dj. F3. $15.00

SPINAZZE, Libera Martina. *Index to the Argonauts of California: Chas Warren Haskins.* 1975. New Orleans. Polyanthos. 514p. prt wrp. D11. $50.00

SPINDLER, Will. *Tragedy Strikes at Wounded Knee.* 1955. Gordon Journal Pub. 1st. sgn. photos. 80p. VG/pict wrp. J2. $85.00

SPINGARN, Amy. *Humility & Pride.* 1926. Harcourt Brace. 1st. ils. NF. B4. $85.00

SPINRAD, Norman. *Agent of Chaos.* 1988. Watts. 1st. F/dj. M2. $15.00

SPINRAD, Norman. *Child of Fortune.* 1985. Bantam. 1st. VG/dj. P3. $20.00

SPINRAD, Norman. *Men in the Jungle.* 1967. Doubleday. 1st. F/dj. M2. $60.00

SPINRAD, Norman. *Men in the Jungle.* 1967. Doubleday. 1st. VG/dj. P3. $50.00

SPINRAD, Norman. *Songs From the Stars.* 1980. S&S. 1st. F/dj. P3. $20.00

SPITZ, Armand N. *Start in Meteorology.* 1943 (1942). NY. Norman Henley. 2nd. 8vo. 97p. VG/dj. K5. $15.00

SPIVACK & STAPLES. *Company of Camelot.* 1994. Greenwood. F. P3. $45.00

SPLIT, S. *Art of Cooking & Serving.* 1929. Proctor & Gamble. mc pl. G+. E6. $15.00

SPOCK, L.E. *Guide to the Study of Rocks.* 1953. Harper. 1st. 256p. F. D8. $15.00

SPOTA, Luis. *Wounds of Hunger.* 1957. Houghton Mifflin. 1st Am. F/F. B4. $150.00

SPOTO, Donald. *Dark Side of Genius: Life of Alf.* 1983. Little Brn. 1st. VG/dj. P3. $20.00

SPRAGUE, Marshall. *Gallery of Dudes.* 1966. Little Brn. 1st. ils. F/dj. C8/M4. $20.00

SPRAT, Thomas. *History of Royal-Society of London.* 1702. London. Scot Chiswell Chapman Sawbridge. 4to. 2 fld pl. cloth. R12. $475.00

SPRATLIN, V.B. *Juan Latino: Slave & Humanist.* 1938. NY. Spinner. 1st. 216p. F. B4. $500.00

SPRATLING, William Philip. *Epilepsy & Its Treatment.* 1904. Phil. Saunders. heavy 8vo. 522p+16p catalog. ruled olive cloth. VG. G1. $175.00

SPRATT, H. Philip. *Transatlantic Paddle Steamers.* 1951. Glasgow. Brn Ferguson. 1st. 9 pl/4 fld tables. 82p. dj. T7. $40.00

SPRING, Agnes Wright. *Caspar Collins, Life & Exploits of an Indian Fighter...* 1927. Columbia. 1st. ils. 187p. VG. J2. $185.00

SPRING, Agnes Wright. *Tales of the 04 Ranch, Recollections of Harold J Cook...* 1968. NE U. 1st. photos. 221p. VG/VG. J2. $90.00

SPRING, Agnes Wright. *70 Years in Cow Country.* 1942. Wyoming Stock Growers. 1st. photos Adams Herd. 273p. VG. J2. $175.00

SPRING, Gardiner. *Glory of Christ: Illustrated in His Character & History...* 1852. Dodd Mead. vol 2 only. 8vo. 312p. gilt stp cloth. H1. $35.00

SPRING, Howard. *Darkie & Co.* 1947 (1932). London. Oxford. rpt. 12mo. 288p. VG. T5. $26.00

SPRING, Norma. *Alaska: The Complete Travel Book.* 1970. Macmillan. xl. dj. A19. $10.00

SPRINGER, Norman. *Dark River.* 1928. Watt. 1st. VG. M2. $35.00

SPROAT, Lin. *Wodehouse at War.* 1981. Ticknor Fields. 1st. NF/dj. P3. $20.00

SPRUILL, Steven. *Paradox Planet.* 1988. Doubleday. 1st. NF/dj. P3. $18.00

SPRUILL, Steven. *Psychopath Plague.* 1978. Doubleday. 1st. F/dj. M2. $15.00

SPRUNGMAN, Ormal I. *Photography Afield.* 1951. Stackpole. 1st. 449p. 4to. A17. $15.00

SPURR, J.E. *Geology Applied to Selenology III.* (1948). Rumford. 253p. xl. K5. $35.00

SPURZHEIM, Johann Gaspar. *Anatomy of the Brain With General View of Nervous System.* 1834 (1826). Boston. Marsh Capen Lyon. 1st Am. 18 pl. 244p. drab brn cloth. G. G1. $325.00

SPURZHEIM, Johann Gaspar. *Observations on Deranged Manifestations of the Mind...* 1836. Boston. Marsh Capen Lyon. 3rd Am. 272p. VG. G1. $175.00

SPURZHEIM, Johann Gaspar. *Physiognomical System of Drs Gall & Spurzheim...* 1815. London. Baldwin Craddock. 2nd. thick 8vo. 19 copper pl. 581p. modern cloth. G1. $350.00

SPYRI, Johanna. *Erick & Sally.* 1921. Boston. 3 mc pl. teg. gilt cloth. VG. M5. $55.00

SPYRI, Johanna. *Eveli the Little Singer.* nd. AL Burt. decor brd. VG. P3. $20.00

SPYRI, Johanna. *Heidi.* 1915. Grosset Dunlap. 318p. cloth. VG/dj. M20. $22.50

SPYRI, Johanna. *Heidi.* 1944. Whitman. ils Arthur Jameson. VG/dj. P3. $15.00

SQUIBB, G.D. *High Court of Chivalry, a Study of Civil Law in England.* 1959. Clarendon. M11. $85.00

SQUIRES, W.H.T. *Through Centuries Three: Short History of Virginia.* 1929. Portsmouth. 1st. sgn/#d. 605p. NF. M4. $40.00

STABLEFORD, Brian M. *Empire of Fear.* 1988. London. 1st. sgn. F/dj. M2. $35.00

STABLEFORD, Brian M. *Man in a Cage.* 1975. John Day. 1st. VG/dj. P3. $20.00

STABLEFORD, Brian M. *Paradox Game.* 1976. London. 1st. sgn. F/dj. M2. $45.00

STABLEFORD, Brian M. *Promised Land.* 1975. Dent. 1st. sgn. F/F. P3. $25.00

STABLER & STAINBACK. *Snake.* 1986. Doubleday. 1st. photos. F/dj. P8/T12. $25.00

STABLES, Gordon. *On to the Rescue: A Tale of the Indian Mutiny.* ca 1898. London. John Shaw. New Ed. 8vo. 374p. teg. gilt pict cloth. T10. $50.00

STACEY, Susannah. *Goodbye, Nanny Gray.* 1987. Summit. 1st. VG/dj. P3. $16.00

STACEY, Susannah. *Knife at the Opera.* 1988. Summit. 1st. F/VG+. N4. $15.00

STACKPOLE, Edouard A. *Voyage of the Huron & the Huntress.* 1955. Mystic. Marine Hist Assc. 86p. prt wrp. P4. $55.00

STACKPOLE, Edward J. *Chancellorsville: Lee's Greatest Battle.* 1958. Bonanza. 384p. cloth. VG/dj. M20. $20.00

STACKPOLE, H. DeVere. *Blue Lagoon.* nd. World Wide. NF/dj. M2. $25.00

STACKPOLE, H. DeVere. *City in the Sea.* 1926. London. 1st. VG. M2. $25.00

STADE, George. *Confessions of a Lady-Killer.* 1980. Muller. 1st. F/dj. P3. $18.00

STADLEY, Pat. *Autumn of a Hunter.* 1971. Collins Crime Club. 1st. VG/dj. P3. $20.00

STAFF, Frank. *Picture Postcard & Its Origin.* 1966. Praeger. 95p. cloth. VG+/dj. M20. $35.00

STAFFORD, Edward P. *Far & the Deep.* 1967. Putnam. 1st. inscr. VG/VG. B11. $65.00

STAFFORD, Jean. *Collected Stories.* 1969. FSG. 1st. F/F. B4. $125.00

STAFFORD, Muriel. *X Marks the Dot.* 1943. DSP. 1st. VG. P3. $25.00

STAFLEU, F.A. *Taxonomic Literature.* 1967. Utrecht. 8vo. 556p. VG. B1. $65.00

STAGG, D.J. *Calendar of New Forest Documents 1244-1334.* 1979. Trowbridge. Hampshire County Council. M11. $50.00

STALKER, John. *Stalker Affair: Shocking True Story of 6 Deaths...* 1988. Viking. 2nd. VG/dj. V4. $20.00

STALLINGS, Penny. *Flesh & Fantasy.* 1981. Bell. 2nd. ils/photos. NF/dj. C9. $35.00

STALLYBRASS, W.T.S. *Salmond's Law of Torts, a Treatise on English Law...* 1945. London. crimson buckram. M11. $45.00

STANDARD, Stella. *Our Daily Bread.* 1970. Bonanza. VG/dj. A16. $12.00

STANDISH, Burt L. *Frank Merriwell's School Days.* 1901 (1896). McKay. 302p. cloth. G. M20. $30.00

STANDISH, Robert. *Elephant Walk.* 1949. Macmillan. 1st. VG. T12. $25.00

STANDLEY, Paul C. *Trees & Shrubs of Mexico. Part 4 of 5.* 1924. WA. GPO. 8vo. gr buckram. xl. A22. $60.00

STANDON. *Gore Vidal: Primary & Secondary Bibliography.* 1978. 247p. VG. A4. $75.00

STANDS IN TIMBER, John. *Cheyenne Memories.* 1967. New Haven. Yale. 1st. photos/mc pl. NF/dj. L3. $85.00

STANEK, V.J. *Pictorial Encyclopedia of Insects.* 1972 (1969). Hamlyn, London. 8vo. 544p. dj. B1. $22.50

STANFORD, Alfred. *Navigator: Story of Nathaniel Bowditch.* 1927. NY. Morrow. 1st. 300p. T7. $35.00

STANFORD, Derek. *Inside the Forties, Literary Memoirs.* 1977. London. 1st. VG/VG. w/3 sgn letters. T9. $50.00

STANFORD, Ernest Elwood. *Mascot Goes Across.* 1929. NY. Century. 1st. ils. VG. K3. $20.00

STANFORD, J.K. *Last Chukker.* 1954. Devin Adair. 1st. VG/VG. O3. $25.00

STANFORTH, Deirdre. *New Orleans Restaurant Cookbook.* 1967. Doubleday. intro/index. VG. A16. $17.50

STANGER, Frank M. *South From San Francisco.* 1963. San Mateo Co Hist Assn. ils/photos. 214p. terra-cotta cloth. F. K7. $50.00

STANHOPE, Hester. *Memoirs of Lady Hester Stanhope...* 1845. ils. 3-quarter leather/marbled brd. VG+. S13. $100.00

STANLEY, Edwin. *Rambles in Wonderland; or, Up the Yellowstone...* 1878. Appleton. 1st. 179p. G. J2. $225.00

STANLEY, Henry M. *In Darkest Africa; or, Quest, Rescue & Retreat...* 1890. Scribner. 2 vol. 1st Am. 8vo. xl/missing 2 maps. VG. W1. $45.00

STANLEY, S.M. *Extinction.* 1987. Scientific. ils. 242p. F/dj. D8. $26.00

STANLEY, Wallace. *Our Week Afloat; or, How We Explored the Pequonset River.* 1890. Chicago. Belford-Clarke. 367p. VG. H7. $12.50

STANS, Maurice. *Terrors of Justice.* 1978. NY. Everest. 3rd. sgn. VG/VG. A23. $40.00

STANTON. *Truman Capote, a Primary & Secondary Bibliography.* 1980. 302p. F. A4. $65.00

STANWOOD, Brooks. *Glow.* 1979. McGraw Hill. 1st. F/dj. P3/T12. $25.00

STANWOOD, Brooks. *Seventh Child.* 1981. Linden. F/dj. P3. $18.00

STAPLEDON, Olaf. *Darkness & Light.* 1974. Hyperion. F. M2. $25.00

STAPLEDON, Olaf. *Far Future Calling.* 1979. Oswald Train. 1st. F/dj. P3. $20.00

STAPLEDON, Olaf. *Flames.* 1947. London. 1st. VG/dj. M2. $35.00

STAPLEDON, Olaf. *Odd John.* 1935. Dutton. 1st Am. VG. M2. $50.00

STAPLEDON, R.G. *Land Now & Tomorrow.* 1934. London. Faber. 336p. fld maps. A10. $22.00

STAPP, Robert. *More Perfect Union.* 1970. Harper. 1st. F/dj. M2. $35.00

STARBUCK, Alexander. *History of the American Whale Fishery.* 1989. Secaucus. Castle. rpt. 779p. NF/dj. P4. $45.00

STARBUCK, Alexander. *History of the American Whale Fishery.* 1989 (1878). Castle. rpt. 779p. F/F. S15. $20.00

STARK, Freya. *Baghdad Sketches.* 1937. London. Murray. 1st. 8vo. 269p. VG. W1. $35.00

STARK, Freya. *Journey's Echo.* 1963. John Murray. 1st. NF/dj. M25. $35.00

STARK, Richard; see Westlake, Donald E.

STARK, Stephen. *Outskirts.* 1988. Algonquin. 1st. author's 1st book. F/F. H11. $20.00

STARKELL, Don. *Paddle to the Amazon.* 1989. CA. Prima Pub. 1st. 319p. dj. F3. $15.00

STARNES, Arthur. *Aerial Maniac.* 1938. Hammond. 1st. sgn pres. ils. 136p. G+. B5. $45.00

STARNES, Richard. *Another Mug for the Bier.* nd. Frederick Muller. 1st. VG/dj. P3. $30.00

STARNES, Richard. *Another Mug for the Bier.* 1950. Lippincott. 1st. author's 2nd book. F/F. H11. $30.00

STARR, Blaze. *Blaze Starr: My Life.* 1974. Praeger. 1st. inscr. NF/NF. B4. $250.00

STARR, Fredrick. *Physical Characters of the Indians of Southern Mexico.* 1902. Chicago. ils/photos/mc chart. 59p. wrp. F3. $75.00

STARR, Jimmy. *Three Short Biers.* 1945. Hollywood. Murray Gee. 1st. inscr. F/F. B4. $200.00

STARR, Louis M. *Bohemian Brigade Civil War Newsmen in Action.* 1987. WI U. 1st. 387p. cloth. as new. M8. $35.00

STARR, Moses Allen. *Brain Surgery.* 1991. Birmingham. facsimile. 295p. tooled purple leather. G1. $65.00

STARR, Moses Allen. *Familiar Forms of Nervous Disease...* 1890. NY. Wm Wood. heavy 8vo. 339p. G. G1. $75.00

STARRETT, Vincent. *Books Alive.* 1940. Random. 1st. 360p. VG/partial dj. K3. $25.00

STARRETT, Vincent. *Penny Wise & Book Foolish.* 1929. Covici Friede. ltd ed. inscr. 200p. G. K3. $75.00

STARRETT, Vincent. *Seaports in the Moon.* 1928. Doubleday. 1st. VG. M2. $27.00

STARRETT, Vincent. *221B: Studies in Sherlock Holmes.* 1940. NY. 1st. 248p+15 pl. ES. xl. G. A17. $30.00

STARRETT, William. *Nurse Blake Overseas.* 1943. NY. Gramercy. 1st. 256p. VG. A25. $10.00

STASHEFF, Christopher. *Company of Stars.* 1991. Del Rey. 1st. F/dj. P3. $20.00

STAUBACH, Roger. *Time Enough To Win.* 1980. Waco. Word. 1st. sgn. F/clip. A23. $48.00

STAUSS, Lehman. *Daniel.* 1969. Loizeaux. 384p. VG/dj. B29. $9.00

STAVELEY, Gaylord. *Broken Waters Sing.* 1971. Boston. 1st. 283p. gr/wht bdg. VG+. F7. $15.00

STAVIS, Barrie. *Man Who Never Died.* 1954. NY. Haven. 1st. sgn. F/NF. B2. $35.00

STAVROULAKIS, Nikos. *Book of Jeremiah: New Translation.* 1973. JPS. folio. ils/woodcuts. 93p. VG. S3. $45.00

STAVROULAKIS, Peter. *Distributed Parameter Systems Theory, Part 1, Control.* 1983. Stroudsburg. 1st. 396p. A17. $35.00

STAWELL, Mrs. Rodolph. *Fabre's Book of Insects.* 1937 (1921). Tudor. 6th. 271p. gilt gr cloth. M20. $40.00

STEADMAN, John. *Best (& Worst) of Steadman.* 1974. Press Box. 1st. VG/G+. P8. $25.00

STEADMAN, Ralph. *Little Red Computer.* 1969. McGraw Hill. 1st Am. 4to. VG/G+. P2. $25.00

STEADMAN, William E. *La Tierra Encantada.* 1969. private prt. ils. 159p. NF/NF. B19. $35.00

STEAM, Jess. *Sisters of the Night: Startling Story of Prostitution...* 1956. NY. Gramercy. 1st. 182p. VG/dj. A25. $18.00

STEARN, William T. *Botanical Masters.* 1990. Prentice Hall. 1st Am. 56 full-p pl. F/dj. A22. $25.00

STEARNS & STEARNS. *Jazz Dance.* 1968. Macmillan. 1st. F/F. B2. $40.00

STEBBING, E.P. *Diary of a Sportsman Naturalist in India.* 1920. London. Jonn Lane. 1st. ils/photos. 298p. G. H7. $45.00

STEBBING, G. *Beating the Record: Story of Life & Times of Geo Stephenson.* ca 1890. London. John Shaw. ils. 8vo. 383p. VG. K3. $30.00

STEBBINS, G. Ledyard. *Flowering Plants: Evolution Above Species Level.* 1974. Cambridge. Harvard. 399p. dj. A10. $30.00

STEBBINS, G. Ledyard. *Variation & Evolution in Plants.* 1963. NY. Columbia. 643p. cloth. A10. $25.00

STEBBINS, Henry M. *Small Game & Varmit Rifles.* 1947. NY. 234p. xl. F. A17. $15.00

STEBEL, S.L. *Narc.* 1976. Constable Crime Club. 1st. sgn. F/F. M19. $25.00

STEEGMULLER, Francis. *Cocteau: A Biography.* 1970. Boston. 1st. 583p. F/dj. A17. $25.00

STEEL, F.A. *Voices in the Night.* 1900. London. 1st. VG. M2. $45.00

STEEL, Kurt. *Imposter.* 1945. Tower. VG/dj. P3. $15.00

STEEL, Kurt. *Murder for What?* 1936. Bobbs Merrill. 1st. F/dj. M15. $90.00

STEELE, Adison; see Lupoff, Richard.

STEELE, Danielle. *Full Circle.* 1984. Delacorte. 1st. F/NF. W2. $25.00

STEELE, Danielle. *Kaleidoscope.* 1987. Delacorte. 1st. 395p. NF/NF. W2. $25.00

STEELE, David J. *Yachtsman in Red China.* 1970. NY. DeGraff. photos. 208p. dj. T7. $22.00

STEELE, Joel Dorman. *New Descriptive Astronomy.* ca 1900. NY. Am Book Co. 326p. cloth. K5. $25.00

STEELE, Matthew Forney. *American Campaigns.* 1922. WA, DC. US Infantry Assn. maps. A19. $100.00

STEELE, Matthew Forney. *American Campaigns. Vol 1.* 1909. Bryon Adams. 1st. 731p. bl cloth. VG. H1. $58.00

STEERE, Douglas V. *On Beginning From Within.* 1943. Harper. 3rd. 149p. VG/dj. V3. $12.50

STEERE, Douglas V. *Prayer & Worship.* 1941. NY. Hazen. 2nd. 70p. VG. V3. $14.00

STEERE, Douglas V. *Time To Spare.* 1949. Harper. 1st. 187p. VG/clip. V3. $14.00

STEERE, Douglas V. *Work & Contemplation.* 1957. Harper. 1st. 148p. VG/clip. V3. $18.00

STEERS, J.A. *Applied Coastal Geomorphology.* 1971. Cambridge. MIT. ils/photos/maps. 227p. cloth. F/F. M12. $15.00

STEFAN, Verena. *Shedding.* 1978. NY. Daughters. 1st Am. trans Johanna Moore/Beth Weckmueller. 118p. VG. A25. $20.00

STEFANSSON, Vilhjalmur. *Adventure of Wrangel Island.* 1925. NY. 1st. 424p. VG. A17. $40.00

STEFANSSON, Vilhjalmur. *Adventure of Wrangel Island.* 1925. NY. Macmillan. 1st. inscr. ils/fld map. 424p. VG. K3. $60.00

STEFANSSON, Vilhjalmur. *Friendly Arctic: Story of 5 Years in Polar Regions.* 1939. NY. later prt. 784p. rear pocket map. A17. $40.00

STEFANSSON, Vilhjalmur. *My Life With the Eskimo.* 1929. Macmillan. later prt. 8vo. 538p. P4. $195.00

STEFANSSON, Vilhjalmur. *Northward Course of Empire.* 1924. NY. 2nd. 274p. fld map. A17. $22.50

STEFANSSON, Vilhjalmur. *Northwest to Fortune: Search...Commercially Route Far East.* 1958. NY. 1st. 356p. F/dj. A17. $20.00

STEFANSSON & WEIGERT. *Compass of the World: A Symposium on Political Geography.* 1945. NY. 2nd. 466p. dj. A17. $16.50

STEGNER, Wallace. *All the Little Live Things.* 1967. Viking. BC. 1st. 248p. NF/dj. W2. $20.00

STEGNER, Wallace. *All the Little Live Things.* 1967. Viking. 1st. F/F. A18. $75.00

STEGNER, Wallace. *All the Little Live Things.* 1967. Viking. 1st. NF/VG+. T11. $60.00

STEGNER, Wallace. *All the Little Live Things.* 1967. Viking. 1st. sgn. VG+/dj. D10. $60.00

STEGNER, Wallace. *Angle of Repose.* 1971. 1st. VG/VG. S13. $50.00

STEGNER, Wallace. *Angle of Repose.* 1971. Garden City. 1st. sgn. F/F. B4. $650.00

STEGNER, Wallace. *Beyond the Hundreth Meridian.* 1954. Houghton Mifflin. 1st. xl. NF/VG+. T11. $195.00

STEGNER, Wallace. *Big Rock Candy Mountain.* 1943. DSP. 1st. author's 3rd novel. VG/VG. B5. $250.00

STEGNER, Wallace. *Big Rock Candy Mountain.* 1943. DSP. 1st. F/VG+ clip. B4. $850.00

STEGNER, Wallace. *Big Rock Candy Mountain.* 1978. Franklin Lib. 1st. sgn. NF/sans. T11. $200.00

STEGNER, Wallace. *City of the Living & Other Stories.* 1956. Houghton Mifflin. 1st. sgn. VG/VG clip. B4. $450.00

STEGNER, Wallace. *Collected Stories of Wallace Stegner.* 1989. Random. 1st. F/F. T11. $50.00

STEGNER, Wallace. *Collected Stories of Wallace Stegner.* 1989. Random. 1st. NF/NF. B3. $40.00

STEGNER, Wallace. *Crossing to Safety.* 1987. Franklin Lib. 1st/ltd. sgn. full leather. F. Q1. $125.00

STEGNER, Wallace. *Crossing to Safety.* 1987. Random. 1st. F/F. B3. $50.00

STEGNER, Wallace. *Gathering Zone.* 1964. McGraw Hill. 1st. NF/VG+. T11. $175.00

STEGNER, Wallace. *On a Darkling Plain.* 1940. Harcourt Brace. 1st. F. A18. $175.00

STEGNER, Wallace. *One Way to Spell Man.* 1982. Doubleday. 1st. NF/NF. B3. $75.00

STEGNER, Wallace. *Recapitulation.* 1979. Doubleday. 1st trade after Franklin Lib. NF/NF. D10. $65.00

STEGNER, Wallace. *Recapitulation.* 1979. Doubleday. 1st trade. blk cloth. F/NF. T11. $80.00

STEGNER, Wallace. *Recapitulation.* 1979. Franklin LIb. true 1st. ils Walter Rane. full leather. F. B3/T11. $95.00

STEGNER, Wallace. *Shooting Star.* 1961. Viking. 1st. F/NF. B4. $150.00

STEGNER, Wallace. *Shooting Star.* 1961. Viking. 1st. NF/dj. from $100 to $125.00

STEGNER, Wallace. *Spectator Bird.* 1976. Franklin Lib. 1st ltd. leather. F/sans. from $65 to $85.00

STEGNER, Wallace. *Where the Bluebird Sings to the Lemonade Springs.* 1992. Random. 1st. F/F. B3. $30.00

STEGNER, Wallace. *Women on the Wall.* 1950. Houghton Mifflin. 1st. NF/VG+. D10. $175.00

STEICHEN, Edward. *Life in Photography.* 1963. NY. 249 photos. dj. A17. $30.00

STEICHEN, Edward. *US Navy War Photographs.* ca 1945. US Camera. 108p. sq 4to. G/wrp. A17. $17.00

STEIG, William. *Amazing Bone.* 1976. FSG. 1st. ils. F/VG. P2. $75.00

STEIG, William. *Farmer Palmer's Wagon Ride.* 1974. FSG. 1st. VG/VG. P2. $40.00

STEIG, William. *Yellow & Pink.* 1984. FSG. 1st. wide 8vo. F/NF. C8. $35.00

STEIN, Aaron Marc. *Days of Misfortune.* 1949. Doubleday Crime Club. 1st. VG/NF. M22. $25.00

STEIN, Aaron Marc. *We Saw Him Die.* 1947. Doubleday. 1st. VG/dj. P3. $20.00

STEIN, Ben. *Croesus Conspiracy.* 1978. S&S. 1st. NF/dj. P3. $10.00

STEIN, Benjamin J. *Manhattan Gambit.* 1983. 1st. NF/dj. K3. $20.00

STEIN, David Lewis. *Living the Revolution: Yippies in Chicago.* 1969. Bobbs Merrill. 1st. F/VG+. B4. $100.00

STEIN, Gertrude. *Have They Attacked Mary? He Giggled.* 1917. np (W Chester, PA). npub (Horace F Temple). 1/200. inscr. NF/wrp. B4. $2,000.00

STEIN, Gertrude. *Portraits & Prayers.* 1934. Random. 1st/1st prt. 1/1800. 8vo. 264p. linen/photo. G. H1. $45.00

STEIN, Gertrude. *Wars I Have Seen.* 1945. London. 1st. VG/VG. T9. $65.00

STEIN, Gertrude. *World Is Round.* 1988. Northpoint. 1st. F/F. B3. $20.00

STEIN, Leonard. *Balfour Declaration.* 1961. S&S. 1st. 8vo. 681p. xl. VG/torn. W1. $35.00

STEIN, Peter. *Character & Influence of the Roman Civil Law...* 1988. London. Hambledon. M11. $60.00

STEIN, Robert H. *Difficult Passages in the New Testament.* 1990. Baker. 392p. VG/dj. B29. $10.00

STEIN, Robert Louis. *French Slave Trade in the Eighteenth Century...* 1979. Madison, WI. dj. A19. $35.00

STEIN, Robert. *Children of Light.* 1986. Knopf. 1st. F/NF. B3. $30.00

STEIN, Robert. *Flag for Sunrise.* 1981. Knopf. 1st. VG/NF. B3. $50.00

STEIN, Sol. *Touch of Treason.* 1985. St Martin. 1st. VG/dj. P3. $15.00

STEINBECK, John. *Cannery Row.* 1945. Viking. 1st/1st issue. buff brd. NF/NF. B4. $750.00

STEINBECK, John. *Cup of Gold.* 1929. McBride. 1st/1st issue. 1/2746. inscr. VG. L3. $6,500.00

STEINBECK, John. *East of Eden.* 1952. Viking. Sears Reading Club Special. gr cloth. NF. W2. $300.00

STEINBECK, John. *Forgotten Village.* 1941. Viking. 1st. F/G. M19. $75.00

STEINBECK, John. *Grapes of Wrath.* 1939. London. Heinemann. 1st. F/VG+. A18. $300.00

STEINBECK, John. *Grapes of Wrath.* 1939. NY. 1st. VG+/dj. B5. $1,000.00

STEINBECK, John. *Log From the Sea of Cortez.* 1951. Viking. ils/photos/map ep. 282p. cloth. VG+/G+. M12. $95.00

STEINBECK, John. *Long Valley.* 1939 (1938). VG/VG. S13. $30.00

STEINBECK, John. *Moon Is Down.* 1942. Viking. 1st. inscr. G+/VG. B4. $2,250.00

STEINBECK, John. *Of Mice & Men.* 1937. Covici Friede. 1st/1st issue. 1/2500. F/F clip. B4. $1,500.00

STEINBECK, John. *Red Pony.* 1937. Covici Freide. 1st. 1/699. sgn. VG/VG+ case. B4. $1,750.00

STEINBECK, John. *Red Pony.* 1945. Viking. 1st. ils Wesley Dennis. 132p. gilt gray cloth. F/case. H3. $50.00

STEINBECK, John. *Russian Journal.* 1948. Viking. 1st. NF/G. M19. $75.00

STEINBECK, John. *Sweet Thursday.* 1954. Viking. 1st. F/VG+ clip. A24. $90.00

STEINBECK, John. *Travels With Charley.* 1962. Viking. VG. W2. $75.00

STEINBECK, John. *Winter of Our Discontent.* 1960. Viking. 1st. NF/G. A24. $45.00

STEINBECK & WALLSTEN. *Steinbeck: A Life in Letters.* 1975. Viking. 1/1000. bl cloth. F/case. w/3 facsimile letters. M25. $200.00

STEINBERG, Avraham. *Jewish Medical Law: Concise Response.* 1980. Israel. Gefen. 180p. VG/dj. S3. $26.00

STEINBERG, I.N. *In the Workshop of the Revolution.* 1953. Rinehart. 1st. G/G. V4. $20.00

STEINBERG, Noach. *Tsu Loyterkayt: Lirishe Proze.* 1931. Dezshey. Yiddish text. 109p. VG. S3. $30.00

STEINBRUNNER, Chris. *Cinema of the Fantastic.* 1972. Saturday Review. 1st. G/dj. P3. $20.00

STEINER, Mona Lisa. *Philippine Ornamental Plants & Their Care.* 1960. Manila. 2nd. 233p. VG. B26. $42.00

STEINER, Ralph. *Point of View.* 1978. Middletown. Wesleyan U. 1st. inscr/dtd. 144p. cloth. dj. D11. $200.00

STEINGRABER, Erich. *Royal Treasures.* 1968. 1st. lg 4to. photos. NF/G+. S13. $30.00

STEINMAN, David B. *Miracle Bridge at Mackinac.* 1957. Grand Rapids. Eerdmans. 2nd. sgn. 208p. G. B11. $35.00

STEKEL, Wilhelm. *Auto-Eroticism: Pyschiatric Study of Onanism & Neurosis.* 1950. Liveright. 1st Am. 289p. VG. A25. $20.00

STELL, Flora Anne. *Tales of Punjab.* 1983. Greenwich House. 1st. F/dj. P3. $15.00

STELLMAN, Louis J. *Vanished Ruin Era.* 1910. SF. Paul Elder. 52 pl. quarter natural burlap/tan sides. F. K7. $125.00

STELLMAN & STRONG. *Chinatown Photographer Louis J Stellman...* 1989. Sacramento. CA State Lib. 1/550. ils. F/gray wrp. R3. $30.00

STEMPEL, John D. *Inside the Iranian Revolution.* 1981. Bloomington, IN. 1st. sgn pres. 8vo. 336p. NF/dj. W1. $22.00

STENDHAL. *Charterhouse of Parma.* 1955. LEC. 1st thus. 1/1500. ils/sgn Rafaello Busoni. F/glassine/case. Q1. $75.00

STENNING, Derrick J. *Savannah Nomads: A Study of Wodaabe Pastoral Fulain...* 1964. Oxford. 2nd. ils/fld map. 266p. VG/dj. W1. $25.00

STEPHEN, David. *Bodach the Badger.* 1983. St Martin. 1st. VG/dj. P3. $11.00

STEPHEN, James Fitzjames. *History of Criminal Law of England.* 1883. London. Macmillan. 3 vol. cloth. M11. $650.00

STEPHENS, H. *Farmer's Guide to Scientific & Practical Agriculture.* 1858. NY. 2 vol. lg 8vo. ils. E6. $125.00

STEPHENS, James. *Crock of Gold.* 1926. London. Macmillan. 1/525. sgn. 12 tipped-in pl. F. T10. $300.00

STEPHENS, James. *Crock of Gold.* 1946. Macmillan. VG. M2. $18.00

STEPHENS, John L. *Incidents of Travel in Central America, Chipas & Yucatan.* 1949. New Brunswick. Rutgers. ils Catherwood. F/dj. O7. $35.00

STEPHENS, W.P. *Canoe & Boat Building.* 1891. NY. Forest Stream. 2 vol. 12mo. w/50 fld pl in envelope. M1. $350.00

STEPHENSON, George. *Puritan Heritage.* 1952. Macmillan. 282p. G/torn. B29. $7.00

STEPTOE, John. *Stevie.* 1969. Harper Row. later ed. author/ils 1st book. NF/dj. M25. $45.00

STEPTOE, John. *Uptown.* 1970. Harper Row. 1st. NF/dj. M25. $60.00

STERCHI, Beat. *Cow.* 1988. NY. Pantheon. 1st Am. author's 1st novel. F/NF. R13. $20.00

STERLING, Bruce. *Crystal Express.* 1989. Arkham. 1st. F/NF. M19. $25.00

STERLING, Bruce. *Crystal Express.* 1990. Legend. 1st. F/dj. P3. $25.00

STERLING, Bryan B. *Will Rogers Scrapbook.* 1976. Bonanza. dj. A19. $30.00

STERLING, Claire. *Time of the Assassins.* 1984. HRW. 1st. VG/VG. W2. $20.00

STERLING, Dorothy. *Ahead of Her Time: Abby Kelley & Politics of Antislavery.* 1991. Norton. 1st. VG/VG. V3. $18.50

STERLING, Dorothy. *Lucretia Mott: Gentle Warrior.* 1964. Doubleday. 237p. dj. V3. $12.00

STERLING, George. *After Sunset.* 1939. SF. Howell. 1/25. 70p. D11. $75.00

STERLING, George. *Beyond the Breakers & Other Poems.* 1914. SF. Robertson. 1st. 141p. gilt cloth. D11. $50.00

STERLING, George. *House of Orchids & Other Poems.* 1911. SF. AM Robertson. 1st. inscr. silver-stp cloth. D11. $100.00

STERLING, George. *Robinson Jeffers, the Man & the Artist.* 1926. NY. Knopf. 1st. blk cloth. F/dj. M24. $85.00

STERLING, George. *Rosamund: A Dramatic Poem.* 1920. SF. AM Robertston. 1/500. sgn/#d. D11. $60.00

STERLING, George. *Sonnets to Craig.* 1928. Boni. 1st. intro Upton Sinclair. 12mo. 120p. NF/dj. T10. $75.00

STERLING, George. *Wine of Wizardry & Other Poems.* 1909. SF. AM Robertson. 1st/1st issue. 137p. gilt cloth. D11. $75.00

STERLING, Gray. *Tooth of Time.* 1955. Marshall Jones. sgn. 151p. VG/dj. M20. $45.00

STERLING, Helen. *Horse That Takes the Milk Around.* 1946. NY. ils Marjorie Hartwell. VG+/dj. M5. $65.00

STERLING, Robert Thayer. *Lighthouses of the Maine Coast & the Men Who Keep Them.* 1935. Battleboro. Stephen Daye. 1st. sgn. 224p. xl. A17. $17.50

STERLING, Stewart. *Dead of Night.* 1950. Dutton. 1st. VG/dj. P3. $25.00

STERLING, W.W. *Trails & Trials of a Texas Ranger.* 1959. private prt. 1st. inscr. VG. A15. $150.00

STERN, H.J. *Rubber: Natural & Synthetic...* 1954. London. 1st. ils. 491p. dj. B18. $65.00

STERN, J. David. *Eidolon.* 1952. Messner. 1st. VG/VG. P3. $20.00

STERN, Madeleine B. *We the Women: Career Firsts of 19th-C America.* 1994. Lincoln, NE. 8vo. ils. pb. R12. $12.95

STERN, Norton B. *California Jewish History: A Descriptive Bibliography.* 1967. Glendale, CA. 1st. NF. O4. $25.00

STERN, Philip Van Doren. *Drums of Morning.* 1942. Doubleday Doran. 1st. VG/dj. P3. $20.00

STERN, Philip Van Doren. *End to Valor: Last Days of the Civil War.* 1958. Houghton Mifflin. 1st. 8vo. 428p. F/dj. H1. $25.00

STERN, Philip Van Doren. *Man Who Killed Lincoln.* 1939. 1st. 408p. O8. $12.50

STERN, Richard Martin. *Flood.* 1979. Doubleday. 1st. VG/dj. P3. $20.00

STERN, Roger. *Death & Life of Superman.* 1993. Bantam. 1st. F/dj. P3. $20.00

STERNBERG & WILSON. *Landscaping With Native Trees.* 1995. Shelburn, VT. Chapters. 288p. cloth. A10. $35.00

STERNE, Lawrence. *Works...* 1815. London. Strahan Wilkie. 4 vol. lg 12mo. 3-quarter vellum/marbled brd. H13. $395.00

STERRETT, Virginia. *Old French Fairy Tales.* 1920. Phil. Penn. 1st. 8 full-p pl. 4to. blk cloth. R5. $225.00

STEVENS, Abel. *Compendious History of American Methodism.* nd. Eaton Mains. abridged. 608p. VG. B29. $10.50

STEVENS, Abel. *History of Religious Movement of 18th C Called Methodism.* 1861. Phillips Hunt. Vol III only. 524p. G. B29. $15.00

STEVENS, Benjamin F. *Cruise on the Constitution.* 1904. NY. rpt. sgn. T7. $50.00

STEVENS, Doris. *En Prison Pour la Liberte! Comment Nous Avons Conquis...* 1936. Paris. A Pedone. 1st French. 359p. F. A25. $60.00

STEVENS, George T. *Illustrated Guide to Flowering Plants of Middle Atlantic...* 1910. NY. 1800+ ils. 749p. gilt olive cloth. VG. B26. $45.00

STEVENS, Henry. *Recollections of James Lenox...* 1951. NY Public Lib. revised. 1/1000. ils. 187p. VG. K3. $20.00

STEVENS, Isaac. *Liberators.* 1908. Dodge. 1st. VG. M2. $32.00

STEVENS, Lyla. *Birds of Australia in Color.* nd. Melbourne. 61p. NF/F. S15. $12.00

STEVENS, Orin. *Handbook of North Dakota Plants.* 1963. Fargo, ND. ND Inst Regional Studies. 3rd. 328p. VG. A10. $22.00

STEVENS, Phillips. *Stone Images of Esie, Nigeria.* 1978. Ibadan. 398p+1581 b&w photos. F/dj. A17. $25.00

STEVENS, Ruth. *Hi-Ya Neighbor.* 1947. Tupper Love. 1st. sgn. 16 photo pl. 122p. G/G. B11. $25.00

STEVENS, Shane. *Anvil Chorus.* 1985. Delacorte. VG/dj. P3. $20.00

STEVENS, Shane. *By Reason of Insanity.* 1979. S&S. 1st. NF/dj. P3. $75.00

STEVENS, Shane. *Dead City.* 1973. HRW. 1st. F/F. T2. $35.00

STEVENS, Stanford. *Plants of Sun & Sand: Desert Growth of Arizona.* 1939. Tucson. 2nd. ils/sgn Gerry Pierce. wood brd/cloth backstrip. B26. $27.50

STEVENS, Wallace. *And the Critical Schools.* 1988. AL U. 1st. F/F. V1. $15.00

STEVENS, Wallace. *Collected Poems.* 1954. NY. Knopf. 1st/1st state bdg (rust brn cloth). 1/2500. dj. M24. $3,000.00

STEVENS, William Oliver. *Charleston, Historic City of Gardens.* 1939. NY. 1st. ils. 331p. VG. B18. $15.00

STEVENSON, Adlai. *Wit & Wisdom of...* 1965. Hawthorn. 1st. ils. NF/clip. Q1. $40.00

STEVENSON, Allan. *Problem of the Missale Speciale.* 1967. London. Bibliographical Soc. 8vo. 400p. F. T10. $75.00

STEVENSON, Burton E. *King in Babylon.* 1917. Sm Maynard. 1st. VG. M2. $25.00

STEVENSON, D.E. *Mrs Tim Gets a Job.* 1974. HRW. 2nd. VG/dj. P3. $18.00

STEVENSON, Janet. *Woman Aboard.* 1969. NY. Crown. 8vo. 312p. VG/dj. P4. $25.00

STEVENSON, M.C. *Zuni Indians: Their Mythology...* 1970. Rio Grande Classic. rpt. 139 pl. F. M4. $35.00

STEVENSON, Robert Louis. *Apology for Idlers.* 1932. NY. Ashlar. 1/200. 8vo. 28p. gilt brd. F. B24. $150.00

STEVENSON, Robert Louis. *Beach of Falesa.* 1956. LA. LEC. 1st thus. 1/1500. ils/sgn Millard Sheets. F/glassine/case. Q1. $60.00

STEVENSON, Robert Louis. *Black Arrow.* 1888. Scribner. 1st (precedes Eng). yel prt wrp. M24. $375.00

STEVENSON, Robert Louis. *Child's Garden of Verses.* (1888). Scribner. early. quarter cloth/paper brd. G. M5. $42.00

STEVENSON, Robert Louis. *Child's Garden of Verses.* 1896. Bodley Head. 1st Eng. ils Charles Robinson. 8vo. aeg. gr cloth. R5. $250.00

STEVENSON, Robert Louis. *Child's Garden of Verses.* 1902. Rand McNally. 1st. ils Mars. VG. S13. $25.00

STEVENSON, Robert Louis. *Child's Garden of Verses.* 1929. 1st. ils Eulalie. VG. S13. $18.00

STEVENSON, Robert Louis. *Child's Garden of Verses.* 1929. Saalfield. ils Clara Burd. folio. stiff sc. M5. $50.00

STEVENSON, Robert Louis. *Child's Garden of Verses.* 1931. London. Harrap. 1st Eng. ils H Willebeek LeMair/12 full-p pl. cloth. dj. R5. $450.00

STEVENSON, Robert Louis. *Child's Garden of Verses.* 1947. Oxford. 1st thus. ils Tasha Tudor. 118p. F/VG-. P2. $250.00

STEVENSON, Robert Louis. *Child's Garden of Verses.* 1978. Golden. 1st. sm 4to. 45p. VG. C14. $12.00

STEVENSON, Robert Louis. *Dr Jekyll & Mr Hyde & an Inland Voyage.* 1912. Tauchnitz. F/wrp. M2. $25.00

STEVENSON, Robert Louis. *Dr Jekyll & Mr Hyde.* 1923. Everleigh Nash/Grayson. VG/fair. P3. $35.00

STEVENSON, Robert Louis. *Footnote to History. Eight Years of Trouble in Samoa.* 1892. London. Cassell. 1st. 8vo. cloth. VG. M23. $50.00

STEVENSON, Robert Louis. *Footnote to History. Eight Years of Trouble in Samoa.* 1892. Scribner. 1st Am. 8vo. 322p. olive gr cloth. F. B24. $75.00

STEVENSON, Robert Louis. *Kidnapped.* 1913. Scribner. 1st. ils NC Wyeth/14 mc pl. 289p. blk cloth/label. M20. $100.00

STEVENSON, Robert Louis. *Kidnapped: Being Memoirs of Adventures of David Balfour...* 1886. Scribner. 1st Am. 12mo. 324p. contemporary bdg. M1. $500.00

STEVENSON, Robert Louis. *La Porte de Maletroit.* 1952. L-D Allen/BC of CA. 1/300. 60p. stiff wrp/glassine/case/chemise. D11. $200.00

STEVENSON, Robert Louis. *Morality of the Profession of Letters.* 1899. Gouverneur, NY. Brothers of the Book. 1st separate. 1/299. gilt cloth. M24. $75.00

STEVENSON, Robert Louis. *Poems, Hitherto Unpublished.* 1921. Bibliophile Soc. 1st. 1/450. 8vo. faux vellum/cloth. F. B24. $150.00

STEVENSON, Robert Louis. *Poems From Child's Garden of Verses.* 1987. London. Orchard. 4 popups. F. P2. $15.00

STEVENSON, Robert Louis. *Songs With Music From a Child's Garden of Verses.* nd. Nelson. ils Margaret Tarrant. 55p. gilt bdg. VG+. P2. $65.00

STEVENSON, Robert Louis. *St Ives, Being the Adventures of a French Prisoner in Eng...* 1898. London. Heinemann. 1st/1st issue. 8vo. 312p. B24. $100.00

STEVENSON, Robert Louis. *Stevenson Medley.* 1899. Chatto Windus. 1st. 1/300. sgn. half morocco/gilt bl cloth. M24. $200.00

STEVENSON, Robert Louis. *Stevenson's Workshop. With Twenty-Nine Facsimiles.* 1921. Bibliophile Soc. 1/450. 8vo. 63p. faux vellum/cloth. F/double case. B24. $175.00

STEVENSON, Robert Louis. *Strange Case of Dr Jekyll & Mr Hyde.* 1886. NY. Scribner. 1st Am/possible 2nd issue. 138p+10p ads. dk gr cloth. B24. $500.00

STEVENSON, Robert Louis. *Travels With a Donkey.* 1957. NY. LEC. 1st thus. 1/1500. ils/sgn Roger Duvoisin. F/glassine/case. Q1. $100.00

STEVENSON, Robert Louis. *Treasure Island.* 1911. Scribner. 1st. ils NC Wyeth's 1st book publication. blk cloth. dj. R5. $1,400.00

STEVENSON, Robert Louis. *Treasure Island.* 1938. Rand McNally. decor brd. NF. P3. $20.00

STEVENSON, Robert Louis. *Treasure Island.* 1941. NY. LEC. 1/1500. ils/sgn Edward Wilson. bl cloth. w/sgn litho. T10. $100.00

STEVENSON, Robert Louis. *When the Devil Was Well.* 1921. Bibliogphile Soc. 1st. 1/450. 8vo. 127p. faux vellum/cloth. B24. $150.00

STEVENSON, W.F. *Wounds in War: Mechanism on Their Production & Treatment.* 1898. NY. 1st. ils/photos. 437p. A13. $200.00

STEVENSON, William G. *Thirteen Months in the Rebel Army.* 1959. VG/VG. M17. $20.00

STEWARD, John F. *Reaper: History of Those Who...Made Bread Cheap.* nd (1931). NY. Greenburg. 1st. 382p. gr cloth. xl. B22. $16.00

STEWART, Charles Samuel. *Visit to the South Seas in the United States Ship Vincennes.* 1833. NY. John P Haven. 2nd. rebound modern cloth. T7. $350.00

STEWART, Desmond. *Middle East. Temple of Janus.* 1971. Doubleday. 1st. 8vo. 414p. cloth. VG. W1. $12.00

STEWART, Desmond. *TE Lawrence.* 1977. Harper Row. 1st. 8vo. 352p. NF/dj. W1. $25.00

STEWART, Edgar. *Custer's Luck.* 1955. Norman, OK. 1st. 522p. VG/dj. J2. $85.00

STEWART, Elihu. *Down the Mackenzie & Up the Ukon in 1906.* 1912. London. John Lane. 2nd. fld map/30 photo pl. 270p. VG. P4. $65.00

STEWART, Fred Mustard. *Pomp & Circumstance.* 1991. Dutton. 1st. F/dj. P3. $20.00

STEWART, Fred Mustard. *Titan.* 1985. S&S. 1st. F/dj. P3. $18.00

STEWART, George R. *California Trail: Epic With Many Heroes.* 1962. McGraw Hill. 10th. F/F. O4. $15.00

STEWART, George R. *Committee of Vigilance: Revolution in San Francisco.* 1851. Houghton Mifflin. 1st. NF/VG clip. O4. $25.00

STEWART, George R. *Earth Abides.* 1949. Random. NF/dj. M2. $50.00

STEWART, George R. *Fire.* 1946. Random. 1st. inscr. F. M19. $25.00

STEWART, George R. *Man, an Autobiography.* 1948. 1st Eng. F/VG. M19. $35.00

STEWART, George R. *North-South Continental Highway Looking South.* 1957. Boston. Houghton Mifflin. 230p. dj. F3. $15.00

STEWART, George R. *Ordeal by Hunger: Story of the Donnor Party.* 1960. Houghton Mifflin. New Ed. VG/G. O4. $15.00

STEWART, George R. *Pickett's Charage: Microhistory of Final Attack Gettysburg.* 1959. Houghton Mifflin. 1st. 354p. cloth. VG/VG. M8. $65.00

STEWART, George R. *Storm.* 1941. Random. 1st. VG. M2. $20.00

STEWART, Gordon T. *Documents Relating to Greata Awakening of Nova Scotia...* 1982. Toronto. Champlain Soc. 299p. gilt red cloth. NF. P4. $95.00

STEWART, Henry. *Domestic Sheep: Its Culture & General Management.* (1900). Chicago. Am Sheep Breeder. photos. 383p. cloth. VG. M12. $25.00

STEWART, Henry. *Shepherd's Manual: A Practical Treatise on the Sheep.* 1876. Orange Judd. 12mo. 252p. cloth. K3. $40.00

STEWART, Ian. *Peking Payoff.* 1975. Macmillan. 1st. F/dj. P3. $15.00

STEWART, Jane L. *Campfire Girl's Adventure.* 1914. Saalfield. 245p. G. W2. $45.00

STEWART, Mary. *Airs Above the Ground.* 1965. Hodder Stoughton. 1st. VG/dj. P3. $35.00

STEWART, Mary. *Crystal Cave.* 1970. Morrow. 1st. NF/NF clip. H11. $30.00

STEWART, Mary. *Gabriel Hounds.* 1967. Hodder Stoughton. 1st. VG/dj. P3. $30.00

STEWART, Mary. *Hollow Hills.* 1973. Morrow. 1st. NF/F. H11. $25.00

STEWART, Mary. *Ivy Tree.* 1961. London. Hodder Stoughton. 1st Eng. NF/VG+. T11. $35.00

STEWART, Mary. *Last Enchantment.* 1979. Hodder Stoughton. 1st. F/dj. P3. $25.00

STEWART, Mary. *Last Enchantment.* 1979. Morrow. 1st. F/dj. M2. $25.00

STEWART, Mary. *Thornyhold.* 1988. Hodder Stoughton. 1st. F/F. P3. $25.00

STEWART, Mary. *Wickey Day.* 1983. Morrow. 1st Am. F/F. B4. $45.00

STEWART, Michael. *Blindsight.* 1987. St Martin. 1st. F/dj. M2. $22.00

STEWART, Michael. *Far Cry.* 1984. Freundlich. 1st. VG/dj. P3. $18.00

STEWART, Michael. *Monkey Shines.* 1983. Freundlich. 1st. F/F. H11. $30.00

STEWART, P. *Winter in the Kitchen: Wine & Cookery of the West.* 1974. ils. easel stand format. VG. E6. $18.00

STEWART, R.J. *Book of Merlin.* 1987. Blanford. 1st. F/dj. P3. $25.00

STEWART, Ramona. *Possession of Joel Delaney.* nd. Little Brn. 2nd. VG/dj. P3. $13.00

STEWART, Watt. *Keith & Costa Rica.* 1964. Albuquerque. 1st. 210p. dj. F3. $25.00

STEWART & STEWART. *Adolph Sutro: A Biography.* 1962. Berkeley. 1st. NF/G+. O4. $15.00

STEWART-BROWN, Ronald. *Sergeants of the Peace of Medieval England & Wales.* 1936. Manchester. gilt blk cloth. VG. M11. $50.00

STEYERMARK, Julian A. *Flora of Missouri.* 1963. Ames. 390 pl/line drawings/distribution maps. F/dj. B26. $100.00

STICK, David. *Graveyard of the Atlantic, Shipwrecks of NC Coast.* 1952. Chapel Hill. sgn. 8vo. 276p. VG/worn. P4. $45.00

STICK, David. *Outer Banks of North Carolina.* 1958. Chapel Hill. 1st. sgn. VG/VG. B11. $60.00

STILL, William. *Underground Railroad.* 1872. Phil. Porter Coates. 1st. 70 engravings. 780p. gilt cloth/rebacked. NF. B4. $500.00

STILLE, Charles. *Northern Interests & Southern Independence.* 1863. Phil. 1st. prt wrp. O8. $45.00

STILLINGFLEET, Edward. *Unreasonableness of Separation; or, Impartial Account...* 1681. London. Mortlock. 2nd corrected. 4to. full red morocco. clamshell box. B24. $3,500.00

STILLMAN, Jacob D.B. *Around the Horn to California in 1849.* 1967. Lewis Osbourne. 1st. 1/1150. F/sans. O4. $25.00

STILLMAN, Jacob D.B. *Wanderings in the Southwest in 1855.* 1990. Clark. Western Frontiersmen Series XXIII. 193p. VG. J2. $65.00

STILLWELL, Norma. *Bird Songs.* 1964. NY. 194p. VG/dj. S15. $10.00

STINE, G. Harry. *ICBM.* 1994. NY. Orion. 1st. 8vo. 291p. VG/dj. K5. $22.00

STINE, G. Harry. *Rocket Power & Space Flight.* 1957. Holt. 1st. 8vo. 182p. VG/partial. K5. $32.00

STIRLING, M.W. *Native Peoples of New Guinea.* 1943. Smithsonian. 8vo. 25p. VG/prt wrp. P4. $25.00

STIRLING, Monica. *Wild Swan: Life & Times of Hans Christian Andersen.* 1965. London. Collins. 1st. 8vo. bl tweed. VG/G. T5. $45.00

STIRTON, R.A. *New Genus of Interatheres From Miocene of Colombia.* 1953. Berkeley. ils/figures/2 maps. F/wrp. M12. $25.00

STOCKING, Charles Francis. *Thou Israel.* 1921. Maestro. 1st. VG. M2. $25.00

STOCKTON, Frank R. *Great Stone of Sardis.* 1899. Harper. VG. M2. $30.00

STOCKTON, Frank R. *Great War Syndicate.* nd. Dodd Mead. VG. M2. $40.00

STOCKTON, Frank R. *Stockton's Stories, First Series. The Lady or the Tiger.* 1886. Scribner. 1st thus. 201p. teg. gr buff cloth. VG. B22. $15.00

STOCKTON, Frank R. *Vizier of the Two-Horned Alexander.* 1899. Century. 1st. NF. M2. $50.00

STOCKTON, Robert F. *Sketch of Life of Com Robert F Stockton...* 1856. NY. Derby Jackson. 1st. 8vo. 131p+2p ads. gilt tan cloth/red leather. K7. $65.00

STODDARD, Charles Warren. *Island of Tranquil Delights.* 1904. Boston. Herbert Turner. 1st. gilt gr cloth. F. M24. $150.00

STODDARD, John L. *John L Stoddard's Lectures. Vol X.* 1904. Balch Bros. VG. O4. $20.00

STODDARD, John L. *John L Stoddard's Lectures. Vol 10.* 1905. Boston. Balch Bros. 8vo. 304p. VG+. F7. $35.00

STODDARD, R.H. *Anecdote Bibliographies of Thackeray & Dickens.* 1874. Scribner. 1st. gilt cream cloth. F. M24. $60.00

STODDARD, S.R. *Midnight Sun...Story of Cruise of the Ohio...1897.* 1901. Glenfalls. self pub. inscr. 200p. A17. $75.00

STODDARD, Sandol. *Doubleday Illustrated Children's Bible.* 1983. Doubleday. ils Tony Chen. 383p. F/dj. B29. $6.50

STODDARD, Theodore Lothrop. *Rising Tide of Color Against White World-Supremacy.* 1920. Scribner. 1st/2nd prt. 320p. cloth. VG. M8. $65.00

STODDART, Anna M. *Elizabeth Pease Nichol.* 1899. London. Dent. 314p. G. V3. $18.00

STOFF, Michael B. *Manhattan Project.* 1991. McGraw Hill. 1st. 298p. VG/wrp. K3. $15.00

STOFFLET. *Dr Seuss From Then to Now, a Catalog.* 1986. San Diego Mus Art. 4to. ils. 96p. F/F. A4. $45.00

STOIKO, Miahael. *Soviet Rocketry.* 1970. HRW. 8vo. 272p. G/dj. K5. $30.00

STOKER, Bram. *Annotated Dracula.* 1975. Potter. 1st. F/dj. M2. $75.00

STOKER, Bram. *Dracula's Guest.* 1937. NY. 1st. G. B5. $40.00

STOKER, Bram. *Dracula.* nd. Modern Lib. VG/fair. P3. $15.00

STOKER, Bram. *Personal Reminiscences of Henry Irving.* 1906. Macmillan. 1st. 2 vol. teg. gilt red cloth. F. M24. $150.00

STOKER, Bram. *Snake's Pass.* Authorized Facsimile (1891 Sampson Low). NF/wrp. M22. $30.00

STOKES, Donald. *Appointment With Fear.* 1950. Coward McCann. 1st. VG/G. P3. $18.00

STOKES, Hugh. *Francisco Goya...Work & Personality.* 1914. London. 1st. 397p+48 full-p pl. cloth. A17. $20.00

STOKES, William. *Honduras.* 1950. Madison, WI. 1st. 315p. dj. F3. $20.00

STOKES, William. *William Stokes: His Life & Work (1804-1878).* 1989. London. Fisher Unwin. 1st. 8vo. 255p. gilt bdg. K3. $40.00

STOLBOV, Bruce. *Last Fall.* 1987. Doubleday. 1st. F/dj. M2/P3. $15.00

STOLTE, Lawrence. *Forgotten Salmon of the Merrimack.* 1981. Dept of Interior. 214p. VG. S15. $18.00

STOLZ, Mary. *Go & Catch a Flying Fish.* 1979. Harper Row. 1st. VG/VG-. P2. $25.00

STOLZ, Mary. *Leftover Elf.* 1952. Harper. probable 1st. ils Peggy Bacon. 48p. VG/G. P2. $30.00

STOLZ, Mary. *Pangur Ban.* 1988. Harper Row. 1st. ils Pamela Johnson. tan brd/brn cloth spine. F/F. T5. $20.00

STONE, Chuck. *King Strut.* 1970. Bobbs Merrill. 1st. inscr. F/VG. B4. $75.00

STONE, Ebenezer. *Digest of Militia Laws of Massachusetts.* 1851. VG. E6. $65.00

STONE, Elizabeth Arnold. *Unita County: Its Place in History.* nd. np. scarce. A19. $85.00

STONE, Hampton. *Kid Who Came Home With a Corpse.* 1972. S&S. 1st. VG/dj. P3. $15.00

STONE, I.F. *War Years 1939-1945: A Nonconformist History of Our Times.* 1988. Little Brn. 1st. VG/G. V4. $12.50

STONE, Irving. *Agony & the Ecstasy.* 1963. Doubleday. 1st ils. inscr/dtd 1965. F/case. w/MTI souvenir book. Q1. $100.00

STONE, Irving. *Depths of Glory.* 1985. Franklin Lib. 1st. sgn. leather. F. B35. $55.00

STONE, Irving. *Manana Land: Irving Stone's Southern California.* 1991. LA. Hist Soc of S CA. rpt. 8vo. M/wrp. T10. $15.00

STONE, Irving. *Passions of the Mind: Biographical Novel of Sigmund Freud.* 1971. Doubleday. 1st trade. inscr. F/NF. M25. $45.00

STONE, Josephine Rector. *Green Is for Galanx.* 1980. Atheneum. 1st. VG/dj. P3. $18.00

STONE, Julius. *Messiah Idea in Jewish History.* 1906. Phil. Jewish Pub. 1st. 347p. brn cloth. B22. $7.00

STONE, Raymond. *Tommy Tiptop & His Boy Scouts (#5).* 1914. Chas E Graham. lists 6 titles. 124p. VG. M20. $16.00

STONE, Reynolds. *Engravings, With an Introduction by the Artist...* 1977. Brattleboro. Stephen Green. 1st. 192p. full buckram. H13. $95.00

STONE, Robert. *Children of Light.* 1986. Knopf. 1st. NF/dj. A24. $25.00

STONE, Robert. *Children of Light.* 1986. Knopf. 1st. sgn. F/F. T11. $75.00

STONE, Robert. *Dog Soldiers.* 1974. Houghton Mifflin. 1st. F/F. from $90 to $100.00

STONE, Robert. *Dog Soldiers.* 1974. Houghton Mifflin. 1st. NF/VG+. A24. $75.00

STONE, Robert. *Dog Soldiers.* 1974. Houghton Mifflin. 1st. sgn. F/F. D10. $125.00

STONE, Robert. *Flag for Sunrise.* 1981. NY. Knopf. 1st. sgn. F/NF. T11. $125.00

STONE, Robert. *Outerbridge Reach.* 1992. NY. Ticknor Fields. 1st. 1/300. sgn/#d/special bdg. F/case. Q1. $125.00

STONE, Stuart B. *Kingdom of Why, Being the Strange Story of Lucile's...* 1913. Bobbs Merrill. 1st. ils Peter Newell. blk cloth/label. VG. M24. $125.00

STONE, Ted. *13 Canadian Ghost Stories.* 1988. Prairie BOoks. 1st. F/dj. P3. $20.00

STONE, Witmer. *Bird Studies at Old Cape May.* 1965 (1937). NY. Dover. rpt. 2 vol. ils/maps. VG. S15. $27.50

STONE, Zackary. *Modigliani Scandal.* 1976. Collins Crime Club. 1st. NF/dj. P3. $25.00

STONEHOUSE, J.H. *Picaddily Notes.* 1933-1938. London. Henry Sotheran Ltd. crude bdg. A17. $45.00

STONER, Dayton. *Rodents of Iowa.* 1918. Des Moines. ils. 172p. VG. S15. $15.00

STONES, E.L.G. *FW Maitland, Letters to George Neilson.* 1976. Glasgow. 56p. sewn wrp. M11. $45.00

STOPES, Marie Carmichael. *Enduring Passion: Further New Contributions...* 1931. Putnam. 1st. 181p. A25. $12.00

STOREY, David. *This Sporting Life.* 1960. Macmillan. 1st Am. author's 1st book. F/NF. B4. $100.00

STORM, Hyemeyohsts. *Seven Arrows.* (19728). Harper Row. 1st. F/dj. M25. $100.00

STORM, Hyemeyohsts. *Song of Heyoehkah.* 1981. Harper Row. 1st. VG/VG. L3. $40.00

STORR, Anthony. *Solitude: Return to the Self.* 1989. Ballantine. 216p. VG. B29. $6.50

STORRS, Les. *Santa Monica: Portrait of a City, Yesterday & Today.* 1974. Santa Monica. 68p. pict brd. D11. $50.00

STORY, Dana. *Hail Columbia.* 1985. Gloucester, MA. Ten Pound Island. VG/VG. B11. $18.00

STORY, Jack Trevor. *Mix Me a Person.* 1960. Macmillan. 1st. VG/dj. P3. $25.00

STOUT, David. *Carolina Skeletons.* 1988. Mysterious. 1st. F/dj. M15. $65.00

STOUT, David. *Hell Gate.* 1990. Mysterious. 1st. VG/dj. P3. $15.00

STOUT, Gardner D. *Shorebirds of North America.* 1967. NY. 32 full-p mc pl. 270p. F/VG. S15. $150.00

STOUT, Rex. *Alphabet Hicks.* 1941. Farrar Rhinehart. 1st. VG/dj. M15. $250.00

STOUT, Rex. *Before Midnight.* 1955. Viking. 1st. F/F. M15. $200.00

STOUT, Rex. *Family Affair.* 1975. Viking. 1st. F/F. M15. $45.00

STOUT, Rex. *Family Affair.* 1975. Viking. 1st. NF/F. B2. $35.00

STOUT, Rex. *Final Deduction.* 1961. Viking. 1st. NF/remnant. M25. $25.00

STOUT, Rex. *Golden Remedy.* 1931. Vanguard. 1st. author's 3rd novel. VG/dj. M15. $400.00

STOUT, Rex. *In the Best of Families.* 1950. Viking. 1st. NF/dj. M25. $150.00

STOUT, Rex. *Mother Hunt.* 1963. Viking. 1st. F/NF. Q1. $125.00

STOUT, Rex. *Mother Hunt.* 1963. Viking. 1st. VG. P3. $20.00

STOUT, Rex. *Murder by the Book.* 1951. Viking. 1st. NF/NF. M22. $125.00

STOUT, Rex. *Nero Wolfe Cook Book.* 1973. Viking. 1st. ES. dj. A16. $70.00

STOUT, Rex. *Please Pass the Guilt.* 1973. Viking. 1st. VG/dj. P3. $40.00

STOUT, Rex. *Prisoner's Base.* 1952. Viking. 1st. NF/dj. M15. $150.00

STOUT, Rex. *Right To Die.* 1974. Viking. 1st. F/NF. B2. $65.00

STOUT, Rex. *Second Confession.* 1973. Tom Stacey. F/dj. P3. $22.00

STOUT, Rex. *Three for the Chair.* 1957. Viking. 1st. VG. P3. $18.00

STOUT, Rex. *Too Many Women.* 1947. Viking. 1st. VG/G. M22. $70.00

STOUT, Rex. *Triple Jeopardy.* 1952. Viking. 1st. VG/VG. M22. $95.00

STOUT, Rex. *Under the Andes.* 1985. Penzler. 1st. VG/dj. P3. $25.00

STOUT, Wesley W. *Bullets by the Billion.* 1946. Detroit, MI. Chrysler Corp. A19. $20.00

STOUT, Wesley W. *Secret.* 1947. Detroit. Chrysler Corp. ils. 67p. K3. $25.00

STOUT, William B. *Boy's Book of Mechanical Models.* 1916. Little Brn. 1st. 8vo. 257p. cloth. VG. T10. $75.00

STOWE, Harriet Beecher. *Earthly Care, a Heavenly Discipline.* 1855. Boston. JP Jewett. 1st/later prt. glazed gr pict wrp. M24. $150.00

STOWE, Harriet Beecher. *Home & Home Papers.* 1865. Ticknor Fields. 1st/A bdg (gilt bl cloth). F. M24. $100.00

STOWE, Harriet Beecher. *Mayflower; or, Scenes & Sketches Among Descendants...* 1853. London. Farrington. 16mo. 154p. old wrp. M1. $100.00

STOWE, Harriet Beecher. *Men of Our Times.* 1868. Hartford. 1st/2nd state. aeg. gilt gr cloth. F. M24. $100.00

STOWE, Harriet Beecher. *My Wife & I; or, Harry Henderson's History.* 1871. NY. JB Ford. 1st. 474p. stp purple cloth. G. H1. $12.00

STOWE, Harriet Beecher. *Palmetto-Leaves.* 1873. Boston. JR Osgood. 1st. gr pict cloth (1st bdg, Osgood imp at foot). M24. $200.00

STOWE, Harriet Beecher. *Story of Topsy From Uncle Tom's Cabin.* 1908. Reilly Britton. ils JR Neill. 12mo. pict brd. R5. $150.00

STOWE, Harriet Beecher. *Uncle Tom's Cabin.* ca 1910. Ward Lock. 12mo. VG. M5. $65.00

STOWELL, Robert E. *Thoreau Gazetteer.* 1970. Princeton. 1st. thin 4to. 56p. F/dj. T10. $75.00

STRAHAN, Kay Cleaver. *Footprints.* 1929. Crime Club. 1st. G. P3. $20.00

STRAHORN, Carrie Adell. *Fifteen Thousand Miles by Stage.* 1911. ils Chas M Russell/others. G+. M17. $100.00

STRAHORN, Robert E. *To the Rockies & Beyond; or, Summer on the Union Pacific...* 1878. Omaha, NE. Omaha Republican Prt. 1st. 8vo. 141p. M1. $250.00

STRAIGHT, Susan. *Blacker Than a Thousand Midnights.* 1994. Hyperion. 1st. sgn. F/F. B3. $40.00

STRAIGHT, Susan. *I Been in Sorrow's Kitchen & Licked Out All the Pots.* 1992. NY. Hyperion. 1st. F/F. H11. $50.00

STRAIN, Frances Bruce. *New Patterns in Sex Teaching: Guide to Answering Children...* 1951. Appleton Century Crofts. revised. photos. 262p. VG. A25. $10.00

STRALEY, John. *Woman Who Married a Bear.* 1992. NY. Soho. 1st. sgn. F/F. B3. $75.00

STRAND, Mark. *Late Hour.* 1978. Atheneum. 1st. assn copy. F/dj. V1. $35.00

STRAND, Mark. *Monument.* 1978. Ecco. 1st. sgn. NF/VG. R14. $275.00

STRAND, Mark. *Mr & Mrs Baby & Other Stories.* 1985. Knopf. 1st. assn copy. F/dj. V1. $25.00

STRANG, Herbert. *Lord of the Seas.* nd. London. 1st. VG. M2. $35.00

STRANGE, Ian. *Bird Man: An Autobiography.* 1976. London. ils. 182p. NF. S15. $15.00

STRANGE, John Stephen. *Night of Reckoning.* 1959. Collins Crime Club. 1st. VG. P3. $20.00

STRANGE, John Stephen. *Strangler Fig.* 1930. Crime Club. 1st. VG. P3. $30.00

STRANGER, Joyce. *Fox at Drummers' Darkness.* 1977. FSG. 1st Am. VG/VG. O3. $25.00

STRANGER, Joyce. *Running Foxes.* 1966. Viking. 1st Am. VG/VG. O3. $25.00

STRAPAROLA. *Italian Novelists.* 1909. London. Soc of Bibliophiles. 7 vol. 1/300. half red morocco. A17. $150.00

STRATEMEYER, Edward. *Colonial Series: At the Fall of Montreal.* 1903. Lee Shepard. 212p. gilt red cloth. VG. M20. $25.00

STRATEMEYER, Edward. *Lakeport Series: Boat Club Boys of Lakeport (#3).* 1908. Lee Shepard. 297p. VG. M20. $25.00

STRATEMEYER, Edward. *Old Glory Series: Under Otis in the Philippines.* 1899. Lee Shepard. 332p+ads. tan cloth. VG. M20. $22.50

STRATEMEYER, Edward. *Stratemeyer Popular Series: Oliver Bright's Search.* 1899 (1895). Lee Shepard. 245p+ads. VG+. M20. $20.00

STRATTON, R.B. *Captivity of the Oatman Girls...* 1982. Time-Life. rpt. 290p. aeg. F. M4. $25.00

STRAUB, Peter. *Floating Dragon.* 1983. London. Collins. 1st. F/dj. P3. $35.00

STRAUB, Peter. *Floating Dragon.* 1983. NY. Putnam. 1st. NF/dj. N4. $40.00

STRAUB, Peter. *Ghost Story.* 1979. CMG. 1st. VG/dj. H11/P3. $45.00

STRAUB, Peter. *Koko.* 1988. Dutton. 1st. F/F. H11. $40.00

STRAUB, Peter. *Koko.* 1988. Dutton. 1st. 562p. NF/F. W2. $35.00

STRAUB, Peter. *Mystery.* 1990. Dutton. 1st. F/dj. P3. $22.00

STRAUB, Peter. *Shadow Land.* 1980. CMG. 1st. F/dj. M2. $25.00

STRAUB, Peter. *Shadow Land.* 1980. CMG. 1st. inscr. F/F. A23. $46.00

STRAUB, Peter. *Throat.* 1993. Dutton. 1st. inscr/sgn. F/F. A23. $46.00

STRAUB, Peter. *Throat.* 1993. Dutton. 1st. sgn. F/dj. Q1. $35.00

STRAUB, Peter. *Wild Animals.* 1984. Putnam. 1st. VG/dj. P3. $35.00

STRAUS, Rachael. *Regensburg & Augsburg.* 1939. JPS. 16mo. ils. 261p. VG+. S3. $35.00

STRAUS, Ralph. *Pengard Awake.* 1920. Appleton. 1st am. F/NF. M15. $125.00

STRAUSS, I. *Paint, Powder & Make-Up.* 1938. NY. 219p. cloth. A17. $20.00

STRAUSS, Lewis L. *Men & Decisions.* 1962. Doubleday. ils. 468p. VG. K3. $20.00

STREATFIELD, Noel. *Beyond the Vicarage.* 1971. London. Collins. 1st. 214p. VG/dj. P2. $35.00

STREATFIELD, Noel. *Vicarage Family.* 1963. London. Collins. 1st. 8vo. 246p. red tweed brd. VG. T5. $45.00

STREET, David. *Horses: A Working Tradition.* 1976. Toronto. McGraw Hill Ryerson. 1st. 4to. VG/VG. O3. $38.00

STREET, Donald M. *Ocean Sailing Yacht.* 1973. Norton. 4th. 703p. F/dj. A17. $20.00

STREET, James. *Look Away: A Dixie Notebook.* 1936. NY. 1st. VG/dj. B5. $50.00

STREET, P. *Animal Reproduction.* 1974. Taplinger. 8vo. 263p. VG/F. B1. $22.50

STREET, P. *Crab & Its Relatives.* 1966. London. Faber. photos/drawings, 167p. dj. B1. $35.00

STREETER, Daniel W. *Camels!* 1927. NY/London. Putnam. 1st. 8vo. 277p. VG. W1. $12.00

STREETER, Thomas. *Bibliography of Texas, 1795-1845.* (1955-60). 5 vol. rpt. 1/150. F. A4. $300.00

STREETS, R.J. *Exotic Forest Trees in the British Commonwealth.* 1962. Oxford. 1st. ils/photos/fld maps. rpr hinge. B26. $87.50

STRETE, Craig. *Bleeding Man.* 1977. Greenwillow. 1st. F/dj. M2. $45.00

STRICKLAND, F. *Manual of Petrol Motors & Motor Cars.* 1907. London. Chas Griffin. 8vo. ils. 376p. VG. K3. $90.00

STRIEBER, Whitley. *Billy.* 1990. Putnam. 1st. F/dj. P3. $20.00

STRIEBER, Whitley. *Black Magic.* 1982. Morrow. 1st. VG/VG. N4. $40.00

STRIEBER, Whitley. *Communion.* 1987. Morrow. 1st. F/dj. M2. $25.00

STRIEBER, Whitley. *Night Church.* 1983. S&S. 1st. F/dj. M2. $20.00

STRIEBER, Whitley. *Transformation.* 1988. London. Century. 1st. VG/VG. M22. $12.00

STRIEBER, Whitley. *Wolf in Shadows.* 1985. Knopf Sierra Club. 1st. VG/dj. P3. $12.00

STRIEBER, Whitley. *Wolfen.* 1978. Morrow. 1st. F/dj. M2. $65.00

STRIEBER, Whitley. *Wolfen.* 1978. Morrow. 1st. NF/VG+. N4. $55.00

STRIEBER, Whitley. *Wolfen.* 1978. Morrow. 1st. VG/dj. P3. $25.00

STRIKER, Fran. *Lone Ranger & the Code of the West (#16).* 1954. Grosset Dunlap. 180p. VG/dj (lists 18 titles). M20. $65.00

STRIMPLE, Helen. *Lindy Lou & the Green Umbrella.* 1946. Broadman. 1st. pict brd. VG. M5. $28.00

STRODE, Hudson. *Jefferson Davis: American Patriot, 1808-1861.* 1955. Harcourt Brace. 1st. 460p. VG/ragged. M20. $25.00

STRODE, Hudson. *Now in Mexico.* 1947 (1946). Harcourt. 1st. dj. F3. $15.00

STRODE, Muriel. *My Little Book of Prayer.* 1906. Open Court. 3rd. inscr/dtd 1911. teg. gilt blk cloth. M24. $475.00

STROM, Sharon Hartman. *Beyond the Typewriter: Gender, Class & Origins...* 1992. IL U. 1st. F/F. V4. $20.00

STRONG, Anna Louise. *Cash & Violence in Laos & Vietnam.* 1962. Mainstream. 1st. NF/wrp. B2. $30.00

STRONG, L.A.G. *Corporal Time.* 1934. Gollancz. VG. P3. $15.00

STRONG, Phil. *Horses & Americans.* 1939. Stokes. 1st. 333p. VG/VG. O3. $48.00

STRONG, Phil. *No-Sitch: The Hound.* 1936. Dodd Mead. 1st. ils Kurt Wiese. 80p. VG+/VG. P2. $75.00

STRONG, Phil. *25 Stories of Mystery & Imagination.* nd. Garden City. VG. P3. $25.00

STRONG, W.C. *Culture of the Grape.* 1866. Boston. Tilton. 355p. A10. $80.00

STRONG, William. *Catalogue of Singularly Choice Collection Rare...Books...* 1843. Bristol. Strong. pres inscr. Strawberry Hill vignette. half calf. R12. $300.00

STRONG, William. *Paracas, Nazca & Tiahuanacoid Cultural Relationships...* 1957. Salt Lake City. photos/fld map. 48p. wrp. F3. $30.00

STRONGIN, Lynn. *Bones & Kim.* 1980. Argyle, NY. Spinsters Inc. 1st. 116p. sc. VG. A25. $10.00

STROOTMAN, Ralph. *History of the 363rd Infantry...* 1947. WA, DC. 1st. photos/maps/roster. 354p. VG. S16. $65.00

STROUD, Carsten. *Sniper's Moon.* 1990. Bantam. 1st. VG/dj. P3. $20.00

STROUD, D.V. *Inscribed Union Swords 1861-1865.* 1983. Kilgore. 1/1500. inscr/#d. photos. 192p. F. M4. $60.00

STROUD, R. *Stroud's Digest on the Diseases of Birds.* 1943. Minneapolis. Marcus/Stroud. ils. 500p. cloth. VG. M12. $37.50

STROUP, Thomas B. *Religious Rite & Ceremony in Milton's Poetry.* 1968. Lexington, KY. sgn. VG/VG. B11. $18.00

STRUGATSKY & STRUGATSKY. *For Rainbow & the Second Invasion From Mars.* 1979. Macmillan. 1st. VG/dj. P3. $15.00

STRUGATSKY & STRUGATSKY. *Hard To Be a God.* 1973. NY. Seabury. 1st Eng language. F/F. T2. $45.00

STRUGATSKY & STRUGATSKY. *Noon: 22nd Century.* 1978. Macmillan. 1st. VG/dj. P3. $18.00

STRUGATSKY & STRUGATSKY. *Time Wanderers.* 1986. NY. Richardson Steirman. 1st Eng-language ed. F/F. T2. $20.00

STRUGATSKY & STRUGATSKY. *Ugly Swans.* 1979. Macmillan. 1st. VG/dj. P3. $15.00

STRUNSKY, Simson. *King Akhnaton.* 1928. Longmans. 1st. NF/dj. M2. $15.00

STRUTHER, Jan. *Sycamore Square.* 1932. Oxford. 1st Am. ils Ernest Shepard. VG-/fair. P2. $30.00

STRYK, Lucian. *Bells of Lombardy.* 1986. IL U. 1st. inscr. F/dj. V1. $20.00

STUART, Alexander. *War Zone.* 1989. Doubleday. 1st. F/dj. M2. $17.00

STUART, Anthony. *Russian Leave.* 1981. Arbor. 1st. VG/dj. P3. $15.00

STUART, Bernard. *How To Become a Successful Engineer.* 1871. Edinburgh. 5th. 127p. VG. B14. $75.00

STUART, Colonel. *Memoir of Indian Wars & Other Occurrences.* 1971. Parsons, WV. 34p. brd. VG. B18. $12.50

STUART, David. *Garden Triumphant.* 1988. Harper Row. 8vo. ils. 316p. F/dj. A22. $25.00

STUART, Dora Jessie. *Return to Thrush Green.* 1979. Houghton Mifflin. 1st Am. ils JS Goodall. 256p. VG+. A25. $8.00

STUART, Henry Logan. *Weeping Cross: Unworldly Story.* 1908. Doubleday. 1st. 497p. purple cloth. VG+. B22. $7.50

STUART, Moses. *Hebrew Grammar Without the Points; Designed As Introduction.* 1813. Andover, MA. Flagg Gould. 1st. 12mo. 123p. contemporary bdg. M1. $850.00

STUART, Sidney; see Avallone, Mike.

STUART & STUART. *Field Guide to the Mammals of Southern Africa.* 1988. Sanibel. Curtis. 100+ mc pl/ils/distribution maps. 272p. NF/F. M12. $20.00

STUART & STUART. *Lost Kingdoms of the Mayas.* 1993. NGS. 1st. 4to. 248p. dj. F3. $35.00

STUBBIER, Adrian. *Road to Revolution in Spain: The Coal Miners of Asters...* 1987. IL U. 1st. F/F. V4. $12.50

STUBBS, Jean. *Dear Laura.* 1973. Macmillan. 1st. VG/fair. P3. $13.00

STUBBS, Jean. *Painted Face.* 1974. Macmillan. 1st. VG/dj. P3. $20.00

STUBBS, Jean. *Painted Face.* 1974. Stein Day. 1st. sgn. 240p. F/VG. W2. $25.00

STUBER, Stanley I. *Illustrated Bible & Church Handbook.* 1966. Assn. 532p. VG/dj. B29. $8.00

STUCKY & STUCKY. *Lithographs of Stow Wengenroth 1931-1972.* 1974. Boston Public Lib. 1st. VG/VG. M17. $75.00

STUEWER, Roger H. *Nuclear Physics in Retrospect.* 1979. NM U. 340p. VG. K3. $20.00

STUFF, Harry S. *Siwash, His Book. Being a Bit of Indian Philosophy...* 1908. Stuff Prt Concern. 8vo. die-cut bdg as house. F/prt tan wrp. B24. $200.00

STUFF, Olive Griffith. *Variations & Relationships in Snakes of Genus Pituophis.* 1940. Smithsonian. 225p. VG. S15. $30.00

STUPHEN, W.G. Van T. *Golficide & Other Tales.* 1898. Harper. 1st. VG. M2. $25.00

STUPKA, Arthur. *Wildflowers in Color.* 1982 (1965). NY. photos. 144p. B26. $14.00

STURGEON, Theodore. *Godbody.* 1986. DIF. 1st. VG/dj. P3. $20.00

STURGEON, Theodore. *Without Sorcery.* 1948. Prime Pr. F/VG. P3. $75.00

STURTEVANT, Edgar H. *Hittite Glossary: Words of Known or Conjectured...* 1936-39. Phil. PA U. 2nd. 2 parts in 1. lg 8vo. VG/wrp. W1. $45.00

STYKES, Christopher. *Troubled Loyalty, a Biography.* 1968. London. 1st. VG/VG. T9. $35.00

STYKES, Jo. *Stubborn Mare.* 1957. Winston. 1st. VG. O3. $15.00

STYRON, William. *Confessions of Nat Turner.* 1967. Random. 1st. sgn. F/F. D10. $145.00

STYRON, William. *Darkness Visible.* 1990. Random. 1st. F/dj. Q1. $25.00

STYRON, William. *Sophie's Choice.* 1979. Random. 1st. F/F. B35. $35.00

STYRON, William. *This Quiet Dust & Other Writings.* 1982. Random. 1st. F/F. B3. $30.00

STYRON, William. *Tidewater Morning.* 1990. Helsinki. Eurographica. 1st. 1/350. sgn/#d. F/stiff wrp/dj. B4. $200.00

STYTHE, R. Margaret. *Art of Illustration 1750-1900.* 1970. London. Lib Assn. 1st. sq 4to. ils/index. T10. $45.00

SUBIK, Rudolf. *Decorative Cacti.* 1972. NY. 132p. VG/dj. B26. $9.00

SUBLETT, Jesse. *Rock Critic Murders.* 1989. Viking. 1st. author's 1st book. F/dj. M25. $35.00

SUBRAMANI. *Indo-Fijan Experience.* 1979. St Lucia. 1st. 8vo. 207p. M/dj. P4. $20.00

SUDHALTER, R. *Bix: Man & Legend.* 1974. Arlington. 1st. VG/VG. B5. $75.00

SUDWORTH, G.B. *Forest Trees of the Pacific Slope.* 1967. Dover. 8vo. 455p. B1. $18.00

SUE, Eugene. *Wandering Jew.* 1844-1845. London. 3 vol. 1st. rebound. VG. M2. $350.00

SUGDEN, John. *Sir Francis Drake.* 1991. NY. Holt. 1st. 8vo. 353p. map ep. half cloth. F/dj. P4. $30.00

SUHL, Yuri. *One Foot in America.* 1951. Macmillan. not stated 1st. author's 1st novel. 252p. F/VG. H1. $15.00

SULLIVAN, Eleanor. *Fifty Years of the Best From Ellery Queen.* 1991. Carroll Graf. VG/dj. P3. $23.00

SULLIVAN, Frank. *Pearl in Every Oyster.* 1938. Little Brn. 1st. sgn. VG. B11. $85.00

SULLIVAN, Katharine. *Girls on Parole.* 1956. Houghton Mifflin. 1st. 243p. VG/dj. A25. $38.00

SULLIVAN, Mary. *Woman Who Went to Alaska.* c 1903. 8th thousand. ils. VG. E6. $35.00

SULLIVAN, Maurice. *Jedediah Smith, Trader & Trailbreaker.* 1936. Pr of Pioneers. 1st. 233p. VG/dj. J2. $225.00

SULLIVAN, May Kellogg. *Woman Who Went to Alaska.* 1910. Boston. JH Earle. photos/maps. 392p. dk olive cloth. VG. P4. $75.00

SULLIVAN, T.R. *Boston Old & New.* 1912. Houghton Mifflin. 1/785. 8vo. teg. gilt blk brd. NF. T10. $100.00

SULLIVAN, T.R. *Hand of Petrarch.* 1913. Houghton Mifflin. 1st. VG. M2. $15.00

SULLIVAN, Walter. *Assault on the Unknown.* 1961. McGraw Hill. 8vo. 460p. dj. K5. $14.00

SULLIVAN, Walter. *Landprints on the Magnificent American Landscape.* 1984. Times. 1st. 384p. NF/VG. W2. $30.00

SULLIVAN, Walter. *Long, Long Love.* 1958. Holt. 1st. F/VG. B4. $50.00

SULLIVAN, Walter. *We Are Not Alone.* 1966 (1964). McGraw Hill. revised. 8vo. 325p. VG/dj. K5. $12.00

SULLY, Langdon. *No Tears for the General, the Life of Alfred Sully...* 1879. Am West Pub. 1st. facsimile/photos. VG/VG. J2. $135.00

SULLY. *Memoires Des Sages et Royalles Oeconomies d'Estat...* 1638. Amstelredam. Aletinosgraphe de Clearetimelee. 2 vols in 1. R12. $1,750.00

SULZBERGER, C.L. *Resistentialists.* 1962. Harper. 1st. F/VG+ clip. B4. $450.00

SULZBERGER, C.L. *Tooth Merchant.* 1973. Quadrangle. 1st. G/dj. P3. $10.00

SUMMER, Charles. *Selected Letters.* 1990. Boston. Northwestern. 1st. 8vo. 2 vol. gray cloth. M/djs. T10. $100.00

SUMMERFIELD. *Fantasy & Reason: Children's Literature in 18th Century.* 1985. ils. 315p. F/F. A11. $55.00

SUMMERHAYS, R.S. *Arabian Horse.* 1976. N Hollywood. Wilshire. 8vo. 103p. VG. O3. $10.00

SUMMERHAYS, R.S. *Problem Horse.* 1959. London. Allen. G/dj. A18. $20.00

SUMMERLIN, Lee B. *Skylab: Classroom in Space.* 1977. NASA. 4to. 182p. VG. K5. $40.00

SUMMERS, Ian. *Tomorrow & Beyond.* 1978. Workman. 1st. NF/dj. P3. $25.00

SUMMERS, Mongague. *Popular History of Witchcraft.* 1973. Causeway Books. VG. P3. $15.00

SUMMERS, Mongague. *Vampire: His Kith & Kin.* 1960. U Books. NF. P3. $25.00

SUMMERS, Montague. *Witchcraft & Black Magic.* 1958. Rider. F/dj. M2. $20.00

SUMMERSELL, C.G. *Journal of George Townley Fullam, Boarding Officer...* 1973. AL U. 1/600. sgn/#d. 229p. bl cloth/leatherette spine. F. M4. $45.00

SUMMERSKILL, Mimi LaFollette. *Aegean Summer: A Family Odyssey.* 1990. Middlebury. PS Eriksson. 1st. ils. 263p. VG/dj. A25. $18.00

SUMMERSON, Henry. *Crown Pleas of the Devon Eyre of 1238.* 1985. Torquay. Devon & Cornwall Record Soc. 163p. prt sewn wrp. M11. $45.00

SUMNER, Charles. *White Slavery in the Barbary States.* 1853. Boston. Jewett. 1st. gilt brn cloth. M24. $650.00

SUMNER, Cid Rickets. *Traveler in the Wilderness.* 1957. NY. Harper. 8vo. blk cloth. NF. F7. $40.00

SUMNER, George. *Compendium of Physiological & Systematic Botany.* 1820. Hartford. 1st. 12mo. 300p. contemporary calf. M1. $150.00

SUMNER, William L. *Organ: Its Evolution, Principles of Construction & Use.* 1958. MacDonald. ils. 466p. fair. B29. $6.00

SUMPTON, Lois. *Cookies & More Cookies.* 1948. IL. Bennet Pub. G/dj. A16. $10.00

SURFACE, Bill. *Roundup at the Double Diamond.* 1974. Houghton Mifflin. 1st. 237p. cloth. VG/dj. M20. $20.00

SURTEES, R.S. *Plain or Ringlets.* 1860. London. Bradbury Evans. 1st. ils. red leather. VG. O3. $250.00

SUSKIND, Patrick. *Pigeon.* 1988. Knopf. 1st Am. F/F. T12. $25.00

SUTCLIFF, Robert. *Travels in Some Parts of North America...1804, 1805 & 1806.* 1811. York. Peacock for Alexander. 8vo. 5 full-p pl. calf/rebacked. R12. $250.00

SUTCLIFF, Rosemary. *Beowulf.* 1962. Dutton. 1st. 8vo. 93p. yel cloth. VG/G+. T5. $30.00

SUTCLIFF, Rosemary. *Knight's Fee.* 1960. London. Oxford. 1st. 8vo. 241p. VG/G. T5. $40.00

SUTCLIFF, Rosemary. *Road to Camlann.* 1982. Dutton. 1st. VG/VG. P3. $20.00

SUTCLIFF, Rosemary. *Sword & the Circle.* 1981. Bodley Head. 1st. F/dj. P3. $20.00

SUTHERLAND, Donald W. *Assize of Novel Disseisin.* 1973. Clarendon. M11. $75.00

SUTHERLAND, Donald W. *Quo Warranto Proceedings in Reign of Edward I, 1278-1294.* 1963. Clarendon. M11. $75.00

SUTHERLAND. *Best in Children's Books, Children's Literature 1973-78.* 1980. 1400 entries/6 indexes. 559p. F/F. A4. $35.00

SUTHERLAND. *Best in Children's Books, University of Chicago Guide...* 1986. 1400 entries. 521p. F/F. A4. $35.00

SUTIN, Lawrence. *Divine Invasions: Life of Philip K Dick.* 1989. Harmony. 1st. NF/dj. M21. $40.00

SUTLEY, Zack T. *Last Frontier.* 1930. Macmillan. VG. A19. $75.00

SUTTER, Barton. *Cedar Home.* 1977. BOA Ed. 1/26 (of 770). sgns. w/poem card. F. V1. $75.00

SUTTON, Ada Louis. *Teddy Bears.* 1907. Saalfield. ils AJ Schaefer. VG. M5. $65.00

SUTTON, George Miksch. *Eskimo Year.* 1934. NY. 1st. 321p+photos. xl. G. A17. $15.00

SUTTON, George P. *Rocket Propulsion Elements.* 1956. John Wiley. 2nd. 8vo. 483p. xl. K5. $40.00

SUTTON, Henry. *Sacrifice.* 1978. Grosset Dunlap. 1st. F/dj. P3. $20.00

SUTTON, Margaret. *Judy Bolton: Discovery at the Dragon's Mouth (#31).* 1960. Grosset Dunlap. lists to Secret Quest. 182p. VG/dj. M2/M20. $80.00

SUTTON, Margaret. *Judy Bolton: Ghost Parade (#5).* nd. Grosset Dunlap. VG/G. P3. $12.00

SUTTON, Margaret. *Judy Bolton: Haunted Attic (#2).* 1932. Grosset Dunlap. 212p. cloth. VG/dj (lists 10 titles). M20. $50.00

SUTTON, Margaret. *Judy Bolton: Phantom Friend (#30).* 1959. Grosset Dunlap. lists to Secret Quest. 174p. VG/dj. M20. $90.00

SUTTON, Margaret. *Judy Bolton: Pledge of the Twin Knights (#36).* 1965. Grosset Dunlap. 1st. 172p. lists to this title. pict brd. VG. M20. $225.00

SUTTON, Margaret. *Judy Bolton: Secret of the Sand Castle (#38).* 1967. Grosset Dunlap. lists to this title. 174p. VG. scarce. M20. $325.00

SUTTON, Margaret. *Judy Bolton: Unfinished House (#11).* 1938. Grosset Dunlap. ils Pelagie Doane. F/NF. P3. $30.00

SUTTON, Margaret. *Judy Bolton: Yellow Phantom (#6).* 1933. Grosset Dunlap. lists 10 titles. 210p. VG/dj. M20. $35.00

SUTTON, Thomas. *Daniells: Artists & Travellers.* 1954. London. Theodore Brun. 1/150 deluxe. 31 pl. gilt leatherette. NF. B24. $250.00

SUTTON & SUTTON. *American West.* nd. NY. Random. 4to. 270p. yel cloth. pict dj. F7. $22.50

SUTTON & SUTTON. *Wilderness World of the Grand Canyon.* 1971. Lippincott. 1st. ils/map ep. 241p. NF/VG+. B19. $25.00

SUTTON & SUTTON. *Wilderness World of the Grand Canyon.* 1971. Lippincott. 1st. 8vo. 241p. salmon cloth. F/dj. F7. $35.00

SUVIN, Darko. *Other Worlds, Other Seas.* 1970. Random. 1st. VG/dj. P3. $22.00

SUYIN, Han. *Enchantress.* 1985. Bantam. 1st. F/dj. M2. $25.00

SUYKER, Betty. *Death Scene.* 1981. St Martin. 1st. F/F. N4. $15.00

SVEND, Otto S. *Ling & the Little Devils.* 1984. London. Pelahm. 1st. 4to. unp. as new. T5. $20.00

SVENDSEN, Linda. *Marine Life.* 1992. FSG. 1st. author's 1st book. F/F. R13. $20.00

SVENSSON, Sam. *Sails Through the Centuries.* 1965. NY. Macmillan. sq 12mo. ils. 115p. dj. T7. $25.00

SVESHNIKOVA, N.M. *Nematode Diseases of Agricultural Plants.* 1967. Moscow. photos/graphs/tables/maps. staple bdg. B1. $26.00

SWAIN, Margaret H. *Historical Needlework: A Study of Influences in Scotland...* 1970. Scribner. 1st. 140p. cloth. VG/dj. M20. $25.00

SWALLOW, Jay. *Pony Care.* 1976. St Martin. 1st. VG. O3. $10.00

SWAN, Joseph. *Demonstration of the Nerves of the Human Body.* 1934. London. 1st 4to ed. 25 pl. half leather/rebacked. A13. $900.00

SWAN, Mark. *Top O' the World.* 1908. Dutton. 1st. 8vo. VG+. M5. $75.00

SWAN, Michael. *Marches of El Dorado.* 1958. Beacon Hill. 1st. 304p. dj. F3. $20.00

SWANBERG, W.A. *Sickles the Incredible.* 1956. 1st. 433p. O8. $21.50

SWANN, Francis. *Brass Key.* 1964. S&S. 1st. VG/dj. P3. $20.00

SWANNER, Charles D. *Santa Ana: Narrative of Yesterday.* 1953. Claremont, CA. Saunder. 1st. sgn. 157p. VG/dj. M20. $40.00

SWANSON, Logan; see Matheson, Richard.

SWANSON, Neil H. *Unconquered.* 1947. Doubleday. 1st. VG/dj. P3. $15.00

SWANWICK, Michael. *In the Drift.* 1989. Legend. 1st Eng. F/F. M19. $25.00

SWARTLEY, John. *Cultivated Hemlock.* 1984. Portland. Timber. 186p. dj. A10. $30.00

SWARUP, Shanti. *Study of the Chinese Communist Movement 1927-1934.* 1966. Oxford. 1st. G/F. V4. $25.00

SWASEY, William F. *Early Days & Men of California...* 1891. Oakland, CA. Pacific Pr. 1st. 8vo. ils. gilt bl cloth. R3. $400.00

SWEELL, Helen. *Belinda the Mouse.* 1944. Oxford. 1st. VG+/VG. P2. $55.00

SWEENEY, B.M. *Rhythmic Phenomena in Plants.* 1973 (1969). London. ils/figures. mottled cloth. B26. $20.00

SWEENEY, Charles. *Naturalist in the Sudan.* 1974. NY. ils. 240p. VG/VG. S15. $12.00

SWEET, Oliver E. *South Dakota Laws.* 1922. Kansas City, MO. Banker Law Pub. A19. $20.00

SWEET, William Herbert. *Not in Our Genes: Biology, Ideology & Human Nature.* 1975. Baltimore. U Park Pr. thick 8vo. 768p. gray cloth. G1. $65.00

SWEETMAN, Luke D. *Back Trailing on Open Range.* 1951. Caldwell. Caxton. A19. $75.00

SWEETSER, Kate Dickinson. *Peggy's Prize Cruise.* 1925. Barse Hopkins. 313p. red silk cloth/pict label. VG. M20. $25.00

SWIFT, Graham. *Learning To Swim & Other Stories.* 1985. Poseidon. 1st Am. F/dj. A24. $30.00

SWIFT, Graham. *Learning To Swim & Other Stories.* 1985. Poseidon. 1st. NF/F. M23. $25.00

SWIFT, Graham. *Out of This World.* 1988. Poseidon. UP. sgn. VG/wrp. B3. $50.00

SWIFT, Graham. *Waterland.* 1983. Poseidon. 1st. F/F. M23. $40.00

SWIFT, Hildegarde Hoyt. *North Star Shining.* 1947. NY. Morrow. 1st. 4to. blk cloth/label. dj. R5. $100.00

SWIFT, Jonathan. *Gulliver's Travels.* 1940. Whitman. ils Erwin L Hess. VG/VG. P3. $20.00

SWIFT, Jonathan. *Gulliver's Travels.* 1947. Crown. 1st thus. 358p. F/VG. H1. $25.00

SWIFT, Jonathan. *Swift's Works.* 1751-1779. London. 27 vol. some detached covers/missing spine labels. G. A15. $300.00

SWIFT, Jonathan. *Tale of a Tub, Written for Universal Improvement of Mankind.* 1710. London. John Nutt. 5th. 8vo. 344p. later bdg. H13. $495.00

SWIFT, Mary A. *First Lessons on Natural Philosophy for Children.* 1875. Hartford. Wm Hamersley. new/enlarged. 12mo. 123p. cloth. R5. $150.00

SWIGART, Rob. *Little America.* 1977. Houghton Mifflin. 1st. VG/dj. P3. $20.00

SWIGART, Rob. *Portal.* 1988. St Martin. 1st. F/dj. P3. $20.00

SWIGART, Rob. *Time Trip.* 1979. Houghton Mifflin. 1st. F/dj. M2. $15.00

SWIHART, Thomas L. *Stellar Atmosphere Theory.* nd. Tucson. 4to. 104p. G. K5. $15.00

SWINBURNE, Algernon Charles. *Lesbia Brandon.* 1952. Falcon. 1st Eng. NF/NF. M19. $25.00

SWINBURNE, Algernon Charles. *Letters.* 1918. London. 2 vol. edit Gosse/Wise. VG/djs. T9. $60.00

SWINBURNE, Algernon Charles. *Love's Cross Currents. A Year's Letters.* 1905. London. Harper. 1st book ed. 8vo. 245p. mauve cloth. H13. $95.00

SWINBURNE, Algernon Charles. *Selected Poems.* 1928. London. John Lane. 1st thus. ils Harry Clarke. gilt blk cloth. F. B24. $150.00

SWINDELLS, P. *Overlook Water Gardener's Handbook.* 1984. Overlook. 172p. VG/VG. B1. $26.50

SWINDOLL, Charles R. *Simple Faith: Do You Feel Confined by the Christian Life?* 1991. Word. 259p. VG/dj. B29. $8.50

SWINGER, S. *Stalking the Ice Dragon: An Alaskan Journey.* 1991. Tucson. 8vo. sgn pres. 219p. F/F. M12. $20.00

SWINGLEHURST, Edmund. *Romantic Journey. Story of Thomas Cook & Victorian Travel.* 1974. Harper Row. 1st Am. 201p. VG/dj. K3. $20.00

SWINK, Floyd. *Plants of the Chicago Region.* 1969. Morton Arboretum. sgn. 445p. VG. A22. $30.00

SWINK & WILHELM. *Plants of the Chicago Region.* 1994. Lisle. IN Academy of Sci. 4th. 921p. dj. B1. $70.00

SWINNERTON, H.H. *New Naturalist: Fossils.* 1973. London. Bloomsbury. ils/pl. 274p. F/F. M12. $20.00

SWINNERTON, Jimmy. *Hosteen Crotchetty.* 1960. Palm Desert. Best West. 1st. sgn. VG/VG. A23. $30.00

SWINTON, George. *Sculpture of the Eskimo.* 1972. Greenwich. NYGS. 255p. gray cloth. VG/clip. P4. $125.00

SWINTON, John. *Striking for Life or Labor's Side of the Labor Question...* 1894. Am Mfg & Pub. VG. V4. $75.00

SWINTON, W.E. *Giants: Past & Present.* 1966. London. Hale. ils/pl/figures. 192p. cloth. F/VG. M12. $30.00

SYKES, John. *Mountain Arabs: A Window in the Middle East.* 1968. Chilton. 1st. 8vo. 229p. NF/dj. W1. $16.00

SYKES, W. Stanley. *Essays on First Hundred Years of Anaesthesia.* 1982. Park Ridge, IL. 1st. 3 vol. A13. $125.00

SYLVESTER, Jerry. *Salt-Water Fishing Is Easy.* 1956. Stackpole. sgn. 208p. VG/dj. M20. $15.00

SYMONDS, John A. *Percy Bysshe Shelley.* 1879. NY. Harper. 1st/1st prt. blk cloth. F. M24. $65.00

SYMONDS, John A. *Sonnets of Michael Angelo Buonarroti.* 1899. Portland, ME. Mosher. 1/935. 12mo. teg. full blk leather. NF. H3. $125.00

SYMONDS, John. *Great Beast.* 1951. London. Rider. 2nd. VG/shabby. B5. $45.00

SYMONS, Julian. *Criminal Comedy.* 1985. Viking. 1st Am. F/F. M22. $15.00

SYMONS, Julian. *General Strike.* 1959. Readers Union. P3. $15.00

SYMONS, Julian. *Name of Annabel Lee.* 1983. Macmillan. 1st. F/dj. P3. $15.00

SYMONS, Julian. *Oscar Wilde: Problem in Biography.* 1980. Council Bluffs. Yel Barn. 1/200. red cloth spine. as new. K7. $100.00

SYMONS, Julian. *Plot Against Roger Rider.* 1973. Harper Row. 1st. VG/dj. P3. $18.00

SYMONS, Julian. *Portraits of the Missing.* 1991. London. Andre Deutsch. ARS. RS. F/dj. A24. $25.00

SYMONS, Julian. *Tigers of Subtopia.* 1983. Viking. 1st Am. VG+. A24. $15.00

SYMONS, Scott. *Helmet of Flesh.* 1986. Toronto. 1st. F/F. T12. $20.00

SYNGE, Patrick M. *In Search of Flowers.* 1973. London. map/pl. VG/dj. B26. $36.00

SYNTAX, Dr. see Combe, William.

SZARKOWSKI, John. *Winogrand: Figments From the Real World.* 1988. NY. MOMA. photos. 260p. cloth. dj. D11. $125.00

SZATHMARY, Louis. *Bakery Restaurant Cookbook.* 1981. Boston. CHI Pub. 1st. inscr. VG/dj. A16. $20.00

SZATHMARY, Louis. *Chef's Secret Cookbook.* 1971. Chicago. Quadrangle. VG/dj. A16. $10.00

SZEKELY, Jozsef I. *Opioid Peptides in Substance Abuse.* 1994. Boca Raton/Ann Arbor. CRC Pr. 277p. wht brd. G1. $60.00

SZILARD, Leo. *Genius in the Shadow.* 1994. Chicago. prt. M/wrp. K3. $20.00

SZILARD, Leo. *His Version of the Facts. Vol 2.* 1978. MIT. 1st. ils. dj. K3. $40.00

SZOLLOSI, Thomas. *Proving.* 1988. Doubleday. 1st. F/dj. P3. $20.00

SZOLNOKI, Rose Namath. *Namath: My Son Joe.* 1975. Oxmoor. 1st. photos. VG+/dj. P8. $35.00

SZYK, Arthur. *New Order.* 1941. Putnam. 1st. 4to. tan cloth. wrp. R5. $225.00

TABER, Gladys. *Conversations With Amber.* 1976. Lippincott. 1st. ils Pamela Carroll. F/F. C8. $20.00

TABER, Gladys. *One Dozen & One.* 1966. Phil. 1st. VG/VG. B5. $30.00

TABER, Gladys. *Still Cover Journal.* 1981. Harper Row. 1st. 223p. VG/dj. M20. $25.00

TABER, Gladys. *Stillmeadow Album.* 1969. Lippincott. 1st. 126p. VG/dj. M20. $30.00

TABER, Louis. *Glimpses of the Life of..., a Recorded Minister...* 1892. Rachel H Taber. 265p. VG. V3. $15.00

TABER, Mary J. *Just a Few Friends.* 1907. Phil. Winston. 1st. sgn. 166p. V3. $40.00

TABER, William P. *Be Gentle, Be Plain: A History of Olney.* 1976. Celo Pr. 1st. 236p. VG. V3. $20.00

TABER, William P. *Eye of Faith: History of Ohio Yearly Meeting...* 1985. Barnesville, OH. VG/dj. V3. $16.00

TACHOLM, Vivi. *Students' Flora of Egypt.* 1956. Cairo. 1st. 81 pl/map/photos. 649p. VG/dj. B26. $55.00

TAFT, L.R. *Greenhouse Construction: A Complete Manual.* 1915 (1893). Orange Judd. 210p. cloth. A10. $35.00

TAFT, Robert. *Artists & Illustrators of the Old West, 1850-1900.* nd. Bonanza. rpt 1953 orig. 8vo. brn cloth. dj. F7. $45.00

TAFT, Robert. *Artists & Illustrators of the Old West, 1850-1900.* 1953. NY. 1st. VG/G+. B5. $30.00

TAGGART, Donald. *History of the 3rd Infantry Division in WWII.* 1947. WA, DC. 1st. photos/maps. 574p. VG. S16. $125.00

TAGNAEUS, Harry. *Blood-Brothers: An Ethno-Sociological Study...* 1952. NY. Philosophical Lib. 1st. folio. 171p. F/NF. B4. $85.00

TAIBO, Paco Ignacio II. *An Easy Thing.* 1990. Viking. 1st Am. F/F. M22. $20.00

TAILLANDIER, Yvon. *Rodin. By Yvon Taillandier.* nd. Milan. ils. VG/VG. M17. $15.00

TAILLEMITE, Etienne. *Bougainville et ses Compagnons Autour de Monde 1766-69...* 1977. Paris. Imp Nationale. 2 vol. 3 lg fld pocket maps. as new/linen case. O7. $350.00

TAINE, John. *Before the Dawn.* 1934. Williams. 1st. VG. M2. $30.00

TAINE, John. *Cosmic Geoids & One Other.* 1949. Fantasy. 1st. F/VG. M19. $45.00

TAINE, John. *Crystal Horde.* 1952. Fantasy. 1st. 1/300. sgn/#d. F/dj. P3. $175.00

TAINE, John. *Forbidden Garden.* 1947. Fantasy. ltd. sgn/#d/inscr. NF/VG. P3. $150.00

TAINE, John. *GOG 666.* 1954. Fantasy. ltd. 1/300. sgn/#d. F/VG. P3. $75.00

TAINE, John. *Gold Tooth.* 1927. Dutton. 1st. VG/fair. P3. $50.00

TAINE, John. *Iron Star.* 1951. Fpci. 1st. VG/dj. P3. $35.00

TAINE, John. *Seeds of Life.* 1951. Fantasy. ltd. sgn/#d/inscr. F/VG. P3. $100.00

TAINE, John. *Time Stream.* 1975. Garland. F. M2. $25.00

TAIT, P.G. *Lectures on Some Recent Advances in Physical Science...* 1876. London. Macmillan. 2nd. ils. 8vo. 363p. K3. $25.00

TAKHAJAN, Armen. *Die Evolution der Angiospermen.* 1959. Jena. sgn. ils. 344p. VG/dj. B26. $45.00

TAL, Uriel. *Christians & Jewis in the Second Reich (1870-1914): A Study.* 1969. Jerusalem. Magnes/Hebrew U/Yad Vashem. Hebrew text. 315p. VG/G+. S3. $26.00

TALBERT, Bill. *Tennis Observed.* 1967. Barre. 1st. ils. VG/dj. P8. $35.00

TALBOT, Frederick A. *Lightships & Lighthouses.* 1913. Lippincott. ils. 325p. T7. $50.00

TALBOT, Godfrey. *Queen Elizabeth: Queen Mother...* 1973. London. Jarrold. F/F. T12. $30.00

TALBOT, J.S. *Foxes at Home & Reminiscences.* 1906. London. Horace Cox. 1st. VG. O3. $35.00

TALBOT, Michael. *Bog.* 1986. Morrow. 1st. NF/dj. M2. $15.00

TALBOT-PONSONBY, J.A. *Art of Show Jumping.* 1955. London. Naldrett. 1st. VG/fair. O3. $15.00

TALBOYS, W.P. *West India Pickles.* 1876. NY. GW Carlton. 16mo. ils. 209p. new ep. T7. $90.00

TALESE, Gay. *Kingdom & the Power.* 1969. World. 1st. 555p. as new/dj. H1. $25.00

TALIAFERRO. *Cartographic Sources in Rosenberg Library.* 1988. TX A&M. 10 maps. 247p. F/F. A4. $45.00

TALLAL, Paula. *Temporal Processing in Nervous System...* 1993. NY Academy Sciences. 1st. ils. F/wrp. G1. $50.00

TALLANT, Robert. *Mrs Candy & Saturday.* 1947. Doubleady. 1st. sgn. 269p. VG/clip. M20. $20.00

TALLENT, Elizabeth. *In Constant Flight.* 1983. Knopf. 1st. author's 1st book. F/F. T11. $30.00

TALLENT, Elizabeth. *Married Men & Magic Tricks: John Updike's Erotic Heroes.* 1982. Creative Arts. 1st. author's 1st collection of stories. F/NF. L3. $150.00

TALLEYRAND-PERIGORD. *Rapport...Relatif a l'Arrete du Departement de Paris...* 1791. Paris. Imprimerie Nationale. 8vo. stitched. R12. $125.00

TALLIS, David. *Music Boxes.* 1971. 1st. NF/NF. S13. $30.00

TAMBO, Oliver. *Oliver Tambo Speaks.* 1988. Braziller. 1st. F/F. A20. $30.00

TAN, Amy. *Chinese Siamese Cat.* 1994. Macmillan. 1st. sgn. ils Gretchen Schields. F/case. B3. $150.00

TAN, Amy. *Joy Luck Club.* 1989. NY. Putnam. 1st. author's 1st book. F/F. L3. $250.00

TAN, Amy. *Joy Luck Club.* 1989. Putnam. 1st. author's 1st book. NF/dj. H11. $160.00

TAN, Amy. *Joy Luck Club.* 1989. Putnam. 1st. F/NF. B2. $200.00

TAN, Amy. *Kitchen God's Wife.* 1991. Putnam. 1st. inscr. author's 2nd adult book of fiction. F/F. T11. $55.00

TAN, Amy. *Moon Lady.* 1992. Macmillan. 1st. ils Gretchen Schields. F/F. B3. $75.00

TANITCH, Robert. *Peggy Ashcroft.* 1987. Hutchinson. ARC. NF/dj. C9. $45.00

TANNAHILL, Reay. *Flesh & Blood.* 1975. Hamish Hamilton. 1st. VG/dj. P3. $20.00

TANNENBAUM, Robert K. *Depraved Indifference.* 1989. NAL. 1st. VG/dj. P3. $20.00

TANNENBAUM, Robert K. *No Lesser Plea.* 1987. NY. Watts. 1st. author's 1st book. F/NF. H11. $30.00

TANNENBAUM & TANNENBAUM. *Elizabethan Bibliographies.* 1967. Kennikat. 10 vol. 8vo. wrp. A17. $60.00

TANNER, John. *Practical Midwifery & Obstetrics, Including Anaesthetics.* 1871. Phil. 1st Am. 237p. A13. $150.00

TANNER, Ralph E.S. *Transition in African Beliefs.* 1967. Maryknoll. 1st. 8vo. 256p. VG/dj. W1. $18.00

TANNER, William. *Book of Bond.* 1965. Jonathan Cape. 1st. VG/dj. P3. $35.00

TANNER, William. *Industrial Robots.* 1979. Dearborn. 2 vol. 1st. 4to. dj. A17. $45.00

TANTAQUIDGEON, Gladys. *Folk Medicine of Delaware & Related Algonquin Indians.* 1972. Harrisburg. inscr/2 sgn. 145p. salmon cloth. F/dj. B14. $125.00

TAPPAN, Eva. *Robin Hood: His Book.* 1905 (1903). ils Charlotte Harding. VG+. S13. $20.00

TAPPLY, William G. *Dead Meat.* 1987. Scribner. 1st. inscr. F/F. M15. $65.00

TAPPLY, William G. *Death at Charity's Point.* 1984. Scribner. 1st. F/NF. M15. $200.00

TAPPLY, William G. *Follow the Sharks.* 1985. Scribner. 1st. F/F. P3. $18.00

TARAKANOFF, Vassili P. *Statement of My Captivity Among the Californians.* 1953. LA. Glen Dawson. 1/200. 47p. decor cloth. D11. $75.00

TARBELL, Harlan. *Tarbell Course in Magic. Vol 4.* 1945. NY. Louis Tannen. inscr/drawing. 8vo. 418p. gilt brd. B11. $65.00

TARBELL, Ida M. *History of the Standard Oil Company.* 1904. McClure Phillips. 1st. 2 vol. photos/ils/diagrams. VG. Q1. $250.00

TARDIF, Adolphe. *Histoire des Sources du Droit Francais, Origines Romaines.* 1890. Paris. Alphonse Picard. tan cloth. xl Cambridge U. M11. $75.00

TARG, William. *Bibliophile in the Nursery.* 1957. ils. 503p. NF/VG. A4. $125.00

TARG, William. *Bibliophile in the Nursery.* 1969 (1957). Scarecrow Rpts. 8vo. photos. xl. NF. C8. $25.00

TARG, William. *Indecent Pleasures: Life & Colorful Times of Wm Targ.* 1975. Macmillan. 1st. ils. 428p. NF/dj. K3. $25.00

TARKINGTON, Booth. *Claire Ambler.* 1928. Doubleday. 1st. F/VG. H11. $30.00

TARKINGTON, Booth. *Penrod Jashber.* 1929. Doubleday Doran. 1st. 321p. cloth. VG/dj. M20. $35.00

TARKINGTON, Booth. *Two Vanrevels.* 1902. McClure Phillips. 1st. VG. A20. $20.00

TARKOVSKY, Andrey. *Scultping in Time, Reflections on the Cinema.* 1987. Knopf. ARC/1st am. photos. w/promo material. C9. $50.00

TARR, Judith. *Dagger & the Cross.* 1991. Doubleday. 1st. F/dj. P3. $22.00

TARTT, Donna. *Secret History.* 1992. Knopf. 1st. author's 1st book. F/dj. A15. $40.00

TATE, James. *Shepherds of the Mist.* 1969. Blk Sparrow. 1/300. sgn/#d. F/sewn wrp. B2. $45.00

TATE, Peter. *Faces in the Flames.* 1976. Doubleday. 1st. VG/dj. P3. $13.00

TATE, Peter. *Greencomber.* 1979. Doubleday. 1st. F/dj. P3. $13.00

TATHAM, Julie. *Vicki Barr: Clue of the Broken Blossom (#5).* 1950. Grosset Dunlap. 1st. VG/dj (lists to this title). M20. $20.00

TATTERSFIELD, Nigel. *Forgotten Trade: Comprising the Log of the Daniel & Henry...* 1991. London. Cape. 1st. 8vo. 460p. map ep. M/dj. P4. $30.00

TAUBE, Karl. *Aztec & Maya Myths.* 1993. Austin, TX. 1st. sm 4to. wrp. F3. $10.00

TAUNAY, Alfredo d'Escragnolle. *La Retraite de Laguna...Imprime par Order de Son Excellence.* 1871. Rio de Janeiro. Typographie Nationale. 1st complete. 224p. recent calf. R15. $2,500.00

TAUSSIG, Charles. *Some Notes on Sugar & Molasses, Story of American Industry.* 1940. Am Molasses Co. 1st. ils. full leather. VG/case. E6. $30.00

TAVENOR-PERRY, J. *Dinanderie: A History & Description of Mediaevel Art...* 1910. NY/London. Macmillan/Allen. 1st. 8vo. ils. NF. Q1. $200.00

TAVERNIER, Jean Baptiste. *Nouvelle Relation de l'Interieur du Serrail...* 1680. Paris. Clouzier. 8vo. calf. R12. $375.00

TAWES, Leonard S. *Coasting Captain.* 1967. Newport News. Mariners Mus. ils. 461p. dj. T7. $60.00

TAYLOR, Airutheus Ambush. *Negro in South Carolina During Reconstruction.* 1924. WA. Assn for Study of Negro Hist. xl. VG. B2. $50.00

TAYLOR, Albert. *Complete Garden.* 1929 (1921). 8vo. 50 pl. VG. E6. $20.00

TAYLOR, Allan. *What Everybody Wants To Know About Wine.* 1934. Knopf. 1st. G. B10. $15.00

TAYLOR, Bayard. *Eldorado; or, Adventures in Path of Empire...* 1850. NY/London. Putnam. 1st/Am issue. 2 vol. 12mo. mc pl. R3. $2,000.00

TAYLOR, Bayard. *Journey to Central Africa...* 1859. NY. Putnam. 10th. sm 8vo. 522p. VG. W1. $35.00

TAYLOR, Baynard. *Story of Kennett.* 1903 (1866). Putnam. 12mo. 469p. gilt bl cloth/photo. G. H1. $20.00

TAYLOR, Bernard. *Reaping.* 1980. Souvenir. 1st. NF/dj. P3. $20.00

TAYLOR, Casey. *Game Plan.* 1975. Atheneum. 1st. F/F. P8. $10.00

TAYLOR, Deems. *Walt Disney's Fantasia.* 1940. S&S. 1st. lg folio. fwd Leopold Stokowski. 15 pl. F/NF. B4. $1,000.00

TAYLOR, Donald S. *Texfake.* 1991. Austin. W Thomas Taylor. 1st. ils. 159p. M. K3. $55.00

TAYLOR, Donald S. *Thomas Chatterton's Art.* 1978. Princeton. 1st. F/dj. K3. $20.00

TAYLOR, E.G. *Regiment for the Sea & Other Writings on Navigation...* 1963. Cambridge. ils. 464p. NF/dj. M4. $20.00

TAYLOR, E.G.R. *Tudor Geography 1485-1583.* 1968. NY. Octagon. ils. F. O7. $65.00

TAYLOR, Ellis. *Salty Lullabies & Sea Chanties.* 1951. Villanova, PA. inscr. 13 drawings/27 chanties/music. 52p. T7. $50.00

TAYLOR, F. Sherwood. *Alchemists.* 1949. NY. Henry Schuman. 1st Am. 246p. VG/dj. K3. $15.00

TAYLOR, Fenton W. *25th Stake of Zion, 1883-1983.* 1983. private prt. 1st. ils. 429p. F/sans. B19. $75.00

TAYLOR, Frederick W. *Principles of Scientific Management.* 1911. Harper. 1st trade/revised. gilt maroon cloth. VG. M24. $400.00

TAYLOR, Geoff. *Court of Honor.* 1966. S&S. 1st. VG/dj. P3. $20.00

TAYLOR, George F. *Aeronautical Meteorology.* 1938. NY. Pitman. sgn. 429p. gilt bl cloth. VG. B11. $75.00

TAYLOR, Georgia Elizabeth. *Death of Jason Darby.* 1970. World. 1st. F/dj. M2. $12.00

TAYLOR, Gordon Rattray. *Natural History of the Mind.* 1979. Dutton. 1st Am. 370p. cloth. VG/dj. G1. $22.50

TAYLOR, Greyton H. *Treasury of Wine & Wine Cookery.* 1963. Harper. 278p. VG/VG. B10. $25.00

TAYLOR, Ida Scott. *Little Quaker Meeting.* nd. London. Raphael Tuck. ils Frances Brundage. V3. $75.00

TAYLOR, James. *Third Reich Almanac.* 1987. NY. photos/maps. 392p. VG/VG. S16. $25.00

TAYLOR, John Russell. *Hitch.* 1978. Pantheon. 1st. VG/dj. P3. $20.00

TAYLOR, John W.R. *Combat Aircraft of the World.* 1969. Putnam. VG/dj. P3. $20.00

TAYLOR, John W.R. *Rockets & Missiles.* 1970. NY. Grosset Dunlap. 8vo. 159p. xl. dj. K5. $8.00

TAYLOR, Judy. *Beatrix Potter: Artist, Storyteller & Country Woman.* 1987 (1986). London. Warne. rpt. sm 4to. 224p. brn brd. VG/dj. T5. $55.00

TAYLOR, Katherine Ames. *Lights & Shadows of Yosemite.* 1926. SF. Croker. 40 photos. 87p. quarter tan cloth. M. K7. $75.00

TAYLOR, Nigel P. *Genus Echinocereus.* 1985. Timber. inscr. 8vo. cloth. VG/dj. A22. $35.00

TAYLOR, Norman. *Vegetation of the Allegany State Part.* 1928. Albany. 12mo. VG/wrp. A22. $15.00

TAYLOR, Norman. *Wild Flower Gardening.* 1955. Princeton. 32p mc pl. 128p. VG/dj. B26. $20.00

TAYLOR, P. Walker. *Murder in the Game Reserve.* 1947. Thornton Butterworth. 1st. VG. P3. $35.00

TAYLOR, Peter. *Old Forest & Other Stories.* 1985. Dial. 1st. F/clip. D10. $45.00

TAYLOR, Peter. *Summons to Memphis.* 1986. Knopf. 1st. F/F. D10. $60.00

TAYLOR, Phoebe Atwood. *Going, Going, Gone.* 1943. Norton. 1st. VG. P3. $35.00

TAYLOR, Phoebe Atwood. *Mystery of the Cape Cod Tavern.* nd. Norton. G. P3. $15.00

TAYLOR, Phoebe Atwood. *Octagon House.* 1937. NY. Norton. ne. F. T12. $60.00

TAYLOR, Phoebe Atwood. *Spring Harrowing.* 1939. Norton. 1st. F/NF. M15. $200.00

TAYLOR, R.L. *Vessel of Wrath: Life & Times of Carry Nation.* 1966. NY. 1st. ils. 373p. F/dj. M4. $20.00

TAYLOR, Raymond Griswold. *Recollection of 60 Years of Medicine in Southern California.* 1953. LA. self pub. typescript, 4 vol in 2. photos. gilt fabricoid. D11. $750.00

TAYLOR, Robert Louis. *Adrift in a Boneyard.* 1947. Doubleday. 1st. NF/dj. M2. $35.00

TAYLOR, Robert N. *Lewis Carroll at Texas.* 1985. Austin. HRC. 1st. ils CL Dodgson. F/wrp. M24. $30.00

TAYLOR, Sam S. *Sleep No More.* 1949. Dutton. 1st. VG/remnant. M25. $50.00

TAYLOR, Samuel W. *Grinning Grismo.* 1951. AA Wyn. 1st. VG/dj. P3. $35.00

TAYLOR, Silas. *History of Gavel-Kind, With Etymology Thereof...* 1663. London. Prt John Starkey. modern cloth. M11. $650.00

TAYLOR, Sydney. *More All-of-a-Kind Family.* 1957 (1954). Follett. 2nd. sm 4to. 160p. gray brd. VG/G. T5. $20.00

TAYLOR, T. *Magnificent Mitscher.* 1954. NY. 1st. VG. B5. $35.00

TAYLOR, T.M.C. *Pea Family (Leguinosae) of British Columbia.* 1974. Victoria. ils/maps. 237p. sc. B26. $12.50

TAYLOR, Vincent. *Gospel According to Mark.* 1957. Macmillan. 696p. G. B29. $30.00

TAYLOR, W. Thomas. *Texfake, an Account of Theft & Forgery of Early Texas...* 1991. TX State Hist Assn. 1st. 158p. M. J2. $50.00

TAYLOR, William. *California Life Illustrated.* 1867. London/NY. Jackson Walford Hodder/Carlton Porter. 1st. 391p. VG. K7. $175.00

TAYLOR, William. *Our South American Cousins.* 1878. NY. Nelson Phillips. 1st. 12mo. 318p. F3. $30.00

TAYLOR & TAYLOR. *Neon Dancers.* 1991. Walker. 1st. F/F. M22. $15.00

TAYLOR & TILLOTSON. *Grand Canyon Country.* 1929. Stanford. 1st. 8vo. orange cloth. VG+. F7. $35.00

TAYLOR & VALUM. *Wildflowers 2: Sagebrush Country.* 1974. Beaverton. 189 mc photos. 139p. sc. VG. B26. $15.00

TAYLOR & WELTY. *Black Bonanza.* 1950. Whittlesey/McGraw Hill. 280p. VG. D8. $35.00

TAYLOR & WINDLE. *Early Architecture of Madison, IN.* 1986. IN Hist Soc. photos. 230p. F/dj. M4. $35.00

TCHITCHINOFF, Zakahar. *Adventures in California of..., 1818-1821.* 1956. LA. Glen Dawson. 1/225. ils. 26p. decor brd/cloth spine. D11. $50.00

TCHOLAKIAN, Arthur. *Majesty of the Black Woman.* 1971. Van Nostrand Reinhold. 1st. ils. 160p. VG/partial. A25. $45.00

TEAGLE, Mike. *Murders in Silk.* 1938. Hillman Curl. 1st. VG. P3. $25.00

TEAGUE, Bob. *Flip Side of Soul: Letters to My Son.* 1989. Morrow. 1st. F/F. B4. $45.00

TEALE, E.W. *Audubon's Wildlife.* 1964. Viking. 1st. F/VG clip. B3. $40.00

TEALE, E.W. *Autumn Across America.* 1956. NY. photos/map. F/dj. M4. $15.00

TEALE, E.W. *Dune Boy: Early Years of a Naturalist.* 1957. IU. 275p. F. M4. $22.00

TEALE, E.W. *Grassroot Jungles.* 1950. photos. VG/VG. M17. $20.00

TEASDALE-BUCKELL, G.T. *Experts on Guns & Shooting.* 1900. London. Sampson Low. 1st. 4to. ils. 590p. VG. H7. $225.00

TEBBEL, J. *Turning the World Upside Down: Inside American Revolution.* 1993. NY. 1st. maps. 448p. F/F. M4. $25.00

TEGNER, Esaias. *Frithiof's Saga.* 1953. Stockholm. LEC. 1st thus. 1/1500. ils/sgn Eric Palmquist. F/case. Q1. $75.00

TEGNER, Henry. *White Foxes of Gorfenletch.* 1954. Morrow. 1st Am. VG/VG. O3. $35.00

TEILHET & TEILHET. *Skwee-Gee.* 1940. Doubleday Doran. 1st. Ils Hardie Gramatky. 4to. pict cloth. dj. R5. $175.00

TEISER, Ruth. *Sudden Empire: California.* 1950. SF. Soc CA Pioneers. 76p. decor gr cloth. as new. K7. $35.00

TEIZERIA DA MOTA, Avelino. *Regimento da Altura de Leste-Oeste de Rui Faleiro.* 1953. Lisboa. Agencia GEral do ultramar. inscr pres. F/wrp. O7. $20.00

TEIZERIA DA MOTA, Avelino. *Viagem de Fernao de Magalhaes e a Questao das Molucas.* 1975. Lisboa. Junta Investigacoes Cientificas Ultramar. 33 maps. F/dj. O7. $175.00

TELANDER, Rick. *Joe Namath & the Other Guys.* 1976. HRW. 1st. F/VG. P8. $30.00

TELFAIR, Raymond Clark II. *Cattle Egret: A Texas Focus & World View.* 1983. College Station. maps/figures. 144p. NF/VG. S15. $10.00

TELLA, Alfred. *Sundered Soul.* 1990. Three Continents. 1st. sgn. F. M2. $27.00

TELLEN, Maurice. *Draft Horse Primer.* 1977. Rodale. 386p. VG. A10. $20.00

TELLER, Edward. *Better a Shield Than Sword.* 1987. NY. Free Pr. 3rd. F/dj. K3. $15.00

TELLER, Edward. *Edward Teller: Giant of the Golden Age of Physics.* 1990. Scribner. 1st. F/dj. K3. $15.00

TELLER, Edward. *Teller's War.* 1992. S&S. F/wrp. K3. $15.00

TELLER, Judd L. *Scapegoat of Revolution.* 1954. Scribner. 352p. VG/G. S3. $25.00

TELLER, Walter. *Five Sea Captains.* 1960. NY. Atheneum. 431p. dj. T7. $30.00

TEMPLE, Shirley. *Shirley Temple's Favorite Tales of Long Ago.* 1958. Random. 1st prt. 4to. unp. C14. $17.00

TEMPLE, William. *Martin Magnus on Mars.* 1956. Muller. 1st. VG/dj. P3. $35.00

TEMPLE, William. *Memoirs of What Past in Christendom, From War Begun 1672...* 1692. London. Chriswell. 8vo. wrp. R12. $125.00

TEMPLE, William. *Works of...* 1757. London. 4 vol. VG. A15. $125.00

TENN & WESTLAKE. *Once Against the Law.* 1968. Macmillan. 1st. VG/dj. P3. $25.00

TENNANT, Joseph F. *Rough Times 1870-1920.* nd. np. Souvenir 50th Anniversary Red River Expedition. 271p. P4. $45.00

TENNEY, Merrill. *Galations: Charter of Christian Liberty.* 1950. Eerdmans. 200p. G/torn. B29. $8.50

TENNYSON, Alfred Lord. *Holy Grail.* 1870. London. Strahan. 1st. 12mo. gr brd. fair. M23. $50.00

TENNYSON, Alfred Lord. *Idylls of the King.* 1952. LEC. 1st thus. 1/1500. ils/sgn Lynd Ward. F/glassine/case. Q1. $150.00

TENNYSON, Alfred Lord. *Maud.* 1869. London. Strahan. 12mo. gr brd. G. M23. $30.00

TENNYSON, Alfred Lord. *Princess & Other Poems.* 1890. Stokes. ils CH Johnson. 400p. teg. maroon cloth. T10. $50.00

TENNYSON, Alfred Lord. *Queen May, a Drama.* 1875. Osgood. 1st. VG. M19. $45.00

TEONGE, Henry. *Diary of Teonge.* 1825. London. Chas Knight. ils. 327p. marbled brd. rebacked blk morocco. T7. $150.00

TEPPER, Sheri S. *Gate to Women's Country.* 1988. Doubleday. 1st. F/clip & dtd 1990. A24. $20.00

TEPPER, Sheri S. *Shadow's End.* 1994. Bantam. 1st. F/dj. P3. $23.00

TERENCE. *Afri Comoediae.* 1772. Birmingham, Eng. Baskerville. Latin text. 4to. aeg. A15. $100.00

TERHUNE, Albert Payson. *Across the Line.* 1945. Dryden. 116p. VG/dj. M20. $15.00

TERHUNE, Albert Payson. *Buff, a Collie & Other Dog Stories.* (1921). Grosset Dunlap. pre-1963 rpt. 12mo. F/VG+. C8. $27.50

TERHUNE, Albert Payson. *Further Adventures of Lad.* (1922). Grosset Dunlap. pre-1943 prt. sm 8vo. NF/VG. C8. $22.50

TERHUNE, Albert Payson. *Lad of Sunnybank.* (1929). Grosset Dunlap. pre-1943 prt. lg 12mo. NF/NF. C8. $25.00

TERHUNE, Albert Payson. *My Friend the Dog.* (1926). Grosset Dunlap. pre-1963 prt. lg 12mo. F/NF. C8. $27.50

TERHUNE, Albert Payson. *Story of Damon & Pythias.* 1915. Grosset Dunlap. VG/dj. P3. $35.00

TERKEL, Studs. *Giants of Jazz.* 1957. NY. 1st. sgn. ils Robert Galster. NF/VG+. A11. $135.00

TERRACE, Vincent. *Complete Encyclopedia of TV 1947-76 Vol 2.* 1976. Barnes. VG/dj. P3. $20.00

TERRELL, John Upton. *War for the Colorado River.* 1965. Arthur H Clark. 1st. 2 vol. NF/NF. B19. $60.00

TERTZ, Abram. *Fantastic Stories.* 1963. Pantheon. 1st. VG/worn. M2. $12.00

TERWILLIGER, Charles. *Horolovar 400-Day Clock Repair Guide.* 1974. Bronxville. Horolovar. 7th. 4to. 183p. VG/dj. K3. $25.00

TESNOHLIDER, Rudolf. *Cunning Little Vixen.* 1985. FSG. 1st thus. 4to. 186p. F/F. T5. $40.00

TEVIS, Walter. *Hustler.* 1959. Harper. 1st. NF/VG. B4. $750.00

TEVIS, Walter. *Queen's Gambit.* 1983. Random. 1st. F/F. H11. $35.00

TEVIS, Walter. *Steps of the Sun.* 1983. Doubleday. 1st. VG/VG. M22. $15.00

THACKERAY, William Makepeace. *Adventures of Philip.* 1862. NY. Harper. 1st Am. gilt blk cloth. M24. $165.00

THACKERAY, William Makepeace. *Newcomes: Memoirs of a Most Respectable Family...* 1954. Cambridge. LEC. 1st thus. 2 vol. 1/1500. ils/sgn Edward Ardizzone. F/case. Q1. $125.00

THAMES, Susan. *As Much As I Know.* 1992. Random. 1st. author's 1st book. F/F. R13. $25.00

THATCHER, Margaret. *Downing Street Years.* 1993. NY. 1/350. sgn. F/box. B5. $105.00

THAYER, Bert Clark. *Thoroughbred.* 1964. DSP. 1st. VG/VG. O3. $25.00

THAYER, Helen. *Polar Dream: Heroic Saga of First Sola Journey...* 1993. NY. S&S. 1st. 8vo. 254p. half cloth. F/dj. P4. $40.00

THAYER, James Stewart. *Pursuit.* 1986. Crown. 1st. VG/dj. P3. $15.00

THAYER, June. *Pussy Who Went to the Moon.* (1960). NY. Morrow. 1st probable. sm 4to. F/VG. C8. $20.00

THAYER, Lee. *Hair's Breadth.* 1946. Dodd Mead. 1st. VG/dj. P3. $25.00

THAYER, Steve. *St Mudd.* 1992. Viking. 1st. author's 1st book. F/NF. B3. $60.00

THAYER, Theodore. *Pennsylvania Politics & Growth of Democracy 1740-1776.* 1953. Harrisburg. PA Hist & Mus Comm. tall 8vo. 234p. dk bl cloth. F. H1. $25.00

THAYER, Tiffany. *Illustrous Corpse.* 1930. Fiction League. 1st. VG. N4. $22.50

THEINER, George. *Let's Go to the Circus.* 1963. London. Bancroft. ils Rudolf Lukes/5 movable pl. unp. T10. $150.00

THELWELL, Norman. *Leg at Each Corner.* 1963. Dutton. 1st Am. VG/VG. O3. $22.00

THEODOR, O. *Fauna Palaestina. Insecta I: Diptera Pupipara.* 1975. Jerusalem. 168p. NF. B1. $40.00

THEROUX, Alexander. *Master Snickup's Cloak.* 1979. Harper Row. 1st Am. 4to. unp. F/F. T5. $30.00

THEROUX, Paul. *Black House.* 1974. Houghton Mifflin. 1st. sgn. F/NF. D10. $75.00

THEROUX, Paul. *Chicago Loop.* 1990. Random. 1st. F/F. H11. $30.00

THEROUX, Paul. *Consul's File.* 1977. Houghton Mifflin. 1st. NF/dj. M25. $25.00

THEROUX, Paul. *Great Railway Bazaar.* 1975. Hamish Hamilton. 1st. VG/dj. M25. $125.00

THEROUX, Paul. *Jungle Lovers.* 1971. Houghton Mifflin. true 1st (1/4500). F/dj. A24. $125.00

THEROUX, Paul. *Kingdom by the Sea.* 1983. Houghton Mifflin. 1st. sgn. NF. M25. $25.00

THEROUX, Paul. *London Snow.* 1980. Houghton Mifflin. 1st. F/NF. T11. $70.00

THEROUX, Paul. *Mosquito Coast.* 1981. Hamish Hamilton. 1st. NF/VG clip. B3. $35.00

THEROUX, Paul. *Mosquito Coast.* 1981. London. Hamish Hamilton. true 1st. inscr. NF/clip. D10. $85.00

THEROUX, Paul. *Mosquito Coast.* 1982. Houghton Mifflin. 1st. F/NF. T11. $25.00

THEROUX, Paul. *Mosquito Coast.* 1982. Houghton Mifflin. 1st. sgn. NF/dj. D10. $65.00

THEROUX, Paul. *Murder in Mount Holly.* 1969. London. Alan Ross. 1st. sgn. F/NF. B4. $2,500.00

THEROUX, Paul. *O-Zone.* 1986. Putnam. 1st. F/dj. A20/P3. $20.00

THEROUX, Paul. *Old Patagonian Express.* 1979. Houghton Mifflin. 1st. F/NF. B3/T11. $50.00

THEROUX, Paul. *Picture Palace.* 1978. Houghton Mifflin. 1st. VG/dj. P3. $20.00

THEROUX, Paul. *Saint Jack.* 1973. Houghton Mifflin. 1st. NF/dj. M25. $45.00

THEROUX, Paul. *Waldo.* 1967. Houghton Mifflin. true 1st. author's 1st book. NF/VG. A24. $185.00

THEROUX, Paul. *World's End & Other Stories.* 1980. Houghton Mifflin. 1st. F/F. T11. $25.00

THESIGER, Wilfred. *Arabian Sands.* 1959. NY. Dutton. 1st. 8vo. ils/fld map. 326p. VG. W1. $28.00

THESIGER, Wilfred. *Marsh Arab.* 1964. NY. 1st. VG/VG. B5. $50.00

THIEL, A.W. *Chinese Pottery & Stoneware.* ca 1953. NY. 1st. NF/attached plastic-covered dj. W3. $75.00

THIEL, Rudolf. *And There Was Light.* 1957. Knopf. 1st Am. VG/poor. M2. $12.00

THIELICKE, Helmut. *Ethics of Sex.* 1964. Harper. 1st. 338p. VG/dj. B29. $8.50

THIELICKE, Helmut. *Silence of God.* 1962. Eerdmans. 92p. G/dj. B29. $7.50

THIERRY, Georges Paul. *Travers und Siecle de Notre Yachting de Course a Voile.* 1948. Paris. Soc d'Editions Geographique. 302 photos. 390p. wrp. T7. $60.00

THIESSEN, Grant. *Science Fiction Collector Vol 1.* 1980. Pandora. 1/140. sgn/#d. F/sans. P3. $45.00

THOBY-MARCELIN, Philippe. *Beast of the Haitian Hills.* 1946. Rinehart. 1st. VG. P3. $20.00

THOMAS, Alfred Barnaby. *Forgotten Frontiers: Study of Spanish Indian Policy...* 1969. Norman, OK. 2nd. 3 fld maps. 420p. cloth. dj. D11. $35.00

THOMAS, Alfred Barnaby. *Teodoro de Croix & Northern Frontier of New Spain 1776...* 1968. OK U. ils/map. 273p. F/dj. M4. $20.00

THOMAS, Antoine Leonard. *Eloge de Maximilien de Bethune, Duc De Sully.* 1763. Paris. Regnard. 8vo. wrp. R12. $125.00

THOMAS, B.P. *Life & Times of Lincoln's Secretary of War.* 1962. np. ils. 642p. O8. $21.50

THOMAS, Craig. *Firefox Down.* 1983. Michael Joseph. 1st. VG/dj. P3. $30.00

THOMAS, Craig. *Jade Tiger.* 1982. Van Nostrand. F/dj. P3. $20.00

THOMAS, Craig. *Sea Leopard.* 1981. Michael Joseph. 1st. F/dj. P3. $25.00

THOMAS, Craig. *Wildcat.* 1989. Putnam. 1st. F/F. W2. $30.00

THOMAS, Craig. *Winter Hawk.* 1987. Collins. 1st. F/dj. P3. $20.00

THOMAS, D. *Nazi Victory, Crete 1941.* 1973. NY. BC. ils. 252p. VG/VG. S16. $16.50

THOMAS, D. Gourlay. *Gladiolus: For Garden & Exhibition.* 1955. London. ils/photos. 94p. VG. B26. $14.00

THOMAS, D.M. *White Hotel.* 1981. Viking. ARC. author's 3rd novel. F/F. T11. $40.00

THOMAS, Dawn C. *Downtown Is.* 1972. McGraw Hill. later prt. NF/dj. M25. $15.00

THOMAS, Dwight. *Poe Log.* 1987. 919p. O8. $27.50

THOMAS, Dylan. *Quite Early One Morning.* 1954. New Directions. 1st. F/NF. B2. $50.00

THOMAS, Dylan. *18 Poems.* 1934. London. Fortune Pr. 1st. author's 1st book. VG/VG. B5. $30,000.00

THOMAS, Eleanor. *Becky & Tatters, a Brownie Scout Story.* 1940. Scribner. ils Gertrude Howe. $35.00

THOMAS, Emory M. *Confederate Nation 1861-1865.* 1979. Harper Row. 1st. 384p. as new/dj. H1. $20.00

THOMAS, Eugene. *Dancing Dead.* 1933. Sears. 1st. G. M2. $10.00

THOMAS, Frank J. *Myths of California Isle.* 1966. LA. Tenfingers. 1/200. 71x56mm. 2 full-p ils. linen-backed brd. F. B24. $150.00

THOMAS, Gary M. *Custer, Scout of April 1867.* 1967. Westport. 1st. 25p. M. J2. $25.00

THOMAS, Herbert. *Classical Contributions to Obstetrics & Gynecology.* 1935. ils. VG. M17. $25.00

THOMAS, Isaiah. *History of Printing in America.* 1810. Worcester. Isaiah Thomas. 1st. 2 vol. 8vo. contemporary bdg. M1. $1,750.00

THOMAS, Isaiah. *Thomas' Almanack for the Year 1784.* 1783. Boston. self pub. A19. $150.00

THOMAS, J. *Blue Ridge Country.* 1942. NY. 1st. 338p. F/dj. M4. $25.00

THOMAS, J.J. *Illustrated Annual Register of Rural Affairs. Vol II.* 1860. Albany. Tucker. 1st. cloth. VG. A10. $50.00

THOMAS, Kathleen. *Gleanie Bird.* 1956. Frederick Warne. 1st. 117p. VG/dj. M20. $25.00

THOMAS, L. *Lives of a Cell.* 1974. Viking. 5th. 153p. clip dj. B1. $15.00

THOMAS, Leslie. *Man With the Power.* 1973. Eyre Methuen. VG/dj. P3. $15.00

THOMAS, Leslie. *Virgin Soldiers.* 1966. Little Brn. 1st. VG/dj. P3. $20.00

THOMAS, Louis. *Good Children Don't Kill.* 1968. Dodd Mead. 1st. F/dj. P3. $15.00

THOMAS, Lowell. *Out of This World.* 1950. Garden City. A19. $15.00

THOMAS, Lowell. *Out of This World.* 1950. Greystone. inscr. 320p. VG. B11. $25.00

THOMAS, Lowell. *Pageant of Life.* 1941. NY. Funk. 1st. sgn. 278p. VG. B11. $32.50

THOMAS, Michael. *Ropespinner Conspiracy.* 1947. Warner. 1st. F/F. T12. $25.00

THOMAS, Oswald. *Heaven & Earth.* 1930. Norton. 8vo. 231p. VG/dj. K5. $30.00

THOMAS, Patricia. *Stand Back, Said the Elephant, I'm Going to Sneeze!* 1971. Lee Shepard. 1st. ils Wallace Tripp. VG/VG-. P2. $25.00

THOMAS, Piri. *Down These Mean Streets.* 1967. Knopf. 1st. F/NF. M23. $100.00

THOMAS, Piri. *Down These Mean Streets.* 1967. Knopf. 1st. inscr. NF/NF. T11. $125.00

THOMAS, Ross. *Briarpatch.* 1984. S&S. 1st. F/dj. from $30 to $40.00

THOMAS, Ross. *Cast a Yellow Shadow.* 1967. Morrow. 1st. F/dj. M15. $175.00

THOMAS, Ross. *Eighth Dwarf.* 1979. London. Hamish Hamilton. 1st. sgn. F/dj. Q1. $75.00

THOMAS, Ross. *Eighth Dwarf.* 1979. S&S. 1st. F/NF. B2. $50.00

THOMAS, Ross. *Fourth Durango.* 1989. Mysterious. 1st. F/F. N4. $20.00

THOMAS, Ross. *Missionary Stew.* 1983. S&S. 1st. VG/dj. P3. $35.00

THOMAS, Ross. *Money Harvest.* 1975. Morrow. 1st. NF/dj. P3. $90.00

THOMAS, Ross. *Out on the Rim.* 1987. Mysterious. ARC. sgn. F/wrp. M25. $35.00

THOMAS, Ross. *Out on the Rim.* 1987. Mysterious. 1st. F/dj. from $25 to $30.00

THOMAS, Ross. *Porkchoppers.* 1972. Morrow. 1st. F/F. M15. $125.00

THOMAS, Ross. *Seercucker Whipsaw.* 1967. Morrow. 1st. VG/dj. M15. $300.00

THOMAS, Ross. *Yellow-Dog Contract.* 1977. Morrow. 1st. VG/dj. P3. $100.00

THOMAS, Tony. *Cinema of the Sea: Critical Survey & Filmology 1925-1986.* 1988. photos. VG. M17. $25.00

THOMAS & WIGGINS. *Flora of the Alaskan Arctic Slope.* 1962. Toronto. tall 8vo. 425p. VG/dj. A22. $70.00

THOMAS & WITTS. *Enola Gay.* 1977. 1st. photos. xl. dj. K3. $15.00

THOMAS & WITTS. *San Francisco Earthquake.* 1971. Stein Day. 316p. F/dj. D8. $15.00

THOMASON, John W. *Fix Bayonets!* 1926. 2nd. lg 8vo. VG. E6. $30.00

THOMASON, John W. *Jeb Stuart.* 1934. Scribner. early prt. 512p. VG/dj. M8. $35.00

THOMPSON, D'Arcy Wentworth. *On Growth & Form.* 1942. Cambridge. later prt. ils/diagrams. VG/dj. M17. $25.00

THOMPSON, Edward. *Roetgen Rays & Phenomena of the Anode & Cathode.* 1896. NY. 1st. 190p. recent blk cloth. A13. $500.00

THOMPSON, Edwin Porter. *History of the First Kentucky Brigade.* 1868. Caxton. 1st. sgn assn. 391p. cloth/expertly recased/rebacked. VG. M8. $350.00

THOMPSON, Ellery. *Draggerman's Haul.* 1950. Viking. map. 277p. dj. T7. $18.00

THOMPSON, Eloise R. *Wildflower Portraits.* 1964. Norman. 1st. 100 mc pl. VG+/dj. B26. $75.00

THOMPSON, Era Bell. *Africa, Land of My Fathers.* 1954. Doubleday. 1st. 281p. VG+/VG. A25. $22.00

THOMPSON, Gerald. *Edward F Beale & the American West.* 1983. Albuquerque. 1st. 8vo. VG+. F7. $35.00

THOMPSON, Hunter S. *Fear & Loathing in Las Vegas.* 1971. Random. 1st. ils Ralph Steadman. VG/VG. M17. $125.00

THOMPSON, Hunter S. *Fear & Loathing in Las Vegas.* 1971. Random. 1st. NF/NF. B2. $225.00

THOMPSON, Hunter S. *Fear & Loathing on the Campaign Trail '72.* 1973. Straight Arrow. 1st. 506p. VG/dj. from $35 to $50.00

THOMPSON, Hunter S. *Generation of Swine.* 1988. Summit. 1st. F/dj. A24. $25.00

THOMPSON, Hunter S. *Generation of Swine.* 1988. Summit. 1st. 304p. NF/dj. M20. $18.00

THOMPSON, Hunter S. *Songs of the Doomed.* 1990. Summit. 1st. F/F. B3. $25.00

THOMPSON, J. Eric. *Maya Archaeologist.* 1963. Norman, OK. 1st. 248p. dj. F3. $35.00

THOMPSON, J. Eric. *Mexico Before Cortez.* 1933. Scribner. 1st. 298p. F3. $45.00

THOMPSON, Jim. *Child of Rage.* 1991. Los Angeles. Blood & Guts. ltd. 1/500. sgn/#d. F/dj/case. M15. $150.00

THOMPSON, Jim. *Killer Inside Me.* 1989. Los Angeles. Blood & Guts. 1st hc. 1/350. sgn. F/dj. M15. $175.00

THOMPSON, Jim. *More Hardcore.* 1987. DIF. 1st. NF/dj. P3. $25.00

THOMPSON, Jim. *Now on Earth.* 1986. Dennis McMillan. ltd. 1/400. F/F. M15. $150.00

THOMPSON, Josiah. *Six Seconds in Dallas.* 1967. NY. 1st. VG/VG. B5. $75.00

THOMPSON, Joyce. *Conscience Place.* 1984. Doubleday. 1st. F/dj. M2. $15.00

THOMPSON, Kay. *Eloise in Moscow.* 1959. S&S. 1st. ils Hilary Knight. orange cloth. VG/VG. D1. $225.00

THOMPSON, Kay. *Eloise in Moscow.* 1959. S&S. 4to. VG/G+. M5. $175.00

THOMPSON, Leonard. *African Societies in Southern Africa.* 1969. NY/WA. Praeger. 1st. 8vo. 336p. NF/dj. W1. $20.00

THOMPSON, Maurice. *Alice of Old Vincennes.* nd. Grosset Dunlap. 1st. F/dj. M2. $15.00

THOMPSON, Neil Baird. *Crazy Horse Called Them Walk-a-Heaps...* 1979. North Star. 150p. VG/VG. J2. $55.00

THOMPSON, Peter. *Thompson's Narrative of the Little Big Horn Campaign 1876...* 1974. Clark. 1st. ils/maps. 339p. VG. J2. $225.00

THOMPSON, Phyllis. *Artichoke & Other Poems.* 1969. HI U. 1st. inscr. F/dj. V1. $25.00

THOMPSON, Ruth Plumley. *Speedy in Oz.* (1934). Reilly Lee. 1st. ils J Neill/12 mc pl. blk cloth. VG. D1. $425.00

THOMPSON, Ruth Plumly. *Captain Salt in Oz.* 1936. Reilly Lee. 1st/1st state. 1st Oz book issued w/o mc pl. 306p. VG. P2. $250.00

THOMPSON, Ruth Plumly. *Grandpa in Oz.* 1924. Reilly Lee. 1st. ils John Neill. VG+. P2. $325.00

THOMPSON, Ruth Plumly. *Hungry Tiger of Oz.* nd. Reilly Lee. decor brd. G. P3. $50.00

THOMPSON, Ruth Plumly. *Hungry Tiger of Oz.* 1926. Reilly Lee. 1st/1st issue. ils John R Neill. olive-drab cloth. R5. $585.00

THOMPSON, Silvanus P. *Elementary Lessons in Electricity & Magnetism.* 1888. Chicago. Thompson Thomas. 43rd thousand. 456p. cloth. VG. M20. $40.00

THOMPSON, Silvanus P. *Light Visibile & Invisible.* 1897. London. 1st. 294p. xl. bl cloth. VG. B14. $375.00

THOMPSON, William. *Reminiscences of a Pioneer.* 1912. SF. private prt. A19. $75.00

THOMPSON & THOMPSON. *Science Fiction & Fantasy Collectibles Price Guide.* 1989. 482p. F. M13. $30.00

THOMSON, Basil. *Case of the Dead Diplomat.* 1935. Crime Club. 1st. xl. VG/dj. P3. $20.00

THOMSON, Christine Campbell. *Not at Night Omnibus.* 1937. London. 1st. G. M2. $35.00

THOMSON, D. *Pair Trawling & Pair Seining...* 1978. Fishery News. ils/tables. 167p. pict brd. VG+. M12. $15.00

THOMSON, David. *Shining Mountains.* 1979. Knopf. A19. $25.00

THOMSON, David. *Showman: Life of David O Selznick.* 1992. NY. 1st. 793p. F/dj. A17. $15.00

THOMSON, H. Douglas. *Great Book of Thrillers.* 1937. Odhams. G. P3. $20.00

THOMSON, H. Douglas. *Mystery Book.* 1934. Odhams. VG. P3. $35.00

THOMSON, J.E. *Grenville Problem: Royal Society of Canada Special Pub 1.* 1956. Toronto. 119p. cloth. NF. D8. $24.00

THOMSON, June. *Question of Identity.* 1977. Crime Club. 1st. F/dj. P3. $25.00

THOMSON, Origen. *Crossing the Plains.* 1983. Ye Galleon. 1st thus. ils. M/sans. A18. $17.50

THOMSON, Richard. *Antique American Clocks & Watches.* 1968. NY. Galahad Books. ils/photos. 192p. brd. dj. D2. $30.00

THOMSON, Samuel. *New Guide to Health; or, Botanic Family Physician...* 1829. Clairsville, OH. Horton Howard. 12mo. 115p. contemporary calf. M1. $375.00

THOMSON, William. *Practical Treatise on Cultivation of Grape Vine.* 1865. London. Blackwood. 77p. cloth. VG. A10. $78.00

THON, Melanie Rae. *Girls in the Grass.* 1991. Random. 1st Am. author's 2nd short stories book. VG/VG. L1. $30.00

THON, Melanie Rae. *Girls in the Grass.* 1991. Random. 1st Am. sgn. author's 2nd book. F/F. D10. $75.00

THON, Melanie Rae. *Girls in the Grass.* 1991. Random. 1st. F/dj. A24. $50.00

THON, Melanie Rae. *Iona Moon.* 1993. Poseidon. 1st. sgn. author's 3rd book. F/F. D10. $45.00

THON, Melanie Rae. *Meteors in August.* 1990. Random. 1st. author's 1st book. F/dj. A24. $60.00

THON, Melanie Rae. *Meteors in August.* 1990. Random. 1st. sgn. F/F. D10. $75.00

THORBURN, Archibald. *British Birds.* 1925-26. Longman Gr. 4 vol. 192 mc pl. red cloth. djs. T10. $400.00

THORBURN, Grant. *Forty Years' Residence in America...* 1834. Boston. Russell. 264p. rebound. A10. $28.00

THOREAU, Henry David. *Henry David Thoreau.* 1967. Viking. 1st. ils James Daugherty. sm 4to. F/F. P2. $25.00

THOREAU, Henry David. *Journal of...* 1984. Salt Lake. GM Smith. 15 vol. F. M12. $125.00

THOREAU, Henry David. *Poems of Nature.* 1895. Boston/NY. Houghton Mifflin/John Lane. 1st/Am issue. 1/750. M24. $450.00

THOREAU, Henry David. *Walden; or, Life in the Woods.* 1854. Ticknor Fields. 1st. gilt brn cloth. F/blk silk box. M24. $8,500.00

THOREAU, Henry David. *Walking.* 1914. Riverside. 1st separate. 1/550. quarter linen. uncut/box. M24. $125.00

THOREAU, Henry David. *Writings of...* 1906. Houghton Mifflin. 20 vol. 1/600. Bliss Perry's copy. gr buckram/paper spine label. C6. $6,000.00

THOREAU, Henry David. *Yankee in Canada.* 1866. Boston. Ticknor Fields. 1st/1st prt/1st bdg. gilt gr cloth. NF. M24. $125.00

THOREK, Max. *Surgical Errors & Safeguards.* 1932. Phil. 1st. ils. 696p. A13. $75.00

THORNBURG, Newton. *Black Angus.* 1978. Little Brn. 1st. VG/dj. P3. $23.00

THORNBURG, Newton. *Lion at the Door.* 1990. Morrow. 1st. F/VG. P3. $20.00

THORNBURY, W.D. *Principles of Geomorphology.* 1969. John Wiley. 2nd. 594p. pict brd. VG. D8. $17.00

THORNDYKE, Helen Louise. *Honey Bunch: Her First Little Treasure Hunt (#18).* 1937. Grosset Dunlap. 183p. cloth. VG/dj. M20. $30.00

THORNE, Anthony. *She Takes a Lover.* 1932. Macmillan. 1st Am. F/F. B4. $85.00

THORNE, Diana. *Diane Thorne's Dogs: Album of Drawings.* 1944. Messner. 1st. sbdg. VG/dj. M20. $75.00

THORNE, Guy. *When It Was Dark.* 1904. Putnam. 1st. VG. P3. $25.00

THORNE, John. *Simple Cooking.* 1987. Viking. 2nd. sgn. 290p. VG/VG. B10. $12.00

THORNE, Paul. *Murder in the Fog.* 1929. Penn. 1st. VG. P3. $40.00

THORNE, S.E. *Discourse Upon Exposicion & Understandinge of Statuetes...* 1942. San Marino. Huntington Lib. M11. $85.00

THORNE, S.E. *Essays in English Legal History.* 1985. London. Hambledon. M11. $50.00

THORNE-THOMSEN, Kathleen. *Why the Cake Won't Rise & the Jelly Won't Set.* 1979. NY. A&W Pub. G/dj. A16. $8.00

THORNTON, A.G. *Astronomer at Large.* 1924. Putnam. 1st. VG. P3. $25.00

THORNTON, B.M. *Steelhead: Supreme Trophy Trout.* 1978. Seattle. Hancock. ils/photos. 159p. VG+/VG. M12. $25.00

THORNTON, J. Quinn. *California Tragedy.* 1945. Biobooks. 1/1500. 4to. F/F. O4. $30.00

THORP, Raymond. *WF Carver, Spirit Gun of the West.* 1957. Clark. 1st. ils. 266p. VG/dj. J2. $185.00

THORP, Roderick. *Rainbow Drive.* 1986. Summit. 1st. VG/dj. P3. $25.00

THORP, W. *Southern Reader.* 1955. VG/VG. M17. $25.00

THRAPP, Dan L. *Al Sieber, Chief of Scouts.* 1964. Norman, OK. 1st. 432p. VG. J2. $195.00

THRAPP, Dan L. *Juh: An Incredible Indian.* 1973. TX W Pr. 1st. 44p. F/wrp. B19. $25.00

THROM, Edward L. *Boy Engineer.* 1959. Golden. 4to. 248p. G. K5. $18.00

THROWER, Norman J.W. *Three Voyages of Edmund Halley in the Paramore 1698-1701.* 1981. London. 2 vol. ils/pl/maps. as issued. K3. $65.00

THRUM, Thomas G. *Hawaiian Folk Tales.* 1907. Chicago. McClurg. 1st. ils/glossary/ads. 284p. VG. P4. $185.00

THUCYDIDES. *De Bello Peloponnesiaco, Libri Octo.* 1594. Frankfurt. Heirs of Andraes Wechel. 16mo. 848p. VG. C6. $375.00

THUNBERG, Carl Peter. *Flora Japonica.* 1975. NY. Oriole. 8vo. 418p. F/VG. A22. $45.00

THURBER, James. *Further Fables of Our Time.* 1956. S&S. 1st. 174p. brd/cloth spine. NF/NF. B22. $12.00

THURBER, James. *Further Fables of Our Times.* 1956 (1956). S&S. Special Ed (on fine paper). 8vo. 174p. wht cloth. VG. H1. $45.00

THURBER, James. *Lanterns & Lances.* 1961. Harper. 1st. NF/VG. M19. $25.00

THURBER, James. *Many Moons.* 1943. Harcourt Brace. 1st. ils Louis Slobodkin. Caldecott Medal. NF/G+. P2. $150.00

THURBER, James. *Thurber Album.* 1952. S&S. 1st. sgn. xl. G. W2. $75.00

THURBER, James. *White Deer.* 1945. Harcourt Brace. 1st. NF/VG+. C8. $50.00

THURBER & WHITE. *Is Sex Necessary? Or, Why You Feel the Way You Do.* 1944. Garden City. 197p. VG/dj. B14. $75.00

THURMAN, Howard. *Growing Edge.* 1956. NY. Harper. 1st. 131p. G+/dj. V3. $15.00

THURMAN, Howard. *Jesus & the Disinherited.* 1949. NY. Abingdon-Cokesbury. 112p. VG/dj. V3. $9.00

THURMAN, Howard. *Negro Spiritual Speaks of Life & Death.* 1947. Harper. VG/VG. B4. $25.00

THURMAN, Sue Bailey. *Pioneers of Negro Origin in California.* ca 1952. SF. Acme. 1st. 70p. sbdg. B4. $150.00

THURMAN, Wallace. *Blacker the Berry.* 1929. Macaulay. 1st. VG/dj. M25. $750.00

THURSTON, P.C. *Geology of Ontario.* 1991. Toronto. 711p. B1. $85.00

THURSTON, Robert. *Alicia II.* 1978. Putnam. 1st. F/dj. P3. $20.00

THWAITE, Mary. *From Primer to Pleasure in Reading: An Introduction...* 1972. Boston. Horn Book. 1st Am. ils. 4to. 350p. F/F. A4. $45.00

THWING, Eugene. *World's Best 100 Detective Stories 1.* 1929. Funk Wagnalls. VG. P3. $15.00

TIBBETS, Paul. *Mission: Hiroshima.* 1985. Stein Day. VG/wrp. K3. $15.00

TICKNER, John. *Tickner's Dogs.* 1988. London. Sportsman's Pr. VG. O3. $18.00

TIDYMAN, Ernest. *Line of Duty.* 1974. Little Brn. 1st. VG/dj. P3. $20.00

TIGER, John; see Wager, Walter.

TILDEN, W.T. *Art of Lawn Tennis.* 1922. Garden City. rpt/enlarged/expanded. G/G. P8. $20.00

TILLICH, Paul. *History of Christian Thought.* 1956. Tillich. edit Peter John. 309p. G/wrp. B29. $11.00

TILLICH, Paul. *Theology of Paul Tillich.* 1952. Macmllan. edit Kegley/Bretall. 370p. VG/dj. B29. $14.00

TILLMAN, Barrett. *Hellcat: The F6F in WWII.* 1979. Annapolis. photos/notes/biblio/index. 265p. VG/VG. S16. $21.50

TILMAN, H.W. *Ice With Everything.* 1974. Sidney. Gray's Pub. 142p. VG/dj. P4. $25.00

TILMAN, H.W. *Mostly Mischief.* 1967. London. Adventurers Club. later prt. 8vo. 191p. P4. $35.00

TILNEY, Frederick. *Form & Function of the Nervous System.* 1921. NY. Hoeber. heavy 4to. 1019p. ruled bl cloth. xl. G1. $50.00

TILTON, Theodore. *True Church. Ils From Designs by Granville Perkins.* 1883. Phil. Claxton. 8vo. gilt pub cloth. F. B24. $125.00

TIME-LIFE EDITORS. *Cosmos.* 1988. Alexandria, VA. Path Through Universe series. 4to. 144p. pict cloth. K5. $12.00

TIME-LIFE EIDTORS. *Spanish West.* 1979. Alexandria, VA. 2nd. leather. A19. $20.00

TIMMIS, R.S. *Modern Horse Management.* nd. London. Cassell. 4to. VG. O3. $25.00

TIMPERLEY, Rosemary. *Child in the Dark.* 1956. Crowell. 1st. VG/dj. P3. $35.00

TIMPERLEY, Rosemary. *Eighth Ghost Book.* 1972. Barrie Jenkins. 1st. xl. VG/dj. P3. $15.00

TINGLEY, Katherine. *Wine of Life: Compilation From Extemporaneous Address...* 1925. Point Loma. Womans Internat Theosophical League. ils. 332p. D11. $50.00

TINKCOM, Harry Marlin. *Republicans & Federalists in Pennsylvania 1790-1801.* 1950. Harrisburg. PA Hist & Mus Comm. tall 8vo. 354p. gilt cloth. F. H1. $25.00

TINKER, F.G. *Some Still Live.* 1937. Funk Wagnalls. 1st. VG/dj. M2. $17.00

TINKHAM, George H. *History of Stockton.* 1880. SF. WM Hinton. A19. $45.00

TINKLE, Lon. *J Frank Dobie, Makings of an Ample Mind.* 1968. Encino. 1st. 1/850. sgn. 57p. VG/box. J2. $140.00

TINSLEY, Jim Bob. *He Was Singin' This Song.* 1981. Orlando. inscr. fwd Gene Autry/S Omar Baker. 255p. F/VG. B11. $75.00

TIONGSON, Nicanor G. *Pilipinas Circa 1907: Production Score for Piano & Voice.* 1985. Quezon City. Philippine Edu Theater Assn. 266p. F/VG. P1. $15.00

TIPPETT, James S. *Crickety Cricket!* 1973. Harper Row. 1st. ils Mary Chalmers. 83p. reinforced cloth. F/F. D4. $35.00

TIPPING, H. Avray. *English Gardens.* 1925. London. folio. 600 ils/photos. 366p. aeg. B26. $200.00

TIPPING, H. Avray. *Gardens Old & New: Country House & Its Garden Environment.* 1900. London. Country Life. 295p. folio. A10. $95.00

TITOV, Gherman. *I Am Eagle!* 1962. Bobbs Merrill. 8vo. photos. 212p. Vg/dj. K5. $30.00

TOBE, John H. *Proven Herbal Remedies.* 1969. Provoker. 304p. VG/VG. M20. $15.00

TOBIAS, Philip V. *Brain in Hominid Evolution.* 1971. Columbia. tall 8vo. 170p. blk cloth. VG/tattered. G1. $50.00

TODD, Barbara. *Earthy Mangold & Worzel Gummidge.* 1954. London. Hollis Carter. 1st. ils JJ Crockford. 200p. NF/VG-. P2. $25.00

TODD, Edwin. *Neuroanatomy of Leonardo da Vinci.* 1983. Santa Barbara. 1st. 189p. A13. $75.00

TODD, Frank Morton. *Eradicating Plague From San Francisco.* 1908. Citizen Health Comm. 1st/only. 313p. maroon cloth. F. K7. $95.00

TODD, John M. *Luther: A Life.* 1982. Crossroad. 396p. VG/dj. B29. $10.00

TODD, Mabel Loomis. *Cycle of Sunsets.* 1910. Boston. Sm Maynard. 1st. teg. gilt gr cloth. VG. M24. $165.00

TODD, Walter E. *Gathered Treasures.* 1912. WA, DC. Murray. 1st. F. B4. $250.00

TODD, William B. *Suppressed Commentaries on Wiseian Forgeries.* 1969. Austin. 1st. 1/750. fld pl. 50p. VG. K3. $60.00

TODER, C.P. *Delaware Canal Journal.* 1972. Bethlehem, PA. 1st. ils/charts. 287p. VG+/dj. B18. $45.00

TODOROFF, A. *Food Buying Today.* 1934. Grocery Trade Pub. ils. VG. E6. $15.00

TOEPPERWEIN & TOEPPERWEIN. *Charcoal & Charcoal Burners.* 1950. Boeme, TX. Highland. 1st. sgns. VG/VG. B11. $40.00

TOEPPERWEIN & TOEPPERWEIN. *Unkle Kris & His Pets.* 1948. Boeme, TX. Higland. 1/200. sgn/#d. VG/VG. B11. $40.00

TOGAWA, Masako. *Lady Killer.* 1986. Dodd Mead. 1st Am. F/F. N4. $27.50

TOKLAS, Alice B. *Alice B Toklas Cookbook.* 1984 (1954). Harper. 1st thus. 8vo. F/F. C8. $25.00

TOKLAS, Alice B. *Aromas & Flavors of Past & Present.* 1958. Harper. 1st. F/clip. B35. $70.00

TOKLAS, Alice B. *What Is Remembered.* 1963. Holt. 1st. F/NF. B2. $45.00

TOLAND, John. *Battle: Story of the Bulge.* 1959. NY. maps/photos/index. 400p. VG/G. S16. $27.50

TOLAND, John. *Last 100 Days: Tumultuous & Controversial Story...* 1966. NY. 622p. VG/G. S16. $23.50

TOLBER, John. *Who's Who in Rock & Roll.* 1991. Mitchell. NF/dj. P3. $20.00

TOLKIEN, Christopher. *Pictures by JRR Tolkien.* 1992. Houghton Mifflin. 1st. unp. cloth. VG+/dj. M20. $50.00

TOLKIEN, J.R.R. *Adventures of Tom Bombadil & Other Verses.* 1962. London. Allen Unwin. true 1st. NF/NF. M22. $75.00

TOLKIEN, J.R.R. *Adventures of Tom Bombadil & Other Verses...* 1962. London. Allen Unwin. 2nd prt. 8vo. NF/NF. C8. $25.00

TOLKIEN, J.R.R. *Film Book of the Lord of the Rings.* 1978. Methuen. MTI. VG/G. P3. $30.00

TOLKIEN, J.R.R. *Hobbit.* 1984. 1st thus. 4to. ils Michael Hague. F/F. A4. $45.00

TOLKIEN, J.R.R. *Letters of JRR Tolkien.* 1981. Houghton Mifflin. 1st. VG/VG. P3. $20.00

TOLKIEN, J.R.R. *Lord of the Rings Part One, the Film Book of...* 1978. Ballantine. 1st thus. ils. obl sm 4to. NF/NF. C8. $45.00

TOLKIEN, J.R.R. *Lord of the Rings.* 1967. Houghton Mifflin. 2nd Am. 3 vol. F/F. B4. $350.00

TOLKIEN, J.R.R. *Return of the Shadow.* 1988. Houghton Mifflin. 1st. VG/dj. P3. $20.00

TOLKIEN, J.R.R. *Road Goes Ever On.* 1967. Houghton Mifflin. 1st. F/VG. M19. $50.00

TOLKIEN, J.R.R. *Road Goes Ever On.* 1967. Houghton Mifflin. 1st. lg 8vo. VG+. M21. $40.00

TOLKIEN, J.R.R. *Silmarillion.* 1977. London. Allen Unwin. 1st. F/F. T12. $30.00

TOLKIEN, J.R.R. *Sir Gawain & the Green Knight, Pearl, Sir Orfeo.* 1975. Houghton Mifflin. 1st Am. 149p. F/dj. H1. $32.00

TOLKIEN, J.R.R. *Smith of Wooten Major.* 1967. Houghton Mifflin. 1st. F/VG. M19. $45.00

TOLKIEN, J.R.R. *Unfinished Tales.* 1980. BC. F/dj. M2. $10.00

TOLKIEN, J.R.R. *Unfinished Tales.* 1980. Houghton Mifflin. 1st. VG/dj. P3. $25.00

TOLKIN, Michael. *Player.* 1988. Atlantic. 1st. author's 1st book. F/F. H11/M22. $40.00

TOLKOWSKY, Samuel. *They Took to the Sea.* 1964. NY. Yoseloff. ils. 316p. dj. T7. $20.00

TOLLES, Frederick B. *James Logan & the Culture of Provincial America.* 1957. Boston. Little Brn. 1st. 228p. VG/dj. V3. $15.00

TOLLES, Frederick B. *Meeting House & Counting House: Quaker Merchants...* 1948. Chapel Hill. 1st. 292p. VG/worn. V3. $18.00

TOLMAN, Richard C. *Relativity, Thermodynamics & Cosmology.* 1962. Clarendon. 6th. 8vo. 501p. G. K5. $60.00

TOLSON, Berneita. *Beer Cookbook.* 1968. Hawthorn. G/dj. A16. $15.00

TOLSON, M.B. *Harlem Gallery.* (1965). Twayne. 1st. VG/dj. M25. $65.00

TOLSON, M.B. *Libretto for the Republic of Liberia.* 1953. Twayne. 1st. VG/dj. M25. $60.00

TOLSTOY, Leo. *Anna Karenina.* 1886. NY. Thomas Crowell. 1st Am. gilt bl cloth. NF. M24. $400.00

TOLSTOY, Leo. *Childhood, Boyhood, Youth.* (1886). NY. Crowell. 1st Am. author's 1st book. gilt brn cloth. F. M24. $225.00

TOLSTOY, Leo. *Ivan Ilyitch & Other Stories.* (1887). Crowell. 1st Am (311p instead of 219p). gilt gr cloth. F. M24. $200.00

TOLSTOY, Leo. *Kreutzer Sonata & Other Stories.* 1890. NY. Ogilvie. 1st Am. VG/bl pict cloth. M24. $100.00

TOLSTOY, Leo. *Letters.* 1978. NY. 1st. 2 vol. VG/VG. T9. $30.00

TOLSTOY, Leo. *War & Peace.* 1889. NY. Crowell. 1st from Russian. 4 vol in 2 (as issued). gilt bl bdg. M24. $450.00

TOLSTOY, Nikolai. *Coming of the King.* 1989. Bantam. 1st. NF/dj. M2. $15.00

TOMAN, Rolf. *High Middle Ages in Germany.* 1990. Cologne. Benedikt Taschen. 4to. 140p. T10. $45.00

TOMKINS, William. *Universal Indian Sign Language.* 1929. San Diego. self pub. A19. $30.00

TOMLINS, Thomas Edlyne. *Law-Dictionary, Examining the Rise, Progress & Present...* 1835. London. contemporary calf. M11. $375.00

TOMLINSON, Everett T. *Washington's Young Aids, a Story of American Revolution.* 1897. Boston. 1st. ils Charles Copeland. 391p. VG. B14. $75.00

TOMLINSON, P.B. *Botany of Mangroves.* 1986. Cambridge, Eng. Cambridge Tropical Biology series. ils. 413p. F/dj. B26. $70.00

TOMMAY, Pat. *Crunch.* 1975. Norton. 1st. photos. VG+/VG. P8. $25.00

TOMPKINS, Ptolemy. *Tree Grows Out of Hell.* 1990. NY. Harper. 1st. 189p. dj. F3. $20.00

TOMPKINS, Stuart Ramsay. *Triumph of Bolshevism-Revolution or Reaction?* 1967. OK U. 1st. xl. VG/dj. V4. $7.50

TOMPKINS, Walter A. *Little Giant of Signal Hill.* 1964. Englewood Cliffs. 1st. NF/NF. O4. $15.00

TONEYAMA, Kojin. *Popular Arts of Mexico.* 1974. NY/Tokyo. Weatherhill/Heibonsha. 2nd. 226p. cloth. dj. D2. $185.00

TONKIN, Peter. *Coffin Ship.* 1990. Crown. 1st. VG/dj. P3. $20.00

TONNESSEN, Johnsen. *History of Modern Whaling.* 1982. Berkeley. thick 8vo. 798p. NF/dj. P4. $65.00

TOOKER, Elva. *Nathan Trotter: Philadelphia Merchant, 1787-1853.* 1955. Cambridge. 1st. 276p. G/tattered. V3. $16.50

TOOKER, L. Frank. *Joys & Tribulations of an Editor.* 1924. Century. 1st. VG. M2. $25.00

TOOLE, John K. *Neon Bible.* 1989. Grove. 1st. F/F. A20. $15.00

TOOLEY, R.V. *English Books With Color Plates 1790 to 1860.* 1954. Boston Book & Art Shop. 8vo. 424p. F/dj. B24. $150.00

TOOLEY, R.V. *Maps & Map-Makers.* 1990. NY. Dorsett. later prt. 140p. M/dj. P4. $40.00

TOOMER, Jean. *Essentials.* 1931. Chicago. private prt. 1/1000. author's 2nd book. M/dj. B4. $1,500.00

TOOR, Frances. *Guide to Mexico.* 1940. McBridge. revised/enlarged. 270p. F3. $15.00

TOPSELL, Edward. *Fowles of Heaven; or, History of Birds.* 1972. Austin. ils. 332p. VG/VG. S15. $30.00

TOREY, B. *Field-Days in California.* 1913. Houghton Mifflin. ils/photos/pl. 235p. gilt cloth. VG+. M12. $37.50

TORGOVNICK, Marianna. *Gone Primitive.* 1990. Chicago. 1st. F/dj. P3. $25.00

TORIBIO MEDINA, Jose. *La Imprenta en Lima, 1584-1824.* 1965 (1904). Amsterdam. Nico Israel. 4 vol. ils. cloth. D11. $100.00

TORME, Mel. *It Wasn't All Velvet.* 1988. Viking. 1st. inscr. F/F. B2. $40.00

TORME, Mel. *It Wasn't All Velvet.* 1988. Viking. 1st. NF/NF. A20. $20.00

TORME, Mel. *Wynner.* 1978. Stein Day. 1st. NF/VG+. A20. $25.00

TORREY, Julia Whitemore. *Old Sheffield Plate.* 1918. ils. VG. M17. $35.00

TOSKI, Bob. *How To Become a Complete Golfer.* 1984. S&S. revised/later prt. inscr. F/NF. B4. $45.00

TOULOUSE, Julian Harrison. *Fruit Jars.* 1969. Thomas Nelson/Everybodys. tall 8vo. 542p. F/dj. H1. $65.00

TOURGEE, Albion W. *Appeal to Caesar.* 1884. NY. 422p. O8. $12.50

TOURGEE, Albion W. *Bricks Without Straw.* 1880. Howard Hulbert. 1st prt. 16mo. 521p. emb brn cloth. G+. O8. $12.50

TOURNIER, Michel. *Golden Droplet.* 1987. Doubleday. 1st. F/NF. B35. $16.00

TOUSEY, Sanford. *Jerry & the Pony Express.* 1936. Doubleday. stated 1st. ils. F/fair. M5. $45.00

TOUSEY, Sanford. *Northwest Mounted Police.* 1941. Chicago. VG. C8. $17.50

TOUSEY, Thomas G. *Military History of Carlisle & Carlisle Barracks.* 1939. Richmond, VA. Dietz. 1st. tall 8vo. 447p. VG. H1. $36.00

TOWNE, Robert D. *Teddy Bears at the Circus.* 1907. Reilly Britton. 1st thus. ils JR Bray. 12mo. mc pict brd. R5. $150.00

TOWNSEND, C.W. *Along the Labrador Coast.* 1907. Boston. 1st. ils/fld map. 289p. VG. B5. $35.00

TOWNSEND, G.W. *Memorial Life of William McKinley.* 1901. np. sm 4to. 520p. emb gilt bdg. VG. H1. $28.00

TOWNSEND, George A. *Rustics in Rebellion.* 1950. 1st/2nd state. 292p. O8. $14.50

TOWNSEND, John Rowe. *Tom Tiddler's Ground.* 1986. Lippincott. 1st Am. 8vo. 170p. rem mk. NF/NF. T5. $20.00

TOWNSEND, Sue. *Adrian Mole Diaries.* 1986. Grove. 1st Am. F/clip. D10. $65.00

TOWNSEND. *Written for Children: Outline of English Language...* 1983. 2nd revised/1st prt. ils. 384p. F/F. A4. $35.00

TOXOPEUS, Klaas. *Flying Storm.* 1954. Dodd Mead. ils. 246p. T7. $20.00

TOYNBEE, Arnold. *Lectures on the Industrial Revolution in England.* 1884. London. Rivington. 1st. 8vo. 256p. gilt gr cloth. VG. T10. $75.00

TOZZER, Alfred M. *Maya Grammar With Bibliography & Appraisement of Works...* 1921. Cambridge. 301p. F3. $40.00

TRACHSEL, Herman H. *Government & Administration of...Wyoming.* 1956. NY. Crowell. A19. $20.00

TRACHTMAN, Paula. *Disturb Not the Dream.* 1981. Crown. 1st. F/dj. M2. $12.00

TRACY, Clarence. *Rape Observed.* 1974. Toronto. 1st. 4to. 101p. gilt red cloth. F/NF. H13. $65.00

TRACY, Louis. *American Emperor.* 1918. Putnam. decor brd. VG. P3. $75.00

TRACY, Louis. *Man With the Sixth Sense.* nd. Hodder Stoughton. G/dj. P3. $25.00

TRACY, Louis. *Pillar of Light.* 1904. Clode. 1st. VG. M2. $15.00

TRAIN, Arthur. *Mr Tutt Comes Home.* 1941. Scribner. 1st. VG/dj. Q1. $60.00

TRAIN, Arthur. *Mr Tutt's Case Book.* 1945. Scribner. VG. P3. $25.00

TRAIN, Arthur. *Old Man Tutt.* 1938. Scribner. 1st. VG/dj. Q1. $60.00

TRALL, R.T. *Digestion & Dyspepsia: A Complete Explanation...* 1873. NY. SR Wells. ils. 160p. xl. VG. K3. $20.00

TRAUB, Charles. *Beach.* 1978. NY. Horizon. photos. 60p. wrp. D11. $30.00

TRAUBEL, Horace L. *Camden's Compliment to Walt Whitman.* 1889. Phil. McKay. 1st. teg. gilt maroon cloth. NF. M24. $250.00

TRAUSCH, William. *Grab Bag.* 1939. Pegasus. 1st. 156p. dj. A17. $20.00

TRAVEN, B. *Rebellion of the Hanged.* 1952. Knopf. 1st Am. NF/dj. M25. $200.00

TRAVER, Robert. *Laughing Whitefish.* 1965. McGraw Hill. 1st. VG/dj. P3. $25.00

TRAVER, Robert. *Trout Madness.* 1960. NY. 1st. 178p. quarter buckram. VG/dj. B18/M20. $35.00

TRAVER, Robert. *Trout Magic.* 1974. NY. 1st. 216p. F/dj. A17. $50.00

TRAVERS, Hugh. *Madame Aubry Dines With Death.* 1967. Harper Row. 1st. VG/dj. P3. $10.00

TRAVERS, Louise A. *Romance of Shells in Nature & Art.* 1962. NY. Barrows. 1/400. sgn. F/F case. B11. $18.00

TRAVERS, P.L. *Friend Monkey.* 1971. HBJ. 1st/2nd prt. inscr. ils Mary Shepard. 122p. VG. T5. $25.00

TRAVERS, P.L. *Mary Poppins From A-Z.* 1962. Harcourt. stated 1st. 8vo. F/VG. M5. $55.00

TRAVERS, P.L. *Mary Poppins in Cherry Tree Lane.* 1982. London. Collins. 1st. ils Mary Shepard. VG+. C8. $15.00

TRAVERS, P.L. *Mary Poppins in the Kitchen.* 1975. HBJ. 1st/B prt. 122p. mauve brd. VG/VG. T5. $45.00

TRAVERS, P.L. *Mary Poppins in the Park.* 1952. Harcourt. stated 1st. ils Mary Shepard. VG+/dj. M5. $60.00

TREASE, Geoffrey. *So Wild the Heart.* 1959. Vanguard. 1st. VG/fair. P3. $12.00

TREAT, Lawrence. *H As in Hangman.* 1944. Books Inc. VG/dj. P3. $20.00

TREAT, Mary. *Injurious Insects of the Farm & Garden.* 1887. Orange Judd. 296p. VG. A10. $35.00

TREATT, Stella Court. *Cape to Cairo. Record of a Historic Motor Journey.* 1927. Little Brn. 1st. 8vo. 251p. xl. G. W1. $12.00

TREATT, Stella Court. *Cape to Cairo. Record of a Historic Motor Journey.* 1927. London. Harrap. 1st. ils. VG. K3. $25.00

TREECE, Henry. *Amber Princess.* 1963. Random. 1st. NF/dj. P3. $25.00

TREECE, Henry. *Golden Strangers.* 1956. Random. 1st. F/dj. M2. $38.00

TREGANOWAN & WEEKS. *Rugs & Carpets of Europe & the Western World.* 1969. Chilton. ils/bibliography/index. cloth. dj. D2. $40.00

TREGARTHEN, Enys. *White Ring.* 1949. harcourt Brace. 1st. ils Nora Unwin. sq 8vo. 65p. VG/VG-. P2. $40.00

TREGASKIS, Richard. *Guadalcanal Diary.* 1943. NY. photos/maps. 263p. VG. S16. $17.50

TREITEL, Jonathan. *Red Cabbage Cafe.* 1990. Pantheon. 1st. author's 1st book. F/F. H11. $25.00

TRELEASE, William. *Winter Botany.* 1918. Urbana. self pub. 1st. 394p. VG. A10. $24.00

TRENHAILE, John. *Mah-Jongg Spies.* 1986. Dutton. 1st. F/NF. H11. $25.00

TRENHAILE, John. *Nocturne for the General.* 1985. Congdon Weed. 1st. VG/dj. P3. $15.00

TRENHOLM, Virginia Cole. *Footprints on the Fontier.* 1945. np. 1st. 284p. VG/dj. J2. $385.00

TRENTO, Joseph J. *Prescription for Disaster.* 1987. NY. Crown. 8vo. 312p. VG/dj. K5. $20.00

TRESSELT, Alvin. *Beaver Pond.* 1970. Lee Shepard. 1st. ils Roger Duvoisin. 4to. VG+/VG. P2. $40.00

TREUTLEIN, Theodore E. *San Francisco Bay, Discovery & Colonization 1769-1776.* 1968. CA Hist Soc. 1st. 4 facsimile maps. quarter bl cloth/gr sides. dj. K7/O4. $25.00

TREVANIAN. *Eiger Sanction.* 1972. Crown. 1st. author's 1st book. F/NF. M25. $100.00

TREVANIAN. *Summer of Katya.* 1983. Crown. 1st. F/F. N4. $25.00

TREVANIAN. *Summer of Katya.* 1983. Granada. 1st. NF/dj. P3. $18.00

TREVER, John C. *Scrolls From Qumran Cave I: Great Isaiah Scroll...* 1972. Jerusalem. Allbright Inst Archaeological Research. 163p. VG+. S3. $75.00

TREVINO, Lee. *Snake in the Sandtrap.* 1985. HRW. 1st. sgn. F/F. A23. $50.00

TREVOR, Elleston. *Blaze or Roses.* 1952. Harper. 1st. 249p. VG/dj. M20. $12.00

TREVOR, William. *News From Ireland & Other Stories.* 1986. Viking. 1st Am. F/F. D10. $45.00

TREVOR, William. *Old Boys.* 1964. NY. Viking. 1st. F/NF. L3. $125.00

TREW, Antony. *Ultimatum.* 1976. St Martin. 1st. VG/VG. M22. $15.00

TRIBUTSCH, H. *When the Snakes Awake.* 1982. Cambridge. MIT. 248p. dj. B1. $25.00

TRIER, Walter. *10 Little Negroes: A New Version.* 1944. London. Sylvan. 1st. obl 8vo. pict brd. R5. $275.00

TRIGGS, J.H. *History of Cheyenne & North Wyoming Embracing Gold Fields...* 1955. Laramie, WY. Powder River Pub. 2 vol. boxed. A19. $45.00

TRIMBLE, Allen. *Autobiography...Allen Trimble, Governor of Ohio.* 1909. np. 240p. G/wrp. B18. $25.00

TRIMBLE, Barbara Margaret. *Fifth Rapunzel.* 1991. Hodder Stoughton. 1st. VG/dj. P3. $20.00

TRIMBLE, Marshall. *Arizona.* 1977. Garden City. dj. A19. $20.00

TRIMBLE, Michael R. *Post-Traumatic Neurosis: From Railway Spine to Whiplash.* 1981. Chichester, Eng. Wiley. 3rd. 8vo. 156p. navy cloth. F/dj. G1. $40.00

TRIMBLE, Vance H. *Sam Walton.* 1990. Dutton. 1st. F/F. W2. $30.00

TRIMBLE, William F. *High Frontier: History of Aeronautics in Pennsylvania.* 1982. Pittsburgh. 344p. VG+/wrp. B18. $17.50

TRIPP, Miles. *Death of a Man-Tamer.* 1987. St Martin. 1st. VG/dj. P3. $15.00

TRIPP, Miles. *Fifth Point of the Compass.* 1967. Macmillan. 1st. VG/dj. P3. $23.00

TRIPP, Wallace. *Sir Toby Jingle's Beastly Journey.* 1976. CMG. 1st. ils. VG-/G. P2. $20.00

TRIPTREE, James Jr. *Her Smoke Rose Up Forever.* 1990. Arkham. 1st. VG/dj. M22. $30.00

TROLLOPE, Anthony. *Barchester Towers.* 1958. NY. LEC. 1st thus. 1/1500. ils/sgn Fritz Kredel. F/case. Q1. $100.00

TROLLOPE, Anthony. *La Vendee: Historical Romance.* June 1874. London. Chapman Hall. rpt. gilt brn cloth. NF. M24. $1,250.00

TROLLOPE, Anthony. *Orley Farm.* 1862. London. Chapman Hall. 2 vol. 1st. lg 8vo. Bumpus bdg. H13. $495.00

TROLLOPE, Anthony. *Rachel Ray, a Novel.* 1868. London. Chapman Hall. so-called 10th. tall 8vo. 347p. Victorian bdg. H13. $195.00

TROLLOPE, Anthony. *Tales of All Countries.* 1861. London. Chapman Hall. 1st. gilt dk bl cloth. w/November 1861 catalog. M24. $1,000.00

TROLLOPE, Anthony. *Travelling Sketches.* 1866. London. Chapman Hall. 1st. gilt red cloth. entirely unopened. M24. $500.00

TROLLOPE, Anthony. *Warden.* 1955. NY. LEC. 1st thus. 1/1500. ils/sgn Fritz Kredel. F/glassine/case. Q1. $100.00

TROLLOPE, Mrs. Frances. *Domestic Manners of the Americans.* 1949. edit D Smalley. VG/VG. M17. $25.00

TROLLOPE, Thomas Adolphus. *Decade of Italian Women.* 1859. London. Chapman Hall. 2 vol. 1st. 8vo. teg. 3-quarter crushed morocco. F. H13. $295.00

TROUT, Kilgore; see Farmer, Philip Jose.

TROWBRIDGE, J.T. *South: A Tour of Its Battle-Fields & Ruined Cities.* 1866. 1st. ils. 590p. O8. $55.00

TROWBRIDGE, W.R.H. *Court Beauties of Old Whitehall.* 1906. Scribner. 1st. F. M19. $65.00

TROY, Simon. *Drunkard's End.* 1961. Walker. 1st. VG/dj. P3. $15.00

TRUAX, Rhoda. *Doctors Warren of Boston: First Family of Surgery.* 1968. Boston. 1st. 369p. A13. $20.00

TRUAX, Rhoda. *Joseph Lister: Father of Modern Surgery.* 1944. Indianapolis. 1st. 287p. A13. $30.00

TRUDEAU, Gary. *Doonesbury Deluxe.* 1987. Holt. sc. F. M13. $19.00

TRUE, Frederick W. *Whalebone Whales of the Western North Atlantic...* 1983. Smithsonian. rpt. 50 pl. 332p. gr cloth. F. P4. $75.00

TRUEBLOOD, Elton. *Abraham Lincoln: Theologian of American Anguish.* 1973. NY. Harper Row. 1st. 149p. VG/dj. V3. $16.00

TRUEBLOOD, Elton. *Company of the Committed.* 1961. Harper. 1st. 113p. VG/dj. V3. $12.00

TRUEBLOOD, Elton. *Doctor Johnson's Prayers.* 1947. Harper. 1st. 66p. VG/G+. V3. $12.00

TRUEBLOOD, Elton. *Lord's Prayers.* 1965. Harper Row. 1st. 128p. VG/dj. V3. $12.00

TRUEBLOOD, Elton. *Signs of Hope in a Century of Despair.* 1950. Harper. 324p. dj. V3. $12.00

TRUEBLOOD, Elton. *Validity of the Christian Mission.* 1972. Harper Row. 1st. 113p. VG/dj. V3. $12.00

TRUEBLOOD, Elton. *While It Is Day: An Autobiography.* 1974. Harper Row. sgn. 170p. VG/dj. V3. $17.50

TRUEBLOOD, Ernest V.; see Faulkner, William.

TRUEMAN, Stuart. *Ghosts, Pirates & Treasure Trove.* 1975. McClelland Stewart. 1st. VG/dj. P3. $15.00

TRUMAN, Margaret. *Murder in Georgetown.* 1986. Arbor. 1st. F/F. B4. $45.00

TRUMAN, Margaret. *Murder in the White House.* 1980. Arbor. 1st. F/NF. M22. $25.00

TRUMBALL, Charles G. *Taking Men Alive.* 1915. Assoc. 199p. G. B29. $6.00

TRUMBO, Dalton. *Night of the Aurochs.* 1979. Viking. 1st. F/F. A20. $30.00

TRUMBULL, Robert. *Nine Who Survived Hiroshima & Nagasaki.* 1965. Dutton. 5th. VG/dj. K3. $25.00

TRUMP, Donald J. *Art of the Deal.* 1987. Random. 1st. F/F. W2. $30.00

TRUMP, Ivana. *For Love Alone.* 1992. Pocket. 1st. F/F. W2. $35.00

TRUMPS. *American Hoyle/Hoyle's Games.* 1907. NY. 18th. 532p. VG. S1. $15.00

TRUSS, Seldon. *Doctor Was a Dame.* 1953. Crime Club. 1st. VG/dj. P3. $20.00

TRUSSLER, D.J. *Early Commercial Vehicles.* 1968. London. 1st. 10 full-p mc pl. 45p. F. M4. $35.00

TRYON, Thomas. *Harvest Home.* 1973. Knopf. 1st. F/F. H11. $40.00

TRYON, Thomas. *Harvest Home.* 1973. Knopf. 1st. NF/dj. M2. $30.00

TRYON, Thomas. *Wings of the Morning.* 1990. Franklin Lib. 1st. sgn. full leather. F. Q1. $40.00

TSCHIRKY, O. *Cook Book by Oscar of the Waldorf.* 1896. 4to. 907p. VG. E6. $95.00

TSE-TUNG, Mao. *Poems.* 1976. Foreign Language Pr. 1st. F/dj. V1. $25.00

TSIOLKOVSKY, K. *Will of the Universe: Intellect Unknown, Mind & Passions.* 1992. Memory. 8vo. 30p. VG/wrp. K5. $10.00

TSUNA, Masuda. *Kodo Zuroku.* 1983. Norwalk, CT. Burndy Lib. ils. wrp. K3. $25.00

TU, A.T. *Martine Toxins & Venoms.* 1988. NY. Marcel Dekker. 8vo. 587p. NF. B1. $125.00

TUCHMAN, Barbara W. *Practicing History.* 1981. Knopf. 1st. ES. as new/F. H1. $20.00

TUCKER, G.C. *Taxonomy of Cyperus (Cyperaceae) in Costa Rica & Panama.* 1983. Ann Arbor. 8vo. 85p. stiff wrp. B1. $22.00

TUCKER, George Fox. *Quaker Home.* 1891. Boston. George Reed. 426p. G. V3. $12.00

TUCKER, Sarah. *Memoirs of Life & Religious Experience.* 1848. Moore Choate. 204p. G. V3. $16.00

TUCKER, William. *Family Dyer & Scourer...Arts of Dyeing & Cleaning...* 1831. Phil. 2nd. 12mo. woodcut. 123p. cloth/lacks label. M1. $250.00

TUCKER, Wilson. *Ice & Iron.* 1974. Doubleday. BC. sgn. VG/G. B11. $20.00

TUCKER, Wilson. *Ice & Iron.* 1974. Doubleday. 1st. NF/dj. M2. $30.00

TUCKER, Wilson. *Ice & Iron.* 1974. Doubleday. 1st. VG/dj. P3. $25.00

TUCKER, Wilson. *Procession of the Damned.* 1965. Crime Club. 1st. VG/dj. P3. $25.00

TUCKERMAN, Edward. *Synopsis of Lichens of New England...* 1848. Cambridge. inscr. 93p. VG. B26. $60.00

TUCKETT, Christopher. *Nag Hammadi & the Gospel Tradition.* 1986. T&T Clark. 194p. VG/dj. B29. $11.50

TUCKEY, H.B. *Dwarfed Fruit Trees.* 1964. Macmillan. 8vo. cloth. B1. $50.00

TUDOR, Tasha. *Advent Calendar From Tasha Tudor.* 1978. NY. 1st. mc ils fld panorama. never opened/F. H3. $100.00

TUDOR, Tasha. *Becky's Birthday.* 1960. Viking. 1st. 4to. xl. VG/dj. M5. $75.00

TUDOR, Tasha. *Corgiville Fair.* 1971. Crowell. 1st. obl 4to. F/VG. P2. $200.00

TUDOR, Tasha. *Dolls' Christmas.* 1950. Oxford. 1st. red cloth/wht pl. G. M5. $95.00

TUDOR, Tasha. *Take Joy! Tasha Tudor Christmas Book.* 1966. World. 1st. obl lg 4to. F/VG. M5. $95.00

TUDOR, Tasha. *Tasha Tudor Book of Fairy Tales.* 1961. Platt Munk. 1st. sgn. 4to. pict brd. R5. $200.00

TUDOR, Tasha. *Tasha Tudor's Old-Fashioned Gifts.* 1979. McKay. 1st. 8vo. VG+/dj. M5. $65.00

TUDOR, Tasha. *Thisly B.* 1949. NY. Oxford. 1st. 12mo. red-brn cloth/label/gilt spine. R5. $100.00

TUDOR, Tasha. *White Goose.* 1943. Oxford. 1st. 12 full-p pl. 12mo. gray cloth. dj. R5. $450.00

TUDOR, Tasha. *White Goose.* 1943. Oxford. 2nd. VG. M5. $125.00

TUDOR, Tasha. *1 Is One.* 1956. NY. Oxford. 1st. sgn. obl 4to. pink cloth. dj. R5. $325.00

TUKE, Samuel. *Plea on Behalf of George Fox & the Early Friends.* 1837. London. Darton Harvey. 41p. V3. $20.00

TUKEY, H. *Pear & Its Culture.* 1928. 1st. photos. xl. VG. E6. $20.00

TULLIUS, F.P. *Out of the Death Bag in West Hollywood.* 1971. Macmillan. 1st. F/F. B4. $100.00

TUNIS, Edwin. *Colonial Living.* 1957. World. dj. A19. $40.00

TUPLING, G.H. *South Lancashire in the Reign of Edward II...* 1949. Manchester. gilt bl cloth. M11. $65.00

TUPPER, Frieda B. *Down in Bull Creek.* 1975. Webster, SD. sgn. A19. $20.00

TURBEVILLE, Deborah. *Wallflower.* 1978. NY. Congreve. photos. 128p. brd. clip dj. D11. $75.00

TURBIN, Carole. *Working Women of Collar City: Gender Class & Community...* 1992. IL U. 1st. F/F. V4. $20.00

TUREK, Leslie. *Noreascon Proceedings Sept 3-6, 1971.* 1976. NESFA. 1st. F/F. P3. $75.00

TURK, H.C. *Black Body.* 1989. Villard. 1st. F/dj. M2. $20.00

TURKLE, Brinton. *Deep in the Forest.* 1976. Dutton. 1st. ils. unp. xl. VG. T5. $25.00

TURNBAUGH, D.B. *Duncan Grant & the Bloomsbury Group: Illustrated Biography.* 1987. ils. VG/VG. M17. $17.50

TURNBULL, Archibald Douglas. *Commodore David Porter 1780-1843.* 1929. NY. Century. 1st. 8vo. 326p. VG/worn. P4. $75.00

TURNBULL, Colin M. *Mountain People.* 1972. S&S. 1st. ils/maps. 309p. VG/dj. W1. $16.00

TURNBULL, Colin M. *Wayward Servants: Two Worlds of African Pygmies.* 1976 (1965). Greenwood. rpt. 8vo. 390p. VG. W1. $25.00

TURNBULL, H.W. *Correspondence of Isaac Newton. Vol 1, 1661-1675.* 1959. Cambridge. fld pl. F/dj. K3. $45.00

TURNER, A. Logan. *Joseph, Baron Lister. Centenary Vol 1827-1927.* 1927. Edinburgh/London. Oliver Boyd. 1st. ils. 182p. VG. K3. $40.00

TURNER, A. Richard. *Vision of Landscape in Renaissance Italy.* 1966. Princeton. 219p. dj. A10. $40.00

TURNER, Ann. *Heron Street.* 1989. Harper Row. 1st. inscr. sm 4to. unp. NF/VG+. C14. $20.00

TURNER, Edward. *Elements of Chemistry Including Recent Discoveries...* 1835. DeSilver Thomas. 5th Am from 5th London. 682p. ES. full leather. VG. H1. $185.00

TURNER, Ethel Duffy. *Revolution in Baja California: Richardo Flores Magon...* 1981. Detroit, MI. Blaine Ethridge. 1st. NF. O4. $20.00

TURNER, Frederick Jackson. *Frontier in American History.* 1937. Holt. A19. $35.00

TURNER, J.V. *Below the Clock.* 1936. Appleton Century. 1st Am. VG/dj. M15. $35.00

TURNER, Joseph. *True Israel.* 1850. Hartford. 8vo. prt yel wrp. R12. $140.00

TURNER, L.M. *Ethnology of the Ungave District, Hudson Bay Territory.* 1984. BAE 11th Annual Report. new cloth. facsimile title p. F. M4. $25.00

TURNER, Lana. *Lady, the Legend, the Truth: Lana.* 1982. Dutton. 1st. ils. 311p. VG/clip. A25. $10.00

TURNER, Nancy Byrd. *Zodiac Town.* 1021. Atlantic Monthly. 1st. ils Winifred Bromhall. gilt bl cloth. VG+/dj. M20. $65.00

TURNER, Ralph V. *English Judiciary in the Age of Glanvill & Bracton...* 1985. Cambrige. M11. $65.00

TURNER, Robert. *Gunsmoke.* 1958. Whitman. TVTI. VG. P3. $20.00

TURNER, Tina. *I, Tina.* 1986. Viking. 1st. F/NF. A20. $15.00

TURNER, W.J. *Duchess of Popocatapetl.* 1939. London. 1st. Vg/dj. M2. $35.00

TURNER, William. *Fruits & Vegetables Under Glass.* 1912. DeLaMare. tall 8vo. 266p. VG. A22. $35.00

TURNER. *Boys Will Be Boys: Story of Sweeney Todd, Deadwood Dick...* 1957. London. Michael Joseph. New ed. ils. 277p. VG/VG. A4. $65.00

TURNILL, Reginald. *Observer's Spaceflight Directory.* 1978. London. Warne. 1st. 384p. VG/dj. K5. $50.00

TUROLLA, Pina. *Beyond the Andes.* 1980. Harper. 1st. 364p. F3. $15.00

TUROW, Scott. *Burden of Proof.* 1990. Franklin Lib. 1st. sgn. full leather. F. Q1. $75.00

TUROW, Scott. *Burden of Proof.* 1990. FSG. F/dj. P3. $25.00

TUROW, Scott. *Presumed Innocent.* 1987. FSG. 1st. author's 1st novel. F/F. D10. $60.00

TUROW, Scott. *Presumed Innocent.* 1987. FSG. 1st. author's 1st novel. VG+/dj. N4. $35.00

TURTLEDOVE, Harry. *Agent of Byzantium.* 1987. 1st. F/F. M19. $35.00

TURTLEDOVE, Harry. *Different Flesh.* 1988. Congdon Weed. 1st. VG/dj. P3. $17.00

TUSKA, Jon. *Films of Mae West.* 1973. Citadel. 1st. VG/dj. P3. $20.00

TUTE, Warren. *Tarnham Connection.* 1971. Dent. 1st. NF/dj. P3. $22.00

TUTTLE, Lisa. *Gabriel.* 1987. Severn. 1st. F/dj. P3. $25.00

TUTTLE, Margaretta. *Feet of Clay.* 1923. Grosset Dunlap. photoplay ed. 368p. VG/dj. M20. $20.00

TUTTLE, S.B. *Miniature Motors for Space Instruments.* 1966. Pasadena. sbdg. K5. $20.00

TUTTLE, William M. *Race Riot: Chicago in Red Summer of 1919.* 1970. Bantam. VG/VG. V4. $17.50

TWAIN, Mark; see Clemens, Samuel L.

TWEED, Thomas F. *Destiny's Man.* 1935. Farrar. 1st. VG/dj. M2. $30.00

TWENHOFEL, W.H. *Principles of Sedimentation.* 1950. McGraw Hill. 2nd. 673p. cloth. VG. D8. $30.00

TWICHELL, Heath. *Northwest Epic: Buildings of the Alaska Highway.* 1992. NY. St Martin. 8vo. 368p. map ep. half cloth. P4. $35.00

TWOMBLY, Wells. *200 Years of Sport in America.* 1976. McGraw Hill. later prt. ils. VG+/dj. P8. $30.00

TYCKARE, Tre. *Lore of Ships.* 1963. NY. HRW. ils. 276p. bl cloth. VG/dj. P4. $95.00

TYLER, Anne. *Accidental Tourist.* 1985. Knopf. 1st. F/F. from $45 to $65.00

TYLER, Anne. *Accidental Tourist.* 1985. Knopf. 1st. sgn. F/F. D10. $90.00

TYLER, Anne. *Breathing Lessons.* 1988. Knopf. 1st. F/F. from $30 to $40.00

TYLER, Anne. *Breathing Lessons.* 1988. Knopf. 1st. sgn. F/F. A23. $46.00

TYLER, Anne. *Celestial Navigation.* 1974. Knopf. 1st. F/NF. M25. $150.00

TYLER, Anne. *Dinner at the Homesick Restaurant.* 1982. Knopf. ARC. sgn. author's 9th novel. F/F. D10. $125.00

TYLER, Anne. *Dinner at the Homesick Restaurant.* 1982. Knopf. 1st. F/F. T11. $80.00

TYLER, Anne. *Dinner at the Homesick Restaurant.* 1982. Knopf. 1st. NF/F. H11. $75.00

TYLER, Anne. *Earthly Possessions.* 1977. Knopf. 1st. NF/NF. T11. $125.00

TYLER, Anne. *Earthly Possessions.* 1977. Knopf. 1st. sgn. NF/NF. R14. $225.00

TYLER, Anne. *If Morning Ever Comes.* 1964. Knopf. 1st. 1/4000. author's 1st novel. F/F. L3. $1,850.00

TYLER, Anne. *Morgan's Passing.* 1980. Knopf. 1st. F/clip. M25. $60.00

TYLER, Anne. *Morgan's Passing.* 1980. Knopf. 1st. F/F. B3. $75.00

TYLER, Anne. *Saint Maybe.* 1991. Knopf. 1st. F/F. T11. $40.00

TYLER, Anne. *Searching for Caleb.* 1976. Knopf. 1st. F/F. B4. $450.00

TYLER, Anne. *Slipping-Down Life.* 1983. Severn House. 1st. F/F. T11. $125.00

TYLER, Anne. *Tin Can Tree.* 1966. Macmillan. 1st Eng. F/F. B4. $750.00

TYLER, David Budlong. *Bay & River Delaware, a Pictorial History.* 1955. Cornell Maritime. 1st. 344p. F/G. H1. $30.00

TYLER, David Budlong. *Steam Conquers the Atlantic.* 1939. NY. Appleton Century. 1st. ils. 425p. VG/dj. K3. $35.00

TYLER, J.E.A. *New Tolkien Companion.* 1979. St Martin. 1st. F/dj. M2. $15.00

TYLER, M.L. *Anne Boleyn, a Tragedy in Six Acts.* 1884. London. Kegan Paul. 12mo. 102p. gilt gr cloth. VG. T10. $50.00

TYLER, Martin. *Olympics 1984.* 1984. Phillips. 1st. ils. F/VG+. P8. $10.00

TYLER, Parker. *Three Faces of the Film.* 1960. NY. Yoseloff. 150p. dj. A17. $15.00

TYLER, Ron. *Alfred Jacob Miller: Artist on the Oregon Trail.* 1982. Ft Worth, TX. Amon Carter Mus. 1st. 4to. 480p. F/F. T10. $45.00

TYMN, Marshall B. *Year's Scholarship in Science Fiction: 1972-1975.* 1979. Kent State. VG. P3. $15.00

TYNAN, Kathleen. *Agatha.* 1978. Ballantine. 1st. VG/dj. P3. $18.00

TYREE, M. *Housekeeping in Old Virginia.* (1879). rpt. VG. E6. $20.00

TYRON, Thomas. *Night of the Moonbow.* 1989. Knopf. 1st. F/F. B4. $45.00

TYRRELL, J.W. *Across the Sub-Arctics of Canada.* (1908). Toronto. Brigs. 3rd revised/enlarged. photos. 280p. cloth. VG. M12. $125.00

TYSON, Ian. *Ian Tyson, I Never Sold My Saddle.* 1994. Gibbs Smith. dj. A19. $23.00

TYSON, Martha E. *Bannecker, the African-American Astronomer.* 1884. Phil. Friends Book Assn. 1st. 12mo. 72p. cloth. F. M1. $250.00

TYSSOT DE PATOT, Simon. *Voyages et Avantures de Jacques Masse.* 1710. Bordeaux. L'Aveugle. 8vo. calf. R12. $600.00

UCCELLO, Linda. *Death of a Renaissance Man.* 1986. St Martin. 1st. NF/dj. P3. $18.00

UDEALL, D.H. *Practice of Veterinary Medicine.* 1954. Ithaca. self pub. VG. O3. $25.00

UDY, M.J. *Chromium Vol I: Chemistry of Chromium & Its Compounds...* 1956. Reinhold. 433p. cloth. VG. D8. $30.00

UEBERROTH, Peter. *Made in America.* 1985. Morrow. 1st. NF/VG. W2. $25.00

UEMATSU & WALKER. *Manual of Echoencephalography.* 1971. Baltimore. 1st. 149p. A13. $125.00

UGARTE, Michael. *Shifting Ground: Spanish Civil War Exile Literature.* 1989. Duke. 1st. as new/dj. V4. $15.00

UHNAK, Dorothy. *False Witness.* 1981. S&S. 1st. VG/dj. P3. $10.00

ULANOV, Ann Belford. *Feminine in Jungian Psychology & Christian Theology.* 1971. Northwestern. 2nd. 8vo. 347p. cream cloth. F. H1. $25.00

ULANOV, Barry. *Incredible Crosby.* 1948. NY. 1st. 336p. VG/dj. B5. $35.00

ULLMANN, Alex. *Afghanistan.* 1991. Ticknor. 1st. author's 1st book. F/F. H11. $20.00

ULLMANN, Walter. *Medieval Idea of Law, As Represented by Lucas de Penna...* 1969 (1946). NY. Barnes Noble. facsimile. M11. $85.00

ULLOM. *Folklore of the North American Indians.* 1969. ils. 136p. F. A4. $55.00

ULLYETT, Kennth. *British Clocks & Clockmakers.* 1987. London. Bracken. 8vo. 8 mc pl/24 b&w ils. 48p. NF. K3. $10.00

ULPH, Owen. *Leather Throne.* 1984. Dream Garden. 1st. sgn. F/F. A18. $50.00

ULRICH, Paul. *Great Mysteries of Vanished Civilizations.* nd. Pleasant Valley Pr. VG. P3. $25.00

ULRICK, Peter. *Brief Sketch of Real Lancasterian System of Education.* (1818). Baltimore. Prt for Author. 1st. 8vo. 24p. M1. $225.00

UMLAND & UMLAND. *Use of Arthurian Legend in Hollywood Film.* 1996. Greenwood. F/sans. P3. $55.00

UNDERBRINK, R.L. *Destination Corregidor.* 1971. MD. ils. 240p. VG/VG. S16. $23.50

UNDERHILL, Harold A. *Jamaica White: Story of the Witch of Rose Hall.* 1968. London. WH Allen. 1st. 256p. NF/NF. B4. $50.00

UNDERHILL, Harold A. *Masting & Rigging: Clipper Ship & Ocean Carrier.* 1976. Glasgow. Brn, Son & Ferguson. rpt. 300p. gr cloth. NF. P4. $55.00

UNDERHILL, J. *Mineral Land Surveying.* 1922. John Wiley. 3rd. 237p. G. D8. $25.00

UNDERWOOD, John. *Spoiled Sport.* 1984. Little Brn. 1st. 287p. NF/NF. W2. $20.00

UNDERWOOD, Kathleen. *Town Building on the Colorado Front.* 1987R. Albquerque. photos. dj. A19. $30.00

UNDERWOOD, L.H. *Fifteen Years Among the Top-Knots or Life in Korea.* 1904. NY. Am Tract Soc. 1st. 271p. VG. W3. $65.00

UNDERWOOD, Michael. *Clear Case of Suicide.* 1980. St Martin. 1st. 190p. red brd. as new/dj. H1. $18.00

UNDERWOOD, Michael. *Goddess of Death.* 1982. St Martin. 1st. VG/dj. P3. $18.00

UNDERWOOD, Peter. *Haunted London.* 1974. Harrap. 2nd. VG. P3. $15.00

UNDERWOOD, Peter. *Vampire's Bedside Companion.* 1975. London. 1st. VG/dj. M2. $50.00

UNDERWOOD, R.S. *Jaunts Into Space.* 1935. Boston. Christopher Pub. 8vo. 79p. VG/dj. K5. $20.00

UNDERWOOD, Tim. *Bare Bones.* 1988. McGraw Hill. 1st. F/dj. P3. $18.00

UNDSET, Sigrid. *Catherine of Sienna.* 1954. Sheed Ward. 1st. F/VG. M19. $35.00

UNGER, Douglas. *El Yanqui.* 1986. Harper Row. 1st. F/F. A20. $30.00

UNGER, Douglas. *Leaving the Land.* 1984. Harper Row. 1st. F/F. A20. $35.00

UNGERER, Tomi. *Hat.* nd (1970). Parents Magazine. possible 1st. VG+/sans. C14. $10.00

UNGERER, Tomi. *Mellop's Go Flying.* 1957. Harper. presumed 1st. ils. obl 4to. pict brd. VG+. M5. $40.00

UNGERER, Tomi. *Orlando the Brave Vulture.* 1966. Harper Row. probable 1st. 4to. 32p. VG/G+. P2. $35.00

UNGERER, Tomi. *Slow Agony.* 1983. Zurich. Diogenes. sm folio. F/F. C8. $75.00

UNITAS, Johnny. *Improving Health & Performance in the Athlete.* 1979. Prentice Hall. 1st. F/VG. P8. $12.50

UNITAS, Johnny. *Pro Quarterback: My Own Story.* 1965. S&S. 1st. photos. VG+/G. P8. $30.00

UNITED STATES EMBASSY. *El Cookbook by the Embassy Women's Group.* 1971. np. Eng/Spanish text. 276p. sbdg. B10. $15.00

UNITT & UNITT. *American & Canadian Goblets, Vol 2.* 1974. Peterborough, Ont. Clock House. 1st. 1/2000. 8vo. F/VG. H1. $65.00

UNSWORTH, Barry. *Mooncranker's Gift.* 1974. Houghton Mifflin. 1st Am. F/NF. M23. $45.00

UNWIN, Charles W.J. *Gladioli & Dahlias.* 1951 (1949). London. photos. 125p. dj. B26. $14.00

UPCHURCH, Boyd. *Slave Stealer.* 1968. Weybright Talley. 1st. VG/dj. P3. $20.00

UPDIKE, John. *Assorted Prose.* 1965. Knopf. 1st. sgn. F/NF. B4. $250.00

UPDIKE, John. *Bech Is Back.* 1982. Knopf. 1st. NF/VG. B35. $32.00

UPDIKE, John. *Bech Is Back.* 1982. Knopf. 1st. VG/dj. P3. $20.00

UPDIKE, John. *Bech Is Back.* 1982. Knopf. 1st. 1/500. sgn. blk cloth. F/dj/case. B24. $150.00

UPDIKE, John. *Bottom's Dream.* 1969. Knopf. 1st. oblong 4to. ils Warren Chappell. F/F. B4. $200.00

UPDIKE, John. *Brazil.* 1994. Knopf. 1st. F/F. H11. $35.00

UPDIKE, John. *Carpentered Hen & Other Tame Creatures.* 1958. Harper. 1st. author's 1st book. F/dj. from $750 to $800.00

UPDIKE, John. *Coup.* 1978. Knopf. 1st. F/F. H11. $45.00

UPDIKE, John. *Getting Older.* 1986. Helsinki. Eurographica. 1st. 1/350. sgn. F/stiff wrp/dj. B4. $250.00

UPDIKE, John. *Hugging the Stone.* 1983. NY. Knopf. 1st. F/dj. Q1. $75.00

UPDIKE, John. *Magic Flute.* (1962). Knopf. ils Warren Chappell. unp. VG. T5. $18.00

UPDIKE, John. *Marry Me.* 1976. Knopf. 1st. F/dj. Q1. $40.00

UPDIKE, John. *Midpoint & Other Poems.* 1969. KNopf. 1st. F/F. B2. $35.00

UPDIKE, John. *Music School.* 1966. Knopf. 1st/2nd state. F/VG. M19. $100.00

UPDIKE, John. *Picked-Up Pieces.* 1975. Knopf. 1st. inscr/dtd 1996. VG/VG. A23. $46.00

UPDIKE, John. *Poorhouse Fair.* 1959 (1958). Knopf. 1st. thin 8vo. 185p. quarter orange cloth. F/1st state. H1. $90.00

UPDIKE, John. *Problems & Other Stories.* 1979. Knopf. 1st. F/F. B35. $30.00

UPDIKE, John. *Rabbit, Run.* 1960. Knopf. true 1st (top edge gr). F/NF. A24. $325.00

UPDIKE, John. *Rabbit at Rest.* 1990. Knopf. 1st. F/dj. H11/Q1. $35.00

UPDIKE, John. *Rabbit Is Rich.* 1981. Knopf. 1st. F/F. B35. $35.00

UPDIKE, John. *Rabbit Redux.* 1971. Knopf. 1st. F/dj. H11/Q1. $40.00

UPDIKE, John. *Rabbit Run.* 1977. Franklin Lib. sgn. F. M19. $75.00

UPDIKE, John. *Recent Poems 1986-1990.* 1990. Helsinki. Eurographica. 1st. 1/350. sgn. F/stiff wrp/dj. B4. $200.00

UPDIKE, John. *S.* 1988. Knopf. 1st. F/dj. Q1. $35.00

UPDIKE, John. *S.* 1988. Knopf. 1st. VG+/F. A20. $20.00

UPDIKE, John. *S: A Novel.* 1988. London. Deutsch. 1st Eng. 1/75 (97 total). sgn/#d. F/case. Q1. $275.00

UPDIKE, John. *Trust Me.* 1987. Knopf. 1st. F/dj. Q1. $35.00

UPDIKE, John. *Twelve Terrors of Christmas.* 1994. Gotham Book Mart. 1st trade. sgn. ils/sgn Gorey. F/gr-gray wrp. A11. $75.00

UPDIKE, John. *Witches of Eastwick.* 1984. Franklin Lib. 1st/ltd. sgn. ils Michael Deas. aeg. full leather. F. Q1. $75.00

UPDIKE, John. *Witches of Eastwick.* 1984. Knopf. 1st. F/dj. from $25 to $35.00

UPDIKE, John. *Witches of Eastwick.* 1984. Knopf. 1st. VG/dj. P3. $20.00

UPDYKE, James; see Burnett, W.R.

UPFIELD, Arthur W. *Bachelors of Broken Hill.* 1969. Heinemann. VG/dj. P3. $25.00

UPFIELD, Arthur W. *Battling Prophet.* 1956. London. Heinemann. 1st. sgn. VG/clip. Q1. $200.00

UPFIELD, Arthur W. *Gripped by Drought.* 1990. Dennis McMillan. 1st Am. F/F. M15. $45.00

UPFIELD, Arthur W. *Venom House.* 1952. Doubleday. 1st. VG/G. P3. $25.00

UPFIELD, Arthur W. *Widows of Broome.* 1950. Doubleday. 1st. VG. P3. $30.00

UPHAM & WRIGHT. *Greenland Icefields & Life in the North Atlantic...* 1896. London. Kegan Paul. 1st Eng. ils/5 maps. 407p. P4. $250.00

UPTON, Bertha. *Adventures of Two Dutch Dolls.* 1898. Longman Gr. 1st. ils F Upton/29 full-p pl. pict brd. VG. D1. $350.00

UPTON, R. *Bird in the Hand: Celebrated Falconers of the Past.* 1980. London. Debrett. ils/photos. 160p. F/VG. M12. $60.00

UPTON, Richard. *Ft Custer on the Big Horn 1877-1898...* 1973. Clark. 1st. ils/maps. 316p. VG/VG. J2. $150.00

UPTON, Robert. *Killing in Real Estate.* 1990. Dutton. 1st. NF/dj. P3. $18.00

URE, Stellanie. *Hawk Lady.* 1980. Doubleday. 216p. NF/dj. S15. $12.00

UREN, L.C. *Petroleum Production Engineering, Oil Field Development.* 1946. McGraw Hill. 764p. VG. D8. $15.00

URIS, Leon. *Battle Cry.* 1953. Putnam. 1st. sgn. author's 1st book. NF/NF. L3. $400.00

URIS, Leon. *Haj.* 1984. Doubleday. 1st. F/G. B35. $14.00

URIS, Leon. *Trinity.* 1976. Doubleday. 1st. F/NF. M25. $25.00

URQUHART, Beryl Leslie. *Rhododendron Vol 1.* 1958. Sharpthorne, Sussex. ils/map ep. NF/dj. B26. $145.00

URQUHART, Fred. *Seven Ghosts in Search.* 1983. Wm Kimber. 1st. VG/dj. P3. $20.00

URRUTIA, Miguel. *Development of the Columbian Labor Movement.* 1969. Bantam. 1st. VG/VG. V4. $17.50

USHER, James. *Body of Divinitie; or, Summe & Substance of Christian...* 1645. London. MF for Theo Downes. 1st. 4to. orig bdg. VG. T10. $400.00

USPENSKII, S.M. *Life in High Latitudes: A Study of Bird Life.* 1984. New Delhi. Amerind Pub. 385p. VG/dj. P4. $65.00

USSHER, Arland. *Magic People: Irishman Appraises the Jews.* 1951. NY. Devin Adair. 177p. VG/G. S3. $27.00

UTLEY, Robert M. *Billy the Kid: A Short & Violent Life.* 1989. NE U. 1st. 302p. cloth. VG/dj. M20. $35.00

UTLEY, Robert M. *Frontier Regulars: United States Army & the Indian 1866-91.* 1973. NY. ils. 466p. F/dj. M4. $20.00

UTLEY, Robert M. *Indian Frontier of the American West 1846-1890.* 1984. Albuquerque. dj. A19. $25.00

UTLEY, Robert M. *Last Days of the Sioux Nation.* 1963. Yale. 1st. 336p. VG/VG. J2. $85.00

UTRILLO, Maurice. *Exposition d'Oeuvres Recentes de Maurice Utrillo.* 1938. Fevrier-Mars. ils/photos. D2. $40.00

UTTLEY, Alison. *Christmas at the Rose & Crown.* 1952. London. Heinemann. 1st. ils Katherine Wigglesworth. 72p. pict brd. R5. $100.00

UTTLEY, Alison. *Fuzzypeg Goes to School.* 1938. London. Collins. 1st. ils Margaret Tempest. 12mo. 100p. pict brd. R5. $100.00

UTTLEY, Alison. *Knot Squirrel Tied.* 1937. London. Collins. 1st. ils Margaret Tempest. 12mo. 101p. pict brd. R5. $100.00

UTTLEY, Alison. *Little Gray Rabbitt's Second Painting Book.* ca 1950. London. Collins. 4to. ils Tempest/8 full-pc mc pl. mc pict limp brd. R5. $175.00

UTTLEY, Alison. *Moldy Warp the Mole.* 1940. London. Collins. 1st. ils Margaret Tempest. 87p. pict brd. R5. $75.00

UTTLEY, Alison. *Sam Pig & the Wind.* 1989 (1940). London. Faber. 1st thus. 12mo. unp. orange brd. VG+. T5. $18.00

UTTLEY, Alison. *Sam Pig's Trousers.* 1989 (1940). London. Faber. 1st thus. 12mo. unp. bl glossy brd. VG+. T5. $18.00

UTTLEY, Alison. *Snug & Serna Meet a Queen.* 1950. London. Heinemann. 1st. ils Katherine Wigglesworth. gray-gr pict brd. R5. $100.00

UZANNE, Octave. *L'Art Dans le Decoration Exterior des Livre.* 1898. Paris. ils. 272p. 3-quarter gilt morocco/orig wrp. C6. $500.00

VACHELL, H.A. *Other Side.* nd. London. VG. M2. $15.00

VACHSS, Andrew. *Another Chance To Get It Right.* 1993. Dk Horse Pub. 1st. F/sans. T2. $35.00

VACHSS, Andrew. *Batman the Ultimate Evil.* 1995. Warner. 1st. F/dj. P3. $20.00

VACHSS, Andrew. *Blossom.* 1990. Knopf. 1st. NF/NF. N4. $25.00

VACHSS, Andrew. *Blossom.* 1990. Knopf. 1st. VG/dj. P3. $18.00

VACHSS, Andrew. *Blue Belle.* 1988. Knopf. 1st. F/F. M19. $25.00

VACHSS, Andrew. *Flood.* 1985. DIF. 1st. author's 1st book. F/dj. Q1. $45.00

VACHSS, Andrew. *Flood.* 1985. DIF. 1st. F/NF. M19. $35.00

VACHSS, Andrew. *Flood.* 1985. DIF. 1st. sgn. F/F. M15. $65.00

VACHSS, Andrew. *Strega.* 1987. Knopf. 1st. author's 2nd book. F/F. H11. $40.00

VACHSS, Andrew. *Strega.* 1987. Knopf. 1st. NF/dj. P3. $20.00

VAGTS, Alfred. *Deutschland und die Vereinigten Staaten in der Weltpolitik.* 1935. Macmillan. 2 vol. NF/dj. O7. $125.00

VAGTS, Alfred. *Hitler's Second Army.* 1943. 1st. F/F. E6. $18.00

VAIL. *Voice of the Old Frontier.* 1949. PA U. 503p. NF. A4. $125.00

VAILLANT, George C. *Aztecs of Mexico: Origin, Rise & Fall of Aztec Nation.* 1950. Doubleday. 8vo. 340p. tan cloth. M/F. K7. $35.00

VAINSTEIN, Yaacov. *Cycle of the Jewish Year: Study of Festivals...* 1953. Jerusalem. WZO. Eng/Hebrew text. 152p. G+/poor. S3. $24.00

VAKILI, H. *Spinal Cord.* 1967. NY. 1st. sgn. 360p. A13. $100.00

VALASEK, Joseph. *Introduction to Theoretical & Experimental Optics.* 1949. John Wiley. ARC. 8vo. 454p. VG. K5. $30.00

VALENTINE, Jean. *Ordinary Things.* 1974. FSG. 1st. sgn. author's 3rd book. F/dj. V1. $55.00

VALENTINOV, Nickolai. *Early Years of Lenin: A Translation of Revealing Manuscript.* 1969. MI U. 1st. F/F. V4. $25.00

VALIN, Jonathan. *Day of Wrath.* 1982. Congdon Lattes. 1st. VG/dj. P3. $25.00

VALIN, Jonathan. *Dead Letter.* 1981. Dodd Mead. 1st. VG/dj. P3. $30.00

VALIN, Jonathan. *Extenuating Circumstances.* 1989. Delacorte. 1st. F/dj. P3. $25.00

VALIN, Jonathan. *Life's Work.* 1986. Delacorte. 1st. sgn. F/dj. P3. $30.00

VALIN, Jonathan. *Second Chance.* 1987. Harper Row. 1st. F/dj. P3. $20.00

VALLEJO, Boris. *Fantastic Art of...* nd. BC. VG/dj. M2. $25.00

VALTON, Emilio. *Impresos Mexicanos de Siglo XVI.* 1935. Mexico. Impresa Universitaria. inscr. buckram/prt wrp bdg in. D11. $75.00

VALVERDE, F. *Studies on the Piriform Lobe.* 1965. Cambridge. 132p. gray cloth. VG/dj. G1. $45.00

VAN ALLSBURG, Chris. *Jumanji.* 1981. Houghton Mifflin. 1st. obl folio. F/F. D1. $225.00

VAN ALLSBURG, Chris. *Just a Dream.* 1990. Houghton Mifflin. 1st. 4to. F/VG. P2. $45.00

VAN ALLSBURG, Chris. *Mysteries of Harry Burdick.* 1984. Houghton Mifflin. 1st. 4to. unp. VG/VG. D1. $135.00

VAN ALLSBURG, Chris. *Stranger.* 1986. Houghton Mifflin. 1st. NF/NF. D1. $85.00

VAN ALLSBURG, Chris. *Stranger.* 1986. Houghton Mifflin. 1st. sgn. F/F. B4. $200.00

VAN ALLSBURG, Chris. *Z Was Zapped.* 1987. Houghton Mifflin. 1st. 4to. unp. F/F. D1. $85.00

VAN ANDEL, T.H. *New Views on an Old Planet.* 1990. Cambridge. 324p. F/dj. D8. $30.00

VAN ARSDALE, G.D. *Hydrometallurgy of Base Metals.* 1953. NY. McGraw Hill. 1st. 370p. F. D8. $25.00

VAN ASH, Clay. *Fires of Fu Manchu.* 1987. Harper. 1st. F/dj. M2. $27.00

VAN CAENEGEM, R.C. *Birth of the English Common Law.* 1973. Cambridge. M11. $65.00

VAN CAENEGEM, R.C. *Law, History, the Low Countries, Europe...* 1994. London. Hambledon. 14 collected essays. M11. $50.00

VAN DE POLL, Willem. *Surinam.* 1951. Hague, Netherlands. 1st. 199p. F3. $15.00

VAN DE WATER, Frederic F. *Glory Hunter: Life of General Custer.* 1934. Indianapolis. 1st. 394p. bl cloth. dj. B18. $95.00

VAN DE WATER, Frederic F. *In Defense of Worms.* 1949. NY. DSP. stated 1st. 182p. NF/VG. H7. $15.00

VAN DE WATER, Frederic F. *Lake Champlain & Lake George.* 1946. Indianapolis. 1st. sgn. VG/dj. B5. $45.00

VAN DE WETTERING, Janwillem. *Blond Baboon.* 1978. Houghton Mifflin. 1st. VG/dj. P3. $20.00

VAN DER ELSKEN, Ed. *Sweet Life.* nd. NY. Abrams. photos. 180p. cloth. dj. D11. $150.00

VAN DER POST, Laurens. *Flamingo Feather.* 1955. London. Hogarth. 1st. NF/clip. Q1. $75.00

VAN DER SLEEN, W.G.N. *Four Months' Camping in the Himalayas.* 1929. London. ils/photos. 213p. VG. M12. $95.00

VAN DERSAL, W. *Native Woody Plants of the US: Their Erosion Control...* 1938. USDA. ils/44 pl/2 fld pocket maps. 362p. VG+. M12. $27.50

VAN DEVENTER, Fred. *Parade to Glory: Story of Shriners & Their Hospitals...* 1959. NY. Morrow. 1st. F/poor. T12. $25.00

VAN DINE, S.S. *Benson Murder Case.* 1928. Scribner. VG. P3. $20.00

VAN DINE, S.S. *Canary Murder Case.* nd. Grosset Dunlap. VG/dj. P3. $23.00

VAN DINE, S.S. *Canary Murder Case.* 1927. Scribner. 1st. VG/dj. M25. $25.00

VAN DINE, S.S. *Garden Murder Case.* 1935. Scribner. 1st. VG/dj. P3. $50.00

VAN DINE, S.S. *Greene Murder Case.* 1928. Scribner. 1st. VG. P3. $25.00

VAN DINE, S.S. *Scarab Murder Case.* 1930. Scribner. 1st. G. P3. $30.00

VAN DINE, S.S. *Scarab Murder Case.* 1930. Scribner. 1st. VG/dj. Q1. $200.00

VAN DOREN, Carl. *Benjamin Franklin's Autobiographical Writings.* 1945. Viking. 1st. 810p. VG/dj. H1. $16.00

VAN DOREN, Carl. *Jane Mecom, the Favorite Sister of Benjamin Franklin...* 1950. Viking. 1st. 15 pl. 255p. F/VG. H1. $18.00

VAN DOREN, Carl. *Mutiny in January.* 1943. Viking. 1st. 288p. VG/dj. M20. $30.00

VAN DOREN, Carl. *Secret History of American Revolution.* 1941. Viking. 1st trade. sgn. 534p. VG/dj. M20. $45.00

VAN DOREN, Carl. *Sinclair Lewis: A Biographical Sketch.* 1933. Doubleday Doran. 1st. 205p. cloth. VG/dj. M20. $125.00

VAN DOREN STERN, Philip. *Confederate Navy: A Pictorial History.* 1962. Doubleday. 4to. ils. 252p. dj. T7. $50.00

VAN DYKE, Henry. *Blue Fowler.* 1902. 1st. ils Howard Pyle. VG. B15. $75.00

VAN DYKE, Henry. *First Christmas Tree.* 1897. Scribner. 1st. ils Howard Pyle. teg. VG+. B15. $175.00

VAN DYKE, Henry. *White Bees & Other Poems.* 1909. Scribner. 1st. sm 8vo. 105p. gilt gr cloth. F. H1. $22.50

VAN DYKE, Theodore S. *Flirtation Camp; or, Rifle, Rod & Gun Club in California.* 1881. NY. Fords Howard Hulbert. 1st. 299p. dk gr cloth. VG. K7. $85.00

VAN GIESON, Judith. *Lies That Bind.* 1993. Harper Collins. 1st. sgn. F/F. A20. $30.00

VAN GIESON, Judith. *Other Side of Death.* 1991. Harper Collins. 1st. sgn. author's 3rd book. F/dj. A24. $75.00

VAN GIESON, Judith. *Raptor.* 1990. Harper Row. 1st. author's 2nd book. F/F. H11. $100.00

VAN GIESON, Judith. *Raptor.* 1990. Harper Row. 1st. sgn. author's 2nd book. F/F. from $135 to $150.00

VAN GULIK, Robert. *Chinese Gold Murders.* 1983. Harper Row. VG/dj. P3. $20.00

VAN GULIK, Robert. *Chinese Lake Murders.* 1960. Harper. 1st Am. NF/dj. M25. $75.00

VAN GULIK, Robert. *Necklace & Calbash.* 1967. Scribner. ils. F/NF. W3. $58.00

VAN GULIK, Robert. *Poets & Murder.* 1968. Scribner. 1st. NF/NF. N4. $65.00

VAN GYTENBEEK, R.P. *Way of a Trout.* 1972. Phil. 1st. 146p. F/dj. A17. $15.00

VAN HINTE, J.E. *Proceedings of 2nd West African Micropaleontological...* 1966. Leiden. EJ Brill. 294p. F/dj. D8. $30.00

VAN HOOSEN, Bertha. *Scopolamine-Morphine Anaesthesia.* 1915. Chicago. 1st. inscr. 216p. A13. $300.00

VAN KLEFFENS, E.N. *Hispanic Law Until the End of the Middle Ages...* 1968. Edinburgh. M11. $75.00

VAN LAREN, A.J. *Succulents Other Than Cacti.* 1934. Los Angeles. sgn John Thomas Howell. ils/woodcut. NF. B26. $125.00

VAN LAREN, A.J. *Vetplanten.* 1932. Zaandam. Dutch text. ils. 4to. VG+. B26. $60.00

VAN LOON, Gerard. *Story of Hendrick Willem VanLoon.* 1972. ils. 410p. F/F. A4. $65.00

VAN LOON, Hendrick Willem. *Christmas Carols.* (1937). S&S. music arranged by Grace Castagnetta. VG. B15. $75.00

VAN LOON, Hendrick William. *Van Loon's Geography.* 1932. S&S. 525p. G. D8. $12.00

VAN LOON, Hendrik Willem. *Invasion.* 1940. Harcourt Brace. 1st. F/dj. M2. $32.00

VAN LOON, Hendrik Willem. *My School Books.* 1939. 1st. 1939 NY World's Fair premium. pict brd. VG+. S13. $20.00

VAN LOON, Hendrik Willem. *Story of Mankind.* 1922 (1921). Boni Liveright. 7th. 8 mc pl/ils. bl cloth/pict label. G. T5. $30.00

VAN LUSTBADER, Eric. *Miko.* 1984. Villard. 1st. NF/dj. P3/W2. $30.00

VAN LUSTBADER, Eric. *Ninja.* 1980. Evans. 1st. F/F. N4. $35.00

VAN LUSTBADER, Eric. *Ninja.* 1980. Villard. 1st. NF/VG. W2. $30.00

VAN LUSTBADER, Eric. *Sirens.* 1981. NY. Evans. 1st. F/G. T12. $20.00

VAN LUSTBADER, Eric. *Zero.* 1988. Random. 1st. F/F. W2. $40.00

VAN NESS, Martha. *Cacti & Succulents Indoors & Outdoors.* 1971. NY. sgn. ils/drawings/photos. 112p. VG/dj. B26. $12.50

VAN NOSTRAND, Jeanne. *Edward Vischer's Drawings of the California Missions...* 1982. BC of CA. 1/600. 44 mc pl. gilt brn cloth. F. R3. $225.00

VAN NOSTRAND, Jeanne. *Pictorial & Narrative History of Monterey...1770-1847.* 1970. John Howell. 1st/only. lg 4to. 77p. F/dj. K7. $85.00

VAN NOSTRAND, Jeanne. *1st Hundred Years of Painting in California 1775-1875.* 1980. John Howell. 4to. ils. gilt bl cloth. F. R3. $125.00

VAN NUYS, Laura Bower. *Family Band.* 1961. Lincoln, NE. sgn. A19. $30.00

VAN PAASSEN, Pierre. *Why Jesus Died.* 1949. NY. Dial. 283p. VG. S3. $23.00

VAN PRAAG, Herman M. *Handbook of Biological Psychiatry in Six Parts.* 1980. NY. Marcel Dekker. 383p. prt brd. G1. $50.00

VAN RJNDT, Philippe. *Blueprint.* 1977. Putnam. 1st. VG/dj. P3. $18.00

VAN RJNDT, Philippe. *Tetramachus Collection.* 1976. Lester Orpen. 1st. VG/dj. P3. $20.00

VAN ROOTEN, Luis d'Antin. *Floriculturist's Vade-Mecum of Exotic & Recondite Plants...* 1973. NY. 126p. dj. B26. $15.00

VAN SCYOC, Sydney. *Cloudcry.* 1977. Putnam. 1st. F/dj. M2. $15.00

VAN SCYOC, Sydney. *Star Mother.* 1976. Berkley. 1st. VG. M2. $10.00

VAN SICKLE, D. *Montana Gothic.* 1979. HBJ. 1st. VG/dj. P3. $20.00

VAN SICKLE, Emogene. *Old York Road & Its Stagecoach Days.* 1960. Flemington. DH Moreau. VG/VG. O3. $68.00

VAN SINDEREN, A. *Foundation Stones.* 1952. 1/700. fld ils. VG. K3. $30.00

VAN SLINGERLAND, Peter. *Something Terrible Has Happened.* 1966. Harper Row. 8vo. blk cloth. VG/dj. P4. $30.00

VAN STOCKUM, Hilda. *Kersti & Saint Nicholas.* 1940. Viking. 1st. 4to. 71p. VG. P2. $30.00

VAN STOCKUM, Hilda. *Mitchells.* 1945. Viking. 1st. 246p. VG/VG. P2. $35.00

VAN THAL, Herbert. *James Agate: An Anthology.* 1961. Hill Wang. 1st. VG/G. P3. $25.00

VAN URK, J. Blan. *Horse, the Valley & the Chagrin Valley Hunt.* 1947. NY. Richard Ellis. 1/700. F/dj/worn case. O3. $225.00

VAN URK, J. Blan. *Little Charlie the Fox.* 1977. Wilmington. Serendipity. 1/1000. VG/VG. O3. $300.00

VAN VECHTEN, Carl. *Nigger Heaven.* 1928. NY. blk cloth. VG. B14. $60.00

VAN VOGT, A.E. *Away & Beyond.* 1952. Pellegrini Cudahy. 1st. VG/dj. P3. $45.00

VAN VOGT, A.E. *Book of Ptath.* 1947. Fantasy. 1st. sgn/#d. F/VG. P3. $250.00

VAN VOGT, A.E. *Book of Ptath.* 1975. Garland. F. M2. $20.00

VAN VOGT, A.E. *Destination: Universe.* 1952. Pellegrini Cudahy. 1st. F/NF. P3. $45.00

VAN VOGT, A.E. *Empire of the Atom.* 1957. SFBC. F/dj. M2. $35.00

VAN VOGT, A.E. *Lan.* 1975. Garland. F. M2. $20.00

VAN VOGT, A.E. *Masters of Time.* 1950. Fantasy. 1st. sgn/#d. F/dj. P3. $175.00

VAN VOGT, A.E. *Slan.* 1951. S&S. 1st. F/VG. P3. $75.00

VAN VOGT, A.E. *Van Vogt Omnibus 2.* 1971. Sidgwick Jackson. 1st. F/dj. P3. $22.00

VAN VOGT, A.E. *Violent Man.* 1962. FSC. 1st. VG/dj. P3. $40.00

VAN VOGT, A.E. *Voyage of the Space Beagle.* 1950. S&S. 1st. VG/dj. P3. $125.00

VAN VOGT, A.E. *Weapon Makers.* 1952. Greenberg. VG/dj. P3. $55.00

VAN VOGT, A.E. *Weapon Makers.* 1952. Greenberg. 1st. F/dj. M2. $70.00

VAN VOGT, A.E. *Weapon Shops of Isher.* 1951. Greenberg. 1st. F/dj. M2. $50.00

VAN VOGT, A.E. *World of Null-A.* 1948. S&S. 1st. NF/dj. M2. $50.00

VAN VOGT, A.E. *World of Null-A.* 1950. Grosset Dunlap. F/dj. P3. $75.00

VAN VORIS, Jacqueline. *Carrie Chapman Catt: A Public Life.* 1987. Feminist Pr. 1st. as new. V4. $10.00

VAN WORMER, Joe. *There's a Marmot on the Telephone.* 1974. Caldwell. sgn pres. ils/photos. 117p. F/F. M12. $17.50

VAN WORMER, Joe. *World of the Black Bear.* 1966. Lippincott. ils. 163p. F/VG. S15. $11.00

VANCE, Jack. *Big Planet.* 1957. Avalon. 1st. F/NF. P3. $250.00

VANCE, Jack. *Ecce & Old Earth.* 1991. Tor. 1st. NF/dj. P3. $22.00

VANCE, Jack. *Palace of Love.* 1968. Dobson. 1st. VG/dj. P3. $40.00

VANCE, Jack. *Throy.* 1992. Underwood Miller. 1st. sgn/#d. F/F. P3. $75.00

VANCE, Louis Joseph. *Street of Strange Faces.* 1939. Caxton. 1st. VG. P3. $30.00

VANCE, Rowland. *They Made Me a Leatherneck.* 1943. NY. 1st. 175p. VG/VG. S16. $35.00

VANCE, Samuel. *Couragous & the Proud: A Black Man in the White Man's Army.* 1970. Norton. 1st. 166p. F/F. B4. $150.00

VANCE, Sutton. *Southward Bound.* 1930. Minton Balch. 1st. VG. M2. $40.00

VANCOUVER, G. *Voyage of Discovery to the North Pacific Ocean...* 1984. London. 4 vol. 46 pl/10 maps. F/dj. M4. $85.00

VANDE VELDE, Vivian. *User Unfriendly.* 1991. HBJ. 1st. F/dj. P3. $17.00

VANDENBELD, John. *Nature of Australia: A Portrait of Island Continent.* 1988. NY. Facts on File. 1st. 292p. NF/dj. B1/P4. $30.00

VANDENBERG, Philipp. *Curse of the Pharoahs.* 1975. Lippincott. dj. A18. $25.00

VANDENBURGH, Jane. *Failure to Zigzag.* 1989. Northpoint. 1st. F/F. B4. $45.00

VANDER WALL, Stephen. *Food Hoarding in Animals.* 1990. Chicago. 445p. F. S15. $17.50

VANDERBILT, Cornelius Jr. *Ranches & Ranch Life in America.* 1968. Crown. dj. A19. $35.00

VANDERDECKEN, William Cooper. *Yachts & Yachting.* 1979 (1873). London. facsimile. 47 pl. 391p. dj. T7. $65.00

VANDERHAEGE, Guy. *Homesick.* 1989. Toronto. 1st Canadian. sgn. F/NF. B3. $60.00

VANDERHAEGE, Guy. *Homesick.* 1990. Ticknor Fields. 1st. F/F. A20. $20.00

VANDERHAEGE, Guy. *My Present Age.* 1985. Ticknor Fields. 1st. F/F. A20. $25.00

VANN, Richard T. *Social Development of English Quakerism, 1655-1755.* 1969. Cambridge. 1st. 259p. VG/dj. V3. $18.00

VARDRE, Leslie. *Nameless Ones.* 1967. John Long. VG/dj. P3. $15.00

VARLEY, John. *Steel Beach.* 1992. Ace/Putnam. 1st. NF/dj. P3. $23.00

VARLEY, John. *Titan.* 1979. Berkeley. 1st. NF/dj. M2. $40.00

VARMA, Devendra P. *Voices From the Vaults.* 1987. Key Porter. 1st. F/dj. P3. $25.00

VARNER & VARNER. *Dogs of the Conquest.* 1983. OK U. 1st. ils. 238p. F/dj. M4. $25.00

VASEY, George. *Grasses of the Pacific Slope.* 1893. GPO. xl. A10. $75.00

VASEY, George. *Grasses of the Southwest.* 1890-91. WA, DC. 2 parts in 1 vol. sgn JM Rusk. 100 pl. newer bdg. VG. B26. $125.00

VASSILIKOS, Vassilis. *Z.* 1968. FSG. 1st Am. F/F. B4. $200.00

VATABLUS, Franciscus. *In hoc Opere Continentvr Totivs Philosophiae Naturalis...* 1533. Paris. Widow of Petit. folio. woodcuts. calf. R12. $1,250.00

VAUGHAN, Beatrice. *Old Cook's Almanac.* 1966. NY. Gramercy. G/dj. A16. $17.50

VAUGHAN, Matthew. *Discretion of Dominick Ayres.* 1980. Linden. 1st. VG/dj. P3. $15.00

VAUGHAN, Norman D. *With Byrd at the Bottom of the World.* 1990. Harrisburg. Stackpole. later prt. ils/map. 196p. M/dj. P4. $40.00

VAUGHN, Agnes. *Akka, Dwarf of Syracuse.* 1940. Longman. 1st. VG. M2. $12.00

VAUX, Patrick. *Shock of Battle.* 1906. Putnam. 1st. VG. M2. $50.00

VAUX, Roberts. *Memoirs of Philadelphia Society for Promoting Agriculture.* 1818. Phil. Warner. 332p. A10. $225.00

VAZ, Edmund W. *Professionalization of Young Hockey Players.* 1982. NE U. 1st. charts/graphs/index. VG+. P8. $15.00

VAZ DE MELLO, Fernando. *Memorial Sobre o Curso dos Rios Pardo, e Mogly...* 1859. Sao Paulo. Imparcial de JR de Azevodo Marques. 1st. 32p. R15. $1,250.00

VAZQUEZ, A.E. *Compendium & Description of the West Indies.* 1942. Smithsonian. 862p. NF. M4. $30.00

VEALL, Donald. *Popular Movement for Law Reform 1640-1660.* 1970. Clarendon. M11. $85.00

VECSEY, George. *Year in the Sun.* 1989. Times. 1st. F/F. P8. $10.00

VEECK, Bill. *Hustler's Handbook.* 1965. NY. 1st. VG/VG. B5. $20.00

VEECK, Bill. *Thirty Tons a Day.* 1972. Viking. 1st. VG/VG. P8. $25.00

VEGSCHEIDER, Sharon. *Another Chance: Hope & Health for the Alcoholic Family.* 1981. Science & Behavior. 256p. VG/dj. B29. $6.50

VELIKOVSKY, Immanuel. *Worlds in Collision.* 1950. Doubleday. VG. M2. $12.00

VENABLE, William Henry. *Cincinnati, a Civic Ode.* 1907. Cincinnati. unp. VG/wrp. B18. $12.50

VENABLES, Bernard. *Baleia! Baleia! Whale Hunters of the Azores.* 1969. NY. Knopf. 16 pl/drawings. 204p. dj. T7. $25.00

VENABLES, Hubert. *Frankenstein Diaries.* 1980. Viking. 1st. VG/dj. P3. $20.00

VENEGAS, Miguel. *Obras Californias del Padre Miguel Venegas, SJ.* 1979. La Paz. Autonoma Baja California Sur. 5 vol+supp. as new. O7. $295.00

VENET, Wendy Hamand. *Neither Ballots Nor Bullets: Women Abolitionists...* 1991. VA U. 1st. as new/dj. V4. $15.00

VENNING, Frank D. *Cacti.* 1974. NY. ils. 12mo. red buckram. F. B26. $12.50

VENNING, Hugh. *End.* 1948. Desmond & Stapleton. 1st. F/dj. M2. $25.00

VENTURI, Lionello. *Modern Painters: Goya, Constable, David, Ingres, Delacroix.* 1947. NY/London. Scribner. 1st. ils. 256p. cloth. D2. $45.00

VER BECK, Frank. *Ver Beck's Book of Bears.* 1906. Lippincott. 2nd. 4to. pict cloth. R5. $335.00

VERCORS. *Battle of Silence.* 1960. HRW. 1st. VG/dj. P3. $20.00

VERCORS. *You Shall Know Them.* 1953. Little Brn. 1st. VG. P3. $13.00

VERDELLE, A.J. *Good Negress.* 1995. Algonquin. 1st. sgn. F/F. A23. $50.00

VERGO, Peter. *Blue Rider.* 1977. ils. VG/VG. M17. $20.00

VERLAINE, Paul. *Forty Poems.* 1948. London. Falcon. 1st. F/dj. A17. $15.00

VERLINDEN, Charles. *Beginnings of Modern Colonization.* 1970. Cornell. trans Yvonne Freccero. F/dj. O7. $35.00

VERNAM, G.R. *Rawhide Years: History of the Cattlemen & Cattle Country.* 1976. Garden City. 1st. ils. 227p. F/dj. M4. $15.00

VERNE, Jules. *Adventures in the Land of the Behemoth.* 1874. Sheperd. VG. M2. $200.00

VERNE, Jules. *Captain Antifer.* 1895. Fenno. VG. M2. $125.00

VERNE, Jules. *Desert of Ice.* 1874. Phil. Porter Coates. A19. $65.00

VERNE, Jules. *Jules Verne.* 1978. Octopus. VG/dj. P3. $15.00

VERNE, Jules. *Mysterious Island.* 1959. Baltimore. LEC. 1st thus. 1/1500. ils/sgn EA Wilson. F/case. Q1. $100.00

VERNE, Jules. *Propeller Island.* 1977. Granada. 1st. VG/dj. P3. $20.00

VERNE, Jules. *Secret of the Island.* 1977. JM Dent. 3rd. VG. P3. $30.00

VERNE, Jules. *Tigers & Traitors.* 1959. Arco. F/dj. M2. $30.00

VERNE, Jules. *Twenty Thousand Leagues Under the Sea.* 1956. LA. LEC. 1st thus. 1/1500. ils/sgn EA Wilson. F/case. Q1. $100.00

VERNE, Jules. *Wreck of the Chancellor.* 1875. Boston. Osgood. 1st. NF. M24. $125.00

VERNON, Arthur. *History & Romance of the Horse.* 1930. Boston. 1st. 525p. F/dj. A17. $20.00

VERNON, Judy. *Cousins.* 1985. Memphis. St Luke's Pr. 1st. F/VG. L3. $45.00

VERNON, Max. *In & Out of Florence.* 1910. Holt. 1st. 370p. teg. gr cloth. VG. B22. $7.00

VERRAL, Charles Spain. *Rin Tin Tin & the Hidden Treasure.* 1958. Golden. TVTI. VG. P3. $10.00

VERRILL, A. Hyatt. *Boy's Book of Buccaneers.* 1927. Dodd Mead. G. P3. $12.00

VERRILL, A. Hyatt. *Bridge of Light.* 1950. Fantasy. 1st. sgn/#d. F/NF. P3. $100.00

VERRILL, A. Hyatt. *Golden City.* 1916. Duffield. 1st. VG. M2. $50.00

VERRILL, A. Hyatt. *Old Civilizations of the New World.* 1942. Home Lib. F/dj. M2. $35.00

VERRILL, A. Hyatt. *Real Story of the Pirate.* 1923. Appleton. 1st. VG. M2. $50.00

VERRILL, A. Hyatt. *Strange Customs, Manners & Beliefs.* 1946. LC Page. 1st imp. ils. 302p. F/G. H1. $17.50

VERSCHAFFELT, Alexandre. *New Iconography of the Camellias.* 1945. Avery Island, LA. trans EA McIhenny. gilt maroon cloth. VG. B26. $45.00

VERTREGT, M. *Principles of Astronautics.* 1960. Amsterdam. Elsevier. 8vo. 221p. VG/dj. K5. $20.00

VERY, Jones. *Essays & Poems.* 1839. Little Brn. 1st. brn cloth/label. VG. M24. $350.00

VERY, Lydia. *Poems.* 1856. Andover. WF Draper. 1st. 12mo. 22p. cloth. M1. $150.00

VESEY, Elizabeth. *Conversations; or, The Bas Bleu.* 1977. Harvard. Sinehour. 1/250. tall 4to. 75p. F/dj. H13. $95.00

VESTAL, Stanley. *Jim Bridger.* 1946. Morrow. 1st. NF/VG+. T11. $65.00

VESTAL, Stanley. *Queen of Cowtowns, Dodge City.* 1952. Harper. 1st. dj. A18. $50.00

VESTAL, Stanley. *Sitting Bull.* 1932. Houghton Mifflin. 1st. 350p. VG/VG. J2. $225.00

VICKER, Ray. *Kingdom of Oil: The Middle East.* 1974. Scribner. 264p. VG/dj. W1. $22.00

VICKERS, Roy. *Best Police Stories.* 1966. Faber. 1st. VG. P3. $15.00

VICKERS, Roy. *Some Like Them Dead.* 1960. Hodder Stoughton. 1st. sgn by contributors. F/NF. M15. $350.00

VICTOR, Orville J. *History of American Conspiracies: A Record of Treason...* 1863. NY. James D Torrey. 1st. VG. B2. $250.00

VIDAL, Gore. *Burr.* 1973. Random. 1st. F/F. B35. $25.00

VIDAL, Gore. *Creation.* 1981. Random. 1st. F/F. M23. $30.00

VIDAL, Gore. *Empire.* 1987. Random. 1st. NF/VG. P3. $25.00

VIDAL, Gore. *Evening With Richard Nixon.* 1972. Random. 1st. F/F. B35. $28.00

VIDAL, Gore. *Hollywood.* 1990. Random. 1/200. sgn. F/case. B35. $70.00

VIDAL, Gore. *Kalki.* 1978. Random. 1st. NF/VG+. N4. $35.00

VIDAL, Gore. *Kalki.* 1978. Random. 1st. VG/dj. P3. $22.00

VIDAL, Gore. *Live From Golgotha.* Random. F/F. B35. $18.00

VIDAL, Gore. *Myron.* 1974. Random. 1st. NF/VG. A20. $20.00

VIDAL, Gore. *Palimpsest: A Memoir.* 1985. Random. 1st. F/F. T12. $40.00

VIDAL, Gore. *Two Sisters.* 1970. Little Brn. 1st. VG/dj. P3. $30.00

VIDOR, King. *Tree Is a Tree.* 1953. Harcourt Brace. photos. rpr dj. C9. $75.00

VIERECK, Leslie. *Alaska Trees & Shrubs.* 1972. GPO. USDA Handbook 40. 265p. w/map. VG. S15. $12.00

VIERTEL, Peter. *White Hunter, Black Heart.* 1953. Doubleday. 1st. F/F. B4. $150.00

VIETZEN, Raymond. *Ancient Man in Northern Ohio.* 1941. Lorain, OH. 1st. sgn. 159p. VG. B5. $35.00

VIGGIANI, Guy. *Hollow Mountains.* 1986. Epimetheus. 1st. F/dj. M2. $15.00

VIGNOLES, C. *Observations Upon the Floridas.* 1977. FL U. Bicentennial series. 184p. F. M4. $20.00

VIGOR, Simon. *Actes de la Dispute...Tenue a Paris, es Mois de Iuillet...* 1566. Strasbourg. Estiard. 8vo. overlapping vellum. R12. $485.00

VIGOUREUX & WILCOX. *Cook It the French Way.* 1940. Roy. torn dj. B10. $15.00

VILDRAC, Charles. *Rose Island.* 1957. Lee Shepard. probable 1st. ils Edy Legrand. VG/G+. T5. $25.00

VILLA, Jose Garcia. *Selected Poems & New.* 1958. NY. McDowell Oolensky. 1st. 236p. M/VG+. P1. $20.00

VILLANO, Anthony. *Brick Agent.* 1977. Quadrangle. 1st. VG. P3. $15.00

VILLIERS, Alan. *Captain James Cook.* 1967. NY. Scribner. 307p. bl cloth. VG/dj. P4. $40.00

VILLIERS, Alan. *Cutty Sark.* 1957. Hodder Stoughton. ils. 96p. dj. T7. $28.00

VILNAY, Zev. *Legends of Galilee, Jordan & Sinai: Sacred Land. Vol 3.* 1978. JPS. ils. 407p. VG. S3. $24.00

VINCENT, Frank. *Through & Through the Tropics: 30,000 Miles of Travel...* 1882. NY. 2nd. 304p. G. A17. $25.00

VINCENT, Gabrielle. *Merry Christmas, Ernest & Celestine.* 1983. NY. Greenwillow. 1st Am. F/VG+. C8. $22.50

VINCENT, Leon H. *Bibliotaph & Other People.* 1898. Boston. Houghton Mifflin. 1st. 8vo. 233p. teg. gilt gr cloth. F. T10. $75.00

VINE, Barbara; see Rendell, Ruth.

VINGE, Joan D. *Fireship.* 1978. SFBC. 1st. F/dj. M2. $10.00

VINGE, Joan D. *Phoenix in the Ashes.* 1985. Bluejay. 1st. VG/dj. P3. $20.00

VINGE, Joan D. *Return of the Jedi Storybook.* 1983. St Michael. MTI. VG. P3. $15.00

VINGE, Joan D. *Summer Queen.* 1991. Warner. 1st. Nf/dj. P3. $22.00

VINGE, Joan D. *World's End.* 1984. Bluejay. 1st. VG/dj. P3. $20.00

VINGE, Vernor. *Fire Upon the Deep.* 1992. Tor. 1st. F/dj. M2. $90.00

VINGE, Vernor. *Peace War.* 1984. Bluejay. 1st. F/dj. P3. $20.00

VINGE, Vernor. *Witling.* 1976. Dobson. 1st. F/dj. P3. $35.00

VINOGRADOFF, Paul. *Collected Papers... With a Memoir...* 1963 (1928). London. Wildy. facsimile. M11. $125.00

VINOGRADOFF, Paul. *Essays in Legal History, Read Before International Congress.* 1913. London. gilt gr cloth. M11. $125.00

VINOGRADOFF, Paul. *Roman Law in Medieval Europe.* 1968 (1929). Cambridge. reissue. M11. $65.00

VINSON, James. *Contemporary Novelists.* 1976. St Martin. 2nd. VG/dj. B2. $65.00

VINSON, Peter. *Diagnosis & Treatment of Diseases of the Esophagus.* 1940. Springfield. 1st. 224p. A13. $100.00

VIOLA, Herman J. *After Columbus.* 1990. Orion. 1st. F/dj. P3. $45.00

VIOLA, Herman J. *Exploring the West.* 1987. Smithsonian. 4to. 256p. brn cloth. F/F. F7. $35.00

VIPONT, Elfrida. *Colin Writes to Friends House.* 1946. London. Friends Book Centre. 2nd. V3. $16.00

VIRAMONTES, Helena Maria. *Under the Feet of Jesus.* 1995. Dutton. 1st. sgn. F/F. B3. $40.00

VIRCHOW, Rudolf. *Cellular Pathology As Based Upon Physiological...Histology.* (1860). NY. 1st Am. 544p. A13. $400.00

VIRGIL (MARO, Publius Virgilu) *Ecologues.* 1960. NY. LEC. 1st thus. 1/1500. ils/sgn Marcel Vertes. F/glassine/case. Q1. $125.00

VIRGIL (MARO, Publius Virgilu) *Georgics.* 1952. Verona. LEC. 1st thus. 1/1500. ils/sgn Giovanni Mardersteig. F/dj/case. Q1. $150.00

VISSCHER, William Lightfoot. *Pony Express.* 1946 (1908). Chicago. Chas Powner Co. rpt. w/ephemera. A19. $55.00

VISSER, Margaret. *Much Depends on Dinner.* 1987. Grove. 1st. VG/dj. A16. $10.00

VIZENOR, Gerald Robert. *Empty Swings.* 1967. Minneapolis. Nodin. NF/wrp. B4. $100.00

VIZENOR, Gerald Robert. *Summer in the Spring.* 1965. Minneapolis. Nodin. 1st. 12mo. F/F. L3. $250.00

VIZETELLY, Ernest Alfred. *My Adventures in the Commune.* 1914. Duffield. 1st. 368p. VG+. B2. $125.00

VLADIMOV, Georgi. *Faithful Ruslan.* 1979. S&S. 1st. F/dj. M2. $15.00

VLADISLAV, Jan. *Italian Fairy Tales.* 1971. Hamlyn. VG. P3. $12.00

VLIET, R.G. *Events & Celebrations.* 1966. Viking. 1st. inscr/dtd 1976. author's 1st book. F/F. L3. $200.00

VOGEL, S. *Role of Scent Glands in Pollination.* 1990. New Delhi. 202p. VG/VG. B1. $48.00

VOIGHT, Cynthia. *Dicey's Song.* 1983. Atheneum. 2nd. 8vo. 196p. brn cloth. G. T5. $20.00

VOLBACH, W. Fritz. *Early Decorative Textiles.* 1969. London. Hamlyn. 1st in Eng. 12mo. 71 mc pl. as new/dj. H1. $12.50

VOLKMAN, Hans. *Cleopatra: Study in Politics & Propaganda.* 1958. NY. Sagamore. 1st. 8vo. 244p. missing 4 pl. VG/torn. W1. $12.00

VOLLMANN, William T. *Father & Crows.* 1992. Viking. 1st. F/F. D10. $45.00

VOLLMANN, William T. *Ice-Shirt.* 1990. Viking. 1st. F/F. T11. $40.00

VOLLMANN, William T. *Rainbow Stories.* 1989. Atheneum. ARC/1st Am. sgn. author's 2nd book. F/F. D10. $125.00

VOLLMANN, William T. *Whores for Gloria.* 1991. Pantheon. 1st. sgn. F/F. B3. $45.00

VOLLMANN, William T. *You Bright & Risen Angels.* 1987. Atheneum. 1st Am. author's 1st book. F/F. from $100 to $135.00

VOLLMANN, William T. *13 Stories & 13 Epitaphs.* 1991. Pantheon. 1st. F/F. A20. $35.00

VOLNEY, C.F. *Lectures on History Delivered in the Norman School of Paris.* 1801. Phil. John Conrad. 1st Am. 16mo. 186p. contemporary calf. M1. $250.00

VOLTAIRE. *An Epistle...Upon His Arrival at His Estate...1755.* 1755. London. Dodsley. 1st Eng. 4to. cloth/brd. R12. $225.00

VOLTAIRE. *History of Charles the Twelfth, King of Sweeden.* 1831. Hartford. leather. G+. M17. $50.00

VOLTAIRE. *History of Zadig; or, Destiny.* 1952. Paris. LEC. 1st thus. 1st thus. 1/1500. F/case. Q1. $150.00

VOLTAIRE. *Virgin of Orleans; or, Joan of Arc.* 1965. Alan Swallow. trans Howard Nelson. F/clip. B35. $55.00

VOLTAIRE. *Voltaire Recueil des Particularites Curieuses...* 1781. Porrentruy. Goetschy. 8vo. calf/brd. R12. $225.00

VON BASSEWITZ, Gert. *Peterchens Mondfahrt.* ca 1920s. Berlin. Hermann Kelemme. 10th. ils Bauluschek. 4to. 126p. VG. D1. $75.00

VON BERGMANN, E. *Surgery of the Pelvis & the Genito-Urinary Organs.* 1904. NY. 1st Eng trans. 354 woodcuts/photos. 789p. A13. $50.00

VON BREITSCHWERT, Wilhelm. *Das Wunderbare Bilderbuch.* ca 1890. Stuttgart. Hoffmann. 9th. 12 full-p litho moveables. R5. $1,500.00

VON BULOW, Prince. *Imperial Germany.* Nov 1916. London/NY. new/revised ed. 8vo. 335p. VG. B14. $35.00

VON CHAMISSO, Adelbert. *Voyage Around the World With the Romanzov Exploring...* 1986. Honolulu. 1st thus. 8vo. 375p. NF/dj. P4. $45.00

VON DANIKEN, Erich. *According to the Evidence.* 1977. Souvenir. 1st. VG. P3. $20.00

VON DANIKEN, Erich. *Gods & Their Grand Design.* 1982. Putnam. 1st. F/dj. M2. $12.00

VON DOBSCHUTZ, Ernst. *Influence of the Bible on Civilization.* 1914. NY. 1st. xl Harvard Divinity School. B14. $30.00

VON GASSNER, Paul. *Figure & Dance Skating.* 1949. A&S Pub. 1st. ils/photos. VG. P8. $12.50

VON GOETHE, Johann Wolfgang. *Faust, by Goethe.* 1925. London. Harrap. 1/1000. ils/sgn Harry Clarke. 254p. teg. VG. B24. $350.00

VON GOETHE, Johann Wolfgang. *Gedichte.* 1906. Venice. S Rosen. 78x56mm. 267p. F/prt wrp. B24. $75.00

VON GOETHE, Johann Wolfgang. *Story of Reynard the Fox.* 1954. LEC. 1/1500. ils/sgn Fritz Eichenberg. F/NF case. T10. $75.00

VON HAGEN, Victor. *Golden Man: Quest for El Dorado.* 1974. London. BC. 1st Am. 346p. dj. F3. $20.00

VON HAGEN, Victor. *Highway of the Sun.* 1955. NY. Duell. 1st. 320p. dj. F3. $25.00

VON HAGEN, Victor. *South American Zoo.* 1946. NY. 182p. F/dj. S15. $15.00

VON HAGEN, Victor. *Sun Kingdom of the Aztecs.* 1958. World. 126p. partial dj. F3. $15.00

VON HOFFMAN, Nicholas. *Citizen Cohn.* 1988. Doubleday. 1st. F/F. A20. $20.00

VON HUMBOLT, Alexander. *Cosmos: Sketch of the Physical Description of the Universe.* 1850. Harper. 2 vol. gr cloth. VG. M20. $80.00

VON HUMBOLT, Alexander. *Letters of Alexander Von Humbolt to Varnhagen Von Ense...* 1860. NY. Rudd Carleton. 8vo. 407p. xl. K3. $20.00

VON KARMAN, Theodore. *Wind & Beyond: Theodore Von Karman.* 1967. Boston. Little Brn. 1st. inscr. VG/dj. K3. $20.00

VON LISINGEN, F.W.B. *Pressure Gauge Murder.* 1930. Dutton. VG. P3. $25.00

VON LOESECKE, Harry W. *Bananas: Chemistry, Physiology, Technology.* 1950 (1949). NY. 2nd/revised. ils/51 tables/2 mc pl. 189p. yel cloth. VG/dj. B26. $40.00

VON MANSTEIN, Erich. *Lost Victories.* 1958. Chicago. maps/index. 574p. G. S16. $30.00

VON MEYER, Ernst. *History of Chemistry From Earliest Times to Present Day.* 1898. London. Macmillan. 2nd Eng. 8vo. 631p. xl. K3. $22.00

VON PUCKLER-MUSKAU, Prince. *Hints on Landscape Gardening.* 1917. 1st Am. ils. NF. A15. $300.00

VON RAD, Gerhard. *Genesis.* 1961. Westminster. Old Testament Lib. 434p. G/dj. B29. $13.00

VON REIS ALTSCHUL, S. *Drugs & Foods From Little-Known Plants...* 1973. Harvard. ils. 366p. F/VG. M12. $45.00

VON SACHS, Julius. *Lectures on the Physiology of Plants.* 1887. Oxford. Clarendon. 836p. cloth. A10. $20.00

VON SALDERN, Axel. *Glass 500 BC to AD 1900. The Hans Cohn Collection.* 1980. Mainz on Rhine. Phillipp vonZabern. 288p. cloth. D2. $55.00

VON TRAPP, Maria. *Creation House.* 1972. Carol Stream, IL. 1st. 16 pl. 203p. as new/F. H1. $25.00

VON ULM, Gerith. *Charlie Chaplin, King of Tragedy.* 1940. Caxton. 39 photos. cloth. VG+. C9. $85.00

VON WELANETZ & VON WELANETZ. *Pleasure of Your Company.* 1976. Atheneum. VG/wrp. A16. $20.00

VONNEGUT, Kurt. *Bluebeard.* 1987. Delacorte. 1st. F/dj. H11. $30.00

VONNEGUT, Kurt. *Bluebird.* 1987. Delacorte. ltd. 1/500. sgn/#d. F/case. Q1. $125.00

VONNEGUT, Kurt. *Bluebird.* 1987. Delacorte. 1st. sgn/drawing. VG/VG. A23. $50.00

VONNEGUT, Kurt. *Breakfast of Champions.* 1973. Delacorte. 1st. F/clip. B35. $32.00

VONNEGUT, Kurt. *Deadeye Dick.* 1982. Delacorte. 1st. NF/F. B3. $60.00

VONNEGUT, Kurt. *Deadeye Dick.* 1982. Delacorte. 1st. sgn. VG/VG. A23. $50.00

VONNEGUT, Kurt. *Galapagos.* 1985. Delacorte. 1st trade after Franklin Lib. sgn. NF/F. D10. $65.00

VONNEGUT, Kurt. *Galapagos.* 1985. Delacorte. 1st. F/NF. H11. $30.00

VONNEGUT, Kurt. *Galapagos.* 1985. Delacorte. 1st. sgn. VG/VG. A23. $50.00

VONNEGUT, Kurt. *Galapagos.* 1985. Franklin Lib. sgn. aeg. gilt full leather. F. from $75 to $100.00

VONNEGUT, Kurt. *God Bless You, Mr Rosewater.* 1965. London. Cape. 1st Eng. NF/dj. Q1. $200.00

VONNEGUT, Kurt. *Hocus Pocus.* 1990. Putnam. 1st. VG/dj. P3. $22.00

VONNEGUT, Kurt. *Jailbird.* 1979. Delacorte. 1st. sgn. F/F. D10. $145.00

VONNEGUT, Kurt. *Jailbird.* 1979. Delacorte. 1st. sgn/dtd. VG/VG. A23. $46.00

VONNEGUT, Kurt. *Jailbird.* 1979. Delacorte. 1st. VG/dj. P3. $30.00

VONNEGUT, Kurt. *Palm Sunday.* 1981. Delacorte. 1st. F/dj. P3. $30.00

VONNEGUT, Kurt. *Player Piano.* 1952. Scribner. 1st. inscr. F/VG+. B4. $2,000.00

VONNEGUT, Kurt. *Slapstick.* 1976. Delacorte. ltd. 1/250. sgn. NF. B3. $200.00

VONNEGUT, Kurt. *Slapstick.* 1976. Delacorte. 1st. NF/dj. P3. $40.00

VONNEGUT, Kurt. *Slapstick; or, Lonesome No More!* 1976. London. Cape. 1st Eng. F/dj. Q1. $40.00

VONNEGUT, Kurt. *Slaughterhouse Five.* 1969. Delacorte. 1st. F/NF. B2. $200.00

VONNEGUT, Kurt. *Sun Moon Star.* 1980. Harper. 1st. NF/NF. C8. $55.00

VONNEGUT, Kurt. *Wampeters, Foma & Granfalloons.* 1974. Delacorte. 1st. VG/dj. M2/P3. $30.00

VONNEGUT, Kurt. *Welcome to the Monkey House.* 1968. Delacorte. 1st. NF. M21. $50.00

VOOUS, K.H. *Atlas of European Birds.* 1960. London. Nelson. 284p. xl. B1. $22.00

VORIS, Emma Frances. *New Columbian White House Cookery.* ca 1893. Potter. 427p. B10. $65.00

VOTH, H.R. *Oraibi Powamu Ceremony.* 1901. Chicago. Field Columbian Mus. 8vo. 37 pl. 158p. limp morocco. VG. K7. $245.00

VRIENDS, Matthew M. *Parakeets of the World.* 1979. TFH. photos. 384p. F. S15. $10.00

VULLIAMY, C.E. *Cakes for Your Birthday.* 1959. British Book Centre. 1st. VG/dj. P3. $25.00

VYNER, R.T. *Notitia Venatica: Treatise on Fox-Hunting...* (1847). London. Ackerman. new revised corrected/enlarged. 172p. VG. M12. $60.00

VYSE, Michael. *Overworld.* 1957. Macmillan. 1st. NF/dj. P3. $23.00

WAAGENAAR, Sam. *Woman of Israel.* 1961. Schocken Books. 1st. 112 pl. 47p. F/dj. H1. $12.00

WACHOLDER, Ben Zion. *Eupolemus: Study of Judaeo-Greek Literature.* 1974. HUC. 332p. VG/VG. S3. $35.00

WACK, Henry Wellington. *Story of the Congo Free State.* 1905. NY/London. Putnam. 1st. 8vo. ils/maps. 634p. teg. xl. W1. $35.00

WADE, Brent. *Company Man.* 1992. Algonquin. 1st. author's 1st book. F/F. H11. $30.00

WADE, Henry. *Litmore Snatch.* 1957. Macmillan. 1st. NF/dj. P3. $23.00

WADE, J.L. *What You Should Know About the Purple Martin.* 1963. Griggsville, IL. ils. 223p. NF. S15. $10.00

WADE, Jonathan. *Back to Life.* 1961. Pantheon. F/dj. P3. $13.00

WADE, Mary Hazelton. *Our Little Jewish Cousin.* 1904. Boston. Page. 1st. ils LJ Bridgman. 12mo. pict cloth. R5. $100.00

WADE-EVANS, A.W. *Welsh Medieval Law, Being a Text of the Laws of Howel...* 1909. Oxford. Clarendon. gilt gr cloth. M11. $125.00

WADSWORTH, Beula. *Design Motifs of the Pueblo Indians.* 1957. Naylor. A19. $35.00

WADSWORTH, Wallace. *Peter Rabbit.* 1960 (1953). Rand McNally. ils Anne Sellers Leaf. folio. F. M5. $20.00

WADSWORTH, William P. *Riding to the Hounds in America.* 1976. Berryville, VA. 8vo. 47p. VG. O3. $12.00

WAFER, Lionel. *New Voyage & Description of Isthmus of America.* 1903 (1699). Cleveland. Burrows. rpt. 1/500. edit GP Winship. teg. F. O7. $150.00

WAFER, Lionel. *New Voyage & Description of Isthmus of America.* 1970. Burt Franklin. rpt. 8vo. 212p. bl cloth. NF. P4. $45.00

WAGENKNECHT, Edward. *Fireside Book of Ghost Stories.* 1947. Bobbs Merrill. 1st. VG. M2. $20.00

WAGENKNECHT, Edward. *Six Novels of the Supernatural.* 1944. Viking. 1st. VG. P3. $35.00

WAGENKNECHT, Edward. *William Dean Howells: The Friendly Eye.* 1969. NY. 1st. 340p. dj. A17. $12.50

WAGER, Walter. *Blue Leader.* 1979. Arbor. VG/dj. P3. $15.00

WAGER, Walter. *Designated Hitter.* 1982. NY. Arbor. 1st. F/F. H11. $20.00

WAGER, Walter. *Otto's Boy.* 1985. Macmillan. 1st. F/dj. P3. $17.00

WAGER, Walter. *Swap.* 1972. Macmillan. 1st. VG/dj. P3. $25.00

WAGER, Walter. *Time of Reckoning.* 1977. Playboy. 1st. VG/dj. P3. $18.00

WAGER, Walter. *Viper Three.* 1971. Macmillan. 1st. F/F. H11. $25.00

WAGER, Walter. *58 Minutes.* 1987. Macmillan. 1st. VG/dj. P3. $25.00

WAGERIN, Walter Jr. *Book of Sorrows.* 1985. Harper Row. 1st. F/dj. P3. $16.00

WAGERIN, Walter Jr. *Book of the Dun Cow.* 1980. Allen Lane. F/dj. P3. $25.00

WAGGONER, Diana. *Hills of Faraway.* 1978. Atheneum. 1st. ils. VG/dj. K3. $10.00

WAGNER, Betty Jane. *Limericks.* 1973. Houghton Mifflin. 1st thus. ils Gorey. 30p. VG/wrp. D1. $30.00

WAGNER, Betty Jane. *Limericks.* 1973. Houghton Mifflin. 1st. ils Gorey. F/wrp. A11. $75.00

WAGNER, Frederick. *Robert Morris.* 1976. Dodd Mead. 1st. NF/NF. W2. $20.00

WAGNER, Henry R. *Collecting, Especially Books.* 1968. Ward Ritchie. 1/400. ils. 25p. F. K3. $85.00

WAGNER, Henry R. *Ernest Hemingway: A Reference Guide.* 1977. 382p. VG. A4. $125.00

WAGNER, Henry R. *Juan Rodriguez Cabrillo: Discoverer of Coast of California.* 1941. SF. CA Hist Soc. Special Pub 17. 1/750. NF. O7. $250.00

WAGNER, Henry R. *One Rare Book.* 1956. Los Angeles. Zamorano Club. 1/250. F/wrp. A4. $125.00

WAGNER, Henry R. *Plains & the Rockies: Bibliography of Original Narratives...* 1921. SF. John Howell. 2nd. 40 tipped-in photostats of title p. 193p. D11. $400.00

WAGNER, Henry R. *Sir Francis Drake's Voyage Around the World.* 1926. SF. John Howell. 1st. 543p. bl cloth. P4. $250.00

WAGNER, Henry R. *Spanish Southwest 1542-1794, an Annotated Bibliography.* nd. 2 vol in 1. 1/150. F. A4. $150.00

WAGNER, Jack R. *Gold Mines of California.* 1980. San Diego. 259p. F/dj. A17. $25.00

WAGNER, Jack R. *Gold Mines of Newmont: A 50-Year History.* 1973. NY. 1st. 344p. F/dj. A17. $12.50

WAGNER, Jon. *Sex Roles in Contemporary American Communes.* 1982. Bloomington, IN. IU. 1st. 242p. VG/dj. A25. $12.00

WAGNER, Karl. *Echoes of Valor II.* 1989. Tor. 1st. F/dj. M2. $25.00

WAGNER, Philip M. *Wine-Grower's Guide.* 1973. Knopf. 2nd. VG/dj. W2. $20.00

WAHL, Jan. *Christmas in the Forest.* 1967. Macmillan. 1st. lg 8vo. NF/VG+. C8. $40.00

WAHL, Jan. *Grandpa's Indian Summer.* 1976. Prentice Hall. 1st. ils Joanne Scribner. obl 8vo. F/F. C8. $20.00

WAHL, Jan. *Little Blind Goat.* 1981. Stemmer. 1st. ils Antonio Frasconi. 32p. VG+/NF. P2. $40.00

WAHL, Jan. *Pleasant Field Mouse.* 1964. Harper Row. 1st. ils Sendak. 66p. NF/dj. P2. $350.00

WAHLOO, Peter. *Assignment.* 1977. Knopf. 1st. VG/dj. P3. $25.00

WAHLOO, Peter. *Generals.* 1974. Pantheon. 1st Am. F/dj. M25. $15.00

WAHLOO, Peter. *Murder on the 31st Floor.* 1966. Michael Joseph. 1st Eng language. F/dj. M25. $25.00

WAHLOO, Peter. *Necessary Action.* 1968. Pantheon. 1st. VG/dj. P3. $20.00

WAHLROOS, Sven. *Mutiny & Romance in the South Seas.* 1989. Topsfield. Salem. 497p. VG/dj. P4. $40.00

WAHLSTEDT, Viola. *Travel Alone, Eva.* 1949. HRW. 1st. 158p. VG/dj. A25. $12.00

WAHRHAFT, Mordecai. *Blue Box the Bold.* ca 1940. Jerusalem. Rubin Mass. 8vo. 22p. F/ils wrp. B24. $250.00

WAIN, Louis. *Cat Alphabet & Picture-Book for Little Folk.* 1913. NY. Dodge. 8vo. brd/label. R5. $1,400.00

WAINER, Cord; see Dewey, Thomas B.

WAINWRIGHT, John. *All Through the Night.* 1985. St Martin. 1st Am. VG+/dj. N4. $15.00

WAINWRIGHT, John. *Bastard.* 1976. St Martin. 1st. NF/dj. P3. $22.00

WAINWRIGHT, John. *Brainwash.* 1979. Macmillan. 1st. NF/dj. P3. $18.00

WAINWRIGHT, John. *Man Who Wasn't There.* 1989. St Martin. 1st. VG/dj. P3. $18.00

WAINWRIGHT, John. *Who Goes Next?* 1976. St Martin. 1st. VG/dj. P3. $18.00

WAKEFIELD, Bob. *Jean Dehaven's Trail of the Jackasses.* 1968. Aberdeen, SD. A19. $20.00

WAKEFIELD, H.R. *Strayers From Sheol.* 1961. Arkham. 1st. F/VG. Q1. $50.00

WAKEFIELD, Ruth. *Ruth Wakefield's Toll House Tried & True Recipes.* 1945. NY. Barrows. G. A16. $10.00

WAKEMAN, Edgar. *Log of an Ancient Mariner.* 1878. SF. Bancroft. 378p. emb cloth. P4. $150.00

WAKEMAN, Frederic. *Shore Leave.* 1944. NY. Farrar Rhinehart. 1st. author's 1st book. F/F. B4. $150.00

WALCOTT, Charles D. *Forest Reserves.* 1900. WA. Dept Interior. 712p. cloth. D11. $500.00

WALCOTT, Derek. *Arkansas Testament.* 1987. FSG. 1st. inscr/dtd 1993. F/F. R14. $75.00

WALCOTT, Derek. *Sea Grapes.* 1976. FSG. 1st Am. sgn/dtd 1994. F/F. R14. $100.00

WALDA, A. *Sequential Analysis.* 1947. John Wiley. 1st. 212p. F/dj. D8. $10.00

WALDEN, Amelia Elizabeth. *Girl Called Hank.* (1951). Morrow. BC. 8vo. 192p. G+/dj. T5. $12.00

WALDEN, Hillary. *Ice Cream.* 1985. S&S. G/dj. A16. $10.00

WALDMAN, Carl. *Who Was Who in Native American History.* 1990. Facts on File. 410p. F/dj. A17. $25.00

WALDMAN, Frank. *Famous American Athletes of Today.* 1949. Page. 1st. photos. VG. P8. $25.00

WALDO, F. *Grenfell: Knight Errant of the North.* 1924. photos. VG. M17. $25.00

WALDO, Myra. *Seven Wonders of the Cooking World.* 1971. Dodd Mead. VG/dj. A16. $10.00

WALDRON, Charles. *Practical Hints for Better Navigation & Guidance...* 1826. London. Norie. ils. 104p. rebound modern cloth. T7. $250.00

WALDROP, Howard. *Night of the Cooters.* 1990. KS City, MO. Ursus. 1/374p. sgn. ils sgns. F/dj/case. M21. $45.00

WALDROP, Howard. *Them Bones.* 1989. Ziesing. 1st. 1/350. sgn/#d. F/dj. P3. $50.00

WALES, George C. *Etchings & Lithographs of American Ships.* 1927. Boston. Goodspeed. 1/500. 4to. 125p. F/VG. C6. $200.00

WALES, Hubert. *Brocklebank Riddle.* 1914. Century. 1st. VG. M2. $28.00

WALFORD, Frank. *Ghost & Albert.* 1945. London. VG/frayed. M2. $25.00

WALFORD, Lionel. *Marine Game Fishes of the Pacific Coast From Alaska...* 1937. CA U. 1st. 70 pl. 205p. bl cloth. VG. S15. $70.00

WALKE, Henry. *Naval Scenes & Reminiscences of Civil War in United States.* 1877. NY. FR Reed. 1st. 38 pl/2 diagrams. 480p. cloth. VG+. M8. $650.00

WALKER, Alice. *Color Purple.* 1982. NY. HBJ. 1st. F/NF clip. B4. $550.00

WALKER, Alice. *Finding the Greenstone.* 1991. HBJ. 1st. ils Catherine Deeter. F/F. B3. $50.00

WALKER, Alice. *Good Night Willie Lee, I'll See You in the Morning.* 1979. NY. Dial. 1st. lg 12mo. VG+. C8. $35.00

WALKER, Alice. *Her Blue Body Everything We Know.* 1991. Harcourt Brace. 1st. sgn. F/F. A23. $40.00

WALKER, Alice. *Her Blue Body Everything We Know.* 1991. San Diego. HBJ. 1st. F/F. R13. $30.00

WALKER, Alice. *In Search of Our Mothers' Gardens.* 1983. HBJ. 1st. NF/VG. A24. $45.00

WALKER, Alice. *Living by the Word.* 1988. HBJ. 1st. sgn. F/dj. A24. $60.00

WALKER, Alice. *Once.* 1968. HBW. 1st. author's 1st book. F/F. L3. $850.00

WALKER, Alice. *Possessing the Secret of Joy.* 1992. London. Cape. 1st. sgn. F/dj. Q1. $75.00

WALKER, Alice. *Temple of My Familiar.* 1989. HBJ. 1st. sgn. F/F. A23. $45.00

WALKER, Alice. *Temple of My Familiar.* 1989. HBJ. 1st. sgn. rem mk. NF/F. B3. $35.00

WALKER, Alice. *Third Life of Grange Copeland.* 1970. HBJ. 1st. author's 2nd book. F/F. L3. $400.00

WALKER, Alice. *Third Life of Grange Copeland.* 1970. HBJ. 1st. sgn. F/dj. B4. $450.00

WALKER, Barbara M. *Little House Cookbook, Frontier Foods From LI Wilder...* 1979. ils. 240p. F/VG. A4. $35.00

WALKER, Danton. *Spooks Deluxe.* 1956. Watts. 1st. VG. M2. $25.00

WALKER, David. *Devil's Plunge.* 1968. Collins. 1st. NF/dj. P3. $22.00

WALKER, David. *Lord's Pink Ocean.* 1972. Collins. 1st. VG/dj. P3. $18.00

WALKER, David. *Lord's Pink Ocean.* 1972. Houghton Mifflin. 1st. F/dj. M2. $20.00

WALKER, David. *Mallabec.* 1965. Collins. 1st. VG/dj. P3. $20.00

WALKER, David. *Oxford Companion to Law.* 1980. Clarendon. M11. $65.00

WALKER, David. *Winter of Madness.* 1964. Collins. 1st. VG/dj. P3. $30.00

WALKER, Dugald Stewart. *Six Who Were Left in a Shoe.* 1923. Volland. 1st. 8vo. mc pict brd. R5. $150.00

WALKER, Eric A. *History of South Africa.* 1940. London/NY/Toronto. Longman Gr. 2nd. 13 maps. 7190p. xl. VG. W1. $20.00

WALKER, Franklin. *Seacost of Bohemia, Account of Early Camel.* 1973. Peregrine Smith. new/enlarged. 30 photos/5 cartoons. 127p. VG/dj. K7. $35.00

WALKER, Fred. *Destination Unknown.* 1935. Lippincott. 1st. 285p. dj. F3. $15.00

WALKER, Ira. *Man in the Driver's Seat.* 1964. Abelard Schuman. 1st. VG/dj. P3. $15.00

WALKER, Irma. *Inherit the Earth.* 1981. Atheneum. 1st. F/dj. M2. $17.00

WALKER, J. Bernard. *America Fallen!* 1915. Dodd Mead. 1st. VG. M2. $75.00

WALKER, Jerry. *Mission Accomplished.* 1947. Cosmos. F/dj. M2. $22.00

WALKER, Joseph A. *River Niger.* 1973. Hill Wang. ARC. RS. NF/dj. M25. $60.00

WALKER, Margaret. *For My People.* 1942. New Haven. 1st. author's 1st book. VG/torn. A15. $150.00

WALKER, Margaret. *For My People.* 1942. New Haven. Yale. 1st. inscr. author's 1st book. F/NF. L3. $750.00

WALKER, Margaret. *Jubilee.* 1966. Houghton Mifflin. 1st. NF/dj. M25. $200.00

WALKER, Marian C. *Dahlias for Every Garden.* 1954. Barrows. 8vo. 128p. VG/torn. A22. $15.00

WALKER, Mary Willis. *Red Scream.* 1994. Doubleday. 1st. F/dj. M25. $75.00

WALKER, Mary Willis. *Under the Beetle's Cellar.* 1995. Doubleday. 1st. sgn. F/F. A23. $45.00

WALKER, Nancy A. *Very Serious Thing: Women's Humor & American Culture.* 1988. MN U. 1st. as new. V4. $12.50

WALKER, Nigel. *Crime & Insanity in England... Historical Perspective.* 1968. Edinburgh. M11. $65.00

WALKER, Sam. *Up the Slot (307th Bomb Group).* 1984. OK City. photos/map/index. 292p. F. S16. $60.00

WALKER, Walter. *Dime To Dance By.* 1983. Harper Row. 1st. F/F. M15. $45.00

WALKER, Walter. *Immediate Prospect of Being Hanged.* 1989. Viking. 1st. VG/dj. P3. $20.00

WALKER, Walter. *Rules of the Knife Fight.* 1986. Harper Row. 1st. F/dj. P3. $20.00

WALKER, William. *Walker's This Race of Mine Poem Book.* 1938. Chicago. self pub. 1st. 22p. VG/stapled wrp. B4. $150.00

WALL, Dorothy. *Blinky Bill Grows Up. Further Adventures of...* 1934. Sydney. Angus Robertson. 1st. 8vo. 84p. tan-beige brd. pict dj. R5. $400.00

WALL, Dorothy. *Blinky Bill: The Quaint Little Australian.* 1933. Angus Robertson. 1st. sm 4to. VG. M5. $75.00

WALL, Dorothy. *Blinky Bill: The Quaint Little Australian.* 1935. Sydney. Angus Robertson. 8vo. rose-pink brd. pict dj. R5. $275.00

WALL, Mervyn. *Return of Fursey.* 1948. London. 1st. VG. M2. $20.00

WALL, Roy. *Contemplative Angler.* 1948. NY. 215p. NF. A17. $12.50

WALLACE, Alexander. *Heather in Lore, Lyric & Lay.* 1903. NY. DeLaMare. 245p. VG. A10. $50.00

WALLACE, Alfred R. *Wonderful Century.* 1898. Toronto. Morang. ils/fld chart. 400p. cloth. VG. M12. $60.00

WALLACE, Andrew. *Grand Canyon.* 1972. Time Life. 1st. ils/index. 184p. NF/VG. B19. $15.00

WALLACE, Andrew. *Pumpelly's Arizona: Excerpt From Across America & Asia...* 1965. Palo Verde. ils/notes/index. 141p. F/VG. B19. $45.00

WALLACE, Anthony F.C. *Death & Rebirth of the Seneca.* 1970. Knopf. 1st. tall 8vo. 384p. F/F. H1/M4. $28.00

WALLACE, Anthony F.C. *King of the Delawares: Teedyuscung 1700-1763.* 1949. PA U. 1st. 8vo. 305p. F/F. H1. $40.00

WALLACE, Archer. *Adventures in the Air.* 1932. Ryerson. sgn. VG. P3. $20.00

WALLACE, Brenton. *Patton & His Third Army.* 1951. Harrisburg. maps/photos/chronology. 232p. VG/VG. S16. $45.00

WALLACE, Cornelia. *O'Nelia.* 1976. Holman. 1st. inscr. full-p photos. 240p. VG/VG. B11. $25.00

WALLACE, David Foster. *Girl With Curious Hair.* 1989. Norton. 1st. F/F. M23. $50.00

WALLACE, David Rains. *Turquoise Dragon.* 1985. Sierra Club. 1st. F/F. M19. $25.00

WALLACE, David Rains. *Wilder Shores.* 1984. SF. Sierra Club. 1/300 for sale. photos M Baer. 162p. loth. F/case. M12. $175.00

WALLACE, Edgar. *Again the Three Just Men.* nd. Hodder Stoughton. VG/dj. P3. $25.00

WALLACE, Edgar. *Avenger.* nd. Leisure Lib. VG/dj. P3. $18.00

WALLACE, Edgar. *Day of Uniting.* 1930. Mystery League. 1st. VG/fair. P3. $25.00

WALLACE, Edgar. *Edgar Wallace Reader of Mystery.* 1943. Tower. VG. P3. $15.00

WALLACE, Edgar. *Feathered Serpent.* 1928. Crime Club. 1st. G. P3. $20.00

WALLACE, Edgar. *Flying Squad.* 1929. Crime Club. 1st. VG. P3. $18.00

WALLACE, Edgar. *Four Just Men.* 1905. Tallis. xl. VG. P3. $75.00

WALLACE, Edgar. *Fourth Plague.* 1928. Ward Lock. VG. P3. $20.00

WALLACE, Edgar. *Fourth Plague.* 1930. Doubleday Crime Club. 1st Am. NF/dj. M15. $100.00

WALLACE, Edgar. *Frightened Lady.* 1933. Musson. 1t. VG. P3. $20.00

WALLACE, Edgar. *Governor of Chi-Foo.* 1933. World Syndicate. 1st. VG. P3. $60.00

WALLACE, Edgar. *Green Archer.* 1924. Sm Maynard. 1st. NF/F later dj. M19. $35.00

WALLACE, Edgar. *Green Rust.* 1919. Ward Lock. 1st Eng. VG/VG. M19. $35.00

WALLACE, Edgar. *Gunman's Bluff.* 1929. Crime Club. 1st. VG. P3. $30.00

WALLACE, Edgar. *Mr Commissioner Sanders.* 1930. Garden City. 1st. VG/VG. B5. $35.00

WALLACE, Edgar. *Unofficial Dispatches (Africana Collectanea, Vol XLIX).* 1975 (1901). Cape Town. Struik. 1/1000. rpt. 332p. VG/dj. W1. $25.00

WALLACE, Edgar. *White Face.* 1932. Musson. 1st. VG. P3. $20.00

WALLACE, F.L. *Address: Centauri.* 1955. Gnome. 1st. NF/dj. P3. $30.00

WALLACE, Ian. *Deathstar Voyage.* 1972. Dobson. 1st. F/dj. P3. $13.00

WALLACE, Ian. *Pan Sagittarius.* 1973. Putnam. NF/dj. P3. $15.00

WALLACE, Ian. *Purloined Prince.* 1971. McCall. 1st. NF/dj. P3. $25.00

WALLACE, Irving. *Mexico Today.* 1936. Boston. Meador. 1st. ils. 364p. map ep. F3. $20.00

WALLACE, Irving. *Pigeon Project.* 1979. S&S. 1st. F/dj. P3. $15.00

WALLACE, Irving. *R Document.* 1976. S&S. 1st. F/dj. P3. $18.00

WALLACE, Irving. *Twenty-Seventh Wife.* 1971. S&S. 1st. 443p. VG/dj. M20. $20.00

WALLACE, Kathleen. *Without a Stair.* 1933. Doubleday Doran. 1st. F/VG+. B4. $85.00

WALLACE, Lew. *Ben-Hur, a Tale of the Christ.* 1880. NY. Harper. 1st/1st prt. lt bl pict cloth (1st bdg). VG. M24. $250.00

WALLACE, Lew. *Fair God; or, Last of the 'Tzins. A Tale of Conquest Mexico.* 1873 (1873). Boston. Osgood. 1st thus. G+. B22. $15.00

WALLACE, Lew. *Fair God; or, Last of the 'Tzins. A Tale of Conquest Mexico.* 1894 (1873). Houghton Mifflin. 586p. gilt cloth. VG. F3. $20.00

WALLACE, Lew. *Prince of India.* 1893. Harper. 1st. 2 vol. sgn. VG. M2. $100.00

WALLACE, Lew. *Prince of India.* 1893. Harper. 1st/1st issue (no dedication). 2 vol. VG. H1. $45.00

WALLACE, Marcia. *Barefoot in the Kitchen.* 1971. St Martin. G/dj. A16. $10.00

WALLACE, Michele. *Black Macho & the Myth of the Superwoman.* 1979. Dial. 2nd. 182p. F/F. B4. $35.00

WALLACE, Paul A.W. *Muhlengers of Pennsylvania.* 1950. PA U. 1st. tall 8vo. 358p. F/VG. H1. $25.00

WALLACE, Paul A.W. *Thirty Thousand Miles With John Heckewelder.* 1958. Pittsburgh. 1st. 2 fld maps. 474p. F/VG. H1. $35.00

WALLACE, Philip B. *Colonial Ironwork in Old Philadelphia.* ca 1965. NY. Bonanza. 147p. dj. A10. $35.00

WALLACE, Philip B. *Colonial Ironwork in Old Philadelphia...* 1970. Dover. rpt. VG. M17. $25.00

WALLACE, Robert. *Seven Men Are Murdered.* 1930. Fiction League. VG. P3. $25.00

WALLACE, W.M. *Traitorous Hero: Life & Fortunes of Benedict Arnold.* 1954. VG/VG. M17. $25.00

WALLACE, Willard M. *East to Gagaduce.* 1963. Chicago. Regnery. 1st. inscr/dtd 1963. NF/VG+. T11. $35.00

WALLACE, Willard M. *Raiders.* 1970. Little Brn. 1st. NF/VG+ clip. T11. $35.00

WALLACE, William N. *Frank Figgord: The Golden Year, 1956.* 1956. Prentice Hall. 1st. photos. VG+/dj. P8. $25.00

WALLACE, Wolf. *Hive.* 1966. NY. Softcover Lib. 1st. 156p. VG. A25. $18.00

WALLACE-DUNLOP. *Fairies, Elves & Flower-Babies.* 1899. Duckworth. 1st. obl 4to. gray cloth. R5. $300.00

WALLACH, Anne Tolstoi. *Women's Work.* 1981. NAL. 1st Canadian. F/VG. T12. $15.00

WALLACH, Carla. *Reluctant Weekend Gardener.* 1973. Macmillan. 1st. inscr. 214p. VG/dj. A25. $12.00

WALLENIUS, K.M. *Men's Sea.* 1955. Staples. 1st. trans from Finnish. 262p. dj. A17. $20.00

WALLER, Effie. *Rhumes From the Cumberland.* 1909. NY. Broadway. 1st. VG. B4. $850.00

WALLER, George. *Saratoga: Sage of an Impious Era.* 1966. Prentice Hall. 1st. 392p. cloth. VG/dj. M20. $30.00

WALLER, Leslie. *Change in the Wind.* 1969. Bernard Geis. 1st. VG/dj. P3. $20.00

WALLER, Robert James. *Bridges of Madison County.* (1992). later prt. sgn. NF/dj. A15. $30.00

WALLER, Robert James. *Bridges of Madison County.* 1992. NY. Warner. 1st. sgn. author's 1st book. VG/F. T11. $150.00

WALLER, Robert James. *Bridges of Madison County.* 1992. Warner. 1st. F/F. D10. $150.00

WALLER, Robert James. *Bridges of Madison County: The Film.* 1995. Warner. 1st thus. F/dj. Q1. $30.00

WALLER, Robert James. *Old Songs in a New Cafe.* 1994. Warner. 1st. F/F. A23. $45.00

WALLER, Robert James. *Slow Waltz in Cedar Bend.* 1993. Warner. 1st. sgn. F/F. A23. $45.00

WALLIN, Homer N. *Pearl Harbor: Why, How, Fleet Salvage & Final Appraisal.* 1968. WA. 377p. G+. B18. $25.00

WALLING, R.A.J. *Corpse With the Eerie Eye.* 1944. Books Inc. VG/G. P3. $12.00

WALLING, R.A.J. *Fatal 5 Minutes.* 1943. Tower. 2nd. VG/dj. P3. $15.00

WALLING, William. *World I Left Behind Me.* 1979. St Martin. 1st. F/dj. M2. $10.00

WALLIS, Dave. *Only Lovers Left Alive.* 1964. Dutton. 1st. VG/dj. P3. $20.00

WALLIS, George A. *Cattle Kings of the Staked Plains.* 1964. Denver Co. dj. A19. $25.00

WALLIS, Helen. *Historians' Guide to Early British Maps...* 1994. London. Royal Hist Soc. 465p. VG. A4. $125.00

WALLIS, Helen. *Voyage of Sir Francis Drake Mapped in Silver & Gold.* 1979. Friends of Bancroft Lib. 29p. gray wrp. P4. $40.00

WALLIS, J.H. *Murder by Formula.* 1932. Jarrolds. 1st. inscr. G. P3. $45.00

WALLIS, M. *Oil Man: Story of Frank Phillips...* 1988. Doubleday. 480p. F/torn. D8. $30.00

WALLMANN, Jeffrey M. *Judas Cross.* 1974. Random. 1st. F/dj. P3. $16.00

WALLS, Ian. *Tomato Growing Today.* 1977. Newton Abbot. 239p. VG/dj. A10. $24.00

WALPOLE, Horace. *Mysterious Mother: A Tragedy.* 1791. Dublin. John Archer. pirated (presumed from Strawberry Hill). H13. $265.00

WALPOLE, Hugh. *All Soul's Night.* 1933. London. Macmillan. 1st. F/NF. M2. $150.00

WALPOLE, Hugh. *Bright Pavilions.* 1940. London. 1st. VG. T9. $10.00

WALPOLE, Hugh. *Captain Nicholas.* 1934. London. 1/275. sgn. VG. T9. $35.00

WALPOLE, Hugh. *Jeremy.* (1919). Grosset Dunlap. rpt. VG/dj. T5. $15.00

WALPOLE, Hugh. *Portrait of a Man With Red Hair.* 1925. Doran. 1st. VG. M2. $25.00

WALSH, Chad. *From Utopia to Nightmare.* 1962. London. 1st. F/dj. M2. $25.00

WALSH, Chad. *Literary Legacy of CS Lewis.* 1979. Harcourt. 1st. F/dj. M2. $25.00

WALSH, James J. *What Civilization Owes to Italy.* 1923. Boston. 8vo. 432p. red cloth. VG. B14. $35.00

WALSH, James Morgan. *Spies Are Abroad.* 1936. Collins. 6th. VG/dj. P3. $20.00

WALSH, James Morgan. *Vandals of the Void.* 1976 (1931). Hyperion. rpt. F. M2. $30.00

WALSH, Jill Paton. *Dawnstone.* 1977 (1973). London. Hamish Hamilton. rpt. ils. VG. T5. $20.00

WALSH, John Evangelist. *Hidden Life of Emily Dickinson.* 1971. S&S. 1st. 286p. VG/dj. A25. $18.00

WALSH, John Evangelist. *Poe the Detective: Curious Circumstances Behind Mystery...* 1968. Rutgers. 1st. VG+/VG. N4. $30.00

WALSH, M.M.B. *Four-Colored Hoop.* 1976. Putnam. 1st. F/dj. P3. $13.00

WALSH, Thomas. *Action of the Tiger.* 1967. S&S. 1st. xl. VG/dj. P3. $5.00

WALSTROM, E.E. *Ingenious Minerals & Rocks.* March 1947. John Wiley. 4th prt. VG. D8. $25.00

WALTARI, Mika. *Egyptian.* 1949. Putnam. 1st Am. F/NF. B4. $125.00

WALTER, Elizabeth. *Dead Woman.* 1975. St Martin. 1st. F/dj. M2. $25.00

WALTER, Elizabeth. *In the Mist.* 1979. Arkham. 1st. F/dj. P3. $15.00

WALTER, Gerard. *Paris Under the Occupation.* 1960. Orion. 1st. 208p. VG/dj. M20. $12.00

WALTER, L. Edna. *Mother Goose's Nursery Tales.* 1923. London. Blk. 1st. ils Folkard/Hartley. pict cloth. R5. $285.00

WALTER, Leibrecht. *Religion & Culture: Essays in Honor of Paul Tillich.* 1959. Harper. 399p. VG. B29. $13.00

WALTER, Richard. *Anson's Voyage Round the World.* 1928. London. Hopkinson. 1/1500. ils/4 charts. teg. T7. $120.00

WALTERS, L.D'O. *Year's at the Spring: An Anthology of Recent Poetry.* 1920. Brentano. Prt Great Britain. 1st Am. 12 mc pl/other ils. 128p. VG. D4. $120.00

WALTERS, Minette. *Scold's Bridle.* 1994. London. Macmillan. 1st. sgn. F/F. D10. $85.00

WALTERS, Minette. *Scold's Bridle.* 1994. St Martin. 1st. F/dj. P3. $22.00

WALTERS, Minette. *Sculptress.* 1993. St Martin. 1st Am. sgn. author's 2nd novel. NF/dj. A24. $50.00

WALTERS, Rachel. *Mountain Bouquet. Wildflowers of Southern Highlands.* 1971. Cullowhee, NC. Greenstone. 71x67mm. ils Benoit. unbound as issued. B24. $385.00

WALTHER, Edvard. *Geographische Charakterbilder.* 1891. Esslingen. JF Schreiber. 4to. 48p. 24 double-p pl. NF. B24. $650.00

WALTON, Alan Hull. *Open Grave.* 1971. Taplinger. VG. P3. $20.00

WALTON, Evangeline. *Cross & the Sword.* 1956. Ryerson. VG/G. P3. $25.00

WALTON, Frank L. *Tomahawks to Textiles.* 1953. Appleton Century Crofts. 1st. 177p. VG/ragged. M20. $25.00

WALTON, Isaak. *Compleat Angler.* nd. Phil. McKay. 1st Am trade. ils Rackham/12 mc pl. 223p. VG+. M20. $160.00

WALTON, John. *Brain's Diseases of the Nervous System.* 1985. Oxford. 9th revised/1st prt. ils. prt bl cloth. G1. $50.00

WAMBAUGH, Joseph. *Black Marble.* 1978. Delacorte. 1st. F/F. A20. $35.00

WAMBAUGH, Joseph. *Black Marble.* 1978. Delacorte. 1st. VG/dj. P3. $20.00

WAMBAUGH, Joseph. *Blooding.* 1989. Morrow. 1st. F/F. A20/W2. $20.00

WAMBAUGH, Joseph. *Blooding.* 1989. Perigord. 1st. VG. P3. $20.00

WAMBAUGH, Joseph. *Echoes in the Darkness.* 1987. Morrow. 1st. F/F. N4. $25.00

WAMBAUGH, Joseph. *Echoes in the Darkness.* 1987. Morrow. 1st. F/NF. W2. $20.00

WAMBAUGH, Joseph. *Fugitive Nights.* 1992. Morrow. 1st. F/F. W2. $30.00

WAMBAUGH, Joseph. *Glitter Dome.* 1981. Morrow. 1st. VG/dj. N4. $25.00

WAMBAUGH, Joseph. *Golden Orange.* 1990. Perigord/Morrow. 1st. VG/dj. P3. $20.00

WAMBAUGH, Joseph. *New Centurions.* 1970. Atlantic/Little Brn. 1st. author's 1st book. F/NF. N4. $40.00

WAMBAUGH, Joseph. *Onion Field.* 1973. Delacorte. 1st. sgn. F/VG+ clip. A24. $60.00

WAMBAUGH, Joseph. *Secrets of Harry Bright.* 1985. Morrow. 1st. VG+/NF. A20. $20.00

WANDREI, Donald. *Web of Easter Island.* 1948. Arkham. 1st. 1/3068. F/dj. P3. $45.00

WANEFSKY, David. *Prophets Speak to Us Anew.* 1952. Philosophical Lib. 232p. xl. G. B29. $7.00

WANGENSTEEN & WANGENSTEEN. *Rise of Surgery From Empiric Craft to Scientific Discipline.* 1978. Minneapolis. 1st. 784p. A13. $85.00

WANGERIN, Walter. *Thistle.* 1983. Harper Row. 1st. sgn. ils Marcia Sewall. VG+/dj. M20. $25.00

WAPLES. D. *Organic Geochemisty for Exploration Geologists.* 1981. Burgess Pub. 151p. xl. F. D8. $35.00

WARD, A. *Grocer's Handbook & Directory for 1883.* 1882. ils. VG. E6. $35.00

WARD, A.C. *Bernard Shaw.* 1951. Longman Gr. ne. VG/dj. V4. $20.00

WARD, Adolphus William. *Dickens.* 1882. London. Macmillan. 1st. blk stp red cloth. M24. $100.00

WARD, Andrew. *Blood Seed.* 1985. Viking. 1st. sgn. F/F. B11. $35.00

WARD, Barbara. *Urban Planet?* 1971. Phil. Girard Bank. 1st. ils Howard Watson. 53p. VG+/case. A25. $10.00

WARD, C.L. *Delaware Continentals 1776-1783.* 1941. Delaware. battle maps. 620p. F. M4. $45.00

WARD, Fay E. *Cowboy at Work.* 1958. Hastings. A19. $35.00

WARD, Fay E. *Cowboy at Work.* 1987. Norman/London. A19. $20.00

Geoffrey C. *Tiger-Wallahs.* 1993. NY. ils. 175p. F/NF. S15. $27.50

WARD, James M. *Deites & Demigods.* 1980. Tsr Advanced D&D. VG. P3. $15.00

WARD, Josiah. *Come With Me to Babylon.* 1902. Stokes. 1st. VG. M2. $27.00

WARD, Lynd. *God's Man.* 1933. NY. Peter Smith. 6th. VG/fair. B5. $75.00

WARD, Lynd. *Silver Pony.* 1973. Houghton Mifflin. 1st. ils. 176p. NF/VG. P2. $85.00

WARD, Maisie. *Robert Browning & His World: Private Face 1821-1861, Vol 1.* 1967. HRW. 1st. tall 8vo. 335p. as new/dj. H1. $17.50

WARD, Margaret. *Testimony of Mrs George R Ward Before US Committee...1883.* 1965. Birmingham, AL. 1st. cloth. NF. M8. $250.00

WARD, R. Gerald. *American Activities in the Central Pacific 1790-1870...* 1966. Ridgewood, NJ. Gregg. 8 vol. fld maps. whit cloth. NF. P4. $295.00

WARD, Robert Plumer. *De Vere; or, Man of Independence.* 1827. London. Henry Colburn. 4 vol. 1st. tall 12mo. w/ALS dtd 1841. H13. $295.00

WARDE, Beatrice. *Stanley Morison, Man of Letters.* nd. Wakefield. Fleece. 1/240. 66x49mm. yel striped cloth/prt label. F. B24. $85.00

WARDEN, Florence. *Mystery of the Thames.* 1913. Ward Lock. G. P3. $25.00

WARDLAW, C.W. *Morphogenesis in Plants: A Contemporary Study.* 1968. London. ils. 451p. VG/dj. B26. $27.50

WARE, Evelyn Woodford. *Islanders. A Romance of Martha's Vineyard.* 1892. Boston. Alfred Mudge. 1st. 12mo. 153p. prt wrp. M1. $125.00

WARE, Wallace. *Charka Memorial.* 1954. Crime Club. VG/dj. P3. $15.00

WARGA, Wayne. *Hardcover.* 1985. Arbor. 1st. sgn. 8vo. F/dj. T10. $50.00

WARHOL, Andy. *A.* 1968. Grove. 1st. NF/G. M19. $85.00

WARHOL, Andy. *Philosophy of Andy Warhol: From A to B & Back Again.* 1975. HBJ. later prt. inscr w/drawing. F/F. M25. $300.00

WARHOL, Andy. *Philosophy of Andy Warhol: From A to B & Back Again.* 1975. HBJ. 1st. inscr. NF/F. T12. $100.00

WARING, G. *Draining for Profit & Health.* 1887 (1886). VG. E6. $40.00

WARING, Holburt. *Surgical Management of Malignant Disease.* 1928. London. 1st. 667p. A13. $75.00

WARING, Robert Lewis. *As We See It.* 1918. WA, DC. Sudwarth. 1st. fair. B4. $275.00

WARINGTON, R. *Chemistry of the Farm.* 1881. London. Bradbury. 128p. xl. VG. A10. $25.00

WARK, Robert R. *Drawings From the Turner Shakespeare.* 1973. San Marino. sgn. 89p. D2. $25.00

WARLOCK, Peter. *English Ayre.* 1926. London. 1st. VG/dj. T9. $45.00

WARMAN, Eric. *Preview Film Album 1963.* 1962. Golden Pleasure. VG. P3. $30.00

WARMINGTON, G.R. *King of Dreams.* 1926. Doran. 1st. F/dj. M2. $75.00

WARNER, C. *My Summer in a Garden.* 1878 (1870). VG. E6. $25.00

WARNER, Charles Dudley. *Being a Boy.* 1878 (1877). Houghton Osgood. 244p. cloth. VG. M20. $25.00

WARNER, Charles Dudley. *Our Italy.* 1892. Harper. 8vo. 226p. F7. $60.00

WARNER, Deborah Jean. *Alvan Clark & Sons.* 1968. Smithsonian. 1st. 8vo. 120p. VG. K5. $100.00

WARNER, Ezra J. *General's in Blue.* 1993. 680p. O8. $27.50

WARNER, Francis. *Physical Expression: Its Modes & Principles.* 1886. NY. Appleton. 1st Am. 12mo. red cloth. G1. $75.00

WARNER, Frank A. *Bobby Blake in Frozen North; or, Old Eskimo's Last Message.* 1923. NY. Barse. 250p. P4. $35.00

WARNER, Matt. *Last of the Bandit Riders.* 1940. Caxton. 1st. photos. 337p. VG. J2. $475.00

WARNER, Oliver. *Crown Jewels.* 1951. King Penguin. 1st. VG/dj. P3. $20.00

WARNER, Oliver. *Nelson.* 1975. Chicago. Follett. 20 mc pl/100 halftones. 231p. dj. T7. $25.00

WARNER, Oliver. *Victory: Life of Lord Nelson.* 1958. ils. VG/VG. M17. $20.00

WARNER, Sylvia Townsend. *Kingdoms of Elfin.* 1977. Viking. 1st. VG/dj. M2. $20.00

WARNER, Sylvia Townsend. *Lolly Willowes.* 1926. Viking. VG. M2. $10.00

WARNER, Sylvia Townsend. *Mr Fortune's Maggot.* 1927. Viking. 1st. VG. M2. $20.00

WARNER. *From the Beast to the Blonde: On Fairy Tales...* 1994. London. Chatto Windus. 458p. NF/NF. A4. $65.00

WARREN, James. *Disappearing Corpse.* 1958. Washburn. 1st. VG/dj. P3. $20.00

WARREN, John Collins. *On an Operation for Cure & Natural Fissure of Soft Palate.* 1828. Boston. 1st. 496p. half leather/marbled brd. xl. A13. $500.00

WARREN, Patricia Nell. *Beauty Queen.* 1978. Morrow. 1st. F/dj. M25. $35.00

WARREN, Patricia Nell. *Fancy Dancer.* 1976. Morrow. 1st. F/dj. M25. $45.00

WARREN, Robert Penn. *All the King's Men.* 1953. Random. 2nd. revised intro. 464p. NF. W2. $50.00

WARREN, Robert Penn. *Homage to Theodore Dreiser.* 1971. Random. 1st. 1/5000. inscr/dtd 1986. F/NF. R14. $90.00

WARREN, Robert Penn. *Legacy of the Civil War Meditations on the Centennial.* 1961. NY. Random. 1st. 190p. cloth. NF/NF. M8. $85.00

WARREN, Robert Penn. *New & Selected Poems 1923-1985.* 1985. Franklin Center. 1st. sgn. full leather. F. Q1. $60.00

WARREN, Robert Penn. *Or Else. Poem/Poems 1968-1974.* 1974. Random. 1st. sgn/dtd 1981. F/clip. D10. $110.00

WARREN, Robert Penn. *Segregation: The Inner Conflict in the South.* 1957. Eyre Spottiswoode. 1st Eng. F/dj. Q1. $75.00

WARREN, Robert Penn. *Selected Poems, New & Old 1923-1966.* 1966. Random. 1st. NF/dj. B35. $28.00

WARREN, W.L. *Henry II. Third Printing.* 1991. Berkeley. 693p. prt wrp. M11. $17.50

WARREN & WARREN. *Helmholtz on Perception: Its Physiology & Development.* 1968. John Wiley. 1st. 8vo. 277p. NF. w/sgn note. K3. $20.00

WARTENBERG, Robert. *Examination of Reflexes: A Simplification.* 1945. Chicago. Year Book Pub. 12mo. 222p. VG. G1. $125.00

WARWICK, Sidney. *Silver Basilisk.* nd. Hodder Stoughton. VG/fair. P3. $10.00

WASHBURN, Cephas. *Reminiscences of the Indians With a Biography...* 1955. Van Buren. 1/990. ils. 192p. F. M4. $40.00

WASHBURN, Cephas. *Reminiscences of the Indians...* (1869). Richmond. Presbyterian Comm of Pub. 1st. 236p. cloth. D11. $250.00

WASHBURN, Mark. *Mars at Last!* 1977. Putnam. 8vo. 291p. VG/dj. K5. $15.00

WASHINGTON, Booker T. *Future of the American Negro.* 1899. Boston. Sm Maynard. 1st. inscr. 244p. F. B4. $1,500.00

WASHINGTON, Booker T. *Tuskegee: Its People...* 1906. Appleton. 3rd. ils. 354p. G+. B18. $45.00

WASHINGTON, Booker T. *Up From Slavery.* 1901. Doubleday Page. 1st. G/VG. B5. $55.00

WASHINGTON, Booker T. *Up From Slavery: An Autobiography by Booker T Washington.* 1901. AL Burt. inscr. VG/dj. V4. $125.00

WASON, Betty. *Encyclopedia of Cheese & Cheese Cookery.* 1966. NY. Galahad. G/dj. A16. $10.00

WASTELL, W.L.F. *Barnet Book of Photography.* 1922. Barnet Herts. new ed. 270p. pict cloth. A17. $20.00

WATERFIELD, Margaret. *Garden Colour.* 1907. London. Dent. 4th. 196p. cloth. VG. A10. $35.00

WATERLOO, Stanley. *Story of AB.* 1914. Doubleday. G+. M2. $20.00

WATERLOO, Stanley. *Story of AB: A Tale of the Time of the Cave Men.* 1897. Chicago. Way Williams. 1st. stp blk cloth. NF. M24. $250.00

WATERMAN, Catharine H. *Flora's Lexicon: Interpretation of Language...Flowers.* 1855 (1839). Boston. Phillips Sampson. 252p. gilt red leather. VG. M20. $45.00

WATERMAN, Charles F. *Fisherman's World.* 1971. NY. 1st. 250p. F/dj. A17. $18.50

WATERS, Alice. *Fanny at Chez Panisse, a Child's Restaurant Adventure...* 1992. Harper. 1st. ils Ann Arnold. F/NF. C8. $25.00

WATERS, D.W. *Elizabethan Navy & Armada of Spain.* 1975. London. Nat Maritime Mus. Maritime Monograph/Reports 17. 4to. NF/wrp. O7. $35.00

WATERS, Ethel. *His Eye Is on the Sparrow.* 1951. Toronto. Doubleday. 1st Canadian. F. T12. $30.00

WATERS, Ethel. *To Me It's Wonderful.* 1972. NY. Harper. 1st. sgn. NF/VG. B4. $45.00

WATERS, Frank. *Colorado.* 1946. 1st. Rivers of Am series. NF/dj. A15. $75.00

WATERS, Frank. *Earp Brothers of Tombstone, Story of Mrs Virgil Earp.* 1931. Neville Spearman. 1st Eng. 520p. VG. J2. $75.00

WATERS, Frank. *Masked Gods: Navajo & Pueblo Ceremonialism.* 1950. Sage Books. 2nd. tall 8vo. gray bdg. NF. F7. $40.00

WATERS, Frank. *Mexico Mystique.* 1975. Chicago. Swallow. 1st. F/F clip. L3. $125.00

WATERS, Frank. *Pike's Peak.* 1971. Chicago. Sage. 1st. NF/NF. T11. $65.00

WATERS, J.M. Jr. *Bloody Winter.* 1967. Princeton. ils/charts. 279p. VG/VG. S16. $20.00

WATERS, John. *Shock Value.* 1985. Delta. 5th. sgn. photos. VG+. C9. $50.00

WATERS, Ralph. *Chloroform: Study After 100 Years.* 1951. Madison. 1st. 138p. VG. A13. $30.00

WATERTON, Charles. *Wanderings in South America.* 1909. NY. Sturgis Walton. 1st. 16 pl. F3. $45.00

WATKINS, Ivor. *Demon.* 1983. MacDonald. 1st. VG/fair. P3. $13.00

WATKINS, John V. *ABC of Orchid Growing.* 1971. Prentice Hall. 3rd/5th prt. 190p. clip. B1. $18.50

WATKINS, John V. *Florida Landscape Plants: Native & Exotic.* 1975. Gainsville. revised. 420p. dj. B26. $24.00

WATKINS, Lura Woodside. *American Glass & Glassmaking.* 1950. Chanticleer. 1st. 104p. cloth. VG/dj. M20. $40.00

WATKINS, Lura Woodside. *Cambridge Glass 1818 to 1888.* 1930. Bramhall. ils. 199p. F/G. H1. $30.00

WATKINS, Lura Woodside. *Cambridge Glass.* 1930. Marshall Jones. 1st. 199p. cloth/pict label. VG/tattered. M20. $50.00

WATKINS, Paul. *Calm at Sunset, Calm at Dawn.* nd. London. Hutchinson. 1st. sgn. author's 2nd book. F/dj. A24. $75.00

WATKINS, Paul. *Calm at Sunset, Calm at Dawn.* 1989. Houghton Mifflin. true 1st. sgn. author's 2nd novel. F/F. D10. $65.00

WATKINS, Paul. *Calm at Sunset, Calm at Dawn.* 1989. Houghton Mifflin. 1st. author's 2nd book. F/F. H11. $60.00

WATKINS, Paul. *Calm at Sunset, Calm at Dawn.* 1989. Houghton Mifflin. 1st. mk Network-Not for Resale. NF/dj. M25. $45.00

WATKINS, Paul. *In the Blue Light of African Dreams.* 1990. Houghton Mifflin. 1st Am. author's 3rd book. F/dj. A24/H11. $40.00

WATKINS, Paul. *In the Blue Light of African Dreams.* 1990. Houghton Mifflin. 1st. sgn. author's 3rd novel. F/F. D10. $50.00

WATKINS, Paul. *Night Over Day Over Night.* 1988. Knopf. 1st Am. author's 1st book. F/dj. A24. $85.00

WATKINS, Paul. *Night Over Day Over Night.* 1988. Knopf. 1st. author's 1st novel. rem mk. F/F. M23. $30.00

WATKINS, Paul. *Promise of Light.* 1992. London. Faber. 1st. author's 4th book. F/NF. B3. $50.00

WATKINS, T.H. *Mark Twain's Mississippi.* 1974. Palo Alto. Am West Pub. ils/halftone. 221p. dj. T7. $22.00

WATKINS, T.H. *On the Shore of the Sundown Sea.* 1973. SF. Sierra Club. 1st. F/NF. O4. $20.00

WATKINS, Thomas G. *Legal Record & Historical Reality...* 1989. London. Hambledon. 13 essays. M11. $60.00

WATKINS, William Jon. *God Machine.* 1973. Doubleday. 1st. VG/dj. P3. $20.00

WATSON, Alan. *Daube Noster, Essays in Legal History of David Daube.* 1974. Edinburgh. Scottish Academic Pr. M11. $65.00

WATSON, Clarissa. *Runaway.* 1985. Atheneum. 1st. F/dj. P3. $20.00

WATSON, Clyde. *Tom Fox & the Apple Pie.* 1972. Crowell. 1st. 8vo. unp. VG. T5. $20.00

WATSON, Colin. *Bump in the Night.* 1961. Walker. 1st. NF/dj. P3. $25.00

WATSON, Edward James. *Pleas of the Crown for the Hundred Swineshead...* 1902. Bristol. W Crofton Hemmons. pres copy. M11. $85.00

WATSON, Frederick. *Hunting Pie: Whole Art & Craft of Foxhunting.* 1931. Derrydale. 1/750. VG. O3. $125.00

WATSON, George E. *Birds of the Antarctic & the Sub-Antarctic.* 1975. WA. ils. 350p. F/VG. S15. $17.00

WATSON, Ian. *Embedding.* 1973. Scribner. 1st. F/dj. M2. $45.00

WATSON, Ian. *Evil Water.* 1987. Gollancz. 1st. F/dj. P3. $22.00

WATSON, Ian. *Fire Storm.* 1988. Gollancz. 1st. sgn. F/F. B11. $35.00

WATSON, Ian. *Flies of Memory.* 1990. Gollancz. 1st. F/dj. P3. $25.00

WATSON, Ian. *Queenmagic, Kingmagic.* 1986. Gollancz. 1st. sgn. F/dj. P3. $30.00

WATSON, Ian. *Slow Birds & Other Stories.* 1985. Gollancz. 1st. sgn. F/dj. P3. $30.00

WATSON, Ian. *Stalin's Teardrops.* 1991. Gollancz. 1st. F/dj. P3. $25.00

WATSON, J.N.P. *World of Polo.* 1986. Topsfield. Salem House. 1st Am. VG/VG. O3. $45.00

WATSON, James B. *Tairora Culture: Contingency & Pragmatism.* 1983. Seattle/London. 6 maps/15 tables/figures. 346p. red cloth. P4. $25.00

WATSON, Lyall. *Heavens' Breath.* 1984. Morrow. 1st. 8vo. 384p. dj. K5. $22.00

WATSON, Margaret G. *Silver Theatre, Amusements of the Mining Frontier...* 1964. Clark. 1st. ils. 387p. VG/VG. J2. $80.00

WATSON, Virginia. *Manhattan Acres.* 1934. Dutton. 1st. B4. $100.00

WATSON, William. *Cactus Culture for Amateurs.* 1920s. London. 4th revised. ils/pl/woodcuts. binding copy. B26. $15.00

WATT, Lauchlan Maclean. *Advocate's Wig.* 1932. Herbert Jenkins. 1st. VG. P3. $30.00

WATTERS, Pat. *Fifty Years of Pleasure.* 1980. Lakeland. Publix. inscr. F/VG. B11. $30.00

WATTERSON, Henry. *Marse Henry.* 1919. 2 vol. 1st. O8. $23.50

WATTS, Alan W. *Cloud-Hidden, Whereabouts Unknown: A Mountain Journal.* 1973. Pantheon. 1st. F/clip. M25. $35.00

WATTS, Alan W. *Reading the Weather.* (1987). Dodd Mead. 4to. 208p. VG. K5. $12.00

WATTS, Alan W. *Two Hands of God: Myths of Polarity.* 1963. Braziller. 1st. NF/clip. M25. $35.00

WATTS, Mabel. *Dozens of Cousins.* 1950. Whittlesey. 1st. ils Roger Duvoisin. VG/G+. M5. $32.00

WATTS, Mabel. *Story of Zachary Zween.* nd (1967). Parents Magazine. sm 4to. ils. NF. C14. $12.00

WATTS, Peter. *Dictionary of the Old West.* 1977. Knopf. 1st. 399p. VG/VG. J2. $65.00

WAUGH, Alec. *Hot Countries.* 1930. ils Lynd Ward. VG. M17. $15.00

WAUGH, Alec. *In Praise of Wine & Certain Noble Spirits.* 1960 (1959). Sloane. 2nd. VG/VG. B10. $12.00

WAUGH, Douglas. *Maudie of McGill: Dr Maude Abbott & Foundations of Heart...* 1942. Toronto. 1st. 142p. A13. $30.00

WAUGH, Evelyn. *Helena.* 1950. Little Brn. 1st. VG/VG. M19. $25.00

WAUGH, Evelyn. *Men at Arms.* 1952. Little Brn. 1st. NF/G. M19. $45.00

WAUGH, Evelyn. *Men at Arms.* 1952. London. Chapman Hall. 1st. F/NF. B2. $85.00

WAUGH, Evelyn. *Officers & Gentlemen.* 1955. Little Brn. 1st. F/VG. M19. $45.00

WAUGH, Evelyn. *When the Going Was Good.* 1947. Little Brn. 1st. F/VG. M19. $65.00

WAUGH, F.A. *American Apple Orchard.* 1911. Orange Judd. 215p. A10. $32.00

WAUGH, F.A. *American Apple Orchard.* 1923. Orange Judd. 215p. dj. A10. $40.00

WAUGH, F.A. *American Apple Orchard.* 1923 (1908). Orange Judd. xl. G+. E6. $18.00

WAUGH, Hillary. *Death in a Town.* 1990. Dodd Mead. 2nd. VG/dj. P3. $17.00

WAUGH, Hillary. *Murder on Safari.* 1987. Dodd Mead. 1st. VG/dj. P3. $16.00

WAUGH, Julia. *Silver Cradle.* 1955. Austin, TX. 1st. 160p. dj. F3. $15.00

WAUMETT, Victor. *Teardown.* 1990. St Martin. 1st. F/dj. P3. $17.00

WAUTERS, A.J. *Stanley's Emin Pasha Expedition.* 1890. NY. Alden. 1st. 8vo. 210p. cloth. VG. W1. $22.00

WAXELL, Sven. *American Expedition.* 1952. London. 1st Eng. 8vo. map ep. bl/gr cloth. VG/dj. P4. $60.00

WAXMAN, Mordecai. *Tradition & Change: Development of Conservative Movement.* 1958. Burning Bush. 34 essays. 477p. VG/poor. S3. $29.00

WAY, Frederick. *Way's Pocket Directory, 1848-1983.* 1983. Athens, OH. ils/over 5000 entries. VG+/dj. B18. $35.00

WAY, Peter. *Belshazzar's Feast.* 1982. Atheneum. 1st. F/dj. M2. $20.00

WAYLAND, John W. *Hopewell Friends History, 1734-1934...Virginia.* 1936. Strasburg, VA. Shenandoah Pub. 1st. 671p. V3. $85.00

WAYNE, Joseph. *By Gun & a Spur.* 1952. Dutton. 1st. VG. P3. $10.00

WEATHERHEAD, Leslie D. *Psychology, Religion & Healing.* 1952. Hodder Stoughton. 544p. G. B29. $6.50

WEATHERMAN, Hazel Marie. *Colored Glassware of the Depression Era, Book 1.* 1970. self pub. 1st/2nd prt. 8vo. 239p. as new/clip. H1. $80.00

WEATHERMAN, Hazel Marie. *Colored Glassware of the Depression Era, Book 2.* 1974. self pub. 1st. sgn. 4to. F. H1. $105.00

WEATHERWAX, Clara. *Marching! Marching!* 1935. John Day. 1st. F/NF. B4. $125.00

WEAVER, D. *Account of Principle Difficulties & Embarrassments...* 1872. Nashville, TN. 1st. 8vo. 37p. prt wrp. M1. $200.00

WEAVER, J.E. *Native Vegetation of Nebraska.* 1965. Lincoln. 1st. 8vo. cloth. F/clip. A22. $17.00

WEAVER, Michael D. *Mercedes Nights.* 1987. St Martin. 1st. F/dj. P3. $17.00

WEAVER, Paul E. *Charlie Dye.* 1981. Los Angeles. dj. A19. $45.00

WEAVER, W.G. *Yankee Doodle Went to Town.* 1959. Ann Arbor. Edwards Bros. 1st. inscr. VG. A23. $40.00

WEBB, Alexander S. *Peninsula.* 1881. NY. 1st. 219p. O8. $21.50

WEBB, Jack. *Bad Blonde.* 1956. Rinehart. 1st. VG/dj. M25. $45.00

WEBB, Jack. *Deadly Sex.* 1959. Rinehart. 1st. xl. VG/dj. P3. $10.00

WEBB, Jack. *Make My Bed Soon.* 1963. HRW. 1st. F/NF. T12. $25.00

WEBB, Jack. *One for My Dame.* 1961. HRW. 2nd. VG/G. P3. $12.00

WEBB, James. *Fields of Fire.* 1978. Prentice Hall. 1st. author's 1st book. 344p. NF/dj. M19/W2. $45.00

WEBB, James. *Spence of Honor.* 1981. Prentice Hall. 1st. F/NF. M19. $25.00

WEBB, Joe. *Care & Training of Tennessee Walking Horse.* nd. Searcy. self pub. 3rd. sgn pres. VG. O3. $35.00

WEBB, Marion St. John. *Forest Faries.* 1932. London. Medici Soc. 4th imp. ils Tarrant. 16mo. gr brd. dj. R5. $100.00

WEBB, Marion St. John. *Little One in Between.* 1929. Harrap. 1st. ils Margaret Tarrant. F/NF. M5. $110.00

WEBB, Marion St. John. *Littlest One Again.* 1923. Harrap. 1st. ils Margaret Tarrant. VG+/VG. M5. $85.00

WEBB, Marion St. John. *Littlest One.* 1919. Harrap. ils Margaret Tarrant. sm 8vo. NF. M5. $65.00

WEBB, Marion St. John. *Pond Fairies.* 1925. London. Modern Arts. 1st. ils Tarrant. 16mo. gray-gr brd/label. R5. $150.00

WEBB, Roy. *Riverman: Story of Bus Hatch.* 1990. Labyrinth. 2nd. 8vo. G+/stiff bl wrp. F7. $12.50

WEBB, Sharon. *Half Life.* 1989. Tor. VG/VG. P3. $18.00

WEBB & WEBB. *Decay of Capitalist Civilization.* 1923. Harcourt. 1st. NF/VG. B2. $45.00

WEBB & WEBB. *Littlest Fairy.* 1910. Dodge. 1st. ils Ruth Clements. 4to. decor brd/pict label. R5. $250.00

WEBBER, Alexander. *Wine: A Series of Notes on This Valuable Product...* nd. London. Simpkins Marshall. aeg. G+. B10. $150.00

WEBBER, C.W. *Wild Scenes & Song-Birds.* 1855. NY. Tiker Thorne. 2nd. 8vo. 347p. pub rose cloth. B24. $225.00

WEBER, Carl J. *Fore-Edge Painting: Historical Survey of Curious Art...* 1966. Irvington-on-Hudson. Harvey. 2nd. F/dj. B24. $275.00

WEBER, Elizabeth Anne. *Duk-Duks.* 1929. Chicago. 1st. 8vo. 142p. F/dj. T10. $75.00

WEBER, Francis J. *California Mission Poetry.* Hong Kong. Libra Pr w/Los Angeles 1978 imp. 1/350. 8vo. NF/wrp. O4. $25.00

WEBER, Francis J. *History of San Buenaventura Mission.* 1977. San Buenaventura. 1st. inscr. NF/F. O4. $25.00

WEBER, Nancy. *Broken-Hearted.* 1989. Dutton. 1st. F/F. T12. $25.00

WEBER, R.L. *Random Walk in Science.* 1973. NY. Crane Russak. ils. VG/dj. K3. $25.00

WEBER, William A. *Handbook of Plants of the Colorado Front Range.* 1953. Boulder. 8vo. 232p. G+. A22. $20.00

WEBER, William A. *Rocky Mountain Flora.* 1976. Boulder, CO. 5th revised. 12mo. 16 mc pl. 479p. VG. B1. $18.00

WEBER. *Art of Babar: Work of Jean & Laurent deBrunhoff.* 1989. Abrams. 1st. ils. 191p. F/F. A4. $40.00

WEBERS, G.F. *Geology & Paleontology of Ellsworth Mountains...* 1992. Boulder. Geological Soc of Am. ils/charts. 459p. NF/dj. P4. $125.00

WEBSTER, A.D. *Tree Wounds & Diseases.* 1916. London. Williams Norgate. 1st. 8vo. 215p. A22. $30.00

WEBSTER, D.K. *Myth & Maneater: Story of the Shark.* 1963. Norton. ils/photos/drawings. 223p. cloth. F/VG+. M12. $17.50

WEBSTER, E.M. *Explorer at Rest: Ludwig Leichhardt Journals.* 1986. Carleton. Melbourne U. 1st. 124p. P4. $20.00

WEBSTER, Frank V. *Two Boys of the Battleship.* 1915. Cupples Leon. 208p. VG/dj. M20. $20.00

WEBSTER, Frank. *Results in Taxidermy, Illustrated by 140 Half-Tone...* (1905). Boston. Marsh. 1st. tall 8vo. ils. unp. VG. H7. $20.00

WEBSTER, H.T. *Best of HT Webster.* 1953. S&S. 1st. VG/dj. P3. $35.00

WEBSTER, H.T. *Who Dealt This Mess?* 1948. Garden City. 1st. bridge cartoons. VG/VG. B5. $25.00

WEBSTER, Noah. *American Dictionary of the English Language.* 1828. NY. Converse. 1st. 2 vol. lacks ftspc. lg/thick 4to. full calf+/ad leaf dtd 1828. M1. $4,750.00

WEBSTER, Noah. *Pay-Off in Switzerland.* 1977. Crime Club. 1st. VG/dj. P3. $15.00

WECHSBERG, Joseph. *Lost World of the Great Spas.* 1979. Harper Row. 1st Am. 208p. cloth. VG/dj. M20. $30.00

WEDDLE, A.E. *Techniques of Landscape Architecture.* 1969. NY. Elsevier. 2nd. dj. A10. $30.00

WEDECK, Harry. *Treasury of Witchcraft.* 1961. Philosophical Lib. 1st. F/dj. M2. $18.00

WEEDEN, Robert B. *Alaska: Promises To Keep.* 1978. Boston. Houghton Mifflin. 1st prt. 8vo. 254p. NF/dj. P4. $25.00

WEEDON, L.L. *Surprise Picture Book.* ca 1890s. London. Nister. ils Hilda Robinson. 5 transformation wheels. R5. $950.00

WEEKES, R.K. *Convict B 14.* 1920. Brentano. VG. P3. $20.00

WEEKLEY, Robert S. *House in Ruins.* 1958. Random. 1st. F/VG+. B4. $85.00

WEEKS, Herbert. *Mystery of Cedar Bluff.* 1928. Colonial. 1st. VG. P3. $30.00

WEEKS, Jim. *Sooners.* 1974. STrode. 1st. photos. F/VG+. P8. $30.00

WEEKS, Morris. *Complete Boating Encyclopedia.* 1964. NY. 560p+500 photos. dj. A17. $15.00

WEEMS, John Edward. *Race for the North Pole.* 1961. NY/London. ils. 240p. dj. T7. $20.00

WEES, Frances Shelley. *Country of Strangers.* 1960. Doubleday. 1st. VG/dj. P3. $20.00

WEESNER, Theodore. *Children's Hearts.* 1992. Summit. 1st. F/F. A20. $15.00

WEHR, Julian. *Animated Animals.* 1943. Saalfield. 4 moveables. VG/dj. D1. $150.00

WEHR, Julian. *Animated Circus Book.* 1943. Grosset Dunlap. 4 moveables. sbdg. VG/dj. D1. $300.00

WEHR, Julian. *Jack & the Beanstalk.* 1944. Duenewald. 5 moveable pl. 8vo. prt paper brd/cbdg. F/dj. T10. $300.00

WEHR, Julian. *Raggedy Ann & Andy.* 1944. Saalfield. ils Gruelle. 8vo. pict brd/sbdg. R5. $175.00

WEHR, Julian. *Snow White.* 1949. Duenewald. 4 moveables. sbdg. VG. D1. $150.00

WEHR, Julian. *Snow White.* 1949. Duenewald. 4 moveables. 8vo. pict brd/sbdg. NF. T10. $75.00

WEHRLE, Joe. *Cauliflower Catnip.* 1981. Teacup. F. M2. $20.00

WEIDEMAN, Polly. *Polly's Kaleidoscope.* nd. Rapid City, SD. Blk Hills Power & Light/KOTA. A19. $35.00

WEIDMAN, Jerome. *Praying for Rain.* 1986. Harper. 1st. F/F. B4. $35.00

WEIGALL, Arthur. *Tutankamen & Other Essays.* 1923. Thornton Butterworth. 1st. VG. P3. $45.00

WEIGHT WATCHERS. *Weight Watchers 365-Day Menu Cookbook.* 1981. Weight Watchers Internat. BC. G/dj. A16. $10.00

WEIGL, Bruce. *Song of Napalm.* 1988. NY. Atlantic Monthly. 1st. inscr. NF/dj. R13. $30.00

WEIGLEY, Russell F. *Eisenhower's Lieutenants.* 1981. IN U. 1st. sm 4to. 800p. bl cloth. as new/dj. H1. $25.00

WEIL, Lisl. *Pandora's Box.* 1986. Atheneum. 1st. lg 8vo. F/NF. C8. $30.00

WEILEN, Helen. *Mein Grosses Teddy Buch.* 1961. Vienna. ils Anny Hoffmann. VG+. M5. $110.00

WEILL, Gus. *Bonnet Man.* 1978. Macmillan. 1st. F/dj. M2. $20.00

WEINBAUM, Stanley G. *Black Flame.* 1948. Fantasy. 1st/ltd. F/NF. P3. $175.00

WEINBAUM, Stanley G. *Martian Odyssey.* nd. Fantasy. ltd/#d. F/VG. P3. $150.00

WEINBAUM, Stanley G. *New Adam.* 1939. Ziff Davis. 1st. VG/dj. P3. $125.00

WEINBAUM, Stanley G. *Red Peri.* 1952. Fantasy. ltd. F/NF. P3. $175.00

WEINBERG, George. *Numberland.* 1987. St Martin. 1st. F/dj. P3. $10.00

WEINBERG, Robert. *Biographical Dictionary Science Fiction & Fantasy Artists.* 1988. Greenwood. 1st. sgn. P3. $75.00

WEINBERG, Robert. *Devil's Auction.* 1988. Owlswick. 1st. F/dj. P3. $20.00

WEINBERG, Robert. *Far Below & Other Horrors.* 1974. Fax. 1st. inscr. F/dj. P3. $45.00

WEINBURG, Steven. *Discovery of Subatomic Particles.* 1983. Scientific Am Lib. 1st. 206p. cloth. VG+/dj. M20. $28.00

WEINBURG, Steven. *First Three Minutes.* 1977. Basic. 1st. F/dj. M2. $10.00

WEINER, Andrew. *Station Gehenna.* 1987. Congdon Weed. 1st. F/dj. M2. $15.00

WEINER, Jonathan. *Planet Earth.* 1986. Bantam. F/dj. M2. $17.00

WEINER, Shirley. *Happy Dieter.* 1974. Regional Ent. 152p. photos. sbdg. B10. $10.00

WEINSTEIN, Frida Scheps. *Hidden Childhood.* 1985. Hill Wang. 151p. F/VG+. S3. $24.00

WEINTRAUB, Stanley. *Last Great Cause, Intellectuals & Spanish Civil War.* 1968. NY. 1st. VG/dj. T9. $18.00

WEINTRAUB, Stanley. *Savoy: Nineties Experiment.* 1966. PA State. 1st. 294p. VG+/dj. M20. $70.00

WEIR & WEIR. *Hostage Bound, Hostage Freed.* 1987. Phil. Westminster. 1st. sgns. VG/VG. B11. $25.00

WEISGARD, Leonard. *Family Mother Goose: Father Goose/Little Goose/Mother Goose.* 1951. Harper. early ed. lg 12mo. VG+/VG. C8. $45.00

WEISHAUPT, C.G. *Vascular Plants of Ohio.* 1971. Dubuque. Kendall/Hunt. 3rd. 293p. B1. $22.00

WEISS, Daniel. *Little Bear Who...* nd. Mill Valley. Figment. 1/150. 68x59mm. ils/prt/sgn Diane Weiss. prt brd. B24. $125.00

WEISS, Diane. *Raven.* nd. Mill Valley. Figment. 1/60. 74x74mm. ils/prt/bdg/inscr Diane Weiss. F. B24. $135.00

WEISS, Hary B. *William Charles: Early Caricaturust, Engraver & Publisher...* 1932. ils. VG/wrp. A4. $45.00

WELCH, Adam C. *Jeremiah: His Time & His Work.* 1928. London. Oxford. index. 263p. G+/fair. S3. $25.00

WELCH, James. *Death of Jim Loney.* 1979. Harper Row. 1st. author's 2nd novel. F/VG. B3. $40.00

WELCH, James. *Fools Crow.* 1986. Viking. 1st. F/F. T11. $40.00

WELCH, James. *Fools Crow.* 1986. Viking. 1st. sgn. F/F. L3. $100.00

WELCH, James. *Indian Lawyer.* 1990. Norton. 1st. sgn. F/F. A18/T11. $50.00

WELCH, James. *Riding the Earthboy 40.* 1971. NY. World. 1st. author's 1st book. F/F. L3. $150.00

WELCH, James. *Winter in the Blood.* 1974. NY. Harper Row. 1st trade. F/F. L3. $150.00

WELCH, William H. *Interdependence of Medicine With Other Sciences of Nature.* 1934. Baltimore. Welch Bibliophilic Soc. 1/225. VG. K3. $40.00

WELCH, William H. *Pathology & Preventive Medicine.* 1920. Baltimore. 1st. 678p. xl. A13. $100.00

WELCOME, H.S. *Story of Metlakahtla.* 1887. London. 1st. ils. 483p. M4. $50.00

WELCOME, John. *Best Crime Stories.* 1964. Faber. 1st. NF/dj. P3. $30.00

WELCOME, John. *Reasons of Hate.* 1990. Collins Crime Club. 1st. F/dj. P3. $20.00

WELDON, Fay. *...And the Wife Ran Away.* 1968. McKay. 1st Am. author's 1st novel. VG/dj. M25. $60.00

WELDON, Fay. *Heart of the Country.* 1988. Viking. 1st Am. sgn. F/dj. A24. $35.00

WELDON, Fay. *Life Force.* 1992. London. Harper Collins. 1st. F/dj. A24. $25.00

WELDON, Fay. *Remember He.* 1976. Hodder Stoughton. 1st. sgn. F/dj. A24. $60.00

WELFARE, Simon. *Arthur C Clarke's Mysterious World.* 1980. A&W. 1st. VG/dj. P3. $20.00

WELKER, WELKER & WELKER. *Cambridge Ohio Glass in Color.* 1969. self pub. 8vo. 15 mc pl+mc pl cover. sbdg. VG. H1. $26.00

WELLARD, James. *Lost Worlds of Africa.* 1967. Dutton. 1st. ils/maps. 214p. VG/dj. W1. $12.00

WELLER, J.M. *Course of Evolution.* 1969. McGraw Hill. ils. 696p. NF. D8. $35.00

WELLER, J.M. *Stratigraphic Principles & Practice.* 1960. NY. Harper. 1st. F/dj. D8. $30.00

WELLER, Philip. *Life & Times of Sherlock Holmes.* 1992. Crescent. F/dj. P3. $20.00

WELLES, Patricia. *Babyhip.* 1967. Dutton. 1st. F/F. B4. $85.00

WELLES, Patricia. *Switch.* 1971. Michael Joseph. 1st. NF/dj. P3. $20.00

WELLMAN, Manly Wade. *After Dark.* 1980. Doubleday. 1st. VG/dj. P3. $25.00

WELLMAN, Manly Wade. *Brave Horse: Story of Janus.* 1968. Colonial Williamsburg. ils Peter Burchard. VG. P3. $15.00

WELLMAN, Manly Wade. *Old Gods Waken.* 1979. Doubleday. 1st. VG/dj. P3. $25.00

WELLMAN, Manly Wade. *Worse Things Waiting.* 1973. Carosa. 1st. sgn. F/dj. P3. $150.00

WELLMAN, Paul I. *Death on Horseback.* 1947. Phil. ils. 484p. G. B18. $22.50

WELLS, Anna Mary. *Sin of Angels.* 1948. S&S. 1st. G. P3. $15.00

WELLS, Anna Mary. *Talent for Murder.* 1942. Knopf. 1st. VG. P3. $25.00

WELLS, Carolyn. *Affair at Flower Acres.* nd. Doubleday Doran. VG. P3. $15.00

WELLS, Carolyn. *All at Sea.* 1927. Lippincott. 1st. VG+. N4. $25.00

WELLS, Carolyn. *Curved Blades.* 1916. Lippincott. 1st. VG. M2. $12.00

WELLS, Carolyn. *Furthest Fury.* 1924. Lippincott. 1st. 320p. VG+/dj. M20. $75.00

WELLS, Carolyn. *Happychaps.* 1908. Century. ils Harrison Cady. 4to. pict cloth. R5. $225.00

WELLS, Carolyn. *Mother Goose's Menagerie.* 1901. Noyes Platt. 1st. ils Peter Newell/12 mc pl. G. C8. $175.00

WELLS, Carolyn. *Ptomaine Street.* 1921. Lippincott. 1st. VG. M20. $20.00

WELLS, Carolyn. *Who Killed Caldwell?* 1942. Lippincott. xl. VG. P3. $12.00

WELLS, Carveth. *Bermuda in Three Colors.* 1938. NY. McBride. 100+photos/map. 271p. cloth. VG+/VG. M12. $17.50

WELLS, Carveth. *Panmexico!* 1937. National Travel Club. 1st. photos/map ep. dj. F3. $15.00

WELLS, David A. *Natural Philosophy for Use of Schools, Academies...* 1865. NY. Iveson Phinney Blakeman. 15th. 375 engravings. xl. K3. $40.00

WELLS, H.G. *Adventures of Tommy.* 1929. NY. Stokes. 1st Am. lg 4to. red cloth/label. pict dj. R5. $225.00

WELLS, H.G. *Anatomy of Frustration.* 1936. Macmillan. 1st. VG. P3. $30.00

WELLS, H.G. *Dream.* 1924. London. Cape. true 1st. F/clip. D10. $265.00

WELLS, H.G. *Experiment in Autobiography.* 1934. Canada. Macmillan. 1st. VG. P3. $35.00

WELLS, H.G. *Food of the Gods.* 1924. Scribner. F. M2. $35.00

WELLS, H.G. *Future in America.* nd. copyright ed. NF. M2. $30.00

WELLS, H.G. *Invisible Man.* 1898. Harper. VG. M2. $95.00

WELLS, H.G. *Joan & Peter.* 1918. Macmillan. 1st. G. P3. $12.00

WELLS, H.G. *Men Like Gods.* 1923. Macmillan. 1st. VG/mc Canon dj. M2. $50.00

WELLS, H.G. *Mr Britling Sees It Through.* 1916. Macmillan. 1st. VG. P3. $40.00

WELLS, H.G. *Outline of History.* 1949. Garden City. VG. P3. $20.00

WELLS, H.G. *Passionate Friends.* 1913. London. 1st. VG. T9. $18.00

WELLS, H.G. *Research Magnificent.* 1915. Macmillan. 1st. G. M2. $22.00

WELLS, H.G. *Secret Places of the Heart.* 1922. London. Cassell. 1st. gilt cloth. dj. B24. $185.00

WELLS, H.G. *Secret Places of the Heart.* 1922. Macmillan. 1st. NF. M2. $20.00

WELLS, H.G. *Seven Famous Novels by...* 1934. Knopf. 1st. VG. P3. $30.00

WELLS, H.G. *Seven Science Fiction Novels of...* nd. Dover. F/dj. M2. $13.00

WELLS, H.G. *Shape of Things To Come.* 1933. London. 1st. VG. M2. $50.00

WELLS, H.G. *Star-Begotten.* 1937. Viking. 1st. VG/dj. M2. $50.00

WELLS, H.G. *Time Machine.* 1931. Random. 1st thus. VG. M2. $12.00

WELLS, H.G. *Tono-Bungay.* 1960. NY. LEC. 1st thus. 1/1500. ils Lynton Lamb. F/case. Q1. $100.00

WELLS, H.G. *War in the Air.* 1908. Macmillan. VG. M2. $75.00

WELLS, H.G. *When the Sleeper Awakes.* 1899. NY. 1st Am. 15 pl. 328p. decor gr cloth. B18. $175.00

WELLS, H.G. *World of William Crissold Vol II.* 1926. Doran. VG. P3. $25.00

WELLS, H.G. *World Set Free.* 1914. Dutton. 1st Am. G. M2. $12.00

WELLS, Helen. *Cherry Ames: Camp Nurse (#19).* 1957. Grosset Dunlap. 182p. VG/dj (lists to #21). M20. $20.00

WELLS, Helen. *Vicki Barr: Secret of Magnolia Manor (#4).* 1949. Grosset Dunlap. 1st. 213p. cloth. VG/dj (lists to this title). M20. $20.00

WELLS, Helen. *Vicki Finds an Answer.* nd. Grosset Dunlap. VG/dj. P3. $8.00

WELLS, Henry P. *Fly-Rods & Fly Tackle, Suggestions As to Their Manufacture.* 1885. Harper. 1st. 364p. NF. H7. $125.00

WELLS, Henry W. *Introduction to Emily Dickinson.* 1947. Packard. 286p. F/dj. H1. $18.00

WELLS, James M. *Chisolm Massacre.* 1878. WA, DC. 331p. decor cloth. G. B18. $35.00

WELLS, Joel. *Grim Fairy Tales for Adults.* 1967. Macmillan. 1st. VG/dj. P3. $25.00

WELLS, Louisa Susannah. *Journal of a Voyage From Charlestown, SC to London.* 1906. NY Hist Soc. 1/200. 121p. teg. gilt bdg. VG. B18. $225.00

WELLS, Peter. *Pirate's Apprentice.* 1943. Winston. 1st. sm 4to. unp. VG/VG. T5. $35.00

WELLS, Stuart W. *Science Fiction & Fantasy Author Index.* 1978. Purple Union. 1st. F. P3. $25.00

WELLS, Tobias. *How To Kill a Man.* 1972. Crime Club. 1st. VG/dj. P3. $15.00

WELLS, Tobias. *Matter of Love & Death.* 1966. Crime Club. 1st. VG/dj. P3. $18.00

WELO, Samuel. *Studio Handbook.* 1931. Letter Design. ils. 232p. VG. B18. $17.50

WELSH, Doris. *History of Miniature Books.* 1987. ils. 160p. F. A4. $135.00

WELSH, Frank. *Building the Trireme.* 1988. London. Constable. ils. 231p. dj. T7. $30.00

WELTON, Paul. *Angels Are Painted Fair.* 1947. Lippincott. 1st. NF/VG. M19. $25.00

WELTON, Paul. *Women Are Skin Deep.* 1948. Lippincott. 1st. NF/VG. M19. $25.00

WELTY, Eudora. *Collected Stories of Eudora Welty.* 1980. Franklin Lib. 1st. aeg/ribbon marker. gilt red leather. F. B2. $50.00

WELTY, Eudora. *Conversations With Eudora Welty.* 1984. Jackson, MS. 1st. 1/2000. inscr. F/F. R14. $125.00

WELTY, Eudora. *Fairy Tale of the Natchez Trace.* 1975. MS Hist Soc. 1/1000. brd. F. M24. $125.00

WELTY, Eudora. *Losing Battles.* 1970. Random. 1st. author's 8th book. NF/dj. D10. $45.00

WELTY, Eudora. *One Writer's Beginnings.* 1984. Harvard. 1st trade. F/dj. M24. $65.00

WELTY, Eudora. *Optimist's Daughter.* 1972. Random. 1st. author's 10th book. NF/clip. D10. $70.00

WELZ, B. *Atomic Absorption Spectroscopy.* 1976. NY. Verlag Chemie. 267p. F/dj. D8. $30.00

WELZI, Jan. *Thirty Years in the Golden North.* 1932. Macmillan. 1st 336p. VG/dj. B18. $22.50

WENDT, Emil. *Buch der Rathsel. Ein Festgeschenk fur die Jugend.* 1842. Leipzig. Dorffling. 12mo. 60p. gr pebbled cloth. NF. B24. $350.00

WENDT, Herbert. *In Search of Adam: Story of Man's Quest for Truth...* 1956. Houghton Mifflin. 1st Am. 540p. VG/torn. W1. $12.00

WENGER, Stephen R. *Flowers of Mesa Verde National Park.* 1976. Mesa Verde Nat Park. photos. 47p. sc. B26. $7.50

WENHAM, Edward. *Old Clocks for Modern Use.* 1951. London. Bell. ils. 174p. VG/dj. K3. $25.00

WENIGER, Del. *Cacti of Texas & Neighboring States.* 1984. Austin. 187 photos. sc. M. B26. $23.00

WENIGER, Del. *Cacti of the Southwest.* ca 1970. Austin. ils/184 mc photos. 249p. VG+/dj. B26. $87.50

WENKAM, Robert. *Maui: Last Hawaiian Place.* nd. Friends of Earth/Seabury. 158p. cloth. VG/dj. M20. $50.00

WENTWORTH, Lady. *Swift Runner: Racing Speed Through the Ages.* 1957. London. Allen Unwin. 1st sm 4to. VG. O3. $65.00

WENTWORTH, Patricia. *Dead or Alive.* 1936. Lippincott. 1st Am. F/dj. M15. $85.00

WENTWORTH, Patricia. *Hue & Cry.* 1927. Lippincott. 1st. VG/dj. P3. $75.00

WENTWORTH, Patricia. *Ivory Dagger.* 1951. Lippincott. 1st. VG. P3. $20.00

WENTWORTH, Patricia. *Miss Silver Comes To Stay.* 1949. Lippincott. 1st. VG. P3. $20.00

WENTWORTH, Patricia. *Pilgrim's Rest.* 1946. Lippincott. 1st. VG. P3. $25.00

WENTWORTH, Patricia. *Red Shadow.* 1932. Lippincott. 1st. VG. N4. $35.00

WENTWORTH, Patricia. *Through the Wall.* 1986. Severn. VG/dj. P3. $20.00

WENTWORTH, Patricia. *Wicked Uncle.* 1947. Lippincott. 1st. VG. P3. $35.00

WERFEL, Franz. *Forty Days of Musa Dagh.* 1934. Viking. 1st. NF. P3. $20.00

WERFEL, Franz. *Song of Bernadette.* 1942. Viking. 1st. VG. M2. $12.00

WERFEL, Franz. *Story of Bernadette.* 1942. London. 1st. VG/dj. T9. $15.00

WERLIN & WERLIN. *Savior.* 1978. S&S. 1st. F/dj. P3. $22.00

WERNER, Eliza Jane. *Patrick.* 1946. Whitman. Fuzzy Wuzzy Book. pict brd. VG/dj. M20. $25.00

WERNER, Helmut. *From the Aratus Globe to the Zeiss Planet Arium.* 1957. Stuttgart. revised/enlarged. 204p. K5. $80.00

WERNER, Jane. *Giant Golden Book of Elves & Fairies.* 1951. S&S. 1st. folio. VG. M5. $165.00

WESCHCKE, Carl. *Growing Nuts in the North.* 1954. St Paul. Webb. 124p. VG/dj. A10. $32.00

WESCHER, Paul. *Time in the Wastebasket: Poems, Collages, Parables...* 1975. Santa Monica. Mary Wescher. private prt. photos. D2. $50.00

WESCOTT, Cynthia. *Gardener's Bug Book.* 1946. Doubleday. 1st. 590p. G/dj. H1. $18.00

WESCOTT, Cynthia. *Westcott's Plant Disease Handbook.* 1979. Van Nostrand. 4th. 8vo. VG/dj. A22. $25.00

WESCOTT, Glenway. *Apple of the Eye.* 1924. Dial. 1st. sgn. F/NF. B4. $300.00

WESLAGER, C.A. *Nanticoke Indians: Refugee Tribal Group of Pennsylvania.* 1948. Harrisburg. PA Hist & Mus Comm. 1st. 8vo. 159p. VG. H1. $48.00

WESLEY, Mary. *Harnessing Peacocks.* 1985. London. Macmillan. 1st. VG/NF. B3. $50.00

WEST, Anthony. *Aspects of a Life.* 1984. London. 1st. VG/dj. T9. $25.00

WEST, Charles E. *Prison-Ship Martyrs.* 1895. Brooklyn. 20p. VG/prt wrp. B11. $35.00

WEST, Edwin; see Westlake, Donald E.

WEST, Herbert Faulkner. *Mind on the Wing.* 1947. Coward McCann. 1st. 308p. VG/dj. M20. $25.00

WEST, Jessamyn. *Except for Me & Thee.* 1969. 1st. sgn. NF/NF. M19. $45.00

WEST, Morris L. *Cassidy.* 1986. Doubleday. 1st. VG/dj. P3. $15.00

WEST, Morris L. *Harlequin.* 1974. Morrow. 1st. F/dj. P3. $23.00

WEST, Morris L. *Proteus.* 1979. Collins. 1st. F/dj. P3. $20.00

WEST, Morris L. *Tower of Babel.* 1968. Morrow. VG/G. P3. $15.00

WEST, Morris L. *World Is Made of Glass.* 1981. Morrow. 1st. NF/NF. W2. $30.00

WEST, Owen; see Koontz, Dean R.

WEST, Pamela. *Yours Truly, Jack the Ripper.* nd. BC. VG/dj. P3. $10.00

WEST, Patrick C. *Resident Peoples & National Parks: Social Dilemmas...* 1991. AZ U. 1st. as new/dj. V4. $22.50

WEST, Ray. *Kingdom of the Saints, Story of Brigham Young & the Mormons.* 1957. Viking. 1st. 389p. VG/VG. J2. $75.00

WEST, Rebecca. *Thinking Reed.* 1936. Viking. 1st. red cloth. F/dj. Q1. $75.00

WEST, Richard. *Gideon Welles: Lincoln's Navy Department.* 1943. 1st. 379p. O8. $23.50

WEST, Richard. *Mr Lincoln's Navy.* 1957. 1st. 328p. O8. $14.50

WEST, Wallace. *Bird of Time.* 1959. Gnome. 1st. VG/dj. P3. $25.00

WESTALL, Robert. *Haunting of Charles McGill.* 1983. Greenwillow. 1st Am. F/NF. T12. $25.00

WESTALL, Robert. *Rachel & the Angel.* 1986. Greenwillow. VG/dj. P3. $18.00

WESTBROOK, Robert. *Nostalgia Kills.* 1988. Crown. 1st. F/dj. P3. $18.00

WESTCOTT, Jan. *Hepburn.* 1950. Crown. 1st. VG/dj. P3. $15.00

WESTERHOFF. *McGuffey & His Readers: Piety, Morality & Education...* 1978. 206p. xl. VG/VG. A4. $45.00

WESTERMAN, Percy F. *Captain Cain.* 1939. Musson. G. P3. $10.00

WESTERMAN, Percy F. *White Arab.* nd. Blackie. ils Henry Coller. VG/dj. P3. $30.00

WESTERMANN, Diedrich. *Shilluk People, Their Language & Folklore.* 1970 (1912). Negro U. rpt. 312p. VG. W1. $35.00

WESTERMEIER, Clifford. *Man, Beast, Dust: The Story of Rodeo.* 1947. World. 1st. 450p. VG/VG. J2. $135.00

WESTERMEIER, Clifford. *Trailing the Cowboy.* 1955. Caxton. 1st. 414p. VG/VG. J2. $100.00

WESTERMEYER, Arthur J. *Udara, Prince of Bidur.* 1913. Dillingham. 1st. NF. M2. $35.00

WESTHEIMER, David. *Von Ryan's Express.* 1964. Doubleday. 1st. F/F. B4. $150.00

WESTHEIMER, David. *Von Ryan's Return.* 1980. London. Michael Joseph. 1st. inscr. A23. $45.00

WESTING, Fred. *Locomotives That Baldwin Built.* 1966. Bonanza. 191p. cloth. VG/dj. M20. $18.00

WESTLAKE, Donald E. *Damsel.* 1967. Macmillan. 1st. VG/dj. P3. $75.00

WESTLAKE, Donald E. *Gangway!* 1986. Mysterious. 1st. NF/dj. P3. $18.00

WESTLAKE, Donald E. *Good Behavior.* 1986. Mysterious. 1st. NF/dj. P3. $16.00

WESTLAKE, Donald E. *Green Eagle Score.* 1986. Allison Busby. VG/dj. P3. $20.00

WESTLAKE, Donald E. *High Adventure.* 1982. Mysterious. 1/250. sgn/#d. F/F. B11. $35.00

WESTLAKE, Donald E. *High Adventure.* 1985. Mysterious. 1st. NF/dj. P3. $20.00

WESTLAKE, Donald E. *I Know a Trick Worth Two of That.* 1986. Tor. 1st. F/F. T12. $20.00

WESTLAKE, Donald E. *Killy.* 1963. Random. 1st. VG/dj. P3. $75.00

WESTLAKE, Donald E. *Levine.* 1984. Mysterious. 1st. VG/dj. P3. $13.00

WESTLAKE, Donald E. *Point Blank.* 1984. Allison Busby. 1st. F/dj. P3. $25.00

WESTLAKE, Donald E. *Sacred Monster.* 1989. Mysterious. 1st. NF/dj. P3. $18.00

WESTLAKE, Donald E. *Score.* 1985. Allison Busby. 1st. NF/dj. P3. $20.00

WESTLAKE, Donald E. *Somebody Owes Me Money.* 1969. Random. 1st. sgn. F/NF. M15. $45.00

WESTLAKE, Donald E. *Trust Me on This.* 1988. Mysterious. 1st. VG/dj. P3. $17.00

WESTLAKE, Donald E. *Up Your Banners.* 1969. Macmillan. 1st. F/dj. M15. $75.00

WESTMORELAND, Billy. *Them Ol' Brown Fish.* 1976. Nashville. 1st. 224p. dj. A17. $15.00

WESTON, Carolyn. *Rouse the Demon.* nd. Random. 2nd. VG/dj. P3. $8.00

WESTON, Edward. *Photographer: From a Motion Picture About Edward Weston.* ca 1946. Monterey. WT Lee Co. photos. 12p. wrp. D11. $200.00

WESTON, Garnett. *Hidden Portal.* 1946. Crime Club. 1st. VG/dj. P3. $20.00

WESTON, George. *His First Million Women.* 1934. Farrar. 1st. VG. M2. $30.00

WESTON, Jack. *Real American Cowboy.* 1985. New Amsterdam. 8vo. 267p. rem mk. F/wrp. T10. $12.00

WESTON & WILSON. *Cats of Wildcat Hill.* 1947. 1st. photos. VG/VG. M17. $100.00

WESTWOOD, Richard E. *Rough-Water Man.* 1992. Reno. 1st. 8vo. 259p. yel cloth. F/dj. F7. $28.00

WETMORE, Alexander. *Observations on the Birds of Northern Venezuela.* 1939. Smithsonian. 88p. VG. S15. $12.00

WETMORE, Claude. *Queen Magi's Little People.* 1913. St Louis. Curran. 1st. 8vo. tan cloth. R5. $75.00

WETMORE, Helen Cody. *Last of the Great Scouts: Buffalo Bill.* 1918. Grosset Dunlap. VG/dj. A19. $45.00

WEVERKA, Robert. *One Minute to Eternity.* 1968. Morrow. VG/VG. P3. $13.00

WEYER, Diane. *Assassin & the Deer.* 1989. Norton. 1st. F/F. H11. $30.00

WEYER, Edward. *Primitive Peoples Today.* 1958. Doubleday. 4to. 288p. F3. $20.00

WEYGOLDT, P. *Biology of Pseudoscorpions.* 1969. Harvard. ils. 145p. cloth. F/NF. M12. $25.00

WEYMAN, Stanley. *Man in Black.* nd. Optimus. VG. M2. $22.00

WEYMOUTH, Richard F. *New Testament in Modern Speech.* 1929. Harper. 5th. 711p. G. B29. $9.00

WHALE, Charles. *Longest Debate: A Legislative History of 1964 Civil Rights.* 1985. Seven Locks. 1st. G/G. V4. $17.50

WHALEN, Philip. *Memoirs of an Interglacial Age.* 1960. SF. Auehahn. 1st. F/wrp. B2. $45.00

WHALEN, Richard E. *Neural Control of Behavior.* 1970. NY. Academic. 301p. gr cloth. VG/dj. G1. $25.00

WHALEY, Gould. *William D Witliff & the Encino Press.* (1989). Dallas. Stillpoint. 1st. 1/500. quarter cloth/gilt label. M24. $75.00

WHALLEY, Joyce. *Cobwebs to Catch Flies: Illustrated Books for Nursery...* 1975. Berkeley. ils. 163p. F/F. A4. $65.00

WHALLEY, Joyce. *Cobwebs to Catch Flies: Illustrated Books for Nursery...* 1975. Berkeley. 1st. 8vo. 163p. bl cloth. NF/NF. D1. $60.00

WHALLEY, Peter. *Crooks.* 1987. Walker. 1st. F/dj. P3. $16.00

WHALLEY, Peter. *Mortician's Birthday Party.* 1988. Walker. F/dj. P3. $20.00

WHALLEY, Peter. *Robbers.* 1986. Walker. 1st. F/dj. P3. $20.00

WHALLEY, Peter. *Rogues.* 1986. Walker. 1st. F/dj. P3. $20.00

WHARTON, Anne Hollingsworth. *Through Colonial Doorways.* 1893. Lippincott. 1st. ils cloth. VG. B14. $45.00

WHARTON, Edith. *Custom of the Country.* 1913. 1st. red cloth. VG. S13. $45.00

WHARTON, Edith. *Ethan Frome.* 1911. Scribner. 1st/1st prt/2nd bdg. teg. gilt red cloth. M24. $200.00

WHARTON, Edith. *Ghost Stories of...* 1973. Scribner. 1st. F/dj. M2. $35.00

WHARTON, Edith. *Gods Arrive.* 1932. NY. Appleton. 1st/1st prt/A bdg. gilt bl cloth. F/NF. M24. $200.00

WHARTON, Edith. *Hudson River Bracketed.* 1930. Appleton. 1st. F/dj. B4. $600.00

WHARTON, Edith. *Son at the Front.* 1923. Scribner. 1st. VG. B4. $125.00

WHARTON, Edith. *Touchstone.* 1900. Scribner. 1st/1st prt. teg. uncut. M24. $300.00

WHARTON, Edith. *Valley of Decision.* 1902. Scribner. 1st/2nd state. 2 vol. teg. cloth. NF. M24. $125.00

WHARTON, Edith. *Xingu.* 1916. Scribner. 1st. VG. Q1. $150.00

WHARTON, William. *Birdy.* 1979. Knopf. 1st. sgn. author's 1st book. F/NF. L3. $250.00

WHARTON, William. *Dad.* 1981. Knopf. 1st. author's 2nd book. F/NF. H11. $30.00

WHARTON, William. *Midnight Clear.* 1982. Knopf. 1st. F/NF. W2. $40.00

WHEAT, Carl I. *Books on the California Gold Rush.* 1949. SF. Colt Pr. 1/500. inscr. decor brd/cloth spine. D11. $225.00

WHEAT, Carl I. *First 100 Years of Yankee California.* 1949. WA. Lib Congress. 1/500. ils. 24p. prt brd. VG. K7. $35.00

WHEAT, Carl I. *Mapping the Transmississippi West, 1540-1861.* 1957-1963. SF. Inst Hist Cartography. 5 vol in 6. 1/1000. cloth. D11. $3,000.00

WHEAT, Carl I. *Pioneer Press of California.* 1948. Oakland. Biobooks. 1/450. 4to. decor mc brd/red cloth spine. F. R3. $200.00

WHEATLEY, Dennis. *Bill for the Use of a Body.* 1964. Hutchinson. 1st. G/G. P3. $15.00

WHEATLEY, Dennis. *Dangerous Inheritance.* 1965. London. 1st. VG. M2. $12.00

WHEATLEY, Dennis. *Dark Secret of Josephine.* 1955. Hutchinson. 1st. VG/dj. P3. $30.00

WHEATLEY, Dennis. *Desperate Measures.* 1974. London. 1st. F/dj. M2. $25.00

WHEATLEY, Dennis. *Devil & All His Works.* 1971. ils. VG/VG. M17. $25.00

WHEATLEY, Dennis. *Gunmen, Gallants & Ghosts.* 1955. London. VG/dj. M2. $17.00

WHEATLEY, Dennis. *Ka of Gifford Hillary.* 1956. Hutchinson. VG. P3. $30.00

WHEATLEY, Dennis. *Malinsay Massacre.* 1986. Magnolia. F. P3. $15.00

WHEATLEY, Dennis. *Murder Off Miami.* 1986. Michael Joseph. decor brd. F. P3. $25.00

WHEATLEY, Dennis. *Shadow of Tyburn Tree.* 1953. London. VG. M2. $10.00

WHEATLEY, Dennis. *Strange Conflict.* 1952. Hutchinson. VG/dj. P3. $25.00

WHEATLEY, Dennis. *Sultan's Daughter.* 1963. Hutchinson. 1st. VG/dj. P3. $25.00

WHEATLEY, Dennis. *Uncharted Seas.* 1938. London. 1st. VG. M2. $30.00

WHEATLEY, Dennis. *V for Vengeance.* 1942. Macmillan. VG/dj. M2. $15.00

WHEATLEY, Dennis. *Vendetta in Spain.* 1961. Hutchinson. 1st. VG/dj. P3. $15.00

WHEATLEY, Dennis. *Worlds Far From Here.* 1952. London. 1st. F/dj. M2. $30.00

WHEELER, Dorothy M. *Three Little Pigs.* 1951. London. Juvenile Prod. 4to. pict brd. R5. $85.00

WHEELER, Francis Rolt. *Boy With the US Survey.* 1909. Lee Shepard. 1st. 8vo. 2-tone cloth. G+. F7. $40.00

WHEELER, George M. *Report Upon US Geographical Surveys West of 100th Meridian.* 1787. GPO. Vol VI. 4to. cloth. A22. $150.00

WHEELER, Harold F. *Story of the British Navy.* 1922. London. Harrap. 1st. 8vo. 384p. gilt bl cloth. P4. $40.00

WHEELER, Harold F. *War in the Underseas.* 1919. London. Harrap. ils. 319p. T7. $45.00

WHEELER, Kate. *Not Where I Started From.* 1993. Houghton Mifflin. 1st. author's 1st book. F/dj. A24. $45.00

WHEELER, Kate. *Not Where I Started From.* 1993. Houghton Mifflin. 1st. sgn. author's 1st book. F/F. D10. $50.00

WHEELER, Keith. *Pacific Is My Beat.* 1943. NY. 1st. 383p. VG/poor. S16. $24.50

WHEELER, Opal. *Sing for Christmas.* 1948 (1943). Dutton. 9th. 4to. VG/VG. C8. $15.00

WHEELER, Opal. *Sing in Praise.* 1946. Dutton. 1st. ils Marjorie Torrey. Caldecott Honor. VG/dj. P2. $60.00

WHEELER, Richard S. *Pagans in the Pulpit.* 1974. Arlington. 137p. VG/dj. B29. $6.50

WHEELER, William Morton. *Ants: Their Structure, Development & Behavior.* 1926 (1910). Columbia. 663p. cloth. VG+. M20. $50.00

WHELAN, Elizabeth. *Sex & Sensibility: A New Look At Being a Woman.* 1975. McGraw Hill. 1st. ils. VG/VG. A25. $8.00

WHELAN & WHELAN. *Making Sense Out of Sex: A New Look At Being a Man.* 1975. McGraw Hill. 1st. 178p. VG/dj. A25. $8.00

WHELEN, Townsend. *Why Not Load Your Own.* 1949. WA. 1st. ils. 216p. VG. B5. $30.00

WHELESS, Joseph. *Is It God's Word? An Exposition of Fables & Mythology...* 1926. Knopf. 474p. VG. S3. $30.00

WHELTON, Paul. *Angels Are Painted Fair.* 1947. Lippincott. 1st. NF/VG. M19. $25.00

WHELTON, Paul. *Women Are Skin Deep.* 1948. Lippincott. 1st. NF/VG. M19. $25.00

WHERRY, Edgar. *Southern Fern Guide.* 1964. Doubleday. 349p. dj. A10. $20.00

WHIDDEN, John D. *Ocean Life in the Old Sailing Ship Days.* 1908. Little Brn. 1st. sgn. 314p. bl cloth. G. B11. $45.00

WHIFFEN, Erwin Thomas. *Outing Lore.* 1928. NY. 1st. 185p. VG. A17. $20.00

WHIPPLE, A.B.C. *Vintage Nantucket.* 1978. Dodd Mead. 1st. 260p. G/VG. V3. $10.00

WHIPPLE, Allen. *Evolution of Surgery in the United States.* 1963. Springfield. 1st. 180p. A13. $75.00

WHISMAN, Fred. *Tiger of Muscovy.* 1904. Longman. 1st. VG. M2. $22.00

WHISTLER, W.A. *Ethnobotany of Tonga: Plants, Their Tongan Names & Uses.* 1991. Honolulu. Bishop Mus. 155p. F/wrp. B1. $35.00

WHISTON, Willima. *Life & Works of Flavius Josephus.* 1957. Winston. 1055p. G/partial. B29. $9.00

WHITAKER, Herman. *West Winds: California's Book of Fiction.* 1914. SF. Paul Elder. 1st. ils. G. O4. $45.00

WHITAKER, Muriel. *Stories From the Canadian North.* 1980. Edmonton. Hurtig. 191p. VG/dj. P4. $35.00

WHITALL, Henry. *Moveable Planisphere of the Heavens at Every Month.* 1871. Phillipsburg. 6th. M1. $275.00

WHITCOMB, Carrie Niles. *Reminiscences of the Springfield Women's Club 1884-1924.* ca 1925. Springfield, MA. 1st. ils. 218p. VG. A25. $25.00

WHITCOMBE, Rick Trader. *Savage Cinema.* nd. Bounty. F/dj. P3. $10.00

WHITE, A. *Attack on America.* 1939. Houghton Mifflin. 1st. NF/dj. M2. $50.00

WHITE, A. *Stapelieae.* 1937. Pasadena. 3 vol. 2nd. 39 mc pl/1233 photos/drawings. VG. B26. $375.00

WHITE, A.R. *Succulent Euphorbieae.* 1941. Pasadena. 2 vol. photos/pl/drawings. new buckram. F. B26. $425.00

WHITE, Alma. *Story of My Life. Vol 1.* 1919. Pillar of Fire. 392p. G. B29. $16.00

WHITE, Anne Terry. *George Washington Carver, Story of a Great American.* 1953. Random. 2nd. sm 8vo. F/NF. C8. $17.50

WHITE, Barbara. *Growing Up Female.* 1985. lists 275 novels. 273p. F/F. A4. $35.00

WHITE, Barbara. *Lady Leatherneck.* 1945. NY. 180p. VG. S16. $28.50

WHITE, Charles. *Life & Times of Little Richard.* 1984. Harmony. dj. A19. $18.00

WHITE, Clarence H. *Symbolism of Light: Photographs of Clarence H White.* 1977. Wilmington/NY. DE Art Mus/Internat Center Photography. 80p. prt wrp. D11. $50.00

WHITE, Colin. *World of the Nursery.* 1984. 4to. ils. 224p. F/F. A4. $55.00

WHITE, David. *Flora of the Hermit Shale, Grand Canyon, Arizona.* 1929. Carnegie Inst. 8vo. 221p. stiff tan wrp. F7. $75.00

WHITE, E.B. *Charlotte's Web.* 1952. Harper Row. 1st. ils Garth William. G+/VG-. M17. $150.00

WHITE, E.B. *Charlotte's Web.* 1952. Harper Row. 1st. ils Garth Williams. VG+/G+. C8. $200.00

WHITE, E.B. *Chrlotte's Web.* 1952. NY. Harper. 1st. F/VG. B4. $675.00

WHITE, E.B. *Essays of EB White.* 1977. Harper. 1st. inscr/dtd 1979. F/VG. B4. $600.00

WHITE, E.B. *Letters of EB White.* 1976. Harper. 1st. sgn tipped-in leaf. F/NF. B2. $45.00

WHITE, E.B. *One Man's Meat.* 1942. NY. 1st. VG/VG. B5. $35.00

WHITE, E.B. *Stuart Little.* 1945. Harper. stated 1st. ils Garth Williams. VG. M5. $75.00

WHITE, E.B. *Stuart Little.* 1945. Harper. 1st. ils Garth Williams. VG/G. M22. $125.00

WHITE, Edmund. *Beautiful Room Is Empty.* 1988. Knopf. 1st. VG/dj. P3. $18.00

WHITE, Edmund. *Caracole.* 1985. Dutton. 1st. F/F. T12. $20.00

WHITE, Eliza Orne. *Ann Francis.* (1935). Houghton Mifflin. 8vo. 126p. VG. T5. $25.00

WHITE, Eliza Orne. *Patty Makes a Visit.* 1939. Houghton Mifflin. 1st. ils Helen Blair. 133p. F/VG-. P2. $25.00

WHITE, Ethel Lina. *Step in the Dark.* 1946. Books Inc. VG. P3. $13.00

WHITE, F. *Panorama of the Tabernacle & Its Service.* nd. London. 12 chromos. G+. E6. $75.00

WHITE, Frank. *Overview Effect.* 1987. Houghton Mifflin. lg 8vo. 318p. Vg/dj. K5. $20.00

WHITE, Fred M. *Crimson Blind.* 1905. Fenno. 1st Am. VG. M2. $22.00

WHITE, Gleason. *English Illustration. The Sixties: 1855-70.* 1897. London. Constable. 4to. ils/5 pl. teg. gilt bdg. VG. B24. $125.00

WHITE, Harvey Elliott. *Intro to Atomic Spectra.* 1934. NY. 457p. A17. $10.00

WHITE, Henry A. *Robert E Lee & the Southern Confederacy.* 1911. NY. ils/index/ads. 467p. G. B5. $50.00

WHITE, J.E. Grant. *Designing a Garden Today.* 1966. NY. 1st Am. ils/pl. 184p. VG+/dj. B26. $22.00

WHITE, James. *Complete System of Farriery & Veterinary Medicine.* 1818. Pittsburgh. Patterson Lambdin. 1st Am. leather. fair. O3. $125.00

WHITE, James. *Genocidal Healer.* nd. BC. F/dj. P3. $8.00

WHITE, James. *Life Span & Reminiscences of Railway Mail Service.* 1973. Bl Letter. facsimile of 1904 ed. 1/500. F. A17. $30.00

WHITE, James. *Watch Below.* 1966. Walker. 1st. VG/dj. P3. $40.00

WHITE, Jane. *Comet.* 1976. Harper. 1st Am. F/dj. M2. $12.00

WHITE, John. *United States Marines in North China.* 1974. Millbrae. 1st. sgn. ils/map. 217p. VG/VG. S16. $50.00

WHITE, Joseph J. *Cranberry Culture.* 1909. Orange Judd. new/enlarged. ils. 12mo. 131p. cloth. K3. $30.00

WHITE, Joseph J. *Cranberry Culture.* 1916. Orange Judd. 131p. F. A10. $32.00

WHITE, Lionel. *Ransomed Madonna.* 1964. Dutton. 1st. VG. P3. $30.00

WHITE, Lionel. *To Find a Killer.* 1954. Dutton. 1st. VG/dj. P3. $40.00

WHITE, Margaret Bourke. *For the World to See: The Life of...* 1983. Viking. 1st. F/dj. Q1. $40.00

WHITE, Margaret Bourke. *Portrait of Myself.* 1963. NY. 1st ed. sgn. F/NF. A17. $100.00

WHITE, Michael. *Lachmi Bai.* 1901. Taylor. 1st. VG. M2. $22.00

WHITE, Patrick. *Twyborn Affair.* 1979. London. 1st. VG/VG. T9. $25.00

WHITE, Philo. *Philo White's Narrative of a Cruise in the Pacific...* 1965. Denver. Old West Pub. 1/1000. 84p. gr cloth. P4. $75.00

WHITE, Randall. *Salute to the Marines.* 1943. NY. 210p. VG. S16. $22.50

WHITE, Randy Wayne. *Batfishing in the Rainforest.* 1991. NY. Burford. 1st. sgn. F/F. B3. $175.00

WHITE, Randy Wayne. *Heat Islands.* 1992. St Martin. 1st. sgn. author's 3rd book. F/F. M15. $100.00

WHITE, Randy Wayne. *Sanibel Flats.* 1990. St Martin. 1st. sgn. author's 1st hc novel. F/NF. B4. $975.00

WHITE, Randy Wayne. *Sanibel Flats.* 1990. St Martin. 1st. VG+/VG+. M22. $425.00

WHITE, Russell H. *Combined Gospels of Matthew, Mark, Luke & John.* 1947. White. complete/chronological pres material in gospels. VG/dj. B29. $9.50

WHITE, Steve. *Privileged Information.* 1991. Viking. 1st. author's 1st novel. F/F. M22. $20.00

WHITE, Stewart Edward. *Arizona Nights.* nd. Grosset Dunlap. G. P3. $10.00

WHITE, Stewart Edward. *Conjuror's House.* 1903. McClure Phillips. A19. $30.00

WHITE, Stewart Edward. *Folded Hills.* 1934. Doubleday Doran. A19. $20.00

WHITE, Stewart Edward. *Forest.* 1903. Outlook. rare. A19. $40.00

WHITE, Stewart Edward. *Leopard Woman.* 1916. Doubleday. 1st. VG. M2. $25.00

WHITE, Stewart Edward. *On Tiptoe.* 1922. Doran. A19. $25.00

WHITE, Stewart Edward. *Riverman.* 1908. NY. McClure. ils NC Wyeth. A19. $35.00

WHITE, Stewart Edward. *Rules of the Game.* 1911. Thomas Nelson. A19. $15.00

WHITE, Stewart Edward. *Westerners.* 1901. Grosset Dunlap. 344p. G. J2. $15.00

WHITE, T.H. *America in Search of Itself.* 1982. Harper Row. 1st. 465p. VG. W2. $30.00

WHITE, T.H. *Book of Merlyn.* 1977. TX U. 1st. F/dj. M2. $30.00

WHITE, T.H. *Book of Merlyn.* 1977. TX U. 2nd. VG/dj. P3. $15.00

WHITE, T.H. *Elephant & the Kangaroo.* 1947. Putnam. VG/dj. P3. $30.00

WHITE, T.H. *Mistress Masham's Repose.* 1946. Putnam. VG/dj. M2. $15.00

WHITE, T.H. *Once & Future King.* 1958. Putnam. 1st Am. F/NF. T12. $200.00

WHITE, T.H. *Verses.* 1962. London. Alderney. 1st. 1/100. inscr. Japanese vellum/cloth. NF/sans. B4. $850.00

WHITE, T.H. *Witch in the Wood.* 1939. Putnam. 1st. VG/dj. M2. $50.00

WHITE, Ted. *Trouble on Project Ceres.* 1971. Westminster. 1st. xl. VG/dj. P3. $8.00

WHITE, Teri. *Bleeding Hearts.* 1984. Mysterious. 1st. F/NF. N4. $25.00

WHITE, Teri. *Bleeding Hearts.* 1984. Mysterious. 1st. NF/NF. P3. $20.00

WHITE, Teri. *Fault Lines.* 1988. Mysterious. 1st. VG/dj. P3. $18.00

WHITE, Teri. *Outlaw Blues.* 1992. Mystery Scene Short Story. 1st. 1/100. sgn/#d. F/sans. P3. $20.00

WHITE, Teri. *Thursday's Child.* 1991. Mysterious. 1st. NF/dj. P3. $20.00

WHITE, Walter. *Man Called White.* 1948. Viking. 1st. VG. M25. $15.00

WHITE, William. *Pale Blonde of Sands Street.* 1946. Viking. 1st. VG/dj. M2. $20.00

WHITECOTTON, Joseph. *Zapotecs: Princes, Priests & Peasants.* 1977. Norman, OK. 1st. ils/maps. 338p. dj. F3. $35.00

WHITEHEAD, Hal. *Voyage to the Whales.* 1990. Post Mills. Chelsea Gr. 195p. 8vo. F/dj. P4. $35.00

WHITEHEAD, Jessup. *Steward's Handbook & Guide to Party Catering in 5 Parts.* 1889. 1st. lg 8vo. 500 double-column p. VG. E6. $65.00

WHITEHEAD, John. *Religious Apartheid: Separation of Religion...* 1994. Moody. sgn. 318p. F. B29. $7.00

WHITEHEAD, John. *Solemn Mockery: Art of Literary Forgery.* 1973. London. Arlington. 1st. ils. 177p. F/VG. K3. $50.00

WHITEHEAD, Paul. *Manners: A Satire.* 1739. London. Dodsley. 1st. sm folio. 20p. recent marbled wrp. H13. $265.00

WHITELEY, George. *Northern Seas, Hardy Sailors.* 1982. NY. Norton. 1st. 8vo. 270p. half cloth. VG/dj. P4. $35.00

WHITELOCK, Dorothy. *Anglo-Saxon Wills.* 1930. Cambridge. gilt olive cloth. M11. $150.00

WHITFIELD, Irene Therese. *Louisiana French Folk Songs.* 1939. LSU. 1st. brn cloth/brn leather labels. F. B2. $85.00

WHITFIELD, Nella. *Kitchen Encyclopedia.* nd. London. Spring Books. G/torn. A16. $25.00

WHITFIELD, Raoul. *Wings of Gold.* 1930. Phil. Penn. 1st. F/VG. B4. $1,250.00

WHITLEY, Cecil. *World of Enameled Carnival Glass Tumblers.* 1985. self pub. unp. sbdg. VG. H1. $30.00

WHITLEY, M.J. *German Coastal Fores of World War Two.* 1992. London. Ams/Armour. 191p. dj. T7. $40.00

WHITLOCK, Herbert. *Story of the Gems.* 1936. NY. 1st. 8vo. ils. 206p. gilt blk cloth. VG. H3. $65.00

WHITLOCK, V.H. *Cowboy Life on the Llano Estacado.* 1970. Norman, OK. 1st. photos. 278p. VG/VG. J2. $135.00

WHITMAN, Royal. *Treatise on Orthopaedic Surgery.* 1901. Phil. 1st. 650p. A13. $100.00

WHITMAN, S.E. *Troopers.* 1962. Hastings. dj. A19. $35.00

WHITMAN, Walt. *Complete Poems & Prose...1855...1888.* 1888. Camden, NJ. 1st complete ed. lg 8vo. gr cloth. M1. $3,250.00

WHITMAN, Walt. *Complete Prose Works.* 1892. McKay. 1st. VG. B4. $125.00

WHITMAN, Walt. *Leaves of Grass.* 1881-1882. Boston. Osgood. 1st prt (of 3). mustard cloth. F. M23. $500.00

WHITMAN, Walt. *Leaves of Grass.* 1913. NY/London. Dutton/Dent. folio. ils Margaret Cook. gr brd. NF. M23. $225.00

WHITMAN, Walt. *Leaves of Grass.* 1920 (1855). Grollier. facsimile (2nd issue). 1/500. gilt gr cloth. M24. $200.00

WHITMAN, Walt. *Poems.* 1868. London. John Camden Hotten. 1st. bl cloth (primary bdg). M24. $450.00

WHITMAN, Walter. *Franklin Evans; or, The Inebriate: A Tale of the Times.* 1929. Random/Merrymount. 1st hc ed. 1/700. NF. B4. $200.00

WHITMORE, Charles. *Winter's Daughter.* 1984. Timescape. 1st. VG/dj. P3. $15.00

WHITMYER & WHITMYER. *Bedroom & Bathroom Glassware of the Depression Era.* 1990. Collector Books. 1st. ils. 253p. as new. H1. $60.00

WHITNEY, Alec. *Armstrong.* 1977. Crime Club. F/dj. P3. $13.00

WHITNEY, C.S. *Bridges: Study in Their Art, Science & Evolution.* 1929. NY. 400 pl. 363p. NF/frayed. M4. $65.00

WHITNEY, Caspar. *Charles Adelbert Canfield.* 1930. NY. private prt. 1/175. 14 full-p photos. brd/leather spine label. D11. $275.00

WHITNEY, Harry. *Hunting With the Eskimos: Unique Record of Sportsman's Year.* 1910. NY. Century. 1st. photos. 453p. teg. VG. H7. $120.00

WHITNEY, J.P. *Silver Mining Regions of Colorado.* 1865. Van Nostrand. 1st. 12mo. 107p. prt wrp. M1. $1,050.00

WHITNEY, Milton. *Field Operations of the Bureau of Soils.* 1910. WA. USDA. 1772p. G. A17. $35.00

WHITNEY, Mrs. Cornelius V. *One Cook's Tour.* nd. np. sbdg. VG. $10.00

WHITNEY, Phyllis A. *Black Amber.* 1965. Robert Hale. 1st. VG/dj. P3. $25.00

WHITNEY, Phyllis A. *Poinciana.* 1980. Doubleday. 1st. G/dj. P3. $12.00

WHITRIDGE, Arnold. *No Compromise!* 1960. FSC. 1st. 212p. VG/dj. M20. $35.00

WHITTAKER, Frederick W. *Samuel Harris, American Theologian.* 1982. Vintage. 268p. VG/dj. B29. $10.00

WHITTEMORE, Edward. *Jericho Mosaic.* 1987. Norton. 1st. NF/dj. M25. $25.00

WHITTEN, L. *Alchemist.* 1973. Charterhouse. 1st. VG/dj. M2. $10.00

WHITTEN, Leslie H. *Moon of the Wolf.* 1967. Doubleday Crime Club. 1st. Harlan Ellison's copy. F/F. M15. $100.00

WHITTIER, John Greenleaf. *Complete Writings...* (1892). Boston. 7 vol. 3-quarter brn morocco. F. C6. $350.00

WHITTIER, John Greenleaf. *Dark Eye Has Left Us, Song of the Indian Women...* 1848. Boston. Oliver Ditson. 1st. sheet music. disbound. M24. $100.00

WHITTIER, John Greenleaf. *Declaration of Sentiments of American Anti-Slavery Society.* 1844. NY. Wm S Dorr. early leaflet prt. F. M24. $200.00

WHITTIER, John Greenleaf. *History of Pennsylvania Hall.* 1838. Phil. Merrihew Gunn. 1st/1st issue. ES. M24. $450.00

WHITTIER, John Greenleaf. *Literary Recreations & Miscellanies.* 1854. Ticknor Fields. 1st/1st catalogue. 1/1500. gilt brn cloth. F. M24. $85.00

WHITTIER, John Greenleaf. *Moll Pitcher & the Minstrel Girl. Poems...Revised Edition.* 1840. Phil. Joseph Healy. 1st complete. 18mo. 44p. prt wrp. M1. $750.00

WHITTIER, John Greenleaf. *Pennsylvania Pilgrim.* 1872. 1st/1st state. F. M19. $65.00

WHITTIER, John Greenleaf. *Snow-Bound.* (1885). Riverside. rpt of 1st ils ed. inscr. aeg. bl-gr cloth. F. M24. $1,250.00

WHITTIER, John Greenleaf. *Supernaturalism of New England.* 1847. London. Wiley Putnam. 1st/Eng issue. gilt gr cloth. uncut. M24. $375.00

WHITTIER, John Greenleaf. *Tent on the Beach & Other Poems.* 1867. Ticknor Fields. 1st/earliest state (N on p172). 12mo. gilt gr cloth. VG. H1. $145.00

WHITTINGHAM, C.P. *Mechanism of Photosynthesis.* 1974. London. Arnold. 125p. stiff wrp. B1. $18.50

WHITTINGTON, Harry. *Bonanza: Treachery Trail.* 1968. Whitman. TVTI. VG. P3. $20.00

WHITTLE, Frank. *Jet: The Story of a Pioneer.* 1953. London. Frederick Muller. 1st. ils. 8vo. 32p. K3. $15.00

WHITTLE, Tyler. *Some Ancient Gentlemen.* 1966. Taplinger. 1st. 8vo. 244p. VG/dj. A22. $20.00

WHITTMAN, George. *Matter of Intelligence.* 1975. Macmillan. 1st. F/dj. P3. $15.00

WHITTON, Blair. *Paper Toys of the World.* 1986. Hobby House. obl 4to. 240p. T10. $25.00

WHITWORTH, Charles. *Account of Russia As It Was in the Year 1710.* 1758. Strawberry Hill. 1st. 1/700. 8vo. brd. R12. $525.00

WHYMPER, Edward. *Scrambles Amongst the Alps.* 1986. Salt Lake City. 262p. F/dj. A17. $20.00

WHYTE, Frederic. *William Heinemann, a Memoir.* 1929. Doubleday Doran. 326p. G. B18. $17.50

WHYTE, Samuel. *Collection of Poems, the Productions of the Kingdom Ireland.* 1773. London. Bladon. 1st thus. 8vo. 272p. contemporary bdg. H13. $450.00

WIBBERLEY, Leonard. *Homeward to Ithaka.* 1977. Morrow. 1st. F/dj. M2. $15.00

WIBBERLEY, Leonard. *Hound of the Sea.* 1969. NY. Washburn. 152p. dj. T7. $20.00

WIBBERLEY, Leonard. *Last Stand of Father Felix.* 1974. Morrow. 1st. xl. VG/dj. P3. $6.00

WICKENDEN, L. *Make Friends With Your Land.* 1949. Devin Adair. 132p. cloth. VG. A10. $20.00

WICKERSHAM, James. *Old Yukon Tales, Trails, Trials.* 1973. St Paul. 514p. F. A17. $30.00

WICKERSHAM, James. *Old Yukon: Tales, Trails, Trials.* 1938. WA Law Book Co. 1st. ils. 514p. gilt cloth. D11. $40.00

WICKS, Mark. *To Mars Via the Moon: An Astronomical Story.* 1911. Lippincott. ARC. 327p. gilt bl cloth. w/pub letter. VG. M20. $160.00

WIDDEMER, Mabel Cleland. *Aleck Bell, Ingenious Boy.* 1947. Bobbs Merrill. 1st. 8vo. orange prt cloth. T10. $50.00

WIDEMAN, John Edgar. *Fever.* 1989. NY. Holt. 1st. F/dj. A24/B3. $25.00

WIDEMAN, John Edgar. *Hiding Place.* 1984. Allison Busby. 1st. F/F. B3. $20.00

WIDEMAN, John Edgar. *Philadelphia Fire.* 1990. Holt. 1st. sgn. F/F. D10. $50.00

WIDEMAN, John Edgar. *Reuben.* 1987. Henry Holt. 1st. sgn. F/F. D10. $50.00

WIDEMAN, John Edgar. *Reuben.* 1987. Holt. 1st. F/F. T11. $30.00

WIDEMAN, John Edgar. *Sent for You Yesterday.* 1984. Allison Busby. 1st. author's 3rd book. F/NF. B3. $25.00

WIDEMAN, John Edgar. *Sent for You Yesterday.* 1984. Allison Busby. 1st. F/F. A24. $35.00

WIDTSOE, J. *Dry Farming: A System of Agriculuture for Countries...* 1912 (1911). ils. VG. E6. $25.00

WIEDERSHEIM, Robert. *Elements of Comparative Anatomy of Vertebrates.* 1897. London. 2nd. 488p. A13. $65.00

WIEGAND, Wayne A. *History of a Hoax: Edmund Lester Pearson...* 1979. Pittsburgh. Beta Phi Mu. 1st. ils. 8vo. 75p. F. K3. $25.00

WIENER, Leo. *Commentary to the Germanic Laws & Medieval Documents.* 1915. Cambridge. M11. $85.00

WIENER, Leo. *History of Yiddish Literature in the 19th Century.* 1972 (1899). NY. Hermon. 2nd. Yiddish/Eng text. 402p. VG. S3. $26.00

WIENER, Norbert. *Ex-Prodigy: My Childhood & Youth.* 1953. S&S. 2nd. ils. 309p. VG/dj. K3. $15.00

WIENER, Willard. *Two Hundred Thousand Flyers.* 1945. WA. Infantry Journal. 1st. 196p. VG/dj. B18. $37.50

WIENPAHL, Robert W. *Gold Rush Voyage on the Bark Orino.* 1978. Arthur Clark. 1st. F/F. O4. $35.00

WIER, Ester. *What Every Air Force Wife Should Know.* 1963. Stackpole. 2nd. 227p. VG/VG. A25. $20.00

WIESE, C. *Expedition in East-Central Africa 1888-91.* 1983. OK U. 1st. photos/maps. 383p. F/dj. M4. $30.00

WIESEL, Elie. *Beggar in Jerusalem.* 1970. Random. 1st. F/F. B35. $18.00

WIESEL, Elie. *Jew Today.* 1978. Random. 208p. VG/dj. S3. $25.00

WIESEL, Elie. *Legends of Our Time.* 1968. HRW. 1st. inscr. NF/NF. R14. $50.00

WIESS, John. *Trail Cooking.* 1981. Van Nostrand Reinhold. 323p. VG/VG. B10. $10.00

WIGGIN, F. *American Farmer's Instructor or Practical Agriculturist.* 1844. ils. 503p. full leather. G+. E6. $75.00

WIGGIN, Kate Douglas. *Affair at the Inn.* Sept 1904. Houghton Mifflin. 1st. 220p. VG. H1. $22.50

WIGGIN, Kate Douglas. *Cathedral Courtship.* 1893. 1st. ils Carleton. VG. M19. $35.00

WIGGIN, Kate Douglas. *Diary of a Goose Girl.* 1902. Houghton Mifflin/Riverside. 1st. ils Claude Shepperson. B15. $55.00

WIGGIN, Kate Douglas. *Old Peabody Pew.* 1907. 1st. ils Stephens. VG. M19. $35.00

WIGGIN, Kate Douglas. *Pinafore Palace: Book of Rhymes for the Nursery.* 1907. McClure. edit Sara Smith. VG. B15. $70.00

WIGGIN, Kate Douglas. *Rebecca of Sunnybrook Farm.* 1903. Houghton Mifflin. 1st/4th issue. state B bdg. F. B24. $225.00

WIGGINS, Marianne. *Gone South.* 1980. Delacorte. 1st. F/F. B4. $175.00

WIGGINTON, Eliot. *Foxfire Book.* 1972. Doubleday. A19. $15.00

WIJNGAARDS, John. *Handbook to the Gospels.* 1979. Servant Books. 301p. F/dj. B29. $7.50

WILBUR, Richard. *Bestiary.* 1983 (1955). rpt. ils Alexander Calder. VG/VG. M17. $20.00

WILBUR, Richard. *Whale & Other Uncollected Translations.* 1982. BOA Ed. 1/26 (of 1200). sgn. w/poem card. F/wrp. V1. $150.00

WILCOX, Collin. *Bernhardt's Edge.* 1988. Tor. 1st. NF/dj. P3. $18.00

WILCOX, Collin. *Dead Aim.* 1973. Robert Hale. 1st Eng. sgn. NF/VG. M19. $35.00

WILCOX, Collin. *Disappearance.* 1970. Random. 1st. sgn. VG/VG. M19. $25.00

WILCOX, Collin. *Third Figure.* 1968. Dodd Mead. 1st. sgn. NF/VG. M19. $25.00

WILCOX, Sylvia. *For Every Hero: Novel of Waves in World War II.* 1961. NY. McKay. 1st. 346p. VG/dj. A25. $22.00

WILCOX. *Japan's Secret War.* 1985. 1st. dj. K3. $25.00

WILD, Peter. *Pioneer Conservationists of Western America.* 1979. Missoula. 246p. dj. A10. $22.00

WILDE, Oscar. *Ballad of Reading Gaol.* 1905. Portland, ME. Mosher. 12mo. 34p+16p end blanks. VG. K7. $95.00

WILDE, Oscar. *Birthday of the Infanta.* 1929. Macmillan. 1st. ils Pamela Bianco. 58p. gray cloth. VG/dj. D1. $85.00

WILDE, Oscar. *Fisherman & His Soul & Other Fairy Tales.* 1929. Farrar Rhinehart. 8vo. 212p. bl cloth. VG. K7. $60.00

WILDE, Oscar. *House of Pomegranates.* nd. Brentano. 1st Am. ils Jessie M King. 162p. VG. D1. $750.00

WILDE, Oscar. *House of Pomegranates.* 1926. Dodd Mead. 1st thus. 180p. VG+. K7. $60.00

WILDE, Oscar. *Picture of Doran Gray.* 1957. LEC. 1st thus. 1/1500. ils/sgn Lucille Corcos. F/remnant glassine/case. Q1. $200.00

WILDE, Oscar. *Picture of Dorian Gray.* 1945. Tower. 4th. VG/dj. P3. $20.00

WILDE, Oscar. *Poems.* 1881. Boston. Roberts Bros. 1st Am/1st bdg (cherub). gilt brn cloth. M24. $250.00

WILDE, Oscar. *Poems.* 1881. London. David Bogue. 1st. gilt full vegetable vellum. M24. $850.00

WILDE, Oscar. *Portrait of Mr WH.* 1921. NY. Mitchell Kennerley. 1/1000. sm 8vo. 133p. M/NF case. K7. $125.00

WILDE, Oscar. *Salome: A Tragedy in One Act.* 1907. Boston. John W Luce. early pirated ed. 36p. gilt blk cloth. K7. $125.00

WILDE, Oscar. *Salome: A Tragedy in One Act.* 1930. Dutton. new ed. 17 ils. bl cloth. VG. K7. $65.00

WILDE, Oscar. *Selfish Giant & Other Tales.* 1986. Mitchell. 1st. decor brd. VG. P3. $20.00

WILDE, Oscar. *Selfish Giant.* 1980. Issaquah, WA. Archive. 1/135. sgn at colophon. unp. w/prospectus. as new/wrp. K7. $95.00

WILDE, Oscar. *Selfish Giant.* 1986. S&S. 1st Am thus. 8vo. unp. F/NF. C14. $15.00

WILDE, Oscar. *Young King & Other Fairy Tales.* 1962. Macmillan. 1st. ils Sandro Nardini/Enrico Bagnoli. F/dj. M5. $75.00

WILDE, Percival. *P Moran, Operative.* 1947. Random. 1st. F/F. M15. $45.00

WILDE, Percival. *Tinsley's Bones.* 1942. Random. 1st. F/NF. M15. $45.00

WILDER, Billy. *Apartment & the Fortune Cookie: Two Screenplays.* 1971. 1st. NF/NF. S13. $20.00

WILDER, Laura Ingalls. *Farmer Boy.* (1933). Harper. not 1st. ils Helen Sewell. VG. M5. $75.00

WILDER, Laura Ingalls. *Farmer Boy.* (1933). Harper. 10th. ils Helen Sewell. VG. C8. $30.00

WILDER, Laura Ingalls. *Little House on the Prairie.* (1935). Eau Claire, WI. EM Hale. rpt. lg 12mo. ils Helen Sewell. G. C8. $45.00

WILDER, Laura Ingalls. *Little Town on the Prairie.* (1941). Harper. 7th. ils Helen Sewell. VG/VG. C8. $45.00

WILDER, Laura Ingalls. *On the Banks of Plum Creek.* 1937. Harper. 1st. ils Sewell/Boyle. 8vo. 239p. tan cloth. R5. $250.00

WILDER, Louise Beebe. *Adventures in My Garden & Rock Garden.* 1925 (1923). Garden City. ils/pl/halftones. 355p. VG. B26. $35.00

WILDER, Louise Beebe. *Colour in My Garden.* 1927. NY. sgn. pl. VG. M17. $25.00

WILDER, Thornton. *American Characteristics & Other Essays.* 1979. Harper Row. 1st. F/F. R14. $30.00

WILDER, Thornton. *Bridge of San Luis Rey.* 1927. London. Longman. 1st. 8vo. bl brd. G. M23. $30.00

WILDER, Thornton. *Bridge of San Luis Rey.* 1927. NY. Boni. 1st. sgn. author's 1st book. olive cloth. VG. B14. $125.00

WILDER, Thornton. *Bridge of San Luis Rey.* 1927. NY. Boni. 1st. 8vo. cloth. NF. M23. $65.00

WILDER, Thornton. *Eighth Day.* 1967. Harper Row. 1st. NF/VG. B35. $16.00

WILDER, Thornton. *Ides of March.* 1948. Harper. 1st. F/VG. M19. $35.00

WILDER, Thornton. *Ides of March.* 1948. Harper. 1st. 8vo. F/dj. T10. $50.00

WILDER, Thornton. *Theophilus North.* 1973. Harper Row. 1/275. sgn/#d. F/dj/case. M25. $100.00

WILDER, Thornton. *Woman of Andros.* 1930. NY. Boni. 1st. 162p. tan cloth. VG+. B22. $15.00

WILDES, Harry Emerson. *Voice of the Lord: Biography of George Fox.* 1965. Phil. 1st. 473p. VG/dj. V3. $20.00

WILDES, Harry Emerson. *William Penn.* 1974. Macmillan. 1st. tall 8vo. 469p. as new/dj. H1. $18.00

WILDING, Philip. *Spaceflight Venus.* 1955. Philosophical Lib. 1st. xl. VG. P3. $10.00

WILDMAN, Rounseville. *Panglima Muda.* 1894. Overland Monthly. VG. M2. $25.00

WILDSMITH, Brian. *Birds.* 1967. London. Oxford. 1st. obl sm 4to. NF/NF. C8. $25.00

WILDSMITH, Brian. *Hare & the Tortoise.* 1966. London. Oxford. 1st. sm 4to. VG+/NF. C8. $35.00

WILDSMITH, Brian. *Maurice Maeterlinck's Blue Bird.* 1976. Franklin Watts. 1st. ils Wildsmith. 37p. VG/dj. M20. $30.00

WILDSMITH, Brian. *Owl & the Woodpecker.* 1971. Oxford. 1st. ils. 4to. NF/F. P2. $50.00

WILDSMITH, Brian. *Python's Party.* 1974. London. Oxford. 1st. ils. 4to. NF/VG+. P2. $60.00

WILEY, Bell Irvin. *Embattled Confederates.* 1964. Bonanza. VG/dj. A19. $45.00

WILEY, Bell Irvin. *Embattled Confederates.* 1964. Bonanza. 290p. VG. O8. $14.50

WILEY, Hugh. *Manchu Blood.* 1927. Knopf. 1st. F/VG. B4. $100.00

WILEY, John L. *History of Monrovia.* 1927. Pasadena. Star-News. ils. 291p. cloth. D11. $100.00

WILEY, Richard. *Festival for Three Thousand Maidens.* 1991. Dutton. 1st. F/F. B4. $65.00

WILEY, Richard. *Fool's Gold.* 1988. Knopf. 1st. F/F. B4. $50.00

WILHELM, Kate. *Clewiston Test.* 1976. Farrar. 1st. F/dj. M2. $20.00

WILHELM, Kate. *Clewiston Test.* 1976. FSG. 1st. VG/dj. P3. $15.00

WILHELM, Kate. *Hamlet Trap.* 1987. St Martin. 1st. NF/dj. P3. $16.00

WILHELM, Kate. *Huysman's Pets.* 1986. Bluejay. 1st. F/dj. M2. $20.00

WILHELM, Kate. *Juniper Time.* 1979. Harper Row. 1st. VG/dj. P3. $20.00

WILHELM, Kate. *More Bitter Than Death.* 1963. NY. S&S. 1st. author's 1st book. F/NF. Q1. $75.00

WILHELM, Kate. *More Bitter Than Death.* 1963. S&S. 1st. NF/dj. M2. $65.00

WILHELM, Kate. *Seven Kinds of Death.* 1992. St Martin. 1st. F/NF. N4. $25.00

WILHELM, Kate. *Somerset Dreams.* 1978. Harper Row. 1st. F/dj. P3. $20.00

WILHELM, Kate. *Welcome, Chaos.* 1983. Houghton Mifflin. 1st. F/dj. P3. $15.00

WILK, Max. *And Did You Once See Sidney Plain?* 1986. NY. ARC. inscr. ils/sgn Hirschfeld. F/F. A11. $55.00

WILK, Max. *And Did You Once See Sidney Plain?* 1986. NY. Norton. 1st. F/F. B4. $45.00

WILKES, Charles. *Narrative of the United States Exploring Expedition Vol IV.* 1845. Phil. Lee Blanchard. ils/maps. half leather. worn. K3. $80.00

WILKES, Charles. *Narrative of the United States Exploring Expedition...* 1845. Phil. Lea Blanchard. 4 vol. 10 fld maps/ils. buckram. D11. $400.00

WILKES, Charles. *Narrative of the US Exploring Expedition...* 1845. Phil. Lea Blanchard. 1/1000. 5 vol+atlas. pl clean/tissue intact. P4. $5,000.00

WILKINS, Cary. *Treasury of Fantasy.* 1981. Avenel. 1st. F/dj. M2/P3. $15.00

WILKINS, Harold. *Mysteries of Ancient South America.* 1956. Citadel. 1st Am. photos/drawings. 216p. dj. F3. $25.00

WILKINS, Mary E. *Jerome: A Poor Man.* 1897. Harper. 1st. 506p. gilt bl cloth. VG. M20. $20.00

WILKINS, W.G. *Charles Dickens in America.* 1911. Scribner. 1st. gilt lavender cloth. uncut. M24. $100.00

WILKINSON, Bud. *Oklahoma Split Football.* 1952. Prentice Hall. 1st. sgn. photos. VG. P8. $45.00

WILKINSON, Doug. *Land of the Long Day.* 1956. London/Toronto. Harrap/Clarke Irwin. 8vo. 261p. map ep. NF/dj. P4. $40.00

WILKINSON, Frederick. *Collecting Military Antiques.* 1984. London. 208p. VG+/dj. B18. $25.00

WILKINSON, Henry C. *Adventures of Bermuda: A History of Island...* 1958. 2nd. ils/fld pocket map. VG/G+. M17. $25.00

WILKINSON, John. *Quakerism Examined in Reply to Letter of Samuel Tuke.* 1836. London. Thomas Ward. 484p. xl. V3. $35.00

WILKINSON, Roderick. *Murder Belongs to Me!* 1956. Museum Pr. 1st. VG/dj. P3. $20.00

WILLARD, Barbara. *Ballad of Biddy Early.* 1987. Knopf. 1st. 4to. unp. NF/VG. T5. $35.00

WILLARD, Barbara. *Three & One To Carry.* 1965 (1964). HBW. 1st Am. 8vo. 197p. VG/G+. T5. $25.00

WILLARD, Frances E. *Glimpses of Fifty Years.* 1889. Boston. Women's Temperance. 1st. 8vo. 698p. VG. T10. $100.00

WILLARD, Mrs. Eugene S. *Life in Alaska. Letters of...* 1884. Phil. Presbyterian Brd Pub. 15 pl/2 maps/ils. emb brn cloth. P4. $150.00

WILLARD, Nancy. *Ballad of Biddy Early.* 1989. Knopf. 1st. ils/sgn Barry Moser. F/F. B3. $45.00

WILLARD, Nancy. *Childhood of the Magician.* 1973. Liveright. 1st. author's 1st book. F/NF. B3. $75.00

WILLARD, Nancy. *East of the Sun & West of the Moon.* 1989. HBJ. 1st. ils Barry Moser. F/F. B3. $30.00

WILLARD, Nancy. *East of the Sun & West of the Moon.* 1989. HBJ. 1st. 64p. VG+/VG. M20. $25.00

WILLARD, Nancy. *Visit to William Blake's Inn.* nd (1982). Methuen Children's Books. possible 1st. 45p. NF/VG. C14. $25.00

WILLARD, Nancy. *Visit to William Blake's Inn.* 1981. HBJ. 1st. ils Provensen. Newbery Medal/Caldicott Honor. NF/VG. P2. $75.00

WILLARD, Wyeth. *Leathernecks Come Through.* 1944. NY. 224p. VG. S16. $25.00

WILLARD, X.A. *Practical Butter Book: A Complete Treatise.* 1875. NY. Rural. 171p. VG. A10. $45.00

WILLCOX, William B. *Portrait of a General: Sir Henry Clinton...* 1964. Knopf. 1st. 526p. VG/clip. M20. $40.00

WILLEFORD, Charles. *Burnt Orange Heresy.* 1971. Crown. 2nd. 2nd. NF/clip. P3. $45.00

WILLEFORD, Charles. *Cockfighter Journal.* 1989. Neville. 1st. 1/300. sgn/#d. F/sans. M15. $100.00

WILLEFORD, Charles. *Miami Blues.* 1984. St Martin. 1st. F/F. D10. $175.00

WILLEFORD, Charles. *Myth of Shakespeare.* 1928. Oxford. 1st. NF. B4. $200.00

WILLEFORD, Charles. *New Hope for the Dead.* 1985. St Martin. 1st. F/F. M15. $200.00

WILLEFORD, Charles. *Off the Wall.* 1980. Montclair. Pegasus Rex. 1st. F/F. M15. $200.00

WILLEFORD, Charles. *Sideswipe.* 1987. St Martin. 1st. VG/dj. P3. $23.00

WILLEFORD, Charles. *Something About a Soldier.* 1986. Random. 1st. F/F. R14. $50.00

WILLEFORD, Charles. *Way We Die Now.* 1988. Hastings-On-Hudson. Ultramarine. 1st. 1/99 special bdg. sgn. F/sans. M15. $150.00

WILLEFORD, Charles. *Way We Die Now.* 1988. NY. Random. 1st. F/F. M22. $40.00

WILLEFORD, Charles. *Way We Die Now.* 1989. London. Gollancz. 1st. F/dj. P3. $25.00

WILLENS, Doris. *Lonesome Traveler: Life of Lee Hays.* 1988. Norton. 1st. VG/VG. V4. $15.00

WILLET, B. *Blood River: Passionate History of South Africa.* 1982. NY. 1st. photos. 255p. F/dj. M4. $15.00

WILLETS, Gilson. *First Law.* 1911. Dillingham. 1st. VG. M2. $22.00

WILLETS, William. *Chinese Art.* 1958. Braziller. 2 vol. 12mo. F/VG case. H1. $35.00

WILLETT, George. *Birds of the Pacific Slope of Southern California.* 1912. Cooper Ornithological Club. 122p. S15. $12.00

WILLETT, John. *Art & Politics in the Weimar Period: New Sobriety...1933.* 1978. Pantheon. 1st Am. 272p. dj. A17. $25.00

WILLIAMS, Alan. *Shah-Mak.* 1976. CMG. 1st. F/dj. P3. $18.00

WILLIAMS, Alan. *Snake Water.* 1965. London. Anthony Blond. 1st. F/F. M15. $45.00

WILLIAMS, Barbara. *Whatever Happened to Beverly Bigler's Birthday?* 1979. Harcourt Brace. 1st. 8vo. VG. C8. $17.50

WILLIAMS, Ben Ames. *Happy End.* 1991. Derrydale. 1/2500. gilt leather. F. A17. $22.50

WILLIAMS, Ben Ames. *House Divided.* 1947. Houghton Mifflin. 1st. F/NF. H11. $25.00

WILLIAMS, Ben Ames. *Pirate's Purchase.* 1931. NY. 1st ed. NF/dj. A17. $15.00

WILLIAMS, C. *Zoological Gardens, Regent Park.* ca 1835. London. C Tilt. 78x64mm. 48 woodcuts. 121p. aeg. gilt cloth. B24. $275.00

WILLIAMS, C.K. *Flesh & Blood.* 1987. FSG. F/dj. V1. $35.00

WILLIAMS, C.K. *Lies.* 1969. Houghton Mifflin. 1st. poet's 1st book. wrp. V1. $100.00

WILLIAMS, Charles. *Aground.* 1960. Viking. 1st. F/NF. M19. $75.00

WILLIAMS, Charles. *All Hallows' Eve.* 1947. Faber. 4th. VG. P3. $20.00

WILLIAMS, Charles. *Descent Into Hell.* 1949. Payson Clarke. 1st. VG/dj. M2. $30.00

WILLIAMS, Charles. *Greater Trumps.* 1950. Payson Clarke. 1st. VG/dj. M2. $35.00

WILLIAMS, Charles. *Man on a Leash.* 1973. Putnam. 1st. F/F. M15. $55.00

WILLIAMS, Charles. *Many Dimensions.* 1947. London. VG/dj. M2. $18.00

WILLIAMS, Charles. *Sailcloth Shroud.* 1960. Viking. 2nd. VG/dj. P3. $25.00

WILLIAMS, Charles. *Scorpion Reef.* 1955. Macmillan. 1st. VG/clip. M15. $85.00

WILLIAMS, Charles. *Shadows of Ectasy.* 1948. Faber. VG/dj. P3. $30.00

WILLIAMS, D.R. *United States & the Philippines.* 1925. Doubleday Page. 335p. VG. P1. $15.00

WILLIAMS, David. *Copper, Gold & Treasure.* 1982. St Martin. 1st. VG/dj. P3. $10.00

WILLIAMS, David. *Murder in Advent.* 1985. St Martin. 1st. NF/dj. P3. $15.00

WILLIAMS, David. *Treasure by Degrees.* 1977. Collins Crime Club. 1st. NF/dj. P3. $20.00

WILLIAMS, Dorian. *Pancho: Story of a Horse.* 1967. Walker. 1st Am. VG. O3. $15.00

WILLIAMS, Emily Wildington. *Homing Pigeon.* 1927. NY. Macaulay. 1st. F/VG+. B4. $100.00

WILLIAMS, Eugenia. *Invitation to Cryptograms.* 1959. NY. 1st. 126p. VG/dj. S1. $15.00

WILLIAMS, Francis. *Roentgen Rays in Medicine & Surgery As Aid in Diagnosis...* 1901. NY. 1st. 658p. xl. A13. $400.00

WILLIAMS, Geoffrey J. *Bibliography of Sierra Leone 1925-1967.* 1971. London/Munich. Africana Pub. 209p. xl. VG. W1. $35.00

WILLIAMS, Gordon. *Hazell Plays Solomon.* 1975. Walker. 1st. NF/dj. P3. $13.00

WILLIAMS, Gordon. *Pomeroy.* 1982. Arbor. 1st. VG/dj. P3. $15.00

WILLIAMS, Harold. *One Whaling Family.* 1964. Houghton Mifflin. 401p. G+/dj. V3. $18.00

WILLIAMS, Hawley. *Rover Boys: At College (#14).* 1910. Grosset Dunlap. 292p. cloth. VG/dj (lists 19 titles). M20. $40.00

WILLIAMS, Helen Maria. *Residence in France During Years 1792, 1793, 1794 & 1795.* 1797. London. Longman. 2nd. 2 vol. 8vo. calf. R12. $375.00

WILLIAMS, Henry Lionel. *Country Furniture of Early America.* 1966. NY/London. 3rd. ils. VG/VG. M17. $25.00

WILLIAMS, J.G. *Field Guide to Birds of East & Central Africa.* 1967. London. Collins. 3rd. 12mo. 288p. dj. B1. $25.00

WILLIAMS, J.H. *Sam Houston: Biography of the Father of Texas.* 1993. NY. 1st. ils. 448p. F/dj. M4. $25.00

WILLIAMS, J.R. *Redrawn by Request.* 1955. NY. 1st. VG/VG. B5. $45.00

WILLIAMS, J.W. *Big Ranch Country.* 1954. Wichita Falls. F. A19. $50.00

WILLIAMS, Jay. *Everyone Knows What a Dragon Looks Like.* 1976. Four Winds. 1st. unp. VG. T5. $25.00

WILLIAMS, Jay. *Practical Princess.* 1969. Parents Magazine Pr. ils Friso Henstra. VG. B15. $45.00

WILLIAMS, Jay. *Time of the Kraken.* 1978. Gollancz. NF/dj. P3. $20.00

WILLIAMS, Jerome. *Tin Box: Story of Texas Cattle & Oil.* 1958. Vantage. 1st. sgn. VG/VG. A23. $34.00

WILLIAMS, Jett. *Ain't Nothin' As Sweet As My Baby.* 1990. Harcourt Brace. 1st. sgn. VG/VG. A23. $30.00

WILLIAMS, John A. *Man Who Cried I Am.* 1967. Little Brn. 1st. NF/dj. M25. $60.00

WILLIAMS, John A. *Most Native of Sons: A Biography of Richard Wright.* 1970. Doubleday. 1st. NF/dj. M25. $45.00

WILLIAMS, John A. *This Is My Country Too.* 1965. NAL. 1st. NF/dj. M25. $75.00

WILLIAMS, John. *Apology for the Pulpits, Being in Answer to a Late Book...* 1688. London. Dorman Newman. 1st. sm 4to. H13. $195.00

WILLIAMS, John. *King God Didn't Save.* 1970. NY. 1st. VG/VG. B5. $20.00

WILLIAMS, Joseph J. *Voodoos & Obeahs: Phases of West India Witchcraft.* 1933 (1932). Dial. 4th. 257p. F/VG. H1. $30.00

WILLIAMS, Kenneth P. *Lincoln Finds a General.* Macmillan. 5 vol. 1st. F. O8. $125.00

WILLIAMS, Kit. *Masquerade.* nd. Schocken. F/frayed. M2. $20.00

WILLIAMS, Leonard. *Granada: Memories, Adventures, Studies & Impressions.* 1906. London/Phil. Heinemann/Lippincott. 1st. 8vo. 213p. teg. VG. W1. $28.00

WILLIAMS, Nigel. *Black Magic.* 1988. Hutchinson. 1st. F/dj. P3. $12.00

WILLIAMS, Paul. *New Homes for Today.* 1946. Murray Gee. 1st. 4to. 96p. tan cloth. VG. A8. $25.00

WILLIAMS, Philip Lee. *Slow Dance in Autumn.* 1988. Peachtree. 1st. F/dj. P3. $20.00

WILLIAMS, R. James. *Pussy-Cats ABC.* ca 1920. London. Deans Rag Book. 12mo. cloth/sewn bdg. R5. $75.00

WILLIAMS, R. James. *Ten Little Niggers With Music.* ca 1910. London. Dean's Rag Book. prt on cloth/sewn bdg. R5. $200.00

WILLIAMS, R. James. *Ten Little Niggers.* ca 1900. Deans Rag Book. 8vo. prt on cloth. VG. D1. $300.00

WILLIAMS, R.P. *Introduction to Chemical Science.* 1888. Boston. Ginn. ils. 106p. gilt brn cloth. G+. H1. $18.00

WILLIAMS, Robert Chadwell. *Klaus Fuchs: Atom Spy.* 1987. Cambridge. Harvard. 1st. ils. VG/dj. K3. $18.00

WILLIAMS, Samuel H. *Voodoo Roads.* 1939. Vienna. Jugend Volk. Eng text. F/NF. B2. $50.00

WILLIAMS, Samuel Howard. *Mammals of Pennsylvania.* 1928. Pittsburg. 1st. 163p. VG. H7. $12.50

WILLIAMS, Samuel. *Daisy or Cautionary Stories in Verse...* ca 1885. London. Griffith Farran. 31st ed. 16mo. plain gray brd. R5. $200.00

WILLIAMS, Sherley Anne. *Some One Sweet Angel Chile.* 1982. Morrow. 1st. F/F. B4. $85.00

WILLIAMS, Sidney Herbert. *Bibliography of the Writings of Lewis Caroll.* 1924. London. Bookman's Journal. 1/700. 4to. 142p. R5. $275.00

WILLIAMS, Stanley T. *Life of Washington Irving.* 1935. Oxford. 1st. 2 vol. F/dj. H1. $45.00

WILLIAMS, Tad. *Stone of Farewell.* 1990. Doran. 1st. sgn. F/F. M19. $25.00

WILLIAMS, Tennessee. *Baby Doll.* 1957. London. Secker Warburg. 1st Eng/photoplay. F/F. B4. $150.00

WILLIAMS, Tennessee. *Baby Doll.* 1957. Secker Warburg. 1st Eng. F/clip. Q1. $100.00

WILLIAMS, Tennessee. *Collected Stories.* 1985. New Directions. 1st. intro Gore Vidal. F/dj. Q1. $40.00

WILLIAMS, Tennessee. *One Arm & Other Stories.* 1954. New Directions. 1st trade. NF/VG. M25. $25.00

WILLIAMS, Tennessee. *Tennessee WIlliams' Letters to D Windham, 1940-65.* 1976. Italy. 1st. 1/500. F/wrp/box. A15. $125.00

WILLIAMS, Tennessee. *Tennessee Williams: An Intimate Biography.* 1983. NY. Arbor. 1st. F/F. T12. $45.00

WILLIAMS, Terry Tempest. *Pieces of White Shell.* 1984. Scribner. 1st. author's 1st solo book. F/NF. L3. $125.00

WILLIAMS, Thomas D. *Cohesion.* 1982. NY. Vantage. 1st. inscr. NF/NF. B4. $150.00

WILLIAMS, Thomas Harry. *Hayes of the 23rd, the Civil War Volunteer Officer.* 1965. Knopf. 1st. 325p. cloth. NF/dj. M8. $45.00

WILLIAMS, Thomas. *Ceremony of Love.* 1955. Bobbs Merrill. 1st. author's 1st book. F/NF. L3. $150.00

WILLIAMS, Ursula Moray. *For Brownies: Stories & Games for the Pack & Everybody Else.* 1935 (1932). London. Harrap. 2nd. sm 8vo. G+/VG. C8. $15.00

WILLIAMS, Valentine. *Crouching Beast.* nd. Grosset Dunlap. VG/dj. P3. $30.00

WILLIAMS, Valentine. *Red Mass.* 1925. Houghton Mifflin. 1st. VG. P3. $30.00

WILLIAMS, Violet M. *Sambo's Party.* ca 1930s. London. Dean. 8vo. pict stiff paper wrp. R5. $150.00

WILLIAMS, W.C. *Pink Church.* 1949. Golden Goose. 1st. 1/400. sgn. uncut. bl prt wrp. M24. $250.00

WILLIAMS, Walter R. *Rich Heritage of Quakerism.* 1962. Grand Rapids. Eerdmans. 279p. G. V3. $15.00

WILLIAMS, Walter. *State of Missouri.* 1904. Columbia, MO. A19. $30.00

WILLIAMS, Whiting. *Horny Hands & Hampered Elbows. The Worker's Mind...* 1922. Scribner. 1st. NF. B2. $35.00

WILLIAMS, William Carlos. *Collected Later Poems.* 1950. New Directions. 1st. NF/NF. w/supplement The Rose. D10. $75.00

WILLIAMS, William Carlos. *Pictures From Brueghel.* 1962. New Directions. 1st. F/wrp. Q1. $75.00

WILLIAMS, William Carlos. *Selected Letters.* 1957. McDowell Obolensky. 1st. F/NF. M25. $35.00

WILLIAMS, William Carlos. *Selected Poems.* 1949. New Directions. 1st/1st imp (tan ep). intro Jarrell. F/NF. A4. $125.00

WILLIAMS, William Carlos. *Something to Say.* 1985. New Directions. 1st. F/dj. Q1. $40.00

WILLIAMS, William. *Journal of the Life, Travels & Gospel Labours...* 1828. Cincinnati. Lodge l'Hommedieu Hammond. 1st. 272p. V3. $75.00

WILLIAMS, William. *Mr Penrose, the Journal of Penrose, Seaman.* 1969. IU. 1st. 8vo. F/NF. T10. $50.00

WILLIAMS. *Books by African-American Authors & Illustrators...* 1991. 1st. 270p. F. A4. $65.00

WILLIAMSON, Chet. *McKain's Dilemma.* 1988. Tor. 1st. VG/dj. P3. $17.00

WILLIAMSON, Chilton Jr. *Roughnecking It, a Brillant Portrait of Life...* 1982. S&S. 1st. 288p. VG/VG. J2. $45.00

WILLIAMSON, Harold E. *American Petroleum Industry: Age of Energy 1899-1959.* 1963. Northwestern. sm 4to. 928p. F/G. H1. $20.00

WILLIAMSON, Hugh Pritchard. *Overland Diary of James A Pritchard.* 1959. San Francisco. Old West Pub. A19. $125.00

WILLIAMSON, J. Bruce. *History of the Temple, London, From the Institution...* 1924. London. gr cloth. M11. $125.00

WILLIAMSON, J.N. *How To Write Horror Fantasy & Science Fiction.* 1987. Writers Digest. F/dj. P3. $18.00

WILLIAMSON, J.N. *Masques II.* 1987. Maclay. 1st. NF. P3. $25.00

WILLIAMSON, J.N. *Masques.* 1984. Maclay. NF/dj. M2. $15.00

WILLIAMSON, Jack. *Brother to Demons, Brother to Gods.* 1979. Bobbs Merrill. 1st. F/dj. P3. $18.00

WILLIAMSON, Jack. *Cometeers.* 1950. Fantasy. 1st. inscr/sgn/#d. NF/VG. P3. $150.00

WILLIAMSON, Jack. *Darker Than You Think.* 1948. Fantasy. 1st. inscr/sgn/#d. F/NF. P3. $300.00

WILLIAMSON, Jack. *Early Williamson.* 1975. Doubleday. 1st. F/dj. M2. $20.00

WILLIAMSON, Jack. *Humanoid Touch.* 1980. Phantasia. 1st. 1/500. sgn/#d. F/dj/case. P3. $45.00

WILLIAMSON, Jack. *Humanoid Touch.* 1989. Holt. 1st. sgn. F/dj. M2. $40.00

WILLIAMSON, Jack. *Humanoids.* 1949. S&S. 1st. VG/dj. P3. $40.00

WILLIAMSON, Jack. *Legion of Time.* 1952. Fantasy. 1st. inscr/sgn/#d. F/NF. P3. $200.00

WILLIAMSON, Jack. *Lifeburst.* 1984. Del Rey. 1st. F/dj. M2. $20.00

WILLIAMSON, Jack. *Lifeburst.* 1984. Del Rey. 1st. VG/dj. P3. $18.00

WILLIAMSON, Jack. *Manseed.* 1982. Del REy. 1st. F/F. M19. $25.00

WILLIAMSON, Jack. *Seetee Ship.* 1951. Gnome. 1st. VG/dj. P3. $60.00

WILLIAMSON, James A. *Age of Drake.* 1946. London. Blk. 2nd. 8 maps. 399p. T7. $45.00

WILLIAMSON, James A. *Maritime Enterprise, 1485-1588.* 1972. NY. Octagon. rpt. 15 ils/maps. F. O7. $50.00

WILLIAMSON, John P. *English-Dakota Dictionary.* 1908. NY. Am Tract Soc. 264p. 3-quarter brn ccalf. F. K7. $150.00

WILLIAMSON, Thames. *Lobster War.* 1935. Lee Shepard. 1st. VG/VG+. B4. $85.00

WILLIAMSON, Tony. *Doomsday Contract.* 1978. S&S. 1st. VG/dj. P3. $20.00

WILLIS, Chester. *Roaring Camp.* 1973. Collins. VG/VG. P3. $12.00

WILLIS, Donald C. *Horror & Science Fiction Films.* 1972. Scarecrow. 1st. VG. P3. $50.00

WILLIS, John. *Screen World 1967 Film Annual.* 1967. Crown. VG/G. P3. $20.00

WILLIS, Stephen. *Weed Control in Farm & Garden.* 1960. London. Garden BC. 184p. VG/dj. A10. $24.00

WILLIS, Ted. *Man-Eater.* 1977. Morrow. 1st. VG/dj. P3. $15.00

WILLMINGTON, Harold L. *Willmington's Complete Guide to Bible Knowledge: NT People.* 1990. Tyndale. 255p. as new/dj. B29. $13.00

WILLMOTT, H.P. *Barrier & the Javelin: Japanese & Allied Pacific Strategies.* 1942. Annapolis. ils. 596p. VG/VG. S16. $22.50

WILLOCKS, Tim. *Green River Rising.* 1994. Morrow. 1st. author's 1st book. F/dj. Q1. $40.00

WILLOUGHBY, Malcolm F. *US Coast Guard in World War II.* 1980. NY. Arno. rpt. 27 maps/diagrams/photos. 347p. T7. $45.00

WILLS, W. David. *Barns Experiment.* 1947. London. Allen Unwin. 2nd. 148p. VG/worn. V3. $20.00

WILLSON, M.W. *Garden Memories.* 1920. poem anthology/pl. G+. M17. $20.00

WILMOT, A. *Monomotapa (Rhodesia): Its Monuments, History...* 1969 (1896). Negro U. rpt. 16mo. ils/fld map. VG. W1. $25.00

WILMOT, Robert Patrick. *Death Rides a Painted Horse.* 1954. Lippincott. 1st. VG/dj. P3. $30.00

WILSIE, Carroll. *Crop Adaptation & Distribution.* 1962. SF. Freeman. 448p. cloth. A10. $22.00

WILSON, A.N. *Laird of Abbotsford, a Side View of Sir Walter Scott.* 1980. Oxford. 1st. VG/VG. T9. $25.00

WILSON, A.N. *Love Unknown.* 1987. Viking. 1st Am. F/F. B4. $50.00

WILSON, A.N. *Tolstoy.* 1988. NY. 1st. VG/VG. T9. $18.00

WILSON, Alan. *Story of the Potato Through Ils Varieties.* 1995 (1993). London. Wilson. 120p. pb. M. A10. $28.00

WILSON, Albert. *How Does Your Garden Grow.* 1955 (1949). Menlo Park. 2nd. photos. 500+p. VG+/dj. B26. $17.50

WILSON, Angus. *Hemlock & After.* 1952. London. 1st. VG/rpr. w/sgn Christmas greeting. T9. $40.00

WILSON, Angus. *No Laughing Matter.* 1967. Viking. 1st. F/dj. Q1. $35.00

WILSON, Barbara M. *Ontario & the First World War, 1914-18. A Collection...* 1977. Toronto. Champlain Soc. 201p. NF. P4. $100.00

WILSON, C.P.H. *Bush Peaches.* 1958. London. Collingridge. 140p. VG/dj. A10. $25.00

WILSON, Carl. *Botany.* 1950. Dryden. 483p. cloth. VG. A10. $12.00

WILSON, Carol Green. *Chinatown Quest: Life Adventures of Donaldina Cameron.* 1931. Stanford. 1st. sgn. stp gr cloth. F/dj. R3. $45.00

WILSON, Carol Green. *Gump's Treasure Trade: Story of San Francisco.* 1965. Crowell. expanded (1st thus). NF/VG. O4. $15.00

WILSON, Charles. *Middle America.* 1944. Norton. 1st. ils/map. 317p. F3. $15.00

WILSON, Colin. *Adrift in Soho.* 1961. Boston. 1st. VG/VG. B5. $35.00

WILSON, Colin. *Afterlife.* 1987. Doubleday Doran. 1st. VG/dj. P3. $20.00

WILSON, Colin. *Dark Dimensions.* 1977. Everest House. 1st. VG/dj. P3. $15.00

WILSON, Colin. *Lingard.* 1970. Crown. 1st. NF/dj. M2. $60.00

WILSON, Colin. *Outsider.* 1950s. Houghton Mifflin. 1st Am. VG/G+. R10. $15.00

WILSON, Colin. *Outsider.* 1956. Gollancz. 1st. VG. P3. $75.00

WILSON, Colin. *Philosopher's Stone.* 1971. Crown. 1st Am. VG/dj. M2. $45.00

WILSON, Colin. *Ritual in the Dark.* 1960. Gollancz. 2nd. VG/G. P3. $35.00

WILSON, Colin. *Schoolgirl Murder Case.* 1975. Hart Davis. 2nd. VG/dj. P3. $15.00

WILSON, Colin. *Space Vampires.* 1976. Random. 1st. F/dj. M2. $60.00

WILSON, Colin. *Space Vampires.* 1976. Random. 1st. NF/F. N4. $45.00

WILSON, Cornwell Baron. *Songs of the Ship.* 1831. London. Barnett. folio. 64p. aeg. rebacked. w/ALS. T7. $200.00

WILSON, D. *Henrietta Robinson.* 1855. NY/Auburn. Miller Orton Mulligan. 1st. 12mo. cloth. M1. $125.00

WILSON, Derek. *Circumnavigators.* 1989. NY. Evans. 1st Am. 345p. half cloth. NF/dj. P4. $35.00

WILSON, Dorothy Clarke. *Bright Eyes: Story of Susette LaFlesche, an Omaha Indian.* 1974. McGraw Hill. 1st. ils. 396p. VG/dj. A25. $8.00

WILSON, E. Raymond. *Thus Far on My Journey.* 1976. IN. Friends United Pr. 308p. G/dj. V3. $12.00

WILSON, E. Raymond. *Uphill for Peace: Quaker Impact on Congress.* 1975. Richmond, IN. Friends United Pr. 432p. VG/dj. V3. $18.00

WILSON, Earl. *Betio Beachhead: US Marines' Own Story of Battle of Tarawa.* 1945. NY. photos/maps. 160p. VG. S16. $30.00

WILSON, Edmund. *Boys in the Back Room: Notes on California Novelists.* 1941. Colt. 1st. 1/1500. NF. A18. $150.00

WILSON, Edmund. *Forties.* 1983. FSG. 1st. F/F. B35. $25.00

WILSON, Edmund. *O Canada: An American's Notes on Canadian Culture.* 1966. FSG. 1st. NF/dj. D10. $45.00

WILSON, Edmund. *Piece of My Mind.* 1956. FSC. 1st. 12mo. 239p. gray cloth. F/dj. H1. $20.00

WILSON, Edmund. *This Room & This Gin & These Sandwiches.* 1937. NY. New Republic. 1st. VG/wrp (no hc issued). Q1. $275.00

WILSON, Edward A. *Book of Edward A Wilson: A Survey of His Work 1916-1948.* 1948. NY. Heritage. 4to. 100 pl. F/dj. B24. $125.00

WILSON, Edward. *Diary of the Terra Nova Expedition to the Antarctic 1910...* 1972. London. Blanford. 1st Eng. 279p. beige cloth. NF/dj. P4. $150.00

WILSON, Ella Grant. *Famous Old Euclid Avenue of Cleveland.* 1937. np. ils/index. 265p. G. B18. $45.00

WILSON, Erica. *Erica Wilson's Embroidery Book.* 1973. Scribner. sgn. 374p. VG/VG. B11. $25.00

WILSON, Ernest H. *Aristocrats of the Trees.* 1930. Boston. 66 halftones. 279p. teg. xl. new buckram. B26. $100.00

WILSON, Ernest H. *Aristocrats of the Trees.* 1930. Boston. Stratford. 279p. VG. A10. $90.00

WILSON, Ernest H. *If I Were To Make a Garden.* 1931. Boston. 38 pl. 295p. teg. cloth. VG. B26. $80.00

WILSON, Everett B. *Fifty Early American Towns.* 1966. AS Barnes. 353p. VG/dj. M20. $20.00

WILSON, F. Paul. *Black Wind.* 1988. Tor. 1st. NF/NF. P3. $30.00

WILSON, F. Paul. *Healer.* 1976. Doubleday. 1st. F/dj. M2. $30.00

WILSON, F. Paul. *Keep.* 1981. Morrow. 1st. NF/dj. M2. $60.00

WILSON, Frazer E. *Arthur St Clair, Rugged Ruler of the Old Northwest.* 1944. Richmond. 1st. 253p. VG/torn. B18. $45.00

WILSON, Gahan. *Eddy Deco's Last Caper.* 1981. Timescape. 1st. F/dj. M2. $15.00

WILSON, Gahan. *Eddy Deco's Last Caper.* 1987. Times Books. 1st. VG. P3. $20.00

WILSON, Hazel. *Herbert's Space Trip.* 1956. Knopf. decor brd. VG. P3. $15.00

WILSON, Jeremy. *TE Lawrence.* 1988. London. 1st. VG/VG. T9. $75.00

WILSON, John Fleming. *Master Key.* nd. Grosset Dunlap. VG. P3. $20.00

WILSON, John. *Cruise of the Gypsy...1838-1843.* 1991. Fairfield. Ye Galleon. rpt. 404p. M/sans. P4. $45.00

WILSON, John. *Somewhere at Sea.* 1924. Dutton. VG. M2. $12.00

WILSON, Jose. *Complete Food Catalogue.* 1977. HRW. VG/dj. A16. $10.00

WILSON, Kenneth M. *New England Glass & Glassmaking.* 1972. Crowell. 1st. 401p. G+/dj. H1. $87.50

WILSON, L.G. *Charles Lyell, the Years to 1841: Revolution in Geology.* 1972. Yale. ils/17 maps. 553p. F/VG. M12. $45.00

WILSON, L.M. *Clothing of the Ancient Romans.* 1938. Baltimore. 95 pl. NF. M4. $20.00

WILSON, Laura. *Good Morning Mexico.* 1937. NY. Suttonhouse. 1st. 75p. F3. $10.00

WILSON, Louis. *Bromeliads for Modern Living.* 1977. Kalamazoo. photos. sc. F. B26. $7.50

WILSON, Mary. *Dream Girl: My Life As a Supreme.* 1986. St Martin. 1st. G/F. W2. $30.00

WILSON, Merzie. *Nealities: Doc Genius & Henry the Stud.* 1980. Vantage. 1st. F/dj. M2. $10.00

WILSON, Mitchell. *American Science & Invention.* 1954. NY. 437p. dj. A17. $20.00

WILSON, P.W. *Newtopia.* 1941. Scribner. 1st. NF/dj. M2. $15.00

WILSON, Richard. *Girls From Planet 5.* 1955. Ballantine. 1st. VG/dj. P3. $60.00

WILSON, Robert Anton. *Earth Will Shake.* 1982. Tarcher. 1st. NF/dj. P3. $30.00

WILSON, Robert C. *Crooked Tree.* 1980. Putnam. 1st. VG/dj. P3. $15.00

WILSON, Ruth. *Here Is Hati.* 1957. Philosophical Lib. 1st. 204p. dj. F3. $20.00

WILSON, Samuel Alexander K. *Neurology.* 1940. Baltimore. Williams Wilkins. 2 vol. 1st Am. pebbled mauve cloth. G1. $250.00

WILSON, Sloan. *Man in the Gray Flannel Suit II.* 1984. NY. Arbor. 1st. sgn. VG/VG. B11. $40.00

WILSON, Steve. *Dealer's Wheels.* 1982. St Martin. F/dj. P3. $15.00

WILSON, Thomas. *Arrowheads, Spears & Knives of Pre-Historic Times.* nd. US National Mus. ils/photos. blk cloth/gr spine. VG. K7. $60.00

WILSON, Thomas. *Brief Journal of Life, Travels & Labors of Love...* 1991. Phil. Friends Bookstore. 124p. VG. V3. $14.00

WILSON, William. *Detour.* 1974. Putnam. 1st. F/F. B4. $150.00

WILSON & WILSON. *Bromeliads in Cultivation Vol 1.* 1963. Coconut Grove, FL. ils/photos/sketches. 126p. F/torn. B26. $50.00

WILSTACH, Paul. *Tidewater Maryland.* 1931. Bobbs Merrill. 1st. 39 ils. 383p. T7. $45.00

WILTSE, David. *Close to the Bone.* 1992. Putnam. 1st. F/dj. P3. $22.00

WILTSEE, Ernest A. *Gold Rush Steamers (of the Pacific).* 1938. Grabhorn. 1st. 1/500. thick 8vo. brn cloth/cream spine. R3. $300.00

WILTZ, Chris. *Diamond Before You Die.* 1987. Mysterious. 1st. VG/dj. P3. $16.00

WINANT, John H. *Keep Business Flying: History of National Business Aircraft.* 1989. WA, DC. 1st. 229p. VG+/dj. B18. $17.50

WINCHESTER, Mark. *In the Hands of the Lamas.* nd. Queensway. VG. P3. $20.00

WIND, Herbert Warren. *Story of American Golf.* 1956. S&S. revised/1st prt. VG+/dj. P8. $40.00

WIND, Herbert Warren. *World of PG Wodehouse.* 1972. Praeger. NF/dj. P3. $20.00

WINDELER, B.C. *Elimus: A Story.* 1923. Three Mtn. 1/300. quarter cloth/prt brd. uncut. M24. $300.00

WINDLE, Ernest. *Windle's History of Santa Catalina Island.* 1931. Avalon. Catalina Islander. 1st. fld linen-backed map. 159p. D11. $150.00

WINDSOR, Kathleen. *Forever Amber.* 1944. Macmillan. 1st. NF/VG+. B4. $300.00

WINFIELD, Arthur M. *Rover Boys in the Jungle (#3).* 1899. Grosset Dunlap. 234p. gr pict cloth. VG/2-color dj. M20. $30.00

WINFIELD, Arthur M. *Rover Boys in the Land of Luck.* 1921. Grosset Dunlap. 1st/4th format. 310p. G/dj. H1. $18.00

WINFIELD, Arthur M. *Rover Boys in the Mountains (#6).* 1902. Grosset Dunlap. 244p+ads. VG/missing most of spine. M20. $20.00

WINFIELD, Dave. *Winfield: A Player's Life.* 1988. Norton. 1st. F/F. P8/T12. $35.00

WINFIELD, P.H. *Cases on the Law of Tort.* 1941. London. gilt bl cloth. M11. $50.00

WINFIELD, P.H. *Chief Sources of English Legal History.* 1925. Cambridge. bl cloth. M11. $125.00

WINFIELD, P.H. *Select Legal Essays.* 1952. London. Sweet & Maxwell. M11. $75.00

WINFIELD, P.H. *Text-Book of the Law of Tort. Second Edition.* 1943. London. Sweet & Maxwell. M11. $65.00

WINGROVE, David. *Broken Wheel.* 1991. Delacorte. 1st. F/F. H11. $25.00

WINGROVE, David. *Chung Kuo.* 1990. Delacorte. 1st. F/NF. H11. $30.00

WINGROVE, David. *White Mountain.* 1992. Delacorte. 1st. F/dj. P3. $23.00

WINKELSTEIN, Asher. *Modern Treatment of Peptic Ulcer.* 1948. NY. 1st. inscr. 205p. A13. $25.00

WINKLEY, J. *John Muir, Naturalist: A Concise Biography.* 1959. Martinez. Muir Hist Park Assn. sgn. w/prospectus. F/VG+. M12. $15.00

WINKS, Robin W. *Modus Operandi.* 1982. Godine. 1st. NF/dj. M25. $35.00

WINN, Dilys. *Murder Ink.* 1977. Workman. 1st. VG/dj. M2. $25.00

WINN, Patrick. *Colour of Murder.* 1965. Robert Hale. 1st. VG/dj. P3. $15.00

WINSLOW, Charles Frederick. *Force & Nature: Attraction & Repulsion.* 1869. Lippincott. 1st. 8vo. 492p. G+. K3. $35.00

WINSLOW, Don. *Cool Breeze on the Underground.* 1991. St Martin. 1st. author's 1st novel. F/dj. M15. $135.00

WINSLOW, Don. *Cool Breeze on the Underground.* 1991. St Martin. 1st. sgn. author's 1st book. F/F. B3. $175.00

WINSLOW, Forbes Benignus. *Obscure Diseases of the Brain & Mind.* 1866. Phil. Lea. 2nd Am. 484p+ads. emb pebbled gr cloth. G1. $275.00

WINSLOW, Pauline. *Copper Gold.* 1978. St Martin. 1st. VG/dj. P3. $15.00

WINSLOW, Pauline. *Death of an Angel.* 1975. St Martin. 1st. F/dj. M2. $12.00

WINSLOW, Richard. *General John Sedgwick.* 1982. 204p. O8. $12.50

WINSOR, Justin. *Narrative & Critical History of America by a Corps...* (1889). Houghton Mifflin. Standard Lib. 8 vol. cloth. xl. VG. M8. $650.00

WINSOR, Kathleen. *Forever Amber.* 1944. London. MacDonald. 1st Eng. NF/VG. B4. $150.00

WINSTER, Owen. *Journey in Search of Christmas.* 1904. Harper. ils Frederic Remington. 93p. red cloth. VG. K7. $55.00

WINSTON, Joan. *Making of Star Trek Conventions.* 1977. Doubleday. 1st. F/dj. M2. $35.00

WINSTON, Robert W. *Robert E Lee, a Biography.* 1934. Morrow. 1st. 428p. cloth. NF. M8. $45.00

WINTER, Douglas E. *Prime Evil.* 1988. NAL. 1st. F/VG+. N4. $25.00

WINTER, Douglas E. *Prime Evil.* 1988. NAL. 1st. NF/dj. P3. $20.00

WINTER, Douglas E. *Stephen King: Art of Darkness.* 1984. NAL. 1st. F/dj. P3. $20.00

WINTER, John Strange. *Magic Wheel.* 1901. Lippincott. 1st. G+. M2. $22.00

WINTER, Milo. *Arabian Nights Entertainments.* 1914. Rand McNally. Windermere series. sm 4to. 12 mc pl. 293p. cloth. W1. $25.00

WINTERBOTHAM, F.W. *Nazi Connection.* 1978. Harper Row. 1st. VG/dj. P3. $15.00

WINTERBOTHAM, Russ. *Joyce of the Secret Squadron.* 1942. Whitman. VG. P3. $12.00

WINTERICH, John T. *Early American Books & Printing.* 1935. Houghton Mifflin. 1st. ils. 253p. VG/dj. K3. $25.00

WINTERICH, John T. *Primer of Book Collecting.* 1935. Greenberg. revised/enlarged. 8vo. 265p. VG. K3. $22.00

WINTERICH, John T. *Three Lantern Slides.* 1949. Urgana. IL U. 1st. 8vo. 109p. VG. K3. $20.00

WINTERS, Shelley. *Shelley II: Middle of My Century.* 1989. S&S. 1st. F/NF. W2. $25.00

WINTERSON, Jeanette. *Art & Lies.* 1994. Knopf. 1st Am. F/F. B3. $30.00

WINTERSON, Jeanette. *Written on the Body.* 1993. Knopf. 1st Am. F/dj. A24. $25.00

WINTHER, Oscar Osburn. *Story of San Jose 1777-1869.* 1935. SF. CA Hist Soc. 1/150. ils. cloth. NF. R3. $165.00

WINTHER, Oscar Osburn. *Transportation Frontier Trans-Mississippi West.* 1964. HRW. A19. $15.00

WINTHROP, Elizabeth. *Belinda's Hurricane.* 1984. Dutton. 1st. sm 8vo. F/F. C8. $22.50

WINTHROP, Theodore. *Canoe & the Saddle; or, Klalam & Klickatat.* 1913. Tacoma. JH Williams. 16 mc pl/100+ ils. vellum-backed cloth. G. B24. $200.00

WINWARD, Walter. *Fives Wild.* 1976. Atheneum. 1st. VG/dj. P3. $15.00

WINWARD, Walter. *Seven Minutes Past Midnight.* 1980. S&S. 1st. VG/dj. P3. $15.00

WIRT, Mildred A. *Brownie Scouts at Silver Beach.* 1952. Cupples Leon. 1st. ils. VG+/VG. A25. $20.00

WIRT, Mildred A. *Brownie Scouts in the Circus (#2).* 1949. Cupples Leon. 212p. cloth. VG/dj (lists 5 titles). M20. $20.00

WIRT, Mildred A. *Courageous Wings.* 1937. Penn. 217p. red cloth. VG+. M20. $50.00

WIRT, Mildred A. *Courageous Wings.* 1940 (1937). Books Inc. 217p. bl cloth. NF/dj. M20. $50.00

WIRT, Mildred A. *Madge Sterling: Deserted Yacht (#2).* 1932. Goldsmith. 123p. VG/dj. M20. $10.00

WIRT, Mildred A. *Painted Shield.* ca 1950s. World. Jr Lib ed. 207p+ad. M20. $25.00

WIRT, Mildred A. *Penny Parker: Behind the Green Door (#4).* 1940. Cupples Leon. 211p. VG/dj. M20. $20.00

WIRT, Mildred A. *Penny Parker: Danger at the Drawbridge (#3).* 1950 (1940). Cupples Leon. 211p. VG/dj. M20. $25.00

WIRT, Mildred A. *Penny Parker: Vanishing Houseboat (#2).* 1939. Cupples Leon. VG/dj. P3. $20.00

WISE, Arthur. *Who Killed Enoch Powell?* 1971. Harper Row. 1st. VG/dj. P3. $20.00

WISE, Daniel. *Young Man's Counsellor; or, Sketches & Illustrations...* 1852. VG. M17. $25.00

WISE, David Burgess. *Illustrated Encyclopedia of World's Automobiles.* 1979. A&W. 1st. 352p. cloth. VG+/dj. M20. $30.00

WISE, Henry A. *Los Gringos; or, Inside View of Mexico & California...* 1849. Scribner. 1st. inscr. 12mo. 3-quarter gr morocco. VG. R3. $300.00

WISE, Herbert A. *Great Tales of Terror & the Supernatural.* 1944. Modern Lib. VG. P3. $20.00

WISE, Thomas J. *Conrad Library: A Catalogue of Printed Books...* 1928. London. Prt for Private Circulation. 1st. 1/180. teg. gilt bdg. M24. $375.00

WISEMAN, Thomas. *Czar.* 1965. London. correct 1st inscr assoc copy. F/F. A11. $85.00

WISEMAN, Thomas. *Day Before Sunrise.* 1976. HRW. 1st. VG/G. P3. $13.00

WISMER, Donald. *Starluck.* 1982. Doubleday. 1st. sgn. F/dj. M2. $23.00

WISTER, Owen. *Lady Baltimore.* 1906. Macmillan. 1st. sm 8vo. 406p. gr cloth. G. H1. $7.50

WISTER, Owen. *Seven Ages of Washington.* 1907. Grosset Dunlap. VG. A19. $25.00

WISTER, Owen. *Virginian.* (1902). Macmillan. 1st. 12mo. VG. C8. $45.00

WITHERS, E.L. *Birthday.* 1962. Crime Club. 1st. VG/dj. P3. $18.00

WITHEY, Lynne. *Dearest Friend: Life of Abigail Adams.* 1981. Free Pr (Macmillan). 1st. 369p. blk cloth. as new/dj. B22. $6.50

WITHEY, Lynne. *Voyages of Discovery: Captain Cook & Exploration of Pacific.* 1987. Morrow. 1st. 512p. map ep. P4. $35.00

WITHGOLL, Coleen K. *Webster's Legal Secretaries' Handbook.* 1981. Meriam-Webster. 1st. F/NF. W2. $50.00

WITNEY, K.P. *Jutish Forest, a Study of Weald of Kent From 450 to 1380AD.* 1976. London. Athlone. M11. $75.00

WITTELS, Fritz. *Jeweller of Bagdad.* 1927. Doran. 1st. VG/worn. M2. $25.00

WITTEN, Barbara Yager. *Isle of Fire Murder.* 1987. Walker. 1st. F/F. N4. $15.00

WITWER, H.C. *Fighting Back.* nd. Grosset Dunlap. VG. P3. $18.00

WITWER, H.C. *Leather Pushers.* 1921. Grosset Dunlap. MTI. VG/G. B5. $25.00

WLLIS, A.B. *Land of Fetish.* 1970 (1883). Negro U. rpt. 316p. VG. W1. $25.00

WODEHOUSE, P.G. *Author! Author!* 1962. S&S. 1st. VG/dj. P3. $50.00

WODEHOUSE, P.G. *Bachelors Anonymous.* 1974. S&S. 1st. F/dj. P3. $25.00

WODEHOUSE, P.G. *Big Money.* 1931. McClelland Stewart. 1st. VG. P3. $60.00

WODEHOUSE, P.G. *Bill the Conqueror.* nd. Goodchild. 1st Canadian. G. P3. $35.00

WODEHOUSE, P.G. *Bring on the Girls.* 1953. S&S. 1st. G. P3. $40.00

WODEHOUSE, P.G. *Catnappers.* 1974. S&S. 1st. 190p. cloth. VG/dj. M20. $25.00

WODEHOUSE, P.G. *Eggs, Beans & Crumpets.* 1940. Doubleday. 1st Am. F/VG. B4. $250.00

WODEHOUSE, P.G. *Full Moon.* 1947. Doubleday. 1st. VG. P3. $40.00

WODEHOUSE, P.G. *Golf Omnibus.* 1973. S&S. 1st. NF/dj. M25. $60.00

WODEHOUSE, P.G. *Heavy Weather.* 1933. McClelland Stewart. 1st Canadian. VG. P3. $60.00

WODEHOUSE, P.G. *Laughing Gas.* 1936. Doubleday Doran. 1st Am. orange brd. VG. M25. $50.00

WODEHOUSE, P.G. *Laughing Gas.* 1936. McClelland Stewart. 1st Canadian. VG. P3. $50.00

WODEHOUSE, P.G. *Luck of the Bodkis.* 1935. McClelland Stewart. 1st Canadian. VG/dj. P3. $75.00

WODEHOUSE, P.G. *Mating Season.* 1949. Didier. 1st. VG. P3. $40.00

WODEHOUSE, P.G. *Mike at Wrykn.* 1953. Meredith. 1st. VG. P3. $25.00

WODEHOUSE, P.G. *Mr Mulliner Speaking.* 1929. McClelland Stewart. 1st Canadian. VG. P3. $50.00

WODEHOUSE, P.G. *Mulliner Nights.* 1933. Herbert Jenkins. 1st. NF. P3. $60.00

WODEHOUSE, P.G. *Nothing Serious.* 1951. Doubleday. 1st. VG/dj. P3. $45.00

WODEHOUSE, P.G. *Pigs Have Wings.* 1952. Doubleday. 1st. F/dj. B24. $150.00

WODEHOUSE, P.G. *Plot That Thickened.* 1973. S&S. 1st. VG/dj. P3. $25.00

WODEHOUSE, P.G. *Plum Pie.* 1967. 1st Am. F/torn. A15. $50.00

WODEHOUSE, P.G. *Psmith Jouralist.* nd. Leipzig. Tauchnitz. 1st. 16mo. 270p. F/buff prt wrp. H3. $200.00

WODEHOUSE, P.G. *Sam in the Suburbs.* 1925. Doran. 1st. 346p. gr cloth. VG. M20. $125.00

WODEHOUSE, P.G. *Sam the Sudden.* 1925. Methuen. 1st. VG. P3. $75.00

WODEHOUSE, P.G. *Something New.* 1930 (1915). Dodd Mead. 346p. VG/dj. M20. $65.00

WODEHOUSE, P.G. *Spring Fever.* 1948. Doubleday. 1st Am. F/VG. B4. $100.00

WODEHOUSE, P.G. *Stiff Upper Lip, Jeeves.* 1963. S&S. 1st. F/dj. B24. $100.00

WODEHOUSE, P.G. *Summer Moonshine.* 1938. McClelland Stewart. 1st. VG/G. P3. $75.00

WODEHOUSE, P.G. *Uncle Fred in the Springtime.* 1939. Doubleday. 1st. F/NF. B4. $350.00

WODEHOUSE, P.G. *Uncle Fred in the Springtime.* 1939. Herbert Jenkins. 1st. VG. P3. $60.00

WODEHOUSE, P.G. *Very Good, Jeeves.* 1930. McClelland Stewart. 1st Canadian. VG. P3. $60.00

WODEHOUSE, P.G. *Wodehouse Nuggets.* 1983. Hutchinson. 1st. F/dj. P3. $18.00

WODEHOUSE, P.G. *World of Ukridge.* 1975. Barrie Jenkins. 1st. VG/dj. P3. $25.00

WOELFEL, Barry. *Through a Glass, Darkly.* 1984. Beaufort. 1st. NF/dj. P3. $20.00

WOIWODE, Larry. *Beyond the Bedroom Wall.* 1975. FSG. 1st. F/NF. A24. $30.00

WOIWODE, Larry. *Even Tide.* 1977. FSG. 1st. F/F. B3. $40.00

WOIWODE, Larry. *What I'm Going To Do, I Think.* 1969. FSG. 1st. inscr. author's 1st novel. F/NF. L3. $225.00

WOLCOTT, Imogene. *New England Yankee Cookbook.* 1939. Coward McCann. ils. VG. A16. $10.00

WOLCOTT, Imogene. *New England Yankee Cookbook.* 1959. Coward McCann. rpt. 398p. B10. $10.00

WOLF, Betty Hartman. *Journey Through the Holy Land.* 1967. Doubleday. 1st. 8vo. 267p. NF/dj. W1. $10.00

WOLF, Blue. *Dwifa's Curse: A Tale of the Stone Age.* 1921. Robert Scott. NF. P3. $60.00

WOLF, David. *Foul!* 1972. HRW. 1st. VG/VG. P8. $35.00

WOLF, Gary. *Generation Removed.* 1977. Doubleday. 1st. NF/dj. M2. $15.00

WOLF, Gary. *Who P-P-Plugged Roger Rabbit?* 1991. Villard. 1st. VG/dj. P3. $20.00

WOLF, George D. *William Warren Scranton: Pennsylvania Statesman.* 1981. PA State. 1st. 220p. F/dj. H1. $22.50

WOLF, Leonard. *Annotated Dracula.* 1975. Clarkson Potter. 4to. 362p. M/dj. B24. $75.00

WOLF, Leonard. *False Messiah.* 1982. Houghton Mifflin. 1st. F/dj. M2. $12.00

WOLF, Leonard. *Wolf's Complete Book of Terror.* 1979. Clarkson Potter. VG/dj. P3. $10.00

WOLFE, Aaron; see Koontz, Dean R.

WOLFE, Alfred. *In Alaskan Waters.* 1943. Caxton. ils. 196p. dj. T7. $28.00

WOLFE, Bernard. *Deep.* 1957. Knopf. 1st. F/NF. B4. $100.00

WOLFE, Bernard. *Limbo.* 1952. Random. 1st. VG/dj. M2. $75.00

WOLFE, Bertram. *Fabulous Life of Diego Rivera.* 1963. NY. 1st. ils. 457p. VG/dj. B5. $47.50

WOLFE, Gene. *Book of the New Sun.* 1981-1983. S&S/Timescape. 1st. 4 vol. F/dj. M2. $260.00

WOLFE, Gene. *Castle of the Otter.* 1982. Willimantic, CT. Ziesing. 1st. 1/100. sgn. il/sgn SE Fabian. F/F. T2. $400.00

WOLFE, Gene. *Castleview.* 1990. Tor. 1st. F/dj. P3. $25.00

WOLFE, Gene. *Citadel of the Autarch.* 1983. Timescape. 1st. F/dj. M2. $30.00

WOLFE, Gene. *Claw of the Conciliator.* 1981. Timescape. 1st. F/dj. P3. $50.00

WOLFE, Gene. *Endangered Species.* 1989. NY. Tor. 1st. sgn. F/F. T2. $35.00

WOLFE, Gene. *Fifth Head of Cerberus.* 1972. Scribner. 1st. F/dj. P3. $35.00

WOLFE, Gene. *Fifth Head of Cerberus.* 1972. Scribner. 1st. VG/dj. M2. $20.00

WOLFE, Gene. *Soldier of the Mist.* 1986. Gollancz. 1st. F/dj. P3. $25.00

WOLFE, Gene. *Sword of Lictor.* 1981. Timescape. 1st. VG/dj. M2. $35.00

WOLFE, Gene. *There Are Doors.* 1988. Tor. 1st. F/dj. M2. $22.00

WOLFE, Gene. *Urth of the New Sun.* 1987. NY. Tor. 1st Am. inscr. F/F. T2. $25.00

WOLFE, Gene. *Urth of the New Sun.* 1987. Tor. 1st. F/dj. P3. $20.00

WOLFE, Theodore F. *Literary Haunts & Homes.* 1899. Phil. Lippincott. 1st. teg. gilt tan cloth. NF. M24. $65.00

WOLFE, Thomas. *Look Homeward, Angel.* 1929. NY. Scribner. 1st. F/dj. B24. $750.00

WOLFE, Thomas. *Look Homeward, Angel.* 1930. London. Heinemann. 1st. author's 1st book. VG/dj. Q1. $750.00

WOLFE, Thomas. *Mannerhouse.* 1948. Harper. 1st. VG/G. M19. $35.00

WOLFE, Thomas. *Of Time & the River.* 1935. NY. 1st. VG/fair. B5. $60.00

WOLFE, Thomas. *Return.* 1976. Asheville. Thomas Wolfe Memorial. 1st ed. F/prt wrp/envelope. Q1. $75.00

WOLFE, Thomas. *Story of a Novel.* 1936. Scribner. 1st. VG/VG. B4. $150.00

WOLFE, Tom. *Bonfire of the Vanities.* 1987. Franklin Lib. 1st. sgn. aeg. full leather. F. Q1. $125.00

WOLFE, Tom. *Bonfire of the Vanities.* 1987. FSG. 1st. NF/NF. N4. $35.00

WOLFE, Tom. *Electric Kool-Aid Acid Test.* 1968. FSG. 1st. NF/dj. Q1. $200.00

WOLFE, Tom. *Kandy-Kolored Tangerine-Flake Streamline Baby.* 1965. FSG. 1st. author's 1st book. F/F. B4. $300.00

WOLFE, Tom. *Radical Chic & Mau-Mauing the Flak Catchers.* 1970. FSG. 1st. F/NF. A24/T11. $40.00

WOLFE, Tom. *Right Stuff.* 1979. FSG. 1st. F/F. M25. $45.00

WOLFE, Tom. *Right Stuff.* 1979. FSG. 1st. F/NF. R14. $35.00

WOLFE, Tom. *Right Stuff.* 1979. FSG. 1st. NF/clip. M23. $25.00

WOLFE & WYSACK. *Handbook for Space Pioneers.* 1978. Grosset Dunlap. 1st. F. M2. $12.00

WOLFERT, Ira. *American Guerrilla in the Philippines.* 1945. NY. sgn Douglas MacArthur. 301p. VG. S16. $250.00

WOLFERT, Ira. *Battle for the Solomons: October-November 1942.* 1943. MA. 200p. VG/G. S16. $23.50

WOLFF, Geoffrey. *Bad Debts.* 1969. S&S. 1st. sgn. NF/clip. R14. $85.00

WOLFF, Geoffrey. *Black Sun.* 1976. Random. 1st. inscr. F/F. T11. $45.00

WOLFF, Geoffrey. *Day at the Beach.* 1992. Knopf. 1st. F/F. B35. $16.00

WOLFF, Geoffrey. *Final Club.* 1990. Knopf. 1st. inscr. F/F. T11. $45.00

WOLFF, Geoffrey. *Inklings.* 1978. Random. 1st. F/F. B35. $25.00

WOLFF, Jacob. *Science of Cancerous Disease From Earliest Times to Present.* 1989. Canton, MA. 1st Eng. 714p. A13. $60.00

WOLFF, John E. *Route of Manly Party of 1849-1850 in Leaving Death Valley...* 1931. Santa Barbara. Pacific Coast Pub. sgn. ils. 29p. prt brd/cloth spine. D11. $150.00

WOLFF, Paul. *My Experiences in Color Photography.* ca 1948. Frankfurt. 43p+54 full-p mc pl. trans from German. 4to. A17. $22.50

WOLFF, Paul. *Skikamerad Toni.* 1936. Frankfurt. 93p+76 full-p b&w photos. sq 4to. cloth. A17. $35.00

WOLFF, Robert Lee. *Strange Stories: Explorations in Victorian Fiction.* 1971. Gambit. 1st. VG/dj. P3. $25.00

WOLFF, Theodore. *Eve of 1914.* 1936. Knopf. 1st Am. 655p. bl silk-type cloth. VG. B22. $9.50

WOLFF, Tobias. *Barracks Thief.* 1984. NY. Ecco. 1st. inscr. F/F. R14. $100.00

WOLFF, Tobias. *In the Garden of the North American Martyrs.* 1981. Ecco. 1st. inscr. F/clip. D10. $135.00

WOLFF, Tobias. *This Boy's Life.* 1989. Atlantic Monthly. 1st. sgn/dtd. F/dj. D10. $95.00

WOLFSON, Theresa. *Woman Worker & the Trade Union.* 1926. NY. Internat'l. 1st. F. B2. $75.00

WOLLASTON, Nicholas. *Red Rumba.* 1964. London. Readers Union. 192p. dj. F3. $15.00

WOLLHEIM, Donald A. *Mike Mars Flies the X-15.* 1961. Doubleday. 1st. VG. P3. $10.00

WOLLHEIM, Donald A. *Portable Novels of Science.* 1945. Viking. 1st. VG/dj. M2. $10.00

WOLLHEIM, Donald A. *Terror in the Modern Vein.* 1955. Hanover. 1st. NF/dj. M2. $22.00

WOLLHEIM, Donald A. *1973 Annual of World's Best Science Fiction.* nd. BC. VG/dj. P3. $8.00

WOLLSTONECRAFT, Mary. *Original Stories From Real Life, With Conversations...* 1791. London. J Johnson. 2nd. sm 8vo. 175p. H13. $395.00

WOLLSTONECRAFT, Mary. *Vindication of Rights of Woman...* 1792. London. Johnson. 4to. modern calf. R12. $1,275.00

WOLO. *Sir Archibald.* 1944. Morrow. 1st. 41p. VG/G. T5. $35.00

WOLPOLE, Horace. *Castle of Otranto.* 1950940s. London. Grey Walls. 8vo. 137p. F/dj. B24. $100.00

WOLTHUYS, J.J. Verbeek. *Enigma of Origin of Monstrosity & Cristation in Succulent...* 1948 (1938). Assen. 2nd enlarged. Dutch/Eng text. ils. 111p. sc. B26. $30.00

WOLTHUYS, J.J. Verbeek. *Het Cactusboex.* 1928. Utrecht. Dutch text. ils/photos. 168p. sc. B26. $40.00

WOLVERTON, C.C. *Fifty Years With Harness Horses.* 1957. Harrisburg. 1st. VG/VG. B5. $30.00

WOMACK, Bob. *Echo of Horsebeats.* 1973. Walking Horse Pub. 1st. VG/VG. O3. $165.00

WOMACK, Jack. *Ambient.* 1987. Weidenfeld Nicholson. 1st. NF/NF. N4. $25.00

WOMACK, Jack. *Heathern.* 1990. Tor. 1st. F/dj. P3. $17.00

WOMEN OF ST. JAMES CHURCH. *300 Favorite Recipes.* nd. NYC. 138p. sbdg. B10. $12.00

WOOD, Bari. *Tribe.* 1981. NAL. 1st. VG/dj. P3. $15.00

WOOD, Charles Erskine Scott. *Poet in the Desert.* 1915. Portland, OR. 1/1000. inscr. 124p. natural linen/tan brd. VG. K7. $35.00

WOOD, Christine. *Safari South America.* 1973. NY. 224p. NF/VG. S15. $12.00

WOOD, Christopher. *Taiwan.* 1981. Michael Joseph. 1st. VG/dj. P3. $15.00

WOOD, Christopher. *Tissot.* 1986. NYGS. ils. VG/VG. M17. $40.00

WOOD, Clement. *Double Jeopardy.* 1947. Arcadia. 1st. VG/fair. P3. $20.00

WOOD, Frank Bradshaw. *Present & Future of the Telescope of Moderate Size.* 1958. Phil. 8vo. 219p. VG. K5. $18.00

WOOD, Henry J. *Pelargoniums: Complete Guide to Their Cultivation.* 1966. London. ils/photos. 168p. F/dj. B26. $22.50

WOOD, James Playsted. *Magazines in the United States.* 1956 (1949). Ronald Pr. 2nd. 390p. cloth. VG/dj. M20. $15.00

WOOD, Oliver. *West Point Scrapbook, a Collection of Stories, Songs...* 1874 (1871). lg 8vo. ils. 339p. VG. E6. $175.00

WOOD, R.G. *Stephen Harriman Long 1784-1864.* 1966. Clark. ils/map. 292p. F. M4. $25.00

WOOD, Robert L. *Men, Mules & Mountains.* 1976. Seattle, WA. Mountaineers. dj. A19. $35.00

WOOD, Robert W. *Physical Optics.* 1934. Macmillan. 3rd. 8vo. 846p. G. K5. $30.00

WOOD, Robert. *Day Trips to Archaeological Mexico.* 1991. Hastings. revised. 174p. wrp. F3. $10.00

WOOD, Stanley. *Over the Range to the Golden Gate.* 1889. Chicago. RR Donnelley. 1st. ils. 351p+29p ads. gilt bl cloth. G. K7. $50.00

WOOD, Ted. *Live Bait.* 1985. Collier Macmillian. 1st Canadian. F/F. P3. $15.00

WOOD, Wallace. *Wizard King.* 1978. Wood. 1st. F/dj. M2. $30.00

WOOD, William. *Manual of Physical Exercise: Comprising Gymnastics...* 1875. NY. 353p. red cloth. G. B14. $275.00

WOOD, Winifred. *We Were Wasps.* 1945. Glade House. 1st. ils Dorothy Swain. 196p. VG. A25. $35.00

WOODARD, Charles L. *Ancestral Voice.* 1989. Lincoln, NE. NE U. 1st. F/F. L3. $35.00

WOODARD, Charles L. *Ancestral Voice: Conversations With N Scott Momaday.* 1989. NE U. 1st. ils/sgn NS Momaday. F/F. D10. $60.00

WOODARD, Lt., M.D.; see Silverberg, Robert.

WOODBERRY, George. *Edgar Allan Poe.* 1885. Houghton Mifflin. 1st. teg. gilt maroon cloth. M24. $50.00

WOODBINE, George E. *Four Thirteenth Century Law Tracts.* 1910. New Haven. Yale. cloth. M11. $125.00

WOODBURNE, Lloyd S. *Neural Basis of Behavior.* 1967. Columbus, OH. Merrill. 378p. beige cloth. VG/dj. G1. $25.00

WOODCOCK, Louise. *Guess Who Lives Here.* (1949). S&S. 2nd/B prt. sq 8vo. unp. G+. T5. $22.00

WOODCOTT, Keith; see Brunner, John.

WOODHOUSE, Barbara. *Barbara's World of Horses & Ponies.* 1984. NY. Summit. 1st Am. VG. O3. $12.00

WOODHOUSE, James. *Young Chemist's Pocket Companion.* 1797. Phil. 56p. marbled wrp. B14. $600.00

WOODING, F.H. *Angler's Book of Canadian Fishes.* 1959. Ontario. 1st. 303 p. F/G. A17. $20.00

WOODLEY, Richard. *Dealer.* 1971. Holt. 1st. F/F. H11. $25.00

WOODMAN, Charles M. *Quakers Find a Way.* 1950. Bobbs Merrill. 1st. 280p. VG/dj. V3. $10.00

WOODRELL, Daniel. *Muscle for the Wing.* 1988. Holt. 1st. F/F. M15. $45.00

WOODRELL, Daniel. *Under the Bright Lights.* 1986. Holt. 1st. author's 1st mystery. F/F. L3. $100.00

WOODRESS, James. *Willa Cather: A Literary Life.* 1987. U NE. VG/dj. P3. $35.00

WOODRUFF, Elizabeth. *Dickey Byrd.* 1928. Springfield, MA. Milton Bradley. 1st. ils Gustaf Tenggren. blk cloth. R5. $550.00

WOODRUFF, Philip. *Call the Next Witness.* 1945. Jonathan Cape. 1st. VG. P3. $30.00

WOODS, Daniel B. *Sixteen Months at the Gold Diggings.* 1851. Harper. 1st. 12mo. brn cloth. VG. R3. $500.00

WOODS, J. *Two Years' Residence on the English Prairie.* 1968. Lakeside Classic. maps. 242p. F. M4. $15.00

WOODS, Sara. *Away With Them To Prison.* 1985. Macmillan. 1st. NF/dj. P3. $20.00

WOODS, Sara. *Bloody Book of Law.* 1984. Macmillan. 1st. VG/dj. P3. $20.00

WOODS, Sara. *Error of the Moon.* 1963. Collins Crime Club. 1st. VG. P3. $20.00

WOODS, Sara. *Weep for Her.* 1980. Macmillan. 1st. F/dj. P3. $20.00

WOODS, Stuart. *Blue Water, Green Skipper.* 1977. Norton. 1st. F/NF. B4. $200.00

WOODS, Stuart. *Deep Lie.* 1986. Norton. 1st. F/NF. Q1. $50.00

WOODS, Stuart. *Grass Roots.* 1989. S&S. 1st. VG/dj. P3. $20.00

WOODS, Stuart. *Palindrome.* 1991. Harper Collins. 1st. VG/dj. P3. $20.00

WOODSON, Carter. *Negro Orators & Their Orations.* 1925. WA. Assoc Pub. 1st. G. B4. $125.00

WOODWARD, Arthur. *Lances at San Pasqual.* 1948. SF. CA Hist Soc. 84p. gilt cloth. D11. $150.00

WOODWARD, Carl R. *Development of Agriculture in New Jersey.* 1927. Brunswick. NJ Agric Exp Sta. 321p. A10. $40.00

WOODWARD, Ian. *Werewolf Delusion.* 1979. Paddington. 1st. VG/dj. P3. $20.00

WOODWARD, W.E. *Meet General Grant.* 1928. 1st. xl. O8. $12.50

WOODWARD, W.E. *Meet General Grant.* 1928. NY. 1st. 512p. F. O8. $18.50

WOODWARD & WOODWARD. *Woodward's Graperies & Horticultural Buildings.* 1865. NY. Woodward. 1st. 139p. A10. $86.00

WOOLCOCK, Helen R. *Rights of Passage. Emigration to Australia...* 1986. London/NY. Tavistock. 8vo. 337p. M/dj. P4. $30.00

WOOLF, Virginia. *Beau Brummell.* 1930. Rimingtom Hooper. 1st. 1/550. sgn. NF/VG case. B4. $1,200.00

WOOLF, Virginia. *Letter to a Young Poet.* 1932. London. Hogarth. 1st. 1/5500. F/wrp. Q1. $100.00

WOOLF, Virginia. *London Scene: Five Essays.* 1975. NY. Frank Hallman. 1st/ltd. F/F. B2. $40.00

WOOLF, Virginia. *Night & Day.* 1920. Doran. 1st Am. gr cloth. F. M24. $125.00

WOOLF, Virginia. *Three Guineas.* 1938. London. Hogarth. 1st. 5 photo pl. NF/dj. B24. $375.00

WOOLF, Virginia. *Three Guineas.* 1938. NY. Harcourt Brace. 1st Am. F/dj. Q1. $250.00

WOOLF, Virginia. *Voyage Out.* 1920. NY. 1st Am. author's 1st book. F/NF/full morocco case. L3. $4,500.00

WOOLF, Virginia. *Waves.* (1931). Harcourt Brace. 1st Am. gilt bl cloth. M24. $35.00

WOOLF, Virginia. *Widow & the Parrot.* 1988. London. Hogarth. 1st. lg 8vo. F/F. C8. $37.50

WOOLF, Virginia. *Writer's Diary.* 1954. London. Hogarth. 1st/2nd prt. assn copy. gilt orange cloth. F/dj. M24. $225.00

WOOLLCOTT, Alexander. *While Rome Burns.* 1934. Viking. 1st. sgn. VG. B11. $75.00

WOOLLCOTT, Alexander. *Woollcott Reader.* 1935. Viking. 1st. VG/dj. P3. $30.00

WOOLLEY, C. Leonard. *Vor 5,000 Jahren.* ca 1932. Stuttgart. Franckch'sche. 118p. xl. VG. W1. $10.00

WOOLLEY, Catherine. *Ginnie & the Mystery House.* 1957. Morrow. 1st. 191p. cloth. VG/dj. M20. $22.00

WOOLLEY, Lazelle T. *Just Alike Twins.* 1912. Dutton. 265p. G. M20. $20.00

WOOLMAN, John. *Journal of John Woolman.* 1871. Boston. Osgood. 1st. gilt terra-cotta cloth. NF. M24. $85.00

WOOLMAN, John. *Journal of Life, Gospel Labours & Christian Experiences...* 1776. Dublin. R Jackson. 1st Irish ed. 434p. worn leather. V3. $185.00

WOOLMAN, John. *Some Considerations on Keeping of Negroes.* 1976. Grossman. 85p. VG/VG. V3. $22.00

WOOLRICH, Cornell. *Deadline at Dawn.* 1946. Tower Books. MTI. F/NF. M25. $25.00

WOOLRICH, Cornell. *Into the Night.* 1988. S&S. completed by Lawrence Block. cloth. NF/dj. C9. $35.00

WOOLRICH, Cornell. *Nightwebs.* 1971. Harper Row. 1st. F/NF. M15. $85.00

WOOLRICH, Cornell. *Rendezvous in Black.* nd. Walter Black. VG. P3. $12.00

WOOLRICH, Cornell. *Ten Faces of Cornell Woolrich.* 1965. S&S. 1st. VG/dj. P3. $45.00

WORCESTER, Hugh M. *Hunting the Lawless.* 1955. Berkeley. Am Wildlife Assn. inscr. dj. A19. $25.00

WORDSWORTH, William. *Prelude; or, Growth of a Poet's Mind.* 1850. Appleton. 1st. 374p. purple cloth. VG. B22. $27.00

WORKMAN, Benjamin. *Gauging Epitomized.* 1788. Phil. Young. 1st. 8vo. 120p. contemporary bdg. M1. $375.00

WORLIDGE, John. *Systema Agriculturae: The Mystery of Husbandry Discovered.* 1970. Los Angeles. Sherwin Freutel. facsimile 1675 2nd. 328p. A10. $48.00

WORM, Piet. *Three Little Horses at the King's Palace.* (1962). Random. 4to. unp. G. T5. $20.00

WORMALD, H. *Diseases of Fruits & Hops.* 1945. London. Lockwood. 294p. cloth. A10. $22.00

WORMSER, Richard. *Trem McRea & the Golden Cinders.* 190. McKay. VG/dj. P3. $15.00

WORNUM, R.N. *Characteristics of Styles: Introduction to Study of History.* 1969. London. ils. VG. M17. $60.00

WORTH, C. Brooke. *Naturalist in Trinidad.* 1967. Lippincott. 1st. ils Don Edkelberry. 291p. F/VG. S15. $20.00

WORTS, George F. *Red Darkness.* 1928. Allen. 1st. VG. M2. $25.00

WOUK, Herman. *Don't Stop the Carnival.* 1965. Doubleday. 1st. F/dj. Q1. $50.00

WOUK, Herman. *War & Remembrance.* 1978. Little Brn. 4th. F/NF. W2. $30.00

WPA WRITERS PROGRAM. *Arizona: A State Guide.* 1956. Hastings. ils/maps/index. 532p. NF/G. B19. $20.00

WPA WRITERS PROGRAM. *Copper Camp: Stories of the World's Greatest Mining Town...* 1943. NY. 1st. ils. 308p. G. B18. $22.50

WPA WRITERS PROGRAM. *Death Valley, a Guide.* 1939. Houghton Mifflin. ils. VG/G. O4. $25.00

WPA WRITERS PROGRAM. *Henderson Home of Audubon.* 1941. Northport. 1st. VG/G. B5. $50.00

WPA WRITERS PROGRAM. *Houston.* 1942. VG. 1st. B5. $45.00

WPA WRITERS PROGRAM. *Lamps on the Prairie: History of Nursing in Kansas.* 1942. Emporia. 1st. ils. 292p. VG/dj. B5. $60.00

WPA WRITERS PROGRAM. *Oklahoma.* 1941. Norman. VG/VG. B5. $85.00

WPA WRITERS PROGRAM. *Pennsylvania Cavalcade.* 1942. PA U. 1st. 8vo. VG/dj. H1. $28.00

WPA WRITERS PROGRAM. *San Francisco: The Bay & Its Cities.* 1947. Hastings. Am Guide series. ils. 531p. VG/dj. K7. $25.00

WPA WRITERS PROGRAM. *University of Louisville History.* 1939. Louisville. 1st. ils/index. 301p. G+. B5. $50.00

WPA WRITERS PROGRAM. *Urbana & Champaign County.* 1942. Urbana. 1st. VG/VG. B5. $85.00

WREDE, Patricia C. *Snow White & Rose Red.* 1989. Tor. 1st. 273p. VG?dj. M20. $20.00

WREN, M.K. *Seasons of Death.* 1984. Firecrest. VG/dj. P3. $18.00

WREN, P.C. *Action & Passion.* 1933. Stokes. 1st. VG. M2. $13.00

WREN, P.C. *Bubble Reputation.* 1936. Longman. 1st. VG. P3. $40.00

WREN, R.C. *Potter's Cyclopaedia of Botanical Drugs & Preparations.* 1950. Potter Clarke. 6th. 12mo. VG. A22. $30.00

WRIGHT, A.J. *Red Demon.* 1933. Putnam. 1st. VG. M2. $20.00

WRIGHT, Adeline. *Life in Lyme.* 1976. np. 3rd vol of Hist of Lyme Township series. 100p. VG. B18. $12.50

WRIGHT, Alan. *Bingo & Babs: A Picture Story.* 1919. London. Blackie. 12 full-p pl. cloth/label. R5. $250.00

WRIGHT, Anna Rose. *Whirligig House.* 1951. Houghton Mifflin. 1st. ils Joshua Tolford. 280p. VG-/dj. P2. $25.00

WRIGHT, Anne Marie. *Life of Hugo the Horse.* 1935. Grosset Dunlap. ils Anne Marie Wright. wide 8vo. VG+. C8. $17.50

WRIGHT, Bart. *Largent.* 1990. D&C Incorp. 1st. photos. VG+. P8. $40.00

WRIGHT, Bruce. *Black Robes.* 1987. Secaucus, NJ. Lyle Stuart. 1st. 214p. F/F. B4. $45.00

WRIGHT, D. Macer. *Gardening With Strawberries.* 1973. NY. Drake. 207p. VG/dj. A10. $20.00

WRIGHT, Dare. *Edith & Midnight.* 1978. Doubleday. stated 1st. lg 4to. VG/dj. M5. $85.00

WRIGHT, Dare. *Lonely Doll.* (1957). Doubleday. 9th. lg 4to. VG. C8. $27.50

WRIGHT, Dare. *Lonely Doll.* 1957. Doubleday. 1st. VG+/dj. M5. $115.00

WRIGHT, Dare. *Look at a Kitten.* 1975. Random. 1st. 4to. unp. T5. $20.00

WRIGHT, Dare. *Take Me Home.* 1965. photos. VG/VG. M17. $30.00

WRIGHT, Dudley. *Book of Vampires.* 1973. Causeway. 1st. VG. P3. $20.00

WRIGHT, Edmond. *Fire of Liberty.* 1983. London. Folio Soc. 1st thus. 8vo. 256p. F/case. T10. $45.00

WRIGHT, Edmond. *History of the World.* 1985. Bonanza. dj. A19. $45.00

WRIGHT, Eric. *Body Surrounded by Water.* 1987. Collins Crime Club. 1st. VG/dj. P3. $15.00

WRIGHT, Eric. *Death in the Old Country.* 1985. Collins Crime Club. 1st. VG/dj. P3. $18.00

WRIGHT, Eric. *Question of Murder.* 1988. Collins Crime Club. 1st. VG/dj. P3. $20.00

WRIGHT, Eric. *Sensitive Case.* 1990. Doubleday. 1st Canadian. NF/dj. P3. $23.00

WRIGHT, Ethel W. *Of Men & Trees.* 1954. NY. Exposition. 1st. F/F. B4. $125.00

WRIGHT, Gene. *Horror Shows.* 1986. Facts on File. 1st. VG/dj. P3. $25.00

WRIGHT, Gordon. *Between the Guillotine & Liberty, Two Centuries of Crime...* 1983. NY. Oxford. M11. $45.00

WRIGHT, Grahame. *Jog Rummage.* 1974. Random. 1st. F/dj. P3. $10.00

WRIGHT, Harold Bell. *Devil's Highway.* 1932. Appleton. VG. M2. $40.00

WRIGHT, Harold Bell. *Eyes of the World.* 1914. 1st. VG/G. M19. $35.00

WRIGHT, Harold Bell. *Their Yesterdays.* 1912. Book Supply. 1st. 8vo. 310p. F. H1. $12.00

WRIGHT, Harold Bell. *When a Man's a Man.* 1916. Book Supply. 1st. 348p. VG+/dj. M20. $85.00

WRIGHT, Harold Bell. *Winning of Barbara Worth.* 1911. AL Burt. photoplay ed. 511p. VG/dj. M20. $12.50

WRIGHT, Helen S. *Old-Time Recipes for Home-Made Wines, Cordials & Liqueurs.* 1900. Dana Estes. 156p. G. B10. $75.00

WRIGHT, Helen. *Great White North: Story of Polar Exploration.* 1910. NY. 1st. 489p. gilt pict cloth. A17. $30.00

WRIGHT, Helen. *James Lick's Monument.* 1987. Cambridge. 8vo. 231p. VG/VG. K5. $75.00

WRIGHT, James W.A. *Cement Hunters: Lost Gold Mine of High Sierra.* 1950. Los Angeles. Dawson. 1/200. ils Margaret Atkinson. 52p. as new. K7. $65.00

WRIGHT, John H. *Compendium of the Confederacy: Annotated Biography.* 1989. Broadfoot. 1326p. 4to. F. A17. $150.00

WRIGHT, L. *Practical Poultry Keeper.* 1857. 5th. VG. E6. $25.00

WRIGHT, L.R. *Among Friends.* 1984. Doubleday. 1st Am. NF/dj. M25. $45.00

WRIGHT, L.R. *Sleep While I Sing.* 1986. Doubleday. 1st Canadian. F/dj. P3. $20.00

WRIGHT, L.R. *Suspect.* 1985. Viking. 1st Am. F/dj. M25. $60.00

WRIGHT, Louis B. *Louis B Wright, a Bibliography & an Appreciation.* 1968. Charlottesville. 1st. VG. w/dinner menu. VG. K3. $15.00

WRIGHT, M. *Candy-Making at Home: 200 Ways.* 1924 (1915). Phil. VG. E6. $20.00

WRIGHT, Mabel Osgood. *Flowers & Ferns in Their Haunts.* 1901. Macmillan. 1st. 358p. VG. M20. $25.00

WRIGHT, Madison. *Plant Adaptation to Mineral Stress in Problem Soils.* 1976. Cornell/USDA. 420p. pb. A10. $20.00

WRIGHT, Mark R. *Heat.* 1893. Longman Gr. ils. 8vo. 336p. G+. K3. $25.00

WRIGHT, Richard. *American Hunger.* 1977. Harper Row. 1st. F/VG. M19. $35.00

WRIGHT, Richard. *Black Boy.* 1945. Harper. 1st. NF/G. M19. $125.00

WRIGHT, Richard. *Black Power.* 1954. Harper. later prt. VG/dj. M25. $25.00

WRIGHT, Richard. *Black Power.* 1954. NY. 1st. 358p. F/NF. B4. $150.00

WRIGHT, Richard. *Bright & Morning Star.* (1941). Internat Pub. 1st thus. VG/yel & blk wrp. M25. $75.00

WRIGHT, Richard. *Early Works.* 1991. Lib of America. 1st. F/dj. P3. $35.00

WRIGHT, Richard. *Outsider.* 1945. 1st Eng. VG/VG. M19. $100.00

WRIGHT, Richard. *Rite of Passage.* 1994. Harper Collins. 1st. F/F. B35. $18.00

WRIGHT, Richard. *12 Million Black Voices: Folk History of the Negro in US.* 1941. Viking. 1st. ils. 152p. cloth. dj. D1. $450.00

WRIGHT, Richardson. *Story of Gardening.* 1934. Dodd Mead. 475p. VG. A10. $30.00

WRIGHT, Richardson. *Story of Gardening.* 1935 (1934). Dodd Mead. 8vo. VG. A22. $30.00

WRIGHT, S. Fowler. *Deluge.* 1928. Cosmopolitan. 1st Am. NF/dj. M2. $50.00

WRIGHT, S. Fowler. *Deluge.* 1928. Cosmopolitan. 1st. G. P3. $15.00

WRIGHT, S. Fowler. *Throne of Saturn.* 1951. London. 1st. F/NF. M2. $35.00

WRIGHT, S. Fowler. *World Below.* 1976 (1930). Hyperion. rpt. F. M2. $25.00

WRIGHT, Stephen. *Meditations in Green.* 1983. Scribner. 1st. sgn. author's 1st book. F/F. D10. $90.00

WRIGHT, Steven. *M31: Family Romance.* 1988. Harmony. 1st. F/dj. P3. $20.00

WRIGHT, T.M. *Place.* 1989. Tor. 1st. NF/dj. P3. $18.00

WRIGHT, T.M. *Strange Seed.* 1978. Everest House. 1st. VG/dj. P3. $20.00

WRIGHT, W.J. *Greenhouses: Their Construction & Equipment.* 1955. Orange Judd. revised. 269p. dj. A10. $30.00

WRIGHT, Walter P. *Ils Encyclopedia of Gardening.* nd. London. Dent Dutton. 16mo. 323p. gilt cloth. NF. A22. $15.00

WRIGHT, William. *Von Bulow Affair.* 1983. Delacorte. 1st. sgn. F/dj. T10. $50.00

WRIGHT & WRIGHT. *Handbook of Frogs & Toads of the United States & Canada.* 1975 (1949). Cornell. 3rd. 640p. F. S15. $32.50

WRIGHTSON, Patricia. *Ice Is Coming.* 1978. Hutchinson. 2nd. NF/dj. P3. $15.00

WRIGHTSON, Patricia. *Nargun & the Stars.* 1974. Hutchinson. 2nd. VG/dj. P3. $7.00

WRYDE, J. Saxby. *British Lighthouses.* 1913. London. Unwin. 73 ils. 383p. marbled ep. gilt full calf. T7. $175.00

WU, William F. *Hong on the Range.* 1989. Walker. 1st. F/dj. P3. $18.00

WUEST, Kenneth S. *New Testament: Expanded Translation.* 1962. Eerdmans. 624p. G. B29. $8.50

WUL, Stefan. *Temple of the Past.* 1973. Seabury. 1st. G/dj. P3. $15.00

WYATT, George. *Brains Benton: Case of the Robing Rolls (#4).* 1961. Whitman. VG. P3. $8.00

WYATT, Joan. *Middle Earth Album.* 1979. S&S. 1st. VG/VG. T12. $30.00

WYATT-BROWN, Bertram. *Lewis Tappan & the Evangelical War Against Slavery.* 1969. Cleveland. 1st. 376p. cloth. VG+/dj. M20. $15.00

WYCKOFF, Nicholas E. *Braintree Mission.* nd. BC. VG/dj. P3. $8.00

WYETH, John. *Text-Book of Surgery.* 1887. NY. 1st. 771 woodcuts. 777p. A13. $250.00

WYETH, N.C. *Great Stories of the Sea & Ships.* 1986. Galahad. VG/dj. P3. $15.00

WYETH, N.C. *John Hay: Pike County Ballads.* 1912. Boston. 1st. VG. B5. $90.00

WYETH, N.C. *Robin Hood.* 1917. McKay. 1st thus. teg. gilt gr cloth/mc pl. VG. B5/M5. $145.00

WYKEHAM. *Historica Descriptio Complectens Vitam Guilielmi Wicami.* 1690. Oxford. The Theatre. 4to. full-p pl. calf. R12. $650.00

WYKES, A. *Dr Cardano: Physican Extraordinary.* 1969. London. Muller. 1st. 8vo. 187p. VG/dj. K3. $25.00

WYKES, Alan. *Pen-Friend.* 1950. Duckworth. 1st. VG/dj. P3. $30.00

WYLIE, Elinor. *Angels & Earthly Creatures.* 1929. Knopf. 1st. 8vo. NF/NF. M23. $50.00

WYLIE, Elinor. *Mr Hodge & Mr Hazard.* 1928. Knopf. 1st. 1/145. sgn. F/F/NF case. B4. $250.00

WYLIE, Francis E. *Tides & the Pull of the Moon.* 1979. Brattleboro, VT. Stephen Greene. 2nd. 246p. VG/dj. K5. $25.00

WYLIE, Philip. *Answer.* 1955. Rhinehart. 1st. VG/dj. M2. $20.00

WYLIE, Philip. *Big Ones Got Away.* 1940. NY. 1st. 271p. VG. A17. $30.00

WYLIE, Philip. *Generation of Vipers.* 1942. Farrar Rhinehart. 1st. F/VG. B4. $125.00

WYLIE, Philip. *Gladiator.* 1930. Knopf. 1st. xl. VG. P3. $15.00

WYLIE, Philip. *Gladiator.* 1974 (1930). Hyperion. rpt. F. M2. $40.00

WYLIE, Philip. *Other Horseman.* 1942. Farrar Rinehart. 1st. xl. VG/dj. P3. $20.00

WYLIE, Philip. *Sons & Daughters of Mom.* 1971. Doubleday. 1st. VG/dj. P3. $20.00

WYLIE, Philip. *Tomorrow!* 1954. Rinehart. 1st. VG. P3. $20.00

WYLIE, Philip. *Triumph.* 1963. Doubleday. 1st. F/dj. M2. $25.00

WYLLIE, John. *Pocket Full of Dead.* 1978. Crime Club. 1st. VG/fair. P3. $13.00

WYLLIE, John. *To Catch a Viper.* 1977. Doubleday. 1st. VG/dj. P3. $15.00

WYMAN, Barry. *Behind the Mask of Tutankhamen.* 1972. Souvenir. 1st Eng. 8vo. 203p. NF/dj. W1. $10.00

WYMAN, L.P. *Golden Boys Along the River Allagash (#7).* 1923. AL Burt. 247p. VG/dj. M20. $30.00

WYMAN, L.P. *Lakewood Boys in Montana (#6).* 1927. AL Burt. lists 7 titles. 241p. cloth. VG/ragged. M20. $20.00

WYND, Oswald. *Black Fountains.* 1947. Doubleday. 1st. VG/dj. P3. $40.00

WYNDHAM, John. *Day of the Triffids.* 1951. Doubleday. 1st Am. NF/dj. Q1. $350.00

WYNDHAM, John. *Midwich Cuckoos.* 1957. Ballantine. 1st. VG/dj. M2. $50.00

WYNDHAM, John. *Midwich Cuckoos.* 1957. London. 1st. F/dj. M2. $85.00

WYNDHAM. *Writing for Children & Teen-Agers.* 1972. revised. 267p. F/VG. A4. $40.00

WYNES, Charles. *Charles Richard Drew: Man & the Myth.* 1988. Urbana. 1st. 132p. A13. $27.50

WYNMALEN, Julia. *Holly: The Education of a Pony.* 1949. Country Life. 1st. VG/G. O3. $20.00

WYNNE, May. *Peter Rabbit's Wedding Day.* 1927. Altemus. 62p+ads. VG/tattered. M20. $35.00

WYSE, Lois. *Grandmothers Are To Love.* 1967. Parents Magazine. probable 1st. unp. VG/dj. T5. $18.00

XIANLIANG, Zhang. *Half of Man Is Woman.* 1988. Norton. 1st Am. trans Martha Avery. F/F. M23. $25.00

XILINAS, Elephteri M. *Le Nil, Son Limon et la Terre Egyptienne...* 1936. Cairo. Noury. 1st. 8vo. 192p. lib buckram. xl. W1. $10.00

XIMENEZ, Fray Francisco. *Historia de la Provincia de San Vincente de Chiapa...* 1929-31. Goathmela. 3 vol. F3. $100.00

XOLSON, Charles. *Body.* 1992. World. 455p. VG/dj. B29. $10.50

YABES, Leopoldo Y. *University of the Philpines & Graduate Education Goals.* 1973. Quezon City. sgn. 66p. P1. $6.00

YADIN, Yigael. *Art of Warfare in Biblical Lands.* 1963. 2 vol. ils. VG/VG case. M17. $100.00

YADIN, Yigael. *Bar-Kokhba.* 1971. RAndom. 1st Am. 271p. VG/G+. S3. $30.00

YAFFE, Alan. *Magic Meatball.* 1979. Dial. 1st. ils KB Andersen. VG/dj. M20. $15.00

YANCEY, Lewis A. *Aerial Navigation & Meteorology.* 1927. self pub. 8vo. 68p. G. K5. $16.00

YANOVSKY, V.S. *Great Transfer.* 1974. Harcourt. 1st. F/dj. M2. $13.00

YAPP, W.B. *Vertebrates: Their Structure & Life.* 1965. Oxford. ils. 525p. VG/VG. S15. $10.00

YARBOROUGH, W.P. *Bail Out Over North Africa: America's First...* 1979. NJ. 1st. ils/map/photos/index. 180p. VG/VG. S16. $27.50

YARBRO, Chelsea Quinn. *Candle for D'Artagnan.* 1989. Tor. 1st. F/dj. P3. $25.00

YARBRO, Chelsea Quinn. *False Dawn.* 1978. Doubleday. 1st. F/dj. P3. $18.00

YARBRO, Chelsea Quinn. *Hotel Transylvania.* 1978. St Martin. 1st. F/dj. M2. $75.00

YARBRO, Chelsea Quinn. *Locadio's Apprentice.* 1984. Harper Row. 1st. F/dj. P3. $15.00

YARBRO, Chelsea Quinn. *Messages From Michael.* 1979. Playboy. 1st. inscr. VG/dj. M2. $35.00

YARBRO, Chelsea Quinn. *Tempting Fate.* 1982. St Martin. 1st. VG/dj. M2. $30.00

YARBROUGH, Steve. *Family Men.* 1990. Baton Rouge. LSU. 1st. author's 1st book. F/dj. A24. $35.00

YARDEN, L. *Tree of Light: Study of the Menorah, 7-Branched Lampstand.* 1971. Cornell. 200 photos/notes/index. 162p. VG/dj. S3. $35.00

YARNALL, Charlton. *Forty Years of Friendship.* 1911. London. Macmillan. 340p. G. V3. $25.00

YARROW, C.H. Mike. *Quaker Experiences in International Conciliation.* 1978. Yale. 1st. 308p. VG/VG. V3. $14.00

YATES, Dornford. *Blind Corner.* 1927. Hodder Stoughton. 3rd. VG. P3. $20.00

YATES, Elizabeth. *Amos Fortune, Free Man.* 1962 (1950). Dutton. 13th. inscr. 8vo. 182p. VG/G. T5. $35.00

YATES, George Worthing. *Body That Wasn't Uncle.* 1941. Triangle. 2nd. VG/dj. P3. $15.00

YATES, Richard. *Revolutionary Road.* 1961. Little Brn. 1st trade. F/NF. L3. $125.00

YAUGHAM, Clark. *Addictive Drinking: Road to Recovery...* 1982. Viking. 313p. VG/dj. B29. $5.50

YAVA, Albert. *Big Falling Snow.* 1978. NY. Crown. 1st. F/VG. L3. $45.00

YEAGER, Chuck. *Press On.* 1988. Bantam. 1st. F/F. T12. $20.00

YEAGER, Chuck. *Press On.* 1988. Bantam. 1st. sgn. VG/VG. A23. $50.00

YEAGER, Chuck. *Yeager: An Autobiography.* 1985. Bantam. 1st. F/F. W2. $35.00

YEAKLEY & YEAKLEY. *Heisey Glass in Color.* 1973. self pub. 2nd. 8vo. cbdg. G. H1. $18.00

YEARNS, W. Buck. *Confederate Governors.* 1985. 295p. O8. $12.50

YEATS, William Butler. *Essays, 1931 to 1936.* 1937. Dublin. Cuala. 1st. 1/300 on paper made in Ireland. F. B24. $200.00

YEATS, William Butler. *Fairy & Folk Tales of the Irish Peasantry.* 1888. London. Walter Scott. 1st. cloth. VG. Q1. $600.00

YEATS, William Butler. *Green Helmet & Other Poems.* 1912. NY. 1st. VG. M17. $85.00

YEATS, William Butler. *Ideas of Good & Evil.* 1903. NY. 1st. VG-. M17. $100.00

YEATS, William Butler. *King's Threshold, a Play in Verse.* 1904. NY. private prt. 1st. 1/100. gilt gray brd. uncut. M24. $850.00

YEATS, William Butler. *Poems of...* 1970. NY. LEC. 1st thus. 1/1500. ils/sgn Robin Jacques. F/remnant glassine/case. Q1. $190.00

YEATS, William Butler. *Poems.* 1901. London. Fisher Unwin. 3rd/1st prt. dk bl cloth. M24. $200.00

YEATS, William Butler. *Secret Rose.* 1897. Dutton. 1st Am. gilt dk bl cloth. uncut. F. M24. $300.00

YEATS, William Butler. *Sophocles' King Oedipus.* 1928. NY. 1st. VG. M17. $40.00

YEE, Chiang. *Silent Traveler in Boston.* 1959. Norton. 1st. 275p. tan cloth. VG/dj. B22. $7.00

YEE, Chiang. *Silent Traveler in San Francisco.* 1946. Norton. inscr/ils author. 8vo. bl stp gray cloth. F/dj. R3. $25.00

YEFREMOV, Ivan. *Andromeda.* 1959. Foreign Language Pub. 1st. VG/dj. P3. $30.00

YENNE, Bill. *All Aboard!: The Golden Age of American Rail Travel.* 1990. Greenwich. rpt. 192p. F/dj. A17. $17.50

YENNE, Bill. *Encyclopedia of US Spacecraft.* 1985. NY. Exeter. 4to. 192p. VG/VG. K5. $25.00

YEP, Laurence. *Child of the Owl.* 1977. Harper Row. VG/G. P3. $15.00

YEP, Laurence. *Seademons.* 1977. Harper Row. 1st. VG/dj. P3. $13.00

YERBY, Frank. *Bride of Liberty.* 1954. Doubleday. 1st. VG/dj. P3. $20.00

YERBY, Frank. *Woman Called Fancy.* 1951. Dial. 1st. F/VG. M19. $25.00

YERUSHALMI, Yosef Hayim. *Haggadah & History: Panorama in Facsimile...* 1975. JPS. 2nd. ils. 494p. VG/dj. S3. $150.00

YEVTUSHENKO, Yevgeny. *Precocious Autobiography.* 1963. Dutton. 1st. F/clip. B35. $45.00

YEVTUSHENKO, Yevgeny. *Stolen Apples.* 1971. Doubleday. 1/250. sgn/#d. F/case. M25. $150.00

YEVTUSHENKO, Yevgeny. *Wild Berries.* 1981. Morrow. 1st. F/F. B35. $18.00

YGLESIAS, Jose. *Truth About Them.* 1971. World. 1st. NF/NF. B4. $125.00

YLLA. *Two Little Bears.* 1954. Harper. photos Ylla. VG/dj. M5. $30.00

YOKOI, Yuho. *Zen Master Dogen.* 1976 (1920). Weatherhill. 1st. 217p. F/F. W3. $48.00

YOLEN, Jane. *All Those Secrets of the World.* 1991. Little Brn. 1st. sm 4to. F/F. C8. $30.00

YOLEN, Jane. *Books of Great Alta.* nd. BC. VG/dj. P3. $10.00

YOLEN, Jane. *Dragon's Blood.* 1982. Julia MacRae. F/dj. P3. $20.00

YOLEN, Jane. *Piggins.* 1987. HBJ. 1st. unp. cloth. VG/dj. M20. $22.00

YOLEN, Jane. *Sleeping Beauty.* 1st. ils/sgn Ruth Sanderson. VG/VG. M17. $20.00

YOLEN, Jane. *Stone Silenus.* 1984. Philomel. 1st. VG/dj. P3. $15.00

YOLEN, Jane. *Tam Lin.* 1990. HBJ. 1st. ils Charles Mikolaycak. F/NF. B3. $15.00

YOLEN, Jane. *Touch Magic.* 1981. NY. Philomel. 1st. 8vo. ils. 96p. VG/VG. T5. $30.00

YOLEN, Jane. *Transfigured Heart.* 1975. Crowell. 1st. VG/VG. P2. $25.00

YOLEN, Jane. *Wizard of Washington Square.* 1969. Cleveland. World. 1st. 8vo. 126p. VG/G+. T5. $25.00

YONGE, C.M. *Sea Shore.* 1990 (1949). London. New Naturalist series. ils. 311p. F/dj. S15. $14.00

YONGE, Charlotte. *Chaplet of Pearls.* 1898. London. Macmillan. sgn. 12mo. gilt bl cloth. G. B11. $65.00

YORK, Andrew. *Tallant for Disaster.* 1978. Crime Club. 1st. VG/dj. P3. $12.00

YORK, Herbert F. *Advisors: Oppenheimer, Teller & the Bomb.* 1989. Stanford. rpt. M/wrp. K3. $10.00

YORK, Jeremy; see Creasey, John.

YORKE, Margaret. *Come-On.* 1979. Harper Row. 1st. NF/dj. P3. $15.00

YORKE, Margaret. *Hand of Death.* 1981. St Martin. 1st. VG/dj. P3. $13.00

YORKE, Margaret. *Silent Witness.* 1975. Walker. 1st. VG/dj. P3. $18.00

YORKE, Margaret. *Small Deceit.* 1991. Hutchinson. 1st. F/dj. P3. $25.00

YOSHIMOTO, Banana. *Kitchen.* 1993. Grove. 1st Am. F/F. B4. $75.00

YOST, Nellie Snyder. *Call of the Range, Nebraska, History of Its Cattle Industry.* 1966. Sage Books. 1st. ils/photos. 437p. VG/VG. J2. $85.00

YOUATT, William. *History, Treatment & Diseases of the Horse.* 1883. Lippincott. rpt. 470p. VG. A10. $45.00

YOUATT, William. *Horse: A New Edition...Together With a General History...* 1843. Phil. Lea Blanchard. 1st Am. leather. G. O3. $85.00

YOUNG, A.S. *Black Champions of the Gridiron.* 1969. HBW. 1st. photos. VG+. P8. $12.50

YOUNG, Andrew. *Retrospect of Flowers.* 1950. London. Cape. 1st. 176p. VG/dj. A10. $28.00

YOUNG, Art. *Art Young's Inferno.* 1934. NY. Delphic Studios. 1st. F. B2. $85.00

YOUNG, Arthur. *Travels During Years 1787-1789...the Kingdom of France.* 1793. Dublin. Cross. 2 vol. rebound. xl. A10. $150.00

YOUNG, C.B. *Overland Sketches. By Lieut CB Young, Bengal Engineers.* ca 1830s. London. Dickinson. 4to. 14 hand-colored lithos. modern cloth. G. B24. $500.00

YOUNG, Charles A. *Lessons in Astronomy.* 1895 (1890). Boston. Ginn. 357p. G. K5. $15.00

YOUNG, Charles R. *Royal Forest of Medieval England.* 1979. Leicester. M11. $50.00

YOUNG, Clarence. *Jack Ranger's Gun Club (#5).* 1910. Cupples Leon. lists 6 titles. 288p. VG+/dj. M20. $50.00

YOUNG, Clarence. *Jack Ranger's School Victories (#1).* 1908. Cupples Leon. lists 6 titles. 286p. VG/dj. M20. $45.00

YOUNG, Clarence. *Jack Ranger's Treasure Box (#6).* June 1926. Cupples Leon. 303p. VG. M20. $20.00

YOUNG, Clarence. *Jack Ranger's Western Trip (#2).* 1908. Cupples Leon. lists 6 titles. 302p. VG/ragged. M20. $45.00

YOUNG, Clarence. *Motor Boys Afloat (#5).* 1908. Cupples Leon. lists 22 titles. 244p. VG/dj. M20. $50.00

YOUNG, Clarence. *Motor Boys Bound for Home (#21).* 1920. Cupples Leon. 246p. G+. M20. $30.00

YOUNG, Clarence. *Motor Boys on the Pacific (#8).* 1909. Cupples Leon. lists 12 titles. VG/dj. M20. $17.50

YOUNG, Clarence. *Motor Boys Overland (#2).* 1906. Cupples Leon. lists 22 titles. 228p. VG/dj. M20. $50.00

YOUNG, Clarence. *Motor Boys: Ned, Bob & Jerry on the Firing Line.* 1919. Cupples Leon. lists to this title. 250p+ads. VG. M20. $25.00

YOUNG, Collier; see Bloch, Robert.

YOUNG, D. *Rommel: Desert Fox.* 1950. NY. ils/maps. 264p. VG/VG. S16. $22.50

YOUNG, David L. *Millions Want To.* 1963. Tucson. Three Flags. 1st. inscr. F/NF. O4. $25.00

YOUNG, Edward. *Brothers, a Tragedy...* 1777. London. John Bell. sm 8vo. recent marbled wrp. H13. $175.00

YOUNG, Francis Brett. *Century of Boys' Stories.* nd. Hutchinson. VG. P3. $30.00

YOUNG, G.O. *Alaskan-Yukon Trophies, Won & Lost.* (1947). Huntington. Standard. 2nd. ils/photos/map ep. 273p. VG. M12. $175.00

YOUNG, G.O. *Alaskan-Yukon Trophies, Won & Lost.* 1947. Huntington. 1st. VG. B5. $145.00

YOUNG, Gordon. *Days of '49.* 1939. Caxton. NF/dj. M2. $15.00

YOUNG, Gordon. *Devil's Passport.* 1942. Triangle. VG/fair. P3. $20.00

YOUNG, Hugh Hampton. *Genital Abnormalities, Hermaphroditism & Related...* 1937. Williams Wilkins. 1st. 649p. G. A17. $18.50

YOUNG, Ian. *Private Life of Islam. Young Doctor's Harrowing Account...* 1974. Liveright. 1st. 8vo. 308p. NF/dj. W1. $18.00

YOUNG, J.Z. *Life of Vertebrates.* 1958 (1950). Oxford. ils. 767p. VG. S15. $24.50

YOUNG, James C. *Roosevelt Revealed.* 1936. NY. 1st. VG+/VG+. A20. $30.00

YOUNG, John Richard. *Schooling for Young Riders.* 1985. Norman. ils Randy Steffen. VG/G. O3. $20.00

YOUNG, John V. *Ghost Towns of the Santa Cruz Mountains.* nd. Santa Cruz. Paper Vision Pr. rpt. F/F. O4. $20.00

YOUNG, John Zachary. *Model of the Brain. Being William Withering Lectures...* 1964. Oxford. Clarendon. 348p. bl cloth. xl. G1. $50.00

YOUNG, Miriam. *If I Drove a Tractor.* 1973. Lee Shepard. 1st possible. lg 8vo. F/VG. C8. $30.00

YOUNG, O.E. *Black Powder & Hand Steel: Miners & Machines...* 1976. OK U. 1st. ils. 196p. F/dj. M4. $20.00

YOUNG, Otis. *West of Philip St George Cooke, 1809-1895.* 1955. Clark. 1st. 393p. VG. J2. $325.00

YOUNG, P. *Revolutionary Ladies.* 1977. NY. 1st. F/dj. M4. $20.00

YOUNG, Percy. *Ding Dong Bell: A First Book of Nursery Songs.* 1957. London. Dobson. 1st. 143p. VG/dj. D4. $85.00

YOUNG, Peter. *Illustrated World War II Encyclopedia.* 1978. Great Britain. 24 vol. ils/maps/photos. VG. S16. $200.00

YOUNG, Ralph W. *Grizzlies Don't Come Easy! My Life As Alaskan Bear Hunter.* (1981). Tulsa. Winchester. 1st. 168p. NF/F. H7. $17.50

YOUNG, Richard S. *Life Beyond Earth.* 1969. Little Brn. 107p. G. K5. $10.00

YOUNG, S. *Practical Pointer Training: Hints on Training...* 1974. NY. ils/photos. 178p. cloth. F/NF. M12. $37.50

YOUNG, Scott. *Boy on Defense.* nd. Little Brn. 12th. F/VG. P3. $10.00

YOUNG, Scott. *Murder in Cold Climate.* 1988. Canada. Macmillan. 1st. F/dj. M25. $35.00

YOUNG. *Most Amazing Science Pop-Up Book.* 1994. 7 popups. F. A4. $45.00

YOUNGBLOOD, Charles L. *Mighty Hunter.* 1890. Chicago. 2nd. 362p. gilt cloth. B18. $150.00

YOUNGER, Edward. *John A Kasson.* 1955. State Hist Soc IA. A19. $25.00

YOUNT, John. *Hardcastle.* 1980. NY. Marek. 1st. F/F. B2. $35.00

YOUNT, John. *Trapper's Last Shot.* 1973. Random. 1st. NF/NF. B2. $30.00

YOUNT, John. *Wolf at the Door.* 1967. Random. 1st. author's 1st book. NF/NF. L3. $125.00

YOURCENAR, Marguerite. *Abyss.* 1976. FSG. 1st. F/NF. D10. $35.00

YOURCENAR, Marguerite. *Coup de Grace.* 1957. FSC. 1st. F/clip. D10. $75.00

YOUSSEF BEY, Amine. *Independent Egypt.* 1940. London. Murray. 1st. 8vo. ils. 272p. VG. W1. $20.00

YUILL, P.B.; see Williams, Gordon.

YUNGBLUT, John R. *Rediscovering Prayer.* 1972. NY. Seabury. 180p. xl. V3. $7.50

YUNGJOHANN, John. *White Gold.* 1989. AZ. Synergetic. 1st. 103p. wrp. F3. $15.00

YURDIN, Betty. *Tiger in the Teapot.* 1968. HRW. 1st. VG+/VG. P2. $35.00

YURICK, Sol. *Warriors.* 1965. HRW. 1st. author's 1st novel. F/dj. L3. $100.00

YURICK, Sol. *Warriors.* 1965. HRW. 1st. VG/dj. P3. $35.00

ZABRISKIE, Geroge A. *Bon Vivant's Companion; or, How To Mix Drinks...* 1948. Ormond Beach. Doldrums. 1/1200. 97p. B10. $45.00

ZACKEL, Fred. *Cocaine & Blue Eyes.* 1978. CMG. 1st. VG/dj. P3. $20.00

ZAGAT, Arthur Leo. *Seven Out of Time.* 1949. Fantasy. 1st/ltd. F/NF. P3. $75.00

ZAHM, Albert F. *Aerial Navigation.* 1911. NY/London. 1st. ils. 496p. VG. B18. $150.00

ZAHN, Timothy. *Cascade Point & Other Stories.* 1986. Bluejay. 1st. F/dj. M2. $20.00

ZAHN, Timothy. *Heir to the Empire.* 1991. Bantam. 2nd. F/dj. M2. $16.00

ZAHN, Timothy. *Star Wars III: The Last Command.* 1993. Bantam. 1st. F/F. B3. $15.00

ZAISER, Marion. *Beneficent Blaze.* 1960. NY. Pageant. 1st. sgn. 347p. VG/VG. B11. $40.00

ZALBEN, Jane Breskin. *Cecilia's Older Brother.* 1973. Macmillan. 1st. 12mo. unp. NF/G. T5. $35.00

ZALBEN, Jane Breskin. *Oliver & Alison's Week.* 1980. FSG. 1st. 4to. 40p. VG. T5. $20.00

ZAMORANO, Agustin V. *Copybook From the Hand of...* 1974. Los Angeles. Zamorano Club. 1/250. unp. blk cloth. F. K7. $95.00

ZAMORANO, Agustin V. *Tablas Para Los Ninos Que Empiezan a Contar.* 1976. Los Angeles. Zamorano Club. 1/200. facsimile. brn cloth. as new. K7. $125.00

ZANELLI, Dario. *Fellini's Satyricon.* 1970. Ballantine. ils. trans Walter/Matthews. NF/lg wrp. C9. $50.00

ZANGWILL, Israel. *Dreamers of the Ghetto.* 1898. 1st. VG. E6. $30.00

ZANGWILL, Israel. *Italian Fantasies.* 1921. Am Jewish Book Co. 408p. VG. S3. $18.00

ZANGWILL, Israel. *Principle of Nationalities.* 1917. Macmillan. 16mo. 116p. G. S3. $20.00

ZAPPLER, Lisabeth. *Natural History of the Nose.* 1976. Doubleday. 1st. lg 8vo. F/NF. C8. $17.50

ZAR, Rubin. *Four Generations.* 1979. CA. self pub. inscr. 87p. VG. S3. $16.00

ZAUGG, Hans. *Decorative Trees & Shrubs.* 1960. NY. lg 4to. ils Schwarzenbach/60 mc pl. F/dj. B26. $32.00

ZAWODNY, J.K. *Death in the Forest: Story of the Katyn Forest Massacre.* 1972. Notre Dame. photos/notes/biblio/index. 235p. VG/torn. S16. $21.50

ZDINAK, Paul. *Bessie's House.* 1976. Carlton. ils/photos. 143p. red cloth. F/dj. H1. $18.00

ZEBROWSKI, George. *Macrolife.* 1979. Harper Row. 1st. F/dj. M2. $20.00

ZEBROWSKI, George. *Macrolife.* 1990. Easton. sgn. leather. F. M2. $45.00

ZEBROWSKI, George. *Stars Will Speak.* 1985. Harper Row. 1st. sgn. F/F. B11. $45.00

ZEBROWSKI, George. *Sunspacer.* 1978. Harper Row. 1st. F/dj. P3. $15.00

ZEEMANN, P. *Progress Recents en Magneto-Optique.* 1907. Fevrier. ils. VG/wrp. K3. $35.00

ZEIGLER, Wilbur G. *Story of the Earthquake & Fire.* 1906. SF. Leon C Osteyee. 1st. 100 half-tone ils. VG/archival case. O4. $20.00

ZEITLIN, Joseph. *Disciples of the Wise: Religious & Social Opinions...* 1947. Columbia Teachers College. 2nd. 233p. VG+/G+. S3. $25.00

ZELAZNY, Roger. *Blood of Amber.* 1986. Arbor. 1st. F/dj. P3. $20.00

ZELAZNY, Roger. *Chronicles of Amber.* nd. BC. 2 vol. VG/dj. P3. $15.00

ZELAZNY, Roger. *Courts of Chaos.* 1978. Doubleday. 1st. F/dj. P3. $35.00

ZELAZNY, Roger. *Doorways in the Sand.* 1977. WH Allen. 1st. F/dj. P3. $20.00

ZELAZNY, Roger. *Eye of Cat.* 1982. Timescape. 1st. NF/dj. P3. $20.00

ZELAZNY, Roger. *Four for Tomorrow.* 1975. Garland. 1st Am. F/sans. M2. $35.00

ZELAZNY, Roger. *Guns of Avalon.* 1974. Faber. NF/dj. P3. $50.00

ZELAZNY, Roger. *Hand of Oberon.* 1978. Faber. 1st. NF/dj. P3. $45.00

ZELAZNY, Roger. *Illustrated Roger Zelazny.* 1978. Baronet. 1st. sgn. F/sans. P3. $60.00

ZELAZNY, Roger. *Last Defender of Camelot.* 1980. SFBC. F/dj. M2. $12.00

ZELAZNY, Roger. *Nebula Award Stories Three.* 1968. Doubleday. 1st. VG/VG. M22. $20.00

ZELAZNY, Roger. *Roadmarks.* 1979. Del Rey. 1st. F/dj. P3. $25.00

ZELAZNY, Roger. *Sign of Chaos.* 1987. Arbor. 1st. F/dj. P3. $16.00

ZELAZNY, Roger. *To Die in Italbar.* 1973. SFBC. F/dj. M2. $12.00

ZELAZNY, Roger. *Trumps of Doom.* 1985. Arbor. 1st. F/NF. R14. $25.00

ZELAZNY, Roger. *Wilderness.* 1994. NY. Forge. 1st. sgn. F/dj. A24. $50.00

ZELIKOFF, M. *Threshold of Space.* 1957. NY. Pergamon. 4to. 342p. G. K5. $25.00

ZELLERS, Parker. *Tony Pastor, Dean of the Vaudeville Stage.* 1971. Ypsilanti, MI. Eastern U. dj. A19. $25.00

ZEMACH, Harve. *Awake & Dreaming.* 1970. FSG. 1st. ils. F/F. D1. $45.00

ZEMACH, Harve. *Mommy, Buy Me a China Doll.* (1966). Chicago. Follett. 2nd. obl 8vo. 32p. G+. T5. $150.00

ZEMACH, Harve. *Salt, a Russian Tale.* 1977 (1965). 1st thus. ils Margot Zemach. as new/F. C8. $25.00

ZEMACH, Margot. *It Could Always Be Worse.* 1976. FSG. 1st. obl sm 4to. F/VG+. C8. $75.00

ZEMACH & ZEMACH. *Duffy & the Devil.* 1973. Harmondsworth Middlesex. Kestrel. 1st. sm 4to. VG/G. C8. $65.00

ZEMPEL, Edward N. *First Editions: A Guide to Identification.* 1985. Spoon River. 2nd. F/dj. P3. $25.00

ZERNER, Henri. *School of Fontainebleau: Etchings & Engravings.* 1969. NY. Abrams. ils/23p fld-out in back. ES. cloth. dj. D2. $175.00

ZEVIN, Israel. *Parables of the Preacher of Doubno.* 1925. NY. Tashrak. Yiddish text. 318p. S3. $19.00

ZHADIN, V.I. *Fauna & Flora of the Rivers, Lakes & Reservoirs of USSR.* 1963. Jerusalem. IPST. ils. 626p. VG+/wrp. M12. $37.50

ZHDANOV, Aleksandr I. *Shadow of Peril.* 1963. Doubleday. 1st. VG/dj. P3. $25.00

ZHUKOV, G. *Marshall Zhukov's Greatest Battles.* 1969. 1st. F/F. E6. $15.00

ZICREE, Marc Scott. *Twilight Zone Companion.* nd. BC. VG/dj. P3. $10.00

ZIEFERT, Harriet. *Measure Me.* 1991. Harper Collins. ils Susan Baum. unp. NF. T5. $22.00

ZIEGLER, Ernst. *Text-Book of General Pathological Anatomy & Pathogenesis.* 1883-1884. NY. 1st Am. 2 vol. 317 woodcuts. A13. $75.00

ZIEGLER, Mel. *Amen: Diary of Rabbi Martin Siegel.* 1971. World. 276p. VG/G. S3. $17.00

ZIEMANN, H. *White House Cookbook.* 1919 (1887). sm 4to. 619p. VG. E6. $50.00

ZIEMANN, Hans Heinrich. *Accident.* 1979. St Martin. 1st. F/dj. P3. $15.00

ZIETLOW, E.R. *Country for Old Men.* 1977. Hermosa, SD. Lame Johnny Pr. A19. $10.00

ZIGMOND, M.L. *Kawaiisu Ethnobotany.* 1981. Salt Lake City. 102p. F/wrp. B1. $37.00

ZIGROSSER, C. *Ars Medica: Collection of Medical Prints...* 1959. Phil Mus Art. ils. 91p. F. M4. $30.00

ZILESKI, George. *Prince in Space.* 1986. Vantage. 1st. F/dj. M2. $25.00

ZILLER, Wolf G. *Tree Rusts of Western Canada.* 1974. Victoria, BC. ils/botanical keys/descriptions/photos. 272p. VG/dj. B26. $22.50

ZIMEN, E. *Wolf: His Place in the Natural World.* 1981. London. Souvenir. ils. 373p. F/F. M12. $37.50

ZIMILES & ZIMILES. *Early American Mills.* 1973. NY. ils. F/dj. M4. $35.00

ZIMMELS, H.J. *Magicians, Theologians & Doctors: Studies in Folk Medicine.* 1952. London. 1st. 293p. VG+. W3. $72.00

ZIMMER, Heinrich. *Philosophies of India.* nd. Princeton. Bollingen series. 687p. F/VG. W3. $86.00

ZIMMER, Joseph. *History of the 43rd Infantry Division.* 1946. Baton Rouge. 1st. maps/photos. 96p. VG. S16. $95.00

ZIMMERMAN, Arthur. *Francisco De Toledo.* 1938. Caxton. 1st. 307p. map ep. F3. $15.00

ZIMMERMAN, Bruce. *Crimson Green.* 1994. Harper Collins. 1st. F/dj. P3. $20.00

ZIMMERMAN, Heinrich. *Third Voyage of Captain Cook.* 1988. Fairfield. 1/500. 128p. gilt bl cloth. P4. $45.00

ZIMMERMAN, John. *Guadalcanal Campaign.* 1990. Nashville. maps/photos. 189p. VG/VG. S16. $32.50

ZIMMERMAN, R.D. *Midscream.* 1989. DIF. VG/dj. P3. $25.00

ZIMMERMANN, A. *Die Morphologie und Physiologie des Pflanzlichen Zellkernes.* 1896. Jena. ils. 188p. detached wrp. B26. $10.00

ZINDEL, Paul. *When Darkness Falls.* 1984. Bantam. VG/G. P3. $13.00

ZIPES, Jack. *Spells of Enchantment.* nd. BC. VG/dj. P3. $15.00

ZIPSER & ZIPSER. *Fire & Grace: Life of Rose Pastor Stokes.* 1989. Athens, GA. 1st. F/F. B2. $25.00

ZITKALSA. *Old Indian Legends.* 1901. Boston. Ginn. 1st. author's 1st book. xl. G. L3. $675.00

ZIVANOVIC, S. *Ancient Diseases: Elements of Palaeopathology.* 1982. London. 1st Eng trans. 285p. dj. A13. $40.00

ZLOTOWITZ, Bernard M. *Septuagint Translation of the Hebrew Terms...* 1981. Ktav. inscr. biblio/index. 196p. VG. S3. $27.00

ZOCHERT, Donald. *Laura: Life of Laura Ingalls Wilder.* 1976. Regnery. 1st. 260p. cloth. VG/dj. M20. $25.00

ZOCHERT, Donald. *Man of Glass.* 1981. HRW. 1st. VG/dj. P3. $13.00

ZOLBROD, Paul G. *Dine Bhane: Navajo Creation Story.* 1985. VG/VG. M17. $20.00

ZOLOTKOFF, Leon. *From Vilna to Hollywood.* 1932. NY. Bloch. 1st. yel brd. NF. M25. $45.00

ZOLOTOW, Charlotte. *Everything Glistens & Everything Sings.* 1987. Harcourt Brace. 1st/1st prt. sm 8vo. F/F. C8. $27.50

ZOLOTOW, Charlotte. *Sleepy Book.* 1988. Harper. 1st probable thus. ils Plume. sm 4to. F/F. C8. $22.50

ZOLOTOW, Charlotte. *Someone New.* 1978. Harper Row. 1st. 32p. VG. T5. $25.00

ZOLOTOW, Charlotte. *Tiger Called Thomas.* (1963). Lee Shepard. 1st. sm 4to. unp. VG/VG. T5. $25.00

ZOLTAN, Janos. *Die Anwendung des Spalthautlappens in der Chirurgie.* 1962. Jena. 1st. ils. 391p. A13. $125.00

ZOMBECK, Martin V. *Handbook of Space Astronomy & Astrophysics.* 1982. Cambridge. 8vo. 326p. VG. K5. $25.00

ZOSS, Joel. *Greatest Moments in Baseball.* 1987. Bison Books. 1st. VG/dj. P3. $10.00

ZUBRO, Mark Richard. *Echo of Death.* 1994. St Martin. 1st. sgn. F/F. M15. $35.00

ZUBRO, Mark Richard. *Simple Suburban Murder.* 1989. St Martin. 1st. inscr. F/NF. N4. $40.00

ZUCKERKANDL, E. *Atlas der Topographischen Anatomie des Menschen.* 1904. Vienna. 1st. 2 vol. 834p. A13. $150.00

ZUCKERKANDL, Otto. *Atlas & Epitome of Operative Surgery.* 1898. Phil. 1st Eng trans. 395p. A13. $100.00

ZUG, C.R. *Lizards of Fiji: Natural History & Systematics.* 1991. Honolulu. Bishop Mus. 136p. B1. $36.00

ZUROY, Michael. *Second Death.* 1992. Walker. 1st. F/dj. P3. $20.00

ZWANZIGER. *Animal Kingdom Fully Illustrated in Colors.* ca 1920. Saalfield. ils/27 double-p lithos. cloth. NF. M12. $95.00

ZWEIG, Arnold. *Education Before Verdun.* 1936. Viking. 447p. VG. S3. $22.00

ZWEMER, Samuel M. *Moslem World.* 1908. NY. Young People's Missionary Movement. 2nd. ils. VG. W1. $25.00

ZWINGER, Ann. *Aspen Blazon of the High Country.* 1991. Salt Lake City. Gibbs Smith. 1st. sgn. F/wrp. B3. $25.00

ZWINGER, Ann. *John Xantus: The Fort Tejon Letters 1857-1859.* 1986. Tucson. 1st. sgn. F/F. B3. $45.00

ZWINGER, Ann. *Wind in the Rock.* 1978. NY. 1st. ils. 258p. F/dj. M4. $20.00

PSEUDONYMS

Listed below are pseudonyms of many paperback and hardcover authors. This information was shared with us by some of our many contributors, and we offer it here as a reference for our readers. This section is organized alphabetically by the author's actual name (given in bold) followed by the pseudonyms he or she been known to use. (It is interesting to note that 'house names' were common with more than one author using the same name for a particular magazine or publishing house.)

If you have additional information (or corrections), please let us hear from you so we can expand this section in future editions.

Aarons, Edward S.
Ayres, Paul
Ronns, Edward

Albert, Marvin H.
Conroy, Albert
Jason, Stuart
Quarry, Nick
Rome, Anthony

Ard, William (Thomas)
Kerr, Ben
Ward, Jonas (some)

Auster, Paul
Benjamin, Paul

Avallone, Mike
Carter, Nick (a few)
Conway, Troy (a few)
Dalton, Priscilla
Jason, Stuart
Noone, Edwina
Stuart, Sidney
Walker, Max

Ballard, W.T.
Hunter, D'Allard
MacNeil, Neil
Shepherd, John

Ballinger, Bill
Sanborn, B.X.

Barnard, Robert
Bastable, Bernard

Barnes, Julian
Kavanagh, Dan
Seal, Basil

Blake, Roger
Sade, Mark

Blassingame, Lurton
Duncan, Peter

Beaumont, Charles
Grantland, Keith

Beck, Robert
Slim, Iceberg

Bedford-Jones, H.
Feval, Paul
Pemjion, L.

Bloch, Robert
Young, Collier

Block, Lawrence
Ard, William
Emerson, Jill
Harrison, Chip
Lord, Sheldon
Morse, Benjamin, M.D.
Shaw, Andrew

Bradley, Marion Zimmer
Chapman, Lee
Dexter, John (some)
Gardner, Miriam
Graves, Valerie
Ives, Morgan

Brunner, John
Woodcott, Keith

Bulmer, Kenneth
Hardy, Adam
Norvil, Manning
Prescot, Dray

Burnett, W.R.
Monachan, John
Updyke, James

Burroughs, William S.
Lee, William

Byrne, Stuart
Bloodstone, John

Cain, Paul
Sims, George

Campbell, Ramsey
Dreadstone, Carl
Ramsay, Jay

Carr, John Dickson
Dickson, Carter
Fairbairn, Roger

Cooper, Basil
Falk, Lee

Cooper, Clarence
Chestnut, Robert

Creasey, John
Ashe, Gordon
Carmichael, Harry
Deane, Norman
Frazier, Robert Caine
Gill, Patrick
Holliday, Michael
Hope, Brian
Hughes, Colin
Hunt, Kyle
Marric, J.J.
York, Jeremy

Crichton, Michael
Lange, John

Cross, David
Chesbro, George B.

Daniels, Norman
Daniels, Dorothy
Wade, David

Davidson, Avram
Queen, Ellery (about 2 titles only)

Derleth, August
Grendon, Stephen

Dewey, Thomas B.
Brandt, Tom
Wainer, Cord

Disch, Thomas
Demijohn, Thomas
Cassandra, Knye
(both with John Sladek)

Duffy, James
Murphy, Haughton

Ellis, Peter Beresford
Tremayne, Peter

Ellison, Harlan
Merchant, Paul

Etchison, Dennis
Martin, Jack

Faust, Fredrick S.
Brand, Max

Fairman, Paul
Paul, F.W.

Fanthorpe, Lionel
Muller, John E.

Farmer, Philip Jose
Norfolk, William
Trout, Kilgore

Fearn, John Russell
Del Martia, Aston

Foster, Alan Dean
Lucas, George

Fox, Gardner F.
Chase, Glen
Cooper, Jefferson
Gardner, Jeffrey
Gardner, Matt
Gray, James Kendricks
Jennings, Dean
Majors, Simon
Matthews, Kevin
Morgan, John Medford
Morgan, Rod
Summers, Bart

Gardner, Erle Stanley
Fair, A.A.
Kendrake, Carleton
Kinney, Charles

Garrett, Randall
Bupp, Walter
Gordon, David
$^1/_2$ of Mark Phillips and
Robert Randall

Geis, Richard
Owen, Robert
Swenson, Peggy

Geisel, Theodore Seuss
Dr. Seuss

Gibson, Walter B.
Brown, Douglas
Grant, Maxwell

Goulart, Ron
Falk, Lee Kains, Josephine
Kearney, Julian
Robeson, Kenneth
Shaw(n), Frank S.
Silva, Joseph

Grant, Charles L.
Andrew, Felicia
Lewis, Deborah

Haas, Ben
Meade, Richard

Haldeman, Joe
Graham, Robert

Hall, Oakley
Hall, O.M.

Halliday, Brett
Shayne, Mike

Hansen, Joseph
Brock, Rose
Colton, James

Harknett, Terry
Hedges, Joseph
Stone, Thomas H.

Harris, Timothy
Hyde, Harris

Heilbrun, Carolyn G.
Cross, Amanda

Highwater, Jamake
Marks, J.
Marks-Highwater, J.

Hochstein, Peter
Short, Jack

Hodder-Williams, C.
Brogan, James

Holt, John Robert
Giles, Elizabeth
Giles, Raymond

Hoppley-Woolrich, Cornell
Hopley, George
Irish, William
Woolrich, Cornell

Hunt, E. Howard
St. John, David

Hunter, Evan
Cannon, Curt
Collins, Hunt
Hannon, Ezra
Marsten, Richard
McBain, Ed

Jackson, J. Denis
Moreau, Julian

Jacks, Oliver
Gandley, Kenneth R.

Jakes, John
Ard, William
Payne, Alan
Scotland, Jay

Jenkins, Will F.
Leinster, Murray

Jones, H. Bedford
Pemjean, Lucien

Kane, Frank
Boyd, Frank

Kane, Henry
McCall, Anthony

Kent, Hal
Davis, Ron

King, Stephen
Bachman, Richard

Klass, Philip K.
Tenn, William

Klavan, Andrew
Peterson, Keith

Knowles, William
Allison, Clyde
Ames, Clyde

Koontz, Dean R.
Axton, David
Coffey, Brian
Dwyer, Deanna
Dwyer, K.R.
Hill, John
Nichols, Leigh
North, Anthony
Paige, Richard
West, Owen
Wolfe, Aaron

Kornbluth, Cyril
Eisner, Simon
Park, Jordan

Kosinski, Jerzy
Somers, Jane

Kubis, P.
Scott, Casey

Kurland, Michael
Plum, Jennifer

L'Amour, Louis
Burns, Tex
Mayo, Jim

Lariar, Lawrence
Knight, Adam

Laumer, Keith
LeBaron, Anthony

Lesser, Milton
Marlowe, Stephen

Lessing, Doris
Somers, Jane

Lewis, Alfred Henry
Quinn, Dan

Linebarger, Paul
Smith, Cordwainer

Long, Frank Belknap
Long, Lyda Belknap

Lovesey, Peter
Lear, Peter

Lucas, Mark
Palmer, Drew

Ludlum, Robert
Ryder, Jonathan
Shepherd, Michael

Lupoff, Richard
Steele, Adison

Lynds, Dennis
Collins, Michael
Crowe, John
Grant, Maxwell (some)
Sadler, Mark

Malzberg, Barry
Berry, Mike
Dumas, Claudine
Johnson, Mel
Johnson, M.L.
O'Donnell, Barrett
O'Donnell, K.M.

Manfred, Frederick
Feikema, Feike

Marshall, Mel
Tayler, Zack

Martin, Robert
Roberts, Lee

Mason, Van Wyck
Coffin, Geoffrey

Masterton, Graham
Luke, Thomas

Matheson, Richard
Swanson, Logan

McGaughy, Dudley
Owen, Dean

Meaker, Marijane
Aldrich, Ann
Packer, Vin

Menken, H.L.
Hatteras, Owen

Mertz, Barbara Gross
Michael, Barbara
Peters, Elizabeth

Millar, Kenneth
MacDonald, Ross
MacDonald, John Ross

Moorcock, Michael
Barclay, Bill
Bradbury, Edward P.

Moore, Brian
Mara, Bernard
Michael, Bryan

Morris, James
Morris, Jan (after sex change)

Nasby, Petroleum
Locke, David R.

Norton, Andre Alice
North, Andrew
Norton, Alice
Norton, Andre

Nuetzel, Charles
Augustus, Albert Jr.
Davidson, John
English, Charles
Rivere, Alec

Oates, Joyce Carol
Smith, Rosamond

Offutt, Andrew
Cleve, John
Giles, Baxter
Williams, J.X. (some)

Patterson, Henry
Fallon, Martin
Graham, James
Higgins, Jack
Patterson, Harry
Marlowe, Hugh

Philips, James Atlee
Atlee, Philip

Phillips, Dennis
Chambers, Peter
Chester, Peter

Phillips, Judson
Pentecost, Hugh

Posner, Richard
Foster, Iris
Murray, Beatrice
Todd, Paul

Pargeter, Edith Mary
Peter, Ellis

Prather, Richard
Knight, David
Ring, Douglas

Radford, R.L.
Ford, Marcia

Pronzini, Bill
Foxx, Jack

Rabe, Peter
MacCargo, J.T.

Rawson, Clayton
Towne, Stuart

Rendell, Ruth
Vine, Barbara

Reynolds, Mack
Belmont, Bob
Harding, Todd
Reynolds, Maxine

Rice, Anne
Rampling, Anne
Roquelaure, A.N.

Rosenblum, Robert
Maxxe, Robert

Ross, W.E.D.
Dana, Rose
Daniels, Jan
Ross, Clarissa
Ross, Dan
Ross, Dana
Ross, Marilyn

Rossi, Jean-Baptiste
Japrisot, Sebastien

Sandford, John
Camp, John

Scoppetone, Sandra
Early, Jack

Sellers, Con
Bannion, Della

Sheldon, Alice Bradley
Bradley, Alice
Sheldon, Raccoona
Tiptree, James

Silverberg, Robert
Beauchamp, Loren
Burnett, W.R. (some only)
Drummond, Walter
Elliott, Don (some)
Ford, Hilary
Hamilton, Franklin
Knox, Calvin
Lt. Woodard, M.D.

Smith, George H.
Deer, J.M.
Hudson, Jan
Jason, Jerry
Knerr, M.E.
Summers, Diana

Stacton, David
Clifton, Bud

Sturgeon, Theodore
Ewing, Frederick R.
Queen, Ellery (1 book only)

Thomas, Ross
Bleeck, Oliver

Tracy, Don
Fuller, Roger

Tralins, Bob
Miles, Keith
O'Shea, Sean

Tubb, E.C.
Kern, Gregory

Vance, Jack
Held, Peter
Queen, Ellery (some/few)

Vidal, Luther
Box, Edgar
Vidal, Gore

Wager, Walter
Tiger, John
Walker, Max

Ward, Harold
Zorro

Webb, Jack
Farr, John

Weiss, Joe
Anatole, Ray
Dauphine, Claude
Mirbeau, Ken

Westlake, Donald E.
Allan, John B.
Clark, Curt
Culver, Timothy
Cunningham, J. Morgan
Holt, Samuel
Marshall, Alan
Stark, Richard
West, Edwin

Williams, Gordon
Yuill, P.B

Whittington, Harry
Harrison, Whit
Shepherd, Shep

Williamson, Jack
Stewart, Will

Wollheim, Don
Grinnell, David

Worts, George F.
Brent, Loring

BOOKBUYERS

In this section of the book we have listed buyers of books and related material. When you correspond with these dealers, be sure to enclose a self-addressed stamped envelope if you want a reply. Do not send lists of books for appraisal. If you wish to sell your books, quote the price you want or send a list and ask if there are any on the list they might be interested in and the price they would be willing to pay. If you want the list back, be sure to send a SASE large enough for the listing to be returned. When you list your books, do so by author, full title, publisher and place, date, edition, and condition, noting any defects on cover or contents.

Advance Review Copies
Paperbacks
The American Dust Co.
47 Park Ct.
Staten Island, NY 10301
718-442-8253 or fax 718-981-0311

Adventure
The Silver Door
P.O. Box 3208
Redondo Beach, CA 90277
310-379-6005

African-American
Children's Book Adoption Agency
P.O. Box 643
Kensington, MD 20895-0643
310-565-2834 or fax 301-585-3091

Fran's Bookhouse
6601 Greene St.
Phil., PA 19119
215-438-2729 or fax 215-438-8997

Monroe Stahr Books
4420 Ventura Canyon, #2
Sherman Oaks, CA 91423
818-784-0870 or fax 818-995-0866

Recollection Books
4519 University Way NE
Seattle, WA 98105
206-548-1346

Alaska
Artis Books
201 N Second Ave.
P.O. Box 822
Alpena, MI 49707
517-354-3401

Albania
W.B. O'Neill-Old & Rare Books
11609 Hunters Green Ct.
Reston, VA 22091
703-860-0782 or fax 703-620-0153

Alcoholics Anonymous
The Book Baron
1236 S Magnolia Ave.
Anaheim, CA 92804
714-527-7022 or fax 714-527-5634

1939-1954
Paul Melzer Fine Books
12 E Vine St.
Redlands, CA 92373
902-792-7299

Americana
Amaranth Books
P.O. Box 421
Wilmette, IL 60091-0421
708-328-2939

The Book Inn
6401 University
Lubbock, TX 79413

The Bookseller, Inc.
174 W Exchange St.
Akron, OH 44302
330-762-3101 or fax 330-762-4413

Bowie & Co. Booksellers, Inc.
314 First Ave. S
Seattle, WA 98104
206-624-4100 or fax 206-223-0966

Woodbridge B. Brown
P.O. Box 445
Turners Falls, MA 01376
413-772-2509 or 413-773-5710

The Captain's Bookshelf, Inc.
P.O. Box 2258
Asheville, NC 28802-2258
704-253-6631

Chapel Hill Rare Books
P.O. Box 456
Carrboro, NC 27510
919-929-8351

Duck Creek Books
Jim & Shirley Richards
P.O. Box 203
Caldwell, OH 43724
614-732-4856 (10 am to 10 pm)

Terry Harper, Bookseller
P.O. Box 312
Vergennes, VT 05491-0312
802-877-9262

Susan Heller, Pages for Sages
22611 Halburton Rd.
Beachwood, OH 44122-3939
216-283-2665

Jim Hodgson Books
908 S Manlius St.
Fayetteville, NY 13066
315-637-6264

M & S Rare Books, Inc.
P.O. Box 2594, E Side Sta.
Providence, RI 02906
401-421-1050 or fax 401-272-0831
(attention M & S)

Parmer Books
7644 Forrestal Rd.
San Diego, CA 92120-2203
619-287-0693 or fax 619-287-6135

Randall House
835 Laguna St.
Santa Barbara, CA 93101
805-963-1909 or fax 805-963-1650

Thorn Books
P.O. Box 1244
Moorpark, CA 93020
805-529-3647 or fax 805-529-0022

18th & 19th C
Gordon Totty
Scarce Paper Americana
347 Shady Lake Pky.
Baton Rouge, LA 70810
504-766-8625

Yesterday's Books
229 Riverview Dr.
Parchment, MI 49004
616-345-1011

Anarchism
Nutmeg Books
354 New Litchfield St. (Rte. 202)
Torrington, CT 06790
203-482-9696

Angling
Book & Tackle Shop
29 Old Colony Rd.
P.O. Box 114
Chestnut Hill, MA 02167
617-965-0459 (winter)
401-596-0700 (summer)

Anthropology
The King's Market Bookshops
P.O. Box 709
Boulder, CO 80306-0709
303-447-0234

Anthologies
Cartoonists from 1890-1960
Craig Ehlenberger
Abalone Cove Rare Books
7 Fruit Tree Rd.
Portuguese Bend, CA 90275

Antiquarian
A.B.A.C.U.S. ®
Phillip E. Miller
343 S Chesterfield St.
Aiken, SC 29801
803-648-4632

Fine, hard-to-find books
Arnold's of Michigan
218 S Water
Marine City, MI 48039
810-765-1350 or fax 810-765-7914

The Book Baron
1236 S Magnolia Ave.
Anaheim, CA 92804
714-527-7022 or fax 714-527-5634

Bowie & Co. Booksellers, Inc.
314 First Ave. S
Seattle, WA 98104
206-624-4100 or fax 206-223-0966

Children's Book Adoption Agency
P.O. Box 643
Kensington, MD 20895-0643
310-565-2834 or fax 301-585-3091

James Tait Goodrich
Antiquarian Books & Manuscripts
135 Tweed Blvd.
Nyack, NY 10960-4913

Terry Harper, Bookseller
P.O. Box 312
Vergennes, VT 05491-0312
802-877-9262

Murray Hudson
Antiquarian Books & Maps
The Old Post Office
109 S Church St.
P.O. Box 163
Halls, TN 38040
901-836-9057 or 800-748-9946

Jeffrey Lee Pressman, Bookseller
3246 Ettie St.
Oakland, CA 94608
510-652-6232

Robert Mueller Rare Books
8124 W 26th St.
N Riverside, IL 60546
708-447-6441

Scribe Company
Attn: Bonnie Smith
427 Hidden Forest S
Longview, TX 75605
903-663-6873

*Also Agriculture, Biographies, Law,
Travel, Turn-of-the-Century Fiction &
Philosophy*
David R. Smith
30 Nelson Circle
Jaffrey, NH 03452
603-532-8666

Printed before 1800
Gordon Totty
Scarce Paper Americana
347 Shady Lake Pky.
Baton Rouge, LA 70810
504-766-8625

Antiques, Collectibles & Reference
Antique & Collectors Reproduction
 News
Box 17774-OB
Des Moines, IA 50325
515-270-8994

Collector's Companion
Perry Franks
P.O. Box 24333
Richmond, VA 23224

Galerie De Boicourt
6136 Westbrooke Dr.
W Bloomfield, MI 48322
248-788-9253

Henry H. Hain III
Antiques & Collectibles
2623 N Second St.
Harrisburg, PA 17110
717-238-0534

Appraisals
J. Sampson Antiques & Books
107 S Main
Harrodsburg, KY 40330
606-734-7829

Lee & Mike Temares
50 Hts. Rd.
Plandome, NY 11030
516-627-8688

Arabian Horses; Arabian Nights
Worldwide Antiquarian
P.O. Box 410391
Cambridge, MA 02141-0004
617-876-6220 or fax 617-876-0839

Archaelogy
Flo Silver Books
8442 Oakwood Ct. N
Indianapolis, IN 46260
317-255-5118

Architecture
Cover to Cover
P.O. Box 687
Chapel Hill, NC 27514

Arctic
Artis Books
201 N Second Ave.
P.O. Box 822
Alpena, MI 49707
517-354-3401

Parmer Books
7644 Forrestal Rd.
San Diego, CA 92120-2203
619-287-0693 or fax 619-287-6135

Armenia
W.B. O'Neill-Old & Rare Books
11609 Hunters Green Ct.
Reston, VA 22091
703-860-0782 or fax 703-620-0153

Art
AL-PAC
Lamar Kelley Antiquarian Books
2625 E Southern Ave., C-120
Tempe, AZ 85282
602-831-3121 or fax 602-831-3193

Book & Tackle Shop
29 Old Colony Rd.
P.O. Box 114
Chestnut Hill, MA 02167
617-965-0459 (winter)
401-596-0700 (summer)

Books West Southwest
Box 6149, University Sta.
Irvine, CA 92616-6149
or
14 Whitman Ct.
Irvine, CA 92612
714-509-7670 or fax 714-854-5102

The Captain's Bookshelf, Inc.
P.O. Box 2258
Asheville, NC 28802-2258
704-253-6631

Fine, applied
L. Clarice Davis Art Books
P.O. Box 56054
Sherman Oaks, CA 91413-1054
818-787-1322

Galerie De Boicourt
6136 Westbrooke Dr.
W Bloomfield, MI 48322
248-788-9253

Edison Hall Books
5 Ventnor Dr.
Edison, NJ 08820
908-548-4455

Heritage Book Shop, Inc.
8540 Melrose Ave.
Los Angeles, CA 90069
213-659-3674

David Holloway, Bookseller
7430 Grace St.
Springfield, VA 22150
703-659-1798

Significant Books
3053 Madison Rd.
P.O. Box 9248
Cincinnati, OH 45209
513-321-7567

Lee & Mike Temares
50 Hts. Rd.
Plandome, NY 11030
516-627-8688

Xanadu Records, Ltd.
3242 Irwin Ave.
Kingsbridge, NY 10463
212-549-3655

Arthurian
Camelot Books
Charles E. Wyatt
P.O. Box 2883
Vista, CA 92083
619-940-9472

Astronomy
Knollwood Books
Lee & Peggy Price
P.O. Box 197
Oregon, WI 53575
608-835-8861 or fax 608-835-8421

Atlases
Murray Hudson
Antiquarian Books & Maps
The Old Post Office
109 S Church St.
P.O. Box 163
Halls, TN 38040
901-836-9057 or 800-748-9946

Before 1870
Gordon Totty
Scarce Paper Americana
347 Shady Lake Pky.
Baton Rouge, LA 70810
504-766-8625

Atomic Bomb
Key Books
P.O. Box 58097
St. Petersburg, FL 33715
813-867-2931

Autobiographies
Herb Sauermann
21660 School Rd.
Manton, CA 96059

Warren's Collector Books
112 Royal Ct.
Friendswood, TX 77546
281-482-7947

Wellerdt's Books
3700 S Osprey Ave. #214
Sarasota, FL 34239
813-365-1318

Autographs
Ads Autographs
P.O. Box 8006
Webster, NY 14580-8006
716-671-2651 or fax 716-671-5727

Michael Gerlicher
1375 Rest Point Rd.
Orono, MN 55364

Susan Heller, Pages for Sages
22611 Halburton Rd.
Beachwood, OH 44122-3939
216-283-2665

Heritage Book Shop, Inc.
8540 Melrose Ave.
Los Angeles, CA 90069
213-659-3674

Historical Newspapers & Journals
Steve & Linda Alsberg
9850 Kedvale
Skokie, IL 60076-1124
847-676-9850

Key Books
P.O. Box 58097
St. Petersburg, FL 33715
813-867-2931

McGowan Book Co.
39 Kimberly Dr.
Durham, NC 27707
919-403-1503 or fax 919-403-1706

Paul Melzer Fine Books
12 E Vine St.
Redlands, CA 92373
909-792-7299

Randall House
835 Laguna St.
Santa Barbara, CA 93101
805-963-1909 or fax 805-963-1650

Aviation
The Book Corner
Michael Tennero
728 W Lumsden Rd.
Brandon, FL 33511
813-684-1133

The Bookseller, Inc.
174 W Exchange St.
Akron, OH 44302
330-762-3101 or fax 330-762-4413

Cover to Cover
P.O. Box 687
Chapel Hill, NC 27514

Baedeker Handbooks
W.B. O'Neill-Old & Rare Books
11609 Hunters Green Ct.
Reston, VA 22091
703-860-0782 or fax 703-620-0153

Barbie
Glo's Books & Collectibles
906 Shadywood
Southlake, TX 76092
817-481-1438

Baseball
Brasser's
8701 Seminole Blvd.
Seminole, FL 33772
813-393-6707

R. Plapinger, Baseball Books
P.O. Box 1062
Ashland, OR 87520
503-488-1200

L. Frank Baum
Alcott Books
Barbara Ruppert
5909 Darnell
Houston, TX 77074-7719
713-774-2202

Bibliographies
About Books
6 Sand Hill Ct.
P.O. Box 5717
Parsippany, NJ 07054
201-515-4591

Books West Southwest
Box 6149, University Sta.
Irvine, CA 92616-6149
or
14 Whitman Ct.
Irvine, CA 92612
714-509-7670 or fax 714-854-5102

Oak Knoll Books
414 Delaware St.
New Castle, DE 19720
800-996-2556 or 302-328-7232
fax 302-328-7274

Big Little Books
Jay's House of Collectibles
75 Pky. Dr.
Syosset, NY 11791

Biographies
Third Time Around Books
Norman Todd
R.R. #1
Mar., Ontario
Canada N0H 1XO
519-534-1382

Herb Sauermann
21660 School Rd.
Manton, CA 96059

Warren's Collector Books
112 Royal Ct.
Friendswood, TX 77546
281-482-7947

Black Americana
Especially Little Black Sambo
Glo's Books & Collectibles
906 Shadywood
Southlake, TX 76092
817-481-1438

History & literature
David Holloway, Bookseller
7430 Grace St.
Springfield, VA 22150
703-569-1798

Mason's Bookstore, Rare Books
& Record Albums
115 S Main St.
Chambersburg, PA 17201
717-261-0541

Black Fiction & Literature
Almark & Co.-Booksellers
P.O. Box 7
Thornhill, Ontario
Canada L3T 3N1
phone/fax 905-764-2665

Black Studies
Recollection Books
4519 University Way NE
Seattle, WA 98105
206-548-1346

Black Hills
James F. Taylor
515 Sixth St.
Rapid City, SD 57701
605-341-3224

Book Search Service
Authors of the West
191 Dogwood Dr.
Dundee, OR 97115
503-538-8132

Avonlea Books
P.O. Box 74, Main Sta.
White Plains, NY 10602
914-946-5923

Bookingham Palace
Rosan Van Wagenen & Eileen Layman
52 North 2500 East
Teton, ID 83451
209-458-4431

Heritage Book Shop, Inc.
8540 Melrose Ave.
Los Angeles, CA 90069
310-659-3674 or fax 310-659-4872

Hilda's Book Search
Hilda Gruskin
199 Rollins Ave.
Rockville, MD 20852
301-948-3181

Lost N' Found Books
Linda Lengerich
3214 Columbine Ct.
Indianapolis, IN 46224
phone/fax 317-298-9077

Passaic Book Center
594 Main Ave.
Passaic, NJ 07055
201-778-6646 or fax 201-778-6738

Recollection Used Books
David Brown
4519 University Way NE
Seattle, WA 98105
206-548-1346

The Silver Door
P.O. Box 3208
Redondo Beach, CA 90277
310-379-6005

Especially children's out-of-print books
Treasures from the Castle
Connie Castle
1720 N Livernois
Rochester, MI 48306
248-651-7317

Book Sets
AL-PAC
Lamar Kelley Antiquarian Books
2625 E Southern Ave., C-120
Tempe, AZ 85282
602-831-3121 or fax 602-831-3193

Books About Books
About Books
6 Sand Hill Ct.
P.O. Box 5717
Parsippany, NJ 07054
201-515-4591

Books West Southwest
Box 6149, University Sta.
Irvine, CA 92616-6149
or
14 Whitman Ct.
Irvine, CA 92616
714-509-7670 or fax 714-854-5102

Bowie & Co. Booksellers, Inc.
314 First Ave. S
Seattle, WA 98104
206-624-4100 or fax 206-223-0966

First Folio
1206 Brentwood
Paris, TN 38242
phone/fax 901-644-9940

Susan Heller, Pages for Sages
22611 Halburton Rd.
Beachwood, OH 44122-3939
216-283-2665

Key Books
P.O. Box 58097
St. Petersburg, FL 33715
813-867-2931

Oak Knoll Books
414 Delaware St.
New Castle, DE 19720
800-996-2556 or 302-328-7232
fax 302-328-7274

Randall House
835 Laguna St.
Santa Barbara, CA 93101
805-963-1909 or fax 805-963-1650

George H. Tweney
16660 Marine View Dr. SW
Seattle, WA 98166
206-243-8243

Botany
Brooks Books
P.O. Box 21473
Concord, CA 94521
510-672-4566 or fax 510-672-3338

Also gardening, horiticulture, etc.
Agave Books
P.O. Box 31495
Mesa, AZ 85275-1495
602-649-9097

Charles Bukowski
Ed Smith Books
P.O. Box 66
Oak View, CA 93022
805-649-2844 or fax 805-649-2863

California
Books West Southwest
Box 6149, University Sta.
Irvine, CA 92616-6149
or
14 Whitman Ct.
Irvine, CA 92616
714-509-7670 or fax 714-854-5102

Paul Melzer Fine Books
12 E Vine St.
Redlands, CA 92373
909-792-7299

Thorn Books
P.O. Box 1244
Moorpark, CA 93020
805-529-3647 or fax 805-529-0022

Canadiana
Third Time Around Books
Norman Todd
R.R. #1
Mar., Ontario
Canada N0H 1XO
519-534-1382

Cartography
Overlee Farm Books
P.O. Box 1155
Stockbridge, MA 01262
413-637-2277

Cartoon Art
Jay's House of Collectibles
75 Pky. Dr.
Syosset, NY 11791

Catalogs
Glass, pottery, furniture, doll, toy, jewelry, general merchandise, fishing tackle
Bill Schroeder
P.O. Box 3009
Paducah, KY 42002-3009

Antiques or other collectibles
Antique & Collectors Reproduction
  News
Box 17774-OB
Des Moines, IA 50325
515-270-8994

Hillcrest Books
961 Deep Draw Rd.
Crossville, TN 38555-9547
phone/fax 615-484-7680

Celtic
Camelot Books
Charles E. Wyatt
P.O. Box 2883
Vista, CA 92083
619-940-9472

Central America
Flo Silver Books
8442 Oakwood Ct. N
Indianapolis, IN 46260
317-255-5118

Marc Chagall
Paul Melzer Fine Books
12 E Vine St.
Redlands, CA 92373
909-792-7299

Children's Illustrated
Noreen Abbot Books
2666 44th Ave.
San Francisco, CA 94116
415-664-9464

Alcott Books
Barbara Ruppert
5909 Darnell
Houston, TX 77074-7719
713-774-2202

Book & Tackle Shop
29 Old Colony Rd.
P.O. Box 114
Chestnut Hill, MA 02167
617-965-0459 (winter)
401-596-0700 (summer)

Books of the Ages
Gary J. Overmann
Maple Ridge Manor
4764 Silverwood Dr.
Batavia, OH 45103-9740
phone/fax 513-732-3456

Bromer Booksellers
607 Boylston St.
Boston, MA 02116
617-247-2818 or fax 617-247-2975

19th & 20th C
Children's Book Adoption Agency
P.O. Box 643
Kensington, MD 20895-0643
301-565-2834 or fax 301-585-3091

Free search service
Steven Cieluch
15 Walbridge St., Ste. #10
Allston, MA 02134-3808
617-734-7778

Ursula Davidson
Children's & Illustrated Books
134 Linden Ln.
San Rafael, CA 94901
414-454-3939 or fax 415-454-1087

Drusilla's Books
859 N Howard St.
Baltimore, MD 21201
401-225-0277

Edison Hall Books
5 Ventnor Dr.
Edison, NJ 08820
908-548-4455

Circa 1850s through 1970s
Encino Books
Diane Yaspan
5063 Gaviota Ave
Encino, CA 91436
818-905-711 or fax 818-501-7711

First Folio
1206 Brentwood
Paris, TN 38242
phone/fax 901-644-9940

Fran's Bookhouse
6601 Greene St.
Phil., PA 19119
215-438-2729 or fax 215-438-8997

*Madeline, Eloise, Raggedy Ann &
Andy, Uncle Wiggly, Wizard of Oz*
Glo's Books & Collectibles
906 Shadywood
Southlake, TX 76092
817-481-1438

Susan Heller, Pages for Sages
22611 Halburton Rd.
Beachwood, OH 44122-3939
216-283-2665

Ilene Kayne
1308 S Charles St.
Baltimore, MD 21230
410-347-7570

Bob Lakin
3021 Lavita Ln.
Dallas, TX 75234
972-247-3291

Marvelous Books
P.O. Box 1510
Ballwin, MO 63022
314-458-3301 or fax 314-273-5452

Much Ado
Seven Pleasant St.
Marblehead, MA 01945
617-639-0400

Nerman's Books
410-63 Albert St.
Winnipeg, Manitoba
Canada R3B 1G4
fax 204-947-0753

Page Books
HCR 65, Box 233
Kingston, AR 72742
870-861-5831

Jo Ann Reisler, Ltd.
360 Glyndon St., NE
Vienna, VA 22180
703-938-2967 or fax 703-938-9057

Scribe Company
Attn: Bonnie Smith
427 Hidden Forest S
Longview, TX 75605
903-663-6873

Barbara Smith Books
P.O. Box 1185
Northampton, MA 01061
413-586-1453

Nancy Stewart, Books
1188 NW Weybridge Way
Beaverton, OR 97006
503-645-9779

Yesterday's Books
229 Riverview Dr.
Parchment, MI 49004
616-345-1011

Treasures from the Castle
Connie Castle
1720 N Livernois
Rochester, MI 48306
248-651-7317

Children's Series
Children's Book Adoption Agency
P.O. Box 643
Kensington, MD 20895-0643
301-565-2834 or fax 301-585-3091

Circa 1900s through 1970s
Encino Books
Diane Yaspan
5063 Gaviota Ave
Encino, CA 91436
818-905-711 or fax 818-501-7711

Judy Bolton, Nancy Drew, Rick Brant, Cherry Ames, etc.; also Dick & Jane readers
Glo's Books & Collectibles
906 Shadywood
Southlake, TX 76092
817-481-1438

Ilene Kayne
1308 S Charles St.
Baltimore, MD 21230
410-347-7570

Bob Lakin
3021 Lavita Ln.
Dallas, TX 75234
972-247-3291

Nerman's Books
410-63 Albert St.
Winnipeg, Manitoba
Canada R3B 1G4
fax 204-947-0753

Scribe Company
Attn: Bonnie Smith
427 Hidden Forest S
Longview, TX 75605
903-663-6873

Lee & Mike Temares
50 Hts. Rd.
Plandome, NY 11030
516-627-8688

Yesterday's Books
229 Riverview Dr.
Parchment, MI 49004
616-345-1011

Christian Faith
Books Now & Then
Dennis Patrick
P.O. Box 337
Stanley, ND 58784
701-628-2084

Christmas
Especially illustrated antiquarian
Drusilla's Books
859 N Howard St.
Baltimore, MD 21201
410-225-0277

Sir W.S. Churchill
Chartwell Booksellers
55 E 52nd St.
New York, NY 10055
212-308-0643

Robert L. Merriam
Rare, Used & Old Books
Newhall Rd.
Conway, MA 01341
413-369-4052

Cinema, Theatre & Films
Cinemage Books
105 W 27th St.
New York, NY 10001
212-243-4919

Xanadu Records, Ltd.
3242 Irwin Ave.
Kingsbridge, NY 10463
212-549-3655

Civil War
Brasser's
8701 Seminole Blvd.
Seminole, FL 33772
813-393-6707

Chapel Hill Rare Books
P.O. Box 456
Carrboro, NC 27510
919-929-8351

Stan Clark Military Books
915 Fairview Ave.
Gettysburg, PA 17325
717-337-1728 or 717-337-0581

Elder's Book Store
2115 Elliston Pl.
Nashville, TN 37203
615-327-1867

Rick Harmon
Military Books & Relics
910 Sullivan Dr.
Belvidere, IL 61008
815-547-7580

Jim Hodgson Books
908 S Manlius St.
Fayetteville, NY 13066
315-637-6264

Mason's Bookstore, Rare Books
    & Record Albums
115 S Main St.
Chambersburg, PA 17201
717-261-0541

K.C. & Jean Owings
Box 389
Whitman, MA 02382
781-447-7850 or fax 781-447-3435

Also ephemera before 1900
Gordon Totty
Scarce Paper Americana
347 Shady Lake Pky.
Baton Rouge, LA 70810
504-766-8625

Cobb, Irvin S.
Always paying $3.00 each plus shipping. Send for immediate payment:
Bill Schroeder
5801 KY Dam Rd.
Paducah, KY 42003

Collectibles, Antiques & Reference
Antique & Collectors Reproduction
    News
Box 1774-OB
Des Moines, IA 50325
515-270-8994

Galerie De Boicourt
6136 Westbrooke Dr.
W Bloomfield, MI 48322
248-788-9253

Henry H. Hain III
Antiques & Collectibles
2623 N Second St.
Harrisburg, PA 17110
717-238-0534

Color Plate Books
Bowie & Co. Booksellers, Inc.
314 First Ave. S
Seattle, WA 98104
206-624-4100 or fax 206-223-0966

Drusilla's Books
859 N Howard St.
Baltimore, MD 21201
410-225-0277

Worldwide Antiquarian
P.O. Box 410391
Cambridge, MA 02141-0004
617-876-6220 or fax 617-876-0839

Comics
Passaic Book Center
594 Main Ave.
Passaic, NJ 07055
201-778-6646 or fax 201-778-6738

Cookery & Cookbooks
Arnold's of Michigan
218 S Water
Marine City, MI 48039
810-765-1350 or fax 810-765-7914

Book & Tackle Shop
29 Old Colony Rd.
P.O. Box 114
Chestnut Hill, MA 02167
617-965-0459 (winter)
401-596-0700 (summer)

Book Broker
P.O. Box 1283
Charlottesville, VA 22902
804-296-2194 or fax 804-296-1566

The Book Corner
Mike Tennero
728 W Lumsden Rd.
Brandon, FL 33511
813-684-1133

RAC Books
R.R. #2
P.O. Box 296
Seven Valleys, PA 17360
717-428-3776

Barbara Smith Books
P.O. Box 1185
Northampton, MA 01061
413-586-1453

Warren's Collector Books
112 Royal Ct.
Friendswood, TX 77546
281-482-7947

Crime
The Silver Door
P.O. Box 3208
Redondo Beach, CA 90277
310-379-6005

Cyprus
W.B. O'Neill-Old & Rare Books
11609 Hunters Green Ct.
Reston, VA 22091
703-860-0782 or fax 703-620-0153

Decorative Arts
Robert L. Merriam
Rare, Used & Old Books
Newhall Rd.
Conway, MA 01341
413-369-4052

Detective
First editions
Karl M. Armens
740 Juniper Dr.
Iowa City, IA 52245

Monroe Stahr Books
4420 Ventura Canyon, #2
Sherman Oaks, CA 91423
818-784-0870 or fax 818-995-0866

Mordida Books
P.O. Box 79322
Houston, TX 77279
713-467-4280 or fax 713-467-4182

Pulphouse
J.H. James
P.O. Box 481
Elberton, GA 30635
706-213-9280

Thomas Books
P.O. Box 14036
Phoenix, AZ 85063
602-247-9289

The Silver Door
P.O. Box 3208
Redondo Beach, CA 90277
310-379-6005

Earth Science
Used, out-of-print, rare
Patricia L. Daniel, Bookseller
13 English Ave.
Wichita, KS 62707-1005
316-683-2079 or fax 316-683-5448

Emily Dickinson
Robert L. Merriam
Rare, Used & Old Books
Newhall Rd.
Conway, MA 01341
413-369-4052

Disney
Cohen Books & Collectibles
Joel J. Cohen
P.O. Box 810310
Boca Raton, FL 33481-0310
561-487-7888

Jay's House of Collectibles
75 Pky. Dr.
Syosset, NY 11791

Documents
McGowan Book Co.
39 Kimberly Dr.
Durham, NC 27707
919-403-1503 or fax 919-403-1706

Dogs
Kathleen Rais & Co.
211 Carolina Ave.
Phoenixville, PA 19460
610-933-1388

Thomas Edison
Edison Hall Books
5 Ventnor Dr.
Edison, NJ 08820
908-548-4455

Ephemera
Antique valentines
Kingsbury Productions
Katherine & David Kreider
4555 N Pershing Ave., Ste. 33-138
Stockton, CA 95207
209-467-8438

The Mulberry Cat
Yvonne Davis
Jan Davis Martel
P.O. Box 3573
Boone, NC 28607
704-963-7693

Equestrine
Books, antiques, art
Artiques, Ltd.
Veronica Jochens
P.O. Box 67
Lonedell, MO 63060
314-629-1374

Espionage
The Silver Door
P.O. Box 3208
Redondo Beach, CA 92077
310-379-6005

Estate Libraries
The Book Collector
2347 University Blvd.
Houston, TX 77005
713-661-2665

Exhibition Catalogs
L. Clarice Davis Art Books
P.O. Box 56054
Sherman Oaks, CA 91413-1054
818-787-1322

Exploration
Western
Terry Harper, Bookseller
P.O. Box 312
Vergennes, VT 05491-0312
802-877-9262

Heritage Book Shop, Inc.
8540 Melrose Ave.
Los Angeles, CA 90069
213-659-3674

Key Books
P.O. Box 58097
St. Petersburg, FL 33715
813-867-2931

Paul Melzer Fine Books
12 E Vine St.
Redlands, CA 92373
909-792-7299

Flo Silver Books
8442 Oakwood Ct. N
Indianapolis, IN 46260
317-255-5118

Fantasy
The Book Baron
1236 S Magnolia Ave.
Anaheim, CA 92804
714-527-7022 or fax 714-527-5634

Camelot Books
Charles E. Wyatt
P.O. Box 2883
Vista, CA 92083
619-940-9472

Farming
First editions
Karl M. Armens
740 Juniper Dr.
Iowa City, IA 52245

Also gardening
Hurley Books
1752 Rt. 12
Westmoreland, NH 03467-4724
603-399-4342 or fax 603-399-8326

Henry Lindeman
4769 Bavarian Dr.
Jackson, MI 49201
517-764-5728

Fiction
Southern
Alice Robbins, Bookseller
3002 Round Hill Rd.
Greensboro, NC 27408
910-282-1964

Third Time Around Books
Norman Todd
R.R. #1
Mar., Ontario
Canada N0H 1XO
519-534-1382

Warren's Collector Books
112 Royal Ct.
Friendswood, TX 77546
281-482-7947

American, European, detective or crime
Ace Zerblonski Books
Malcolm McCollum, Proprietor
1419 North Royer
Colorado Springs, CO 80907
719-634-3941

Bob Lakin
3021 Lavita Ln.
Dallas, TX 75234
972-247-3291

19th & 20th-C American
Mason's Bookstore, Rare Books
   & Record Albums
115 S Main St.
Chambersburg, PA 17201
717-261-0541

Financial
Warren's Collector Books
112 Royal Ct.
Friendswood, TX 77546
281-482-7947

Fine Bindings & Books
The Book Collector
2347 University Blvd.
Houston, TX 77005
713-661-2665

Bromer Booksellers
607 Boylston St.
Boston, MA 02116
617-247-2818 or fax 617-247-2975

Dad's Old Bookstore
Green Hills Ct.
4004 Hillsboro Rd.
Nashville, TN 37215
615-298-5880

Heritage Book Shop, Inc.
8540 Melrose Ave.
Los Angeles, CA 90069
310-659-3674 or fax 310-659-4872

Terry Harper, Bookseller
P.O. Box 312
Vergennes, VT 05491-0312
802-877-9262

George Robert Kane Fine Books
252 Third Ave.
Santa Cruz, CA 95062
phone/fax 408-426-4133

Kenneth Karimole, Bookseller, Inc.
509 Wilshire Blvd.
Santa Monica, CA 94001
310-451-4342 or 310-458-5930

Mason's Bookstore, Rare Books
   & Record Albums
115 S Main St.
Chambersburg, PA 17201
717-261-0541

Paul Melzer Fine Books
12 E Vine St.
Redlands, CA 92373
909-792-7299

Also sets
Randall House
835 Laguna St.
Santa Barbara, CA 93101
805-963-1909 or fax 805-963-1650

David R. Smith
30 Nelson Circle
Jaffrey, NH 03452
603-532-8666

Fine Press

Susan Heller, Pages for Sages
22611 Halburton Rd.
Beachwood, OH 44122-3939
216-283-2665

Heritage Book Shop, Inc.
8540 Melrose Ave.
Los Angeles, CA 90069
310-659-3674 or fax 310-659-4872

Randall House
835 Laguna St.
Santa Barbara, CA 93101
805-963-1909 or fax 805-963-1650

Firearms

Melvin Marcher, Bookseller
6204 N Vermont
Oklahoma City, OK 73112

First Editions

A Tale of Two Sisters
2509 Stone Hollow Dr.
Bedford, TX 76021

After 1937
A.B.A.C.U.S.®
Phillip E. Miller
343 S Chesterfield St.
Aiken, SC 29801
803-648-4632

Hyper-modern
Almark & Co.-Booksellers
P.O. Box 7
Thornhill, Ontario
Canada L3T 3N1
phone/fax 905-764-2665

Modern or signed
AL-PAC
Lamar Kelley Antiquarian Books
2625 E Southern Ave., C-120
Tempe, AZ 85282
602-831-3121 or fax 602-831-3193

Modern or signed
Alcott Books
Barbara Ruppert
5909 Darnell
Houston, TX 77074-7719
713-774-2202

Amaranth Books
P.O. Box 421
Wilmette, IL 60091-0421
708-328-2939

Karl M. Armens
740 Juniper Dr.
Iowa City, IA 52245

Modern
Bella Luna Books
P.O. Box 260425
Highlands Ranch, CO 80163
800-497-4717 or fax 303-791-7342

Between the Covers
35 W Maple Ave.
Merchantville, NJ 08109
609-665-2284 or fax 609-665-3639

The Book Baron
1236 S Magnolia Ave.
Anaheim, CA 92804
714-527-7022 or fax 714-527-5634

Modern
Chapel Hill Rare Books
P.O. Box 456
Carrboro, NC 27510
919-929-8351

Modern
Tom Davidson, Bookseller
3703 Ave. L
Brooklyn, NY 11210
718-338-8428

Modern
Bernard E. Goodman, Bookseller
7421 SW 147 Ct.
Miami, FL 33193
305-382-2464

Edison Hall Books
5 Ventnor Dr.
Edison, NJ 08820
908-548-4455

Modern
Susan Heller, Pages for Sages
22611 Halburton Rd.
Beachwood, OH 44122-3939
216-283-2665

Modern
David Holloway, Bookseller
7430 Grace St.
Springfield, VA 22150
703-569-1798

Ruth Heindel Associates
First Editions, Rare & Used Books
2629 Cranberry Cir.
Harrisburg, PA 17110
717-657-0047

Heritage Book Shop, Inc.
8540 Melrose Ave.
Los Angeles, CA 90069
310-659-3674 or fax 310-659-4872

Modern
Ken Lopez, Bookseller
51 Huntington Rd.
Hadley, MA 01035
413-584-4827 or fax 413-584-2045

Also presentation or association copies
MacDonnell Rare Books
9307 Glenlake Dr.
Austin, TX 78730
512-345-4139

Monroe Stahr Books
4420 Ventura Canyon, #2
Sherman Oaks, CA 91423
818-784-0870 or fax 818-995-0866

Much Ado
Seven Pleasant St.
Marblehead, MA 01945
617-639-0400

Robert Mueller Rare Books
8124 W 26th St.
N Riverside, IL 60546
708-447-6441

Jeffrey Lee Pressman, Bookseller
3246 Ettie St.
Oakland, CA 94608
510-652-6232

Pulphouse
J.H. James
P.O. Box 481
Elberton, GA 30635
706-213-9280

American & British
Quill & Brush
Box 5365
Rockville, MD 20848
301-460-3700 or fax 301-871-5425

Alice Robbins, Bookseller
3002 Round Hill Rd.
Greensboro, NC 27408
910-282-1964

Especially fiction, cookery, children's, business, sports & illustrated
Eileen Serxner
Box 2544
Bala Cynwyd, PA 19004
610-664-7960

Modern
Ed Smith Books
P.O. Box 66
Oak View, CA 93022
805-646-2844 or fax 805-649-2863

Scribe Company
Attn: Bonnie Smith
427 Hidden Forest S
Longview, TX 75605
903-663-6873

20th-century authors of nature, natural history, 20th-century Americana, historical & nautical fiction
Town's End Books
John D. & Judy A. Townsend
132 Hemlock Dr.
Deep River, CT 06417
860-526-3896

Modern; especially British & European literature
The Typographeum Bookshop
246 Bennington Rd.
Francestown, NH 03043
603-547-2425

Modern
The Early West/Whodunit Books
P.O. Box 9292
College Sta., TX 77842
409-775-6047 or fax 409-764-7758

Harrison Fisher
Parnassus Books
218 N 9th St.
Boise, ID 83702

Fishing
Artis Books
201 N Second Ave.
P.O. Box 208
Alpena, MI 49707
517-354-3401

Edison Hall Books
5 Ventnor Dr.
Edison, NJ 08820
908-548-4455

Jim Hodgson Books
908 S Manlius St.
Fayetteville, NY 13066
315-637-6264

Melvin Marcher, Bookseller
6204 N Vermont
Oklahoma City, OK 73112

Mason's Bookstore, Rare Books
   & Record Albums
115 S Main
Chambersburg, PA 17201
717-261-0541

Yesterday's Books
229 Riverview Dr.
Parchment, MI 49004
616-345-1011

Florida
The Book Corner
Michael Tennero
728 W Lumsden Rd.
Brandon, FL 33511
813-684-1133

Brasser's
8701 Seminole Blvd.
Seminole, FL 33772
813-393-6707

Football
Brasser's
8701 Seminole Blvd.
Seminole, FL 33772
813-393-6707

Fore-Edge Painted Books
Susan Heller, Pages for Sages
22611 Halburton Rd.
Beachwood, OH 44122-3939
216-283-2665 or fax 316-991-2665

George Robert Kane Fine Books
252 Third Ave.
Santa Cruz, CA 95062
phone/fax 408-426-4133

Freemasonry
Mason's Bookstore, Rare Books
   & Record Albums
115 S Main St.
Chambersburg, PA 17201
717-261-0541

Gambling & Gaming
Gambler's Book Shop
630 S Eleventh St.
Las Vegas, NV 89101
800-634-6243

Games
Card or board; Whist & Bridge
Bill & Mimi Sachen
927 Grand Ave.
Waukegan, IL 60085
847-662-7204

Gardening
The American Botanist Booksellers
P.O. Box 532
Chillicothe, IL 61523
309-274-5254

The Book Corner
Mike Tennero
728 W Lumsden Rd.
Brandon, FL 33511
813-684-1133

Brooks Books
P.O. Box 21473
Concord, CA 94521
510-672-4566 or fax 510-672-3338

The Captain's Bookshelf, Inc.
P.O. Box 2258
Asheville, NC 28802-2258
704-253-6631

Gazetteers
Murray Hudson
Antiquarian Books & Maps
The Old Post Office
109 S Church St.
P.O. Box 163
Halls, TN 38040
901-836-9057 or 800-748-9946

Genealogy
Elder's Book Store
2115 Elliston Pl.
Nashville, TN 37203
615-327-1867

General Out-of-Print
Best-Read Books
122 State St.
Sedro-Wooley, WA 98284
206-855-2179

Bicentennial Book Shop
820 S Westnedge Ave.
Kalamazoo, MI 49008
616-345-5987

The Book Baron
1236 S Magnolia Ave.
Anaheim, CA 92804
714-527-7022 or fax 714-527-5634

Book Den South
2249 First St.
Ft. Myers, FL 33901
813-332-2333

The Bookseller, Inc.
174 W Exchange St.
Akron, OH 44302
330-762-3101 or fax 330-762-4413

Cinemage Books
105 W 27th St.
New York, NY 10001

Antiquarian
Eastside Books & Paper
P.O. Box 1581, Gracie Sta.
New York, NY 10028-0013
212-759-6299

Edison Hall Books
5 Ventnor Dr.
Edison, NJ 08820
908-548-4455

Fran's Bookhouse
6601 Greene St.
Phil., PA 19119
215-438-2729 or fax 215-438-8997

Grave Matters
P.O. Box 32192-08
Cincinnati, OH 45232
513-242-7527 or fax 513-242-5115

George Robert Kane Fine Books
252 Third Ave.
Santa Cruz, CA 95062
phone/fax 408-426-4133

McGowan Book Co.
39 Kimberly Dr.
Durham, NC 27707
919-403-1503 or fax 919-403-1706

Robert L. Merriam
Rare, Used & Old Books
New Hall Rd.
Conway, MA 01341
413-369-4052

The Mulberry Cat
Yvonne Davis
Jan Davis Martel
P.O. Box 3573
Boone, NC 28607
704-963-7693

Passaic Book Center
594 Main Ave.
Passaic, NJ 07055
201-778-6646 or fax 201-778-6738

RAC Books
R.R. #2
P.O. Box 296
Seven Valleys, PA 17360
717-428-3776

J. Sampson Antiques & Books
107 S Main
Harrodsburg, KY 40330
606-734-7829

Significant Books
3053 Madison Rd.
P.O. Box 9248
Cincinnati, OH 45209
513-321-7567

A.A. Vespa
P.O. Box 637
Park Ridge, IL 60068
708-692-4210

Genetics
The King's Market Bookshops
P.O. Box 709
Boulder, CO 80306-0709
303-447-0234

Geographies
Murray Hudson
Antiquarian Books & Maps
The Old Post Office
109 S Church St.
P.O. Box 163
Halls, TN 38040
901-836-9057 or 800-748-9946

Overlee Farm Books
P.O. Box 1155
Stockbridge, MA 01262
413-637-2277

Golf
Brasser's
8701 Seminole Blvd.
Seminole, FL 33772
813-393-6707

David Goodis
The American Dust Co.
47 Park Ct.
Staten Island, NY 10301
718-442-8253 or fax 718-981-0311

Sue Grafton
Glo's Books & Collectibles
906 Shadywood
Southlake, TX 76092
817-481-1438

Thomas Books
P.O. Box 14036
Phoenix, AZ 85063
602-247-9289

Grand Canyon & Colorado River
Five Quail Books — West
P.O. Box 9870
Phoenix, AZ 85068-9870
602-861-0548

The Great Lakes
Artis Books
201 N Second Ave.
P.O. Box 822
Alpena, MI 49707
517-354-3401

Greece
W.B. O'Neill-Old & Rare Books
11609 Hunters Green Ct.
Reston, VA 22091
703-860-0782 or fax 703-620-0153

Zane Grey
British Stamp Exchange
12 Fairlawn Ave.
N Weymouth, MA 02191
871-335-3075

Health
Warren's Collector Books
112 Royal Court
Friendship, TX 77546
281-482-7947

Herbals
The American Botanist Booksellers
P.O. Box 352
Chillicothe, IL 61523
309-274-5254

Brooks Books
P.O. Box 21473
Concord, CA 94521
510-672-4566 or fax 510-672-3338

Heritage Press
Lee & Mike Temares
50 Hts. Rd.
Plandome, NY 11030
516-627-8688

History
American & natural
Ace Zerblonski Books
Malcolm McCollum, Proprietor
1419 North Royer
Colorado Springs, CO 80907
719-634-3941

Science & medicine
Amaranth Books
P.O. Box 421
Wilmette, IL 60091-0421
708-328-2939

Especially US military, US Marine Corps & American Civil War
Stan Clark Military Books
915 Fairview Ave.
Gettysburg, PA 17325
717-337-1728 or 717-337-0581

Camelot Books
Charles E. Wyatt
P.O. Box 2883
Vista, CA 92083
619-940-9472

Early American & Indian
Duck Creek Books
Jim & Shirley Richards
P.O. Box 203
Caldwell, OH 43724
614-732-4856 (10 am to 10 pm)

Postal & postal artifacts
McGowan Book Co.
39 Kimberly Dr.
Durham, NC 27707
919-403-1503 or fax 919-403-1706

Local & regional
Significant Books
3053 Madison Rd.
P.O. Box 9248
Cincinnati, OH 45209
513-321-7567

General as well as Civil & Revolutionary Wars
David R. Smith
30 Nelson Cir.
Jaffrey, NH 03452
603-532-8666

Hollywood
Cinemage Books
105 W 27th St.
New York, NY 10001
212-243-4919

Horror
The Book Baron
1236 S Magnolia Ave.
Anaheim, CA 92804
714-527-7022 or fax 714-527-5634

Kai Nygaard
19421 Eighth Pl.
Escondido, CA 92029
619-746-9039

Pandora's Books, Ltd.
P.O. Box BB-54
Neche, ND 58265
204-324-8548 or fax 204-324-1628

Horse Books
October Farm
2609 Branch Rd.
Raleigh, NC 27610
919-772-0482 or fax 919-779-6265

Horticulture
The American Botanist Booksellers
P.O. Box 532
Chillicothe, IL 61523
309-274-5254

Ornamental
Brooks Books
P.O. Box 21473
Concord, CA 94521
510-672-4566 or fax 510-672-3338

Woodbridge B. Brown
P.O. Box 445
Turners Falls, MA 01376
413-772-2509 or 413-773-5710

L. Ron Hubbard
AL-PAC
Lamar Kelley Antiquarian Books
2625 E Southern Ave., C-120
Tempe, AZ 85282
602-831-3121 or fax 602-831-3193

Humanities
Reprint editions
Dover Publications
Dept. A 214
E Second St.
Mineola, NY 11501

Hunting
Artis Books
201 N Second Ave.
P.O. Box 822
Alpena, MI 49707
517-354-3401

Edison Hall Books
5 Ventnor Dr.
Edison, NJ 08820
908-548-4455

Jim Hodgson Books
908 S Manlius St.
Fayetteville, NY 13066
315-637-6264

Melvin Marcher, Bookseller
6204 N Vermont
Oklahoma City, OK 73112

Yesterday's Books
229 Riverview Dr.
Parchment, MI 49004
616-345-1011

Idaho
Parnassus Books
218 N 9th St.
Boise, ID 83702

Illustrated
Noreen Abbot Books
2666 44th Ave.
San Francisco, CA 94116
415-664-9464

Bowie & Co. Booksellers, Inc.
314 First Ave. S
Seattle, WA 98104
206-624-4100 or fax 206-223-0966

Books of the Ages
Gary J. Overmann
Maple Ridge Manor
4764 Silverwood Dr.
Batavia, OH 45103-9740
phone/fax 513-732-3456

Bromer Booksellers
607 Boylston St.
Boston, MA 02116
617-247-2818 or fax 617-247-2975

George Robert Kane Fine Books
252 Third Ave.
Santa Cruz, CA 95062
phone/fax 408-426-4133

Old or new; many subjects
Gary R. Smith
517 Laurel Ave.
Modesto, CA 95351

Barbara Smith Books
P.O. Box 1185
Northampton, MA 01061
413-586-1453

Randall House
835 Laguna St.
Santa Barbara, CA 93101
805-963-1909 or fax 805-963-1650

Irvin S. Cobb
Always paying $3.00 each plus shipping. Send for immediate payment to:
Bill Schroeder
5801 KY Dam Rd.
Paducah, KY 42003

Indians
Wars
K.C. & Jean Owings
Box 389
Whitman, MA 02382
781-447-7850 or fax 781-447-3435

Plains, Black Hills, etc.
Flo Silver Books
8442 Oakwood Ct. N
Indianapolis, IN 46260
317-255-5118

Iowa
Karl M. Armens
740 Juniper Dr.
Iowa City, IA 52245

Will James
British Stamp Exchange
12 Fairlawn Ave.
N Weymouth, MA 02191
871-335-3075

Jazz
Chartwell Booksellers
55 E 52nd St.
New York, NY 10055
212-308-0643

John Deere
Henry Lindeman
4769 Bavarian Dr.
Jackson, MI 49201
517-764-5728

James Joyce
Paul Melzer Fine Books
12 E St.
Redlands, CA 92373
909-792-7299

Judaica
Stanley Schwartz
1934 Pentuckett Ave.
San Diego, CA 92104-5732
619-232-5888 or fax 619-233-5833

Juvenile
Cover to Cover
P.O. Box 687
Chapel Hill, NC 27514

Edison Hall Books
5 Ventnor Dr.
Edison, NJ 08820
908-548-4455

Susan Heller, Pages for Sages
22611 Halburton Rd.
Beachwood, OH 44122-3939
216-283-2665

Page Books
HRC 65, Box 233
Kingston, AR 72742
870-861-5831

Jo Ann Reisler, Ltd.
360 Glyndon St., NE
Vienna, VA 22180
703-938-2967 or fax 703-938-9057

Nancy Stewart, Books
1188 NW Weybridge Way
Beaverton, OR 97006
503-645-9779

Lee & Mike Temares
50 Hts. Rd.
Plandome, NY 11030
516-627-8688

John F. Kennedy
British Stamp Exchange
12 Fairlawn Ave.
N Weymouth, MA 02191
871-335-3075

Kentucky Authors
Bill Schroeder
P.O. Box 3009
Paducah, KY 42002-3009

Kentucky History
Bill Schroeder
P.O. Box 3009
Paducah, KY 42002-3009

King Arthur
Also early Britain
Thorn Books
P.O. Box 1244
Moorpark, CA 93020
805-529-3647 or fax 805-529-0022

Labor
A\K\A Fine Used Books
4124 Brooklyn Ave. NE
Seattle, WA 98107

Volume I Books
One Union St.
Hillsdale, MI 49242
517-437-2228

Lakeside Classics
Linda Holycross
109 N Sterling Ave.
Veedersburg, IN 47987
fax 765-793-2249

Landscape Architecture
The American Botanist Booksellers
P.O. Box 532
Chillicothe, IL 61523
309-274-5254

Brooks Books
P.O. Box 21473
Concord, CA 94521
510-672-4566 or fax 510-672-3338

Latin American Literature
Almark & Co.-Booksellers
P.O. Box 7
Thornhill, Ontario
Canada L3T 3N1
phone/fax 905-764-2665

Flo Silver Books
8442 Oakwood Ct. N
Indianapolis, IN 46260
317-255-5118

Law & Crime
Meyer Boswell Books, Inc.
2141 Mission St.
San Francisco, CA 94110
415-255-6400 or fax 415-255-6499

T.E. Lawrence
Denis McDonnell, Bookseller
653 Park St.
Honesdale, PA 18431
717-253-6706 or fax 717-253-6785

Lawrence of Arabia
Denis McDonnell, Bookseller
653 Park St.
Honesdale, PA 18431
717-253-6706 or fax 717-253-6785

Lebanon
W.B. O'Neill-Old & Rare Books
11609 Hunters Green Ct.
Reston, VA 22091
703-860-0782 or fax 703-620-0153

Lewis & Clark Expedition
George H. Tweney
16660 Marine View Dr. SW
Seattle, WA 98166
206-243-8243

Literature
Amaranth Books
P.O. Box 421
Wilmette, IL 60091-0421
708-328-2939

In translation
Almark & Co.-Booksellers
P.O. Box 7
Thornhill, Ontario
Canada L3T 3N1
phone/fax 905-764-2665

First editions
Karl M. Armens
740 Juniper Dr.
Iowa City, IA 52245

18th & 19th-C English
The Book Collector
2347 University Blvd.
Houston, TX 77005
713-661-2665

First editions
Bromer Booksellers
607 Boylston St.
Boston, MA 02116
617-247-2818 or fax 617-247-2975

African-American
Between the Covers
35 W Maple Ave.
Merchantville, NJ 08109
609-665-2284 or fax 609-665-3639

The Captain's Bookshelf, Inc.
P.O. Box 2258
Asheville, NC 22802-2258
704-253-6631

Chapel Hill Rare Books
P.O. Box 456
Carrboro, NC 27510
919-929-8351

Southern
Elder's Book Store
2115 Elliston Pl.
Nashville, TN 37203
615-327-1867

18th century
Hartfield Rare Books
Ruth Inglehart
117 Dixboro Rd.
Ann Arbor, MI 48105
phone/fax 313-662-6035

Susan Heller, Pages for Sages
22611 Halburton Rd.
Beachwood, OH 44122-3939
216-283-2665

Ken Lopez, Bookseller
51 Huntington Rd.
Hadley, MA 01035
413-584-4827 or fax 413-584-2045

Mason's Bookstore, Rare Books
    & Record Albums
115 S Main St.
Chambersburg, PA 17201
717-261-0541

Much Ado
Seven Pleasant St.
Marblehead, MA 01945
617-639-0400

Magazines
Mystery only
Grave Matters
P.O. Box 32192-08
Cincinnati, OH 45232
513-242-7527 or fax 513-242-5115

Robert A. Madle
4406 Bestor Dr.
Rockville, MD 20853
301-460-4712

Relating to decorative arts
Mordida Books
P.O. Box 79322
Houston, TX 77279
713-467-4280 or fax 713-467-4182

Passaic Book Center
594 Main Ave.
Passaic, NJ 07055
201-778-6646 or fax 201-778-6738

Manuscripts
Susan Heller, Pages for Sages
P.O. Box 2219
Beachwood, OH 44122-3939
216-283-2665

Heritage Book Shop, Inc.
8540 Melrose Ave.
Los Angeles, CA 90069
310-659-3674 or fax 310-659-4872

Key Books
P.O. Box 58097
St. Petersburg, FL 33715
813-867-2931

Asiatic languages
Worldwide Antiquarian
P.O. Box 410391
Cambridge, MA 02141-0004
617-876-6220 or fax 617-876-0839

Randall House
835 Laguna St.
Santa Barbara, CA 93101
805-963-1909 or fax 805-963-1650

Maps
State, pocket-type, ca 1800s
The Bookseller, Inc.
174 W Exchange St.
Akron, OH 44302
330-762-3101 or fax 330-762-4413

Bowie & Co. Booksellers, Inc.
314 First Ave. S
Seattle, WA 98104
206-624-4100 or fax 206-223-0966

Pre-1900 Florida
Brasser's
8701 Seminole Blvd.
Seminole, FL 33772
813-393-6707

Elegant Book & Map Company
815 Harrison Ave.
P.O. Box 1302
Cambridge, OH 43725
614-432-4068

Maritime
Including pirates, treasure, ship-wrecks, oceanliners, the Caribbean, Cuba & Panama
The Book Corner
Michael Tennero
728 W Lumsden Rd.
Brandon, FL 33511
813-684-1133

Book & Tackle Shop
29 Old Colony Rd.
P.O. Box 114
Chestnut Hill, MA 02167
617-965-0459 (winter)
401-596-0700 (summer)

Overlee Farm Books
P.O. Box 1155
Stockbridge, MA 01262
413-637-2277

J. Tuttle Maritime Books
1806 Laurel Crest
Madison, WI 53705
608-238-SAIL (7245)
fax 608-238-7249

Martial Arts
Nutmeg Books
354 New Litchfield St. (Rte. 202)
Torrington, CT 06790
203-482-9696

Masonic History
Mason's Bookstore, Rare Books
    & Record Albums
115 S Main St.
Chambersburg, PA 17201
717-261-0541

Mathematics
Significant Books
3053 Madison Rd.
P.O. Box 9248
Cincinnati, OH 45209
513-321-7567

Cormac McCarthy
Alice Robbins, Bookseller
3002 Round Hill Rd.
Greensboro, NC 27408
910-282-1964

Medicine
Amaranth Books
P.O. Box 421
Wilmette, IL 60091-0421
708-328-2939

Book & Tackle
29 Old Colony Rd.
P.O. Box 114
Chestnut Hill, MA 02167
617-965-0459 (winter)
401-596-0700 (summer)

Antiquarian Medical Books
W. Bruce Fye
1607 N Wood Ave.
Marshfield, WI 54449-1298
715-384-8128 or fax 715-389-2990

Key Books
P.O. Box 58097
St. Petersburg, FL 33715
813-867-2931

M & S Rare Books, Inc.
P.O. Box 2594, E Side Sta.
Providence, RI 02906
401-421-1050 or fax 401-272-0831
(attention M & S)

Smithfield Rare Books
20 Deer Run Trail
Smithfield, RI 02917
401-231-8225

Medieval
Camelot Books
Charles E. Wyatt
P.O. Box 2883
Vista, CA 92083
619-940-9472

Metaphysics
AL-PAC
Lamar Kelley Antiquarian Books
2625 E Southern Ave., C-120
Tempe, AZ 85282
602-831-3121 or fax 602-831-3193

Meteorology
Knollwood Books
Lee & Peggy Price
P.O. Box 197
Oregon, WI 53575
608-835-8861 or fax 608-835-8421

Mexico
Flo Silver Books
8442 Oakwood Ct. N
Indianapolis, IN 46260
317-255-5118

Michigan
Artis Books
201 N Second Ave.
P.O. Box 822
Alpena, MI 49707
517-354-3401

Yesterday's Books
229 Riverview Dr.
Parchment, MI 49004
616-345-1011

Middle Eastern Countries
Denis McDonnell, Bookseller
653 Park St.
Honesdale, PA 18431
717-253-6706 or fax 717-253-6785

Worldwide Antiquarian
P.O. Box 410391
Cambridge, MA 02141-0004
617-876-6220 or fax 617-876-0839

Militaria
The Book Corner
Mike Tennero
728 W Lumsden Rd.
Brandon, FL 33511
813-684-1133

The Bookseller, Inc.
174 W Exchange St.
Akron, OH 44302
330-762-3101 or fax 330-762-4413

Brasser's
8701 Seminole Blvd.
Seminole, FL 33772
813-393-6707

Edison Hall Books
5 Ventnor Dr.
Edison, NJ 08820
908-548-4455

Rick Harmon
Military Books & Relics
910 Sullivan Dr.
Belvidere, IL 61008
815-547-7580

Robert L. Merriam
Rare, Used & Old Books
Newhall Rd.
Conway, MA 01341
413-369-4052

Significant Books
3053 Madison Rd.
P.O Box 9248
Cincinnati, OH 45209
513-321-7567

Before 1900
Gordon Totty
Scarce Paper Americana
347 Shady Lake Pky.
Baton Rouge, LA 70810
504-766-8625

Histories
Tryon County Bookshop
2071 State Hwy. 29
Johnstown, NY 12905
518-762-1060

Volume I Books
One Union St.
Hillsdale, MI 49242
517-437-2228

Miniature Books
Bromer Booksellers
607 Boylston St.
Boston, MA 02116
617-247-2818 or fax 617-247-2975

Foreign atlases
Murray Hudson
Antiquarian Books & Maps
The Old Post Office
109 S Church St.
P.O. Box 163
Halls, TN 38040
901-836-9057 or 800-748-9946

Hurley Books
1752 Rt. 12
Westmoreland, NH 03467-4724
603-399-4342 or fax 603-399-8326

Gary R. Smith
517 Laurel Ave.
Modesto, CA 95351

Movies
Cinemage Books
105 W 27th St.
New York, NY 10001
212-243-4919

Mysteries
Alcott Books
Barbara Ruppert
5909 Darnell
Houston, TX 77074-7719
713-774-2202

Karl M. Armens
740 Juniper Dr.
Iowa City, IA 52245

First editions
Island Books
P.O. Box 19
Old Westbury, NY 11568
516-759-0233

Mordida Books
P.O. Box 79322
Houston, TX 77279
713-467-4280 or fax 713-467-4182

Mail order; primarily first editions
Norris Books
2491 San Ramon Vly. Blvd.
Ste. #1-201
San Ramon, CA 94583
phone/fax 510-867-1218

Pandora's Books, Ltd.
P.O. Box BB-54
Neche, ND 48265
204-324-8548 or fax 204-324-1628

Pulphouse
P.O. Box 481
Elberton, GA 30635-0481
706-213-9280
e-mail: Pulpmaster@msn.com

RAC Books
R.R. #2
P.O. Box 296
Seven Valleys, PA 17360
717-428-3776

The Silver Door
P.O. Box 3208
Redondo Beach, CA 90277
310-379-6005

Napoleonic Memorabilia
The Book Collector
2347 University Blvd.
Houston, TX 7005
713-661-2665

Narcotics
Nutmeg Books
354 New Litchfield St. (Rte. 202)
Torrington, CT 06790
203-482-9696

Natural History
Agave Books
P.O. Box 31495
Mesa, AZ 85275-1495
602-649-9097

Thomas C. Bayer
85 Reading Ave.
Hillsdale, MI 49242
517-439-4134 or fax 517-439-5661

Woodbridge B. Brown
P.O. Box 445
Turners Falls, MA 01376
413-772-2509 or 413-773-5710

Noriko I. Ciochon
Natural History Books
1025 Keokut St.
Iowa City, IA 52240
319-354-4844

Melvin Marcher, Bookseller
6204 N Vermont
Oklahoma City, OK 73112

Snowy Egret Books
1237 Carroll Ave.
St. Paul, MN 55104
612-641-0917

Nautical
Much Ado
Seven Pleasant St.
Marblehead, MA 01945
617-639-0400

Overlee Farm Books
P.O. Box 1155
Stockbridge, MA 01262
413-637-2277

Needlework
Galerie De Boicourt
6136 Westbrooke Dr.
W Bloomfield, MI 48322
248-788-9253

Stanley Schwartz
1934 Pentuckett Ave.
San Diego, CA 92104-5732
619-232-5888 or fax 619-233-5833

Neuroscience
John Gach Books
5620 Waterloo Rd.
Columbia, MD 21045
410-465-9023 or fax 410-465-0649

New England
Book & Tackle
29 Old Colony Rd.
P.O. Box 114
Chestnut Hill, MA 02167
617-965-0459 (winter)
401-596-0700 (summer)

Newspapers & Periodicals
From 1660s to 1960s; by appointment only
Historical Newspapers & Journals
Steve & Linda Alsberg
9850 Kedvale
Skokie, IL 60076-1124
847-676-9850

Significant & unusual American
Periodyssey
151 Crescent St.
Northampton, MA 01060
413-585-1010 or fax 413-585-1074

Randall House
835 Laguna St.
Santa Barbara, CA 93101
805-963-1909 or fax 805-963-1650

Thorn Books
P.O. Box 1244
Moorpark, CA 93020
805-529-3647 or fax 805-529-0022

Wellerdt's Books
3700 S Osprey Ave. #214
Sarasota, FL 34239
813-365-1318

Xanadu Records, Ltd.
3242 Irwin Ave.
Kingsbridge, NY 10463
212-549-3655

Nonfiction
Pre-1950
Brasser's
8701 Seminole Blvd.
Seminole, FL 33772
813-393-6707

Warren's Collector Books
112 Royal Court
Friendship, TX 77546
281-482-7947

Novels
The Silver Door
P.O. Box 3208
Redondo Beach, CA 90277
310-379-6005
Date 02/25/98Page 3

Occult & Mystics
AL-PAC
Lamar Kelley Antiquarian Books
2625 E Southern Ave., C-120
Tempe, AZ 85282
602-831-3121 or fax 602-831-3193

British Stamp Exchange
12 Fairlawn Ave.
N Weymouth, MA 02191
871-335-3075

Ohio
The Bookseller, Inc.
174 W Exchange St.
Akron, OH 44302
330-762-3101 or fax 330-762-4413

Omar Khayyam
Worldwide Antiquarian
P.O. Box 410391
Cambridge, MA 02141-0004
617-876-6220 or fax 617-876-0839

Oriental Books & Art
Ruth Woods Oriental Books
266 Arch Rd.
Englewood, NJ 07631
201-567-0149 or fax 201-567-1419

Original Art
By children's illustrators
Kendra Krienke
230 Central Park W
New York, NY 10024
201-930-9709 or 201-930-9765

Paperbacks
The American Dust Co.
47 Park Ct.
Staten Island, NY 10301
718-442-8253 or fax 718-981-0311

Michael Gerlicher
1375 Rest Point Rd.
Orono, MN 55364

Bernard E. Goodman, Bookseller
7421 SW 147 Ct.
Miami, FL 33193
305-382-2464

Vintage
Grave Matters
P.O. Box 32192
Cincinnati, OH 45232
513-242-7527 or fax 513-242-5115

Modern Age Books
P.O. Box 325
E Lansing, MI 48826
517-351-9334

Originals
Mordida Books
P.O. Box 79322
Houston, TX 77279
713-467-4280 or fax 713-467-4182

Olde Current Books
Daniel P. Shay
356 Putnam Ave.
Ormond Beach, FL 32174
904-672-8998

Pandora's Books, Ltd.
P.O. Box BB-54
Neche, ND 58265
204-324-8548 or fax 204-324-1628

Pulphouse
J.H. James
P.O. Box 481
Elberton, GA 30635
706-213-9280

Also trades; want lists welcomed
Roger Reus
9412 Huron Ave.
Richmond, VA 23294
Mail order only

Tom Rolls
230 S Oakland Ave.
Indianapolis, IN 46201

Andrew Zimmerli
5001 General Branch Ct.
Sharpsburg, MD 21781
301-432-7476

Robert B. Parker
Thomas Books
P.O. Box 14036
Phoenix, AZ 85063
602-247-9289

Pennsylvania
Mason's Bookstore, Rare Books
  & Record Albums
115 S Main
Chambersburg, PA 17201
717-261-0541

Performing Arts
Bowie & Co. Booksellers, Inc.
314 First Ave. S
Seattle, WA 98104
206-624-4100

Philosophy
The Book Corner
Mike Tennero
728 W Lumsden Rd.
Brandon, FL 33511
813-684-1133

John Gach Books
5620 Waterloo Rd.
Columbia, MD 21045
410-465-9023 or fax 410-465-0649

Photography
Cary Loren
The Captain's Bookshelf, Inc.
P.O. Box 2258
Asheville, NC 28802-2258
704-253-6631

Significant Books
3053 Madison Rd.
P.O. Box 9248
Cincinnati, OH 45209
513-321-7567

19th-C Middle & Far East Countries
Worldwide Antiquarian
P.O. Box 410391
Cambridge, MA 02141-0004
617-876-6220 or fax 617-876-0839

Playing Cards
Bill & Mimi Sachen
927 Grand Ave.
Waukegan, IL 60085
847-662-7204

Poetry
Edison Hall Books
5 Ventnor Dr.
Edison, NJ 08820
908-548-4455

Ed Smith Books
P.O. Box 66
Oak View, CA 93022
805-649-2844 or fax 805-649-2863

David R. Smith
30 Nelson Cir.
Jaffrey, NH 03452
603-532-8666

VERSEtility Books
P.O. Box 1133
Farmington, CT 06034-1133
860-677-0606

Polar Explorations & Ephemera
Alaskan Heritage Bookshop
174 S Franklin, P.O. 22165
Juneau, AK 99802

Parmer Books
7644 Forrestal Rd.
San Diego, CA 92120-2203
619-287-0693 or fax 619-287-6135

Political
Realm of Colorado
P.O. Box 24
Parker, CO 80134

Radical
Volume I Books
One Union St.
Hillsdale, MI 49242
517-437-2228

Postcards
Book & Tackle Shop
29 Old Colony Rd.
P.O. Box 114
Chestnut Hill, MA 02167
617-965-0459 (winter)
401-596-0700 (summer)

Posters
The Mulberry Cat
Yvonne Davis
Jan Davis Martel
P.O. Box 3573
Boone, NC 28607
704-963-7693

Pre-Colombian Art
Flo Silver Books
8442 Oakwood Ct. N
Indianapolis, IN 46260
317-255-5118

Press Books
Heritage Book Shop, Inc.
8540 Melrose Ave.
Los Angeles, CA 90069
213-659-3674

Randall House
835 Laguna St.
Santa Barbara, CA 93101
805-963-1909 or fax 805-963-1650

Prints
The Mulberry Cat
Yvonne Davis
Jan Davis Martel
P.O. Box 3573
Boone, NC 28607
704-963-7693

Private Presses
First Folio
1206 Brentwood
Paris, TN 34842
phone/fax 901-644-9940

Susan Heller, Pages for Sages
22611 Halburton Rd.
Beachwood, OH 44122-3939
216-283-2665

Promoters of Paper, Ephemera & Book Fairs
Kingsbury Productions
Katherine and David Kreider
4555 N Pershing Ave., Ste. 33-138
Stockton, CA 95207
209-467-8438

Psychedelia
Nutmeg Books
354 New Litchfield St. (Rte. 202)
Torrington, CT 06790
203-482-9696

Psychiatry
John Gach Books
5620 Waterloo Rd.
Columbia, MD 21045
410-465-9023 or fax 410-465-0649

Psychoanalysis
Also related subjects
John Gach Books
5620 Waterloo Rd.
Columbia, MD 21045
410-465-9023 or fax 410-465-0649

Psychology
John Gach Books
5620 Waterloo Rd.
Columbia, MD 21045
410-465-9023 or fax 410-465-0649

The King's Market Bookshops
P.O. Box 709
Boulder, CO 80306-0709
303-447-0234

Pulps
Science fiction & fantasy before 1945
Robert A. Madle
4406 Bestor Dr.
Rockville, MD 20853
301-460-4712

Quaker
Vintage Books
181 Hayden Rowe St.
Hopkinton, MA 01748
517-437-2228

Also Shakers, Christians & Collectivists
Duck Creek Books
Jim & Shirley Richards
P.O. Box 203
Caldwell, OH 43724
614-732-4856 (10 am to 10 pm)

Quilt Books
Bill Schroeder
P.O. Box 3009
Paducah, KY 42002-3009

Galerie De Boicourt
6136 Westbrooke Dr.
W Bloomfield, MI 48322
248-788-9253

R.R. Donnelley Christmas Books
Linda Holycross
109 N Sterling Ave.
Veedersburg, IN 47987
fax 765-793-2249

Arthur Rackham
Books of the Ages
Gary J. Overmann
Maple Ridge Manor
4764 Silverwood Dr.
Batavia, OH 45103-9740
phone/fax 513-732-3456

Railroading
Mason's Bookstore, Rare Books &
 Record Albums
115 S Main St.
Chambersburg, PA 17201
717-261-0541

Rare & Unusual Books
First Folio
1206 Brentwood
Paris, TN 38242
phone/fax 901-644-9940

Susan Heller, Pages for Sages
22611 Halburton Rd.
Beachwood, OH 44122-3939
216-283-2665

Kenneth Karimole, Bookseller, Inc.
509 Wilshire Blvd.
Santa Monica, CA 94001
310-451-4342 or 310-458-5930

M & S Rare Books, Inc.
P.O. Box 2594, E Side Sta.
Providence, RI 02906
401-421-1050 or fax 401-272-0831
(attention M & S)

Reprint editions
Dover Publications
Dept. A 214
E Second St.
Mineola, NY 11501

Terry Harper, Bookseller
P.O. Box 312
Vergennes, VT 05491-0312
802-877-9262

Heritage Book Shop, Inc.
8540 Melrose Ave.
Los Angeles, CA 90069
213-659-3674

Paul Melzer Fine Books
12 E Vine St.
Redlands, CA 92373
909-792-7299

Richard C. Ramer
Old & Rare Books
225 E 70th St.
New York, NY 10021
212-737-0222 or 212-737-0223
fax 212-288-4169

Revere Books
P.O. Box 420
Revere, PA 18953
610-847-2709 or fax 610-847-1910

Leona Rostenberg & Madeleine
   Stern
Rare Books
40 E 88th St.
NY, NY 10128
212-831-6628 or fax 212-831-1961

Thorn Books
P.O. Box 1244
Moorpark, CA 93020
805-529-3647 or fax 805-529-0022

Reference
About Books
6 Sand Hill Ct.
P.O. Box 5717
Parsippany, NY 07054
201-515-4591

Religion
Books Now & Then
Dennis Patrick
P.O. Box 337
Stanley, ND 58784
701-628-2084

Chimney Sweep Books
419 Cedar St.
Santa Cruz, CA 94060-4304
408-458-1044

David R. Smith
30 Nelson Cir.
Jaffrey, NH 03452
603-532-8666

Reptiles
Mason's Bookstore, Rare Books
   & Record Albums
115 S Main St.
Chambersburg, PA 17201
717-261-0541

Revolutionary War
K.C. & Jean Owings
Box 389
Whitman, MA 02382
781-447-7850 or fax 781-447-3435

Scholarly Books
Reprint editions
Dover Publications
Dept. A 214
E Second St.
Mineola, NY 11501

Science & Technology
Thomas C. Bayer
85 Reading Ave.
Hillsdale, MI 49242
517-439-4134 or fax 517-439-5661

Book & Tackle Shop
29 Old Colony Rd.
P.O. Box 114
Chestnut Hill, MA 02167
617-965-0459 (winter)
401-596-0700 (summer)

Key Books
P.O. Box 58097
St. Petersburg, FL 33715
813-867-2931

M & S Rare Books, Inc.
P.O. Box 2594, E Side Sta.
Providence, RI 02906
401-272-0831 or fax 401-272-0831
(attention M & S)

Smithfield Rare Books
20 Deer Run Trail
Smithfield, RI 02917
401-231-8225

Science Fiction
AL-PAC
Lamar Kelley Antiquarian Books
2625 E Southern Ave., C-120
Tempe, AZ 85282
602-831-3121 or fax 602-831-3193

Karl M. Armens
740 Juniper Dr.
Iowa City, IA 52245

Bernard E. Goodman, Bookseller
7421 SW 147 Ct.
Miami, FL 33193
305-382-2464

First editions
Island Books
P.O. Box 19
Old Westbury, NY 11568
516-759-0233

Horror & Occult
Bob Lakin
3021 Lavita Ln.
Dallas, TX 75234
972-247-3291

Robert A. Madle
4406 Bestor Dr.
Rockville, MD 20853
301-460-4712

Also fantasy
Kai Nygaard
19421 Eighth Pl.
Escondido, CA 92029
619-746-9039

Pandora's Books, Ltd.
P.O. Box 54
Neche, ND 58265
204-324-8548 or fax 204-324-1628

Pulphouse
P.O. Box 481
Elberton, GA 30635-0481
706-213-9280

Also fantasy
Xanadu Records, Ltd.
3242 Irwin Ave.
Kingsbridge, NY 10463
212-549-3655

Sciences
Cover to Cover
P.O. Box 687
Chapel Hill, NC 27514

Reprint editions
Dover Publications
E Second St.
Mineola, NY 11501

Significant Books
P.O. Box 9248
3053 Madison Rd.
Cincinnati, OH 45209
513-321-7567

Series Books
Glo's Children's Series Books
906 Shadywood
Southlake, TX 76092
817-481-1438

Set Editions
AL-PAC
Lamar Kelley Antiquarian Books
2625 E Southern Ave., C-120
Tempe, AZ 85282
602-831-3121 or fax 602-831-3193

Bowie & Weatherford, Inc.
314 First Ave. S
Seattle, WA 98104
206-624-4100

Sherlockiana
The Silver Door
P.O. Box 3208
Redondo Beach, CA 90277
310-379-6005

Ships & Sea
Book & Tackle Shop
29 Old Colony Rd.
P.O. Box 114
Chestnut Hill, MA 02167
617-965-0459 (winter)
401-596-0700 (summer)

Parmer Books
7644 Forrestal Rd.
San Diego, CA 92120-2203
619-287-0693 or fax 619-287-6135

J. Tuttle Maritme Books
1806 Laurel Crest
Madison, WI 53705
608-238-SAIL (7245)
fax 608-238-7249

Signed Editions
Chapel Hill Rare Books
P.O. Box 456
Carrboro, NC 27510
919-929-8351

Dan Simmons
Thomas Books
P.O. Box 14036
Phoenix, AZ 85063
602-247-9289

Socialism
Volume I Books
One Union St.
Hillsdale, MI 49242
517-437-2228

South America
Flo Silver Books
8442 Oakwood Ct. N
Indianapolis, IN 46260
317-255-5118

South Dakota
Also any pre-1970 Western-related books
James F. Taylor
515 Sixth St.
Rapid City, SD 57701
605-341-3224

Space Exploration
Knollwood Books
Lee & Peggy Price
P.O. Box 197
Oregon, WI 53575
608-835-8861 or fax 608-835-8421

Speciality Publishers
Arkham House, Gnome, Fantasy, etc.
Robert A. Madle
4406 Bestor Dr.
Rockville, MD 20853
301-460-4712

Sports
Baseball or boxing
Ace Zerblonski Books
Malcolm McCollum, Proprietor
1419 North Royer
Colorado Springs, CO 80907
719-634-3941

Adelson Sports
13610 N Scottsdale Rd. #10
Scottsdale, AZ 85254
602-596-1913 or fax 602-598-1914

Rare & out-of-print baseball; sports in general
R. Plapinger, Baseball Books
P.O. Box 1062
Ashland, OR 97520
541-488-1220

Randall House
835 Laguna St.
Santa Barbara, CA 93101
805-963-1909 or fax 805-963-1650

Statue of Liberty
Mike Brooks
7335 Skyline
Oakland, CA 94611

Surveying
Also tools, instruments & ephemera
David & Nancy Garcelon
10 Hastings Ave.
Millbury, MA 01527-4314
508-754-2667

Technology
Thomas C. Bayer
85 Reading Ave.
Hillsdale, MI 49242
517-439-4134 or fax 517-439-5661

Cover to Cover
P.O. Box 687
Chapel Hill, NC 27514

Significant Books
3053 Madison Rd.
P.O. Box 9248
Cincinnati, OH 45209
513-321-7567

Tennessee History
Elder's Book Store
2115 Elliston Pl.
Nashville, TN 37203
615-327-1867

Tennis
Brasser's
8701 Seminole Blvd.
Seminole, FL 33772
813-393-6707

Texana Fiction & Authors
Alcott Books
Barbara Ruppert
5909 Darnell
Houston, TX 77074-7719
713-774-2202

Bob Lakin
3021 Lavita Ln.
Dallas, TX 75234
972-247-3291

Textiles
Galerie De Boicourt
6136 Westbrooke Dr.
W Bloomfield, MI 48322
248-788-9253

Stanley Schwartz
1934 Pentuckett Ave.
San Diego, CA 92104-5732
619-232-5888 or fax 619-233-5833

Theology
Books Now & Then
Dennis Patrick
P.O. Box 337
Stanley, ND 58784
701-628-2084

Chimney Sweep Books
419 Cedar St.
Santa Cruz, CA 94060-4304
408-458-1044

Hurley Books
1752 Rt. 12
Westmoreland, NH 03467-4724
603-399-4342 or fax 603-399-8326

Jim Thompson
The American Dust Co.
47 Park Ct.
Staten Island, NY 10301
718-442-8253 or fax 718-981-0311

Trade Catalogs
Eastside Books & Paper
P.O. Box 1581, Gracie Sta.
New York, NY 10028-0013
212-759-6299

Trades & Crafts
19th C
Cover to Cover
P.O. Box 687
Chapel Hill, NC 27514

Hillcrest Books
961 Deep Draw Rd.
Crossville, TN 38555-9547
phone/fax 615-484-7680

Travel
19th century
The Book Corner
Michael Tennero
728 W Lumsden Rd.
Brandon, FL 33511
813-684-1133

Also exploration
Duck Creek Books
Jim & Shirley Richards
P.O. Box 203
Caldwell, OH 43724
614-732-4856 (10 am to 10 pm)

Terry Harper, Bookseller
P.O. Box 312
Vergennes, VT 05491-0312
802-877-9262

Heritage Book Shop, Inc.
8540 Melrose Ave.
Los Angeles, CA 90069
213-659-3674

Jim Hodgson Books
908 S Manlius St.
Fayetteville, NY 13066
315-637-6264

Flo Silver Books
8442 Oakwood Ct. N
Indianapolis, IN 46260
317-255-5118

Discoveries before 1900
Gordon Totty
Scarce Paper Americana
347 Shady Lake Pky.
Baton Rouge, LA 70810
504-766-8625

Tasha Tudor
Books of the Ages
Gary J. Overmann
Maple Ridge Manor
4764 Silverwood Dr.
Batavia, OH 45103-9740
phone/fax 513-732-3456

Turkey
W.B. O'Neill-Old & Rare Books
11609 Hunters Green Ct.
Reston, VA 22091
703-860-0782 or fax 703-620-0153

UFO
AL-PAC
Lamar Kelley Antiquarian Books
2625 E Southern Ave., C-120
Tempe, AZ 85282
602-831-3121 or fax 602-831-3193

Vargas
Parnassus Books
218 N 9th St.
Boise, ID 83702

Vietnam War
A\K\A Fine Used Books
4124 Brooklyn Ave. NE
Seattle, WA 98107
206-632-5870

Rick Harmon
Military Books & Relics
910 Sullivan Dr.
Belvidere, IL 61008
815-547-7580

Voyages, Exploration & Travel
Chapel Hill Rare Books
P.O. Box 456
Carrboro, NC 27510
919-929-8351

Terry Harper, Bookseller
P.O. Box 312
Vergennes, VT 05491-0312
802-877-9262

Heritage Book Shop, Inc.
8540 Melrose Ave.
Los Angeles, CA 90069
213-659-3674

Jim Hodgson Books
908 S Manlius St.
Fayetteville, NY 13066
315-637-6264

Key Books
P.O. Box 58097
St. Petersburg, FL 33715
813-867-2931

Overlee Farm Books
P.O. Box 1155
Stockbridge, MA 01262
413-627-2277

George H. Tweney
16660 Marine View Dr. SW
Seattle, WA 98166
206-243-8243

Weapons
All edged types
Knife Readables
115 Longfellow Blvd.
Lakeland, FL 33810
813-666-1133

Western Americana
Bowie & Co. Booksellers, Inc.
314 First Ave. S
Seattle, WA 98104
206-624-4100

Dawson's Book Shop
535 N Larchmont Blvd.
Los Angeles, CA 90004
213-469-2186 or fax 213-469-9553

Terry Harper, Bookseller
P.O. Box 312
Vergennes, VT 05491-0312
802-877-9262

Rare & historical ephemera
Jordon Gallery
1349 Sheridan Ave.
Cody, WY 82414
307-587-6689 or fax 307-527-4944

K.C. & Jean Owings
Box 389
Whitman, MA 02382
781-447-7850 or fax 781-447-3435

Thorn Books
P.O. Box 1244
Moorpark, CA 93020
805-529-3647 or fax 805-529-0022

George H. Tweney
16660 Marine View Dr. SW
Seattle, WA 98166
206-243-8243

Nonfiction 19th-C outlaws, lawmen, etc.
The Early West/Whodunit Books
P.O. Box 9292
College Sta., TX 77842
409-775-6047 or fax 409-764-7758

Charles Willeford
The American Dust Co.
47 Park Ct.
Staten Island, NY 10301
718-442-8253 or fax 718-981-0311

Wine
Second Harvest Books
Warren R. Johnson
P.O. Box 3306
Florence, OR 97439
phone/fax 541-902-0215

Warren's Collector Books
112 Royal Ct.
Friendswood, TX 77546
281-482-7947

Women Authors
Alice Robbins, Bookseller
3002 Round Hill Rd.
Greensboro, NC 27408
910-282-1964

Women's History
Also related areas of everyday life
An Uncommon Vision
1425 Greywall Ln.
Wynnewood, PA 19096-3811
610-658-0953 or fax 610-658-0961

Volume I Books
One Union St.
Hillsdale, MI 49242
517-437-2228

World War I
The Book Corner
Mike Tennero
728 W Lumsden Rd.
Brandon, FL 33511
813-684-1133

Denis McDonnell, Bookseller
653 Park St.
Honesdale, PA 18431
717-253-6706 or fax 717-253-6785

World War II
Cover to Cover
P.O. Box 687
Chapel Hill, NC 27514

BOOKSELLERS

This section of the book lists names and addresses of used book dealers who have contributed the retail listings contained in this edition of *Huxford's Old Book Value Guide*. The code (A1, S7, etc.) located before the price in our listings refers to the dealer offering that particular book for sale. (When more than one dealer has the same book listing their code is given alphabetically before the price.) Given below are the dealer names and their codes.

Many book dealers issue catalogs, have open shops, are mail order only, or may be a combination of these forms of business. When seeking a book from a particular dealer, it would be best to first write (enclose SASE) or call to see what type of business is operated (open shop or mail order).

A1
A-Book-A-Brac Shop
6760 Collins Ave.
Miami Beach, FL 33141
305-865-0092

A2
Aard Books
31 Russell Ave.
Troy, NH 03465
603-242-3638

A3
Noreen Abbot Books
2666 44th Ave.
San Francisco, CA 94116-2635
415-664-9464

A4
About Books
6 Sand Hill Ct.
P.O. Box 5717
Parsippany, NJ 07054
201-515-4591

A5
Adelson Sports
13610 N Scottsdale Rd. #10
Scottsdale, AZ 85254
602-596-1913 or fax 602-596-1914

A6
Ads Autographs
P.O. Box 8006
Webster, NY 14580-8006
716-671-2651 or fax 716-671-5727

A7
Avonlea Books Search Service
P.O. Box 74, Main Sta.
White Plains, NY 10602
914-946-5923
fax 914-946-5924 (allow 6 rings)

A8
AL-PAC
Lamar Kelley Antiquarian Books
2625 E Southern Ave., C-120
Tempe, AZ 85282
602-831-3121 or fax 602-831-3193
al-pac@juno.com or alpac2625@aol.com

A9
Amaranth Books
P.O. Box 421
Wilmette, IL 60091-0421
708-328-2939

A10
The American Botanist
P.O. Box 532
Chillicothe, IL 61523

A11
The American Dust Co.
47 Park Ct.
Staten Island, NY 10301
718-442-8253 or fax 718-981-0311

A13
Antiquarian Medical Books
W. Bruce Fye
1607 N Wood Ave.
Marshfield, WI 54449-1298
715-384-8128 or fax 715-389-2990
bfye@tznet.com

A14
Almark & Co.-Booksellers
P.O. Box 7
Thornhill, Ontario
Canada L3T 3N1
phone/fax 905-764-2665

A15
Karl M. Armens
740 Juniper Dr.
Iowa City, IA 52245
319-337-7755

A16
Arnold's of Michigan
Judith A. Herba
218 S Water St.
Marine City, MI 48039
810-765-1350 or fax 810-765-7914
arnodlbk@ees.eesc.com

A17
Artis Books
201 N Second Ave.
P.O. Box 822
Alpena, MI 49707-0822
517-354-3401

A18
Authors of the West
191 Dogwood Dr.
Dundee, OR 97115
503-538-8132
lnash@georgefox.edu

A19
Aplan Antiques & Art
HC 80, Box 793-25
Piedmont, SD 57769-9403
605-347-5016 or fax 605-347-9336
alpanpeg@rapid.net.com

A20
Ace Zerblonski Books
Malcolm McCollum, Proprietor
1419 North Royer
Colorado Springs, CO 80907
719-634-3941

A21
Artiques Ltd.
Veronica Jochens
P.O. Box 67
Lonedell, MO 60360
314-629-1374

A22
Agave Books
P.O. Box 31495
Mesa, AZ 85275-1495
602-649-9097
agavebks@interloc.com

A23
Alcott Books
5909 Darnell
Houston, TX 77074-7719
713-774-2202
BRuppert@webtv.net

A24
A Tale of Two Sisters
2509 Stone Hollow Dr.
Bedford, TX 76021

A25
An Uncommon Vision
1425 Greywall Ln.
Wynnewood, PA 19096-3811
610-658-0953 or fax 610-658-0961

B1
Thomas C. Bayer
85 Reading Ave.
Hillsdale, MI 49242-1941
phone/fax 517-439-5661

B2
Beasley Books
Paul and Beth Garon
1533 W Oakdale, 2nd Floor
Chicago, IL 60657
312-472-4528 or fax 312-472-7857
beasley@mcs.com
www.abaa-booknet.com/usa/beasley/

B3
Bela Luna Books
P.O. Box 260425
Highlands Ranch, CO 80163-0425
800-497-4717 or fax 303-791-7342
Bellalun@aol.com

B4
Between the Covers
35 W Maple Ave.
Merchantville, NJ 08109
609-665-2284 or fax 609-665-3639
BetweenCov@aol.com

B5
Bicentennial Book Shop
820 S Westnedge Ave.
Kalamazoo, MI 49008
616-345-5987

B6
Bibliography of the Dog
The New House
216 Covey Hill Rd.
Havelock, Quebec
Canada J0S 2C0
514-827-2717 or fax 514-827-2091

B7
Best-Read Books
122 State St.
Sedro-Woolley, WA 98284
206-855-2179

B9
The Book Baron
1236 S Magnolia Ave.
Anaheim, CA 92804
714-527-7022 or fax 714-527-5634

B10
Book Broker
P.O. Box 1283
Charlottesville, VA 22902
804-296-2194 or fax 804-296-1566
bookbrk@cfw.com

B11
The Book Corner
Michael Tennero
728 W Lumsden Rd.
Brandon, FL 33511
813-684-1133
bookcrnr@worldnet.att.net

B13
The Book Inn
6401-D University
Lubbock, TX 79413

B14
Book & Tackle Shop
29 Old Colony Rd.
P.O. Box 114
Chestnut Hill, MA 02167
617-965-0459 (winter)
401-596-0700 (summer)

B15
Book Treasures
P.O. Box 121
E Norwich, NY 11732

B16
The Book Den South
Nancy Costello
2249 First St.
Ft. Myers, FL 33901
813-332-2333

B17
Books of the Ages
Gary J. Overmann
Maple Ridge Manor
4764 Silverwood Dr.
Batavia, OH 45103-9740
phone/fax 513-732-3456
e-overman@ix.netcom.com

B18
The Bookseller, Inc.
174 W Exchange St.
Akron, OH 44302
330-762-3101 or fax 330-762-4413
Booklein@Interloc.com

B19
Books West Southwest
Box 6149, University Station
Irvine, CA 92616-6149
714-509-7670 or fax 714-854-5102
bkswest@ix.netcom.com

B20
Bowie & Co. Booksellers, Inc.
314 First Ave. S
Seattle, WA 98104
206-624-4100 or fax 206-223-0966

B21
Brasser's
8701 Seminole Blvd.
Seminole, FL 33772
813-393-6707

B22
Bridgman Books
906 Roosevelt Ave.
Rome, NY 13440
315-337-7252

B23
British Stamp Exchange
12 Fairlawn Ave.
N Weymouth, MA 02191
871-335-3075

B24
Bromer Booksellers
607 Boylston St.
Boston, MA 02116
617-247-2818 or fax 617-247-2975
books@bromer.com
www.xensei.com/users/books/ho
me.htm

B25
Mike Brooks
7335 Skyline
Oakland, CA 94611

B26
Brooks Books
Phil and Marty Nesty
1343 New Hampshire Dr.
P.O. Box 21473
Concord, CA 94521
510-672-4566 or fax 510-672-3338
brooksbk@interloc.com

B27
The Bookstall
570 Sutter St.
San Francisco, CA 94102
fax 415-362-1503

B28
Woodbridge B. Brown
312 Main St.
P.O. Box 445
Turner Falls, MA 01376
413-772-2509 or 413-773-5710

B29
Books Now & Then
Dennis Patrick
P.O. Box 337
Stanley, ND 58784
701-628-2084

B30
Burke's Bookstore
1719 Poplar Ave.
Memphis, TN 38104-6447
901-278-7484

B35
Brillance Books
Morton Brillant, Bookseller
313 Meeting St. #21
Charleston, SC 29401
803-722-6643
brillbooks@aol.com

C1
Camelot Books
Charles E. Wyatt
P.O. Box 2883
Vista, CA 92083
619-940-9472

C2
The Captain's Bookshelf, Inc.
Cary Loren
31 Page Ave.
Asheville, NC 22801
704-254-5733 or fax 704-253-4917

C3
Cattermole
20th-C Children's Books
9880 Fairmount Rd.
Newbury, OH 44065

C4
Bev Chaney, Jr. Books
73 Croton Ave.
Ossining, NY 10562
914-941-1002

C5
Chimney Sweep Books
419 Cedar St.
Santa Cruz, CA 95060-4304
408-458-1044

C6
Chapel Hill Rare Books
P.O. Box 456
Carrboro, NC 27510
919-929-8351

C7
Chartwell Booksellers
55 E 52nd St.
New York, NY 10055
212-308-0643

C8
Children's Book Adoption Agency
P.O. Box 643
Kensington, MD 20895-0643
301-565-2834 or fax 301-585-3091
KIDS_BKS@interloc.com

C9
Cinemage Books
105 W 27th St.
New York, NY 10001
212-243-4919

C10
Cohen Books & Collectibles
Joel J. Cohen
P.O. Box 810310
Boca Raton, FL 33481-0310
561-487-7888

C11
Cover to Cover
P.O. Box 687
Chapel Hill, NC 27514

C12
Noriko I. Chichon
Natural History Books
1025 Keokut St.
Iowa City, 52240
319-354-4844

C14
Steven Cieluch
15 Walbridge St. Ste. #10
Allston, MA 02134-3808
617-734-7778
steve.cath@juno.com

D1
Ursula Davidson
Children's & Illustrated Books
134 Linden Ln.
San Rafael, CA 94901
415-454-3939 or fax 415-454-1087

D2
L. Clarice Davis
Fine & Applied Art Books
P.O. Box 56054
Sherman Oaks, CA 91413-1054
818-787-1322 or fax 818-780-3281

D3
Harold B. Diamond, Bookseller
Box 1193
Burbank, CA 91507
818-846-0342

D4
Carol Docheff, Bookseller
1390 Reliez Vly. Rd.
Lafayette, CA 94549
510-935-9595

D5
Dover Publications
Dept. A 214
E Second St.
Mineola, NY 11501

D6
Drusilla's Books
859 N Howard St.
P.O. Box 16
Baltimore, MD 21201
410-225-0277

D7
Duck Creek Books
Jim & Shirley Richards
P.O. Box 203
Caldwell, OH 43724
614-732-4856

D8
Patricia L. Daniel, Bookseller
13 English Ave.
Wichita, KS 62707-1005
316-683-2079 or fax 316-683-5448
pldaniel@Southwind.net

D9
Dad's Old Bookstore
Green Hills Ct.
4004 Hillsboro Rd.
Nashville, TN 37215
615-298-5880

D10
Tom Davidson, Bookseller
3703 Ave. L
Brooklyn, NY 11210
718-338-8428

D11
Dawson's Book Shop
535 N Larchmont Blvd.
Los Angeles, CA 90004
213-469-2186 or fax 213-469-9553
dawsonbk@ix.netcom.com

E1
The Early West/Whodunit Books
P.O. Box 9292
College Sta., TX 77842
409-775-6047 or fax 409-764-7758

E2
Edison Hall Books
5 Ventnor Dr.
Edison, NJ 08820
908-548-4455

E4
Elder's Book Store
2115 Elliston Pl.
Nashville, TN 37203
615-327-1867

E5
Elegant Book & Map Company
815 Harrison Ave.
P.O. Box 1302
Cambridge, OH 43725
614-432-4068

E6
Eastside Books & Paper
P.O. Box 1581, Gracie Sta.
New York, NY 10028-0013
212-759-6299

F1
First Folio
1206 Brentwood
Paris, TN 38242-3804
phone/fax 910-944-9940

F2
Fisher Books & Antiques
345 Pine St.
Williamsport, PA 17701

F3
Flo Silver Books
8442 Oakwood Ct. N
Indianapolis, IN 46260
phone/fax 317-255-5118

F5
Fran's Bookhouse
6601 Greene St.
Phil., PA 19119
215-438-2729 or fax 215-438-8997

F6
Frontier America
P.O. Box 9193
Albuquerque, NM 87119-9193

F7
Five Quail Books — West
P.O. Box 9870
Phoenix, AZ 85068-9870
602-861-0548
5quail@futureone.com

G1
John Gach Fine & Rare Books
5620 Waterloo Rd.
Columbia, MD 21045
410-465-9023 or fax 410-465-0649
john.gach@clark.net

G2
Galerie De Boicourt
6136 Westbrooke Dr.
W Bloomfield, MI 48322
248-788-9253

G3
Gambler's Book Shop
630 S Eleventh St.
Las Vegas, NV 89101
800-634-6243

G4
David & Nancy Garcelon
10 Hastings Ave.
Millbury, MA 01527-4314

G5
Michael Gerlicher
1375 Rest Point Rd.
Orono, MN 55364

G6
Glo's Children's Series Books
Gloria Stobbes
906 Shadywood
Southlake, TX 76092
817-481-1438

G7
James Tait Goodrich
Antiquarian Books & Manuscripts
135 Tweed Blvd.
Nyack, NY 10960-4913

G8
Grave Matters
P.O. Box 32192-08
Cincinnati, OH 45232
513-242-7527 or fax 513-242-5115
GraveMatrs@aol.com

G10
Bernard E. Goodman, Bookseller
7421 SW 147 Ct.
Miami, FL 33193
305-382-2464

H1
Henry F. Hain III
Antiques & Collectibles
2623 N Second St.
Harrisburg, PA 17110
717-238-0534
antcolbks@ezonline.com

H2
Rick Harmon
Military Books & Relics
910 Sullivan Dr.
Belvidere, IL 61008
815-547-7580

H3
Terry Harper, Bookseller
P.O. Box 312
Vergennes, VT 05491-0312
802-877-9262

H4
Susan Heller, Pages for Sages
22611 Halburton Rd.
Beachwood, OH 44122-3939
216-283-2665
hellersu@cyberdrive.net

H5
Heritage Book Shop, Inc.
8540 Melrose Ave.
Los Angeles, CA 90069
310-659-3674 or fax 310-659-4872

H6
Hillcrest Books
961 Deep Draw Rd.
Crossville, TN 38555-9547
phone/fax 615-484-7680

H7
Jim Hodgson Books
908 S Manlius St.
Fayetteville, NY 13066
315-637-6264

H9
Murray Hudson
Antiquarian Books & Maps
The Old Post Office
109 S Church St.
P.O. Box 163
Halls, TN 38040
901-836-9057 or 800-748-9946

H10
Hurley Books/Celtic Cross Books
1753 Rt. 12
Westmoreland, NH 03467
603-399-4342 or fax 603-399-8326

H11
Ken Hebenstreit, Bookseller
813 N Washington Ave.
Royal Oak, MI 48067
phone/fax 810-548-5460
KHBooks@ibm.net

H12
Historical Newspapers & Journals
Steve & Linda Alsberg
9850 Kedvale
Stokie, IL 60076
847-676-9850

H13
Hartfield Rare Books
Ruth Inglehart
117 Dixboro Rd.
Ann Arbor, MI 48105
phone/fax 313-662-6035

H14
Ruth Heindel Associates
First Editions, Rare & Used Books
2629 Cranberry Cir.
Harrisburg, PA 17110
717-657-0047

I1
Island Books
P.O. Box 19
Old Westbury, NY 11586
516-759-0233

J1
Jay's House of Collectibles
75 Pky. Dr.
Syosset, NY 11791

J2
Jordan Gallery
1349 Sheridan Ave.
Cody, WY 82414
307-587-6689 or fax 307-527-4944

J3
Pricilla Juvelis
1166 Massachusetts Ave.
Cambridge, MA 02138

K1
Kenneth Karmiole, Bookseller, Inc.
509 Wilshire Blvd.
Santa Monica, CA 90401
310-451-4342 or fax 310-458-5930

K2
Ilene Kayne
1308 S Charles St.
Baltimore, MD 21230
410-347-7570
IleneGold@aol.com

K3
Key Books
P.O. Box 58097
St. Petersburg, FL 33715-8097
813-867-2931

K4
The King's Market Bookshop
P.O. Box 709
Boulder, CO 80306-0709
303-447-0234

K5
Knollwood Books
Lee and Peggy Price
P.O. Box 197
Oregon, WI 53575-0197
608-835-8861 or fax 608-835-8421
books@tdsnet.com

K6
Kendra Krienke
230 Central Park West
New York, NY 10024
201-930-9709 or 201-930-9765

K7
George Robert Kane Fine Books
252 Third Ave.
Santa Cruz, CA 95062
phone/fax 408-426-4133

L1
Bob Lakin
3021 Lavita Ln.
Dallas, TX 75234
972-247-3291

L2
Henry Lindeman
4769 Bavarian Dr.
Jackson, MI 49201
517-764-5728

L3
Ken Lopez, Bookseller
51 Huntington Rd.
Hadley, MA 01035
413-584-4827 or fax 413-584-2045
klopez@well.com
abaa-booknet.com/usa/lopez

M1
M & S Rare Books, Inc.
P.O. Box 2594, E Side Sta.
Providence, RI 02906
401-421-1050 or fax 401-272-0831
(attention M & S)
mns@tiac.net

M2
Robert A. Madle
4406 Bestor Dr.
Rockville, MD 20853
301-460-4712

M4
Melvin Marcher, Bookseller
6204 N Vermont
Oklahoma City, OK 73112

M5
Marvelous Books
Dorothy (Dede) Kern
P.O. Box 1510
Ballwin, MO 63022
314-458-3301 or fax 314-273-5452
marvlous@interloc.com

M6
Mason's Bookstore, Rare Books
  & Record Albums
115 S Main St.
Chambersburg, PA 17201
717-261-0541

M7
Denis McDonnell, Bookseller
653 Park St.
Honesdale, PA 18431
717-253-6706 or fax 717-253-6786

M8
McGowan Book Co.
39 Kimberly Dr.
Durham, NC 27704
919-403-1503 or fax 919-403-1706

M9
Paul Melzer Fine & Rare Books
12 E Vine St.
Redlands, CA 92373
909-792-7299

M10
Robert L. Merriam
Rare & Used Books
39 Newhall Rd.
Conway, MA 01341-9709
413-369-4052

M11
Meyer Boswell Books, Inc.
2141 Mission St.
San Francisco, CA 94110
415-255-6400 or fax 415-255-6499
rarelaw@myerbos.com

M12
Frank Mikesh
1356 Walden Rd.
Walnut Creek, CA 94596
510-934-9243

M13
Ken Mitchell
710 Conacher Dr.
Willowdale, Ontario
Canada M2M 3N6
416-222-5808

M14
Modern Age Books
P.O. Box 325
E Lansing, MI 48826
517-351-9334

M15
Mordida Books
P.O. Box 79322
Houston, TX 77279
713-467-4280 or fax 713-467-4182

M16
The Mulberry Cat
Yvonne Davis
Jan Davis Martel
P.O. Box 3573
Boone, NC 28607
704-963-7693

M17
Much Ado
Seven Pleasant St.
Marblehead, MA 01945
617-639-0400

M19
My Book Heaven
2212 Broadway
Oakland, CA 94612
510-893-7273 or 510-521-1683

M20
My Bookhouse
27 S Sandusky St.
Tiffin, OH 44883
419-447-9842
mybooks@bright.net

M21
Brian McMillan, Books
1429 L Ave.
Traer, IA 50675
319-478-2360 (Mon.-Sat., 9 am to
9pm CDT)
Brianbks@netins.net

M22
M/S Books
53 Curtiss Rd.
New Preston, CT 06777
860-868-0627 or fax 860-868-0504

M23
McGee's First Varieties
8012 Brooks Chapel Rd., Ste. 247
Brentwood, TN 37027
615-373-5318
TMcGee@BellSouth.net

M24
MacDonnell Rare Books
Kevin MacDonnell
9307 Glenlake Dr.
Austin, TX 78730
512-345-4139

M25
Monroe Stahr Books
4420 Ventura Canyon, #2
Sherman Oaks, CA 91423
818-784-0870 or fax 818-995-0866
MStahrBks@aol.com

N1
Nerman's Books
410-63 Albert St.
Winnipeg, Manitoba
Canada R3B 1G4
fax 204-947-0753

N2
Nutmeg Books
354 New Litchfield St. (Rte. 202)
Torrington, CT 06790
203-482-9696

N3
Kai Nygaard
19421 Eighth Pl.
Escondido, CA 92029
619-749-9039

N4
Norris Books
2491 San Ramon Vly. Blvd.
Ste. #1-201
San Ramon, CA 94583
phone/fax 510-867-1218
norrisbooks@slip.net

O1
David L. O'Neal, Antiquarian
Bookseller
234 Clarendon St.
Boston, MA 02116

O2
W.B. O'Neill
Old & Rare Books
11609 Hunters Green Ct.
Reston, VA 22091
703-860-0782 or fax 703-620-0153

O3
October Farm
2609 Branch Rd.
Raleigh, NC 27610
919-772-0482 or fax 919-779-6265
octoberfarm@bellsouth.net

O4
The Old London Bookshop
P.O. Box 922
Bellingham, WA 98227-0922
360-733-RARE or fax 306-647-8946
OldLondon@aol.com
www.ABAA-Booknet.com/USA/
OldLondon

O5
The Old Map Gallery
Paul F. Mahoney
1746 Blake St.
Denver, CO 80202
303-296-7725

O6
Old Paint Lick School Antique Mall
Raymond P. Mixon
11000 Hwy. 52 West
Paint Lick, KY 40461
606-925-3000 or 606-792-3000

O7
Overlee Farm Books
P.O. Box 1155
Stockbridge, MA 01262
413-637-2277

O8
K.C. & Jean C. Owings
Box 389
Whitman, MA 02382
781-447-7850 or fax 781-447-3435

O9
Olde Current Books
Daniel P. Shay
356 Putnam Ave.
Ormond Beach, FL 32174
904-672-8998
PEAKMYSTER@aol.com
members.aol.com/peakmyster/
aolwp.htm

O10
Oak Knoll Books
414 Delaware St.
New Castle, DE 19720
800-996-2556 or 302-328-7232
fax 302-328-7274
oakknoll@wakknoll.com
www.oakknoll.com

P1
Pacific Rim Books
Michael Onorato
P.O. Box 30575
Bellingham, WA 98228-2575
206-676-0256
PACRIMBKS@AOL.COM

P2
Maggie Page
Page Books
HCR 65, Box 233
Kingston, AR 72742
870-861-5831

P3
Pandora's Books Ltd.
P.O. Box 54
Neche, ND 58265
204-324-8548 or fax 204-324-1628

P4
Parmer Books
7644 Forrestal Rd.
San Diego, CA 92120-2203
619-287-0693 or fax 619-287-6135
ParmerBook@aol.com

P5
Parnassus Books
218 N 9th St.
Boise, ID 83702

P6
Passaic Book Center
594 Main Ave.
Passaic, NJ 07055
201-778-6646 or fax 201-778-6738

P7
Pauper's Books
206 N Main St.
Bowling Green, OH 43402-2420
419-352-2163

P8
R. Plapinger, Baseball Books
P.O. Box 1062
Ashland, OR 97520
541-488-1220

P9
Prometheus Books
59 John Glenn Dr.
Buffalo, NY 14228-2197
716-691-0133 or fax 716-691-0137

P10
Pulphouse
J.H. James
P.O. Box 481
Elberton, GA 30635
706-213-9280
Pulpmaster@msn.com

P11
Pelanor Books
7 Gaskill Ave.
Albany, NY 12203

P12
Popek's Pages Past
R.D. 3, Box 44-C
Oneonta, NY 13820

P13
Periodyssey
151 Crescent St.
Northampton, MA 01060
413-585-1010 or fax 413-585-1074
richard.west@the-spa.com

Q1
Quill & Brush
Patricia & Allen Ahearn
Box 5365
Rockville, MD 20848
301-460-3700 or fax 301-871-5425
firsts@qb.com

R1
Raintree Books
432 N Eustis St.
Eustis, FL 32726
904-357-7145

R2
Kathleen Rais & Co.
Rais Place Cottage
211 Carolina Ave.
Phoenixville, PA 19460
610-933-1388

R3
Randall House
Pia Oliver
835 Laguna St.
Santa Barbara, CA 93101
805-963-1909 or fax 805-963-1650
pia@piasworld.com
www.piasworld.com/randall/

R5
Jo Ann Reisler, Ltd.
360 Glyndon St., NE
Vienna, VA 22180
703-938-2967 or fax 703-938-9057
Reisler@clark.net.

R6
Wallace Robinson Books
RD #6, Box 574
Meadville, PA 16335
800-653-3280 or 813-823-3280
814-724-7670 or 814-333-9652

R7
Tom Rolls
230 S Oakland Ave.
Indianapolis, IN 46201

R8
RAC Books
R.R. #2
P.O. Box 296
Seven Valleys, PA 17360
717-428-3776

R9
Realm of Colorado
P.O. Box 24
Parker, CO 80134

R10
Roger Reus
9412 Huron Ave.
Richmond, VA 23294
Mail order only

R11
Recollection Books
4519 University Way NE
Seattle, WA 98105
206-548-1346
www.mediastream.com/mpayson
/recollection/

R12
Leona Rostenberg and Madeleine
   Stern
Rare Books
40 E 88th St.
NY, NY 10128
212-831-6628 or fax 212-831-1961

R13
Alice Robbins, Bookseller
3002 Round Hill Rd.
Greensboro, NC 27408
910-282-1964

R14
Revere Books
P.O. Box 420
Revere, PA 18953
610-847-2703 or fax 610-847-1910

R15
Richard C. Ramer
Old & Rare Books
225 E 70th St.
New York, NY 10021
212-737-0222 or 212-737-0223
fax 212-288-4169
5222386@mcimail.com

S1
Bill and Mimi Sachen
927 Grand Ave.
Waukegan, IL 60085-3709
847-662-7204

S2
J. Sampson Antiques & Books
107 S Main
Harrodsburg, KY 40330
606-734-7829

S3
Stanley Schwartz
1934 Pentuckett Ave.
San Diego, CA 92104-5732
619-232-5888 or fax 619-233-5833
Schwartz@cts.com

S4
Scribe Company
Attn: Bonnie Smith
427 Hidden Forest S
Longview, TX 75605
903-663-6873

S5
Significant Books
3053 Madison Rd.
P.O. Box 9248
Cincinnati, OH 45209
513-321-7567
www.iac.net/~signbook

S6
The Silver Door
P.O. Box 3208
Redondo Beach, CA 90277
310-379-6005

S7
K.B. Slocum Books
P.O. Box 10998 #620
Austin, TX 78766
800-521-4451 or fax 512-258-8041

S8
Barbara Smith Books
P.O. Box 1185
Northampton, MA 01061
413-586-1453

S9
Ed Smith Books
P.O. Box 66
Oak View, CA 93022
805-649-2844 or fax 805-649-2863
edsbooks@aol.com

S10
Smithfield Rare Books
20 Deer Run Trail
Smithfield, RI 02917
401-231-8225

S11
Nancy Stewart, Books
1188 NW Weybridge Way
Beaverton, OR 97006
503-645-9779

S12
Sweet Memories
Sharyn Laymon
400 Mulberry St.
Loudon, TN 37774
615-458-5044

S13
Eileen Serxner
Box 2544
Bala Cynwyd, PA 19004
610-664-7960

S14
Second Harvest Books
Warren R. Johnson
P.O. Box 3306
Florence, OR 97439
phone/fax 541-902-0215
2harvest@presys.com

S15
Snowy Egret Books
1237 Carroll Ave.
St. Paul, MN 55104
612-641-0917
snowy@mr.net

S16
Stan Clark Military Books
915 Fairview Ave.
Gettysburg, PA 17325
717-337-1728 or 717-337-0581

S17
David R. Smith
30 Nelson Circle
Jaffrey, NH 03452
603-532-8666
Bookinc@Cheshire.net

T1
Lee and Mike Temares
50 Hts. Rd.
Plandome, NY 11030
516-627-8688

T2
Thomas Books
4425 W Olive, Ste. 168
Glendale, AZ 85302
602-435-5055 or 602-247-9289
tom@poisonedpen.com

T3
Gordon Totty
Scarce Paper Americana
347 Shady Lake Pky.
Baton Rouge, LA 70810
504-766-8625

T4
Trackside Books
8819 Mobud Dr.
Houston, TX 77036
713-772-8107

T5
Treasures From the Castle
Connie Castle
1720 N Livernois
Rochester, MI 48306
248-651-7317
treasures3@juno.com

T6
H.E. Turlington Books
P.O. Box 190
Carrboro, NC 27510

T7
J. Tuttle Maritime Books
1806 Laurel Crest
Madison, WI 53705
608-238-SAIL (7245)
fax 608-238-7249

T8
George H. Tweney
16660 Marine View Dr. SW
Seattle, WA 98166
206-243-8243

T9
Typographeum Bookshop
246 Bennington Rd.
Francestown, NH 03043
603-547-2425

T10
Thorn Books
P.O. Box 1244
Moorpark, CA 93020
805-529-36647 or fax 805-529-0022
thornbooks@earthlink.net

T11
Town's End Books
John D. & Judy A. Townsend
132 Hemlock Dr.
Deep River, CT 06417
860-526-3896
townsend@ct2.nai.net
hhtp://w3.nai.net-townsend

T12
Third Time Around Books
Norman Todd
R.R. #1
Mar., Ontario
Canada N0H 1XO
519-534-1382

V1
VERSEtility Books
P.O. Box 1133
Farmington, CT 06034-1133
860-677-0606
versebks@tiac.net

V2
A.A. Vespa
P.O. Box 637
Park Ridge, IL 60068
708-692-4210

V3
Vintage Books
Nancy and David Haines
181 Hayden Rowe St.
Hopkinton, MA 01748
508-435-3499
vintage@gis.net

V4
Volume I Books
One Union St.
Hillsdale, MI 49242
517-437-2228
volume1book@dmci.net

W1
Worldwide Antiquarian
P.O. Box 410391
Cambridge, MA 02141-0004
617-876-6220 or fax 617-876-0839
mbalwan@aol.com

W2
Warren's Collector Books
Warren Gillespie, Jr.
112 Royal Ct.
Friendswood, TX 77546
281-482-7947

W3
Ruth Woods Oriental Books & Art
266 Arch Rd.
Englewood, NJ 07631
201-567-0149 or fax 201-567-1419

Y1
Yesterday's Books
229 Riverview Dr.
Parchment, MI 49004
616-345-1011

X1
Xanadu Records, Ltd.
3242 Irwin Ave.
Kingsbridge, NY 10463
718-549-3655

COLLECTOR BOOKS

Informing Today's Collector

*For over two decades we have been keeping collectors informed
on trends and values in all fields of antiques and collectibles.*

BOOKS ON GLASS AND POTTERY

4927	ABC Plates & Mugs, Lindsay	$24.95
4929	American Art Pottery, Sigafoose	$24.95
1312	Blue & White Stoneware, McNerney	$9.95
1959	Blue Willow, 2nd Ed., Gaston	$14.95
4937	Coll. Glassware from the 40's, 50's, 60's, 4th Ed., Florence	$19.95
1373	Collector's Ency. of American Dinnerware, Cunningham	$24.95
3815	Coll. Ency. of Blue Ridge Dinnerware, Newbound	$19.95
2272	Collector's Ency. of California Pottery, Chipman	$24.95
3811	Collector's Ency. of Colorado Pottery, Carlton	$24.95
3312	Collector's Ency. of Children's Dishes, Whitmyer	$19.95
2133	Collector's Ency. of Cookie Jars, Roerig	$24.95
3723	Coll. Ency. of Cookie Jars-Volume II, Roerig	$24.95
4938	Collector's Ency. of Depression Glass, 13th Ed., Florence	$19.95
5040	Collector's Ency. of Fiesta, 8th Ed., Huxford	$19.95
1439	Collector's Ency. of Flow Blue China, Gaston	$19.95
3812	Coll. Ency. of Flow Blue China, 2nd Ed., Gaston	$24.95
3813	Collector's Ency. of Hall China, 2nd Ed., Whitmyer	$24.95
2334	Collector's Ency. of Majolica Pottery, Katz-Marks	$19.95
1358	Collector's Ency. of McCoy Pottery, Huxford	$19.95
3313	Collector's Ency. of Niloak, Gifford	$19.95
3837	Collector's Ency. of Nippon Porcelain, Van Patten	$24.95
2089	Collector's Ency. of Nippon Porcelain, 2nd Series, Van Patten	$24.95
1665	Collector's Ency. of Nippon Porcelain, 3rd Series, Van Patten	$24.95
4712	Collector's Ency. of Nippon Porcelain, 4th Series, Van Patten	$24.95
1447	Collector's Ency. of Noritake, Van Patten	$19.95
1034	Collector's Ency. of Roseville Pottery, Huxford	$19.95
1035	Collector's Ency. of Roseville Pottery, 2nd Ed., Huxford	$19.95
3314	Collector's Ency. of Van Briggle Art Pottery, Sasicki	$24.95
2339	Collector's Guide to Shawnee Pottery, Vanderbilt	$19.95
1425	Cookie Jars, Westfall	$9.95
3440	Cookie Jars, Book II, Westfall	$19.95
2275	Czechoslovakian Glass & Collectibles, Barta	$16.95
4716	Elegant Glassware of the Depression Era, 7th Ed., Florence	$19.95
3725	Fostoria - Pressed, Blown & Hand Molded Shapes, Kerr	$24.95
3883	Fostoria Stemware - The Crystal for America, Long	$24.95
3886	Kitchen Glassware of the Depression Years, 5th Ed., Florence	$19.95
4772	McCoy Pottery, Coll. Reference & Value Guide, Hanson	$19.95
4725	Pocket Guide to Depression Glass, 10th Ed., Florence	$9.95
3825	Puritan Pottery, Morris	$24.95
1670	Red Wing Collectibles, DePasquale	$9.95
1440	Red Wing Stoneware, DePasquale	$9.95
1958	So. Potteries Blue Ridge Dinnerware, 3rd Ed., Newbound	$14.95
5035	Std. Encyclopedia of Carnival Glass, 6th Ed., Edwards/Carwile	$24.95
3327	Watt Pottery – Identification & Value Guide, Morris	$19.95
2224	World of Salt Shakers, 2nd Ed., Lechner	$24.95

BOOKS ON DOLLS & TOYS

4707	A Decade of Barbie Dolls and Collectibles, 1981 - 1991, Summers	$19.95
2079	Barbie Fashion, Vol. 1, 1959-1967, Eames	$24.95
3310	Black Dolls – 1820 - 1991 – Id. & Value Guide, Perkins	$17.95
1529	Collector's Ency. of Barbie Dolls, DeWein	$19.95
2338	Collector's Ency. of Disneyana, Longest & Stern	$24.95
3727	Coll. Guide to Ideal Dolls, Izen	$18.95
4645	Madame Alexander Price Guide #21, Smith	$9.95
4723	Matchbox Toys, 1947 to 1996, Johnson	$18.95
4647	Modern Collector's Dolls, 8th series, Smith	$24.95
1540	Modern Toys, 1930 - 1980, Baker	$19.95
4640	Patricia Smith's Doll Values – Antique to Modern, 12th ed.	$12.95
4728	Schroeder's Coll. Toys, 3rd Edition	$17.95
3826	Story of Barbie, Westenhouser, No Values	$19.95
2028	Toys, Antique & Collectible, Longest	$14.95
1808	Wonder of Barbie, Manos	$9.95
1430	World of Barbie Dolls, Manos	$9.95

OTHER COLLECTIBLES

1457	American Oak Furniture, McNerney	$9.95
3716	American Oak Furniture, Book II, McNerney	$12.95
4704	Antique & Collectible Buttons, Wisniewski	$19.95
2333	Antique & Collectible Marbles, 3rd Ed., Grist	$9.95
1748	Antique Purses, Holiner	$19.95
1426	Arrowheads & Projectile Points, Hothem	$7.95
1278	Art Nouveau & Art Deco Jewelry, Baker	$9.95
1714	Black Collectibles, Gibbs	$19.95
4708	B.J. Summers' Guide to Coca-Cola, Summers	$19.95
1128	Bottle Pricing Guide, 3rd Ed., Cleveland	$7.95
3717	Christmas Collectibles, 2nd Ed., Whitmyer	$24.95
1752	Christmas Ornaments, Johnson	$19.95
3718	Collectible Aluminum, Grist	$16.95
2132	Collector's Ency. of American Furniture, Vol. I, Swedberg	$24.95
2271	Collector's Ency. of American Furniture, Vol. II, Swedberg	$24.95
3720	Coll. Ency. of American Furniture, Vol III, Swedberg	$24.95
3722	Coll. Ency. of Compacts, Carryalls & Face Powder Boxes, Mueller	$24.95
2018	Collector's Ency. of Granite Ware, Greguire	$24.95
3430	Coll. Ency. of Granite Ware, Book 2, Greguire	$24.95
1441	Collector's Guide to Post Cards, Wood	$9.95
1716	Fifty Years of Fashion Jewelry, Baker	$19.95
4568	Flea Market Trader, 10th Ed., Huxford	$12.95
3819	General Store Collectibles, Wilson	$24.95
3436	Grist's Big Book of Marbles, Everett Grist	$19.95
2278	Grist's Machine Made & Contemporary Marbles	$9.95
1424	Hatpins & Hatpin Holders, Baker	$9.95
4721	Huxford's Collectible Advertising – Id. & Value Gd., 3rd Ed	$24.95
4648	Huxford's Old Book Value Guide, 8th Ed.	$19.95
1181	100 Years of Collectible Jewelry, Baker	$9.95
2216	Kitchen Antiques – 1790 - 1940, McNerney	$14.95
4724	Modern Guns – Id. & Val. Gd., 11th Ed., Quertermous	$12.95
2026	Railroad Collectibles, 4th Ed., Baker	$14.95
1632	Salt & Pepper Shakers, Guarnaccia	$9.95
1888	Salt & Pepper Shakers II, Guarnaccia	$14.95
2220	Salt & Pepper Shakers III, Guarnaccia	$14.95
3443	Salt & Pepper Shakers IV, Guarnaccia	$18.95
4727	Schroeder's Antiques Price Guide, 15th Ed.	$14.95
4729	Sewing Tools & Trinkets, Thompson	$24.95
2096	Silverplated Flatware, 4th Ed., Hagan	$14.95
2348	20th Century Fashionable Plastic Jewelry, Baker	$19.95
3828	Value Guide to Advertising Memorabilia, Summers	$18.95
3830	Vintage Vanity Bags & Purses, Gerson	$24.95

Reach **Thousands** with Your **Free Listing** in Our Next Edition!

✏ **Book Sellers!** If you publish lists or catalogs of books for sale, take advantage of this *free* offer. Put us on your mailing list right away so that we can include you in our next edition. We'll not only list you in our Bookbuyers section under the genre that best represents your special interests (please specify these when you contact us), but each book description we choose to include from your catalog will contain a special dealer code that will identify you as the book dealer to contact in order to buy that book. Please send your information and catalogs or lists right away, since we're working on a first-come, first-served basis. Be sure to include your current address, just as you'd like it to be published. You may also include a fax number or an e-mail address. Our dealers tell us that this service has been very successful for them, both in buying and selling.

Send your listings to:

_____

Huxford's Old Book Value Guide
1202 Seventh Street
Covington, IN 47932-1099

_____

Schroeder's
ANTIQUES
Price Guide

. . . is the #1 best-selling antiques & collectibles value guide on the market today, and here's why . . .

Schroeder's ANTIQUES Price Guide

OUR #1 BEST SELLER!

Identification & Values Of Over 50,000 Antiques & Collectibles

8½ x 11, 608 Pages, $12.95

• *More than 450 advisors, well-known dealers, and top-notch collectors work together with our editors to bring you accurate information regarding pricing and identification.*

• *More than 45,000 items in almost 550 categories are listed along with hundreds of sharp original photos that illustrate not only the rare and unusual, but the common, popular collectibles as well.*

• *Each large close-up shot shows important details clearly. Every subject is represented with histories and background information, a feature not found in any of our competitors' publications.*

• *Our editors keep abreast of newly developing trends, often adding several new categories a year as the need arises.*

If it merits the interest of today's collector, you'll find it in *Schroeder's*. And you can feel confident that the information we publish is up to date and accurate. Our advisors thoroughly check each category to spot inconsistencies, listings that may not be entirely reflective of market dealings, and lines too vague to be of merit. Only the best of the lot remains for publication.

Without doubt, you'll find
SCHROEDER'S ANTIQUES PRICE GUIDE
the only one to buy for
reliable information and values.

COLLECTOR BOOKS
A Division of Schroeder Publishing Co., Inc.